EIGHTH EDITION, COMPLETELY REVISED

GUIDE TO AMERICAN GRADUATE SCHOOLS

Harold R. Doughty

PENGUIN BOOKS

PENGUIN BOOKS
Published by the Penguin Group
Penguin Books USA Inc., 375 Hudson Street,
New York, New York 10014, U.S.A.
Penguin Books Ltd, 27 Wrights Lane,
London W8 5TZ, England
Penguin Books Australia Ltd, Ringwood,
Victoria, Australia
Penguin Books Canada Ltd, 10 Alcorn Avenue,
Toronto, Ontario, Canada M4V 3B2
Penguin Books (N.Z.) Ltd, 182–190 Wairau Road,
Auckland 10, New Zealand

Penguin Books Ltd, Registered Offices:
Harmondsworth, Middlesex, England

First edition published in the United States of America by
The Viking Press 1967
Viking Compass edition published 1967
Second edition published 1970
Third edition published 1975
Published in Penguin Books 1976
Fourth edition published 1982
Fifth edition published 1986
Sixth edition published 1990
Seventh edition published 1994
This eighth edition published 1997

1   3   5   7   9   10   8   6   4   2

ISBN 0 14 04.6986 9

Printed in the United States of America
Set in Times Roman

PENGUIN HANDBOOKS

GUIDE TO AMERICAN GRADUATE SCHOOLS

Harold R. Doughty is currently a Management and Educational Consultant. He was formerly Executive Vice President and Chief Operating Officer at American Commonwealth University; Vice President for Admissions, Financial Aid and Enrollment at United States International University; Director of Admissions and Summer Sessions at New York University; and Director of Admissions and Freshmen Development at Adelphi University.

CONTENTS

PREFACE TO
THE EIGHTH EDITION

"Crisis" is a word grown impotent from overuse.

That sentence has opened every edition of this *Guide* since it was first published in 1967. Many of the traumata that inspired the remark are now so dated as to seem almost quaint. Some remain, festering. And still others, thought to be in remission, have returned to haunt us. The original observation continues to be valid, then, both for the American educational system and the larger society that supports it and receives its benefits.

Yet, despite a lingering propensity to react to challenges, rather than to anticipate them, our colleges and universities have managed to transform themselves in meaningful ways. This is especially true on the postbaccalaureate level. From 1975 to 1994, for example, the number of women enrolled in graduate programs increased by 180 percent, and total minority group registrations tripled. These advances show some sign of leveling or even reversing, however, in the face of the backlash implicit in widely publicized legal suits alleging reverse discrimination. Even with the moderation occurring in the 1980s, a century-long history of overt and *de facto* exclusionary practice has been reversed.

Problems persist, of course. Task forces of educators doggedly debate overproduction of doctorates, although the much-bemoaned "Ph.D. glut" is still confined primarily to the humanities, and demand is still high for the products of most other disciplines. Complicating the anxieties of those same graduate faculties is the slowdown in the rate of increase of students pursuing advanced study. There is no *decline* in graduate enrollments, it must be understood. But after doubling every ten years since the turn of the century and tripling in the 1960s, graduate enrollments increased "only" from 985,000 in 1970 to 1,680,000 in 1979 and leveled off at 2,100,000 in 1994. The rush to advanced education has cooled, it is true, but it long threatened to boil over, so the results are not entirely negative. Unrestricted growth has been curtailed, costs are being contained, and some marginal academic operations are being eliminated or absorbed by those in which demand remains high. Under such circumstances—which should prevail throughout this decade—the quality of facilities and instruction should improve as universities learn to live within their means and focus on those areas in which they can best serve their client students.

Despite these contractions, applications for admission in most fields have remained constant. As education beyond high school has become a commonplace expectation, the demand for further training intensifies, if only to give a competitive edge in an ever-more-credentialed and specialized marketplace now being governed by consumer-oriented licensure requirements and regulations. That this is true is exemplified by the marked upswing in candidates for the master's degree, especially in business administration, computer application, and other narrowly defined and specialized programs. In spite of this, the current graduate student is being torn between the perceived need for graduate study and the immediate desire for career or job and instant financial gratification. The burdensome overabundance of applications of the past, which swamped understaffed administrative offices, has been greatly reduced. Higher application fees, earlier and earlier deadlines, and more stringent entrance standards, long a hallmark of the oversubscribed, have given way to the need for many graduate schools to market programs via Web sites, use direct mail solicitations, and actively recruit students in order to maintain an adequate applicant pool. Full-time study has given way to part-time. Indeed, full-time faculty has in many cases had to give way to more specialized part-time or adjunct associates. It is fair to say that only a few prestigious institutions can hold to and enforce the high academic requirements of just a few years ago.

Those full-time applicants who gain entrance to the fabled colleges of their choice are now confronted by financial difficulties substantially greater than those experienced in their undergraduate years. The belief that ample financial aid funds await the use of every graduate student is quickly dispelled. Inflation, tight money, and parents who often are unable or just unwilling to subsidize further education forces many students to assume staggering financial burdens just when he or she is least able to afford them. This may be the first confrontation with the practical reality that graduate students must have alternative financial means in order to afford the graduate education they desire. This scenario further reinforces the belief that to find employment now will give the needed direction to pursue graduate study on one's own, the direction that is so often missing in undergraduate study.

Although college guidance is fully developed at the

high-school level, no equivalent counseling structure exists for the potential graduate student. Such advisement as is available is provided by a small number of placement officers and faculty members concerned that able students realize their full potential. Unfortunately, no single individual can keep abreast of current offerings at even the major institutions. Indeed, it is difficult to keep track of developments within a single large university. Despite these obstacles, it remains true that most students who hold bachelor's degrees can gain admission to some graduate school in any section of the country.

This volume is designed to provide the kind of basic information students need to reach sound decisions in the selection of appropriate institutions at which to continue their education. It describes more than twelve hundred institutions throughout the United States providing graduate and professional study. All have been surveyed once again for this eighth edition of the *Guide to American Graduate Schools,* and still more complete information has been sought.

Listed are programs in all areas of the liberal arts and sciences, education, medicine, dentistry, veterinary medicine, pharmacy, nursing, law, social work, agriculture, theology, the applied arts, engineering, and business. Admission and degree requirements, standards, enrollment and faculty figures, tuition charges, financial aid opportunities, and research and housing facilities are given whenever possible. While this book has been prepared with the student in mind, it is hoped that counselors, faculty, and administrative officers will find it of value, as well.

It should be noted that the *Guide to American Graduate Schools* is intended only as a first source of information. Careful use of the data summarized should enable the student to become more fully aware of the opportunities available and then to narrow selections to the geographical area and then the institutions he or she is likely to find most suitable. The student is encouraged to seek the advice of undergraduate faculty, especially those who teach in the proposed field of graduate study. Catalogues, bulletins, departmental brochures, and Web sites should be used when possible. Most important, the applicant must be brutally frank in self-appraisal of ability, objectives, and motives for undertaking graduate study.

The author wishes to express his indebtedness to the graduate deans, admission officers, and their assistants in the nation's colleges and universities who provided the information presented. Further revisions of this volume are planned, and corrections and suggestions are welcomed.

H.R.D

INTRODUCTION

The Graduate School

Many students believe graduate study to be essentially an extension of undergraduate work, "only harder." On the contrary, the basic character and objectives of graduate and undergraduate study differ in many important particulars. The doctorate, and to a certain extent the master's degree, signifies the attainment of a high level of expertise in a given academic or professional field as well as the mastery of the investigative techniques of the scholar. Achievement of these goals relies upon the cultivation of habits of rigorous self-discipline and diligent thoroughness of mind.

The ensuing pages attempt to outline in forthright terms what a student can anticipate in graduate school, what will be demanded of him, and what he can expect in return. Since graduate education in the United States is simultaneously the target of severe criticism and the recipient of bountiful favor, the following remarks attempt to offer a balanced view of both the strengths and deficiencies of the system. This is not meant to suggest that these words constitute a complete analysis of graduate study. It is hoped, however, that these notes will help the student approach the decisions that face him with realism and some precision.

THE FIRST HUNDRED AND TWENTY-FIVE YEARS

Graduate education in the United States is barely seven generations old. The attitudes and social conditions that characterized this predominantly rural young nation in the first half of the nineteenth century simply were not favorable to the extension of education beyond the college years. Despite the encouragement of many leaders, among them George Washington and Thomas Jefferson, several attempts to establish graduate education failed. The start of a tragic war sped the development of national maturity, and with it the first formal graduate program. Yale awarded three doctorates to students of its Scientific School in 1861.

Resistance to the founding of graduate programs dwindled as concern mounted over the numbers of American students flocking to German universities for postbaccalaureate study. Harvard announced in 1872 the availability of work leading to the Master of Arts, Doctor of Science, and Doctor of Philosophy. With the establishment of Johns Hopkins in 1876, and that university's avowed mission to bring its substantial resources to bear upon its graduate programs, higher education made its first firm commitment to advanced study beyond college.

With this recognition of responsibility, graduate education grew rapidly. By the end of the century, dozens of public and private universities enrolled graduate students. Soon the American penchant for standardization led quite naturally to the formation of the Association of American Universities. Harvard, Princeton, Columbia, Chicago, Johns Hopkins, California, Catholic, Pennsylvania, Michigan, Wisconsin, Clark, Cornell, and Yale were the charter members. As conceived, the organization was to encourage greater uniformity of conditions for successful work leading to higher degrees, to make representations to foreign universities regarding their admission of American students, and to improve European opinion of American degrees. Inevitably, since its membership included many of the most highly regarded universities, the Association became a prestigious organization into which invitation was eagerly sought. By World War I, ten additional institutions had been admitted.

After a period of stabilization in enrollment, during which acceptable standards for graduate study were defined, rapid growth resumed. Graduate enrollments, more than doubling every decade, went from 5800 in 1900 to 106,000 in 1940. World War II brought the demands for trained scientists and attendant governmental support that remain with us today, and the booming college enrollments of the 1950s intensified the need for college teachers. As a result of these and other pressures, graduate enrollment had surpassed the one-million mark by the midseventies and now the two-million mark.

Although the prestige of the Ph.D. and the other badges of completion of programs of graduate study has grown steadily over the last century, the increase in stature has been accompanied by rising criticism. The graduate school is often named as the assassin of the liberal arts college, and is said to have promoted professional proficiency at the expense of scholarship. Many critics feel that the value of the Ph.D. is demeaned by the practice of conferring this degree in fields other than those traditionally felt to be worthy of serious study. The graduate school is also accused, with justice, of enforcing archaic degree requirements simply because they have become the "keys to the club" of scholars.

Others have attacked graduate schools for emphasizing research over the training of college teachers (and vice versa), for promoting academic snobbery, for adopting allegedly second-rate "professional" or "specialized" master's and doctoral degrees. Undoubtedly, debate will continue in the years to come, and along essentially the same lines as in the past. Witness this warning from the North Central Association: "The crowding of graduate schools has become so great as to raise some question as to the quality of work done and the value of the degree." This statement was issued in 1926.

Criticism notwithstanding, it is evident that increasing proportions of college graduates will seek the prestige of graduate degrees and the advantages, both intellectual and material, which accrue to those fortunate enough to be able to add those magic letters to their names.

SELECTING A GRADUATE SCHOOL

Once the student decides that graduate study will be of sufficient value to justify one or more years of hard work, major expenses, and the possible delay of personal plans or obligations, he or she must begin the often torturous task of making a choice of schools and opportunities. Once the choice of the proposed field of study is made, a number of considerations assume importance.

COST, SIZE, LOCATION. Contrary to widely held beliefs, financial aid for graduate students is by no means ample. Most students have to manage their support through means other than fellowships or similar awards. The most common solution is part-time study while employed full-time outside the graduate school. Whatever the method, the cost of attending graduate school is a primary factor in most students' deliberations. Fortunately, at least half of the most highly regarded institutions are publicly supported. Tuition costs therefore remain affordable, although usually somewhat higher than on the undergraduate level. Even the substantially higher charges normally set for out-of-state students at public universities are customarily less than the charges at private institutions. Furthermore, some public institutions are permitted to waive fees for nonresident graduate students under certain circumstances, or a student can establish residency in a relatively short period of time, thereby reducing tuition enormously, and these features should be checked.

Annual fees or tuition for residents in public institutions range from about $1800 to $7500, and from about $2400 to $15,000 for nonresidents. At most private colleges and universities the student can expect tuition charges of from $4000 to $21,000, although some church-related schools are less expensive. Private institutions rarely make distinctions between resident and nonresident students. Housing expenses vary widely, of course, depending upon sections of the country, rural or urban location, and the student's accustomed standard of living. Very roughly, married students can anticipate rents of from $3200 to $11,000 annually, while single students will usually be charged between $2100 and $6500 for institutional housing, exclusive of board.

Size of a graduate school is an important factor, but caution must be observed in weighing this consideration.

Even in a graduate school with a very large enrollment, students in many fields can enjoy the advantages of small classes and close faculty-student rapport. Since graduate study is pursued primarily in a single field of study, the size of the major department may determine the closeness of faculty-student relationships as well as class enrollments. This is not meant to suggest that departments with large enrollments do not offer these benefits, but rather to warn against the assumption that large enrollments mean an impersonal, factory-like atmosphere in contrast to the presumed warmth and individual attention of smaller schools. It must be remembered, too, that larger institutions generally offer the extensive facilities required for *many* fields of study, while smaller institutions are more likely to specialize in fewer areas to permit them to provide equivalent research opportunities. In either case, care must be exercised in selecting not only a graduate school, but also the individual department in question.

Geographical location and type of environment can significantly influence choice of school. Institutions in urban centers offer distinct advantages, including cultural resources and greater research and employment opportunities than may customarily be found in rural locations. On the other hand, students who have spent most of their lives in nonurban environments may well find the tensions of the city too difficult, living costs too high, and distractions too numerous. The study of many fields is enhanced in obvious ways by the environment and by the availability of raw material for research. Sociology can have either an urban or rural emphasis, but other fields, such as public administration and art history, or animal husbandry and geology, are clearly oriented to specific environments. The student must weigh both his own background and preferences. Graduate study is demanding enough without the additional stress of unfamiliar surroundings or inadequate research opportunities.

THE QUESTION OF QUALITY. By the time a student is ready to consider graduate study, he knows that no thoroughly reliable measure of quality in education has been devised, including the latest attempts by *U.S. News and World Report.* Viewed through this screen of healthy cynicism, the selection of a graduate school can prove to be a less agonizing task than one might imagine. Recognizing that no two students can be equally served by one institution or program, the potential graduate student is nevertheless in a position to make certain basic judgments that will strengthen his chances for a satisfactory experience in graduate school.

The five factors most likely to influence estimations of quality are faculty resources, facilities, student body, reputation, and placement success. The question of reputation is most subject to challenge and yet apparently is most unshakable as it is assigned to particular institutions. This fact is evidenced in several evaluations of quality in graduate education dating from 1925 to the most recent in 1996. In these compilations of academic opinion, the same twenty to twenty-five graduate schools have appeared consistently as the most distinguished institutions. While schools within this group shift position somewhat in each new study, and occasionally a newer school makes the grade, this cluster of top-rated schools varies only slightly.

A relationship clearly exists between *perceived* quality and prestige. For many reasons, however, these listings of academic departments in order of presumed merit inevitably favor the older institutions. Most of the individuals queried in these surveys of opinion are senior professors or deans, for the quite logical reason that they possess sufficient experience to enable them to draw distinctions between departments. On the other hand, it must be remembered that until 1970 only twenty graduate schools gave over half the doctorates awarded annually. Since it can be assumed that most faculty members participating in these studies received their doctorates from these same twenty schools, some narrowness in scope of representation persists as a result of institutional background and loyalties.

Despite these and other limitations, these studies, undertaken by reputable agencies, serve as valuable guides to students seeking strong programs in certain fields. Other criteria for assessing quality are available, however. School catalogues and departmental brochures are valuable sources of information and are well worth the fee now charged for them. Many graduate schools list the institutions that awarded the highest degrees held by each member of the faculty. It is often possible to discover the number and kind of publications produced by a professor by referring to such volumes as *Who's Who in America,* the *Directory of American Scholars,* and reports provided by the professional associations representing each academic field. Since the most distinguished members of every faculty are eagerly sought by industry, government, and other institutions, the catalogue often states whether professors are on leave or sabbatical, and, of course, whether they are still employed by the university. Since graduate students often seek the opportunity to study under noted scholars, it should be determined whether particular faculty members are to be available during the student's period of attendance. This is particularly true of students taking only the master's degree.

Examination of the catalogue also reveals the number of courses in each department that are open to undergraduate as well as graduate students. While course requirements often differ in such cases, depending upon the status of each student, effectiveness and content of a course may be impaired because of disparities in student backgrounds. Further, the number of courses and breadth of material

covered can be important, allowing for the tendency to offer too many courses that might overlap.

Reports in general and academic news media are additional sources of information. These list the institutions attended by the recipients of the many prestigious fellowships, such as the National Science Foundation Fellowship program, as well as the grants of federal and state governments. Since the competition for these awards is keen, the institutions selected by these honored few can be assumed to offer well-regarded programs in specific fields. The simple fact that clusters of fellowship recipients attend specific schools at the very least reflects favorably upon the composition of their student bodies.

Most graduate students agree that the capability of their colleagues is very important in their assessments of the effectiveness of their programs. In fact, many observers suggest that it is difficult to determine whether a school or department is good because the training is better than elsewhere or because the students enrolled are stronger. This suggests a relationship between competitiveness of admission standards and quality of program. The potential graduate student can indeed reach valid conclusions about the makeup of a school's student body by determining the levels of competition resulting from admission policies.

It must be emphasized, however, that difficulty of admission *cannot be equated* with quality of program. As observed elsewhere, students exercise self-selection in applying to the more prestigious institutions, but often little restraint is evident in applications to more lightly regarded schools. This may result in the former group of schools accepting more than two-thirds of their applicants, while the latter rejects a much larger percentage. Also, small departments with excellent faculties and facilities sometimes find they must employ "soft" admission policies to build their enrollments, and thus their contribution to institutional budgets, while larger departments in more popular fields often must restrict admission because of limited faculties and facilities.

Availability and scope of research facilities provide another clue to the quality of individual schools. The nature and breadth of facilities can be indicative of a school's commitment to serious research and of its ability to attract support. The manner in which funds are allocated suggests something of the priorities established by an institution. Elaborate stadia and athletic arenas casting shadows across aging classroom buildings may not only be symptoms of the enthusiasms of misguided alumni, but the situation may also be evidence of misplaced emphasis by the administration.

The size of an institution's library holdings and the manner in which these resources are made available to students can be assumed to have considerable bearing upon quality. Virtually all of the highly regarded universities have library holdings well in excess of two million volumes, and several have more than three million. The only significant exceptions are a few leading technological institutions. Large numbers of volumes, microforms, and periodicals do not in themselves insure the quality of library resources, of course. A major portion of the collections should be on open stacks, or at least permission for access should be easily obtainable. Ideally, individual alcoves or carrels are made available to graduate students. Students are wise to seek information about the nature of specialized collections in their particular fields of interest.

Older institutions with large libraries may have weaker collections in the modern disciplines, while newer universities often possess holdings of less breadth. Institutional resources are often supplemented by nearby public libraries and research institutes, and this is to be borne in mind when considering graduate schools. Finally, some groups of institutions have arrangements pooling their libraries for the common use of their combined student bodies.

Other criteria are useful in assessing quality, though perhaps not as important as those discussed above. Among these are faculty salaries, eminence of alumni, number of recipients of major fellowships among both the graduate students and the faculty, the number of Nobel Prize winners on the faculty, institutional rank in production of doctorates and in size of annual gifts. Most of these factors are weighted in favor of the larger institutions, which makes it again necessary to stress the importance of investigating individual departments within graduate schools as well as the schools themselves.

GUIDANCE. Counseling services for prospective graduate students are largely informal and unorganized at most undergraduate colleges, with the exception of a few institutions that send large percentages of their graduates on to advanced study. Some universities have established regular series of interviews for those undergraduates who have demonstrated particular promise for graduate work. In addition, representatives of professional schools, especially those offering study in law and business administration, often visit colleges and universities as part of recruitment efforts. Unfortunately, this practice is rare on the part of graduate schools.

The best sources of specialized information about graduate study continue to be the members of the faculty in the student's proposed field of graduate study. Most professors can readily list the five to ten graduate schools offering what they believe to be the strongest programs in their disciplines. They can also aid the student in planning for financial aid and in discussing career opportunities. If the student is able to obtain some consensus on these matters from several faculty members, so much the better.

Some college placement offices make efforts to gather material about opportunities for graduate study and financial aid, and libraries and admissions offices generally keep files of graduate catalogues.

ADMISSION

It may be reassuring to know at the outset that most college graduates can gain admission to some graduate school somewhere in the section of the country they prefer. There are, of course, exceptions to this rule in some fields of specialization, but the statement remains valid for the vast majority of applicants. The reason this is true is the tendency on the part of most graduate schools to screen students more vigorously *following* entrance rather than before. This results in the common distinction made between admission to study and admission to candidacy. The latter procedure is typical on the doctoral level, and preliminary or qualifying examinations are usually employed to determine eligibility for continuance toward the degree. Applicants for the master's degree often are expected to meet requirements for formal candidacy, but the practice is less standard at this level.

Although admission policies and procedures vary widely from school to school and between departments, there are general requirements that have become fairly standard.

PREPARATION. Graduate schools of arts and science, education, business, and the like nearly always expect applicants to possess an appropriate bachelor's degree at the time of entrance. Although it is occasionally possible to gain admission without this degree, compensatory strength in previous academic performance or experience is customarily demanded.

The specific kind of undergraduate preparation necessary for individual fields of graduate study is much less subject to uniformity. Some social science departments are willing to consider applicants who do not present undergraduate majors in a particular social science discipline, but who have accumulated course work in several social science fields. While sociology departments are often liberal on this point, economics departments generally demand full undergraduate preparation. Because of the often greater-than-usual curricular requirements on the graduate level in psychology, many psychology departments accept applications from students with as few as twelve semester hours of undergraduate study in psychology, assuming substantial work was completed in the natural and social sciences. While it is not possible to note all these variations here, it is usually true that natural and physical science departments demand extensive undergraduate preparation in the proposed field of graduate study, and departments of business, political science, sociology, and education place less emphasis on specific training on the college level. The humanities and older social sciences are likely to fall somewhere in the middle range in this regard.

CREDENTIALS. Every graduate institution requires that at least one official transcript of the undergraduate record be provided in support of the application for admission. If a student has attended more than one college or university, a single official transcript from the institution conferring the baccalaureate, showing courses accepted in transfer, is often adequate. More often, graduate schools request submission of transcripts from *each* undergraduate institution attended. Since admission procedures on the graduate level are often coordinated efforts between the offices of the dean, the departments, and/or admissions, it is not unusual for two or even three copies of each transcript to be required. Applicants are of course expected to provide official transcripts of any graduate study completed elsewhere, in addition to undergraduate records.

Letters of recommendation are typically required, usually from one to three persons, but often from as many as four or five. Generally, the letters are to be provided by members of the applicant's faculty who are in a position to assess his aptitude and motivation for graduate study. In the case of elementary and secondary teachers seeking further study, references may be required from a school supervisor. While potential for graduate study is customarily the basis for the letter of recommendation, some graduate schools desire evaluations of the character of the applicant as well.

Special departmental applications must be submitted on occasion if it is felt that a particular area of specialization is not adequately served by the general graduate school application. This is characteristically true of departments or schools offering programs of a more professional nature within larger graduate divisions empowered to grant all or most graduate degrees. This might include majors in social work, business administration, education, urban planning, or architecture, among others.

ENTRANCE EXAMINATIONS. Contrary to widely held opinion, the submission of results of entrance examinations is by no means a standard graduate school admission requirement. Accordingly, a student should ascertain whether he must meet this entrance requirement for the specific department of the particular graduate school in which he is interested. Those who intend to apply for national fellowships must also determine whether an examination is required for consideration.

Very few graduate schools have flat, divisionwide entrance exam requirements. Individual departments may specify single parts of exams, such as the general or appropriate subject test of the Graduate Record Examination. Others accept either the GRE or the Miller Analogies Test or require both. Many departments have no stated exam requirement but *strongly recommend* submission of test results. (In this case, the prudent applicant will take the suggested exams.) In still other schools, there is a minimum test requirement for all applicants, with the department stipulating additional exams when felt to be appropriate.

It must be noted that the reason for this lack of uniformity in entrance exam requirements is the divergence of opinion on the relative value of these tests as predictors of success in graduate study. Many graduate schools and departments use the tests essentially as a screening device when confronted with the problem of selecting a limited number of students from a much larger group of highly qualified applicants. It is further suspected that some schools utilize the tests more to satisfy notions of status or prestige than to measure aptitude.

The examinations most commonly used are the Graduate Record Examination (referred to here as the GRE), the Miller Analogies Test (MAT), and the Graduate Management Admissions Test (GMAT). On occasion, individual schools supplement or replace these exams with tests of their own creation. Arrangements often can be made to take the exam at the applicant's present institution if it is inconvenient to travel to the school requiring the special exam.

The Graduate Record Examination has a general test plus subject tests in twenty-five fields of graduate study. The general test has verbal and quantitative sections, scored separately, and is designed to determine scholastic ability in those two general areas. The general test is two and one-half hours long, the subject test in each field takes three hours. While there is no minimum "passing" score, scores below 450 on the 200 to 800 scale are rarely considered adequate by most graduate schools with this requirement.

The Miller Analogies Test attempts to measure verbal and reasoning ability and takes only fifty minutes to complete.

The Graduate Management Admissions Test measures abilities and skills developed over a long period of time. It requires you to think clearly and systematically.

Information about these examinations may be obtained from graduate admissions offices or from the Psychological Corporation, 7500 Old Oak Blvd., Cleveland, Ohio 44130 (MAT), and the Educational Testing Service in Princeton, N.J., or Los Angeles, Calif. (GRE and GMAT). Both examinations are given at colleges and universities across the country.

OTHER REQUIREMENTS. Some departments offering certain forms of advanced study set additional admission requirements. Applicants for graduate study in music are usually expected to audition for performance and music education programs or to provide samples of work for composition programs. Creative art majors typically are asked to supply either portfolios or photographs of finished work. Other departments or schools require statements of purpose for graduate study, which may include projected plans for the thesis or final project. Interviews are often requested, either for students with marginal records or for entrance to certain departments.

STANDARDS. Although graduate schools commonly specify a minimum "B−" average for entrance, the manner in which this standard is interpreted or applied varies substantially. It may refer to the cumulative grade average of all four years of undergraduate study, or to just the junior and senior years. The school may have in mind the average for all study completed, or only the courses in the proposed field of graduate study. Still another distinction is in the degree of rigidity with which the stated minimum average is observed. Some schools make no exceptions to the minimum, others regard the average as simply a point of guidance and regularly admit students whose records fall below it.

Further, some schools interpret the "B" as "B−." In other words, "B" to one school may be a 3.0 average on the customary four-point scale (A = 4, B = 3, C = 2), while another school might regard a 2.5 as essentially a "B" average. In practice, therefore, the "B" average stipulation can mean either the admission of virtually any college graduate or of a limited number of superior applicants. Despite the elusive manner in which this standard is interpreted, specific minimum grade-point averages are listed, when available, for each graduate institution in this revised *Guide.* Due caution should be exercised in interpreting this information.

Most schools give greatest weight to the undergraduate performance in the proposed field of graduate study, assuming the total average is not significantly out of line with that in the courses in the major area of concentration.

The reputation of the undergraduate college undeniably has some bearing upon admission to the more highly selective graduate schools. It is not unusual for departments to offer admission more readily to graduates of institutions of substantial national prestige than to students applying from little-known colleges. Unhappy experiences with graduates of particular colleges often cause departmental suspicion of subsequent applicants. Some graduate departments are known to deny admission even to honors graduates of colleges they view with disfavor. Generally, however, applicants are judged upon the merits of their individual records. Among the students of the most highly regarded graduate schools are found many alumni of obscure colleges.

DEADLINES. Students are urged to make their inquiries about admission and financial aid at least a year in advance of the date of anticipated enrollment. While closing dates for receipt of applications for admission are rarely as early as for undergraduate colleges, the deadlines for financial-aid applications for the more selective institutions are generally set for midwinter, and some fall as early as December 1. Schools state their closing dates in different ways. Some of the highly selective schools simply give the date by which applications for financial aid *and* admission must be filed, indicating that applications solely for admission are considered after that date as long as spaces continue to exist. Most graduate schools give separate closing dates for each type of application, noting that those applying for particular forms of aid must file both applications by the same stated deadline.

Since the award of most assistantships and some service fellowships depends upon vacancies created by the anticipated graduation of present recipients, departments may accept applications later in the spring for these particular awards than for scholarships and most fellowships.

The fragmented organizational structure of graduate schools often makes it difficult to determine to which office inquiries should be directed. Most often, requests for information are answered by the office of the dean of the graduate school or by the admissions office of the school or university. Sometimes the head of the proposed major department is the proper person to query about assistantships as well as admission. Students are advised to contact the specific individuals or offices noted in the institutional entries of this book.

FINANCIAL ASSISTANCE

Many types of financial assistance are available through federal and state governmental agencies, private foundations, and civic organizations. While space does not permit a listing here of specific grants and awards, the following paragraphs should enable students to identify sources for further exploration.

The customary distinction drawn between fellowships and scholarships is that the former type of grant often requires some service in exchange for a stipend, while the latter carries no obligation other than satisfactory academic performance. Increasingly, however, graduate schools use the term "fellowship" to cover both outright awards and service grants, since "fellowships" are more readily associated with graduate study. Whatever label is used, it is worth noting that grants that require no service function are tax-free, while those demanding some form of work must be reported on income tax forms. However, IRS regulations and the interpretation of the regulations sometimes change the way income is reported and therefore all students receiving some type of stipend should verify how this remuneration will be reported for tax purposes.

Traineeships, assistantships, and internships provide stipends for performance of a variety of tasks. These include classroom teaching, proctoring in residence halls, laboratory research, and duties of a more or less clerical nature, such as grading undergraduate test papers or gathering and filing research materials.

An aura of status often surrounds the fellowship, and this characteristic may be enhanced by larger stipends and perhaps more engaging tasks than are normally associated with assistantships. Fellowship stipends range on the average from $2500 to $12,000, and in private institutions carry tuition remission privileges as well. Allowances for dependents of married fellows may range from $1000 to $3500. Assistantships normally carry grants on a somewhat lower scale than fellowships, from perhaps $1000 to $8000 plus free tuition or tuition waivers. Stipends for some fellowships and/or for married students with two or more dependents occasionally reach highs of over $15,000. At the other end of the scale, awards of an essentially honorary nature may pay as little as $100. Fellowships, assistantships, traineeships, and similar grants are available through the graduate schools or through individual departments, either from their own funds or from outside funds administered by them.

Although fellowships traditionally were reserved for doctoral candidates, many of those mentioned above and those available from other sources are open to students seeking the master's degree. Further information can be obtained through the office of the dean of the graduate school or designated members of the faculty representing various agencies. Students should also note the announcements of fellowships and other forms of assistance customarily posted on bulletin boards at central points in most colleges.

Students should not forget the possibility of full-time employment in the administrative offices of the institution in which they wish to study. Clerical positions are usually available in the offices of the Registrar, Dean of Admissions, Student Housing, Personnel, and others, and often carry a limited tuition remission privilege for part-time graduate study.

Most students must continue to find their solutions in combinations of outside employment, part-time study, loans, and support by parents or working spouses. This situation continues to run counter to the generally accepted conviction that graduate work is best accomplished through full-time study, but it does recognize the practical reality that graduate students must have alternative financial means in order to afford the graduate education they desire.

THE STRUCTURE OF GRADUATE STUDY

Anxiety and doubt often attend a student's embarkation on the path to the master's and doctoral degrees. The candidate is confronted by a maze of course options, language and research tool requirements, oral and written examinations, thesis proposals and faculty committees, and academic standards. While no one is likely to suggest that successful negotiation of these obstacles can be accomplished with ease, certain patterns of expected performance can be anticipated prior to entrance.

THE PROGRAMS. Perhaps the first surprise for the beginning student is the realization that graduate study, especially on the master's level, is not necessarily a series of intimate seminars conducted by brilliant scholars and famous professors. In many universities, a number of courses are open to both graduate and undergraduate students, and these are likely to be conducted as lectures rather than discussion groups. In the more popular majors or in classes taught by senior members of the faculty, more than half the courses for the master's may have enrollments in excess of one hundred students. Even courses billed as seminars may have twenty or thirty students, which makes the free-discussion format difficult, or the professor may simply choose to conduct the class on a lecture basis.

For most master's degrees, the customary course requirement is the equivalent of two semesters (or three quarters) of full-time study. In some cases, however, the professional master's extends over two academic years. In many graduate schools this is true of the Master of Fine Arts and the Master of Business Administration, for example. In the data disciplines, the necessary time for the master's often includes a full year of course work plus up to one additional year for research for the thesis. A great many graduate schools have two plans for the master's degree, one including the thesis or final project, the other without a thesis.

The candidate planning to continue to the doctorate is wise to make his preliminary decision for his doctoral dissertation early in the master's program. The exercise of this foresight may permit him to accomplish basic research for the dissertation while working on the master's thesis.

Although some cross-disciplinary programs are available for both the master's and doctorate, permitting some flexibility in course work, the graduate student must realize that he is subject to what might be described as "instant commitment"; that is, all or nearly all of his courses will be in one area of specialization or in fields bearing directly upon his major field of study. Interdepartmental programs such as American Studies or biochemistry allow somewhat more latitude in course work, but a common objective serves to emphasize a particular aspect of even the broadest interdisciplinary study. Students cannot expect, therefore, to make decisions about their major following entrance, as may have been the case when they began undergraduate study.

In the second and third years of study, course work becomes more advanced than in the first year of essentially introductory work. Seminars in more specialized areas are increasingly the rule, and large lecture classes are generally less common. The doctoral candidate can expect to be required to complete a minimum of two years of course work beyond the master's, in full-time attendance or the equivalent in parttime study.

EXAMINATIONS, CANDIDACY, AND RESIDENCE. Some departments conduct placement exams at the time of initial registration for the master's program. This is characteristic of chemistry and music departments, among others, and the test is used essentially for guidance purposes. Others set the exam later in the first semester of registration and use it for the dual purpose of placement and formal matriculation. In either case, the test varies greatly in duration, content, and format from school to school. It may measure general English usage, or knowledge in specific areas of the major field, or simply aptitude for graduate study. The requirement is often waived altogether if the student presents acceptable results of the GRE, MAT, or GMAT taken prior to entrance. Only some departments and schools make this requirement for the master's, however.

An exam in the initial stages of doctoral study is much more common, although not universal. Again, the test may simply determine the student's acceptability for advanced doctoral study, in which case it is usually referred to as a "preliminary" examination. An exam more comprehensive in content is generally required following completion of a majority of formal course work for the doctorate. Satisfactory performance on this test often precedes admission to doctoral candidacy. At many schools, these tests are combined in a variety of ways, and in form they can be written, oral, or both. Terminology is also mixed, even between departments within schools. As a result, exams may be labeled as "qualifying," "candidacy," or "comprehensive."

In any event, a student can anticipate at least one examination before he is admitted to formal candidacy for the doctorate. Less standard is an exam for master's degree candidacy. Candidacy may be withheld further, especially on the doctoral level, until satisfaction of the language or research tool requirements, submission of an acceptable dissertation proposal, and/or appointment of a dissertation advisory committee.

Finally, presentation of the master's thesis or doctoral dissertation is usually followed by an oral and/or written examination, the oral portion of which is customarily a defense of the thesis or dissertation itself. A final written exam is typically required if the "candidacy" or "comprehensive" was oral in form.

Potential students should determine prior to entrance the graduate school's interpretation of the term "residence." At minimum, it refers to the number of semester or quarter hours which must be completed at the school itself, exclusive of advanced standing awarded for work completed at other graduate schools. However, "residence" is sometimes interpreted to mean only work completed while in *full-time* attendance at the institution awarding the degree. Graduate schools are often rather obscure in their explanations of this requirement. An impression may be given in their catalogues that only full-time study is permitted, but the qualification "or its equivalent" may be found tucked away in the text.

Most master's programs demand that at least 24 semester hours of a 30-hour requirement (or 36 *quarter* hours of a 45-hour total) be completed at the institution granting the degree. If the thesis or final project is included in the total credit-hour requirement, the stated residence still applies. Some schools expect only one summer session in full-time attendance, so the attendance and residence requirements obviously differ. Schools or departments requiring full-time residence for the master's during the regular academic year are in the minority. Periods of full-time attendance are increasingly expected for the Ph.D., less commonly for "professional" doctorates such as the Ed.D., Psy.D., and D.B.A.

It is difficult to make definitive statements regarding residence requirements for the doctorate. However, while the trend toward increased full-time residence is clear in the most prestigious schools, most graduate schools still permit students to complete most or all course work while in attendance as part-time students. A number of schools refuse to make flat statements about the doctoral credit-hour requirement, preferring instead to state this in terms of total semesters, quarters, term units, or years. In general, students are expected to complete at least three years of full-time study or its equivalent beyond the bachelor's, including course work applied toward the master's. Time needed for the writing of the dissertation usually extends beyond this minimum period of course work. Indeed, the average total period of work for recipients of the Ph.D. is estimated to be well over seven years. This includes, of course, time for the master's degree, research for the dissertation, and interruptions in attendance. It might be noted that this "Ph.D. stretch-out" is a subject of much academic controversy, since lingering students tie up faculty and facilities, cause substantial administrative problems, and contribute to the oversupply of ABDs.

THE LANGUAGE REQUIREMENT. Perhaps twenty percent of the nation's graduate schools require some sort of ability in at least one foreign language for the master's degree. A diminishing number of schools, however, demand knowledge of at least one language, and sometimes two, for the doctorate. The language requirement has evolved from the traditional French, German and/or Russian of the early years of graduate study in the United States to a variety of present forms.

For the master's degree, the language requirement is generally stated as a "reading knowledge of one modern foreign language, usually French, German, or Russian." The requirement is usually not schoolwide, but some departments may stipulate a reading knowledge when their schools do not. On the doctoral level, two of the above-named languages may be specified. Several variations of this customary requirement for the doctorate have cropped up in recent years, however. These include: (1) a reading, speaking, and writing knowledge of one foreign language, *or* reading knowledge only of two languages; (2) a proficiency in one foreign language or in two languages; (3) a reading knowledge of one language plus proven ability to use another appropriate research tool such as statistical methods; (4) reading knowledge of only one language.

Although some graduate schools adhere to the traditional French, German, or Russian requirement for the doctorate, most now permit substitution of another language deemed appropriate for a particular area of specialization for at least one of the two languages. A substantial number of graduate schools, responding to the criticism that the language requirement is no longer justifiable as a research tool in most fields, have either eliminated the language requirement altogether or have reduced it for the

doctorate to one language, permitting individual departments to set additional requirements as they feel appropriate. This trend appears to be accelerating. Thus, three or more languages may be stipulated for the Ph.D. in the art history or comparative literature departments, while only one language may be mandatory for the history department; or appropriate languages may be required for particular specializations within a single academic discipline and not for others.

While the language requirement, in its various forms, remains a part of most Ph.D. programs in the arts and sciences, other doctoral programs, notably in education, business, and psychology, have reduced or eliminated the requirement. In these cases, additional course work is sometimes substituted or computer literacy has become an acceptable substitute.

Criticisms of the foreign language requirement are many—that it is no longer a functional tool, that the "general culture" justification is out-of-date, that it serves to discourage able students—and modifications will continue to be made. The admonition to examine departmental rather than institutional standards thus gains strength.

THE THESIS, PROJECT, AND DISSERTATION. When a thesis is required for the master's degree, its purpose is often described as a "comprehensive survey of a specific area of knowledge." The doctoral thesis or dissertation, on the other hand, is typically expected to be the result of substantial research in an area of interest providing an "original contribution to the advancement of knowledge" in a given discipline. The distinction is essentially in the "original contribution" stipulation of the dissertation as compared to the "survey" nature of the master's thesis.

As with all other graduate degree requirements, however, variety abounds. The master's thesis may actually be an essay or an essay-length report of a research or creative project, or a recital, or an exhibition of art works, or a musical composition, or a combination of almost any of these. Schools which use the terms "essay," "paper," or "report" are generally implying a more limited length or depth of content than suggested by the term "thesis." As indicated above, the thesis or similar requirement is made only by some schools and departments, and nonthesis options of additional course work are usually available. As a rule, the thesis is included in total credit-hour requirements; that is, three to six semester hours (or the equivalent in quarter hours) are given for the completed thesis toward the thirty-two hours customarily required. Exceptions are theses or projects for the two-year professional master's degrees, where more credit is typically assigned toward the total semester or quarter-hour requirement.

The length of a master's thesis may be anywhere from fifty to three hundred and fifty pages, but the average is probably around one hundred pages. The doctoral dissertation is rarely less than one hundred pages and ranges up to five hundred pages or more. Although some professors are fond of relating stories about superb dissertations ten pages long, the student is advised not to cling to such fragile hopes.

With diligence and careful planning, the dissertation can be written in less than a year, especially if research material is gathered and sorted while the candidate is still engaged in course work. Unfortunately, the temptation to delay commencement of research or writing until completion of other degree requirements is strong, obviously resulting in increased difficulty when the project is finally begun.

The "contribution to knowledge" aspect of the doctoral dissertation has been increasingly diluted in favor of "significance and relevance." This trend is intended to counter the tendency to seek novelty of concept or subject matter, a practice that often leads to dissertations that are "islands of minutiae in a sea of trivia." To compensate for the peripheral quality of many dissertation topics, departments may emphasize the interpretive and critical approach in preference to pure research.

Whatever the faults or virtues of the master's thesis and doctoral dissertation, there is little doubt that it is for most students the single most satisfying experience in graduate study.

SIXTH-YEAR PROGRAMS. Some mention must be made of the certificates of advanced study available in certain professional fields, notably education and engineering, but occasionally in other areas. These programs fill the need for refresher training beyond the master's, and, it must be said, salary increments often reward those who complete this additional work.

The sixth-year certificate/diploma customarily requires at least one year of full-time study in residence, or the equivalent in part-time attendance. There is usually no language or thesis requirement, but a final project of a type promoting professional proficiency in specific areas is often required. The certificate of advanced study does not attempt to replace the doctorate, but is instead an intermediate program of graduate training.

The Professional School

All study beyond the undergraduate college is essentially "professional" in nature. The graduate school of arts and science was created primarily to train college teachers and scholars, even though most of those who hold master's and doctoral degrees do not enter higher education. But graduate training in fields other than the humanities and sciences is clearly designed for readily identifiable occupations.

Although there are no agreed demarcations, it can be fairly stated that some sixteen disciplines are the predominant arenas of postbaccalaureate professional study: architecture, business, dentistry, education, engineering, forestry, law, library science, medicine, nursing, optometry, pharmacy, public health, social work, theology, and veterinary medicine. Cases can be made for including under this label such fields as journalism and physical therapy, but for the purposes at hand these sixteen are most relevant.

Even this list could be winnowed further. The origins of formal education for just three professions predate those of all others by many decades. Training for these—law, medicine, theology—has developed independently of most forms of graduate study. Indeed, law schools still speak of work for the first law degree as "undergraduate," as if candidates could enter directly from high school. Many of the other programs still struggle for acceptance to fully recognized professional status for themselves, but remain as mere departments of larger divisions.

And make no mistake—the designation of an academic subdivision as a department or institute or school or college is a distinction important beyond simple academic snobbery. Professional "schools" within broader institutions have more stature than departments. They have more independent administrations and faculties, sometimes even their own boards of trustees. Often, they are able to detach their fund-raising activities from their parent institutions and thus have greater latitude in distribution of moneys separated from contributors. There is greater unity of purpose in, say, a graduate school of business administration than in a graduate school of arts and science, which is more often a collection of thirty or more mini-colleges pulling in separate directions. Faculties of *schools* are typically better paid than those of *departments* in the same fields. There is less jockeying for internal political advantage, because academic apples are not thrown together with professional oranges.

And in the current atmosphere of student specialization and vocationalism, professional schools have the upper hand in determining the direction of their institutions, while many liberal arts programs struggle with enrollment and fiscal problems. The following pages outline these schools and programs and briefly survey factors to be considered in selection, admission and degree requirements, and sources of financial aid. Much of the descriptive material contained in the previous section applies to professional schools as well, so these remarks are concerned only with the distinctive characteristics of these programs.

SELECTING A PROFESSIONAL SCHOOL

Professional schools often have been accused of unduly restricting enrollments at times of expanding need. Now, having rushed to meet urgently expressed national needs, educational institutions find themselves the targets of the reverse criticism: they went too far.

There are now oversupplies of teachers in some areas of the country; some say two for every job. New members of the bar are encountering stiffer competition, and there looms the previously unbelievable prospect of a surplus of doctors, dentists, and nurses. According to one estimate, if the United States merely sustains current output, by 1996 there will be half again as many doctors as in 1980, a slight decrease in dentists, and 30 percent more nurses. In a nation headed toward zero population growth, this prediction has been used as justification by federal agencies to attempt to limit aid for professional education to just loan programs.

The result of these trends will be to make professional

study even more difficult to undertake than it is already. Medical schools, for example, are talking tentatively about charging tuition that actually covers instructional expenses, meaning annual tuition could soon reach as high as $31,000 at some private institutions! This, not even counting living expenses, and when financial aid is far from munificent and federal cutbacks can be anticipated. Admission standards, too, may escalate still further, putting even the least glossy law and medical schools out of reach of all but the most capable applicants.

In the very short-lived meantime, students of above-average, if unspectacular, aptitude and credentials have reason to be hopeful about gaining entrance to some school in their chosen fields—as long as they are not unrealistically fussy about location and "image."

COST, SIZE, LOCATION. As with graduate schools of arts and science, costs for professional study vary widely, depending principally upon the field and the type of institutional or state support. Nearly all schools of veterinary medicine and forestry are affiliated with public institutions, so tuition expenses are correspondingly lower for state residents in those majors. The other professional schools are as likely to be under private sponsorship as public, so costs can differ substantially. Annual tuition ranges from about $1800 to $9000 at publicly supported schools, from

$15,000 to $25,000 at private schools, all escalating at an average rate of nearly 5 percent a year. The exceptions are the theological seminaries and schools of divinity. These are all privately controlled, yet tuitions may be as little as $1500 or as much as $7500. In general, tuition has been increasing by 6 to 7 percent each year. Always check with the institution in question regarding current tuition charges.

Student bodies of professional schools are customarily in the 200 to 500 range, but some exceed 3000 in enrollment and some seminaries have as few as 25 students. The great majority of professional schools are affiliated with universities, but divinity schools are more frequently parts of colleges or are autonomous. Increasingly, formerly independent law and medical schools are being absorbed into larger institutions or are joining with other institutions to form new entities.

Only the most populous states have schools offering all sixteen types of professional study. There are law schools in forty-eight states, medical and dental schools in forty-five, and veterinary schools in twenty-six. On the other hand, there is at least one graduate school of education and one theological school in every state. Under the circumstances, most full-time professional students can expect to enroll at institutions at much greater distance from their homes than their undergraduate colleges.

ADMISSION

The professional schools of law, medicine, dentistry, and veterinary medicine set rigorous entrance requirements and thus avoid the separate step of "admission to candidacy," not to mention the high attrition rate, of most graduate schools. It is not possible, therefore, to suggest that *any* college graduate can gain admission to some professional school in his chosen field. Nevertheless, admission is not always as difficult as is commonly supposed, if students are willing to consider professional schools without regard to location or to presumed reputation. (Since most types of professional schools must meet fairly high minimum criteria to retain accreditation by appropriate professional associations, it is probably safe to say that few truly "bad" schools exist.) Several factors influence the decisions of admission committees, and these should be understood by the potential applicant.

PREPARATION. Some professional schools are willing to consider applicants who do not hold a bachelor's degree certifying completion of a four-year undergraduate program. Schools of veterinary medicine and dentistry, for example, sometimes admit students with as little as two years of undergraduate study, though nearly all medical and law schools now require the bachelor's degree.

Undergraduate preparation need not have followed the curricula laid down in preprofessional programs. However, applicants to schools of medicine, dentistry, public health, engineering, nursing, pharmacy, and veterinary medicine should have completed programs that permitted substantial emphasis upon the natural and/or physical sciences. This does not mean, of course, that the diversity of background provided by study in the humanities and social sciences is to be minimized. In fact, basic work in English, humanities, and the social sciences are required for

medical school admission nearly as often as biology, chemistry, and physics.

Schools of law, business, social work, and theology are less likely to require specific undergraduate preparation. These schools emphasize in their catalogues that general liberal arts studies are more important for their students than specialized majors in fields thought to be closely related to the professions in question. Applicants to a law school, for example, might hold majors in economics, history, English, sociology, or even business administration.

CREDENTIALS. In addition to transcripts of undergraduate study completed, applicants to the types of professional schools discussed here are nearly always expected to provide one to four letters of recommendation and the scores on the standard tests available for each professional field (except theology). In many cases, the letters of recommendation may be replaced totally or in part by the recommendations of the undergraduate preprofessional faculty committees. Professional schools, particularly those in theology, often request character references as well as estimations of potential for study in the particular field.

Nearly all schools of dentistry, medicine, law, business, nursing, and veterinary medicine demand the results of the appropriate entrance examinations prepared and/or administered by the professional associations. These are as follows:

Dental Aptitude Test (DAT)—applications available from either the chosen dental school or from the Department of Testing Services, American Dental Association, 211 East Chicago Avenue, Suite 1840, Chicago, Ill. 60611-2678; (312)440-2689.

Graduate Management Admissions Test (GMAT)—applications available from Graduate Management Admissions Test, P.O. Box 6101, Princeton, N.J. 08541-601; (601) 771-7330.

Graduate Record Examination (GRE)—application available from Graduate Record Examinations, Education Testing Service, P.O. Box 6000, Princeton, N.J. 08541-6000; (609)771-7670 or in the California Bay Area (510) 654-1200.

Law School Admission Test (LSAT)—applications from Law School Council, Box 2000, Newtown, Pa. 18940; (215) 968-1001.

Medical College Admission Test (MCAT)—applications available from MCAT Program Office, P.O. Box 4065, Iowa City, Ia. 52243; (319)337-1276.

Miller Analogies Test (MAT)—applications available from The Psychological Corporation, 555 Academic Court, San Antonio, Tx. 78204; (800)622-3231 or (210) 299-1061.

National League of Nursing Graduate Nursing Examination (NLNGNE)—information from nursing schools offering graduate study.

Optometry Admission Test (OAT)—applications from Optometry Admission Testing Program, 211 East Chicago Avenue, Suite 1840, Chicago, Ill. 60611-2678; (312)440-2693.

Pharmacy College Admission Test (PCAT)—applications available from The Psychological Corporation, 555 Academic Court, San Antonio, Tx. 78204; (800)622-3231 or (210)299-1061.

Praxis Series Tests (Includes NTE and PPST)—applications available from The Praxis Series, P.O. Box 6051, Educational Testing Service, Princeton, N.J. 08541-6051; (800)772-9476 or (609)771-7395.

Test of English as a Foreign Language, Test of Written English (TOEFL, TSE, TWE)—applications available from TOEFL, P.O. Box 6151, Princeton, N.J. 08541-6151; (609)771-7100.

Veterinary College Admission Test (VCAT)—applications from The Psychological Corporation, 555 Academic Court, San Antonio, Tx. 78204; (800)622-3231 or (210) 299-1061.

A majority of professional schools require a qualifying interview by invitation for the semifinalist applicants, but this is not universal. For medical and dental schools, the interview usually follows preliminary screening of applications.

DEADLINES. Medical and dental schools customarily accept applications for admission starting in July of the year preceding the proposed term of entrance. Most medical schools set closing dates for receipt of completed applications in January or February, although these dates are now often flexible. Dental schools accept applications as late as May. Preliminary applications are sometimes required, followed by formal applications from those who pass the initial screening.

The other types of professional schools generally accept applications well into the summer preceding the term of entrance, although some of the more prestigious schools have deadlines in January. It is to be remembered that most professional schools restrict entrance for beginning students to the Fall term, or occasionally to the Summer and Fall terms.

COMMON APPLICATION SERVICES. In an effort to ease the burden on students intent on applying for admission—and to cut their own clerical cost—most law, medical, and dental schools have subscribed to the services of centralized processing agencies. These offices accept academic credentials and other data from applicants, summarizing them in uniform formats and passing them on to the designated schools. The clearinghouses do not offer advisement and do not make admission decisions; that remains the province of the schools themselves. After ascertaining whether the schools in which the student is interested employ the relevant service, he or she should write to it as follows:

Law School Admission Council (LSAC)—or write the Law Services, Box 2000, 661 Penn Street, Newtown, Pa. 18940-0977; (215) 968-1314.

American Association of Colleges of Osteopathic Medicine Application Service (AACOMAS)—for applications information contact AACOMAS, 6110 Executive Boulevard, Suite 405, Rockville Md. 20852; (301)468-0990.

American Medical College Application Service (AMCAS)—obtain an AMCAS Application Request Card from participating medical schools or from premedical advisers in the undergraduate college, or by writing directly to AMCAS, Section for Student Services. AAMC, 2450 N St. NW, Suite 2011, Washington, D.C. 20037-1131; (202)828-0600.

American Association of Dental Schools Application Service (AADSAS)—request an AADSAS Application Request Card from participating dental schools or write to AADSAS, 1625 Massachusetts Ave., NW, #101, Washington, D.C. 20036.

There is a fee associated with these applications, usually escalating with the number of schools to which the materials are to be sent. Some of the schools require supplementary materials and/or an interview. A few expect payment of additional application fees.

STANDARDS. It is probably safe to say that at least between 40% and 50% of the applicants to professional schools are accepted for admission, a little less than that for law, medicine, and dentistry and higher for the other professional schools. Allowing for duplication of applications, available statistics suggest that an even larger percentage of students eventually gain entrance to some school, perhaps as many as two-thirds of all applicants.

Most professional schools seek students with undergraduate grade-point averages of "B." Depending on the degree of competition created by numbers of applicants, this may be interpreted to mean an average as low as "C plus" or as high as "A minus." It is generally agreed, in any event, that the grade average is the single most reliable predictor of success in postbaccalaureate professional studies. While the scores on the various entrance exams are undeniably important in the deliberations of admissions committees, students should not expect strong scores to outweigh mediocre grades in undergraduate course work, even if the degree is from a prestigious institution.

FINANCIAL ASSISTANCE

Professional study is expensive, and although various forms of aid are available, most students must plan to meet costs through loans or their own resources. Most professional schools provide limited numbers of scholarships and fellowships from institutional funds. Low-cost loans are widely available through governmental agencies, professional associations, and private or community groups, in addition to the schools themselves.

The Federal Health Professions Educational Assistance Act has established scholarship and loan programs. Students apply for these through the individual schools to which they seek admission. Research fellowships are awarded by many medical and dental schools in exchange for laboratory assistance during the summer months. Most professional schools assist the spouses of students in obtaining local or institutional employment. Although part-time employment is usually discouraged for students, this possibility should be explored. Finally, some schools have teaching or research assistantships or fellowships for advanced students.

THE STRUCTURE OF PROFESSIONAL STUDY

Programs leading to first degrees require four years of full-time study for the medical, veterinary, and dental professions, three years of full-time study or the equivalent in part-time attendance (when permitted) for law, and usually two years for the other fields.

Since practice in the medical/veterinary/dental professions demands both clinical skills and thorough understanding of the physical and natural sciences, students in these fields can expect balanced study in both these aspects of training. The first two years are spent in work in the basic and preclinical sciences, while the last two are devoted largely to clinical work. There are no language or thesis requirements as in the graduate school, and summers are usually free.

Law students can anticipate a beginning year of introductory work, usually conducted in lecture classes. The following two years permit more latitude in course selection, and seminars are more commonly available. Course work is generally supplemented by tutorial work emphasizing training in research and various forms of legal writing. First professional degrees in religion usually follow this same pattern, but variations are many.

In the other professions, a full-time two-year program (or its equivalent) is the norm, with the exception of those fields in which graduate study is primarily a continuation of undergraduate work, as in architecture and pharmacy. In many areas, undergraduate study in the field will reduce credit requirements for the graduate degree.

Most medical, dental, and veterinary schools offer advanced study beyond the first degree in both clinical and research specializations. Graduate study in law and religion is also available, though proportionally less common. Such programs are generally administered by the graduate schools of the institutions with which the professional schools are affiliated, and students usually must meet admission and degree requirements established by both the graduate and professional divisions. Sometimes graduate work is given through the professional school itself, especially if the school is located at a medical center separated from the main campus of the institution.

Programs leading to professional degrees are demanding, and standards of performance are rigorous, but the rewards are substantial. If the potential student is realistic in selecting a school consistent with his interests and aptitudes, the experience will test his mind and spirit and lead to the kind of lifelong fulfillment few others are fortunate to enjoy.

UNDERSTANDING THE ENTRIES

The information on the following pages describes the structure and content of the institutional entries that make up the main portion of this volume. For the entries to be of maximum value, it is important that the reader properly interpret the data provided.

The entries contain the kinds of basic information a potential applicant is likely to seek in choosing a graduate school. Careful examination of the school descriptions should aid the student in reaching realistic preliminary decisions. Since admission standards and requirements, course offerings, and financial-aid opportunities are subject to frequent revision, it is not to be assumed that the entries can replace individual school bulletins.

Several points must be kept in mind. The listed institutions were asked to supply figures on enrollment and faculty and percentages of applications accepted and grants of financial aid awarded. When possible, estimates for the 1996–97 academic year were supplied. Generally, however, these are actual statistics for 1995–96.

All institutions in this *Guide* are accredited by the appropriate national, regional, and/or professional accrediting associations. Although no agency is specifically charged with the accreditation of graduate schools, those schools which are part of properly approved colleges and universities are all included. Among the associations that assign accreditation of independent professional schools as well as those affiliated with larger institutions are the Liaison Committee on Medical Association, the Commission on Accreditation of the Council on Social Work Education, the American Dental Association, and the American Veterinary Medical Association.

Every effort has been made to render these data understandable without reference to elaborate indexes of codes and abbreviations. However, some symbols, other than abbreviations for degrees and commonly required entrance examinations, have been used. For example, the names of some colleges and universities and of some divisions of universities are followed by two asterisks (**). This means that these institutions did not take advantage of the opportunity to revise their entries from the last edition of the *Guide*. One asterisk denotes incomplete information.

Another symbol regularly used throughout this book is the "diacritical" or "stroke" mark, as in "teaching/research." As employed here, the stroke means *only* "and/or."

The following pages describe in detail the kinds of information to be found under each entry, in the same order. The items listed below are not included in every entry, either because they are not relevant or because specific data were not available.

GENERAL CHARACTERISTICS OF THE INSTITUTION

Name of the institution. The colleges and universities are arranged in alphabetical order according to the most important word in the title. Separate institutional entries are provided for individual university centers that are either autonomously administered or distinct in character or offerings. An institutional index for further assistance is at the back of the book.

Mailing address of the main campus. The name of the city and state in which the main campus offering graduate study is located, plus the zip code. When individual graduate or professional departments or schools are located in other towns or cities, that fact is noted in the body of the text. Internet Web sites are also included when available.

Founding date. Usually the year the institution was chartered, but sometimes the year classes were started or the year of the opening of another institution from which the present one developed.

Location in direction and miles from nearest major city. Direction from nearest major city is given in appropriate capital letters (NW, SE). The mileage given is approximate road distance. Often the city named is relatively small but sufficiently well known, and is given only to establish the location of the main campus.

Coed, men only, or women only. Relatively few institutions limit their graduate enrollments to students of one sex. When the undergraduate program is thus restricted, and the graduate programs are not, it is stated: "Coed on the graduate level."

Type of control. If the institution is supported primarily by public funds, the level of government is specified, whether state, county, or municipal. Occasionally, institutions receive substantial amounts of financial support from the state or city government but decision-making powers are retained by the board of trustees. In other cases, individual divisions of universities are totally or mostly supported by public funds. In these instances, control is often shared. When appropriate, these situations are noted.

Many private institutions are sponsored by religious denominations, and this affiliation is mentioned. Although few such colleges and universities restrict their enrollments to members of the sponsoring churches, students may be expected to adhere to certain basic social or curricular requirements. Institutions that are open only to members of particular denominations or to the clergy are not listed in this book unless they are divisions of larger institutions that are not otherwise restricted. This is also true of colleges offering training only for the clergy of particular churches.

Semester, quarter, or trimester system. The semester system provides study during two terms of a nine-month academic year and, usually, during one or more summer sessions. The quarter system divides the calendar year into four equal terms, the trimester into three. Under all three systems, students typically attend classes for about nine months. For no apparent historical reason, Western colleges and universities most often operate on the quarter system, those in the East on the semester. The trimester is still relatively uncommon but has met favor in some sections.

Major research facilities. Special institutes, laboratories, interdepartmental and interinstitutional programs and resources are mentioned. The list is not intended to be exhaustive, but only to note distinctive offerings or equipment and to suggest their scope. Since this information is not always available, its absence does not necessarily mean that special facilities do not exist at any given institution.

Library. This figure is the total number of bound volumes in the institution's collections; when available, a figure for microforms and current periodicals are also included when available. When special collections or several libraries at different centers are available, the figure represents the combined number of volumes. If the term "capacity" is used, it can be assumed that fewer volumes are actually in stock and that this figure is not available. If "items" is used instead of "volumes," the figure includes periodicals and similar materials in addition to books.

Annual tuition charges for full-time students. Many public institutions use the term "fees" rather than "tuition," often with additional "tuition" for out-of-state students. This semantic distinction is often employed to maintain the illusion of tuition-free institutions. As used here, "fees" refers only to basic expense of course work and does not include the additional charges for use of laboratory and similar facilities. Generally, the cost of tuition and/or fees at public institutions is greater for nonresidents than for residents, while there is usually no such distinction at private colleges and universities. On occasion, still a third level of tuition is charged foreign students. When no flat-rate tuition is set for full-time students, the per hour charge is given.

Throughout this book, "annual" refers to the academic, not the calendar, year. It also should be remembered that tuition charges are constantly on the rise, increasing at an annual rate at most institutions. This fact has been anticipated when possible, and the charges indicated are customarily for the 1996–97 year.

Part-time tuition charges. Schedules of charges are either per credit (or semester or quarter) hour, or according to varying ranges of hours, *i.e.,* $100 for 1–4 hours, $200 for 5–8 hours, and so on. As above, charges are indicated for both resident and nonresident students, when appropriate. Charges indicated are for graduate or professional students only. Tuition scales for undergraduate students sometimes differ and are not listed. If charges are mainly the same for most divisions of a university, any specific difference is noted under this heading *or* under the divisional heading. Unless so indicated, the tuition stated in the general institutional paragraph applies to all divisions.

On-campus housing available. Many institutions are unable to provide separate statistics for housing available to graduate students only. Therefore, unless noted as "for 100 graduate men," the figures given are for all students, both undergraduate and graduate. In this event, it may be assumed that graduate students are eligible for such housing. The figure given for married student housing should be interpreted as family units, while the figure for men and women refers to individual spaces only. "On-campus housing" means institutionally owned or controlled housing and does not include private accommodations. Only one or two colleges indicate that nearby privately owned, off-campus housing is *not* available. Graduate students who choose to live in institutional housing must remember that they are usually expected to observe the restrictions in force for all residents.

Average academic year housing cost. This is for the academic year only. When housing is available to graduate students only during the summer, the summer housing cost is provided. These figures relate only to the cost of university-owned or operated housing, not to private accommodations. The cost described is generally for the middle range, and variations depend upon the nature of accommodations. Unless otherwise specified, figures are for rent or room charges only, not board.

Title of housing officer. This notes the titles of the officers to contact for on- and off-campus housing information. If only one officer is named, he provides information for both institutional and private accommodations unless otherwise indicated.

GRADUATE AND PROFESSIONAL DIVISION REQUIREMENTS AND OFFERINGS

Name of division. The full proper name is usually given. If there is no separate graduate or professional school within the institution, this section is simply headed "Graduate Study" or "Graduate Program."

Founding date. The year graduate study began or when the division was established or affiliated may be given.

Location if other than main campus. In the case of professional schools, graduate study may be offered at two or more centers or in a different city.

Tuition and housing. These are given only if they are different from those indicated in the general institutional paragraph. This is most often true of professional schools.

Enrollment. Figures are for graduate or postbaccalaureate students only, if the division offers undergraduate courses as well. In rare cases, the statistics are for all enrolled students in the division, both graduate and undergraduate. If so, this fact is noted. The figures are usually broken down into full- and part-time enrollments, and the percentages of men and women for the combined total. On occasion, the latter figures refer either to the full- or part-time figure.

Faculty. This is the total number of faculty teaching graduate courses on a full- and/or parttime basis. This is often the least reliable statistic of all, for it is not always possible for institutions to make cut-and-dried distinctions between faculty members teaching primarily graduate or undergraduate students. Where possible, some clarification has been noted.

Types of degrees conferred. All master's, sixth-year, and doctoral level degrees are listed. Abbreviations often differ for the same degree, as in M.A. or A.M., D.Sc. or Sc.D. In the engineering master's degree, the subject field is often part of the formal title, such as "M.S. in Chemical Engineering." To conserve space when many such master's degrees are offered, the subject field has been deleted. Abbreviations have been used wherever possible, such as C.A.S. (Certificate of Advanced Standing); consult the list beginning on page xxvii.

ADMISSION REQUIREMENTS

Credentials required in support of application. This paragraph lists all documents, entrance examinations, interviews, and other requirements for admission to all programs and degrees. Since virtually all graduate schools expect applicants to hold a bachelor's degree, only exceptions to this normal requirement are mentioned. Professional schools, on the other hand, may admit students with fewer than four years of undergraduate study. The minimum number of pre-professional years is usually indicated in law, medical, dental, and veterinary school entries. Transcripts of previous undergraduate and graduate study (when applicable) are always required in support of applications for admission. Generally, applicants must submit one transcript from each college or university attended. In some cases, however, transcripts must be provided in duplicate. The opening words "Two transcripts . . ." refer to this requirement.

Many schools request one or more letters of recommendation. Ordinarily, the applicant is asked to have the letters sent directly to the school. In other cases, the names of the persons willing to send recommendations are requested in the application, and the school takes the responsibility of obtaining the letters.

When the Graduate Record Examination (GRE) is required, the specific test, whether General and/or Subject, is noted wherever possible.

Many graduate schools accept students in special or nonmatriculant categories without prior submission of these credentials. In this *Guide,* degree and admission requirements refer only to those students intending to seek degrees.

Additional requirements for admission. Individual programs, schools, or departments sometimes request supplementary credentials in addition to those mentioned above. This is generally due to the professional nature of the program in question or to the need to have more data available. Entrance examinations such as the Miller Analogies Test (MAT) or the Graduate Management Admissions Test (GMAT) are typical of these extra requirements. Potential art majors often must submit portfolios of their work, and music majors may have to audition. Mention is made of additional requirements only if they pertain to two or more departments. Otherwise, special notice is made in the appropriate departmental listing under the *Fields of Study* section.

Transfer applicants. Most graduate and professional schools accept transfer applicants from similar institutions. Generally speaking, no more than 20 to 25 percent of the total course work for the master's degree is allowed for work completed at other graduate schools. The amount of advanced standing permitted toward the doctorate varies widely, but usually at least the equivalent of the master's degree is granted as transfer credit. Some schools are willing to consider transfer applicants, but not with advanced standing. Graduate schools often give advanced standing only after a student has completed study in residence.

Graduates of unaccredited institutions. Most graduate schools are willing to consider applicants from colleges or universities that do not hold approval from one of the six regional accrediting associations. Therefore, *only* those graduate schools that do *not* consider such applicants have statements to that effect. Special testing is often demanded of graduates of unaccredited colleges, or formal admission may be conditional upon satisfactory performance in residence.

Restrictions upon terms of entrance. Individual departments of graduate schools may restrict entrance to only the Fall semester, or to the Fall and Summer terms. Medical and dental schools nearly always admit only for the Fall, whereas law schools often permit initial entrance to other terms as well. It is usually preferable to begin in the Fall, whether or not such restrictions are set.

Title of admitting officer and dates of application. This refers to the officer of the college from whom application forms can be obtained. The completed forms and supporting documents are customarily returned to the same officer. Closing dates for filing applications follow, and should be carefully observed. These dates are generally final, and all supporting credentials must be received with the application by these deadlines for the terms indicated. In some cases, no firm deadlines are set but *preferred* dates are suggested. The applicant is advised to apply well in advance in any event, and both the applications for admission *and* financial aid should be submitted by the date indicated in the *Financial Aid* section. Information on closing dates for all terms is not always available, so it should not be implied that no summer term exists simply because no closing date is mentioned for that term.

Application fee. This information is not always available. Its absence here does not necessarily mean that no fee is required.

Telephone and fax numbers and E-mail addresses. The number listed in both the Admission Requirements and the Financial Aid sections is a general contact number and is being supplied for a preliminary applicant's convenience only.

ADMISSION STANDARDS

These are characterized as "very competitive," "competitive," "very selective," "selective," or "relatively open." The schools were asked to specify whether they accepted less than 10% of their applicants (very competitive), or 10% to 20% (competitive), 20% to 50% (very selective), or 50% to 75% (selective). Those schools indicating they accepted nearly all applicants with the appropriate undergraduate baccalaureate are categorized as "relatively open." Since standards vary from department to department within graduate schools, this item often will be stated as, for example, "Very competitive for some departments, competitive for the others," or some similarly appropriate combination. It must be recognized that the quality of credentials of the groups of applicants to different institutions varies widely, and the degree of difficulty of admission must be interpreted accordingly. In other words, the most highly regarded institutions naturally attract applications from superior students in greater numbers than do less favored schools. Therefore, "competitive" standards at a top graduate school cannot be assumed to be dealing with the same level of applicants as "competitive" admissions policies at less prestigious institutions.

Caution must be taken in equating difficulty of admission with quality of program. While there is clearly some relationship between the strength of the student body and the effectiveness of the program, this is less true on the graduate than on the undergraduate level. Limited facilities may restrict enrollment and therefore produce an image of quality due to the resultant low number of applicants accepted. On the other hand, departments offering study in fields that do not require substantial special facilities may be willing to accept larger proportions of applicants without reduction in the quality of the student body.

One more point: the statement of degree of selectivity of admission standards is generally that reported by the institutions listed. On occasion, graduate schools may overestimate the difficulty of their standards. Statistics may have been interpreted differently from school to school in responding to this inquiry. When other available data clearly have indicated that the stated admission standards of particular institutions do not accurately reflect the standards actually employed, this statement has been altered accordingly. In the main, however, statements of standards are presented in the entries as reported by the institutions.

Usual minimum undergraduate average. The schools were asked to specify the overall, or cumulative, undergraduate grade-point average they customarily require. For these purposes, all reported averages were converted to the most widely used 4-point system (A = 4, B = 3, C = 2, D = 1). Normally, graduate schools expect somewhat higher averages in the proposed field of graduate study. Since this requirement varies with departments, lack of space has not permitted inclusion of this information. It must be remembered that the grade-point average stated here is not necessarily the absolute "floor" but that typically required for unconditional matriculation. Many schools offer limited matriculation to students below the reported grade-point average. As with the characterizations of admissions policies above, this information is offered merely as a guide. Some institutions overestimate their selectivity; others receive most of their applications from colleges with very difficult grading systems. Thus, it is possible to be described as "selective" (accepting up to 75% of all applicants) and have a 3.0 minimum grade average, or to be "competitive" with a 2.25 required average.

In the case of professional schools, often exceedingly competitive, the usual minimum average required is replaced here by a statement as to the number of total annual applications accepted to fill each new first-year class.

FINANCIAL AID

Types of aid other than loans. Scholarships, fellowships, internships, assistantships, tuition waivers, and traineeships are the most common forms of aid available. As given here, they are grants offered from institutional funds or from aid programs administered by the college or university in question. This line also specifies the type of service required of the recipient, when appropriate. For this revision, the actual number of each type of grant annually awarded is given, when available. Since these figures generally include renewals to old students, it cannot be assumed that all those listed are solely for entering students. Nevertheless, some conclusions can be drawn about actual aid available. Scholarships rarely have service requirements, and the term "fellowship" is often used in lieu of "scholarship." Thus, an entry reading "Scholarships, fellowships, teaching/research assistantships" means that no service is required in exchange for the first two forms of aid, while those who hold assistantships are expected to assume either teaching or research responsibilities, or both. Duties may involve direct assistance in research to a particular faculty member, or general responsibilities within a department, such as grading papers or assisting in laboratory experiments or demonstrations. Fellowships and assistantships typically carry a tuition remission privilege plus an annual stipend. Since fellowships are generally regarded as the more prestigious of the two types of award, the stipend is often larger than for assistantships and the tasks assigned may be more challenging in nature. This is subject to broad variations between departments and schools, however. In medical and dental schools, scholarships are usually the only form of aid other than loans available during the academic year. Many of these schools also award research fellowships for intervening summer sessions when regular classes are not in session.

To whom to apply, and the closing date. It is often necessary to apply to different persons or offices for the kinds of aid available. If no deadline date is set, it is wise to apply by February 1 or earlier to receive maximum consideration. Scholarships and fellowships are often awarded through a central committee of a graduate school, while assistantships are typically granted by the department offering study in the proposed major field. As a result, it may be necessary to contact as many as three or four persons or offices to obtain information about various forms of aid. All graduate and professional schools require interested students to apply for financial aid using the Free Application for Federal Student Aid (FAFSA) and the Graduate and Professional School Financial Aid Service (GAPSFAS), Box 2614, Princeton, NJ 08540, or other financial aid services.

Percentage of students receiving aid other than loans. The percentage given here relates to the number of students awarded scholarships, fellowships, assistantships, and other grants (but not loans) from *both* internal *and* external sources. The latter includes grants provided by private and governmental agencies. Unfortunately, it is not always possible to determine whether the percentages refer to the total graduate enrollment, both full- and part-time, or solely to the full-time student body. Normally, however, the figures are for the entire student group, regardless of full- or part-time status. In any event, this factor changes so rapidly from year to year that the percentages must be considered only as rough estimates.

Aid available to part-time students. It is by no means universal practice to make aid, even loans, available to part-time students. This line states whether or not such aid, including loans, is offered.

DEGREE REQUIREMENTS

For master's degrees. This section begins with the minimum total number of credit (or semester or quarter) hours that must be completed for the master's, followed by the minimum number of hours to be completed in residence at the institution granting the degree. As used here, and throughout this book, "residence" refers to *credit hours completed while in full-* or *part-time attendance at the institution granting the degree.* Therefore, the difference in credit hour requirements between the minimum number for the degree and the number to be completed "in residence" is the number of hours accepted in transfer from other graduate or professional schools. In those cases where residence credit hours must be completed while in attendance as a full-time student, the entry reads "at least 24 in full-time residence." If the residence and full-time attendance requirements differ, this is normally stated as "at least 24 in residence and 18 in full-time attendance."

If a student may elect whether or not to complete a thesis in partial fulfillment of degree requirements, both options are stated in terms of minimum total and residence credit hours. For example: "24 credit hours plus thesis, at least 18 in residence, *or* 30 hours without thesis, at least 24 in residence." These options are stated in different ways, generally in accordance with the terminology of the school being reported.

Listed next are additional degree requirements: qualifying, candidacy, or final exams; thesis or final projects; language or other research tools. If any of these requirements are only for particular majors or departments, this fact is noted: "thesis for most departments; final oral exam for some departments," etc. Most graduate schools stress that the requirements specified are minimums only, and that additional credit hours, exams, or the like may be stipulated, depending upon the candidate's previous background, his performance in, or the special nature of, a particular program. In practice, such variations are more likely to occur at the doctoral rather than the master's level.

Schools always point out that admission to study does not imply automatic admission to candidacy. Advancement to formal candidacy for the degree depends upon successful completion of a variety of requirements, such as the filing of an acceptable thesis plan, appointment of a faculty thesis committee, and/or language tests or candidacy exams. This is true for both the master's and doctoral degrees.

For sixth-year degrees or certificates. The number of credit hours required is generally given as a minimum total "beyond the bachelor's" *or* "beyond the master's." Ordinarily, there are relatively few requirements other than course work, but a thesis or project and/or final exam may be expected. Sixth-year certificates are given primarily in the fields of education and engineering.

For doctoral degrees. As with the sixth-year certificate, the number of hours is given as a minimum total beyond the bachelor's or master's. However, many institutions do not specify a set number of credits for the doctorate, choosing instead to state the residence requirements in terms of semesters or years. (This is occasionally true of the master's as well.) In this case, it can be assumed that the years or semesters of residence required may be completed in equivalent part-time attendance, unless otherwise specified. As mentioned above, "residence" refers to hours completed while in full- *or* part-time attendance at the institution granting the degree. In those cases where residence credit must be completed while in full-time attendance, the entry specifies "in full-time residence." Further, the number of hours (or semesters or years) to be completed in residence is the total required for the doctorate minus maximum possible transfer credit beyond the master's or bachelor's, as indicated.

The nature and scope of the doctoral dissertation and/or project vary for each type of degree. The dissertation for the Ph.D. is normally expected to show technical mastery of the major field and to offer an original contribution to the existing body of knowledge in the field. For the Ed.D. and other professional doctorates, the dissertation is likely to be based upon a specific project designed to fully develop research skills and to contribute new knowledge to the professional field.

FIELDS OF STUDY

Areas of concentration or academic departments. These are arranged alphabetically, usually in the manner listed in the school bulletin; that is, if several divisions contribute programs to the graduate school, the fields of study are noted under each division. Since titles of major fields or departments vary from school to school, the reader should look carefully for the programs that interest him or her. For instance, various engineering majors are listed *either* individually *or* under one department heading. This is often true of education programs as well. To take another example, a biological sciences department may include majors in biochemistry, microbiology, zoology, or these may be in a variety of other combinations. "Art history" is sometimes called "history of art" or "fine arts"; "political science" might be "government" or simply "politics." Further, the Ph.D. in a particular field might be offered by one division while the master's in the same field is offered by another school within the university. Still another complication is the fact that some majors are offered by more than one school or department or even at two or more centers of an institution.

Special majors. Following each departmental listing, if necessary, is a clarification of available majors. The name of the department may not be self-explanatory, so it might be stated, for example: *"Art.* Studio art, art history, art education," or *"Modern Languages.* French, German, Span-

ish." In other cases, special notice is made of unusual majors or of majors not ordinarily found under a particular departmental heading. This is then stated: *"English.* Includes creative writing." The "includes" gives notice that the other more common majors of the field are available. It is important to remember that only fields which offer programs leading to at least one degree are listed. Departments that simply contribute courses to degrees are not mentioned.

Special degree or admission requirements. Notation is made of degree or admission requirements which deviate from those outlined in the general paragraphs, whether in addition to, or in lieu of, those stated above. This can include special entrance examinations, such as the MAT, or extra credit hours for the degree. If no such mention is made, it can be assumed that the general requirements apply.

Types of degrees awarded. This is stated only if appropriate degrees are not awarded in particular departments on all levels conferred by the school. For example, if both master's and doctoral degrees are granted by the school, but the Music Department offers only the M.F.A., the listing reads *"Music.* M.F.A. only." Without this notation, it can be assumed the department offers all the degrees appropriate to the field in question. Occasionally, an additional degree not listed under the general headings is mentioned here, but only if of a special nature.

KEY TO ABBREVIATIONS

MASTER'S DEGREES

A.M.	Master of Arts
E.M.B.A.	Executive Master of Business Administration
LL.C.M.	Master of Comparative Law
LL.M.	Master of Law
M.A.	Master of Arts
M.A.A.	Master of Applied Art, Master of Administrative Arts, Master of Aeronautics and Astronautics
M.A.A.A.	Master of Arts in Arts Administration
M.A.A.B.S.	Master of Arts in Applied Behavioral Sciences
M.A.A.E.	Master of Arts in Applied Economics, Master of Aeronautical and Astronautical Engineering, Master of Arts in Art Education
M.A.Am.St.	Master of Arts in American Studies
M.A.A.O.M.	Master of Arts in Applied Organizational Management
M.A.A.T.	Master of Arts in Art Therapy
M.Acc.	Master of Accounting
M.Accy.	Master of Accountancy
M.A.B.S.	Master of Arts in Behavior Science
M.A.C.	Master of Arts in Communications
M.A.C.A.	Master of Arts in Computer Applications
M.A.C.E.	Master of Arts in Computer Education
M.A.C.P.	Master of Arts in Community Psychology, Master of Arts in Counseling Psychology
M.A.C.T.A.	Master of Arts in Computer Teaching Applications
M.A.C.C.T.	Master of Arts in Community College
M.Ad.	Master of Administration
M.A.Ad.Ed.	Master of Arts in Adult Education
M.A.C.T.	Master of Arts in College Teaching
M.A.E.	Master of Agricultural Extension, Master of Agricultural Engineering, Master of Aerospace Engineering
M.A.Ed.	Master of Arts in Education
M.Ag.	Master of Agriculture
M.Ag.Ed.	Master of Agricultural Education
M.Ag.Ext.	Master of Agricultural Extension
M.Aq.	Master of Aquacultures
M.A.FC.	Master of Arts in Family Counseling
M.A.H.	Master of Arts in Humanities
M.A.H.E.	Master of Arts in Human Ecology
M.A.H.E.& FE.	Master of Arts in Home Economics and Family Ecology
M.A.H.R.M.	Master of Arts in Human Resource Management
M.A.H.S.	Master of Human Services
M.A.H.S.M.	Master of Arts in Human Service Management
M.A.I.A.	Master of Arts in International Affairs
M.A.I.C.	Master of Arts in International Communication
M.A.I.D	Master of Arts in International Diplomacy, Master of Arts in Interior Design
M.A.I.R.	Master of Arts in International Relations
M.A.I.S.	Master of Arts in International Studies, Master of Arts in Interdisciplinary Studies
M.A.J.	Master of Arts in Journalism
M.A.L.A.	Master of Arts in Liberal Arts
M.A.L.D.	Master of Arts in Law and Diplomacy
M.A.L.S.	Master of Arts in Library Science, Master of Arts in Liberal Studies
M.A.L.T.	Master of Arts in Language Teaching
M.A.M.	Master of Arts Management, Master of Animal Medicine, Master of Aviation Management, Master of Agriculture and Management
M.A.M.B.	Master of Arts in Molecular Biology
M.A.M.C.	Master of Arts in Mass Communication
M.A.M.FC.	Master of Arts in Marriage and Family Counseling
M.A.M.F.C.C.	Master of Arts in Marriage, Family, and Child Counseling
M.A.M.F.T.	Master of Arts in Marriage and Family Therapy
M.A.M.R.D.	Master of Agricultural Management and Resource Development
M.A.O.M.	Master of Aerospace Operations Management
M.A.P.A.	Master of Arts in Public Administration, Master of Arts in Public Affairs
M.A.P.E.	Master of Arts in Physical Education
M.Appl.M.	Master of Applied Mathematics
M.Ap.Sc.	Master of Applied Science
M.A.P.P.	Master of Arts in Public Policy
M.A.P.R.S.	Master of Arts in Pacific Rim Studies
M.A.P.S.	Master of Arts in Pastoral Studies
M.A.Psych.	Master of Art in Psychology
M.A.R.	Master of Arts in Religion, Master of Arts in Research
M.Arch.	Master of Architecture
M.Arch.E.	Master of Architectural Engineering
M.Arch.H.	Master of Architectural History
M.Arch.U.D.	Master of Architecture in Urban Design

M.A.S.	Master of Actuarial Science, Master of Aeronautical Science, Master of Applied Statistics, Master of Archival Studies
M.A.S.A.C.	Master of Arts in Substance Abuse Counseling
M.A.T.	Master of Arts in Teaching
M.A.U.A.	Master of Arts in Urban Affairs
M.A.U.D.	Master of Arts in Urban Design
M.A.U.R.P	Master of Arts in Urban and Regional Planning
M.A.W.	Master of Arts in Writing
M.B.A.	Master of Business Administration
M.B.A.I.B.	Master of Business Administration in International Business
M.B.E.	Master of Business Education, Master of Business Economics, Master of Bilingual Education
M.B.I.	Master of Biological Illustration
M.B.S.	Master of Basic Science, Master of Behavioral Science, Master of Building Science
M.B.T.	Master of Business Taxation
M.C.	Master of Counseling, Master of Communication
M.C.A.	Master of Communication Arts
M.C.D.	Master of Communication Disorders
M.C.E.	Master of Chemical Engineering, Master of Civil Engineering
M.C.Ed.	Master of Continuing Education
M.Ch.E.	Master of Chemical Engineering
M.C.H.	Master of Community Health
M.C.I.S.	Master of Computer Information Systems
M.C.J.	Master of Comparative Jurisprudence, Master of Criminal Justice
M.C.J.A.	Master of Criminal Justice Administration
M.C.L.	Master of Comparative Law, Master of Civil Law
M.C.M.	Master of Church Music
M.C.P.	Master of City Planning, Master of Community Planning, Master of Counseling Psychology, Master of Community Psychology
M.Crim.	Master of Criminology
M.C.R.P.	Master of City and Regional Planning
M.C.S.	Master of Computer Science
M.C.Sc.	Master of Commercial Science
M.C.S.E.	Master of Computer Science and Engineering
M.Des.	Master of Design
M.Des.S.	Master of Design Studies
M.Div.	Master of Divinity
M.D.S.	Master of Dental Science, Master of Decision Sciences
M.E.	Master of Engineering
M.E.A.	Master of Engineering Administration, Master of Engineering Architecture
M.Ed.	Master of Education
M.C.E.	Master of Electrical and Computer Engineering
M.E.D.	Master of Environmental Design, Master of Education of the Deaf
M.E.E.	Master of Electrical Engineering
M.E.M.	Master of Engineering Management
M.E.M.S.	Master of Engineering in Manufacturing Systems
M.Eng.	Master of Engineering
M.E.PC.	Master of Environmental Pollution Control
M.E.Sc.	Master of Engineering Science
M.Env.Des.	Master of Environmental Design
M.Env.S.	Master of Environmental Science
M.Ex.St.	Master of Experimental Statistics
M.Ext.Ed.	Master of Extension Education
M.E.P	Master of Environmental Planning
M.E.R.	Master of Energy Resources
M.E.S.S.	Master of Exercise and Sports Science
M.E.T.	Master of Education in Teaching
M.F.	Master of Forestry, Master of Finance
M.F.A.	Master of Fine Arts
M.F.E.	Master of Forest Engineering
M.F.R.	Master of Forest Resources
M.F.S.	Master of Family Studies, Master of Foreign Service, Master of Forest Science, Master of Forensic Science
M.F.T.	Master of Family Therapy
M.G.A.	Master of Government Administration
M.G.E.	Master of Geological Engineering
M.G.S.	Master of General Studies, Master of Gerontological Studies
M.H.	Master of Health, Master of Humanities
M.H.A.	Master of Health Administration, Master of Hospital Administration
M.H.A.M.S.	Master of Historical Administration and Museum Studies
M.H.C.A.	Master of Health Care Administration
M.H.E.	Master of Health Education, Master of Higher Education, Master of Home Economics
M.H.E.	Master of Health Education, Master of Higher Education, Master of Human Ecology
M.H.K.	Master of Human Kinetics
M.H.M.	Master of Hotel Management
M.H.P	Master of Heritage Preservation, Master of Historical Preservation
M.H.R.	Master of Human Resources
M.H.R.M.	Master of Human Resources Management
M.H.S.	Master of Health Services, Master of Human Services, Master of Hispanic Studies
M.H.S.A.	Master of Health Services Administration
M.I.	Master of Insurance
M.I.A.	Master of International Affairs
M.I.B.	Master of International Business
M.I.B.A.	Master of International Business Administration
M.I.D.	Master of Industrial Design, Master of Interior Design
M.I.E.	Master of Industrial Engineering
M.I.L.R.	Master of Industrial and Labor Relations
M.I.L.S.	Master of Information and Library Science
M.Ind.Adm.	Master of Industrial Administration
M.Ind.Ed.	Master of Industrial Education
M.I.M.	Master of Industrial Management, Master of International Management
M.I.P.A.	Master of International Public Administration
M.I.P.P.	Master of International Public Policy
M.I.R.	Master of Industrial Relations
M.I.S.	Master of Individualized Studies, Master of Information Services, Master of Interdisciplinary Studies
M.J.	Master of Journalism Management
M.J.S.	Master of Juridical Science
M.L.	Master of Librarianship
M.L.A.	Master of Landscape Architecture, Master of Liberal Arts
M.L.A.U.D.	Master of Landscape Architecture in Urban Development
M.L.I.R.	Master of Labor and Industrial Relations
M.Lib.	Master of Librarianship
M.L.I.S.	Master of Library and Information Science
M.Lit.M.	Master of Liturgical Music
M.L.L.	Master of Law Librarianship
M.L.S.	Master of Legal Studies, Master of Liberal Studies, Master of Library Science, Master of Life Science
M.L.S.P.	Master of Law and Social Policy
M.L.&T.	Master of Law and Taxation
M.M.	Master of Music, Master of Management, Master of Mathematics

M.M.A.	Master of Marine Affairs, Master of Manpower Administration, Master of Medical Art, Master of Musical Art
M. Mat. E.	Master of Materials Engineering
M.M.B.	Master of Medical Biochemistry
M.M.C.	Master of Mass Communication
M.M.E.	Master of Material Engineering, Master of Mechanical Engineering, Master of Mineral Engineering
M.M.Ed.	Master of Music Education
M.M.F.C.C.	Master of Marriage, Family, and Child Counseling
M.M.F.T.	Master of Marriage and Family Therapy
M.Mgt.	Master of Management
M.M.I.S.	Master of Management Information Systems
M.M.M.E.	Master of Metallurgical and Materials Engineering
M.M.P.	Master of Marine Policy, Master of Museum Practice
M.M.R.	Master of Marketing Research
M.M.S.	Master of Management Science, Master of Marine Science, Master of Materials Science
M.M.Sc.	Master of Management Science, Master of Marine Science, Master of Medical Science
M.Mu.	Master of Music
M.Mus.	Master of Music
M.M.T	Master of Movement Therapy, Master of Music Teaching
M.N.	Master of Nursing
M.N.A.	Master of Nursing Administration, Master of Nonprofit Administration
M.Nat.Sci.	Master of Natural Science
M.N.E.	Master of Nuclear Engineering
M.N.Ed.	Master of Nursing Education
M.N.S.	Master of Nursing Science, Master of Nutritional Sciences, Master of Natural Sciences, Master of Nuclear Science
M.Nuc.Sc.	Master of Nuclear Science
M.O.B.	Master of Organizational Behavior
M.Oc.E.	Master of Oceanographic Engineering
M.Opt.	Master of Optometry
M.O.D.	Master of Organizational Development
M.O.E.	Master of Ocean Engineering
M.O.R.	Master of Operations Research
M.O.T.	Master of Occupational Therapy
M.P.	Master of Pharmacy, Master of Planning
M.P.A.	Master of Pubic Administration, Master of Public Affairs, Master of Professional Accounting
M.P.Acc.	Master of Public Accounting, Master of Professional Accounting
M.P.C.	Master of Professional Counseling, Master Public Communication
M.P.E.	Master of Physical Education
M.P.E.R.	Master of Personnel and Employee Relations
M.Pet.E.	Master of Petroleum Engineering
M.P.H.	Master of Public Health
M.P.H.Ed.	Master of Public Health Education
M.Pharm.	Master of Pharmacy
M.Phil.	Master of Philosophy
M.P.H.&T.M.	Master of Public Health and Tropical Medicine
M.P.I.A.	Master of Public and International Affairs
M.P.M.	Master of Personnel Management, Master of Public Management
M.P.M.&P.H.	Master of Preventive Medicine and Public Health
M.P.N.	Master in Psychiatric Nursing
M.P.P	Master of Public Policy
M.P.P.U.P.	Master of Public Policy and Urban Planning
M.Prof.Acc.	Master of Professional Accounting
M.P.P.P.M.	Master of Plant Protection and Pest Management

M.Pr.Met.	Master of Professional Meteorology
M.PR.T.M.	Master of Park, Recreation, and Tourism Management
M.Ps.Sc.	Master of Psychological Science
M.P.S.	Master of Personnel Services, Master of Political Science, Master of Public Service
M.P.T.	Master of Physical Therapy
M.P.V.M.	Master of Preventive Veterinary Medicine
M.Q.S.	Master of Quantitative Systems
M.R.A.	Master of Recreation Administration, Master of Rehabilitation Administration, Master of Resource Administration
M.R.C.	Master of Rehabilitation Counseling
M.R.C.P.	Master of Regional and Community Planning
M.R.E.	Master of Religious Education
M.R.Ed.	Master of Recreation Education
M.Rel.Ed.	Master of Religious Education
M.R.E.C.M.	Master of Real Estate and Construction Management
M.R.E.D.	Master of Real Estate Development
M.R.M.	Master of Resource Management
M.R.P	Master of Regional Planning
M.R.P.A.	Master of Recreation and Parks Administration
M.R.T.P.	Master of Rural and Town Planning
M.S.	Master of Science
M.S.A.	Master of Science in Accounting, Master of Science in Administration, Master of Sports Administration, Master of School Administration
M.S.A.A.E.	Master of Science in Aeronautical and Astronautical Engineering
M.S.A.C.M.	Master of Science in Acquisition and Contracts Management
M.S.A.E.	Master of Science in Aerospace Engineering, Master of Architectural Engineering
M.S.Ag.	Master of Science in Agriculture
M.S.Agr.E.	Master of Science in Agricultural Engineering
M.S.A.I.	Master of Science in Artificial Intelligence
M.S.A M.	Master of Science in Applied Mathematics
M.San.Sc. &P.H.	Master of Sanitary Science and Public Health
M.S.Ap.Sc.	Master of Science in Applied Science
M.S.A.S.	Master of Science in Architectural Studies
M.S.B.A.	Master of Science in Business Administration
M.S.B.E.	Master of Science in Biomedical Engineering
M.S.B.M.	Master of Science in Business Management
M.S.C.	Master of Speech Communication, Master of Science in Counseling
M.Sc.A.	Master of Social Administration
M.S.Ch.E.	Master of Science in Chemical Engineering
M.S.C.E.	Master of Science in Civil Engineering, Master of Science in Computer Engineering
M.S.C.E.E.	Master of Science in Civil and Environmental Engineering
M.Sc.D.	Master of Science in Dentistry
M.S.C.Ed.	Master of Science in Continuing Education
M.S.Ch.E.	Master of Science in Chemical Engineering
M.S.Cer.E.	Master of Science in Ceramic Engineering
M.S.C.I.S.	Master of Science in Computer Information Systems
M.S.C.J.	Master of Science in Criminal Justice
M.Sc.T.	Master of Science Teaching, Master of Science in Teaching
M.S.C.P.	Master of Science in Counseling Psychology
M.S.C.S.	Master of Science in Computer Science
M.S.D.	Master of Science in Dentistry, Master of Dietetics, Master of Science in Design
M.S.E.	Master of Science Education, Master of Science in Education, Master of Science in Engineering, Master of Software Engineering

M.Sec.Sch.Sci.	Master of Secondary School Science	M.S.P.A.	Master of Science in Public Administration
M.S.Ed.	Master of Science Education, Master of Science in Education	M.S.Pet.E.	Master of Science in Petroleum Engineering
		M.S.P.Ex.	Master of Science in Physiology of Exercise
M.S. in Ed.	Master of Science in Education	M.S.P.H.	Master of Science in Public Health
M.S.E.E.	Master of Science in Electrical Engineering, Master of Science in Environmental Engineering	M.S.PNG.E.	Master of Science in Petroleum and Natural Gas Engineering
		M.S.P.S.	Master of Science in Psychological Services
M.S.E.M.	Master of Science in Engineering and Mining, Master of Science in Engineering Management	M.S.P.T	Master of Science in Physical Therapy
		M.S.Rad.Sc.	Master of Science in Radiation Science
M.S.E.Mech.	Master of Science in Engineering Mechanics	M.S.S.	Master of Science in Safety, Master of Social Service, Master of Sports Science
M.S.E.Mgt.	Master of Science in Engineering Management		
M.S.E.R.	Master of Science in Energy Resources	M.S.S.A.	Master of Science in Social Administration
M.S.Envr.E.	Master of Science in Environmental Engineering	M.S.S.E.	Master of Science in Systems Engineering
		M.S.S.PA.	Master of Science in Speech Pathology and Audiology
M.S.E.S.S.	Master of Science in Exercise and Sports Studies		
M.S.F.	Master of Science in Finance, Master of Science in Forestry	M.S.Stat.	Master of Science in Statistics
		M.S.S.T	Master of Science in Science Teaching
M.S.F.S.	Master of Science in Forensic Science, Master of Science in Foreign Service	M.S.S.W	Master of Science in Social Work
		M.S.T.	Master of Science in Taxation, Master of Science Teaching, Master of Science in Teaching, Master of Speech Therapy, Master of Science in Tourism
M.S.G.	Master of Science in Gerontology		
M.S.H.S.	Master of Science in Health and Safety, Master of Science in Health Systems		
M.S.Hyg.	Master of Science in Hygiene	M.S.T.E.	Master of Science in Technical Education, Master of Science in Transportation Engineering
M.S.I.A.	Master of Institutional Administration, Master of Science in International Affairs		
		M.S.T.Ed.	Master of Science in Technical Education
M.S.I.B.	Master of Science in International Business	M.S.Text.	Master of Science in Textiles
M.S.I.E.	Master of Science in Industrial Engineering	M.S.T.M.	Master of Science in Technology Management, Master of Science in Tropical Medicine
M.S.I.E.O.R.	Master of Science in Industrial Engineering and Operations Research		
M.S.I.M.	Master of Science in Information Management		
M.S.I.R.	Master of Science in Industrial Relations	M.S.U.D.	Master of Science in Urban Design
M.S.I.S.	Master of Science in Information Science	M.S.W.	Master of Social Work
M.S.J.	Master of Science in Journalism	M.T.	Master of Taxation, Master of Teaching, Master of Technology
M.S.J.P.S.	Master of Science in Justice and Public Service		
M.S.K.	Master of Science in Kinesiology	M.T.A.	Master of Tax Accounting, Master of Teaching Arts, Master of Theater Arts
M.S.L.S.	Master of Science in Library Science		
M.S.M.	Master of Sacred Music, Master of Science in Management	M.Tech.	Master of Technology
		M.T.E.S.L.	Master of Teaching English as a Second Language
M.S.Mat.S.E.	Master of Science in Materials Science Engineering		
		M.Th.	Master of Theology
M.S.M.C.	Master of Science in Mass Communication, Master of Science in Marketing Communication	M.T.M.H.	Master of Tropical Medicine and Hygiene
		M.Tox.	Master of Toxicology
		M.T.P.W.	Master of Technical and Professional Writing
M.S.M.E.	Master of Science in Manufacturing Engineering, Master of Science in Mechanical Engineering		
		M.T.S.	Master of Teaching of Science
		M.T.S.C.	Master of Teaching Speech Communication, Master of Technical and Scientific Communication
M.S.Met.E.	Master of Science in Metallurgical Engineering		
M.S.Mgt.	Master of Science in Management	M.U.A.	Master of Urban Affairs, Master of Urban Architecture
M.S.M.I.	Master of Science in Medical Illustration		
M.S.M.S.Ed.	Master of Science in Mathematics and Science Education	M.U.D.	Master of Urban Design
		M.U.P.	Master of Urban Planning
M.S.M.T.	Master of Science in Medical Technology	M.U.P.P.	Master of Urban Planning and Policy
M.S.N.	Master of Science in Nursing	M.U.R.P.	Master of Urban and Regional Planning, Master of Urban and Rural Planning
M.S.N.A.	Master of Science in Nursing Administration, Master of Science in Nurse Anesthesia		
		M.U.S.	Master of Urban Studies
M.S.N.E.	Master of Science in Nuclear Engineering	M.V.A.	Master of Visual Arts
M.S.O.	Master of Science in Orthodontics	M.Vet.Sc.	Master of Veterinary Science
M.S.O.B.	Master of Science in Organizational Behavior	M.V.S.	Master of Valuation Sciences
M.S.O.D.	Master of Science in Organizational Development	M.V.T.E.	Master of Vocational Technical Education
		M.W.P.S.	Master of Wood and Paper Science
M.S.O.E.	Master of Science in Ocean Engineering	M.W.R.A.	Master of Water Resource Administration
M.S.O.L.M.	Master of Science in Organizational Leaderships and Management	M.W.S.	Master of Women's Studies
		M.Z.S.	Master of Zoology Science
M.S.O.R.	Master of Science in Operations Research	Phil.M.	Master of Philosophy
M.S.O.T.	Master of Science in Occupational Therapy	S.T.M.	Master of Sacred Theology
M.S.P.	Master in School Psychology, Master of Science in Planning, Master in Social Psychology, Master of Speech Pathology	Th.M.	Master of Theology
		X.M.B.A.	Executive Master of Business Administration

SIXTH-YEAR DEGREES

A.C.E.	Advanced Certificate in Education	G.D.T.	Graduate Diploma Taxation
A.D.	Artist's Diploma	Op.S.	Specialist in Optical Science
Ad.M.Ed.	Advanced Master of Education	P.D.	Professional Diploma
Ad.M.L.S.	Advanced Master of Library Science	Psy.S.	Specialist in Psychology
A.G.C.	Advanced Graduate Certificate	S.A.S.	School Administrator and Supervisor
A.G.S.	Advanced Graduate Specialist	S.C.C.T.	Specialist in Community College Teaching
A.S.Ed.Cert.	Advanced Specialist in Education Certificate	Sc.S.	Specialist in Science
C.A.G.S.	Certificate of Advanced Graduate Studies	S.Ed.	Specialist in Education
C.A.G.S.B.	Certificate in Advanced Study in Business	S.G.C.	Specialist in Guidance and Counseling
C.A.P.S	Certificate in Advanced Professional Studies	Sp.A.	Specialist in Art
C.A.S.	Certificate of Advanced Standing, Certificate of Advanced Study	Sp.App.Biol.	Specialist in Applied Biology
		S.L.S.	Specialist in Library Science
C.E.	Civil Engineer	S.P.A.	Specialist in Public Administration
Ch.E	Chemical Engineer	Sp.C.	Specialist in Counseling
C.S.E.	Computer Science Engineer	S.C.G.	Specialist Certificate in Gerontology
Ed.A.	Advanced Degree in Education	Sp.Ed.	Specialist in Education
E.E.	Electrical Engineer	Sp.E.S.	Special Education Specialist
Ed.S.	Specialist in Education	Sp.S.	Specialist in Science
Eng.	Engineer	S.S.A.	Specialist in School Administration
G.D.M.	Graduate Diploma in Management	S.S.P.	Specialist in School Psychology
G.D.P.A.	Graduate Diploma in Public Administration	S.S.P.A.	Specialist in Speech Pathology and Audiology

DOCTORAL DEGREES

A.Mus.D.	Doctor of Musical Arts	D.Min.	Doctor of Ministry
D.A.	Doctor of Arts, Doctor of Accounting	D.M.L.	Doctor of Modern Languages
D.A.I.S.	Doctor of Arts in Information Science	D.M.Sc.	Doctor of Medical Science
D.Arch.	Doctor of Architecture	D.Mus.	Doctor of Music
D.A.T.L.	Doctor of Arts in Training and Learning	D.Mus.Ed.	Doctor of Music Education
D.B.A.	Doctor of Business Administration	D.N.	Doctor of Nursing
D.C.L.	Doctor of Comparative Law, Doctor of Civil Law	D.N.Sc.	Doctor of Nursing Science
		D.O.	Doctor of Osteopathy
D.Chem.	Doctor of Chemistry	D.P.A.	Doctor of Public Administration
D.C.S.	Doctor of Computer Science	D.P.E.	Doctor of Physical Education
D.D.S.	Doctor of Dental Surgery	D.PH.	Doctor of Public Health
D.E.	Doctor of Engineering	Dr.P.H.	Doctor of Public Health
D.E.D.	Doctor of Environmental Design	D.Sc.	Doctor of Science
D.Ed.	Doctor of Education	D.Sc.D.	Doctor of Science in Dentistry
D.Eng.	Doctor of Engineering	D.Sc.V.M.	Doctor of Science in Veterinary Medicine
D.Eng.Sc.	Doctor of Engineering Science		
D.Env.Des.	Doctor of Environmental Design	D.S.M.	Doctor of Sacred Music
D.E.S.	Doctor of Engineering Science	D.S.Sc.	Doctor of Social Science
D.F.	Doctor of Forestry	D.S.W.	Doctor of Social Work
D.F.A.	Doctor of Fine Arts	D.Th.	Doctor of Theology
D.F.E.S.	Doctor of Forestry and Environmental Systems	D.V.M.	Doctor of Veterinary Medicine
		Ed.D.	Doctor of Education
D.H.S.	Doctor of Health and Safety, Doctor of Human Services	J.D.	Doctor of Jurisprudence
		J.S.D.	Doctor of Judicial Science
D.I.B.A.	Doctor of International Business Administration	L.L.D.	Doctor of Laws
		P.Ed.	Doctor of Physical Education
D.I.T.	Doctor of Industrial Technology	Pharm. D.	Doctor of Pharmacy
D.L.I.S.	Doctor of Library and Information Sciences	Ph.D.	Doctor of Philosophy
D.L.S.	Doctor of Library Science	Psy.D.	Doctor of Psychology
D.M.	Doctor of Music, Doctor of Management	Re.D.	Doctor of Recreation
D.M.A.	Doctor of Musical Arts	Rh.D.	Doctor of Rehabilitation
D.M.D.	Doctor of Medical Dentistry, Doctor of Dental Medicine	Sc.D.	Doctor of Science
		Sc.D.Hyg.	Doctor of Science in Hygiene
D.M.Ed.	Doctor of Music Education	S.J.D.	Doctor of Judicial Science

EXAMINATIONS AND OTHER ABBREVIATIONS

AACOMAS	American Association of Colleges of Osteopathic Medicine Application Service
AADSAS	American Association of Dental Schools Application Service
AACSB	American Assembly of Collegiate Schools of Business
AMCAS	American Medical College Application Service
AOA	American Optometric Association
CGS	Council of Graduate Schools
COPA	Council on Postsecondary Accreditation
DAT	Dental Aptitude Test
EDP	Early Decision Program
EMSAP	Early Medical School Acceptance Program
ETS	Educational Testing Service
FAF	Financial Aid Form
FAFSA	Free Application for Federal Student Aid
FFS	Family Financial Statement
GAPSFAS	Graduate and Professional School Financial Aid Service
GMAT	Graduate Management Admissions Test
GRE	Graduate Record Exam
LAAB	Landscape Architectural Accreditation Board
LSAT	Law School Aptitude Test
LSDAS	Law School Data Assembly Service
MAT	Miller Analogies Test
MCAT	Medical College Admissions Test
MELAB	Michigan English Language Assessment Battery
MMPI	Minnesota Multiphasic Personality Inventory
NCATE	National Council for Accreditation of Teacher Education
NLNGNE	National League of Nursing Graduate Nursing Examination
NTE	National Teaching Examination
OAT	Optometry Admissions Test
PAEG	Prueba de Admisiones para Estudios Graduados
PCAT	Pharmacy College Admissions Test
TOEFL	Test of English as a Foreign Language
TSE	Test of Spoken English
TWE	Test of Written English
VMAT	Veterinary Medicine Aptitude Test
WICHE	Western Interstate Commission for Higher Education

GUIDE TO
AMERICAN GRADUATE SCHOOLS

ABILENE CHRISTIAN UNIVERSITY
Abilene, TX 89699
http//www.acu.edu/

Coed. Independent/religious. Semester system. Library: 1,000,000 items. Special facilities: Center for Restoration Studies, Center for Aging, Center for Adolescent Studies.

Tuition: per credit $274. On-campus housing available. Annual room and board expenses: single students $4200, married students $2925 (room only). Apply to the Graduate Housing Office by May 1. Phone: (915)674-2066. Day care facilities available.

Graduate School

Enrollment: full- and part-time 663. University faculty teaching graduate students: full- and part-time 131. Degrees conferred: M.A., M.B.A., M.Div., M.Ed., M.L.A., M.M.F.T., M.P.A., M.S., M.S.N., D.Div.

ADMISSION REQUIREMENTS. Transcripts, GRE/MAT/GMAT, personal interview, three letters of recommendation required in support of application. TOEFL or other evidence of English ability required of foreign students. Accepts transfer applicants. Apply to Office of University Admission by March 1 (Summer and Fall admission), October 15 (Spring). Application fee $25. Phone: (915)674-2355.

ADMISSION STANDARDS. Selective for most departments. Usual minimum average: 2.75 (A = 4).

FINANCIAL AID. Annual awards from institutional funds: scholarships, research/teaching assistantships, internships, Federal W/S, loans. Apply to the University of Financial Aid by April 1. Use FAFSA.

DEGREE REQUIREMENTS. For M.A., M.S., M.Div., M.L.A.: 30–36 credit hours depending upon program; thesis, nonthesis option/professional paper/synthesis project, depending upon major; comprehensive exam; reading knowledge of one foreign language for some majors; practicum (M.S.). For M.A. (Psychology), M.M.F.T.: 45 credit program; practicum; thesis. For M.B.A.: 33 credit hour program for students holding undergraduate degrees in business, other students may need to enroll in up to 39 additional credits; no comprehensive exam. For M.P.A.: 42 credit hour program; internship; comprehensive exam. For D.Min.: 45–72 credit hours beyond master's depending upon program; reading knowledge of at least two foreign languages; preliminary exam; dissertation; final oral/written exam.

FIELDS OF STUDY.

COLLEGE OF ARTS AND SCIENCES:
American Religious History.
Counseling and Clinical Psychology.
Educational Diagnostician.
Elementary Teaching.
English.
History and Theology. Includes History of Christian Thought, Restoration History, Theology.
Human Communication.
Journalism and Mass Communication.
Liberal Arts.
Organizational and Human Resource Administration.
Public Administration.
Reading Specialist.
Religious Communication.
Religious Journalism.
School Psychology.
School Supervisor.
School Superintendent.
School Counselor.
Secondary Teaching.

COLLEGE OF BIBLICAL AND FAMILY STUDIES:
Biblical Studies. Includes New Testament, Old Testament, Greek New Testament.
Biblical and Related Studies.
Christian Ministry. Includes Christian Education, Congregational Ministry, Youth and Family.
Family Studies.
Gerontology.
Missions.

COLLEGE OF BUSINESS ADMINISTRATION:
Business Administration. GMAT for admission. M.B.A. only.

SCHOOL OF NURSING:
Nursing. M.S.N. only.

ADAMS STATE COLLEGE
Alamosa, Colorado 81102
http://www.adams.edu

Founded 1921. Located 220 miles SW of Denver. Coed. State control. Semester system. Special facilities: Luther Bean Historical Museum, Hatfield Art Gallery, Zachers Observatory. Library: 466,351 volumes.

Tuition: per credit $262, nonresident $314. On-campus housing for 114 married students, 170 single graduate students. Average annual housing cost: $6000 for married students, $5240 (including board) for single students. Apply to Director of Housing. Phone: (719)589-7522.

Division of Graduate Studies

Enrollment: full-time 46, part-time 426, summer 1106. Degree conferred: M.A.

ADMISSION REQUIREMENTS. Transcripts, GRE/MAT, a letter of intent required in support of application. TOEFL required for international applicants. Accepts transfer applicants. Apply to Office of the Dean at least two weeks prior to registration. Application fee $25. Phone: (719)587-7011; E-mail: pjmelgar@adams.edu.

ADMISSION STANDARDS. Selective. Usual minimum average: 2.75 (A = 4): MAT score 37, GRE combined score 1250.

FINANCIAL AID. Annual awards from institutional funds: seventeen graduate assistantships, one internship, Federal W/S, loans. Approved for VA benefits. Apply by March 1 to Dean for assistantships; to Financial Aid Office for all other programs. Use FAFSA. Phone: (719)587-7306. About 10% of students receive aid other than loans from College and outside sources.

DEGREE REQUIREMENTS. For M.A.: 30–36 semester hours, at least 24–30 in residence; thesis/nonthesis option/creative project; final comprehensive exam; no language requirement.

FIELDS OF STUDY.
Art. Art portfolio for admission.
Community Counseling. Autobiography essay for admission.
Elementary Education.
Health, Physical Education, and Recreation. Autobiographical statement for admission.
School Counseling. Autobiography essay for admission. Includes elementary and secondary.

Secondary Education. Active teaching license, two letters of recommendations for admission. Includes art, business, English, health, physical education, recreation, history, government, industrial arts, science.

Special Education, Teacher I—Moderate Need. Active teaching license, two letters of recommendations for admission. Includes bilingual education, ESL.

ADELPHI UNIVERSITY
Garden City, New York 11530

Founded 1896. Located 20 miles E of New York City. Coed. Private control. Semester system. Library: 624,000 volumes, 623,500 microforms. Special facilities: Hy Weinberg Center for Communicative Disorders, Adelphi Institute for Prevention of Drug Abuse, Center for Social Policy.

Tuition: per credit $425. No on-campus housing. Annual room and board expenses: $6400. Apply to Director of Housing for off-campus housing information. Phone: (516)877-3650. Day care facilities available.

Graduate School of Arts and Sciences

Enrollment: full- and part-time 200 (men 58%, women 42%). University faculty teaching graduate students: full- and part-time 194. Degrees conferred: M.A., M.S., D.A.

ADMISSION REQUIREMENTS. Transcripts, two letters of recommendation required in support of application. GRE required by some departments. TOEFL required of foreign students. Interview by invitation. Accepts transfer applicants. Apply to Office of University Admission two months prior to registration. Foreign students must apply by February 1 (Fall admission only). Application fee $50. Phone: (516)877-3033.

ADMISSION STANDARDS. Selective for most departments. Usual minimum average: 2.75 (A = 4).

FINANCIAL AID. Annual awards from institutional funds: partial scholarships, 100 research/teaching assistantships, 10 internships, Federal W/S, loans. Apply to the University Office of Financial Aid by April 1. Use FAFSA. About 50% of full-time students receive aid other than loans from University and outside sources.

DEGREE REQUIREMENTS. For M.A., M.S.: 30–36 credit hours depending upon program; thesis optional, depending upon major; reading knowledge of one foreign language for some M.S. majors. For D.A.: 45–72 credit hours beyond master's depending upon program; reading knowledge of at least two foreign languages for mathematics and language majors, one language or knowledge of computer programming for psychology majors; preliminary exam; dissertation; final oral/written exam.

FIELDS OF STUDY.
Art, Studio. Thirty-three credits for M.A.
Biochemistry.
Biology. Thirty-three hours for M.S.
Chemistry. M.S. only.
Earth Science. M.S. only.
English. M.A. only.
Mathematics and Applied Sciences. M.S., D.A.
Mathematics Education. M.S. only.
Physics and Energy Studies. M.S. only.

School of Business and Management

Tuition: per credit $ 425.

Enrollment: full-time 74, part-time 660 (men 60%, women 40%). Graduate faculty: full-time 24, part-time 19. Degrees conferred: M.B.A., M.S.Acct.

ADMISSION REQUIREMENTS. Transcripts, three recommendations, GMAT required in support of application. TOEFL required for foreign applicants. Accepts transfer applicants. Admits Fall and Spring semester. Apply to the Office of Admissions at least one month prior to semester of registration. Application fee $50. Phone: (516)877-4688.

ADMISSION STANDARDS. Selective. Usual minimum average: 3.0 (A = 4).

FINANCIAL AID. Annual awards from institutional funds: 8 assistantships, Federal W/S, loans. Apply to the Financial Aid Office by August 15 (Fall); December 15 (Spring). Use FAFSA. Phone: (516)877-3364. About 5% of students receive aid other than loans from School and outside sources.

DEGREE REQUIREMENTS. For M.B.A.: 66 credit hour program. For M.S. in Accounting: 42 credit hour program.

FIELDS OF STUDY.
Accounting.
Administrative Sciences.
Banking and Money Management.

School of Education

Enrollment: full- and part-time 300 (men 40%, women 60%). University faculty teaching graduate students: full- and part-time 60. Degrees conferred: M.A., M.S., P.D.

ADMISSION REQUIREMENTS. Transcripts, three letters of recommendation required in support of School's application. MAT required by some departments. TOEFL required of international applicants. Interviews encouraged. Accepts transfer applicants. Apply to Office of University Admission two months prior to registration. Foreign students must apply by February 1 (Fall admission only). Application fee $50. Phone: (516)877-3033.

ADMISSION STANDARDS. Selective for most departments. Usual minimum average: 2.75 (A = 4).

FINANCIAL AID. Annual awards from institutional funds: partial scholarships, research/teaching assistantships, Federal W/S, loans. Apply to the University of Financial Aid by April 1. Use FAFSA. About 20% of full-time students receive aid other than loans from University and outside sources.

DEGREE REQUIREMENTS. For M.A., M.S.: 30–36 credit hours depending upon program; thesis/nonthesis option, depending upon majors. For P.D.: 30 credit hours beyond master's depending upon program.

FIELDS OF STUDY.
Art Education.
Coaching.
Communicative Disorders.
Early Childhood Special Education.
Elementary Education.
English Education.
Mathematics Education.

Music Education.
Physical Education.
Reading.
School Health Education.
Secondary Education. Usual subject areas.
Special Education.
Sports Management.
Teaching English to Speakers of Other Languages.

School of Nursing–Graduate Division

Graduate study since 1949. Tuition: per credit $425. On-campus housing available. Enrollment: full- and part-time 266. Graduate Faculty: full-time 15, part-time 7. Degree conferred: M.S.

ADMISSION REQUIREMENTS. Transcripts, two years experience in nursing, GRE, letters of reference required in support of application. TOEFL required for foreign applicants. Accepts transfer applicants. Apply to Office of University Admissions by May 1 (Fall), November 1 (Spring). Application fee $50. Phone: (516)877-3020.

ADMISSION STANDARDS. Selective. Usual minimum average: 3.0 (A = 4). FINANCIAL AID. Annual awards from institutional funds: 25 Federal Nursing traineeships, Federal W/S, loans. Apply to Director, Graduate Studies by March 1. Use FAFSA. Phone: (516)877-4541. About 75–90% of students receive aid other than loans from all sources.

DEGREE REQUIREMENTS. For M.S.: 48 credit hours minimum; master's project.

FIELDS OF STUDY.
Clinical Nursing. Includes adult health, mental health/psychiatric, parent-child.
Nurse Practitioner.
Nursing Service Administration.
Teaching of Nursing.

School of Social Work

Founded 1949. Annual tuition: $14,500; per credit $425. On-campus housing available. Contact Director of Housing. Phone: (516)877-3650.
Enrollment: full-time 500, part-time 500. Faculty: full-time 28, part-time 35. Degree conferred: M.S.W., D.S.W.

ADMISSION REQUIREMENTS. Transcript, three professional references, minimum of twenty semester hours in social sciences required in support of application. TOEFL score of 585 required for foreign applicants. Interview sometimes required. Accepts transfer applicants. Apply to Director of Admissions. Rolling admissions process. Application fee $50. Phone: (516)877-3020; fax: (516)877-3039.

ADMISSION STANDARDS. Competitive. Usual minimum average: 3.0 (A = 4).

FINANCIAL AID. Annual awards from institutional funds: assistantships, Federal W/S, loans. Apply to Director of Admissions by March 1. Use FAFSA. Phone: (516)877-3080; fax: (516)877-3380. About 20% of students receive aid other than loans from School and outside sources.

DEGREE REQUIREMENTS. For M.S.W.: 64 credit hours minimum, at least one year in full-time residence. For D.S.W.: 48 doctoral-level credits beyond master's degree; candidacy exam; dissertation; oral exam.
Note: Accelerated one year program available for qualified applicants with undergraduate Social Work degree.

AIR FORCE INSTITUTE OF TECHNOLOGY
Wright-Paterson Air Force Base, Ohio 45433-6583

Founded 1919 as the Air School of Application to provide education and research to meet Air Force requirements. Located adjacent to Dayton. Coed. Federal control. Quarter system. Library: 85,000 volumes.
Tuition paid by U.S. Government. Air Base has facilities for limited number of single and married students.
Enrollment: full-time 737. Participation in Institute by military personnel and Federal Civil Service employees is on a voluntary basis. Faculty: full-time 257, part-time 2. Degrees conferred: M.S., Ph.D.

ADMISSION REQUIREMENTS. Transcripts, GRE/GMAT required in support of application. Apply to the Director of Admission/Registrar Directorate. Phone: (513)225-7168.

ADMISSION STANDARDS. Very selective for most majors, competitive for others. Usual minimum average: for M.S. in management programs 2.5, for M.S. in engineering/technical 3.0, for Ph.D. 3.5 (A = 4).

FINANCIAL AID. All students are military officers or Federal or Civil Service employees drawing full pay.

DEGREE REQUIREMENTS. For M.S.: 48 quarter hours, 36 in residence; thesis. For Ph.D.: 3 consecutive quarters of full-time course work, 48 quarter hours residence; dissertation; final oral exam.

FIELDS OF STUDY.

SCHOOL OF CIVIL ENGINEERING AND SERVICES:
Engineering.
Environmental Science.

SCHOOL OF ENGINEERING:
Aeronautical Engineering.
Applied Mathematics.
Astronautical Engineering.
Civil Engineering.
Computer Engineering.
Computer Systems.
Electrical Engineering.
Engineering Management.
Engineering Physics.
Mechanical Engineering.
Nuclear Engineering.
Operations Research.
Physics.
Space Operations.
System Engineering.

SCHOOL OF LOGISTICS AND ACQUISITION MANAGEMENT:
Acquisition Management.
Contract Management.
Cost Analysis.

Logistics Management.
Software Systems Management.
Systems Management.

UNIVERSITY OF AKRON
Akron, Ohio 44325-0001

Founded 1870. Coed. Municipal control. Semester system. Library: 1,078,000 volumes, 1,626,100 microforms; 75 computer workstations. Special facilities: Institute of Polymer Science, Polymer Engineering Institute, Institute for Biomedical Engineering, Oak Hill Center for Environmental Studies, Center for Urban Studies, Bliss Institute for Applied Politic.

Tuition: per credit, resident $159, nonresident $297. Limited on-campus housing available. Annual housing costs: $5016 (including board). For off-campus housing contact the Off-Campus Housing Office. Phone: (216)972-6936.

Graduate School

First graduate degree conferred 1880. Enrollment: full-time 1600, part-time 2026. University faculty teaching graduate students: full-time 516, part-time 186. Degrees conferred: M.A., M.A.Ed., M.A.H.E.&F.E., M.S., M.S.Ed., M.S.A., M.S.M., M.B.A., M.T., M.S.T.Ed., M.S.E., M.S.E.E., M.S.C.E., M.S.M.E., M.S.Ch.E., M.S.N., M.M., Ed.D., Ph.D.

ADMISSION REQUIREMENTS. Transcripts, departmental exam may be required in support of application. TOEFL for foreign students. Accepts transfer applicants. Graduates of unaccredited institutions not considered. Apply to Director of Admissions at least six weeks prior to registration. Rolling admissions process. Application fee $25, International application fee $50. Phone: (216)375-6308.

ADMISSION STANDARDS. Selective for most departments. Usual minimum average: 2.75 (A = 4).

FINANCIAL AID. Annual awards from institutional funds: 101 academic scholarships, 423 research assistantships, 369 teaching assistantships, Federal W/S, loans. Approved for V.A. benefits. Apply to Director of Financial Aid by March 1. Phone (216)375-7032. About 50% of students receive aid other than loans from both University and outside sources.

DEGREE REQUIREMENTS. For master's: 30–36 semester hours minimum; thesis required by some departments; advancement to candidacy; final/cumulative exams for most departments. For M.B.A.: 58 credit hour program; some foundation courses may be waived. For Ph.D.: at least two academic years beyond the master's; one year minimum in full-time residence; reading knowledge of two languages or comprehensive knowledge of one language; or language option in selected departments; preliminary/cumulative exams for many departments; advancement to candidacy; dissertation; final oral exam. For Ed.D.: essentially the same as for Ph.D. except no language requirement.

FIELDS OF STUDY.

BUCHTEL COLLEGE OF ARTS AND SCIENCES:
Applied Mathematics. Thesis optional. Master's only.
Biology. Thesis for master's.
Chemistry. Includes analytical, inorganic, organic, physical. Thesis for master's.
Computer Science. M.S. only.
Earth Science. Thesis. Master's only.
English. Thesis or two essays for master's. Master's only.
French. Thesis/nonthesis options for master's. Master's only.
Geography/Urban Planning. Thesis for M.A. Master's only.

Geology. Thesis. Master's only.
Geophysics. Thesis. Master's only.
History. Master's, Ph.D. (temporarily suspended).
Home Economics and Family Ecology. Master's only.
Mathematical Sciences. Thesis optional. Master's only.
Physics. Thesis optional. Master's only.
Political Science. Thesis for master's. Master's only.
Psychology. Includes industrial, general; M.A., Ph.D.
Sociology. Thesis for master's.
Spanish. Thesis/nonthesis option for master's. Master's only.
Statistics. Final paper of thesis for master's. Master's only.
Urban Studies. Includes urban studies/public administration 40 credits; urban studies/urban planning 45 credits. Ph.D.

COLLEGE OF BUSINESS ADMINISTRATION:
Accounting. Master's only.
Business Administration. Master's only.
Business Administration/Law. J.D./M.B.A.
Finance. Master's only.
International Business.
Management. Master's only.
Marketing. Master's only.
Taxation. Master's only.
Taxation/Law. J.D./M.Tax.

COLLEGE OF EDUCATION:
Athletic Training for Sports. M.A.Ed.
Classroom Guidance and Counseling. M.A., M.S.
Counseling Psychology. Ph.D.
Educational. M.A.Ed.
Elementary Administration. M.A., M.S.
Elementary Education.
Elementary School Counseling. M.A., M.S.
Health and Physical Education. M.A.Ed., M.S.Ed.
Higher Educational Administration. Ed.D.
Marriage and Family Therapy. M.A., M.S.
Outdoor Education. M.A.Ed., M.S.Ed.
Reading Supervisor. M.A.Ed., M.S.Ed.
School Psychology. M.A., M.S.
Secondary School Education. M.A.Ed., M.S., Ph.D.
Secondary School Administration. M.A.Ed., M.S.Ed.
Special Education.

COLLEGE OF ENGINEERING:
Biomedical Engineering.
Chemical Engineering.
Civil Engineering.
Electrical Engineering.
Mechanical Engineering.

COLLEGE OF FINE AND APPLIED ARTS:
Accompaniment.
Arts Management.
Audiology.
Clothing, Textile, and Interior.
Communication.
Composition.
Music Education.
Performance.
Speech Pathology.
Theater.
Theory.

COLLEGE OF NURSING:
Nursing Administration.
Nursing Clinical Specialist.
Nursing Education.

COLLEGE OF POLYMER SCIENCE AND POLYMER ENGINEERING:
Polymer Engineering.
Polymer Science.

School of Law (44325-2901)

Founded 1921. Law library 228,504 volumes, has LEXIS, NEXIS, WESTLAW, OhioLINK. Semester system.

Annual tuition: resident full-time $5851, part-time $4565; nonresident full-time $9979, part-time $7790. On- and off-campus housing available. Contact Housing Office. Phone: (216)972-6936.

Enrollment: first-year class 100 day, 107 evening; total day and evening 564 (Men 65%, Women 35%). Faculty; full-time 23, part-time 22. Degree conferred: J.D., J.D.-M.P.A., J.D.-M.B.A.

ADMISSION REQUIREMENTS. LSDAS Law School report, LSAT, two recommendations, bachelor's degree required in support of application. Interview not required. Accepts transfer applicants. Graduates of unaccredited colleges not considered. Apply to Admission Director as early as possible after October 1. Fall admission only. Application fee $35. Phone: (216)375-7331; fax: (216)258-2343.

ADMISSION STANDARDS. Selective. Admits 30% of total annual applicants.

FINANCIAL AID. Limited. Apply prior to April 1 to University Financial Aid Office. Use FAFSA. Phone: (216)972-7032. About 30% of students receive aid, including loans. Aid available for part-time students.

DEGREE REQUIREMENTS. For J.D.: 87 semester hours minimum. For M.P.A., M.B.A.: see Graduate School listing above.

ALABAMA AGRICULTURAL AND MECHANICAL UNIVERSITY
Normal, Alabama 35762

Founded 1875. Located in Huntsville. Coed. State control. Semester system. Library: 396,000 volumes, 528,000 microforms. Special facilities: Optics Center, Agriculture Research Center, Biological Research Center, Remote Sensor Center.

Tuition: per semester hour residents $111, nonresidents $222. Limited on-campus housing available for single graduate students, none for married students. Average annual housing cost: $3300 (including board) for single students. Apply to Director of Housing. Phone: (205)851-5797.

Graduate Program

Enrollment: full- and part-time 1499 (men 36%, women 64%). Graduate faculty: full-time 59. Degrees conferred: M.S., M.Ed., M.B.A., Ed.S., Ph.D.

ADMISSION REQUIREMENTS. Transcripts, GRE General/Subject Tests, GMAT for business required in support of application. TOEFL required for foreign applicants. Admits Spring, Fall, Summer. Apply one month prior to registration. International students must apply six months in advance. Application fee $15. Phone: (205)859-7415; fax: (205)859-3641.

ADMISSION STANDARDS. Selective. Usual minimum average: 2.5 (A = 4).

FINANCIAL AID. Annual awards from institutional funds: 30 research fellowships, 10 internships, Federal W/S, loans. Apply to Office of Financial Aid. Use FAFSA. Phone: (205)851-5400; fax: (205)851-5407. About 10% of students receive aid other than loans from University and outside sources.

DEGREE REQUIREMENTS. For master's: 30 semester hours minimum; thesis, or 6 additional hours and research paper. For Ed.S.: 30 semester hours beyond the master's; thesis. For Ph.D.:

at least 45 credits beyond the master's degree; preliminary exam; reading knowledge of two foreign languages or one language and approved appropriate research technique substitution; dissertation; final oral exam.

FIELDS OF STUDY.
Applied Physics.
Art Education.
Biology.
Business Administration.
Clinical Psychology.
Computer Science.
Counseling Psychology.
Early Childhood Education.
Educational Administration.
Elementary Education.
Food Science and Animal Industry.
Guidance Counseling.
Home Economics.
Industrial Technology.
Music Education.
Personnel Administration.
Physical Education.
Physics.
Psychometry.
Reading.
School Psychology.
Secondary Education. Includes agribusiness education, biology, business education, chemistry, English, general science, home economics, education, industrial arts, language arts, mathematics, physics, social science, trade and industrial.
Social Work.
Soil and Plant Science. Includes plant physiology, remote sensing, soil physics, biotechnology.
Special Education. Includes emotional conflict, learning disabilities, mental retardation.
Speech Pathology.
Trade and Industrial Education.
Urban Planning.

UNIVERSITY OF ALABAMA
Box 870118
University, Alabama 35487

Founded 1831. Main campus located 50 miles SW of Birmingham. Coed. State control. Semester system. Special facilities: Alabama Business Research Council, Alabama Law Institute, Alabama Museum of Natural History, Alabama Oil and Gas Board, Belser-Parton Reading Laboratory, Brewer-Porch Children's Center, Bureau of Education Services and Research, Bureau of Engineering, Research Bureau of Legal Research, Capstone International Program Center, Cartographic Laboratory Center for Administrative and Policy Studies, Center for Alcohol and Drug Education, Center for Business and Economic Research, Center for Communication Research and Service, Center for Developmental and Learning Disorders, Center for Economic Education, Center for Government and Public Service, Center for Law and Public Policy, Center for Southern Regional Folk Life Studies, Center for the Study of Aging, Center for the Study of Southern History and Culture, Child Development Laboratories, Computer Center, Early Childhood Day Care Center, Electron Microscope Laboratory, Evaluation and Assessment Laboratory, Geological Survey of Alabama, Herbarium, Human Development Laboratory, Human Resources Institute, Institute of Higher Education Research and Services, Inter-University Consortium for Political Research, J. Nicholene Bishop Biological Station, Legal Aid Clinic, Marine Environmental Services Consortium Incorporated, Mineral Resources Institute—State Mine Experimental Station, Minority Culture Archives,

Mound State Monument, Museum of Natural History, Natural Resources Center, Office for Archeological Research, Office of Education Media, Psychological Clinic, Remote Sensing Laboratory, Research Laboratory of Human Nutrition, Ridgecrest Center, Rochester Products Applied Research Facility, Rose Tower Learning Center, School of Mines and Energy Development, Speech and Hearing Center, Teaching and Learning Center, Transportation Research Group, Tuscaloosa Metallurgical Laboratory, U.S. Bureau of Mines, University of Alabama Arboretum, University of Alabama Art Gallery, University of Alabama Icthyological Collection, University of Alabama Press, University of Alabama Theatre, University of Alabama Television Service, William B. Bennett International Trade Center. Library: 1,860,000 volumes, 2,560,000 microforms, plus access to online retrievals services.

Annual tuition: full-time, resident $2470, nonresident $6268. On-campus housing for 300 married students, 500 men, 500 women. Average housing cost: $350 monthly for married students, $845–$1077 per semester for single students. Apply to Director of Housing. Phone: (205)348-8086. Day care facilities available.

Graduate School

Organized 1924. Enrollment: full-time 1950, part-time 1640. Graduate faculty: full-time 560, part-time 120. Degrees conferred: M.A., M.S., M.B.A., M.C.R., M.F.A., M.L.S., M.P.A., M.S.W., Ed.S., D.M.A., D.P.A., Ed.D., D.S.W., Ph.D.

ADMISSION REQUIREMENTS. Two transcripts, references, GRE required in support of application. GRE Advanced Test required by many departments. GMAT required for Manderson Graduate School of Business. GRE or MAT or NTE for College of Education. GRE or MAT for School of Human Environmental Sciences. GRE for College of Engineering. Interview sometimes required. Accepts transfer applicants. Apply to Dean of the Graduate School six weeks prior to registration. Application fee $25. Phone: (205)348-5921.

ADMISSION STANDARDS. Very selective for some departments, selective for the others. Usual minimum average: 3.0 (A = 4). Usual minimum test score, 50th percentile.

FINANCIAL AID. Annual awards from institutional funds; 57 graduate council fellowships, 1250 departmental teaching and research assistantships, Federal W/S, loans. All full-time fellowships and departmental assistantships accompanied by full-tuition scholarships. Apply to Dean of the Graduate School by March 1. Phone: (205)348-6756. Use FAFSA. About 30% of the students receive aid other than loans from University and outside sources.

DEGREE REQUIREMENTS. For master's: Plan I—24 semester hours minimum; reading knowledge of one foreign language for some departments; thesis; final written/oral exam. Plan II—30 semester hours minimum; reading knowledge of one foreign language for some departments; no thesis; final written/oral exam. For Ed.S.: 30 semester hours minimum beyond master's. For Ph.D.: 48 semester hours minimum beyond the bachelor's, at least 18 in full-time residence; preliminary exam; dissertation; reading knowledge of two foreign languages or one language and appropriate research technique/tool or other approved substitution; final written/oral exam. For other Doctoral programs: 90 semester hours minimum beyond the bachelor's, at least 45 in residence; preliminary exam; final oral exam; no language requirement; dissertation.

FIELDS OF STUDY.

ARTS AND SCIENCES:
American Studies. M.A.
Anthropology. M.A.
Art. M.A., M.F.A.

Audiology. M.S.
Biology. M.S., Ph.D., Ed.S.
Chemistry. M.S. Ph.D., Ed.S.
Creative Writing. M.F.A.
Criminal Justice. M.S., M.C.J.
Economics. M.A., Ph.D.
Education of the Hearing Impaired. M.S.
English. M.A.
French. M.A.
Geography. M.S.
Geology. M.S., Ph.D.
German. M.A.
Historical Preservation. M.A., Ph.D.
History. M.A., Ph.D.
Marine Science. M.S. (Biology)
Mathematics. M.A., Ph.D.
Music. M.M.
Music (Applied). M.M.
Music Management. M.M.
Music (Performance and Composition). M.M.
Physics. M.S., Ph.D.
Political Science. M.S., Ph.D.
Psychology. M.A., Ph.D., Psychological Spec.
Public Administration. M.P.A., D.P.A.
Romance Languages. M.A., Ph.D.
Spanish. M.A.
Speech-Language Pathology. M.S.
Theatre. M.A., M.F.A.
Women's Studies. M.A.

MANDERSON GRADUATE SCHOOL OF BUSINESS:
Accounting. M.A., M.Acct., M.S.C., Ph.D.
Business Administration. M.B.A.
Economics. M.A., M.S.C., Ph.D.
Finance. M.A., M.S.C ., Ph.D.
Human Resource Management. M.S., M.S.C, Ph.D.
Management Science. M.A., M.S.C., Ph.D.
Marketing. M.A., M.S.C., Ph.D.
Statistics. M.A. M.S.C., Ph.D.
Tax Accounting. M.T.A.

SCHOOL OF COMMUNICATION:
Advertising and Public Relations. M.A.
Broadcast and Film Communication. M.A.
Journalism. M.A.
Mass Communication. Ph.D.
Speech Communication. M.A.

COLLEGE OF EDUCATION:
Adapted and Therapeutic Physical Education. M.A.
Administration of Vocational Education. M.A., Ed.S.
Adult Basic Education. M.A., Ed.S.
Art Education. M.A.
Business Education. M.A.
Counselor Education. M.A. in community, elementary, rehabilitation, secondary, student personnel counseling. Ed.D., Ph.D., Ed.S.
Distributive Education. M.A.
Early Childhood Education. M.A.
Educational Administration: Higher Education. M.A., Ed.D., Ph.D.
Educational Psychology. M.A., Ed.D., Ph.D., Ed.S.
Educational Research. Ed.D., Ph.D., Ed.S.
Elementary Education. M.A. Ed.D., Ph.D., Ed.S.
Health, Physical and Recreation Education. M.A., Ed.D., Ed.S.
Home Economics Education. M.A.
Instructional Leadership. M.A., Ed.D., Ph.D., Ed.S.
Middle School Education. Includes biology, chemistry, earth and space science, economics, English, French, general science, geography, history, language arts, mathematics, physics, political science, sociology, Spanish, speech communication/theater. M.A., Ed.S.

Music Education. M.A.
Secondary Education. M.A., Ed.D., Ph.D., Ed.S. offered in all areas except as indicated: anthropology, M.A. only; art, Ed D., Ph.D., Ed.S.; biology, business education, E.D., Ph.D., Ed.S.; chemistry, earth science, M.A., Ed.S.; economics, English, French, geography, German, M.A. only; history, home economics, Ed.D., Ph.D., Ed.S.; language arts, M.A., Ed.S.; Latin American studies, mathematics, music, Ed.D., Ph.D., Ed.S.; physics, political science, psychology, M.A., Ed.S.; social science, sociology, Spanish, rhetoric and speech communication.
Speech Education. Ed.D., Ed.S.; M.A in emotional conflict, gifted and talented, learning disabilities, mental retardation, multiple disabilities, special education administration.
Supervision of Health Education. M.A., Ed.S.
Supervision of Physical Education. M.A., Ed.S.
Supervision of Reading. M.A., Ed.S.
Supervision of Special Education. M.A., Ed.S.
Teaching of Reading. M.A., Ed.S.
Trade and Industrial Education. M.A.

COLLEGE OF ENGINEERING:
Aerospace Engineering. M.S.
Chemical Engineering. M.S., Ph.S.
Civil Engineering. M.S., Ph.D., Ed.S.
Computer Science. M.S.
Electrical Engineering. M.S., Ph.D.
Engineering. M.S.
Engineering (Coastal). M.S.
Engineering (Environmental). M.S.
Engineering Hydrology. M.S.
Engineering Mechanics. M.S., Ph.D.
Industrial Engineering. M.S.
Mechanical Engineering. M.S., Ph.D.
Metallurgical Engineering. M.S.
Mineral Engineering. M.S.

SCHOOL OF HUMAN ENVIRONMENTAL SCIENCES:
Clothing, Textiles and Interior Design. M.S.
Consumer Sciences. M.S.
Foods, Nutrition and Institutional Management. M.S.
General Home Economics. M.S.
Human Development and Family Life. M.S.

GRADUATE SCHOOL AND INTERDISCIPLINARY:
Applied Statistics. M.S., Ph.D.
Interdisciplinary. M.A., M.S., Ph.D., Ed.S.
Latin American Studies. M.A.
Materials Science. Ph.D.

School of Library and Information Studies

Semester tuition: resident $1187, nonresident $2962. On-campus housing available for married students, graduate men and women. Apply to Office of Residential Life, P.O. Box 87052.
Enrollment: full-time 70, part-time 113. Faculty: full-time 11, part-time 13. Degrees conferred: M.L.S., Ed.S. (sixth year), M.F.A., Ph.D. Day care facilities available.

ADMISSION REQUIREMENTS. Transcripts, bachelor's degree, GRE General Test/MAT required in support of application. TOEFL required for foreign applicants. Accept transfer students. Graduates of unaccredited colleges not considered. Apply to Dean at least six weeks prior to registration. Application fee $25. Phone: (205)348-4610.

ADMISSION STANDARDS. Selective. Usual minimum average: 3.0 (A = 4).

FINANCIAL AID. Three teaching fellowships, twenty-one teaching assistantships, Federal W/S, loans. Apply to Director of Financial Aid by July 15. Use FAFSA. Phone: (205)348-6756.

About 10% of students receive aid other than loans from both University and outside sources.

DEGREE REQUIREMENTS. For M.L.S.: 36 semester hours minimum; thesis not required. For M.F.A.: 48 semester hours. For Ph.D.: 48 semester hours beyond master's minimum; research tool; dissertation.

FIELDS OF STUDY.
Book Arts. M.F.A. only.
Information Studies.
Library Science.

School of Social Work

School and M.S.W. program established in 1965; D.S.W. established in 1975, changed to Ph.D. in 1992. Tuition: per semester full-time resident $1187, nonresident $2962. On-campus housing available.
Enrollment: M.S.W. full-time 151, part-time 24; Ph.D. full-time 16, part-time 6. Faculty: full-time 20, part-time 7. Degrees conferred: M.S.W., Ph.D.

ADMISSION REQUIREMENTS. Transcripts, GRE or MAT, three letters of reference required in support of application. Advanced Standing requires B.S.W. from C.S.W.E. accredited program. For Ph.D., M.S.W is recommended. Interviews may be requested. For M.S.W.: apply by February 1 (Fall), April 10 (Summer). For Ph.D.: apply by July 1 (Fall). Application fee $25. Phone: (205)348-7027.

ADMISSION STANDARDS. For M.S.W.: regular admission, 3.0 (A = 4) overall or for last 60 hours. Conditional admission considered for 2.5 overall and either 50 MAT or 1500 GRE. For Ph.D.: 3.0 overall or in last 60 hours of previous program and 50 MAT or 1500 GRE.

FINANCIAL AID. Master's level: three research assistantships, three teaching assistantships, twenty-six academic scholarships, sixteen grants, stipends and tuition grants from School and agency funds, Federal W/S, loans. Apply to the school by February 15 for master's level assistance, to University's Financial Aid Office by February 15 for all other aid. Use FAFSA and institutional financial aid form. Phone: (205)348-6756.

DEGREE REQUIREMENTS. For M.S.W.: 42 credits with Advanced Standing, or 60 credits for two-year program. For Ph.D.: minimum 51 credit hours (including up to 12 hours for M.S.W.); comprehensive exam; dissertation (minimum of 24 dissertation research credits); final oral exam.
Note: Semester program in Washington, D.C., available.

School of Law

Established 1872. Located at Tuscaloosa (35487-0382). Law library 227,900; has LEXIS, NEXIS, WESTLAW, DIALOG, OCLC. Annual tuition: resident $3198, nonresident $6776. On-campus housing available.
Enrollment: first-year class 101; total full-time 500 (men 62%, women 38%); no part-time students. Faculty: full-time 28, part-time 31. Degree conferred: J.D., J.D.-M.B.A., J.D.-M.P.A., LL.M., M.C.L. (international lawyers only).

ADMISSION REQUIREMENTS. LSDAS Law School report, two transcripts, LSAT required in support of application. Applicants must have received bachelor's degree prior to entrance. Interview not required but may be requested by School. Graduates of unaccredited colleges not considered. Apply to Admission Office after September 1, before March 1. First-year students admitted Fall only. Application fee $25. Phone: (205)348-5440.

ADMISSION STANDARDS. Selective. Admits 30% of total annual applicants.

FINANCIAL AID. Scholarships, loans. Apply by March 1 to Chair, Scholarship Committee, University Office of Financial Aid. Phone: (205)348-6756. About 25% of students receive aid other than loans from School.

DEGREE REQUIREMENTS. For J.D.: 90 semester hours minimum, at least three semesters in full-time residence. For LL.M., M.C.L.: 24 graduate semester hours beyond the J.D.

School of Medicine
(Box 100-UAB Station)

Founded 1859 in Mobile; located in Birmingham (35294) since 1945. Branch campuses created in 1969 at Huntsville and Tuscaloosa. Medical library 150,000 volumes. Annual tuition: resident $6180, nonresident $18,324; student fees $927. Very limited on-campus housing available. Contact Director of Auxiliary Services.

Enrollment: first-year class 165 (8 were M.D.-Ph.D.); approximately 15 EDP; total full-time 684 (men 70%, women 30%). Faculty: full-time 314, part-time 80. Degree conferred: M.D., M.D.-Ph.D. The Ph.D. conferred through the Graduate School.

ADMISSION REQUIREMENTS. AMCAS report, transcripts, MCAT, recommendations, interview required in support of application. Has EMSAP. Preference given to Alabama residents. Graduates of unaccredited institutions not considered. Does have EDP. Apply to Director of Admissions after June 15, before November 1. Application fee $50. Phone: (205)934-2330; fax: (205)934-8724.

ADMISSION STANDARDS. Competitive. Accepts about 20% of total annual applicants. Approximately 80% of class are state residents.

FINANCIAL AID. Scholarships, summer stipends, summer fellowships, loans. Apply to Director of Financial Aid after acceptance; no specified closing date. 67% of students receive financial aid.

DEGREE REQUIREMENTS. For M.D.: satisfactory completion of four-year program. For Ph.D., see Graduate School listing above.

FIELDS OF GRADUATE STUDY:
Anatomy.
Biochemistry.
Biophysics.
Cell Biology.
Genetics.
Immunology.
Microbiology.
Neurosciences.
Pathology.
Pharmacology.
Physiology.

School of Dentistry
(Box 16-SDB)

Established 1945. Located in Birmingham (35294-0007). Library (combined with School of Medicine) 150,000 volumes. Tuition: resident $5163, nonresident $15,489. Housing: very limited. Total average cost for all other first-year expenses $5800.

Enrollment: first-year class 55; total full-time 217 (men 160, women 57). Faculty: full-time 76, part-time 78. Degree conferred: D.M.D., M.S.

ADMISSION REQUIREMENTS. For D.M.D.: AADSAS transcripts showing completion of at least three years of undergraduate study, DAT, four recommendations required in support of School's application. Interview by invitation only. Accepts transfer applicants for second and third years only. Preference given to Alabama and SREB residents. Graduates of unaccredited colleges not considered. For M.S., M.P.H., Ph.D.: students may apply after completion of second year of program. Apply to AADSAS after June 1 and before April 1. Application fee $25. Phone: (205)934-3387.

ADMISSION STANDARDS. Competitive. Admits 40% of total annual applicants. Approximately 80% are state residents.

FINANCIAL AID. Scholarships, loans. Apply to School's Office of Financial Aid; no specified closing date. About 79% of students receive aid other than loans from School.

DEGREE REQUIREMENTS. For D.M.D.: satisfactory completion of four-year program. For M.S., M.P.H., Ph.D.: See Graduate School listing above.

FIELDS OF GRADUATE STUDY.
Anatomy. Ph.D.
Biochemistry. Ph.D.
Dentistry. M.S. only.
Microbiology. Ph.D.
Pharmacology. Ph.D.
Physiology and Biophysics. Ph.D.
Public Health. M.P.H.

UNIVERSITY OF ALABAMA AT BIRMINGHAM
Birmingham, Alabama 35294-1203

Founded 1966. Coed. Quarter system. Libraries: 1,174,161 volumes, 980,000 microforms, 5290 periodicals, plus access to online data retrieval services. Special facilities: Center for Urban Affairs, Small Business Development Center.

Tuition: per credit hour, residents $91, nonresidents $182. Limited on-campus housing for married and single students. Average housing cost: ranges from $150 to $400 per month. Contact UAB Student Housing and Residential Life Office, 1604 Ninth Ave., South Birmingham, AL 35294-1230. Phone: (205)934-2092. Day care facilities available.

Graduate School

Enrollment: 3846. Faculty: full- and part-time 1200. Degrees conferred: M.S.N.A., M.P.A., M.S.O.T., M.S.H.A., M.S.F.S., M.A., M.Ac., Ph.D., M.S., M.B.A., M.S.C.L.S., M.S.C.J., M.A.Ed., Ed.S., Ed.D., M.S.B.E., M.S.C.E., M.S.E.E., M.S.Mte., M.S.M.E., M.S.H.I.M., D.S.N., M.S.N.

ADMISSION REQUIREMENTS. Two transcripts, references, GRE (some UAB graduate programs require, or are willing to accept, other recognized national tests) required in support of application. TOEFL and TWE required of foreign students. Interview required for some departments. Accepts transfer applicants. Apply to Dean of the Graduate School at least six weeks prior to registration; some graduate programs admit only at certain times of the year and have specific deadlines. Application fee $30, international applicants $55. Phone: (205)934-8243, or (800)975-GRAD.

ADMISSION STANDARDS. Competitive for most departments.

FINANCIAL AID. Partial tuition waivers, assistantships, fellowships, Federal W/S, loans. Financial Aid Office administers loan, grant, and work-study programs, students in certain programs may participate in UAB's Coop Ed program. Contact Office of Student Financial Aid. Phone: (205)934-8223; fax: (205)934-8941. Apply to the specific graduate program director.

DEGREE REQUIREMENTS. For master's: Plan I—24 hours minimum, at least 18 in major and 6 in related minor; thesis; reading knowledge of one foreign language for some departments; final written/oral exam. Plan II—30 hours minimum, at least 18 in major; no thesis; reading knowledge of one foreign language for some departments; final written/oral exam for some programs. For Ed.S.: 30 hours beyond the master's; final oral/written exam. For doctoral programs: preliminary exam; dissertation; reading knowledge of one language, a research tool, or computer technique; research project for some programs; final oral exam.

FIELDS OF STUDY.
Accounting. M.Ac.
Administration—Health Services. Ph.D.
Anthropology. M.A.
Applied Mathematics. Ph.D.
Art History. M.A.
Biochemistry. Ph.D.
Biology. M.S., Ph.D.
Biomedical Engineering. Ph.D., M.S.B.E.
Biophysical Sciences. Ph.D.
Biostatistics. M.S., Ph.D.
Business Administration. M.B.A.
Cell Biology. Ph.D.
Chemistry. M.S., Ph.D.
Civil Engineering. M.S.C.E.
Clinical Laboratory Sciences. M.S.C.L.S.
Clinical Nutrition. M.S.
Computer & Information Sciences. M.S., Ph.D.
Criminal Justice. M.S.C.J.
Dentistry. M.S.
Education—Early Childhood. Ph.D.
Education (all areas). M.A.Ed., Ed.S.
Educational Leadership. Ph.D., Ed.D.
Electrical and Computer Engineering. M.S.E.E.
English. M.A.
Environmental Health Sciences. Ph.D.
Epidemiology. Ph.D.
Forensic Science. M.S.F.S.
Health Education/Health Promotion. Ph.D.
Health Information Management. M.S.H.I.M.
Health Services Administration. M.S.H.A.
History. M.A.
Materials Engineering. M.S.Mt.E., Ph.D.
Materials Science. Ph.D.
Mathematics. M.S.
Mechanical Engineering. M.S.M.E.
Medical Genetics. Ph.D.
Medical Sociology. Ph.D.
Microbiology. Ph.D.
Nursing. D.S.N.
Nurse Anesthesia. M.N.A.
Nutrition. Ph.D.
Occupational Therapy. M.S.
Oral Biology. M.S.
Pathology. Ph.D.
Pharmacology. Ph.D.
Physical Therapy. M.S.
Physics. M.S., Ph.D.
Physiology and Biophysics. Ph.D.

Psychology. Includes Behavioral Neuroscience, Developmental, Medical. Ph.D.
Public Administration. M.P.A.
Sociology. M.A.
Vision Science. M.S., Ph.D.

UNIVERSITY OF ALABAMA IN HUNTSVILLE
Huntsville, Alabama 35899

Established 1950. Coed. Public control. Semester system. Special facilities: Alabama Solar Research Center, Center for Applied Optics, Johnson Research Center, Center for Microgravity and Materials Research, Center for Robotics, Center for Space Plasma and Aeronomic Research. Library: 426,000 volumes, 613,000 microforms, 3100 current periodicals.

Annual tuition: resident $3386, nonresident $6418. On-campus housing available for 160 married students, for 700 single graduate students. Average academic year housing costs: $3500 (including board) for single students, $4920 for married students. Contact Director of University Housing for both on- and off-campus housing information. Phone: (205)895-6108. Day care facilities available.

School of Graduate Studies

Enrollment: full-time 390, part-time 792. Faculty: full-time 251, part-time 109. Degrees conferred: M.A., M.S., M.Admin.Sci., M.S.E, M.S.O.R., Ph.D.

ADMISSION REQUIREMENTS. Two official transcripts, bachelor's degree, GRE (subject for some departments)/GMAT/MAT, three recommendations required in support of School's application. TOEFL required for international applicants. Accepts transfer applicant. Graduates of unaccredited institutions not considered. Apply to Graduate Office by July 1 (Fall), December 1 (Spring); international students must apply three months prior to registration. Rolling admissions process. Application fee $20. Phone: (205)895-6070; fax: (205)895-6073.

ADMISSION STANDARDS. Relatively open. Usual minimum average 3.0 (A = 4).

FINANCIAL AID. Annual awards from institutional funds: 10 scholarships, 13 grants, 11 fellowships, 124 research assistantships, 119 teaching assistantships, Federal W/S, loans. Approved for VA benefits. Use FAFSA. About 36% of students receive aid other than loans from both University and outside sources.

DEGREE REQUIREMENTS. For master's: 24 semester hours minimum plus thesis; or 36 semester hours without thesis; final comprehensive exam. For Ph.D.: three years of study beyond the bachelor's, at least one year in full-time residence; qualifying exam; dissertation; final exam; additional requirements determined by appropriate department advisor.

FIELDS OF STUDY.
Administrative Science.
Aerospace Engineering.
Applied Mathematics.
Atmospheric Science.
Biological Sciences.
Business Administration.
Chemical Engineering.
Chemistry.
Civil Engineering.
Computer Engineering.
Computer Science.

Electrical Engineering.
Engineering Management.
English.
History.
Industrial Engineering.
Materials Science.
Mathematics.
Mechanical Engineering.
Nursing.
Operations Research.
Optical Science and Engineering.
Physics.
Psychology.
Public Affairs.
System Engineering.

UNIVERSITY OF ALASKA FAIRBANKS
Fairbanks, Alaska 99775-0820

Founded 1917. Located 4 miles NW of Fairbanks. Coed. State control. Semester system. Special research units: Alaska Cooperative Wildlife Research Unit, Alaska Coop Fisheries Research Unit; Center for Cross-Cultural Studies, Institute of Arctic Biology, Geophysics Institute, Marine Science, Water Resources, and Institute of Northern Engineering; Mineral Industry Research Laboratory, Petroleum Development Laboratory. State and federal agencies on campus include the Branch of Alaskan Geology of the U.S. Geological Survey, Alaska Division of Geological and Geophysical Survey, Institute of Northern Forestry (U.S. Forest Service), and College Observatory (U.S. Dept. of Commerce). Library: 750,000 volumes, 880,000 microforms, plus access to online data retrieval services.

Semester tuition/fees: full-time, resident $1748, per credit $150; nonresident $3098, per credit $300. On-campus housing for 180 married students, housing available as needed for single graduate students. Average academic-year housing cost: $5000 for married students, $3320 for single students. Apply to Director of Housing. Phone: (907)474-7247. Day care facilities available.

Graduate School

Graduate study since 1950. Enrollment: full-time 466, part-time 325 (men 452, women 339). Faculty teaching graduate students: full-time 300, part-time 40. Degrees conferred: M.A., M.A.T., M.B.A., M.F.A., M.Ed., M.M.E., M.C.E., M.E.E., M.S., Ed.S., Ph.D.

ADMISSION REQUIREMENTS. Transcripts, three letters of recommendation required in support of application. GRE/GMAT required. TOEFL required for all foreign students. Interview not required. Accepts transfer applicants. Apply to Director of Admissions and Records; no specified closing dates. Application fee $35. Phone: (907)474-7464.

ADMISSION STANDARDS. Selective for most departments. Usual minimum average: 3.0 (A = 4).

FINANCIAL AID. Annual awards from institutional funds: 25 scholarships, 12 fellowships, 340 assistantships, grants, Federal W/S, loans. Apply to Dean of the appropriate College for assistantships; closing date early spring; for all other aid apply by February 15 for Fall semester. Use FAFSA and institutional FAF. About 50% of students receive aid other than loans from University and outside sources. Aid sometimes available to part-time students. Phone: (907)474-7256.

DEGREE REQUIREMENTS. For master's: 30 semester credits minimum, at least 21 in residence; thesis or project for most de-

partments; final written/oral exam. For Ed.S.: 36 semester hours beyond the master's; final oral exam. For Ph.D.: number of credits determined by the advisory committee, but usually at least two years beyond the master's; minimum 18 credit thesis; preliminary exam; reading knowledge of one foreign language or other research-tool competence; dissertation; final oral exam.

FIELDS OF STUDY.
Anthropology. M.A., Ph.D.
Biochemistry/Molecular Biology. M.S., Ph.D.
Biological Sciences. M.S., Ph.D.
Business Administration. M.B.A.
Chemistry. M.S.
Economics. M.S.
Education. Includes administration, counseling and guidance, cross-cultural. M.Ed., Ed.S.
Engineering. Includes arctic, civil, geological, electrical, environmental quality, management, mechanical, mineral preparation, mining, petroleum.
English. M.A., M.F.A.
Fisheries. M.S.
Geology. M.S., Ph.D.
Geophysic. M.S., Ph.D.
Interdisciplinary. M.S., Ph.D.
Marine Biology. M.S.
Mathematics. M.S., Ph.D.
Music. M.A. only.
Natural Resources Management. M.S.
Northern Studies. M.A.
Oceanography. M.S., Ph.D.
Physics. M.S., Ph.D.
Space Physics. M.S., Ph.D.
Wildlife Management. M.S., Ph.D.
Zoology. M.S., Ph.D.

ALBANY MEDICAL COLLEGE
Albany, New York 12208-3479

Founded 1839. Co-ed. Library: 110,000 volumes.
Annual tuition: M.D. program resident $25,278, non-resident $26,613; graduate study, full-time $11,550. Limited on-campus housing available. Total average figure for all other expenses: $7500.

Enrollment: M.D. program, first-year class 132; total 522 (men 52%, women 48%); graduate study, full-time 136, part-time 3. Faculty: M.D., full-time 351, part-time 31; Graduate Study, full-time 68, part-time 39. Degrees conferred: M.D., M.D.-Ph.D., Ph.D.

ADMISSION REQUIREMENTS. For M.D. program: AMCAS report, transcripts, MCAT required in support of application. Interview by invitation only. Applicants must have completed at least three years of college study. Preference given to state residents. Does not have EDP. Apply to Secretary of Admissions after June 15, before November 15 (Fall). Application fee $70. Phone: (518)445-5253; fax: (518)445-5183. For graduate study: transcripts, two letters of recommendation, interview required in support of application. GRE recommended. Accepts transfer applicants. Apply to Office of Admissions at least forty-five days prior to registration. Application fee $70.

ADMISSION STANDARDS. Very competitive. Accepts 3–4% total annual applicants. Approximately 47% are state residents.

FINANCIAL AID. For M.D. program: scholarships. Apply to Financial Aid Committee on Scholarships and Loans by January 15. For graduate study: research fellowships/assistantships. Apply to Office of Admissions, Graduate School; no specified closing date. Use FAFSA. About 80% of medical students, 35% of graduate students receive some aid from College.

DEGREE REQUIREMENTS. For M.D.: satisfactory completion of four-year program. For M.D.-Ph.D.: Completion of 6-year program. For Ph.D.: 90 hours minimum beyond the bachelor's; preliminary exam; dissertation; final oral/written exam.

FIELDS OF GRADUATE STUDY.
Anatomy.
Biochemistry.
Cell Biology.
Immunology.
Microbiology.
Molecular Biology.
Neurosciences.
Pathology.
Pharmacology.
Physiology.

UNIVERSITY AT ALBANY, STATE UNIVERSITY OF NEW YORK
Albany, New York 12222-0001

Founded 1844. Coed. State control. Semester system. Special facilities: Albany Center for Learning Disabilities, Atmospheric Sciences Research Center, Center for Biological Macromolecules, Child Research and Study Center, Hindelang Criminal Justice Center, Center for Molecular Genetics, Center for Neuro-Biological Research, Center for Executive Development, Instructional Resources Center, Local Government Studies Center, New York State Writer's Institute, Performing Arts Center, Center for Social and Demography Analysis, Center for Stress and Anxiety Disorders, Dudly Observatory, Wadsworth Center for Laboratories and Research. Library: 1,800,000 volumes, 2,600,000 microforms, 7000 current periodicals, 87 PCs in all libraries.

Annual tuition; resident full-time $5100, per credit $213; nonresident full-time $8416, per credit $351. On-campus housing for 100 graduate men, 100 graduate women; none for married students. Average annual housing cost: $4135 (including board). Contact Housing Office for both on- and off-campus housing information. Phone: (518)442-5875. Day care facilities available.

School of Graduate Studies

Graduate study since 1913. Enrollment: full-time 1900, part-time 2270 (men 45%, women 55%). University faculty: full-time 600, part-time 50. Degrees conferred: M.A., M.S., M.B.A., M.L.S., M.P.A., M.P.H., M.F.A., M.R.P., M.S.W., C.A.S., D.A., Ed.D., D.P.A., Ph.D., Psy.D.

ADMISSION REQUIREMENTS. Official transcripts required in support of School's application. GRE General/Subject Tests required for University Certificate and doctoral applicants, GMAT for business applicants. Interview required by some departments. TOEFL required for international applicants. Accepts transfer applicants. Graduates of unaccredited institutions not considered. master's applicants apply to appropriate School or College by August 15 (Fall), January 1 (Spring), April 15 (Summer). Doctoral and University Certificate applicants apply to School of Graduate Studies by April 30 (Fall), November 15 (Spring), March 1 (Summer). International applicants apply to School of Graduate Studies by February 1 (Fall). Application fee $50. Phone: (518)442-3980.

ADMISSION STANDARDS. Competitive for most departments, selective for the others. Usual minimum average: 3.0 (A = 4).

FINANCIAL AID. Annual awards from institutional funds: 226 external assistantships, 669 internal assistantships, 100 internal fellows, 115 external fellows, Federal W/S, loans. Approved for VA benefits. Apply by February 15 to appropriate department chair for fellowships, assistantships; to Financial Aid Office for all other programs. Phone: (518)442-5757. Use FAFSA. About 35% of students receive aid other than loans from School and outside sources. No aid for part-time students.

DEGREE REQUIREMENTS. For M.A., M.S.: 30 semester hours minimum, at least 24 in residence; reading knowledge of one foreign language required by some departments; thesis/nonthesis option for some departments; comprehensive exam required by some departments. For M.B.A.; 30–60 semester hours, depending on previous preparation. For M.L.S.: 36 semester hours minimum. For M.F.A.: 48 credits minimum, at least 40 in residence, For M.P.H.: 51 semester hours, at least 30 in residence; two internships required. For M.P.A.: 12 graduate courses minimum; comprehensive exam. For M.S.W.: 60 semester hours minimum, at least 30 in residence, one year in full-time attendance; research project. For C.A.S.: 48 semester hours minimum, at least 30 in residence, one semester or equivalent in full-time attendance; comprehensive exam. For Ed.D.: 75 semester hours minimum, at least 38 in residence, one year in full-time attendance; qualifying exam; dissertation. For D.P.A.: 60 credit hours minimum beyond the bachelor's; dissertation. For Ph.D.: 60 semester hours minimum, at least 30 in residence, one year in full-time attendance; competency in one or two research tools; qualifying exam; dissertation. For D.A.: 60 semester hours minimum, at least 30 in residence; research project; supervised college teaching internship; research tool; written/oral comprehensive exam.

FIELDS OF STUDY.

COLLEGE OF ARTS AND SCIENCE:
Africana Studies.
Anthropology.
Art.
Atmospheric Sciences.
Cellular and Developmental Biology.
Chemistry.
Classics.
Clinical Psychology.
Communication.
Computer Science.
Demography.
Ecology and Animal Science.
Economics.
English.
French Studies.
General/Experimental Psychology.
Geography.
Geological Sciences.
History.
Humanistic Studies.
Italian.
Latin American and Caribbean Studies.
Liberal Studies.
Mathematics.
Molecular Biology.
Neurobiology.
Philosophy.
Physics.
Public History.
Regional Planning.
Secondary Teaching.
Sociology.
Sociology and Communication.
Spanish.
Statistics.

Theater.
Urban Policy.

SCHOOL OF BUSINESS:
Accounting.
Business Administration.
Finance.
Management.
Management Science and Information Systems.
Marketing.
Organizational Studies.
Taxation.

SCHOOL OF EDUCATION:
Counseling Psychology.
Curriculum and Instruction.
Curriculum Planning and Development.
Educational Administration.
Educational Communication.
Educational Psychology.
Educational Psychology and Statistics.
Measurement and Evaluation.
Reading.
Rehabilitation Counseling.
School Psychology.
Special Education.

NELSON A. ROCKEFELLER COLLEGE OF PUBLIC AFFAIRS AND POLICY:
Administrative Behavior.
Comparative and Development Administration.
Criminal Justice.
Human Resource.
Information Science and Policy.
Legislative Administration.
Planning and Policy Analysis.
Political Science.
Public Administration.
Public Affairs and Policy.
Public Finance.
Public Management.
Social Welfare.

SCHOOL OF PUBLIC HEALTH:
Biochemistry, Molecular and Genetics.
Biometry and Statistics.
Cell and Molecular Structure.
Environmental and Occupational Health.
Environmental Chemistry.
Epidemiology.
Health Policy and Management.
Immunobiology and Immunochemistry.
Molecular Pathogenesis.
Neurosciences.
Public Health.
Toxicology.

ALFRED UNIVERSITY
Alfred, New York 14802
http://www.alfred.edu/

Founded 1836. Located 70 miles S of Rochester. Coed. Private control. The New York State College of Ceramic is located on campus. Special facility: College of Ceramics Library, Center for Advanced Ceramic Technology, Center for Glass Research. Library: 350,000 volumes, 98,000 microforms.

Annual tuition: full-time $18,498. For College of Ceramics, annual tuition: $11,466. Contact Assistant Dean for Student Life for on- and off-campus housing information. Phone: (607)871-2186. Total annual average additional costs: $5,500.

Graduate Division

Graduate study since 1938. Enrollment: full-time 205, part-time 150. University faculty teaching graduate students: full-time 72, part-time 17. Degrees conferred: M.A., M.S. in Ed., M.P.S., M.S., M.F.A., Ph.D.

ADMISSION REQUIREMENTS. Transcripts, GRE/GMAT, personal statement of objectives, two letters of recommendation required in support of application. TOEFL required of foreign students. Interview required for some Programs. Accepts transfer applicants. Apply to Office of Graduate Admissions, rolling admissions process. Application fee $50. Phone: (607)871-2141, (800)541-9229; fax: (607)871-2198.

ADMISSION STANDARDS. Very selective for some departments, selective for the others. Usual minimum average: 3.0 (A = 4).

FINANCIAL AID. Annual awards from institutional funds: scholarships, full and partial tuition grants, teaching assistantships, Federal W/S, loans. Apply to the Graduate Admissions Office. Use FAFSA. Phone: (607)871-2159. About 80% of students receive aid from University and outside sources.

DEGREE REQUIREMENTS. For M.A. (Psychology): 70 hours minimum; oral/written qualifying exam, thesis. For M.B.A.: 55 hours minimum. For M.S. in Ed., M.P.S.: 30 hours minimum; thesis or final document recommended; final oral/written exam.

College of Ceramics. For M.S.: 30 hours minimum; thesis; final oral exam. For M.F.A.: 60 hours minimum, at least two years in residence; thesis. For Ph.D.: 90 hours minimum beyond the bachelor's, at least two years in residence; written/oral comprehensive exam; dissertation; final oral exam.

FIELDS OF STUDY.
Art. M.F.A., M.S. in Ed.
Biology. M.S. in Ed. only.
Ceramic Engineering. M.S., Ph.D.
Ceramic Science. M.S.
Chemistry. M.S. in Ed.
Community Services Administration. M.P.S.
Education. Includes art, college student development, counselor education, elementary, secondary, reading.
English. M.S. in Ed.
Glass Science. M.S., Ph.D.
Industrial Engineering. M.S.
Mathematics. M.S. in Ed.
School Psychology. M.A., Ph.D.
Social Studies. M.S. in Ed.

AMERICAN GRADUATE SCHOOL OF INTERNATIONAL MANAGEMENT
Glendale, Arizona 85306-3236

Founded 1918. Coed. Private control. Semester system. Library: 60,000 volumes, 5000 microforms, 1200 periodicals, 40 PCs.

Annual tuition: full-time $18,800. On-campus housing available for single students only. Average academic year housing costs: $4580 (including board). Contact the Housing Office for off-campus housing information. Phone: (602)978-7132.

Graduate Programs

Enrollment: full-time 1421, part-time 0. Graduate faculty: full-time 83, part-time 33. Degrees conferred: M.I.H.M., M.I.M., M.I.M.O.T., M.I.M.-M.B.A.

ADMISSION REQUIREMENTS. Official transcripts, GMAT, required in support of School's application. TOEFL required for international applicants. Accepts transfer applicants. Graduates of unaccredited institutions not considered. Apply by January 15 (Fall), July 31 (Spring) to Dean of Admissions. Rolling admission process. Application fee $50. Phone: (602)978-7210; fax: (602)439-5432.

ADMISSION STANDARDS. Selective. Usual minimum average: 2.75 (A = 4).

FINANCIAL AID. Five hundred and seventy scholarships, 10 fellowships, 120 assistantships, partial tuition waivers, Federal W/S, loans. Approved for VA benefits. Apply by April 1 to appropriate program chair for fellowships, assistantships; to Financial Aid Office for all other programs. Use FAFSA. About 65% of students receive aid from School and outside sources.

DEGREE REQUIREMENTS. For master's: 45–60 semester credits minimum, all in full-time residence; language proficiency for some programs; final oral/written exam.

FIELDS OF STUDY.
International Health Management.
International Management.
International Technology Management.
Note: Joint degree programs are with Arizona State University, Case Western Reserve University, University of Colorado, Drury College, University of Florida, University of Houston.

THE AMERICAN UNIVERSITY
Washington, D.C. 20016-8111

Founded 1893. Coed. Private control. Methodist affiliation. Semester system. University participates in Joint Graduate Consortium with Catholic, Georgetown, George Washington, Howard Universities. Library: 850,000 volumes, 1,384,000 on microfiche, plus access to online data retrieval services.

Tuition: per credit $627. On-campus housing for single and married students. Average annual cost $6000–$11,000. Apply to Housing Office. Phone: (202)885-3370. Day care facilities available.

College of Arts and Sciences—Graduate Division

Enrollment: full-time 696, part-time 860. Faculty: full-time and part-time 235. Degrees conferred: M.A., M.S., M.F.A., Ph.D.

ADMISSION REQUIREMENTS. Transcripts, two letters of recommendation required in support of application. GRE General Test, interview for some departments. TOEFL required for foreign students. Accepts transfer applicants. Apply to Office of Graduate Admissions by August 1 (Fall), December 1 (Spring), April 15 (Summer). Application fee $50. Phone: (202)885-1098, (202)885-6000 or (202)885-3406.

ADMISSION STANDARDS. Selective for most departments. Usual minimum average: 3.0 (A = 4).

FINANCIAL AID. Annual awards from institutional funds: 45 scholarships, 186 fellowships, 198 assistantships, Federal W/S, loans. Apply by January 15 to Financial Aid Office. Phone: (202)885-1098. About 60% of students receive aid other than loans from College and outside sources.

DEGREE REQUIREMENTS. For master's: 30 hours minimum, at least 24 in residence; reading knowledge of one foreign language for some departments; thesis for some departments; written comprehensive exam. For Ph.D.: 72 hours minimum beyond the bachelor's, at least 42 in residence; research tool; three writ-

ten comprehensives; one oral comprehensive; dissertation; final oral defense.

FIELDS OF STUDY.
Anthropology. Thesis, oral exam for M.A. M.A., Ph.D.
Applied Anthropology. M.A.
Applied Sociology: Social Policy. M.A.
Art. Thesis/final project for M.A., M.F.A. Includes painting, sculpture, printmaking, art history.
Biology. Thesis, oral exam for M.S. M.A., M.S. only.
Chemistry. One language, thesis, oral exam for M.S. M.S., Ph.D.
Computer Science and Information Systems. M.S. only. Weekend option.
Economics. Includes applied, developmental banking, financial economics for public policy. M.A., Ph.D.
Education. M.A.T.(includes elementary, secondary); M.A. (includes special education, learning disabilities); Ph.D.
Environmental Policy. M.A.
Environmental Science. M.S.
Health/Fitness Management. M.S.
History. One language for M.A. M.A., Ph.D.
Language and Foreign Studies. M.A. includes French, Russian, Spanish, foreign language, media, TESOL.
Literature. Includes literary studies, creative writing. M.A., M.F.A.
Mathematics. Includes statistics, mathematics education, statistics for policy analysis. M.A., Ph.D.
Performing Arts. Includes dance, arts management. M.A. only.
Philosophy and Religions.
Philosophy and Social Policy. M.A. only.
Physics. Thesis, oral exam for M.S. M.A., M.S., Ph.D.
Psychology. Includes clinical, experimental, general. M.A., Ph.D.
Sociology. Includes applied sociology, international training and education. Thesis, oral exam for M.A. M.A., Ph.D.

Kogod College of Business Administration

Established 1955. Enrollment: full-time 350, part-time 250. Graduate faculty: full-time 60, part-time 15. Tuition: $707 per credit. Housing is available for single and married students. Degrees conferred: M.B.A., M.S.(Acc.), M.S.(Tax), M.S.(Finance). M.B.A.-J.D., M.B.A.-M.A.I.A.

ADMISSION REQUIREMENTS. Transcripts, GMAT required in support of application. TOEFL recommended for international students. Graduates of unaccredited institutions not considered. Apply to the Director of Graduate Admission by June 1. Application fee $50. Phone: (202)885-1907; fax: (202)885-1078.

ADMISSION STANDARDS. Selective. Accepts about 50% of total annual applicant pool.

FINANCIAL AID. Annual awards from institutional funds: scholarships, internships, loans. Apply to the Director of Financial Aid by February 1. Use FAFSA. Phone: (202)985-6000; fax: (202)885-6014. About 40% of students receive aid other than loans from School and outside sources.

DEGREE REQUIREMENTS. For M.B.A.: 54 semester hour program.

FIELDS OF STUDY.
Accounting. M.B.A., M.S.
Business Management Information Systems.
Entrepreneurship and Management.
Finance.
Human Resource Management.
International Business. Tracks in finance, marketing, and management.
Marketing.
Real Estate and Urban Development.
Taxation. M.S.

School of International Service

Established 1958. Tuition: $60 per credit hour. On-campus housing available. Contact Director, Residential Life. Phone: (202)885-3370. Day care facilities available.

Enrollment: full-time 465, part-time 228. Faculty: full-time 555, part-time 23. Degrees conferred: M.A., M.S., Ph.D., M.A.-M.B.A., M.A.-J.D.

ADMISSION REQUIREMENTS. Transcripts, two letters of recommendation, GRE General required in support of application. TOEFL required for non–English-speaking foreign students. Graduates of unaccredited institutions not considered. Apply to the Office of Admissions by January 15 (Fall), October 15 (Spring). Application fee $50. Phone: (202)885-6000; fax: (202)885-6014.

ADMISSION STANDARDS. Selective. Usual minimum average: 3.45, 3.0 average last 60 credits (A = 4).

FINANCIAL AID. Scholarships, fellowships, assistantships, all federal financial aid programs. Apply to Dean of the School before March 1 for all non-Federal programs; to the Financial Aid Office before April 1 for all Federal programs. Use FAFSA. No aid for part-time students.

DEGREE REQUIREMENTS. For master's: 36–42 semester hours minimum, at least 24 in residence; proficiency in one foreign language; written comprehensive exams; thesis or two research papers. For Ph.D.: 72 semester hours, at least 30 in residence; proficiency in one foreign language; oral and written exams; dissertation; final oral exam.

FIELDS OF STUDY.
Comparative and Regional Studies.
Development Management. Forty-two semester hours for M.S.
International Affairs. Thirty-six to thirty-nine semester hours for M.A.
International Communication. M.A. only.
International Development. Forty-three semester hours for M.A. M.A., Ph.D.
International Economic Policy.
International Law and Organization. J.D.-M.A.
International Peace and Conflict Resolution.
International Politics.
International Relations. Ph.D. only.
Note: Dual degrees available with Ritsuoneikan University (Kyoto, Japan), Korea University (Seoul, Korea).

School of Public Affairs

Established 1958.
Tuition: per credit hour $605.
Enrollment: full-time 219, part-time 342. Faculty: full-time 53, part-time 32. Degrees conferred: M.A., M.P.A., Ph.D.

ADMISSION REQUIREMENTS. Official transcripts, GRE, two letters of recommendation required in support of application. TOEFL required of international students. GRE General/Subject Tests recommended for those who desire consideration for financial aid. Accepts transfer applicants. Graduates of unaccredited institutions not considered. Apply to the Office of Admissions by February 1. Application fee $50. Phone: (202)885-1098.

ADMISSION STANDARDS. Selective. Usual minimum average: 2.75, 3.0 average last 60 credits (A = 4).

FINANCIAL AID. Fellowships, scholarships, assistantships, Federal W/S, loans. Approved for VA benefits. Apply by March 1 to School for assistantships, fellowships; to Financial Aid Office for all other programs. No aid for part-time students.

DEGREE REQUIREMENTS. For M.A.: 33 semester hours minimum, at least 24 in residence; written comprehensive exams; thesis or two research papers. For M.P.A.: 42 semester hours minimum, at least 33 in residence; written comprehensive exam. For Ph.D.: 60–72 semester hours, at least 30 in residence; proficiency in one foreign language or proficiency in statistics, computer science; written exam; dissertation; final oral exam.

FIELDS OF STUDY.
American Politics.
Comparative Politics.
Justice, Law and Society.
Policy Analysis.
Political Science.
Public Administration.

Washington College of Law

Founded 1896. Law library 352,800 volumes. Library has LEXUS, WESTLAW.

Annual tuition: full-time $21,618; per credit $761. On-campus housing limited. Total annual additional expense $8441.

Enrollment: first-year full-time 271, part-time 93; total 1167 (men 52%, women 48%). Faculty: full-time 48, part-time 90 (men 70%, women 30%). Degrees conferred: J.D., J.D.-M.A. (International Service), J.D.-M.B.A.(Kogod College), J.D.M.S. (Justice), LL.M. (International Legal Studies).

ADMISSION REQUIREMENTS. LSDAS Law School report, transcripts, LSAT, bachelor's degree required in support of application. Interview not required. Accepts transfer applications. Graduates of unaccredited colleges not considered. Apply to Director of Admission of the College after October 1, before March 1. Fall admission only. Application fee $55. Phone (202)885-2606.

ADMISSION STANDARDS. Selective. Accepts 15–20% of total annual applicants.

FINANCIAL AID. Scholarships, loans. Apply to Director of Financial Aid by February 15. Use FAFSA. Phone: (202)885-6100. About 5% of students receive aid other than loans from College. Aid sometimes available to part-time students.

DEGREE REQUIREMENTS. For J.D.: 86 semester hours minimum, at least 28 in residence. Transfer credit individually considered. For LL.M.: at least 24 graduate credits beyond J.D. For M.A., M.B.A., M.S.: see Graduate School listing above.

ANDREWS UNIVERSITY
Berrien Springs, Michigan 49104

Founded 1874. Located 25 miles N of South Bend, Indiana. Coed. Private control. Seventh-Day Adventist. Quarter system. Library: about 805,309 volumes, including microforms.

Tuition: per quarter hour $265. On-campus housing for 460 married students, 100 graduate men, 100 graduate women. Annual housing costs: per month $350–$455 efficiency and one-bedroom apartments for single students. Apply to Housing Manager. Phone: (616)471-6979. Day care facilities available.

School of Graduate Studies

Coordinates programs for College of Arts and Sciences, School of Business, School of Education, and SDA Theological Seminary. Enrollment: full-time 335, part-time 289. University faculty teaching graduate: full-time 98, part-time 30. Degrees conferred: M.A., M.S., M.S.M.T., M.S.P.T., M.A.T., M.B.A., Ed.S., Ed.D., Ph.D., Th.D.

ADMISSION REQUIREMENTS. Transcripts, GRE, recommendations required in support of application. GMAT required for business programs. TOEFL/MELAB required for foreign applicants. Accepts transfer applicants. Apply to Director of Admissions at least one month prior to registration. Application fee $30. Phone: (616)471-3490 or (800)253-2874.

ADMISSION STANDARDS. Selective. Usual minimum average: 2.6 (A = 4); doctoral: 3.5 (A = 4).

FINANCIAL AID. Annual awards from institutional funds: 57 scholarships, 97 research/teaching fellowships, Federal W/S, loans. Apply to Office of Financial Aid; no specified closing date. Use FAFSA and Institutional FAF. Phone: (616)471-3334.

DEGREE REQUIREMENTS. For master's: 44–72 quarter credits minimum, at least 35 in residence; candidacy; thesis; comprehensive exam/project paper, depending upon major and degree. For Doctoral Degrees: three years of study beyond bachelor's minimum, at least three quarters in residence; appropriate research tool; comprehensive exam; dissertation; final oral defense.

FIELDS OF STUDY.
Biology.
Business Administration.
Communication.
Computer Science.
Education. Includes administration, supervision, counseling psychology, education and developmental psychology, community counseling, school counseling, curriculum and instruction, reading.
English.
History.
Human Nutrition.
Medical Technology.
Music.
Physical Therapy.
Religion. Includes Old and New Testament, church history, Adventist studies.
Software Engineering.

ANGELO STATE UNIVERSITY
San Angelo, Texas 76909
http://www.angelo.edu

Formerly Angelo State College, created in 1963. Coed. Semester system. Library: 262,000 volumes, 607,000 microforms, 2000 current periodicals, 37 PCs.

Annual tuition: per semester resident $415, nonresident $1243. Housing available for 82 married, single graduate students. Annual housing cost: $6640 (including board). Some day care facilities available.

Graduate School
http://www.angelo.edu/grad/

Graduate study since 1970. Enrollment: full-time 81, part-time 315. Faculty: full-time 98, part-time 13. Degrees conferred: M.A., M.A.T., M.B.A., M.Ed., M.M.Ed., M.M.E., M.P.A., M.S., M.S.N.

ADMISSION REQUIREMENTS. Two official transcripts, GRE/GMAT required in support of School's application. TOEFL required for international applicants. Accepts transfer applicants. Graduates of unaccredited institutions not considered. Apply to Dean of Graduate School by August 15 (Fall), January 5 (Spring). Application fee, none; $50 fee for international applicants. Phone: (915)942-2169; fax: (915)942-2078.

ADMISSION STANDARDS. Selective. Usual minimum average: 2.5 (A = 4); or 3.0 for last 60 semester hours.

FINANCIAL AID. Seventy-nine fellowships, eleven teaching assistantships, six graduate assistantships, Federal W/S, loans. Approved for VA benefits. Apply by July 15 to Dean of Graduate School for fellowships, assistantships; to Financial Aid Office for all other programs. Use FAFSA and University's FAF. Phone: (915)942-2246.

DEGREE REQUIREMENTS. For master's: 30–36 semester hours minimum; written/oral comprehensive exam; thesis/nonthesis option in some programs. For M.B.A.: Plan I—39 semester hours minimum; capstone course: Plan II—36 semester hours (accounting concentration).

FIELDS OF STUDY.
Animal Science.
Biology.
Business Administration. Includes accounting, computer science, management.
Educational Diagnostician.
Elementary Education.
English.
Guidance and Counseling.
History.
Interdisciplinary Studies.
International Studies.
Kinesiology.
Mathematics.
Music Education. Includes all-level, elementary.
Nursing.
Physical Education.
Psychology. Includes general, counseling.
Public Administration.
Reading Specialist.
School Administration.
Supervision.

ANTIOCH UNIVERSITY
Yellow Springs, Ohio 45387

Founded 1852. Located 20 miles E of Dayton. Coed. Private control. Quarter system. Library: over 268,000 volumes, 43,000 microforms. University has graduate campuses in Keene, New Hampshire; Los Angeles and Santa Barbara, California; Seattle, Washington.

Tuition: full-time per quarter $1344; per credit $275 (tuition varies by program). No campus housing available.

The McGregor School

Graduate study since 1964. Enrollment: full- and part-time 240 (men 83, women 157). Graduate faculty: varies by program. Degree conferred: M.A.

ADMISSION REQUIREMENTS. Two transcripts, three letters of recommendation, goal statement, interview required in support of application. Apply to Director of Admissions at least one month prior to quarter of registration. Admits to Fall, Winter, Spring, and Summer quarters. Application fee $35. Phone (513)767-6325; fax: (513)767-6461.

ADMISSION STANDARDS. Selective. Usual minimum average: 2.5 (A = 4).

FINANCIAL AID. Scholarships, assistantships, Federal W/S, loans. Apply to Director of Admissions and Financial Aid: no specified closing date. Use FAFSA.

DEGREE REQUIREMENTS. For M.A.(Management): two years in full-time residence; program offered on Saturdays only. For other M.A.: 45–60 quarter hours; residency requirements vary by program.

FIELDS OF STUDY.
Conflict Resolution.
Environment and Community.
Individualized Study.
Intercultural Relations.
Management.

ANTIOCH NEW ENGLAND GRADUATE SCHOOL
Keene, New Hampshire 03431-3516

Coed. Private control. Semester system. Library: 10,000 volumes, 29,000 microforms, 23 PCs and access to online bibliographic databases, union catalogs, and interlibrary loan networks. The main University campus is located in Yellow Springs, Ohio. It also has graduate campuses in Los Angeles and Santa Barbara, California; Seattle, Washington.

Tuition: per credit master's $340, Doctoral program $515. Only off-campus housing is available. Average academic year housing costs: $1100 per month.

Graduate School

Enrollment: full-time 802, part-time 113. Graduate faculty: full-time 46, part-time 100. Degrees conferred: M.A., M.Ed., M.S.H.A., M.S., Psy.D.

ADMISSION REQUIREMENTS. Two transcripts, three letters of recommendation, goal statement, interview required in support of application. Accepts transfer applicants. Graduates of unaccredited institutions not considered. Apply to Director of Admissions by December 31 (Winter), August 31 (Fall); January 15 for doctoral programs. Admits Winter, Summer, Fall for master's; Fall only for Doctoral programs. Application fee $35. Phone: (603)357-3122, ext. 287; fax: (603)357-0718.

ADMISSION STANDARDS. Selective. Usual minimum average: 2.5 (A = 4).

FINANCIAL AID. Annual awards from institutional funds: twenty-seven fellowships, traineeships, scholarships for ethnic and racial groups which are historically underrepresented, Federal W/S, loans. Apply to Director of Financial Aid by April 1. Use FAFSA.

DEGREE REQUIREMENTS. For master's: 40–60 credits, at least 30 in residence; thesis/nonthesis option or special project. For Psy.D.: 60 credits beyond an approved master's: qualifying exam; advancement to candidacy; dissertation; final oral exam.

FIELDS OF STUDY.
Administration and Supervision. M.S. only.
Applied Psychology.
Clinical Psychology. Psy.D. only.
Counseling Psychology. Includes substance abuse and addiction, marriage and family therapy, dance/movement therapy. M.A. only.
Elementary/Early Childhood Education. Includes integrated day, Waldorf, science.
Environmental Studies.
Foundation of Education for Experienced Educators. M.Ed.
Human Services Administration. M.H.S.A. only.

Interdisciplinary Studies. M.A. only.
Management. M.S. only.
Resource Management and Administration. M.S. only.

ANTIOCH SOUTHERN CALIFORNIA LOS ANGELES
Marina del Rey, California 90292

Established 1972. Coed. Private control. Quarter system. Library: access to online bibliographic databases, union catalogs, and interlibrary loan networks. The main University campus is located in Yellow Springs, Ohio. It also has graduate campuses in Keene, New Hampshire; Santa Barbara, California; Seattle, Washington.

Tuition: per credit $320. Only off-campus housing is available.

Graduate School

Enrollment: full-time 233, part-time 152. Graduate faculty: full-time 8, part-time 58. Degree conferred: M.A.

ADMISSION REQUIREMENTS. Transcripts, two letters of recommendation, goal statement, interview required in support of application. TOEFL required for all international applicants. Apply to Director of Admissions by August 4 (Fall); rolling for other quarters. Admits Fall, Winter, Spring, and Summer. Application fee $50. Phone: (310)578-1090; fax: (310)822-4824.

ADMISSION STANDARDS. Selective. Usual minimum average: 2.5 (A = 4).

FINANCIAL AID. Scholarships, Federal W/S, loans. Apply to Director of Financial Aid by August 4. Phone: (310)578-1080; fax: (310)822-4824. Use FAFSA and GAPSFAS.

DEGREE REQUIREMENTS. For M.A.: 60–72 quarter units; thesis/nonthesis option or special project.

FIELDS OF STUDY.
Clinical Psychology.
Organizational Management.
Psychology.

ANTIOCH SOUTHERN CALIFORNIA SANTA BARBARA
Santa Barbara, California 93101-1580

Coed. Private control. Quarter system. Library: access to online bibliographic databases, union catalogs, and interlibrary loan networks. The main University campus is located in Yellow Springs, Ohio. It also has graduate campuses in Keene, New Hampshire; Los Angeles, California; and Seattle, Washington.

Tuition: full-time $12,200, half-time $1830 per quarter. Only off-campus housing is available.

Graduate School

Enrollment: full-time 241, part-time 85. Graduate faculty: full-time 4, part-time 19. Degree conferred: M.A.

ADMISSION REQUIREMENTS. Transcripts, two letters of recommendation, goal statement, interview required in support of application. TOEFL required of international applicants. Accepts transfer applicants. Apply to Director of Admissions by August 16 (Fall); rolling admissions process. Admits Fall, Winter only. Application fee $50. Phone: (805)962-8179; fax: (805)962-4786.

ADMISSION STANDARDS. Selective. Usual minimum average: 2.5 (A = 4). TOEFL score of 600 required of international applicants.

FINANCIAL AID. Limited to Federal W/S, loans. Apply to Director of Financial Aid by August 1. Use FAFSA and GAPSFAS.

DEGREE REQUIREMENTS. For M.A.(Management): 56–60 quarter units; thesis/nonthesis option, or special project. For M.A. (Psychology): 72 quarter units; thesis.

FIELDS OF STUDY.
Clinical Psychology.
Organizational Management.
Psychology.

ANTIOCH UNIVERSITY SEATTLE
Seattle, Washington 98121-1211

Coed. Private control. Semester system. Library: 5130 volumes and has access to online bibliographic databases, union catalogs, and interlibrary loan networks. The main University campus is located in Yellow Springs, Ohio. It also has graduate campuses in Keene, New Hampshire; Los Angeles, and Santa Barbara, California.
Tuition: per credit $315. Only off-campus housing is available.

Graduate Programs

Enrollment: full-time 336, part-time 256. Graduate faculty: full-time 32, part-time 39. Degree conferred: M.A.

ADMISSION REQUIREMENTS. Two transcripts, three letters of recommendation, goal statement, interview required in support of application. Accepts transfer applicants. Apply to Director of Admissions by August 16 (Fall); rolling for other semesters. Admits Winter, Summer, Fall. Application fee $50. Phone: (206)441-5352.

ADMISSION STANDARDS. Selective. Usual minimum average: 2.5 (A = 4).

FINANCIAL AID. Limited to Federal W/S, loans. Apply by June 15 to Director of Financial Aid. Use FAFSA.

DEGREE REQUIREMENTS. For M.A.: 40 credits, at least 30 in residence; thesis/nonthesis option or special project.

FIELDS OF STUDY.
Education.
Management.
Psychology.
Whole System Design.

APPALACHIAN STATE UNIVERSITY
Boone, North Carolina 28607
http://www.appstate.edu

Founded 1899. Located 120 miles NW of Charlotte. Coed. State control. Semester system. Special facilities: Dark Sky Observatory, Center for Appalachian Studies, Early Childhood Learning Center, Center for Management Development, Western Carolina Research Center. Library: 510,000 volumes.
Annual tuition: resident $1694, nonresident $8848. On-campus housing available for both single and married students. Average academic year housing cost $2340–$3100. Contact Director of Residential Life for both on- and off-campus housing information. Phone: (704)262-2160.

Cratis D. Williams Graduate School

Graduate study since 1948. Enrollment: full-time 626, part-time 428 (men 35%, women 65%). Graduate faculty: full-time 325. Degrees conferred: M.A., M.S., M.M., M.L.S., M.B.A., M.P.A., Ed.S., Ed.D.

ADMISSION REQUIREMENTS. Transcripts, three letters of recommendation, GRE/GMAT required in support of the School's application. Interview required by some departments. TOEFL required for international applicants. Accepts transfer applicants. Graduates of unaccredited institutions not considered. Apply to the Office of the Dean of Graduate Studies by August 1 (Fall); international applicants apply by April 1 (Fall). Application fee $25. Phone: (704)262-2130; fax: (704)262-2709.

ADMISSION STANDARDS. Selective. Use 2,000 point formula (Undergraduate GPA × 400)+GRE – V + GRE – Q = 2000. Use 1,000 point formula for M.B.A. (Undergraduate GPA × 200) + GMAT=Total. TOEFL minimum score 550.

FINANCIAL AID. Fellowships, assistantships, Federal W/S, loans. Approved for VA benefits. Apply by March 15 to Office of the Dean of Graduate Studies for fellowships, assistantships; to Director of Student Financial Aid for all other programs. Use FAFSA. Phone: (704)262-2190. About 60% of students receive aid other than loans from University and outside sources.

DEGREE REQUIREMENTS. For M.A., M.L.S.: 30–36 semester hours, exclusive of the thesis, 24 in residence; thesis/nonthesis option; reading knowledge of one foreign language or statistics and/or computer science; comprehensive exam. For M.B.A.: 36 semester hour program. For M.S.: 30 credit hours minimum with thesis. For Ed.S.: 30–36 hours beyond the master's degree. For Ed.D.: 60 hours beyond master's, one year of full-time study; comprehensive exam; dissertation; oral/written exam.

FIELDS OF STUDY.
Accounting.
Appalachian Studies.
Applied Physics.
Biology.
Business Administration.
Chemistry.
Counseling.
Curriculum and Instruction.
Educational Administration.
Educational Media.
Educational Supervision.
Elementary Education.
English.
Exercise Science.
Family and Consumer Affairs.
French.
Geography.
Gerontology.
Higher Education.
History.
Industrial Arts.
Junior College Education.
Library Science.
Management.
Mathematics.
Music.
Physical Education.
Political Science.
Psychology. Includes theoretical, clinical, school.

Public Administration.
Reading Specialization.
School Administration.
School Supervision.
Secondary Education.
Social Science.
Sociology.
Spanish.
Special Education. Includes mental retardation.
Speech Pathology. Includes communication disorders.
Student Personnel.
Supervision of Student Teaching.

ARIZONA STATE UNIVERSITY
Tempe, Arizona 85287-1003

Founded 1885. Located 10 miles E of Phoenix. Coed. State control. Semester system. Special facilities: Architecture Library, Bureau of Broadcasting with Public Broadcasting Station KAET, Center for Asian Studies, Center for Executive Development, Center for Latin American Studies, Center for Medieval and Renaissance Studies, Institute for Studies in the Arts, Cancer Research Institute, Center for Research in Engineering and Applied Sciences, Center for Environmental Studies, Exercise and Sport Research Center, Center for Meteorite Studies with Miniger Meteorite Collection, Center for Solid State Science, Fine Arts Center, Grady Gammage Center for the Performing Arts, Law Library, Music Library, Research Park, University Art Collection Library: 2,712,000 volumes; 4,150,000 microforms.

Annual tuition: full-time resident $2010, nonresident $8378; per credit resident $99, nonresident $330. On-campus housing for 98 graduate men and 98 graduate women; none for married students. Average annual housing cost: $4850. Apply to Residential Life. Phone: (602)965-3515.

Graduate College

Organized 1937. Enrollment: full-time 5315, part-time 5757. University faculty: full- and part-time 2000. Degrees conferred: M.A., M.S., M.Acc., M.Arch., M.Ed., M.E.P., M.T., M.B.A., M.C., M.C.S., M.F.A., M.H.S.A., LL.M., M.M., M.M.C., M.N.S., M.P.A., M.S.D., M.S.E., M.S.W., M.Tax., M.T.E.S.L., Ed.D., Ph.D., D.M.A., D.P.A.

ADMISSION REQUIREMENTS. Official application, two official transcripts. Some academic departments may require additional information, i.e., GRE, GMAT, MAT. TOEFL required for international applicants. Accepts transfer students. Apply to the Admissions Office, Graduate College at least two months prior to registration, earlier for international applicants. Application fee $35. Phone: (602)965-6116; fax: (602)965-2012.

ADMISSION STANDARDS. Selective to very competitive. Generally students must have a minimum junior/senior average: 3.0 (A = 4). Some academic departments may require higher averages.

FINANCIAL AID. Annual awards from institutional funds: 750 scholarships, 32 fellowships, 2049 assistantships. Approved for VA benefits. Apply to Director of Financial Aid by July 15. Use FAFSA. Phone: (602)965-3355.

DEGREE REQUIREMENTS. For most master's: 30 semester hours minimum, at least 24 in residence; reading knowledge of one foreign language for some departments; thesis often required; final written/oral exam. For Ph.D.: normally 84 hours minimum beyond the bachelor's, at least 30 in residence, plus 24 hours dissertation and two semesters in continuous full-time attendance; comprehensive oral/written exams; dissertation; final oral exam.

FIELDS OF STUDY.
Accounting. M.Acc. only.
Aerospace Engineering. M.S., M.S.E., Ph.D.
Agribusiness. Includes agribusiness management and marketing, food quality assurance. M.S. only. (Courses offered at ASU East Site.)
Anthropology. Includes archaeology, bioarchaeology, linguistic, medical anthropology, museum studies, physical anthropology, social-cultural anthropology. M.A., Ph.D.
Architecture. M.Arch. only.
Art. Includes art education, art history, ceramics, drawing, fibers, jewelry, painting, photography, printmaking, sculpture, wood. M.A., M.F.A.
Bioengineering. M.S., Ph.D.
Biological Sciences. M.S. only.
Botany. M.S., M.N.S., Ph.D.
Building Design. Includes computer-aided design, energy performance of buildings, facilities development and management, solar architecture. M.S. only.
Business Administration. M.B.A., Ph.D.
Chemical Engineering. Includes biomedical and clinical, chemical processing, chemical reactor, energy and material conversion, environmental control, solid state processing, transport phenomena. M.S., M.S.E., Ph.D.
Chemistry. Includes analytical, biochemistry, geochemistry, inorganic, organic, physical, solid state. M.S., M.N.S., Ph.D.
Civil Engineering. Includes environmental/sanitary, geo-technical/soil mechanics, structure, transportation, water resources/hydraulics. M.S., M.S.E., Ph.D.
Communication. M.A., Ph.D.
Communication Disorders. M.S. only.
Computer Science. M.C.S., M.S., Ph.D.
Construction. Includes facilities, management. M.S. only.
Counseling. M.C. only.
Counseling Psychology. Ph.D. only.
Counselor Education. M.Ed., Ed.D. only.
Creative Writing. M.F.A. only.
Curriculum and Instruction. M.A., M.Ed., Ed.D., Ph.D.
Dance. M.F.A. only.
Decision and Information Systems. M.S. only.
Design. Includes industrial, interior. M.S.D. only.
Economics. M.S., Ph.D. only.
Educational Administration and Supervision. M.Ed., Ed.D.
Educational Leadership and Policy Studies. Ph.D. only.
Educational Media and Computers. M.Ed. only.
Educational Psychology. M.A., M.Ed., Ph.D.
Electrical Engineering. M.S., M.S.E., Ph.D.
Engineering Sciences. M.S., M.S.E., Ph.D.
English. Includes comparative literature, English linguistics, literature and language. M.A., Ph.D.
Environmental Design and Planning. Ph.D. only.
Environmental Planning. Includes urban. M.E.P. only.
Environmental Resources. M.S. only.
Exercise Science. Includes biomechanics, physiology of exercise, psychology of exercise and sport. Ph.D. only.
Exercise Science/Physical Education. M.S. only.
Family Resources and Human Development. M.S. only.
Family Science. Ph.D. only.
French. Includes comparative literature, language and culture, literature. M.A. only.
Geography. M.A., Ph.D.
Geology. M.S., M.N.S., Ph.D.
German. M.A. only.
Health Services Administration. M.H.S.A. only.
Higher and Adult Education. M.Ed., Ed.D. only.
History. Includes Asian, British, European, Latin, Public, United States, U.S./Western. M.A., Ph.D.
Humanities. M.A. only.

Industrial Engineering. Includes human factor, information systems, operations research, organization control, quality control/reliability. M.S., M.S.E., Ph.D.

Justice Studies. M.S., Ph.D.

Laws. LL.M. only.

Learning and Instructional Technology. M.A., M.Ed., Ed.D., Ph.D.

Mass Communication. M.M.C. only.

Mathematics. M.A., M.N.S., Ph.D.

Mechanical Engineering. M.S., M.S.E., Ph.D.

Microbiology. M.S., M.N.S., Ph.D.

Molecular and Cellular Biology. M.S., Ph.D.

Music. Includes ethnomusicology, history, choral, instrumental, performance, theory and composition. M.A., M.M., D.M.A.

Nursing. Includes administration, adult health, community health, community mental health/psychiatric, parent-child nursing. M.S. only.

Philosophy. M.A. only.

Physics. M.S., M.N.S., Ph.D.

Political Science. Includes American politics, comparative politics, international relations, political theory. M.A., Ph.D.

Psychology. Includes clinical, developmental, environmental, experimental, physiological, social. Ph.D. only.

Public Administration. M.P.A., D.P.A.

Recreation. Includes outdoor, administration, social/psychological aspects of leisure, tourism, and commercial. M.S. only.

Religious Studies. M.A. only.

School Library Sciences. M.A., M.Ed.

Social and Philosophical Foundations of Education. M.A. only.

Social Work. M.S.W., Ph.D.

Sociology. M.A., Ph.D.

Spanish. Includes comparative literature, language and culture, linguistics, literature. M.A., Ph.D.

Special Education. Includes gifted, mildly handicapped, multicultural exceptional, severely/multiply handicapped. M.A. only.

Speech and Hearing Sciences. Includes developmental neurolinguistic disorders, neuroauditory processes, neurogerontologic communication disorders. Ph.D. only.

Statistics. M.S. only.

Taxation. M.Tax. only.

Teaching English as a Second Language. M.TESL only.

Technology. Includes aeronautical engineering, aeronautical management, electronics engineering, graphic communication, industrial management and supervision, manufacturing engineering, mechanical engineering, welding engineering. M.T. only. (Courses offered at ASU East site.)

Theater. Includes scenography, theater for youth. M.A., M.F.A., Ph.D.

Zoology. M.S., M.N.S., Ph.D.

GRADUATE SCHOOL OF SOCIAL WORK

Created 1961. Tuition: residents $99 per credit, nonresident $330 per credit. Enrollment: full-time 345, part-time 123 (men 16%, women 84%). Faculty: full-time 28, part-time 25. Degree conferred: M.S.W.

ADMISSION REQUIREMENTS. Two transcripts, three letters of reference, GRE/MAT required in support of application. Accepts transfer applicants. TOEFL required of international applicants. Graduates of unaccredited institutions not considered. Apply to Graduate College by March 1. Fall admission only. Application fee $35. Phone: (609)965-6113.

ADMISSION STANDARDS. Very selective. Usual minimum average: 3.0 (A = 4).

FINANCIAL AID. Annual awards from University funds: approximately 32 scholarships, 5 research assistantships, 2 teaching assistantships, Federal W/S, loan. Apply to Graduate School by March 1. Use FAFSA. No aid for part-time students. Phone: (602)695-3355.

DEGREE REQUIREMENTS. For M.S.W.: 60 semester hours minimum, at least 30 (the second year) in full-time residence.

College of Law (85287-0604)

Established 1966. Special facilities: Center for the Study of Law, Science and Technology, Indian Legal Program. Library: 319,000 volumes. Library has LEXUS, WESTLAW.

Tuition: per semester, resident $4010, nonresident $10,378. On- and off-campus housing available for single graduate students. Total annual cost for all other expenses: $7000.

Enrollment: first-year 160; full-time 501 (men 57%, women 43%). Faculty: full-time 31, part-time 10. Degree conferred: J.D., J.D.-M.B.A., J.D.-M.H.S.A. (Health Administration), J.D.-Ph.D. (Justice Studies).

ADMISSION REQUIREMENTS. LSDAS Law School report, transcripts, LSAT, bachelor's degree required in support of application. Interview not required. Preference given to state residents. Accept transfer applicants. Graduates of unaccredited colleges not considered. Apply to Office of Admissions after September 1, before March 1. Applicants admitted Fall only. Application fee nonresident $35. Phone (602)965-7207.

ADMISSION STANDARDS. Selective. Accepts 15% of total annual applicants. Nonresidents are 24% of entering class.

FINANCIAL AID. Scholarships, fellowships, assistantship, Federal W/S, state grants, loans. About 25% of student receive aid other than loans from College funds. Apply to Financial Aid Office by March 1.

DEGREE REQUIREMENTS. For J.D.: 87 semester hours minimum, transfer credit individually considered. For M.B.A., M.H.S.A., Ph.D.: see Graduate School listing above.

ARIZONA STATE UNIVERSITY WEST
Box 37100
Phoenix, Arizona 85069-7100

Founded 1984. Located in northwest Phoenix. Coed. State control. Semester system. Library: 250,000 volumes; 1,300,000 microforms, 3300 current periodicals.

Annual tuition: full-time resident $1940, nonresident $8308; part-time per semester resident $306, nonresident $1038. No on-campus housing available.

Graduate College

Enrollment: full-time 38, part-time 225. University faculty: full-time 31, part-time 17. Degrees conferred: M.B.A., M.Ed.

ADMISSION REQUIREMENTS. Official application, two official transcripts. GMAT/MAT required for some departments. TOEFL required for international applicants. Accepts transfer students. Apply to the Admissions Office, Graduate College at least two months prior to registration, earlier for international applicants. Application fee $35. Phone: (602)543-4567; fax: (602)543-4561.

ADMISSION STANDARDS. Selective. Generally students must have a minimum junior/senior average: 2.75 (A = 4). Some departments may require higher averages.

FINANCIAL AID. Annual awards from institutional funds: scholarships, assistantships, full and partial tuition waivers, Federal W/S, loans. Apply to Financial Aid Services Office by July 15. Use FAFSA.

DEGREE REQUIREMENTS. For M.Ed.: 30–36 semester hours minimum, at least 24 in residence; thesis/nonthesis option; final written/oral exam. For M.B.A.: 45 semester hour program.

FIELDS OF STUDY.
Business Administration.
Educational Administration.
Elementary Education.
Secondary Education.

THE UNIVERSITY OF ARIZONA
Tucson, Arizona 95721

Founded 1885. Coed. State control. Semester system. Special facilities: Agricultural Experiment Station, Arizona Arthritis Center, Arizona Cancer Center, Arizona Center on Aging, Arizona Center for Mathematical Sciences, Arizona Cooperative Fish and Wildlife Research Unit, Arizona Cooperative National Park Resources Studies Unit, Arizona Emergency Medicine Research Center, Arizona Institute for Neurogenic Communication Disorders, Arizona Poison and Drug Information Center, Arizona Remote Sensing Center, Arizona Research Laboratories, Arizona State Museum, Arizona Transportation and Traffic Institute, Arizona Veterinary Diagnostic Laboratory, Boyce Thompson Southwestern Arboretum, Bureau of Applied Research in Anthropology, Bureau of Mineral Technology, Center for Computing and Information Technology, Center for Creative Photography, Center for Electronic Packaging Research, Center for Insect Science, Center for Microcontamination Control, Center for Middle Eastern Studies, Center for Pharmaceutical Economics, Center for the Management of Information, Center for the Study of Complex Systems, Center for the Study of Higher Education, Center for Toxicology, Cooperative Extension System, Division of Economic and Business Research, Division of Neural Systems, Memory and Aging, Division of Neurobiology, Division of Social Perspectives in Medicine, Economic Science Laboratory, Engineering Experiment Station, Flandrau Science Center and Planetarium, Institute for the Study of Planet Earth, Institute of Atmospheric Physics, Jeffrey M. Golding Clinical Research Unit, Karl Eller Center for the Study of the Private Market Economy, KUAT Communications Group, Laboratory of Tree-Ring Research, Latin American Area Center, Lunar and Planetary Laboratory, Mexican American Studies and Research Center, Mineral Museum, Office of Arid Land Studies, Optical Sciences Center, Respiratory Sciences Center, Ruth E. Golding Clinical Pharmacokinetics Laboratory, Sematech Center of Excellence for Contamination/Defect Control and Assessment, Social and Behavioral Sciences Research Institute, Southwest Center, Southwest Institute for Research on Women, Southwest Retail Center, Steele Memorial Children's Research Center, Steward Observatory, USDA Forest Service Cooperative Research Unit, University Animal Care, University Heart Center, University of Arizona Museum of Art, University of Arizona Press, Water Resources Research Center, Extended University, Summer Sessions, Guadalajara Summer School in Mexico. The University Library System, 7,000,000 catalogued volumes consisting of the Main Library, Science Library, Music Collection, the Center for Creative Photography, the Library Science Collection: College of Law Library, Health Sciences Center Library, and several others.

Annual tuition: resident 1–6 units, $99 per unit registration fee. 7 or more units, $942, per semester; nonresident 1–6 units, $330 per unit registration fee. Seven or more units $2342–$3989 per semester registration fee. On-campus housing for a limited number of graduate students, some housing for married students. Average annual (9 month) housing cost: $2520–$4680 for married students or single students. Apply to Director of Resident Life. Phone: (520)621-6500.

Graduate College

Graduate study since 1898. Enrollment: full-time 5277, part-time 3020, Graduate faculty, teaching and research: 1602. Degrees conferred: M.A., M.S., M.Acc., M.Ag.Ed., M.H.E.Ed., M.Arch., M.B.A., M.Ed., M.F.A., M.L.S., M.M., M.P.A., M.T., Ed.S., Ed.D,, Ph.D.

ADMISSION REQUIREMENTS. One transcript from each institution attended required in support of application. GRE General/Subject Tests/GMAT, interview required for some majors. TOEFL required of all non–English-speaking international applicants. Graduates of unaccredited colleges not considered. Accepts transfer applicants. Apply to the Dean of Graduate College at least by June 1 (Fall), considerably earlier for most departments. Application fee for degree program $35, nondegree status $10. Phone: (520)621-3132; fax: (520)621-4101.

ADMISSION STANDARDS. Selective. Usual minimum average: 3.0 (A = 4).

FINANCIAL AID. Annual awards from institutional funds: approximately 1043 academic scholarships, 1271 teaching assistantships, and 1100 research assistantships, 156 unspecified assistantship, Federal W/S, loans. Approved for VA benefits. Apply to appropriate department head by February 1. Use FAFSAS and University FAF. Phone: (520)621-1858. About 33% of students receive aid other than loans from University and outside sources. Aid sometimes available for part-time students.

DEGREE REQUIREMENTS. For M.A., M.S.: 30 units minimum, at least 15 in residence; thesis required by many departments; reading knowledge of one or more foreign language(s) in some departments (options available in lieu of second language in some cases); final exam. For M.Acc.: 30 units minimum, at least 15 in residence; thesis optional; GMAT required. For M.Ag.Ed., M.H.E.Ed.: 32 units minimum; final research problem. For M.Arch.: 32 units minimum; three-part thesis; final oral exam. For M.B.A.: 60 units minimum, at least 30 units in residence; research project instead of thesis. Prerequisites are Mathematics 119 (Finite Mathematics) and Mathematics 123 (Elements of Calculus) or the equivalent. For M.Ed.: 32 units minimum; final exam may be written, oral, or both. For M.F.A.: major in Art—60 units minimum; thesis or original work or group of such work presented to the public. For major in Creative Writing—36 units minimum; original book-length work of fiction or poetry; final exam. For major in Drama—60 units minimum, in lieu of thesis, monograph/rehearsal, performance journal/original designer production project; final oral exam. For M.L.Arch.: 30 units minimum; thesis. For M.P.H.: a minimum of 33 units including a minimum of 3 units of internships. For M.M.: 30 units minimum; public recital for Applied Music Majors only; reading knowledge of German or French for Music History majors. For M.P.A.: 54 units minimum; optional internship or thesis. For M.T.: 32 units minimum; final written exam. For Ph.D.: 6 semesters minimum beyond bachelor's; at least 2 semesters and 30 units in full-time residence; qualifying exam; language requirement varies; preliminary and oral exam; dissertation; final oral exam. For Ed.D.: essentially the same as for the Ph.D.; reading knowledge of one foreign language is required only when deemed necessary. For A.Mus.D.: essentially the same as for the Ed.D. For Ed.S.: 60 units minimum; GRE General required.

FIELDS OF STUDY.
Accounting. GMAT for admission. M.Acc. only.
Aerospace Engineering. Thesis optional for M.S.
Agricultural Economics. Thesis for M.S. M.S. only.
Agricultural Education. One year's teaching experience for admission. M.S., M.Ag.Ed. only.
Anatomy. GRE for admission.

Animal Science. Thesis for M.S. M.S. only.

Anthropology. GRE General for admission.

Applied Mathematics.

Architecture. Bachelor's degree in architecture for admission; three-part thesis for M.Arch. M.Arch. only.

Arid Lands Resource Sciences. Ph.D. only.

Art. Portfolio for admission; thesis optional. M.A. only.

Art Education. Portfolio for admission; thesis optional. M.A. only.

Art History. One language for M.A. M.A. only.

Astronomy. GRE General/Subject (Physics) for admission; written document for M.S.

Atmospheric Sciences. GRE admission. Thesis for M.S.

Bilingual/Multicultural Education. M.A., M.Ed.

Biochemistry.

Botany. GRE General/Subject for admission.

Business Administration. GMAT or GRE for admission.

Cancer Biology.

Chemical Engineering. Thesis for M.S.

Chemistry. Thesis for M.S.; reading knowledge of one foreign language and thesis for M.S.

Civil Engineering. Thesis or Engineering Report for M.S.

Communication. GRE for admission.

Comparative Literature and Literary Theory.

Computer Science.

Counseling and Guidance. M.A. only.

Creative Writing. M.F.A. only.

Dairy Science. Thesis for M.S.; M.S. only.

Dietetics. GRE for admission; M.S. only.

Drama. Thesis for theater history and criticism. M.A., M.F.A.

East Asian Studies. M.A. only.

Ecology and Evolutionary Biology. GRE General/Subject for admission.

Economics. GRE General/Subject for admission.

Educational Administration. Thesis for M.A.; GRE General/Subject for Ph.D., Ed.D., Ed.S.

Educational Media. MAT for M.Ed., GRE for Ed.S.

Educational Psychology. GRE for admission.

Electrical Engineering. Thesis option for M.S.

Engineering Mechanics. Thesis or Engineering Report for M.S.

English. GRE General/Subject for admission.

English as a Second Language. Language proficiency required for admission. M.A. only.

Entomology. GRE General/Subject for admission. Thesis for M.S.

Epidemiology. M.S., Ph.D.

Exercise and Sport Sciences.

Family and Consumer Resources. M.S., Ph.D. only.

Finance. GMAT for admission; thesis or report for M.S. M.S. only.

Food Science. Thesis for M.S. M.S. only.

Foundations of Education. GRE for admission.

French. GRE Subject for admission.

General Biology. GRE General/Subject for admission.

Genetics. Thesis for M.S.

Geography. GRE General/Subject for admission; thesis option for M.S.

Geological Engineering. GRE General/Subject for admission; thesis for M.S.

Geosciences. GRE General/Subject for admission; thesis/nonthesis optional for M.A.

German. M.A., M.Ed. only.

Health Education. M.Ed only.

Higher Education. MAT or GRE for admission to doctoral programs.

History. GRE General Subject for admission; one language; thesis optional for M.A.

Home Economics Education. GRE Subject for admission; thesis for M.S. M.S., M.H.E.Ed. only.

Hydrology. Thesis for M.S.

Industrial Engineering. M.S. only.

Journalism. M.A. only.

Landscape Architecture. Thesis for M.L.Arch. M.L.Arch. only.

Latin American Studies. GRE Subject for admission; oral and written proficiency in Spanish/Portuguese. M.A. only.

Library Science. GRE or MAT for admission. M.L.S. only.

Linguistics.

Management. Ph.D.

Management and Policy. GMAT for admission; thesis for M.S. M.S. only.

Management Information Systems. GMAT or GRE for admission; proficiency in programming language. M.S. only.

Marketing. GMAT for admission. M.S. only.

Materials Science and Engineering.

Mathematics. Computer programming exam for master's.

Mechanical Engineering. Thesis optional for M.S.

Microbiology. GRE for admission; thesis for M.S.

Mining Engineering. GRE Subject (Engineering); thesis for M.S.

Molecular and Cellular Biology. GRE General/Subject for admission.

Music. Includes applied music, theory, music education, musicology, composition; conducting large-scale composition for A.Mus.D. in composition; three years' experience for admission to A.Mus.D. in music education; four recitals in lieu of dissertation for A.Mus.D. in performance and conducting.

Near Eastern Studies.

Neuroscience. M.S., Ph.D. only.

Nuclear Engineering. Thesis for M.S.

Nursing. GRE for admission.

Nutritional Sciences.

Optical Sciences. GRE for admission; thesis for M.S.

Pharmaceutical Sciences.

Pharmacology. GRE for admission; thesis for M.S.

Pharmacy. Thesis for M.S.

Philosophy. GRE General/Subject for admission.

Physic. GRE General/Subject for admission; thesis for M.S.

Physiological Sciences. GRE for admission.

Planetary Sciences. GRE General/Subject for admission; thesis for M.S.

Planning. M.S. only.

Plant Pathology. Thesis for M.S.

Plant Protection. M.S. only.

Political Science. GRE for admission.

Poultry Science. Thesis for M.S. M.S. only.

Psychology. GRE for admission.

Public Administration. GRE for admission; thesis or internship for M.P.A. M.P.A. only.

Range Management. GRE for admission.

Reliability and Quality Engineering. M.S. only.

Rhetoric, Composition and the Teaching of English. Ph.D. only.

Russian. M.A., M.Ed. only.

Second Language Acquisition and Teaching.

Sociology. GRE General/Subject for admission.

Soil and Water Science. Thesis for M.S.

Spanish. GRE General/Subject for admission.

Special Education and Rehabilitation. GRE General/Subject for Ph.D., Ed.D. Ed.S.; thesis for M.A.

Speech and Hearing Sciences. GRE General for admission.

Statistics. Thesis for M.S. M.S. only.

Systems and Industrial Engineering. Ph.D. only.

Systems Engineering. Thesis for M.S. M.S. only.

Teaching and Teacher Education.

Toxicology. GRE for admission; thesis for M.S. M.S. only.

Water Resources Administration. Thesis for M.S.

Watershed Management. GRE for admission; thesis for M.S.

Wildlife and Fisheries Science. GRE General/Subject for admission; thesis or professional paper for M.S. M.S., Ph.D.

College of Law

Law instruction since 1915. Library: 340,000 volumes. Library has LEXUS, NEXUS, WESTLAW, DIALOG, OCLC. Annual tuition: resident $4010, nonresident $10,378. On-campus housing available for single graduate students. Total annual cost for all other expenses: single students $9000, married students $12,000. Enrollment: first-year 150; full-time 465 (men 54%, women 46%). Faculty: full-time 30, part-time 28. Degree conferred: J.D., J.D.-M.A.(Economics), J.D.-M.B.A., J.D.-M.P.H., J.D.-Ph.D. (Philosophy, Psychology, Economics), LL.M.

ADMISSION REQUIREMENTS. LSDAS Law School report, transcripts, LSAT, bachelor's degree, two letters of recommendation required in support of application. Interview not required. Preference given to state residents. Accept transfer applicants. Graduates of unaccredited colleges not considered. Apply to Admissions Office after September 1, before March 1. Beginning and nonresident applicants admitted Fall only. Application fee $35. Phone (602)621-3477.

ADMISSION STANDARDS. Selective. Accepts 15% of total annual applicants.

FINANCIAL AID. Scholarships, cash awards, fellowships, research assistantships, partial tuition waivers, loans. Apply to Financial Aid Office by March 1. Use FAFSA. Some preference given to minority group students. About 17% of students receive aid other than loans from College funds.

DEGREE REQUIREMENTS. For J.D.: 6 semester minimum, at least the final 2 semesters in residence; 85 units. For LL.M.: at least 24 units beyond J.D. For M.A., M.B.A., M.P.A., Ph.D.: see Graduate School listing above.

College of Medicine (58724)

First class entered 1967. Library: 70,000 volumes. Annual tuition: resident $6760. On-campus housing for 480 married students, for single students very limited. Average figure for all other expenses $8250.

Enrollment: first-year class, 100; total 390 (men 50%, women 50%). School faculty: full-time 247, part-time 642. Degree conferred: M.D., M.D.-Ph.D.

ADMISSION REQUIREMENTS. AMCAS report, transcripts, MCAT, Preprofessional committee evaluation, letters of recommendation, interview required in support of application. Applicants must have completed at least ninety semester units of college study. All candidates must be residents of Arizona or WICHE certified residents. Graduates of unaccredited institutions not considered. Does not have EDP. Apply to College Admissions Office after June 15, before November 1. Application fee, none. Phone: (602)626-6214; fax: (606)626-4554.

ADMISSION STANDARDS. Competitive. Accepts 41% of total resident applicants. 100% are state residents or certified WICHE funded residents.

FINANCIAL AID. Scholarships, loans. About 87% of students receive aid other than loans from College. Apply after acceptance, before May 15, to Financial Aid Officer.

DEGREE REQUIREMENTS. For M.D.: satisfactory completion of four-year program.

FIELDS OF GRADUATE STUDY.
Anatomy.
Biochemistry.
Cell Biology.
Genetics.
Immunology.
Microbiology.
Molecular Biology.
Neurosciences.
Pharmacology.
Physiology.

ARKANSAS STATE UNIVERSITY
State University, Arkansas 72467

Founded 1909. Located 60 miles NW of Memphis, Tennessee. Coed. State control. Semester system. Library: 596,300 volumes; 397,300 microforms.

Annual tuition: resident $2340, nonresident $6120. On-campus housing for 217 married students, 1000 men, 1000 women. Average annual housing cost: $2000 for married students, $3030 for single students. Apply to Director of Housing. Phone: (501)972-2042.

Graduate School

Graduate study since 1995. Enrollment: full-time 256, part-time 811 (men 371, women 696). College faculty: full-time 404, part-time 49. Degrees conferred: M.A., M.S., M.S. in Ed., M.M.E., M.M., M.R.C., M.B.A., M.P.A., M.S.Agric., M.S.M.C., M.S.N., M.C.D., S.C.C.T., Ed.S., Ed.D.

ADMISSION REQUIREMENTS. Transcripts required in support of application. MAT/GRE/GMAT required by some departments. Interview required for Specialist and Doctoral programs. TOEFL required for international applicants. Accepts transfer applicants. Apply to Graduate Dean at least six weeks prior to registration. Application fees: $15, for international applicants $25, for doctoral applicants $35. Phone: (510)972-3209.

ADMISSION STANDARDS. Selective. Usual minimum average: 2.5 overall or 2.75 last 60 hours.

FINANCIAL AID. Annual awards from institutional funds: 175 teaching assistantships, 25 internships, Federal W/S, loans. Apply to Dean six weeks prior to registration. Use FAFSA. Phone: (501)972-2310. About 60% of full-time students receive aid loans from other than University funds. No aid for part-time students.

DEGREE REQUIREMENTS. For M.A.: 30 semester hours minimum, at least 24 residence; thesis for 6 semester hours; reading knowledge of one foreign language; final oral/written exam. For M.S.M.C.: same as M.A., except no language requirement. For M.S.: 30–36 semester hours minimum including thesis; reading knowledge of one foreign language or research tool; final written/oral exam. For M.B.A.; M.M., M.M.E., M.S.Agric., M.S.Ed., M.S.N., M.C.D.: 30–39 hours minimum, at least 24 in residence; thesis optional; no language requirement. For M.R.C.: 48–54 hours. For M.P.A.: 42 hours. For Ed.S., S.C.C.T.: 30 hours beyond the master's, including internship or field study; final written comprehensive.

FIELDS OF STUDY.
Agriculture.
Art.
Biology.
Business.
Chemistry.
Communicative Disorders.
Computer Science.
Counselor Education. Includes rehabilitation counseling.
Early Childhood Education.
Educational Administration.
Elementary Education.
English.
History.
Journalism.
Mathematics.
Music. Includes education, performance.
Nursing.
Physical Education.
Political Science.

Public Administration.
Radio/Television.
Reading.
Secondary Education. Most subject fields.
Special Education.
Speech Communication and Theater Arts.
Sociology.

UNIVERSITY OF ARKANSAS
Fayetteville, Arkansas 72701-1201
http://www.uark.edu

Founded 1871. Main campus at Fayetteville, 200 miles NW of Little Rock. In Little Rock (72201): University of Arkansas for Medical Sciences, includes College of Health-Related Professions, Medicine, Nursing, Pharmacy, Graduate Institute of Technology (72203). Coed. State control. Semester system. Special facilities: Agricultural Experiment Station, Engineering Experiment Station, Bureau of Business and Economic Research, Water Resources Research Center. Sponsoring university of the Oak Ridge Institute of Nuclear Studies in Tennessee. Library: 1,400,000 volumes, 1,720,000 microforms, 16,000 current periodicals, 150 PCs in all libraries, plus access to online data retrieval services.

Annual tuition: full-time, resident $3384, nonresident $7752; per credit, resident $141, nonresident $323. On-campus housing for 334 married students, unlimited for single graduate students. Average annual housing cost: $1940–$4340 (including board) for single students, $3000 for married students. Contact the Residence Life and Dining services for both on- and off-campus housing information. Phone: (501)575-3951.

Graduate School
http://www.uark.edu/depts/gradinfo

Graduate study since 1927. Enrollment: full-time 992, part-time 1363 (men 60%, women 40%). University faculty: full-time 808, part-time 76. Degrees conferred: M.A., M.Acc., M.B.A., M.F.A., M.M., M.Ed., M.S., M.S.C.E., M.S.Ch.E., M.S.E.E., M.S.I.E., M.S.M.E., M.P.A., Ed.S., Ed.D., Ph.D.

ADMISSION REQUIREMENTS. Official transcripts, three letters of recommendations required in support of School's application. GRE for marginal applicants. Interview not required. TOEFL required for international applicants. Accepts transfer applicants. Graduates of unaccredited institutions not considered. Apply to Office of Graduate Admissions; no specified closing dates. Application fee $25; $35 for international applicants. Phone: (501)575-4401; fax: (501)575-5908.

ADMISSION STANDARDS. Selective for most departments. Usual minimum average: 2.75 (A = 4).

FINANCIAL AID. Annual awards from institutional funds: 45 scholarships, 946 teaching/research assistantships, Federal W/S, loans. Approved for VA benefits. Apply to appropriate department head, normally before March 1 for assistantships; to Financial Aid Office for all other programs. Phone: (501)575-3806; fax: (501)575-7790. Use FAFSA and University's FAF. About 35% of students receive aid other than loans from University and outside sources. Aid available for part-time students.

DEGREE REQUIREMENTS. For M.A., M.S., M.M.: 24 semester hours minimum and thesis, or 30 hours minimum, without thesis, at least 30 weeks in residence; final written/oral exam; no language requirement in most cases. For M.B.A.: 30 hours minimum, at least 30 weeks in residence, final exam. For M.Ed.: 33 hours minimum, at least 30 weeks in residence, final exam. For

M.F.A.: 60 hours minimum in residence; thesis and creative project; final written/oral exam. For Ed.S.: 60 hours minimum beyond bachelor's, 30 weeks in residence. For Ed.D.: at least three years of full-time residence beyond bachelor's or the equivalent; preliminary written/oral exam; dissertation; final oral exam. For Ph.D.: same as for Ed.D., except reading knowledge of two foreign languages required by some departments.

FIELDS OF STUDY.
Accounting. M.Acc. only.
Adult Education.
Agricultural Economics. M.S. only.
Agronomy. M.S., Ph.D. only.
Anatomy. At U. of A. M.S., Ph.D.
Animal Science. M.S., Ph.D. only.
Anthropology. M.A. only.
Bacteriology.
Biochemistry. At U. of A. M.S.
Biology.
Biometry. At U. of A. M.S.
Botany.
Business Administration.
Chemistry.
Communication.
Communicative Disorders. At U. of A. M.S. only.
Comparative Literature. M.S. only.
Counselor Education.
Creative Writing. M.F.A. only.
Curriculum and Instruction.
Drama. M.A., M.F.A.
Economics.
Educational Administration.
Educational Technology.
Elementary Education. M.Ed., Ed.S. only.
Engineering. Includes agricultural, chemical, civil, computer systems, electrical, engineering sciences, environmental, industrial, mechanical, transportation.
English.
Entomology.
Food Science.
Foreign Languages and Literature. Includes French, German, Spanish. M.A.
Geography. M.A. only.
Geology. M.S. only.
Health Education.
Health Science.
Higher Education.
History.
Home Economics. M.S. only.
Horticulture. M.S. only.
Interdisciplinary Toxicology. At U. of A. M.S.
Journalism.
Kinesiology.
Mathematics.
Microbiology and Immunology. At U. of A. M.S.
Music. M.M. only.
Music Education. M.Ed only.
Nursing. At U. of A. M.S. only.
Operational Research. M.S. only.
Pathology. At U. of A. M.S.
Pharmaceutical Sciences. At U. of A. M.S.
Pharmacology. At U. of A. M.S.
Philosophy.
Physical Education. M.A.T. only.
Physics.
Physiology & Biophysics. At U. of A. M.S.
Plant Pathology.
Political Science.
Poultry Science.
Psychology.
Public Administration. M.P.A. only.

Recreation. M.Ed. only.
Rehabilitation Education.
Secondary Education. M.Ed., Ed.S. only.
Sociology.
Special Education. M.Ed. only.
Speech Pathology-Audiology. M.S. only.
Statistics. M.S. only.
Translation. M.F.A. only.
Vocational Education.

School of Law

Established 1924. Library: 220,000 volumes. Library has LEXUS, WESTLAW. Annual tuition: resident $3496, nonresident $7528. On- and off-campus housing available. Total annual cost for all other expenses: $6300.

Enrollment: first-year 157; full-time 400 (men 63%, women 37%), part-time 25. Faculty: full-time 31, part-time 11. Degrees conferred: J.D., J.D.-M.B.A., LL.M. (Agricultural Law).

ADMISSION REQUIREMENTS. LSDAS Law School report, transcripts, LSAT (no later than February) required in support of application. Interview not required. Preference given to state residents. Accepts transfer applicants. Graduates of unaccredited colleges not considered. Apply to Director of Admissions after September 1, before April 1. Applicants admitted Fall only. Application fee nonresident $35. Phone: (501)575-3102.

ADMISSION STANDARDS. Selective. Accepts 30% of total annual applicants.

FINANCIAL AID. Scholarships, grants, Federal W/S, loans. Apply by April 1 to the University's Office of Student Financial Aid. Use FAFSA. About 8% of students receive aid other than loans from School.

DEGREE REQUIREMENTS. For J.D.: satisfactory completion of three-year program: 90 semester hours; transfer credit individually considered. For LL.M.: at least 24 credits beyond the J.D. For M.B.A.: see Graduate School listing above.

School of Medicine

Established 1879. Located in Little Rock (72205-7199). Library: 55,000 volumes. Annual tuition: residents $7712, nonresidents, $15,424. Total average figure of other expenses, $6000. Average figure for all other expenses $8250. On-campus housing available.

Enrollment: first-year class 140; total full-time 465 (men 60%, women, 40%). Faculty: full-time 190, part-time 190. Degrees conferred: M.D., M.D.-Ph.D. The M.S. and Ph.D. are offered through the Graduate School.

ADMISSION REQUIREMENTS. AMCAS, transcripts, MCAT, interview (all state residents), recommendations required in support of application. Admission to first-year class given almost exclusively to state residents. Apply to the Dean or AMCAS after June 15, before November 15. Transfers from foreign medical schools to apply COTRANS. Does not have EDP. Application fee $10. Phone: (501)686-5354; fax: (501)686-5873.

ADMISSION STANDARDS. Selective. Accepts 30–40% of total annual applicants. Approximately 97% are state residents.

FINANCIAL AID. Scholarships, loans, grants. Apply to Dean after notification of acceptance. About 80% of students receive aid other than loans from School.

DEGREE REQUIREMENTS. For M.D.: satisfactory completion of four-year program. For M.S., Ph.D.: see Graduate School listing above.

FIELDS OF GRADUATE STUDY.
Anatomy.
Biochemistry.
Biophysics.
Immunology.
Microbiology.
Molecular Biology.
Pharmacology.
Physiology.

School of Law (72202-5142)

Located in Little Rock. Law library 230,000 volumes. Library has LEXUS, NEXUS, WESTLAW, DIALOG.

Annual tuition: resident $3718, nonresident, $8424, per credit resident $143, nonresident $324. No on-campus housing.

Enrollment: first-year class 130, total 271 (men 55%, women 45%). Faculty: full-time 26, part-time 16. Degrees conferred: J.D., J.D.-M.B.A.

ADMISSION REQUIREMENTS. LSDAS Law School report, LSAT, transcripts, bachelor's degree, three recommendations required in support of applications. Preference given to state residents. Accepts transfer applicants. Graduates of unaccredited colleges not considered. Apply to the Director of Admissions by April 1. Admits to Fall semester only. Application fee $40. Phone: (501)324-9439.

ADMISSION STANDARDS. Accepts 45% of total annual applicants.

FINANCIAL AID. Scholarships available to second- and third-year students, Federal W/S, loans. Apply to Director of Financial Aid by May 1. Use FAFSA. Phone: (501)569-3130.

DEGREE REQUIREMENTS. For J.D.: 87 semester hours, at least two years in residence. For M.B.A.: see Graduate School listing above.

ARMSTRONG ATLANTIC STATE UNIVERSITY
Savannah, Georgia 31419

Founded 1935. Public control. Quarter system. Coed. Library: 145,000 volumes, 435,000 microforms.

Annual tuition: full-time resident $1650, nonresident $4587; per credit: resident $47, nonresidents $114. On-campus housing available for single graduate students. Average academic year housing costs: $4500 (includes board). Contact Office of Student Affairs for both on- and off-campus housing information. Phone: (912)927-5271.

Graduate Studies

Graduate study since 1971. Enrollment: full-time 100, part-time 300. College faculty: full-time 137, part-time 15. Degrees conferred: M.A., M.Ed., M.S.C.J., M.H.S., M.S.N., M.S.P.T.

ADMISSION REQUIREMENT. Two official transcripts, GRE/MAT/GMAT required in support of application. TOEFL required for international applicants. Accepts transfer applicants. Graduates of unaccredited institutions not considered. Apply to Admissions Office at least one month prior to registration. Application fee $15. Phone: (912)927-5377; fax: (912)921-5586.

ADMISSION STANDARDS. Relatively open. Usual minimum average: 2.5 (A = 4). Minimum scores GRE 800, MAT 40, GMAT 450.

FINANCIAL AID. Two Regent's Opportunity Scholarships, twenty assistantships, Federal W/S, loans. Approved for VA benefits. Apply to the Dean's Office for assistantships; to Financial Aid Office for all other programs. Use FAFSA. Phone: (912)927-5272; fax: (912)921-7357.

DEGREE REQUIREMENTS. For master's: 45–60 quarter hours minimum; at least 30 in residence; candidacy; comprehensive exam.

FIELDS OF STUDY.
Criminal Justice.
Elementary Education.
Health Science.
History.
Middle School Education.
Nursing.
Physical Therapy.
Secondary Education.
Special Education.

ARMSTRONG UNIVERSITY
Berkeley, California 94704-1489

Founded 1918. Located 10 miles NE of San Francisco. Coed. Private control. Quarter system. Library: 24,000 volumes, 5000 microforms, 150 periodicals, 5 PCS.
Tuition: per quarter hour $205. No on-campus housing available. Contact the Student Services Office for off-campus housing information. Phone: (510)848-2500.

Graduate School of Business Administration

Enrollment: full time 108, part time 5. Graduate faculty: full-time 6, part-time 5. Degree conferred: M.B.A.

ADMISSION REQUIREMENTS. Official transcripts, interview required in support of School's application. TOEFL required for international applicants. Accepts transfer applicants. Apply to Director of Admissions, preferably one month prior to registration. Rolling admission process. Application fee $35 domestic, $50 international. Phone: (510)848-2500; fax: (510)848-9438.

ADMISSION STANDARDS. Relatively open. Usual minimum average: 2.5 (A = 4).

FINANCIAL AID. Limited loans. Approved for VA benefits. Contact the Financial Aid Office for current information. Phone: (510)848-2500; fax: (510)848-9438.

DEGREE REQUIREMENTS. For M.B.A.: 56 units minimum, all in residence; final written exam.

FIELDS OF STUDY.
Accounting.
Finance.
International Business.
Management.
Marketing.

THE SCHOOL OF THE ART INSTITUTE OF CHICAGO
Chicago, Illinois 60603-3103
http://www/saic/saichome.html

Founded 1866. Coed. Private control. Semester system. Associated with The Art Institute of Chicago, the Ryerson and Burn-

ham libraries. Special facilities: Museum of the Art Institute, Center for Advanced Studies in Art and Technology. Library: 216,000 volumes, 2225 current periodicals.
Annual Tuition: full-time $17,760; per credit $592. On-campus housing available for single students only. Contact the Student Affairs Office for off-campus housing information. Phone: (312)345-3527.

Graduate Program

Enrollment: full-time 342, part-time 133. School faculty: full-time 41, part-time 30. Degrees conferred: M.F.A., M.A.A.H., M.A.A.T., P.B.C., M.A.A.E., M.S.H.P., M.A.A.A.

ADMISSION REQUIREMENTS. Official transcripts, three letters of recommendation, portfolio (preferably 20 piece, on slides) required in support of application. GRE required for Art History applicants. Photographs, videocassette, film for Time Arts, Video and Filmmaking. TOEFL required for international applicants. Apply to Office of Admission by February 1 for M.F.A. (Studio); at least two months prior to registrations for all other programs. Application fee $45. Phone: (312)889-5219, (312)899-1840.

ADMISSION STANDARDS. Very selective. Decision based primarily on general creativity and visual perception displayed in portfolio.

FINANCIAL AID. 53 Scholarship, 285 grants, 75 teaching assistantships, Federal W/S, loans. Approved for VA benefits. Apply to the Director of Financial Aid; no specified closing date. Use FAFSA and institutional FAF. About 65% of students receive aid other than loans from Institute.

DEGREE REQUIREMENTS. For the M.F.A., M.A.A.T., M.S.H.P., 60 semester hours minimum, at least 30 in full-time residence (programs worked out with adviser); 48 semester hours in studio work, and 12 semester hours in advanced art history. For M.A.A.H., M.A.A.E.: 36 semester hours. For M.A.A.A.: 48 semester hours. For P.B.C.: 30 semester hours.

FIELDS OF STUDY.
Art and Technology.
Art Education.
Arts Administration.
Art Therapy. Master's only.
Ceramics.
Fiber.
Filmmaking.
Historic Preservation.
Interior Architecture.
Modern Art History, Theory and Criticism.
Painting and Drawing.
Performance Art.
Photography.
Printmaking.
Sculpture. Includes electronics, kinetics, holography, laser.
Time Arts.
Video.
Visual Communication.
Writing.

ASSUMPTION COLLEGE
Worcester, Massachusetts 01615-0005

Established 1904. Private control. Roman Catholic. Semester system. Library: 240,000 volumes. Tuition: per credit $272. No on-campus housing. Apply to Director of Residential Life for off-campus housing information. Phone (508)767-7505.

Graduate School

Established 1951. Enrollment: full-time 57, part-time 205. Graduate faculty: full-time 37, part-time 31. Degrees conferred: M.A., M.B.A., C.A.G.S., C.A.P.S., C.P.S.

ADMISSION REQUIREMENTS. Transcripts, two letters of recommendation (three for Psychology) required in support of application. TOEFL required for international applicants. Graduates of unaccredited colleges not considered. Accepts transfer applicants. Apply at least one month prior to registration. Application fee $20, Phone: (508)767-7387; fax: (508)799-4412.

ADMISSION STANDARDS. Selective. Usual minimum average: 2.75 overall, last 60 credits 3.0 (A = 4).

FINANCIAL AID. Assistantships, loans. Approved for VA benefits. Use FAFSA. Apply for assistantships to the department chair by July 1. Phone: (508)767-7387.

DEGREE REQUIREMENTS. For master's: 36 credits minimum, at least 30 in residence; final oral/written exam. For C.A.G.S., C.A.P.S.: 30 credits beyond the master's. For C.A.P.S.: 15 credits beyond master's.

FIELDS OF STUDY.
Business Administration. GMAT for admission.
Counseling Psychology.
Education.
Marital and Family Counseling.
Pastoral Counseling.
Rehabilitation Counseling.
Religious Education.
Special Education.
Theology.
Theology/Youth Ministry.

AUBURN UNIVERSITY
Auburn University, Alabama 36849-0001

Founded 1856. Located 60 miles NE of Montgomery. Coed. State control. Quarter system. Library: 1,900,000 volumes, 2,000,000 microforms.

Annual tuition: full-time resident $2235, nonresident $7065. On-campus housing for 384 married students, 700 men, 2500 women. Average annual housing cost: $4000 for married students, $1800 ($3600 including board) for single students. Apply to Director of Housing. Phone: (334)844-4580.

Graduate School

Graduate study since 1870. Enrollment: full-time 1700, part-time 1362. Graduate faculty: 1010. Degrees Conferred: M.S. M.A., M.Acc., M.Ag., M.Ag., M.A.C.T., M.A.E., M.B.A., M.B.C., M.C., M.C.D., M.Ch.E., M.C.E., M.C.P., M.Ed., M.E.E., M.F.A., M.F., M.F.S., M.H.S., M.I.D., M.I.E., M.Mat.E., M.M.E., M.M.I.S., M.Mu., M.P.S., M.Z.S., Ed.S., Ed.D., Ph.D.

ADMISSION REQUIREMENTS. Transcripts, GRE required in support of application. GRE Subject Test required for some master's applicants, for most doctoral applicants. GMAT required for M.B.A. Letters of recommendation required by some departments. Accepts transfer applicants. Apply to Graduate School at least three weeks prior to first day of class. Application fee $25. Phone: (334)844-4700.

ADMISSION STANDARDS. Selective; competitive for some departments.

FINANCIAL AID. Annual awards from institutional funds: 455 teaching assistantships, 245 research assistantships. Apply by February 15 to Dean of the Graduate School for fellowships, to appropriate department head for assistantships. Use FAFSA and institutional FAF. About 50% of students receive aid other than loans from University and outside sources.

DEGREE REQUIREMENTS. For master's: 45–60 quarter hours, at least one quarter in residence; thesis/final paper; final written/oral exam. For Ed.D.: 120 hours beyond the bachelor's, at least three quarters in full-time residence; preliminary exam; dissertation; final written/oral exam. For Ph.D.: 92–120 hours beyond the bachelor's, at least three quarters in full-time residence; preliminary exam; dissertation; final written/oral exam; reading knowledge of foreign language required by some departments.

FIELDS OF STUDY.
Accountancy. M.S., M Acc.
Aerospace Engineering. M.A.E., M.S., Ph.D.
Agricultural Economics. M.S., M.Ag., Ph.D.
Agricultural Engineering. M.S., Ph.D.
Agronomy and Soils. M.S., M.Ag., Ph.D.
Anatomy and Histology. M.S., Ph.D.
Animal and Dairy Sciences. M.S., M.Ag., Ph.D.
Art. M.F.A.
Botany and Microbiology. M.S., M.A.C.T., Ph.D.
Building Science. M.B.C.
Business. M.B.A., M.S.
Chemical Engineering. M.Ch.E., M.S., Ph.D.
Chemistry. M.A.C.T., M.S., Ph.D.
Civil Engineering. M.C.E., M.S., Ph.D.
Communication. M.C., M.A.
Communication Disorders. M.C.D., M.S.
Community Planning. M.C.P.
Computer Science-Engineering. M.C.S.E., M.S., Ph.D.
Consumer Affairs. M.S., M.A.C.T.
Counseling Psychology. Ph.D.
Economics. M.S., Ph.D.
Education. Includes counseling and counseling psychology, educational foundations, leadership, and technology, elementary education, health and human performance, rehabilitation and special education, secondary education, vocational and adult education. M.Ed., M.S., Ed.S., Ed.D.
Electrical Engineering. M.E.E., M.S., Ph.D.
English. M.A., M.A.C.T., Ph.D.
Entomology. M.Ag., M.S., Ph.D.
Family and Child Development. M.S., M.A.C.T., Ph.D.
Finance. M.S.
Fisheries and Allied Aquacultures. M.S., M.Ag., Ph.D.
Forestry. M.S., M.F., Ph.D.
French. M.A., M.A.C.T., M.F.S.
Geology. M.S.
History. M.A., Ph.D.
Horticulture. M.S., M.Ag., Ph.D.
Industrial Design. M.I.D.
Industrial Engineering. M.S., M.I.E., Ph.D.
Large Animal Surgery and Medicine. M.S., Ph.D.
Management. M.S., M.M.I.S., Ph.D.
Marketing and Transportation. M.S.
Materials Engineering. M.Mtl.E., M.S., Ph.D.
Mathematics. M.S., M.A.M., Ph.D.
Mechanical Engineering. M.S., M.M.E., Ph.D.
Music. M.Mu.
Nutrition and Food Science. M.S., M.A.C.T., Ph.D.
Pathobiology. M.S., Ph.D.
Pharmacal Science. M.S.

Pharmaceutical Sciences. Ph.D.
Pharmacy Care System. M.S.
Physics. M.S., M.A.C.T., Ph.D.
Physiology and Pharmacology. M.S., interdepartmental Ph.D.
Plant Pathology. M.Ag., M.S., Ph.D.
Political Science. M.A., M.A.C.T.
Poultry Science. M.S., M.Ag., Ph.D.
Psychology. M.S., Ph.D.
Public Administration. M.P.A., Ph.D.
Radiology. M.S., Ph.D.
Small Animal Surgery and Medicine. M.S., Ph.D.
Sociology. M.A.C.T., M.S., M.A., interdepartmental Ph.D.
Spanish. M.A., M.A.C.T., M.H.S.
Statistics. M.S., M.P.S.
Wildlife Science. M.S., Ph.D.
Zoology. M.S., M.A.C.T., M.Z.S., Ph.D.

College of Veterinary Medicine (36949-5517)

College began as a department in 1892, became a college in 1907.

Annual tuition: full-time resident and nonresident contract $3168, nonresident $7128. Total other expenses: $6000.

Enrollment: first-year class 90, total full-time 360, postgraduate 60. Faculty: full-time 807, part-time 10. Degree conferred: D.V.M., D.V.M.-M.S., D.V.M.-Ph.D. M.S., Ph.D. is offered though the Graduate School.

ADMISSION REQUIREMENTS. VMCAS report, two transcripts (prerequisite courses must be completed by June 1), letters of recommendation, GRE (October Test) required in support of application. Interview by invitation only. Does not accept transfer applicants. Applicants must have completed at least three years of college study. Preference given to Kentucky and state residents. Apply to the Dean after August 1, but before November 1. Application fee $35. Phone: (334)844-2685.

ADMISSION STANDARDS. Competitive. Accepts about 30% of annual applicant and only 3–5% of nonresident applicants. Nonresident quota 10 acceptees, U.S. citizens only.

FINANCIAL AID. Scholarships, loans. Apply to Office of Financial Aid by March 15. About 20% Of students receive aid other than loans.

DEGREE REQUIREMENTS. For D.V.M.: satisfactory completion of four-year program. For M.S. and Ph.D.: see Graduate School listing above.

FIELDS OF GRADUATE STUDY.
Anatomy and Histology.
Large Animal Surgery.
Pathobiology.
Pharmacology.
Physiology.
Radiology.
Small Animal Surgery.

AUBURN UNIVERSITY AT MONTGOMERY

Montgomery, Alabama 36117-3596

Founded 1969. Coed. State control. Quarter system. Library: 675,000 volumes, 790,000 microforms, 3000 current periodicals, 5 PCs.

Annual tuition: full-time resident $2130, nonresident $6390; per credit, resident $52, nonresident $156. On-campus housing available. Annual housing cost: $1913 (room only) for single student; $3825 for married students. Phone: (334)244-3572. Day care facilities available.

Graduate Studies

Enrollment: full-time 434, part-time 453 (men 40%, women 60%). Faculty: full-time 142, part-time 29. Degrees conferred: M.B.A., M.P.A., M.Ed., M.P.S., M.S.J.P.S., M.P.G., Ed.S., M.L.A. (Master of Liberal Arts). Joint Ph.D. with Auburn main campus in Public Administration.

ADMISSION REQUIREMENTS. Official transcripts, GRE/MAT/GMAT required in support of application. Interview sometimes required. Accepts transfer applicants. Graduates of unaccredited institutions not considered. Apply to Director of Admissions at least three weeks prior to registration. Application fee, none. Phone: (334)244-3621; fax: (334)244-3762.

ADMISSION STANDARDS. Selective. Usual minimum average: 2.75 (A = 4).

FINANCIAL AID. Fellowships, assistantships, loans. Approved for VA benefits. Apply to appropriate department for fellowships, assistantships; to Financial Aid for all other programs. No specified closing date. Use FAFSA. Phone: (334)244-3564.

DEGREE REQUIREMENTS. For master's: 45–60 quarter hours minimum, at least 35 credits in residence; thesis/nonthesis option/project; final written/oral exam.

FIELDS OF STUDY.
Administration. Includes educational, non-school.
Art Education Counseling.
Biology. Includes medical technology.
Business Administration. Includes accounting, finance, information systems nursing administration, personnel management.
Chemistry.
Early Childhood Education/Elementary Physical Education. Includes general, non-school physical education.
Gerontology.
Justice and Public Safety. Includes correction, juvenile justice, judicial administration, law enforcement administration, security administration.
Liberal Arts. Interdisciplinary. Includes communication, English, fine arts, history, music, philosophy, political science, sociology, theater.
Mathematics.
Political Science.
Psychology.
Public Administration. Includes health care administration, state and local administration.
Reading Education.
Secondary Education. Includes biology, English, history, language arts, mathematics, physical science, social studies.
Special Education. Includes early childhood special education, learning disabilities, mental retardation, mild learning disabilities.

AUGUSTANA COLLEGE

Sioux Falls, South Dakota 57197
http//www.augie.edu/

Founded 1860. Coed. Private control. Lutheran affiliation. 4-1-4 system. Library: 240,000 volumes.

Tuition: per credit hour $220. Limited on-campus housing available. Contact Dean of Graduate Study. Has on-campus day care facilities.

Graduate Division

Enrollment: full-time 2, part-time 100. College faculty teaching graduate students: full-time 80, part-time 0. Year-round program. Degree conferred: M.A.

ADMISSION REQUIREMENTS. Transcripts, two letters of recommendation required in support of college's application. TOEFL required for foreign applicants. Accepts transfer applicants. Apply to Dean of Graduate Study at least two weeks prior to registration. Application fee $50. Phone: (605)336-4126; fax: (605)336-4450.

ADMISSION STANDARDS. Selective. Usual minimum average 3.0 (A = 4).

FINANCIAL AID. Limited to scholarships Federal W/S, loans. Apply to office of Financial Aid: no specified closing date. Phone (605)336-5216. Use FAFSA.

DEGREE REQUIREMENTS. For M.A.: 32 credits minimum, at least 16 in residence; written English proficiency; written/oral comprehensive exam; a graduate paper. No language requirement.

FIELDS OF STUDY.
Communication Disorders.
Nursing.
Secondary Education.
Selected Studies.
Special Education.
Teaching.

AUGUSTA STATE UNIVERSITY

Augusta, Georgia 30910-2200
http://www.Peachnet.edu:80/ borweb/inst/augusta.html

Founded 1925. Public control. Coed. Quarter system. Library: 463,154 volumes, 1,506,685 microforms, 2000 current periodicals.

Annual tuition: full-time, resident $2054, nonresident $7936, per credit resident $47, nonresident $114. No on-campus housing available. For off-campus housing information contact the Office of Student Affairs. Phone: (706)773-1411.

Graduate Studies

Graduate study since 1971. Enrollment: full-time 166, part-time 265 (men 144, women 287). Faculty: full-time 45, part-time 2. Degrees conferred: M.Ed., M.B.A., M.S., Ed.S.

ADMISSION REQUIREMENTS. Transcripts, NTE/WCET/ GRE/MAT (Education), GMAT (Business Administration) required in support of application. TOEFL required for international applicants. Accepts transfer applicants. Graduates of unaccredited institutions not considered. Apply to Admissions Office at least four week, prior to beginning of quarter. Application fee $10. Phone: (706)737-1405.

ADMISSION STANDARDS. Selective. Usual minimum average: 2.5 (A = 4).

FINANCIAL AID. Scholarships, Federal W/S, loans. Approved for VA benefits. Apply to the Office of Financial Aid; no specified closing date. Use FAFSA. Phone: (706)737-1431; fax: (706)737-1777. About 3% of students receive aid other than loans from College and outside sources.

DEGREE REQUIREMENTS. For master's: 60 quarter hours minimum; comprehensive exam. For Ed.S.: 45 quarter hours minimum beyond the master's.

FIELDS OF STUDY.
Business Administration. Includes accounting, management.
Education. Includes early childhood, administration, elementary, English, mathematics, middle grades, health and physical education, social science, special.
Psychology. GRE for admission.

AUSTIN PEAY STATE UNIVERSITY

Clarksville, Tennessee 37040-0001
http://APSU.APSU.EDU

Founded 1927. Coed. State control. Semester system.
Annual tuition: full-time resident $2300, nonresident $6636; per credit, resident $116, nonresident $306. On-campus housing available for both married and single graduate students. Average academic year housing costs: $4000 for married students, $1540–$3050 for single students. Contact Director of Housing for both on- and off-campus housing information. Phone: (615)648-7444. Day care facilities available.

Graduate School

Graduate study since 1952. Enrollment: full-time 110, part-time 331. Faculty: full-time 69, part-time 12. Degrees conferred: M.A., M.S., M.A.Ed., M.M., Ed.S.

ADMISSION REQUIREMENTS. Two official transcripts, GRE required in support of School's application. Interview not required. TOEFL required of international students. Accepts transfer applicants. Graduates of unaccredited institutions not considered. Apply to Dean of Graduate School by July 1 (Fall), December 1 (Spring), May 15 (Summer). Application fee $5. Phone: (615)648-7414; fax: (615)648-7641.

ADMISSION STANDARDS. Relatively open. Usual minimum average: 2.5 (A = 4).

FINANCIAL AID. Annual awards from institutional funds: Minority scholarships, fifty teaching assistantships, Federal W/S, loans. Approved for VA benefits. Apply by March 1 to Dean of Graduate School and appropriate chair. Use FAFSA. Phone: (615)648-7907; fax: (615)648-6305. About 20% of students receive aid from University and outside sources. No aid for part-time students.

DEGREE REQUIREMENTS. For master's: 32 semester hours minimum, at least 24 in residence and one semester full-time attendance; research course; thesis or research paper; final written/oral exam. For Ed.S.: 30 semester hours minimum beyond the master's; special project.

FIELDS OF STUDY.
Administration and Supervision.
Biology.
Education.
Elementary Education.
English.
Guidance and Counseling.
Health and Physical Education.
Music.
Psychology.
Reading.

AZUSA PACIFIC UNIVERSITY
Azusa, California 91702-7000

Founded 1899. Located 25 miles E of Los Angeles. Coed. Private control. Library: 130,000 volumes, 450,000 microforms, 944 current periodicals, 10 PCs.

Tuition: per credit hour $325 minimum; some degree programs cost more. No on-campus housing for graduate students. Average monthly off-campus housing costs: $700.

Graduate Studies Division

Enrollment: full-time 358, part-time 1411. College faculty reaching graduate students: full-time 56, part-time 75. Degrees conferred: M.A., M.Ed., M.M., M.S., M.A.M.F.T., M.Div., M.H.R.D., M.S., M.A.P.S., M.B.A., Ed.D.

ADMISSION REQUIREMENTS. Official transcripts, references required in support of application. Interviews may be requested by some departments. TOEFL required for international applicants. Accepts transfer applicants. Graduates of unaccredited institutions not considered. Apply to the Graduate Admissions Office; no specified closing date. Application fee $45 (domestic), $75 (international). Phone: (818)812-3037; fax: (818)815-3867.

ADMISSION STANDARDS. Selective. Usual minimum average for full admission: 3.0 (A = 4) ; 2.5–2.9 needed for provisional admission.

FINANCIAL AID. Limited to loans. Contact the Office of Student Financial Services for further information. Use FAFSA.

DEGREE REQUIREMENTS. For master's: 32–48 semester hours, at least 26–42 hours in residence; thesis/nonthesis option; final written/oral exam, varies according to program. For Ed.D.: 60 semester hours minimum beyond the master's, at least one year in full-time residence; qualifying exam; dissertation; final oral exam.

FIELDS OF STUDY.
Applied Computer Science and Technology. M.S.
Business Administration. Includes strategic, international, general.
College Student Affairs. M.A.Ed.
Education. Includes administration, computer, language development, physical education, pupil personnel, special education, teaching. M.Ed.
Educational Leadership and Administration. Ed.D.
Human Resource Development. M.H.R.D.
Leadership Studies. M.A.
Marital and Family Therapy. M.A.M.F.T.
Music. M.M.
Nursing. Includes administration, child care, psychiatric. M.S.
Pastoral Studies. M.A.
T.E.S.O.L. M.A., Certificate.

BABSON COLLEGE
Babson Park, Massachusetts 02157-0310
http://www.babson.edu

Founded 1919. Located 12 miles from Boston. Coed. Small independent college. Semester system. Library: 125,000 volumes, 346,000 microforms, 1500 current periodicals.

Tuition: per course $1885. On-campus housing for married and single students. Contact the Office of Campus Life for both on- and off-campus housing information. Phone: (617)239-4438.

F.W. Olin Graduate School of Business

Enrollment: full time 372, part-time 1281. Faculty: full-time 120. Degree conferred: M.B.A.

ADMISSION REQUIREMENTS. Official transcripts, undergraduate degree, GMAT, resume, reference, essays, interview required in support of School's application. TOEFL and official English translation of all pertinent academic documents required of international applicants. Apply to M.B.A. Admissions Office by January 15 (Spring), March 1 (Fall). Rolling admission process. Application fee $50. Phone: (800)488-4512; fax: (617)239-4194.

ADMISSION STANDARDS. Selective. Usual minimum average: 3.0 (A = 4).

FINANCIAL AID. Several forms of financial assistance for full-time M.B.A. students who are U.S. citizens or permanent residents. These awards include grants, graduate assistantships, loans. Apply to the Office of Financial Aid; no specified closing date. Use FAFSA.

DEGREE REQUIREMENTS. For M.B.A.: 45–60 credits hours, depending on previous degree, experience. Advanced standing may be granted for prior business coursework. Program can be completed on a full- or part-time basis.

FIELDS OF STUDY.
Accounting.
Economics.
Entrepreneurial Studies.
Finance and Investments.
International Business.
Management.
Management Information System.
Marketing.
Operations Management.
Quantitative Methods.
Real Estate.
Taxation.

BALL STATE UNIVERSITY
Muncie, Indiana 47306-1099

Founded 1918. Located 55 miles NE of Indianapolis. Coed. State control. Semester system. Library: 1.4 million volumes, 700,000 microforms, plus access to online data retrieval services.

Annual tuition: full-time resident $3188, nonresident $8448; fees for part-time students vary according to number of credits: on-campus 0–3 credits $478, off-campus $141 per credit. On-campus housing for 600 married students, about 2700 men, 4300 women. Average annual housing cost: $3312 for married students, $3872 (including board) for single student. Apply to Director of Housing. Phone: (317)285-1678. Day care facilities available.

Graduate School

Graduate study since 1932. Enrollment: full-time 845, part-time 1157. Graduate faculty: full-time 644, part-time 0. Degrees conferred: M.A., M.A. in Ed., M.S., M.P.A., M.Arch., M.L.A., M.U.R.P., M.B.A., M.M., Ed.S., D.A., Ed.D., Ph.D.

ADMISSION REQUIREMENTS. Transcripts required in support of application. For Ed.S. and doctoral Programs: GRE, letters of recommendation required. TOEFL required for foreign applicants. Accepts transfer applicants. Graduates of unaccredited colleges not considered. Apply to Graduate School's Office of Admissions at least one month prior to registration. Application fee $15. Phone (317)285-1300.

ADMISSION STANDARDS. Selective. Usual minimum average: 2.8 (A = 4)

FINANCIAL AID. Annual awards from institutional funds: 5 doctoral fellowships, 600 master's graduate assistantships for teaching, research, or appropriate assignment, Federal W/S, loans. Apply to Dean of Graduate School by April 15. Phone: (317)285-5600; fax: (317)285-2173. Use FAFSA. About 10–15% of students receive aid other than loans from University and outside sources. No aid other than loans for part-time students.

DEGREE REQUIREMENTS. For master's: 30 semester hours minimum, thesis, research paper, creative project or departmental designated research course included in 30 hours. For Ed.S.: 30 semester hours minimum beyond the master's, at least 24 in residence and one semester in full-time attendance; thesis included in 30 hours; final written/oral exams. For D.A., Ed.D., Ph.D.: 90 semester hours beyond the bachelor's, at least 48 in residence and two consecutive semesters, in full-time attendance; dissertation included in 90 hours; preliminary, final written/oral exam.

FIELDS OF STUDY.
Accounting.
Actuarial Science. M.A. only.
American History.
Anthropology. M.A. only.
Architecture. M.Arch. only.
Art. Studio, art education, art history.
Audiology. M.A. only.
Biology. Master's only.
Business Administration and Management. M.B.A. only.
Business Education. Master's only.
Chemistry. Master's only.
City and Regional Planning.
Classics.
Clinical Psychology.
Computer Science.
Economics. M.A. only.
Education. Adult, community, distributive, reading, administration and supervision curriculum, elementary, guidance and counseling, student personnel administration, management, junior high/middle school, early childhood.
Educational Psychology. Master's only.
English.
Executive Development for Public Services.
Foreign Languages. French, German, Latin, Russian, Spanish. Master's only.
Geography. Master's only.
Government and Political Sciences.
Health and Safety. Master's only.
History. Master's only.
Home Economics. Master's only.
Human Bioenergenics. Ph.D. only.
Industrial Education and Technology. Master's only.
Journalism. Master's only.
Landscape Architecture. M.Arch., M.L.A. only.
Linguistics.
Management. M.S. only.
Mathematics and Statistics. Master's only.
Medical Technology. M.S. only.
Music. Music education, history, literature, performance, theory and composition.
Natural Resources. Master's only.
Nursing. Master's only.
Physical Education and Athletics. Master's only.
Physics. Master's only.
Physiology and Health Science.
Political Science. Master's only.

Psychology. Includes preclinical, precounseling, school, social.
Public Administration. M.P.A. only.
Public Relations. Master's only.
Sociology. Master's only.
Special Education. Includes deaf, E.D.C., M.R., orthopedically handicapped, neurologically impaired, learning disabled. M.A. only.
Speech Communications. Includes audiology, journalism, radio and television, speech and hearing therapy, theater. M.A. only.
Teaching English as a Foreign Language. M.A. only.
Urban and Regional Planning. M.U.R.P. only.
Wellness Management. M.S. only.

UNIVERSITY OF BALTIMORE
Baltimore, Maryland 21201-5779
http://www.ubalt.edu

Founded 1925. Coed. Public. Semester system. Special facilities: Hoffberger Center for Professional Ethic, Institute for Publication Design, William Donald Schaefer Center for Public Policy Studies. Library: 389,000 volumes, 278,000 microforms, 1400 current periodicals.

Tuition: per credit hour Business $208, per credit hour Liberal Arts $283. No on-campus housing available.

Graduate School

Enrollment: full-time 299, part-time 1240. Faculty: full- and part-time 171. Degrees conferred: M.A., M.B.A., M.P.A., M.S., Certificate.

ADMISSION REQUIREMENTS. Official transcripts, three letters of recommendations, GMAT (Business) required in support of School's application. TOEFL required for international applicants. Accepts transfer applicants. Graduates of unaccredited schools not considered. Apply to the Office of Graduate Admission by July 15 (Fall), November 15 (Spring). Application fee $30. Phone: (410)837-4777.

ADMISSION STANDARDS. Selective for most departments. Usual minimum average: 3.0 (A = 4).

FINANCIAL AID. Fellowships, assistantships, Federal W/S, loans. Approved for VA benefits. Apply by April 15 to Director of Financial Aid. Use FAFSA.

DEGREE REQUIREMENTS. For M.A., M.P.A., M.S.: 30–42 credits minimum, at least 24 in residence; thesis/research paper/field experience; final written exam. For M.B.A.: 30 credits minimum, at least 24 in residence. For Certificate: at least 30 credits beyond master's.

FIELDS OF STUDY.
Business Administration and Management.
Criminal Justice and Criminology.
Economics.
Finance and Banking.
Gerontology.
Graphic Design.
Information Science.
Management Information Systems.
Psychology.
Public Policy and Administration.
Taxation.

School of Law (21201-5779)

Full-time day division established 1969. Semester system. Law library 260,000 volumes. Library has LEXIS, CARL, and WESTLAW.

Annual tuition: full-time resident $7166, nonresident $12,788; part-time per credit, resident $296, nonresident $500. On-campus housing only.

Enrollment: first-year class, day 199, evening 134. Day division 630, evening division 448. Faculty: full-time 46, part-time 61. Degrees conferred: J.D., J D.-M.B.A., J.D.-M.P.A., J.D.-M.S. (Criminal Justice), LL.M. (Taxation), J.D.-Ph.D. (Policy Science).

ADMISSION REQUIREMENTS. LSDAS Law School report, transcripts, LSAT, at least three years of college work required in support of application. Interview not required. Accepts transfer applications. Graduates of unaccredited colleges not considered. Apply to Director of Admission of the School after September 1, before April 5. Admits Fall and Spring. Application fee $35. Phone: (410)837-4459; fax: (410)837-4450. For LL.M., Phone: (410)837-4200.

ADMISSION STANDARDS. Selective. Accepts 30%–35% of total annual applicants.

FINANCIAL AID Scholarships, assistantships, Federal W/S, loans. Apply to Office of Financial Aid by April 1. Use FAFSA.

DEGREE REQUIREMENTS. For J.D.: satisfactory completion of three-year (day) or four-year (evening) program; 90 semester hours. Transfer credit individually considered. For LL.M.: at least 24 graduate hours beyond J.D. For other master's degrees, see Graduate School listing above.

BANK STREET COLLEGE OF EDUCATION

New York, New York 10025-1120
http://www.bnkst.edu/

Founded 1916. Private control. Semester system. Special facilities: Nursery/Elementary School (ages 3–13), Infant Center. Library: 112,000 volumes, 339,000 microfilms.

Tuition: per Credit, $510. No on-campus housing. For off-campus housing information: Contact Dean's Office. Phone: (212)875-4404.

Graduate Division

Graduate study since 1930. Enrollment: full- and part-time 909. Faculty: full-time 77, part-time 62. Degrees conferred: M.S. in Ed., Ed.M.

ADMISSION REQUIREMENTS. Transcripts, references, personal essay, interview required in support at application. TOEFL required for foreign applicants. Accepts transfer applicants. Apply to Director of Admissions prior to registration. Application fee $50. Phone: (212)875-4404; fax: (212)875-4678.

ADMISSION STANDARDS. Selective. Usual minimum average: 3.0 (A = 4).

FINANCIAL AID. Scholarships, internships, Federal W/S, loans. Apply to the Director of Financial Aid by March 1. Phone: (212)875-4408; fax: (212)875-4678. Use FAFSA. About 50% of students receive aid other than loans from College and outside sources.

DEGREE REQUIREMENTS. For M.S. in Ed.: 30 credit hours minimum in graduate courses and seminars; 12 credit hours in supervised field work; integrative independent study. For Ed.M.: 36 credits beyond the master's.

FIELDS OF STUDY.
Bilingual Education.
Computers in Education.
Early Adolescence Education.
Early Childhood Leadership.
Early Childhood and Elementary Education.
Educational Leadership.
Infant/Parent Development.
Museum Education.
Museum Leadership.
Reading.
Special Education.

BARRY UNIVERSITY

Miami, Florida 33161-6695
http://www/barry.edu/

Founded 1940. Coed. Private control. Roman Catholic. Semester system. Library: 750,000 volumes/items.

Tuition: per credit hour $390, for M.S.W. $405, Ph.D. $510. On-campus housing for single students only. Apply to Director, Residential Life. Phone (305)899 3875, or (800)756 6000, ext. 3875. Annual housing cost: $5980.

Graduate Programs

Enrollment: full-time 900, part-time 1800. Faculty: full-time 74, part-time 40. Degrees conferred: M.A., M.S., M.S.N., M.S.W., M.B.A., or M.B.A.-M.S.N., Ed.S., Ph.D.

ADMISSION REQUIREMENTS. Transcripts, GRE/MAT/MCAT/ GMAT, three letters of recommendation required in support of University's application. No admission test required for Social Work. TOEFL required for foreign applicants. Interview may be required. Accepts transfer applicants. Apply to Graduate Admissions Office by August 1 (Fall), December 1 (Spring), May 1 (Summer). Application fee $30. Phone: (800)695-2279, (305)899-3127; fax: (305)899-3104.

ADMISSION STANDARDS. Selective. Usual minimum average 3.0 (A = 4).

FINANCIAL AID. Limited to scholarships (M.S.W.), Federal W/S, loans. Approved for VA benefits. Apply to Director of Financial Aid by March 1. Phone: (305)899-3113; fax: (305)899-3104. Use FAFSA.

DEGREE REQUIREMENTS. For M.A., M.S., M.S.N., M.B.A.: 30–60 semester hours minimum; final comprehensive exam for some programs. For M.S.W.: 60 semester hours, at least 30 in residence; thesis optional. For Ph.D. in Education: 62 semester hours beyond master's; dissertation; final oral/written exam. For Ph.D. in Social work: essentially the same as for Education except 45 semester hours.

FIELDS OF STUDY.
Anesthesiology.
Biology.
Biomedical Sciences.
Business Administration.
Clinical Psychology.
Communication.
Educational Computing and Technology.
Educational Leadership.
Elementary Education.
Exceptional Student Education.
Guidance and Counseling.
Health Services Administration.
Higher Educational Administration.

Human Resources Development and Administration. Includes leadership of Not-for-Profit/Religious organizations.
Management Information Systems.
Mental Health Counseling.
Ministry. D.Min. only.
Montessori Elementary Education.
Nurse Practitioner.
Nursing Administration.
Nursing Education.
Pastoral Ministry of Hispanics.
Physical Therapy.
Primary Care Nurse Practitioner.
Psychology.
Reading.
Rehabilitation Counseling.
School Psychology.
Social Work.
Sport Management.
Theology.

BERNARD M. BARUCH COLLEGE OF THE CITY UNIVERSITY OF NEW YORK

New York, New York 10010-5585

http://bus-baruch.cuny.edu

Established 1919. Formerly a branch of City College, became independent unit in 1968. Coed. Municipal control. Semester system. Library: over 410,000 volumes, 1,740,000 microforms, 2000 current periodicals.

Tuition: per credit, city resident $185, non-city resident $320. No on-campus housing.

Graduate Study

Graduate study since 1920. Enrollment: full-time 696, part-time 1639. College faculty: full-time 240, part-time about 36. Degrees conferred: M.B.A., M.P.A., M.S. in Ed., M.S. in Business, Ph.D., M.B.A.-J.D. (with New York Law or Brooklyn Law).

ADMISSION REQUIREMENTS. Transcripts, letters of recommendation, essay, GMAT (M.B.A.), GRE General Test (M.P.A.) required in support of application. TOEFL required for international applicants. Accepts transfer applicants. Apply to Office of Graduate Admissions by June 1 (Fall), December 20 (Spring). Application fee $40. Phone: (212)802-2300; fax: (212)802-2340.

ADMISSION STANDARDS. Very selective. Usual minimum average: 3.0 (A = 4). Average GMAT: 540.

FINANCIAL AID. Annual awards from institutional funds: 60 scholarships, 120 assistantships, Federal W/S, loans. Approved for VA benefits. Apply to Office of Financial Aid by May 15 (Fall), December 20 (Spring). Use FAFSA and CUNY Supplemental FAF. Phone: (212)802-2240; fax: (212)802-2256.

DEGREE REQUIREMENTS. For M.B.A.: 54 semester hours minimum, depending on previous academic work. For M.P.A.: 42–45 semester hours minimum, depending on previous academic work, thesis/nonthesis options. For M.S.: 30–36 semester hours, including specialization courses; thesis/nonthesis option. For Ph.D.: 60 semester hours minimum, at least 38 in residence and two consecutive semesters in full-time residence, one may be required in some departments; oral/written exam; research methodology; dissertation; final exam.

FIELDS OF STUDY.
Accountancy.
Advertising and Public Relations.
Business Administration and Policy.

Business Education.
Computer Systems.
Early Childhood Education.
Economics. Includes quantitative economics.
Education.
Educational Administration.
Finance.
Finance and Investments.
Health Care Administration.
Health Care Policy.
Higher Education.
Industrial Labor Relations.
Industrial and Organizational Psychology.
International Business.
Management.
Marketing.
Operations Research.
Organizations and Policy Studies.
Organizational Behavior.
Personnel and Human Resource Management.
Public Administration.
Statistics.
Taxation.

BAYLOR COLLEGE OF DENTISTRY

PO Box 660677

Dallas, Texas 75266-0677

Founded in 1905. Affiliated with Baylor University from 1918–1971. Became independent corporation in 1971. Joined the Texas A & M System in 1996. Quarter system. Library: 26,800 volumes, 3100 microforms, 500 current periodicals, 16 PCs.

Annual tuition: resident $5400, nonresident $16,200. Off-campus housing available. Average academic year housing costs: $10,000. Contact the Housing Office for housing information. Phone: (214)828-8210. Total average cost for all other expenses in first year: $4200.

Enrollment: D.D.S. program, first-year class 90; full-time 360 (men 65%, women 35%), graduate study 39. Faculty: full-time 99, part-time 130. Degrees conferred: D.D.S., M.S., M.S.D.

ADMISSION REQUIREMENTS. For D.D.S. program: official transcripts, three letters of recommendation, DAT, personal interview required in support of College's application. Accepts transfer applicants. Applicants must have completed at least three years of college study. Apply to Registrar of the College after June 1, before December 1 (flexible). Application fee $35. Phone: (214)828-8230.

For graduate study: official transcripts, three letters of recommendation, GRE, interview required in support of College's application. Accepts transfer applicants. Graduates of unaccredited colleges not considered. Apply to Registrar of the College after June 1, no specified closing date. Application fee $35.

ADMISSION STANDARDS. For D.D.S. program: competitive. Accepts 30% of total annual applicants. Approximately 90% are state residents. For graduate study: competitive. Usual minimum average: 3.0 (A = 4).

FINANCIAL AID. For D.D.S. program: scholarships, grants, tuition waivers, loans. Apply to Office Financial Aid; no specified closing date. Use FAFSA. Phone: (214)828-8236. For graduate study: fellowships, assistantships for teaching/research. Apply as soon as possible to Head of Department. Use FAFSA and GAPSFAS. About 20% of students receive aid other than loans from University and outside sources.

DEGREE REQUIREMENTS. For D.D.S.: satisfactory completion of 45-month program. For M.S., M.S.D.: 45 quarter hours minimum (90 for Clinical Dentistry) ; thesis; comprehensive oral exam. For Ph.D.: 117 quarter hours minimum beyond the master's; preliminary exam; reading knowledge of two foreign languages; final written exam; dissertation; final oral exam.

FIELDS OF GRADUATE STUDY.
Dental Materials.
Endodontics.
General Dentistry.
Oral and Maxillofacial Surgery.
Orthodontics.
Pediatric Dentistry.
Pedodontics.
Periodontics.
Prosthodontics.

BAYLOR COLLEGE OF MEDICINE
Houston, Texas 77030-3498

Founded 1903. Quarter system. Library: 183,000 volumes. Special program: Medical Scientist Training Program.

Annual tuition: M.D. program, resident $6550, nonresident $19,650; student fees $1559; graduate program, $6000. No on-campus housing. Total average figure for other expenses $12,000.

Enrollment: M.D. program, first-year class 168 (5 EDP) (men 60%, women 40%) ; total 665. Graduate enrollment: full-time 136, post-doctoral fellows 106. Faculty: full-time and part-time 1284. Degrees conferred: M.D., M.D.-Ph.D., Ph.D.

ADMISSION REQUIREMENTS. For M.D. program: transcripts, MCAT required in support of application. Interview required of final candidates. Preference given to state residents. Accepts transfer applicants from both U.S. and foreign schools. Graduates of unaccredited colleges not considered. Does have EDP; apply between June 15–Aug. 1. Apply to Director of Admissions after June 1, before November 1. Application fee $35. Phone: (713)799-4841.

For graduate study: transcripts, letters of recommendation, GRE General/Subject Tests required in support of application. Interview required. Accepts transfer applicants. Graduates of unaccredited colleges not considered. Apply to Office of Admissions April 30. Application fee $35.

ADMISSION STANDARDS. Competitive. Accepts about 15% of total annual applicants. Approximately 65% are state residents.

FINANCIAL AID. For M.D. program: limited. Apply to Financial Aids Officer after acceptance. For graduate study: fellowships, teaching/research assistantships; apply to appropriate department chair after acceptance. About 90% of students receive aid other than loans from College.

DEGREE REQUIREMENTS. For M.D.: satisfactory completion of four-year program. For Ph.D.: 108 quarter hours minimum, preliminary exam; thesis; final oral exam.

FIELDS OF GRADUATE STUDY.
Audiology and Speech Pathology.
Biochemistry.
Biomedical Engineering.
Biophysics.
Cardiovascular Sciences.
Cell Biology.
Genetics.
Immunology.
Microbiology.

Neuroscience.
Pharmacology.
Virology.

BAYLOR UNIVERSITY
Waco, Texas 76798
http://www.baylor.edu

Founded 1845. Located 90 miles S of Dallas/Fort Worth. Coed. Private control. Semester system. Special facilities: Glassock Energy Center, Institute of Environmental Studies, Institute for Famine Research and Alternative Agriculture, Van de Graaff accelerator laboratory. Library: 1,531,000 volumes, 1,047,000 microforms, 10,500 current periodicals, 67 PCs.

Annual tuition: full-time $6456, per credit $269. On-campus housing available for graduate students. Average academic year housing costs: $4254 (including board) for single students, $3200 for married students. Contact Office of Student Life for both on- and off-campus housing. Phone: (817)755-3642.

Graduate School

Enrollment: full-time 736, part-time 615. Faculty: full-time 350, part-time 0. Degrees conferred: M.A., M.B.A., M.B.A.-M.I.M., M.C.G., M.E.S., M.F.A., M.H.A., M.M., M.S., M.S.G., M.S.Ed., M.S.E.C., M.S.S.P.A., M.T., M.P.P.A., M.P.T., M.I.J., Ed.S., Ed.D., Psy.D., Ph.D.

ADMISSION REQUIREMENTS. Official transcripts required in support of School's application. GRE required for many departments, GRE Subject Test for some departments, GMAT for business. Interview required for some departments. TOEFL required for international students. Accepts transfer students. Graduates of unaccredited institutions not considered. Apply to Office of Graduate School at least thirty days prior to registration. Rolling admission process. Application fee $25. Phone: (817)755-3588.

ADMISSION STANDARDS. Selective to very competitive. Usual minimum average: 2.75 (A = 4).

FINANCIAL AID. Annual awards from institutional funds: 65 fellowships, 172 teaching assistantships, 62 research assistantships, 183 general duties assistantships, full and partial tuition waivers, Federal W/S, loans. Approved for VA benefits. Apply to appropriate department chair for fellowships, assistantships; to Director of Student Financial Aid for all other programs. No specified closing date. Use FAFSA. Phone: (817)755-2611. About 708 of students receive aid from School and outside sources.

DEGREE REQUIREMENTS. For M.A., M.M., M.S.: 30 credit hours minimum, at least 24 in residence; thesis/nonthesis option, comprehensive oral exam; reading knowledge of one foreign language for some programs. For M.S. in professional fields: 30 credit hours minimum, at least 24 in residence; thesis/nonthesis option; comprehensive exam. For M.B.A.: 36 credit hours minimum, at least 30 in residence. For Ed.S.: 30 credit hours minimum beyond master's. For Ph.D.: 78 credit hours minimum beyond the bachelor's, at least 48 in residence and two consecutive semesters in full-time attendance; reading knowledge of one foreign language; preliminary exam; dissertation; final oral exam. For Ed.D.: 60 credit hours minimum beyond the master's, at least two consecutive semesters in full-time residence; preliminary exam; dissertation; final oral exam. For Psy.D.: 107 credit hours minimum beyond the bachelor's, plus one year of internship; at least nine consecutive semesters of residence study; no foreign language or dissertation; comprehensive written and oral exam at end of third year to qualify for internship.

FIELDS OF STUDY.
American Studies. M.A. only.
Anthropology. M.A. only.
Applied Sociology. Ph.D. only.
Biology. M.A., M.S., Ph.D.
Biomedical Studies. M.S., Ph.D.
Business Administration. GMAT for admission. Includes information systems management, international management. M.B.A., M.I.M., M.B.A.-M.I.M.
Chemistry. M.S., Ph.D.
Christian Theology. M.C.T.
Church-State Studies. M.A., Ph.D.
Clinical Gerontology. M.C.G.
Clinical Psychology. Psy.D.
Communication Sciences and Disorders. M.A. only.
Communication Studies. M.A. only.
Computer Science. M.S.
Earth Science. M.A.
Economics. M.A., M.E.C.
Education. Includes administration, curriculum and instruction, educational psychology, health, human performance and recreation. M.S.Ed., M.A., Ph.D.
English. M.A., Ph.D.
Environmental Biology. M.S.
Environmental Chemistry. M.S.
Environmental Economics. M.S.
Environmental Studies. M.S., M.E.S. only.
Fine Arts (Theater Arts). M.F.A.
Geology. M.S., Ph.D.
Gerontology. M.S.G.
Health Care Administration. M.H.A. only. For military personnel only. Offered in San Antonio.
History. M.A. only.
International Journalism. M.I.J. only.
International Management. M.I.M.
International Relations. M.A.
Limnology. M.S.L.
Mathematics. M.A., M.S. only.
Museum Studies. M.A.
Music. Includes church music, composition, conduction, education, history and literature, theory, performance, piano pedagogy, string pedagogy; qualifying exam. M.M. only.
Neuroscience. Ph.D. only.
Philosophy. M.A. only.
Physical Education, Health, and Recreation. M.S. Ed. only.
Physical Therapy. M.P.T. only. For military personnel only. Offered in San Antonio.
Physics. M.S., Ph.D.
Political Science. Includes international relations, public policy and administration. M.A., M.I.M., M.P.P.A.
Psychology. M.A., Psy.D., Ph.D. only.
Public Policy and Administration. M.P.P.
Religion. M.A., Ph.D.
Sociology. M.A. only.
Spanish. M.A.
Speech Pathology and Audiology. Includes communications disorder. M.S.P.
Statistics. M.A., Ph.D.
Taxation. M.T.
Theater Arts. M.A.

School of Law

Founded 1857. Quarter system. Law library 165,000 volumes. Library has LEXIS, WESTLAW, DIALOG, OCLC.

Annual tuition: $9758. On-campus housing available. Apply to Baylor Rental properties.

Enrollment: first-year class 57 (Fall), 70 (Spring), 30 (Summer); total full-time 403 (men 62%, women 38%), part-time 5. Faculty: full-time 22, part-time 33. Degrees conferred: J.D., J.D.-M.B.A., J.D.-M.Tax.

ADMISSION REQUIREMENTS. LSDAS Law School report, transcripts indicating at least 90 semester hours of college study LSAT required in support of application. Interview not required. Accepts transfer applications. Graduates of unaccredited colleges not considered. Apply to Director of Admissions and Scholarship Coordinator by November 1 (Spring), February 1 (Summer), March 1 (Fall). Application fee $40 Phone: (817)755-1911, (800) BAYLOR U.

ADMISSION STANDARDS. Selective. Accepts 20–25% of total annual applicants.

FINANCIAL AID. Scholarships (⅓ full tuition), Texas Tuition Equalization grants, Federal W/S, loans. About 60% of students receive aid other than loans from school funds. For all financial aid, apply by May 1 to the Director of Admissions and Scholarship Coordinator. Use FAFSA.

DEGREE REQUIREMENTS. For J.D.: satisfactory completion of three-year program, at least 120 quarter hours minimum. Transfer credit individually considered. For other master's: see Graduate School listing above.

BEMIDJI STATE UNIVERSITY
Bemidji, Minnesota 56601

Founded 1919. Located 230 miles NW of Minneapolis. Coed. State control. Quarter system. Library: 250,000 volumes, 721,000 microforms. Special facilities: Freshwater Aquatics Laboratory, Center for Environmental Studies, UNIVAC 1100/80, CDC CYBER 172.

Tuition: per credit, resident $75, nonresident $99.85. On-campus housing for 40 men, 32 women; none for married students. Average annual housing cost: $2800 (including board). Apply to Director of Housing. Phone: (218)755-3750. Day care facilities available.

Graduate Studies

Enrollment: full-time 14, part-time 141 (men 50%, women 50%). Degrees conferred: M.S., M.A.

ADMISSION REQUIREMENTS. Transcripts, GRE required in support of application. TOEFL required for foreign applicants. Interview not required. Accepts transfer applicants. Apply to Director of Graduate Studies prior to registration. Application fee $20. Phone: (218)755-2027; fax: (218)755-3788.

ADMISSION STANDARDS. Selective for some departments, relatively open for most. Usual minimum average: 2.75 (A = 4)

FINANCIAL AID. Annual awards from institutional funds: approximately 16 teaching research assistantships, Federal W/S, loans. Apply to department chair; no specified closing date. Use FAFSA. Phone: (218)755-2034. Less than 10% of students receive aid other than loans from University and outside sources. No aid for part-time students.

DEGREE REQUIREMENTS. For M.A., M.S.: 45 quarter hours minimum, at least 30 in residence; research paper or thesis; final oral exam.

FIELDS OF STUDY.
Biology.
Education. Includes elementary, administration, curriculum and instruction, mathematics, music, special, vocational/technical.
English Language and Literature.
Environmental Policy and Resource Management.
Physical Education.
Science and Mathematics. Includes biology, chemistry, mathematics, general science, environmental studies.
Social Sciences.

BENNINGTON COLLEGE
Bennington, Vermont 05201-9993
http://www.bennington.edu

Founded 1932. Located 40 miles E of Albany, New York. Coed. Private control. Semester system. Special facilities: Regional Center for Language and Culture, Visual and Performing Arts Center. Library: 116,000 volumes, 5800 microforms, 600 current periodicals.

Annual tuition: $12,400. On-campus housing available. Average academic year housing costs: approximately $4100 (including board) for single student; $2100 for married students. Contact Director of Residential Life for both on- and off-campus housing information. Phone: (802)442-5401.

Graduate Programs

Enrollment: full-time 94, part-time 0. Faculty: full-time 10, part-time 11. Degree conferred: M.A., M.A.L., M.F.A.

ADMISSION REQUIREMENTS. Official transcript, references, interview/audition in support of application. Accepts transfer applicants. Apply to Assistant Director of Admission. Application fee $45. Phone: (800)833-6845 or (802)442-5401, ext. 198; E-mail: admission@bennington.edu.

ADMISSION STANDARDS. Selective. Usual minimum average: 2.75 (A = 4).

FINANCIAL AID. Teaching assistantships, Federal W/S, loans. Apply to the appropriate department for assistantships; to Financial Aid office for all other programs. Use FAFSA.

DEGREE REQUIREMENTS. For master's: four semesters of study, master's project.

FIELDS OF STUDY.
Art.
Creative Writing.
Dance.
Drama.
Liberal Arts.
Literature.
Literature/Creative Writing.
Music.
Visual Arts.

BERRY COLLEGE
Mount Berry, Georgia 30149-0159

Founded 1902. Coed. Semester system. Library: 158,500 volumes, 397,000 microforms, 1250 current periodicals, 10 PCs.

Annual tuition: $9678; per credit $323. No on-campus housing available for graduate students. Contact Director of Residence Life for off-campus housing information. Phone: (706)232-2209.

Graduate Studies

Enrollment: full-time 8, part-time 90. Faculty: full-time 0, part-time 17. Degrees conferred: M.B.A., M.Ed.

ADMISSION REQUIREMENTS. Official transcript, bachelor's degree, two letters of reference, GMAT (Business) required in support of application. TOEFL required for international applicants. Accept transfer applicants. Graduates of unaccredited institutions not considered. Apply to Dean of Admissions at least thirty days prior to the beginning of semester. Rolling admission process. Application fee $20. Phone: (404)232-3745, ext. 2215; fax: (706)236-2248.

ADMISSION STANDARDS. Selective. Usual minimum average: 3.0 (A = 4), with above average scores.

FINANCIAL AID. Assistantships, loans. Apply to Office of Financial Aid; no specified closing date. Phone: (706)236-2244.

DEGREE REQUIREMENTS. For M.B.A.: 36 semester hours minimum; thesis not required. For M.Ed.: 33 semester hours minimum; thesis/nonthesis option.

FIELDS OF STUDY.
Business Administration.
Early Childhood Education.
Family and Consumer Sciences.
Middle Grades Education.
Reading.

BLACK HILLS STATE UNIVERSITY
Spearfish, South Dakota 57799-9502

Founded 1883. Located 50 miles NW of Rapid City. Coed. State control. Semester system. Library: 230,000 volumes, 450,000 microfiche and microfilm.

Tuition per credit, resident $124, nonresident $251. On-campus housing for married and single students. Apply to Housing Office. Phone: (605)642-6590. Day care facilities available.

Graduate Division

Graduate study since 1959. Enrollment: full- and part-time 30, 200 in summer. Graduate faculty: part-time 64. Degrees conferred: M.S.C.I., M.S.T.

ADMISSION REQUIREMENTS. Transcripts, GRE required in support of application. TOEFL required for International applicants. Interview not required. Accepts transfer applicants. Apply to Office of Admissions and Director of Graduate Studies six months prior to registration. Application fee $15; $100 for international applicants. Phone: (605)642-6270.

ADMISSION STANDARDS. Selective. Usual minimum average: 2.75 (A = 4).

FINANCIAL AID. Limited to three research assistantships, Federal W/S, loans. Apply to Director of Financial Aid; no specified closing date. Use FAFSA. Phone: (605)642-6254.

DEGREE REQUIREMENTS. For M.S.C.I.: 35 credit hours minimum, at least 22 in residence; thesis/final project; final oral exam. For M.S.T.: 32–35 credit hours minimum, at least 22 in residence; thesis/creative component; final oral exam.

FIELDS OF STUDY.
Curriculum and Instruction.
Tourism.
Note: Cooperative degrees in English and Speech. Students take 12 credits at BHSU and transfer to the receiving institution.

BLOOMSBURG UNIVERSITY OF PENNSYLVANIA
Bloomsburg, Pennsylvania 17815-1905
http://www.bloomu.edu

Founded 1839. Located 70 miles N of Harrisburg. Coed. State control. Semester system. Special facilities: Institute for Comparative and International Management Studies, Institute for Interactive Technologies, Reading Clinic, Speech and Hearing

Clinic. Library: 340,000 volumes, 1,750,000 microforms, 1600 current periodicals.

Tuition: per hour, resident $187, nonresident $336. Limited on-campus housing for graduate students. Average academic year housing costs: $2854 (including board). Contact Office of Residence Life for both on- and off-campus housing information. Phone: (717)389-4088.

School of Graduate Studies

http://www.bloomu.edu/academic/graduate/pages/graduate.html

Graduate study since 1960. Enrollment: full-time 183, part-time 423. College faculty teaching graduate students: full-time 225. Degrees conferred: M.A., M.B.A., M.Ed., M.S., M.S.N. Supervisory Certificates are also granted.

ADMISSION REQUIREMENTS. Transcripts, MAT, GRE, NTE, GMAT (Business Administration), interview required in support of School's application. TOEFL required for international applicants. Accepts transfer applicants. Graduates of unaccredited institutions not considered. Apply to Office of Graduate Studies and Research at least six weeks prior to registration. Application fee $25. Phone: (717)389-4015; fax: (717)389-3054.

ADMISSION STANDARDS. Relatively open. Usual minimum average 2.5 for admission, 3.0 for degree candidacy (A = 4).

FINANCIAL AID. Scholarships, research assistantships, teaching assistantships, Federal W/S, loans. Apply to Assistant Vice President Graduate Studies and Research at least one month prior to registration for assistantships; contact the Financial Aid Office for all other programs. Use FAFSA. Phone: (717)389-4498; fax: (717)389-4795. About 5% of students receive aid other than loans from College and outside sources.

DEGREE REQUIREMENTS. For M.A., M.Ed., M.S.: 30 credits minimum; thesis or research project; final oral/written exam. For M.S.N.: 39 credits minimum; thesis. For M.B.A.: 36 credits minimum.

FIELDS OF STUDY.
Accounting.
Art. Includes art studio, art history.
Audiology.
Biology.
Business Administration.
Business Education.
Communications.
Early Childhood Education.
Education of the Deaf/Hard of Hearing.
Elementary Education.
Exercise Science and Adult Fitness.
Instructional Technology.
Nursing.
Reading.
Special Education. Includes mentally retarded, learning disabilities, behavioral disorders, and exceptional persons.
Speech Pathology.

BOISE STATE UNIVERSITY
Boise, Idaho 83725-0399

Established 1932. Coed. Public control. Semester system. Library: 480,000 volumes, 1,000,000 microforms.

Annual tuition: resident $2578; nonresident $7924; per credit for both $108. There are 170 units available for full-time married students. Annual housing cost for single students: $3600. Monthly housing cost for married students: $465–502. Phone: (208)385-3986.

Graduate College

Graduate study since 1969. Enrollment: full-time 628; part-time 3350. Graduate faculty: full-time 265, part-time 99. Degrees conferred: M.A., M.B.A., M.H.P., M.S., M.M., M.P.A., M.S.W., Ed.D.

ADMISSION REQUIREMENTS. Transcripts, GMAT/GRE/MAT required in support of application. TOEFL required for foreign applicants. Accepts transfer applicants. Graduates of unaccredited institutions not considered. Apply to Graduate Admissions Office at least two months prior to registration. Application fee $20. Phone: (208)385-3903 or (208)385-4204; fax: (208)385-4061.

ADMISSION STANDARDS. Selective. Usual minimum average: 2.75 (3.0 last two years) (A = 4).

FINANCIAL AID. Ninety-nine graduate assistantships, Federal W/S, loans. Apply to Dean, Graduate College (Phone: (208)385-3647) or Department chair for assistantships; to Director of Financial Aid for W/S, loans; no specified closing date. Use FAFSA. Phone: (208)385-1644.

DEGREE REQUIREMENTS. For master's: 30 semester hours minimum, at least 21 in residence; thesis/project; final oral written exam. For Ed.D.: six semesters minimum beyond the bachelor's, at least two in residence; qualifying exam; dissertation; final oral exam.

FIELDS OF STUDY.
Business Administration. GMAT for admissions.
Communication.
Education. Includes curriculum and instruction (Ed.D., GRE for admission), educational technology, early childhood, reading, special education, art, earth science, mathematics, school counseling.
English. GRE for admission.
Exercise and Sport Studies.
Geology. GRE for admission.
Geophysics. GRE for admission.
Health Policy. GRE for admission.
History. GRE for admission.
Instructional & Performance Technology. MAT for admission.
Interdisciplinary Studies.
Music.
Public Administration. GRE for admission.
Raptor Biology. GRE for admission.
Social Work. GRE for admission.
Technical Communication.

BOSTON COLLEGE
Chestnut Hill, Massachusetts 02167-9991
http:/infoeagle.bc.edu/

Founded 1863. Coed. Private control. Catholic affiliation, semester system. Library: 1,500,000 volumes, 2,500,000 microforms, plus online data retrieval service. Special facilities: Weston observatory, social welfare institute, VAX-11/780, IBM 4341.

Tuition: per hour $566. No on-campus housing for graduate students. Apply to Housing Office for off-campus housing information. Phone: (617)552-3075.

Graduate School of Arts and Sciences

Enrollment: full-time 750, part-time 750. Faculty: full- and part-time 350. Degrees conferred: M.A., M.S., M.A.T., M.S.T., C.A.G.S., Ph.D.

ADMISSION REQUIREMENTS. Transcripts, two letters of recommendation required in support of application. GRE General/ Subject Tests, MAT required by some departments. Interview not required. TOEFL required for international applicants. Accepts transfer applicants. Apply to the Graduate Office by February 15, contact departments for Spring admissions deadlines. Application fee $40. Phone: (617)552-3265; fax: (617)552-3700.

ADMISSION STANDARDS. Selective for most departments, relatively open to very competitive for the others. Usual minimum average: 3.0 (A = 4).

FINANCIAL AID. Scholarships, teaching fellowships, assistantships, Federal W/S, loans. Apply to the University Financial Aid Office by April 1. Phone: (617)552-4987. Use FAFSA. About 30% of students receive aid other than loans from School and outside sources. No aid for part-time students.

DEGREE REQUIREMENTS. For master's: 30 semester hours minimum, at least 24 in residence; language requirement varies by department; final oral/written exam. For C.A.G.S.: 30 credits beyond the master's; final exam. For Ph.D.: 60 hours minimum beyond bachelor's, at least one year in full-time residence; comprehensive exam; dissertation; final oral exam.

FIELDS OF STUDY.
Biology. GRE for admission; 34 credits minimum for nonthesis M.S. option. M.S., Ph.D.
Chemistry. Includes analytical, inorganic, organic. M.S., Ph.D.
Classical Languages. M.A., M.A.T., M.A., Ph.D.
Economics. GRE General/Subject for admission; Ph.D. only.
English. GRE for admission; thesis optional for M.A. M.A., Ph.D.
French. M.A., Ph.D.
Geology and Geophysics. Thesis optional. M.S. only.
History. Thesis optional for M.A. M.A., Ph.D.
Linguistics. M.A. only.
Mathematics. Thesis, language optional. M.A. only.
Medieval Studies. Interdepartmental.
Modern Languages. French, Italian, Spanish, Slavic and Far Eastern; thesis optional, one language in addition to major for M.A.; no thesis for M.A.T.; no Ph.D. in Slavic, Far Eastern Languages, or Italian.
Philosophy. GRE for admission; prefers admitting to Ph.D. only; two years of full-time residence for Ph.D.
Physics. Thesis optional for M.S. M.S., Ph.D.
Political Science. M.A., Ph.D.
Psychology. GRE General/Subject, interview for admission. Ph.D. only.
Religious Education and Pastoral Ministry. M.A., Ph.D.
Russian and Slavic Languages.
Sociology. M.A., Ph.D.
Spanish. M.A., Ph.D
Theology. M.A., Ph.D.

Wallace E. Carroll School of Management
http://www.bc.edu/

Graduate study since 1957. Semester system. Tuition: per course $1938.
Enrollment: full-time 210, part-time 550. Faculty: full-time 71, part-time 10. Degrees conferred: M.B.A., M.S. (Finance), M.B.A.-Ph.D. (Sociology, Finance, Organization Studies).

ADMISSION REQUIREMENTS. Transcripts, GMAT, two letters of recommendation required in support of college's applica-

tion. TOEFL, TSE, TWE required for foreign applicants. Interview recommended. Accepts transfer students. Graduates of un-accredited institutions not considered. Apply to the Director of Admissions by April 15 (Fall), December 1 (Spring). Application fee $45. Phone: (617)552-3920; fax: (617)552-8087.

ADMISSION STANDARDS. Selective. Usual minimum average: 3.1 (A = 4).

FINANCIAL AID. Annual awards from School funds: seven academic scholarships, seven AHANA scholarships, and forty-three research assistantships, Federal W/S, loans. Apply to the Director of Financial Aid by March 1. Use FAFSA. Phone: (617)552-3320. About 25% of students receive aid other than loans from School and outside sources. No aid for part-time students.

DEGREE REQUIREMENTS. For M.B.A.: 55 semester hours, 21 courses including 15 required courses in the common body of knowledge and 8 electives. For M.S.: 36 semester hours.

FIELDS OF STUDY.
Accounting.
Business Law.
Computer Science.
Finance.
Human Resource Management/Organization Studies.
International Management.
Management of Financial Institutions.
Marketing.
Operations of Strategic Management.
Public Management.
Note: International exchange program in France, Spain, Ireland, New Zealand.

Graduate School of Social Work
gopher://infoeagle.bc.edu:70/00/g...s_of_BC/Soc_Work_at_BC/about GSSW

Established 1936. Annual tuition: full-time $16,740; per credit $454. Enrollment: full-time 375, part-time 125. Faculty: full-time 22, part-time 27. Degrees conferred: M.S.W., D.S.W., M.S.W.-M.B.A., M.S.W.-J.D., M.S.W.-M.A. (Pastoral Ministry).

ADMISSION REQUIREMENTS. Official transcripts, three letters of reference, GRE or MAT required in support of School's application. TOEFL required for international applicants. Interview not required. Apply to Office of Admissions by March 1. Application fee $40. Phone: (617)552-4024.

ADMISSION STANDARDS. Multidimensional: MAT/GRE or UG content and GPA, related experience, references, and statement of purpose weighted.

FINANCIAL AID. College-administered Federal W/S, loans. School-administered work-study internships, VA stipends, Forensic grant, graduate assistantships, minority scholarships, and various grants on funds-available basis. Apply to School's Director of Financial Aid; no specified closing date. Use FAFSA. Phone: (617)552-4982.

DEGREE REQUIREMENTS. For M.S.W.: 81 semester hours, including field work; thesis. For D.S.W.: 51 semester hours beyond master's; comprehensive exam; dissertation; oral exam.

FIELDS OF STUDY.
Clinical Social Work. M.S.W., D.S.W.
Social Planning. D.S.W.
Social Planning and Administration. M.S.W.

Law School

Established 1929. Semester system. Located at Newton (02159). Law library 285,000 volumes. Library has LEXIS, NEXIS, WESTLAW, DIALOG, 25 Macintosh computers.

Annual tuition: full-time $21,230. No housing on-campus. Total average annual expenses: $10,000. Enrollment: first year class 282; total full-time 800 (men 50%, women 50%). Faculty: full-time 44, part-time 36. Degrees conferred: J.D., J.D.-M.B.A., J.D.-M.S.W.

ADMISSION REQUIREMENTS. LSDAS Law School report, transcripts, LSAT, recommendation, bachelor's degree required in support of application. Interview not required. Accepts transfer applicants. Graduates of unaccredited colleges not considered. Apply to the Director of Admissions; closing date March 1. Application fee $50. Phone: (617)552-4350.

ADMISSION STANDARDS. Selective. Accepts 15–20% of total annual applicants.

FINANCIAL AID. Scholarships, resident assistantships, Federal W/S, loans. About 75% receive aid other than loans from School funds. Apply by March 1 to the Boston College Office of Financial Aid. Use FAFSA.

DEGREE REQUIREMENTS. For J.D.: 85 credit hours minimum, at least the last four semesters in residence. For other master's degrees: see Graduate School listing above.
Note: Semester-abroad program (University of London) available.

BOSTON UNIVERSITY
Boston, Massachusetts 02215

Founded 1839. Coed. Private control. Methodist affiliation. Semester system. Special facilities: African studies center, audiovisual resources center, Center for applied social science, Center for Asian development, reading clinic. computer center, counseling and special education clinics, demonstration classroom, physical therapy clinic, radio, television, film, and photography studios. Library: 1,000,000 volumes, 2,000,000 microforms. 85 computer workstations.

Annual tuition: full-time $20,570; per credit $643. Limited on-campus housing. Average annual housing cost: $7100 (includes board). Contact off-campus housing office. Phone: (617)353-3523.

Graduate School of Arts and Sciences

Graduate study since 1874. Enrollment: full- and part-time 2000. Arts and Science faculty: 600. Degrees conferred: M.A., Ph.D.

ADMISSION REQUIREMENTS. Transcripts, two to three letters of recommendation required in support of application. GRE General/ Subject Tests for most departments, GMAT/MAT for some departments. TOEFL required for foreign applicants. Interviews may be requested. Graduates of unaccredited institutions not considered. Apply to Office of Admissions by January 15 (Fall), October 15 (Spring). Application fee $50. Phone: (617)353-2693.

ADMISSION STANDARDS. Selective for most departments. Usual minimum average: 3.0 (A = 4).

FINANCIAL AID. Annual awards from institutional funds: 166 scholarships, 225 research; 43 graduate assistantships, 321 fellowships, Federal W/S, loans. Apply to Director of Financial

Aid; no specified closing date. Use FAFSA. Phone: (617)353-2697. About 65% of full-time students receive aid from School.

DEGREE REQUIREMENTS. For most M.A. programs: eight semester courses; thesis or final comprehensive exam; students who have not completed two years of undergraduate language study must make up deficiency. For most Ph.D. Programs: eight semester courses beyond the master's; residency requirements of a minimum of two consecutive regular semesters of full-time study; qualifying exam; dissertation; final oral exam; reading knowledge of one or more foreign language.

FIELDS OF STUDY.
African-American Studies. M.A. only.
American and New England Studies. Ph.D. only.
Anthropology.
Applied Linguistics. Ph.D. only.
Archaeological Studies.
Art History.
Astronomy.
Biology.
Biostatistics.
Cellular Biophysics.
Chemistry.
Classical Studies.
Cognitive and Neural Systems.
Computer Science.
Earth Sciences.
Economics.
Energy and Environmental Studies. Includes Environmental Remote Sensing and Geographic Information. M.A. only.
English. Includes English and American literature, creative writing. M.A. only.
Geography.
History.
International Relations. Includes joint programs in international, relations and international communication, and international relations, and resource environmental management.
Mathematics. Includes statistics.
Modern Foreign Languages and Literatures. Includes French, Hispanics.
Music. Includes musicology; 12 semester courses for Ph.D.
Philosophy.
Physics.
Political Science.
Preservation Studies. M.A. only.
Psychology. Includes clinical, community, developmental, experimental, social.
Religion and Theological Studies.
Sociology. Includes joint Ph.D. in Sociology/Social Work.

School for the Arts

Annual tuition: $20,570. Graduate enrollment: full-time 332, part-time 21. Graduate faculty: full-time 68, part-time 34. Degrees conferred: M.F.A., Mus.M., Mus.A.D., Diploma

ADMISSION REQUIREMENTS: Transcripts, three letters of recommendation required in support of School's application. Audition, interview, or portfolio required, depending upon major. TOEFL required for international applicants. Accepts transfer applicants. Applications should be filed by February 1 with the Office of Graduate Admissions of the School for the Arts. Application fee $45. Phone: (617)353-3350.

ADMISSION STANDARDS. Competitive for most departments. Usual minimum average of 3.0 (A = 4) in undergraduate studies.

FINANCIAL AID. Over two hundred annual awards, including teaching fellowships, graduate assistantships, Director's Awards,

Federal W/S, loans. Application for aid should be submitted with application for admission but before February 15. Use FAFSA.

DEGREE REQUIREMENTS. For Mus.M. and M.F.A.: 32 credits minimum; recitals, thesis, or terminal project. For Mus.D.A.: 48 credits minimum beyond the master's, at least two semesters in full-time residence; qualifying examinations; reading knowledge of French and German; dissertation/terminal project; final oral examination.

FIELDS OF STUDY.
Applied Music. Instruction in all major instruments; audition for admission.
Art Education. Portfolio for admission.
Collaborative Piano.
Composition. Manuscripts of music composition for admission.
Conducting. Audition and interview for admission.
Costume Design. Portfolio for admission.
Costume Production. Portfolio for admission.
Directing. Interview for admission.
Graphic Design. Portfolio for admission.
Historical Performance. Audition for admission.
History & Literature of Music. Research paper for admission.
Lighting Design. Interview for admission.
Music Education. Audition for admission.
Music History and Literature.
Opera Performance. Certificate only.
Painting. Portfolio for admission.
Performance. Audition for admission.
Scene Design. Portfolio for admission.
Sculpture. Portfolio for admission.
Studio Teaching. Portfolio for admission.
Technical Production. Interview for admission.
Theater Education. Audition/interview for admission.
Theory of Music. Research paper for admission.
Vocal Accompaniment. Audition for admission.

School of Management
http://management.bu.edu/

Graduate study since 1974. Special facilities: Center for Team Learning. Tuition: full-time, per semester $10,285, per course $2572.
Enrollment: full-time 567, part-time 783 (men 60%, women 40%). Faculty: full-time 116, part-time 48. Degrees conferred: M.B.A., E.M.B.A M.S.M.I.S., D.B.A.

ADMISSION REQUIREMENTS. Transcripts, two letters of recommendation, GMAT required in support of School's application. Interview not required. TOEFL required for foreign applicants. Accepts transfer applicants. Graduates of unaccredited institutions not considered. Apply to Office of Admissions by April 1 (international applicants), May 1 (full-time, begins Fall semester only), July 15 (part-time), December 1 (January admissions), January 5 (D.B.A. admission Fall only). Application fee $50. Phone: (617)353-2670; fax: (617)353-7368.

ADMISSION STANDARDS. Competitive. Usual minimum average: 3.0 (A = 4).

FINANCIAL AID. Scholarships, Federal W/S, loans. Apply to Financial Aid Office by March 15. Use FAFSA. Phone: (617)353-2670.

DEGREE REQUIREMENTS. For A.M.B.A., E.M.B.A., M.B.A.: 64 semester hours maximum; advanced standing for previous academic background is possible. For D.B.A.: fourteen courses minimum, at least eight in residence; teaching/applied research internships; dissertation.

FIELDS OF STUDY.
Accounting.
Entrepreneurial Management.
Executive M.B.A.
Finance.
Health Care Management.
International Business.
Management Information System.
Marketing.
Operations Management.
Organization Behavior.
Public and Not-for-Profit Management.
Note: Dual degrees offered are M.B.A.-M.A.(Economics, International Relations, Medical Sciences), M.B.A.-M.S.(Broadcast Administration, Information Sciences, Manufacturing Engineering), M.B.A.-J.D.

School of Education

Tuition: full-time $20,570; per credit $643. Graduate enrollment: full-time 300, part-time 449 (men 30%, women 70%). Faculty: full-time 47, part-time 52. Degrees conferred: Ed.M., M.A.T., C.A.G.S., Ed.D.

ADMISSION REQUIREMENTS. Transcripts, MAT/GRE, three letters of recommendation required in support of School's application. Interview not required. TOEFL required for international applicants. Accepts transfer applicants. Graduates of unaccredited institutions not considered. Apply by March 1 to Office of Graduate Admissions. Rolling admission process. Application fee $45. Phone: (617)353-4237; fax: (617)353-8937.

ADMISSION STANDARDS. Selective for most departments.

FINANCIAL AID. One hundred fifty scholarships, three fellowships, sixty-six teaching/research assistantships, Federal W/S, loans. Approved for VA benefits. Apply by March 1 (Fall), November 1 (Spring) to Graduate School for fellowships, assistantships; to the Office of Graduate Financial Assistance for all other programs. Use FAFSA. Phone (617)353-4238. About 45% of full-time students receive aid from School and outside sources. No aid for part-time students.

DEGREE REQUIREMENTS. For Ed.M.: 32 credits minimum. For C.A.G.S.: 30 credits minimum beyond the master's, at least 24 in residence; final written/oral exam; no language requirement. For Ed.D.: 60 credits minimum beyond the master's, at least 45 in residence and 24 in full-time attendance; preliminary exam; dissertation; no language requirement.

FIELDS OF STUDY.
Bilingual Education.
Counseling.
Counseling Psychology.
Curriculum and Instruction.
Early Childhood Education.
Educational Media and Technology.
Education of Deaf.
Elementary Education.
English and Language Arts Education.
English Education.
Health Education.
Hearing-Impaired Education.
Higher Educational Administration.
Human Development and Education.
Human Movement.
Human Resource Education.
International Educational Development.
Latin and Classical Humanities.
Leisure Education.
Mathematics Education.

Modern Foreign Language Education.
Policy, Planning and Administration.
Reading.
Science Education.
Social Studies Education.
Special Education.
TESOL (Teaching English to Speakers of Other Languages).
Therapeutic Recreation.

College of Engineering
110 Cummington Street

Enrollment: full-time 326, part-time 182 (men 90%, women 10%). Faculty: full-time 87, part-time 13. Degrees conferred: M.S., M.S.-M.B.A., Ph.D.

ADMISSION REQUIREMENTS: Transcripts, GRE, two letters of recommendation, statement of personal and research goals required in support of application. TOEFL required for international applicants. Accepts transfer applicants. Graduates of unaccredited institutions not considered. Apply to Graduate Admission Office by July 1 (Fall), November 1 (Spring). Application fee $45. Phone: (617)353-9760; fax: (617)353-5769.

ADMISSION STANDARDS. Competitive for most departments, selective for the others. Usual minimum average: 2.75 (A = 4).

FINANCIAL AID. Annual awards from institutional funds: 90 scholarships, 108 fellowships, 61 research assistantships, 59 teaching assistantships, Federal W/S, loans. Approved for VA benefits. Apply to Dean by January 15. Use FAFSA and University's FAF. Phone: (617)353-8970.

DEGREE REQUIREMENTS. For M.S.: 32–36 semester hours minimum, at least 24 in residence. For Ph.D.: see Graduate School listing above.

FIELDS OF STUDY.
Aerospace Engineering.
Biomedical Engineering.
Computer Engineering.
Electrical Engineering.
Engineering Sciences.
Manufacturing Engineering.
Mechanical Engineering.
Systems Engineering. Includes software engineering.
Note: Joint Program is with School of Management and Manufacturing Department. M.S.-M.B.A.

College of Communication

Graduate study since 1947. Annual tuition: $20,570. Graduate enrollment: full-time 400, part-time 127. Faculty: full-time 86, part-time 43. Degrees conferred: M.S., J.D.-M.S., M.B.A.-M.S.

ADMISSION REQUIREMENTS. Official transcripts, three letters of recommendation, MAT/GMAT/GRE/LSAT required in support of College's application. Interview not required. TOEFL/TSE/TWE required for international applicants. Transfer students not accepted. Graduates of unaccredited institutions not considered. Apply to Admissions Officer, preferably by February 1 (Fall). Application fee $50. Phone: (617)353-3481.

ADMISSION STANDARDS. Very selective to competitive. Usual minimum average: 3.0 (A = 4).

FINANCIAL AID. Annual awards from institutional funds: fifty scholarships, two grants, twenty-five research assistantships, thirty administrative assistantships, eighty teaching assistantships, one hundred internships, Federal W/S, loans. Approved for

VA benefits. Apply by April 1 to Graduate Financial Aid Coordinator. Use FAFSA. Phone: (617)353-4658. Seventy-five percent of students receive aid other than loans from School and outside sources. No aid for part-time students.

DEGREE REQUIREMENTS, For M.S.: 32–48 credits minimum; thesis, creative project, analytical project or comprehensive exam.

FIELDS OF STUDY.

SCHOOL OF BROADCASTING AND FILM:
Broadcast Administration.
Broadcasting.
Film.

SCHOOL OF JOURNALISM:
Broadcast Journalism.
Business and Economics Reporting.
Journalism.
Science Journalism.

SCHOOL OF MASS COMMUNICATION AND PUBLIC RELATIONS:
Mass Communication.
Public Relations.

DUAL DEGREE PROGRAMS:
J.D.-M.S. in Mass Communication.
M.B.A.-M.S. in Broadcast Administration.

School of Social Work

Annual tuition: $16,240, per credit $507. On-campus housing available. Contact Housing Office. Phone: (617)353-3511. Enrollment: full-time 294, part-time 312. School faculty: full-time 28, part-time 60. Day care facilities available. Degree conferred: M.S.W.

ADMISSION REQUIREMENTS. Transcripts, references, MAT/GRE, personal statement required in support of School's application. TOEFL required for international applicants. Interview not required. Accepts transfer applicants. Graduates of unaccredited colleges not considered. Apply to the School's Admissions Office by March 1. Application fee $45. Phone: (617)353-3765; fax: (617)353-5612.

ADMISSION STANDARDS. Selective. Usual minimum GPA: 2.7. Average GPA: 3.2 (A = 4).

FINANCIAL AID. Annual awards form institutional funds: 150 Scholarships, Federal W/S, loans. Apply to School's Financial Aid Office. Use FAFSA and School's application. Phone: (617)353-3765. About 70% of students receive aid other than loans from School and outside sources. Aid available for part-time students.

DEGREE REQUIREMENTS. For M.S.W.: 65 credit programs, advance standing may be awarded for candidates with a bachelor's degree in Social Work.

FIELDS OF STUDY.
Social Work. Includes major in either Clinical Social Work practice with individuals, families, and groups, or Macro practice, which includes community organizing, management and planning.

School of Theology

Graduate study since 1839. Coed. Semester system.
Annual tuition: $8480, per credit $265.
Graduate enrollment: full-time 200, part-time 150. Faculty: full-time 21, part-time 14. On-campus housing available. Day

care facilities available. Degrees conferred: M.Div., M.T.S., D.Min., S.T.M., M.S.M., Th.D. The A.M. and Ph.D. are offered through the Graduate School.

ADMISSION REQUIREMENTS. Official transcripts, four letters of recommendation required in support of application. GRE required for some degrees. TOEFL, TWE required for international applicants. Interview not required. Accepts transfer applicants. Apply to Director of Admissions by August 1 (Fall). For A.M. or Ph.D., apply by November 1 (Fall) for February 1 (Spring). Application fee $50. Phone: (617)353-3036; fax: (617)353-3061.

ADMISSION STANDARDS. Very selective. Usual minimum average: 3.0 M.Div.; 3.3 D.Min; 3.3 Th.D. (A = 4).

FINANCIAL AID. Annual awards from institutional funds: 182 scholarships, 10 internships, 16 research, 12 teaching assistantships, Federal W/S, loans. Approved for VA benefits. Apply by July 15 to the Director of Financial Aid. Use FAFSA. Phone: (617)353-3053; fax: (617)353-3061. All D.Min. students and 50% of Ph.D. students receive aid other than loans from School; 80% of all students.

DEGREE REQUIREMENTS. For M.Div.: 96 credits minimum, at least 32 in residence and two semesters in full-time attendance; functional competence in one Biblical language for Biblical Studies majors. For M.T.S.; 64 credits minimum, at least 32 in residence. For S.T.M.: 32 credits minimum beyond the M. Div., at least 24 in residence and two semesters in full-time attendance; final comprehensive exam or thesis. For M.S.M.: 60 credits minimum, at least 32 in residence and two semesters in full time attendance; thesis or research project or composition or two recitals. For D.Min.: 40 credits minimum beyond the M.Div., at least two semesters in full-time residence. For Th.D.: 48 credits minimum; language and/or research competence; qualifying exam; dissertation; final oral exam.

FIELDS OF STUDY:
Biblical Studies.
Church History.
Church Ministries and Administration.
Liturgical Studies.
Missions and Evangelism.
Philosophical and Systematic Theology.
Psychology of Religion and Pastoral Counseling.
Religious Education.
Sacred Music.
Sociology of Religion and Social Ethics.

School of Law

Founded 1872. Semester system. Special facilities: Morin Co. for Banking Law Studies, Center for Law and Health, Center for Law and Technology. Library: 475,000 volumes. Library has LEXIS, NEXIS, WESTLAW, DIALOG.

Annual tuition: $18,666. On-campus housing available. Apply to Office of Housing. Total average annual expenses: $11,500. Enrollment: first-year class 400; total full-time 1185 (men 57%, women 43%). Faculty: full-time 58, part-time 70. Degrees conferred: J. D., J.D.-M.B.A.(Management, Health Care Management), J.D.-M.S.(Mass Communication), J.D.-M.A. (Preservation Studies, International Relations), LL.M. (Taxation, American Banking Law, International Banking Law).

ADMISSION REQUIREMENTS. LSDAS Law School report, transcripts, LSAT, letter of recommendation required in support of application. Interview not required, but visits encouraged. Accepts transfer applicants. Graduates of unaccredited colleges not considered. Apply to the Office of Admissions after September

15, before March 1. Admits to Fall semester only. Application fee $50. Phone: (617)353-3100.

ADMISSION STANDARDS. Selective. Accepts 25–30% of total annual applicants.

FINANCIAL AID. Partial tuition grants, 5 fellowships, 405 scholarships, Federal W/S, loans. Apply by April 1 to the Assistant Dean. Use FAFSA. About 30% of students receive aid including loans from School funds.

DEGREE REQUIREMENTS. For J.D.: satisfactory completion of 3-year program; 84 semester units. For LL.M.: at least 24 credits beyond the J.D.; one year in full-time residence. *Note*: Study abroad available in France, England, Israel.

School of Medicine

Established 1848. Located in Boston (02118). Acquired by Boston University in 1873. Library: 100,000 volumes. Annual tuition: $31,500. Off-campus housing only. Total average figure all other expenses: $13,500. Enrollment: first year class 135 (3 EDP); total 629 (men 58%, women 42%). Degrees conferred: M.D., M.D-Ph.D., M.D.-M.P.H. The M.P.H. and Ph.D. are offered through Graduate School.

ADMISSION REQUIREMENTS. AMCAS, transcripts, MCAT, interview, recommendations, and bachelor's degree from an approved college of arts and science required in support of application. Candidates of unusual ability sometimes accepted after three years in undergraduate school (90 semester hours required). Does have EDP. Apply to School Office of Admissions after June 15, before November 15. Application fee $95. Phone: (617)638-4630.

ADMISSION STANDARDS. Very competitive. Accepts 3% total annual applicants. Approximately 40% are state residents.

FINANCIAL AID. Scholarships, loans available for accepted students. Apply to Financial Aid Office after acceptance. 40% receive aid other than loans from institutional funds.

DEGREE REQUIREMENTS. For M.D.: satisfactory completion of four-year program. For M.P.H., Ph.D.: see Graduate School listing above.

FIELDS OF GRADUATE STUDY.
Anatomy.
Biochemistry.
Biomedical Engineering.
Biophysics.
Genetics.
Immunology.
Microbiology.
Neurosciences.
Pathology.
Pharmacology.
Physiology.

School of Graduate Dentistry

Founded 1963. D.M.D. program established 1972. Annual tuition $29,500. Total average cost for all other first-year expenses $6,310.

Enrollment: first-year class 75, total full-time 499 (men 80%, women 20%); full-time study only. Faculty: full-time 62, part-time 110. Degrees conferred: D.M.D., M.Sc., M.S., C.A.G.S., D.Sc.

ADMISSION REQUIREMENTS. AADSAS report, transcripts, DAT (no later than October), two letter of reference required in support of School's application. Interview by invitation only. Applicants must have completed at least three years of undergraduate study for D.M.D. Graduates of unaccredited colleges not considered. TOEFL required of international applicants. Does not have EDP. Apply to Admissions Committee after June 1 and before March 1 for all programs. Application fee $40. Phone: (617)638-4787, (617)638-4798.

ADMISSION STANDARDS. Competitive. Accepts 25% of total applicants. Usual minimum average: 3.0 (A = 4). Approximately 10% are state residents.

FINANCIAL AID. Scholarships, grants, tuition waivers, loans. Apply by April 1 to the Dean for scholarships; to Office of Financial Management, Medical Center for all other programs. Use FAFSA. Phone: (617)638-5130. About 75% of students receive aid other than loans from School and outside sources.

DEGREE REQUIREMENTS. For D.M.D.: satisfactory completion of forty-four month program. For M.S., M.Sc.: 36 credits minimum in residence; final oral exam; research project. For C.A.G.S.: same as M.S., except no research project. For D.Sc.: 54 credits minimum, at least three years in residence; research project; final written/oral exam.

FIELDS OF STUDY.
Dental Care Management. C.A.G.S. only.
Dental Public Health.
Endodontics.
Nutritional Science. D.Sc. only.
Operative Dentistry.
Oral Biology.
Oral and Maxillofacial Surgery.
Oral Pathology.
Orthodontics.
Pediatric Dentistry.
Pedodontics.
Periodontology.
Prosthodontics.
Note: Ph.D. programs available through the Department of Medical and Dental Sciences, School of Medicine.

BOWIE STATE UNIVERSITY
Bowie, Maryland 20715-3318

Established 1865. Located 25 miles N of Washington, D.C. Coed. Public control. Semester system. Evening session only. Library: 180,000 volumes, 317,000 microforms, 1150 current periodicals.

Tuition: per credit, resident $144, nonresident $244. On-campus housing for single student only. Average academic year housing costs: $4455 (including board). Contact Housing Department for both on- and off-campus housing information. Phone (301)464-7135.

Division of Graduate Studies

Graduate study since 1970. Enrollment: full-time 304, part-time 1354. Faculty: full-time 31, part-time 43. Degrees conferred: M.A., M.S., M.Ed., M.A.Mgt.

ADMISSION REQUIREMENTS. Official transcripts required in support of application. TOEFL required for international applicants. Accepts transfer applicants. Graduates of unaccredited institutions not considered. Apply to Graduate Office by June 29 (Fall), December 7 (Spring). Rolling admission process. Application fee $30. Phone: (301)464-6586; fax: (301)464-7786.

ADMISSION STANDARDS. Selective. Usual minimum average: 2.5 (A = 4).

FINANCIAL AID. Eight fellowships, twenty-five assistantships, Federal W/S, loans. Approved for VA benefits. Apply to Dean's Office for fellowships, assistantships; to Financial Aid Office for all other programs. No specified closing date. Use FAFSA. Phone: (301)464-6544.

DEGREE REQUIREMENTS. For most master's: 36 semester hours minimum; advancement to candidacy; seminar paper; comprehensive exam. For M.A.Mgt.: 45 semester hours minimum. For M.S. in Nursing: 43 semester hours minimum.

FIELDS OF STUDY.
Administrative Management. M.A.Mgt.
Computer science. M.S.
Counseling Psychology. M.A.
Elementary Education. M. Ed.
Family Nurse Practitioner. M.S.
Management Information Systems. M.S. only.
Nursing. M.S.
Organizational Communication. M.A.
Public Administration. M.A.Mgt.
Reading Education. M.Ed.
Secondary Education. M.Ed.
Special Education. M.Ed.

BOWLING GREEN STATE UNIVERSITY
Bowling Green, Ohio 43403-0180

Founded 1910. Located 23 miles S of Toledo. Coed. State assisted. Semester system. Special facilities: Center for Archival Collections, Center for the Study of Popular Culture, Center for Photo Chemical Sciences, Center for Microscopy and Microanalysis, Institute for Great Lakes Research, Environmental Study Center, Laboratory of Marine Studies, Population and Society Research Center, Center for Governmental Research, Public Service Management Center, Institute for Psychological Research and Application, Social Philosophy and Policy Center. Library: 1,903,000 volumes, 1,772,000 microforms, 5427 current periodicals, 167 PCs in all libraries.

Tuition: per credit, resident $256, nonresident $482. On-campus housing available for graduate students. Average academic year housing costs: $4400. Contact Director of Student Housing and Residential Programs for both on- and off-campus housing information. Phone: (419)372-2456.

Graduate College

Enrollment: full-time 1550, part-time 934. University faculty: full-time 567, part-time 165. Degrees conferred: M.A., M.A.T., M.M., M.B.A., M.O.D., M.P.A., M.R.C., M.S., M.F.A., M.Ed., M.A.H.E., M.I.T., Specialist, Ed.S., Ph.D.

ADMISSION REQUIREMENTS. Two official transcripts, GRE/GMAT, three letters of recommendation to department required in support of College's application. TOEFL/MELAB required of international applicants. Accepts transfer students. Apply at least six months prior to semester of registration (Ph.D.), three month prior to semester of registration (Masters). Application fee $30. Phone: (419)372-2791.

ADMISSION STANDARDS. Competitive. Usual minimum average: 2.6 (A = 4).

FINANCIAL AID. Annual awards from institutional funds: 208 Ph.D. fellowships, 433 research assistantships, 598 teaching assistantships, Federal W/S, loans. Approved for VA benefits. Admission process must be completed by January 15. Apply by February 15 to appropriate department chair for fellowships, assistantships; to Financial Aid Office for all other programs. Use

FAFSA. Phone: (419)372-2651. About 60% of students receive aid from Institution in the form of assistantships or fellowships.

DEGREE REQUIREMENTS. General requirements for master's: Plan I—30 hours minimum, minimum of 24 hours in residence thesis; final written/oral exam. Plan II—30 hours minimum, minimum of 24 hours in residence; final comprehensive exam. For M.A.: Plan I or II available. For M.Ed.: 30 hours minimum; thesis or written exam; 33 hours minimum; comprehensive exam. For M.A.T.: 35 hours minimum;; final written comprehensive. For M.M.: 34 hours minimum; option of thesis, recital and research document or composition. For M.B.A.: Phase I—for students with little or no previous work in business administration or economic; required work must be completed, but not to exceed the 30 hours of Phase II courses. For M.I.T.: 33 hours minimum; thesis or major project. For M.S.: 30 hours minimum; Plan I or Plan II available. For M.F.A.: in Art, 62 hours; thesis; exhibition; in Creative Writing, 40 hours minimum; thesis. For M.A.H.E.: 33 hours minimum; applied or research option. For M.O.D.: 33 hours minimum; thesis. For M.P.A.: 42 hours minimum; thesis; final written/oral exam. For M.R.C.; 48 hours minimum; thesis; final comprehensive exam. For Specialist: 30 hours minimum beyond the master's; comprehensive oral exam. For Ph.D.: 90 hours minimum beyond the bachelor's; proficiency in one foreign language, proficiency in computer research applications; preliminary exam; dissertation; final/oral written exam.

FIELDS OF STUDY.
American Culture Studies. M.A., M.A.T., Ph.D.
Applied Biology. Specialist.
Applied Human Ecology. Includes human development, family studies, food and nutrition, textile and clothing. M.A.H.E.
Applied Philosophy. M.A., Ph.D.
Applied Statistics (Mathematics). M.S., Ph.D.
Applied Statistics and Operation Research. M.S.
Art. M.A., M.F.A.
Biological Sciences. M.A., Ph.D.
Business Administration. M.B.A.
Career and Technology Education. M.Ed.
Chemistry. M.S., M.A.T.
College Student Personnel. M.A., M.Ed.
Communication Disorders. M.S., Ph.D.
Computer Science. M.S.
Creative Writing. M.F.A.
Curriculum and Instruction. Includes elementary, library and educational media, mathematics supervision, secondary, reading.
Economics. M.A.
Education. Includes elementary, secondary. M.Ed., Ph.D.
Educational Administration and Supervision. M.Ed., Ed.S., Ph.D.
English. Includes creative, interpersonal, technical writing. teaching.
English as a Second Language. M.A., Ph.D.
French. M.A.
Geology. M.S., M.A.T.
German. M.A., M.A.T.
Guidance and Counseling. M.A., M.Ed.
Health, Physical Education and Recreation. Includes adapted physical education, elementary, health secondary. M.Ed.
History. M.A., M.A.T., Ph.D.
Industrial Technology. M.I.T.
Interpersonal Communication. M.A., Ph.D.
Mass Communication. M.A., Ph.D.
Mathematics. M.A., Ph.D.
Mathematics Supervision. Ed.S.
Music. Includes performance, music education, instrumental specialist, music composition, music theory, music history. M.M.
Organizational Development. M.O.D.
Philosophy. M.A.
Photochemical Sciences. Ph.D.
Physics. M.A.T., M.S.

Political Science. M.A., M.A.T.
Popular Culture. M.A., Ph.D.
Psychology. Includes clinical, developmental, experimental, industrial, social. M.A., Ph.D.
Public Administration. M.P.A.
Reading. M.Ed.
Rehabilitation Counseling. M.R.C.
School Psychology. M.Ed.
Sociology. M.A., Ph.D.
Spanish. M.A.
Special Education. Includes educable mentally retarded, trainable mentally retarded, learning/behavioral disorders. M.Ed.
Theater. M.A., Ph.D.

BRADLEY UNIVERSITY
Peoria, Illinois 61625-0002

Founded 1897. Located 163 miles SW of Chicago. Coed. Private control. Semester system. Library: 530,000 volumes, 762,000 microforms, 1800 current periodicals, 112 PCs in all libraries. Special facilities: Center for Learning Resources (includes on-campus CCTV and satellite, teleproduction capacity, computer center), Materials Testing and Research Lab, Institute for Urban Affairs and Business Research.

Annual tuition: full-time $12,010, per credit $326; for M.L.S. per credit $164. No on-campus housing available. Average academic year housing costs: $550 per month. Contact Director of Housing for off-campus housing information. Phone: (309)677-3218.

Graduate School

Enrollment: full-time 135, part-time 686. Graduate faculty: full-time 256, part-time 30. Degrees conferred: M.A.. M.S., M.F.A., M.B.A., M.M.E., M.M., M.S.C.E., M.S.E.E., M.S.I.E., M.S.M.E., M.S.M.E., M.L.S., M.S.N., M.N.S.

ADMISSION REQUIREMENTS. Two official transcripts, two references required in support of School's application. Interview, GRE required by some departments. GMAT for M.B.A. applicants, MAT for all Education programs. Portfolio for Art program. TOEFL and evidence of financial resources required of international applicants. Accepts transfer applicants. Graduates of unaccredited institutions not considered. Apply to Dean of the Graduate School at least six weeks prior to registration. Rolling admission process. Application fee $35. Phone: (309)677-2371; fax: (309)677-3343.

ADMISSIONS STANDARDS. Selective. Usual minimum average: 2.5 (2.75 major areas) (A = 4). Non-degree students permitted.

FINANCIAL AID. Scholarships, assistantships, Federal W/S, loans. Approved for VA benefits. Apply by March 1 to Dean of the Graduate School for assistantships; to Financial Aid Office for all other programs. Use FAFSA. Phone: (309)677-3215.

DEGREE REQUIREMENTS. For master's: 30 semester hours minimum; thesis/nonthesis option; final comprehensive exam.

FIELDS OF STUDY.
Art. Includes Ceramics, painting, photography, printmaking, sculpture. M.A., M.F.A.
Biology.
Business Administration. M.B.A.
Chemistry. M.S.
Civil Engineering.
Computer Information System.
Computer Science. M.S. only.
Curriculum and Instruction.

Educational Administration.
Electrical Engineering.
English.
Human Development Counseling.
Human Services Administration.
Industrial Engineering.
Learning Disabilities.
Liberal Studies. M.L.S. only.
Manufacturing Engineering.
Music. M. M. only.
Music Education.
Nursing. Includes administration, nurse-administered anesthesia.

BRANDEIS UNIVERSITY
Waltham, Massachusetts 02254-9110
http:/gsas.brandeis.edu/

Founded 1953. Located 8 miles NW of Boston. Coed. Private control. Semester system. Special facilities: research centers for biology, biochemistry, chemistry, mathematics, social sciences, physics; Judaic Center, American Civilization Center, Humanities Center, art museum, music center, Rosenstiel Basic Medical Sciences Research Center, Center for Health Policy Analysis and Research, Levinson Policy Institute, Center for Employment and Income Studies, Center for Aging and Income Maintenance, theater arts center. Library: 1,000,000 volumes, 760,000 microforms, 100 PCs.

Annual tuition: full-time $21,440. Some on-campus housing for graduate students. Annual housing costs: $5600. Apply to Housing Office for off-campus housing information. Phone: (617)736-3550.

Graduate School of Arts and Sciences

Graduate study since 1953. Enrollment: full-time 980, part-time 56 (men 50%, women 50%). Faculty: full-time 345, part-time 58. Degrees conferred: M.A., M.F.A., Ph.D.

ADMISSION REQUIREMENTS. Transcripts, two letters of recommendation required in support of application. GRE General/Subject Test or MAT, GMAT, interview for some departments. GRE recommended for all departments. TOEFL required of all foreign applicants. Accepts transfer applicants. Graduates of unaccredited colleges not considered. Apply to the Associate Dean of the School by January 15, earliest deadline (Fall). Application fee $40 (before December 1), $60 (after December 1). Phone: (617)736-3410.

ADMISSION STANDARDS. Very competitive. Usual minimum average: 3.0 (A = 4).

FINANCIAL AID. Scholarships, fellowships, assistantships for teaching/research, Federal W/S, loans. Apply to the Associate Dean of the School by February 1. Use FAFSA. Phone: (617)736-3410. Aid sometimes available to part-time students.

DEGREE REQUIREMENTS. For M.A.: 24 semester hours minimum in residence; reading knowledge of one foreign language; thesis sometimes required; final written/oral exam. For M.F.A. in Music: 36 hours minimum in residence; reading knowledge of one or two foreign languages; moderate instrumental proficiency; general exams; composition for composers, thesis for music history or theory majors. For M.F.A. in Theater Arts: acting and dramatic writing; 48 semester hours in residence; thesis play for dramatic writing; design-technical, 54 semester hours in residence; thesis. For Ph.D.: 48 hours minimum beyond the bachelor's, at least one year in residence; reading knowledge of at least one foreign language for most departments; qualifying exams; dissertation; final oral exam.

FIELDS OF STUDY.
Anthropology. GRE for admission; apply by February 16.
Biochemistry. GRE, three letters of recommendation for admission. Apply by January 15, rolling admissions.
Biology. GRE, three letters of recommendation for admission. Rolling admission.
Biophysics. GRE, three letters of recommendation for admission. Rolling admission.
Chemistry. GRE for admission. Apply by March 15.
Comparative History. For M.A.: writing sample for admission; apply July 30. For Ph.D.: GRE, writing sample. Apply by February 1.
Computer Science. GRE, three letters of recommendation. Apply by March 1.
English and American Literature. GRE General/Subject, writing sample. Apply by February 15.
Genetic Counseling. GRE, three letters of recommendation. Apply by February 15.
History of American Civilization. For M.A.: GRE, writing sample for admission. Apply by July 30.
International Economics and Finance. GRE or GMAT, three letters of recommendation for admission. Apply by March 1.
Jewish Communal Services. GRE or GMAT, interview, writing sample for admission. Apply by February 15.
Literary Studies. Writing sample for admission. Apply by March 15.
Mathematics. GRE General/Subject. Apply by February 15.
Music. For musicology, GRE and writing sample for admission; Composition, sample of work. Apply by January 31.
Near Eastern and Judaic Studies. GRE suggested. Apply by February 1.
Physics. GRE General/Subject Test for admission. Apply by February 15.
Politics. GRE, writing sample, three letters of recommendation for admission.
Psychology and Cognitive Science. GRE General/Subject Test for admission. For Ph.D.: apply by February 15; for M.S., apply by June 1.
Sociology. Writing sample for admission. Apply by February 15. M.A., Ph.D.
Theater Arts. For admission: Designers, portfolio; Actors, audition; writers, sample of work.

The Florence Heller Graduate School for Advanced Studies in Social Welfare
http://www.brandeis.edu/Heller/heller.html

Organized for training in social policy and health, and human services management 1959. Semester system. Annual tuition: full-time $20,410, part-time evening $1770 per course. On-campus housing available. Day care facilities available.

Enrollment: full-time 104, part-time 5. Faculty: full-time 25, part-time 15. Degrees conferred M.M.H.S., Ph.D.

ADMISSION REQUIREMENTS. Transcripts, successful academic and professional experience, writing sample, statement of purpose, three letters of recommendation, GMAT/GRE required in support of application. Interviews suggested. Apply no later than February 15 (Ph.D.), March 15 (Master's), priority given to early applicants. Master's academic year starts in June. Application fee $50. Phone (617)736-3800.

ADMISSIONS STANDARDS. Competitive. Usual minimum average: 3.0 (A = 4).

FINANCIAL AID. Ten academic scholarships, twenty grants, fifteen fellowships, ten teaching assistantships, loans. Apply to Director of Financial Aid by February 15. Use FAFSA profile. Phone (617)736-3811.

DEGREE REQUIREMENTS. For master's: (day) 19 semester courses; field practicum; (evening) program 12 semester courses;

final paper thesis. For Ph.D.: 14–18 semester courses minimum; qualifying exam; dissertation.

FIELDS OF STUDY.
Health Care and Children, Youth and Family Services. M.M.H.S. only.
Social Policy. Ph.D.

UNIVERSITY OF BRIDGEPORT
Bridgeport, Connecticut 06601

Founded 1927. Located 60 miles NE of New York. Coed. Private control. Semester system. Special facilities: Bernhard Center for Arts and Humanities, Carlson Art Gallery, Connecticut Technology Institute, Center for Venture Management and Entrepreneurial Studies. Library: 310,000 volumes, 970,000 microforms, 1610 current periodicals.

Tuition: per credit School of Education and Human Resources $290, School of Business $310, School of Science, Engineering and Technology $320. On-campus housing for single students, none for married students. Average academic year housing costs: $3700 ($6610 including board). Contact Office of Residential Life for both on- and off-campus housing information. Phone: (203)576-4461.

Graduate Studies

Enrollment: full-time 333, part-time 434. Faculty: full-time 47, part-time 89. Degrees conferred: M.S., M.B.A., Sixth Year Professional Diplomas, Ed.D.

ADMISSION REQUIREMENTS. Official transcripts, three letters of recommendation required in support of application. GRE/GMAT/MAT required by some departments. Supplemental application, personal statement, and/or an interview may be requested. TOEFL required for international applicants. Accepts transfer applicants. Apply to Office of Admissions at least thirty days (60 days for Business) prior to registration. Admits Fall, Spring, and Summer. Application fee $35. Phone: (800)898-8278, (203)576-4552; fax: (203)576-4941. E-mail: admit@cse.bridgeport.edu.

ADMISSION STANDARDS. Selective. Usual minimum average: 2.5 (A = 4).

FINANCIAL AID. Twenty-six assistantships, endowed scholarships, ninety-eight internships, co-op, residence hall directors, Federal W/S, loans. Approved for VA benefits. Apply to Financial Aid Office; no specified closing date. Use FAFSA. Phone: (203)576-4568.

DEGREE REQUIREMENTS. For master's: 30–33 credits minimum, at least 27 in residence; thesis/nonthesis options. For Sixth-Year Professional Certificate: 30 credits beyond master's, at least 24 in residence. For Ed.D.: at least two years in residence; qualifying exam; dissertation; final oral exam.

FIELDS OF STUDY.

SCHOOL OF BUSINESS:
Accounting. M.Acc. only.
Business Economics.
Finance.
Information Systems.
International Business.
Management.
Marketing.

SCHOOL OF EDUCATION AND HUMAN RESOURCES:
Counseling. Includes agency, human resources development, school.
Education. Includes elementary, secondary, educational management.
Human Nutrition.

SCHOOL OF SCIENCE, ENGINEERING AND TECHNOLOGY:
Computer Engineering.
Computer Science.
Electrical Engineering.
Management Engineering.
Mathematics.
Mechanical Engineering.

BRIDGEWATER STATE COLLEGE
Bridgewater, Massachusetts 02324-0001

Founded 1840. Located 35 miles S of Boston. Coed. State control. Semester system. Library: 250,000 volumes.

Tuition and fees: per hour, resident $140, nonresident $307. No on-campus housing available.

Graduate School

Enrollment: approximately 1500 full- and part-time. Graduate faculty: approximately 175. Degrees conferred: M.A., M.A.T., M.Ed., M.P.A., M.S., C.A.G.S.

ADMISSION REQUIREMENTS. Official transcripts, three letters of references, GRE required in support of School's application (GRE Subject Test for M.A. Only). Interview required for some programs. TOEFL required for international applicants. Accept transfer applicants. Apply to the Graduate School Office by April 1 (Fall), October 1 (Spring). Application fee $25. Phone (508)697-1300.

ADMISSION STANDARDS. Selective for most departments. Usual minimum average: 2.75 (A = 4).

FINANCIAL AID. Limited to assistantships, Federal W/S, loans. Apply to Graduate School Dean for assistantships; to Financial Aid for all other programs. Use FAFSA.

DEGREE REQUIREMENTS. For M.A.: 30 semester hours minimum; research proficiency test; comprehensive exam; thesis. For M.A.T., M.S., M.Ed., M.P.A.: 30–36 semester hours minimum; thesis/nonthesis option; comprehensive exam. For C.A.G.S.: 30 semester hours beyond the master's degree; special project.

FIELDS OF STUDY.
Biology.
Chemistry.
Communication.
Computer Science.
Education. Includes elementary administration, counseling, early childhood, health, library, media, reading, secondary, special education.
English.
Health Promotion.
History.

Physical Education.
Psychology.
Public Administration.

BRIGHAM YOUNG UNIVERSITY
Provo, Utah 84602-1001
http//www.byu.edu:80/home-ns.html

Founded 1875. Located 50 miles S of Salt Lake City. Coed. Private control; Church of Jesus Christ of Latter-day Saints. Trimester system. Library: 12,500,000 volumes, 356 PCS in all libraries.

Annual tuition and fees: full-time, LDS church members $2980, nonchurch members $4470; per credit, LDS church member $165, nonchurch member $248. On-campus housing for 1048 married students, 2210 for men, 2950 for women. Average annual housing cost: $4320 for married students, $3620 for single students (includes room and board). Apply to Assistant Director Housing Services. Phone: (801)378-2611. For off-campus housing information, contact Off-Campus Housing Manager. Phone: (810)378-5506.

Graduate Studies

Graduate study since 1918. Total enrollment 2840. Graduate faculty: full-time 1241, no part-time. Degrees conferred: M.A., M.S., M.P.A., M.Acc., M.B.A., M.Ed., M.E.A., M.E.M., M.M., M.T.M., Ed.Spec. Cert., Ed.D., Ph.D., TESL Certificate.

ADMISSION REQUIREMENTS. Two transcripts, three letters of recommendation required in support of application, GRE/GMAT/MAT required by some departments. TOEFL required of foreign applicants. Interview required by some departments. Accepts transfer applicants. Graduates of unaccredited colleges not considered. Usual deadline February 1 (Fall), June 30 (Winter), February 1 (Spring), March 15 (Summer) Apply to Office of Graduate Studies, B-356 ASB by published department deadlines. Application fee $30. Phone: (801)378-4091; fax: (801)378-5238.

ADMISSION STANDARDS. Selective for most departments. Usual minimum average: 3.0 (A = 4).

FINANCIAL AID. Scholarships, research fellowships, teaching/research assistantships, Federal W/S, loans. Apply to by application deadline to department of specialization for scholarships and assistantships; to Office of Financial Aid for all other aid. Phone: (801)378-4104; fax: (801)378-4264. Use FAFSA.

DEGREE REQUIREMENTS. For master's: 30 semester hours minimum, at least 20 in residence for most programs; thesis/nonthesis option; final oral/written exam. For Certificate; Ed.Spec.Cert.: 30 semester hours beyond master's. For Ed.D.: three years minimum of full-time study or its equivalent beyond the bachelor's, two consecutive semesters in residence; qualifying exam; research project; final oral/written exam. For Ph.D.: ordinarily two years of full-time course work or research or its equivalent to be taken in residence; language/research tool; comprehensive exam; dissertation; final oral exam.

FIELDS OF STUDY.

COLLEGE OF BIOLOGY AND AGRICULTURAL SCIENCES:
Agronomy and Horticulture.
Animal Science.
Botany and Range Science. Includes biological science education, botany, range science, wildlife and range resources.
Food Science and Nutrition.

Microbiology.
Zoology.

COLLEGE OF EDUCATION:
Educational Leadership.
Educational Psychology. Includes audiology, counseling, psychology, school psychology, special education, speech-language pathology.
Elementary Education. Includes teaching and learning, reading.
Instructional Science. Includes instructional psychology and instructional science.

COLLEGE OF ENGINEERING AND TECHNOLOGY:
Chemical Engineering.
Civil Engineering.
Electrical Engineering.
Engineering Management.
Manufacturing Engineering and Engineering Technology. Includes computer-integrated manufacturing, manufacturing engineering, MFE-industrial.
Mechanical Engineering.
Technology Education.
Technology Management.

COLLEGE OF FAMILY, HOME AND SOCIAL SCIENCES:
Anthropology.
Family Sciences. Includes family studies; marriage and family therapy.
Geography.
History.
International and Area Studies.
Psychology. Includes clinical psychology.
Social Work.
Sociology.

COLLEGE OF FINE ARTS AND COMMUNICATIONS:
Mass Communication.
Music. Includes composition, conducting music education, musicology, pedagogy, performance.
Theater and Film.
Visual Arts. Includes art education, art history, studio art.

COLLEGE OF HUMANITIES:
English.
French.
German Literature.
Humanities and Comparative Literature.
Language Acquisition. Includes Arabic, Chinese, French, German, Japanese, Korean, Portuguese, Russian, Scandinavian.
Linguistics and TESL.
Spanish and Portuguese Language and Literature.

COLLEGE OF NURSING:
Nursing. Includes nursing administration, family nurse practitioner, pediatric nurse practitioner.

COLLEGE OF PHYSICAL AND MATHEMATICAL SCIENCES:
Chemistry. Includes biochemistry.
Computer Science.
Geology.
Mathematics. Includes Mathematics Education.
Physics and Astronomy.
Statistics.

COLLEGE OF PHYSICAL EDUCATION:
Dance.
Health Sciences.
Physical Education. Includes exercise science/wellness, PE administration, curriculum and instruction.
Recreation Management and Youth Leadership.

THE J. WILLARD AND ALICE S. MARRIOTT SCHOOL OF MANAGEMENT:
Accountancy. Includes professional accountancy, accounting information systems, tax.
Business Administration.
Managerial Economics.
Organizational Behavior.
Public Administration.

J. Reuben Clark Law School

Established 1971. Semester system. Law library 315,000 volumes. Library has LEXIS, NEXIS, RLIN, and WESTLAW.

Annual tuition: church members $4760, nonmembers $7140. On-campus housing available, contact University Housing Office. Total average cost for all other expenses $11,300–$13,190.

Enrollment: first-year class 150; total 487 (men 67%, women 33%). Faculty: full-time 32, part-time 28. Degrees conferred: J.D., J.D.-M.B.A., J.D.-M.P.A., J.D.-M.Acc., S.D.M.O.B.

ADMISSION REQUIREMENTS. LSDAS Law School report, transcripts, LSAT, three recommendations, interview with a clergyman or bishop required in support of application. Accepts transfer applicants. Apply to Director of Admissions by February 15. Fall admission only. Application fee $30. Phone: (801)378 4277.

ADMISSION STANDARDS. Selective. Accepts about 30–35% of total annual applicants.

FINANCIAL AID. Scholarships, assistantships, Federal W/S, loans, church loans. Apply to Student Financial Aid Office; no specified closing date. Use FAFSA. About 25% of students receive merit scholarships.

DEGREE REQUIREMENTS. For J.D.: satisfactory completion of three-year program; 90 semester credits. For other master's degrees: see Graduate listing above.

BROOKLYN COLLEGE OF THE CITY UNIVERSITY OF NEW YORK

Brooklyn, New York 11210-2889

Founded 1930. Coed. Municipal control. Semester system. Special facilities: Africana Research Institute, Applied Science Institute, Archaeological Research Institute, Computer Center, Dynamitron, Electronic Music Studio, Graduate Center for Worker Education, Center for Health Promotion, Center for Human Relations Training, Wolfe Institute for the Humanities, Infant Studies Center, Center for Italian-American Studies, Center for Puerto Rican Studies, Center for Nuclear Theory, Institute for Studies in American Music, Television Center, Speech and hearing Clinic, Library: 1,174,470 volumes, 1,495,800 microforms, 4800 current periodicals, 150 PCs in all libraries.

Tuition: per semester, State residents $2150, non-State residents $3800; per credited State resident $185, non-State $320. No on-campus housing available.

Division of Graduate Studies

Graduate study since 1935. Enrollment: full-time 246, part-time 1966. Faculty: full-time 567, part-time 372. Degrees conferred: M.A., M.F.A., M.S., M.S. in Ed., Advanced Certificate.

ADMISSION REQUIREMENTS. Official transcripts, two letters of reference required in support of application. GRE General/ Subject Tests, interview required by some departments. Accepts transfer applicants. Graduates of unaccredited colleges not considered. Apply to Office of Admissions by March 1 (Summer and Fall), November 1 (Spring), by March 1 for selected teacher-education programs. Application fee $30. Phone: (718)951-5914.

ADMISSION STANDARDS. Competitive. Usual minimum average: 2.75 overall, 3.0 in the major (A = 4).

FINANCIAL AID. Teaching/research fellowships, lectureships, internships, Federal W/S, loans. Approved for VA benefits. Apply to appropriate department for fellowships and internships; to Office of Financial Aid for all other programs. No specified closing date. Use FAFSA and City University's FAF.

DEGREE REQUIREMENTS. For all master's: 30 credits minimum, at least 24 in residence; thesis/nonthesis option; comprehensive exam. For liberal arts and science majors: thesis/written comprehensive exam; reading knowledge of one foreign language required in some programs. For Advanced Certificate: 30 credits beyond the master's degree; special project.

FIELDS OF STUDY.
Accounting.
Applied Physics.
Art. Portfolio required for admission. Includes drawing and painting, graphics, photography, sculpture.
Art History. Two languages for master's.
Bilingual and Bicultural Education.
Biology. One language for master's.
Chemistry. One language for master's.
Community Health.
Computer and Information Science.
Computer Science and Health Science.
Creative Writing. Includes fiction, playwriting, poetry.
Economics.
Education.
   Elementary. Special concentrations in early childhood, home economics, comparative and industrial education art, bilingual teaching, social science, mathematics, music, reading, science, teaching of Spanish-speaking children.
   Secondary. All junior and senior high-school subjects.
   Special Education. Education of children with retarded mental development/emotional handicaps/neuropsychological learning disabilities; education of the speech and hearing handicapped; speech improvement.
   Sixth-Year Certificate Program. Includes administration and supervision, guidance and counseling, school psychologist, educational use of computers.
English. One language for master's.
French.
General Science.
Geology.
Gerontological Studies.
Health and Nutrition Sciences.
History.
Judaic Studies.
Liberal Studies.
Management Information Systems.
Mathematics.
Modern Languages. French or Spanish.
Music. One language for master's. Includes composition, performance.
Nutrition.
Philosophy.
Physics.
Political Economy.
Political Science. One language for master's. Includes urban policy and administration.
Psychology. Includes experimental, forensic, human relations, industrial organization.
Social Studies.
Sociology.

Spanish.

Speech. Includes public communication (M.A.); audiology, pathology, speech and hearing science (M.S.).

Theater. Includes criticism, history (M.A.); acting, design, technical production, directing, performing arts management (M.F.A.).

TV/Radio. Includes television production.

Urban Studies.

BROOKLYN LAW SCHOOL

250 Joralemon Street

Brooklyn, New York 11201-3798

Established 1901. Coed. A Private control. Semester system. Special facility: Center for the Study of International Law. Library: 439,000 volumes, 840,000 microforms. Library has LEXIS, NEXIS, WESTLAW, DIALOG.

Annual tuition: full-time $19,660, part-time $14,745. Total average cost for all other expenses: $9000-$11,000. Enrollment: first-year class full-time 280, part-time 185; total full and part-time 1457 (men 55%, women 45%). Faculty: full-time 62, part-time 56. No on-campus housing, but six Law School residence halls in close proximity to campus. Degrees conferred: J.D., combined J.D.-Master's program with Baruch College, Hunter College, Brooklyn College, and Pratt Institute.

ADMISSION REQUIREMENTS. LSDAS Law School report, transcripts, LSAT, bachelor's degree required in support of application. Interview not required. Graduates from unaccredited colleges not considered. Apply to the Office of Admissions after October 15, before April 1. Admits Fall only. Application fee $50. Phone: (718)780-7906.

ADMISSION STANDARDS. Accepts 30–35% of total annual applicants.

FINANCIAL AID. Scholarships, fellowships, assistantships, Federal W/S, loans. Apply to the Financial Aid Office by April 1. About 25% of students receive aid other than loans from school. Use FAFSA.

DEGREE REQUIREMENTS. For J.D.: three-year program (full-time), four-year program (part-time), 84 semester hours minimum. For master's program: see other institutional listings.

BROWN UNIVERSITY

Providence, Rhode Island 02912

Founded in 1764. Coed. Private control. Semester system. Special facilities: Biomedical Center, Computing Laboratory, East Asia Language and Area Center, Geology-Chemistry research centers, Graduate Center (dormitories and administrative offices), Haffenreffer Museum of Anthropology, herbarium, Hunter Psychological Laboratory, Institute of Life Sciences, Ladd Observatory, Lefschetz Center for Dynamic Systems, Population Studies and Training Center, Prince Engineering Laboratory, University Library (2,225,000 items), John Carter Brown Library (Americana, 40,000 volumes), Annmary Brown Memorial Library (Renaissance and Medieval culture). Library: 2,200,000 volumes.

Annual tuition: full-time $21,592. On-campus housing available. Average annual housing cost: $4800 ($9000 including board). Apply to Housing Office, Box 1864. Phone: (401)863-2251.

Graduate School

Graduate study since 1887. Enrollment: full-time 1800, part-time 200. Faculty: full-time 500, part-time 30. Degrees conferred: A.M., Sc.M., M.A.T., M.M.C., Ph.D., M.D.-Ph.D.

ADMISSION REQUIREMENTS. Transcripts, three letters of recommendation required in support of application and letter from the student stating plans for graduate study. GRE General/Subject required for biochemistry, biology and medical science, comparative literature, computer science, English, French studies, Hispanic and Italian studies, mathematics, psychology. GRE for most other departments. TOEFL required of foreign applicants. Accepts transfer applicants. Graduates of unaccredited colleges not considered. Apply to Graduate School by January 2. Application fee $60. Phone: (401)863-2600.

ADMISSION STANDARDS. Competitive. Usual minimum average: 3.0 (A = 4).

FINANCIAL AID. Seventy-five scholarships, 100 fellowships, 250 research assistantships, 400 teaching assistantships, proctorships, grants, endowed awards, Federal W/S, loans. Apply to the Office of Financial Aid by January 1. Use FAFSA. About 75% of students receive aid other than loans from school and outside sources. No aid for part-time students.

DEGREE REQUIREMENTS. For master's: 8 semester courses minimum, additional courses required by some programs; thesis, special projects, special exams required by some departments. For Ph.D.: three years of full-time study or equivalent beyond master's, at least two semesters in residence; preliminary exam; final exam; dissertation.

FIELDS OF STUDY.

American Civilization. A.M., Ph.D.

Anthropology. A.M., Ph.D.

Applied Mathematics. Sc.M., Ph.D.

Biology and Medical Sciences. Sc.M., Ph.D., M.M.S., M.D.-Ph.D.

Biomedical Engineering. Sc.M.

Chemistry. Sc.M., Ph.D.

Classics. A.M., Ph.D.

Cognitive and Linguistic Sciences. Sc.M., Ph.D.

Comparative Literature. A.M., Ph.D.

Comparative Study of Development. A.M.

Computer Science. Sc.M., Ph.D.

Creative Writing. M.F.A.

Economics. A.M., Ph.D.

Education. M.A.T.

Egyptology. A.M., Ph.D.

Engineering. Sc.M., Ph.D.

English. A.M., Ph.D.

Environmental Studies. A.M.

French Studies. A.M., Ph D

Geological Sciences. A.M., Sc.M., Ph.D.

German. A.M., Ph.D.

History. A.M., Ph.D.

History of Art and Architecture. A.M., Ph.D.

History of Mathematics. A.M., Ph.D.

Italian Studies. A.M., Ph.D.

Judaic Studies. A.M., Ph.D.

Mathematics. A.M., Sc.M., Ph.D.

Music. A.M., Ph.D.

Neuroscience. A.M., Ph.D.

Old World Archaeology and Art. A.M., Ph.D.

Philosophy. A.M., Ph.D.

Physics. Sc.M., Ph.D.

Political Science. A.M., Ph.D.

Portuguese and Brazilian Studies. A.M.

Psychology. A.M., Sc.M., Ph.D.

Religious Studies. A.M., Ph.D.

Slavic Languages. A.M., Ph.D.
Sociology. A.M., Ph.D.
Theater, Speech, and Dance. A.M.

Medical School (02912-9706)

Program in medicine leading to the M.D. began in 1975. Majority of each class admitted into freshman 7-8 year program of the University.

Annual tuition: $24,984. Student fees $1548. On-campus housing available. Total average figure of other expenses: $8000.

Enrollment: first-year class 60; total 263 (men 50%, women 50%). Faculty: full-time 296, part-time 672. Degree conferred: M.D., M.D.-M.M.Sc., M.D.-Ph.D. The M.M.Sc. and Ph.D. are offered through the Graduate School.

ADMISSION REQUIREMENTS. MCAT or GRE (general and subject exams), transcripts, three letters of recommendation required in support of application. Accepts transfer applicants. Preference given to Rhode Island residents. Apply to Office of Admissions, Box G, after August 15, before March 15. Application fee $60. Phone: (401)863-2149; fax: (401)863-2660.

ADMISSION STANDARDS. Competitive. Accepts about 50% of total annual applicants. Approximately 20% are state residents.

FINANCIAL AID. Scholarships, loans, awards. No qualified student will be denied admission solely because of financial disability. About 50% of students receive financial assistance. Apply to Dean; no specified closing date.

DEGREE REQUIREMENTS. For M.D.: satisfactory completion of seven- to eight-year program in Liberal Medical Education; at least two years in full-time residence for students admitted with advanced standing. For M.M.Sc., Ph.D.: see Graduate School listing above.

FIELDS OF GRADUATE STUDY.
Biochemistry.
Cell Biology.
Immunology.
Molecular Biology.
Neurosciences.
Pathology.
Physiology.

BRYANT COLLEGE

Smithfield, Rhode Island 02917-1287

Located 12 miles N of Providence. Coed. Private control. Semester system. Day and evening programs. Special facilities: Center for International Business and Economic Development. Library: 122,000 volumes, 16,500 microforms, 1250 current periodicals, 16 PCs.

Tuition: per course $840. On-campus housing for single students. Average academic year housing costs: $4600; off-campus housing costs: $600 per month. Contact housing office for both on and off-campus housing information. Phone: (401)232-6140.

Graduate School

Enrollment: full-time 58, part-time 607. Faculty: full-time 81, part-time 20. Degrees conferred: M.B.A., M.S.A., M.S.T.

ADMISSION REQUIREMENTS. Official transcripts, GMAT, statement of objectives, three letters of recommendation required in support of School's application. Accepts transfer applicants. Apply by August 1 (Fall), December 12 (Spring) to Director of

Graduate Admissions. Rolling admission process. Application fee $35. Phone: (401)232-6231.

ADMISSION STANDARDS. Selective. Usual minimum average: 2.5 (2.75 last two years) (A = 4).

FINANCIAL AID. Limited to ten research assistantships, Federal W/S, loans. Approved for VA benefits. Apply by August 1 to Director of Financial Aid. Phone: (401)232-6020.

DEGREE REQUIREMENTS. For master's: 30–61 semester hours; no thesis or foreign language requirement.

FIELDS OF STUDY.
Business Administration. Concentration in accounting, computer information systems, finance, general business, health services management, international business, management, management of operation technology, marketing, taxation.

BRYN MAWR COLLEGE

Bryn Mawr, Pennsylvania 19010-2899
http://www.brynmawr.edu

Founded 1885. Located 11 miles W of Philadelphia. Coed on graduate level. Private control. Semester system. Special facility: Ella Riegel Museum of Classical Archaeology. Library: 850,000 volumes, 2500 current periodicals.

Annual tuition: full-time $18,480, per course $3150. Campus housing available at Glenmede Graduate Residence Center for men and women. Average annual housing cost: $7085 (including board). Contact Director of Graduate Housing for both on- and off-campus housing information. Phone: (610)526-7334.

Graduate School of Arts and Sciences

http://www.brynmawr.edu/Adm/grads.html#gsas

Graduate study since 1885. Enrollment: full-time 62, part-time 148. College faculty: full-time 106, part-time 40. Degrees conferred: M.A., Ph.D.

ADMISSION REQUIREMENTS. Official transcripts, three letters of recommendation (including at least one from a professor in applicant's major field), GRE (Subject for Biology, Chemistry, Physics, Psychology, and Russian) required in support of School's application. TOEFL required for international applicants. Applicants for Financial aid should apply by January 1 (Science programs), January 25 (Humanities), February 1 (Clinical Development), January 25 for foreign applicants, all others must be completed by June 20. Application fee $40. Phone: (215)526-5072; E-mail: sbernhar@brynmawr.edu.

ADMISSION STANDARDS. Competitive. Usual minimum average: 3.0 (A = 4).

FINANCIAL AID. Annual awards from institutional funds: 115 scholarships, 3 research fellowships, 47 teaching assistantships, loans. Apply by February 1 (January 25 for foreign applicants) to the Dean of the School for fellowships, assistantships; to Financial Aid Office for all other programs. Phone: (215)526-5349. Aid for part-time study available.

DEGREE REQUIREMENTS. For M.A.: one year minimum in full-time residence; thesis; final oral/written exam. For Ph.D.: three years minimum, at least two in full-time residence; reading knowledge of foreign languages/computer languages/special techniques as required by individual departments; preliminary exam; dissertation; final oral exam.

FIELDS OF STUDY.
Biochemistry.
Biology.
Chemistry.
Classical and Near Eastern Archaeology.
Classical Languages.
Classical Studies.
Clinical Development Psychology. Apply by February 1; admits Fall only.
French. M.A. only.
Geology.
Greek.
Greek Studies.
History of Art.
Latin.
Mathematics.
Neural and Behavioral Sciences. Interdisciplinary.
Physics.
Roman Studies.
Russian.

Graduate School of Social Work and Social Research (19010-1697)

http://www.brynmawr.edu/Adm/swsr

Annual tuition: $17,734, per course $2031 (Master's), $2980 (Doctoral). Enrollment: full-time 216, part-time 75. Faculty: full-time 16, part-time 25. Degrees conferred: M.L.S.P., M.S.S., Ph.D.

ADMISSION REQUIREMENTS. Official transcripts, three letters of recommendation required in support of School's application. TOEFL required for international applications. Accepts transfer applicants. Graduates of unaccredited institutions not considered. Apply to Assistant Dean and Director of Admission. Applications must be completed by March 1. Rolling admissions process. Application fee $40. Phone: (610)520-2601.

ADMISSION STANDARDS. Competitive. Usual minimum average: 2.75 (A = A), 3.0 (Doctoral programs).

FINANCIAL AID. Annual awards from institutional fund; sixteen fellowships, two research assistantships, six teaching assistantships, Federal W/S, loans. Approved for VA benefits. Apply by March 1 to Assistant Dean for fellowships, assistantships; to Financial Aid Office for all other programs. Use FAFSA. Phone: (215)527-5403.

DEGREE REQUIREMENTS. For master's: 45–60 credits minimum, at least one year in full-time residence; field placement; thesis/special project; final exam. For Ph.D.: three years minimum, at least two in full-time residence; advance practice internship; dissertation; final oral exam.

FIELDS OF STUDY.
Law and Social Policy.
Social Science.
Social Work.

BUCKNELL UNIVERSITY

Lewisburg, Pennsylvania 17837

Founded 1846. Located 155 miles NW of Philadelphia. Coed. Private control. Semester system. Library: 230,000 volumes.

Tuition: per course $2315. Limited on-campus housing available for single students, none for married students. Average annual housing cost: $4925 (including board). Apply to Residential Life Director. Phone: (717)524-1195.

Graduate Studies

Enrollment: full-time 166, part-time 50, total 216 (men 102, women 114). University faculty teaching graduate students: full-time 16 part-time 0. Degrees conferred: M.A., M.S.

ADMISSION REQUIREMENTS. Transcripts, GRE General/Subject Tests, GMAT (Business), two letters of recommendation required in support of application. TOEFL required for international applicants. Accepts transfer applicants. Graduates of unaccredited colleges not considered. Apply to Director of Graduate Studies by June 15 (Fall), December 1 (Spring), April 15 (Summer). Application fee $25. Phone: (717)524-1304; fax: (717)524-3760.

ADMISSION STANDARDS. Selective for most departments, very selective for some. Usual minimum average: 2.8 (A = 4).

FINANCIAL AID. Annual awards from institutional funds: sixty-five scholarships, fifty-two assistantships, Federal W/S, loans. Apply by March 1 to Graduate Office. Use FAFSA and University's FAF. Phone: (717)524-1304. About 50% of students receive aid other than loans from University and outside sources. Aid sometimes available to part-time students.

DEGREE REQUIREMENTS. For M.A., M.S.: 28 credit hours minimum, at least 22 in residence; thesis; final exam; reading knowledge of one foreign language required for M.A.(English).

FIELDS OF STUDY.
Animal Behavior.
Biology.
Business Administration.
Chemical Engineering.
Chemistry.
Civil Engineering.
Education.
Electrical Engineering.
English.
Management.
Mathematics.
Mechanical Engineering.
Psychology.

BUTLER UNIVERSITY

Indianapolis, IN 46208-3485
gopher://Gopher.Butler.edu:70/

Founded 1855. Coed. Private control. Semester system. Special facility: Holcomb Observatory and Planetarium. Library: 320,000 volumes, 235,000 microforms 2900 current periodicals, 49 PCs.

Tuition: $210 per credit. On-campus housing available for graduate students. Average academic year housing costs: $4450 (including board). Contact Director of Residential Life for both on- and off-campus housing information. Phone: (317)283-9570.

Division of Graduate Studies

Graduate study since 1932. Enrollment: full-time 83, part-time 655. University faculty: full-time 105, part-time 62. Degrees conferred: M.A., M.S., M.M., M.B.A., Ed.S.

ADMISSION REQUIREMENTS. Two official transcripts, GRE/GMAT required in support of application. Interview not required. TOEFL required for international applicants. Accepts transfer applicants. Graduates of unaccredited institutions not considered. Apply to Office of Graduate Admissions by August 15. Application fee $30. Phone: (800)972-2882, (317)283-9310; fax: (317)921-6433.

ADMISSION STANDARDS. Selective. Usual minimum average: 2.75 (A = 4). TOEFL score required 550.

FINANCIAL AID. Twenty-five scholarships, four teaching fellowships, two teaching assistantships, ten music awards, Federal W/S, loans. Apply to the Office of Graduate Studies for fellowships, assistantships; to Financial Aid Office for all other programs. No specified closing date. Use FAFSA. Phone: (800)972-2882.

DEGREE REQUIREMENTS. For master's; 30–36 hours for most programs; final written/oral exam for some majors; comprehensive exam. For Specialist: 30 credits beyond the master's; special project.

FIELDS OF STUDY.

COLLEGE OF LIBERAL ARTS AND SCIENCES:
Chemistry. M.S.
English. M.A.
History. M.A.

COLLEGE OF EDUCATION:
Administration. M.S.
Counseling. Includes administration for pupil personnel. Ed.S.
Educational Administration. Ed.S.
Elementary Education. M.S.
Reading. M.S., Ed.S.
School Counseling.
School Psychology.
Secondary Education.

COLLEGE OF BUSINESS ADMINISTRATION:
Business Administration. Up to 12 additional prerequisite hours for M.B.A., depending upon previous preparation; GMAT for admission. M.B.A.
Economics. Thesis for M.S.

COLLEGE OF PHARMACY:
Medicinal chemistry.
Pharmaceutics.
Pharmacology.
Pharmacy Administration.

JORDAN COLLEGE OF FINE ARTS:
Composition.
Conducting.
Music Education.
Music History.
Performance.
Piano Pedagogy.
Theory.

CALIFORNIA COLLEGE OF ARTS AND CRAFTS
Oakland, California 94618

Founded 1907. Located adjacent to San Francisco. Private control. semester system. Special facilities: Graduate Center Gallery; MFA Student Gallery. Library: 42,000 volumes, 450 microforms; 42 PC workstations.

Annual tuition: per credit $623. No on-campus housing. For off-campus housing information, contact Student Services Office. Phone: (510)597-3672.

Graduate Division

Graduate study since 1956. Enroll full-time $70. Faculty: full-time 1, part-time 22. Degree conferred: M.F.A.

ADMISSION REQUIREMENTS. Transcripts, portfolio, slides/photographs of art work required in support of College's application. TOEFL required of foreign applicants. Interview not required. Graduates of unaccredited colleges not considered. Apply to Director of the Graduate Division by February 15 (Fall). Application fee $30, $45 for Internationals. Phone: (510)597-3667; fax: (510)428-1346.

ADMISSION STANDARDS. Selective. Admission based on talent.

FINANCIAL AID. Annual awards from institutional funds: twenty to twenty-five scholarships, twenty assistantships, Federal W/S, loans. Apply to Director of Graduate Division by April 1. Use FAFSA and institutional FAF. Phone: (510)597-3684. About 75% of students receive aid other than loans from College and outside sources. No institutional aid for part-time students.

DEGREE REQUIREMENTS. For M.F.A.: 60 units minimum, at least 48 in residence; final oral exam; art project.

FIELDS OF STUDY.
Ceramics.
Drawing.
Film/Video/Performance.
Glass.
Metal Arts.
Painting.
Photography.
Printmaking.
Sculpture.
Textile Arts.

CALIFORNIA INSTITUTE OF TECHNOLOGY
Pasadena, California 91125-0001
http://www.caltech.edu

Founded 1891. Coed. Private control. Quarter system. Special facilities: well-equipped laboratories in fields of specialization, computing center (computing support services for IBM, DEC, Apple, Sun, NeXT; INTEL Touchstone Delta, Cray Y-MP), large telescopes at Big Bear Solar, Caltech Submillimeter (Mauna Kea, Hawaii) and Palomar Observatories, radio telescopes at Bishop and Palomar Observatories, seismological laboratory at Pasadena, Kerckhoff Marine Laboratory at Corona del Mar, Environmental Quality Laboratory, Kellog Radiation Laboratory, Graduate Aeronautics laboratory, Jet Propulsion Lab at Pasadena. Library: 520,000 volumes, 532,200 microforms, 4600 current periodicals, 64 PCs in all libraries.

Annual tuition: full-time $17,370. On- and off-campus housing available for single and married students. Average academic year housing costs: $5400–8500. Apply to Housing Office before May 1. Phone: (818)356-6178. Day care facilities available.

Graduate Study (Mail Code 02-31)
http://www.cco.caltech.edu/~gradofc/graduate/

Graduate study since 1916. Enrollment: full-time 1065 (men 90%, women 20%); no part-time study except in unusual cases.

Institute faculty, research and teaching: full-time 726, part-time 27. Degrees conferred: M.S., Engineer, Ph.D.

ADMISSION REQUIREMENTS. Transcripts, three letters of recommendation required in support of application. GRE General/Subject Tests required by some divisions, strongly recommended by all. Interview not required. TOEFL required for international applicants, TSE strongly recommended. Graduates of unaccredited institutions not considered. Apply to Dean of Graduate Studies by January 15; applications received later considered as long as vacancies exist. Admits September only. Application fee, none. Phone: (818)395-6346; fax: (818)577-9246.

ADMISSION STANDARDS. Very competitive. Usual minimum average: 3.5 (A = 4).

FINANCIAL AID. Five hundred and one research fellowships, 200 teaching assistantships, full and partial scholarships, loans. Most scholarships and fellowships have no teaching or research requirements. Apply to Dean of Graduate Studies by January 15. Use FAFSA and University's FAF. Phone: (818)356-3811. Most students receive aid other than loans from Institute and outside sources.

DEGREE REQUIREMENTS. For M.S.: at least 3 quarters in full-time residence; candidacy; thesis required by some divisions. For Engineer: at least 6 quarters in full-time residence beyond the bachelor's; candidacy; thesis; final exam for some divisions. For Ph.D.: at least 9 quarters in full-time residence beyond the bachelor's; candidacy; foreign languages proficiency required by some programs; thesis; final oral exam.

FIELDS OF STUDY.
Aeronautics.
Applied Mathematics. Ph.D. only.
Applied Mechanics.
Applied Physics. Ph.D. only.
Astronomy. Ph.D. only.
Biochemistry. Ph.D. only.
Biology. Ph.D. only.
Biophysics. Ph.D. only.
Biotechnology. Ph.D. only.
Cellular Biology. Ph.D. only.
Cellular and Molecular Biology. Ph.D. only.
Chemical Engineering.
Chemistry. Ph.D. only.
Civil Engineering.
Computation and Neural Systems. Ph.D. only.
Computer Science.
Control and Dynamical Systems. Ph.D. only.
Developmental Biology. Ph.D. only.
Engineering Sciences.
Environmental Engineering Science.
Genetics. Ph.D. only.
Geochemistry.
Geology and Planetary Sciences. Ph.D. only.
Geophysics. Ph.D. only.
Government and Political Sciences.
Immunology. Ph.D. only.
Integrative Neurobiology. Ph.D. only.
Materials Sciences.
Mathematics. Ph.D.
Mechanical Engineering.
Molecular Biology and Biochemistry. Ph.D. only.
Physics.
Planetary Sciences. Ph.D. only.
Social Science. Ph.D. only.

CALIFORNIA LUTHERAN UNIVERSITY
Thousand Oaks, California 91360
http://www.clunet.edu

Founded in 1959. Coed. Located 50 miles NW of Los Angeles. Church sponsored—Lutheran. Library: 85,000 volumes.
Tuition: per credit, $380 M.B.A., $300 others. No on-campus housing available. For off-campus information contact Housing Office. Phone: (805)493-3220.

Graduate Studies

Graduate study since 1970. Enrollment: full-time 100 part-time 900. Faculty: full-time 26 part-time 89. Degrees conferred: M.A., M.S., M.B.A., M.P.A.

ADMISSION REQUIREMENTS. Transcripts, GRE/GMAT, three letters of recommendation, interview required in support of application. TOEFL required for foreign applicants. Apply to Graduate Enrollment Services Office six weeks prior to registration. Application fee $35. Phone: (805)493-3127; fax: (805)493-3543.

ADMISSION STANDARDS. Selective. Usual minimum average 3.0 (A = 4).

FINANCIAL AID. Limited to scholarships, graduate assistantships, Federal W/S, loans. Apply to the Office of Financial Aid; no specified closing date. Use FAFSA and Institutional FAF. Phone: (805)493-3115; fax: (805)493-3114.

DEGREE REQUIREMENTS. For master's: 30–48 credits minimum; thesis/nonthesis option.

FIELDS OF STUDY.
Business Administration.
Clinical Psychology.
Counseling and Guidance.
Curriculum and Instruction.
Educational Administration.
Marriage and Family Therapy.
Public Administration.
Special Education.

CALIFORNIA POLYTECHNIC STATE UNIVERSITY
San Luis Obispo, California 93407
http://www.calpoly.edu/

Founded 1901. Located 200 miles N of Los Angeles. Coed. Public control. Quarter system. Special facilities: Agricultural Safety Institute, Applied Research and Development facilities, Brock Center for Agricultural Communication, Center for Practical Politics, Coastal Resource Institute, Computer-Integrated Manufacturing Center, Dairy Products Technology Center, Design and Construction Institute, Electric Power Institute, Irrigation Training and Research Center, Small Business Institute, Library: 650,000 volumes, 1,500,000 microforms.
Tuition: residents $0, nonresident per credit $164. Fees: full-time (more than 6 units) $690 per quarter, part-time (6 units or less), $486 per quarter. No on-campus housing available. For off-campus housing, call (805)756-1226.

Research and Graduate Program

Enrollment: full-time 696, part-time 384. University faculty: full-time 623, part-time 242. Degrees conferred: M.A., M.S., M.B.A., M.C.R.P., teacher credential.

ADMISSION REQUIREMENTS. Transcripts required in support of application. GRE/GMAT required for some pro grams. TOEFL, TWE required for foreign applicants, Accepts transfer applicants. Apply to Office of Admissions by July 1 (Fall), November (Winter), March 1 (Spring), April 1 (Summer). Application fee $55. Phone: (805)756-2328; fax: (805)756-1725; E-mail: du628@oasis.calpoly.edu.

ADMISSION STANDARDS. Selective. Minimum average: 2.5 (A = 4). For foreign applicants: 550 on TOEFL, 4.5 on TWE required.

FINANCIAL AID. Annual awards from institutional funds: 25 scholarships, Federal W/S, loans. Apply by March 1 to Financial Aid Office. Use FAFSA. Phone: (805)756-2927; fax: (805)756-7243.

DEGREE REQUIREMENTS. For master's: 45 quarter units minimum except for M.C.R.P. (72 units), English (48), Psychology (90), Business (48–96), at least 32 in residence; thesis, project or culminating exam.

FIELDS OF STUDY.
Aeronautical Engineering. M.S.
Agriculture. Includes dairy products technology, engineering technology, food science and nutrition, international agriculture development, soil science. M.S.
Architecture. M.S.
Biological Sciences. M.S.
Business Administration. M.B.A.
City and Regional Planning. M.C.R.P.
Civil and Environental Engineering. M.S.
Computer Science. M.S.
Credentials Programs. Include single subject, multiple subject, educational administration.
Education. Includes counseling and guidance, curriculum and instruction, education administration, reading, special education. M.A.
Electrical Engineering. Includes computer engineering, electronic. M.S.
Engineering. Includes biochemical, industrial, materials, mechanical, water. M.S.
Engineering Management. M.B.A.-M.S.
English. M.A.
Industrial and Technical Studies. M.A.
Mathematics. M.S.
Physical Education. M.S.
Psychology. M.A.

CALIFORNIA STATE POLYTECHNIC UNIVERSITY

Pomona, California 91768-2557
http://www.csupomona.edu

Established 1938. Located 30 miles from Los Angeles. Coed. Public control. Quarter system. Special facilities: Institute for Advanced Systems Studies, Center for Community Affairs, W.K. Kellogg Arabian Horse Center, Landlab—Center for Education and Research in the Sustainable Use of Resources, Institute for Cellular and Molecular Biology, Small Business Institute. Library: 592,000 volumes, 2,000,000 microforms, 2900 current periodicals, 147 PCs in all libraries.

Tuition per unit: resident $0, no resident $164. Fees: $1584. On-campus housing for single graduate students: $2420 ($4760 including board). Contact Director of Marketing for both on- and off-campus housing information. Phone: (909)869-3308.

Graduate School

Graduate study since 1968. Enrollment: full-time 198, part-time 840. Faculty: full-time 334. Degrees conferred: M.A., M.S., M.Arch., M.B.A., M.L.A., M.S.E., M.S.E.E., M.S.B.A., M.U.P.

ADMISSION REQUIREMENTS. Transcripts, GRE General/Subject Tests, GMAT (business) required in support of School's application. Interview required for Architecture, Urban and Regional Planning, and Landscape Architecture. TOEFL required of international applicants. Accepts transfer applicants. Graduates of unaccredited Colleges not considered. Apply to Admissions Office. Application fee $55. Phone: (909)869-2000; fax: (909)869-4529.

ADMISSION STANDARDS. Selective. Usual minimum average: 3.0 (A = 4).

FINANCIAL AID. Graduate presidential fellowships, teaching assistantships, internships, Federal W/S, loans. Use FAFSA. Apply to Dean's Office for fellowships, assistantships; to Financial Aid Office for all other programs. Phone: (909)869 3700; fax: (909)869-4757.

DEGREE REQUIREMENTS. For master's: 45 units minimum, at least 32 units residence; reading knowledge of one foreign language may be required; thesis, project, or comprehensive examination, varies by program.

FIELDS OF STUDY.
Agricultural Sciences.
Applied Mathematics.
Architecture.
Biological Sciences.
Business Administration.
Chemistry.
Computer Science.
Economics.
Education.
Engineering and Applied Sciences.
English.
Environmental Design.
Landscape Architecture.
Management Information Systems Auditing.
Mathematics.
Nutrition and Food Management.
Physical Education and Human Movement.
Urban and Regional Planning.

CALIFORNIA STATE UNIVERSITY, BAKERSFIELD

Bakersfield, California 93311-1022
http://www.csubak.edu

Established 1970. Located 125 miles N of Los Angeles. Coed. Public control. Quarter system. Special facilities: Applied Research Center, Archaeological Information Center, California Well Core Repository, Center for the Study of Classical Economics, Direct Marketing Institute, Center for International

Studies, Center for Environmental Studies, Center for Mathematical and Statistical Studies, Center for Physiological Research, Kegley Institute of Ethics. Library: 250,000 volumes, 343,000 microforms, 2600 current periodicals.

Tuition per unit: resident $0, nonresident $164. Fees: $1584. On-campus housing for single and married students. Average academic year housing costs: $4070 (including board). Contact Director of Housing for both on- and off-campus housing information. Phone: (805)664-3014.

Division of Graduate Studies and Research

http://www.csubak.edu/on_campus.html

Enrollment: full-time 427, part-time 645. Faculty: full-time 75, part-time 100. Degrees conferred: M.A., M.S., M.B.A., M.H.A., M.P.A.

ADMISSION REQUIREMENTS. Transcripts, GRE/GMAT/MAT required in support of School's application. GRE Subject Test, letters of recommendation, interview required by some departments. TOEFL required for international applicants. Accepts transfer applicants. Graduates of unaccredited institutions not considered. Apply to Admissions Office at least two months prior to registration. Late admission will be considered. Application fee $35. Phone: (805)664-2231.

ADMISSION STANDARDS. Selective. Usual minimum average: 2.75 (A = 4).

FINANCIAL AID. Scholarships, teaching assistantships, Graduate Equity Fellowships, Federal W/S, loans. Approved for VA benefits. Apply by March 1 to Dean, School of Graduate Studies for assistantships, fellowships; to Office of Financial Aid for all other programs. Phone: (805)664-2231. Use FAFSA. About 10% of students receive aid other than loans from College, 21% from all sources. Aid sometimes available for part-time students.

DEGREE REQUIREMENTS. For master's: 60–90 units minimum, at least 45 in residence; candidacy; final written/oral exam for most majors; reading knowledge of one foreign language for some majors; thesis/creative/research project.

FIELDS OF STUDY.
Anthropology.
Bilingual/Bicultural Education.
Business Administration. GMAT for admission. M.B.A.
Counseling. M.S. only.
Early Childhood Education.
Educational Administration.
English. Includes creative writing; thesis or project for master's.
Geology.
Health Care Administration. M.H.A. only.
History.
Nursing. Includes administration, child care, clinical, education, supervision.
Psychology. GRE Subject for admission; qualifying exam, thesis or project for master's.
Public Administration. M.P.A.
Pupil Personnel Services.
Reading.
Sociology.
Special Education.

CALIFORNIA STATE UNIVERSITY, CHICO

Chico, California 95929-0150

Founded 1887. Located 100 miles N of Sacramento. Coed. State control. Semester system. Special facilities: Eagle Lake Bi-ological Field Station, Instructional Media Center, Survey Research Center, Vertebrate Museum. Library: 1,365,000 volumes, 927,000 microforms, 3700 current periodicals, 56 PCs.

Tuition: per semester, resident $0, nonresident $246 for each semester unit. Fees: full-time $2006, part-time $1340. On-campus housing for single students only. Average academic year housing costs: $4364 (including board); average off-campus housing costs: $225 per month. Contact Director Of University Housing and Food Service for both on- and off-campus housing information. Phone: (916)898-6328.

Graduate School

Enrollment: full-time 480, part-time 322. University faculty: full-time 651, part-time 215. Degrees conferred: M.A., M.S., M.B.A., M.P.A., M.R.T.P., M.S.A.

ADMISSION REQUIREMENTS. Two official transcripts, GRE, letters of recommendation required in support of application. GRE Subject/MAT/GMAT required for some departments. Interview not required. TOEFL required for international students. Accepts transfer applicants. Graduates of unaccredited institutions not considered. Apply to Graduate School by April 1 (Fall), October 18 (Spring), June 15 (Summer). Rolling admissions process. Application fee $55. Phone: (916)898-5391; fax: (916)898-6804.

ADMISSION STANDARDS. Selective. Usual minimum average: 2.5 in last 60 units. 3.0 in last 30 units (A = 4).

FINANCIAL AID. Annual awards from institutional funds: scholarships, research fellowships, teaching assistantships, Federal W/S, loans. Approved for VA benefits. Apply by February 15 to the Dean's Office for fellowships, assistantships; to the Office of Financial Aid for all other programs. About 50% of students receive aid other than loans from College and outside sources.

DEGREE REQUIREMENTS. For master's: 30 semester units minimum, at least 24 in residence; thesis/nonthesis option for most majors; final written/oral exam.

FIELDS OF STUDY.
Accountancy.
Agricultural Sciences. GRE for admission.
Anthropology. Two letters of recommendation for admission.
Art/Fine Arts. Portfolio for admission.
Biological Sciences. GRE, two letters of recommendation for admission.
Botany and Plant Sciences.
Business Administration. GMAT for admission.
Computer Science. GRE, two letters of recommendation for admission.
Counseling Psychology.
Earth Sciences.
Education.
Electrical Engineering.
Engineering and Applied Sciences.
English. Two letters of recommendation for admission.
Geography. GRE for admission.
Geology.
Health Services Management.
History. GRE for admission.
Information and Communication Studies. MAT or GRE, two letters of recommendation for admission.
Interdisciplinary Studies.
Mechanical Engineering.
Museum Studies.
Music. Includes education, performance; GRE Subject Test for admission.
Nursing. MAT, three letters of recommendation for admission.
Nutritional Science.

Physical Education and Human Movement Studies. GRE, two letters of recommendation for admission.

Political Science. Two letters of recommendation for admission.

Psychology. GRE/MAT for admission.

Public Administration. Two letters of recommendation for admission.

Reading.

Recreation Administration. GRE, two letters of recommendation for admission.

Rural and Town Planning.

Special Education.

Speech-Language Pathology and Audiology. MAT or GRE, three letters of recommendation for admission.

CALIFORNIA STATE UNIVERSITY, DOMINGUEZ HILLS

Carson, California 90747-0001

Founded 1965. Located in Los Angeles County. Coed. Public control. Semester system. Special facilities: Desert Studies Center; Social Systems Research Center, Southern California Ocean Studies Center; art gallery. Library: 411,000 volumes, 572,000 microforms, 2220 current periodicals.

Tuition: full-time, resident $0, nonresidents $246 per unit. Fees: full-time $2006, part-time $1340. On-campus housing for married or graduate students. Average academic year housing costs: $2598 (room only) for single students; $3390 for married students. Contact Office of Dean of Student Affairs for both on- and off-campus housing information.

Division of Graduate Studies and Research

Graduate enrollment: full-time 415, part-time 1327. University faculty teaching graduate students: full-time 69, part-time 31. Degrees conferred: M.A., M.S., M.B.A., M.P.A.

ADMISSION REQUIREMENTS. Two official transcripts required in support of application. GRE may be required by some departments. TOEFL required for international applicants. Graduates of unaccredited institutions not considered. Accepts transfer applicants. Apply to Office of Admission and Records by June 1 (Fall), November 30 (Spring). Application fee $55. Phone: (310)516-3613.

ADMISSION STANDARDS. Selective. Usual minimum average: 2.5 overall, 2.75 in last two years (A = 4).

FINANCIAL AID. Scholarships, teaching/research assistantships, graduate equity fellowships, Federal W/S, loans. Apply to Financial Aid Office; no specified closing dates. Use FAFSA. Phone: (310)516-3647. About 30% of students receive aid from University and outside sources. Aid sometimes available to part-time students.

DEGREE REQUIREMENTS. For master's: 30–48 semester hours minimum, at least 21 in residence; thesis/nonthesis option; final written/oral exam or project.

FIELDS OF STUDY.

Arts Administration. M. A.

Biology and Biomedical Sciences. M.A.

Business Administration. Includes general business, computer information systems.

Child and Family Studies.

Clinical Psychology.

Conflict Resolution and Mediation.

Education. Includes computer-based, education, counseling, curriculum, educational administration, multilingual and multicultural, physical, reading. M.A.

English. Includes literature, rhetoric, and composition, TESL. M.A.

Genetics.

Gerontology.

Historic Preservation.

Humanities. M.A.

Industrial and Management Engineering.

Marriage, Family and Child Counseling. M.S.

Nursing. M.S.

Psychology. Includes general, clinical, social. M.A.

Public Administration. M.P.A.

Public History and Historic Preservation. M.A.

Sociology. Includes general, research skills. M.A.

Special Education. Includes learning handicapped, severely handicapped. M.A.

TESOL.

Writing.

CALIFORNIA STATE UNIVERSITY, FRESNO

Fresno, California 93740-0051

http://www.csufresno.edu/gradstudies

Founded 1911. Located 185 miles SE of San Francisco. Coed. Public control. Semester system. Special facility: California Agricultural Technology Institute, Center for Agricultural Business, Center for Irrigation Technology, Computer Integrated Manufacturing Center, Moss Landing Marine Laboratory (shared by five state colleges), Small Business Development Center, University Business Center, Viticulture and Enology Research Center. Library: 775,000 volumes, 925,000 microforms.

Tuition: full-time, resident $0, nonresident $246 per unit. Fees: full-time $906, part-time $573. On-campus housing for 555 men, 660 women; none for married students. Average annual housing cost: $4000 (including board). Off-campus moderate priced housing is also available. Apply to Director of Housing. Phone: (209)278-2345.

Division of Graduate Studies and Research

Graduate study since 1946. Enrollment: full-time 1659, part-time 1340. Faculty: full-time 703, part-time 297. Degrees conferred: M.A., M.S., M.B.A., M.S.W., M.P.A., M.P.T., M.P.H.

ADMISSION REQUIREMENTS. Transcripts, GRE required in support of University's application. Letters of recommendation, GMAT, interview required by some departments. TOEFL required for foreign applicants. Accepts transfer applicants. Apply to Admissions Office at least two month prior to date of entrance. Late admission will be considered. Application fee $55. Phone: (209)278-2448.

ADMISSION STANDARDS. Selective. Usual minimum average: 2.75 (A = 4), TOEFL score of 550 required of non-English speaking applicants

FINANCIAL AID. Scholarships, 137 teaching assistantships, Federal W/S, loans. Approved for VA benefits. Apply to Office of Financial Aid by February 1 for scholarships, to Department Chairperson, for assistantships. Use FAFSA. Phone: (209)278-2183. About 20% of students receive aid other than loans from University. Aid sometimes available for part-time students.

DEGREE REQUIREMENTS. For master's: 30 units minimum, at least 21 in residence; GRE or GMAT for accountancy, M.P.A., and M.B.A. Advancement to candidacy; final written/oral exam for most majors; reading knowledge of one foreign language for some majors; thesis/creative/research project.

FIELDS OF STUDY.

Accountancy.

Agriculture. Includes agricultural chemistry, animal science, food science, nutrition.

Art. Includes art history, theory; thesis or project for master's.

Biology. Includes marine, microbiology.

Business.

Chemistry. GRE Subject; thesis for master's.

Communicative Disorders. Includes speech-language pathology, education of the deaf.

Computer Science.

Criminology. Includes law enforcement, corrections.

Education. Includes early childhood, elementary, secondary, curriculum and instruction, educational theory, administration, counselor, health, home economics, music, physical, special.

Engineering.

English. Includes creative writing; thesis or project for master's.

Geography.

Geology.

History. One language; GRE Subject, thesis for master's.

International Relations. Includes government; one language, GRE Subject, project for master's.

Linguistics. Includes English as a second language.

Marine Science.

Mass Communication.

Mathematics. GRE Subject, thesis for master's.

Music. Includes performance, music education.

Nursing. Includes clinical, primary nurse practitioner.

Physical Therapy.

Physics. GRE Subject, thesis or project for master's.

Plant Science.

Psychology. GRE Subject, qualifying exam, thesis or project for master's.

Public Administration.

Public Health.

Rehabilitation Counseling.

Social Work. Admits Fall only; two years full-time, thesis for master's.

Spanish.

Special Education.

Special Major.

Speech. Includes, speech communicat ion; GRE Subject, thesis or project for master's.

CALIFORNIA STATE UNIVERSITY, FULLERTON

Fullerton, California 92634-9480

Founded 1957. Located 35 miles SE of Los Angeles. Coed. Public control. Semester system. Special facilities: Desert Studies Consortium, Center for Economic Education, Institute for Economics and Environmental Studies, Center for Governmental Studies, Center for International Business, Ruby Gerontology Center, Social Science Research Center, Twins Study Center. Library: 750,000 volumes, 947,000 microforms, 3900 current periodicals.

Tuition: resident $0; nonresident $246 per unit. Fees: full-time $1420, part-time $1254. No on-campus housing for graduate students. Contact the Housing Office for off-campus housing information. Phone: (714)773-2168.

Graduate Study

Graduate study since 1960. Enrollment: full-time 680, part-time 2967 (men 39%, women 61%). College faculty; full-time 617, part-time 614. Degrees conferred: M.A., M.S., M.B.A., M.P.A., M.M., M.F.A., M.A.T.

ADMISSION REQUIREMENTS. Two official transcripts required with application. GRE required for some programs; GMAT for M.B.A., Accountancy, Taxation, Management Science. TOEFL required for international applicants. Accepts transfer applicants. Graduates of unaccredited institutions not considered. Apply to Office of Admissions and Records by July 1 (Fall), December 1 (Spring); earlier deadlines exist for some programs. Application fee $55. Phone: (714)773-2618.

FINANCIAL AID. Annual awards from institutional funds: 120 assistantships, Federal W/S, loans. Approved for VA benefits. Apply by March 1 to appropriate department chair for assistantships; to Financial Aid Office for all other programs. Use FAFSA. Phone: (714)773-3125. Aid sometimes available for part-time students

DEGREE REQUIREMENTS. For master's: 30 units minimum, at least 21 in residence; advancement to candidacy; thesis, project, or comprehensive exam required for all programs.

FIELDS OF STUDY.

Accountancy. Project for M.S.

American Studies. Thesis or final exam for M.A.

Anthropology. Thesis or project for M.A.

Art. Includes studio and art history programs; thesis or project for M.A., M.F.A.

Biology. GRE General/Subject for admission; thesis for M.A.

Business Administration. Final exam or thesis for M.B.A.

Chemistry. Departmental exams for classified standing; thesis for M.S.

Communications. GRE for admission; thesis or project for M.A.

Communicative Disorders. Thesis option; comprehensive exam required for M.A.

Comparative Literature. Thesis or final exam for M.A.

Computer Science. GRE for admission; project or thesis for M.S.

Counseling. Project required for M.S.

Economics. GRE for classified standing; thesis for M.A.

Education. Includes bilingual/bicultural education (Spanish/English), elementary curriculum/instruction, reading, special education, administration, TESOL; teaching experience required for classified standing; project/thesis/final exam as determined by concentration for M.S.

Engineering. Includes electrical, mechanical, civil, engineering mechanics systems, engineering science; thesis/project option; final exam for M.S.

English. Project option; final exam for M.A.

Environmental Studies. Thesis for M.S.

Foreign Languages. Includes French, German, Spanish; thesis option; final exam for M.A.

Geography. Project or thesis for M.A.

History. Thesis/project/final exam option for M.A.

Interdisciplinary Studies. M.A. only.

Kinesiology. Thesis or project; final exam for M.S.

Linguistics. Thesis option; final exam for M.A.

Management Science. Final exam for M.S.

Mathematics. Final exam for M.A.

Music. Includes history and literature, performance, theory-composition, music education, proficiency exams for classified standing; thesis or project for M.M., M.A.

Physics. Final exam or thesis for M.S.

Political Science. Project, final exam for M.A.

Psychology. Includes clinical experimental. GRE General/Subject Test for admission; thesis for M.A.; final exam for M.S.

Public Administration. GRE for classified standing; project/thesis/final exam option for M.P.A.

Radio, TV, and Film.

Science. Thesis or project for M.A.T.

Social Science. Thesis or project for M.A.

Sociology. Thesis for M.A.

Speech. Thesis option; final exam for M.A.

Taxation. Project for M.S.

Theater Arts. Includes acting, directory, technical theater and design. Thesis/project and final exam for M.A.; two projects for M.F.A. (technical theater and design, theater for children, acting).

CALIFORNIA STATE UNIVERSITY, HAYWARD

Hayward, California 94542-3000
hhtp://www.csuhayward.edu/

Founded 1957. Located in San Francisco Bay Area, 12 miles SE of Oakland. Coed. State controls. Quarter system. Special facilities: Moss Landing Marine Laboratory, C.F. Smith Museum of Anthropology. Library: 800,000 volumes, 667,000 microforms, 49 PC workstations.

Tuition: resident $0, nonresident $164 per unit. Fees: full-time $1776, part-time $1119. On-campus apartments available. Annual housing cost: $2845. No on-campus housing for married students. Contact Director of Housing and Residential Life for off-campus housing information. Phone (510)582-4745. Day care facilities available.

Graduate Study

Enrollment: full-and part-time 2748. College faculty teaching graduate students: approximately 378. Degrees conferred: M.A., M.B.A., M.P.A., M.S.

ADMISSION REQUIREMENTS. Transcripts required in support of application. GRE, GMAT or MAT required by some departments. TOEFL required of foreign students. Interview required by some departments. Accepts transfer applicants. Graduates of unaccredited institutions not considered. Apply to the Office of Admissions. Application fee $55. Phone: (510)885-3817.

ADMISSION STANDARDS. Competitive. Minimum undergraduate GPA for postbaccalaureate status is 2.5 in last 90 quarter units (A = 4).

FINANCIAL AID. Scholarships, grants, fellowships, internships, Federal W/S, loan. Apply to Director of Financial Aid by March 1. Use FAFSA and institution FAF. Phone: (510))885-3616. About 10% of students receive aid other than loans from University and outside sources.

DEGREE REQUIREMENTS. For master's: 45 quarter hours minimum, at least 32 in residence; thesis, project, or comprehensive exam; foreign language for several majors.

FIELDS OF STUDY
Anthropology. Thesis and comprehensive exam.
Biological Science. Includes botany, zoology; thesis.
Business Administration. M.B.A., M.S.; thesis or comprehensive exam; ten options.
Chemistry. Thesis or comprehensive exam for M.S.
Computer Science. M.S.; thesis or comprehensive exam.
Counseling. Includes clinical and school; thesis, project, or comprehensive exam.
Economics. M.A.; thesis or comprehensive exam.
Education. Includes children's literature, ESL, environmental, mathematics, science, reading instruction, educational psychology, pupil personnel, curriculum, early childhood, special; thesis or project.
Educational Leadership. Thesis or project.
English. One language for M.A.; comprehensive exam required; thesis optional.
Geography. Thesis or project for M.A.

Geology. M.S.; thesis.
History. Thesis, project, or comprehensive exam; one language in most options.
Marine Science. M.S.; thesis.
Mathematics. Includes teaching, applied, pure math options for M.S.; comprehensive exam.
Multimedia. M.A. Interdisciplinary; project.
Music. Includes history-literature, education, performance, theory, composition; proficiency exams for admission; thesis/project; comprehensive exam.
Physical Education. Thesis/project; comprehensive exam.
Public Administration. Options in public policy development, public management, organizational change, health care administration; comprehensive exam.
Sociology. Thesis/project; comprehensive exam.
Special Major. Self-designed M.A. or M.S., thesis/project; comprehensive exam.
Speech. M.A.; Communication; thesis/project; comprehensive exam.
Speech Pathology. M.S. Thesis optional; comprehensive exam.
Statistics. M.S.; comprehensive exam.
Taxation. M.S.; thesis for M.S.

CALIFORNIA STATE UNIVERSITY, LONG BEACH

Long Beach, California 90840-0118
http://www.csulb.edu/

Founded 1949. Located between Los Angeles and Orange County. Coed. Public control. Semester systems. Special facilities: Performing Art Center. Library: 1,000,000 volumes plus 2,000,000 items, 200 PCs.

Tuition: resident $0, nonresident $246. Fees: full-time $1816, part-time $1150. On-campus housing for 725 men, 1075 women; none for married students. Average annual housing cost: $5250 (including board). Apply to Director of Housing. Dance Center. Day care facilities available.

Graduate Studies

Enrollment: full-time 1703, part-time 3436. College faculty: full-time 500, part-time 100. Degrees conferred: M.A., M.S., M.F.A., M.P.A., Ph.D. (Engineering Mathematics with Claremont Graduate School).

ADMISSION REQUIREMENTS. Transcripts, GRE/GMAT required in support of University's application. TOEFL required for foreign applicants. Accept transfer applicants. Graduates of unaccredited institutions not considered. Apply to Office Of Admissions and Records by August 1 (Fall), December 1 (Spring). Application fee $55. Phone: (310)985-4128; fax: (310)985-1680.

ADMISSION STANDARDS. Very selective for some departments, relatively open for others. Minimum average: 2.5 in last 60 units attempted (A = 4).

FINANCIAL AID. Annual awards from institutional funds; 20 scholarships, 170 assistantships, Federal W/S, loans. Apply to the Office of Financial Aid between February 1 and March 1 for scholarships, loans, W/S; to appropriate department chair for assistantships. Use FAFSA. No aid for part-time students. Phone: (310)985-4641.

DEGREE REQUIREMENTS. For master's: 30 units minimum, at least 24 in residence; reading knowledge of one foreign language for some major; candidacy exam; thesis/Project or final written/oral exam. For Ph.D.: see degree requirements in Claremont Graduate School listing.

FIELDS OF STUDY.
Aerospace Engineering.
Anthropology.
Art. Includes studio, education, art history.
Asian Studies.
Biochemistry.
Biology.
Business Administration.
Chemistry.
Civil Engineering.
Communicative Disorders.
Computer Engineering.
Computer Sciences.
Counseling.
Criminal Justice.
Dance.
Design.
Economics.
Education. Includes administration, psychology and social foundations; elementary, secondary.
Electrical Engineering.
Engineering Mathematics.
English.
French.
Geography.
Geological Sciences.
German.
Gerontology.
Health Care Administration.
Health Science.
History.
Home Economics.
Interdisciplinary Studies.
Linguistics.
Mathematics.
Mechanical Engineering.
Microbiology.
Music. Includes applied, musicology, performance.
Nursing.
Nutritional Science.
Philosophy.
Physical Education.
Physics.
Political Science.
Psychology. Includes industrial, clinical.
Public Administration.
Public Health.
Recreation Administration.
Social Work.
Spanish.
Special Education.
Speech Communication.
Theater Arts.
Vocational Education.

CALIFORNIA STATE UNIVERSITY, LOS ANGELES

Los Angeles, California 90032-8350

Founded 1947. Public control. Quarter system. Special facilities: Center for the Study of Business in Society, Chinese Studies Center, Center for Korean-American Studies, Center for Armament and Disarmament, Desert Studies Center. Library: 1,100,000 volumes, 800,000 microforms, about 100 PC workstations.

Tuition: resident $0, nonresident $164 per quarter unit. Fees per quarter: full-time $580, part-time $358. On-campus housing available. Total annual cost: $2900. For off-campus housing, contact Housing and Residence Life. Phone: (213)343-4800. Day care facilities available.

Graduate Program

Enrollment: full-time 1533, part-time 2750. Faculty: full-time 540, part-time 503. Degrees conferred: M.A., M.F.A., M.S., M.B.A., Ph.D. (Special Education) offered jointly with UCLA.

ADMISSION REQUIREMENTS. Two transcripts required in support of University's application. GRE and interview required by some departments. TOEFL required for international applicants. Accepts transfer applicants. Graduates of unaccredited institutions not considered. Apply to Office of Admissions and Records. Application fee $55. Phone: (213)343-3891.

ADMISSION STANDARDS. Relatively open. Usual minimum average: 2.5 (A = 4).

FINANCIAL AID. Limited to Federal W/S, loans. Approved for VA benefits. Apply to Office of Student Financial Services. Use FAFSA. Phone: (213)343-3240.

DEGREE REQUIREMENTS. For master's: 45 quarter units minimum, at least 32 in residence; foreign language competency for some departments; thesis for some majors; advancement to candidacy; comprehensive; oral/written exam for some major. For Ph.D.: 32 quarter units in residence; for additional Ph.D. requirements, see UCLA listing.

FIELDS OF STUDY.
Accountancy.
Anthropology.
Art.
Biochemistry.
Business Administration. Includes accounting, business economics, business education, finance, international, management, marketing.
Chemistry.
Child Development.
Communicative Disorders.
Counseling. Includes school counseling and school psychology, rehabilitation counseling, community college counseling, applied behavior analysis.
Criminal Justice.
Criminalistics.
Economics.
Education. Includes elementary, secondary, computer education, educational foundation, reading, special interests.
Educational Administration.
Engineering. Includes civil, electrical, mechanical.
English.
French.
Geography.
Geology. Offered jointly with California State University, Long Beach, California State University, Northridge.
Health Care Management.
Health Science.
History.
Home Economics. Option in nutrition and food.
Industrial and Technical Studies.
Latin-American Studies.
Mathematics. Includes applied and pure.
Mexican-American Studies.
Microbiology.
Music. Includes music composition, performance, musicology.
Music Education.
Nursing. Includes mental and community health.
Philosophy.
Physical Education.
Physics.

Political Science.
Psychology.
Public Administration.
Sociology.
Spanish.
Special Communication.
Special Education. Ph.D. offered jointly with UCLA.
Special Major.
Theater Arts.
Urban Education.
Vocational Education.

CALIFORNIA STATE UNIVERSITY, NORTHRIDGE

Northridge, California 91330

Founded 1958. Located near Los Angeles. Coed. Public control. Semester system. Special facilities: Cancer Research Center, San Fernando Valley Teaching Center, Northridge Center for public Archaeology. Urban Archives Center. Library: 1 million volumes, 7500 current periodicals.

Tuition: full-time, resident $0; nonresident $246 per unit. Fees: fulltime $1970, part-time $1304. On-campus housing for single students only. Average academic year housing costs: $5840 (including board). Contact Housing Office for both on- and off-campus housing information. Phone: (818)885-2160.

Graduate School

Enrollment: full-time 422, part-time 2167. Faculty: full-time 829, part-time 632. Degrees conferred: M.A., M.B.A., M.P.A., M.P.H., M.S.

ADMISSION REQUIREMENTS. Two official transcripts, GRE/MAT/GMAT required in support of School's application. TOEFL required for international applicants. Interview required for some departments. Separate departmental applications required in some departments. Accepts transfer applicants. Apply to Admissions Office by August 1 (Fall), January 1 (Spring). Application fee $55. Phone: (818)885-2138.

ADMISSION STANDARDS. Selective for most departments. Usual minimum average: 2.5 (A = 4).

FINANCIAL AID. Annual awards from institutional funds: fellowships, assistantships, partial tuition waivers, Federal W/S, loans. Approved for VA benefits. Use FAFSA. Phone: (919)995-2374. About 5% of students receive aid from University and outside sources. No aid for part-time students.

DEGREE REQUIREMENTS. For master's: 30 units minimum, at least 21 in residence; thesis/project; comprehensive exam; reading knowledge of one foreign language for some departments. For M.B.A.: 33 units.

FIELDS OF STUDY.
Accounting.
Aerospace/Aeronautical Engineering.
Anthropology.
Art. Includes applied, 2-D, 3-D, history. Portfolio, creative project for M.A.
Bioengineering and Biomedical Engineering.
Biology. GRE Subject for M.S.
Business Administration. GMAT required for admission. M.S., M.B.A.
Chemistry. Departmental proficiency exam for M.S. Option I Chemistry; Option II Environmental Chemistry.
Civil Engineering.

Computer Engineering.
Computer Science.
Counselor. M.S. for M.F.C.C.
Education. Includes supervision and higher education; educational psychology, counseling and guidance; elementary education, secondary education, social, philosophical foundations, foundations of education.
Educational Administration. M.A. only.
Electrical Engineering.
Engineering Management.
English.
French.
Geography.
Geology. M.S. offered cooperatively with CSU, Long Beach, and CSU, Los Angeles.
Health Science. Applications for health education (M.P.H.) option accepted Fall only; application by March 1.
History. One language required in area of concentration for M.A.
Home Economics.
Industrial Management Engineering.
Interdisciplinary Studies. M.A., M.S.
Journalism.
Linguistics. One language required for M.A.
Marketing.
Mass and Organizational Communication. Option I—news communication, Option II—radio-TV-film.
Materials Engineering.
Mathematics.
Mechanical Engineering.
Mexican-American Studies.
Music. Includes theory, composition, performance, music education. Placement tests in theory and history for M.A. and M.M.
Physical Education and Human Movement Studies.
Physics. Departmental proficiency exam.
Political Science.
Psychology. GRE subject for M.S.; Fall applications February 15 deadline; Spring applications November 1 deadline.
Public Administration. Departmental qualifing exam for M.P.A.
Public Policy and Administration. Applications accepted for Fall only; March 1 deadline.
Recreation and Leisure Studies. Departmental qualifying exam for M.A.
Sociology.
Spanish.
Special Education.
Speech Communication.
Speech-Language Pathology and Audiology.
Taxation.
Theater Arts. Departmental qualifying exam for M.A.

CALIFORNIA STATE UNIVERSITY, SACRAMENTO

Sacramento, California 95819-6048

Founded 1947. Coed. Public control. Semester system. Library: 806,000 volumes, 32,000 microforms, 5200 current periodicals.

Tuition: resident $0, nonresident $246 per unit. Fees: full-time $1970, part-time $1304. On-campus housing for single students. Average academic year housing costs: $4583 (including board). Contact to Office of Residence Hall Life for both on- and off-campus housing information.

Graduate Division

Enrollment: full- and part-time 2761. Graduate faculty: full-time 793, part-time 454. Degrees conferred: M.A., M.S., M.B.A., M.P.P.A., M.S.W.

ADMISSION REQUIREMENTS. Two official transcripts required in support of application. GRE/GMAT required by some departments. Interview may be requested. TOEFL required for international applicants. Accepts transfer applicants. Graduates of unaccredited institutions not considered. Apply April 15 (Fall), November 1 (Spring) to Office of Admissions. Application fee $55. Phone: (916)278-6470.

ADMISSION STANDARDS. Selective. Usual minimum average: 2.5 (A = 4).

FINANCIAL AID. Assistantships, Federal W/S, loans. Apply to the Dean for assistantships; to Financial Aid Office for all other programs. No specified closing dates. Use FAFSA.

DEGREE REQUIREMENTS. For most master's: 30 semester hours minimum, at least 21 in residence; thesis/nonthesis option for many majors; final written/oral exam for some majors. For M.B.A., M.P.A.: 30–57 hours, depending upon previous preparation. For M.S.W.: satisfactory completion of two-year program, at least one year in residence.

FIELDS OF STUDY.
Accounting.
Anthropology. M.A.
Art. Includes fine arts, art history. M.A.
Biological Sciences. M.A., M.S.
Biology and Biomedical Engineering. M.S.
Business Administration. M.B.A.
Business Administration. Includes management information systems. M.S.
Chemistry. M.S.
Civil Engineering. M.S.
Communication Studies. M.A.
Computer Science. Includes software engineering, scientific and engineering applications, computer systems. M.S.
Counseling. Includes career counseling, generic counseling, school counseling, school psychology, vocational rehabilitation counseling. M.S.
Criminal Justice. Includes forensic science. M.A.
Drama. M.A.
Economics. M.A.
Education. Includes behavioral sciences in education, art, bilingual/cross-cultural education, curriculum and instruction, early childhood education, educational administration, English language development, gifted/talented education, guidance, reading specialist, special education. M.A.
Electrical Engineering. M. S.
English. Includes creative writing, teaching English to speakers of other languages. M.A.
French. M.A.
German. M.A.
Government. M.A.
History. Includes public history. M.A.
Human Services.
Interdisciplinary Studies.
International Affairs. M.A.
Management Information Systems. M.I.S.
Marine Science. M.S.
Mathematics. M.A.
Mechanical Engineering. M.S.
Music. M.A.
Nursing. M.S.
Occupational Therapy.
Psychology. M.A.
Public Administration. M.P.A.
Public and Community Health. M.S.
Recreation Administration. M.A.
School Psychology.
Social Science. Includes anthropology, communication studies, economics, government, history, psychology, sociology. M.A.

Social Work. Includes family and children's services, health care, mental health, social justice and corrections. M.S.W.
Sociology. M.A.
Software Engineering.
Spanish. M.A.
Speech Pathology and Audiology. Includes speech pathology, audiology. M.S.
TESOL. M.A.
Writing.

CALIFORNIA STATE UNIVERSITY, SAN BERNARDINO
San Bernardino, California 92407-2397

Established 1965. Located 60 miles NE of Los Angeles. Coed. Public control. Quarter system. Special facilities: Desert Research Center, Institute for Social and Public Policy Research. Library: 550,000 volumes, 585,000 microforms, 1650 current periodicals, 12 PCs.

Tuition: resident $0 per quarter; nonresident $264 per quarter unit. Fees: full-time $1384, part-time $1816. On-campus housing for single students only. Average academic year housing costs including board $4108–$5078. Contact Housing Director for both on-and off-campus housing information. Day care facilities available.

Graduate Studies

Graduate study since 1972. Enrollment: full-time 898, part-time 1960. Graduate faculty: full-time 100, part-time 21. Degrees conferred: M.A., M.S., M.B.A., M.P.A., M.S.W.

ADMISSION REQUIREMENTS. Transcripts GRE/GMAT required in support of application. TOEFL, TWE required for international applicants. Accepts transfer applicants. Graduates of unaccredited institutions not considered. Apply to the Office of Admissions by September 15 (Fall), December 15 (Winter), March 15 (Spring). Application fee $55. Phone: (909)880-5200.

ADMISSION STANDARDS. Selective. Usual minimum average: 2.5 in last 90 quarter/60 semester credits (A = 4).

FINANCIAL AID. Annual awards from institutional funds: scholarships, assistantships, Federal W/S, loans. Approved for VA benefits. Apply to Director of Financial Aid by July 1. Use FAFSA. Phone: (909)880-7800.

DEGREE REQUIREMENTS. For master's: 45 quarter hours minimum, 36 in residence; thesis/nonthesis option; 3.0 GPA required.

FIELDS OF STUDY.
Administration. Includes business, public.
Biology.
Computer Science.
Criminal Justice.
Education. Includes bilingual/cross-cultural, counseling and guidance, early childhood education, educational administration, elementary, English, environmental education, history, middle school, physical education, reading, secondary, special education, vocational education, teaching English as a second language.
English Composition. Includes ESL.
Health Services Administration.
Interdisciplinary Studies.
Mathematics.
National Security Studies.
Psychology. Includes counseling, general, industrial-organizational, lifespan developmental.

Rehabilitational Counseling.
Social Sciences.
Social Work.

CALIFORNIA STATE UNIVERSITY, STANISLAUS
Turlock, California 95382

Founded 1965. Located 13 miles S of Modesto. Coed. Public control. 4-1-4 system. Library: 290,000 volumes, 770,000 microforms. Special facilities: Moss Landing Marine Laboratories.

Tuition: resident $0, nonresident $246 per unit. Fees: full-time $1925, part-time $1739. On-campus housing for single and married graduate students. Annual room and board cost: $5623. Apply to Director of Housing. Phone: (209)667-3675. Day care facilities available.

Graduate Division

Enrollment: full-and part-time 1174. Faculty: full-time 262, part-time 70. Degrees conferred: M.A., M.S., M.B.A., M.P.A.

ADMISSION REQUIREMENTS. Two transcripts, GRE Subject Test (History, Education, Psychology, Marine Science, English), GRE (International Relations, Interdisciplinary Studies), GMAT (Business) required in support of University's application. TOEFL required for foreign applicants. Accepts transfer applicants. Apply to Admissions and Records Office; no specified closing date. Application fee $55. Phone: (209)667-3129; fax: (209)667-3788.

ADMISSION STANDARDS. Selective. Usual minimum average: 3.0 (A = 4).

FINANCIAL AID. Twenty-five scholarships, four research assistantships, loans. Approved VA benefits. Apply to Office of Financial Aid; no specified closing date. Use FAFSA and University's FAF. Phone: (209)667-3336.

DEGREE REQUIREMENTS. For master's 30 units minimum, at least 24 in residence; thesis/project or final written/ oral exam.

FIELDS OF STUDY.
Business Administration.
Education. Includes administration and supervision, school counseling, curriculum and instruction (elementary, secondary, reading, special education), physical education.
English.
History.
Interdisciplinary Studies.
International Relations. (Concentration in M.A., History)
Marine Science.
Psychology.
Public Administration.
Social Work.

CALIFORNIA UNIVERSITY OF PENNSYLVANIA
California, Pennsylvania 15419-1394

Founded 1852. Located 40 miles S of Pittsburgh. Coed. Public control. Semester system and two 5-week Summer terms. Library: 330,400 volumes, 1,297,000 microforms, 1500 current periodicals, 60 PCs.

Tuition: full-time, resident $3368, per credit $187; nonresident $6054, per credit $336. On-campus housing for single students only. Average academic year housing cost: $3890 (including

board). Contact Director of Housing for both on- and off-campus housing information. Phone: (412)938-4439. Day care facilities available.

School of Graduate Studies

Enrollment: full-time 416, part-time 481 (men 38%, women 62%). Faculty: full-time 11, part-time 86. Degrees conferred: M.A., M.S., M.Ed., M.S.

ADMISSION REQUIREMENTS. Transcripts, teacher certification for M.Ed. programs, MAT/GRE/GMAT interview required for some programs in support of application. TOEFL required for foreign applicants. Accepts transfer applicants. Graduates of unaccredited colleges not considered. Apply by August 23 (Fall), January 10 (Spring), April 27 (Summer). Phone: (412)938-4187.

ADMISSION STANDARDS. Selective. Usual minimum average: 2.50 (A = 4), some programs are higher.

FINANCIAL AID. Annual awards from institutional funds: 150 nonteaching graduate assistantships, Federal W/S, loans. Apply to the Graduate Dean for assistantships; to Financial Aid Office for all other programs. No specified closing date. Phone: (412)938-4415. Use FAFSA. About 5% of students receive aid other than loans from College and outside sources.

DEGREE REQUIREMENTS. For master's: 30–36 credits minimum, 24 in residence; thesis/nonthesis option; final oral/written exam.

FIELDS OF STUDY.
Athletic Training. M.S. only.
Biology. M.Ed., M.S. only.
Business Administration. M.S.
Communication. M.A. only.
Communication Disorders. M.S.
Computer Science. M.Ed.
Counselor Education. Includes elementary, secondary; M.Ed. only; business and industry counseling, M.S. only.
Early Childhood Education. M.Ed. only.
Earth Science. M.S. only.
Educational Administration. Includes elementary, secondary principal, superintendent's letter of eligibility.
Elementary Education. M.Ed. only.
English. M.A., M.Ed. only.
Geography. M.A., M.Ed. only.
Mathematics Education. M.Ed. only.
Reading Specialist. M. Ed. only.
School Psychology. M.S. only.
Science Education. M.Ed., M.A.
Social Science. M.A.
Special Education. M.Ed.
Technology Education. M.Ed. only.

UNIVERSITY OF CALIFORNIA AT BERKELEY
Berkeley, California 94720
http://www.berkeley.edu

Founded 1868. Located 12 miles E of San Francisco. Coed. Public control. Semester system. Special facilities: Lawrence Berkeley and Livermore National Laboratories, Bodega Marine Laboratory, Center for Pure and Applied Mathematics, Mathematical Sciences Research Institute, Space Sciences Laboratory, Virus Laboratory, Naval Biomedical Laboratory, International House, Low-Density Wind-Tunnel Facility; Laboratories for

Electronics Research, Hydraulic Engineering, Sea Water Conversion, Structural and Sanitary Engineering; Institutes of Transportation, Traffic Engineering, Personality Assessment and Research, Business and Economic Research, Governmental Studies, Human Development, Human Learning, Industrial Relations, International Studies, Library Research, Marine Resources, Basic Research in Science, Urban and Rural Development; Operations Research Center, White Mountain Research Station, Lick Observatory; centers for study of Law and Society, Study of Higher Education, Research in Management Science, Survey Research; Chinese Studies, Japanese and Korean Studies, Latin American Studies, Planning Development and Research; computer facilities. The twenty-six Berkeley campus libraries house more than 7,000,000 volumes, 3,000,000 microforms, plus online data retrieval services.

Annual fees/tuition: full-time, resident $4395, nonresident $12,094. Fifteen residence halls for graduate and upper division students. Rooms are double occupancy. 994 apartments for married and single students. Apply to Housing Services. Phone: (510)642-7781. For off-campus information, phone (510)643-6544.

Graduate Division

Graduate study since 1868. Enrollment: 8454 (men 4870, women 3584). Faculty: full-time 1790, part-time 0. Degrees conferred: M.A., M.S., M.A.T., M.Arch., M.B.A., M.C.P., M.Eng., M.F., M.J., M.F.A., LL.M., M.L.A., M.P.A., M.P.P., M.S.W., Ed.D., D.Eng., J.D., J.S.D., Dr.P.H., Ph.D.

ADMISSION REQUIREMENTS. Transcripts, GRE/GMAT required in support of University's application. Interview normally not required. TOEFL required for all non-English speaking applicants. Graduates of unaccredited colleges not considered. Request application materials directly from department. Deadline range: December 15–February 10 (Fall); September 1 (Spring). Many departments admit for the Fall only. Application fee $40. Phone: (510)642-7404; fax: (510)643-1524.

ADMISSION STANDARDS. Very selective for most departments.

FINANCIAL AID. Fifteen hundred fellowships, 2500 research assistantships, 1750 teaching assistantships, 630 readers, Federal W/S, loans. Apply to appropriate department; no specified closing date. For Federal programs apply to Financial Aid Office. Phone: (510)642-0485. Use FAFSA.

DEGREE REQUIREMENTS. For M.A.. M.S.: Plan I–20 semester units minimum plus thesis, at least two semesters (one year) in residence. Plan II—24 semester units minimum without thesis, at least two semesters (one year) in residence, comprehensive exam. For other master's: the same requisites outlined above normally apply. For Ph.D.: normally at least two years minimum in residence beyond the bachelor's degree; reading knowledge of at least one foreign language required by most departments; qualifying exams; dissertation; final oral exam. For other doctorates: essentially the same minimum requisites as for Ph.D., except no foreign language requirement.

FIELDS OF STUDY.
Agricultural and Environmental Chemistry.
Agricultural and Resource Economics and Policy. Ph.D. only.
Ancient History and Archaeology.
Anthropology. Ph.D. only.
Applied Mathematics. Ph.D. only.
Applied Science and Technology.

Architecture.
Art. Studio; portfolio for admission; M.F.A. only.
Asian Studies. Emphasis on East Asia, Southeast Asia, South Asia, Northeast Asia studies for M.A.
Astronomy. Ph.D. only.
Bioengineering (with UCSF). Ph.D. only.
Biophysics.
Biostatistics.
Buddhist Studies. Ph.D. only.
Business Administration. GMAT for admission; M.B.A. normally two-year program.
Chemical Engineering. Chemistry. Ph.D. only.
City and Regional Planning.
Classical Archaeology.
Classics.
Comparative Biochemistry.
Comparative Literature.
Computer science.
Demography.
Design (Visual). M.A. only.
Dramatic Art. Ph.D. only.
East Asian Languages. Chinese, Japanese.
Economics. Ph.D. only.
Education.
Endocrinology.
Energy and Resources.
Engineering and Engineering Science. Includes civil engineering, electrical engineering and computer sciences, industrial engineering and operations research, mechanical engineering, naval architecture and offshore engineering, nuclear engineering, materials science and mineral engineering.
English.
Entomology.
Environmental Health Sciences.
Environmental Planning. Ph.D. only.
Environmental Science Policy and Management.
Epidemiology.
Ethnic Studies. Ph.D. only.
Folklore. M.A. only.
Forestry. M.F. only.
French.
Geography.
Geology.
Geophysics.
German.
Greek. M.A. only.
Health and Medical Sciences. Dual degree option; genetic counseling, M.S.; medical program (with UCSF), M.S., M.D.
Health Services and Policy Analysis. Ph.D. only.
Hispanic Languages and Literatures.
History.
History of Art. Ph.D. only.
Information Management and Systems.
Integrative Biology.
Italian.
Jewish Studies. Joint program with Graduate Theological Union.
Journalism. M.J. only.
Jurisprudence and Social Policy. Ph.D. only.
Landscape Architecture. M.L.A. only.
Latin. M.A. only.
Latin American Studies.
Linguistics.
Logic and the Methodology of Science. Ph.D. only.
Mathematics.
Medical Anthropology (with UCSF). Ph.D. only.
Medical Physics. Ph.D. only.
Microbiology.
Molecular and Cell Biology.
Music. Includes performance, musicology.
Near Eastern Religions. Joint program with Graduate Theological Union.

Near Eastern Studies.
Neurobiology. Ph.D. only.
Nutrition.
Optometry. Certificate only. Must have O.D. degree.
Parasitology.
Philosophy. Ph.D. only.
Physical Education. M.A. only.
Physics.
Plant Biology.
Political Science. Ph.D. only.
Psychology. Ph.D. only.
Public Health.
Public Policy.
Range Management. M.S. only.
Rhetoric. Ph.D. only.
Romance Languages and Literatures. Includes French, Italian, Spanish; Ph.D. only.
Romance Philology. Ph.D. only.
Scandinavian Languages and Literatures. Includes Danish, Norwegian, Old Norse, Swedish.
Science and Mathematics Education. Ph.D. only.
Slavic Languages and Literatures. Includes Russian, Polish, Czech, Serbo-Croatian.
Sociology. Ph.D. only.
South and Southeast Asian Studies. Includes Hindu-Urdu, Malay-Indonesian Sanscrit, South Asian Archaeology.
Special Education.
Urban Design. M.U.D.
Visual Science.
Wildland Resource Science.
Wood Science and Technology.

Boalt Hall School of Law (94720-7200)

Established 1912. Coed. Semester system. Law library: 650,000 volumes. Library has LEXIS, NEXIS, WESTLAW, INNOPAC, MELVYL.

Annual tuition: resident $7801, nonresident $16,195. On-campus housing available. Enrollment: first-year class 269; full-time 870 (men 52%, women 48%); post-graduates 50. Faculty: full-time 75, part-time 48. Degrees conferred: J.D., J.D.-M.A.(Asian Studies, Economics, Journalism), J.D.-M.B.A., J.D.-M.P.H., J.D.-M.S.W., J.D.-M.C.P., J.D.-Ph.D. (Economics, Legal History), J.D.-M.A.L.O. (Fletcher School of Law, Tufts University), J.D.-M.P.P. (J.F.K. School of Government, Harvard University), LL.M.

ADMISSION REQUIREMENTS. LSDAS Law School report, transcripts, LSAT (no later than December), two references recommended in support of application. Applicants must have received the bachelor's prior to entrance. Accepts transfer applicants. Preference given to state residents. Graduates of unaccredited colleges not considered. Apply to Admissions Office after September, before February 1; early filing strongly recommended. Admission on full-time basis only; admits fall only. Application fee $40. Phone: (510)642-2273.

ADMISSION STANDARDS. Competitive. Accepts about 15% of total annual applicants.

FINANCIAL AID. Scholarships, fellowships, research assistantships, grants, Federal W/S, loans. All financial aid based on need. Apply to Office of Financial Aid by March 1. Use FAFSA. About 40% of students receive aid other than loans from institution and outside sources.

DEGREE REQUIREMENTS. For J.D.: 6 terms minimum, at least 2 terms in full-time residence; 81 units. For LL.M.: 24 units

minimum in full-time residence; final research project. For other master's, Ph.D. programs: see Graduate School listing above or other institutional programs.

UNIVERSITY OF CALIFORNIA, DAVIS
Davis, California 95616

Founded 1868. Located 12 miles W of Sacramento. Coed. State control. Quarter system. Special facilities: Arboretum and Natural Reserve System, Agricultural Experiment Stations, Agricultural History Center, Agricultural issues Center. Adult Fitness Laboratory, Bodega Marine Laboratory (off-campus), Botany Department Herbarium, California Regional Primate Research Center, Center for Consumer Research, Center for Image Processing and Integrated Computing Research (CIPICR), Computer Center, Crocker Nuclear Laboratory, Embryological Collection from Carnegie Institution, Facility for Advanced Instrumentation, Institute for Environment Health Research, Institute of Governmental Affairs, Humanities Institute, Institute of Marine Resources, Lawrence Livermore Laboratory, Nuclear Magnetic Resonance Facility, Plant Growth Laboratory, Serology Laboratory, Institute of Transportation Studies. Library: 2,655,000 volumes, 3,315,000 microforms, 49,000 current periodicals.

Annual fees/tuition: full-time, resident $4422, nonresident $12,120. On-campus housing for 476 married students, 180 single students. Average annual housing cost: $5000–$6500 for married students, $6200 (including board) for single students. Contact Housing Office for both on- and off-campus housing information. Phone: (916)752-2033. Day care facilities available.

Graduate Studies

Graduate study since 1924. Enrollment: full- and part-time 3299, (men 65%, women 35%). University faculty teaching graduate students: full-time 1600. Degrees conferred: M.A., M.A.T., M.B.A., M.Ed., M.E., M.F.A., M.S., M.A.M., M.Admin., D.Engr., Ed.D., Ph.D.

ADMISSION REQUIREMENTS. Transcripts, three letters of recommendation required in support of application. GRE/Subject Tests, GMAT required by most departments. TOEFL required for international applicants. Interview not required. Accepts transfer applicants. Graduates of unaccredited institutions not considered. Apply to the Office of the Graduate Studies by April 1 (Fall). Rolling admission process. Application fee $40. Phone: (916)752-9292.

ADMISSION STANDARDS. Selective. Usual minimum average: 3.0 (A = 4).

FINANCIAL AID. Annual awards from institutional funds: scholarships, research assistantships, teaching assistantships, nonresident tuition fellowships, Federal W/S, loans. Approved for VA benefits. Apply by January 15 to appropriate department for fellowships, assistantships; to Financial Aid Office for all other programs. Use FAFSA. Phone: (916)752-2390. About 35–45% of students receive aid other than loans from University and outside sources.

DEGREE REQUIREMENTS. For master's: Plan I—30 units minimum in residence plus thesis, reading knowledge of one foreign language for some departments; Plan II—36 units minimum in residence, reading knowledge of one foreign language for some, departments, final comprehensive exam. For Ph.D.: two years minimum in residence; dissertation; preliminary, final oral exams; reading knowledge of two foreign languages for some departments. For Ed.D., D.Eng.: essentially the same as for the Ph.D., except no foreign language requirement.

FIELDS OF STUDY.
Aerospace Engineering. M.E., D. Eng., Ph.D.
Agricultural Economics and Agribusiness. M.S., Ph.D.
Agricultural Science. M.S.
Agronomy. M.S. only.
Animal Behavior. M.S., Ph.D.
Animal Science. M.S., M.A.M.
Anthropology. M.A., Ph.D.
Applied Mathematics. M.S., Ph.D.
Art. Includes art only; portfolio for admission; M.F.A. only.
Atmospheric Science. M.S., Ph.D.
Biochemistry. Molecular biology, M.S., Ph. D.
Bioengineering and Biomedical. M.S., Ph.D.
Biophysics. M.S., Ph.D.
Botany and Plant Sciences. M.S., Ph.D.
Cell and Developmental Biology. Ph.D.
Chemical Engineering. M.S., D.Engr., Ph.D.
Chemistry. M.S., Ph.D.
Child and Family Studies. M.S. only.
Civil Engineering. M.S., D.Engr., Ph.D.
Classics. M.A. only.
Community Development. M.S. only.
Comparative Literature. M.A., Ph.D.
Comparative Pathology. M.S., Ph.D.
Computer Engineering. M.S., Ph.D.
Computer Science. M.S., Ph.D.
Dramatic Art. Production; M.A.; M.F.A., Ph.D.
Ecology. M.S., Ph.D.
Economics. M.A., Ph.D.
Education. M.A., M.Ed., Ph.D.
Educational Psychology. Ed. D.
Electrical Engineering. M.S., D.Engr., Ph.D.
Endocrinology. M.S., Ph.D.
English. M.A., Ph.D.
Entomology. M.S., Ph.D.
Environmental Engineering. M.Engr., M.S., D.Engr., Ph.D.
Epidemiology. M.S., Ph.D.
Food Science and Technology. M.S., Ph.D.
French. M.A., Ph.D.
Genetics. M.S., Ph.D.
Geography. M.A., Ph.D.
Geology. M.S., Ph.D.
German. M.A., Ph.D.
History. M.A., M.A.T., Ph.D.
History of Art. M.A. only.
Horticulture. M.S. only
Human Development. Ph.D. only.
Hydrologic Sciences. M.S., Ph.D.
Immunology. M.S., Ph.D.
International Agricultural Development. M.S. only.
Linguistics. Interdepartmental; M.A. only.
Management. M.B.A.
Materials Sciences. M.S., Ph.D.
Mathematics. M.A., M.A.T., Ph.D.
Mechanical Engineering. M.Engr., M.S., D.Engr., Ph.D.
Microbiology. M.S., Ph.D.
Music. Includes composition, musicology; M.A., M.A.T., Ph.D.
Neurobiology. Ph.D.
Nutrition. M.S., Ph.D.
Pharmacology and Toxicology. M.A., Ph.D.
Philosophy. M.A., Ph.D.
Physical Education. M.A. only.
Physics. M.A., Ph.D.
Physiology. M.S., Ph.D.
Plant Biology. M.S., Ph.D.
Plant Pathology. M.S., Ph.D.

Plant Protection and Pest Management. M.S. only.
Political Science. M.A., Ph.D.
Population Biology. M.S., Ph.D.
Psychology. Ph.D.
Rhetoric and Communication. M.A. only.
Sociology. M.A., Ph.D.
Spanish. M.A., Ph.D.
Statistics. M.S., Ph.D.
Textiles Design. M.S. only.
Water Resources. M.S. only.
Writing. M.A.
Zoology. M.A., Ph.D.

School of Law (95616-5201)

Opened 1965. Coed. Library: 377,210 volumes. Library has LEXIS, NEXIS, WESTLAW, MELVYL. Annual tuition: resident $10,796, nonresident $19,190. On-campus housing available. Apply well in advance of April 1 deadline. Total average annual additional expenses: $9700. Enrollment: first-year class 151; full-time 468 (men 51%, women 49%); no part-time study. Facility: full-time 27, part-time 17. Degrees conferred; J.D., J.D.-M.B.A. (School of Management).

ADMISSION REQUIREMENTS. LSDAS Law School report, transcripts indicating award of bachelor's degree, references, LSAT (no later than December) required in support of application. Interview not required. Accepts transfer applicants. Graduates of unaccredited colleges not considered. Apply to the Admissions office of the School by February 1. Fall admission only. Application fee $40. Phone: (916)752-6477.

ADMISSION STANDARDS. Selective. Accepts 20% of total annual applicants.

FINANCIAL AID. Fellowships, grants, Federal W/S, loans. Apply to Financial Aid office by March 1. Use FAFSA. About 65% of students receive aid other than loans from School.

DEGREE REQUIREMENTS For J.D.: 88 credit minimum; three years in full-time residence. For master's programs: see Graduate School listing above.

School of Medicine

Founded 1968. Coed. State Control, Quarter System. First class entered 1968. Annual tuition and fees: resident $8837, nonresident $17,231. Average figure for all other expense: $8200. Enrollment: first-year class 93; total full-time 400 (men 60%, women 40%). Faculty: full-time 253, part-time 23. Degrees conferred: M.D., M.D.-Ph.D.

ADMISSION REQUIREMENTS. AMCAS report, transcripts, MCAT required in support of application. Usually, bachelor's degree from an accredited U.S. or Canadian school required for admission. Preference given to state and WICHE residents. Interview required for all accepted candidates. Transfer applicants may be considered. Does not have EDP. Apply through AMCAS after June 15, before November 1. Application fee $40. Phone: (916)752-2717.

ADMISSION STANDARDS. Competitive. Accepts about 4% of total annual applicants.

FINANCIAL AID. Scholarships, fellowships, grants, loans. Apply to Financial Aid Office following admission. Phone: (916)752-6618. About 85% of students receive aid other than loans from institutional funds.

DEGREE REQUIREMENTS. For M.D.: satisfactory completion of four-year program. For Ph.D., see graduate listing above.

FIELDS OF GRADUATE STUDY.
Biochemistry.
Biomedical Engineering.
Cell Biology.
Genetics.
Immunology.
Microbiology.
Neurosciences.
Pharmacology.
Physiology.

School of Veterinary Medicine (95616-8731)

Annual fees/tuition: full-time, resident and WICHE contract students $8394, nonresident $16,893. On-campus housing available. Total living expenses $10,500. Enrollment: first-year class 108; total full-time 721 (men 280, women 80). School faculty: full- and part-time 242. Degrees conferred: D.V.M., D.V.M.-M.P.V.M.

ADMISSION REQUIREMENTS. VMCAS report, transcripts, GRE/Subject in biology (October test), three letters of evaluation, Veterinary/Animal experience required in support of application. Accepts transfer applicants if openings exist (priority to state residents). Interviews by invitation only. Applicants must have completed at least three years of college study. Apply to the Admissions Office after July 1, before November 1. For transfer applicants after December 1, before May 1. Application fee $40. Phone: (916)752-1383.

ADMISSION STANDARDS. Competitive. Accepts 25% of total annual applicants. Accepts no more than 2 applicants from WICHE states.

FINANCIAL AID. Scholarships, fellowships, teaching assistantships, loans. Apply to UCD Financial Aid office. Use FAFSA. About 8% of students receive aid other than loans from School funds.

DEGREE REQUIREMENTS. For D.V.M.: satisfactory completion of four-year program. M.V.P.H. offered through the Graduate Division.

UNIVERSITY OF CALIFORNIA, HASTINGS COLLEGE OF LAW

San Francisco, California 94102-4978

Established 1878. Coed. Is now the Law Department of the University of California. Semester system. Library: 548,919 volumes. Library has LEXIS, NEXIS, WESTLAW, DIALOG, INFOTRAC, DATATIMES, LEGITECH, FIRST SEARCH, EPIC.
Annual tuition: resident $11,167, nonresident $19,559. On-campus housing available for 480 students. Enrollment: first-year class 418; total 1262 (men 50%, women 50%). Faculty: full-time 67, part-time 49. Degree conferred: J.D., J.D.-M.A. with Berkeley (Asian Studies, Business Administration, City and Regional Planning, Economics, History, Journalism, and Public Policy).

ADMISSION REQUIREMENTS. LSDAS Law School report, bachelor's degree, LSAT (no later than December), transcripts required in support of application. Personal statements and recommendations are considered. Graduates of unaccredited colleges not considered. Apply to Office of Admissions before February 1. Application fee $40. Phone: (415)565-4623.

ADMISSION STANDARDS. Selective. Admits about 25% of total annual applications.

FINANCIAL AID. Scholarships, full and partial tuition waivers, Federal W/S, loans. Apply by February 1 to Office of Admissions. Use FAFSA and Student Financial Aid Supplement. About 70% of students receive some form of aid.

DEGREE REQUIREMENTS. For J.D.: satisfactory completion of three-year program.
Note: Exchange programs with Nihon University, Leiden University, University of British Columbia, Vermont Law School.

UNIVERSITY OF CALIFORNIA, IRVINE

Irvine, California 92717
http://www.rgs.uci.edu/grad/

Opened 1965. Located 40 miles S of Los Angeles. Coed. Public control. Quarter system. Special facilities: Cancer Research Institute, Center for Neurobiology of Learning and Memory, DEC system -10, Developmental Biology Center, Honeywell DPS-8/49C, Institute Transportation Studies, Laser Microbeam facility, Public Policy Research Organization, Thesaums Linguae Graecae project, Transportation Studies. Library: 1,450,000 volumes, 1,676,000 microforms.
Annual fees/tuition: full-time, resident $4830, nonresident $12,529. Oncampus housing includes 862 one-, two-, and three-bedroom apartments for married and single graduate students; 203 unit complex for full-time graduate, medical and postdoctoral students; residence hall for 60 single graduate student. Average annual housing cost: $6500 (excluding board). Apply to Housing Office. Phone: (714)824-6811. Day care facilities available.

Office of Research and Graduate Studies

Enrollment: approximately 2200. Faculty: full- and part-time 997. Degrees conferred: M.A., M.S., M.B.A., M.F.A., M.A.T., M.U.R.P., ED.D., Ph.D.

ADMISSION REQUIREMENTS. Transcripts, three letters of recommendation required in support of University's application. GRE required for most majors. TOEFL required of foreign applicants. Interview not required. Accepts transfer applicants. Graduates of unaccredited institutions not considered. Apply to Office of Graduate Studies by February 1 (Fall), October 15 (Winter), January 15 (Spring). Application fee $40. Phone. (714)824-6761; fax: (714)824-2095.

ADMISSION STANDARDS. Very competitive to relatively open. Usual minimum average: 3.0 (A = 4)

FINANCIAL AID. Annual awards include fellowships, teaching and research assistantships, need-based grants, Federal W/S, loans. Approved for VA benefits. Apply by February 1 on Graduate Application form to appropriate academic unit. Apply to the Financial Aid Office for Federal programs. Phone: (714)824-6261. Use FAFSA. Most students receive aid other than loans from University and outside sources.

DEGREE REQUIREMENTS. For most master's': three quarters minimum, at least 80% of courses in residence; full-time attendance is normally expected, but part-time study is possible; thesis or final comprehensive exam. For M.F.A. (Creative Writing): six quarters minimum in residence; book-length thesis in recognized genre (poetry, short stories, plays, novel); final comprehensive exam. For Ph.D.: normally six quarters minimum in residence; one foreign language for some departments; qualifying exam and advancement to candidacy; dissertation; final oral exam. For Ed.D.: at least six quarters in residence; qualifying exam and advancement to candidacy; dissertation; final oral exam.

FIELDS OF STUDY.
Accounting and Regional Planning.
Administration.
Aerospace/Aeronautical Engineering.
Anatomy.
Anthropology.
Art.
Art History.
Biochemistry.
Biological Chemistry.
Biological Sciences.
Biophysics and Biophysical Chemistry.
Biopsychology.
Business Administration.
Cell Biology.
Chemical Engineering.
Chemistry.
Civil Engineering.
Classics.
Cognitive Science.
Comparative Literature.
Computer Engineering.
Creative Writing.
Criminal Justice.
Dance.
Developmental Biology.
Drama.
Earth System Science.
East Asian Languages and Literatures.
Ecology.
Economics.
Educational Administration.
Education Credentials. Includes administrative services, bilingual/cross-cultural specialist, early childhood education specialist, multiple-subject instruction (elementary), pupil personnel service, single-subject instruction (secondary), special education (learning handicapped, physically handicapped, severely handicapped).
Electrical Engineering.
Engineering and Applied Sciences.
English and American Literature.
Environmental Analysis.
Environmental Engineering.
Environmental Toxicology.
Evolutionary Biology.
Fine Arts.
French.
Genetics.
Genetic Counseling.
German.
Government.
History.
Humanities.
Information and Computer Science.
Interdisciplinary Studies.
Management.
Materials Science and Engineering.
Mathematics.
Mechanical Engineering.
Medical Physics.
Microbiology.
Molecular Biology.
Molecular Genetics.
Music.
Neurobiology.
Pharmacology and Toxicology.

Philosophy.
Physics and Biophysics.
Physiology.
Political Science.
Politics and Society.
Protein Engineering.
Psychobiology.
Psychology.
Radiological Sciences.
Social Behavior.
Social Ecology.
Social Networks.
Social Relations.
Social Science.
Sociology.
Spanish.
Studio Art.
Urban and Regional Planning.
Writing.

College of Medicine (92717-3952)

Founded in 1896, merged with University of California at Irvine in 1965. State control. Quarter system.

Annual tuition/fee: resident $9297, nonresident $17,691. Totoal average figure for all expenses $8158. Enrollment: first-year class 92; total 386 (men 60% women 40%), 100 graduate students. Faculty: full-time 83, part-time 250. Degrees conferred: M.D., M.D.-Ph.D.

ADMISSION REQUIREMENTS. AMCAS report, transcripts, letters of recommendation, MCAT requiredin support of application. Applicants must have completed at least three years of college study. Interview required for all final candidates. Preference given to California residents. Accepts transfer applicants. Does not have EDP. Apply to the Director of Admissions after June 15, before November 1. Application fee $40. Phone (714)824-5388; fax: (714)824-2083.

ADMISSION STANDARDS: Competitive. Accepts about 3% of total annual applicants; 98% are state residents.

FINANCIAL AID. Scholarships, fellowships, grants, loans, summer research fellowships. Apply to the Office of Medical Student Financial Aid; no closing date. About 87% of students receive aid of some type. Phone: (714)824-4606.

DEGREE REQUIREMENTS. For M.D.: satisfactory completion of four-year program. For M.S., Ph.D.: see Graduate Division listing above for degree requirements.

FIELDS OF GRADUATE STUDY.
Anatomy.
Biochemistry.
Biophysics.
Microbiology.
Molecular Biology.
Pharmacology.
Physiology.
Radiological Sciences.

UNIVERSITY OF CALIFORNIA, LOS ANGELES

Los Angeles, California 90024-1301
http://WWW.UCLA.EDU

Founded 1919. Coed. State control. Quarter system. Special facilities: Center for the Study of Comparative Folklore and

Mythology, Center for Medieval and Renaissance Studies, Center for African Studies, Institute of Archaeology, Center for Latin American Studies, Gustave E. Von Grunebaum Center for Near Eastern Studies, Institute of Social Science Research, Dental Research Institute, Jules Stein Eye Institute, Mental Retardation Center, Brain Research Institute, Institute of American Cultures, Afro-American Studies Center, Asian American Studies Center, Chicano Studies Research Center, Institute of Geophysics and Planetary Physics, Institute of Industrial Relations, Laboratory of Biomedical and Environmental Sciences, Molecular Biology Institute, Institute of Medical Engineering, University Elementary School, Grunwald Center for the Graphic Arts, Frederick S. Wight Art Gallery, Mildred E. Mathias Botanical Gardens, Fernald School, Center for Plasma Physics and Fusion Technology, Dental Clinic, Cancer Research Center, Cardiovascular Research Laboratory, Reed Neurological Research Center, Committee on International and Comparative Studies, Neuropsychiatric Institute, Museum of Cultural History, UCLA Hospital and Clinics. Library: over 6,200,000 volumes, 6,300,000 microforms, 94,000 current periodicals.

Annual fees/tuition: full-time, resident $3795, nonresident $11,493. University maintains 1183 units for married graduate students five miles from campus, one residence hall on campus to house 334 single graduate students. Average academic year housing costs: $9703 (including board) for single students; $12,000 for single students off-campus; $3500–$5000 for married students. Contact the Office of Residential Life for both on- (310-825-4941) and off-campus (310-390-1274) housing information. Day care facilities available.

Graduate Division
http://WWW.GDNET.UCLA.EDU

Graduate study since 1933. Enrollment: full-time 9302. Faculty: full-time 1526. Degrees conferred: M.A., M.S., M.B.A., M.A.T., M.Ed., M.Engr., M.F.A., M.P.H., M.S.W., M.Arch., M.L.S., M.M., M.N., Ed.D., C.Phil., D.M.A., D.N.Sc., Dr.P.H., D.Env., Engr.

ADMISSION REQUIREMENTS. Two transcripts, statement of purpose, required in support of application. Additional application, supplementary information form, two letters of recommendation, GRE/MAT required by some departments. Interview sometimes required. TOEFL required for international applicants. Accepts transfer applicants. Apply to Graduate Admissions/Student and Academic Affairs by December 15 (Fall), October 1 (Winter), December 31 (Spring). Application fee $40. Phone: (310)825-1711; fax: (310)206-4627.

ADMISSION STANDARDS. Selective for most departments, very competitive or competitive for the others.

FINANCIAL AID. Annual awards from institutional funds: 3000 fellowships and grants, 2285 research assistantships, 2477 teaching assistantships, Federal W/S, loans. Approved for VA benefits. Apply by March 1 to the appropriate department for assistantships, fellowships; to Financial Aid Office for all Federal programs. Use FAFSA and University's Supplemental FAF. Phone: (310)206-0400. About 52% of students receive aid other than loans from University and outside sources.

DEGREE REQUIREMENTS. For M.A., M.S.: nine graduate courses, at least seven in residence and three in full-time attendance; thesis or final written/oral exam; reading knowledge of one foreign language for some majors. For other master's': the same minimum requisites outlined normally apply. For Ph.D.: normally three years minimum in residence beyond the bachelor's; preliminary exam; reading knowledge of one or two foreign languages; qualifying exam; dissertation; final oral exam. For other Doctorates: essentially the same minimum requisites as for the Ph.D., except no foreign language requirement.

FIELDS OF STUDY.

Aerospace Engineering. GRE General/Subject in engineering, mathematics or related area, departmental application for admissions; M.S., Ph.D.; admits Fall only; offered by School of Engineering and Applied Science.

African Area Studies. Interdepartmental. GRE, research paper for admission; one language (African) for M.A. M.A. only.

Afro-American Studies. Interdepartmental. GRE, writing sample for admission; one language for M.A. M.A. only; admits Fall only.

American Indian Studies. Interdepartmental. GRE recommended, not required. M.A. only; admits Fall only.

Anatomy. GRE/Subject in biology for admission; M.S., C.Phil., Ph.D.

Anthropology. GRE for admission; one language for M.A., one language special proficiency for Ph.D.; admits Fall only.

Applied Linguistics. Interdepartmental. GRE for admission; two languages or one language special proficiency for Ph.D. C.Phil., Ph.D.; admits Fall only.

Archaeology. Interdepartmental. GRE, three research papers for admission; one language for M.A., two languages for Ph.D. M.A., C.Phil., Ph.D.; admits Fall only.

Architecture. Portfolio, GRE (Ph.D.) for admission; M.Arch. I and II, M.A., Ph.D.; urban design program; offered by Graduate School of Architecture and Urban Planning.

Art. Twenty slides due January 15 for admission. M.A., M.F.A.; admits Fall only; offered by School of the Arts.

Art History. GRE, thesis or three research papers for admission; two languages for M.A. and Ph.D.

Asian American Studies. Interdepartmental. Writing sample for admission; one language or research tool for M.A. M.A. only; admits Fall only.

Astronomy. GRE/Subject in physics for admission. Ph.D. only; admits Fall only.

Atmospheric Sciences. GRE for admission. M.S., C.Phil., Ph.D.

Biochemistry. GRE/Subject in chemistry for admission. M.S., C.Phil. Ph.D.; admits Fall only; offered by Department of Chemistry and Biochemistry.

Biology. GRE/Subject biology for admission. M.S., C.Phil., Ph.D.; admits Fall only.

Biomathematics. GRE/Subject for admission. M.S., Ph.D.

Biomedical Physics. GRE for admission. M.S., Ph.D.; usually admits in Fall; offered by Department of Radiological Sciences.

Biostatistics. GRE for admission. M.S., Ph.D.; offered by School of Public Health.

Chemical Engineering. GRE/Subject in engineering, mathematics or related area, Departmental application for admission. M.S., Ph.D.; admits Fall only; offered by School of Engineering and Applied Science.

Chemistry. Apply by January 15; GRE/Subject for admission; one language for MS, and Ph.D. M.S., C.Phil., Ph.D.; admits Fall only.

Civil Engineering. GRE/Subject in engineering or mathematics or related area, departmental application for admission. M.S., Ph.D.; admits Fall only; offered by School of Engineering and Applied Science.

Classics. Apply by January 15; GRE, term paper for admission; one language for M.A., two languages for Ph.D. M.A., C.Phil., Ph.D.

Comparative Literature. Interdepartmental. Apply by January 15; GRE, writing sample for admission; two languages for M.A. and Ph.D. M.A., C.Phil., Ph.D.

Computer Science. Apply by January 15; GRE/Subject in mathematics or computer science for admission; M.S., Ph.D.; admits Fall only; offered by School of Engineering and Applied Science.

Dance. Audition, interview for admission. M.A. M.F.A.; admits Fall only; offered by School of the Arts.

Dance Movement Therapy. Audition, interview for admission. M.A. only; admits Fall only; offered by the School of the Arts.

Design. Twenty slides for admission, due January 15; admits Fall only. M.A., M.F.A.

East Asian Languages and Cultures. GRE, writing sample for admission; one year Japanese (Chinese majors) or one year Chinese (Japanese majors) for M.A., two languages for Ph.D. M.A., C.Phil., Ph.D.

Economics. GRE General for admission; one language for Ph.D. M.A., C.Phil., Ph.D.; admits Fall only.

Education. GRE, departmental application for admission; M.Ed., M.A., Ed.D., Ph.D.; Ph.D. in Special Education with CSULA, certificate (credential) program; admits Fall only for credential; offered by Graduate School of Education.

Electrical Engineering. GRE/Subject in engineering, mathematics or related area, departmental application for admission. M.S., Ph.D.; admits Fall only; offered by School of Engineering and Applied Science.

English. GRE General/Subject in literature for admission; one language for M.A., two languages for Ph.D. M.A., C. Phil., Ph.D.

Environmental Health Sciences. GRE for admission. M.S., Ph.D.; offered by School of Public Health.

Environmental Science and Engineering. Interdepartmental. GRE/Subject for admission. D. Env. only.

Epidemiology. GRE for admission. M.S., Ph.D; offered by School of Public Health.

Ethnomusicology and Systematic Musicology. Biographical/purpose statement, sample work for admission; apply by December 30. M.A., Ph.D., offered by School of the Arts.

Experimental Pathology. GRE for admission. Ph.D. only.

Film and Television. GRE for admission. M.A., M.F.A., C.Phil., Ph.D.; offered by School of Theater, Film and Television.

Folklore and Mythology. Interdepartmental. GRE recommended; one language for M.A., two languages for Ph.D.

French. GRE, research paper or thesis for admission; one language for M.A., two languages for Ph.D. M.A., C.Phil., Ph.D.

Geochemistry. GRE/Subject for admission. M.S., C.Phil., Ph.D.; offered by Department of Earth and Space Sciences.

Geography. GRE for admission; research tool for M.A. and Ph.D. M.A., C.Phil., Ph.D.

Geology. GRE for admission; M.S., C.Phil., Ph.D.; offered by Department of Earth and Space Sciences.

Geophysics and Space Physics. GRE/Subject in physics for admission. M.S., Ph.D.; offered by Department of Earth and Space Sciences.

German. GRE, writing sample for admission; one language for M.A.; M.A. only; offered by Department of Germanic Languages.

Germanic Languages. GRE, writing sample for admission; one language for Ph.D., C.Phil., Ph.D.; offered by Department of Germanic Languages.

Greek. GRE, term paper for admission; one language for M.A. M.A. only; offered by Department of Classics.

Health Services. GRE for admission. M.S., Ph.D.; offered by School of Public Health.

Hispanic Languages and Literatures. GRE, term paper for admission; two languages for Ph.D. C.Phil., Ph.D.; offered by the Department of Spanish and Portuguese.

History. GRE for admission; one language for M.A., two languages for Ph.D. M.A., C.Phil., Ph.D.; admits Fall only.

Indo-European Studies. Interdepartmental. Two languages for Ph.D. C.Phil., Ph.D.

Islamic Studies. Interdepartmental. GRE for admission, recommended for international applicants; one language for M.A.; two languages for Ph.D.

Italian. GRE for admission, recommended for international applicants; one language for M.A., two languages for Ph.D. M.A., C.Phil., Ph.D.

Latin. GRE, term paper for admission, one language for M.A. M.A. only.

Latin American Studies. Interdepartmental. GRE for admission; two languages for M.A. M.A. only.

Library and Information Science. GRE for admission; two research papers for Ph.D. M.L.S., Certificate, Ph.D.; admits Fall only.

Linguistics. GRE, sample of work for admission; one language for M.A., two languages or one language special proficiency for Ph.D. M.A., C.Phil., Ph.D.; admits Fall only.

Management. GMAT (M.B.A.), GMAT or GRE (M.S., Ph.D.) for admission. M.B.A., M.S., C.Phil., Ph.D.; admits Fall only.

Manufacturing Engineering. GRE/Subject in engineering, mathematics or related area, departmental application for admission; M.S. only; admits Fall only; offered by School of Engineering and Applied Science.

Material Science and Engineering. GRE for admission. M.A., Ph.D.; admits Fall only; offered by School of Engineering and Applied Science.

Mathematics. GRE/Subject, departmental application for admission; two languages for Ph.D. M.A., M.A.T., C.Phil., Ph.D.; admits Fall only.

Mechanical Engineering. GRE/Subject in engineering, mathematics or related area, departmental application for admission. M.A., Ph.D.; admits Fall only; offered by the School of Engineering and Applied Science.

Microbiology and Immunology. GRE/Subject in biology for admission; apply by January 15. Ph.D. only; admits Fall only.

Microbiology and Molecular Genetics. GRE/Subject in biology or chemistry for admission. M.A., Ph.D.; admits Fall usually.

Molecular Biology. Interdepartmental. GRE for admission. Ph.D. only.

Music. Departmental exam, sample work, biographical/purpose statement for admission; apply by December 30; one language for M.A. and M.F.A., two languages for Ph.D. M.A., M.F.A., M.M., D.M.A., Ph.D.; admits Fall only; offered by the School of Arts.

Musicology. Department exam, sample work, biographical/purpose statement for admission; apply by December 30. M.A., Ph.D.

Near Eastern Languages and Cultures. GRE, recent term paper for admission; one language for M.A., two languages for Ph.D. M.A., C. Phil., Ph.D.

Neuroscience. Interdepartmental. GRE for admission; apply by January 5. Ph.D. only; admits Fall only.

Nuclear Engineering. GRE/Subject in engineering, mathematics or related field, departmental application for admission; admits Fall only; offered by the school of Engineering and Applied Science.

Nurse Anesthesia. GRE for admission; apply by December 5. M.S. only; admits Fall only; offered by the Department of Anesthesiology.

Nursing. GRE (D.N.Sc.), CGFNS exam for admission. M.N., D.N.Sc.; admits Fall only.

Oral Biology. Apply by January 15. M.S., Ph.D.; offered by School of Dentistry.

Pharmacology. GRE, personal statement for admission. Ph.D. only; admits Fall only.

Philosophy. GRE sample work, departmental application for admission; apply by January 10; one language for M.A., one language special proficiency for Ph.D. M.A., C.Phil., Ph.D.; admits Fall only.

Physics. GRE/Subject for admission. M.A.T., Ph.D.; admits Fall usually.

Physiological Science. GRE for admission. M.S., Ph.D.

Physiology. GRE/Subject for admission. M.S., Ph.D.; admits Fall only for Ph.D.

Political Science. GRE, sample work for admission; one language for Ph.D. (or substitute program). M.A., C.Phil, Ph.D.; admits Fall only.

Portuguese. GRE, personal statement, recent term paper for admission; one language for M.A. M.A. only.

Psychology. GRE/Subject, personal statement for admission. M.A., M.A.T., C.Phil., Ph.D.; admits Fall only to Ph.D.

Public Health. GRE for admission. M.P.H., M.S., Dr.P.H., Ph.D.; admits Fall only; offered by School of Public Health.

Romance Linguistics and Literature. Interdepartmental. GRE, writing sample, one language (M.A.), two languages (Ph.D.) for admission. M.A, C.Phil., Ph.D.

Scandinavian. One language for M.A. M.A., Ph.D.; offered by Department of Germanic Languages.

Slavic Languages and Literatures. GRE, personal statement for admission; one language for M.A., two languages for Ph.D. M.A., C.Phil., Ph.D.

Social Welfare. GRE, personal statement for admission. M.S.W., Ph.D. admits fall only.

Sociology. GRE, writing sample for admission; one language for Ph.D. M.A., C.Phil., Ph.D.; admits Fall only.

Spanish. GRE, personal statement, recent term paper for admission; one language for admission. M.A. only.

Teaching English as a Second Language. GRE, research paper for admission. M.A., Certificate only; admits Fall only.

Theater. GRE for admission; apply by December 1; one language for Ph.D. M.A., M.F.A., Ph.D.; admits Fall only.

Urban Planning. Departmental application for admission. M.A., Ph.D.; admits only; offered by Graduate School of Architecture and Urban Planning.

School of Law (90024-1445)

Established 1947. Law library 480,500 volumes. Library has LEXIS, NEXIS, WESTLAW.

Annual fees: residents $9722, nonresidents $16,952.

Enrollment: first-year class 377; full-time 995 (men 54%, women 46%); no part-time study. Faculty: full-time 7460, part-time 27. Degrees conferred: J.D., LL.M., J.D.-M.A. (Urban planning); J.D.-M.B.A.

ADMISSION REQUIREMENTS. LSDAS Law School report, transcripts, LSAT (no later than December) required in support of application. Interview not required. Accepts transfer applicants. Graduates of unaccredited colleges not considered. Apply to Admissions and Records Office after October 1, before February 1, transfer applicants May 1. First-year students admitted Fall only. Application fee $40. Phone: (310)825-4041.

ADMISSION STANDARDS. Selective. Accepts 15–20% of total annual applicants. About 25% of class are nonresidents.

FINANCIAL AID. Scholarships, grants, Federal W/S, loans available. All financial aid, except for second- and third-year students, is administered by the campus-wide Office of Financial Aid. Apply after acceptance. Use FAFSA.

DEGREE REQUIREMENTS. For J.D.: satisfactory completion of three-year program. For LL.M.: at least 24 credits beyond J.D.: one year in full-time residence. For M.A.: Course work divided in second and third year between both schools. M.A. awarded after fourth year in school of Architecture and upon acceptance of thesis. For M.B.A.: see Graduate School listing above.

School of Medicine (90095-1720)

Established 1951. State control. Quarter system. Annual tuition and fees: resident $7144, nonresident $14,800. Total average for all other expenses $10,024. Enrollment: first-year class 145, full-time 575 (men 58%, women 42%). Faculty: full-time 250. Degrees conferred: M.D., Ph.D. Graduate study (Medical Scientist Training Program) in preclinical departments, degrees offered through Graduate Division.

ADMISSION REQUIREMENTS. AMCAS report, transcripts, MCAT, letters of recommendation, interview required in support of application. Bachelor's is ordinarily required, but students who have completed three academic years may be admitted. Preference given to state residents. Accepts transfer applicants. Graduates of unaccredited colleges not considered. Does not have EDP. Apply to Office of Student Affairs Division of Admissions after June 15, before November 1, transfer applicants by January 1. Fall admission only. Screening fee $40. Phone: (310)825-6081.

ADMISSION STANDARDS. Very competitive. Accepts about 2% of total annual applicants. Approximately 88% are state residents.

FINANCIAL AID. Scholarships, 125 fellowships, 116 research assistantships, loans. Apply after acceptance to Office of Student Affairs before March 1. Use FAFSA.

DEGREE REQUIREMENTS. For M.D.: 12 quarters minimum, at least the last 6 in residence. Candidates must be 21 years old. For M.S., Ph.D.: see Graduate Division listing above for degree requirements.

FIELDS OF GRADUATE STUDY.
Anatomy.
Biochemistry.
Biomedical Engineering.
Biophysics.
Cell Biology.
Genetics.
Immunology.
Microbiology.
Molecular Biology.
Neurosciences.
Pathology.
Pharmacology.
Physiology.

School of Dentistry (90095-1762)

Founded in 1960. Annual tuition fees: residents $6707, nonresidents $14,406. Limited on-campus housing available. Total average cost for all other first-year expenses: $6720. Phone: (310)825-4491.

Enrollment: first-year class 88, total 391 (men 70%, women 30%). Faculty: full-time 72, part-time 168. Degrees conferred: D.D.S., D.D.S.-M.S., D.D.S.-Ph.D.

ADMISSION REQUIREMENTS. AADSAS, transcripts, DAT, substantive letters of recommendation, comprehensive bibliography and personal statement required in support of application. Applicants must have completed at least three years of college study. Preference given to state and WICHE residents. Graduates of unaccredited colleges not considered. Apply to Office of Admissions or AADSAS after June 1, before January 1. Application fee $40. Phone: (310)794-7971.

ADMISSION STANDARDS. Competitive. Accepts about 20% of total annual applicants. Approximately 95% are state residents.

FINANCIAL AID. Limited number of scholarships, fellowships, loans, summer work study. Apply to Financial Aids Office by May 1. Use FAFSA. Phone: (310)825-6994. About 91% of students receive some aid from School.

DEGREE REQUIREMENTS. For D.D.S.: satisfactory completion of forty-five-month program. For D.D.S.-M.S.: Satisfactory completion of fifth-year program. For D.D.S.-Ph.D.: Satisfactory completion of six to seven year program; research project.

UNIVERSITY OF CALIFORNIA, RIVERSIDE
Riverside, California 92521-0102
http://cnas,ucr,edu/graddiv/home.html

Founded 1954. Located 60 miles E of Los Angeles. Coed. State control. Quarter system. Special facilities: California Museum of Photography, Centers for agricultural research, air pollution research, bibliographic studies, citrus research, dry lands research, geophysics and planetary physics, social and behavioral science research, extensive botanic gardens and natural area reserve system; entomological teaching and research collection, and academic computing center, laboratory for historic research. Library: 1,700,000 volumes, 1,313,000 microforms.

Annual tuition/fees: resident $4848, nonresident $12,546. University housing for 268 married students, 600 men, 600 women. Additionally, there are 316 University-owned apartments available for either married students without children or single students. Phone: (909)787-4307. For off-campus information: Phone (909)787-3770. Day care facilities available.

Graduate Division

Established 1960. Enrollment: full-time 1256, part-time 100 (men 55%, women 45%). University faculty: full-time 600. Degrees conferred: M.A., M.S., M.B.A., Ph.D.

ADMISSION REQUIREMENTS. Two transcripts, GRE/Subject Test, GMAT, three letters of recommendation required in support of University's application. Interview required for some departments. TOEFL or MELPE required for foreign applicants. Graduates of unaccredited colleges not considered. Apply to Graduate Division by May 1 (Fall), September 1 (Winter), December 1 (Spring). Application fee $40. Phone: (909)787-3313; fax: (909)787-2380; E-mail: graduadmis@ucracl.usr.edu.

ADMISSION STANDARDS. Selective. Usual minimum average: 3.2 (A = 4).

FINANCIAL AID. Annual awards from institutional funds: scholarships, teaching assistantships, research assistantships, Federal W/S, loans. Approved for VA benefits. GRE Test is required of all fellowship applicants. Apply to appropriate departments and Financial Aid Office by February 1. Use FAFSA. About 60% of students receive aid other than loans from University and outside sources. No aid for part-time students. Phone: (909)787-3878.

DEGREE REQUIREMENTS. For M.A., M.S.: 36 quarter units minimum; thesis or comprehensive exam. For M.B.A.: 92 quarter units; thesis or case project. For Ph.D.: two years minimum beyond the bachelor's; written and qualifying exams; dissertation, final oral defense of dissertation.

FIELDS OF STUDY.
Anthropology.
Applied Statistics. Ph.D. only.
Art History. Two languages for M.A. M.A. only.
Biochemistry. M.S., Ph.D.
Biology. M.A., Ph.D.
Biomedical Sciences. Ph.D. only.
Botany. M.S., Ph.D.
Comparative Literature. M.A., Ph.D.
Computer Science. M.S., Ph.D.
Dance History. Ph.D. only.
Economics. M.A., Ph.D.
Education. M.A., Ph.D
English. One language for M.A., two languages for Ph.D.
Entomology. One language for Ph.D.
Environmental Toxicology. M.S., Ph.D.

French. M.A. only. Current moratorium on program.
Genetics. Ph.D. only.
Geography. M.S., Ph.D.
Geological Sciences. One language for Ph.D.; M.S., Ph.D.
German. One language for M.A. M.A. only. Current moratorium on program.
History. One language for M.A., two languages for Ph.D.
Management. M.B.A. only.
Mathematics. One language for Ph.D.
Microbiology. M.S., Ph.D.
Music. Includes musicology, theory, composition; one language for M.A. M.A. only.
Philosophy. One language for M.A., two languages for Ph.D.
Physics. M.S., Ph.D.
Plant Pathology. M.S., Ph.D.
Plant Science. M.S. only.
Political Science. One language for Ph.D.
Psychology. Ph.D. only.
Sociology. Ph.D. only.
Soil Science. M.S., Ph.D.
Spanish. One language for M.A., two languages for Ph.D.
Statistics. One language for M.S.

UNIVERSITY OF CALIFORNIA, SAN DIEGO
La Jolla, California 92093-5003

Founded in 1964. Coed. State control. Quarter system. Special facilities: California Space Institute, Cancer Center, Center for Astrophysics and Space Sciences, Center for Energy and Combustion Research, Center for Human Information Processing, Center for Iberian and Latin American Studies, Center for Magnetic Recording Research, Center for Research in Computing and the Arts, Center for Molecular Genetics, Center for Research in Language, Center for United States-Mexican Studies, Cray C90, Intel paragon supercomputer, Thinking Machine CM-Z, DEC Alpha Fany, Institute for Biomedical Engineering, Institute on Global Conflict and Cooperation, Institute for Geophysics and Planetary Physics, Institute for Neural Computation, Institute for Nonlinear Science, Institute for Pure and Applied Physical Sciences, Institute for Research on Aging, Intercampus Institute for Research and Particle Accelerators, Laboratory for Comparative Human Cognition, Laboratory for Mathematics and Statistics, Scripps Institution of Oceanography, International House, San Diego Supercomputer Center. Library: 2,300,000 volumes, 2,416,000 microforms, 200 PC workstations in all libraries.

Annual tuition/fees: resident $4800, nonresident $12,600. On-campus housing for about 500 graduate students. Average annual housing cost: $5000 (room only) for single students. Apply to Housing Office. Phone: (619)534-2952. Limited day care facilities available.

Graduate Division

Graduate study since 1965. Enrollment: full-time 2100, part-time 200. University faculty: 1200. Degrees conferred: M.A., M.S., M.F.A., M.P.I.A., C.Phil., Ph.D.

ADMISSION REQUIREMENTS. Transcripts, GRE/GMAT, three letters of recommendation required in support of University's application. GRE Subject Test recommended for most departments. TOEFL required for foreign applicants. Interview not required. Accepts transfer applicants. Graduates of unaccredited institutions not considered. Apply to the prospective major department and Office of Graduate Admission by January 15. Application fee $40. Phone: (619)534-1193; fax: (619)534-4722.

ADMISSION STANDARDS. Selective. Minimum average: 3.0 (A = 4).

FINANCIAL AID. Annual awards from institutional funds: 400 fellowships, 600 research assistantships/fellowships, 800 teaching assistantships/fellowships. Fellowship and assistantships applicants must take GRE no later than December. Apply to appropriate department and Financial Aid Office; no specified closing date. Use FAFSA. About 80% of students receive aid from University and outside sources. Aid available to part-time students. Phone: (619)534-3807.

DEGREE REQUIREMENTS. For master's: requirements vary but normally include one year of course work; thesis or comprehensive exam; one year in residence. For Ph.D.: requirements vary but normally includes a minimum of two years beyond the master's; preliminary exam; dissertation; final oral exam.

FIELDS OF STUDY.
Anthropology. Ph.D. only.
Biology. Ph.D. only.
Biomedical Sciences. Ph.D. only.
Chemical Engineering.
Chemistry. Ph.D. only.
Clinical Psychology. Ph.D. only.
Cognitive Science. Ph.D. only.
Communication. Ph.D. only.
Computer Science and Engineering.
Earth Sciences. Ph.D. only.
Economics. Ph.D. only.
Electrical Engineering.
Engineering Sciences. Includes aerospace engineering, applied mechanics, bioengineering, mechanical engineering, structural engineering, engineering physics, advanced manufacturing.
History.
International Affairs. Ph.D. only.
Latin American Studies. M.A. only.
Linguistics. Ph.D. only.
Literature, Comparative. M.A. only.
Literature, English and American. M.A. only.
Literature, French. M.A. only.
Literature, German. M.A. only.
Literature, Spanish. M.A. only.
Marine Biology. Ph.D. only.
Materials Science.
Mathematics.
Molecular Pathology. Ph.D. only.
Music.
Neurosciences. Ph.D. only.
Oceanography. Ph.D. only.
Pacific International Affairs. M.P.I.A. only.
Philosophy. Ph.D. only.
Physics. Ph.D. only.
Physics (Biophysics). Ph.D. only.
Political Science. Ph.D. only.
Psychology. Ph.D. only.
Sociology. Ph.D. only.
Teaching and Learning. M.A. only.
Theater. M.F.A.
Visual Arts. M.F.A.

School of Medicine (92093-0621)

Opened 1968. State control. Quarter system. Annual tuition/fees: resident $7,250, nonresident $14,000. On-campus housing available. Total average figure all other expenses: $8000.

Enrollment: first-year class 122; total full-time 515 (men 56%, women 44%). Faculty: full-time 170, part-time 500. Degree conferred: M.D. Graduate study (Medical Scientist Training Program) degrees offered through Graduate School.

ADMISSION REQUIREMENTS. AMCAS report, transcripts, MCAT, letters of recommendation, interview required in support of application. Applicants must have completed at least three years of college study. Graduates of unaccredited colleges not considered. Preference given to state and WICHE residents. Does not have EDP. Apply to Director of Admissions after June 15 and before November 1. Application fee $40. Phone: (619)534-3880; fax: (619)534-8282.

ADMISSION STANDARDS. Very selective. Accepts 3–5% of total annual applicants. Approximately 96% are state residents.

FINANCIAL AID. Scholarships, fellowships, grants, loans. About 75% of students receive aid other than loans from School funds. Apply to Financial Aids Officer as soon as possible after acceptance.

DEGREE REQUIREMENTS. For M.D.: satisfactory completion of four-year program. Senior thesis or equivalent required. For Ph.D.: see graduate listing above.

FIELDS OF GRADUATE STUDY.
Biochemistry.
Biomedical Engineering.
Biophysics.
Cell Biology.
Genetics.
Immunology.
Microbiology.
Molecular Biology.
Neurosciences.
Pathology.
Pharmacology.
Physiology.

UNIVERSITY OF CALIFORNIA, SAN FRANCISCO
San Francisco, California 94143

Founded 1864. Coed. State control. Special facilities: Cardiovascular Research Institute, Cancer Research Institute, Francis I. Proctor Foundation for Research in Ophthalmology, Hormone Research Laboratory, Institute for Health and Aging, Institute of Health Policy Studies, Laboratory of Radiobiology, Langley Porter Psychiatric Institute, Metabolic Research Unit, Reproductive Endocrinology Center, George Williams Hooper Foundation for Medical Research. Library: 691,041 volumes, 160,000 microforms.

Tuition/fees: full-time, resident $4800, nonresident $12,600. On-campus housing for 165 married students. Average monthly housing cost: $600 for one bedroom, $700 for two bedrooms for married students, $252–$460 per month for single students. Apply to Housing Officer. Phone: (415)476-2211.

Graduate Division

Enrollment: full-time 1047. Faculty: full-time 1200, part-time 30. Degrees conferred: M.S., M.A., M.P.T. (Physical Therapy), Ph.D.

ADMISSION REQUIREMENTS. Transcripts, GRE, letters of recommendation required in support of application. Interview required by some programs. Accepts transfer applicants. Graduates of unaccredited colleges not considered. Apply to graduate program by the deadline established by each department. Admits Fall only. Application fee $40. Phone: (415)476-2310.

ADMISSION STANDARDS. Very selective for most departments. Minimum average: 3.0 (A = 4).

FINANCIAL AID. Annual awards from institutional funds: fellowships, scholarships, traineeships, teaching/research assistantships, Federal W/S, loans. Application for fellowships and assistantships should be filed with the application for admission, but prior to January 10. For all other aid apply to Office of Financial Aid: no specified closing date. Use FAFSA.

DEGREE REQUIREMENTS. For master's: Plan I—30 quarter units minimum plus thesis; Plan II—36 quarter units minimum without thesis, final comprehensive exam. For Ph.D.: at least six quarters in full-time residence; qualifying exams; dissertation; final oral exam.

FIELDS OF STUDY.
Biochemistry.
Bioengineering.
Biomedical Sciences. Includes anatomy, endocrinology, experimental pathology, physiology.
Biophysics.
Cell Biology.
Genetics.
History of Health Sciences. One language for M.S.
Medical Anthropology.
Microbiology Immunology.
Neurosciences.
Nursing. M.S., Ph.D.
Oral Biology. M.S., Ph.D.
Pharmaceutical Chemistry.
Physical Therapy.
Sociology.

School of Pharmacy
http://cgl.ucsf.edu

Tuition/fees: full-time resident $6337, nonresident $14,731. On-campus housing available for single and married students. Average annual housing cost: $5500. Apply to Housing office. Phone: (415)476-2231.

Enrollment: Full-time 78, part-time 0. Faculty: full-time 33, part-time 39. Degrees conferred: Ph.D.

ADMISSION REQUIREMENTS. Transcripts, GRE, letters of recommendation required in support of School's application. TOEFL required for foreign applicants. Graduates of unaccredited institutions not considered. Apply to the Department of Pharmaceutical Chemistry by January 15. Admits Fall quarter only. Application fee $40. Phone: (415)476-1914; E-mail: crosse@cgl.ucsf.edu.

ADMISSION STANDARDS. Competitive. Usual minimum average: 3.0 (A = 4).

FINANCIAL AID. Fourteen teaching assistantships, sixty-five research assistantships, forty-eight supplemental fellowships. Apply to Department; no specified closing date. Most doctoral candidates receive funding at the standardized level of $15,200.

DEGREE REQUIREMENTS. For Ph.D.: curriculum is individualized to meet student's needs; at least two years in residence; oral qualifying exam; full-time dissertation research; 1-year teaching experience as teaching assistant; proficiency in biostatistics for pharmaceutics pathway, and toxicology pathway; dissertation; final oral exam.

FIELDS OF STUDY.
Medicinal Chemistry.
Pharmaceutics.
Toxicology.

School of Medicine

Established as Toland Medical College in 1864, affiliated with UCSF 1873. State Control. Quarter system. Annual tuition/fees:

resident $8753, nonresident $17,147. Total average cost for all other expenses: $9000.

Enrollment: first-year class 141; total 580 (men 50%, women 50%). Degrees conferred: M.D., M.D.-M.S., M.D.-M.P.H., M.D.-Ph.D. Graduate study, Medical Scientist Training Program, joint M.S. program with University of California, Berkeley.

ADMISSION REQUIREMENTS. AMCAS report, transcripts, MCAT, recommendations required in support of application. Interview by invitation. Preference given to state WICHE residents. Graduates of unaccredited colleges not considered. Does not have EDP. Apply to Admissions Office after June 15, before November 1. Application fee $40. Phone: (415)476-4044.

ADMISSION STANDARDS. Very competitive. Admits about 5% of total annual applications. Approximately 77% are state residents.

FINANCIAL AID. Limited scholarships, grants, loans (all need-based). Apply after acceptance to Financial Aid Office.

DEGREE REQUIREMENTS. For M.D.: satisfactory completion of four-year program. For M.D.-M.S.: satisfactory completion of five-year programs. For M.D.-Ph.D.: satisfactory completion of six to seven-year program.

FIELDS OF GRADUATE STUDY.
Anatomy.
Biochemistry.
Biophysics.
Cell Biology.
Genetics.
Immunology.
Microbiology.
Molecular Biology.
Neurosciences.
Pathology.
Physiology.

School of Dentistry (94143-0430)

Established 1881. Annual tuition: resident $8388, nonresident $16,782. Fees: $5031 per year. Housing available. Average academic year housing costs: $11,200. Total average cost for all first-year expenses: $6080. Contact Housing Office for both on- and off-campus housing information. Phone: (415)476-2231.

Enrollment: D.D.S. program, first-year class 80, total 350 (men 65%, women 35%). Graduate enrollment: 49. Faculty: full-time 105, part-time 35. Degree conferred: D.D.S., D.D.S.-M.S. The M.S. is offered through the Graduate Division.

ADMISSION REQUIREMENTS. AADSAS report, two official transcripts, DAT, three recommendations required in support of School's application. Supplemental application required by November 1. Interview sometimes requested by School. Applicants must have completed at least three years of college study. Preference given to state and WICHE residents. Does not accept transfer applicants. Does not have EDP. Apply after June 1, before November 1, to Dental Admissions Office, Room S-630. Application fee $40. Phone: (415)476-2737.

ADMISSION STANDARDS. Competitive. Accepts about 25% of total annual applicants.

FINANCIAL AID. Scholarships, limited grant, loans. Apply to Financial Aid Office after acceptance. Phone: (415)476-4181. About 52% of first-year students receive some aid from School.

DEGREE REQUIREMENTS. For D.D.S.: satisfactory completion of forty-eight-month program. For M.S.: see Graduate Division listing above.

FIELDS OF STUDY.
Dental Public Health.
Oral and Maxillofacial Surgery.
Oral Biology.
Orthodontics.
Pediatric Dentistry.
Periodontology.
Prosthodontics.

UNIVERSITY OF CALIFORNIA, SANTA BARBARA
Santa Barbara, California 93106

Founded 1891. Located 100 miles NW of Los Angeles. Coed. State control. Quarter system. Special facilities: Federally Funded Research Centers: Center for Quantized Electronic Structures, Institute for Theoretical Physics, Materials Research Laboratory, National Center for Ecological Analysis & Synthesis, National Center for Geographic Information and Analysis, National Nanofabrication Users Network, Southern California Earthquake Center, Optoelectronics Technology Center; Other Federally Funded Research Centers: ARPA Center for Optical Communications, Center for Computational Modeling & Systems, Center for Non-Stoichiometric Semiconductors, High Performance Composites Center, Multidisciplinary Optical Switching Technology, Long-Term Ecological Research on the Antarctic Marine Ecosystem, Research Project on Forty Gigabit Per Second WDM Fiber Optic Components and Architecture for Telecommunication and Supercomputing, Robust Nonlinear Control of Stall and Flutter in Aeroengines; Organized Research Units: Center for Chicano Studies, Community and Organization Research Institute, Institute for Computational Earth Systems Science, Institute for Crustal Studies, Institute for Polymers and Organic Solids, Marine Science Institute, Neuroscience Research Institute, Quantum Institute; Multi-Campus Research Units: Linguistic Minority Research Institute, Institute for Nuclear Particle Astrophysics & Cosmology; Engineering Research Centers: Center for Computational Modeling & Systems, Center for Control Engineering & Computation, Center for High-Speed Image Processing, Center for Information Processing Research, Center for Macro-Molecular Science & Engineering, Center for Risk Studies and Safety, Compound Semiconductor Research Center, Ocean Engineering Laboratory, other Research Groups: Center for Black Studies, Interdisciplinary Humanities Center, The Writings of Henry D. Thoreau, Five Natural Land and Water Reserves. Library: 2,200,000 volumes, 24,325 current periodicals.

Annual fees/tuition: full-time, resident $4917, nonresident $13,311. On-campus housing available, average academic year housing cost: $3300. Apply to Housing Office for University housing. Phone: (805)893-4501 (on-campus apartment living), (805)893-4371 (off-campus housing). Day care facilities available.

Graduate Division
http://graddiv.uscb.edu

Graduate study since 1954. Enrollment: full-time 2300, part-time 102 (men 60%, women 40%). Faculty: full-time 650. Degrees conferred: M.A., M.Ed., M.E.S.M., M.S., M.F.A., M.M., Certificate Programs, D.M.A., Ph.D.

ADMISSION REQUIREMENTS. Transcripts, three letters of recommendation required in support of application. GRE/MAT required for most departments. GRE required of all fellowship applicants. TOEFL required for foreign applicants. Interview not required. Graduates of unaccredited colleges not considered. Apply by May 1 (Fall), November 1 (Winter), February 1 (Spring), May 1 (Summer—earlier deadline for some majors and fellowships consideration). Application fee $40. Phone: (805)893-2277; fax: (805)893-8259.

ADMISSION STANDARDS. Selective for all departments. Usual minimum average: 3.0 (A = 4).

FINANCIAL AID. Annual awards from institutional funds: 80 scholarships, 600 teaching assistantships, 300 research fellowships, 130 nonresident waivers, Federal W/S, loans. Approved for VA benefits. Apply by mid-January to Graduate Division for scholarships, to appropriate department chair for assistantships and fellowships; to Financial Aid Office for all other programs. Use FAFSA. Phone: (805)893-2432.

DEGREE REQUIREMENTS. For master's: Plan I—30 units minimum, thesis; final written exam; Plan II—36 units minimum, final written exam; reading knowledge of one foreign language for some majors. For Ph.D.: two years minimum in residence, including three consecutive quarters; dissertation; preliminary, final oral exams; reading knowledge of one or two foreign languages.

FIELDS OF STUDY.
Anthropology. M.A., Ph.D.
Applied Mathematics. M.A.
Art History. M.A., Ph.D.
Art Studio. M.F.A.
Asian Studies. M.A.
Biochemistry and Molecular Biology. Ph.D.
Chemical Engineering. M.S., Ph.D.
Chemistry. M.A., M.S., Ph.D.
Classics. M.A., Ph.D.
Communication Studies. M.A., Ph.D.
Comparative Literature. M.A., Ph.D.
Computer Science. M.S., Ph.D.
Counseling, Clinical, School Psychology. Ph.D.
Counseling Psychology. M.A.
Dramatic Art. M.A., Ph.D.
Ecology, Evolution, and Marine Biology. M.A., Ph.D.
Economics. M.A., Ph.D.
Education. M.A., M.Ed., Credential Certificate, Ph.D.
Electrical and Computer Engineering. M.S., Ph.D.
English. M.A., Ph.D.
Environmental Science and Management. M.E.S.M.
French. M.A., Ph.D.
Geography. M.A., Ph.D.
Geological Science. M.A., Ph.D.
Geophysics. M.S.
Germanic Languages and Literatures. M.A., Ph.D.
Hispanic Languages and Literatures. Ph.D.
History. M.A., Ph.D.
Latin American and Iberian Studies. M.A.
Materials Engineering. M.S., Ph.D.
Mathematics. M.A., Ph.D.
Mechanical Engineering. M.S., Ph.D.
Molecular, Cellular, and Developmental Biology. M.A., Ph.D.
Music. M.A., M.M., D.M.A., Ph.D.
Nuclear Engineering. M.S.
Philosophy. Ph.D.
Physics. Ph.D.
Political Science. M.A., Ph.D.
Portuguese. M.A.
Psychology. M.A., Ph.D.
Religious Studies. M.A., Ph.D.
Sociology. M.A., Ph.D.
Spanish. M.A.
Statistics. M.A., Ph.D.
Statistics and Applied Probability. Ph.D.

UNIVERSITY OF CALIFORNIA, SANTA CRUZ

Santa Cruz, California 95064

Opened 1965. Located in the redwoods of California's central coast, 75 miles S of San Francisco. Coed. Public control. Quarter system. Special facilities: Syntax Research Center, Lick Observatory, forest ecology and marine environments, Center for Non-Linear Science, Santa Cruz Institute for Particle Physics, Tectonics Institute, Third World Teaching Resource Center. Library: over 1,000,000 volumes, 600,000 microforms, 9100 current periodicals.

Annual tuition/fees: residents $4885, nonresidents $13,279. On-campus housing consists of 199 apartments for graduate men and women with priority given to married couples. Average academic year housing cost: $4470 (room only), $6600 for married students. Phone: (408)459-2394.

Graduate Division

Graduate study initiated in 1966. Enrollment: full- and part-time 1047. University faculty for graduate students: full-time 500. Degrees conferred: M.A., M.S., Professional Certificate, Ph.D.

ADMISSION REQUIREMENTS. Transcripts, letters of recommendation required in support of application. GRE required for most programs, recommended for others. TOEFL required for international applicants. Interview not required. Accepts transfer applicants. Graduate program deadlines vary: December 15–May 1. Fall admission only. Rolling admission process. Application fee $40. Phone: (408)459-2301.

ADMISSION STANDARDS. Very selective or competitive for most departments. Usual minimum average: 3.0 (A = 4).

FINANCIAL AID. Annual awards from institutional funds: 100 scholarships, 250 teaching assistantships, 200 research assistantships, loans. Apply by February 1 to Graduate Office for assistantships; to the Financial Aid Office for all other programs. Use FAFSA. Phone: (408)429-2963. About 65% of students receive aid other than loans from University and outside sources.

DEGREE REQUIREMENTS. For master's: requirements vary, but normally include one year of course work; thesis/nonthesis option; final written exam. Some programs require reading knowledge of one foreign language. For Certificates: varies by program. For Ph.D.: requirements vary, but normally include two years of course work beyond the master's; preliminary exam; reading knowledge of one foreign language; dissertation; final written/oral exam.

FIELDS OF STUDY.
Anthropology. Ph.D. only.
Astronomy and Astrophysics. Ph.D. only.
Biology. Ph.D. only.
Chemistry and Biochemistry. M.S., Ph.D.
Computer and Information Sciences. M.S., Ph.D.
Computer Engineering. M.S., Ph.D.
Earth Sciences. M.S., Ph.D. only.
Economics. Includes applied, international. M.S., Ph.D.
Education. M.A. only.
Environmental Studies. Ph.D.
History. Ph.D. only.
History of Consciousness. Ph.D. only.
Linguistics. M.A., Ph.D.
Literature. M.A., Ph.D. only.
Marine Sciences. M.S. only.
Mathematics. M.A., Ph.D.
Music. M.A. only.
Physics. M.S., Ph.D. only.

Psychology. Includes developmental, experimental, social. Ph.D. only.
Science Communication. Certificate only.
Sociology. Ph.D. only.
Theater Arts. Certificate only.

CALIFORNIA WESTERN SCHOOL OF LAW

225 Cedar Street
San Diego, California 92101-3046

Established 1958. Library: 240,000 volumes. Library has LEXIS, NEXIS, WESTLAW, DIALOG. 12 PCs in library.

Annual tuition: $19,100. No on-campus housing available. Total average annual additional expenses: $12,650.

Enrollment: first-year class 282; total full-time 800 (men 57%, women 43%); no part-time students. Faculty: full-time 46, part-time 28. Degree conferred: J.D., J.D.-M.A.(Psychology), J.D.-M.B.A., J.D.-M.S.W.

ADMISSION REQUIREMENTS. LSDAS Law School report, transcripts, LSAT, three recommendations, bachelor's degree required in support of application. Interview granted on request. Accepts transfer applicants from ABA accredited law schools only. Apply to Director of Admissions after September 1, before June 1. Beginning students admitted Fall only. Application fee $35. Phone: (619)239-0391, (800)255-4252.

ADMISSION STANDARDS. Accepts 45–50% of total annual applicants.

FINANCIAL AID. Scholarships, full and partial tuition grants, Federal W/S, loans. Apply to Director of Financial Aid after acceptance but before March 31. Use FAFSA. About 80% of students receive some aid from School.

DEGREE REQUIREMENTS. For J.D.: Ninety semester hours minimum, at least forty-five hours and three semesters in residence. Optional two-year program is also available. For master's degrees: see San Diego State University's institutional listing.

CAMPBELL UNIVERSITY

Buies Creek, North Carolina 27506

Founded in 1887. Located 30 miles south of Raleigh. Coed. Private control. Southern Baptist. Semester system. Library: 180,000 volumes, 8 PCs in library.

Tuition: per semester hour $155. On-campus housing for single and married students. Annual housing cost: $3200. Apply to Director of Housing. Phone: (910)893-1200, ext. 2226. Day care facilities available

Graduate Studies

Enrollment: full- and part-time 1000. Faculty: 35 full- and part-time. Degrees conferred: M.B.A., M.S., M.Ed., Ed.S.

ADMISSION REQUIREMENTS. Transcripts, GRE/MAT, letters of recommendation required in support of University's application. GMAT required for business programs. TOEFL required for international applicants. Graduates of unaccredited colleges not considered. Apply to the Director of Graduate Admissions at least forty-five days prior to expected semester of entrance. Application fee $25. Phone: (910)893-1200, ext. 1318; fax: (910)893-9850.

ADMISSION STANDARDS. Relatively open. Usual minimum average: 2.5 (A = 4).

FINANCIAL AID. Scholarships, assistantships, Federal W/S, loans. Apply to the Director of Financial Aid; no specified closing date. Phone: (910)893-1315. Use FAFSA.

DEGREE REQUIREMENTS. For M.Ed., M.S.: 33–48 credits minimum, at least 24 in residence; thesis/research paper/field experience/final written exam. For Ed.S.: 30 credits minimum beyond master's; final written exam. For M.B.A.: 33 credits minimum; comprehensive oral exam.

FIELDS OF STUDY.
Business Administration and Management.
Community Counseling. M.A.
Counselor Education.
Curriculum and Instruction. Master's and Ed.S.
Early Childhood Education. Master's and Ed.S.
Educational Administration. Master's and Ed.S.
Elementary Education.
English Education.
Mathematics Education.
Middle School Education.
Pharmacy.
Physical Education and Human Movement Studies.
Science Education.
Secondary Education.
Social Science Education.

Norman Adrian Wiggins School of Law
Box 158

Established 1976. Private control. Semester system. Library: 139,000 volumes. Library has LEXIS, NEXIS, WESTLAW.
Annual tuition: resident $12,400. Enrollment: first-year class 110; total 320 (men 60%, women 40%). Faculty: full-time 20, part-time 15. Degree conferred: J.D., J.D.-M.B.A.

ADMISSION REQUIREMENTS. LSDAS Law School report, transcripts, bachelor's degree, LSAT, recommendations required in support of application. Interview upon request. Graduates of unaccredited colleges not considered. Apply to Director of Admissions. No specified closing date. Application fee $40. Phone: (910)893-1754.

ADMISSION STANDARDS. Selective. Admits about 15% of total annual applications.

FINANCIAL AID. Full and partial scholarships, grants, assistantships, Federal W/S, loans. Apply by May 1 to Director of Admissions. Use FAFSA. About 20–30% of students receive some aid from School.

DEGREE REQUIREMENTS. For J.D.: satisfactory completion of 90 semester hour program. For M.B.A.: see Graduate School listing above.

CANISIUS COLLEGE
Buffalo, New York 14208-1098

Founded 1870. Coed. Private control. Roman Catholic Jesuit. Semester system. Library: 280,000 volumes, 502,300 microforms, 1150 current periodicals, 68 PCs in all libraries.
Tuition: per credit (Education)$375, (M.B.A.)$400. On-campus housing for 100 graduate students. Average academic year housing costs: $5800 (including board). Contact Office of Residence Life for both on- and off-campus housing information. Phone: (716)888-2220.

Graduate Division

Graduate study since 1919. Enrollment: full-time 450, part-time 1000. Faculty teaching graduate students: full-time 40, part-time 100. Degrees conferred: M.S., M.B.A., M.S. in Education.

ADMISSION REQUIREMENTS. Two official transcripts, GRE, two letters of recommendation required in support of application. For Education program, two transcripts for admission. TOEFL required for international applicants. Accepts transfer applicants. Graduates of unaccredited institutions not considered. Apply to Director of Admissions by July 1 (Fall), November 1 (Spring), April 15 (Summer). Application fee $20. Phone: (800)950-2505 or (716)888-2545; fax: (716)888-3290.

ADMISSION STANDARDS. Selective. Usual minimum average: 2.5 (A = 4).

FINANCIAL AID. Limited to assistantships, Federal W/S, loans. Apply to Office of Financial Aid; no specified closing date. Use FAFSA. Phone: (716)888-2300.

DEGREE REQUIREMENTS. For master's: 33–39 credits for most majors; thesis/nonthesis options for all majors; total score of GRE and GPA plus a zero must equal 3600.

FIELDS OF STUDY.
Accounting.
Business Administration.
College Student Personnel Administration.
Education.
Elementary Education.
General Education.
Montessori Education.
Physical Education.
Public Administration.
Reading.
School Administrator and Supervisor.
School Counselor.
Secondary Education.
Special Education.
Sport Administration.
Taxation.
Teacher of the Deaf and Hard of Hearing.
Teacher of Reading.

CAPITAL UNIVERSITY
2199 E. Main Street
Columbus, Ohio 43209-2394

Founded 1830. Coed. Lutheran. Semester system. Library: 376,000 volumes, 90,000 microforms, 55 PC workstations; OHIONET.
Annual tuition: per credit hour $245. Evening program only. No on-campus housing.

Graduate School of Administration

Enrollment: part-time 300 (men 150, women 150). Faculty: full-time 7, part-time 18. Degree conferred: M.B.A.

ADMISSION REQUIREMENTS. Transcripts, GMAT, interview required in support of application. Accepts transfer applicants and graduates of accredited colleges. Applicants must have two years' work experience and be employed full-time. Preference given to Central Ohio residents. TOEFL required for international applicants. Apply to Director of Admissions; no specified closing date. Admits Fall and Spring. Application fee $25. Phone: (614)236-6679.

ADMISSION STANDARDS. Selective. Usual minimum average. 3.0 (A = 4).

FINANCIAL AID. Federal W/S, loans only. Apply to Financial Aid Office; no specified closing date. Use FAFSA.

DEGREE REQUIREMENTS. For M.B.A.: 40 credits in residence.

Law and Graduate Center (43215)

Established 1903 as Columbus College of Law, affiliated with Capital University in 1966. Library: 225,300 volumes. Library has LEXIS, NEXIS, WESTLAW, INFOTRAC.

Annual tuition: full-time $15,407, part-time per credit $497. Limited off-campus housing available. Total average annual additional expense: $9500. Enrollment: first-year class 180 (day), 30 (evening); total 805 (men 58%, women 42%). Faculty: full-time 34, part-time 46. Degree conferred: J.D., J.D.-M.B.A., J.D.-M.S.(Nursing), J.D.-M.S.A.(Sports Administration with Ohio University), LL.M. (Taxation).

ADMISSION REQUIREMENTS. LSDAS Law School report, transcripts, LSAT, essay required in support of application. Interview by invitation only. Preference is given to state residents. Graduates of unaccredited colleges not considered. Apply to Director of Admissions by May 1. Application fee $35. Phone: (614)445-8836; fax: (614)445-7125.

ADMISSION STANDARDS. Selective. Accepts about 50% of total annual applications. Approximately 45% of enrolled students are nonresidents.

FINANCIAL AID. Scholarships, research and teaching assistantships, Federal W/S, loans. Apply as early as possible after application has been filed to Director of Admissions before April 1. Use FAFSA. About 30% of students receive some aid from School.

DEGREE REQUIREMENTS. For J.D.: satisfactory completion of 85-semester hour program. For LL.M.: satisfactory completion of one year program beyond J.D. For master's degree: see Graduate School listing above and Ohio University listings.

School of Nursing

Enrollment: full-time 7, part-time 18. School's Faculty: full-time 14, part-time 5. Degree conferred: M.S.N.

ADMISSION REQUIREMENTS. Transcripts, interview required in support of application. Accepts transfer applicants and graduates of accredited colleges. Preference given to Central Ohio residents. TOEFL required for international applicants. Apply to Director of Admissions; no specified closing date. Admits Fall and Spring. Application fee $25. Phone: (614)236-6361; fax: (614)236-6157.

ADMISSION STANDARDS. Selective. Usual minimum average. 3.0 (A = 4).

FINANCIAL AID. Federal W/S, loans only. Apply to Financial Aid Office; no specified closing date. Use FAFSA.

DEGREE REQUIREMENTS. For M.S.N.: at least 36 credits in residence; thesis.

FIELDS OF STUDY.
Administration.
Family and Community.
Nursing.

CARDINAL STRITCH COLLEGE
Milwaukee, Wisconsin 53217-3985
http://www.strich.edu

Chartered 1937. Coed. Private control. Roman Catholic. Semester system. Library: 773,000 volumes, 108,000 microforms, 1200 current periodicals.

Tuition: per credit $290. On-campus single housing limited to a space-available basis; none for married students. Average academic year housing costs: $3600 (including board). Phone: (414)352-5400, ext. 347. Day care facilities available.

Graduate Division
http://www.strich.edu/csc/gradcat.html

Graduate study since 1956. Enrollment: full- and part-time 2300. Graduate faculty: full-time 19, part-time 249. Degrees conferred: M.A., M.B.A., M.B.A.-I., M.Ed., M.Ed.P.D., M.S.H., M.S.M.

ADMISSION REQUIREMENTS. Official transcripts, GMAT (Business), MAT (Education) required in support of application. TOEFL required for international applicants. Interview not required. Accepts transfer applicants. Graduates of unaccredited colleges not considered. Apply to Graduate Admission Officer, at least three weeks prior to registration. Application fee $20. Phone: (414)352-5400, ext. 212.

ADMISSION STANDARDS. Relatively open. Usual minimum average: 2.5 (A = 4).

FINANCIAL AID. Annual awards from College funds: 4 assistantships, Federal W/S, loans. Approved for VA benefits. Apply by May 1 to Chair of the Graduate Committee for assistantships; to Financial Aid Office for all other programs. Use FAFSA. Phone: (414)352-5400, ext. 227. About 5% of students receive aid other than loans from College and outside sources.

DEGREE REQUIREMENTS. For M.B.A., M.S.M., M.S.H.: 33–36 credits minimum, at least 24 in residence; thesis, research paper/field experience; final written exam. For M.A.: 35 credits minimum; practice/research option. For M.Ed.P.D.: 36 credits minimum, at least 27 credits in residence; comprehensive portfolio. For M.Ed., M.S.: 30–31 credits minimum; thesis/nonthesis option; comprehensive exam.

FIELDS OF STUDY.
Business Administration. Includes international business administration.
Computer Science Education.
Educational Computing.
Educational Leadership.
English as a Second Language.
Health Services Management.
Management.
Ministry. M.Ed.
Professional Development. M.Ed.P.D.
Reading/Language Arts.
Writing.

CARNEGIE MELLON UNIVERSITY
Pittsburgh, Pennsylvania 15213-3891
http://www.hss.cmu.edu/

Founded 1900. Coed. Private control. Semester system. Special facilities: Center for the Materials of the Artist and Conservator, Center for Building Performance and Diagnostics, Center for Machine Translation, Center for the Management of Technology, Center for Molecular Genetics, Center for the Study of Public Policy, Communications Design Center, Engineering Design Center, Laboratory for Computational Linguistics, Mellon Institute, National Center for the Study of Writing, Robotics Institute, Software Engineering Institute, Statistical Center for Quality Improvement. Library: 783,000 volumes, 639,000 microforms, 220 PC workstations in all libraries.

Annual tuition; full time $19,400, per credit $269. No on-campus housing available. For off-campus housing: phone (412)268-2139. Day care facilities available.

College of Humanities and Social Sciences

Enrollment: full-time 153 part-time 95. Faculty: full-time 111, part-time 8. Degrees conferred: M.A., M.S., Ph.D.

ADMISSION REQUIREMENTS. Transcripts, additional application form, three letters of recommendation, GRE required in support of College's application. TOEFL required for foreign applicants; TSE and TOEFL required for foreign applicants in psychology. Interview not required. Accepts transfer applicants. Apply to individual departmental chairs by April 15 (Fall) in History: February; in English: March 1; prior to registration for other sessions. Application fee: generally $35, but varies by department. Dean's Phone: (412)268-2830.

ADMISSION STANDARDS. Selective to very selective. Usual minimum average: 3.0 (A = 4).

FINANCIAL AID. Annual awards from institutional funds: 90 scholarships, 3 teaching fellowships, 24 research fellowships, 26 research assistantships, 124 teaching assistantships, Federal W/S, loans. Apply to the appropriate Departmental chairman and to Financial Aid Office by April 15. Use FAFSA. Phone: (412)268-2068. 100% of students receive aid other than loans from College and outside sources.

DEGREE REQUIREMENTS. Determined by each department and vary by program.

FIELDS OF STUDY.
Economics. Provided by faculty of the Graduate School of Industrial Administration.
English. Includes rhetoric, literary and cultural theory, professional writing, creative writing.
History. Includes history and policy, social history.
Modern Languages.
Philosophy. Includes logic and computation, computational linguistics.
Psychology. Includes cognitive psychology, social psychology, developmental psychology, cognitive neuroscience.
Second Language Acquisition.
Social and Decision Sciences. Includes behavioral decision making, organizational behavior.
Statistics.
Theoretical, Applied, and Computational Statistics.

Carnegie Institute of Technology
Graduate Engineering
http://www.cit.cmu.edu/

Tuition: full-time $18,850, per credit $785. No on-campus housing available. For off-campus information, contact housing office. Phone: (412)268-2139.

Enrollment: full-time 470, part-time 86. Faculty: full-time 114. Degrees conferred: M.S., M.E., Ph.D.

ADMISSION REQUIREMENTS. Transcripts, three letters of recommendation, GRE/Subject tests required in support of Institute's application. TOEFL required of foreign applicants. Interview not required. Accepts transfer applicants. Graduates of unaccredited institutions not considered. Apply to department of interest by February 1 (Fall), one month prior to registration for other sessions. Application fee $35. Phone: (412)268-2482.

ADMISSION STANDARDS. Selective. Usual minimum average: 3.0 (A = 4).

FINANCIAL AID. Sixty-one teaching assistantships, 51 fellowships, 232 research assistantships/fellowships, Federal W/S, loans. Approved for VA benefits. Apply by February 1 (preferably) to department of interest for scholarships, fellowships, and assistantships; to Financial Aid Office for Federal Funds, for priority consideration by February 1. USE FAFSA and CMU FAF. Phone: (412)269-2478.

DEGREE REQUIREMENTS. For M.S.: one year full-time study beyond bachelor's degree; comprehensive final oral/written exam; thesis for some departments. For M.E.: two years full-time study beyond bachelor's; comprehensive exam; project. For Ph.D.: three years minimum beyond the bachelor's degree, at least one in full-time residence; qualifying exam; dissertation; final oral exam.

FIELDS OF STUDY.
Biomedical Engineering.
Chemical Engineering.
Civil and Environmental Engineering.
Electrical and Computer Engineering.
Engineering and Public Policy.
Manufacturing Engineering.
Materials Science and Engineering.
Mechanical Engineering.
Metallurgical Engineering and Materials Science.

Graduate School of Industrial Administration
http:/www.gsia.cmu.edu

Established 1949. Annual tuition: $22,100; for M.S.C.F. (three semesters) $33,750 (Pittsburgh), $38,750 (New York). Enrollment: full-time 503, part-time 175 (men 75%, women 25%). Faculty teaching graduate students: full-time 69, part-time 27. Degrees conferred: M.S.I.A., M.S.C.F., Ph.D.

ADMISSION REQUIREMENTS. Transcripts, three letters of recommendation required in support of application. GMAT required for M.S.I.A. applicants, GRE required for Ph.D. applicants. TOEFL required for international applicants. Interview required. Transfer applicants considered. Graduates of unaccredited institutions not considered. Apply to Director of Admissions of the School by March 15. Rolling admission process. Fall admission only. Application fee $50. Phone: (412)268-2272.

ADMISSION STANDARDS. Very selective. Usual minimum average: mean 3.4 (A = 4), GMAT 640.

FINANCIAL AID. Annual awards available to U.S. citizens and permanent residents from institutional funds, need- and merit-based scholarships, and federal as well as private loan programs. Apply by March 31. Use FAFSA. About 80% of students receive some form of Financial Aid.

DEGREE REQUIREMENTS. For M.S.I.A.: four semesters in residence (full-time). For M.S.C.F.: either three semesters in full-time study or six semesters in part-time study. For Ph.D.: program by advisement; first- and second-summer research papers; written qualifying exam; dissertation; final oral exam.

FIELDS OF STUDY.
Accounting. Ph.D. only.
Computational Finance. M.S.C.F.

Economics. Ph.D. only.
Financial Economics. Ph.D. only.
Industrial Administration. M.S.I.A. only.
Information Systems. Ph.D. only.
Manufacturing and Operating Systems. Ph.D. only.
Operation Research. Ph.D. only.
Organizational Behavior and Theory. Ph.D. only.
Note: The following joint Ph.D. programs are available. *Algorithms, Combinatorics,* and *Optimization* (with Mathematics and Computer Science departments), *Mathematical Finance* (with the Mathematics department), *Management of Manufacturing and Automation* (with the Robotics Institute).

College of Fine Arts—Graduate Division
http://artsnet.cmu.edu

Tuition: $18,600. Enrollment: full-time 148, part-time 51. College faculty teaching graduate students: full-time 66, part-time 7. Degrees conferred: M.S., M.A.M., M.F.A., Ph.D.

ADMISSION REQUIREMENTS. Transcripts, letters of recommendation, portfolio/audition, GRE may be required in support of application. Interview for most departments. Accepts transfer applicants. Apply to the Department by March 1. Fall admission only. Application fee varies by departments. Phone: (412)268-2349.

ADMISSION STANDARDS. Very competitive.

FINANCIAL AID. Annual awards from institutional funds: scholarships, fellowships, research assistantships, Federal W/S, loans. Apply by April 1 to appropriate department chair for fellowships, assistantships; to Financial Aid Office for all other programs. Use FAFSA. About 50% of students receive aid other than loans from College and outside sources. Phone: (412)268-2068.

DEGREE REQUIREMENTS. For master's: 30 semester hours minimum; final project; thesis/nonthesis option; final written/oral exam. For Ph.D.: two years minimum in residence; qualifying exam; dissertation; final oral exam.

FIELDS OF STUDY.
Architecture. M.S., Ph.D.
Art. M.F.A.
Arts Management. M.A.M. (joint degree with School of Public Policy and Management).
Design/Production.
Directing.
Music. M.F.A. in performance, composition, conducting.
Playwriting. M.F.A.

CASE WESTERN RESERVE UNIVERSITY
Cleveland, Ohio 44106

University formed with merger in 1967 of Case Institute of Technology (founded 1880) and Western Reserve University (1826). Coed. Private control. Semester system. Special facilities: Alzheimer Center, Center on Aging and Health, Center for Applied Polymer Research, Center for Automation and Intelligent Systems Research, Biology Field Station, Center for Biomedical Ethics, Cancer Research Center, Case Center for Adhesives, Sealants & Coatings, Case Center for Electrochemical Sciences, Center for Management Development and Research, Center for International Health, Mental Development Center, Institute of Pathology, Cleveland Hearing and Speech Center, Electronics Design Center, Genetics Center, Health Systems Management Center, Mandel Center for Non-profit Organizations, Center for Urban Poverty and Social Change. Joint programs with Cleveland Museum of Art, Institute of Art, Institute of Music, Cleveland Playhouse. Library: 1,871,260 volumes, 2,141,154 microforms.

Annual tuition: full-time $17,100, per credit $713. On-campus housing for single students only; 120 co-ed units. Average annual housing cost: $5200. Married students, contact University Off-Campus Housing Bureau. Phone: (216)368-3780. Day care facilities available near campus.

School of Graduate Studies

Graduate study since 1926. Enrollment: full-time 922 (men 518, women 404), part-time 1459 (men 861, women 598). University faculty teaching graduate students: full-time 1800, part-time 79. Degrees conferred; M.A., M.S., M.F.A., D.M.A., Ph.D.

ADMISSION REQUIREMENTS. Transcripts, letters of recommendation required in support of application. GRE required for some departments. Interview generally not required. TOEFL required for international applicants. Accepts transfer applicants. Graduates of unaccredited institutions not considered. Apply to Office of Graduate Studies Admissions at least one month prior to registration. Application fee $25. Phone: (216)368-4390; fax: (216)368-4250.

ADMISSION STANDARDS. Very selective to very competitive. Usual minimum average: 3.0 (A = 4).

FINANCIAL AID. Nine hundred assistantships for teaching/research, Federal W/S, loans. Apply by March 1 to Office of Graduate Studies Admissions. Phone: (216)368-4530. Use FAFSA; program FAFs may be requested. About 45% of students receive aid other than loans from University and outside sources. Limited aid for part-time students.

DEGREE REQUIREMENTS. For M.A., M.S.: 27 semester hours minimum, at least 21 semester hours in residence; thesis/comprehensive exam. For M.F.A.: 60 semester hours minimum; comprehensive exam; monograph. For D.M.A., Ph.D.: three years minimum beyond the bachelor's, at least one year in full-time residence; reading knowledge of one or two foreign languages and statistics for some departments; qualifying exam; dissertation; final oral defense.

FIELDS OF STUDY.
American Studies. GRE for admission.
Anatomy. GRE/Subject for admission.
Anesthesiology. GRE for admission. M.S. only.
Anthropology. GRE for admission.
Art. Includes art education.
Astronomy. GRE for admission. Thesis required for M.S., two languages for Ph.D.
Biochemistry. GRE for admissions.
Bioethics. GRE for admission. M.A. only.
Biology. Includes zoology; GRE/Subject for admission.
Chemistry. GRE/Subject for admission.
Communication Sciences. Includes speech-language, pathology, and audiology. GRE for admission.
Comparative Literature. M.A. only.
Dentistry. D.D.S. for admission; M.S.D. only.
Engineering. Includes biomedical engineering, ceramics, chemical engineering, civil engineering, clinical engineering, computer engineering, environmental engineering, fluid, thermal and aerospace sciences, electrical engineering, macromolecular science, mechanical engineering, materials science, systems engineering. GRE for admission.
English. GRE for admission.
Environmental Health Sciences. GRE for admission.
Epidemiology and Biostatistics. GRE for admission.

Family Medicine. M.S. only; apply to program chairman.
Genetics. GRE/Subject for admission.
Geological Sciences. GRE/Subject for admission.
History. Includes history of science and technology. GRE for admission.
Management. Ph.D. only; GMAT for admission.
Mathematics. GRE/Subject for admission.
Molecular Biology and Microbiology. GRE/Subject for admission.
Molecular Virology. GRE/Subject for admission.
Music. Includes music education, music history and research, Ph.D. in Musicology, D.M.A. in performance or composition.
Neurosciences. GRE/Subject for admission.
Nursing. GRE for admission. Ph.D. only.
Nutrition. Includes Dietetic Internship Program.
Operations Research. GRE for admission.
Organizational Behavior.
Pathology. GRE for admission.
Pharmacology. GRE for admission.
Physics.
Physiology and Biophysics. GRE for admission.
Political Science. GRE/Subject for admission.
Psychology. GRE for admission.
Reproductive Biology. Ph.D. only.
Romance Languages. French. GRE General/Subject for admission.
Social Welfare. M.S.W. required; MAT or GRE for admission; Ph.D. only.
Sociology. GRE/Subject for admission.
Statistics. GRE for admission.
Theater Arts. Includes acting, contemporary dance. M.F.A. only.

Mandel School of Applied Social Sciences

http://www.cwru.edu/aurora-home.html

Established 1916. Semester system. Annual tuition: full-time $17,100, per credit hour $713. Graduate study only. On-campus housing available for single students only. Apply to Director of Residence Life. Phone: (216)368-3780.

Enrollment: full-time 195, part-time 12. Faculty: full-time 33, part-time 40. Degrees conferred: M.S.S.A., Ph.D.

ADMISSION REQUIREMENTS. Transcripts, letters of reference required in support of School's application. GRE/MAT required for Ph.D. and applicants with G.P.A. below 2.7 (A = 4). Interview optional. TOEFL required of foreign students. Accepts transfer applicants. Graduates of unaccredited institutions not considered. Apply to Mandel School of Applied Social Sciences at least two months prior to registration. Fall admission only. Application fee $25 (not required of foreign students). Phone: (800)944-2290, ext. 2280; fax: (216)368-5065.

ADMISSION STANDARDS. Usual minimum average: 2.7 (A = 4). Personal suitability for human services and experience evaluated.

FINANCIAL AID. Annual awards from institutional fund: 19 scholarships, 343 MSASS grants, Federal W/S, loans. Apply to Admissions Office of the School; no specified closing date. Use FAFSA. Phone: (216)368-22103; fax: (216)368-5065. About 60% of students receive aid other than loans from School and outside sources.

DEGREE REQUIREMENTS. For M.S.S.A. (Master of Science in Social Administration): 60 credits minimum. For Ph.D. : 54 credits minimum beyond the master's; qualifying exam; dissertation; final oral exam.

FIELDS OF STUDY.
Applied Social Sciences.
Social Administration.
Social Welfare.

Weatherhand School of Management

http://nexus.som.cwru.edu/

Annual tuition: $19,300, per credit $804.

Enrollment: Full-time 276, part-time 669 (men 62%, women 38%). Graduate faculty: full-time 75, part-time 18. Degrees conferred: M.B.A., M.Acct., M.S.M.(Information Science), M.N.O. (Nonprofit Organizations), E.D.M.(Executive Doctorate in Management), Ph.D.

ADMISSION REQUIREMENTS. Transcripts, GMAT required in support of application. TOEFL required for foreign applicants. Accepts transfer applicants. Apply to Admissions Office by April 15 for both 60-hour and 42-hour programs. Application fee $35. Phone: (216)368-2030; fax: (216)368-5548.

ADMISSION STANDARDS. Selective. Usual minimum average 3.12 (A = 4), GMAT 590.

FINANCIAL AID. Annual awards from institutional funds: sixty scholarships, Federal W/S, loans. Apply by March 15 to Admissions Office. Phone: (216)368-8907. Use FAFSA and University's FAF. About 30% of students receive aid other than loans from School and outside sources.

DEGREE REQUIREMENTS. For MBA: 42–60 credit hours minimum. For Ph.D., at least two years beyond master's; two years in full-time study; qualifying exam; dissertation; final oral exam. For M.S.M., E.D.M.: individualized programs, contact the School directly.

FIELDS OF STUDY.
Banking and Finance.
Economics.
Entrepreneurship.
Health Systems Management.
Human Resource & Labor Policy.
International Management.
Management Information Systems.
Management Policy.
Management of Technology.
Marketing.
Nonprofit Management.
Operations Management.
Operations Research.
Organizational Behavior.

School of Medicine (44106-4920)

Organized 1843. Annual tuition: $24,500. Total average figure for all other expenses $9,600.

Enrollment: first-year class 138; full-time 571 (men 55%, women 45%). Faculty: full-time 350, part-time 700. Degrees conferred: M.D., M.D.-M.S., M.D.-Ph.D. (Medical Scientist Training program).

ADMISSION REQUIREMENTS. AMCAS report, transcripts, MCAT. Interviews at the discretion of Admissions Committee required in support of application. Applicants must have completed at least three years of college study. At least 50% are residents of Ohio. Accepts transfer applicants. Does have EDP; approximately 20–25 per year. Apply to AMCAS after June 15, before November 11. Application fee $40. Phone: (216)368-3450; fax: (216)368-4621.

ADMISSION STANDARDS. Very competitive. Accepts about 5% of total annual applicants. Approximately 65% are state residents.

FINANCIAL AID. Scholarships, research fellowships, loans. Apply through GAPSFAS to Office of the Dean of the School before April 1. About 30% of students receive aid other than loans from School, 75% from all sources.

DEGREE REQUIREMENTS. For M.D.: satisfactory completion of four-year program, at least three years in residence. Combined M.D./M.S., M.D./Ph.D. offered in most basic science departments. See Graduate School listing above.

FIELDS OF GRADUATE STUDY.
Biochemistry.
Biomedical Engineering.
Biophysics.
Cell Biology.
Genetics.
Immunology.
Microbiology.
Molecular Biology.
Neurosciences.
Pathology.
Pharmacology.
Physiology.

School of Dentistry

Organized 1892. Annual tuition: $23,900. On-campus housing available. Average academic year housing costs: $9000. Contact Director of Housing for housing information. Phone (216)368-3780. Total average cost for all other first-year expenses $6271.

Enrollment: first-year class 62, total full-time 240 (men 70%, women 30%). Faculty: full-time 32, part-time 250. Degrees conferred: D.D.S., M.S.

ADMISSION REQUIREMENTS. AADSAS report, transcripts, DAT, letters of recommendation required in support of application. Interview by invitation only. Applicants must have completed at least two years of college study, prefer four years of college work. TOEFL required of international students. Accepts transfer applicants. Apply to Committee on Admissions after June 1, before April 1. Fall admission only. Application fee $35 (not required of foreign students). Phone: (216)368-2460.

ADMISSION STANDARDS. Competitive. Accepts 15–18% of total annual applicants. Approximately 40% are state residents.

FINANCIAL AID. Scholarships, grants, tuition waivers, Federal W/S, loans. Students should not depend on aid from School for first semester of attendance. Apply by July 15 to Financial Aid Office. Use FAFSA. Phone: (216)368-3256. About 73% of students receive some aid from school and outside sources.

DEGREE REQUIREMENTS. For D.D.S.: satisfactory completion of 46-month program, at least 36 months in residence. For M.S.: see Graduate School listing above.

FIELDS OF GRADUATE STUDY.
Endodontics.
General Dentistry.
Oral Medicine.
Oral Surgery.
Orthodontics.
Pedodontics.
Periodontics.

Frances Payne Bolton School of Nursing (44106-4804)

http:cwru.edu/CWRU/Bulletin/FPB/

Established 1898. Semester system.
Annual tuition: $17,100; per credit $713.

Graduate enrollment: full-time 261, part-time 220. Faculty: full-time 87, part-time 14. Degrees conferred: M.S.N., M.S.N.-M.A., M.S.N.-M.B.A., N.D.

ADMISSION REQUIREMENTS. Transcripts, three letters of reference, MAT or GRE for M.S.N., GRE for N.D. required in support of School's application. Interview strongly recommended; required for N.D. applicants. TOEFL required for international applicants. Accepts transfer applicants. Graduates of unaccredited institutions not considered. Apply to Assistant Dean by April 1 (Fall), December 1 (Spring), May 1 (Summer). Application fee $75. Phone: (216)368-2541; fax: (216)368-3542.

ADMISSION STANDARDS. Selective. Usual minimum average: 3.0 (A = 4).

FINANCIAL AID. Fellowships, research assistantships, teaching assistantships, partial tuition waivers, Federal W/S, loans. Approved for VA benefits. Apply when requesting admission but prior to June 30. Phone: (216)368-4530. Use FAFSA. About 85% of students receive financial assistance.

DEGREE REQUIREMENTS. For M.S.N.: 36 semester hours minimum; thesis or research project. For N.D.: completion of four levels of program; Licensure exam; thesis. For M.S.N.-M.A.: 45 credit hours, a minimum of 18 credits in each school. For M.S.N.-M.B.A.: 72 credits, a minimum of 30 credits in each school.

FIELDS OF STUDY.
Community Health Nursing.
Critical Care Nursing.
Geriatric Mental Health Nursing.
Gerontological Nursing.
Medical-Surgical Nursing.
Nurse Anesthesia.
Nurse-Midwifery.
Nurse Practitioner. Includes acute, adult, neonatal, pediatric, women's health.
Nursing Administration.
Nursing Care of Childbearing Families.
Primary Health Nursing Care of Women.

THE CATHOLIC UNIVERSITY OF AMERICA

Washington, D.C. 20064
http://www.cua.edu

Founded 1887. Coed. Private control. Semester system. University participates in Joint Graduate Consortium with American, Georgetown, George Washington, Howard Universities. Special facilities: Center for Advanced Training in Cell and Molecular Biology, Latin American Center for Graduate Studies in Music, Life Cycle Institute; Center for the Study of Youth Development, Computer Center—VT320 terminals at various campus locations; fiber optics network; two VAX 4000 computers; laboratories for fluid mechanics, solid state, solid mechanics, acoustics, member Folger Institute of Renaissance and Eighteenth-Century Studies, Institute of Christian Oriental Research. Library: over 1,300,000 volumes, 1,125,000 microforms, 9310 current periodicals, 76 PCs in libraries.

Annual tuition: full-time $15,562, part-time $600 per credit. On-campus housing for single graduate students. Annual cost: $6208–7962 (including board). Contact Director of Housing for both on- and off-campus housing information. Phone: (202)319-5615.

School of Arts and Sciences

Graduate study since 1895. Enrollment: full-time 223, part-time 543. School faculty teaching graduate students: full-time 167, part-time 87. Degrees conferred: M.A., M.F.A., M.S., Ph.D.

ADMISSION REQUIREMENTS. Transcripts, GRE, two letters of recommendation required in support of application. GRE Subject/MAT/interviews required by some departments. TOEFL required of international applicants. Accepts transfer applicants. Apply to Office of Graduate Students Services at least one month prior to registration. Application fee $30. Phone: (202)319-5057.

ADMISSION STANDARDS. Competitive for most departments, selective for others. Usual minimum average: 3.0 (A = 4).

FINANCIAL AID. Annual awards from institutional funds: scholarships, teaching assistantships, research assistantships, Federal W/S, loans. Apply by February 1 to Committee on Fellowships and Scholarships, to appropriate department head for assistantships; to Office of Financial Aid for all other programs. Use FAFSA. About 50% of students receive aid other than loans from University and outside sources.

DEGREE REQUIREMENTS. For master's: 30-36 semester hours, 24 credits in residence; thesis/nonthesis option; reading knowledge of one language for some majors; final written exam. For M.F.A.: same as above except no language and creative project instead of thesis. For Ph.D.: 53 credits minimum including the master's, at least 6 full-time semesters in residence; comprehensive exam; reading knowledge of one foreign language; dissertation; final oral exam.

FIELDS OF STUDY.
Anthropology. Includes anthropology, archaeology. M.A., Ph.D.
Art. Includes creative art; M.F.A.
Biochemistry. Interdepartmental. M.S. only.
Biology. Includes cell biology, microbiology, medical technology teaching; GRE Subject, M.S., Ph.D. for admission.
Chemistry. GRE Subject for admission.
Comparative Literature. Interdepartmental. Two literatures for M.A., three literatures for Ph.D.
Drama. M.A.: drama; M.F.A.: acting, directing, design, and playwriting.
Early Christian Studies. M.A.
Economics. M.A. in accounting, economics, management; joint programs with Law School and Politics Department.
Education. Includes administration, counseling and guidance, curriculum and instruction, educational psychology and evaluation, and foundations of education. M.A., Ph.D.
English Language and Literature. Sample of research required of doctoral applicants for admission. M.A., Ph.D.
Greek and Latin. M.A. in classics, Latin; Ph.D.
History. Includes American, Latin American, medieval, modern European; ecclesiastical history; joint M.A.-J.D. with School of Law; joint M.A.-M.S.L.S. with Library Science. M.A., Ph.D.
Irish Studies. M.A.
Mathematics. M.A., M.S.
Medieval and Byzantine Studies. M.A., Ph.D.
Modern Languages and Literatures. Includes French, Spanish; Ph.D.; also in German, Celtic, Iberian studies; comparative philology and romance philology.
Physics. M.S., Ph.D.
Politics. Includes congressional studies; M.A. only. Joint M.A.-J.D. with School of Law. M.A., Ph.D.
Psychology. Includes clinical, counseling, human development, human factors, social. MAT, GRE Subject (Ph.D.) for admission; M.A., Ph.D. Joint M.A.-J.D. with School of Law.
Semitic and Egyptian Languages and Literatures. Arabic, Coptic, Syriac, Hebrew, Islamic literature, Akkadian. Joint M.A.-S.T.L. with department of theology. M.A., Ph.D.
Sociology. M.A., Ph.D.

School of Engineering and Architecture
http://www.ee.cua.edu/

Graduate study since 1896. Semester system. Annual tuition: $15,692, per credit hour $600. On-campus housing available. For costs: See University listing above.
Enrollment: full-time 40, part-time 287 (men 90%, women 10%). School faculty: full-time 26, part-time 20. Degrees conferred: M.S.E., D.Arch., D.Eng., Ph.D.

ADMISSION REQUIREMENTS. Transcripts, two letters of recommendation required in support of School's application. GRE strongly recommended; required by some departments. TOEFL required of international applicants. Interview not required. Accepts transfer applicants. Graduates of unaccredited colleges not considered. Apply to University Admissions Office by August 1. Fall admission only. Application fee $30. Phone: (202)319-5097; fax: (202)319-4499.

ADMISSION STANDARDS. Selective. Usual minimum average: 2.5 (A = 4).

FINANCIAL AID. Annual awards from institutional funds: eight scholarships, twelve teaching assistantships, eight research assistantships, Federal W/S, loans. Apply by March 1 to the Registrar for scholarships, to the Dean for assistantships, to Financial Aid Office for all other programs. Phone: (202)319-5185. Use FAFSA. About 50% of full-time students receive aid other than loans from School and outside sources. No aid other than loans for part-time students.

DEGREE REQUIREMENTS. For M.S.E.: 24 semester hours minimum, at least 18 in residence; thesis or 30 semester hours minimum, at least 18 in residence; no thesis. For Ph.D.: 54 hours minimum beyond the master's, at least four semesters in residence; preliminary exam for some departments; reading knowledge of one foreign language; dissertation; final written/oral exams. For D.Arch., D.Eng.: essentially the same as for the Ph.D.

FIELDS OF STUDY.
Architecture. Portfolio for admission to architectural design.
Civil Engineering.
Design and Robotics.
Electrical Engineering.
Fluid Mechanics.
Material Sciences.
Mechanical Engineering.
Mechanics.

Columbus School of Law

Founded 1897. Semester system. Special facilities: Institute for Communications Law, the Comparative and International Law Institute. Law library 220,000 volumes. Library has LEXIS, NEXIS, WESTLAW, DIALOG.
Tuition: full-time $20,875, per credit $751. Total average cost for all other expenses: $11,979. Enrollment: first-year class 200 (day), 56 (night); total full-time 659, part-time 256 (men 53%, women 47%). Faculty: full-time 47, part-time 77. Degrees conferred: J.D., J.D.-M.A., J.D.-M.L.S., J.D.-M.S.W.

ADMISSION REQUIREMENTS. LSDAS Law School report, transcripts, two character references, LSAT (not later than December), bachelor's degree required in support of application. Interview not required. Accepts transfer applicants. Applicants from unaccredited institutions not considered. Apply to the Dean after October 1, before March 1; part-time, May 1. Admits first-year students Fall only. Application fee $55. Phone: (202)319-5151.

ADMISSION STANDARDS. Accepts 30% of total annual applicants.

FINANCIAL AID. Scholarships, grants, Federal W/S, loans. Apply to the Financial Aid Office by March 1. Use FAFSA. About 11% of full-time students receive aid other than loans from School.

DEGREE REQUIREMENTS. For J.D.: 84 semester hours in residence. Advanced standing from other law schools will be considered. Combined programs available in economics, accounting, history, management, philosophy, psychology, politics, social work, library science. For degree requirements: see Graduate School listing above.

The Benjamin T. Rome School of Music
http://www.cua.edu/www/musu/

Graduate study since 1887. School established 1950. Annual tuition: fulltime $14,617, per credits $563. On-campus housing available. See University listing above.

Enrollment: full-time 74, part-time 107. Graduate faculty: full-time 16, part-time 100. Degrees conferred: M.A., M.M., M.Lit.M., Ph.D., D.M.A., M.A.-M.S.L.S.

ADMISSION REQUIREMENTS. Transcripts, two letters of recommendation required in support of School's application. Additional requirements vary by program. TOEFL required for international applicants. GRE and interview recommended for some programs. GRE required for University scholarship consideration. Apply to Dean at least forty-five days prior to beginning of semester. Application fee $30. Phone: (202)319-5057; fax: (202)319-5199.

ADMISSION STANDARDS. Competitive. Usual minimum average: 3.0 (A = 4).

FINANCIAL AID. Fifteen scholarships, four research assistantships, eight teaching assistantships, fifty-four performance awards, Federal W/S, loans. Apply to Dean and Financial Aid Office by February 1. Use FAFSA and University's FAF. Phone: (202)319-5185.

DEGREE REQUIREMENTS. For master's: 30–36 credits, at least one year in residence; language and thesis for M.A.; thesis optional for M.S.Mus.Ed.; performance for M.M. For D.M.A. (degree individualized): 70–90 credits beyond bachelor's, at least three years in residence; dissertation; composition; recital. For Ph.D.: 54 credits minimum, at least three years in residence; two foreign languages; dissertation; written/oral exam.

FIELDS OF STUDY.
Composition.
Instrumental Conducting.
Liturgical Music.
Music Education.
Musicology.
Performance. Includes piano, organ, voice, voice and piano, pedagogy, chamber music, and accompanying.
Note: A concentration in Latin American Music is available for all Fields of Study in cooperation with the School's Latin American Center for Graduate Studies in Music.

School of Nursing

Graduate study since 1951. Semester system. Annual tuition: full-time $14,734, per credit $563.
Enrollment: full-time 60, part-time 72. School faculty: full-time 26, part-time 5. Degrees conferred: M.S.N., M.S.N.-M.A.

(Health Services Management with George Washington University), Certificates, D.N.Sc.

ADMISSION REQUIREMENTS. Transcripts, letters of recommendation, GRE required in support of School's application. TOEFL for international applicants. Interview for some majors. Accepts transfer applicants. Graduates of unaccredited institutions not considered. Apply to School's Admissions Office by August 1 (Fall); no specified closing dates for Spring or Summer. Application fee $30. Phone: (202)319-6466; fax: (202)319-6485.

ADMISSION STANDARDS. Selective. Usual minimum average: 3.0 (A = 4).

FINANCIAL AID. Twenty partial scholarships, four internships, Federal traineeships, Federal W/S, loans. Apply to Dean and Financial Aid Office by April 1. Use FAFSA and institutional FAF. Phone: (202)319-5185.

DEGREE REQUIREMENTS. For M.S.N.: 40–46 semester hours; thesis/nonthesis option; comprehensive exam. For M.S.N.-M.A.: 61 semester hours required. For certificates: varies by program, at least 18 semester hours. For D.N.Sc.: 66 semester hours beyond the bachelor's; dissertation; final oral exam.

FIELDS OF STUDY.
Adult Health Nusing.
Adult Nurse Practitioner.
Advanced Practice Psychiatric—Mental Health Nursing.
Community Health Nursing.
Family Nurse Practitioner.
Maternal-Child Health Nursing.
Nurse Educator.
Nurse Manager.
Pediatric Nurse Practitioner.
School Nurse Practitioner.

School of Philosophy

Founded 1895. Annual tuition: $14,612. Off-campus housing available. Annual housing cost: $4012, plus $2884 board. Apply to Office of Off-Campus Housing. Phone: (202)319-5680. Day care facilities available.

Graduate enrollment: full-time 72, part-time 52. School faculty: full-time 12, part-time 2. Degrees conferred: M.A., Ph.L., Ph.D.

ADMISSION REQUIREMENTS. Transcripts, recommendations, GRE required in support of School's application. TOEFL required for foreign applicants. Interview not required. Accepts transfer applicants. Apply to University Admissions Office; no specified closing dates. Application fee $30. Phone: (202)319-5259.

ADMISSION STANDARDS. Very competitive. Usual minimum average: 3.0 (A = 4).

FINANCIAL AID. Eighteen scholarships, five research fellowships, five teaching assistantships, Federal W/S, loans. Apply by February 1 to the Registrar for scholarships, to the Dean for fellowships and assistantships, to the Financial Aid Office for all other programs. Use FAFSA. Phone: (202)319-5057. About 50% of students receive aid other than loans from School and outside sources. Aid other than loans sometimes available to part-time students.

DEGREE REQUIREMENTS. For M.A., Ph.L.: 24 semester hours in residence; transfer credit not accepted for M.A.; thesis and reading knowledge of one foreign language; final written/oral exam. For Ph.D.: 60 semester hours minimum beyond the bachelor's, at least 36 in residence; preliminary exam; reading knowledge of two foreign languages; dissertation, final oral exam.

FIELDS OF STUDY.
Ancient Philosophy.
Aquinas.
Husserl; Heidegger.
Logic and Epistemology.
Medieval Philosophy.
Metaphysics.
Modern Philosophy.
Moral Philosophy.
Phenomenology.
Philosophical Anthropology.
Philosophy of Science.

School of Religious Studies

Annual tuition: full-time $14,612, per credit hour $563.

Enrollment: full-time 186, part-time 201. Faculty: full-time 48, part-time 15. Degrees conferred: J.C.L., J.C.D., M.R.E., M.Div., M.A., D.Min., Ph.D., S.T.B., S.T.L., S.T.D.

ADMISSION REQUIREMENTS. Transcripts, bachelor's degree, three letters of recommendation, GRE required in support of application. TOEFL required for foreign applicants. Admission open to all qualified applicants. Apply by August 1 (Fall), December 1 (Spring). Application fee $30. Phone: (202)319-5057.

ADMISSION STANDARDS. Selective. Usual minimum average: 2.75 (A = 4).

FINANCIAL AID. Annual awards from institutional funds: 110 scholarships, 12 teaching assistantships, 14 fellowships, Burses, Federal W/S, loans. Use FAFSA and institutional FAF. Apply to the Dean and Financial Aid Office by February 1. Phone: (202)319-5185.

DEGREE REQUIREMENTS. For M.A., Ph.D.: requirements same as for School of Arts and Sciences, above. For other degrees, write Dean, School of Religious Studies, The Catholic University of America, Washington, D.C. 20064.

FIELDS OF STUDY.
Biblical Studies.
Canon Law.
Church History.
History of Religion.
Liturgical Studies.
Pastoral Studies.
Religion and Religious Education.
Theology.

The National Catholic School of Social Service

Established 1918. Annual tuition: full-time $14,612, per credit $563. On-campus housing available. See University listing above.

Enrollment: full-time 180, part-time 190. Faculty: full-time 21, part-time 17. Degrees conferred: M.S.W., Ph.D.

ADMISSION REQUIREMENTS. Transcripts, GRE or MAT, three letters of recommendation, personal statement, resume required in support of School's application. TOEFL required for foreign applicants. Accepts advanced standing and M.S.W. transfer students. Interview sometimes required. Graduates of unaccredited institutions not considered. Apply to Director of Admissions by May 1. Fall admission only. Application fee $50. Phone: (202)319-5496; fax: (202)319-5093.

ADMISSION STANDARDS. Selective. Usual minimum average: 3.0 (A = 4).

FINANCIAL AID. Limited assistance available. Scholarships, fellowships, graduate assistantships (Ph.D.), loans. Approved for VA benefits. Apply by March 1 to Director of Admissions. Use FAFSA. About 35% of students receive aid other than loans.

DEGREE REQUIREMENTS. For M.S.W.: 60 credits and four semesters minimum, at least two semesters in full-time residence; thesis or major paper. For Ph.D.: 24 credits beyond the master's minimum, at least four semesters in residence and two semesters in full-time attendance; qualifying exam; reading knowledge of one foreign language; written/oral comprehensive exams; dissertation; final oral exam.

UNIVERSITY OF CENTRAL ARKANSAS
Conway, Arkansas 72035-0001

Founded 1907. Located 30 miles NW of Little Rock. Coed. State control. semester system. Library: 376,000 volumes, 572,000 microforms, 10 PC workstations.

Tuition: per hour, resident $120, nonresident $235. Limited on-campus housing graduate students. Annual housing cost $3175. Apply to Director of Housing. Phone: (501)450-3124.

Graduate School

Graduate study since 1955. Enrollment: full-time 388; part-time 413. College faculty teaching graduate students: full-time 245; part-time 54. Degrees conferred: M.A., M.S. in Ed., M.S., M.S.N., M.M.E., M.M., M.B.A., Ed.S.

ADMISSION REQUIREMENTS. Transcripts, GRE/MAT, three references required in support of application. TOEFL required for foreign applicants. Accept transfer applicants. Graduates of unaccredited institutions not considered. Apply to Office of Graduate Dean by March 1 (Summer and Fall), October 1 (Spring). Phone: (501)450-3124; fax: (501)450-5066.

ADMISSION STANDARDS. Selective. Usual minimum average: 2.7 (A = 4).

FINANCIAL AID. Annual awards from institutional funds: 107 assistantships, Federal W/S, loans. Apply to Dean of Graduate School for assistantship information; March 1 (Fall), October 1 (Spring). Use FAFSA. Phone: (501)450-3140. About 10% of students receive aid other than loans from School and outside sources.

DEGREE REQUIREMENTS. For master's: 30 semester hours minimum (48 for counseling, 60 for counseling psychology, 60 for school psychology), at least 24 in residence; thesis/nonthesis options; final written and/or oral exam. For Ed.S.: 33 semester hours beyond master's; project.

FIELDS OF STUDY.
Biology.
Business Administration.
Business Education.
Early Childhood Education.
Elementary Education.
Elementary School Leadership.
English.
Family and Consumer Sciences.
Foreign Language.
Health Education.
History.

Kinesiology and Physical Education.
Library Media.
Mathematics.
Music.
Nursing.
Occupational Therapy.
Physical Sciences.
Physical Therapy.
Psychology and Counseling.
Secondary School Leadership.
Sociology.
Special Education.
Speech-Language Pathology.
Technology Education.

CENTRAL CONNECTICUT STATE UNIVERSITY

New Britain, Connecticut 06050-4010
http://wwgs.ccsu.ctstateu.edu/

Founded 1849. Located 13 miles SW of Hartford. Coed. State control. Semester system. Library: 500,000 volumes.

Annual tuition: resident $3985, nonresident $9057. Limited on-campus housing. Average annual housing cost: $4953 (including board). Contact the Director of Residence Life for on- and off-campus accommodations. Phone: (860)832-1660. Limited day care facilities available.

Graduate Division

Graduate study since 1955. Enrollment: full-time 327, part-time 1980. Graduate faculty: full-time 252, part-time 217. Degrees conferred: M.A., M.S., M.B.A., sixth-year certificate (Reading and Educational Leadership).

ADMISSION REQUIREMENTS. Transcripts, GMAT (International Business only) required in support of University's application. References, TOEFL, and proof of financial capability required for international applicants. Apply to Assistant Dean of Graduate Studies at least one month prior to semester of entrance. Rolling admission process. Application fee $20. Phone: (860)832-2350; fax: (869)832-2522.

ADMISSION STANDARDS. Moderately selective. Minimum average: 2.7 (A = 4).

FINANCIAL AID. Annual awards from institutional funds: fifty scholarships, eighty assistantships, two internships, Federal W/S, loans. Apply to Dean and Director of Financial Aid by March 15 (Fall), November 15 (Spring). Use FAFSA. Phone: (860)832-2205.

DEGREE REQUIREMENTS. For master's: 30–36 semester hours minimum, at least 21 in residence; thesis or final written exam or special project/capstone; no language requirement in most programs. For Sixth-Year program: 30 credits beyond master's, at least 21 in residence. Some programs requires capstone project.

FIELDS OF STUDY.
Art. Includes studio, education.
Biology. Includes general biology, environmental studies, nurse anesthesia, health sciences.
Chemistry.
Communication.
Counseling. Includes marriage/family therapy, rehabilitation, school guidance, student development in higher education.
Criminal Justice.
Education. Includes business, early childhood, educational foundations, educational leadership and administration, educa-
tional media, elementary, marketing/distributive education, modern languages, physical education, reading, science, special, technology education for regular or vocational environments.
English.
Geography.
History.
Industrial Technical Management.
International Business Administration.
International Studies.
Mathematics.
Modern Languages. Includes French, Spanish.
Physics-Earth Sciences.
Psychology. Includes community and general.
Science.
Social Science.
TESOL.

UNIVERSITY OF CENTRAL FLORIDA

Box 160112
Orlando, Florida 32816-0112

Founded 1963. Coed. Public control. Semester system. Library: 960,000 volumes, 936,000 microforms, 5000 current periodicals.

Annual tuition: residents $2808, nonresidents $4280; per credit, resident $117, nonresident $387. On-campus housing available for single students only. Average academic year housing costs: $4305 (including board). Contact to Housing Office for both on- and off-campus housing.

Graduate Programs

Enrollment: full- and part-time 3133. Graduate faculty: full- and part-time 520. Degrees conferred: M.A., M.S., M.Ed., M.S.A., M.B.A., M.A.A.E., M.P.H., M.S.T., M.S.W., M.C.E., M.S.E., M.S.I.E., M.S.M.E., M.S.Mfg.E., Ed.S., Ed.D., Ph.D.

ADMISSION REQUIREMENTS. Transcripts, GRE, GMAT required in support of application. Three letters of recommendation for most programs. TOEFL required for international students. Accepts transfer applicants. Graduates of unaccredited institutions not considered. Apply to the Graduate Admissions Office at least six months prior to the date of registration. Rolling admission process. Application fee $20. Phone: (407)823-2766.

ADMISSION STANDARDS. Selective. Usual minimum average: 2.75 (A = 4).

FINANCIAL AID. Scholarships, fellowships, assistantships, partial tuition waivers, Federal W/S, loans. Approved for VA benefits. Apply by March 15 to appropriate Dean's Office for fellowships, assistantships, to Financial Aid Office for all other programs. Use FAFSA. About 20% students receive aid from University and outside sources. Aid available for part-time students.

DEGREE REQUIREMENTS. For master's: 30–45 semester hours minimum, at least one year in residence for most departments; however some departments require two or more years of full-time study; thesis/nonthesis option; reading knowledge of one foreign language for some departments; written/oral exam; completion of degree no later than five years from date of entrance. For Ed.S.: 30 semester credits minimum beyond the master's degree; special project. For Ed. D.: 90 semester hours, at least three years minimum in residence; written comprehensive exam; dissertation; final oral exam; completion of all requirements no later than seven years from date of entrance. For Ph.D.: 60 semester hours minimum beyond the bachelor's, and three years of full-time study or equivalent in residence; written comprehensive exam; advancement to candidacy; dissertation; final oral exam; completion of all requirements no later than seven years from date of entrance.

FIELDS OF STUDY.

COLLEGE OF ARTS AND SCIENCES:
Applied Sociology. M.A.
Clinical Psychology. M.S.
Communication. M.A.
Computer Sciences. M.S., Ph.D.
Creative Writing. M.A.
History. M.A.
Human Factors Psychology. Ph.D.
Industrial Chemistry. M.S.
Industrial/Organizational Psychology. M.S.
Literature. M.A.
Mathematics. Ph.D.
Physics. M.S., Ph.D.
Political Science. M.A.
Statistical Computing. M.S.
Technical Writing. M.A.

COLLEGE OF BUSINESS ADMINISTRATION:
Accounting. M.S.A.
Business Administration. M.B.A., Ph.D.
Economics (Applied). M.A.A.E.
Taxation. M.S.T.

COLLEGE OF EDUCATION:
Art Education. M.A., M.Ed.
Counseling. Ed.D.
Counselor Education. M.A., M.Ed.
Curriculum & Instruction. S.Ed., Ed.D.
Educational Administration. M.A., M.Ed., Ed.S., Ph.D.
Educational Media. M.Ed.
Elementary Education. M.A., M.Ed.
Music Education. M.A., M.Ed.
Physical Education. M.A., M.Ed.
Reading. M.Ed.
School Psychology. Ed.S.
Secondary Education. M.A., M.Ed.

COLLEGE OF ENGINEERING:
Civil Engineering. M.C.E., M.S., M.S.E., Ph.D.
Computer Engineering. M.S.E. , Ph.D.
Computer-integrated Manufacturing. M.S.
Electrical Engineering. M.S.E., Ph.D.
Engineering Management. M.S.
Manufacturing Engineering. M.S.Mfg.E.
Mechanical Engineering. M.S.M.E.

COLLEGE OF HEALTH AND PUBLIC AFFAIRS:
Communicative Disorders. M.A.
Health Sciences. M.S.
Social Work. M.S.W.

CENTRAL MICHIGAN UNIVERSITY
Mount Pleasant, Michigan 48859
http://www.cmich.edu/

Founded 1892. Located 70 miles N of Lansing. Coed. State control. Semester system. Special facilities: Beaver Island Neckercut Wood, Center for Computer Vision and Robotics, Center for Polymer Chemistry, Michigan Geographic Alliance. Library: 847,900 volumes, 1,154,454 microforms, 59 PC workstations.

Tuition: per credit, resident $126.90, nonresident $251.75. On-campus housing for married and single students. Annual cost for single students $3300–$4388 (including board), for married students $3948–5004 (room only). Apply to Director of Housing. Phone: (517)774-3112. Day care facilities available.

College of Graduate Studies

Graduate study since 1939. Enrollment: full-time 668, part-time 1202 (men 50%, women 50%). Faculty: full-time 537, part-time 145. Degrees conferred: M.A., M.S., M.B.A., M.F.A., M.M., M.S.A., Specialist, Psy.D., Au.D.

ADMISSION REQUIREMENTS. Transcripts, GRE/GMAT/MAT required in support of College's application. TOEFL required for foreign applicants; TWE required for some programs. Interview required for some programs. Accepts transfer applicants. Graduates of unaccredited institutions not considered. Apply to Graduate Office by July 15 (Fall), January 6 (Spring). Application fee $30. Phone: (517)774-GRAD; fax: (517)774-3439; E-Mail:grad@cmich.edu.

ADMISSION STANDARDS. Selective. Usual minimum average: 2.5 (A = 4).

FINANCIAL AID. Annual awards from University funds: 180 teaching assistantships, 28 internships, Federal W/S, loans. Apply by February 6 to Dean of College of Graduate Studies for fellowships, to appropriate department chair for assistantships, to Financial Aid office for all other programs. Use FAFSA. Phone: (517)774-3674. About 30% of students receive aid other than loans from University. Aid sometimes available for part time students.

DEGREE REQUIREMENTS. For master's: 30 semester hours minimum; thesis or two research papers. For Specialist: 30 semester hours beyond the master's; thesis or field study; final oral exam. No language requirements. For Psy.D.: at least 60 credit hours beyond the master's; two years in full-time residence; qualifying exam; full-year internship; case study; final exam.

FIELDS OF STUDY.
Accounting.
Administrative Services and Business Teacher's Education.
Art.
Biology.
Broadcast and Cinematic Arts.
Business Administration. Includes accounting, finance, management, marketing; GMAT for admission.
Business Education.
Business Law and Regulation.
Chemistry. Joint program with Michigan Molecular Institute.
Clinical Psychology.
Communication Disorders.
Computer Science.
Counseling/Special Education.
Economics.
Education. Includes elementary, secondary, community college teaching, audio-visual, administration and supervision, curriculum, guidance and counseling, special education, early childhood.
Educational Administration and Community Leadership.
English.
Finance.
Foreign Languages, Literatures, and Cultures.
Geology.
Health Education and Health Science.
History.
Home Economics, Family Life-Consumer Education.
Humanities.
Industrial and Engineering Technology.
Information Systems and Analysis.
Journalism.

Library Media.
Management.
Marketing and Hospitality Services Administration.
Mathematics.
Music.
Philosophy.
Physical Education and Sport.
Physical Science.
Physical Therapy.
Physician Assistant.
Physics.
Political Science.
Polymer Science. Joint program with Michigan Molecular Institute.
Psychology.
Public Administration.
Recreation and Park Administration.
School Librarianship.
Sociology, Anthropology, and Social Work.
Speech Communication and Dramatic Arts.
Sports Administration.
Teacher Education and Professional Development.

CENTRAL MISSOURI STATE UNIVERSITY
Warrensburg, Missouri 64093

Founded 1871. Located 50 miles SE of Kansas City. Coed. State control. Semester system. Library 1,100,700 volumes, 992,000 microforms.

Tuition per credit: resident $126, nonresident $252. On-campus housing for about 200 married students, 3000 men, 3000 women. Housing cost: $355–$455 per month for married students, $1800 per term (including board) for single students. Apply to Director of Residential Life. Phone: (816)543-4515.

Graduate Study

Graduate study since 1947. Enrollment: full-time 500, part-time 1200. Graduate faculty: full-time 300, part-time 50. Degrees conferred: M.A., M.S., M.S.E., M.B.A., Ed.Specialist.

ADMISSION REQUIREMENTS. Transcripts, bachelor's degree required in support of University's application. GRE/GMAT/MAT may be required by some departments. Accepts transfer applicants. Interview not required. Graduates from unaccredited institutions not considered. Apply to Admissions Office by August 15 (Fall), January 5 (Spring), June 1 (Summer).

ADMISSION STANDARDS. Relatively open. Usual minimum average 2.0 (A = 4).

FINANCIAL AID. Annual awards from institutional funds: fifty scholarships, two fellowships, twenty administrative assistantships, twenty research assistantships, seventy teaching assistantships, Federal W/S, loans. Apply to chair of proposed major for assistantships, fellowships; to financial aid office for W/S, loans. Phone: (816)543-4040; fax: (816)543-8080. Use FAFSA. About 10% of students receive aid other than loans from College funds. Aid other than loans, sometimes available to part-time students.

DEGREE REQUIREMENTS. For master's: 32 credits minimum; some departments require thesis. For Ed.Specialist: 30 credits minimum beyond the master's; thesis or research project.

FIELDS OF STUDY.
Accountancy.
Adult Education.

Agriculture Technology.
Art.
Aviation Safety.
Biology.
Business Administration.
Business/Office Education.
Criminal Justice.
Curriculum and Instruction.
Economics.
Elementary Education.
English.
History.
Home Economics.
Industrial Hygiene.
Industrial Management.
Industrial Safety Management.
Industrial Technology.
Industrial Vo-Tech Education.
K-12 Education.
Library Science and Information Services.
Mass Communication.
Mathematics.
Music.
Physical Education, Exercise, and Sports Science.
Psychology.
Public Services Administration.
Reading.
Safety Education.
School Administration.
School Counseling.
Secondary Education.
Security.
Social Gerontology.
Social Studies.
Sociology.
Special Education.
Speech Communication.
Speech Pathology and Audiology.
Student Personnel Administration.
Teaching English as a Second Language.
Theater.
Transportation Safety.
Note: Ed. Specialist available in most education-related programs.

UNIVERSITY OF CENTRAL OKLAHOMA
Edmond, Oklahoma 73034-5209

Founded 1800. Located 12 miles N of Oklahoma City. Coed. State control. Semester system. Library: 850,000 volumes.

Tuition: per hour, resident $72.20, nonresident $167.20. On-campus housing for 158 married students, 592 men, 716 women. Average annual housing cost: $3600 for married students, $2311 (including board) for single students. Apply to Director of Housing for on-campus housing; to Vice President, Student Services for off-Campus housing information. Phone: (405)341-2980, ext. 3368.

Graduate College

Graduate study since 1954. Enrollment: full-time 1782, part-time 1504. Faculty: full-time 283, part-time 47. Degrees conferred: M.A., M.S., M.B.A., M.Ed., M.M.

ADMISSION REQUIREMENTS. Transcripts, GRE, GMAT (for business) required in support of College's application. TOEFL required for international applicants. Interview not required. Accepts transfer applicants. Graduates of unaccredited colleges not considered. Apply to Dean of the Graduate College at least one month prior to registration. Application fee, $15. Phone: (405)341-2980, ext. 3341; fax: (405)330-3830.

ADMISSION STANDARDS. Relatively open. Usual minimum average: 2.5 (2.5, last 60 hours) (A = 4).

FINANCIAL AID. Sixty assistantships, Federal W/S, loans. Apply to appropriate department chair for assistantships. For W/S, loans, apply to Office of Financial Aid. Phone: (405)341-2980, ext. 3336.

DEGREE REQUIREMENTS. For master's: 32–36 semester hours minimum, at least 24 in residence.

FIELDS OF STUDY.
Adult Education.
Applied Mathematical Sciences.
Biology.
Business Administration.
Community Counseling.
Criminal Justice Administration.
Elementary Education and Early Childhood Education.
English.
Guidance and Counseling.
History.
Human Environmental Sciences.
Industrial and Applied Physics.
Instructional Media.
Music.
Physics.
Political Science.
Professional Health Occupations.
Psychology.
Reading.
School Administration.
Secondary Education. Usual subject areas.
Southwestern Studies.
Special Education. Includes learning disabilities, mental retardation, emotionally disturbed, multi-handicapped.
Speech Pathology.

CENTRAL WASHINGTON UNIVERSITY
Ellensburg, Washington 98926

Founded 1890. Located 36 miles N of Yakima and 100 miles E of Seattle. Coed. State control. Quarter system. Special facilities: educational television in conjunction with Ellensburg public schools, computer center, Geographic Information System Lab, Chimpanzee and Human Communication Institute. Library: 435,000 volumes, 757,880 microforms.

Annual tuition: full-time resident $3885, nonresident $11,817; per credits resident $130, nonresident $393. On-campus housing for married, single students. Average annual housing cost: $4500 (including board) for single students. Apply to Housing Office. Phone: (509)963-1831.

Graduate School

Graduate study since 1949. Enrollment: full-time 201, part-time 134. (men 42%, women 58%). Graduate faculty: full-time 220. Degrees conferred: M.A., M.Ed., M.S., M.A.T., M.M., M.F.A.

ADMISSION REQUIREMENTS. Transcripts, GRE required in support of University's application. TOEFL required for foreign applicants. Accepts transfer applicants. Apply to Office of Graduate Admissions by July 1 (Fall), October 1 (Winter), Janu-

ary 1 (Spring). Application fee $35. Phone: (509)963-3103; fax: (509)963-1799.

ADMISSION STANDARDS. Relatively open. Required minimum average: 3.0 (A = 4).

FINANCIAL AID. Annual awards from College funds: ninety-five graduate assistantships, minority fellowships, Federal W/S, loans. Apply by February 1 to Dean of Graduate School. Use FAFSA and institutional FAF. Phone: (509)963-1611. About 40% of students receive aid other than loans from College and outside sources.

DEGREE REQUIREMENTS. For M.A., M.Ed., M.S., M.A.T., M.M.: 45 credit hours minimum; thesis or project; final oral/written exam. For M.F.A.: 90 credit hours minimum; at least three quarters in residence.

FIELDS OF STUDY.
Art.
Biological Sciences.
Business and Marketing Education.
Counseling Psychology.
Educational Administration.
English. Includes TESOL, TEFL.
English Language Learning.
Experimental Psychology.
Geology.
History.
Individualized Studies.
Master Teacher.
Music.
Nutrition, Family, and Consumer Studies.
Organization Development.
Physical Education, Health Education, and Leisure Studies.
Reading Specialist.
Resource Management.
School Counseling.
School Psychology.
Special Education.
Supervision and Curriculum.
Theater. For secondary school teachers only.

CHADRON STATE COLLEGE
Chadron, Nebraska 69337

Founded 1911. Located 300 miles NE of Denver, Colorado. Coed. State control. Semester system. Library: 280,000 volumes, 125,000 microforms, 38 PC workstations.

Tuition: per hour, resident $69, nonresident $138. On-campus housing for 62 married students, 800 single students. Annual housing cost including board: $3508. Apply to Director of Housing. Phone: (800)CHA-DRON. Day care facilities available.

Graduate Program

Graduate study since 1955. Average enrollment per year: full-time 25, part-time 600. Graduate faculty: full-time 65, part-time 15. Degrees conferred: M.B.A., M.S. in Ed., M.A. in Ed., Specialist in Education.

ADMISSION REQUIREMENTS. Two transcripts, references, GRE or MAT required in support of College's application. TOEFL required for foreign applicants. Interview required for Specialist Degree only. Accepts transfer applicants. Graduates of unaccredited institutions not considered. Apply to Chair of the Graduate Council. Application fee $10. Phone: (800)CHA-DRON; fax: (308)432-4451.

ADMISSION STANDARDS. Selective. Usual minimum average: 2.75 (A = 4).

FINANCIAL AID. Scholarships, seventeen teaching assistantships, two internships, Federal W/S, loans. Apply to Financial Aids Officer for scholarships, Federal W/S, loans, to Chair of the Graduate Council for assistantships. Use FAFSA. Phone: (800)CHA-DRON. About 5% of students receive aid other than loans from College, 20% from all sources. Aid sometimes available for part-time students.

DEGREE REQUIREMENTS. For M.B.A., M.S., M.A. in Ed.: 36 credits minimum, at least 12 in residence; thesis/nonthesis option; final oral exam. For Specialist in Education Degree: 30 credits minimum, at least 15 in residence; thesis or field study option; final oral/written exams.

FIELDS OF STUDY.
Business Administration.
Education. Includes elementary, secondary teaching, administration; computer education, fine arts, language arts, mathematics, physical education, reading, science, social studies, guidance, supervision, reading.

CHAPMAN UNIVERSITY
Orange, California 92666-1011

Founded 1861. Located 35 miles SE of Los Angeles. Coed. Private control. Disciples of Christ affiliation. Semester system. Special facilities: Center for Economic Research, Center for International Business. Library: 150,000 volumes, 13,000 Microforms, 1250 current periodicals, 20 PCs in library.

Tuition: per credit M.B.A. $410, M.P.T. $430, Education $320, all other programs $400. On-campus housing for married students, single graduate students. Average academic year housing costs: $6070–$9028 (including board) for single students; $634–$940 per month for married students. Contact Director of Residence Life for both on- and off-campus housing information. Phone: (714)997-6604.

Division of Graduate Studies

Enrollment: full-and part-time 1150. Faculty teaching graduate students: full-time 134, part-time 350. Degree conferred: M.A., M.B.A., M.F.A., M.H.A., M.P.T., M.S.

ADMISSION REQUIREMENTS. Official transcripts, GRE, two letters of recommendation required in support of application. GRE Subject/GMAT/MAT/NTE required for some programs. TOEFL or Institutionally administered TOEFL required for international applicants. Accepts transfer applicants. Graduates of unaccredited institutions not considered. Apply to Office of Graduate Admissions. Application fee $30. Phone: (714)997-6613.

ADMISSION STANDARDS. Competitive. Usual minimum average: 3.0 (A = 4).

FINANCIAL AID. Graduate assistantships, fellowships, tuition awards, Federal W/S, loans. Approved for VA benefits. Apply by March 1 to Graduate Dean for fellowships, assistantships; to Financial Aid Office for all other programs. Use FAFSA. Phone: (714)997-6741.

DEGREE REQUIREMENTS. For master's: 33–60 credits at least 24 credits in residence; candidacy; thesis/nonthesis/project option; comprehensive exam; internship for some programs.

FIELDS OF STUDY.
Art. Includes interior and environmental design.
Business Administration.
Career Counseling.
Communication. Include theater and film studies.
Computer Science.
Creative Writing.
Criminal Justice.
Education.
Educational Psychology.
English.
Film Studies.
Film and Television Production.
Food Science and Nutrition.
Health Administration.
Human Resource.
Organizational Leadership.
Physical Therapy.
Psychology.
School Counseling.
Special Education.
Sports Medicine.

CHICAGO STATE UNIVERSITY
Chicago, Illinois 60628

Founded 1867. Coed. State control. Semester system. Library: 323,000 volumes, 100,000 microforms, 300 current periodicals, 25 PCs.

Annual tuition: full-time, resident $2220, nonresident $6400; per hour, resident $88.75, nonresident $266.25. Limited on-campus housing available for single graduate students. Average academic year housing cost: $5140 (includes board). Contact Director, Student Housing for on-campus housing information. Phone: (312)995-dorm. Day care facilities available.

Graduate School

Graduate study since 1938. Enrollment: full-time 103, part-time 1120. Graduate faculty: full-time 83, part-time 25. Degrees conferred: M.A., M.S., M.S. in Ed.

ADMISSION REQUIREMENTS. Official transcripts required in support of School's application. Interview recommended by some departments. TOEFL required for international applicants. Accepts transfer applicants. Graduates of unaccredited institutions not considered. Apply to Dean of Graduate Studies at least two months prior to registration. Rolling admissions process. Students may enroll on a nondegree basis pending formal admission. Application fee, none. Phone: (312)995-2404.

ADMISSION STANDARDS. Selective. Usual minimum average: 2.75 (A = 4).

FINANCIAL AID. Limited. Twenty-five scholarships, ten research fellowships, tuition waivers, Federal W/S, loans. Approved for VA benefits. Apply to the Director of Financial Aid; no specified closing date. Use FAFSA. Phone: (312)995-2304.

DEGREE REQUIREMENTS. For M.A., M.S.: 30–36 semester hours minimum, at least 21–27 in residence; thesis optional; final written/oral exam. For M.A. in Ed.: same as above, except 32 hours minimum.

FIELDS OF STUDY.
Biological Science.
Corrections and Criminal Justice.
Education. Includes elementary, secondary, early childhood, bilingual, administration and supervision, teaching in non-school settings.
English.
Geography.
History.
Library Science.
Mathematics.
Occupational Education. Includes business, industrial, industrial supervision.
Psychology. Includes guidance, counseling.
Special Education. Includes teaching of mentally retarded, learning disabled, emotionally disturbed, gifted.

THE UNIVERSITY OF CHICAGO

Chicago, Illinois 60637
http://www.uchicago.edu/

Founded 1890. Coed. Private control. Quarter system. Special facilities: Amdahl 470/7, DECSYSTEM 20, Oriental Institute Museum, Comparative Law Research Center, Center for Studies in Criminal Justice, Ben May Laboratory for Cancer Research, Center for International Studies, special book collections of English Bibles, Lincolniana, modern poetry, anatomical illustration, Cromwelliana, official depository for U.S. Government documents, Section on Nuclear Medicine, Center for Balkan and Slavic Studies, Center for Middle Eastern Studies, Enrico Fermi Institute for Nuclear Studies, Institute for Study of Metals, Institute for Computer Research, Yerkes Observatory (Williams Bay, Wisconsin), 1.6 and 3.6 Mev van de Graaff Accelerators, Franklin McLean Memorial Research Institute, Laboratory for Astrophysics and Space Research, Argonne National Laboratories, Map Library, Center for Urban Studies, Center for International Studies, National Opinion Research Center, Population Research Training Center, Social Psychology, Community and Family Study Center. Library: 5,710,000 volumes, 2,039,000 microforms; 130 PC workstations.

On-campus housing available, 1080 apartments, 660 single rooms. Average annual housing cost: $6000–$8500 for married students, $6500 for single students. Apply to Office of Single Students Housing or Office of Married Student Housing by July 1. Phone: (312)753-2200.

Graduate School of Business

Annual tuition: full-time $23,930.
Enrollment: full-time 1316, part-time 1460. Faculty: full-time 122, part-time 35.
Degrees conferred: M.B.A., M.B.A.-J.D., M.B.A.-M.A., M.B.A.-M.D., M.B.A.-S.M., I.M.B.A., Ph.D.

ADMISSION REQUIREMENTS. Transcripts, two letters of recommendation, GRE or GMAT required in support of school's application. Interview strongly encouraged. TOEFL required for all non-English speaking international applicants. Graduates of unaccredited institutions not considered. Apply to the Director of Admissions and Aid by March 1 for full-time Program, three months prior to registration for part-time program. Full-time M.B.A. applicants admitted Autumn and Summer only. Application fee $100. Phone: (312)702-7369.

ADMISSION STANDARDS. Highly competitive.

FINANCIAL AID. One hundred scholarships, Federal W/S, loans. Apply to the Director of Admissions and Aid by January 4. Use FAFSA and institutional FAF. Phone: (312)702-3076.

DEGREE REQUIREMENTS. For M.B.A.: 20 courses minimum, at least five quarters in residence and normally in full-time attendance. For Ph.D.: usually 27 courses and three years beyond the bachelor's, at least three quarters in full-time residence; qualifying exam; dissertation; final oral exam.

FIELDS OF STUDY.
Accounting.
Behavioral Science.
Business Economics.
Econometrics.
Financial Management.
Foreign Language and Culture.
International Business.
Management Science and Information System.
Management Studies.
Marketing Management.
Policy Studies.
Production and Operations Management.
Quality Management.
Relations and Human Resource Management.
Statistics.
Note: Joint M.B.A. programs are offered in Area Studies, International Relations, Library Science, Social Service Administration, Public Policy, Physical Science, Law, and Medicine.

Division of the Biological Sciences

Graduate study since 1892. Tuition: full-time $27,080.
Graduate enrollment: full- and part-time 350. Graduate faculty: full-time 736; no part-time faculty. Degrees conferred: S.M., Ph.D., M.D.-Ph.D.

ADMISSION REQUIREMENTS. Transcripts, GRE, three letters of recommendation required in support of application. TOEFL required for foreign applicants. Interview recommended. Accepts transfer applicants. Apply to Associate Dean for Graduate Affairs by January 5. Application fee $50, $55 for foreign applicants. Phone: (312)702-5883; fax: (312)702-2598.

ADMISSION STANDARDS. Very selective for most departments, competitive to very competitive for the others. Usual minimum average 3.0 (A = 4).

FINANCIAL AID. Twenty scholarships, one hundred research assistantships, fellowships, Federal W/S, loans. Apply to Associate Dean for Graduate Affairs; no specified closing date. Use FAFSA. 100% of students receive aid other than loans from University and outside sources.

DEGREE REQUIREMENTS. For S.M.: Individual degree granting units set requirements; thesis; final written/oral exam. For Ph.D.: completion of Research Residency; preliminary exam; dissertation; final written/oral exam. For M.D.: see School of Medicine listing below.

FIELDS OF STUDY.
Anatomy.
Biochemistry and Molecular Biology.
Biopsychology.
Cancer Biology.
Developmental Biology.

Ecology and Evolution.
Evolutionary Biology.
Genetics.
Human Nutrition and Nutritional Biology.
Immunology.
Molecular Genetics and Cell Biology.
Neurobiology.
Ophthalmology.
Pathology.
Pharmacological and Physiological Science.
Radiology.
Virology.

Division of the Humanities

Graduate study since 1892.

Tuition: full-time $21,420. Graduate enrollment: full-time 923, part-time 12 (358 men, 380 women). Division faculty: full-time 203, part-time 10. Degrees conferred: A.M., M.F.A., Ph.D.

ADMISSION REQUIREMENTS. Transcripts, GRE/Subject Test, three letters of recommendation, evidence of satisfactory training in one foreign language required in support of application. TOEFL required for foreign applicants. Interview not required. Graduates of unaccredited institutions not considered. Apply to the Dean of Students, Division of the Humanities by January 5. Application fee $50, $55 for foreign applicants. Phone: (312)702-8499.

ADMISSION STANDARDS. Competitive for most departments, very competitive for others. Usual minimum average: 3.5 (A = 4).

FINANCIAL AID. One hundred eighty scholarships, eighty fellowships, tuition waivers, Federal W/S, loans. Apply by January 5 to the Dean of Students. Use FAFSA. About 70% of students receive aid other than loans from University and outside sources.

DEGREE REQUIREMENTS. For A.M.: 3 quarters minimum in residence; thesis/essay/similar project; final written/oral exam. For M.F.A.: 18 courses, final creative project and paper instead of thesis. For Ph.D.: 12 quarters minimum beyond the bachelor's, at least 3 quarters in residence; preliminary exam; reading knowledge of foreign languages set by individual departments; dissertation; final written/oral exam.

FIELDS OF STUDY.
Ancient Mediterranean World. Interdisciplinary.
Art. Includes practice and teaching, history and theory; photographs/slides of work for admission to M.F.A.; one language for A.M.; two languages for Ph.D.
Art and Design. M.F.A. only.
Classical Languages and Literature. Greek, Latin, classical archaeology; reading knowledge of Greek, Latin, one other language for A.M., two other languages for Ph.D.
Comparative Studies in Literature.
Conceptual Foundation of Science.
East Asian Languages and Civilizations. GRE for admission.
English Language and Literature. Includes creative writing program; GRE/Subject for admission; samples of work for admission to creative writing.
General Studies in the Humanities. A.M. only.
Germanic Languages and Literatures. Includes German, Scandinavian; one language in addition to major for A.M.; specialization available in medieval studies.
History of Culture. Includes study of cultures of various geographic areas and historical periods.
Humanities. Master of Arts in Humanities program; M.A. only.
Jewish Studies. M.A. only.
Latin American Studies. M.A. only.
Linguistics. Includes Indo-European and Balkan studies.

Middle Eastern Studies. M.A. only.
Music. Includes composition, theory, history; term essay for admission; apply for fellowships before January 1; two languages (German required) for A.M.; 3 languages (German required) for Ph.D. in theory and history.
Near Eastern Languages and Literatures. Includes Western Asia, Egypt, Judaic, Islam.
New Testament and Early Christian Literature. Competence in Greek for A.M., Greek and Hebrew for Ph.D.
Philosophy.
Romance Languages and Literatures. Includes French, Spanish, Italian; GRE for admission; one language in addition to major for A.M., two in addition to major for Ph.D.
Slavic Languages and Literatures. Includes Russian, Polish, Czech, and Slovak literatures, Slavic linguistics.
South Asian Languages and Civilization. Includes Bengali, Hindi, Sanskrit, Tamil, Urdu languages, literatures, and cultures; French and German in addition to major for A.M. and Ph.D.

Division of the Physical Sciences

Graduate study since 1892.

Tuition: full-time $21,420. Enrollment: full- and part-time 515. Degrees conferred: M.S., Ph.D.

ADMISSION REQUIREMENTS. Transcripts, GRE, three letters of recommendation required in support of application. TOEFL required for foreign applicants. Interview not required. Accepts transfer applicants. Apply to Department Chair before January 15 (priority date). Application fee $50, $55 for international applicants. Phone: (312)702-8789.

ADMISSION STANDARDS. Competitive. Usual minimum average: 3.0 (A = 4).

FINANCIAL AID. Scholarships, fellowships, assistantships, Federal W/S, loans. Apply to department chair for scholarships, fellowships, assistantships, to Office of Financial Aid for federal programs; priority application date February 15. About 99% of students receive aid other than loans from University and outside sources.

DEGREE REQUIREMENTS. For M.S.: 9 courses and 3 quarters minimum in residence; full-time attendance normally expected. For Ph.D.: course requirements vary by department; candidacy qualifying exam sometimes required; reading knowledge of foreign languages in some departments; dissertation; final dissertation defense.

FIELDS OF STUDY.
Astronomy and Astrophysics.
Atmospheric sciences.
Chemistry.
Computer Sciences.
Divisional Master's Program.
Earth Sciences.
Geophysical Sciences.
Mathematics.
Physics.
Planetary and Space Sciences.
Statistics.

Division of Social Sciences.

Graduate study since 1992.

Tuition: full-time $21,420. Graduate enrollment: full- and part-time 1700. Division faculty: full-time 225. Degrees conferred: A.M., M.A.T., M.S.T., Ph.D.

ADMISSION REQUIREMENTS. Transcripts, three letters of recommendation required in support of application. TOEFL required for international applicants. GRE General/Subject Tests required for most departments. Interview not required. Accepts transfer applicants. Graduates of unaccredited institutions not considered. Application deadline for U.S. citizens and nationals is January 5, for international citizens January 1. Application fee $50, international applicants $55. Phone: (312)702-8415.

ADMISSION STANDARDS. Competitive for most departments, very competitive for others.

FINANCIAL AID. Scholarships, teaching assistantships, fellowships, tuition waivers, Federal W/S, loans. Apply by January 1 to Dean for fellowships, assistantships; to the University's Financial Aid Office for all other programs. Use FAFSA. About 70% of students receive aid from both Division and outside sources.

DEGREE REQUIREMENTS. For A.M.: 9 courses and 3 quarters minimum in residences, thesis or research paper, final comprehensive exam. For Ph.D.: 18 courses or 6 quarters in full-time residence; reading knowledge of at least one foreign language; preliminary exam; dissertations final oral exam.

FIELDS OF STUDY.
Anthropology. GRE for admission. A.M. through divisional master's; joint Ph.D. in Anthropology and Linguistics available; social, cultural, and psychological anthropology, archaeology, linguistic anthropology, physical anthropology, and museology. Ph.D. only.
Behavioral Sciences. GRE required. Subject Test recommended for admission. Biopsychology, cognition and communication, developmental, educational, research methodology and quantitative psychology. Ph.D. only.
Divisional A.M. in Social Sciences. Interdepartmental. Concentrations in individual and society, urban studies, philosophy and history of the social sciences, communication, policy dimensions of social change, industrial relations, area and language studies, evaluation and survey research, economics and policy, individualized study; 9 courses and paper required for A.M.; admissions every quarter. A.M. only.
Economics. GRE for admission; A.M. through divisional master's; joint degree in law and economics; price theory, theory of income, employment, and price level, mathematical economic theory, monetary theory and banking, economic history, econometrics and statistics, history of economic thought, labor economics, agricultural economics, public finance, international economic relations, urban economics, industrial organization, economic development. Ph.D. only.
Education. GRE for admission. Includes educational administration, curriculum and instruction, educational psychology; mathematics, measurement, evaluation, and statistical analysis; education and social order; elementary- and secondary-level teacher training, and higher education; C.A.S. available in addition to M.A. and Ph.D.; year beyond M.A. for C.A.S.
Geography. GRE for admission. Includes spatial organization, earth environment and cultures and societies; A.M., Ph.D.
History. GRE for admission. High competence in reading either German or French required for admission; United States history, ancient history, medieval history, Byzantine history, Russian history, Renaissance and Reformation history, modern European history, British history, history of science and/or medicine, and the histories of the Chinese, Indian and Islamic civilizations.
International Relations. GRE for admission. Interdepartmental: includes international politics, organization, economics; American foreign policy; international theory; economic development; strategic studies; international law and communism; and political geography.
Latin American and Caribbean Studies. Five-quarter A.M. program leads to competency in one of the Latin American or Caribbean languages in addition to studying history, culture, civilization, and current problems of the area. A.M. only.

Middle Eastern Studies. Five-quarter A.M. program leads to competency in one of the Middle Eastern languages in addition to studying history, culture, civilization, and current problems of the area. A.M. only.
Political Science. GRE for admission. Includes political theory; politics and parties; public administration and bureaucracy; international relations; public law and jurisprudence; comparative politics; and political sociology.
Social Thought. GRE for admission. Interdepartmental; application deadline is January 1. Ph.D. only.
Sociology. GRE for admission. Includes community structure; demography; human ecology; deviance; economic and work institutions; family and socialization; formal organization; educational institutions; mathematical sociology; medical sociology; methodology; modernization; personality and social structure; political organization; race and ethnic relations; small groups; social change and social movements; social psychology; social stratification; and urban sociology.

Divinity School

All study at the graduate level. Tuition: $14,300 for M.Div., $18,735 for A.M., Ph.D. students. Enrollment: full-time 997. Faculty: full-time 31. Degrees conferred: A.M., Ph.D., M.Div.

ADMISSION REQUIREMENTS. Transcripts, four letters of recommendation, GRE Test required in support of application. TOEFL required for foreign applicants. Interview not required. Apply to Dean of Students of the School, preferably by January 1. Application fee $45, $50 international applicant. Phone: (312)702-8217; fax: (312)702-6048.

ADMISSION STANDARDS. Very competitive. Usual minimum average: 3.0 (A = 4).

FINANCIAL AID. Scholarships, Federal W/S, loans. Apply to Dean of Students of the School by January 1. Phone: (312)702-8217. Use FAFSA. About 90% of students receive aid other than loans from school.

DEGREE REQUIREMENTS. For A.M.: Two years of full-time residence; reading knowledge of French or German; three course sequence on the Modern Study of Religion. For Ph.D.: three years of full-time residence beyond A.M.; reading knowledge of French and German; qualifying exams; dissertation. For M.Div.: three years of full-time residence beyond B.A. (27 courses); one Biblical language; M.Div. paper.

FIELDS OF STUDY.
Bible.
Ethics.
History of Christianity.
History of Judaism.
History of Religions.
Philosophy of Religions.
Religion and Literature.
Psychology and Sociology of Religion.
Theology.

The Irving B. Harris Graduate School of Public Policy

Established 1987.
Annual tuition: full-time $20,580. On-campus housing available. Enrollment: full-time 163, part-time none. Faculty: full-time 20, part-time none. Degrees conferred: A.M., Ph.D.

ADMISSION REQUIREMENTS. Official transcripts, three letters of recommendation, GRE or GMAT required in support of School's application. TOEFL required for international applicants. Accepts transfer applicants. Graduates of unaccredited colleges may not be considered. Rolling admission process. Early application encouraged. Application fee $100. Phone: (312)702-8401; fax: (312)702-0926.

ADMISSION STANDARDS. Selective. Usual minimum average: 2.75 (A = 4), 3.0 in major field of undergraduate study.

FINANCIAL AID. One hundred and four fellowships, eight assistantships, Federal W/S, loans. Apply by February 1 to appropriate department chair for fellowships, assistantships; to Office of Financial Aid for all other programs. Use FAFSA. Phone: (312)702-6062.

DEGREE REQUIREMENTS. For A.M.: 9 courses and 3 quarters minimum in residence; candidacy; thesis or essay, reading knowledge of one foreign language usually required; final written/oral exam. For Ph.D.: 27 courses and 9 quarters minimum beyond the bachelor's, at least 3 quarters in residence; preliminary exam; reading knowledge of at least one foreign language; dissertation; final written/oral exam.

FIELD OF STUDY.
Public Policy Studies.

School of Social Service Administration

Chartered 1908.
Tuition: full-time $18,480; per course $2482. Graduate enrollment: full-time 207, part-time 118. Faculty: full-time 29, part-time 20. Degrees conferred: A.M., Ph.D.

ADMISSION REQUIREMENTS. Transcripts required in support of School's application. TOEFL required for international applicants. Interview not required. Accepts transfer applicants. Graduates of unaccredited institutions not considered. Apply to the School by February 1 (priority date). Fall admission only. Rolling admission process. Application fee $45. Phone: (312)702-1250.

FINANCIAL AID. Annual awards from School funds: scholarships, teaching assistantships, Federal W/S, loans. Apply by April 15 to Dean's Office for assistantships; to Financial Office for all other programs. Use FAFSA. Phone: (312)702-1126. About 80% of students receive aid from School and outside sources.

DEGREE REQUIREMENTS. For A.M.: 18 courses, at least 3 quarters in full-time residence. For Ph.D.: minimum of 13 courses beyond the master's; evidence of research and statistics competency; written preliminary exam; dissertation; final oral exam.

FIELDS OF STUDY.
The Master of Arts Program. Includes advanced clinical social work practice, community work, social planning, policy analysis for social welfare, or management. Specialization in health, criminal and juvenile justice, mental health, or target populations (children, the aged, etc.).
The Doctor of Philosophy Program. A program of advanced study for students preparing for careers in scholarship and research. Specializations are available in social development; includes policy, planning, and management; social treatment; and combined social development and social treatment. Individualized programs are tailored to the student's scholarly and research interests.
Note: Joint degree programs available with Business School and Divinity School.

Law School

Opened 1902. Quarter system. Law library 570,000 volumes. Library has LEXIS, NEXIS, WESTLAW, DIALOG. Annual tu-

ition: $22,425. Total average cost for all other expenses: $12,400. Off-campus housing available (two blocks from School).
Enrollment: first-year 175, total full-time 550 (men 60%, women 40%); no part-time students. Postgraduates 5. Faculty: full-time 39, part-time 21. Degrees conferred: J.D., J.D.-M.A. (Economics, History, International Relations, Public Policy), J.D.-M.B.A., LL.M., J.S.D., M.C.L., D.C.L.

ADMISSION REQUIREMENTS. LSDAS Law School report, LSAT (not later than December), letters of recommendation required in support of application. Interview used in a number of cases; by invitation only. LSAT recommended but not required of graduate law applicants. Applicants must hold a bachelor's degree. Accepts about 10 transfer applicants annually. Graduates of unaccredited colleges not considered. Apply to Law School Admissions office after September 1 and preferably by January 1. Beginning students admitted Fall only. Application fee $45. Phone: (312)702-9484.

ADMISSION STANDARDS. Very competitive. Accepts 10–15% of total annual applicants.

FINANCIAL AID. Scholarships, tutorial and research fellowships. Apply to Admissions Office by March 15 for scholarships. No closing date for loans. Use FAFSA. About 75 of students receive aid other than loans from School.

DEGREE REQUIREMENTS. For J.D.: 9 full quarters and 140 credit hours minimum. For LL.M.: 3 consecutive quarters in full-time residence; final research paper. For J.S.D.: at least 3 consecutive quarters in full-time residence; dissertation; final oral exam. For M.C.L.: 3 consecutive quarters in full-time residence. For D.C.L.: at least 3 consecutive quarters in full-time residence; dissertation. The M.C.L. and D.C.L. programs available to law graduates primarily from foreign legal institutions.

Pretzker School of Medicine (60637-5416)

Established 1927. Annual tuition: $21,660. Total average figure for all other expenses $9500. Enrollment (M.D. program): first-year class 104 (5 EDP); total 400 (men 55%, women 45%). Faculty: same as for Division of the Biological Sciences. Degrees conferred: M.D., M.D.-Ph.D. (Medical Scientist Training program).

ADMISSION REQUIREMENTS. AMCAS report, transcripts, three letters of recommendation, MCAT, interview required in support of application. Applicants must have completed at least three years of college study. Has EDP (apply between June 15–August 1). Apply to University Director of Admissions after June 15, before November 15. Application fee $55. Phone: (312)702-1939; fax: (312)702-2598.

ADMISSION STANDARDS. Very competitive. Accepts 3% of total annual applicants. Approximately 45% are state residents.

FINANCIAL AID. Scholarships, tuition awards, loans. Apply by February 1 to Dean of Students of the School of Medicine. Use GAPSFAS. About 70% of medical students receive aid other than loans from School.

DEGREE REQUIREMENTS. For M.D.: satisfactory completion of four-year program, or a three-year program for students who already have Ph.D. For Ph.D.: see Division of the Biological Sciences listing above.

FIELDS OF GRADUATE STUDY.
Anatomy.
Biochemistry.
Biophysics.
Cell Biology.

Genetics.
Immunology.
Microbiology.
Molecular Biology.
Neurosciences.
Pathology.
Pharmacology.
Physiology.

UNIVERSITY OF CINCINNATI
Cincinnati, Ohio 45221
http://www.cu.edu

Founded 1819. Coed. Public control. Quarter system. Cooperative graduate program in social work with Ohio State University. Special facilities: Biomedical Chemistry Research Center, Center for Computational Fluid Dynamics, Center for Cultural Resources, Center for Hazardous Waste Research, Center for Economic Education, Environmental Health Center, Center for Geographic Informational Systems and Spatial Analysis, Center for Neighborhood and Community Studies, Institute of Policy Research, Center for Women's Studies. Library: 2,035,164 volumes, 2,919,096 microforms, 350 PCs in all libraries.

Annual tuition: Cincinnati residents $7256, per credit $181; nonresidents $13,840, per credit $346. On-campus housing for 656 single men or women. Average annual housing cost: $3188 (including board) for single students. Apply to Housing Office. Phone: (513)556-0682; for off-campus information (513)566-7375.

Division of Research and Advanced Studies

Established 1906. Enrollment: full-time 3660, part-time 3199. Graduate faculty: full and part-time 750. Degrees Conferred: M.A., M.S., M.Ed., M.A.T., M.B.A., M.C.P., M.Des., M.F.A., M.S.Arch., M.S.N., Ed.D., D.M.A., M.M., Pharm.D., Ph.D.

ADMISSION REQUIREMENTS. Transcripts required in support of application. Interview, GRE required by some departments. Accepts transfer applicants. TOEFL, TSE, TWE required for all international students. Graduates of unaccredited institutions not considered. Apply to appropriate Dean prior to registration. Foreign students apply to Foreign Students Office. Application fee $30. Phone: (513)556-4335; (513)556-0128.

ADMISSION STANDARDS. Selective. Usual minimum average: 2.75 (A = 4).

FINANCIAL AID. Scholarships, fellowships, 850 research assistantships, 850 teaching assistantships, Federal W/S, loans. Apply by February 15 to appropriate Dean for scholarships and fellowships, to appropriate department chair for assistantships, to the Office of Financial Aid for all other programs. Use FAFSA. Phone: (513)556-6982; fax: (513)556-9171. About 90% of full-time students receive aid other than loans from School and outside sources. No aid for part-time students.

DEGREE REQUIREMENTS. For master's: 45–90 quarter hours minimum, at least one year in residence for some departments; however some departments require two or more years of full-time study; thesis; reading knowledge of one foreign language for some departments; completion of degree no later than seven years from date of entrance; written/oral exam. For Ed.D.: three years minimum in residence; written comprehensive exam; dissertation. For Ph.D.: 135 quarter hours minimum and three years of full-time study or equivalent in residence; written comprehensive exam; advancement to candidacy; dissertation; final oral exam; completion of all requirements no later than nine years from date of entrance.

FIELDS OF STUDY.

MCMICKEN COLLEGE OF ARTS AND SCIENCES:
Anthropology. M. A.
Biological Sciences. M.S., Ph.D.
Chemistry. M.S., Ph.D.
Classics. M.A., Ph.D.
Communication. M.A.
Communication Sciences and Disorders. M.A., Ph.D.
Economics. M.A., M.A.L.E.R., Ph.D.
English and Comparative Literature. M.A., Ph.D.
Geography. M.A., Ph.D.
Geology. M.S., Ph.D.
Germanic Languages and Literature. M.A., Ph.D.
History. M.A., M.A.T., Ph.D.
Mathematics. M.S., M.A.T., Ph.D.
Philosophy. M.A., Ph.D.
Physics. M.S., Ph.D.
Political Science. M.A., M.P.A., Ph.D.
Psychology. M.A., Ph.D.
Romance Languages and Literature. Includes French, Spanish; M.A., Ph.D.
Sociology. M.A., Ph.D.
Women's Studies. M.A.

COLLEGE OF BUSINESS ADMINISTRATION:
Finance. M.B.A., Ph.D.
International Business. M.B.A.
Management. M.B.A., Ph.D.
Marketing. M.B.A., Ph.D.
Operations Management. M.B.A., Ph.D.
Quantitative Analysis. M.S. M.B.A., Ph.D.
Real Estate. M.B.A.

COLLEGE OF DESIGN, ARCHITECTURE, ART AND PLANNING:
Architecture. M.S.
Art Education. M.A.
Art History. M.A.
Community Planning. M.C.P.
Design. M.Des.
Fine Arts. M.F.A.
Health Planning/Administration. M.S.

COLLEGE OF EDUCATION:
Community Counseling. M.A.
Counselor Education. M.Ed., Ed.D.
Criminal Justice. M.S., Ph.D.
Curriculum & Instruction. M.Ed., Ed.D.
Early Childhood. M.Ed.
Educational Foundation. M.Ed., Ed.D.
Elementary Education. M.Ed., Ed.D.
Health Promotion. M.Ed.
Literacy. M.Ed., Ed.D.
Nutrition. M.Ed.
School Counseling. M. Ed.
School Psychology. M.Ed., Ed.D.
Secondary Education. M.Ed.
Special Education. M.Ed., Ed.D.

COLLEGE OF ENGINEERING:
Aerospace Engineering. M.S., Ph.D.
Chemical Engineering. M.S., Ph.D.
Civil Engineering. M.S., Ph.D.
Computer Engineering and Computer Science. M.S., Ph.D.
Electrical Engineering. M.S., Ph.D.
Engineering Mechanics. M.S., Ph.D.
Environmental Engineering. M.S., Ph.D.
Environmental Science. M.S., Ph.D.
Health Physics. M.S., Ph.D.
Industrial Engineering. M.S., Ph.D.
Materials Science. M.S., Ph.D.

Mechanical Engineering. M.S., Ph.D.
Metallurgical Engineering. M.S., Ph.D.
Nuclear Engineering. M.S., Ph.D.
Solid State Electronics. M.S., Ph.D.

COLLEGE OF NURSING AND HEALTH:
Community Health Nursing. Includes community, occupational health nursing. M.S.N.
Medical-Surgical Nursing. Includes adult, critical care (trauma), nurse anesthesia. M.S.N.
Nursing Service Administration. Includes nursing service administration, M.S.N.; nursing, Ph.D.
Parent and Child Health. Includes family nurse practitioner, pediatric nurse practitioner, perinatal health, neonatal nursing. M.S.N.
Psychiatric Mental Health. Includes psychiatric nursing. M.S.N.

COLLEGE OF PHARMACY:
Pharmaceutical Sciences. M.S.
Pharmaceutical Sciences/Biopharmaceutics. Ph.D.
Pharmacy. Pharm.D.

SCHOOL OF SOCIAL WORK:
Social Work. M.S.W.

College of Law (45221-0040)

Established 1833. Coed. Semester system. Special facilities: the Center for Dispute Resolution, Urban Morgan Institute for Human Rights. Library 347,000 volumes. Library has LEXIS, NEXIS, WESTLAW, UCLIO, OHIOLINK, OCLC, DIALOG, EPIC, DATATIMES.

Annual tuition: full-time, residents $6900, nonresidents $13,407. Limited on-campus housing available. Apply to University Office for Resident Living for both on- and off-campus housing. Total average cost for all other expenses: $9325.

Enrollment: first-year class 130; full-time 410 (men 58%, women 42%). Faculty: full-time 51, part-time 25. Degree conferred: J.D., J.D.-M.B.A., J.D.-M.C.P. (Community Planning).

ADMISSION REQUIREMENTS. LSDAS Law School report, transcripts, bachelor's degree, two letters of recommendation, LSAT required in support of application. Interview not required. Accepts transfer applicants. Applicants from unaccredited colleges not considered. Apply to College after October 1, before April 1. Fall admission. Application fee $35. Phone: (513)556-6805.

ADMISSION STANDARDS. Accepts 25% of total annual applicants.

FINANCIAL AID. Scholarships, fellowships, assistantships, Federal W/S, loans. Apply by March 1. Use FAFSA. About 60% of students receive aid other than loans from College.

DEGREE REQUIREMENTS. For J.D.: 88 semester hours minimum, at least one year in full-time residence.

College of Medicine (45267-0552)

Established 1819. Annual tuition: residents $11,478, nonresidents $21,039. Total average figure for all other expenses $6000.

Enrollment: first-year class 160; total full-time 613 (men 65%, women 35%). Faculty: full-time 400. Degrees conferred: M.D., M.D.-M.S., M.D.-Ph.D.

ADMISSION REQUIREMENTS. AMCAS, transcripts, letters of recommendation, MCAT secondary application required in support of application. Applicants must have completed at least three years of college study. Interview required of final candidates. Has EDP; apply between June 15 and August 1. Accepts

transfer applicants. Graduates of unaccredited colleges not considered. Apply to Admissions Committee of the College after June 15, before November 15. Application fee $25. Phone: (513)558-7341; fax: (513)558-1165.

ADMISSION STANDARDS. Very competitive. Accepts 5% of total annual applicants. Approximately 83% are state residents.

FINANCIAL AID. Scholarships, loans. Apply by May 1 to the Associate Dean. Use FAFSA. Phone: (513)558-6797. About 67% of students receive some aid from College.

DEGREE REQUIREMENTS. For M.D.: satisfactory completion of four-year program. For M.S., Ph.D.: see graduate school listing above.

FIELDS OF GRADUATE STUDY.
Anatomy.
Biochemistry.
Biophysics.
Blood Transfusion Medicine.
Cardiovascular Biology.
Cell Biology.
Cell Biophysics.
Developmental Biology.
Environmental Health.
Genetics.
Immunology.
Microbiology.
Molecular Biology.
Neurosciences.
Pathology.
Pharmacology.
Physiology.
Radiology.
Surgery.

College-Conservatory of Music, Graduate Division

Graduate study since 1929, doctoral study since 1971. Coed. Quarter system.

Annual tuition; resident $5442, nonresident $10,380; per credit, resident $181, nonresident $346.

Enrollment: full-time 400, part-time 175. Total college faculty: full-time 90, part-time 30. Degrees conferred: M.A., M.F.A., Artist Diploma, M.M., D.M.A., D.M.E., Ph.D.

ADMISSION REQUIREMENTS. Official transcripts, three letters of recommendation, audition/interview, GRE Subject Test required in support of College's application. GMAT required for Art Administration. TOEFL required for international applicants. Accepts transfer applicants. Apply to Assistant Dean for Admissions and Student Services by February 15 for priority consideration. Application fee $65. Phone: (513)556-5463, Fax: (513)556-1028.

ADMISSION STANDARDS. Selective on basis of demonstrated talent and academic background. Usual minimum average: 3.0 (A = 4).

FINANCIAL AID. Annual awards from institutional funds: 275 scholarships, 130 teaching assistantships, Federal W/S, loans. Approved for VA benefits. Apply by February 15 to Assistant Dean for Admissions and Student Services. Use FAFSA. Phone: (513)556-6982; fax: (513)556-9171.

DEGREE REQUIREMENTS. For master's: 50 quarter hours minimum (theory 66 quarter hours, music history 65 quarter hours); at least one year in residence; recitals where appropriate; final oral exam; knowledge of one foreign language for some programs. For D.M.A., D.M.E.: 90 quarter hours minimum beyond master's; preliminary exam; final document; reading knowledge of one foreign language for D.M.A. For Ph.D.: 90 quarter hours, minimum beyond the master's; reading knowledge of two foreign languages; outside-of-field cognate; preliminary exam; dissertation; final oral exam.

FIELDS OF STUDY.
Accompanying. M.M.
Arts Administration. M.A.
Bassoon. M.M., D.M.A.
Choral Conducting. M.M., D.M.A.
Clarinet. M.M., D.M.A.
Classical Guitar. M.M.
Composition. M.M., D.M.A.
Directing. M.F.A.
Double Bass. M.M., D.M.A.
Euphonium. M.M.
Flute. M.M., D.M.A.
French Horn. M.M., D.M.A.
Harp. M.M.
Harpsichord. M.M., D.M.A.
Instrumental Conducting. Emphasis in orchestral, wind. M.M., D.M.A.
Music Education. M.M.
Music History. M.M.
Oboe. M.M., D.M.A.
Percussion. M.M., D.M.A.
Piano. M.M., D.M.A.
Saxophone. M.M.
Theater Design and Production. M.F.A.
Theater Performance. M.F.A.
Theory. M.M.
Trombone. M.M., D.M.A.
Trumpet. M.M., D.M.A.
Tuba. M.M.
Viola. M.M., D.M.A.
Violin. M.M., D.M.A.
Violoncello. M.M., D.M.A.
Voice. M.M., D.M.A.
Woodwinds. M.M., D.M.A.

THE CITADEL
Charleston, South Carolina 29409

Founded 1842. Located 100 miles S of Columbia. Coed on graduate level. State control. Semester system. Library: 197,000 volumes, 935,000 microforms; 12 PC workstations.
Tuition: per credit hour $130. No on-campus housing for graduate students.

Graduate Studies

Graduate study since 1968. Enrollment: full-time 167, part-time 953. Faculty teaching graduate students: full-time 69, part-time 20. Degrees conferred: M.A., M.A. Ed., M.A.T., M.B.A., M.Ed., Ed.S.

ADMISSION REQUIREMENTS. Transcripts, interview, MAT/GRE/GMAT required in support of application. TOEFL required for international applicants. Accepts transfer applicants. Graduates of unaccredited institutions not considered. Apply to Dean, Graduate Studies or Director of M.B.A. Program at least one month prior to registration. Application fee for Graduate Education and M.B.A. is $25. Phone: (803)953-5189; fax: (803)953-7630.

ADMISSION STANDARDS. Selective. Usual minimum average: 2.75 (A = 4).

FINANCIAL AID. Limited to 28 graduate assistantships, Federal W/S, loans. Apply to Financial Aid office; no specified closing date. Phone: (903)792-5187. Use FAFSA.

DEGREE REQUIREMENTS. For M.A., M.A. Ed., M.A.T., M.Ed.: 39–45 semester hours minimum, at least 24 in residence; no language or thesis requirements. For M.B.A.: 30 semester hours minimum, at least 24 in residence; no language or thesis requirements; comprehensive exam. For Ed.S.: 39 semester hours beyond the master's.

FIELDS OF STUDY.
Biology.
Business Administration.
Counselor Education.
Curriculum and Instruction.
Education.
English.
General Business. GMAT for admission. M.B.A. only.
History.
Marine Biology.
Mathematics.
Physical Education.
Reading.
School Administration.
School Psychology.
School Superintendency.
Secondary Education. (For initial Certification only.)
Social Sciences.
Special Education.

THE CITY COLLEGE OF THE CITY UNIVERSITY OF NEW YORK
New York, New York 10031-6977
http://www.ccny.cuny.edu/

Founded 1847. Coed. Municipal control. Semester system. Library: 1,187,470 volumes, 746,547 microforms.
Tuition: New York City and State residents $185 per credit, nonresidents $320. No on-campus housing.

College of Liberal Arts and Sciences— Graduate Division

Graduate study since 1944. Enrollment: full-and part-time 500 (men 310, women 190). College faculty: full-time 588, part-time 552. Degrees conferred: M.A., M.S., M.F.A., Ph.D. (offered through CUNY Graduate).

ADMISSION REQUIREMENTS. Transcripts, three letters of recommendation required in support of application. TOEFL or evidence of proficiency in English required of international students. Interview not required. Accepts transfer applicants. Apply to Graduate Admissions Unit by June 1, May 1 international applicants (Fall). December 1 (Spring). Application fee $40. Phone: (212)650-6980; fax: (212)650-6417.

ADMISSION STANDARDS. Relatively open for some departments, selective for others. Usual minimum average: 2.75 (A = 4).

FINANCIAL AID. Annual awards from institutional funds: five scholarships, thirty assistantships, full and partial tuition waivers, Federal W/S, loans. Apply by February 1 to University's Financial Aid Office for scholarships, fellowships, Federal funds;

by March 1 to appropriate department chair for assistantships. Phone: (212)650-5812. Use FAFSA and CUNY's FAF. About 5–10% of students receive aid other than loans from University and outside sources. Aid not available to part-time students.

DEGREE REQUIREMENTS. For master's: 30–48 credit hours minimum, at least two semesters in residence; thesis or comprehensive exam in many fields. For Ph.D.: two years minimum, at least one year in residence; preliminary exam; reading knowledge of one or two foreign languages; and proficiency in one research tool; dissertation; final oral exam.

FIELDS OF STUDY.
Applied Urban Anthropology.
Architecture. Includes urban design.
Art History.
Biochemistry.
Biology.
Chemistry.
Clinical Psychology.
Computer Sciences in Engineering.
Creative Writing.
Earth and Environmental Science. Includes oceanography.
Economics.
English and American Literature.
Fine Arts. M.F.A. only.
Geology.
History.
International Relations.
Language and Literacy.
Mathematics.
Meteorology.
Museum Studies.
Music.
Painting.
Physics.
Psychology.
Sociology.
Spanish.

School of Education—Graduate Division
http://www.ccny.cuny.edu/

Graduate study since 1921. Semester system.
Tuition: per credit, New York State resident $185, nonresident and international $320. Enrollment: full-time 30, part-time 975. Faculty: full-time 84, part-time 75. Degrees conferred: M.A., M.S., Advanced Certificate.

ADMISSION REQUIREMENTS. Transcripts, GRE required in support of School's application. TOEFL required for international applicants. Interview required by some departments. Accepts transfer applicants. Graduates of unaccredited institutions not considered. Apply to Admissions Office of the School by April 15 (Summer, Fall), November 15 (Spring). Application fee $40. Phone: (212)650-6236; fax: (212)650-6970.

ADMISSION STANDARDS. Selective. Usual minimum average: 2.5, 3.0 for Administration and Supervision, School Psychology (A = 4).

FINANCIAL AID. Graduate assistantships, Federal W/S, loans. Approved for VA benefits. Apply to Financial Aid Office. Use FAFSA and University's FAF. Phone: (212)650-6656.

DEGREE REQUIREMENTS. For M.A., M.S.: 30 credit hours minimum, at least 19 in residence; thesis optional. For Advanced Certificate: 30 credit hours beyond master's.

FIELDS OF STUDY.
Administration and Supervision.
Art.

Bilingual Education.
Bilingual Special Education.
Curriculum and Teaching in the Elementary School.
Developmental and Remedial Reading.
Early Childhood Education.
English.
Environmental Studies. Includes science and social studies.
Mathematics Education.
Reading.
Secondary Science Education.
Social Studies.
Teachers of the Emotionally Disturbed.
Teachers of the Mentally Retarded.

School of Engineering—Graduate Division

Tuition: N.Y.S. resident $185–$245 per credit, to a maximum of $2175 per semester; nonresident (including foreign students) $320–$425 per credit to a maximum of $3800 per semester.
Enrollment: full-time 210, part-time 476 (men 84%, women 16%). Graduate faculty: full-time 72, part-time 24. Degrees conferred: M.E., M.S., Ph.D.

ADMISSION REQUIREMENTS. Transcripts, letters of recommendation, GRE (for Ph.D.) required in support of application. Interview not required. TOEFL required for international applicants. Accepts transfer applicants. Apply to Admission Office of the School by May 15 (Fall), December 15 for Spring. Application fee $40. Phone: (212)650-6447, 642-2812 (Ph.D.).

ADMISSION STANDARDS. Selective. Usual minimum average 2.75 (A = 4).

FINANCIAL AID. For Ph.D. students only: Scholarships, fellowships, assistantships for teaching/research. Minority fellowships, Federal W/S, loans for both master's and Ph.D. candidates. Apply by May 1 to Dean for scholarship, fellowships, assistantships, to Financial Aid Office for all other aid. Use FAFSA. Aid sometimes available for part-time students.

DEGREE REQUIREMENTS. For M.E., M.S.: 30 credit hours minimum, at least 24 in residence; thesis. For Ph.D.: 60 credit hours minimum, at least 30 in residence; Knowledge of tools of research; first and second exams; candidacy; dissertation; final oral exam.

FIELDS OF STUDY.
Chemical Engineering.
Civil Engineering.
Computer Sciences.
Electrical Engineering.
Mechanical Engineering.

CLAREMONT GRADUATE SCHOOL
Claremont, California 91711-6163

Established 1925. Located 35 miles E of Los Angeles. Coed. Private control. Semester system. Special facilities: Rancho Santa Ana Botanic Garden, affiliated with the Francis Bacon Foundation, the Blaisdell Institute for Advanced Study in World Cultures and Religions. Library: 2,000,000 volumes, 1,000,000 microforms.
Annual tuition: full-time $18,650, per credit $840. Limited on-campus housing for married students, men, and women. Average annual living expenses: $15,309. Apply to Housing Office. Phone: (909)621-8036.

Graduate School

Enrollment: full-time 500, part-time 1500 (men 54%, women 46%), Faculty: full-time 85, part-time 85. Degrees conferred: M.A., M.B.A., M.F.A., M.S., D.C.M., M.Phil., Ph.D., D.M.A.

ADMISSIONS REQUIREMENTS. Transcripts, GRE/GMAT, three letters of recommendation required in support of School's application. TOEFL required for foreign applicants. Accepts transfer applicants. Graduates of unaccredited institutions not considered. Apply to Office of Admissions by February 15 (priority consideration date). Rolling admissions process. Application fee $40. Phone: (909)621-8069; fax: (909)621-8390.

STANDARDS. Very competitive for most programs. Usual minimum average: 3.0 (A = 4).

FINANCIAL AID. Fellowships, assistantships, Federal W/S, loans. Apply to Office of Financial Aid by February 15 for fellowships, assistantships; for other aid September 1 (Fall), January 15 (Spring). Use FAFSA and institution's FAF. Phone: (909)621-8337; fax: (909)621-8390.

DEGREE REQUIREMENTS. For M.A., M.S.: 30 credits minimum, at least one semester of 12 credits for residence; thesis or critique; qualifying or final exam. For M.B.A., M.F.A.: 60 credits program. For Ph.D.: 3 years of full-time enrollment, or equivalent beyond the bachelor's (72 units); at least one year of full-time study for residence requirement; reading knowledge of two foreign languages or two optional research tools required; oral/written qualifying exam; dissertation; final oral exam.

FIELDS OF STUDY.
Art. Portfolio, one introductory, one advanced art history course for M.F.A.; one-year full-time attendance required; undergraduate major in art, one semester of full-time study required for M.A. M.A., M.F.A. only.
Botany. Emphasis on the systematics and evolution of higher plants and fungi; sub-fields including monographic and revisionary study of specific plant groups, cytotaxonomy, biochemical systematics, plant anatomy, comparative morphology, ecology, plant geography, physiology. M.A., Ph.D.
Cultural Studies. M.A. Ph.D.
Economics. Micro, Macro Theory and Econometrics emphasized; two languages or one language and mathematics for Ph.D. M.A., Ph.D.
Education. Includes administrative studies, curriculum, philosophy, instructional theory, language and learning, behavioral studies in human development, evaluation and research; study focusing on preschool and early childhood, elementary and secondary, higher education; elementary and secondary internship program and certification; administrative and professional credentials. M.A., Ph.D.
English. Includes English and American literature, literature and film; two foreign languages for Ph.D. M.A., M.Phil., Ph.D.
History. Emphasizes United States, including Colonial period; Great Britain; Medieval Europe; Modern Europe; Latin America; new interdisciplinary Ph.D. program in European intellectual history. M.A., Ph.D.
Human Resource Design. M.S.H.R.D.
Information Science. M.I.S., M.S., Ph.D.
Management. Emphasis on practice of management. M.B.A., Executive M.B.A., Ph.D. in Management.
Mathematics. Includes applied mathematics, computer science and scientific computing, operations research, junior college teaching, M.A. Ph.D. research interests include functional analysis, differential equations, applied mathematics, stochastic processes, algebra, number theory, and topology.
Music. Entrance audition required; one language required; major in music history, composition, performance and music educa-

tion, music criticism, medieval studies, music librarianship, church music. M.A., Ph.D., D.M.A, D.C.M.
Philosophy. Concentration in Plato, Aristotle, Epistemology, Logic, Ethics, Phenomenology, philosophical topics; 2 foreign languages required. M.A., Ph.D.
Political Science. Includes American government and politics, public law and criminal justice, political theory, public administration, methodology, comparative government and area studies. M.A., Ph.D., international relations, international political economy, foreign and defense policy, public policy, political philosophy, environmental and natural resources policy.
Psychology. Emphasis in social and environmental psychology, cognitive psychology, with sub-fields in attitudes and opinions, group processes, personality theory and research, environmental ecological psychology, human learning and memory, perception, attention and sensory psychology, problem-solving and conceptual behavior, language and thought. M.A., Ph.D.
Religion. Affiliated with institute for Antiquity and Christianity, The School of Theology at Claremont. German and French required, additional languages as necessary. Concentration in Old and New Testament, Church History, Philosophy of Religion and Theology, Women's Studies in Religion. M.A., Ph.D.

CLARION UNIVERSITY OF PENNSYLVANIA
Clarion, Pennsylvania 16214

Founded 1887. Located 85 miles N of Pittsburgh. Coed. State control. Semester system. Library: 304,285 volumes, 1.38 million nonprint items.

Tuition: per credit hour resident $187, nonresident $336. On-campus housing for 30 graduate men, 40 graduate women, none for married students. Average annual housing cost: $1740 (room only), $1530 (board). Apply to Student Affairs Housing Office. Phone: (814)226-2352.

Graduate College

Enrollment: full-time 194, part-time 276. Faculty: part-time 144. Degrees conferred: M.A., M.B.A., M.Ed., M.S., M.S. in L.S., M.S.N. (Joint program with Slippery Rock University of PA).

ADMISSION REQUIREMENTS. Transcripts, references, recommended in support of application. Interview recommended. TOEFL required for foreign applicants. GRE required of graduates of unaccredited institutions and for Biology, English, Speech Pathology, and Nursing programs. GMAT required for Business program. Accepts transfer applicants. Apply to Dean of Graduate College by August 1 (Fall), December 1 (Spring), June 1 (Summer). Application fee $25. Phone: (814)226-2337.

ADMISSION STANDARDS. Selective to relatively open. Usual minimum average: 2.75 (A = 4). S.P.A., Reading and Library Science require a minimum of 3.0.

FINANCIAL AID. Annual awards from institutional funds: one hundred graduate assistantships, loans. Apply to Graduate College by March 1. Phone: (814)226-2315.

DEGREE REQUIREMENTS. For master's: 30–45 semester hours minimum, 21–27 hours in residence (depending upon program); thesis optional in some programs.

FIELDS OF STUDY.
Biology.
Business Administration.

Communication.
Elementary Education.
English.
Library Science.
Mathematics.
Nursing.
Reading.
Science Education.
Special Education.
Speech Pathology and Audiology.

CLARK ATLANTA UNIVERSITY
Atlanta, Georgia 30314

Founded 1865. Name change 1988. Coed. Private control. Semester system. Special facilities: Resource Center for Science and Engineering, Center for Computational Science, Center for Polymer and Material Research, Institute for Community Development, Center on Aging, Criminal Justice Institute, Institute for International Affairs, Center for Afro-American Studies. Library: 800,000 items.

Annual tuition: $8640, per credit $360. On-campus housing for 400 graduate men and women; none for married students. Annual housing cost: $3740 (room only). Apply to Director of Graduate Residential Complex. Phone: (404)880-8072.

Graduate School

Graduate study since 1929. Enrollment: full- and part-time 1225. Graduate faculty: full- and part-time 290. Degrees conferred: M.A., M.S., M.B.A., M.S.L.S., M.S.W., Specialist in Ed., Ph.D.

ADMISSION REQUIREMENTS. Transcripts, GRE, references required in support of application. TOEFL required for foreign applicants. Interview not required. Graduates of unaccredited institutions not considered. Accepts transfer applicants. Admits September (Fall), January (Winter), June (Summer). Apply to Registrar at least one month prior to registration. Application fee $40. Phone: (800)688-3228, (404)880-8784.

ADMISSION STANDARDS. Selective for most departments. Usual minimum average: 2.75 (A = 4).

FINANCIAL AID. Limited. Scholarships, grants, fellowships, assistantships, Federal W/S, loans. Apply to the Office of Financial Aid by April 30. Use FAFSA. Phone: (404)653-8429. About 20% of students receive aid other than loans from University and outside sources.

DEGREE REQUIREMENTS. For M.A., M.S.: 24–36 semester hours, at least 24 in residence; reading knowledge of one foreign language; thesis; final written/oral exam. For M.B.A.: 60 semester hours; no language requirement. For M.S.L.S.: same as for M.A., except thesis is optional. For M.S.W.: 53 semester hours minimum, at least 24 in full-time residence, including fieldwork experience; thesis; final exam. For M.A. in Ed.: 30–48 semester hours; final exam. For Specialist: 30 semester hours beyond the master's; research project; final oral exam. For Ph.D.: 72 semester hours minimum beyond the bachelor's, at least one year in full-time residence; preliminary exam; reading knowledge of two foreign languages; dissertation; final written/oral exam.

FIELDS OF STUDY.
African Women's Studies.
African and African American Studies.
Biology. M.S., Ph.D.
Business Administration. M.B.A. only.
Chemistry. M.S. only.
Computer Science.

Criminal Justice Administration. M.A. only.
Decision Sciences and Information System.
Economics. M.A. only.
Education. Includes elementary, secondary, educational psychology, guidance and counseling, administration and supervision, special education (mentally retarded), reading, school librarianship. Ph.D. available in guidance and counseling, and administration; Specialist program available in most fields.
English. M.A. only.
Finance.
French. M.A. only.
History. M.A. only.
Humanities.
International Affairs. Ph.D. only.
Library Science. Includes academic, public school, special librarianship. M.S.L.S. and Specialist.
Marketing.
Mathematics and Computer Sciences. M.S. only.
Physics. M.S. only.
Political Sciences. M.A., Ph.D.
Public Administration. M.P.A. only.
Social Policy. Ph.D.
Social Sciences. Interdepartmental. M.A. only.
Social Work. M.S.W., Ph.D.
Sociology and Anthropology. M.A. only.

CLARK UNIVERSITY
Worcester, Massachusetts 01610-1477

Founded 1887. Located 40 miles W of Boston. Coed. Private control. Semester system. Library: 500,000 volumes, 58,000 microforms, 20 PCs.

Annual tuition: full-time $19,600, part-time $2470 per course. No on-campus housing. Apply to Building and Grounds Office for off-campus housing information. Phone: (508)793-7453.

Graduate School

Graduate study since 1887. Enrollment; full- and part-time 700 (men 60%, women 40%). Faculty: full-time 176, part-time 20. Degrees conferred: M.A., M.A. in Ed., M.B.A., M.H.A., Ph.D.

ADMISSION REQUIREMENTS. Transcripts, two letters of recommendation required in support of University's application. TOEFL required for foreign applicants. Some departments require, most others recommend GRE Subject Tests/ GMAT. Interview usually not required. Accepts transfer applicants. Apply to chair of proposed major department by February 15 (Fall), January 15 (Spring). Application fee $40. Phone: (508)793-7676; fax: (508)793-8834.

ADMISSION STANDARDS. Competitive for most departments. Usual minimum average: 2.75 (A = 4).

FINANCIAL AID. Annual awards from institutional funds: sixty-seven scholarships, sixty teaching assistantships, Federal W/S, loans. Apply to chair of proposed major department by February 15. Use FAFSA. About 60% of students receive aid other than loans from University and outside sources.

DEGREE REQUIREMENTS. For M.A., M.B.A., M.H.A.: 30 semester hours minimum, at least 24 in full-time residence; reading knowledge of one foreign language; thesis; final oral exam. For M.A. in Ed.: same as above, except thesis may be replaced by six additional hours or by election of double seminar. For Ph.D.: 48 semester hours minimum beyond the bachelor's, at least 24 in full-time residence; reading knowledge of foreign language as set by department; preliminary written/oral exam; dissertation; final oral exam.

FIELDS OF STUDY.
Biochemistry.
Biology. GRE Subject for admission; M.A. usually requires three or four semesters.
Business Administration. Includes accounting, economics and finance, management and personnel, marketing.
Cell Biology.
Chemistry. Includes inorganic, organic, physical.
Clinical Psychology.
Developmental Psychology.
Ecology.
Economics.
Education. Includes elementary, secondary, counseling, one- or two-year M.A. program, interview usually required for admission; GRE Subject for Ph.D. admission.
English.
Environmental Policy and Resource Management.
Genetics.
Geography. GRE for admission; full-time only.
Health Services Management.
History.
International Affairs.
Liberal Studies.
Mathematics. Two languages for Ph.D.
Microbiology.
Molecular Biology.
Neurobiology.
Physics.
Psychology. GRE Subject, interview for admission; admits Fall only; full-time only.
Public Policy and Administration.
Social Psychology.

CLARKE COLLEGE
Dubuque, Iowa 52001-3198

Founded 1843. Located 185 miles W of Chicago. Graduate coed. Private control. Roman Catholic. Semester system. Library: 97,000 volumes, 7600 microforms, 550 current periodicals.

Tuition: per semester credit $315. On-campus housing available for single students. Average academic year housing costs: $3525 (including board). Contact Office of Residential Life for both on- and off-campus housing information. Phone: (319)588-6313.

Graduate Studies

Graduate study since 1964. All degree programs offered in conjunction with Loras College and University of Dubuque through the Tri-College Cooperative Effort. College enrollment about 33. College faculty teaching graduate students: full-time 4, part-time 4. Degree conferred: M.A.

ADMISSION REQUIREMENTS. Official transcripts, two letters of recommendation, eligibility for School Certification, MAT required in support of application. TOEFL required for international applicants. Accepts transfer applicants. Apply to Coordinator of Graduate Studies at least one month prior to registration. Application fee $20. Phone: (319)588-6331; fax: (319)588-6789.

ADMISSION STANDARDS. Selective. Usual minimum average: 2.5 (A = 4).

FINANCIAL AID. None other than loans and area Professional Development Grants. Use FAFSA and Institutional FAF. Phone: (319)599-6316.

DEGREE REQUIREMENTS. For M.A.: 36 semester credits minimum, at least 30 in residence; thesis/nonthesis option.

FIELDS OF STUDY.
Counseling. Includes elementary and secondary.
Educational Administration. Includes elementary and secondary.
Educational Media. Includes elementary and secondary.
Reading. Elementary only.
Special Educational. Includes multicategorical.
Technology in Education.

CLARKSON UNIVERSITY
Potsdam, New York 13699
http://www.clarkson.edu/

Founded 1896. Located 150 NE of Syracuse. Coed. Private control. Semester system. Special facilities: Center for Advanced Materials Processing, computer center. Library: 475,000 print and microfilm items.

Annual tuition: per credit hour $584. Very limited on-campus housing. Average annual off-campus housing cost: $6400 (includes room and board). Apply to Residence Life Office. Phone: (315)268-6442.

Graduate Division

Enrollment: full-time 325, limited part-time study. College teaching faculty: full-time 107, part-time 1. Degrees conferred: M.E., M.S., M.B.A., Ph.D.

ADMISSION REQUIREMENTS. Transcripts required in support of University's application. GRE Test recommended. TOEFL required for foreign applicants. Interview not required. Accepts transfer applicants. Apply to Dean of Graduate School, preferably by March 15 (Fall), prior to registration for other terms. Application Fee $25; $35 for application sent from outside the U.S. Phone: (315)268-6442; fax: (315)268-7994.

ADMISSION STANDARDS. Selective in some departments, competitive in others. Usual minimum average: 3.0 (A = 4).

FINANCIAL AID. Annual awards from institutional funds: 149 teaching assistantships, 190 research assistantships, 11 graduate assistantships, 15 industrial fellowships, Federal W/S, loans. Apply to the Dean of the Graduate School by March 1. Use FAFSA. About 80% of students receive aid other than loans from University and outside sources.

DEGREE REQUIREMENTS. For M.S., M.E.: 30 credit hours minimum, at least 20 in residence; thesis (6–10 credit hours); nonthesis option in some departments. For M.B.A.: 32 credit hours beyond foundation requirements. For Ph.D.: 90 credit hours minimum beyond the bachelor's, at least two years in residence; language/research tool may be required; dissertation; comprehensive exam; final exam.

FIELDS OF STUDY.
Business Administration. M.B.A. only.
Chemical Engineering.
Chemistry.
Civil Engineering.
Electrical Engineering.
Engineering Science. Includes fluid and thermal science, solid mechanics, systems engineering, environment science and engineering.
Management Systems. M.S. only.
Mathematics.
Mechanical Engineering.
Physics.

CLEMSON UNIVERSITY

Clemson, South Carolina 29634

http://www.clemson.edu/

Founded 1889. Located 25 miles SW of Greenville. Coed. Land grant, state assisted. Semester system. Special facilities: Archbold Tropical Research Center (Dominica), Belle W. Baruch Forest Science Institute, Center for Advanced Engineering Fibers, Center for Advanced Manufacturing, Center for Computer Communication, Center for Engineering Ceramic Manufacturing, Center for Semiconductor Device Reliability Research, Division of Computing and Information Technology, Electron Microscope, Institute of Wildlife and Environment Toxicology, Lee Hall Art Gallery, Daniel Center (Genoa, Italy), Nursing and Wellness Center, Recreation, Travel and Tourism Center, South Carolina Energy Research and Development Center, South Carolina Water Resources Research Institute, Strom Thurman Institute of Government and Public Policy. Library: 1,637,000 volumes, 1,982,000 microforms, 100 PC workstations.

Annual tuition: resident full-time $2922; per credit $120; non-resident $5844, per credit $240. On-campus housing for 100 married students, 200 graduate men, 200 graduate women. Average annual housing cost: $1510–$2200 (room only) for single students; $1960–$2380 (apartment rent only) for married students. Apply to Housing Office. Phone: (803)656-2295.

Graduate Division

Enrollment: full-time 1852, part-time 2338 (men 50%, women 50%). University faculty teaching graduate students: full-time 1074, part-time 151. Degrees conferred: M.A., M.S., M.B.A., M.Ed., M.Ag.Ed., M.Arch., M.C.R.P., M.C.S.M., M.F.A., M.E.R., M.P.Acc., M.H.R.D., M.P.R.T.M., M.in.Ed., M.N.S., M.Engr., M.Ag., Ed.S., Ed.D., Ph.D.

ADMISSION REQUIREMENTS. Transcripts required in support of University's application. GRE required for M.A,, M.S., Ed.D., Ph.D, GMAT required for M.B.A., M.P.Acc. and M.S. in Industrial Management. TOEFL required for non-English-speaking international applicants. Interview not required. Graduates of unaccredited institutions not considered. Accepts transfer applicants. Apply to Graduate School Office by July 1 (Fall); for international applicants all application materials must arrive at least four months prior to anticipated semester of enrollment. Application fee $30. Phone: (803)656-3195; fax: (803)656-5344.

ADMISSION STANDARDS. Very competitive for some departments, competitive or selective for the others. Usual minimum average: 2.75 (A = 4).

FINANCIAL AID. Annual awards from institutional funds: 113 scholarships, 705 teaching assistantships, 518 research assistantships, 230 other assistantships. Apply by March 1 to appropriate department. Use FAFSA. About 90% of full-time students receive aid other than loans from University and outside sources. Aid rarely available for part-time students.

DEGREE REQUIREMENTS. For master's: 30 credit hours minimum; final oral/written exam. For M.A., M.S.: 30 hours may include 6 in research; thesis. For Ed.D., Ph.D.: three years minimum beyond the bachelor's, at least two consecutive semesters in residence; preliminary written/oral exam; reading knowledge of foreign language required for some departments; final oral defense of dissertation.

FIELDS OF STUDY.

COLLEGE OF AGRICULTURAL SCIENCES:
Agricultural Applied Economics. M.S.
Agricultural Education. M.Ag.Ed.
Agriculture. M.Ag.
Agronomy. M.S., Ph.D.
Animal and Food Industries. M.S.
Animal Physiology. M.S., Ph.D.
Applied Economics. M.S., Ph.D.
Aquaculture Fisheries and Wildlife Biology. M.S.
Entomology. M.S., Ph.D.
Environmental Toxicology. M.S., Ph.D.
Food Technology. Ph.D only.
Genetics. M.S., Ph.D.
Horticulture. M.S. only.
Nutrition. M.S., Ph.D.
Plant Pathology. M.S., Ph.D.
Plant Physiology. M.S., Ph.D.

COLLEGE OF ARCHITECTURE:
Architecture. M.Arch., M.S.
City and Regional Planning. M.C.R.P.
Construction Science and Management. M.C.S.M.
Planning Administration. M.C.R.P.
Visual Studies. M.F.A.

COLLEGE OF COMMERCE AND INDUSTRY:
Accounting. M.P.Acc.
Applied Economics. Ph.D.
Business Administration. M.B.A.
Economics. M.A.
Industrial Management. M.S., Ph.D.
Management Science. Ph.D.
Textile Chemistry. M.S.
Textile and Polymer Science. Ph.D.
Textile Science. M.S.

COLLEGE OF EDUCATION:
Administration and Supervision. M.Ed., Ed.S.
Counseling and Guidance Services. M.Ed.
Curriculum and Instruction. Ph.D.
Elementary Education. M.Ed.
English. M.Ed.
History and Government. M.Ed.
Human Resource Development. M.H.R.D.
Industrial Education. M.Ind.Ed.
Mathematics. M.Ed.
Natural Sciences. M.Ed.
Reading. M.Ed.
Secondary Education. M.Ed.
Special Education. M.Ed.
Vocational/Technical Education. Ed.D.

COLLEGE OF ENGINEERING:
Agricultural Engineering. M.Engr., M.S., Ph.D.
Bioengineering. M.S., Ph.D.
Ceramic Engineering. M.Engr., M.S., Ph.D.
Chemical Engineering. M.Engr., M.S. Ph.D.
Civil Engineering. M.Engr., M.S., Ph.D.
Computer Engineering. M.S., Ph.D.
Electrical Engineering. M.Engr., M.S. Ph.D.
Engineering Mechanics. M.S., Ph.D.
Environmental Systems Engineering. M.Engr., M.S., Ph.D.
Industrial Engineering. M.S., Ph.D.
Materials Science and Engineering. M.S., Ph.D.
Mechanical Engineering. M.Engr., M.S., Ph.D.

COLLEGE OF FOREST AND RECREATION RESOURCES:
Forest Resources. M.F.R., M.S., Ph.D.
Parks, Recreation and Tourism Management. M.P.R.T.M., M.S., Ph.D.

COLLEGE OF LIBERAL ARTS:
Applied Psychology. M.S.
Applied Sociology. M.S.
English. M.A.

History. M.A.
Industrial Organization Psychology. Ph.D.
Professional Communication. M.A.
Public Administration. M.P.A.

COLLEGE OF NURSING:
Nursing. M.S.

COLLEGE OF SCIENCES:
Biochemistry. M.S., Ph.D.
Botany. M.S.
Chemistry. M.S., Ph.D.
Computer Science. M.S., Ph.D.
Genetics. M.S., Ph.D.
Hydrogeology. M.S.
Mathematical Sciences. M.S., Ph.D.
Microbiology. M.S. Ph.D.
Operations Research. M.S., Ph.D.
Physics. M.S., Ph.D.
Plant Physiology. Ph.D.
Statistics. M.S., Ph.D.
Zoology. M.S., Ph.D.

CLEVELAND STATE UNIVERSITY
Cleveland, Ohio 44115

Formerly private, Fenn College became state university in 1965. Coed. Quarter system. Special facilities: Advanced Manufacturing Center, the Urban Center. Library: 879,000 volumes, 633,000 microforms, 6500 current periodicals, 143 PCs in all libraries.

Tuition: per quarter hour, resident $119, nonresident $238. Limited on-campus housing. Average academic housing costs: $4053 (three quarters). Contact Residence Life Office for both on- and off-campus housing information. Phone: (216)697-7330.

College of Graduate Studies

Enrollment: full-time 794, Part-time 3694. Faculty: full-time 527, part-time 99. Degrees conferred: M.A., M.Ed., M.S., M.B.A., M.M., M.C.I.S., M.L.R.H.R., M.P.A., M.S.U.S., M.S.W., M.U.P.D.D., Ed.S., D.B.A., D. Engr., Ph.D.

ADMISSION REQUIREMENTS. Transcripts, two letters of recommendation required in support of College's application. GRE Subject Tests required by most departments. TOEFL required for international applicants. Accepts transfer applicants. Apply to College of Graduate Studies at least four weeks prior to registration. Application fee: none. Phone: (216)687-3594.

ADMISSION STANDARDS. Selective for most majors. Usual minimum average: 2.75 (A = 4)

FINANCIAL AID. Three hundred graduate assistantships, Federal W/S, loans. Approved for VA benefits. Apply by May 15 to appropriate department chair for assistantships; to Financial Aid for all other programs. Use FAFSA. Phone: (216)687-3764.

DEGREE REQUIREMENTS. For master's: 45 quarter hours minimum, at least 33 in residence; thesis (for up to 8 credits) or final comprehensive exam. No language requirement. For D.B.A.: 92 quarter credits beyond master's; oral/written qualifying exam; dissertation; final oral exam. For Ph.D.: Biology and Chemistry 130 credits, Education 100 credits, engineering 90 credits beyond the master's; oral/written qualifying exam; dissertation; final oral exam.

FIELDS OF STUDY.
Accountancy and Financial Information Systems.
Applied Communication Theory and Methodology.

Art History.
Biology. M.S., Ph.D.
Business Administration. M.B.A., D.B.A.
Chemical Engineering.
Chemistry. Includes analytical, inorganic, organic, physical, M.S., Ph.D.
City and Regional Planning.
Civil Engineering.
Computer Information Systems.
Computer Science.
Economics.
Education. Includes administration, counselor, curriculum and institution, early childhood, exercise science, multiply handicapped, health, physical, reading, secondary, special, sports management. M.Ed., Ph.D.
Educational Specialist.
Electrical Engineering.
Engineering and Applied Science. D. Engr. only.
English.
History.
Industrial Engineering.
Management and Labor Relations.
Mathematics. Includes applied. M.A., M.S.
Mechanical Engineering.
Music.
Optical Sciences.
Philosophy.
Physics.
Psychology. Includes clinical, counseling, experimental, industrialized organizational.
Public Administration.
Recreation.
Social Work.
Sociology.
Speech Pathology and Audiology.
Urban Education. Ph.D. only.
Urban Planning Design and Development.
Urban Studies. M.A., Ph.D.

Cleveland-Marshall College of Law

Cleveland Law School established 1887, John Marshall Law School established 1916. Merged into university 1969. Semester system. Library 290,000 volumes. Library has LEXIS, NEXIS, WESTLAW.

Tuition: full-time, day resident $6894, day nonresident $13,788; per credit, evening resident $265, evening nonresident $530. Enrollment: first-year class days 180, evening 120. Total full- and part-time 1100 (men 59%, women 41%). Faculty: full-time 58, part-time 30. Degrees conferred: J.D., J.D.-M.B.A., LL.M.

ADMISSION REQUIREMENTS. LSDAS Law School report, transcripts, bachelor's degree, LSAT (no later than December), three letters of recommendation, writing sample required in support of application. Applicants must have completed at least four years of college study. Apply to the Assistant Dean after September 1, before March 1. Application fee $35. Phone: (216)687-2304.

ADMISSION STANDARDS. Accepts 40% of total annual applicants. Approximately 20–25% of enrolled students are nonresidents.

FINANCIAL AID. Scholarships, loans. Apply to the Dean by March 1; use FAFSA. About 20% of students receive aid other than loans from College funds.

DEGREE REQUIREMENTS. For J.D.: Three academic years minimum (day), or four years minimum (evening), at least one year or equivalent in residence; 87 semester hours. For LL.M.: at least 32 quarter hours beyond J.D., one year minimum in residence; final essay.

COLGATE UNIVERSITY
Hamilton, New York 13346-1386

Founded 1819. Located 38 miles SE of Syracuse. Coed. Private control. Semester system. Library: 452,000 volumes, 274,000 microforms, 2500 periodicals.

Tuition: per course $2392. No on-campus housing available. For off-campus housing, contact Director of Residential Life. Phone: (315)824-7367.

Graduate Studies

Enrollment: full-time 16, part-time 8. Faculty: 22 full-time. Degrees conferred: M.A., M.A.T.

ADMISSION REQUIREMENTS. Transcripts, GRE, writing sample, three letters of recommendation, personal statement required in support of application. Interview required by most departments. Accepts transfer applicants. Graduates of unaccredited institutions not considered. Apply by March 15 to Director of Graduate Studies. Application fee $50. Phone: (315)824-7220.

ADMISSION STANDARDS. Competitive. Usual minimum average: 3.0 (A = 4).

FINANCIAL AID. Annual awards from institutional funds: scholarships, research assistantships, Federal W/S, loans. Apply by April 1 to Director of Financial Aid. Phone: (315)824-7431. Use FAFSA. About 90% of students receive aid from University and outside sources. Aid sometimes available for part-time students.

DEGREE REQUIREMENTS. For M.A. in an academic subject: 7 graduate courses minimum, for counseling 9–10 courses; thesis; final oral exam. For M.A.T. Programs with internships: 9 courses; special project; final oral exam. For other M.A.T. programs: 8 courses; special project; final oral exam.

FIELDS OF STUDY.
Counseling—Internship Program.
English.
Geology.
History.
Mathematics.
Philosophy.
Religion.
Secondary School Teaching.

COLORADO SCHOOL OF MINES
Golden, Colorado 80401

Founded 1874. Located 10 miles W of Denver. Coed. State control. Semester system. Special facilities: Colorado Advanced Materials Institute, Advanced Steel Processing and Products Center, Center for Ground Water Research, Center for Research on Hydrates and Other Solids, Center for Wave Phenomena, Center for Waste Management, Center for Directional Drilling, Energy and Mineral Field Institute, Excavation Engineering and Earth Mechanics Institute, Kroll Institute for Extractive Metallurgy, Center for Welding and Joining Research, Colorado Center for Advanced Ceramics. Library 144,900 volumes, 194,000 microforms.

Annual tuition: full-time, resident $4384, nonresident $13,442; part-time, per credit, resident $146, nonresident $448. On-campus housing for married students and for single graduate students. Average annual housing cost: $4210 for single students;

$365–$450 per month for married students. Apply to Director of Student Housing. Phone: (303)273-3350.

Graduate School

Enrollment: full-time 538 (men 461, women 77), part-time 367. Faculty: full-time 189, part-time 81. Degrees conferred: M.Eng., M.S., Ph.D., Professional Engr.

ADMISSION REQUIREMENTS. Two transcripts, three of recommendations, GRE, GRE Subject Test in some departments, required in support of School's application. TOEFL required for foreign applicants. Interview not required. Accepts transfer applicants. Graduates of unaccredited colleges not considered. Apply to Graduate Office preferably by April 15 (Fall). Rolling admission process. Application fee $30, $45 for international applicants. Phone: (800)245-1064 (toll-free in state), (800)446-9488 (toll-free outside state); fax: (303)273-3244; E-Mail: grad-school@mines.colorado.edu.

ADMISSION STANDARDS. Very selective. Usual minimum average: 3.0 (A = 4).

FINANCIAL AID. Annual awards from institutional funds: 20 scholarships, 33 fellowships, 141 research assistantships, 99 teaching assistantships, 10–15 internships, Federal W/S, loans. Apply by April 15 to Dean of the Graduate School. Use FAFSA. About 75% of students receive aid other than loans from School and outside sources. No aid for part-time students.

DEGREE REQUIREMENTS. For M.S.: 24 semester hours minimum, at least 14 in residence; qualifying exam; thesis; final oral exam. For M.S. (nonthesis): at least 39 credits. For Ph.D.: 90 hours minimum beyond the bachelor's, at least 30 in residence and two semesters in full-time attendance; preliminary exam; foreign language is a department option; comprehensive exams; dissertation; final written/oral exam.

FIELDS OF STUDY.
Applied Mechanics.
Applied Physics.
Ceramic Sciences and Engineering.
Chemical and Petroleum Refining Engineering.
Chemistry.
Ecological Engineering.
Environmental Sciences and Engineering.
Geochemistry.
Geological Engineering and Geology.
Geophysical Engineering.
Materials Engineering.
Materials Sciences.
Mathematics.
Metallurgical Engineering.
Mine Health and Safety.
Mineral Economics.
Mining Engineering.
Operations Research Management Science.
Petroleum Engineering.
Physics.

COLORADO STATE UNIVERSITY
Fort Collins, Colorado 80523-0015
http://www.ColoSTATE.EDU

Founded 1879. Located 65 miles N of Denver. Coed. Public control. Semester system. Special facilities: Archaeomagnetic Laboratory, Engineering Research Center, Electron Microscope, Radiological Health Lab, National Seed Storage Lab, Colorado

Water Resource Center, Rocky Mountain Forest and Range Experimental Station. Library: 1,600,000 volumes, 2,183,000 microforms, 21,000 current periodicals, 187 PCs.

Annual tuition: full-time, resident $2562, nonresident $9556, part-time, per credit, resident $106, nonresident $398. On-campus housing for 700 married students, 200 graduate men or women. Average academic year housing costs: $3000/single, $5400 married. Apply to Office of Housing and Food Service for both on- (970-491-7427) and off-campus (970-491-2248) housing information. Day care facilities available.

Graduate School

http://www.ColoSTATE.EDU/Depts/Grad

Graduate study since 1893. Enrollment: full-time 2135, part-time 1270 (men 1885, women 1520). University faculty: full-time 987. Degrees conferred: M.A., M.Ag., M.A.T., M.B.A., M.Ed., M.F., M.F.A., M.M., M.S., M.S.W., Ph.D.

ADMISSION REQUIREMENTS. Two official transcripts, GRE, GMAT, three letters of recommendation required in support of School's application. Interview not required. TOEFL required for international applicants. Accepts transfer applicants. Graduates of unaccredited institutions not considered. Apply to proposed major department and Graduate School by March 1 (Fall), August 1 (Spring), December 1 (Summer); some departments may have earlier deadlines. Application fee $30. Phone: (970)291-6817.

ADMISSION STANDARDS. Very competitive for some departments, competitive or selective for the others. Usual minimum average: 3.0 (A = 4).

FINANCIAL AID. Annual awards from institutional funds: 662 teaching assistantships, 492 research assistantships, approx. 160 internships and fellowships, Federal W/S, loans. Apply by February 1 to appropriate department for fellowships, internships, assistantship; to Financial Aid Office for all other aid. Use FAFSA and University's FAF. Phone: (303)491-6321. About 55% of students receive aid other than loans from University and outside sources. Aid sometimes available for part-time students.

DEGREE REQUIREMENTS. For most master's: 30–32 credits minimum, at least 24 in residence; thesis required for many majors, optional for others; reading knowledge of one foreign language for some majors; final written/oral exam. For M.M.: 33 credits minimum. For M.S.W.: 45–63 credits minimum. For M.F.A.: 48–60 credits minimum. For Ph.D.: 72 credits minimum beyond the bachelor's, at least 32 in residence; preliminary exam; dissertation; final written/oral exam.

FIELDS OF STUDY.
Agricultural and Resource Economics. M.S., Ph.D.
Agricultural Engineering. M.S., Ph.D.
Agricultural Sciences. M.Ag.
Agronomy. M.S., Ph.D.
Anatomy. M.S., Ph.D.
Animal Sciences. M.S., Ph.D.
Anthropology. M.A.
Art. M.F.A.
Atmospheric Science. M.S., Ph.D.
Biochemistry. M.S., Ph.D.
Botany. M.S., Ph.D.
Business. M.B.A., M.S.
Cell and Molecular Biology. M.S., Ph.D.
Chemical Engineering. M.S., Ph.D.
Chemistry. M.S., Ph.D.
Civil Engineering. M.S., Ph.D.
Clinical Sciences. M.S., Ph.D.
Computer Science. M.S., Ph.D.
Creative Writing. M.F.A.

Design, Merchandising and Consumer Science. M.A., M.S.
Earth Resources. M.S., Ph.D.
Economics. M.A., Ph.D.
Electrical Engineering. M.S., Ph.D.
English. M.A.
Entomology. M.S., Ph.D.
Environmental Health. M.S.
Exercise and Sport Sciences. M.S.
Fishery and Wildlife Biology. M.S., Ph.D.
Food Science and Nutrition. M.S., Ph.D.
Foreign Languages and Literatures. M.A.
Forest and Wood Sciences. M.F., M.S., Ph.D.
Geology. M.S.
History. M.A.
Home Economics. M.H.Ec.
Horticulture. M.S., Ph.D.
Human Development and Family Studies. M.S.
Industrial Sciences. M.S.
Mathematics. M.S., Ph.D.
Mechanical Engineering. M.S., Ph.D.
Microbiology. M.S., Ph.D.
Music. M.M.
Occupational Therapy. M.S.
Pathology. M.S., Ph.D.
Philosophy. M.A.
Physics. M.S., Ph.D.
Physiology. M.S., Ph.D.
Plant Pathology and Weed Science. M.S., Ph.D.
Political Science. M.A., Ph.D.
Psychology. M.S., Ph.D.
Radiological Health Science. M.S., Ph.D.
Rangeland Ecosystems Science. M.S., Ph.D.
Recreation Resources. M.S., Ph.D.
Social Work. M.S.W.
Sociology. M.A., Ph.D.
Speech Communication. M.A.
Statistics. M.S., Ph.D.
Student Affairs in Higher Education. M.S.
Technical Communication. M.S.
Vocational Education. M.Ed., Ph.D.
Watershed Sciences. M.S.
Zoology. M.S., Ph.D.

College of Veterinary Medicine and Biomedical Sciences

Annual tuition for the professional school: WICHE and state resident $8340, nonresident $28,240. Living expenses approximately $8000. Enrollment: first-year class 132; total full-time 496. Faculty: full-time 155. Degrees conferred: D.V.M., D.V.M.-M.S., D.V.M.-Ph.D.

ADMISSION REQUIREMENTS. VMCAS report, transcripts, GRE, recommendations, animal/veterinary experience required in support of application. Will consider international applicants. Interview by invitation only. Applicants must have completed at least three years of college study. State residents and WICHE residents given preference. Accepts transfer applicants if opening exists. Has EAP, applicants must have at least 68 credits, G.P.A. 3.8, GRE combined score of 1750. Apply to the Office of the Dean of the College after August before November 1. Transfer applicants apply by May 1. Application fee $40. Phone: (303)491-7051; fax: (303)491-2250.

ADMISSION STANDARDS. Selective. Accepts 33% of total annual applicants. Nonresident quota 15–20. Approximately 50% are state residents.

FINANCIAL AID. Scholarships, assistantships, fellowships, and loans. Apply to the Office of Financial Aid following admission.

DEGREE REQUIREMENTS. For B.S.: satisfactory completion of two-year program. For D.V.M.: satisfactory completion of four-year program. For M.S., Ph.D.: see Graduate School listing above.

FIELDS OF GRADUATE STUDY.
Anatomy.
Environmental Health.
Microbiology.
Neurobiology.
Pathology.
Physiology.
Public Health.
Radiation Biology.

UNIVERSITY OF COLORADO, BOULDER

Boulder, Colorado 80309
http://www.colorado.edu/

Founded 1876. Located 28 miles NW of Denver. Coed. State control. Semester system. Library 2,000,000 volumes, 4,230,000 microforms, 174 PC workstations in all libraries.

Annual tuition: full-time, resident $3084, nonresident $13,698. Limited on-campus housing available. Annual average housing cost: $8650. Off-campus Housing Office. Phone: (303)492-7053. Family Housing Office: Phone: (303)292-6384. Day care facilities available.

Graduate School

Graduate study since 1892. Enrollment: full- and part-time 4800. University faculty: approx. 1000. Degrees conferred: M.A., M.S., M.F.A., M.E., M.Mus., M.Mus.Ed., M.B.S., M.B.A., D.Mus.A., Ph.D.

ADMISSION REQUIREMENTS. Two transcripts, four letters of reference required in support of School's application. GRE/GMAT, three letters of recommendation required for many departments. TOEFL required for international applicants. Interview not required. Accepts transfer applicants. Graduates of unaccredited colleges not considered. Apply to office of the major department at least 120 days before term admission is sought. Application fee $40, $50 for international. Phone: (303)492-6301.

ADMISSION STANDARDS. Selective to competitive. Usual minimum average: 2.75 (A = 4), 3.0 in some departments.

FINANCIAL AID. Annual awards from institutional funds: scholarships, fellowships, teaching/research assistantships, traineeships, Federal W/S, loans. Number of awards varies. Apply by January 15 through appropriate department. Use FAFSA. Aid sometimes available for part-time students.

DEGREE REQUIREMENTS. For most master's: 24 semester hours minimum with thesis or 30 semester hours minimum without thesis, at least two semesters in residence; qualifying exam; up to 9 semester hours in transfer; final written/oral exam. For M.F.A.: 48 hours minimum; written, creative thesis. For M. Mus.: same as for the master's, except final creative or performance project. Some departments require foreign languages for master's. For Ph.D., D.Mus.A.: 30 hours minimum beyond the master's, at least 6 semesters in residence; preliminary exam; final written/oral exam; dissertation. Some departments require foreign language for Ph.D.

FIELDS OF STUDY.
Aerospace Engineering Sciences.
Anthropology.
Applied Mathematics.
Art Education.
Art History.
Astrophysical, Planetary and Atmospheric.
Biology. Includes environmental, population, organistic, molecular, cellular, developmental.
Business. Includes accounting, finance, information systems, management, marketing.
Chemical Engineering.
Chemical Physics.
Chemistry and Biochemistry.
Chinese.
Civil Engineering.
Classics.
Communication.
Communication Disorders and Speech Science.
Comparative Literature.
Computer Science.
Dance.
Economics.
Education. Includes curriculum and instruction, educational psychology, research and evaluation methodology; social, multi-cultural, and bilingual foundations.
Electrical and Computer Engineering.
Engineering Management.
English.
Fine Arts.
French.
Geography.
Geological Sciences.
Geophysics.
German.
History.
Journalism and Mass Communication.
Kinesiology.
Linguistics.
Mathematical Physics.
Mathematics.
Mechanical Engineering.
Music.
Musical Arts.
Music Education.
Philosophy.
Physics.
Political Science.
Psychology.
Religious Studies.
Sociology.
Spanish.
Telecommunication.
Theater.

Graduate School of Business Administration

Graduate study since 1965. Annual tuition: full-time resident $3574, nonresident $13,590; per credit resident $149, nonresident $566. Enrollment: full-time 160, part-time 58. Faculty: full-time 35, part-time 2. Degrees conferred: M.B.A., M.S., Ph.D.

ADMISSION REQUIREMENTS. Two transcripts, GMAT, current resume, three letters of recommendation (four letters for Ph.D.), and typewritten essay (personal statement for Ph.D.). TOEFL required for international applicants. All applicants required to have two or more years work experience, one semester of college calculus and must appear for personal interview (no interview for M.S.). Apply to Director of Graduate Student Services by April 1. Application fee $40, $60 for international students. Phone: (303)492-1831; fax: (303)492-1727.

ADMISSION STANDARDS. Competitive. Minimum average 3.2 (A = 4) for master's programs. Selective for Ph.D., minimum average 3.3. GMAT: 590 M.S. and M.B.A., 650 Ph.D.

FINANCIAL AID. Limited to Federal W/S, loans. Apply to the Financial Aid Office by May 1. Use FAFSA.

DEGREE REQUIREMENTS. For M.B.A.: 52 semester hours. For M.S.: 24–30 semester hours; comprehensive exam. For Ph.D.: 60 semester hours minimum; comprehensive exam; research internship; dissertation; final oral exam.

FIELDS OF STUDY.
Accounting. M.S. only.
Finance. M.B.A., Ph.D.
Information Systems. Ph.D.
Marketing. M.B.A., Ph.D.
Operations Management. Ph.D.
Operations Research. Ph.D.
Organization Management. M.B.A. only.
Self-designed option. Includes entrepreneurial studies. M.B.A. only.
Taxation. M.S. only.
Technology and Innovation Management. M.B.A. only.
Note: Joint programs available with the School of Law and College of Engineering.

School of Law (80309-0403)

Organized 1892. Semester System. Library 301,000 volumes. Library has LEXIS, NEXIS, WESTLAW, LEGISLATE. Special facilities: Natural Resources Law Center, Indian Law Clinic, National Wildlife Federation's Natural Resources Litigation Clinic. Annual tuition: resident $4286, nonresident $14,742. On-campus housing available for single and married students. Apply to University Housing Office. Total average cost for all other expenses: $9500.

Enrollment: first-year class 170, full-time 480 (men 58%, women 42%); no part-time study. Faculty: full-time 32, part-time 34. Degrees conferred: J.D., J.D.-M.B.A., J.D.-M.P.H.

ADMISSION REQUIREMENTS. LSDAS Law School report, two transcripts, LSAT, recommendations required in support of application. Applicants must have received bachelor's prior to admission. Accepts 5–10 transfer applicants each year. Graduates of unaccredited colleges not considered. Apply to School by February 15. Entering students admitted Fall only. Application fee $40. Phone: (303)492-3084.

ADMISSION STANDARDS. Selective. Accepts 20% of total annual applicants.

FINANCIAL AID. Scholarships, grants-in-aid, Federal W/S, loans; research assistantships for advanced students only. For best aid packages apply by January 1. Financial Aid deadline, April 1. Use FAFSA. About 20% of students receive aid other than loans from School. Priority given to state residents.

DEGREE REQUIREMENTS. For J.D.: 6 semesters minimum; 89 semester hours; advanced standing for work completed at other approved law schools. For M.B.A., M.P.A.: see Graduate School listing above.

School of Medicine (80262)

Opened 1883. Located in Denver at the University Health Science Center. Medical library 100,000 volumes.

Annual tuition: resident $10,621, nonresident $49,849, student fees $1529. No student housing. Total average figure for all other expenses: $8500.

Enrollment: first-year class 131 (10 EDP), total 525 (men 59%, women 41%). Faculty: full-time 1200, part-time volunteers 2000. Degree conferred: M.D. The M.S. and Ph.D. (medical) are offered through the Graduate School.

ADMISSION REQUIREMENTS. AMCAS report, transcripts, MCAT, letters of recommendation required in support of application. Interviews for final selections. Applicants must have completed 120 semester hours of college study. Accepts transfer applicants. Preference given to residents of Colorado, Wyoming and Montana. Has EDP; apply between June 15 and August 1. Apply to Office of Admissions and Records of School after June 15, before November 15. Application fee $50. Phone: (303)270-7361; fax: (303)270-8494.

ADMISSION STANDARDS. Competitive. Accepts 15% of total annual applicants. Approximately 85% are state residents.

FINANCIAL AID. Scholarships, grants, loans. Apply by May 31 to the Associate Dean. Phone: (303)270-8364. About 50% of students receive aid other than loans from College.

DEGREE REQUIREMENTS. For M.D.: satisfactory completion of four-year program. For M.S., Ph.D.: See Graduate Division listing above.

FIELDS OF GRADUATE STUDY.
Biochemistry.
Cell Biology.
Developmental Biology.
Genetics.
Immunology.
Molecular Biology.
Neurosciences.
Pharmacology.
Physiology.
Public Health.

School of Dentistry (80262)

Established 1967. Located at University Health Science Center. Annual tuition: resident $6980, nonresident $23,668. Off-campus housing only. Average academic year housing costs: $10,740. Average first-year academic costs: $8730.

Enrollment: first-year class 35; total 140 (men 70%, women 30%). Degree conferred: D.D.S.

ADMISSION REQUIREMENTS. AADSAS, official transcripts, DAT (no later than October), two letters of recommendation required in support of School's application. Applicant must have completed at least three years of study; prefer four years of study. Interview by invitation. Accepts transfer applicants. Preference given to state residents and WICHE participating states. Graduates of unaccredited colleges not considered. Apply after June 1, before January 1 to Admission Committee, Room C-284. Application fee $35. Phone: (303)270-7259.

ADMISSION STANDARDS. Competitive. Admits about 15–20% of total annual applications. Approximately 60% are state residents.

FINANCIAL AID. Scholarships, grants, tuition waivers, loans. Apply to Director, Student Financial Aid Office of Medical Center after acceptance. Phone: (303)270-8364. About 91% of students receive some aid from School and outside sources. Reduced tuition for residents who will upon graduation practice in underserved areas of Colorado.

DEGREE REQUIREMENTS. For D.D.S.: satisfactory completion of forty-five-month program.

COLUMBIA UNIVERSITY
New York, New York 10027
http://www.columbia.edu/

Founded 1754. Coed. Private control, Semester system. Special facilities: Institute of Nutrition Sciences, Lamont Geological Observatory, Russian Institute, East Asian Institute, Institute on Western Europe, Middle East Institute, Institute on East Central Europe, Institute of African Studies, Institute of Latin American and Iberian Studies, Nevis Synchrocyclotron Laboratory, Armstrong Field Laboratories for Microwave Research, Cooperative Industrial Reactor Laboratories, Institute of Administrative Research, Institute of Field Studies, Institute of Psychological Research, Horace Mann-Lincoln Institute of School Experimentation, Institute of Research and Service in Nursing Education, Institute of Language Arts, Curriculum Service Center, Evaluation and Measurement Service Center, Institute of Higher Education, Institute of Educational Technology, Institute of Philosophy and Politics of Education, Institute of the Education of the Handicapped, Nevis Biological Station, Columbia Radiation Laboratory. University libraries have more than 4,000,000 volumes, 3,388,000 microforms.

On-campus housing for married students, 611 graduate men, 391 graduate women. Average annual housing cost: $6000–$8000 for married students, $2500–$5500 for single students. Apply to Livingston Hall (on-campus housing for single and married students), to Housing Office for off-campus housing information. Phone: (212)854-3923.

Graduate School of Arts and Sciences

Graduate study since 1880. Annual tuition: full-time $21,132. Enrollment: full-time 3200, part-time 100. Faculty: full- and part-time 700. Degrees conferred: M.A., M. Phil., Ph.D.

ADMISSION REQUIREMENTS. Transcripts, GRE General/Subject Tests, three letters of recommendation required in support of School's application. TOEFL required for international applicants from non-English-speaking countries. Interview not required. Accepts transfer applicants. Graduates of unaccredited institutions not considered. Apply to Graduate School of Arts and Sciences Office of Admissions by January 3 (for priority consideration for both admissions and Financial Aid) April 30 for regular consideration (Fall). Application fee $60. Phone: (212)854-4737; fax: (212)854-2863.

ADMISSION STANDARDS. Very competitive for some departments, competitive or very selective for the others. Usual minimum average: 3.0 (A = 4).

FINANCIAL AID. Annual awards from institutional funds: 466 scholarships, 347 fellowships (80 available for entering students), 488 teaching assistantships, 943 research assistantships, Federal W/S, loans. Apply by the first Monday in January (for priority consideration) to Office of Student Affairs for scholarships and fellowships. Use FAFSA. Phone: (212)854-3808. About 90% of students receive aid other than loans from University and outside sources. Aid usually not available to part-time students.

DEGREE REQUIREMENTS. For M.A.: Two semesters minimum in full-time residence; reading knowledge of one foreign language for some departments; essay required by many departments. For M.Phil.: essentially the same as Ph.D., except no dissertation requirement. For Ph.D.: six semesters minimum beyond the master's in full-time residence; reading knowledge of two foreign languages; qualifying exam; dissertation; final oral exam.

FIELDS OF STUDY.
American Studies.
Anatomy and Cell Biology.
Ancient Studies.
Anthropology. Includes interdisciplinary programs in applied anthropology (Ph.D. only), ecology, medical anthropology.
Applied Mathematics.
Applied Physics.
Art History and Archaeology.
Astronomy.
Biochemistry and Molecular Biophysics.
Biological Sciences.
Biostatistics.
Chemical Engineering, Material Science and Mining Engineering.
Chemical Physics. Ph.D. only.
Chemistry.
Civil Engineering and Engineering Mechanics.
Classics.
Computer Science.
East Asian Languages and Cultures. Includes Chinese, Japanese, Korean, Buddhist Studies.
Economics.
Electrical Engineering.
Engineering. Ph.D. only. The M.S., D.Eng.Sc., professional degrees are under the jurisdiction of the School of Engineering and Applied Science.
English and Comparative Literature.
Epidemiology.
French and Romance Philology.
Genetics and Development.
Geological Sciences.
Germanic Languages.
History.
Industrial Engineering and Operations Research.
Italian.
Mathematics.
Mechanical Engineering.
Microbiology.
Middle East and Asian Languages and Cultures. Includes Akkadian, Caucasian, Iranian, Turkic.
Music.
Neurobiology and Behavior.
Nutrition.
Pathology.
Pharmacology.
Philosophy.
Physics.
Physiology and Cellular Biophysics.
Political Science.
Psychology.
Religion.
Slavic Languages.
Sociology.
Sociomedical Sciences.
South Asian Studies.
Spanish and Portuguese.
Statistics.

School of the Arts
http://www.columbia.edu/cu/arts/

Established 1965. Annual tuition: full-time $21,132, per credit $704. Enrollment: full-time 545, Faculty: full-time 36, part-time 69. Degrees conferred: M.F.A., D.M.A.

ADMISSION REQUIREMENTS. Transcripts, portfolio or samples of work, audition/interview (depending upon major), at least three years of relevant professional experience required in support of application. TOEFL required for international applicants. Accepts transfer applicants. Apply to Office of the Dean for Admission and Financial Aid, 305 Dodge Hall. Application deadlines vary, depending on field of study. Fall and Spring admissions, except in Painting and Sculpture (Fall only). Application fee $60. Phone: (212)854-2134.

ADMISSION STANDARDS. Competitive or very competitive. Usual minimum average: 3.25 (A = 4).

FINANCIAL AID. Tuition waivers, twelve research assistantships, forty teaching assistantships, Federal W/S, loans. Apply by February 7. Use FAFSA. Phone: (212)854-2875. About 80% of students receive aid other than loans from School and outside sources.

DEGREE REQUIREMENTS. For M.F.A.: 60 credit program, four semesters in full-time residence; program by advisement; final project or thesis project. For D.M.A.: usually six semesters beyond the bachelor's or 30 credits beyond the M.F.A., at least four semesters in residence; final project/dissertation.

FIELDS OF STUDY.
Acting.
Arts Administration.
Directing.
Dramaturgy.
Drawing.
Film. M.F.A.
Painting and Sculpture. M.F.A. only.
Theater Arts. M.F.A.
Writing. Includes fiction, nonfiction, poetry. M.F.A. only.
Note: Joint J.D.-M.F.A. program in Entertainment Law.

Graduate School of Business

Annual tuition: $23,830. Trimester system. Graduate study only. Enrollment: full-time 1283 (men 880, women 403); no part-time students. Faculty: full-time 99, part-time 76. Degrees conferred; M.B.A., Ph.D.

ADMISSION REQUIREMENTS. Transcripts, one letter of reference for M.B.A. applicants, two letters for Ph.D. applicants, GMAT required in support of School's application. Interview not required. TOEFL required for international applicants. Graduates of unaccredited institutions not considered. Apply by February 1 to the Dean of Admissions and Financial Aid. Application fee: M.B.A. $75, Ph.D. $80. Phone: (212)854-6083; fax: (212)932-2545.

ADMISSION STANDARDS. Competitive. Usual minimum average: 3.3 (M.B.A.), 3.5 (Ph.D.) (A = 4).

FINANCIAL AID. Scholarships, Ph.D. fellowships, research/teaching assistantships, Federal W/S, loans. M.B.A. candidates apply by February 15 (Fall, Summer), November 15 (Spring) to Office of Admissions; Ph.D. candidates by March 1 (Fall) to Office of Doctoral Studies. Use FAFSA and University's FAF. About 40% of M.B.A. and 100% of Ph.D. students receive aid other than loans from School and outside sources.

DEGREE REQUIREMENTS. For M.B.A.: 20 courses minimum, noncredit course in personal computing. For Ph.D.: 20 courses minimum, at least 10 courses in residence; reading knowledge of one foreign language; research paper; preliminary written exams; oral qualifying exam; dissertation and defense.

FIELDS OF STUDY.
Accounting.
Business Economics and Public Policy.
Corporate Relations and Public Affairs.
Executive Management.
Finance and Economics.
Human Resource Management.
International Business.
Management of Organizations.
Management Science.
Marketing.
Money and Financial Markets.
Operations Management.
Production and Operations Management.
Public and Nonprofit Management.

School of Engineering and Applied Science— Graduate Division

Special facilities: Center for Advanced Technology in Computers and Information Systems, Center for Telecommunications Research, Microelectronics Sciences Laboratories, Schapiro Center for Engineering and Physical Science Research.

Annual tuition: full-time $22,700, per credit $696. On-campus housing available. See housing information above. Enrollment: full-time 475, part-time 261. Faculty: full-time 100, part-time 20. Degrees conferred: M.S., Eng., Sc.D., Ph.D., Prof. Engr.

ADMISSION REQUIREMENTS. Official transcripts, two letters of recommendation required in support of School's application. GRE required in most programs. TOEFL required for international applicants. Accept transfer applicants. Graduates of unaccredited institutions not considered. Apply to Office of Engineering Admissions by January 1 (Fall), October 1 (Spring). Application fee $45. Phone: (212)854-2931.

ADMISSION STANDARDS. Very selective. Usual minimum average: 3.0 (A = 4).

FINANCIAL AID. Annual awards from institutional funds: 90 scholarships, 26 fellowships, 168 research assistantships, 89 teaching assistantships, Federal W/S, loans. Approved for VA benefits. Apply by January 15 (Fall) to Office of Admission of the School for scholarships, fellowships, assistantships; to the Office of Financial Aid for all other programs. Use FAFSA. Phone: (212) 854-3442.

DEGREE REQUIREMENTS. For master's: 30 semester hours of approved graduate courses beyond the bachelor's; thesis at discretion of department or division program. For Eng.Sc.D.: 30 semester hours of approved graduate courses beyond the master's, or residence units beyond the bachelor's; foreign language proficiency at discretion of department/division; departmental qualifying exam; thesis and research required. For Ph.D.: see Graduate School of Arts and Sciences listing above.

FIELDS OF STUDY.
Applied Chemistry.
Applied Physics. Includes applied mathematics, medical physics, plasma physics, quantum electronics, solid state physics.
Bioengineering.
Chemical Engineering.
Civil Engineering.
Computer Science.
Electrical Engineering.
Environmental Control Engineering.
Industrial Engineering.
Materials Science.
Mechanical Engineering.
Mechanics.
Metallurgical Engineering.
Mineral Engineering.
Nuclear Engineering.
Operations Research.
Solid State Science and Engineering.

School of International and Public Affairs and the Regional Institutes

Established 1946. Graduate study only. Annual tuition: full-time $21,910; per credit $913.

Enrollment: full- and part-time 650. Faculty: full-time 134. Degrees conferred: M.I.A., M.P.A.

ADMISSION REQUIREMENTS. Transcripts, three letters of recommendation required in support of School's application. GRE recommended. TOEFL required for international applicants. Graduates of unaccredited institutions not considered. Apply to Office of University Admission, Low Memorial Library, by January 15. Application fee $65. Phone: (212)854-4737.

ADMISSION STANDARDS. Competitive. Usual minimum average: 3.5 (A = 4).

FINANCIAL AID. Annual awards from institutional funds: fellowships, assistantships, Federal W/S, and career-related internships. Apply by January 15 to Director of Admissions of the School. Use FAFSA. About 35% of students receive aid other than loans from School.

DEGREE REQUIREMENTS. For M.I.A., M.P.A.: 54 credits minimum, at least 30 in residence; proficiency in one foreign language; thesis.

FIELDS OF STUDY.

REGIONAL STUDIES:
African Studies.
East Asian.
East Central Europe.
Latin American and Iberian Studies.
Middle East.
Russia CIS.
Southern Asian.
Uralic Studies.
Western Europe.

FUNCTIONAL SPECIALIZATIONS:
Economic and Political Developments.
Environmental Policy Studies.
Human Rights and Humanitarian Affairs.
International Economic Policy.
International Finance and Business.
International Media and Communications.
International Security Policy.

Graduate School of Journalism

Established 1912. Annual tuition: $20,130. Graduate study only. Enrollment: full-time 180, part-time 15. Faculty: full-time 19, part-time 78. Degree conferred: M.S.

ADMISSION REQUIREMENTS. Official transcripts, up to three letters of recommendation, essays required in support of School's application. TOEFL required for international applicants. Transfer applicants not considered. Graduates of unaccredited institutions not considered. Apply to Office of Journalism Admissions by December 15. Application fee $60. Phone: (212)854-3828.

ADMISSION STANDARDS. Competitive. Decisions based on professional promise, academic excellence and writing test.

FINANCIAL AID. Annual awards from institutional funds: 100 scholarships, loans, on- and off-campus employment. Apply to Office of Journalism Admissions. Use FAFSA. Phone: (212)854-3829. About 80% of students receive aid from School and outside sources.

DEGREE REQUIREMENTS. For M.S.: 30 credits minimum; major paper or tape of publishable or broadcast quality.

FIELD OF STUDY.
Journalism. Include news-editorial in all print and broadcast aspects of professional journalism.

School of Public Health.
http://cpmcnet.columbia.edu/dept/sph/

Graduate study since 1921. Semester system.
Annual tuition: full-time $19,890; per credit $663.
Enrollment: full-time 269, part-time 345. Faculty: full-time 86, part-time 206. Degrees conferred: M.P.H., Executive M.P.H., M.S., Dr.P.H. The Ph.D. is administered by the Graduate Faculties.

ADMISSION REQUIREMENTS. Official transcripts, GRE or another appropriate objective test required in support of School's application. Interview sometimes required. M.P.H. or equivalent master's, internship required for Dr.P.H. applicants. TOEFL required for international applicants. Accepts transfer applicants. Graduates of unaccredited institutions not considered. Apply to Office of Admissions of the School before April 15 (Fall), November 15 (Spring). Application fee $60. Phone: (212)305-3927, Fax: (212)305-6450.

ADMISSION STANDARDS. Competitive. Usual minimum average: 3.0 (A = 4).

FINANCIAL AID. Assistantships, traineeships, Federal W/S, loans. Apply to Financial Aid Office; no specified closing date. Use FAFSA. Phone: (212)305-4113; fax: (212)305-6450. About 50% of students receive aid from all sources.

DEGREE REQUIREMENTS. For M.P.H.: 45 credits minimum, at least one year in residence; practicum. For M.S.: 21-month program minimum, at least one year in residence. For Dr.P.H.: 2-year program minimum, at least one year in residence; comprehensive exam; dissertation; final oral exam. For Ph.D.: see Graduate Faculties listing above.

FIELDS OF STUDY.
Biostatistics.
Environmental Health Sciences.
Epidemiology.
Health Policy and Management.
Population and Family Health.
Sociomedical Sciences.

School of Social Work

Annual tuition: Full-time $17,220; per credit $547. On-campus housing available. See Housing listing above. Enrollment: full-time 595, part-time 139 (men 15%, women 85%). Faculty: full-time 44, part-time 53. Degrees conferred: M.S.S.W., D.S.W.

ADMISSION REQUIREMENTS. Official transcripts, three letters of reference, required in support of School's application. Interviews sometimes requested by School. TOEFL required for international applicants. Accepts transfer applicants. Especially interested in minority group applicants. Apply to Office of Admissions by February 15 (Fall) for full-time; September 1 (Fall) for part-time. Full-time Students admitted Fall only Application fee $50. Phone: (212)954-2856; fax: (212)854-2975.

ADMISSION STANDARDS. Selective. Usual minimum average: 3.0 (A = 4).

FINANCIAL AID. Annual awards from institutional funds: scholarships, teaching assistantships, internships, Federal W/S, loans. Apply by June 15 (Fall) to Office of Admissions. Use FAFSA. No aid for part-time students. About 60% of students receive aid from School and outside sources.

DEGREE REQUIREMENTS. For M.S.S.W: 60 credits minimum. For D.S.W: 30 credits minimum beyond the master's, at least two consecutive terms in full-time residence; preliminary exam; dissertation; final oral/written exam.

FIELDS OF STUDY.

Generalist Social Work Practice.
Organizing, Planning, and Management.
Services to Individuals, Families, and Groups.
Note: Joint degree programs with Jewish Theological Seminary of America; Bank Street College of Education.

Teachers College

Founded 1887. Graduate study only. Affiliated with the University since 1898 and is designated the Graduate Faculty of Education. Semester system. Special facilities: Center for Health Promotion, Center for Infants and Parents, Institute for Urban and Minority Education, Institute of Higher Education, Institute of Philosophy and Politics of Education, Institute for Learning Technologies, Institute for Education and Economy, International Center for Cooperation and Conflict Resolution, Center for the Study and Education of the Gifted, Institute of International Education, Center for Community Colleges, Center for Nursing Leadership Development, National Center for Restructuring Education, Schools and Teaching, Institute of Research and Service in Nursing Education. Milbank Library houses the largest American collection on education, psychology, and health services.

Tuition: per credit $580.

Enrollment: full-time 1797, part-time 2751 (men 30%, women 70%). Faculty: full-time 123, part-time 381. Degrees conferred: M.A., M.S., Ed.M., Sixth-Year Professional Diploma, Ed.D., Ph.D.

ADMISSION REQUIREMENTS. Official transcripts, personal statement, two letters of recommendation required in support of application. Interview, GRE/MAT required by some departments. TOEFL required for international applicants. Accepts transfer applicants. Graduates of unaccredited institutions not considered. Apply to Teachers College Admissions Office by February 1 (Fall, for some programs and scholarships), July 1 (Fall), December 15 (Spring), April 15 (Summer). Application fee $50. Phone: (212)678-3710; fax: (212)678-4171.

ADMISSION STANDARDS. Competitive for most departments, very competitive for the others. Usual minimum average: 3.0 (A = 4).

FINANCIAL AID. Annual awards from institutional funds: 670 scholarships, 25 teaching fellowships, 80 research assistantships, Tuition Assistance Awards, Federal W/S, loans. Apply by February 1 to appropriate department chair for assistantships, scholarships, fellowships; to Director of Student Aid of the College for all other programs. Use FAFSA. Phone: (212)678-3714. About 25% of students receive aid other than loans from College and outside sources.

DEGREE REQUIREMENTS. For M.A., M.S.: 30 credits minimum, at least one year in residence; thesis or essay. For Ed.M.: 60 credits minimum, at least 30 in residence. For Ed.D.: 90 credits minimum beyond the bachelor's, at least 45 in residence; certification exam; dissertation; final oral/written exam. For Sixth-Year Diploma: 60 semester hours beyond bachelor's; research project. For Ph.D.: 75 credits minimum beyond the bachelor's, at least 45 in residence; certification exam; Proficiency in foreign languages for some programs; dissertation; final oral/written exam.

FIELDS OF STUDY.

DIVISION OF EDUCATIONAL INSTITUTIONS:
Adult Education.
Behavior Disorders.
College Teaching and Academic Leadership.
Community College Education.
Curriculum and Teaching.
Early Childhood Education.
Early Childhood Special Education.

Educational Administration.
Elementary Education.
Family and Community Education.
Higher Education.
Secondary Education.
Special Education. Includes hearing impaired, behaviorally disturbed, emotionally disturbed, gifted, learning disabled, mentally retarded, physically handicapped, visually impaired, administration and supervision.
Student Personnel Administration.

DIVISION OF HEALTH SERVICES, SCIENCES, AND EDUCATION:
Health Education.
Nursing, Executive Role.
Nursing, Nonexecutive Roles.
Nutrition Education.
Nutrition Education and Public Health Nutrition.

DIVISION OF INSTRUCTION:
Applied Linguistics.
Applied Physiology.
Art Education.
Bilingual and Bicultural Education.
Communication, Computing, and Technology in Education.
Dance Education.
Educational Media/Instructional Technology.
English Education.
Mathematics Education.
Motor Learning.
Music Education.
Physical Education.
Science Education.
Social Studies Education.
TESOL.
Teaching of Spanish.

DIVISION OF PHILOSOPHY, THE SOCIAL SCIENCES, AND EDUCATION:
Anthropology.
Comparative and International Education.
Economics.
Educational Policy.
History in Education.
International Educational Development.
Philosophy of Education.
Politics in Education.
Religious Education.
Sociology.

DIVISION OF PSYCHOLOGY AND EDUCATION:
Applied Educational Psychology.
Audiology.
Clinical Psychology.
Counseling Psychology.
Developmental Psychology.
Educational Measurement and Evaluation.
Educational Psychology.
Neurosciences and Education.
Organizational Psychology.
Psychology in Education.
School Psychology.
Social Psychology.
Speech-Language Pathology.

School of Law

Established 1858. Semester system. Law library 1,262,000 volumes. Special facilities: Center for Chinese Legal Studies, Center for Japanese Legal Studies.

Annual tuition: full-time $24,353. Total average for all other expenses: $11,650. Enrollment: first-year class 337; total full-time 1050 (men 50%, women 50%). Faculty: full-time 68, part-time 37. Degrees conferred: J.D., LL.M., J.S.D.

ADMISSION REQUIREMENTS. For J.D. program: LSDAS report, transcripts, LSAT required in support of application. Interview not required. Accepts transfer applicants. Apply to Law Admissions Office after September 1, before February 15. Application fee $65. Phone: (212)854-2670. For graduate program: transcripts required in support of application. Apply to Office of Graduate Legal Studies of the School by January 15. Fall admission only. Accepts full-time students only. Application fee $65. Phone: (212)854-2670.

ADMISSION STANDARDS. Competitive. Accepts about 15% of total annual applicants.

FINANCIAL AID. For J.D. program: scholarships, fellowships, assistantships, Federal W/S, apply for financial aid at time of application for admission, but before March 1. Use FAFSA. For graduate program: apply for fellowships by March 1 to Office of Graduate Legal Studies of the School. About 40% of students receive aid other than loans from School.

DEGREE REQUIREMENTS. For J.D.: satisfactory completion of three-year program; 83 credits. For LL.M.: 24 credits minimum, at least one year in residence. For J.S.D.: at least one year in residence; dissertation; oral exam.

FIELDS OF GRADUATE STUDY.
Civil Procedure.
Commercial Law.
Constitutional Law.
Corporation Securities Law.
Criminal Law.
Government Service.
Human Rights Law.
International Law.
Labor Law.
Legal History.
Legal Philosophy.
Property.
Taxation.
Note: School has joint programs with the Graduate Schools of the Arts, Arts and Sciences, Business, Journalism, International Affairs, Social Work; programs in Public Affairs, Urban Planning, with Princeton University's Woodrow Wilson School of Public and International Affairs.

College of Physicians and Surgeons

Established 1767. Annual tuition: $25,154. Enrollment: first-year class 150; total 600 (men 60%, women 40%). Housing available. Total average figure for all other expenses $10,200. College faculty: full-time 800, part-time 900. Degrees conferred: M.D., M.D.-M.S., M.D.-M.P.H., M.D.-Ph.D. The M.S. and Ph.D. are offered through Graduate Faculties. Graduate study, Medical Scientist Training Program.

ADMISSION REQUIREMENTS. Transcripts, MCAT, recommendations required in support of application. Interview may be required. Applicants must have completed at least three years of college study. Does not have EDP. Apply to Office of the Dean of the College after June 15, before October 15. Application fee $65. Phone: (212)305-3595.

ADMISSION STANDARDS. Very competitive. Accepts 8% of total annual applicants. Approximately 32% are state residents.

FINANCIAL AID. Scholarships, loans. Apply after acceptance. Phone: (212)305-4100. About 68% of students receive some aid from institutional funds.

DEGREE REQUIREMENTS. For M.D.: satisfactory completion of four-year program. For M.S., M.P.H., Ph.D.: see Graduate Faculties listing above.

FIELDS OF GRADUATE STUDY.
Acute Adult Care.
Acute Pediatrics.
Anatomy.
Biochemistry.
Biomedical Sciences.
Biostatistics.
Cell Biology.
Epidemiology.
Genetics and Development.
Geriatrics and Gerontology.
Microbiology.
Neurology and Behavior.
Neurosciences.
Pathobiology
Pathology.
Pharmacology-Toxicology.
Physiology and Cellular Biology.

School of Dental and Oral Surgery

Established 1852. Private control. Semester system. Annual tuition: full-time $25,000. Off-campus housing only. Average academic year housing costs: $11,100. Total average cost for all first-year expenses $5460.

Enrollment: D.D.S. program, first-year class 70 (men 50%, women 50%) full-time 280, none part-time; postgraduate program, full-time 48, part-time 4. Faculty: full-time 39, part-time 4. Degrees conferred: D.D.S., D.D.S.-M.P.H., D.D.S.-M.S. (Health Care Management), D.D.S.-M.A. (Education).

ADMISSION REQUIREMENTS. AADSAS, official transcripts, three letters of recommendation, DAT required in support of School's application. Interview by invitation only. Applicants must have completed at least three years of college study. Graduates of unaccredited institutions not considered. Does not have EDP. Apply to Director of Student Affairs of the School after July 1, before March 1. Application fee $50. Phone: (212)305-3478.

ADMISSION STANDARDS. Very competitive. Accepts about 20% of total annual applicants. Approximately 60% are state residents.

FINANCIAL AID. Scholarships, grants, tuition waivers, loans. Apply to Director of Student Affairs of the School. Use FAFSA and GAPSFAS. Phone: (212)305-4100. No specified closing date. About 96% of students receive aid other than loans from School and outside sources.

DEGREE REQUIREMENTS. For D.D.S.: satisfactory completion of forty-five-month program.

COLUMBUS STATE UNIVERSITY
Columbus, Georgia 31907-5645

Founded in 1963. Public control. Coed. Quarter system. Library 242,000 volumes, 742,000 microforms, 1400 current periodicals, 36 PCs.

Annual tuition: full-time resident $1845, nonresident $5724; per credit, resident $82, nonresident $190. Limited on-campus housing for single students only. Average academic year housing costs: $3255–$3660. Contact Office of Residential Life for both on- and off-campus housing information. Phone: (706)568-2026.

Graduate Studies

Graduate program since 1973. Enrollment: full-time 345, part-time 409 (men 35%, women 65%). Faculty: full-time 53, part-time 23. Degrees Conferred: M.B.A., M.Ed., M.M., M.S.A., Ed.S.

ADMISSION REQUIREMENTS. Transcripts, GRE/MAT/GMAT required in support of application. Audition required for M.M. TOEFL/MTELP required for international applicants. Accepts transfer applicants. Graduates of unaccredited institutions not considered. Apply to Admissions Office before August 31 (Fall), November 30 (Winter), February 28 (Spring). Application fee $10. Phone: (706)568-2079; fax: (706)568-2462; E-mail: ccinfo@mercury.csg.peachnet.edu.

ADMISSION STANDARDS. Selective. Usual minimum average: 2.75 (A = 4).

FINANCIAL AID. Scholarships, thirty-four administrative assistantships, twenty-two internships, Federal W/S, loans. Approved for VA benefits. Apply to Director of Financial Aid before July 15. Use FAFSA. Phone: (706)568-2036, Fax: (706)568-2230. About 1% of students receive aid other than loans from University and outside sources.

DEGREE REQUIREMENTS. For M.Ed., M.M.: 60 quarter credit hours minimum, at least 45 in residence. For M.B.A.: 60–80 quarter credit hours minimum, depending upon previous preparation; at least 45 quarter hours in residence. For M.S.A.: 60 quarter credit hours minimum, at least 45 in residence. For Ed.S.: at least 45 quarter hours beyond master's.

FIELDS OF STUDY.
Art Education.
Business Administration.
Criminal Justice and Criminology.
Early Childhood Education.
Educational Administration.
English Education.
Health Services Administration.
Leisure and Sport Fitness Management.
Mathematics Education.
Middle Grades Education.
Music Education.
Public Administration.
Reading.
Recreation.
Science Education.
Secondary Education. Includes biology, English, general science, history, mathematics, political science, social science.
Social Psychology.
Special Education. Includes behavioral disorders, learning disabilities, mental retardation.

CONCORDIA COLLEGE
Seward, Nebraska 68434-1599
http://www.ccsn.edu

Founded 1894. Located 20 miles NW of Lincoln. Coed. Private control, Lutheran-Missouri Synod. Semester system. Library: 165,000 volumes.

Tuition: per credit hour $115. On-campus housing for 200 graduate men, 200 graduate women, 30 married students. Housing cost: (2½-week session) $120. Apply to Student Life Office for on-campus information. Phone: (402)643-7411, for off-campus information (402)643-7239.

Graduate Studies

Enrollment: full-time 36, part-time 197. College faculty: full-time 40, part-time 8. Degrees conferred: M.Ed., M.S., M.P.Ed.

ADMISSION REQUIREMENTS. Transcripts, three letters of recommendations, MAT required in support of College's application. TOEFL required for international applicants. Interview not required. Accepts transfer applicants. Graduates of unaccredited institutions not considered. Apply to Director of Admissions by June 1 (Summer), August 1 (Fall). Application fee 15. Phone: (800)535-5494, Fax: (402)643-4073.

ADMISSION STANDARDS. Selective. Usual minimum average: 3.0 (last two years) (A = 4).

FINANCIAL AID. Eighty scholarships, Federal W/S, loans. Apply to Financial Aid Officer by April 15. Use FAFSA and College's FAF. Phone: (402)643-7270; fax: (402)643-4073.

DEGREE REQUIREMENTS. For M.Ed.: 36 credit hours minimum, at least 24 residence; thesis option; final written/oral exam.

FIELDS OF STUDY.
Family Life Ministry.
Parish Education.
Teacher Education. Includes early childhood, elementary, administration, reading.

CONCORDIA UNIVERSITY
River Forest, Illinois 60305-1499

Founded 1864. Located 10 miles W of Chicago. Coed. Private control, Lutheran-Missouri Synod. Quarter system. Library: 164,000 volumes, 460,000 microforms, 21 PC workstations.

Tuition: per hour $236. On-campus housing available. Annual housing cost: $4443 (includes board). Apply to Director of Housing for on- and off-campus housing information. Phone: (708)209-3006. Day-care facilities available.

School of Graduate Studies

Enrollment: full- and part-time 1100. College faculty: full-time 57, part-time 30. Degrees conferred: M.A., C.A.S.

ADMISSION REQUIREMENTS. Transcripts, recommendations, GRE required in support of University's application. TOEFL required for international applicants. Interview not required. Accepts transfer applicants. Graduates of unaccredited institutions not considered. Apply to Dean of the School of Graduate Studies; no specified closing dates. Rolling admissions process. Application fee, none. Phone: (708)209-4093; fax: (708)209-3176.

ADMISSION STANDARDS. Selective. Usual minimum average 2.85 (A = 4).

FINANCIAL AID. Annual awards from institutional funds: five scholarships, thirty-four assistantships, Federal W/S, loans. Apply by April 1 to Dean of Graduate Studies. Use FAFSA. About 45% of students receive aid other than loans from School and outside sources. Aid sometimes available to part-time students.

DEGREE REQUIREMENTS. For M.A.: 48 quarter hours minimum, at least 39 in residence; research project optional; final written/oral exam. For C.A.S.: 48 quarter hours beyond master's.

FIELDS OF STUDY.
Church Music.
Curriculum and Instruction.
Early Childhood Education.
Gerontology.
Human Services.
Mathematics Education.

Music Education.
Psychology.
Reading Instruction.
School Administration.
School Counseling.
Supervision of Instruction.
Theology and Education.
Note: Programs in school administration, supervision of instruction, special education, school counseling, and reading lead to Illinois Certification by entitlement.

CONNECTICUT COLLEGE
New London, Connecticut 06320-4196

Founded 1911. Located 40 miles W of Providence, R.I. Coed. Private control. Semester system. Day-care facilities available. Library: 460,000 volumes, 277,000 microforms, 1400 current periodicals.

Tuition per course: $880. No on-campus housing for graduate students. Contact Office of Continuing Education. Phone: (203)439-2060.

Graduate Studies

Enrollment: full-time 20, part-time 61. College faculty: full-time 143, part-time 9. Degrees conferred: M.A., M.A.T.

ADMISSION REQUIREMENTS. Official transcripts, interview, three references required in support of application. GRE or MAT for some programs. TOEFL required for international applicants. Accepts transfer applicants. Graduates of unaccredited colleges not considered. Apply to Graduate Studies Program by February 1 (Fall) for Psychology; for other programs March 15 (Fall), October 15 (Spring). Rolling admission process. Application fee $40. Phone: (203)439-2060.

ADMISSION STANDARDS. Competitive. Usual minimum average: 3.0 (A = 4).

FINANCIAL AID. Limited to five teaching assistantships, Federal W/S, loans. Apply to Office of Financial Aid; no specified closing date. Phone: (203)439-2057. Use FAFSA and Connecticut College FAF.

DEGREE REQUIREMENTS. For M.A.: 9–12 semester courses minimum (32 credits), at least 5 courses in residence. Thesis usually required and counted as 2-semester course; final comprehensive exam when thesis is not required; reading knowledge of one foreign language for some majors. For M.A.T.: 8 or 9 semester courses minimum, at least 5 courses in residence.

FIELDS OF STUDY.
Botany.
Chemistry.
Child Development.
Classics.
Dance.
Economics.
English.
French.
Human Relations.
International Relations.
Mathematics.
Music. Includes performance.
Physics.
Psychology. GRE Subject for admission.
Religious Studies.
Secondary Education. Includes English, history-social studies, French, German, Spanish, Italian, mathematics, biology, chemistry, general science, physics.

Theater.
Urban Studies.
Zoology.

THE UNIVERSITY OF CONNECTICUT
Box U-6-A
Storrs, Connecticut 06269

Founded 1881. Located 30 miles E of Hartford. The Schools of Law and Social Work are located in West Hartford; the Schools of Dental Medicine and Medicine are located at the University's Health Center in Farmington. Part-time evening M.B.A. programs offered at off-campus centers in Hartford and Stamford. Coed, State control. Semester system. Special facilities: Institute of Materials Science, Marine Science Institute, Institute of Water Resources, Institute of Social Inquiry. Library: 2,444,000 volumes, 2,465,000 items in microform, 131 PC workstations in all libraries.

Annual tuition/fees: maximum per semester, resident $4968, nonresident $12,910. On-campus housing limited. Average annual housing cost: $3688, board charges $2520. Apply to Division of Housing and Food Services, Housing Services Officer. Phone: (860)486-2926.

Graduate School

Graduate study since 1920. Enrollment: full-time 3332, part-time 2381 (men 50%, women 50%). University faculty: full-time 1150, part-time 48. Degrees conferred: M.A., M.S., M.B.A., M.M., M.P.A., M.F.A., M.P.H., M.Dent.Sc., M.S.W., D.M.A., Ph.D.

ADMISSION REQUIREMENTS. Transcripts, two or three letters of recommendation required in support of School's application. GRE Subject Tests required by many departments, recommended for all. TOEFL required for international students. Interview required by some departments. Accepts transfer applicants. Graduates of unaccredited institutions not considered. Apply to the Graduate Admissions Office by June 1 (Fall), November 1 (Spring); international applicants by April 1 (Fall), October 1 (Spring). Apply directly to professional schools, Application fee $40, international applicants $45. Phone: (860)486-3617.

ADMISSION STANDARDS. Selective for most departments. Usual minimum average: 3.0 (last 2 years) (A = 4).

FINANCIAL AID. Annual awards from institutional funds: scholarships, research fellowships, research assistantships, Federal W/S, loans. Apply by February 15 to appropriate department head on forms available from Graduate Admissions Office. Use FAFSA and institutional FAF. About 50% of students at Storrs receive aid other than loans from University and outside sources. Aid sometimes available to part-time students.

DEGREE REQUIREMENTS. For M.A., M.S.: 15 credits minimum plus thesis or 24 credits minimum without thesis; final written/oral exam. For M.B.A.: 57 credits, which may be reduced depending upon previous registration, at least 24 credits in residence; final written/oral exam. For M.S.W.: 60 credits minimum, at least one year in full-time residence; final paper and group project; final written/oral exam. For M.F.A.: 2 years' full-time study minimum; final project. For Ph.D.: 3 year's minimum beyond the bachelor's, at least one year in full-time residence; general exam.; final written/oral exam; dissertation.

FIELDS OF STUDY.
Adult and Vocational Education. Ph.D. only.
Agricultural and Resource Economics.
Allied Health.

Animal Science.
Anthropology.
Art.
Biobehavioral Science.
Biochemistry.
Biological Engineering. Interdisciplinary.
Biophysics.
Biotechnology. M.S. only.
Botany.
Business Administration. Full-time program at Storrs, part-time evening programs at Hartford and Stamford; GMAT for admission to Storrs program; September admission only; apply by March 15; M.B.A., Ph.D.
Cell Biology.
Chemical Engineering.
Chemistry.
Civil Engineering.
Communication Science.
Comparative Literature. Interdisciplinary.
Computer Science.
Curriculum and Instruction. Ph.D. only.
Dental Science. M.Dent.Sc. only.
Dramatic Arts. Includes acting, directing, designing, puppetry, history, and criticism. M.A., M.F.A.
Ecology.
Economics.
Education. Includes secondary, elementary, guidance, counseling and personnel, special education, administration, supervision and curriculum development, technical and industrial education, evaluation and measurements, foundations, educational psychology, professional higher education administration; GRE, MAT, STEP Writing Test required for admission to Ph.D.
Educational Administration. Ph.D. only.
Educational Psychology. Ph.D. only.
Electrical Engineering.
English. GRE Subject for admission; apply by May 1 (Fall), December 1 (Spring)
Entomology.
Environmental Engineering. Interdisciplinary.
Family Studies. Ph.D. only.
French.
Genetics.
Geography.
Geological Sciences. Includes geology, geophysics.
German.
History.
Human Development and Family Relations. M.A. only.
Instructional Media and Technology. Ph.D. only.
International Studies. M.A. only.
International Studies and Business Administration. M.A., M.B.A. only.
Italian.
Linguistics.
Materials Science. Interdisciplinary.
Mathematics.
Mechanical Engineering.
Medieval Studies. Interdisciplinary.
Metallurgy.
Microbiology.
Music. Audition during first semester of enrollment.
Natural Resources: Land, Water, and Air. M.S. only.
Nursing.
Nutritional Science.
Ocean Engineering. M.S. only.
Oceanography.
Pathobiology. D.V.M. for admission to comparative pathology major.
Pharmaceutical Sciences.
Philosophy.
Physics.
Physiology.

Plant Science.
Political Science.
Polymer Science.
Professional Higher Education Administration. Ph.D. only.
Psychology. GRE Subject, MAT for admission. M.A., Ph.D. only.
Public Affairs. M.P.A. only.
Public Health. M.P.H. only.
Social Work. Interviews required; offered in Hartford; M.S.W. only.
Sociology.
Sport and Leisure Studies. Ph.D. only.
Statistics.
Zoology.

School of Law

Founded in 1921. Semester system. Located in Hartford (06105-2296). Library 382,700 volumes. Library has LEXIS, NEXIS, WESTLAW.

Annual tuition and fees: full-time, resident $10,320, nonresident New England Higher Education Compact residents $15,482, other nonresidents $19,840; per credit resident $360, nonresident NEHEC $540, other nonresident $692. No on-campus housing information. Total average cost for all other expenses: $9450.

Enrollment: first-year class day 130, evening 70; full-time 422 (men 50%, women 50%), part-time 220. Faculty: full-time 42, part-time 51. Degrees conferred: J.D., J.D.-M.B.A., J.D.-M.P.A., J.D.-M.S.W., J.D.-M.L.S. (with Southern Connecticut State University), J.D.-M.A. (with Trinity College), LL.M.

ADMISSION REQUIREMENTS. LSDAS Law School report, bachelor's degree, transcript, LSAT, two letters of recommendation required in support of application. Interview not required. Accepts transfer applicants. Graduates of unaccredited colleges not considered. Apply to the Dean of Admissions after October 1, before March 1. Application fee: day or evening $30; day and evening $45. Phone: (203)241-4696.

ADMISSION STANDARDS. Selective. Accepts 20% of total day applicants; 25% of total evening applicants.

FINANCIAL AID. Scholarships, tuition remission, grants, loans. About 33% of students receive aid other than loans from School funds. Apply by March 1. Use FAFSA and school forms. No aid for part-time students.

DEGREE REQUIREMENTS. For J.D.: 86 semester hours minimum; advanced standing for work completed at other law school individually considered. For LL.M.: at least 24 credits beyond the J.D.

UNIVERSITY OF CONNECTICUT HEALTH CENTER
Farmington, Connecticut 06030

Coed. State control. Semester system. No on-campus housing available.

Graduate School

Annual tuition: full-time $4800, nonresident $12,274; per course, resident 800, nonresident $2079. Enrollment: full-time 100, part-time 40. Faculty: full-time 20, part-time 141. Degrees conferred: M.P.H., M.D.S., Ph.D.

ADMISSION REQUIREMENTS. Official transcripts, three letters of recommendation, GRE required in support of College's application. TOEFL required for international applicants. Interviews may be arranged. Accepts transfer applicants. Graduates of unaccredited institutions not considered. Apply to Office of Graduate Admissions by April 1. Rolling admission process. Application fee $25. Phone: (203)679-3150.

ADMISSION STANDARDS. Competitive. Usual minimum average: 3.0 (A = 4).

FINANCIAL AID. Fellowships, research assistantships, teaching assistantships, tuition waivers, Federal W/S, loans. Approved for VA benefits. Apply by April 1 to the office of the Graduate School for fellowships, assistantships; to the Financial Aid Office for all other programs. Use FAFSA. Aid available to part-time students.

DEGREE REQUIREMENTS. For M.D.S.: 30 credit hours, at least 24 in residence; thesis/nonthesis option. For M.P.H.: 36 credit hours minimum, at least 30 in residence; thesis. For Ph.D.: 60 credit hours minimum beyond the bachelor's, 30 credit hours in full-time residency; qualifying exam; dissertation defense.

FIELDS OF STUDY.
Cell Biology. Ph.D.
Dental Science. M.D.S.
Immunology. Ph.D.
Molecular and Cellular Pharmacology. Ph.D.
Molecular Biology and Biochemistry. Ph.D.
Neuroscience. Ph.D.
Oral Biology. Ph.D.
Pharmacology. Ph.D.
Public Health. M.P.H.

School of Medicine

Located in Farmington at the Health Center (06030-1905). First class entered September 1968. Public control. Library: 130,000 volumes. Annual tuition fees: resident $8400, nonresident $19,100; student fees $3125. For off-campus housing, apply to Student Affairs Office. Total average figure for all other expenses $9100.
Enrollment: first-year class 80; full-time 328 (men 50%, women 50%). School faculty: full-time 203, part-time 90. Degrees conferred: M.D., M.D.-Ph.D.

ADMISSION REQUIREMENTS. AMCAS report, transcripts, MCAT, recommendations required in support of application. Accepts transfer applicants. Preference given to state residents. Has EDP; apply between June 15 and August 1. Apply to Admissions Office after June 15, before December 15. Application fee $60. Phone: (203)679-2152; fax: (203)679-1282.

ADMISSION STANDARDS. Competitive. Accepts about 10% of annual applicants. Approximately 86% are state residents.

FINANCIAL AID. Scholarships, Federal W/S, loans. Information regarding financial aid applications provided following admission from Director of Financial Aid. Use FAFSA. About 85% of students receive some aid from School funds.

DEGREE REQUIREMENTS. For M.D.: satisfactory completion of four-year program. For Ph.D., see Graduate School listing above.

GRADUATE FIELDS OF STUDY.
Biochemistry.
Cell Biology.
Immunology.
Molecular Biology.
Neurosciences.
Pharmacology.

School of Dental Medicine

Located in Farmington (06030). First class entered September 1968. Public control. Semester system. Annual tuition fee: resident $7300, New England resident $8750, other state residents $18,700. No on-campus housing. Average off-campus academic year housing costs: $11,000. Total average academic cost for all other first-year expenses excluding instruments $6350.
Enrollment: first-year class 40; total 163 (men 65%, women 35%); postgraduates 67. School faculty: full-time 18, part-time none. Degrees conferred: D.M.D., D.M.D.-Ph.D.

ADMISSION REQUIREMENTS. AADSAS, transcripts, DAT (not later than October), three letters of recommendation required in support of School's application. Applicants must have completed at least three years of college study. Preference given to state residents. Accepts transfer students. Has EDP for state and New England residents only. Apply to the Associate Dean, Student Affair, after June 1, before April 1. Application fee $60. Phone: (203)679-3748.

ADMISSION STANDARDS. Competitive. Accepts 15% of total annual applicants. Approximately 35% are state residents.

FINANCIAL AID. Scholarships, grants, tuition waivers, loans. Apply by April 1 to Office Financial Aid Office. Use FAFSA and GAPSFAS. Phone: (203)679-3574. About 85% of students receive some aid from School funds.

DEGREE REQUIREMENTS. For D.M.D.: satisfactory completion of four-year program. For D.M.D.-Ph.D.: a minimum of three additional years.

CONVERSE COLLEGE
Spartanburg, South Carolina 29301-0006

Established 1889. Located 70 miles SW of Charlotte, North Carolina. Coed on graduate Level. Private independent. Semester system. Library: 139,360 volumes, 10,533 microforms, 680 current periodicals, 4 PCs.
Tuition: per credit hour $165. No on-campus housing for graduate students.

Graduate Division

Enrollment: full-time 118, part-time 333. College faculty: full-time 62, part-time 24. Degrees conferred: M.M., M.Ed., Ed.S.

ADMISSION REQUIREMENTS. Official transcripts, GRE/NTE, research paper required in support of application. Audition/composition required for some programs. Accepts transfer applicants. Apply to the Director of the Graduate Education May 1 (Fall), January 30 (Spring). Phone: (803)596-9021 (Music); (803)596-9082 (Education). Rolling admissions process. Application fee $35.

ADMISSION STANDARDS. Selective. Usual minimum average: 2.75 (A = 4).

FINANCIAL AID. Annual awards from institutional funds: 8 assistantships, grants, Federal W/S, loans. Approved for VA benefits. Apply to Graduate Office of appropriate programs for assistantships, grants to Director of Financial Aid for all other programs. Use FAFSA. Phone: (803)596-9019.

DEGREE REQUIREMENTS. For M.Ed.: 36 semester hours minimum, at least two summer sessions in residence. For M.M.: 30 semester hours minimum, at least two semesters in residence; thesis/final project, or performance in music. For Ed.S.: 36 semester hours minimum, at least two summer sessions in residence.

FIELDS OF STUDY.
Administration. Ed.S.
Elementary Education.
Gifted Education.
Music. Includes vocal/instrumental performance, music education, musicology, piano pedagogy, music theory, composition, vocal; two languages for M.M. in musicology.
Secondary Education.
Special Education.

CORNELL UNIVERSITY
Ithaca, New York 14850
http://www.gradschool.cornell.edu

Founded 1865. Located 220 miles NW of New York City. Coed. Private control. Some graduate divisions are statutory colleges of the State University of New York. Semester system. Special facilities: Africana Studies and Research Center; American Indian Program; American Studies; Center for Applied Mathematics; Full-Year Asian Language Concentration (FALCON); Laboratory of Atomic and Solid State Physics; James A. Baker Institute for Animal Health; Biophysics Program; Boyce Thompson Institute for Plant Research; Bronfenbrenner Life Course Center; Community and Rural Development Institute; Institute for Comparative and Environmental Toxicology; Program of Computer Graphics; Institute for the Study of Continents; Cornell Institute for Social and Economics Research; Cornell International Institute for Food, Agriculture and Development; East Asia Program; Mario Einaudi Center for International Studies; Center for the Environment; Program on Ethics and Public Life; Institute for European Studies; Exchange Scholar Program; International Network for Graduate Student Exchange; Family Life Development Center; Farming Alternatives Programs; Center for High-Energy Synchrotron Studies; Society for the Humanities; Program in International Nutrition; Latin American Studies Program; Latino Studies Program; Center for Manufacturing Enterprise; Materials Science Center; National Nanofabriction Facility (NNF); New York State Agricultural Experiment Stations; Floyd R. Newman Laboratory of Nuclear Studies; Northeast Regional Climate Center; Peace Studies Program; Laboratory of Plasma Studies; Center for Radiophysics and Space Research; Renaissance Studies; Rural Development; South Asia Program; Southeast Asia Program; Center for Statistics; Center for Theory and Simulation in Science and Engineering; Ward Laboratory of Nuclear Engineering; Library: over 5,000,000 volumes, 5,000,000 Microforms, 400 PCs in all libraries.

Annual tuition, for endowed divisions $20,000; for state-supported divisions (Colleges of Agriculture and Life Sciences, Human Ecology, and School of Industrial and Labor Relations), $10,000; Veterinary Medicine, $10,600. On-campus housing for 411 married students and 262 single students. Inquire at Campus Life Office. Phone: (607)255-5368.

Graduate School

Enrollment: full-time 4352. University faculty teaching graduate students: full-time 1600. Degrees conferred: M.A., M.S., M.Arch., M.L.A., M.A.T., M.F.A., M.F.S., M.H.A., M.I.L.R., M.M.H., M.P.A., M.P.S., M.R.P., M.S.T., M.Eng., LL.M., D.M.A., Ph.D., J.S.D.

ADMISSION REQUIREMENTS. Transcripts, two or three letters of recommendation (depending on the field) required in support of School's application. GRE required by most fields. TOEFL required for international applicants unless he or she (1) has received a degree from a college or a university in a country where the native language is English or (2) has studied for two or more years in an undergraduate or graduate program in a country where the native language is English. Accepts transfer students. Graduate of unaccredited institutions not considered. Apply to the Graduate School by January 10 for Fall admission (some fields have later deadlines). Application fee $65. Phone: (607)255-4884.

ADMISSION STANDARDS. Very competitive to very selective. Usual minimum average: 3.0 (A = 4).

FINANCIAL AID. Annual awards from institutional funds: 458 fellowships, 953 teaching assistantships, 1088 research assistantships, Federal W/S, loans. Apply by January 10 for Fellowships, assistantships; most programs use this deadline date, some are later. Apply to Financial Aid Office for other federal programs. Use FAFSA. About 75% of students receive primary support from University and outside sources.

DEGREE REQUIREMENTS. For master's: Two semester minimum in full-time residence; for research master's degrees, thesis and final oral/written exam; for professional master's degrees, usual course requirements, no thesis. Additional requirements may vary by field. For doctorate: Six semester minimum in full-time residence; admission to candidacy examination; dissertation; final oral exam. Additional requirements vary by field.

FIELDS OF STUDY.

HUMANITIES:
Architecture. M.S., M.A., M.Arch., Ph.D.
Art. M.F.A.
Classics. M.A., Ph.D.
Comparative Literature. Ph.D.
East Asian Literature. M.A., Ph.D.
English. M.A., M.F.A., Ph.D.
Germanic Studies. M.A., Ph.D.
History. M.A., Ph.D.
History of Art and Archaeology. Ph.D.
Medieval Studies. Ph.D.
Music. M.F.A., M.A., Ph.D., D.M.A.
Near Eastern Studies. M.A., Ph.D.
Philosophy. M.A., Ph.D.
Romance Studies. M.A., Ph.D.
Science and Technology Studies. M.A., Ph.D.
Slavic Studies. M.A., Ph.D.
Theater Arts. M.A., Ph.D.

BIOLOGICAL SCIENCES:
Animal Breeding. M.S., Ph.D.
Animal Science. M.S., Ph.D., M.P.S. (Agr.).
Biochemistry, Molecular and Cell Biology. Ph.D.
Biometry. M.S., Ph.D.
Ecology and Evolutionary Biology. M.S., Ph.D.
Entomology. M.S., Ph.D.
Environmental Toxicology. M.S., Ph.D.
Floriculture and Ornamental Horticulture. M.S., Ph.D., M.P.S. (Agr.).
Food Science and Technology. M.S., Ph.D., M.P.S. (Agr.), M.E.S.
Genetics and Development. Ph.D.
Immunology. M.S., Ph.D.
Microbiology. Ph.D.
Natural Resources. M.S., Ph.D., M.P.S. (Agr.).
Neurobiology and Behavior. Ph.D.
Nutrition. M.S., M.P.S. (Hu.Ec.), Ph.D.
Pharmacology. M.S., Ph.D.
Physiology. M.S., Ph.D.
Plant Biology. Ph.D.
Plant Breeding. M.S., Ph.D., M.P.S. (Agr.).
Plant Pathology. M.S., Ph.D., M.P.S. (Agr.).

Plant Protection. M.P.S.(Agr.).
Pomology. M.S., Ph.D., M.P.S. (Agr.).
Psychology. Ph.D.
Soil, Crop, and Atmospheric Sciences. M.S., Ph.D., M.P.S. (Agr.).
Vegetable Crops. M.S., M.P.S. (Agr.), Ph.D.
Veterinary Medicine. M.S., Ph.D.
Zoology. M.S., Ph.D.

PHYSICAL SCIENCES:
Aerospace Engineering. M.S., Ph.D., M.Eng.
Agricultural and Biological Engineering. M.S., Ph.D., M.Eng., M.P.S. (Agr.).
Applied Mathematics. Ph.D.
Applied Physics. M.S., Ph.D., M.Eng.
Astronomy and Space Sciences. M.S., Ph.D.
Chemical Engineering. M.S., Ph.D., M.Eng.
Chemistry. Ph.D.
Civil Engineering. M.S., Ph.D., M.Eng.
Computer Sciences. Ph.D., M.Eng.
Electrical Engineering. M.S., Ph.D., M.Eng.
Geological Sciences. M.S., Ph.D., M.Eng.
Materials Science and Engineering. M.S., Ph.D., M.Eng.
Mathematics. Ph.D.
Mechanical Engineering. M.S., Ph.D., M. Eng.
Nuclear Science and Engineering. M.S., Ph.D., M.Eng.
Operations Research. Ph.D., M.Eng.
Physics. M.S., Ph.D.
Textiles. M.A., M.S., Ph.D., M.P.S. (Hu.Ec.).
Theoretical and Applied Mathematics. M.S., Ph.D., M.Eng.

SOCIAL SCIENCES:
African and Afro-American Studies. M.P.S. (A.A.A.).
Agricultural Economics. M.S., Ph.D., M.P.S. (Agr.).
Anthropology. M.A., Ph.D.
Archaeology. M.A.
Asian Studies. M.A.
City and Regional Planning. Ph.D., M.R.P., M.A.
Communication Arts. M.S., Ph.D., M.P.S.
Consumer Economics and Housing. M.S., Ph.D.
Design and Environmental Analysis. M.A., M.P.S. (Hu.Ec.), M.S.
Developmental Sociology. M.S., Ph.D., M.P.S. (Agr.).
Economics. Ph.D.
Education. M.S., Ph.D., M.P.S. (Agr.), M.A.T.
Government. Ph.D.
Hotel Administration. M.S., Ph.D., M.P.S. (H.Ad.), M.M.H.
Human Development and Family Studies. M.A., Ph.D.
Human Service Studies. M.S., Ph.D., M.P.S. (Hu.Ec.), M.H.A.
Industrial and Labor Relations. M.S., Ph.D., M.I.L.R., M.P.S. (I.L.R.).
International Agricultural and Rural Development. M.P.S. (Agr.).
International Development. M.P.S. (I.D.).
Landscape Architecture. M.L.A.
Law. LL.M., J.S.D.
Linguistics. M.A., Ph.D.
Management. Ph.D.
Public Affairs. M.P.A.
Real Estate. M.P.S.
Regional Science. M.A., M.S., Ph.D.
Sociology. M.A., Ph.D.
Statistics. M.S., Ph.D.

College of Human Ecology

Tuition: $10,000. Enrollment: full-time 239 (men 70, women 169), none part-time. Faculty: full-time 102, none part-time. Degrees conferred: M.A., M.S., M.P.S.; Ph.D. offered in conjunction with Graduate School.

ADMISSION REQUIREMENTS. Transcripts, GRE (except for interior design) required in support of College's application. Interview not usually required. Accepts transfer applicants. Gradu-

ates of unaccredited colleges not considered. Apply to Cornell Graduate School by January 10. Application fee $65. Phone: (607)255-2138.

ADMISSION STANDARDS. Very competitive in some departments, selective to competitive in others. Usual minimum average: 3.0 (A = 4).

FINANCIAL AID. Annual awards from institutional funds: 110 teaching/research assistantships, 36 fellowships, 15 traineeships, tuition waiver, Federal W/S, loans. Applications received by January 15 will receive consideration for all financial aid. Use FAFSA. About 80% of students receive aid other than loans from College and outside sources.

DEGREE REQUIREMENTS. For master's: Two residence units minimum; thesis; final exam. For M.P.S.: 30 credits beyond master's. For Ph.D.: Six residence units minimum; qualifying exam; dissertation; final exam. For M.A.T., Ed.D.: see Graduate School offerings above.

FIELDS OF STUDY.
Animal Nutrition.
Apparel Design.
Clinical Nutrition.
Clothing.
Consumer and Household Economics.
Design and Environmental Analysis.
Facility Planning and Management.
Family Resource Management.
Family Studies and the Life Cause.
Fiber Science.
Foods.
General Nutrition.
Human Development and Family Studies.
Human Ecology.
Human Environmental Relations.
Human Nutrition.
Human Service Administration.
Interior Design.
International Nutrition.
Nutritional Biochemistry.
Polymer Sciences.
Textile Science.
Textile, Economics, and Marketing.

New York State School of Industrial and Labor Relations
http://www.cornell.edu/

Graduate study since 1945. Annual tuition: $10,500. On-campus housing for married, single students. Average academic year housing costs: $9000. Contact Housing Office. Phone: (607)255-5511.

Graduate enrollment: full-time 135 (men 50%, women 50%). Faculty: full-time 50. Degrees conferred: M.I.L.R., M.P.S., M.S., Ph.D.

ADMISSION REQUIREMENTS. Official transcripts, three letters of recommendation, GRE (if degree is from English-speaking institution) required in support of School's application. Interview not required. TOEFL required for international applicants. Graduates of unaccredited institutions not considered. Apply to Dean of Graduate School by January 15 (Fall), November 1 (Spring). Application fee $65. Phone: (607)225-2227; fax: (607)255-7774.

ADMISSION STANDARDS. Competitive. Usual minimum average: 3.0 (A = 4).

FINANCIAL AID. Annual awards from institutional funds: Fifteen scholarships, six fellowships, thirty research assistantships, thirty teaching assistantships, loans. Approved for VA benefits. Apply by January 15 (Fall), November 1 (Spring), to Graduate department for fellowships, assistantships; to Director of Financial Aid for all other programs. Phone: (607)255-4884, Fax: (607)255-1816. Use FAFSA. About 70% of students receive aid other than loans from University/School and outside sources.

DEGREE REQUIREMENTS. For M.I.L.R.: 13 courses (45 credit hours), one year minimum in full-time residence. For M.P.S.: 30 credits, minimum; one year minimum in full-time residence. For M.S.: one year minimum in full-time residence; thesis; final oral/written exam. For Ph.D.: four semesters minimum in full-time residence; thesis; qualifying and candidacy exams; final exam.

FIELDS OF STUDY.
Collective Bargaining, Labor Law and Labor History.
Economic and Social Statistics.
Human Resource Studies.
Industrial Labor Relations. M.I.L.R. only.
International and Comparative Labor Relations.
Labor Economics.
Organizational Behavior.
Note: A special 1 year (9 course) M.I.L.R. program is available for applicants with either M.B.A. or J.D.

School of Law (14853-4901)

Library 415,500 volumes, 380,000 microforms. Library has LEXIS, NEXIS, WESTLAW, DIALOG.
Annual tuition: $23,135. Total average cost for all other expenses: $11,000, single, $16,000 married. On-campus housing available.
Enrollment: first-year class 180, total full-time 570 (men 62%, women 38%). School faculty: full-time 40, part-time 16. Degrees conferred: J.D., J.D.-M.A., J.D.-M.B.A., J.D.-M.P.A., J.D.-M.I.L.R., J.D.-Ph.D., J.D.-LL.M. (International and Comparative Law), LL.M., J.S.D.

ADMISSION REQUIREMENTS. LSDAS Law School report, bachelor's degree, transcripts, LSAT (not later than December) required in support of application. Accepts transfer applicants from other law schools. Graduates of unaccredited colleges not considered. Apply to Director of Admissions of the School after September 1 and before February 1. Application fee $65. Phone: (607)255-3527.

ADMISSION STANDARDS. Selective. Accepts 10–12% of total annual applicants.

FINANCIAL AID. Scholarships, grants-in-aid, fellowships, assistantships, Federal W/S, loans. About 50% of students receive aid other than loans from School. Apply to Director of Admissions of the School by March 15. Use GAPSFAS or FAFSA.

DEGREE REQUIREMENTS. For J.D.: satisfactory completion of three-year program. For LL.M.: 2 semesters beyond J.D.; oral exam. For J.S.D.: 4 semesters beyond J.D.; thesis; final exam.

Medical College

Founded 1898. Located in New York City (10021). On-campus housing for married, single students. Contact Assistant Dean, 445 East 69th Street. Annual tuition: full-time $21,300. Total average figure for all other expenses $8500.
Enrollment: first-year class 101 (2 EDP); total full-time 405 (men 54%, women 46%); postgraduates 150. Faculty: full-/part-time approximately 1500. Degrees conferred: M.D., M.D.-Ph.D. (coordinated with Graduate School of Medical Sciences, Memorial Sloan Kettering Cancer Center and Rockefeller University).

Medical Scientist Training program in cooperation with Rockefeller University.

ADMISSION REQUIREMENTS. AMCAS report, transcripts, letters of recommendation, interview required in support of application. MCAT recommended. Has EDP; apply between June 15 and August 1. Apply to Chair of the Admissions Committee after June 1, before October 15. Application fee $65. Phone: (212)746-1067. Phone for M.D.-Ph.D. program: (212)746-6565.

ADMISSION STANDARDS. Very competitive. Accepts 2% of total annual applicants. Approximately 40% are state residents.

FINANCIAL AID. Grants, loans. Apply upon notification of acceptance to Committee on Financial Aid of the College. No closing date. About 55% receive aid other than loans from School funds.

DEGREE REQUIREMENTS. For M.D.: satisfactory completion of four-year program.

FIELDS OF GRADUATE STUDY.
Biochemistry.
Biophysics.
Cell Biology.
Genetics.
Immunology.
Molecular Biology.
Neurosciences.
Pharmacology.
Physiology.

New York State College of Veterinary Medicine

Professional graduate study since 1894. Coed. State supported. Special facilities: On-campus Teaching Hospital, Regional Veterinary Laboratories for Poultry Disease Diagnosis, New York State Mastitis Control Program Laboratories, James A. Baker Institute for Animal Health, Equine Research Park. Library 70,000 volumes.
Annual tuition: resident $13,800, nonresident $18,600 and Contract nonresidents $13,080. Living expenses $9540. Enrollment: first-year class 80; full-time 320 (women 60%, men 40%). Faculty: full-time 125, part-time 3. Degrees conferred: D.V.M., D.V.M.-Ph.D.

ADMISSION REQUIREMENTS. VMCAS report, transcripts, prerequisite course work: English composition, 6 credits; Biology (with laboratory), 6 credits; Inorganic Chemistry (with laboratory), 6 credits; Organic Chemistry (with laboratory), 6 credits; Biochemistry, 4 credits; Physics (with laboratory), 6 credits; GRE, experience with animals and the veterinary profession, essay, three recommendations (one from an academic advisor), required in support of application. At least three years of undergraduate college study leading to a bachelor's degree. Interview by invitation. Preference given to state or contract state residents. Accepts transfers only if vacancies exist. Apply to the Office of Admissions beginning August 15 for an application, deadline of November 1. For transfer April 1. Fall admission only. Application fee $60. Phone: (607)253-3700.

ADMISSION STANDARDS. Selective. Accepts 16% of total annual applicants. Minimum GPA 3.0; minimum GRE score 1200. 60 places reamed for state residents.

FINANCIAL AID. Loans, grants, scholarships, fellowships, assistantships. Apply to College Financial Aid Office. Use FAFSA. Apply by March 15.

DEGREE REQUIREMENTS. Satisfactory completion of four-year D.V.M. program. For Ph.D.: see Graduate School listing.

CRANBROOK ACADEMY OF ART

Box 801
Bloomfield Hills, Michigan 48303-0801

Located 20 miles from Detroit. Coed. Private control. Semester system. Special facility: semiprivate studios in most. Library: 27,000 volumes, 4 PC workstations.

Annual tuition: full-time $15,150. Limited on-campus housing for 95 students; none for married students. Average annual housing cost: $4950 (including board) for single students. Apply to the Dean of Admission for housing information. Phone: (810)645-3300.

Graduate Program

Enrollment: full-time 140 (men 70, women 70); no part-time students. Academy faculty: full-time 9, part-time 0. Degrees conferred: M.F.A., M.Arch.

ADMISSION REQUIREMENTS. Transcripts, references, portfolio required in support of application. TOEFL required for foreign applicants. Interview not required. Accepts transfer applicants, but two years' residence still required for degree. Apply to Dean of Admission by March 1 (Fall). Application fee $50. Phone: (810)645-3300, (810)646-0046.

ADMISSION STANDARDS. Competitive.

FINANCIAL AID. Fifteen scholarships, twenty-four departmental assistantships, limited need-based aid for U.S. citizens. Apply by February 1 to the Registrar. Phone: (313)645-3303. Use FAFSA. Assistantships reserved for second-year students. About 70% of students receive aid from the Academy.

DEGREE REQUIREMENTS. For M.F.A., M.Arch.: 60 semester hours minimum in full-time residence; thesis including photographic record of work.

FIELDS OF STUDY.
Architecture.
Ceramics.
Design. Includes graphic design, industrial, interior, packaging design.
Fiber.
Metalsmithing.
Painting.
Photography.
Printmaking.
Sculpture.

THE CREIGHTON UNIVERSITY

Omaha, Nebraska 68178-0150

Founded 1878. Coed. Private control, Roman Catholic affiliation. Semester system. Library 826,488 items.

Tuition: per credit $366. On-campus housing for both married and single students. Average annual housing cost: $4548. Apply to Housing Office. Phone: (402)280-3016.

Graduate School

Enrollment: full-time 138, part-time 379. Faculty; full-time 170, part-time 0. Degrees conferred: M.A., M.B.A., M.S., M.C.S., M.C.S.M., Ph.D.

ADMISSION REQUIREMENTS. Transcripts, GRE, letters of reference required in support of School's application. TOEFL required for international applicants. Interview varies by department. Apply to Graduate School Office by July 15 (Fall), December 15 (Spring), May 15 (Summer). Application fee $30. Phone: (402)280-2870; fax: (402)280-5762.

ADMISSION STANDARDS. Selective. Usual minimum average: 3.0 (A = 4).

FINANCIAL AID. Limited to Federal W/S, loans. Apply by March 15 to Dean of the Graduate School. Phone: (402)280-2731. Use FAFSA. About 15% of students receive aid other than loans from University and outside sources. No aid for part-time students.

DEGREE REQUIREMENTS. For most master's: 30 credit hours minimum; thesis; reading knowledge of one foreign language; comprehensive oral/written exam; or 33 credit hours minimum; written comprehensive exam. For M.B.A.: 33 credit hours minimum. For Ph.D.: 90 credits beyond the bachelor's, one year in full-time study; two foreign languages or one language and alternative tool for some departments; comprehensive exam; dissertation.

FIELDS OF STUDY.
Atmospheric Sciences.
Biomedical Sciences.
Business Administration. GMAT for admission: M.B.A. only.
Christian Spirituality.
Computer Systems Management.
Counseling.
Elementary School Administration.
English.
International Relations.
Mathematics/Computer Science.
Microbiology. 2 years minimum in full-time residence for M.S.
Ministry.
Nursing.
Pharmacology.
Physics.
Secondary School Administration.
Theology.

School of Law

Organized 1904. Semester system. Law library 161,000 volumes. Library has LEXIS, NEXIS, WESTLAW.

Annual tuition: full-time $14,326. On-campus housing available. Total average annual additional expenses: $10,450.

Enrollment: first-year class 180, total full-time 536 (men 56%, women 44%). Faculty: full-time 25, part-time 36. Degrees conferred: J.D., J.D.-M.B.A.

ADMISSION REQUIREMENTS. LSDAS Law School report, transcripts, LSAT, bachelor's degree required in support of application. Two letters of recommendation suggested. Accepts transfer applicants. Graduates of unaccredited colleges not considered. Apply to University Admissions Office after August 31, before May 1. Application fee $40. Phone: (402)280-2872; fax: (402)280-2244.

ADMISSION STANDARDS. Selective, Accepts 25–30% of total annual applicants.

FINANCIAL AID. Scholarships, fellowships, assistantship, partial tuition waiver, Federal W/S, loans. Apply by April 1 to Dean of the School. Use FAFSA. About 40% of students receive aid other than loans from School.

DEGREE REQUIREMENTS. For J.D.: 94 hours minimum, at least final two semesters in residence.

School of Medicine

Established 1892. Annual tuition: $24,254; student fees $770. On-campus housing available. Total average figure for all other expenses $9000. Enrollment: first-year class 119 (20 EDP); total full-time 473 (men 67%, women 33%), postgraduates 128. Faculty: full-time 318, part-time 210. Degrees conferred: M.D., M.D.-M.S., M.D.-Ph.D.

ADMISSION REQUIREMENTS. AMCAS report, transcripts, MCAT, interview required in support of application. Applicants must have completed at least three years of college study. Preference given to residents of midwestern states. Has EDP; apply between June 15 and August 1. For regular admission apply between June 15 and December 1. Application fee $50. Phone: (402)280-2798; fax: (402)280-1241.

ADMISSION STANDARDS. Competitive. Accepts 2% of total annual applicants. Approximately 9% are state residents.

FINANCIAL AID. Scholarships, grants, fellowships, assistantships, loans. Apply to Office of the Dean, preferably before January 15. About 87% of students receive some aid from School.

DEGREE REQUIREMENTS. For M.D.: satisfactory completion of four-year program. For M.S., Ph.D.: see Graduate School listing above.

FIELDS OF GRADUATE STUDY.
Anatomy.
Biochemistry.
Microbiology.
Parasitology.
Pharmacology.
Physiology.

School of Dentistry

Founded 1905. Annual tuition: $19,578. Some housing for single students only. Average academic year housing costs: $9725. Contact Student Personnel Office for housing information. Phone: (402)280-3016. Total average cost for all other first-year expenses: $4949.

Enrollment: first-year class 80 (men 68, women 7). Total enrollment 316 (men 75%; women 25%). Faculty: full-time 51, part-time 78. Degree conferred: D.D.S.

ADMISSION REQUIREMENTS. AADSAS, official transcripts, three letters of recommendation, DAT required in support of application. Applicants must have completed at least three years of college study; prefer four years of study. Interview not required. Graduates of unaccredited colleges not considered. Preference given to educational compact states of Idaho, New Mexico, Utah, and Wyoming. Apply to Director of Admissions after July 15, before April 1. Application fee $35. Phone: (402)280-2695, (800)544-5072.

ADMISSION STANDARDS. Competitive. Accepts about 15–20% of total annual applicants. Approximately 15% are state residents.

FINANCIAL AID. Scholarships, grants, tuition waivers, loans. Apply by June 1 to the Director of Financial Aid. Use FAFSA. Phone: (402)280-2731. About 94% of students receive some aid from School.

DEGREE REQUIREMENTS. For D.D.S.: satisfactory completion of four-year program.

UNIVERSITY OF DALLAS
Irving, Texas 75062-4799

Founded 1955. Coed. Private control. Roman Catholic. Semester for Braniff Graduate School. Trimester for Graduate School of Management. Library: 278,000 volumes, 107,600 microforms, 70 PCs.

Tuition: per credit $350. On-campus housing for 750 single students. Average annual housing cost: $4420.46 (room and board with tax and phone) for single students. Apply to Director of Housing. Phone: (214)721-5387.

Graduate Divisions

Enrollment: full-time 400, part-time 1500. Graduate faculty: full-time 58, part-time 85. Degrees conferred: M.A., M.B.A., M.F.A., M. Pol., M.R.E., M.Eng., M.H., M.Mgt., M.Th., M.T.S., Ph.D.

ADMISSION REQUIREMENTS. Transcripts, letter of intent, two letters of recommendation, resume, portfolio for Art programs required in support of University's applications. GMAT required for Business. TOEFL required for foreign applicants. GRE Subject Test recommended. Accepts transfer applicants. Graduates of unaccredited institutions not considered. Apply to Graduate Office by August 6 (Fall). Application fee $30. Phone: (214)721-5166; Graduate School of Management: (214)714-5174; fax: (214)721-4009.

ADMISSION STANDARDS. Selective. Usual minimum average: 3.0 (A = 4).

FINANCIAL AID. 85 scholarships, assistantships, Federal W/S, loans. Apply by August 5 to Graduate Dean. Use FAFSA. Phone: (214)721-5266.

DEGREE REQUIREMENTS. For master's: 30 semester hours, minimum, at least 24 in residence and 12 in full-time attendance; language requirement for some programs; thesis; final oral exam. For M.B.A.: 37–49 credit hours and attendance at 10 lectures in GSM's Ethics & Management Lecture series. For M. Mgt.: 25 credit hours (8 courses and attendance at 10 lectures in GSM's Ethics & Management Lecture series) Ph.D.: 84 Semester hours, at least 40 in full-time residence; qualifying exam; dissertation; final written/oral exam.

FIELDS OF STUDY.

BRANIFF GRADUATE SCHOOL OF LIBERAL ARTS:
Art. M.A., M.F.A.
Art Education. M.A. only.
Education.
English. M.A., M.Eng.
Literature. M.A., Ph.D.
Philosophy. Ph.D. only.
Politics. M.A., M. Pol.
Psychology.
Theology. M.A., M.S.T., M.R.E., M.Th.

GRADUATE SCHOOL OF MANAGEMENT:
Business Management.
Corporate Finance.
Engineering Management.
Financial Planning Management.
Health Services Management.
Human Resource Management.
Industrial Management.
Information Systems.
International Accounting.
International Management.
Marketing.
Purchasing and Contract Management.
Telecommunications Management.

DARTMOUTH COLLEGE
Hanover, New Hampshire 03755

Founded 1769. Located 135 miles NW of Boston. Coed on all levels. Private control. Year-round operation. Special facilities:

Fairchild Science Center, Expanded Medical School. Library over 1.7 million volumes.

On-campus housing for 136 married students, a few available rooms for single students. Average monthly housing cost: $550–$850 for married students, $450–$600 for single students. Apply to Director of Rental Housing. Phone: (603)646-2170.

School of Arts and Sciences

Graduate study since 1960. Tuition per year: $29,128. Enrollment: full-time 297, (men 174, women 123), part-time 150. Faculty teaching graduate students: full-time 200. Degrees conferred: M.A., M.S., M.A.L.S., Ph.D.

ADMISSION REQUIREMENTS. Transcripts, letters of recommendation, GRE required in support of School's application. TOEFL required of foreign students. Interview not required. Accepts transfer applicants. Graduates of unaccredited institutions not considered. Apply by February 1 to department of study. Application fee, varies by field of study. General information number: Phone: (603)646-2106.

ADMISSION STANDARDS. Competitive for most departments, very competitive for others. Usual minimum average: 3.0 (A = 4).

FINANCIAL AID. Annual awards from institutional funds: three hundred tuition scholarships, ninety fellowships, one hundred research assistantships, loans. Apply to Financial Aid Office by February 15. Use FAFSA. Phone: (603)646-2451. All applicants for graduate program simultaneously considered for financial aid and all financial resources available at College. All Ph.D. students are supported by College funds.

DEGREE REQUIREMENTS. Vary by department, but generally for M.A., M.S.: Eight courses minimum, at least three terms in residence; thesis; final oral exam. For M.A.L.S.: two to three summers in residence. For Ph.D.: Eight courses minimum, at least six terms in residence; language requirement established by department; qualifying exam; dissertation; final oral exam.

FIELDS OF STUDY.
Biochemistry.
Biological Sciences.
Chemistry.
Comparative Literature.
Computer Science.
Earth Sciences.
Electro-Acoustic Music.
Engineering Sciences.
Evaluative Clinical Sciences.
Liberal Studies.
Mathematics.
Molecular and Cell Biology.
Pharmacology.
Physics.
Physiology.
Psychology.

The Tuck School of Business Administration

The first graduate business school, founded in 1900. On-campus housing available during first year.

Annual tuition: $23,700. Average academic year housing costs: $8000 for single students (including board), $11,650 for married students (including board). Enrollment: full-time 360. Faculty: full-time 36, part-time 5. Degree conferred: M.B.A.

ADMISSION REQUIREMENTS. Official transcripts, GMAT, recommendations required in support of School's application. TOEFL required for international applicants. Transfer applicants

not considered. Graduates of unaccredited institutions not considered. Apply to the Director of Admissions by April 15. Fall admission only. Application fee $75. Phone: (603)646-2460; fax: (603)646-1308.

ADMISSION STANDARDS. Very selective. Usual minimum average: 3.3 (A = 4).

FINANCIAL AID. Annual awards from institutional funds: 167 fellowships, Federal W/S, loans. Use FAFSA. Phone: (603)646-3748. About 70% of students receive aid from School and outside sources. Low-interest loans available from College.

DEGREE REQUIREMENTS. For M.B.A.: 25 courses minimum, all in full-time residence.
Note: Joint programs in medicine, international affairs and engineering available.

Thayer School of Engineering—Graduate Division
http://www.dartmouth.edu/thayer

Established 1871. Tuition: $20,805 for three terms. Annual room and board $9660. Enrollment: full-time 134 (men 100, women 34). Faculty: full-time 32, part-time 8, Degrees conferred: B.E., M.E., M.S.-M.B.A., M.S., Ph.D., M.D.-Ph.D.

ADMISSION REQUIREMENTS. Transcripts, two letters of reference, GRE Test required in support of School's application. TOEFL required for foreign applicants. Graduates of unaccredited institutions not considered. Apply to Graduate Admission by January 1. Application fee $40. Phone: (603)646-2606; fax: (603)646-3856.

ADMISSION STANDARDS. Competitive. Usual minimum average 3.0 (A = 4).

FINANCIAL AID. Fellowships and teaching assistantships are available from institutional funds; 45 research assistantships are available from contract research. Such support normally covers tuition plus a monthly stipend. Approved for VA benefits. Apply to Director of Financial Aid by February 1. Phone: (603)646-3844; fax: (602)646-3856. Use FAFSA.

DEGREE REQUIREMENTS. For B.E.: 9 courses, proficiency in design, analytical and experimental work, and economic analysis of engineering problems. For M.E.: nonthesis option requires 18 courses with distribution in engineering, design and manufacturing, and management. For M.S.: 6–10 courses minimum, at least three consecutive terms in residence; thesis; final oral exam. For Ph.D.: Two-year minimum in residence; oral exam; dissertation.

FIELDS OF STUDY.
Biomedical Engineering.
Biotechnology/Biochemical Engineering.
Electrical and Computer Engineering.
Engineering Management.
Environmental Engineering.
Materials Science and Engineering.
Mechanical Engineering.

Medical School

Founded 1797. Annual tuition: $23,260; student fees $1765. Total average figure for all other expenses $7150. Enrollment: first-year class 88, total 401 (men 56%, women 44%). Faculty: full-time 410, part-time 354. 20 Rhode Island residents admitted each year to Brown-Dartmouth program. Faculty: full- and part-time 900. Degrees conferred: M.D., M.D.-M.B.A., M.D.-Ph.D.

ADMISSION REQUIREMENTS. AMCAS report, transcripts indicating completion of three years of college work, letters of recommendation, MCAT, interview required in support of application. Transfer applicants, graduates of unaccredited colleges not considered. Preference given to residents of New Hampshire and Rhode Island. Apply to Admissions Office of the School after June 15, before November 1. Application fee $55. Phone: (603)650-1505; fax: (603)650-1614.

ADMISSION STANDARDS. Very competitive. Accepts about 3% of total annual applications. Approximately 13% are state residents.

FINANCIAL AID. Scholarships, part-time jobs, loans. Apply to Office of Financial Aid of the School after acceptance. Use FAFSA. About 75% of students receive some aid from School.

DEGREE REQUIREMENTS. For M.D.: completion of 4-year program.

FIELDS OF GRADUATE STUDY.
Biochemistry.
Biomedical Engineering.
Biophysics.
Cell Biology.
Genetics.
Immunology.
Microbiology.
Molecular Biology.
Neurosciences.
Pharmacology.
Physiology.
Toxicology.

UNIVERSITY OF DAYTON
Dayton, Ohio 45469-1611

Founded 1850. Coed. Private control. Roman Catholic affiliation. Semester system. Library: about 1,150,463 volumes, 15 PCs.

Graduate School

Tuition, per credit: $379. University fee $25. Limited on-campus housing for graduate students; 88 for single men, 42 for single women, 8 for married students. Apply to Residents Services. Phone: (523)229-3317.

Enrollment: full-time 693, part-time 2143. Graduate faculty: full-time 245, part-time 165. Degrees conferred: M.A., M.B.A., M.C.L.T., M.C.S., M.P.A., M.S., M.S.Ed., M.S.T., Ed.S., Ph.D., D.E.

ADMISSION REQUIREMENTS. Transcripts, three letters of recommendation, GMAT for M.B.A., GRE/MAT for Psychology, Biology and Clinical Laboratory Technology required in support of School's application. TOEFL or evidence of proficiency in English required of international students. Accepts transfer applicants. Graduates of unaccredited colleges not considered. Apply to the Graduate School by August 1 (Fall), December 1 (Spring), April 1 (Third Term), June 1 (Third Term-Summer Session). Application fee $25. Phone: (513)229-2343; fax: (513)229-4545.

ADMISSION STANDARDS. Varies for each program, usually 3.0 in areas desired for graduate study (A = 4).

FINANCIAL AID. Two hundred and ten teaching/research assistantships. Apply to Graduate School at time of application. No aid for part-time students.

DEGREE REQUIREMENTS. For master's: 30–36 semester hours minimum (includes 6 in research if thesis required), at least 24 in residence; thesis/comprehensive oral/written exam/internship or project required by some departments. For Ed.S.: at least 30 semester hours beyond the master's. For Ph.D.: 60 semester hours minimum, at least two years in residence; preliminary exam; qualifying exam; candidacy exam; dissertation; research tool. For D.E.: essentially the same as for the Ph.D., except one year internship.

FIELDS OF STUDY.

COLLEGE OF ARTS AND SCIENCES:
American Studies.
Applied Mathematical Systems.
Biology.
Chemistry.
Clinical Laboratory Technology.
Communication Arts.
Computer Science.
English.
History.
Mathematics.
Pastoral Ministries.
Philosophy.
Physics/Electro-Optics.
Political Science/International Studies.
Psychology. Includes clinical, experimental, general, human factors.
Public Administration.
Theological Studies.

SCHOOL OF BUSINESS ADMINISTRATION:
Business Administration. M.B.A.

SCHOOL OF EDUCATION:
Counselor Education and Human Services.
Educational Administration.
Educational Leadership. Ph.D. only.
Educational Specialist in Educational Leadership.
Elementary Education. Usual subject areas.
Physical and Health Education.
Secondary Education. Usual subject areas.

SCHOOL OF ENGINEERING:
Aerospace Engineering.
Chemical Engineering.
Civil Engineering.
Electrical Engineering.
Electro-Optics.
Engineering Management.
Management Science.
Materials Engineering.
Mechanical Engineering.

School of Law (45469-1320)

Established 1974. Library 208,000 volumes.
Annual tuition: $16,900. Limited on-campus housing available. Total average annual additional expenses: $5500–7500.
Enrollment: first-year class 180; total 485 (men 60%, women 40%). Faculty: full-time 24, part-time 28. Degree conferred: J.D., J.D./M.B.A., J.D./M.S. (Educ. Admin.).

ADMISSION REQUIREMENTS. LSDAS Law School report, bachelor's degree, transcripts, LSAT, recommendations required in support of application. Accepts transfers from other ABA approved School. Graduates of unaccredited colleges not considered. Apply to Admissions Office by May 1. Application fee $35. Phone: (513)229-3555.

ADMISSION STANDARDS. Selective. Accepts about 40–45% of total annual applications.

FINANCIAL AID. Partial scholarships, grants, Federal W/S, loans. Apply by May 1 to Financial Aid Office. Use FAFSA of GAPSFAS. About 30 of students receive some aid from School.

DEGREE REQUIREMENTS. For J.D.: Satisfactory completion of three-year program. For master's degrees: see Graduate School listing above.

UNIVERSITY OF DELAWARE

Newark, Delaware 19716-1501

http://www.udel.edu

Established 1743, degree granting since 1834. Located 15 miles SW of Wilmington. Coed. State-related. Semester system. Special facilities: Institute of Applied Mathematics, Center for the Study of Catalysts, Center for the Study of Composite Materials, University Computing Center, Agricultural Experiment Station, Institute for Energy Conversion, Science Teaching Center, Mathematics, Teaching Center, Mt. Cuba Astronomical Observatory, Marine Biology Field Station; cooperative program in American Studies and related fields with the Henry Francis du Pont Winterthur Museum and in American technological, business and Labor History with the Hagley Museum. Library: 2,100,000 volumes, 2,600,000 microforms, 24,000 current periodicals.

Annual tuition: full-time, resident $3990, nonresident $11,250; per credits, resident $222, nonresident $625; for M.B.A./ E.M.B.A. resident $270, nonresident $596. On-campus housing for both married and single students. Average academic year housing costs: $6120 (including board) single students; $6360 for married students. Contact Office of Housing and Residence Life for both on- and off-campus housing information. Phone: (302)831-6573.

Graduate Studies

Graduate study since 1900. Enrollment: full-time 1686, part-time 1661. University faculty teaching graduate students: full-time 950, part-time none. Degrees conferred: M.A., M.S., M.B.A., M.Ed., M.C.E., M.E.E., M.M.S., M.M.E., M.A.S., M.P.A., M.C., M.F.A., M.M., M.P.T., M.M.P., M.I., M.S.N., Ph.D., Ed.D.

ADMISSION REQUIREMENTS. Transcripts, GRE, GMAT (Business), three letters of recommendation required in support of application. TOEFL required of international applicants. Accepts transfer applicants. Graduates of unaccredited institutions not considered. Apply to the Office of Graduate Studies before July 1 (Fall), December 1 (Spring), April 1 (Summer). Application fee $40. Phone: (302)831-2129; fax: (302)831-8745; E-mail: john.cavanaugh @mvs.udel.edu.

ADMISSION STANDARDS. Selective to very competitive.

FINANCIAL AID. Annual awards from institutional funds: 416 University fellowships, 407 teaching assistantships, 412 research assistantships, traineeships, Federal W/S, loans. Approved for VA benefits. Apply by March 1 to appropriate department chair in each Graduate College for assistantships, fellowships; to the Financial Aid Office for all other programs. Use FAFSA. Phone: (302)931-9761. About 70% of students receive aid from University.

DEGREE REQUIREMENTS. For master's: 30–48 semester hours minimum; proficiency in one language for some departments thesis/nonthesis option/special project. For Ph.D.: three years minimum beyond the bachelor's, at least one year in continuous residence; language proficiency for some programs; oral/written qualifying exam; dissertation; final oral exam.

FIELDS OF STUDY.

COLLEGE OF AGRICULTURAL SCIENCES:
Agricultural Economics.
Animal Science and Agricultural Biochemistry. M.S., Ph.D.
Entomology.
Food and Resource Economics. M.S. only.
Food Science. M.S. only.
Plant and Soil Sciences. M.S., Ph.D.
Plant Science.
Public Horticulture Administration. M.S. only.

COLLEGE OF ARTS AND SCIENCE:
American Civilization.
Applied Mathematics.
Art. M.A., M.F.A. only.
Art Conservation. Ph.D.
Art History.
Biological Sciences. Interdepartmental. Includes marine biology, morphology, ichthyology, botany, zoology, microbiology; one language for master's. M.S., Ph.D.
Chemistry and Biochemistry. M.A., M.S., Ph.D.
Climatology. Ph.D. only.
Communication.
Computer and Information Science. M.S., Ph.D.
Criminology.
Early American Culture. Two-year program; M.A. only.
Ecology. M.S., Ph.D.
English. One language; general qualifying exam for M.A.
Foreign Languages and Literatures. M.A.
Foreign Languages and Pedagogy.
French. M.A. only.
Geography. M.A., M.S.
Geology. M.S., Ph.D.
German. M.A. only.
History. M.A., Ph.D.
International Relations. M.A.
Liberal Studies. M.A.
Linguistics. M.A., Ph.D.
Mathematics. M.A., M.S., Ph.D.
Music. Includes performance, teaching. M.M. only.
Neuroscience. Ph.D.
Operations Research. M.S., Ph.D.
Physical Therapy. M.P.T.
Physics. Oral exam for M.S.
Political Science. M.A. only.
Psychology. Includes clinical, cognitive, social, neuroscience. Ph.D. only.
Public Administration.
Sociology. M.A., Ph.D.
Statistics. M.S., Ph.D.
Theater. Includes acting, stage management, technical production. M.F.A. only.

COLLEGE OF BUSINESS AND ECONOMICS:
Accounting. M.S. only.
Business Administration. GMAT for admission. M.B.A. only.
Economics. M.A., M.S., Ph.D.
Economic-Business Administration. M.A.-M.B.A.

COLLEGE OF EDUCATION:
Applied Human Development. M.A., Ph.D.
Cognition and Instruction. M.A., Ph.D.
College Counseling. M.Ed.
Curriculum and Instruction. M.Ed., Ph.D.
Educational Leadership. M.Ed., Ed.D.
Educational Policy. M.A., Ph.D.
ESL/Bilingualism. M.A.
Exceptional Children. M.Ed.
Instruction. M.I.
Measurement, Statistics and Evaluation. M.A., Ph.D.

School Counseling. M.A., M.Ed.
School Psychology. M.A.
Secondary Education. M.Ed.

COLLEGE OF ENGINEERING:
Applied Sciences. M.A.s only.
Chemical Engineering. M.CH.E., Ph.D.
Civil Engineering. M.C.E., Ph.D.
Electrical Engineering. M.E.E., Ph.D.
Materials Science and Engineering. M.M.S.E., Ph.D.
Mechanical Engineering. M.M.E., Ph.D.

COLLEGE OF HUMAN RESOURCES:
Applied Nutrition. M.S.
Family Studies. Ph.D. only.
General Human Nutrition. M.S only.
Individual and Family Studies. M.S.
Life Span Development. M.S. only.
Nutrient Metabolism and Utilization. M.S.

COLLEGE OF MARINE STUDIES:
Marine Policy. M.M.P. only.
Marine Studies. M.A., M.S., Ph.D.
Oceanography. Ph.D. only.

COLLEGE OF NURSING:
Nursing. M.S. only.

COLLEGE OF PHYSICAL EDUCATION, ATHLETICS AND RECREATION:
Biomechanics. M.S.
Cardiac Rehabilitation. M.S.
Exercise Physiology. M.S.
Physical Education. M.A., M.S.
Professional Development. M.A., M.S.

COLLEGE OF URBAN AFFAIRS AND PUBLIC POLICY:
Public Administration. M.P.A.
Urban Affairs and Public Policy. M.A., Ph.D.

DELTA STATE UNIVERSITY

Cleveland, Mississippi 38733-0001
http://www.deltast.edu/

Founded 1924. Located 100 miles S of Memphis, Tennessee. Coed. State control. Semester system. Library: 208,855 volumes, 717,867 microforms.

Annual tuition: resident $2294; nonresident $4888. On- and off-campus housing available. Annual on-campus housing cost: $2180. Phone: (601)846-4151. Day care facilities available.

Graduate Studies

Graduate study since 1964. Enrollment: full-time 196, part-time 411. Faculty: full-time 42, part-time 11. Degrees conferred: M.B.A., M.C.A., M.Ed., M.S., M.M.E., M.S.N., M.P.A., M.S.C.J., Ed.S., Ed.D.

ADMISSION REQUIREMENTS. Two transcripts, GRE/GMAT/MAT required in support of application. TOEFL required for international applicants. Graduates of unaccredited colleges not considered. Accepts transfer applicants. Apply to Dean of Graduate Studies at least thirty days prior to registration. Application fee none. Phone: (601)946-4310; fax: (601)946-4016.

ADMISSION STANDARDS. Selective. Usual minimum average: 2.5 (A = 4).

FINANCIAL AID. Six hundred and nine scholarships, 1500 grant 120 graduate assistantships, Federal W/S, loans. Apply to the Office of Student Financial Assistance: no specified closing date. Phone: (601)846-4670. Use FAFSA and institutional FAF. About 80% of students receive aid from all sources.

DEGREE REQUIREMENTS. For master's: 33 semester hours minimum, at least 27 in residence and one semester in full-time attendance; thesis optional; final oral/written exam. For Ed.S.: 30 semester hours beyond the master's; paper, final oral/written exam. For Ed.D.: 90 semester hours beyond the bachelor's degree; dissertation and residency requirement.

FIELDS OF STUDY.
Accountancy.
Administration and Supervision.
Biological Science.
Business Administration.
Commercial Aviation.
Counseling.
Criminal Justice.
Curriculum and Supervision.
Elementary Education.
Elementary Supervision.
English.
Guidance.
Health, Physical Education, and Recreation.
History.
Nursing.
Mathematics.
Secondary Education.
Secondary Supervision and Principalship.
Social Science.
Special Education.

UNIVERSITY OF DENVER

Denver, Colorado 80208
http://www.du.edu

Founded 1864. Coed. Private. Quarter system. Special Facilities: Humanities Institute, Echo Lake Lab, Mount Evans Observatory, Denver Research Institute, Child Study Center, Center of Marital Studies, Center for Policy and Contemporary Issues. Library: 2.9 million volumes. Over 50 PC workstations and multimedia computers available.

Tuition: per credit $465 up to 12 credit hours, no additional charge for 13 through 18 credit hours. On-campus housing for single and married students. Housing cost: One bedroom $4,053 (9-month academic year); meal plan available: $1,965 (9-month academic year). Two-bedroom units and suites available. Contact Graduate Housing Office. Phone: (303)871-2246; fax: (303)871-4064.

Faculties of Art and Humanities, Social and Natural Sciences, Mathematics and Engineering

Enrollment: full- and part-time graduate students: 448 (men 41%, women 59%). Faculty: full-time 212. Degrees Conferred: M.A., M.M., M.F.A., M.S., Ph.D.

ADMISSION REQUIREMENTS. Two transcripts, GRE (Subject Test for some programs) required in support of application. Contact department for additional requirements. TOEFL required for international students. TSE required for some programs. TSE is required for all international graduate teaching assistants. The TWE required by Communications. Application fee: $40. Phone: Graduate Admissions (303)871-2305, or request application materials directly http://www.du.edu/`bhughes/gradadm.html.

ADMISSION STANDARDS. Selective to competitive for most departments. Usual minimum average: 2.75 (A = 4).

FINANCIAL AID. Annual awards from institutional funds: 77 scholarships, 170 teaching assistantships, Federal W/S, loans. Apply by March 1 to departments for scholarships and assistantships, to Financial Aid Office for all other programs. Phone: (303)871-2681. Use FAFSA.

DEGREE REQUIREMENTS. For M.A., M.M., M.S.: 45–75 quarter hours; qualifying exam; reading knowledge of one foreign language for some departments; comprehensive exam; thesis required by many departments, optional in others, final oral/written exam required by some programs. For M.F.A.: 90 quarter hours, at least two years in residence; qualifying exam, advancement to candidacy, thesis, oral exam; gallery exhibition. For Ph.D.: 135 quarter hours minimum beyond bachelor's degree or 90 quarter hours beyond master's; Biological Sciences, Chemistry, Engineering (Materials Science) and Physics require minimum of 90 credit hours beyond bachelor's degrees; at least six quarters in residence, including two consecutive quarters of full-time attendance; reading knowledge of two foreign languages or advanced proficiency in one language; preliminary exam; advancement to candidacy; dissertation, final oral exam.

FIELDS OF STUDY.
Advertising Management. M.S.
Anthropology. M.A.
Art History. Includes museum studies. M.A.
Biological Sciences. M.S. Ph.D.
Chemistry. M.A., M.S., Ph.D.
Composition (Music). M.M.
Computer Science. M.S.
Conducting (Music). M.M.
Economics. M.A.
Electrical Engineering. M.S.
English. Includes literary studies, creative writing. M.A., Ph.D.
French. M.A.
Geography. M.A., Ph.D.
German. M.A.
History. M.A.
Human Communication Studies. M.A., Ph.D.
International and Intercultural Communication. M.A.
Judaic Studies. M.A.
Management and Engineering. M.S.
Mass Communications and Journalism Studies. M.A.
Materials Science. Ph.D.
Mathematics. M.A., M.S.
Mechanical Engineering. M.S.
Music History and Literature. M.A.
Music Performance. M.M.
Music Theory. M.A.
Philosophy. M.A.
Physics. M.S., Ph.D.
Piano Pedagogy. M.M.
Psychology. Includes child, clinical, experimental, developmental. Ph.D.
Public Relations. M.S.
Religious Studies. M.A. (Joint Ph.D. program with Iliff School of Theology.)
Sociology. M.A.
Studio Art. M.F.A.
Suzuki Pedagogy. M.M.
Note: University offers Flexible Dual Degrees; students design their own programs.

Daniels College of Business—Graduate School
http://www.dcb.du.edu

Graduate study since 1950. Quarter system. Annual tuition: full-time $15,948, per credit $443. Limited housing available.

Enrollment: full-time 350, part-time 250 (men 58%, women 42%). Faculty teaching graduate students: full-time 51, part-time 5. Degrees conferred: M.Acc., M.B.A., M.I.M., M.R.E.C.M., M.S.F., M.S.M., M.B.A.-J.D., M.I.M.-J.D.

ADMISSION REQUIREMENTS. Transcripts, GMAT two letters of recommendation, essay responses required in support of College's application. TOEFL required for international applicants. Accepts transfer applicants. Graduates of unaccredited colleges not considered. Admits Fall and Spring quarters; M.S.T. program Fall only, M.S.M. programs, all four quarters. Apply to Office of Admission by May 1 (Fall), January 1 (Spring). Rolling admissions process. Application fee $50. Phone: (303)871-3416; fax: (303)871-4466.

ADMISSION STANDARDS. Competitive for most programs. Usual minimum average 2.75 (A = 4). TOEFL score of 550 required for international applicants.

FINANCIAL AID. Annual awards from institutional funds: scholarships, twenty-three research assistantships, Federal W/S, loans. Apply by February 15 to the Student Services Office. Phone: (303)871-3416. Use FAFSA. About 20% of Students receive aid other than loans from University and outside sources.

DEGREE REQUIREMENTS. For M.B.A.: 72 quarter hour program. For M.S.F., M.R.E.C.M.: 64 quarter hour program. For M.I.M.: 79 quarter hour program. For other master's: 52–60 quarter hour programs. Additional quarter hours and thesis for some degree programs.

FIELDS OF STUDY.
Accounting.
Business Administration.
Entrepreneurship.
Finance.
International Management.
Management Information System.
Marketing.
Real Estate and Construction Management.
Real Estate Appraisal.
Real Estate Finance.

Graduate School of International Studies

Graduate study since 1929. Annual tuition: full-time $15,948, per credit $443. Graduate housing available. Enrollment: full- and part-time 225 (men 51%, women 49%). Faculty teaching graduate students: full-time 20, part-time 6. Degrees conferred: M.A., M.A.I.I.C., M.I.M., M.P.P., M.A.–M.S.W., M.A.–J.D., Ph.D.

ADMISSION REQUIREMENTS. Transcripts, 3 letters of recommendation, GRE (GMAT or LSAT may be substituted), statement of purpose required in support of the school's application. TOEFL required for international applicants. Accepts transfer applicants. Graduates of unaccredited institutions not considered. Apply to the Office of Admission by February 15 (priority date). Application fee $40. Phone: (303)871-2544; fax: (303)871-2456.

ADMISSION STANDARDS. Competitive. Usual minimum average: 3.0 (A = 4), TOEFL 550 required.

FINANCIAL AID. Annual awards from institutional funds: Eighty fellowships (includes Foreign Language and Area Studies Fellowships), thirty graduate research/teaching assistantships, Federal W/S, loans. Apply to department chair by February 15 for all non-Federal programs; to Financial Aid Office for all Federal programs. Phone: (303)871-2681. Use FAFSA and Departmental FAF.

DEGREE REQUIREMENTS. For M.A., M.A.I.I.C.: 90 quarter hour program (must include the core, one field, one concentration, and two methodology courses); thesis; foreign language proficiency. For M.P.P.: 90 quarter hour program (must include the core, one policy analysis area, one policy issue area, and a participant-observer experience). For Ph.D.: 135 quarter hour beyond bachelor's, at least three consecutive quarters in residence; most programs include the core, two fields, one concentration, three methodology courses; research tool; advancement to candidacy; one foreign language proficiency; written/oral comprehensive exam; dissertation.

FIELDS OF STUDY.
Comparative Politics.
International Economics.
International Political Economy.
International Political Theory. Concentration in Development or Human Rights.
International Politics.
International Security.
International Technology Analysis and Management.
Policy Analysis.

Graduate School of Social Work

Enrollment: full- and part-time 387 (men 15%, women 85%). Faculty teaching graduate students: full-time 21, part-time 0. Degrees conferred: M.S.W., Ph.D.

ADMISSION REQUIREMENTS. Official transcripts, three letters of recommendation required in support of School's application. A personal interview may be requested by School. TOEFL, TSE required for international applicants. Accepts transfer applicants. Graduates of unaccredited colleges not considered. Apply to Office of Admissions by May 31. Rolling admission process. Application fee $30. Phone: (303)871-2841; fax: (303)871-2845.

ADMISSION STANDARDS. Competitive. Usual minimum average: 2.75 (A = 4)

FINANCIAL AID. Annual awards from institutional funds: 6 fellowships, 17 teaching assistantship, Federal W/S, loans. Apply by February 20 to the Financial Aid Office. Phone: (303)871-2681. Use FAFSA. About 10% of students receive aid from School and outside sources.

DEGREE REQUIREMENTS. For M.S.W.: 90 quarter hours minimum, at least three quarters in full-time study; advancement to candidacy; six quarters of field practicum. For Ph.D.: 135 quarter hours minimum beyond the bachelor's degree, at least 75 quarter hours in full-time study; preliminary exam; advancement to candidacy; research tool; dissertation; final oral exam.

FIELDS OF STUDY.
Children, Youth and Families.
Community Mental Health.
Drug Dependency.
Gerontology.
Health.

College of Education

Enrollment: full-time 110, part-time 80. Faculty teaching graduate students: full-time 16, part-time 8. Degrees conferred: M.A., Ph.D.

ADMISSION REQUIREMENTS. Transcripts, letters of recommendation required in support of application. TOEFL required for international applicants. Accepts transfer applicants. Graduates of unaccredited colleges not considered. Apply to Office of Admission by January 1 (priority date). Rolling admission

process. Application fee $40. Phone: (303)871-2305, Fax: (303)871-4566.

ADMISSION STANDARDS. Competitive. Usual minimum average 2.75 (A = 4).

FINANCIAL AID. Annual awards from institutional funds: Fifty-five scholarships, ten research assistantships, nine teaching assistantships, Federal W/S, loans. Apply by March 1 to the Financial Aid Office. Phone: (303)871-2681. Use FAFSA. About 30% of students receive aid other than loans from University and outside sources.

DEGREE REQUIREMENTS. For M.A.: 45 quarter hours minimum, at least 35 in residence; thesis or extra credit required for some departments; final written/oral exam. For Ph.D.: 135 quarter hours minimum beyond the bachelor's degree, at least 90 quarter hours in full-time study; qualifying exam; comprehensive exam; advancement to candidacy; research tool; dissertation; final oral exam.

FIELDS OF STUDY.
Child and Family Studies.
Counseling Psychology. Includes guidance and counseling, mental health counseling.
Curriculum and Instruction.
Educational Psychology.
Higher Education.
International Studies.
School Administration
School Psychology.

Graduate School of Professional Psychology

Graduate study since 1976. Tuition: per credit $443. Enrollment: full- and part-time 100 (men 25%, women 75%). Faculty teaching graduate students: full-time 3, part-time 31. Degree conferred: Psy.D.

ADMISSION REQUIREMENTS. Transcripts, GRE Subject Test, four letters of recommendation required in support of School's application. TOEFL, TSE required for international applicants. Accepts transfer applicants. Graduates of unaccredited colleges not considered. Apply to Office of Admission by January 15. Application fee $40. Phone: (303)871-3873.

ADMISSION STANDARDS. Competitive. Usual minimum average 3.0 (A = 4).

FINANCIAL AID. Annual awards from institutional funds: Six teaching assistantships, loans. Apply by March 1 to the Financial Aid Office. Phone: (303)871-2681. Use FAFSA. About 20% of students receive aid other than loans from University and outside.

DEGREE REQUIREMENTS. For Psy.D.: 135 quarter hours minimum beyond the bachelor's degree, at least two years minimum in full-time study; clinical experience; advancement to candidacy; research tool; practicum; twelve-month clinical psychology internship; doctoral paper.

FIELD OF STUDY.
Clinical Psychology.

College of Law (80220)

Established 1892. Semester system. Library 300,000 volumes. Library has LEXIS, NEXIS, WESTLAW, DIALOG, INFOTRAC. Annual tuition: full-time $16,089, part-time $10,380. Total average annual additional expenses: $9,044.

Enrollment: first-year class 350, total full-time 800 (men 56%, women 46%), part-time 320. Faculty: full-time 43, part-time 60.

Degrees conferred: J.D., LL.M. (Taxation), M.S.L.A. (Legal Administration).

ADMISSION REQUIREMENTS. LSDAS Law School report, bachelor's degree, transcripts, LSAT, written statement required in support of application. Interview discouraged. Accepts transfer applicants. Graduates of unaccredited colleges not considered. Apply to Admissions Committee after November 1, before May 1 (flexible). Admits Fall only. Application fee $45. Phone: (303)871-6135.

ADMISSION STANDARDS. Competitive. Accepts 30–35% of total annual applicants.

FINANCIAL AID. Scholarships, fellowships, Federal W/S, loans, internships, externships. Apply by February 15 to Scholarship Committee Use GAPSFAS or FAFSA. About 14% of students receive aid other than loans from College.

DEGREE REQUIREMENTS. For J.D.: satisfactory completion of three-year program. For dual degrees in History, International Studies, International Management, Mineral Economics, Psychology, Social Work, Sociology. For LL.M., M.S.L.A.: satisfactory completion of two-semester program.

DEPAUL UNIVERSITY
Chicago, Illinois 60604-2287

Founded 1898. Coed. Private control. Roman Catholic affiliation. Quarter system. Graduate study at Loop, Lincoln Park, O'Hare and Oakbrook campuses. Special facilities: Institute for Applied Artificial Intelligence, Chicago Area Studies Center, Center for Church/State Studies, DePaul Performance Center, Hispanic Research Center, Center for the Studies of Values, Institute for Business Ethics, Kellstadt Center for Marketing Analysis and Planning, Mental Health Clinic, Blackstone Theatre, Psychological Testing Center. Library 665,000 volumes, 300,500 microforms, 9700 current periodicals, 245 PCs in libraries.

Tuition: per credit $290. No on-campus housing available. Average academic year off-campus housing costs: $7000–$10,500.

Graduate Study

Enrollment: full-time 3133, part-time 3501 (men 60%, women 40%). Faculty teaching graduate students: full-time 494, part-time 670. Degrees conferred: M.A., M.S., M.M., M.F.A., M.B.A., M.Ed., M.S.A., M.S.T., M.Acc., M.S.-M.I.S., Ph.D.

ADMISSION REQUIREMENTS. Official transcripts required in support of application. Letters of recommendation, GRE/GMAT interview required for some departments. TOEFL required for international applicants. Accepts transfer applicants. Graduates of unaccredited colleges not considered. Apply to appropriate Graduate School at least one month prior to registration. Rolling admission process. Application fee $25. Phone: Business (312)362-8810; Liberal Arts and Sciences (312)362-8880; Computer Science (312)362-8366; Education (312)362-8106; Music (312)362-8373; School for New Learning (312)362-8001; Theater School (312)325-8375.

ADMISSION STANDARDS. Selective to competitive for most departments. Usual minimum average 2.75 (A = 4).

FINANCIAL AID. Annual awards from institutional funds: scholarships, research assistantships, teaching assistantships, tuition waivers, Federal W/S, loans. Approved for VA benefits. Apply by May 1 to head of appropriate department for scholarships, assistantships; to Financial Aid Office for all other programs.

Phone: (312)362-8526. Use FAFSA and institutional FAF. About 20% of students receive aid other than loans from University and outside sources. Aid available for part-time students.

DEGREE REQUIREMENTS. For master's: 48–60 quarter hours minimum, at least three quarters in residence for full-time students, five quarters in residence for part-time student; reading knowledge of one or two foreign languages for some department; thesis required by many departments, optional in others; final oral/written exam required by some programs. For Ph.D.: 90 quarter hours minimum, at least six quarters in residence; comprehensive exam; advance to candidacy; dissertation; final oral exam.

FIELDS OF STUDY.

COLLEGE OF LIBERAL ARTS AND SCIENCES:
Biological Sciences.
Chemistry.
Communications.
Economics.
English.
History.
Interdisciplinary Studies.
International Studies.
Liberal Studies.
Mathematical Sciences.
Mathematics Education.
Nursing.
Philosophy. M.A., Ph.D.
Physics.
Psychology. Includes clinical, experimental, general, industrial, school. GRE/Subject for admission; additional departmental application for admission. M.A., Ph.D.
Public Services.
Rehabilitation Services.
Sociology.
Women's Studies.
Writing.

CHARLES H. KELLSTADT GRADUATE SCHOOL OF BUSINESS:
Accounting.
Association Management.
Business Administration.
Economics.
Entrepreneurship.
Finance.
Human Resource Management.
International Business.
International Markets and Finance.
Management.
Management of Information Systems.
Marketing Research.
Operations Management.
Quantitative Methods.
Taxation. M.S.T. only.

SCHOOL OF COMPUTER SCIENCE TELECOMMUNICATION AND INFORMATION SYSTEMS:
Computer Science.
Information Systems.
Management of Information Systems.
Software Engineering.
Telecommunication Systems.

SCHOOL OF EDUCATION:
Adolescent Learning Disabilities.
Bilingual Multicultural Learning Disabilities.
Business Education.
Catholic School Leadership.
Computers in Education.
Curriculum Development.

Diagnosis and Treatment of Reading Disabilities.
Educational Administration, Supervision and Curriculum.
Elementary Education.
Human Development and Learning.
Human Services Management.
Physical Education.
Secondary Schools.

SCHOOL OF MUSIC:
Applied Music.
Composition.
Jazz Studies.
Music Education.
Performance.

SCHOOL FOR NEW LEARNING:
Program for Working Professionals. M.A.

THEATER SCHOOL:
Acting.
Costume Design.
Directing.
Lighting Design.
Scenic Design.

College of Law

Founded 1912. Semester system. Located at Loop Campus. Library 283,000 volumes. Library has LEXIS, NEXIS, WEST-LAW, DIALOG, ILLINET; 95 PCs. Special facilities: International Human Rights Law Institute, Center for Church/State Studies, Health Law Institute.

Tuition: day $17,500, evening $11,300. On-campus housing limited. Contact Director of Housing. Total average annual additional expenses: $10,200.

Enrollment: first-year class 260 day, 45 evening; total full- and part-time 980 (men 52%, women 48%). Faculty: full-time 45, part-time 52. Degrees conferred: J.D., J.D.-M.B.A., J.D.-M.S. (Accounting), LL.M. (Taxation, Health Law).

ADMISSION REQUIREMENTS. LSDAS Law School report, bachelor's degree, transcripts, LSAT required in support of application. Letters of recommendation helpful. Accepts transfer applications. Graduates of unaccredited colleges not considered. Apply to Director of Admissions after September 1, before April 1. Application fee $40. Phone: (312)362-6813, outside Illinois (800)428-7453.

ADMISSION STANDARDS. Selective. Accepts 30–35% of total applicants.

FINANCIAL AID. Scholarships, Federal W/S, loans. Apply to Office of Financial Aid by May 1. Use FAFSA. Aid available to part-time students. 9% of students receive aid other than loans from the College.

DEGREE REQUIREMENTS. For J.D.: 86 semester hours, 6 semesters (day) or 8 semesters (evening) in residence; acceleration possible through attendance at two summer sessions; "C" average required. For LL.M.: at 24 credits beyond J.D.

DETROIT COLLEGE OF LAW AT MICHIGAN STATE UNIVERSITY
N-210 N. Business Complex
East Lansing, Michigan 48824

Founded 1891. Private control. Semester system. Law library: 200,000 volumes. Library has LEXIS, NEXIS, WESTLAW, OCLC, INFOTRAC; 24 PCs, 6 Macintosh.

Annual tuition: $13,000, part-time $9750.

Enrollment: first-year class, full-time 110, part-time 60; full- and part-time 693 (men 65%, women 35%). Faculty: full-time 32, part-time 35. Degree conferred: J.D.

ADMISSION REQUIREMENTS. LSDAS Law School report, transcripts, LSAT, bachelor's degree required in support of application. Interview may be required. Accepts transfer applicants. Graduates of unaccredited colleges not considered. Apply to the Dean by April 15 (Fall), October 15 (Spring). Beginning students admitted Fall or Spring. Application fee $50. Phone: (313)226-0100; fax: (313)965-5097; E-mail: heat/eya@pilot.msu.edu.

ADMISSION STANDARDS. Selective. Accepts about 20–25% of total annual applicants.

FINANCIAL AID. Scholarships, grants, Federal W/S, loans. Apply to Financial Aid Office by February 15 (Fall), September 15 (Spring). Use FAFSA.

DEGREE REQUIREMENTS. For J.D.: satisfactory completion of three-year program (day), four year program (evening); 85 semester hours minimum.

UNIVERSITY OF DETROIT MERCY
Detroit, Michigan 48219-0900

Founded 1877. In 1990 the University of Detroit and Mercy College consolidated to form a new university. Private control. Roman Catholic affiliation. Coed. Semester system. The Colleges of Business Administration, Engineering and Sciences, and Liberal Arts are at the McNichols Campus; the Colleges of Health Services, and Education and Human Services, and Housing are at Outer Drive Campus. Special facilities: Center for the Study of Development and Aging, Manufacturing Institute, Institute for Business and Community Services, Kellstadt Consumer Research Center, Polymer Institute, Center for Excellence in Environmental Engineering and Science. Library: 645,000 volumes, 777,000 microforms, 5500 current periodicals.

Tuition: per credit $428–$450. On-campus housing for 200 single students, 30 married student accommodations. Apply to Director of Residential Life for on-campus housing, to Director of Students Activities for off-campus housing information. Phone: (313)993-1230.

Graduate Studies

Graduate study since 1885. Enrollment: full-time 1279, part-time 1591 (men 55%, women 45%). Graduate faculty: full-time 165, part-time 32. Degrees conferred: M.A., M.S., M.B.A., S.Sec., M.A.T.M., M.P.A., M.Engr.Mgt., M.A.C.S., Ed.S., M.E., M.C.S., Ph.D., D.E.

ADMISSION REQUIREMENTS. Official transcripts, GRE/GMAT required in support of application. Proof of English proficiency required for international applicants. Interview not required. Accepts transfer applicants. Graduates of unaccredited institutions not considered. Apply to Graduate Office of the College or School listed below at least six weeks prior to registration. Application fee $25, $35 for international applicants. Phone: (313)993-1000; E-mail: admission@udmercy.edu.

ADMISSION STANDARDS. Selective to competitive. Usual minimum average: 3.0 (A = 4).

FINANCIAL AID. Annual awards from institutional funds: scholarships, twenty-five teaching fellowships, thirty-five graduate assistantships, two residence assistantships, one coaching assistantship, eight internships, Federal W/S, loans. Approved for

VA benefits. Apply by April 1 to appropriate department chair for fellowships, assistantships; to Scholarships and Financial Aid Office for all other programs. Phone: (313)993-3350. Use FAFSA.

DEGREE REQUIREMENTS. For master's: 30 semester hours minimum, at least 18 in residence; six hours for thesis when required or elected; final written/oral exam in some programs. For Ed.S.: 30 semester hours minimum beyond master's. For D.E.: two-year minimum beyond master's (total of 51 hours including dissertation), usually at least 30 hours in full-time residence, must be in residence in the trimester in which the final qualifying exam is taken; dissertation; oral exam. For Ph.D.: about 60–65 hours beyond the master's, at least 30 in full-time residence; language proficiency for some departments; preliminary exam; dissertation; final oral exam.

FIELDS OF STUDY.

COLLEGE OF BUSINESS ADMINISTRATION:
Business Administration. Thirty-six hours minimum for M.B.A.

COLLEGE OF ENGINEERING AND SCIENCE:
Automotive Engineering. D.E.
Biology. Thesis for M.S.
Chemical Engineering. M.E., D.E.
Civil Engineering. M.E., D.E.
Computer Science. M.E., D.E.
Economic Aspects of Chemistry. M.S.E.C.
Electrical Engineering. M.E., D.E.
Elementary Mathematics Education. M.A.T.M.
Engineering Management. M.E.M.
Junior High Mathematics Education. M.A.T.M.
Macromolecular Chemistry. M.S., Ph.D.
Manufacturing Engineering. M.E., D.E.
Mathematics. M.A.
Plastics Engineering. M.E., D.E.
Polymer Chemistry.
Secondary Mathematics Education. M.A.T.M.

COLLEGE OF LIBERAL ARTS:
Economics. M.A.
History. Thesis option; teaching plan. M.A.
International Politics and Economics. M.A.
Liberal Studies. Interdepartmental. M.A.
Political Science. M.A.
Psychology. Includes clinical, industrial/organizational, school. M.A., Specialist. Ph.D.
Public Administration. M.P.A.
Religious Studies. M.A.
Social Sciences. Interdisciplinary. M.A., Thesis option.

SCHOOL OF EDUCATION AND HUMAN SERVICES:
Counseling.
Criminal Justice Studies. M.A., M.C.S. only.
Curriculum and Instruction. M.A.
Early Childhood Education. M.A.
Educational Leadership. M.A., Ed.S.
Guidance and Counseling. M.A., Ed.S.
Health-Care Education. M.S.
Health Services Administration. M.S.
Science Education. M.S. Interdepartmental.
Security Administration. M.S.
Special Education/Learning Disabilities/Emotionally Impaired. M.A., Ed.S.
Teaching of Reading. M.A., Ed.S.

SCHOOL OF NURSING:
Nurse Anesthesiology.
Nursing Administration.

School of Law (48226)

Established 1912. Semester system. Law library 190,000 volumes. Library has NEXIS, WESTLAW. Tuition: per credit $490. Limited on-campus housing for single and married students available. Total average annual additional expense: 9,034.

Enrollment: first-year class 250, part-time 60; total full- and part-time 800 (men 56%, women 44%). Faculty: full-time 28, part-time 29. Degrees conferred: J.D. (special J.D. for Canadian lawyers), J.D.-M.B.A.

ADMISSION REQUIREMENTS. LSDAS Law School report, bachelor's degree, transcripts, two letters of recommendation, LSAT, required in support of application. Interview not required. Accepts transfer applicants. Apply to Director of Admissions after September 1, before April 15. Fall admissions only. Application fee $50. Phone: (313)596-0200.

ADMISSION STANDARDS. Selective. Accepts about 40% of total annual applicants.

FINANCIAL AID. Scholarships, grants, Federal W/S, loans. Apply to Director of Financial Aid before April 15 (flexible). Use FAFSA. About 32% of students receive aid other than loans from institutional funds.

DEGREE REQUIREMENTS. For J.D.: 86 hours required. For J.D.-M.B.A.: 108–111 hours required, 72 hours of law, 36–39 boom of M.B.A.
Note: Study-abroad programs available.

School of Dentistry (48207-4282)

Established 1932. Private control. Annual tuition: $15,500. Contact Office of Student Affairs for housing information. Phone: (313)446-1825. Total average cost for all other first-year expenses $3228.

Enrollment: first-year class 63; total 274 (men 80%, women 20%); postgraduates 7. Faculty: full-time 52; part-time 120. Degree conferred: D.D.S.

ADMISSION REQUIREMENTS. AADSAS, official transcripts, DAT (October date preferred), three letters of recommendation required in support of School's application. Interview may be requested by applicant. Applicants must have completed at least three years of college study. Accepts transfer applicants. Preference given to state residents. Apply to Director of Admissions after July 1, before April 1 Fall admission only. Application fee $25. Phone: (313)446-1859.

ADMISSION STANDARDS. Competitive. Accepts about 20–25% of total annual applicants. Approximately 95% are state residents.

FINANCIAL AID. Scholarships, grants, tuition waivers, loans. Apply after acceptance to the University Financial Aids office. Use FAFSA. Phone: (313)993-3350/446-1950. About 85% of Michigan students receive some aid from School and outside sources.

DEGREE REQUIREMENTS. For D.D.S.: satisfactory completion of forty-five-month program.

THE DICKINSON SCHOOL OF LAW
Carlisle, Pennsylvania 17013

Founded 1834. Located 20 miles SW of Harrisburg. Private control. Semester system. Library: 340,000 volumes, 554,000 microforms, 42 PCs. Library has LEXIS, NEXIS, WESTLAW, OCLC, RLIN, EPIC.

Annual tuition: $14,500. On-campus housing for 100 single students. Total average cost for all other expenses: $18,850. Apply to Director of Housing. Phone: (717)243-4611, ext. 220.

Enrollment: first-year class 180; full-time 530 (men 52%, women 48%); no part-time study. Faculty: full-time 27, part-time 38. Degrees conferred: J.D., LL.M. (Comparative Law).

ADMISSION REQUIREMENTS. LSDAS Law School report, bachelor's degree, transcripts, two letters of recommendation, LSAT required in support of application. Interview not required. Accepts transfer applicants. Graduates of unaccredited colleges not considered. Apply to Office of Admissions preferably after September 1, before February 15, before June 15 (transfers). Fall admission only. Application fee $50. Phone: (800)840-1122; fax: (717)243-4443.

ADMISSION STANDARDS. Selective. Accepts about 30–40% of total annual applicants.

FINANCIAL AID. Scholarships, grants, Federal W/S, loans. Apply to Chair, Scholarship Committee, by February 15. Use GAPSFAS or FAFSA. About 30% of students receive aid other than loans from School.

DEGREE REQUIREMENTS. For J.D.: satisfactory completion of 88 semester hours minimum, summer session abroad available. For LL.M.: at least 24 credits beyond J.D.; thesis.
Note: Special summer program in Florence, Vienna, and Strasbourg.

DISTRICT OF COLUMBIA SCHOOL OF LAW
719 13th Street, N.W.
Washington, D.C. 20005

Established 1986. Public control. Semester system. Library: 182,000 volumes. Library has LEXIS, WESTLAW, DIALOG.

Annual tuition: DC resident $3500, nonresidents $10,950. No on-campus housing available. Total average annual additional expense: $16,100.

Enrollment: first-year class 106; full-time 280 (men 50%, women 50%); no part-time study. Faculty: full-time 26, part-time 10. Degrees conferred: J.D.

ADMISSION REQUIREMENTS. LSDAS Law School report, bachelor's degree, transcripts, letters of recommendation, LSAT required in support of application. Interview not required. Accepts transfer applicants. Graduates of unaccredited colleges not considered. Apply to Office of Admissions preferably before April 1. Fall admission only. Application fee $35. Phone: (202)727-5232.

ADMISSION STANDARDS. Accepts about 60% of total annual applicants.

FINANCIAL AID. Scholarships, grants, Federal W/S, loans. Apply to the Office of Financial Aid by April 30. Use FAFSA. About 50% of students receive aid other than loans from School.

DEGREE REQUIREMENTS. For J.D.: satisfactory completion of eighty-five-semester hour program.

DOMINICAN COLLEGE
San Rafael, California 94901-8008

Founded 1890. Coed. Private control, Roman Catholic. Semester system. Library: 95,000 volumes, 2300 microforms, 300 current periodicals, 10 PCs.

Annual tuition: full-time $11,630, part-time $485 per credit. On-campus housing for single students only. Average academic year housing cost: $6240–$6700 (including board); off-campus housing costs: $700 per month. Contact the Dean of Student Services. Phone: (415)485-3277.

Graduate Division

Graduate study since 1950. Enrollment: full-time 215, part-time 177. Faculty: full-time 15, part-time 3. Degrees conferred: M.A., M.B.A., M.B.A.-S.L., M.B.A.-Pacific Basin Studies, M.S.

ADMISSION REQUIREMENTS. Official transcripts, three letters of recommendation, interview required in support of application. TOEFL required for international applicants. Accepts transfer applicants. Graduates of unaccredited institutions not considered. Apply to Chair of appropriate Department. Admissions deadlines vary by departments. Application fee $35. Phone: (415)485-3291; fax: (415)485-3205.

ADMISSION STANDARDS. Selective. Usual minimum average: 2.75 (A = 4).

FINANCIAL AID. Annual awards from institutional funds: scholarships, fellowships, grants, assistantships, Federal W/S, loans. Approved for VA benefits. Apply by March 2 to Financial Aid Office. Phone: (415)485-3204; fax: (415)485-3205. Use FAFSA. About 20% of students receive aid other than loans from College and outside sources.

DEGREE REQUIREMENTS. For master's: 30–60 units depending on degree, at least 24 in residence; reading knowledge of one foreign language for some programs; thesis for M.S. in Education; final comprehensive exam or internship.

FIELDS OF STUDY.
Counseling Psychology.
Humanities. Includes history, literature, art history, religion, philosophy.
International Business.
International Economic and Political Assessment in the Pacific Basin.
Strategic Leadership.

DRAKE UNIVERSITY
Des Moines, Iowa 50311-4516

Founded 1881. Coed. Private control. Semester system. Special facilities: Agricultural Law Center, Center for Hypertension Research, Health Issues Research Center, Information System Research Center, Insurance Research and Professional Development Center, Center for the Study of Urban Problems, Library 700,000 volumes, 1,006,000 microforms, 5500 current periodicals, 240 PCs in all libraries.

Annual tuition: full time $14,780; M.B.A. $14,730; per credit $415–$510. On-campus housing available for both single and married students. Average academic year housing costs: $3300 for single students; $3600 for married students; off-campus $200–$350 per month. Contact Housing Office for both on- and off-campus housing information. Phone: (515)271-2196.

Graduate Study

Graduate study since 1881. Enrollment full-time 100, part-time 1387. Faculty: full-time 276. Degrees conferred: M.A., M.S., M.S.T., M.A.T., M.S. in Education, M.S.N., Ed.S., Ed.D., Doctor of Pharmacy. Joint programs: M.B.A.-J.D., M.P.A.-J.D., M.A.(Mass Communication)-J.D., M.B.A.-Pharmacy.

ADMISSION REQUIREMENTS. Official transcripts, GRE or MAT required in support of application. GMAT is required for M.B.A. degree program. Interview usually not required. TOEFL required for international applicants. Accepts transfer applicants. Graduates of unaccredited institutions not considered. Apply to the Office of Graduate Admissions at least six weeks prior to registration; Doctoral applicants apply by February 1. Application fee $25. Phone: (515)271-3871 or toll-free (800)44-DRAKE; fax: (515)271-2831; E-mail: admitinfo@acad.drake.edu

ADMISSION STANDARDS. Competitive for some departments, selective for the others. Usual minimum average: 2.5 (3.0 last two years in major) (A = 4).

FINANCIAL AID. Assistantships, fellowships, Federal W/S, loans. Approved for VA benefits. Apply to appropriate department chair for assistantships, fellowships; to Office of Student Financial Planning. Priority deadline March 1. Use FAFSA. Phone: (515)271-2905.

DEGREE REQUIREMENTS. For master's: 30–36 semester hours minimum, at least two-thirds of the course work in residence; 3–8 hours are given for graduate project, usually a thesis, field report, or creative project; final written/oral exam. For Ed.S.: 30 hours minimum beyond the master's. For Ed.D.: 60 hours minimum beyond master's, at least 2 semesters in residence; written/oral exam; dissertation; internship experience.

FIELDS OF STUDY.
Art. Includes creative, education, painting, printmaking.
Biology.
Business Administration.
Education. Includes elementary and secondary, administration and supervision, counseling, counselor education, higher education, special education (mental disabilities, behavioral disorders, learning disabilities and multicategorical with integration, multicategorical resource), adult education training and development, rehabilitation.
English.
Journalism. Includes mass communication.
Music. Includes applied, conducting, education, voice and instrumental.
Nursing.
Pharmacy.
Physical Science.
Physics.
Psychology.
Public Administration.

Law School

Founded 1865. Private control. Semester system. Library 240,000 volumes. Library has LEXIS, NEXIS, WESTLAW. Special facilities: Constitutional Law Resource Center, the Agricultural Law Center. Annual tuition: $15,200. Limited on-, off-campus housing available. Total average annual additional expense: $8325.

Enrollment: first-year class 186; total full-time 500 (men 61%, women 39%). Faculty: full-time 23, part-time 31. Degrees conferred: J.D.; J.D.-M.B.A., J.D.-M.A. (Mass Communications, Political Science—Iowa State University), J.D.-M.P.A., J.D.-M.S., (Agricultural Economics—Iowa State University).

ADMISSION REQUIREMENTS. LSDAS Law School report, bachelor's degree, transcripts, letters of recommendation, LSAT, writing sample required in support of application. Interview not required. Accepts transfer applicants. Graduates of unaccredited colleges not considered. Apply to Admissions Director after September 1, before March 1 (Fall admission). Fall and Summer admission (Conditional Admission programs only). Application fee $35. Phone: (800)44-DRAKE, Ext. 2782, (515)271-2782.

ADMISSION STANDARDS. Selective. Accepts 50% of total annual applicants.

FINANCIAL AID. Scholarships, merit awards, fellowships, Federal W/S, loans. Apply by March 1 to Director, Financial Aid Office. Use FAFSA. About 35% of students receive aid other than loans from School funds.

DEGREE REQUIREMENTS. For J.D.: 90 hours minimum, at least three semesters in residence.

DREW UNIVERSITY
Madison, New Jersey 07940-1493
http://www.drew.edu

Founded 1867. Located 25 miles W of New York City. Coed. Private control. Semester system. Library about 500,000 volumes, 364,000 microforms.

Annual tuition: full-time $19,400; per credit $1030. Limited on-campus housing for single and married students. Average academic year housing cost: $3672–$3880 (excluding board); for married students: $4170–$9834. Apply to University Housing Office. Phone: (201)408-3037. Day care facilities available.

Graduate School

Graduate study 1912. Enrollment: full-time 111, part-time 267 (men 178, women 200. Graduate faculty: full-time 61, part-time 17. Degrees conferred: M.A., C.M.H., M.M.H., M.Litt., Ph.D.

ADMISSION REQUIREMENTS. Transcripts, GRE General Test (for U.S. and Canadian citizens), 4 letters of reference, writing sample required in support of School's application. Interview recommended. Accepts transfer applicants. Graduates of Unaccredited Institutions not considered. Apply to Office of Graduate Admissions by February 1. For Spring application deadline contact Admissions Office. Application fee $35. Phone: (201)408-3110; fax: (201)408-3242.

ADMISSION STANDARDS. Selective. Usual minimum average: 3.3 (A = 4).

FINANCIAL AID. Scholarships, merit awards, Federal W/S, loans. Apply to the Financial Aid Office by February 15. Use FAFSA. Phone: (201)408-3112; fax: (201)408-3188. About 70% of students receive aid other than loans from University and outside sources. Aid available to part-time students.

DEGREE REQUIREMENTS. For master's: one year minimum in residence; reading knowledge of French or German or substitute; thesis. For Ph.D.: three years in full-time residence beyond the bachelor's; reading knowledge of French and German or substitute for one; final comprehensive; dissertation.

FIELDS OF STUDY.
Biblical Studies and Early Christianity. M.A., Ph.D.
English Literature. M.A., Ph.D.
Liturgical Studies. M.A., Ph.D.
Master of Letters. M.Litt.
Medieval Humanities. C.M.H., M.M.H.
Modern History and Literature.
Religion and Society. Includes Christian social ethics; sociology and anthropology of religion; psychology and religion. M.A., Ph.D.
Theological and Religious Studies. Includes philosophic, theology, historical, theology and church history, theological studies, Methodist and Wesley studies, American religious studies, contemporary theology. M.A., Ph.D.

DREXEL UNIVERSITY
Philadelphia, Pennsylvania 19104-2875
http://www.drexel.edu

Founded 1891. Coed. Private control. Quarter system. Special facilities: Art Museum, Center for Applied Neurogerontology, Image Processing Center, Bioelectrode Research Laboratory, Center for Multidisciplinary Study and Research, Biomedical Engineering and Science Institute, Environmental Studies Institute, Survey Research Center. Library 450,000 volumes, 700,000 microforms.

On- and off-campus housing available. Apply to Dean of Students Office. Phone: (215)895-3507.

College of Arts and Sciences

Tuition: per credit $502 (sciences)/$439 (humanities). Enrollment: 181 part-time 330 (men 54%, women 46%). College faculty: full-time 44, part-time 21. Degrees conferred: M.S., Ph.D.

ADMISSION REQUIREMENTS. Transcripts, letters of recommendation required in support of application. GRE General Test/Subject suggested for some departments. TOEFL required for international applicants. Accepts transfer applicants. Graduates of unaccredited institutions not considered. Apply to University Office of Admissions, Box P by August 20 (Fall), November 2 (Winter), March 1 (Spring), May 31 (Summer); International students June 20 (Fall), September 25 (Winter), January 3 (Spring), March 31 (Summer). Application fee $25. Phone: (215)895-6700; fax: (215)895-5939.

ADMISSIONS STANDARDS. Selective for most departments. Usual minimum average: 3.0 (A = 4) for last two years, 2.75 (A = 4) may be admitted on a probationary basis, departmental approval required.

FINANCIAL AID. Annual awards from institutional funds, 10 research assistantships, 108 teaching assistantships, 5 research fellowships, tuition waivers, Federal W/S, loans. USE FAFSA. Phone: (215)895-29064. Apply to appropriate department chair by March 1. About 50% of full-time students receive aid from University and outside sources. Aid not available to part-time students.

DEGREE REQUIREMENTS. For M.S.: 45 quarter credits minimum, at least 30 in residence; comprehensive exam. For Ph.D.: three-year minimum beyond the bachelor's, at least one year in full-time residence; preliminary exam; advancement to candidacy; dissertation; final oral exam.

FIELDS OF STUDY:
Arts Administration. M.S. only.
Atmospheric Science.
Biomedical Science.
Bioscience and Biotechnology.
Chemistry.
Computer Science. M.S. only.
Human Nutrition. M.S. only.
Mathematics.
Neuropsychology. M.S. only.
Nutrition and Food Sciences.
Physics.
Psychology. Ph.D. only.
Science of Instruction. M.S. only.

College of Business and Administration— Graduate Division

Tuition: per credit $369. Enrollment: full-time 299, part-time 503 (men 75%, women 25%). College faculty: full-time 69, part-time 21. Degrees conferred: M.B.A., M.S., Ph.D.

ADMISSION REQUIREMENTS. Official transcripts, two letters of recommendation, GMAT required in support of College's application. TOEFL required for international applicants. Accepts transfer applicants. Graduates of unaccredited institutions not considered. Apply by February 1 Office of Admissions. Rolling admission process. Application fee $35. Phone: (215)895-2111.

ADMISSIONS STANDARDS. Selective. Normally higher than AACSB guidelines.

FINANCIAL AID. Annual awards from institutional funds: 207 teaching assistantships, 72 graduate assistantships, tuition waivers, loans. Approved for VA benefits. Apply by February 1 to Dean of the College for assistantships; to the Office of Aid for all other programs. Use FAFSA and University's FAF. Phone: (215)895-6676. About 40% of full-time students receive aid from College and outside sources. Aid not available to part-time students.

DEGREE REQUIREMENTS. For M.B.A.: 48–60 advanced credit hours minimum, at least 39 in residence. For M.S.: 45 credit hour minimum, at least 39 credits in residence; thesis/non-thesis option. For Ph.D.: three-year minimum beyond the bachelor's, at least one year in full-time residence: preliminary exam; advancement to candidacy; dissertation; final oral exam.

FIELDS OF STUDY.
Accounting. M.S.
Decision Sciences. Ph.D.
Economics. M.B.A., Ph.D.
Finance. M.B.A., Ph.D.
Legal Studies. M.B.A.
Management. M.B.A.
Marketing. M.B.A., Ph.D.
Organizational Sciences. Ph.D.
Quantitative Methods. M.S.
Strategic Management. Ph.D. only.
Taxation. M.S.

College of Engineering

Annual tuition: full-time $13,878 (three terms); per credit $502. Enrollment: full-time 300, part-time 644 (men 84%, women 16%). Faculty: full-time 100, part-time 20. Degrees conferred: M.S., Ph.D.

ADMISSION REQUIREMENTS. Transcripts, two letters of recommendation required in support of College's application. GRE strongly recommended for applicants requesting assistantships. TOEFL required for international applicants. Accepts transfer applicants. Graduates of unaccredited institutions not considered. Apply to University Office of Admissions by August 20 (Fall), November 2 (Winter), March 1 (Spring), May 30 (Summer); international students June 20 (Fall), September 25 (Winter), January 3 (Spring), March 31 (Summer). Application fee $35. Phone: (215)895-6706; fax: (215)895-5939.

ADMISSION STANDARDS. Selective for most departments. Usual minimum average: 3.0 (A = 4) for last two years; 2.75 may be admitted on a probationary basis; departmental approval required.

FINANCIAL AID. Annual awards from institutional funds: ninety research assistantships, seventy-two teaching assistantships, nine fellowships, tuition waivers, Federal W/S, loans. Approved for VA benefits. Apply by March 1 to appropriate department chair for fellowships, assistantship; to Financial Aid Office for all other programs. Phone: (215)895-2964. About 50% of full-time students receive aid from University and outside sources. Aid available to part-time students.

DEGREE REQUIREMENTS. For M.S.: 45 credit hours minimum, at least 30 in residence; comprehensive exam. For Ph.D.: three-year minimum beyond the bachelor's, at least one year in residence (requirement varies by Department); preliminary exam; candidacy; dissertation; final oral exam.

FIELDS OF STUDY.
Biochemical Engineering. M.S. only.
Biomedical Engineering.
Biomedical Engineering and Sciences. Multidisciplinary.
Chemical Engineering.
Civil Engineering.
Electrical and Computer Engineering.
Engineering Geology. M.S. only.
Engineering Management. M.S. only.
Environmental Engineering.
Environmental Engineering and Science. Multidisciplinary.
Materials Engineering.
Mechanical Engineering and Mechanics.

College of Information Science and Technology

Founded 1892. Tuition: per credit $406. Enrollment: full-time 47, part-time 542. Faculty: full-time 15, part-time 17. Degrees conferred: M.S., M.S.I.S., Ph.D.

ADMISSION REQUIREMENTS. Official transcripts, GRE required in support of College's application. TOEFL required for international applicants. Interview not required. Accepts transfer applicants. Graduates of unaccredited institutions not considered. Apply to Office of Graduate Admissions of the College at least one month prior to registration. Application fee $35. Phone: (215)895-2474.

ADMISSION STANDARDS. Competitive. Usual minimum average: 3.0 (A = 4).

FINANCIAL AID. Annual awards from institutional funds: two scholarships, eleven graduate assistantships, seven library assistantships, loans. Apply by February 1 to Office of the Dean for assistantships; to Financial Aid Office for all other programs. Use FAFSA. Phone: (215)895-2474. About 20% of students receive aid other than loans from School and outside sources. Aid available to part-time students.

DEGREE REQUIREMENTS. For M.S., M.S.I.S.; 60 quarter hours minimum, at least 30 in residence. For Ph.D.: one year, full-time residence; approved plan of study; dissertation; final oral exam.

FIELDS OF STUDY.
Information Studies. Ph.D. only.
Information Systems. M.S.I.S. only.
Library and Information Science. M.S. only.

Nesbitt College of Design Arts

Graduate study since 1952. Tuition: per credit $439. Enrollment: full-time 60, part-time 80. Graduate faculty: full-time 35, part-time 19. Degree conferred: M.S.

ADMISSION REQUIREMENTS. Transcripts, two letters of recommendation required in support of application. TOEFL required for international applicants. Interview recommended. Accepts transfer applicants and a limited number of nonmatriculants. Graduates of unaccredited institutions not considered. Apply to Dean of Graduate Admissions. Application fee $25. Phone: (215)895-6700; fax: (215)895-5939.

ADMISSION STANDARDS. Very selective. Usual minimum average: 3.0 (A = 4).

FINANCIAL AID. First-year students limited to Federal W/S, loans. 15 graduate assistantships for second-year students. Apply to Dean of Graduate Admission; no specified closing date. Phone: (215)895-6700.

DEGREE REQUIREMENTS. For M.S.: 45 quarter credits minimum, at least 30 in residence; major comprehensive project.

FIELDS OF STUDY.
Fashion Design.
Interior Design.
Publication Management. Includes publishing, printing, business and writing courses.

DRURY COLLEGE
Springfield, Missouri 65802-3791

Founded 1873. Located 180 miles SE of Kansas City. Coed. Private control, United Church of Christ Congregational Church. Semester system. Library: 240,000 volumes.

Tuition; M.B.A., per semester hour $210; M.Ed., per semester hour $158. On-campus housing for single students only. During Summer terms (two 5-week terms): single person $295 per term. Apply to Dean of Students. Phone: (417)873-7215.

Graduate Program

Enrollment: 425, most are part-time. College faculty teaching graduate students: full-time 25, part-time 20. Degrees conferred: M.B.A., M.Ed.

ADMISSION REQUIREMENTS: Transcripts, MAT or GMAT (depending on major) required in support of application. TOEFL required for international applicants. Accepts transfer applicants. Graduates of unaccredited institutions not considered. Apply to Director of appropriate program well in advance of registration. Application fee $20. Phone: (417)873-7271; fax: (417)873-7432.

ADMISSION STANDARDS. Selective. Usual minimum average: 2.75 (A = 4).

FINANCIAL AID. Limited to ten fellowships, three teaching assistantships, Federal W/S, loans. Apply to Director of appropriate program for fellowships, assistantships; to Financial Aid Office for federal programs; no specified closing dates. Phone: (417)873-7312. Use FAFSA.

DEGREE REQUIREMENTS. For M.Ed.: 36 semester hours for degree. For M.B.A.: 31 semester hours required, 25 in residence plus 24 hours of undergraduate prerequisite courses.

FIELDS OF STUDY.
Business Administration. Includes joint program with American Graduate School of International Management (Thunderbird).
Education. Includes elementary, English, social science, science, middle school, gifted education.

UNIVERSITY OF DUBUQUE
Dubuque, Iowa 52001-5050
http://www.dbq.edu

Founded 1852. Located 185 miles W of Chicago. Coed. Private control. Affiliated with the Presbyterian Church (U.S.A.). Semester system. Library: 165,000 volumes, 27,000 microforms, 800 current periodicals, 10 PCs.

Tuition: per semester credit $300. On-campus housing available for single students, but limited for married students. Average academic year housing costs: single students $4340 (including board). Contact the Director of Housing for both on- and off-campus housing information. Phone: (319)589-3583.

Graduate Studies

Graduate study since 1964. Education courses offered through the Dubuque Tri-College Cooperative Effort, in conjunction with Clarke College and Loras College. Enrollment: full-time 117, part-time 120. College faculty teaching graduate students: full-time 22, part-time 8. Degrees conferred: M.A., M.B.A., M.Ed.

ADMISSION REQUIREMENTS. Transcripts, two letters of recommendation, eligibility for School Certification (Education), GRE/MAT/GMAT required in support of application. TOEFL required for international applicants. Accepts transfer applicants. Apply to Graduate Studies at least one month prior to registration. Application fee $25. Phone: (319)589-3200; fax: (319)556-8633.

ADMISSION STANDARDS. Selective. Usual minimum average: 2.5 (A = 4).

FINANCIAL AID. None other than loans and area Professional Development Grants. Use FAFSA and Institutional FAF. Phone: (319)589-3596, Fax: (319)556-8633.

DEGREE REQUIREMENTS. For master's: 36–45 semester credits minimum, at least 30 in residence; thesis/nonthesis option.

FIELDS OF STUDY.
Business Administration.
Counseling. Includes elementary and secondary, early childhood education.
Educational Administration. Includes elementary and secondary.
Educational Media. Includes elementary and secondary.
Integrated Language.
Reading. Elementary only.
Special Educational. Includes multicategorical.
Technology in Education.

DUKE UNIVERSITY
Durham, North Carolina 27708-0065

Founded 1838. Private control. Semester system. Special facilities: Animal Behavior Station, Asian-Pacific Institute, Botanical and Zoological Laboratories, Canadian Studies program, Center for Demographic Studies, Center for Documentary Studies, Center on East-West Trade Investments and Communications, Center for Emerging Cardiovascular Technologies, Center for Health Policy Research and Education, Center for International Development Research, Center for International Studies, Center for Mathematics and Computation in Life Sciences and Medicine, Center for the Study of Aging and Human Development, Center for Tropical Conservation, Center for Research on Women, Duke Forest with 7700 acres, Marine Laboratory, Morphometrics Laboratory, Oak Ridges National Laboratory, Organization for Tropical Studies, Phytotron, Primate Facilities, Program in Integrative Biology, Program in Latin-American Studies, Program in Political Economy, Program in Russian and East European Studies. Library: 4,300,000 volumes, 9,500,000 manuscripts, over 2,000,000 public documents, 31,800 current periodicals, 300 PCs in all libraries.

Annual tuition: full-time $15,324 (Ph.D. students); per unit $600 (master's students). On-campus apartments: 206 available for single students. Average cost per academic year of an on-campus apartment: $2869–$4423. Contact Office of Housing

Administration for both on- and off-campus housing information. Phone: (919)684-4304.

The Graduate School

Enrollment: full-time 2099, part-time 190. Faculty: full-time 1079, part-time 190. Degrees conferred: A.M., M.S., M.A.T., Ph.D.

ADMISSION REQUIREMENTS. Two copies of official transcript from each college, university, or seminary attended, three letters of recommendation, GRE required in support of School's application. GRE Subject Test required for some programs. International applicants must submit evidence of English proficiency and a financial statement. Accepts transfer applicants. Graduates of unaccredited colleges not considered. Apply to the Dean of the Graduate School by December 31 (Fall), November 1 (Spring). For Summer Session apply to the Dean of the Graduate School and to the Director of the Summer Session by April 15 (Summer Session I), May 15 (Summer Session II). Application fee $65. Phone: (919)684-3913; E-mail: grad-admission@acpub.duke.edu.

ADMISSION STANDARDS. Competitive for most departments, very competitive for the other. Usual minimum average: 3.0 (A = 4).

FINANCIAL AID. Annual awards: Scholarships, fellowships, teaching assistantships, research assistantships, Federal W/S, loans. Apply to the Dean of the Graduate School. The application form for admission is also the application for financial aid, and should be completed by December 31. Use FAFSA. About 80% of full-time students receive aid other than loans from University and outside sources.

DEGREE REQUIREMENTS. For A.M., M.S., M.A.T.: 30 credits minimum; thesis; final oral exam; nonthesis option in some departments. For Ph.D.: 60 credits minimum beyond the bachelor's, at least one year full-time in residence; language requirements vary by department; preliminary exam; dissertation; final oral exam.

FIELDS OF STUDY.
Art History. A.M., Ph.D.
Biochemical Engineering. M.S., Ph.D.
Biochemistry. Ph.D. only.
Biological Anthropology and Anatomy. Ph.D.
Biomedical Engineering. Ph.D.
Botany. Ph.D.
Business Administration. Ph.D.
Cell Biology. Ph.D.
Chemistry. Ph.D.
Civil and Environmental Engineering. M.S., Ph.D.
Classical Studies. Ph.D.
Computer Science. Ph.D.
Cultural Anthropology. Ph.D.
Economics. A.M., Ph.D.
Electrical Engineering. M.S., Ph.D.
English. Ph.D.
Environmental Engineering. A.M., M.S., Ph.D.
Genetics. Ph.D.
Geology. M.S., Ph.D.
Germanic Studies. Ph.D.
History. Ph.D.
Humanities Program. A.M.
Immunology. Ph.D.
International Development Policy. A.M.
Liberal Studies. A.M.
Literature Program. Ph.D.
Mathematics. Ph.D.
Mechanical Engineering and Materials Science. M.S., Ph.D.
Microbiology. Ph.D.

Molecular Cancer Biology.
Music. A.M., Ph.D.
Musicology. Ph.D.
Neurobiology. Ph.D.
Pathology. Ph.D.
Pharmacology. Ph.D.
Philosophy. Ph.D.
Physical Therapy. M.S.
Physics. Ph.D.
Political Science. A.M., Ph.D.
Psychology. Includes experimental, social and health science. Ph.D. only.
Public Policy Studies. A.M. only.
Religion. Ph.D.
Romance Studies. Ph.D.
Slavic Languages and Literatures. Ph.D.
Sociology. A.M., Ph.D.
Statistics and Decision Sciences. Ph.D.
Zoology. Ph.D. only.

Divinity School

Founded 1926. Annual tuition: full-time $9000; per course $1125. Enrollment: full-time 403, part-time 48. Faculty: full-time 28, part-time 12. Degrees conferred: M.Div., M.C.M., M.T.S., Th.M.

ADMISSION REQUIREMENTS. Transcripts, five letters of recommendations, required in support of School's application. TOEFL, TSE required for international applicants. Interview not required. Accepts transfer applicants. Apply to Director of Admissions by April 1 (Fall), November 1 (January). Application fee $25. Phone: (919)660-3436; fax: (919)660-3474.

ADMISSION STANDARDS. Selective. Usual minimum average: 2.7 (A = 4).

FINANCIAL AID. Tuition grants, field education grants, scholarships, loans. Apply to Financial Aid Office by May 1. Phone: (919)660-3442; fax: (919)660-3473. Use FAFSA. No aid for nondegree candidates.

DEGREE REQUIREMENTS. For M.Div.: 24 course units plus 2 field education credits. For M.C.M.: 16 course units plus 1 field education credit. For M.T.S.: 16 course units with a 2.5 GPA average. For Th.M.: 8 course units with a B average.

Nicholas School of the Environmental

PO Box 90330
http://www.env.duke.edu

Graduate study since 1938. School moved into a new Research Center (Levine Science Research Center in 1994. Annual tuition: $16,500; per credit $700. Graduate enrollment: full-time 205, part-time 10 (men 48%, women 52). Faculty: full-time 60 (includes Durham at Marine Laboratory), part-time 12. Degrees conferred: M.F., M.E.M.; M.S., A.M., Ph.D. through the Graduate School.

ADMISSION REQUIREMENTS. Transcripts, three letters of recommendation, GRE General Test required in support of School's application. TOEFL required for international applicants. Interview not required. Graduates of unaccredited institutions not considered. Apply to Office of Enrollment Services by December 31 for M.S., A.M., Ph.D.; February 15 for M.F., M.E.M. Application fee $65. Phone: (919)613-8070; fax: (919)684-8741; E-mail: admission @env.duke.edu.

ADMISSION STANDARDS. Average of all accepted applicants: 3.4 (A = 4), 650 score on each section of GRE.

FINANCIAL AID. Scholarships, fellowships, assistantship, Federal W/S, loans. Apply by February 15 to Office of Enrollment Services. Use FAFSA. Phone: (919)613-8070.

DEGREE REQUIREMENTS. For M.F., M.E.M.: 48 semester credits (with a possible exception for professionals in the field), at least four semesters in residence; master's project. For A.M., M.S., Ph.D.: see Graduate School listing above.

FIELDS OF STUDY.
Biohazard Sciences.
Coastal Environmental Management.
Environmental Law. M.F./M.E.M.-J.D., A.M.-J.D.
Environmental Management and Business. M.F./M.E.M.-M.B.A.
Environmental Management and Public Policy. M.F./M.E.M.-M.P.P.
Environmental Toxicology, Chemistry and Risk Assessment.
Forest Resource Management.
Ocean Sciences.
Resource Ecology.
Resource Economics and Policy.
Water and Air Resources.

School of Law (Box 90393)

Founded 1904. Semester System. Law library 400,000 volumes. Annual tuition: $22,300. Total average cost for all other expenses: $11,000–$13,000. Housing available.

Enrollment: first-year class 200. Total full-time 595 (men 60%, women 40%). Faculty: full-time 40, part-time 36. Degrees conferred: J.D., J.D.-LL.M. (International and Comparative Legal Studies), LL.M., S.J.D., M.L.S.

ADMISSION REQUIREMENTS. LSDAS Law School report, bachelor's degree, transcripts, LSAT (no later than December), two recommendations required in support of application. Interview not required. Transfer applicants considered. Graduates of unaccredited colleges not considered. Applications should be completed by January 15. Fall admission only. Application fee $65. Phone: (919)613-7200.

ADMISSION STANDARDS. Selective. Accepts about 15-20% of total annual applications.

FINANCIAL AID. Scholarships, Federal W/S, loans. Submit financial aid application with admission application. Use FAFSA. About 30% of students receive aid other than loans from School, 50% from all sources. A loan forgiveness plan is available.

DEGREE REQUIREMENTS. For J.D.: 84 semester hours minimum, at least four semesters in residence. For LL.M., S.J.D., M.L.S.: programs arranged on an individual basis. School offers joint master's programs in Business Administration, Economics, English, Environmental Management, Mechanical Engineering, Policy Science, Medicine and Health Administration, Public Policy, Ph.D. in Political Science.

School of Medicine (27710)

Established 1930. Located at Durham. Library 239,000 volumes. Annual tuition: $24,650; student fees $1341. Total average figure for all other expenses $7631.

Enrollment: first-year class 104; total full-time 446 (men 57%, women 43%). Faculty: full-time 551, part-time 1. Degrees conferred: M.D., M.D.-J.D., M.D.-M.A., M.D.-Ph.D. [Medical Scientist Training Program], M.D.-M.P.H., M.D.-M.H.A.

ADMISSION REQUIREMENTS. AMCAS report, transcripts, MCAT, interview required in support of application. Applicants must have completed at least three years of college study. Accepts transfer applicants. Graduates of unaccredited colleges not considered. Special consideration given to North Carolina residents. Does not have EDP. Apply to Committee on Admissions after June 15, before October 15. Application fee $55. Phone: (919)684-2985; fax: (919)684-8893.

ADMISSION STANDARDS. Very competitive. Accepts about 4% of total annual applicants. Approximately 32% are state residents.

FINANCIAL AID. Scholarships, loans, summer research fellowships. Apply to Coordinator, Financial Aid after acceptance, before April 1; Use FAFSA. About 75% of students receive some aid from School.

DEGREE REQUIREMENTS. For M.D.: satisfactory completion of four-year program.

FIELDS OF GRADUATE STUDY.
Biochemistry.
Biomedical Engineering.
Cell Biology.
Genetics.
Health Administration.
Immunology.
Law.
Medical History.
Microbiology.
Molecular Biology.
Neurosciences.
Pathology.
Pharmacology.
Public Health.
Public Policy Sciences.

DUQUESNE UNIVERSITY
Pittsburgh, Pennsylvania 15282-0001

Founded 1878. Coed. Private control. Roman Catholic affiliation. Semester system. Library: 648,000 volumes, 421,000 microforms, 5500 current periodicals. Tuition: per credit $444. On-campus housing for single students only. Average annual housing cost: $5418 (including board). Contact Housing Director for both on- and off-campus housing information. Phone: (412)396-5028.

Graduate School of Liberal Arts

Enrollment: full-time 390, part-time 281. Faculty: full-time 84, part-time 26. Degrees conferred: M.A., M.L.S., M.S., Ph.D.

ADMISSION REQUIREMENTS. Official transcripts, GRE/GMAT/MAT, three letters of recommendation required in support of School's application. TOEFL required for international applicants. Interview required by some departments. Accepts transfer applicants. Graduates of unaccredited institutions not considered. Apply to Office of Graduate School by August 1 (Fall), May 1 (Fall for financial aid applicants), January 1 (Spring). Application fee $40. Phone: (412)396-6400; fax: (412)396-5644.

ADMISSION STANDARDS. Selective to very competitive. Usual minimum average: 3.0 (A = 4).

FINANCIAL AID. Annual awards from institutional funds: 69 scholarships, 23 research assistantships, 64 teaching assistantships, Federal W/S, loans. Apply by May 1 to Dean of School for assistantships, scholarships; to Financial Aid Office for all other programs. Use FAFSA. Phone: (412)396-6607. About 25% of students receive aid other than loans from School and outside sources.

DEGREE REQUIREMENTS. For master's: 24 credit hours minimum, at least one year in residence; reading knowledge of one foreign language in some departments; thesis; comprehensive exam; or 30 credit hours minimum, at least one year in residence; reading knowledge of one foreign language in some departments; comprehensive exam. For Ph.D.: 56 credits hours minimum, at least one year in residence; preliminary exam; reading knowledge of two foreign languages or one language and one language equivalency; dissertation; final oral/written exam.

FIELDS OF STUDY.
Archival, Museum, and Editing Studies. M.A.
Church Administration and Canon Law. M.A.
Conflict Resolution. M.A.
Corporate Communications. M.A.
English. M.A., Ph.D.
Health-Care Ethics. M.A.
History. M.A.
Liberal Studies. M.L.S.
Pastoral Ministry. M.A.
Pharmaceutical Sciences. Apply by April 1 (Fall); two-year program including residency; thesis for M.S.; Ph.D. in pharmaceutical chemistry only.
Philosophy. M.A., Ph.D.
Psychology. Essay, two letters of recommendation for admission; 30 hours minimum; thesis for M.A.; 48 hours minimum beyond the master's for Ph.D. Admits Fall semester only.
Religion and Personality. Offered by Institute of Formative Spirituality; 30–48 hours minimum, nonthesis program for M.A.; Ph.D., 54 credits plus 6 credit dissertation.
Rhetoric and Philosophy of Communication. M.A.
Social and Public Policy. M.A.
Theology. M.A., Ph.D.

Graduate School of Business and Administration

Established 1913. Graduate study since 1958.
Tuition: per credit $438. Enrollment: full-time 120, part-time 430 (men 330, women 220). Faculty: full-time 36, part-time 10. Degrees conferred: M.B.A., M.S., M.B.A.-J.D., M.B.A.-M.S. (Environmental Science, Health Management Systems), M.S.-Pharm., M.S. in M.I.S., M.B.A.-M.S. (Nursing).

ADMISSION REQUIREMENTS. Official transcripts, GMAT, three letters of reference required in support of School's application. TOEFL required for international applicants. Accepts transfer applicants. Apply to Associate Dean of the School by June 1 (Fall), November 1 (Spring). Application fee $40 for domestic; $40 for international applicants. Phone: (412)396-6276; fax: (412)396-5304.

ADMISSION STANDARDS. Selective. Usual minimum average: 3.0 (A = 4); Average GMAT: 510.

FINANCIAL AID. Annual awards from institutional funds: 27 assistantships. Apply by June to Associate Dean of School. Phone: (412)396-6607, Fax: (412)396-5284. About 80% of students receive aid other than loans. Aid available for part-time students.

DEGREE REQUIREMENTS. For master's: maximum 56 credits; thesis optional.

FIELDS OF STUDY.
Accounting.
Economics.
Finance.
Human Resources.
International Business.
Management.
Management Information Systems.

Marketing.
Taxation.

School of Education—Graduate Division

School established 1929. Enrollment: full-time 217, part-time 621. Graduate faculty: full-time 30, part-time 17. Degrees conferred: M.S.Ed., C.A.G.S., Ed.D.

ADMISSION REQUIREMENTS. Official transcripts required in support of School's application. MAT, three letters of recommendation, interviews sometimes required. TOEFL required for international applicants. Accepts transfer applicants. Graduates of unaccredited institutions not considered. Apply to the School by August 1 (Fall), January 1 (Spring), June 1 (Summer). Application fee $40. Phone: (412)396-6091; fax: (412)396-5585.

ADMISSION STANDARDS. Selective. Usual minimum average: 2.50 (A = 4).

FINANCIAL AID. Limited to seventeen assistantships, Federal W/S, loans. Approved for VA benefits. Apply to Dean's Office for assistantships; to Financial Aid Office for all other programs. No specified closing date. Use FAFSA and institution's FAF. Phone: (412)396-6607; fax: (412)396-5284.

DEGREE REQUIREMENTS. For master's: 30 credit hours minimum, at least 24 in residence; comprehensive exam in some programs. For C.A.G.S.: 30 credit hour minimum beyond master's. For Ed.D.: 60 credit hours minimum beyond the master's; qualifying exam; candidacy; dissertation; final oral exam.

FIELDS OF STUDY.
Counselor Education.
Educational Studies. Interdisciplinary Doctoral Program for Educational Leaders (IDPEL).
Elementary Education.
Reading and Language Arts.
Religious Education/CCO.
School Administration. Includes elementary and secondary.
School Psychology.
School Supervision.
Secondary Education.
Special Education. Includes mentally/physically handicapped.

School of Law

Established 1911. Semester system. Law library 166,000 volumes. Library has LEXIS, WESTLAW.

Annual tuition: day $12,975, evening $9773. On-campus housing available. Total average annual additional expense: $6500.

Enrollment: first-year class day 102 evening 97; total full- and part-time 640 (men, 59%, women 41%). Faculty: full-time 22, part-time 38. Degrees conferred: J.D., J.D.-M.B.A., J.D.-M.Div.

ADMISSION REQUIREMENTS. LSDAS Law School report, bachelor's degree, transcripts, LSAT, two letters of recommendation required in support of application. Interview sometimes required. Transfer applicants considered. Apply to Office of Admissions after September 1, before May 1 (rolling admission process). Fall admission only. Application fee $45. Phone: (412)396-6296.

ADMISSION STANDARDS. Competitive, Accepts 20% of total annual applicants. About 30% of entering class are nonresidents.

FINANCIAL AID. Scholarships, grants-in-aid, Federal W/S, loan. Apply to University's Financial Aid Office by May 1. Use FAFSA or PHEAA, or GAPSFAS. About 8% of students receive aid other than loans from School funds.

DEGREE REQUIREMENTS. For J.D.: satisfactory completion of three-year (day), or four-year (evening) program; 86 credit hours minimum.

EAST CAROLINA UNIVERSITY
Greenville, North Carolina 27834-4353

Founded 1907. Located 85 miles E of Raleigh. State control. Semester system. Special facilities: Center on Aging, Center for Coastal and Marine Resources, Mental Health Training Institute, East Carolina Development Institute. Library: 1,112,000 volumes, 1,588,000 microforms, 7000 current periodicals, 348 PCs.

Annual tuition: full-time resident $1557, nonresident $8041. On-campus housing for single students. Average academic year housing costs: $2490–$3190 (room only) for single students. Contact the Housing office for both on- and off-campus housing information. Phone: (919)328-6450.

Graduate School

Graduate study since 1929. Enrollment: full-time 926, part-time 1159. Graduate faculty: full-time 526, part-time 4. Degrees conferred: M.A., M.A.Ed., M.B.A., M.S.A., M.P.A., M.S.E.H., M.F.A., M.M., M.S., M.Physics, Ed.S., C.A.S., Ph.D. (Medical Sciences), Ed.D. (Educational Leadership).

ADMISSION REQUIREMENTS. Two official transcripts, GRE/GMAT (Business) required in support of School's application. MAT/GRE subject Tests, interviews, letters of reference sometimes required. TOEFL required for international applicants. Accepts transfer applicants. Graduates of unaccredited institutions not considered. Apply to Graduate School June 1 (Fall), October 15 (Spring). Rolling admission process. Application fee $35. Phone: (919)329-6012; fax: (919)328-6071.

ADMISSION STANDARDS. Selective for most departments. Usual minimum average: 2.5 (3.0 in major or senior year) (A = 4).

FINANCIAL AID. Annual awards from institutional funds: assistantships, fellowships, Federal W/S, loans. Approved for VA benefits. Apply by April 15 to appropriate department chair for assistantships, fellowships; to Financial Aid Office for all other programs. Use FAFSA. Phone: (919)328-6610. About 20% of students receive aid other than loans from University and outside sources.

DEGREE REQUIREMENTS. For M.A., M.S., M.F.A.: 30 semester hours minimum; reading knowledge of one foreign language or other research skill; thesis for most programs; final oral/written exam. For M.A. in Ed., M.B.A., M.M., M.S.H.E., M.Physics: same as for M.A., except no thesis or language requirement. For C.A.S., Ed.S.: 30 credits minimum beyond the master's; comprehensive exam. For Ed.D.: 60 semester hours beyond the master's, at least one year in full-time residency; internships, candidacy exam; dissertation. For Ph.D.: 40 semester hours; candidacy exam; dissertation; final oral exam.

FIELDS OF STUDY.
Accounting. M.S.A. only.
Adult Education. M.A.Ed. only.
Art. Includes art education. M.A., M.F.A., M.Ed.
Biology. M.S. only.
Business Administration. M.B.A. only.
Business and Marketing Education. M.A.Ed., C.A.S. only.
Chemistry. M.S. only.
Child Development and Family Relations. M.S. only.
Communication Sciences and Disorders. M.S.
Counselor Education.

Educational Administration and Supervision.
Educational Leadership. Ed.D. only.
Elementary Education.
English.
Environmental Health. M.S.E.H.
Geography. M.A. only.
Geology. M.S. only.
Health Education.
History. Includes maritime history.
Home Economics. M.S.
Home Economics Education. M.S., C.A.S.
Industrial and Technical Education. M.A.Ed. only.
Industrial Technology. M.S.
Instructional Technology Specialist—Computers. M.A. Ed. only.
Library Science. M.L.S., M.A.Ed.
Marriage and Family Therapy. M.S.
Mathematics.
Middle Grades Education.
Molecular Biology and Biotechnology.
Music. Includes accompaniment, church, composition, education, therapy, performance, piano pedagogy. M.M. only.
Nursing. M.S.N. only.
Physical Education. M.A., M.A.Ed.
Physics.
Political Science. M.A. only.
Psychology. Includes clinical, general, school; M.A., C.A.S.
Public Administration. M.P.A. only.
Reading Education.
Rehabilitation Studies. Includes substance abuse, vocational evaluation. M.S. only.
Science Education.
Social Work. M.S.W. only.
Sociology. M.A. only.
Special Education. Includes learning disabilities, mental retardation.

School of Medicine (27858-4354)

Four-year program established 1977. Annual tuition: resident $1876, nonresident $19,308; student fees $793. Average expense for all other costs: $5641. Enrollment: first-year class 72 (EDP 9); total 299 (men 49%, women 51%). Faculty: full-time 88, part-time 2. Degrees conferred: M.D., M.D.-Ph.D.

ADMISSION REQUIREMENTS. AMCAS report, transcripts, MCAT, recommendations required in support of application. Interview by invitation only. Preference given to state residents. Graduates of unaccredited colleges not considered. Has EDP for North Carolina residents only; apply between June 15 and August 1. Apply to Office of Admissions after June 15, before November 15. Application fee $35. Phone: (919)816-2202.

ADMISSION STANDARDS. Selective. Admits about 30% of total annual applications. 100% are state residents.

FINANCIAL AID. Limited scholarships, loans. Apply after acceptance to Financial Aid Office. About 65% of student receive some financial assistance.

DEGREE REQUIREMENTS. For M.D.: satisfactory completion of four-year program.

FIELDS OF GRADUATE STUDY.
Anatomy.
Biochemistry.
Cell Biology.
Immunology.
Microbiology.
Pathology.
Pharmacology.
Physiology.

EAST CENTRAL UNIVERSITY
Ada, Oklahoma 74820-6899

Established 1909. Located 90 miles SE of Oklahoma City. Coed. state control. Semester system. Library 221,000 volumes, 793,000 microforms, 12 PC workstations.

Tuition: per semester hour resident $70, nonresident $165. On-campus housing for 95 married students, 418 single men, 558 single women. Academic year housing cost: $2068. Apply to Director of Housing. Phone: married housing information (405)332-8000, ext. 226; single housing information (405)332-8000, ext. 208. Day care facilities available.

Graduate Program

Enrollment: full-time 50, part-time 550 (academic year), about 575 (Summer). College faculty teaching graduate students: full-time 50, part-time 10. Degrees conferred: M.Ed., M.S. in Psychological Services, M.S. in Human Resources.

ADMISSION REQUIREMENT. Transcripts, GRE/MAT required in support of application. Departmental writing exam for Education. TOEFL required for foreign applicants. Accepts transfer applicants. Apply to Graduate Dean prior to registration. Phone: (405)332-8000, ext. 709.

ADMISSION STANDARDS. Selective. Usual minimum average: 2.5 (M.Ed. M.S.H.R.), 3.0 (M.S.P.S.) (A = 4).

FINANCIAL AID. Awards from institutional funds: thirty scholarships, six assistantships, Federal W/S, loans; no specified closing date. Use FAFSA. Phone: (405)322-8000, ext. 242.

DEGREE REQUIREMENTS. For M.Ed.: 32 semester hours minimum, at least 24 in residence; thesis optional. For M.S.P.S.: 36 semester hours minimum; thesis optional. For M.S.H.R.: 36 semester hours minimum; rehabilitation counselor option 51 semester hours.

FIELDS OF STUDY.
Elementary Counselor.
Elementary Principal.
Elementary Teaching.
Human Resources Administration.
Human Resources Counseling.
Human Resources Criminal Justice.
Human Resources Rehabilitation Counseling.
Psychological Services.
Reading Specialist.
Secondary Counselor.
Secondary Principal.
Secondary Teaching.
Special Education (LD).

EAST STROUDSBURG UNIVERSITY OF PENNSYLVANIA
East Stroudsburg, Pennsylvania 18301

Founded 1893. Located 85 miles W of New York City. Coed. State control. Semester system. Library: 411,000 volumes, 1,146,000 microforms.

Tuition: per credit resident $179, nonresident $322. Limited on-campus housing for graduate students. Average academic year cost: $3224. On-campus housing in Summer only for single students. Average Summer cost: $100 per week (including board). Apply to director of Housing. Phone: (717)422-3461.

Graduate School

Enrollment: full-time 225, part-time 800. Faculty: full-time 111, part-time 10. Degrees conferred: M.A., M.S., M.Ed., M P.H.

ADMISSION REQUIREMENTS. Two official transcripts required in support of School's application. GRE required for some programs. TOEFL required for international applicants. Interview required by some departments. Accepts transfer applicants. Apply to Dean of Graduate School at least six weeks prior to registration. Admits to Fall and Spring semesters. Application fee $15. Phone: (717)424-3536; fax: (717)422-3506.

ADMISSION STANDARDS. Selective. Usual minimum average: 2.5, 3.0 major field (A = 4).

FINANCIAL AID. Annual awards from institutional funds: seventy research assistantships, Federal W/S, loans. Apply to the Graduate School by March 1. Use FAFSA and University's FAF. Phone: (717)422-3340. About 95% of full-time students receive aid other than loans from College and outside sources. Aid sometimes available for part-time students.

DEGREE REQUIREMENTS. For M.A.: 30 credit hours minimum, at least 24 in residence; thesis. For M.Ed. or M.S.: 30 credits minimum, at least 24 in residence, plus thesis; or 34 credits, at least 28 in residence, and research project; written comprehensive exam; final oral exam. For M.P.H.: 48 credit hours, at least 32 credits in residence; thesis.

FIELDS OF STUDY.
Biological Science.
Cardiac Rehabilitation and Exercise Science.
Computer Science.
Elementary Education.
General Science.
Health and Physical Education.
Health Education.
History.
Physical Education.
Political Science.
Reading. For Reading Specialist, 36 credit hours.
Secondary Education.
Special Education.
Speech Language Pathology.

EAST TENNESSEE STATE UNIVERSITY

Johnson City, Tennessee 37614-0734

http://www.east-tenn-st.edu

Founded 1911. Located 100 miles NE of Knoxville. Coed. State control. Semester system. Library: 550,000 volumes.

Graduate tuition fees: resident, per semester hour $127, not to exceed $1128 per semester; nonresident per semester hour $308, not to exceed $3262 per semester. On-campus housing available for both single and married students. Average academic year cost: $3000. Apply to Director of Housing. Phone: (615)929-4446. Day care facilities available.

Graduate School

Enrollment: full-time 936, part-time 1369. University faculty: full-time 651, part-time 289. Degrees conferred: M.A., M.B.A., M.S., M.S.E.H., M.F.A., M.A.T., M.C.M., M.P.H., Ed.S., Ed.D., Ph.D.

ADMISSION REQUIREMENTS. Transcripts, personal essay required in support of School's application. GRE/GMAT, letters of recommendation required in some departments. Interview sometimes required. TOEFL required for international applicants. Accepts transfer applicants. Graduates of unaccredited institutions not considered. Apply to Dean, School of Graduate Studies by August 1 (Fall), December 1 (Winter), March 1 (Spring), May 1 (Summer). Application fee $5. Phone: (423)929-4221; fax: (423)929-5624.

ADMISSION STANDARDS. Selective. Usual minimum average: 2.5 (A = 4).

FINANCIAL AID. Annual awards from institutional funds: one hundred scholarships, two hundred graduate assistantships, one hundred research assistantships, Federal W/S, loans. Approved for VA benefits. Apply by May 1 to appropriate department chair. Use FAFSA and University's FAF. About 50% of students receive aid other than loans from School and outside sources. Aid sometimes available to part-time students.

DEGREE REQUIREMENTS. For all master's: 30 semester hours minimum; thesis, final oral/written exam; or 36 semester hours minimum, final oral exam. For Ed. S.: 30 semester hours beyond the master's; dissertation. For Ed.D.: 90 semester hours minimum, at least one year in full-time study; preliminary exam; qualifying exam; final exam; dissertation. For Ph.D.: 60 semester hours beyond the master's; preliminary and qualifying exam; language/computer option; final exam; dissertation.

FIELDS OF STUDY.
Accountancy. M.A.
Art. M.A., M.F.A.
Biology. M.S.
Biomedical Sciences. M.S., Ph.D.
Business Administration. GMAT for admission. M.B.A.
Chemistry. M.S.
Clinical Nutrition.
Communicative Disorders. M.S.
Computer and Information Science. M.S.
Counseling. M.A., M.Ed.
Criminal Justice and Criminology. M.A.
Education. Includes administration and supervision, early childhood, elementary, secondary, media services, curriculum and instruction, reading, storytelling. M.A., M.Ed., Ed.D., Ed.S.
English. M.A.
Environmental Health. M.S.E.H.
History. M.A.
Library Service.
Mathematical Science. M.S.
Music Education.
Nursing. M.S.N.
Physical Education, Exercise and Sport Science. M.A., M.Ed.
Political Science.
Psychology. M.A.
Public and City Management.
Public Health. M.P.H.
Sociology. M.A.
Special Education. Includes EMR.
Technology. M.S.

James H. Quillen College of Medicine (37614-0580)

Established 1978. Annual tuition: resident $8750; nonresident $16,484. Total average cost of all other expenses: $8100. Enrollment: first-year class 60 (EDP 9); total 234 (men 55%, women 45%). Faculty: full-time 146; part-time, 17; volunteers 425. Degrees conferred: M.D., M.D.-Ph.D.

ADMISSION REQUIREMENTS. AMCAS report, transcripts, MCAT, recommendations required in support of application. Interview by invitation. Preference given to state residents and veterans of U.S. military service. Graduates of unaccredited colleges not considered. Has EDP; apply between June 15 and

August 1. Apply to Admissions Office/Registrar after June 15, before December 1. Application fee, $25. Phone. (615)929-6221; fax: (615)461-7040.

ADMISSION STANDARDS. Competitive. Admits about 10% of total annual applications. Approximately 100% are state residents.

FINANCIAL AID. Scholarships, grants, loans. Apply after acceptance to Financial Aid Officer. Use FAFSA.

DEGREE REQUIREMENTS. For M.D.: satisfactory completion of four-year program.

FIELDS OF GRADUATE STUDY.
Anatomy.
Biochemistry.
Biophysics.
Cell Biology.
Immunology.
Microbiology.
Pathology.
Pharmacology.
Physiology.

EAST TEXAS STATE UNIVERSITY
Commerce, Texas 75429
http://etsu.edu

Founded 1889. Located 65 miles NE of Dallas. Coed. State control. Semester system. Library: 1,500,219 volumes, 422,000 microforms, 48 PCs.

Annual tuition: resident $1640, nonresident $5096. On-campus housing for 250 married students, 1558 single students. Average academic year housing cost: $2475 for married students, $4055 (including board) for single students. Apply to Director of Housing. Phone: (903)886-5797. Day care facilities available.

Graduate School

Graduate study since 1936. Enrollment: full-time 584, part-time 1995. Faculty: full-time 200, part-time 15. Degrees conferred: M.A., M.S., M.M., M.F.A., M.Ed., M.B.A., M.S.L.S., Ph.D., Ed.D.

ADMISSION REQUIREMENTS. Transcript, GRE GMAT, four recommendations (Ph.D.) required in support of School's application. TOEFL required for foreign applicants. Interview not required. Accepts transfer applicants. Graduates of unaccredited institutions not considered. Apply to the Graduate School at least one month prior to registration. Phone: (903)886-5167; fax: (903)886-5165.

ADMISSION STANDARDS. Selective. Usual minimum average 2.75 (A = 4).

FINANCIAL AID. One hundred seventy assistantships for teaching/research, Federal W/S, loans. Approved for VA benefits. Apply to Financial Aid Office at least four months before aid is needed. Use FAFSA and institutional FAF. Phone: (903)886-5096.

DEGREE REQUIREMENTS. For M.A.: ten graduate courses minimum, at least eight in residence; reading knowledge of one foreign language; thesis; final oral exam. For M.S., M.M., M.B.A., M.S.L.S.: ten graduate courses minimum, at least eight in residence; thesis and final oral exam; or twelve graduate courses without thesis. For M.Ed.: twelve courses minimum. For

Ph.D.: 90 semester hours minimum beyond the bachelor's, at least one year in residence; reading knowledge of two foreign languages; qualifying exam; dissertation; final oral exam. For Ed.D.: generally the same as for the Ph.D., except proficiency in computer science, statistics or foreign language.

FIELDS OF STUDY.
Agricultural Education.
Agriculture.
Art. Includes graphic design.
Biology.
Business Administration.
Chemistry.
Computer Science.
Counseling and Guidance.
Earth Science.
Economic.
Educational Administration.
Elementary Education. Includes supervision, curriculum, and instruction at elementary, early childhood, reading.
English.
History.
Industry and Technology.
Mathematics.
Music.
Physical and Health Education. Includes recreation.
Physics.
Psychology. Includes applied, educational, school.
Secondary Education. Includes supervision, curriculum and instruction, higher education, learning technology.
Sociology.
Spanish.
Special Education. Includes mentally retarded, handicapped, brain injured, learning disabilities.

EASTERN CONNECTICUT STATE UNIVERSITY
Willimantic, Connecticut 06226-2295

Founded 1889. Located 30 miles E of Hartford. Coed. State control. Semester system.

Tuition: per hour $147. No on-campus housing for married or single graduate students. Apply to Student Affairs office for off-campus housing information. Phone: (860)465-5369.

Graduate Studies

Enrollment: full-time 20, part-time 274. College faculty teaching graduate courses: full-time 16, part-time 4. Degree conferred: M.S.

ADMISSION REQUIREMENTS. Transcripts, two recommendations required in support of application. TOEFL required for international applicants. Accepts transfer applicants. Apply to Dean of Graduate Studies. No specified closing date. Admits Fall, Spring. Application fee $20. Phone: (860)465-5192; fax: (890)465-4538.

ADMISSION STANDARDS. Selective. Usual minimum average: 2.7 (A = 4).

FINANCIAL AID. Annual awards from institutional funds: two assistantships, Federal W/S, loans. Apply to Dean by March 15. Use FAFSA and institutional FAF. Phone: (860)456-5205.

DEGREE REQUIREMENTS. For M.S.: 36 semester hours minimum, at least 21 in residence; thesis or comprehensive exam.

FIELDS OF STUDY.

Education. Includes early childhood, elementary, reading, science.

Organizational Relations. Interdisciplinary.

EASTERN ILLINOIS UNIVERSITY
Charleston, Illinois 61920-3099

Founded 1895. Located 180 miles S of Chicago. Coed. State control. Semester system. Library: 950,000 volumes, 1,600,000 microforms, 3100 current periodicals, 62 PCs.

Annual tuition/fees: full-time, resident $3019.10, nonresident $7351.10; per credit resident $90.25, nonresident $270.75. On-campus housing for 100 married students, 600 graduate men, 600 graduate women. Average academic year housing costs: $3800 for married students, $3434 (including board) for single graduate students. Contact Director, University Housing for both on- and off-campus housing information. Phone: (217)581-3923.

Graduate School

Enrollment: full-time 525, part-time 754. University faculty teaching graduate students: full-time 362, part-time 25. Degrees conferred: M.A., M.S., M.S. in Ed., M.B.A., Ed.S., S.S.P.

ADMISSION REQUIREMENTS. Transcripts, GRE or MAT, GMAT for business, may be required in support of application. Interview not required. TOEFL required for international applicants. Accepts transfer applicants. Graduates of unaccredited institutions not considered. Apply to Graduate School's Admissions Office at least ten days prior to registration. Application fee $25. Phone: (217)581-2220, Fax: (217)581-6020.

ADMISSION STANDARDS. Relatively open. Usual minimum average: 2.75 (A = 4); higher in some programs.

FINANCIAL AID. Annual awards from institutional funds: research assistantships, teaching assistantships, residence hall assistantships, Federal W/S, loans. Approved for VA benefits. Apply by February 15 to Dean of Graduate School. Use FAFSA. Phone: (217)581-3713. About 25% of students receive aid other than loans from University and outside sources.

DEGREE REQUIREMENTS. For master's: 30–32 semester hours; final oral/written exam. For Ed.S., S.S.P.: 64 semester hours minimum beyond the bachelor's; final oral/written exam/special project.

FIELDS OF STUDY.

Art.

Biological Sciences.

Business Administration.

Chemistry.

Communication Disorders and Science.

Economics.

Education. Includes business, administration, elementary, mathematics, physical science, biological science, physical education, special.

English.

Family and Consumer Sciences.

Gerontology.

Guidance and Counseling.

History.

Mathematics.

Music.

Political Science.

Psychology. Includes experimental, school.

Speech Communication.

Technology.

EASTERN KENTUCKY UNIVERSITY
Richmond, Kentucky 40475-3101

Founded 1906. Located 26 miles SE of Lexington. Coed. State control. Semester system. Library: about 811,000 volumes, 1,151,000 microforms, 4000 current periodicals. Special facilities: Hummel Planetarium, Lilley Cornett Woods, Oral History Center, Spenser Morton Preserves.

Annual tuition: full-time, resident $2150, nonresident $5998; per hour, resident $120, nonresident $333. On-campus housing for married students: 292 units, single on-campus housing available for about 3000 men, 4000 women. Average academic year housing costs: $648–$1009 per semester for single students, about $180–$305 per month for married students. Contact Director of Housing for both on- and off-campus housing information. Phone: (606)622-1520.

Graduate School

Graduate study since 1935. Enrollment: full-time 446, part-time 1521 (men 439, women 1082). Graduate faculty: full-time 350, part-time 10. Degrees conferred: M.A., M.A.Ed., M.S., M.B.A., M.P.A., M.M., M.S.N., Ed.S., joint doctoral programs available.

ADMISSION REQUIREMENTS. Official transcripts, GRE Subject Tests, GMAT (Business) required in support of application. Interview required for some programs. TOEFL required for international applicants. Accepts transfer applicants. Graduates of unaccredited institutions not considered. Apply to Graduate Office at least two weeks prior to registration. Foreign students must be clearly admitted thirty days prior to the beginning of the semester of attendance. Application fee, none. Phone: (606)622-1742.

ADMISSION STANDARDS. Selective. Usual minimum average: 2.5 (A = 4).

FINANCIAL AID. Annual awards from institutional funds: 150 teaching/research assistantships, Federal W/S, loans. Approved for VA benefits. Apply by March 1 to Graduate Office for assistantships; to Financial Aid Office for all other programs. Use FAFSA and University's FAF. About 50% of full-time students receive aid other than loans from University and outside sources.

DEGREE REQUIREMENTS. For most master's: 24 semester hours plus thesis, or 30 semester hours without thesis; final oral/comprehensive exam. For M.A.Ed.: same as for M.A., except candidates are required to hold the teaching certificate. For Ed.S.: 30–39 semester hours beyond the master's; special project.

FIELDS OF STUDY.

Administration and Supervision. Ed.S., joint Ed.D. with University of Kentucky.

Agriculture Education. M.A.Ed. only.

Allied Health Education (non-teaching). M.A.Ed. only.

Art Education. M.A.Ed. only.

Biology. Includes ecology. M.S. Joint Ph.D. with University of Kentucky.

Business Administration. M.B.A. only.

Business Education. M.A.Ed. only.

Chemistry. M.A.Ed., M.S.

Communication Disorders. M.A.Ed. only.

Community Counseling. M.A. only.

Community Nutrition. M.S. only.

Counseling. Includes community, elementary, school, secondary. M.A.Ed. only.

Criminal Justice. Includes corrections and juvenile services, police administration. M.S. only.

Earth Science. M.A.Ed. only.

Educational Policies, Studies and Evaluation. Joint Ed.D. with University of Kentucky only.

Educational Psychology. Joint Ed.D. with University of Kentucky only.

Elementary Education. Includes early elementary, middle grades, M.A. Ed. only.

English. M.A., M.A.Ed.

General Science Education. M.A.Ed. only.

Geography Education. M.A.Ed. only.

Geology. M.S. only.

Health, Physical Education and Recreation. Joint Ed.D. with University of Kentucky only.

History. M.A., M.A.Ed. Home Economics Education. M.A. Ed. only.

Industrial Education.

Library Science. Includes elementary, secondary. M.A.Ed. only.

Loss Prevention and Safety. M.S. only.

Manufacturing Technology. M.S. only.

Mathematical Sciences. Includes computer science, statistics. M.S. only.

Music. Includes choral/instrumental conducting, general, performance, theory, composition. M.M. only.

Music Education. M.M. only.

Nursing. Includes rural health family nurse practitioner, rural community health care nursing. M.S.N.

Occupational Therapy. M.S. only.

Physical Education. Includes sports administration.

Physics. M.A.Ed., M.S.

Political Science. M.A., M.A.Ed.

Psychology. Includes clinical, education, school (Psy.D. and joint Ph.D. with University of Kentucky).

Reading Education. Includes elementary, secondary. M.A. Ed. only.

Recreation and Park Administration. M.S. only.

School Health Education. M.A. Ed.

Sociology Education. M.A.Ed. only.

Special Education. Includes early childhood (non-teaching), LBD, TMH, hearing impaired. Joint Ed.D. with University of Kentucky.

Student Personnel Services. M.A.

Vocational Education. Joint Ed.D. with University of Kentucky only.

EASTERN MICHIGAN UNIVERSITY
Ypsilanti, Michigan 48197

Founded 1849. Located 30 miles W of Detroit. Coed. State control. Semester system. Library: 623,000 volumes 732,000 microforms, 150 PCs.

Tuition: per hour, resident $154, nonresident $340. On-campus housing for married students, graduate men and women. Average academic year housing cost: $4800, apt. $450 per month for married students; $4300 per academic year (including board) for single students. Apply to Director of Auxiliary Services. Phone: (313)487-1300.

Graduate School

Graduate study since 1953. Enrollment: full-time 1186, part-time 4460 (men 40%, women 60%). University faculty: full- and part-time 672. Degrees conferred: M.A., M.S., M.S.A. M.B.A., M.L.S., M.P.A., M.B.E., M.F.A., M.S.E.S., M.S.N., M.S.W., Sp.A., C.A.S., Ed.D.

ADMISSION REQUIREMENTS. Transcripts, GRE/MAT/GMAT, letters of recommendation required in support of School's application. Interview not required. TOEFL required for international applicants. Accepts transfer applicants. Graduates of unaccredited institutions not considered. Apply to Graduate School Office at least sixty days before registration. Application fee $25. Phone: (313)487-0042; fax: (313)487-0050.

ADMISSION STANDARDS. Selective. Usual minimum average: 2.75 (A = 4).

FINANCIAL AID. Annual awards from institutional funds: 425 assistantships, Federal W/S, loans. Apply to appropriate department head; no specified closing date. Apply to Financial Aid Officer for federal funds. Use FAFSA. Phone: (313)487-0455. Aid sometimes available for part-time students.

DEGREE REQUIREMENTS. For master's: 30 semester hours minimum (maximum varies by department), at least 6 in residence; thesis/nonthesis option; research paper may be included; final written/oral exam may be required. For Sp.A., C.A.S.: normally 32 hours beyond the master's, at least 16 in residence. For Ed.D.: 28 hours beyond University's specialist degree; all in residence; major project; written/oral exam.

FIELDS OF STUDY.

COLLEGE OF ARTS AND SCIENCES:

Applied Economics.

Art Education.

Biology. Includes general biology, aquatic biology, community college teaching, physiology.

Chemistry.

Communication.

Criminology and Criminal Justice.

Development, Trade and Planning.

Drama.

Economics.

English. Includes literature, English language and composition, children's literature.

Fine Arts. M.F.A. only.

Foreign Languages. French, Spanish, German.

General Science.

Geography. Includes environmental studies, man and his works.

Historic Preservation Planning.

History.

Language and International Trade.

Liberal Studies. Includes women's studies, social studies, American culture.

Literature.

Mathematics.

Music. Includes music education, music literature, music theory-literature, performance, choral conducting.

Physics. Includes physics education.

Psychology. Includes general psychology, clinical psychology.

Public Administration.

School Psychology.

Social Science.

Social Work.

Sociology.

Spanish. Includes bilingual-bicultural education.

Speech and Dramatic Arts. Includes communication–public address, dramatic arts for the young, oral interpretation.

Teaching English to Speakers of Other Languages.

Theater Arts.

Women's Studies.

Written Communication.

COLLEGE OF BUSINESS:

Accounting.

Business Administration.

Computer Information Systems.

Finance.

Management.

Marketing.

COLLEGE OF EDUCATION:

Community Counseling.

Curriculum and Instruction.

Early Childhood Education.

Educational Leadership.

Educational Psychology. Includes development and personality, research and technology.

Elementary Education. Includes general elementary, language arts, open education, educational media.

Guidance and Counseling. Includes school counselor endorsement, college and community personnel.

K-12 Curriculum.

Middle School Education.

Physical Education.

Reading.

School Psychology.

Secondary School Teaching.

Social Foundations.

Special Education. Includes mentally impaired, hearing impaired, emotionally impaired, visually impaired, speech and language impaired, learning impaired, physically impaired.

COLLEGE OF HUMAN SERVICES

Associated Health Professions.

Human Environmental and Consumer Resources. Includes general home economics, clothing, textiles, family and child development, food and nutrition, consumer affairs, occupational therapy.

Nursing Education.

Social Work.

COLLEGE OF TECHNOLOGY

Business and Technology Education.

Industrial Technology. Includes CAD/CAM, construction, manufacturing.

Interdisciplinary Technology.

Liberal Studies in Technology.

Polymer Technology.

EASTERN NEW MEXICO UNIVERSITY
Portales, New Mexico 88130

Founded 1927. Coed. State control. Branches located in Roswell, Ruidoso. Semester system. Library: 270,000 volumes, 688,100 microforms, 2750 current periodicals, 33 PCs.

Annual tuition: full-time, resident $1850, nonresident $6346; per credit, resident $77, nonresident $264. On-campus housing for 181 married students, 540 graduate men, 918 graduate women. Average academic year housing costs: $1268–$1888 for single students; $260–$300 per month for married students. Contact Director of Housing for both on- and off-campus housing information. Phone: (505)562-2631.

Graduate School

Enrollment: full-time 163, part-time 394. University faculty: full-time 57, part-time 39. Degrees conferred: M.A., M.S., M.B.A., M.Ed., M.M., M.S., M.Sp.Ed.

ADMISSION REQUIREMENTS. One official transcript, GMAT (business) required in support of School's application. Interview not required. TOEFL required for international applicants. Accepts transfer applicants. Graduates of unaccredited institutions not considered. Apply to Dean of Graduate School at least 30 days prior to registration. Application fee $10. Phone: (505)562-2147.

ADMISSION STANDARDS. Relatively open. Usual minimum average: 3.0 (regular), 2.5 (provisional) (A = 4).

FINANCIAL AID. Annual awards from institutional funds; fifty-two research assistantships, fifty teaching assistantships, fellowships for minorities, women and handicapped, tuition waivers, Federal W/S, loans. Approved for VA benefits. Apply by March 1 to appropriate department chair for assistantships; to the Financial Aid Office for all other programs. Use FAFSA and University's FAF. Phone: (505)562-2147. About 65% of students receive aid from University and outside sources. No aid for part-time students.

DEGREE REQUIREMENTS. For master's: 30 credit hours minimum, at least 24 in residence; thesis; final oral exam; or 32 credit hours minimum, at least 16 in residence; final oral written exam.

FIELDS OF STUDY.

Anthropology. M.A.

Biology. M.S.

Business Administration. M.B.A.

Chemistry. One language for M.S.

Communication. M.A.

Communicative Disorders. M.Ed.

Counseling. M.A.

Counseling and Guidance. M.Ed.

Education. M.Ed.

English. M.A.

Mathematics. M.S.

Music. M.M.

Physical Education. M.S.

Psychology. M.A.

Special Education. M.Sp.Ed.

EASTERN OREGON STATE COLLEGE
La Grande, Oregon 97850-2899

Founded 1929. Located 265 miles E of Portland. Coed. State control. Quarter system. Library: 150,000 volumes, 1300 current periodicals.

Annual tuition: full-time, resident $4629, nonresident $7851; per credit, resident $106, nonresident $175. On-campus housing for married and single students. Average academic year housing costs: $3000 (including board) for single students. Contact Director of Campus Housing for both on- and off-campus housing information. Phone: (541)962-3553.

Graduate Division

Established 1952. Enrollment: full-time 40, part-time 120. Faculty: full-time none, part-time 20, Degrees conferred: M.T.E. for Interns, M.T.E. for Practitioners.

ADMISSION REQUIREMENTS. Transcripts, NTE required in support of application. TOEFL required for international applicants. Accepts transfer applicants. Apply to Office of Admission well in advance of registration. Application fee $50. Phone: (541)962-3393.

ADMISSION STANDARDS. Relatively open. Usual minimum average: 2.5 (A = 4).

FINANCIAL AID. Limited to loans. Approved for VA benefits. Apply to Financial Aid Officer with admission application. Use FAFSA.

DEGREE REQUIREMENTS. For master's: 45 quarter hours minimum, at least 30 in residence; qualifying exam; written/oral comprehensive exam. M.T.E. Intern, during academic year; M.T.E. Practitioner, primarily summers.

FIELDS OF STUDY.
Education for Elementary School Teachers.
Education for Secondary School Teachers.

EASTERN VIRGINIA MEDICAL SCHOOL OF THE MEDICAL COLLEGE OF HAMPTON ROADS
Norfolk, Virginia 23507-2000

Established 1973. Library 66,000 volumes, 20,000 microforms. Annual tuition: resident $13,000, nonresident $23,000; student fees $1819. Total average figure for all other expenses $9100. No on-campus housing available, for off-campus housing. Phone: (804)446-5812.

Enrollment: first-year class 100 (15 EDP); total 381 (men 54%, women 46%). Faculty: full-time 283, part-time and volunteers 900. Degrees conferred: M.D., M.D.-Ph.D., M.D.-Psy.D.

ADMISSION REQUIREMENTS. AMCAS report, transcripts, MCAT, two letters of recommendation, interview required in support of application. Preference given to residents of Tidewater area. Transfer applicants and graduates of unaccredited colleges not considered. Has EDP; apply between June 15 and August 1. Apply to Chair of Admissions Committee after June 15, before November 15. Application fee $80. Phone: (804)446-5812; fax: (804)446-5817.

ADMISSION STANDARDS. Selective. Accepts about 89% of total annual applicants. Approximately 62% are state residents.

FINANCIAL AID. Scholarships, loans available. Apply to Financial Aid Office after acceptance, before March 15. Phone: (804)446-5813. Use FAFSA. About 90% of students receive financial assistance.

DEGREE REQUIREMENTS. For M.D.: satisfactory completion of four-year program.

GRADUATE FIELDS OF STUDY.
Biomedical Sciences. With Old Dominion University. Ph.D.
Psychology. With the College of William and Mary. Psy.D.

EASTERN WASHINGTON UNIVERSITY
Cheney, Washington 99004-2431

Founded 1882. Located 16 miles SW of Spokane. Coed. State control. Quarter system. Library: 700,000 volumes, 1,120,000 microforms.

Annual tuition: full-time resident $3885, nonresident $11,817: part-time resident $129 per credit, nonresident $394 per credit. On-campus housing for 143 married students, 1749 single students. Average academic year housing cost: $3000 married students, $4160 for single students. Apply to Director of Residential Life. Day care facilities available.

Graduate Studies

Graduate study since 1947. Enrollment: full-time 500, part-time 550. College faculty teaching graduate students: full-time 230, part-time 16. Degrees conferred: M.A., M.S., M.Ed., M.B.A., M.F.A., M.N., M.P.A., M.P.T., M.S.W., M.U.R.P.

ADMISSION REQUIREMENTS. Transcripts, letters of recommendation required in support of application. GRE General/Subject Tests, interview for some programs, GMAT for business.

TOEFL required for international applicants. Accepts transfer applicants. Apply to Graduate Program Office at least 1 month prior to beginning of quarter. Application fee $25. Phone: (509)359-6296.

ADMISSION STANDARDS. Selective. Minimum average: 3.0 (A = 4).

FINANCIAL AID. Annual awards from institutional funds: 85 assistantships, Federal W/S, loans. Apply by March 1 to appropriate department for assistantships, to Financial Aid Office for federal programs. Use FAFSA. Phone: (509)359-2314. Aid sometimes available for part-time student. About 45% of students receive aid from University and outside source.

DEGREE REQUIREMENTS. For M.A., M.S.: 45 quarter hours minimum, at least 34 credits in residence; final oral exam; thesis, reading knowledge of one foreign language sometimes required. For M.Ed., M.B.A.: 49 quarter hours minimum, at least 36 credits in residence; final comprehensive exam. For M.P.A.: 60 quarter hours minimum, at least 45 in residence; final comprehensive exam. For M.P.T.: 133 quarter hours minimum, at least 100 credits in residence: final comprehensive exam. For M.S.W.: 84 quarter hours minimum, 63 in residence; final comprehensive exam. For M.F.A., M.U.R.P.: 72 quarter hours minimum, 54 in residence; thesis (M.F.A.); final comprehensive exam. For M.N.: 59 quarter hours minimum, 44 in residence; thesis; final comprehensive exam.

FIELDS OF STUDY.
Art.
Biology.
Biology-Medical Technology Option.
Business Administration.
Business Education.
College Instruction.
Communications.
Communications Disorders.
Computer Science.
Creative Writing.
Curriculum and Instruction.
Early Childhood Education.
Elementary Teaching.
English. Includes English in the public school, literature, rhetoric and composition, teaching English as a second language, technical and professional writing.
Foundations of Education.
Geology.
History.
Instructional Communications.
Interdisciplinary.
Literacy Specialist.
Marketing Education.
Mathematics.
Music.
Nursing.
Physical Education.
Physical Therapy.
Psychology. Includes clinical, developmental, experimental, mental health counseling, school counseling.
Public Administration.
School Administration.
Science Education.
Social Science Education.
Social Work.
Special Education.
Supervising (Clinic) Teaching.
Technology.
Urban and Regional Planning.
Vocational Administration.

EDINBORO UNIVERSITY OF PENNSYLVANIA
Edinboro, Pennsylvania 16444

Founded 1857. Located 20 miles S of Erie. State control. Semester system. Library: 417,518 volumes, 1,249,000 microforms, 1900 current periodicals.

Tuition: per credit, resident $206.25, nonresident $343.25. On-campus housing available for single and married graduate students. Average academic year housing costs: $1720–2145 (including board) for single students; $3600 for married students. Off-campus housing cost; $400 per month. Contact Housing Office for both on- and off-campus housing information. Phone: (814)732-2818.

Graduate Studies

Graduate study since 1957. Enrollment: full-time 256, part-time 400. College faculty teaching graduate students: full-time 95. Degrees conferred: M.Ed., M.A., M.S., M.F.A., M.S.N.

ADMISSION REQUIREMENTS. Transcripts, interview required in support of application. MAT/GRE required for some departments. TOEFL required for international applicants. Accepts transfer applicants. Graduates of unaccredited institutions not considered. Apply to Coordinator of Graduate Studies admissions at least one month prior to registration. Rolling admission process. Application fee $25. Phone: (814)732-2720; fax: (814)732-2680

ADMISSION STANDARDS. Relatively open. Usual minimum average: 2.5 (A = 4).

FINANCIAL AID. Annual awards from institutional funds: 135 assistantships, Federal W/S, loans. Apply to Financial Aid Office; no specified closing date. Use FAFSA and institutional FAF for graduate assistantship. Phone: (814)732-2821.

DEGREE REQUIREMENTS. For M.A., M.S., M.Ed.: 30 semester hours minimum, at least 21 in residence; thesis/nonthesis option. For M.F.A.: 60 semester hours, at least 45 in residence. For M.S.N.: 42 semester hours, at least 30 in residence.

FIELDS OF STUDY.
Art. M.A.
Biology. M.S.
Clinical Psychology. M.A.
Communication Studies. M.A.
Educational Psychology. M.Ed.
Elementary Education. M.Ed.
Elementary School Administration. M.Ed.
Guidance. Includes elementary, secondary; 39 hours for M.A.
Nurse Practitioner. M.S.N.
Reading. M.Ed.
Rehabilitation Counseling. M.A.
School Counseling. M.A.
Secondary School Administration. M.Ed.
Social Science. M.A.
Special Education. M.Ed.
Speech-Language Pathology. M.A.
Student Personnel Services. M.A.
Studio Art. Includes ceramics, painting printmaking, sculpture. M.F.A.

ELMIRA COLLEGE
Elmira, New York 14901

Founded 1855. Located 54 miles SW of Binghamton, New York. Coed. Private control. 12-12-6-6 term. Special facility: off-campus graduate centers at Oswego, Bath, Corning, Ithaca, Rome, Watkins Glen, N.Y.; multimedia learning center, Center for Mark Twain Studies at Quarry Farms. Library: 160,000 volumes.

Graduate tuition: per credit $312. Limited on-campus housing available for single students only. Annual housing cost: $5845 (including board). Apply to Coordinator of Housing.

Graduate Study

Enrollment: about 618 (evening and summer sessions only). College faculty teaching graduate students: about 25. Degrees conferred: M.S.Ed.

ADMISSION REQUIREMENTS. Transcripts required in support of College's application. Accepts transfer applicants. Apply to Dean of Continuing Education before or at the time of registration. Phone: (607)735-1825; fax: (607)735-1758.

ADMISSION STANDARDS. Relatively open. Usual minimum average 2.5 (A = 4).

FINANCIAL AID. Limited to Federal W/S, Loans. Approved for VA benefits. Apply to Financial Aid Office at time of application. Use FAFSA.

DEGREE REQUIREMENTS. For master's: 36 semester hours, at least 30 on campus; research experience required.

FIELDS OF STUDY.
Adult Education.
Elementary and Secondary Education.
General Education.
Reading Specialist (K-12).

EMERSON COLLEGE
Boston, Massachusetts 02116-1511

Founded 1880. Coed. Private control. Semester system. Special facilities: one television and two radio stations, speech clinic, theatre facilities. Library: 167,000 volumes, 10,000 microforms, 11 current periodicals.

Annual tuition: per credit $520. On-campus housing available. Average academic year housing costs: $7782 (including board). Off-campus housing costs: $300–$500 per month. Contact Office of Housing for both on- and off-campus housing information. Phone: (617)578-8620.

Graduate Division

Enrollment: full-time 533, part-time 220. Faculty: full-time 59, part-time 55. Degrees conferred: M.A., M.F.A., M.S., Ph.D.

ADMISSION REQUIREMENTS. Official transcripts, three letters of recommendation, GRE/GMAT required in support of application. Interview required by some departments. TOEFL required for international applicants. Accepts transfer applicants. Graduates of unaccredited institutions not considered. Apply to Director of Graduate Admission by July 15 (Fall), December 15 (Spring). Application fee $40, $75 for international students. Phone: (617)578-8610; fax: (617)578-8609; E-mail: gradapp@emerson.edu.

ADMISSION STANDARDS. Selective. Usual minimum average: 3.0 (A = 4), 2.7 for provisional admission.

FINANCIAL AID. Annual awards from institutional funds: one hundred assistantships, twenty-eight scholarships, Federal W/S, loans. Approved for VA benefits. Apply by July 1 to the appropriate department for assistantships; to Office of Financial Aid for all other programs. Use FAFSA. Phone: (617)578-8655.

DEGREE REQUIREMENTS. For M.A.: 36–40 credits: thesis/nonthesis program; final written/oral exam. For M.S.: 49 credits. For M.F.A.: 52 credits; thesis/nonthesis program; final written/oral exam. For Ph.D.: 60 credits beyond the master's, at least 45 in residence; practicum; qualifying exam; dissertation; final oral exam.

FIELDS OF STUDY.
Business Communication and Public Relations. M.A.
Communication Disorders. M.S., Ph.D.
Communication Industries Management. M.A.
Communication Studies. Includes communication education, oral interpretation, rhetoric and public address. M.A.
Creative Writing. M.F.A.
Health Communication. M.A.
Marketing Communication. M.A.
Mass Communication. Includes broadcast journalism and radio, television and video production. M.A.
Performing Arts. Includes community and educational theater, secondary drama, theater for children. M.A.
Political Communication. M.A.
Writing and Publishing. M.A.

EMORY UNIVERSITY
Atlanta, Georgia 30322-1100
http://www.emory.edu

Founded 1836. Coed. Private control. Semester system. Special facilities: Institute of the Liberal Arts, Yerkes Regional Primate Research Center, Michael C. Carlos Museum, Winship Cancer Center, Center for Research in Social Change, The Carter Center of Emory University. Library: 2,200,000 volumes, 2,400,000 microforms

Annual tuition: full-time $19,870. On-campus graduate housing: approximately 272 units. Average academic year housing cost: $6000. Apply to Graduate and Family. Phone: (404)727-8830.

Graduate School of Arts and Sciences

Graduate study since 1919. Enrollment: full- and part-time 1500 (708 men, 852 women). Faculty: 325. Degrees conferred: M.A., M.S., M.A.T., M.Ed., M.M., M.S.M., Ph.D.

ADMISSION REQUIREMENTS. Two copies of transcripts, three letters of recommendation, and GRE required in support of School's application. International applicants whose native language is not English must demonstrate proficiency in English as specified by the individual department. Accepts transfer applicants. Graduates of unaccredited institutions not considered. Apply to Graduate School at least one month prior to registration. (To be considered for Financial Aid in the Fall, apply by January 20.) Application fee $45. Phone: (404)727-6028.

ADMISSION STANDARDS. Competitive to selective for most departments. Usual minimum average: 3.0 in major (A = 4).

FINANCIAL AID. Annual awards from institutional funds: 628 tuition scholarships, 108 graduate assistantships, 65 teaching assistants, 501 nonservice fellowships, Federal W/S, loans. Apply by January 20 to the Financial Aid Office. Use FAFSA. Phone: (404)727-1141. About 60% of students receive aid. These awards available on a competitive basis.

DEGREE REQUIREMENTS. For M.A., M.S.: 24 semester hours minimum; thesis, final oral/written exam. For M.A.T.,

M.Ed., M.M., M.S.M.: 40 semester hours minimum; no thesis or language requirement. For Ph.D.: 48 semester hours beyond the master's; comprehensive exam; reading knowledge of one or more foreign languages in some departments; dissertation; final oral exam.

FIELDS OF STUDY.
Anthropology. Ph.D. only.
Art History. M.A., Ph.D.
Biological and Biomedical Sciences. Includes biochemistry and molecular biology, cell and developmental biology, genetic and molecular biology, immunology and molecular pathogenesis, microbiology and molecular genetics, neuroscience, nutrition and health sciences, physiological and pharmacological sciences. Ph.D. only.
Biostatistics. M.S., Ph.D.
Chemistry. M.S., Ph.D.
Comparative Literature. Ph.D. only.
Economics. Ph.D. only.
Educational Studies. M.A., M.A.T., M.Ed., D.A.S.T., Ph.D.
English. M.A., Ph.D.
Epidemiology and Biostatistics. M.S., Ph.D.
Film Studies. M.A. only.
French. Ph.D. only.
History. Ph.D. only.
Jewish Studies. M.A. only.
Liberal Arts, Graduate Institute of the. Includes American and African-American culture, history and theory.
Mathematics and Computer Science. M.S., Ph.D.
Music. Includes choral conducting, organ performance, sacred music. M.M., M.S.M.
Philosophy. Ph.D. only.
Physics. Ph.D. only.
Political Science. Ph.D. only.
Psychology. Includes clinical, cognitive and developmental, psychobiology. Ph.D. only.
Religion. Includes Old Testament, New Testament, historical, theological, ethics and society, theology and personality. Ph.D. only.
Sociology. Ph.D.
Spanish. Ph.D.
Women's Studies. Ph.D. only.

Goizueta Business School
http://www.emory.edu/BUS/

Semester system. Special facilities: Center for Leadership and Career Studies, Center for Relationship marketing.
Annual tuition: $21,250
Enrollment: full-time 290. Faculty: full-time 55, part-time 10. Degree conferred: M.B.A., M.B.A.-J.D., M.B.A.-M.Div., M.B.A.-M.P.H., M.B.A.-M.N.

ADMISSION REQUIREMENTS. Transcripts, three letters of reference, GMAT required in support of School's application. TOEFL required for international applicants. Interview recommended but not required. Accepts transfer applicants. Graduates of unaccredited institutions not considered. Apply to Director of Admissions by April 15. Admits Fall only. Application fee $45. Phone: (404)727-6311; fax: (404)727-4612.

ADMISSION STANDARDS. Highly selective. Usual minimum average: 3.2 (A = 4). Average GMAT: 626

FINANCIAL AID. One hundred twenty fellowships, forty research assistantships, Federal W/S, loans. Approved for VA benefits. Apply by March 1 to Financial Aid Office. Phone: (404)727-1141. Use FAFSA.

DEGREE REQUIREMENTS. For M.B.A.: 63 semester hours. Core may be reduced through waivers in business and economics.

AREA CONCENTRATIONS.
Customer Business Development.
Latin American Studies.
Soviet and Eastern European Studies.

The School of Law

Founded 1916. Semester system. Law library 250,000 volumes. Library has LEXIS, NEXIS, WESTLAW, DOBIS.

Annual tuition $27,000. Limited on-campus housing available. Total average cost for all other expenses: $9800

Enrollment: first-year class 260; total full-time 740 (men 57%, women 43%); postgraduates 112. Faculty: full-time 40, part-time 38. Degrees conferred: J.D., J.D.-M.B.A., J.D.-M.Div., J.D.-M.T.S., LL.M. (Taxation, Litigation).

ADMISSION REQUIREMENTS. LSDAS report, transcripts, letters of recommendation, LSAT (not later than December), bachelor's degree required in support of application. Interview not required. Accepts transfer applicants. Apply to Director of Admissions after September 1, before March 1. Beginning students admitted Fall only. Application fee $45. Phone: (404)727-6801

ADMISSION STANDARDS Selective. Accepts about 25–30% of total annual applicants.

FINANCIAL AID Scholarships, fellowships (advanced students only), assistantships, Federal W/S, loans. Apply to Director of Admissions by March 1, Use FAFSA. About 10% of students receive aid other than loans from School funds.

DEGREE REQUIREMENTS, For J.D.: 88 semester hours minimum. For LL.M.: 24 semesters beyond the J.D.; one-year minimum in residence. For the master's degrees: see Graduate School listing above.

School of Medicine (30322-4510)

Founded as Atlanta Medical College in 1854. Library 107,000 volumes.

Annual tuition: $19,500; student fees $700. On-campus housing for married students only. Apply to University Housing Office. Total average figure for all other expenses $7590.

Enrollment: first-year class 110; total full-time 444 (men 53%, women 47%); postgraduates 650; fellows 95. Faculty: approximately 1200 full- and part-time. Degree conferred: M.D.; M.M.Sc., M.D.-M.P.H. is offered through Division of Allied Health Professions. The combined degree programs, M.S. and Ph.D. (Medical Scientist Training Program) are offered through the Graduate School of Arts and Sciences.

ADMISSION REQUIREMENTS. AMCAS report, transcripts, letters of reference, MCAT (preferably in Spring), supplemental application, interview required in support of application. Applicants must have completed at least three years of college study. Accepts transfer applicants. Does not have EDP. Apply to Office of the Dean, School of Medicine, after June 15, before October 15. Application fee $50. Phone: (404)727-5660; fax: (404)727-0045.

ADMISSION STANDARDS. Very competitive. Accepts 3% of total annual applicants. Approximately 52% are state residents.

FINANCIAL AID. Scholarships, fellowships, assistantships, Federal W/S, loans. Use FAFSA. About 71% of students receive aid other than loans from School funds. Apply to Financial Aid Office.

DEGREE REQUIREMENTS. For M.D.: satisfactory completion of four-year program. For M.P.H. see Division of Allied Health

Professions listing below. For M.S., Ph.D., see Graduate School of Arts and Sciences listing above.

FIELDS OF GRADUATE STUDY.
Anatomy.
Anesthesiology.
Biochemistry.
Biomedical Engineering.
Biophysics.
Cell Biology.
Genetics.
Immunology.
Microbiology.
Molecular Biology.
Neurosciences.
Pathology.
Pharmacology.
Physiology.
Public Health.

Rollins School of Public Health
http://www.sph.emory.edu

Semester system. Annual tuition: $12,192, per credit $508. On-campus housing available. Apply to University Housing Office. Phone: (404)727-5481; fax: (404)727-3996. Degree conferred: M.P.H.

Enrollment: full-time 291, part-time 220 (men 29%, women 71%). Faculty: full-time 90, part-time 213.

ADMISSION REQUIREMENTS. Transcript, GRE, bachelor's degree required in support of School's application. TOEFL required for foreign applicants. Graduates of unaccredited institutions not considered. Apply to School by March 15. Application fee $35. Phone: (404)727-5481; fax: (404)727-3996.

ADMISSION STANDARDS. Selective. Usual minimum average: 3.0 (A = 4).

FINANCIAL AID. Eight scholarships, eight grants, two fellowships, thirty-two teaching assistantships, Federal W/S, loans. Apply to the Financial Aid Office and to Program Director; no specified closing date. Use FAFSA. Phone: (404)727-3958.

DEGREE REQUIREMENTS. For M.P.H.: 42 semester hours minimum, at least two in residence; comprehensive written exam or thesis.

FIELDS OF STUDY.
Biostatistics.
Environmental and Occupational Health.
Epidemiology.
Health Policy and Management.
International Health.

Nell Hodgson Woodruff School of Nursing
http://www.emory.edu

Annual tuition: $16,450, per credit $678. Enrollment: full- and part-time 277. School faculty: full-time 40, part-time 12. Degrees conferred: M.S.N., M.S.N.-M.P.H., M.S.N.-M.B.A.

ADMISSION REQUIREMENTS. Transcripts, B.S.N., MAT or GRE, one year experience in a clinical area required in support of School's application. TOEFL required for international applicants. Accepts transfer applicants. Graduates of unaccredited institutions not considered. Apply by June 1 to Office of Student Affairs. Application fee $35. Phone: (404)727-7980 or (800)222-3879; fax: (404)727-0536.

ADMISSION STANDARDS. Selective. Usual minimum overall average: 3.0; average for nursing courses: 3.3 (A = 4).

FINANCIAL AID. Scholarships, fellowships, assistantships, Federal W/S, loans. Approved for VA benefits. Apply by February 1 to the Programs Director for scholarships, fellowships, assistantships; to the Financial Aid Office for all other programs. Phone: (404)727-6039. Use FAFSA and CSS Profile.

DEGREE REQUIREMENTS. For M.S.N.: 48 semester hours minimum, all in residence; thesis option. Part-time study available.

FIELDS OF STUDY.
Adult Critical Care.
Adult Medical Surgical Nurse Practitioner.
Adult Nurse Practitioner.
Adult Oncology.
Family Nurse Practitioner.
Gerontological Nurse Practitioner.
Nurse Midwifery.
Nursing Administration.
Pediatric Nurse Practitioner.
Perinatal and Neonatal.

EMPORIA STATE UNIVERSITY
Emporia, Kansas 66801-5087
http://www.emporia.edu

Founded 1863. Located 55 miles SW of Topeka. Coed. State control. Semester system. special facilities: Ross Natural History Reservation, Butcher Laboratory School, Charles Coughlen Tall Grass Preserve, Reading Woods. Library: 711,000 volumes, 937,000 microforms.

Tuition: per semester, full-time resident $1039, nonresident $2732, per credit resident $89, nonresident $230. On-campus housing for 93 married students, unlimited for single students. Average academic year housing cost: $1890 for married students, $1550–$3150 for single students. Apply to Residential Life and Housing Coordinator. Phone: (316)343-5264, (316)341-5909. Day care facilities available.

Graduate Division

Enrollment: full-time 462, part-time 1036. College faculty teaching graduate students: full-time 194, part-time 4. Degrees conferred: M.A., M.A.T., M.B.A., M.M., M.L.S., M.S., Ed.S., Ph.D.

ADMISSION REQUIREMENTS. Transcript, letters of recommendation required in support of University's application. GRE/GMAT/MAT required by some departments. TOEFL required for international applicants. Interview required for library science major. Accepts transfer applicants. Graduates of unaccredited institutions not considered. Apply to Graduate Office by August 16. Application fee $20, $30 (Ph.D.). Phone: (316)341-5403.

ADMISSION STANDARDS. Relatively open. Usual minimum average: 2.5 (A = 4).

FINANCIAL AID. Annual awards from institutional funds: 10 fellowships, 10 research assistantships, 101 teaching assistantships, 6 graduate aides, 10 special graduate assistantships, Federal W/S, loans. Approved for VA benefits. Apply to Graduate Office by March 15. Use FAFSA. Phone: (316)343-5457. About 12% of students receive aid other than loans from University and outside sources. No aid for part-time students.

DEGREE REQUIREMENTS. For M.A., M.B.A., M.M., M.S.: 30 semester hours with thesis, or 32–38 hours without thesis, at least 22 in residence and one semester in full-time attendance; final written/oral exams. For M.A.T.: 36 semester hours minimum, at least 22 in residence and one semester in full-time attendance; thesis/nonthesis option; final written/oral exam. For M.L.S.: 42 specified hours; thesis/nonthesis option; final written/oral exam. For Ed.S.: 22 hours minimum in residence beyond the master's, thesis included, at least one semester in full-time attendance; GRE for candidacy; final written/oral exam. For Ph.D.: 60 semester hours beyond master's minimum, at least 42 in full-time residence; advancement to candidacy; research tool; comprehensive exam; dissertation; final oral exam.

FIELDS OF STUDY.
Biology.
Business.
Business Education.
Cell Biology.
Education. Includes art, early childhood, education of the gifted, elementary, reading, secondary, counselor education, rehabilitation counseling, administration, curriculum and instruction.
English.
Health, Physical Education and Recreation.
History. Includes American and world.
Library and Information Management. Ph.D.
Marketing.
Mathematics.
Music. Includes music education, performance; recital for performance majors.
Physical Science. Includes chemistry, earth science, physics.
Psychology. Includes art therapy, clinical, organizational, school psychology, special education.
Social Science.

UNIVERSITY OF EVANSVILLE
Evansville, Indiana 47722-0002

Founded 1854. Located 300 miles S of Chicago, Coed. Private control, Methodist affiliation. Semester system. Library: 238,533 volumes, 317,500 microforms, 1150 current periodicals, 10 PCs.

Tuition: per hour $350. On-campus housing for both single and married students. Contact Director of Student Housing for information. Phone: (812)479-2956. Day care facilities available.

Graduate programs

Enrollment: full-time 10, part-time 66 (men 10%, women 90%), Graduate faculty: full-time 7, part-time 7. Degrees conferred: M.A., M.S., M.S.N.

ADMISSION REQUIREMENTS. Official transcripts, three letters of reference required in support of application. NTE/MAT required for some programs. TOEFL required for international applicants. Interview not required. Accepts transfer applicants. Apply to individual program directors at least sixty days prior to registration. Application fee $25. Phone: (812)479-2000.

ADMISSION STANDARDS. Selective. Usual minimum average: 2.75 (A = 4).

FINANCIAL AID. Limited to assistantships, loans. Apply to individual schools by July 1 for assistantships; to Financial Aid Office for all other programs. Use FAFSA. About 5% of students receive aid other than loans from University. Aid available for part-time students.

DEGREE REQUIREMENTS. For master's: 33 semester hours minimum, at least 24 in residence and 9 in full-time attendance; thesis/nonthesis option.

FIELDS OF STUDY.

DEPARTMENT OF NURSING:
Gerontology.
Health Service Administration. M.S.
Nursing. M.S., M.S.N.

SCHOOL OF EDUCATION:
Counseling. M.A., M.S.
Special Education. M.A.

FAIRFIELD UNIVERSITY
Fairfield, Connecticut 06430-5195

Founded 1942. Located 50 miles NE of New York City. Coed on graduate level. Private control. Roman Catholic. Semester system. Library: 260,000 volumes, 466,290 microforms, 20 PC workstations.

Tuition: per credit hour $320. Limited on-campus housing available.

Graduate School of Education

Graduate study since 1950. Enrollment: full-time 111, part-time 537. University faculty teaching graduate students: full-time 17, part-time 26. Degrees conferred: M.A., C.A.S.

ADMISSION REQUIREMENTS. Transcripts, two letters of recommendation, PRAXIS I CBT or waiver required in support of School's application. TOEFL required for international applicants. Graduates of unaccredited institutions not considered. Apply to Graduate School Office; no specified closing date except for MMTP and Counselor Education program. Rolling admission process. Application fee $35. Phone: (203)254-4250; fax: (203)254-4241.

ADMISSION STANDARDS. Relatively open. Usual minimum average: 2.67 (A = 4).

FINANCIAL AID. Annual awards from institutional funds: eight to twelve graduate assistantships, Federal W/S, loans. Apply to Dean by May 1 (Fall) December 15 (Spring). Use FAFSA and University's FAF. Phone: (203)254-4125. Loans available for part-time students.

DEGREE REQUIREMENTS. For M.A.: 33–54 credits; comprehensive examination or thesis. For C.A.S.: 30 credits minimum beyond the master's, at least 24 in residence. No thesis or language requirement.

FIELDS OF STUDY.
Counselor Education. Includes community, school, student affairs practice in higher education.
Marriage and Family Therapy.
Media/Educational Technology.
School and Applied Psychology.
Special Education. Includes bilingual special education, S.E. consulting teacher, education of gifted and talented.
Teaching and Foundations. Includes early childhood, computers in education, media and educational technology.
TESOL and Bilingual Education.

FAIRLEIGH DICKINSON UNIVERSITY
Florham-Madison Campus, Madison, New Jersey 07940-1099
http://www.fdu.edu

Established 1942. Private control. Coed. Semester system. Library: 182,000 volumes, 114,387 microforms, 923 current periodicals, 22 PCs.

Tuition: $471 graduate credit. Contact Office of Student Life for off-campus housing. Phone: (201)593-8586. Day care facilities available.

Graduate Studies

Enrollment: full-time 190, part-time 1199. Faculty: full-time 62, part-time 84. Degrees conferred: M.A., M.A.T., M.B.A., M.P.A., M.S., M.S.T.

ADMISSION REQUIREMENTS. Official transcripts required in support of application. Three letters of recommendation, GRE/GMAT/MAT/PRAXIS required for some programs. TOEFL required for international applicants. Accepts transfer applicants. Graduates of unaccredited institutions may not be considered. Rolling admissions process. Early application encouraged. Application fee $35. Phone: (201)593-8905; fax: (201)593-8088.

ADMISSION STANDARDS. Selective. Usual minimum average: 2.5, 3.0 in major field of undergraduate study (A = 4).

FINANCIAL AID. Limited to fellowships, loans. Approved for VA benefits. Apply to appropriate department chair for fellowships; to Office of Financial Aid for loans. Phone: (201)593-8700. Use FAFSA.

DEGREE REQUIREMENTS. For master's: 32–60 semester credits minimum, at least 26 in residence; final written exam: thesis/nonthesis option; other requirements vary by department.

FIELDS OF STUDY.

MAXWELL BECTON COLLEGE OF ARTS AND SCIENCES:
Applied Social and Community Psychology. M.A.
Biological Sciences. M.A.T.
Biology. M.S.
Chemistry. M.S.
Clinical Psychology. M.A.
Computer Science. M.S.
Corporate & Organizational Communications. M.A.
Elementary Education. M.A.T.
English as a Second Language. M.A.T.
English Language and Literature. M.A.T.
ESL/Bilingual Education. M.A.T.
Foreign Languages. M.A.T.
General Experimental Psychology. M.A.
Industrial Psychology. M.A.
Mathematics. M.S.
Organizational Behavior for Managers. M.A.
Personnel Psychology. M.A.
Physical Science. M.A.T.
Science. M.A.T.
Social Studies. M.A.T.
Substance Abuse. M.A.

SAMUEL J. SILBERMAN COLLEGE OF BUSINESS ADMINISTRATION:
Accounting.
Accounting (for Non-Accountants).
Economics.
Finance.
Human Resource Management.

Industrial and Operations Management.

International Business.

Management. Includes entrepreneurial studies, information systems professional, managers of technology.

Marketing.

Pharmaceutical Chemical Studies.

Public Administration. M.P.A.

Quantitative Analysis.

Taxation. M.S.T.

FAIRLEIGH DICKINSON UNIVERSITY

Teaneck-Hackensack Campus

Teaneck, New Jersey 07666-1914

http://www.fdu.edu

Established 1942. Private control. Coed. Semester system. Library: 264,112 volumes, 190,769 microforms, 1600 current periodicals, 17 PCs.

Tuition: per credit $471. No on-campus housing available. Contact the Office of Student Life for off-campus housing information. Phone: (201)692-2231.

Graduate Studies

Enrollment: full-time 575, part-time 1419. Faculty: full-time 107, part-time 67. Degrees conferred: M.A., M.A.T., M.B.A., M.S., M.P.A., M.S., M.S.E.E., M.S.N., M.S.T., Ph.D. (Clinical Psychology).

ADMISSION REQUIREMENTS. Transcripts, three letters of recommendation, GRE/GMAT/MAT/PRAXIS required in support of applications. TOEFL required for international applicants. Accepts transfer applicants. Graduates of unaccredited institutions may not be considered. Rolling admissions process. Early application encouraged. Application fee $35. Phone: (800)338-8803.

ADMISSION STANDARDS. Selective. Usual minimum average: 2.5 (A = 4), 3.0 in major field of undergraduate study.

FINANCIAL AID. Scholarships, research fellowships, teaching fellowships, M.P.A., M.A.T. paid internships, loans. Approved for VA benefits. Apply to appropriate department chair for fellowships; to Office of Financial Aid for all other programs. Phone: (201)692-2362. Use FAFSA.

DEGREE REQUIREMENTS. For master's: 32–60 semester credits minimum, at least 26 in residence; final written exam; thesis/nonthesis option; other requirements vary by department. For Ph.D.: 60 semester credits beyond the master's; qualifying exam; internship; dissertation; final exam.

FIELDS OF STUDY.

UNIVERSITY COLLEGE:

Biological Sciences. M.A.T.

Biology. M.S.

Chemistry. M.S.

Clinical Psychology. Ph.D.

Computer Science. M.S.

Corporate and Organizational Communication. M.A.

Electrical Engineering. M.S.E.E.

English as a Second Language. M.A.T.

English and Comparative Literature/Technical Writing. M.A.

English Language and Literature. M.A.T.

Foreign Language. M.A.T.

General/Experimental Psychology. M.A.

History. M.A.

Learning Disabilities. M.A.

Management Information Systems. M.S.

Mathematics. M.A.T.

Medical Technology. M.S.

Multilingual Education. M.A.

Nursing. M.S.

Physical Sciences. M.A.

Political Science. M.A.

School Psychology. M.A.

Science. M.A.T.

Social Studies. M.A.T.

System Science/Pollution Studies. M.S.

SAMUEL J. SILBERMAN COLLEGE OF BUSINESS ADMINISTRATION:

Accounting.

Accounting (for Non Accountants).

Economics.

Finance.

Financial Economics. M.A.

Human Resource Management.

Industrial and Operations Management.

International Business.

Management.

Management for:—entrepreneurial studies; executives; information systems; hospitality managers; managers of technology.

Marketing.

Pharmaceutical Chemical Studies.

Public Administration. M.P.A.

Quantitative Analysis.

Taxation. M.S.T.

FINCH UNIVERSITY OF HEALTH SCIENCES/ THE CHICAGO MEDICAL SCHOOL

3333 Green Bay Road

North Chicago, Illinois 60064-3037

Founded in 1912. University established in 1968, with Chicago Medical School as core component of three allied units. Private control. Quarter system. Special facilities: Electron-microscope facility, Protein Sequence Laboratory, Special Pathogen-Free Swine Facility, Computer Center, and Medical Library. Library: 87,000 volumes, 5790 microforms, 1084 journal titles, 3 academic computer labs.

Off-campus housing available. Average living expenses: $1000 per month. Contact Office of Student Affairs.

School of Graduate and Postdoctoral Studies

Graduate study since 1968. Tuition: full-time $4188 per quarter; part-time $350 per unit.

Enrollment: full- and part-time 328. Faculty: full- and part-time 99. Degrees conferred: M.S., Ph.D.

ADMISSION REQUIREMENTS. Completed application, transcripts, three letters of recommendation, GRE required in support of School's application. Graduates of unaccredited institutions not considered. Early application advised for applicants seeking fellowships. All applications must be completed by June 1. Apply to the Office of Admissions. Application fee $25. Phone: (708)578-3209.

ADMISSION STANDARDS. Competitive for most departments. Usual minimum average: 3.0 (A = 4).

FINANCIAL AID. Fifty-four fellowships, teaching assistantships, research grants, loans. Apply to chairman of department for fellowships and assistantships; to the Office of Financial Aid for loans. Phone: (708)578-3216. Use FAFSA. Almost all students in basic medical science doctoral programs who are in good standing receive some sort of financial aid through University fellowships, research grants, and/or other sources.

DEGREE REQUIREMENTS. For M.S. (research master's): minimum of 30 units of course work and 15 units of research; minimum of one year of full-time residence; thesis; final oral exam. For Ph.D.: minimum of 60 units of course work and 75 units of research credit; minimum of two years of full-time residence; preliminary exam; thesis; final oral exam.

FIELDS OF STUDY.
Applied Physiology.
Biological Chemistry.
Cell Biology and Anatomy.
Clinical Psychology.
Medical Radiation Physics.
Microbiology and Immunology.
Neurosciences.
Pathology.
Pharmacology and Molecular Biology.
Physiology and Biophysics.

Chicago Medical School

Founded 1912. Annual tuition: $29,160. Total average cost for all other expenses: $9900. Enrollment: first-year class 150 (EDP 3); total full-time 624 (men 65%, women 35%). School faculty: full-time 349, part-time 35. Degrees conferred: M.D., M.D.-M.S., M.D.-Ph.D.

ADMISSION REQUIREMENTS. AMCAS report, transcripts, references, MCAT, interview required in support of application. Applicants must have completed at least four years of college study. Has EDP; apply between June 15 and August 1. Apply to Office of Admissions after June 15, before December 15 (firm). Application fee $65. Phone: (708)578-3206; fax: (708)578-3284.

ADMISSION STANDARDS. Very competitive. Accepts 3% of total annual applications. Approximately 30% are state residents.

FINANCIAL AID. Scholarships, loans. Apply to Associate Dean (Student Affairs); no specified closing date. Use GAPSFAS. About 75% of students receive aid other than loans from School funds.

DEGREE REQUIREMENTS. For M.D.: satisfactory completion of three-, four-, or five-year program. For M.D.-M.S.: satisfactory completion of five-year program. For M.D.-Ph.D.: satisfactory completion of program.

FIELDS OF GRADUATE STUDY.
Anatomy.
Biochemistry.
Cell Biochemistry.
Immunology.
Microbiology.
Neurosciences.
Pathology.
Pharmacology.
Physiology.

FISK UNIVERSITY
Nashville, Tennessee 37208-3051

Established 1867. Coed. Private control. Semester system. Library: 260,000 volumes, 5600 microforms, 350 current periodicals.

Annual tuition: full-time $6615; $393 per credit. On-campus housing for single and married students. Average academic year housing cost: $3690 (including board) for single students; $4000 for married students. Contact Dean of Students for both on- and off-campus housing information. Phone: (615)329-8557.

Graduate Programs

Graduate study since 1889. Enrollment: about 40. Degree conferred: M.A.

ADMISSION REQUIREMENTS. Transcripts, letters of recommendation required in support of application. GRE recommended for most programs. TOEFL required for international applicants. Accepts transfer applicants. Apply to Office of Admissions at least one month prior to date of registration. Rolling admission process. Application fee $25. Phone: (615)329-8665.

ADMISSION STANDARDS. Selective. Usual minimum average: 2.5 (A = 4).

FINANCIAL AID. Fellowships, assistantships, loans. Apply to appropriate Department; for fellowships, assistantships; to Office of Financial Aid for all other programs. No specified closing date. Use FAFSA. Phone: (615)329-8737.

DEGREE REQUIREMENTS. For M.A.: 30 semester hours minimum full-time; thesis; final written/oral exam.

FIELDS OF STUDY.
Biology.
Chemistry. Reading knowledge of one foreign language for M.A.
Clinical Psychology. GRE for admission.
Physics.
Psychology. GRE for admission.
Sociology.

FITCHBURG STATE COLLEGE
160 Pearl Street
Fitchburg, Massachusetts 01420-2697

Founded 1894. Located 26 miles N of Worcester. Coed. State control. Semester system. Library: 194,000 volumes, 410,000 microforms, 1800 current periodicals, 9 PCs.

Tuition: per hour, resident $140, nonresident $140. Limited on-campus housing available. Average academic year housing costs: $3700–$4000 (including board). Contact Office of Residence Life for both on- and off-campus housing information. Phone: (508)665-3219. Day care facilities available.

Division of Graduate and Continuing Education

Enrollment: full-time 0, part-time 767. Graduate faculty: part-time 164. Degrees conferred: M.A.T., M.B.A., M.Ed. M.S., C.A.G.S.

ADMISSION REQUIREMENTS. Transcripts, MAT/GMAT required in support of application. TOEFL required for international applicants. Accepts transfer applicants. Graduates of unaccredited institutions not considered. Apply to Director of Admission at least one month prior to entrance. Rolling admission process. Application fee $10, $40 for international applicants. Phone: (508)655-3181; fax: (508)655-3658; E-mail: dgce@fscvax.fsc.mass.edu.

ADMISSION STANDARDS. Selective. Usual minimum average: 2.8 (A = 4). Minimum GMAT score 400, MAT 50th percentile.

FINANCIAL AID. Scholarships, twenty research and twenty-two graduate assistantships, loans. Apply to the Graduate Office by September 15 (Fall), January 15 (Spring) for scholarships; by May 15 (Fall) for assistantships; to Financial Aid Office for all other programs. Use FAFSA. Phone: (508)665-3185.

DEGREE REQUIREMENTS. For master's: 33–36 semester hours minimum, at least 30 in residence; no language requirement; thesis/nonthesis option. For C.A.G.S.: 30 semester hours beyond the master's; special project/final exam.

FIELDS OF STUDY.
Biology. M.A.T.
Business Administration and Management. M.B.A.
Communication and Media Management. M.S.
Computer Science. M.S.
Consultation and Peer Leadership. C.A.G.S.
Counseling. Includes psychological, school. M.S.
Criminal Justice. M.S.
Early Childhood Education. M.Ed.
Educational Leadership and Management. C.A.G.S.
Educational Staff Development. C.A.G.S.
Elementary Education. M.Ed.
English. M.A.T.
History. M.A.T.
Interdisciplinary Studies. C.A.G.S.
Middle School Education. M.Ed.
Occupational Education. M.Ed.
Science Education. M.Ed.
Secondary Education. M.Ed.
Special Education. M.Ed.

FLORIDA AGRICULTURAL AND MECHANICAL UNIVERSITY
Tallahassee, Florida 32307

Founded 1887. Coed. State control. Semester system. Library: 466,000 volumes, 82,000 microforms.

Tuition: per hour, resident $110.80, nonresident $363.82. On-campus housing for 85 married students. Average per semester housing cost: $1592 per single occupancy. Apply to Business Manager for on-campus housing; to Dean of Men or Dean of Women for off-campus housing information. Phone: (904)599-3992.

School of Graduate Studies

Graduate study since 1945. Enrollment: full-time 800, part-time 1,591. Graduate faculty: full-time 200, part-time 20. Degrees conferred: M.S., M.Ed., M.B.A., M.A.S.S., M.S.S.C.P., Pharm.D., Ph.D.

ADMISSION REQUIREMENTS. Transcripts, GRE/GMAT required in support of School's application. TOEFL required for international applicants. Interview not required. Accepts transfer applicants. Graduates of unaccredited colleges not considered. Apply by July 22 (Fall), April 2 (Summer), November 30 (Spring). Application fee $20. Phone: (904)599-3796.

ADMISSION STANDARDS. Selective. Usual minimum average: 2.5 (A = 4).

FINANCIAL AID. Two hundred fifty scholarships, fifteen fellowships, Federal W/S, loans. Apply to Graduate Dean at least thirty days prior to registration for fellowships and scholarships; to Financial Aid Office for Federal programs. Phone: (904)599-3730. About 20% of students receive aid other than loans from School and outside sources. No aid other than loans for part-time students.

DEGREE REQUIREMENTS. For master's: 36 hours minimum including thesis, at least 30 in residence; final written/oral exam.

For Pharm. D.: series of clinical clerkships, covering approximately 2000 hours; written comprehensive exam; clinical research project.

FIELDS OF STUDY.
Accounting.
Adult Education.
Agricultural Sciences.
Applied Social Science.
Architectural Studies.
Biology. Includes cell and molecular, physiology, ecological sciences, space life science.
Business Administration.
Business Education.
Chemical Engineering.
Chemistry.
Civil Engineering.
Counselor Education.
Criminal Justice.
Economics.
Educational Leadership.
Electrical Engineering.
Engineering.
Finance.
Health and Physical Education.
History.
Industrial Engineering.
Journalism.
Management Information Systems.
Marketing.
Mechanical Engineering.
Pharmaceutical Science. Includes environmental toxicology, medicinal chemistry, pharmaceutics, pharmacology and toxicology.
Physics.
Political Science.
Psychology.
Public Administration.
School/Community Psychology.
Secondary Education. Includes biology, chemistry, English, emotionally handicapped, French, physics, school psychology, social studies, Spanish.
Vocational Education.

FLORIDA ATLANTIC UNIVERSITY
PO Box 3091
Boca Raton, Florida 33431-0991

Opened 1964. Main campus located midway between Ft. Lauderdale and West Palm Beach just off I-95, other campus in Broward County. Coed. State control. Semester system. Library: 543,000 volumes, 1,960,000 microforms, 100 PCs.

Tuition: per semester hour, resident $119, nonresident $389. On-campus housing for graduate single men and women; none for married students. Annual housing cost: $3450. Apply to Director of Housing. Phone: (407)367-2880.

Graduate Studies

Enrollment: degree-seeking students full-time 764, part-time 1625, nondegree 1853. University faculty teaching graduate students: full-time 600. Degrees conferred: M.Ed., M.S., M.A., M.A.T., M.F.A., M.S.T., M.E., M.P.A., M.B.A., M.S.Eng., M.Acc., M.B.S., M.C.S., M.C.E., Ed.S., M.S.N., Ed.D., Ph.D.

ADMISSION REQUIREMENTS. Transcripts, letters of recommendation, GRE Subject Tests/GMAT required in support of application. TOEFL required for foreign applicants. Accepts transfer applicants. Graduates from unaccredited institutions not considered. Apply to Director of Admissions at least ninety days prior to registration, Application fee $20. Phone: (407)367-3040.

ADMISSION STANDARDS. Selective. Usual minimum average: 3.0 (A = 4), and combined score of 1000 on GRE, 500 GMAT.

FINANCIAL AID. Four scholarships, 223 assistantships, 70 fellowships, 137 teaching/research assistantships, nonresident tuition waivers, Federal W/S, loans. Apply to the Financial Aid Office; no specified closing date. Use FAFSA. Phone: (407)367-3530.

DEGREE REQUIREMENTS. For master's: 30 semester hours minimum, thesis, nonthesis option. For Ed.D.: 90 semester hours minimum beyond the bachelor's degree; essentially the same as for the Ph.D., except no language requirement. For Ph.D.: 90 semester hours minimum; one foreign language or research tool; qualifying exam; dissertation; final oral exam.

FIELDS OF STUDY.
Accounting.
Anthropology.
Art.
Biological Sciences.
Biology.
Business Administration.
Chemistry.
Civil Engineering.
Communication.
Computer Engineering.
Computer Science.
Economics.
Education. Includes educational foundations and technology, counselor education, curriculum and instruction, elementary, exceptional student, educational leadership, early childhood, exercise science and wellness.
Electrical Engineering.
English and Comparative Literature.
Geography.
Geology.
German.
History.
Languages and Linguistics. Includes French, German, Spanish.
Manufacturing Systems Engineering.
Mathematics.
Mechanical Engineering.
Music.
Nursing.
Ocean Engineering.
Physics.
Political Science.
Psychology.
Public Administration.
Reading Education.
Sociology.
Teacher Education.
Theater.
Urban and Regional Planning.

FLORIDA INSTITUTE OF TECHNOLOGY

Melbourne, Florida 32901-6975
http://www.fit.edu

Located within an hour's drive of Kennedy Space Center and Disney World. Coed. Private control. Semester system. Special facilities: Vero Beach Marine Research Center, Center of Electronics Manufacturability, Claude Pepper Institute for Aging and Therapeutic Research, Infectious Diseases Laboratory. Library: 210,000 volumes, 114,500 microforms.

Tuition: per credit $518. Limited on-campus housing for married and single graduate students. Average academic year housing cost: $4264 (includes board). Apply to Assistant Dean of Students. Phone: (407)768-8000, ext. 8080.

Graduate School

Enrollment: full-time 477, part-time 1975. Faculty teaching graduate students: full-time 158, part-time 122. Degrees conferred: M.B.A., M.S., Ed.S., Psy.D., Ph.D.

ADMISSION REQUIREMENTS. Transcripts required in support of School's application. GRE/GMAT required for some majors. TOEFL required for international applicant. Accepts transfer students. Graduates of unaccredited institutions not considered. Apply to Graduate Admissions office; no specified closing date. Rolling admission process. Application fee $40, for international applicants $50. Phone: (407)768-8000, ext. 7118, or (800)944-4348; fax: (407)723-9468.

ADMISSION STANDARDS. Usual master's level minimum average: 3.0 (A = 4).

FINANCIAL AID. Annual awards from institutional funds: 250 assistantships, Federal W/S, loans. Apply to Graduate School Admissions Office by March 1. Use FAFSA. Phone: (407)768-8000, ext. 8070. About 80% of students receive aid other than loans from institute and outside sources.

DEGREE REQUIREMENTS. For master's: 32–48 credits minimum, at least 24–36 credits in residence; thesis option; final written/oral exam in some program. For Ph.D.: 60 credits minimum, at least 32 credit, in full-time study; preliminary exam; advancement to candidacy; one foreign language or research tool; dissertation; final oral exam. For Psy.D.: essentially the same as Ph.D., except no foreign language requirement; special project may be substituted for dissertation.

FIELDS OF STUDY.
Aerospace Engineering.
Applied Mathematics.
Aviation Management.
Biological Sciences.
Business Administration.
Chemical Engineering.
Chemistry.
Clinical Psychology.
Coastal Resource Management.
Communication.
Computer Engineering.
Computer Science.
Contract and Acquisition Management.
Electrical Engineering.
Engineering Psychology.
Environmental Engineering.
Environmental Resources Management.
Industrial/Organizational Psychology.
Interdisciplinary Science.
Management of Technology.
Mechanical Engineering.
Meteorology.
Ocean Engineering.
Oceanography. Includes bio-environmental, chemical, geological, physical-environments.
Operations Research.
Personnel Psychology.
Physics.
Science Education.
Space Sciences.

FLORIDA STATE UNIVERSITY

Tallahassee, Florida 32306

http://www.fsu.edu

Founded 1857. Coed. State control. Semester system. Special facilities: The National High Magnetic Field Laboratory, The Center for Materials Research and Technology (MARTECH), 9 Mev Super FN tandem Van de Graaff accelerator, Florida State University Marine Laboratory, Center for Music Research, Antarctic Research Facility, Two Supercomputers: The Cray Y-MP and a Connection Machine, FSU Proton-Induced X-Ray Emission (PIXE) Laboratory, Supercomputer Computations Research Institute (SCRI), Institute of Science and Public Affairs, Institute for Social Research, Geophysical Fluid Dynamics Institute, Institute of Molecular Biophysics, Creative Writing Program, Educational Research Center for Child Development, Center for Information Systems Research, Beaches and Shores Resource Center. Library: 2,065,507 volumes, 4,253,891 microforms.

Tuition: per credit, resident $118, nonresident $389. Capacity for on-campus housing for graduate students is 791. Average academic year housing costs. $5004 for married students, $3072 (includes board) for single students. Contact Office of Resident Student Development for both on- (904-644-0089) and off-campus (904-644-2860) housing information.

Graduate School

Enrollment: full-time 3740, part-time 2116. Graduate faculty: full-time 852, part-time 136. Degrees conferred: M.A., M.S., M.Acc., M.B.A., M.M., M.M.Ed., M.S.N., M.S.P., M.S.W., Adv.M., Ed.Sp., Ad.M.L.S., M.F.A., M.P.A., Ed.D., D.Mus., Ph.D.

ADMISSION REQUIREMENTS. Two transcripts, GRE required in support of School's application. TOEFL/TSE required for international applicants. Interview/GRE Subject Test/GMAT required for some departments. Accepts transfer applicants. Graduates of unaccredited institutions not considered. Apply to Office of Admissions by July 16 (Fall), November 25 (Spring), April 2 (Summer), Application fee $20. Phone: (904)644-3420; fax: (904)644-0197.

ADMISSION STANDARDS. Competitive or very selective for some departments, selective for most. Usual minimum average 3.0 (A = 4).

FINANCIAL AID. Annual awards from institutional funds that meet the minimum University requirements for tuition waivers: 100 graduate fellowships, 555 research and service assistantships, 503 assistantships with instructional responsibility, 447 assistantships assisting faculty with instruction, Federal W/S, loans. Approved for VA benefits. Apply by March 1 to appropriate department chair for fellowships, assistantships; to University's Office of Financial Aid for all other programs. Phone: (904)644-5871; fax: (904)644-6404. Use FAFSA. About 45% of students receive aid other than loans from University and outside sources.

DEGREE REQUIREMENTS. For M.A., M.S.: 30 semester hours minimum including thesis or 32 hours minimum without thesis, reading knowledge of one language for M.A. sometimes required for M.S.; final written/oral exams required by some departments. For M.Acc.: 33 hours minimum. For M.B.A., M.P.A.: 39 hours minimum. For M.M., M.M.Ed., M.P.: 30 hours minimum, including thesis, recital, or composition, or 36 hours minimum without thesis. For M.S.W.: 4 semesters (Fall and Spring consecutively), 60 hours minimum; 36 hours on-campus instruction, 24 hours field instruction. For M.F.A.: 75 hours minimum in Creative Art; 60 hours minimum in Theater; includes creative project and final exhibition; final written/oral exams sometimes required. For Ph.D.: at least 24 hours during any one-year period after completion of 30 hours or master's degree, additional hours may be required by departments; a minimum of 24 hours of dissertation credit; preliminary exam; dissertation; final oral exam. For D.Mus.: 80 hours minimum beyond the bachelor's; diagnostic exam; five recitals: two public, one studio, three chamber work, one performance with a large ensemble for performance majors: for theory/composition majors, 70 hours minimum beyond the bachelor's, diagnostic exam, public performance of original chamber works, dissertation (which must be a major work for composition majors); final written/oral exams.

FIELDS OF STUDY.

COLLEGE OF ARTS AND SCIENCES:

Anthropology.

Biological Sciences. Includes microbiology, botany, ecology, genetics, physiology, zoology, marine, molecular. Thesis, one language for M.A., M.S.; GRE Subject for admission.

Chemical Physics.

Chemistry.

Classical Language and Literature. Includes Latin, Greek. One language in addition to major for M.A., M.A. only.

Computer Science.

English.

Geology. Thesis for master's.

Geophysical Fluid Dynamics. Ph.D. only.

History. GRE Subject for admission; thesis for M.A.

Mathematics.

Meteorology.

Modern Languages. Includes French, German, Russian, Slavic, Spanish. GRE Subject for admission.

Molecular Biophysics. Ph.D. only.

Neuroscience.

Oceanography. Includes physical, biological, geological.

Philosophy. Thesis; one language for M.A.

Physics.

Psychology. Three recommendations, GRE Subject for admission; thesis for M.A.

Religion. One or more languages for M.A., Ph.D.

Statistics.

COLLEGE OF BUSINESS:

Accounting.

Business Administration.

Finance.

Management.

Marketing.

COLLEGE OF COMMUNICATION:

Audiology and Speech Pathology.

Communication.

SCHOOL OF CRIMINOLOGY AND CRIMINAL JUSTICE:

Criminology.

COLLEGE OF EDUCATION:

Adult Education.

Comprehensive Vocational Education.

Counseling and Human Systems. Master's only.

Counseling Psychology and Human Systems. Ed.D. only.

Early Childhood.

Educational Administration/Leadership.

Educational Psychology.

Educational Research.

Elementary Education.

Emotional Disturbances and Learning Disabled. Master's only.

English Education.

Evaluation and Measurement.

Foundations of Education.

Health Education.

Higher Education.

Instructional Systems.
Leisure Services and Studies. Master's only.
Mathematics Education.
Mental Retardation. Master's only.
Multilingual and Multicultural Education.
Physical Education.
Reading Education.
Rehabilitation Services.
Science Education.
Social Studies Education.
Special Education.
Visual Disabilities.

COLLEGE OF ENGINEERING:
Chemical Engineering.
Civil Engineering.
Electrical Engineering.
Industrial Engineering.
Mechanical Engineering.

SCHOOL OF MOTION PICTURE, TELEVISION, AND RECORDING ARTS.
Motion Picture, Television, and Recording Arts.

SCHOOL OF MUSIC:
Music Education.
Music Theory.
Music Therapy. Master's only.
Musicology. Master's only.
Opera Production. Master's only.
Performance.

SCHOOL OF NURSING:
Nursing. Master's only.

COLLEGE OF SOCIAL SCIENCES:
Demography. Master's only.
Economics.
Geography.
Political Science.
Public Administration.
Sociology.
Urban and Regional Planning.

SCHOOL OF SOCIAL WORK:
Social Work.

SCHOOL OF THEATER:
Theater. Includes acting, costume technology, directing, technical production, theatre management.

SCHOOL OF VISUAL ARTS AND DANCE:
Art Education.
Art History and Criticism.
Dance. Master's only.
Interior Design. Master's only.
Studio Art. Master's only.

COLLEGE OF HUMAN SCIENCES:
Clothing and Textiles.
Family, Child, and Consumer Sciences.
Home Economics Education.
Human Sciences.
Marriage and the Family.
Movement Science Education.
Nutrition and Food Science.

SCHOOL OF LIBRARY AND INFORMATION STUDIES:
Library Science.

INTERDISCIPLINARY PROGRAMS:
American Studies. Master's only.
Asian Studies. Master's only.

Humanities.
International Affairs. Master's only.
Marriage and Family Living.
Russian and East European Studies.
Social Sciences.

College of Law (32306-1034)

Established 1965. Semester system. Library 360,000 volumes. Library has LEXIS, NEXIS, WESTLAW, OCLC. Annual tuition, full-time resident $3951, nonresident $12,411. On-campus housing available. Total average annual additional expenses: $9525. Apply to Director of Housing.

Enrollment: first-year class 205; total full-time 625 (men 52%, women 48%). Faculty: full-time 42, part-time 9. Degrees conferred: J.D., J.D.-M.B.A., J.D.-M.A., J.D.-M.P.A., J.D.-M.S.

ADMISSION REQUIREMENTS. LSDAS Law School report, bachelor's degree, transcripts, LSAT, personal statement, letters of recommendation required in support of application. Accepts transfer applicants. Graduates of unaccredited colleges not considered. Apply to Office of Admissions after September 1, before March 1. Admits first-year student, Fall only; transfers Fall and Summer. Application fee $20, Phone: (909)644-3787.

ADMISSION STANDARDS. Selective. Accepts about 20–25% of total applicants.

FINANCIAL AID. Scholarships, fellowships, Federal W/S, loans. Apply to University Office of Financial Aid by March 1. Use FAFSA. About 15% of students receive aid other than loans from College and outside sources.

DEGREE REQUIREMENTS. For J.D.: satisfactory completion of three-year program; 88 semester hours. J.D.-M.B.A. offered with School of Business, J.D.-M.A./M.S. with the departments of Economics, International Affairs, Public Affairs, Urban and Regional Planning, Graduate School of Arts and Science. The J.D.-M.P.A. with the School of Criminology and Criminal Justice.

UNIVERSITY OF FLORIDA
Gainesville, Florida 32611-8140
http://www.orge.ufl.edu

Founded 1953. Located 75 miles SW of Jacksonville. Coed. State control. Semester system. Member of the Association of American Universities (AAU). Sponsoring University of Oak Ridge associated universities. Special facilities: Agricultural Research Center, Florida Engineering and Experiment Station, Center for Applied Thermodynamics and Corrosion, Center for Aquatic Sciences, Clinical Research Center, Center for Gerontological Studies, Human Development Center, Center for Information Research, Center for Intelligent Machines and Robotics, Center for International Studies, Center for Latin American Studies, Center for Research on Human Prosthesis, Florida Museum of Natural History, Florida Water Resources Research Center. Library: over 3,000,000 volumes, 4,200,000 microforms.

Annual tuition: resident, per credit hour $115, nonresident $386. On-campus housing for 980 married students, graduate men, women. Annual housing cost: $2400–$5400. Apply to Division of On-Campus Housing; to Division of Off-Campus Housing for information. Phone: (352)392-2161.

Graduate School

Graduate study since 1906. Enrollment: full-time 4250 (men 65%, women 35%), part-time 2449 (men 50%, women 50%).

University faculty: full- and part-time 2500. Degrees conferred: M.A., M.S., M.A.T., M.S.T., M.Ag., M.Arch., M.Acc., M.A.E., M.H.S.E., M.S.H.S.E., M.A.M.C., M.A.M.R.D., M.A.U.R.P., M.ER.C., M.S.R.S., M.H.S., M.Nsg., M.S.B.C., M.S.Nsg., M.S.P., M.Stat., M.S.Stat., M.B.C., M.E., M.Ed., M.B.A., M.F.A., Ed.S., Engr., M.S.A.S., M.C.E., M.S.E.S.S., M.E.S.S., M.L.A., M.M., LL.M., Ed.D., Ph.D.

ADMISSION REQUIREMENTS. Two transcripts, letters of recommendation, GRE/GMAT/LSAT required in support of School's application. GRE Subject Test recommended. Interview required by some departments. TOEFL required for international applicants. Accepts transfer applicants. Graduates of unaccredited institutions not considered. Apply to Director of Admissions by June 9 (Fall), November 1 (Spring), March 1 (Summer). Anthropology, Architecture, Business Administration, Clinical Health Psychology, Counseling Education, Counseling Psychology, History Programs have earlier deadline dates. Application fee $20. Phone: (352)392-1365; fax: (352)392-3987.

ADMISSION STANDARDS. Very selective for most departments. Usual minimum G.P.A.: 3.0 (A = 4).

FINANCIAL AID. Annual awards from institutional funds: 250 research fellowships, 2600 assistantships, Federal W/S, loans. Approved for VA benefits. Apply by February 15 to appropriate department chair for fellowships, assistantships; to Office of Student Aid for all other aid. Use FAFSA. Phone: (352)392-1275. About 44% of students receive aid other than loans from University and outside sources. No aid for part-time students.

DEGREE REQUIREMENTS. For master's: 30 credits minimum, thesis, final written/oral exam; 32 minimum nonthesis option, written comprehensive exam; reading knowledge of one foreign language required for many majors. Exceptions to the above include: LL.M. in Tax: 24 credits; M.Acc.: 34 credits; M.Ag.: 32 credits; M.Arch.: 52 credits; M.A.M.R.D.: 32 credits; M.A.T.: 36 credits; M.A.U.R.P.: 52 credits; M.B.A.: 48 credits; M.B.C.: 33 credits; M.Ed.: 36 credits; M.E.S.S.: 34 credits; M.F.A.: 60 credits for art and theatre; 48 credits for English; M.F.R.C.: 32 credits; M.H.S.: 36 credits for occupational therapy, 43 credits for rehabilitation counseling; M.H.S.E.: 36 credits; M.L.A.: 48 credits; M.M.: 32 credits; M.S.R.S.: 34 credits; M.Nsg. and M.S.Nsg.: 48 credits; M.S.T.: 36 credits; M.Stat.: 36 credits; Engr.: 30 credits beyond the master's; Ed.S.: 36 credits beyond the master's. For Ph.D. and Ed.D.: 90 credits beyond the bachelor's, 30 credits in one calendar year, qualifying written and oral exam, dissertation, final written/oral exam.

FIELDS OF STUDY.

COLLEGE OF AGRICULTURE:
Agricultural Education and Communication.
Agricultural Engineering.
Agronomy.
Animal Science.
Botany.
Dairy Science.
Entomology and Nematology.
Fisheries and Aquatic Sciences.
Food and Resource Economics.
Food Science and Human Nutrition.
Forest Resources and Conservation.
Horticultural Science. Includes fruit crops, environmental horticulture, vegetable crops.
Microbiology and Cell Science.
Plant Molecular and Cellular Biology.
Plant Pathology.
Poultry Science.
Soil and Water Science.

COLLEGE OF ARCHITECTURE:
Architecture.
Building Construction.
Landscape Architecture.
Urban and Regional Planning.

COLLEGE OF LIBERAL ARTS AND SCIENCES:
Anthropology.
Astronomy.
Botany.
Chemistry.
Classics.
Communication Processes and Disorders.
Computer and Information Sciences.
Counseling Psychology.
Creative Writing.
English.
French.
Geography.
Geology.
Germanic and Slavic Languages and Literatures.
History.
Latin.
Latin American Studies.
Linguistics.
Mathematics.
Philosophy.
Physics.
Political Science.
Political Science–International Relations.
Psychology.
Religion.
Romance Languages and Literatures.
Sociology.
Spanish.
Statistics.
Zoology.

COLLEGE OF BUSINESS ADMINISTRATION:
Accounting.
Business Administration. Includes decision and information sciences, finance and insurance, management, marketing, real estate.
Economics.

COLLEGE OF EDUCATION:
Curriculum and Instruction.
Early Childhood Education.
Education of the Emotionally Disturbed.
Education of the Mentally Retarded.
Educational Leadership.
Educational Psychology.
Elementary Education.
English Education.
Foreign Language Education.
Foundation of Education.
Higher Education Administration.
Marriage and Family Counseling.
Mathematics Education.
Mental Health Counseling.
Reading Education.
Research and Evaluation Methodology.
School Counseling and Guidance.
School Psychology.
Science Education.
Social Studies Education.
Special Education.
Specific Learning Disabilities.
Speech Pathology.
Student Personnel in Higher Education.
Vocational, Technical, and Adult Education.

COLLEGE OF ENGINEERING:
Aerospace Engineering.
Agricultural and Biological Engineering.
Chemical Engineering.
Civil Engineering.
Coastal and Oceanographic Engineering.
Computer and Information and Engineering.
Electrical and Computer Engineering.
Engineering Mechanics.
Engineering Science.
Environmental Engineering Sciences.
Industrial and Systems Engineering.
Materials Science and Engineering.
Mechanical Engineering.
Nuclear Engineering Sciences.

COLLEGE OF DENTISTRY:
Endodontic.
Orthodontics.
Periodontics.
Prosthodontics.

COLLEGE OF FINE ARTS:
Art.
Art Education.
Art History.
Music.
Music Education.
Theater.

COLLEGE OF HEALTH-RELATED PROFESSIONS:
Clinical.
General Health Psychology.
Health and Hospital Administration.
Occupational Therapy.
Physical Therapy.
Rehabilitation Counseling.

COMMUNICATIONS:
Mass Communication.

COLLEGE OF LAW
Comparative Law.
Taxation.

COLLEGE OF MEDICINE:
Biochemistry and Molecular Biology.
Medical Sciences. Includes anatomical sciences, molecular genetics and microbiology, neuroscience, oral biology, pathology, pharmacology, physiology.

COLLEGE OF NURSING:
Nursing Science.

COLLEGE OF PHARMACY:
Pharmaceutical Sciences. Includes medicinal chemistry, pharmacodynamics, pharmacy.

COLLEGE OF HEALTH AND HUMAN PERFORMANCE:
Exercise and Sport Science.
Health Science Education.
Health and Human Performance.
Recreational Study.

INTERDISCIPLINARY PROGRAMS:
Animal Molecular and Cellular Biology.
Hydrology Sciences.
Jewish Studies.
Mammalian Genetics.
Toxicology.
Women's/Gender Studies.

Note: The Graduate Catalog, Graduate Coordinators for each program are listed on University's homepage noted above.

College of Law (PO Box 117622)

Founded 1909. Semester system. Law library 550,000 volumes. Library has LEXIS, WESTLAW, DIALOG, PLATO. Tuition per credit hour: resident $129; nonresidents $411. Total average annual additional expenses: $8500.

Enrollment: first-year class 200 (Fall), 200 (Spring), full-time 1210 (men 60%, women 40%); no part-time study. Faculty: full-time 80, part-time 2. Degrees conferred: J.D., J.D./M.B.A., J.D./M.A. (Accounting, Political Science, Sociology, Urban and Regional Planning), J.D.-Ph.D. (History), LL.M. (Comparative Law [Foreign Lawyers], Taxation).

ADMISSION REQUIREMENTS. LSDAS Law School report, transcript showing bachelor's degree completion, LSAT (no later than December) required in support of application. Interview not required. Accepts transfer applicants. Graduates of unaccredited colleges not considered. Apply to Assistant Dean for Admission and Financial Aid by February 1 (Fall), July 1 (Spring). Application fee $15. Phone: (904)392-2087; fax: (904)392-8727.

ADMISSION STANDARDS. Selective. Accepts 30% of total annual applicants.

FINANCIAL AID. Limited scholarship, loans available; most funds directed toward loans. Use FAFSA and College's Financial Aid form. Applications should be completed no later than March 1. About 15% of students receive aid other than loans.

DEGREE REQUIREMENTS. For J.D.: 88 hours minimum; transfer credit from other law school considered. For LL.M.: 24 credits of study beyond J.D.

College of Medicine (32610)

Established 1956. Annual tuition: full-time, resident $8703, nonresident $22,612. Total cost for all other expenses: $8500.

Enrollment: first-year class 85; total full-time 500 (men 55%, women 45%); postgraduate 446. Faculty: full-time 799, part-time 185. Degrees conferred: B.S.-M.D. (junior honors program and bachelor's completion program with FSU and FAMU). M.D., M.D.-M.S., M.D.-Ph.D. Medical Scientist Training Program. The M.S. and Ph.D. are offered through the Graduate School.

ADMISSION REQUIREMENTS. AMCAS report, transcripts, MCAT, recommendations, interview required in support of application. Florida residents given preference. Graduates of unaccredited colleges not considered. Bachelor's normally required for admission. Does not have EDP. Apply to Chairman, Medical Selection Committee after June 15, before December 1 (flexible). Admits Fall only. Application fee $20. Phone: (904)392-4514; fax: (904)392-6482.

ADMISSION STANDARDS. Competitive. Accepts 10% of total annual applicants. Approximately 98% are state residents.

FINANCIAL AID. Scholarships, summer fellowships, assistantships, loans. Apply to Associate Dean after acceptance and prior to June 1. About 55% of students receive aid other than loans from College.

DEGREE REQUIREMENTS. For B.S.-M.D.: satisfactory completion of either a six-year or seven-year program. For M.D.: satisfactory completion of four-year program. Advanced standing for work completed in another school will be considered. For M.S., Ph.D.: see Graduate School listing above.

FIELDS OF GRADUATE STUDY.
Anatomy.
Biochemistry.
Cell and Developmental Biology.
Immunology.
Microbiology.
Molecular Biology.
Neurosciences.
Oral Biology.
Pathology.
Pharmacology.
Physiology.

College of Dentistry (32610-0445)

Established 1972. Annual tuition: resident $7749, nonresident $19,901. On-campus housing available. Average academic year housing costs: $10,165. Contact Housing Office for both on- and off-campus housing information. Phone: (904)392-2161. Total average academic cost for all other first-year expenses: $5864.

Enrollment: first-year class 78, total 279 (men 75%, women 25%). Faculty: full-time 98, part-time 34. Degree conferred: D.M.D.

ADMISSION REQUIREMENTS. AADSAS report, official transcripts, DAT (not later than October), three letters of recommendation, at least three years of college required in support of application. Accepts transfer applicants. Interview by invitation only. Preference given to state residents. Graduates of unaccredited colleges not considered. Apply after June 1, before October 15 to Director of Admissions. Application fee $20. Phone: (904)392-4866.

ADMISSION STANDARDS. Selective. Accepts about 50% of total annual applicants. Approximately 99% are state residents.

FINANCIAL AID. Scholarships, grants, loans. Apply to Office of Dental Admissions after acceptance; no specified closing date. Use FAFSA. Phone: (904)846-1384.

DEGREE REQUIREMENTS. For D.M.D.: satisfactory completion of 11-semester program.

College of Veterinary Medicine (32610-0125)

Annual tuition: full-time resident $6612, nonresident $16,820. Total other expenses: $9482.

Enrollment: first-year class 80, total full-time 365, postgraduate 60. Faculty: full-time 88, part-time 10. Degree conferred: D.V.M. The M.S. and Ph.D. are offered through the Graduate School.

ADMISSION REQUIREMENTS. VMCAS report, two transcripts, animal/veterinary experience, GRE, three letters of recommendation (one from an academic advisor) required in support of application. Interview by invitation only. Transfer applicants for second-year class rarely considered. Applicants must have completed at least three years of college study. Preference given to state residents. Apply to the Dean after July 1, before November 1. Application fee $15. Phone: (904)392-4700, ext. 5300; fax: (904)392-8351.

ADMISSION STANDARDS. Competitive. Accepts about 30% of annual applicants. Not more than 15% of class can be nonresidents.

FINANCIAL AID. Scholarships, fellowships, assistantships, loans. Apply to Office of Financial Aid by February 15. Use FAFSA. About 20% of students receive aid other than loans.

DEGREE REQUIREMENTS, For D.V.M.: satisfactory completion of four-year program. For M.S. and Ph.D.: see Graduate School listing above.

FORDHAM UNIVERSITY
Rose Hill Campus
Bronx, New York 10458

Founded in 1841. Coed. Independent institution. Semester system. Library: 1,413,331 volumes, 1,295,800 microforms.

Tuition: per credit $500. Limited on-campus housing for single graduate students only. Annual housing cost: $5400. Apply to Director of Residential Life. Phone: (718)817-3080.

Graduate School of Arts and Sciences

Established in 1916. Enrollment: full-time 300, part-time 815. Graduate faculty: full-time 220, part-time 20. Degrees conferred: M.A., M.S., Ph.D.

ADMISSION REQUIREMENTS. Transcripts, two letters of recommendation, GRE Subject Tests required in support of School's application. MAT required in Psychology. Evidence of Proficiency in English or TOEFL required of all international applicants. Interview not required. Accepts transfer applicants. Graduates of unaccredited institutions not considered. Apply to Office of Graduate Admission by April 1 (Summer), May 1 (Fall), December 1 (Spring). Psychology applications must be completed by January 15. Application fee $50. Phone: (718)817-4416.

ADMISSION STANDARDS. Very competitive for some departments, competitive or selective for others. Usual minimum average: 3.0 (A = 4).

FINANCIAL AID. Awards from institutional funds: 200 scholarships, 25 teaching fellowships, 125 research assistantships, Federal W/S, loans. Apply to Office of Graduate Admissions by January 30 for most departments. Phone: (718)817-3800. No aid for part-time students.

DEGREE REQUIREMENTS. For master's: 30 credits minimum, up to six transfer credits accepted; thesis optional in some departments; comprehensive exam required; reading knowledge of one foreign language or demonstrated computer/research skill required. For Ph.D.: 60 credits minimum; at least two years in residence; reading knowledge of two foreign languages or one computer/research skill and one language; comprehensive exam; dissertation required; final oral exam.

FIELDS OF STUDY.
Biological Sciences. M.S., Ph.D.
Classical Languages and Literatures. M.A., Ph.D.
Clinical Psychology. Ph.D. only.
Communication. M.A.
Computer Science. M.S.
Developmental Psychology. Ph.D. only.
Economics. M.A., Ph.D.
English Language and Literature. M.A., Ph.D.
History. M.A., Ph.D.
International Political Economy and Development. M.A.; interdisciplinary.
Liberal Studies. M.A.; interdisciplinary.
Medieval Studies Program. M.A.; interdisciplinary.
Philosophy. M.A., Ph.D.
Political Science. M.A., Ph.D. only.
Psychometrics. Ph.D. only.
Sociology. M.A., Ph.D.
Theology. M.A., Ph.D.

Graduate School of Education

Located at Lincoln Center Campus, New York City (10023).

Tuition: per credit $450. On-campus housing available. Average academic year housing cost: $5800–6900. Contact University's Residential Life Office for both on- and off-campus housing information. Phone: (212)579-2327.

Enrollment: full-time 144, part-time 946. Graduate faculty: full-time 34, part-time 150. Degrees conferred: M.S.Ed., M.A.T., Advance Certificate, Ed.D., Ph.D.,

ADMISSION REQUIREMENTS. Official transcripts required in support of School's application. GRE required for Ed.D. and Ph.D. applicants. Evidence of proficiency in English required of international students. Accepts transfer applicants. Graduates of unaccredited institutions not considered. Apply to Office of Admissions by May 15 (Fall), October 15 (Spring), March 15 (Summer). Rolling admissions process. Application fee $40. Phone: (212)636-6400.

ADMISSION STANDARDS. Selective. Usual minimum average: 2.75 (A = 4).

FINANCIAL AID. Annual awards from institutional funds: scholarships, assistantships, Federal W/S, loans. Approved for VA benefits. Apply by February 1 to Dean's Office for assistantships; to the Financial Aid Office for all other programs. Phone: (212)636-6700. Use FAFSA. About 20% of students receive aid other than loans from School and outside sources. Aid available for part-time students.

DEGREE REQUIREMENTS. For master's: 30–36 credits minimum; thesis/nonthesis option; comprehensive exam. For Professional Diploma: 30 credits beyond the master's; comprehensive exam. For Ph.D.: 39–57 credits minimum beyond the master's; matriculation exam; reading knowledge of one foreign language or proficiency in a computer language and statistics; written comprehensive exam; dissertation; final oral exam. For Ed.D.: 66 credits minimum beyond the master's; requirements essentially the same as Ph.D. except no foreign language requirement.

FIELDS OF STUDY.
Administration and Supervision.
Administration and Supervision for Church Leaders.
Adult Education.
Bilingual Teacher Education.
Counseling and Personnel Services.
Counseling Psychology. Fall admission only.
Curriculum and Teaching. Includes elementary and secondary.
Early Childhood Education.
Education Administration and Supervision.
Educational Psychology.
Human Resource Management.
Language, Literacy, and Learning.
Reading.
School Psychology. Includes urban bilingual.
Secondary Education.
Special Education.
Teaching English as a Second Language.

Graduate School of Social Service

Established 1916. Tuition: per credit $449. On-campus housing for single students only. Enrollment: full-time 300, part-time 450. Faculty: full-time 35, part-time 6. Degrees conferred: M.S.W., D.S.W.

ADMISSION REQUIREMENTS. Transcripts, three letters of recommendation, autobiographical statement, interview required in support of School's application. TOEFL required for international applicants. Accepts transfer applicants. Graduates of unac-

credited institutions not considered. Apply to Office of Admissions by June 1 (Fall), prior to registration for other sessions. Full-time students admitted Fall only. Application fee $40. Phone: (212)636-6600; fax: (212)636-6613.

ADMISSION STANDARDS. Competitive. Usual minimum average: 3.0 (A = 4).

FINANCIAL AID. Scholarships, fellowships, assistantships, grants, loans. Approved for VA benefits. Apply to Financial Aid Office by April 1. Use FAFSA. Phone: (212)636-6700. About 5% of students receive aid other than loans from School, 98% from all sources. Aid available to part-time students.

DEGREE REQUIREMENTS. For M.S.W.: 60 credits minimum, at least one year in full-time residence; thesis optional. For D.S.W.: 30 credits minimum beyond M.S.W., at least two semesters in residence; preliminary exam; dissertation; final oral/written exam.

School of Law

Founded 1905. Semester system. Located at Lincoln Center Campus, New York City (10023). Law library: 410,000 volumes. Library has LEXIS, NEXIS, WESTLAW, DIALOG; 36 PCs. Special facilities: Center on European Community Law and International Antitrust, Stein Institute on Law and Ethics. No on-campus housing.

Annual tuition: $20,400 (Day Division), $15,300 (Evening Division).

Enrollment: first-year class 335 (day), 105 (evening); total 1525 (men 55%, women 45%). Faculty: full-time 51, part-time 158. Degrees conferred: J.D., J.D.-M.B.A., LL.M. (International Business; Banking, Corporate, and Finance Law).

ADMISSION REQUIREMENTS. LSDAS Law School report, bachelor's degree, transcripts, LSAT required in support of application. Interview not required. Accepts transfer applicants. Graduates of unaccredited colleges not considered. Apply to Office of Admissions of School after September 1, before March 1. Application fee $50. Phone: (212)636-6875.

ADMISSION STANDARDS. Accepts about 20% of total annual applicants.

FINANCIAL AID. Scholarships, grants, loans. Apply by February 1 to Financial Aid Office of School. Use FAFSA or GAPS-FAS. About 10% of students receive aid other than loans from School. Aid sometimes available to part-time students. A Public Service loan forgiveness program available.

DEGREE REQUIREMENTS. For J.D.: three-year program for day students; four-year program for evening students; 83 credits minimum. For LL.M.: 2 semesters beyond J.D.

FORT HAYS STATE UNIVERSITY
Hays, Kansas 67601

Founded 1902. Located 300 miles W of Kansas City. Coed. State control. Semester system. Library: 500,000 volumes, 30 PCs in library.

Tuition: per credit, resident $85.20, nonresident $226.30. On-campus housing for 92 married students, unlimited for single graduate students. Annual academic year average cost: single room $2228–$3761; double room $1682–$3215; apartments per month $168–$195. Apply to Housing Director. Phone: (913)628-4245.

Graduate School

Graduate study since 1929. Enrollment: full-time 214, part-time 467; about 1500 students during Summer session. Faculty: full-time 239, part-time 26. Degrees conferred: M.A., M.S., M.A.T., M.B.A., M.S.N., M.F.A., Ed.S.

ADMISSION REQUIREMENTS. Official transcripts, letter of recommendation, GRE Subject Tests (Psychology, Counseling, Speech Language, and Pathology), MAT (Administration, Education, Nursing, Specialist in Educ. Ed.S.), GMAT (M.B.A.) required in support of School's application. Interview not required. Accepts transfer applicants. Graduates of unaccredited institutions not considered. Apply to Dean of Graduate School; no specified closing dates. Application fee none, international applicants $35.

ADMISSION STANDARDS. Selective for most departments. Usual minimum average. 2.5 (A = 4). Some departments require 3.0 G.P.A. minimum.

FINANCIAL AID. Annual awards from institutional funds: 2100 scholarships, 900 grants, 70 teaching assistantships, 26 research assistantships, 10 administrative assistantships, Federal W/S, loans. Apply to Dean of Graduate School for scholarships, assistantships; for all other aid apply to the Office of Financial Aid; no specified closing date. Use FAFSA. Phone: (913)628-4408. No aid for part-time students.

DEGREE REQUIREMENTS. For M.A., M.F.A., M.S.: 30 semester hours minimum; thesis or research paper for most majors; final written exam; final oral exam for thesis writers. For Ed.S.: 30 semester hours minimum beyond the master's; field study or research project; final written/oral exams.

FIELDS OF STUDY.
Art. M.F.A.
Biology.
Business.
Communication.
Education. Includes elementary, secondary, administration, counseling, and special education.
English.
Geology.
Health, Physical Education, and Recreation.
History.
Nursing.
Psychology.
Speech Pathology.

FORT VALLEY STATE UNIVERSITY
Fort Valley, Georgia 31030-3262

Founded 1895. Located 25 miles from Macon, Georgia. Coed. State control. Quarter system. Library: 190,000 volumes, 187,000 microforms, 880 current periodicals, 10 PCs.

Tuition: per hour, resident $47, nonresident $161. On-campus housing for single students only. Average academic year housing cost: $2625 (including board); off-campus housing cost: $250 per month. Contact Dean of Students for both on- and off-campus housing information. Phone: (912)825-6293. Day care facilities available.

Graduate Division

Graduate study since 1957. Enrollment: full-time 87, part-time 99. Faculty: full-time 7, part-time 15. Degree conferred: M.S.

ADMISSION REQUIREMENTS. Official transcripts, MAT or GRE required in support of application. TOEFL required for international applicants. Accepts transfer applicants. Apply to Admissions Office in month prior to beginning of registration. Application fee none. Phone: (912)825-6307.

ADMISSION STANDARDS. Selective. Usual minimum average: 2.5 (A = 4).

FINANCIAL AID. Annual awards from institutional funds: assistantships, Federal W/S, loans. Apply to Graduate Dean; no specified closing date. Use FAFSA. Phone: (912)825-6351. Aid available for part-time students.

DEGREE REQUIREMENTS. For M.S.: 45 quarter hours minimum, at least 36 in residence: thesis/nonthesis option; written exam/oral exam.

FIELDS OF STUDY.
Early Childhood Education.
Elementary Education.
Guidance and Counseling.
Mental Health Counseling.
Middle Grades Education.
Rehabilitation Counseling.

FRAMINGHAM STATE COLLEGE
Framingham, Massachusetts 01701-9101

Founded 1839. Located 20 miles W of Boston. Coed. State control. Semester system. Library: 100,000 volumes, 50 PCs.

Annual tuition: full-time resident $1763, nonresident $5542; part-time resident $588, nonresident $1848. Limited on-campus housing available for single students only. Contact Housing Office for both on- and off-campus housing information. Phone: (508)626-4636.

Office of Graduate Studies

Graduate study since 1961. Enrollment: full-time 100, part-time 500 (men 40%, women 60%). Graduate faculty: full-time 30, part-time 40. Degrees conferred: M.A., M.A.A., M.S., M.Ed.

ADMISSION REQUIREMENTS. Two transcripts, two letters of recommendation, MAT required in support of application. Interview not required. Accepts transfer applicants. Graduates of unaccredited colleges not considered. Apply to Office of Graduate Studies by April 1 (Fall), October 1 (Spring). Application fee $25. Phone: (508)626-4550.

ADMISSION STANDARDS. Selective. Usual minimum average: 3.0 (A = 4).

FINANCIAL AID. Limited to loans. Apply to Financial Aid Office by March 1. Use FAFSA. Phone: (508)626-4534. About 5% of students receive aid other than loans from College and outside sources.

DEGREE REQUIREMENTS. For master's: ten courses or seminars minimum; final oral exam; no thesis or language requirement.

FIELDS OF STUDY.
Business Administration.
Counseling. Includes alcohol, substance abuse, community, families.
Educational Administration.
Elementary Education. Includes mathematics, reading and language arts. M.Ed. only.

English.
Food and Nutrition. M.S. only.
Health Care Administration.
Home Economics.
Human Resources Administration.
Museum Administration.
Public Administration.
Reading and Language Arts. Part-time only.
Secondary Education. Includes biology, English, history, home economics, mathematics. M.Ed. only.
Special Education.

FRANKLIN PIERCE LAW CENTER
Concord, New Hampshire 03301

Established 1973. Semester system. Library: 187,000 volumes. Library has LEXIS, NEXIS, WESTLAW, DIALOG: 22 personal computers. Special facilities: The Institute for Health, Law and Ethics.

Annual tuition: resident $14,955. Total average annual additional expense: $12,500.

Enrollment: first-year class 130; total 400 (men 64%, women 36%). Faculty: full-time 21, part-time 35. Degree conferred: J.D., J. D.-M.I.P. (Intellectual Property).

ADMISSION REQUIREMENTS. LSDAS Law School report, bachelor's degree, transcripts, LSAT, recommendations, personal statement, resume required in support of application. Accepts transfer applicants. TOEFL required of foreign students. Apply to Admissions Office by April 1 (flexible), rolling admissions process. Phone: (603)228-9217.

ADMISSION STANDARDS. Selective. Accepts about 30% of total annual applications.

FINANCIAL AID. Scholarships, Federal W/S, loans. Apply to Financial Aid office by April 1. Use FAFSA and FPLC Financial Aid Application. About 40% of students receive some aid from School.

DEGREE REQUIREMENTS. For J.D.: satisfactory completion of three-year program. For G J.D.-M.I.P.: satisfactory completion of three- or four-year program.

FROSTBURG STATE UNIVERSITY
Frostburg, Maryland 21532
http://fre.psu.umd.edu

Founded 1898. Located 110 miles S of Pittsburgh and 150 miles from both Baltimore and Washington, D.C. Coed. State control. Semester system. Library: 510,000 volumes, 152,700 microforms.

Tuition: per credit resident $156, nonresident $171. On-campus housing for limited number of graduate students, none for married students. Average academic year housing cost: $4500 (board included). Apply to Director of Residence Life. Phone: (301)687-4121. Day care facilities available.

Graduate Study

Enrollment: full-time 167, part-time 635. University faculty: full- and part-time 90. Degrees conferred: M.A., M.Ed., M.S., M.B.A.

ADMISSION REQUIREMENTS. Transcripts required in support of application. TOEFL required for international applicants.

Accepts transfer applicants. Apply to Office of Graduate Admissions at least sixty days prior to registration. Application fee $30. Phone: (301)687-7053; fax: (310)687-4597.

ADMISSION STANDARDS. Relatively open. Minimum average: 2.5 (A = 4).

FINANCIAL AID. Seventy-three graduate assistantships, Federal W/S, loans. Apply to Director of Financial Aid; no specified closing date. Use FAFSA. Phone: (301)689-4301; fax: (310)687-4937.

DEGREE REQUIREMENTS. For M.A., M.Ed.: 33 semester hours minimum. For M.S.: 36–42 semester hours. For M.B.A.: 45 semester hours.

FIELDS OF STUDY.
Applied Ecology and Conservation Biology. M.S.
Biology. M.Ed.
Business Administration. M.B.A.
Counseling Psychology. M.S.
Curriculum and Instruction. M.Ed.
Education. M.Ed. only.
Elementary Administration. M.Ed.
Guidance and Counseling. M.Ed.
Health and Physical Education. M.Ed.
Human Performance. M.S.
Interdisciplinary. M.Ed.
Modern Humanities. M.A.; Summer only.
Reading. M.Ed.
Science Education. M.Ed.
Secondary Administration. M.Ed.
Secondary Education. M.Ed.
Wildlife/Fisheries Biology. M.S.

FURMAN UNIVERSITY
Greenville, South Carolina 29613

Founded in 1826. Coed. Private control. Three-term system. Library has 300,000 volumes.

Tuition: per credit, $155. No on-campus housing available.

Graduate Division

Enrollment: full-time 42, part-time 256. University faculty teaching graduate students: full-time 50, part-time 10. Degrees conferred: M.A. in Ed., M.S. in Chemistry.

ADMISSION REQUIREMENTS. Transcripts, bachelor's degree, twelve hours in undergraduate education for Ed. majors, GRE for Chemistry required in support of application. Accepts transfer students. Graduates of unaccredited institutions not considered. Application fee $25. Phone: (803)294-2213.

ADMISSION STANDARDS. Usual minimum average: 3.0 (A = 4).

FINANCIAL AID. None.

DEGREE REQUIREMENTS. For M.A. in Ed.: admission to candidacy; completion of 30 hours (education 12 hours, concentration 12 hours, electives 6 hours), comprehensive exam. For M.S. in Chem.: admission to candidacy; completion of prescribed courses; B average on all course work; comprehensive exam.

FIELDS OF STUDY.
Chemistry.
Education. Includes early childhood, elementary, physical education, reading, social studies, special, school administration.

GALLAUDET UNIVERSITY
Washington, D.C. 20002-3625

Founded 1864. Coed. Private control. Semester system. Special facilities: Center for Auditory and Speech Sciences, Gallaudet Research Institute, Genetic Counseling Center, Fendall Demonstration School, Model Secondary School for the Deaf, Center for Assessment and Demographic Studies, Center for Studies in Education and Human Development. Library: 220,000 volumes, 372,000 microforms, 1700 current periodicals, 5 PCs.

Tuition: $3605 per semester, per credit $343. On-campus housing for single students only. Average housing cost: $1625–$2850 per semester. Contact Director of Housing for both on- and off-campus housing information. Phone: (202)651-5255.

Graduate Studies

Enrollment: full-time 258 (men 45, women 213), part-time 114. Graduate faculty: full-time 55, part-time 20. Degrees conferred: M.A., M.S., M.S.W., Ph.D.

ADMISSION REQUIREMENTS. Official transcripts, three letters of recommendation, GRE or MAT required in support of application. Accepts transfer applicants. Apply by February 15 to Director of Admissions. Application fee $50. Phone: (202)651-5253; fax: (202)651-5744; E-mail: adm_bennetti@gallua.gallaudet.edu.

ADMISSION STANDARDS. Competitive. Usual minimum average: 3.0 (A = 4).

FINANCIAL AID. Scholarships, partial tuition waiver, grants-in-aid, Federal W/S, loans. Apply by April 1 to Director of Financial Aid. Use FAFSA. About 60% of students receive aid other than loans from College and outside sources. Limited aid for part-time students.

DEGREE REQUIREMENTS. For master's: 42 hours minimum full-time study; sign language proficiency for some programs; final oral/written exam. For Ph.D.: two years minimum beyond the master's, two consecutive semesters in residence; comprehensive exam; sign language proficiency for some programs; internship; dissertation; final written exam.

FIELDS OF STUDY.
Administration and Supervision. M.S.
Audiology. M.S.
Clinical Psychology. Ph.D.
Counseling of the Hearing Impaired. Includes school, guidance, mental health, rehabilitation. M.A.
Developmental Psychology. M.A.
Education of the Hearing Impaired and Multihandicapped Hearing Impaired. Includes preschool, elementary, secondary, parent-infant, multihandicapped. M.A., Ph.D.
Educational Technology. M.A.
Interpreting. M.A.
Linguistics and Sign Language. M.A.
School Psychology. M.A., Ed.S.
Social Work. M.S.W.
Special Education Administration and Supervision. Ph.D.
Speech/Language Pathology. M.S.
Teacher Training. M.A.

GANNON UNIVERSITY
Erie, Pennsylvania 16541
http://www.gannon.edu

Founded 1925. Private control. Roman Catholic. Semester system. Library: 248,938 volumes, 402,238 microforms, 8 CD ROM databases, and online card catalog.

Tuition: per semester credit: Nursing and Engineering $400, other programs $365; Physical Therapy per semester $6215. Limited on-campus housing for graduate single students. Contact Director of Student Living. Phone: (814)871-7660.

School of Graduate Studies

Enrollment full-time 149, part-time 388. College faculty teaching graduate students full-time 94, part-time 91. Degrees conferred: M.A., M.S., M.Ed., M.B.A., M.P.A., M.S.N., M.P.T., M.S.N.-M.B.A.

ADMISSION REQUIREMENTS. Transcripts, GRE Subject Tests or GMAT, letters of recommendation required in support of School's application. Interviews required for some programs. TOEFL required for international applicants. Accepts transfer applicants. Graduates of unaccredited institutions not considered. Apply to Director of Admissions well in advance of registration. Application fee $25 for most programs. Phone: (814)871-7407; fax: (814)871-5803.

ADMISSION STANDARDS. Relatively open. Usual minimum average 2.5 (A = 4).

FINANCIAL AID. One scholarship, 187 grants, 5 teaching assistantships, 19 administrative assistantships, Federal W/S, loans. Apply to Director of Financial Aid by March 1 (Fall), November 1 (Spring). Use FAFSA. Phone: (814)871-7337; fax: (814)871-5803.

DEGREE REQUIREMENTS. For M.A., M.S.: 30–48 credit hours; statistics or reading knowledge of one foreign language; thesis/nonthesis option/research project; comprehensive exam. For M.B.A.: 48 credit hours minimum, at least 36 in residence; research thesis. For M.Ed.: 30 credit hours minimum, at least 24 in residence; research essay or project; comprehensive exam. For M.P.T.: 63 credit hours; research thesis; plus clinical practicum. For M.S.N.: 42–48 credit hours; clinical practicum; research thesis.

FIELDS OF STUDY.
Business Administration.
Counseling Psychology.
Education. Includes early intervention and computing technology.
Engineering.
English.
Health Services Administration.
Natural Environmental Science.
Nursing. Includes administration, anesthesia, medical/surgical, rural nurse practitioner.
Pastoral Studies.
Physical Therapy.
Public Administration.

GEORGE MASON UNIVERSITY
Fairfax, Virginia 22030-4444

Established 1957. Coed. Public. Semester system. Library: 353,000 volumes, 660,000 microforms. Special facilities: Pyramid 90x, CDC CYBER 180/830, DEC/VAX 8500 and 8920, Center for Applied Research and Development in Education, Center for Conflict Analysis and Resolution, Center for Constitutional Rights, Federal Theatre Archives, Institute for Information Technology, Center for Innovative Technology, Center for Market Process, Photographic Archives, Performing Arts Archives, Institute for Computational Sciences and Informatics, Center for Artificial Intelligence, Center for Robotics and Control, Center for Public Choice, Center for Software Engineering. Day-care facilities available. Library: 635,700 volumes, 1,683,000 microforms, 9100 current periodicals.

Tuition: per credit resident $125, nonresident $445. On-campus housing for both single and married students. Average academic year housing cost: $4670–$4220 (including board) for single students, $3950 for married students. Contact Director of Housing for both on- and off-campus housing information. Phone: (703)993-2720.

Graduate School

Graduate study since 1972. Enrollment: full-time 1300, part-time 5200 (men 45%, women 55%). Faculty: full-time 720, part-time 504. Degrees M.A., M.A.I.S., M.B.A., M.Ed., M.F.A., M.P.A., M.S., M.S.N., Certificate, D.A.Ed., Ph.D.

ADMISSION REQUIREMENTS. Two official transcripts required in support of School's applications. GRE Subject Tests/GMAT/MAT, interview required by some departments. TOEFL required of international applicants. Apply to Graduate School's Admissions Office MSN 3A4 by May 1 for most departments. Rolling admissions process. Application fee $30. Phone: (703)933-2400.

ADMISSION STANDARDS. Competitive for many departments, selective for others. Usual minimum average: 2.5/4.0 for master's, 3.0 for doctoral studies. Minimum TOEFL score 575.

FINANCIAL AID. Scholarships and tuition waivers (limited), fellowships, assistantships, career-related internships, Federal W/S, loans. Apply by April 1 to the Dean, Graduate School for fellowships, assistantships, scholarships, and tuition waivers; to Director of Financial Aid for all other programs. Phone: (703)933-4350. Use FAFSA. Aid available for part-time students.

DEGREE REQUIREMENTS. For master's: 24 semester hours minimum plus thesis; reading knowledge of one foreign language for some programs; final exam/final project for some programs. For D.A.Ed.: 72 credits minimum beyond the bachelor's, at least 32 in residence; written preliminary exam; three comprehensive written exams, dissertation, final oral exam. For Ph.D.: a minimum of 72 semester hours beyond the bachelor's (or 50 beyond the master's); completion of foreign language requirements (if applicable); preliminary exam, dissertation; final written/oral exam.

FIELDS OF STUDY.
Accounting. M.S.
Applied and Engineering Physics. M.S.
Applied and Engineering Statistics. M.S.
Biology. M.S.
Business Administration. M.B.A.
Chemistry. M.S.
Community College Education. D.A.Ed.
Computational Sciences and Informatics. Ph.D.
Computer Science. M.S.
Conflict Analysis and Resolution. M.S., Ph.D.
Counseling and Development. Includes school, nonschool. M.Ed.
Curriculum and Instruction. Includes early, middle secondary, bilingual/multicultural, instructional applications of microcomputers, reading, teaching of English as a second language. M.Ed.
Economics. M.A., Ph.D.
Education. Ph.D.
Educational Leadership. M.Ed.
Electrical Engineering. M.S.
English. M.A.
Environmental Science and Public Policy. Ph.D.
Exercise Science and Health. M.S.
Foreign Languages and Literature. Includes French, German, Spanish. M.A.
Geography and Cartographic Sciences. M.S.
History. M.A.

Information Science. M.S.
Information Technology. Ph.D.
Interdisciplinary Studies. Includes tracks in archaeology, gerontology, video-based production, regional economic development and technology. M.A.I.S.
International Transaction. M.A.
Liberal Studies. M.A.L.S.
Mathematics. M.S.
Music. M.A.
Nursing. M.S., Ph.D.
Operations Research and Engineering. M.S.
Psychology. Includes clinical, school. M.A., Ph.D.
Public Policy. Ph.D.
Sociology. M.A.
Software Systems Engineering. M.S.
Special Education. M.Ed.
Studio Art. Includes creative writing, dance, visual information technology. M.F.A.
Tax. M.S.
Telecommunication. M.A.
Visual Information Technology. M.S.

School of Law (22201-4498)

Affiliated in 1979. Located at the Metro Campus, Arlington. Library: 300,000 volumes. Library has LEXIS, NEXIS, WESTLAW, LEGALTRAK.

Annual tuition: resident $7280, per credit $260; nonresident $17,920, per credit $882. Limited on-campus housing available. Total average annual additional expense: $9000.

Enrollment: first-year class, full-time 175, part-time 45; total 582 (men 60%, women 40%). Faculty: full-time 33, part-time 28. Degree conferred: J.D.

ADMISSION REQUIREMENTS. LSDAS Law School report, bachelor's degree, transcripts, LSAT, writing sample, personal statement, letters of recommendation required in support of application. Preference given to state residents. Graduates of unaccredited colleges not considered. Apply to Admissions Office by March 15. Application fee $35. Phone: (703)993-8000.

ADMISSION STANDARDS. Competitive. Admits about 25% of total annual applications.

FINANCIAL AID. Limited to fellowships, Federal W/S, loans. Apply to Admissions Office by March 1. Use FAFSA and institutional Financial Aid Application.

DEGREE REQUIREMENTS. For J.D.: satisfactory completion of three-year program.

THE GEORGE WASHINGTON UNIVERSITY
Washington, D.C. 20052

Founded 1821. Coed. Private control. Semester system. Member of consortium of universities of the Washington Metropolitan Area. Library: 1.6 million volumes, 1,685,000 microforms.

Annual tuition: per semester hour $625.

Columbian School of Arts and Sciences

Graduate study since 1886. Enrollment: full-time about 450, part-time 1350. Graduate faculty: full-time 275. Degrees conferred: M.A., M.F.A., M.F.S., M.S.F.S., M.S., Psy.D., Ph.D.

ADMISSION REQUIREMENTS. Transcripts, GRE, letters of reference required in support of School's application. TOEFL required for international applicants; TWE recommended, TSE required for international applicants applying for graduate assistantships. GRE subject test required by some departments. Accepts transfer applicants. Apply to Office of Graduate Admissions by May 1 (Fall), October 1 (Spring), March 1 (Summer). Earlier submission required by some programs. Application fee $45. Phone: (202)994-6210; fax: (202)994-6213; E-mail: asgrad@acad.ccgs.gwu.edu.

ADMISSION STANDARDS. Very selective for most departments, competitive or selective for the others. Usual minimum average: 3.0 (A = 4). Recommended minimum TOEFL score for international students: 550.

FINANCIAL AID. Annual award from institutional funds: 200 fellowships, 150 assistantships, Federal W/S, loans. Apply by February 1 to Office of Student Financial Assistance (January 15 for students in clinical psychology). Use FAFSA. Phone: (202)994-6210. About 20% of students receive aid from School and outside sources.

DEGREE REQUIREMENTS. For master's: 30–36 semester hours; thesis/nonthesis option; comprehensive exam. For Ph.D.: 72 semester hours beyond the bachelor's; general exam for candidacy; dissertation; final oral exam.

FIELDS OF STUDY.
Administrative Science. M.A. only.
American Civilization.
American Literature.
American Religious History. Ph.D. only.
Anthropology. M.A. only.
Applied Mathematics.
Art. Includes ceramics, design, printmaking, painting, photography, sculpture, visual communications. M.F.A. only.
Art History.
Art Therapy. M.A. only.
Biochemistry.
Biological Sciences. Includes biology, botany, zoology.
Biostatistics.
Chemical Toxicology. M.S. only.
Chemistry.
Criminal Justice. M.A. only.
Economics.
English Literature.
Environmental and Resource Policy. M.A. only.
Epidemiology.
Forensic Sciences. M.F.S., M.S.F.S. only.
Genetics.
Geobiology.
Geochemistry. M.S. only.
Geography. M.A. only.
Geology.
History.
Human Sciences. Ph.D. only.
Industrial and Engineering Statistics. M.S only.
Legislative Affairs. M.A. only.
Mathematics.
Microbiology.
Molecular and Cellular Oncology. Ph.D. only.
Museum Studies. M.A. only.
Neuroscience. Ph.D. only.
Pharmacology.
Philosophy and Social Policy. M.A. only.
Physics.
Political Science.
Professional Psychology. Psy.D. only.
Psychology.
Public Policy. Ph.D. only.
Radiological Sciences. Ph.D. only.
Religion. M.A. only

Sociology. M.A. only.
Speech-Language Pathology and Audiology. M.A. only.
Statistics.
Telecommunications. M.A. only.
Theater. Includes a concentration in scenic design. M.F.A. only.
Women's Studies. M.A. only.

School of Education and Human Development

Tuition: per hour $625. Graduate enrollment: full-time 362, part-time 802. School faculty: full-time 57, part-time 61. Degrees conferred: M.A. in Ed., M.Ed., Ed.S., Ed.D.

ADMISSION REQUIREMENTS. Transcripts, GRE/MAT, two letters of recommendation (out-of-area applicants), interview required in support of School's application. TOEFL required for international applicants. Accepts transfer applicants. Graduates of unaccredited institutions not considered. Apply to Dean of the School by March 1 (Fall), October 1 (Spring), February 1 (Summer Session). Application fee $45. Phone: (202)994-6160; fax: (202)994-7207.

ADMISSION STANDARDS. Selective. Usual minimum average 2.75 (A = 4); 2.3 to 2.74 for provisional admission.

FINANCIAL AID. Thirteen assistantships are available at Ed.D. level, Federal W/S, loans. Apply to school by February 15. Use FAFSA. Phone: (202)994-6620. Some employment opportunities are available at the University. Information is available through the Personnel Office.

DEGREE REQUIREMENTS. For M.A. in Ed., M.Ed.: 24 semester hours minimum in residence; thesis optional for 6 semester hours; comprehensive exam for some programs; additional courses in lieu of comprehensive in some programs. For Ed.S.: 30 semester hours minimum beyond the master's, at least 21 in residence; comprehensive exams; final oral. For Ed.D.: usually about 75 to 90 semester hours beyond the bachelor's, about 60 semester hours in residence and at least one semester in full-time attendance; preliminary exams; dissertation; final oral exam.

FIELDS OF STUDY.
Community Counseling.
Curriculum and Instruction.
Early Childhood Special Education.
Educational Policy Studies.
Educational Technology Leadership.
Elementary/Secondary Administration and Supervision.
Elementary Education.
Higher Education Administration.
Human Development.
Human Resource Development.
Infant Special Education.
International Education.
Museum Education.
Rehabilitation Counseling.
School Counseling.
Secondary Education.
Special Education. Includes seriously emotionally disturbed students, transitional.

School of Engineering and Applied Science
http://www.seas.gwu.edu

Graduate enrollment: full-time 547, part-time 1309. Graduate faculty: full-time 83, part-time 101.
Tuition: per credit hour $600. Degrees conferred: M.S., M.E.M., professional degrees of Engineer and Applied Scientist; D.Sc.

ADMISSION REQUIREMENTS. Transcripts required in support of School's application. GRE Subject Tests recommended;

GRE required for Financial Aid applicants. Interview not required, but desirable for doctoral applicants. TOEFL required for international applicants. Accepts transfer applicants. Graduates of unaccredited institutions not considered. Apply to School Admissions Office by March 1 (Fall), October 1 (Spring), March 1 (1st Summer Session), April 1 (2nd Summer Session). Application fee $45. Phone: (202)994-3096; fax: (202)994-4522.

ADMISSION STANDARDS. Selective. Usual minimum average: 3.0 (A = 4).

FINANCIAL AID. Annual awards from institutional funds: a number of research/teaching assistantships and fellowships are available based on previous academic performance; Federal W/S, loans. Approved for VA benefits. Apply to the Office of Financial Services by February 1 (Summer and Fall), September 1 (Spring). Phone: (202)994-6620; fax: (202)994-7221. Use FAFSA. Aid sometimes available for part-time students.

DEGREE REQUIREMENTS: For M.S. (Electrical Engineering and Computer Science): 30 credit hours including thesis; M.S. (Civil, Mechanical, and Environmental and Operations Research): 33 credit hours including thesis; M.S., M.E.M. (Engineering Management): 36 semester hours including thesis. For the Professional Engineering degree: 30 semester hours beyond the master's. For D.Sc.: 30 hours minimum beyond the master's; 54 credit hours beyond the baccalaureate; qualifying exam; dissertation; final oral exam.

FIELDS OF STUDY.
Civil and Environmental Engineering. Includes engineering mechanics, environmental engineering, geotechnical engineering, structural engineering, water resources engineering.
Computer Science. Includes algorithms and theory, artificial intelligence and computer vision, computer and communications security, computer engineering and architecture, graphics and multimedia, industrial engineering, parallel and distributed computing, software engineering and systems.
Electrical Engineering. Includes biomedical engineering, communications, controls, systems, and signal processing, electrical power and engineering management, electrophysics and fiber optics, energy conversion, power, and transmission, industrial engineering, microelectronics and VLSI systems.
Engineering Management. Includes domain-specific engineering management; economics, finance, and cost engineering; engineering management principles, practices, and methods; industrial engineering; information and process engineering; systems engineering; and quantitative analysis.
Mechanical Engineering. Includes aerospace engineering, design of mechanical engineering systems, fluid mechanics, thermal sciences and energy, industrial engineering, solid mechanics and materials science, transportation safety engineering.
Operations Research. Includes general operations research, industrial and engineering statistics, industrial engineering, management science, mathematical optimization, stochastic modeling.
Telecommunications and Computers.

School of Business and Public Management

Graduate study since 1928. Semester system.
Tuition: per credit $625.
Graduate enrollment: full-time 934, part-time 1095. School faculty: full-time 110, part-time 62. Degrees conferred: M.Acct., M.B.A., M.P.A., M.S.F., M.S.H.S.A., M.S. Info. Systems, M.S.P.M., M.Tax., M.T.A., Ph.D.

ADMISSION REQUIREMENTS. Transcripts, GMAT/GRE required in support of School's application. Interview not required. Three references for doctoral applicants. TOEFL required for international applicants. Accepts transfer applicants. Graduates of unaccredited institutions not considered. Apply to Graduate Admission Office by April 1 (Fall), October 1 (Spring). Application fee $45. Phone: (202)944-6584; fax: (202)944-6382.

ADMISSION STANDARDS. Highly selective.

FINANCIAL AID. Limited to Federal W/S, loans. Approved for VA benefits. Apply by June 1 (Fall), October 1 (Spring) to the Director of Financial Aid. Use FAFSA. Phone: (202)994-6620; fax: (202)994-0906.

DEGREE REQUIREMENTS. For M.Acct.: 60 semester hours maximum; may be reduced to 33 hours depending upon previous preparation. For M.B.A.: 60 semester hours maximum; may be reduced to 36 hours depending upon previous preparation. For M.T.A., M.S.P.M.: 36 semester hours minimum. For M.P.A.: 42 semester hours minimum. For M.S.H.S.A.: 54 credits minimum. For M.S.F., M.Tax.: 48 semester hours minimum; written comprehensive exam. For M.S. Info. Systems Tech.: 30 semester hours minimum; comprehensive exam. For Ph.D.: 30 hours minimum beyond master's; additional course work often required; foreign proficiency for some programs; general exam for candidacy; dissertation; final oral exam.

FIELDS OF STUDY.
Accountancy.
Business, Economics, and Public Policy.
Finance. M.S.F.
Finance and Investments.
Health Services Administration.
Human Resource Management.
Information Systems. Includes information systems development, information systems project management.
Information Systems Management.
International Business.
Logistics, Operations, and Materials Management.
Management Decision Making.
Management of Science, Technology, and Innovation.
Marketing.
Organizational Behavior and Development.
Project Management. M.S.P.M.
Public Administration.
Real Estate and Urban Development.
Small Business Entrepreneurship.
Taxation. M.Tax.
Tourism Administration. M.T.A.

The Elliott School of International Affairs

Established 1898. Name change in 1988.
Tuition: $10,800, per credit $600.
Enrollment: full- and part-time 706. School faculty: full-time 87, part-time 25. Degrees conferred: M.A., M.A.-M.B.A., M.A.-J.D. The Ph.D. is offered through the Graduate School of Arts and Sciences.

ADMISSION REQUIREMENTS. Transcripts, GRE, letters of recommendation, foreign language proficiency, work experience, personal essay required in support of School's application. TOEFL required for international applicants. TWE is recommended for international applicants. Graduates of unaccredited institutions not considered. Admits Fall only. Apply to Graduate Admissions Office by February 1. International, graduate fellowship and assistantship applicants apply by January 15. Application fee $45. Phone: (202)994-7050; fax: (202)994-0335.

ADMISSION STANDARDS. Very selective. Usual minimum average: 3.0 (A = 4).

FINANCIAL AID. Fellowships, assistantships, off-campus employment, Federal W/S, loans. Apply to the Director of Financial

Aid by January 1. Use FAFSA. Phone: (202)994-6620; fax: (202)994-0906.

DEGREE REQUIREMENTS. For M.A.: 2 options (except in Security Policy studies); 30 semester hours minimum in residence including thesis, or 36 semester hours of course work; reading knowledge of one foreign language or specified level of statistics; final comprehensive exam(s).

FIELDS OF STUDY.
East Asian Studies.
European Studies.
International Affairs. Includes fields in comparative politics, economic development, international law and organizations, international business, international economics, international politics, political psychology, strategy and military, U.S. foreign policy, regional studies (Africa, Asia, Europe, Latin America, Middle East, former Soviet Union/Russia).
International Development Studies.
Latin American Studies.
Russian and East European Studies.
Science Technology and Public Policy.
Security Policy Studies.

The National Law Center (20052)

Established 1865. Semester system. Law library 426,000 volumes. Library has LEXIS, NEXIS, WESTLAW, DIALOG, ALADIN.

Annual costs: $19,700, per credit $690. On- and off-campus housing available. Contact University Housing Office. Total annual average additional expense: $13,500.

Enrollment: first-year class 420 day, 75 evening; full-time 1251, part-time 350 (men 54%, women 46%); postgraduates 275. Faculty: full-time 61, part-time 75. Degrees conferred: J.D., J.D.-M.A., J.D.-M.B.A., J.D.-M.P.A., J.D.-M.II.S.A., LL.M., LL.M.-M.P.H., M.C.L., S.J.D.

ADMISSION REQUIREMENTS. LSDAS Law School report, bachelor's degree, transcripts, LSAT (no later than December), three letters of recommendation required in support of application. Interview not required. Accepts very limited number of transfer applicants. Graduates of unaccredited colleges not considered. Apply to Office of the Dean after October 1, before March 1. Beginning students admitted Fall only. Application fee $55. Phone: (202)994-7230.

ADMISSION STANDARDS. Selective. Accepts 20–25% of total annual applicants.

FINANCIAL AID. Scholarships, teaching fellowships (for LL.M. candidates), assistantships, Federal W/S, loans. Apply to Office of Financial Aid by March 1. Use FAFSA or GAPSFAS. About 40% of students receive aid other than loans from Law Center.

DEGREE REQUIREMENTS. For J.D.: 94 semester hours minimum, at least 28 in resident. For LL.M.: 24 hours and 2 semesters minimum in residence. For M.C.L. (Foreign Practice): 24 hours and 2 semesters minimum in residence; designed for foreign lawyers intending to return to their countries. For M.C.L. (American Practice): 32 hours and 2 semesters minimum in residence; designed for foreign lawyers who intend to remain in United States. For S.J.D.: two semesters minimum in residence beyond the master's; dissertation; oral defense of dissertation required.

School of Medicine and Health Sciences (20037)

First class in 1825. Annual tuition: $30,500, student fees $720. Total average figure for all other expenses $10,200. Enrollment: first-year class 150 (2 EDP), full-time 600 (men 55%, women 45%). Faculty: full-time 536, part-time and volunteers 1500. Degrees conferred: M.D., M.D.-M.P.H. The M.S. and Ph.D. are offered through the Graduate School.

ADMISSION REQUIREMENTS. AMCAS report and supplemental application, transcripts, MCAT, interview required in support of application. Applicants must have completed at least three years of college study. Has EDP; apply between June 15 and August 1. Accepts transfer applicants. First-year students apply AMCAS after June 15, before November 15. Advanced standing students apply to Admissions Office by December 1. Application fee $55. Phone: (202)994-3506.

ADMISSION STANDARDS. Very competitive. Accepts 1% of total annual applicants. Approximately 2% are district residents.

FINANCIAL AID. Scholarships, Federal W/S, loans. About 78% of students receive aid other than loans from School. Apply to the Director of Financial Aid after acceptance but by April 15. Use FAFSA.

DEGREE REQUIREMENTS. For M.D.: satisfactory completion of four-year program. For M.S., M.P.H., Ph.D.: see the Graduate listings above.

FIELDS OF GRADUATE STUDY.
Anatomy.
Biochemistry.
Biomedical Engineering.
Biophysics.
Cell Biology.
Genetics.
Immunology.
Microbiology.
Molecular Biology.
Neurosciences.
Pathology.
Pharmacology.
Physiology.

GEORGETOWN COLLEGE
Georgetown, Kentucky 40324-1696

Founded 1829. Located 12 miles N of Lexington. Coed. Private control. Baptist. Semester system. Library: 130,000 volumes, 120,000 microforms, 8 PCs.

Tuition: per hour $150. No on-campus housing for graduate students.

Graduate Study

Enrollment: full-time 2, part-time 306. Faculty: full-time 4, part-time 10. Degree conferred: M.A. in Ed.

ADMISSION REQUIREMENTS. Transcripts, letters of recommendation required in support of School's application. GRE is strongly recommended. Interview sometimes required. Accepts transfer applicants. Graduates of unaccredited colleges not considered. Apply to Dean of Graduate Study at least thirty days prior to start of semester. Application fee none. Phone: (502)863-8176; fax: (502)868-8888.

ADMISSION STANDARDS. Relatively open. Minimum average: 2.7 (A = 4).

FINANCIAL AID. Limited to Federal W/S, loans. Approved for VA benefits. Apply to Director of Financial Aid; no specified closing date. Use FAFSA CSS. Phone: (502)863-8027.

DEGREE REQUIREMENTS. For M.A. in Ed.: 30 semester hours minimum, at least 24 in residence; final comprehensive exam.

FIELD OF STUDY.
Education. Includes elementary, secondary, middle grades, kindergarten endorsement, gifted endorsement for K–12.

GEORGETOWN UNIVERSITY
Washington, D.C. 20057
http://www.georgetown.edu

Founded 1789. Coed. Private control. Roman Catholic. Semester system. Special facilities: Center for Contemporary Arab Studies, computation center, Joseph and Rose Kennedy Institute of Ethics, Lombardi Cancer Research Center, Center for Child Development, Center for German and European Studies, Center for Latin American Studies, Center for Muslim-Christian Understanding: History and International Affairs, Institute for the Study of Diplomacy. Participates in the Consortium of Universities of the Washington Metropolitan Area, includes the American, Catholic, Gallaudet, George Mason, George Washington, and Howard Universities, the University of the District of Columbia, the University of Maryland College Park, Mt. Vernon and Trinity Colleges. Library: 2,071,000 volumes, 2,747,000 microforms, 12,800 current periodicals.

Annual tuition: full-time $16,992; per credit $708. No on-campus housing available for graduate students. Contact Director of Campus Housing for off-campus housing information. Phone: (202)687-4560.

Graduate School of Arts and Sciences
http://www.georgetown.edu/grad/

Graduate study since 1820. Enrollment: full-time 2089, part-time 786. Graduate faculty: full-time 1320, part-time 406. Degrees conferred: M.A., M.S., M.A.T., M.B.A., M.P.P., Ph.D.

ADMISSION REQUIREMENTS. Official transcripts, three letters of reference required in support of School's application. GRE/GMAT/MAT required by some departments. TOEFL required for international applicants. Interview not required. Accepts transfer applicants. Graduates of unaccredited institutions not considered. Apply by February 1 to the Graduate School's Admission Office. Application fee $50 for students with an undergraduate degree from a U.S. institution, $55 for students with an undergraduate degree from a non-U.S. institution. Phone: (202)687-5568; fax: (202)687-6802.

ADMISSION STANDARDS. Competitive for most departments. Minimum average: 3.0 (A = 4).

FINANCIAL AID. Annual awards from institutional funds: 300 scholarships, approximately 350 scholarship awards requiring teaching research, administrative duties; Federal W/S, loans. Approved for VA benefits. Apply by February 1 to the Graduate School Office for scholarships; to Financial Aid Office for all other programs. Phone: (202)687-4547; fax: (202)687-6542. Use FAFSA and graduate student supplement. About 50% of full-time students receive aid other than loans from School and outside sources.

FIELDS OF STUDY.
Arab Studies. GRE for admission. CERT., M.A. only.
Arabic Language, Literature, and Linguistics. M.S., M.S.-Ph.D., Ph.D.
Biochemistry and Molecular Biology. GRE Subject in biology, biochemistry, or chemistry for admission. Ph.D. only.
Biology. GRE Subject for admission. M.S., Ph.D.

Biostatistics and Epidemiology. GRE for admission. M.S. only.
Business Administration. GMAT for admission. M.B.A. only.
Cell Biology. GRE for admission. Ph.D. only.
Chemistry. GRE for admission. M.S., M.S.-Ph.D., Ph.D.
Communication, Culture, and Technology. GRE for admission. M.A. only.
Demography. GRE for admission. M.A. only.
Economics. GRE for admission. Ph.D. only.
English. GRE for admission. M.A. only.
Foreign Service. GRE for admission. M.S. only.
German. M.S., M.S.-Ph.D., Ph.D.
German and European Studies. GRE for admission. M.A. only.
Government. GRE for admission. M.A., Ph.D.
History. GRE for admission. Ph.D. only.
Latin American Studies. GRE for admission. M.A. only.
Liberal Studies. M.A. only.
Linguistics. CERT, M.A.T., M.S., Ph.D.
Microbiology and Immunology. GRE for admission. Ph.D. only.
National Security Studies. GRE or MAT for admission. M.A. only.
Neuroscience. GRE for admission. Ph.D. only.
Nursing. GRE or MAT for admission. M.S. only.
Pathology. GRE for admission. M.S., M.S.-Ph.D., Ph.D.
Pharmacology. GRE for admission. Ph.D. only.
Philosophy. GRE for admission. M.A., Ph.D.
Physiology and Biophysics. GRE or MCAT for admission. M.S., Ph.D.
Psychology. GRE Subject for admission. Ph.D. only.
Public Policy. GRE for admission. M.P.P. only.
Radiation Science. M.S. only.
Russian and East European Studies. GRE for admission. M.A. only.
Spanish and Portuguese. M.S., M.S.-Ph.D., Ph.D.

Law Center (20001)

Founded 1902. Semester system. Law library: 768,700 volumes. Library has LEXIS, NEXIS, WESTLAW, DIALOG.

Annual tuition: $22,430; per credit $765. No on-campus housing available. For off-campus housing contact Student Life Office. Phone: (202)661-9292. Total average cost for all other expenses: $13,700.

Enrollment: first-year class 625; day 506, evening 119; total full-time 1660 (men 54%, women 46%); total part-time 459; postgraduates 509. Faculty: full-time 84, part-time 155. Degrees conferred: J.D., L.L.M., S.J.D., M.L.T., M.C.L., D.C.L.

ADMISSION REQUIREMENTS. LSDAS Law School report, bachelor's degree, transcripts, three references, LSAT required in support of application. Interview not required. Graduates of unaccredited colleges not considered. Part-time study available. Apply to Law Center Director of Admissions after September 1, before February 1 (Day), March 1 (Evening). First-year students admitted Fall only. Application fee $60. Phone: (202)662-9010.

ADMISSION STANDARDS. Selective. Accepts 20% of total annual applicants.

FINANCIAL AID. Scholarships including Public Interest Law Scholars Program, Federal W/S, loans. Apply to the Office of Financial Aid by February 1. Use FAFSA and institutional FAF. About 20% of students receive aid other than loans from Center. No University aid for part-time students except for students with extreme need.

DEGREE REQUIREMENTS. For J.D.: 83 semester hours required minimum, at least two in residence. For LL.M.: 24 credits beyond the J.D.; one year in residence, two research papers. For M.L.D.: same as LL.M., except at least 20 credits must be in tax courses. For S.J.D.: two years of residence, first year in full-time attendance; publishable thesis.

FIELDS OF GRADUATE STUDY.
Common Law Studies.
International and Comparative Law.
Labor and Employment Law.
Securities Regulation.
Taxation.
Note: Combined degree programs offered in conjunction with the School of Business, the School of Foreign Service, and the Johns Hopkins School of Public Health.

School of Medicine

Opened 1851. Medical library 100,000 volumes. Annual tuition: $23,600. Total average figure for all other expenses $10,500.

Enrollment: M.D. program, first-year class 165 (EDP 10); total 1006 (men 65%, women 35%); graduate program, full-time 72. Faculty: full-time 425, part-time 1000. Degrees conferred: M.D., M.D.-Ph.D. The M.S. and Ph.D. are offered in cooperation with the Graduate School of Arts and Sciences.

ADMISSION REQUIREMENTS. AMCAS report, transcripts, two references, MCAT (Spring test date) required in support of application. Interview by invitation only. Accepts transfer applicants. Has EDP; apply between June 15 and August 1. Apply to Office of Admissions after June 15, before November 15 (credentials by February 15). Admits Fall only. Application fee $60. Phone: (202)687-1154.

ADMISSION STANDARDS. Very competitive. Accepts 4% of total annual applicants. Approximately 3% are district residents.

FINANCIAL AID. Limited scholarships, loans, work-study. Apply, after acceptance, to Financial Aid Administrator. About 95–98% of students receive aid from School and outside sources.

DEGREE REQUIREMENTS. For M.D.: satisfactory completion of four-year program. For M.S., Ph.D., see Graduate School listing above.

FIELDS OF GRADUATE STUDY.
Anatomy.
Biochemistry.
Bioethics.
Biophysics.
Biostatistics and Epidemiology.
Cell Biology.
Community and Family Medicine.
Experimental Pathology.
Microbiology.
Molecular Biology.
Neurosciences.
Pathology.
Pharmacology.
Physiology.
Note: Special program for fourth-year students to travel in Third World countries to gain practical experience.

GEORGIA COLLEGE
Milledgeville, Georgia 31061
http://www.gac.peachnet.edu

Founded 1889. Located 100 miles SE of Atlanta. State control. Quarter system. Library: 170,000 volumes, 511,000 microforms.

Annual tuition and fees: resident $2000, nonresident $6071; per quarter part-time $240, nonresident $810. Limited on-campus housing available. Apply to Associate Director of Residence Life. Phone: (912)453-5160.

Graduate School

Graduate study since 1958. Graduate study available at Macon, Warner Robins, and Dublin campuses. Enrollment: full-time 444, part-time 743. Faculty: full-time 90, part-time 10. Degrees conferred: M.A., M.A.T., M.S., M.Ed., M.B.A., M.I.S., M.P.A., M.S.A., M.S.L.S., M.S.N., Ed.S., M.S.N.-M.B.A.

ADMISSION REQUIREMENTS. Transcripts, GRE/GMAT/MAT required in support of School's application. TOEFL required for foreign applicants. T-5 Georgia Certification or equivalent for Specialist. Interview may be requested. Accepts transfer applicants. Graduates of unaccredited institutions not considered. Apply to Director of Admissions at least one month prior to quarter of entrance. Application fee $10. Phone: (912)453-6285 or (800)342-0471.

ADMISSION STANDARDS. Relatively open.

FINANCIAL AID. Annual awards from institutional funds: twenty-seven academic scholarships, nine scholarships, sixty assistantships, unlimited internships, Federal W/S, loans. Approved for VA benefits. Apply to Dean of Graduate School; no specified closing date. Use FAFSA and institutional FAF. Phone: (912)471-2063.

DEGREE REQUIREMENTS. For M.A., M.A.T., M.P.A., M.S., M.S.A., M.Ed.: 60 quarter hours, at least 30 in residence; admission to candidacy; knowledge of one foreign language required by some departments; thesis/nonthesis option.

FIELDS OF STUDY.
Administration and Supervision.
Biology.
Business Administration.
Early Childhood Education.
English.
Health and Physical Education.
History.
Instructional Technology—Library Media.
Instructional Technology—Technology Coordination.
Logistics Management.
Logistics Systems.
Management Information Systems.
Mathematics.
Middle Grades Education.
Natural Science (Biology).
Nursing.
Psychology.
Public Administration.
Social Science.
Special Education. Includes behavior disorders, interrelated, mental retardation, and teaming disabilities.

THE GEORGIA INSTITUTE OF TECHNOLOGY
Atlanta, Georgia 30332-0001

Founded in 1885. Coed. State control. Quarter system. Special facilities: Georgia Tech Research Institute and over 40 interdisciplinary research centers on campus, including Microelectronics Research Center, Manufacturing Research Center, Bioengineering Research Center, Multimedia Technology Laboratory, video-based master's programs; various mainframe and microcomputing environments; graduate cooperative program; research affiliations Oak Ridge National Labs, Emory University Medical Center, Skidaway Institute of Oceanography. Library: more than 2,700,00 volumes, 12,000 serials, 135 PCs in all libraries.

Annual tuition: full-time resident $2220, nonresident $8223; per credit, resident $60, nonresident $245. On-campus housing for 300 married students. Average academic year housing cost: single students $1063 per quarter on-campus, off-campus $1100 per quarter; married students from $514 per month for one-bedroom apartments. Apply to Director, Housing Office. Phone: (404)894-2470.

Division of Graduate Studies and Research

Graduate study since 1922. Enrollment: full-time 2730, part-time 833. Graduate faculty: full-time 595, part-time 12. Degrees conferred: M.S., Ph.D.

ADMISSION REQUIREMENTS. Transcripts, three letters of recommendation required in support of application. GRE General/Subject Tests or GMAT for most programs. Additional materials required by some departments. TOEFL required for international applicants. Interview not required. Accepts transfer applicants. Graduates of unaccredited colleges not considered. Apply directly to individual Schools or Graduate Admissions no later than June 1 (Fall), February 1 recommended for financial aid and international applicants. Application fee $15. Phone: (404)894-4612.

ADMISSION STANDARDS. Selective. Usual minimum average: 3.0 (A = 4).

FINANCIAL AID. Annual awards from institutional and sponsored funds: 350 fellowships, 340 teaching assistantships, 1250 research assistantships, out-of-state tuition waivers, Federal W/S, loans. Apply to appropriate School Directors; no specified closing dates. Use FAFSA for Federal W/S, loans. Phone: (404)894-4160. About 60% of students receive aid other than loans from Institute and outside sources.

DEGREE REQUIREMENTS. For master's: 45 quarter hours minimum; candidacy; reading knowledge of one foreign language for some departments; thesis, nonthesis option for some departments. For Ph.D.: normally 45 quarter hours minimum beyond the master's, at least three quarters in residence; preliminary exam; reading knowledge of one foreign language for some departments; dissertation; final oral/written exams.

FIELDS OF STUDY.
Aerospace Engineering. GRE for admission.
Algorithms, Combinatorics and Optimization. GRE for admission. Ph.D. only.
Architecture. GRE for admission to some programs. Portfolio, one year's, experience in an architectural firm for admission.
Atmospheric Sciences. GRE for admission.
Bioengineering. GRE for admission.
Biology. GRE for admission.
Ceramic Engineering. GRE for admission.
Chemical Engineering. GRE for admission.
Chemistry. GRE Subject for admission.
City Planning. GRE for admission.
Civil Engineering. GRE for Financial Aid.
Computer Science. GRE Subject for admission.
Economics. GRE for admission.
Electrical Engineering. GRE for admission.
Engineering Science and Mechanics. GRE for Financial Aid.
Environmental Engineering. GRE for Financial Aid.
Executive Management of Technology. GRE for admission.
Geophysical Sciences. GRE for admission.
Health Physics. GRE for admission.
Health Systems. GRE for admission.
History of Technology. GRE for admission.
Industrial and Systems Engineering. GRE for admission.
Information Design and Technology. GRE for admission.
Management. GMAT for admission.

Mathematics. GRE Subject for admission.
Mechanical Engineering. GRE for admission.
Metallurgy. GRE for admission.
Nuclear Engineering. GRE for admission.
Operations Research. GRE for admission.
Physics. GRE for admission.
Polymers. GRE for admission.
Psychology. GRE Subject for admission.
Public Policy. GRE for admission.
Statistics. GRE for admission.
Textiles. GRE for admission.
Textiles Engineering and Science. GRE for admission.

MEDICAL COLLEGE OF GEORGIA
Augusta, Georgia 30912-1003
http://www.emcg.edu

Chartered 1828. Coed. State control. Quarter system. Special facilities: Alzheimer's Disease Center, Sickle Cell Center, Gene Data Bank. Medical library: 163,000 volumes.
Annual tuition: graduate program, full-time resident $2960, nonresident $10,212; per hour, resident $62, nonresident $214. On-campus housing for 108 graduate men, 195 graduate women, 64 married students, Average annual housing cost: $3000–$4000. Apply to Director of Housing. Phone: (706)721-3471. Day care facilities available.

School of Graduate Studies

Enrollment: full-time 112, part-time 109 (men 35%, women 65%). Faculty: full-time 187. Degrees conferred: M.S., M.S.N., M.H.E., Ph.D.

ADMISSION REQUIREMENTS. Transcripts, three letters of recommendation, GRE Subject Tests required in support of School's application. Interview required for some departments. TOEFL required of all international applicants. Accepts transfer applicants. Apply to the Dean of School of Graduate Studies: deadlines vary by program. Application fee none. Phone: (706)721-3278; fax: (706)721-4183.

ADMISSION STANDARDS. Competitive for most departments. Usual minimum average: 3.0 (A = 4).

FINANCIAL AID. Fifty assistantships, traineeships, Federal W/S, loans. Apply to Financial Aid Office with admissions application. Phone: (706)721-4901. Use FAFSA. About 80% of students receive aid other than loans from College and outside sources. Aid available to part-time students.

DEGREE REQUIREMENTS. For M.S., M.S.N., M.H.E.; 45 quarter hours minimum, at least 36 in full-time residence; reading knowledge of one foreign language; comprehensive exam; thesis, final oral exam. For M.S. in Medical Illustration: same as above, except graphics project may be submitted in lieu of thesis and language not required. For Ph.D.: 90 hours and three full years minimum beyond the bachelor's, at least three consecutive quarters or equivalent in full-time residence; preliminary exams; dissertation; final oral exam.

FIELDS OF STUDY.
Adult Nursing. M.S.N. only.
Biochemistry and Molecular Biology. M.S., Ph.D.
Cellular Biology and Anatomy. M.S., Ph.D.
Clinical Nutrition. M.S. only.
Community Nursing. M.S.N. only.
Dental Hygiene. M.S., M.H.E.
Diagnostic Medical Sonography. M.S. only.
Endocrinology. M.S., Ph.D.

Health Information Management. M.S., M.H.E.
Medical Illustration. GRE for admission; apply by March 1. Fall admission only; M.S. only.
Medical Technology. M.S., M.H.E.
Mental Health-Psychiatric Nursing. M.S.N. only.
Nuclear Medicine Technology. M.S. only.
Nurse Anesthetist. M.N. only.
Nurse Practitioner. Includes adult/family, pediatric, neonatal. M.S. only.
Occupational Therapy. M.S., M.H.E.
Oral Biology. M.S., Ph.D.
Parent-Child Nursing. M.S.N. only.
Pharmacology and Toxicology. M.S., Ph.D.
Physical Therapy. M.S., M.H.E.
Physician Assistant. M.S. only.
Physiology. M.S., Ph.D.
Radiation Therapy Technology. M.S. only.
Radiography. M.S. only.
Respiratory Therapy. M.S. only.

School of Medicine (30912-4760)

Founded 1828.
Tuition: residents $6300, nonresidents $19,000. Total average figure for all other expenses: $8500. Enrollment: first-year class 180 (EDP 45); total 721 (men 70%, women 30%). Faculty: full-time 241, part-time 39. Degrees conferred: M.D., M.D.-Ph.D.

ADMISSION REQUIREMENTS. AMCAS report, transcripts, references, MCAT, interview required in support of application. Applicants must have completed at least three years of college study. Preference given to Georgia residents. Has EDP, state residents only. Apply between June 15 and August 1. Apply to Associate Dean for Admissions after June 15, before November 1. Application fee none. Phone: (706)721-3186; fax: (706)721-0959.

ADMISSION STANDARDS. Selective. Accepts 15% of total annual applicants. Approximately 96% are state residents.

FINANCIAL AID. Scholarships, loans. Apply to Office of Financial Aid; no closing date. Less than 20% of students receive aid other than loans from School.

DEGREE REQUIREMENTS. For M.D.: satisfactory completion of four-year program, at least one year in residence.

FIELDS OF GRADUATE STUDY.
Biochemistry.
Immunology.
Molecular Biology.
Neurosciences.
Pharmacology.
Physiology.

School of Dentistry (30912)

First class entered 1969. Quarter system. Tuition: residents $5292, nonresidents $18,261. On-campus housing available. Contact Director of Housing for housing information. Phone: (706)721-3471. Total average academic costs for all other first-year expenses: $3157.
Enrollment: first-year class 50 (men 65%, women 35%), total 194; postgraduates 15. Faculty: full-time 83, part-time 32. Degrees conferred: D.M.D., D.M.D.-M.S. (oral biology).

ADMISSION REQUIREMENTS. Official transcripts, DAT (not later than October), two letters of reference, a pre-dental adviser's recommendation required in support of School's application. Preference given to state residents. Applicants must have completed at least three years of college study. Interviews by in-

vitation only. Apply to Associate Director of Student Affairs after July 1, before November 1. Application fee none. Phone: (706)721-3587; fax: (706)721-6276.

ADMISSION STANDARDS. Competitive. Accepts 65% of total annual applicants. 100% are state residents.

FINANCIAL AID. Scholarships, loans, grants. Apply between January 1 and March 31 to Director of Financial Aid. Use FAFSA. Phone: (706)721-4901. About 91% of students receive aid other than loans from School.

DEGREE REQUIREMENTS. For D.M.D.: satisfactory completion of 45-month program.

GEORGIA SOUTHERN UNIVERSITY
Statesboro, Georgia 30460-8033

Founded 1906. Located 50 miles E of Savannah. Coed. State control. Quarter system. Library: 463,000 volumes, 759,000 microforms, 200 PCs in all libraries.
Annual tuition: resident $2022, nonresident $6092. On-campus housing for 1370 men, 1818 women. Average academic year housing cost: $2500. Apply to Director of Housing. Phone: (912)681-5406.

Graduate School

Enrollment: full- and part-time 1856 (men 30%, women 70%). University faculty teaching graduate students: full-time 140, none part-time. Degrees conferred: M.A., M.S., M.B.A., M.F.A., M.S.N., M.P.A., M.Ed., Ed.S., M.R.A., M.T., Ed.D.

ADMISSION REQUIREMENTS. Two transcripts, GRE (M.A., M.S., M.P.A., M.R.A., M.S.N., M.T., Ed.D.), GMAT (M.B.A.), MAT (M.Ed., Ed.S., M.S.N.) required in support of School's application. TOEFL required for international applicants. Interview not required. Accepts transfer applicants. Graduates from unaccredited institutions not considered. Apply to Graduate School at least one month prior to registration. Application fee, none. Phone: (912)681-0634; fax: (912)681-0740.

ADMISSION STANDARDS. Selective. Usual minimum average: 2.5 (A = 4).

FINANCIAL AID. Annual awards from institutional funds: 128 teaching assistantships, 46 research assistantships, Federal W/S, loans. Apply to chair of appropriate division for assistantships; to Financial Aid Office for all other programs. Phone: (912)681-5413. About 20% of students receive aid other than loans from College and outside sources. No aid for part-time students other than loans.

DEGREE REQUIREMENT. For M.A., M.S.: 40 quarter hours minimum, final comprehensive exam. For M.Ed., M.R.A.: 60 quarter hours minimum, final comprehensive exam. For Ed.S.: 40 quarter hours minimum; final comprehensive exam. For M.B.A.: 48 quarter hours minimum. For M.P.A.: 60 quarter hours minimum; internship; final oral exam. For M.T.: 40 quarter hours minimum; thesis; final oral exam. For M.F.A.: 90 quarter hours; thesis. For M.S.N.: 60 quarter hours minimum; thesis or project; final exam. Minimum residence requirement for a master's degree is one academic year or three summer sessions. For Ed.D.: 90 quarter hours beyond the master's; preliminary exam; advancement to candidacy; dissertation; final oral exam.

FIELDS OF STUDY.
Adult and Vocational Education. M.Ed.
Art. M.F.A., M.Ed.

Biology. M.S.
Business. M.B.A.
Business Education. M.Ed.
Counselor Education. M.Ed., Ed.S.
Early Childhood Education. M.Ed., Ed.S.
English. M.A., M.Ed., Ed.S.
Exercise Science. M.S.
French. M.Ed.
German. M.Ed.
Health and Physical Education. M.Ed., Ed.S.
History. M.A.
Home Economics. M.Ed., M.S.T.
Instructional Media. M.Ed.
Mathematics. M.S., M.Ed., Ed.S.
Middle Grades Education. M.Ed., Ed.S.
Music. M.Ed., Ed.S.
Nursing. M.S.N.
Political Science. M.A.
Psychology. M.S.
Public Administration. M.P.A.
Reading Specialist. M.Ed., Ed.S.
Recreation Administration. M.R.A.
School Administration and Supervision. M.Ed., Ed.S.
School Psychology. M.Ed., Ed.S.
Science. M.Ed., Ed.S.
Secondary Subject Matter Supervision. M.Ed.
Social Science. M.Ed., Ed.S.
Sociology. M.A.
Spanish. M.Ed.
Special Education for Exceptional Children. M.Ed., Ed.S.
Sport Management. M.S.
Technology. M.T.
Technology Education (Industrial Arts). M.Ed., M.S.T., Ed.S.

GEORGIA STATE UNIVERSITY

Atlanta, Georgia 30303-3083
http://www.gsu.edu

Founded 1913. Coed. State control. Quarter system. Special facilities: Center for Biotechnology and Drug Design, Center for Brain Sciences and Health, Center for Creative Writing, Center for Ethics, Center for Environmental Research, Center for Ethics and Public Affairs, Center for Health Policy, Center for High Angular Resolution Astronomy, Center for Integrative Neurosciences and Health, Center for International Media Research and Training, Center for Latin American Studies, Center for Learning Disorders, Center for Learning and Teaching, Center for Neural Communication and Computation, Center for Professional Communication, Center for Sports Medicine, Gerontology Center, Language Research Center. Library: 1,572,000 volumes, 1,871,000 microforms.

Tuition: per quarter hour, resident $50, nonresident $196, $82 activity fee each quarter. No on-campus housing. Apply to Dean of Students for off-campus housing information.

Division of Graduate Studies—College of Arts and Sciences

Enrollment: full- and part-time 1360. Faculty: full-time 380, part-time 45. Degrees conferred: M A., M.A.Ed., M.H.P., M.S., M.A.T., M.F.A., M.Mu., Certificate, Ph.D.

ADMISSION REQUIREMENTS. Transcripts, GRE required in support of College's application. Some programs require letters of recommendation, portfolio, audition, resume, interview, writing sample, or list of references. TOEFL required for international applicants. Accepts transfer applicants. Graduates of unaccredited institutions not considered. Apply to the Office of Graduate Admissions; application deadlines vary by department. Application fee $25. Phone: (404)651-2297; fax: (404)651-1032.

ADMISSION STANDARDS. Competitive. Usual minimum average: 3.0 (A = 4).

FINANCIAL AID. Annual awards from institutional funds: scholarships (includes five to ten minority scholarships), 412 graduate assistantships, Federal W/S, loans. Approved for VA benefits. Apply to head of proposed major department prior to registration; to Office of Financial Aid for all other programs. Phone: (404)651-2227; fax: (404)651-1519. Use FAFSA.

DEGREE REQUIREMENTS. For M.A., M.S.: 40 quarter hours minimum, at least 30 hours in residence; thesis/nonthesis option; reading knowledge of one foreign language; research tool may be substituted in some departments; written/oral exam. For Certificates: 45 quarter hours minimum beyond the master's. For M.A.T.: 50 quarter hours minimum; final written/oral exam. For M.F.A.: 80 quarter hours minimum; final written/oral exam. For Ph.D.: six quarters in residence, at least three consecutive quarters in full-time attendance; ordinarily, reading knowledge of two foreign languages; research skill may be substituted for one or two languages in some departments; general exam; dissertation; final exam.

FIELDS OF STUDY.
Anthropology. M.A. Includes health policy and planning, urban policy and planning, community development, ethnicity, ethnomedicine, health behavior, urban development, social impact assessment.
Art and Design. M.A., M.A.Ed., M.F.A. Includes ceramics, drawing and painting, interior design, jewelry design and metalsmithing, photography, printmaking, sculpture.
Astronomy. Ph.D. Includes astronomy, astrophysics.
Biology. M.S., Ph.D. Includes microbiology, molecular genetics, neurobiology and behavior, physiology.
Chemistry. M.S., Ph.D. Includes analytical, biochemical, inorganic, organic, and physical chemistry.
Communication. M.A. Includes print journalism, public relations, broadcast journalism, film and video, speech.
Economics. M.A.
English. M.A., M.F.A., Ph.D. Includes American and British literature, creative writing, rhetoric, and composition.
Geography. M.A. Includes metropolitan area studies, cartography, physical geography/environmental studies.
Geology. M.S. Includes geochemistry, environmental geology, hydrogeology (M.S. and Certificate).
Gerontology. Certificate only.
Heritage Preservation. M.H.P., Certificate. Includes archaeology, planning, architectural history, historical research, urban history.
History. M.A., Ph.D. Includes United States, European, Asian, Latin American, African, and Middle Eastern history.
Mathematics and Computer Science. M.S., M.A.T. Includes mathematics, computer information systems, computer science, statistics.
Modern and Classical Languages. M.A. Includes French, German, Spanish.
Music. M.Mu. Includes music education, performance, music theory, choral conducting, instrumental conducting, composition, jazz studies, piano pedagogy, sacred music.
Philosophy. M.A. Includes applied ethics, history of philosophy, Wittgenstein, religious studies.
Physics. M.S., Ph.D. Includes atomic physics, biophysics, molecular physics, nuclear physics, condensed matter physics.
Political Science. M.A., Ph.D. Includes electoral politics, international relations.
Psychology. Ph.D. Includes clinical psychology, community psychology, neuropsychology and behavioral neurosciences, psychological foundations.

Sociology. M.A., Ph.D. Includes family, life course, social inequality, conflict.
Translation/Interpretation. Certificate only.
Women's Studies. M.A.

College of Business Administration— Graduate Programs

http://cbasun.gsu.edu/www.oaa/public-html

Graduate study since 1958. Quarter system.
Tuition: per credit hour; resident $50, nonresident $1961.
Enrollment: full-time 1388, part-time 982. Faculty: full-time 190. Degrees conferred: M.B.A., M.A.S., M.P.A., M.H.A., M.S., M.S.R.F., M.Tax., Ph.D.

ADMISSION REQUIREMENTS. Two transcripts, references, GMAT required in support of College's application. Interview may be required for some programs. TOEFL required for international applicants. Accepts transfer applicants and some transfer credit. For master's program, apply to Office of Academic Assistance. For doctoral programs, apply to the Office of Doctoral Programs. Applications must be completed two months prior to registration. Application fee $25. Phone: for master's (404)651-1958, for Ph.D. (404)651-3379; fax: (404)651-1184.

ADMISSION STANDARDS. Selective for most majors. Average GPA: 3.0 (A = 4), average GMAT 560.

FINANCIAL AID. Limited number of assistantships for master's candidates, ninety teaching/research fellowships for Ph.D., Federal W/S, loans. Approved for VA benefits. Apply at least thirty-five days prior to registration to Doctoral Programs Office for fellowships; to University Financial Aid Office for all other programs. Use either FAFSA. Phone: (404)651-2227; fax: (414)651-1419. Aid sometimes available for part-time students.

DEGREE REQUIREMENT. For M.B.A.: 60–95 quarter hours. For M.H.A.: 95–120 quarter hours minimum. For all other master's: 45–75 quarter hours minimum, no language requirements; no thesis. For Ph.D.: 95 quarter hours minimum in full-time; preliminary exam; dissertation; final oral exam.

FIELDS OF STUDY.
Accountancy.
Actuarial Science.
Computer Information Systems.
Decision Sciences.
Economics.
Finance.
Health Administration.
International Business.
Management.
Marketing.
Personal Financial Planning.
Personnel and Employment Relations.
Real Estate.
Risk Management and Insurance.
Taxation.

College of Education

Tuition: per credit resident $50, nonresident $196.
Enrollment: full-time 563, part-time 1250. College faculty: full-time 48, part-time 33. Degrees conferred: M.Ed., M.B.E., M.S., Ed.S., Ph.D.

ADMISSION REQUIREMENTS. Official transcripts, three letters of recommendation, handwritten autobiography, GRE/MAT/GSTEP (Georgia State Test of English Proficiency) required in support of College's application. TOEFL, GSTEP required for international applicants. Interviews may be required. Accepts transfer applicants. Apply for master's 90 days prior to registration. For Ph.D., application deadlines vary by major; usually accepted once or twice yearly. Rolling admissions process. Application fee $10. Phone: (404)651-2525.

ADMISSION STANDARDS. Usual minimum average master's: 2.5 GPA, GRE 800, MAT 44; Specialist: 3.25 GPA, GRE 900, MAT 48; Ph.D.: varies by degree.

FINANCIAL AID. Five fellowships, one hundred research assistantships, thirteen teaching assistantships, Federal W/S, loans. Approved for VA benefits. Apply to chairman of appropriate department for fellowships, assistantships; to Director of Financial Aid for all other programs. No specified closing date. Use FAFSA. Phone: (402)651-2227. About 20% of students receive aid from University and outside sources. Aid available for part-time students.

DEGREE REQUIREMENTS. For M.Ed.: 60 quarter hours minimum; final written/oral exams. For Ed.S.: 50 quarter hours minimum; final written/oral exams/projects. For Ph.D.: 90 quarter hours minimum; qualifying exam; candidacy; dissertation; final oral exam.

FIELDS OF STUDY.
Art Education.
Communication Disorders.
Community Counseling.
Early Childhood Education.
Education of the Behavior/Learning Disabled.
Education of the Hearing Impaired.
Educational Administration and Supervision.
Educational Psychology.
English Education.
Exercise Science.
Health and Physical Education.
Health Occupations Education.
Human Resource Development.
Instructional Technology.
Library Media Technology.
Mathematics Education.
Middle Childhood Education.
Music Education.
Pastoral Counseling.
Physical Education.
Reading.
Rehabilitation Counseling.
Research, Measurement, and Statistics.
School Counseling.
School Psychology.
Science Education.
Social Foundations of Education.
Social Studies Education.
Special Education—Early Childhood.
Special Education Administration.
Sports Administration.
Sports Medicine.
Sports Science.
Vocational Leadership.

College of Law (30303-4049)

Established 1982. Library: 180,000 volumes. Library has LEXIS, NEXIS, WESTLAW.
Tuition: per credit hour, resident $106, nonresident $345. No on-campus housing available. Off-campus housing costs range from $375–$500 per month. Total average annual additional expense: $7500.
Enrollment: first-year class, full-time 76, part-time 101; total 620 (men 53%, women 47%). Faculty: full-time 38, part-time 5. Degrees conferred: J.D., J.D./M.B.A.

ADMISSION REQUIREMENTS. LSDAS Law School report, bachelor's degree, transcripts, LSAT, letters of recommendation, personal statement required in support of application. Accepts transfer applicants. Preference given to state residents. Apply to Admissions Office by April 1. Application fee $10. Phone: (404)651-2048.

ADMISSION STANDARDS. Selective. Accepts about 20–25% of total annual applicants.

FINANCIAL AID. Scholarships, tuition waiver, research assistantships, grants, Federal W/S, loans. Apply by May 1 to Office of Financial Aid. Use FAFSA. About 25% of students receive some aid from School.

DEGREE REQUIREMENTS. For J.D.: satisfactory completion of 135 quarter hours program. For M.B.A.: see Graduate School listing above.

THE UNIVERSITY OF GEORGIA
Athens, Georgia 30602-7402

Founded 1785. Located 70 miles E of Atlanta. Coed. State control. Quarter system. Sponsoring university of the Oak Ridge Associated Universities. Special facilities: Institute of Behavioral Research, Complex Carbohydrate Research Center, Institute of Ecology, Institute of Higher Education, Marine Institute on Sapelo Island, Poultry Disease Research Center, Institute of Remote Sensing and Mapping, Skidaway Institute of Oceanography, Social Science Research Institute, Organization of Tropical Studies. Library: 3,200,000 volumes, 5,204,000 microforms, 47,600 current periodicals, 240 PCs.

Tuition: full-time resident per quarter $836, nonresident $2265. On-campus housing for 545 married students, unlimited for single students. Average housing costs: per quarter $1152–$1397 (including board) for single students; per month $195–$260 for married students. Contact University Housing Office for both on- and off-campus housing information. Phone: (706)542-1421.

Graduate School

Graduate study since 1868. Enrollment: full-time 3886, part-time 1729. Graduate faculty: full-time 1338, part-time none. Degrees conferred: M.A., M.S., M.Acc., M.A.E., M.B.A., M.A.Ed., M.Ed., M.F.A., M.H.E., M.L.A., M.S.W., M.Ag.Ext., M.A.M.S., M.A.T., M.A.M., M.H.P., L.L.M., M.M.C., M.M.R., M.M., M.M.Ed., M.F.R., M.P.P.P.M., M.S.T., M.P.A., Ed.S., Ph.D., Ed.D., D.P.A., D.M.A.

ADMISSION REQUIREMENTS. Two official transcripts, two copies of GRE/GMAT/MAT/LSAT, three letters of recommendation required in support of School's application. TOEFL required for international applicants. Interview not required. Accepts transfer applicants. Graduates of unaccredited institutions not considered. For international applicants apply to Graduate Admissions Office June 15 (Fall), October 15 (Winter), January 1 (Spring), March 15 (Summer); for domestic applicants apply August 1 (Fall), November 15 (Winter), February 15 (Spring), May 1 (Summer). Application fee $30. Phone: (706)542-1787.

ADMISSION STANDARDS. Selective for most departments. Usual minimum average: 3.0 (A = 4).

FINANCIAL AID. Annual awards from institutional funds: fellowships, 220 scholarships, 250 graduate assistantships, Federal W/S, loans. Approved for VA benefits. Apply by February 15 to Graduate School Office for assistantships; to Financial Aid Office for all other programs. Use FAFSA. Phone: (706)542-6147. Aid available for part-time students.

DEGREE REQUIREMENTS. For M.A., M.S.: 40 quarter hours minimum, at least 30 in residence; thesis; reading knowledge of one foreign language for some majors; final oral exam. For M.Acc.: 47 quarter hours minimum. For M.B.A.: 63 hours minimum, additional hours may be required depending upon previous preparation. For M.A.Ed.: 55–60 hours minimum, at least 45 in residence; final written/oral exam. For M.A.E., M.Ed.: 55 or 64 hours minimum depending upon program, at least 40 in residence; final written/oral exam. For M.F.A.: 90 hours minimum; creative project, depending upon major; final written/oral exam. For M.H.E.: 55 hours minimum, at least 45 in residence; final written report; final written/oral exam. For M.L.A.: 65 hours minimum; thesis; final written/oral exam. For M.S.W.: typically six academic quarters, including instruction and field work; problems course or thesis; final written/oral exam. For M.Ag.Ext.: 60 hours minimum; written problem. For M.A.M.S.: 55 hours minimum; 12 technical reports. For M.A.T.: 40 hours minimum in subject area; 15 hours minimum in education; comprehensive exam. For M.A.M.: 65 hours minimum; oral exam. For M.H.P.: 90 hours minimum; internship; thesis. For L.L.M.: 27 semester hours; thesis; oral. For M.M.R.: 56 hours minimum including internship. For M.M.: 50 hours minimum and final project. For M.M.Ed.: 50–60 hours minimum. For M.P.P.P.M.: 62 hours minimum; two internships; final written and oral exams. For Ph.D.: three years beyond the bachelor's, at least three consecutive quarters in residence; preliminary exam, research skills requirements; dissertation; final oral exam. For Ed.D., D.M.A., D.P.A.: essentially the same as for the Ph.D., except no research skills requirement.

FIELDS OF STUDY.
Accountancy. M.Acc.
Agricultural Economics. M.S., Ph.D.
Agricultural Engineering. Includes technology. M.S.
Agriculture Extension.
Agronomy. M.S.
Anatomy (Veterinary). M.S.
Animal Sciences. Includes animal nutrition, dairy science. Ph.D.
Anthropology. M.A., Ph.D.
Applied Mathematical Science.
Art Education.
Art History. M.A., Ph.D.
Artificial Intelligence. M.S.
Avian Medicine.
Biochemistry and Molecular Biology. M.S., Ph.D.
Biological and Agricultural Engineering. Ph.D.
Botany. M.S., Ph.D.
Business Administration. Includes accounting, banking and finance, business law, economics, management, management sciences, marketing, real estate, risk management, and insurance. M.A., Ph.D.
Chemistry. M.S., Ph.D.
Child and Family Development. Ph.D.
Classics. M.A.
Communication Sciences and Disorders. Ph.D.
Comparative Literature. M.A., Ph.D.
Computer Science. M.S.
Conservation Ecology and Sustainable Development. M.S.
Counseling and Student Personnel Services. Ph.D.
Counseling Psychology. Ph.D.
Dairy Science. M.S.
Drama. M.F.A.
Economics. M.A.
Education. M.A., Ed.S., Ed.D., Ph.D.
English. M.A., Ph.D.
Entomology. M.S.
Exercise Science. Ph.D.
Fine Arts. M.F.A.
Food Science. M.S., Ph.D.
Foods and Nutrition. Ph.D.
Forest Resources. M.S.

French. M.A.
Genetics. M.S., Ph.D.
Geography. Includes human, regional, physical. M.A., Ph.D.
Geology. M.S., Ph.D.
German. M.A.
Greek. M.A.
Health Promotion and Behavior. Ph.D.
Historic Preservation. M.H.P.
History. M.A., Ph.D.
Home Economics. M.S.
Horticulture. M.S., Ph.D.
Housing and Consumer Economics. Ph.D.
Instructional Technology. Ph.D.
Journalism. M.A.
Landscape Architecture. M.L.A. only.
Latin. M.A.
Law. LL.M. only.
Linguistics. M.A., Ph.D.
Market Research. M.A.
Mass Communication. Ph.D.
Mathematics. M.A., Ph.D.
Mathematics. Nonthesis option available. M.A., Ph.D.
Medical Microbiology. M.S., Ph.D.
Microbiology. M.S., Ph.D.
Music. Includes applied, composition, education, musicology,
    music literature. M.A., D.M.A., Ph.D.
Music Education.
Pharmacology (Veterinary). M.S., Ph.D.
Pharmacy. M.S., Ph.D.
Philosophy. M.A., Ph.D.
Physics. M.S., Ph.D.
Physiology (Veterinary). M.S., Ph.D.
Plant Pathology. M.S., Ph.D.
Plant Protection and Pest Management. M.P.P.P.M.
Political Science. M.A., Ph.D.
Poultry Science. M.S., Ph.D.
Psychology. M.S., Ph.D.
Public Administration. M.P.A., D.P.A.
Religion. M.A. only.
Romance Languages. Includes French, Italian, Portuguese,
    Spanish. M.A., Ph.D.
Science Technology. M.A.
Social Work. M.S.W., Ph.D.
Sociology. M.A., Ph.D.
Spanish. M.A.
Speech Communication. M.A., Ph.D.
Statistics. M.S., Ph.D.
Textile Science. Ph.D.
Veterinary Parasitology. M.S., Ph.D.
Veterinary Pathology. M.S., Ph.D.
Zoology. M.S., Ph.D.

School of Law (30602-6012)

Established 1859. Semester system. Law library: 459,000 volumes. Library has LEXIS, NEXIS, WESTLAW, INFOTRAC, INNOPAC. Special facilities: The Dean Rusk Center for International and Comparative Law.

Annual tuition: resident $3315, nonresident $10,017. On- and off-campus housing available. Total average annual additional cost: $7500.

Enrollment: first-year class 209; full-time 692 (men 59%, women 41%). Faculty: full-time 42, part-time 14. Degrees conferred: J.D., LL.M., J.D.-M.B.A., J.D.-M.H.P. (Historic Preservation).

ADMISSION REQUIREMENTS. LSDAS Law School report, bachelor's degree, transcripts, LSAT (not later than December), three references required in support of application. Some priority given State residents after January. Interview not required. Four-year undergraduate degree required. May accept transfer applicants. Apply to the Director of Admissions prior to March 15. First-year students admitted Fall only. Application fee $30. Phone: (706)542-7060.

ADMISSION STANDARDS. Competitive. Accepts 20–25% of total annual applicants.

FINANCIAL AID. Scholarships, tuition Equalization scholarships, grants, Federal W/S, loans. Apply to Office of Admissions; use FAFSA and School FAF, preferably by January 31. About 9% of students receive aid from School.

DEGREE REQUIREMENTS. For J.D.: 88 semester hours minimum, at least 30 semester hours in full-time residence. For LL.M.: at least 24 semester hours beyond the J.D.; 2 semesters of graduate study in residence; final thesis.

Note. There are formal exchange agreements with the University of Regensberg (Germany), Southhampton University (Great Britain), and the University of Brussels (Belgium).

College of Veterinary Medicine

Professional and graduate study since 1930. Tuition: resident $3250, contract nonresident $10,500. Living expenses approximately: $8000–9000. Enrollment: first-year class 80; total full-time 344 (men 60%, women 40%); graduate program, full-time 100. Faculty: full-time 77. Degrees conferred: D.V.M. The M.S. and Ph.D. are offered through the Graduate School.

ADMISSION REQUIREMENTS. Professional program: transcripts, GRE General, VAT, animal experience, three recommendations (one from an academic advisor), essay required in support of application. At least three years of undergraduate study prior to entrance. Interview by invitation. Admission limited to residents of Georgia, South Carolina, West Virginia, and U.S. citizens. Apply to Dean after July 15, before November 1. Admits Fall only. Graduate program: transcripts, GRE, recommendations required in support of application. Apply to individual department at least thirty days prior to beginning of quarter of entry. Application fee $30. Phone: (706)542 5728; fax: (706)542-8254.

ADMISSION STANDARDS. Selective. Accepts 35% of total annual applicants. Approximately 10 places for nonresident (at-large) applicants.

FINANCIAL AID. Scholarships, assistantships, partial fee waivers, Federal W/S, loans. Apply to Office of Student Aid at least two months prior to entrance; for graduate program, apply to appropriate department; no specified closing date. About 60% of students receive aid other than loans from School.

DEGREE REQUIREMENTS. For D.V.M.: Four years in residence. For M.S., Ph.D., see Graduate School listing.

FIELDS OF GRADUATE STUDY.
Medical Microbiology.
Parasitology.
Pathology.
Pharmacology.
Physiology.

GODDARD COLLEGE
Plainfield, Vermont 05667
http://sun.goddard.edu

Founded 1938, began offering graduate study leading to the M.A. in 1940. Located 200 miles NW of Boston. Coed. Semester system. Library: 70,000 volumes, 300 active periodicals, on-line databases (DIALOG).

Annual tuition: resident $13,470, nonresident $14,632. On-campus housing available. Annual academic year housing cost: $4520 (room and board).

Graduate Program

Enrollment: full- and part-time 220. Combined faculty: full-time 44, part-time 47. Degrees conferred: M.A., M.F.A.

ADMISSION REQUIREMENTS. Self-initiated study plan, transcripts, interview, letters of recommendation, preliminary bibliography required in support of application. Accepts transfer applicants. Apply to Director of Admissions; no specified closing date. Rolling admissions process. Application fee $40. Phone: (802)454-8311; fax: (802)454-8017.

ADMISSION STANDARDS. Selective. Usual minimum average: 2.75 (A = 4).

FINANCIAL AID. Graduate/teaching assistantships, Federal W/S, loans. Apply to Financial Aid Office; no specified closing date. Use FAFSA and CSS Profile. About 50% of students receive aid other than loans from both College and outside sources.

DEGREE REQUIREMENTS. For M.A., M.F.A.: satisfactory completion of individually planned program supervised by a study supervisor and a second reader drawn from the Goddard faculty as a whole.

FIELDS OF STUDY.
Counseling Psychology.
Education.
Feminist Studies.
Individualized. Includes psychology, social ecology, writing (M.F.A.).
Mass Communication.
Multicultural Studies.
Music.
Studio Art.
Theater.

GOLDEN GATE UNIVERSITY
San Francisco, California 94105-2968
http://www.ggu.edu

Founded 1853. Coed. Private control. Trimester system. Library: 126,500 volumes, 703,300 microforms, 1500 current periodicals, 25 PCs.

Tuition: per unit $392, except Information Systems, Taxation, and Telecommunications $412. No on-campus housing available. Contact Student Affairs Office for off-campus housing information. Phone: (415)442-7294.

Graduate Programs

Graduate study since 1950. Enrollment: full-time 1326, part-time 3280 (men 2397, women 2209). Graduate faculty: full-time 57, part-time 200. Degrees conferred: M.A., M.B.A., M.P.A., M.S., D.B.A., D.P.A. (C.P.A. exam preparation program also available).

ADMISSION REQUIREMENTS. Transcripts required in support of application. GMAT required for M.B.A. applicants. TOEFL required for international applicants. Interview not required. Accepts transfer applicants. Graduates of unaccredited institutions not considered. Apply to the Office of Enrollment and Prospective Student Services at least one month prior to registration. Rolling admissions process. Application fee $55,

doctoral $75, $65 for international applicants. Phone: (415)442-7800; fax: (415)442-7807.

ADMISSION STANDARDS. Selective. Usual minimum average: 2.5 for M.P.A., M.B.A., M.S.; 3.5 in graduate work for D.B.A., D.P.A. (A = 4).

FINANCIAL AID. Annual awards from institutional funds: one hundred scholarships, Federal W/S, loans. Approved for VA benefits. Apply to Director of Financial Aid; no specified closing date. Use FAFSA, Student loan application. Phone: (415)442-7270; fax: (415)442-7807.

DEGREE REQUIREMENTS. For M.A.: 30 units minimum; thesis; foreign language required by some departments. For M.B.A.: 36 units minimum plus 12 units in general business or undergraduate units if not completed before entrance; thesis optional for 3 units. For M.S.: 30 units minimum, plus 6 general business units if not completed before entrance. For M.P.A.: 39 units minimum plus 9 undergraduate units if act completed before entrance. No language or thesis requirement for master's degrees; limited number of transfer credits considered. For D.B.A., D.P.A.: 56 units in graduate core requirements beyond master's; qualifying exam; dissertation; final oral/written exam.

FIELDS OF STUDY.

SCHOOL OF ARTS AND SCIENCES:
Applied Psychology. Includes counseling, industrial/organizational, marriage, family and child counseling. M.A.
Liberal Studies. M.A.

SCHOOL OF BUSINESS:
Accountancy. M.Acc.
Accounting. M.B.A., M.S.
Economics. M.S.
Entrepreneurship. M.B.A.
Finance. M.B.A., M.S.
Human Resources Management. M.B.A., M.S.
International Business. M.B.A.
Management. M.B.A.
Manufacturing Management. M.S.
Marketing. M.B.A.
Operations Management. M.B.A.
Organizational Behavior and Development. M.B.A., M.S.
Procurement and Logistics Management. M.S.
Project and Systems Management. M.S.
Public Relations. M.S.

SCHOOL OF TAXATION:
Taxation. M.S.

SCHOOL OF TECHNOLOGY AND INDUSTRY:
Hospitality Administration. M.B.A.
Information Systems. M.B.A., M.S.
Management of Technology. M.S.
Telecommunications. M.B.A., M.S.

SCHOOL OF URBAN AND PUBLIC AFFAIRS:
Arts Administration. M.A., M.B.A.
Health-care Management. M.B.A., M.P.A.
International Relations. M.A.

School of Law

Established 1901. Semester system. Law library: 200,000 volumes. Library has LEXIS, WESTLAW, CALI.

Annual tuition: $18,700, part-time $11,700. On-campus housing available. Total average annual additional expense: $13,500.

Enrollment: first-year class full-time 180, part-time 65; total 720 (men 51%, women 49%). Faculty: full-time 31, part-time 82.

Degrees conferred: J.D., LL.M. (Taxation, International Legal Studies).

ADMISSION REQUIREMENTS. LSDAS Law School report, bachelor's degree, transcripts, LSAT personal statement, letters of recommendation required in support of application. Interview not required. Accepts transfer applicants. Graduates of unaccredited colleges not considered. Apply to Admissions Office by April 15. Admits Fall only. Application fee $30. (415)442-6630.

ADMISSION STANDARDS. Selective. Accepts 40–45% of total annual applicants.

FINANCIAL AID. Scholarships, fellowships, assistantships, full and partial tuition waivers, Federal W/S, loans. Apply to Financial Aid Officer by April 15. Use FAFSA.

DEGREE REQUIREMENTS. For J.D.: 86 semester hours minimum. For LL.M.: at least 24 semester hours beyond the J.D.
Note: School has exchange program with Chulalongkorn University (Bangkok), the University of Bologna (Italy), University of Paris at Nantere (France).

GONZAGA UNIVERSITY
Spokane, Washington 99258-0001

Founded 1887. Coed. Private control. Jesuit, Roman Catholic. Semester system. Library: 550,000 volumes, 290,000 microforms, 4200 current periodicals, 120 PCs.
Annual tuition: full-time $5575; per credit $385. Limited on-campus housing for single graduate students; none for married students. Average annual housing cost: $4200 (double room including board). Contact Residence Life Office for both on- and off-campus housing information. Phone: (509)328-4220, ext. 4103.

Graduate School

Enrollment: full-time 937, part-time 426. University faculty teaching graduate students: full-time 23, part-time 57. Degrees conferred: M.A., M.Acc, M.B.A., M.B.A.-J.D., M.A.P., M.A.A., M.A.C.E., M.Anthes.Ed., M.Ed., M.E.S., M.P.E., M.T.A., M.I.T., M.S.M.E., M.O.L., M.S.N., M.E.L., M.S.E.E., Ph.D.

ADMISSION REQUIREMENTS. Two official transcripts required in support of School's application. GRE/MAT/GMAT, recommendation/reference letters and interview required by some departments. TOEFL required for international applicants. Accepts transfer applicants. Graduates of unaccredited institutions not considered. Rolling admissions process. Application $40. Phone: (509)328-4220, ext. 3546; fax: (509)324-5399.

ADMISSION STANDARDS. Selective. Usual minimum average: 3.0 G.P.A.; 3.5 G.P.A. for doctoral applicants (A = 4).

FINANCIAL AID. Fellowships, teaching assistantships, Federal W/S, loans. Approved for VA benefits. Apply to appropriate department chair for fellowships, assistantships; to Financial Aid Office for all other programs. Use FAFSA. Phone: (509)328-4220, ext. 3182. Aid sometimes available for part-time students.

DEGREE REQUIREMENTS. For master's: 30 semester hours minimum, at least 24 in residence; thesis required for some programs; final oral/written exam; one research skill; reading knowledge of one foreign language for programs in arts. For Ph.D.: 60 credits minimum beyond the bachelor's, at least 45 in residence; qualifying exam; proficiency in one foreign language; dissertation; final oral exam.

FIELDS OF STUDY.
Accounting. M.Acc. only.
Administration and Curriculum. M.A.A.
Administration of Physical Education and Athletics. M.P.E.
Anesthesia Education. M.Anesth.Ed.
Business Administration. M.B.A., M.B.A.-J.D.
Computer Education. M.A.C.E.
Counseling Psychology. M.A.P.
Educational Leadership. Ph.D.
Electrical Engineering. M.S.E.E.
English. M.A., M.E.L.
Initial Teaching. M.I.T.
Mechanical Engineering. M.S.M.E.
Nursing. M.S.N.
Organizational Leadership. M.O.L.
Pastoral Ministry. M.A.
Philosophy. M.A.
Religious Studies. M.A., M.Div.
Special Education. M.E.S.
Spirituality. M.A.
Teaching. M.Ed., M.T.A.

School of Law (Box 3528)

Established 1912. Semester system. Law library: 200,000 volumes. Library has LEXIS, NEXIS, WESTLAW, DIALOG, CARL.
Tuition: per credit $520. Evening program available. No on-campus housing available. Total average annual additional expense: $11,500.
Enrollment: first-year class 204; total 544 (men 65%, women 35%). Faculty: full-time 33, part-time 10. Degrees conferred: J.D., J.D.,-M.B.A., J.D.-M.Acc.

ADMISSION REQUIREMENTS. LSDAS Law School report, bachelor's degree, transcripts, LSAT required in support of application. Interview not required. Accepts transfer applicants. Graduates of unaccredited colleges not considered. Apply to Dean by March 15. Admits Fall only. Application fee $40. Phone: 1-900-572-9658 (within Washington state), 1-800-523-9712 (Continental U.S.), (509)328-4220.

ADMISSION STANDARDS. Selective. Accepts 40–45% of total annual applicants.

FINANCIAL AID. Scholarships, full and partial tuition waivers, fellowships, assistantships, Federal W/S, loans. Apply to Law School Financial Aid Office by May 1. Use FAFSA.

DEGREE REQUIREMENTS. For J.D.: 90 semester hours minimum, at least one year in residence.

GOUCHER COLLEGE
Baltimore, Maryland 21204-2794
http://www.goucher.edu

Private control. Coed. Semester system. Library: 269,000 volumes, 58,000 microforms.
Tuition: per credit $225. No housing for graduate students.

Graduate Program

Enrollment: full- and part-time 200. Graduate faculty: full- and part-time 36. Degree conferred: M.Ed., M.A.T.

ADMISSION REQUIREMENTS. Transcripts, two letters of recommendation, bachelor's required in support of application. TOEFL required for international applicants. Accepts transfer students. Apply to the Office of Graduate Studies; no specified closing date. Rolling admissions process. Application fee $25. Phone: (410)337-6047; fax: (410)337-6405.

FINANCIAL AID. Limited to grants, loans. Approved for VA benefits. Apply to the Office of Financial Aid. Use FAFSA and institutional FAF. Phone: (410)337-6500

DEGREE REQUIREMENTS. For M.Ed.: 35 semester credits; action research project; thesis; internship. For M.A.T.: 36 credits; year-long student teaching internships.

FIELD OF STUDY.
Education. Includes urban education, middle school, the at-risk student, school mediation, school improvement leadership.

GOVERNORS STATE UNIVERSITY
University Park, Illinois 60466

Established 1969. Located 30 miles S of Chicago. Coed. Trimester system. Library: 235,000 volumes, 644,000 microforms, 2500 current periodicals.

Tuition: resident, per hour $89, or $1038 full-time, per term (12 hours or more); nonresident, per hour $267 or $3114 per term (12 hours or more). No on-campus housing available. Day care facilities available.

Graduate Studies

Enrollment: full-time 140, part-time 1711 (men 35%, women 65%). Faculty: full-time 136, part-time 160. Degrees conferred: M.A., M.S., M.B.A., M.P.A., M.P.T., M.H.S., M.H.A., M.S.N.

ADMISSION REQUIREMENTS. Official transcripts, bachelor's degree required in support of application. TOEFL required for international applicants. Accepts transfer applicants. Graduates of unaccredited colleges not considered. Apply by July 1 (Fall), November 1 (Spring) to Office of Admissions. Applications and credentials required approximately 2 months prior to registration. Rolling admissions process. Application fee none. Phone: (708)534-4490; fax: (708)534-8951.

ADMISSION STANDARDS. Relatively open for some departments, selective for others. Usual minimum average: 2.5 (A = 4).

FINANCIAL AID. Annual awards from institutional funds: scholarships, research assistantships, teaching assistantships, Federal W/S, loans. Approved for VA benefits. Apply by May 1 to Director of Financial Aid; no specified closing date. Phone: (708)534-5000. Use FAFSA. About 44% of students receive aid from University and outside sources. Aid available for part-time students.

DEGREE REQUIREMENTS. At least 32–48 credit hours in graduate-level courses; thesis/nonthesis option; at least 2 credit hours are designated as master's final project.

FIELDS OF STUDY.
Accounting. M.S.
Addiction Studies. M.H.S.
Analytical Chemistry. M.S.
Art. M.A.
Business Administration. M.B.A.
Communication Disorders. M.H.S.
Communication Studies. M.A.
Computer Science. M.S.
Counseling. M.A.
Education. M.A.
Educational Administration. M.A.

English. M.A.
Environmental Biology. M.S.
Health Administration. M.H.A.
Instructional and Training Technology. M.A.
Multicategorical Special Education. M.A.
Nursing. M.S.N.
Physical Therapy. M.P.T.
Political Studies and Justice Studies. M.A.
Psychology. M.A.
Public Administration. M.P.A.

HAMLINE UNIVERSITY*
St. Paul, Minnesota 55104-1284

Coed. Private control. United Methodist Church. Hamline is the oldest institution of higher learning in the state of Minnesota. Library: 313,732 volumes, 167,000 microform, 3700 current periodicals, 70 PCs.

Tuition: per course $926. On-campus housing for single students only. Average academic year housing cost: $2152 (room only). Contact Office of Residential Life for both on- and off-campus housing information. Phone: (612)641-2061.

Graduate School

Enrollment: full-time 115, part-time 527. Faculty; full-time 14, part-time 50. Degrees conferred: M.A., M.A.Ed., M.A.P.A., Certificate.

ADMISSION REQUIREMENTS. Official transcripts, three letters of recommendation required in support of School's application. TOEFL required for international applicants. Accepts transfer applicants. Apply by July 1 (Fall), December 15 (Spring) to Graduate Studies Office. Rolling admissions process. Application fee $35. Phone: (612)641-2900; fax: (612)641-2956.

ADMISSION STANDARDS. Selective. Usual minimum average: 2.9 (A = 4).

FINANCIAL AID. Limited to Federal W/S, loans. Approved for VA benefits. Apply to the Office of Financial Aid; no specified closing date. Use FAFSA. Phone: (612)641-2280. Aid sometimes available for part-time students.

DEGREE REQUIREMENTS. For M.A. Liberal Arts: 30 semester credits; final project. For M.A. Public Administration: seven required core courses; independent problem analysis; three noncredit one-day public management seminars. For Certificate of Advanced Liberal Studies: nine courses beyond the master's.

FIELDS OF STUDY.
Education.
Liberal Arts.
Public Administration.

School of Law

Established 1972. Semester system. Library: 204,000 items. Library has LEXIS, NEXIS, WESTLAW, DIALOG.

Annual tuition: $14,500. On-campus housing available. Housing cost: $3500–$5000. Apply to Director of University Housing for off-campus housing.

Enrollment: first-year class 209; total 476 (men 52%, women 48%). Faculty: full-time 29, part-time 44. Degrees conferred: J.D., J.D.-M.A.P.A., J.D.-M.B.A. (with University of St. Thomas).

ADMISSION REQUIREMENTS. LSDAS Law School report, bachelor's degree, transcripts, LSAT, recommendations required in support of application. Preference given to state residents. Graduates of unaccredited colleges not considered. Apply to Admissions Office by May 15. Phone: (612)641-2461.

ADMISSION STANDARDS. Selective. Admits about 25–30% of total annual applicants.

FINANCIAL AID. Scholarships, Federal W/S, loans. Apply by April 15. Use FAFSA. About 50% of students receive some aid from School. Public Law forgiveness program available.

DEGREE REQUIREMENTS. For J.D.: satisfactory completion of 88-semester-hour program.

HAMPTON UNIVERSITY
Hampton, Virginia 23668

Founded 1868. Located SE of Richmond. Coed. Private control. Semester system. Special facilities: Marine Science Center for Coastal and Environmental Studies, Center for Non-linear Analysis, Nuclear/High Energy Physics Research Center of Excellence, Research Center for Optical Physics, National Center for Minority Special Education Research, Hampton University Museum. Library: 400,000 volumes, 380,000 microforms, 1500 current periodicals, 75 PCs.

Annual tuition: full-time $8198; per credit $200. Limited on-campus housing for single students. Average academic year off-campus housing cost: $4800 excluding board. Contact Office of Auxiliary Enterprises for off-campus housing information. Phone: (804)727-5210.

Graduate College

Graduate study since 1928. Enrollment: full-time 178 (men 30%, women 70%), part-time 135. Graduate faculty: full-time 90, part-time 11. Degrees conferred: M.A., M.S., M.B.A., Ph.D.

ADMISSION REQUIREMENTS. Transcripts, GRE/GMAT required in support of College's application. TOEFL required for international applicants. Accepts transfer applicants. Apply to Dean of Graduate College at least 6 weeks prior to registration. Application fee $15. Phone: (804)727-5454 or -5496; fax: (804)727-5084.

ADMISSION STANDARDS. Competitive. Usual minimum average: 2.8 (A = 4).

FINANCIAL AID. Fellowships, traineeships, assistantships, Federal W/S, loans. Approved for VA benefits. Apply by May 1 to Dean of Graduate College for fellowships, assistantships; to the Office of Financial Aid for all other programs. Use FAFSA. Phone: (804)727-5332.

DEGREE REQUIREMENTS. For M.A.: 30–32 hours, at least 24 hours in residence; thesis/special project/comprehensive exam. For M.S.: 32–45 hours; thesis/nonthesis option/comprehensive exam. For M.B.A.: 36–60 semester hours. For Ph.D.: 72 semester hours; qualifying exam; dissertation; final oral exam.

FIELDS OF STUDY.
Applied Mathematics. M.S.
Biology. M.A., M.S.
Business Administration. M.B.A.
Chemistry. M.S.

Communicative Sciences and Disorders. M.A.
Counseling. Includes college student development, community agency counseling. M.A.
Elementary Education. M.A.
Museum Studies. M.A.
Nursing. Includes education, administration, practitioner, community health, community mental health/psychiatric, advanced adult nursing. M.S.
Physics. M.S., Ph.D.
Special Education. Includes emotionally disturbed/re-education specialist, learning disabilities. M.A.

HARDIN-SIMMONS UNIVERSITY
Abilene, Texas 79698-0001

Founded 1891. Coed. Private control, Baptist. Semester system. Library: 413,000 volumes, 17,000 microforms, 5 PCs.

Tuition: per credit $240. On-campus housing for 55 married students, 59 graduate men, 67 graduate women. Average academic year housing cost: $3000. Apply to Director of Housing. Phone: (915)670-1329.

Graduate School

Graduate study since 1926. Enrollment: full-time 97, part-time 266. University faculty: full-time 60, part-time 15. Degrees conferred: M.A., M.B.A., M.Ed., M.M.

ADMISSION REQUIREMENTS. Transcript, GRE/GMAT/MAT required in support of School's application. TOEFL required for international applicants. Accepts transfer applicants. Graduates of unaccredited institutions not considered. Apply to Dean of the Graduate School at least two weeks prior to registration. Application fee $25. Phone: (915)670-1298; fax: (915)670-1564.

ADMISSION STANDARDS. Selective for most departments. Usual minimum average: 3.0 (A = 4)

FINANCIAL AID. Annual awards from institutional funds: scholarships, graduate assistantships, Federal W/S, loans. Approved for VA benefits. Apply at least one month prior to registration to Dean of the Graduate School. Phone: (915)670-1331. About 10% of students receive aid other than loans from University and outside sources. Aid sometimes available to part-time students.

DEGREE REQUIREMENTS. For M.A.: 30–36 credit hours minimum, at least 24 in residence; thesis; comprehensive oral exam. For M.Ed.: 36 credit hours minimum, at least 24 in residence; comprehensive oral exam. For M.M.: by advisement. For M.B.A.: 36 credit hours; oral/written exam.

FIELDS OF STUDY.
Business Administration. M.B.A. only.
Counselor Education. M.Ed. only.
Education. Includes elementary, secondary, physical. M.Ed. only.
English. M.A. only.
Family Ministry. M.A. (60-credit-hour program).
Family Psychology. M.A. (54-credit-hour program).
Guidance Education. M.Ed. only.
History. M.A. only.
Music. Includes applied literature, music education, theory-composition. M.M. only.
Reading Specialist. M.Ed. only.
Religion. M.A. only.

HARDING UNIVERSITY
Searcy, Arkansas 72143-0001

Founded 1924. Located 50 miles N of Little Rock. Coed. Private control. Church of Christ. Semester system. Library: 407,000 volumes, 174,000 microforms.

Tuition: per credit $190. On-campus housing for 99 married students. Average academic year housing cost: $3600 for single students. Per month $225–$350 per month for married students. Apply to Director of Housing. Phone: (510)270-4256.

Graduate Program

Enrollment: full-time 80, part-time 68. University faculty: full-time 42, part-time 5. Degrees conferred: M.Ed., M.S.E.

ADMISSION REQUIREMENTS. Two transcripts, letter of recommendation required in support of application. TOEFL required for international applicants. Accepts transfer applicants. Apply to Director of Graduate Studies prior to registration. Application fee none. Phone: (501)279-4315; fax: (501)279-4951.

ADMISSION STANDARDS. Selective. Usual minimum average: 2.5 (A = 4).

FINANCIAL AID. Annual awards from institutional funds: one hundred academic scholarships, thirty fellowships, Federal W/S, loan. Approved for VA benefits. Apply to Director of Graduate Program; no specified closing date. Phone: (501)279-4315. About 25% of students receive aid other than loans from University and outside sources. Aid sometimes available for part-time students.

DEGREE REQUIREMENTS. For M.Ed., M.S.E.: 35 semester hours minimum, at least 29 in residence; final written exam; thesis/nonthesis option (thesis may replace 3–6 hours of course work); comprehensive exam.

FIELDS OF STUDY.
Arkansas Elementary Principal. Certificate only.
Elementary Education.
Reading.
Secondary Education. Includes school administration, English and humanities, natural sciences, social sciences.

UNIVERSITY OF HARTFORD
West Hartford, Connecticut 06117-1500
http://www.hartford.edu

Established 1957. Private control. Semester system. Library: 397,000 volumes. 59,500 microforms.

Tuition: Arts and Sciences, per credit $270, Business and Public Administration, per credit hour $320, Engineering per credit hour $350, Education, Nursing, and Health, per credit hour $275, Hartt School of Music, per credit hour $240. On-campus housing for graduate students. Monthly room charge: $300–$500 for single students, $400–$600 for married students. Phone: (860)768-7793.

Graduate Studies

Graduate enrollment: full-time 499, part-time 1529. Faculty: full-time 130, part-time 83. Degrees conferred: M.A., M.A.T., M.Ed., M.Mus., M.M.Ed., M.B.A., M.P.A., M.S.O.B., M.S.T., M.S.I., M.S., M.S.P.A., M.F.A., Certificate, C.A.G.S. Specialist diploma, Sixth-year Certificate.

ADMISSION REQUIREMENTS. Transcripts, GRE/GMAT/MAT required in support of application. Letters of recommendation, auditions required for some programs. TOEFL required for international applicants. Accepts transfer applicants. Graduates of unaccredited institutions not considered. Apply to Admissions Office by July 1 (Fall), November 15 (Spring). Application fee $35. Phone: (203)768-4371.

ADMISSION STANDARDS. Selective for most departments. Usual minimum average: 3.0 (A = 4).

FINANCIAL AID. Annual awards from institutional funds: eighteen teaching assistantships, eight to ten research fellowships, fifteen to twenty internships, Federal W/S, loans. Apply to Dean of appropriate school for assistantships, fellowships by May 1; to the Office of Financial Aid for all other programs: no specified closing date. Use FAFSA and institutional FAF. Phone: (860)768-4296. Very few students receive aid other than loans from University.

DEGREE REQUIREMENTS. For most master's: 30–45 semester hours minimum, at least two semesters in residence; thesis/nonthesis option. For M.B.A.: 4.8 semester hours maximum, at least two semesters in residence. For C.A.G.S., Specialist, Certificate: 30 credit hours minimum beyond the master's; research paper; comprehensive exam.

FIELDS OF STUDY.

BARNEY SCHOOL OF BUSINESS AND PUBLIC ADMINISTRATION:
Accounting.
Business Administration.
Finance.
Health Administration.
Human Resources Management.
Insurance. Includes life, property, casualty.
International Business.
Management Information Systems.
Organizational Development.
Public Administration.
Taxation.
Urban and Regional Planning.

COLLEGE OF ARTS AND SCIENCES:
Biology.
Biopsychology.
Chemistry.
Communication.
Health Psychology.
Industrial Psychology.
Neurosciences.
School Psychology.

COLLEGE OF EDUCATION, NURSING, AND HEALTH PROFESSIONS:
Administration and Supervision.
Early Childhood Education.
Educational Computing and Technology.
Elementary Education.
Guidance and Counseling.
Nursing.
Secondary Education.

HARTT SCHOOL OF MUSIC:
Applied Music. Includes accompanying, pedagogy, performance.
Choral Conducting.
Composition.
Instrumental Conducting.
Kodaly Training.
Liturgical Music.
Music Education.
Music History. Includes performance, research.

Music Theory.
Opera.
Voice.

HARVARD UNIVERSITY
Cambridge, Massachusetts 02138

Founded 1636. Located adjacent to Boston. Coed. Private control. Semester system. Special facilities: Astronomical and Blue Hill meteorological observatories; Peabody Museum of Archaeology and Ethnology; several art museums; Harvard Forest, geological laboratories; seismograph station; research centers/institutes in International Affairs and Russian, Middle Eastern, East Asian Studies, Jewish Studies, World Religions, Japanese Studies, International Development, Afro-American Studies, Urban Studies, American Political Studies; rare book and manuscript collection; biological, chemical, psychological, and social relations laboratories; biological museums, Herbaria, computer center; engineering and physics laboratories. Library: more than 12,850,000 volumes, 5,555,000 microforms.

On-campus housing for about 350 single graduate students from Graduate School of Arts and Sciences. Approximately 1400 apartment units for which graduate students are eligible. Annual housing cost: $2100–$3100 (room only); apartments $517–$1600 per month. Contact Harvard Real Estate, Inc., Housing Office, 7 Holyoke Street for both on- and off-campus housing. Phone: (617)495-5060. Day care facilities available.

Graduate School of Arts and Sciences

Graduate study since 1872. Annual tuition: full-time $20,038. Enrollment: 3460 (men 65%, women 35%). Faculty teaching graduate students: 800. Degrees conferred: A.M., S.M., M.F.S., M.E., Ph.D.

ADMISSION REQUIREMENTS. Transcripts, three letters of recommendation, personal statement required in support of College's application. Many departments require GRE. Interview not required. Transfer credit for work done elsewhere considered only for Ph.D. Admits Fall only. Apply by December 15 Natural Sciences, December 29 Social Sciences and Humanities, to the Office of Admissions and Financial Aid. Application fee $60. Phone: (617)495-5315; E-mail: adm@hugsas.harvard.edu.

ADMISSION STANDARDS. Very competitive for most departments.

FINANCIAL AID. Annual awards from institutional funds: 1300 scholarships, 1000 research assistantships, 1500 teaching assistantships, Federal W/S, loans. File for financial aid with application for admission. FAFSA and institutional FAF. Phone: (617)495-5396. About 85% of students receive aid and/or loans from College and outside sources.

DEGREE REQUIREMENTS. For A.M.: two terms minimum in full-time residence; reading knowledge of one foreign language for most majors; thesis normally not required; final written/oral exam. For S.M., M.E., M.S.F.: two terms minimum in full-time residence; final written/oral exam; no language or thesis requirement. For Ph.D.: minimum of two years in full-time residence and sixteen half courses minimum beyond the bachelor's; general or qualifying exam; reading knowledge of two foreign languages for most majors; thesis; final written/oral exam.

FIELDS OF STUDY.
African History.
American History.
Anthropology. Includes archaeology, biological anthropology, social anthropology. Ph.D. only.

Applied Sciences. Includes applied mathematics, applied physics, engineering. S.M., M.E., Ph.D.
Art History.
Asian Studies.
Astronomy. Ph.D. only.
Biochemistry. Ph.D. only.
Biology. Includes cellular and developmental biology, organismic and evolutionary biology. Ph.D. only.
Biophysics. Includes structural molecular biology, cell and membrane biophysics, molecular genetics, physical biochemistry, mathematical biophysics. Ph.D. only.
Business Economics. Ph.D. only.
Business Studies. Includes decision sciences and organizational behavior; Ph.D. only.
Celtic Languages and Literatures. Irish, Welsh; A.M., Ph.D.
Chemical Physics. Ph.D. only.
Chemistry. Includes chemistry, inorganic chemistry, biological chemistry, physical chemistry. Ph.D. only.
Classics. Includes classical philology, classical philosophy, classical archaeology, Byzantine Greek, medieval Latin. Ph.D.
Comparative Literature. Ph.D. only.
Decision Sciences. Ph.D. only.
Earth Sciences.
East Asian Languages and Civilizations. Includes Chinese, Japanese, Korean, Mongolian. Ph.D. only.
Economics. Ph.D. only.
English and American Literature and Language. Includes English literature to 1500, English literature 1660–1825, English literature 1800–present, American literature. Ph.D. only.
Fine Arts. Includes ancient art, medieval art, Renaissance art, Baroque art, 17th- and 18th-century art, modern art, Islamic art, Oriental art. Ph.D.
Forest Science. M.F.S.
Genetics.
Geological Sciences. Includes geology, geophysics. A.M., Ph.D.
Germanic Languages and Literatures. Ph.D.
Government. Includes political thought and its history, American government, law and administration, comparative government, international relations, quantitative methods for political science. Ph.D.
History. Includes ancient history, medieval history, early modern European history, American history, African history, East Asian history, English history, Latin American history, Russian history. Ph.D.
History and East Asian Languages. Ph.D.
History and Middle Eastern Studies. Ph.D.
History of American Civilization. Ph.D.
History of Science Department. Ph.D.
Inner Asian and Altaic Studies. Ph.D.
Linguistics. Includes linguistic theory, descriptive linguistics, historical linguistics, linguistics anthropology, psycholinguistics, sociolinguistics, comparative philology. Ph.D.
Mathematics. Ph.D.
Medical Sciences. Includes anatomy, biochemistry, cell and developmental biology, experimental pathology, genetics, immunology, microbiology and molecular genetics, neurobiology, experimental pathology, pharmacology, physiology, virology. Ph.D.
Middle Eastern Studies. Includes regional studies, Middle East anthropology and Middle Eastern studies, economics and Middle Eastern studies, history and Middle Eastern studies, fine arts and Middle Eastern studies. Ph.D.
Molecular Biology. Ph.D. only.
Music. Includes musicology, composition. Ph.D.
Near Eastern Languages and Civilizations. Includes Akkadian and Sumerian, Arabic, Armenian, Biblical history and Northwest Semitic philology, Indo-Muslim culture, Iranian, Persian, post-Biblical Jewish history and literature, Syro-Palestinian archaeology, Turkology. Ph.D.
North American Studies.
Oral Literature.

Paleontology. See Biology and Geological Sciences.

Philosophy. Ph.D.

Physics. Includes theoretical physics, experimental physics. Ph.D.

Planetary Sciences.

Political Economy and Government. Open only to holders of Harvard M.P.A.; write to Kennedy School for instructions; Ph.D.

Political Science.

Psychology and Social Relations. Includes experimental psychology, personality and developmental studies, social psychology. Ph.D.

Public Policy. Open only to holders of Harvard M.P.P.; write to Kennedy School for instructions; Ph.D.

Regional Studies. China, Japan, Korea, Mongolia, Vietnam. A.M.

Regional Studies—Middle East. See Middle Eastern Studies.

Regional Studies—Soviet Union Committee. A.M.

Religion. Ph.D.

Romance Languages and Literatures. Includes French, Italian, Portuguese, Spanish; A.M., Ph.D.

Sanskrit and Indian Studies. A.M., Ph.D.

Slavic Languages and Literatures. Ph.D.

Sociology. Ph.D.

Statistics. A.M., Ph.D.

Urban Planning. Ph.D.

Graduate School of Business Administration
Soldiers Field Road, 02163

http://www.hbs.harvard.edu

Graduate study since 1908. Semester system. Annual tuition: $23,700, fees $2420. On- and off-campus housing available for both single and married graduate students.

Enrollment: full-time 1500 (women 27%, minorities 18%, international 25%). Faculty: full-time 162. Degrees conferred: M.B.A., D.B.A.

ADMISSION REQUIREMENTS. For M.B.A.: completed application form, essays, transcripts, three letters of recommendation. Interviews not required and by invitation only. TOEFL required, TWE strongly recommended for international applicants. Apply to Admissions Board by March 1 for September admissions (two-year program), September 1 for January admissions (sixteen-month program). Application fee $150. Phone: (617)495-6127; fax: (617)496-9272. For D.B.A.: completed application form, three letters of recommendation, GRE or GMAT scores; application fee $75. Fall admission only. Phone: (617)495-6101; fax: (617)496-9272, E-mail: admission@hbs.edu.

ADMISSION STANDARDS. Very competitive. Usual minimum average: 3.2 (A = 4).

FINANCIAL AID. Scholarships, fellowships, loans available based on demonstrated need. Approved for VA benefits. Apply to the Office of Financial Aid when applying for admission. Use FAFSA and institutional FAF. Phone: (617)495-6640; fax: (617)496-3955. About 70% of students receive financial aid, primarily in the form of loans. International students are eligible for some financial assistance.

DEGREE REQUIREMENTS. For M.B.A.: either two years in full-time residence (beginning in September) or 16 months in full-time residence (beginning in January). For D.B.A.: normally two years of course work and one year of thesis work; general examination; special field exam; six-month full-time research assistantship; dissertation.

Graduate School of Design

Annual tuition: full-time $20,240.

Enrollment: full-time 525 (men 61%, women 39%). Faculty: full-time 32, part-time 66. Degrees conferred: M.Arch., M.L.A., M.Des.S., M.Arch. in Urban Design, M.L.A. in Urban Design, M.U.P., Dr. Design.

ADMISSION REQUIREMENTS. Transcripts, three letters of recommendation, GRE required in support of School's application. TOEFL required for international applicants. Interview not required. Apply to Graduate School of Design by January 3. Fall admission only. Application fee $60. Phone: (617)495-5453.

ADMISSION STANDARDS. Very selective.

FINANCIAL AID. Grants, Federal W/S, loans (master's candidates); grants, fellowships, teaching/research assistantships (doctoral candidates). Apply to the Dean's Office or appropriate department chair: no specified closing date. Use FAFSA and institutional FAF. No aid for special students.

DEGREE REQUIREMENTS. For M.Arch.: (first professional degree): 3½ years minimum in residence; terminal project. For M.Des.S., M.U.P.: 2 years minimum in residence. For M.Arch. (second professional degree): B.Arch. required for admission; 1½ years minimum in residence; terminal project. For M.L.A.: normally 3 years in residence; terminal project.

FIELDS OF STUDY.

Architecture.

Design Studies.

Landscape Architecture.

Urban Design and Planning.

Divinity School

Theology study since 1636. Coed. Annual tuition: full-time $12,830.

Enrollment: full-time 416, part-time 78 (men 35%, women 65%). Faculty: full-time 30, part-time 48. Degrees conferred: M.Div., M.T.S., Th.M., Th.D. The Ph.D. is offered through the Graduate School of Arts and Sciences.

ADMISSION REQUIREMENTS. Official transcripts, three letters of recommendation, personal statement required in support of School's application. Interview not required. Accepts transfer applicants. Apply by February 1 (Fall), December 1 (Spring) to Dean of Admissions of School. Rolling admissions process. Application fee $45. Phone: (617)495-5796; fax: (617)495-9489.

ADMISSION STANDARDS. Selective. Usual minimum average: 3.0 (A = 4).

FINANCIAL AID. Annual awards from institutional funds: scholarships, teaching fellowships (for advanced students only), Federal W/S, loans. Apply to Dean of Admission by January 10 for Th.M., Th.D.; by February 15 for M.Div. Use FAFAS and institutional supplementary form. Phone: (617)495-5772. About 81% of students receive aid in the form of grants and/or loans. Aid rarely available to part-time students or Th.M. students.

DEGREE REQUIREMENTS. For M.Div.: 24 half-courses minimum, at least two years in full-time residence; distribution and arts of ministry requirements, senior thesis; reading knowledge of either Hebrew, Greek, Latin, German, French, or Spanish. For M.T.S.: 16 half-courses minimum, two years in full-time residence; distribution requirements; reading knowledge of one language of theological scholarship. For Th.M.: eight half-courses minimum in residence; reading knowledge of two of Hebrew, Greek, Latin, German, French, or Spanish; one major or two smaller research papers; final oral exam. For Th.D.: two years minimum beyond the M.Div. in full-time residence; seven-year limit for degree; knowledge of one classical and two modern languages indicated for M.Div., Th.M.; general exam; dissertation; final oral exam.

Graduate School of Education

Established 1920. Tuition: per semester $9230. Limited on-campus housing available. Contact Director of Student Affairs for on- and off-campus information. Phone: (617)495-8035. Day care facilities available.

Enrollment: full-time 869, part-time 270. Faculty: full-time 42, part-time 52. Degrees conferred: Ed.M., C.A.S., Ed.D.

ADMISSION REQUIREMENTS. Transcripts, GRE or MAT, three academic/professional references, statement of purpose required in support of School's application. Interview not required. TOEFL, TWE required for international applicants. Graduates of unaccredited institutions and transfer applicants not considered. Doctoral applicants apply to the Office of Admissions by January 2; January 10 for all others. Admits Fall only. Application fee $60. Phone: (617)495-3414; fax: (617)496-3577; E-mail: admit@hugse2.harvard.edu.

ADMISSION STANDARDS. Competitive to very selective.

FINANCIAL AID. Five hundred thirteen grants, 91 fellowships, 50 research assistantships, 220 teaching assistantships, Federal W/S, loans. Approved for VA benefits. Apply to the Office of Financial Aid; no specified closing date. Phone: (617)495-3416; fax: (617)495-0840. Use FAFSA, institutional FAF, CSS profile (doctoral candidates). Students enrolled half-time or more in the Ed.D., Ed.M., and C.A.S. programs are eligible to receive financial aid.

DEGREE REQUIREMENTS. For Ed.M.: One year or equivalent in residence; no transfer of credit permitted; no language, thesis, or comprehensive exam requirement; ordinarily, requirements must be met through full-time study during the academic year. For C.A.S.: one year or equivalent in residence beyond the master's; full-time study during academic year ordinarily required, but exceptions are considered; no language or thesis requirement. For Ed.D.: two years or equivalent beyond the bachelor's, at least two semesters in full-time attendance; written qualifying paper; thesis; final oral exam; no language requirement.

FIELDS OF STUDY.
Administration Planning and Social Policy. Ed.D., C.A.S., Ed.M.
Human Development and Psychology. Ed.D., C.A.S., M.Ed.
Individualized. Ed.M. only.
International Education.
Language and Literacy.
Learning and Teaching. Ed.D., C.A.S., M.Ed.
Risk and Prevention.
Teacher Certification Programs. Ed.M., C.A.S. only.
Technology Education.
Urban Superintendents Program.

John Fitzgerald Kennedy School of Government

Annual tuition: full-time $19,770.
Enrollment: full-time about 700; no part-time. Faculty: full-time 70. Degrees conferred: M.P.A., M.P.P., M.P.P.-M.U.P., Ph.D.

ADMISSION REQUIREMENTS. Transcripts, three letters of reference, GRE or GMAT, responses to essay questions required in support of School's application. Seven years of administrative public interest work required for Mid-Career M.P.A. TOEFL required for foreign applicants. Interview not required. Graduates of unaccredited colleges normally not considered. Apply to Admissions Office by January 8 for M.P.P. and Ph.D.; Mid-Career M.P.A. has rolling admissions from January 15 through May 14. Admits Fall only. Application fee $80. Phone: (617)495-1155.

ADMISSION STANDARDS. Competitive.

FINANCIAL AID. Scholarships, assistantships, fellowships, Federal W/S, loans. Apply to Office of Financial Aid by February 12 for M.P.P. and April 16 for Mid-Career M.P.A. Use FAFSA and CSS profile. Phone: (617)495-1152.

DEGREE REQUIREMENTS. For M.P.P.: two years of full-time study; 18 units of academic credit, 10 in required courses. For the M.P.A.: one year of full-time study; 8 semester-length courses.

FIELDS OF STUDY.
City Planning and Public Policy.
Political Economy and Government.
Public Administration.
Public Policy.
Note: Students choose courses from Kennedy School of Government, as well as from other Harvard graduate and professional schools, the Fletcher School of Law and Diplomacy at Tufts University, and MIT.

School of Public Health

Founded 1922. Annual tuition: full-time $19,800, half-time $9420. On-campus housing available. See housing listing above.
Enrollment: full-time 526, part-time 156 (men 45%, women 55%). Faculty: full-time 155, part-time 115. Degrees conferred: S.M., M.P.H., M.O.H., S.D., Dr.P.H.

ADMISSION REQUIREMENTS. Official transcripts, three letters of reference, GRE (requests to substitute MCAT/DAT/GMAT/LSAT are normally approved) required in support of School's application. TOEFL required for international applicants. Graduates of unaccredited institutions not considered. Apply by January 1 (priority deadline) to Office of Admissions. Admits Fall only. Application fee $60. Phone: (617)432-1031.

ADMISSION STANDARDS. Competitive. Usual minimum average: 2.75 (A = 4).

FINANCIAL AID. Fellowships, research/teaching assistantships, tuition grants, Federal W/S, loans. Apply by March 15 to Director of Financial Aid. Use FAFSA. Phone: (617)432-1867. Aid rarely available to part-time or foreign students.

DEGREE REQUIREMENTS. For M.P.H.: 40 credit units minimum in residence; applicants ordinarily must be graduates of schools of medicine, dental medicine, veterinary health, law, or hold a doctorate in field related to public health. For S.M.: 40 units minimum in residence for students with prior doctoral (and some master's) degree or 80 units minimum in residence for students with relevant bachelor's degrees. For M.O.H.: 40 units minimum in residence; applicants must hold M.D. For S.D.: two years in residence; applicants must hold bachelor's or master's degree depending on department; qualifying exam; thesis; final oral exam. For Dr.P.H.: essentially the same as the S.D.; applicants must be graduates of schools of medicine, dental medicine, or veterinary medicine, or hold another doctorate in field related to public health; applicants must also hold M.P.H.

FIELDS OF STUDY.
Biological Sciences.
Biostatistics.
Cancer Biology.
Carcinogenesis.
Environmental and Occupational Health.
Epidemiology.
Health and Social Behavior.
Health Care and Organizational Management.
Health Policy and Management.
Immunology.
International Health.
Maternal and Child Health.

Molecular & Cellular Toxicology.
Molecular Genetics.
Nutritional Biochemistry.
Occupational Health.
Population and International Health.
Public Management and Community Health.
Quantitative Methods.
Radiobiology.
Radiological Health.
Respiratory Biology.
Tropical Public Health.
Virology.

Law School

Established 1817. Semester system. Law library: over 1,500,000 volumes.

Annual tuition: $21,700. Total average cost for all other expenses: $13,500.

Enrollment: first-year class 550. Total full-time J.D. students 1646 (men 60%, women 40%) LL.M. and S.J.D. students 160. Faculty: full-time 101, part-time 53. Degrees conferred: J.D., LL.M., S.J.D.

ADMISSION REQUIREMENTS. LSDAS Law School report, bachelor's degree, transcripts, references, LSAT, personal statement required in support of application. Interview not required. Accepts transfer applicants. Graduates of unaccredited colleges not considered. Apply to Admissions Office of School after September 15, before February 1. Admits Fall only. Application fee $65 (J.D. applicants only). Phone: (617)495-3109.

ADMISSION STANDARDS. Competitive. Accepts about 10–12% of total annual applicants.

FINANCIAL AID. Scholarships, fellowships, assistantships, Federal W/S, loans. Apply by March 1 to Financial Aid Office (entering J.D. students), by February 1 to Chair of Division of Graduate Studies (postbaccalaureate students). Use FAFSA. All students receive aid who demonstrate need according to a combination of Federal and institutional guidelines.

DEGREE REQUIREMENTS. For J.D.: three years minimum in residence; advanced standing for study completed in other law schools considered in exceptional cases; final written paper. For LL.M.: at least 24 credits beyond the J.D.; one year in full-time residence; final written essay or thesis. For S.J.D.: one year minimum in full-time residence; dissertation; final oral exam.

Medical School

Established 1782. Located in Boston (02115-6092).

Annual tuition: $24,150, student fees $1610. Total average figure for all other expenses: $9055. Limited housing available. Enrollment: first-year class 165; total 688 (men 47%, women 53%). Faculty: full- and part-time 3000. Degrees conferred: M.D., M.D.-M.P.H., M.D.-Ph.D. (Medical Scientist Training Program in cooperation with Massachusetts Institute of Technology.)

ADMISSION REQUIREMENTS. Transcripts, MCAT, recommendations, essay required in support of application. Interview by invitation. Applicants must have completed at least two years of college study, but four recommended. Does not have EDP. Apply after June 15, before October 15 to Director of Admissions. Application fee $70. Phone: (617)432-1550; fax: (617)432-3307.

ADMISSION STANDARDS. Competitive. Accepts about 7% of total annual applicants. Approximately 9% are state residents.

FINANCIAL AID. Scholarships, loans. Apply to Director of Financial Aid after acceptance. Use GAPSFAS.

DEGREE REQUIREMENTS. For M.D.: satisfactory completion of four-year program. For M.P.H., Ph.D.: see Graduate School listing above.

FIELDS OF GRADUATE STUDY.
Biochemistry.
Biomedical Engineering.
Biophysics.
Cell Biology.
Genetics.
Immunology.
Microbiology.
Molecular Biology.
Neurobiology.
Neurosciences.
Pathology.
Pharmacology.
Public Administration.
Public Health.
Toxicology.
Virology.

School of Dental Medicine

Established 1867. Located in Boston (02115). Medical-dental library: 412,000 volumes. Annual tuition: residents $23,192, nonresidents $32,192. Total average academic costs for all other first-year expenses: $2319. Limited on-campus housing for single students only. Average academic year housing cost: $11,905. For off-campus housing, contact Assistant Dean for Student Affairs.

Enrollment: first-year class 25 (men 60%, women 40%); postgraduates 65. No part-time students. Faculty: full-time 14, part-time 123. Degrees conferred: D.M.D., D.M.D.-M.P.H., D.M.D.-M.P.P., D.M.D.-M.M.Sc., D.M.D.-D.M.Sc., D.M.D.-M.D.

ADMISSION REQUIREMENTS. AADSAS, official transcripts, high school and college faculty evaluations, SAT and DAT required in support of School's application. Interview by invitation only. Students with three years undergraduate preparation are considered, but normally four years of college are expected. Accepts transfer applicants from other dental and medical schools. Graduates of unaccredited colleges not considered. Apply to Assistant Dean after June 1, before January 1. Application fee $50. Phone: (617)432-1443.

ADMISSION STANDARDS. Competitive. Usual minimum average: 2.8 (A = 4). Accepts 15–20% of total annual applicants. Approximately 20% are state residents.

FINANCIAL AID. Scholarships, grants, tuition waivers, loans. Apply by July 1 to Office of Financial Aid. Use FAFSA and GAPSFAS. Phone: (617)432-1527. About 60% of students receive aid other than loans from School.

DEGREE REQUIREMENTS. For D.M.D.: 53 months minimum, normally at least two years in full-time residence; transfer students occasionally permitted to enter in fourth year. For M.P.H., M.P.P., M.M.Sc., D.M.Sc.: see Graduate Schools listings above.

FIELDS OF GRADUATE STUDY.
Endodontics.
Maxillofacial Surgery.
Oral Biology.
Oral Pathology.
Oral Surgery.
Orthodontics.
Pediatric Dentistry.
Periodontology.
Prosthetic Dentistry.

HAWAII PACIFIC UNIVERSITY
Honolulu, Hawaii 98623-2785

Coed. Private control. Semester system. Library: 122,000 volumes, 200,000 microforms, 1700 current periodicals, 40 PCs.

Annual tuition: full-time $7100; per credit $296. On-campus housing for single graduate students; none for married students. Average academic year housing cost: $66 (including board). Contact Director of Residence Life for both on- and off-campus housing information. Phone: (808)233-3184.

Graduate Studies

Enrollment: full-time 408, part-time 526. University faculty teaching graduate students: full-time 33, part-time 31. Degrees conferred: M.B.A., M.A. in H.R.M., M.S.I S.

ADMISSION REQUIREMENTS. Official transcripts, GMAT required in support of application. TOEFL required for international applicants. Accepts transfer applicants. Graduates of unaccredited institutions not considered. Apply to the Graduate Admissions Coordinator at least one month prior to the date registration. Rolling admissions process. Application $50. Phone: (808)544-1120, fax. (808)544-0280.

ADMISSION STANDARDS. Selective. Usual minimum average: 3.0 (A = 4).

FINANCIAL AID. Assistantships, Federal W/S, loans. Approved for VA benefits. Apply after January 1 to Financial Aid Office; no specified closing date. Use FAFSA. Aid sometimes available for part-time students.

DEGREE REQUIREMENTS. For master's: 36–45 semester hours minimum, at least 30 in residence; thesis/nonthesis option.

FIELDS OF STUDY.
Accounting.
Finance.
Human Resource Management. M.A. in H.R.M.
Information Systems. M.S.I.S.
International Business.
Management.
Marketing.
Not-for-Profit Management.
Travel Industry Management.

UNIVERSITY OF HAWAII AT MANOA
Honolulu, Hawaii 96822

Founded 1907. Coed. State control. Semester system. Special facilities: Institute for Astronomy; Computing Center; English Language Institute; Environmental Center; Foreign Languages Laboratories; Hawaii Agricultural Experiment Station; Hawaii Cooperative Fisheries Unit; Hawaii Institute of Geophysics; Hawaii Institute of Marine Biology; Industrial Relations Center; Institute for Astronomy; Instructional Resources Service Center; Laboratory of Sensory Sciences; JKK Look Laboratory of Oceanographic Engineering; Harold L. Lyon Arboretum; Pacific and Asian Linguistics Institute; Pacific Biomedical Research Center; Population Genetics Laboratory; Social Science Research Institute; Social Welfare Development and Research Center; Speech and Hearing Clinic; Survey Research Office; University of Hawaii Press; Waikiki Aquarium; Water Resources Research Center. Library: 2,718,000 volumes, 5,488,718,000 microforms, 23,000 current periodicals, 105 PCs.

Annual tuition: full-time, resident $3174, nonresident $8688. On-campus housing for about 1300 single students, with preferences given to Hawaii residents. No on-campus housing facilities for married students. Average academic year housing cost: $4090 (including board) for single students, $8100 (including board) for married students. Contact Student Housing Office for both on- and off-campus housing information. Phone: (808)956-8177.

Graduate Division

Enrollment: full-time 2400 (men 45%, women 55%), part-time 2500 (men 40%, women 60%). University faculty: full- and part-time 1765. Degrees conferred: M.Arch., M.A., M.Acc., M.B.A., M.Ed., M.Ed.T., M.F.A., M.L.S., M.M., M.Mus., M.P.A., M.P.H., M.P.S., M.S., M.S.W., M.U.R.P., Ed.D., Dr.P.H., Ph.D.

ADMISSION REQUIREMENTS. Two official transcripts required in support of application. MAT required for some departments; GMAT required by College of Business Administration. GRE required by some fields of study, recommended in others. Letters of recommendation required by some departments. Interview not required. TOEFL required for international applicants. Accepts transfer applicants. Graduates of unaccredited colleges not considered. Apply to Admissions Office, Graduate Division for most programs before January 15; internationals, February 1, U.S. citizens and permanent residents (Fall); August 1, internationals, September 1, U.S. citizens and permanent residents (Spring). Phone: (808)956-8544.

ADMISSION STANDARDS. Selective. Usual minimum average: 3.0 (A = 4).

FINANCIAL AID. Scholarships; fellowships, assistantships for teaching/research, Federal W/S, loans. Approved for VA benefits. Apply to Dean of Graduate Division for scholarships, fellowships; for East-West Center scholarships, write to East-West Center; to appropriate department chair by February 1 for assistantships; to Financial Aid Office for all other programs. Use FAFSA. About 32% of students receive aid other than loans from University, about 50% from all sources. Aid available for part-time students.

DEGREE REQUIREMENTS. For M.A., M.S., M.Ed.: 28 credit hours minimum plus thesis, or 30 credit hours minimum without thesis, at least half of credits in residence; qualifying exam; final written/oral exam. For M.F.A.: 30–34 credits minimum depending on field of study, final exhibition of creative work. For M.B.A.: 54 credits, thesis/nonthesis option. For M.L.S.: 36 credit hours minimum, thesis/nonthesis program. For M.S.W.: 52 credit hours minimum; final group project or thesis. For M.M.: 28 credit hours minimum plus thesis/composition, or 30 credit hours; performance; final oral exam. For M.P.H.: 30 credit hours minimum; nonthesis program; qualifying exam; final oral exam. For M.Arch., M.U.R.P.: 36 credit hours minimum; thesis. For Ph.D.: 3 semesters minimum in full-time residence beyond the master's; no specific credit requirements; reading knowledge of one foreign language is an optional requirement determined by each field of study; dissertation; final written/oral exam.

FIELDS OF STUDY.
Accounting. GMAT required for admission.
Agricultural Economics and Agribusiness. GRE recommended for admission; one language for Ph.D.
Agricultural Engineering. M.S. only.
Agronomy and Soil Science. GRE required for admission. M.S., Ph.D.
American Studies. GRE recommendations for admission. M.A., Ph.D.
Anatomy and Reproductive Biology. GRE Subject required for admission; Ph.D. only.
Animal Sciences. GRE Subject recommended for admission. M.S. only.

Anthropology. GRE required for admission; admits Fall only.

Architecture. ETS Architectural School Test, samples of work, documented evidence of 600 hours of supervised architecture work experience required for admission. M.Arch. only.

Art. M.A. in Asian, Pacific art history; M.F.A. (thesis program only) for creative studio work. M.A., M.F.A. only.

Asian Studies. GRE required for admission; interdepartmental program. M.A. only.

Astronomy. GRE Subject required for admission. M.S., Ph.D.

Biochemistry. GRE Subject required for admission. M.S., Ph.D.

Biomedical Engineering. M.S., Ph.D.

Biophysics. GRE Subject required for admission. M.S., Ph.D.

Botanical Sciences. GRE required for admission; one language for Ph.D.; fields include botany, plant pathology, plant physiology. M.S., Ph.D.

Business Administration. GMAT for admission. M.B.A. only.

Chemistry. GRE Subject required for admission of international applicants, recommended for domestic applicants; one language for Ph.D.

Civil Engineering. M.S. only; GRE required for admission.

Classics. M.A.

Clinical Psychology. GRE for admission. Ph.D. only.

Communication. M.A. only; GRE recommended.

Communication and Information Sciences. GRE for admission. Ph.D. only.

Computer Science. M.S., Ph.D.

Counselor and Guidance. GRE for admission. M.Ed. only.

Dance. M.A., M.F.A.

Drama and Theater. GRE required for admission. M.A. in theater. Ph.D.

Earth Science. M.S., Ph.D.

East Asian Languages and Literature. Includes Chinese, Japanese, Korean. GRE for admission. M.A., Ph.D.

Economics. GRE Subject required for admission.

Educational Administration. Course work or professional experience in education required for admission. Fall admission only. M.Ed.

Educational Psychology. GRE required for admission; proficiency in computer language for Ph.D.; Fall admission only for Ph.D.

Educational Technology. GRE Subject for admission. M.Ed. only.

Electrical Engineering. GRE required for admission to Ph.D. program, recommended for M.S. program.

Elementary Education. GRE Subject for admission. M.Ed. only.

English. GRE for M.A., GRE Subject for Ph.D.

Entomology. GRE Subject recommended. One language for Ph.D.

Environmental and Occupational Health. M.P.H.

Environmental Engineering. M.S.

European Languages and Literature. Includes classics, French, German, Russian, Spanish. M.A. only.

Food Science and Technology. GRE Subject recommended. M.S. only.

Genetics. M.S., Ph.D.

Geography. GRE required for admission; one language for Ph.D., M.A., Ph.D.

Geology and Geophysics. GRE Subject required for admission; one language for Ph.D.

Health Services Management and Hospital Administration. M.S.

History. GRE required for admission; one language for M.A.; two languages for Ph.D.

Horticulture. GRE for M.S., GRE Subject required for Ph.D.

Information Sciences. GRE Subject recommended, knowledge of programming language required for admission; M.S. only.

International Health. M.P.H.

Library Studies and Information Studies. GRE required for admission. M.L.I.S. only.

Linguistics. GRE required for admission; one language for M.A. Two languages for Ph.D.

Marine Biology. M.S., Ph.D.

Mathematics. GRE Subject recommended for admission; two languages for Ph.D.

Mechanical Engineering. GRE Subject required.

Meteorology. GRE required for Ph.D.; one language for Ph.D. M.S., Ph.D.

Microbiology. GRE Subject required for admission; one language for Ph.D.

Music. GRE recommended for admission; thesis program only for M.A. in dance ethnology, ethnomusicology, musicology, music education, theory; nonthesis program for M.A. in performance only; M.Mus. in composition and performance; one language for M.A. thesis program. M.A., M.Mus. only.

Nursing. Bachelor's degree in nursing, licensure in Hawaii for practice of nursing, GRE required for admission; areas of specialization for M.S.: mental-health–maternal-child nursing, medical-surgical nursing. M.S. only.

Nursing Administration. M.S.

Nutritional Sciences. GRE recommended for admission. M.S. only.

Ocean Engineering. GRE Subject required for admission to M.S. program; master's degree, GRE required for admission to Ph.D. program; one language for Ph.D.

Oceanography. GRE Subject required for admission; one language, digital computing for Ph.D.

Pacific Islands Studies. GRE required for admission; one language for M.A. M.A. only.

Philosophy. GRE recommended for native English speakers. Areas: Western, Asian, Comparative; two Western languages for Ph.D.

Physics. GRE Subject required for admission. M.S., Ph.D.

Political Science. GRE required for admission.

Psychology. GRE Subject required for admission; admits Fall only.

Public Administration. M.P.A. only.

Public and Community Health. GRE recommended for admission; admits Fall only; M.P.H. only.

Religion (Asian). M.A. only.

Second Language Acquisition. GRE for admission. Ph.D. only.

Secondary Education. GRE Subject required for admission. M.Ed. only.

Social Work. GRE for admission for Ph.D.; 52 credits for M.S.W.

Sociology. GRE required for admission. M.A., Ph.D. only.

Speech. GRE for admission. M.A. only.

Speech Pathology and Audiology. GRE for admission. Thirty-three credits plus thesis or 44 credits for nonthesis program for M.S. M.S. only.

Teaching English as a Second Language. GRE required for admission; one semester of a new language required; M.A. only.

Travel Industry Management. GMAT for admission. M.P.S. only.

Urban and Regional Planning. GRE recommended for admission. M.U.R.P. only.

Zoology. GRE Subject required for admission; one language for Ph.D. M.S., Ph.D.

William S. Richardson School of Law

Established 1973. Semester system. Located at Manoa (96822). Library: 242,400 volumes. Library has LEXIS, NEXIS, WESTLAW, CALI.

Annual tuition: resident $4800, nonresident $12,744. Limited on-campus housing. Apply to Director of Student Housing; for off-campus housing, apply to Off-campus Housing Office. Total average annual additional expense: $8500.

Enrollment: first-year class 77; total 243 (men 49%, women 51%). Faculty: full-time 16, part-time 27. Degrees conferred: J.D., J.D.-M.A. (Asian Studies), J.D.-M.B.A., J.D.-M.U.R.P.

ADMISSION REQUIREMENTS. LSDAS Law School report, bachelor's degree, transcripts, LSAT, recommendations required in support of application. Accepts transfer applicants on a space available basis only. Graduates of unaccredited institutions are not considered. Preference given to state residents. Apply to Office of Admissions by February 16 (firm). Application fee none. Phone: (808)956-3000.

ADMISSION STANDARDS. Selective. Admits about 20% of total annual applicants.

FINANCIAL AID. Scholarships, Federal W/S, loans. Apply by March 1 to Director of Financial Aid. Use FAFSA. About 90% of students receive some aid from School.

DEGREE REQUIREMENTS. For J.D.: satisfactory completion of 89 credit hours of study.

John A. Burns School of Medicine

First class entered September 1967. Located on Manoa Campus. Annual tuition: resident $9107, nonresident $23,373. Total average figure for all other expenses: $9000. Enrollment: first-year class 56 (2 EDP), total 235 (men, 46%, women 54%); post-graduates 188. Faculty: full-time 107, part-time 101. Degrees conferred: M.D., M.D.-M.S., M.D.-Ph.D.

ADMISSION REQUIREMENTS. AMCAS report, MCAT, three years of college, recommendations, and the completion of at least 90 credits are required. Interview by invitation. An evaluation of what the potential student might contribute to the health profession in the Pacific is an integral part of the selection process. Has EDP; apply between June 15 and August 1. Apply through AMCAS after June 15, before December 1. AMCAS application fee only. Phone: (808)956-5446; fax: (808)956-9547.

ADMISSION STANDARDS. Competitive. Accepts about 10% of total annual applicants. Approximately 95% are state residents.

FINANCIAL AID. Scholarships, loan fund. Apply after acceptance to University of Hawaii Financial Aids Office. About 60% of students receive some aid from School and outside sources.

DEGREE REQUIREMENTS. For M.D.: satisfactory completion of four-year program and passing Parts I and II of National Boards.

FIELDS OF GRADUATE STUDY.
Anatomy.
Biochemistry.
Biophysics.
Genetics.
Molecular Biology.
Pharmacology.
Physiology.
Reproductive Biology.
Tropical Medicine.

UNIVERSITY OF HEALTH SCIENCES
Kansas City, Missouri 64124-2395

College of Osteopathic Medicine

Founded 1916, relocated to current location in 1921. Coed. Private control. Library: 60,000 volumes, has MEDLINE, CANCERLINE, BIOETHIC, HEALTH, TOXLINE, DIALOG, OCLC. No on-campus housing available. Average academic year housing cost: $350 per month. Contact the Admissions Office for off-campus housing information.

Annual tuition: $22,200. Enrollment: first-year class 180, total 640 (men 74%, women 26%). Faculty: full-time 28, part-time 70. Degree conferred: D.O.

ADMISSION REQUIREMENTS. AACOMAS report, bachelor's degree preferred, transcripts, MCAT, letters of recommendation from premed advisory committee, evaluation from a

physician (preferably a D.O.) required in support of College's application. Interview by invitation only. Graduates of unaccredited college not considered. Apply by March 1. Admits first-year students Fall only. Application fee: $35. Phone: (800)234-4UHS, (816)283-2300; fax: (816)283-2303.

ADMISSION STANDARDS. Selective. Accepts approximately 15% of annual applicants. Usual minimum average: 2.75. Mean GPA: 3.2 (A = 4).

FINANCIAL AID. Scholarships, fellowships, loans. Apply after acceptance to Office of Financial Aid. Use FAFSA.

DEGREE REQUIREMENT. For D.O.: satisfactory completion of four-year program.

HEBREW COLLEGE
Brookline, Massachusetts 02146-5495
http://shamash.org/hc

Founded 1921. Located adjacent to Boston. Coed. Private control. Semester system. Library: 100,000 volumes, 2500 microforms.

Tuition: $295 per credit. No on-campus housing. For off-campus information: Phone: (617)279-4944.

Department of Graduate Studies

Graduate study since 1951. Enrollment: full-time 20, part-time 40. Graduate faculty: full-time 4, part-time 14. Degrees conferred: M.A. Judaic Studies, M.J.Ed.

ADMISSION REQUIREMENTS. Transcripts, GRE, three letters of reference, essay, bachelor's degree required in support of department's application. Interview recommended for admission. TOEFL required for international applicants. Phone: (617)278-4944; fax: (617)264-9264.

FINANCIAL AID. Internal scholarships, loans available. Approved for VA benefits. Financial aid; aid available for part-time students. Phone: (617)278-4944.

DEGREE REQUIREMENTS. For MA: 39 credit hours minimum, thesis. For M.J.Ed.: 45 credit hours minimum; program normally requires 2½–3 years of study.

FIELDS OF STUDY.
Hebrew Literature.
Jewish Education.
Jewish History.
Jewish Thought and Philosophy.
Rabbinics.

HENDERSON STATE UNIVERSITY
Arkadelphia, Arkansas 71999-0001
http://www.hsu.edu

Founded 1890. Located 75 miles SW of Little Rock. Coed. State control. Semester system. Library: 250,000 volumes, 192,00 microforms.

Tuition: per semester hour, resident $100, nonresident $199. On-campus housing for 600 men, 600 women, 27 married students. Average academic year housing cost: $1500 (room and board) for single students. $275 per month for married students. Apply to Dean, Residence Life. Phone: (501)230-5070.

Graduate Program

Graduate study since 1954. Enrollment: full- and part-time 330. Faculty teaching graduate students: full-time 110, part-time 4. Degrees conferred: M.S.E., M.S., M B.A.

ADMISSION REQUIREMENTS. Transcripts, GRE/GMAT/MAT required in support of application. TOEFL required for foreign applicants. Accepts transfer applicants. Graduates of unaccredited institutions not considered. Apply to Dean well in advance of registration. Application fee none. Phone: (501)230-5126; fax: (501)230-5094.

ADMISSION STANDARDS. Selective. Usual minimum average: 2.7 (A = 4).

FINANCIAL AID. Annual awards from institutional funds: 250 scholarships, 35 teaching/research assistantships, Federal W/S, loans. Approved for VA benefits. Apply to Dean of Graduate School; no specified closing date. Use FAFSA. Phone: (501)230-5094; fax: (501)230-5144.

DEGREE REQUIREMENTS. For master's: 30–48 semester hours minimum, at least 24–42 in residence.

FIELDS OF STUDY.
Business Administration.
Community Counseling.
Education. Includes art, biology, counseling, elementary, English, mathematics, physical, school administration, social sciences, special.
Sociology.

HOFSTRA UNIVERSITY

Hempstead, New York 11550-1090
http://www.Hofstra.Edu

Founded 1935. Located 25 miles E of New York City. Coed. Private control. Semester system. Library: more than 1,427,000 volumes, 1,000,000 microforms, 5637 periodicals.

Tuition: per credit $423. On-campus housing for both single and married students. Average academic year housing cost: $4300 (including board). Contact Specialty Housing Coordinator. Phone: (516)463-6936. Day care facilities available.

Graduate Division

Graduate study since 1951. Enrollment: full-time 528, part-time 2616. Faculty teaching graduate students: full-time 174, part-time 143. Degrees conferred: M.A., M.S., M.B.A., M.P.S., J.D.-M.B.A., C.A.S., Professional Diploma, Ed.D., Psy.D., Ph.D.

ADMISSION REQUIREMENTS. Transcripts, GRE/MAT/NTE/NYSTLE required in support of Divisional application. TOEFL required for international applicants. Interview, recommendations required by some departments. Accepts transfer applicants. Graduates of unaccredited institutions not considered. Apply to Admissions Office at least sixty days prior to registration. Application fee $40, $75 for international applicants. Phone: (516)463-6700, fax: (516)560-7600.

ADMISSION STANDARDS. Competitive to very competitive. Usual minimum average: 3.0 (A = 4).

FINANCIAL AID. Scholarships, twenty teaching assistantships, Federal W/S, loans. Approved for VA benefits. Apply to appropriate department chairman for scholarships or assistantships; to the Financial Aid Office of all other programs. Use FAFSA. Phone: (516)463-6680; fax: (516)463-4936. Aid available to part-time students.

DEGREE REQUIREMENTS. For M.A.: 30–36 semester hours minimum, at least 24 in residence; master's essay; one language or knowledge of statistics for many majors; oral/written comprehensive exam. For M.S.: 30–37 semester hours minimum, at least 24 in residence; comprehensive exam or alternative. For M.B.A.: 36 hours minimum, at least 24 in residence; thesis/nonthesis option; comprehensive exam. For C.A.S., Professional Diploma: 30 hours beyond the master's. For Ed.D.: 90 semester hours minimum; preliminary exam, research project; final oral exam. For Ph.D.: 93 semester hours minimum, at least one year in full-time residence; preliminary exam; reading knowledge of one foreign language; dissertation; final oral exam.

FIELDS OF STUDY.
Biology. Includes electron microscopy, human cytogenetics, molecular biology, oral biology.
Business Administration. Includes accounting, banking and finance, business computer information systems, international business, management, marketing, taxation. GMAT for admission. M.B.A. only.
Computer Science. GRE for admission. M.A., M.S.
Counselor Education. GRE interview, three recommendations, essay on professional objectives for admission. M.S., Professional Diploma.
Creative Arts Therapy. Competency in art; three recommendations for admission.
Education. M.A., M.S. in 12 areas.
Educational Administration. MAT, GRE, three recommendations, statement of career goals, resume. M.S., Professional Diploma, Ed.D.
Elementary Education. M.A., M.S. only.
English. M.A., English literature, full-time; M.A., English and American literature, part-time only.
Foundations of Education. Interview for admission. M.S. only.
Health Administration. Minimum 2.5 GPA, interview for admission. M.A.
Health Education. Teacher certification required, 2.5 GPA minimum for admission. Twenty-four hours in full-time residence. M.S. only.
Humanities. M.A. only.
Liberal Arts and Education. M.A. in twenty-four areas.
Marriage and Family Counseling. M.A.
Mathematics. 2 recommendations for admission. M.A., M.S.
Psychology. GRE/Subject, interview (Ph.D. programs) for admission. Application deadline February 1. Includes industrial, organization (M.A. only); clinical, school (Ph.D. only).
Reading. MAT or GRE or NTE or NYSTCE, two recommendations, interview for admissions. Complete application by January 15 for doctoral programs (admits Fall only). M.A., M.S., Professional Diploma, Ed.D., Ph.D.
Rehabilitation Counselor. Four recommendations, essay, resume, interview for admission. M.S. only.
School-Community Psychology. Psy.D.
Secondary Education. M.A., M.S. only.
Special Education. Three recommendations, interview for admission. Includes emotionally disturbed, physically handicapped, mentally retarded. M.S., M.S., Professional Diploma.
Speech Pathology and Audiology. Three recommendations, interview for admission. M.A. only.

School of Law

First class entered 1970. Semester system. Library: 395,000 volumes. Library has LEXIS, NEXIS, WESTLAW, DIALOG.

Annual tuition: $19,840. On-campus housing available for single and married students. Average housing cost: $5900–$7000. Apply to Director, Housing Office. Phone: (516)468-6930.

Enrollment: first-year class 294; total enrollment 835 (men 59%, women 41%). Faculty: full-time 42, part-time 2. Degrees conferred: J.D., J.D.-M.B.A.

ADMISSION REQUIREMENTS. LSDAS Law School report, bachelor's degree, transcripts, LSAT required in support of application. Graduates of unaccredited colleges not considered. Apply to Admissions Office after October 1, before April 15. Admits Fall only. Application fee $50. Phone: (516)463-5916.

ADMISSION STANDARDS. Selective. Accepts about 20% of total annual applicants.

FINANCIAL AID. Scholarships, grants, full and partial tuition waivers, assistantships, Federal W/S, loans. Apply to University Financial Aid Office by May 15. Use FAFSA.

DEGREE REQUIREMENTS. For J D.: satisfactory completion of three-year (87 credit hours) program.

HOLLINS COLLEGE
Roanoke, Virginia 24020-1688
http://www.hollins.edu

Established 1842. Located 6 miles N of Roanoke. Coed. Private control. Semester system. Library: 220,000 volumes, 175,000 microforms.

Annual tuition: full-time $14,560, per credit varies by program. No on-campus housing for graduate students.

Graduate School

Enrollment: full-time 76, part-time 168 (men 10%, women 90%). Graduate faculty: full-time 36, part-time 9. Degrees conferred: M A., M.A.L.S., M.A.T., C.A.S.

ADMISSION REQUIREMENTS. Transcripts, GRE Subject Tests required in support of School's application. Interview not required. TOEFL required for international applicants. Transfer applicants, graduates of unaccredited colleges not considered. Apply to Office of Admissions by March 15, one month prior to registration for other sessions. Application fee $25. Phone: (540)362-6575; fax: (540)362-6288.

ADMISSION STANDARDS. Competitive. Usual minimum average: 3.0 (A = 4)

FINANCIAL AID. Fifteen scholarships, twenty-three grants, ten research fellowships, eleven work stipends, Federal W/S, loans. Approved for VA benefits. Apply by April 15 to Chair of Graduate Council for scholarships, grants, fellowships; to Financial Aid Office for all other programs. Phone: (540)362-6332; fax: (540)362-6093. Use FAFSA and Institutional FAF. All M.A. graduate students receive aid from College. About 50% of students receive aid other than loans from College and outside sources.

DEGREE REQUIREMENTS. For M.A., M.A.L.S., M.A.T.: 30 semester hours minimum; final oral/written exam; thesis/final document. For C.A.S.: 30 semester hours minimum beyond master's; special project.

FIELDS OF STUDY.
Children's Literature. Primarily a summer program. Four to five summer sessions for completion of degree requirements.
Computer Science.
Creative Writing.
English. One language for M.A.

Humanities.
Liberal Studies.
Psychology.
Social Science.
Teaching. At least three years of teaching experience required for admissions.

HOLY NAMES COLLEGE
Oakland, California 94619-1699

Founded 1868. Private control. Roman Catholic. Semester system. Library: 109,557 volumes, 36,570 microforms, 10 PC workstations in library.

Tuition: per credit $375. On-campus housing for single students only. Average academic year room and board cost: $5930. Apply to Director of Residents for off-campus housing information. Phone: (510)436-1292.

Graduate Division

Graduate study since 1956. Enrollment: full-time 111, part-time 182 (men 73, women 220). College faculty teaching graduate students: full-time 21, part-time 31. Degrees conferred: M.A., M.S., M.M. in Mus. Ed., M.Ed., M.B.A.

ADMISSION REQUIREMENTS. Two transcripts, two letters of recommendation required in support of Divisional application. TOEFL required for international applicants. Interview and NTE required for Education, Clinical Psychology, Pastoral Counseling. Graduates of unaccredited colleges not considered. Apply to Graduate Admission Office at least six to eight weeks prior to registration. Application fee $30. Phone: (510)436-1317; fax: (510)436-1325.

ADMISSION STANDARDS. Selective. Minimum average: 2.6 cumulative, 3.0 in major (A = 4).

FINANCIAL AID. Annual awards from institutional funds: Kodaly grants, Federal W/S, loans. Apply to Director of Financial Aid by March 2. Use FAFSA. Phone: (510)436-1327. About 80% of students receive financial aid. Aid sometime available for part-time students.

DEGREE REQUIREMENTS. For master's: 30–36 semester hours; thesis, project or final comprehensive exam, recital.

FIELDS OF STUDY.
Business Administration.
Counseling Psychology.
Culture and Spirituality.
Education.
English.
Music. Includes performance, piano pedagogy, music education with Kodaly emphasis; preliminary qualifying exam.
Pastoral Counseling.

HOOD COLLEGE
Frederick, Maryland 21701-8587
http://www.hood.edu

College founded 1895. Located 45 miles from Washington, D.C. Private. Semester system. Library: 165,000 volumes, 385,000 microforms.

Tuition: per credit hour $245. No on-campus housing available.

Graduate School

Enrollment: full-time 28, part-time 903 (men 372, women 559). Faculty: full-time 24, part-time 6. Degrees conferred: M.A., M.B.A., M.S.

ADMISSION REQUIREMENTS. Transcripts required in support of application. GMAT required for Business applicants. TOEFL required for international applicants. Interview recommended. Accepts transfer applicants. Graduates of unaccredited colleges not considered. Apply to Dean of Graduate School. Application fee $30. Phone: (301)696-3600; fax: (301)696-3597.

ADMISSION STANDARDS. Selective. Usual minimum average: 2.5 (A = 4).

FINANCIAL AID. Limited to loans. Phone: (301)696-3411.

DEGREE REQUIREMENTS. For M.A., M.S.: 30 credit hours minimum; thesis required in some programs; comprehensive written exam. For M.B.A.: 36 credit hours minimum.

FIELDS OF STUDY.
Administration and Management.
Applied Behavioral and Social Research.
Biomedical Sciences.
Business Administration.
Computer and Information Sciences.
Early Childhood Education.
Elementary Education.
Elementary School Science and Mathematics.
Environmental Biology.
Gerontology.
Home Economics.
Psychology.
Reading Specialist.
Secondary Education.
Special Education.

UNIVERSITY OF HOUSTON
Houston, Texas 77004
http://www.uh.edu.

Founded 1934. Coed. State control. Semester system. Special facilities: Blaffer Gallery, Center for Critical Cultural Studies, Institute for Molecular Design, Institute for Public History, Center for Public Policy, Southwest Center for International Business, Space Vacuum Epitaxy Center, Center for Study of Issues Management, Texas Center for Superconductivity, Institute for Texas German Studies. Library: 1.8 million, 3,600,000 microforms, 14,100 current periodicals, depository for U.S. and Texas government documents.

Annual tuition: full-time resident $1344, nonresident $5904; per credit, resident $60, nonresident (U.S. citizen) $258. On-campus housing for 2600 single students; for 200 married students. Average academic year housing cost: $4435 (including board) for single students; $6900 (including board) for married students. Contact Director of Housing for both on- and off-campus housing information. Phone: (800)247-7184. Day care facilities available.

Graduate Division

Graduate study since 1939. Enrollment: full-time 3573, part-time 3675. Graduate faculty: full-time 1137, part-time 281. Degrees conferred: M.A., M.S., M.S.A., M.B.A., M.Ed., M.M., M.Arch., M.S. Accy., M.S.A., M.S.Ch.E., M.Ch.E., M.S.C.E., M.C.E., M.S.E.E., M.E.E., M.S.I.E., M.I.E., M.S.M.E., M.M.E., M.F.A., M.S.Phar., M.S.O.T., Ed.D., Ph.D., D.M.A., O.D.

ADMISSION REQUIREMENTS. Two official transcripts, GRE/GMAT/MAT required in support of application. Interview required for some departments. Departmental applications in some cases. TOEFL required for international applicants. Accepts transfer applicants. Graduates of unaccredited colleges not considered. Apply to Director of Admissions; deadlines vary by Schools. Rolling admissions process. International applicants should apply to International Student Office by May 1. Application fees vary by Schools. Phone: (713)743-9090.

ADMISSION STANDARDS. Very competitive for some departments, selective for others. Usual minimum average: 3.0 for most departments, 2.6 for conditional admission to most departments (A = 4).

FINANCIAL AID. Annual awards from institutional funds: fellowships, assistantships, Federal W/S, loans. Approved for VA benefits. Apply by March 1 to appropriate department chair for assistantships, fellowships; to the Financial Aid Office for all other programs. About 20% of students receive aid from University and outside sources. Aid available for part-time students.

DEGREE REQUIREMENTS. For M.A., M.S.: 30 semester hours minimum, at least 24 in residence; qualifying exam; thesis, final exam; or 36 hours minimum, at least 27 in residence; qualifying exam; final comprehensive exam. For M.B.A.: 36 semester hours minimum, at least 27 in residence. For M.Ed.: 36 semester hours minimum, at least 27 in residence; comprehensive written exam; or 30 semester hours minimum, at least 24 in residence; written comprehensive exam; thesis; final oral exam. For M.M.: 30 semester hours minimum, at least 24 in residence; thesis; final oral exam. For M.S.O.T.: 30–36 semester hours; thesis. For M.F.A.: 60 semester hours; one year in residence; written and oral comprehensive exam. For M.S.W.: 63 semester hours. For Ed.D.: 66 semester hours minimum beyond the master's, at least 30 in residence and 24 consecutive hours in full-time attendance; qualifying exam; dissertation; final written/oral exams. For D.M.A.: 60 semester hours minimum beyond master's; four public performances, written and oral comprehensive exams; research document. For Ph.D.: 24 years beyond the master's, at least one year in full-time residence; reading knowledge of one or two foreign languages; qualifying exam; dissertation; final oral exams.

FIELDS OF STUDY.

COLLEGE OF ARCHITECTURE:
Architecture.

COLLEGE OF BUSINESS ADMINISTRATION:
Accountancy.
Business Administration.
Finance.
International Business.
Management.
Management Information Systems.
Marketing.
Operations Research.
Taxation.

COLLEGE OF EDUCATION:
Art Education.
Bilingual Education.
Counseling Psychology.
Curriculum and Instruction.
Early Childhood Education.
Education of the Gifted.
Educational Administration.
Educational Psychology.
Elementary Education.
Exercise Science.

Health Education.
Higher Education.
Instructional Technology.
Mathematics Education.
Physical Education.
Reading and Language Arts.
Science Education.
Second Language Education.
Secondary Education.
Special Education.

COLLEGE OF ENGINEERING:
Biomedical Engineering.
Chemical Engineering.
Civil and Environmental Engineering.
Electrical and Computer Engineering.
Industrial Engineering.
Materials Engineering.
Mechanical Engineering.
Petroleum Engineering.

CONRAD HILTON COLLEGE OF HOTEL AND RESTAURANT
MANAGEMENT:
Hospitality Management.

COLLEGE OF HUMANITIES, FINE ARTS, AND COMMUNICATION:
Accompanying.
Applied Music.
Ceramics.
Communication.
Communication Disorders.
Composition.
Conducting.
Drama.
French.
German.
History.
Interior Design.
Literature and Creative Writing.
Mass Media Studies.
Music Education.
Music Literature.
Music Theory.
Organizational and Interpersonal Studies.
Painting.
Performance.
Philosophy.
Photography.
Public Relations.
Sculpture.
Spanish.
Speech Communication.

COLLEGE OF NATURAL SCIENCE AND MATHEMATICS:
Biochemical Sciences.
Biochemistry.
Biology. Includes evolutionary.
Chemical Physics.
Chemistry. Includes analytical, biological, inorganic, organic,
   physical, theoretical.
Computer Science.
Geophysics.
Geosciences.
Marine Biology.
Mathematics. Includes applied.
Physics.

COLLEGE OF OPTOMETRY:
Optometry.
Physiological Optics.
Vision Science.

COLLEGE OF PHARMACY:
Hospital Pharmacy.
Pharmaceutics.
Pharmacology.

COLLEGE OF SOCIAL SCIENCES:
Anthropology.
Economics.
Political Science.
Psychology. Includes clinical, developmental, industrial, organi-
   zational, social.
Public Administration.
Sociology.

SCHOOL OF SOCIAL WORK:
Social Work.

COLLEGE OF TECHNOLOGY:
Construction Management.
Industrial Education.
Information Systems.
Manufacturing Systems.
Microcomputer Systems.

Law Center (77204-6390)

Library: 300,000 volumes. Library has NEXIS, WESTLAW.
Special facilities: Health Law and Policy Institute, the Institute
for Higher Educational Law and Governance, International Law
Institute.

Annual tuition: full-time resident $7595, nonresident $12,245.
Limited on-campus housing available.

Enrollment: first-year class 395; 315 (day), 80 (evening); total
full- and part-time 1100 (men 60%, women 40%), LL.M.. total
120. Faculty: full-time 50, part-time 54. Degrees conferred: J.D.,
J.D.-M.A. (history and urban studies), J.D.-M.B.A., J.D.-M.P.H.,
J.D.-Ph.D. (medical humanities), LL.M.

ADMISSION REQUIREMENTS. LSDAS Law School report,
bachelor's degree, transcripts, LSAT (not later than December)
required in support of application. Interview not required. Accepts transfer applicants. Graduates of unaccredited colleges not
considered. Apply to College after September 1, before February
1. Application fee $50. Phone: (713)743-1070.

ADMISSION STANDARDS. Selective. Accepts about 20–25%
of total annual applicants.

FINANCIAL AID. Scholarships, teaching assistantships, Federal W/S, loans. Apply after acceptance, by April 1 to Financial
Aid Office. Use FAFSA. About 3% of students receive aid other
than loans from College. Aid available to part-time students.

DEGREE REQUIREMENTS. For J.D.: 88 semester credits minimum, at least 44 in residence. For LL.M.: 24 semester credits,
18 in residence (concentrations in Energy, Environmental, and
Natural Resources Law; Health Law; Intellectual Property Law;
International Law; Taxation Law).

HOWARD UNIVERSITY
Washington, D.C. 20059-0002

Founded 1867. Private control. Seventeen schools and colleges.
Howard participates in Joint Graduate Consortium with George
Washington, Georgetown, and Catholic universities, the Univer-
sity of the District of Columbia, and three Associate Members
(Gallaudet, Mount Vernon, and Trinity colleges). Founders Library
for graduate students ranks among top 100 in the United States

and Canada. Special facilities: Computer Center, Laser Chemistry Laboratory, Solid-State Electronics Laboratory, Center for Hypertension Control, 5 specialized research institutes, Cancer Research Center, Center for Sickle Cell Disease, modern 500-bed teaching hospital, 5-million-watt public educational television station (WHMM, Channel 32), 24-thousand-watt commercial radio station (WHUF-FM, 96.3 MHZ), and the Moorland-Spingarn Research Center, which houses the world's most comprehensive collection of materials on Africa and persons of African descent. Library: 1,729,875 volumes, 1,453,000 microforms.

Annual tuition: full-time $14,860; part-time, per credit hour, $517. On-campus housing usually unavailable. Off-campus academic year cost: $8000–$15,000 including board. Contact Supervisor of Off-Campus Housing. Phone: (202)806-5749.

Graduate School of Arts and Sciences

Graduate study since l919. Enrollment: full- and part-time 1200. Graduate faculty: full- and part-time 300. Degrees conferred: M.A., M.S., M.Eng., M.S.C.S., Ph.D.

ADMISSION REQUIREMENTS. Transcripts, GRE required in support of School's application. Interview not required. Transfer applicants accepted. Graduates from unaccredited institutions not considered. Apply to the Office of Student Relations and Enrollment Management by February 1 (Fall), November 1 (Spring), March 1 (Summer). Application fee $25. Phone: (202)806-7469/6800; fax: (202)462-4053.

ADMISSION STANDARDS. Selective. Usual minimum average: 3.0 (A = 4).

FINANCIAL AID. More than fifty scholarships; more than three hundred graduate assistantships. Apply by April 1 (Fall), November 1 (Spring), March 15 (Summer) to appropriate department for assistantships; to Financial Aid Office for scholarships and other financial aid programs. Use FAFSA. About 43% of students receive aid other than loans from University and outside sources. No aid for part-time students.

DEGREE REQUIREMENTS. For master's: 30 semester hours minimum, at least two semesters in residence; thesis/nonthesis option; reading knowledge of one foreign language in some departments; final/oral exam. For Ph.D.: 72 semester hours minimum beyond the bachelor's degree, at least four semesters in full-time residence (two of which are consecutive); reading knowledge of two foreign languages in some departments; dissertation; demonstrated proficiency in expository writing, final written/oral exam.

FIELDS OF STUDY.
African Studies. M.A., Ph.D.
Anatomy. M.S., Ph.D.
Art. Includes history, design, education. M.A. only.
Biochemistry. M.S., Ph.D.
Biology. M.S., Ph.D.
Chemical Engineering. M.S. only.
Chemistry. Includes analytical. M.S., Ph.D.
Civil Engineering. M.Eng. only.
Communication Science and Disorders. M.S., Ph.D.
Economics. M.A., Ph.D.
Electrical Engineering. M.Eng., Ph.D.
English. M.A., Ph.D.
Genetics and Human Genetics. M.S., Ph.D.
History. M.A., Ph.D.
Human Communication Studies. M.A., Ph.D.
Mathematics. M.S., Ph.D.
Mechanical Engineering. M.Eng., Ph.D.
Microbiology. Ph.D.
Modern Languages and Literatures. M.A.

Nutritional Sciences. M.S., Ph.D.
Pharmacology. M.S., Ph.D.
Philosophy. M.A. only.
Physical Education and Recreation. M.S
Physics and Astronomy. M.S., Ph.D.
Physiology and Biophysics. M.S., Ph.D.
Political Science. M.A., Ph.D.
Psychology. Includes clinical, developmental, personality, social. M.S., Ph.D.
Sociology and Anthropology. M.A., Ph.D.
Systems and Computer Sciences. M.C.S.

School of Social Work

Organized 1945. Semester system. Tuition: full-time $10,500. Limited on-campus housing available. Contact Dean of Residence Life. Phone: (202)806-6131.

Enrollment: full- and part-time 358. Faculty: full-time 24, part-time 18. Degrees conferred: M.S.W., D.S.W.

ADMISSION REQUIREMENTS. Transcripts, three letters of recommendations required in support of School's application. TOEFL required for international applicants. Accepts transfer applicants. Apply to School by October 1 (Spring), February 1 (Fall). Application fee $25. Phone: (202)806-6450; fax: (202)387-4309.

ADMISSION STANDARDS. Selective. Usual minimum average: 2.5 (A = 4).

FINANCIAL AID. Very limited scholarships, fellowships, and graduate assistantships, federal grants. Apply to Financial Aid Office; no specified closing date. Use FAFSA. Phone: (202)806-2800.

DEGREE REQUIREMENTS. For M.S.W.: satisfactory completion of 60-hour program, at least 30 hours in residence. For D.S.W.: satisfactory completion of 48 semester credit hours beyond the master's; dissertation.

School of Law (20008)

Organized 1868. Law library: 245,000 volumes. Library has LEXIS, NEXIS, WESTLAW, CALI, OCLC, LEGALTRAC.

Annual tuition: $11,560. Total average annual additional expense: $10,650.

Enrollment: first-year class 140 (men 53%, women 47%). Faculty: full-time 33, part-time 22. Degrees conferred: J.D., J.D.-M.B.A., M.C.J.

ADMISSION REQUIREMENTS. LSDAS Law School report, bachelor's degree, LSAT (GMAT for J.D.-M.B.A. program), transcripts, two letters of recommendation required in support of application. Applicants must have completed at least four years of college study. Accepts transfer applicants. Graduates of unaccredited colleges not considered. Apply to University Office of Admissions after September 1, before April 30. Application fee $60. Phone: (202)806-8008.

ADMISSION STANDARDS. Selective. Accepts 20% of total annual applicants.

FINANCIAL AID. Scholarships, grant, Federal W/S, loans. Apply to Chairman, Financial Aid Committee. Use FAFSA. About 50% of students receive aid other than loans from School.

DEGREE REQUIREMENTS. For J.D.: satisfactory completion of 3-year program, 88 semester hours minimum. For M.C.J., at least 24 credit hours beyond J.D.; thesis.

College of Medicine

Organized 1868. Annual tuition: $15,500. Total average figure for all other expenses: $10,349. Very limited housing available. Contact Dean, Resident Life.

Enrollment: first-year class 110; total 415 (men 51%, women 49%). Faculty: full-time 240, part-time 350. Degrees conferred: M.D., M.D.-M.S., M.D.-Ph.D. The M.S. and Ph.D. are offered through the Graduate School.

ADMISSION REQUIREMENTS. AMCAS report, transcripts, letters of recommendation, MCAT required in support of application. Interview by invitation. Applicants must have completed at least three years of college study. Accepts transfer applicants. Does not have EDP. Apply to AMCAS after June 15, before December 15. Application fee $25. Phone: (202)806-6270; fax: (202)806-7934.

ADMISSION STANDARDS. Very competitive. Accepts 5% of total annual applicants. Approximately 10% are District residents.

FINANCIAL AID. Scholarships, loans. Apply to Office of the Dean before May 1. Use GAPSFAS. About 85% of students receive some aid.

DEGREE REQUIREMENTS. For M.D.: satisfactory completion of four-year program, at least the final two years in residence; passing of Step II FUSMLE. For M.S., Ph.D., see Graduate School listing above.

FIELDS OF STUDY.
Anatomy.
Biochemistry.
Genetics.
Microbiology.
Pharmacology.
Physiology.

College of Dentistry
600-W Street, N.W. 20008

Organized 1881. Library: 85,000 volumes. Annual tuition: $11,600. No on-campus housing available. Off-campus housing cost: $12,500. Total average cost for all other first-year expenses: $6967.

Enrollment: first-year class 87 (men 50%, women 50%); total full-time 462, postgraduates 25. Faculty: 140. Degrees conferred: B.S.-D.D.S. (with Howard University's College of Liberal Arts), D.D.S.

ADMISSION REQUIREMENTS. AADSAS, transcripts, three letters of recommendation, DAT required in support of College's application. Applicants must have completed at least two years of college study. Apply to Dean after June 1, before April 1. Application fee $25. Phone: (202)806-0400.

ADMISSION STANDARDS. Competitive. Usual minimum average: 2.3 in sciences. Accepts about 20–25% of total annual applicants. Approximately 90% are District residents.

FINANCIAL AID. Limited scholarships, loans. Apply to Financial Aid Committee by July 1. 95% of needy students receive some aid from Institution. Phone: (202)806-0374.

DEGREE REQUIREMENTS. For D.D.S.: satisfactory completion of forty-two-month program.

FIELDS OF STUDY.
Oral and Maxillofacial Surgery. Certificate only.
Orthodontics. Certificate only.
Pediatric Dentistry. Certificate only.

HUMBOLDT STATE UNIVERSITY
Arcata, California 95521-8299

Founded 1913. Located 300 miles N of San Francisco. Coed. State control. Semester system. Special facilities: Arts Center, Marine Biological and Oceanography Station, Natural History Museum, Center for Indian Community Development, Center for the Resolution of Environmental Disputes, Lamphere Dunes, Schatz Tree Farm Experimental Forest, fish hatchery. Library: 900,000 volumes, 460,000 microforms, 25 PCs.

Annual tuition/fees: full-time, resident $2106, nonresident $246 per semester unit plus $2106. On-campus housing for graduate students. Average academic year housing cost: $5195 (including board) for single students. Apply to Director of Housing. Phone: (707)826-3451.

Graduate Studies

Enrollment: full- and part-time 450. Faculty teaching graduate students: 350. Degrees conferred: M.A., M.S., M.B.A., M.F.A.

ADMISSION REQUIREMENTS. Transcripts required in support of application. GRE Subject Tests for some departments; letters of recommendation for some departments. TOEFL required for international applicants. Interview not required. Accepts transfer applicants. Graduates of unaccredited institutions not considered. Call for application deadlines for individual programs. Application fee $55. Phone: (707)826-4402.

ADMISSION STANDARDS. Very selective for most departments. Usual minimum average: 2.5 for last 60 credits (A = 4).

FINANCIAL AID. Annual awards from institutional funds: ten scholarships, ten research fellowships, fifty teaching assistantships, fifty research assistantships, Federal W/S, loans. Apply by August 1 to appropriate department or division chair for fellowships and assistantships; to Financial Aid Office for all other programs. Phone: (707)826-4321. Use FAFSA. About 25% of students receive aid other than loans from College and outside sources. No aid for part-time students.

DEGREE REQUIREMENTS. For M.A., M.S., M.B.A.: 30 semester units minimum, at least 21 in residence; thesis/nonthesis option. For M.F.A.: 60 semester units, at least 42 in residence; creative project.

FIELDS OF STUDY.
Acting.
Biology.
Business Administration. M.B.A. only.
Children's Theater.
Directing.
Engineering.
English.
Environmental Resource Engineering.
Environmental System–Math Modeling.
Film History.
Fisheries.
Forestry.
Geology.
International Development.
Math Modeling.
Natural Resources.
Physical Education.
Playwriting.
Psychology.
Sociology.
Teaching of Writing.
Theater Arts. M.F.A., M.A.

Waste Water Utilization.
Watershed Management.
Wildlife Management.

HUNTER COLLEGE OF THE CITY UNIVERSITY OF NEW YORK
New York, New York 10021-5085

Founded 1870. Coed. Municipal control. Semester system. Special facilities: Brookdale Center on Aging, Center for AIDS, Drugs and Community Health, Center for Biomolecular Structure and Function, Center for Communication Disorders, Center for Occupational and Environmental Health, Center for Puerto Rican Studies, Urban Research Center. University libraries: 708,000 volumes, 992,000 microforms, 2100 current periodicals, 80 PCs.

Annual tuition: resident $4350, per credit $185; nonresident $7600, per credit $320. No on-campus housing. Contact Graduate Housing Office for off-campus housing information. Phone: (212)481-4311.

Graduate School

Enrollment: full-time 824, part-time 2750 (men 30%, women 70%). Graduate faculty: full-time 674, part-time 547. Degrees conferred: M.A., M.S., M.U.P., M.S.W., M.F.A., M.S.Ed., M.P.H., Advanced Certificate. The Ph.D. is offered through the University's Graduate Center.

ADMISSION REQUIREMENTS. Official transcripts, three letters of recommendation, GRE (Arts and Sciences areas) required in support of School's application. Interview required for some departments. TOEFL required for international applicants; TWE for some programs. Accepts transfer applicants. Graduates of unaccredited colleges not considered. Apply to Office of Graduate Admissions by March 1 (Fall), November 1 (Spring). Application fee $35. Phone: (212)772-4490.

ADMISSION STANDARDS. Competitive for most departments, very competitive or selective for others. Usual minimum average: 2.75 (A = 4).

FINANCIAL AID. Scholarships, fellowships, assistantships for teaching/research, tuition waivers, Federal W/S, loans. Approved for VA benefits. Apply by April 1 to Office of Graduate Fellowships and Scholarships; to Office of the Dean of Humanities, Sciences, and Mathematics, or Social Sciences for assistantships; to the Office of Financial Aid for all other programs. Phone: (212)772-4820. Closing dates subject to change; consult Financial Aid Office for specific dates. Use FAFSA and CUNY FAF. No aid for part-time students.

DEGREE REQUIREMENTS. For master's: 30–45 semester hours minimum; reading knowledge of one foreign language normally required; thesis/nonthesis option; final comprehensive written exam for most departments.

FIELDS OF STUDY.
Administration and Supervision. Advanced certificate.
Anthropology.
Applied Mathematics.
Art. Includes history, studio, education.
Biochemistry.
Biological Sciences.
Chemistry.
City and Regional Planning.
Classics.
Communication Sciences. Includes speech pathology, audiology, speech, and hearing sciences.

Communications.
Community Health Education. M.P.H.
Computer Science.
Counselor Education.
Dance, Drama, Music Therapy.
Economics.
Education. Includes elementary, reading, bilingual, gifted, foreign languages, health, secondary, guidance and counseling, reading, rehabilitation counseling, science, social sciences, special, speech and hearing, TESL.
English Literature.
Environmental and Occupational Health Science.
Geography.
History.
Mass and Organizational Communication.
Mathematics.
Music. Includes composition, ethnomusicology, history, performance.
Nursing. Includes medical-surgical, psychiatric, administration, maternity-child health, gerontological practitioner, public and community health nursing.
Nutrition.
Physical Sciences.
Physics.
Psychology. Includes clinical, developmental, experimental.
Romance Languages. Includes French, Italian, Spanish.
Russian Area Studies.
Social Work.
Theater.
Urban Planning.
Urban Studies.

IDAHO STATE UNIVERSITY
Pocatello, Idaho 83201
http://www.isu.edu/

Founded 1901. Located 165 miles N of Salt Lake City. Coed. State control. Semester system. Library: 406,000 volumes, l,355,000 microforms, 30 PCs in all libraries.

Annual tuition/fees: full-time, resident $2399, nonresident $7509. On-campus housing for 150 married and 1200 single students. Average academic year housing cost: $2730–$5000 for married students; $2850–$3140 (including board) for single students. Apply to Housing Office. Phone: (208)236-2120.

Graduate School

Enrollment: full-time 622, part-time 1401 (men 40%, women 60%). Graduate faculty: full-time 219, part-time 0. Degrees conferred: M.A., M.S., M.Ed., M.H.E., M.P.E., M.F.A., M.Coun., M.P.T., Ed.S., D.A., M.N.S., Ph.D., Ed.D.

ADMISSION REQUIREMENTS. Two transcripts, GRE/GMAT/MAT required in support of School's application. TOEFL required for international applicants. Interview not required. Accepts transfer applicants. Graduates from unaccredited institutions not considered. Apply to Office of Registrar and Admissions by August 15 (Fall), December 15 (Spring), May 1 (Summer). Application fee $25. Phone: (208)236-2150; fax: (208)236-4529.

ADMISSION STANDARDS. Relatively open for most departments. Usual minimum average: 2.75 (A = 4), 35th percentile on at least one GRE subscore.

FINANCIAL AID. Annual awards from institutional funds: 150 scholarships, 100 teaching and research assistantships, 27 fellowships, Federal W/S, loans. Approved for VA benefits. Apply by March 1 to appropriate department chair for fellowships and assistantships; to Financial Aid Office for all other programs. Use FAFSA. Phone: (208)236-2756, fax: 236-4231. About 60% of students receive aid other than loans from University and outside sources. Aid sometimes available for part-time students.

DEGREE REQUIREMENTS. For master's: 30 semester hours minimum, at least 22 in residence; reading knowledge of one foreign language for some departments; thesis/nonthesis options; final written/oral exam. For Ed.S.: 30 semester hours beyond master's; project. For D.A.: 60 credits minimum beyond master's, at least 30 in residence; professional project; final oral exam. For Ph.D.: 72 credits minimum beyond bachelor's, at least 30 in residence; reading knowledge of one foreign language for some departments; qualifying exam; dissertation; final oral exam.

FIELDS OF STUDY.
Anthropology. Thesis for M.A., M.S.
Art. One-person show for M.F.A.
Audiology.
Biological Sciences. Includes botany, zoology, microbiology, biochemistry; thesis/nonthesis options. M.S., Ph.D., D.A., M.N.S.
Business Administration. Thesis/nonthesis options for M.B.A.
Chemistry. Combine B.S./M.S. with entry at junior level. Thesis/nonthesis for M.N.S.
Civil Engineering.
Deaf Education.
Education. Includes administration, student personnel work in higher education, curriculum and supervision, guidance and counseling; elementary, secondary, school psychology; home economics, special education, and psychological services; two years' experience for master's in administration, curriculum and supervision, one year for guidance counseling; no language requirement.
Engineering and Nuclear Science. Includes measurements and controls. M.S., Ph.D.
English. Thesis for M.A., D.A.
Environmental Engineering.
Geology. Thesis for M.S., no thesis for M.N.S.
Hazardous Waste Engineering.
Hazardous Waste Management. Interdisciplinary.
Health and Nutrition Sciences.
Mathematics. Nonthesis program for M.S., M.N.S.; thesis for D.A.
Microbiology.
Nursing. Thesis for M.S.
Operations Research.
Pharmacy. Includes pharmacognosy, pharmaceutical chemistry, pharmacology; thesis, 35 hours minimum for M.S.
Physical Education and Health Education. Thesis/nonthesis option for M.P.E., M.H.E.
Physical Therapy.
Physics. Thesis for M.S., nonthesis for M.N.S.
Political Science. M.A., M.P.A., D.A.
Psychology. M.S.
Public Policy and Administration.
Sociology. Thesis for M.A.
Speech Languages Pathology. Thesis/nonthesis options for M.S.
Speech Theater. M.A.
Zoology.

UNIVERSITY OF IDAHO
Moscow, Idaho 83844-3017

Founded 1889. Located 85 miles SE of Spokane, Wash. Coed. State control. Semester system. Special facilities: Cooperative Fishery Research Unit, Cooperative Park Studies Unit, Cooperative Wildlife Research Unit, Microelectronics Research Center, Institute for Molecular and Agricultural Genetic Engineering,

Laboratory of Anthropology, Remote Sensing Research Unit, Graduate Center at Idaho Nuclear Engineering Laboratory, cooperative graduate course program and library usage exchange with Washington State University, Computer Center, Agricultural Experiment Station, Center for Business Development and Research, Bureau of Education Research and Service, Bureau of Mines and Geology, Bureau of Public Affairs Research, Engineering Experiment Station, Forest, Wildlife and Range Experiment Station, Materials Testing Laboratory, U.S. Forest Service, Intermountain Forest Sciences Laboratory, Water Resources Research Institute. Library: 957,000 volumes, 1,333,000 microforms, 159 PCs.

Annual tuition fee: full-time, resident $2308, nonresident $7960; part-time per credit, resident $108, nonresident $198. On-campus housing for 276 married students, 1700 men, 1040 women. Housing cost: $285–$356 per month for married students, $3096 per year (including board) for single students. Apply to Director of Housing. Phone: (208)885-7961. Day care facilities available.

College of Graduate Studies

Graduate study since 1896. Enrollment: full-time 1100, part-time 1250. University faculty: full-time 431, part-time 10. Degrees conferred: M.A., M.S., M.Arch., M.F.A., M.M., M.Ed., M.Nat.Sc., M.A.T., M.Nuc.Sc., M.Engr., M.P.A., Ed.D., Ed.S., Ph.D.

ADMISSION REQUIREMENTS. Transcript required in support of College's application. GRE required by some departments. TOEFL required for international applicants. Interview not required. Accepts transfer applicants. Graduates of unaccredited colleges not considered. Apply to Admissions Officer by August 1 (Fall), January 1 (Spring). International application deadline: June 1 (Fall), December 1 (Spring). Application fee $20. Phone: (208)885-4001; fax: (208)885-6198.

ADMISSION STANDARDS. Selective for most departments. Usual minimum average: 2.8 (A = 4). Some departments require higher GPA.

FINANCIAL AID. Annual awards from institutional funds: scholarships, research fellowships, 236 teaching assistantships, 236 research assistantships, Federal W/S, loans. Apply by March 1 to appropriate department head for fellowships, assistantships; to Financial Aid Office for all other aid. Use FAFSA and institutional FAF. Phone: (208)885-6312. About 50% of students receive aid other than loans from University and outside sources. Aid available for part-time students.

DEGREE REQUIREMENTS. For M.A., M.S., M.Arch., M.F.A.: 30 credits minimum, at least 18 in residence; thesis; final oral exam. For M.Nuc.Sc., M.Nat.Sc.: 30 credits minimum, at least 22 in residence; final written exam. For M.M.: 30 credits minimum, at least 22 in residence; thesis, composition, or recital; final written exam. For M.B.A.: 30 credits; calculus and computer proficiency. For M.P.A.: 30 credits minimum, at least 18 in residence; comprehensive exam. For M.Engr.: 30 credits minimum; final document. For Ed.S.: 30 credits beyond the master's. For Ph.D.: 78 credits minimum beyond the bachelor's; at least one year in residence; preliminary exam; reading knowledge of one foreign language required by some departments; dissertation; final written/oral exam. For Ed.D.: essentially the same as for the Ph.D., except no language requirement.

FIELDS OF STUDY.
Agricultural Economics. M.S. only.
Agricultural Education. M.S. only.
Agricultural Engineering.
Animal Physiology. Ph.D.
Animal Sciences. M.S.
Anthropology. Master's only.

Architecture.

Art. M.A., M.F.A.

Biological Sciences. M.Nat.Sc.

Biology.

Botany.

Business Education.

Chemical Engineering.

Chemistry.

Civil Engineering.

Computer Engineering. M.S. only.

Computer Science.

Counseling and Human Services.

Earth Science. M.A.T. only.

Economics. M.S. only.

Education. Includes elementary, secondary, special education; business, administration, guidance and counseling, distributive.

Educational Administration.

Electrical Engineering.

Elementary Education.

English. M.A., M.A.T. only.

English as a Second Language.

Entomology.

Environmental Science. M.S. only.

Family and Consumer Sciences. M.S. only.

Fishery Resources.

Food Sciences.

Forest Products.

Forest Resources.

Forestry, Wildlife, and Range Sciences.

Geography. M.S., Ph.D.

Geological Engineering.

Geology.

Geophysics.

History.

Hydrology.

Industrial Education.

Interdisciplinary Studies. M.A., M.S. only.

Mathematics.

Mechanical Engineering.

Metallurgical Engineering.

Metallurgy.

Microbiology, Molecular and Biochemistry. M.S., Ph.D.

Mining Engineering.

Mining Engineering–Metallurgy.

Music. Includes performance, history and literature, composition, applied; M.A., M.M. only.

Nuclear Engineering.

Physical Education.

Physics.

Plant Sciences.

Political Science.

Psychology. M.S. only.

Public Administration.

Range Resources.

Recreation.

Resource Recreation and Tourism.

School Psychology.

Secondary Education.

Soil Science.

Special Education.

Theater Arts. M.F.A. only.

Veterinary Science. M.S. only.

Vocational Education.

Wildlife Resources.

Zoology.

School of Law

Established 1909. Semester system. Library: 156,000 volumes. Library has LEXIS, NEXIS, WESTLAW, DIALOG.

Annual tuition: resident, no tuition charge, but mandatory fees $2466 per year, nonresident $6974. On-campus housing available.

Enrollment: first-year class 122; total full-time 298 (men 50%, women 50%). Faculty: full-time 20, part-time 2. Degree conferred: J.D.

ADMISSION REQUIREMENTS. LSDAS Law School report, bachelor's degree, transcripts, LSAT required in support of application. Interview not required. Preference given to state residents. Graduates of unaccredited colleges not considered. Apply to Admissions Officer after September 1, before February 1. Admits to Fall only. Application fee $30. Phone: (208)885-6422.

ADMISSION STANDARDS. Selective. Accepts 30–35% of total annual applicants. Approximately 20% of first-year class are nonresidents.

FINANCIAL AID. Scholarships, assistantships, Federal W/S, loans. Apply by February 1 to Financial Aid Office. Use FAFSA. About 16% of students receive aid other than loans from institutional funds.

DEGREE REQUIREMENTS. For J.D.: satisfactory completion of three-year program; 89 semester hours.

ILLINOIS INSTITUTE OF TECHNOLOGY
Chicago, Illinois 60616

Formed in 1940 by merger of Armour Institute and Lewis Institute. Coed. Private control. Semester system. Special facilities: Center for the Study of Ethics and the Professions, National Center for Food Safety and Technology, Hazardous Waste Management Center, Center for Research on Industrial Strategy and Policy, Centers for Biotechnology, Energy Technology, Fluid Dynamics, Industrial Waste Elimination, Railroad Engineering. Library: 500,000 volumes, 177,000 microforms, 750 current periodicals.

Annual tuition: full-time $16,350; per credit $545. On-campus housing for 360 married graduate students, 132 graduate men, 45 graduate women. Average academic year housing cost: $6500 for married students, $5500 (including board) for single students. Contact Director of Housing for both on- and off-campus housing information. Phone: (312)567-5075.

Graduate School

Enrollment: full-time 1652, part-time 2938. Institute faculty: full-time 202, part-time 114. Degrees conferred: M.S., M.Arch., M.B.A., M.Ch.E., M.C.E., M.C.R.P., M.Met.E., M.M.E., M.P.A., Ph.D.

ADMISSION REQUIREMENTS. Transcripts, two letters of recommendation required in support of application. GRE General/Subject Tests required in chemistry, psychology, electrical engineering. TOEFL required for international applicants. Interview not required. Accepts transfer applicants. Graduates of unaccredited institutions not considered. Apply to appropriate department by July 1 (Fall), November 15 (Spring). Rolling admissions process. Application fee $30. Phone: (312)567-3024.

ADMISSION STANDARDS. Very selective for most departments. Usual minimum average: 3.0 (A = 4).

FINANCIAL AID. Annual awards from institutional funds: 50 scholarships, 25 fellowships, 157 teaching assistantships, 90 research assistantships, 20 internships, Federal W/S, loans. Approved for VA benefits. Apply by March 1 to appropriate department chair for scholarships, fellowships, assistantships; to Director of Financial Aid for all other programs. Use FAFSA and institutional FAF. Phone: (312)567-3303. About 50% of students receive aid other than loans from Institute and outside sources. No aid for part-time students.

DEGREE REQUIREMENTS. For master's: 32–36 semester hours minimum; includes 6–8 hours for thesis (when required); final written/oral exam. For Ph.D.: usually 96 semester hours beyond the bachelor's, two semesters in full-time residence; preliminary exam; dissertation; final oral exam.

FIELDS OF STUDY.
Architecture. Admits Fall only; M.Arch. only.
Biology. Includes biochemistry, microbiology, physiology. M.S., Ph.D.
Business Administration. GMAT for admission; M.B.A.
Chemical Engineering. M.S., Ph.D.
Chemistry. One language for Ph.D.; M.S., M.C.E., Ph.D.
City and Regional Planning. Admits Fall only; M.C.R.P. only.
Civil Engineering. M.S., Ph.D.
Computer Science. M.S., Ph.D.
Design, Institute of. Includes photography, product design, visual design. M.S., Ph.D.
Electrical and Computer Engineering. M.E.E.
Environmental Engineering. M.S., Ph.D.
Food Safety and Technology. M.F.S.
Manufacturing Engineering. M.M.E.
Mechanical and Aerospace Engineering. M.S., Ph.D.
Metallurgical Engineering. M.M.E.
Personnel and Human Resources Development. M.S.
Physics. M.S., Ph.D.
Psychology. M.S., Ph.D.
Public Administration. M.P.A.
Rehabilitation Counseling. M.S.

Chicago-Kent College of Law (60661-36912)

Founded in 1887, became an integral Part of IIT in 1969. Semester system. Library: 477,000 volumes, 80 PCs. Library has LEXIS, NEXIS, WESTLAW, DIALOG.

Annual tuition: $18,850 (day), $13,600 (evening). Housing available on main campus. Total average annual additional expense: $10,000.

Enrollment: first-year class approximately 400, full-time 300, part-time 100. Total enrollment approximately 975 (men 53%, women 47%). Faculty: full-time 70, part-time 73. Degrees conferred: JD., J.D.-M.B.A., J.D.-LL.M. (Taxation and Financial Services) LL.M., (Tax and Financial Service Law).

ADMISSION REQUIREMENTS. LSDAS Law School report, bachelor's degree, transcripts, LSAT, two letters of recommendation required in support of application. Minority and disadvantaged applicants encouraged to apply. Transfer applicants accepted from ABA-approved law school only. Apply by April 1, rolling admissions process. Application fee $40. Phone: (312)906-5020.

ADMISSION STANDARDS. Selective. Accepts 25–30% of total annual applicants.

FINANCIAL AID. Scholarships, grants, Federal W/S, loans. Apply to Financial Aid Office after acceptance before April 3. Use FAFSA and institutional FAF.

DEGREE REQUIREMENTS. For J.D.: satisfactory completion of three-year program; 90 semester hours. For LL.M., M.A.L.: at least 24 credits beyond the J.D.; 20 credits in residence. For M.B.A. requirements: see Graduate School listing above.

ILLINOIS STATE UNIVERSITY
Normal, Illinois 61761-2000
http://www.istu.edu

Founded 1857. Located 130 miles S of Chicago. Coed. State control. Semester system. Library: 1,442,135 volumes, 1,258,000 microforms, 112 PCs.

Annual tuition/fees: full-time, resident $3030 (12 hours each semester), Fall, Spring semester, nonresident $7384; per credit resident $120, nonresident $303. On-campus housing for 292 married students, 125 single men, and 125 single women. Average academic year cost: $3403 for single. Apply to Office of Residential Life. Phone: (309)438-8611 or (800)366-4675. Day care facilities available.

The Graduate School

Graduate study since 1943. Enrollment: full-time 1289, part-time 1342. University faculty: full- and part-time 700. Degrees conferred: M.A., M.S., M.S. in Ed., M.M.Ed., M.F.A., M.B.A., S.S.P., Ed.D., D.A., Ph.D.

ADMISSION REQUIREMENTS. Two transcripts required in support of School's application. Applicants to degree programs must submit scores of GRE for some departments. Applicants to the Departments of Psychology and Sociology and Anthropology must submit scores on the GRE Subject Test in their field of study. Applicants for Business should submit the GMAT. Doctoral applicants must submit three letters of recommendation. TOEFL required for international applicants. Interview sometimes required. Accepts transfer applicants. Graduates of unaccredited institutions not considered. Apply to Office of Admissions at least three weeks (master's) or two months (doctoral programs) prior to registration. Application fee none. Phone: (309)438-2181; fax: (309)438-3932.

ADMISSION STANDARDS. Selective. Usual minimum average: 2.6 (A = 4).

FINANCIAL AID. Annual awards from institutional funds: five fellowships, eight hundred assistantships, Federal W/S, loans. Approved for VA benefits. Apply March 15 to Graduate Office for fellowships, to head of proposed major department for assistantships; to Financial Aid Office for all other programs. Use FAFSA. Phone: (309)438-2231; fax: (309)438-3755. About 60% of students receive aid other than loans from University and outside sources. No aid for students-at-large or part-time students with less than 5 hours in a degree-seeking program. Departmental tuition waivers are available to part-time students (in-state) on a limited basis.

DEGREE REQUIREMENTS. For master's: 32 semester hours minimum, at least 24 in residence and one semester in full-time attendance for selected majors; optional thesis for 4–6 hours, final oral exam; without thesis, final written exam; reading knowledge of one foreign language (for M.A.). For S.S.P.: 30 semester hours minimum. For Ed.D., Ph.D., D.A.: approximately 60 semester hours minimum beyond the master's; research project; final written/oral exam. Knowledge of two foreign languages for Ph.D., or approved substitute; approved alternate research tool for Ed.D. Residency requirements vary.

FIELDS OF STUDY.

COLLEGE OF APPLIED SCIENCE AND TECHNOLOGY:
Agribusiness. M.S.
Applied Computer Science. M.S.
Criminal Justice Sciences. M.A., M.S.
Family and Consumer Sciences. M.A., M.S.
Health and Physical Education. M.A., M.S.
Industrial Technology. M.S.

COLLEGE OF ARTS AND SCIENCES:
Biological Sciences. M.S., Ph.D.
Chemistry. M.S.
Communication. M.A., M.S.
Economics. M.A., M.S.
English. M.A., M.S., D.A.
Foreign Languages. M.A.
Geohydrology. M.S.
History. M.A., M.S., D.A.
Mathematics. M.A., M.S.
Mathematics Education. Ph.D.
Political Science. M.A., M.S.
Psychology. M.A., M.S.
School Psychology. S.S.P., Ph.D.
Sociology. M.A., M.S.
Speech Pathology and Audiology. M.A., M.S.
Writing. M.A., M.S.

COLLEGE OF BUSINESS:
Accounting. M.S.
Business Administration. Includes finance and law; management, quantitative methods, marketing. M.B.A.

COLLEGE OF EDUCATION:
Counselor Education. M.S., M.S. in Ed.
Curriculum and Instruction. M.S. in Ed., Ed.D.
Educational Administration. M.S., M.S. in Ed., Ed.D., Ph.D.
Reading. M.S. in Ed.
Special Education. M.S. in Ed., Ed.D.

COLLEGE OF FINE ARTS:
Art. M.A., M.S., M.F.A.
Music. M.M., M.M.Ed.
Theater. M.A., M.S., M.F.A.

UNIVERSITY OF ILLINOIS AT CHICAGO

Chicago, Illinois 60680
http://www.uic.edu

Created in 1992 by combining the resources and facilities of the two University of Illinois campuses in Chicago: the 20-year-old Chicago Circle and the Medical Center in existence for over 100 years. Coed. Public control. Semester system. Special facilities: Anatomy Museum, Institute for Humanities, Pathology Museum, Research and Educational Hospitals, Neuropsychiatric Institute, Molecular Biology Research Facility, Biologic Resource Laboratory, Electron Microscope Facility, Energy Resources Center, Engineering Research Facility, Environmental Stress Facility, Center for Urban Transportation, Center for Women's Studies, Institute for the Study of Developmental Disabilities, Survey Research Laboratory. Day-care facilities available. Library: 1.6 million volumes; 225,00 volumes in Medical Library.

On-campus housing for single students only. Apply to Director of Housing for on-campus information to the Housing Listing Office, 704 CCC, 503 S. Halsted, Chicago, Illinois 60607-7014. Phone: (312)413-5418.

Graduate College

Annual tuition and fees: full-time resident $4518; nonresident $10,534.

Enrollment: full-time 2486, part-time 2844. Faculty: full- and part-time 1100. Degrees conferred: M.A., M.Arch., M.A.T., M.B.A., M.Ed., M.F.A., M.P.A., M.S., M.S.W., M.H.P.Ed., M.A.M.S., D.A., Ph.D.

ADMISSION REQUIREMENTS. Transcripts, 3 letters of recommendation, GRE/GMAT required in support of College's application. TOEFL required for international applicants. Accepts transfer applicants. Graduates of unaccredited colleges not considered. Apply to Office of Admissions by February 15 (Fall). Application fee $30, $40 for international applicants. Phone: (312)996-4350.

ADMISSION STANDARDS. Competitive for most departments, selective for others. Usual minimum average: 2.75 (A = 4).

FINANCIAL AID. One hundred and twenty scholarships, three hundred research assistantships, three hundred teaching assistantships, tuition waivers, Federal W/S, loans. Approved for VA benefits. Special support programs exist for minority students. Apply by February 15 to appropriate departments for assistantships, scholarships; to Director of Financial Aid for all other programs. Use FAFSA and institutional FAF. Phone: (312)996-5563.

DEGREE REQUIREMENTS. For most master's: 32 semester hours minimum; thesis/nonthesis option; language required for some departments. For M.Ed.: same as most master's programs except no thesis. For M.F.A.: 64 semester hours minimum in residence; written report required for majors in design, painting and printmaking, sculpture, art history; reading knowledge of one foreign language for art history majors. For M.P.A.: 54 semester hours minimum; no thesis. For M.S.W.: 60 semester hours minimum, three semesters in residence; field work experience. For M.H.P.Ed.: 32 semester hours minimum; thesis; final oral exam. For M.A.M.S.: 45–47 semester hours minimum. For D.A., Ph.D.: 96 semesters hours minimum beyond the bachelor's, at least three consecutive semesters in residence; preliminary exam; dissertation; final oral exam.

FIELDS OF STUDY.
Accounting. M.S.
Anatomy. M.S., Ph.D.
Anthropology. M.A.
Architecture. M.Arch.
Art, Design and Studio. M.F.A.
Art Therapy. M.A.
Associated Medical Sciences. M.S., M.A.M.S.
Biochemistry. M.S., Ph.D.
Bioengineering. M.S., Ph.D.
Biological Chemistry. M.S., Ph.D.
Biological Sciences. Includes cell, developmental, evolutionary, microbiology, molecular, neurobiology, radiation, M.S., D.A., Ph.D.
Business Administration. M.B.A., Ph.D.
Chemical Engineering. M.S., Ph.D.
Chemistry. M.S., Ph.D.
Civil Engineering. M.S., Ph.D.
Communication. M.A.
Criminalistics. M.S.
Criminal Justice. M.A.
East European and Soviet Studies.
Economics. Includes urban, quantitative, information, and decision science.
Education. Includes administration, curriculum and instruction, elementary, secondary. TESOL, policy and evaluation, reading, special.
Electrical Engineering and Computer Science. M.S., Ph.D.
English. M.A., Ph.D.
Finance.
French. M.A.
Genetics. Ph.D.
Geography. M.A.
Geological Sciences. M.S.
Geotechnical Engineering and Geosciences. Ph.D.
German. M.A., Ph.D.

Gerontological Nursing.
Health Professions Education. M.H.P.E.
History. M.A., M.A.T., Ph.D.
Human Resources Management.
Industrial and System Engineering. M.S.
Industrial Engineering and Operations Research. Ph.D.
Kinesiology. M.S.
Linguistics. M.A.
Management Information Systems. M.S., Ph.D.
Marketing. Ph.D.
Materials Engineering. M.S., Ph.D.
Maternity Nursing. M.S.N.
Mathematics. Includes applied. M.A., M.S., M.S.T., D.A., Ph.D.
Mechanical Engineering. M.S., Ph.D.
Medical Laboratory Sciences. M.S.
Medicinal Chemistry. M.S., Ph.D.
Microbiology and Immunology. M.S., Ph.D.
Nursing. Includes maternity, adult health, administration, medical-surgical, pediatric, psychiatric, public health. M.S., Ph.D.
Occupation Therapy. M.S.
Pathology. M.S., Ph.D.
Pharmacognosy. M.S., Ph.D.
Pharmacology. M.S., Ph.D.
Philosophy. M.A., Ph.D.
Physics. M.S., D.A., Ph.D.
Physiology and Biophysics. M.S., Ph.D.
Political Science. M.A., Ph.D.
Psychology. M.A., Ph.D.
Public Administration. M.P.A.
Public Health Sciences. M.P.H., Dr.P.H., M.S., Ph.D.
Public Policy Analysis. Ph.D.
Slavic and Baltic Languages and Literature. M.A., Ph.D.
Social Work. M.S.W., Ph.D.
Sociology. M.A., Ph.D.
Spanish-Hispanic Studies. M.A.
Surgery. M.D. for admissions; M.S.
Urban Planning and Policy. M.U.P.P., Ph.D.

College of Medicine (60612-7302)

Founded 1881. College of Medicine has campuses at Champaigne-Urbana, Peoria, Rockford. Annual tuition: resident $11,250, nonresident $32,780. Total average figure for all other expenses: $10,853.

Enrollment: first-year class 300, total full-time 1319 (men 66%, women 34%). Faculty; full-time 250, part-time 2500. On-campus housing for 132 single students; none for married students. Average annual housing cost: $5000 for single students. Contact Housing Office, Medical Center. Phone: (312)413-5418. Degrees conferred: M.D., M.D.-M.S., M.D.-Ph.D.

ADMISSION REQUIREMENTS. AMCAS report, transcripts, letters of recommendation, MCAT required in support of application. Interview may be requested. Preference given to state students. Applicants must have completed bachelor's or equivalent. Has EDP; apply between June 15 and August. Apply to Office of Admissions and Records after June 15, before December 1. Application fee $30. Phone: (312)996-5635; fax: (312)996-6693.

ADMISSION STANDARDS. Competitive. Accepts 15% of total annual applicants. Approximately 90% are state residents.

FINANCIAL AID. Scholarships, awards, loans. About 17% of students receive aid other than loans from College funds. Apply to Office of Student Affairs by July 1. Use FAFSA. Phone: (312)413-0127.

DEGREE REQUIREMENTS. For M.D.: satisfactory completion of four-year program. For M.S., Ph.D. requirements refer to Graduate College listing above.

FIELDS OF GRADUATE STUDY.
Anatomy.
Biochemistry.
Biophysics.
Cell Biology.
Genetics.
Immunology.
Microbiology.
Pathology.
Pharmacology.
Physiology.
Public Health.
Toxicology.

College of Dentistry (60612-7211)

Founded 1898. Annual tuition: resident $7448, nonresident $19,580. On-campus housing for single students only. Average academic year housing cost: $11,000. Total average cost for all other first-year expenses: $11,000.

Enrollment: first-year class 57; total full-time 333 (men 70%, women 30%). Faculty: full-time 72, part-time 171. Degrees conferred: D.D.S., D.D.S.-M.S., D.D.S.-Ph.D.

ADMISSION REQUIREMENTS. AADSAS report, transcripts, DAT, recommendations required in support of application. Interview often required. Applicants must have completed at least 2 years of college study, preferably 3 years of study. Apply to Office of Admissions and Records after July 1, before April 1. Application fee $30. Phone: (312)996-1020.

ADMISSION STANDARDS. Selective. Usual minimum average: 2.25. Accepts 60% of total annual applicants. Approximately 85% are state residents.

FINANCIAL AID. Scholarships, loans. Apply to Office of Student Financial and Services of Health Science Center; no specified closing date. About 86% of students receive some aid from College. Phone: (312)996-5563/4940.

DEGREE REQUIREMENTS. For D.D.S.: satisfactory completion of forty-five-month program. The D.D.S.-M.S. program can normally be completed during four-year period.

FIELDS OF GRADUATE STUDY.
Endodontics.
Oral Surgery.
Orthodontics.
Pediatric Dentistry.
Periodontics.
Prosthodontics.

UNIVERSITY OF ILLINOIS AT URBANA-CHAMPAIGN

Urbana-Champaign, Illinois 61820
http://www.grad.uiuc.edu

Founded 1967. Located 125 miles S of Chicago. Coed. State control. Semester system. Special facilities: Beckman Institution for Advanced Science and Technology, Biotechnology Center, Center for Advanced Construction Technology, Center for African Studies, Center for Latin American and Caribbean Studies, Center for Russian and East European Studies, Center for Complex System Research, Center for Cement Composite Materials, Center for Composite Materials Research, Center for Compound Semiconductor Microelectronics, Center for East Asian and Pacific Studies, Center for South and West Asian Studies,

Center for the Study of Reading, National Center for Supercomputing Applications, Illinois Electron Paramagnetic Research Center, Institute for Environmental Studies, Krannert Art Museum, World Heritage Museum. Library (third largest university library): 8,000,000 volumes, 3,000,000 microtexts, 10,000 periodicals, serials, newspapers.

Annual tuition fees: full-time, resident $4408–$4908, nonresident $10,492–$10,892; part-time, resident $1562–$1696, nonresident $3580–$3714. On-campus housing: 750 married student apartments; 1000 graduate dormitory rooms (mixed sex). Average academic year housing cost: $3200–$4500 (plus utilities) for married students, $5175 (including board) for single students. Apply to Division of Housing. Phone: (217)333-1752 (on-campus information), (217)333-1420 (off-campus information).

Graduate College

Graduate study since 1867. Enrollment: full-time 8687, part-time 135. Graduate teaching faculty: full-time about 2200, part-time figures not available. Degrees conferred: A.M., M.S., M.A.S., M.Arch., M.F.A., M.B.A., Ed.M., M.L.A., LL.M., M.C.S., M.M., M.Ext.Ed., M.S.B.A., M.S.W., M.U.P., A.C.Ed., C.A.S., Ed.D., D.M.A., Ph.D.

ADMISSION REQUIREMENTS. Transcript required in support of College's application. GRE/MAT/GMAT/recommendations/interview required by some departments. TOEFL required for international applicants. Accepts transfer applicants. Graduates of unaccredited institutions not considered. Apply to Office of Admissions and Records at least three months in advance of registration, international applicants at least six months in advance of registration. Application fee $30 domestic students, $40 international students. Phone: (217)333-0302.

ADMISSION STANDARDS. Competitive for most departments. Usual minimum average: 3.0 (A = 4).

FINANCIAL AID. Annual awards from institutional funds: 500 academic tuition scholarships, 500 fellowships, 800 administrative assistantships, 2300 teaching assistantships, 3200 research assistantships, Federal W/S, loans. Approved for VA benefits. Apply by February 15 to appropriate department head for fellowships, assistantships; for other aid programs apply to Office of Financial Aid. Phone: (217)333-0100. Use FAFSA. About 65% of students receive aid other than loans from University and outside sources. No aid for part-time students.

DEGREE REQUIREMENTS. One unit = 4 semester hours. For most master's: 8 units minimum, at least 4 units in residence; thesis/nonthesis option; language required for some departments. For M.A.S., Ed.M.: same as for most master's, except no thesis requirement. For M.M.: same as for most master's, except reading knowledge of one foreign language for musicology majors. For M.F.A.: 16 units minimum in residence; written report required for majors in design, painting and printmaking, sculpture, art history; no thesis for A.M. in Art Education; reading knowledge of one foreign language for art history majors. For M.B.A.: 18 units minimum; no thesis. For LL.M.: 8 units minimum, at least 2 for research; thesis. For M.S.W.: 16 months in residence and field work. For M.U.P.: normally 2 years in residence; thesis. For A.C.Ed.: 8 units beyond the master's, at least 4 in residence. For Ph.D.: 24 units minimum beyond the bachelor's, at least 16 in residence; preliminary exam; dissertation; final oral exam. For Ed.D.: essentially the same as for the Ph.D. For D.M.A.: essentially as for the Ph.D., except special performance or composition projects in addition to dissertation.

FIELDS OF STUDY.
Accounting.
Advertising. M.S. only.

Aeronautical and Astronautical Engineering. Thesis for M.S.
African Studies.
Agricultural and Consumer Economics.
Agricultural Education. M.S. only.
Agricultural Engineering.
Animal Sciences.
Anthropology. Thesis for A.M.
Architecture. Portfolio for admission. M.Arch. only.
Art and Design. Includes applied, creative, art education, art history, graphic design; portfolio for admission to creative majors; Ed.D. in art education; Ph.D. in art history.
Astronomy. Includes astrophysics.
Atmospheric Sciences.
Biochemistry.
Biological Engineering.
Biology. Interdepartmental.
Biophysics.
Business Administration.
Cell and Structural Biology.
Ceramic Engineering. Thesis for M.S.
Chemical Engineering. Thesis for M.S.
Chemical Physics. Ph.D. only.
Chemistry. Includes biophysical chemistry.
Civil Engineering. Eight units plus thesis or nine units without thesis for M.S.
Classics. Includes Latin, Greek, classics; Ph.D. in classical philology only.
Communications. Ph.D. only.
Community Health. Thesis normally required for M.S.
Comparative Literature. Interdepartmental.
Computer Engineering.
Computer Science.
Crop Sciences.
Dance. Performance; M.F.A. only.
East Asian Languages and Culture.
Ecology.
Economics. GRE for admission; thesis optional for A.M., M.S.
Education. Includes elementary, secondary teaching; administration and supervision, adult curriculum, exceptional children, bilingual education, educational psychology, early childhood teaching, reading research, guidance and counseling, rehabilitation counseling, educational policy studies, history and philosophy, measurement and evaluation, research methods, school psychology; vocational and technical education; all subject fields; thesis for A.M., M.S.
Electrical Engineering. Thesis for M.S.
Engineering Design.
English. One language for A.M.; thesis optional.
English as International Language. A.M. only.
Entomology. Thesis required for M.S.
Extension Education. Eight units plus thesis or nine units without thesis for M.Ext.Ed.; M.Ext.Ed. only.
Finance. Eight units with thesis or ten units without thesis for master's.
Food Science and Human Nutrition.
French.
General Engineering. M.S. only.
Genetics. Interdepartmental; Ph.D. only.
Geography.
Geology.
Germanic Languages and Literatures. Thesis, one language in addition to German for A.M.; two additional languages for Ph.D.
History. One language for A.M.
Human Development and Family Ecology. M.S. or A.M. only; thesis optional.
Industrial Engineering.
Journalism. Thesis or special project for M.S.; M.S. only.
Kinesiology. GRE, MAT for admission; thesis for M.S.
Labor and Industrial Relations. Eight units with thesis, 10 units without thesis for M.S.

Landscape Architecture. Twelve units for M.L.A.; M.L.A. only.

Latin American and Caribbean Studies.

Law. J.D. admission.

Leisure Studies.

Library and Information Science. GRE for admission; 10 units required for M.S.

Linguistics. One language, final essay for A.M.

Materials Engineering.

Mathematics. Includes applied, statistics.

Mechanical Engineering. Thesis required for M.S.

Metallurgical Engineering. Thesis for M.S.

Microbiology.

Molecular and Integrative Physiology.

Music. Includes performance, musicology, music education, composition; qualifying exam for admission, including performance when appropriate; one language for M.M. in musicology.

Natural Resources and Environmental Science.

Neuroscience.

Nuclear Engineering. Eight units with thesis, nine units without thesis for M.S.

Nutritional Science.

Philosophy. GRE for admission; essay for A.M.

Physics.

Physiology.

Plant Biology.

Plant Pathology. Thesis for M.S.

Political Science. Thesis or research paper for A.M.

Psychology. GRE for admission; thesis for A.M.

Rehabilitation Education.

Russian.

Russian and East European Studies.

Slavic Languages and Literatures.

Social Work. Ten units required for M.S.W.

Sociology. GRE for admission.

Spanish, Italian, and Portuguese. A.M., Ph.D. in all three languages.

Speech and Hearing Science. Includes education of the deaf.

Speech Communication. GRE for admission; thesis for A.M.

Statistics.

Theater. Fourteen units required for M.F.A.

Theoretical and Applied Mechanics. Eight units with thesis, nine units without thesis for M.S.

Urban and Regional Planning. Thesis or master's project required; 12–13½ units for M.U.P.; Ph.D. in regional planning.

Veterinary Medical Science. Includes veterinary biosciences, clinical medicine, pathology, and hygiene; D.V.M. or appropriate B.S. for admission.

College of Law

Established 1897. Semester system. Law library: 593,400 volumes. Library has LEXIS, NEXIS, WESTLAW.

Annual tuition: resident $5750, nonresident $15,342. Total average annual additional expense: $8000.

Enrollment: first-year class 213; total full-time 630 (men 59%, women 41%); postgraduates 25; no part-time study. Faculty: full-time 37, part-time 17. Degrees conferred: J.D., J.D.-M.D., J.D.-M.Acc., J.D.-M.B.A., J.D.-M.A. (Labor and Industrial Relations, Urban Planning), J.D.-M.Ed., J.D.-Ed.D. The LL.M., J.S.D. are offered through the Graduate College.

ADMISSION REQUIREMENTS. LSDAS Law School report, bachelor's degree, transcripts, LSAT required in support of application. Interview not required. Accepts transfer applicants. Apply to Admission Office of the College by May 1 (preference given to applications received by January 15). Admits first-year students Fall only. Application fee $30. Phone: (217)244-6415.

ADMISSION STANDARDS. Selective. Accepts 20% of total annual applicants.

FINANCIAL AID. Scholarships, fellowships, assistantships, full and partial tuition waiver, loans. Apply to Financial Aid Office, preferably by March 15. Use FAFSA. Graduate students apply through Graduate College and use University FAF. About 25% of students receive aid other than loans from College.

DEGREE REQUIREMENTS. For J.D.: 90 hours minimum, at least 6 semesters in full-time residence. Transfer credit from other law schools individually considered. For LL.M.: at least 2 semesters beyond J.D. For J.S.D.: first professional degree required; 16 courses, individually arranged. Refer to Graduate College listings for joint degree requirements.

College of Veterinary Medicine

Established 1944. Annual tuition: resident $7098, nonresident $18,678. Total average cost for other expenses: $7842.

Enrollment: first-year class 86; total full-time 340 (men 45%, women 55%); no part-time students; graduate students 100. Faculty: full-time 100. Degrees conferred: D.V.M.-Ph.D., D.V.M.-Law. The Ph.D. is offered through the Graduate College.

ADMISSION REQUIREMENTS. VMCAS report, transcripts, VCAT, essay, animal/veterinary experience, three recommendations (one from an academic advisor) required in support of application. Interview by invitation only. Applicants must have completed at least two years of college study. Preference given to residents and to nonresidents from states that do not have veterinary schools. Apply to Assistant Dean after August 15 but before November 1 for nonresidents, by December 15 for residents. Fall admission only. Application fee $30. Phone: (217)333-1192.

ADMISSION STANDARDS. Selective. Accepts 45% of total annual applicants. 20–30% nonresidents are offered admission each year.

FINANCIAL AID. Scholarships, research fellowships, reaching/research assistantships, full and partial; tuition waivers, CWSP. Apply to University Office of Student Financial Aid by January 15. Use FAFSA.

DEGREE REQUIREMENTS. For D.V.M.: 153 semester hours in full-time residence. For Ph.D.: see Graduate College listing above.

FIELDS OF GRADUATE STUDY.

Veterinary Biosciences.

Veterinary Pathobiology.

UNIVERSITY OF THE INCARNATE WORD

San Antonio, Texas 78209

Founded 1881. Coed. Private control. Semester system. Library: 200,000 volumes, 44,000 microforms, computerized retrieval service, 30 PCs.

Tuition: per credit $350. On-campus housing for graduate men and women. Annual academic year housing cost: $4000–$5000. Apply to Director of Admissions. Phone: (210)829-6034.

Graduate Division

Graduate study since 1950. Enrollment: full-time 103, part-time 442. College faculty: full-time 68, part-time 31. Degrees conferred: M.A., M.S., M.B.A., M.S.N., M.Ed.

ADMISSION REQUIREMENTS. Transcripts, GRE/MAT/GMAT required in support of application. Interview required for some disciplines. TOEFL required for foreign applicants. Accepts transfer applicants. Graduates of unaccredited colleges usually not considered. Apply to Admissions Office at least 6 weeks prior to registration. Application fee $20. Phone: (210)829-6005; fax: (210)829-3921.

ADMISSION STANDARDS. Selective. Usual minimum average: 2.5 (3.0 in major) (A = 4).

FINANCIAL AID. Annual awards from institutional funds: Five research assistantships, eight administrative assistantships, six internships, Federal W/S, loans. Approved for VA benefits. Apply to the Financial Aid office; no specified closing date. Use FAFSA and institutional FAF. Phone: (210)829-6008.

DEGREE REQUIREMENTS. For M.A., M.Ed., M.S., M.S.N.: 36 credit hours minimum, at least 24 in residence; thesis/nonthesis option. For M.B.A.: 48 credit hours minimum, at least 36 in residence (specific undergraduate prerequisites required).

FIELDS OF STUDY.
Biology.
Business Administration. Joint M.B.A./M.S.N. program.
Communication Arts.
Education. Includes reading, special, educational diagnostician, education for hearing impaired, curriculum, teaching, early childhood, adult.
English.
Management.
Mathematics.
Multidisciplinary Studies.
Nursing. Joint M.S.N./M.B.A. program.
Nutrition.
Physical Education.
Religious Studies.
Social Gerontology.
Sports Management.

INDIANA STATE UNIVERSITY
Terre Haute, Indiana 47809-1401
http://www.indstate.edu

Founded 1865. Located 170 miles S of Chicago. Coed. State control. Semester system. Special facilities: Biotech Center, Center for Governmental Studies, Hearing Disorder Center, School Psychology Center, Special Education Center, Speech Pathology Center, Technology Services Center, Turman Art Gallery, Center for Urban-Regional Studies. Library: 1,000,000 volumes, 712,000 microforms, 120 PCs.

Tuition: per credit, resident $132, nonresident $299. On-campus housing for 393 married students, limited number of graduate men, women. Average academic year housing cost: $3624–$5820 for married students, $3859–$4845 (including board) for single students. Apply to Director, University Housing. Phone: (812)237-7697. Day care facilities available.

School of Graduate Studies

Graduate study since 1927. Enrollment: full-time 692 (men 353, women 339); part-time 948. University faculty teaching graduate students: full-time 343, part-time 12. Degrees conferred: M.A., M.M., M.M.E., M.S., M.B.A., M.P.A., M.F.A., Ed.S., Ph.D., Psy.D.

ADMISSION REQUIREMENTS. Transcript required in support of School's application. Interview required for all Ph.D. applicants. GRE required for some M.A. departments, all doctoral applicants, five letters of recommendation for doctoral applicants. TOEFL required for international applicants. Accepts transfer applicants. Graduates of unaccredited colleges considered. Apply to Dean, School of Graduate Studies one month prior to registration. Application fee none. Phone: (812)237-3111; fax: (812)237-8060.

ADMISSION STANDARDS. Selective. Usual minimum average: 2.5 (A = 4).

FINANCIAL AID. Annual awards from institutional funds: 92 research fellowships, 327 assistantships, Federal W/S, loans. Apply by March 1 to appropriate department chair for fellowships, assistantships; to Director of Financial Aid for all other programs. Phone: (812)237-2215. About 50% of full-time students receive aid other than loans from University and outside sources.

DEGREE REQUIREMENTS. For M.A., M.M., M.M.E., M.S., M.B.A., M.P.A., M.F.A.: 32 semester hours minimum; reading knowledge of one foreign language for some departments; GMAT for M.B.A. candidacy; final oral exam with thesis. For Ed.S.: 30 semester hours minimum beyond the master's, at least 20 in residence and one semester in full-time attendance; research project; final oral exam. For Ph.D., Psy.D.: 83–90 semester hours minimum beyond the bachelor's, at least 30 in residence and two consecutive semesters in full-time attendance; preliminary exam; reading knowledge of two foreign languages or one language and statistics or computer science; dissertation final oral exam.

FIELDS OF STUDY.
Agency Counseling.
Art. Includes history, graphic design. M.A., M.F.A.
Business Administration.
Business Education.
Chemistry.
Clinical Laboratory Science.
Clinical Psychology. Admits Fall only.
College Student Personnel Services.
Communication.
Communication Disorders. Includes speech-language pathology.
Criminology.
Drama/Theater Arts.
Economics.
Education. Includes educational administration, elementary, secondary (business, industrial arts, usual subject fields), gifted, health, guidance and psychological services, guidance and counseling, media and instructional technology, student personnel services in higher education, school psychology.
Engineering and Applied Sciences.
English.
Foreign Languages. Includes French, Spanish, Latin.
Geography. Includes economic, physical.
Geology.
Health and Safety.
History.
Home Economics and Human Development.
Human Resource Development.
Humanities. Interdisciplinary.
Industrial and Professional Technology.
Library Science.
Life Sciences. Includes microbiology, systematics, ecology, physiology.
Marriage and Family Therapy.
Mathematics.
Music.
Music Education.
Nursing.
Physical Education. Includes athletic training.
Physics.
Political Science. Includes public administration.
Psychology.
Public Policy and Administration.

Social Psychology.

Social Studies.

Sociology.

Special Education. Includes LD, M.I.M.H., S.E.H., E.D. interdisciplinary school psychology program.

Technology Education.

Vocational-Technical Education.

INDIANA UNIVERSITY

Bloomington, Indiana 47405

http://www.indiana.edu

Founded 1820. Main campus in Bloomington; Medical Center campus and Law School in Indianapolis. Coed. State control. Semester system. Special facilities: Center for American Studies, Bowen Research Center, CDC CYBER 170/855, Dec VAX-11/780, Geological Field Station in Montana, observatory, biological research station, participant in CIC Traveling Scholar Program with other Big Ten universities, Cyclotron facility, East Asian Languages and Cultures Center, Russian and East European Institute, Fine Arts Museum, Center for Health and Safety Studies, Hilltop and Garden Center, Center for the Study of Law in Action, Indiana Business Research Center, Indiana Museum (anthropology, archaeology, history), Lilly rare book library, Kinsey Sex Institute, Glen Black Archaeological Laboratory, Archives of Traditional Music, Folklore Institute, Nuclear Magnetic Resonance Laboratory, Institute of Psychiatric Research, Institute for Social Research, Semiotics Institute, Transportation Research Center. Library: 5,500,000 volumes, 3,442,000 microforms.

Tuition: per unit, resident $140, nonresident $408. On-campus housing for 1467 married students, 850 graduate men, 850 graduate women. Average academic year housing cost $5100 for married students, $425 per month; $7728 (including board) for single students. Apply to University Halls of Residence. Phone: (812)855-5601. Day care facilities available.

Graduate School

http://www.indiana.edu/~grdschl/index.html

Graduate study since 1881. Enrollment: full-time 3200, part-time 800 (men 65%, women 35%). Graduate faculty: full-time 1887. Degrees conferred: M.A., M.S., M.A.T., M.F.A., M.H.A., D.B.A., Ph.D., LL.M.

ADMISSION REQUIREMENTS. Two transcripts, three reference letters required in support of School's application. GRE or other entrance exams may be required. Interview not required. Accepts transfer applicants. Graduates of unaccredited institutions not considered. Apply to Office of Graduate School by January 15 (Fall), August 15 (Spring), January 1 (Summer). Application fee $35, $50 for international applicants. Phone: (812)855-8853; fax: (812)855-4266.

ADMISSION STANDARDS. Varies, from relatively open to very competitive. Usual minimum average: 3.0 (A = 4).

FINANCIAL AID. Scholarships; 185 research assistantships, 814 graduate assistantships, 36 faculty assistants, 1665 associate instructors, 247 counselors. Apply by February 1 to proposed major department for fellowships, assistantships; to Financial Aid Office for all other programs. Use FAFSA. About 50% of students receive aid other than loans from University and outside sources. Aid sometimes available to part-time students.

DEGREE REQUIREMENTS. For M.A., M.S.: 30 hours minimum, at least one semester or two summer sessions in full-time attendance; thesis for up to 6 hours' credit; reading knowledge of one foreign language; final written or oral exam may be required. For M.A.T., M.H.A.: 36 hours minimum, at least 24 in residence and one semester in full-time attendance. For M.F.A.: 60 hours minimum in residence, at least one semester in full-time attendance; final creative project in chosen studio area. For LL.M.: 30 hours minimum in residence; thesis; final oral exam sometimes required. For Ph.D., D.B.A.: 90 hours minimum beyond the bachelor's, at least 60 in residence and two consecutive semesters in full-time attendance; proficiency in depth in one foreign language, reading knowledge in two foreign languages, or reading proficiency in one language and research skill may be required; qualifying exam; dissertation for up to 30 hours' credit; final oral exam.

FIELDS OF STUDY.

American Studies. Ph.D. is combined with related major field.

Anthropology. Thesis or exam required for M.A.

Apparel Merchandising and Interior Design. M.S. only.

Applied Mathematics.

Arabic.

Archaeology.

Arts Administration. M.A. only.

Astronomy. Thesis ordinarily required for M.A.

Astrophysics. Ph.D. only.

Biochemistry. Interdepartmental; programs at Bloomington and Indianapolis campuses; thesis for M.S.; Ph.D.

Biology. M.A.T.; genetics, Ph.D.; microbiology, M.A., Ph.D.; molecular and cellular biology, Ph.D.; plant sciences, M.A., Ph.D.; zoology, M.A., Ph.D.; environmental and evolutionary biology, M.A., Ph.D.

Business. Ph.D. only.

Central Eurasian Studies. M.A., Ph.D.

Ceramics.

Chemistry. Thesis for M.S., M.A.T., Ph.D.

Classical Studies. Includes Greek, Latin; thesis for M.A., M.A.T.; GRE for admission to Ph.D.

Clinical Psychology. GRE for admission.

Cognitive Science. Ph.D. is combined with related major field.

Comparative Literature. Proficiency in one, fluency in one foreign language; thesis for M.A., M.A.T.; fluency in two, proficiency in three foreign languages for Ph.D.

Computer Science. M.S., Ph.D.

Creative Writing.

Criminal Justice.

Dentistry. Program at Indianapolis campus; apply to Secretary of Dental Graduate Program; thesis for Ph.D.

East Asian Languages and Cultures. Includes Chinese, Japanese, East Asian Studies (M.A. only); one East Asian language for admission; thesis, two languages for M.A.; two languages for Ph.D.

Economics. GRE Subject for admission. M.A., Ph.D.

Education. Includes adult, art, business, counseling and counselor education, curriculum, educational inquiry and methodology, English, international and comparative, math, occupational, science, urban and overseas education, educational psychology, elementary, higher, history, instructional systems technology, philosophy, reading research, school administration, secondary, special; M.A., Ph.D. through Graduate School; M.S. in Ed., Ed.S., Ed.D. through School of Education.

English. Includes creative writing major for M.A.; one language for M.A., M.A.T.; two languages for admission to Ph.D. in English language.

Environmental Risk Analysis.

Environmental Science. Ph.D. only.

Evolution and Ecology.

Fine Arts. Includes studio, art history; one language for M.A. in art history, portfolio for admission to M.F.A., M.A.T.; Ph.D. in art history only.

Folklore. Thesis optional; one language for M.A., Ph.D.

French and Italian. GRE for admission; three languages for Ph.D.; French M.A., M.A.T., Ph.D.; Italian M.A., Ph.D.

General Science. M.A.T. only.

Genetics. Interdepartmental; Ph.D.

Geochemistry.

Geography. M.A., M.A.T., Ph.D.

Geophysics.

Germanic Languages. M.A., M.A.T., Ph.D.

Graphic Design.

Health Administration.

Health, Physical Education, Recreation. Ph.D. only; others through School of HPER.

History. GRE, one language for admission. M.A., M.A.T., Ph.D.

History and Philosophy of Science. M.A., Ph.D.

Hungarian Studies. Certificate only.

Journalism. Thesis or project for M.A., M.A.T. only.

Latin American Studies. One language for M.A.

Law and Social Science.

Library Science. M.L.S. offered by School of Library and Information Sciences, Ph.D. by Graduate School.

Linguistics. One language; thesis optional for M.A., Ph.D.

Mass Communication. Interdepartmental; GRE for admission. Ph.D. only.

Mathematical Physics. Interdepartmental. Ph.D. only.

Mathematics. M.A., M.A.T., Ph.D. only.

Medical Sciences (Bloomington). Includes anatomy, M.A., Ph.D.; pathology, M.S., Ph.D.; physiology, M.A., Ph.D.; pharmacology, M.S., Ph.D.; (Indianapolis) anatomy, M.S., Ph.D.; medical biophysics, M.S., Ph.D.; medical genetics, M.S., Ph.D.; medical neurobiology, M.S., Ph.D.; microbiology and immunology, M.S., Ph.D.; pharmacology, M.S., Ph.D.; physiology, M.S., Ph.D.; toxicology, M.S., Ph.D.

Medical Sciences Combined Degree Program (Bloomington and Indianapolis). M.S. or Ph.D., and M.D.

Medieval Studies. Certificate only.

Microbiology. M.A., Ph.D.

Music. Includes Composition, M.A.; musicology, theory, education, M.A., M.A.T. (music education only), Ph.D. offered by Graduate School; for M.M., M.S.Mus., M.M.Ed., D.Mus.Ed., D.Mus., admission is through School of Music; entrance exams required; thesis for M.A.; several years' experience for admission to M.A.T.

Near Eastern Languages and Cultures. Includes Arabic, Hebrew; for Ph.D.: thesis, one language in addition to Arabic, Hebrew.

Neural Sciences. Ph.D. only.

Painting.

Philosophy. GRE for admission; thesis, one language for M.A., Ph.D.

Physics. M.S., M.A.T., Ph.D.

Physiological Optics. Thesis for M.S., Ph.D.

Plant Science. M.A., Ph.D.

Political Science. M.A., M.A.T., Ph.D.

Psychology. Thesis for M.A., Ph.D.

Public Affairs. Ph.D. only.

Public Policy. Ph.D. only.

Slavic Languages and Literatures. Includes Russian major for M.A., M.A.T., Russian literature or Slavic linguistics for Ph.D., one language in addition to Russian for M.A., two languages in addition to Russian for Ph.D. in Russian literature; comprehensive knowledge of one Slavic language, reading knowledge of French, German, and one other Slavic language for Ph.D. in Slavic linguistics.

Social Psychology.

Social Studies. M.A.T. only.

Sociology. Special project for M.A., Ph.D.

Spanish and Portuguese. Includes Spanish major for M.A., M.A.T.; Hispanic literature or Spanish linguistics for Ph.D.; some knowledge of Latin plus two other languages in addition to Spanish for Ph.D.

Speech and Hearing Sciences. Includes speech pathology and audiology; thesis for M.A.; thesis may be creative in nature; M.A.T., Ph.D.

Speech Communication. M.A., M.A.T., Ph.D.

Telecommunication. Thesis for M.A., M.S.

Theater and Drama. M.A., M.A.T., M.F.A., Ph.D.

Western European Studies. Thesis, comprehensive knowledge of one language, reading knowledge of one other. M.A. only.

Zoology.

Graduate School of Business

http://www.bus.indiana.edu/MBA

Graduate study authorized 1936. Annual tuition: resident $7738, nonresident $15,282. Enrollment: M.B.A. full-time 564, Ph.D. 85. Faculty: full-time 186. Degrees conferred: M.B.A., D.B.A.-Ph.D., J.D.-M.B.A.

ADMISSION REQUIREMENTS. Transcripts, recommendations, work experience, GMAT required in support of School's application. TOEFL required for international applicants. Interview recommended for D.B.A.-Ph.D., M.B.A. programs. Apply to Graduate School of Business Admissions by January 6 (M.B.A.), March 1 (Ph.D.); international applicants February 1. Fall entry only. Application fee $35; international application fee $65. Phone: (812)855-8006 (M.B.A.), (812)855-3476 (doctoral).

ADMISSION STANDARDS. Very selective for M.B.A. and D.B.A.-Ph.D. Usual average: 3.2 (A = 4). Average GMAT 620, 664 (doctoral).

FINANCIAL AID. Annual awards from institutional funds: Seventy scholarships, two hundred graduate assistantships, forty fellowships, loans. Apply to Director of Admissions and Financial Aid; no specified closing date. Use FAFSA and institutional FAF. Phone: (812)855-8006. About 50% of students receive aid other than loans from School and outside sources.

DEGREE REQUIREMENTS. For M.B.A.: 54 semester hours minimum, at least 47 in residence. For D.B.A./Ph.D.: three to four years minimum in residence beyond the M.B.A.; dissertation for up to 24 hours, including research seminars; final oral exam. For J.D. requirements: see School of Law listing below.

FIELDS OF STUDY.

M.B.A. program. Includes accounting and information systems, entrepreneurship, design, finance, human resource management, international business administration, management, marketing, operations and decision technology, production/operations leaders program.

Ph.D. program. Includes accounting, business economics and public policy, decision sciences, management information systems, and operations management.

School of Education—Graduate Studies

http://education.indiana.edu

Graduate degrees since 1930. Semester system. Tuition: per credit resident $140, nonresident $408. Enrollment: full-time 1013, part-time 186. Graduate faculty: full-time 105, part-time 41. Degrees conferred: M.S. in Ed., Ed.S., Ed.D. The M.A. and Ph.D. are awarded by the Graduate School.

ADMISSION REQUIREMENTS. Transcripts, GRE, three letters of recommendation, goal statement required in support of School's application. Interview may be required. TOEFL required for international applicants. Accepts transfer applicants. Graduates of unaccredited institutions not considered. Apply to Office of Graduate Studies by June 1 (Fall), November 1 (Spring), March 1 (Summer). Application fee $35. Phone: (812)856-8504; fax: (812)856-8518.

ADMISSION STANDARDS. Selective for most departments. Usual minimum average: 2.75 (A = 4) (master's applicants), average GRE combined score 1640; 3.30 (doctoral applicants), average GRE combined score 1700.

FINANCIAL AID. Annual awards from institutional funds: 30 grants, 42 fellowships, 56 research assistantships, 119 teaching assistantships, 50 internships, 103 other assistantships, Federal W/S, loans. Apply by February 15 to Director of Financial Aid. Use FAFSA, FAC sheet. Phone: (812)855-FAST. About 15% of students receive aid other than loans from both School and outside sources.

DEGREE REQUIREMENTS. For M.S. in Ed.: 36 semester hours minimum without thesis, at least 27 in residence, 15 credits at the campus awarding the degree. For Ed.S.: 65 hours minimum beyond the bachelor's, at least 35 in residence at the Bloomington or Indianapolis campus; 9 credits in full-time attendance in either one semester, or summer. For Ed.D., Ph.D.: 90 hours minimum beyond the bachelor's or 60 credits with a master's degree, at least two consecutive semesters in residence; qualifying written/oral exams; thesis for up to 15 hours; final oral exam.

FIELDS OF STUDY.

ADULT EDUCATION:
Adult Education. M.S.

COUNSELING AND EDUCATIONAL PSYCHOLOGY:
Counseling and Counselor Education. M.S.
Counseling Psychology. Ph.D.
Educational Psychology. M.S., Ph.D.
School Psychology. Ed.S., Ph.D.

CURRICULUM AND INSTRUCTION:
Art Education. M.S.
Curriculum and Instruction. Ed.D., Ph.D.
Elementary Education. M.S., Ed.S.
Secondary Education. Includes mathematics, science; M.S., Ed.S.
Social Studies. M.S., Ed.S.
Special Education. M.S., Ed.S., Ed.D., Ph.D.

EDUCATIONAL LEADERSHIP AND POLICY STUDIES:
Higher Education. Ed.D., Ph.D.
Higher Education and Student Affairs. M.S.
History, Philosophy, and Policy Studies. M.S.
International and Comparative Education. M.S.
School Administration. M.S., Ed.S., Ed.D., Ph.D.

INSTRUCTIONAL SYSTEMS TECHNOLOGY:
Instructional Systems Technology. M.S., Ed.S., Ed.D., Ph.D.

LANGUAGE EDUCATION:
Language Education. M.S., Ed.S., Ed.D., Ph.D.

School of Health, Physical Education, and Recreation—Graduate Division

In operation since 1946. Tuition: per credit, resident $140.00, nonresident $408. Enrollment: full- and part-time 330. Faculty teaching graduate students: full-time 50, part-time 12. Degrees conferred: M.S., M.P.H., Director, H.S.D., P.E.D., Re.D., Ph.D.

ADMISSION REQUIREMENTS. Transcripts, GRE, letters of recommendation required in support of School's application. TOEFL required for international applicants. Interview usually not required. Accepts transfer applicants. Apply to Associate Dean for Academic Services; no specified closing dates. Application fee $20. Phone: (812)855-1561; fax: (812)855-4983.

ADMISSION STANDARDS. Selective. Usual minimum average: for M.S. 2.8; for doctoral degree 3.0 (A = 4).

FINANCIAL AID. Annual awards from institutional funds: 120 students academic appointments, Federal W/S, loans. Apply to

Dean for academic appointments; to Financial Aid Office for all other programs. Use FAFSA. Phone: (812)855-0321.

DEGREE REQUIREMENTS. For M.S.: 35 semester hours minimum, at least 25–30 in residence. For M.P.H.: 40 credit hours minimum, at least 25–30 in residence. For Director's degree: 65 hours minimum beyond the bachelor's, at least 35 in residence; final project; one year of professional experience; final written exam. For H.S.D., P.E.D., Re.D.: normally 90 hours beyond the bachelor's, at least 45 in residence and two semesters in full-time attendance; qualifying exam; dissertation for 15 hours; two years of practical experience; language/statistics options; final oral exam. For Ph.D. human performance: 90 hours beyond the bachelor's, at least 60 hours in residence; qualifying exams; dissertation; language/statistics option; final oral exam.

FIELDS OF STUDY.
Applied Health Science. Includes public health, human development and family studies, nutrition and dietetics, safety management, school health education, health behavior, health promotion.
Kinesiology. Includes adapted physical education, administration/curriculum/instruction, applied sport science, athletic administration/sport management, athletic training, biomechanics, exercise physiology, motor learning and control, clinical exercise physiology, social science of sport.
Recreation and Park Administration. Includes general administration, leisure behavior, outdoor and resource management, recreational sports administration, therapeutic recreation.

School of Library and Information Science
http://www-slis.lib.indiana.edu

Organized library and information science study since 1930. Semester system.
Tuition: per credit, resident $140, nonresident $408. On-campus housing available. Enrollment: full-time 170, part-time 479 (men 30%, women 70%). Faculty: full-time 22. Degrees conferred: M.L.S., M.I.S., Specialist. The Ph.D. is offered by the Graduate School.

ADMISSION REQUIREMENTS. Transcripts, letters of reference, professional goals statement required in support of School's application. GRE required for applicants with less than 3.0 GPA. TOEFL required for international applicants. Interview may be required. Accepts transfer applicants. Graduates of unaccredited colleges not considered. Apply to Office of School by June 15 (Fall), November 15 (Spring), March 15 (Summer). Application fee $35. Phone: (812)855-2018; fax: (812)855-6166.

ADMISSION STANDARDS. Selective. Usual minimum average: 3.0 (A = 4).

FINANCIAL AID. Annual awards from institutional funds: Thirty academic scholarships, fellowships, graduate assistantships, fee reduction assistance for nonresidents also available; Federal W/S, loans. Approved for VA benefits. Apply by February 1 to appropriate department for scholarships, fellowships, assistantships; to Office of Scholarships and Financial Aid for all other programs. Use FAFSA and institutional FAF. Phone: (812)855-7787. About 10% of students receive aid from University and outside sources. Aid available to part-time students; part-time work opportunities in the library generally available.

DEGREE REQUIREMENTS. For M.L.S.: 36 hours minimum with entire program available in Bloomington, Indiana University–Purdue, Indiana University Indianapolis, Indiana University South Bend. Courses offered in the Fall, Spring, and during two Summer Sessions. For M.I.S.: 42 hours minimum; entire program available in Bloomington and IUPUI. For Specialist: 30

hours minimum beyond the master's. For Ph.D.: see Graduate School listing above.

School of Music

Organized music study since 1910. Semester system. On-campus housing available.

Tuition: per credit, resident $140, nonresident $408. Graduate enrollment: full-time 730. School faculty: full-time 120, part-time 25. Degrees conferred: M.M., M.M.Ed., M.S., D.Mus.Ed., D.Mus. The M.A., M.A.T., and Ph.D. are offered through the Graduate School.

ADMISSION REQUIREMENTS. Transcripts, references required in support of application. GRE Music Subject Test strongly recommended for all applicants. GRE scores are required for applicants in Music Education, Music Theory, and Musicology. TOEFL required for international applicants. Audition and/or interview required for most degree and diploma programs. Entrance exams at time of first registration. Accepts transfer applicants. Apply to Director of Admissions by June 15 (Fall), December 1 (Spring), May 1 (Summer). Application fee $20. Phone: (812)855-7998; fax: (812)855-4936.

ADMISSION STANDARDS. Selective. Usual minimum average: 3.0 (A = 4).

FINANCIAL AID. Annual awards from institutional funds: 66 research assistantships, 202 teaching assistantships, 12–15 fellowships, full and partial tuition waivers. Apply to Dean by March 15. Phone: (812)855-1352. Use FAFSA and institutional FAF. About 35% of students receive aid other than loans from School and outside sources.

DEGREE REQUIREMENTS. For master's: 30–35 semester hours minimum, at least 30 in residence and one year or four summer sessions in full-time attendance; reading knowledge of one or more foreign languages for some majors; thesis required for some majors, optional for others. For D.Mus.Ed., D.Mus.: 90 semester hours minimum beyond the bachelor's, at least 30 hours and two consecutive semesters in full-time residence; reading knowledge of one to three foreign languages/research techniques, depending upon program; qualifying exam; recitals or other public performance for most majors; dissertation or final document; final oral exam. For M.A., M.A.T., Ph.D.: see Graduate School listing above.

FIELDS OF STUDY.
Applied Music. Includes instrumental, vocal, early music; audition for admission; knowledge of three languages for M.M. in voice.
Ballet.
Church Music.
Composition. Sample compositions for admission.
Conducting. Includes choral, instrumental, wind.
Music Education.
Musicology.
Music Theater Scenic Techniques.
Music Theory.
Stage Direction for Opera.

School of Nursing

Located at Indianapolis campus (46202). Annual tuition: full-time resident $2508, nonresident $7650; per credit, resident $139, nonresident $425.

Graduate enrollment: full-time 92, part-time 421. Faculty full-time 47, part-time 1. Degrees conferred: M.S.N., D.N.S.

ADMISSION REQUIREMENTS. Official transcripts, GRE, three letters of references, interview, current Indiana R.N. license required in support of School's application. TOEFL required for international applicants. Accepts transfer applicants. Graduates of unaccredited institutions not considered. Apply to Graduate Admissions, School of Nursing by June 15 (Fall), December 15 (Spring), April 15 (Summer). Rolling admissions process. Application fee $25, $50 for international applicants. Phone: (317)274-2806; fax: (317)274-2996.

ADMISSION STANDARDS. Selective. Usual minimum average: 3.0 (A = 4).

FINANCIAL AID. Eighty-six scholarships, sixteen fellowships, forty-two research assistantships, fifteen teaching assistantships, Federal W/S, loans. Apply by May 1 to School of Nursing for fellowships, assistantships, to Traineeships Program for traineeships; to Director of Scholarships and Financial Aid IUPUI for scholarships and all other programs. Use FAFSA. Phone: (317)274-4162. Aid available for part-time students.

DEGREE REQUIREMENTS. For M.S.N.: 36–42 hours minimum, at least 20 in residence; final document. For D.N.S.: Three years minimum beyond the master's, at least one year in full-time residence; qualifying exam; comprehensive exam; dissertation; final oral exam.

FIELDS OF STUDY.
Administration of Nursing Services.
Community Health Nursing.
Nursing of Adults.
Parent Child Nursing.
Primary Health Care Nursing.
Psychiatric Mental Health Nursing.

School of Medicine (46202-5113)

Founded 1903. In 1971 became the hub of statewide medical system. After admission, students select which center they will attend. Centers located at Indianapolis, Bloomington, Gary, South Bend, Fort Wayne, Muncie, Terre Haute, Lafayette, Evansville.

Annual tuition: resident $11,040, nonresident $25,252. Total average figure for all other expenses $7000–$9000. Medical Center housing for 175 married students, 160 men, 130 women.

Enrollment: first-year class 280 (50 EDP) (men 60%, women 40%); total 1060. Faculty: full-time 550, part-time 200. Degrees conferred: M.D., M.D.-M.S., M.D.-Ph.D. The M.S. and Ph.D. are offered through the Graduate School at either Bloomington or Indianapolis.

ADMISSION REQUIREMENTS. AMCAS report, transcripts, letters of recommendation, MCAT required in support of application. Interview by invitation. Applicants must have completed at least three years of college study. Does have EDP; apply between June 15 and August 1. Preference given to Indiana residents. Accepts transfer applicants. Apply to School Admissions Office after June 15, before December 15. Application fee $35, $45 for international applicants. Phone: (317)274-3772.

ADMISSION STANDARDS. Selective. Accepts 25% of total annual applicants. Approximately 90% are state residents.

FINANCIAL AID. Scholarships, fellowships, assistantships, full and partial fee waivers, loans. Use FAFSA. About 50% of students receive aid other than loans from School.

DEGREE REQUIREMENTS. For M.D.: satisfactory completion of four-year program. For M.S. and Ph.D.: see Graduate School listing above.

FIELDS OF GRADUATE STUDY.
Anatomy.
Biochemistry.

Biophysics.
Genetics.
Immunology.
Microbiology.
Molecular Biology.
Neurosciences.
Pathology.
Pharmacology.
Physiology.

PROGRAMS WITH PURDUE UNIVERSITY AT LAFAYETTE:
Engineering.
Medicinal Chemistry.
Molecular Biology.
Neurosciences.

School of Dentistry

Established 1879. Located at Indianapolis campus (46202). Medical Center housing for 99 married students. Average academic year housing cost: $13,900. Contact Housing Office for both on- and off-campus housing information. Phone: (317)274-5159.

Annual tuition: resident $9856, nonresident $21,120. Total average cost for all other first-year expenses: $5930.

Enrollment: first-year class 98; total 475 (men 65%, women 35%), postgraduates 91. Faculty: full-time 112, part-time 113. Degrees conferred: D.D.S., M.S.D. The M.S. and Ph.D. are offered through the Graduate School.

ADMISSION REQUIREMENTS. AADSAS report, transcripts, DAT (no later than October), three letters of recommendation required in support of School's application. Applicants must have completed at least three years of college study, prefer four years of study. Interview by invitation only. Preference given to Indiana residents. Accepts transfer applicants from foreign schools at the second-year level on a space available basis. Graduates of unaccredited institutions not considered. Apply to Director of Admissions after June 1, before February 1. Application fee $25, $50 for international applicants. Phone: (317)274-8173.

ADMISSION STANDARDS. Selective. Accepts 20–25% of total annual applicants. Approximately 85% are state residents.

FINANCIAL AID. Scholarships, fellowships, loans. Apply to the Loan and Scholarship Committee after acceptance, before February 15. Phone: (317)274-4162. About 80% of students receive aid from School.

DEGREE REQUIREMENTS. For D.D.S.: satisfactory completion of four-year program. For M.S.D.: 30 hours minimum in residence; thesis; final written/oral exam. For M.S., Ph.D.: see Graduate School listing above.

FIELDS OF GRADUATE STUDY.
Dental Materials.
Oral Diagnosis and Oral Medicine.
Oral Pathology.
Orthodontics.
Pediatric Dentistry.
Periodontics.
Preventive Dentistry.
Prosthodontics.

School of Law (47405-1001)

Established 1842. Semester system. Located in Bloomington. Library: 520,000 volumes. Library has LEXIS, NEXIS, WESTLAW, DIALOG, LEGISLATE, Wilson-ONLINE.

Tuition: per credit hour, resident $178, nonresident $463. Total average annual additional expense: $9500.

Enrollment: first-year class 234; total 623 (men 56%, women 44%). Faculty: full-time 34, part-time 19. Degrees conferred: J.D., J.D./M.B.A., J.D.-M.L.S., J.D./M.P.A., J.D./M.S. (Environ. Sci.), LL.M., M.C.L.

ADMISSION REQUIREMENTS. LSDAS Law School report, bachelor's degree, transcripts, LSAT, recommendations required in support of application. Graduates of unaccredited colleges not considered. Apply to Admissions Office; no specified closing date. Priority given to applications received before March 1, rolling admissions process. Application fee $35. Phone: (812)335-4765.

ADMISSION STANDARDS. Selective. Admits about 25–30% of total annual applications.

FINANCIAL AID. Scholarships, fellowships, assistantships, Federal W/S, loans. Apply to Admissions Office for fellowships, to Office of Scholarships and Financial Aid for loans; no specified closing date. Use FAFSA. About 25% of students receive some aid from School.

DEGREE REQUIREMENTS. For J.D.: satisfactory completion of an eighty-six-credit-hour program or accelerated twenty-seven-month program is also available. For LL.M., M.C.L.: at least 24 credits minimum beyond J.D.; M.C.L. is limited to graduates of foreign law schools.
Note: Study abroad in London (Great Britain) available.

School of Law—Indianapolis (46202)

Semester system. Law library: 410,000 volumes. Library has LEXIS, NEXIS, WESTLAW.

Tuition: per credit hour, residents $178, nonresidents $463. Limited on-campus housing available.

Enrollment: first-year class, full-time 180, part-time 85; total full- and part-time 830 (men 55%, women 45%). Faculty: full-time 40, part-time 25. Degrees conferred: J.D., J.D.-M.B.A., J.D.-M.H.A., S.D.-M.P.A.

ADMISSION REQUIREMENTS. LSDAS Law School report, bachelor's degree, transcripts, LSAT, personal statement, letters of recommendations required in support of application. Interview not required. Transfer applicants accepted. Applicants must have completed 90 credits prescribed by ABA. Graduates of unaccredited colleges not considered. Apply after September 1, before March 1 to Admissions Office. Beginning part-time students admitted May or August only. Application fee $35. Phone: (317)274-2459.

ADMISSION STANDARDS. Selective. Accepts 40% of total annual applicants.

FINANCIAL AID. Scholarships, fellowships, assistantships, partial tuition waivers, Federal W/S, loans. Apply to Office of Student Financial Aid by February 15. Use FAFSA. About 20% of students receive aid other than loans from School.

DEGREE REQUIREMENTS. For J.D.: 90 semester hours and 6 semesters in full-time residence or 8 semesters in part-time residence. For master's degree: see Graduate School listing above.
Note: Summer program in Shanghai, China, available.

INDIANA UNIVERSITY OF PENNSYLVANIA
Indiana, Pennsylvania 15705-1081

Founded 1875. Located 60 miles NE of Pittsburgh. Coed. State control. Semester system. Day-care facilities available. Library: 742,000 volumes, 578,000 microforms, 8500 filmstrips, 6000 phonograph records, 40,000 current periodicals. A designated Federal Depository.

Annual tuition: full-time resident $3668, nonresident $6054; per credit, resident $187, nonresident $336. Limited on-campus housing available. Average academic year housing cost: $1822–$3060 (including board). Contact Housing and Residence Life Office for on- and off-campus housing information. Phone: (412)357-2696.

Graduate School and Research

Graduate study since 1957. Enrollment: full-time 699, part-time 873. University faculty teaching graduate students: full- and part-time 366. Degrees conferred: M.A., M.S., M.B.A., M.Ed., M.F.A. Ed.D., Psy.D., Ph.D.

ADMISSION REQUIREMENTS. Transcripts, letters of recommendation, GRE/GMAT required in support of application. Interview required by some departments. TOEFL required for international applicants. Accepts transfer applicants. Graduates of unaccredited institutions not considered. Apply to Dean of Graduate School by July 1 (Fall), November 1 (Spring), April 1 (Summer). Application fee $20. Phone: (412)357-2222.

ADMISSION STANDARDS. Selective. Usual minimum average: 2.75 (A = 4).

FINANCIAL AID. Annual awards from institutional funds: 26 scholarships (based on merit and need), 230 research fellowships, 23 teaching assistantships, 40 internships, tuition waiver, Federal W/S, loans. Approved for VA benefits. Apply by March 15 to Assistant Dean of Graduate School for assistantships, fellowships; to Director of Financial Aid for all other programs. Use FAFSA. Phone: (412)357-2218. About 30% of students receive aid other than loans from University.

DEGREE REQUIREMENTS. For master's: 30–36 credit hours minimum for most, at least 24 in residence; thesis/nonthesis option. For Ed.D., Ph.D., Psy.D.: minimum of 60 credits beyond the bachelor's degree; qualifying exam; dissertation; final oral exam.

FIELDS OF STUDY.
Adult/Community Education.
Art.
Art Education.
Biology.
Business Administration.
Chemistry.
Counseling Services. Includes certifications in elementary school counselor, secondary school counselor, and supervisor of guidance services.
Criminology.
Early Childhood Education.
Educational Psychology.
Education of Exceptional Children.
Elementary Education.
Elementary School Guidance.
English. Includes English education, literature, teaching English to speakers of other languages.
Fine Arts.
Food and Nutrition.
Geography and Regional Planning.
History.
Industrial and Labor Relations.
Mathematics.
Music.
Nursing.
Physics.
Political Science.
Professional Growth.
Psychology. Includes school psychology certification.
Public Affairs.
Safety Science.
Secondary School Guidance.
Sociology.
Special Education/Exceptionality.
Special Learning Disabilities.
Speech Pathology.
Sports Sciences.
Student Personnel Services in Higher Education.

UNIVERSITY OF INDIANAPOLIS
Indianapolis, Indiana 46227-3697
http://www.Uindy.edu

Founded 1902. Private control. United Methodist. Semester system. Library: 153,000 volumes, 22,000 microforms, 24 PCs in library.
Tuition: $192–$380 per credit. No on-campus housing for graduate students.

Graduate Division

Graduate enrollment: full-time 313, part-time 591. Faculty teaching graduate students: full-time 19, part-time 42. Degrees conferred: M.A., M.B.A., M.Acc., M.S., M.S.N., Psy.D.

ADMISSION REQUIREMENTS. Transcripts, GRE/GMAT, interview required in support of Divisional application. TOEFL required for international applicants. Accepts transfer applicants. Apply to Office of the Graduate Division. Rolling admission. Application fee $20. Phone: (317)788-3216; fax: (317)788-3399.

ADMISSION STANDARDS. Relatively open.

FINANCIAL AID. None from the University except Federal W/S, loans. Approved for VA benefits. Apply to Financial Aid Office; no specified closing date. Use FAFSA.

DEGREE REQUIREMENTS. For M.A.: 32 semester hours and thesis, or 36 semester hours, without thesis, at least 24 in residence. For M.Acc.: 30 semester hours. For M.S.: 36 semester hours. For M.B.A.: 42 semester hours minimum. For M.S.N.; 40-semester-hour program. For Psy.D.: 108-semester-hour program: final year internship. All master's degrees must be completed within five years.

FIELDS OF STUDY.
Accounting.
Art.
Biology.
Business and Economics.
Education.
English.
History and Political Sciences.
Nursing.
Occupational Therapy.
Physical Therapy.
Psychology.
Social Sciences.

COLLEGE OF INSURANCE
New York, New York 10007-2165

Founded 1962. Private control (sponsored by more than 350 companies in the insurance and financial services industry). Semester system. Library: 96,000 volumes, 10,000 microforms, 466 current periodicals.
Tuition: per semester $510 (or $475 for employees of corporate sponsors), on-campus housing for graduate students. Aver-

age academic year housing cost: $8100. Contact Housing Office for both on- and off-campus housing information. Phone: (212)815-9292.

Graduate Program

Enrollment: evening only; full- and part-time 165 (men 104, women 61). College faculty: full-time 20, part-time 18. Degree conferred: M.B.A.

ADMISSION REQUIREMENTS. Official transcripts, GMAT required in support of College's application. TOEFL required for international applicants. Accepts transfer applicants. Apply to Office of Admissions by May 1 (Fall), October 1 (Spring). Application fee $30. Phone: (212)815-9232; fax: (212)964-3381.

ADMISSION STANDARDS. Selective. Usual minimum average: 3.0 (A = 4), plus 500 GMAT. Minimum TOEFL score 550.

FINANCIAL AID. Annual awards from institutional funds: ten graduate assistantships, two research assistantships, two internships, loans. Approved for VA benefits. Apply to Director of Financial Aid; no specified closing date. Use FAFSA. Phone: (212)815-9221; fax. (212)964-3381.

DEGREE REQUIREMENTS. For M.B.A.: completion of 51-credit program with at least a 3.0 (A = 4); 27 credits in core curriculum, 9 credits in major, 15 credits of electives.

FIELDS OF STUDY.
Actuarial Science.
Finance.
Insurance.
Risk Management.

INTER AMERICAN UNIVERSITY
San German, Puerto Rico 00683-5008

College-level study since 1921. Coed. Private control. Semester system. Main campuses at San German and San Juan. Regional colleges at Aguadilla, Arecibo, Barranquitas, Fajardo, Guayama, and Ponce. Library: 157,000 volumes, 57,000 microforms, 2400 current periodicals, 21 PCs.

Tuition: per graduate credit hour $140. On-campus housing available only at San German campus for single students. Average academic year housing cost: $2060 (including board). Contact Dean of Students Office for both on- and off-campus housing information. Phone: (809)264-1912, ext. 215.

Graduate Study

Offered at San German campus and San Juan campus. Enrollment: full-time 100, part-time 754. Graduate faculty: full-time 23, part-time 24. Degrees conferred: M.A., M.A.Ed., M.B.A., M.L.S., M.S., M.S.Ed.

ADMISSION REQUIREMENTS. Official transcripts, two letters of recommendations, PAEG or GRE required in support of application. Accepts transfer applicants. Apply by May 1 (Fall), December 1 (Spring), April 1 (Summer) to the Admissions Director. Rolling admissions process. Application fee $25. Phone: (809)892-3090.

ADMISSION STANDARDS. Selective. Usual minimum average: 3.0 (last 60 credits) or 2.75–2.99 (last 60 credits plus GRE) for full standing (A = 4).

FINANCIAL AID. Limited to assistantships, loans. Apply to appropriate department chair well in advance of registration. Use

FAFSA and University's FAF. Phone: (809)264-1912. Aid available for part-time students.

DEGREE REQUIREMENTS. For master's: 36–45 credit hours minimum, at least 30 credits in residence; thesis/nonthesis option; comprehensive exam for some programs.

FIELDS OF STUDY.
Administration of Higher Education.
Business Administration. Includes accounting, finance, human resources, industrial relations, marketing.
Curriculum and Instruction.
Educational Administration.
English.
Library Science.
Medical Technology.
Psychology. Fifty-one credits for M.A.
Special Education.
TESOL.

School of Law (P.O. Box 70351)

Established 1961. Semester system. Located in Santurce (00910). Library: 162,000 volumes. Library has LEXIS, NEXIS, DIALOG, DOBIS/LUVEN, MICRO JURIS.

Tuition: per credit hour, resident $240. No on-campus housing available. Total average annual additional expense: $7403.

Enrollment: first-year class, full-time 90, part-time 85; total full- and part-time 625 (men 60%, women 40%). Faculty: full-time 29, part-time 16. Degree conferred: J.D.

ADMISSION REQUIREMENTS. Transcripts, bachelor's degree, LSAT, PAEG, three letters of recommendation, personal interview required in support of application. Interview by invitation. Proficiency in Spanish required. Graduates of unaccredited colleges not considered. Application fee $25. Phone: (809)751-1912, ext. 2012, 2013.

ADMISSION STANDARDS. Selective. Admits approximately 25–30% of total annual applicants.

FINANCIAL AID. Scholarships, grants, Federal W/S, loans, and a deferred payment plan available. Apply to Financial Aid Office by March 31. Use FAFSA. About 90% of students receive some aid from School.

DEGREE REQUIREMENTS. For J.D.: satisfactory completion of three-year (full-time), four-year (part-time) program, 92 credits hours.

IONA COLLEGE
New Rochelle, New York 10801

Founded 1940. Located 16 miles NE of New York City. Coed. Private control. Roman Catholic. Semester and trimester systems. Library: 313,000 volumes, 90,000 microforms, 90 Pentium PCs.

Tuition: per credit $335–$415. No on-campus housing available. Apply to Off-Campus Office for off-campus housing information. Phone: (914)633-2336.

Graduate Study

Graduate enrollment: full- and part-time 1450. Faculty teaching graduate students: full-time 88, part-time 40. Degrees conferred: M.A., M.S., M.S. in Ed., M.B.A.

ADMISSION REQUIREMENTS. Transcripts required in support of application. GMAT required in business. GRE and interview required for some programs. TOEFL required for international applicants. Accepts transfer applicants. Apply to Graduate School of Arts and Science for Education and Arts and Sciences, or Hagan School of Business for Business and Management; no specified closing date. Admit to Fall, Spring, Summer trimesters. Application fee $25. Phone: (800)231-IONA, (914)633-2328 (Arts & Science), (914)633-2288 (Business).

ADMISSION STANDARDS. Selective. Usual minimum average: 2.75 (A = 4).

FINANCIAL AID. Limited to approximately forty graduate assistantships, loans. Approved for VA benefits. Apply to the Office of Financial Aid: no specified closing date. Use FAFSA. Phone: (914)633-2497.

DEGREE REQUIREMENTS. For master's: 30–61 credit hours minimum, at least 24 in residence; written/oral comprehensive exam in some programs.

FIELDS OF STUDY.
Biology Education.
Business Administration.
Business Education.
Communication Arts.
Computer Science.
Criminal Justice.
Economics.
Education.
Educational Computing.
Elementary Education. Includes specialization in science.
English.
English Education.
Family Counseling.
Financial Management.
Health Services Administration.
History.
Human Resource Management.
Journalism.
Management.
Management Information Systems.
Marketing.
Mathematics Education.
Multicultural Education.
Operations Management.
Organizational Behavior.
Pastoral Counseling.
Psychology.
School Administration and Supervision.
Secondary Education.
Social Studies Education.
Spanish.
Spanish Education.
Telecommunications.

IOWA STATE UNIVERSITY OF SCIENCE AND TECHNOLOGY

Ames, Iowa 50011
http://www.iastate.edu

Founded 1859. Located 40 miles N of Des Moines. Coed. State control. Semester system. Special facilities: Ames Laboratory, National Soil Tilth Laboratory, National Animal Disease Center, Institute for Physical Research and Technology, Iowa Agriculture and Home Economics Experiment Station, Leopold Center for Sustainable Agriculture, Center for Agricultural and Rural Development, Center for Nondestructive Evaluation, Industrial Relations Center, Iowa Transportation Center, Veterinary Medical Research Institute, Social and Behavioral Research Center, Uti-

lization Center for Agricultural Products, Center for Immunity Enhancement in Domestic Animals, Computation Center, Center for Designing Foods to Improve Nutrition, Iowa Energy Center. Library: 2,500,000 volumes, 2,000,000 microforms.

Annual tuition: resident $2934, nonresident $8636. Unlimited on-campus housing for married and single students. Housing costs range from $932 per semester (double occupancy) to monthly apartment rates of $182–$503. Apply to Director of Residential Life. Phone: (515)294-2900.

Graduate College

Graduate study since 1877. Enrollment: full- and part-time 4,223. Graduate faculty: full-time 1300. Degrees conferred: M.A., M.S., M.Agr., M.Arch., M.B.A., M.C.R.P., M.Ed., M.Eng., M.F.A., M.F.C.S., M.L.A., M.P.A., specialist, Ph.D.

ADMISSION REQUIREMENTS. Transcripts, letters of reference required in support of College's application. GRE required for most departments. Interview not required. Accepts transfer applicants. Graduates of unaccredited colleges not considered. Apply to Director of Admissions and Records at 2 months prior to beginning of term (some departments have earlier deadlines); international applicants should apply between nine and twelve months before entering term. Application fee $20, $30 for international applicants. Phone: (800)262-3810.

ADMISSION STANDARDS. Very competitive for most departments, competitive for some. Usual minimum average: 2.75 (A = 4).

FINANCIAL AID. Scholarships, fellowships, teaching/research assistantships, Federal W/S, loans; deferred payment plan. Approved for VA benefits. Apply to head of proposed major department for scholarships, fellowships, assistantships, preferably by March 15; to Financial Aid Office for all other programs. Use FAFSA and institutional FAF. About 50% of students receive aid other than loans from University and outside sources. Aid available for part-time students.

DEGREE REQUIREMENTS. For master's: 30 credits minimum, at least 22 credits in residence; reading knowledge of one foreign language for some majors; thesis for most majors; final oral exam. For M.Arch.: 90 credits minimum beyond bachelor's, or 45 credits beyond B.Arch. For M.B.A.: 48 credits minimum (a combination of integrated core modules and advanced electives). For Ph.D.: 72 credits minimum with 36 credits under supervision of Student's Program of Study Committee; at least 24 credits must be earned during two consecutive semesters or a continuous period of two semesters in a summer term; preliminary exam; dissertation; final written/oral exam.

FIELDS OF STUDY.
Aerospace Engineering.
Agricultural and Biosystems Engineering.
Agricultural Education.
Agronomy.
Animal Ecology.
Animal Science.
Anthropology.
Architecture. M.Arch.; M.S. in architectural studies; M.F.A. in graphic design, interior design; M.A. in art and design.
Biochemistry and Biophysics.
Biomedical Engineering.
Botany.
Business Administration. M.B.A. only.
Business Administrative Sciences. M.S. only.
Chemical Engineering.
Chemistry.
Civil and Construction Engineering.
Community and Regional Planning. M.C.R.P. only.

Computer Engineering.
Computer Science.
Ecology and Evolutionary Biology.
Economics.
Education. Includes adult, agricultural, administration, curriculum and instructional technology, counselor education, elementary, industrial education, research and evaluation, higher, history, philosophical and comparative studies, special, vocational.
Electrical Engineering.
Engineering Mechanics.
English.
Entomology.
Family and Consumer Sciences. M.F.C.S.
Family and Consumer Science Education and Studies.
Food Science and Human Nutrition.
Forestry.
General Graduate Studies. Interdepartmental program; M.A., M.S. only.
Genetics.
Geological and Atmospheric Science.
Gerontology. Minor only.
Health and Human Performance.
History.
Horticulture.
Hotel, Restaurant, and Institutional Management.
Human Development and Family Studies.
Immunobiology.
Industrial Education and Technology.
Industrial and Manufacturing Systems Engineering.
Industrial Relations. M.S. only.
Journalism and Mass Communication.
Landscape Architecture. M.L.A. only.
Material Science and Engineering.
Mathematics.
Mechanical Engineering.
Microbiology, Immunology, and Preventive Medicine.
Molecular, Cellular, and Developmental Biology.
Neuroscience.
Nuclear Engineering.
Physics and Astronomy.
Plant Pathology.
Plant Physiology.
Political Science. M.A., M.P.A. only.
Professional Agriculture. M.Agr. only.
Psychology.
Sociology.
Statistics.
Technology and Social Change. Minor only.
Textiles and Clothing.
Toxicology.
Transportation Planning. M.S. only.
Veterinary Anatomy.
Veterinary Clinical Sciences.
Veterinary Pathology.
Veterinary Physiology and Pharmacology.
Water Resources.
Zoology.

College of Veterinary Medicine (50011)

Established 1879. Annual tuition: resident and contract students $6345, nonresident $14,842. Total average cost for all other expenses: $17,280. On-campus housing available.

Enrollment: first-year class 105, total full-time 450 (men 50%, women 50%). Faculty: full-time 119, part-time 22. Degree conferred: D.V.M. The M.S. and Ph.D. are offered through the Graduate College.

ADMISSION REQUIREMENTS. VMCAS report, transcripts, GRE, three letters of recommendation (from an academic advisor) required in support of application. Applicants must have completed at least three years of college study. Early Decision Option available. Accepts transfer applicants on space available basis only. Preference given to state, North Dakota, and South Dakota residents. Apply to University Director of Admissions and Records after June 1, before December 22. Fall admission only. Application fee $20. Phone: (515)294-5836, toll-free outside Iowa (800)247-3965.

ADMISSION STANDARDS. Competitive. Accepts about 30% of total applicants. Accepts approximately 25 nonresidents (at large) applicants.

FINANCIAL AID. Scholarships, fellowships, teaching assistantships, Federal W/S, loans. Apply by March 1 to Student Financial Aid Office, to appropriate department head for fellowships and assistantships. About 50% of students receive aid other than loans from College funds.

DEGREE REQUIREMENTS. For D.V.M.: satisfactory completion of four-year program. For M.S., Ph.D.: see Graduate College listing above.

FIELDS OF GRADUATE STUDY.
Biomedical Engineering.
Immunobiology.
Microbiology.
Pharmacology.
Physiology.
Veterinary Anatomy.
Veterinary Clinical Sciences.
Veterinary Microbiology and Preventive Medicine.
Veterinary Pathology.

THE UNIVERSITY OF IOWA

Iowa City, Iowa 52242
http://www.uiowa.edu/

Founded 1847. Located 250 miles SW of Chicago. Coed. State control. Semester system. Special facilities: Computer-assisted Image Analysis Facility, Electron Microscopy Facility, High Field Nuclear Magnetic Facility, High Resolution Mass Spectrometry Facility, Institute of Hydraulic Research, Laser Science Research Facility, Large Scale Fermentation Facility, Museum of Art, Museum of Natural History, Public Policy Center, Social Science Institute. Library: 3,567,000 volumes.

On-campus housing for 749 married students, 5356 for single students. Average academic year housing cost: $1908–$3519 for married students, $3550–$4426 (including board) for single students. Apply to Family Housing Office. Phone: (319)335-9199 or Housing Assignment Office (319)335-3009; for off-campus housing, the University Housing Clearinghouse (319)335-3055.

Graduate College

Graduate study since 1900. Academic year tuition: resident $2934, nonresident $9452. Enrollment: full-time 296, part-time 3232. University faculty teaching graduate students: full-time 1747, part-time 56. Degrees conferred: M.A., M.S., M.Ac., M.F.A., M.A.T., M.P.A., M.P.T., M.S.W., M.S.N., Ed.S., D.M.A., Ph.D.

ADMISSION REQUIREMENTS. Transcripts, three letters of recommendation required in support of College's application. Interview, GRE Subject Tests, GMAT required by some departments. TOEFL required for international applicants. Accepts transfer applicants. Graduates of unaccredited institutions not considered. Apply to University Director of Admissions by July

15 (Fall), December 1 (Spring), April 15 (Summer). Application fee $20. Phone: (319)335-1525; fax: (319)335-1535.

ADMISSION STANDARDS. Very selective or competitive for most departments. Usual minimum average: 2.5 (A = 4).

FINANCIAL AID. Annual awards from institutional funds: 1135 scholarships, 375 fellowships, 1447 teaching assistantships, 1121 research assistantships, Federal W/S, loans. Approved for VA benefits. Apply by February 1 to appropriate department for scholarships, fellowships, assistantships: to Director of Financial Aid for all other programs. Use FAFSA and institutional FAF. Phone: (319)335-1450; fax: (319)335-3060. Approximately 50% of students receive aid other than loans from College and outside sources. Aid sometimes available for part-time students.

DEGREE REQUIREMENTS. For M.A., M.S., M.Ac.: 30 semester hours minimum with or without thesis, at least 24 in residence; final written/oral exam; no language for most majors. For M.F.A.: ordinarily two years of full-time residence, but requirement may be reduced to a minims of one year at discretion of department head; thesis/creative project. For M.A.T.: 38 hours minimum, at least 24 in residence; final written/oral exam. For M.S.W.: 36–60 hours required, at least 24 in residence; final written/oral exam. For M.P.T.: 67 hours minimum, four semesters of full-time residence plus internship; written/oral exam. For M.P.A.: 92 hours minimum, at least 24 in residence; final project/comprehensive exam. For M.S.N.: 40–52 hours required, at least 24 in residence; thesis/nonthesis option; final written/oral exam. For Ed.S.: ordinarily two years, at least one year in residence and 1 semester in full-time attendance; final written/oral exam. For Ph.D.: 72 hours minimum, at least 18 in full-time residence; preliminary written/oral exam; dissertation; knowledge of foreign languages or knowledge of special research tools, as determined by department; final oral exam. For D.M.A.: same as for the Ph.D., except qualifying recital and doctoral essay instead of dissertation.

FIELDS OF STUDY.
Accounting. M.Ac.
Afro-American Studies. M.A.
American Studies. M.A., Ph.D.
Anatomy. M.S., Ph.D.
Anthropology. M.A.
Applied Mathematical and Computational Sciences. Ph.D.
Art. M.A., M.F.A.
Art History. M.A., Ph.D.
Asian Civilizations. M.A.
Astronomy. M.S.
Biochemistry. M.S., Ph.D.
Biology. M.S., Ph.D.
Biomedical Engineering. M.S., Ph.D.
Botany. M.S., Ph.D.
Business Administration. M.A., Ph.D.
Chemical and Biochemical Engineering. M.S., Ph.D.
Chemistry. M.S., Ph.D.
Civil and Environmental Engineering. M.S., Ph.D.
Classics. No thesis for M.A.; M.A., Ph.D.
Communication Studies. M.A., Ph.D.
Comparative Literature. M.A., M.F.A., Ph.D.
Computer Science. M.S., Ph.D.
Criminal Justice and Corrections. No thesis; M.A.
Dance. M.F.A.
Dental Public Health. M.S.
Economics. M.A., Ph.D.
Education. No thesis for M.A.T. or Ed.S.; M.A., M.A.T., Ed.S., Ph.D.
Electrical and Computer Engineering. M.S., Ph.D.
Endodontics. M.S.
English. M.A., M.F.A., Ph.D.

Exercise Science. M.S., Ph.D.
Film and Video Production. M.F.A.
French. M.A., Ph.D.
Genetics. Ph.D.
Geography. M.A., Ph.D.
Geology. M.S., Ph.D.
German. M.A., Ph.D.
Greek. No thesis; M.A.
History. M.A., Ph.D.
Hospital and Health Administration. M.A., Ph.D.
Immunology. Ph.D.
Industrial Engineering. M.S., Ph.D.
Journalism. M.A.
Latin. No thesis; M.A.
Leisure Studies. M.A.
Library and Information Science. M.A.
Linguistics. M.A., Ph.D.
Mass Communications. Ph.D.
Mathematics. M.S., Ph.D.
Mechanical Engineering. M.S., Ph.D.
Microbiology. M.S., Ph.D.
Molecular Biology. Ph.D.
Music. M.A., M.F.A., D.M.A., Ph.D.
Neuroscience. Ph.D.
Nursing. M.S.N.
Operative Dentistry. M.S.
Oral and Maxillofacial Surgery. M.S.
Oral Science. M.S., Ph.D.
Orthodontics. M.S.
Pathology. M.S.
Pediatric Dentistry. M.S.
Periodontology. M.S.
Pharmacology. M.S., Ph.D.
Pharmacy. M.S., Ph.D.
Philosophy. M.A., Ph.D.
Physical Education. M.A., Ph.D.
Physical Therapy. No thesis for M.P.T.; M.A., M.P.T.
Physician Assistant Studies. No thesis for M.P.A.; M.P.A.
Physics. M.S., Ph.D.
Physiology and Biophysics. M.S., Ph.D.
Political Science. M.A., Ph.D.
Preventive Medicine and Environmental Health. M.S., Ph.D.
Prosthodontics. M.S.
Psychology. M.A., Ph.D.
Quality Management and Productivity. M.S.
Radiation Biology. M.S., Ph.D.
Religion. M.A., Ph.D.
Russian. M.A.
Science Education. M.S., Ph.D.
Social Studies. M.A.
Social Work. M.S.W.
Sociology. M.A., Ph.D.
Spanish. M.A., Ph.D.
Speech Pathology and Audiology. M.A., Ph.D.
Sports, Health, Leisure, and Physical Studies. M.A., Ph.D.
Statistics. M.S., Ph.D.
Stomatology. M.S.
Theater Arts. M.F.A.
Third World Development Support. M.A.
Urban and Regional Planning. M.A., M.S.

College of Law

Founded 1865. Semester system. Law library: 773,000 volumes. Library has LEXIS, NEXIS, WESTLAW, ILP.

Annual tuition: residents $5166, nonresidents $15,360. Total cost for all other expenses: $9000.

Enrollment: first-year class 244 (Fall), 45 (Summer) full- and part-time total 700 (men 56%, women 44%). Faculty: full-time 49, part-time 3. Degrees conferred: J.D., J.D.-M.A., LL.M. (International and Comparative Law).

ADMISSION REQUIREMENTS. LSDAS Law School report, bachelor's degree, transcripts, LSAT required in support of application. Interview not required. Accepts transfer applicants. Preference given to state residents. Graduates of unaccredited colleges not considered. Apply to Director of Admissions after September 1, before March 1. Fall and Summer admission only. Application fee $20, foreign application fee $30. Phone: (800)553-IOWA; fax: (319)335-9071.

ADMISSION STANDARDS. Selective. Accepts less than 30–35% of total annual applicants. Limited to no more than 30% nonresidents.

FINANCIAL AID. Scholarships, fellowships, assistantships, full and partial tuition waivers, Federal W/S, loans. Apply by March 1 to Office of the Dean. Use FAFSA. About 85% of students receive some aid from College.

DEGREE REQUIREMENTS. For J.D.: 90 credit hours minimum, at least two years in residence. For LL.M.: at least 24 credits minimum beyond the J.D.

College of Medicine (52242-1101)

Founded 1850. Annual tuition: resident $8722, nonresident $23,360. Total average figure for all other expenses: $7000. On-campus housing for married students only.

Enrollment: first-year class 175; total 650 (men 56%, women 44%). Faculty: full- and part-time 500. Degrees conferred: M.D., M.D.-Ph.D. (Medical Scientist Training Program). The M.A., M.S., and Ph.D. are offered through the Graduate College.

ADMISSION REQUIREMENTS. AMCAS report, transcripts, letters of evaluation, MCAT required in support of application. Interviews may be requested. Preference given to Iowa residents. Has EDP; apply between June 15 and August 1. Accepts transfer applicants. Applicants must have completed at least three years of college study. Graduates of unaccredited colleges not considered. Apply after June 15, before November 1. Application fee $20. Phone: (319)335-8052; fax: (319)335-8049.

ADMISSION STANDARDS. Selective. Accepts 15% of total annual applicants. Approximately 88% are state residents.

FINANCIAL AID. Scholarships, summer fellowships, grants, loans. Apply to Associate Dean by June 1. Use FAFSA. Less than 5% of students receive aid from College.

DEGREE REQUIREMENTS. For M.D.: satisfactory completion of four-year program. For M.A., M.S., Ph.D., see Graduate College listing above.

FIELDS OF GRADUATE STUDY.
Anatomy.
Biochemistry.
Biomedical Engineering.
Biophysics.
Cell Biology.
Genetics.
Immunology.
Microbiology.
Molecular Biology.
Neurosciences.
Pathology.
Pharmacology.
Physiology.

College of Dentistry

Organized 1882. Annual tuition: Iowa and Arkansas residents $5442, nonresident $16,664. On-campus housing available. Contact University Housing Assignment Office. Phone: (319)335-9199. Total average academic cost for all other first-year expenses: $6392.

Enrollment: first-year class 75; total full-time 351 (men 60%, women 40%); postgraduates 60. Faculty: full-time 83, part-time 60. Degrees conferred: D.D.S., M.S., D.D.S.-Ph.D.

ADMISSION REQUIREMENTS. AADSAS report, transcripts, DAT (not later than October), three letters of recommendation, interview required in support of application. Preference given to Iowa and Arkansas residents. Applicants must have completed at least three years of college study. Apply to Associate Dean for Academic Affairs after June 1, before February 1. Application fee $20. Phone: (319)335-7157; fax: (319)335-7155.

ADMISSION STANDARDS. Competitive. Usual minimum average: 2.5 (A = 4). Accepts about 25–30% of total annual applicants. Approximately 60% are state residents.

FINANCIAL AID. Scholarships, federal programs, loans. Apply by November 30 to University Office of Student Aid. Use FAFSA. Phone: (319)335-1450. About 89% of students receive aid from College.

DEGREE REQUIREMENTS. For D.D.S.: satisfactory completion of forty-five-month program. For M.S.: thirty-hour minimum in residence, final exam. For Ph.D.: see Graduate College listing above.

FIELDS OF GRADUATE STUDY.
Community Dentistry.
Dental Hygiene.
Endodontics.
Operative Dentistry.
Oral and Maxillofacial Surgery.
Oral Pathology/Diagnosis.
Orthodontics.
Pediatric Dentistry.
Pedodontics.
Periodontics.
Prosthodontics.

ITHACA COLLEGE
Ithaca, New York 14850-7020
http://www.ithaca.edu

Founded 1892. Located 50 miles SW of Syracuse. Coed. Private control. Semester system. Library: 335,000 volumes, 198,000 microforms, 2500 current periodicals, 6 PCs.

Tuition: per credit $504. No on-campus housing for graduate students. Contact Room Assignments Coordinator of Residential Life for off-campus housing information.

Graduate Studies

Enrollment: full-time 200, part-time 13. Degrees conferred: M.S., M.M.

ADMISSION REQUIREMENTS. Official transcripts, 2 letters of recommendation (4 letters if applying for an assistantship), GRE scores (for Speech Pathology, Audiology, and Exercise and Sport Science applicants) required in support of application. Auditions required for Music applicants. TOEFL required for international applicants. Accepts transfer applicants. Graduates of unaccredited institutions not considered. Apply to Dean of Graduate Studies by June 1 (Fall), November 26 (Spring). Application fee $30. Phone: (607)274-3527; fax: (607)274-1263.

ADMISSION STANDARDS. Selective. Usual minimum average: 3.0. (A = 4).

FINANCIAL AID. Annual awards from institutional funds: teaching assistantships, Federal W/S, loans. Approved for VA benefits. Apply with admission application to Dean of Graduate Studies for assistantships; to Financial Aid Office for all other programs. Phone: (607)274-3131; fax: (607)274-1895. Use FAFSA. About 40% of students receive aid other than loans from College. No aid for part-time students.

DEGREE REQUIREMENTS. For M.S.: 30–39 credits minimum; thesis; 36–39 credit hours nonthesis; final oral/written exam. For M.M.: 30 credits minimum; recital; final oral/written exam.

FIELDS OF STUDY.
Communication.
Exercise and Sports Sciences.
Music. Includes composition, conducting, music education, theory, string, woodwinds, brass.
Speech-Language, Pathology and Audiology.
Teacher of the Speech and Hearing Handicapped.

JACKSON STATE UNIVERSITY
Jackson, Mississippi 39217

Founded 1877. Coed. State control. Semester system. Library: 370,000 volumes, 472,000 microforms.

Tuition: per semester hour $132, or $1190 per semester. Out-of-state students pay an additional fee of $1297 per semester. On-campus housing. Average academic year housing cost: $2988 (including board) for single students. Contact the Director of Housing for both on- and off-campus information. Phone: (601)968-2326.

Graduate Program

Enrollment: full- and part-time about 1000. University faculty teaching graduate students: full-time 200, part-time 0. Degrees conferred: M.A., M.S., M.M.Ed., M.S.Ed., M.S.T., M.A.T., M.B.A., M.Bus.Ed., M.P.A., M.P.P.A., Ed.S., Ed.D., Ph.D.

ADMISSION REQUIREMENTS. Transcripts, GRE/GMAT required in support of application. TOEFL required for international students. Accepts transfer applicants. Apply to Office of Admissions before March 15 (Summer), March 1 (Fall), October 1 (Spring). Application fee $20 for nonresidents. Phone: (601)968-2455; fax: (601)973-3664.

ADMISSION STANDARDS. Relatively open. Usual minimum average: 2.5 (A = 4).

FINANCIAL AID. One hundred and thirty scholarships, thirty assistantships, Federal W/S, loans. Approved for VA benefits. Apply to department of interest before March 1 (Summer), May 1 (Fall), November 1 (Spring) for scholarships, assistantships; to the Office of Aid for all other programs. Use FAFSA. Phone: (601)968-2227.

DEGREE REQUIREMENTS. For master's: 30 semester hours, 36 hours without thesis or project; thesis or project option, written comprehensive exam/final oral exam. For Ed.S.: 30 semester hours beyond the master's. For M.S.W.: 60 semester hours beyond the bachelor's degree. For Ed.D.: 60–66 semester hours. For Ph.D.: 60 semester hours; comprehension exam; dissertation; final oral exam.

FIELDS OF STUDY.
Accounting. M.P.A.
Biology. M.S.T., M.S.
Business Administration. M.B.A.
Business Education. M.B.Ed.
Chemistry. M.S.
Clinical Psychology. Ph.D.
Communicative Disorders. M.S.
Computer Science. M.S.
Criminology and Justice Services. M.A.
Early Childhood. M.S.Ed., Ed.D.
Educational Administration. Ph.D.
Educational Administration and Supervision. M.S.Ed., Ed.S.
Elementary Education. M.S.Ed., Ed.S.
English. M.A.T., M.A.
Environmental Science. M.S., Ph.D.
Guidance and Counseling. M.S.Ed., M.S., Ed.S.
Hazardous Materials Management. M.S.
Health, Physical Education, and Recreation. M.S.Ed.
History. M.A.
Industrial Arts Education. M.S.Ed.
Mass Communication. M.S.
Mathematics. M.S.T., M.S.
Music Education. M.M.Ed.
Political Science. M.A.
Public Administration. Ph.D.
Public Policy and Administration. M.P.P.A.
Rehabilitation Services. M.S.
Science Education. M.S.Ed., Ed.S.
Secondary Education. M.S.
Social Work. M.S.W.
Sociology. M.A.
Special Education. M.S.

JACKSONVILLE STATE UNIVERSITY
Jacksonville, Alabama 36265-9982

Founded 1883. Located 76 miles NE of Birmingham. Coed. Public control. Semester system.

Annual tuition: resident, full-time $2985, nonresident $4479; per credit hour, resident $95, nonresident $143. On-campus housing for all graduate men and women who apply; none for married students. Average academic year housing cost: $2200–4400 (including board). Apply to Director of University Housing. Phone: (205)782-5122.

College of Graduate Studies

Graduate study since 1957. Enrollment: full-time 269, part-time 815 (men 430, women 654). Faculty teaching graduate students: full-time 124. Degrees conferred: M.S. in Ed., M.S., M.B.A., M.A., M.M., M.M.Ed., M.P.A.

ADMISSION REQUIREMENTS. Transcripts, GRE General/Subject Tests/GMAT/MAT required in support of College's application. Interview not required. TOEFL required for international applicants. Accepts transfer applicants. Apply to College of Graduate Studies; no specified closing date. Application fee $20. Phone: (205)782-5329; fax: (205)782-5321; E-mail: RPARKER@jsu.edu.

ADMISSION STANDARDS. Unconditional admissions; 450 x UGPA + GRE = 2000 or more; or 15 x UGPA + MAT = 60 or more; or 200 x UGPA + GMAT = 950 or more.

FINANCIAL AID. Limited to twenty teaching assistantships, Federal W/S, loans. Approved for VA benefits. Apply to Financial Aid Office; no specified closing date. Phone: (205)782-5006.

DEGREE REQUIREMENTS. For M.A., M.M.Ed., M.M., M.P.A., M.S., M.S. in Ed.: Plan I, 24–36 semester hours plus thesis. For M.B.A.: Plan II, 30–42 semester hours without thesis. Under both plans, final oral/comprehensive exam.

FIELDS OF STUDY.
Biology.
Business Administration.
Counselor Education.
Criminal Justice.
Early Childhood Education.
Early Childhood Special Education.
Educational Administration.
Elementary Education.
English.
General Studies.
Health Education.
History.
Library Media.
Mathematics.
Music.
Music Education
Physical Education.
Political Science.
Psychology.
Public Administration.
Secondary Education. Eight subject areas.
Special Education.

JACKSONVILLE UNIVERSITY
Jacksonville, Florida 32211-3394

Founded 1934. Coed. Private control. Semester system. Library: 294,000 volumes, 201,000 microforms, 800 current periodicals, 27 PCs.

Tuition: per hour $240; for M.B.A. $410. No on-campus housing for married students. Annual housing cost: $2120–$4598 (including board). Contact Dean of Students Office for both on- and off-campus housing information. Phone: (904)744-3950.

Graduate Program

Enrollment: full-time 130, part-time 208. Graduate faculty: full-time 60, part-time 20. Degrees conferred: M.A.T., M.B.A.

ADMISSION REQUIREMENTS. Transcripts, GRE, three letters of recommendation (two for M.B.A.), GMAT (M.B.A.) required in support of application. Interview required for most departments. TOEFL required for international applicants. Accepts transfer applicants. Apply to Director of M.A.T. or M.B.A. program at least 30 days prior to registration. Application fee $25. Phone: (904)744-3950, ext. 5416.

ADMISSION STANDARDS. Selective. Usual minimum average: 3.0 (A = 4).

FINANCIAL AID. Limited to eight scholarships, assistantships, Federal W/S, loans. Approved for VA benefits. Apply to the Office of Financial Aid; no specified closing date. Use FAFSA. Phone: (904)744-3950.

DEGREE REQUIREMENTS. For M.A.T.: 36 semester hours, at least 30 in residence; six semester hours of internship or three years of teaching; final written exam. For M.B.A.: 30 semester hours, which must be completed within five years of completion of first graduate course.

FIELDS OF STUDY.
Art.
Business Administration.
Computer Education.
Education.
Elementary Education.
English.
Guidance Counseling.
Health Care Administration.
International Business.
Management.
Management/Marketing.
Marketing.
Mathematics.
Music.
Physical Education.
Reading.
Social Sciences.

JAMES MADISON UNIVERSITY
Harrisonburg, Virginia 22807
http://www.jmu.edu

Established 1908. Located approximately 2½ hours from Washington, D.C. Coed. Public control. Semester system. Special facilities: Center for Economics Education, Center for Entrepreneurship, Human Development Center, Speech and Hearing Center. Library: 587,400 volumes, 1,294,000 microforms, 95 PCs in library.

Tuition: per credit, resident $131, nonresident $363. Limited on-campus housing for graduate students.

Graduate School

Graduate study since 1954. Enrollment: 850 (men 300, women 550). University faculty: full-time 145, part-time 34. Degrees conferred: M.A., M.S., M.S.Ed., M.B.A., M.A.T., M.Ed., M.M., M.P.A., M.F.A., Ed.S., Psy.D.

ADMISSION REQUIREMENTS. Transcripts, GRE Subject Tests (for some majors), GMAT for M.B.A. required in support of School's application. TOEFL required for international applicants. Interview required by some departments. Accepts transfer applicants. Graduates of unaccredited institutions not considered. Apply to Office of Dean at least 60 days prior to registration. Application fee $50. Phone: (540)568-6131; fax: (540)568-6266.

ADMISSION STANDARDS. Selective. Usual minimum average: 2.5 (A = 4).

FINANCIAL AID. Annual awards from institutional funds: ten scholarships, fifty-five teaching assistantships, forty-six research assistantships, twenty-eight service assistantships, Federal W/S, loans. Approved for VA benefits. Apply to Dean of Graduate School; no specified closing date. Use FAFSA and University's FAF. Phone: (540)568-7820; fax: (640)568-7994. About 30% of students receive aid other than loans from both College and outside sources.

DEGREE REQUIREMENTS. For master's: 30 semester credits minimum; thesis optional for many departments; final written/oral exam. For Ed.S.: 30 semester credits minimum; thesis optional for many departments, final written/oral exam. For Psy.D.: 60 semester credits minimum beyond master's degree; qualifying exam; advancement to candidacy; internship; special project; final written/oral exam.

FIELDS OF STUDY.
Accounting. M.S.
Art. M.F.A., M.A.
Biology. M.S.
Business Administration. Includes concentrations in accounting, economics, finance, health administration, management, marketing. M.B.A.
Computer Science. M.S.
Counseling Psychology. Ed.S., Psy.D.
Early Childhood Education. M.Ed.
Elementary Education. M.Ed.
English. M.A.T.
Fine Arts. Includes ceramics, drawing and painting, jewelry and metalwork, photography, printmaking, sculpture, weaving. M.F.A.
Health Education. M.S.Ed.
Health Science. M.S.
Hearing Disorders. M.Ed.
History. M.A., M.A.T.
Human Resource Development. M.Ed.
Kinesiology. M.S.
Music. M.M.
Psychology. M.A.
Public Administration. Includes nonprofit organizations. M.P.A.
Reading Education. M.Ed.
School Administration. M.Ed.
School and Counseling Psychology. M. A., Psy.D.
School Guidance Counseling. M.Ed.
School Library Media Services. M.Ed.
School Psychology. M.Ed., Ed.S.
Secondary Education. M.Ed.
Special Learning Disabilities. M.Ed.
Speech Pathology. M.S.

JERSEY CITY STATE COLLEGE
Jersey City, New Jersey 07305-1957

Founded 1927. Coed. Public control. Semester system. Special facilities: ADA Technology Center, Center for the Advancement of Teaching and Learning, Peter W. Rodino Jr. Institute of Criminal Justice. Library: 250,000 volumes, 500,000 microforms, 1550 current periodicals.

Tuition: per credit, resident $170, nonresident $213. No on-campus housing for graduate students. Contact Director of Student Services for off-campus housing information. Phone: (201)200-2338. Day care facilities available.

Graduate Division

Graduate study since 1960. Enrollment: full-time 49, part-time 1275. Graduate faculty: full-time 87, part-time 22. Degrees conferred: M.A., M.F.A., M.S., Professional Diploma, Specialist.

ADMISSION REQUIREMENTS. Official transcripts, 2 letters of recommendation, interview, GRE General/MAT/NTE required in support of application. TOEFL required for all international applicants. Accepts transfer applicants. Graduates of unaccredited institutions not considered. Apply to Director of Graduate Studies by August 1 (Fall), December 1 (Spring), May 1 (Summer). Application fee none. Phone: (201)200-3413,-3410.

ADMISSION STANDARDS. Selective. Usual minimum average: 2.75 (A = 4).

FINANCIAL AID. 15 assistantships, Federal W/S, loans. Approved for VA benefits. Apply by June 1 to Office of Graduate Studies. Use FAFSA and institutional FAF. About 4% of students receive aid from all sources. Aid sometimes available to part-time students.

DEGREE REQUIREMENTS. For M.A., M.S.: 32 credit hours minimum, at least 24 in residence; thesis or final document; practicum or comprehensive exam. For M.F.A.: 60 credits hours minimum, at least 45 in residence; special project. For Professional Diploma, Specialist: 33 minimum credits beyond the master's.

FIELDS OF STUDY.
Art Education.
Counseling.
Criminal Justice. M.S.
Early Childhood Education.
Educational Psychology.
Fine Arts. M.F.A.
Health Sciences. M.S.
Mathematics Education.
Music Education.
Reading. M.A., Specialist.
School Psychology. Professional Diploma.
Special Education.
Student Personnel Services–Guidance.
Urban Education. Includes administration and supervision, bilingual and bicultural, ESL, basics and urban studies; Specialist available for some programs.

JOHN CARROLL UNIVERSITY
Cleveland, Ohio 44118-4581

Founded 1986. Coed. Private control. Roman Catholic. Semester system. Library: 565,000 volumes, 178,000 microforms, 5 PCs.

Tuition: per credit $405, M.B.A. $500. No separate on-campus housing for graduate students. Apply to Dean of Students Office for off-campus housing. Phone: (216)397-4401.

Graduate School

Enrollment: full-time 149, part-time 705. Graduate faculty: full-time 229, part-time 157. Degrees conferred: M.A., M.S., M.B.A., M.Ed.

ADMISSION REQUIREMENTS. Transcripts required in support of application. GRE Subject Tests/MAT recommended. TOEFL required of international students. Accepts transfer applicants. Deadline to Admissions Office, 30 days prior to registration. Application fee $25, $35 for international applicants. Phone: (216)397-4284.

ADMISSION STANDARDS. Selective. Usual minimum average: 2.5. Some programs require 3.0 (A = 4).

FINANCIAL AID. Scholarships, sixty-seven teaching and research assistantships, Federal W/S, loans. Apply by March 1 to Dean, Graduate School. Use FAFSA. Phone: (216)397-4248. About 30% of students receive aid other than loans from School.

DEGREE REQUIREMENTS. For M.A., M.S., M.Ed.: 30–33 semester hours, counseling 40 semester hours minimum, at least 24 in residence; reading knowledge of one foreign language for M.A. in some departments; thesis/research essay; oral/written comprehensive exam. For M.B.A.: 40 semester hours.

FIELDS OF STUDY.
Biology. GRE Subject in Biology for admission.
Business. GMAT for admission.
Chemistry.
Classical Languages.
Counseling and Human Services. MAT for admission.

Education. Includes school guidance and counseling, school psychology, administration and supervision, professional teacher, guidance, school-based program, certificate programs.

English. GRE for admission to degree programs.

History.

Humanities.

Mathematics.

Physics.

Religious Studies. MAT or GRE for admission.

JOHN JAY COLLEGE OF CRIMINAL JUSTICE
New York, New York 10019-1093

Established 1965. A unit of the City University of New York. Coed. Municipal control. Semester system. Special facilities: Center for Study of Law and Society in China, Center on Violence and Human Survival, Fire Science Institute, Institute on Alcohol and Substance Abuse. Library: 220,000 volumes, 13,100 microforms.

Tuition: per credit, resident $185, nonresident $320. No on-campus housing. Apply to Dean of Students for off-campus housing information. Phone: (212)237-8737.

Graduate Division

Program intended for students seeking careers in public services, for personnel in various criminal justice agencies. Enrollment: full-time 128, part-time 627. Faculty: full-time 45, part-time 14. Degrees conferred: M.A., M.S., M.P.A.

ADMISSION REQUIREMENTS. Transcripts, GRE, letters of recommendation required in support of College's application. Accepts transfer applicants. Apply to Graduate Office of Admissions by June 30 (Fall), December 15 (Spring). Application fee $40. Phone: (212)237-8863; fax: (212)237-8777.

ADMISSION STANDARDS. Selective. Usual minimum average: 3.0 in major area of concentration (A = 4).

FINANCIAL AID. Limited to Federal W/S, loans. Approved for VA benefits. Apply to Director of Financial Aid for all programs. Phone: (212)237-8151. Use CUNY's FAFSA. About 80% of students receive aid other than loans from College and outside sources. Aid available to part-time students.

DEGREE REQUIREMENTS. For master's: credit hours vary from 36–42 credit hours, depending on the selected major.

FIELDS OF STUDY.

Criminal Justice. M.A.

Forensic Psychology. M.A.

Forensic Science. M.S.

Protection Management. M.S.

Public Administration. M.P.A.

JOHN MARSHALL LAW SCHOOL
315 South Plymouth Court
Chicago, Illinois 60604-3968

Founded 1899. Private control. Semester system. Law library: 260,000 volumes. Library has LEXIS, NEXIS, WESTLAW, CALI, and 242 personal computers.

Tuition: per semester hour $520. No on-campus housing available. Total average annual additional expense: $14,000.

Enrollment: first-year class, full-time 200, part-time 62; total full- and part-time 981 (men 66%, women 37%); postgraduates

125. Faculty: full-time 54, part-time 136. Degrees conferred: J.D., J.D.-M.A. (Political Sciences, with Roosevelt University), J.D.-M.B.A. (in cooperation with Rosary College), LL.M. (Taxation, Intellectual Property).

ADMISSION REQUIREMENTS. LSDAS Law School report, bachelor's degree, transcripts, LSAT, letters of recommendation required in support of application. Accepts transfer applicants. Apply after October 1, before April 1 (Fall), October 1 (Spring) to Director of Admissions, Application fee $40. Phone: (312)987-1406; outside Chicago (900)537-4280.

ADMISSION STANDARDS. Selective. Accepts 35–40% of total annual applicants.

FINANCIAL AID. Scholarships, grants, loans. Apply by May 1 to Financial Aid Office. Use FAFSA and JMLS financial aid form.

DEGREE REQUIREMENTS. For J.D.: satisfactory completion of eighty-six-semester-hour program. For master's degree: see Rosary College, Roosevelt University listing for requirements. For LL.M.: at least 24 credits minimum beyond J.D.

THE JOHNS HOPKINS UNIVERSITY
Baltimore, Maryland 21218
http://www.jhu.edu

Founded 1876, Coed. Private control. Semester system. Special facilities: Center for Astrophysical Sciences, Applied Physics Laboratory, Bologna Center (Italy), Carnegie Institute, Center for Social Organization of Schools, Center for Non-Destructive Testing, Geology Field Station, Homewood Computing Center, McCollum-Pratt Institute, Nanjing Center (PRC), Oceanographic Research Vessels, Space Telescope Science Institute, Villa Spelman (Italy). Library over: 2,200,000 volumes, 2,400,000 microforms, 135 PCs.

Annual tuition: full-time $20,740. On-campus housing for married students, single men and women. Average academic year housing cost: $5220–$7020 for married students; $5000 for single students. Apply to Director of Housing. Phone: (410)516-7960.

School of Arts and Science

Enrollment: full-time 923, part-time 24. Graduate faculty: full-time 59, part-time 83. Degrees conferred: M.A., Ph.D.

ADMISSION REQUIREMENTS. Two transcripts, letters of recommendation required in support of School's application. GRE Subject Tests strongly recommended. TOEFL required for international applicants. Accepts transfer applicants. Graduates of unaccredited institutions not considered. Admission requirements vary by department and applicants should first contact the individual department to obtain pertinent formation. Submit applications as directed. Application fee $50. Dean's Phone: (410)516-8212.

ADMISSION STANDARDS. Very competitive.

FINANCIAL AID. Scholarships, 95 fellowships, 241 research assistantships, 352 teaching assistantships, full and partial tuition waivers, Federal W/S, loans. Apply January 15 (for priority consideration) to appropriate department chair for fellowships, assistantships, scholarships; to Financial Aid office for all other programs. Use FAFSA. Phone: (410)338-8724.

DEGREE REQUIREMENTS. For M.A.: One year minimum in full-time residence; reading knowledge of one foreign language optional by department; thesis or comprehensive exam for some departments. For Ph.D.: generally three years minimum beyond the bachelor's; at least one year in full-time residence; reading knowledge of one foreign language optional by department; preliminary oral exam; dissertation; final oral/written exam.

FIELDS OF STUDY.
Anatomy. Ph.D. only.
Art. Includes art history, architecture.
Astronomy.
Astrophysics.
Biochemistry. Ph.D. only. The D.Sc., D.P.H. are offered by School of Hygiene and Public Health.
Biology. Includes chemical biology, developmental biology, genetic biology. Ph.D. only.
Biomedical Engineering. Ph.D. and postdoctoral study only.
Biophysics. Ph.D. only.
Biostatistics. Two years minimum of full-time residence for Ph.D.
Cell Biology.
Chemistry. Generally Ph.D. only.
Classics. Knowledge of Greek and Latin in addition to French, Italian, or German for M.A.; German and French or Italian for admission to Ph.D.
Earth and Planetary Sciences. Includes petrology and geochemistry. GRE.
Economics. Essay, oral exam for M.A.
English.
French.
Geology.
German. Oral/written exam for M.A.; qualifying exam for Ph.D.
Hispanic and Italian Studies.
History. Includes American studies, medieval history.
History of Art.
History of Medicine. Offered by School of Medicine; comprehensive written exam, oral qualifying exam for Ph.D.
History of Science. Ph.D. only.
Human Genetics.
International Studies. Generally admits to Ph.D. only.
Mathematical Science.
Mathematics.
Medical and Biological Illustration. Offered by School of Medicine; M.A. only.
Microbiology. Offered by School of Medicine.
Near Eastern Studies.
Pharmacology and Experimental Therapeutics. Offered by School of Medicine.
Philosophy. Apply to department chair; two years minimum in full-time residence; Ph.D. only.
Physics and Astronomy.
Physiological Chemistry. Offered by School of Medicine; Ph.D. only.
Physiology. Offered by School of Medicine; Ph.D. only.
Political Science. Includes public law and jurisprudence, public administration; oral/written exam for M.A.
Psychology. Comprehensive exam for M.A.
Sociology. Includes sociology and public health; Ph.D. only.
Writing. Interdepartmental; M.A. only.

G.W.C. Whiting School of Engineering

Annual tuition; full-time $19,750.

Enrollment: full-time 457, part-time 44. Faculty: full-time 112, part-time 78. Degrees conferred: M.A., M.M.S.E., M.S., M.S.E., Ph.D.

ADMISSION REQUIREMENTS. Official transcripts, GRE, three letters of reference required in support of School's application. TOEFL required for international applicants. Interview not required. Accepts transfer applicants. Graduates of unaccredited institutions not considered. Apply to the Office of Admission by February 1. Application fee $50. Phone: (410)516-8174.

ADMISSION STANDARDS. Selective. Usual minimum average: 3.0 (A = 4).

FINANCIAL AID. Sixty-six fellowships, 207 research assistantships, 90 teaching assistantships, tuition waivers, Federal W/S, loans. Approved for VA benefits. Apply by March 15 to Office of Students Financial Services. Use FAFSA. Phone: (410)516-8028.

DEGREE REQUIREMENTS. For master's: One year minimum in full-time residence; thesis or comprehensive exam for some departments. For Ph.D.: generally three years minimum beyond the bachelor's, at least one year in full-time residence; preliminary exam; dissertation; Graduate Board oral exam.

FIELDS OF STUDY.
Biomedical Engineering. Ph.D.
Chemical Engineering. M.S., Ph.D.
Civil Engineering. M.S., Ph.D.
Computer Science. M.S., Ph.D.
Electrical and Computer Engineering. M.S., Ph.D.
Engineering. Ph.D.
Geography and Environmental Engineering. M.S., Ph.D.
Materials Science and Engineering. M.S., Ph.D.
Mathematical Science and Engineering. M.S., Ph.D.
Mechanical Engineering. M.S., Ph.D.

Paul H. Nitze School of Advanced International Studies

Established 1943. Located in Washington, D.C. Special facilities: European Center in Bologna, Italy; Center in Nanjing, P.R.C.; Washington Center of Foreign Policy Research, Center for Canadian Studies. Library: 85,000 volumes.

Annual tuition: full-time $20,000. Graduate enrollment: full-time 441, part-time 41. School faculty: full-time 45, part-time 105. No on-campus housing available. Average academic year cost for off-campus housing: $7000. Degrees conferred: M.A., M.I.P.P., Ph.D.

ADMISSION REQUIREMENTS. Official transcripts, three letters of recommendation required in support of School's application. GRE, interview recommended. TOEFL required for international applicants. Graduates of unaccredited colleges not considered. Apply to Director of Admissions by February 1 (Fall), November 1 (Spring). Rolling admissions process. Application fee $50. Phone: (202)663-5700.

ADMISSION STANDARDS. Competitive. Usual minimum average: 3.5 (A = 4).

FINANCIAL AID. Annual awards from institutional funds: 171 fellowships, research/teaching assistantships, internships, Federal W/S, loans. Apply by February 1 to Office of Admissions. Use FAFSA. Phone: (202)663-5706. About 50% of students receive aid from School and outside sources. Aid available for part-time students.

DEGREE REQUIREMENTS. For M.A.: Two-year program; speaking and reading knowledge of one foreign language; final oral exam. For M.I.P.P.: one-year program (mid-career); completion of eight courses within the nine-month period. For Ph.D.: Three years minimum beyond the bachelor's; reading knowledge of two foreign languages; written exam; dissertation; final oral exam.

FIELDS OF STUDY.
American Foreign Policy.
Area Studies. Includes Africa, Asian, Canada, Chinese, European, Japanese, Latin American, Middle Eastern, Russian, and East European.

International Economics.
International Law and International Organizations.
International Politics.
Social Change and Development.
Note: Joint programs are available. M.A.-M.B.A. with Wharton School at the University of Pennsylvania; M.A./J.D. with Stanford Law School; M.A./M.H.S. with School of Hygiene and Public Health.

School of Hygiene and Public Health
HTTP://PHWEB.SPH.JHU.EDU

Established 1916. Quarter system.

Annual tuition: full-time $25,625 (M.P.H.), per credit $428. All other programs full-time $20,740, per credit $433. Graduate enrollment: full-time 941, part-time 531 (men 39%, women 61%). School faculty: full-time 400, part-time 447. Degrees conferred: M.P.H., Sc.M., M.H.S., Dr.P.H., Sc.D., Ph.D.

ADMISSION REQUIREMENTS. Official transcripts, GRE, three letters of reference required in support of School's application. TOEFL or evidence of proficiency in English required of international students. Interview not required. Accepts transfer applicants. Apply to Admissions Office of School by February 1. Rolling admissions process from October 1 to February 1. Application fee $60. Phone: (410)955-3543; fax: (410)955-0464.

ADMISSION STANDARDS. Selective for most departments. Usual minimum average: 3.0 (A = 4).

FINANCIAL AID. Seven hundred and eighty full and partial scholarships, Federal W/S, loans and federal training grants are offered. Approved for VA benefits. Apply to appropriate department chairperson or Master of Public Health Office for scholarships and traineeships support; the Office of Student Financial Services for all other aid. Phone: (410)955-3004; fax: (410)955-0464. Approximately 70% of students receive either school scholarships, loans, or FWS; 19% receive federal training grants and 50% receive other aid.

DEGREE REQUIREMENTS. For full-time M.P.H.: Eleven months minimum in residence and satisfactory completion of approved schedule of studies. For part-time M.P.H.: 80 credit units within three years. For Sc.M.: Two years minimum, one in residence; thesis; written exam. For M.H.S.: One to two academic years in residence; thesis and field studies vary by department. For Dr.P.H.: Three years minimum beyond the bachelor's, one year minimum in residence. For Dr.P.H. students who do not already have the M.P.H., the first eleven months of study is for M.P.H. degree; preliminary oral exam; comprehensive written exam; thesis; oral defense of thesis. For Sc.D.: Two years minimum in residence; preliminary oral exam; comprehensive written exam; thesis; oral defense of thesis. For Ph.D.: One year minimum in residence; comprehensive written exam; preliminary oral exam; thesis; oral defense of thesis. For the doctoral degrees, some departments may require reading knowledge of one foreign language.

FIELDS OF STUDY.
Biochemistry.
Biostatistics.
Clinical Investigation.
Environmental Health Sciences. Includes toxicological sciences, physiology, environmental chemistry and biology, radiation health sciences, environmental health engineering, occupational health.
Epidemiology.
Health Policy and Management. Includes behavioral sciences and health education, health finance and management, health policy, public health.

International Health. Includes disease control, vaccine sciences, human nutrition, health systems.
Maternal and Child Health.
Mental Hygiene.
Molecular Microbiology and Immunology.
Population Dynamics.

The Peabody Institute of The Johns Hopkins University (21202)
http://www.peabody.jhu.edu

Founded 1868. Coed. Private control. Semester system. Music library: 70,000 volumes; audio visual library: 13,510 discs.

Annual tuition: full-time $18,700, per credit $512. On-campus housing available. Apply to Director of Admissions. Graduate enrollment: full-time 308, part-time 34. Institute faculty: full-time 74, part-time 73. Degrees conferred: M.M., M.M.Ed., D.M.A., Graduate Performance Diploma, Artist Diploma.

ADMISSION REQUIREMENTS. Official transcripts, entrance audition and entrance exams in music history, theory, and ear training required in support of application. TOEFL required for international applicants. Apply to Director of Admissions by December 15. Application fee $45. Phone: (800)368-2521, (410)659-8110; fax: (410)659-8102.

ADMISSION STANDARDS. Selective.

FINANCIAL AID. Seventy scholarships, twenty-seven assistantships, grants, Federal W/S, loans. Apply by February 15 to Director of Admissions. Use FAFSA and institutional FAF. Approximately 40% of students receive aid other than loans from Institute; 77% from all sources.

DEGREE REQUIREMENTS. For M.M., M.M.Ed.: 32 semester hours minimum; recital. For D.M.A.: 90 hours beyond the bachelor's, at least one year in full-time residence; preliminary exam; final written/oral exam; final dissertation or lecture-recital document for all majors; six public recitals; reading knowledge of languages required.

FIELD OF STUDY.
Music. Performance, conducting, theory, composition, music history, music criticism, and music education.

School of Medicine (21205-2196)

Annual tuition: $22,800; student fees $2180. Total average figure for all other expenses: $10,663. On-campus housing available. Library: 300,000 volumes.

Enrollment: first-year class 120 (EDP 6); total full-time 716 (men 55%, women 45%). Faculty: full-time 1100, part-time 1200. Degrees conferred: B.A./M.D., M.D., M.D.-M.P.H., M.D.-Ph.D. (Medical Scientist Training Program).

ADMISSION REQUIREMENTS. Transcripts, one test score from a single SAT, ACT, GRE, letters of recommendation, interview required in support of application. Has EDP; apply between June 15 and August 1. Applicants must have completed at least two years of college study. Apply to Committee on Admission after July 1, before November 15. Application fee $60. Phone: (410)955-3182; Website: http://infonet.welch.jhu.edu.

ADMISSION STANDARDS. Competitive. Accepts 7% of total annual applicants. Approximately 15% are state residents.

FINANCIAL AID. Scholarships, summer fellowship, loans. MSTP funded by NIH. Apply to Committee on Admission; no specified closing date. About 60% of students receive some aid from School funds.

DEGREE REQUIREMENTS. For M.D.: satisfactory completion of four-year program for those who enter with bachelor's; satisfactory completion of five- or six-year program for those who enter with less than four years of undergraduate study. For M.P.H., Ph.D.: see Graduate School listing above.

FIELDS OF GRADUATE STUDY.
Anatomy.
Biochemistry.
Biomedical Engineering.
Biophysics.
Cell Biology.
Genetics.
Immunology.
Molecular Biology.
Neurosciences.
Pharmacology.
Physiology.
Public Health.

THE JUILLIARD SCHOOL
New York, New York 10023-6588

Founded 1905. Located at Lincoln Center. Coed. Private control. Semester system. Library: 63,617 volumes, 45,105 musical scores.

Annual tuition: full-time $13,600. On-campus housing for 350 students. Annual acádemic year housing cost: $6300. Apply to Office of Students Affairs for on- and off-campus housing information. Phone: (212)799-5000, ext. 7400 (on-campus), ext. 200 (off-campus).

Graduate Study

Graduate study since 1924. Enrollment: full-time 316; part-time 32 (women, 65%, men 35%). Degrees conferred: M.M., D.M.A.

ADMISSION REQUIREMENTS. Transcripts, recommendations, interview, performance audition entrance exam required in support of School's application. TOEFL, TWE required for international applicants. Apply to Admissions Office by December 15. Fall admission only. Application and entrance exam fees $85. Phone: (212)799-5000, ext. 223; fax: (212)769-6420.

ADMISSION STANDARDS. Very competitive.

FINANCIAL AID. Scholarships, teaching fellowships, Federal W/S, loans. Approved for VA benefits. Apply by February 17 to Financial Aid Office. Use FAFSA and institutional FAF. Phone: (212)799-5000.

DEGREE REQUIREMENTS. For M.M.: 54 semester hours minimum, at least two years in full-time residency; graduation performance; final exam. For D.M.A.: 98 semester hours minimum beyond the bachelor's, at least 60 in full-time residence; preliminary exam; reading knowledge of one foreign language; final project/recital/document, depending upon major; final oral exam.

FIELDS OF STUDY.
Accompanying.
Composition.
Conducting.
Guitar. M.M. only.
Harpsichord.
Organ.
Piano.
Stringed and Orchestral Instruments.
Voice.

KANSAS STATE UNIVERSITY
Manhattan, Kansas 66506
http://www.ksu.edu

Founded 1863. Located 55 miles from Topeka. Coed. State control. Semester system. Special facilities: nuclear reactor, Flight Research Laboratory, Higuch Biosciences Center, 12 MEV Van de Graaff accelerator, observatory, fish hatchery, botanical garden, Kansas Geological Survey, Konza Prairie Research Area, Natural Science Museum, Wheat Genetics Resource Center, Institute for Environmental Research, Food and Feed Grain Institute, computer center, environmental laboratory, Cereal Technology Laboratory, engineering and agriculture experiment stations. Library: 3,292,000 volumes, 2,750,000 microforms, 250 PCs.

Annual tuition: full-time, resident $2256, nonresident $7416; per credit hour, resident $94, nonresident $309. On-campus housing for 625 married students, 400 graduate men, 200 graduate women. Average academic year housing cost: $2115–$2673 for married students, $3370 (including board) for single students. Apply to Director of Housing. Phone: (813)532-6453 (on-campus), (913)539-2097 (off-campus). Day care facilities available.

Graduate School

Graduate study since 1868. Enrollment: full-time 2508, part-time 4180. University faculty: full-time 1006, part-time 97. Degrees conferred: M.A., M.S., M.Acc., M.B.A., M.F.A., M.M., M.Arch., M.P.A., M.R.P., M.L.A., Ed.D., Ph.D.

ADMISSION REQUIREMENTS. Two transcripts, GRE required in support of School's application. GMAT required for M.B.A., M.Acc. TOEFL required for international applicants. Interview sometimes required. Accepts transfer applicants. Graduates of unaccredited institutions not considered. Apply to head of the department concerned at least 3 months prior to registration. Application fee none, $25 for international applicants. Phone: (913)532-6191; fax: (913)532-6944.

ADMISSION STANDARDS. Selective for most departments. Usual minimum average: 2.75 (A = 4).

FINANCIAL AID. Annual awards from institutional funds: scholarships, 578 teaching assistantships, 611 research assistantships, Federal W/S, loans. Apply by March 15 to Dean of Graduate School for assistantships; to the Financial Aid Office for all other programs. Use FAFSA. Phone: (913)532-6420; fax: (913)532-7628. About 65% of students receive aid other than loans from University and outside sources. Aid available for part-time students.

DEGREE REQUIREMENTS. For most master's: 30 semester hours minimum including thesis, at least one academic year in full-time residence; transfer credit from other graduate schools individually considered; final oral exam. For M.R.P.: 48 hours minimum, at least one academic year in full-time residence. For M.F.A.; 60 hours minimum. For Ph.D.: 90 semester hours minimum beyond the bachelor's, at least one year in full-time residence; preliminary exam; language requirements vary; dissertation; final written/oral exam. For Ed.D.: essentially the same as Ph.D. except no language requirement.

FIELDS OF STUDY.

Accounting. M.Acc.

Agricultural Economics. M.S.

Agricultural Engineering. Ph.D.

Agronomy. M.S., Ph.D.

Animal Science. M.S.

Architectural Engineering. M.S.

Architecture. Includes design, structures, interior design; M.Arch. only.

Art. Creative only; final studio project and exhibition. M.F.A. only.

Biochemistry. M.S., Ph.D.

Biological and Agricultural Engineering. M.S.

Biology. M.S., Ph.D.

Business Administration. M.B.A.

Chemical Engineering. M.S., Ph.D.

Chemistry. M.S., Ph.D.

Civil Engineering. M.S., Ph.D.

Clothing, Textiles, and Interior Design. M.S. only.

Computer and Information Science. M.S., Ph.D.

Economics. M.A., Ph.D.

Education. Includes adult, elementary, secondary, administration, student counseling and personnel services, special; three recommendations for admission; GRE for continuance in program.

Electrical and Computer Engineering. M.S., Ph.D.

Engineering. Includes energy processes, materials, systems engineering, bioenvironmental engineering, information processing; Ph.D. only.

English. Creative writing major available for M.A.; GRE for continuance in program.

Entomology. M.S., Ph.D.

Family Studies and Human Services. M.S. only.

Food Science. M.S., Ph.D.

Genetics. M.S., Ph.D.

Geography. M.A., Ph.D.

Geology. M.S., Ph.D.

Grain Science. M.S., Ph.D.

History. Two languages for Ph.D. M.A., Ph.D.

Horticulture. M.S., Ph.D.

Human Ecology. Ph.D.

Industrial Engineering. M.S., Ph.D.

Industrial Management. M.S.

Journalism and Mass Communication. M.S. only.

Kinesiology. M.S.

Landscape Architecture. M.L.A. only.

Mass Communication. M.S.

Mathematics. M.S., Ph.D.

Mechanical Engineering. M.S., Ph.D.

Microbiology. M.S., Ph.D.

Modern Languages. Includes German, French, Spanish; one language in addition to major.

Music. Includes applied, music education, music literature; recital for master's. M.M. only.

Nuclear Engineering. M.S., Ph.D.

Operations Research. M.S.

Physics. M.S., Ph.D.

Plant Pathology. M.S.

Political Science. M.A. only.

Psychology. M.S., Ph.D.

Public Administration. M.P.A.

Regional and Community Planning. Interdepartmental. M.R.P. only.

Sociology. M.A., Ph.D.

Software Engineering. M.S. Eng.

Speech. Includes radio-television, theater, speech pathology and audiology. M.A. only.

Statistics. M.S., Ph.D.

Veterinary Anatomy and Physiology. M.S., Ph.D.

Veterinary Laboratory Medicine. M.S.

Veterinary Pathology. M.S., Ph.D.

College of Veterinary Medicine

Annual tuition: resident and contract state resident $34,783; nonresident $15,733. Total average costs for all other expenses: $6500. On-campus housing available.

Enrollment: first-year class 107; total 428 (men 60%, women 40%); postgraduates 65. Faculty: full-time 75, part-time 16. Degree conferred: D.V.M. The M.S. and Ph.D. are offered through the Graduate School.

ADMISSION REQUIREMENTS. VMCAS report, transcripts showing completion of seventy hours of preprofessional college work, GRE, animal/veterinary experience, essay, three names and addresses for potential recommendations (one from an academic advisor) required in support of application. Interview by invitation only. Accepts transfer applicants, on a space-available basis. Preference given to state, contract residents, and U.S. residents. Apply to Assistant Dean after September 1, prior to January 15. Application fee $20. Phone: (913)532-5660.

ADMISSION STANDARDS. Selective. Accepts 40% of total annual applicants. Approximately 15–20% of class from nonresident (at-large) applicants.

FINANCIAL AID. Assistantships, Federal W/S, loans. Apply to Dean after acceptance.

DEGREE REQUIREMENTS. For D.V.M.: 152 semester hours and four years in residence. For M.S. and Ph.D.: see Graduate School listing above.

UNIVERSITY OF KANSAS

Lawrence, Kansas 66045

http://www.ukans.edu

Founded 1866. Main campus is 40 miles W of Kansas City. College of Health Sciences and Hospital located at Kansas City. State control. Semester system. Special facilities: Museum—anthropology, art, invertebrate paleontology, natural history, entomological; Herbarium, computer facilities, Kansas Geological Survey, Higuchi Biosciences Center, Bureau of Child Research, Flight Research Laboratory, Infant Research Laboratory, Retardation Research Center, Gerontology Center, Institute for Social and Environmental Studies, Institute for Economic and Business Research, Transportation Research Group, Space Technology Center, Biological Anthropology Laboratory, Enzyme Laboratory, Chemical Biology Laboratory, Nuclear Reactor Center, field facilities, Water Resources Institute, Paleontological Institute, Tertiary Oil Recovery Project, mineral resources research, animal care units, health and safety research, center for research, children's rehabilitation unit, cancer center program, drug design program. Library: 3,292,000 volumes, 2,797,000 microforms, 33,000 current periodicals, 250 PCs in all libraries. Day care facilities available.

Annual tuition: full-time, resident $2534, nonresident $7412; per credit hour, resident $118, nonresident $322. On-campus housing for 300 married students. Average academic year housing cost: $3544–$4524 (including board) for single students, $2500 for married students. Contact Director of Student Housing for both on- and off-campus housing information. Phone: (913)864-7224.

Graduate School

http://www.research.ukans.edu/gradhome.html

Organized 1894. Enrollment: full-time 2098, part-time 3539. Graduate faculty: full-time 1021, part-time 95. Degrees conferred: M.A., M.S., M.B.A., M.S.Ed., M.F.A., M.M., M.E.,

M.M.Ed., M.M.E., M.H.D., M.F.A., M.U.P., M.Arch., Ed.S., D.M.A., D.E., Ed.D., Ph.D.

ADMISSION REQUIREMENTS. Two official transcripts required in support of School's application. GRE/MAT, letters of recommendation required by some departments. Interview not required. TOEFL required for international applicants. Accepts transfer applicants. Graduates of unaccredited institutions not considered. Apply to Graduate Advisor of proposed major department by July 1 (Fall), December 1 (Spring), May 1 (Summer); some departments have earlier deadlines. Application fee varies by department $10–$40, $40–$55 for international applicants. Phone: (913)864-3301; fax: (913)864-5272.

ADMISSION STANDARDS. Competitive for most departments, very competitive for others. Usual minimum average: 3.0 (A = 4).

FINANCIAL AID. Annual awards from institutional funds: 45 scholarships, 58 fellowships, 1050 teaching assistantships, 650 research assistantships, Federal W/S, loans. Approved for VA benefits. Apply by February 1 (earlier for some departments) to appropriate department chair for fellowships, assistantships; to Financial Aid Office for all other programs. Use FAFSA. Phone: (913)864-4700, (913)864-5469. About 50% of students receive aid other than loans from University and outside sources.

DEGREE REQUIREMENTS. For master's: 30 credit hours minimum, at least 24 in residence; research component; thesis/nonthesis options for some departments. For M.Arch.: 60 credit hours; project/thesis; final exam. For M.B.A.: 60 credit hours; final exam. For M.E., M.M.E.: 36 credit hours; project; internships; final exam. For M.F.A.: 48–60 credit hours; thesis/exhibition; final exam. For M.H.D.: 36 credit hours; practicum experience; thesis option; final exam. For M.M.: 30 credit hours; thesis/recital/project; final exam. For M.M.Ed.: 30 credit hours; thesis; final exam. For M.P.A.: 30 credit hours; internship; project; final exam. For M.U.P.: 50 credit hours; thesis/nonthesis option; final exam. For Ed.S.: 60 credit hours beyond bachelor's; special project. For Ed.D., D.E., D.M.A.: some variations but all basically the same as for the Ph.D. For Ph.D.: three years beyond the baccalaureate; at least one year in full-time residence; foreign language or other research skills; comprehensive oral exam; dissertation; final oral exam.

FIELDS OF STUDY.

SCHOOL OF ARCHITECTURE AND URBAN DESIGN:
Architectural Engineering. M.S. only.
Architecture. M.Arch. only.
Urban Planning. M.U.P. only.

SCHOOL OF BUSINESS:
Accounting.
Business.
Business Administration. M.B.A. only.
Finance.
Marketing.
Petroleum Management. M.S. only.

COLLEGE OF LIBERAL ARTS AND SCIENCES:
American Studies.
Anthropology.
Applied Mathematics and Statistics.
Atmospheric Sciences.
Biology. Includes cell, physiology.
Botany.
Chemistry.
Child Clinical Psychology.
Classics. M.A. only.
Clinical Psychology.
Communication Studies.
Computer Science. M.S. only.

East Asian Languages and Cultures. M.A. only.
Economics.
English.
Entomology.
French.
Geography.
Geology.
Germanic Languages and Literature.
History.
History of Art.
Human Development and Family Life.
Latin American Studies. M.A. only.
Linguistics.
Mathematics.
Microbiology.
Philosophy.
Physics.
Political Science.
Psychology.
Public Administration.
Religious Studies. M.A. only.
Slavic Languages and Literature.
Sociology.
Soviet and East European Studies. M.A. only.
Spanish.
Speech and Hearing Science. Ph.D. only.
Speech Pathology and Audiology.
Systematics and Ecology.
Theater and Film.

SCHOOL OF EDUCATION:
Art Education.
Counseling Psychology.
Early Childhood Education.
Education for the Gifted.
Educational Administration.
Foundations of Education.
Health Education.
Higher Education.
Music Education.
Physical Education.
Recreation.
School Psychology.
TESL.

SCHOOL OF ENGINEERING:
Aerospace Engineering.
Architectural Engineering.
Chemical Engineering.
Civil Engineering.
Electrical and Computer Engineering.
Engineering.
Engineering Management. M.S. only.
Mechanical Engineering.
Petroleum Engineering.
Petroleum Management.

SCHOOL OF FINE ARTS:
Art. M.F.A. only.
Design. Includes interior, textiles. M.F.A. only.
Music. Includes composition, conducting, performance, musicology, theory.
Musical Arts.
Visual Communication.

SCHOOL OF JOURNALISM:
Journalism.

SCHOOL OF PHARMACY:
Health Services Administration.
Hospital Pharmacy. M.S. only.

Medicinal Chemistry.
Pharmaceutical Chemistry.
Pharmacology.
Toxicology.

SCHOOL OF SOCIAL WORK:
Social Work.

School of Law

Founded 1891. Semester system. Law library: 280,000 volumes. Library: has LEXIS, NEXIS, WESTLAW, DIALOG.

Annual tuition: full-time resident $3268, nonresident $7826. On-campus housing available for both single and married students. Total average cost for all other expenses: $10,000.

Enrollment: first-year class 180; full-time 492 (men 59%, women 41%); no part-time students. Faculty: full-time 29, part-time 9. Degrees conferred: J.D., J.D.-M.B.A., J.D.-M.P.A., J.D.-M.A. (Economics, Philosophy), J.D.-M.U.P., J.D.-M.S. (Health Services Administration, Urban Planning).

ADMISSION REQUIREMENTS. LSDAS Law School report, bachelor's degree, transcripts, LSAT required in support of application. Interview not required. Accepts transfer applicants. Preference given to state residents. Graduates of unaccredited colleges not considered. Apply to Director of Law Admission before March 15 for both Summer and Fall admission. Admits Summer and Fall only. Application fee $40. Phone: (913)864-4378.

ADMISSION STANDARDS. Selective. Accepts about 30–35% of total annual applicants. 82% of class are state residents.

FINANCIAL AID. Scholarships, assistantships, Federal W/S, loans. Apply to Office of Student Financial Aid by March 1. Use FAFSA. About 10% of students receive aid from School.

DEGREE REQUIREMENTS. For J.D.: 90 hours minimum, at least 30 in full-time residence. For master's degree: see Graduate School listings above.

UNIVERSITY OF KANSAS MEDICAL CENTER
Kansas City, Kansas 66103

Medical study since 1905. Includes Allied Health, Nursing, Medical School, Graduate School (administered by University's Graduate School). Library: 179,130 volumes, 9668 microforms.

Graduate School

Annual tuition: resident $2256, nonresident $7416; per credit, resident $94, nonresident $309. Enrollment: full-time 271, part-time 380. Faculty: full-time 235, part-time 40. Degrees conferred: M.A., M.N., M.P.H., M.S., Ph.D.

ADMISSION REQUIREMENTS. Official transcripts, three letters of recommendation, GRE Subject Tests required in support of application. TOEFL required for international applicants. Accepts transfer applicants. Graduates of unaccredited institutions not considered. Apply by July 1 (Fall), December 1 (Spring). Rolling admissions process. Application fee none. Phone: (913)588-1238.

ADMISSION STANDARDS. Competitive. Usual minimum average: 3.0 (A = 4).

FINANCIAL AID. Scholarships, fellowships, assistantships, Federal W/S, loans. Approved for VA benefits. Apply by May 1 to appropriate department for assistantships, fellowships; to Financial Aid Office for all other programs. Use FAFSA. Aid available for part-time students.

DEGREE REQUIREMENTS. For M.S., M.A., M.N., M.P.H., Ph.D.: see University of Kansas Graduate School listing above.

FIELDS OF GRADUATE STUDY.
Anatomy.
Audiology.
Biochemistry.
Biology.
Cell Biology.
Developmental and Child Psychology.
Dietetics and Nutrition. M.S. only.
Education of Deaf.
Immunology.
Microbiology.
Molecular Genetics.
Nurse Anesthesia. M.S.
Nursing. M.N., Ph.D.
Nutrition.
Occupational Therapy. M.S.
Pathology and Oncology.
Pharmacology.
Physical Therapy. M.S.
Physiology.
Preventive Medicine.
Public and Community Health.
Speech and Hearing Science.
Speech-Language Pathology.
Toxicology. Ph.D.

School of Medicine

Founded 1899. Located in Kansas City (66160-7301). Annual tuition: resident $8830, nonresident $21,738. Total average figure for all other expenses $6500. Enrollment: first-year class 175 (EDP 40); total full-time 700 (men 65%, women 35%). Faculty: full-time 407, part-time 112. Degrees conferred: M.D., M.D.-Ph.D. Library: 170,000 volumes.

ADMISSION REQUIREMENTS. AMCAS, transcripts, recommendation from premedical advisor, MCAT, required in support of application. Interview by invitation. Has EDP; apply between June 15 and August 1. Accepts transfer applicants. Bachelor's degree required for admission. Preference given to Kansas residents. Apply to Office of Student Admissions and Records after June 15, before November 1. Application fee: nonresidents $40. Phone: (913)588-5245; fax: (913)588-5259.

ADMISSION STANDARDS. Competitive. Accepts 12% of total annual applicants. Approximately 92% are state residents.

FINANCIAL AID. Scholarships, assistantships, fellowships, loans. Apply to Office of Student Financial Aid. Phone: (913)588-5170. About 75% of students receive aid from School.

DEGREE REQUIREMENTS. Satisfactory completion of four-year program. Advanced standing for medical study completed elsewhere considered on individual basis. For Ph.D.: see Graduate School listing above.

FIELDS OF GRADUATE STUDY.
Anatomy.
Biochemistry.
Microbiology.
Pathological.
Pharmacology.
Physiology.

KEAN COLLEGE OF NEW JERSEY
Union, New Jersey 07083

Founded 1855. Located 15 miles W of New York City. Coed. State control. Semester system. Library: 265,000 volumes, 92,000 microforms, 1300 current periodicals.

Annual tuition: full-time, resident $4939, nonresident $6067; per hour, resident $206, nonresident $253. No on-campus housing available for graduate students.

Graduate School

Graduate study since 1954. Enrollment: full-time 152, part-time 1092. Faculty: full-time 280, part-time 40. Degrees conferred: M.A., M.P.A., M.S., M.S.N., M.A.L.S., Professional Diploma in School Psychology.

ADMISSION REQUIREMENTS. Official transcripts, recommendations, GRE/MAT/GMAT required in support of School's application. Interview is usually required. TOEFL required for international applicants. Accepts transfer applicants. Graduates of unaccredited institutions not considered. Apply to Office of Graduate Admissions, T-106 by June 15 (Fall), November 1 (Spring). All documents including test scores must be received by deadline in order for application to be reviewed. Application fee $20. Phone: (908)527-2665.

ADMISSION STANDARDS. Selective for most departments. Usual minimum average: 2.75 (A = 4).

FINANCIAL AID. Annual awards from institutional funds: Seventy-five assistantships; scholarships, loans. Approved for VA benefits. Apply to Office of Financial Aid; no specified closing date. Phone: (908)572-2050. About 50% of full-time students receive aid other than loans from both College and outside sources. Aid sometimes available for part-time students.

DEGREE REQUIREMENTS. For master's: 33 credits minimum; comprehensive exam; thesis/nonthesis option. For Professional Diploma: 30 credits minimum beyond master's.

FIELDS OF STUDY.
Behavioral Sciences. M.A.
Communication Sciences.
Counselor Education. M.A.
Early Childhood Education. M.A.
Educational Administration. M.A.
Educational Psychology. M.A.
Fine Arts. M.A.
Instruction and Curriculum. M.A.
Liberal Studies. M.A.
Management Systems Analysis. M.S.
Mathematics Education. M.A.
Nursing. M.S.N.
Public Administration. M.P.A.
Reading. M.A.
School Psychology. Professional Diploma.
Special Education. M.A.
Speech Education. M.A.

KEENE STATE COLLEGE
Keene, New Hampshire 03431-1701

Founded 1909. Located 90 miles NW of Boston. Coed. Semester system. State control. Library: 185,000 volumes.

Tuition: per credit hour, resident $140, nonresidents $412. On-campus housing for single and married students. Annual housing cost: $3214–$4700 single students, $5000 married students. Apply to Director of Residential Life Phone: (603)358-2339. Day care facilities available.

Graduate Studies

Graduate study since 1947. Enrollment: full-time 24, part-time 107. College faculty: full-time 160, part-time 50. Degrees conferred: M.Ed., M.A.T.

ADMISSION REQUIREMENTS. Transcripts, three letters of recommendations, essay required in support of application. TOEFL required for international applicants. Accepts transfer applicants. Graduates of unaccredited institutions not considered. Apply to Dean of Graduate Studies; no specified closing date. Application fee $25 resident, $35 nonresident. Phone: (603)358-2332.

ADMISSION STANDARDS. Selective. Usual minimum average: 2.90 (A = 4).

FINANCIAL AID. Limited to 1 scholarship, eight to fifteen assistantships, Federal W/S, loans. Apply to Office of Student Financial Management; no specified closing date. Use FAFSA. Phone: (603)358-2280.

DEGREE REQUIREMENTS. For master's: 36–39 credit hours minimum.

FIELD OF STUDY.
Education. Includes administration, counseling, curriculum and instruction, special education.

KENT STATE UNIVERSITY
Kent, Ohio 44242-0001

Founded 1910. Located 35 miles SE of Cleveland. Coed. State control. Semester system. Special facilities: Center for Aquatic Ecology, Editing Center for the Study of World Musics, Liquid Crystal Institute, Center for NATO Studies, Center for Nuclear Physics. Library: 1,800,000 volumes, 1,000,000 microforms, 8000 current periodicals.

Annual tuition: resident $4568, nonresident $8856; per credit, resident $208, nonresident $403. On-campus housing for 250 single students, 259 married students. Average academic year housing cost: $4344 for married students, $2298 for single students. Contact Director of Residence Services for both on- and off-campus housing information. Phone: (216)672-7000.

Division of Research and Graduate Schools

Graduate study since 1935. Enrollment: full-time 2136, part-time 2650. University faculty teaching graduate students: full-time 765. Degrees conferred: M.Arch., M.A., M.A.T., M.B.A., M.Ed., M.F.A., M.L.S., M.M., M.P.A., M.S., M.S.Acct., M.S.N., Ed. Specialist, Ph.D. Graduate work is administered by the Division of Research and Graduate Studies.

ADMISSION REQUIREMENTS. Official transcripts, three letters of recommendation required in support of application. GRE/GMAT required for some programs. Interview not required. Accepts transfer applicants. Graduates of unaccredited institutions not considered. Apply to appropriate Graduate School at least one month prior to registration. Application fee $25. Phone: (216)672-2660.

ADMISSION STANDARDS. Very selective for most departments, competitive for others. Usual minimum average: 2.75 (A = 4).

FINANCIAL AID. Annual awards from institutional funds: fellowships, research/teaching assistantships, Federal W/S, loans. Approved for VA benefits. Apply by March 1 to appropriate department chair for fellowships, assistantships; to the Financial Aid Office for all other programs. Use FAFSA. Phone: (216)672-2972. About 25% of full-time students receive aid other than loans from School and outside sources.

DEGREE REQUIREMENTS. For M.A.: 32 semester hours minimum; thesis in most departments; final exam in some. For M.S.: 32 semester hours; thesis. M.S.Acct.: 33 semester hours beyond the bachelor's in accounting or 64 semester hours beyond other bachelor's; internship. For M.Ed.: 32 semester hours minimum; one year teaching experience required in most programs. For M.F.A.: 60 semester hours; studio thesis; qualifying exam. For M.M.: 32 semester hours; recital; essay. For M.L.S.: 36 semester hours; thesis or research paper. For M.S.N.: 36–40 semester hours. For M.P.A.: 45 semester hours; thesis/nonthesis option. For M.Arch.: 32 semester hours minimum. For Ed.S.: 60 semester hours beyond the bachelor's or 30 semester hours beyond the master's; comprehensive exam; final oral exam. For Ph.D.: 60 semester hours beyond the bachelor's minimum, at least two years in residence; qualifying exam; one foreign language for some programs; dissertation; final oral exam.

FIELDS OF STUDY.

COLLEGE OF ARTS AND SCIENCES:
American Politics.
Analytical Chemistry.
Applied Mathematics.
Biochemistry.
Botany.
Chemistry.
Clinical Psychology.
Comparative Literature.
Computer Science.
Criminal Justice.
Ecology.
English.
Exercise Physiology.
Experimental Psychology.
French.
Geography.
Geology.
German.
History.
International Politics.
Liberal Studies.
Philosophy.
Physical Education.
Physiology.
Political Theory.
Public Administration.
Spanish.
Zoology.

COLLEGE OF FINE AND PROFESSIONAL ARTS:
Architecture.
Art Education.
Communication Studies.
Composition.
Conducting.
Ethnomusicology.
Fiber Arts.
Graphic Design/Illustration.
Journalism.
Library and Information Science.
Mass Communication.
Music Education.

Musicology.
Performance.
Piano Pedagogy.
Speech Pathology and Audiology.
Theater.
Theory.

SCHOOL OF EDUCATION:
Community Counseling.
Counseling.
Counseling and Human Development.
Curriculum and Instruction.
Early Childhood Education.
Educational Psychology.
Gifted Education.
Health Education.
Higher Education Administration and Student Personnel.
Instructional Technology.
K–12 Leadership.
Organizational Development.
Reading.
Rehabilitation Counseling.
School Counseling.
School Psychology.
Secondary Education.
Special Education.

GRADUATE SCHOOL OF MANAGEMENT:
Accounting.
Economics.
Finance.
Marketing.

SCHOOL OF BIOMEDICAL SCIENCES:
Biological Anthropology.
Cellular and Molecular Biology.
Neuroscience.
Pharmacology.
Physiology.
Note: Programs offered in cooperation with Northeastern Ohio Universities College of Medicine.

SCHOOL OF NURSING:
Clinical Nursing. Includes nursing of the adult; psychiatric mental health nursing.
Nursing Administration.
Nursing Education.
Parent-Child Nursing.

UNIVERSITY OF KENTUCKY
Lexington, Kentucky 40506-0027
http://www.uky.edu

Founded 1865. Coed. State control. Semester system. Sponsoring university of Oak Ridge Institute of Nuclear Studies in Tennessee. Special facilities: Appalachian Center, Center for the Arts, Center for Business and Economic Research, Maxwell H. Gluck Equine Research Center, Gaines Center for the Humanities, Lucille Parker Mackey Cancer Research Center, Multidisciplinary Center on Gerontology, Institute for Mining/Minerals Research, Sanders-Brown Center for Aging, Survey Research Center, Kentucky Transportation Center, Water Resources Institute. Library: more than 2,200,000 volumes, 5,200,000 microforms, about 1000 PCs in all libraries.

Annual tuition: full-time, resident $2916, nonresident $8076; per credit, resident $150, nonresident $436. No on-campus housing available. Day care facilities available.

Graduate School

Graduate study since 1870. Enrollment: full-time 2454, part-time 2671. Graduate faculty: full-time 900, none part-time. Degrees conferred: M.A., M.S., M.S.Acc., M.S.Agr.E., M.S.Ch.E., M.S.C.E., M.S.C.N., M.S.Ed., M.S.E., M.S.E.M., M.S.F.S., M.S.M.E., M.S.R.M.P., M.S.N., M.S.O.R., M.S.R.H., M.S.B.E., M.S.P.H., M.B.A., M.A.T., M.M., M.P.A., M.S.D., M.S.L.S., M.F.A., M.S.W., Ed.S., D.M.A., D.B.A., Ed.D., Ph.D.

ADMISSION REQUIREMENTS. Two official transcripts from each school attended, GRE/GMAT required in support of School's application. TOEFL required for international applicants. Interview not required. Accepts transfer applicants. Graduates of unaccredited institutions not considered. Apply to Graduate Admissions Office by July 15 (Fall), November 1 (Spring), April 1 (Summer). Application fee none. Phone: (606)257-4613; fax: (606)323-1928.

ADMISSION STANDARDS. Relatively open for some departments, selective to very selective for others. Minimum average: 3.0 (A = 4).

FINANCIAL AID. Annual awards from institutional funds: 20 academic scholarships, 1100 research/teaching assistantships, 200 fellowships, Federal W/S, loans. Apply by March 1 to Graduate Dean for fellowships, to appropriate department chair for assistantships; to Financial Aid Office for all other programs. Use FAFSA. Phone: (606)257-3172.

DEGREE REQUIREMENTS. For M.A., M.A.T., and all M.S. programs: 30–36 credit hours minimum with or without thesis; final written/oral exam; reading knowledge of one language for some majors. For M.B.A., M.P.A.: same as for M.A. except comprehensive exam instead of thesis. For M.M.: same as M.A., except recital for applied music major, composition for composition major, in lieu of thesis; thesis optional for music education or theory majors. For M.F.A.: 48 credits minimum, at least 40 in residence. For M.S.W.: 60 credits minimum, at least 1½ years in residence; thesis. For Ed.S.: 30 credit hours minimum beyond the master's, research problem and written report included; final written/oral exam. For Ph.D.: three years minimum beyond the bachelor's, at least two semesters in full-time residence; qualifying exam; reading knowledge of one or two foreign languages; dissertation; final written/oral exam. For Ed.D., D.B.A.: same as for Ph.D., except at least 72 credit hours minimum beyond the bachelor's; no foreign language requirement.

FIELDS OF STUDY.

COLLEGE OF AGRICULTURE:
Agricultural Economics.
Agronomy.
Animal Sciences.
Entomology.
Forestry.
Plant and Soil Science.
Plant Pathology.
Plant Physiology.
Veterinary Science.

COLLEGE OF ALLIED HEALTH PROFESSIONS:
Clinical Nutrition.
Communication Disorders.
Physical Therapy.
Radiation Sciences.

COLLEGE OF ARTS AND SCIENCES:
Anthropology.
Biology.
Chemistry.
Classical Languages.

Clinical Psychology.
English.
French.
Geography.
Geology.
German.
History.
Mathematics.
Philosophy.
Physics and Astronomy.
Political Science.
Psychology.
Sociology.
Spanish.
Statistics.

COLLEGE OF BUSINESS AND ECONOMICS:
Accounting.
Business Administration.
Economics.

COLLEGE OF COMMUNICATIONS AND INFORMATION STUDIES:
Communication.
Library Science.

COLLEGE OF EDUCATION:
Administration.
Business Education.
Counseling Psychology.
Curriculum and Instruction.
Early Childhood Education.
Educational Psychology.
Elementary Education.
Guidance and Counseling.
Higher Education.
Kinesiology and Health Promotion.
Reading.
Rehabilitation Counseling.
Secondary Education. Includes English, mathematics, science, social science.
Special Education.
Vocational Education.

COLLEGE OF ENGINEERING:
Agricultural Engineering.
Biomedical Engineering.
Chemical Engineering.
Civil Engineering.
Computer Science.
Electrical Engineering.
Engineering Mechanics.
Manufacturing Systems Engineering.
Materials Science and Engineering.
Mechanical Engineering.
Mining Engineering.

COLLEGE OF FINE ARTS:
Art Education.
Art History.
Art Studio.
Composition.
Music.
Music Education.
Music Theory.
Musicology.
Performance.
Theater Arts.

COLLEGE OF HUMAN ENVIRONMENTAL SCIENCE:
Design Textiles.
Family Studies.

Interior Design, Merchandising, and Textiles.
Nutrition and Food Science.

COLLEGE OF DENTISTRY:
Dentistry.

COLLEGE OF MEDICINE:
Anatomy.
Behavioral Science.
Biochemistry.
Health Administration.
Microbiology.
Pharmacology.
Physiology.
Public Health.
Toxicology.

COLLEGE OF NURSING:
Nursing.

COLLEGE OF PHARMACY:
Pharmaceutical Science.

COLLEGE OF SOCIAL WORK:
Social Work.

MARTIN SCHOOL OF PUBLIC ADMINISTRATION:
Public Administration.

PATTERSON SCHOOL OF DIPLOMACY AND INTERNATIONAL
  COMMERCE:
Diplomacy.
International Commerce.

College of Law (40506-0048)

Established 1908. Semester system. Law library: 349,000 volumes. Library has LEXIS, NEXIS, WESTLAW, DIALOG. Special facilities: The Mineral Law Center.

Annual tuition: resident $4440, nonresident $12,614. Limited on-campus housing available. Total average annual additional expense: $8500.

Enrollment: first-year class 147; total full-time 400 (men 65%, women 35%); no part-time study. Law faculty: full-time 28, part-time 24. Degrees conferred: J.D., J.D.-M.B.A., J.D.-M.P.A.

ADMISSION REQUIREMENTS. LSDAS Law School report, bachelor's degree, transcripts, LSAT (not later than February), letters of recommendations required in support of application. Interview not required. Accepts transfer applicants. Graduates of unaccredited colleges not considered. Approximately 85% of students are state residents. Apply to Associate Dean for Admissions by March 1. Admits Fall only. Application fee $25. Phone: (606)257-1678; (606)257-7938 for catalogs only.

ADMISSION STANDARDS. Selective. Accepts about 30–35% of total annual applicants.

FINANCIAL AID. Scholarships, full and partial tuition waivers, Federal W/S, loans. Apply to University's Student Financial Aid Office by April 1. Use FAFSA. About 8% of students receive aid other than loans from both College and outside sources.

DEGREE REQUIREMENTS. For J.D.: 90 semester hours minimum. Note: transfer credit from other ABA-accredited law schools considered.

College of Medicine (40536-0084)

First class admitted 1960. Medical Center library: 100,000 volumes. Annual tuition: resident $8250, nonresident $19,420; student fees $330. Total average figure for all other expenses: $9294. On-campus housing for both married and single students available.

Enrollment: first-year class 95 (EDP 30); total full-time 489 (men 68%, women 32%); postgraduates 12. Faculty: full-time $45, part-time 64. Degrees conferred: M.D., M.D.–M.S., M.D.–Ph.D. The M.S. and Ph.D. are offered through the Graduate School.

ADMISSION REQUIREMENTS. AMCAS report, transcripts, MCAT, interview required in support of application. Accepts transfer applicants. Has EDP; apply between June 15 and August 1. Preference given to state residents. Apply to Office of Admissions after June 15, before November 1. Phone: (606)233-6161; fax: (606)323-2076.

ADMISSION STANDARDS. Selective. Accepts about 15% of total annual applicants. Approximately 87% are state residents.

FINANCIAL AID. Limited number of scholarships; summer fellowships, assistantships, loans. Apply to Office of Student Services after acceptance. About 85% of students receive aid from College and outside sources.

DEGREE REQUIREMENTS. For M.D.: satisfactory completion of four-year program. For M.S., Ph.D.: see Graduate School listing above.

FIELDS OF GRADUATE STUDY.
Anatomy and Neurobiology.
Biochemistry.
Biomedical Engineering.
Biophysics.
Immunology.
Microbiology.
Neurosciences.
Nutritional Sciences.
Pathology.
Pharmacology.
Physiology.
Public Health Toxicology.

College of Dentistry (40536-0084)

First classes 1962. Medical Center library: 100,000 volumes. Annual tuition: resident $6765, nonresident $17,700. On-campus housing available. Contact Housing Office. Phone: (606)257-3721. Total average cost for all other first-year expenses: $6744.

Enrollment: first-year class 53, total 196 (men 60%, women 40%); postgraduates 32. Faculty: full-time 66, part-time 42. Degrees conferred: B.S.-D.M.D. (with the University's College of Arts and Sciences), D.M.D.

ADMISSION REQUIREMENTS. AADSAS report, transcripts, DAT (not later than October), three letters of recommendation, interview required in support of application. Accepts transfer applicants. Graduates of unaccredited institutions are not considered. Preference given to state residents. Apply to Admissions Office after June 1, before April 1. Application fee: residents none, nonresidents $10. Phone: (606)233-6071.

ADMISSION STANDARDS. Selective. Usual minimum average: 3.0 (A = 4). Accepts 80% of state residents, 1% of nonresidents. Approximately 90% are state residents.

FINANCIAL AID. Limited number of scholarships, loans. Apply to Financial Aid Office after acceptance. Use FAFSA. About 92% of students receive some aid from College and outside sources.

DEGREE REQUIREMENTS. For D.M.D.: satisfactory completion of forty-month program.

FIELDS OF GRADUATE STUDY.
General Practice Residency.
Geriatric Dentistry.
Oral and Maxillofacial Surgery.
Orofacial Pain.
Orthodontics.
Pediatric Dentistry.
Periodontics.

KIRKSVILLE COLLEGE OF OSTEOPATHIC MEDICINE
Kirksville, Missouri 63501-1497

Founded 1892 by Andrew Taylor Still, the founder of Osteopathic Medicine. Coed. Private control. Library: 78,000 volumes, 650 microforms, 1000 current periodicals, 36 PCs; has MEDLINE and interlibrary loan. On-campus housing available. Average academic year housing cost: $3500 (room only) for single students; $4000 for married students. Contact Student Affairs Office for both on- and off-campus housing information. Phone: (816)626-2236.

Annual tuition: $21,900. Enrollment: first-year class 140, total 583 (men 72%, women 28%). Faculty: full-time 78, part-time 43. Degree conferred: D.O.

ADMISSION REQUIREMENTS. AACOMAS report, supplemental school application, bachelor's degree preferred, transcripts, MCAT, letters of recommendation from premed advisory committee. Interview by invitation only. Graduates of unaccredited college not considered. Apply by February 1. Admits first-year students Fall only. Application fee: $50. Phone: (816)626-2237.

ADMISSION STANDARDS. Selective. Accepts approximately 15% of annual applicants. Usual minimum average: 3.0 (A = 4). Mean GPA: 3.3.

FINANCIAL AID. Institutional scholarships, National Health Services Corps Scholarships, loans include HEAL, Stafford, primary care, Perkins. Special loan programs for minorities and rural students. Apply by May 1 to Students Affairs Office. Use FAFSA.

DEGREE REQUIREMENT. For D.O.: satisfactory completion of four-year program.

KUTZTOWN UNIVERSITY OF PENNSYLVANIA
Kutztown, Pennsylvania 19530

Founded 1866. Located 15 miles NE of Reading. Coed. State control. Semester system. Library: 418,000 hardcover volumes, 1,100,000 microforms, 50 PCs.

Tuition: per credit, resident $187, nonresident $336. On-campus housing generally not available to graduate students. For information contact Director of Off-Campus Housing: (610)683-4022.

College of Graduate Studies

Graduate study since 1959. Enrollment: full-time 100, part-time 746. Faculty: full-time 5, part-time 150. Degrees conferred: M.A., M.S., M.Ed., M.L.S., M.P.A., M.B.A.

ADMISSION REQUIREMENTS. One transcript from all post-secondary institutions attended, three letters of recommendation,

interview, GRE/GMAT required in support of College's application. TOEFL, TSE required for international applicant. Resume and statement of goals are needed when applying for M.B.A. Accepts transfer applicants. Graduates of unaccredited institutions not considered. Apply to Dean of Graduate Studies by February 1 (Fall), July 1 (Spring). Application fee $25. Phone: (610)693-4200.

ADMISSION STANDARDS. Selective. Usual minimum average: 2.5 plus test scores (A = 4).

FINANCIAL AID. Thirty-six assistantships, Federal W/S, loans. Approved for VA benefits. Apply to Director of Financial Aid. Use FAFSA. Phone: (610)683-4077. Less than 5% of students receive aid other than loans from University.

DEGREE REQUIREMENTS. For master's: 30–57 credit hours minimum, at least 24 in residence (for most programs); thesis/nonthesis option; final written/oral exam.

FIELDS OF STUDY.
Art Education. M.Ed.
Business Administration. M.B.A.
Computer and Information Science. M.S.
Counseling Psychology. M.A.
Counselor Education. Includes elementary, secondary, student affairs in higher education. M.Ed.
Elementary Education. M.Ed.
English. M.A.
Library Science. M.L.S.
Mathematics. M.A.
Public Administration. M.P.A.
Reading Specialist. M.Ed.
Secondary Education. Includes biology, curriculum and instruction. English, mathematical social studies. M.Ed.
Telecommunications. M.S.

LAGRANGE COLLEGE
LaGrange, Georgia 30240-2999
http://www.lgc.peachnet.edu

Founded 1831. Coed. Private. Methodist. Quarter system. Library: 130,000 volumes, 17,200 microforms, 48 PCs in library.

Annual tuition: full-time $5460, part-time, per credit $182. No on-campus housing available for graduate students. Average academic year off-campus housing cost: $5000–$6500. Contact Dean of Students for off-campus information. Phone: (706)882-2911.

Graduate Program

Enrollment: full-time 13, part-time 48. Faculty: full-time 3, part-time 12. Degrees conferred: M.Ed., M.B.A.

ADMISSION REQUIREMENTS. Transcripts, GRE/MAT/GMAT, 3 references, interview required in support of application. TOEFL required for international applicants. Accepts transfer applicants. Apply to Director of Admissions by August 31 (Fall), December 31 (Spring). Application fee $20, $25 for international students. Phone: (706)812-7290; fax: (706)884-6567.

ADMISSION STANDARDS. Selective. Usual minimum average: 2.5, 3.0 for last 90 quarter hours, 60 semester hours. (A = 4).

FINANCIAL AID. Limited to Federal W/S, loans. Approved for VA benefits. Apply to the Financial Aid Office; no specified closing date. Phone: (706)812-7241. Use FAFSA and Institutional FAF.

DEGREE REQUIREMENTS. For M.Ed.: 60 quarter hours minimum; candidacy; final exam. For M.B.A.: 65–90 quarter hours minimum; comprehensive exam.

FIELDS OF STUDY.
Business Administration.
Early Childhood Education.
Middle Childhood.

LAMAR UNIVERSITY
Beaumont, Texas 77705

Founded 1923. Coed. State control. Semester system. Special facilities: Dishman Art Gallery, Center for Criminal Justice, Gulf Coast Hazardous Substance Research Center, Center for Public Policy Studies, Space Exploration Center. Library: 628,000 volumes, 1,003,000 microforms, 58 PCs.

Annual tuition: full-time resident $2050, nonresident $6900, part-time tuition varies according to credit hours. On-campus housing for married, single students. Average annual housing cost: $6000 for married students, $3900 (including board) for single students. Apply to Associate Dean, Student Development. Phone: (409)880-2314.

College of Graduate Studies

Graduate study since 1962. Enrollment: full-time 400, part-time 400. Graduate faculty: full-time 164, part-time 11. Degrees conferred: M.A., M.E.M., M.B.A., M.Ed., M.S., M.E.Sc., M.E., M.M., M.P.A., D.Egr., Ed.D.

ADMISSION REQUIREMENTS. Transcripts, GRE/GMAT required in support of College's application. Interview not required. TOEFL required for international applicants. Accepts transfer applicants. Graduates of unaccredited colleges not considered. Apply to Dean of College of Graduate Studies at least 4 weeks prior to registration. Application fee none. Phone: (409)880-8350, or (800)443-5638.

ADMISSION STANDARDS. Selective. Usual minimum average: 2.5 (A = 4).

FINANCIAL AID. Annual awards from institutional funds: Fifty scholarships, eighteen research fellowships, seven teaching fellowships, Federal W/S, loans. Approved for VA benefits. Apply to Dean of College of Graduate Studies for scholarships, fellowships, assistantships; to the Financial Aid Office for all other programs. No specified closing date. Use FAFSA. Phone: (409)880-8450. About 15% of students receive aid.

DEGREE REQUIREMENTS. For M.A., M.E.Sc., M.M.: 30 credit boom minimum, at least 24 in residence; thesis; final oral exam; reading knowledge of one foreign language required for M.A. only. For M.S., M.B.A., M.E., M.E.M., M.P.A., M.Ed.: 30 credit hours minimum, at least 24 in residence; thesis; final oral exam, or 36 credit hours minimum and final written exam in lieu of thesis. For D.Egr.: 30 credit hours minimum beyond master's; thesis; final oral exam. For Ed.D.: at least 60 credit hours beyond master's; qualifying exam; dissertation; final written/oral exam.

FIELDS OF STUDY.
Art Education.
Biology.
Business Administration.
Chemistry.
Communication.
Computer Science.

Education. Includes elementary, secondary, counseling, English, foreign language, music, science, social sciences, special education, supervision, public school administration.
Engineering and Applied Science.
Engineering Management.
Engineering Science.
English.
Government.
Health Education.
History.
Home Economics and Human Development.
Mathematics.
Music.
Physical Education and Human Movement Studies.
Psychology.
Public Administration.
Reading.
Speech, Hearing and Deafness. Includes audiology, deaf education.
Speech-Language Pathology.

UNIVERSITY OF LA VERNE
La Verne, California 91750-4443

Founded 1891. Located 30 miles E of Los Angeles. Coed. Independent. Semester system. Library: 250,000 volumes.

Tuition: per hour $335 (master's), $475 (doctorate). No on-campus housing available.

Graduate Program

Enrollment: full-time 400, part-time 652. Graduate faculty: full-time 40, part-time 25. Degrees conferred: M.Ed., M.S., M.A., M.H.A., M.P.A., M.B.A., Ed.D., D.P.A.

ADMISSION REQUIREMENTS. Transcripts, 3 letters of reference required in support of application. GRE/GMAT/MAT for some programs. Accepts transfer applicants. TOEFL required for international applicants. Graduates of unaccredited institutions not considered. Apply to Graduate Studies Office; specified closing date. Application fee $25 (master's), $75 (doctorate). Phone: (714)593-3511, ext. 4244.

ADMISSION STANDARDS. Selective. Usual minimum average: 2.5–3.0 for master's programs, 3.0 for doctoral (A = 4).

FINANCIAL AID. Annual awards from institutional funds: departmental scholarships, assistantships, Federal W/S, loans. Apply by May 1 to Financial Aid Office. Phone: (714)543-3511, ext. 4135. Use FAFSA. No aid for part-time students carrying less than half of full program.

DEGREE REQUIREMENTS. For master's: 32–50 semester hours minimum (6–12 credits may be transferred into program); thesis or graduate seminar. For Ed.D.: 54 semester hours beyond master's. For D.P.A.: 54 semester hours beyond master's.

FIELDS OF STUDY.
Business Administration. M.B.A.
Child Development.
Counseling.
Educational Management. M.Ed., Ed.D.
Health Care Administration.
Leadership and Management.
Learning Handicapped.
Marriage and Family Therapy.
Operations Management.
Public Administration. M.P.A., D.P.A.

Reading.
School Counseling.
Special Education.

LEHIGH UNIVERSITY
Bethlehem, Pennsylvania 18015-3094

Founded 1865. Located 60 miles N of Philadelphia. Coed. Private control. Semester system. Special facilities: Research centers in Chemical Process Modeling and Control, Design and Manufacture Innovation, Economic Education, Innovation Management Studies, International Studies, Molecular Bioscience and Biotechnology, Polymer Science and Engineering Social Research, Energy Research, Advanced Technology for Large Structural Systems, Environmental Studies, Jewish Studies, Study of Private Enterprise, Materials Research, Business Communications, Solid State Studies, Small Business Development, Technology Studies, Surface Studies; Research institutes in Emulsion Polymers, Fracture and Solid Mechanics, Metal Forming, Study of the High-Rise Habitat, Thermo-Fluid Engineering and Science, 18th-Century Studies, Studies of Commodities, Health Science, Biomedical Engineering and Mathematical Biology. Library: 1,000,000 volumes, 1,700,000 microforms, 137 PCs. Day care facilities available.

Annual tuition: full-time $18,760, per credit $770. Limited on-campus housing for both married and single students. Average academic year housing cost: $6020 for single graduate students, $7500 for married students. Apply to Coordinator of Graduate and Off-Campus Housing. Phone: (610)758-3500.

Graduate Studies

Graduate study since 1866. Enrollment: full-time 950, part-time 1117. University faculty: full-time 425, part-time 85. Degrees conferred: M.A., M.B.A., M.Ed., M.S., Ed.D., D.A., Ph.D.

ADMISSION REQUIREMENTS. Transcripts, GRE/GMAT/MAT required in support of application. International students must submit evidence of competence in English or TOEFL. Interview not required. Accepts transfer applicants. Graduates of unaccredited colleges not considered. Apply to appropriate colleges; no specified closing date. Application fee $40. Graduate Studies phone: (610)758-4500; fax: (610)758-4244.

ADMISSION STANDARDS. Competitive for some departments, very selective for others. Minimum average: 2.75 (A = 4).

FINANCIAL AID. Annual awards from institutional funds: 65 scholarships, 210 research assistantships, 200 teaching fellowships, 10 internships, Federal W/S, loans. Approved for VA benefits. Apply by January 15 to appropriate department chair for scholarships, fellowships, assistantships; to the Financial Aid Office for all other programs. Use either FAFSA. Phone: (610)758-3181. About 75% of students receive aid from University and outside sources.

DEGREE REQUIREMENTS. For master's: 30 credit hours minimum, at least 24 in residence; thesis/comprehensive exam. For Ph.D.: three years minimum beyond the bachelor's, at least one year in residence; reading knowledge of foreign languages varies with department; written/oral general exam; dissertation; final oral exam. For Ed.D.: same as for Ph.D., except no language requirement. For D.A.: same as for Ph.D., except college teaching internship, appropriate project instead of dissertation.

FIELDS OF STUDY.
Applied Mathematics.
Applied Social Research.

Business Administration. M.B.A. only.
Business and Economics.
Chemical Engineering.
Chemistry.
Civil Engineering.
Clinical Chemistry.
Counseling Psychology.
Education Administration.
Educational Specialist.
Educational Technology.
Electrical Engineering and Computer Science.
Elementary Education.
English.
Geology.
Government.
History.
Industrial Engineering.
Management Science.
Manufacturing System Engineering.
Materials Science and Engineering.
Mathematics.
Mechanical Engineering and Mechanics.
Molecular Biology.
Molecular Bioscience and Biotechnology.
Physics.
Physiological Chemistry.
Polymer Science and Engineering.
Psychology.
Reading.
School Psychology.
Secondary Education.
Social Relations.
Special Education.

HERBERT H. LEHMAN COLLEGE OF THE CITY UNIVERSITY OF NEW YORK
Bronx, New York 10468-1589

Founded in 1932 as branch of Hunter College, became independent unit of City University in 1968. Coed. Municipal control. Semester system. Library: 450,000 volumes, 400,000 microforms. Day care facilities available.

Tuition: per credit, state resident $185, nonresident $320. No on-campus housing available.

Graduate Division

Enrollment: full-time 102, part-time 1500. Faculty: full-time 230, part-time 40. Degrees conferred: M.A., M.A.T., M.S., M.S. in Ed., M.F.A.

ADMISSION REQUIREMENTS. Transcripts, letters of recommendation, TOEFL required for all international applicants. Accepts transfer applicants. Graduates of unaccredited institutions not considered. Apply to Office of Admissions by April 1 (Fall), November 1 (Spring). Application fee $40. Phone: (718)960-8702.

ADMISSION STANDARDS. Competitive. Usual minimum average: 2.75 (A = 4).

FINANCIAL AID. Limited to graduate TAP, loans. Apply to Student Financial Aid Office by December 1. Use FAFSA and University's FAF. Phone: (718)960-8545.

DEGREE REQUIREMENTS. For master's: 30 credit hours minimum; thesis and/or comprehensive exams for most majors.

FIELDS OF STUDY.
Accounting. GMAT for admission.
Art. M.A., M.F.A.
Biological Sciences.
Computer Science.
Education. Includes elementary and secondary teaching; subject fields include art, music, biology (7–12), reading, mathematical (7–12), health, social studies (7–12), early childhood education; guidance and counseling, physical education, teaching of emotionally disturbed, mentally retarded, learning disabled, recreation, science education, English, Spanish.
English and English Literature.
History.
Mathematics.
Nursing. Includes psychiatric.
Nutrition.
Speech Pathology and Audiology.
Teacher of Handicapped Bilingual Students. M.S.Ed.
TESOL. M.S.Ed.

LEWIS AND CLARK COLLEGE
Portland, Oregon 97219-7879

Founded 1867. Coed. Private control. Presbyterian. Quarter system. Library: 270,000 volumes, 222,000 microforms, 1900 current periodicals, 54 PCs.

Tuition: $382 per quarter hour. No on-campus housing available.

Graduate School of Professional Studies

Enrollment: full- and part-time 749. Faculty teaching graduate students: full-time 35, part-time 63. Degrees conferred: M.A., M.S., M.A.T., M.Ed., M.P.A.

ADMISSION REQUIREMENTS. Official transcripts, GRE/NTE or MAT required in support of School's application. TOEFL required for international applicants. Accepts transfer applicants. Graduates of unaccredited institutions not considered. Apply to the program chairman at least 2 weeks prior to registration for part-time applicants. Applicants in some programs admitted quarterly. Teacher Education applicants apply by January 15. Rolling admissions process. Application fee $40. Phone: (503)768-7700.

ADMISSION STANDARDS. Selective. Usual minimum average: 3.0 (A = 4).

FINANCIAL AID. Limited to Federal W/S, loans. Apply to Office of Student Financial Services. Phone: (503)768-7090. Use FAFSA.

DEGREE REQUIREMENTS. For master's: 10–15 courses minimum, at least 8–12 in residence; thesis/nonthesis option.

FIELDS OF STUDY.
Counseling Psychology.
Educational Administration.
Elementary Education.
Music Education.
Public Administration.
School Psychology.
Secondary Education.
Special Education–Hearing Impaired.

Northwestern School of Law

Established 1884. Semester system. Lewis and Clark 1965. Library: 350,000 volumes. Library has LEXIS, NEXIS, WEST-LAW, DIALOG, CALI, FIRSTSEARCH, QLSYSTEMS. No on-campus housing.

Annual tuition: $16,485 (day), $12,365 (evening). Total average annual additional expense: $7000.

Enrollment: first-year class, day 160, evening 70; total 700 (men 55%, women 45%). Faculty: full-time 29, part-time 54. Degrees conferred: J.D., LL.M. (Environmental and Natural Resources Law).

ADMISSION REQUIREMENTS. LSDAS Law School report, bachelor's degree, transcripts, LSAT, short essay, letters of recommendation required in support of application. Accepts transfer applicants. Personal visit encouraged. Graduates of unaccredited colleges not considered. Apply to Assistant Dean for Admissions by March 15. Admits Fall only. Application fee $45. Phone: (503)768-6613.

ADMISSION STANDARDS. Selective. Accepts about 30–35% of total annual applications.

FINANCIAL AID. Scholarships, grants, fellowships, full and partial tuition waivers, Federal W/S, loans. Apply to Financial Aids Office by February 1. Use FAFSA.

DEGREE REQUIREMENTS. For J.D.: satisfactory completion of three-year (day), four-year (evening) program; 86 credit hours.

LINCOLN UNIVERSITY
Jefferson City, Missouri 65102

Founded 1866. Located 125 miles W of St. Louis. Coed. State control. Semester system. Library: 141,000 volumes, 27,000 microforms.

Tuition: per hour, resident $107, nonresident $214. On-campus housing for single students available. Housing cost per semester: $1349 (includes board). Apply to Director of Residential Life. Phone: (314)681-5478.

Graduate Studies and Continuing Education

Enrollment: full-time 34, part-time 337 (men 111, women 260). University faculty teaching graduate students: full-time 51, part-time varies by semester. Degrees conferred: M.A., M.Ed., M.B.A.

ADMISSION REQUIREMENTS. Transcripts, three letters of recommendation required in support of application. GRE/MAT required for M.A., M.Ed.; GMAT required for M.B.A. TOEFL required for international applicants. Accepts transfer applicants. Apply to Office of Graduate Studies and Continuing Education by July 15 (Fall), November 30 (Spring). Application fee $17. Phone: (314)681-5207; fax: (312)681-5209.

FINANCIAL AID. Limited to Federal W/S, loans. Approved for VA benefits. Use FAFSA. Phone: (314)681-6156; fax: (314)681-5566. Aid for part-time students carrying at least six credits.

DEGREE REQUIREMENTS. For M.A.: 33 semester hours minimum; thesis/nonthesis option. For M.Ed.: 36 semester hours minimum. For M.B.A.: 36 semester hours minimum.

FIELDS OF STUDY.
Agency Counseling.
Business Administration.
Elementary Education.
Elementary Principalship.
Guidance and Counseling.
History.

Secondary Education.
Secondary Principalship.
Social Science. Includes sociology, history, and political science.
Sociology.
Sociology/Criminal Justice.

LOMA LINDA UNIVERSITY
Loma Linda, California 92350

Founded in 1905. Located in the San Bernardino Redlands area about 5 miles from each city. Coed. Quarter system. Loma Linda University offers programs in graduate professional education through the Graduate School. The programs utilize resources in the Schools of Allied Health Professions, Dentistry, Medicine, Nursing, and Public Health. The University is operated by the Seventh-Day Adventist Church with approximately 40% of its student body belong to other religious faiths. Library: 299,867 volumes, 74,224 microforms, 75 PCs.

Tuition: per unit $350, graduate dental programs full-time $17,000–$40,000. On-campus housing for 100 graduate men, 32–64 graduate women, none for married students. Average academic year cost: $5450–$6250. Apply to Dean of Students. Phone: (909)824-4510. Day care facilities available.

Graduate School

Opened 1954. Enrollment: full-time 355, part-time 154. University faculty: full-time 116, part-time 64. Degrees conferred: M.A., M.S., M.S.W., M.P.H., Psy.D., Dr. P.H., Ph.D.

ADMISSION REQUIREMENTS. Two transcripts, letters of reference, GRE/Subject Tests required in support of School's application. TOEFL required for foreign applicants. Interview not required for most programs. Accepts transfer applicants. Apply to Dean of Graduate School by August 1. Most department prefer Fall entrance. Application fee $50. Phone: (909)824-4529; fax: (909)824-4859.

ADMISSION STANDARDS. Very selective for some departments, selective for others. Usual minimum average: 3.0 (A = 4).

FINANCIAL AID. Annual awards from institutional funds: 12 scholarships, 22 fellowships, 125 stipends, 27 teaching assistantships, full and partial tuition waiver, Federal W/S, loans. Approved for VA benefits. Apply by March 1 to appropriate department chair for scholarships, fellowships, assistantships; to Financial Aid Office for all other programs. Use FAFSA and institutional FAF. Phone: (909)824-4509, (800)422-4558.

DEGREE REQUIREMENTS. For master's: 48 quarter units minimum, at least 12 in residence; thesis/nonthesis option; final written/oral exams. For Ph.D.: three years minimum beyond the bachelor's, at least two years in residence and 30 units in full-time attendance; some require reading knowledge of two foreign languages; dissertation; final oral exam. For Psy.D.: essentially the same as Ph.D., except no foreign language; internship; special research project.

FIELDS OF STUDY.
Anatomy.
Biochemistry.
Biology.
Biomedical Ethics. M.A. only.
Clinical Ministry. M.A. only.
Dentistry. Includes endodontics, implant dentistry, oral surgery, orthodontics, pediatrics, periodontics. Apply by October 1; D.D.S. or D.D.M. for admission. M.S. only.
Family Life Education.
Family Studies. M.A. only.

Geology. M.S. only.
Marriage and Family Therapy. M.S. only.
Medical Scientist Program. M.D.-M.S., M.D.-Ph.D., D.D.S.-Ph.D.
Microbiology.
Nursing. Includes adult critical care, adult nurse practitioner, family nurse practitioner, the growing family, neonatal critical care/practitioner, nurse management, school nurse, the adult and aging family. M.S. only.
Nutrition. M.S.
Paleontology. M.S.
Pharmacology.
Physiology.
Psychology.
Social Work. M.S.W.
Speech Language Pathology. M.S. only.

School of Medicine

Organized 1909. Annual tuition: $23,946. Total average figure for all other expenses: $9100. Enrollment: first-year class 150 (EDP 10); total 600 (men 53%, women 47%). Faculty: full-time 138, part-time 15. Degree conferred: M.D. The M.S., Ph.D. is offered through the Graduate School.

ADMISSION REQUIREMENTS. AMCAS report, transcripts, recommendations, MCAT, supplementary form, required in support of application. Interview by invitation. Has EDP: apply between June 1 and August 1. Applicants must have completed at least three years of college study. Some preference to members of Seventh-Day Adventist Church. Apply to Dean of Admissions after June 15, before November 15. Application fee $55. Phone: (909)824-4467; fax: (909)824-4146.

ADMISSION STANDARDS. Very competitive. Accepts 8% of total annual applicants. Approximately 60% are state residents.

FINANCIAL AID. Loans. Apply to Director of Student Finance.

DEGREE REQUIREMENTS. For M.D.: satisfactory completion of four-year program. For M.S.-Ph.D.: see Graduate School listing above.

FIELDS OF GRADUATE STUDY.
Anatomy.
Biochemistry.
Microbiology.
Pharmacology.
Physiology.

School of Dentistry

Annual tuition: $21,310. Quarter system. On-campus housing for single graduate students only. Apply to Dean, Student Services. Phone: (714)824-4510. Total average cost for all other first-year expenses: $6860.

Enrollment: first-year class 82; total 320 (men 65%, women 35%). School faculty: full-time 90, part-time 82. Degrees conferred: D.D.S., D.D.S.-M.P.H., D.D.S.-M.S., D.D.S.-Ph.D. The M.S., Ph.D. is offered through the Graduate School.

ADMISSION REQUIREMENTS. AADSAS report, Loma Linda supplemental form, official transcripts, three letters of recommendation, DAT (preference given to October test takers), dexterity test required in support of School's application. Interview by invitation only. Applicants must have completed at least three years of college study, preferably four years of study. Preference given to Seventh-Day Adventist Church members. Graduates of unaccredited institutions not considered. Apply to AADSAS after June 1, before January 1. Application fee $50. Phone: (909)824-4683, (800)422-4558.

ADMISSION STANDARDS. Competitive. Accepts about 20% of total annual applicants. Approximately 80% are state residents.

FINANCIAL AID. Scholarships, loans. Apply to Office of Student Aid and Finance by May 1 after acceptance. Phone: (909)824-4509. About 76% receive aid from School.

DEGREE REQUIREMENTS. For D.D.S.: satisfactory completion of 45-month program. For D.D.S.-M.P.H.: usually requires two additional quarters. For M.S., Ph.D. see Graduate School listing above.

FIELDS OF GRADUATE STUDY.
Endodontics.
Oral Implantology.
Oral and Maxillofacial Surgery.
Orthodontics.
Pediatric Dentistry.
Periodontics.
Prosthodontics.

LONG ISLAND UNIVERSITY, BROOKLYN CAMPUS

Brooklyn, New York 11201

Founded 1926. Coed. Private control. Semester system. Library: 400,000 volumes, 300 PCs.

Tuition: per credit, $425. Rooms and apartments available for single and married students. Average academic year housing cost: single student $6000 (including board), married $6000 (room only). Apply to Director of Housing. Phone: (718)488-1549.

Enrollment: full-time 694, part-time 1098. Faculty: full-time 143, part-time 148. Degrees conferred: M.A., M.S., M.B.A., M.S.Acc., M.P.A., M.S.Ed., Pharm.D., Ph.D.

Graduate Programs

ADMISSION REQUIREMENTS. Transcripts, GRE/GMAT, 2 letters of recommendation required in support of application. TOEFL required for international applicants. Interview not required. Accepts transfer applicants. Graduates of unaccredited institutions not considered. Apply to Graduate Admissions Office at least 1 month prior to beginning of semester. Application fee $30. Phone: (718)403-1011; fax: (718)797-2399.

ADMISSION STANDARDS. Competitive to relatively open. Usual minimum average 2.75 (A = 4).

FINANCIAL AID. Twenty scholarships, thirty fellowships, forty research assistantships, forty administrative assistantships, forty teaching assistantships, Federal W/S, loans. Approved for VA benefits. Apply by May 1 (Fall), November 1 (Spring), March 1 (Summer) to appropriate department chair for scholarships, fellowships, assistantships; to Graduate Admissions Office for all other programs. Use FAFSA and institutional FAF. Phone: (718)488-1037; fax: (718)488-3343.

DEGREE REQUIREMENTS. For M.A., M.S., M.S.Ed.: 30–36 semester hours minimum, at least 24 in residence; thesis for many departments; final oral/written exam. For M.B.A., M.P.A.: 36 credits beyond core; thesis/nonthesis option; comprehensive exam. For Ph.D.: by advisement.

FIELDS OF STUDY.
Accounting and Taxation. M.S.Acc., M.B.A.
Alcohol Counseling. Includes bilingual school counselor, alcoholism counselor.

Athletic Training and Sports Sciences. M.A.
Biology. Includes cellular, microbiology, molecular, physiology, medical microbiology. M.S.
Business Administration. M.B.A.
Chemistry. M.S.
Community Health. M.S.
Computer Science. M.S.
Counseling and Development. M.S., M.S.Ed.
Economics. M.A.
Education. Includes bilingual, business, computers in education, early childhood and elementary, educational technology, reading, school psychology, special, school administration, secondary, TESOL. M.S., M.S.Ed.
English. M.A.
Finance. M.B.A.
Health Administration. M.P.A.
Health Science. Includes athletic training and sports sciences, exercise physiology, physical therapy, adapted physical education, therapeutic recreation. M.S.
History. M.A.
International Business. M.B.A.
Management. M.B.A.
Marketing. M.B.A.
Pharmacy. Arnold and Marie Schwartz College of Pharmacy and Health Sciences. M.S., Ph.D., Pharm.D.
Physical Therapy. B.S.-M.S., M.S.
Political Science. M.A.
Psychology. M.A., Ph.D. in Clinical Psychology.
Public Administration. M.P.A.
Social Science. M.S.
Sociology. M.A.
Speech-Language Pathology. M.S.
Taxation. M.B.A.
TESOL.
United Nations Program. Certificate only.
Urban Studies. M.A.
Writing.

LONG ISLAND UNIVERSITY, C. W. POST CAMPUS

Brookville, New York 11548-1300

Established 1954. Coed. Private control. Semester system. Special facilities: Hillwood Art Museum, Center for Aging, Tilles Center for Performing Arts, Accounting and Tax Research Library, Center for Economic Research, Center for Business Research. Library: 1,297,800 volumes, 678,500 microforms, 9600 current periodicals.

Tuition: per credit $427. Rooms and apartments available for single and married students. Average academic year housing cost: $1835 (room only), $2395 (including board). Contact Director of Housing for both on- and off-campus housing information. Phone: (516)299-2326.

Graduate Division

Graduate study since 1954. Enrollment: full-time 827, part-time 2292. Faculty: full-time 470. Degrees conferred: M.A., M.S., M.B.A., M.F.A., M.P.A., C.A.S., Ph.D., Psy.D.

ADMISSION REQUIREMENTS. Official transcripts, GRE/GMAT, 2 letters of recommendation required in support of applications. Department interview may be required. All requirements vary by department. TOEFL or ASPECT program required for international applicants. Accepts transfer applicants. Graduates of unaccredited institutions not considered. Apply to Graduate Admissions Office at least 1 month prior to beginning of semester. Application fee $30. Phone: (516)299-2417; fax: (516)299-2137; E-mail: admission@collegehall.livnet.edu.

ADMISSION STANDARDS. Selective to relatively open. Usual minimum average: 2.5 (A = 4).

FINANCIAL AID. Scholarships, research/teaching assistantships, fellowships, internships, Federal W/S, loans. Approved for VA benefits. Apply by June 1 (Fall), October 1 (Spring), April 1 (Summer) to appropriate department chair for fellowships, assistantships; to Graduate Admissions Office for scholarships; to Financial Aid Office for all other programs. Use FAFSA, TAP for NY State residents. Phone: (516)299-2338.

DEGREE REQUIREMENTS. For M.A., M.S., 30–36 semester hours minimum, at least 24 in residence; thesis/nonthesis option for many departments; final oral/written exam. For M.B.A., M.P.A.: 36 credits beyond core; thesis/nonthesis option; comprehensive exam. For M.F.A.: 60 credits minimum beyond bachelor's, at least 45 in residence; project.

FIELDS OF STUDY.

COLLEGE OF ARTS AND SCIENCES:
Applied Mathematics.
Biology.
Clinical Psychology. Psy.D. only.
Computer Science Education.
English.
Environmental Studies.
Experimental Psychology.
History.
Interdisciplinary Studies.
Management Engineering.
Math for Secondary School Teachers.
Political Science.
Spanish.

SCHOOL OF BUSINESS, PUBLIC ADMINISTRATION, AND PROFESSIONAL ACCOUNTANCY:
Accounting.
Criminal Justice.
Finance.
Fraud Examination. Certificate.
Health Administration.
Health Administration—Gerontology.
Health Systems Finance.
International Business.
Management and Information Systems.
Marketing.
Public Administration.
Security Administration.
Strategic Management—Accounting.
Taxation.

SCHOOL OF EDUCATION:
Art Education.
Bilingual Education. Includes elementary, secondary.
Biology Education.
College Student Development Counseling.
Computers in Education.
Earth Science Education.
Elementary Education.
English Education.
Mathematics Education.
Mental Health Counseling.
Middle School Education.
Music Education.
Reading Teacher.
School Administration Supervisor.
School Business Administration.
School Counselor.
School District Administration.
Social Studies Education.

Spanish Education.
Speech-Language Pathology.
Teacher of Gifted and Talented.
Teacher of Special Education.
Teaching English to Speakers of Other Languages.

SCHOOL OF VISUAL AND PERFORMING ARTS:
Art.
Art Education.
Art Therapy.
Fine Art and Design.
Music.
Music Education.
Theater.

SCHOOL OF HEALTH PROFESSIONS:
Clinical Laboratory Management.
Dietetics.
Medical Biology.
Nutrition.

Palmer School of Library and Information Science

Tuition: per credit, $405.
Enrollment: full-time 57, part-time 229. Faculty: full-time 11, part-time 15. Degrees conferred: M.S.L.S., Certificate (Archives and Records Management).

ADMISSION REQUIREMENTS. Official transcripts, GRE/MAT, statement of career objectives, three letters of recommendation, interview required in support of School's application. TOEFL required for international applicants. Accepts transfer applicants. Graduates of unaccredited institutions not considered. Apply by May 15 (Fall), October 15 (Spring), to Graduate Admission. Rolling admissions process. Application fee $30. Phone: (516)299-2417; fax: (516)626-2665.

ADMISSION STANDARDS. Selective. Usual minimum average: 3.0 (A = 4).

FINANCIAL AID. Scholarships, fellowships, assistantships, Federal W/S, loans, tuition reductions for students with a 3.5 or higher undergraduate average. Apply to Dean's Office for fellowships, assistantships; to Office of Financial Aid for all other programs. No specified closing date. Use FAFSA. Phone: (516)299-2338.

DEGREE REQUIREMENTS. For master's: 36 semester hours minimum, at least 12 in residence; thesis. For Certificate: 15–30 semester hours beyond master's; special project.

FIELDS OF STUDY.
Archives.
Library Sciences.
Records Management.

LONGWOOD COLLEGE
Farmville, Virginia 23909-1800

Founded 1839. Located 65 miles W of Richmond. Coed. State control. Semester system. Library: 830,000 print and nonprint items.
Tuition: per credit, resident $127, nonresident $340. Limited housing for graduate students in Fall and Spring semesters. Contact Director of Housing for on- and off-campus information. Phone: (804)395-2080.

Graduate Division

Graduate study since 1954. Enrollment: full- and part-time 405. College faculty: full-time 40, part-time 20. Degrees conferred: M.A., M.S.

ADMISSION REQUIREMENTS. Transcripts, 2 letters of recommendation, essay required in support of application. TOEFL required for international applicants. Accepts transfer applicants. Graduates of unaccredited colleges not considered. Apply to the Graduate Division; no specified closing date. Application fee $25. Phone: (804)395-2060.

ADMISSION STANDARDS. Selective. Usual minimum average: 2.5 (A = 4).

FINANCIAL AID. Assistantships, loans. Apply to the appropriate department for assistantships; to the Office of Financial Aid for loans. No specified closing date. Use FAFSA.

DEGREE REQUIREMENTS. For M.A.: 30 credit hours minimum, at least 24 in residence; thesis. For M.S.: 30 credit hours minimum, at least 24 in residence; thesis/nonthesis option; comprehensive exam for nonthesis option.

FIELDS OF STUDY.
Community and College Counseling.
Curriculum and Instruction Specialist. Includes elementary, environmental science, English, modern languages, mild disabilities, physical education, speech, theater.
English.
Guidance and Counseling.
Reading.
School Librarian/Media Specialist
Supervision.

LORAS COLLEGE
Dubuque, Iowa 52004-0178

Founded 1839. Coed. Private control. Roman Catholic. Semester system. Special facilities: Bioethics Resource Center, Center for Business and Research, Center for Dubuque Area History, Center for Environmental Research. Library: 340,000 volumes, 77,000 microforms.

Tuition: per credit hour $320. On-campus housing for graduate students during summer only; none for married students. Average summer housing cost: $600 for six-week summer session. Contact Dean of Students for housing information.

Graduate Division

All courses offered through Tri College Department of Education. Graduate enrollment: Summer, part-time 125. Faculty teaching graduate students: full-time 22, part-time 3. Degree conferred: M.A.

ADMISSION REQUIREMENTS. Official transcripts, GRE/MAT, 2 letters of recommendation required in support of application. Interview required by some departments. TOEFL required for international applicants. Accepts transfer applicants. Apply to Director of Graduate Division at least 6 weeks prior to registration. Application fee $25. Phone: (319)588-7139; fax: (319)588-7964.

ADMISSION STANDARDS. Selective. Usual minimum average: 2.5 (A = 4).

FINANCIAL AID. Limited to loans. Use FAFSA. Phone: (319)588-7339.

DEGREE REQUIREMENTS. For M.A.: 30 semester hours minimum, at least 24 in residence; written/oral exam (varies by department); reading knowledge of one foreign language (History); thesis/nonthesis option.

FIELDS OF STUDY.
Education. Includes curriculum and instruction, early childhood education, elementary counseling, secondary counseling, elementary administration, secondary administration, special education.
English.
History.
Physical Education.
Psychology.

LOUISIANA STATE UNIVERSITY AND AGRICULTURAL AND MECHANICAL COLLEGE
Baton Rouge, Louisiana 70803

Established 1860. Coed. State control. Semester system. Member institution of Organization for Tropical Studies. Special facilities: Coastal Studies Institute, System Network Computer Center, Center for French and Francophone Studies, Center for Life Course and Population Studies, Southern Regional Climate Center, Louisiana Office of State Climatology, The U.S. Civil War Center, Eric Voegelin Institute for American Renaissance Studies, Public Management Program, Louisiana Real Estate Research Institute, Louisiana Education Policy Research Center, Center for Scientific and Mathematical Literacy, Hazardous Waste Research Center, Louisiana Transportation Research Center, Louisiana Water Resource Research Institute, Institute for Recyclable Materials, Remote Sensing and Image Processing Laboratory, Center for Coastal Energy and Environmental Resources, Basin Research Institute, Center for Energy Studies, Coastal Ecology Institute, Coastal Fisheries Institute, Mining and Mineral Resources Research Institute, Wetland Biogeochemistry Institute, National Ports and Waterways Institute, Office of Sea Grant Development, Louisiana Space Consortium, Museum of Art, Vascular Plant Herbarium, Mycological Herbarium, Rural Life Museum, LSU Agricultural Center, Pennington Biomedical Research Center, Museum of Natural Science, Nuclear Science Center, Center for Advanced Microstructures and Devices, T. Henry Williams Center for Oral History. Founding member of the Council of Sponsoring Institutions of Oak Ridge Associated Universities. Library: 2,700,000 volumes, more than 4,000,000 microforms, more than 11,000,000 manuscripts.

Annual tuition: full-time resident $3267, nonresident $7392. On-campus housing for 578 married students, unlimited for graduate men and women. Average academic year housing cost: $2500 for married students, $3813 (including board) for single students. Apply to Director of Housing. Phone: (504)388-8663.

Graduate School

Graduate study since 1868. Enrollment: full-time 3400, part-time 1900. Faculty teaching graduate students: full-time 1122, part-time 61. Degrees conferred: M.A., M.B.A., M.Ed., M.L.A., M.M.Ed., M.M., M.N.S., M.A.H., M.F.A., M.Ap.Stat., M.E., M.P.A., M.S.W., Ed.S., D.M.A., D.V.M., M.M.E., M.L.I.S., C.L.I.S., Ph.D.

ADMISSION REQUIREMENTS. Transcripts, GRE/GMAT required in support of School's application. TOEFL required for international applicants. TSE required of international students seeking financial aid. Interview not required. Accepts transfer applicants. Graduates of unaccredited institutions not considered.

Apply to the School by May 15 (Fall), October 15 (Spring), May 15 (Summer). Application fee $25. Phone: (504)388-8663.

ADMISSION STANDARDS. Selective for most departments, very selective for others. Usual minimum average: 2.5 (A = 4).

FINANCIAL AID. Annual awards from institutional funds: 200 scholarships, 1744 research assistantships/teaching assistantships, 403 fellowships, Federal W/S, loans. Approved for VA benefits. Apply to appropriate department chair for scholarships, fellowships, assistantships; to Office of Financial Aid for all other programs. No specified closing date. Use FAFSA. Phone: (504)388-3103; fax: (504)388-6300. About 60% of students receive aid other than loans from University and outside sources. Aid sometimes available to part-time students.

DEGREE REQUIREMENTS. For master's: 30 semester hours minimum, at least 24 in residence; thesis; final oral/written exam; or 36 semester hours minimum, at least 30 in residence; final oral/written exam in some department; reading knowledge of one foreign language for some departments. For Ph.D.: 60 semester hours minimum beyond the master's, at least one year in continuous residence; oral/written qualifying exam in some departments; oral/written general exam; dissertation; final oral exam.

FIELDS OF STUDY.
Accounting.
Administrative and Foundational Services.
Agricultural Economics and Agribusiness.
Agronomy.
Architecture.
Art (School of). Includes art education, art history, photography, studio art.
Biochemistry.
Biological and Agricultural Engineering.
Business Administration.
Chemical Engineering.
Chemistry.
Civil and Environmental Engineering.
Communication Sciences and Disorders.
Comparative Literature.
Computer Science. Includes systems science.
Curriculum and Instruction.
Dairy Science.
Economics.
Electrical and Computer Engineering.
Engineering Sciences.
English.
Entomology.
Environmental Studies.
Epidemiology and Community Health.
Experimental Statistics.
Finance.
Food Science.
Forestry, Wildlife, and Fisheries.
French.
Genetics.
Geography and Anthropology.
Geology and Geophysics.
Health, Physical Education, Recreation, and Dance (School of).
History.
Horticulture.
Human Ecology.
Humanities.
Industrial and Manufacturing Systems Engineering.
Kinesiology.
Landscape Architecture (School of).
Library and Information Science (School of).
Linguistics.
Management.
Marketing.

Mass Communication.
Mathematics.
Mechanical Engineering.
Microbiology.
Music (School of).
Natural Sciences.
Nuclear Science (Center). Includes nuclear engineering.
Oceanography and Coastal Sciences.
Petroleum Engineering.
Philosophy.
Physics.
Plant Biology.
Plant Pathology and Crop Physiology.
Plant Physiology.
Political Science.
Poultry Science.
Psychology. Includes clinical, developmental, industrial and organizational, school.
Public Administration.
Quantitative Business Analysis.
Social Work (School of).
Sociology.
Spanish.
Speech Communication.
Systematics and Evolutionary Biology.
Theater.
Veterinary Anatomy and Cell Biology.
Veterinary Microbiology and Parasitology.
Veterinary Pathology.
Veterinary Physiology, Pharmacology, and Toxicology.
Vocational Education (School of). Includes extension education, industrial education, vocational agricultural education, vocational home economics education.
Zoology.

Paul M. Hebert Law Center

Established 1907. Semester system. Located Baton Rouge (70803). Law library: 522,400 volumes. Library has LEXIS, NEXIS, WESTLAW, DIALOG. Annual tuition: resident $3922, nonresident $8542.

Enrollment: first-year class 275; total full-time 691 (men 57%, women 43%). Faculty: full-time 33, part-time 12. Degrees conferred: J.D., J.D.-M.P.A., LL.M., M.C.L.

ADMISSION REQUIREMENTS. For J.D. program: LSDAS Law School report, bachelor's degree, transcripts, LSAT (not later than December) required in support of application. Preference given to state residents. Accepts transfer applicants. Graduates from unaccredited institutions not considered. Apply to Admissions Office after November 1, before February 1. Admits Fall only. Application fee $25. For Graduate Program: transcripts required in support of application, TOEFL required for foreign applicants. Apply to Office of Admissions. Phone: (504)388-8646.

ADMISSION STANDARDS. Selective. Accepts 45–50% of total annual applicants. Highly selective for LL.M., M.C.L.

FINANCIAL AID. Limited scholarships, loans. Apply to Office of Financial Aid by March 1. Use FAFSA.

DEGREE REQUIREMENTS. For J.D.: 87 semester hours minimum, at least 29 in residence. For LL.M., M.C.L.: 24 semester hours minimum, at least two semesters in residence; thesis.
Note: A summer program at the University of Aix-Marseille III (France) Law School available.

School of Social Work

Graduate study since 1937. Semester system. Annual tuition: resident $2654, nonresident $5954.

Enrollment: full-time 150, part-time 50. School faculty: full-time 22, part-time 10. Degree conferred: M.S.W., Ph.D.

ADMISSION REQUIREMENTS. Transcripts, GRE required in support of School's application. TOEFL required for international applicants. Interview may be required. Accepts transfer applicants. Graduates of unaccredited institutions not considered. Apply to Office of Admissions by March 1. Application fee $25. Phone: (504)388-5875; fax: (504)388-1357.

ADMISSION STANDARDS. Selective. Usual minimum average: 3.0 (A = 4). GRE combined score (analytic section not included): 1000.

FINANCIAL AID. Child Welfare Stipends, Corrections Stipends, eleven scholarships, seven teaching assistantships, minority student tuition waivers, Federal W/S, loans. Approved for VA benefits. Apply to Office of Admissions; no specified closing date. Use FAFSA. Phone: (504)388-3103; fax: (504)388-6300. About 30% of students receive aid from School and outside sources.

DEGREE REQUIREMENTS. For M.S.W.: 60-hour program, including internship. Advanced standing awarded to qualified B.S.W. degree holders. For Ph.D.: 39 semester hours beyond the master's; qualifying exam; dissertation; final oral exam.

School of Veterinary Medicine

Annual tuition: resident and contract state resident $4458; nonresident $15,408. Total average cost for all other expenses: $6800. On-campus housing available.

Enrollment: first-year class 80; total 320 (men 50%, women 50%); postgraduates 65. Faculty: full-time 95, part-time 14. Degrees conferred: D.V.M., D.V.M.-M.S., D.V.M.-Ph.D. The M.S. and Ph.D. are offered through the Graduate School.

ADMISSION REQUIREMENTS. VMCAS report, transcripts showing completion of sixty-six hours of preprofessional college work, MCAT or GRE recommendations, animal/veterinary experience, essay required in support of application. Interview always required. Accepts transfer applicants. Preference given to state and contract residents. Apply to Assistant Dean after September 1, prior to November 1. Application fee $50. Phone: (504)346-3155; fax: (504)346-3295.

ADMISSION STANDARDS. Selective. Accepts 40% of total annual applicants. Accepts nine from Arkansas, two from Puerto Rico, ten from outside state.

FINANCIAL AID. Fellowships, assistantships, full tuition waivers, federal W/S, loans. Apply to Office of Financial Aid after acceptance.

DEGREE REQUIREMENTS. For D.V.M.: 152 semester hours and four years in residence. For M.S. and Ph.D.: see Graduate School listing above.

LOUISIANA STATE UNIVERSITY MEDICAL CENTER
New Orleans, Louisiana 70112-2223

Founded 1967. Coed. State control. Semester system. Special facilities: Pennington Biomedical Research Center, LSU Eye Center. Library: 320,100 volumes, 8500 microforms, 3500 current periodicals.

Annual tuition: full-time, resident $2828, nonresident $5953. On-campus housing available for both single and married stu-

dents. Average academic year housing cost: $6000–$9000 (including board); off-campus housing $350 per month. Contact Director of Housing for both on- and off-campus housing information. Phone: (504)568-6260.

School of Graduate Studies

Graduate study since 1967. Enrollment: full-time 115, part-time 6. Faculty teaching graduate students: full-time 123, part-time 1. Degrees conferred: M.S., Ph.D.

ADMISSION REQUIREMENTS. Transcripts, letters of recommendation, GRE required in support of School's application. TOEFL required of international applicants. Interview not required. Accepts transfer applicants. Apply to the Office of Graduate Studies; no specified closing date. Rolling admissions process. Application fee $30. Phone: (504)568-4804; fax: (504)568-5588.

ADMISSION STANDARDS. Selective. Usual minimum average: 2.75 (A = 4).

FINANCIAL AID. 4 fellowships, 59 research assistantships, 41 teaching assistantships, Federal W/S, loans. Apply to appropriate department chair for assistantships, fellowships; to Office of Financial Aid for all other programs. No specified closing date. Use FAFSA and institutional FAF. About 20% of students receive aid other than loans from University and outside sources. Aid sometimes available to part-time students.

DEGREE REQUIREMENTS. For M.S.: 30–36 semester hours minimum, at least 24–36 in residence; thesis/nonthesis option; final written/oral exam for some programs. For Ph.D.: 42 semester hours minimum beyond the master's degree, at least two years in full-time residence; qualifying exam; foreign language proficiency for some programs; dissertation; final oral exam.

FIELDS OF STUDY.
Anatomy.
Biochemistry and Molecular Biology.
Biometry.
Human Genetics.
Microbiology and Immunology.
Neuroscience. Ph.D. only.
Pharmacology and Experimental Therapeutics. Ph.D. only.
Physiology.

School of Medicine (70112-1393)

Established 1931. Annual tuition: resident $6776. Enrollment: first-year class 175 (EDP 10), total 703 (men 60%, women 40%). Faculty: full-time 283, part-time 659. Degrees conferred: M.D., M.D.-Ph.D.

ADMISSION REQUIREMENTS. AMCAS report, transcripts, MCAT required in support of application. Interview by invitation only. Has EDP; apply June 15–August 1. Applicants must have completed at least three years of college study. Accepts state residents only. Accepts transfer applicants. Apply after June 15, before December 15 to Admissions Office. Application fee $50. Phone: (504)568-6262; fax: (504)568-7701.

ADMISSION STANDARDS. Competitive. Accepts 35% of total annual applicants. 100% are state residents.

FINANCIAL AID. Scholarships, CWSP, loans. Apply to Student Financial Aid Office.

DEGREE REQUIREMENTS. For M.D.: satisfactory completion of four-year program.

FIELDS OF GRADUATE STUDY.
Anatomy.
Biochemistry.
Genetics.
Immunology.
Microbiology.
Molecular Biology.
Neurosciences.
Pathology.
Pharmacology.
Physiology.

School of Medicine—Shreveport

Established 1966. Located in Shreveport (71130–3932).
Annual tuition: resident $7850. Total average cost for all other expenses: $9500. On-campus housing available.
Enrollment: first-year class 100; total 387 (men 70%, women 30%). Faculty: full-time 25, part-time 9. Degrees conferred: M.D., M.D.-Ph.D.

ADMISSION REQUIREMENTS. AMCAS reports, transcripts, MCAT, recommendations, interview required in support of application. Accepts transfer applicants. Graduates of unaccredited colleges are considered. Accepts state residents only. Does not have EDP. Apply to Admission Committee after June 15, before November 15. Application fee $50. Phone: (318)675-5190; fax: (318)675-5244.

ADMISSION STANDARDS. Selective. Accepts about 20% of total annual applicants. 100% are state residents.

FINANCIAL AID. Scholarships, long-term loans. Apply to Office of Student Affairs after acceptance, before March 31. About 80% of students received are from school and outside sources.

DEGREE REQUIREMENTS. For M.D.: satisfactory completion of four-year program.

FIELDS OF GRADUATE STUDY.
Anatomy.
Biochemistry.
Cell Biology.
Immunology.
Microbiology.
Pharmacology.
Physiology.

School of Dentistry

Established 1968. Annual tuition: resident $5736, nonresident $10,486. No on-campus housing available. Average off-campus housing cost: $9000. Total average cost for all other expenses: $1651.
Enrollment: first-year class 57 (men 75%, women 25%). Degree conferred: D.D.S.

ADMISSION REQUIREMENTS. Transcripts, DAT, interview, recommendations, at least three years of college required in support of School's application. Preference given to residents of Louisiana and Arkansas. Graduates of unaccredited colleges not considered. Apply to Assistant Dean of Admissions after September 15, before February 28. Application fee $50. Phone: (504)949-3579.

ADMISSION STANDARDS. Selective. Accepts about 60% of total annual applicants. Approximately 88% are state residents.

FINANCIAL AID. Limited. Scholarships, loans. Apply to Medical Center's Office of Financial Aid after acceptance. Phone: (504)948-8556. About 80% of students receive aid from School and outside sources.

DEGREE REQUIREMENTS. For D.D.S.: satisfactory completion of four-year program.

School of Nursing—Graduate Program
http://www.lsumc.edu

Graduate study since 1972. Semester system. Annual tuition: resident $722, nonresident $1556. On-campus housing available. Enrollment: full-time 73, part-time 135. Faculty: full-time 11, part-time 5. Degrees conferred: M.N., D.N.S.

ADMISSION REQUIREMENTS. Transcripts, Louisiana license, GRE/MAT, two letters of recommendation required in support of School's application. TOEFL required for foreign applicants. Accepts transfer applicants. Graduates of unaccredited institutions not considered. Apply to Graduate Program by March 15. Application fee $50. Phone: (504)568-4141.

ADMISSION STANDARDS. Selective. Usual minimum average: 3.0 (A = 4).

FINANCIAL AID. Limited to three graduate assistantships, fifteen grants, Federal W/S, loans. Approved for VA benefits. Apply to the Graduate Program for assistantships, grants; to the Financial Aid Office for all other programs. Use FAFSA and institutional FAF. Phone: (504)568-4820; fax: (504)568-5545.

DEGREE REQUIREMENTS. For M.N.: 39 credit minimum, at least three semesters of full-time study; up to 12 credits may be transferred; thesis optional. For D.N.S.: 54 credits minimum, four semesters of full-time study; up to 15 credits may be transferred; candidacy; comprehensive exam; dissertation.

FIELDS OF STUDY.
Adult Health and Nursing.
Neonatal/Nurse Practitioner.
Nursing Service Administration.
Parent-Child Health Nursing.
Primary Care/Nurse Practitioner.
Psychiatric-Community Mental Health.
Public Health/Community Health Nursing.

LOUISIANA STATE UNIVERSITY IN SHREVEPORT
Shreveport, Louisiana 71115
http://www.prysm.com/n/suscba

Founded 1967. Coed. State control. Semester system. Special facilities: Life Science Museum, Pioneer Heritage Center, Social Science Research and Analysis Unit. Library: 225,100 volumes, 230,000 microforms.
Tuition: per credit, resident $95, nonresident $240. Limited on-campus housing. Contact Director, University Court Apartments for housing information. Phone: (318)797-8588.

Graduate Studies

Graduate study since 1978. Enrollment: full-time 84, part-time 518. Faculty teaching graduate students: full-time 80, part-time 4. Degrees conferred: M.A.L.S., M.B.A., M.Ed., M.S.T.

ADMISSION REQUIREMENTS. Transcripts, letters of recommendation, GRE/GMAT required in support of application. TOEFL required of international applicants. Interview not required. Accepts transfer applicants. Apply to the Office of Admissions; no specified closing date. Application fee $10, $20 for international applicants. Phone: (318)797-5061; fax: (318)797-5286.

ADMISSION STANDARDS. Selective. Usual minimum average: 2.5 (A = 4).

FINANCIAL AID. Limited to eighteen graduate assistantships, Federal W/S, loans. Approved for VA benefits. Apply to appropriate department chair for assistantships; to Office of Financial Aid for all other programs. No specified closing date. Use FAFSA and institutional FAF. Phone: (318)797-5363; fax: (318)797-5180. About 10% of students receive aid other than loans from University and outside sources. Aid sometimes available to part-time students.

DEGREE REQUIREMENTS. For master's: 30–48 semester hours minimum, at least 24–36 in residence; thesis/nonthesis option; final written/oral exam for some programs.

FIELDS OF STUDY.
Business Administration.
Education. Includes elementary, secondary, administration.
Liberal Studies
School Psychology.
Systems Management.

LOUISIANA TECH UNIVERSITY
Ruston, Louisiana 71272

Founded 1894. Located 72 miles E of Shreveport. Coed. State control. Quarter system. Special facilities: Biomedical Engineering Center, Water Resource Center, Center for Robotics and Automated Manufacturing, Rehabilitation Engineering Research and Development Training Center, Small Business Institute. Library: more than 981,000 volumes, 2,265,000 microforms, 39 PCs.

Annual tuition: resident $2358, nonresident $4353. On-campus housing for 42 married students, 2052 men, 1860 women. Average academic year housing cost: per month, $215 plus electricity for married students, for 3 quarters $2385 (including board) for single students. Apply to Director of Housing by July 15. Phone: (318)257-4917.

Graduate School

Authorized 1958. Enrollment: full-time 862, part-time 711. Faculty: full- and part-time 270. Degrees conferred: M.A., M.S., M.B.A., M.P.A., M.F.A., Specialist, D.B.A., Ph.D., D.Engr.

ADMISSION REQUIREMENTS. Transcripts, GRE/GMAT required in support of School's application. TOEFL required for foreign applicants. Interview not required. Accepts transfer applicants. Graduates of unaccredited institutions not considered. Apply to Admissions Office at least one month prior to registration. Application fee $20. Phone: (318)257-2924; fax: (318)257-4487.

ADMISSION STANDARDS. Selective. Usual minimum average: 2.5 (A = 4).

FINANCIAL AID. Scholarships, teaching fellowships, research fellowships, Federal W/S, loans. Approved for VA benefits. Apply at least five months prior to registration to department concerned for scholarships, fellowships; to Financial Aid Office for all other programs. Use FAFSA and institutional FAF. Phone: (318)257-2641. About 20% of students receive aid other than loans from University and outside sources. Aid sometimes available for part-time students.

DEGREE REQUIREMENTS. For master's: 30 semester hours minimum without thesis or creative project or including thesis or creative project, at least 24 in residence; final written/oral exam; reading knowledge of one foreign language for some majors. For D.B.A., Ph.D.: 60 credits minimum beyond the bachelor's, at least 24 in residence; qualifying exam; language requirement for some majors; dissertation; final oral exam.

FIELDS OF STUDY.
Accounting.
Applied Computational Analysis and Modeling.
Art. Includes applied arts, fine arts, interior design, philosophy, science, social sciences.
Bacteriology (Microbiology).
Biomedical Engineering.
Botany.
Business Administration.
Chemical Engineering. Thesis for M.S.
Chemistry. One language, thesis for M.S.
Civil Engineering. Thesis for M.S.
Computer Science.
Counseling and Guidance.
Dietetics.
Economics.
Education. Includes business, elementary, English.
Electrical Engineering.
Engineering.
Engineering Mechanics.
English. One language; thesis or 6 additional credits for M.A.
Finance.
French.
Health and Physical Education.
History.
Home Economics.
Industrial Engineering.
Life Sciences.
Management.
Manufacturing Systems Engineering.
Marketing.
Mathematics.
Mechanical Engineering.
Nutrition and Food.
Operations Research.
Physics.
Psychology.
Quantitative Analysis.
Reading.
Secondary Education.
Special Education.
Speech.
Speech Pathology and Audiology.
Statistics.
Zoology. Thesis for M.S.
Note: Doctoral degrees available only in applied computational analysis and modeling, business administration, education, engineering.

UNIVERSITY OF LOUISVILLE
Louisville, Kentucky 40292-0001

Founded 1798. Coed. State control. Semester system. Special facilities: sponsoring university of Oak Ridge Institute of Nuclear Studies in Tennessee, Applied Microcirculation Center, Cancer Center, Center for the Humanities, Institute for the Environment and Sustainable Development, Center for Leadership

Studies, Performance Research Laboratory, Water Resources Laboratory, Archaeology Survey, Computer Science Center, Center for Urban and Economic Research. Library: 1,232,000 volumes, 12,260 current periodicals.

Annual tuition: resident $2580, nonresident $7740; per credit hour, resident $149.50, nonresident $425. On-campus housing for 110 married students, 46 graduate women, 82 graduate men. Average academic year housing cost: $1740–$2230 (room only) for single students; $445–$540 per month for married students. Contact Director of Residential Life for both on- and off-campus housing information. Phone: (502)852-6636. Day care facilities available.

Graduate School

Graduate study since 1907. Enrollment: full-time 1341, part-time 1922. Graduate faculty: full-time 549, part-time 302. Degrees conferred: M.A., M.A.T., M.Ed., M.S., M.Eng., M.M., M.B.A., M.F.A., M.S.N., M.P.A., Ed.S., Ed.D., Ph.D.

ADMISSION REQUIREMENTS. Official transcripts, two letters of recommendation, GRE/MAT required in support of application. GRE Subject required for some departments. GMAT for business. TOEFL required of international applicants. Accepts transfer applicants. Graduates of unaccredited institutions not considered. Apply to Office of Research and Graduate Programs at least three months prior to date of entrance. Application fee none. Phone: (502)588-6525.

ADMISSION STANDARDS. Relatively open for most departments. Usual minimum average: 2.75 (A = 4).

FINANCIAL AID. Annual awards from institutional funds: scholarships, 173 assistantships, 64 research assistantships, 42 fellowships in doctoral programs, Federal W/S, loans. Approved for VA benefits. Apply to appropriate department for assistantships, fellowships; to Office of Financial Aid for all other programs. No specified closing date. Use FAFSA. Phone: (502)588-5511. About 50% of students receive aid other than loans from School and outside sources.

DEGREE REQUIREMENTS. For most master's: 30 semester hours minimum, at least 24 in residence; qualifying exam; thesis for 6 hours required in most departments; final written/oral exam. For M.M.: same as above, except final recital for applied music majors, composition for composition majors in lieu of thesis. For M.F.A. (Theater): 72 hours minimum. For M.S.S.W. (one year advanced-standing program): 42 semesters hours minimum in full-time residence; supervised fieldwork experience. For M.S.S.W. (two-year regular program): 60 semester hours minimum, at least 45 in residence; supervised fieldwork experience. For Ed.S.: 30 hours minimum beyond the master's. For Ph.D., Ed.D.: three years minimum beyond the bachelor's, at least two years in residence and one year in full-time attendance; reading knowledge of two foreign languages or one language and computer science required by some departments; preliminary exam; dissertation; final oral exam.

FIELDS OF STUDY.
Anatomical Sciences and Neurobiology. Ph.D. only.
Art History. Ph.D. only.
Biochemistry. Ph.D. only.
Biology. M.S. only.
Business and Economics. M.B.A. only.
Chemical Engineering. Ph.D. only.
Chemistry. Ph.D. only.
Clinical Psychology. Ph.D. only.
Education. Includes elementary, secondary, higher, special education, guidance and counseling, administration and supervision, psychology, special, reading. M.Ed., M.A., Ed.S., Ed.D.

Engineering. Includes chemical, civil, electrical, mechanical, computer science. M.S. only; chemical engineering, industrial engineering, computer science and engineering. Ph.D. only.
English. Includes M.A. in creative writing; Ph.D. in Rhetoric and Composition.
Environmental Biology. Ph.D. only.
Experimental Psychology. Ph.D. only.
Expressive Therapies. M.A.
Fine Arts. Includes creative, art history; one language for M.A. in art history; studio project and paper instead of thesis for M.A. in creative art; M.A., M.A.T.
Health Promotion.
History. M.A., M.A.T. only.
Humanities.
Interdisciplinary Studies.
Justice Administration.
Linguistics.
Mathematics.
Microbiology and Immunology. Ph.D. only.
Modern Languages. M.A.T. in French, German, Spanish; M.A. in French, German. M.A., M.A.T.
Music. Includes theory and composition, applied music, music education. M.A., M.M., M.A.T.; Ph.D. in musicology offered in cooperation with U. Kentucky.
Nursing. M.S.N.
Occupational Training and Development.
Oral Biology. D.D.S. or equivalent for admission. M.S. only.
Pharmacology. Ph.D. only.
Philosophy.
Physics.
Physiology and Biophysics. Ph.D. only.
Political Science.
Psychology. Ph.D. only.
Public Administration. M.P.A. only.
Social Work. M.S.S.W.
Sociology. M.A.T.
Sports Studies.
Theater Arts. M.A., M.F.A.
Urban Education. Ed.D. only.
Urban and Public Affairs. Ph.D. only.
Visual Sciences. Ph.D. only.

School of Law (40292)

Established 1846. Semester system. Law library: 244,678 volumes. Library has LEXIS, WESTLAW, OCLC. Limited on-campus housing available, moderate cost housing near campus.

Annual tuition: full-time; resident $4440, nonresident $12,040; evening, resident $3700, nonresident $9000. Total average annual additional expense: $10,210.

Enrollment: first-year class 135 (day), 40 (evening); total approximately 500. Faculty: full-time 37, part-time 22. Degrees conferred: J.D., J.D.-M.B.A., J.D.-M.Div. (with Louisville Presbyterian Theological Seminary).

ADMISSION REQUIREMENTS. LSDAS Law School report, bachelor's degree, transcripts, LSAT (not later than December) required in support of application. Interview not required. Accepts transfer applicants. Graduates of unaccredited colleges not considered. Preference given to state residents. Apply to Law School Admissions Office after October 1, before February 1. Fall admission only. Application fee $30. Phone: (502)852-6364.

ADMISSION STANDARDS. Selective. Accepts 30–35% of total annual applicants.

FINANCIAL AID. Scholarships, assistantships, loans. For scholarships, apply to Associate Dean by April 1. Use FAFSA. Students seeking financial aid should contact University's Student Financial Aid Office.

DEGREE REQUIREMENTS. For J.D.: 90 semester hours minimum, at least the last 28 in residence.

Note: School has an exchange program with law schools in England, France, Germany, Japan, Australia.

School of Medicine (40292)

Founded 1833.

Annual tuition: resident $8300, nonresident $19,420. Medical-dental housing for married and single students. Total average figure for all other expenses: $9608.

Enrollment: first-year class 136 (EDP 15); total 500 (men 53%, women 47%). Faculty: full-time 458; part-time 55. Degree conferred: M.D. The M.S. and Ph.D. are offered through the Graduate School.

ADMISSION REQUIREMENTS. AMCAS report, transcripts, recommendations, MCAT required in support of application. Interview by invitation only. Applicants must have completed at least three years of college study. Preference given to four-year college graduates and state residents. Accepts transfer applicants. Has EDP; apply between June 15 and August 1. Apply to Director of Admissions after June 15, before November 1. Application fee $15. Phone: (502)582-5193.

ADMISSION STANDARDS. Competitive. Accepts about 15% of total annual applicants. Approximately 90% are state residents.

FINANCIAL AID. Scholarships, summer research scholarships. 90% of students receive some financial aid. Apply to Office of Student Affairs by June 1.

DEGREE REQUIREMENTS. For M.D.: satisfactory completion of four-year program. For M.S., Ph.D.: see Graduate School listing above.

FIELDS OF GRADUATE STUDY.
Anatomy.
Biochemistry.
Immunology.
Microbiology.
Neurosciences.
Pharmacology.
Physiology.

School of Dentistry (49292–0001)

Organized 1886. State supported. Semester system. Annual tuition: resident $6400, nonresident $16,680. Medical-dental housing for married and single students. Average academic year housing cost: $9000. Total average cost for all other first-year expenses: $2900.

Enrollment: first-year class 72, total 200 (men 60%, women 40%). School faculty: full-time 71, part-time 65. Degree conferred: D.M.D. The M.S. (Oral Biology) is offered through the Graduate School.

ADMISSION REQUIREMENTS. AADSAS report, official transcripts, recommendations, DAT (October date preferred) required in support of School's application. Interview often required. Applicants must have completed at least three, preferably four, years of college study. Ninety percent of class must be residents. Accepts transfer applicants. Apply to Committee on Admissions between June 1 and April 1. Application fee, none for residents, nonresident $10. Phone: (502)588-5293, (800)334-8635, ext. 5081.

ADMISSION STANDARDS. Competitive. Usual minimum average: 2.75 (A = 4). Accepts about 20% of total annual applicants. 90% are state residents.

FINANCIAL AID. Scholarships, tuition waivers, loans. Apply to Student Affairs Office after acceptance. Phone: (502)588-5081. About 95% of students receive some aid from School.

DEGREE REQUIREMENTS. For D.M.D.: satisfactory completion of forty-five-month program. For M.S., see Graduate School listing above.

LOYOLA COLLEGE
Baltimore, Maryland 21210-2699

Founded 1852. Coed. Private control. Roman Catholic. Semester system. Library: 307,000 volumes, 397,000 microforms, 2000 current periodicals.

Tuition: per credit $197. No on-campus housing for graduate students. Contact Dean of Students for off-campus housing information.

Graduate Division

Graduate study since 1949. Enrollment: full-time 643, part-time 2243. Graduate faculty: full-time 97, part-time 160. Degrees conferred: M.A., M.Ed., M.S., M.M.S., M.B.A., M.I.B., M.S.F., M.M.S., M.E.S., C.A.S.

ADMISSION REQUIREMENTS. Official transcripts in support of application. GMAT required for M.B.A., M.S.E, and M.P.A. Two letters of recommendation required for M.E.S., three letters for M.A. or M.S. in psychology. Accepts transfer applicants. Graduates of unaccredited institutions not considered. Apply to Graduate Admissions Office by May 15 (Summer), August 15 (Fall), January 15 (Spring). Application fee $35. Phone: (410)617-5020.

ADMISSION STANDARDS. Selective. Usual minimum average: 3.0 (A = 4).

FINANCIAL AID. Sixty graduate assistantships, loans. Approved for VA benefits. Apply to appropriate department for assistantships; to Financial Aid Office for all other programs. Use FAFSA. Less than 1% of students receive aid other than loans from College and outside sources.

DEGREE REQUIREMENTS. For master's: 30–36 semester hours minimum, at least 24 in residence; thesis for M.A., no language requirement. For C.A.S.: 30 hours beyond the master's; no language; thesis or final exam.

FIELDS OF STUDY.
Business Administration. Includes accounting, economics, decision sciences, finance, management, marketing, quantitative analysis.
Education. Includes classroom teaching, curriculum and instruction, educational management and supervision, foundations of education, guidance and counseling, reading, special education.
Employment Assistance and Substance Abuse.
Engineering Science. Includes digital systems, computer science.
Finance. M.B.A., M.S.F.
International Business. M.I.B.
Modern Studies.
Psychology. Includes clinical, counseling, drug and alcohol abuse counseling, general, pastoral counseling, substance abuse.
Speech Pathology and Audiology.

LOYOLA MARYMOUNT UNIVERSITY
Los Angeles, California 90045-8350

Founded 1911. Coed. Private control. Roman Catholic. Library: 351,000 volumes, 101,000 microforms, 2900 current periodicals, 30 PCs.

Tuition: per unit $450–$560, depending on program. No on-campus housing available for graduate students. Average academic year off-campus housing cost: $600 per month. Contact Student Housing Office for housing information. Phone: (310)338-2963.

Graduate Programs

Graduate Study since 1948. Enrollment: full-time 688, part-time 317. Graduate faculty: full-time 154, part-time 243. Degrees conferred: M.A., M.A.T., M.B.A., M.Ed., M.S., M.S.E.

ADMISSION REQUIREMENTS. Two official transcripts, letters of recommendation, GRE, GMAT (for M.B.A. applicants) required in support of applications. Two letters of recommendation required for Counseling Psychology. TOEFL required for international applicants. Accepts transfer applicants. Graduates of unaccredited institutions not considered. Apply to Graduate Admissions Office. Application fee $35. Phone: (310)338-2721; fax: (310)338-6086.

ADMISSION STANDARDS. Competitive. Usual minimum average: 3.0 (A = 4).

FINANCIAL AID. Scholarships, grants, assistantships, loans. Apply by March 1 to appropriate department chair for assistantships; to Office of Financial Aid for all other programs. Use FAFSA. Phone: (310)338-2753. About 10% of students receive some aid other than loans from University and outside sources. Aid available to part-time students.

DEGREE REQUIREMENTS. For most master's: 10 courses minimum, at least 8 in residence; thesis/nonthesis option or final written/oral exam. For M.B.A.: 10–18 courses depending on previous degree; project. For M.F.A.: 18 courses, at least 15 in residence; final project.

FIELDS OF STUDY.
Art Therapy.
Biology. M.A.T.
Business Administration. M.B.A.
Communication Arts. M.A.T.
Communications. Includes film production, TV production, screenwriting. M.A., M.A.T.
Computer Science. M.S.
Counseling Psychology. Includes marital, family and child counseling, general, chemical dependency counseling. M.A.
Education. Includes counseling, educational psychology, school psychology, special education, M.A.; reading, school administration, student-devised master's, M.Ed.; elementary, secondary, administrative services, reading, and special education credentials; California state credential recommendation programs.
Engineering. Includes civil, environmental, electrical, mechanical.
Engineering and Production Management. M.S.
English. M.A., M.A.T.
Environmental Science. M.S.
History. M.A.T.
Latin. M.A.T.
Learning and Teaching. M.A.T.
Mathematics. M.A.T.
Social Studies. M.A.T.

School of Law (90015–3980)

Established 1920. Semester system. Law library: 360,600 volumes. Library has LEXIS, NEXIS, WESTLAW, DIALOG, C.CALI. Special facilities: Western Center for Disability Rights.

Annual tuition: $19,406 (day), $12,978 (evening). No on-campus housing available.

Enrollment: first-year class 375 (day), 100 (evening); total full-time 1378 (men 55%, women 45%). Faculty: full-time 56, part-time 49. Degree conferred: J.D.

ADMISSION REQUIREMENTS. LSDAS Law School report, bachelor's degree, transcripts, LSAT (no later than December), letters of recommendation required in support of application. Interview not required. Accepts transfer applicants. Graduates of unaccredited colleges not considered. Apply to Office of Admissions by February 1 (Fall, day), April 17 (Fall, evening). Evaluation fee $50. Phone: (213)736-1180.

ADMISSION STANDARDS. Selective. Accepts about 20–25% of total annual applicants.

FINANCIAL AID. Scholarships, full and partial tuition waivers, assistantships, Federal W/S, loans. Apply to Financial Aid Office after acceptance. Preference given to applications received by March 2. Use FAFSA. Fellowships available only to advanced students. About 80% of students receive some aid from School. Aid sometimes available for part-time students.

DEGREE REQUIREMENTS. For J.D.: 87 semester units minimum; completion of three-year program (day), four-year program (evening).
Note: Summer program in Central America.

LOYOLA UNIVERSITY
New Orleans, Louisiana 70118-6195

Established 1912. Coed. Private control. Roman Catholic. Semester system. Library: 437,000 volumes, 930,000 microforms.

Tuition: per credit $475. On-campus housing for 24 graduate men, 24 graduate women; none for married students. Average academic year housing cost: $4365 (including board). Apply to Director of Residential Life. Phone: (504)865-3736. Day care facilities available.

Graduate School

Graduate study since 1912. Enrollment: full-time 90, part-time 1200. Faculty: full-time 64, part-time 20. Degrees conferred: M.A., M.B.A., M.C.M., M.M., M.M.T., M.S., M.S.T., M.R.E., M.P.S., J.D.-M.A., J.D.-M.B.A., J.D.-M.C.M.

ADMISSION REQUIREMENTS. Application, transcripts, statement of intent, resume, letters of recommendation, GMAT (Business), GRE (Mass Communications), MAT (Education) required in support of School's application. TOEFL required for international applicants. An interview is required for education programs, recommended for other programs. Accepts transfer applicants. Application deadlines: Mass Communications, July 1 (Fall), November 1 (Spring); Education, August 1 (Fall), December 1 (Spring), May 1 (Summer); other programs August 1 (Fall), December 1 (Spring), and May 1 (Summer). Application fee $20. Phone: (504)865-3240 or (800)4-LOYOLA; fax: (504)865-3383.

ADMISSION STANDARDS. Selective for most departments. Usual minimum average: 3.0 (A = 4).

FINANCIAL AID. Limited to two music scholarships, Federal W/S, loans. Use the Federal Student Aid Form (FAFSA). Phone: (504)865-3231. Aid sometimes available for part-time students.

DEGREE REQUIREMENTS. For master's: 30–36 semester hours minimum, at least 24 in residence; thesis; final written/oral exam for some departments.

FIELDS OF STUDY.
Business Administration.
Elementary Education.
Mass Communications.
Mathematics. M.S.T.
Music (Performance).
Music Education.
Music Therapy.
Pastoral Studies.
Quality Management.
Reading.
Religious Education.
Religious Studies.
Secondary Education.

School of Law

Established 1914. Semester system. Law library: 235,000 volumes. Library has LEXIS, NEXIS, WESTLAW, DIALOG. Special facilities: Public Law Center.

Annual tuition: full-time $16,585 (day), $11,235 (evening). Limited on-campus housing. Total average annual additional expense: $10,200.

Enrollment: first-year class, full-time 170, evening 60; total full and part-time 750 (men 52%, women 48%). Faculty: full-time 36, part-time 41. Degrees conferred J.D., J.D.-M.A. (Communications, Religious Studies), J.D.-M.B.A.

ADMISSION REQUIREMENTS. LSDAS Law School report, bachelor's degree, transcripts, LSAT required in support of application. Interview not required. Graduates of unaccredited colleges not considered. Accepts transfer applicants. Apply to Director of Admissions after September 1, before April 1 for priority consideration. Rolling admission process. For part-time study, apply by June 1. Admits beginning students Fall only. Application fee $20. Phone: (504)861-5575.

ADMISSION STANDARDS. Competitive. Accepts about 25–30% of total annual applicants.

FINANCIAL AID. Scholarships, assistantships, full and partial tuition waivers, Federal W/S, loans. Apply to Office of Financial Aid by May 1. Use FAFSA. Aid available for part-time study.

DEGREE REQUIREMENTS. For J.D.: 90 credit hours minimum, at least one year in residence. For M.B.A. and M.A.: see Graduate School listing above.
Note: Summer study programs in Mexico, Japan, and Eastern Europe available.

LOYOLA UNIVERSITY OF CHICAGO
Chicago, Illinois 60626-2196
http://www.lsu.edu

Established 1870. Coed. Private control. Roman Catholic. Semester system. Library: 1.2 million volumes, 650,000 microforms, 245 PCs. Limited on-campus housing available. Contact Dean, Residence Life for off-campus information. Phone: (312)508-3300.

Graduate School

Graduate study since 1918. Tuition: per credit $408. Enrollment: full- and part-time 5537. Faculty teaching graduate students: full-time 519. Degrees conferred: M.A., M.S., M.B.A., M.Div., M.Ed., M.J., M.P.S., M.R.E., M.S.I.R., M.S.O.D., M.S.N., Ed.D., Ph.D.

ADMISSION REQUIREMENTS. Transcripts required in support of School's application. GRE/Subject tests/GMAT for some departments. Interview required in some departments. TOEFL required for international applicants. Accepts transfer applicants. Graduates of unaccredited institutions not considered. Apply to Dean of Graduate School at least eight weeks prior to registration. Application fee $35. Phone: (312)508-3396; fax: (312)508-2460.

ADMISSION STANDARDS. Competitive. Usual minimum average: 3.0 (A = 4).

FINANCIAL AID. Annual awards from institutional funds: 233 assistantships, Federal W/S, loans. Approved for VA benefits. Apply by February 1 to Dean of School. Use FAFSA and institutional FAF. About 35% of students receive aid other than loans from School and outside sources. No aid for part-time students.

DEGREE REQUIREMENTS. For master's: generally 30 semester hours minimum; research tool requirement for some departments; final oral/written exam. For Ed.D., Ph.D.: 60 semester hours minimum beyond the bachelor's, at least two semesters in residence; research tool requirement in most departments; preliminary exam; dissertation; final oral exam.

FIELDS OF STUDY.
Cell Biology, Neurobiology, and Anatomy.
Biology.
Business Administration.
Chemistry.
Classical Studies.
Computer Science.
Counseling Psychology.
Criminal Justice.
Education.
English.
History.
Human Resources and Industrial Relations.
Mathematical Sciences.
Microbiology and Immunology.
Molecular Biology.
Molecular and Cellular Biochemistry.
Neuroscience.
Nursing.
Organizational Development.
Pastoral Studies.
Pharmacology.
Philosophy.
Physiology.
Political Science.
Psychology. Apply by January 1 for Fall admission to clinical psychology and counseling psychology.
Sociology.
Spanish.
Theology.

Institute of Human Resources and Industrial Relations

Graduate study since 1941. Quarter system. Tuition: $1455 per course. On-campus housing available. Contact Dean, Residence Life. Phone: (312)508-3300.

Enrollment: full-time 35, part-time 290. Faculty teaching graduate students: full-time 7, part-time 7. Degree conferred: M.S.I.R.

ADMISSION REQUIREMENTS. Transcripts, GRE or GMAT, personal statement, three letters of reference required in support of Institute's application. TOEFL required for international applicants. Transfer applicants considered. Institute operates on a quarter calendar consisting of ten weeks. Students may enter in any quarter: Fall, Winter, Spring, or Summer. No specified closing date. Application fee $35. Phone: (800)424-3983 or (312)915-6595; fax: (312)915-6231; E-mail: f-daly@luc.edu

ADMISSION STANDARDS. Selective. Usual minimum average: 3.0 (A = 4).

FINANCIAL AID. Annual awards from institutional funds: six research assistantships, Federal W/S, loans. Use FAFSA. Apply to University's Financial Aid Office; no specified closing date. Phone: (312)915-6639. About 80% of students receive aid other than loans from Institute and outside sources.

DEGREE REQUIREMENTS. For M.S.I.R.: Fourteen graduate courses; optional thesis; at least one academic year in residence (part-time students must fulfill the equivalent of one year's residence by part-time attendance, which may not be protracted for more than five years).

FIELDS OF STUDY.
Compensation and Benefits.
Global Human Resources.
Human Resource Management.
Industrial Relations.
Organization Development.

School of Social Work

Semester system. Annual tuition: full-time $10,250. Limited on-campus housing for single students only. Apply to Dean, Residence Life (60626). Phone: (312)508-3300.
Enrollment: full-time 275, part-time 285. Graduate faculty: full-time 25, part-time 30. Degrees conferred: M.S.W., D.S.W.

ADMISSION REQUIREMENTS. Transcripts, letters of recommendation, personal statement required in support of School's application. TOEFL required for international applicants. Accepts transfer applicants. Graduates of unaccredited institutions not considered. Apply to School by July 15. Application fee $30. Phone: (312)915-7038; fax: (312)915-7645.

ADMISSION STANDARDS. Selective. Usual minimum average: 3.0 (A = 4) plus knowledge of the values of the field and experience in working with people.

FINANCIAL AID. Annual awards from institutional funds: ten scholarships, fourteen research fellowships, forty internships, loans. Apply by July 15 to School. Use FAFSA and institutional FAF. About 37% of students receive aid other than loans from School and outside sources. Aid available to part-time students.

DEGREE REQUIREMENTS. For M.S.W.: 55 semester hours minimum; internships. For D.S.W.: 60 semester hours minimum; comprehensive exam; dissertation; final oral exam.
Note: Program emphasis is on the Clinical Practice of Social Work.

School of Law

Established 1908. Semester system. Library: 345,000 volumes. Library has LEXIS, NEXIS, WESTLAW. Special facilities: Civitas Child Law Center, Institute for Health Law, Institute of Human Resources and Industrial Relations.

Annual tuition: $17,472 (day), $14,530 (evening). Total average annual additional expense: $9400.
Enrollment: first-year class, 200 day, 77 evening; total full-time, 545 day, 162 evening; total 710 (men 51%, women 49%). Faculty: full-time 34, part-time 120. Degrees conferred: J.D., J.D.-M.A., J.D.-M.B.A., J.D.-M.I.R., J.D.-M.H. (Health Law), J.D.-M.S.W., LL.M.

ADMISSION REQUIREMENTS. LSDAS Law School report, bachelor's degree, transcripts, LSAT required in support of application. Interview sometimes required. Accepts transfer applicants. Apply to Director of Admission after September 1, before April 1. Fall admission only for beginning students. Application fee $45. Phone: (312)915-7170, (800)545-5744.

ADMISSION STANDARDS. Selective. Accepts 20–25% of total annual applicants.

FINANCIAL AID. Scholarships, partial tuition waivers, Federal W/S, loans. Apply to Financial Aid Office April 1. Use FAFSA or GAPSFAS. About 10% of students receive aid other than loans from School.

DEGREE REQUIREMENTS. For J.D.: satisfactory completion of eighty-six-semester-hour program. For LL.M.: at least 24 credits minimum beyond the J.D. For master's degrees: see Graduate school listing above.
Note: Summer programs available in Rome, London, and at McGill University (Canada).

Stritch School of Medicine (60153)

Established 1920. Located in Maywood, Illinois. Annual tuition: $27,150. Limited on-campus housing available. Apply to Director of Student Personnel Services for off-campus housing. Total average figure for all other expenses: $9000.
Enrollment: first-year class 130 (EDP 10); full-time 516 (men 60%, women 40%); postgraduate 93. Faculty: full-time 545, part-time 45. Degrees conferred: M.D., M.D.-M.S., M.D.-Ph.D.

ADMISSION REQUIREMENTS. AMCAS report, transcripts, MCAT required in support of application. Interview by invitation only. Applicants must have completed at least 3 years of college study. Has EDP; apply between June 15 and August 1. Preference given to residents of Illinois and the Midwest. Apply to Committee on Admissions of School after June 15, before November 15. Application fee $35. Phone: (708)216-3229.

ADMISSION STANDARDS. Very competitive. Accepts 5% of total annual applicants. Approximately 50% are state residents.

FINANCIAL AID. Limited to scholarships, loans. Apply to Director of Financial Aid as soon as possible after acceptance. About 90% of students receive aid from School and outside sources.

DEGREE REQUIREMENTS. For M.D.: satisfactory completion of three-year program. For M.S., Ph.D.: see Graduate listing above.

FIELDS OF GRADUATE STUDY.
Anatomy.
Biochemistry.
Cell Biology.
Immunology.
Microbiology.
Molecular Biology.
Neurosciences.
Pharmacology.
Physiology.

LYNCHBURG COLLEGE*
Lynchburg, Virginia 24501-3199

Founded 1903. Located 120 miles W of Richmond. Coed. Private control. Semester system. Special facilities: Center for Advanced Engineering, Belle Boone Beard Gerontology Center, Earl Childhood Special Education Technical Assistance Center, Center for Economics Education. Library: 218,000 volumes.

Tuition: per credit $150–$175, depending on program. On-campus housing for single students only. Average academic year housing cost: $4245. Contact Office of Residential Living for both on- and off-campus housing. Phone: (804)522-8320.

Graduate Studies

Graduate study since 1964. Enrollment: full-time 88, part-time 413. Faculty teaching graduate students: full-time 48, part-time 20. Degrees conferred: M.Ad., M.B.A., M.Ed.

ADMISSION REQUIREMENTS. Official transcripts, three letters of recommendation, GMAT (Business) required in support of application. TOEFL required for international applicants. Interview not required. Accepts transfer students. Graduates of unaccredited institutions not considered. Apply to Director of specific graduate program at least thirty days prior to desired date of entrance. Application fee $25. Phone: (804)522-8238 (Education), (804)522-8256 (Business).

ADMISSION STANDARDS. Selective. Usual minimum average: 3.0 (A = 4).

FINANCIAL AID. Limited to Federal W/S, loans. Apply to the Office of Financial Aid; no specified closing date. Use FAFSA. Phone: (804)522-8228.

DEGREE REQUIREMENTS. For M.Ed.: 36 semester hours minimum, at least 30 in residence; optional final project. For M.B.A.: 48 semester hours. For M.Ad.: 30 semester hours.

FIELDS OF STUDY.
Administration. Includes industrial management, personnel management. M.Ad.
Agency Counseling.
Business Administration. M.B.A.
Curriculum and Instruction. Includes early childhood, middle school, reading specialist, secondary.
English Education.
Gerontology.
Physical Education.
School Administration.
School Counseling.
Special Education. Includes early childhood, mental retardation, learning and behavior problems, severe/profound handicaps.
Supervision.
Teaching Children with Learning Disabilities.
Teaching the Emotionally Disturbed.

UNIVERSITY OF MAINE
Orono, Maine 04469-5703

Founded 1865. Located 8 miles N of Bangor. Coed. State control. Semester system. School of Law in Portland (04102). Special facilities: Center for Marine Studies, Canadian American Center, Migratory Fish Research Institute, Institute for Quaternary Studies, College of Forest Resources, computer facilities, Darling Center for Research, Teaching, and Service (marine laboratory at Walpole). Library: 880,000 volumes, 6700 periodicals.

Tuition: per credit, resident $179, nonresident $509. Housing for 40 married students, 100 single students. Average housing cost: per semester $2370 (including board), single students, $2000 married students (room only). Apply to Housing Office, Hilltop Complex. Phone: (207)581-4580.

Graduate School

Graduate study since 1881. Enrollment: total full- and part-time 2150. Graduate faculty: full- and part-time 600. Degrees conferred: M.A., M.S., M.Ed., M.A.T., M.B.A., M.Eng., M.M., M.P.A., M.P.S., M.S.W., C.A.S., Ph.D., Ed.D.

ADMISSION REQUIREMENTS. Transcripts, three letters of reference, GRE required in support of School's application. GRE Subject Test, interview required for some programs. GMAT required for M.B.A. TOEFL required for international applicants. Accepts transfer applicants. Application and all credentials required six weeks prior to registration. Apply to the Graduate School; no specified closing date. Application fee $35. Phone: (207)581-3218.

ADMISSION STANDARDS. Selective for some departments, competitive or relatively open for others. Usual minimum average: 2.75 (A = 4).

FINANCIAL AID. Annual awards from institutional funds: 50 scholarships, 275 teaching assistantships, 250 research assistantships, Federal W/S, loans. Apply by December 15 to department chair for scholarships, assistantships, and fellowships; to Financial Aid Office for all other programs. Use FAFSA. Phone: (207)581-1324; fax: (207)581-3085. About 45% of students receive aid other than loans from School and outside sources. No aid for part-time students.

DEGREE REQUIREMENTS. For M.A., M.S.: 30 semester hours minimum; thesis; final oral exam; nonthesis option in some programs. For M.Ed.: 33 hours minimum. For M.B.A.: 30 hours minimum; additional course work required for those with little or no undergraduate work in business. For M.A.T.: 33 hours minimum. For M.Eng., M.P.S., M.M.: essentially same as M.A., except thesis not required. For M.P.A.: 36 hours minimum. For M.S.W.: 60 hours total; advanced standing for B.S.W. For C.A.S.: 30 hours minimum. For Ed.D., Ph.D.: two consecutive academic years beyond the bachelor's or one year beyond the master's; comprehensive exam; dissertation; final exam. Foreign language requirements in some fields of study. Language requirements vary by department.

FIELDS OF STUDY.
Agricultural and Resource Economics. M.S., M.P.S. only.
Animal Veterinary and Aquatic Sciences. M.S., M.P.S.
Biochemistry. M.S., M.P.S.
Biochemistry and Molecular Biology. Ph.D.
Biological Sciences. Ph.D.
Bio-Resource Engineering. M.S.
Botany and Plant Pathology. M.S. only.
Business Administration. M.B.A. only.
Chemical Engineering. M.E., M.S., Ph.D.
Chemistry. M.S., Ph.D.
Civil Engineering. M.E., M.S., Ph.D.
Communication Disorders. M.A.
Community Development. M.S., M.P.S. only.
Computer Science. M.S. only.
Ecology and Environmental Science. Ph.D.
Economics. M.A. only.
Education. M.A., M.S., Ed.D.
Electrical Engineering. M.E., M.S. only.
English. M.A. only.
Entomology. M.S. only.
Food and Nutrition. Ph.D.
Food Science and Human Nutrition. M.S. only.

Forest Resources. Ph.D. only.
Forestry. M.S. only.
French. M.A., M.A.T.
Geological Sciences. M.A., Ph.D.
German. M.A.T.
History. M.A., Ph.D.
Human Development. M.S. only.
Individualized Program. Ph.D. only.
Liberal Studies. M.A. only.
Manufacturing Management. M.M.M. only.
Marine Bio-Resources. M.S., Ph.D.
Mathematics. M.A. only.
Mechanical Engineering. M.S., M.E.
Microbiology. M.S., Ph.D.
Music. M.M.
Nursing. M.S.
Oceanography. M.S., Ph.D.
Physics. M.S., Ph.D.
Plant Science. Ph.D.
Plant, Soil, and Environmental Sciences. M.S.
Psychology. M.A., Ph.D.
Public Administration. M.P.A.
Quaternary Studies. M.S.
Resource Utilization. M.S.
Social Work. M.S.W.
Spanish. M.A.T. only.
Spatial Information Sciences and Engineering. M.S., Ph.D.
Speech Communication. M.A. only.
Surveying Engineering. M.S. only.
Theater. M.A.
Wildlife. Ph.D.
Wildlife Management. M.S., M.W.M.
Zoology. M.S., Ph.D.

School of Law

Reestablished 1961. Located on the University of Southern Maine Campus in Portland (04102). Semester system. Library: 280,000 volumes. Library has LEXIS, NEXIS, WESTLAW. Special facilities: Marine Law Institute.

Tuition: per credit, resident $276, nonresident $548. Total average annual additional expense: $7500.

Enrollment: first-year class 93; full-time 260 (men 53%, women 47%); no part-time or evening study. Faculty: full-time 16, part-time 7. Degrees conferred: J.D., J.D.-M.A. (Public Policy and Management).

ADMISSION REQUIREMENTS. LSDAS Law School report, bachelor's degree, transcripts, LSAT, letter of recommendation required in support of application. Accepts transfer applicants. Graduates of unaccredited colleges not considered. Apply to Registrar of School after September 1, before February 15. Transfer applications due June 1. Fall admission only. Application fee: $25. Phone: (207)780-4341.

ADMISSION STANDARDS. Selective. Accepts 30–35% of total annual applicants.

FINANCIAL AID. Full and partial tuition waivers, Federal W/S, loans. Apply to Financial Aid Office by March 1. Approximately 30% receive aid other than loans from School and outside sources. Use FAFSA. New England students may qualify for a special rate under the NEBHE Compact. NEBHE is in-state tuition plus 50%.

DEGREE REQUIREMENTS. For J.D.: satisfactory completion of eighty-nine credit-hour program. For M.A.: see Graduate School listing under the University of Southern Maine.

MANHATTAN COLLEGE
Bronx, New York 10471

Founded 1853. Private control. Library: 236,266 volumes, 1590 current periodicals.

Tuition: per semester hour $360 (Education), $430 (Business), $460 (Engineering). Limited on-campus housing available for single graduate students. Average academic year housing cost: $6800; $550 per month for off-campus housing. Apply to Director of Residence Life for both on- and off-campus housing information. Phone: (212)920-0932.

Graduate Division

Enrollment: full-time 92, part-time 506. Faculty: full-time 63, part-time 14. Degrees conferred: M.A., M.S.Ed., M.B.A., M.E., M.S.

ADMISSION REQUIREMENTS. Transcripts, GRE/GMAT required in support of application. TOEFL required for international applicants. Accepts transfer applicants. Graduates of unaccredited institutions not considered. Apply to Dean of Admissions before May 2 (Fall—Business, Engineering, Biotechnology), August 10 (Fall—all other programs), January 7 (Spring). Application fee $50. Phone: (212)920-0199.

ADMISSION STANDARDS. Competitive. Usual minimum average; 3.0 (A = 4).

FINANCIAL AID. Twenty scholarships and assistantships, five research fellowships, Federal W/S, loans. Apply by February 1 to appropriate departmental chair for scholarships, assistantships, fellowships; to Director of Financial Aid for all other programs; no specified closing date for these programs. Use FAFSA. Phone: (212)920-0939.

DEGREE REQUIREMENTS. For master's: 30–34 credits minimum, at least 24 in residence; thesis/nonthesis option/major research paper/project; internship for some programs. For M.B.A.; 39 credits minimum; master's project.

FIELDS OF STUDY.
Biotechnology. Interdisciplinary. M.S.
Business Administration. Includes accounting, finance, international business, management, management information systems. Part-time only. M.B.A.
Chemical Engineering. M.S.
Civil Engineering. M.S.
Computer Engineering. M.S.
Counseling. M.A.
Electrical Engineering. M.S.
Environmental Engineering. M.E.
Mechanical Engineering. M.S.
School Administrators and Supervisors. M.S.Ed.
Special Education. Includes adaptive physical education. M.A.

MANHATTAN SCHOOL OF MUSIC
120 Claremont Avenue
New York, New York 10027-4698

Founded 1917. Coed. Private control. Semester system. Special facilities: one thousand seat auditorium, three recital halls, two electronic music studios, one recording studio. Library: 80,000 volumes, 20,000 recordings.

Annual tuition: full-time $16,000. On-campus housing for single students only. Average academic year housing cost: $4500. Contact Director of Campus and Residential Life. Phone: (212)749-2802, ext. 462.

Graduate Division

Enrollment: full-time 391, part-time 75. Faculty: full-time 25, part-time 225. Degrees conferred: M.M., D.M.A.

ADMISSION REQUIREMENTS. Official transcripts, interview, school entrance exam and audition required in support of application. Accepts transfer applicants. Apply to Office of Admission at least one month prior to one of the four separately scheduled audition dates, but no later than April 1. Application fee $85. Phone: (212)749-2802, ext. 510; fax: (212)749-5471.

ADMISSION STANDARDS. Very competitive for some departments, competitive for others. Talent basis for admission.

FINANCIAL AID. One hundred seventy-five scholarships, tuition waivers, twelve fellowships, six teaching assistantships, Federal W/S, loans. Apply four weeks prior to the scheduled audition date. Use FAFSA. Phone: (212)749-2802. About 50% of students receive aid from School and outside sources.

DEGREE REQUIREMENTS. For M.M.: 60 semester credits minimum, at least 54 in residence; recital. For D.M.A.: 54 semester credits minimum, at least 54 in residence; dissertation; three recitals; orals; comprehension exam.

FIELDS OF STUDY.
Accompanying.
Commercial Music.
Composition.
Jazz.
Performance. Includes instrumental, orchestral, vocal.

MANHATTANVILLE COLLEGE

2900 Purchase Street
Purchase, New York 10577-2132

Founded 1841. Located 25 miles NE of midtown New York City and 5 miles from Greenwich, CT. Coed. Private control. Nondenominational. Semester system. Library: 273,000 volumes, 379,000 microforms, 30 PCs.

Tuition: per credit $390. On-campus housing for men, women. Average academic year housing cost: $4480 (including board), $620 for summer. For housing information, phone: (914)694-2200.

Graduate Program

Enrollment: full-time 50, part-time 720. Graduate faculty: full-time 12, part-time 20. Degrees conferred: M.A.T., M.P.S., M.A. in Liberal Studies and Writing, M.S. in Human Resources and Organizational Management.

ADMISSION REQUIREMENTS. Transcripts, two letters of recommendation required in support of application. TOEFL required for international applicants. Accepts transfer applicants. Graduates of unaccredited institutions not considered. For Education, contact School of Education (914)323-5214; for Liberal Studies and Writing, contact Special Programs (914)323-5300; no specified application closing date. Application fee $40.

ADMISSION STANDARDS. Competitive. Usual minimum average: 2.75 (A = 4).

FINANCIAL AID. Fellowships, tuition reduction program for recently unemployed, Federal W/S, loans. Apply by April 15 to Committee on Financial Aid. Use FAFSA. Phone: (914)323-

5357. About 20% of students receive aid from College and outside sources.

DEGREE REQUIREMENTS. For master's: 36 credit hours minimum; final written/oral exam/project.

FIELDS OF STUDY.
Elementary and Special Education.
Organizational Management and Human Resource Development.
Reading and Writing.
Secondary and Special Education.

MANKATO STATE UNIVERSITY

Mankato, Minnesota 56002-8400
http://www.mankato.msus.edu

Founded 1867. Located 80 miles SW of Minneapolis–St. Paul. Coed. State control. Quarter system. Special facilities: Biotechnology Research Center, Andreas and Standeford Astronomy Observatories, Performing Arts Center, Trafton Science Center, Water Resource Center, Urban Studies Institute, Conkling Art Gallery. Library: 985,000 volumes, 609,000 microforms, 3500 current periodicals, 90 PCs.

Tuition: per credit hour, resident $91, nonresident $137 (out-of-state students may be eligible for reciprocity or an out-of-state tuition scholarship). On-campus housing available for single students only. Average academic year housing cost: $3179 (including board). Contact the Office of Residential Life for both on- and off-campus housing information. Phone: (507)389-1011.

College of Graduate Studies

Graduate degrees authorized in 1953. Enrollment: full-time 972, part-time 1002. Graduate faculty: full- and part-time 571. Degrees conferred: M.A., M.B.A., M.S., M.A.T., M.F.A., M.M., Specialist.

ADMISSION REQUIREMENTS. Two official transcripts required in support of application. GRE/Subject/MAT/ GMAT required for some majors. TOEFL required for international applicants. Accepts transfer applicants. Graduates of unaccredited institutions not considered. Apply to Graduate Studies Office by August 15 for Fall, two weeks prior to registration for other quarters. Applicants for Graduate assistantships apply by February 3 for the Fall. Application fee $15. Phone: (800)772-0544 or (507)389-2321; fax: (507)389-5974; E-mail: grad@mankato.msus.edu.

ADMISSION STANDARDS. Selective for most departments, relatively open for others. Usual minimum average: 2.75 (A = 4).

FINANCIAL AID. Annual awards from institutional funds: five hundred assistantships, ten Affirmative Action assistantships, tuition waivers, twenty-five internships, Federal W/S, loans. Approved for VA benefits. Apply by February 1 to the Dean for assistantships; to Financial Aid Office for all other programs. Use FAFSA. Phone: (507)389-1185. About 50% of full-time students receive aid other than loans from College and outside sources. Aid sometimes available for part-time students.

DEGREE REQUIREMENTS. For M.A.: 45 quarter hours with thesis, or 51 quarter hours plus research paper; final written/oral exams. For M.S.: same as for M.A., no language requirement. For M.B.A.: 45 quarter hours; research paper. For M.A.T.: similar to M.A., but includes teaching internships. For Specialist: 45 hours beyond master's. For M.F.A.: 72 quarter hours; special project.

FIELDS OF STUDY.
Accounting.
Art. Includes education, studio; creative or investigative project for master's.
Biology.
Business Administration.
Business Education.
Chemistry. Thesis required.
Communication Disorders.
Computer Science.
Counseling and Student Personnel. Includes college student affairs, elementary school, secondary school, community.
Economics.
Education. Includes elementary, secondary, experiential, environmental, counseling, special, foundations, administration, reading, education technology, library media.
Educational Psychology.
English. Includes literature, technical communication, TESL.
Environmental Science.
French.
Geography.
German.
Gerontology.
Health Science. Includes chemical dependency, community health, school health.
History.
Home Economics.
International Business.
Manufacturing.
Mathematics.
Mathematics and Computer Science.
Music. Includes applied, composition, theory, history; recital, original composition, orchestration, or thesis for master's.
Nursing.
Physical Education.
Physics. Thesis required.
Political Science.
Psychology. Includes clinical, industrial.
Public Administration.
Rehabilitation Counseling.
Sociology. Includes corrections, human services planning and administration.
Spanish.
Speech Communication.
Technology Education.
Theater Arts.
Urban and Regional Studies.
Women's Studies.

MANSFIELD UNIVERSITY OF PENNSYLVANIA
Mansfield, Pennsylvania 16933
http://www.mnsfld.edu

Founded 1857. Located in north-central Pennsylvania. Coed. State control. Semester system. Library: 238,181 volumes, 1,100,000 microforms, 141 PCs.

Tuition: per credit, resident $187, nonresident $336. On-campus housing for single graduate students; none for married students. Annual academic year housing cost: $2409.50 including board. Apply to Director of Residence Life for off-campus housing information. Phone: (717)662-4933.

Graduate Division

Graduate study since 1966. Enrollment: full-time 62, part-time 223. Faculty: full-time 1, part-time 35. Degrees conferred. M.Ed., M.A., M.S., M.M.

ADMISSION REQUIREMENTS. Transcript required in support of Division's application. GRE/MAT for Psychology only. Audition required for music students. TOEFL required for international applicants. Accepts transfer applicants. Apply to Associate Provost at least 2 weeks prior to registration. Application fee $25. Phone: (717)662-4806; fax: (717)662-4995.

ADMISSION STANDARDS. Selective. Usual minimum average: 2.5 (A = 4).

FINANCIAL AID. Annual awards from institutional funds: twenty-four assistantships, Federal W/S, loans. Approved for VA benefits. Apply to Associate Provost prior to entrance. Use FAFSA. Phone: (717)662-4129; fax: (717)662-4112. About 70% of students receive aid other than loans from University and outside sources.

DEGREE REQUIREMENTS. For master's: 30–40 credit hour minimum; thesis/nonthesis option; final oral/written exam.

FIELDS OF STUDY.
Art Education. M.Ed.
Community Psychology. M.A.
Education. M.S.
Elementary Education. M.Ed.
Exceptional Persons. M.S.
Music. M.M.
Reading. Specialist Certificate only.
Special Education. M.Ed.

MARQUETTE UNIVERSITY
Milwaukee, Wisconsin 53233-1881
http://www.mu.edu

Founded 1881. Coed. Private control. Roman Catholic. Semester system. Special facilities: Biological and Biomedical Research Institute, Institute of the Catholic Media, Center for Citizenship Public Policy, Center for Ethical Resources, Institute for Family Studies, Parenting Center, Center for Psychological Services. Library: 900,000 volumes, 268,000 microforms, 70 PCs.

Tuition: per credit $427, $468 for M.B.A. program, $550 for M.S. programs in Dentistry. On-campus housing, 260 units for graduate students. Average monthly cost: $375 (apartments and single rooms). Apply to Office of Residence Life. Phone: (414)288-7208. For off-campus housing information: (414)288-7281.

Graduate School

Established 1922. Enrollment: full- and part-time 2237. Faculty: full-time 501, part-time 113, emeritus 43. Degrees conferred: M.A., M.S.A.E., M.A.T., M.B.A., M.Ed., M.S., M.S.N., M.S.E.M., M.S.H.R., M.S.A., Ed.D., Ph.D.

ADMISSION REQUIREMENTS. Transcripts required in support of School's application. GRE/Subject Test/MAT/ GMAT, three letters of recommendation required in many programs. Evidence of proficiency in English or TOEFL required of international students. Accepts transfer applicants. Apply to Graduate School at least six weeks prior to registration. Application fee $40. Phone: (414)288-7137; fax: (414)288-1902.

ADMISSION STANDARDS. Competitive for most departments, very competitive or selective for others. Usual minimum average: 3.0 (A = 4).

FINANCIAL AID. Annual awards available from institutional funds: research assistantships, teaching assistantships, fellowships and scholarships, loans. Approved for VA benefits. Apply by February 15 to Graduate School for fellowships, assistantships, scholarships; to Financial Aid Office for all other programs. Phone: (414)288-7390; fax: (414)288-1718.

DEGREE REQUIREMENTS. For M.A., M.S., M.A.T.: 30 semester hours minimum, at least 24 in residence; thesis; comprehensive oral/written exam; or 30 semester hours minimum; master's essay; comprehensive oral/written exam written exam in some departments. For M.B.A.: 33 semester hours minimum. For M.Ed.: 30 semester hours minimum; comprehensive oral/written exam. For Ph.D.: 60 semester hours minimum beyond the bachelor's; two semesters in full-time residence within an eighteen-month period carrying at least nine credits; qualifying exam; dissertation; final oral exam. For Ed.D.: 60 semester hours minimum beyond the bachelor's, at least one year in full-time residence; qualifying exam; dissertation; dissertation defense.

FIELDS OF STUDY.
Biology. Three letters of recommendation for admission.
Biomedical Engineering. GRE for admission.
Business Administration. M.B.A. only; GMAT for admission.
Chemistry.
Civil Engineering.
Communication. Includes advertising, broadcast and electronic communication, communication statistics, journalism, mass communication, theater arts. GRE for admission. M.A. only.
Dentistry. M.S. only.
Economics. M.S.A.E. only; GRE or GMAT for admission.
Education. Includes curriculum and instruction, educational psychology, educational foundations, administration and supervision, counseling, counseling psychology; GRE/MAT for admission.
Electrical and Computer Engineering.
Engineering Management. M.S.E.M. only; GRE or GMAT for admission.
English. GRE for admission.
History. GRE for admission.
Human Resources. M.S.H.R. only; GRE or GMAT for admission.
International Affairs. M.A. only; GRE for admission.
Materials Science and Engineering.
Mathematics, Statistics, and Computer Science.
Mechanical and Industrial Engineering. Includes materials science.
Medieval Studies. M.A. only; GRE for admission.
Nursing. M.S.N. only; GRE for admission.
Philosophy. GRE for admission.
Political Science. M.A. only; GRE for admission.
Psychology. GRE General/Subject, MAT for admission; 36 hours for M.S. (clinical).
Public Service. M.A.P.S. only; GRE for admission.
Spanish Language and Literature.
Speech Pathology and Audiology. M.S.; GRE for admission.
Theology. Ph.D. in religious studies; GRE for admission.

Law School

Established 1892. Semester system. Law library: 228,700 volumes. Library has LEXIS, NEXIS, WESTLAW, DIALOG, LEGALTRAC, CALI, WISCAT, OCLC.

Annual tuition: full-time $15,310. No on-campus housing available. Off-campus housing available; contact Office of Residential Life. Phone: (414)288-7208. Total average annual additional expense: $9000.

Enrollment: first-year class 160, total 495 (men 59%, women 41%). Faculty: full-time 21, part-time 30. Degrees conferred: J.D., J.D.-M.B.A., J.D.-M.A. (Political Science, International Affairs).

ADMISSION REQUIREMENTS. LSDAS Law School report, bachelor's degree, transcripts, LSAT required in support of application. Interview not required. Accepts transfer applicants. Graduates of unaccredited colleges not considered. Apply to Registrar after September 1, before March 15. Fall admission only. Application fee $40. Phone: (414)299-6767.

ADMISSION STANDARDS. Selective. Accepts 30–35% of total annual applicants.

FINANCIAL AID. Scholarships, Federal W/S, loans. Apply to the Office of Financial Aid by March 1. Phone: (414)288-7390. Use FAFSA. About 10% of students receive aid other than loans from School.

DEGREE REQUIREMENTS. For J.D.: satisfactory completion of ninety semester-hour program. For master's degree: see Graduate School listing above.

School of Dentistry

Established 1894. Semester system. Annual tuition: residents $15,325, nonresidents $26,995. No on-campus housing available. Average academic year housing cost: $9450. For off-campus housing, apply to Office of Student Affairs. Phone: (414)288-7208. Total average cost for all other first-year expenses: $5555.

Enrollment: first-year class 71; total full-time 260 (men 65%, women 35%). Faculty: full-time 92, part-time 28. Degrees conferred: D.D.S., M.S.

ADMISSION REQUIREMENTS. AADSAS report, transcripts, three letters of recommendation, DAT required in support of School's application. Interview by invitation only. Applicants must have completed at least three years of college study. Preference given to Wisconsin, North and South Dakota residents. Apply to Director of Admissions after June 1, before April 1. Application fee $25. Phone: (414)288-3532, (800)445-5385; fax: (414)288-3586.

ADMISSION STANDARDS. Selective. Accepts 10–15% of total annual applicants. Approximately 20% are state residents.

FINANCIAL AID. Scholarships, awards, loans. Apply by April 1 to University Office of Financial Aid. Use FAFSA. Phone: (414)288-7390.

DEGREE REQUIREMENTS. For D.D.S.: satisfactory completion of forty-five-month program. For M.S.: satisfactory completion of one-year program.

FIELDS OF GRADUATE STUDY.
Dental Biomaterials.
Endodontics.
Oral Surgery.
Orthodontics.
Pediatric Dentistry.
Pedodontics.
Periodontics.
Prosthodontics.

MARSHALL UNIVERSITY
Huntington, West Virginia 25755-2020
http://www.marshal.edu

Founded 1837. Coed. State control. Semester system. Special facilities: WMUL-FM, WPBY-TV, Robert C. Byrd Institute for Advanced Flexible Manufacturing Systems, Research and Economic Development Center. Library: 422,025 volumes, 189,065 microforms, 32 PCs, and CD ROMs. Library is repository for

General Chuck Yeager memorabilia and Blake Collection of antebellum American literary materials.

Annual tuition and fees; full-time, resident $2226, nonresident $6200; per credit resident $104.25, local metro counties resident $213.50, nonresident $325. On-campus housing for 84 married students, 1050 graduate men, 1050 graduate women. Average academic year housing cost: approximately $3800–$5400 for married students, $3870 for single students (including board). Apply to Director of Student Housing. Phone: (304)696-3171; (304)696-2564 (off-campus housing information).

Graduate School

Graduate study since 1938. Graduate School established 1948. Enrollment: full-time 650, part-time 1350. Graduate faculty: full-time 200, part-time 20. Degrees conferred: M.A., M.B.A., M.S., M.A.J., M.A.T., M.S.N., Ph.D.

ADMISSION REQUIREMENTS. Transcript, GRE, GMAT (for M.B.A.) required in support of School's application. TOEFL required of international students. Interview required by some departments. Accepts transfer applicants. Graduates of unaccredited institutions not considered. Apply to Admissions Office at least one month prior to registration. Application fee residents $10, nonresidents $25. Phone: (800)642-3499 or (304)696-3160; fax: (304)696-3135.

ADMISSION STANDARDS. Vary by department. Usual minimum average: 2.75 (A = 4).

FINANCIAL AID. Ten scholarships, one hundred grants, two hundred academic tuition waivers, one hundred research assistantships, seventy-five teaching assistantships, one hundred administrative assistantships, one hundred internships, Federal W/S, loans. Approved for VA benefits. Apply to Director of Financial Aid; no specified closing date. Use FAFSA and institutional FAF. Phone: (304)696-3162; fax: (304)696-3242.

DEGREE REQUIREMENTS. For master's: 32 credit hours minimum including thesis or 36 credit hours minimum without thesis; final written/oral exam. For Ph.D.: at least 60 credits beyond the master's; reading knowledge of one foreign language for some departments; qualifying exam; dissertation; final oral exam.

FIELDS OF STUDY.
Adult Fitness Cardiac Rehabilitation.
Allopathic Medicine.
Art.
Biological Sciences.
Biomedical Science.
Business Administration and Management. Includes accounting, finance, management, marketing.
Chemistry.
Communication Disorders.
Communication Studies.
Counselor Education.
Criminal Justice.
Education. Includes adult and technical education, art, early childhood, administration, elementary, health and physical education, family and consumer sciences, reading, secondary, social studies, special.
English.
Forensic Science.
Geography.
History.
Journalism.
Mathematics.
Music.
Nursing.
Physical Science and Recreation.
Political Science.

Psychology. Includes clinical psychology.
Safety.
Sociology.
Teaching. M.A.T. only.
Technology Management.

School of Medicine (25704)

Established 1972. Annual tuition: resident $7784, nonresident $8,210. Total average figure for all other expenses: $7500. Enrollment: first-year class 48 (EDP 12); total full-time 202 (men 65%, women 35%). Degree conferred: M.D.

ADMISSION REQUIREMENTS. AMCAS report, transcripts, MCAT, recommendations required in support of application. Interview by invitation only. Preference given to state residents. Has EDP; apply between June 15 and August 1. Apply to Admissions Office after June 15, before November 15. Application fee $20. Phone: (304)696-7312; (800)544-8514.

ADMISSION STANDARDS. Competitive. Admits about 15% of total annual applicants. Approximately 90% are state residents.

FINANCIAL AID. Scholarships, tuition waiver, loans. Apply after acceptance to University's Office of Financial Assistance. Approximately 90% of students receive some financial assistance.

DEGREE REQUIREMENTS. For M.D.: satisfactory completion of four-year program.

MARYCREST INTERNATIONAL UNIVERSITY

Davenport, Iowa 52804-4096
http://www.mcrest.edu

Founded 1939. Coed. Private control. Catholic tradition. Semester system. Library: 108,000 volumes, 23,000 microforms, 523 current periodicals, 10 PCs.

Tuition: per credit $380, $179 for teachers. Limited on-campus housing available. Average academic year housing cost: $4772 (including board) single room, $4128 double room. Contact Housing Office for both on- and off-campus housing information. Phone: (319)326-9204. Day care facilities available.

Graduate Program

Enrollment: full-time 7, part-time 278 (men 20%, women 80%). Faculty: full-time 8, part-time 3. Degrees conferred: M.A., M.S., M.A.T.

ADMISSION REQUIREMENTS. Transcripts, three letters of recommendation required in support of application. TOEFL required for international applicants. Accepts transfer applicants. Applicants from unaccredited colleges not considered. Apply to Admissions Office one month prior to beginning of semester. Application fee $25. Phone: (800)728-9705, (319)326-9225; fax: (319)327-9620; E-mail: tmcdonough@acc.mcrest.edu.

ADMISSION STANDARDS. Usual minimum average: 2.8 (A = 4), conditional acceptance 2.4.

FINANCIAL AID. Sixty academic scholarships, 140 grants, 2 assistantships, 4 internships, Federal W/S, loans. Approved for VA benefits. Apply to Director of Financial Aid; no specified closing date. Use FAFSA. Phone: (800)728-9705; fax: (319)327-9620.

DEGREE REQUIREMENTS. For master's: 30 credit minimum; comprehensive exam; thesis/nonthesis option.

FIELDS OF STUDY.
Computer Science.
Education. (Noncertification).
Elementary Education.
Reading. Specialist K–12.
Secondary Education.

MARYGROVE COLLEGE
Detroit, Michigan 48221-2599

Founded 1910. Moved to Detroit in 1927. Coed. Private control. Roman Catholic. Semester system. Library: 187,000 volumes, 16,000 microforms.

Tuition: per credit $325. On-campus housing available for single students only. Annual academic year housing cost: $4160–$5000. Apply to Residence Director. Phone: (313)862-8000, ext. 412.

Graduate Division

Enrollment: full- and part-time 250. College faculty: full-time 9, part-time 18. Degrees conferred: M.A. M.Ed., M.A.T.

ADMISSION REQUIREMENTS. Transcripts, MAT, interview required in support of application. TOEFL required for international applicants. Accepts transfer applicants. Apply to Graduate Admissions Office; no specified closing dates. Application fee $25. Phone: (313)862-8000, ext. 446.

ADMISSION STANDARDS. Selective. Usual minimum average: 3.00 (A = 4).

FINANCIAL AID. Limited to tuition grants, Federal W/S, loans. Approved for VA benefits. Apply to Financial Aid Office; no specified closing date. Phone: (313)862-8000, ext. 436; fax: (313)862-0973.

DEGREE REQUIREMENTS. For M.Ed., M.A.T.: 30 semester hours minimum, at least 24 in residence; no language or thesis requirement. For M.A. (Pastoral Ministry): 36 semester hours minimum, internship; final project. For M.A. (Administration): 36 semester hours minimum.

FIELDS OF STUDY.
Administration. Includes educational administration and human resources administration.
Art of Teaching. M.A.T. only.
Pastoral Ministry.
Teacher Education. Includes educational psychology, early childhood, foreign language, reading, special education (learning disabilities).

MARYLAND INSTITUTE COLLEGE OF ART
Baltimore, Maryland 21217

Founded 1826. Coed. Private control. Semester system. Library: 80,000 volumes.

Annual tuition: full-time $14,950. Limited on-campus housing. Annual academic year housing cost: $4690. Apply to Housing and Residence Life Office for on- and off-campus housing information. Phone: (410)225-2398.

Graduate Studies

Enrollment: full-time 72, part-time 25. Faculty: full-time 5, part-time 3. Degree conferred: M.F.A.

ADMISSION REQUIREMENTS. Transcripts, three letters of recommendation, portfolio required in support of application. TOEFL required for international applicants. Apply by March 1 for painting, ceramics, sculpture, printmaking, and photography. Fall admission for all majors except art education. Application $50. Phone: (410)225-2256.

ADMISSION STANDARDS. Competitive for most departments, relatively open for others. Usual minimum average: 2.75 (A = 4).

FINANCIAL AID. Scholarships, grants, 52 teaching assistantships, loans. Apply to Dean, Graduate Studies, before March 1. Use FAFSA. Phone: (410)225-2285; fax: (410)669-9206. About 65% of students receive aid other than loans from College. No aid for part-time students.

DEGREE REQUIREMENTS. For M.F.A.: 60 semester hours minimum, at least 54 in full-time residence; thesis/creative project; no language requirement.

FIELDS OF STUDY.
Art Education. Portfolio required for admission to all programs.
M.F.A. for Art Educators. Four summers in residence.
Mixed Media.
Painting. Private studios for full-time students.
Photography. Private studios for full-time students.
Sculpture. Private studios for full-time students; large shop and foundry.

UNIVERSITY OF MARYLAND
College Park, Maryland 20742-5121
http://www.umcp.umd.edu

Established 1856. College Park campus located 10 miles N of Washington, D.C.; Schools of Medicine, Dentistry, Nursing, Pharmacy, Social Work, and Law are located in Baltimore. Coed. State control. Semester system. Special facilities: Center for Aging, Automation Research Center, Institute for Criminal Justice and Criminology, Center for Estuarine and Environmental Sciences, Center for Language, Institute for Philosophy and Public Policy, Institute for Physical Science and Technology, Center for Renaissance and Baroque Studies, Survey Research Center, electron microscope, linear accelerator, wind tunnel, marine laboratory, research farms, laboratory-equipped vessels for water research, Transportation Studies Center. Library: more than 2,452,000 volumes, 4,939,000 microforms, 18,600 current periodicals.

Tuition: per hour, resident $250, nonresident $375. On-campus housing for 476 married students, limited number of single graduate students. Average academic year housing cost: $400–$600 per month. Contact Office of Residential Life. Phone: (301)314-2100, (301)314-5274 (off-campus housing information).

Graduate School

Established 1919. Enrollment: full-time 4158, part-time 4377 (men 50%, women 50%). Graduate faculty: full-time more than 1700, part-time under 100. Degrees conferred: M.A., M.S., M.Ed., M.F.A., M.L.S., M.M., M.B.A., M.C.P., M.A.A., M.Arch., M.Eng. A.G.S., Ed.D., D.M.A., Ph.D.

ADMISSION REQUIREMENTS. Transcripts, GRE/MAT/GMAT, three letters of recommendation required in support of School's application. GRE Subject Test for many programs. TOEFL, TWE required for international applicants. Interview usually not required. Accepts transfer applicants. Graduates of unaccredited institutions not considered. Apply to Director of Graduate Admission and Records by March 1 (Fall), November 1 (Spring), May 1 (Summer); international February 1 (Fall), June 1 (Spring). Application fee $50, $70 international applicants. Phone: (301)405-4198; fax: (301)314-9305.

ADMISSION STANDARDS. Selective for most departments. Usual minimum average: 3.0 (A = 4).

FINANCIAL AID. Annual awards from institutional funds: 65 grants, 95 academic scholarships, 2770 teaching/research/administrative assistantships, 350 research fellowships, tuition waivers, Federal W/S, loans. Approved for VA benefits. Apply by February 1 to appropriate department for scholarships, assistantships, fellowships; to Financial Aid Office for all other programs. Use FAFSA and FATS. Phone: (301)314-8313; fax: (301)314-9587. About 31% of students receive aid other than loans from School and outside sources.

DEGREE REQUIREMENTS. For most master's: 30–39 semester hours minimum, at least 24 in residence: thesis/nonthesis option; final oral exam. For M.L.S.: 36 hours minimum. For A.G.S.: 30 semester hours beyond the master's. For Ph.D.: three years minimum beyond the bachelor's, at least one in residence; preliminary exam; dissertation; final oral exam. For D.M.A.: essentially the same as for the Ph.D., except reading knowledge of one language required; composition/final recital.

FIELDS OF STUDY.
Aerospace Engineering. M.S., M.E., Ph.D.
Agricultural and Resource Economics. M.S., Ph.D.
Agronomy. M.S., Ph.D.
American Studies. M.A., Ph.D.
Animal Sciences. M.S., Ph.D.
Anthropology. M.A.A.
Applied Mathematics. M.A., Ph.D.
Architecture. M.Arch.
Art. Includes studio. M.F.A.
Art History and Archaeology. M.A., Ph.D.
Astronomy. M.S., Ph.D.
Biochemistry. M.S., Ph.D.
Biological Sciences. M.S., Ph.D.
Business and Management. GMAT for admission. M.S., M.B.A., Ph.D.
Chemical Engineering. M.S., M.E., Ph.D.
Chemical Physics. Interdepartmental. M.S., Ph.D.
Chemistry. M.S., Ph.D.
Civil Engineering. M.E., Ph.D.
Classics. M.A.
Comparative Literature. M.A., Ph.D.
Computer Science. M.S., Ph.D.
Counseling and Personnel Services. M.Ed., M.A., Ph.D., A.G.S.
Creative Writing. M.F.A.
Criminal Justice and Criminology. M.A., Ph.D.
Curriculum and Instruction. Includes elementary and secondary. M.Ed., M.A., Ed.D., Ph.D., A.G.S.
Dance. M.F.A.
Economics. M.A., Ph.D.
Education Policy, Planning, and Administration. M.A., M.Ed., Ed.D., Ph.D., A.G.S.
Electrical Engineering. M.S., M.E., Ph.D.
English Language and Literature. M.A., Ph.D.
Entomology. M.S., Ph.D.
Family Studies. M.S.
Fire Protection Engineering. M.S., M.E.

Food Science. M.S., Ph.D.
French Language and Literature. M.A., Ph.D.
Geography. M.A., Ph.D.
Geography/Library and Information Systems. M.A., M.L.S.
Geology. M.S., Ph.D.
Germanic Language and Literature. M.A., Ph.D.
Government and Politics. M.A., Ph.D.
Health Education. M.A., Ph.D.
Hearing and Speech Science. M.A., Ph.D.
History. M.A., Ph.D.
History/Library and Information. M.A., M.L.S.
Horticulture. M.S., Ph.D.
Human Development. M.Ed., M.A., Ed.D., Ph.D., A.G.S.
Journalism. M.A.
Kinesiology. M.A., Ph.D.
Library and Information Services. M.L.S., Ph.D.
Linguistics. M.A., Ph.D.
Marine-Estuarine-Environmental Sciences. M.S., Ph.D.
Mass Communications. Ph.D.
Material Sciences and Engineering. M.S., M.E., Ph.D.
Mathematical Statistics. M.A., Ph.D.
Mathematics. M.A., Ph.D.
Measurement, Statistics, and Evaluation. M.A., Ph.D.
Mechanical Engineering. M.S., M.E., Ph.D.
Meteorology. M.S., Ph.D.
Microbiology. M.S., Ph.D.
Music. M.M., M.A., M.Ed., D.M.A., Ph.D., Ed.D.
Nuclear Engineering. M.S., M.E., Ph.D.
Nutrition. M.S., Ph.D.
Philosophy. M.A., Ph.D.
Physics. M.S., Ph.D.
Plant Biology. M.S., Ph.D.
Policy Studies. Ph.D. only.
Poultry Science. M.S., Ph.D.
Psychology. Ph.D.
Public Management. M.P.M.
Public Policy. M.P.P.
Reliability Engineering. M.S., M.E., Ph.D.
Russian Language and Linguistics. M.A.
Sociology. M.A., Ph.D.
Spanish Language and Literature. M.A., Ph.D.
Special Education. M.Ed., M.A., Ed.D., Ph.D., A.G.S.
Speech Communication. M.A., Ph.D.
Survey Methodology. M.S., Ph.D.
Sustainable Development and Conservation Biology. M.S.
Systems Engineering. M.S., M.E.
Telecommunications. M.S.
Theater. M.A., M.F.A., Ph.D.
Toxicology. M.S., Ph.D.
Zoology. M.S., Ph.D.

UNIVERSITY OF MARYLAND AT BALTIMORE

Baltimore, Maryland 21201-1627
http://www.umbc.edu

Founded 1807. Coed. Semester system. Special facilities: Aquatic Pathology Center, Cancer Center, Clinical Stroke Research Center, Biotechnology Research Center, Center for Health Policy Research, Center for Human Virology, Center for Drugs and Public Policy, Center for Vaccine Development. Library: 410,000 volumes, 530,000 microforms, 2900 journal titles.

Tuition: per credit, resident $231, nonresident $416. On-campus housing available for graduate men and women. Annual academic year average cost: $3500 (room only). Apply to Office of Residential Life. Phone: (410)706-7766.

Graduate School

http://www.umbc.edu.edu/umgsb

Enrollment: full- and part-time 1320. Faculty: full-time 146, part-time 4. Degrees conferred: M.S., Ph.D.

ADMISSION REQUIREMENTS. Transcripts, GRE, three letters of recommendation required in support of School's application. TOEFL required of international applicants. Accepts transfer applicants. Graduates of unaccredited colleges not considered. Apply to Graduate Admission and Records Office; no specified closing date. Application fee $40. Phone: (410)766-7131; fax: (410)706-5035.

ADMISSION STANDARDS. Selective in some departments, competitive in others. Usual minimum average: 3.0 (A = 4).

FINANCIAL AID. Annual awards from institutional funds: 39 fellowships, 82 teaching assistantships, 125 research assistantships, Federal W/S, loans. Approved for VA benefits. Use FAFSA. Phone: (410)455-7347; fax: (410)706-0824. About 30% of students receive aid other than loans from both University and outside sources.

DEGREE REQUIREMENTS. For M.S.: 30 semester hours minimum; thesis/nonthesis option; final exam. For Ph.D.: three years of full-time study, at least one year in residence; preliminary exam; dissertation; final exam.

FIELDS OF STUDY.
Anatomy.
Biochemistry.
Biological Sciences.
Dental Hygiene.
Emergency Health Services.
Epidemiology and Preventive Medicine.
Forensic Toxicology.
Human Genetics.
Marine-Estuarine-Environmental Sciences.
Medical and Research Technology.
Medicinal Chemistry and Pharmacognosy.
Microbiology and Immunology.
Molecular and Cell Biology.
Nursing.
Oral Biology.
Pathology.
Pharmaceutics.
Pharmacology and Experiment Therapeutics.
Physiology.
Social Work and Community Planning.
Toxicology.

School of Law

Founded 1816. Located in Baltimore (21201). Semester system. Law library: 346,000 volumes. Library has LEXIS, WESTLAW, DIALOG, CARL, UNCOVER, OCLC.

Annual tuition: full-time resident $8987, nonresident $15,722; part-time resident $6460, nonresident $11,400. No on-campus housing is available.

Enrollment: full-time first-year class 180, part-time 75; total full- and part-time 850 (men 50%, women 50%). Faculty: full-time 53, part-time 42. Degrees conferred: J.D., J.D.-Master's (Business Administration, Criminal Justice, Marine and Environmental Sciences, Policy Sciences, Public Management, Social Work).

ADMISSION REQUIREMENTS. LSDAS Law School report, bachelor's degree, transcript, LSAT (no later than February) required in support of application. Interview not required. Accepts transfer applicants. Graduates of unaccredited colleges not con-

sidered. Apply to Director of Admissions after September 1, before February 15 (priority deadline). Fall admission only for beginning students. Application fee $40. Phone: (410)706-3492.

ADMISSION STANDARDS. Selective. Accepts 25–30% of total annual applicants.

FINANCIAL AID. Scholarships, grants, loans. Apply by March 15 to Financial Aid Office. Use FAFSA. About 60% of students receive aid other than loans from School. Aid sometimes available for part-time students.

DEGREE REQUIREMENTS. For J.D.: satisfactory completion of three-year program, at least one year in residence; 85 semester-hours program. For J.D.-Masters: see Graduate School listing above.

School of Medicine

Chartered 1808. Located in Baltimore (21201). Annual tuition: resident $10,751, nonresident $20,851; student fees $1700. Total average figure for all other expenses: $8500. Enrollment: first year 145 (EDP 10), total 411 (men 50%, women 50%). Faculty: full- and part-time 426. Degrees conferred: M.D., M.D.-Ph.D. The M.S. and Ph.D. are awarded by the Graduate School.

ADMISSION REQUIREMENTS. AMCAS report, transcripts, MCAT, letters of recommendation required in support of application. Interview by invitation only. Applicants must have completed at least three years of college study. Preference given to Maryland residents. Accepts transfer applicants in second and third years only. Graduates of unaccredited colleges not considered. Has EDP for Maryland residents only; apply between June 15 and August 1. Apply to Director of Admissions after June 15, before November 15. Application fee $40. Phone: (410)706-7478.

ADMISSION STANDARDS. Competitive. Accepts 8% of total annual applicants. Approximately 82% are state residents.

FINANCIAL AID. Scholarships, Summer fellowships, loans. About 70% of students receive some aid from School. Apply by June 1 to Office of Financial Aid.

DEGREE REQUIREMENTS. For M.D.: satisfactory completion of four-year program, at least one year in residence. For M.S., Ph.D., see Graduate School listing above.

FIELDS OF GRADUATE STUDY.
Anatomy.
Biochemistry.
Biomedical Engineering.
Biophysics.
Cell Biology.
Genetics.
Immunology.
Microbiology.
Molecular Biology.
Neurosciences.
Pathology.
Pharmacology.
Physiology.

Baltimore College of Dental Surgery

Founded 1840. Located in Baltimore (21201). Annual tuition: resident $8961, nonresident $19,732. Average academic year housing cost: $200. Total average cost for all other first-year expenses: $5100.

Enrollment: first-year class 98; total 400 (men 60%, women 40%). Faculty: full-time 125, part-time 96. Degrees conferred:

B.S.-D.D.S., D.D.S. The Ph.D. (Physiology) is awarded through the Graduate School.

ADMISSION REQUIREMENTS. AADSAS report, transcripts, DAT (not later than October), three letters of recommendation required in support of application. Interviews by invitation only. Applicants must have completed at least three but preferably four years of study in an accredited college of arts and sciences. Transfer applicants accepted. Preference given to state residents. Apply after June 1, before February 1 to the Office of Admissions of the Dental School. Application fee $40. Phone: (410)706-7472.

ADMISSION STANDARDS. Competitive. Usual minimum average: 3.0 (A = 4). Accepts about 25% of annual applicants. Approximately 65% are state residents.

FINANCIAL AID. Scholarships, work-study; Federal, state, and private loans. Apply to Office of Student Financial Aid, University of Maryland at Baltimore; priority consideration given applications received by February 15. Use FAFSA. Phone: (410)706-7347. About 76% of students receive some aid from the School.

DEGREE REQUIREMENTS. For B.S.-D.D.S.: satisfactory completion of seven-year program. For D.D.S.: satisfactory completion of forty-five-month program. For Ph.D.: see Graduate School listing above.

UNIVERSITY OF MARYLAND BALTIMORE COUNTY
Baltimore, Maryland 21228-5398
http://www.umbc.edu

Founded 1807. Coed. Semester system. Special facilities: Bioimaging Center, Center for Educational Research and Development, Bradley Center for Employment and Training, Center for Fluorescience Spectrocopy, Molecular Graphic Center, Institute for Policy Analysis and Research, Sargent and Eunice Shriver Center, Structural Biochemistry Center. Library: 650,000 volumes, 850,000 microforms, 4000 current periodicals, 40 PCs.

Tuition: per credit, resident $231, nonresident $416. On-campus housing for single students only. Average academic year housing cost: $4546 (including board). Contact Office of Residential Life for both on- and off-campus housing information.

Graduate School
http:// www.umbc.edu/umgsb

Enrollment: full- and part-time 1500. Faculty: full-time 346, part-time 17. Degrees conferred: M.A., M.F.A., M.P.S., M.S., Ph.D.

ADMISSION REQUIREMENTS. Transcripts, GRE, three letters of recommendation required in support of School's application. TOEFL required of international applicants. Accepts transfer applicants. Graduates of unaccredited colleges not considered. Apply to Director, Graduate Admissions and Records Office; no specified closing date. Application fee $40. Phone: (410)455-2537; fax: (410)455-1130.

ADMISSION STANDARDS. Selective in some departments, competitive in others. Usual minimum average: 3.0 (A = 4).

FINANCIAL AID. Annual awards from institutional funds: fellowships, teaching assistantships, research assistantships, Federal W/S, loans. Approved for VA benefits. Apply by April 1 to the Dean's Office for fellowships, assistantships; to the Financial Aid Office for all other programs. Use FAFSA. About 30% of students receive aid other than loans from both University and outside sources. Aid available for part-time students.

DEGREE REQUIREMENTS. For master's: 30–39 semester hours minimum; thesis/nonthesis option; final exam. For M.F.A.: 60 semester hours minimum, all in full-time residence or equivalent; special final project. For Ph.D.: three years of full-time study, at least one year in residence; preliminary exam; dissertation; final exam.

FIELDS OF STUDY.
Applied Molecular Biology.
Applied Physics.
Biochemistry.
Biological Sciences.
Chemistry.
Computer Science.
Education.
Emergency Health Services.
Engineering. Includes chemical, electrical, mechanical.
Engineering Management.
Historical Studies.
Imaging and Digital Arts.
Instructional Systems Development.
Marine-Estuarine-Environmental Sciences.
Operations Analysis.
Policy Sciences.
Psychology. Includes developmental, human service.
Sociology.
Statistics.

MARYVILLE UNIVERSITY OF SAINT LOUIS
St. Louis, Missouri 63141-7299

Founded 1872. Coed. Semester system. Library: 149,483 volumes, 325,893 microforms.

Annual tuition: $10,280; per credit $309. On-campus housing semi-private and private accommodations. Annual academic year housing cost: $4750 (includes board). Apply to Director of Residential Life. Phone: (314)529-9505.

Graduate Studies

Graduate study for Education since 1982, for Business since 1990. Enrollment: full-time 38, part-time 505 (men 162, women 381). Faculty: full-time 23, part-time 12. Degrees conferred: M.A., M.B.A.

ADMISSION REQUIREMENTS. Transcripts required in support of application. For Business: GMAT, personal letter explaining qualifications for graduate study. For Education: three letters of recommendation, essay. TOEFL required for international applicants. Accepts transfer applicants. Graduates of unaccredited institutions not considered. Apply to Admission Office of appropriate school; no specified closing date. Application fee $20. School of Education, phone: (314)529-9542; fax: (314)519-9921, E-mail: rush@maryville.edu. School of Business, phone: (314)529-9382; fax: (314)529-9975; E-mail: beggs@ maryville.edu.

FINANCIAL AID. Professional educator scholarships, corporate reimbursement, Federal W/S, loans. Approved for VA benefits. Apply to Financial Aid Office; no specified closing date. Use FAFSA. Phone: (314)576-9360; fax: (314)542-9085, E-mail: fin_aid@maryville.edu.

DEGREE REQUIREMENTS. For M.A.: 30 credits minimum; thesis/nonthesis option. M.B.A.: 36 credits.

FIELDS OF STUDY.

SCHOOL OF EDUCATION:
Art Education.
Early Childhood.
Elementary Generalist.
Environmental Education.
Gifted Education.
Middle Level Teacher.
Multicultural Classroom.
Secondary Generalist.

JOHN E. SIMON SCHOOL OF BUSINESS:
Business Administration. Includes accountancy, health care management, information systems, marketing, management.

MARYWOOD COLLEGE
Scranton, Pennsylvania 18509-1598

Founded 1915. Located approximately 100 miles W of New York City and 100 miles N of Philadelphia. Coed. Private control. Roman Catholic. Semester system. Library: 202,000 volumes, 221,000 microforms, 1192 current periodicals, 100 PCs.

Tuition: per credit $400; $410 for M.F.A. On-campus housing for single students only. Average academic year housing cost: $4800 (including board). Contact Office of Student Affairs for on- and off-campus housing information. Phone: (717)348-6246.

Graduate School of Arts and Sciences

Enrollment: full-time 136, part-time 440 (men 25%, women 75%). Graduate faculty: full-time 46, part-time 97. Degrees conferred: M.A., M.S., M.P.A., M.B.A., M.F.A., M.P.A.-M.S.W., C.A.G.S., Ph.D.

ADMISSION REQUIREMENTS. Transcripts, two letters of recommendation, GRE or MAT, GMAT (Business) required in support of School's application. TOEFL required for international applicants. Accepts transfer applicants. Graduates of unaccredited institutions not considered. Apply by July 1 (Fall), December 1 (Spring), April 15 (Summer). Application fee $20. Phone: (717)348-6230.

ADMISSION STANDARDS. Selective. Usual minimum average: 3.0 (A = 4).

FINANCIAL AID. Annual awards from institutional funds: two hundred scholarships, twenty-four assistantships, loans. Apply by March 15 to Dean of Graduate School of Arts and Sciences for scholarships, assistantships; to Financial Aid Office for loans. Use FAFSA. Phone: (717)348-6225. About 55% of students receive aid other than loans from College and outside sources. Aid available to part-time students.

DEGREE REQUIREMENTS. For master's: 30–60 credits; thesis/professional contribution; comprehensive exams. For C.A.G.S.: 30 credits beyond the master's; special project. For Ph.D.: 60 credits beyond the master's minimum, at least one year in full-time residence; qualifying exam; dissertation; final oral exam.

FIELDS OF STUDY.
Art. Includes two-dimensional, three-dimensional. M.F.A.
Art Education. M.A.
Art Therapy. M.A.
Business Administration. M.B.A.
Church Music. M.A.
Communication Arts. M.A.
Counseling. Includes addictions, agency, pastoral. M.A.
Counseling. Includes elementary, secondary. M.S.
Criminal Justice. M.P.A.
Dietetics.
Education. Includes school leadership, early childhood, elementary, instructional technology, reading. M.S.
Finance and Investments. M.B.A.
Fine Arts.
Foods and Nutrition. Includes nutrition, sports nutrition, critical care/nutritional support, food systems management, gerontology. M.S.
Gerontology. M.P.A.
Health Services Administration. M.B.A., M.P.A.
Human Development. Interdisciplinary. Ph.D. only.
Industrial Management. M.B.A.
Information Systems Technology. M.B.A.
International Business. M.B.A.
Management Information Systems. M.S.
Management of Nonprofit Organizations. M.P.A.
Music Education. M.A.
Musicology. M.A.
Psychology. Includes clinical services, general/theoretical, school/child. M.A.
Public Administration. M.P.A.
Special Education. M.S.
Studio Art. M.A.
Teaching. M.A.
Theological Studies. M.A.

School of Social Work

Established 1968. Coed. Annual tuition: full-time $11,550; per credit hour $410 main campus, $415 Lehigh Valley campus.
Enrollment: full-time 197, part-time 35. Faculty: full-time 15, part-time 11. Degree conferred: M.S.W.

ADMISSION REQUIREMENTS. Transcripts, three letters of reference, personal statement required in support of School's application. TOEFL required for international applicants. Interview may be required. Accepts transfer applicants. Apply to Coordinator of Admissions by May 30 (flexible). Application fee $20. Phone: (717)348-6282; fax: (717)348-4742.

ADMISSION STANDARDS. Selective. Usual minimum average: 3.0 (A = 4).

FINANCIAL AID. More than thirty-three partial scholarships, twenty-four research/administrative assistantships, loans. Apply to Coordinator of Financial Aid Office by June 1. Use FAFSA and institutional FAF. Phone: (717)348-6225.

DEGREE REQUIREMENTS. For M.S.W.: 60 credit hours minimum including fieldwork. Advanced standing for graduates of accredited undergraduate social work programs.

FIELDS OF STUDY.
Administration.
Gerontology.
Interpersonal Intervention.

MASSACHUSETTS COLLEGE OF ART
Boston, Massachusetts 02115-3393

Founded 1873. Coed. State control. Semester system. Library: 92,000 volumes, 65,000 microforms, 10 PCs.
Tuition: per credit $170. Limited on-campus housing available for graduate students. Contact Housing Office for off-campus housing information. Phone: (617)232-1555, ext. 513.

Graduate Program

Enrollment: full-time 82, part-time 30. Faculty: full-time 16, part-time 15. Degrees conferred: M.S., M.S.A.E., M.F.A.

ADMISSION REQUIREMENTS. Transcripts, bachelor's degree, three letters of recommendation, statement of purpose, portfolio required in support of application. TOEFL required for international applicants. Accepts transfer applicants. Apply to Admissions Office by February 1. Application fee $50. Phone: (617)232-1555, ext. 375; fax: (617)566-4934.

ADMISSION STANDARDS. Competitive. Portfolio/talent-based selection process.

FINANCIAL AID. Annual awards from institutional funds: eight administrative assistantships, twenty teaching assistantships, ten technical assistantships, Federal W/S, loans. Apply to the Financial Aid Office; no specified closing date. Use FAFSA. Phone: (617)232-1555, ext. 236.

DEGREE REQUIREMENTS. For M.S., M.S.A.E.: 36 semester hours. For M.F.A.: 60 semester hours.

FIELDS OF STUDY.
Art Education. M.S.A.E.
Design. M.F.A.
Fine Arts. Includes painting, printmaking, sculpture, ceramics, fibers, glass, metalsmithing, photography, film, studio for interrelated media; M.F.A.

MASSACHUSETTS COLLEGE OF PHARMACY AND ALLIED HEALTH SCIENCES

Boston, Massachusetts 02115-5896

Founded 1823. Coed. Private control. Special facilities: Samuel M. Best Research Laboratory, Pfeiffer Pharmaceutics Laboratory. Library: 75,000 volumes, 48 PCs.

Tuition: per hour $413. Housing on nearby campus. Annual academic year housing cost: approximately $9000.

Graduate Study

Enrollment: full-time 32, part-time 4. Graduate faculty: full-time 18, part-time 3. Degrees conferred: M.S., Ph.D.

ADMISSION REQUIREMENTS. Transcripts, GRE, three letters of recommendation required in support of application. TOEFL, TSE required for international applicants. Interview not required. Accepts transfer applicants. Graduates of unaccredited colleges not considered. Apply by February 1 for September admission. Admits normally to Fall only. Application fee $50. Phone: (617)732-2850; fax: (617)732-2801.

ADMISSION STANDARDS. Selective. Usual minimum average: 3.0 (A = 4).

FINANCIAL AID. Annual awards from institutional funds: seventeen teaching fellowships, two research assistantships, Federal W/S, loans. Approved for VA benefits. Apply to appropriate department by March 30 for assistantships, fellowships; to Financial Aid Office for all other programs. Use FAFSA. Phone: (617)732-2861; fax: (617)732-2801. About 25% of students receive aid other than loans from the College, 30% from other sources. No aid for part-time students.

DEGREE REQUIREMENTS. For M.S.: 30 semester hours minimum, normally in full-time residence; thesis; final oral exam.

For Ph.D.: 50 semester hours minimum beyond bachelor's, normally in full-time residence; one language or research skill; preliminary exam; dissertation; final written/oral exam.

FIELDS OF STUDY.
Chemistry.
Industrial Pharmacy.
Pharmaceutics.

MASSACHUSETTS INSTITUTE OF TECHNOLOGY

Cambridge, Massachusetts 02139
http://WEB.MIT.EDU

Founded 1861. Located adjacent to Boston. Coed. Private control. 4-1-4 system. Special facilities: Biotechnology Process Engineering Center, Center for Cognitive Science, Center for Environmental Health Sciences, Center for Global Change Science, Center for Information Systems Research, Center for International Studies, Center for Materials Science and Engineering, Materials Processing Center, Center for Space Research, Center for Transportation, Computation Center, Joint Center for Urban Studies with Harvard University, Laboratory for Nuclear Science, Haystack Observatory, Lincoln Laboratory for Research and Development in Advanced Electronics, media laboratory, Leaders for Manufacturing, National Magnet Laboratory, Operations Research Center, Research Laboratory of Electronics, nuclear reactor, Whitehead Institute for Biomedical Research, MIT–Japan Science and Technology, spectroscopy laboratory. Library: 2,395,000 volumes, 2,041,000 microforms, 310 PCs.

Annual tuition: full-time $22,000, per credit $365. On-campus housing for 40 married students, 800 graduate men and women. Average annual housing cost: $7000–$11,500 for married students, $3000–$8500 for single students. Apply to Manager of Ashdown House (single students) or to Campus Housing Office (married students). Phone: (617)253-5148; apply to Off-Campus Housing Service for off-campus housing information. Phone: (617)253-4449.

Graduate School

Graduate study since 1886. Enrollment: full-time 5090 (men 75%, women 25%). Faculty: full-time 956, part-time 375. Degrees conferred: M.Arch., M.B.A., M.S., M.Eng., Engineer, Sc.D., M.Arch.A.S., M.C.P., Ph.D.

ADMISSION REQUIREMENTS. Transcripts, three references required in support of School's application. GRE required by some departments, recommended for the others. Interview not required. TOEFL required of international students. Accepts transfer applicants. Graduates of unaccredited institutions not considered. Apply to Director of Admissions by January 15 (Fall or Summer), November 1 (Spring). Later applications are considered if vacancies still exist. Application fee $50. Phone: (617)253-4897.

ADMISSION STANDARDS. Competitive. Usual minimum average: 3.5 (A = 4).

FINANCIAL AID. Annual awards from institutional funds: 303 scholarships, 429 teaching assistantships, 2021 research assistantships, 350 traineeships, loans. Apply by January 15 to Director of Admissions for scholarships or traineeships, loans; to appropriate department chair for assistantships. Use FAFSA and institutional FAF. Phone: (617)253-4971; fax: (617)258-8301. About 80% of students receive aid other than loans from School and outside sources. No aid for part-time students.

DEGREE REQUIREMENTS. For master's: 66 subject units minimum, at least one term in residence; thesis. For M.Arch.: 164 subject units minimum, at least 96 in residence; thesis. For Engineering: 162 units minimum beyond the bachelor's, at least one year in residence; thesis. For Sc.D., Ph.D.: three years minimum beyond the bachelor's, at least three terms in residence; qualifying written exam; language requirements vary with department; dissertation; final oral exam.

FIELDS OF STUDY.

SCHOOL OF ARCHITECTURE AND PLANNING:
Architecture. M.Arch., M.Arch.A.S.; no doctorate.
Urban Studies and Planning.

SCHOOL OF ENGINEERING:
Aeronautics and Astronautics.
Chemical Engineering.
Civil and Environmental Engineering.
Computer Science.
Electrical Engineering.
Environmental Engineering.
Materials Science and Engineering.
Mechanical Engineering.
Nuclear Engineering.
Ocean Engineering.
Technology and Policy.

SCHOOL OF HUMANITIES AND SOCIAL SCIENCE:
Economics.
Linguistics.
Philosophy.
Political Science.
Science, Technology, and Society

SCHOOL OF SCIENCE:
Biology.
Brain and Cognitive Sciences.
Chemistry.
Earth, Atmospheric, and Planetary Sciences.
Mathematics.
Physics.

WHITAKER COLLEGE:
Health Sciences and Technology.
Toxicology.

UNIVERSITY OF MASSACHUSETTS, AMHERST

Amherst, Massachusetts 01003-0001

Founded 1863. Located 90 miles W of Boston. Amherst campus is primary graduate school location. State control. Semester system. Special facilities: University Computing Center, Labor Relations and Research Center, Environmental Institute, Water Resources Center, Hampshire Inter-Library Center, Marine Station, Suburban Experiment Station, University of Massachusetts Abroad, Center for Instructional Resources and Improvement, Office of Research Services, University Press, Institute for Governmental Service, Center for Business and Economic Research, Polymer Research Institute. Five-College (Amherst, Hampshire, Mount Holyoke, Smith, University of Massachusetts) cooperative undergraduate and graduate programs. Library: 4,700,000 volumes, 2,800,000 microforms, 24,000 current periodicals.

Annual tuition: full-time, resident $2778, nonresident $8568; per hour, resident $115.75, nonresident $357. On-campus housing for 300 graduate single students; 345 married students. Average academic year housing cost: $4010 (including board) for single students; $5000–$7000 for married students. Apply to Housing Office. Phone: (413)545-2100.

Graduate School

Graduate study since 1876. Enrollment: full-time 2400, part-time 3700. University faculty: full-and part-time 1150. Degrees conferred: M.A., M.S., M.S.E.C.E., M.R.P., M.A.T., Ch.E., M.S.C.E., M.S.Envr.E., M.S.I.E.O.R., M.S.M.E., M.P.A., M.P.H., M.Ed., M.B.A., M.F.A., M.L.A., M.M., C.A.G.S., Ed.D., Ph.D., Five-College Ph.D.

ADMISSION REQUIREMENTS. Transcripts, two recommendations, GRE or GMAT, proof of residency form required in support of School's application. Interview not required. TOEFL required for international applicants. Graduates of unaccredited institutions not considered. Apply to Graduate Admissions Office by March 1 (Fall and Summer), October 1 (Spring). Some programs may have earlier deadline. Application fee $40. Phone: (413)545-0721; fax: (413)577-0010.

ADMISSION STANDARDS. Very selective for most departments. Usual minimum average: 3.0 (A = 4).

FINANCIAL AID. Annual awards from institutional funds: 600 fellowships and internships, 1700 teaching assistantships, 1450 research assistantships, Federal W/S, loans. Apply to Financial Aid Office; no specified closing date. Phone: (413)545-0801. Use FAFSA. About 50% of students receive aid other than loans from University and outside sources.

DEGREE REQUIREMENTS. For most master's: 30 credits; thesis; final general exam. For M.A.T.: 39–45 credits. For M.Ed.: 33 credits. For M.B.A.: 55 credits. For M.F.A.: 60 credits; final M.F.A. creative project (English, Art, Theater). For M.R.P., M.L.A.: 46 credits; internships; research project; thesis optional. For M.M.: 33 credits; one original composition in lieu of thesis for composition majors. For C.A.G.S.: 30 credits beyond master's. For Ph.D., Ed.D.: course work as specified by program, at least two consecutive semesters in full-time residence; comprehensive exam; foreign language requirement varies by program; dissertation; final oral exam. The Statute of Limitations (maximum time allowed in which to earn the degree) is six years for the doctorate, four years for the M.F.A., and three years for all other master's degree programs; a part-time student may apply for an additional year in which to complete a program.

FIELDS OF STUDY.
Accounting.
Afro-American Studies.
Animal Science.
Anthropology.
Applied Mathematics.
Art.
Art History.
Astronomy.
Biochemistry.
Biology.
Chemical Engineering.
Chemistry.
Chinese.
Civil Engineering.
Communication.
Communication Disorders.
Comparative Literature.
Computer Science.
Consumer Studies.
Counseling Psychology.
Economics.
Education.
Electrical and Computer Engineering.
Engineering Management.
English.
Entomology.

Environmental Engineering.
Exercise Science.
Food Science.
Forestry and Wood Technology.
French.
Geography.
Geology.
Germanic Language and Literatures.
Hispanic Literature and Linguistics.
History.
Hotel, Restaurant, and Travel Administration.
Industrial Engineering and Operations Research.
Italian.
Japanese.
Labor Studies.
Landscape Architecture.
Latin and Classical Humanities.
Linguistics.
Management.
Manufacturing Engineering.
Mathematics and Statistics.
Mechanical Engineering.
Microbiology.
Molecular and Cellular Biology.
Music.
Neuroscience and Behavior.
Nursing.
Nutrition.
Organismic and Evolutionary Biology.
Philosophy.
Physics.
Plant and Soil Sciences.
Plant Biology.
Plant Pathology.
Political Science.
Polymer Science and Engineering.
Psychology.
Public Administration.
Public Health.
Regional Planning.
Resource Economics.
Sociology.
Sport Studies.
Theater.
Wildlife and Fisheries Conservation.

Medical School

Founded 1970. Located in Worcester (01655). Annual tuition: resident $8792, nonresident not applicable; student fees $1470. Total average cost for all other expenses: $11,800. Very limited housing available.

Enrollment: first-year class 100 (EDP 10); total 400 (men 50%, women 50%). Faculty: approximately 500 full- and part-time. Degrees conferred: M.D., M.D.-Ph.D.

ADMISSION REQUIREMENTS. Transcripts, MCAT, recommendations, interview required in support of application. Non-Massachusetts residents, graduates of unaccredited colleges not considered. Has EDP; apply between June 15 and August 1. Apply after June 15, before December 1. Application fee $50. Phone: (508)856-2323.

ADMISSION STANDARDS. Selective. Accepts about 20% of total annual applicants. 100% are state residents.

FINANCIAL AID. Scholarships, loans. Use FAFSA. Apply to Dean of School after acceptance, but before March 1. About 75% of students receive some form of financial assistance.

DEGREE REQUIREMENTS. For M.D.: satisfactory completion of four-year program. For Ph.D.: requirements refer to Graduate School listing above.

FIELDS OF GRADUATE STUDY.
Anatomy.
Biochemistry.
Biomedical Engineering.
Biophysics.
Cell Biology.
Genetics.
Immunology.
Microbiology.
Molecular Biology
Pathology.
Pharmacology.
Physiology.

UNIVERSITY OF MASSACHUSETTS, BOSTON

Boston, Massachusetts 02125-3393
http://www.umb.edu

Founded 1964. Coed. State control. Semester system. Special facilities: Center for the Advancement of Teaching in the Sciences, Asian-American Institute, Gerontology Institute, Gaston Institute for Latino Affairs, Institute for Learning and Teaching, McCormack Institute of Public Affairs, Center for Survey Research, Joiner Center for the Study of War and Social Consequences, Trotter Institute for the Study of Black Culture, Urban Harbors Institute. Library: 559,885 volumes, 727,750 microforms.

Tuition: per credit, resident $116, nonresident $357. No on- or off-campus housing available (commuter institution).

Graduate Studies and Research

Enrollment: full-time 711, part-time 1894 (men 982, women 1623). University faculty: full-time 464, part-time 371. Degrees conferred: M.A., M.S., M.Ed., M.B.A., C.A.G.S., Ph.D., Ed.D., Graduate Certificate.

ADMISSION REQUIREMENTS. Transcripts, GRE/MAT/GMAT required in support of application. TOEFL required for international applicants. Accepts transfer applicants. Graduates of unaccredited institutions not considered. Apply to Office of Graduate Admissions and Records. Application deadlines vary by program. Application fee $20 (residents), $35 (nonresidents). Phone: (617)287-6400; fax: (617)287-6236.

ADMISSION STANDARDS. Selective. Usual minimum average: 2.75 (A = 4).

FINANCIAL AID. Four academic scholarships, 299 grants, 131 research assistantships, 48 administrative assistantships, 70 teaching assistantships, Federal W/S, loans. Approved for VA benefits. Apply to Director of Financial Aid. No specified closing date. Use FAFSA and institutional FAF. Phone: (617)287-6300; fax: (617)287-6323.

DEGREE REQUIREMENTS. For master's: 30 credits minimum; thesis and general exam for some departments. For Ph.D.: 60 credits beyond the master's minimum; two semesters in full-time residence; qualifying exam; one foreign language required for some departments; dissertation; final oral exam. For Ed.D.: essentially the same as Ph.D. except no foreign language requirement.

FIELDS OF STUDY.
American Studies. M.A.
Applied Physics. M.S.
Applied Sociology. M.A.
Bilingual Education. M.A.
Biology. M.S.
Biotechnology and Biomedical Science. M.S.
Business Administration. M.B.A.
Chemistry. M.S.
Clinical Psychology. Ph.D.
Computer Science. M.S., Ph.D.
Counselor Training Education. M.Ed., C.A.G.S.
Critical and Creative Thinking. M.A., Graduate Certificate.
Dispute Resolution. M.A., Graduate Certificate.
Education (Elementary and Secondary). M.Ed., C.A.G.S.
Education/Higher Educational Administration. Ed.D.
Education/Leadership in Urban Schools. Ed.D.
Educational Administration. M.Ed., C.A.G.S.
English. M.A.
English as a Second Language. M.A.
Environmental Sciences. M.S., Ph.D.
Environmental Sciences/Environmental Biology. M.S., Ph.D.
Gerontology. Ph.D.
History. M.A.
History/Archival Methods. M.A.
History/Historical Archaeology. M.A.
Human Services. M.S.
Instructional Design. M.Ed.
Nursing. M.S., Ph.D.
Nursing/Business Administration. M.S.
Public Affairs. M.S.
Public Policy. Ph.D.
School Psychology. M.Ed., C.A.G.S.
Special Education. M.Ed.
Women in Politics. Graduate Certificate.

UNIVERSITY OF MASSACHUSETTS, DARTMOUTH

North Dartmouth, Massachusetts 02747-2300

Founded 1895. Located 50 miles S of Boston. Coed. State control. Semester system. Special facilities: Center for Marine Science and Technology (CMAST), Northeast Regional Aquaculture Center; research affiliations with Brookhaven National Lab (physics), Marine Biological Lab (marine sciences), and Woods Hole Oceanographic Institute (marine sciences); 2 Digital VAX 6610 mainframe computers; 150 IBM and Macintosh personal computers in cluster labs. Library: 334,000 volumes, 596,000 microforms, 2750 current periodicals, 40 PCs.

Annual tuition/fees: full-time, resident $3308, nonresident $10,378. Limited on-campus housing for graduate students. Average academic year housing cost: $3088. Contact Office of Residential Life for both on- and off-campus housing information. Phone: (508)999-8140.

Graduate School

Enrollment: full-time 181, part-time 270, Graduate faculty: full-time 134, part-time 5. Degrees conferred: M.A., M.S., M.F.A., M.B.A., M.A.E.

ADMISSION REQUIREMENTS. Official transcripts, three letters of recommendation required in support of School's application. GRE Subject Test/GMAT/MAT required by some programs. Interview not required. TOEFL required for international applicants. Accepts transfer applicants. Graduates of unaccredited institutions not considered. Apply to Graduate Admissions Office by April 20 (September), November 20 (January); international

applicants apply by February 20 (September), September 15 (January). Application fee resident $20, nonresident $40. Phone: (508)999-8604; fax: (508)999-8025.

ADMISSION STANDARDS. Selective. Usual minimum average: 2.75 (A = 4).

FINANCIAL AID. Limited to research fellowships, teaching assistantships, tuition waivers, Federal W/S, loans. Approved for VA benefits. Apply to Dean, Graduate School for fellowships, assistantships; to Financial Aid Office for all other programs. No specified closing date. Use FAFSA and University's FAF. Phone: (508)999-9632. About 20% of students receive aid other than loans from University. Aid available for part-time study.

DEGREE REQUIREMENTS. For master's: 30 credits minimum, at least 24 in residence; comprehensive exam; thesis/nonthesis option.

FIELDS OF STUDY.
Art Education.
Artisanry/Visual Design.
Biology/Marine Biology.
Business Administration.
Chemistry.
Computer Science.
Design. Portfolio for admission.
Electrical Engineering.
Fine Arts.
Graphic Design.
Nursing.
Physics.
Professional Writing.
Psychology.
Textile Chemistry.
Textile Technology.

UNIVERSITY OF MASSACHUSETTS, LOWELL

Lowell, Massachusetts 01854-2881
http://www.uml.edu

Founded 1897. Located 25 miles N of Boston. State control. Semester system. Special facilities: Center for the Arts, Center for Criminal Justice, Center for Family and Community Studies, Center for Field Service, Center for Health Promotion, Center for Lowell History, Pinaski Energy Center, Institute for Plastics Innovation, Center for Productivity Enhancement, Toxic Use Reduction Center, Tsongas Industrial History Center. Library: 388,000 volumes, 611,000 microforms.

Annual tuition/fees: full-time, resident $4982, nonresident $9173, per credit, resident $219, nonresident $427. On-campus housing available. Average academic year housing cost: $4800 (including board). Contact Housing Officer for on- and off-campus housing information. Phone: (508)934-2107.

The Graduate School

Founded 1935. Enrollment: full-time 1100, part-time 1850 (men 1700, women 1250). Faculty: full-time 450, part-time 50. Degrees conferred: M.S., M.Ed., M.B.A., M.M.S., M.S.Eng., M.A., C.A.G.S., M.M., Ph.D., D.Sc., D.Eng., D.Ed., Certificate.

ADMISSION REQUIREMENTS. Transcripts, three references, GRE Subject Tests/GMAT/MAT required in support of School's application. TOEFL required for international applicants. Interview not required. Accepts transfer applicants. Graduates of unaccredited institutions not considered. Apply to Graduate School Office by April 1 (Fall), November 1 (Spring). Phone: (800)656-GRAD or (508)934-5380.

ADMISSION STANDARDS. Selective. Usual minimum average: 2.75 (A = 4).

FINANCIAL AID. Annual awards from institutional funds: four hundred teaching assistantships, two hundred research fellowships, Federal W/S, loans. Approved for VA benefits. Apply by April 1 to appropriate department chair for assistantships; to Financial Aid Office for all other programs. Use FAFSA. Phone: (508)934-4220. About 10% of students receive aid other than loans from University and outside sources. No aid for part-time students.

DEGREE REQUIREMENTS. For master's: 30 credit hours minimum including thesis, at least one year in residence; final written/oral exam. For C.A.G.S.: 30 credits beyond the master's; project for some programs. For Certificates: twelve credits minimum; all credits applicable to master's degree. For Ph.D.: two to three years minimum in residence beyond the master's, depending upon previous preparation; preliminary exam; qualifying exam; dissertation; final oral exam. For D.Sc., D.Eng.: requirements are essentially the same as for Ph.D.

FIELDS OF STUDY.

COLLEGE OF ARTS AND SCIENCES (GRE FOR ALL PROGRAMS):
Biological Sciences. Includes biotechnology. M.S. only.
Chemistry. Includes biochemistry, environmental studies. M.S., Ph.D.
Community Social Psychology. M.A., M.A.T.
Computer Science. Includes Mathematical Science. M.S., D.Sc.
Criminal Justice. M.A.
Mathematics. Includes applied, mathematics for teachers, scientific computing, statistics and operators research. M.S. only.
Physics. Includes applied mechanics, energy engineering, optical sciences, radiological sciences. M.S., Ph.D.
Polymer Science. Includes plastics engineering. Ph.D. only.
Radiological Sciences and Protection. M.S. only.

COLLEGE OF EDUCATION (GRE OR MAT FOR ALL PROGRAMS):
Curriculum and Instruction. Includes ESL, teacher certification. M.Ed., C.A.G.S.
Educational Administration. M.Ed.
Educational Administration, Planning, and Policy. C.A.G.S. only.
Language Arts and Literacy. Ed.D.
Leadership in Schooling. Ed.D.
Mathematics and Science Education. Ed.D.
Reading and Language. M.Ed., C.A.G.S.

COLLEGE OF ENGINEERING (GRE FOR ALL PROGRAMS):
Civil Engineering. Includes environmental, geoenvironmental, geotechnical, structural, transportation. M.S.Eng.
Computer Engineering. M.S.Eng.
Electrical Engineering. Includes opto-electronics. M.S.Eng.
Energy Engineering. Includes nuclear, solar. M.S.Eng., Eng.D.
Environmental Studies. M.S.
Materials Sciences and Engineering. Includes electronic and photonic materials. M.S.Eng.
Mechanical Engineering. Includes manufacturing, mechanics and materials, thermo/fluid/energy, vibrations and dynamics. M.S.Eng., Eng.D.

Plastics Engineering. Includes coatings/adhesives, fibers/composites, synthetic fibers. M.S.Eng., Eng.D.
Work Environment. Includes epidemiology, industrial hygiene, occupational ergonomics, work environment policy. M.S., D.Sc.

COLLEGE OF FINE ARTS:
Music Performance. Includes conducting. M.M. only.

COLLEGE OF HEALTH PROFESSIONS (GRE FOR ALL PROGRAMS):
Clinical Laboratory Science. M.S.
Health Services Administration. M.S.
Nursing. Includes adult psychiatric/mental health nursing, family and community health nursing, gerontological nursing, occupational health nursing. M.S.
Physical Therapy. M.S.

COLLEGE OF MANAGEMENT:
Business Administration. GMAT for admission. M.B.A.
Management Science in Manufacturing. GMAT or GRE for admission. M.M.S.
Management Science in Sound Recording Technology. GMAT or GRE for admission. M.M.S.

MAYO MEDICAL SCHOOL
Rochester, Minnesota 55905

Established 1972. Graduate program affiliated with University of Minnesota since 1914. Special facilities: CDC CYBER 120/770, Digital PDP-11/44, Cancer Center. Library: 337,000 volumes, 3527 microforms, 16 PCs.

Annual tuition: residents of Arizona, Florida, and Minnesota $9925, nonresidents: $19,800. Off-campus housing available. Total average figure for all other expenses: $7820. Enrollment: first-year class 42 (EDP 2); total full-time 156 (men 52%, women 48%). Faculty: full-time 839, part-time 25. Degrees conferred: M.D., M.D.-M.S., M.D.-Ph.D.

ADMISSION REQUIREMENTS. AMCAS report, transcripts, MCAT, bachelor's degree, interview, recommendations required in support of application. Preference given to state residents. Graduates of unaccredited colleges not considered. Has EDP; apply between June 15 and August 1. Apply to Director of Admissions after June 15, before November 15. Application fee $40. Phone: (507)284-3671; fax: (507)284-2634.

ADMISSION STANDARDS. Very competitive. Accepts 4% of total annual applicants. Approximately 12% are state residents.

FINANCIAL AID. Limited. Scholarships, loans. Apply to Office of Student Affairs after appointment. There are special merit scholarships for residents of Arizona, Florida, and Minnesota. Use GAPSFAS. Phone: (507)284-4839.

DEGREE REQUIREMENTS. For M.D.: satisfactory completion of four-year program. For M.S.: one year beyond M.D.; knowledge of one foreign language; thesis/nonthesis option. For Ph.D.: at least two years beyond M.D.; knowledge of two foreign languages; one language/research tool; preliminary oral/written exam thesis; final oral exam.

FIELDS OF GRADUATE STUDY.
Biochemistry.
Biophysics.
Immunology.
Molecular Biology.

Neurosciences.
Pharmacology.
Physiology.

MCNEESE STATE UNIVERSITY
Lake Charles, Louisiana 70609-2495

Founded 1938. Located 130 miles W of Baton Rouge. Coed. State control. Semester system. Library: 249,000 volumes, 483,000 microforms.

Annual tuition, depending upon credit load: $1650 resident, nonresident $5180; 0–3 credits, resident $436, nonresident $824. On-campus housing for 116 married students, 1177 men, 425 women. Average annual housing cost: $4500 married students, $2500 (including board) for single students. Apply to Dean of Student Life for housing information. Phone: (318)475-5706.

Graduate School

Enrollment: full-time 203, part-time 955. Graduate faculty: full-time 130, part-time 20. Degrees conferred: M.A., M.S., M.F.A., M.Eng., M.B.A., M.Ed., M.M., Ed.S.

ADMISSION REQUIREMENTS. Transcripts, GRE required in support of School's application. TOEFL required for international applicants. Interview not required. Accepts transfer applicants. Graduates of unaccredited colleges not considered. Apply to Office of Registrar at least thirty days prior to registration. Application fee $10, foreign students $25. Phone: (318)475-5147.

ADMISSION STANDARDS. Relatively open. Usual minimum average: 2.0 (A = 4).

FINANCIAL AID. Ten scholarships, thirty research assistantships, sixty teaching assistantships, Federal W/S, loans. Apply to appropriate department head for scholarships, assistantships; to Office of Financial Aid for all other programs; no specified closing date. Use FAFSA and University's FAF. Phone: (319)475-5065. About 3% of students receive aid other than loans from University and outside sources. Aid available to part-time students.

DEGREE REQUIREMENTS. For master's: 30 semester hours minimum, at least 24 in residence; thesis required (for 6 hours) for M.A., M.S., optional for other master's; reading knowledge of one foreign language for some majors; final oral exam for all majors; final written exam for some majors. For Ed.S.: 30 semester hours minimum beyond the master's in residence; three years' teaching experience.

FIELDS OF STUDY.
Biology.
Business.
Business Administration.
Chemistry. One language for M.S.
Education, Administration, and Supervision. Includes guidance, elementary, health and physical education, early childhood education, educational technology, secondary education, special education, speech.
Engineering. Includes chemical, electrical, civil.
English. One language for M.A.
Environmental Sciences.
Fine Arts.
Mathematics, Computer Science, and Statistics. Final written exam for M.S.
Microbiology.

Music. Includes applied, education; audition and piano competency for admission to M.M.; public recital for M.M.; thesis/recital for M.M.Ed.
Psychology. Includes counseling, experimental, psychometric, school.

UNIVERSITY OF MEDICINE AND DENTISTRY OF NEW JERSEY
Newark, New Jersey 07103-2400

Established 1970. Coed. State control. Quarter system. Special facilities: Center for Advanced Biotechnology and Medicine, Environmental and Occupational Health Science Center, New Jersey Cancer Institute, New Jersey Eye Institute. Library: 192,000 volumes, 3900 current periodicals, 95 PCs. No on-campus housing available. Average academic year housing cost: $9634. Contact off-campus Housing Office for housing information. Phone: (201)982-5362.

New Jersey Dental School

Established 1956. Located in Newark. Annual tuition: resident $14,492, nonresident $22,679. Total average cost for all other first-year expenses: $3443.

Enrollment: first-year class 75; total 323 (men 65%, women 35%); postgraduates 23. Faculty: full-time 70, part-time 81: Degrees conferred: D.M.D., Certificates.

ADMISSION REQUIREMENTS. AADSAS report, transcripts, 3 letters of recommendation, DAT required in support of application. Interview by invitation only. Preference given to state residents. Applicants must have completed at least 3 but preferably 4 years of college study; most applicants have bachelor's degree. Apply to AADSAS after June 1, before March 1. Application fee $50. Phone: (201)982-4583.

ADMISSION STANDARDS. Competitive. Accepts 20–25% of total annual applicants. Approximately 85% are state residents.

FINANCIAL AID. Scholarships, fellowships. Apply after acceptance to Office of Financial Aid. Use FAFSA. Phone: (201)982-4376. About 99% of students receive aid from School.

DEGREE REQUIREMENTS. For D.M.D.: satisfactory completion of four-year program.

CERTIFICATE PROGRAMS.
Endodontics.
Oral and Maxillofacial Surgery.
Orthodontics.
Pediatric Dentistry.
Periodontics.
Prosthodontics.

New Jersey Medical School

Located in Newark (07103). Annual tuition: resident $14,092, nonresident $22,679; student fees $1106. Total average figure for all other expenses: $9000.

Enrollment: first-year class 170 (EDP 3); total 705 (men 60%, women 40%); postgraduates 318. School faculty: full-time 608. Degrees conferred: M.D., M.D.-Ph.D.

ADMISSION REQUIREMENTS. AMCAS report, transcripts, MCAT required in support of application. Applicants must have completed at least three years of college study. Preference given to New Jersey residents. Interviews by invitation only. Has EDP;

apply between June 15 and August 1. Apply to Director of Admissions after June 15, before December 15. Application fee $50. Phone: (201)982-4631; fax: (201)982-7986.

ADMISSION STANDARDS. Competitive. Accepts 10% of total annual applicants. Approximately 90% are state residents.

FINANCIAL AID. Scholarships and loans. Apply to Financial Aid Office after acceptance. Use FAFSA. About 70% of the students receive some form of financial aid.

DEGREE REQUIREMENTS. For M.D.: satisfactory completion of four-year program.

FIELDS OF GRADUATE STUDY.
Anatomy.
Biochemistry.
Microbiology.
Neurosciences.
Pathology.
Pharmacology.
Physiology.

Robert Wood Johnson Medical School

Established 1966. Located at Piscataway (08854-5635) and a division at Camden. Annual tuition: resident $14,492, nonresident $22,679, student fees $939. Total average figure for all other expenses: $8890.

Enrollment: first-year class 142 (EDP 6); total 598 (men 63%, women 37%). Faculty: full- and part-time 636. Degrees conferred: M.D., M.D.-M.P.H., M.D.-Ph.D.

ADMISSION REQUIREMENTS. AMCAS report, transcripts, MCAT required in support of application. Interview by invitation only. Applicants should have completed four years of college study. Has EDP; apply between June 15 and August 1. Apply to Committee on Admissions of School after June 15, before December 15 (Fall). Application fee $50. Phone: (908)235-4576; fax: (908)235-5078.

ADMISSION STANDARDS. Competitive. Accepts 10–12% of total annual applicants. Approximately 90% are state residents.

FINANCIAL AID. Scholarships, grants, loans. About 75% of students receive some aid from School. Apply to Financial Aid Office; no specified closing date.

DEGREE REQUIREMENTS. For M.D.: satisfactory completion of four-year program. For Ph.D., see Graduate School listing for Rutgers University.

FIELDS OF GRADUATE STUDY.
Anatomy.
Biochemistry.
Biomedical Engineering.
Biophysics.
Cell Biology.
Genetics.
Immunology.
Microbiology.
Molecular Biology.
Pathology.
Pharmacology.
Physiology.

School of Osteopathic Medicine

Founded 1976. Located in Stratford (08084-1504). No on-campus housing available.

Annual tuition: resident $13,295, nonresident $17,445. Enrollment: first-year class 75, total 250 (men 56%, women 44%), 90%

state residents. Faculty: full-time 107, part-time 18. Degree conferred: D.O.

ADMISSION REQUIREMENTS. AACOMAS report, bachelor's degree, transcripts, MCAT, letters of recommendation from premed advisory committee, evaluation from a physician (preferably a D.O.). Preference given to state residents. Interview by invitation only. Has EDP. Graduates of unaccredited colleges not considered. Apply by February 1. Admits first-year students Fall only. Application fee $25. Phone: (609)566-7050; fax: (609)566-6895.

ADMISSION STANDARDS. Selective. Accepts approximately 15% of annual applications. Usual minimum average: 3.0 (A = 4). Mean GPA: 3.4

FINANCIAL AID. Scholarships, HEAL, HPSL, Federal W/S, loans. Apply after acceptance to Financial Aid Office. Use FAFSA.

DEGREE REQUIREMENTS. For D.O.: satisfactory completion of four-year program.

MEHARRY MEDICAL COLLEGE
Nashville, Tennessee 37208-9989

Founded 1976. Coed. Private control. Semester system. Library: 80,000 volumes.

On-campus housing for single students only. Average academic year housing cost: $6130 (including board).

School of Graduate Studies

Annual tuition: $7700. Enrollment: full-time 144, part-time 11. Faculty: full-time 9. Degrees conferred: M.S.P.H., Ph.D.

ADMISSION REQUIREMENTS. Official transcripts, GRE, two letters of recommendation, statement summarizing research interests and career plans required in support of School's application. TOEFL required for international applicants. Accepts transfer applicants. Graduates of unaccredited institutions not considered. Apply to Director of Admissions and Records by June 1. Application fee $25. Phone: (615)327-6533.

ADMISSION STANDARDS. Competitive. Usual minimum average: 3.0 (A = 4).

FINANCIAL AID. Annual awards from institutional funds: scholarships, assistantships, Federal W/S, loans. Apply to Financial Aid Office by April 1. Use FAFSA.

DEGREE REQUIREMENTS. For M.S.P.H.: 60 credits minimum; thesis and extensive fieldwork. For Ph.D.: 40 credits minimum beyond the bachelor's, at least 30 in residence; qualifying exam; dissertation; final oral exam.

FIELDS OF STUDY.
Biochemistry.
Biomedical Sciences.
Community Health Sciences. M.S.P.H.
Microbiology.
Pharmacology.
Physiology.

School of Medicine

Founded 1876 as Medical Department of Central Tennessee College; became independent in 1915. Annual tuition: $17,820. Total average cost for all other expenses: $7900. Enrollment:

first-year class (EDP 6); total 322 (men 48%, women 52%). Degree conferred: M.D.

ADMISSION REQUIREMENTS. AMCAS, transcripts, MCAT, interview required in support of application. Applicants must have completed at least three years of college study. Accepts transfer applicants. Has EDP; apply between June 15 and August 1. Apply to Director of Admissions after June 1, before December 15. Application fee $25. Phone: (615)327-6223; fax: (615)327-6228.

ADMISSION STANDARDS. Very competitive. Accepts about 3% of total applicants. Approximately 10% are state residents.

FINANCIAL AID. Scholarships, loans. Apply to Director, Student Financial Aid by April 15. About 85% of students receive some aid.

DEGREE REQUIREMENTS. For M.D.: satisfactory completion of four-year program.

School of Dentistry

Organized 1886. Annual tuition: $18,025. Housing for 158 married students, 100 single graduate students. Average academic year housing cost: $7113. Apply to Director of Housing Services. Total average cost for all other first-year expenses: $4051.

Enrollment: first-year class 51; total 180 (men 35%, women 65%). School faculty: full-time 62, part-time 39. Degree conferred: D.D.S.

ADMISSION REQUIREMENTS. AADSAS report, transcripts, three letters of recommendation, DAT, supplemental application required in support of School's application. Applicants must have completed at least three years of college study. Interview not required. Preference given to SREB member states. Accepts transfer applicants from U.S. and Canadian dental schools. Apply to Office of Admissions and Records after April 1. Application fee $25. Phone: (615)327-6223.

ADMISSION STANDARDS. Selective. Accepts 15–20% of total annual applicants. Approximately 10% are state residents.

FINANCIAL AID. Scholarships, grants, loans. Apply to Director of Financial Aid after acceptance. Use FAFSA. Phone: (615)327-8626. About 95% of students receive some aid from School funds.

DEGREE REQUIREMENTS. For D.D.S.: satisfactory completion of forty-four-month program.

THE UNIVERSITY OF MEMPHIS
Memphis, Tennessee 38152
http://www.memphis.edu

Established 1912, name changed from Memphis State University in 1994. Coed. State control. Semester system. Library: more than 1 million volumes, more than 2.7 million microforms.

Annual tuition: resident $2674, nonresident $7010. On-campus housing for single students and families. Apply to Director of Residence Life. Phone: (901)678-2295.

Graduate School

Graduate study since 1951. Enrollment: full-time 1880, part-time 2555 (men 1886, women 2549). Faculty: full-time 973, part-time 212. Degrees conferred: M.A., M.A.T., M.B.A., M.H.A., M.S., M.F.A., M.P.A., M.C.R.P., D.M.A., M.Mu., Ed.S., Ed.D., Ph.D.

ADMISSION REQUIREMENTS: Transcripts, GRE/GMAT/MAT required in support of School's application. For additional requirements contact individual program chair. TOEFL required of international students. Accepts transfer applicants. Graduates of unaccredited colleges not considered. Graduate School application deadlines: August 1 (Fall), December 1 (Spring), May 1 (Summer). Some programs may have earlier deadlines. Application fee $5. Phone: (901)678-2911; fax: (901)678-3003; E-mail: MSCHAFER@UMEM.MEMPHIS.EDU.

ADMISSION STANDARDS. Selective for most departments, very selective for some departments. Usual minimum average: 2.75 (A = 4).

FINANCIAL AID. Limited fellowships, 448 research assistantships, 1268 administrative assistantships, 333 teaching assistantships, Federal W/S, loans. Apply to individual chairs for assistantships; to Financial Aid Office for all other programs. Use FAFSA. Phone: (901)678-4825; fax: (901)678-3590.

DEGREE REQUIREMENTS. For master's: 30 semester hours minimum; thesis; final oral/written exam; or 33 semester hours minimum; no thesis; final oral/written exam for most departments. For Doctorates: three years, at least one year in full-time residence; reading knowledge of one foreign language or statistics/ research tool or both; preliminary exam; dissertation; final oral exam. Contact program chair for additional degree requirements.

FIELDS OF STUDY.

COLLEGE OF ARTS AND SCIENCES:
Anthropology. M.A. only.
Biology. M.S., Ph.D.
Chemistry. M.S., Ph.D.
City and Regional Planning. M.C.R.P.
Creative Writing. M.F.A. only.
Criminal Justice. M.A. only.
English. M.A. only.
Geography. M.A., M.S.
Geology. M.S. only.
Geophysics. Ph.D. only.
Health Administration. M.H.A. only.
History. M.A., Ph.D.
Mathematics. M.S., Ph.D.
Philosophy. M.A., Ph.D.
Physics. M.S. only.
Political Science. M.A. only.
Psychology. M.S., Ph.D.
Public Administration. M.P.A. only.
Romance Languages. M.A. only.
School Psychology. M.A. only.
Sociology. M.A. only.

FOGELMAN COLLEGE OF BUSINESS AND ECONOMICS:
Accounting. M.S. only.
Business Administration. M.S., M.B.A., Ph.D.
Economics. M.A. only.

COLLEGE OF COMMUNICATION AND FINE ARTS:
Art. M.F.A. only.
Art History. M.A. only.
Communication. M.A. only.
Journalism. M.A. only.
Music. M.M., D.M.A., Ph.D.
Theater. M.F.A. only.

COLLEGE OF EDUCATION:
Clinical Nutrition. M.S. only.
Consumer Science and Education. M.S. only.
Counseling and Personnel Services. M.S., Ed.D.

Counseling Psychology. Ph.D. only.
Education. Ed.S. only.
Educational Psychology and Research. M.S., Ed.D.
Exercise Science and Health Promotion. M.S. only.
Higher and Adult Education. Ed.D. only.
Instruction and Curriculum Leadership. M.S., Ed.D.
Leadership and Policy Studies. M.S., Ed.D.
Teaching. M.A.T. only.

HERFF COLLEGE OF ENGINEERING:
Biomedical Engineering. M.S. only.
Civil Engineering. M.S. only.
Electrical Engineering. M.S. only.
Engineering. Ph.D. only.
Engineering Technology. M.S. only.
Industrial and Systems Engineering. M.S. only.
Mechanical Engineering. M.S. only.

SCHOOL OF AUDIOLOGY AND SPEECH-LANGUAGE PATHOLOGY:
Audiology and Speech Pathology. M.A., Ph.D.

Cecil C. Humphreys School of Law (38152)

Founded 1962. Semester system. Law library: 245,300 volumes. Library has LEXIS, NEXIS, WESTLAW, DIALOG.

Annual tuition: full-time, resident $3852, nonresident $9680. On-campus housing available; expenses: $4500 (includes room and board). Apply to Director of Residence Life.

Enrollment: first-year class 157; total 425 (men 53%, women 47%). Faculty: full-time 22, part-time 21. Degrees conferred: J.D., J.D.-M.B.A.

ADMISSION REQUIREMENTS. LSDAS Law School report, bachelor's degree, transcripts, LSAT required in support of application. Interview not required. Accepts transfer applicants. Graduates of unaccredited colleges not considered. Apply by February 1. Fall admission only. Application fee $10. Phone: (901)678-2073.

ADMISSION STANDARDS. Selective. Accepts 30–35% of total annual applicants.

FINANCIAL AID. Scholarships, assistantships, Federal W/S, loans. Apply to Financial Aid Office by April 1. About 25% of students receive aid other than loans from School. Use FAFSA.

DEGREE REQUIREMENTS. For J.D.: satisfactory completion of three-year program; 90 credit-hour program.

MERCER UNIVERSITY
Macon, Georgia 31207-0003

Founded 1833. Located 92 miles S of Atlanta. Private control. Baptist. Quarter system. Library: 404,800 volumes, 242,000 microforms, 35 PCs.

Tuition: per credit hour, Liberal Arts $90, Engineering $210, Business $150, University College $137. On-campus housing for 70 married students, 650 men, 510 women. Average academic year housing cost: $3900–$5000 for married students, $2085 (room only), $4365 (includes full board) for single students. Phone: (912)752-2687.

Graduate Programs

Enrollment: full- and part-time 1074. University faculty teaching graduate students: full-time 386, part-time 147. Degrees conferred: M.Ed., M.B.A., M.S.E., M.S., M.S.M., M.F.S., S.Ed.

ADMISSION REQUIREMENTS. Transcripts, letters of reference, GRE/NTE/MAT/GMAT tests required in support of application. TOEFL required for international applicants. Interview not required. Accepts transfer applicants. Graduates of unaccredited institutions sometimes considered. Apply to Director of Graduate Programs; no specified closing dates. Application fee none. Phone: (912)752-4151.

ADMISSION STANDARDS. Selective for most departments. Usual minimum average: 3.0 (A = 4); GRE score: 35th percentile.

FINANCIAL AID. Limited to ten supervising teacher scholarships (Summer only), Federal W/S, loans (academic year). Approved for VA benefits. Apply to the Financial Aid Office; no specified closing date. Use FAFSA. Phone: (912)752-2670.

DEGREE REQUIREMENTS. For M.Ed., M.B.A.: 60 quarter hours minimum. For M.S.E., M.S.: 48 quarter hours minimum. For M.S.M., M.F.S.: 62 quarter hours minimum. For S.Ed.: 35 quarter hours minimum; special project.

FIELDS OF STUDY.
Biomedical Engineering.
Computer and Information Systems.
Education. Includes early childhood, English, mathematics, middle grades, reading, science, social science.
Electrical Engineering.
Engineering Management.
Family Studies/Family Therapy.
Finance.
General Business.
Management/Marketing.
Mechanical Engineering.
Service Management.
Technical Management.

Walter F. George School of Law

Established 1873. Semester system. Law library: 260,000 volumes. Library has LEXIS, NEXIS, WESTLAW, DIALOG.

Annual tuition: full-time $17,490. No on-campus housing available.

Enrollment: first-year class 160; total full-time 420 (men 60%, women 40%); no part-time students. Faculty: full-time 29, part-time 19. Degrees conferred: J.D., J.D.-M.B.A.

ADMISSION REQUIREMENTS. LSDAS Law School report, bachelor's degree, transcripts, LSAT, three letters of recommendation required in support of application. Interviews are encouraged. Accepts transfer applicants. Graduate of unaccredited colleges not considered. Apply to Director of Admissions after September 1, before April 1. Beginning students admitted Fall only. Application fee $35. Phone: (800)MERCER-U, ext. 2605.

ADMISSION STANDARDS. Selective. Accepts 25–30% of total annual applicants.

FINANCIAL AID. Scholarships and loans. Apply by May 1 (flexible) to Director of Admissions. Use FAFSA.

DEGREE REQUIREMENTS. For J.D.: satisfactory completion of three-year program; 90 credit-hour program. For M.B.A.: see Graduate School listing above.

School of Medicine

Established 1982. Annual tuition: resident $18,890. Enrollment: first-year class 56 (EDP 10): total 175 (men 59%, women 41%). Faculty: full-time 186, part-time 81. Degree conferred: M.D.

ADMISSION REQUIREMENTS. AMCAS report, transcripts, MCAT, two letters of recommendation or one premedical committee evaluation, essay, Certificate of Georgia residency required in support of application. Interview by invitation only. Accepts only state residents. Has EDP; apply between June 15 and August 1. Graduates of unaccredited colleges not considered. Apply to Office of Admissions and Student Affairs after June 15, before December 1. Application fee $25. Phone: (912)752-2524.

ADMISSION STANDARDS. Competitive. Admits about 20% of total annual applicants. 100% are state residents.

FINANCIAL AID. Scholarships, loans. Apply after acceptance to Office of Admissions and Student Affairs. Use FAFSA. About 20% of students receive some aid from School.

DEGREE REQUIREMENTS. For M.D.: satisfactory completion of four-year program.

MIAMI UNIVERSITY
Oxford, Ohio 45056

Founded 1809. Located 35 miles NW of Cincinnati. Coed. State control. Semester system. Special facilities: academic centers located in Hamilton, Middletown; Bachelor Wildlife Reserve, Willard Sherman Turrell Herbarium, Institute of Environmental Sciences, Scripps Gerontology Center. Library: 1,200,000 volumes, 1,800,000 microforms.
Annual tuition: full-time, resident $5110, nonresident $10,500. Limited on-campus housing available. Annual academic year housing cost: $5000. Apply to Office of Student Housing for housing information. Phone: (513)529-5000.

Graduate School

Graduate study since 1820, became Graduate School 1947. Enrollment: full-time, 996, part-time 835. Faculty teaching graduate students: full-time 600, part-time 40. Degrees conferred: M.A., M.A.T., M.B.A., M.Ed., M.F.A., M.M., M.S., M.Arch., M.Env.Sci., M.G.S., M.S. in Stats., M.T.S.C., M.Acc., Specialist, Ph.D.

ADMISSION REQUIREMENTS. Two transcripts, GRE/MAT/GMAT required in support of School's application. Proof of proficiency in English or TOEFL required of international applicants. Accepts transfer applicants. Graduates of unaccredited institutions not considered. Apply to School at least three months prior to registration. Application fee $35. Phone: (513)529-4125; fax: (513)529-3762.

ADMISSION STANDARDS. Selective for all departments. Minimum average: 2.75 (A = 4).

FINANCIAL AID. Annual awards from institutional funds: 10 scholarships, 56 grants, 30 tuition waivers, 100 research assistantships, 150 administrative assistantships, 600 teaching assistantships, 10 fellowships, Federal W/S, loans. Apply by March 1 to Dean of Graduate School. Use FAFSA. Phone: (513)529-8734. About 75% of full-time students receive aid other than loans from both School and outside sources. Aid sometimes available for part-time students.

DEGREE REQUIREMENTS. For M.A.: 30 credit hours minimum, at least 15 in residence; preliminary oral/written exam; thesis; final oral/written exam. For M.A.T.: 30 credit hours minimum, at least 15 in residence; thesis; preliminary oral/written exam; final oral/written exam. For M.B.A.: 76 credit hours minimum, all in residence; oral/written comprehensive exam. For M.Env.Set.: 36 credit hours minimum; written comprehensive exam; thesis. For M.Ed.: 30 credit hours minimum; field study; preliminary oral/written exam; comprehensive oral/written exam. For M.F.A., M.Arch.: 60 credit hours minimum; preliminary oral/written exam; thesis; final project; final oral/written exam. For M.M.: 33 credit hours generally required. For M.S.,

M.S. in Stats.: 30 hours minimum, at least 15 in residence; preliminary oral/written exam; final oral/written exam. For M.T.S.C.: 32 credit hours minimum, at least 16 in residence; thesis or internship; qualifying exam; final oral/written exam. For M.Acc.: 33 credit hours minimum, at least 17 in residence; oral/written comprehensive exam. For M.G.S., Specialist: 30 credits beyond the master's, at least 24 in residence. For Ph.D.: 60 credit hours beyond the master's, at least 48 in residence; oral/written comprehensive exam; dissertation; final exam.

FIELDS OF STUDY.
Accountancy. GMAT for admission. Master's only.
Architecture. Master's only.
Art. Master's only.
Art Education. Master's only.
Biological Sciences Education. Master's only.
Botany. M.A., M.S., M.A.T., Ph.D.
Business. GMAT for admission. Master's only.
Chemistry. M.S., Ph.D.
Child and Family Studies. Master's only.
Economics. Master's only.
Education. Includes educational administration, student personnel services, curriculum and leadership, elementary, secondary, reading, sport studies, exercise and health studies, educational psychology; Ph.D./Ed.D. in administration and curriculum only.
English. M.A., M.A.T., M.T.S.C., Ph.D.
Environmental Sciences. MAT for admission. Master's only.
Finance. GMAT for admission. Master's only.
French. Master's only
Geography. Master's only.
Geology. M.A., M.S., Ph.D.
Gerontological Studies. Master's only.
History. Master's only.
Management. GMAT for admission. Master's only.
Management Information Systems. Master's only.
Marketing. GMAT for admission. Master's only.
Mass Communication. Master's only.
Mathematics. Master's only.
Microbiology. M.A., M.S., Ph.D.
Music. Includes music education, performance. Master's only.
Paper Science and Engineering. Master's only.
Philosophy. Master's only.
Physics. Master's only.
Political Science. M.A., M.A.T., Ph.D.
Psychology. GRE for admission. Ph.D. only.
Religion. Master's only.
School Psychology. Nine-month internship for M.S.; M.S., Ed.S.
Spanish. Master's only.
Special Education. Master's only.
Speech Communication. Master's only.
Speech Pathology and Audiology. Master's only.
Statistics. Master's only.
System Analysis. Master's only.
Technical and Scientific Communication. M.A. only.
Theater. Master's only.
Zoology. M.A., M.S., M.A.T., Ph.D.

UNIVERSITY OF MIAMI
Coral Gables, Florida 33124

Founded 1925. Located 12 miles SW of Miami. Coed. Private control. Semester system. Special facilities: Lowe Art Museum, Bascome Palmer Eye Institute, Comprehensive Cancer Center for Florida, Rosenstiel School of Marine and Atmospheric Sciences, Graduate School International Studies, Mailman Center for Child Development, the Ungar Computing Center; Organization for Tropical Studies, Inc., sponsoring university of the Oak Ridge Associated Universities in Oak Ridge, Tennessee, special environmental-ecology field stations, Long Pine Key, Fairchild Tropical Gardens. Library: 2,030,000 volumes, 3,020,000 microforms.

Tuition: per credit $746. On-campus housing for married and single students. Average academic year housing cost: $6935. Apply to Director, Residence Halls. Phone: (305)284-4505.

Graduate School

Organized 1941. Enrollment: full-time 2514, part-time 736. Graduate faculty: full-time 1884, part-time 502. Degrees conferred: M.A., M.S., M.B.A., M.S.Ed., M.Arch., M.M., M.F.A., M.P.Acc., M.S.Tax., M.P.H., M.S.P.H., M.P.A., M.P.T., M.S.P.T., M.S.N., M.S.B.E., M.S.I.E., M.S.C.E., M.S.M.E., M.S.E.C.F., M.S.O.E., Spec.M., Ed.S., Ed.D., Ph.D., D.M.A., D.A.

ADMISSION REQUIREMENTS. Transcripts, letters of recommendation, GRE Subject Tests required in support of School's application. GMAT for M.B.A. TOEFL required for international applicants. Interview required for some programs. Graduates of unaccredited institutions not considered. Apply to individual program directors. Admissions by February 1 (Fall). Application fee $35. Phone: (305)284-4154.

ADMISSION STANDARDS. Selective for most departments, very competitive for others. Usual minimum average: 3.0 (A = 4).

FINANCIAL AID. Annual awards from institutional funds: 22 scholarships, 60 fellowships, 250 research assistantships, 400 teaching assistantships, Federal W/S, loans. Approved for VA benefits. Apply by February 1 to individual program directors for scholarships, assistantships, fellowships; to Financial Aid Office for all other programs. Use FAFSA. Phone: (305)284-5212; fax: (305)284-4082. About 50% of students receive aid other than loans from University and outside sources.

DEGREE REQUIREMENTS. For M.A., M.S.: 30 semester credits minimum, at least 24 in residence; reading knowledge of one foreign language for many departments; thesis/comprehensive exam; up to 6 credits for thesis if required. For M.B.A.: 39 credits minimum, at least 30 in residence; additional study may be required, depending upon previous preparation. For M.S.Ed.: 30–60 credits, depending on department, at least 30 in residence. For M.M.: 30 credits minimum, at least 24 in residence; thesis for up to 6 credits for majors in music education or theory-composition; recital for three credits for applied music major; final oral exam in defense of thesis for music education majors. For M.F.A.: 36–60 credits, depending on department. For D.M.A.: 90 credits beyond the bachelor's, essentially the same as for the Ph.D., except a creative effort/performance and doctoral essay instead of dissertation. For D.A.: essentially the same as for the Ph.D., except a college teaching internship and scholarly investigation replace the dissertation. For Ph.D.: 60 credits minimum beyond the bachelor's, at least 24 in residence and two consecutive semesters in full-time attendance; qualifying exam; dissertation for at least 12 credits; final oral exam; final written exam sometimes required. For Ed.D.: 85 credits minimum beyond the bachelor's, at least 30 in residence and two consecutive semesters in full-time attendance; preliminary exam; written comprehensive exam; proficiency in four research tools, which may include language, statistics, or similar methods; research project; final oral exam.

FIELDS OF STUDY.

COLLEGE OF ARTS AND SCIENCES:
Art. Includes art history (M.A.), painting, sculpture, weaving, graphic design, printmaking, art studio; M.F.A.
Behavioral Medicine.
Biology.
Chemistry.
Computer Science.
Ecology.
English.
Foreign Languages. Includes French, German, Portuguese, Russian, Spanish; three languages for M.A.
History.
Liberal Studies.
Mathematics.
Philosophy.
Physics.
Psychology.
Romance Languages.
Sociology.
Spanish.
Tropical Biology.

SCHOOL OF BUSINESS ADMINISTRATION:
Accounting.
Applied Statistics and Computer Models. M.S. only.
Business Administration.
Computer Information System.
Economics.
Management Science.
Operations Research.
Public Administration.

SCHOOL OF EDUCATION AND ALLIED PROFESSIONS:
Administration, Curriculum, and Instruction. Includes elementary, secondary, general, school-based management, health, public agency management, higher, college student personnel services.
Counseling Psychology/Counselor Education.
Educational Psychology.
Elementary Education.
Exceptional Citizen. Includes behavior disorders, deafness, learning disabilities, mental retardation, motor disabilities, varying exceptionalities.
Exercise Physiology.
Health, Physical Education, and Recreation.
Instructional Technology.
Reading.
Recreation Therapy.
Research, Evaluation and Statistics.
Sports Administration.
Sports Health/Athletic Training.

COLLEGE OF ENGINEERING:
Architectural Engineering.
Biomedical Engineering.
Civil Engineering.
Electrical Engineering.
Ergonomics.
Industrial Engineering.
Mechanical Engineering.

SCHOOL OF MEDICINE-LIFE SCIENCES:
Anatomy.
Biochemistry.
Cellular and Molecular Biology.
Epidemiology and Public Health.
Microbiology and Immunology.
Neuroscience.
Pharmacology.
Physical Therapy.
Physiology and Biophysics.
Radiological Science.

ROSENSTILL SCHOOL OF MARINE AND ATMOSPHERIC SCIENCES:
Applied Marine Physics.
Marine Affairs and Policy.

Marine and Atmospheric Chemistry.
Marine Biology and Fisheries.
Marine Geology and Geophysics.
Meteorology and Physical Oceanography.
Ocean Engineering.
Joint Degree. Programs with Engineering and Law schools available.

SCHOOL OF MUSIC:
Jazz Composition.
Music Business and Entertainment Industries.
Music Education.
Music Engineering.
Musicology.
Music Performance.
Music Theory and Composition.

SCHOOL OF NURSING:
Adult Health.
Transcultural Nursing.

SCHOOL OF COMMUNICATION:
Communication Studies.
Journalism.
Motion Picture.
Public Relations Administration.

SCHOOL OF ARCHITECTURE:
Architecture.

GRADUATE SCHOOL OF INTERNATIONAL STUDIES:
Inter-American Studies.
International Studies.

School of Law

Established 1928 Semester system. Law library: 412,100 volumes. Library has LEXIS, NEXIS, WESTLAW, LEGALTRAC. Annual tuition: $20,712 (day), $15,100 (evening). Limited on-campus housing available. Total average annual additional expense: $13,500.

Enrollment: first-year class 410 (day), 60 (evening); total 1500 (men 58%, women 42%); postgraduates: 118. Faculty: full-time 54, part-time 76. Degrees conferred: J.D., LL.M. (Inter-American Law, International Law, Ocean and Coastal Law, Taxation, Estate Planning, Real Property Development and Finance Law), M.C.L.

ADMISSION REQUIREMENTS. LSDAS Law School report, bachelor's degree, transcripts, LSAT, three letters of recommendation required in support of application. Interview not required. Accepts transfer applicants. Graduates of unaccredited colleges not considered. Apply to Director of Law Admissions after September 1, before March 6. Application fee $40. Phone: (305)284-2523.

ADMISSION STANDARDS. Selective. Accepts 40–45% of total annual applicants.

FINANCIAL AID. Scholarships, Federal W/S, loans. Apply to Financial Aid Office by March 1 (Fall). Use FAFSA. About 11% of students receive aid other than loans from School funds.

DEGREE REQUIREMENTS. For J.D.: 88 credits minimum, at least the last 28 credits and 36 weeks in residence. For LL.M.: at least 24 credits minimum beyond the J.D. and 36 weeks in resident; thesis.
Note: Summer program at University College (London) available.

School of Medicine (33101)

Opened 1952. Annual tuition: $21,940. Limited on-campus housing available. Total average figure for all other expenses: $13,200.

Enrollment: first-year class 138 (EDP 10); total 561 (men 60%, women 40%). Faculty: full-time 971, part-time 60. Degrees conferred: B.S.-M.D., M.D., M.D.-M.S., M.D.-Ph.D. The M.S. and Ph.D. are offered through the Graduate School.

ADMISSION REQUIREMENTS. AMCAS, transcripts, undergraduate faculty evaluation, two personal references, MCAT (preferably in spring) required in support of application. Interview by invitation only. Applicants must have completed at least three years of college study. Preference given to Florida residents. Has EDP; apply between June 15 and August 1. Accepts transfer applicants. Apply to Office of Admissions after July 1, before December 1. Application fee $50. Phone: (305)547-6791; fax: (305)547-6548. For M.D.-Ph.D. program GRE required. Application fee $50.

ADMISSION STANDARDS. Selective. Accepts 15% of total annual applicants. Approximately 90% are state residents.

FINANCIAL AID. Limited. Scholarships, loans. Apply to Office of Financial Aid after acceptance, before April 1. Phone: (305)547-6211. Use FAFSA. About 80% of students receive aid from School and outside sources.

DEGREE REQUIREMENTS. For B.S.-M.D.: satisfactory completion of seven-year program. For M.D.: satisfactory completion of four-year program. For Ph.D. to M.D.: satisfactory completion of two-year M.D. program. For M.S., Ph.D., see Graduate School listing above.

FIELDS OF GRADUATE STUDY.
Anatomy.
Biochemistry.
Biophysics.
Cell Biology.
Immunology.
Microbiology.
Molecular Biology.
Neurosciences.
Pharmacology.
Physiology.

MICHIGAN STATE UNIVERSITY
East Lansing, Michigan 48824-1020
http:WEB.MSU.EDU/

Founded 1855. Located 80 miles NW of Detroit. Coed. State control. Semester system. Special facilities: Abrams Planetarium, African Studies Center, Agricultural Experiment Station, Alumni Memorial Chapel, Animal Health Diagnostic Laboratory, Asian Studies Center, Bioelectromagnetics Laboratory, Biological Research Center, Breslin Student Events Center, Carcinogenesis Laboratory, Career Information Center, Center for Advanced Study of International Development, Center for Electron Optics, Center for Environmental Toxicology, Center for International Programs, Center for International Transportation Exchange, Center for Remote Sensing, Center for Urban Affairs, Clinical Center (outpatient facility), Cooperative Extension Service, Counseling Center, English Language Center, Fairchild Theater, Forest Akers Golf Courses, Genetics Clinic, Hematology Oncology Clinic, Hidden Lake Gardens, Institute for Research on Teaching, Institute for Water Research, Institute of Agricultural Technology, Institute of International Agriculture, Institute of Nutrition, Institute of Public Utilities, IPTV (3 TV stations, TV teaching auditorium, closed-circuit TV), Jenison

Gymnasium and Fieldhouse, Journalism/Law Institute, Kellogg Center (hotel/restaurant), Kellogg Center for Continuing Education, Kresge Art Center and Museum, Laboratory Animal Care Service, Language Laboratory, Latin American Studies Center, Learning Resources Center, Livestock Pavilion, Living-Learning (dorm-classroom) Centers, MSU/DOE Plant Research Laboratory, MSU Laboratory Preschool, MSU Union, Munn Ice Arena, National Superconducting Cyclotron, Olin Health Center, Pesticide Research Center, Psychological Clinic, Service-Learning Center (volunteers), Social Science Research Bureau, Spartan Nursery School, Spartan Stadium, Speech and Hearing Clinic, University Auditorium, University Center for International Rehabilitation, University Museum, university radio stations (AM/FM), Veterinary Clinical Center, Wharton Center for Performing Arts (Festival Stage and Great Hall), W. J. Beal Botanical Garden and Campus Plant Collection, and W. K. Kellogg Biological Station. Graduate study available through many of 7 off-campus extensions centers. Library: approximately 3,900,000 volumes, 4,800,000 microforms.

Annual tuition (academic year): full-time, resident $5034, nonresident $10,182; per credit, resident $203, nonresident $412. On-campus housing: Owen Graduate Center (476 graduate men and 396 graduate women at $3193 per academic year with minimum board included) and 2175 apartments available to undergraduate and graduate single and married students (1160 one-bedroom apartments, each available to 1–2 students at average monthly cost of $340 per apartment, and 1025 one- and two-bedroom family apartments at average monthly cost of $365 per apartment). Apply to University Housing Office or University Apartments for on-campus housing or to Off-Campus Housing Office. Phone: (517)355-7457. Day care facilities available.

Graduate School

Graduate study since 1863. Enrollment: full- and part-time 7825. University faculty teaching students: full- and part-time 2670. Degrees conferred: M.A., M.A.T., M.B.A., M.F.A., M.L.R.H.R., M.Mus., M.P.A., M.S., M.S.N., M.S.W., M.U.P., Ed.S., D.M.A., Ed.D., D.O., D.V.M., M.D., Ph.D.

ADMISSION REQUIREMENTS. Transcripts, three letters of recommendation required in support of School's application. TOEFL required for international applicants. GRE/GMAT/MAT required by some departments. Interview usually not required. Accepts transfer applicants. Graduates of unaccredited institutions not considered. Apply to Office of Admissions and Scholarships at least forty-five days prior to registration. Application fee $30, $40 for international applicants. Phone: (517)355-8332; fax: (517)353-1674.

ADMISSION STANDARDS. Selective or very selective for most departments, competitive for others. Usual minimum average: 3.0 (A = 4).

FINANCIAL AID. Annual awards from institutional funds: 3211 grants/scholarships, 714 fellowships, 1604 teaching, 1705 research assistantships, Federal W/S, loans. Approved for VA benefits. Apply by February 15 to appropriate department chair for assistantships, fellowships; to Financial Aid Office for all other programs. Use FAFSA. Phone: (517)353-5940; fax: (517)432-1155. About 57% of students receive aid other than loans from School and outside sources. Aid sometimes available for part-time students.

DEGREE REQUIREMENTS. For M.A., M.F.A., M.L.R.H.R., M.Mus., M.P.A., M.S.: 30 credits minimum, at least 6 in residence; thesis/nonthesis options; oral exam required with thesis option; final written and/or oral certifying exam may be required with nonthesis option; no language requirements for most majors. For M.S.N.: 37 credits minimum, at least 6 in residence; thesis/nonthesis option; final written and/or oral certifying exam

(oral exam when thesis is offered). For M.B.A.: 37 credits minimum, at least 27 in residence. For M.U.P.: 48 credits minimum, at least 24 in residence. For M.S.W.: 57 credits minimum, at least 29 in residence (Social Work Plan I), and 61 credits minimum, at least 6 in residence (Social Work Plan II). For M.A.T.: 30 credits minimum, at least 9 in residence; completion of requirements for the secondary provisional certificate; thesis usually not required. For Ed.S.: normally two years beyond bachelor's; 30 credits minimum beyond the master's, at least 22 in residence; competence in statistics or a reading knowledge of a foreign language may be required. For Ph.D.: normally at least three years beyond the bachelor's, at least 12 credits or one year in residence; qualifying exam for some departments; written and/or oral comprehensive exams; language requirements vary by department; thesis; final oral exam. For D.M.A., Ed.D.: essentially the same as for the Ph.D. For D.O.: completion of eleven-term professional program, including 6 semesters of clerkships; endorsement of the Committee on Student Evaluation; an affirmative vote from College faculty. For D.V.M.: completion of 12 semesters professional program (minimum of 163 credits), including three terms (minimum of 60 credits) of clerkships. For M.D.: completion of three-phase professional program (normally extending from 10 to 13 semesters), including clinical clerkships in community hospitals; preclinical comprehensive exams (NBME Exams, Parts I and II).

FIELDS OF STUDY.

COLLEGE OF AGRICULTURE AND NATURAL RESOURCES:
Agricultural Economics. GRE for admission. M.S., Ph.D.
Agricultural Engineering. Thesis required for M.S., Ph.D.
Agricultural and Extension Education. GRE or MAT for admission. M.S., Ph.D.
Agricultural Technology and Systems Management. Thesis required for M.S.; M.S., Ph.D.
Animal Science. M.S., Ph.D.
Building Construction Management. Thesis required for M.S.; M.S. only.
Crop and Soil Sciences. M.S., Ph.D.
Ecology and Evolutionary Biology. Includes crop and soil sciences, fisheries and wildlife, forestry, horticulture. M.S., Ph.D.
Environmental Toxicology. Includes animal science, crop and soil sciences, fisheries and wildlife, food science, resource development. M.S., Ph.D.
Fisheries and Wildlife. GRE Subject (biology) for admission. M.S., Ph.D.
Food Science. Includes food science and foods, human nutrition and institution administration; GRE for admission. M.S., Ph.D.
Forestry. M.S., Ph.D.
Horticulture. M.S., Ph.D.
Packaging. GRE for admission. M.S., Ph.D.
Park, Recreation, and Tourism Resources. GRE for admission. M.S., Ph.D.
Plant Breeding and Genetics. Includes crop and soil sciences, forestry, horticulture or botany, plant pathology. Thesis required for M.S., Ph.D.
Resource Development. GRE for admission. M.S., Ph.D.
Resource Economics. Includes agricultural economics, fisheries and wildlife, forestry, park, recreation, and tourism resources, resource development. M.S., Ph.D.
Urban Studies. Includes forestry, park, recreation, and tourism resources, resource development. M.S., Ph.D.
Note: Oral final exam required for all M.S. degrees.

COLLEGE OF ARTS AND LETTERS:
Acting. M.F.A. only.
American Studies. M.A., Ph.D.
Applied Music. Language requirement for admission to Applied Voice program; audition or tape for admission to D.M.A. or Ph.D. programs; public recital and final written and/or oral

exam required for M.Mus.; four recitals and document required for D.M.A.; M.Mus., D.M.A.

Comparative Literature. GRE for admission; qualifying exam for M.A.; M.A. only.

English. GRE Subject (English literature or a cognate area) for admission; GPA of 3.5 in English courses for admission to M.A. program; two years of college-level foreign language for admission; predissertation exam required for Ph.D.; M.A., Ph.D.

English: Community College Teaching. GRE Subject (English literature or cognate area) and GPA of 3.5 in English courses for admission; thesis/oral required for M.A. M.A. only.

English: Creative Writing. Portfolio of poems, fiction, or plays for admission; thesis/oral required for M.A. M.A. only.

English: Secondary School Teaching. Thesis/oral required for degree. M.A. only.

English: Teaching of English to Speakers of Other Languages. GRE Subject (English literature or a cognate area) and overall GPA of 3.25 for admission. M.A. only.

French. GRE Subject (French) and department proficiency exam in French for admission. M.A. only.

French Language and Literature. GRE Subject (French) and qualifying exam for admission; reading proficiency in two languages other than major language required. Ph.D. only.

French Secondary School Teaching. GRE Subject (French) and department proficiency exam in French for admission. M.A. only.

German. Oral and written exams, nonthesis option for M.A. M.A. only.

German Language and Literature. Reading knowledge of one language appropriate for research in addition to German and English required. Ph.D. only.

History. Includes urban studies. GPA of 3.5 in history courses, GRE Subject (history) and term paper for admission; oral exam and competence in one foreign language required for M.A.; competence in two foreign languages and written and oral comprehensive required for Ph.D.

History of Art. GRE for admission. Two years college-level French, German, Italian and minimum of 18 credits in History of Art upper-level courses or the equivalent for admission. M.A. only.

History: Secondary School Teaching. One year secondary school teaching experience and overall GPA of 3.0 for admission. M.A. only.

Linguistics. Two years of a college-level foreign language for admission; major linguistic research paper and qualifying exam required for admission to Ph.D. program; written exam required for M.A.; nonthesis option; demonstrated ability in two foreign languages required for Ph.D.

Music Composition. Two original compositions for admission to M.M., Ph.D.; original composition and final written and/or oral exam required for M.Mus., Ph.D. M.Mus. and Ph.D.

Music Education. GRE or MAT and orientation exam for admission to Ph.D. program; final written exam; oral exam required for M.Mus.; dissertation, written and/or oral exam for Ph.D. M.Mus., Ph.D.

Music Theory. Writing or sample composition for admission to M.Mus., Ph.D.; thesis and final written and/or oral exam required for M.Mus.; dissertation, written exams, oral exam for Ph.D. M.Mus., Ph.D.

Music Therapy. Thesis and final written and/or oral exam required. M.Mus. only.

Musicology. Reading knowledge of one foreign language for admission to M.A. program; thesis/dissertation, final written and/or oral exam required for M.A. and Ph.D. M.A., Ph.D.

Philosophy. Sample of philosophic writing for admission; GRE optional. Public demonstration of philosophic competence required for M.A. with nonthesis option; reading knowledge of one foreign language, written comprehensive exam for Ph.D.

Russian. Oral and written exams and reading knowledge of another foreign language required. M.A. only.

Spanish. GRE Subject (Spanish) and department proficiency exam in Spanish for admission. M.A. only.

Spanish Language and Literature. GRE Subject (Spanish) and qualifying exam for admission; reading proficiency in two languages other than major language required. Ph.D. only.

Spanish: Secondary School Teaching. GRE Subject (Spanish) for admission. M.A. only.

Studio Art. Includes ceramics, graphic design, painting, printmaking, sculpture. 10–15 color slides and or other media (CDs, video) of creative work, and B.F.A. for admission to M.F.A. program; qualifying and terminal reviews required for M.F.A. M.A. and M.F.A. only.

TESL. M.A. only.

Theater. Audition required for admission to M.F.A., program; written and oral exams required for M.A. nonthesis option. M.A., M.F.A. (production design, acting).

Note: GRE and personal statement required for admission for most programs.

ELI BROAD GRADUATE SCHOOL OF MANAGEMENT:

Accounting. M.B.A. and Ph.D. only.

Economics. Includes econometrics, development, history, international labor. GRE for admission to Ph.D. program; written comprehensive required for M.A. M.A. and Ph.D.

Finance. Ph.D. only.

Financial Administration. M.B.A. only.

Food Systems Economics and Management. M.B.A. only.

Hotel, Restaurant, and Institutional Management. M.B.A. only.

Industrial Organization and Public Policy. M.A., Ph.D.

Management Policy and Strategy. Ph.D. only.

Management Science. M.B.A.

Marketing. M.S., Ph.D.

Materials and Logistics Management: Operations Management. M.B.A. only.

Materials and Logistics Management: Purchasing Management. M.B.A. only.

Materials and Logistics Management: Transportation/Physical Distribution Management. M.B.A. only.

Operations Research Management. Comprehensive oral exam in course work required. M.S. only.

Organizational Behavior: Personnel. Ph.D. only.

Personnel: Human Relations. M.B.A. only.

Production and Operations Management. Ph.D. only.

Professional Accounting. Minimum overall GPA of 3.25 and personal statement for admission. M.B.A. only.

Transportation Distribution. M.B.A. and Ph.D. only.

Note: GMAT required for admission to M.B.A. program; oral and written comprehensive exams required for D.B.A. and Ph.D. programs.

COLLEGE OF COMMUNICATION ARTS AND SCIENCES:

Advertising. Minimum third- and fourth-year undergraduate GPA of 3.25 for admission. M.A. only.

Audiology and Speech Sciences. M.A., Ph.D.

Communication. M.A., Ph.D.

Communication Arts and Sciences: Mass Media. Ph.D. only.

Communication: Urban Studies. M.A. only.

Journalism. GRE, autobiography, and personal statement for admission. M.A. only.

Public Relations. Minimum third- and fourth-year undergraduate GPA of 3.25 for admission. M.A. only.

Telecommunication. Minimum third- and fourth-year undergraduate GPA of 3.25 for admission. M.A. only.

Note: Written and oral exams required for nonthesis option.

COLLEGE OF EDUCATION:

Administration and Supervision of Student Teaching. Interview and scholarly writing samples for admission; personal statement for admission to Ed.S. program; internship required for Ed.D. and Ph.D. Ed.S., Ed.D., and Ph.D. only.

Adult and Continuing Education. Personal statement for admission.

College and University Administration. Personal statement and interview for admission; minimum cumulative GPA of 3.5 of graduate work and at least two years full-time work experience for admission to Ph.D. program. M.A. and Ph.D. only.

Counseling. Interview and one year counseling experience for admission to Ed.S. program; internship (21 credits) required for M.A. in rehabilitation counseling; one major and two minor field exams, prepracticum, three terms of practicum, and one year internship required for Ed.D. and Ph.D.

Curriculum and Teaching. M.A. only.

Educational Psychology. M.A. only.

Educational System Development. Interview required for admission to M.A., Ed.S., Ed.D., and Ph.D. programs, scholarly writing sample required for admission to Ed.D. and Ph.D. programs.

Health Education and Human Performance. MAT and master's thesis or other acceptable written materials required for admission to Ed.D. and Ph.D. programs. M.A., Ed.D., and Ph.D. only.

K–12 Educational Administration. Personal statement for admission; interview and short, written essay exam for admission to Ed.S., Ed.D., and Ph.D. programs.

Measurement, Evaluation, and Research Design.

Physical Education and Exercise Science.

Reading Instruction. Experience with elementary or secondary school-age children for admission. M.A. only.

Rehabilitation Counselor Education.

Special Education. Elementary or secondary teaching credential, eligibility for additional endorsement as a teacher of severely or mildly impaired learner, and 1 full year of successful teaching experience for admission to M.A. program; interview and samples of both scholarly and spontaneous writing required for admission to Ed.D. and Ph.D. programs; internship (1 term) required for Ed.S.

Note: GRE required for Ed.S., Ed.D., and Ph.D. admission; M.A., M.A.T. (joint with College of Natural Science); Ed.S., Ed.D. and Ph.D.

COLLEGE OF ENGINEERING:

Chemical Engineering.

Civil Engineering.

Civil Engineering: Urban Studies. M.S. only.

Computer Science.

Electrical Engineering.

Environmental Engineering.

Environmental Engineering: Urban Studies. M.S. only.

Materials Science.

Mechanical Engineering.

Mechanics.

Note: GRE required for all international applicants, GRE strongly recommended for domestic applicants; certifying exam or thesis defense for M.S. degrees; qualifying exams for all Ph.D. degrees.

COLLEGE OF HUMAN ECOLOGY:

Apparel and Textiles. M.A. only.

Child Development. M.A. only.

Community Services. M.S. only.

Family and Child Ecology. GRE for admission. Ph.D. only.

Family Studies. M.A. only.

Food Science. GRE for admission.

Home Economics Education and Outreach. M.A. only.

Human Environment: Design and Management. M.A. only.

Human Nutrition. GRE for admission. M.S., Ph.D.

Interior Design and Facilities Management. M.A. only.

Marriage and Family Therapy. M.A. only.

Merchandising Management. M.S. only.

Note: Oral or written comprehensive exam required for master's nonthesis option.

COLLEGE OF HUMAN MEDICINE:

Anatomy. GRE for admission; publishable manuscript required for Ph.D.

Biochemistry. GRE Subject or MCAT (M.D.-Ph.D.) for admission.

Cell and Molecular Biology. GRE Subject for admission.

Genetics. GRE Subject for admission.

Microbiology. GRE Subject (biology) and personal statement for admission; participation in lab teaching, predissertation oral exam, and publishable manuscript required for Ph.D.; M.S., Ph.D.

Neuroscience. GRE Subject for admission.

Pathology. Publishable manuscript required.

Pharmacology. GRE for admission to Ph.D. program.

Zoology. GRE for admission.

Note: Thesis/oral exam required for master's degrees.

COLLEGE OF NATURAL SCIENCE:

Analytical Chemistry.

Applied Mathematics.

Biochemistry. GRE Subject for admission.

Biological Science. Interdepartmental. Teacher's certificate, or candidacy for, required for admission to M.A.T. program; reading knowledge of one foreign language and one term's residency at a recognized biological station required for M.S. M.S., M.A.T. only.

Biotechnology. Interdepartmental.

Botany and Plant Pathology. Certifying exam required for M.S.

Cell and Molecular Biology. Interdepartmental. GRE for admission.

Chemical Physics. GRE for admission.

Chemistry. Orientation exam required for admission; teacher's certificate, or candidacy for certificate, required for admission to M.A.T. program; qualifying exam required for M.S. and M.A.T. degrees and for admission to Ph.D. program; reading knowledge of German, Russian, or French and preoral exam required for Ph.D. M.S., M.A.T., and Ph.D.

Clinical Laboratory Science.

Computational Mathematics.

Earth Science. Interdepartmental. Teacher's certificate, or candidacy for certificate, required for admission. M.A.T. only.

Ecology and Evolutionary Biology. Interdepartmental.

Entomology. GRE for admission; appropriate master's degree with thesis required for admission to Ph.D. program; final oral exam required for M.S.; qualification exam and written and oral comprehensive required for Ph.D.

Entomology: Urban Studies. Admission and degree requirements same as for Entomology.

Environmental Geoscience.

Environmental Toxicology. Interdepartmental.

General Science. Interdepartmental. Teacher's certificate, or candidacy for certificate, required for admission; M.A.T. only.

Genetics. Interdepartmental. Ph.D. only.

Geology. GRE for admission. M.S., M.A.T., Ph.D.

Inorganic Chemistry.

Mathematics. Reading knowledge of two foreign languages required for Ph.D.; M.A., M.S., M.A.T., Ph.D.

Mathematics Education.

Microbiology. GRE Subject (biology) and personal statement for admission; final oral exam required; M.S. only.

Nuclear Chemistry. M.S., Ph.D.

Operations Research Statistics. M.S. only.

Pathology. Ph.D. only.

Physical Science. Interdepartmental. Certifying exam required for M.S.; M.S., M.A.T. only.

Physics. Qualifying exam required for M.S. and Ph.D.; one term of half-time teaching required for Ph.D. M.S., M.A.T., Ph.D.

Physiology. GRE for admission; thesis/oral exam required for M.S.; qualifying exam required for Ph.D.

Statistics. Qualifying exam and reading ability in French, German, or Russian required for Ph.D. M.A., M.S., Ph.D.

Theoretical Chemistry. Ph.D. only.

Zoology. GRE for admission. M.S., M.A.T., Ph.D.

Note: Requirements for secondary provisional certificate must be met for M.A.T.

COLLEGE OF NURSING:

Nursing. Includes family and gerontological nursing. GRE (within the last five years), personal interview, statistics course, B.S.N. from accredited nursing program with GPA of 3.0 for years three, four, one-year work experience as R.N. during previous five years or the equivalent, current licensure to practice nursing in the U.S., and eligibility for Michigan licensure required for admission. M.S.N. only.

COLLEGE OF OSTEOPATHIC MEDICINE:

Anatomy. GRE for admission; thesis or publishable manuscript required for M.S.; thesis and publishable manuscript required for Ph.D.

Biochemistry. GRE Subject for admission.

Microbiology. GRE Subject (biology) and personal statement for M.S., in addition to lab teaching, predissertation oral exam, publishable manuscript for Ph.D. M.S. Ph.D.

Neuroscience. Interdepartmental. GRE for admission; Ph.D. only.

Pathology. Thesis/oral exam, publishable manuscript for M.S., Ph.D.; M.S., Ph.D.

Pharmacology. GRE for admission to Ph.D.

Physiology. GRE for admission; thesis/oral exam required for M.S.; qualifying exam required for Ph.D.

Zoology. GRE for admission. Ph.D. only.

Note: Final oral exam required for M.S.

COLLEGE OF SOCIAL SCIENCE:

Anthropology. Thesis/oral exam required for M.A. (can substitute qualifying exam or doctoral comprehensive exam if directly admitted to doctoral program without M.A.).

Criminal Justice. GRE or MAT (social science professional scale) and minimum overall undergraduate GPA of 3.2 for admission; policy paper and oral exam required for nonthesis option; M.S. only.

Geography. GRE and a minimum GPA of 3.4 in all geography courses and all junior-senior courses for admission to M.A. or M.S. programs; minimum GPA of 3.6 for admission to Ph.D. M.A., M.S., Ph.D.

Geography: Urban Studies. GRE and a minimum GPA of 3.4. M.A. only.

Labor and Industrial Relations. Includes collective bargaining and employment relations, and employment and training programs options; GRE for admission. M.L.R.H.R. only.

Political Science. GRE and 3.2 GPA for admission to M.A., Ph.D. M.A., Ph.D.

Political Science: Urban Studies. GRE and 3.2 GPA for admission; M.P.A. Ph.D. only.

Psychology. GRE Subject (psychology) for admission to M.A., Ph.D. thesis/oral exam required for M.A. M.A., Ph.D.

Psychology: Urban Studies. GRE Subject (psychology) for admission. M.A., Ph.D.

Public Administration. GRE for admission. M.P.A. only.

Social Science: Criminal Justice. GRE for admission. Ph.D. only.

Social Science: Industrial Relations and Human Resources. GRE for admission. Ph.D. only.

Social Science: Social Work. GRE for admission. Ph.D. only.

Social Science: Urban and Regional Planning. GRE for admission. Ph.D. only.

Social Work. Includes administration and program evaluation and interpersonal intervention; MSWI (two-year) and MSWII (one-year) program options; bachelor's in social work from CSEW-accredited program and full-time student status required for admission to MSWII program. M.S.W. only.

Social Work: Urban Studies. Includes administration and pro-gram evaluation and interpersonal intervention; no thesis option. M.S.W. only.

Sociology. GRE for admission; master's thesis or original research paper for admission to Ph.D. program.

Sociology: Urban Studies. GRE for admission; master's thesis or original research paper for admission to Ph.D. program; thesis/oral exam required for M.A.

Urban and Regional Planning. M.U.R.P. only.

COLLEGE OF VETERINARY MEDICINE:

Note: Also see separate listing on page 270.

Anatomy. GRE for admission; thesis/oral exam or publishable manuscript required for M.S.; publishable manuscript required for Ph.D.

Environmental Toxicology. Multidisciplinary program, granting a Ph.D. only: anatomy (GRE for admission), microbiology (GRE Subject [biology] for admission), pathology, pharmacology (GRE for admission), physiology (GRE General/Subject for admission).

Large-Animal Clinical Sciences. M.S., Ph.D.

Microbiology. GRE Subject (biology) and personal statement for admission; final oral exam required. M.S., Ph.D.

Pathology. Thesis/oral exam and publishable manuscript required for M.S.; publishable manuscript required for Ph.D.

Pharmacology and Toxicology. GRE for admission to Ph.D. program.

Physiology. GRE Subject for admission; thesis/oral exam required for M.S.; qualifying exam required for Ph.D.

Small Animal Clinical Sciences. M.S. only.

College of Human Medicine (48824–1317)

First class entered 1969. Tuition: resident $13,233, nonresident $29,079. On-campus housing available. Total average figure for all other expenses: $9500.

Enrollment: first-year class 105; total 454 (men 50%, women 50%). Faculty: full-and part-time approximately 2000. Degrees conferred: M.D., M.D.-Ph.D. The M.S. and Ph.D. are available through the Graduate School.

ADMISSION REQUIREMENTS. AMCAS report, transcripts, letters of recommendation, MCAT, autobiographical statement required in support of application. Interview by invitation only. Has EDP; apply between June 15 and August 1. Applicants must have completed at least three years of college study. Preference given to state residents. Apply to Office of Admissions after June 15, before November 15. Application fee $50. Phone: (517)353-9620; fax: (517)432-1051.

ADMISSION STANDARDS. Competitive. Accepts 12% of total annual applicants. Approximately 90% are state residents.

FINANCIAL AID. Limited to scholarships, loans. Apply to the Office of Financial Aid after acceptance.

DEGREE REQUIREMENTS. For M.D.: satisfactory completion of three- or four-year program. For M.S., Ph.D., see Graduate School listing above.

FIELDS OF GRADUATE STUDY.

Anatomy.

Biochemistry.

Biomedical Engineering.

Cell Biology.

Genetics.

Microbiology.

Molecular Biology.

Neurosciences.

Pathology.

Pharmacology.

Physiology.

College of Veterinary Medicine (48824–1316)

Annual tuition: resident $10,186, nonresident $20,973. Total average cost for all other expenses: $6952.

Enrollment: first-year class 100; total full-time 469 (men 50%, women 50%); no part-time students. Faculty: full-time 180. Degree conferred: D.V.M. The M.S. and Ph.D. are offered through the Graduate School.

ADMISSION REQUIREMENTS. VMCAS report, completion of required preveterinary courses, transcripts, MCAT or GRE (General), interview, autobiography, three recommendations required in support of application. Has EDP; apply after August 1, before October 15. Equal preference given to Michigan residents and nonresidents. Graduates of unaccredited colleges not considered. All application materials must be received by the Office of Admissions and Scholarships by November 1. Application fee $65. Phone: (517)355-9793; fax: (517)432-2391.

ADMISSION STANDARDS. Selective. Accepts 30–35% of total annual applicants. Accepts 15–20% of nonresident applicants.

FINANCIAL AID. Fellowships, research assistantships, Federal W/S, loans. Apply to Office of Admissions and Scholarships. Use FAFSA.

DEGREE REQUIREMENTS. For D.V.M.: satisfactory completion of three-year, year-round, professional curriculum. For M.S., Ph.D., see Graduate School listing above.

FIELDS OF GRADUATE STUDY.
Anatomy.
Environmental Toxicology.
Large-Animal Clinical Sciences.
Microbiology.
Pathology.
Pharmacology.
Physiology.
Small-Animal Clinical Sciences.

MICHIGAN TECHNOLOGICAL UNIVERSITY
Houghton, Michigan 49931-1295

Founded 1885. Located 400 miles N of Chicago. Coed. State control. Quarter system. Special facilities: A. E. Seaman Mineralogical Museum, National Center for Clean Industrial and Treatment Technologies, Environmental Engineering Center, Keweenaw Research Center, Center for Clean Manufacturing and Research, Ford Forestry Center, Institute of Wood Research, Institute of Materials Processing, Regional Groundwater Education in Michigan Center. Library: 786,000 volumes, 415,000 microforms, 10,000 current periodicals, 32 PCs.

Annual tuition: full-time, resident $3959, nonresident $8959. On-campus housing for 300 married units, 110 single units. Average academic year housing cost: $3978 (including board) for single students; $4816 for married students. Contact Director of Housing for both on- and off-campus housing information. Phone: (906)487-2682.

Graduate School

Enrollment: full-time 650, part-time 34. University faculty: full-time 316. Degrees conferred: M.S., Ph.D.

ADMISSION REQUIREMENTS. Official transcripts, GRE, GMAT required in support of School's application. TOEFL required for international applicants. Interview not required. Accepts transfer applicants. Graduates of unaccredited institutions not considered. Apply to Graduate School Office at least six weeks prior to the desired quarter of registration. Application fee $30, $35 for international applicants. Phone: (906)487-2327.

ADMISSION STANDARDS. Selective. Usual minimum average: 2.7 (A = 4).

FINANCIAL AID. 135 research fellowships, 175 research assistantships, 197 teaching assistantships, Federal W/S, loans. Approved for VA benefits. Apply March 1 to Dean, Graduate School for fellowships, assistantships; to Financial Aid Office for all other programs. Use FAFSA. Phone: (906)487-2622. About 71% of students receive aid other than loans from University and outside sources. No aid for part-time students.

DEGREE REQUIREMENTS. For M.S.: 45 credits minimum, at least 30 in residence; 9–15 credits of the 45 may be assigned to thesis; final oral exam. For Ph.D.: total number of credits variable, at least six quarters in residence; preliminary written/oral exam; foreign language proficiency recommended by some departments; dissertation; final oral exam.

FIELDS OF STUDY.
Biological Sciences. M.S., Ph.D.
Chemical Engineering. M.S., Ph.D.
Chemistry. M.S., Ph.D.
Civil Engineering. M.S., Ph.D.
Computational Science. Interdepartmental. Ph.D. only.
Computer Science. M.S. only.
Electrical Engineering. M.S., Ph.D.
Engineering Mechanics. M.S. only.
Environmental Engineering. Interdepartmental. Ph.D. only.
Forest Science. Ph.D. only.
Forestry. M.S. only.
Geological Engineering. M.S. only.
Geology. M.S., Ph.D.
Geophysics. M.S. only.
Industrial Archaeology. M.S. only.
Mathematics. M.S. only.
Mechanical Engineering. M.S.
Mechanical Engineering/Engineering Mechanics. Ph.D. only.
Metallurgical Engineering. M.S., Ph.D.
Mineral Economics. M.S. only.
Mining Engineering. M.S., Ph.D.
Physics. M.S., Ph.D.
Rhetoric and Technical Communication. M.S., Ph.D.
Sensing and Signal Processing. Interdepartmental. Ph.D. only.
Structural Engineering. Interdepartmental. Ph.D. only.

THE UNIVERSITY OF MICHIGAN
Ann Arbor, Michigan 48109

Founded 1817. Located 40 miles W of Detroit. Coed. State control. Trimester system. Special facilities: computer center; four astronomical laboratories; experimental school; nuclear reactor; statistical research laboratory; installations for handling radioisotopes and high-intensity radiation sources; centers for ancient and modern studies, Afro-American and African studies, Chinese studies, Near Eastern and North African studies, Russian and East European studies, South and Southeast Asian studies, Western European studies, research on economic development, human growth and development, research on learning and teaching; institutes for environmental quality, labor and industrial relations, mental health research, public policy, science and technology, social research. Library: 6,000,000 volumes, 3,470,000 microforms.

Annual tuition: full-time (9 or more credits), resident $9322, nonresident $18,940. On-campus housing for 2100 married students, 750 graduate men, 750 graduate women. Average academic year housing cost: $6103 for married students, $3816 for 8 months (including board) for single students. Apply to Housing Office. Phone: (313)763-3164.

Horace H. Rackham School of Graduate Studies

Graduate study since 1849. Enrollment: 6463 (men 3681, women 2782). Graduate faculty: full-time 2010. Degrees conferred: A.M., M.S., M.F.A., M.I.L.S., M.L.Arch., M.L.S., M.P.A., M.P.P., M.S.Pharm., M.U.P., M.S.E., Engineer, Ed.S., Ed.D., A.Mus.D., Ph.D.

ADMISSION REQUIREMENTS. Transcripts, letters of reference required in support of School's application. GRE either required or strongly recommended for most departments. TOEFL or MELAB required of international students. Interview not required. Accepts transfer applicants. Graduates of unaccredited institutions not considered. Apply by January 15. Application fee $55. Phone: (313)747-4537; fax: (313)763-2447.

ADMISSION STANDARDS. Selective to competitive for most departments. Usual minimum average: 3.0 (A = 4).

FINANCIAL AID. Annual awards from institutional funds: approximate total of 4987 fellowships, 3573 assistantships, Federal W/S, loans. Approved for VA benefits. Apply by February 1 to Fellowships, Assistantships Office; to Financial Aid Office for all other programs. Use FAFSA and University's FAF. 1040 IRS form must be submitted. Phone: (313)763-6600; fax: (313)747-3801. About 75% of students receive aid other than loans from University and outside sources. Aid sometimes available for part-time students.

DEGREE REQUIREMENTS. For master's: 24 hours minimum, at least 18 in residence; thesis, final written/oral exam for most majors; reading knowledge of one foreign language for some majors. For M.S.E.: 30 hours minimum, at least 24 in residence. For Engineering: 30 hours minimum beyond the bachelor's, at least 24 in residence. For Ed.S.: 54 hours minimum beyond the bachelor's, at least 48 in residence; final research report. For Ph.D.: six terms of study/research minimum beyond the bachelor's, at least two terms of not less than eight hours each in residence; no specific hour requirement except 60 hours minimum for education; language requirements vary by major; preliminary exam; dissertation; final oral exam. For Ed.D.: 72 hours minimum beyond the bachelor's, at least two terms in residence; preliminary exam; dissertation; final oral exam. For A.Mus.D.: essentially the same as for the Ph.D.

FIELDS OF STUDY.
Aerospace Engineering. GRE for admission. M.S., A.E., Ph.D.
Aerospace Science. M.S., Ph.D.
American Culture. GRE for admission; interdepartmental.
Anthropology. GRE for admission. A.M., Ph.D.
Anthropology and History. GRE for admission; interdepartmental. Ph.D.
Applied Economics. A.M. only.
Applied Mechanics. M.S.E., Ph.D.
Applied Physics. GRE for admission.
Applied Social Research. A.M. only.
Applied Statistics. A.M.
Architecture. M.S., Ph.D.
Art. Includes photography, art education; portfolio for admission; M.A., M.F.A.
Asian Languages and Culture. GRE for admission; includes Chinese, Japanese, Buddhist studies; one language for M.A. candidacy, plus two years' study in Far Eastern language.

Asian Studies. GRE for admission. interdepartmental; includes China, Japan, South and Southeast Asia. A.M.
Astronomy. GRE Subject for admission.
Atmospheric and Space Sciences. GRE recommended.
Bioengineering. GRE for admission; interdepartmental.
Biological Chemistry. GRE for admission. Ph.D.
Biology. GRE for admission; Ph.D. only.
Biophysics. Interdepartmental; Ph.D. only.
Biostatistics. GRE for admission. M.S., Ph.D.
Botany. Ph.D. only.
Business Administration. M.B.A., M.A.S., M.H.A. granted by School of Business Administration; Ph.D. only.
Cell Development and Neural Biology. Ph.D.
Cellular and Molecular Biology. GRE for admission; interdepartmental. Ph.D. only.
Chemical Engineering. GRE for admission. M.S.E., Ph.D.
Chemistry. GRE for admission. Ph.D. only.
Civil Engineering. Includes construction, public works, sanitary, and water resources; GRE for admission.
Classical Art and Archaeology. GRE for admission; interdepartmental.
Classical Studies. GRE for admission; M.A. in Greek, Latin; Ph.D. in Classical Studies.
Clinical Research Design and Statistical Analysis. M.S. only.
Communication. Includes radio, TV, film, journalism. GRE for admission.
Comparative Literature. Interdepartmental; one language for admission; substantial knowledge of two languages, some facility in another for Ph.D.
Computer Science and Engineering. M.S., M.S.E., Ph.D.
Construction Engineering and Management. M.S.E.
Creative Writing. M.F.A.
Dance. M.F.A.
Dentistry. D.D.S. for admission, except in dental hygiene and biomaterials.
Economics. GRE Subject for admission. Ph.D.
Education. Includes curriculum, teaching and psychological studies, educational foundations, policy and administration, higher and adult continuing education; GRE for admission.
Education and Psychology. GRE for admission; interdepartmental; Ph.D. only.
Electrical Engineering. GRE for admission. M.S., M.S.E., E.E., Ph.D. only.
Electrical Engineering and Atmospheric, Oceanic, and Space Science. Includes computer sciences and engineering, electrical engineering, electrical. GRE for admission.
English and Education. GRE for admission; interdepartmental. Ph.D.
English and Women's Studies. Ph.D. only.
English Language and Literature. Includes creative writing; one language, GRE, writing sample for admission. Ph.D. only.
Environmental Engineering. Includes sixty-hour combined program leading to dual master's; environmental health and sanitary engineering (M.P.A., M.S.E.); environmental planning and water development (M.P.S., M.S.); GRE for admission.
Environmental Health Science. M.S., Ph.D.
Epidemiologic Science. Normally admits to Ph.D. only; GRE for admission.
Geology. GRE for admission.
Germanic Languages and Literatures. GRE for admission.
Health Behavior and Health Education. GRE for admission. Ph.D. only.
Health Services Management/Industrial Engineering. M.S. only.
Health Services Organization and Policy. Ph.D.
History. GRE for admission. A.M., Ph.D.
History of Art. One language for M.A. GRE for admission.
Human Genetics. GRE for admission. M.S., Ph.D.
Industrial and Operations Engineering. GRE for admission.
Information and Library Studies. M.I.L.S., Ph.D.
Journalism. A.M.
Kinesiology. A.M., M.S., Ph.D.

Landscape Architecture. M.L.Arch., Ph.D.

Linguistics. GRE for admission. Ph.D. only.

Macromolecular Science and Engineering. GRE for admission; interdepartmental. M.S., Ph.D.

Manufacturing Systems Engineering (Dearborn campus).

Materials Science and Engineering. GRE for admission. M.S.E., Ph.D.

Mathematics. GRE for admission. A.M., M.S., Ph.D.

Mechanical Engineering. Also offered at Dearborn Campus.

Medical and Biological Illustration. M.F.A. only.

Medical Scientist Training Program. M.D.-Ph.D. program.

Medicinal Chemistry. GRE for admission; interdepartmental.

Microbiology and Immunology. GRE for admission. Ph.D. only.

Mineralogy. M.S., Ph.D.

Modern Middle Eastern and North African Studies. GRE for admission; interdepartmental.

Music. Includes composition, conducting, performance, theory, music education, musicology; M.A., Ph.D., A.Mus.D., Dance, M.F.A.; theater, M.A., M.F.A., Ph.D.

Natural Resources. Includes forestry, administration, fisheries, wildlife management, outdoor education, landscape architecture, resource management. GRE for admission. M.S., Ph.D.

Naval Architecture and Marine Engineering. GRE for admission.

Near Eastern Studies. GRE for admission. M.S., Ph.D.

Neuroscience. GRE for admission; interdepartmental. Ph.D. only.

Nuclear Engineering.

Nuclear Science. M.S., Ph.D.

Nursing. GRE for admission. M.S., Ph.D.

Nutritional Science. M.S. only.

Oceanography: Marine Geology and Geochemistry. M.S., Ph.D.

Pathology. Ph.D. only.

Pharmaceutical Chemistry. GRE for admission. M.S., Ph.D.

Pharmaceutics. GRE for admission. M.S., Ph.D.

Pharmacognosy. GRE for admission. M.S., Ph.D.

Pharmacology. GRE for admission. Ph.D. only.

Pharmacy. GRE for admission. M.S. Pharm., Ph.D.

Philosophy. GRE, writing sample for admission. A.M., Ph.D.

Physics. GRE for admission. M.S., Ph.D.

Physiology. GRE for admission. Ph.D. only.

Political Science. GRE for admission. A.M., Ph.D.

Population Planning. GRE for admission. M.S., Ph.D.

Psychology. GRE for admission. Ph.D. only, additional departmental application required for admission.

Psychology and Women's Studies. Ph.D. only.

Public Administration. GRE for admission; M.P.A.

Public Policy Studies. GRE for admission; interdepartmental. M.P.A., M.P.P., Ph.D.

Romance Languages and Literature. Includes French, Spanish, Italian, Romance linguistics. GRE for admission. A.M., Ph.D.

Russian and East European Studies. Interdepartmental. GRE for admission. A.M. only.

Scientific Computing. Ph.D. only.

Slavic Languages and Literatures. GRE for admission. A.M., Ph.D.

Social Work and Social Science. Ph.D. only.

Sociology. GRE Subject for admission. A.M., Ph.D.

Statistics. Includes applied statistics; A.M. only. GRE for admission. A.M., Ph.D.

Telecommunication Arts. A.M. only

Theater. A.M., Ph.D.

Toxicology. M.S., Ph.D.

Urban Planning. GRE for admission. M.U.P. only.

Urban, Technological, and Environmental Planning. GRE for admission. Ph.D. only.

Graduate School of Business Administration

Established 1924. Tuition: full-time resident $16,450, nonresident $23,300. Enrollment: full-time 850, part-time 1000. Degree conferred: M.B.A. The Ph.D. is offered through the Rackham School of Graduate Studies.

ADMISSION REQUIREMENTS. Transcripts, GMAT required in support of School's application. Apply to Director of Admissions by March 1 (Fall), November 1 (Winter—part-time only). Application fee $100. Phone: (313)763-5796.

ADMISSION STANDARDS. Very selective. Usual average: 3.3 (A = 4).

FINANCIAL AID. Annual awards from institutional funds: 75 fellowships, Federal W/S, loans. Approved for VA benefits. Apply by March 1 to Director of Financial Aid. Use FAFSA and University's FAF. Phone: (313)764-5139; fax: (313)763-7804. About 30% of students receive scholarships from School and outside sources.

DEGREE REQUIREMENTS. For M.B.A.: 60 credit hours minimum, all in residence. For Ph.D.: see School of Graduate Studies listing above.

FIELDS OF STUDY.

Accounting.

Business Economics and Public Policy.

Corporate Strategy/Operations Management.

Finance.

International Business.

Management.

Marketing.

Operations Management.

Organizational Behavior and Human and Resource Management.

Statistics.

School of Music

http://www.music.umich.edu

Organized 1880. Annual tuition: resident $8508, nonresident $17,668; per credit, resident $462, nonresident $971.

Enrollment: full-time 286, part-time 25 (men 50%, women 50%). Faculty: full-time 80, teaching fellows 10. Degrees conferred: M.M., Specialist in Music. The M.A., M.F.A., D.M.A., Ph.D. are offered through the School of Graduate Studies

ADMISSION REQUIREMENTS. Varies by department, but generally one official transcript, audition, or tape (for M.M., D.M.A.), GRE (for some majors) required in support of School's application. MELAB required for international applicants. Accepts transfer applicants. Apply to Associate Dean by February 15 (Fall), November 15 (Winter); February 1 for Composition, Music History, and Conducting. Application fee $50. Phone: (313)764-0593; fax: (313)763-5097.

ADMISSION STANDARDS. Selective for most programs, very selective for others. Usual minimum average: 3.0 (A = 4).

FINANCIAL AID. Annual awards from institutional funds: one hundred full or partial scholarships, one hundred teaching assistantships, Federal W/S, loans. Approved for VA benefits. Apply February 15 to Associate Dean for scholarships, assistantships; to Financial Aid Office for all other programs. Use FAFSA. Phone: (313)763-6600; fax: (313)747-3081. About 40% of students receive aid other than loans from School and outside sources. No aid for part-time students.

DEGREE REQUIREMENTS. For M.M.: 30–36 semester hours minimum; placement exam in theory; thesis, composition, final exam, or public recital, depending upon major. For other degree requirements, consult the Associate Dean, or see the School of Graduate Studies listing above.

FIELDS OF STUDY.
Composition.
Conducting.
Dance.
Music Education.
Musicology. Includes ethnomusicology.
Performance.
Theater.
Theory.

School of Public Health

http://www.sph.umich.edu

Established 1941. Annual tuition: resident $8878, nonresident $18,088.

Enrollment: full- and part-time 762. Faculty: full-time 109. Degrees conferred: M.P.H., M.H.S.A., Dr.P.H. The M.S. and Ph.D. are offered through the School of Graduate Studies.

ADMISSION REQUIREMENTS. Transcript, three letters of recommendation, GRE required in support of School's application. Interview required for M.P.H. only. TOEFL required for international applicants. Apply to Office of Student Affairs. School-wide application deadline is March 1. Application fee $55. Phone: (313)764-5425; fax: (313)763-5455.

ADMISSION STANDARDS. Very selective for most programs, selective for others. Usual minimum average: 3.0 (A = 4).

FINANCIAL AID. Grants, Federal W/S, loans. Approved for VA benefits. Apply to the Office of Student Affairs and to the University of Michigan Office of Financial Aid. Use FAFSA. Phone: (313)763-0931.

DEGREE REQUIREMENTS. For M.P.H.: 60 credit hours; field experience. For M.H.S.A.: 60 credit hours; field experience. For Dr.P.H.: two-year minimum beyond master's; preliminary exam; dissertation; final oral exam. For M.S., Ph.D., see Horace H. Rackham School of Graduate Studies listing above.

FIELDS OF STUDY.
Biostatistics.
Dental Public Health.
Environmental and Industrial Health.
Epidemiology.
Health Behavior/Health Education.
Health Management and Policy.
Human Nutrition.
International Health.

School of Social Work (48109-1285)

Established 1921. Semester system. Annual tuition: resident $9412, nonresident $18,940.

Enrollment: full-time 570, part-time 23. School faculty: full-time 43, part-time 8. Degrees conferred: M.S.W., M.S.W.-Ph.D. (Anthropology, Economics, Political Science, Psychology, Sociology). The Ph.D. is offered through the Horace H. Rackham School of Graduate Studies.

ADMISSION REQUIREMENTS. Transcripts, letters of reference, supplementary statement dealing with applicant's career objectives and personal qualifications required in support of School's application. TOEFL or MELAB TSE (recommended) required for international applicants. Apply to M.S.W. program director by March 1 (Fall), Ph.D. application January 2 (Fall). Application fee $50. Phone: (313)764-3309.

ADMISSION STANDARDS. Very selective. Usual minimum average: 3.0 (A = 4).

FINANCIAL AID. Grants, scholarships, traineeships, Federal W/S, loans. Apply at the same time as admission to program. Use FAFSA. Phone: (313)763-6600.

DEGREE REQUIREMENTS. For M.S.W.: 56 hours minimum; research papers. For Ph.D.: see Horace H. Rackham School of Graduate Studies listing above.

Law School (48109-1215)

Opened 1859. Semester system. Law library: 750,000 volumes. Library has LEXIS, NEXIS, WESTLAW, LEXCALIBUR. Annual tuition: residents $16,498, nonresidents $22,498. On-campus housing available for single students only. Total average annual additional expenses: $11,650.

Enrollment: first-year class 360; total full-time 1146 (men 57%, women 43%); postgraduate 31; no part-time study. Faculty: full-time 61, part-time 44. Degrees conferred: J D., J.D.-M.B.A., J.D.-M.A.(Modern Middle Eastern and North African Studies, Natural Resources, World Politics, Public Policy Studies, Russian and East European Studies), J.D.-M.H.S.A., J.D.-M.S.W., J.D.-Ph.D. (Economics), LL.M., M.C.L., S.J.D.

ADMISSION REQUIREMENTS. LSDAS Law School report, bachelor's degree, transcripts, LSAT, letters of recommendation required in support of application. TOEFL required of international students. Interview not required. Accepts transfer applicants. Graduates of unaccredited colleges not considered. Apply to Director of Admissions after September 1, before February 15. Application fee $70. Phone: (313)764-0537.

ADMISSION STANDARDS. Competitive. Accepts about 10–15% of total annual applicants. Approximately 36% of entering class are nonresidents.

FINANCIAL AID. Scholarships, grants, fellowships (overseas travel fellowships for legal studies abroad), assistantships, Federal W/S, loans. Apply for financial aid by February 1. Use FAFSA. Apply to Director of Advanced Studies for fellowships for advanced degrees. About 50% of students receive aid from School. Most state residents with need are aided.

DEGREE REQUIREMENTS. For J.D.: three years minimum, at least two in full-time residence; 83 credit-hour program. For LL.M.: at least 24 credits and one year in full-time residence. For M.C.L.: one year in full-time residence beyond the J.D.; research project. For S.J.D.: one year in full-time residence beyond the master's; original research project; final oral exam.

Medical School (48109-0611)

First class in 1850. Medical Center library: 200,000 volumes. Annual tuition: resident $16,040, nonresident $25,140. Total average figure for all other expenses: $7800.

Enrollment: first-year class 125 (EDP 10); total 845 (men 60%, women 40%). Faculty: full- and part-time approximately 1200. Degrees conferred: M.D., M.D.-M.S., M.D.-Ph.D. The M.S. and Ph.D. are offered through the School of Graduate Studies. Graduate study, Medical Scientist Training Program.

ADMISSION REQUIREMENTS. AMCAS report, transcripts, references, MCAT, interview required in support of application. Applicants must have completed at least 90 semester hours of university work. Has EDP; apply between June 15 and August 1. Accepts transfer applicants. Apply after June 15, before November 15. Application fee $56, after initial screening procedure. Phone: (313)764-6317; fax: (313)936-3510.

ADMISSION STANDARDS. Competitive. Accepts 8% of total annual applicants. Approximately 75% are state residents.

FINANCIAL AID. Scholarships, assistantships, fellowships, work-study, loans. Based on need. Accepted applicants are advised on procedures for acquiring financial aid.

DEGREE REQUIREMENTS. For M.D.: four years minimum, at least two in full-time residence. For M.S., Ph.D., see School of Graduate Studies listing above.

FIELDS OF GRADUATE STUDY.
Anatomy.
Biochemistry.
Biomedical Engineering.
Biophysics.
Cell Biology.
Genetics.
Immunology.
Microbiology.
Molecular Biology.
Neurosciences.
Pathology.
Pharmacology.
Physiology.

School of Dentistry (48109-1078)

Originated 1875. Annual tuition: resident $13,658, nonresident $24,870. On-campus housing available. Average academic year cost: $9140. Housing Office phone: (313)763-3164. Total average cost for all other first-year expenses: $3900.

Enrollment: first-year class 90; full-time 450 (men 65%, women 35%). Degree conferred: D.D.S. The M.S., M.P.H., and Ph.D. are offered through the School of Graduate Studies.

ADMISSION REQUIREMENTS. AADSAS, transcripts, three letters of recommendation, DAT (not later than October) required in support of School's application. Interview often required. Applicants must have completed at least two but preferably three years of college study. Preference given to state residents. Accepts transfer applicants from U.S. and Canadian dental schools. Apply to AADSAS after July 1, before March 1. Application fee $50. Phone: (313)763-3316.

ADMISSION STANDARDS. Selective. Usual minimum average: 2.75 (A = 4). Accepts 20–25% of total annual applicants. Approximately 80% are state residents.

FINANCIAL AID. Scholarships, fellowships, externships, loans. Apply to the Office of Financial Aid before April 1 after acceptance. Use FAFSA. Phone: (313)763-3313. About 74% of students receive aid from School and outside sources.

DEGREE REQUIREMENTS. For D.D.S.: satisfactory completion of four-year program. For M.S., M.P.H., Ph.D.: see Graduate School listing above.

FIELDS OF GRADUATE STUDY.
Dental Hygiene. Undergraduate degree in dental hygiene required for admission. M.S. only.
Dental Materials. M.S., Ph.D.
Dental Public Health. M.P.H., Ph.D.
Endodontics. M.S. only.
Oral Diagnosis. M.S. only.
Oral Pathology. M.S. only.
Oral Surgery. three years of full-time study; M.S. only.
Orthodontics. M.S. only.
Pedodontics. M.S. only.
Periodontics. M.S. only.
Prosthodontics. Includes crown and bridge prosthodontics, occlusion, operative dentistry; M.S. only.
Note: All programs require thesis.

MIDDLEBURY COLLEGE
Middlebury, Vermont 05753-6002
http://www.middlebury.edu/~is

Founded 1800. Located 35 miles S of Burlington. Coed. Private control. 4-1-4 system. Special facilities: Music Library, Performing Arts Center, Museum of Art. Library: 580,000 volumes.

Tuition: summer study (includes room and board) on campus $2780, academic year abroad at Language Schools (Florence, Italy; Madrid, Spain; Mainz, Germany; Paris, France) $10,610, (Moscow, Russia) $16,480.

Graduate Study

Graduate study since 1915. Enrollment: full- and part-time 700. Faculty: full-time 100. Degrees conferred: M.A., D.M.L. The M.A. and D.M.L. may be earned either during a series of summers in Vermont, or by combining summer study in Vermont with an academic year at one of College's five schools abroad.

ADMISSION REQUIREMENTS. For M.A.: transcripts, proficiency in the language equivalent to an undergraduate major required in support of College's application. For D.M.L.: transcripts, equivalent of an M.A. in the primary language. Apply to Language School Office of the primary language of interest. Rolling admissions process. Application fee $40. Phone: (802)388-3711, ext. 5552; fax: (802)388-1253.

FINANCIAL AID. Awards from institutional funds: limited number of scholarships, Federal W/S, loans. Approved for VA benefits. Apply to Office of Financial Aid as soon as possible after January 1. Use FAFSA. Phone: (802)388-3711, ext. 5158.

DEGREE REQUIREMENTS. For M.A. in foreign languages: twelve course units. Transfer credits limited to three approved course units. For D.M.L.: 12 units beyond the M.A.; teaching experience; residence in country of primary language; proficiency in one other language in addition to primary language; dissertation; final written/oral exams.

FIELDS OF STUDY.

ACADEMIC YEAR LANGUAGE PROGRAMS:
French.
German.
Italian.
Russian.
Spanish.

INTENSIVE SUMMER PROGRAMS:
Arabic.
Chinese.
French.
German.
Italian.
Japanese.
Russian.
Spanish.

MIDDLE TENNESSEE STATE UNIVERSITY
Murfreesboro, Tennessee 37132
http://www.mtsu.edu/~graduate

Founded 1911. Located 30 miles SE of Nashville. Coed. State control. Semester system. Library: 1,000,000 volumes, 20 PCs.

Annual tuition: full-time, resident $2538, nonresident $6874;

per hour, resident $116, nonresident $306. Annual academic year housing cost for single students: $1460–$1660 (excluding board). Contact Housing Office for both on- and off-campus housing information. Phone: (615)898-2660. Day care facilities available.

Graduate School

Enrollment: full-time 1250, part-time 800. Faculty teaching graduate students: full-time 350, part-time 50. Degrees conferred: M.A., M.A.T., M.B.A., M.B.E., M.C.J., M.Ed., M.S., M.S.T., M.V.T.E., Ed.S., D.A.

ADMISSION REQUIREMENTS. Transcripts, three letters of reference, MAT/GRE/GMAT in support of School's application. TOEFL required for international applicants. Accepts transfer applicants. Graduates of unaccredited institutions not considered. Apply to Dean of Graduate School, by August 1. Application fee $5. Phone: (615)898-2840; fax: (615)904-8020.

ADMISSION STANDARDS. Selective. Usual minimum average: 3.0 (A = 4).

FINANCIAL AID. Twenty-five fellowships, fifty research assistantships, twenty-five administrative assistantships, two hundred teaching assistantships, Federal W/S, loans. Approved for VA benefits. Contact the Office of Financial Aid; no specified closing date. Use FAFSA and University's FAF. Phone: (615)898-2830.

DEGREE REQUIREMENTS. For M.A., M.S.: 30 semester hours minimum; admission to candidacy; reading knowledge of one foreign language or approved research tool; thesis (three semester hours minimum). For M.A.T., M.S.T., M.V.T.E.: 30 semester hours minimum; teaching certification; admission to candidacy; comprehensive exam. For M.Ed.: 33 semester hours; admission to candidacy; comprehensive exam. For M.B.A.: 36 semester hours; admission to candidacy; comprehensive exam. For M.B.E.: 32 semester hours; admission to candidacy; comprehensive exam. For M.C.J.: 36 semester hours; admission to candidacy; comprehensive exam. For Ed.S.: 30 semester hours; admission to candidacy; comprehensive exam. For D.A.: 48 semester hours beyond master's; qualifying exam; admission to candidacy; 3 hours externship, 3 hours internship; dissertation (6 semester hours minimum); defense of dissertation.

FIELDS OF STUDY.
Accounting.
Administration and Supervision.
Aerospace Education.
Biology.
Business Administration.
Business Education. Includes marketing education, office management.
Chemistry.
Computer Information Systems.
Computer Science.
Criminal Justice Administration.
Curriculum and Instruction.
Economics.
English.
Foreign Language.
Guidance and Counseling.
Health, Physical Education, Recreation, and Safety.
History. Includes historic preservation.
Human Sciences.
Industrial Studies.
Mass Communications.
Mathematics.
Music.
Physical Education.
Psychology.
Reading.

Sociology.
Special Education.
Vocational-Technical Education.
Wellness and Fitness.

MIDWESTERN STATE UNIVERSITY
Wichita Falls, Texas 76308-2096
http://www.nexus.mwsu.edu

Founded 1922. Coed. State control. Semester system. Library: 500,000 items.

Annual tuition: full-time, resident $1826, nonresident $8246; per credit, resident $38, nonresident $181. On-campus housing for single students. Average academic year housing cost: $3026 (including board). Apply to Director of Housing. Phone: (817)689-4217.

Graduate School

Graduate study since 1952. Enrollment: full-time 162, part-time 539 (men 336, women 365). Graduate faculty: full-time 55, part-time 7. Degrees conferred: M.A., M.S., M.Ed., M.S.K., M.B.A.

ADMISSION REQUIREMENTS. One official transcript from each institution attended, GRE or GMAT required in support of School's application. TOEFL required for international applicants. Accepts transfer applicants. Graduates of unaccredited institution. Admission deadlines: August 7 (Fall), December 15 (Spring), May 15 (Summer I), June 15 (Summer II). International applications must be received 5 months prior to registration. Phone: (817)689-4321.

ADMISSION STANDARDS. Varies with program. Usual minimum average: 3.0 (A = 4). Must meet index GRE/GMAT + (200 times the GPA on last 60 hours of undergraduate work.)

FINANCIAL AID. Annual awards from institutional funds: 860 scholarships, 20 teaching assistantships, Federal W/S, loans. Approved for VA benefits. Apply by March 1 to Division Director of major field. Use FAFSA. Phone: (817)689-4214. Aid sometimes available to part-time students.

DEGREE REQUIREMENTS. For M.A.: 30 semester hours minimum, at least 24 in residence; reading knowledge of one foreign language; thesis; final comprehensive exam. For M.Ed., M.B.A., M.S., M.S.K.: 36 hours minimum, at least 30 in residence; final comprehensive exam; substantial research paper.

FIELDS OF STUDY.
Biology.
Business Administration.
Computer Science.
Education. Includes counseling, administration, elementary, physical, reading, secondary, special.
English.
Family Nurse Practitioner.
History.
Kinesiology.
Nurse Educator.
Nursing.
Political Science.
Psychology.
Radiologic Administration.
Radiologic Education.

MIDWESTERN UNIVERSITY
Downers Grove, Illinois 60515-1235

Chicago College of Osteopathic Medicine

Founded 1900. Coed. Private control. Semester system. Library: 84,000 volumes, 1400 current periodicals, 41 PCs; has MEDLINE, CANCERLINE, BIOETHIC, HEALTH, TOXLINE, DIALOG, OCLC.

Annual tuition: resident $17,602, nonresident $21,343. On-campus housing available. Average academic year housing cost: $5575 (including board) for single students; $5716 for married students. Enrollment: first-year class 125, total 591 (men 65%, women 35%). Faculty: full-time 231, part-time 69. Degree conferred: D.O.

ADMISSION REQUIREMENTS. AACOMAS report, bachelor's degree, official transcripts, MCAT, three recommendations (one from premed advisory committee, one evaluation from a physician, preferably a D.O.), supplemental college form required in support of application. Interview by invitation only. Graduates of unaccredited colleges not considered. Preference given to state residents. Apply by February 1 to the Director of Admissions and Marketing. Admits first-year students Fall only. Rolling admissions process. Application fee $50. Phone: (800)458-6253.

ADMISSION STANDARDS. Selective. Accepts approximately 5% of total annual applicants. Usual minimum average: 3.0 (A = 4). Mean GPA: 3.36.

FINANCIAL AID. Scholarships, full and partial tuition waivers, Federal W/S, loans. Apply by June 1 to the Financial Aid Office. Use FAFSA and institutional FAF.

DEGREE REQUIREMENT. For D.O.: satisfactory completion of four-year program.

MILLERSVILLE UNIVERSITY OF PENNSYLVANIA
Millersville, Pennsylvania 17551-0302

Founded 1850. Located 3 miles SW of Lancaster. Coed. Semester system. State control. Library: 472,098 volumes, 440,000 microforms.

Tuition: per credit, resident $187, nonresident $336. On-campus housing for single graduate students. Housing cost: $3900 (including board). Apply to Office of Resident Life. Phone: (717)872-3162.

Graduate Division

Graduate study since 1959. Enrollment: full-time 150, part-time 750. Faculty: full-time 150, part-time 10. Degrees conferred: M.Ed., M.S., M.A.

ADMISSION REQUIREMENTS. Transcripts, statement of academic and professional goals, three recommendations, GRE or MAT required in support of application. TOEFL required for international applicants. Accepts transfer applicants. Graduates of unaccredited incitations not considered. Apply to Graduate Office by May 1. Rolling admissions process. Application fee $25. Phone: (717)872-3030; fax: (717)871-2022.

ADMISSION STANDARDS. Selective for most departments, Usual minimum average: 2.75 (A = 4).

FINANCIAL AID. Annual awards from institutional funds: eighty assistantships, Federal W/S, loans. Approved for VA benefits. Apply to Dean, Graduate School for assistantships; to Financial Aid Office for all other aid. Use FAFSA. Phone: (717)872-3026. About 20% of students receive aid other than loans from College and outside sources. Loans available for part-time students.

DEGREE REQUIREMENTS. For M.Ed.: 30 credit hours minimum, 36 credit hours without research papers; qualifying exam; research paper. For M.A., M.S.: 30 credit hours minimum; qualifying exam; thesis/nonthesis option by program.

FIELDS OF STUDY.
Biological Science.
Counselor Education. Includes elementary, secondary; post-master's program available.
Earth Sciences.
Education Supervision. Post-master's program only.
Elementary Education.
English.
Foreign Language. Includes French, German, Latin, Spanish.
Gifted Education.
History.
Industrial Arts.
Mathematics.
Psychological Services.
Psychology.
Reading Supervision. Post-master's program only.
School Psychology. Post-master's program.
Special Education.

MILLS COLLEGE
Oakland, California 94613-1000
http://www.mills.edu

Founded 1852. Located 12 miles E of San Francisco. Coed on graduate level. Private control. Semester system. Library: 193,000 volumes, 7657 microforms, 17 PCs.

Annual tuition: full-time $9260; per course $2340. On-campus housing for single graduate students. Average academic year cost: $6100 (including board). Contact Director of Residence Life. Phone: (510)430-2130. Day care facilities available.

Graduate Programs

Enrollment: full-time 261, part-time 48. College faculty teaching graduate students: full-time 40, part-time 35. Degrees conferred: M.A., M.F.A.

ADMISSION REQUIREMENTS. Two transcripts, GRE, three letters of recommendations required in support of application. Samples of creative work required for art, music, and writing majors. Interview required for some programs. TOEFL required for international applicants. Apply to Director of Graduate Study by February 1 (Fall), November 1 (Spring). Application fee $50. Phone: (510)430-3309; fax: (510)430-3314.

ADMISSION STANDARDS. Very selective. Usual minimum average: 3.2 (A = 4).

FINANCIAL AID. Limited annual awards from institutional funds: eighty academic scholarships, ninety teaching assistantships, special scholarships, music lesson scholarships, Federal W/S, loans. Apply to Director of Graduate Study by February 1 for scholarships, assistantships; to Financial Aid Office for all other programs. Use FAFSA and FAF of CSS. Phone: (415)430-2134. About 46% of students receive some form of financial aid, including loans.

DEGREE REQUIREMENTS. For M.F.A., M.A.: 10-12 semester course credits minimum, two years in residence; thesis or final project; final written/oral exam. Thesis is credited as a two-semester courses.

FIELDS OF STUDY.
American and English Literature. M.A. only.
Art. Includes ceramics, painting, sculpture, photography; admits Fall term only. M.F.A. only.
Creative Writing. Includes fiction, nonfiction, poetry. M.F.A. only.
Dance. Includes performance. M.A., M.F.A.
Education. Includes elementary, secondary, child life in hospitals. M.A., teaching credentials.
Interdisciplinary Computer Science. M.A.
Liberal Studies. M.A. (part-time evening program).
Music. Composition; M.A. Performance, electronic music; M.F.A.

MILWAUKEE SCHOOL OF ENGINEERING
Milwaukee, Wisconsin 53201-3109

Founded 1903. Coed. Private control. Quarter system. Graduate study available on part-time evening basis only. Special facilities: Applied Industrial Research Institute, Applied Technology Center, Biomedical Research Center, Fluid Power Institute. Library: 53,000 volumes, 48,600 microforms.

Tuition: per credit $325. Limited on-campus housing as most students are part-time evening. Contact Housing Office for information. Phone: (414)277-7400.

Graduate School

Enrollment: part-time only, about 400. Faculty teaching graduate students: 30. Degrees conferred: M.S., M.S.E.E., M.S.E.M., M.S.P.

ADMISSION REQUIREMENTS. Transcripts, GRE/GMAT, interview required in support of School's application. TOEFL required for international applicants. Accepts transfer applicants. Apply to Graduate School by July 1. Application fee $25. Phone: (414)277-7155 or (800)321-6763; fax: (414)277-7475.

ADMISSION STANDARDS. Selective. Usual minimum average: 2.75 (A = 4).

FINANCIAL AID. Limited to three research assistantships, loans.

DEGREE REQUIREMENTS. For master's: 50 quarter hours minimum, at least 41 in residence.

FIELDS OF STUDY.
Engineering.
Engineering Management.
Environmental Engineering. M.S.E.E.
Perfusion. M.S.P.

UNIVERSITY OF MINNESOTA
Minneapolis, Minnesota 55455-0213

Established 1851. Coed. State control. Quarter system. Special facilities: Bell Museum of Natural History, member of Committee on Institutional Cooperation with other Big Ten universities and the University of Chicago. Graduate study also offered at the Duluth campus. Library: more than 5,000,000 volumes, 3,000,000 microforms.

Annual tuition: full-time, resident $4680, nonresident $9390; part-time per quarter, resident $905, nonresident $1359. On-campus housing for married students, single men and women. Average academic year housing cost: $325–$395 per month for married students; $1800 per quarter (including board) for single students. Apply to the Housing Office. Phone: (612)624-2994.

Graduate School

Graduate study since 1879. Enrollment: full-time 6000, part-time 5600. Faculty: full- and part-time 3300. Degrees conferred: M.A., M.S., M.Arch., M.B.A., M.F.A., M.E., M.F., M.S.W., Ed.D., Ph.D., and many other designated degrees.

ADMISSION REQUIREMENTS. Transcripts required in support of School's application. GRE Subject Tests, MAT, GMAT required for some departments. TOEFL required for international applicants. Accepts transfer applicants. Graduates of unaccredited institutions not considered. Apply to Graduate School by July 15 (Fall), October 25 (Winter), December 15 (Spring), April 15 (Summer 1), May 15 (Summer 11). Application fee $40, $50 for international applicants. Phone: (612)625-3014.

ADMISSION STANDARDS. Acceptance ratios vary among degree programs; admission based on competition generated by spaces available and applications received.

FINANCIAL AID. Individual departments award and administer graduate assistantships. Limited number of fellowships; program nomination is required for consideration. Apply to individual department.

DEGREE REQUIREMENTS. For master's: 45 quarter hours minimum; reading knowledge of one foreign language for most departments; thesis/nonthesis option for some departments; final design project for some departments; final written/oral exam. For Ph.D.: 90 quarter hours minimum; reading knowledge of two foreign languages or one language/research tool/collateral field in some departments; preliminary oral and written exam; thesis; final oral. For Ed.D.: 90 quarter hours minimum; supervised internship/clinical experience; preliminary written/oral exam; project; final oral exam.

FIELDS OF STUDY.
Aerospace Engineering.
Agricultural and Applied Economics.
Agricultural Education.
Agronomy.
American Studies.
Ancient and Medieval Art and Archaeology.
Anesthesiology.
Animal Sciences.
Anthropology.
Arabic.
Architecture.
Art.
Art Education.
Art History.
Astronomy.
Astrophysics.
Biochemistry, Molecular Biology, and Biophysics.
Biomedical Engineering.
Biomedical Science.
Biophysical Sciences and Medical Physics.
Biophysics.
Biostatistics.
Biosystems and Agricultural Engineering.
Business Administration.
Business and Marketing Education.
Business Taxation.
Cellular and Integrative Physiology.
Chemical Engineering.
Chemical Physics.

Chemistry.
Child Psychology.
Chinese.
Civil Engineering.
Classics.
Clinical Laboratory Science.
Communication Disorders.
Comparative Literature.
Comparative Studies in Discourse and Society.
Computer and Information Sciences.
Conservation Biology.
Control Science and Dynamical Systems.
Creative Writing.
Dentistry.
Dermatology.
Design, Housing and Apparel.
East Asian Studies.
Ecology.
Economics.
Education.
Educational Administration.
Educational Policy and Administration.
Educational Psychology.
Educational Psychology.
Electrical Engineering.
Elementary Education.
English.
English as a Second Language.
Entomology.
Environmental Health.
Epidemiology.
Experimental Surgery.
Family Education.
Family Planning Administration.
Family Practice and Community Health.
Family Social Science.
Fisheries.
Fluid Mechanics.
Food Science.
Forestry.
French.
Geography.
Geological Engineering.
Geology.
Geophysics.
Geotechnology.
German.
Germanic Philology.
Greek.
Health Informatics.
Hispanic and Luso-Brazilian Literature.
Hispanic and Luso-Brazilian Literature and Linguistics.
Hispanic Linguistics.
Hispanic Literature.
History.
History of Medicine and Biological Sciences.
History of Science and Technology.
Health Services Research and Policy.
Health Services Research, Policy, and Administration.
Horticulture.
Hospital Pharmacy.
Industrial Education.
Industrial Engineering.
Industrial Relations.
Interdisciplinary Archaeological Studies.
Italian.
Japanese.
Kinesiology.
Landscape Architecture.
Latin.
Liberal Studies.

Linguistics.
Luso-Brazilian Literature.
Management of Technology.
Mass Communication.
Materials Science and Engineering.
Mathematics.
Mathematics Education.
Mechanical Engineering.
Mechanics.
Medical Microbiology.
Medicinal Chemistry.
Medicine.
Microbial Engineering.
Microbiology, Immunology, and Molecular Pathobiology.
Mineral Engineering.
Molecular, Cellular, Developmental Biology and Genetics.
Music.
Music Education.
Musicology.
Neurology.
Neuroscience.
Neurosurgery.
Nursing.
Nutrition.
Obstetrics and Gynecology.
Operations Research.
Ophthalmology.
Oral Biology.
Orthopedic Surgery.
Otolaryngology.
Pathology.
Pediatrics.
Pharmaceutics.
Pharmacognosy.
Pharmacology.
Pharmacy Administration.
Philosophy.
Physical Chemistry.
Physical Medicine and Rehabilitation.
Physical Therapy.
Physics.
Physiological Hygiene.
Planning.
Plant Biological Sciences.
Plant Breeding.
Plant Pathology.
Plastic Surgery.
Political Science.
Portuguese.
Psychiatry.
Psychology.
Public Affairs.
Radiology.
Recreation, Park, and Leisure Studies.
Rhetoric and Scientific and Technical Communication.
Russian Area Studies.
Scandinavian Studies.
Science and Technology Policy.
Scientific Computation.
Scientific and Technical Communication.
Secondary Education.
Social and Administrative Pharmacy.
Social Work.
Sociology.
Soil Science.
South Asian Languages.
Spanish.
Speech-Communication.
Statistics.
Surgery.
Theater Arts.

Therapeutic Radiology.
Theriogenology.
Toxicology.
Urology.
Veterinary Biology.
Veterinary Medicine.
Veterinary Pathobiology.
Veterinary Surgery, Radiology, and Anesthesiology.
Vocational Education.
Water Resources Science.
Wildlife Conservation.
Zoology.

Law School

Established 1888. Semester system. Law library: 800,000 volumes. Library has LEXIS, NEXIS, WESTLAW, LUMINA. Special facilities: Center for Computer Assisted Legal Invention.

Annual tuition: full-time, resident $8448, nonresident $14,344. Limited on-campus housing available. Total average annual additional expense: $9500.

Enrollment: first-year class 270; total full-time 810 (men 53%, women 47%); no part-time students. Faculty: full-time 50, part-time 70. Degrees conferred: J.D., J.D.-M.B.A., J.D.-M.P.A., LL.M., S.J.D.

ADMISSION REQUIREMENTS. LSDAS Law School report, bachelor's degree, transcripts, LSAT, personal statement, letters of recommendation required in support of application. Interview not required. Occasionally accepts transfer applicants. Graduates of unaccredited colleges not considered. Apply to the Director of Admission after October 1, before March 1. Application fee $30. Phone: (612)625-5005.

ADMISSION STANDARDS. Selective. Accepts 25–30% of total annual applicants.

FINANCIAL AID. Scholarships, full and partial tuition waivers, Federal W/S, loans. Apply to the University's Office of Financial Aid by February 15. Use FAFSA. About 85% of students receive some aid from School.

DEGREE REQUIREMENTS. For J.D.: satisfactory completion of three-year program; 88 credit hours. For LL.M.: at least 24 credit hours beyond the J.D.; one year in full-time residence. For S.J.D.: one year in full-time residence beyond the master's; original research project; final oral exam.

Note: Summer study available at Université Jean Moulin, Lyon (France), and Uppsala University Law School (Sweden). Joint degree programs exist with Hubert H. Humphrey Institute of Public Affairs and Curtis L. Carlson School of Management.

Medical School (55455-0310)

Founded 1888. Annual tuition: resident $14,092, nonresident $28,184. On-campus housing available. Apply to Admissions Office, Medical School. Total average figure for all other expenses: $7500.

Enrollment: first-year class 185 (EDP 20), total 857 (men 53%, women 47%). Faculty: full-time 919, part-time 1642. Degrees conferred: M.D., M.D.-M.S., M.D.-Ph.D. Medical Scientist Training Program. The M.S. and Ph.D. are offered through the Graduate School.

ADMISSION REQUIREMENTS. AMCAS report, transcripts, letters of evaluation, MCAT required in support of application. Applicants must have completed bachelor's degree. Preference given to residents of Minnesota. Interview by invitation only. Accepts transfer students from University of Minnesota-Duluth. Has EDP; apply between June 15 and August 1. Apply to AMCAS after June 15, before November 15. Application fee none. Phone: (612)624-1122; fax: (612)624-6800.

ADMISSION STANDARDS. Selective. Accepts 16% of total annual applicants. Approximately 90% are state residents.

FINANCIAL AID. Loans. Apply to Financial Aid Office after acceptance. Use FAFSA.

DEGREE REQUIREMENTS. For M.D.: satisfactory completion of three- or four-year program. For M.S. and Ph.D., see Graduate School listing above.

FIELDS OF GRADUATE STUDY.
Biochemistry.
Biomedical Engineering.
Cell Biology.
Genetics.
Immunology.
Microbiology.
Molecular Biology.
Neurosciences.
Pathobiology.
Pharmacology.
Physiology.

School of Dentistry

Founded 1888. Quarter system. Annual tuition: resident $9920, nonresident $13,968. On-campus housing available. Average academic year housing cost: $6762. Contact Housing Office at (612)624-2994. Total average cost for all other first-year expenses: $2957.

Enrollment: first-year class 86, total 30 (men 70%, women 30%); postgraduates: about 800. Degrees conferred: B.D., D.D.S. The M.S. and Ph.D. are offered through the Graduate School.

ADMISSION REQUIREMENTS. AADSAS, transcripts, three letters of recommendations, DAT (not later than October) required in support of School's application. TOEFL, TWE required for non-native speakers of English. Applicants must have completed at least three years of college study. Has early admission program. Interview by invitation only. Accepts transfer applicants from U.S. and Canadian dental schools. Preference given to residents of Minnesota, nearby states, and Manitoba. Apply to Associate Dean after June 1, before February 1. Application fee $50. Phone: (612)625-7149.

ADMISSION STANDARDS. Selective. Usual minimum average: 2.5 (A = 4). Accepts 25–30% of total annual applicants. Approximately 60% are state residents.

FINANCIAL AID. Scholarships, summer research fellowships, loans. Apply to University Student Financial Aid Office after acceptance; no specified closing date. Use FAFSA. Phone: (612)626-2290. 100% of students demonstrating need receive financial assistance.

DEGREE REQUIREMENTS. For B.D.: satisfactory completion of three-year undergraduate program and one year at School. For D.D.S.: satisfactory completion of forty-five-month program. For M.S., Ph.D.: requirements vary with department; see Graduate School listing above.

FIELDS OF GRADUATE STUDY.
Endodontics.
Oral and Maxillofacial Surgery.
Oral Biology.
Oral Microbiology.
Oral Pathology.
Oral Radiology.
Orthodontics.
Pediatric Dentistry.

Periodontics.
Prosthodontics.

College of Veterinary Medicine

Established in 1947. Located in St. Paul (55108). Annual tuition: resident and nonresident contract $8652, nonresident $13,162. Off-campus housing only. Annual living expenses: $3500–$5500.

Enrollment: first-year class 76; full-time 300 (men 50%, women 50%); postgraduates 80. Faculty: full-time 80, part-time 10. Degrees conferred: D.V.M., D.V.M.-Ph.D.

ADMISSION REQUIREMENTS. VMCAS report, transcripts, GRE General, animal/veterinary knowledge required in support of application. Interview not required. Applicants must have completed at least three years of college study (by Spring prior to entrance) with a specific area distribution. Accepts a limited number of transfer applicants. Apply to the Office of Student Affairs and Admissions after August 1, before November 15. Admits Fall only. Preference given to state and contract residents. Application fee $50. Phone: (612)624-4747.

ADMISSION STANDARDS. Selective. Accepts about 40% of total annual applicants. Accepts not more than 20% of nonresident applicants.

FINANCIAL AID. Awards, scholarships, fellowships, assistantships, Federal W/S, loans. Apply to University Office of Student Financial Aid by March 1. Use FAFSA. Most students receive loans or have part-time employment.

DEGREE REQUIREMENTS. For D.V.M.: satisfactory completion of four-year program. For M.S., Ph.D.,: see Graduate School listings above.

FIELDS OF GRADUATE STUDY.
Veterinary Biology.
Veterinary Medicine.
Veterinary Parasitology.
Veterinary Pathology.
Veterinary Radiology and Anesthesiology.
Veterinary Surgery.
Veterinary Theriogenology.
Note: M.P.H. in Veterinary Public Health through the School of Public Health.

UNIVERSITY OF MINNESOTA

Duluth, Minnesota 55812-2596
http://www.d.umn.edu/academic.html

Founded in 1895. State control. Quarter system. Special facilities: Alworth Institute for International Studies, Large Lakes Observatory, Marshall Performing Arts Center, Natural Resource Research Institute, Small Business Development Center, Tweed Museum of Art. Library: 421,100 volumes, 373,100 microforms, 113 PCs.

Annual tuition: resident $4350, nonresident $9390; per credit, resident $233, nonresident 473. On-campus housing for single graduate men and women; none for married students. Average academic year housing cost: $8100 (including board) for single students. Phone: (219)726-9119.

Graduate School

Graduate study since 1957. Enrollment: full-time 200, part-time 158. Faculty teaching graduate students: 380. Degrees conferred: M.A., M.S., M.B.A., M.L.S., M.M., M.S.W.

ADMISSION REQUIREMENTS. Two transcripts required in support of School's application. GRE/GMAT/MAT required for some departments. TOEFL required for international applicants. Accepts transfer students. Apply to Associate Dean of Graduate School at least eight weeks prior to registration. Application fee $40, $50 for international applicants. Phone: (218)726-7523; fax: (218)726-6970.

ADMISSION STANDARDS. Selective. Usual minimum average: 3.0 (A = 4).

FINANCIAL AID. Annual awards from institutional funds: 3 fellowships, 110 teaching assistantships, 20 research assistantships, tuition remission for TA, RA, and fellowship recipients, loans. Approved for VA benefits. Apply to director of each program for fellowships, assistantships; to director of Financial Aid for loans. No specified closing date. Use FAFSA. About 60% of students receive aid other than loans from University and outside sources.

DEGREE REQUIREMENTS. For master's Plan A: 44 quarter hours minimum; thesis; final written/oral exam. Plan B: 44 quarter hours minimum without thesis; major project; final written/oral exam.

FIELDS OF STUDY.
Applied and Computational Mathematics. M.S. (Plans A and B).
Art. Includes studio, education. M.A. (Plan B).
Biology. Includes botany, zoology, environmental, cellular, physiological. M.S. (Plans A and B).
Business Administration. M.B.A. (Plan B).
Chemistry. Includes analytical, inorganic, physical, organic, biochemistry. M.S. (Plans A and B).
Communication Disorders. M.A. (Plan B).
Computer Science. M.S. (Plans A and B).
Educational Psychology. M.A. (Plan B).
English. Includes teaching of English; M.A. (Plan B).
Geology. M.S.
Liberal Studies. M.L.S. (Plan B).
Music. M.M. (Plan B).
Physics. M.S. (Plan A and B).
Social Work. M.S.W. (Plan B).
Toxicology. M.S. (Plans A and B); Ph.D.
Water Resources Science. M.S. (Plans A and B); Ph.D.

Duluth Campus School of Medicine (55812)

Established 1972. Annual tuition: resident $14,092, nonresident $28,684. Total average cost for all other expenses: $7500.

Enrollment: first-year class 50; total 103 (men 60%, women 40%); postgraduates 24. Faculty: full-time 45, part-time and volunteers 250. Two-year transfer program.

ADMISSION REQUIREMENTS. AMCAS report, transcripts, MCAT, recommendations required in support of application. Interview by invitation only. Preference given to state residents and residents of North Dakota, South Dakota, Iowa, and northern Wisconsin. Has EDP; apply between June 15 and August 1. Graduates of unaccredited colleges not considered. Apply to Associate Dean after June 15, before November 15 (firm). Application fee none. Phone: (218)726-8511; fax: (218)726-6235.

ADMISSION STANDARDS. Selective. Accepts about 15% of total annual applicants. Approximately 87% are state residents.

FINANCIAL AID. Scholarships, loans. Apply to University Financial Aid Program following admission. About 93% of students eligible for aid receive assistance.

DEGREE REQUIREMENTS. Satisfactory completion of two-year program. All students transfer to University of Minnesota Medical School in Minneapolis to complete studies for M.D.

MINOT STATE UNIVERSITY
Minot, North Dakota 58702-0002

Founded 1913. Coed. State control. Semester system. Library: 289,000 volumes.

Annual tuition: resident $2578, nonresident $6462; per credit, resident $107.45, nonresident $269.25. Limited on-campus housing available. Average academic year housing cost: $3200 for married students, $1960 for single students. Contact Housing Office for both on- and off-campus housing information. Phone: (701)858-3360.

Graduate School and Continuing Education

Enrollment: full- and part-time 267. University faculty teaching graduate students: full-time 30, part-time 9. Degrees conferred: M.S., M.M.E., M.A.T.

ADMISSION REQUIREMENTS. Official transcripts from all colleges/universities attended, GRE/GMAT, three letters of recommendation, autobiography required in support of School's application. TOEFL required for international applicants. Apply to the Dean of the Graduate School at least four weeks prior to registration. Application fee $25. Phone: (701)858-3484.

ADMISSION STANDARDS. Selective. Usual minimum average: 3.00 (A = 4).

FINANCIAL AID. Annual awards from institutional funds: scholarships, Federal W/S, loans. Approved for VA benefits. Apply to Financial Aid Office; no specified closing date. Use FAFSA. Phone: (701)858-3375.

DEGREE REQUIREMENTS. For master's: 30–36 semester hours minimum; thesis option/written comprehensive exam; oral exam.

FIELDS OF STUDY.
Audiology.
Criminal Justice.
Elementary Education.
Management. M.S.
Mathematics. M.A.T.
Music. M.M.E.
School Psychology.
Science. M.A.T.
Special Education—Early Childhood.
Special Education—Education of the Deaf.
Special Education—Learning Disabilities.
Special Education—Severely Multihandicapped.
Speech-Language Pathology.

MISSISSIPPI COLLEGE
Clinton, Mississippi 39058

Founded 1826. Located 5 miles W of Jackson. Coed. Private control. Semester system. Library: 240,000 volumes, 900 current periodicals, 20 PCs.

Tuition: per hour $240. On-campus housing for single students only. Average academic year housing cost: $3000 (including board); off-campus housing cost: $500–$700 per month. Contact the Dean of Students Office for both on- and off-campus housing information. Phone: (601)925-3248.

Graduate School

Enrollment: full- and part-time 658. College faculty: full-time 92, part-time 41. Degrees conferred: M.A., M.Ed., M.B.A., M.M., M.C.C., M.C.P., M.C.S., M.H.S., M.S., M.S.S.

ADMISSION REQUIREMENTS. Two transcripts, two photographs, GRE/NTE/GMAT required in support of application. GRE Subject for some programs. Interview required for most departments. TOEFL required for foreign applicants. Accepts transfer applicants. Graduates of unaccredited colleges not considered. Apply to Graduate Office by August 20 (Fall), May 15 (Summer). Rolling admissions process. Application fee $25, $75 for international applicants. Phone: (601)925-3225; fax: (601)925-3804; E-mail: graduate@mc.edu.

ADMISSION STANDARDS. Relatively open. Usual minimum average: 2.75 (A = 4).

FINANCIAL AID. Annual awards from institutional funds: ten teaching assistantships; tuition waivers; loans. Apply by May 1 to appropriate department chair; to Financial Aid Office for all other programs. Use FAFSA. About 20% of students receive aid other than loans from College and outside sources. Aid sometimes available for part-time students.

DEGREE REQUIREMENTS. For master's: 30–36 semester hours minimum, at least 24–36 in residence; thesis or final project; reading knowledge of one foreign language for M.A.; final oral/written comprehensive exam.

FIELDS OF STUDY.
Accounting. M.B.A.
Art. M.A.
Art Education. M.Ed.
Biology Education. M.Ed.
Business Administration. M.B.A.
Business Education. M.Ed.
Combined Sciences. M.C.S.
Community Psychology. M.Ed.
Computer Science. M.S.
Computer Science Education. M.Ed.
Elementary Education. M.Ed.
English. M.A.
Health Care Administration. M.H.S.
History. M.A., M.Ed., M.S.S.
Marriage and Family Therapy. M.S.
Mass Communication. M.S.
Mathematics. M.S.
Mathematics Education. M.Ed.
Music. Includes applied, education, performance, accompanying. M.M.
School Administration. M.Ed.
Science Education. M.Ed.
Secondary Education. M.Ed.
Social Sciences. M.S.S.
Sociology. Includes general. M.S.S.

School of Law (39201-1391)

Established 1975. Semester system. Library: 220,000 volumes.

Annual tuition: full-time $11,400. No on-campus housing available. Total average annual additional expenses: $12,500.

Enrollment: first-year class, full-time 155; total 383 (men 65%, women 35%). Faculty: full-time 18, part-time 21. Degree conferred: J.D.

ADMISSION REQUIREMENTS. LSDAS Law School report, bachelor's degree, transcripts, LSAT (not later than March), recommendations required in support of application. Graduates of unaccredited colleges not considered. Apply to Office of Admissions by May 1. Application fee $25. Phone: (601)353-3907.

ADMISSION STANDARDS. Accepts about 40–45% of total annual applications.

FINANCIAL AID. Full and partial scholarships, Federal W/S, loans. Apply to Office of Financial Aid by May 1. Phone: (601)925-3254. Use FAFSA. About 90% of students receive some aid from School.

DEGREE REQUIREMENTS. For J.D.: satisfactory completion of three-year (full-time), four-year (extended division) program; 88 credit hours.

MISSISSIPPI STATE UNIVERSITY
Mississippi State, Mississippi 39762
http://www.mstate.edu

Founded 1878. Located 130 miles NE of Jackson. Coed. State control. Semester system. Special facilities: Institute for Humanities, Cobb Institute for Archaeology, Center for Robotics, Automation, and Artificial Intelligence, electron microscope, Mississippi Energy Research Center, Mississippi State Chemical Laboratory, Radiological Safety Office, Water Resource Research Institute, Center for International Security and Strategic Studies, Mississippi Alcohol Safety Education Program, John C. Stennis Institute of Government, Social Science Research Center, Gulf Coast Research Laboratory at Ocean Springs. Library: 850,000 volumes, 2,067,000 microforms, 7380 current periodicals, 44 PCs.

Annual tuition: full-time, resident $2631, nonresident $5451, per credit, resident $111, nonresident $268. On-campus housing for 268 married students. Average academic year housing cost: $3000 for married students, $1500–$2240 (room only) for single students. Contact Housing Director. Phone: (601)325-3557. Day care facilities available.

Graduate School

Graduate study since 1893. Enrollment: full-time 1521, part-time 941 (men 55%, women 45%). University faculty: full-time 779. Degrees conferred: M.A., M.S., M.Ag., M.A.B.M., M.B.A., M.F.A., M.P.P.A., M.Prof.Acc., M.Tax., Ed.S., D.B.A., Ed.D., Ph.D.

ADMISSION REQUIREMENTS. Official transcripts, GRE, GMAT, three letters of recommendation required in support of School's application. Interview not required. TOEFL required of international students. Accepts transfer applicants. Apply to Office of Admissions at least twenty days prior to registration. Application fee $25. Phone: (601)325-7400; fax: (601)325-1967.

ADMISSION STANDARDS. Selective for some departments, relatively open for others. Usual minimum average: 2.5 for master's, 3.0–3.5 for Ed.S., Ed.D., Ph.D. (A = 4).

FINANCIAL AID. Annual awards from institutional funds: scholarships, grants, teaching assistantships, research assistantships, Federal W/S, loans. Approved for VA benefits. Apply by March 1 to Dean of the Graduate School for assistantships; to Financial Aid Office for all other programs. Use FAFSA and institutional FAF. Phone: (601)325-2450; fax: (601)325-0702. About 40% of students receive aid other than loans from University and outside sources. Aid sometimes available for part-time students.

DEGREE REQUIREMENTS. For M.A., M.S.: 30 semester hours minimum, at least 24 in residence; reading knowledge of one foreign language for majors in English, physical and biological sciences; final oral exam. For M.Ag.: same as for M.A., except thesis is optional; no language requirement; final written/oral exam. For M.B.A., M.Prof.Acc.: 30 semester hours minimum, at least 24 in residence; no thesis or language requirement; final written/oral exam. For Ed.S.: 30 semester hours beyond the master's, at least 24 in residence; special problem or thesis included; final written/oral exam. For Ph.D.: three years beyond the bachelor's, at least one year in full-time residence, preliminary exam; foreign language proficiency for some programs; qualifying exam; dissertation; final oral exam. For D.B.A., Ed.D.: essentially the same as for the Ph.D., except no language requirement.

FIELDS OF STUDY.
Accounting.
Aerospace Engineering.
Agribusiness Management. M.Agri.Bus.Mgt. only.
Agricultural Economics.
Agricultural and Extension Education.
Agricultural Pest Management. M.Ag. only.
Agronomy.
Animal Physiology. Interdepartmental.
Architecture.
Biochemistry.
Biological/Biomedical Engineering.
Biological Engineering.
Biological Sciences.
Business Administration.
Business Education.
Chemical Engineering. M.S. only.
Chemistry. Includes analytical, inorganic, organic, physical. Placement exam; one language for M.S.
Civil Engineering.
Computational Engineering.
Computer Engineering.
Computer Science.
Counselor Education.
Economics.
Education.
Educational Psychology.
Electrical Engineering.
Electronic Visualization. M.F.A. only.
Elementary Education.
Engineering.
Engineering Mechanics.
Engineering Physics.
English. One language for M.A.; M.A. only.
Entomology.
Food Science and Technology.
Foreign Languages. French, German, Spanish; M.A. only.
Forest Products.
Forest Resources.
Forestry. M.F., M.S. only.
General Engineering.
Genetics. Interdepartmental; one language for M.S.
Geosciences.
History.
Horticulture.
Industrial Engineering. M.S. only.
Instructional Technology.
Mathematics. One language for M.S.
Mechanical Engineering.
Molecular Biology.
Nuclear Engineering. M.S. only.
Nutrition.
Physical Education.
Physics. One language for M.S.
Plant Pathology.
Political Science. Master's only.
Poultry Science.
Psychology. Master's only.
Public Administration.
Public Policy and Administration. M.P.P.A. only.
School Administration.
Secondary Education.
Sociology.
Special Education. Master's, Ed.S. only.

Statistics.
Taxation. Master's only.
Technology.
Veterinary Medical Science.
Weed Science.
Wildlife Ecology.

College of Veterinary Medicine (PO Box 9825)

Annual tuition: resident $5215, nonresident $12,706. Total average costs for all other expenses: $4500. On-campus housing available.

Enrollment: first-year class 45; total 206 (men 50%, women 50%); postgraduate, 65. Faculty: full-time 62, part-time 11. Degrees offered: D.V.M., D.V.M.-M.S., D.V.M.-Ph.D. The M.S. and Ph.D. are offered through the Graduate School.

ADMISSION REQUIREMENTS. VMCAS report, transcripts showing completion of sixty-five hours of preprofessional college work, VCAT, recommendations, animal/veterinary experience, essay required in support of application. Interview by invitation only. Accepts transfer applicants on a space-available basis. Preference given to state residents. Apply to Assistant Dean after August 1, prior to November 1. Application fee $25. Phone: (601)325-1129.

ADMISSION STANDARDS. Selective. Accepts 40% of total annual applicants. Approximately 20% are nonresidents.

FINANCIAL AID. Research assistantships, Federal W/S, loans. Apply to Dean after acceptance. Use FAFSA.

DEGREE REQUIREMENTS. For D.V.M.: 152 semester hours and four years in residence. For M.S. and Ph.D.: see Graduate School listing above.

MISSISSIPPI UNIVERSITY FOR WOMEN
Columbus, Mississippi 39701-9998

Founded 1894. State control. Semester system. Library: 250,000 volumes, 652,000 microforms, 1600 current periodicals, 17 PCs.

Annual tuition: resident $2244, nonresident $4200. On-campus housing for 250 graduate students. Average academic year housing cost: $2090 (including meals). Apply to Graduate Housing Office for both on- and off-campus housing. Phone: (601)329-7142. Day care facilities available.

Graduate School

Enrollment: full-time 21, part-time 110. College faculty teaching graduate students: full-time 5, part-time 3. Degrees conferred: M.Ed., M.S., M.S.N.

ADMISSION REQUIREMENTS. Official transcripts, letters of recommendation, GRE required in support of School's application. TOEFL and Graduate English Proficiency required of international applicants. Accepts transfer applicants. Apply to the Dean of the Graduate School by April 1. Application fee none. Phone: (601)329-7142.

ADMISSION STANDARDS. Selective. Usual minimum average: 2.5; 3.0 in area of study (A = 4).

FINANCIAL AID. Annual awards from institutional funds: Federal traineeships (when available), in-state scholarships, Federal W/S, loans. Apply to Dean of the Graduate School; no specified closing date. Phone: (601)329-7142. About 80% of students receive aid other than loans from College and outside sources.

DEGREE REQUIREMENTS. For master's: 30–36 semester hour minimum, at least 30 in residence; written/oral final exam; thesis/nonthesis option; language optional with department/student.

FIELDS OF STUDY.
Gifted Studies. M.Ed.
Nursing. Includes family, gerontological practitioner.
Speech/Language Pathology. M.S.

THE UNIVERSITY OF MISSISSIPPI
University, Mississippi 38677

Founded 1848. Located 76 miles SE of Memphis, Tenn. Coed. State control. Semester system. New Science Center complex. Special facilities: Center for Computational Hydroscience and Engineering, Center for the Study of Southern Culture, Mary Buie Museum, National Center for Physical Acoustics, Research Institute for Pharmaceutical Sciences. Library: 917,000 volumes, 2,724,000 microforms, 14,100 current periodicals, 166 PCs.

Annual tuition: full-time, resident $1996, nonresident $5366; per credit, resident $111, nonresident $268. On-campus housing for both single and married students. Average academic year housing cost: $2015 (room only) for single students; $2300 for married students. Contact Director of Housing for both on- and off-campus housing. Phone: (601)232-7328.

Graduate School

Graduate study since 1870. Enrollment: full-time 1193, part-time 529. Graduate faculty: full- and part-time 400. Degrees conferred: M.A., M.S., M.B.A., M.Ed., M.F.A., M.M., M.Acc., M.S.S., M.Tax., D.A., Ed.Sp., Ed.D., Ph.D.

ADMISSION REQUIREMENTS. Official transcripts, three letters of recommendation, GRE, GMAT (Business), NTE (Education) required in support of School's application. Interview usually not required. TOEFL required for international applicants. Accepts transfer applicants. Graduates of unaccredited institutions not considered. Apply by April 1 to the Registrar's Office. Rolling admissions process. Phone: (601)232-7226.

ADMISSION STANDARDS. Selective. Usual minimum average: 3.0, 2.75 for last 60 credits (A = 4).

FINANCIAL AID. Scholarships, fellowships, special minority fellowships, teaching/research assistantships, Federal W/S, loans. Approved for VA benefits. Apply to Graduate School for Honors Fellowships and Minority Fellowships; to appropriate department for assistantships; to Office of Financial Aid for all other programs. No specified closing date. Use FAFSA. Phone: (601)232-7175. About 55% of students receive aid other than loans from University and outside sources. Aid available to part-time students.

DEGREE REQUIREMENTS. For M.A., M.S., M.S.S., M.Acc., M.Tax.: 30 semester hours minimum, at least 24 in residence; thesis included for six hours; reading knowledge of one foreign language for some majors; final oral exam. For M.B.A.: one year minimum in residence; specific number of hours depends upon previous preparation. For M.Ed.: 30 hours minimum, at least 24 in residence; final oral exam. For M.F.A.: 60 hours minimum, at least two years in residence; creative project included for six hours; final exhibition and final oral exam may be required. For M.M.: 30 hours minimum, at least 24 in residence; recital, composition, or thesis; final oral exam. For Ed.Sp.: 30 hours beyond the master's; special project; final oral exam. For D.A., Ed.D.: 60 hours of course work beyond the master's degree; one year of continuous full-time attendance; internship; doctoral essay; comprehensive exam. For Ph.D.: three years minimum beyond the bachelor's, at least two years in residence, and one year of continuous full-time attendance; preliminary exam; written, oral comprehensive exam; dissertation; final oral exam.

FIELDS OF STUDY.

Accountancy. GMAT for admission. M.Acc., Ph.D.

Anthropology. M.A.

Art. Includes art education. M.A., M.F.A. only.

Art History. M.A.

Biological Sciences. M.S., Ph.D.

Business Administration. GMAT required for admission. M.B.A., Ph.D.

Chemistry. M.S., Ph.D., D.A.

Classics. Greek, Latin, classical archaeology; one language in addition to major. M.A. only.

Communicative Disorders. Includes audiology, speech pathology. M.S., Sp.Ed.

Computational Engineering Science. M.S., Ph.D.

Economics. Ph.D.

Education. Includes curriculum and instruction, educational leadership, educational psychology. M.A., M.Ed., Ed.Sp., Ph.D.

Engineering. Includes civil, environmental engineering, computer science, geology and geological engineering, mechanical engineering, chemical engineering, electrical engineering.

English. M.A., Ph.D., D.A.

Exercise Science. M.S. only.

French. M.A.

Geology. M.S.

German. M.A.

Higher Education and Student Personnel. M.A.

History. One language for M.A., Ph.D., Ed.Sp.

Journalism. M.A. only.

Leisure Management. M.A. only.

Mathematics. M.A., M.S., Ph.D.

Medicinal Chemistry. Ph.D.

Music. Includes applied, composition, performance, theory, opera production, music education. M.M., D.A.

Pharmacy. Includes pharmacology, medicinal chemistry, pharmaceutics, pharmacognosy, pharmacy administration, hospital pharmacy. M.S., Ph.D.

Philosophy. M.A. only.

Physics. One language for M.A., M.S., Ph.D.

Political Science. M.A., Ph.D.

Psychology. M.A., Ph.D.

Secondary Education. M.A.

Sociology. One language or research tool for M.A. M.A., M.S.S. only.

Southern Studies. M.A. only.

Spanish. M.A.

Theater Arts. M.A., M.F.A. only.

Wellness. M.A.

School of Law

Established 1854 as a Department of Law. Semester system. Law library: 288,000 volumes. Library has LEXIS, NEXIS, WESTLAW, DIALOG. Annual tuition: resident $3118, nonresident $7844. On-campus housing available. Total average annual expense: $7500.

Enrollment: full-time, J.D. program, first-year class 179, total full-time 500 (men 65%, women 35%); graduate program 25. School faculty: full-time 26, part-time 5. Degrees conferred: J.D., J.D.-M.B.A., M.M.L.S., LL.M., M.C.L., J.S.D.

ADMISSION REQUIREMENTS. For J.D.: LSDAS Law School report, bachelor's degree, transcripts, LSAT, five letters of recommendation required in support of application. Accepts a lim-

ited number of transfer applicants. Apply to Law School Director of Admissions by March 1 (nonresidents for Summer, Fall), April 1 (residents for Summer). Fall or Summer admission only. Preference given to state residents. Application fee $20. Phone: (601)232-7361. For graduate degrees: transcripts required in support of application. Applicants should have graduated in upper half of law school class. Apply to Chair of the Graduate Program at least twenty days prior to registration.

ADMISSION STANDARDS. Selective. Accepts 20–25% of total applicants.

FINANCIAL AID. Scholarships, fellowships, assistantships, Federal W/S, loans. Apply to University Financial Aid Officer for loans, to Scholarship Coordinator for all others by March 1; to Chair of Graduate Programs by March 1. Use FAFSA. About 50% of students receive aid other than loans from School.

DEGREE REQUIREMENTS. For J.D.: satisfactory completion of ninety credit-hour program. For M.C.L., LL.M., M.M.L.S.: 24 hours minimum beyond the J.D.; thesis included for 6 hours. M.C.L. is designed for graduates of international law schools. For J.S.D.: 24 hours minimum beyond the LL.M.; thesis. For M.B.A.: see Graduate School listing above.

Note: Summer program at Dowling College, Cambridge (England), available.

UNIVERSITY OF MISSISSIPPI MEDICAL CENTER

Jackson, Mississippi 39216-4505

Includes Schools of Medicine, Nursing, Health-Related Professions, Dentistry, and University Hospital. Library: 100,000 volumes.

School of Medicine

Founded 1903, became four-year school in 1955.

Annual tuition: resident $6600, nonresident $13,200. Total average cost for all other expenses: $7908. Housing for 95 married students, 114 single graduate students.

Enrollment: M.D. program, first-year class 100 (EDP 10); total 398 (men 70%, women 30%); graduate program, total full-time 150 (men 85%, women 15%); part-time 102. Faculty: full-time 343; part-time 117. Degrees conferred: M.D., M.S., Ph.D.

ADMISSION REQUIREMENTS. For M.D. program: AMCAS report, transcripts, MCAT, recommendations required in support of application. Interview by invitation only. Applicants must have completed at least three years of college study. Preference given to state residents only. Has EDP; apply between June 15 and August 1. For graduate program: transcripts, five references, GRE General/Subject Tests required in support of application. Interview required for most departments. Accepts transfer applicants for M.D. and graduate program. Graduates of unaccredited colleges not considered. Apply to Registrar after June 15, before December 1 (M.D.). Application fee none. Phone: (601)984-5010; fax: (601)984-5008.

ADMISSION STANDARDS. Selective for M.D., selective for most graduate programs. Accepts 30% of total annual applicants for M.D. 100% are state residents.

FINANCIAL AID. Scholarships and loans available to medical students; research fellowships and teaching/research assistantships for graduate programs. Apply to Division of Student Services and Records for scholarships and loans, to appropriate department chair for fellowships and assistantships; no specified closing date, April 15 suggested.

DEGREE REQUIREMENTS. For M.D.: satisfactory completion of four-year program; advanced standing for work completed at other medical schools considered. For M.S.: 45 quarter hours minimum, at least one year in full-time residence; thesis; final oral exam for many departments. For Ph.D.: 82 quarter hours minimum, at least two years in full-time residence; preliminary exam; dissertation; final written/oral exams; reading knowledge of one language for many departments.

FIELDS OF GRADUATE STUDY.
Anatomy.
Biochemistry.
Microbiology.
Nutrition.
Obstetrics-Gynecology.
Parasitology.
Pathology.
Pharmacology.
Physiology.
Preventive Medicine.

School of Dentistry

Established 1973. State control.
Annual tuition: resident $4400, nonresident $10,400. No on-campus housing available. Average academic year housing cost: $11,940. Total average cost for all other first-year expenses: $3457.
Enrollment: first-year class 33; total 123 (men 70%, women 30%). Faculty: full-time 44, part-time 27. Degree conferred: D.M.D.

ADMISSION REQUIREMENTS. Transcripts, DAT, three letters of recommendation required in support of School's application. Interview by invitation only. Applicants must have completed at least three years of college study. Strong preference given to state residents. Accepts transfer applicants. Apply to Office of Student Services and Records after July 1, before March 1. Application fee: resident $25, nonresident $50. Phone: (601)984-6009.

ADMISSION STANDARDS. Selective. Accepts about 80% of total annual applicants. 100% are state residents.

FINANCIAL AID. Scholarships, grants, tuition waivers, loans. Apply to Office of Student Services and Records; no specified closing date. Preference given to applications received before April 15. Phone: (601)984-1117. About 61% of students receive aid from School and outside sources.

DEGREE REQUIREMENTS. For D.M.D.: satisfactory completion of forty-five-month program; advanced standing for work completed at other dental schools considered.

School of Nursing
http://www.USNSmed.edu

Graduate program began in 1970. Tuition: full-time resident $1996, nonresident $4315; per credit, resident $111, nonresident $239.83. On-campus housing available for single and married students. Average academic year cost: single room $1860, double room $1240. Contact Housing Office for married student information. Phone: (601)984-1490.
Enrollment: full-time 22, part-time 81. Faculty with graduate appointment: full-time 6, part-time 2. Degree conferred: M.S.N.

ADMISSION REQUIREMENTS. Transcript, B.S.N., GRE, license (R.N.), at least one year of nursing experience, one page biography, three letters of recommendation required in support of School's application. Accepts transfer applicants. Applicants accepted for admission each semester. Apply to Registrar. Application fee $10. Phone: (601)984-1087; fax: (601)984-1099.

ADMISSION STANDARDS. Selective. Usual minimum average; 2.75 cumulative; 3.0 for nursing courses (A = 4). Combined GRE 900.

FINANCIAL AID. Sixteen grants, Federal Nurse Traineeships, loans. Approved for VA benefits. Apply to Director of Student Financial Aid; no specified closing date. Preferred date April 1. Use FAFSA. Phone: (601)984-1117; fax: (601)984-1099.

DEGREE REQUIREMENTS. For M.S.N.: 40 credits minimum; accepts up to 9 hours in transfer; thesis or non-thesis option.

FIELDS OF STUDY.
Nurse Clinician.
Nurse Educator.
Nurse Manager.
Note: A R.N.-B.S.N.-M.S.N. program is available for qualified students.

UNIVERSITY OF MISSOURI AT COLUMBIA
Columbia, Missouri 65211

Founded 1839. Located 120 miles W of St. Louis. Coed. State control. Semester system. Special facilities: Center for Aging, Agricultural Experiment Station Research Farms, Business and Public Administration Research Center, Capsule Pipeline Research Center, Dalton Center for Cardiovascular Research, Financial Research Institute, Freedom of Information Center, Geographic Resource Center, Nuclear Magnetic Resonance Center, Power Electronics Research Center, Research Reactor Center, Center for Research in Social Behavior, Space Sciences Center, Water Resources Research Center; Museums of Anthropology Art and Archaeology, Entomology, Geological Sciences; herbarium; extensive acreage for research in soils, field crops, horticulture; art collections. Library: 2,680,304 volumes, 5,000,000 microforms.
Tuition: per credit, resident $168, nonresident $461. On-campus housing for 352 married students, 2100 single men, 2880 single women. Average academic year housing cost: $3620 (double room, including board). Apartments $242–$328 per month. Apply to Residential Life Office. Phone: (314)882-7275.

Graduate School

Graduate study since 1846. Enrollment: full- and part-time 4400. Faculty: full-time 1550, part-time 50. Degrees conferred: M.A., M.S., M.Acc., M.P.A., M.H.A., M.H.S., M.A.P.E., M.S.W., M.S.P.H., M.B.A., M.S.T., M.F.A., M.Ed., M.M., Ed.Sp., Ed.D., Ph.D.

ADMISSION REQUIREMENTS. Transcripts required in support of School's application. GRE/GMAT/MAT, recommendations required by some departments. Interview not required. TOEFL required for international applicants. Accepts transfer students. Graduates of unaccredited institutions not considered. Apply to Director of Admissions by July 1 (Fall), December 1 (Winter), May 1 (Summer). Two-part application process; 1 application for Graduate School, second part for departments. Some departmental application deadlines may be earlier. Application fee $25, $50 for international applicants. Phone: (314)882-6311; fax: (314)884-5454.

ADMISSION STANDARDS. Very selective for most departments, selective to very competitive for others. Usual minimum average: 3.0 (A = 4).

FINANCIAL AID. Annual awards from institutional funds: 40 academic scholarships/fellowships, 1200 teaching assistantships,

600 research assistantships, Federal W/S, loans. Approved for VA benefits. Apply by January 1 to appropriate department chair for assistantships; to Financial Aid Office for all other programs. Use FAFSA. Aid sometimes available for part-time study.

DEGREE REQUIREMENTS. For master's: 30 hours minimum; thesis required for many majors; final written/oral exam. For Ed.Sp.: 30 hours minimum beyond the master's; final written/oral exam. For Ph.D.: 72 credits beyond the bachelor's (all in residence), at least 18 semester hours within an 18-month period; language requirements vary by department; comprehensive exam; dissertation; final oral exam. For Ed.D.: 82 hours minimum beyond the bachelor's (all in residence), at least 18 semester hours within an 18-month period; knowledge of statistics; matriculation exam; no language requirement; dissertation; final oral exam.

FIELDS OF STUDY.
Accountancy.
Agricultural Economics.
Agricultural Engineering.
Agricultural Mechanization. M.S. only.
Agronomy.
Anatomy and Neurobiology.
Animal Sciences.
Anthropology.
Applied Mathematics.
Art. M.F.A. only.
Art History and Archaeology.
Atmospheric Science.
Biochemistry.
Biological Sciences.
Black Studies (Minor).
Business Administration.
Chemical Engineering.
Chemistry.
Civil Engineering.
Classical Languages. M.A. only.
Classics and Classical Archaeology. Ph.D. only.
Communication.
Communicative Disorders. Includes speech-language pathology.
Computer Science. M.S. only.
Consumer and Family Economics.
Curriculum and Instruction.
Economics.
Educational Administration.
Educational Counseling and Psychology.
Electrical and Computer Engineering.
English.
Entomology.
Environmental Design.
Fisheries and Wildlife.
Food Science and Human Nutrition.
Forestry.
French. M.A. only.
Genetic Area Program.
Geography. M.S. only.
Geological Sciences.
German, Russian, and Asian Studies. M.A. only.
Health and Physical Education.
Health Services Management. M.H.A. only.
Higher and Adult Education.
History.
Horticulture.
Industrial Engineering.
International Development (Minor).
Journalism.
Laboratory Animal Medicine Area. M.S. only.
Library and Informational Science. M.A. only.
Mathematics.
Mechanical and Aerospace Engineering.

Medieval and Renaissance Studies (Minor).
Molecular Biology and Immunology.
Museum Studies (Minor).
Music. Includes Musicology.
Nuclear Engineering.
Nursing. M.S. only.
Nutrition Area Program.
Parks, Recreation, and Tourism. M.S. only.
Pathology. M.S. only.
Pharmacology.
Philosophy.
Physics and Astronomy.
Physiology—Medicine.
Plant Pathology.
Political Science.
Practical Arts and Vocational-Technical Education.
Psychological Statistics and Methods (Minor).
Psychology.
Public Administration. M.P.A. only.
Public Health. Includes family and community medicine; M.S.P.H. only.
Romance Languages.
Rural Sociology.
Social and Philosophical Foundations of Education.
Social Work. M.S., M.S.W. only.
Sociology.
South Asian Language and Area Studies (Minor).
Spanish. M.A. only.
Special Education.
Statistics.
Textile and Apparel Management.
Theater.
Veterinary Biomedical Sciences.
Veterinary Medicine and Surgery.
Veterinary Microbiology.
Veterinary Pathology.

School of Law

Established 1872. Semester system. Law library: 288,000 volumes. Library has LEXIS, WESTLAW, INFOTRAC, LUMIN/OCLC. Special facilities: Center for the Study of Dispute Resolution.

Annual tuition/fee: resident $7792, nonresident $15,582. Total average annual additional expense: $9100.

Enrollment: first-year class 150; total full-time 451 (men 58%, women 42%). Faculty: full-time 23, part-time 10. Degree conferred: J.D.

ADMISSION REQUIREMENTS. LSDAS Law School report, bachelor's degree, transcripts, LSAT required in support of application. Interview not required. Accepts transfer applicants. Graduates of unaccredited colleges not considered. Apply to Admissions Office, preferably by March 1. Students accepted for Fall only. Application fee $25. Phone: (314)882-6042.

ADMISSION STANDARDS. Selective. Accepts about 30–35% of total annual applicants.

FINANCIAL AID. Scholarships, assistantships, Federal W/S, loans. Apply to School of Law Scholarship Committee by March 1. Use FAFSA. About 20% of students receive aid other than loans from School.

DEGREE REQUIREMENTS. For J.D.: 89 hours minimum, at least two years in residence.
Note: One-semester study abroad program in London, England, available.

School of Medicine (65212)

Founded 1872 as a two-year school, expanded to four years in 1956. Annual tuition: resident $13,216, nonresident $26,579. On-campus housing available. Apply to Housing Office. Total average figure for all other expenses: $7560.

Enrollment: first-year class 96 (EDP 10), full-time 534 (men 60%, women 40%); postgraduates 317. Medical faculty: 444; part-time 120. Degrees conferred: M.D., M.D.-Ph.D. The M.S. and Ph.D. are offered through the Graduate School.

ADMISSION REQUIREMENTS. AMCAS report, transcripts, letters of recommendation, MCAT required in support of application. Applicants must have completed at least three years of college study. Interview by invitation only. Has EDP; apply between June 15 and August 1. Preference given to Missouri residents. Accepts transfer applicants. Apply to Assistant Dean after June 15, before November 15. Application fee none. Phone: (314)882-2933; fax: (314)884-4808.

ADMISSION STANDARDS. Competitive. Accepts about 15% of total annual applicants. Approximately 95% are state residents

FINANCIAL AID. Scholarships, loans. Apply to Financial Aid Office. Use FAFSA. Phone: (314)882-2923. About 85% of students receive some aid from School.

DEGREE REQUIREMENTS. For M.D.: satisfactory completion of four-year program and passing step 2 of USMLE. For M.S., Ph.D., see Graduate School listing above.

FIELDS OF GRADUATE STUDY.
Biochemistry.
Microbiology.
Pathology.
Pharmacology.
Physiology.

College of Veterinary Medicine

Established 1949. Annual tuition: resident $9290, nonresident $16,463. On-campus housing available; estimated living expenses: $18,112.

Enrollment: first-year class 64; full-time 296 (men 45%, women 55%); no part-time students. Faculty: full-time 170, part-time 20. Degree conferred: D.V.M. The M.S. and Ph.D. are offered through the Graduate School.

ADMISSION REQUIREMENTS. Transcripts, VCAT (must be received by February 1), two recommendations, animal/veterinary experience, essay, interview required in support of application. For combined programs, a bachelor's degree is required. Accepts transfer applicants on a space-available basis. Will consider American students with two years in foreign college of veterinary medicine. Graduates of unaccredited colleges not considered. Applicants must have completed at least two years of preprofessional college study. Preference given to state residents. Apply to Dean, School of Veterinary Medicine after September 1, before November 1. Fall admission only. Application fee $50. Phone: (314)882-3554.

ADMISSION STANDARDS. Selective. Accepts 30% of total annual applications. Can enroll eight nonresident applicants.

FINANCIAL AID. Scholarships, fellowships, assistantships, Federal W/S, loans, grants. Apply to Director of Student Aids; no specified closing date. Use FAFSA.

DEGREE REQUIREMENTS. For D.V.M.: satisfactory completion of four-year program. For M.S., Ph.D., see Graduate School listing above.

FIELDS OF GRADUATE STUDY.
Pathology. Ph.D.
Physiology. Ph.D.
Veterinary Anatomy. M.S.
Veterinary Biochemistry and Nutrition.
Veterinary Medicine and Surgery.
Veterinary Microbiology.
Veterinary Pathology. M.S.
Veterinary Pharmacology. M.S.
Veterinary Physiology. M.S.

UNIVERSITY OF MISSOURI AT KANSAS CITY
Kansas City, Missouri 64110-2499

Founded 1929. Coed. State control. Semester system. Special facilities: Institute for Study in American Music, Electronic Music Laboratory, Center for Underground Space Studies, Drug Information Center, Biopharmacokinetics Laboratory, Hormone Research Laboratory, Family Study Center, Center for the Study of Metropolitan Problems in Education, Center for Labor Studies, Institute for Human Development. Library: 942,000 volumes, 1,773,000 microforms, 8700 current periodicals.

Tuition and fees: per credit hour, resident $186.20, nonresident $462.40 plus prorated tuition 7–10 hours. On-campus housing for single students only. Average academic year housing cost: $3690 (including board). Contact University Housing Office for both on- and off-campus housing information. Phone: (816)235-2800.

Graduate Studies

Graduate study since 1939. Enrollment: full-time 1928, part-time 2105. University faculty teaching graduate students: full-time 489, part-time 233. Degrees conferred: M.A., M.S., M.A. in Ed., M.Ed., M.B.A., M.P.A., LL.M., M.M., M.M.Ed., Ed.S., D.M.A., Ph.D.

ADMISSION REQUIREMENTS. Two official transcripts, GRE/GMAT required in support of application. Interview not required. TOEFL required of international applicants whose first language is not English. Accepts transfer applicants. Graduates of unaccredited institutions not considered. Apply to the Admissions Office by February 1 (Summer and Fall), September 1 (Winter). Application fee none. Phone: (816)235-1111; fax: (816)235-1717.

ADMISSION STANDARDS. Selective for some departments, competitive for most departments. Usual minimum average: 3.0; probationary status: 2.75 (A = 4).

FINANCIAL AID. One hundred Chancellor nonresident awards, scholarships, 120–170 teaching assistantships, 6 internships, full and partial fee waiver, Federal W/S, loans. Apply by March 1 to appropriate department chair for assistantships, scholarships; to the Financial Aid Office for all other programs. Use FAFSA. About 10% of students receive aid other than loans from University. No aid for part-time students.

DEGREE REQUIREMENTS. For M.A., M.S.: 30 semester hours minimum, at least 24 in residence; reading knowledge of one foreign language for some departments; qualifying exam for many departments; thesis/nonthesis option; final written/oral exam. For M.A. in Ed., M.Ed.: 30 semester hours minimum, at least 24 in residence; thesis not required. For M.B.A.: 36 hours minimum or 43 hours minimum, depending upon previous education, at least 30 or 37 hours in residence; thesis sometimes required for 6 hours. For M.P.A.: 36 hours minimum, at least 30 in residence; thesis optional for 6 hours. For LL.M.: 24 hours minimum beyond the J.D.; thesis for 8 hours. For M.M.: 30 semester hours minimum, at least 24 in residence, qualifying exam sometimes required; thesis/recital/research project; final oral/written exam. For M.M.Ed.; 30 semester hours minimum, at least 24 in residence; thesis for 4–6 hours; final written/oral exam. For Ed.S.: 60 hours minimum beyond the bachelor's, at least 20 in residence and one semester in full-time attendance; field project; final oral exam; offered in counseling and guidance, educational administration, and reading. For Ph.D.: usually 90 hours minimum beyond the bachelor's, at least 45 hours in residence and two consecutive semesters in full-time attendance; preliminary exam; reading knowledge of two foreign languages or one language and one other acceptable research tool; dissertation; final oral exam. For D.M.A.: essentially the same as for the Ph.D., except composition/recitals replace thesis in appropriate fields.

FIELDS OF STUDY.
Accounting. M.S. only.
Administration of Justice. M.A. only.
Art. Includes art history, graphic design, photography. Portfolio and interview required. M.A. only.
Biochemistry.
Biology. M.A., M.S. only.
Business Administration. GMAT for admission. M.B.A. only.
Cell Biology and Biophysics. Ph.D.
Chemistry. Includes analytical, inorganic, organic, physical. M.S., Ph.D.
Communication Studies. M.A.
Computer Networking. Ph.D.
Computer Science. M.S.
Counseling and Guidance. M.A.
Criminal Justice.
Dental Hygiene Education. B.S. in dental hygiene for admission. M.S. only.
Dentistry. Includes anatomy, biochemistry, microbiology, oral histology and embryology, oral medicine and diagnosis, oral radiology, periodontics, restorative dentistry, oral surgery, orthodontics, pedodontics, prosthodontics, oral pathology; D.D.S. for admission. M.S. only.
Economics. GRE for admission. M.A., Ph.D.
Education. Includes elementary and secondary curriculum and instruction, administration and community leadership, adult foundations and philosophy of education. M.A., Ed.S.; Ph.D. in curriculum and instruction, administration and community leadership, counseling, and guidance.
Engineering. Includes civil, electrical, industrial, mechanical; degrees awarded by University of Missouri-Columbia. M.S., Ph.D.
English Language and Literature. One language for M.A. M.A., Ph.D.
History. M.A., Ph.D.
Mathematics. M.S., Ph.D.
Microbiology. Interdivisional. M.S. only.
Molecular Biology and Biochemistry. Ph.D.
Music. Includes applied music, theory, composition, sacred music, music education; GRE Subject, audition for admission. M.M., Ph.D.
Nursing. Includes child-care nursing.
Oral Biology. M.S., Ph.D.
Pharmaceutical Sciences. M.S., Ph.D.
Pharmacology. Ph.D.
Philosophy. Ph.D.
Physics. M.S., Ph.D.
Policy Studies in Education. Ph.D.
Political Science. GRE for admission. M.A., Ph.D.
Psychology. M.A., Ph.D.
Public Administration. GRE for admission. M.P.A. only.
Public Affairs and Administration. Ph.D.
Reading. M.Ed.
Romance Languages and Literature. M.A. only.

Sociology. M.A., Ph.D.
Special Education. M.Ed.
Studio Art.
Taxation.
Telecommunications. Ph.D.
Theater. Includes acting, directing, design and technology. Production thesis or new play may replace thesis. M.A. only.
Urban Environmental Geology. M.S. only.
Urban Studies. M.S., Ph.D.
Virology.

School of Law

Founded 1895. Semester system. Law library: 255,000 volumes. Library has LEXIS, NEXIS, WESTLAW, DIALOG.

Annual tuition, fees: resident $7792, nonresident $15,582. No on-campus housing available. Total average annual additional expense: $9500.

Enrollment: first-year class 175; total enrollment 457 (men 51%, women 49%). LL.M. candidates 70. Faculty: full-time 28, part-time 37. Degrees conferred: J.D., J.D.-M.B.A., J.D.-LL.M. (Taxation), LL.M. (Taxation and Urban Affairs).

ADMISSION REQUIREMENTS. LSDAS Law School report, bachelor's degree, transcripts, LSAT required in support of application. Interview not required. Accepts transfer applicants. Preference given to state residents. Graduates of unaccredited institutions not considered. Apply to Office of the Associate Dean; no closing date. Fall admission only for beginning law students. Application fee $25. Phone: (816)235-1644.

ADMISSION STANDARDS. Selective. Accepts about 40-45% of total applicants.

FINANCIAL AID. Scholarships, loans. Apply to Office of the Dean for scholarships, to University's Financial Aid Office for loans. Use FAFSA and UMKC FAF.

DEGREE REQUIREMENTS. For J.D.: 90 credit hours minimum, at least the last year in residence. For LL.M.: at least 24 credit hours beyond the J.D., at least one year in residence. For M.B.A.: see Graduate School listing above.

School of Medicine (64108)

Established 1969. Six-year baccalaureate, medical program only. Annual tuition: resident $13,385, nonresident $27,137. Limited on-campus housing available for married and single students. Total average figure for all other expenses: $7500.

Enrollment: first-year class 101; total 387 (men 50%, women 50%). Faculty: full-time 40, part-time 65. Degree conferred: B.A.-M.D. (six calendar year program).

ADMISSION REQUIREMENTS. Transcripts, ACT, three letters of recommendation, screening interview required in support of application. Preference given to state residents. Accepts a limited number of upper division applicants. Graduates of unaccredited colleges not considered. Apply to Director of Admissions and Registrar after August 1, before November 15. Application fee: resident none, nonresident $25. Phone: (816)235-1870; fax: 235-5277.

ADMISSION STANDARDS. Selective. Accepts about 50% of total annual applicants. Approximately 85% are state residents.

FINANCIAL AID. Scholarships, CWSP, loans. Apply to University's Financial Aid Office by February 15. Use FAFSA or CSS.

DEGREE REQUIREMENTS. For M.D.: satisfactory completion of six-year program.

School of Dentistry

Founded 1881. In 1963 Dental School joined University of Missouri. Annual tuition: resident $12,663, nonresident $24,964. No on-campus housing available. Average academic year housing cost: $9560. Contact Housing Office for off-campus housing information. Phone: (816)235-1428. Total average cost for all other first-year expenses: $6100.

Enrollment: first-year class 80; total 350 (men 65%, women 35%). Faculty: full-time 70, part-time 65. Degree conferred: D.D.S. The M.S. (Oral Biology) is offered through the School of Graduate Studies.

ADMISSION REQUIREMENTS. AADSAS report, official transcripts, DAT (no later than October), three letters of recommendation required in support of School's application. Interviews of students under serious consideration are required. Applicants must have completed at least two years of college study. Accepts transfer applicants. Preference given to residents of Missouri, Arkansas, Kansas, New Mexico, Hawaii. Apply to Office of Student Affairs after June 1, before January 1. Application fee $25. Phone: (816)235-2080 (local), (800)776-8652.

ADMISSION STANDARDS. Selective. Accepts 20–25% of total annual applicants. Approximately 50% are state residents.

FINANCIAL AID. Limited scholarships, grants, loans. Apply to Student Financial Aid Office. Use FAFSA. Phone: (816)235-1154.

DEGREE REQUIREMENTS. For D.D.S.: satisfactory completion of forty-month program. For M.S.: see School of Graduate Studies listing above.

FIELDS OF GRADUATE STUDY.
Diagnostics Sciences
General Dentistry.
Maxillofacial Prosthetics.
Oral and Maxillofacial Surgery.
Orthodontics.
Pediatric Dentistry.
Periodontics.
Prosthodontics.

UNIVERSITY OF MISSOURI—ROLLA

Rolla, Missouri 65401-0249
http://www.umr.edu

Founded 1871. Located 100 miles SW of St. Louis. Coed. State control. Semester system. Special facilities: nuclear reactor, Graduate Center for Materials Research, Graduate Center for Cloud Physics Research, Rock Mechanics and Explosives Research Center, Institute for River Studies, fully equipped mine for research and study. Library: 440,000 volumes, 365,000 microforms, 1450 current periodicals, 20 PCs.

Annual tuition and fees: full-time, resident $3677, nonresident $11,054; per credit, resident $141, nonresident $417. On-campus housing for 50 married students, 1340 single students. Average academic year housing cost: $3500 (including board) for single students; $3150 per for married students. Off-campus housing cost: $350–$450 per month. Contact Housing office for on- and off-campus housing information. Phone: (314)341-4218.

Graduate School

Enrollment: full- and part-time 1145. University faculty: full-time 252, part-time 52. Degrees conferred: M.S., M.S.T., Ph.D., D.E.

ADMISSION REQUIREMENTS. Official transcripts required in support of School's application. Interview not required. GRE and TOEFL required of international students. Accepts transfer applicants. Graduates of unaccredited institutions not considered. Apply to the Admission Office by July 1 (Fall), December 1 (Spring), May 1 (Summer). Rolling admissions process. Application fee $20, $50 for international applicants. Phone: (314)341-4315; fax: (314)341-4062.

ADMISSION STANDARDS. Competitive for most departments. Usual minimum average: 2.75 (A = 4).

FINANCIAL AID. One hundred academic scholarships, 113 fellowships, 198 teaching and research assistantships, Federal W/S, loans. Approved for VA benefits. Apply to chair of proposed major department for fellowships, assistantships; to Financial Aid Office for all other programs. No specified closing date. Use FAFSA. Phone: (314)341-4282. About 35% of students receive aid. Aid sometimes available for part-time students.

DEGREE REQUIREMENTS. For M.S.: 30 semester hours with thesis, 33 without thesis; final oral exam. For M.S.T.: 36 semester hours minimum, at least 24 in residence; final written exam; no thesis. For Ph.D., D.E.: about 90 semester hours beyond the bachelor's, at least two semesters in full-time residence; proficiency in foreign language for Ph.D.; dissertation; final oral exam.

FIELDS OF STUDY.
Aerospace Engineering.
Applied Mathematics.
Ceramic Engineering.
Chemical Engineering.
Chemistry.
Civil Engineering.
Computer Science.
Construction Engineering.
Electrical Engineering.
Engineering Management.
Engineering Mechanics.
Environmental Engineering.
Geochemistry.
Geological Engineering.
Geology and Geophysics.
Geotechnical Engineering.
Mathematics.
Mechanical Engineering.
Metallurgical Engineering.
Mineral and Mining Engineering.
Nuclear Engineering.
Petroleum Engineering.
Physics.
Statistics.
Structural Engineering.
Water Resources.

UNIVERSITY OF MISSOURI AT ST. LOUIS

St. Louis, Missouri 63121-4499
http://www.umsl.edu/

Founded 1963. Coed. State control. Semester system. Special facilities: Art Gallery 210, Center for Humanities, Center for International Studies, Center for Molecular Electronics, International Center for Tropical Ecology, Joint Center for East Asian Studies (in cooperation with Washington University), Public Policy Research Center, Center for Science and Technology, St.

Louis Historical Research Center. Library: 600,000 volumes, 1,000,000 microforms, 2800 periodicals.

Tuition: per credit hour, resident $153, nonresident $461. On-campus housing available for single graduate students only. Apartments located approximately three blocks from campus. Average academic year housing cost: $4816 (including board). Day care facilities available.

Graduate School

Graduate study since 1968. Enrollment: full-time 368, part-time 2231 (men 32%, women 68%). Faculty: full-time 401. Degrees conferred: M.A., M.S., M.B.A., M.M.E., M.Ed., M.P.P.A., M.Acc., Ed.D., Ph.D.

ADMISSION REQUIREMENTS. Transcripts, GRE/GMAT required in support of School's application. TOEFL required of all foreign students. Accepts transfer applicants. Graduates of unaccredited colleges not considered. Apply to Director of Admissions by July 1 (Fall), December 1 (Spring), May 1 (Summer). Application fee none. Phone: (314)516-5458; fax: (314)516-5310.

ADMISSION STANDARDS. Selective. Usual minimum average: 2.75 (A = 4).

FINANCIAL AID. Annual awards from institutional funds: 12 scholarships, 110 teaching assistantships, 74 research assistantships, 4 graduate-school–funded dissertation fellowships, 8 summer research fellowships, Federal W/S, loans. Approved for VA benefits. Apply by July 1 to department chair for fellowships, assistantships; to Financial Aid Office for all other programs. Use FAFSA. Phone: (314)516-5526; fax: (314)516-5310.

DEGREE REQUIREMENTS. For master's: 30 credits minimum, at least 21 credits in residence; thesis required by some departments; final written/oral exam. For Ph.D.: at least three academic years of full-time study or equivalent, at least two years in residence; two consecutive semesters full-time; qualifying exam; reading knowledge of two foreign languages or one language and one research skill; dissertation; final exam.

FIELDS OF STUDY.
Biology. M.S., Ph.D.
Business Administration. GMAT for admission; 39–60 credits. M.B.A., M.S., M.Acc.
Chemistry. M.S., Ph.D.
Criminology. M.A., Ph.D.
Economics. M.A. only.
Education. Includes counseling, educational administration, elementary education, secondary education, special education, learning-instructional processes, and behavioral developmental processes. M.Ed., Ed.D.
English. M.A. only.
Gerontology. M.A. only.
History. M.A. only.
Mathematics. M.A.
Music Education. M.M.E. only.
Nursing. M.S., Ph.D.
Physiological Optics. M.S., Ph.D.
Political Science. Includes urban and regional politics, American politics, political process and behavior, international public administration, M.A.; politics, comparative politics, Ph.D.
Psychology. M.A., Ph.D.
Public Policy Administration. Includes policy analysis, public administration, management, accounting and economics.
Sociology. M.A. only.

MONMOUTH UNIVERSITY
West Long Branch, New Jersey 07764-1898
http://www.monmouth.edu

Founded in 1933. Located 50 miles S of New York City, 75 miles NE of Philadelphia. Semester system. Library: 243,000 volumes, 1,331,000 microforms, 1336 periodicals.

Tuition: per credit hour $419. Limited on-campus housing for graduate students but available for international students. Annual academic year housing cost: $3786–$4206. For off-campus housing contact Director, Residential Life. Phone: (908)571-3465.

Graduate Division

Graduate study since 1967. Enrollment: full-time 100, part-time 1100. Degrees conferred: M.B.A., M.A., M.A.L.S., M.S., M.A.T., M.S.Ed.

ADMISSION REQUIREMENTS. Transcripts, two letters of recommendation, GRE, GMAT Test (for M.B.A.) required in support of Divisional application. TOEFL required for foreign applicants. Accepts transfer applicants. Graduates of unaccredited institutions not considered. Apply to Director of Graduate Admissions at least two months prior to registration. Rolling admissions process. Application fee $35. Phone: (908)571-3452; fax: (908)571-3629.

ADMISSION STANDARDS. Selective. Usual minimum average: 2.5 overall, 3.0 in major. For M.B.A. program only: GPA x 200 + GMAT = 1000.

FINANCIAL AID. Limited to Federal W/S, loans. Apply to Financial Aid Office; no specified closing date. Use FAFSA. Phone: (908)571-3463; fax: (908)571-3629.

DEGREE REQUIREMENTS. For M.B.A.: 30–60 semester hours depending upon previous preparation. For M.S. Computer Science: 33 semester hours. For M.S. Software Engineering: 36 semester hours depending upon previous preparation. For M.S. Electronic Engineering: 30 semester hours. For M.A.L.S., M.A. (History): 36 semester hours. For M.A.T. with certification, M.A.T. Advanced, M.S.Ed. Student Personnel Services: 36 semester hours. For M.S.N.: 40 semester hours. For the M.A. Psychological Counseling: 30 semester hours. For the M.A. Criminal Justice: 36 semester hours.

FIELDS OF STUDY.
Business Administration. M.B.A.
Computer Science. M.S.
Criminal Justice. M.A.
Education. Includes elementary, secondary, supervision, principal, school administrator, school business administrator, special education, student personnel services, reading; M.S.Ed.
Electronic Engineering. M.S.
History. M.A.
Liberal Studies. M.A.L.S.
Nursing. M.S.N.
Psychological Counseling. M.A.
Secondary Education.
Software Engineering. M.S.
Special Education.
Student Personnel Services.

MONTANA STATE UNIVERSITY
Billings, Montana 59101-0298

Founded 1927. Coed. State control. Semester system. Special facilities: Montana Center for Disabilities, Native American Cultural Institute, Red Mountain Biological Field Station. Library: 150,000 volumes, 660,000 microforms, 12 PCs.

Annual tuition: resident $2756, nonresident $6928. On-campus housing for graduate men, women; none for married students. Average academic year housing cost: $2000–$6000. Apply to Director of Resident Life for both on-campus housing and off-campus information. Phone: (408)657-2333.

Graduate Program

Established 1954. Enrollment: full-time 72, part-time 325. University faculty teaching graduate students: full-time 72. Degrees conferred: M.Ed., M.S.Sp.Ed., M.S.R.C., M.S.I.P.C.

ADMISSION REQUIREMENTS. Transcripts, GRE/MAT, required in support of application. TOEFL required for international applicants. Accepts transfer applicants. Graduates of unaccredited institutions not considered. Apply to Director of Graduate Studies at least 1 month prior to registration. Phone: (406)657-2338; fax: (406)657-2299.

ADMISSION STANDARDS. Selective for most departments. Usual minimum average: 3.0 (A = 4).

FINANCIAL AID. Annual awards from institutional funds: grants, fellowships, graduate assistantships, Federal W/S, loans. Approximately thirty resident fee waivers and five nonresident fee waivers available. Approved for VA benefits. Apply to Director of Graduate Studies for fellowships, assistantships; to Office of Financial Aid for all other programs. Use FAFSA. Phone: (406)657-2188; fax: (406)657-2302. About 30% of students receive aid other than loans from both University funds and outside sources.

DEGREE REQUIREMENTS. For M.Ed., M.S.: 36–45 semester hours minimum, at least 30 in residence; thesis/nonthesis options. For M.S.R.C.: 60 semester hours.

FIELDS OF STUDY.
Education. Includes reading, school counseling, curriculum, early childhood, teaching as a second career (secondary, K–12), self-design.
Information Processing and Communication. M.S.I.P.S.
Rehabilitation Counseling. M.S.R.C.
Special Education. Includes emotional disturbances, learning disabilities, mental retardation, multi-handicapped, community counseling, and self design. M.S.Sp.Ed.
Teaching Endorsement. Includes K–12.

MONTANA STATE UNIVERSITY
Bozeman, Montana 59717
http://www.montana.edu

Founded 1893. Located 90 miles N of Yellowstone Park. Coed. State control. Quarter system. Special facilities: Animal Research Center, Engineering Research Center, Local Government Center, Marsh Laboratory, Water Center. Library: 569,000 volumes, 1,300,000 microforms, 40 PCs.

Annual tuition: full-time, resident $2500, nonresident $5000. On-campus housing for 704 married students, 50 single students. Average academic year housing cost: $3710 (including board) for single students; $3500 for married students. Apply to Housing Office. Phone: (406)994-2661.

College of Graduate Studies

Graduate study since 1898. Enrollment: full-time 600 (men 75%, women 25%); part-time 300. Graduate faculty: 425, part-time 20. Degrees conferred: M.A., M.Ed., M.N., M.S., Ed.D., Ph.D.

ADMISSION REQUIREMENTS. Transcripts, GRE, three letters of recommendation required in support of College's application. Interview may be required by some departments. TOEFL and GRE required for international applicants. Apply to College of Graduate Studies by August 1 (Fall), November 1 (Winter), February 1 (Spring), May 1 (Summer). Late applicants considered as nondegree students. Rolling admissions process. Application fee $30. Phone: (406)994-4145; fax: (406)994-4733.

ADMISSION STANDARDS. Selective. Usual minimum average: 3.0 (A = 4).

FINANCIAL AID. Annual awards from institutional funds: 10 scholarships, 194 teaching assistantships, 147 research assistantships, 34 internships, Federal W/S, loans. Approved for VA benefits. Apply prior to registration to appropriate department chair for fellowships, assistantships; to Financial Aid Office for all other programs. Use FAFSA. Phone: (406)994-2845; fax: (406)994-6962. About 70% of students receive aid from College and outside sources.

DEGREE REQUIREMENTS. For M.S., M.A.: 36 quarter hours minimum, at least 20 in residence; thesis, or 45 quarter hours minimum without thesis, at least 35 in residence (available in some departments). For M.A. in Art: 45 quarter hours minimum, at least 35 in residence; professional paper/thesis. For M.Ed.: 45 quarter hours minimum. For M.N.: 70 quarter hours minimum including thesis, or 76 nonthesis. For all master's degrees: final written/oral exam. For Ed.D.: 90 quarter hours beyond the master's, at least 45 credits in residence; reading knowledge of one foreign language required by some departments; written/oral comprehensive exam; thesis; final written/oral exam. For Ph.D.: normally three years minimum beyond the bachelor's, at least 45 credits in residence; qualifying exam may be required; language requirements vary by department; oral/written comprehensive exam; dissertation; final written/oral exam.

FIELDS OF STUDY.
Agricultural Economics. M.S. only.
Agricultural Education. M.S. only.
Agricultural Engineering. M.S. only.
Agronomy. M.S. only.
Animal Science. M.S. only.
Applied Economics. M.S. only.
Art. Portfolio required for admission. M.A. only.
Biochemistry.
Biological Science. GRE for admission. M.S., Ph.D.
Botany and Plant Sciences.
Business Education. M.S. only.
Chemical Engineering. M.S., Ph.D.
Chemistry. M.S., Ph.D.
Civil Engineering. M.S., Ph.D.
Computer Science. M.S. only.
Crop and Soil Sciences. Ph.D. only.
Earth Sciences. Includes geography, geology, meteorology; GRE for admission. M.S. only.
Economics. M.A. only.
Education. Includes adult and higher, elementary administration, curriculum and instruction, guidance and counseling, sec-

ondary administration, secondary teaching, general administration, vocational and technical; GRE for admission.

Electrical Engineering. M.S., Ph.D.

Engineering Mechanics. M.S. only.

Entomology. M.S. only.

Environmental Engineering. M.S. only.

Fine Arts. Thesis for M.F.A.; includes studio.

Fish, Game, and Wildlife Management. GRE for admission. M.S. only.

History. GRE for admission. M.A. only.

Land Rehabilitation. GRE required for admission. M.S. only.

Mathematics. M.S., Ph.D.

Mechanical Engineering. M.S., Ph.D.

Microbiology. GRE required for admission.

Nursing. GRE for admission. M.N. only.

Physical Education. GRE required for admission. M.S. only.

Physics. M.S., Ph.D.

Plant Pathology. M.S., Ph.D.

Political Science. M.A. only.

Professional Accountancy. M.P.A.

Public Administration. GRE required for admission. M.P.A. only.

Range Science. M.S. only.

Statistics. M.S., Ph.D.

Technology Education. M.S. only.

Veterinary Science. Seventy credits minimum for Ph.D.

Zoology. GRE for admission.

MONTANA TECH OF THE UNIVERSITY OF MONTANA

Butte, Montana 59701-8997

http://www.mtech.edu

Founded in 1893. Located 300 miles E of Spokane, Washington, and 400 miles N of Salt Lake City. Coed. State control. Semester system. Special facilities: Mineral Research Center for Advanced Mining Processing, Montana Bureau of Mines and Geology. Library: 93,533 volumes, 376,016 microforms, 19 PCs.

Annual tuition: full-time, resident $2787, nonresident $8325. On-campus housing limited. Housing for married students both on- and off-campus. Average academic year housing cost: $3500 double (includes board) for single students; $2430 for married students (60 apartments on campus). Apply to Director, Resident Life. Phone: (406)496-4425. Day care facilities available.

Graduate School

Graduate study since 1929. Enrollment: full-time 69, part-time 30. Faculty teaching graduate students: full-time 48, part-time 6. Degree conferred: M.S.

ADMISSION REQUIREMENTS. Transcripts, GRE Subject Tests, three references required in support of application. Interview not required. TOEFL required for international applicants. Accepts transfer applicants. Apply to Administrator of Graduate School before March 31. Application fee $30 (for U.S./Canada), $90 for international applicants. Phone: (406)496-4128; fax: (406)496-4334.

ADMISSION STANDARDS. Very competitive. Usual minimum average: 3.0 (A = 4).

FINANCIAL AID. Annual awards from institutional funds: three fellowships, thirty-seven teaching assistantships, twenty-seven research assistantships, forty-two fee waivers, Federal W/S, loans. Approved for VA benefits. Apply Administrator, Graduate School. Use FAFSA and institutional FAF. Phone: (406)496-4212; fax: (406)496-4133. Aid available for part-time students.

DEGREE REQUIREMENTS. For M.S.(thesis required): 30 semester hours. For M.S. (nonthesis): 36 semester hours.

FIELDS OF STUDY.

Engineering Science.

Environmental Engineering.

Geoscience. Includes geochemistry, hydrogeology, hydrogeological engineering, geology, geological engineering, geophysical engineering, mineral economics.

Industrial Hygiene.

Metallurgical/Mineral Processing Engineering.

Mining Engineering.

Petroleum Engineering.

UNIVERSITY OF MONTANA

Missoula, Montana 59812

http://umt.edu/nss/gradcat

Established 1893. Coed. State control. Semester system. Special facilities: University Biological Station, Wood Chemistry Laboratories, Animal Behavior Laboratory, Bureau of Business and Economic Research, Computer Center, Lubrecht Forestry Camp, Montana Forest and Conservation Experiment Station, Performing Arts and Radio/TV Center, Institute for Social Science Research, Bureau of Government Research, Wildlife Research Unit, Division of Educational Research and Services, Bureau of Press and Broadcasting, Stella Duncan Memorial Institute for Respiratory Disease Research Center, Mansfield Center of Ethics and Asian Affairs. Library: 700,000 volumes, 555,000 microforms, 4500 periodicals.

Annual tuition, fees: full-time, resident $2800, nonresident $6454. On-campus housing for 394 married students, limited number for single graduate students. Average academic year housing cost: $3500 for married students. Apply to Family Housing Office. Phone: (406)549-0134 (married students); to Off-Campus Housing Clearinghouse. Phone: (406)243-4636 (off-campus housing information).

Graduate School

Enrollment: full-time 900, part-time 400 (men 65%, women 35%). Faculty: full-time 380, part-time 10. Degrees conferred: M.A., M.Acc., M.A.S., M.A.T., M.B.A., M.Ed., M.F., M.S.T., M.M.Ed., M.I.S., M.F.A., M.M., M.P.A., M.S., Ed.S., Ed.D., Ph.D.

ADMISSION REQUIREMENTS. One official transcript, GRE, three letters of recommendation required in support of School's application. GMAT required for business. Interview not required. TOEFL required for international applicants. Accepts transfer applicants. Graduates of unaccredited institutions not considered. Apply to department concerned at least two months prior to registration. Some departments have earlier deadlines. Application fee $30. Phone: (406)243-2572; fax: (406)243-4593.

ADMISSION STANDARDS. Very competitive for some departments, competitive or selective for others. Usual minimum average: 3.0 (A = 4).

FINANCIAL AID. Annual awards from institutional funds: 30 scholarships, 50 research assistantships, 150 teaching assistantships, Federal W/S, loans. Approved for VA benefits. Apply by February 1 to department for assistantships; to Financial Aid Office for all other programs. Use FAFSA. Phone: (406)243-5373. About 40% of students receive aid other than loans from School and outside sources. Aid sometimes available for part-time students.

DEGREE REQUIREMENTS. For master's: 30 semester credits minimum, at least 12 in residence; final oral/written exam; thesis/final project; reading knowledge of one foreign language required by some departments. For Ed.D.: 90 semester credits minimum, at least 30 in residence; comprehensive exam; dissertation; final oral exam. For Ph.D.: three years minimum beyond the bachelor's, at least three semesters in residence; language requirement varies with department; comprehensive exam; dissertation; final oral exam.

FIELDS OF STUDY.
Accounting. M.Acc.
Administrative Services.
Anthropology.
Art. Portfolio for admission to M.F.A. program. M.A., M.F.A.
Biochemistry. M.S.
Biochemistry-Microbiology. Ph.D.
Biological Sciences. M.S.T.
Business Administration.
Chemistry. M.S., M.S.T., Ph.D.
Communication Studies. M.A.
Computer Science. M.S.
Creative Writing. M.F.A.
Drama. M.A., M.F.A.
Economics.
Education. M.A., M Ed., Ed.S., Ed.D.
English. M.A. only.
Environmental Studies.
Foreign Languages. Includes French, Spanish, German.
Forestry. M.S., M.F., Ph.D.
Geography.
Geology. M.S., Ph.D.
Guidance and Counseling. M.A., Ed.S.
Health and Physical Education.
History.
Interdisciplinary Studies. M.I.S.
Journalism.
Mathematical Sciences. M.A., M.A.T., Ph.D.
Microbiology. M.S.
Music. M.A., M.M., M.M.F.
Organismal Biology and Ecology. M.S., Ph.D.
Pharmacy. M.S., Ph.D.
Philosophy.
Physical Therapy. M.S.
Political Science. M.A.
Psychology. M.A., Ph.D.
Public Administration.
Recreation Management.
Resource Conservation.
School Psychology. M.A., Ed.S.
Sociology. M.A.
Wildlife Biology.

School of Law

Established 1911. Semester system. Law library: 125,000 volumes. Library has LEXIS, WESTLAW.

Annual tuition: full-time, resident $5091, nonresident $10,252. On-campus housing available. Total average annual additional expense: $7000.

Enrollment: first-year class 75; total full-time 225 (men 60%, women 40%). Faculty: full-time 17, part-time 15. Degrees conferred: J.D., J.D.-M.P.A.

ADMISSION REQUIREMENTS. LSDAS Law School report, bachelor's degree, transcripts, LSAT (not later than February) required in support of application. Interview not required. Preference given to state residents. Graduates of unaccredited colleges not considered. Apply to Dean of the Law School after September 1, before March 15. Fall admission only. Application fee $60. Phone: (406)243-4311.

ADMISSION STANDARDS. Selective. Accepts 25% of total annual applicants.

FINANCIAL AID. Limited to loans; research assistantships for third-year students only. Apply by March 1 to Financial Aid Office. Use FAFSA and Montana FAF. About 27% of students receive aid other than loans from School.

DEGREE REQUIREMENTS. For J.D.: satisfactory completion of three-year program; 90 credit-hour program.

MONTCLAIR STATE COLLEGE
Upper Montclair, New Jersey 07043-1624

Founded 1908. Located 15 miles W of New York City. Coed. State control. Semester system. Library: 434,872 volumes, 1,115,000 microforms, 3800 current periodicals.

Tuition: per credit, resident $163.50, nonresident $203.50. Limited on-campus housing for graduate students. Contact Office of Residence Life for both on- and off-campus housing information. Phone: (201)893-5284. Day care facilities available.

Graduate Studies

Graduate study since 1932. Enrollment: full-time 466, part-time 1933. College faculty: full- and part-time 419. Degrees conferred: M.A., M.B.A., M.A.T., M.Ed., M.S.

ADMISSION REQUIREMENTS. Official transcripts, GRE/GMAT/MAT/NTE, interview required in support of application. Portfolios required for some programs. TOEFL required for international applicants. Accepts transfer applicants. Graduates of unaccredited institutions not considered. To be considered for matriculation, applications and credentials need to be received by the Graduate Office before April 1 (Summer and Fall), November 1 (Spring). Some programs have earlier deadlines. Application fee $35. Phone: (800)331-9207, (201)893-5147; E-mail: gradstudies@saturn.montclair.edu.

ADMISSION STANDARDS. Admission decisions based on combination of GPA and standardized test score. Usual minimum average: 2.75 (A = 4).

FINANCIAL AID. Annual awards from institutional funds: approximately 100 graduate assistantships, Federal W/S, loans. Apply by April 1 to the Office of Graduate Studies for assistantships; to Office of Financial Aid for all other programs. Use FAFSA. Phone: (201)893-4461.

DEGREE REQUIREMENTS. For M.A., M.S.: 32 semester hours minimum, at least 30 in residence; additional hours may be required depending on undergraduate major; thesis/special project/comprehensive exam. For M.A.T.: 45 semester hours minimum, at least 30 in residence. For M.B.A.; 45–60 semester hours depending on undergraduate major, at least 30 in residence.

FIELDS OF STUDY.
Accounting. M.B.A.
Administration and Supervision. Includes educator, trainer. M.A.
Applied Linguistics. M.A.
Applied Sociology. M.A.
Biology. M.S.
Business Education. Includes distributive. M.A.
Chemistry. M.S.
Communication Sciences and Disorders. Includes audiology, early childhood special education, learning disabilities, speech/language pathology. M.A.
Computer Science. Includes applied mathematics, applied statistics. M.S.

Counseling and Guidance. Includes human services. M.A.
Critical Thinking. M.Ed.
Education. M.Ed. only.
Educational Psychology. M.A.
English and Comparative Literature. M.A.
Environmental Studies. Includes education, health, management, science. M.A.
Finance. M.B.A.
Fine Arts. Includes art history, studio. M.A.
French. M.A.
Geoscience. M.S.
Health Education. M.A.
Home Economics. Includes family life education, family relations/ child development, education, home management/consumer economics. M.A.
Human Services. M.A.
Industrial Studies. M.A.
Management. M.B.A.
Marketing. M.B.A.
Mathematics. Includes computer science, education, pure and applied mathematics, statistics. M.S.
Music. Includes education, performance, theory/composition. M.A.
Philosophy for Children. M.Ed.
Physical Education. Includes coaching and sports administration, exercise science, teaching and administration of physical education. M.A.
Practical Anthropology. M.A.
Psychology. Includes clinical for Spanish-English bilinguals, industrial and organizational, school. M.A.
Quantitative Analysis. M.B.A.
Reading. M.A.
Social Sciences. Includes anthropology, economics, geography, history, sociology, urban studies. M.A.
Spanish. M.A.
Speech and Theater. Includes communication arts. M.A.
Statistics. M.S.

MONTEREY INSTITUTE OF INTERNATIONAL STUDIES

Monterey, California 93940-2691
http://www.miis.edu

Founded 1955. Located 124 miles S of San Francisco. Coed. Private control. Semester system. Library: 64,000 volumes.
Annual tuition: full-time $16,200, per credit $640. No on-campus housing available for graduate students.

Graduate Program

Enrollment: full-time 702, part-time 38. Faculty: full-time 65, part-time 3. Degrees conferred: M.A., M.B.A., M.P.A.

ADMISSION REQUIREMENTS. Transcripts, 2 letters of recommendation required in support of application. GRE for native English speakers for M.A. Translation and Interpretation applicants. GMAT required for M.B.A. applicants. TOEFL required for international applicants. Campus visits/interviews recommended. Apply to the Admissions Office; no specified closing date. Application fee $50. Phone: (408)647-4123; fax: (408)647-6405.

ADMISSION STANDARDS. Selective. Usual minimum average: 3.0 (A = 4).

FINANCIAL AID. Annual awards from institutional funds: 110 scholarships, assistantships, Federal W/S, loans. Approved for VA benefits. Apply by March 1 to Financial Aid Office. Use FAFSA. Phone: (408)647-4119; fax: (408)647-4199. About 65%

of full-time students receive aid other than loans from Institute and outside sources.

DEGREE REQUIREMENTS. For master's: 32–64 units depending upon program; proficiency in one or more foreign languages.

FIELDS OF STUDY.
International Environmental Policy. M.A.
International Management. M.B.A., M.P.A.
International Policy. M.A.
International Public Administration. M.P.A.
Teaching English to Speakers of Other Languages. M.A.
Teaching Foreign Language. M.A.
Translation and Interpretation. M.A.

UNIVERSITY OF MONTEVALLO

Montevallo, Alabama 35115

Founded 1896. Located 32 miles from Birmingham. Coed. State control. Semester system. Library: 200,000 volumes, 116,000 microforms, 25 PCs.
Annual tuition: full-time, resident $3390, nonresident $6780; per credit hour, resident $95, nonresident $190; Summer session $90 per credit hour. On-campus housing in Summer for 200 men, 200 women; none for married students. Annual academic year housing cost: $2100. Single students apply to Director of Housing and Residence Life. Phone: (205)665-6235. Married students make own arrangements for off-campus housing.

Graduate Program

Enrollment: full-time 124, part-time 295. University faculty teaching graduate students: full- and part-time 97. Degrees conferred: M.A., M.S., M.Ed., M.M., M.A.T.

ADMISSION REQUIREMENTS. Transcripts, GRE/MAT required in support of application. Interview not required. TOEFL required for international applicants. Accepts transfer applicants. Graduates of unaccredited colleges not considered. Apply to Office of Graduate Studies one month prior to registration. Application fee $10. Phone: (205)665-6350; fax: (205)665-6353.

ADMISSION STANDARDS. Relatively open. Usual minimum average: 2.5 (A = 4).

FINANCIAL AID. Limited to Federal W/S, loans. Approved for VA benefits. Apply to Office of Financial Aid; no specified closing date. Phone: (205)665-6050. Use FAFSA.

DEGREE REQUIREMENTS. For master's: 30–36 semester hours minimum; thesis/nonthesis option.

FIELDS OF STUDY.
Communication Arts.
Education. Includes school administration, early childhood, elementary education, secondary education, counseling and guidance, physical education, traffic safety and driver's education.
English.
History.
Home Economics.
Music. Includes composition, music education, performance, theory-composition.
Speech Pathology and Audiology.

MOORHEAD STATE UNIVERSITY
Moorhead, Minnesota 56563-0002
http://www.moorhead.msus.edu

Founded 1887. Located 260 miles NW of Minneapolis. Coed. State control. Semester system. Library: 360,000 volumes, 684,394 microforms, 1,500 periodical titles, 85 PCs.

Tuition: per credit hour, MN residents $124, North Dakota residents with reciprocity $144, South Dakota and Manitoba residents with reciprocity $124, Wisconsin residents with reciprocity $125; nonresidents $189. No on-campus housing available. Contact Housing Office for off-campus housing information. Phone: (218)236-2118.

Graduate Studies

Graduate study since 1952. Enrollment: full-time 89 (men 39%, women 61%); part-time 133. Graduate faculty: full-time 198. Degrees conferred: M.A., M.S., M.B.A., M.F.A., M.L.A., Specialist.

ADMISSION REQUIREMENTS. Transcripts required in support of application. GRE/GMAT/MAT may be required by some programs. Immunization record required for all applicants. TOEFL required for international applicants. Interview required for some programs. Accepts transfer applicants. Apply to Graduate Admissions Office by May 1 (Fall semester), September 1 (Spring semester). International students accepted Fall semester only. Application fee $15.00, $35 for international applicants. Phone: (218)236-2164; fax: (218)236-2168.

ADMISSION STANDARDS. Selective. Usual minimum average: 2.75 or 3.25 (A = 4) in last 30 semester hours of graded course work.

FINANCIAL AID. Annual awards from institutional funds: 40 graduate assistantships, Federal W/S, loans. Approved for VA benefits. Apply by July 1 to Dean of Academic Services for assistantships; to Financial Aid Office for all other programs. Use FAFSA and institutional FAF. About 20% of students receive aid from all sources. Aid available for part-time students.

DEGREE REQUIREMENTS. For master's: 30–35 semester hours minimum; thesis or final project; final written/oral exam. For Specialist: 31 semester hours minimum beyond master's, at least 30 in residence.

FIELDS OF STUDY.
Art Education. M.S.
Business Administration. M.B.A. only.
Counseling and Student Affairs. M.S.
Creative Writing. M.F.A.
Elementary Education. M.S.
Liberal Studies. M.L.S.
Music. M.A.
Music Education. M.S.
Public and Human Service Administration. M.S.
Reading. M.S.
School Psychology. M.S., Specialist.
Special Education. M.S.
Speech/Language Pathology. M.S.
Studio Art. M.A.
Note: Cooperative program in Educational Administration (M.S., Ed.S.) with Tri-College University; in Nursing (M.S.N.), Social Work (M.S.W.) with University of Minnesota.
Master of Science with a Major in Nursing (University of Minnesota-MSU partnership)
Master of Social Work Option. (via distance education, University of Minnesota-MSU partnership)

MOREHEAD STATE UNIVERSITY
Morehead, Kentucky 40351

Founded 1922. Located 65 miles E of Lexington. Semester system. Library: 400,000 volumes, 650,000 microforms, 2000 current periodicals, 200 PCs.

Annual tuition: full-time, resident $2976, nonresident $8112; per credit, resident $124, nonresident $338. On-campus housing for married and single students. Average academic year housing cost: $2800 (including board) for single students; $3000 for married students. Contact Director of Housing for both on- and off-campus housing information. Phone: (606)783-2060.

Graduate Programs

Enrollment: full-time 174, part-time 695. Faculty: full-time 159, part-time 24. Degrees conferred, M.A., M.B.A., M.S., M.M., M.A.Ed., M.S.W., Ed.S., Ed.D., Ph.D.

ADMISSION REQUIREMENTS. Official transcripts, GRE required in support of application. TOEFL required for international applicants. Accepts transfer applicants. Graduates of unaccredited colleges not considered. Apply to Graduate Admissions Office at least two months prior to registration. Rolling admissions process. Application fee none. Phone: (606)783-2039; fax: (606)763-2678.

ADMISSION STANDARDS. Selective. Usual minimum average: 2.5 (A = 4).

FINANCIAL AID. Annual awards from institutional funds: One hundred research/teaching assistantships, Federal W/S, loans. Approved for VA benefits. Apply by March 15 to Dean of Graduate and Extended Campus Programs for assistantships; to Financial Aid Office for all other programs. Use FAFSA and University's FAF. Phone: (606)783-2039. About 15% of students receive aid from University. No aid for part-time students.

DEGREE REQUIREMENTS. For master's: 33–45 semester hours minimum, at least 37–36 in residence; thesis/nonthesis optional final written/oral exams. For Ed.S.: 30 semester hours beyond the master's. For Ph.D.: 60 credits minimum, at least one year in full-time residence; qualifying exam; proficiency in one foreign language for some programs; dissertation; final oral exam.

FIELDS OF STUDY.
Adult and Higher Education.
Biology.
Business Administration.
Clinical Psychology.
Communications.
Education. Includes administration, art, business, curriculum and instruction, elementary, secondary, guidance and counseling, health, special education reading, early childhood education.
Educational Psychology.
English.
Experimental Psychology.
Music.
Physical Education.
Psychology.
Recreation.
Social Work.
Sociology.
Vocational and Technical Education.

MOREHOUSE SCHOOL OF MEDICINE
Atlanta, Georgia 30310-1495

Established 1978. Primary mission is to provide physicians for medically underserved rural and inner-city areas. Library: 25,000 volumes, 10 PCs.

Annual tuition and fees: $17,708; student fees $1,833. There is no medical school housing. Total average cost for all other expenses: $9502. Enrollment: first-year class 35 (EDP 1), total 145 (men 45%, women 55%). Faculty: full-time 90; part-time and volunteers 130. Degree conferred: M.D.

ADMISSION REQUIREMENTS. AMCAS report, transcripts, MCAT, three letters of recommendation, biographical questionnaire, personal statement required in support of application. Has EDP; apply between June 15 and August 1. Interview by invitation. Preference given to state residents. Apply to Office of Admissions and Student Affairs after June 15, before December 1. Application fee $45. Phone: (404)752-1650; fax: (404)752-1512.

ADMISSION STANDARDS. Very competitive. Admits about 10% of total annual applications. Approximately 70% are state residents.

FINANCIAL AID. Limited scholarships, loans. Apply after acceptance to Office of Student Fiscal Affairs. Use FAFSA. About 87% of students receive some aid from School.

DEGREE REQUIREMENTS. For M.D.: satisfactory completion of four-year program and passing step 2 of USMLE.

MORGAN STATE UNIVERSITY
Baltimore, Maryland 21239
http://www.morgan.edu/

Founded 1867. Coed. State control. Semester system. Library: 652,000 volumes, 300,000 microforms, 12 PCs.

Tuition: per credit, resident $145, nonresident $240. On-campus housing for graduate students during academic year, some housing during Summer session. Annual academic year housing cost: $3950 (including board). Apply to Director, Residence Life. Phone: (410)319-3217.

School of Graduate Studies

Graduate study since 1964. Enrollment: full-time 157, part-time 246. Graduate faculty: full-time 70, part-time 2. Degrees conferred: M.A., M.S., M.B.A., M.Arch., M.L.A., M.C.R.P., M.E., D.E., Ed.D., Ph.D.

ADMISSION REQUIREMENTS. Transcripts, GRE/GMAT/MAT required in support of School's application. Interview not required. TOEFL required for international applicants. Accepts transfer applicants. Apply to Graduate School by August 1 (Fall), December 1 (Spring), June 1 (Summer). Application fee none. Phone: (410)319-3185; fax: (410)319-3837.

ADMISSION STANDARDS. Selective. Usual minimum average: 3.0 (unconditional), 2.5 (conditional) (A = 4).

FINANCIAL AID. Annual awards from institutional funds: scholarships, teaching assistantships, minority fellowships, Federal W/S, loans. Approved for VA benefits. Use FAFSA and University's FAF. Phone: (410)319-3170; fax: (410)319-3852.

DEGREE REQUIREMENTS. For M.A., M.S.: 30–42 semester hours, depending upon major, at least 25–36 hours in residence; thesis/final written/oral exam. For M.B.A.: 30–51 hours depend-

ing upon academic background. For M.C.R.P.: 51 semester hours. For M.Arch.: 30–90 semester hours, depending on academic background. For M.L.A.: 90 semester hours, depending on academic background. For D.E., Ed.D.: 60 semester hours minimum beyond the master's. For Ph.D.: 60 semester hours minimum beyond the master's, qualifying exam; one foreign language and research tool for some programs, dissertation; final oral exam.

FIELDS OF STUDY.
African-American Studies.
Architecture.
Business Administration. Includes accounting, finance, international, management, marketing.
City and Regional Planning.
Economics.
Educational Administration and Supervision.
Elementary Education.
English.
History. Ph.D.
International Studies.
Landscape Architecture.
Mathematics.
Mathematics Education. Ed.D.
Music. Includes choral and instrumental conducting, musicology, theory, performance.
Science Education. Ed.D.
Sociology.
Transportation Studies.
Urban Educational Leadership. Ed.D. only.

MORNINGSIDE COLLEGE
Sioux City, Iowa 51106-1751

Founded 1894. Coed. Private control. Methodist affiliation. Semester system. Library: 130,000 volumes, 133,500 microforms, 16 PCs.

Tuition: per semester hour $255 ($90 rebate to qualified students). On-campus housing for graduate men, women; some for married students. Contact Director of Housing for on- and off-campus information. Phone: (712)274-5104.

Graduate Program

Summer study with evening program during academic year. Enrollment: part-time only, 300 (men 10%, women 90%). College faculty teaching graduate students: full-time 18, part-time 3. Degree conferred: M.A.T.

ADMISSION REQUIREMENTS. Transcripts, writing sample, MAT required in support of application. TOEFL required for international applicants. Accepts transfer applicants. Apply to Director of Graduate Study at least one month prior to registration. Application fee: $15. Phone: (712)274-5375.

ADMISSION STANDARDS. Relatively open. Minimum average: 2.7 (A = 4).

FINANCIAL AID. Rebates for qualified students, Federal W/S, loans. Apply to Director of Graduate Studies; no specified closing date. Use FAFSA. Phone: (712)274-5104.

DEGREE REQUIREMENTS. For M.A.T.: 33 semester hours minimum; final written comprehensive exam; three final research papers.

FIELDS OF STUDY.
Behavior Disorders.
Elementary Education.

Learning Disabilities.
Multicategorical Disabilities.
Reading Specialist.
Technology-Based Learning.

MOUNT HOLYOKE COLLEGE
South Hadley, Massachusetts 01075-1414

Founded 1837. Located 90 miles W of Boston. Coed on graduate level. Private control. Cooperative Ph.D. program with the University of Massachusetts, Amherst College, Hampshire College, Smith College. (Apply through the University of Massachusetts.) Library: 602,000 volumes, 1800 current periodicals.

Tuition: per credit $665. On-campus housing for a limited number of graduate students. Average academic year housing cost: $5880 (including board). Contact Director of Residential Life for both on-campus housing and off-campus housing information. Phone: (413)538-2088.

Graduate Studies

Enrollment: full-time 14, part-time 4. Faculty: full-time 36, part-time 4. Degrees conferred: M.A., M.A.T.

ADMISSION REQUIREMENTS. Official transcripts, GRE, three letters of recommendation required in support of application. TOEFL required for international applicants. Interview usually not required. Accepts transfer applicants. Graduates of unaccredited colleges not considered. Apply through chair of department of field of study by February 15. Phone: (413)538-2481; fax: (413)538-2584.

ADMISSION STANDARDS. Competitive to very competitive. Usual minimum average: 3.0 (A = 4).

FINANCIAL AID. Research assistantships, teaching assistantship, loans. Apply by February 15 to Chair of department of field of study; to Director of Residential Life for residence hall staff positions.

DEGREE REQUIREMENTS. For master's: 28–32 credits; up to eight credits may be accepted for work completed elsewhere; thesis; reading knowledge of one foreign language; final written/oral exam.

FIELDS OF STUDY.
Chemistry.
Education.
Psychology.

MOUNT ST. MARY'S COLLEGE
Los Angeles, California 90049-1597

Founded 1925. Coed. Private control. Roman Catholic. Semester system. Library: 135,000 volumes, 7900 microforms.
Tuition: per credit $375. No on-campus housing.

Graduate Division

Enrollment: full-time 75, part-time 148. Graduate faculty: full-time 16, part-time 23. Degrees conferred: M.A., M.S.

ADMISSION REQUIREMENTS. Transcripts, MAT, letters of recommendation required in support of application. TOEFL required of foreign students. Accepts transfer applicants. Apply to Director of Admissions at least one month prior to registration. Application fee $50. Phone: (213)746-9450, ext. 2205.

ADMISSION STANDARDS. Relatively open. Usual minimum average: 2.5 (A = 4).

FINANCIAL AID. Limited to loans. Approved for VA benefits. Apply to Financial Aid Office; no specified closing date. Use FAFSA. Phone: (213)746-0450, ext. 2210; fax: (213)744-0833.

DEGREE REQUIREMENTS. For master's: 30 units minimum, at least 24 in residence; final written/oral exams; final project or thesis.

FIELDS OF STUDY.
Counseling Psychology.
Education. Includes administrative studies; special education (learning handicapped).
Individually Designed Program.
Religious Studies. M.A.

MURRAY STATE UNIVERSITY
Murray, Kentucky 42071-0009

Founded 1922. Located 110 miles W of Nashville, Tenn. Coed. State control. Semester system. Library: 831,000 volumes, 160,500 microforms.
Annual tuition: full-time, resident $2240, nonresident $6080; per credit, resident $108, nonresident $311. On-campus housing for 144 married students, 1383 men, 1449 women. Average annual housing cost: $3720 for married students, $1330–$2910 for single students. Contact Housing Office for on- and off-campus information. Phone: (502)762-2310.

The Graduate School

Graduate study since 1936. Enrollment: full-time 491, part-time 898. University faculty: full-time 305, part-time 6. Degrees conferred: M.A., M.S., M.B.A., M.A.Ed., M.S.N., M.M.E., M.A.T., M.P.A., Ed.S.

ADMISSION REQUIREMENTS. Transcripts, GRE Subject Tests GMAT required in support of School's application. TOEFL required for international applicants. Interview required by some departments. Accepts transfer applicants. Graduates of unaccredited colleges not considered. Apply to Graduate Office at least one month prior to registration. Application fee $15. Phone: (502)762-3741; fax: (502)762-3050.

ADMISSION STANDARDS. Relatively open. Usual minimum average: 2.5 (A = 4).

FINANCIAL AID. Annual awards from institutional funds: 23 scholarships, 102 teaching fellowships, 145 research assistantships, Federal W/S, loans. Apply by April 15 to chair of proposed major department for fellowships and assistantships; to Financial Aid Office for all other programs. Use FAFSA. Phone: (502)762-2546. About 10% of students receive aid other than loans from University and outside sources. Aid available for part-time students.

DEGREE REQUIREMENTS. For master's: 30–45 semester hours, at least 18–33 in residence; final written/oral exams; reading knowledge of one foreign language for some degrees, majors; thesis usually required for M.A., M.S.; for Ed.S.: 30 semester hours minimum beyond master's.

FIELDS OF STUDY.
Agriculture.
Biology. One language for M.S. Joint doctoral program with the University of Louisville.
Business Administration. GMAT for admission.

Chemistry.
Communications. Includes advertising, journalism, public relations, radio-TV.
Economics.
Education. Includes elementary, middle school, secondary, educational administration and supervision, guidance and counseling, special education, reading. M.A.Ed.: 27 hours with thesis, 33 without. Joint doctoral program with University of Kentucky.
English.
Fine Arts. Includes music education.
Geography.
Health, Physical Education, and Recreation.
History. One language for M.A.
Human Services.
Industrial Education.
Management of Technology.
Mathematics.
Music.
Nursing.
Occupational Safety and Health.
Organizational Communication.
Physics.
Psychology. Includes clinical, general.
Public Administration.
Recreation and Leisure Services.
Speech Language Pathology.
Teaching English to Speakers of Other Languages (TESOL).
Vocational and Technical Education.
Water Science.

NATIONAL-LOUIS UNIVERSITY
Evanston, Illinois 60201-1730

Founded 1886 as National College of Education. Name change in 1992. Four campuses—Evanston, Chicago, Wheaton, Wheeling. Coed. Private control. Quarter system. Library: 160,000 volumes, 1,200,000 microforms, 31 PCs.

Annual tuition: part-time $370 per semester hour. On-campus housing for limited number of men, women; none for married students. Apply to Director of Housing. Phone: (847)475-1100.

Foster G. McGaw Graduate School

Graduate study since 1951. Enrollment: full-time 1490, part-time 3283. Graduate faculty: full-time 125, part-time 456. Degrees conferred: M.Ed., M.A.T., M.S.Ed., Ed.S., Ed.D.

ADMISSION REQUIREMENTS. Transcripts, three letters of recommendation, MAT required in support of School's application. GRE for Ed.S. and doctoral program. TOEFL required for international applicants. Accepts transfer applicants. Graduates of unaccredited institutions not considered. Apply to Director of Admission; no specified closing date. Rolling admissions process. Application fee $25. Phone: (847)475-1100, ext. 2479.

ADMISSION STANDARDS. Selective. Usual minimum average: 3.0 (A = 4).

FINANCIAL AID. Annual awards from institutional funds: fifty fellowships, Federal W/S, loans. Apply to Office of Financial Assistance; no specified closing date. Use FAFSA. Phone: (847)465-0575, ext. 5770. Aid sometimes available for part-time students.

DEGREE REQUIREMENTS. For master's: 32 credits minimum; thesis/nonthesis option. No language requirement. For Ed.S.: at least 30 credits beyond master's. For Ed.D.: 63 credits minimum; qualifying exam; dissertation; final oral exam.

FIELDS OF STUDY.
Administration and Supervision.
Curriculum and Instruction.
Early Childhood Education.
Educational Leadership.
Elementary Education.
Human Resource Development.
Management.
Mathematics.
Reading/Writing Specialist.
School Psychology.
Science Education.
Special Education.
Technology in Education.
Writing.

NATIONAL UNIVERSITY
San Diego, California 92108-4107

Chartered 1971. Eight branch campuses—North San Diego, Irvine, Riverside, Los Angeles, Sacramento, San Jose, Fresno, Stockton. Coed. Private control. One-course-per-month format, quarter system. Library: 138,000 volumes, 1,366,000 microforms, 2500 current periodicals, 37 PCs.

Tuition: $755 per 5 quarter-hour course. No on-campus housing available.

Graduate Studies

Graduate study since 1975. Enrollment: full-time 2118, part-time 900. Graduate faculty: full-time 100, part-time 560. Degrees conferred: M.A., M.B.A., M.F.S., M.P.A., M.S.

ADMISSION REQUIREMENTS. Official transcripts, three letters of recommendation required in support of application. TOEFL required for international applicants. Accepts transfer applicants. Graduates of unaccredited institutions not considered. Apply to Admission Office: no specified closing date. Rolling admissions process. Application fee $60, $100 for international applicants. Phone: (800) NAT-UNIV or (619)563-7100; fax: (619)563-7393.

ADMISSION STANDARDS. Relatively open. Usual minimum average: 2.5 (A = 4).

FINANCIAL AID. Annual awards from institutional funds: fellowships, Federal W/S, loans. Approved for VA benefits. Apply to Office of Financial Assistance; no specified closing date. Use FAFSA. Aid available for part-time students.

DEGREE REQUIREMENTS. For master's: 45–60 credits minimum, at least 35 in residence; thesis/nonthesis option; no foreign language requirement.

FIELDS OF STUDY.

SCHOOL OF EDUCATION:
Counseling Psychology. M.A.
Curriculum and Instruction. M.S.
Educational Counseling. M.S.
Educational Leadership. M.S.
Educational Technology. M.S.
Human Behavior. M.A.
Instructional Leadership. Includes adult and higher education, early childhood, educational administration.
School Psychology. M.S.
Special Education. M.S.

SCHOOL OF MANAGEMENT AND TECHNOLOGY:

Business Administration. Includes accountancy, financial management, human resource management, marketing, technology. M.B.A.

Forensic Sciences. M.F.S.

Government Relations and Politics. M.P.A.

Human Resource Management. M.A.

International Business Administration. M.A.

Management. M.A.

Software Engineering. M.S.

Taxation. M.S.

Technology Management. M.S.

Telecommunication. M.S.

NAVAL POSTGRADUATE SCHOOL

Monterey, California 93943

Organized 1909. Located 125 miles S of San Francisco. Enrollment limited to military officers and sponsored civilian federal employees and selected international officers. Federal control. Quarter system. Library: 500,000 volumes, 520,000 microforms, 1700 current periodicals.

Annual tuition: fully funded. On-campus housing for single and married students. Average academic year housing cost: $9200. Day care facilities available.

Enrollment: full-time 1714; no part-time students. Faculty: full-time 318; part-time 15. Degrees conferred: M.A., M.S., Engr., D.Eng., Ph.D.

ADMISSION REQUIREMENTS. Official transcripts, recommendations required in support of application. Interview not required. TOEFL, TWE required for international applicants. Officers on active duty with all branches of the armed services eligible for enrollment. Apply to branch personnel division; no specified closing dates. Phone: (408)646-3093.

ADMISSION STANDARDS. Competitive. Usual minimum average: 2.5 (A = 4).

DEGREE REQUIREMENTS. For M.A., M.S.: 45 quarter hours minimum in full-time residence; thesis; no language requirement. For Engineering: 45 quarter hours beyond the master's; special project. For Ph.D.: three years minimum beyond the bachelor's, at least two years in full-time residence; preliminary exam; reading knowledge of one foreign language; dissertation; final oral exam. D.Eng.: essentially the same as Ph.D., except no foreign language requirement.

FIELDS OF STUDY.

Aeronautical and Astronautical Engineering. M.S., D.Eng., Engr., Ph.D.

Command, Control, and Communications. M.S.

Computer Science. M.S., Ph.D.

Electronic Warfare Systems Technology. M.S.

Engineering Acoustics. M.S., Ph.D.

Engineering Science. M.S., Ph.D.

Mathematics. M.S., Ph.D.

Mechanical Engineering. M.S., Engr., Ph.D.

Meteorology. M.S., Ph.D.

National Security Affairs. M.A., M.S.

Oceanography. M.S., Ph.D.

Operations Research. M.S., Ph.D.

Physics. M.S., Ph.D.

Space Systems. M.S.

Systems Management. M.S., Ph.D.

Undersea Warfare. M.S.

UNIVERSITY OF NEBRASKA AT KEARNEY

Kearney, Nebraska 68849-0001

Founded 1903. Located 125 miles W of Lincoln. Coed. State control. Semester system. Special facilities: Center for Economic Education, Center for Rural Research, Museum of Nebraska Art, Nebraska Business Development Center, Nebraska State Arboretum, Safety Center. Library: 250,000 volumes, 845,000 microforms.

Tuition: per credit hour, resident $75, nonresident $142. Limited on-campus housing available for single graduate students, about 100 apartments for married students. Housing cost: $1350 per semester for single students; $1550 per semester for married students. Contact Director of Residence Life for on- and off-campus housing information. Phone: (308)865-8519.

College of Graduate Study

Graduate study since 1956. Enrollment full-time 250, part-time 1000. Graduate faculty: full-time 170, part-time 50. Degrees conferred: M.S. in Ed., M.A. in Ed., M.B.A., Specialist.

ADMISSION REQUIREMENTS. Transcripts, GRE/GMAT required in support of College's application. TOEFL required for foreign applicants. Interview not required. Accepts transfer applicants. Graduates of unaccredited institutions not considered. Apply to Dean of Graduate School prior to registration. Application fee $25. Phone: (308)865-8838; fax: (308)865-8837.

ADMISSION STANDARDS. Selective. Usual minimum average: 2.75 (A = 4), GRE minimum 750–950.

FINANCIAL AID. Annual awards from institutional funds: ten academic scholarships, ten non-resident tuition scholarships, five grants, eighty teaching/research assistantships, Federal W/S, loans. Approved for VA benefits. Apply to Dean of Graduate Studies for scholarships, assistantships; to Financial Aid Office for all other programs. Apply one month prior to registration. Use FAFSA. Phone: (308)865-8520; fax: (308)865-8096. About 5% of students receive aid from College and outside sources. Aid sometimes available to part-time students.

DEGREE REQUIREMENTS. For M.A. and M.S. in Ed.: 36 credit hours minimum, at least 27 in residence; optional thesis included; comprehensive written exam. For M.B.A.: 36 credit hours; final exam. For Specialist: 30 credits beyond the master's.

FIELDS OF STUDY.

Art.

Biology.

Business Administration.

Communication Disorders.

Community Counseling.

Educational Administration.

Elementary/Early Childhood Education.

English.

Exercise Science.

Foreign Languages. Includes French, German, Spanish.

History.

Industrial Technology.

Instructional Technology.

Mathematics.

Middle School.

Music.

Physical Education.

School Counseling.

School Principalship.

School Psychology. Specialist only.

Science Teaching.

Special Education.
Speech Communication.
Teaching the Secondary School. Usual subject fields.
Vocational and Technical Education.

UNIVERSITY OF NEBRASKA AT LINCOLN

P.O. Box 880434
Lincoln, Nebraska 68588-0434
http://www.unl.edu

Founded 1869. Coed. State control. Semester system. Special facilities: Barkley Memorial Center, G.W. Beadle Center for Genetics and Biomaterial Research, Bureau of Sociological Research, Government Research Institute, Lied Center for Performing Arts, Midwestern Center for Mass Spectrometry, Nebraska State Museum of Natural History, Sheldon Art Gallery. Library: 2,200,000 volumes, 3,829,000 microforms.

Annual tuition: full-time, resident $2190, nonresident $4840; per credit hour, resident $99, nonresident $245. On-campus housing for single graduate students. Apartment housing for 70 married students. Average monthly housing cost: $300–$375 for married students. Average academic year housing cost for single students: $3990. Contact Office of University Housing for both on- and off-campus housing information. Phone: (402)472-3561.

Graduate College

http://www.unl.edu/gradstud/undex.html.

Graduate study since 1886. Graduate enrollment: full- and part-time 4500. Graduate faculty full-time 1500, part-time none. Degrees conferred: M.A., M.S., M.Arch., M.Ed., M.A.T., M.Sc.T., M.F.A., M.B.A., M.L.S., M.P.A., M.M., M.P.E., M.C.R.P., M.S.T., Ed.S., Ed.D., D.M.A., Ph.D.

ADMISSION REQUIREMENTS. Two transcripts required in support of College's application. GRE General/Subject Tests/ MAT required by some programs. GMAT required for business programs. TOEFL required for international applicants. Interview not required. Accepts transfer applicants. Graduates of unaccredited institutions not considered. Apply to Graduate Office by March 1 (Fall), September 1 (Spring), February 1 (Summer). Admission fee $25. Phone: (800)742-8800, (402)472-2875.

ADMISSION STANDARDS. Competitive for most departments, very competitive or selective for the others. Usual minimum average: 2.5 for master's, 3.0 for doctoral candidates (A = 4).

FINANCIAL AID. Two thousand teaching and research assistantships, Federal W/S, loans. Approved for VA benefits. Apply by February 15 to Office of Graduate Studies for information regarding fellowships, to appropriate department chair for assistantships; to Office of Financial Aid for all other programs. Use FAFSA. Phone: (402)472-2030. About 33% of students receive aid other than loans from College. Aid sometimes available for part-time students.

DEGREE REQUIREMENTS. For M.A., M.S., M.S.T., M.Sc.T.: 30 semester credits minimum, at least 12 in residence; thesis; final oral/written exams; or 36 credits minimum, at least 18 in residence; final oral/written exam in some departments. For M.Ed., M.A.T., M.P.E.: 30 semester hours minimum, at least 12 in residence; qualifying exam; thesis; final oral/written comprehensive exam; or nonthesis option, 36 semester hours minimum, at least 18 in residence. For M.F.A., M.Arch., M.C.R.P.: 60 semester hours minimum; final project; final exam. For M.B.A., M.P.A.: 48 hours minimum, at least 18 in residence. For Ed.S.: 64 hours beyond bachelor's. For Ed.D., Ph.D., D.M.A.: three full years

minimum; 90 semester hours; reading knowledge of one foreign language, plus reading knowledge of second language or comprehensive knowledge of one foreign language or proficiency in research techniques or evidence of knowledge of a collateral field; residency, 27 hours graduate work within a consecutive 18-month period or less; comprehensive exam; dissertation; final oral exam.

FIELDS OF STUDY.
Accountancy. M.P.A.
Actuarial Science. M.S. only.
Agricultural Economics. M.S., Ph.D.
Agricultural Education. M.S. only.
Agronomy. M.S., Ph.D.
Animal Science. M.S., Ph.D.
Anthropology. M.A. only.
Architecture. M.Arch. only.
Art and Art History. M.F.A. only.
Biochemistry. M.S., Ph.D.
Biological Sciences. M.A., M.S., Ph.D.
Biometry. M.S. only.
Business. GMAT for admission. M.A., M.B.A., Ph.D.
Chemistry. M.S., Ph.D.
Classics. M.A. only.
Communication Studies and Theater Arts. M.A., Ph.D.
Community and Regional Planning. M.C.R.P.
Computer Science. M.S., Ph.D.
Economics. M.A., Ph.D.
Education. M.A., M.Ed., M.P.E., M.S.T., M.S., Ed.S., Ed.D., Ph.D. Includes administration, curriculum and instruction, adult and continuing, community and human resources, health, physical education and recreation, psychological and cultural studies, special, speech language pathology and audiology, vocational, vocational and adult.
Engineering. M.S., Ph.D. Includes agricultural and biological systems, chemical, civil, computer science, electrical, engineering mechanics, industrial and management systems, manufacturing systems engineering, mechanical.
English. M.A., Ph.D.
Entomology. M.S., Ph.D.
Family and Consumer Sciences. M.S. only.
Food Science and Technology. M.S., Ph.D.
Forestry, Fisheries, and Wildlife. M.S. only.
Geography. M.A., Ph.D.
Geology. M.S., Ph.D.
History. M.A., Ph.D.
Horticulture. M.S. only.
Horticulture and Forestry. Ph.D. only.
Human Nutrition and Food Service Management. M.S. only.
Human Resources and Family Sciences. M.S., Ph.D.
Journalism. M.A. only.
Legal Studies. M.L.S. only.
Mathematics and Statistics. M.A., M.S., M.A.T., M.Sc.T., Ph.D.
Mechanized Systems Management. M.S. only.
Modern Language and Literature. M.A., Ph.D.
Museum Studies. M.A., M.S.
Music. M.M., D M.A.
Nutrition. M.S., Ph.D.
Philosophy. M.A., Ph.D.
Physics and Astronomy. M.S., Ph.D.
Political Science. M.A., Ph.D.
Psychology. M.A., Ph.D.
Sociology. M.A., Ph.D.
Textiles, Clothing and Design. M.A., M.S.
Theater Arts and Dance. M.F.A. only.
Veterinary Science. M.S. only.

College of Law (68583-0902)

Established 1888. Semester system. Law library: 345,000 volumes. Library has LEXIS, NEXIS, WESTLAW, DIALOG.

Tuition: per semester hour, resident $98, nonresident $250. On-campus housing for single students only.

Enrollment: first-year class 137; total full-time 436 (men 57%, women 43%). Faculty: full-time 26, part-time 22. Degrees conferred: J.D., J.D.-M.A. (Economics, Political Sciences, Psychology), J.D.-M.B.A., J.D.-M.P.A., J.D.-M.C.R.P., J.D.-Ph.D. (Educational Administration).

ADMISSION REQUIREMENTS. LSDAS Law School report, bachelor's degree, transcripts, LSAT, letters of recommendation required in support of application. Interview not required. Transfer applicants and graduates of unaccredited colleges not considered. Apply to Dean of College after September 1, before March 1 for preferred consideration. First-year students admitted September only. Application fee $25. Phone: (402)472-2161.

ADMISSION STANDARDS. Accepts about 40–45% of total annual applicants.

FINANCIAL AID. Scholarships, fellowships, assistantships, Federal W/S, loans. Apply to the University Financial Aid Office by March 1. Use FAFSA and College's need-based grant application.

DEGREE REQUIREMENTS. For J.D.: satisfactory completion of three-year program, last two semesters required in residence; 96 credit-hour program. For J.D.-master's and doctoral programs: see Graduate school listing above.

College of Dentistry (68583-0740)

Founded 1889. Affiliated with University in 1917.

Annual tuition: full-time, resident $8862, nonresident $20,525. On-campus housing available. Average academic year housing cost: $13,200. Contact Housing Office for both on- and off-campus housing information. Phone: (402)472-3561. Total average cost for all other first-year expenses: $3250.

Enrollment: first-year class 40 (men 75%, women 25%); total 250; postgraduates 50. College faculty: full-time 79, part-time 54. Degree conferred: D.D.S. Graduate study (Oral Biology) is offered through the Graduate College.

ADMISSION REQUIREMENTS. AADSAS report, transcripts, DAT (no later than October) required in support of application. TOEFL and Certification of Financial Support required of international students whose first language is not English. Interview not required. At least three years of college preferred. Preference given to Nebraska residents and nearby states without dental schools. Apply to Admissions Committee after June 1, before March 1. Phone: (402)472-1366.

ADMISSION STANDARDS. Selective. Accepts 20–25% of total annual applicants. TOEFL score required: 575. Approximately 65% are state residents.

FINANCIAL AID. Scholarships, grants, tuition waivers, loans. Apply to Office of Financial Aid; no specified closing date. Use FAFSA. Phone: (402)559-4199. About 90% of students receive aid from College.

DEGREE REQUIREMENTS. For D.D.S.: satisfactory completion of forty-four-month program. For graduate study, see Graduate College listing above.

FIELDS OF GRADUATE STUDY.
Endodontics.
General Dentistry.
Oral and Maxillofacial Surgery.
Orthodontics.

Pediatric Dentistry.
Periodontics.
Prosthodontics.

UNIVERSITY OF NEBRASKA AT OMAHA
Omaha, Nebraska 68101
http://www.unomaha.edu/graduate

Founded 1908. Coed. State control. Semester system. Special facilities: Center for Afghanistan Studies, Aviation Institute, Center for Faculty Development, Center for International Telecommunications Management, Center for Urban Education, Small Business Development Center. Library: 691,000 volumes, 1,619,000 microforms.

Tuition: per credit hour, resident $86, nonresident $206. No on-campus housing. For off-campus housing, contact Office of Student Housing. Day care facilities available.

Graduate College

Graduate study since 1931. Enrollment: full-time 628, part-time 2142. Faculty teaching graduate students: full-time 286, part-time 15. Degrees conferred: M.A., M.S., M.B.A., M.M., M.P.A., M.S.W., Ed.S., Ph.D.

ADMISSION REQUIREMENTS. Transcripts, GRE/MAT/GMAT required in support of College's application. Evidence of English proficiency or TOEFL required of international students. Accepts transfer applicants. Graduates of unaccredited institutions not considered. Apply to Director of Admissions by July 1 (Fall), December 1 (Spring), May 1 (Summer). Application fee $25. Phone: (402)554-2341.

ADMISSION STANDARDS. Selective for most departments. Usual minimum average: 3.0 (A = 4).

FINANCIAL AID. Annual awards from institutional funds: 150 graduate assistantships, Federal W/S, loans. Approved for VA benefits. Apply by March 31 to appropriate department chair for assistantships; to Financial Aid Office for all other programs. Phone: (402)554-2327. Use FAFSA. Aid sometimes available to part-time students.

DEGREE REQUIREMENTS. For M.A.: 30 semester hours minimum, at least 24 in residence; thesis included; final written/oral exam. For M.B.A., M.S., M.M., M.P.A., M.S.W.: 36 semester hours minimum, at least 30 in residence; final written/oral exam. For Ed.S.: one year minimum beyond the master's, at least one semester and one summer in full-time residence; field project; final oral exam. For Ph.D.: three years minimum, 90 semester hours, 27 hours graduate work within a consecutive 18-month period or less; reading knowledge of one foreign language, plus reading knowledge of one foreign language or proficiency in research techniques or evidence of knowledge of a collateral field; comprehensive exam; dissertation; final oral exam.

FIELDS OF STUDY.
Biology.
Business Administration.
Communication.
Computer Science.
Criminal Justice.
Dramatic Arts.
Economics.
Education. Includes counseling and guidance, teaching of the hearing impaired and mentally retarded, speech pathology, elementary education, secondary, educational administration, urban education, health, physical education and recreation, re-

source teaching and learning disabilities, teaching the emotionally disturbed, reading.
Educational Psychology.
English.
Geography.
Gerontology.
History.
Management Information Systems.
Mathematics.
Music.
Professional Accounting.
Psychology. Includes educational, school industrial, organizational.
Public Administration.
Social Work.
Sociology.
Urban Studies.

Medical Center–Graduate College

http://www.unmc.edu/grad.html

Located in Omaha (68198). Library: 241,000 volumes. Tuition: per semester-hour credit, resident $99, nonresident $245. For on- and off-campus housing information. Phone: (402)559-5201.

Enrollment: full-time 164, part-time 249. Graduate faculty: 350. Degrees conferred: M.S., Ph.D.

ADMISSION REQUIREMENTS. Transcripts, GRE required in support of College's application. TOEFL required for foreign applicants. Accepts transfer applicants. Graduates of unaccredited colleges not considered. Deadlines for applications vary by program. Application fee $25. Phone: (402)559-4206; fax: (402)559-9671.

ADMISSION STANDARDS. Selective. Usual minimum average: 3.0 for M.S. and Ph.D. (A = 4).

FINANCIAL AID. Scholarships, fellowships, assistantships for teaching and research, loans. Approved for VA benefits. Use FAFSA. Phone: (402)559-4199; fax: (402)559-9671. About 50% of students receive aid other than loans from all sources.

DEGREE REQUIREMENTS. For M.S.: six didactic courses; seminars; thesis/final document; final oral/written exam. For Ph.D.: three years minimum; reading knowledge of foreign language(s)/research tool may be required; dissertation; final oral/written exam.

FIELDS OF STUDY.
Anatomy.
Biochemistry and Molecular Biology.
Cell Biology.
Dentistry. Interdepartmental. M.S. only.
Medical Sciences. Interdepartmental.
Nursing.
Pathology and Microbiology.
Pharmaceutical Sciences.
Pharmacology.
Physiology.

College of Medicine

Established 1880. Located in Omaha (68198-4430) since 1913. Annual tuition: resident $10,814, nonresident $20,908. Total average figure for all other expenses: $9500.

Enrollment: first-year class 120, total 496 (men 53%, women 47%); resident training 285. College faculty: full-time 395, part-time and volunteers 1100. Degree conferred: M.D.

ADMISSION REQUIREMENTS. AMCAS report, transcripts, MCAT, screening interview required in support of application.

Applicants must have completed at least three years of college study but degree recommended. Does not have EDP. Preference given to state residents. Apply to Office of Dean of College after June 15, before November 15. Application fee $25. Phone: (402)559-4205; fax: (402)559-4104.

ADMISSION STANDARDS. Selective. Accepts 15% of total annual applicants. Approximately 99% are state residents.

FINANCIAL AID. Scholarships, grants, loans. Apply to Office of Financial Aid by March 1. About 60% of students receive some aid from College and outside sources.

DEGREE REQUIREMENTS. For M.D.: satisfactory completion of four-year program.

UNIVERSITY OF NEVADA, LAS VEGAS
Las Vegas, Nevada 89154-9900

Founded 1955. Coed. State control. Semester system. Special facilities: Desert Biology Research Center, Education Equity Resource Center, Center for Energy Research, Harry Reid Center, Information Science Research Center, Center for In-Service Training and Educational Research, International Gaming Institute, Limnological Research Center, Nevada Small Business Development Center, Arnold Shaw Popular Music Research Center, Center for Public Data Research, Supercomputing Center for Energy and the Environment, Center for the Study of Public Policy, Sports Injury Research Center, Transportation Research Center, Center for Volcanic and Tectronic Studies. Library: 752,657 volumes, 1,391,880 microforms.

Tuition: per credit full-time, resident $87, nonresident $129 plus $2550 per semester. Summer registration fees assessed at $84 per hour. Limited on-campus housing. Room and board: $2433–$2746 per semester. Contact the Office of Student Personnel Services for both on- and off-campus information. Phone: (702)895-3489.

Graduate College

Enrollment: admitted students 2168, specials 1966. Faculty: full-time 500, part-time 200. Degrees conferred: M.A., M.S., M.Ed., M.Arch., M.B.A., Ed.S., M.M., M.F.A., M.P.A., Ed.D., Ph.D.

ADMISSION REQUIREMENTS. Transcripts, two letters of recommendation; appropriate undergraduate background required in support of College's application. Individual departments may impose special requirements such as GRE or GMAT. Interview not normally required. TOEFL required for international applicants. Transfer applicants considered. Graduates of unaccredited institutions not considered. Apply to Dean, Graduate College; deadlines vary by department for U.S. applicants; May 1 (Fall), October 1 (Spring) for international applicants. Application fee $40, $95 for international applicants. Phone: (702)895-4391; fax: (702)895-4180.

ADMISSION STANDARDS. Selective. Usual minimum average: 2.75; 3.0 for last two years (A = 4).

FINANCIAL AID. Three fellowships, 19 partial scholarships, 325 assistantships, Federal W/S, loans. Approved for VA benefits. Apply to Graduate Dean by March 1 for fellowships, scholarships, assistantships; to Financial Aid Office for all other programs. Phone: (702)895-3424. Use FAFSA and institutional FAF. No financial aid for part-time students.

DEGREE REQUIREMENTS. Minimum of 30 hours. Varies with department and degree. Final examination required in all programs except M.B.A. Thesis required in most programs. For Ph.D., Ed.D.: 72 semester credits (Ph.D.), 90 credits (Ed.D.) beyond the bachelor's degree; seven-year time limit; at least two successive semesters in full-time residence; qualifying exam; comprehensive exam; dissertation; final oral exam.

FIELDS OF STUDY.
Accounting. M.S.
Anthropology. M.A. only.
Architecture. M.Arch.
Art. M.F.A.
Biological Sciences. M.S., Ph.D.
Business Administration. M.B.A.
Chemistry. M.S.
Civil Engineering. M.S.
Communication. M.A.
Computer Science. M.S., Ph.D.
Counseling, Educational Psychology, and Foundations. M.S., M.Ed.
Criminal Justice. M.A.
Economics. M.A.
Educational Administration and Higher Administration. M.Ed., Ed.S., Ed.D.
Electrical Engineering. M.S.
Engineering. Includes civil, electrical, mechanical. Ph.D.
English. M.A., Ph.D.
Ethics and Policy Studies. M.A.
Foreign Languages. Includes French, Spanish. M.A.
Geoscience. M.S.
Health Physics. M.S.
History. M.A., Ph.D.
Hospitality Administration. Ph.D.
Hotel Administration. M.S.
Human Performance and Development. Includes sport and leisure services, exercise physiology, kinesiology. M.S.
Instructional and Curricular Studies. M.S., M.Ed., Ed.S., Ed.D.
Liberal Studies. M.A.
Mathematical Science. M.S.
Mechanical Engineering. M.S.
Music. M.M.
Nursing. Includes adult health nursing, family nurse practitioner. M.S.
Physics. M.S., Ph.D.
Political Science. M.A.
Psychology. M.A.
Public Administration. M.P.A.
Science. M.A.
Social Work. M.S.W.
Sociology. M.A., Ph.D.
Special Education. M.S., M.Ed., Ed.S., Ed.D.
Theater. M.A., M.F.A.
Transportation. M.S.T.
Water Resources Management. M.S.

UNIVERSITY OF NEVADA, RENO
Reno, Nevada 89557-0035

Founded 1864. Coed. State control. Semester system. Special facilities: Center for Advanced Study, Agricultural Experiment Station; Biological Science Center, Bureaus of Business, Economics, and Government Research; Desert Research Institute; Engineering Research and Development Center, Energy and Environmental Engineering Center, Fleischmann Atmospherium-Planetarium; nuclear reactor; Nevada Mining Analytical Laboratory; Mackay Mineral Resource Research Institute; Nevada Bureau of Mines; Reno Metallurgy Research Center, Water Resource Center. Library: 861,000 volumes, 2,720,000 microforms, 6700 current periodicals, 122 PCs.

Tuition: full-time, resident $84 per credit hour; nonresident, $129 per credit plus $5100 per year. On-campus housing for both single and married students. Average academic year housing cost: $7440–$10,125. Contact Housing Services Office for both on- and off-campus housing information. Phone: (702)784-6107.

Graduate School

Semester enrollment: full-time 1105, part-time 855. University faculty teaching graduate students: full-time 485, part-time 32. Degrees conferred: M.A., M.S., M.Ed., M.B.A., M.J.S., M.M., M.S.W., Ph.D., Ed.D.

ADMISSION REQUIREMENTS. Two official transcripts from each college or institution, GRE General/Subject Tests, GMAT (for M.B.A.) required in support of School's application. TOEFL, financial statement, and medical history and exam for international applicants. Accepts transfer applicants. Graduates of unaccredited institutions not considered. Apply to Office of Admissions and Records three weeks prior to registration. Many departments have earlier deadlines. Application fee $20. Phone: (702)784-6869; fax: (702)784-6064.

ADMISSION STANDARDS. Selective, for most departments. Usual minimum average: 2.75 for master's; 3.0 for doctoral programs (A = 4).

FINANCIAL AID. Annual awards from institutional funds: 20 scholarships, 214 teaching assistantships, 517 research assistantships, 30 internships, Federal W/S, loans. Apply to Chair of Scholarships, Committee for Scholarships; to Dean of College for internships and fellowships; to department concerned for assistantships; to Financial Aid Office for all other programs. Use FAFSA. Phone: (702)784-4666. About 50% of full-time students receive aid other than loans from School and outside sources.

DEGREE REQUIREMENTS. For M.A., M.S., M.B.A., M.M.: 30 semester credits minimum, at least 21 in residence; thesis/nonthesis option; reading knowledge of one foreign language required by some departments; final oral/written exam. For M.Ed., M.S.W.: 32 credits minimum, at least 24 in residence; two years' educational experience; final paper or comprehensive exam; final oral/written exam; six-year time limit. For Ph.D., 72 semester credits, Ed.D. 90 semester credits minimum beyond the bachelor's; eight-year time limit; at least two successive semesters in full-time residence; qualifying exam; comprehensive exam; dissertation; final oral exam.

FIELDS OF STUDY.
Agricultural Economics. Master's only.
Animal Science. Master's only.
Anthropology. M.A., Ph.D.
Basque Studies. Ph.D. only.
Biochemistry. Ph.D. only.
Biology.
Botany.
Business Administration. M.B.A. only.
Cellular and Molecular Biology. Ph.D.
Cellular and Molecular Pharmacology. Ph.D.
Chemical Physics. Ph.D.
Chemistry. M.S., Ph.D.
Civil Engineering. Master's only.
Clinical Psychology.
Computer Science. M.S.
Counseling and Educational Psychology. M.A., Ph.D.
Ecology. Ph.D.
Economics. Master's only.
Educational Leadership. M.S., Ph.D.
Electrical Engineering. Master's only.
Elementary Education. Master's only.
Engineering. Ph.D.
English. M.A., Ph.D.
Entomology. M.S. only.

Environmental Science and Health. M.S., Ph.D.
Foreign Languages and Literature. (French, German, Spanish). Master's only.
Geochemistry. Ph.D.
Geological Engineering. Master's only.
Geology.
Geophysics. Ph.D.
History. M.A., Ph.D.
Human Development and Family Studies.
Hydrology and Hydrogeology. M.S., Ph.D.
Journalism. Master's only.
Judicial Studies.
Land Use Planning.
Mathematics. Master's only.
Mechanical Engineering. Master's only.
Metallurgical Engineering. M.S., Ph.D.
Mining Engineering. Master's only.
Music. Master's only.
Nursing. Master's only.
Nutrition. Master's only.
Pharmacology. Ph.D.
Philosophy. Master's only.
Physical Education. Master's only.
Physics. M.S., Ph.D.
Political Science. Master's only.
Psychology. M.A., Ph.D.
Public Administration and Policy. Master's only.
Secondary Education. Master's only.
Social Psychology. Ph.D. only.
Social Work.
Sociology.
Special Education. Master's only.
Speech Communication. Master's only.
Speech Pathology and Audiology. Master's only.
Systems Engineering.
Teaching of English. M.A. only.
Water Resources.
Zoology. Master's only.

School of Medicine (89557)

Established 1969. Annual tuition: resident $8947, nonresident $16,976, student fees $1616. Limited on-campus housing. Total average figure for all other expenses: $8100. Enrollment: first-year class 52 (EDP 2) full-time 200 (men 63%, women 37%). Faculty: full-time 30, part-time none. Degrees conferred: M.D., M.D.-Ph.D.

ADMISSION REQUIREMENTS. AMCAS report, transcripts, MCAT, three letters of evaluation required in support of application. Interview by invitation only. Graduates of unaccredited colleges not considered. Preference given to residents of Nevada and residents of Alaska, Idaho, Montana, and Wyoming. Has EDP; apply between June 15 and August 1. Apply to Admissions Office after June 15, before November 1. Application fee $35. Phone: (702)784-6063; fax: (702)784-6096.

ADMISSION STANDARDS. Selective. Accepts 20–25% of total annual applicants. Approximately 80% are state residents.

FINANCIAL AID. Scholarships, loans. Apply to Director of Student Affairs; no specified closing date. About 80% of students receive some aid from School and outside sources.

DEGREE REQUIREMENTS. For M.D: satisfactory completion of four-year program. Third and fourth years are spent in Reno, Las Vegas, and rural Nevada. For Ph.D.: see Graduate School listing above.

FIELDS OF GRADUATE STUDY.
Biochemistry.
Biophysics.

Cell Biology.
Molecular Biology.
Pathology.
Pharmacology.

NEW ENGLAND CONSERVATORY OF MUSIC
Boston, Massachusetts 02115-5000

Founded 1867. Coed. Private control. Semester system. Library: 65,000 volumes.
Annual tuition: full-time $17,100. On-campus housing available for single students. Average academic year housing cost: $7600 (including board).

Graduate Program

Enrollment: full-time 378, part-time 47. Faculty: full-time 55, part-time 123. Degrees conferred: M.M., Graduate Diploma, Artist Diploma, D.M.A.

ADMISSION REQUIREMENTS. Transcripts, bachelor's, three letters of recommendation, audition required in support of application. Interview required by some departments. TOEFL required for international applicants. Apply by January 15 (Fall). Application fee $75. Phone: (617)262-1120.

ADMISSION STANDARDS. Selective. Usual minimum average: 3.0 (A = 4).

FINANCIAL AID. Scholarships, teaching fellowships, teaching assistantships, Federal W/S, loans. Apply to the Financial Aid Office; no specified closing date. Use FAFSA and institutional FAF. Phone: (617)262-1120. 60% of students receive aid other than loans from School. Aid sometimes available for part-time study.

DEGREE REQUIREMENTS. For master's: 32 credits. For diplomas: at least 30 credits beyond the master's; public performance; special project for some programs. For D.M.A.: 90 semester hours beyond the bachelor's degree, at least 30 credits in full-time residence; reading knowledge of one foreign language/research technique, depending on program; qualifying exam; recitals or other public performance for most programs; dissertation or final document; final oral exam.

FIELDS OF STUDY.
Accompaniment.
Classical Performance. Includes brass, strings, harp, guitar, organ, piano, percussion, woodwinds, voice.
Composition.
Conducting. Includes choral, orchestral, wind ensemble.
Contemporary Improvisation.
Historical Performance.
Jazz Studies. Includes performance and composition.
Music Education. Concentration in supervision.
Musicology.
Theoretical Studies.
Vocal Pedagogy.

NEW ENGLAND SCHOOL OF LAW
154 Stuart Street
Boston, Massachusetts 02116

Founded 1908 as Portia Law School; name changed 1969. Semester system. Library: 250,000 volumes, 50 PCs. Library has LEXIS, NEXIS, WESTLAW, DIALOG, OCLC.

Annual tuition: day $13,350, evening $10,010. No on-campus housing available. Total average annual additional expense: $11,200.

Enrollment: first-year class, day 220, evening 130; total 1186 (men 57%, women 43%). Faculty: full-time 40, part-time 61. Degree conferred: J.D.

ADMISSION REQUIREMENTS. LSDAS Law School report, bachelor's degree, transcripts, LSAT, two letters of recommendation required in support of application. Accepts transfer applicants. Graduates of unaccredited colleges not considered. Apply to Director of Admissions by March 15. Application fee $45. Phone: (617)422-7210.

ADMISSION STANDARDS. Selective. Accepts about 30–35% of total annual applicants.

FINANCIAL AID. Minority and disadvantaged scholarships, Federal W/S, loans. Apply to Office of Financial Aid by April 15. Use FAFSA and NESL financial aid application.

DEGREE REQUIREMENTS. For J.D.: satisfactory completion of 84 credit-hour program.

UNIVERSITY OF NEW ENGLAND
Biddeford, Maine 04005-9526

College Of Osteopathic Medicine

College established 1970. Formed University 1978. 20 minutes' drive from Portland. Coed. Private control. Library: 86,000 volumes, 570 current periodicals; has MEDLINE, CANCER LINE, BIOETHIC, HEALTH, TOXLINE, DIALOG, OCLC.

Annual tuition: $21,150. On-campus housing available. Average academic year housing cost: $6130 (including board) for single students; $4500 for married students. Contact Student Affairs Office for both on- and off-campus housing information. Phone: (207)283 0171, ext. 2272.

Enrollment: first-year class 80, total 325 (men 65%, women 35%). Faculty: full-time 15, part-time 50. Degree conferred: D.O.

ADMISSION REQUIREMENTS. AACOMAS report, bachelor's degree, official transcripts, MCAT (no later than September), three letters of recommendation, one from premed advisory committee, evaluation from a physician (preferably a D.O.), supplemental form required in support of application. Interview by invitation only. Graduates of unaccredited college not considered. Apply by January 1 to the Office of Admissions. Admits first-year students Fall only. Application fee: $50. Phone: (800)477-4UNE, (207)283-0171, ext. 475.

ADMISSION STANDARDS. Selective. Accepts approximately 5% of annual applications. Usual minimum average: 2.75 (A = 4). Mean GPA: 3.2.

FINANCIAL AID. Scholarships, fellowships, tuition waivers, loans. Apply by April 15 to the Financial Aid Office. Use FAFSA.

DEGREE REQUIREMENTS. For D.O.: satisfactory completion of four-year program.

UNIVERSITY OF NEW HAMPSHIRE
Durham, New Hampshire 03824-3547
http://www.gradschool.unh.edu

Founded in 1866. Located 60 miles N of Boston. Coed. State control. Semester system. Special facilities: Agricultural Experi-

ment Station, Center for Business and Economics Research, Family Research Center, Center for Humanities, Institute on Disabilities, Environmental Research Group, Manchester Manufacturing Management Center, New Hampshire Small Business Development Center, Institute for Policy and Social Science Research, Institute for the Study of Earth, Oceans and Space, Center for Venture Research. Library: more than 1,000,000 volumes, 6500 periodicals.

Annual tuition: full-time, resident $4320, nonresident $13,290; part-time, resident $234 per credit, nonresident $523. On-campus housing available for married students (154 units) and single students (180 rooms). Average academic year housing cost: $7000. For on-campus housing, apply to Residential Life, Pettee House. Phone: (603)862-2120; for off-campus housing, contact Commuter Transfer Center. Phone: (603)862-3612.

Graduate School

Graduate study since 1928. Enrollment: full-time 965, part-time 829. Graduate faculty: 540. Degrees conferred: M.A., M.S., M.A.T., M.S.W., M.S.T., M.A.O.E., M.B.A., M.Ed., M.H.A., M.P.A., C.A.G.S., Ph.D.

ADMISSION REQUIREMENTS. Transcripts, three letters of recommendation required in support of School's application. GRE required by some departments; GMAT required for M.B.A. applicants. TOEFL required for international applicants. Apply to Dean of the Graduate School by July 1 (Fall), December 1 (Spring), April 1 (Summer), by February 15 to ensure financial aid consideration (earlier applications encouraged). Application fee $45. Phone: (603)862-3000; fax: (603)862-3617.

ADMISSION STANDARDS. Selective to competitive. Usual minimum average: 2.75 (A = 4).

FINANCIAL AID. Annual awards from institutional funds: 120 academic scholarships, 57 tuition scholarships, 153 teaching assistantships, Federal W/S, loans. Approved for VA benefits. Apply to Graduate School for scholarships, assistantships; to Financial Aid Office for all other programs. Use FAFSA. Phone: (603)862-3600. Financial aid available for part-time students.

DEGREE REQUIREMENTS. For master's: 30 credits minimum; thesis/nonthesis option in some departments. For C.A.G.S.: 32-40 credits beyond master's. For Ph.D.: three years beyond bachelor's, at least one year in residence; written exam; language required in some programs.

FIELDS OF STUDY.
Adult and Occupational Education. M.A.O.E.
Animal and Nutritional Sciences. M.S., Ph.D.
Biochemistry. M.S., Ph.D.
Biology. M.S.
Business Administration. M.B.A.
Chemical Engineering. M.S.
Chemistry. M.S., M.S.T., Ph.D.
Civil Engineering. M.S.
Communication Disorders. M.S.
Computer Science. M.S.
Earth Sciences. M.S., Ph.D.
Economics. M.A., Ph.D.
Education. Includes counseling, administration/supervision, elementary, secondary, early childhood, reading, reading/writing instruction, special. M.A., M.A.T., C.A.G.S., M.Ed., Ph.D.
Electrical and Computer Engineering. M.S.
Engineering. Ph.D.
English. M.A., M.S.T., Ph.D.
Family and Consumer Studies. M.S.
Genetics. M.S., Ph.D.
History. M.A., Ph.D.
Hydrology. M.S.

Mathematics. M.S., M.S.T. (Summer only), Ph.D.
Mechanical Engineering. M.S.
Microbiology. M.S., Ph.D.
Music. M.A., M.S.
Natural Resources. M.S., Ph.D.
Nursing. M.S., Ph.D.
Occupational Therapy. M.S.
Ocean Engineering. M.S.
Physical Education. M.S.
Physics. M.S., Ph.D.
Plant Biology. M.S., Ph.D.
Political Science. M.A.
Psychology. Ph.D.
Public Administration. M.P.A.
Resource Administration and Management. M.S.
Resource Economics. M.S.
Social Work. M.S.W.
Sociology. M.A., Ph.D.
Spanish. M.A.
Zoology. M.S., Ph.D.

UNIVERSITY OF NEW HAVEN
West Haven, Connecticut 06516-1916
http://www.newhaven.edu

Established 1920. Coed. Trimester system. Private control. Library: 300,000 volumes.

Tuition: per credit $340. Limited on-campus housing available. Contact the Director of Residential Life for on- and off-campus housing information. Phone: (203)932-7176.

Graduate School

Graduate study since 1969. Enrollment: full-time 647, part-time 1787 (men 54%, women 46%). Faculty: full-time 250, part-time 150. Degrees conferred: M.A., M.S., M.B.A., M.P.A., M.S.I.E., Sc.D., M.B.A.-M.S.I.E., M.B.A.-M.P.A.

ADMISSION REQUIREMENTS. Transcripts, letters of recommendation required in support of School's application. GRE required for M.S.-Forensic Science, GMAT for business. TOEFL required of all international applicants. Accepts transfer applicants. Graduates of unaccredited colleges not considered. Apply to Dean by June 15 (Fall), October 1 (Winter), January 15 (Spring). Application fee $50. Phone: (800)DIAL-UNH, ext. 7133, (203)932-7133; fax: (203)932-7137.

ADMISSION STANDARDS. Competitive. Usual minimum average: 2.75 (A = 4).

FINANCIAL AID. Annual awards from institutional funds: thirty-five fellowships, twenty-seven administrative assistantships, eighteen research assistantships, nineteen teaching assistantships, Federal W/S, loans. Approved for VA benefits. Apply by April 15 to Dean for fellowships, assistantships; to Director of Financial Aid for all other programs. Use FAFSA. Phone: (203)932-7315. About 15% of students receive aid other than loans from University and outside sources. Aid sometimes available for part-time students.

DEGREE REQUIREMENTS. For M.A., M.S.: 36–48 credit hours minimum, depending on program; 30 credits in residence; thesis/nonthesis option. For M.P.A.: 42 credit hours minimum, 30 credits in residence; internship; special project. For M.B.A.: 57 credit hours minimum, at least 30 in residence; thesis/nonthesis option. For Sc.D.: 30 credits beyond the master's minimum; dissertation; final oral exam.

FIELDS OF STUDY.
Accounting.
Business Administration.
Cellular and Molecular Biology.
Community Psychology.
Computer and Informational Science.
Criminal Justice.
Electrical Engineering.
Environmental Engineering.
Environmental Science.
Executive M.B.A.
Finance and Financial Services.
Fire Science.
Forensic Science.
Health Care Administration.
Hospitality and Tourism.
Human Nutrition.
Industrial Engineering.
Industrial Hygiene.
Industrial/Organizational Psychology.
Industrial Relations.
Management Systems. Sc.D. only.
Mechanical Engineering.
Occupational Safety and Health Management.
Operations Research.
Public Administration.
Taxation.

COLLEGE OF NEW JERSEY
Hillwood Lakes CN4700
Trenton, New Jersey 08625-4700

Established 1855. Coed. State control. Semester system. Library: 560,000 volumes, 700,000 microforms, 1700 periodicals.

Tuition: per credit, resident $269, nonresident $363. No on-campus housing available. Contact Housing Office for off-campus information. Phone: (609)771-2466. Day care facilities available.

Graduate Division

Enrollment: full-time 129, part-time 530 (men 35%, women 65%). Graduate faculty: full-time 126, part-time 10. Degrees conferred: M.A., M.S., M.Ed., M.A.T., M.S.N., Ed.S.

ADMISSION REQUIREMENTS. Transcripts, GRE or MAT, letters of recommendation required in support of application. TOEFL required for international applicants. Accepts transfer applicants. Graduates of unaccredited institutions are not considered. Apply to the Office of Graduate Admission by June 1 (Fall), November 1 (Spring). Application fee $50. Phone: (609)771-2300; fax: (609)771-3357.

ADMISSION STANDARDS. Selective. Usual minimum average: 2.75 (A = 4).

FINANCIAL AID. Eighty graduate assistantships, loans. Apply by May 1 to Dean of Graduate Study for assistantships, Financial Aid Office for all other programs. Phone: (609)771-2211. Use FAFSA. About 2–5% of students receive aid other than loans from College and outside sources. Aid available for part-time students.

DEGREE REQUIREMENTS. For master's: 30 credits minimum; final written exam. For M.A.T.: 40–56 credits; final written exam. For M.S.N.: 36 credits; final written exam.

FIELDS OF STUDY.
Audiology.
Education. Includes developmental reading, elementary, secondary, counseling and personnel services.
English.
Health Education.
Music. Includes applied, composition, conducting, education.
Nursing.
Physical Education.
Special Education. Includes teaching developmentally handicapped, learning disabilities; Ed.S. only.
Speech. Includes speech correction, pathology.
Speech Pathology.

NEW JERSEY INSTITUTE OF TECHNOLOGY
Newark, New Jersey 07102-1982

Founded 1881. Coed. State control. Semester system. Special facilities: Biomedical Engineering Center for Manufacturing Systems, Hazardous Substance Management Research Center, Center for Transportation Studies and Research. Library: 204,471 volumes, 4700 microforms, 1250 current periodicals, 25 PCs.

Annual tuition: full-time, resident $7824, nonresident $10,824; per credit, resident $324, nonresident $451. Limited on-campus housing available. Average academic year housing cost: $3764–$5364. Contact the Office of Residence Life for both on- and off-campus housing information. Phone: (201)596-3041.

Graduate Studies

Enrollment: full-time 615, part-time 1465. Faculty: full-time 308, part-time 196. Degrees conferred: M.Arch., M.F.S., M.S., Ph.D.

ADMISSION REQUIREMENTS. Two official transcripts, GRE, three letters of recommendation required in support of application. TOEFL required for international applicants. Interview not required. Accepts transfer applicants. Graduates of unaccredited institutions not considered. Apply to Office of University Admissions by June 5 (Fall), November 5 (Spring); Architecture applicants apply by April 1 (fall), October 15 (Spring). Application fee $30. Phone: (201)596-3300; fax: (201)596-3461.

ADMISSION STANDARDS. Selective for most departments. Usual minimum average: master's: GPA of at least 2.5; doctoral: GPA of at least 3.5.

FINANCIAL AID. More than four hundred annual awards from institutional funds: teaching/research assistantships, tuition remission, Federal W/S, loans. Approved for VA benefits. Apply by March 1 to appropriate department chair for assistantships; to Financial Aid Office for all other programs. Use FAFSA. Phone: (201)596-3479. About 50% of full-time students receive aid other than loans from College and outside sources.

DEGREE REQUIREMENTS. For master's: 30 credit hours minimum; thesis/project. For Ph.D.: 60 credit hours minimum beyond the master's degree, at least one year in residence; qualifying exam; thesis/research design; final oral exam.

FIELDS OF STUDY.
Applied Chemistry. M.S.
Applied Math. Ph.D.
Applied Physics. Ph.D.
Architectural Studies. M.S.
Biomedical Engineering. M.S.
Building Science. M.Arch.
Chemical Engineering. M.S., Ph.D.
Chemistry. Ph.D.
Civil Engineering. Ph.D.
Community and Urban Design. M.Arch.
Computer Engineering. M.S.
Computer Science. Ph.D.
Electrical Engineering. Ph.D.
Engineering Science. M.S.
Environmental Policy Studies. Ph.D.
Environmental Science. M.S., Ph.D.
Industrial Engineering. M.S., Ph.D.
Information Systems. Ph.D.
Infrastructure Planning. M.F.S.
Management. M.S.
Management Engineering. M.S.
Management and Organizational Studies.
Manufacturing Systems Engineering. M.S.
Mechanical Engineering. M.S., Ph.D.
Occupational Safety and Health Engineering. M.S.
Professional and Technical Communication. Ph.D.
Transportation. M.S., Ph.D.

NEW MEXICO HIGHLANDS UNIVERSITY
Las Vegas, NM 87701
http://www.nmhu.edu

Founded 1893. Located 60 miles E of Santa Fe. Coed. State control. Semester system. Library: 551,276 volumes.

Annual tuition: full-time resident $1708, nonresident $6682; per credit, resident $69, nonresident $275. On-campus housing for 64 married and 154 single graduate students. Average academic year housing cost: $3420 for married students; $2599 for single students. Apply to Coordinator of Housing. Phone: (505)454-3197.

Graduate Division

Enrollment: full-time, 300; part-time, 528. University faculty teaching graduate students: full-time 93. Degrees conferred: M.A., M.S., M.B.A., M.S.W.

ADMISSION REQUIREMENTS: Transcripts required in support of Divisional application. TOEFL required for international applicants. Interview required for some programs. Accepts transfer applicants. Graduates of unaccredited institutions not considered. Apply to Graduate Division, Office of the Vice President for Academic Affairs at least 60 days prior to registration. Application fees: Social Work, $50; all others $15. Phone: (505)454-3220 (Social Work); (505)454-3266; fax: (505)454-3558, E-mail: portega@merlin.nmhu.edu.

ADMISSION STANDARDS: Selective for some disciplines, relatively open for others. Usual minimum average: 3.0 in major field (A = 4).

FINANCIAL AID: Awards from institutional funds: eleven academic scholarships; seventy-three assistantships, stipends, Federal W/S, loans. Approved for VA benefits. Apply by March 1 to Office of Vice President for assistantships; to Financial Aid Office for all other programs. Use FAFSA. Phone: (505)454-3318; fax: (505)454-3398. About 80% of students receive aid from University and outside sources. Aid sometimes available to part-time students.

DEGREE REQUIREMENTS: For master's: 34 credits minimum; thesis/nonthesis option; case/field study; comprehensive exam.

FIELDS OF STUDY.

SCHOOL OF BEHAVIORAL SCIENCES:
Psychology. M.S.
Public Affairs. Interdisciplinary and interschool. Includes social and organizational processes. M.A.
Southwest Studies. Interdisciplinary and interschool. Includes Anthropology. M.A.

SCHOOL OF BUSINESS:
Business Administration. M.B.A.
Public Affairs. Interdisciplinary and interschool. Includes economic process. M.A.

SCHOOL OF EDUCATION:
Counseling and Guidance. Includes agency counseling, school counseling, professional counseling. M.A.
Curriculum and Instruction. Includes English, math, history, elementary education, bilingual education. M.A.
Educational Administration. M.A.
Human Performance and Sport. Includes business sport administration, school athletic administration, teacher education. M.A.
Special Education. M.A.

SCHOOL OF HUMANITIES:
Public Affairs. Interdisciplinary and interschool. Includes political and governmental processes, historical and cross-cultural perspectives. M.A.
Southwest Studies. Interdisciplinary and interschool. Includes history/political science, Hispanic language and literature. M.A.

SCHOOL OF NATURAL SCIENCES:
Applied Chemistry. M.S.
Life Sciences. Includes biology, environmental science and management. M.S.

SCHOOL OF SOCIAL WORK:
Social Work. Includes mental health, social gerontology, children and family services. M.S.W.

NEW MEXICO INSTITUTE OF MINING AND TECHNOLOGY
Saceur, New Mexico 87801

Founded 1889. Located 75 miles S of Albuquerque. State control. Special facilities: Center for Explosive Technology Research, Geophysical Research Center, Joint Observatory for Cometary Research, Waldo Experimental Mine, Petroleum Recovery Research Center, New Mexico Bureau of Mines and Mineral Resources, Langmuir Laboratory for Atmospheric Physics, Very Large Array radio telescope, Very Large Baseline Array. Cooperative research opportunities with Sandia National Laboratories. Day care facilities available. Library: 137,000 volumes, 130,000 microforms, 10 PCs.

Tuition: per credit, resident $83, nonresident $342. On-campus housing for 36 married students, 10 graduate dorms for men, 10 graduate dorms for women. Average academic year housing cost: $5250 for married students, $4046 (including board) for single students. Apply to Office of Auxiliary Services. Phone: (505)835-5900.

Graduate Studies

Graduate study since 1946. Enrollment; full-time 230, part-time 12 (men 85%, women 15%). Institute faculty: full-time 83, part-time 3. Degrees conferred: M.S., Ph.D.

ADMISSION REQUIREMENTS. Transcripts, GRE, three letters of reference required in support of application. TOEFL re-

quired for international applicants. Interview not required. Accepts transfer applicants. Graduates of unaccredited institutions not considered. Apply to Dean of Graduate Studies by March 15 (Fall). Application fee $16. Phone: (505)835-5513 or (800)428-8324; fax: (505)835-5476.

ADMISSION STANDARDS. Selective for most departments. Usual minimum average: 3.0 (A = 4).

FINANCIAL AID. Annual awards from institutional funds: thirty teaching fellowships, sixty-one research fellowships, 5 HEW fellowships, Federal W/S, loans. Approved for VA benefits. Apply by March 15 to Dean of Graduate Studies for fellowships, assistantships; to Financial Aid Office for all other programs. Use FAFSA. Phone: (505)835-5300. About 70% of students receive aid from Institute and outside source.

DEGREE REQUIREMENTS. For M.S.: 30 credit hours minimum, at least 24 in residence; thesis/nonthesis option; final oral exam; faculty review. For Ph.D.: three years minimum beyond the bachelor's, at least two in residence; reading knowledge of one foreign language; dissertation; preliminary exam/ faculty review; oral defense.

FIELDS OF STUDY.
Chemistry. M.S., Ph.D.
Computer Science. M.S., Ph.D.
Geological Engineer. M.S. only.
Geoscience. Includes geochemistry, geology, geophysics, hydrology; M.S., Ph.D.
Materials Engineer. M.S., Ph.D.
Mathematics. M.S. only.
Petroleum Engineering. M.S., Ph.D.
Physics. M.S., Ph.D.
Science Teaching. M.S. only.

NEW MEXICO STATE UNIVERSITY
Las Cruces, New Mexico 88003-8001
http://www.nmsu.edu

Established 1899. Located 40 miles N of El Paso, Texas. Coed. State control. Semester system. Special facilities: Agricultural Experiment Station, Arts and Sciences Research Center, Astrophysical Research Consortium, Border Research Institute, Center for Business Research and Services, Center for Educational Development, Center for Latin American Studies, Computer Center, Computing Research Laboratory, Consortium for International Development, Cooperative Extension Service, Educational Research Center, Engineering Research Center, Branson Hall Library and New Library, New Mexico Department of Agriculture, New Mexico Regional Primate Research Laboratory, New Mexico Water Resources Research Institute, Physical Science Laboratory, Plant Genetic Engineering Laboratory, Southwest Technology Development Institute, United States Department of Agriculture (Cotton Genetics, Ars-Jornada Experimental Range, Southwest Cotton Ginning Research Laboratory, Economics Research), University Statistics Center, cooperative program with White Sand Missile Range. Library: 1,254,000 volumes, 1,269,000 microforms, 101 PCs.

Annual tuition: full-time, resident $2352, nonresident $7344; per credit resident $99, nonresident $306. On-campus housing for married students, single men and women. Average academic year housing cost: $330 per month for married students, $1650–$3042 for single students (including board). Contact the Director of Housing for on- and off-campus housing information. Phone: (505)646-3203. Day care facilities available.

Graduate School

http://www.nmsu.edu/~gradcolg

Graduate study since 1895. Enrollment: full-time 1491, part-time 1064. University faculty teaching graduate students: full- and part-time 615. Degrees conferred: M.A., M.B.A., M.Acc., M.Ag., M.A.G., M.C.J., M.F.A., M.A.T., M.S., M.M., M.S.N., M.P.H., M.P.A., M.S.W., Ed.S., Ed.D., Ph.D.

ADMISSION REQUIREMENTS. Two transcripts, letters of recommendation required in support of School's application. Interview, GRE/Subject Tests/GMAT/MAT required by some departments. TOEFL required for international applicants. Accepts transfer applicants. Graduates of unaccredited colleges not considered. Apply to Dean of Graduate School by July 1 (Fall), November 1 (Spring), April 1 (Summer). Application fee $15. Phone: (505)646-2733; fax: (505)646-7721.

ADMISSION STANDARDS. Selective for most departments. Usual minimum average: 3.0 (A = 4).

FINANCIAL AID. Annual awards from institutional funds: 4 minority assistantships, 21 minority/women fellowships, 870 teaching/research assistantships, 170 other grants, Federal W/S, loans. Approved for VA benefits. Apply by March 15 to appropriate department chairman for assistantships, fellowships; to Financial Aid Office for all other programs. Use FAFSA. Phone: (505)646-4205; fax: (505)646-7381.

DEGREE REQUIREMENTS. For master's: 30–36 semester hours minimum, at least 24 in residence; reading knowledge of one foreign language for some departments; thesis; final oral/written exam. For Doctorate: three years minimum beyond the bachelor's, at least one year in residence: language requirements and psychometric tools vary by department; preliminary exam; dissertation; final oral/written exam.

FIELDS OF STUDY.
Accountancy.
Agricultural Biology.
Agricultural Extension and Education.
Agriculture.
Agronomy.
Animal Science and Range Science.
Anthropology.
Applied Geography.
Art.
Astronomy.
Biology.
Business Administration.
Chemical Engineering.
Chemistry.
Civil Engineering.
Computer Science.
Counseling and Guidance.
Counseling Psychology.
Counselor Education.
Criminal Justice.
Curriculum and Instruction.
Economics.
Education. Includes elementary, secondary, administration, educational psychology.
Electrical Engineering.
English.
Experimental Statistics.
Government.
History.
Home Economics.
Horticulture.
Industrial Engineering.
Interdisciplinary.

Mathematics.
Mechanical Engineering.
Molecular Biology.
Music.
Physics.
Psychology.
Public Administration.
Reading.
Rhetoric and Professional Communication.
Sociology.
Spanish.
Special Education/Communication Disorders.
Speech.
Wildlife Science.

THE UNIVERSITY OF NEW MEXICO
Albuquerque, New Mexico 87131-2039

Founded 1889. State control. Semester system. Coed. Special facilities: Bureau of Engineering Research, Bureau of Business and Economic Research, Office of Contract Archeology, Maxwell Museum of Anthropology, Museum of Southwestern Biology, New Mexico Engineering Research Center, Technology Application Center; Centers for Advanced Studies, Alcohol and Substance Abuse, Design and Assistance, Economic Development, Communications, Health Sciences, High Performance Computing and Education and Research, High Technology Materials, Microelectronics Research, MicroEngineering Ceramics, Radioactive Waste Management; Institutes for Applied Research Services, Astrophysics, Environmental Education, Meteoritics, Modern Optics, Organizational Communication, Plastics, Public Policy, Social Research, Space and Nuclear Power Studies, Southwest Hispanic Research, Manufacturing Engineering and Development; UNM Business Link, Latin American Institute, Tamarind Institute. Library system: 1.6 million volumes, 5 million microforms, 17,000 periodicals. Off-Campus Graduate Centers: Los Alamos, Santa Fe, and Taos.

Tuition and fees: per semester hour, resident $95; nonresident $325. Housing available for single and married graduate students; 200 apartments for married students. Annual academic year housing cost: $3500. Contact Housing Reservations for both on and off-campus housing information. Phone: (505)277-2606.

Graduate Studies

Graduate study since 1916. Enrollment: full-time 3275, part-time 1896. Faculty: full- and part-time 1483. Degrees conferred: M.A., M.S., M.B.A., M.F.A., M.P.A., M.P.H., M.Mu., M.Arch., M.C.R.P., M.E.M.E., M.W.R.A., E.M.B.A., Ed.D., Ph.D.

ADMISSION REQUIREMENTS. Transcripts required in support of application. GRE/Subject Tests/GMAT recommended or required by some departments. TOEFL required for international students. Interview generally not required. Accepts transfer applications. Graduates of unaccredited institutions not considered. U.S. applicants apply to Graduate Studies by published departmental deadline dates. Application fee $25. Phone: (505)277-2711. International applicants apply to International Admissions, Student Services Center. Phone: (505)277-3136.

ADMISSION STANDARDS. Selective for most departments. Usual minimum average: 3.0 (A = 4).

FINANCIAL AID. Annual awards from institutional funds: 100 scholarships, 300 research fellowships, 708 research assistantships, 800 teaching assistantships, Federal W/S, loans. Apply to the appropriate departmental chair for fellowships, assistantships; to Student Financial Aid Office for all other programs. Application dates vary by department. Use FAFSA. Phone: (505)277-2041. About 33% of students receive aid through loans from School and outside sources.

DEGREE REQUIREMENTS: For master's: thesis/nonthesis options offered by many departments, others designate one of the two plans. PLAN I: minimum of 24 semester hours of course work, thesis; final oral/written exam. PLAN II: minimum of 32 semester hours of course work, no thesis; final oral/written exam. Some programs require demonstration of competence in one or more foreign languages. For Ph.D., Ed.D., M.F.A.: minimum of 48 semester hours of course work beyond the bachelor's degree; at least 18 semester hours exclusive of dissertation credit must be earned in courses numbered 500 or above at UNM (some programs require more course work). Ph.D. requires at least three years of intensive study and research beyond the bachelor's degree.

FIELDS OF STUDY.
American Studies. M.A., Ph.D.
Anthropology. M.A., M.S., Ph.D.
Architecture. M.Arch.
Art. Includes art history. M.A., Ph.D.; studio art M.F.A.
Biology. M.S., Ph.D.
Biomedical Sciences. M.S., Ph.D.
Buddhist Philosophy. M.A.
Business and Administrative Services. Ph.D.
Chemistry. M.S., Ph.D.
Communication. M.A., Ph.D.
Communicative Disorders. M.S.
Community and Regional Planning. M.C.R.P.
Comparative Literature. M.A.
Earth and Planetary Sciences. M.S., Ph.D.
Economics. M.A., Ph.D.
Education. Includes administration and supervision, art, counseling, educational administration, educational linguistics, educational thought and sociocultural studies, elementary, family studies, foundations of education, health, physical education, and recreation, multicultural teacher and childhood, nutrition, psychological foundations, secondary, special, training and learning technologies. M.A., M.S., Ed.D., Ph.D.
Engineering. Includes chemical, civil, computer science, electrical and computer, engineering, manufacturing, mechanical, nuclear.
English. M.A., Ph.D.
French. M.A.
Geography. M.A.
German Studies. M.A.
History. M.A., Ph.D.
Latin American Studies. M.A., Ph.D.
Linguistics. M.A., Ph.D.
Management. M.B.A., E.M.B.A.
Mathematics. M.A., Ph.D.
Music. M.Mu.
Nursing. M.S.
Optical Sciences. Includes physics. Ph.D.
Pharmaceutical Sciences. Includes hospital pharmacy, pharmacy administration, radiopharmacy, toxicology.
Philosophy. M.A., Ph.D.
Philosophy of Literature. M.A.
Philosophy of Science. M.A.
Physics. M.S., Ph.D.
Political Science. M.A., Ph.D.
Portuguese. M.A.
Psychology. M.S., Ph.D.
Public Administration. M.P.A.
Public Health. M.P.H.
Romance Languages. Ph.D.
Sociology. M.A., Ph.D.
Spanish. M.A.
Studio Art. M.F.A.

Theater and Dance. M.A.
Water Resources Administration. M.W.R.A.

School of Law

Founded in 1947. Semester system. Law library: 350,000 volumes. Library has LEXIS, NEXIS, WESTLAW, DIALOG, Q/L. Special facilities: American Indian Law Center, the Institute of Public Law, the Natural Resource Center. Annual tuition: resident $3251, nonresident $10,983. Total average annual additional expense: $8500.

Enrollment: first-year class 107, total full-time 330 (men 45%, women 55%). Faculty: full-time 30, part-time 11. Degree conferred: J.D., J.D.-M.A. (Latin American Studies), J.D.-M.B.A., J.D.-M.P.A.

ADMISSION REQUIREMENTS. LSDAS Law School report, bachelor's degree, two transcripts, LSAT (no later than December), personal statement, letters of recommendation required in support of application. Interview not required. Accepts transfer applicants. Graduates of unaccredited institutions not considered. Preference given to state residents. Apply to School of Law after September 1, before February 1. Admits beginning students Fall only. Application fee $40. Phone: (505)277-0572.

ADMISSION STANDARDS. Selective. Accepts 15–20% of total annual applicants.

FINANCIAL AID. Scholarships; grants for Native Americans; loans. Apply to Financial Aid Office, School of Law, by March 1. Use FAFSA and UNM supplemental application. About 20% of students receive aid other than loans from school.

DEGREE REQUIREMENTS. For J.D.: 86 semester hours program, at least two years in full-time residence.

School of Medicine

Medical study since 1964. Library: 100,000 volumes. Annual tuition: resident $4835, nonresident $13,922. Total average figure for all other expenses: $8200.

Enrollment: first-year class 73 (EDP 20); total 301 (men 46%, women 54%). Faculty: full-time 408, part-time 117. Degrees conferred: M.D., M.D.-Ph.D.

ADMISSION REQUIREMENTS. AMCAS report, transcripts, MCAT required in support of application. Interview by invitation only. Applicants must have completed at least three years of college study. Preference given to New Mexico and WICHE residents. Accepts transfer applicants. Has EDP; apply between June 15 and August 1. Graduates of unaccredited colleges not considered. Apply to Director of Admissions after June 15, before November 15. Application fee $25. Phone: (505)277-4766; fax: (505)277-2755.

ADMISSION STANDARDS. Selective. Accepts 25% of total annual applicants. Approximately 90% are state residents.

FINANCIAL AID. Scholarships, loans (short-term, and no-interest). Apply after acceptance to Office of Student Affairs Graduate Committee. Use FAFSA. About 10% of students receive aid other than loans from School and outside sources.

DEGREE REQUIREMENTS. For M.D.: satisfactory completion of four-year program.

FIELDS OF GRADUATE STUDY.
Anatomy.
Biochemistry.
Cell Biology.
Immunology.

Microbiology.
Neurosciences.
Pathology.
Pharmacology.
Physiology.

UNIVERSITY OF NEW ORLEANS

New Orleans, Louisiana 70148

Opened 1958. Formerly Louisiana State University at New Orleans. Coed. State control. Semester system. Special facilities: Center for Energy Resource Management, Energy and Environmental Materials Research Institute, Environmental Social Science Research Institute, Gulf Coast Region Maritime Technology Center, Center for the Industrial Application of Electric Power and Instrumentation, Small Business Development Center, Urban Waste Management and Research Center, Computer Research Center. Library: 1,000,000 volumes, 12 PCs.

Annual tuition: per semester, resident $1181, nonresident $2577. On-campus housing for 360 graduate men, 252 graduate women; 120 apartments for married students. Annual cost: single student $1500, married $4200. Contact Director, Auxiliary Enterprises for both on- and off-campus housing information. Phone: (504)286-6590.

Graduate School

Enrollment: full-time 960, part-time 2750. University faculty teaching graduate students: full- and part-time 500. Degrees conferred: M.A., M.A.E.T., M.A.S.T., M.S., M.B.A., M.F.A., M.Ed., M.E.D., M.U.R.P., Ph.D., Ed.D.

ADMISSION REQUIREMENTS. Official transcripts required in support of application. GRE Subject Tests required by many departments; GMAT for M.B.A., M.S. in accounting majors. Interview for some departments. TOEFL required for international applicants. Accepts transfer applicants. Graduates of unaccredited institutions not considered. Apply to Dean of Graduate School by July 1 (Fall), November 15 (Spring), May 1 (Summer). Application fee $20. Phone: (504)286-6237.

ADMISSION STANDARDS. Very selective for some departments. Usual minimum average: 2.5 (A = 4).

FINANCIAL AID. Annual awards from institutional funds: 160 teaching assistantships, 80 research assistantships, Federal W/S, loans. Approved for VA benefits. Apply by April 15 to the appropriate department chairman for assistantships; to Financial Aid Office for all other programs. Use FAFSA. Phone: (504)286-6689. About 30% of students receive aid other than loans from University and outside sources. Aid sometimes available for part-time students.

DEGREE REQUIREMENTS. For master's: 30–48 credits, at least 24 in residence; thesis for most majors; reading knowledge of one foreign language in some programs; final written/oral exam. For Ph.D., Ed.D.: 60 credits minimum beyond the bachelor's, normally at least one year in residence; reading knowledge of one or two foreign languages; qualifying exam; general exam; dissertation; final oral exam.

FIELDS OF STUDY.
Accounting. Tax option available; M.S. only.
Art. Includes fine arts, graphic design, photography. M.A., M.F.A.
Arts Administration. M.A.
Biological Sciences. M.S. only.
Biopsychology.
Business Administration. Additional study may be required for students lacking previous preparation in the field. M.B.A. only.

Chemistry.
Drama and Communications. M.A., M.F.A.
Economics. M.A., Ph.D.
Education. Includes elementary, secondary, physical, special, administration and supervision, measurement and evaluation, guidance and counseling. M.E.D., Ed.D., Ph.D.
Engineering. Includes civil and environmental, naval architecture and marine, electrical, mechanical. M.S., Ph.D.
English. M.A. only.
English Teaching. M.A.E.T. only.
Geography. M.A. only.
Geology and Geophysics.
History. M.A. only.
Mathematics. M.S. only.
Music. M.M. only.
Physics. Includes applied. M.S. only.
Political Science. M.A., Ph.D.
Psychology. M.S., Ph.D.
Public Administration. M.P.A. only.
Romance Languages. Options in French and Spanish; M.A. only.
Science Teaching. M.A.S.T only.
Sociology. M.A. only.
Urban and Regional Planning. M.U.R.P.
Urban Studies. M.S. only.

COLLEGE OF NEW ROCHELLE

New Rochelle, New York 10805-2308

Founded 1904. Composed of 4 schools. Located 16 miles NE of New York City. Coed. Private control. Semester system. Special facilities: Education Center: supervised experience for graduate students in Reading/Special Education working with children/persons who are having difficulties in learning. Library: 220,000 volumes, 286,000 microforms, 1500 current periodicals, 16 PCs.

Tuition: per credit $304, $348 for Administration and Supervision, Communication Arts. On-campus housing available for single students only. Average academic year housing cost: $3125 plus $450 declining food balance (5 months), $5650 plus a $900 declining food balance (9 months). Contact Director Residence for both on- and off-campus housing information. Phone: (914)654-5365.

Graduate School

Established 1967. Enrollment: full-time 126, part-time 924. Faculty: full-time 16, part-time 67. Degrees conferred: M.A., M.S. in Ed., M.S.

ADMISSION REQUIREMENTS. Transcripts, three references, interview required in support of School's application. TOEFL required for international applicants. Accepts transfer applicants. Graduates of unaccredited colleges not considered. Apply by August 2 (Fall), December 1 (Spring) to the Office of the Dean. Rolling admissions process. Application fee $35. Phone: (914)654-5334; fax: (914)654-5554.

ADMISSION STANDARDS. Selective. Usual minimum average: 2.7, 3.0 in major field (A = 4).

FINANCIAL AID. Forty scholarships, ten research assistantships, forty staff assistantships, grants, Federal W/S, loans. Apply to the Office of the Dean for assistantships; to the financial Aid Office for all other programs. No specified closing date. Phone: (914)654-5224. Use FAFSA and College's FAF.

DEGREE REQUIREMENTS. For master's: 33–45 credits minimum (depending on program), at least 28–35 in residence.

FIELDS OF STUDY.
Art Education. M.A.
Art Therapy. M.S.
Career Development. M.S.
Communication Arts. M.S.
Community/School Psychology. M.S.
Early Childhood Education. M.S.Ed.
Gerontology. M.S.
Gifted Education. M.S.Ed.
Guidance and Counseling. M.S.
Reading/Adult Communication Skills. M.S.Ed.
Reading/Special Education. M.S.Ed.
School Administration and Supervision. M.S.Ed.
Special Education. M.S.Ed.
Studio Arts. M.
TESL. M.S.Ed.
Therapeutic Education. M.S.Ed.

THE NEW SCHOOL FOR SOCIAL RESEARCH
New York, New York 10011-8603

Founded 1919. Coed. Private control. Semester system. Special facilities: Center for Studies of Social Change, Community Development Research Center, Center for the Study of Politics, Theory, and Policy, Environmental Simulation Center. Library: 4,063,000 volumes, 1,849,000 microforms, 21,000 current periodicals, 36 PCs.

Tuition: full-time per credit $838. Off-campus housing for graduate students. Average academic year housing cost: $5450. Contact Director of Housing for both on- and off-campus housing information. Phone: (212)229-5459.

Graduate Faculty of Political and Social Science

Enrollment: full-time 410, part-time 878. Graduate faculty: full-time 74, part-time 55. Degrees conferred: M.A., Ph.D., D.S.Sc.

ADMISSION REQUIREMENTS. Transcripts, letters of reference, GRE required in support of application. TOEFL required for international applicants. Interview not required. Accepts transfer applicants. Graduates of unaccredited institutions not considered. Apply to Director of Admissions by August 1 (Fall), December 1 (Spring), May 1 (Summer). Rolling admissions process. Application fee $30. Phone: (212)229-5710; fax: (212)229-7102.

ADMISSION STANDARDS. Selective for most departments. Usual minimum average: 3.0 (A = 4).

FINANCIAL AID. One hundred fifty scholarships, 55 teaching/research assistantships, Federal W/S, loans. Approved for VA benefits. Apply by February 1 to the department chair for scholarships and assistantships; to the Office of Financial Aid for all other aid. Phone: (212)741-5714. Use FAFSA. About 30% of students receive aid other than loans from School, 50% from all sources. Loans available for part-time study.

DEGREE REQUIREMENTS. For M.A.: 30–36 credits, thesis/nonthesis option; other requirements vary by department. For Ph.D.: 60 credits minimum beyond the bachelor's, at least 30 credits in full-time residence; written qualifying exam; oral comprehensive exam; reading knowledge of one foreign language, computer/statistics substitute possible; dissertation; final oral defense. For D.S.Sc.: 92 credits minimum beyond the bachelor's; other requirements essentially the same as for Ph.D.

FIELDS OF STUDY.
Anthropology.
Clinical Psychology.
Criticism.
Economics.
Gender Studies.
General Psychology.
Historical Studies.
Liberal Studies.
Philosophy.
Political Economy.
Political Science.
Psychology.
Sociology.

Robert J. Milano Graduate School of Management and Urban Policy

Graduate study since 1975. Semester system. Annual tuition: full-time $11,550; per credits $550. Enrollment: full-time 106, part-time 880. Graduate faculty: full-time 24, part-time 79. Degrees conferred: M.S., Adv.C.

ADMISSION REQUIREMENTS. Transcripts, letters of reference required in support of School's application. GMAT considered if available. TOEFL required for international applicants. Accepts transfer students. Graduates of unaccredited institutions not considered. Apply to Admission Office by August 1 (Fall), December 1 (Spring), May 1 (Summer). Application fee $30. Phone: (212)229-5462; fax: (212)229-8935.

ADMISSION STANDARDS. Selective for most departments. Usual minimum average: 3.0 (A = 4).

FINANCIAL AID. One hundred twenty-eight academic scholarships, ninety-seven grants, sixteen fellowships, seven research assistantships, five administrative assistantships, five teaching assistantships, Federal W/S, loans. Approved for VA benefits. Apply by March 1 to department chair for scholarships, fellowships, assistantships; to the Office of Financial Aid for all other programs. Use FAFSA and CSS/FA Profile. Phone: (212)229-5462; fax: (212)229-8935.

DEGREE REQUIREMENTS. For M.S.: 42 credits minimum; internship (strongly encouraged); thesis/nonthesis option. For Adv.C.: 18 credits minimum beyond master's.

FIELDS OF STUDY.
Health Services Management and Policy.
Human Resources Management.
Nonprofit Management.
Urban Policy Analysis and Management.

Parsons School of Design
http://www.parson@newschool.edu

Annual tuition: $17,530; per credits $622. Enrollment: full-time 82; part-time 41. Faculty: full-time 0, part-time 30. Degrees conferred: M.A., M.Arch., M.F.A.

ADMISSION REQUIREMENTS. Transcripts, three letters of recommendation, resume, statement of intent, portfolio of 15–20 pieces of work required in support of School's application. Interview sometimes required. TOEFL required for international applicants. Apply to Admissions Committee by March 1. Application fee $30. Phone: (800)252-0852 or (212)229-8910.

ADMISSION STANDARDS. Selective. Admission based on portfolio review.

FINANCIAL AID. Annual awards from institutional funds: scholarships, assistantships, Federal W/S, loans. Apply to Financial Aid Office; no specified closing date. Use FAFSA, institutional FAF and CSS profile. Phone: (212)229-8930; fax: (212)229-8975. About 20% of students receive aid other than loans from School and outside sources.

DEGREE REQUIREMENTS. For M.A.: 32 credits minimum, at least 24 in residence; thesis option. For M.Arch.: 30-36 credits minimum, at least 24 in residence; master's project. For M.F.A.: 48 credits minimum, at least 40 in residence; departmental requirements determined by portfolio review; final essay; applied project, gallery exhibition.

FIELDS OF STUDY.
Architecture.
History of Decorative Arts.
Lighting Design.
Painting.
Sculpture.

THE CITY UNIVERSITY OF NEW YORK
The Graduate School and University Center
New York, New York 10036-8099

Established 1962. Public control. Semester system. Special facilities: Center for Advanced Study in Education, Center for Jewish Studies, Center for Research in Cognition and Affect, Center for Research in Speech and Hearing Sciences, Center for Social Research, Center for Urban and Policy Studies, Center for the Study of Women and Sex Roles. Library: 204,000 volumes, 409,000 microforms.

Tuition: per credit, state residents $245 (maximum $4350), nonresidents $425 (maximum $7600). No on-campus housing available.

Graduate Studies

Enrollment: full-time 3586, part-time 478 (men 1911, women 2153). Faculty: full-time 100, part-time 1600. Degrees conferred: M.A., M.Phil., D.M.A., D.S.W., Ph.D.

ADMISSION REQUIREMENTS. Official transcripts, GRE, GMAT (Business Ph.D. program only), two faculty recommendations required in support of application. TOEFL required for international applicants. Accepts transfer applicants. Apply to Admissions Office by March 1 for most programs (Fall), November 15 (Spring). Application fee $40. Phone: (212)642-2812.

ADMISSION STANDARDS. Selective. Usual minimum average: 3.0 (A = 4).

FINANCIAL AID. Fellowships (service and nonservice), grants, assistantships, traineeships, Federal W/S, loans. Apply to the Office of Financial Aid by February 1. Use CUNY Student Aid form. Phone: (212)642-2811.

DEGREE REQUIREMENTS. For M.A., M.Phil.: 30 credits minimum, at least 24 in residence; final comprehensive exam; thesis. For D.S.W.: 30 credits minimum beyond the master's, at least two terms in residence; preliminary exam; dissertation; final oral/written exam. For D.M.A., Ph.D.: 60 credits minimum, at least 30 in residence and two consecutive semesters in full-time residence; preliminary exam; candidacy exam; dissertation; final defense of dissertation.

FIELDS OF STUDY.
Anthropology. Admits Fall only. Apply by January 15.
Art History.
Biochemistry.

Biology.
Biomedical Sciences. At Mount Sinai Graduate School of Biological Sciences.
Business. Admits Fall only.
Chemistry.
Classics.
Comparative Literature.
Computer Science.
Criminal Justice. Admits Fall only. Apply by March 15.
Earth and Environmental Sciences.
Economics.
Education.
Educational Psychology. Admits Fall only. Apply by February 15 for school psychology.
Engineering.
English. Admits Fall only. Apply by April 1.
French.
Germanic Languages and Literature.
Hispanic and Luso-Brazilian Literature.
History.
Liberal Studies.
Linguistics Admits Fall only.
Mathematics.
Music. Admits Fall only. Apply by January 15.
Philosophy.
Physics.
Political Science.
Psychology. Admits Fall only. Apply by March 1, January 1 for clinical and neuropsychology, February 1 for social-personality, March 15 for learning processes.
Social Welfare. Admits Fall only. D.S.W. only.
Sociology.
Speech and Hearing Sciences.
Theater.

Mount Sinai School of Medicine (10029-6574)

First class entered Fall 1968. Private control. Affiliated with City University of New York. Semester system.

Annual tuition: $21,000. Total average cost for all other expenses: $9800. Enrollment: first-year class 115 (EDP 5); total 490 (men 52%, women 48%). School faculty: full-time 1000, part-time 250. On-campus housing for 50 married students, 100 single students. Total average cost for all other expenses: $10,800. Apply to Office for Student Affairs. Degrees conferred: M.D., M.D.-Ph.D. (Medical Scientist Training Program).

ADMISSION REQUIREMENTS. AMCAS report, transcripts, MCAT, references, interview required in support of application. Has EDP; apply between June 15 and August 1. Accepts transfer applicants. Applicants must have completed at least three years of college study. Apply to Office for Admissions after June 15, before November 1. Application fee $75. Phone: (212)241-6696; fax: (212)369-6013.

ADMISSION STANDARDS. Very competitive. Accepts about 5% of total applicants. Approximately 65% are state residents.

FINANCIAL AID. Scholarships, loans. Apply to Financial Aid Officer after acceptance. MSTP funded by NIH. About 70% of students receive aid other than loans from School; over 75% receive some form of financial assistance.

DEGREE REQUIREMENTS. For M.D.: satisfactory completion of four-year program.

FIELDS OF GRADUATE STUDY.
Anatomy.
Biochemistry.
Biophysics.
Cell Biology.

Genetics.
Immunology.
Microbiology.
Molecular Biology.
Neuroscience.
Pathology.
Pharmacology.
Physiology.

NEW YORK INSTITUTE OF TECHNOLOGY
Old Westbury, New York 11568-8000

Main campus located 35 miles E of New York City; other branches are located in NYC and Islip, Long Island, New York. Coed. Private control. Semester system. Special facilities: Center for Labor and Industrial Relations, Management Information Systems Center, Science and Technology Research Center, Video Center. Library: 110,000 volumes, 441,000 microforms, 2000 current periodicals.

Tuition: per credit $370. On-campus housing available. Average academic year housing cost: $5500 (including board) for single students; $2904 for married students. Off-campus housing cost: $600 per month. Contact Office of Residential Life for both on- and off-campus housing information. Phone: (516)348-3340.

Graduate Division

Enrollment: full-time 772, part-time 1355. University faculty teaching graduate students: full-time 90, part-time 145. Degrees conferred: M.A., M.B.A., M.P.S., M.S.

ADMISSION REQUIREMENTS. Transcripts, GMAT (Business) required in support of application. GRE required by some programs. TOEFL required for international applicants. Interview not required. Accepts transfer applicants. Graduates of unaccredited institutions not considered. Apply to Graduate Admissions Office at least one month prior to registration. Rolling admission process. Application fee $50. Phone: (516)686-7519; fax: (516)626-0419.

ADMISSION STANDARDS. Selective. Usual minimum average: 2.85 (A = 4).

FINANCIAL AID. Scholarships, assistantships, grants, Federal W/S, loans. Apply to appropriate dean for assistantships; to Financial Aid Office for all other programs. No specified closing date. Use FAFSA. Aid available for part-time students.

DEGREE REQUIREMENTS. For master's: 33–45 credit hours minimum; at least 30 credit hours in residence; thesis/nonthesis option; final oral exam for some programs.

FIELDS OF STUDY.
Business Administration. Includes accounting, finance, general management, international business, management of information systems, marketing, personnel and industrial relations. M.B.A.
Clinical Nutrition. M.S.
Communication Arts. M.A.
Computer Science. M.S.
Electrical Engineering. M.S.
Elementary Education. M.S.
Energy Management. M.S.
Environmental Technology. M.S.
Human Relations. M.P.S.
Human Resources Management. M.S.

Instructional Technology. M.S.
Labor Relations. M.S.

New York College of Osteopathic Medicine

25 miles E of New York City. Coed. Private control. Library: 60,000 volumes, has MEDLINE, BIOETHIC, HEALTH, TOXLINE, DIALOG, OCLC.

Annual tuition: $20,000. No on-campus housing available. Enrollment: first-year class 80, total 325 (men 65%, women 35%). Faculty: full-time, 40. Degree conferred: D.O.

ADMISSION REQUIREMENTS. AACOMAS report, bachelor's degree, official transcripts, MCAT (no later than September), three letters of recommendation, one from premed advisory committee, evaluation from a physician (preferably a D.O.), supplemental form required in support of application. Interview by invitation only. Graduates of unaccredited college not considered. Apply by February 1 to the Director of Admissions. Admits first-year students Fall only. Application fee: $60. Phone: (516)626-6947.

ADMISSION STANDARDS. Selective. Accepts approximately 15% of annual applicants. Usual minimum average: 2.75 (A = 4). Mean GPA: 3.2.

FINANCIAL AID. Scholarships, fellowships, tuition waivers, loans. Apply by April 1 to the Financial Aid Office. Use GAPSFAS.

DEGREE REQUIREMENT. For D.O.: satisfactory completion of four-year program.

NEW YORK LAW SCHOOL
57 Worth Street
New York, New York 10013-2960

Established 1891. Private control. Semester system. Library: 330,000 volumes, 17,000 microfilms. Library: LEXIS, NEXIS, WESTLAW, OCLC, RLIN.

Annual tuition: full-time, $20,541 (day); part-time, $15,041 (evening). On-campus housing for 480 single students. Annual housing cost: $8400. Contact Director of Residential Life. Phone: (212)431-8166.

Enrollment: first-year class, full-time 340, part-time 133; total 1390 (men 59%, women 41%). School faculty: full-time 52, part-time 99. Degrees conferred: J.D., J.D.-M.B.A., J.D.-M.P.A. (with Baruch College of CUNY).

ADMISSION REQUIREMENTS. LSDAS Law School report, bachelor's degree, transcripts, LSAT required in support of application. Applicants must have completed four years of college. Accepts transfer applicants. Graduates of unaccredited institutions not considered. Apply to Admissions Office after September 1. No specified closing date. Admits full-time students in Fall and Spring. Application fee $50. Phone: (212)431-2888.

ADMISSION STANDARDS. Selective. Accepts approximately 10–15% of total annual applicants.

FINANCIAL AID. Scholarships, grants, Federal W/S, loans. Apply to Office of Financial Aid, preferably by July 1. Use FAFSA. About 35% of students receive aid other than loans from School.

DEGREE REQUIREMENTS. For J.D.: satisfactory completion of three-year day program or four-year evening program; 86 credit hour program. For M.B.A., M.P.A.: see appropriate Graduate School listing in Baruch College, CUNY.

NEW YORK MEDICAL COLLEGE

Valhalla, New York 10595

Established 1860. Coed. Private control. Semester system. Library: 148,000 volumes, 851 microforms, 1200 current periodicals, 20 PCs.

Annual tuition: graduate program, per credit $360. On-campus housing available. Average academic year housing cost: $6000 for married students, $4600 for single students; off-campus cost: $450 per month. Contact Housing Office for both on- and off-campus housing information. Phone: (914)993-4532.

Graduate School of Basic Medical Sciences

Tuition: per credit $340. Enrollment: full-time 115, part-time 70. Faculty: full- and part-time 83. Degrees conferred: M.S., Ph.D.

ADMISSION REQUIREMENTS. Official transcripts, GRE, three letters of recommendation required in support of School's application. GRE Subject required for some programs. TOEFL, or evidence of proficiency in English required of international applicants. Accepts transfer applicants. Apply to Dean of the School by April 1. Application $35, $60 for international applicants. Phone: (914)993-4110.

ADMISSION STANDARDS. Competitive. Usual minimum average: 3.3 (A = 4).

FINANCIAL AID. Scholarships, fellowships, assistantships, loans. Apply to Dean of the School; no specified closing date. Phone: (914)993-4521. Use FAFSA.

DEGREE REQUIREMENTS. For M.S.: 30–36 credits minimum, at least 24–30 credits in residence; qualifying exam; thesis. For Ph.D.: 60 credits minimum beyond the bachelor's; at least two years in full-time residence; reading knowledge of one foreign language or research tool; qualifying exam; dissertation; final oral exam.

FIELDS OF STUDY.
Anatomy.
Biochemistry.
Cell Biology.
Experimental Pathology.
Immunology.
Microbiology.
Molecular Biology.
Neuroscience.
Pathology.
Pharmacology.
Physiology.

Graduate School of Health Sciences

Enrollment: full-time 28, part-time 348. Faculty: full-time 10, part-time 50. Degrees conferred: M.S., M.P.H.

ADMISSION REQUIREMENTS. Official transcripts, GRE, two letters of recommendation required in support of School's application. TOEFL or evidence of proficiency in English required for international students. Accepts transfer applicants. Graduates of unaccredited institutions not considered. Apply by July 15 (Fall), December 1 (Spring) to Associate Dean of School. Rolling admissions process. Application fee $35, $60 for international applicants. Phone: (914)993-4531.

ADMISSION STANDARDS. Competitive for some departments, selective for all others. Usual minimum average: 3.0 (A = 4).

FINANCIAL AID. Six traineeships; fifty assistantships; loans. Apply by June 15 to Dean for assistantships; to Financial Aid Office for all other programs. Use FAFSA. Phone: (914)993-4491.

DEGREE REQUIREMENTS. For M.S., M.P.H.: 1½ years minimum, at least 24–30 credits in residence; thesis and defense/research report/qualifying exam.

FIELDS OF STUDY.
Behavioral Sciences and Health Promotion. M.P.H.
Biostatistics. M.P.H.
Developmental Disabilities. M.P.H.
Emergency Medical Services. M.S., M.P.H.
Environmental and Occupational Health Services. M.S., M.P.H.
Epidemiology. M.S.
Exercise Physiology. M.S.
General Public Health. M.P.H.
Gerontology. M.P.H.
Health Policy and Management. M.S., M.P.H.
International Health. M.S., M.P.H.
Maternal and Child Health. M.P.H.
Nutrition. M.S., M.P.H.
Physical Therapy. M.S.

Medical College

Established 1860. Located in Valhalla (10595).

Annual tuition: $26,000; student fees $415. Total cost of all other expenses: $12,389. Enrollment: first-year class 186 (EDP 10); total 781 (men 65%, women 35%). Faculty: full-time 1000, part-time and volunteers 1800. Degrees conferred: M.D., M.D.-Ph.D.

ADMISSION REQUIREMENTS. AMCAS report, transcripts, MCAT, screening interview, recommendations required in support of application. Applicants must possess bachelor's degree. Has EDP; apply between June 15 and August 1. Apply to Admissions Office after June 15, before December 1. Application fee $60. Phone: (914)993-4507.

ADMISSION STANDARDS. Very competitive. Accepts 3% of total annual applicants. Approximately 23% are state residents.

FINANCIAL AID. Scholarships, loans. Apply to Director of Financial Aid; no specified closing date. Use FAFSA. About 85% of students receive some aid from College.

DEGREE REQUIREMENTS. For M.D.: satisfactory completion of four-year program.

STATE UNIVERSITY OF NEW YORK AT BINGHAMTON

Binghamton, New York 13902-6000

Founded 1950. Coed. State control. Special facilities: Center for Cognitive and Psycholinguistic Sciences, Center for Developmental Psychobiology, Center for Global Cultural Studies, Integrated Electronic Engineering Center, Center for Leadership Studies, Center for Medieval and Early Renaissance Studies, Center for Research in Translation, Center for Women's Studies, Institute for Research on Multicultural and International Labor. Library: 1,600,977 volumes, 1,460,000 microforms, 9,729 periodical subscriptions.

Annual tuition: residents $5100, nonresidents $8416; per credit, residents $213, nonresidents $351. On-campus housing available in a new graduate apartment complex consisting of three- and four-person apartments each with living room, dining area, kitchen, and bathroom. Annual academic year housing cost:

$3710 for a single, $5990 for family apartment. Apply to Coordinator, Graduate Community. Phone: (607)777-2904. Day care facilities available.

Graduate School

Graduate study since 1961. Enrollment: full-time 1300, part-time 1300. University faculty teaching graduate students: full-time 467, part-time 196. Degrees conferred: M.A., M.S., M.A.T., M.M., M.S.Ed., M.S.T., M.B.A., M.P.A., Certificate, Ed.D., Ph.D.

ADMISSION REQUIREMENTS. Transcripts, two letters of recommendation required in support of School's application. GRE GMAT required for School of Management. GRE Subject required by some departments. Interview is not required. TOEFL required for international applicants. Accepts transfer applicants. Graduates of unaccredited institutions not considered. Apply to Graduate School Admissions Office at least one month prior to registration. Application fee $50. Phone: (607)777-2151.

ADMISSION STANDARDS. Competitive. Usual minimum average: 3.0 (A = 4).

FINANCIAL AID. Annual awards from institutional funds: 800 tuition scholarships, 250 teaching assistantships, 80 research assistantships, 100 fellowships, 10 internships, Federal W/S, loans. Approved for VA benefits. Apply by February 15 to appropriate Academic Program Directors for assistantships, fellowships, internships; to Director of Student Financial Aid for all other programs. Phone: (607)777-2428. Use FAFSA. About 64% of students receive aid other than loans from University and outside sources.

DEGREE REQUIREMENTS. For master's: 30 credit hours minimum, at least 24 in residence; thesis and nonthesis options; final oral/written exam; most departments require reading knowledge of one foreign language. For Ph.D.: 60 credit hours, at least 24 in full-time residence; knowledge of at least one foreign language; dissertation; final written/oral exam.

FIELDS OF STUDY.
Accounting.
Advanced Technology. Includes computer science, electrical engineering, mechanical engineering, industrial engineering, systems science, computer science. M.S., Ph.D.
Applied Science. M.S.
Art History. M.A., Ph.D.
Biological Sciences. M.A., M.A.T., M.S.T., M.S.Ed., Ph.D.
Chemistry. M.A., M.S., Ph.D.
Comparative Literature. M.A., Ph.D.
Computer Science. M.S., Ph.D.
Creative Writing. Certificate, M.A.
Economics. M.A., Ph.D.
Education. Includes early childhood elementary, reading, secondary, special. M.S.Ed.
Educational Theory and Practice. Ed.D.
Electrical Engineering. M.S., Ph.D.
English. M.A., M.A.T., M.S.T., M.S.Ed., Ph.D.
Environmental Policy and Resource Management.
Family Nurse Practitioner. Certificate only.
Geography. M.A.
Geological Sciences. Includes earth science. M.A., M.A.T., M.S.T., M.S.Ed., Ph.D.
Geophysics.
History. M.A., Ph.D.
Industrial Engineering. M.S.
Interdepartmental Publishing. Certificate only.
Latin American and Caribbean Area Studies. Certificate only.
Management. M.B.A., M.S., Ph.D.
Mechanical Engineering. M.S., Ph.D.

Medieval and Early Renaissance Studies. Certificate only.
Modern Drama and Theater. Certificate only.
Music. M.A., M.M.
Nursing. M.S. Includes family nurse practitioner, Certificate; gerontological nurse practitioner, Certificate; community health/primary care nurse practitioner, Certificate.
Philosophy. M.A., Ph.D.
Physics. M.A., M.A.T., M.S., M.S.T., M.S.Ed.
Political Science. M.A., M.P.A., Ph.D.
Professional Accounting. M.S.
Psychology. Includes general experimental psychology, clinical psychology, and psychobiology. M.A., Ph.D.
Reading and Language Arts. Certificate of Advanced Study.
Romance Languages and Literatures. Includes French (M.A., M.A.T., M.S.T.), Italian (M.A.), Spanish (M.A., M.A.T., M.S.T.).
Social Sciences. M.A., M.A.T., M.S.T., M.S.Ed.
Sociology. M.A., Ph.D.
Southwest Asian (Middle East) and North African (Maghreb) Studies. Certificate only.
Systems Science. M.S., Ph.D.
Theater. M.A., M.F.A.
Women's History.

OTHER PROGRAMS:
M.B.A. Management with M.A. History. M.B.A.-M.A.
M.B.A. with Specialization in Arts Administration. M.B.A.

STATE UNIVERSITY OF NEW YORK AT BUFFALO
Buffalo, New York 14260-1608

Founded 1846. Coed. State control. Semester system. Special facilities: Center for Studies in American Culture, Center for Assistive Technology, Center for Comparative and Global Studies in Education, Center for Critical Languages, Center for Curriculum Planning, Superconductivity, National Center for Earthquake Engineering Research, Center for Electronic and Electropoptic Materials, Center for Applied Molecular Biology and Immunology, Center for Research in Special Environments, New York Center for Hazardous Waste Management, Center for Studying of Aging, Baldy Center for Law and Social Policy, Center for Behavioral and Social Aspects of Health, Center for Cognitive Sciences, Center for the Study of Psychoanalysis and Culture, Center for Research in Special Environments, Center for Hearing and Deafness, Research Center for Law and Jurisprudence, Research Institution on Addiction, Toxicology Research Center. Library: 2,500,000 volumes, 3,600,000 microforms, 20,000 current periodicals.

Annual tuition: full-time, resident $5100, nonresident $8416. Unlimited on-campus housing available for single graduate students. Average academic year housing cost: $4622–$5872 (including board). Contact Director of Residence Life for both on- and off-campus housing information. Phone: (716)645-2171.

Graduate School

Graduate study since 1923. Enrollment: full-time 4805, part-time 3349. Graduate faculty: full- and part-time 2146. Degrees conferred: M.A., M.B.A., M.S., M.Arch., M.U.P., M.M., M.F.A., M.E., Ed.M., Ed.D., Ph.D., M.D., D.D.S., Pharm.D., D.N.S.

ADMISSION REQUIREMENTS. Transcripts required in support of application. GRE/MAT, letters of recommendation required by some departments. Interview not required. TOEFL required for foreign applicants. Accepts transfer applicants. Graduates of unaccredited institutions not considered. Contact individual program regarding deadlines for admission. Application fee $50. Phone: (716)645-6142; or (716)645-2000, ask for individual department chair.

ADMISSION STANDARDS. Relatively open to very competitive. Usual minimum average varies by department.

FINANCIAL AID. Annual awards from institutional funds: 200 fellowships, 824 teaching assistantships, 349 graduate assistantships, 512 research assistantships. Approved for VA benefits. Apply to the appropriate department chair for fellowships, assistantships; to the Financial Aid Office for all other programs. Use FAFSA. Phone: (716)645-3724. About 55% of full-time students receive aid other than loans from School and outside sources. Aid available to part-time students.

DEGREE REQUIREMENTS. For most master's: 30 semester hours minimum, at least 24 in residence; comprehensive exam; thesis/nonthesis option/special project; oral exam requirements vary by departments. For Ph.D.: three years minimum, at least one year in full-time residence; preliminary exam; dissertation; final oral exam. Contact individual programs for other requirements.

FIELDS OF STUDY.
American Studies. M.A., Ph.D.
Anthropology. M.A., Ph.D.
Architecture. M.Arch.
Art. M.F.A. only.
Art History. M.A. only.
Biological Sciences. M.A., Ph.D.
Biomaterials. M.S.
Biometry. M.S. only.
Chemistry. M.A., Ph.D.
Classics. M.A., Ph.D.
Communication. M.A., Ph.D.
Communicative Disorders and Sciences. M.A., Ph.D.
Comparative Literature. M.A., Ph.D.
Computer Science. M.S., Ph.D.
Economics. M.A., Ph.D.
Engineering. Includes aerospace, chemical, civil, electrical, environmental science (M.S.), industrial, mechanical. M.E., M.S., Ph.D.
English. M.A., Ph.D.
Exercise Science. M.S., Ed.D.
Fine Art/Art. M.F.A.
Geography. M.A., Ph.D.
Geology. M.A., Ph.D.
Health Education. Ed.M., Ed.D.
Health Science Education and Evaluation. M.S. only.
History. M.A., Ph.D.
Humanities. Interdisciplinary. M.A. only.
Linguistics. M.A., Ph.D.
Mathematics. M.A., Ph.D.
Medical Technology. M.S. only.
Modern Languages and Literature. Includes French, Spanish, German. M.A., Ph.D.
Music. Includes music history, music composition. M.A., Ph.D.
Music Education. M.A., M.M.
Music Performance. M.M.
Natural Sciences. M.S. only.
Nursing. Includes child health care, maternity and women's health, education, rehabilitation, administration. M.S., D.N.S.
Nutrition. M.S. only.
Occupational Therapy. Includes hand rehabilitation. M.S.only.
Philosophy. M.A., Ph.D.
Physics. M.A., Ph.D.
Planning and Design. M.U.P.
Policy Studies. Ph.D. only.
Political Science. M.A., Ph.D.
Psychology. M.A., Ph.D.
Social Sciences. M.A., Ph.D.

Sociology. Includes medical sociology. M.A., Ph.D.
Urban Planning. M.U.P. only.

Graduate School of Education

Graduate study since 1931. Tuition: per credit, resident $213, nonresident $351. Graduate housing available. Apply to Office of Housing Services, 106 Spaulding Quad, Ellicott Housing. Phone: (716)645-2171. For off-campus housing, apply to Off-Campus Housing, 100 Allen. Phone: (716)829-2224.

Enrollment: full- and part-time 1200. Faculty: full-time 55, part-time 14. Degrees conferred: Ed.M., Ed.D. The M.A., M.S., and Ph.D. are offered through the Graduate School.

ADMISSION REQUIREMENTS. Transcripts, GRE/MAT, letters of reference required in support of all doctoral applications. Consult departments for additional requirements. TOEFL required for international applicants. Accepts transfer applicants. Graduates of unaccredited institutions not considered. Deadlines vary with the department. Application fee $50. Phone: (716)636-2491.

ADMISSION STANDARDS. Competitive. Usual minimum average: 3.0 (A = 4).

FINANCIAL AID. Limited to ten teaching assistantships, fifty-seven graduate assistantships, Federal W/S, loans. Approved for VA benefits. Apply to Director of Financial Aid; no specified closing date. Use FAFSA and TAP. Phone: (716)829-3724.

DEGREE REQUIREMENTS. For master's: 32 semester hours minimum; comprehensive exam. For Certificate: 30 credits beyond the master's. For Ed.D., Ph.D.: 72 semester hours minimum, at least two semesters in continuous full-time residence; preliminary exams; dissertation; final oral exam.

FIELDS OF STUDY.
Counseling and Educational Psychology. Includes counseling psychology, counselor education, educational psychology, rehabilitation counseling, school counseling, school psychology. Phone: (716)645-2484.
Educational Organization, Administration, and Policy. Includes educational administration, social foundations of education, specialist in educational administration (leading to permanent certification as school district administrator). Phone: (716)645-2471.
Learning and Instruction. Includes bilingual education, elementary education, English education, foreign and second language education, mathematics education, reading education, science education, social studies education, school administration and supervision, special education, teaching English to speakers of other languages. Phone: (716)645-2455.

School of Information and Library Studies

Annual tuition: resident $5100, nonresident $8416. Enrollment: full-time 115, part-time 142. Faculty: full-time 11, part-time 6. Degree conferred: M.L.S.

ADMISSION REQUIREMENTS. Transcripts, bachelor's degree required in support of School's application. TOEFL required for international applicants. Accepts transfer applicants. Graduates of unaccredited institutions not considered. Apply to School by September 15 (Spring), February 1 (Summer), April 1 (Fall). Application fee $35. Phone: (716)645-2412; fax: (716)645-3775.

ADMISSION STANDARDS. Selective. Usual minimum average: 3.0 (A = 4).

FINANCIAL AID. Annual awards from institutional funds: three to six scholarships, four to five fellowships, eight internships,

Federal W/S, loans. Apply to Director of Financial Aid; no specified closing date. Use FAFSA. Phone: (716)645-2412.

DEGREE REQUIREMENTS. For M.L.S.: 36 credit hours minimum, at least 30 credits in residence.

FIELDS OF STUDY.
Information Science.
Library Studies.

School of Management
http://wings.buffalo.edu

Established 1927. Tuition: per credit, resident $213, nonresident $351. Enrollment: full-time M.B.A. 320, Ph.D. 65, part-time M.B.A. 350. Faculty: full-time 65, part-time 2. Degrees conferred: M.B.A., Ph.D.

ADMISSION REQUIREMENTS. Transcripts, GMAT required in support of School's application. TOEFL required for international applicants. Does not consider transfer applicants. Apply to Office of Academic Programs Administration in the School. Application fee $50. Phone: (716)645-3204; fax: (716)645-2341.

ADMISSION STANDARDS. Selective. Usual minimum average: 3.2 (A = 4); GMAT 575 (M.B.A.), 645 (Ph.D.).

FINANCIAL AID. Seventy-five administrative assistantships, Federal W/S, loans. Approved for VA benefits. Apply as early as possible to the Dean's Office for assistantships; to Financial Aid Office for all other programs. Use FAFSA. Phone: (716)829-3724; fax: (716)829-2022. About 41% of full-time students receive some form of financial aid.

DEGREE REQUIREMENTS. For M.B.A.: 60-hour program, 30 hours in residence. For Ph.D.: formal requirements are primarily qualitative; second-year research paper; dissertation; final oral exam.

FIELDS OF STUDY.
Business Administration. Includes corporate financial management, financial institutions and markets, health care systems management, human resources management, international management, management information systems, management science, manufacturing and operations management, marketing management, management skills, professional accounting; M.B.A. program (full-time).
Business Management. Includes accounting, finance, industrial relations/human resources, management science, management systems, managerial economics and policy, marketing, organization; Ph.D. program.

Roswell Park Cancer Institute (14263)

Annual tuition: resident $5100, nonresident $8416.
Enrollment: full-time 340, part-time 90. Faculty: full-time 250. Degrees offered through the graduate school: M.A., M.S., Ph.D.

ADMISSION REQUIREMENTS. Transcripts. GRE, recommendations required in support of application. TOEFL required for foreign applicants. Apply by February 1. Application fee $35. Phone: (716)845-2339; fax: (716)845-8178.

ADMISSION STANDARDS. Usual minimum average: 3.0 (A = 4). TOEFL 600 minimum.

FINANCIAL AID. Annual awards from insititutional funds: 150 tuition scholarships, 20 research fellowships, 130 research assistantships, Federal W/S, loans. Apply after acceptance to appropriate department. Use FAFSA. Phone: (716)831-3724. About 66% of students receive aid other than loans from Institute and outside sources.

DEGREE REQUIREMENTS. For M.A., M.S.: 30 semester hours minimum, at least 24 in residence; thesis, oral exam required by some departments. For Ph.D.: three years minimum, at least one year in full-time residence; preliminary exam; dissertation; final oral exam.

FIELDS OF STUDY.
Biochemistry.
Biometry. M.S. only.
Biophysics/Radiation Biology.
Cellular-Molecular Biology.
Cellular Physiology.
Chemistry. Includes medicinal chemistry.
Experimental Pathology.
Microbiology/Immunology.
Natural Sciences. Includes epidemiology and oncology for nurses. M.S. only.
Pharmacology/Experimental Therapeutics.

School of Social Work

Established 1934. Annual tuition: resident $5100, nonresident $8416, per credit resident $213, nonresident $351. On-campus housing available. Day care facilities available.
Enrollment: full-time 268, part-time 214. Faculty: full-time 16, part-time 25. Degree conferred: M.S.W.

ADMISSION REQUIREMENTS. Transcripts, GRE, three letters of reference, personal statement required in support of School's application. TOEFL required for international applicants. Accepts transfer applicants and advanced-standing applicants. Graduates of unaccredited institutions not considered for advanced standing. Apply to Director of Admissions by April 1. Admits Fall only, for both full- and part-time programs. Application fee $35. Phone: (716)645-3381, ext. 224; fax: (716)645-3883.

ADMISSION STANDARDS. Selective. Usual minimum average: 3.0 (A = 4).

FINANCIAL AID. Limited to loans. Use FAFSA. Phone: (716)829-3724.

DEGREE REQUIREMENTS. For M.S.W.: 60 credit hours minimum, for full-time at least two years in residence, for part-time one year in residence with advanced standing.

School of Pharmacy

Established 1886. Annual tuition: full-time resident $5900, nonresident $10,350; per credit resident $246, nonresident $432. Graduate enrollment: full-time 57, part-time 40 (men 65%, women 35%). Faculty: full-time 32; part-time 10. Degrees conferred: M.S., Ph.D., Pharm.D.

ADMISSION REQUIREMENTS. Transcripts, GRE required in support of School's application. TOEFL required for international applicants. Accepts transfer applicants. Graduates of unaccredited institutions not considered. Apply to appropriate department at least 60 days prior to registration. Pharm.D. admits Fall only. Application fee $35. Phone: (716)645-2828; fax: (714)645-2886.

ADMISSION STANDARDS. Competitive. Usual minimum average: 3.0 (A = 4).

FINANCIAL AID. Assistantships, tuition waivers, Federal W/S, loans. Apply by February 1 to appropriate department chair for assistantships; to Office of Financial Aid for all other programs. Use FAFSA.

DEGREE REQUIREMENTS. For M.S.: 30 semester hours minimum, at least 24 in residence; thesis, oral exam required by some departments. For Ph.D.: three years minimum, at least one year in full-time residence; preliminary exam; dissertation; final oral exam. For Pharm.D.: essentially the same as for Ph.D., except no foreign language requirement.

FIELDS OF STUDY.
Biochemical Pharmacology. M.S., Ph.D.
Medicinal Chemistry. M.S., Ph.D.
Pharmaceutics. M.S., Ph.D.
Pharmacy. Pharm.D.

School of Law

Established 1887. Located at Amherst campus (14260). Semester system. Library: 310,000 volumes. Library has LEXIS, NEXIS, WESTLAW, DIALOG, LRS, QL. Special facilities: Baldy Center for Law and Social Policy. Annual tuition: resident $6100, nonresident $10,750. Limited on-campus housing for single students only. Annual housing cost: $4000–$5000. Apply to Director of University Housing for both on- and off-campus housing. Total average annual additional expense: $6000–$7000.

Enrollment: first-year class 225, full-time 771 (men 52%, women 48%). Faculty: full-time 39, part-time 32. Degrees conferred: J.D., J.D.-M.A., J.D.-Ph.D.

ADMISSION REQUIREMENTS. LSDAS Law School report, bachelor's degree, transcript, LSAT, three recommendations required in support of application. Interview not required. Transfer applicants considered. Apply to Admissions Office after September 1, before February 1. Admits Fall only. Application fee $50. Phone: (716)645-2061.

ADMISSION STANDARDS. Selective. Accepts about 40–45% of total annual applicants.

FINANCIAL AID. TAP, SUSTA (N.Y. State residents only), fellowships, assistantships, Federal W/S, loans. Apply to Financial Aid Office by March 15. Use FAFSA.

DEGREE REQUIREMENTS. For J.D.: satisfactory completion of six-semester program or five semesters plus two summer sessions; 82 credit hour program. For M.A., Ph.D. degrees: see Graduate School listing above.

School of Medicine and Biomedical Sciences.

Founded 1846. Located in Buffalo (14214-3013). Annual tuition: resident $10,840, nonresident $21,940; student fees $359. Limited on-campus housing for single medical students only. Total average for all other expenses: $10,300.

Enrollment: first-year class 135 (EDP 10); total 585 (men 58%, women 42%). Faculty: full-time 593, part-time 108. Degrees conferred: M.D., M.D.-Ph.D. (Medical Scientist Training Program).

ADMISSION REQUIREMENTS. AMCAS report, transcripts, MCAT, letters of recommendation, interview required in support of application. Applicants must have completed at least three years of college study. Preference given to state residents. Has EDP; apply between June 5 and August 1. Accepts very few transfer applicants. Supplement application for MSTP. Apply to AMCAS after June 15, before December 1. Application fee $65. Phone: (716)829-3465.

ADMISSION STANDARDS. Competitive. Accepts about 7–8% of total annual applicants. Approximately 98% are state residents.

FINANCIAL AID. Scholarships, fellowships, loans. Apply to Office of Financial Aid after acceptance, but prior to May 15, Use FAFSA.

DEGREE REQUIREMENTS. For M.D.: satisfactory completion of four-year program. For Ph.D. requirements refer to Graduate School listing above.

FIELDS OF GRADUATE STUDY.
Anatomy.
Biochemistry.
Biomedical Engineering.
Biophysics.
Cell Biology.
Immunology.
Microbiology.
Molecular Biology.
Pathology.
Pharmacology.
Physiology.

School of Dental Medicine

Organized 1892. Annual tuition: resident $10,840, nonresident $21,940. On-campus housing available. Average academic year housing cost: $8477. For housing, apply to SUNYAB, Housing Office. Phone: (716)636-2181. Total average cost for all other first-year expenses: $4800.

Enrollment: first-year class 86; total full-time 357 (men 75%, women 25%); postgraduates 40. Faculty: full-time 138, part-time 65. Degree conferred: D.D.S.

ADMISSION REQUIREMENTS. AADSAS report, transcripts, DAT, three letters of recommendation required in support of School's application. Interviews by invitation only. Applicants must have completed at least three years of college, prefer four years of college. Accepts transfer students from U.S. and Canadian dental schools. Graduates of unaccredited colleges not considered. Apply to Admissions Office after July 1, before March 1. Application fee $50. Phone: (716)829-2839, or (716)829-2826.

ADMISSION STANDARDS. Selective. Usual minimum average: 2.8 (A = 4). Accepts 25–30% of total annual applicants. Approximately 85% are state residents.

FINANCIAL AID. Scholarships, grants, loans. Apply to the Financial Aid Office by June 1. Use FAFSA. Phone: (716)831-2839. About 80% of students receive some aid from School.

DEGREE REQUIREMENTS. For D.D.S.: satisfactory completion of forty-five-month program.

FIELDS OF GRADUATE STUDY.
Oncology.
Oral Biology.
Oral and Maxillofacial Surgery.
Oral Medicine.
Pediatric Dentistry.
Restorative Dentistry.

STATE UNIVERSITY OF NEW YORK AT STONY BROOK (WEST CAMPUS)
Stony Brook, New York 11794-4433

Founded 1957. Located 60 miles E of New York City on Long Island's north shore. Coed. State control. Semester system. Special facilities: Humanities Institute, Institute for American Studies, Institute for Decision Sciences, Institute for Mathematical

Science, Institute for Theoretical Physics, Nuclear Structure Laboratory, Marine Sciences Research Center, Institute for Pattern Recognition, Health Sciences Center. Library: 1,700,000 bound volumes, 3,000,000 microforms.

The Graduate School

http://www.grad.sunsb.edu

Annual tuition: full-time, resident $5100, nonresident $8416; per credit, resident $213, nonresident $351. On-campus housing available for married and singe graduate students. Housing application mailed with acceptance to degree program. Monthly housing cost: $237–$741 per person per bed, including most utilities.

Enrollment: full-time 1873, part-time 770. Graduate faculty: full-time approximately 714, part-time approximately 238. Degrees conferred: M.A., M.M., M.F.A., M.S., D.M.A., D.A., Ph.D.

ADMISSION REQUIREMENTS. Two transcripts from all undergraduate and graduate programs (Certified English translations of all international transcripts), GRE, three letters of recommendation required in support of School's application. GRE Subject Test required for some programs. TOEFL or TSE required for international applicants. Apply by January 15 (Fall), October 1 (Spring). Application fee $50. Phone: (516)632-7040; fax: (516)632-7243.

ADMISSION STANDARDS. Competitive. Minimum GPA of 2.75 (A = 4), a GPA of 3.0 in the major or related courses. Very competitive programs require higher GPA. For international applicants: minimum TOEFL scored 550 or TSE of 240.

FINANCIAL AID. Current awards from institutional funds: 1750 tuition scholarships, 754 teaching and graduate assistantships, 638 graduate research assistantships, 89 state supported fellowships, Federal W/S, loans. Approved for VA benefits. Apply to the Graduate Office for scholarships, fellowships, assistantships; to Financial Aid Office for all other programs. Use FAFSA and CSS Profile. About 134 students supported on stipends from outside sources. No aid for part-time students.

DEGREE REQUIREMENTS. For master's: 30 credits minimum with a 3.0 GPA, time limit of three years; reading knowledge of one foreign language for some programs; practicum in teaching; thesis/comprehensive exam/written exam varies by program. For doctoral degrees: at least three years in residence, a minimum of two semesters in full-time study, time limit of seven years after completion of the first 24 credits; GPA of 3.0; preliminary exam; reading knowledge of two foreign languages for some programs; advancement to candidacy; disscrtation, dissertation defense; practicum in teaching; final oral/written examination varies by program.

FIELDS OF STUDY.
Anatomical Sciences. Ph.D.
Anthropology. M.A., Ph.D.
Applied Mathematics and Statistics. M.S., Ph.D.
Art History and Criticism. M.A., Ph.D.
Basic Health Sciences. M.S.
Biological Science. M.A.
Biopsychology. Ph.D.
Cellular and Developmental Biology. Ph.D.
Cellular and Molecular Pathology. Ph.D.
Chemistry. M.S., Ph.D.
Clinical Psychology. Ph.D.
Coastal Oceanography. Ph.D.
Computer Science. M.S., Ph.D.
Dramaturgy. M.F.A.
Earth and Space Science. M.S., Ph.D.
Ecology and Evolution. Ph.D.
Economics. M.A., Ph.D.

Electrical Engineering. M.S., Ph.D.
English. M.A., Ph.D.
Experimental Psychology. Ph.D.
Foreign Language Instruction. D.A.
Genetics. Ph.D.
Germanic Languages and Literature. M.A.
Hispanic Languages and Literature. M.A., Ph.D.
History. M.A., Ph.D.
Information System Management. Advance Certificate.
Linguistics. M.A., Ph.D.
Management and Policy Sciences. M.S.
Marine Environmental Science. M.S.
Materials Science and Engineering. M.S., Ph.D.
Mathematics. M.A., Ph.D.
Mechanical Engineering. M.S., Ph.D.
Molecular Biology and Biochemistry. Ph.D.
Molecular and Cellular Pharmacology. Ph.D.
Molecular Microbiology. Ph.D.
Music. M.A., Ph.D.
Music Performance. M.M., D.M.A.
Neurobiology and Behavior. Ph.D.
Oral Biology and Pathology. Ph.D.
Philosophy. M.A., Ph.D.
Physics. M.A., M.S., Ph.D.
Physiology and Biophysics. Ph.D.
Political Science. M.A., Ph.D.
Psychology. M.A.
Romance Languages and Literature. M.A.
Slavic Languages and Literature. M.A.
Social/Health Psychology. Ph.D.
Sociology. M.A., Ph.D.
Studio Art. M.F.A.
Teaching of English to Speakers of Other Languages (TESOL). M.A.
Technological Systems Management. M.S.
Theater. M.A.
Women's Studies. Advance Certificate.

School of Health Technology and Management

Graduate study since 1974. Annual tuition: resident $5100, nonresident $8416.

Enrollment: M.S. part-time 54; Advanced Certificate part-time 11. Faculty: full-time 27, part-time 7. Degree Conferred: M.S., Advance Certificate.

ADMISSION REQUIREMENTS. Transcripts, GRE or other relevant admission exam, three letters of reference, essay, registration, certification or licensure; at least one year of full-time practice in the professional field required in support of School's application. TOEFL required for international applicants. Accept transfer applicants. Apply to the Office of Student Services by April 1. Application fee $35. Phone: (516)444-2111.

ADMISSIONS STANDARDS. Selective. Usual minimum average: 3.0 (A = 4).

FINANCIAL AID. Limited to Federal W/S, loans. Apply to the Financial Aid Office with admissions application. Use FAFSA.

DEGREE REQUIREMENTS. For master's: 36 credits minimum with 3.0 GPA; core and track requirement; practicum; thesis. Must maintain minimum 3.0 GPA. For Advanced Certificate: 18 credits minimum with 3.0 GPA; a health care management focus; two generic management courses.

FIELDS OF STUDY.
Allied Health Science. M.S.
Health Care Management. Advance Certificate

The School of Professional Development and Continuing Studies

Annual tuition: full-time resident $5100, nonresident $8416; per credit resident $213, nonresident $351.

Enrollment: full-time 300, part-time 1541. Faculty: full-time 25, part-time 48. Degrees conferred: M.A., M.A.T., M.P.S., Advance Certificate.

ADMISSION REQUIREMENTS. Transcripts, essay, three letters of recommendation required in support of School's application. GRE and undergraduate major in related field is required for the MAT candidates. TOEFL required for international applicants. Accepts transfer applicants. Apply to Director of Admissions and Advisement by May 1. Application fee $50. Phone: (516)632-7050; fax: (516)632-9046.

ADMISSION STANDARDS. Selective. Usual minimum average: 2.75 (A = 4). TOEFL score of 550 for international applicants.

FINANCIAL AID. Limited to Federal W/S, loans. Apply to the Financial Aid Office with admissions application. Use FAFSA.

DEGREE REQUIREMENTS. For master's: 30–36 credits minimum with a 3.0 GPA; time limit five years. For certificates: 18–24 credits with a 3.0 GPA; time limit five years.

FIELDS OF STUDY.
Chemistry 7–12. M.A.T.
Coaching. Advance Certificate.
Earth Science 7–12. M.A.T.
Educational Computing. Advance Certificate.
English 7–12. M.A.T.
Environmental and Occupational Health and Safety. Advance Certificate.
French 7–12. M.A.T.
German 7–12. M.A.T.
Italian 7–12. M.A.T.
Liberal Arts. M.A.
Long Island Regional Studies. Advance Certificate.
Physics 7–12. M.A.T.
Russian 7–12. M.A.T.
School Administrator and Supervisor. Advance Certificate.
School District Administration. Advance Certificate.
Social Science and the Professions/Labor Management Studies. M.P.S.
Social Science and the Professions/Public Affairs. M.P.S.
Social Science and the Professions/Waste Management. M.P.S.
Social Studies 7–12. M.A.T.
Waste Management. Advance Certificate.

School of Social Welfare

Graduate study since 1971. Semester system. Annual tuition: resident $5100, nonresident $8416; per credit resident $213, nonresident $351.

Enrollment: full-time 277, part-time 52. Faculty: full-time 21, part-time 10. Degree conferred: M.S.W.

ADMISSION REQUIREMENTS. Transcript, three letters of reference, essays, evidence of commitment to profession and social concern required in support of School's application. Accepts transfer students. Apply to Office of Admissions by March 1. Application fee $50.

ADMISSION STANDARDS. Selective. Usual minimum average: 2.5 (A = 4).

FINANCIAL AID. Limited to Federal W/S, loans. Apply to the Office of Financial Aid. Use FAFSA.

DEGREE REQUIREMENTS. For M.S.W.: 64 credits minimum, 16 in field instruction; master's project; 3.0 GPA.

School of Medicine (11794-8434)

Established 1971. Annual tuition: resident $10,840, nonresident $21,940. Total average cost for all other expenses: $11,000. Enrollment: first-year class 100 (EDP 5); total 426 (men 62%, women 38%). Faculty: full-time 500, part-time 40, volunteers 1600. Degrees conferred: M.D., M.D.-Ph.D.

ADMISSION REQUIREMENTS. AMCAS report, transcript, MCAT, letter of evaluation, recommendations required in support of application. Interview by invitation only. Has EDP; apply between June 15 and August 1. Apply to Committee on Admissions after June 1, before December 15. Application fee $65. Phone: (516)444-2113; fax: (516)444-2202.

ADMISSION STANDARDS. Competitive. Admits about 5–8% of total annual applications. Approximately 92% are state residents.

FINANCIAL AID. Scholarships, grants, Federal W/S, loans. Apply after acceptance to Office of Student Affairs. About 25% of students receive some aid from school.

DEGREE REQUIREMENTS. For M.D.: satisfactory completion of four-year program. For M.D.-Ph.D.: satisfactory completion of six to eight-year program. For Ph.D. requirements see Graduate School listing above.

School of Dental Medicine

Graduate study since 1973. Annual tuition: resident $10,840, nonresident $21,940. On-campus housing available. Average academic year housing cost: $13,417. Total average cost for all other first-year expenses: $4566.

Enrollment: first-year class 38, total 143 (men 55%, women 45%); postgraduates 14. Faculty: full-time 34, part-time 50. Degree conferred: D.D.S.

ADMISSION REQUIREMENTS. AADSAS, transcripts, DAT (no later than October), three letters of recommendation from science faculty, personal interviews required in support of application. Applicants must have completed at least three years of college work. Preference given to state residents. Accepts transfer applicants from U.S. and Canadian dental schools. Graduates of unaccredited institutions not considered. Apply through AADSAS after July 1, before January 15. Application fee $50. Phone: (516)632-8980.

ADMISSION STANDARDS. Competitive. Accepts about 15-20% of total annual applicants; 99% are state residents.

FINANCIAL AID. Full and partial scholarships, Federal W/S, loans. Apply to Financial Aid Office after acceptance. Use FAFSA. Phone: (516)632-8980. 100% of students receive aid from School and outside sources.

DEGREE REQUIREMENTS. For D.D.S.: satisfactory completion of forty-six-month program.

POSTGRADUATE CERTIFICATE.
Dental Care for the Developmentally Disabled. Postdoctoral program.
General Dentistry. Postdoctoral program.
Orthodontics. Advance certificate, postdoctoral program.
Periodontics. Advance certificate, postdoctoral program.

School of Nursing

Graduate study since 1970. Annual tuition: resident $5100, nonresident $8416; per credit $213 resident, nonresident $351.

Enrollment: full-time and part-time 504. Faculty: full-time 22, part-time 24. Degrees conferred: M.S., B.S./M.S., Post Master's Advance Certificate.

ADMISSION REQUIREMENTS. Transcripts, three letters of reference, personal statement, registered professional nurse licensure within one year of admission, CPR certification, B.S. with major in nursing required in support of Schools application. Midwives' M.S. completion program applicants must be ACC certified. Neonatal M.S. applicants must have at least two years of full-time nursing experience in the neonatal intensive care setting. Non-nursing B.S. degree applicants to the M.S. Nursing programs must pass Regents College Examination in Health Restoration I and II, and Health Support I and II within one year of admission. Accepts transfer applicants. Graduates of unaccredited institutions not considered. Apply to Admissions Office by May 1. Application fee $50. Phone: (516)444-3262.

ADMISSIONS STANDARDS. Selective. Usual minimum average: 3.0 (A = 4).

FINANCIAL AID. Partial tuition scholarships for full-time study, Federal W/S, loans. Apply at time of Admissions. Use FAFSA.

DEGREE REQUIREMENTS. For master's: 45 credits in required core courses in clinical specialty; minimum 3.0 GPA. Certificates of Advanced Standing: 18–24 credits in required courses and clinicals; minimum 3.0 GPA.

FIELDS OF STUDY.
Adult Health: Primary, Acute, and Critical Care Nursing. M.S.
Child Health Nursing. M.S
Gerontological Nursing. M.S.
Mental Health/Psychiatric Nursing. M.S.
Neonatal Nursing. M.S.
Nursing Midwifery. M.S.
Perinatal/Women's Health Nursing. M.S.

POST MASTER'S ADVANCE CERTIFICATES:
Addictions Nursing. Advance Certificate.
Adult Health Nurse Practitioner. Advance Certificate.
Child Health Nurse Practitioner. Advance Certificate.
Mental Health Nurse Practitioner. Advance Certificate.
Neonatal Nurse Pracitioner. Advance Certificate.
Nurse Midwifery. Advance Certificate.
Perinatal/Women's Health Nurse Practitioner. Advance Certificate.

Graduate Studies

Graduate study since 1948. Enrollment: full-time 300, part-time 1577. Faculty teaching graduate students: full-time 112, part-time 71. Degrees conferred: M.A., M.F.A., M.S., M.S.Ed., M.P.A., C.A.S.

ADMISSION REQUIREMENTS. Transcripts, three letters of recommendations required in support of application. GRE required for some programs. Portfolio in lieu of GRE for M.F.A. TOEFL required for international applicants. Accepts transfer applicants. Closing date varies by program. Application fee $50. Phone: (716)395-2751.

ADMISSION STANDARDS. Selective. Usual minimum average: 3.0 (A = 4).

FINANCIAL AID. Annual awards from institutional funds: nineteen scholarships, nineteen fellowships, seven research assistantships, thirty-one teaching assistantships, nineteen minority fellowships, Federal W/S, loans. Approved for VA benefits. Apply by April 15 to academic department for fellowships, assistantships; to Financial Aid Office for all other programs. Use FAFSA. Phone: (800)295-9150, (716)395-2501; fax: (716)395-5445.

DEGREE REQUIREMENTS. For master's: 30 credits minimum. For C.A.S., M.F.A.: 60 credits minimum beyond the bachelor's.

FIELDS OF STUDY.
Biological Sciences. (Botany, Zoology).
Communication.
Counselor Education. M.S.Ed., C.A.S.
Dance. M.F.A.
Educational Administration. Includes school administration, school business administration. M.S.Ed., C.A.S.
Educational and Human Development. Includes bilingual, elementary, reading teacher, secondary (English, mathematics, science, social studies).
English.
Health Science.
History.
Liberal Studies.
Mathematics.
Physical Education.
Psychology.
Public Administration.
Recreation and Leisure Studies.
Special Physical Education.
Visual Studies. Includes book arts, computer imaging, photography, video.

STATE UNIVERSITY OF NEW YORK COLLEGE AT BROCKPORT
Brockport, New York 14420-2997
http://www.Brockport.edu

Founded 1841. Located 18 miles W of Rochester. Coed. State control. Semester system. Library more than 410,000 volumes, 1,900,000 microforms.

Annual tuition: full-time, resident $5100, nonresident $8416; per credit, resident $231, nonresident $351. On-campus housing for single graduate students. Average academic year housing cost: $5680. Contact Director of Residential Life for on- and off-campus housing information. Phone: (716)395-2122.

STATE UNIVERSITY OF NEW YORK COLLEGE AT BUFFALO
Buffalo, New York 14222-1095
http://www.snybuf.edu

Established 1871. Coed. State control. Semester system. Special facilities: Burchfield Center, Center for Development of Human Services, Great Lakes Center for Environmental Research and Education, Prevention Resources Center, Center for Study in Creativity. Library: 600,000 volumes, 800,000 microform.

Annual tuition: full-time, resident $5100, nonresident $8416; per semester hour, resident $213, nonresident $351. On-campus housing for men and women; none for married students. Average annual housing cost: $4620. Apply to Director of Residential Life. Phone: (716)878-6806. Day care facilities available.

Graduate Division

Established 1945. Enrollment: full-time 322, part-time 1479. College faculty teaching graduate students: full-time 273, part-time 15. Degrees conferred: M.A., M.S., M.S.Ed., M.P.S., C.A.S.

ADMISSION REQUIREMENTS. Transcripts required in support of application. TOEFL required for international applicants. Accepts transfer applicants. Apply to Office of Graduate Studies by May 1 (Fall), October 1 (Spring), March 1 (Summer). Application fee $50. Phone: (716)878-5601.

ADMISSION STANDARDS. Relatively open. Usual minimum average: 2.75 for M.A.; 2.5 for M.S., M.S.Ed. for last two years (A = 4).

FINANCIAL AID. Sixty-nine research assistantships, nineteen minority fellowships, Federal W/S, loans. Approved for VA benefits. Apply to individual graduate departments for assistantships; to Office of Financial Aid for all other programs. No specified closing date. Use FAFSA. Phone: (716)878-4901. About 50% of students receive aid other than loans from outside agencies.

DEGREE REQUIREMENTS. For master's: 30 semester hours minimum, at least 24 in residence; comprehensive exam/thesis for M.A. For C.A.S.: 30 semester hours beyond master's, at least 27 in residence.

FIELDS OF STUDY.
Art Conservation.
Biology.
Chemistry.
Creative Studies.
Criminal Justice.
Education. Includes elementary, early secondary, school administration and supervision, teaching of exceptional children, art, biology, chemistry, earth science, English, mathematics, educational computing, speech-language pathology, vocational-technical, business, distributive, social studies, teaching bilingual exceptional individuals, technology.
English.
History.
Industrial Technology.
Multidisciplinary Studies.
Reading.
Student Personnel Administration.

STATE UNIVERSITY OF NEW YORK COLLEGE AT CORTLAND

Cortland, New York 13045
http://snycorva.cortland.edu

Founded 1868. Located 35 miles S of Syracuse. Coed. State control. Semester system. Library: 631,000 volumes, 575,000 microforms. Annual tuition: resident, full-time $5100, nonresident $8416, per credit $213; nonresident $351. No on-campus housing for graduate students. Apply to Office of Student Housing for off-campus housing information.

Graduate Division

Graduate study since 1947. Enrollment: full- and part-time 2600. Faculty: full- and part-time 155. Degrees conferred: M.A., M.S., M.S.E., M.A.T., C.A.B., C.A.S.

ADMISSION REQUIREMENTS. Transcripts required in support of application. GRE/MAT required by some departments.

TOEFL required for international applicants. Interview not required. Accepts transfer applicants. Graduates of unaccredited institutions not considered. Apply to Office of Graduate Admissions by August 15 (Fall), December 31 (Spring), May 15 (Summer). Application fee $50. Phone: (607)753-4711; fax: (607)753-5999.

ADMISSION STANDARDS. Selective. Usual minimum average: 3.0 (A = 4).

FINANCIAL AID. Annual awards from institutional funds: 26 teaching fellowships, Federal W/S, loans. Approved for VA benefits. Apply to Director of Financial Aid by March 15. Use FAFSA and TAP application. Phone: (607)753-4717; fax: (607)753-5999.

DEGREE REQUIREMENTS. For master's: 30 semester hours minimum, at least 24 in residence; admission to candidacy; written comprehensive exam/thesis/special project. For C.A.S., C.A.B.: 30 semester hours beyond the master's.

FIELDS OF STUDY.
Elementary Education.
English. M.A., M.A.T.
Health Education.
History.
Physical Education.
Reading.
Recreation Education.
School Administration and Supervisor. C.A.S. only.
Secondary Education. Includes the teaching of French, biology, chemistry, earth science, English, geology, mathematics, social studies, physics, speech, and general science.
Speech Education.

STATE UNIVERSITY OF NEW YORK COLLEGE AT FREDONIA

Fredonia, New York 14063

Established 1948. Located 45 miles from Buffalo. Coed. State control. Semester system. Library: 381,000 volumes, 964,800 microforms.

Annual tuition: full-time, resident $5100, nonresident $8416; per credit, resident $213, nonresident $351. On-campus housing for single students only. Annual academic year housing cost: $2500–$2900. Contact Director of Housing for off-campus housing information. Phone: (716)673-3341.

Graduate Studies

Graduate study since 1956. Enrollment: full-time 70, part-time 216 (men 40%, women 60%). Graduate faculty: full-time 37, part-time 8. Degrees conferred: M.A., M.S., M.S. in Ed., M.M., C.A.S.

ADMISSION REQUIREMENTS. Transcripts, two letters of recommendation required in support of application. TOEFL required for international applicants. Interview sometimes required. Accepts transfer applicants. Apply to Graduate Admissions, Fenner House, by July 5 (Fall), December 5 (Spring), April 20 (Summer). Application fee $50. Phone: (716)673-3251.

ADMISSION STANDARDS. Relatively open for most departments. Usual minimum average: 2.5 (A = 4).

FINANCIAL AID. Annual awards from institutional funds: twelve graduate assistantships, various research assistantships, tuition waivers; free tuition for disadvantaged students, Federal W/S, loans. Approved for VA benefits. Apply by March 15 to appropriate department chair for fellowships and assistantships; to Financial Aid Office for all other programs. Use FAFSA. Phone: (716)673-3253. About 12% of students receive aid other than loans from College and outside sources.

DEGREE REQUIREMENTS. For master's: 30 credits minimum, at least 15 in residence; thesis/final oral/written exam for some departments. For C.A.S.: 30 hours beyond the master's; internship; research paper.

FIELDS OF STUDY.
Biology.
Chemistry.
Education. Includes elementary, secondary teaching; most subject fields; speech pathology and audiology; reading.
Educational Administration.
English.
Mathematics.
Music. Includes music education, performance, theory/composition.
Special Studies. Interdisciplinary.
Speech Pathology and Audiology.

STATE UNIVERSITY OF NEW YORK COLLEGE OF ARTS AND SCIENCES AT GENESEO
Geneseo, New York 14454-1401

Founded 1871. Located 30 miles S of Rochester. Coed. State control. Semester system. Library: 419,000 volumes, 582,000 microforms, 100 PCs.
Annual tuition: full-time resident $5100, nonresident $8416; per credit, resident $213, nonresident $351. No on-campus housing available. Day care facilities available.

Graduate Division

Graduate study since 1952. Enrollment: full-time 100, part-time 400. Graduate faculty: full-time 200, part-time 20. Degrees conferred: M.A., M.S. in Ed.

ADMISSION REQUIREMENTS. Transcripts, two letters of recommendation, interview, GRE required in support of application. TOEFL required for international applicants. Accepts transfer applicants. Apply to Graduate Studies by July 1 (Fall), November 1 (Spring), May 1 (Summer). Application fee $35. Phone: (716)245-5546; fax: (716)245-5005; E-mail: harke@uno.cc.geneseo.edu.

ADMISSION STANDARDS. Selective. Usual minimum average: 2.75 (A = 4).

FINANCIAL AID. Annual awards from institutional funds: eleven teaching assistantships, Federal W/S, loans. Apply by April 1 to appropriate department chair for assistantships; to Financial Aid Office for all other programs. Use FAFSA and TAP application. Phone: (716)245-5731. About 65% of students receive aid from College and outside sources. Aid available to part-time students.

DEGREE REQUIREMENTS. For master's: 33–42 credit hours minimum; final written/oral exam or thesis.

FIELDS OF STUDY.
Biology.
Education of the Hearing Impaired. (Presently not admitting to program.)
Elementary Education.
Reading Teacher.

Secondary Education.
Special Education.
Speech Pathology.

STATE UNIVERSITY OF NEW YORK COLLEGE AT NEW PALTZ
New Paltz, New York 12561-2449

Founded 1885. Located 80 miles N of New York City. Coed. State control. Semester system. Library: 900,000 volumes, 800,000 microforms, 1300 periodicals.
Tuition: full-time, resident $5100, nonresident $8416; per credit, resident $213, nonresident $351. On-campus housing for single students; none for married students. Average annual housing cost: $2900–$4900. Apply to Director of Residence Life. Phone: (914)257-4444. Day care facilities available.

Graduate Division

Graduate study since 1947. Enrollment: full-time 300, part-time 1400. Faculty teaching graduate students: full-time 270, part-time 10. Degrees conferred: M.S., M.S. in Ed., M.A.T., M.A., M.F.A., M.P.S., C.A.S.

ADMISSION REQUIREMENTS. Transcripts, GRE/MAT/GMAT required in support of application. Provisional or permanent teaching certificate for M.S. in Ed. TOEFL required for international applicants. Interview not required. Accepts transfer applicants. Graduates of unaccredited colleges not considered. Apply to Director of Graduate Admissions at least one month prior to registration. Application fee $50. Phone: (914)257-3286; fax: (914)257-3284.

ADMISSION STANDARDS. Selective. Usual minimum average: 3.0 (A = 4).

FINANCIAL AID. Annual awards from institutional funds: minority student scholarships, fifty teaching assistantships, Federal W/S, loans. Approved for VA benefits. Apply one month prior to registration to Division chair for scholarships, assistantships; to Director of Financial Aid for all other programs. Use FAFSA. Phone: (914)257-3250. About 4% of students receive aid other than loans from School. No aid for part-time students.

DEGREE REQUIREMENTS. For master's: 30–36 semester hours minimum, at least 24 in residence; final comprehensive exam. For C.A.S.: 30 hours minimum beyond the master's.

FIELDS OF STUDY.
Art Education.
Art Studio.
Biology.
Business—International. M.S. only.
Chemistry.
Communication Disorders.
Computer Sciences.
Early Secondary. Includes English, French, mathematics, general science.
Elementary Education.
English.
English as a Second Language.
Geology.
Humanistic Education. M.P.S. only.
Mathematics.
Nursing.
Physics.
Psychology.
Reading. (K–12).

School Administration and Supervision.
Secondary Education. Includes French, German, Spanish, social studies, mathematics, biology, chemistry, earth science, physics.
Sociology.
Special Education.

STATE UNIVERSITY OF NEW YORK COLLEGE AT ONEONTA

Oneonta, New York 13820

Founded 1889. Located 200 miles NW of New York City. Coed. State control. Semester system. Library: 530,000 volumes, 750,000 microforms, 40 PCs.

Annual tuition: full-time, resident $5100, nonresident $8416; per credit, resident $213, nonresident $351. Limited dormitory housing for single students. No housing for married students. Average academic year housing cost: $5658 (including board). Contact Housing Office for both on- and off-campus housing information. Phone: (607)436-3725. Day care facilities available.

Graduate Studies

Established 1948. Enrollment: full-time 80, part-time 381. College faculty teaching graduate students: full-time 6. Degrees conferred: M.A., M.S., M.S.Ed., C.A.S.

ADMISSION REQUIREMENTS. Transcripts, GRE required in support of application. TOEFL required for international applicants. Accepts transfer applicants. Graduates of unaccredited institutions not considered. Apply to Graduate Office by March 1 (Summer and Fall), October 1 (Spring). Application fee $50. Phone: (800)786-9123, or (607)436-2523.

ADMISSION STANDARDS. Selective. Usual minimum average: 2.8 (A = 4).

FINANCIAL AID. Annual awards from institutional funds: four teaching assistantships, Federal W/S, loans. Apply to Financial Aid Office by April 15. Use FAFSA and TAP application. Financial aid largely in form of federal and state loan programs.

DEGREE REQUIREMENTS. For M.A., M.S.: 30–48 semester hours minimum, at least 24 in residence; reading knowledge of one foreign language sometimes required for M.A.; thesis sometimes required; written/oral comprehensive exam. For C.A.S.: 27 semester hours beyond master's, thesis required for some programs.

FIELDS OF STUDY.
Biology.
Business Economics. M.S.
Earth Science.
Education. Includes early childhood annotation, elementary, secondary (usual subject fields), counselor education.
History.
History Museum Studies. Forty hours for M.A.; program located at Cooperstown Graduate Center.
Reading.

STATE UNIVERSITY OF NEW YORK COLLEGE AT OSWEGO

Oswego, New York 13126

Founded 1861. Located 35 miles NW of Syracuse. Coed. State control. Semester system. Library: 405,000 volumes, 185,000 government documents, 1,500,000 microforms, 41 PCs.

Annual tuition: full-time, resident $5100, nonresident $8416; per credit, resident $213, nonresident $351. On-campus dormitory housing available. Average academic year housing cost: $3190–$5230. Contact Director of Housing for both on- and off-campus housing information. Phone: (315)341-2246. Day care facilities available.

Division of Graduate Studies and Research

Graduate study since 1948. Enrollment: full-time 260, part-time 980. Faculty: full-time 60, part-time 20. Degrees conferred: M.A., M.S., M.S. Ed., C.A.S., M.S.-C.A.S.

ADMISSION REQUIREMENTS. Transcripts, letters of recommendation, GRE Subject Test, GMAT required in support of application. Interview required by some departments. TOEFL required for international applicants. Accepts transfer applicants. Graduates of unaccredited colleges not considered. Apply to Office of Graduate Studies at least one month prior to registration. Application fee $50. Phone: (315)341-3152; fax: (315)341-3577.

ADMISSION STANDARDS. Selective. Usual minimum average: 3.0 (A = 4).

FINANCIAL AID. Annual awards from institutional funds: ten scholarships, twenty-five teaching assistantships, four research fellowships, four internships, Federal W/S, loans. Approved for VA benefits. Apply by November 15 (Spring), May 15 (Fall) to Graduate Office for scholarships, fellowships, assistantships; to Financial Aid Office for all other programs. Use FAFSA and TAP application. Phone: (315)341-2248. About 20% of students receive aid other than loans from College and outside sources.

DEGREE REQUIREMENTS. For master's: 30–36 credit hours minimum; thesis required for some programs. For C.A.S.: 60 credit hours minimum; thesis required for some programs.

FIELDS OF STUDY.
Art.
Business Administration.
Chemistry.
Counseling and Guidance.
Educational Administration and Supervision.
Elementary Education.
English.
History.
Human Services Counseling.
Reading Education.
School Psychology.
Secondary Education. Includes English, mathematics, science, social science.
Special Education.
Technology Education.
Vocational Education.

STATE UNIVERSITY OF NEW YORK COLLEGE AT PLATTSBURGH

Plattsburgh, New York 12901
http://BIO444.beaumont.plattsburg.edu

Organized 1889. Located 60 miles S of Montreal, Canada, 160 miles N of Albany, New York. Coed. State control. Semester system. Library: 300,000 volumes, 122,000 microforms, 30 PCs.

Annual tuition: full-time, resident $5100, nonresident $8416; per credit, resident $213, nonresident $351. On-campus housing for single students only. Annual academic year housing cost: $2620–$3340. Contact the Office of Campus Life/Housing for housing information. Phone: (518)564-3824.

Graduate Program

Graduate study since 1950. Enrollment: full-time 205, part-time 523. Faculty: full-time 49, part-time 7. Degrees conferred: M.A., M.S., C.A.S.

ADMISSION REQUIREMENTS. Transcripts, statement of purpose, three recommendations, GRE Subject Tests in support of application. Interview required for some departments. TOEFL required for international applicants. Accepts transfer applicants. Apply to Admissions Office by March 1 (Fall) School Psychology, Counseling, Speech-Language Pathology; May 1 (Fall) Education, Liberal Studies; October 15 (Spring) Liberal Studies, Education, Counseling; February 15 (Summer) Counseling, Speech-Language Pathology. Application fee $50. Phone: (518)564-2040; fax: (518)564-2045.

ADMISSION STANDARDS. Selective. Usual minimum average: 2.5 (A = 4).

FINANCIAL AID. Annual awards from institutional funds: twenty assistantships. Federal W/S, loans. Approved for VA benefits. Apply to Office of Financial Aid; no specified closing date. Use FAFSA and TAP application. Phone: (519)564-2072; fax: (518)564-4079. About 1% of students receive aid other than loans from College, 27% from all sources.

DEGREE REQUIREMENTS. For M.A., M.S.: 30 credits minimum, at least 18 in residence. For C.A.S.: 60 credits.

FIELDS OF STUDY.
Education. Includes elementary teaching, elementary reading specialist, French, Spanish, N-9 education specialties, secondary teaching in English, mathematics, social science, science, administration and supervision, curriculum and instruction, special education (elementary and secondary), biology, chemistry, earth science, physics.
Liberal Studies.
School Counseling.
School Psychology.
Speech-Language Pathology.
Student Affairs in Higher Education.

STATE UNIVERSITY OF NEW YORK COLLEGE AT POTSDAM

Potsdam, New York 13676

Founded 1816. Located 120 miles NW of Albany. Coed. State control. Semester system. Library: 370,000 volumes, 604,000 microforms, 60 PCs.

Annual tuition: full-time, resident $5100, nonresident $8416; per credit, resident $213, nonresident $351. On-campus housing available for graduate students. Annual housing cost: $2300–$4000. Apply to Director of Residence Life. Phone: (315)267-2350. On-campus day care facilities available.

Graduate Studies

Enrollment: full-time 146, part-time 336. College faculty teaching graduate students: full-time 57. Degrees conferred: M.A, M.S. in Ed., M.M., M.S.T.

ADMISSION REQUIREMENTS. Transcripts, NYSTCE required in support of application. TOEFL required for international applicants. Accepts transfer applicants. Graduates of unaccredited institutions not considered. Apply to Dean of Graduate Studies; by April 1 (Summer and Fall), October 15 (Spring) for M.S. Ed., M.S.T.; no specified closing date for M.A., M.M. Application fee $50. Phone: (315)267-2165; fax: (315)267-4802.

ADMISSION STANDARDS. Usual minimum average: 2.75 (A = 4) final 60 semester credits of undergraduate studies.

FINANCIAL AID. Limited to six graduate assistantships, minority graduate fellowships, Federal W/S, loans. Approved for VA benefits. Apply to the Dean of Graduate Studies; no specified closing date. Use institutional FAF. Phone: (315)267-2162.

DEGREE REQUIREMENTS. For master's: 30–33 credits minimum, 24 in residence. For M.S.T.: 42 credits minimum.

FIELDS OF STUDY.
Elementary Education (Nursery-6th Grade).
English.
Instructional Technology and Media Management.
Mathematics.
Music. Includes composition, music education, music history and literature, music theory, performance.
Reading.
Secondary Education. Includes English, mathematics, science (biology, chemistry, geology, physics), social studies.
Special Education.
Note: M.S.T. is for students whose bachelor's degrees are not in education.

STATE UNIVERSITY OF NEW YORK COLLEGE OF ENVIRONMENTAL SCIENCE AND FORESTRY AT SYRACUSE

Syracuse, New York 13210-2779
http://www.esf.edu

Coed. State control. Semester system. Special facilities: Archer and Anna Huntington Wildlife Forest, Adirondack Ecological Center, Cranberry Lake Biological Station, Empire State Paper Research Institute, Heiberg Memorial Forest, Wanakena Campus, Institute of Environmental Program Affairs, State University Polymer Research Center, U.S. Forest Service Cooperative Research Unit. Library supports 115,000 cataloged items, 1,800 serials and abstracts, extensive bibliographic databases and interlibrary loans.

Annual tuition (9 months): resident $5100, nonresident $8416; per credit, resident $213, nonresident $351. On-campus housing available for married and single students. Housing cost: married students $500–$640 per month, single $1500–$3120 per semester. Phone: (315)443-2567.

Graduate Studies

Graduate study since 1913. Enrollment: full-time 268, part-time 346. College faculty: full- and part-time 127. Degrees conferred: M.L.A., M.P.S., M.S., Ph.D.

ADMISSION REQUIREMENTS. Transcripts, GRE Subject tests, bachelor's degree, three letters of reference required in support of application. Interview desirable. TOEFL required of international students. Accepts transfer applicants. Apply to Office of Instruction and Graduate Studies by April 15 (Fall), November 15 (Spring). Application fee $50. Phone: (315)470-6599; fax: (315)470-6779; E-mail: esfgrad@esfedu.

ADMISSION STANDARDS. Very selective for most departments. Usual minimum average: 3.0 (A = 4.0).

FINANCIAL AID. Annual awards from institutional funds: sixty teaching assistantships, seventy-seven research assistantships, twelve fellowships, Federal W/S, loans. Apply to Financial Aid

Office; no specific closing date. Use FAFSA. Phone: (315)470-6670. About 70% of students receive aid other than loans from outside sources.

DEGREE REQUIREMENTS. For M.S. and M.L.A.: 30–37 semester hours minimum; thesis; project; oral exam. For M.P.S.: 30–39 semester hours minimum; course work and comprehensive exam or terminal experience depending on area of study. For Ph.D.: three years total study beyond the bachelor's; written/oral candidacy exam; advancement to dissertation; oral exam. Additional requirements upon decision of student's program director.

FIELDS OF STUDY.
Environmental and Forest Biology. Includes ecology, entomology, environmental physiology, fish and wildlife biology and management, forest pathology and mycology, plant science and biotechnology, and chemical ecology.
Environmental and Forest Chemistry. Includes forest chemistry, biochemistry, environmental chemistry, organic chemistry of natural products, and polymer chemistry.
Environmental and Resource Engineering. Includes forest engineering, paper science engineering, and wood products engineering.
Environmental Science. Includes environmental land planning, environmental policy and democratic processes, environmental modeling and risk analysis, and water resources management.
Forest Resources Management. Includes forest management, recreation and tourism, policy and administration, forest economics, quantitative methods, silvics, silviculture, forest soil science, tree improvement, international forestry, urban forestry, watershed management/hydrology, and forest information management.
Landscape Architecture. Includes course work in social/behavioral studies, natural/physical applied science, design process, methods and management.

STATE UNIVERSITY OF NEW YORK HEALTH SCIENCE CENTER AT BROOKLYN
Brooklyn, New York 11203-2098

Founded 1860; merged with State University of New York in 1950. Name changed 1986. Coed. State control. Semester system. Medical library: 330,000 volumes.

College of Graduate Studies

Annual tuition: resident $5100, nonresident $8416. Enrollment: full-time 120, part-time 1 (men 66%, women 33%). Faculty: full-time 117, part-time none. Degree conferred: M.S., Ph.D.

ADMISSIONS REQUIREMENTS. Transcripts, three letters of recommendation, GRE required in support of application. TOEFL, TSE required for international applicants. Interview may be arranged. Accepts transfer applicants. Apply to Office Graduate Studies by July 1. Application fee $35. Phone: (212)270-1155; fax: (212)270-3378.

ADMISSION STANDARDS. Competitive. Usual minimum average: 3.0 (A = 4).

FINANCIAL AID. Fellowships, research assistantships, teaching assistantships, full and partial tuition waivers, Federal W/S, loans. Apply to Office of Financial Aid, no specified closing date. Use FAFSA.

DEGREE REQUIREMENTS. For M.S.: 30 credit hours; no residency required; thesis defense. For Ph.D.: 90 credit hours beyond bachelor's, 24 credit hours in full-time residency; qualifying exam; dissertation defense.

FIELDS OF GRADUATE STUDY.
Anatomy.
Biochemistry.
Biophysics.
Cell Biology.
Immunology.
Microbiology.
Neurosciences.
Pathology.
Pharmacology.
Physiology.

College of Medicine

Enrollment: first-year class 185 (EDP 20), total 844 (men 58%, women 42%), postgraduates 712. Faculty: full- and part-time and volunteers approximately 2500. Degrees conferred: B.A.-M.D. (with Brooklyn College), M.D., M.D.-Ph.D.

ADMISSION REQUIREMENTS. AMCAS report, transcripts, letters of recommendation, MCAT required in support of application. Has EDP; apply between July 15 and August 15. Interviews by invitation only. Applicants must have completed at least three years of college study. Preference given to state residents. Apply to Office of Admissions after June 15, before December 15. Application fee $60. Phone: (718)270-2446.

ADMISSION STANDARDS. Competitive. Accepts 8% of total annual applicants. Approximately 90% are state residents.

FINANCIAL AID. Scholarships, fellowships, loans, work-study. Apply to Student Financial Assistance Office after acceptance. Use FAFSA and institutional application. About 85% of students receive some aid from College.

DEGREE REQUIREMENTS. For M.D.: satisfactory completion of four-year program.

STATE UNIVERSITY OF NEW YORK HEALTH SCIENCE CENTER AT SYRACUSE
Syracuse, New York 13210-2334

Founded 1834; merged with State University of New York in 1950. Name changed in 1986. Coed. State control. Semester system. Library: 167,000 volumes, 26 PCs. On-campus housing available for both single and married students. Annual academic year housing cost: $4200 for single students, $4800 for married students.

College of Graduate Studies

Annual tuition: resident $5100, nonresident $8416. Enrollment: full-time 32, part time 55 (men 48%, women 52%). Center faculty: 80. Degrees conferred: M.S., Ph.D., M.D.-Ph.D.

ADMISSION REQUIREMENTS. Transcripts, three letters of recommendation, GRE required in support of College's application. TOEFL, TSE required for international applicants. Interviews may be arranged. Accepts transfer applicants. Graduates of unaccredited institutions not considered. Apply to Office of Graduate Studies by April 1. Application fee $40. Phone: (315)464-4538; fax: (315)464-4544.

ADMISSION STANDARDS. Competitive. Usual minimum average: 3.0 (A = 4).

FINANCIAL AID. Predoctoral fellowships, graduate/research assistantships, tuition waivers, loans. Approved for VA benefits. Contact Office of the Dean for information. Use FAFSA.

DEGREE REQUIREMENTS. For M.S.: 30 credit hours; no residency required; thesis defense. For Ph.D.: 90 credit hours, 24 credit hours in full-time residency; qualifying exam; dissertation defense. For M.D. requirements refer to College of Medicine listing below.

FIELDS OF GRADUATE STUDY.
Anatomy and Cell Biology.
Biochemistry and Molecular Biology.
Cell Biology and Molecular Biology.
Microbiology and Immunology.
Neuroscience.
Pharmacology.
Physiology.

College of Medicine

Annual tuition; resident $10,840, nonresident $21,940. Total average cost for all other expenses: $7500. On-campus housing for 235 married students, 90 men, 90 women. Apply to Director of Housing. Phone: (315)464-6498.
Enrollment: first-year class 150 (EDP 5); total 656 (men 57%, women 43%). Faculty: about 700. Degrees conferred: M.D., M.D.-Ph.D. (Medical Scientist Training Program).

ADMISSION REQUIREMENTS. AMCAS report, transcripts, MCAT, recommendations required in support of application. Interview by invitation only. Applicants must have completed at least three years of college study. Preference given to state residents. Has EDP; apply between June 15 and August 1. Apply to Admissions Committee after June 15, before November 1 (firm). Application fee $60. Phone: (315)464-4570; fax: (315)464-8867.

ADMISSION STANDARDS. Competitive. Accepts 10% of total annual applicants. Approximately 90% are state residents.

FINANCIAL AID. Scholarships, loans. Apply to Office of Admissions and Student Affairs by May 1. Use FAFSA. Phone: (315)464-4329. About 35% of students receive aid other than loans from College.

DEGREE REQUIREMENTS. For M.D.: satisfactory completion of four-year program.

NEW YORK UNIVERSITY
New York, New York 10012-1019

Founded 1831. Coed. Private control. Semester system. Special facilities: Center for Latin American and Caribbean Studies, Institute for Developmental Studies, Maison Française, Courant Institute of Mathematical Sciences, National Academy of Television Arts and Sciences Archives, Institute of French Studies, Institute of Physical Medicine and Rehabilitation, Grey Art Gallery, Institute of Fine Arts, Murray and Leonie Guggenheim Foundation, Institute for Dental Research, C.J. Devine Institute of Finance, C.V. Starr Center for Applied Economics, Hargop Kevorkian Center for Near Eastern Studies, Institute of Retail Management, Institute of Planning and Housing, Institute of Labor Relations, Institute of Environmental Medicine, Henry W. and Albert A. Berg Institute for Experimental Physiology, Surgery, and Pathology, Institute of Judicial Administration, Institute of International Law, Copyright Publications Center, Onassis Center for Hellenic Studies. University libraries: 3,600,000 volumes, 3,326,000 microforms, 300 PCs.

Limited on-campus housing for married students, 602 graduate men and women. Housing cost: $450–$675 per month for married students, $4800 per semester for single students. Apply to Office of Director of Housing. Phone: (212)998-4600.

Graduate School of Arts and Sciences

Graduate study since 1886. Tuition: per credit $636. Enrollment: full-time 3045, part-time 1603. School faculty: full-time 832, part-time 30. Degrees conferred: M.A., M.Phil., M.S., Ph.D.

ADMISSION REQUIREMENTS. Transcripts, three letters of recommendation required in support of School's application. Interview, GRE, TSE required for some departments. TOEFL required for international applicants. Accepts transfer applicants. Graduates of unaccredited institutions not considered. Apply to Office of Graduate Enrollment Services by January 4 (priority deadline). International applicants apply to International Student Center by December 15. Application fee $60. Phone: (212)998-8050; fax: (212)995-4557.

ADMISSION STANDARDS. Selective to very competitive. Usual minimum average: 3.3 (A = 4).

FINANCIAL AID. Annual awards from institutional funds: 50 scholarships, 15 grants, 125 fellowships, 800 teaching/research/administrative assistantships, Federal W/S, loans. Multi-year fellowships available for Ph.D. students. Approved for VA benefits. Apply by January 4 to Fellowship Office for scholarships, internships, and fellowships; to appropriate department head for assistantships; to Financial Aid Office for Federal W/S, loans. Use FAFSA. Phone: (212)998-4486. About 30% of students receive aid other than loans from School.

DEGREE REQUIREMENTS. For M.A., M.S., M.Phil.: 32 credits minimum, at least 24 in residence; reading knowledge of one foreign language; thesis for most departments; final written exam for some departments. For Ph.D.: 72 credits minimum beyond the bachelor's, at least 32 in residence; reading knowledge of two foreign languages for most departments; qualifying exam; dissertation; final oral exam.

FIELDS OF STUDY.
Africana Studies.
American Studies.
Anthropology. Research papers, oral exam for M.A.
Asian Studies.
Basic Medical Sciences. Includes anatomy, biochemistry, biophysics, microbiology, pathology, pharmacology, physiology; combined M.D.-Ph.D. programs available.
Biology. Includes training program in basic cancer research, cell and molecular, developmental, environmental, evolutionary, physiology, neurobiology, population biology; preliminary oral exam for Ph.D.
Chemistry.
Cinema Studies.
Classics. Includes Greek, Latin, Byzantine and Hellenic studies.
Comparative Literature. Three languages for Ph.D.
Computer Science.
Dental Materials Science. M.S. only.
Earth System Science.
Economics.
English. Essay required for M.A. in lieu of thesis.
Environmental Health Sciences.
European Studies. M.A. only.
Fine Arts. Includes history of art, archaeology, conservation, anatorial studies; creative art major offered by School of Education; French and German for M.A.; for Ph.D. in Far Eastern art and archaeology, competence in Chinese/Japanese for Ph.D. in Near Eastern art and archaeology, reading knowledge of Ara-

bic and Persian, or Akkadian/Sumerian; written comprehensive exam for M.A.; final oral/written exam for Ph.D.

French Studies.
Germanic Languages and Literatures.
Hebrew and Judaic Studies.
History.
Italian.
Journalism. M.A. only.
Latin American and Caribbean Studies. M.A. only.
Liberal Studies. Interdepartmental. M.A. only.
Linguistics.
Mathematics. Thesis/nonthesis options for M.S.
Middle Eastern Studies.
Museum Studies. Certificate program only.
Music. Includes musicology, theory, composition.
Near Eastern Studies. M.A. only.
Neural Science. Ph.D. only.
Performance Studies.
Philosophy. M.A. only.
Physics.
Politics. Includes international relations; regional study programs are available.
Psychology. Includes chemical, developmental, individual and organizational, social.
Religious Studies. M.A. only.
Slavic Languages and Literatures. Includes Russian; written comprehensive exam for M.A. in Russian; qualifying exam for Ph.D. in Slavic philology and linguistics.
Sociology.
Spanish and Portuguese Languages and Literatures.
Theory and Culture.

Tisch School of the Arts—Graduate Division
721 Broadway, 7th Floor, 10003-6807

Graduate study since 1968. Semester system.
Annual tuition: full-time $21,458. On-campus housing available. Average academic year housing cost: $9500.
Enrollment: 700. School faculty teaching graduate students: full-time 72. Degrees conferred: M.F.A., M.P.S. The M.A., Ph.D. awarded through the Graduate School of Arts and Science.

ADMISSION REQUIREMENTS. Transcripts, two or three letters of recommendation, interview/audition or portfolio required in support of School's application. Deadlines vary. Please consult Office of Graduate Admissions at (212)998-1918. Application fee $45. Admits Fall only. Apply to: Director of Graduate Admission, 721 Broadway, 7th Floor, New York, NY 10003-6807. Phone: (212)998-1914; fax: (212)995-4060; E-mail: ipdbs@uccvm.nyu.edu.

ADMISSION STANDARDS. Competitive. Evidence of professional promise.

FINANCIAL AID. Annual awards from institutional funds: over 110 graduate teaching assistantships, 113 funded awards, Federal W/S, loans. Apply to Financial Aid Office; no specified closing date. Use FAFSA and Tisch FAF. Phone: (212)998-1900; fax: (212)995-4060.

DEGREE REQUIREMENTS. For M.F.A.: Design, 108 credits; Dance, 72 credits; Acting, 108 credits; Dramatic Writing, 70 credits; Film, 108 credits; Musical Theater, 72 credits. For M.P.S.: Interactive Telecommunications, 60 credits. For M.A., Ph.D., see Graduate School of Arts and Sciences listing above.

FIELDS OF STUDY.
Cinema Studies. M.A., Ph.D.
Dramatic Writing. Includes writing for film, theatre, television.
Film and Television. Includes film production-direction, cinematography, animation degree program by advisement.

Interactive Telecommunications. Focus on application of new media and telecommunications technologies.
Performance Studies. M.A., Ph.D.
Theater. Includes acting, dance, design, musical.

Leonard N. Stern School of Business Administration, Graduate Division
http://www.stern.nyu.edu/

Graduate study since 1916. Semester system. Located at 44 West 4th Street, New York, NY 10012-1126. Tuition: first credit $1143, each additional credit $854. Enrollment: full-time 900, part-time 2400. Faculty: full-time 200, part-time 90. Degrees conferred: M.S. (Accounting), M.B.A., Ph.D.

ADMISSION REQUIREMENTS. Transcripts, letters of recommendation, GMAT, personal essay, resume required in support of application. Interview by invitation only. TOEFL required for international applicants. Graduates of unaccredited colleges not considered. Apply to Admissions Office of the School by March 15 (Fall), May 15 (part time only Fall), October 15 domestic (part-time only Spring). Application fee domestic $60, international $75. Phone: (212)998-0600; fax: (212)995-4231.

ADMISSION STANDARDS. Very selective. Mean undergraduate average: 3.32 (A = 4); mean GMAT: 640; minimum TOEFL score 600.

FINANCIAL AID. Annual awards from institutional funds; scholarships, research fellowships, graduate assistantships, loans. Approved for VA benefits. Apply by January 31 to the Office of Financial Aid. Use FAFSA. About 40% of students receive aid other than loans from School and outside sources. Loans available to part-time students.

DEGREE REQUIREMENTS. For M.B.A.: 60 credits (20 courses) plus comprehensive business project; calculus, computer economics and business writing proficiencies. For M.S. in Accounting: 60 credits. For Ph.D.: 72 credits.

FIELDS OF STUDY.
Accounting.
Economics.
Finance.
Information Systems.
International Business. Multidisciplinary program.
Management.
Marketing.
Operations Management.
Statistics and Operations Research.
Taxation.

School of Education—Graduate Division
http://www.nyu.edu/edschool.html

Graduate study since 1980. Semester system. Special facilities: Center for Research and Community Service, Center for Nursing Research, Center for the Study of American Culture and Education, Center for Urban Community College Leadership, Metropolitan Center for Urban Education, New York University Institute for Education and Social Policy, Reading Recovery Teacher Leader Training Center. Tuition: per credit $578. Enrollment: full-time 1400, part-time 2800. School faculty: full-time 182, part-time 600. Degrees conferred: M.A., M.S., M.P.H., Sixth-Year Certificate, D.A., Ed.D., Psy.D., Ph.D.

ADMISSION REQUIREMENTS. Transcripts required in support of application. GRE required for all doctoral applicants.

TOEFL required for all non-native speakers of English. Interview required for some graduate applicants. Apply to School of Education, Graduate Admissions, by March 1 for master's and February 1 for doctoral programs (Fall), and December 1 for master's only (Spring). Application fee $40, foreign students $60. Phone: (212)998-5030; fax: (212)995-4328.

ADMISSION STANDARDS. Selective to very selective (varies by program).

FINANCIAL AID. Annual awards from institutional funds: fifty-three fellowships, fifty-five teaching and research assistantships, sixty-nine graduate assistantships, Federal W/S, loans. Approved for VA benefits. Apply by March 1 for Fall term and by November 1 for Spring term to Office of Graduate Admissions. Use FAFSA and New York State residents use TAP application. Phone: (212)998-4480. About 44% of full-time students receive aid other than loans from University and outside sources. Aid available to part-time students.

DEGREE REQUIREMENTS. For M.A.: 34 credits minimum without thesis, at least 24 in residence; or 30 credits minimum plus thesis, at least 24 in residence. For Sixth-Year Certificate: 30 credits minimum beyond a 34-credit master's degree, at least 24 credits in residence. For Ph.D., Ed.D., Psy.D., D.A.: 30 credit basic core, plus department requirements, at least 54 credits in residence beyond bachelor's, at least 30 credits in residence beyond master's; departmental candidacy exam; final oral exam; tool requirement for research; research proposal; dissertation; one or two semesters in full-time residence for some departments.

FIELDS OF STUDY.
Administration, Leadership, and Technology. Includes business education, educational communication and technology, educational administration, educational sociology, higher education.
Applied Psychology. Includes counseling and guidance, counseling psychology, educational psychology, psychological development, psychological foundations of reading, school psychology.
Art and Art Professions. Includes studio art, art education, visual arts administration, decorative arts, art therapy.
Culture and Communication. Includes environmental conservation education, graphic communications management and technology, history of education, media ecology, philosophy of education, religious education, speech and interpersonal communication.
Health Studies. Includes rehabilitation counseling, deafness rehabilitation, health education, recreation and leisure studies.
Music and Performing Arts Professions. Includes dance education, educational theatre, music education, music entertainment professions, music performance and composition, jazz and vocal studies, music technology, performing arts administration, performing arts therapy.
Nursing. Includes nursing, nursing and management, advanced practice nursing (adult), advanced practice nursing (elderly), advanced practice nursing (infants, children and adolescents), nursing midwifery, advanced certificate programs for advanced nursing practice, research and theory development in nursing science.
Nutrition and Food Studies. Includes clinical nutrition, foods and nutrition, food service management, public health nutrition.
Occupational Therapy. Includes professional and post-professional programs, ergonomics and biomechanics.
Physical Therapy.
Speech-Language Pathology and Audiology.
Teaching and Learning. Includes bilingual, early childhood and elementary education; foreign language, international, math, science, and social studies education; TESOL, quantitative studies, and special education.

Robert F. Wagner Graduate School of Public Service
http://www.nyu.edu/wagner

Established 1938. Semester system. Tuition: per credit $461. Enrollment: full-time 321, part-time 523 (men 318, women 526). Faculty: full-time 27, part-time 40. Degrees conferred: M.S., M.P.A., M.U.P., Ph.D., Advanced Professional Certificates.

ADMISSION REQUIREMENTS. Transcripts required in support of application. GRE required for doctoral students. Interview not required. TOEFL, TWE required for international applicants. Accepts transfer applicants. Graduates of unaccredited institutions not considered. Apply to Office of Admissions of School by August 1 (Fall), December 1 (Spring). Application fee $40. Phone: (212)998-7414.

ADMISSION STANDARDS. Selective. Usual minimum average: 3.0 (A = 4); 3.3–3.5 for doctoral applicants.

FINANCIAL AID. Annual awards from institutional funds: 290 scholarships, 12 research assistantships, Federal W/S, loans. Approved for VA benefits. Apply by March 1 to Office of Admissions. Use FAFSA. Phone: (212)998-4486. About 40% of students receive aid other than loans from School and outside sources. Aid available to part-time minority-group students.

DEGREE REQUIREMENTS. For M.P.A., M.U.P.: 60 credits minimum, at least 32 in residence; capstone project. For Ph.D.: 72 credits minimum beyond the bachelor's, at least 32 in residence; written preliminary exam; three comprehensive written exams; foreign language or advanced statistics; dissertation; final oral exam. For Adv. Prof. Cert.: 20 credits minimum beyond the master's, at least 15 in residence.

FIELDS OF STUDY.
Health Policy and Management. Includes management, financial management, policy analysis; customized specialization.
Public and Nonprofit Management and Policy. Includes inter alia, financial management, management of nonprofit organizations, policy analysis, comparative and international policy and management, environmental policy and management.
Urban Planning. Includes inter alia, urban government administration and organization, urban economics and public finance, housing and urban renewal, transportation, and other urban infrastructure.

Shirley M. Ehrenbranz School of Social Work

Established in 1960. Semester system. Annual tuition: full-time $16,224, per credit $507. Enrollment: full-time 608, part-time 413. Faculty: full-time 41, part-time 95. Degrees conferred: M.S.W., Ph.D.

ADMISSION REQUIREMENTS. Transcripts, personal essay required in support of School's application. Interview may be required. TOEFL required for international applicants. Accepts limited number of transfer applicants. Graduates of unaccredited colleges not considered. Apply to Director of Admissions of School. Fall admission for full-time program. Rolling admissions process. Application fee $35. Phone: (212)998-5910; fax: (212)995-4171.

ADMISSION STANDARDS. Competitive. Usual minimum average: 3.0 (A = 4).

FINANCIAL AID. Internships, tuition remission program, Federal W/S, loans. Apply to the Director of Admissions; no specified closing date. Use FAFSA and in New York State residents use TAP application. About 85% of students receive aid other than loans from School and outside sources. Only loans available to part-time students.

DEGREE REQUIREMENTS. For M.S.W.: 65 credits minimum, at least one year in full-time residence. For Ph.D.: 60 credits beyond the master's.

School of Law

Founded 1935. Semester system. Law library: 888,100 volumes. Library has LEXIS, NEXIS, WESTLAW, DIALOG. Special facilities: Center for International Studies, Center for Research in Crime and Justice, the Public Interest Center, Institute for Judicial Administration.

Annual tuition: $23,400. On-campus housing for about 800 students. Total average annual additional expense: $13,600.

Enrollment: J.D. program, first-year class 420; total 1299 (men 57%, women 43%); graduate program, full-time 300. Faculty: full-time 95, part-time 97. Degrees conferred: J.D., J.D.-M.A. (Economics, French, History, Politics, Philosophy, Sociology), J.D.-M.B.A., J.D.-M.U.P., J.D.-M.P.A., J.D.-M.S.W., J.D.-LL.M. (Taxation), LL.M., M.C.J., J.S.D.

ADMISSION REQUIREMENTS. For J.D.: LSDAS Law School report, bachelor's degree, transcripts, LSAT, three letters of recommendation required in support of application. Interview not required or encouraged. Evidence of proficiency in English required for international applicants. Accepts transfer applicants. Apply to Committee on Admissions of the School by February 1. Accepts full-time students only. Application fee $65. Phone: (212)998-6060. For graduate program: transcripts in support of application. English language proficiency evaluation by American Language Institute at NYU for international applicants. Apply to Graduate Office of School by August 10 (Fall), December 10 (Spring), May 10 (Summer).

ADMISSION STANDARDS. Very competitive for J.D. Accepts 15–20% of total annual applications. For graduate programs: accepts 65% of total annual applicants.

FINANCIAL AID. For J.D.: scholarships, Federal W/S, loans. Apply to Committee on Admissions by March 1. About 50% of students receive aid other than loans from School. For graduate program: fellowships, assistantships; apply to Financial Aid Office of the School by May 1. Use FAFSA. About 25% of students receive aid other than loans from School. Public service loan forgiveness plan available.

DEGREE REQUIREMENTS. For J.D.: 82 semester hours minimum, six semesters in full-time residence. For LL.M.: at least 24 credit hours beyond the J.D. minimum, at least 16 in residence. For M.C.J.: at least one year in full-time residence; essay; for foreign lawyers other than those trained in Common Law countries. For J. S.D.: 36 credit hours minimum, at least one year in full-time residence; oral exam; dissertation. Refer to other Graduate School listings for joint degree requirements.

FIELDS OF GRADUATE STUDY.
Administrative and Constitutional Law.
Advanced Property Law.
Corporation.
Criminal Justice.
International Legal Studies.
Jurisprudence, Legal History, and Legal Education.
Labor Law.
Taxation.
Trade Regulation.
Urban Affairs and Poverty Law.

Note: Joint degree program in public affairs with Woodrow Wilson School, Princeton University, also available.

School of Medicine

Organized 1841. Located 550 First Avenue, New York 10016. Annual tuition: $24,620, student fees $3,070. On-campus housing for married students, men and women. Apply to Housing Department, New York University Medical Center. Total average figure for all other expenses: $8500.

Enrollment: first-year class 160 (men 62%, women 38%); total 595. Faculty: full-time 663, part-time 105. Degrees conferred: M.D., M.D.-Ph.D. (Medical Scientist Training Program).

ADMISSION REQUIREMENTS. Transcripts, two letters of recommendation, MCAT, screening interview required in support of application. Interview for serious candidates only. Applicants must have completed at least three years of college study. TOEFL required for foreign applicants. Does not have EDP. Accepts transfer applicants. Graduates of unaccredited colleges not considered. Apply to Office of Admissions of School after August 15, before December 1. Foreign students apply to International Student Center. Fall admission only. Application fee $65. Phone: (212)263-5290; fax: (212)725-2140.

ADMISSION STANDARDS. Competitive. Accepts about 10–12% of total annual applicants. Approximately 55% are state residents.

FINANCIAL AID. Scholarships, research fellowships, assistantships, Federal W/S, loans, MSTP funded by NIH. Apply to Office of the Assistant Dean; no specified closing date. Use FAFSA. About 20% of students receive aid other than loans from School.

DEGREE REQUIREMENTS. For M.D.: satisfactory completion of four-year program, at least two years in residence. For M.D.-Ph.D.: consult Director, Institute of Graduate Biomedical Sciences.

FIELDS OF GRADUATE STUDY.
Biochemistry.
Biophysics.
Cell Biology.
Genetics.
Microbiology.
Molecular Biology.
Neurosciences.
Pathology.
Pharmacology.
Physiology.

College of Dentistry—David B. Kriser Dental Center

Founded 1865. Located 345 East 24th St, New York 10010.

Annual tuition: $32,950. On-campus housing for married students, men, women. Average academic year housing cost: $9000. Apply to Office of the Manager, Hall of Residence, New York University Medical Center. Total average cost for all other first-year expenses: $8500.

Enrollment: D.D.S. program: first-year class 180 (men 60%, women 40%); total 618; postgraduates 80. Faculty: full-time 131, part-time 455. Degrees conferred: A.B.-D.D.S., D.D.S., D.D.S.-M.S. (Management), D.D.S.-M.B.A., Certificate.

ADMISSION REQUIREMENTS. For D.D.S. program: AADSAS, transcripts, three letters of recommendation, DAT required in support of College's application. Interviews by invitation only. Applicants must have completed at least three years of college study. TOEFL required for international applicants. Accepts transfer applicants from U.S. and Canadian dental schools. International transfer applicants accepted into a three year program only. Apply to Director of Admissions after December 1, before June 1. Fall admission only. Application fee $35. Phone: (212)998-9818. For Certificate programs: official transcripts, two letters of recommendation, D.D.S. or D.M.D., interview required in support of College's application. Apply to Director of Advanced Education of School by March 31. Fall admission only.

ADMISSION STANDARDS. Selective. Usual minimum average: 3.0 (A = 4). Accepts 25–30% of total annual applicants. Approximately 65% are state residents.

FINANCIAL AID. Scholarships, grants, loans. Apply to Dental Center Financial Aid Office after acceptance. Use FAFSA. Phone: (212)998-9826. About 95% of students receive some aid from College and outside sources.

DEGREE REQUIREMENTS. For A.B.-D.D.S.: satisfactory completion of seven-year program. For D.D.S.: satisfactory completion of forty-five-month program. For Certificate: varies by program.

FIELDS OF GRADUATE STUDY.
Endodontics.
Implant Dentistry.
Oral and Maxillofacial Surgery.
Orthodontics.
Pedodontics.
Periodontics.
Prosthodontics.

NIAGARA UNIVERSITY
Niagara University, New York 14109

Founded 1856, located 25 miles NW of Buffalo. Coed. Private control. Roman Catholic. Semester system. Library: exceeds 288,000 volumes, 74,000 microforms.
Tuition: per credit $291 Education and Arts and Sciences; $371 Nursing and M.B.A. Limited on-campus housing. Annual academic year housing cost: $5084. Apply to Director of University Housing. Phone: (716)285-8568.

Graduate Division

Enrollment: full-time 302, part-time 338 (men 268, women 325). University faculty: full-time 9, part-time 20. Degrees conferred: M.S., M.B.A., M.S.Ed.; Professional Diploma in Educational Administration, School Counseling.

ADMISSION REQUIREMENTS. Transcripts, two letters of recommendation, GRE Subject Tests/MAT/GMAT scores, Statement of Intent required in support of application. Interview may be required by some departments. TOEFL required for international applicants. Accepts transfer applicants. Graduates of unaccredited institutions not considered. Apply to Dean of Education (phone: 716-886-8557); Nursing (phone: 716-286-8312); Business (phone: 716-286-8050); Criminal Justice (phone: 716-286-9081) at least one month prior to registration. Application fee: Education and Arts and Sciences $10; Nursing and M.B.A. $25.

ADMISSION STANDARDS. Selective. Usual minimum average: 3.0 (A = 4).

FINANCIAL AID. Six scholarships, one research assistantship, Federal W/S, loans. Apply by March 1 to Financial Aid Office; no specified closing date. Use FAFSA. Phone: (716)286-8686.

About 40% of students receive aid other than loans from University and outside sources.

DEGREE REQUIREMENTS. For M.S.: 33–36 semester hours minimum; thesis/oral exam; comprehensive exam. For M.S. Ed.: 36 semester hours; comprehensive exam. For M.B.A.: 48 semester hours. For Professional Diplomas: 30 hours beyond the master's.

FIELDS OF STUDY.

GRADUATE DIVISION OF ARTS AND SCIENCES:
Criminal Justice. M.S.

GRADUATE DIVISION OF NURSING:
Family Nurse Practitioner. M.S.

GRADUATE DIVISION OF BUSINESS:
Business Administration. M.B.A. only.

GRADUATE DIVISION OF EDUCATION:
Educational Administration and Supervision.
Foundations and Teaching.
Mental Health Counseling.
School Counselor.
Teacher Education.

NORTH ADAMS STATE COLLEGE*
North Adams, Massachusetts 01247-4100

Founded 1894. Located 40 miles E of Albany, N.Y. Coed. State control. Semester system. Library: 180,500 volumes, 212,000 microforms, 552 current periodicals.
Tuition: per credit, resident $130, nonresident $145. No on-campus housing available. Contact Dean of Graduate and Continuing Education.

Graduate Studies

Enrollment: part-time 149. Faculty: full-time 8, part-time 4. Degree conferred: M.Ed.

ADMISSION REQUIREMENTS. Transcripts required in support of application. Accepts transfer applicants. Apply to Dean, Graduate and Academic Affairs; no specified closing dates. Rolling admissions process. Application fee $25. Phone: (413)662-5381.

ADMISSION STANDARDS. Selective. Usual minimum average: 2.5 (A = 4).

FINANCIAL AID. None.

DEGREE REQUIREMENTS. For M.Ed.: 33 hours minimum, at least 27 in residence; final written exam.

FIELDS OF STUDY.
Education. Includes elementary, secondary, curriculum and instruction.

UNIVERSITY OF NORTH ALABAMA
Florence, Alabama 35632-0001

Founded 1830. Located 120 miles N of Birmingham. Coed. State control. Semester system. Library: 269,000, 666,000 microforms, 2517 current periodicals, 50 PCs.

Tuition: per credit, resident $84, nonresident $168. On-campus housing for 50 married students, unlimited for single graduate men and women. Average annual housing cost: $2550 (including board) for single students; $2904 for married students. Contact Office of Student Affairs for both on- and off-campus housing information. Phone: (205)760-4280.

Graduate Division

Enrollment: full-time 48, part-time 453. University faculty teaching graduate students: full-time 96. Degrees conferred: M.A., M.A.Ed., M.B.A.

ADMISSION REQUIREMENTS. Transcripts, GRE Subject Tests or MAT/GMAT required in support of application. TOEFL required for international applicants. Interview not required. Accepts transfer applicants. Apply to Director of Admissions at least one month prior to registration. Application fee $25. Phone: (205)760-4621.

ADMISSION STANDARDS. Selective. Usual minimum average: 2.75 unconditional, 2.0 conditional (A = 4).

FINANCIAL AID. Limited to sixty scholarships, Federal W/S, loans. Apply to Financial Aid Office; no specified closing date. Phone: (205)760-4278. Use FAFSA.

DEGREE REQUIREMENTS. For master's: 33 credit hours minimum; at least 24 credit hours in residence; thesis/nonthesis option; final oral exam.

FIELDS OF STUDY.
Administration and Supervision.
Business Administration.
Counseling.
Early Childhood.
Elementary Education.
N–12 education.
Non–School-based counseling.
Secondary. Includes usual subject fields.
Special Education. Includes learning disabilities, mental retardation, mild learning handicapped.

NORTH CAROLINA AGRICULTURAL AND TECHNICAL STATE UNIVERSITY
Greensboro, North Carolina 27411

Founded 1891. Coed. State control. Semester system. Library: 390,000 volumes, 612,000 microforms, 1900 current periodicals.
Annual tuition: full-time, resident $874, nonresident $8026. On-campus housing for single students only. Average academic year housing cost: $3120 (including board). Contact Dean of Students for both on- and off-campus housing information. Phone: (910)334-7920. Day care facilities available.

Graduate School

Graduate study since 1939. Enrollment: full-time 365, part-time 631. Faculty: full-time 261, part-time none. Degrees conferred: M.A., M.S., M.S.E., M.S.A.E., M.S.E.E., M.S.I.T.

ADMISSION REQUIREMENTS. Two official transcripts, GRE required in support of School's application. TOEFL required for international applicants. Interview not required. Accepts transfer applicants. Graduates of unaccredited institutions not considered. Apply to Graduate Office by June 1 (Fall), December 1 (Spring). Rolling admissions process. Application fee $25. Phone: (910)334-7920.

ADMISSION STANDARDS. Selective. Usual minimum average: 2.5 (A = 4).

FINANCIAL AID. Nineteen fellowships, sixty-five research assistantships, fifteen teaching assistantships, Federal W/S, loans. Approved for VA benefits. Apply to Dean of Graduate School for fellowships, assistantships; to Financial Aid Office for all other programs. No specified closing date. Use FAFSA. About 10% of students receive aid other than loans from School. Aid available to part-time students.

DEGREE REQUIREMENTS. For master's: 30–36 semester hours minimum, at least 22 in residence; qualifying exam; thesis/nonthesis option; final oral/written exam.

FIELDS OF STUDY.

COLLEGE OF ARTS AND SCIENCES:
Biology.
Chemistry.
English.
English and Afro-American Literature.
French.
History.
Mathematics.
Social Work.
Sociology.

SCHOOL OF AGRICULTURE:
Agricultural Economics.
Agricultural Education.
Food and Nutrition.
Plant Science.

SCHOOL OF EDUCATION:
Adult Education.
Art Education.
Biology Education.
Chemistry Education.
Early Childhood Education.
Educational Administration.
Educational Media.
Educational Supervision.
English Education.
Guidance and Counseling.
Health and Physical Education.
History Education.
Human Resources.
Reading.
Social Science Education.

SCHOOL OF ENGINEERING:
Architectural Engineering.
Chemical Engineering.
Civil Engineering.
Computer Science.
Electrical Engineering.
Engineering.
Industrial Engineering.
Mechanical Engineering.

SCHOOL OF TECHNOLOGY:
Industrial Arts Education.
Industrial Technology.
Safety and Driver Education.
Technology Education.
Vocational-Industrial Education.

NORTH CAROLINA CENTRAL UNIVERSITY

Durham, North Carolina 27707-3129

Founded 1910. Coed. State control. Semester system. Library: 614,000 volumes, 860,000 microforms, 4500 current periodicals, 30 PCs.

Annual tuition: full-time, resident $1754, nonresident $8902. On-campus housing for single students only. Average academic year housing cost: $3009 (including board). Contact Director of Residence Operations for both on- and off-campus for housing information. Phone: (919)560-6517. Day care facilities available.

Division of Graduate Studies

Enrollment: full-time 617, part-time 799. Faculty: full-time 247, part-time 74. Degrees conferred: M.A., M.S., M.Ed., M.B.A., M.I.S., M.L.S., M.P.A.

ADMISSION REQUIREMENTS. Official transcripts, three letters of reference required in support of application. TOEFL required for international applicants. Interview not required. Accepts transfer applicants. Graduates of unaccredited institutions not considered. Apply to the Admissions Office at least one month prior to registration. Application fee $15. Phone: (919)560-6230.

ADMISSION STANDARDS. Selective. Usual minimum average: 2.5, 3.0 in undergraduate major (A = 4).

FINANCIAL AID. Thirty assistantships, twenty teaching/research fellowships, Federal W/S, loans. Approved for VA benefits. Apply by April 30 to the Vice Chancellor's Office for assistantships, fellowships; to the Financial Aid Office for all other programs. Use FAFSA and University's FAF. Phone: (919)560-6202. About 25% of students receive aid other than loans from College and outside sources. Aid available for part-time students.

DEGREE REQUIREMENTS. For master's: 30–42 semester hours minimum with at least three summers in full-time attendance; thesis/nonthesis option or research project; reading knowledge of one foreign language or other research tool for some programs; final oral/written exam.

FIELDS OF STUDY.
Biology. M.S.
Business Administration. M.B.A.
Chemistry. M.S.
Communication Disorders. M.Ed.
Counselor Education. Includes agency counseling, career, school. M.A.
Criminal Justice. M.S.
Earth Science. M.S.
Educational Leadership. M.A.
Elementary Education. M.Ed.
English. M.A.
French. M.A.
History. M.A.
Human Sciences. M.S.
Information Science. M.I.S.
Instructional Media. M.A.
Library Science. M.L.S.
Mathematics. M.S.
Middle Level Education. M.A., M.Ed.
Music. M.A.
Physical Education. M.S.
Psychology. M.A.
Public Administration. M.P.A.
Recreation Administration. M.S.

Sociology. M.A.
Special Education. M.S.
Speech-Language Pathology and Audiology. M.S.
Therapeutic Recreation. M.S.

School of Law

Established 1939. Semester system. Law library: 166,000 volumes. Library has LEXIS, NEXIS, WESTLAW, DIALOG. On-campus housing available for single students only. Apply to Director of Housing. Phone: (919)560-6227.

Annual tuition: resident $1891, nonresident $10,843. Total average annual additional expense: $13,438.

Enrollment: first-year class, 65 (day),16 (evening); full-time 231, part-time 89 (men 46%, women 54%). Faculty: full-time 20, part-time 5. Degrees conferred: J.D., J.D.-M.L.S.(Law Librarianship).

ADMISSION REQUIREMENTS. LSDAS Law School report, bachelor's degree, transcript, two letters of recommendation, LSAT required in support of application. Interview not required. Accepts transfer applicants. Graduates of unaccredited colleges not considered. Apply to School after September 1, before April 15. Application fee $15. Phone: (919)560–6247.

ADMISSIONS STANDARDS. Accepts about 15% of total annual applicants.

FINANCIAL AID. Scholarships, assistantships, Federal W/S, loans. Apply to Director of Student Financial Aid by February 1. Use FAFSA. About 20% of students receive aid other than loans from School. Aid sometimes available to part-time students.

DEGREE REQUIREMENTS. For J.D.: satisfactory completion of three-year program; 88 semester hour program.

NORTH CAROLINA STATE UNIVERSITY AT RALEIGH

Raleigh, North Carolina 27695

Established 1987. Coed. State control. Semester system. Special facilities: Center for Electric Power Research, Center for Sound and Vibration, Electron Microscope Facilities, Highlands Biological Station, Reproductive Physiology Research Laboratory, Phytotron, Triangle Universities Nuclear Laboratory, Mars Mission Research Center, Nuclear Reactor Program Facilities, Pesticide Residue Research Laboratory, Precision Engineering Center, Southeastern Plant Environment Laboratories, Sea Grant College Program, Triangle Universities Computation Center, Institute of Statistics, member Institution Research Program at Oak Ridge, Water Resources Research Institute. Library: 2,398,000 volumes, 3,992,000 microforms, 18,500 current periodicals, 246 PCs.

Annual tuition/fees: full-time, resident $2206, nonresident $10,738; part-time, graduated scale depending upon number of credits. On-campus housing for 300 married students, 4000 men, 1500 women. Average academic year housing cost: $3374 for married student housing; $2290 for single students. Off-campus housing cost: $590 per month. Contact Director of Student Housing for both on- and off-campus housing information. Phone: (919)515-2410.

Graduate School

Graduate study since 1993. Enrollment: full-time 3336, part-time 1756. University faculty: full-time 1800. Degrees conferred: M.S., M.A., Master of a Designated Field, Ed.D., Ph.D.

ADMISSION REQUIREMENTS. Official transcripts, GRE/MAT/GMAT required in support of School's application. GRE Subject Test recommended for some programs. TOEFL required for international applicants. Interview not required. Accepts transfer applicants. Graduates of unaccredited institutions not considered. Apply to Graduate Admissions Office at least 60 days prior to registration. Application fee $45. Phone: (919)737-2871.

ADMISSION STANDARDS. Selective. Usual minimum average: 3.0 (A = 4).

FINANCIAL AID. Annual awards from institutional funds: 200 scholarships, 122 fellowships, 1266 research assistantships, 727 teaching assistantships, Federal W/S, loans. Approved for VA benefits. Apply by March 1 to appropriate department chair for fellowships, assistantships; to Financial Aid Office for all other programs. Use FAFSA and University's FAF. Phone: (919)737-2421. About 50% of students receive aid other than loans from School and outside sources.

DEGREE REQUIREMENTS. For master's: 33–48 credits minimum, at least one academic year in residence; thesis/nonthesis option; final oral/written exam. For professional degrees: 30–36 credits, at least one academic year in residence; project paper required by some departments; final oral exam. For Ph.D.: 6 semesters beyond the bachelor's, at least two semesters in full-time residence; reading knowledge of at least one foreign language required by some departments; dissertation; oral/written qualifying exam; final oral exam. For Ed.D.: essentially the same as Ph.D., except no language requirement.

FIELDS OF STUDY.
Accounting.
Adult and Community College Education.
Aerospace Engineering.
Agricultural Economics.
Agricultural Education.
Agricultural Engineering.
Agricultural Sciences.
Agronomy.
Animal Science.
Architecture.
Archival Management.
Art. Includes applied, graphics design, historic preservation.
Biochemistry.
Biomedical Engineering.
Biometrics.
Botany and Plant Sciences.
Business Administration.
Cell Biology.
Chemical Engineering.
Chemistry.
Civil Engineering.
Computer Engineering.
Computer Science.
Counselor Education.
Curriculum and Instruction.
Earth Sciences.
Ecology.
Economics.
Educational Administration.
Electrical Engineering.
English.
Entomology.
Environmental Policy and Resource Management.
Food Science and Technology.
Forestry.
Genetics.
Geography.
Geology.
Geophysics.
History.
Horticultural Science.
Industrial Design.
Industrial Engineering.
International Affairs.
Landscape Architecture.
Liberal Studies.
Management.
Management Information System.
Manufacturing Engineering.
Marine Sciences.
Material Engineering.
Materials Science and Engineering.
Mathematics. Includes applied.
Mathematics Education.
Mechanical Engineering.
Meteorology and Atmospheric Sciences.
Microbiology.
Middle School Education.
Nuclear Engineering.
Nutrition.
Operations Research.
Paper and Pulp Engineering.
Pathology.
Pharmacology.
Physics.
Physiology.
Plant Pathology.
Political Science.
Psychology.
Public Policy and Administration.
Recreation.
Rural Sociology.
Science Education.
Sociology.
Sports Administration.
Statistics.
Technical Writing.
Telecommunications.
Textiles Sciences and Engineering.
Toxicology.
Veterinary Medical Sciences.
Vocational and Technical Education.
Zoology.

College of Veterinary Medicine (27606)

Annual tuition: resident $4408, nonresident $18,896. Total average cost for all other expenses: $8070.

Enrollment: first-year class 72; total full-time 333 (men 65%, women 35%); postgraduates 40. Faculty: full-time 120. Degrees conferred: D.V.M., D.V.M.-Ph.D. The M.S. and Ph.D. are offered through the Graduate School.

ADMISSION REQUIREMENTS. VMCAS report, transcripts, recommendations, personal essay, animal/veterinary experience, interview required in support of application. Preference given to state and South Carolina residents. Graduates of unaccredited colleges not considered. Considers transfer applicants on a space available basis. Apply to the College after July 31. Application packets distributed in October must be completed and returned by November 1. Application fee $45. Phone: (919)829-4205; fax: (919)829-4222.

ADMISSION STANDARDS. Selective. Accepts 30–35% of qualified applicants. Approximately twelve are nonresident (at large) applicants.

FINANCIAL AID. Scholarships, fellowships, assistantships, Federal W/S, loans available. Apply to the Financial Aid Office after acceptance; no specified closing date. Use FAFSA.

DEGREE REQUIREMENTS. For D.V.M., satisfactory completion of four-year program. For Ph.D., see Graduate School listing above.

FIELDS OF GRADUATE STUDY.
Veterinary Medical Sciences.

THE UNIVERSITY OF NORTH CAROLINA AT CHAPEL HILL

Chapel Hill, North Carolina 27599
http://www.adp.unc.edu/sis/admissions/grad/
gradhome/html

Chartered 1789. Located 20 miles NW of Raleigh. Coed. State control. Semester system. Special facilities: Biological Sciences Research Center, Cancer Research Center, Center for Urban and Regional Studies, Center for Alcohol, Institute for Research in Social Science, Institute for Environmental Studies, Child Development Institute, Institute of Statistics, Institute of Marine Science, Institute of Government, Institute of Latin American Studies, Research Laboratories of Anthropology, Member of the Research Triangle Institute of North Carolina. Library: 3,500,000 volumes, 2,700,000 microforms.

Annual tuition: full-time, resident $1677, nonresident $9793. On-campus housing for 306 married students, 325 men, 325 women. Average academic year housing cost: $4560 (housing only) for married students, $7340 for single students. Contact the Director of Housing for both on- and off-campus housing information. Phone: (919)966-5661.

Graduate School

Graduate study since 1853. Enrollment: full-time 6800 (men 3000, women 3800), part-time 250. Graduate faculty: 1500. Degrees conferred: M.A., M.B.A., M.M., M.Ed., M.P.H., M.R.P., M.S., M.S.L.S., M.S.S.E., M.S.P.H., M.S.W., M.P.A., M.F.A., M.A.T., Ed.D., D.P.H., Ph.D.

ADMISSION REQUIREMENTS. Two transcripts, three letters of reference, GRE Subject Tests/GMAT required in support of School's application. Interview required by some departments. TOEFL required for international applicants. Accepts transfer applicants. Graduates of unaccredited institutions not considered. Apply to Office of the Dean by January 31 (Fall), October 15 (Spring). Application fee $55. Phone: (919)966-2611; fax: (919)966-4010.

ADMISSION STANDARDS. Selective to competitive. Usual minimum average: 3.0 (A = 4).

FINANCIAL AID. Annual awards from institutional funds: 600 fellowships or traineeships, 1600 teaching/research fellowships, Federal W/S, loans. Approved for VA benefits. Apply by January 31 to the Graduate School. Use FAFSA. Phone: (919)962-8396; fax: (919)962-2716. About 57% of students receive aid other than loans from University and outside sources. Aid sometimes available to part-time students.

DEGREE REQUIREMENTS. For M.A., M.S.: 30 semester hours minimum, at least two semesters in residence; reading knowledge of one foreign language or approved options in some departments; thesis or acceptable option; written/oral compre- hensive exam. For M.B.A.: two years minimum. For M.Ed.: 30 semester hours minimum; written comprehensive exam. For M.A.T., M.P.H., M.S.P.H., M.S.S.E.: 30 semester hours minimum, at least two semesters in residence; final written/oral exam. For M.F.A.: 40 semester hours minimum, at least two semesters in residence; oral exam. For M.S.L.S., M.S.S.: 48 semester hours minimum, at least two semesters in residence; final written exam. For M.P.A.: 45 semester hours minimum, at least two semesters in residence; oral exam. For M.S.W.: 53 semester hours minimum, at least two semesters in residence; final written/oral exam. For Ph.D.: four semesters minimum in residence, at least two semesters in continuous attendance; reading knowledge of two foreign languages or approved options in some departments; doctoral oral exam; written exam; dissertation; final oral exam. For D.P.H., Ed.D.: requirements essentially the same as for the Ph.D., except no language requirement.

FIELDS OF STUDY.
Anthropology.
Art. Includes creative art, art history; Ph.D. in art history only.
Biochemistry and Geophysics.
Biology.
Biomedical Engineering and Mathematics.
Business Administration. GMAT for admission to M.B.A.
Cell Biology and Anatomy.
Chemistry.
City and Regional Planning. Two years for M.R.P.
Classics.
Comparative Literature. Latin for Ph.D.
Computer Science.
Dramatic Art. M.F.A.
Ecology.
Economics.
Education. M.A.T., M.A. in college teaching; internship, comprehensive written exam for M.A.; includes administration and supervision, adult education, curriculum and instruction, educational media, elementary, higher education, educational psychology, educational leadership, counseling, school psychology, reading and language arts, physical education, social foundations of education, special education.
English. Latin for Ph.D.
Folklore. M.A. only.
Genetics. Interdepartmental.
Geography.
Geology.
German Languages. French for M.A., Ph.D.
History.
Information and Library Science. Thirty-six hours for M.S.L.S., Ph.D.
Journalism. M.A. only; interdepartmental program, mass communications research for Ph.D.
Leisure Studies and Recreation Administration. M.S. only.
Linguistics.
Marine Sciences.
Mathematics. Written qualifying exam for M.S.; apply by February 11 (Fall).
Microbiology and Immunology.
Music. Original composition for M.S.; other requirements as for M.A.
Neurobiology. Ph.D. only.
Nursing.
Occupational Therapy. M.S. only.
Operations Research.
Pathology.
Pharmacology.
Pharmacy.
Philosophy.
Physical Education. M.A. only.
Physical Therapy. M.S. only.
Physics and Astronomy.
Physiology.

Political Science. Includes public administration; M.P.A. only; 40 hours, internship, comprehensive written exam, final oral exam.

Psychology. GRE, MAT for admission.

Public Health. Includes environmental sciences and engineering, biostatistics, epidemiology, maternal and child health, health behavior and health education, public health nursing, nutrition, health policy and administration.

Public Policy Analysis. Ph.D. only.

Radio, Television, and Motion Pictures. M.A.

Rehabilitation Counseling. M.S. only.

Religious Studies.

Romance Languages. Includes Spanish; Latin, German for Ph.D.

Slavic Languages.

Social Work. GRE, MAT for admission; four semesters, one Summer term in residence for M.S.W.; M.S.W., Ph.D.

Sociology.

Speech Communications. M.A. only.

Speech and Hearing Science. M.S. only.

Statistics.

Toxicology.

School of Law (27599-3380)

Opened 1845. Semester system. Law library: 385,000 volumes.

Annual tuition: resident $2123, nonresident $11,539. Total average annual additional expense: $5824.

Enrollment: first-year class 235; total 705 (men 57%, women 43%). Faculty: full-time 31, part-time 11. Degrees conferred: J.D., J.D.-M.B.A., J.D.-M.P.A., J.D.-M.R.P.

ADMISSION REQUIREMENTS. LSDAS Law School report, bachelor's degree, transcripts, LSAT (not later than December) required in support of application. Accepts transfer applicants. Graduates of unaccredited institutions not considered. Preference is given to state residents. Apply to Admissions Office after September 1, before February 1. Application fee $55. Phone: (919)962-5106.

ADMISSION STANDARDS. Competitive. Accepts about 15–20% of total annual applicants.

FINANCIAL AID. Scholarships, research assistant grants, Federal W/S, loans. Apply to Student Aid Office by January 15 (fellowships), March 1 (grants and loans). Use FAFSA.

DEGREE REQUIREMENTS. For J. D.: satisfactory completion of three-year program; 86 credit hour program. For master's degrees, see Graduate School listing above.

School of Medicine (27599-7000)

Established 1879. Medical library: 263,000 volumes. Annual tuition: resident $2430, nonresident $21,890, student fees $734. Total average figure for all other expenses: $6500.

Enrollment: first-year class 160, total 656 (EDP 10) (men 59%, women 41%). Faculty: full-time 290, part-time 335. Degrees conferred: M.D., M.D.-Ph.D., M.D.-M.P.H.

ADMISSION REQUIREMENTS. AMCAS report, transcripts, two letters of recommendation, MCAT, supplementary application, interview required in support of application. Applicants must have completed at least three years of college study. Preference given to state residents. Has EDP; apply between June 15 and August 1. Accepts transfer applicants. Graduates of unaccredited colleges not considered. Apply to Office of the Dean after June 15, before November 15. Application fee $55. Phone: (919)962-8331.

ADMISSION STANDARDS. Competitive. Accepts 8–10% of total annual applicants. Approximately 90% are state residents.

FINANCIAL AID. Scholarships, loans. Apply after acceptance to Chair, Student Aid Committee. Use FAFSA. Phone: (919)962-8335. About 54% of students receive aid other than loans from School.

DEGREE REQUIREMENTS. For M.D.: satisfactory completion of four-year program. Refer to other Graduate School listings above for joint degree requirements.

FIELDS OF GRADUATE STUDY.
Anatomy.
Biochemistry.
Biomedical Engineering.
Cell Biology.
Genetics.
Immunology.
Microbiology.
Neurosciences.
Pathology.
Physiology.
Public Health.

School of Dentistry (27599-7450)

Established 1950. Annual tuition: D.D.S., resident, first and second year $3868; nonresident, first and second year $26,134. Total average cost for all other first-year expenses: $3271.

Enrollment: D.D.S., first-year class 75; total 386 (men 70%, women 30%); graduate study 45. Faculty: full-time 80, part-time 15. Degrees conferred: D.D.S., M.S., D.D.S.-Ph.D., D.D.S.-M.P.H.

ADMISSION REQUIREMENTS. For D.D.S.: AADSAS report, official transcripts, DAT (April test in Junior year preferred) required in support of School's application. Applicants must have completed at least three years of college study, prefer four years of study. TOEFL required for international applicants. Preference given to state residents. Interview by invitation only. Accepts transfer students. Apply to Office of Admission, School of Dentistry after June 1, before November 1. Application fee $55. Phone: (919)966-4565. For graduate study: official transcripts, GRE required in support of School's application. Graduates of unaccredited colleges not considered.

ADMISSION STANDARDS. Selective. Usual minimum average: 3.0 (A = 4). Accepts 25–30% of total applicants. Approximately 80% are state residents.

FINANCIAL AID. For D.D.S.: Limited to state, federal scholarships, loans. Apply to Office of Financial Aid after acceptance, but prior to April 1. Use FAFSA. About 63% of students receive aid from School. Graduate study: fellowships, assistantships, loans. Apply after acceptance to Office of Admissions, School of Dentistry. About 52% of graduate students receive aid from School and outside sources. No aid for part-time students.

DEGREE REQUIREMENTS. For D.D.S.: satisfactory completion of four-year program. For M.S.: 45–60 credits; thesis; final oral exam. Refer to other Graduate School listings above for joint degree requirements.

FIELDS OF GRADUATE STUDY.
Dentistry. Language not required for M.S. M.S., Certificate only. (See School of Dentistry Listing.)
Endodontics.
Oral and Maxillofacial Surgery. Fall admission only; two years and one summer session for M.S.
Orthodontics. Nineteen months including two summer sessions for M.S.
Pedodontics. Two years and two summer sessions for M.S.

Periodontics. Summer session admission only; two years and two summer sessions for M.S.

Prosthodontics. Fall admission only; two years and one summer session for M.S.

THE UNIVERSITY OF NORTH CAROLINA AT CHARLOTTE

Charlotte, North Carolina 28223

http://www.uncc.edu

Established 1965. Coed. State control. Semester system. Special facilities: Cameron Applied Research Center, Small Business and Technology Development Center, Urban Institute. Library: 557,000 volumes, 1,033,000 microforms, 5000 current periodicals.

Annual tuition: full-time, resident $1880, nonresident $9820; per credit, graduated scale for resident, nonresident students. Limited on-campus housing for graduate men and women, none for married students. Average academic year housing cost: $3260–$4784 (including board). Contact the Director of Residence Life for both on- and off-campus housing information. Phone: (704)547-2585.

Graduate School

Enrollment: full-time 475, part-time 1448. University faculty: full-time 500, part-time 84. Degrees conferred: M.A., M.A.L.S., M.B.A., M.Ed., M.S.A., M.S.E., M.S.C.E., M.S.E.E., M.S.M.E., M.L.S., M.S.N., M.P.A., C.A.S., Ph.D.

ADMISSION REQUIREMENTS. Transcripts, GRE, three letters of recommendation, statement of purpose required in support of School's application. MAT/NTE/GMAT required by some departments. Interview/auditions/portfolio required by some departments. TOEFL required for international applicants. Accepts transfer applicants. Apply to the Assistant Dean for Graduate Admissions at least sixty days prior to date of desired registration, many programs have early deadlines. Application fee $35. Phone: (704)547-3366.

ADMISSION STANDARDS. Competitive. Usual minimum average: 2.75 (A = 4).

FINANCIAL AID. Annual awards from institutional funds: 3 fellowships, 286 teaching assistantships, 122 research assistantships, 4 administrative assistantships, Federal W/S, loans. Approved for VA benefits. Apply to appropriate department chair for fellowships, assistantships; to Office of Financial Aid for all other programs. No specified closing date. Use FAFSA. About 40% of students receive aid from School and outside sources. Aid available to part-time students.

DEGREE REQUIREMENTS. For master's: 30 semester hours minimum; thesis; written/oral exam; reading knowledge of one foreign language for many departments. For M.Ed.: 32 semester hours minimum; final written exam. For M.L.S.: 36 semester hours minimum; written/oral exam. For M.B.A., M.P.A.: 36 semester hours minimum; written exam. For M.S.N.: 36 semester hours minimum; thesis; written/oral exam. For C.A.S.: 30 semester hours beyond the master's. For Ph.D.: six full semesters minimum beyond the bachelor's, at least two consecutive semesters or equivalent in full-time resident; reading knowledge of one or more foreign languages or equivalent in some departments; preliminary exam; dissertation; final oral exam.

FIELDS OF STUDY.

Applied Mathematics. M.S., Ph.D.

Applied Physics. M.S.

Applied Statistics. M.S.

Architecture. M.S.A.

Biology. M.A., M.S.

Business Administration. M.B.A.

Chemistry. M.S.

Civil Engineering. M.S.C.E.

Computer Science. M.S.

Counselor Education. M.A.

Criminal Justice. M.S.

Curriculum and Instruction. Includes elementary, middle grades, secondary. M.Ed., C.A.S.

Economics. M.S.

Educational Administration. M.Ed., C.A.S.

Electrical Engineering. M.S.E.E., Ph.D.

Engineering. M.E., M.S.E.

English. M.A.

Geography. M.A.

Health Promotion and Kinesiology. M.Ed.

History. M.A.

Liberal Studies. M.A.L.S.

Mathematics. M.A.

Mathematics Education. M.A.

Mechanical Engineering. M.S.M.E., Ph.D.

Nursing. M.S.N.

Psychology. M.A.

Public Administration. M.P.A.

Reading. M.Ed.

Social Work. Interinstitutional program with UNC at Chapel Hill. M.S.W.

Sociology. M.A.

Special Education. M.Ed., C.A.S.

Teaching English as a Second Language. M.Ed.

THE UNIVERSITY OF NORTH CAROLINA AT GREENSBORO

Greensboro, North Carolina 27412-5001

http://www.uncg.edu

Established 1891. Coed. State control. Semester system. Special facilities: Three College Observatory, Center for Applied Research, Center for Critical Inquiry into the Liberal Arts, Center for Educational Research and Evaluation, Center for Social Research, Center for Social Welfare, Center for Applied Research, Weatherspoon Art Gallery. Library: 850,000 volumes, 810,000 microforms.

Annual tuition: full-time, resident $1995, nonresident $10,273; per credit, graduated scale for resident, nonresident students. Limited on-campus housing for graduate men and women, none for married students. Average academic year housing cost: $3900 (including board, medical services fee). Contact the Director of Residence Life for both on- and off-campus housing information. Phone: (910)334-5636.

Graduate School

First graduate degree conferred in 1922. Enrollment: full-time 1595, part-time 1202. University faculty: full-time 500, part-time 84. Degrees conferred: M.A., M.Ed., M.F.A., M.M., M.S., M.A.L.S., M.L.S., M.S.N., M.P.A., Ed.S., Ph.D., Ed.D., D.M.A.

ADMISSION REQUIREMENTS. Transcripts, GRE required in support of School's application. MAT/NTE/ GMAT required by some departments. Interview/auditions/portfolio required by some departments. TOEFL required for international applicants. Accepts transfer applicants. Apply to Graduate School at least sixty days prior to date of desired registration, many programs have early deadlines. Application fee $35. Phone: (910)334-5596.

ADMISSION STANDARDS. Competitive. Usual minimum average: 2.75 (A = 4).

FINANCIAL AID. Annual awards from institutional funds: 36 academic scholarships, 50 grants, 190 teaching assistantships, 500 research assistantships, 100 administrative assistantships, 60 internships, Federal W/S, loans. Approved for VA benefits. Apply to appropriate department chair for assistantships; to Office of Financial Aid for all other programs. No specified closing date. Phone: (910)334-5702; fax: (910)334-3010. Use FAFSA. About 90% of students receive aid other than loans from School and outside sources. Aid not available to part-time students.

DEGREE REQUIREMENTS. For M.A., M.S.: 30 semester hours minimum; thesis; written/oral exam; reading knowledge of one foreign language for many departments. For M.Ed.: 32 semester hours minimum; final written exam. For M.F.A.: 60 semester hours minimum (except for creative writing 36 semester hours); final written/oral exam; thesis/final project. For M.M.: 30 semester hours minimum; recital. For M.A.L.S., M.L.S.: 36 semester hours minimum; written/oral exam. For M.P.A.: 36 semester hours minimum; written exam. For M.S.N.: 36 semester hours minimum; thesis; written/oral exam. For Ed.S.: 30 semester hours beyond the master's. For Ph.D., Ed.D.: six full semesters minimum beyond the bachelor's, at least two consecutive semesters or equivalent in full-time resident; reading knowledge of one or more foreign languages or equivalent in some departments; preliminary exam; dissertation; final oral exam. For D.M.A.: requirements essentially the same as for Ph.D. except a final project/recital/performance required.

FIELDS OF STUDY.
Accounting.
Art. Includes fine arts, interior design, studio, art education.
Biology.
Business Administration.
Business Education.
Chemistry.
Clothing and Textile.
Communication Studies.
Counseling and Development.
Creative Arts. Includes studio, creative writing, modern dance, music composition.
Curriculum and Teaching.
Dance.
Drama. Includes film/video, acting, directing, design, theatre for youth.
Economics.
Educational Administration.
Educational Research, Measurement, and Evaluation.
Educational Supervision.
Elementary Education.
English.
Exercise and Sport Science.
Food, Nutrition, and Food Service Management.
French.
Geography.
Health Education.
History.
Home Economics in Education and Business.
Human Development and Family Studies.
Interior Design.
Liberal Studies.
Library Information Studies.
Mathematics.
Middle Grades Education.
Music. Includes composition, education, performance, theory.
Nursing. Includes nurse anesthesia, administration, gerontological.
Parks and Recreation Management. Includes therapeutic recreation.
Physics.

Political Science.
Psychology. Includes clinical.
Public Affairs.
Secondary Education. Includes the usual majors.
Sociology.
Spanish.
Special Education.
Speech Pathology and Audiology.

THE UNIVERSITY OF NORTH CAROLINA AT WILMINGTON
Wilmington, North Carolina 28401-3201

Established 1975. Coed. State control. Semester system. Special facilities: Center for Marine Science Research. Library: 389,000 volumes, 837,000 microforms, 5000 current periodicals.

Annual tuition: full-time, resident $1880, nonresident $9820; per credit, graduated scale for resident, nonresident students. Limited on-campus housing for graduate men and women, none for married students. Average academic year housing cost: $3800 (including board). Contact the Housing Office for both on- and off-campus housing information. Phone: (910)395-3241.

Graduate Programs

Enrollment: full-time 95, part-time 273. University faculty: full-time 87, part-time 3. Degrees conferred: M.A., M.A.T., M.B.A., M.Ed.

ADMISSION REQUIREMENTS. Transcripts, GRE, three letters of recommendation, a statement of purpose required in support of School's application. MAT/NTE/GMAT required by some departments. Interview required by some departments. TOEFL required for international applicants. Accepts transfer applicants. Apply to the Assistant Dean for Graduate Admissions at least 60 days prior to date of desired registration; some programs have early deadlines. Rolling admissions process. Application fee $35. Phone: (910)350-3311.

ADMISSION STANDARDS. Competitive. Usual minimum average: 2.75 (A = 4).

FINANCIAL AID. Annual awards from institutional funds: six fellowships, eighty teaching assistantships, six research assistantships, four administrative assistantships, Federal W/S, loans. Approved for VA benefits. Apply to appropriate department chair for fellowships, assistantships; to Office of Financial Aid for all other programs. No specified closing date. Use FAFSA. About 20% of students receive aid from School and outside sources. Aid available to part-time students.

DEGREE REQUIREMENTS. For M.A: 30 semester hours minimum; thesis; written/oral exam; reading knowledge of one foreign language for some departments. For M.Ed.: 32 semester hours minimum; final written exam. For M.B.A.: 36 semester hours minimum; written exam.

FIELDS OF STUDY.
Biological Oceanography. M.S.
Biology. M.A., M.S.
Business Administration. M.B.A.
Chemistry. M.S.
Coastal Biology. M.S.
Educational Administration and Supervision. M.Ed.
Elementary Education. M.Ed.
English. M.A.

Geology. M.S.
History. M.A.
Marine Biology. M.S.
Mathematical Sciences. M.A., M.S.
Psychology. M.A.
Reading. M.Ed.
Special Education. M. Ed.
Teaching. M.A.T.

NORTH DAKOTA STATE UNIVERSITY
Fargo, North Dakota 58105

Founded 1889. Coed. State control. Semester system. Special facilities: Agricultural Experiment Station, North Dakota Institute for Regional Studies, United States Department of Agriculture Metabolism and Radiation Research Laboratory. Library: 486,000 volumes, 242,000 microforms, 5200 current periodicals, 65 PCs.

Annual tuition: full-time, resident $2700, nonresident $6500; per credit, resident $128, nonresident $290. On-campus housing for 305 married students, limited housing for single students. Average academic year housing cost: $1020 for single students, $2744 with seven day meals; $2880 for married students. Contact the Director of Housing for both on- and off-campus information. Phone: (701)231-7557. On-campus day care facilities available.

Graduate School

Graduate study since 1895. Enrollment: full-time 629, part-time 364. Faculty: full-time 400, part-time 26. Degrees conferred: M.A., M.S., M.Ed., M.B.A., Ed.S., Ph.D.

ADMISSION REQUIREMENTS. Official transcript required in support of School's application. GRE or MAT or GMAT required by some departments. TOEFL required for foreign applicants. Interview not required. Accepts transfer applicants. Graduates of unaccredited institutions not considered. Apply to Graduate School Admission Office at least one month prior to registration. Application fee $25. Phone: (701)237-8643.

ADMISSION STANDARDS. Very selective for most departments. Usual minimum average: 3.00 (A = 4).

FINANCIAL AID. Annual awards from institutional funds: 45 scholarships, 250 teaching assistantships, 250 research assistantships, Federal W/S, loans. Approved for VA benefits. Apply by March 15 to Graduate Dean for scholarships, to appropriate department chair for assistantships; to Financial Aid Office for all other programs. Phone: (701)237-7533. Use FAFSA. About 35% of students receive aid other than loans from University and outside sources. Aid available for part-time students.

DEGREE REQUIREMENTS. For all master's: 30 semester hours minimum, at least 20 in residence; thesis/nonthesis option; final oral exam. For M.Ed.: two seminar papers. For M.B.A.: 30 semester hours minimum. For Ed.S.: 30 semester hours beyond the master's, at least 24 in residence. For Ph.D.: normally three years beyond the bachelor's; preliminary exam; dissertation; final written/oral exam.

FIELDS OF STUDY.
Agricultural Economics. M.S. only.
Agricultural Education. M.S. only.
Agricultural Engineering. M.S. only.
Agricultural Management Systems. M.S. only.
Agronomy.
Animal Sciences.

Biochemistry.
Botany and Plant Sciences.
Business Administration. M.B.A.
Cellular and Molecular Biology.
Chemistry.
Child Development and Family Relations. GRE for admission; master's only.
Civil Engineering. Master's only.
Computer Science.
Counseling and Guidance. Master's only (option in education).
Education. Includes personnel, counseling and guidance, school administration, physical education, secondary education; MAT or cooperative English test (CET); for admission. M.Ed., M.S. only.
Educational Administration. M.S. only.
Electrical Engineering. Master's only.
Engineering and Applied Engineering.
English. M.A. only.
Entomology.
Environmental Engineering. M.S. only.
Environmental Policy and Resource Management.
Food Science and Technology. GRE for admission. Master's only.
History. GRE for admission; master's only.
Horticulture and Forestry. M.S. only.
Industrial Engineering. M.S. only.
Mass and Organizational Communication.
Mathematics.
Mechanical Engineering. M.S. only.
Microbiology. M.S. only.
Natural Resource Management. M.S. only.
Operations Research.
Pharmaceutical Sciences.
Pharmacology.
Physical Education and Human Movement Science.
Physics.
Plant Pathology.
Polymer Science/Plastics Engineering.
Psychology. M.S. only.
Range Science.
Speech and Interpersonal Communication. Master's only.
Statistics.
Toxicology.
Veterinary Sciences.
Zoology.

UNIVERSITY OF NORTH DAKOTA
Grand Forks, North Dakota 58201

Established 1883. Located 300 miles NW of Minneapolis. Coed. State control. Semester system. Special facilities: Center for Aerospace Studies, Ireland Cancer Research Laboratory, Energy and Environmental Research Center, biological field stations. Library: 2,000,000 items, 150 PCs.

Annual tuition: full-time, resident $2700, nonresident $6500; per credit, resident $129, nonresident $290. On-campus housing for 892 married students, 3100 single students. Average academic year housing cost: single students $2700 (including board); married students $3300. Contact the Director of Housing for both on- and off-campus housing information. Phone: (701)777-4251. Day care facilities available.

Graduate School

Graduate study since 1883. Enrollment: full-time 800, part-time 700. University faculty: full-time 413, part-time none. Degrees conferred: M.A., M.S., M.Ed., M.B.A., M.P.A., M.F.A., M.Engr., Specialist, Ed.D., D.A., Ph.D.

ADMISSION REQUIREMENTS. Transcripts, GRE/MAT/ GMAT/NTE, letters of recommendation required in support of School's application. Interview not required. TOEFL required for international applicants. Accepts transfer applicants. Graduates of unaccredited institutions not considered. Apply to Graduate School at least one month prior to registration. Application fee $20. Phone: (701)777-2784; fax: (701)777-3619.

ADMISSION STANDARDS. Selective for most departments. Usual minimum average: 3.0 (A = 4).

FINANCIAL AID. Annual awards from institutional funds: six academic scholarships, seven fellowships, three hundred teaching assistantships, sixty research assistantships, Federal W/S, loans. Approved for VA benefits. Apply to Dean of Graduate School for fellowships, assistantships; to Financial Aid Office for all other programs. No specified closing date. Use FAFSA. Phone: (701)777-3121.

DEGREE REQUIREMENTS. For master's: 30–32 credits minimum; thesis and nonthesis programs; comprehensive exam; final oral/written exam. For Ed.D.: 96 credits minimum beyond the bachelor's, at least two consecutive semesters in full-time residence; preliminary exam; dissertation for 10 credits; final oral exam. For D.A.: 90 semester hours, two years in residence; comprehensive exam; research project/oral exam. For Ph.D.: 90 credits minimum beyond the bachelor's, at least two consecutive semesters in full-time residence; competence in scholarly tools as specified by department; preliminary exam; dissertation; final oral exam.

FIELDS OF STUDY.
Anatomy.
Art. Includes fine arts.
Biochemistry.
Biology.
Botany and Plant Sciences.
Business Administration.
Chemistry.
Communication.
Computer Science.
Drama.
Ecology.
Economics.
Education. Includes early childhood, business, measurement and evaluation, elementary, music, physical, secondary, special, vocational and technical.
Education Administration.
Energy Engineering.
Engineering. Includes chemical, civil, electrical, environmental, mechanical, mineral/mining, structural, applied sciences.
English.
Entomology.
Environmental Biology.
Fish, Game, and Wildlife Management.
Genetics.
Geography.
Geology.
History.
Linguistics.
Mathematics.
Medical Technology.
Microbiology.
Music.
Nursing.
Pharmacology.
Physical Therapy.
Physics.
Physiology.
Psychology. Includes clinical, counseling.
Public Policy and Administration.

Reading.
Social Work.
Sociology.
Space Studies.
Speech-Language Pathology and Audiology.
Zoology.

School of Law (58202)

Established 1899. Semester system. Law library: 250,000 volumes. Library has LEXIS, WESTLAW.
 Annual tuition: full-time, resident $2530, nonresident $6756.
 Enrollment: first-year class 100; total full-time 240 (men 60%, women 40%). Faculty: full-time 13, part-time 10. Degree conferred: J.D.

ADMISSION REQUIREMENTS. LSDAS Law School report, bachelor's degree, transcripts, LSAT required in support of application. Interview not encouraged. Accepts transfer applicants. Preference given to state residents. Graduates of unaccredited colleges not considered. Admits beginning students in Fall only. Apply to Office of the Dean after August 15, before April 1. Application fee $20. Phone: (701)777-2260.

ADMISSION STANDARDS. Selective. Accepts 50–60% of total annual applicants.

FINANCIAL AID. Scholarships, full and partial tuition waivers, Federal W/S, loans. Apply to Dean of the School for scholarships by May 1; for loans apply to the University's Financial Aid Office. Use FAFSA. About 10% of students receive aid other than loans from School. No aid for part-time students.

DEGREE REQUIREMENTS. For J.D.: 90 credits minimum, at least one year in residence. Up to 30 transfer credits of advance standing may be accepted from another accredited school.
Note: An exchange program at the University of Oslo in Norway is available.

School of Medicine (58201)

Established 1905. Library: 75,000 volumes. Annual tuition: resident $8466; nonresident $22,588, student fees $318. Total average figure for all other expenses $9250.
 Enrollment: first-year class 55, total 226 (men 65%, women 35%). School faculty: full-time 163, part-time 91. Degrees conferred: M.D., M.D.-Ph.D.

ADMISSION REQUIREMENTS. Transcripts, letters of recommendation. MCAT, interview required in support of application. Has special program for Native Americans wishing to enter medicine (In Med). Special consideration of residents of Minnesota and WICHE states. Does not have EDP. Apply to Secretary of Admissions of School after July 1, before November 1. Application fee $35. Phone: (701)777-4221; fax: (701)777-4942.

ADMISSION STANDARDS. Selective. Accepts 60% of total annual applicants. Approximately 67% are state residents.

FINANCIAL AID. Scholarships, loans. Apply to Office of the Dean of the School after acceptance. Use FAFSA. About 85% of students receive aid from School. Phone: (701)777-2849.

DEGREE REQUIREMENTS. For M.D.: successful completion of four-year program. For Ph.D. requirements refer to Graduate School listing above.

FIELDS OF GRADUATE STUDY.
Anatomy.
Biochemistry.
Immunology.

Microbiology.
Pharmacology.
Physiology.

UNIVERSITY OF NORTH FLORIDA

Jacksonville, Florida 32216-2645

http://www.unf.edu

Authorized by Florida Legislature in 1965 and opened in 1972. Coed. Public control. Semester system. Special facilities: Center for Membrane Physics, Florida Institute of Education, Center for Local Government, Small Business Development Center. Library: over 495,000 volumes, 715,000 microforms.

Tuition: per semester hour, resident $118, nonresident $389. On-campus housing for 100 married students and unlimited housing for single students. Annual academic year housing costs: $1900–5200. Contact the Director of Residential Life for both on- and off-campus housing information. Phone: (904)646-2636. On-campus day care facilities available.

Graduate Studies

Enrollment: full-time 232, part-time 956 (men 50%, women 50%). University faculty: full-time 220, part-time 20. Degrees conferred: M.A., M.P.A., M.S., M.B.A., M.Ed., M.H.A., M.H.R.M., M.Acc.

ADMISSION REQUIREMENTS. Transcripts, bachelor's degree, GRE/GMAT required in support of application. TOEFL required for international applicants. Accepts transfer applicants. Graduates of unaccredited institutions not considered. Apply at least six weeks prior to registration for the desired term. Application fee $20. Phone: (904)646-2524.

ADMISSION STANDARDS. Selective. Usual minimum average: 3.0 (A = 4), a composite score of 1000 or more on GRE (College of Education and Human Services), a score of 500 or more on GMAT (College of Business Administration). TOEFL score of 500 or more for international applicants.

FINANCIAL AID. Annual awards from institutional funds: fifteen to twenty graduate assistantships, Federal W/S, loans. Approved for VA benefits. Apply by April 1 to Financial Aid Office. Use FAFSA and University's FAF. Phone: (904)646-2604; fax: (904)646-2703.

DEGREE REQUIREMENTS. For M.A. in Mathematical Sciences: 30 semester hours. M.P.A.: 36 credit hours for those with significant government experience or 39 credit hours for those who do not have background. For M.S. Criminal Justice: 37 credit hours. For M.A. in Counseling: 40 semester hours. For M.B.A.: Part I—a foundation for regular graduate study; Part II—36 semester hours. For M.Acc.: 36 semester hours. For M.H.R.M.: 36 credit hours. For M.Ed.: 36–39 hours selected from component cores. For M.S. in Allied Health Services: 36 semester hours.

FIELDS OF STUDY.
Accountancy.
Administration and Supervision.
Allied Health Sciences.
Art Education.
Business Administration.
Computer and Information Sciences.
Computer Science.
Counseling Psychology.
Counselor Education.
Criminal Justice.
Drug and Alcohol Abuse Counseling.

Educational Administration and Supervision.
Elementary Education.
English.
Gerontology.
Health and Physical Education.
History.
History. Joint program with University of Florida.
Human Ecology and Nutrition.
Human Resources Management.
Mathematics.
Mathematics Education.
Music Education.
Physical Education and Human Movement Studies.
Psychology.
Public Administration.
School Psychology.
Science Education.
Secondary Education.
Special Education.
Statistics.
Vocational and Technical Education.

UNIVERSITY OF NORTH TEXAS

Denton, Texas 76203-5446

http://www.unt.edu

Founded 1890. Located 38 miles NW of Dallas. Coed. State control. Semester system. Special facilities: Institute for Studies in Addiction, Institute for Applied Sciences, Institute of Criminal Justice, Center for Economic Education, Center for Environmental Economic Studies and Research, Center for Inter-American Studies and Research, Center for Network Neuroscience, Center for Organometallic Research and Education, Center for Public Service, Center for Remote Sensing and Land-Use Analysis, University Center for Texas Studies. Library: 1,206,000 volumes, 2,190,000 microforms, 8750 current periodicals, 124 PCs in all libraries.

Tuition: per credit, resident $38, nonresident $164. On-campus housing for 50 married students, unlimited for single students. Average academic year housing costs: $3654 (including board) for single students; $2200 for married students. Contact Director of Housing for both on- and off-campus housing information. Phone: (817)565-2605.

Robert B. Toulouse School of Graduate Studies

Graduate study since 1935. Enrollment: full-time 2227, part-time 2810. Graduate faculty: full-time 500, part-time 200. Degrees conferred: M.A., M.S., M.B.A., M.F.A., M.J., M.P.A., M.Ed., M.L.S., M.M., M.M.Ed., Ed.D., D.M.A., Ph.D., D.F.A.

ADMISSION REQUIREMENTS. Official transcripts, GRE/MAT/GMAT (for business) required in support of School's application. TOEFL required for international applicants. Interview not required. Accepts transfer applicants. Graduates of unaccredited institutions not considered. Apply to Dean of Graduate School at least six weeks prior to registration, some departments have earlier deadlines.

Application fee: $25 (U.S. students), $50 (international students). Phone: (817)565-2383.

ADMISSION STANDARDS. Selective. Usual minimum average: 2.80, 3.0 on last 60 hours of undergraduate study (A = 4).

FINANCIAL AID. Annual awards from institutional funds: One hundred scholarships, four hundred teaching fellowships, four hundred research assistantships, Federal W/S, loans. Approved for VA benefits. Apply by March 1 to appropriate department chair for fellowships and assistantships; to Financial Aid Office for all other programs. Use FAFSA. Phone: (817)565-2016. About 25–30% of students receive aid other than loans from University and outside sources. Aid generally not available for part-time students.

DEGREE REQUIREMENTS. For M.A., M.S.: 30–36 credit hours minimum, depending upon program and degree; comprehensive oral/written exam; reading knowledge of one foreign language for some departments; for 30-hour M.A. program, thesis or research problem. For M.B.A.: 36 credit hours minimum; final oral/written exam. For M.Ed., M.L.S., M.P.A.: 36 credit hours minimum; final oral/written exam. For M.M.: 32 credit hours; thesis; reading knowledge of one foreign language; final oral/written exam. For M.F.A.: 60 credit hours minimum; final oral/written exam. For M.M.Ed.: 36 credit hours minimum; final written/oral exam. For D.M.A., Ph.D., D.F.A.: normally 60 credit hours or three years in residence beyond the bachelor's and at least two consecutive semesters in full-time attendance; reading knowledge of one or two foreign languages or completion of tool subject; qualifying exam; dissertation; final written/oral exam. For Ed.D.: 60 credit hours beyond the master's, at least 2 consecutive semesters in full-time residence; qualifying exam; dissertation; final oral exam.

FIELDS OF STUDY.

COLLEGE OF ARTS AND SCIENCES:
Art. M.A., M.F.A., Ph.D.
Behavior Analysis. M.S.
Biochemistry. M.S., Ph.D.
Biology. M.S., Ph.D.
Chemistry. M.S., Ph.D.
Computer Science. M.S., Ph.D.
Drama. M.A., M.S.
Economics. M.A., M.S.
Engineering Technology. M.S.
English. M.A., Ph.D.
Foreign Languages. Spanish or French major. M.A.
History. M.A., M.S., Ph.D.
Journalism. M.A., M.J.
Mathematics. M.A., M.S., Ph.D.
Molecular Biology. Ph.D.
Physics. M.S., Ph.D.
Psychology. Includes clinical, counseling, experimental, industrial, school. M.A., M.S., Ph.D.
Sociology. M.A., M.S., Ph.D.
Speech/Language Pathology. M.A., M.S.

COLLEGE OF BUSINESS ADMINISTRATION:
Business Administration. M.B.A., M.S. (Accounting), Ph.D., three letters of reference for admission to Ph.D. program; reading knowledge of one language plus a demonstrated proficiency in mathematics, statistics, or computer programming for Ph.D.

SCHOOL OF COMMUNITY SERVICE:
Applied Economics. M.S.
Economic Education. M.S.
Labor and Industrial Relations. M.S.
Public Administration. M.P.A.
Rehabilitation Studies. M.S.
Studies in Aging. M.A., M.S.

SCHOOL OF EDUCATION:
Computer Education. M.S.
Counseling and Student Services. M.Ed., M.S., Ph.D.
Curriculum and Instruction. Ed.D., Ph.D.
Early Childhood Education. M.Ed., M.S., Ph.D.
Educational Administration. M.Ed., M.S., Ph.D.
Health Promotion. M.S.
Higher Education. Ed.D., Ph.D.

Human Development and Family Studies. M.S.
Kinesiology. M.S.
Reading. M.S.
Secondary Education. M.Ed., M.S.
Special Education. M.Ed., M.S., Ph.D.

SCHOOL OF MERCHANDISING AND HOSPITALITY MANAGEMENT:
Hotel and Restaurant Management. M.S.
Merchandising. M.S.

SCHOOL OF LIBRARY AND INFORMATION SCIENCE:
Information Science. M.S., Ph.D.
Library Science. M.S.L.S., Ph.D.

SCHOOL OF MUSIC:
Applied Music. M.M., D.M.A.
Composition. M.M., Ph.D., D.M.A.
Jazz Studies. M.M.
Music Education. M.M., Ph.D.
Musicology. M.M., Ph.D.
Performance. Includes conducting. M.M., D.M.A.
Theory. M.M., Ph.D.

SCHOOL OF VISUAL ARTS:
Art Education. M.A., M.F.A., Ph.D.
Art History. M.A., M.F.A.
Ceramics. M.F.A.
Communication Design. M.F.A.
Fashion Design. M.F.A.
Interior Design. M.F.A.
Metalsmithing and Jewelry. M.F.A.
Painting and Drawing. M.F.A.
Photography. M.F.A.
Printmaking. M.F.A.
Sculpture. M.F.A.

College of Osteopathic Medicine

Founded 1970. Coed. State control. Semester system. Library; 38,000 volumes, 520 current periodicals, has MEDLINE, CANCERLINE, BIOETHIC, HEALTH, PALINET, TOXLINE, DIALOG, OCLC.

Annual tuition: resident $6550, nonresident $19,650. Total of all other first year expenses $19,511. Enrollment: first-year class 100, total 435 (men 65%, women 35%). Faculty: full-time 170, part-time 300. Degree conferred: D.O.

ADMISSION REQUIREMENTS. AACOMAS report, bachelor's degree preferred, official transcripts, MCAT (no later than the Spring of junior year), three recommendations (one from premed advisory committee, one evaluation from a physician, preferably a D.O.), supplemental form required in support of application. Has EDP (apply September 1). Interview by invitation only. Graduates of unaccredited colleges not considered. Preference given to state residents. Apply by December 15 to the Office of Medical Student Admissions. Admits first year students Fall only. Application fee $50. Phone: (800)735-TCOM, (817)735-2204; fax: (817)735-5098.

ADMISSION STANDARDS. Selective. Accepts approximately 25% of total annual applicants. Usual minimum average: 3.0 (A = 4). Mean GPA: 3.4. 90% are state residents.

FINANCIAL AID. Scholarships, fellowships, assistantships, loans. Apply by May 1 to the Financial Aid Office. Use FAFSA and institutional FAF.

DEGREE REQUIREMENT. For D.O.: satisfactory completion of four year program.

NORTHEAST LOUISIANA UNIVERSITY
Monroe, Louisiana 71209-0600

Founded 1931. Located 100 miles E of Shreveport. Coed. State control. Semester system. Special facilities: Cancer Research Center, Louisiana Drug and Poison Information Center, Small Business Development Center, Center for Educational Research and Services, Herbarium, Human Performance Laboratory, Marriage and Family Counseling Center, Institute of Gerontology, Pharmaceutics Research and Technical Service center, Speech and Hearing center, Institute of Toxicology. Library: 539,000 volumes, 502,000 microforms, 2900 current periodicals.

Annual tuition: full-time, resident $1932, nonresident $4272; per credit, resident $324, nonresident $325. On-campus housing for single students only. Average academic year housing costs: $2000 (including board) for single students. Contact Director of University Housing for both on- and off-campus housing information. Phone: (318)342-5240. Day care facilities available.

Graduate Studies

Established 1961. Enrollment: full-time 562, part-time 417. Graduate faculty: full-time 222, part-time 36. Degrees conferred: M.A., M.S., M.B.A., M.M., M.M.Ed., Ed.S., Ed.D., Ph.D.

ADMISSION REQUIREMENTS. Official transcripts, GRE required in support of application. TOEFL required for international applicants. Interview not required. Accepts transfer applicants. Graduates of unaccredited institutions not considered. Apply to Registrar at least thirty days prior to date of enrollment. Application fee $15, $25 for non-U.S. citizens. Phone: (318)342-1036; fax: (318)342-1042.

ADMISSION STANDARDS. Selective. Usual minimum average: 2.75 (A = 4).

FINANCIAL AID. Annual awards from institutional funds: 75 teaching assistantships, 113 research assistantships, 85 laboratory, 184 non-teaching, Federal W/S, loans. Approved for VA benefits. Apply to Dean of Graduate Studies for assistantships; to Financial Aid for all other programs. No specified closing date. Use FAFSA. Phone: (318)342-5320. About 15% of students receive aid other than loans from University. No aid for part-time students.

DEGREE REQUIREMENTS. For M.A., M.S., M.M.: 30 semester hours minimum, at least 20 in residence; thesis/nonthesis option or final project (Pharmacy only); final or written/oral exam. For M.B.A.: 33 hours minimum, at least 27 in residence. For M.Ed.: same as for M.A., except thesis is optional. For M.M.Ed.: same as for M.A., except recital for three hours or thesis for six may be elected. For Ed.S.: 60 semester hours minimum beyond the bachelor's, at least two semesters in residence; final written/oral exam. For Ph.D. (Pharmacy only): 60 semester hours minimum beyond the bachelor's, at least two semesters in residence; qualifying exam; reading knowledge of at least one foreign language; dissertation; final oral exam.

FIELDS OF STUDY.
Biology. M.S.
Business Administration. M.B.A.
Chemistry. One language or computer science for admission. M.S.
Communication. M.A.
Communicative Disorders. M.A.
Criminal Justice. M.A.
Curriculum and Instruction. Ed.D.
Education. Includes administration and supervision, counseling, elementary, health and physical education, reading, special, marriage and family therapy, business, secondary (usual subject fields), special education. M.Ed.

Educational Leadership. Ed.D.
English. One language for admission. M.A.
Geosciences. M.S.
Gerontology. M.A.
History. M.A.
Marriage and Family Therapy. M.A.
Music. Includes applied music, education. M.M.
Pharmacy. Includes hospital pharmacy, medicinal chemistry, pharmaceutics, pharmacology, pharmacy administration, toxicology. M.S., Ph.D.
Psychology. M.S.
Substance Abuse Counseling. M.A.

NORTHEASTERN ILLINOIS UNIVERSITY
Chicago, Illinois 60625-4699

Founded 1896, this campus 1961. Coed. State control. Trimester system. Special facilities: Mazon Creek Paleontological Collection, Center for Exercise Science and Cardiovascular Research, Center for Inner Cities Studies. Library: 630,900 volumes, 722,000 microforms, 3600 current periodicals, 88 PCs.

Tuition: per credit, resident $90, nonresident $269. No on-campus housing. Day care facilities available.

Graduate College

Graduate study since 1961. Enrollment: full-time 164, part-time 1360. Graduate faculty: full-time 241, part-time 99. Degrees conferred M.A., M.B.A., M.Ed., M.S.

ADMISSION REQUIREMENTS. Official transcripts required in support of College's application. TOEFL required for international applicants. Interview not required. Accepts transfer applicants. Graduates of unaccredited institutions not considered. Apply to Graduate Office by April 1 (Fall), October 15 (Spring). Application fee, none. Phone: (312)583-4050; fax: (312)794-6670.

ADMISSION STANDARDS. Competitive. Usual minimum average: 2.75 (A = 4).

FINANCIAL AID. Annual awards from institutional funds: thirty-six research assistantships, twenty-two teaching assistantships, tuition waivers, Federal W/S, loans. Apply to appropriate department chair for assistantships; to Financial Aid Office for all other programs. No specified closing date. Use FAFSA. About 5–10% of students receive aid other than loans from College and outside sources. Aid sometimes available for part-time students.

DEGREE REQUIREMENTS. For master's: 30–48 hours minimum, at least 24–42 in residence; thesis or final paper for most majors; final written/oral exam.

FIELDS OF STUDY.
Accounting. M.B.A.
American Studies.
Biology. M.S.
Business Administration. M.B.A.
Chemistry. M.S.
City and Regional Planning. M.S.
Computer Science. M.S.
Earth Science. M.S.
Education. Includes counselor, media and instructional technology, gifted, English, physical.
Educational Administration. M.A.
English. Final paper(s) for M.A.; M.A. only.
Exercise Sciences and Cardiac Rehabilitation. M.S.

Finance. M.B.A.

Gerontology. M.A.

Guidance and Counseling. Includes elementary, secondary, vocational; 36 hours for M.A.

History. M.A.

Human Resource Development. M.A.

Inner City Studies Education. M.A. only.

Instructional Media. M.A.

Linguistics. M.A.

Literature. M.A.

Management. M.B.A.

Marketing. M.B.A.

Mathematics. M.S.

Music. M.A.

Physics. M.S.

Political Science. M.A.

Reading. M.A. only.

Special Education. Includes culturally disadvantaged, mentally handicapped, trainable, emotionally disturbed, socially maladjusted, learning disabilities, behavior disorders, gifted and talented; 30 hours plus 6-hour practicum for M.A.; M.A. only.

Speech. M.A. only.

NORTHEASTERN OHIO UNIVERSITIES

Rootstown, Ohio 44272-0095

College of Medicine

Established 1973 as a medical school consortium. Public control. Coed. Library: 80,000 volumes, 6300 microforms.

Annual tuition: resident $9255, nonresident $18,510, student fees $699. Total average cost for all other expenses: $6825. Enrollment: first year class, B.S.-M.D. 105, M.D. 15 (EDP 5); total 405 (men 59%, women 41%). Faculty: full-time 50, part-time 1300. Degrees conferred: B.S.-M.D., M.D.

ADMISSION REQUIREMENTS. AMCAS report, transcripts, MCAT, recommendations required in support of application. Interview by invitation only. Preference given to state residents. For B.S.-M.D.: preference given to applicants from Kent State, University of Akron, Youngstown State University. Has EDP; apply between June 15 and August 1. Graduates of unaccredited colleges not considered. For M.D.: apply to Office of Student Affairs after June 15, before November 1. Application fee $30. Phone: (800)686-2511 (in Ohio); (216)325-2511 (outside Ohio).

ADMISSION STANDARDS. Very competitive. For M.D. program: admits about 3% of total annual applicants. Approximately 100% are state residents.

FINANCIAL AID. Scholarships, loans. Apply after acceptance to Fellowships and Awards Committee. Use FAFSA. About 75% of students receive some aid from School.

DEGREE REQUIREMENTS. For B.S.-M.D.: satisfactory completion of six-year program. For M.D.: satisfactory completion of four-year program.

NORTHEASTERN STATE UNIVERSITY

Tahlequah, Oklahoma 74464-7099

Founded 1846. Located 75 miles SE of Tulsa. Coed. State control. Semester system. Library: 500,000 volumes, 365,000 microforms, 60 PCs.

Tuition: per credit, resident $70, nonresident $165 plus fees. On-campus housing for 140 married students, 800 men, 800

women. Cost varies with type of accommodation; approximate costs: $2200–$2400 per year. Contact Director of Housing for both on- and off-campus housing information. Phone: (918)456-5511, ext. 6004.

Graduate College

Graduate study since 1954. Enrollment: full- and part-time 1223. College faculty teaching graduate students: full-time 22, part-time 111. Degrees conferred: M.A., M.B.A., M.Ed., M.S.

ADMISSION REQUIREMENTS. Official transcripts, three letters of reference, GRE/MAT/GMAT required in support of College's application. TOEFL required for international applicants. Interview not required. Accepts transfer applicants. Graduates of unaccredited institutions not considered. Apply to Office of Graduate Dean by June 1 (Fall), December 1 (Spring), May 1 (Summer). Application fee: none. Phone: (918)456-5511, ext. 3690; fax: (918)458-2149.

ADMISSION STANDARDS. Relatively open. Usual minimum average: 2.5 overall (A – 4), 2.75 (for last 60 hours).

FINANCIAL AID. Annual awards from institutional funds: sixty scholarships, five research assistantships, thirty-five teaching assistantships, Federal W/S, loans. Approved for VA benefits. Apply to Dean of Graduate College for assistantships; to Financial Aid Office for all other programs. Use FAFSA. Phone: (918)456-5511.

DEGREE REQUIREMENTS. For master's: 32–36 semester hours minimum, at least 24 hours including the last 8 in residence.

FIELDS OF STUDY.

American Studies. M.A.

Business Administration. M.B.A.

College Teaching. M.S.

Communication. M.A.

Counseling Psychology. M.S.

Criminal Justice. M.S.

Curriculum and Instruction. M.Ed.

Early Childhood Education. M.Ed.

Educational Administration. M.Ed.

Elementary Education. M.Ed.

Industrial Technology. M.S.

Optometry. O.D.

Reading. M.Ed.

School Counseling. M.Ed.

Secondary Education. M.Ed.

Special Education.

NORTHEASTERN UNIVERSITY

Boston, Massachusetts 02115-5096

Founded 1898. Coed. Private control. Quarter system. Special facilities: Center for Applied Social Research, Barnett Institute of Chemical Analysis and Materials Science, Center for Biotechnology Engineering, Center for Digital Signal Processing, Center for European Economic Studies, Center for Labor Market Studies, Marine Science Center, Center for the Study of Sport, Center for Innovation in Urban Education, Institute on Writing and Teaching. Library: 777,000 volumes, 1,803,000 microforms, 8800 current periodicals. Both day and evening classes offered.

Tuition varies with program; see school listing below. On-campus housing for single students only. Housing costs per quarter: $1465–$1615. Apply to Director of Residential Life for both on- and off-campus housing information. Phone: (617)373-2814.

Graduate School of Arts and Sciences

Tuition: per quarter hour $390. Enrollment: full-time 627, part-time 331. School faculty: full-time 200, part-time 53. Degrees conferred: M.A., M.A.T., M.S., M.P.A., M.S.H.S., M.S.E.P.P., M.J.N.M.M., M.T.P.W., C.A.G.S., Ph.D.

ADMISSION REQUIREMENTS. Official transcripts, two or three letters of recommendation required in support of School's application. GRE Subject Tests required for many departments. TOEFL and certification of finances required from international applicants. Accepts transfer applicants. Graduates of unaccredited institutions not considered. Apply by March 15 (in many cases) to the Graduate School of Arts and Sciences. Application fee $40. Phone: (617)373-3982; fax: (617)373-2942; E-mail: a&sgradinfo@casdn.neu.edu.

ADMISSION STANDARDS. Selective for most departments. Usual minimum average: 2.75 (A = 4).

FINANCIAL AID. Annual awards from institutional funds: approximately 40 research fellowships, approximately 230 teaching assistantships, approximately 100 Northeastern tuition assistantships, minority fellowships and MLK scholarships, Federal W/S, loans. Approved for VA benefits. Apply by March 15 to Graduate School for assistantships, fellowships; to the Financial Aid Office for all other programs. Use FAFSA. Phone: (617)373-3982.

DEGREE REQUIREMENTS. For master's: 40 quarter hours minimum, at least 29 in residence; thesis/final comprehensive exam/language required for most departments. For Ph.D.: normally 40 quarter hours beyond the master's, at least one year in residence; qualifying exam; final written/oral exams; reading knowledge of one or two foreign languages; dissertation; final oral exam. For C.A.G.S.: 45 quarter hours beyond the master's degree; comprehensive exam.

FIELDS OF STUDY.
American Government and Politics.
Biology. GRE Subject, three references for admission; M.S. in biology, research, or literature, thesis required; M.S. in health science, thesis optional; M.S. full- or part-time; two languages for Ph.D. or research tool.
Chemistry. Includes analytical, clinical, organic, inorganic, physical; two references for admission, M.S. full- and part-time; one language for Ph.D.
Economics. Includes economic policy and planning; two references for admission, comprehensive exam for M.A., M.S.E.P.P.; thesis optional for M.A., M.S.E.P.P.
English. Includes linguistics, literature, writing. Three references for admission; one language for M.A., thesis optional, Master of Technical and Professional Writing, C.A.G.S. in humanistic literary study also offered.
History. GRE Subject, two references for admission; one language and comprehensive exam for M.A., thesis optional; includes historical agencies and administration.
Journalism. Includes news media management, technical and professional writing, technical writing, writing; GRE, two references for admission. M.A., M.J.N.M.M.; comprehensive exam for both degrees.
Law, Policy, Society, and Political Theory. M.S., Ph.D.; interdisciplinary programs; one language for Ph.D.
Mathematics. Includes applied and pure mathematics; three references for admission, one language for Ph.D.
Operations Research. Offered jointly with the School of Engineering.
Physics. GRE recommended, two references for admission. M.S. full- and part-time.
Political Science. Includes comparative government, international relations. Three references for admission; comprehen-

sive exam for M.A., thesis optional. M.P.A. full- and part-time study.
Psychology. GRE Subject, MAT for Ph.D.; three references for admission; includes applied behavior analysis, experimental; thesis required for M.A.
Public Administration. Includes development, public policy, personnel administration, policy and planning, public financing, health administration.
Sociology-Anthropology. GRE, three references for admission; thesis optional for M.A.; comprehensive, dissertation, research tool for Ph.D.; full- and part-time study.

Graduate School of Professional Accounting

Graduate study since 1965. Quarter system. Fifteen-month cooperative program includes 3-month internship where student is able to earn $8000–$10,000.

Total tuition costs for M.S.-M.B.A. $25,000; for M.S.T. $17,000. On-campus housing available. Contact University's Housing Office. Phone: (617)373-5877.

Enrollment: full-time 70, part-time 150. School faculty: full-time 20, part-time 2. Degree conferred: M.S. in Accounting, M.B.A., M.S.T.

ADMISSION REQUIREMENTS. Transcripts, three letters of reference, interview, GMAT or LSAT required in support of School's application. TOEFL required for international applicants. Applicants cannot be undergraduate accounting majors. Apply to Director of School, preferably before March 1. Classes start in June. Application fee $50. Phone: (617)373-3244; fax: (617)373-8890; E-mail: GSPA@neu.edu.

ADMISSION STANDARDS. Very selective. Usual minimum average: 3.2 (A = 4).

FINANCIAL AID. Annual awards from institutional funds: twenty to twenty-five scholarships, ten research assistantships, ten teaching assistantships, ten administrative assistantships, seventy internships, Federal W/S, loans. Approved for VA benefits. Apply by March 1 to Director of School. Use FAFSA and institutional FAF. About 75% of students receive aid other than loans from School and outside sources.

DEGREE REQUIREMENTS. For M.S.-M.B.A.: 97 quarter hours minimum and successful completion of internship. For M.S.T.: 42 quarter hours; 6 required, seven electives; successful completion of internship.

Graduate School of Business Administration

Special facilities: DEC VAX 8650 computer, 300 IBM PCs.
Tuition: per quarter hour $450.
Enrollment: full-time 384, part-time 557. Faculty: full-time 118, part-time 30. On-campus housing available. Degree conferred: M.B.A., E.M.B.A., M.S.F.

ADMISSION REQUIREMENTS. Official transcripts, GMAT, references required in support of School's application. TOEFL required for international applicants. Accepts transfer applicants. Graduates of unaccredited institutions not considered. Apply by May 1 to the Director of Admission. Rolling admissions process. Application fee $50. Phone: (617)373-5992; fax: (617)373-8564.

ADMISSION STANDARDS. Selective. Usual minimum average: 3.2 (A = 4); average GMAT 540.

FINANCIAL AID. Annual awards from institutional funds: twelve fellowships, eighteen teaching assistantships, fifty-five research assistantships, Federal W/S, loans. Approved for VA benefits. Apply April 1 to appropriate department chair for fellowships, assistantships; to the Director of Financial Aid for all other programs. Use FAFSA. Phone: (617)373-3190. About 25% of students receive aid other than loans from School and outside sources.

DEGREE REQUIREMENTS. For master's: 84–90 credits minimum, at least 54 in residence.

FIELD OF STUDY.
Business Administration. Includes, finance, marketing, production, human relations, quantitative methods, economics, management, management systems, international business.

Graduate School of Computer Science
http://www.ccs.neu.edu

Graduate study since 1988. Tuition: $425 per quarter hour. On-campus housing available. Contact University's Housing Office for both on- and off-campus housing information. Phone: (617)373-5877.
Enrollment: full-time 170, part-time 30. Faculty: full-time 17, part-time 3. Degrees conferred. M.S., Ph.D.

ADMISSION REQUIREMENTS. Transcripts, three letters of recommendation, GRE required in support of School's application. TOEFL required for international applicants. Accepts transfer applicants. Graduates of unaccredited institutions not considered. Apply to Graduate School Office by August 15. Application fee $40. Phone: (617)373-2462; fax: (617)373-5121.

ADMISSION STANDARDS. Selective. Usual minimum average: 3.0 (A = 4).

FINANCIAL AID. Annual awards from institutional funds: one fellowship, ten research assistantships, fifteen teaching assistantships, Federal W/S, loans. Approved for VA benefits. Apply by February 15 to Graduate School Office for fellowships, assistantships; to Financial Aid Office for all other programs. Use FAFSA. Phone: (617)373-3190; fax: (617)373-8735.

DEGREE REQUIREMENTS. For M.S.: 48 quarter hours minimum, including required courses and concentration area. For Ph.D.: normally 60 quarter hours beyond master's, at least one year in residence; qualifying exam, reading knowledge of one foreign language; dissertation; final oral exam.

FIELD OF STUDY.
Computer Science. Includes artificial intelligence, communications and networks, data bases, distributed systems, programming languages, operating systems, theory.

Graduate School of Criminal Justice

Graduate study since 1974. Quarter system. Tuition: $365 per quarter hour.
Enrollment: full-time 40, part-time 10. Faculty: full-time 10, part-time 4. Degree conferred: M.S.

ADMISSION REQUIREMENTS. Official transcripts, three letters of recommendation from academic and professional sources, GRE or LSAT, essay expressing academic and personal objectives required in support of School's application. TOEFL required for international applicants. Accepts transfer applicants. Apply by June 1, full-time (admits Fall only); June 1, part-time (Fall), November 1 (Winter), February 1 (Spring). Application fee $40. Phone: (617)373-3327; fax: (617)373-8723.

ADMISSION STANDARDS. Selective. Usual minimum average: 3.0 (A = 4), but lower considered for provisional admission.

FINANCIAL AID. Annual awards from institutional funds: nine teaching assistantships, Federal W/S, loans. Approved for VA

benefits. Apply to the Graduate School for assistantships; to Financial Aid Office for all other programs. Use FAFSA and institutional FAF. Phone: (617)372-3190; fax: (617)373-8735. Aid available to part-time students.

DEGREE REQUIREMENTS. For master's: 42 quarter hours minimum; comprehensive exam; thesis optional. Full-time students may complete program in one year.

FIELDS OF STUDY.
Criminology.
Juvenile Justice.

Bouve College of Pharmacy and Health Sciences Graduate School
http://www.neu.edu/gradschool/bouve.html

Tuition: per credit $390. Enrollment: full-time 461, part-time 218. Faculty: full-time 63. Degrees conferred: M.S., C.A.G.S., M.H.P., Ph.D., Pharm.D.

ADMISSION REQUIREMENTS. Official transcripts, references, essay, test (vary by program and degree), required in support of School's application. TOEFL scores are required of those applicants whose native language is not English. Accepts transfer applicants. The application deadline for the Pharm.D. program is February 1; Ph.D. program deadline is April 15. All application materials for master's program must be submitted to the Director of Graduate Admissions at least one month prior to registration. Application fee $40. Phone: (617)373-2708; fax: (617)266-6756; E-mail: jweber@lynx,dac.neu.edu.

ADMISSION STANDARDS. Selective for most departments. Usual minimum average: 3.0 (A = 4); TOEFL score of 600.

FINANCIAL AID. Scholarships, fellowships, assistantships, a limited number of minority fellowships and Martin Luther King, Jr. scholarships, Federal W/S, loans. Approved for VA benefits. Need based financial aid is available only to American citizens or permanent residents of the United States. Apply by March 1 to appropriate department for assistantships, fellowships; to Office of Financial Aid for all other programs. Use FAFSA. Phone: (617)373-5899.

DEGREE REQUIREMENTS. For M.S.: 45–76 quarter hours minimum; comprehensive exam. For C.A.G.S.: one year beyond the master's; qualifying exam; comprehensive exam. For Pharm.D.: 76 quarter hours beyond the master's; qualifying exam; comprehensive exam; dissertation; final oral exam. For Ph.D.: normally 60 quarter hours beyond master's, at least one year in residence; qualifying exam; dissertation; final oral exam.

FIELDS OF STUDY.
Applied Behavior Analysis. M.S.
Applied Educational Psychology. Includes school counseling, school psychology. M.S., C.A.G.S.
Audiology. M.S.
Biomedical Science. Includes general, pharmaceutics, toxicology. M.S.
Cardiopulmonary Science—Perfusion Technology. M.S.
Clinical Exercise Physiology. M.S.
College Student Development and Counseling. M.S.
Counseling Psychology. M.S., C.A.G.S., Ph.D.
Health Professions. Includes general, health policy, physician assistant, regulatory toxicology. M.H.P. only.
Hospital Pharmacy. M.S., Pharm.D.
Human Resource Counseling. M.S.
Intensive Special Needs. M.Ed.
Medical Laboratory Science. Includes clinical microbiology education management, hematology, immunahematology, immunology. M.S.

Medicinal Chemistry. M.S., Ph.D.
Pharmaceutics. Ph.D.
Pharmacology. M.S., Ph.D.
Rehabilitation Counseling. M.S., C.A.G.S.
Special Needs. M.Ed.
Speech-Language Pathology. M.S.
Toxicology. M.S., Ph.D.

Graduate School of Engineering

http://www.neu.edu/gradschool/engineering.html

Tuition: $415 per quarter hour. Enrollment: full-time 471, part-time 593. Faculty: full-time 106. Degrees conferred: M.S., M.S.C.E., M.S.C.S.E., M.S.E.E., M.S.E.M., M.S.I.E., M.S.I.S., M.S.M.E., M.S.O.R., Ph.D., E.Engr., I.Engr., M.Engr.

ADMISSION REQUIREMENTS. Transcripts, GRE, two letters of recommendation required in support of School's application. For Ph.D.: statement of purposes required. TOEFL required for international applicants. Accepts transfer applicants. Graduates of unaccredited colleges not considered. Apply to Graduate School Admissions Office by April 15. Rolling admissions process. Application fee $40. Phone: (617)373-2711; fax: (617)373-2501.

ADMISSION STANDARDS. Selective. Usual minimum average: 2.8 (A = 4).

FINANCIAL AID. Annual awards from institutional funds: 8 fellowships, 43 tuition assistantships, 83 teaching assistantships, 106 research assistantships, Federal W/S, loans. Approved for VA benefits. Apply by February 15 to appropriate department chair for fellowships, assistantships; to Financial Aid Office for all other programs. Use FAFSA. Phone: (617)373-3190. About 35% of students receive aid other than loans from School and outside sources. Aid available for part-time students.

DEGREE REQUIREMENTS. For master's: 40–48 quarter hours minimum, at least 28 in residence; thesis/nonthesis option in most programs. For Ph.D.: credit requirements vary; reading knowledge of one foreign language; qualifying exam; final written/oral exam; thesis; final oral exam.

FIELDS OF STUDY.
Chemical Engineering. Apply by April 15 for Ph.D.; one language for Ph.D. M.S., M.S.C.E., Ph.D.
Civil Engineering. Includes construction, environmental, geotechnical/geoenvironmental, public works engineering management, transportation; thesis option for M.S.; apply by April 15 for Ph.D. M.S., M.S.C.E., Ph.D.
Computer Systems Engineering. Includes CAD/CAM, engineering software design, robotics. M.S.C.S.E.
Electrical Engineering. Includes communications and signal processing, computer, control systems and signal processing, electromagnetics, plasma and optics, electronic circuits and semiconductor devices, power systems; thesis option for M.S.; apply by April 15 for Ph.D.; one language for Ph.D. M.S., M.S.E.E., Ph.D., E.Engr.
Engineering Management. Includes computer and information systems, manufacturing, operations research, quality control and reliability analysis; thesis for M.S.E.M.; M.S.E.M.
Industrial Engineering. Includes computer and information systems, manufacturing, operations research, quality control and reliability analysis; thesis for M.S., M.S.I.E.; apply by April 15 for Ph.D. M.S., M.S.I.E., Ph.D., I.Engr.
Information Systems. Thesis for M.S.I.S.; M.S.I.S.
Interdisciplinary Engineering. Ph.D. only.
Mechanical Engineering. Includes materials science and engineering, mechanics and design, thermofluids; thesis normally required for M.S.; apply by April 15 for Ph.D.; one language for Ph.D. M.S., M.S.M.E., Ph.D., M.Engr.
Operations Management. M.S.O.R. only.

School of Law (02117-0728)

Established 1968. Based on cooperative plan of legal education. Law library: 220,000 volumes. Library has LEXIS, NEXIS, WESTLAW, DIALOG.

Annual tuition: $20,150. No on-campus housing available. Total average annual additional expense: $12,000–$13,000.

Enrollment: first-year class 200; total full-time 830 (men 40%, women 60%). Faculty: full-time 32, part-time 30. Degrees conferred: J.D., J.D.-M.S. (Accounting), J.D.-M.B.A.

ADMISSION REQUIREMENTS. LSDAS Law School report, bachelor's degree, transcripts, LSAT required in support of application. Accepts transfer applicants. Graduates of unaccredited colleges not considered. Apply to Director of Admissions by March 1. Admits first-year students Fall only. Begin study in August. Application fee $55. Phone: (617)373-2395.

ADMISSION STANDARDS. Selective. Accepts about 25% of total annual applicants.

FINANCIAL AID. Full and partial tuition waivers, fellowships, assistantships, Federal W/S, loans. Apply to Director of Financial Aid by March 1. Use FAFSA. About 20% of students receive aid other than loans from School and outside sources.

DEGREE REQUIREMENTS. For J.D.: satisfactory completion of two year, ninemonth continuous coop program. Cooperative legal education program integral part of J.D. For M.B.A.: see Graduate School listing above.

NORTHERN ARIZONA UNIVERSITY
P.O. Box 4125
Flagstaff, Arizona 86011-4125
http://www.nau.edu

Founded 1899. Coed. State control. Semester system. Special facilities: Arizona Center for Research in Vocational Education, Arizona Earthquake Center, Bilby Research Center, Center for Colorado Plateau Studies, Center for Excellence in Education, Institute for Human Development, Center for Ecological Research, Center for Quaternary Studies. Library: 1,742,000 volumes, 336,000 microforms.

Annual tuition: full-time, resident $2009, nonresident $7100; per credit, $111, nonresident $320. On-campus housing with attractive options available for single students. Annual academic year housing costs: $3200. On-campus family housing limited (one year waiting list). Phone: (520)523-3978.

Graduate School

Enrollment: full-time 1500, part-time 4300. University faculty: full-time 550, part-time 200. Degrees conferred: M.A., M.A.T., M.Ed., M.B.A., M.M., M.P.A., M.P.T., M.V.E., M.S., M.S.N., Ph.D., Ed.D.

ADMISSION REQUIREMENTS: Transcripts, GRE/GMAT/MAT required in support of application. TOEFL required for international applicants. Accepts transfer applicants. Graduates of unaccredited institutions not considered. Apply to Director of Admissions by March 1. Application fee $35. Phone: (520)523-4348, (520)523-8950.

ADMISSION STANDARDS. Selective. Usual minimum average: 2.9 (A = 4).

FINANCIAL AID. Annual awards from institutional funds: One hundred academic scholarships, fifty administrative assistantships, one hundred research assistantships, one hundred teaching assistantships, Federal W/S, loans. Approved for VA benefits. Apply March 1 to department chair for assistantships; to Financial Aid Office for all other programs. Use FAFSA. Phone: (520)523-4951. Loans and part-time work available.

DEGREE REQUIREMENTS. For master's: Thesis Plan—32 hours including thesis or practicum; Comprehensive Examination Plan—33 hours plus written comprehensive exam; Extended Coursework Plan—36–45 hours, 8–10 hours of transfer credit may be accepted. For Ed.D.: 90 semester hours beyond bachelor's; residence requirement; dissertation; final oral exam. For Ph.D.: 75 semester hours, two semesters in full-time study; foreign language; dissertation; final oral exam.

FIELDS OF STUDY.
Anthropology.
Applied Linguistics. Ph.D.
Applied Sociology.
Biology. M.S., Ph.D.
Business Administration.
Chemistry.
Clinical Speech Pathology.
Counseling.
Criminal Justice.
Education. Includes elementary, secondary, bilingual/multicultural, early childhood, reading-learning disabilities, special education, administration and supervision, curriculum and instruction, usual subject fields.
English.
Forestry. M.S., Ph.D.
Geology.
History. M.A., Ph.D.
Mathematics.
Music.
Nursing.
Physical Education.
Physical Therapy.
Political Science. M.A., Ph.D.
Psychology.
Public Administration.
Quaternary Studies.
Rural Geography.
School Psychology.
Teaching English as a Second Language.
Vocational Education.

UNIVERSITY OF NORTHERN COLORADO
Greeley, Colorado 80639

Founded 1890. Located 50 miles N of Denver. Coed. State control. Semester system. Special facilities: Center for Educational Technology, Mathematics and Science Teaching Center, Laboratory School (K–12). Library: 942,000 volumes, 969,000 microforms, 4100 current periodicals.

Annual tuition: full-time, resident $2264, nonresident $8958. On-campus housing for 94 married students, 20 graduate men, 20 graduate women. Average academic year housing costs: $2000 (room only) for single students; $392 per month for married students; off-campus housing $400–$700 per month. Contact Director of Residence Life for both on- and off-campus housing information. Phone: (970)351-2721.

Graduate School

Graduate study since 1913. Enrollment: full-time 1100, part-time 372 (men 35%, women 65%). Graduate faculty: full-time 295, part-time 27. Degrees conferred: M.A., M.S., M.P.H., Ed.S., D.A., D.M.E., Ed.D., Psy.D., Ph.D.

ADMISSION REQUIREMENTS. Two transcripts, GRE, three letters of reference (Ed.S., D.A., Psy.D. applicants) required in support of School's application. TOEFL required for international applicants. Accepts transfer applicants. Graduates of unaccredited institutions not considered. Apply to Dean of Graduate School, preferably at least sixty days prior to registration. Application fee $35, $50 for international applicants. Phone: (800)776-GRAD, or (970)351-2831; fax: (970)351-2371.

ADMISSION STANDARDS. Selective. Usual minimum average 2.7, 3.0 for doctoral applicants (A = 4).

FINANCIAL AID. Annual awards from institutional funds: 99 fellowships, 276 teaching/graduate assistantships with stipend and partial/full tuition waiver, Federal W/S, loans. Approved for VA benefits. Apply by March 1 to appropriate department chair for fellowships, assistantships; to Financial Aid Office for all other programs. Phone: (970)351-2502. Use FAFSA. About 30% of students receive aid other than loans from University and outside sources. Limited aid for part-time students.

DEGREE REQUIREMENTS. For M.A., M.S.: 30 semester hours minimum; thesis or creative project/internship; comprehensive exams of capstone project. For Ed.S.: 30 semester hours beyond the master's; practicum report; final written exam. For Ph.D., Ed.D., D.A., D.M.E., Psy.D.: 64 semester hours minimum beyond the master's, at least 18 hours residence and two semesters in full-time attendance; dissertation; final written/oral exam. Ph.D. students must also demonstrate competency in using two research tools (foreign language, applied statistics, mathematical statistics, or computer languages/application).

FIELDS OF STUDY.
Agency Counseling. M.A.
Applied Statistics and Research Methods. M.S., Ph.D.
Biological Science. M.A.
Biological Sciences Education. Ph.D.
Chemical Education. Ph.D.
Chemistry. M.A.
College Student Personnel Administration. Ph.D.
Communication Disorders—Audiology. M.A.
Communication Disorders—Speech/Language Pathology. M.A.
Community Health Education. M.P.H.
Counseling Psychology. Psy.D.
Counselor Education. Ed.D.
Early Childhood Special Education. M.A.
Earth Sciences. M.A.
Educational Leadership. M.A., Ed.S., Ed.D.
Educational Mathematics. Ph.D.
Educational Psychology. M.A., Ph.D.
Educational Technology. M.A., Ph.D.
Elementary Education. M.A., Ed.D.
Elementary Education—Early Childhood Education. M.A., Ed.D.
Elementary Education—Middle School. M.A.
English. M.A.
Foreign Languages (Teaching). M.A.
Gerontology. M.A.
Human Rehabilitation. Ph.D.
Interdisciplinary Studies. M.A., Ed.S., D.A., Ed.D.
Mathematical Sciences. M.A., Ph.D.
Mathematics—Teaching. M.A.
Music. M.M., M.M.E., D.A., D.M.E.
Music Education. M.M.E., D.M.E.
Nursing. M.S.
Physical Education. M.A., Ed.D.
Psychology. M.A.
Reading. M.A., Ed.D.
Recreation. M.A.
Rehabilitation Counseling. M.A.
School Counseling. M.A.
School Psychology. Ed.S., Ph.D.

Secondary Science Teaching. M.A.
Social Sciences—Clinical Sociology. M.A.
Special Education. Includes moderate need, profound need, severe needs (affective, cognitive, communications, hearing vision). M.A., Ed.D.
Speech Communication. M.A.
Teaching Gifted and Talented. M.A.
Visual Arts. M.A.

NORTHERN ILLINOIS UNIVERSITY
De Kalb, Illinois 60115-2854

Founded 1895. Located 65 miles W of Chicago. Coed. State control. Semester system. Special facilities: Center for Black Studies, Center for Governmental Studies, Plant Molecular Biology Center, Regional History Center, Social Science Research Center, Center for Southeast Asian Studies, Library: 2,000,000 volumes.

Tuition: per credit, resident $130, nonresident $322. On-campus housing for 80 married students, 3400 single men, 3200 single women. Average academic year housing costs: $7862 (including board) for single students; $4000 for married students. Contact the Office of Housing Services for information on both on- and off-campus housing. Phone: (815)753-1525.

Graduate School

Graduate study since 1951. Enrollment: full-time 1676, part-time 4342. Graduate faculty: full-time 745, part-time 88. Degrees conferred: M.A., M.S., M.B.A., M.A.S., M.M., M.S.Ed., M.F.A., M.P.A., M.P.H., Ed.S., Performer's Certificate, Ed.D., Ph.D.

ADMISSION REQUIREMENTS. Transcripts, GRE (GMAT for business), two letters of recommendation for master's (three for doctorate) required in support of School's application. TOEFL required for applicants whose native language is not English; TSE for international applicants applying for teaching assistantships and M.A. program in Communication Studies. GRE Subject Test required by Department of Biological Sciences. Interview typically not required. Accepts transfer applicants. Graduates of unaccredited institutions not considered. Apply to Graduate School by June 1 (Fall), November 1 (Spring), April 1 (Summer); international applicant deadlines May 1 (Fall), October 1 (Spring). Application fee: $30. Phone: (815)753-0395; fax: (815)753-6366.

ADMISSION STANDARDS. Selective. Usual minimum average: 2.75 (A = 4).

FINANCIAL AID. Annual awards from institutional funds: 340 academic scholarships, 75 fellowships, 1200 assistantships, Federal W/S, loans. Approved for VA benefits. Apply to specific department for fellowships, assistantships; to Office of Financial Aid for all other programs. No specified closing date. Use FAFSA and institutional FAF. Phone: (815)753-1395; fax: (815)753-9475. Aid sometimes available for part-time students.

DEGREE REQUIREMENTS. For most M.A.'s, M.M., M.P.A., M.P.H., M.M., M.S., M.S.Ed.: 30 semester hours minimum; final comprehensive exam in most programs; some departments require thesis; some require a reading knowledge of one foreign language. For M.B.A., M.A.S.: 30 semester hours plus 0–18 hours of deficiencies; no thesis required. For M.F.A.: 60 semester hours beyond the bachelor's degree; qualifying exam; final written/oral exam; final individual show or project. For Ed.S.: 30 semester hours minimum beyond the master's; final written/oral exam. For Performer's Certificate: 24 semester hours; two public recitals. For Ed.D., Ph.D.: about 90 semester hours beyond the bachelor's degree; qualifying exam in some programs; candidacy exam; final oral exams; proficiency in foreign language/research tool for Ph.D.; dissertation.

FIELDS OF STUDY.
Accountancy. GMAT for admission. M.A.S.
Adult-Continuing Education. Thesis optional for M.S.Ed. M.S.Ed., Ed.D.
Allied Health Profession. See Public Health.
Anthropology. Thesis optional. M.A.
Applied Probability and Statistics. Thesis optional. M.S.
Art. Includes studio, art history, art education, art therapy; studio art M.A., M.F.A; one language, thesis for art history M.A., M.F.A.
Biochemistry and Biophysics. Interdepartmental.
Biological Sciences. GRE Subject Test in Biology for admission; thesis optional for M.S. M.S. Ph.D.
Business Administration. GMAT for admission; M.B.A.; joint M.B.A.-J.D.
Chemistry. Thesis required for M.S. M.S., Ph.D.
Communication Studies. Thesis optional. M.A.
Communicative Disorders. Includes speech language pathology, audiology, deafness rehabilitation counseling; thesis optional. M.A.
Community Health. See Public Health.
Computer Science. No thesis. M.S. only.
Counseling. Thesis optional for M.S.Ed. M.S.Ed., Ed.S., Ed.D.
Criminology. See Sociology.
Curriculum and Instruction. Thesis optional for M.S.Ed. M.S.Ed., Ed.S., Ed.D.
Curriculum and Supervision. Thesis optional for M.S.Ed. M.S.Ed., Ed.S., Ed.D.
Early Childhood Education. Thesis optional. M.S.Ed.
Economics. Thesis optional for M.A. M.A., Ph.D.
Educational Administration. Thesis optional for M.S.Ed. M.S.Ed., Ed.S., Ed.D.
Educational Psychology. Thesis optional for M.S.Ed. M.S.Ed., Ed.D.
Electrical Engineering. Thesis required; M.S.
Elementary Education. Thesis optional; M.S. Ed.
English. Thesis optional for M.A. M.A., Ph.D.
Family and Child Studies. See Human and Family Resources.
Finance. GMAT for admission; thesis optional. M.S.
Foreign Languages and Literatures. Includes French, Spanish; thesis optional. M.A.
Foundation of Education. Thesis optional. M.S. Ed.
Geography. Thesis optional. M.S.
Geology. Thesis optional for M.S. M.S., Ph.D.
Gerontology. Interdepartmental program.
Higher Education. Interdepartmental.
History. Thesis optional for M.A. M.A., Ph.D.
Human and Family Resources. Includes applied family and child studies; home economics, resources and services; marriage and family therapy; nutrition and dietetics; thesis optional. M.S.
Industrial Engineering. Thesis required. M.S.
Industrial Management. Thesis optional. M.S.
Instructional Technology. Thesis optional for M.S.Ed. M.S.Ed., Ed.D.
Law. Joint M.B.A.-J.D.
Management. See Business Administration.
Management Information Systems. M.S.
Marketing. See Business Administration.
Marriage and Family Therapy. See Human and Family Resources.
Mathematical Sciences. Thesis optional for M.S. M.S., Ph.D.
Mechanical Engineering. Thesis required. M.S.
Music. Includes music education, theory and composition, history and literature, performance and pedagogy; individualized major, thesis or recital required. M.M., Performer's Certificate.
Nursing. Thesis optional. M.S.
Nutrition and Dietetics. See Human and Family Resources.

Outdoor Teacher Education. Thesis optional. M.S.Ed.
Philosophy. Thesis optional. M.A.
Physical Education. Thesis optional. M.S.Ed.
Physics. Thesis optional. M.S.
Political Science. Includes public administration (M.P.A.); no thesis for M.P.A.; thesis optional for M.A. M.A., M.P.A., Ph.D.
Psychology. Thesis optional for M.A. M.A., Ph.D.
Public Administration. No thesis. M.P.A. only.
Public Health. Thesis optional. M.P.H. only.
Reading. Thesis optional for M.S.Ed. M.S.Ed., Ed.D.
School Business Management. Thesis optional. M.S.Ed.
Secondary Education. Thesis optional. M.S.Ed., Ed.S., Ed.D.
Sociology. Thesis optional. M.A.
Southeast Asian Studies. Interdepartmental.
Special Education. Thesis optional. M.S.Ed. only.
Speech Communication. For M.A. see Communication Studies.
Statistics. Thesis optional. M.S. only.
Theater Arts. Thesis optional. M.A., M.F.A.
Women's Studies. Interdepartmental.

College of Law (60115-2890)

Established 1975. Semester system. Library: 225,000 volumes. Library has LEXIS, WESTLAW, LIS.

Annual tuition: resident $4272, nonresident $8544. On-campus housing available. Total average annual additional expenses: $6500.

Enrollment: first-year class 110; total 327 (men 56%, women 44%). Faculty: full-time 33, part-time 10. Degrees conferred: J.D., J.D.-M.B.A.

ADMISSION REQUIREMENTS. LSDAS Law School report, bachelor's degree, transcripts, recommendation, LSAT required in support of application. Preference given to state residents. Graduates of unaccredited institutions not considered. Apply by June 1. Rolling admissions process. Application fee $35. Phone: (815)753-1420 or (815)753-9485.

ADMISSION STANDARDS. Selective. Admits about 30–35% of total annual applications.

FINANCIAL AID. Scholarships, grants, assistantships, loans. Apply by May 1 to Financial Aid Office. Use FAFSA. About 90% of students receive some aid from School.

DEGREE REQUIREMENTS. For J.D.: satisfactory completion of three-year program. For M.B.A.: see Graduate School listing above.

UNIVERSITY OF NORTHERN IOWA
Cedar Falls, Iowa 50614

Founded 1876. Located 96 miles NE of Des Moines. Coed. State control. Semester system. Special facilities: Iowa Teachers Conservation Camp, Iowa Lakeside Laboratory, Institute for Environmental Education. Library: 735,000 volumes, 690,000 microforms, 3030 current periodicals.

Annual tuition: full-time, resident $2932, nonresident $7230; per hour, resident $163, nonresident $402. On-campus housing for 365 married graduate students, limited for single graduate students. Average academic year housing costs: $2930 (including board) for single students; $2400 for married student apartments. Apply to Director of Housing for both on- and off-campus housing information. Phone: (319)273-2333.

The Graduate College

Graduate study since 1951. Enrollment: full-time 482, part-time 471 (men 35%, women 66%). Graduate faculty: full-time

410. Degrees conferred: M.A., M.A.Ed., M.M., M.B.A., M.S., Ed.S., D.I.T., Ed.D.

ADMISSION REQUIREMENTS. Official transcripts required in support of College's application. GRE/GMAT required for some programs. Interview not required. TOEFL required for international applicants. Accepts transfer applicants. Apply to Registrar by August 10 (Fall), January 15 (Spring). Rolling admissions process. Application fee $20, $30 for international applicants. Phone: (319)273-2748.

FINANCIAL AID. Annual awards from institutional funds: 150 scholarships, fellowships, assistantships, tuition waivers, Federal W/S, loans. Approved for VA benefits. Apply by March 1 to major department for fellowships, assistantships; to Financial Aid Office for all other aid. Phone: (319)273-2700. About 40% of students receive aid other than loans from College and outside sources. Aid sometimes available for part-time students.

DEGREE REQUIREMENTS. For master's: 30 or 32 semester hours minimum; qualifying exam; thesis/nonthesis option; final written exam for nonthesis plan. For Ed.S.: 30 hours minimum beyond the master's, at least 20 in residence and one semester or two Summer sessions in full-time attendance; final written exam often required; final oral exam. For Ed.D.: 60 semester hours minimum beyond the master's, at least 45 in residence; GRE required prior to starting dissertation; dissertation; final oral exam. For D.I.T.: 64 semester hours minimum beyond the master's, at least 52 in residence; GRE required prior to starting dissertation; dissertation; final oral exam.

FIELDS OF STUDY.
Art. Includes studio, education; final creative project optional. M.A.
Audiology. M.A.
Biology. M.A.
Business Administration.
Chemistry. M.A.
College/University Student Services. M.A.Ed.
Communication Studies. M.A.
Communications and Training Technology. M.A.Ed.
Composition. M.M.
Computer Science Education. M.A.
Conducting. M.M.
Counseling. M.A., Ed.D.
Curriculum and Instruction. M.A.Ed., Ed.D.
Early Childhood Education. M.A.Ed.
Education for the Gifted. M.A.Ed.
Educational Administration. Ed.D.
Educational Media. M.A.Ed.
Educational Psychology. M.A.Ed.
Elementary/Secondary Principalship. M.A.Ed.
English. M.A.
Environmental Science/Technology. M.S.
French. M.A.
Geography. M.A.
German. M.A.
Health Education. M.A.
History. M.A.
Industrial Technology. M.A., D.I.T.
Jazz Pedagogy. M.M.
Library Science. M.A.
Mathematics. M.A.
Mathematics for Elementary and Middle School. M.A.
Middle School/Junior High Education. M.A.
Music. M.M.
Music Education. M.M.
Music History. M.M.
Performance. M.M.
Physical Education. M.A.
Political Science. M.A.
Psychology. M.A.

Reading. M.A.Ed.
School Counseling. M.A.Ed.
School Psychology. Ed.S.
Science Education. M.A.
Sociology. M.A.
Spanish. M.A.
Special Education. M.A. Ed.
Two Languages. Includes French/German, Spanish/French, German/Spanish. M.A.
Youth Agency Administration. M.A.

SALMON P. CHASE COLLEGE OF LAW OF NORTHERN KENTUCKY UNIVERSITY
Highland Heights, Kentucky 41076

Established 1893. State control. Semester system. Law library: 233,500 volumes. Library has LEXIS, NEXIS, WESTLAW, DIALOG.

Annual tuition: resident $4728, nonresident $12,336. On-campus housing available. Total average annual additional expense: $3600–$10,800.

Enrollment: first-year class, full-time 90, part-time 30; total 340 (men 58%, women 42%). Faculty: full-time 20, part-time 27.

Degrees conferred: J.D., J.D.-M.B.A.

ADMISSION REQUIREMENTS. LSDAS Law School report, bachelor's degree, transcripts, LSAT required in support of application. Transfer applicants accepted. Preference given to state residents. Graduates of unaccredited colleges not considered. Apply to the Office of Admissions, after October 1, before May 15. Rolling admissions process. Application fee $25. Phone: (606)572-6476.

ADMISSION STANDARDS. Selective. Accepts about 25–30% of total annual applicants.

FINANCIAL AID. Scholarships, tuition waivers, Federal W/S, loans. Apply to Financial Aid Office of University by February 1. Use FAFSA.

DEGREE REQUIREMENTS. For J.D.: satisfactory completion of three-year (full-time) or four-year (part-time) program; 90 credit hour program.

NORTHERN MICHIGAN UNIVERSITY
Marquette, Michigan 49855-5301

Founded 1899. Located 300 miles N of Milwaukee. Coed. State control. Semester system. Library: 511,000 volumes, 574,000 microforms, 2500 current periodicals.

Tuition: per semester hour, resident $120, nonresident $171. On-campus housing for 3200 students, 200 apartments for married students. Average academic year housing costs: $3772 (room and board) for single students; $2202 for married students. Contact Director of Housing for both on- and off-campus housing information. Phone: (906)227-2622.

School of Graduate Studies

Graduate study since 1960. Enrollment: full-time 120, part-time 254. University faculty: full-time 98, part-time 7. Degrees conferred: M.A., M.A.Ed., M.M.E., M.P.A., M.S.

ADMISSION REQUIREMENTS. Official transcripts required in support of School's application. GRE required for all educa-

tion programs. TOEFL required for international applicants. Suggest international students allow one year to complete all application procedures. Accepts transfer applicants. Apply to Dean of Graduate Studies at least one month prior to entrance. Rolling admissions process. Application fee: $25. Phone: (906)227-2204.

ADMISSION STANDARDS. Selective. Usual minimum average: 2.5 (A = 4). May be higher for some departments.

FINANCIAL AID. Sixty-three graduate assistantships, tuition waivers, Federal W/S, loans. Approved for VA benefits. Apply by March 1 to Director of Financial Aid. Use FAFSA. Phone: (906)227-2327.

DEGREE REQUIREMENTS. For master's: 32 semester hours minimum, at least 28 in residence and one semester or one Summer session in full-time residence; thesis/nonthesis option/special project.

FIELDS OF STUDY.
Administration and Supervision.
Administrative Service.
Biology.
Chemistry.
Communication Disorders.
Community College Education.
Elementary Education.
English.
Exercise Science.
Health Education.
History.
Nursing.
Public Administration.
Secondary Education.
Special Education.

NORTHERN STATE UNIVERSITY
Aberdeen, South Dakota 57401-7198

Founded 1801. Located 288 miles W of Minneapolis. Coed. State control. Semester system. Library: 260,000 volumes, 92,600 microforms, 6 PCs.

Annual tuition: per hour, resident $78, nonresident $217. On-campus housing for 411 graduate men and 582 graduate women; none for married students. Annual academic year housing costs: $2600–$3185. Apply to Director of Student Housing. Phone: (605)626-3007.

Graduate Study

Graduate study since 1956. Enrollment: full-time 77, part-time 347; Summer, full-time 200. College faculty teaching graduate students: full-time 87. Degrees conferred: M.A.T., M.S. in Ed.

ADMISSION REQUIREMENTS. Transcripts required in support of application. GRE required for some programs. TOEFL required for international applicants. Accepts transfer applicants. Apply to Director of Graduate Studies at least two weeks prior to registration. Application fee $15. Phone: (605)626-2558; fax: (605)626-2542.

ADMISSION STANDARDS. Selective. Usual minimum average: 2.75 (A = 4).

FINANCIAL AID. Annual awards from institutional funds: fifteen graduate assistantships, Federal W/S, loans. Approved for VA benefits. Apply by March 1 to Director of Graduate Studies for assistantships; to Financial Aid Office for all other programs. Use FAFSA. Phone: (605)622-2640; fax: (605)626-3022.

DEGREE REQUIREMENTS. For master's: 24 semester hours minimum plus 6-hour thesis, or 27 semester hours and a 3-hour project paper, or 32 semester hours; final oral exam. Guidance and Counseling: 48-hour program.

FIELDS OF STUDY.
Art. M.A.T.
Business Education. M.A.T.
Elementary and Secondary Administration. M.S. in Ed.
Elementary and Secondary Education. M.S. in Ed.
English. M.A.T.
Guidance. Includes elementary and secondary; M.S. in Ed.; 48-credit program only.
Health, Physical Education, and Recreation. M.A.T.
Industrial Education. M.A.T.
Mathematics. M.A.T.
Natural Science. M.A.T.
Social Science. M.A.T.

NORTHWEST MISSOURI STATE UNIVERSITY

Maryville, Missouri 64468-6001

Founded 1905. Located 95 miles N of Kansas City. Coed. State control. Semester system. Special facilities: Alternative Crop Center, Biomass Applied Research Center, Institute for Quality Productivity, Poultry Compost Research Center. Library: 335,000 volumes, 689,000 microforms, 80 PCs in library.

Tuition: per credit hour, resident $102, nonresident $180. On-campus housing available for graduate students. Annual academic year housing costs; $900–$1100 (excluding board). Apply to Housing Office. Phone: (816)562-1363.

Graduate School

Enrollment: full-time, Summer 400, academic year 150; part-time, Summer 850, academic year 650 (men 40%, women 60%). Faculty teaching graduate students: full-time, Summer 30, academic year 118; part-time, Summer 40, academic year 100. Degrees conferred: M.A., M.S., M.S. in Ed., M.B.A., Ed.S.

ADMISSION REQUIREMENTS. Transcripts, GRE required in support of School's application. GMAT for M.B.A. applicants. TOEFL required for international applicants. Accepts transfer applicants. Graduates of unaccredited institutions not considered. Apply to Dean of Graduate School by July 1 (Fall), November 1 (Spring), April 1 (Summer). Application fee none. Phone: (816)562-1145.

ADMISSION STANDARDS. Relatively open. Usual minimum average: 2.5 (A = 4).

FINANCIAL AID. Annual awards from institutional funds: eighty-six assistantships, fifteen teaching assistantships, Federal W/S, loans. Approved for VA benefits. Apply by March 1 to Dean of the Graduate School for assistantships; to Director of Financial Aid for all other programs. Use FAFSA. Phone: (816)562-1363. About 10% of students receive aid other than loans from University and outside sources.

DEGREE REQUIREMENTS. For master's: 32 semester hours minimum, at least 24 in residence; thesis optional; final comprehensive exam; no language requirement. For Ed.S.: 32 credits beyond the master's, at least 24 in residence.

FIELDS OF STUDY.
Agriculture.
Biology.

Business.
Business Education.
Counseling Psychology.
Elementary School Administration and Supervision.
Elementary School Reading.
Elementary School Teaching.
English.
Guidance and Counseling.
Health and Physical Education.
History.
Science Education.
Secondary School Administration and Supervision.
Special Education. Includes mental retardation and learning disabilities.
Teaching.

NORTHWESTERN OKLAHOMA STATE UNIVERSITY

Alva, Oklahoma 73717-2799

Founded 1897. Located 150 miles NW of Oklahoma City. Coed. State control. Library: 217,000 volumes, 350,000 microfiche, 100,000 government documents, 26 PCs.

Tuition: per credit, resident $67, nonresident $162. On-campus housing available for graduate students. Average academic year housing costs: $1876 (including board). Apply to Housing Director. Phone: (405)327-8418.

Graduate School

Graduate study since 1954. Enrollment: full-time 12, part-time 112. College faculty: full-time 45, part-time 9. Degrees conferred: M.Ed., M.B.S.

ADMISSION REQUIREMENTS. Transcripts, GRE or MAT required in support of School's application. Interview not required. Accepts transfer applicants. Apply to Dean, Graduate School; no specified closing dates. Phone: (405)327-8410.

ADMISSION STANDARDS. Selective. Usual minimum average: 2.75 overall or 3.0 in last 60 hours (A = 4).

FINANCIAL AID. Limited to Oklahoma tuition grants, Federal W/S, loans. Apply to Director of Financial Aid; no specified closing date. Use FAFSA. Phone: (405)327-8542.

DEGREE REQUIREMENTS. For M.Ed.: 32 credit hours minimum, optional paper; final written/oral exam. For M.B.S.: 45 credits minimum; National Counselor Examination.

FIELDS OF STUDY.
Elementary Education.
Guidance and Counseling. Includes elementary and secondary.
Library Media Specialist.
Licensed Professional Counselor.
Reading Specialist.
School Psychometrist.
Secondary Education.

NORTHWESTERN STATE UNIVERSITY OF LOUISIANA

Natchitoches, Louisiana 71497

Founded 1884. Located 75 miles SW of Shreveport. Coed. State control. Semester system. Special facilities: Northwest

Louisiana Lignite Institute, Southern Studies Institute, Williamson Museum. Library: 296,000 volumes, 595,000 microforms, 15 PCs.

Annual tuition: full-time resident $2027, nonresident $4247. On-campus housing for 40 married students, 1000 men, 1240 women. Average academic year housing costs: $2000 for married students, $2216 (including board) for single students. Apply to Director of Housing. Phone: (318)357-6703. On-campus day care facilities available.

Graduate Studies and Research

Graduate work since 1954. Enrollment: full-time 248, part-time 655. Graduate faculty: full-time 61, part-time 27. Degrees conferred: M.A., M.B.A., M.Ed., M.S., M.M., M.M.Ed., M.S.N., Ed.S.

ADMISSION REQUIREMENTS. Transcripts, GRE required in support of application. GMAT required for Business. Interview not required. TOEFL required of international students. Accepts transfer applicants. Apply to Dean of Graduate School thirty days prior to registration. Application fee $5, foreign students $15. Phone: (318)357-6171; fax: (318)357-5823.

ADMISSION STANDARDS. Selective. Usual minimum average: 2.5 (A = 4).

FINANCIAL AID. Annual awards from institutional funds: eighty teaching assistantships, thirty service assistantships, five research assistantships, Federal W/S, loans. Approved for VA benefits. Apply by July 15 to appropriate department head for assistantships; to Financial Aid Office for all other programs. Use FAFSA. About 75% of full-time and 30% of all students receive aid other than loans from School and outside sources. Aid available for part-time students.

DEGREE REQUIREMENTS. For master's: 30 semester hours minimum including thesis, at least 24 in residence; final written exam. For M.A. in Ed., M.S. in Ed., M.M.Ed., M.Ed.: same as above, except student may elect 33 semester hour program and special research report instead of thesis. For M.B.A.: 36 semester hour program, at least 30 in residence. For Ed.S.: 60 hours minimum beyond the bachelor's degree; one semester or two consecutive summers of full-time residence; thesis.

FIELDS OF STUDY.
Art.
Business Administration. M.B.A.
Clinical Psychology.
Education. Includes elementary, early childhood, secondary, reading, administration, business, English, distributive, health, home economics, mathematics, reading, guidance, student personnel services, media, library.
Educational Technology.
English.
Health, Physical Education, and Recreation.
History.
Music. Includes applied, education, composition, theory.
Nursing.
Psychology.
Special Education.

NORTHWESTERN UNIVERSITY
Evanston, Illinois 60208

Founded 1851. Located 12 miles N of Chicago. Coed. Private control. Quarter system. Special facilities: Basic Industry Research Laboratory, Biomedical Engineering laboratory, Center for Experimental Animal Resources, Materials Science Research Center, Center for Mathematical Studies in Economic and

Management, Center for Urban Affairs and Policy, Vogelback Computing Center, Van de Graaff accelerator, cooperative arrangement with Argonne National Laboratory, Gas Dynamics Laboratory, Transportation Center. On the Chicago campus are the Medical School, School of Law, Dental School, Kellogg Graduate School of Management. Library: 3,900,000 volumes, 2,200,000 microforms, 28,000 current periodicals (both campuses), 200 PCs in all libraries.

Annual tuition: full-time $18,108, per course $2148. On-campus housing for limited number of graduate students. Average academic year housing costs: $6720 for married students, $4425 for single students. Apply to Director of Graduate Housing. Phone: (847)491-5127.

Graduate School

Graduate study since 1893. Enrollment: full-time 2538, part-time 204. Faculty: full- and part-time 248. Degrees conferred: M.A., M.E.M., M.S., M.F.A., Ph.D.

ADMISSION REQUIREMENTS. Transcripts, two letters of recommendation required in support of School's application. TOEFL required for international applicants. GRE required for financial aid applicants, recommended for admission; GRE or GMAT required for management. Interview required for some departments. Accepts transfer applicants, but no advanced standing toward master's degree. Apply to Admissions Office of the Graduate School at least four weeks prior to registration, by January 15 for financial aid consideration. Application fee $40, international students $45. Phone: (847)491-7264.

ADMISSION STANDARDS. Selective for most departments, very competitive for some.

FINANCIAL AID. Fifty traineeships, 554 research assistantships, 453 teaching, 308 academic fellowships, Federal W/S, loans. Apply by January 15 to Office of the Graduate School for scholarships, to appropriate chairperson for assistantships; to Financial Aid Office for all other programs. Use FAFSA. Phone: (847)491-7264. About 60% of students receive aid other than loans from University and outside sources. No aid for part-time students.

DEGREE REQUIREMENTS. For master's: equivalent of three quarters of full-time study; thesis required by many departments; no language requirement; final written/oral exam. For Ph.D.: equivalent of nine quarters of full-time study with at least three consecutive quarters in full-time study with at least three consecutive quarters in full-time attendance; qualifying exam; dissertation; final oral exam.

FIELDS OF STUDY.
Anthropology.
Art. Six full-time quarters for M.F.A.
Art History. M.A., Ph.D.
Art Theory.
Astronomy.
Biological Sciences. Includes biochemistry and molecular biology, cell biology, microbiology-immunology, neurobiology, physiology, tumor cell biology (offered at Evanston and Chicago campuses).
Chemistry. Includes biochemistry; one language for Ph.D.
Classics. Proficiency in Greek or Latin for M.A.; both Latin and Greek plus two modern languages for Ph.D.
Clinical Dentistry. At Dental School in Chicago; prosthodontics, endodontics, oral surgery, orthodontics, pediatric dentistry, periodontics, diagnosis and radiography, dental education; D.D.S. for admission; final research project for M.S.
Comparative Literature.
Economics. Elementary mathematics for Ph.D.

Education. Includes administration and policy studies, counseling psychology, teaching and learning processes, human development, social policy.

Engineering. Includes biomedical, biosolid mechanics, chemical, civil, electrical computer, computer sciences, electrical, environmental health, industrial, mechanical and nuclear, material science and engineering, structural transportation systems.

English. One or two languages for Ph.D.

French and Italian.

Geography.

Geological Sciences.

German Language and Literature. One language in addition to German for Ph.D.

Hispanic Studies.

History.

History and Literature of Religions. Thesis may be required for M.A.; one language for Ph.D.

Linguistics. One language for Ph.D.

Mathematics. Includes applied.

Medicine. Clinical; includes otolaryngology, head and neck, clinical psychology, physical therapy, radiology; thesis for M.S. in all fields; M.D. for admission to most majors.

Music. Ph.D. through the Graduate School; M.M., M.S.M., D.Mus. through the School of Music; degrees in education, history and literature, theory; two languages for Ph.D.

Neuroscience. Interdepartmental.

Philosophy. Two languages for Ph.D.

Physics and Astronomy.

Political Science.

Probability and Statistics. Interdepartmental.

Psychology. Admits to Ph.D. only, no terminal master's.

Religion. Includes history, literature. Offered in cooperation with the Garrett Theological Seminary; both B.A. and B.D. or equivalents for admission; one to four languages for Ph.D., depending upon specialization.

Slavic Languages and Literature.

Sociology.

Speech. Includes radio, television, and film; theater; learning disabilities; speech and language pathology; audiology and hearing impairment; communication studies; performance studies; theatre and drama, directing; stage design.

Statistics.

Telecommunication. Interdepartmental.

Transportation and Operations Analysis. Interdepartmental.

Medill School of Journalism

Evanston campus. Annual tuition: $21,644. Graduate enrollment: full-time 260 (men 45%, women 55%). School faculty: full-time 45, part-time 29. Degrees conferred: M.S.I.M.C., M.S.J.

ADMISSION REQUIREMENTS. Transcripts, three recommendations, five hundred-word autobiography, five hundred-word report on a news event or marketing campaign, news writing test clip of any published material (editorial candidates) required in support of School's application. GRE required for editorial applicants, GRE/GMAT required for integrated marketing communications applicants. TOEFL required for international applicants. Interview required for domestic I.M.C. applicants. Graduates of unaccredited colleges not considered. Apply to Office of Graduate Admissions by March 1. Application fee $50. Phone: (847)491-5228; fax: (847)467-1238.

ADMISSION STANDARDS. Competitive. Usual minimum average: 3.0 (A = 4).

FINANCIAL AID. Sixty-five scholarships, fellowships, Federal W/S, loans. Approved for VA benefits. Apply by February 1 to Office of Graduate Admissions. Use FAFSA and Medill's FAF.

Phone: (847)491-5228; fax: (847)467-2319. About 26% of students receive aid other than loans from School and outside sources.

DEGREE REQUIREMENTS. For M.S.J.: twelve month programs. For M.S.I.M.C.: fifteen month program; includes a summer residency.

FIELDS OF STUDY.

Advertising Management.

Broadcast Journalism.

Corporate Public Relations.

Direct Marketing.

Magazine Publishing.

Marketing Communications.

Newspaper Management.

Reporting and Writing.

J. L. Kellogg Graduate School of Management

Quarter system. Annual tuition: $23,022. Full-time program located on Evanston campus, part-time (evening) program on Chicago campus. On-campus housing for single, married students. Contact Assistant Director of Student Affairs for housing information. Phone: (708)491-3300.

Enrollment: full-time 1100, part-time 1300. Faculty: full-time 115, no part-time faculty. Degrees conferred: M.M., M.M. Manufacturing (combined program with School of Engineering). The Ph.D. is offered through the Graduate School.

ADMISSION REQUIREMENTS. Transcripts, GMAT, (GRE required for doctoral applicants) interview, letters of reference required in support of School's application. TOEFL required of international applicants. Transfer applicants not accepted. Apply to Office of Admissions by March 30 for M.M.; for Ph.D. by February 1. Admission June or September quarters only. Application fee $100. Phone: (708)491-3308; fax: (708)491-4960.

ADMISSION STANDARDS. Very selective. No minimum G.P.A. or GMAT required.

FINANCIAL AID. Annual awards are from government, institutional, and corporate funds, including minority fellowship. Apply by February 15 to Office of Admission. Use FAFSA. Phone: (708)491-3308. Ph.D. students who wish financial aid should apply by January 15; there are approximately 20 research assistantships. About 67% of students receive aid. Very little aid for part-time students.

DEGREE REQUIREMENTS. For M.M.: four quarters in residence, beginning in June, for AACSB-accredited business school graduates; six quarters in residence, beginning in September, for candidates other than graduates of accredited business schools. Evening M.M. program also available. For Ph.D., see Graduate School listing above.

FIELDS OF STUDY.

Accounting and Information Systems.

Decision Sciences.

Entrepreneurship and Innovation.

Finance.

Health Services Management.

Human Resources Management.

Industrial Relations.

Information Management.

International Business.

Management and Strategy.

Managerial Economics.

Marketing.

Operations Management.

Organizational Behavior.

Public and Nonprofit Management.
Quantitative Methods.
Real Estate.
Transportation Management.

School of Music

Annual tuition: full-time $18,100, per course $1509. On-campus housing is available for graduate students. Graduate enrollment 25 M.M., 15 post-master's certificate in performance, 20 D.M., 15 Ph.D. School of Music faculty: 16 full-time, none part-time. Degrees conferred: M.M., D.M., Ph.D. (The Ph.D. is offered by the Graduate School.)

ADMISSION REQUIREMENTS. Transcripts and two recommendations required in support of School's application. GRE required for Ph.D. applicants only. TOEFL required for international applicants. Accepts transfer applicants. For M.M.: audition or recording for performance majors, scores for composition majors, research papers for theory majors, music history and literature majors, essays for music education majors. For D.M.: theory and music history exams; interview and audition for performance majors; scores and tape recording of compositions for composition majors. Transfer credits for M.M. not accepted. Limited transfer credit for D.M. from an accredited college accepted. Apply to Office of Music Admission and Financial Aid; no specified closing date, early filing is given preference. Application $40. Phone: (847)491-3141; fax: (847)491-5260.

ADMISSION STANDARDS. Highly selective. Minimum usual average 3.0 (A = 4).

FINANCIAL AID. Annual awards from institutional funds: 150 grants, 3 fellowships, 120 graduate assistantships, Federal W/S, loans. Approved for VA benefits. Financial Aid application sent out after admissions application is received. Apply by January 15 for D.M., February 15 for M.M. applicants to Office of Admissions and Financial Aid. Use FAFSA and institutional FAF. About 80% of students receive aid other than loans from School of Music and outside sources. No aid is offered part-time students.

DEGREE REQUIREMENTS. For M.M.: 12 units minimum in residence; recital for performance and conducting majors; large composition for composition majors; comprehensive exams for music theory, music history, and music education majors; optional thesis or project for music education majors. For D.M.: 18 units minimum in residence, at least 9 units in full-time attendance; recitals-projects, lecture-recitals or document, depending on major; reading knowledge of one or two foreign languages, depending on major; qualifying exam; final oral exam.

FIELDS OF STUDY.
Music Education. M.M., Ph.D.
Musicology. M.M., Ph.D.
Music Technology. M.M.
Music Theory. M.M., Ph.D.
Performance. Includes conducting, jazz, voice, winds, percussion, strings, piano, organ. M.M., D.M., Certificate in performance.

School of Law

Founded 1859. Chicago campus (60611-3069). Semester system. Law library: 586,000 volumes. Library has LEXIS, NESTS, WESTLAW, CCH Access, DIALOG. Special facilities: Center for Urban Affairs and Research. Annual tuition: $21,316. On-campus housing available for both single and married students. Living expenses for single students: approximately $11,900.

Enrollment: first-year class 200; total 600 (men 56%, women 44%); postgraduates 9; no part-time study. Faculty: full-time 59, part-time 103. Degrees conferred: J.D., J.D.-M.M.(Management), J.D.-Ph.D.(Social Sciences), LL.M., J.S.D.

ADMISSION REQUIREMENTS. LSDAS Law School report, bachelor's degree, transcripts, LSAT (not later than December), two recommendations, personal statement required in support of application. Graduates of unaccredited colleges not considered. Apply after October 1, before February 1. Candidates for LL.M. and J.S.D. must submit two additional recommendations, but not the LSAT. Apply to Law School Office of Admissions preferably no later than February 1. Admits first-year students Fall only. Application fee $60 ($75 after February 1). Phone: (312)503-8465.

ADMISSION STANDARDS. Competitive. Accepts 20% of total annual applicants.

FINANCIAL AID. Scholarships, minority scholarships, research fellowships, teaching assistantships, Federal W/S, loans. Apply to Office of Admissions by March 15. Use FAFSA. About 60% of students receive aid other than loans from School. Loan Repayment Assistance Programs available.

DEGREE REQUIREMENTS. For J.D.: satisfactory completion of 86 semester hour program. For LL.M.: at least 24 credits beyond the J.D.; one year in full-time residence; thesis; final written/oral exam. For J.S.D.: at least one year in residence beyond the J.D., but more time normally required; thesis; final written/oral exam. Refer to Graduate School listings above for joint degree requirements.

Medical School

Founded 1859. Chicago campus (60611). Medical library: 250,000 volumes. Annual tuition: $26,592, student fees $720. Total average figure for all other expenses $9500.

Enrollment: first-year class 170 (EDP 5) (men 51%, women 49%), total 678. Faculty: more than 2200 full- and part-time. Degrees conferred: B.A.-M.D., B.S. (Engineering)-M.D., M.D., M.D.-M.M., M.D.-Ph.D., (Medical Scientist Training Program) M.P.H., M.D.-M.P.H. The M.M. (Kellogg Graduate School of Management) and Ph.D, are offered through the Graduate School.

ADMISSION REQUIREMENTS. AMCAS report, transcripts, two letters of recommendation, MCAT required in support of application. At least three years of premedical work required for admission. Has EDP; apply between June 15 and August 1. Interview required for all applicants under serious consideration. Accepts transfer applicants. Apply to Office of Admissions after June 15, before October 15. Application fee (after screening): $50. Phone: (312)503-8206.

ADMISSION STANDARDS. Very competitive. Accepts 3% of total annual applicants. Approximately 50% are state residents.

FINANCIAL AID. Scholarships, fellowships, loans. Apply to Financial Aid Committee after acceptance. Use FAFSA. MSTP funded by NIH. About 60% of students receive some aid from School.

DEGREE REQUIREMENTS. For B.A., B.S.-M.D.: satisfactory completion of seven-year program. For M.D.: satisfactory completion of four-year program. For M.M.: see J. L. Kellogg Graduate School of Management listing above. For M.P.H.: one year beyond M.D., in certain cases it can be accomplished during four-year M.D. program; see Graduate School listing above. For Ph.D., see the Graduate School listing above.

FIELDS OF GRADUATE STUDY.
Anatomy.
Biochemistry.

Biomedical Engineering.
Cell Biology
Immunology.
Management.
Microbiology.
Molecular Biology.
Neuroscience.
Pathology.
Pharmacology.
Physiology.
Public Health.

Dental School

Established in 1851. Chicago campus (60611-2909). Quarter system. Dental library: 40,000 volumes. Annual tuition: $24,894. On-campus housing available. Average academic year housing costs: $9540. Phone: (312)503-8514. Total average cost for all other first-year expenses: $3776.

Enrollment: first-year class 70 (men 65%, women 35%); total 112. Faculty: full-time 29, part-time 60. Degrees conferred: D.D.S., Certificates.

ADMISSION REQUIREMENTS. AADSAS, official transcripts, essay, three letters of references, DAT (not later than October) required in support of School's application. At least two years of college study required for admission. Interview highly recommended. Transfer from other dental schools is not encouraged. Apply to Office of Admissions and Records after June 1, before February 1. Admits Fall only; transfer applicants at beginning of the sophomore or junior year. Application fee $45. Phone: (312)503-8334; fax: (312)503-3831.

ADMISSION STANDARDS. Competitive. Accepts 10-15% of total annual applicants. Approximately 40% are state residents.

FINANCIAL AID. Scholarships, grants-in-aid, loans. Apply to Office of Financial Aid; no specified closing date. Phone: (312)503-8722. Use FAFSA. About 79% of students receive aid other than loans from School.

DEGREE REQUIREMENTS. For D.D.S.: satisfactory completion of forty-five-month program.

FIELDS OF GRADUATE STUDY.
Dental Education.
Endodontics.
Oral Dental Science.
Oral Pathology.
Oral Surgery.
Orthodontics.
Pediatric Dentistry.
Periodontics.
Prosthodontics.

COLLEGE OF NOTRE DAME
Belmont, California 94002-1997

Established 1851. Located 25 miles S of San Francisco. Coed. Private control. Roman Catholic affiliation. 4-4-4 system. Library: 108,000 volumes, 16,000 microforms, 550 current periodicals.

Tuition: per credit $423. On-campus housing available. Annual cost: $7500. Contact Director of Housing for both on- and off-campus housing information. Phone: (415)508-3513.

Graduate Study

Enrollment: full-time 253, part-time 508 (men 215, women 546). College faculty: full-time 17, part-time 82. Degrees con-

ferred: M.A., Eng.M.A.T., M.M., M.Ed., M.B.A., M.P.A., M.A.-A.T.; M.A.-C.P, M.S.S.M., M.A.-Geron.

ADMISSION REQUIREMENTS. Official transcripts, GMAT (business), three letters of recommendations required in support of application. Interview required for some programs. TOEFL required for international applicants. Accepts transfer applicants. Graduates of unaccredited colleges not considered. Apply to Graduate Office at least one month prior to date of registration. Rolling admissions process. Application fee $50. Phone: (415)508-3523.

ADMISSION STANDARDS. Selective. Usual minimum average: 2.5 (A = 4).

FINANCIAL AID. Limited scholarships, Federal W/S, loans. Apply to Director of Financial Aid; no specified closing date. Use FAFSA. Phone: (415)508-3580.

DEGREE REQUIREMENTS. For master's: 30 credits minimum, at least 24 in residence; thesis/nonthesis option.

FIELDS OF STUDY.
Art Therapy.
Business Administration.
Counseling Psychology.
Education. Includes elementary, multicultural, secondary, Montessori theory, educational administration, teaching of art, English, French, social science, biology, music, and religious studies.
English.
Gerontology.
Music. Includes pedagogy, performance.
Public Administration.
Systems Management.

UNIVERSITY OF NOTRE DAME
Notre Dame, Indiana 46556
http://www.nd.edu

Founded 1842. Located 80 miles SE of Chicago. Coed on graduate level. Private control. Roman Catholic affiliation. Semester system. Library: 2,000,000 volumes, 1,471,000 microforms, 100 PCs in all libraries. Special facilities: Center for Applied Mathematics, Center for Bioengineering and Pollution Control, Computing Center with IBM 3033 (16-megabyte memory) system with peripheral equipment, Center for the Study of Contemporary Society, Hessert Center for Aerospace Research, Institute for Pastoral Liturgy, Joan B. Kroc Institute of International Peace Studies, Helen Kellog Institute for International Studies, Lobund Laboratory (germfree life equipment), Radiation Laboratory, Medieval Institute Library, Center for the Study of Man in Contemporary Society, new Graduate Student Housing Faculty. Day care facilities available.

Annual tuition: full-time $18,700, per credit $1039. On-campus housing for 132 married students and 253 single students. Average academic year housing cost: $5000 for married students, $3750 (including board) for single students. Apply to Director of Student Residences. Phone: (219)631-5878.

Graduate School

Organized 1918. Enrollment: full-time 1395, part-time 100. University faculty: 1193. Degrees conferred: M.A., M.B.A., M.S., M.Div., M.F.A., M.M., M.Arch., M.M.S., Ph.D.

ADMISSION REQUIREMENTS. Transcripts, three letters of recommendation, GRE Subject Tests required in support of

School's application. TOEFL required for international applicants. Interview not required. Accepts transfer applicants. Graduates of unaccredited institutions not considered. Apply to Director of Graduate Admissions, preferably by February 1. New students normally begin Fall only. Application fee $50. Phone: (219)631-7706; fax: (219)239-6630.

ADMISSION STANDARDS. Selective for most departments. Usual minimum average: 3.0 in area of concentration (A = 4).

FINANCIAL AID. Annual awards from institutional funds: 550 scholarships, 440 teaching assistantships, 70 research assistantships, 40 fellowships, Federal W/S, loans. Apply to Director of Graduate Admissions by February 1. Use FAFSA. Phone: (219)631-6436. About 85% of students receive aid other than loans from University and outside sources. No aid for part-time students.

DEGREE REQUIREMENTS. Degree programs are all determined by departmental advisement. The following are illustrative degree programs. For M.A., M.S.: Plan I—30 semester hours minimum; thesis (6 semester boom), final written/oral exam; Plan II—30 semester hours minimum; no thesis or language requirement; normally a terminal degree. For M.A. (Art): 32 semester hours minimum; final portfolio and essay. For M.B.A.: 60 semester hours minimum in residence. For M.F.A.: 60 semester boom minimum; final portfolio; studio thesis. For M.M.: 36 semester hours minimum; final music project. For M.M.S.: 38 semester hours minimum and knowledge of Latin required for entrance. For M.Div.: 72 semester hours. For Ph.D.: 72 semester hours, at least one year in full-time residence; candidacy exam; dissertation; defense of dissertation.

FIELDS OF STUDY.
Aerospace—Mechanical Engineering.
American Studies. Interdepartmental; master's only.
Architecture. M.Arch. only.
Art. M.F.A. and master's.
Biochemistry and Biophysics. Interdisciplinary.
Biological Sciences.
Chemical Engineering.
Chemical Physics. Interdisciplinary.
Chemistry.
Civil Engineering.
Computer Science and Engineering.
Economics.
Electrical Engineering.
English.
German Language and Literature. Master's only.
Government and International Studies.
History.
History and Philosophy of Science.
Mathematics.
Medieval Studies.
Music. Master's only.
Peace Studies. Master's only.
Philosophy.
Physics.
Romance Languages and Literature. Master's only.
Sociology.
Theology.

Law School (46556-0959)

Established 1869. Semester system. Library: 340,000 volumes. Library has LEXIS, NEXIS, VU/Text, DIALOG, WESTLAW. Special facilities: Center for Civil and Human Rights, Thomas J. White Center on Law and Government.

Annual tuition: $19,400. On-campus housing available. Apply to University Housing Office. Total average annual additional expenses: $6500.

Enrollment: first-year class 205, total full-time 597 (men 60%, women 40%). Faculty: full-time 24, part-time 25. Degrees conferred: J.D., J.D.-M.B.A., LL.M. (Comparative and International Law), J.S.D.

ADMISSION REQUIREMENTS. LSDAS Law School report, bachelor's degree, transcripts, LSAT required in support of application. Interview usually not required. Accepts transfer applicants. Apply to the Director of Admission for the School after September 1, before April 1. Application fee $45. Phone: (219)631-6626; fax: (219)631-7371.

ADMISSION STANDARDS. Selective. Accepts 20% of total annual applicants.

FINANCIAL AID. Scholarships, fellowships, resident assistantships, Federal W/S, loans. Apply to the Financial Aid Office by April 1. Use FAFSA. About 20% of students receive aid other than loans from School.

DEGREE REQUIREMENTS. For J.D.: satisfactory completion of three-year program. For LL.M., J.S.D.: at least 24 credit hours beyond the J.D.; thesis; for J.S.D. one year in full-time study and a final written/oral exam. For M.B.A., see Graduate School listing above.
Note: Academic year and summer program in London for J.D. candidates.

NOVA SOUTHEASTERN UNIVERSITY
Fort Lauderdale, Florida 33314-7721

Chartered 1964. Merged with Southeastern University of Health Sciences in 1994. Offers degree programs throughout United States and four foreign countries. Coed. Private control. Special facilities: Family Center for Child Development, Institute for Marine and Coastal Studies, Institute for Social Services to Families, Center for Youth Policy. Library: 224,000 volumes, 524,000 microforms, 6500 current periodicals, 88 PCs.

Tuition: per credit $225–$525, varies by program. On-campus housing for married and single graduate students. Average academic year housing costs: $6142 (including board), $4280 for married students. Contact Director of Residential Life for both on- and off-campus housing information. Phone: (305)475-7052.

Graduate Programs

Enrollment: full-time 2854, part-time 5610. Faculty: full-time 290, part-time 569. Degrees conferred: M.S., M.B.A., M.P.A., M.Acc, M.C.C.A., M.A., M.I.B.A., M.O.T., M.P.T., M.P.H., D.I.B.A., Sc.D., Psy.D., D.S., D.A., D.P.A., D.O.T., Ed.S., Ed.D., Ph.D., D.B.A.

ADMISSION REQUIREMENTS. Official transcripts, letters of recommendation required in support of application. GRE Subject Tests, GMAT required for some programs. Accepts transfer applicants. Graduates of unaccredited institutions not considered. Apply to Office of Admissions for the program of interest, or the Registrar's Office. Closing date varies with the program; rolling admissions for most programs. Application fee $40. Phone: (800)541-6682, or (305)475-7400.

ADMISSION STANDARDS. Selective. Usual minimum average: 3.0 (A = 4).

FINANCIAL AID. Scholarships, research fellowships, research assistantships, Federal W/S, loans. Approved for VA benefits. Apply to appropriate department for fellowships/assistantships; to Financial Aid Office for all other programs. Use FAFSA. Phone: (800)541-6682. About 20% of students receive aid other than loans from both University and outside sources.

DEGREE REQUIREMENTS. For master's: generally 36–45 hours minimum, varies with program; thesis/nonthesis option. For Ed.S.: 36 hours beyond the master's. For doctorate: satisfactory completion of core instructional sequence, areas of specialization and research experiences; dissertation; final exam. Residence requirements: varies with program; Ph.D. and other doctoral programs require three to four years.

FIELDS OF STUDY.
Accounting. M.Acc., Ph.D.
Adult Education. Ed.D.
Business Administration. M.B.A.
Child and Youth Administration. M.S.
Child and Youth Studies. Ed.D.
Child-Care Administration. M.S.
Clinical Psychology. Psy.D.
Coastal Zone Administration. M.S.
Computer Information Systems. M.S., Ph.D.
Computer Sciences. M.S., Ph.D.
Computer Technology in Education. M.S., Ed.D., Ph.D.
Computing and Information Technology. Ed.D.
Dispute Resolution. M.S., Ph.D.
Educational Leadership. M.S., Ed.D.
Educational Media. M.S.
Elder-Care Administration. M.S.
Elementary Education. M.S., Ed.S.
Exceptional Child Education. M.S., Ed.S.
Family Support Studies. M.S.
Family Therapy. M.S., Ph.D.
Finance. Ph.D.
Financial Services Management. M.F.S.M.
Health-Care Education. Ed.D.
Health Service Administration. M.S., Ph.D.
Higher Education. Ed.D.
Human Resources Management. M.S., Ph.D.
Human Services. M.S.
Information Systems and Science. Ph.D.
International Business. M.I.B.A.
International Management. Ph.D.
Management Information Systems. M.S.
Marine Biology. M.S.
Marketing. Ph.D.
Medical Management. M.S.
Mental Health Counseling. M.S.
Occupational Therapy. M.O.T., D.O.T.
Oceanography. Ph.D.
Physical Therapy. M.P.T.
Psychology. Ph.D.
Public Health. M.P.A.
Public Policy and Administration. M.P.A., D.P.A.
School Guidance and Counseling. M.S.
Secondary Education. M.S.
Special Education. M.S., Ed.S.
Speech and Language Pathology. M.S.
Teacher Education. Includes seventeen majors. M.S.
Teaching English as a Second Language. M.S.
Vocational, Technical, and Occupational Education. Ed.D.

Shepard Broad Law Center (33315)

Established 1974. Semester system. Library: 268,000 volumes. Library has LEXIS, NEXIS, WESTLAW, DIALOG, CALI. Special facilities: Disability Law Institute, Center for the Study of Youth Policy.

Annual tuition: full-time $17,990, part-time $14,500. On-campus housing available. Total average annual additional expense: $7000–$12,000.

Enrollment: first-year class 250; total full- and part-time 940 (men 60%, women 40%). Faculty: full-time 42, part-time 52. Degree conferred: J.D., J.D.-M.B.A., J.D.-M.S.(Psychology), J.D.-M.U.R.P.

ADMISSION REQUIREMENTS. LSDAS Law School report, bachelor's degree, transcripts, LSAT, personal statement required in support of application. Accepts transfer students. Apply to Office of Admissions by March 1. Rolling admissions process. Application fee $45. Phone: (305)451-6117.

ADMISSION STANDARDS. Selective. Admits about 30–35% of total annual applications.

FINANCIAL AID. Scholarships, grants, partial tuition waivers, assistantships, Federal W/S, loans. Apply to the Financial Aid Office by April 1. Use FAFSA. About 50% of students receive some aid from School.

DEGREE REQUIREMENTS. For J.D.: satisfactory completion of 87 credit hour program. For master's degrees, see Graduate School listing above.

College of Osteopathic Medicine

Founded 1979. Coed. Private control. Semester system. Library: 35,000 volumes, 480 current periodicals, has MEDLINE, CANCERLINE, BIOETHIC, HEALTH, TOXLINE, DIALOG, OCLC.

Annual tuition: in-state $16,850, out-of-state $21,250. Enrollment: first-year class 140, total 528 (men 70%, women 30%). Faculty: full-time 45, part-time 145. Degree conferred: D.O.

ADMISSION REQUIREMENTS. AACOMAS report, bachelor's degree, official transcripts, MCAT (no later than the Spring of junior year), three recommendations (one from premed advisory committee, one evaluation from a physician, preferably a D.O.), supplemental form required in support of application. Interview by invitation only. Graduates of unaccredited colleges not considered. Preference given to state residents. Apply by February 1 to the Director of Admissions. Rolling admissions process. Admits first year students Fall only. Application fee $50. Phone: (305)949-4000, ext. 1110.

ADMISSION STANDARDS. Selective. Accepts approximately 15% of total annual applicants. Usual minimum average: 2.75 (A = 4). Mean GPA: 3.1.

FINANCIAL AID. Scholarships, fellowships, Federal W/S, loans. Apply by April 1 to the Financial Aid Office. Use FAFSA and institutional FAF.

DEGREE REQUIREMENT. For D.O.: satisfactory completion of four-year program.

OAKLAND UNIVERSITY
Rochester, Michigan 48309-4401

Founded 1957. Located 25 miles N of Detroit. Coed. State control. Trimester system. Special facilities: Eye Research Institute, Biochemistry and Biotechnology Institute. Library: 593,000 volumes, 1,016,000 microforms, 2000 current periodicals, 350 PCs.

Annual tuition: full-time resident $3600, nonresident $7992; per credit, resident $200, nonresident $444. On-campus housing for graduate men and women, 48 units for married students. Average academic year housing costs: $4304 (including board) for single students; $4560 for married students. Contact Director, Residence Halls for both on- and off-campus housing information. Phone: (810)370-3570.

Graduate Studies

Enrollment: full-time 613, part-time 1907 (men 40%, women 60%). University faculty: full-time 286, part-time 36. Degrees conferred: M.A., M.Ed., M.S., M.A.T., M.M., M.P.A., M.P.T., M.B.A., M.S.N., Ed.S., Ph.D.

ADMISSION REQUIREMENTS. Official transcripts, two recommendations required in support of application. GRE/GMAT required for some programs. Interview not required. TOEFL and GRE required for international applicants. Accepts transfer applicants. Apply to Office of Admission by July 15 (Fall), November 20 (Winter), April 4 (Spring), May 15 (Summer). Application fee $30. Phone: (810)370-3168.

ADMISSION STANDARDS. Selective for some departments, competitive for others. Usual minimum average: 3.0 (A = 4).

FINANCIAL AID. Annual awards from institutional funds: teaching assistantships, research assistantships, full tuition waivers, Federal W/S, loans. Apply to appropriate department chairman by March 15. Use FAFSA and University's FAF. Phone: (810)370-3370. About 10% of students receive aid other than loans from University and outside sources. Aid sometimes available to part-time students.

DEGREE REQUIREMENTS. For master's: 36–45 semester hours minimum, at least 30 in residence; candidacy; thesis/nonthesis option. For Ed.S.: 30 semester hours beyond master's. For Ph.D.: 60 credits beyond the bachelor's minimum, at least one year in full-time residence; proficiency in at least one foreign language for some programs; qualifying exam; dissertation; final oral exam.

FIELDS OF STUDY.
Accounting. M.S.
Biological Sciences. M.S., Ph.D.
Biomedical Sciences. Includes cellular biology, health and environmental chemistry, medical physics. Ph.D.
Business Administration. M.B.A.
Cellular Biology. M.S., Ph.D.
Chemistry. M.S., Ph.D.
Computer Education. M.Ed.
Computer Science and Engineering. M.S.
Counseling. M.A.
Curriculum, Instruction, and Leadership. M.Ed.
Early Childhood. M.Ed.
Educational Administration. Ed.S.
Electrical and Computer Engineering. M.S.
Engineering Management. M.S.
English. M.A.
History. M.A.
Linguistics. M.A.
Mathematics. Includes applied and statistics. M.S., M.A.
Mechanical Engineering. M.S.
Music. M.M.
Nursing. M.S.N.
Physical Therapy. M.P.T.
Physics. M.S., Ph.D.
Public Administration. M.P.A.
Reading Instruction. M.A.T., Ph.D.
School Administration. Ed.S.
Special Education. M.Ed.
Systems Engineering. M.S., Ph.D.

OCCIDENTAL COLLEGE
Los Angeles, California 90041-3392

Founded 1887. Coed. Private control. Semester system. Library: 500,000 volumes, 200,000 microforms.

Annual tuition: full-time $19,406; part-time, per unit $675. No on-campus housing for graduate students. Contact Residence Life Office for off-campus housing information. Phone: (213)259-2531.

Graduate Study

Enrollment: full-time 17 (men 8, women 9). College faculty: full-time 134, part-time 50. Degrees conferred: M.A., M.A.T.

ADMISSION REQUIREMENTS. Official transcripts, three recommendations, GRE required in support of application. GRE Subject Test required for some majors. TOEFL and GRE required for international applicants. Interview not required. Does not accept transfer applicants. Graduates of unaccredited institutions not considered. Apply to Graduate Office by March 1 (Fall), October 1 (Spring), March 1 (Summer). Application fee $30. Phone: (213)259-2921.

ADMISSION STANDARDS. Selective. Usual minimum average: 3.0 (A = 4), minimum TOEFL score 625.

FINANCIAL AID. Limited to Federal W/S, loans. Apply by March 1 to Financial Aid Office. Use FAFSA and institutional FAF. Phone: (213)259-2548. About 90% of students receive aid other than loans from College and outside sources. Aid sometimes available for part-time students.

DEGREE REQUIREMENTS. For M.A., M.A.T.: a minimum of 6 courses (30 units) including thesis, internships, or creative project, final written/oral exam.

FIELDS OF STUDY.
Biology. Thesis for M.A.; M.A. only.
Elementary Education. M.A.T. only.
Secondary Education. M.A.T. only.

OGLETHORPE UNIVERSITY
Atlanta, Georgia 30319-2797

Founded 1835. Coed. Private control. Semester system. Library: 150,000 volumes, 752 current periodicals, 12 PCs.
Tuition: $460 per course. On-campus housing for single students only. Average academic year housing costs: $4040 (including board). Contact Housing office for both on- and off-campus housing information. Phone: (404)261-1441.

Graduate Study

Graduate study since 1971. Enrollment: full- and part-time 59 (men 5%, women 95%). Faculty: full-time 4, part-time 5. Degree conferred: M.A.

ADMISSION REQUIREMENTS. Transcripts, GRE/MAT/NTE, two recommendations required in support of application. TOEFL required for international applicants. Accepts transfer applicants. Graduates of unaccredited colleges not considered. Apply to Director of Graduate Studies by mid-April (Summer), 15 days prior to other semesters. Rolling admissions process. Application fee $25. Phone: (404)364-8307.

ADMISSION STANDARDS. Selective. Usual minimum average: 2.8 (A = 4).

FINANCIAL AID. Limited to loans.

DEGREE REQUIREMENTS. For M.A.: 36 semester hours minimum, at least 30 in residence; comprehensive final exam.

FIELD OF STUDY.
Elementary Education. Concentrations in early childhood (K–4), or middle grades (4–8).

OHIO NORTHERN UNIVERSITY
Ada, Ohio 45810-1599

Founded 1885. Located 85 miles SE of Toledo. Private control. Methodist affiliation. Semester system. Special facilities: Pharmacy Law Institute.

Claude W. Pettit College of Law

Established 1884. Law library: 235,000, volumes. Library has LEXIS, NEXIS, WESTLAW.

Annual tuition: $18,200. On-campus housing available. Total average annual additional expense: $7000.

Enrollment: first-year class 138; total 366 (men 65%, women 35%); no part-time students. College faculty: full time 25, part-time 14. Degree conferred: J.D.

ADMISSION REQUIREMENTS. LSDAS Law School report, bachelor's degree, transcripts, four character references, LSAT required in support of application. Interview not required. Accepts transfer applicants. Graduates of unaccredited colleges not considered. Apply to Director of Admissions, preference given to applications received by March 15. Rolling admissions process. Admits first-year students in Fall only. Application fee $40. Phone: (419)772-2211.

ADMISSION STANDARDS. Selective. Accepts 40–45% of total annual applicants.

FINANCIAL AID. Scholarships, need-based grants, assistantships, Federal W/S, loans. Apply to Financial Aid Office, by March 15. Use FAFSA. About 15% of students receive aid other than loans from College.

DEGREE REQUIREMENTS. For J.D.: satisfactory completion of required 87 semester hour program.
Note: Exchange program with the University of Iceland.

THE OHIO STATE UNIVERSITY
Columbus, Ohio 43210
http://www.gradsch.ohio-state.edu

Established 1870. Coed. State control. Quarter system. Special facilities: Advanced Computing Center for the Arts and Design, Center for Advanced Study in Telecommunication, Atmospheric Sciences Program, Ohio State Biochemistry Program, Laboratory for Artificial Intelligence Research, Biomedical Engineering Center, Biostatistics Program, Byrd Polar Research Center, Campus Chemical Instrument Center, Chemical Physics Program, Center for Cognitive Science, Criminal Justice Research Center, Electroscience Laboratory, Engineering Research Center for Net Shape Manufacturing, Environmental Biology Program, Center for Human Resource Research, International Area Studies, Center for Lake Erie Area Research, Center for Mapping, Center for Materials Research, Center for Medieval and Renaissance Studies, Mershon Center for Research and Education in National Security and Public Policy, Molecular, Cellular, and Developmental Biology Program, National Regulatory Research Institute, OSU Comprehensive Cancer Center, OSU Nisonger Center for Mental

Retardation and Developmental Disabilities, Ohio Supercomputer Center, Physiological Optics Program, Slavic and East European Studies Program, Comprehensive Program in Vocational Education, Water Resources Center. Library: 4,517,095 volumes, 3,380,000 microforms, 126 PCs in all libraries.

Annual tuition: full-time, resident $4707, nonresident $12,222. On-campus housing for 396 married students, 890 single students. Average annual housing cost: $4755 (including board) for single students. Apply to the Office of Contracts and Assignments. Phone: (614)292-8266.

Graduate School

Graduate study since 1878. Enrollment; full-time 7278, part-time 3116. Graduate faculty: 2877. Degrees conferred: M.Appl.Stat., M.Arch., M.A., M.B.A., M.C.R.P., M.Ed., M.F.A., M.H.A., M.L.H.R., M.Land.Arch., M.Mus., M.P.A., M.P.H., M.S., M.S.W., D.M.A., Ph.D., Cert.Sp'l., Edu'l.Adm., Cert.Sp'.I.L.Am.S., Cert.Sp'l. (Russian Area Studies), Cert.Sp'l. (Medieval and Renaissance Studies).

ADMISSION REQUIREMENTS. Transcripts, three letters of recommendation, autobiography required in support of School's application. Additional items may be required by individual departments. GRE Subject Tests for most departments. GMAT required for some departments. Interview required by some departments. Evidence of proficiency in English required of international applicants. Accepts transfer applicants. Graduates of unaccredited institutions not considered. Apply to Admissions Office by August 15 (Autumn), December 1 (Winter), March 1 (Spring), May 1 (Summer); prior to February 1 if a fellowship applicant. Application fee $30; international applicants $40. Phone: (614)292-5995; fax: (614)292-4818.

ADMISSION STANDARDS. Very competitive for some departments, competitive for the others. Minimum average required (unless otherwise specified by individual graduate program): 2.7 (A = 4).

FINANCIAL AID. Annual awards from institutional funds: 250 fellowships, 1750 research associateships, 395 administrative associateships, 2323 teaching associateships, Federal W/S, loans. Apply before February 1 (prior to the intended academic year of enrollment) to Admissions Office for fellowships; by April 1 to appropriate department chair for associateships; to Office of Financial Aid for all other programs. Use FAFSA. Phone: (614)292-0300; fax: (614)292-9264. About 47% of students receive aid other than loans from institution and outside sources. Aid sometimes available to part-time students.

DEGREE REQUIREMENTS. For master's: 45 quarter hours minimum, at least 36 in residence; either a thesis and an oral and/or written exam or a four-hour written comprehensive exam which may include an oral portion. For Ph.D.: 135 quarter hours minimum beyond the bachelor's degree, at least one full-time year in residence; foreign language requirement for some departments; general comprehensive exam; dissertation; final oral exam. For D.M.A.: essentially the same as for Ph.D., except a D.M.A. document and performance for some areas.

FIELDS OF STUDY.
Accounting and Management Information Systems. GMAT and additional requirements for admission; contact department for additional materials. M.A., Ph.D.
Aeronautical and Astronautical Engineering. GRE required for admission, additional department materials required; contact department. Admits primarily for Autumn quarter, apply by January 15. M.S., Ph.D.
Agricultural Economics and Rural Sociology. GRE or GMAT required for admission, GRE required for fellowship applicants.

Agricultural Education. Includes rural sociology (50-hour M.S., if nonthesis); GRE/GMAT required for admission. M.S., Ph.D.

Agricultural Engineering. GRE Subject Test strongly recommended. Fifty-hour M.S., if nonthesis.

Agronomy. GRE required for admission. M.S., Ph.D.

Allied Medical Professions. GRE required for all applicants whose GPA is below 3.5. Health professions certification, registration, or licensure required. M.S. only.

Anatomy. GRE Subject Test in Biology required for admission. M.S., Ph.D.

Animal Science. GRE required for admission. Thesis for M.S. M.S., Ph.D.

Anthropology. GRE required for admission. Prefer Autumn quarter applicants.

Architecture. Admits Autumn quarter only. Applicants for three-year plus (90 hour) program admitted Summer quarter. GRE, portfolio required for admission. Thesis (45 hour program)/nonthesis (50 hours).

Art. Admits Autumn quarter only. Application completed by January 20. For additional admission requirements contact department. Ninety hour program; public exhibition of studio work, thesis.

Art Education. Apply by April 5 (Autumn), January 5 (Summer). GRE for fellowship applicants and Art Administration. For additional admissions requirements contact department. Sixty or 70 hour master's; thesis.

Astronomy. Admits Summer and Autumn quarters only; apply by January 15. GRE Subject Test in Physics for admission. Thesis required. M.S., Pd.D.

Atmospheric Sciences. Autumn quarter preferred. Apply by February 1 for associateships. GRE required for admission; thesis required for M.S. M.S., Ph.D.

Biochemistry Program (OSBP). Autumn quarter applications strongly recommended; apply by February 1. GRE required for admission. Thesis for M.S. M.S., Ph.D.

Biomedical Engineering. GRE required for admission; thesis required for M.S. Statement of purpose, title and abstract of master's thesis for Ph.D.; M.S., Ph.D.

Biophysics. GRE recommended for all applicants, required if GPA is below 3.0. M.S., Ph.D.

Biostatistics. GRE required for admission; Summer quarter applications strongly recommended; January 15 deadline for fellowship consideration. Ph.D. only.

Black Studies. GRE required of all domestic applicants and international fellowship applicants. Thesis (45 hours)/nonthesis (50 hours). M.A. only.

Business Administration. Admits Autumn quarter only. GMAT for admission, except for organizational behavior, GRE may be substituted; 104-hour full-time M.B.A. program. M.B.A. applicants apply by March 1, February 1 for Financial Aid; Ph.D. applicants apply by February 1. M.B.A., Ph.D.

Chemical Engineering. GRE recommended for all applicants and required of graduates of foreign universities, holders of nonengineering degrees and applicants whose GPA is below 3.0; thesis required for M.S. M.S., Ph.D.

Chemical Physics. Summer and Fall quarters preferred. GRE Subject Test in Physics or Chemistry required of graduates of foreign universities and highly recommended for all other applicants particularly if GPA is below 3.0. M.S., Ph.D.

Chemistry. Admits Summer (international applicants preferred) and Autumn (domestic applicants preferred). Apply by February 1. GRE Subject Test in Chemistry required. M.S., Ph.D.

City and Regional Planning. GRE for master's applicants with GPA below 3.0 and all Ph.D.s and fellowship applicants. 90 hours for M.C.R.P. M.C.R.P., Ph.D.

Civil Engineering. No Summer quarter admission. GRE required of all applicants with undergraduate GPA below 2.7 and of applicants with graduate GPA below 3.0, of non-engineering majors, of fellowship applicants and of engineering graduates from non-ABET-accredited or non-CAB-accredited institutions. GPA of 3.6 of fellowships. M.S., Ph.D.

Classics. GRE required for admission. Apply January 29 for teaching associateships, 60 hours for M.A., M.A., Ph.D.

Communication. Admits Autumn quarter only. Apply by May 15, by March 1 for associateships consideration. GRE required for admission. Contact department for additional requirements. Fifty hour M.A. M.A., Ph.D.

Comparative Literature. Apply by April 1 (Summer and Autumn quarter), January 1 (for financial aid consideration), November 1 (Winter), January 15 (Spring). GRE required for admission. Fifty hours M.A. M.A. only.

Computer and Information Science. Admits Autumn quarter only. GRE Subject Test required for admission. M.S., Ph.D.

Dairy Science. GRE required for admission. Thesis required for M.S. M.S., Ph.D.

Dance. Admits Autumn quarter only. Qualifying audition required for admission. Ninety hours for M.F.A.; M.A., M.F.A.

Dentistry. Admits Summer quarter only. Apply by October 1. GRE; D.D.S. or D.M.D. required for admission, except those wanting dental materials or oral biology. Thesis required. M.S. only.

East Asian Languages and Literature. No Summer quarter admission; prefer Autumn quarter. Apply by February 15, prefer earlier submission. GRE for financial aid consideration and if GPA is less than 3.0. 65 hour M.A. M.A., Ph.D.

Economics. Admits Autumn quarter only. Apply by February 15 for priority financial aid consideration. GRE required for admission; Subject Test in Economics recommended. M.A., Ph.D.

Education. No Summer quarter admission. GRE/MAT required for most programs. Includes educational policy and leadership; educational services and research; educational studies: humanities, science, technological and vocational; educational theory and practice. Contact the School of Education for specific program listing for requirements and contact information. M.Ed., M.A., Ph.D., Certificate of Specialist in Education Administration.

Electrical Engineering. GRE required of M.S. applicants and if GPA is less than 3.0. and of all graduates of foreign universities. Ph.D. applicants should submit thesis or thesis abstract (in English) and letter of recommendation from thesis advisor. Fifty hours required for nonthesis M.S. M.S. Ph.D.

Engineering Mechanics. GRE required of graduates of foreign universities and for all fellowship applicants; GRE recommended for all applicants. Thesis/50 hour nonthesis M.S. option. M.S., Ph.D.

English. Admits Autumn quarter only. Apply by January 15. GRE, sample of critical writing required of M.A., Ph.D. applicants; subject test recommended. Fifty hours for M.A. Sixty-five hours for M.F.A. M.A., M.F.A., Ph.D.

Entomology. GRE Subject Test in Biology, curriculum vitae required for admission. M.S., Ph.D.

Environmental Science. Admits Autumn quarter only. Apply by May 1 (preferably by March 1), February 15 for financial aid consideration. GRE required for admission. Contact department for additional application materials. M.S., Ph.D.

Family Resource and Human Development. Admits Autumn quarter only. Apply by February 1. GRE required for admission. Fifty hour nonthesis option for M.S.; M.S., Ph.D.

Family Resource Management. GRE required for admission. M.S., Ph.D.

Food Science and Nutrition. GRE required for admission. Fifty hours required for nonthesis M.S. M.S., Ph.D.

French and Italian. Admits Autumn quarter only. Apply by February 15 for associateships consideration. GRE required for all applicants with degrees from American universities. Scholarly paper required for Ph.D. applicants. M.A., Ph.D.

Geodetic Science and Surveying. Autumn quarter preferred; Summer quarter if prerequisites required. Mathematics through differential and integral calculus required for admission; one course in linear algebra and knowledge of computer programs recommended. M.S., Ph.D.

Geography. Autumn quarter admission preferred. GRE required for admission. Statement of purpose for Ph.D. applicants; contact department for details. M.A., Ph.D.

Geological Sciences. GRE Subject Test in Geology or allied science in undergraduate area of study required for admission; thesis required for M.S. M.S., Ph.D.

German. Autumn quarter strongly recommended. Apply by January 15 for priority consideration. GRE required for admission. M.A., Ph.D.

Health, Physical Education, and Recreation. Exercise science, health education, sport management; admits Autumn quarter only. Apply by February 15 for associateships; January 1 for fellowships. GRE required for admission. Fifty hour nonthesis option for M.A. M.A., M.Ed., Ph.D.

Health Services Management and Policy. Admits Autumn quarter only. Apply by March 15 for priority consideration. GRE/GMAT required for admission. Contact department for additional admission materials. Eighty-four hour M.H.A. M.H.A. only.

History. Admits Summer and Autumn quarter only. Apply by January 10. GRE required for all U.S. citizens. Sample of written work required. M.A., Ph.D.

History of Art. Admits Summer and Autumn quarters only. Apply by January 15 for associateship or fellowship consideration. GRE, writing sample required for admission. Fifty hour nonthesis option for M.A. M.A., Ph.D.

Home Economics Education. Apply by February 1 for associateship, fellowship consideration. Fifty hour nonthesis option for M.S. M.S., Ph.D.

Horticulture. GRE required for admission. M.S., Ph.D.

Human Ecology. Includes family relations and human development, family resource management, home economics education, human nutrition and food management, and textiles and clothing. Contact School of Human Ecology for specific admission requirements. M.S., Ph.D.

Human Nutrition and Food Management. GRE required for admission. M.S., Ph.D.

Industrial and System Engineering. Admits Autumn quarter only. Apply by March 1; February 1 for financial aid consideration. GRE required for admission. M.S., Ph.D.

Industrial Design. Admits Autumn only. Apply by April 15. Portfolio of recent academic or professional visual work required. Contact department for additional admission requirements. Sixty hour nonthesis option for M.A. M.A. only.

Journalism. Admits Autumn and Winter quarters only. Apply by June 1 (Autumn), October 1 (Winter). GRE required for admission. Fifty hour nonthesis option for M.A. M.A. only.

Labor and Human Resources. Admits Ph.D. applicants to Autumn quarter only; apply by February 1. Apply for M.L.H.R. by July 1 (Autumn), October 1 (Winter), February 1 (Spring), April 1 (Summer). GRE/GMAT required for admission. 50 hour nonthesis option for M.L.H.R. M.L.H.R., Ph.D.

Landscape Architecture. Prefer applicants for Autumn quarter. Apply by March 31. Applicants with landscape architecture or allied field may apply for Winter or Spring quarter. GRE, portfolio, statement of intent required for admission. Contact department for additional admission requirements. M.Land, Arch. only.

Linguistics. Admits Autumn quarter only. Apply by December 15. GRE required for admission. M.A., Ph.D.

Materials Science and Engineering. GRE required for graduates of foreign universities and of holders of nonengineering degrees. M.S., Ph.D.

Mathematics. Prefer applicants for Summer quarter. GRE Subject Test in mathematics required for admission. Contact department for additional admission requirement. 51 hour M.A.; writing project. Fifty hour nonthesis M.S. M.A., M.S., Ph.D.

Mechanical Engineering. Apply by July 1 (Autumn), November 1 (Winter), February 1 (Spring), May 1 (Summer); January 1 for associateship consideration. GRE required for M.S. applicants with below 3.3 GPA. M.S. application who hold nonengineer-

ing baccalaureate and or degrees from a foreign university; all doctoral applicants with GPA below 3.7, applicants with a master's degree from a foreign university, and fellowships applicants. M.S., Ph.D.

Medical Biochemistry. GRE required for admission. Subject Test in Biochemistry recommended. Thesis required for M.S. M.S., Ph.D.

Medical Microbiology and Immunology. Autumn quarter applications strongly recommended. Apply by March 1 for priority consideration; by February 1 for associateships, fellowships. GRE required for admission; Subject Test in Biology recommended. M.S., Ph.D.

Microbiology. Autumn quarter application strongly recommended. Apply by February 1. GRE required for admission. Subject Test in Biology or Biochemistry recommended. Sixty hour nonthesis M.S. option. M.S., Ph.D.

Molecular, Cellular and Developmental Biology. Prefer Autumn quarter applicants. GRE General and Subject Test (Biology, Chemistry, or Biochemistry, Cell and Molecular Biology preferred) required for admission. Thesis required for M.S. M.S., Ph.D.

Molecular Genetics. Includes genetics. GRE Subject Test (Biology or Biochemistry, Cell and Molecular Biology) required for admission. Thesis required for M.S. M.S., Ph.D.

Music. GRE required for M.A., Ph.D. applicants in music education, music history and music theory; and for M.Mus. D.M.A. in music composition. Contact department for additional requirements. Fifty hour nonthesis M.A. option. Forty-five hours required for M.Mus., plus tape-recorded recital. M.A., M.Mus., D.M.A., Ph.D.

Natural Resources. Apply by February 15. GRE required for admission. Fifty-five hour nonthesis M.S. option. M.S. only.

Near Eastern, Judaic, and Hellenic Languages and Literature. GRE recommended. M.A. only.

Neuroscience. GRE/Subject Test (Biology, Psychology, Biochemistry, Cell and Molecular Biology) required for admission. Contact department for Statement of Purpose guidelines. Ph.D. only.

Nuclear Engineering. GRE required for admission. Fifty hours nonthesis M.S. option, plus written task report. M.S., Ph.D.

Nursing. Admits M.S. May 1 (Autumn), November 1 (Winter), February 1 (Spring). Admits Ph.D. January 15 (Autumn only). GRE required for admission. Applicants must hold or be eligible for licensure as an RN in Ohio. Contact department for additional admission requirements. Fifty-two hours nonthesis M.S. option. M.S., Ph.D.

Oral Biology. Admits Autumn quarter only. GRE required for admission. Ph.D. only

Pathology. GRE Subject (Biology, Cell and Molecular-Biology required for admission. Contact department for additional admission requirements. Thesis required M.S. M.S., Ph.D.

Pharmacology. Admits Autumn quarter only. GRE Subject (Biology or Chemistry, Cell and Molecular) required for admission. MCAT scores in lieu of GRE for M.D.-Ph.D. applicants. M.S., Ph.D.

Pharmacy. Includes pharmaceutical administration (admits Autumn quarter only, GRE or GMAT for applicants with GPA below 3.0), pharmacology (GRE for admission), pharmaceutical chemistry (GRE for admission), medicinal chemistry and Pharmacognosy (GRE for admission). M.S., Ph.D.

Philosophy. Autumn quarter strongly recommended. Apply by February 1 for priority consideration. GRE, sample of work required for admission. M.A., Ph.D.

Physics. Admits Summer and Autumn quarters; Summer preferred. GRE Subject Test in Physics required for admission. 50 hour nonthesis M.S. option. M.S., Ph.D.

Physiological Optics. Contact program for admission requirements. Thesis required for M.S. M.S., Ph.D.

Physiology. GRE required for admission. M.S., Ph.D.

Plant Biology. Apply by March 15 for associateship consideration. GRE Subject Test in Biology required for admission.

TOEFL, TSE required for applicants whose native language is not English. Fifty-five hour nonthesis M.S. option. M.S., Ph.D.

Plant Pathology. GRE required for admission. M.S., Ph.D.

Political Science. Admits Autumn quarter only. Apply by March 1; January 1 for fellowships consideration. GRE required for admission. M.A., Ph.D.

Poultry Science. GRE required for admission. M.S., Ph.D.

Preventive Medicine. Admits Autumn quarter only (M.S., Ph.D.); Summer quarter only (M.P.H.). GRE required for admission. M.P.H., M.S., Ph.D.

Psychology. Admits Autumn quarter only. Apply by February 1; January 1 for fellowship consideration. GRE Subject Test in Psychology required for admission. Contact department for additional admission requirements. Thesis required for M.A. M.A., Ph.D.

Public Policy and Management. Autumn quarter applicants preferred. GRE/GMAT (all M.P.A. applicants), GRE/GMAT (M.A. applicants with GPA below 2.7), GRE (for all Ph.D. applicants) required for admission. Fifty hour M.A., 74 hour M.P.A. M.A., M.P.A., Ph.D.

Slavic and East European Languages and Literature. Autumn quarter applicants preferred. GRE required for admission. M.A., Ph.D.

Slavic and East European Studies. GRE recommend for admission. 50 hour M.A.; M.A. only.

Social Work. Admits M.S.W. Autumn and Summer quarters; Ph.D. Autumn quarter only (apply by April 1). Contact programs for additional admission requirements. Ninety hour M.S.W.; 60 hour M.S.W. for applicants with advance standing available. M.S.W., Ph.D.

Sociology. Admits Autumn quarter only. Apply by March 1 for associateship consideration. GRE required for admission. Contact department for additional admissions requirements. Thesis required for M.A. M.A., Ph.D.

Spanish and Portuguese. Autumn Quarter application strongly recommended. Apply by March 1 for associateship consideration. GRE (for all graduates from U.S. and Canadian Universities), TSE (for all applicants required to take TOEFL/MELAB; minimum score 230 for teaching associateships), tape recordings (for all non-native Spanish speakers); telephone interview, scholarly paper required for Ph.D. applicants. M.A., Ph.D.

Speech and Hearing Science. Admits M.A. Autumn quarter only; Ph.D. all quarters. Apply by January 15 for financial aid consideration. GRE required for admission. Fifty-seven hour nonthesis M.A. option. M.A., Ph.D.

Statistics. Summer quarter strongly recommended. Apply by January 15 for fellowship consideration. GRE required for admission. Fifty hour M.Appl.Stat. M.Appl.Stat., M.S., Ph.D.

Textiles and Clothing. Admits Autumn quarter only. Apply by February 1. GRE required for admission. Contact program for statement of purpose guidelines. Fifty hours nonthesis M.S. option. M.S., Ph.D.

Theater. Admits mainly Autumn and Winter quarters for M.A., Ph.D. programs. Apply by January 1 (fellowship consideration), February 15 (associateships); April 15 (M.F.A. acting and design associateships). Acting program accepting for Autumn 1996, 1997. GRE required for M.A., Ph.D. applicants; audition for M.F.A.(acting), portfolio (design). Thesis required for M.A.; M.F.A. in design. Ninety-nine hour M.F.A. M.A., M.F.A., Ph.D.

Veterinary Anatomy. D.V.M. or equivalent required. GRE required for applicants with GPA below 3.0 (unless they have a completed master's degree at time of evaluation) and of all graduates of foreign universities. Thesis required for M.S. M.S., Ph.D.

Veterinary Clinical Sciences. D.V.M. or equivalent required. Most applicants admitted through AAVC's Residency MATCH Program. Contact program for admission procedures. GRE required of all graduates of foreign universities and to theriogenology and equine exercise physiology. Thesis required for M.S. M.S., Ph.D.

Veterinary Pathobiology. D.V.M. or equivalent B.S. with training in microbiology, immunology or virology required. GRE required of all graduates of non-AVMA-accredited veterinary colleges. Thesis required for M.S. M.S., Ph.D.

Veterinary Physiology and Pharmacology. D.V.M. or equivalent and GRE, letter of intent required for admission. Contact department for letter of intent guidelines. Thesis required for M.S.; M.S., Ph.D.

Veterinary Preventive Medicine. D.V.M. or equivalent required. GRE required of all graduates of non-AVMA-accredited veterinary colleges. Thesis required for M.S. M.S., Ph.D.

Vocational Education, Comprehensive Program. Curriculum undergoing review. Contact program for admission requirements and deadlines. Ph.D. only.

Welding Engineering. GRE Subject Test in Engineering required for applicants with GPA below 2.7. M.S., Ph.D.

Women's Studies. Admits Autumn quarter only. Apply by January 15. GPA of 3.0 and at least four women's studies courses required for admission. Duplicate copies of all application materials must be sent to program. M.A. only.

Zoology. Prefer Autumn quarter applicants. Apply by March 1; preference given to applications received by February 1. GRE Subject Test in Biology, statement of purpose required for admission. Contact program for statement of purpose. M.S., Ph.D.

College of Law

Founded 1891. Semester system. Law Library: 603,000 volumes. Library has LEXIS, NEXIS, WESTLAW, DIALOG. Special facilities: Comprehensive National Resources Center.

Annual tuition: full-time resident $6164, nonresident $14,686. On-campus housing available for married and single students. Total average annual additional expense: $7800.

Enrollment: first-year class 220, total full-time 650 (men 55%, women 45%). Faculty: full-time 35, part-time 20. Degrees conferred: J.D., J.D.-M.B.A., J.D.-M.H.A., J.D.-M.P.A.

ADMISSION REQUIREMENTS. LSDAS Law School report, bachelor's degree, transcripts, writing sample, letters of recommendation, resume, LSAT (not later than February) required in support of application. Interview required for final selection. Accepts transfer applicants. Graduates of unaccredited institutions not considered. Apply to Director of Admissions after October, before March 15. Admits first-year students Fall only. Application fee $30. Phone: (614)292-8810; fax: (614)292-1383.

ADMISSION STANDARDS. Selective. Accepts 20% of total annual applicants.

FINANCIAL AID. Scholarships, grants, Federal W/S, loans. Apply to the Financial Aid Office by March 1. Use FAFSA. About 45% of students receive aid other than loans from College.

DEGREE REQUIREMENTS. For J.D.: 88 semester hours minimum, three years in residence.

Note: Has summer programs with Oxford University (Great Britain).

College of Medicine (43210-1238)

Established 1914. Library: 155,000 volumes. Annual tuition: resident $9174, nonresident $28,059, student fees $246. Total average figure for all other expenses: $6078.

Enrollment: M.D. program, first-year class 210 (EDP 15); total 890 (men 63%, women 37%). Faculty: full- and part-time 1700. Degree conferred: M.D. The M.S. and Ph.D. are offered through the Graduate School.

ADMISSION REQUIREMENTS. For M.D. program: AMCAS report, transcripts, letters of recommendation, bachelor's degree,

MCAT, interview required in support of application. Has EDP; apply between June 15 and August 1. Accepts transfer applicants. Preference given to Ohio residents. Apply to AMCAS after June 15, before November 1. Application fee $30. Phone: (614)292-7137; fax: (614)292-1544.

ADMISSION STANDARDS. Selective.. Accepts 6–8% of total applications. Approximately 80% are state residents.

FINANCIAL AID. Scholarships, assistantships, loans. About 35% of students receive aid other than loans from College. Apply to the Dean.

DEGREE REQUIREMENTS. For M.D.: satisfactory completion of four-year program. For M.S., Ph.D., see Graduate School listing above.

FIELDS OF GRADUATE STUDY.
Allied Medical Professions. M.S only.
Anatomy.
Biochemistry.
Biomedical Engineering.
Biophysics.
Cell Biology.
Genetics.
Health Administration.
Immunology.
Microbiology.
Molecular Biology.
Neurosciences.
Obstetrics and Gynecology. M.S. only.
Ophthalmology. M.S. only.
Pathology.
Pediatrics. M.S. only.
Pharmacology.
Physical Medicine M.S. only.
Physiology.
Preventive Medicine.
Radiology. M.S. only.
Surgery. M.S. only.
Toxicology. M.S. only.

College of Dentistry

Organized 1890. Joined Ohio State University in 1914. Annual tuition: resident $8400, nonresident $24,609. On-campus housing available. Average academic year housing costs: $7500. Contact the Housing Office. Phone: (614)292-8266. Total average cost for all other first-year expenses: $3142.

Enrollment: first-year class 90, total 181 (men 65%, women 35%); postgraduates 65. Faculty: full-time 91, part-time 134. Degrees conferred: D.D.S.-B.A./B.S., D.D.S., D.D.S.-M.S. The M.S. is offered through the Graduate School.

ADMISSION REQUIREMENTS. AADSAS, transcripts, DAT (not later than October) required in support of application. Interview by invitation only. Accepts transfer applicants. Applicants must have completed at least two years of college study. Preference given to state residents. Apply to Director of Admissions after June 1, before February 1. Application fee $30. Phone: (614)292-3361.

ADMISSION STANDARDS. Selective. Accepts 20–25% of total annual applicants. Approximately 85% are state residents.

FINANCIAL AID. Scholarships, grants, loans. Apply to University's Financial Aid Office after acceptance, before July 1. Use FAFSA. Phone: (614)292-7764. About 85% of students receive some aid from College-controlled and outside sources.

DEGREE REQUIREMENTS. For D.D.S.-B.A./B.S.: satisfactory completion of seven-year program. For D.D.S.: satisfactory

completion of forty-five-month program. For M.S., see Graduate School listing above.

College of Veterinary Medicine

Established 1885. Third oldest veterinary college. Annual tuition: resident and contract nonresident $7506, nonresident $23,460. On-campus housing available. Annual living expenses: single $9826; married $12,826.

Enrollment: first-year class 133; total full-time 590 (men 50%, women 50%); postgraduates 54. Faculty: full-time 110, part-time 11. Degrees conferred: D.V.M., D.V.M.-M.S., D.V.M.-Ph.D. The M.S. and Ph.D. are offered through the Graduate School.

ADMISSION REQUIREMENTS. Transcripts, VCAT or GRE or MCAT, two recommendations, animal/veterinary experience, required in support of application. Interview by invitation only. Preference given to state and contract state residents. Applicants must have completed at least 101 quarter hours of college study. Accepts transfer applicants on a space available basis. Apply to Chairperson, Admissions Committee, by November 1. Application fee $30. Phone: (614)292-8831; fax: (614)262-6989.

ADMISSION STANDARDS. Selective. Accepts 30–40% of total annual applicants. Fifteen to thirty spaces available for nonresidents.

FINANCIAL AID. Scholarships, grants, fellowships, assistantships, Federal W/S, loans. Apply to Financial Aid Officer of the College after acceptance, before March 15. About 50% of students receive aid other than loans from College. Aid available to part-time students.

DEGREE REQUIREMENTS. For D.V.M.: satisfactory completion of four-year program. For M.S., Ph.D.: successful completion of first year of veterinary curriculum required for consideration; see Graduate School listing above.

FIELDS OF GRADUATE STUDY.
Anatomy.
Pathobiology.
Pharmacology.
Toxicology.
Veterinary Anatomy.
Veterinary Pathobiology.
Veterinary Physiology.
Veterinary Preventive Medicine.

OHIO UNIVERSITY
Athens, Ohio 45701

Chartered 1804. Located 76 miles SE of Columbus. Coed. State control. Quarter system. Library: 2,800,000 volumes, 2,200,000 microforms, 50 PCs.

Annual tuition: full-time, resident $4695, nonresident $9189; per credit, resident, $195, nonresident, $381. Limited on-campus housing for married and single graduate students. Average annual housing cost: $5080 (12 months, room only) for married students; $2013–$4095 (12 months) for single students. Phone: (614)593-4090.

Graduate College

Graduate study since 1950. Enrollment: full-time 2051, part-time 4024 (men 55%, women 45%). University faculty: full-time 718, part-time 99. Degrees conferred: M.A., M.S., M.M., M.B.A., M.Ed., M.F.A., M.H.S.A., M.P.A., M.P.T., M.S.A., Ph.D.

ADMISSION REQUIREMENTS. Transcripts required in support of School's application. GRE Subject Tests, MAT, GMAT, interview required for some departments. TOEFL required for international applicants; TSE required by some departments. Accepts transfer applicants. Graduates of unaccredited institutions not considered. Apply to Office of Graduate Student Services at least six weeks prior to registration; international application at least six months prior to registration. Application fee $25. Phone: (614)593-2800; fax: (614)593-4625.

ADMISSION STANDARDS. Relatively open for many departments, competitive or very competitive for the others. Usual minimum GPA: 2.75 (A = 4).

FINANCIAL AID. Five hundred scholarships, two hundred research assistantships, five hundred teaching assistantships, Federal W/S, loans. Approved for VA benefits. Apply to the individual departmental Graduate Committee chairman for scholarships, assistantships; to the Financial Aid Office for all other programs. Use FAFSA. Phone: (614)543-4141; fax: (614)593-4140. About 50% of students receive aid other than loans from College and outside sources.

DEGREE REQUIREMENTS. For master's: 45–60 quarter hours minimum; thesis; final oral exam; nonthesis option in some departments. For M.B.A.: 90 quarter hours minimum. For Ph.D.: 9 quarters minimum beyond the bachelor's, at least 3 quarters in full-time residence; comprehensive exam; scholarly disciplines are determined by department; dissertation; final oral exam.

FIELDS OF STUDY.
Accountancy. M.S. only.
Art. Includes art history, art education, ceramics, painting, photography, printmaking, sculpture. M.F.A., M.A. only.
Art Education. M.A. only.
Biological Sciences. M.S., Ph.D.
Business Administration. M.B.A.
Chemical Engineering. M.S., Ph.D.
Chemistry. M.S., Ph.D.
Civil Engineering. M.S. only.
Comparative Arts. Ph.D. only.
Counselor Education. M.Ed., Ph.D.
Curriculum and Instruction. M. Ed., Ph.D.
Economic Education. M.A., Ph.D.
Economics. M.A. only.
Educational Leadership. M.Ed., Ph.D.
Electrical Engineering. M.S., Ph.D.
Elementary Education. M.Ed., Ph.D.
English Language and Literature. M.A., Ph.D.
Environmental and Plant Biology. M.S., Ph.D.
Environmental Sciences. M.S.
Film. M.F.A., M.A. only.
French. M.A. only.
Geology. M.S. only.
Health, Physical Education, and Recreation. Includes sports administration, physiology of exercise. M.S., M.Ed.
Health Services Administration. M.H.S.A. only.
Hearing and Speech Science. M.A., Ph.D.
History. M.A., Ph.D.
Home Economics. M.S. only.
Individual Interdisciplinary Programs. M.A., M.S., Ph.D.
Industrial and System Engineering. M.S. only.
Integrated Engineering. Ph.D.
International Affairs. M.A. only.
Interpersonal Communication. M.A., Ph.D.
Journalism. M.A., Ph.D.
Linguistics. M.A. only.
Mass Communication. Includes journalism, telecommunication. Ph.D. only.
Mathematics. M.S., Ph.D.

Mechanical Engineering. M.S. only.
Music. Includes performance, music education, history and literature, therapy, theory and composition. M.F.A., M.A.
Philosophy. M.A. only.
Physical Therapy. M.P.T. only.
Physics. M.S., Ph.D.
Political Science. M.A. only.
Psychology. M.S., Ph.D.
Public Administration. M.A., M.P.A. only.
Sociology. M.A. only.
Spanish. M.A. only.
Telecommunications. M.A. only.
Theater. M.A., M.F.A. only.

College of Osteopathic Medicine

Coed. Public control. Library: 65,000 volumes, has MEDLINE, CANCERLINE, BIOETHIC, HEALTH, TOXLINE, DIALOG, OCLC.

Annual tuition: resident $10,560, nonresident $14,970. Enrollment: first-year class 100, total 381 (men 55%, women 45%). Faculty: full-time 71, part-time 400. Degrees conferred: D.O., D.O.-Ph.D.

ADMISSION REQUIREMENTS. AACOMAS report, bachelor's degree preferred, official transcripts, MCAT (no later than September), three letters of recommendation, one from premed advisory committee, evaluation from a physician (preferably a D.O.), supplemental form required in support of application. Interview by invitation only. Graduates of unaccredited colleges not considered. Preference given to state residents. Apply by February 1 to the Director of Admissions. Admits first year students Fall only. Application fee: $25. Phone: (800)345-1560, or (614)593-2147; fax: (614)593-2256.

ADMISSION STANDARDS. Selective. Accepts approximately 35% of annual applications. 80% of class are state residents. Usual minimum average: 3.0 (A = 4), mean GPA: 3.4.

FINANCIAL AID. Scholarships, fellowships, Federal W/S, loans. Apply by April 1 to the Financial Aid Office. Use FAFSA and institutional FAF. About 80% of students receive aid from College and outside sources.

DEGREE REQUIREMENT. For D.O.: satisfactory completion of four-year program. For Ph.D., see Graduate College listing above.

MEDICAL COLLEGE OF OHIO AT TOLEDO
Toledo, Ohio 43699-0008

School of Medicine

Established 1968. Annual tuition: resident $9534, nonresident $12,963. On-campus housing available. Total average figure for all other expenses: $8500.

Enrollment: first-year class 135 (EDP 15) total 537 (men 60%, women 40%). Faculty: full-time 286, part-time 26. Degrees conferred: M.D.-M.S., M.D.-Ph.D.

ADMISSION REQUIREMENTS. AMCAS report, transcripts, MCAT, recommendations required in support of application. Interviews by invitation only. Preference given to state residents. Has EDP; apply between June 15 and August 1. Graduates of unaccredited colleges not considered. Apply to Director of Admissions after June 15, before December 1. Application fee $30. Phone: (419)381-4229; fax: (419)381-4005.

ADMISSION STANDARDS. Selective. Accepts about 6–8% of total annual applicants. Approximately 78% are state residents.

FINANCIAL AID. Limited, based on need. Apply to Admissions Office; no specified closing date. Use FAFSA.

DEGREE REQUIREMENTS. For M.D.: satisfactory completion of four-year program. For M.S.: 32 semester hours minimum; thesis or comprehensive exam. For Ph.D.: at least 90 credits beyond bachelor's. Foreign language required by some departments; comprehensive exam; dissertation; final oral exam.

FIELDS OF GRADUATE STUDY.
Anatomy.
Biochemistry.
Microbiology.
Neurosciences.
Pathology
Pharmacology.
Physiology.

OKLAHOMA CITY UNIVERSITY

Oklahoma City, Oklahoma 73106-1402
http://www.okcu.edu

Founded 1904. Coed. Private control. Methodist affiliation. Semester system. Library: 274,000 volumes, 577,000 microforms, 4150 current periodicals, 36 PCs.

On-campus housing for married and single graduate students. Average 5 academic year housing costs: $3472 for married students, $2858 (including board) for single students. Contact Dean of Students Office for both on- and off-campus housing information. Phone: (405)744-9164.

Petree College of Arts and Science

Tuition: per credit $280. Enrollment: full-time 34, part-time 387. Faculty: full-time 13, part-time 25. Degrees conferred: M.A.C.P., M.Ed., M.L.A., M.C.J.A.

ADMISSION REQUIREMENTS. Official transcripts, two letters of recommendation required in support of College's application. Interview sometimes required. TOEFL required for international applicants. Accepts transfer applicants. Graduates of unaccredited institutions not considered. Apply by August 25 (Fall), January 15 (Spring) to Office of Graduate Admissions. Rolling admissions process. Application fee $35, $55 for international applicants. Phone: (405)521-5351 or (800)633-7242, ext. 2; fax: (405)521-5356.

ADMISSION STANDARDS. Selective for some programs, very selective for others. Usual minimum average: 3.0 (A = 4).

FINANCIAL AID. Thirteen fellowships, full and partial tuition waivers, Federal W/S, loans. Approved for VA benefits. Apply by August 1 to the Deans Office for fellowships; to Financial Aid Office for all other programs. Use FAFSA. Phone: (800)633-7242, ext. 5211. About 35% of students receive aid from University and outside sources. Aid available to part-time students.

DEGREE REQUIREMENTS. For master's: 36–45 semester hours minimum, at least 27 in residence; thesis/nonthesis option.

FIELDS OF STUDY.
Computer Science. M.S.
Counseling. M.A.C.P.
Criminal Justice Administration. M.C.J.A.
Early Childhood Education. M.Ed.
Elementary Education. M.Ed.
Gifted and Talented Education. M.Ed.
Liberal Arts. M.L.A.
Science Education. Includes biology, chemistry, physics. M.Ed.
Secondary Education. Includes art, business, health, physical education and recreation, mathematics, music, social studies, language arts. M.Ed.
TESOL. M.Ed.

Meinders School of Management and Business Science

http://www.okcu.edu

Graduate study since 1904. Semester system. Tuition: per credit $310. Enrollment: full-time 617, part-time 523. Graduate faculty: full-time 33, part-time 20. Degrees conferred: M.B.A., M.S.A.

ADMISSION REQUIREMENTS. Transcripts, GMAT required in support of School's application. TOEFL required for international applicants. Interview not required. Accepts transfer applicants. Apply to Director of M.B.A. Program by July 31 (Fall), prior to registration for other sessions. Application fee $35. Phone: (800)683-7242, ext. 2; fax: (405)521-5356.

ADMISSION STANDARDS. Relatively open. Usual minimum average: 2.75 (A = 4).

FINANCIAL AID. Three hundred thirty-three academic scholarships, Federal W/S, loans. Approved for VA benefits. Apply to Financial Aid Office; no specified closing date. Use FAFSA. Phone: (405)521-5211; fax: (405)521-5466.

DEGREE REQUIREMENTS. For M.S. Accounting: 30 semester hours, 24 in residence. For M.B.A.: 36 semester hours minimum, at least 24 in residence; comprehensive written exam.

FIELDS OF STUDY.
Accounting. M.S.A. only.
Arts Management.
Business Administration.
Finance.
Health Administration.
Information Systems.
International Business.
Management.
Public Management.
Note: M.B.A./J.D. available.

School of Law (73146-1310)

Opened 1952. Semester system. Law library: 222,400 volumes. Library has LEXIS, NEXIS, WESTLAW, OCLC.

Annual tuition: full-time $12,900, part-time $8600. Limited on-campus housing available. Total average annual additional expense: $7000.

Enrollment: first-year class 170 (day), 80 (evening); total full- and part-time 439 (men 63%, women 37%). Faculty: full-time 30, part-time 21. Degrees conferred, J.D., J.D.-M.B.A., J.D.-M.Div.

ADMISSION REQUIREMENTS. LSDAS Law School report, bachelor's degree, transcripts, LSAT, recommendation required in support of application. Accepts limited transfer applicants. Graduates of unaccredited colleges not considered. Apply to the School; no specified closing date. Beginning students Fall admission only. Application fee $35. Phone: (800)663-7242, ext. 5354, (405)521-5354.

ADMISSION STANDARDS. Accepts 40–45% of total annual applicants.

FINANCIAL AID. Scholarships, tuition remission, fellowships, assistantships, Federal W/S, loans. Apply to the Director of Financial Aid by April 1. Use FAFSA. About 20% of students receive aid other than loans from School.

DEGREE REQUIREMENTS. For J.D.: day students may complete the J.D. degree in 24 months by year-round attendance, evening students in 33 months by year-round attendance; 90-hour semester program.

OKLAHOMA STATE UNIVERSITY
Stillwater, Oklahoma 74078

Founded 1890. Located in NC Oklahoma approximately one hour from Tulsa and Oklahoma City. Special facilities: Laser Center, Twenty-first Century Center for Agriculture and Renewable Natural Resources, University Center for Water Research, Center for Global Studies, Center for Local Government and Technology, Institute for Energy Analysis, Remote Sensing Center, Laser Center, Center for International Trade and Development, Virgin Prairie and Woodland Study and Research Site. Library: 1,900,000 volumes, 2,100,000 microforms, 15,000 current periodicals.

Tuition: per credit hour, resident $74, nonresident $234. On-campus housing available for graduate students. Average academic year housing costs: $2858 (including board) for single students; $3473 for married student housing. Contact the Graduate Student Housing Office for both on- and off-campus housing information. Phone: (405)744-9164.

Graduate College

Graduate study since 1905. Enrollment: full-time 1286, part-time 1955. Faculty: full-and part-time 1137. Degrees conferred: M.A., M.Ag., M.M.S.E., M.S., M.Arch., M.Arch.Eng., M. Eng., M.B.A., Ed.S., Ed.D., Ph.D.

ADMISSION REQUIREMENTS. Two official transcripts required in support of College's application. GRE/MAT/GMAT required for some programs. TOEFL required of international applicants. Accepts transfer applicants. Graduates of unaccredited institutions not considered. Apply to Graduate College at least thirty days prior to the semester of expected enrollment; international students 60 days prior to enrollment. Application fee $25. Phone: (405)744-6501.

ADMISSIONS STANDARDS. Competitive for most departments, selective for the others. Usual minimum average: 2.75 (A = 4).

FINANCIAL AID. Scholarships, research assistantships, teaching assistantships, Federal W/S, loans. Approved for VA benefits. Apply directly to the academic department or unit in which the student desires the appointment for assistantships. Contact individual department for date. Apply to the Office of Financial Aid for all other programs. Use FAFSA. Phone: (405)744-6604. Approximately 35% of students receive aid from both College and outside agencies. Aid available for part-time students.

DEGREE REQUIREMENTS. For master's: Plan I—30 credit hours including 6 hours for thesis, 21 hours in residence; thesis. Plan II—32 credit hours including 2 credit hours for special re-

port, 23 credit hours in residence; special report. Plan III—32 credit hours, 23 credit hours in residence; creative component/project. For Ed.S.: 60 credit hours beyond the bachelor's degree; one year or equivalent in residency; qualifying exam; thesis with final exam. For Ed.D.: 90 hours beyond the bachelor's degree; 75% of course work at 5000 and 6000 level; 10-hour thesis; maintain B average; qualifying exams; thesis defense. For Ph.D.: 60 hours minimum beyond the bachelor's degree or 30 hours minimum beyond the master's degree; one year in residence; one or two foreign languages for some departments; qualifying exam; dissertation (minimum 15 credit hours); final oral exam.

FIELDS OF STUDY.
Accounting.
Aerospace Engineering.
Agricultural Economics and Agribusiness.
Agricultural Engineering.
Agricultural Sciences.
Agronomy and Soil Sciences.
Animal Breeding.
Animal Nutrition.
Animal Science.
Applied Behavioral Studies.
Applied Mathematics.
Architectural Engineering.
Architecture.
Biochemistry.
Botany and Plant Sciences.
Business Administration.
Business Education.
Chemical Engineering.
Chemistry.
Child and Family Studies.
Civil Engineering.
Clinical Psychology.
Clothing, Textiles, and Merchandising.
Computer Education.
Computer Engineering.
Computer Science.
Counseling and Student Personnel.
Crop Science.
Curriculum and Instruction.
Ecology.
Economics.
Educational Administration.
Educational Media.
Educational Psychology.
Electrical Engineering.
Elementary Education.
English.
Entomology.
Environmental Engineering.
Environmental Science.
Experimental Psychology.
Finance.
Food Science and Technology.
Forestry.
Genetics.
Geography.
Geology.
Health, Physical Education, and Recreation.
Higher Education.
History.
Home Economics.
Home Economics Education.
Horticulture.
Hospitality Administration.
Human Development.
Industrial Engineering and Management.
Landscape Architecture.
Manufacturing System Engineering.

Marketing.
Marriage and Family Therapy.
Mass Communications.
Mathematics.
Mechanical Engineering.
Microbiology.
Molecular Biology.
Pathology.
Philosophy.
Physics.
Physiology.
Plant Pathology.
Political Science.
Psychology.
Range Science.
Reading.
Secondary Education.
Social Work.
Sociology.
Speech. Includes speech communication, speech-language pathology and audiology; theater.
Statistics.
Systems Engineering.
Technical Education.
Veterinary Parasitology.
Veterinary Pathology.
Zoology.

College of Veterinary Medicine (74078-0353)

Annual tuition: resident $6000, nonresident $15,000. Total average cost for all other annual expenses: $7000.

Enrollment: first-year class 71; total full-time 260 (men 50%, women 50%); postgraduates 40. Faculty: full-time 65. Degrees conferred: D.V.M., D.V.M.-M.S. The M.S. and Ph.D. are offered through the Graduate College.

ADMISSION REQUIREMENTS. VMCAS, transcripts, GRE General and Subject Biology, recommendations, personal essay, animal/veterinary experience, required in support of application. Interview by invitation only. Preference given to state residents. Accepts transfer applicants on a space available basis only. Graduates of unaccredited colleges not considered. Apply to the College after July 1, before November 1. Application fee $15. Phone: (405)744-6653.

ADMISSION STANDARDS. Selective. Accepts 33–50% of qualified applicants. Accepts up to fourteen nonresidents.

FINANCIAL AID. Scholarships, fellowships, assistantships, partial tuition waivers, Federal W/S, loans available. Apply to Office of Financial Aid by March 1.

DEGREE REQUIREMENTS. For D.V.M.: satisfactory completion of four-year program. For M.S., Ph.D., see Graduate College listing above.

FIELDS OF GRADUATE STUDY.
Public Health.
Veterinary Microbiology.
Veterinary Parasitology.
Veterinary Pathology.

OKLAHOMA STATE UNIVERSITY
Tulsa, Oklahoma 74107-1898

College of Osteopathic Medicine

Founded 1972. Coed. Public control. Semester system. Library: 22,000 volumes, 24,000 microforms, 500 current periodicals, 22 PCs; has MEDLINE, CANCERLINE, BIOETHIC, HEALTH, TOXLINE, DIALOG, OCLC.

Annual tuition: resident $7550, nonresident $18,660. No on-campus housing available. Enrollment: first-year class 88, total 316 (men 65%, women 35%). Faculty: full-time 80, part-time 400. Degree conferred: D.O.

ADMISSION REQUIREMENTS. AACOMAS report, bachelor's degree preferred, official transcripts, MCAT (no later than Spring of year prior to application) from premed advisory committee, evaluation from a physician (preferably a D.O.), supplemental form required in support of application. Interview by invitation only. Graduates of unaccredited college not considered. Preference given to state residents. Apply by January 1 to the assistant Dean of Students. Admits first year students Fall only. Rolling admissions process. Application fee $25. Phone: (800)677-1972, or (918)528-1972; fax: (918)561-8412.

ADMISSION STANDARDS. Selective. Accepts about 5% of total annual applications. Usual minimum average: 3.0 (A = 4), mean GPA: 3.42.

FINANCIAL AID. Scholarships, grants, partial tuition waivers, Federal W/S, loans. Apply by June 1 to the Financial Aid Office. Use FAFSA and institutional FAF.

DEGREE REQUIREMENT. For D.O.: satisfactory completion of four-year program.

UNIVERSITY OF OKLAHOMA
Norman, Oklahoma 73019
http://GPADNT.GRAD.UOKNOR.EDU

Founded 1890. Located 18 miles S of Oklahoma City. Coed. State control. Special facilities: Center for the Investigation of Mesoscale Meteorological Systems; permanent biological station on Lake Texoma; earth sciences observatory at Leonard; geological field camp at Canon City, Colo.; aquatic biology and fisheries research center in Noble; virgin prairie and woodland plots for study and research; Sarkey's Energy Center; Surfactant Institute; Rock Mechanics Institute; Ground Water Institute; cooperative program with Oak Ridge Institute of Nuclear Studies; library features the Western History Collection, Degolyer Collection in the History of Science and Technology and the Bass Business History Collection. Library: over 2,400,000 volumes, 3,000,000 microforms, 49 PCs in all libraries.

Tuition: per credit, resident $80.15, nonresident $240.15. On-campus housing for 922 married students, 100 men, list women. Average annual housing cost: $2500–$5000 for married students, $3526 (including board) for single students. Apply to Director of the Office of Housing. Phone: (405)325-2511.

Graduate College

Graduate study since 1892. Enrollment: full-time 3000, part-time 2000. Graduate faculty: full-time 700. Degrees conferred: M.Ac., M.A., M.Arch., M.A. in Art, M.A. in L.Sci., M.P.A., M.B.A., M.Ed., M.Ed. in HPER., M.Env.Sci., M.F.A. in Art, M.F.A. in Dance, M.F.A. in Design, M.F.A. in Drama, M.H.R., M.L.S., M.Land.Arch., M.L.Sc., M.Mus., M.Mus.Ed., M.Nat.Sci., M.P.H., M.R.C.P., M.S., M.S. in Const.Set., M.S. in Metr., M.Soc.Sci., M.Soc.Work, D.Mus.Arts, Ed.D., Ph.D., Dr.P.H., D.P.A.

ADMISSION REQUIREMENTS. Transcripts required in support of College's application. GRE/GMAT/MAT/interview for some departments. TOEFL required for international applicants. Accepts transfer applicants. Graduates of unaccredited institutions not considered. Apply to Office of Admissions and Records as soon as possible before registration. Application fee $25. Phone: (405)325-3811; fax: (405)325-5346.

ADMISSION STANDARDS. Selective for most departments, very selective for others. Usual minimum average: 3.0 (A = 4).

FINANCIAL AID. Annual awards from institutional funds: 1000 fee waiver scholarships, 450 teaching assistantships, 450 research assistantships, Federal W/S, loans. Approved for VA benefits. Apply by March 31 to Graduate College and appropriate department chair for scholarships, assistantships; to Financial Aid Office for all other programs. Use FAFSA. Phone: (405)325-4521; fax: (405)325-7608. About 30% of students receive aid other than loans from College and outside sources. Aid sometimes available for part-time students.

DEGREE REQUIREMENTS. For most master's: 30 semester hours minimum, at least 22 in residence; thesis; comprehensive oral/written exam sometimes required; 32 semester hours minimum, at least 24 in residence; comprehensive oral/written exam for some departments. For M.Ac.: 33 hours minimum; comprehensive oral/written exam. For M.B.A.: 36 hours minimum; comprehensive written exam. For M.R.C.P.: 54 hours minimum, final project. For M.S.W.: 60 hours minimum; field work; thesis/final project. For M.L.A.: 62 hours minimum; research project. For M.F.A.: 60 hours minimum; final project/exhibition. For Ph.D.: 3 years minimum and at least 90 semester hours beyond the bachelor's degree, at least 2 semesters in residence; general oral/written exam, dissertation; final oral exam. For Ed.D.: evidence of proficiency in statistics/methods of research or reading knowledge of one foreign language; other requirements essentially the same as the Ph.D. For D.P.A., D.Mus.Arts, essentially the same as for the Ph.D.

FIELDS OF STUDY.

NORMAN CAMPUS:
Accounting. M.Ac., M.A.
Aerospace and Mechanical Engineering. M.S., Ph.D.
Anthropology. M.A., Ph.D.
Architecture. M.Arch. only.
Art. Portfolio for admission; master's only.
Biochemistry.
Biomedical Library Sciences.
Botany. M.S., Ph.D.
Business Administration. M.B.A., Ph.D.
Chemical Engineering and Materials Science. M.S., Ph.D.
Chemistry. M.S., Ph.D.
Civil Engineering and Environmental Science. M.S., Ph.D.
Communication.
Computer Science. M.S., Ph.D.
Dance. M.F.A. only.
Design. M.F.A.
Drama. M.A., M.F.A. only.
Economics. M.A., Ph.D.
Education. Includes adult and community education; counseling psychology; educational psychology; educational technology; elementary education; elementary school administration; general educational administration; school counseling; geographic education; guidance and counseling; community counseling; higher education (including student personnel administration; historical, philosophical, and social foundations); reading education; science education; secondary education; secondary school administration; special education. M.Ed., Ed.D., Ph.D.
Electrical Engineering. M.S., Ph.D.
Engineering. M.S., Ph.D.
English. M.A., Ph.D.
Fisheries Biology. M.S. only.
French. M.A., Ph.D.
Geography. M.A., Ph.D.
Geology. M.S., Ph.D.

Geophysics. M.S. only.
German. M.A.
Health, Physical Education, and Recreation. Master's only.
History. M.A., Ph.D.
History of Science. M.A., Ph.D.
Human Relations. M.H.R. only.
Industrial Engineering. M.S., Ph.D.
Journalism and Mass Communication. M.A. only.
Landscape Architecture. M.L.A. only.
Liberal Studies. M.L.S. only.
Library Science. M.A. in L.Sci., M.L.S. only.
Mathematics. M.A., M.S., Ph.D.
Meteorology. M.S., Ph.D.
Microbiology. M.S., Ph.D.
Modern Languages. Includes French, German, Spanish; M.A. only in German.
Music. Includes music history, theory, music education, performance, conducting, composition. M.Mus., D.M.A., Ph.D.
Natural Science. Emphasis on earth science, botany, physical. M.Nat.Sci. only.
Petroleum and Geological Engineering. M.S., Ph.D.
Philosophy. M.A., Ph.D.
Physics and Astronomy. M.S., Ph.D.
Political Science. M.A., Ph.D.
Psychology. M.S., Ph.D.
Public Administration. M.P.A.
Regional and City Planning. M.R.C.P. only.
Social Science. M.Soc.Sci. only.
Social Work. M.S.W. only.
Sociology. M.S., Ph.D.
Spanish. M.A., Ph.D.
Zoology. GRE Subject for admission. M.S., Ph.D.

HEALTH SCIENCES CAMPUS:
Anatomical Sciences. M.S., Ph.D.
Behavior. M.S., Ph.D,
Biochemistry and Molecular Biology. M.S., Ph.D.
Biological Psychology. M.S., Ph.D.
Biostatistics and Epidemiology. M.S., Ph.D.
Communication Disorders. M.S., Ph.D.
Dental Sciences (Orthodontics). M.S.
Environmental Health. M.S., Ph.D.
Health Administration. M.S., Ph.D.
Immunology. Ph.D.
Medical Microbiology. M.S., Ph.D.
Medical Physiology and Biophysics. M.S., Ph.D.
Nursing. M.S.
Pathology. M.S., Ph.D.
Pharmaceutical Sciences. M.S., Ph.D.
Pharmacology. M.S., Ph.D.
Public Health. M.P.H.
Radiological Sciences. M.S., Ph.D.
Social Sciences and Health. M.S., Ph.D.

College of Law (73019)

Organized 1909. Semester system. Library: 296,300 volumes. Library has LEXIS, WESTLAW, OLIN. Special facilities: American Indian Law and Policy Center.

Annual tuition: full-time, resident $3274, nonresident $10,216. On-campus housing available. Total average annual additional expense: $7800.

Enrollment: first-year class 216; total 658 (men 60%, women 40%). Faculty: full-time 42, part-time 36. Degrees conferred: J.D., J.D.-M.B.A., J.D.-M.P.A., J.D.-M.S. (Health Administration, Environmental Management, Occupational Health).

ADMISSION REQUIREMENTS. LSDAS Law School report, bachelor's degree, transcripts, LSAT required in support of application. Accepts transfer applicants. Graduates of unaccredited colleges not considered. Apply to the Admissions Office by

March 15. Application fee $15 (nonresident only). Phone: (405)325-4699.

ADMISSION STANDARDS. Selective. Accepts 30–35% of total annual applicants.

FINANCIAL AID. Scholarships, full and partial tuition waivers, fellowships, assistantships, Federal W/S, loans. Apply to the Office of Financial Aid preferably by March 15, but no later than June 1. Use FAFSA. About 20% of students receive aid other than loans from College.

DEGREE REQUIREMENTS. For J.D.: 90 boom minimum, at least final year in residence. For master's degrees, see Graduate College listing above.
Note: Summer study abroad at Oxford University (Great Britain) available.

UNIVERSITY OF OKLAHOMA HEALTII SCIENCES CENTER

Oklahoma City, Oklahoma 73190
http://www.uokhsc.edu

Coed. State control. Semester system. Special facilities: Alcohol Research Center, Child Study Center, John W. Keys Speech and Hearing Center, Oklahoma Center for Neurosciences, Toxicology Center. Library: 233,000 volumes, 2600 current periodicals, 41 PCs; has MEDLINE, HEALTHLINE. No on-campus housing available.

Graduate College

Tuition: per credit, resident $74, nonresident $234. Enrollment: full-time 695, part-time 320 (men 20%, women 80%). Faculty: full-time 320, part-time 141. Degrees conferred: M.P.H., M.S., Dr.P.H., Ph.D., M.D.-Ph.D.(Biomedical Sciences), M.P.H.-M.B.A. (with Oklahoma State University).

ADMISSION REQUIREMENTS. Official transcripts, three letters of recommendation, GRE Test required in support of College's application. TOEFL required for international applicants. Interviews may be arranged. Accepts transfer applicants. Graduates of unaccredited institutions not considered. Apply to Office of Graduate Admissions by April 1. Rolling admissions process. Application fee $25. Phone: (405)271-2085, fax, (405)271-1155.

ADMISSION STANDARDS. Competitive. Usual minimum average: 3.0 (A = 4).

FINANCIAL AID. Fellowships, research assistantships, teaching assistantships, tuition waivers, Federal W/S, loans. Approved for VA benefits. Apply by April 1 to the Office of the Dean for fellowships, assistantships; to the Financial Aid Office for all other programs. Use FAFSA. Aid available to part-time students.

DEGREE REQUIREMENTS. For M.S.: 30 credit hours; no residency required; thesis defense. For M.P.H.: 36 credit hours minimum, at least 30 in residence; thesis. Dr.P.H.: at least one and up to three years in full-time residence, depending upon previous preparation and experience; qualifying exam; dissertation; final oral exam. For Ph.D.: 60 credit hours minimum beyond the bachelor's, 30 credit hours in full-time residency; qualifying exam; dissertation defense. For M.D. requirements refer to College of Medicine listing below.

FIELDS OF STUDY.
Anatomical Sciences. M.S., Ph.D.
Audiology. M.S., Ph.D.

Biostatistics. M.P.H., M.S.
Education of the Deaf. M.S.
Epidemiology. M.P.H., M.S., Dr.P.H., Ph.D.
Health Administration. M.P.H., M.S., Dr.P.H., Ph.D.
Immunology. M.S., Ph.D.
Molecular Biology. M.S., Ph.D.
Nursing. M.S.
Nutritional Sciences. M.S.
Occupational and Environmental Health. M.P.H., M.S., Dr.P.H., Ph.D.
Orthodontics. M.S.
Pathology. Ph.D.
Periodontics. M.S.
Pharmacology. Ph.D.
Pharmacy. M.S., Ph.D.
Physical Therapy. M.S.
Physiology. M.S., Ph.D.
Speech and Language Pathology. M.S., Ph.D.

School of Medicine (P.O. Box 26901)

Established 1900. Located in Oklahoma City (73190). Annual tuition: resident $7550, nonresident $19,050, student fees $307. Total average figure for all other expenses: $8000.
Enrollment: first-year class 150; total 650 (men 51%, women 49%) Faculty: full-time 150, part-time 250. Degree conferred: M.D. The M.S. and Ph.D. are offered through the Graduate College.

ADMISSION REQUIREMENTS. AMCAS report, transcripts, letters of recommendation, MCAT required in support of application. Interview by invitation only. Applicants must have completed at least three years of college study. Preference given to state residents. Does not have EDP. Apply to Assistant Dean for Admissions after June 15, before October 15. Application fee $50. Phone: (405)271-2331; fax: (405)271-3032.

ADMISSION STANDARDS. Selective. Accepts about 30% of total applicants. Approximately 90% are state residents.

FINANCIAL AID. Scholarships, fee waivers, loans. Apply to Director of Financial Aids; no specified closing dates. About 94% of students receive some financial assistance.

DEGREE REQUIREMENTS. For M.D.: satisfactory completion of four-year program. For M.S., Ph.D., see Graduate College listing above.

FIELDS OF GRADUATE STUDY.
Anatomical Sciences.
Biochemistry.
Biophysics.
Cell Biology.
Immunology.
Microbiology.
Neurosciences.
Pathology.
Pharmacology.
Physiology.

School of Dentistry

Established 1972. Located in Oklahoma City (73190). Annual tuition: resident $6260, nonresident $15,534. No on-campus housing available. Average academic year off-campus housing costs: $11,075. Contact Office for off-campus housing information. Phone: (405)325-2511. Total average cost for all other expenses: $5909.
Enrollment: first-year class 50; total 195 (men 50%, women 50%). Faculty: full-time 62, part-time 75. Degrees conferred: D.D.S., M.S.

ADMISSION REQUIREMENTS. AADSAS, official transcripts, three letters of recommendation, DAT (no later than October) required in support of School's application. Applicants must have completed at least two years of college study. Interviews by invitation only. Preference given to state residents. Apply to Office of Admissions after July 1, before December 1. Application fee $15. Phone: (405)271-3530.

ADMISSION STANDARDS. Selective. Accepts about 30–35% of total annual applicants. Approximately 80% are state residents.

FINANCIAL AID. Limited to scholarships, tuition waivers, grants, loans. Apply to Director, University Office of Financial Aid after acceptance and before May 1. Use FAFSA. Phone: (405)271-2118. About 75% of students receive some aid from School and outside sources.

DEGREE REQUIREMENTS. For D.D.S.: satisfactory completion of forty-five-month program. For M.S.: satisfactory completion of one-year program.

FIELDS OF GRADUATE STUDY.
Oral and Maxillofacial Surgery.
Orthodontics.
Periodontics.
Prosthetic Dentistry.

OLD DOMINION UNIVERSITY
Norfolk, Virginia 23529

Established 1930. Coed. State control. Semester system. Special facilities: Center for Coastal Physical Oceanography. Library: 842,000 volumes, 1,110,000 microforms, 78 PCs in all libraries.

Tuition: per credit, resident $171, nonresident $453. On-campus housing for 750 graduate men, 750 graduate women; none for married students. More housing available on competitive basis with undergraduate students. Average annual housing cost; $4500 (including board). Apply to Housing Office. Phone: (804)683-3843.

School of Graduate Studies

Enrollment: full-time 3885, part-time 2100. Faculty teaching graduate students: full-time 500, part-time 200. Degrees conferred: M.A., M.S., M.B.A., M.E., M.S.Ed., M.U.S., M.P.A., M.E.M., M.F.A., C.A.S., Psy.D., Ph.D., D.B.A.

ADMISSION REQUIREMENTS. Transcripts, three references (depending on program) required in support of School's application. GRE/GMAT required for certain programs. TOEFL required for international applicants. Accepts transfer applicants. Graduates of unaccredited institutions not considered. Apply to appropriate graduate program director at least two months prior to registration. Application fee $30. Phone: (804)683-3637, e-mail: aus100u@shawnee.odu.edu.

ADMISSION STANDARDS. Selective. Usual minimum average: regular status 2.5, 3.0 for major (A = 4).

FINANCIAL AID. Scholarships, assistantships, grants-in-aid (over one thousand of all kinds), Federal W/S, loans. Approved for VA benefits. Apply to appropriate graduate program director for fellowships, assistantships; to Financial Aid Office for all other programs; no specified closing date. Use FAFSA and institutional FAF. Phone: (804)683-3638; fax: (804)683-5920.

DEGREE REQUIREMENTS. For master's: 30–33 semester hours minimum, at least 24 in residence; thesis/nonthesis option;

final oral/written exam. For C.A.S.: 30 semester hours beyond the master's. For Ph.D.: up to 48 semester hours beyond the master's; preliminary exam; language requirement; research tool; dissertation; final oral defense.

FIELDS OF STUDY.,
Biology. M.S.
Biomedical Sciences. Ph.D.
Business Administration. M.B.A., D.B.A.
Business and Distributive Education. M.S.Ed.
Chemistry. M.S.
Civil Engineering. M.E., M.S., Ph.D.
Clinical Psychology. Psy.D.
Community Health Education. M.S.
Computational and Applied Mathematics. M.S., Ph.D.
Computer Science. M.S.
Dental Hygiene. M.S.
Early Childhood Education. M.S.Ed.
Ecological Sciences. Ph.D.
Economics. M.A.
Educational Administration. M.S.Ed., C.A.S.
Electrical Engineering. M.E., M.S., Ph.D.
Elementary Education. M.S.Ed.
Engineering Management. M.E.M., Ph.D.
Engineering Mechanics. M.E., M.S., Ph.D.
English. M.A.
Geology. M.S.
Guidance and Counseling. M.S.Ed., C.A.S.
History. M.A.
Humanities. M.A.
International Studies. M.A., Ph.D.
Mechanical Engineering. M.E., M.S., Ph.D.
Medical Technology. M.S.
Nursing. M.S.
Oceanography. M.S., Ph.D.
Physical Education. M.S.Ed.
Physics. M.S.
Physics (Applied). Ph.D.
Psychology. M.S., Ph.D.
Public Administration. M.P.A.
Reading. M.S.Ed.
Secondary Education. Includes biology, chemistry, English, mathematics, physics, social studies. M.S.Ed.
Sociology (Applied). M.A.
Special Education. M.S.Ed.
Speech Pathology and Audiology. M.S.Ed.
Urban Health Services. Ph.D.
Urban Studies. M.U.S.
Visual Studies. M.A., M.F.A.

OLIVET NAZARENE UNIVERSITY
Kankakee, Illinois 60901-0592
http://www.olivet.edu/

Founded 1907. Located 50 miles S of Chicago. Coed. Semester system. Private control. Church of the Nazarene affiliation. Library: 155,000 volumes, 88,000 microforms, 25 PCs.

Annual tuition: full-time $6000, per credit $200. Limited on-campus housing for graduate students. Contact the Admissions Office for housing information. Phone: (815)939-5203.

Graduate Program

Graduate study since 1961. Enrollment: full-time 273, part-time 32. Graduate faculty: full-time 48, part-time 119. Degrees conferred: M.A. M.A.E., M.A.T., M.B.A., M.C.M., M.P.C.

ADMISSION REQUIREMENTS. Official transcripts, three references, interview, photograph required in support of application. GRE required for some programs. TOEFL required for international applicants. Accepts transfer applicants. Apply by July 1 (Fall), December 1 (Spring), May 1 (Summer). Phone: (815)939-5291; fax: (815)935-4991.

ADMISSION STANDARDS. Selective. Usual minimum average: 2.5 (A = 4).

FINANCIAL AID. Thirty-seven grants, three teaching assistantships, Federal W/S, loans. Approved for VA benefits. Apply to Office of Financial Aid; no specified closing date. Use FAFSA and institutional FAF. Phone: (815)939-5249; fax: (815)935-4990.

DEGREE REQUIREMENTS. For M.A., M.A.E., M.C.M., M.P.C.: 30 semester hours minimum; thesis or scholarly option of 2–4 credits. For M.B.A., M.A.T.: 36 semester hours minimum.

FIELDS OF STUDY.
Business Administration.
Church Management.
Education. Includes elementary, English, reading, science, social studies.
Marriage and Family Counseling.
Pastoral Counseling.
Professional Counseling.
Religion.
Teaching. Includes elementary and secondary.

ORAL ROBERTS UNIVERSITY
Tulsa, Oklahoma 74171-0001
http://oru.edu

Founded 1965. Coed. Private control. Semester system. Library: 650,000 volumes, 300,000 microforms. Limited on-campus housing available. Rooms/apartments for both single and married students. Average academic year on- and off-campus housing costs: $4474–$6750. Apply to Director, Residential Life. Phone: (918)495-7700.

School of Business

Graduate study since 1978. Tuition: per credit $215. Enrollment: full-time 45, part-time 18. Faculty: full-time 7, part-time 3. Degree conferred: M.B.A.

ADMISSION REQUIREMENTS. Transcripts, letters of recommendation, GMAT required in support of School's application. TOEFL required for international applicants. Accepts transfer students. Apply at least one month prior to the beginning of each semester. Application fee $35. Phone: (918)495-6117; fax: (918)495-6033.

ADMISSION STANDARDS. Selective. Usual minimum average: 3.0 (A = 4). GMAT score required 500, TOEFL score required 600.

FINANCIAL AID. Scholarships, grants, assistantships, fellowships, career-related internships, Federal W/S, loans. Approved for VA benefits. Apply by March 15 to Director of University Financial Aid. Use FAFSA. Phone: (918)495-7035; fax: (918)395-6803. About 30% of the students receive aid other than loans from University and outside sources.

DEGREE REQUIREMENTS. For M.B.A.: 34–40 credits minimum; final exam.

FIELDS OF STUDY.
Accounting.
Business Administration.
Finance.
Health Care Management.
International Business.
Management.
Marketing.

School of Education

Graduate study since 1965. Tuition: per credit $215. Enrollment: full-time 65, part-time 85. Faculty: full-time 7, part-time 8. Degree conferred: M.A.Ed.

ADMISSION REQUIREMENTS. Transcripts, letters of recommendation, GRE/MAT required in support of School's application. TOEFL required for international applicants. Accepts transfer students. Apply at least one month prior to the beginning of each semester. Application fee $35. Phone: (800)678-8876, (918)495-6665; fax: (918)495-6050; E-mail: GRADEDU@ORU.EDU.

ADMISSION STANDARDS. Selective. Usual minimum average: 2.5 (A = 4). TOEFL score required 550.

FINANCIAL AID. Twenty-two scholarships, seventeen grants, twenty assistantships, Federal W/S, loans. Approved for VA benefits. Apply by March 15 to Director of University Financial Aid. Use FAFSA. Phone: (918)495-6510; fax: (918)395-6803. About 30% of the students receive aid other than loans from University and outside sources.

DEGREE REQUIREMENTS. For M.A.Ed.: 30–36 credit hours depending upon program; thesis optional.

FIELDS OF STUDY.
Christian School Teaching. Includes public school certification.
Curriculum and Instruction.
Early Childhood Education.
School Administration.
TESOL.

Graduate School of Theology and Missions

Graduate study since 1965. Tuition: per credit $170. Enrollment: full-time 400, part-time 235. Faculty: full-time 24, part-time 27. Degrees conferred: M.A., M.Div., D.Min.

ADMISSION REQUIREMENTS. Transcripts, letters of recommendation, GRE/MAT required in support of School's application. TOEFL required for international applicants. Accepts transfer students. Apply at least six months prior to the beginning of each semester. Application fee $35. Phone: (800)678-8876, (918)495-6127; fax: (918)495-6259.

ADMISSION STANDARDS. Selective. Usual minimum average: 2.5 (A = 4).

FINANCIAL AID. Limited to Federal W/S, loans. Approved for VA benefits. Apply by March 15 to Director of University Financial Aid. Use FAFSA. Phone: (918)495-6510; fax: (918)395-6803. About 30% of the students receive aid other than loans from University and outside sources.

DEGREE REQUIREMENTS. For M.A.: 36 credits hours depending upon program; thesis/nonthesis option. For M.Div.: 72 credits minimum in full-time residence; final comprehensive exam or research paper. For D.Min.: 32 credits minimum beyond M.Div., at least two semesters in full-time residence; thesis.

FIELDS OF STUDY.
Advanced Languages.
Biblical Literature.
Charismatic/Pentecostal Studies.
Christian Counseling.
Christian Education.
Divinity.
Marriage and Family Therapy.
Ministry and Missions.
Practical Theology.
Sacred Music.
Substance Abuse.
Theological Historical Studies.

OREGON GRADUATE INSTITUTE OF SCIENCE AND TECHNOLOGY
Portland, Oregon 97291-1000

Graduate study only. Coed. Quarter system. Special facilities: Center for the Application of Advanced Materials Science and Engineering Concepts, Center for Coastal and Land-Margin Research, Center for Groundwater Research, Center for Molecular Cardiology, Center for Semiconductor Research, Center for Spoken Language Understanding, Data-Intensive Systems Center, Change Research Center, Pacific Software Research Center. Library: 31,000 volumes, 13 microforms, 8 PCs.

Annual tuition: $15,000, per credit $375. No on-campus housing available. Off-campus monthly housing cost: approximately $650. Enrollment: full-time 227, part-time 130. Faculty: full-time 72, part-time 71. Degrees conferred: M.S., Ph.D.

ADMISSION REQUIREMENTS. Transcripts, GRE, letters of recommendations required in support of Institute's application. TOEFL required for international applicants. Accepts transfer applicants. Graduates of unaccredited institutions not considered. Apply to the Director of Admissions and Records at least two months prior to the date of registration. Rolling admissions process. Application fee $50. Phone: (800)685-2423; fax: (503)690-1285.

ADMISSION STANDARDS. Selective for most departments, competitive for the others. Usual minimum average: 3.0 (A = 4).

FINANCIAL AID. Fellowships, assistantships, Federal W/S, loans. Apply to the appropriate department chair for fellowships, assistantships; to Financial Aid Office for all other programs. Use FAFSA. About 65% of students receive aid from Institute and outside sources.

DEGREE REQUIREMENTS. For M.S.: 45 credit hours minimum, at least 30 credits in residence; thesis/nonthesis option; final written/oral exam. For Ph.D.: three years minimum beyond the bachelor's degree; residency requirement; qualifying exam; candidacy; dissertation; final exam.

FIELDS OF STUDY.
Applied Physics. M.S., Ph.D.
Computer Engineering. M.S., Ph.D.
Computer Science. M.S., Ph.D.
Electrical Engineering. M.S., Ph.D.
Environmental Science. Includes atmospheric sciences. M.S., Ph.D.
Management in Science and Technology. M.S.
Materials Science and Engineering. M.S., Ph.D.

Note: Joint degree programs are offered with Pacific University, Willamette University, Reed College, Lewis & Clark University.

OREGON HEALTH SCIENCES UNIVERSITY
Portland, Oregon 97201-3098

Oregon's Medical School was founded in 1887. In 1974 the University of Oregon's Schools of Medicine, Dentistry and Nursing were unified at the University of Oregon Health Sciences Center; in 1981 it was renamed the Oregon Health Sciences University. Library: 200,000 volumes, 32 PCs.

School of Medicine

Established 1887. Annual tuition: M.D. program, resident $13,466, nonresident $28,339, student fees $2097. On-campus housing available. Phone: (503)494-7747. Total average figure for all other expenses: $8000.

Enrollment: M.D. program, first-year class 90; total full-time 494 (men 60%, women 40%); graduate programs 117. Faculty: full-time 350, part-time 50. Degrees conferred: M.D., M.D.-Ph.D., M.S., Ph.D.

ADMISSION REQUIREMENTS. For M.D. program: AMCAS report, transcripts, letters of recommendation, MCAT, interview required in support of application. Applicants must have completed at least three years of college study. Preference given to Oregon residents and residents of WICHE states without medical schools. Does not have EDP. Apply to Office of Admissions after June 15, before November 15. Application fee $60. Phone: (503)494-2998; fax: (503)494-3400. For graduate study: transcripts, letters of recommendation, GRE Subject Tests required in support of application. Interview sometimes required. Accepts transfer applicants. Graduates of unaccredited colleges not considered. Apply to Director of Admissions at least three months prior to date of expected entrance.

ADMISSION STANDARDS. For M.D. program: selective. Accepts 15–20% of total annual applicants. Approximately 85% are state residents. For graduate study: very competitive for some departments, competitive for the others.

FINANCIAL AID. For M.D. program: Sixty scholarships, loans. Apply to Financial Aid Office; no specified closing date. For graduate study: research fellowships, assistantships. Apply to appropriate department chair; no specified closing date. About 75% of students receive some aid from School.

DEGREE REQUIREMENTS. For M.D.: satisfactory completion of four-year program. For M.S.: 45 credit hours minimum, at least three terms in residence; thesis; final oral exam. For Ph.D.: 135 credit hours minimum, at least six terms in residence; reading knowledge of one foreign language; written qualifying exam; thesis; final oral exam.

FIELDS OF GRADUATE STUDY.
Biochemistry.
Biopsychology.
Cell Biology and Anatomy.
Genetics.
Immunology.
Medical Psychology. Ph.D. only.
Medical Technology. M.S. only.
Microbiology.
Molecular Biology.
Molecular and Medical Genetics.

Neurosciences.
Pathology.
Pharmacology. Ph.D. only.
Physiology.

School of Dentistry (97201-3097)

Founded 1900. Joined state system in 1945. Quarter system. Library: 20,000 volumes. Annual tuition: resident $8521, nonresident $17,654. Total average cost for all other expenses: $6349. Enrollment: first-year class 70; total 296 (men 80%, women 20%). Faculty: full-time 72, part-time 91. Degrees conferred: D.M.D., M.S., Certificates.

ADMISSION REQUIREMENTS. Official transcripts, three letters of recommendation, DAT (no later than October) required in support of School's application. Applicants must have completed at least three years of college study. Interview may be required. Preference given to Oregon residents; WICHE residents second. Apply to Office of Admission after June 1, before November 15. Application fee $40. Phone: (503)494-5274; fax: (503)494-4666.

ADMISSION STANDARDS. Selective. Accepts 30–35% of total annual applicants. Approximately 60% are state and WICHE residents.

FINANCIAL AID. Grants, scholarships, loans. Apply to Financial Aid Office by March 1; Financial Aid interview required. Phone: (503)494-8249. About 92% of students receive some aid from School and outside sources.

DEGREE REQUIREMENTS. For D.M.D.: satisfactory completion of forty-five-month program. For M.S.: 45 quarter hours minimum, at least three quarters in residence; thesis; final oral exam.

FIELDS OF GRADUATE STUDY.
Oral and Maxillofacial Surgery.
Orthodontics.
Pediatric Dentistry
Periodontics.
Prosthodontics.

OREGON STATE UNIVERSITY

Corvallis, Oregon 97331
http://www.orst.edu

Founded 1868. Located 85 miles S of Portland. Coed. State control. Quarter system. Special facilities: Agricultural Experiment Station, Center for Advanced Materials Research, Center for Gene Research and Biotechnology, Center for Analysis of Environmental Change, Computer Center, Cooperative Center for Marine Resources Studies, Engineering Experiment Station, Environmental Health Sciences Center, Environmental Remote Sensing Laboratory, Forest Research Laboratory, Center for Humanities, Integrated Plant Protection Center, Mark O. Hatfield Marine Science Center, Nuclear Science and Engineering Institute, Nutrition Research Institute, Radiation Center, Sea Grant College Program, Survey Research Center, Transportation Research Institute, Water Resources Research Institute, and the Western Rural Development Center. Library: 1,225,000 volumes, 1,700,000 microforms.

Annual tuition: full-time, resident, $5796, nonresident $9811; per credit, resident $198, nonresident $356. On-campus housing includes dormitories, cooperative living groups, apartments for married students, and miscellaneous rental properties owned by the University. Average annual (12 month) housing costs: $5700 (including board). Apply to Director of Housing and Dining Services. Phone: (541)737-4771.

Graduate School
http://www.orst.edu/Dept/grad_school

Graduate study since 1876. Enrollment: full-time 2158 (men 1318, women 846). Graduate faculty: full-time 1800. Degrees conferred: M.A., M.Agr., M.A.I.S., M.A.T., M.B.A., Ed.M., M.Eng., M.F., M.Oc.E., M.P.H., M.S., Ed.D., Ph.D.

ADMISSION REQUIREMENTS. Transcripts, letters of recommendation, statement indicating special fields of interest required in support of School's application. GRE/GMAT/NTE required by some departments. TOEFL and certification of financial support required for international applicants. Accepts transfer applicants. Graduates of unaccredited institutions not considered. Apply to Office of Admission and Orientation as soon after January 1 as possible for Fall admission. Departments may establish their own deadlines. Application fee $50. Phone: (541)737-4411; fax: (541)737-2482.

ADMISSION STANDARDS. Selective. Usual minimum average: 3.0 (A = 4) on the last 90 graded quarter hours of undergraduate work.

FINANCIAL AID. Annual awards from institutional funds: 625 teaching assistantships, 725 research assistantships, Federal W/S, loans. Approved for VA benefits. Apply to appropriate department chair for assistantships; to Financial Aid Office for all other programs. Use FAFSA. Phone: (541)737-2241; fax: (541)737-2400.

DEGREE REQUIREMENTS. For master's: 45 credit hours minimum, at least 30 in residence; thesis/nonthesis option; final exam for some programs. For Ph.D.: three years minimum beyond the bachelor's; residency requirement; preliminary exam; thesis; final exam. For Ed.D.: two years teaching experience; other requirements essentially the same as for the Ph.D.

FIELDS OF STUDY
Adult Education. Ed.M.
Agricultural and Resource Economics. M.S., Ph.D.
Agricultural Education. M.S.
Agriculture. M.Agr.
Animal Science. M.S., Ph.D.
Apparel, Interiors, and Merchandising. M.A., M.S., Ph.D.
Applied Anthropology. M.A.
Atmospheric Sciences. M.A., M.S., Ph.D.
Biochemistry and Biophysics. M.A., M.S., Ph.D.
Bioresource Engineering. M.S., Ph.D.
Botany and Plant Pathology. M.A., M.S., Ph.D.
Business Administration. M.B.A.
Chemical Engineering. M.S., Ph.D.
Chemistry. M.A., M.S., Ph.D.
Civil Engineering. M.S., Ph.D.
College Student Services Administration. Ed.M., M.S.
Comparative Veterinary Medicine. Ph.D.
Computer Science. M.A., M.S., Ph.D.
Counseling. M.S., Ph.D.
Crop Science. M.S., Ph.D.
Economics. M.A., M.S., Ph.D.
Education. Ed.M., M.S., Ed.D., Ph.D.
Electrical and Computer Engineering. M.S., Ph.D.
English. M.A.
Entomology. M.A., M.S., Ph.D.
Environmental Health Management. M.S.
Family Resource Management. M.S., Ph.D.
Fisheries Sciences. M.S., Ph.D.
Food Science and Technology. M.S., Ph.D.
Forest Engineering. M.F., M.S., Ph.D.
Forest Products. M.F., M.S., Ph.D.
Forest Resources. M.F., M.S., Ph.D.

Forest Science. M.F., M.S., Ph.D.
General Science. M.A., M.S., Ph.D.
Genetics. M.A., M.S., Ph.D.
Geography. M.A., M.S., Ph.D.
Geology. M.A., M.S., Ph.D.
Geophysics. M.A., M.S., Ph.D.
Health Education. M.S.
Health and Safety Administration. M.S.
Home Economics. M.S.
Horticulture. M.S., Ph.D.
Human Development and Family Studies. M.S., Ph.D.
Human Performance. M.S., Ph.D.
Industrial Engineering. M.S., Ph.D.
Interdisciplinary Studies. M.A.I.S.
Manufacturing Engineering. M.Eng.
Marine Resource Management. M.A., M.S.
Materials Science. M.S.
Mathematics. M.A., M.S., Ph.D.
Mathematics Education. M.A., M.S., Ph.D.
Mechanical Engineering. M.S., Ph.D.
Microbiology. M.A., M.S., Ph.D.
Molecular and Cellular Biology. Ph.D.
Movement Studies in Disability. M.S.
Nuclear Engineering. M.S., Ph.D.
Nutrition and Food Management. M.S., Ph.D.
Ocean Engineering. M.Oc.E.
Oceanography. M.A., M.S., Ph.D.
Operations Research. M.A., M.S.
Pharmacy. M.S., Ph.D.
Physics. M.A., M.S., Ph.D.
Plant Physiology. M.S., Ph.D.
Poultry Science. M.S., Ph.D.
Public Health. M.P.H., M.S., Ph.D.
Radiation Health Physics. M.A., Ph.D.
Rangeland Resources. M.S., Ph.D.
Science Education. M.A., M.S., Ph.D.
Scientific and Technical Communication. M.A., M.S.
Soil Science. M.S., Ph.D.
Statistics. M.A., M.S., Ph.D.
Teaching. M.A.T.
Toxicology. M.S., Ph.D.
Veterinary Science. M.S.
Wildlife Science. M.S., Ph.D.
Zoology. M.A., M.S., Ph.D.

College of Veterinary Medicine (97331-4801)

Established 1949. Annual tuition: resident and contract non-residents $9168, nonresident $17,200. On-campus housing available; estimated living expenses: $7000.

Enrollment: first-year class 36; full-time 150 (men 60%, women 40%); no part-time students. Faculty: full-time 29, part-time 15. Degree conferred: D.V.M. The M.S. and Ph.D. are offered through the Graduate School.

ADMISSION REQUIREMENTS. VMCAS report, transcripts, VCAT or GRE, two recommendations, animal/veterinary experience, essay required in support of application. Interview by invitation only. Accepts transfer applicants on a space-available basis only. Graduates of unaccredited college not considered. Applicants must have completed at least two years of preprofessional college study. Preference given to state and Western Regional Compact state residents. Apply to Dean, College of Veterinary Medicine after July 1, before November 1. Fall admission only. Application fee $40. Phone: (503)737-2098; fax: (503)737-4245.

ADMISSION STANDARDS. Selective. Accepts 50% of total annual applications. Accepts up to a maximum of 8 nonresident applicants.

FINANCIAL AID. Scholarships, loans, grants. Apply to Director of Student Aids; no specified closing date.

DEGREE REQUIREMENTS. For D.V.M.: satisfactory completion of four-year program. For Compact state residents: first year at OSU, second and third year at Washington State University, fourth year back at OSU. For M.S., Ph.D., see Graduate School listing above.

FIELDS OF GRADUATE STUDY.
Comparative Veterinary Medicine.
Laboratory Animal Medicine.
Microbiology.
Parasitology.
Pathology.
Pharmacology.
Physiology.
Toxicology.
Veterinary Biochemistry and Nutrition.

UNIVERSITY OF OREGON

Eugene, Oregon 97403
http://www.uoregon.edu

Established 1871. Coed. State control. Quarter system. Special facilities: Institute for Chemical Physics, Humanities Center, Institute for Molecular Biology, Institute for Neuroscience, Institute of Theoretical Science, Computing Center, Advanced Science and Technology Institute, Bureau of Government Research, Institute on Violence and Destructive Behavior, Center for the Study of Women in Society, Oregon Institute of Marine Biology, Solar Energy Center. Library: 2,064,000 volumes, 1,973,000 microforms, 17,900 current periodicals, 75 PCs.

Annual tuition: full-time, resident $5889, nonresident $10,062; part-time resident $781, nonresident $1248. On-campus housing for married students and single students. Average academic year housing costs: $2368 for married students off-campus; $3949 (including board) for single students on-campus. Contact Housing Office for both on- and off-campus housing information. Phone: (503)346-4277.

Graduate School

Organized 1900. Enrollment: full-time 2695, part-time 571. Faculty: full-time 539, part-time 55. Degrees conferred: M.A., M.Arch., M.B.A., M.Ed., M.F.A., M.Mus., M.S., M.U.P., Ed.D., D.M.A., Ph.D.

ADMISSION REQUIREMENTS. Official transcripts, GRE/GMAT/MAT, three letters of recommendation required in support of School's application. Interview not required. TOEFL required for international applicants. Accepts transfer applicants. Graduates of unaccredited institutions not considered. Apply to appropriate department or school at least one month prior to registration. Rolling admissions process. Application fee $50. Phone: (503)346-5129.

ADMISSION STANDARDS. Selective. Usual minimum average: 3.0 (A = 4).

FINANCIAL AID. Annual awards from institutional funds: 1183 research/teaching assistantships, full tuition waiver, Federal W/S, loans. Approved for VA benefits. Apply by February 1 to appropriate department for fellowships, assistantships; to the Office of Student Financial Aid for all other programs. Phone:

(503)346-3221. Use FAFSA. About 30% of students receive aid other than loans from School. Aid sometimes available for part-time students.

DEGREE REQUIREMENTS. For most master's: 45 quarter hours minimum, at least 39 in residence; reading knowledge of one foreign language for M.A.; qualifying exam/final exam/thesis required for some departments. For M.F.A.: two years minimum, at least one year in full-time residence; final project; oral/written final exam. For M.Arch., M.L.A., M.U.P.: 45 quarter hours minimum, at least 39 in residence; thesis/final project. For Ph.D.: three years minimum beyond the bachelor's, at least one year in residence; qualifying exam; oral/written comprehensive exam; thesis; oral/written final exam. For Ed.D.: essentially the same as for the Ph.D., except no specified language requirement.

FIELDS OF STUDY.

COLLEGE OF ARTS AND SCIENCES:
Anthropology. Includes archaeology, cultural, linguistics, physical.
Asian Studies. Interdisciplinary. Includes China, Japan, Southeast Asia. M.A., M.S.
Biochemistry.
Biology. Includes cell, developmental, ecology, genetics, marine, microbiology, molecular, neuroscience.
Chemistry. Includes biochemistry, cell biology, chemical physics, materials science, organic, physical, theoretical.
Classics. Includes classics, Greek, Latin. M.A. only.
Comparative Literature. Interdisciplinary.
Computer Science and Information Science.
Creative Writing.
Ecology and Evolution.
Economics. Includes advanced macroeconomics, applied econometrics, economic growth and development, industrial organization, international, labor, public finance, urban-regional.
English. Includes American literature, creative writing, English literature. M.A., Ph.D.
Environmental Studies. M.A., M.S.
Exercise and Movement Science. Includes biomechanics, motor control, physiology of exercise, social psychology of sport, sport medicine.
Geography. Includes biogeography, cultural, physical, quaternary geography.
Geological Sciences. Includes mineral deposits, mineralogy–petrology, geochemistry stratigraphy–sedimentary petrology paleontology, structural geology–geophysics, volcanology.
Germanic Languages and Literature. M.A., Ph.D.
History. Includes ancient, Britain and its empire, East Asia and Southeast Asia, German-speaking world, Latin American, medieval, early modern and modern Europe, Soviet Union, United States. M.A., Ph.D.
Individualized Program. Interdisciplinary. Includes applied information management, environmental studies, folklore. M.A., M.S.
International Studies. Interdisciplinary. M.A. only.
Linguistics. Includes applied, general. M.S., Ph.D.
Mathematics. Includes algebra, analysis, combinatorics, differential and algebraic geometry, geometry, mathematical physics, numerical analysis, probability, statistics, topology.
Philosophy. M.A., Ph.D.
Physics. Includes astronomy, astrophysics, cosmology; atomic and molecular, and optical physics; biophysics; condensed-matter; elementary-particle; fluid and superfluid mechanics; nuclear.
Political Science. Includes American government, classical and contemporary political theory, comparative politics, international relations, public policy, research methodology.
Psychology. Includes clinical, cognitive, developmental, physiological-neuroscience, social and personality.

Romance Languages. Includes French, Italian, Spanish language and literature. M.A., Ph.D.
Russian. M.A.
Sociology. Includes sex and gender, labor, organization, and political, environment, social psychology, language and culture, theory.
Speech. Includes theater arts.

SCHOOL OF ARCHITECTURE AND ALLIED ARTS:
Architecture. M.Arch. only.
Art History. M.A., Ph.D.
Arts Management.
Community and Regional Planning. M.C.R.P. only.
Fine and Applied Arts. Includes ceramics, jewelry and metalsmithing, painting, printmaking, sculpture, visual design, fibers. M.F.A. only.
Historic Preservation. M.S. only.
Interior Architecture. M.I.Arch.
Landscape Architecture. Includes planing, public policy and management. M.L.A. only.
Public Affairs. M.A., M.S.

COLLEGE OF BUSINESS ADMINISTRATION:
Accounting. Ph.D. only.
Decision Sciences. Includes business statistics, production, operations management.
Finance.
Industrial Relation. M.A., M.S.
Information Management. M.S.
Management. Includes corporate strategy and policy (Ph.D.), general business (M.B.A.), human resources management (Ph.D.), organizational studies (Ph.D.).
Marketing.

COLLEGE OF EDUCATION:
Communication Disorders and Sciences.
Computer and Education.
Counseling. Includes community and other agency settings, early intervention, employment and vocational, individual and family.
Counseling Psychology. Ph.D. only.
Educational Administration.
Educational Policy and Management.
Higher Education.
Management and Leadership.
School Psychology.
Special Education. Includes developmental disabilities, handicapped learner, rehabilitation.
Speech Pathology and Audiology.
Teaching Foreign Languages.

SCHOOL OF JOURNALISM AND COMMUNICATION:
Journalism. Includes advertising, magazine, news-editorial, public relations, radio-television. M.A., M.S. only.

SCHOOL OF MUSIC:
Choral Conducting. M.Mus.
Composition. M.Mus., D.M.A.
Dance. M.A., M.S.
Music Education.
Music History.
Music Theory.
Performance.
Piano Pedagogy.
Wind Ensemble Conduction.

School of Law (97403-1221)

Established 1884. Located in Eugene. Semester system. Law library: 300,000 volumes. Library has LEXIS, NEXIS, WESTLAW; 21 computer workstations. Summer study available.

Annual tuition: resident $9090, nonresident $13,572. On-campus housing available. Total average annual additional expense: $6800.

Enrollment: first-year class 157; total full-time 426 (men 54%, women 46%). Faculty: full-time 40, part-time 11. Degrees conferred: J.D., J.D.-M.B.A., J.D.-M.S. (Environmental Studies).

ADMISSION REQUIREMENTS. LSDAS law school report, bachelor's degree, transcripts, LSAT required in support of application. Written recommendations and personal statements encouraged. Accepts transfer applicants. Graduates of unaccredited institutions not considered. Apply to Admissions Office after September 1, before April 1. Fall admission only. Application fee $50. Phone: (503)346-3846.

ADMISSION STANDARDS. Selective. Accepts 25–30% of total annual applicants.

FINANCIAL AID. Scholarships, partial tuition waivers, Federal W/S, loans, grants for second- and third-year students Apply to Office of Financial Aid by March 1. Use FAFSA. About 40% of students receive aid other than loans from School.

DEGREE REQUIREMENTS. For J.D.: satisfactory completion of three-year program. For M.B.A., M.S., see Graduate School listing above.

COLLEGE OF OSTEOPATHIC MEDICINE OF THE PACIFIC
Pomona, California 91766-1889

Founded 1977. Coed. Private control. Semester system. Library: 10,000 volumes, 400 current periodicals; has MEDLINE.
Annual tuition: $20,815. No on-campus housing available.
Enrollment: first-year class 170, total 682 (men 68%, women 32%). Faculty: full-time 42, part-time 1000. Degree conferred: D.O.

ADMISSION REQUIREMENTS. AACOMAS report, bachelor's degree preferred, official transcripts, MCAT, three recommendations (one from premed advisory committee, one evaluation from a physician, preferably a D.O.), supplemental form required in support of application. Interview by invitation only. Graduates of unaccredited colleges not considered. Apply by February 1 (earlier applications encouraged) to the Director of Admissions. Admits first year students Fall only. Rolling admissions process. Application fee $50. Phone: (800)477-COMP, or (909)469-5335.

ADMISSION STANDARDS. Selective. Accepts approximately 5% of total annual applicants. Usual minimum average: 2.8 (A = 4), mean GPA: 3.2.

FINANCIAL AID. Scholarships, Federal W/S, loans. Apply by June 1 to the Financial Aid Office. Use FAFSA and institutional FAF.

DEGREE REQUIREMENT. For D.O.: satisfactory completion of four-year program.

UNIVERSITY OF OSTEOPATHIC MEDICINE AND HEALTH SCIENCES
Des Moines, Iowa 50312-4104

College of Osteopathic Medicine and Surgery

Founded 1898. Coed. Private control. Semester system. Library: 28,000 volumes, 500 current periodicals, 40 PCs; has

MEDLINE, CANCERLINE, BIOETHIC, HEALTH, TOXLINE, DIALOG, OCLC.
Annual tuition: $20,500. No on-campus housing available. Average academic year housing costs: $525 per month. Contact the Dean of Students Office for off-campus housing information. Phone: (515)271-1504.
Enrollment: first-year class 200, total 795 (men 65%, women 35%). Faculty: full- and part-time 59. Degree conferred: D.O.

ADMISSION REQUIREMENTS. AACOMAS report, bachelor's degree, official transcripts, MCAT, three recommendations (one from premed advisory committee, one evaluation from a physician, preferably a D.O.), supplemental form required in support of application. Interview by invitation only. Graduates of unaccredited colleges not considered. Preference given to state resident. Apply by March 1 to the Director of Admissions. Admits first year students Fall only. Rolling admissions process. Application fee $50. Phone: (515)271-1450/1614; fax: (515)271-1578.

ADMISSION STANDARDS. Selective. Accepts approximately 31% of total annual applicants. Usual minimum average: 2.75 (A = 4), mean GPA: 3.32.

FINANCIAL AID. Scholarships, Federal W/S, loans. Apply by July 15 to the Financial Aid Office. Use FAFSA and institutional FAF.

DEGREE REQUIREMENT. For D.O.: satisfactory completion of four-year program.

OTIS COLLEGE OF ART AND DESIGN
Los Angeles, California 10057

Founded 1918. Coed. Private control. Semester system. Library: 27,000 volumes.
Annual tuition: full-time $15,900; per credit $530. On-campus housing for single students only. Annual academic year housing costs: $2700 (double occupancy). Contact Assistant Dean Student Services for both on- and off-campus housing information. Phone: (213)251-0547.

Graduate Study

Enrollment: full-time 20, part-time 1. Faculty: full-time 1, part-time 14. Degree conferred: M.F.A.

ADMISSION REQUIREMENTS. Transcripts, three letters of recommendation, portfolio of fifteen to twenty pieces of work (can be photographs or color slides) required in support of application. Interview sometimes required. TOEFL required for international applicants. Accepts transfer applicants. Apply to Admissions Committee by April 15. Application fee $40. Phone: (213)251-0577; fax: (213)480-0059.

ADMISSION STANDARDS. Selective. Admission based on talent. TOEFL score a minimum of 600.

FINANCIAL AID. Annual awards from institutional funds: seven scholarships, six to eight teaching assistantships, Federal W/S, loans. Approved for VA benefits. Apply to Financial Aid Office; no specified closing date. Use FAFSA and institutional FAF. Phone: (213)251-0541. About 60% of students receive aid other than loans from College and outside sources.

DEGREE REQUIREMENTS. For M.F.A.: at least four semesters in full-time residence; departmental requirements determined by portfolio review; final essay; applied project; gallery exhibition.

FIELDS OF STUDY.
Ceramics.
Drawing.
Painting.
Photography.
Printmaking.
Sculpture.

OUR LADY OF THE LAKE UNIVERSITY

San Antonio, Texas 78207-4666

Founded 1985. Coed. Independent. Roman Catholic. Semester system, except Weekend College's M.B.A. is on trimester system. Library: 166,000 volumes, 106,000 microform, 10 PCs.

Tuition: $7333; per credit hour $333. On-campus housing available for single and married students. Average academic year housing costs: $2140–$3756. Apply to Office of Campus Activities and Services. Phone: (210)434-6711.

College of Art and Sciences

Graduate study since 1911. Enrollment: full-time 10 and part-time 25. Graduate faculty: full-time 5, part-time 3. Degrees conferred: M.A., Psy.D.

ADMISSION REQUIREMENTS. Transcripts, GRE required in support of application. TOEFL required for foreign applicants. Accepts transfer applicants. Apply to Director of Admissions by August 15 (Fall), December 15 (Spring), May 5 (Summer). Application fee $15. Phone: (210)434-6711; fax: (210)436-9028.

ADMISSION STANDARDS. Selective. Usual minimum average: 2.5, or 3.0 (A = 4) in last 60 undergraduate credits.

FINANCIAL AID. Scholarships, assistantships, Federal W/S, loans. Approved for VA benefits. Apply to the Office of Financial Aid; no specified closing date. Use FAFSA. Phone: (512)434-6711.

DEGREE REQUIREMENTS. For M.A.: 30–36 credits minimum; thesis/nonthesis. For Psy.D.: 54 credits in residence beyond master's degree, at least 30 credits in residence; candidacy; clinical case study; final oral exam.

FIELDS OF STUDY.
Communication Art.
Counseling Psychology.
English Education.
English Language and Literature.
Note: Cooperative programs with University of the Incarnate Word and St. Mary's University.

School of Business and Public Administration

Graduate study since 1978. Coed. Trimester system. A weekend instructional format.

Tuition: per credit $314. Enrollment: full-time 9, part-time 441. Graduate faculty: full-time 12, part-time 3. Degree conferred: M.B.A.

ADMISSION REQUIREMENTS. Transcripts, GRE/MAT/GMAT, two letters of recommendation, detailed resume required in support of School's application. TOEFL required for international applicants. Accepts transfer applicants. Graduates of unaccredited institutions not considered. Apply to Director of Admission by at least one week prior to Weekend College orientation for the trimester of registration. Application fee $15. Phone: (210)434-6711, ext. 491; fax: (210)436-0821.

ADMISSION STANDARDS. Selective. Usual minimum average: 2.5, or 3.0 (A = 4) in last 60 undergraduate credits.

FINANCIAL AID. Limited to loans. Approved for VA benefits. Apply to the Office of Financial Aid; no specified closing date. Use FAFSA. Phone: (210)434-6711, ext. 319.

DEGREE REQUIREMENTS. For M.B.A.: 36 credits minimum; thesis/professional project option in lieu of six semester hours of electives.

FIELDS OF STUDY.
Business Administration.
Health Care Management.

School of Education and Clinical Studies

Graduate study since 1950. Tuition: per credit $314; doctoral tuition per credit $357.

Enrollment: full-time 96, part-time 170 (men 19%, women 81%). Graduate faculty: full-time 30, part-time 20. Degrees conferred: M.A., M.Ed., M.S., Psy.D.

ADMISSION REQUIREMENTS. Transcripts, GRE/MAT, two letters of recommendation required in support of School's application. TOEFL required for foreign applicants. Accepts transfer applicants. Apply to School of Education by August 6 (Fall), January 4 (Spring), May 5 (Summer); some programs have earlier deadlines. Application fee $15. Phone: (210)434-6711, ext. 372; fax: (210)436-2314.

ADMISSION STANDARDS. Selective. Usual minimum average: 2.5, or 3.0 (A = 4) in last 60 undergraduate credits.

FINANCIAL AID. Fellowships, assistantships for teaching/research, Federal W/S, loans. Approved for VA benefits. Apply to the Office of Financial Aid; no specified closing date. Use FAFSA. Phone: (210)434-6711, ext. 319.

DEGREE REQUIREMENTS. For M.A.: 36 credits minimum, at least 24 in residence; final oral/written exam. For M.Ed.: 36 credits minimum, at least 30 in residence; final written exam. For M.S. (Psychology): 60 credits minimum; comprehensive exam. For Psy.D.: 119 credits beyond the bachelor's degree, two consecutive 9-hour semesters in residence; dissertation; written/oral exam.

FIELDS OF STUDY.
Administration and Supervision.
Bilingual Education.
Communication Disorders.
Curriculum and Instruction.
Early Childhood Education.
General Counseling.
Human Sciences.
Learning Resources.
Psychological Counseling.
School Counseling.
School Psychology.
Special Education.

Worden School of Social Services

Graduate study since 1942. Coed. Semester system.

Enrollment: full-time 121, part-time 50. Graduate faculty: full-time 12, part-time 3. Degree conferred: M.S.W.

ADMISSION REQUIREMENTS. Transcripts, GRE/MAT, three letters of recommendation required in support of School's application. TOEFL required for international applicants. Interview may be required. Accepts transfer applicants. Graduates of unaccredited institutions not considered. Apply to Director of Admission by April 2 (Fall), November 2 (Spring). Application fee $15. Phone: (210)434-6711, ext. 231; fax: (210)436-2314.

ADMISSION STANDARDS. Selective. Usual minimum average: 2.5, or 3.0 (A = 4) in last 60 undergraduate credits.

FINANCIAL AID. Limited to Federal W/S, loans. Approved for VA benefits. Apply to the Office of Financial Aid; no specified closing date. Use FAFSA. Phone: (210)434-6711, ext. 319.

DEGREE REQUIREMENTS. For M.S.W.: 58 credits minimum, at least one year in residence; field practicum; final oral/written exam.
Note: A 36 credit hour program is available for eligible undergraduates with a B.S.W. from a CSWE accredited program.

PACE UNIVERSITY
New York, New York 10038

Founded 1906. Westchester campuses at Pleasantville/Briarcliff and White Plains. Private control. Semester system. Special facilities: Center for Applied Research, Center for International Business, Center for Nursing Research and Clinical Practice. Library: 825,000 volumes, 666,000 microforms.

Tuition: per credit $485. On-campus housing for single students at all campuses. Average academic year housing costs: $3420–$4500.

Lubin School of Business
Graduate Programs

Graduate study since 1906. Enrollment: full-time 300, part-time 2600 (men 55%, women 45%). Graduate faculty: full-time 65, part-time 55. Degrees conferred: M.S., M.B.A., Advanced Professional Certificate, D.P.S.

ADMISSION REQUIREMENTS. Transcript, GMAT required in support of School's application. TOEFL required for international applicants. Interview may be required. Accepts transfer applicants. Graduates of unaccredited colleges not considered. Apply to Graduate Admissions Office by August 15 (Fall), December 15 (Spring), March 15 (May Term), May 1 (Summer). Application fee $60. Phone: (212)346-1531.

ADMISSION STANDARDS. Selective. Usual minimum average: 3.0 (A = 4).

FINANCIAL AID. Scholarships, 160 research/administrative assistantships, Federal W/S, loans. Approved for VA benefits. Apply to Graduate Admissions Office by March 15 (Summer and Fall), December 15 (Spring). Phone: (212)346-1300. Use FAFSA. About 65% of students receive aid from University and outside sources. Aid available to part-time students.

DEGREE REQUIREMENTS. For M.B.A.: 36 credits minimum, at least 33 in residence. For M.S.: 36 credit hours minimum, at least 30 in residence. For D.P.S.: 57 credits beyond the master's; written/oral exam; dissertation. For A.P.C.: 18 credits minimum.

FIELDS OF STUDY.
Accounting. M.B.A., M.S.
Banking and Finance. M.B.A.
Business Economics. M.B.A., M.S.
Corporate Financial Management. M.B.A.
Financial Economics. M.B.A.
Information Systems. M.B.A.

International Business. M.B.A.
Investment Management. M.B.A., M.S.
Management Science. M.B.A.
Managerial Accounting. M.B.A.
Marketing Management. M.B.A.
Operations Management. M.B.A.
Taxation. M.B.A., M.S.
Note: Special degree programs include J.D./M.B.A., International Exchange Programs; M.S. Accounting/Internship Program; Dual concentration M.B.A.

Dyson College of Arts and Science

Graduate study since 1906. Enrollment: full-time 95, part-time 332. Graduate faculty: full-time 26, part-time 49. Degrees conferred: M.S., M.S.Ed., M.P.A., Psy.D.

ADMISSION REQUIREMENTS. Transcript, GRE/MAT required in support of College's application. TOEFL required for international applicants. Interview may be required. Accepts transfer applicants. Graduates of unaccredited colleges not considered. Apply to Graduate Admissions Office by August 15 (Fall), December 15 (Spring), March 15 (May Term), May 1 (Summer). Rolling admissions process. Application fee $60. Phone: (212)346-1531.

ADMISSION STANDARDS. Selective. Usual minimum average: 3.0 (A = 4).

FINANCIAL AID. Scholarships, research assistantships, teaching assistantships, tuition waivers, Federal W/S, loans. Approved for VA benefits. Apply to Graduate Admissions Office by March 15 (Summer and Fall), December 15 (Spring). Phone: (212)346-1300. Use FAFSA. About 25% of students receive aid from University and outside sources. Aid available to part-time students.

DEGREE REQUIREMENTS. For M.P.A.: 36 credits minimum, at least 33 in residence. For M.S.: 36 credit hours minimum, at least 30 in residence. For Psy.D.: 57 credits beyond the master's; qualifying exam; internship; written/oral exam; special research project.

FIELDS OF STUDY.
Counseling-Substance Abuse. M. S.
Government Management. M.P.A.
Health Care Administration. M.P.A.
Publishing. M.S.
School-Community Psychology. M.S.Ed., Psy.D.

School of Law

Established 1976. Located in White Plains (10603). Semester system. Library: 293,000 volumes. Library has LEXIS, NEXIS, WESTLAW, DIALOG, VUTEXT, EPIC, RLIN, OCLC, PALS.

Tuition: full-time $19,394, part-time $14,522. On-campus housing available. Total average annual additional expense: $9395.

Enrollment: first-year class, full-time 160, part-time 93; total full- and part-time 720 (men 53%, women 47%). Degrees conferred: J.D., J.D.-M.B.A., J.D.-M.P.A., LL.M. (Environmental Law).

ADMISSION REQUIREMENTS. LSDAS Law School report, bachelor's degree, transcripts, LSAT, two letters of recommendation, a personal statement required in support of application. Accepts transfer applicants. Graduates of unaccredited institutions not considered. Apply to Office of Admissions by March 15 for priority consideration. Rolling admissions process. Application fee $50. Phone: (914)681-4210.

ADMISSION STANDARDS. Selective. Admits about 30% of total annual applications. Summer conditional program available.

FINANCIAL AID. Limited scholarships, grants, Federal W/S, loans. Apply to Admissions Office by March 15. Use FAFSA or GAPSFAS. About 50% of students receive some aid from School.

DEGREE REQUIREMENTS. For J.D.: satisfactory completion of three-year (full-time), four-year (part-time) program; 90 credit hour program. For LL.M.: at least 24 credits minimum beyond the J.D. For M.B.A., M.P.A., see graduate school listing above. *Note:* School has summer program in conjunction with the University of London (Great Britain).

PACIFIC LUTHERAN UNIVERSITY
Tacoma, Washington 98447

Founded 1890. Coed. Private control. Lutheran affiliation. 4-1-4 calendar system. Library: 247,757 volumes, 75,000 microforms, 21 PCs.

Tuition: $455 per credit hour. On-campus housing for 27 married students; single students accommodated in dormitories. Average academic year housing cost: $4644 (including board) for single students. Contact Assistant Director for Residential Life for both on- and off-campus housing information. Phone: (206)535-7200.

Division of Graduate Studies

Enrollment: full-time 126, part-time 176. Faculty: full-time 60, part-time 20. Degrees conferred: M.A., M.A. in Computer Application, M.A. in Ed., M.A. in Social Sci., M.B.A., M.P.E., M.S. in Computer Sci., M.S. in Nursing, M.A., in Physical Education.

ADMISSION REQUIREMENTS. Transcripts, two references, MAT or GRE (Education) required in support of application. GMAT for admission to M.B.A. program. TOEFL required for international applicants. Interview required for M.A.S.S. (Marriage and Family Therapy) and M.A.E. Accepts transfer applicants. Apply to Dean of Graduate Studies at least one month prior to registration. Rolling admissions process. Application fee $35. Phone: (800)274-6758, (206)535-7151; fax: (206)535-8320; E-mail: admission@plu.edu.

ADMISSION STANDARDS. Selective for most departments. Usual minimum average: 2.75 (A = 4).

FINANCIAL AID. Annual awards from institutional funds: summer scholarships, 14 research fellowships, Federal W/S, loans. Approved for VA benefits. Apply to Dean of Graduate Studies by March 31. Use FAFSA. Phone: (206)535-7161. No aid for part-time students.

DEGREE REQUIREMENTS. For master's: 32 semester hours minimum, at least 24 in residence; thesis or research paper; final oral/written exam.

FIELDS OF STUDY.
Business Administration. M.B.A.
Computer Science. M.A.C.A., M.S.C.S.
Education. Includes concentrations in administration, educational psychology, classroom teaching, literacy education, special education; teaching experience required. M.A.
Nursing. Includes continuity of care administration, nurse practitioner. M.S.N.

Physical Education. Includes sports administration, teaching, exercise science. M.P.E.
Social Sciences. Includes concentrations in marriage and family therapy, organizational systems, individualized study.

PACIFIC UNION COLLEGE
Angwin, California 94508
http://www.pac.edu

Founded 1882. Located 76 miles NE of San Francisco. Coed. Quarter system. Private control. Seventh-day Adventist. Library: 123,000 volumes, 78,000 microforms, 10 PCs.

Annual tuition: full-time $12,960; per credit $375. Limited on-campus housing for married and single students. Single students need permission to live off-campus. Average academic year housing costs: $4050 (including board) for single students. Apply to the Office of Enrollment Services. Phone: (800)862-7080.

Graduate Division

Graduate study since 1933. Enrollment: full- and part-time 16. College faculty: 128; graduate faculty full-time 4, part-time none. Degree conferred: M.A.

ADMISSION REQUIREMENTS. Official transcripts, GRE, written essay, two letters of recommendation, MSAT (as required), CBEST, interview required in support of application. All applicants must possess a teaching credential. Accepts transfer applicants. Graduates of unaccredited colleges considered on an individual basis. Apply to Office of Enrollment Services; no specified closing date. Application fee $30. Phone: (800)862-7080.

ADMISSION STANDARDS. Selective. Usual minimum average: 3.0 (overall), 3.0 (U.G. major), 3.0 (Education courses) (A = 4).

FINANCIAL AID. Limited. Two assistantships, Federal W/S, loans. Apply to Student Financial Services; no specified closing date. Use FAFSA. Phone: (800)862-7080; fax: (707)965-6400.

DEGREE REQUIREMENTS. For master's: 45 quarter hours minimum including graduate project, at least 33 hours in residence; final oral exam. Teacher training emphasis.

FIELD OF STUDY.
Education. Includes a reading emphasis.

PACIFIC UNIVERSITY
Forest Grove, Oregon 97116-1797

Founded 1842. Located 23 miles W of Portland. Coed. Private control. United Church of Christ. Semester system. Special facilities: Malheur Field Station, Blodget Arboretum. Library: 219,000 volumes, 20,200 microforms, 1000 current periodicals, 10 PCs.

Annual tuition: Education, full-time $12,960; per credit $270; Physical Therapy, full-time $13,998, per credit $466; Professional Psychology, full-time $15,120, per credit $375. On-campus housing for graduate men and women; none for married students. Average academic year housing costs: $4100 (including board) for single students. Contact Dean of Students Office for both on- and off-campus housing information. Phone: (503)357-6151, ext. 2200.

Graduate Division

Enrollment: full-time 557; part-time 149. University faculty teaching graduate students: full-time 47, part-time 64. Degrees conferred: M.S., M.A. in Ed., M.A.T., M.S.P.T., M.S.T.

ADMISSION REQUIREMENTS. Official transcripts required in support of application. TOEFL required for international applicants. Accepts transfer applicants. Apply to Director of Admissions for Professions programs; no specified closing dates for School of Education (rolling admission process), January 15 (Fall) for School of Physical Therapy, December 15 (Fall) for School of Professional Psychology. Application fee $40. Phone: (503)359-2900; fax: (503)359-2975.

ADMISSION STANDARDS. Selective or relatively open. Usual minimum average: 2.5 (A = 4).

FINANCIAL AID. Annual awards from institutional funds: research/teaching assistantships, Federal W/S, loans. Approved for VA benefits. Apply by April 1 to Director of the Professional Programs for assistantships; to Financial Aid Office for all other programs. Use FAFSA. About 35% of students receive aid other than loans from University and outside sources. Aid available for part-time students.

DEGREE REQUIREMENTS. For master's: 30 semester hours minimum, at least 21 in residence; GRE for candidacy; thesis/final project. For Psy.D.: 45 semester hours beyond the master's, at least two years in residence or equivalent; qualifying exam; internship; research paper; final exam.

FIELDS OF STUDY.
Clinical Optometry.
Clinical Psychology.
Elementary Education.
Physical Therapy.
Professional Psychology.
Secondary Education.
Visual Function in Learning.

UNIVERSITY OF THE PACIFIC

Stockton, California 95211-0197
http://www.uop.edu

Founded 1851. Located 90 miles E of San Francisco. Coed. Private control. Semester system. Library: 444,000 volumes, 531,000 microforms, 48 PCs in all libraries.

Annual tuition: full-time $17,910; per unit charge $560. On-campus housing available. Average academic year housing costs: $5300 (including board). Apply to Director of Housing. Phone: (209)946-2331.

Graduate School

Enrollment: full-time 450, part-time 150. University faculty: full-time 210, part-time 10. Degrees conferred: M.A., M.S., M.Ed., M.A.T., Mus.M., Ed.D., D.A., Ph.D.

ADMISSION REQUIREMENTS. Transcripts, references, GRE Subject Tests required in support of School's application. TOEFL score of 550 required for international applicants. Accepts transfer applicants. Apply to Dean of Graduate School by March 1 (Summer, Fall), November 15 (Spring). Application fee $50. Phone: (209)946-2261; fax: (209)946-2858.

ADMISSION STANDARDS. Selective. Usual minimum average: 3.0 (A = 4).

FINANCIAL AID. Annual awards from institutional funds: scholarships, twelve grants, sixty-eight teaching assistantships, Federal W/S, loans. Approved for VA benefits. Apply March 1 to the Dean for assistantships; to Financial Aid Office for all other programs. Use FAFSA. Phone: (209)946-2421. About 20% of students receive aid other than loans from University and outside sources. Aid sometimes available for part-time students.

DEGREE REQUIREMENTS. For master's: 28–32 units minimum, at least 24 in residence; thesis/nonthesis option; final oral exam. For Ph.D.: 45 units beyond master's; preliminary written/oral, reading knowledge of 2 foreign languages; dissertation; final oral exam. For Ed.D., D.A.: 65 units minimum beyond the bachelor's, at least 36 in residence and 2 semesters in full-time attendance; preliminary written/oral exam; foreign language usually not required; dissertation; final oral exam.

FIELDS OF STUDY.
Biological Sciences. Includes microbiology, botany, zoology. M.S. only.
Business. M.B.A. only.
Chemistry.
Communication. M.A. only.
Communicative Disorders. M.A. only.
Education. Includes administration and supervision, curriculum and instruction, educational counseling, social foundations, special education.
Electrical Engineering. M.S. only.
English. 1 language for M.A.
History. M.A. only.
Music (Pacific Conservatory of Music). Includes applied music, theory and composition, music education, music therapy. M.A., Mus.M. only.
Pharmaceutical Sciences. Includes pharmaceutics, clinical pharmacy, medicinal chemistry, physiology-pharmacology.
Physical Therapy. M.S. only.
Physics. M.S. only.
Psychology. M.A. only.
Religion. M.A. only.
Sociology. M.A. only.
Sport Sciences. M.A. only.

McGeorge School of Law

Founded 1924, amalgamated with the University in 1966. Located at Sacramento (95817). Semester system. Law library: 390,000 volumes. Library has LEXIS, NEXIS, WESTLAW, DIALOG. Day and evening programs. Annual tuition: day $16,820, evening $9714. On-campus housing available. Apply to the Housing Office. Early applications advised. Total average annual additional expense: $13,910.

Enrollment: first-year class, day 315, evening 81; total full- and part-time 1225 (men 56%, women 44%). Faculty: full-time 50, part-time 40. Degrees conferred: J.D., J.D.-M.B.A., J.D.-M.P.P.A., LL.M. (Taxation, Business and Taxation, Transnational Business Practice).

ADMISSION REQUIREMENTS. LSDAS Law School report, bachelor's degree, transcripts, LSAT, three letters of recommendation required in support of application. Applicants must have completed at least three years of college study. Interview not required. Accepts transfer applicants. Apply to Admissions Committee; no specified closing date; early applications encouraged. Application fee $40. Phone: (916)739-7105.

ADMISSION STANDARDS. Selective. Accepts about 40–45% of total annual applicants.

FINANCIAL AID. Scholarships, Federal W/S, loans. Apply to Financial Aid Office by April 1. Use FAFSA and institutional financial aid form. About 85% of students receive aid other than loans from School and outside sources.

DEGREE REQUIREMENTS. For J.D.: 88 credit hour program, at least 84 in residence. LL.M.: at least 24 credit hours beyond the J.D.; one year in residence; thesis.

School of Dentistry

Established 1896. Quarter system. Located in San Francisco, 2155 Webster Street (94115).

Annual tuition: $27,747. Off-campus housing only. Average academic year housing costs: $12,040. Contact Off-campus Housing Office. Phone: (415)929-6491. Total average cost for all other first year expenses: $11,212.

Enrollment: first-year class 125; total 400 (men 55%, women 45%); postgraduates 12. School faculty: full-time 50, part-time 75. Degrees conferred: B.A.-D.D.S., D.D.S., M.S. (Orthodontics).

ADMISSION REQUIREMENTS. AADSAS report, official transcripts, DAT (no later than November) required in support of School's application. TOEFL, TSE, TWE required for international applicants whose native language is not English. Interview by invitation only. Applicants must have completed at least three years of college study. Preference given to Asia Pacific Islanders and state residents. Apply to Office Admission, after June 1, before April 1. Application fee $50. Phone: (415)929-6491.

ADMISSION STANDARDS. Selective. Accepts 30% of total annual applicants. Approximately 90% are Asia Pacific Islanders and state residents.

FINANCIAL AID. Scholarships, grants, loans. Apply to Office of Financial Aid after acceptance. Use FAFSA. Phone: (415)929-6452. About 85% of students receive aid from School and outside sources.

DEGREE REQUIREMENTS. For D.D.S.: satisfactory completion of thirty-six-month program.

MEDICAL COLLEGE OF PENNSYLVANIA AND HAHNEMANN UNIVERSITY
Philadelphia, Pennsylvania 19102-1192

The Medical College of Pennsylvania, established 1850, and Hahnemann University, established 1848, consolidated in 1993, and are now the educational anchor of Allegheny Health, Education and Research Foundation (AHERF), a statewide health care system. Campuses in Philadelphia and Pittsburgh and clinical affiliate hospitals in Pennsylvania and New Jersey. More than 3,500 faculty and 3,100 students. Libraries: 185,000 volumes, 3,000 journals, online catalogs. Limited on-campus housing. Average academic year housing costs: $7200–$8500. Contact Office of Student Housing. Phone: (215)762-8495.

Graduate School

Enrollment: full-time 624, part-time 231, total 855 (men 33%, women 67%). Graduate School faculty: full-time 235, part-time 100. Annual Tuition: full-time $10,120, part-time $563 per credit (some programs higher). Degrees conferred: M.A., M.S., M.F.T., M.P.T., M.E.M.S., M.L.A.S., M.G.P.G.P., M.M.S., Ph.D., J.D.-Ph.D., M.D.-Ph.D.

ADMISSIONS REQUIREMENTS. Official transcripts, three letters of recommendation, GRE General (some programs accept MAT in lieu of GRE) required in support of School's application.

Interview required for some programs. TOEFL required for international applicants. Accepts transfer applicants. Graduates of unaccredited institutions not considered. Application deadlines: Biomedical Science programs April 1; Clinical Psychology January 15; Art Therapy March 1; Family Therapy April 1; Foreign Applicants April 1; Law-Psychology February 15; M.D./Ph.D. November 15; master's in Physical Therapy December 15; all others June 1. Application fee $50. Biomedical Science applicants: phone: (215)991-8570. Professional programs: phone: (215)762-8388.

ADMISSIONS STANDARDS. Very selective. Usual minimum average: 3.0 (A = 4).

FINANCIAL AID. Scholarships, stipends, research assistantships, teaching assistantships, Federal W/S, loans. Biomedical Science students apply to Biomedical Science Office; all others to Financial Aid Office. Use FAFSA. Phone: (215)762-7739. About 70% of students receive some form of financial aid.

DEGREE REQUIREMENTS. For M.A. and M.S.: 48 semester hours minimum; comprehensive exam; thesis. For all other master's degree programs: 48 semester hours minimum; some programs require comprehensive exam and thesis. For Ph.D.: 96 semester hours minimum, at least four semesters in residence; qualifying exam; dissertation.

FIELDS OF STUDY.

BIOMEDICAL SCIENCE PROGRAMS:
Anatomy and Neurobiology. Ph.D.
Biochemistry. Ph.D.
Microbiology and Immunology. M.S., Ph.D.
Molecular and Cell Biology. M.S., Ph.D.
Molecular Pathobiology. Ph.D.
Neuroscience. Ph.D.
Pharmacology. M.S., Ph.D.
Physiology. Ph.D.
Radiation Sciences. M.S., Ph.D.

PROFESSIONAL PROGRAMS:
Clinical Microbiology. M.S.
Clinical Psychology. Ph.D.
Creative Arts in Therapy. M.A.
Emergency Medical Services. M.E.M.S.
Family Therapy. M.F.T.
Group Process and Group Psychotherapy. M.S., M.G.P.G.P.
Hand/Upper Quadrant Rehabilitation. M.S.
Laboratory Animal Sciences. M.L.A.S.
Law/Psychology. J.D.-Ph.D. in conjunction with Villanova University Law School.
Orthopedic Physical Therapy. M.S., Ph.D.
Pediatric Physical Therapy. M.S., Ph.D.
Physical Therapy. M.P.T. (entry-level master's)

School of Medicine (19129)

Medical College of Pennsylvania founded 1850. Hahnemann University School of Medicine founded 1848. Coed. Private control. Semester system.

Annual tuition: $22,500. Total average cost for all other expenses: approximately $12,400.

Enrollment: first-year class 250 (EDP 12), total full-time 692 (men 62%, women 38%). Faculty: approximately 4000 full- and part-time and volunteers. Degrees conferred: M.D., M.D.-Ph.D.

ADMISSION REQUIREMENTS. AMCAS report, transcripts, letters of reference, MCAT, interview required in support of application. Has EDP; apply between June 1 and August 1. Apply to Committee on Admission by November 1. Application fee $50. Phone: (215)991-8202; fax: (215)843-1766.

ADMISSION STANDARDS. Very selective. Accepts about 5% of total applicants. Approximately 50% are state residents.

FINANCIAL AID. Scholarships, fellowships, loans. Apply to Committee on Admissions after acceptance before May 31. Phone: (215)762-7734. Use PHEAA and FAFSA. About 90% of students receive aid from School.

DEGREE REQUIREMENTS. For M.D.: satisfactory completion of four-year program. For Ph.D.: see Graduate School listing above.

FIELDS OF GRADUATE STUDY.
Anatomy.
Biochemistry.
Immunology.
Microbiology.
Molecular Biology.
Neurosciences.
Pathology.
Pharmacology.
Physiology.

Medical College of Pennsylvania Medical School

Tuition: $16,500. Enrollment: first-year class 136; total full-time 470 (men 50%, women 50%). Faculty: full-time 600. Degrees conferred: B.A., B.S.-M.D. (Joint programs with Leigh University and Villanova University), M.D., M.D.-M.S., M.D.-Ph.D.

ADMISSION REQUIREMENTS. AMCAS report, transcripts, MCAT, interview required in support of application. Has EDP; apply between June 15 and August 1. Applicants must have completed at least three years of college study. Preference given to state residents. Apply to Office of Student Affairs after June 15, before December 1 (Fall). Application fee $55. Phone: (215)842-7009.

ADMISSION STANDARDS. Very competitive. Accepts about 3% of total annual applicants. Approximately 30% are state residents.

FINANCIAL AID. Scholarships, loans, CWSP. Apply to School's Financial Aid Office after acceptance.

DEGREE REQUIREMENTS. For B.A./B.S.-M.D.: satisfactory completion of either six- or seven-year program. For M.D.: satisfactory completion of four-year program. For M.S., Ph.D., see graduate listing above.

PENNSYLVANIA COLLEGE OF OPTOMETRY
Philadelphia, Pennsylvania 19141-3323

Founded 1919. Coed. Private control. Quarter system. Library: 12,000 volumes, 325 periodicals, 25 PCs.

Annual tuition: full-time $11,400–$18,800. On-campus housing, 111 apartments. Average academic year housing costs: $5700 for married students, $3300 for single students. Board costs: single $1500, married $3000. Apply to Office of Student Affairs. Phone: (215)276-6262.

Enrollment: O.D.: full-time 616; M.S./M.Ed. part-time 33. College faculty: full-time 41, part-time 33. Degrees conferred: O.D., M.S., M.Ed.

ADMISSION REQUIREMENTS. O.D. program: transcripts, OAT, essay, letters of recommendation required in support of College's application. Graduates of unaccredited institutions not

considered. Apply to the Office of Admissions by March 31 for priority consideration. Rolling admissions process. For M.S./M.Ed.: O.D. required for admission. Apply by May 20 for priority consideration. Application fee $50. Phone: (215)276-6262; fax: (215)276-6081.

ADMISSION STANDARDS. Competitive.

FINANCIAL AID. Scholarships, Federal W/S, loans. Some surrounding states have contractual arrangements with College. Contact Admissions Office for pertinent information. For other aid apply by May 1 to Office of Admissions. Use FAFSA. About 55% of students receive aid other than loans from College and outside sources.

DEGREE REQUIREMENTS. For O.D.: four years beyond minimum three years of pre-optometry college study; final written exam; passage of National Board of Examiners in Optometry part 1 and part 2.

FIELDS OF STUDY.
Education of the Visually Handicapped.
Optometry. O.D.
Orientation and Mobility.
Rehabilitation Teaching.
Vision Rehabilitation.

PENNSYLVANIA STATE UNIVERSITY
University Park, Pennsylvania 16802

Founded 1855. Located 90 miles NW of Harrisburg. Coed, State control. Semester system. Special facilities: Agricultural Experiment Station, Agricultural and Home Economics Extension Services, Computation Center, Nuclear Reactor, Psychology Clinic, Reading Center, Institute of Public Administration, Ionosphere Research Laboratory, Materials Research Laboratory, Earth and Mineral Sciences Experiment Station, Applied Research Laboratory, Petroleum Refining Laboratory. Graduate work is offered in the Milton S. Hershey Medical Center in Hershey, Penn State Great Valley Center in Malvern near Philadelphia, Penn State Harrisburg, and the Penn State Erie; cooperative program with the Jefferson Medical College of Philadelphia. Library: 3,500,000 volumes, 1,300,000 government documents, 2,000,000 other biographical items.

Annual tuition: full-time resident $6078, nonresident $12,516; per credit, resident $256, nonresident $523. On-campus housing available for graduate students. Annual academic year housing costs: $3900–$4620 (including board) for single students, $3870 for one and two bedroom apartments. Apply to Assignment Office for Campus Residences, 101 Shields Building. Phone: (814)865-7501.

Graduate School

Graduate study since 1862. Enrollment: full-time 4387, part-time 2469. Graduate faculty: 2000. Degrees conferred: M.A., M.S., M.Agr., M.B.A., M.C.P., M.Ed., M.Eng., M.E.P.C., M.F.A., M.F.R., M.H.A., M.J., M.H.R.I.M., M.L.A., M.P.A., M.Mgt., M.Mus., D.Ed., Ph.D.

ADMISSION REQUIREMENTS. Two transcripts, GRE/GMAT/MAT (varies by department) required in support of School's application. TOEFL required for international applicants. Accepts transfer applicants. Apply to Office of Graduate Admissions; completed forms must be received at least one month prior to registration. Application fee $40. Phone: (814)865-1795; fax: (814)863-4627.

ADMISSION STANDARDS. Usual minimum average: 3.0 (A = 4).

FINANCIAL AID. Annual awards from institutional funds: 230 fellowships, 3000 graduate assistantships, Federal W/S, loans. Approved for VA benefits. Apply to departments for assistantships, fellowships; to the Financial Aid Office for all other aid. Use FAFSA. Phone: (814)865-6301. About 65% of students receive aid other than loans from both School and outside sources.

DEGREE REQUIREMENTS. For M.A., M.S.: 30 credits minimum, at least 20 in residence; thesis for most M.S. and M.A. candidates. For M.Agr.: 30 credits minimum, at least 20 in residence; final paper/report of internship training. For M.B.A.: 48 credits minimum; project paper. For M.C.P.: 36 credits minimum, at least 20 in residence. For M.Ed.: 30 credits minimum, at least 20 in residence. For M.Eng.: 30 credits minimum; final document. For M.E.P.C.: 30 credits minimum, at least 20 in residence; thesis/paper. For M.F.A.: 48 credits minimum; professional project plus monograph. For M.H.A.: 51 credits minimum; professional paper. For M.H.R.I.M.: 36 credits minimum; professional paper. For M.J.: 30 credits minimum. For M.L.A.: 44 credits minimum, at least 34 in residence; individual project. For M.Mgt.: 33 credit minimum. For M.P.A.: 45 credits minimum; professional paper. For M.Mus.: 36 credits minimum, at least 30 in residence; paper. For M.F.R.: 30 credits minimum. For Ph.D.: two consecutive semesters minimum in residence; candidacy exam; language requirement varies by department; comprehensive oral/written exam; final oral exam; thesis. For D.Ed.: minimum six semesters full-time or equivalent; 30 credits in residence; comprehensive exam; final oral exam; thesis.

FIELDS OF STUDY.
Acoustics.
Adult Education.
Advertising.
Aerospace Engineering.
Agricultural and Biological Engineering.
Agricultural Economics.
Agricultural Education.
Agronomy.
American Studies.
Anatomy.
Animal Science.
Anthropology.
Applied Psychology.
Architectural Engineering.
Architecture.
Art.
Art Education.
Art History.
Astronomy and Astrophysics.
Biobehavioral Health.
Biochemistry and Molecular Biology.
Biochemistry, Microbiology and Molecular Biology.
Bioengineering.
Biology.
Business Administration.
Cell and Molecular Biology.
Chemical Engineering.
Chemistry.
Civil Engineering.
Communication Disorders.
Community Psychology.
Community System Planning and Development.
Comparative and International Education.
Comparative Literature.
Composition/Theory.
Computer Science and Engineering.
Conducting.
Counseling Psychology.
Counselor Education.
Crime, Law and Justice.
Curriculum and Instruction.
Demography.
Earth Sciences.
Ecology.
Economics.
Educational Administration.
Educational Psychology.
Educational Theory and Policy.
Electrical Engineering.
Engineering Mechanics.
Engineering Science.
Engineering Science and Mechanics.
English.
Entomology.
Environmental Engineering.
Environmental Pollution Control.
Extension Education.
Film and Video.
Food Science.
Forest Resources.
French.
Genetics.
Geography.
Geosciences.
German.
Health Education.
Health Policy and Administration.
Higher Education.
History.
Horticulture.
Hotel, Restaurant, and Institutional Management.
Human Development and Family Studies.
Humanities.
Industrial Engineering.
Industrial Relations and Human Resources.
Information Science.
Information Systems.
Instructional Systems.
Journalism.
Kinesiology.
Laboratory Animal Medicine.
Landscape Architecture.
Leisure Studies.
Linguistics.
Man-Environment Relations.
Management.
Mass Communications.
Materials.
Materials Science and Engineering.
Mathematics.
Mechanical Engineering.
Medieval Studies.
Meteorology.
Microbiology and Immunology.
Mineral Economics.
Mineral Engineering Management.
Mineral Processing.
Mining Engineering.
Music.
Music Theory and History.
Neuroscience.
Nuclear Engineering.
Nursing.
Nutrition.
Operations Research.
Pathobiology.
Performance.
Petroleum and Natural Gas.
Pharmacology.

Philosophy.
Physics.
Physiology.
Piano Pedagogy and Performance.
Plant Pathology.
Plant Physiology.
Political Science.
Psychology.
Public Administration.
Quality and Manufacturing Management.
Rural Sociology.
School Psychology.
Sociology.
Soil Science.
Spanish.
Special Education.
Speech Communication.
Statistics.
Teaching and Curriculum.
Teaching English as a Second Language.
Telecommunications Studies.
Theater Arts.
Training and Development.
Voice Performance and Pedagogy.
Wildlife and Fisheries Science.
Workforce Education and Development.

College of Medicine

Founded 1964. Located at Hershey (17033-2360). Medical library: 125,000 volumes. Annual tuition: resident $15,960, nonresident $22,981; student fees $998. Off-campus housing available. Annual housing costs: single students $3000; married students $6500 (room only).

Enrollment: first-year class 110 (10 EDP); total 526 (men 55%, women 45%); postgraduates 10. Faculty: full-time 485; part-time 40. Degrees conferred: M.D., M.D.-Ph.D.

ADMISSION REQUIREMENTS. AMCAS report, transcripts, MCAT, interview required in support of application. Applicants must have completed at least three years of college study. Has EDP; apply between June 15 and August 1. Preference given to Pennsylvania residents. Apply to Admissions Committee after June 15, before November 15. Application fee $40. Phone: (717)531-8755; fax: (717)531-6225.

ADMISSION STANDARDS. Competitive. Accepts 5–6% total annual applicants. Approximately 60% are state residents.

FINANCIAL AID. Scholarships, CWSP, loans. Apply to Office of Student Affairs; no specified closing date. Use GAPSFAS. About 60% of students receive aid other than loans from College.

DEGREE REQUIREMENTS. For M.D.: satisfactory completion of four-year program. Combined M.D.-M.S. and M.D.-Ph.D. program available; see Graduate School listing above.

FIELDS OF GRADUATE STUDY.
Anatomy.
Biochemistry.
Biomedical Engineering.
Cell Biology.
Immunology.
Microbiology.
Molecular Biology.
Neurosciences.
Pharmacology.
Physiology.

PENNSYLVANIA STATE UNIVERSITY AT HARRISBURG— THE CAPITAL COLLEGE

Middletown, Pennsylvania 17057-4898

Established 1966. Public. Coed. Semester system. Library: 213,000, 1,100,000 microforms.

Annual tuition: resident $6078, nonresident 12,516; per credit resident $256, nonresident $523. On-campus housing for single and 20 married students. Annual academic year housing costs: $2800–$5100 single students, $4300 for married students.

Enrollment: full- and part-time 1335. Faculty: full-time 83, part-time 5. Degrees conferred: M.A., M.B.A., M.E.P.C., M.Ed., M.E.E., M.Eng., M.P.A., M.S., Ph.D., Ed.D., M.Com.Psy.

ADMISSION REQUIREMENTS. Transcripts, GRE/GMAT, recommendations required in support of College's application. TOEFL required for international applicants. Accepts transfer applicants. Apply to Office of Enrollment Services. Application fee $40. Phone: (717)948-6250.

ADMISSION STANDARDS. Selective. Usual minimum average: 2.5 (A = 4).

FINANCIAL AID. Limited to two scholarships, five research assistantships, Federal W/S, loans. Approved for VA benefits. Apply to Financial Aid Office; no specified closing date. Use FAFSA. Phone: (717)654-7728. About 1% of students receive aid other than loans from both College and outside sources.

DEGREE REQUIREMENTS. For master's: 30 credits minimum; research paper. For Doctorate: 90 credits minimum; qualifying exam; dissertation; final oral exam.

FIELDS OF STUDY.
American Studies.
Applied Psychology.
Business Administration.
Community Psychology.
Education.
Electrical Engineering.
Engineering Science.
Environmental Pollution Control.
Health Education.
Humanities.
Information Systems.
Public Administration.
Teaching and Curriculum.
Training and Development.

UNIVERSITY OF PENNSYLVANIA

Philadelphia, Pennsylvania 19104
http://www.upenn.edu

Founded 1740. Coed. Private control. Semester system. Special facilities: University Museum, Institute for Environmental Studies. Center for Health, Achievement, Neighborhood, Growth and Ethnic Studies (CHANGE), International Literacy Institute, National Center on Fathers and Families, National Institute on Adult Literacy, Institute of Neurological Sciences, Lauder Institute, Population Studies Center, Leonard Doves Institute of Health Economics, Center for the Study of Aging, Early American Studies Center, Center for Urban Ethnography, Wistar Institute of Anatomy and Biology. Library: 4,200,000 volumes, 1,500,000 microforms, 33,000 current periodicals.

Average academic year housing costs: $4500–$7900 for single students. Apply to Director of Residential Living for on-campus housing, to office of Off-Campus Living for off-campus housing. Phone: on-campus information, (215)989-3676, off-campus information (215)898-8500.

School of Arts and Sciences

Annual tuition: $20,846, per course $2478.

Enrollment: full-time 1688, part-time 500. Faculty: 850. Degrees conferred: A.M., M.S., Ph.D., postdoctoral study in most departments.

ADMISSION REQUIREMENTS. Transcripts, letters of recommendation, GRE General Tests required in support of School's application. GRE Subject Tests for fellowships. Evidence of proficiency in English, TOEFL/TSE required for international applicants. Accepts transfer applicants. Graduates of unaccredited institutions not considered. Apply by January 15 (for fellowships), July 15 (Fall), December 1 (Spring), May 1 (First Summer Session), June 1 (Second Summer Session). Application fee $55. Phone: (215)898-5720; fax: (215)898-0821.

ADMISSION STANDARDS. Very selective. Usual minimum average: 3.0 (A = 4).

FINANCIAL AID. Annual awards from institutional funds: grants, 603 fellowships, 1521 assistantships for teaching/research, loans. Apply by January 15 for fellowships. GRE required of all financial aid applicants. Use FAFSA. Phone: (215)898-1988; fax: (215)898-5428. About 60% of students receive aid other than loans from School. Generally no aid for part-time students.

DEGREE REQUIREMENTS. For A.M., M.S.: 8 units minimum in residence; thesis/final project; oral/written exam. For Ph.D.: 20 units minimum, at least 12 in residence; reading knowledge of two foreign languages for most departments; preliminary exam; dissertation; final oral/written exam.

FIELDS OF STUDY.
American Civilization.
Anatomy and Structural Biology.
Ancient History.
Anthropology.
Astronomy.
Astrophysics.
Biochemistry.
Biology. Includes cell, molecular, developmental.
Biophysics.
Chemistry.
Classical Archaeology.
Classical Studies.
Comparative Literature.
Demography.
East Asian Studies.
Ecology.
Economics.
Energy Management and Power.
English.
Folklore and Folklife.
French.
Geology.
Germanic Languages and Literatures.
Hellenistic Judaism.
Hillinistic Judaism.
Historic Preservation.
History.
History and Sociology of Science.
History of Art.
Immunology.
International Studies. A.M. only.
Italian.
Liberal Studies. M.S. only.
Linguistics.
Literary Theory.
Mathematics.
Molecular Biology. Includes genetics, microbiology.
Music.
Near Eastern Studies.
Neurosciences.
Philosophy.
Physics.
Plant Sciences.
Political Science.
Psychology.
Regional Science.
Religious Studies.
Social System Sciences.
Sociology.
South Asia Regional Studies.
Spanish.

Annenberg School for Communication

Founded 1959. Annual tuition: full time $16,146. Enrollment: full-time 75, part-time 15. Faculty: full-time 12, part-time 12. Degrees conferred: M.A.C., Ph.D.

ADMISSION REQUIREMENTS. Transcripts, three letters of recommendation, GRE required in support of application. Evidence of proficiency in English required of international applicants. Transfer applicants not accepted. Apply to School by January 15 (Fall). Application fee $55. Phone: (215)898-7041.

ADMISSION STANDARDS. Competitive. Usual minimum average: 3.0 (A = 4).

FINANCIAL AID. Scholarships, fellowships, assistantships, Federal W/S, loans. Approved for VA benefits. Apply at date of application for admission. Use FAFSA. Phone: (215)898-2046. About 80% of students receive aid other than loans from School and outside sources.

DEGREE REQUIREMENTS. For M.A.C.: 12 courses minimum; thesis. For Ph.D.: 20 courses minimum; preliminary exam; dissertation.

FIELD OF STUDY.
Communication.

Graduate School of Education

Graduate study since 1930. Annual tuition: $21,992, per course unit $2614.

Enrollment: full-time 513, part-time 371. Faculty: full-time 37, part-time 75. Degrees conferred: M.S.Ed., Ed.D., Ph.D.

ADMISSION REQUIREMENTS. All undergraduate and graduate transcripts, three letters of recommendation, GRE Subject Test/MAT required in support of School's application. Evidence of proficiency in English required of international applicants. Interview not required. Accepts transfer applicants. Graduates of unaccredited institutions not considered. Apply to Graduate School of Education by July 15 (Fall), December 1 (Spring), May 1 (Summer). Application fee $55. Phone: (215)898-6455; fax: (215)573-2166.

ADMISSION STANDARDS. Competitive. Usual minimum average: 3.0 (A = 4).

FINANCIAL AID. Twenty-seven fellowships, 173 teaching assistantships, Federal W/S, loans. Apply by February 1 to the appropriate department for fellowships, assistantships; to Financial Aid Office for all other programs. Use FAFSA and institutional FAF. Phone: (215)898-1501; fax: (215)573-2166. About 80% of students receive aid other than loans from School and outside sources. Aid available to part-time students.

DEGREE REQUIREMENTS. For M.S.: 10 units minimum; specialization exam; comprehensive exam. For Ph.D.: 20 units minimum, at least 10 in residence; qualifying exam; written major exam; written comprehensive exam; thesis; final oral exam. For Ed.D.: essentially the same as for the Ph.D.

FIELDS OF STUDY.
Counseling Psychology.
Early Childhood Education.
Education, Culture and Society.
Educational Linguistics.
Elementary and Secondary Counseling.
Elementary Education.
Higher Education.
Human Sexuality Education.
Intercultural Communication.
Policy and Leadership.
Policy Research and Educational Measurement (PREM).
Reading, Writing and Literacy.
School Psychology.
Science Education.
Secondary Education.
TESOL.

School of Engineering and Applied Science—Graduate

http://www.seas.Upenn.edu

Annual tuition: full-time $20,644, part-time $2614 per course.
Enrollment: full- and part-time 620. Graduate faculty: full-time 99, part-time none. Degrees conferred: M.S.E., Ph.D.

ADMISSION REQUIREMENTS. Transcripts, GRE, two letters of recommendation required in support of School's application. TOEFL score of 600 required for international applicants. Accepts transfer applicants. Graduates of unaccredited institutions not considered. Apply to Graduate Education and Research Office by July 1 (Fall), November 1 (Spring). Application fee $55. Phone: (218)898-9650; fax: (215)898-2245.

ADMISSION STANDARDS. Competitive. Usual minimum average: 3.0 (A = 4).

FINANCIAL AID. Fellowships, teaching assistantships, research fellowships, Federal W/S, loans. Approved for VA benefits. Apply by February 1 to Office of Student Financial Services. Use FAFSA and institutional FAF. Phone: (215)898-2046.

DEGREE REQUIREMENTS. For M.S.E.: 10 course units; thesis optional for some departments. For Ph.D.: 20 course units; dissertation; preliminary exam; final oral/written exam.

FIELDS OF STUDY.
Bioengineering.
Chemical Engineering.
Computer and Information Science.
Electrical Engineering.
Materials Science and Engineering.
Mechanical Engineering.
Systems Engineering.
Telecommunications.

Wharton School

Annual tuition: full-time $22,700. Enrollment: full- and part-time 1942. Graduate faculty: full-time 184, part-time 85. Degrees conferred: A.M., M.B.A., Exec. M.B.A., Ph.D.

ADMISSION REQUIREMENTS. Official transcripts, three letters of recommendation, GRE/GMAT required in support of School's application. TOEFL required for international applicants. Interview desirable. Graduates of unaccredited institutions not considered. Apply to Director of Admissions of the Graduate Division by April 1 (Fall), December 1 (Spring). Application fee $60. Phone: (215)898-7601.

ADMISSION STANDARDS. Very selective. Usual minimum average: master's 3.0 (A = 4); Ph.D. 3.3.

FINANCIAL AID. Scholarships, fellowships, assistantships, Federal W/S, loans. Apply by February 1 to the Office of the Dean for assistantships, fellowships; to the Financial Aid Office for all other programs. Use FAFSA. About 48% of students receive aid from School and outside sources.

DEGREE REQUIREMENTS. For Exec. M.B.A., M.B.A.: 18 units minimum in residence; thesis/final project. For A.M.: 10 units in residence; oral/written exam. For Ph.D.: 24 units minimum in residence; preliminary exam; reading knowledge of one foreign language and computer tool; dissertation; final oral exam.

FIELDS OF STUDY.
Accounting.
Decision Science.
Finance.
Health Care Systems.
Insurance and Risk Management.
International Studies.
Legal Studies.
Management.
Marketing.
Operations and Information Management.
Public Policy and Management.
Statistics.

Graduate School of Fine Arts

Library: 68,000 volumes.
Annual tuition: full-time $19,560.
Enrollment: full-time 551, part-time 128. School faculty: full-time 36, part-time 130. Degrees conferred: M.Arch., M.C.P., M.L.A., M.F.A., M.G.A., M.R.P., M.S., Ph.D.

ADMISSION REQUIREMENTS. Official transcripts, three letters of recommendation, portfolio required in support of application. TOEFL required for international applicants. Interview not required. Transfer applicants considered. Graduates of unaccredited institutions not considered. Apply to appropriate department chair by March 1 (February 1 for Architecture). Fall admission only. Application fee $55. Admissions Coordinator's phone: (215)898-6520.

ADMISSION STANDARDS. Competitive for most departments. Usual minimum average: 3.0 (A = 4).

FINANCIAL AID. Three hundred fifty-seven fellowships, seven research assistantships, fifty-three teaching assistantships, full and partial tuition waivers, Federal W/S, loans. Apply by March 1 to Graduate School of Fine Arts for fellowships, assistantships; for Financial Aid Office for all other programs. Use FAFSA. About 75% of students receive aid other than loans from School and outside sources.

DEGREE REQUIREMENTS. For M.S.: one year in full-time residence; thesis/nonthesis option; final exam. For M.Arch.: two to four years, depending upon previous education; thesis. For M.C.P., M.R.P.: four terms minimum of full-time study; one summer of office practice; thesis. For M.L.A.: generally two-year program, including one summer semester; thesis. For M.F.A.: two to three years, depending upon previous education. For Ph.D.: three to four years, depending upon previous education; at least two years in residence; reading knowledge of two foreign languages or one language and research tool; preliminary exam; dissertation; final oral/written exam.

FIELDS OF STUDY.
Architecture. M.Arch., M.S., Ph.D.
City and Regional Planning.
Fine Arts. Includes painting and sculpture.
Historic Preservation.
Landscape Architecture.
Regional Planning.
Urban Design.

School of Social Work

Established 1909. Annual tuition: $18,699; per course $2337. Enrollment: full-time 250, part-time 70. Faculty: full-time 16, part-time 31. Degrees conferred: M.S.W, Ph.D., M.S.W.-M.B.A., M.S.W.-M.S.Ed., M.S.W.-M.C.P., M.S.W.-J.D.

ADMISSION REQUIREMENTS. Official transcript, three references required in support of School's application. Interview may be required. Accepts transfer applicants. Graduates of unaccredited institutions not considered. Apply March 15 to Office of Admissions before. Application fee $40. Phone: (215)898-5521; fax: (215)573-2099.

ADMISSION STANDARDS. Selective. Usual minimum average: 3.0 (A = 4).

FINANCIAL AID. Fellowships, research assistantships, teaching assistantships, grants, Federal W/S, loans. Apply by April 1 to the Dean's Office for fellowships, assistantships; to the Financial Aid Office for all other programs. Use FAFSA. Fifty percent of students receive aid from University and outside sources.

DEGREE REQUIREMENTS. For M.S.W.: 65 credits minimum, at least one year in full-time residence; thesis. For Ph.D.: one year minimum beyond M.S.W.; qualifying exam; field practice; dissertation; final oral exam.

Law School

Established 1852. Semester system. Law library: 560,000 volumes. Library has LEXIS, NEXIS, WESTLAW, DIALOG, BRS, VUTEXT.
Annual fees/tuition: $21,800. On-campus housing for 166 single students. Apply to Office of Graduate Housing. Total average annual additional expense: $10,733.
Enrollment: first-year class 275; total 778 (men 60%, women 40%); postgraduates 25; no part-time students. Faculty: full-time 41, part-time 50. Degrees conferred: J.D., J.D.-M.A. (Economics, Middle Eastern Studies, Public Policy Analysis), J.D.-M.B.A., J.D.-M.C.P., J.D.-Ph.D., LL.M., S.J.D.

ADMISSION REQUIREMENTS. For J.D. program: LSDAS Law School report, bachelor's degree, transcripts, two letters of recommendation, LSAT required in support of application. TOEFL required of international student. Interview not required. Accepts transfer applicants. Graduates of unaccredited institutions not considered. Apply to Assistant Dean for Admissions and Student Aid after August 30, before February 1. Fall admission only. Application fee $60. Phone: (215)898-7400. For

graduate programs: apply to the Chair, Committee on Graduate Studies, Law School.

ADMISSION STANDARDS. Selective. Accepts 20–25% of total annual applicants.

FINANCIAL AID. For J.D. program: scholarships, Federal W/S, loans. Apply to Dean Admissions and Student Aid by February 1. Use FAFSA and institutional financial aid application. For graduate program: apply to the Assistant Dean, Graduate Studies and Research before February 1. About 75% of J.D. students receive some aid from School. A loan forgiveness program for those who work in the public sector is available.

DEGREE REQUIREMENTS. For J.D.: satisfactory completion of three-year program. For LL.M.: at least 24 credits minimum beyond the J.D.; one year in full-time residence. For S.J.D.: one year minimum in full-time residence; thesis. For M.A., M.B.A., M.C.P., Ph.D.: see Graduate School listing above.

School of Medicine (19104-6056)

Established 1765; the first in U.S. Annual tuition: $25,880; student fees $1129. Limited on-campus housing. Apply to Residence Office. Total average figure for all other expenses: $9710.
Enrollment: first-year class 150; total 650 (men 55%, women 45%). Faculty: full-time 1000, part-time 1000. Degrees conferred: M.D., M.D.-Ph.D. (Medical Scientist Training Program).

ADMISSION REQUIREMENTS. AMCAS report, transcripts, two letters of recommendation (one from premed advisor), MCAT required in support of application. Bachelor's required for matriculation. Does not have EDP. Interview by invitation only. Accepts transfer applicants. Apply to Director of Admissions of School after June 15, before November 1 (Fall). Application fee $55. Phone: (215)898-8001; fax: (215)898-0833.

ADMISSION STANDARDS. Very competitive. Accepts 3–5% of total annual applicants. Approximately 30% are state residents.

FINANCIAL AID. Scholarships, loans. Apply to Director of Admissions after admission. MSTP-funded by NIH. Use FAFSA. About 75% of students receive some aid from School.

DEGREE REQUIREMENTS. For M.D.: satisfactory completion of four-year program. For Ph.D.: see Graduate School listing above.

FIELDS OF GRADUATE STUDY.
Anatomy.
Biochemistry.
Biophysics.
Cell Biology.
Genetics.
Immunology.
Microbiology.
Molecular Biology.
Neurosciences.
Pathology.
Pharmacology.
Physiology.

School of Dental Medicine (19104-6003)

Founded 1878. Library: 55,000 volumes.
Annual tuition: $30,100. On-campus housing available. Average academic year housing costs: $11,670. Contact Graduate Housing Advisor for housing information. Phone: (215)898-8271. Total average cost for all other first-year expenses: $5231.
Enrollment: first-year class 90 (men 60%, women 40%); total D.M.D. 350; postgraduates 72. Faculty: full-time 83, part-time

300. Degrees conferred: D.M.D., D.M.D.-M.S. (Education), M.S., Ph.D. (Bioengineering and Basic Sciences).

ADMISSION REQUIREMENTS. AADSAS, official transcript indicating completion of at least six semesters or their equivalent of college work, three letters of recommendation, DAT (April test of junior year preferred) required in support of School's application. Interviews by invitation only. Accepts transfer applicants from U.S. schools only. Graduates of unaccredited institutions not considered. Apply to Director of Admissions after June 1, before January 15. Application fee $35. Phone: (215)898-8943.

ADMISSION STANDARDS. Competitive. Usual minimum average: 3.0 (A = 4). Accepts 15–20% of total annual applicants.

FINANCIAL AID. Scholarships, grants, loans. Apply after acceptance to Director of Student Affairs. Phone: (215)898-4550. Use FAFSA. About 77% of students receive some aid from School and outside sources.

DEGREE REQUIREMENTS. For D.M.D.: satisfactory completion of four-year program. For M.S., see School of Education listing above. For M.S., Ph.D., see Graduate School of Arts and Sciences listing above.

School of Nursing—Graduate Division

http://www.upenn.edu/nursing

Graduate study since 1961. Annual tuition: full-time $19,226, per course $2424. Enrollment: full-time 100; part-time 300. Degrees conferred: M.S.N., M.S.N./M.B.A., Ph.D., Ph.D./M.B.A.

ADMISSION REQUIREMENTS. Transcripts, three letters of reference, interview, GRE required in support of School's application. GMAT required for M.S.N./M.B.A. applicants. TOEFL required for international applicants. Accepts transfer applicants. Graduates of unaccredited institutions not considered. Application fee $55. Phone: (215)898-3301; fax: (215)898-8439.

ADMISSION STANDARDS. Usual minimum average for M.S.N. applicants: 3.0 (A = 4). Usual minimum average for doctoral applicants: 3.2 (A = 4) at the master's level.

FINANCIAL AID. Limited to teaching/research assistantships, Federal W/S, loans. Approved for VA benefits. Apply by April 15 to School for assistantships; to the Office of Student Financial Services for all other programs. Use FAFSA and institutional FAF. Phone: (215)898-8191.

DEGREE REQUIREMENTS. For M.S.N.: 12 course units minimum. 16 course units for Nurse-Midwifery, Nursing Administration, Family Nurse Practitioner and Occupational Health Nursing programs. For Ph.D.: maximum seven calendar years allowed beyond master's, one year or more of full-time study recommended; candidacy exam; dissertation; related field final oral exam.

FIELDS OF STUDY.
Adult Health and Illness. Includes tertiary nurse practitioner, critical care, oncology.
Gerontological Nurse Practitioner.
Health Care of Women. Includes perinatal nurse practitioner, neonatal practitioner, nurse-midwifery.
Nursing Administration. In cooperation with the Wharton School. M.S.N./M.B.A., Ph.D./M.B.A.
Nursing of Children. Includes acute/chronic care practitioner, pediatric critical care practitioner.
Primary Care. Includes pediatric nurse practitioner, adult nurse practitioner, family nurse practitioner, home care nurse practitioner, occupational health practitioner.

Psychiatric Mental Health Nursing. Includes adult and special populations, child and family, geropsychiatry.

School of Veterinary Medicine (19104-6044)

Established 1884. Annual tuition: full-time, resident and nonresident contract students $20,318, nonresident $24,364. On-campus housing available. Apply to Graduate Housing. Total average cost for all other expense: $10,000–$12,000.

Enrollment: first-year class 109 (men 40%, women 60%); full-time 433 (men 40%, women 60%); no part-time students. Faculty: full-time 230, part-time 5. Degrees conferred: V.M.D., V.M.D.-M.B.A., V.M.D.-Ph.D. (Veterinary Medical Scientist Training Program).

ADMISSION REQUIREMENTS. VMCAS report, transcript, completion of 90 credits or three years of college study with prescribed courses, animal/veterinary experience, three recommendations, GRE General required in support of application. Interview by invitation only. Graduates of unaccredited colleges not considered. Transfer accepted on a space available basis. Apply to Dean of School after July 1, before November 1. Application fee $50. Phone: (215)898-5434, (215)898-5435.

ADMISSION STANDARDS. Selective. Accepts 18–20% of total annual applicants. Accepts forty-five to fifty nonresidents, includes international applicants.

FINANCIAL AID. Scholarships, fellowships, Federal W/S, loans available. VMSTP funded by NIH. Apply after acceptance to Associate Dean for Student Affairs. Use FAFSA. About 50% of students receive aid other than loans from all sources.

DEGREE REQUIREMENTS. For V.M.D.: satisfactory completion of four-year program. For M.B.A., Ph.D., see Graduate School listings above.

PEPPERDINE UNIVERSITY
Culver City, California 90230-7615

Founded 1937. Coed. Private control. Church of Christ. Trimester system. Library: 110,000 volumes, 280,000 microforms, 555 current periodicals.

Tuition: per unit, varies from $495. No on-campus housing available.

Graduate Programs

Enrollment: full-time 1304, part-time 2881. Faculty: full-time 100, part-time 135. Degrees conferred: M.A., M.S., M.S.O.D., M.S.T.M., M.B.A., M.I.B., Ed.D., Psy.D.

ADMISSION REQUIREMENTS. Official transcripts, GRE/GMAT/MAT, recommendations required in support of application. TOEFL required for international applicants. Interview may be required. Accepts transfer applicants. Graduates of unaccredited institutions not considered. Apply to the Director of Admission for appropriate School. Application fee $45. Phone: (310)568-5600.

ADMISSION STANDARDS. Selective. Usual minimum average: 2.5 (A = 4).

FINANCIAL AID. Scholarships, research assistantships, teaching assistantships, Federal W/S, loans. Approved for VA benefits. Apply by July 1 to appropriate department chair for assistantships; to Financial Aid Office for all other programs. Use FAFSA. Aid is sometimes available for part-time students.

DEGREE REQUIREMENTS. For master's: 30 semester units minimum and at least 24 in residence; thesis/nonthesis option. For M.B.A.: 48 units, at least 40 in residence. For Ed.D., Psy.D.: GRE Subject Tests for candidacy; thesis or research project; final written/oral exam.

FIELDS OF STUDY.

GRADUATE SCHOOL OF EDUCATION AND PSYCHOLOGY:
Administration and Educational Technology. M.S.
Clinical Psychology. M.A., Psy.D.
Educational Computing. M.S.
Institutional Management. Ed.D.
Psychology. M.A.
School Business Administration. M.S.
School Management and Administration. M.S.
Special Education. M.S.

SCHOOL OF BUSINESS AND MANAGEMENT:
Business Administration. M.B.A.
Executive Business Administration. M.B.A.
International Business. M.I.B.
Organizational Development. M.O.D.
Technology Management. M.S.T.M.

PEPPERDINE UNIVERSITY
Pacific Coast Highway,
Malibu, California 90263-0001
http://www.pepperdine.edu

Founded 1937. Coed. Private control. Church of Christ. Trimester system. Special facilities: Ira Sherman Center for Ethical Awareness, Center for Educational Leadership, National School Safety Center, Institute for the Study of Asian Culture, Library: 640,972 volumes, 800,454 microforms, 2500 current periodicals.

Tuition: per unit, varies from $600. On-campus housing available for single students only. Average academic year housing costs: $3570–$6750. Contact the Office of Residential Life for both on- and off-campus housing information. Phone: (310)456-4104.

Seaver College

Enrollment: full-time 12, part-time 91. Faculty: full-time 38, part-time 5. Degrees conferred: M.A., M.S., M.Div.

ADMISSION REQUIREMENTS. Transcripts, GRE, three recommendations required in support of College's application. TOEFL required for international applicants. Interview may be required. Accepts transfer applicants. Graduates of unaccredited institutions not considered. Apply by May 1 (Fall), September 1 (Spring) to Admissions Office. Rolling admissions process. Application fee $45. Phone: (310)456-4392.

ADMISSION STANDARDS. Selective. Minimum average: 2.5 (A = 4).

FINANCIAL AID. Scholarships, research assistantships, teaching assistantships, Federal W/S, loans. Approved for VA benefits. Apply to Dean's Office for assistantships; to Financial Aid Office for all other programs. Use FAFSA. Phone: (310)456-4301. Aid is sometimes available for part-time students.

DEGREE REQUIREMENTS. For master's: 30 semester units minimum and at least 24 in residence; thesis/nonthesis option; comprehensive exam.

FIELDS OF STUDY.
American Studies. M.A.
Communication. M.A.
English. M.A.
History. M.A.
Ministry. M.S.
Religion. M.Div, M.S.

School of Law

Formerly Orange University College of Law. Affiliated 1969. Located in Malibu (90263). Semester system. Library: 235,000 volumes. Library has LEXIS, NEXIS, WESTLAW, DIALOG. Special facilities: Institute for Dispute Resolution.

Annual tuition: $20,850. University housing available near campus. Total average annual additional expense: $15,156.

Enrollment: first-year class 250; total full-time 715 (men 53%, women 47%). Faculty: full-time 35, part-time 21. Degrees conferred: J.D., J.D.-M.B.A.

ADMISSION REQUIREMENTS. LSDAS Law School report, bachelor's degree, transcripts, LSAT, two letters of reference required in support of application. Accepts transfer applicants. Graduates of unaccredited colleges not considered. Apply to Admissions Office by March 1. Application fee $40. Phone: (310)456-4631.

ADMISSION STANDARDS. Selective. Accepts about 30–35% of total annual applicants.

FINANCIAL AID. Scholarships, assistantships, Federal W/S, loans. Apply to Director of Financial Aid by May 1. Use FAFSA. About 83% of students receive some aid from School.

DEGREE REQUIREMENTS. For J. D.: satisfactory completion of three-year program; 88 credit hour program.
Note: Study abroad program in London (Great Britain) available each Fall term for second- and third-year students.

PHILADELPHIA COLLEGE OF OSTEOPATHIC MEDICINE
Philadelphia, Pennsylvania 1913-1696

Founded 1899. Largest of the 15 Osteopathic Schools. Coed. Private control. Semester system. Library: 71,000 volumes, 785 current periodicals, 25 PCs; has MEDLINE, CANCERLINE, BIOETHIC, HEALTH, PALINET, TOXLINE, DIALOG, OCLC.

Annual tuition: $21,000. No on-campus housing available.

Enrollment: first-year class 235, total 895 (men 63%, women 37%). Faculty: full-time 101, part-time 600. Degrees conferred: D.O., M.Sc., D.O.-M.B.A. (Saint Joseph's University), D.O.-M.P.H. (Temple University).

ADMISSION REQUIREMENTS. AACOMAS report, bachelor's degree, official transcripts, MCAT, three recommendations (one from premed advisory committee, one evaluation from a physician, preferably a D.O.), supplemental form required in support of application. Interview by invitation only. Graduates of unaccredited college not considered. Preference given to state residents. Apply by February 1 to the Assistant Dean for Admissions and Enrollment. Admits first year students Fall only. Rolling admissions process. Application fee: $10, $50 for nonresidents. Phone: (215)871-6700.

ADMISSION STANDARDS. Selective. Accepts approximately 15% of total annual applicants. Usual minimum average: 2.75 (A = 4), mean GPA: 3.1.

FINANCIAL AID. Scholarships, fellowships, assistantships, Federal W/S, loans. Apply by April 1 to the Financial Aid Office. Use FAFSA and institutional FAF.

DEGREE REQUIREMENT. For D.O.: satisfactory completion of four-year program. For joint degree requirements, consult Graduate School listing.

THE PHILADELPHIA COLLEGE OF PHARMACY AND SCIENCE
Philadelphia, Pennsylvania 19104-4495

Founded 1821. Coed. Private control. Semester system. Special facilities: McNeil Laboratory, Pharmacology/Toxicology Research Center. Library: 71,600 volumes, 26,500 microforms, 814 current periodicals, 29 PCs.

Annual tuition: full-time $18,495. No on-campus housing available for graduate students. Contact Dean of Student Affairs for off-campus housing information. Phone: (215)596-8844.

Graduate School

Graduate study since 1921. Enrollment: full-time 53, part-time 24. Graduate faculty: full-time 39, part-time none. Degrees conferred: M.S., Ph.D.

ADMISSION REQUIREMENTS. Official transcripts, GRE, three letters of recommendation required in support of School's application. TOEFL and certification of finances required for international applicants. Interview, GRE Subject Tests recommended. Accepts transfer applicants. Graduates of unaccredited institutions not considered. Apply to Dean of Graduate School. Admits to Fall and Spring. Application fee $25. Phone: (215)596-8937.

ADMISSION STANDARDS. Very selective. Usual minimum average: 3.0 (A = 4).

FINANCIAL AID. Annual awards from institutional funds: ten fellowships, thirty-five teaching assistantships, tuition scholarships, tuition waivers, Federal W/S, loans. Apply to appropriate department chair for fellowships, assistantships; to Financial Aid Office for all other programs. No specified closing date. Use FAFSA and PHEAA. Phone: (215)596-8894; fax: (215)895-1100. About 80% of students receive aid other than loans from College and outside sources.

DEGREE REQUIREMENTS. For M.S. (nonthesis): 30 semester hours of didactic credit. For M.S. (thesis): 20 semester hours of didactic credit; 24 semester hours of credit in research; thesis; proficiency exam may be required. For Ph.D.: 20 semester hours of didactic credit; 48 semester hours of credit in research; at least eight months in full-time residence; proficiency exam may be required; dissertation; final oral/written exam.

FIELDS OF STUDY.
Chemistry.
Pharmaceutics. Thesis/nonthesis option.
Pharmacognosy.
Pharmacology and Toxicology.
Pharmacy Administration.
Physical Therapy.

PHILLIPS UNIVERSITY
Enid, Oklahoma 73701-6439
http://www.phillips.edu

Founded 1907. Located 80 miles NW of Oklahoma City. Coed. Private control. Disciples of Christ. Semester system. Library: 400,000 volumes, 50,000 microforms.

Tuition: per credit $97. On-campus housing for married and single students. Average academic year housing costs: $2400 for married students, $3900 (including board) for single students. Apply to Director of Housing and Student Activities. Phone: (405)548-2265.

Graduate Division

Enrollment: full-time 17, part-time 52. Graduate faculty: full-time 9, part-time none. Degrees conferred: M.Ed., M.B.A.

ADMISSION REQUIREMENTS. Transcripts, three letters of reference (Education only) required in support of application. GMAT required for M.B.A. TOEFL required for international applicants. Interview not required. Accepts transfer applicants. Graduates of unaccredited colleges not considered. Apply to Director of Graduate Studies by August 1 (Fall), December 1 (Spring). Application fee none. Phone: (405)548-2203; fax: (405)237-1607.

ADMISSION STANDARDS. Relatively open. Usual minimum average: 2.5 (A = 4). For Business: 2.5 (A = 4) with GMAT of 450.

FINANCIAL AID. None except Federal W/S, federal loans. Use FAFSA. Phone: (405)548-2201; fax: (405)237-1607.

DEGREE REQUIREMENTS. For master's: 36 credit hours minimum, at least 24 in residence; final oral exam; thesis may be required or elected for some majors.

FIELDS OF STUDY.
Business Administration. GMAT for admission.
Elementary Education.
Secondary Education.

UNIVERSITY OF PHOENIX
Phoenix, Arizona 85072-2069
http://www.uophx.edu

Chartered 1970. University offers programs in Arizona, California, Colorado, Commonwealth of Puerto Rico, Hawaii, Louisiana, Michigan, Nevada, New Mexico, Utah. Coed. Private proprietary (Apollo Group) control. One-course-per-month format, six weeks in duration. Special facilities: Center for Distance Learning, Center for Higher Education and Economic Development. Library: Electronic, 1,366,000 microforms, 2500 current periodicals, several hundred PCs in all Learning Resource Centers.

Tuition: $270 per semester credit; directed study $320 per semester credit course. No on-campus housing available.

Graduate Programs

Graduate study since 1975. Enrollment: full- and part-time 6875. Graduate faculty: full-time 30, part-time 1100. Degrees conferred: M.A.Ed., M.A.O.M., M.B.A., M.C., M.N., M.S.C.I.S.

ADMISSION REQUIREMENTS. Official transcripts required in support of application. TOEFL required for international applicants. Accepts transfer applicants. Graduates of unaccredited institutions not considered. Apply to appropriate Admission Office at least one month prior to date of registration. Rolling admissions process. Application fee $50. Contact website for appropriate Admissions Office number.

ADMISSION STANDARDS. Relatively open. Usual minimum average: 2.5 (A = 4).

FINANCIAL AID. Annual awards from institutional funds: Federal W/S, loans. Most sites are approved for VA benefits. Apply to Office of Financial Assistance at each site; no specified closing date. Use FAFSA. Aid available for part-time students.

DEGREE REQUIREMENTS. For master's: 36–51 credits minimum, at least 30–45 in residence; thesis/nonthesis option; no foreign language requirement; final exams/internships in some programs.

FIELDS OF STUDY.
Business Administration. M.B.A.
Computer Information Systems. M.S.C.I.S.
Counseling. Includes marriage, family and child counseling, mental health. M.C.
Education. M.A.Ed.
Nursing. Includes women's health nurse practitioner. M.N.
Organizational Management. M.A.O.M.
Technology Management. M.B.A.-T.M.

DEGREE REQUIREMENTS. For master's: 30–36 semester hours minimum; research problem or thesis/nonthesis option. For Ed.S.: 30 semester hours minimum beyond the master's.

FIELDS OF STUDY.
Accounting.
Art.
Biological Science. Includes zoology, botany, biology.
Business Administration.
Chemistry.
Communications.
Community College Education.
Counseling Psychology.
Drama.
Education.
Educational Administration.
Elementary Education.
English.
History.
Mathematics.
Music.
Music Education.
Nursing.
Physical Education.
Physics.
Psychology.
Reading.
School Psychology.
Secondary Education.
Special Education.
Technology and Public Policy.
Technology Education.

PITTSBURG STATE UNIVERSITY
Pittsburg, Kansas 66762-5880

Founded 1903. Located 125 miles S of Kansas City. Coed. State control. Semester system. Library: 350,000 volumes, 327,000 microforms, 1200 current periodicals.
Annual tuition: resident $2102, nonresident $5488; per credit, resident $90, nonresident $231. On-campus housing for 47 married students, 630 men, 700 women. Average academic year housing costs: $375 per month (room and board). Apply to Director of Residence Life. Phone: (316)235-4245.

Graduate Studies

Graduate study since 1929. Enrollment: full-time 400, part-time 923. College faculty teaching graduate students: 200. Degrees conferred: M.A., M.S., M.B.A., M.M., M.S.N., Ed.S.

ADMISSION REQUIREMENTS. Official transcripts, GRE/GMAT, recommendations required in support of application. TOEFL required for international applicants. Accepts transfer applicants. Apply to Dean, Graduate Studies and Research; no specified closing date. Rolling admissions process. Application fee $40. Phone: (316)235-4221.

ADMISSION STANDARDS. Selective. Usual minimum average: 2.5 (A = 4).

FINANCIAL AID. Annual awards from institutional funds: teaching assistantships, research assistantships, Federal W/S, loans. Approved for VA benefits. Apply to Graduate Office for assistantships; to Financial Aid Office for all other programs. Use FAFSA. Phone: (316)235-7000. About 60% of students receive aid other than loans from College and outside sources.

UNIVERSITY OF PITTSBURGH
Pittsburgh, Pennsylvania 15261

Chartered 1787. Coed. State related. Trimester system. Regional campuses in Titusville, Bradford, Greensburg, Johnstown. Special facilities: Applied Research Center, Center for Biotechnology and Bioengineering, Cleft-Palate-Craniofacial Center, Frick Fine Arts Building, Center for International Studies, Learning Research and Development Center, Mid-Atlantic Technology Application Center, Center for Neuroscience, Center for Philosophy of Science, Pittsburgh Cancer Institute, Center for Social and Urban Research, Surface Science Center. Library: 3,200,000 volumes, 3,100,000 microforms, 23,000 current periodicals.
Annual tuition: full-time resident $7378, nonresident $15,048; per credit resident $304, nonresident $620. No on-campus housing. For off-campus housing, contact Graduate Housing Office. Phone: (412)624-7115.

Faculty of Arts and Sciences

Former Divisions of Humanities, Natural Sciences, and Social Sciences combined into Faculty of Arts and Sciences. Graduate enrollment: full-time 1376, part-time 398 (men 55%, women 45%). Faculty teaching graduate students: full-time 620, part-time 234. Degrees conferred: M.A., M.F.A., M.S., Ph.D.

ADMISSION REQUIREMENTS. Transcripts required in support of application. GRE required for some departments. TOEFL required for international applicants. Accepts transfer applicants. Graduates of unaccredited institutions not considered. Apply to chair of proposed graduate department by August 1 (Fall), December 1 (Winter), April 1 (Spring), June 1 (Summer). Earlier deadlines may be applicable for some programs. Application fee

$30, $40 for international applicants. Phone: (412)624-6094; fax: (412)624-5299.

ADMISSION STANDARDS. Selective for most departments, competitive for the others. Usual minimum average: 3.0 (A = 4).

FINANCIAL AID. Annual awards from institutional funds: 250 scholarships, 112 fellowships, 248 research assistantships, 781 teaching assistantships, 20 internships, 40 Mellon fellowships, full and partial tuition waivers, Federal W/S, loans. Approved for VA benefits. Apply by April 1 to departmental chairperson for fellowships, assistantships; to the Financial Aid Office for all other programs. Use FAFSA and institutional FAF. About 60% of full-time students receive aid other than loans from University and outside sources.

DEGREE REQUIREMENTS. For master's: 8 courses minimum; comprehensive exam; thesis/nonthesis. For Ph.D.: 24 courses minimum beyond the bachelor's; preliminary, comprehensive exams; dissertation; final oral exam; additional requirements may be determined by each department.

FIELDS OF STUDY.
Analytical Chemistry.
Anthropology.
Applied Mathematics.
Applied Statistics.
Astronomy.
Biological Sciences.
Chemistry.
Classics.
Communication Disorders.
Computer Science.
Crystallography.
East Asian Languages and Literatures.
East Asian Studies.
Ecology and Evolution.
Economics.
English.
Fine Arts.
French and Italian Languages and Literature.
Geology and Planetary Sciences.
Geophysics.
Germanic Languages and Literatures.
Hispanic Languages and Literatures. Includes Spanish.
History.
History and Philosophy of Science.
History of Art and Architecture.
Linguistics.
Mathematics and Statistics.
Music.
Neuroscience.
Philosophy.
Physics.
Political Science.
Psychology.
Religion.
Rhetoric and Communication.
Slavic Languages and Literatures.
Sociology.
Theater Arts.
Writing.

The Joseph M. Katz Graduate School of Business

Established 1960. Special facilities: Center for Economic Development, Small Business Development Center, Center for International Business, Strategic Management Institute, Program in Corporate Culture, Business, Society and Government Research Institute, and Center for Research on Contracts and the Structure of Enterprise.

Annual tuition: resident $12,345, nonresident $20,427.
Enrollment: full-time 474, part-time 439. Faculty: full-time 69, part-time 49. Degrees conferred: M.B.A., E.M.B.A., M.S. in MOIS, M.H.A., M.B.A.-J.D., Ph.D., M.I.B., M.B.A.-M.S.N., M.B.A.-M.P.I.A.

ADMISSION REQUIREMENTS. Baccalaureate or higher degree; introductory calculus; GMAT required in support of School's application. TOEFL required for international applicants. Accepts transfer applicants. Graduates of unaccredited institutions not considered. Apply prior to May 1 (Fall), November 1 (Spring) to the Admission Office. Full-time M.B.A. applicants admitted Fall only. Part-time applicants admitted Fall, Spring, Summer terms. Application fee $50. Phone: (412)648-1556; fax: (412)648-1552.

ADMISSION STANDARDS. Very selective. Usual minimum average: 3.1 (A = 4), usual GMAT range 550–650.

FINANCIAL AID. Annual awards from institutional funds: scholarships, tuition fellowships, research assistantships, teaching assistantships, Federal W/S, loans. Approved for VA benefits. Apply to Dean's Office for fellowships, assistantships; to Financial Aid Office for all other programs. Submit FAFSA and completed institutional application with GMAT scores by March 15. Phone: (412)624-PITT. No scholarship aid is available for part-time students or international students in M.B.A. program.

DEGREE REQUIREMENTS. For master's: 39–51 credit hours depending on previous degree and experience; thesis/nonthesis option; final comprehensive exam for some programs. For Ph.D.: 72 credit hours; comprehensive exam in major and minor fields; dissertation; final oral exam.

FIELDS OF STUDY.
Accounting.
Business Administration.
Health Administration.
International Business. Includes concentrations in East Asian, Eastern European, Latin American, Western European.
Management of Information Systems.

School of Education
http://www.pitt.edu/education.html

Graduate study since 1910. Semester system.
Annual tuition: full-time resident $7062, nonresident $14,200, per credit resident $291, nonresident $594.
Enrollment: full-time 658, part-time 811. Faculty: full-time 95, part-time 52. Degrees conferred: M.A., M.Ed., M.A.T., M.S., Ed.D., Ph.D.

ADMISSION REQUIREMENTS. Official transcripts, GRE required in support of School's application. Interview/MAT required by some departments. TOEFL required for international applicants. Accepts transfer applicants. Graduates of unaccredited institutions not considered. Apply to the Office of Student Personnel Services, School of Education, by February 1 (Fall), November 15 (Spring). Application fee $30, international applicants $40. Phone (412) 648-2330; fax (412) 648-1899.

ADMISSION STANDARDS. Selective for master's, usual minimum average 3.0; 3.3 (A=4) for doctorate.

FINANCIAL AID. Five scholarships, 109 teaching assistantships, 44 research assistantships, Federal W/S, loans. Approved for VA benefits. Apply to department chair for fellowships, assistantships; to Office of Financial Aid for all other programs. Use FAFSA and institutional FAF. Phone: (412) 624-PITT.

DEGREE REQUIREMENTS: For master's: 36 credit hours minimum; comprehensive exam. For Ed.D., Ph.D.: 90 credit hour minimum beyond bachelor's degree, at least 60 credits in residence; comprehensive written exam; dissertation; final oral exam.

FIELDS OF STUDY

Administrative Studies. Includes higher education administration and K–12 administration.
Counseling. Includes school counseling, cross-cultural.
Counseling Psychology.
Developmental and Educational Psychology.
Health, Physical, and Recreation Education. Includes exercise physiology, health promotion, and education.
Humanities Education. Includes English, communications, foreign language, reading, social studies.
Instructional Design and Technology.
Mathematics and Science Education.
Policy, Planning, and Evaluation Studies.
Research Methodology.
Social and Comparative Analysis in Education. Includes international, development education; social, philosophical, and historical foundations of education.
Special Education. Includes education of the mentally and physically handicapped, of the visually impaired, early education of the handicapped, severe disabilities, deaf, and hard of hearing.
Teacher Education. Includes early childhood, elementary education.

School of Engineering

Annual tuition: resident $8808, nonresident $17,964; per credit resident $423, nonresident $855.

Enrollment: full-time 349, part-time 470. Faculty: full-time 105, part-time 8. Degrees conferred: M.S., M.E.R., M.S.B.Eng., M.S.C.E.E., M.S.Ch.E., M.S.E.E., M.S.E.R., M.S.I.E., M.S.M.E., M.S.Met.E., M.S.Mf.S.E., M.S.M.S.E., M.S.P.E., Ph.D.

ADMISSION REQUIREMENTS. Official transcript, GRE required in support of School's application. GRE Subject Test required for some programs. Interview not required. TOEFL required for international applicants. Accepts transfer applicants. Graduates of unaccredited institutions not considered. Apply to appropriate department chair by August 1 (Fall), December 1 (Spring), April 1 (Summer). Rolling admission process. Application fee $30, international applicants $40. Phone: (412) 624-9809; fax (412) 624-1108.

ADMISSION STANDARDS. Selective. Usual minimum average: 3.0 (A = 4) from ABET-accredited undergraduate institution. Applicants with lower averages considered on limited and exceptional basis.

FINANCIAL AID. Seventy-one teaching assistantships, 188 research assistantships, fellowships, Federal W/S, loans. Approved for VA benefits. Apply by March 1 to appropriate department chair for assistantships, fellowships; to Financial Aid Office for all other programs. Use FAFSA. Phone: (412) 624-7488.

DEGREE REQUIREMENTS. For Master's: 30 credit hours minimum; comprehensive exam; thesis/nonthesis option; final exam. For M.E.R.: 42 credit hours minimum; comprehensive exam; thesis optional. For Ph.D.: 72 credit hours minimum, at least two consecutive terms in residence; qualifying exam; comprehensive exam; dissertation; final oral exam.

FIELDS OF STUDY.
Bioengineering. M.S.B.Eng., Ph.D.
Chemical Engineering. M.S.Ch.E., Ph.D.
Civil and Environmental Engineering. M.S.C.E.E., Ph.D.
Electrical Engineering. M.S.E.E., Ph.D.

Energy Resources. M.E.R., M.S.E.R.
Industrial Engineering. M.S.I.E., Ph.D.
Manufacturing system Engineering. M.S.Mf. S.E. only.
Materials Science and Engineering. M.S.M.E., Ph.D.
Mechanical Engineering. M.S.M.E., Ph.D.
Metallurgical Engineering. M.S.Met.E., Ph.D.
Petroleum Engineering. M.S.P.E.

School of Health and Rehabilitation Sciences
4019 Forbes Tower(15260)

Annual tuition: full-time per term, resident $4327, nonresident $8879; per credit, resident $358, nonresident $729.

Enrollment: full-time 85, part-time 81. Faculty: full-time 32, part-time 16. Degrees conferred: M.S., M.P.T., Ph.D.

ADMISSION REQUIREMENTS. Official transcripts, three recommendations required in support of School's application. GRE required for M.P.T., Ph.D. applicants. TOEFL required for international applicants. Accepts transfer applicants. Application deadlines: M.S.; June I (Fall), November 15 (Spring); M.P.T. January 31; Ph.D. April 1 (Fall), September 1 (Spring) Application fee $30, international applicants $40, M.T.P., application fee $50. Phone: (412) 674-1252; fax (412) 647-1255.

FINANCIAL AID. Six grants, one teaching fellowships, four teaching assistantships, Federal W/S, loans. Approved for VA benefits. Apply to departmental chair for fellowships, assistantships; to Financial Aid Office for all other programs. Use FAFSA and institutional FAF. Phone: (412) 624-7488, fax (412) 648-8815. Financial assistance also available for selected minority students. About 50% of students receive aid other than loans from both School and outside sources.

DEGREE REQUIREMENTS. For M.S., M.P.T.: 8-course minimum; comprehensive exam; thesis/nonthesis option. For Ph.D.: 90 credit hours minimum beyond the bachelor's degree, at least 60 credits in residence; qualifying exam; candidacy; dissertation; final oral exam.

FIELDS OF STUDY.
Clinical Dietetics.
Communication Science and Disorders.
Entry Level Master's of Physical Therapy. M.P.T.
Health Care Supervision and Management.
Health Information Systems.
Musculoskeletal Physical Therapy.
Neuromuscular Physical Therapy.
Occupational Therapy.
Rehabilitation Sciences and Technology. M.S., Ph.D.

School of Library and Information Science
http:///www.lis.pitt.edu

Established 1962.
Annual tuition: full-time, resident $11,139, nonresident $22,716; per credit, resident $308, nonresident $629.

Enrollment: full-time 239, part-time 341. Faculty: full-time 32, part-time 12. Degrees conferred: M.L.S., M.S.I.S., M.S.T., C.A.S., Ph.D.

ADMISSION REQUIREMENTS. Official transcripts, GRE, letters of recommendation required in support of School's application. TOEFL required for international applicants. Accepts transfer applicants. Graduates of unaccredited institutions not considered. Apply to School at least two months prior to registration. Application fee $30, international applicants $40. Phone: (412) 624-5230; fax (412) 624-5231.

FINANCIAL AID. Annual awards from institutional funds: Twenty-five fellowships, three assistantships, Federal W/S, loans. Approved for VA benefits. Apply to the School for fellowships, assistantships; to the Office of Financial Aid for all other programs. Use FAFSA and institutional FAF. Phone: (412) 624-7488; fax (412) 648-8815. Financial assistance also available for selected minority students.

DEGREE REQUIREMENTS. M.L.S., M.S.I.S.,: 36 credit hours minimum, at least 30 in residence. For M.S.T.: 48 credit hours minimum, at least 36 in residence. For Ph.D. in L.S.: 54 credit hours minimum beyond the Master's; preliminary exam; comprehensive exam; proficiency in language determined by Committee on Doctoral Studies; dissertation. For Ph.D. in I.S.: 60 credit hours minimum beyond the Master's; 6 credits in linguistics; preliminary exam; comprehensive exam; 18 dissertation credits. For Certificate: 24 credit hours minimum beyond the master's.

FIELDS OF STUDY.
Academic, School, Public, and Special Librarianship.
Archives, Book Arts, and Preservation.
Children and Youth Services.
Medical Informatics.
Photonics.
System Analysis.
Technical Services.
Telecommunication Networking.

Graduate School of Public and International Affairs
http://WWW.PITT.EDU/~GSPIA/

Graduate study since 1957. Coed. Semester system.
Annual Tuition: full-time resident $7062, nonresident $14,400, per credit resident $291, nonresident $594.
Enrollment: full-time 340, part-time 120 (men 51%, women 49%). Faculty: full-time 42, part-time 8. Degrees conferred: M.P.A., M.P.I.A., M.U.R.P., Ph.D.

ADMISSION REQUIREMENTS. Transcripts, essay, letters of reference required in support of School's application. GRE and a major paper required of doctoral applicants, recommended for master's applicants. Evidence of proficiency in English required of international students. Interview not required. Accepts transfer applicants. Graduates of unaccredited institutions not considered. Apply to Office of Admissions by March 1 (Fall), October 1 (Spring). Rolling admission process. Application fee $30, international applicants $40. Phone: (412) 648-7640; fax (412) 648-2605.

ADMISSION STANDARDS. Selective. Usual minimum average: 3.0 (A=4).

FINANCIAL AID. Fifty scholarships, five to ten minority scholarships, five fellowships, eighteen research fellowships, two teaching assistantships, six internships, Federal W/S, loans. Apply by March 1 to Admissions Office of School for scholarships, fellowships, assistantships; to the Financial Aid Office for all other programs. Use FAFSA and institutional FAF. Phone: (412) 648-7647; fax (412) 648-2605. About 41% of students receive aid other than loans from School.

DEGREE REQUIREMENTS. For M.P.A., M.P.I.A., M.U.R.P.: 48 hours minimum in residence; policy seminar, and internship. For Ph.D.: 78 credit hours minimum, at least four terms in residence; proficiency in advanced research and quantitative analysis; preliminary exam; comprehensive exam; dissertation; final oral exam.

FIELDS OF STUDY.
Economic and Social Development. M.P.I.A., Ph.D.
Environmental Management and Policy.
International Affairs. M.P.I.A., Ph.D.

International Political Economy. M.P.I.A., Ph.D.
International Security Studies. M.P.I.A., Ph.D.
Management of Non-Profit Organizations.
Personnel and Labor Relations. M.P.A.
Public Management and Policy. M.P.A., Ph.D.

School of Pharmacy–Graduate Studies (15261)

Founded 1878. Coed. Semester system.
Tuition: per credit resident $291, nonresident $594.
Enrollment: full-time 25, part-time 2. Faculty full-time 25, part-time 4. Degrees conferred: M.S., Ph.D.

ADMISSION REQUIREMENTS. Transcripts, GRE, personal statement outlining goals, letters of reference required in support of School's application. TOEFL, TSE, TWE required for international applicants. Interview not required, but may be requested. Accepts transfer applicants. Apply to Director of Graduate Programs by March 31 (Fall). Admits Fall only. Application fee $30, international students $40. Phone: (412) 648-1104; fax (412) 648-1086.

ADMISSION STANDARDS. Very selective. Usual minimum average: 3.0 (A=4).

FINANCIAL AID. Fourteen scholarships, fourteen teaching assistantships, Federal W/S, loans. Apply by March 31 to Director of Graduate Programs for scholarships, assistantships; to the Financial Aid Office for all other programs. Use FAFSA and institutional FAF. Phone: (412) 648-7488. Nearly 100% of students receive aid from School or outside sources.

DEGREE REQUIREMENTS. For M.S.: at least 24 credits, but usually 30 credits of approved graduate study; comprehensive written exam; thesis; final oral exam. For Ph.D.: at least 72 credits; thesis; preliminary exam; dissertation; final oral exam.

FIELDS OF STUDY.
Biopharmaceutics/Pharmacokinetics.
Clinical Pharmaceutical Science.
Medicinal Chemistry.
Pharmaceutical Analysis.
Pharmacognosy/Natural Products Chemistry.

Graduate School of Public Health

Established 1948.
Annual tuition: resident $10,600, nonresident $21,550. No on-campus housing available.
Enrollment: full-time 231, part-time 333 (men 206, women 358). Faculty: full-time 72, part-time 15. Degrees conferred: M.P.H., M.H.A., M.S., M.H.P.E., D.P.H., Ph.D.

ADMISSION REQUIREMENTS. Transcripts, two letters of recommendation, GRE, GMAT (Health Administration) required in support of application. TOEFL, statement of financial responsibility required of all international applicants. Interview not required for most programs. Accepts transfer applicants. Graduates of unaccredited colleges not considered. Apply to Admissions Office of the School; deadlines vary by program. Fall and Winter admission for most programs. Application fee $30; international fee $40. Phone (412) 624-3002; fax (412) 624-3755.

ADMISSION STANDARDS. Competitive. Usual minimum average: 3.0 (A = 4).

FINANCIAL AID. Annual awards from institutional funds vary from year to year; 20 scholarships, 110 research assistantships, 5 teaching assistantships, 30 internships, 10 postdoctoral positions, loans. Approved for VA benefits. Apply to appropriate department chairman for scholarships, assistantships, internships, postdoctoral positions; to the Financial Aid Office for all other programs. Use FAFSA and institutional FAF. Phone: (412) 624-3002. About 50% of Students receive aid other than loans from School and outside sources. Limited aid for part-time students.

DEGREE REQUIREMENTS. For Master's program by advisement: thesis/final document; final oral/written exam. For Doctoral programs by advisement: knowledge of one computer language; preliminary exam; comprehensive exam; dissertation; final oral exam.

FIELDS OF STUDY.
Biostatistics.
Community Health Services.
Environmental and Occupational Health.
Epidemiology.
Genetic Counseling.
Health Administration.
Health Promotion and Education. M.H.P.E.
Human Genetics.
Infectious Diseases and Microbiology.
Radiation Health.
Note: Joint programs with Joseph M. Katz School of Business, the School of Social Work and the School of Education.

School of Social Work—Graduate Division

Graduate study since 1942.
Annual tuition: full-time resident $7935, nonresident $16192; per credit, resident $291, nonresident $594.
Enrollment: full-time 261, part-time 160. Faculty: full-time 33, part-time 30. Degrees conferred: M.S.W., Ph.D.

ADMISSION REQUIREMENTS. Transcripts required in support of School's application. Interview may be required. TOEFL required for international applicants. Accepts transfer applicants. Graduates of unaccredited colleges not considered. Apply to the School by March 31. Fall admission only. Application fee $30, $40 for international applicants. Phone: (412) 624-6302; fax (412) 624-6323.

ADMISSION STANDARDS. Competitive. Usual minimum average: 3.0 (A = 4).

FINANCIAL AID. One hundred six grants, five research assistantships, sixteen teaching assistantships, eighteen internships, Federal W/S, loans. Approved for VA benefits. Apply by June 1 to Assistant Dean of Admissions of the School for assistantships; to Financial Aid Office for all other programs. Use FAFSA and School's FAF. Phone: (412) 624-6302. About 45% of students receive aid other than loans, No aid for part-time students.

DEGREE REQUIREMENTS. For M.S.W.: 58 credits minimum, including 18 credits field practicum. For Ph.D.: 42 credits minimum beyond the Master's; comprehensive exam; dissertation; final oral defense.

FIELDS OF STUDY.
Child Development and Child Care.
Family Therapy.
Gerontology.
Social Work.

School of Law (15260)

Founded 1895. Semester system. Library: 295,100 volumes. Library has LEXIS, NEXIS, WESTLAW.
Annual tuition: resident $10,490, nonresident $16,240. On-campus housing available. Total average annual additional expense: $9800.
Enrollment: first-year class 235, full-time 700 (men 60%,

women 40%). Faculty: full-time 37, part-time 28. Degrees conferred: J.D., J.D.-M.A., J.D.-M.B.A., J.D.-M.P.A., J.D.-M.P.I.A., J.D.-M.P.H., J.D.-M.S. (Carnegie Mellon's Schools of Industrial Management and Urban and Public Affairs), J.D.-M.S.I.A., J.D.-M.U.R.P., LL.M.

ADMISSION REQUIREMENTS. LSDAS Law School report, bachelor's degree, transcripts, LSAT required in support of application. Accepts transfer applicants. Graduates of unaccredited institutions not considered. Apply to Director of Admissions after September 1, before March 1. Application fee $40 Phone: (412) 649-1412.

ADMISSION STANDARDS. Accepts about 45–50% of total annual applicants.

FINANCIAL AID. Scholarships, fellowships, assistantships, Federal W/S, loans. Apply to the Financial Aid Office by March 1. Use FAFSA and institutional financial aid form.

DEGREE REQUIREMENTS. For J.D.: three years minimum, at least the final year in full-time residence; 88 credit hour program. For LL.M.: at least 24 credit hours minimum beyond J.D.; final project.

Note: School has a faculty exchange program with the University of Augsburg (Germany).

School of Medicine (15261)

Established 1883.
Annual tuition: resident $17,556, nonresident $23,478, student fees $425. Total average figure for all other expenses: $12,200.
Enrollment: first-year class 140 (EDP 4); total 665 (men 51%, women 49%). Faculty: about 1350. Degrees conferred: M.D., M.S., M.D.-M.S., M.D.-Ph.D. (Medical Scientist Training Program in Cooperation with Carnegie-Mellon University.)

ADMISSION REQUIREMENTS. AMCAS report, transcripts, letters of recommendation, preprofessional committee evaluation, MCAT, interview required in support of application. Has EDP; apply between June 15 and August 1. Apply to Office of the Associate Dean of the School after June 15, before November 1 (firm). Application fee $50. Phone: (412) 648-9891; fax (412) 648-8768. M.D.-Ph.D. (412) 648-2324.

ADMISSION STANDARDS. For M.D. program: competitive. Accepts about 3–5% of total annual applicants. Approximately 65% are state residents.

FINANCIAL AID. Scholarships, loans, research fellowships. MSTP funded by NIH. FAFSA. Apply after acceptance to Financial Aid Committee.

DEGREE REQUIREMENTS. For M.D.: satisfactory completion of four-year program. For M.S.: 32 credit hours minimum; final project/thesis.

FIELDS OF GRADUATE STUDY.
Anatomy.
Biochemistry.
Biomedical Engineering.
Biophysics.
Cell Biology.
Diagnostic Medical Computerization.
Flow Cytometry and Imaging.
Genetics.
Immunology.
Medical Informatics.
Medical Robotics.
Microbiology.

Molecular Biology.
Neurosciences.
Nuclear Magnetic Resonance.
Pathology.
Pharmacology.
Physiology.

School of Dental Medicine (15261–1945)

Founded 1896.

Annual tuition: resident $16,000, nonresident $23,575. Limited on-campus housing available. Average academic year housing costs: $9500. Contact Assistant Director of Housing. Phone: (412) 648-8422. Total average cost for all other first-year expenses: $6630.

Enrollment: D.M.D. program: full-time 34, part-time 35. Faculty: full-time 98, part-time 70. Degrees conferred: D.M.D., M.D.S., M.S., Ph.D.

ADMISSIONS REQUIREMENTS. For D.M.D. program: AADSAS report, official high school and college transcripts, three letters of recommendation, essay, DAT (April test in junior year preferred) required in support of School's application. Interview by invitation only. Applicants must have completed at least three years of college study. Preference given to state residents. Apply to Office of Admissions after August 1, before February 15. Application fee $35. Phone: (412) 648-8424, (800) 833-3204, Fax (412)648-8219. For graduate program: official transcripts, three letters of recommendation required in support of School's application. Apply to Director, Graduate Education by December 1.

ADMISSION STANDARDS. For D.M.D. program: Selective. Accepts about 40% of total annual applicants. Approximately 90% are state residents. For graduate program: competitive for most departments, very competitive, selective for the others.

FINANCIAL AID. D.M.D. programs: Scholarships, grants, loans. Apply to University Office of Financial Aid after acceptance. For Graduate students: fellowships, assistantships, loans. Apply April 1 to Financial Aid Office. Use FAFSA. Phone: (412)648-8422, (800)833-3204.

DEGREE REQUIREMENTS. For D.M.D.: satisfactory completion of four-year program. For Master's degrees: see program listing below. For Ph.D.: 60 credit hours minimum; preliminary exam; dissertation; final oral exam.

GRADUATE FIELDS OF STUDY.
Endodontics. Twenty-four months minimum; thesis. M.D.S. and/or certification.
General Dentistry. Twenty-four months minimum. M.S. only.
Oral Diagnosis. Twenty-four months minimum; thesis. M.S. only.
Oral and Maxillofacial Surgery. Hospital certification.
Orthodontics. Apply by December 1; Summer admission; minimum thirty-six months. M.D.S. and/or certification,
Pediatric Dentistry. Twenty-four months minimum; thesis. M.D.S. and/or certification.
Periodontics. Twenty-four months minimum. M.D.S. and/or certification.
Prosthodontics. Twenty-four months minimum. M.D.S. and/or certification.

POINT LOMA NAZARENE COLLEGE
San Diego, California 92106-2899

Founded 1902 in Los Angeles, California; located in Pasadena, California, 1910–1973. Formerly Pasadena College. Coed. Private control. Church of the Nazarene. Quarter system. Library: 151,000 volumes, 35,000 microforms.

Tuition: per unit $416. On-campus housing for a limited number of single graduate students. Average annual housing cost: $4190 (including board) for single students. Apply to Associate Dean for Residential Life. Phone: (619)221-2482.

Graduate Studies

Enrollment: full-time 250, part-time 139. College faculty teaching graduate students: full-time 17, part-time 40. Degrees conferred: M.A., M.Min., Ed.S.

ADMISSION REQUIREMENTS. Transcripts, interview, three recommendations, MAT or GRE General/Subject Tests required in support of application. TOEFL required of international applicants. Accepts transfer applicants. Apply to Director of Admissions by May 15 (priority Fall consideration), November 1 (Spring). Rolling admissions process. Application fee $25. Phone: (619)221-2273; fax: (619)221-2579.

ADMISSION STANDARDS. Selective. Usual minimum average: 2.5 (A = 4).

FINANCIAL AID. Limited to Federal W/S, loans. Apply to the Office of Financial Aid; no specified closing date. Phone: (619)221-2296. Use FAFSA.

DEGREE REQUIREMENTS. For M.A., M.Min.: 52 quarter units without thesis, at least 43 in residence; or 46 including thesis, at least 37 in residence; reading knowledge of Greek for M.A. in Religion. For Ed.S.: 46 quarter hours beyond the master's; internship; written comprehensive exam.

FIELDS OF STUDY.
Education. Includes administration, counseling and guidance, curriculum and supervision, leadership, multicultural education, special education, teaching and learning.
Religion. Includes Christian education, theology, and church administration.

POLYTECHNIC UNIVERSITY
6 Metrotech Center
Brooklyn, New York 11201-2990

Founded 1854 as Polytechnic Institute of Brooklyn, became Polytechnic University in 1973. Polytechnic is the second oldest private institution of science and engineering in the United States. Coed. Private control. Semester system. Three campuses: Brooklyn, Long Island, Westchester. The Brooklyn Center is the focus of an exciting new environment with the arrival of Metrotech, a joint University-industry development. Four major industrial companies now share a common campus with Polytechnic University, with the university as its core. Specialized facilities: Center for Advanced Technology in Telecommunications, Aerospace Research Laboratories, Center for Applied Large-Scale Computing, Center for Digital Systems, Center for Transportation Research, Dibner Library/Center for Advanced Technology in Communications, Microwave Research Institute, Philosophy and Technology Center, Polymer Research Institute, Institute for Imaging Sciences, and the Weber Research Institute. Library: 200,000 volumes.

Annual tuition: full-time $17,890; per unit $615. On-campus housing for 150 students. Average academic year housing costs: $4700 (including board). Apply to Dean of Student Life. Phone: (718)260-3800.

Graduate Studies

Graduate study since 1902. Enrollment: full- and part-time 2200 (men 85%, women 15%). Faculty: full-time 176, part-time 145. Degrees conferred: M.S., Engineer, Ph.D.

ADMISSION REQUIREMENTS. Transcripts, two letters of recommendation required in support of application. TOEFL required for international applicants. Accepts transfer applicants. Graduates of unaccredited colleges not considered. Apply to Office of Admissions by August 1 (Fall), November 1 (Spring), May 1 (Summer). Application fee $45. Phone: (800) POLYTECH, (718)260-3200.

ADMISSION STANDARDS. Competitive. Usual minimum average: 2.75 (A = 4).

FINANCIAL AID. Annual awards from institutional funds: fourteen teaching assistantships, sixty-seven teaching fellowships, forty-five research fellowships; stipends, Federal W/S, loans. Apply by March 1 to Office of Financial Aid or major department. Phone: (718)260-3300. Use FAFSA. No aid for part-time students.

DEGREE REQUIREMENTS. For M.S.: 36 semester units minimum, at least 27 in residence; thesis/project optional. For Engineer: 36 semester units beyond the M.S., at least 27 in residence; thesis/project, required; final oral exam. For Ph.D.: three years minimum, at least one year in residence; reading knowledge of one foreign language, two foreign languages required by some departments; qualifying oral/written exam; dissertation; final oral defense.

FIELDS OF STUDY.
Aeronautics and Astronautics. M.S.
Chemical Engineering. Includes polymer science. M.S., Ph.D.
Chemistry. M.S., Ph.D.
Civil Engineering. M.S., Ph.D.
Computer Science. M.S., Ph.D.
Distributed Information Systems Engineering. M.S. only.
Electrical Engineering. M.E., Ph.D.
Electrophysics. M.S., Ph.D.
Environment Engineering. M.S., Ph.D.
Environmental Health Science. M.S. only.
Industrial Engineering. M.S. only.
Management. M.S. only.
Management of Technology. M.S. only.
Manufacturing Engineering. M.S. only.
Materials Science. M.S., Ph.D.
Mathematics. M.S., Ph.D.
Mechanical Engineering. M.S., Ph.D.
Metallurgical Engineering. M.S. only.
Operations Management. M.S. only.
Organizational Behavior. M.S. only.
Physics. M.S., Ph.D.
System Engineering. M.S. only.
Telecommunications and Computing Management. M.S. only.
Transportation Management. M.S. only.
Transportation Planning and Engineering. M.S., Ph.D.

PONCE SCHOOL OF MEDICINE
P. O. Box 7004
Ponce, Puerto Rico 00732-7004

Formerly Catholic University of Puerto Rico School of Medicine, reorganized 1980. Annual tuition: resident $16,973, nonresident $23,304, student fees, $1763. Enrollment: first-year class 60 (EDP 5); total 190 (men 55%, women 45%). Degree conferred: M.D.

ADMISSION REQUIREMENTS. AMCAS report, transcripts, MCAT, recommendations required in support of application. Interview by invitation. Has EDP (for Puerto Rico students only); apply between June 15 and August 1. Fluency in Spanish required. Preference given to residents of Puerto Rico. Apply to

Admissions Office after June 15, before December 15. Application fee $50. Phone: (809)840-2511; fax: (809)844-3085.

ADMISSION STANDARDS. Competitive. Admits about 20% of total annual applicants. Approximately 75% are residents.

FINANCIAL AID. Scholarships, loans. Apply after acceptance to Student Financial Aid Office. About 82% of students receive some aid from School.

DEGREE REQUIREMENTS. For M.D.: satisfactory completion of four-year program.

PONTIFICAL CATHOLIC UNIVERSITY OF PUERTO RICO
Ponce, Puerto Rico 00732-6382

Established 1948. Located 140 miles S of San Juan. Coed. Private control. Roman Catholic. Semester system.
Tuition: per credit $190. On-campus housing available for single students only. Apply to Director of Housing for on/off-campus housing information.

Law School

Founded 1961. Law library: 160,600 volumes. Library has LEXIS, NEXIS, WESTLAW.
Enrollment: first-year class 135; total 434 (men 50%, women 50%). Faculty: full-time 21, part-time 13. Degrees conferred: J.D., J.D.-M.B.A.

ADMISSION REQUIREMENTS. Transcripts, interview, two letters of recommendation, LSAT, PAEG required in support of application. Bachelor's degree required for matriculation. Fluency in both written and spoken Spanish essential. Accepts transfer applicants. Graduates of unaccredited colleges not considered. Apply to School by May 15. Beginning students accepted Fall and Spring (part-time only). Application fee $25. Phone: (809)941-2000, ext. 339, 340.

ADMISSION STANDARDS. Selective. Accepts 68% of total annual applications. Most enrolled students are from Puerto Rico.

FINANCIAL AID. Scholarships, loans. Apply by May 15 to Student Aid Office. Use FAFSA. About 6% of students receive aid other than loans from School.

DEGREE REQUIREMENTS. For J.D.: 94 semester hours minimum, at least two years in residence, including last two semesters.

PORTLAND STATE UNIVERSITY
Portland, Oregon 97270-0751
http://www.pdx.edu

Established 1946. Coed. State control. Quarter system. Library: over 1,000,000 volumes, 2,130,000 microforms.
Annual tuition: resident $5700, nonresident $9795. Limited on- and off-campus housing for married and graduate students. Annual academic year housing costs: $2700 single students, $4572 for married students. Apply through College Housing Northwest, 1802 SW 10th Ave. (97201). Phone: (800)547-8887, ext. 4333, (503)725-4333.

Graduate Studies

Enrollment: full-time 1509, part-time 2623. University faculty: full-time 510; part-time 171. Degrees conferred: M.A., M.E., M.I.M., M.S., M.Ed., M.P.A., M.P.H., M.T., M.U.S., M.U.R.P., M.A.T., M.S.T., M.B.A., M.F.A., M.S.W., Ed.D., Ph.D.

ADMISSION REQUIREMENTS. Two official transcripts required in support of application. GRE required for most programs, GMAT required for M.B.A., M.I.M., M.T. TOEFL required for international applicants. Accepts transfer applicants. Apply to Office of Graduate Admissions prior to registration. Application fee $50. Phone: (503)725-3511; fax: (503)725-5525.

ADMISSION STANDARDS. Relatively open or selective. Usual minimum average: 2.75, or 3.0 for last 2 years (A = 4).

FINANCIAL AID. Annual awards from institutional funds: 867 academic scholarships, 137 research assistantships, 262 teaching assistantships, Federal W/S, loans. Approved for VA benefits. Apply to Graduate Office; no specified closing dates. Use FAFSA and institutional FAF. Phone: (503)725-3461; fax: (503)725-5965. About 18% of students receive aid other than loans from University and outside sources. Aid sometimes available to part-time students.

DEGREE REQUIREMENTS. For master's: 45–90 term hours depending on degree program, at least 30 in residence; thesis/final exam varies by department. Reading knowledge of one foreign language for M.A., M.A.T. For Ed.D., Ph.D.: three years beyond the bachelor's, at least three consecutive terms in full-time residence; competency in at least one foreign language (Ph.D. only); comprehensive written/oral exam; dissertation; final oral exam.

FIELDS OF STUDY.
Administration of Justice.
Anthropology.
Biology.
Business Administration.
Chemistry.
Civil Engineering.
Computer Science.
Economics.
Education. Includes counseling, curriculum and instruction, educational policy, foundations and administration, media/librarianship, special.
Electrical and Computer Engineering.
Engineering Management.
English.
Environmental Sciences and Resources.
Fine Arts.
Foreign Languages. Includes French, German, Spanish.
Foreign Literature and Language.
General Arts and Letters.
General Science.
General Social Science.
Geography.
Geology. Includes geohydrology.
Health Education.
History.
International Management.
Manufacturing Engineering.
Mathematics.
Mechanical Engineering.
Music Education.
Painting.
Physics.
Political Science.
Postsecondary Education.
Psychology.

Public Administration. Includes Health Administration.
Public Administration and Policy.
Public Health. Includes health education/health promotion, health administration and policy.
Sculpture.
Secondary Education.
Social Work.
Sociology.
Speech Communication.
Speech and Hearing Science.
System Science.
Taxation.
TESOL.
Theater Arts.
Urban and Regional Planning. Includes regional science.
Urban Studies.

UNIVERSITY OF PORTLAND
Portland, Oregon 97203-5798

Founded 1901. Coed. Private control. Semester system. Library: 310,000 volumes, 210,000 microforms.

Tuition: per credit $455. Limited on-campus housing for graduate students during academic year. Average academic year housing costs: $4200 (including board). Apply to Dean of Students for both on- and off-campus information. Phone: (503)283-7205.

Graduate School.

Graduate study since 1936. Enrollment: full-time 105, part-time 226 (men 50%, women 50%). Graduate faculty: full-time 72, part-time 26. Degrees conferred: M.A., M.Ed., M.F.A., M.M., M.M.Ed., M.B.A., M.A.T., M.S.M.E., M.S.E.E., M.S.C.E., M.S.N.

ADMISSION REQUIREMENTS. Transcripts, three letters of recommendation, GRE/GMAT/MAT/NTE required in support of School's application. TOEFL required for international applicants. Accepts transfer applicants. Apply to Dean of Graduate School at least one month prior to registration. Application fee $30. Phone: (503)283-7107; fax: (503)283-7399.

ADMISSION STANDARDS. Competitive for some departments, selective for others. Usual minimum average: 3.0 (A = 4).

FINANCIAL AID. Limited to Federal W/S, loans. Approved for VA benefits. Apply to the Office of Financial Aid; no specified closing date. Use FAFSA. Phone: (503)283-7311.

DEGREE REQUIREMENTS. For master's: 30 semester hours minimum, at least 21 in residence; comprehensive exam; thesis or final research project required for M.A.; final oral/written exam.

FIELDS OF STUDY.
Business Administration. M.B.A.
College Student Personnel. M.S.
Communications. M.A., M.S.
Drama. M.F.A.
Education. Thirty-six hours minimum for M.Ed., M.A.T., M.A.
Engineering. Includes civil, electrical, mechanical. M.S.M.E., M.S.E.E., M.S.C.E.
History and Government. M.A.
Music. Includes theory, performance, education. M.A., M.M.Ed.
Nursing. M.S.N.
Theology. M.A.

PRAIRIE VIEW A&M UNIVERSITY
Prairie View, Texas 77446-0188

Founded 1876. Located 45 miles NW of Houston. Coed. State control. Semester system. A unit of the Texas A&M University system. Special facilities: Cooperative Agricultural Research Center, Particle Detector Research Center, Center for Social and Economic Research. Library: 284,000 volumes, 372,000 microforms, 1200 current periodicals, 48 PCs.

Annual tuition: full-time, resident $958, nonresident $3476; per credit, resident $36, nonresident $144. On-campus housing for single students only. Average academic year housing costs: $2800 (including board). Average off-campus housing costs: $300–$450 per month. Contact the Housing Office for both on- and off-campus housing information.

Graduate School

Founded 1938. Enrollment: full-time 250, part-time 900. Degrees conferred: M.A., M.Ed., M.S., M.S.Eng., M.B.A.

ADMISSION REQUIREMENTS. Official transcripts, three letters of recommendation, GRE/GMAT (Business) required in support of application. TOEFL required for international applicants. Accepts transfer applicants. Graduates of unaccredited institutions not considered. Apply by July 1 (Fall), November 1 (Spring) to Dean of Graduate School. Rolling admissions process. Application fee $10. Phone: (409)857-2315; fax: (409)857-4521.

ADMISSION STANDARDS. Relatively open. Usual minimum average: 2.75 ($\Lambda = 4$).

FINANCIAL AID. Fifty teaching assistantships, twenty-five research assistantships, Federal W/S, loans. Apply by April 1 to the Dean of the Graduate School for assistantships; to Financial Aid Office for all other programs. Use FAFSA. About 65% receive aid from School and outside sources.

DEGREE REQUIREMENTS. For master's: 30–36 semester hours minimum (depending upon program), at least 20 hours in residence; thesis usually required for M.A., M.S.

FIELDS OF STUDY.
Agriculture. Includes economics, education, extension education, animal science, soil science.
Agronomy and Soil Sciences.
Art.
Biology.
Business Administration. M.B.A. only.
Chemistry.
Drama.
Economics.
Education. Includes elementary, secondary teaching, business, industrial, health, physical, counselor education, special education, administration, supervision, educational technology, history, home economics, curriculum and foundations.
Educational Technology.
Engineering and Applied Sciences.
English.
History.
Marketing.
Mathematics-Computer Science.
Music. Includes applied, theory, education.
Physics.
Plant Science.
Political Science.
Sociology.
Soils.

PRATT INSTITUTE
Brooklyn, New York 11205-3899

Founded 1887. Coed. Private control. Semester system. Special facilities: Center for Community and Environmental Development, Printmaking/Fine Arts Center, Schaffler Art Gallery. Library: 220,000 volumes, 50,000 microforms, 100,000 pictures and prints, 500 current periodicals, 10 PCs.

Annual tuition: full-time $13,738; per credit $573. On-campus housing for married and single students. Average academic year housing costs: $4666 for married students, $7266 (including board) for single students. Contact Residential Life Office for both on- and off-campus housing information. Phone: (708)636-3509.

Graduate Programs

Graduate study since 1950. Enrollment: full-time 660, part-time 589. Faculty: full- and part-time 134. Degrees conferred: M.Arch., M.S., M.S.C.R.P., M.I.D., M.S.U.E.S.M., M.S.U.D., M.F.A., M.L.S.

ADMISSION REQUIREMENTS. Official transcripts, three letters of reference required in support of application. Interview often required. GRE Subject Tests recommended. Portfolio required for Art, Design, and Architecture Departments. TOEFL recommended for international applicants. Accepts transfer applicants. Graduates of unaccredited institutions not considered. Apply to Graduate Admissions Office by March 1 (Fall), December 1 (Spring). Rolling admissions process. Application fee $35, $80 for international applicants. Phone: (718)636-3669; fax: (718)636-3670.

ADMISSION STANDARDS. Very competitive for some departments, very selective for most. Usual minimum average: 2.5 ($A = 4$).

FINANCIAL AID. Scholarships, fellowships, assistantships, Federal W/S, loans. Approved for VA benefits. Apply by May 1 to Director of Graduate Program of the appropriate program for fellowships, assistantships; to Financial Aid Office for all other programs. Use FAFSA. About 20–25% of students receive aid from Institute and outside sources. No aid for part-time students.

DEGREE REQUIREMENTS. For M.Arch.: 36 credits minimum, at least 22 in residence. For M.S.: 36 credits minimum, at least 24 in residence. For M.I.D.: 34 credits minimum, at least 26 in residence. For M.L.S.: 36 credits minimum, at least 30 in residence. For M.F.A.: 48 credits minimum, at least 40 in residence. For M.S.C.R.P., M.S.U.E.S.M., M.S.U.D.; 62 credits minimum, at least 45 in full-time residence; special project.

FIELDS OF STUDY.
Architecture. M.Arch.
Art and Design Education. M.S.
Art History. M.S.
Art Therapy. M.P.S.
City and Regional Planning. M.S.C.R.P.
Communication Design. M.S.
Computer Graphic Design. M.F.A.
Facilities Management. M.S.
Graphic Design. M.F.A.
Industrial Design. M.I.D.
Interior Design. M.S.
Library and Information Science. M.L.S.
Package Design. M.S.
Painting. M.F.A.
Photography. M.F.A.
Printmaking. M.F.A.

Sculpture. M.F.A.
Urban Design. M.S.U.D.
Urban Environmental Systems Management. M.S.U.E.S.M.

PRINCETON UNIVERSITY
Princeton, New Jersey 08544-1019

Founded 1746. Located 50 miles SW of New York City. Private control. Semester system. Special facilities: cooperative with the Institute for Advanced Study, Center for Human Values, Geophysical Fluid Dynamics Lab of NOAA, Plasma Physics Fusion Research Laboratory; affiliation with Princeton Theological Seminary, Office for Survey Research and Statistical Studies, Princeton Materials Institute, Textile Research Institute, Center for Studies in Twentieth-Century American Statecraft and Public Policy, Center of International Studies. Library: 4,000,000 volumes, 1,500,000 microforms.

Annual tuition: full-time $22,640. On-campus housing for more than 400 married students, 570 single students. Average academic year housing costs: $1296 per month plus $525 for each child for married students, $1029 per month plus partial board for single students. Apply to Assistant Director for Graduate Housing. Phone: (609)258-3720.

Graduate School

Enrollment: full-time 1769 (men 1122, women 647); no part-time students. Faculty: full-time 693, part-time 69. Degrees conferred: M.A., M.F.A., M.Public Affairs, M.S., M.Arch., M.S.E., Ph.D.

ADMISSION REQUIREMENTS. Transcripts, three letters of recommendation, GRE Test required in support of School's application. GRE Subject Test strongly recommended or required according to department. TOEFL required of international applicants. Apply by the first Wednesday in January. Admits full-time students only. Fall admission only. Application fee $55 domestic, $60 international. Phone: (609)258-3034; fax: (609)258-6180.

ADMISSION STANDARDS. Very competitive for some departments, competitive for the others.

FINANCIAL AID. Annual awards from institutional funds: 650 fellowships, 700+ teaching/research assistantships, Federal W/S, loans. Apply by first Wednesday in January to Graduate School Office for fellowships, assistantships; to Financial Aid Office for all other programs. Phone: (609)258-3028; fax: (609)258-6180. Use FAFSA and University's FAF. About 95% of students receive aid other than loans from School and outside sources.

DEGREE REQUIREMENTS. For master's: one year minimum in full-time residence; general exam (one year minimum full-time before sitting for general exam); thesis for M.S. and for M.A. in Near Eastern Studies; M.A. generally regarded as incidental degree. For Ph.D.: one year minimum in full-time residence; oral/written general exam; dissertation; final public oral exam.

FIELDS OF STUDY.
African Studies. Interdepartmental.
Afro-American Studies. Interdepartmental program in combination with an established discipline.
Anthropology. Ph.D. in cultural anthropology; competence in one foreign language, usually French.
Applied and Computational Mathematics. Interdepartmental in combination with science and engineering departments.
Architecture. two- and three-year M.Arch. program; design project and oral exam for M.Arch.

Art and Archaeology. Includes joint program in classical archaeology; two languages for Ph.D.
Astrophysical Sciences. Includes astronomy, astrophysics, plasma physics.
Biology and Neuroscience.
Chemistry. Includes cooperative program in physics and chemical physics; Ph.D. applicants given preference for admission; one language appropriate to study of chemistry for Ph.D.
Chinese and Japanese Art and Archaeology. Interdepartmental; proficiency in classical and modern Chinese, reading knowledge of Japanese for Chinese concentration; proficiency in Japanese, reading knowledge of Chinese for Japanese concentration; also French or German for Ph.D.
Classical Archaeology. Interdepartmental; proficiency in Greek, Latin, French, and German for Ph.D.
Classical Philosophy. Interdepartmental; Greek and Latin for Ph.D.
Classics. Competence in Greek and Latin plus French and German for Ph.D.
Comparative Literature. Competence in two foreign languages plus Greek or Latin for Ph.D.
Demography. Admission to Ph.D. program granted to students in economics, sociology, statistics; language requirement of that department must be fulfilled.
East Asian Studies. High degree of competence in Chinese or Japanese plus one European language for Ph.D.
Ecology and Evolutionary Biology.
Economics. Strong mathematical/statistical background recommended.
Engineering and Applied Science-Mechanical and Aerospace Engineering. Includes interdepartmental programs in nuclear engineering, mechanical engineering, chemical engineering, civil engineering and operations, electrical engineering, and computer science.
English. Reading knowledge of Latin or Greek and reading knowledge of German and French.
Geological and Geophysical Sciences.
Germanic Languages and Literatures. Two languages in addition to German for Ph.D.
History. Reading knowledge of at least one language; more may be required depending on area of study.
History of Science. French and German required for students of history of science; French or German for students of philosophy of science; for medieval or ancient periods, Latin/Greek.
International and Regional Studies.
Latin American Studies. Interdepartmental program.
Mathematics. Reading knowledge of mathematical texts in German or Russian for Ph.D.
Molecular Biology.
Music. Includes music history, theory, composition; reading knowledge of at least one of the following: German, French, or Italian for Ph.D.
Near Eastern Studies.
Neurosciences. Interdepartmental with biology and psychology.
Philosophy. Reading knowledge of French or German for Ph.D.
Physics. Includes mathematical, chemical, plasma.
Political Philosophy. Interdepartmental.
Politics.
Polymer Science and Materials. Interdepartmental program.
Population Studies. Interdepartmental.
Psychology.
Public Affairs. Two-year M.P.A.
Religion. Two languages in addition to competence in biblical, classical, Oriental languages as required in field of specialization.
Romance Languages and Literatures. Includes French, Spanish; reading knowledge of French, German, and simple Latin for Ph.D.
Slavic Languages and Literature.
Sociology. One language and knowledge of general sociological theory, statistical theory and procedure, competence in research methodology including computer application for Ph.D.

Statistics and Operations Research.
Transportation. Interdepartmental.
Water Resources. Interdepartmental.

Woodrow Wilson School of Public and International Affairs

http://www.wws.princeton.edu

Established 1930. Graduate enrollment: full-time, M.P.A. 130, Ph.D. 25. Faculty: full-time 53, adjunct 20. Degrees conferred: M.P.A., M.P.A.-J.D., M.P.A.-U.R.P., Ph.D., Certificate.

ADMISSION REQUIREMENTS. Transcripts, three letters of reference, public policy essay, personal statement, GRE required in support of School's application. TOEFL required for international applicants. Accepts transfer applicants. Graduates of unaccredited institutions not considered. Apply to Office of Graduate Admissions by January 8. Fall admission only. Application fee $55, $60 if mailed outside the United States, Canada and Mexico. Phone: (609)258-4836; fax: (609)258-2095.

ADMISSION STANDARDS. Very competitive. Usual minimum average: 3.6 (A = 4).

FINANCIAL AID. One hundred twenty academic scholarships, ten research fellowships, ten teaching fellowships, five research assistantships, one hundred internships, Federal W/S, loans. Approved for VA benefits. Apply in early January to Graduate School for scholarships, fellowships, assistantships; to Financial Aid Office for all other programs. Use FAFSA and University's FAF. Phone: (609)258-3037. 92% of M.P.A.'s and 100% of Ph.D.'s receive aid from School and outside sources.

DEGREE REQUIREMENTS. For M.P.A.: one year in residence; two qualifying examinations. For M.P.A. J.D.: three semesters in residence. For M.P.A.-U.R.P.: four semesters in residence. For Ph.D.: reading knowledge of one foreign language; dissertation; final oral exam.

FIELDS OF STUDY.
Demography. Certificate.
Development Studies.
Domestic Policy.
Economics and Public Policy.
International Relations.
Science Technology and Public Policy. Certificate.

PROVIDENCE COLLEGE

Providence, Rhode Island 02918

Founded 1917. Private control. Roman Catholic affiliation. Semester system. Library: 296,000 volumes, 27,800 microforms, 5 PCs.
Tuition: per course $570–$650, depending on program. Limited on-campus housing available. Contact Director of Life for both on- and off-campus housing information. Phone: (401)865-2392.

Graduate School

Graduate study since 1965. Enrollment: full-time 45, part-time 880 (men 240, women 640). Faculty teaching graduate students: full-time 36, part-time 43. Degrees conferred: M.A., M.A.T. (Math), M.B.A., M.Ed.

ADMISSION REQUIREMENTS. Transcripts, two letters of recommendation, GMAT/MAT required in support of School's application. TOEFL required for foreign applicants. Accepts

transfer applicants. Apply to Office of Admissions; no specified closing date. Application fee $30. Phone: (401)865-2247; fax: (401)865-2057.

ADMISSION STANDARDS. Selective. Usual minimum average: 3.0 (A = 4).

FINANCIAL AID. Annual awards from institutional funds limited to twenty-eight assistantships, loans. Approved for VA benefits. Apply by March 15 to appropriate department chair for assistantships; to Financial Aid Office for all other programs. Phone: (401)865-2286. About 10% of students receive aid other than loans from School and outside sources.

DEGREE REQUIREMENTS. For M.A. (History), M.S.: 30 credit hours minimum; reading knowledge of one foreign language; comprehensive exam; thesis/final document. For M.B.A., M.Ed.: 36 credit hours; comprehensive exam.

FIELDS OF STUDY.
Business Administration.
Education.
History.
Mathematics. M.A.T. only.
Religious Studies.

UNIVERSITY OF PUERTO RICO, MAYAGUEZ

Mayaguez, Puerto Rico 00680-5000

Established in 1911. Public control. Coed. Semester system. Formerly the College of Agriculture and Mechanic Arts. Special facilities: Center for Energy and Environmental Research, Engineering Research Center, Magueyes Island Marine Station, Agricultural Experimental Station, Water Resource Research Institute. Library: 849,000 volumes, 544,000 microforms, 25 PCs.
Tuition: U.S. citizens, residents of Puerto Rico, $75 per credit; U.S. nonresidents of Puerto Rico $75 per credit plus additional amount equivalent to what a Puerto Rican student would pay in the public university in the applicant's state of origin. Foreign students: $3500 per year. There are also applicable regular or special fees. Limited on-campus housing available. Average off-campus housing costs: $400–$800 per month. Contact Office of Residential Life for on- and off-campus housing information. Phone: (809)834-0589.

Graduate Studies

Graduate study since 1957. Graduate enrollment: full-time 675, part-time 50. Graduate faculty: 400. Degrees conferred: M.A., M.B.A., M.S., M.E., Ph.D.

ADMISSION REQUIREMENTS. Bachelor's degree, transcript, working knowledge of Spanish and English required in support of application. GRE/GMAT required for some programs. Interview required for some departments. Apply to the Office of Admission by March 15 (Fall), December 15 (Winter). Application fee $15. Phone: (809)265-3809; fax: (809)831-1115.

ADMISSION STANDARDS. Selective. Usual minimum average: 2.5 (A = 4).

FINANCIAL AID. Annual awards from institutional funds: 75 research assistantships, 450 teaching assistantships, Federal W/S, loans. Approved for VA benefits. Apply to Director of Financial Aid; no specified closing date. Use FAFSA and institutional FAF. Phone: (809)265-3683; fax: (809)265-3683.

DEGREE REQUIREMENTS. Master's: 36 credits minimum, at least 24 in residence; candidacy; thesis; final oral exam. For Ph.D.: 72 credits beyond the bachelor's minimum; at least 30 credits in residence; comprehensive exam; candidacy; dissertation; final exam.

FIELDS OF STUDY.

Agriculture. Includes agricultural economics, agricultural education, agronomy-crops, animal industry, crop protection, extension education, horticulture, plant pathology.

Biology. Includes botany, ecology, entomology, genetics, molecular biology, zoology.

Business Administration.

Chemistry. Includes biochemistry, organic chemistry, physical chemistry, radiochemistry.

Engineering. Includes chemical, civil, computer science, electrical, mechanical, industrial management systems.

Geology.

Latin American Studies.

Marine Science. Includes biological, chemical, geological, physical oceanography.

Mathematics. Includes statistics, computer sciences, applied mathematics.

Physics. Includes nuclear, solid state, theoretical physics.

UNIVERSITY OF PUERTO RICO
Rio Piedras, Puerto Rico 00931

Founded 1903. Located 8 miles S of San Juan. Coed. Public control. Semester system. Special facilities: Center for Studies of American Arts, Center for Archaeological Research, Caribbean Studies Institute, Institute of Cooperativism, Economic Research Center, Center for Historical Research, Natural Science Academic Computer Center, Resource Center for Scientific Engineering, Social Science Research Center. Library: 4,091,000 volumes, 1,637,000 microforms, 4900 current periodicals.

Annual tuition: full-time $2202; per credit $75. Limited on-campus housing for single graduate students. Average academic year housing costs: $1400 (room only). Contact Dean of Students Office for both on- and off-campus housing information. Phone: (809)764-0000, ext. 5651.

Graduate Division

Graduate study since 1927. Enrollment: full-time 897, part-time 2260. Graduate faculty: full-time 195, part-time 146. Degrees conferred: M.A., M.S., M.B.A., M.L.S., M.Ed., M.P., M.P.A., M.S.W., M.Arch., M.C.R., Ed.D., Ph.D.

ADMISSION REQUIREMENTS. Two official transcripts required in support of application. GRE, interview required for some departments. Accepts transfer applicants. Apply February 15 to Office of Admissions of appropriate College/School. Earlier application deadline for some departments. Application fee $45. Phone: Education (809)764-0000, ext. 3346; Humanities (809)764-4300; Social Sciences (809)764-2040; Natural Science (809)763-5101; Business (809)764-0000, ext. 4142; Librarianship, (809)764-0000, ext. 5828; Planning (809)764-0000, ext. 5010; Architecture (809)764-0000, ext. 3449; Communication (809)764-0000, ext. 5043.

ADMISSION STANDARDS. Competitive. Usual minimum average: 3.0 (A = 4).

FINANCIAL AID. Scholarships, fellowships, assistantships, partial tuition waivers, Federal W/S, loans. Apply to appropriate department chair for fellowships, assistantships; to Financial Aid Office for all other programs. Phone: (809)764-0000, ext. 3148. Use FAFSA and University's FAF. About 60% of students receive aid from University and outside sources.

DEGREE REQUIREMENTS. For master's: one year minimum in residence; thesis/nonthesis; final oral exam; final written exam. For Ph.D.: 30 semester hours minimum beyond the master's, at least two semesters in full-time attendance; reading knowledge of two foreign languages for most programs; qualifying written exam; dissertation; final oral exam. For Ed.D. essentially the same as Ph.D., except no language requirement.

FIELDS OF STUDY.

SCHOOL OF ARCHITECTURE:
Architecture. M.Arch.

GRADUATE SCHOOL OF BUSINESS ADMINISTRATION:
Business Administration. M.B.A.

COLLEGE OF EDUCATION:
Biology Education. M.Ed.
Chemistry Education. M.Ed.
Child Education. M.Ed.
Curriculum and Teaching. Ed.D.
Educational Research and Evaluation. M.Ed.
English Education. M.Ed.
Guidance and Counseling. M.Ed., Ed.D.
History Education. M.Ed.
Mathematics Education. M.Ed.
Physics Education. M.Ed.
School Administration. M.Ed., Ed.D.
Special Education. M.Ed.

COLLEGE OF HUMANITIES:
Comparative Literature. M.A.
English. M.A.
Hispanic Studies. M.A., Ph.D.
History. M.A., Ph.D.
Linguistics. M.A.
Philosophy. M.A. only.
Translation. M.A.

COLLEGE OF SOCIAL SCIENCES:
Economics. M.A. only.
Psychology. M.A., Ph.D.
Public Administration. M.P.A.
Rehabilitation Counseling. M.C.R.
Social Work. M.S.W.
Sociology. M.A.

FACULTY OF NATURAL SCIENCES:
Applied Physics. M.S.
Biology. M.S., Ph.D.
Chemical Physics. Ph.D.
Chemistry. M.S., Ph.D.
Mathematics. M.A. only.
Physics. M.S. only.

GRADUATE SCHOOL OF LIBRARIANSHIP:
Library Science. M.L.S.

GRADUATE SCHOOL OF PLANNING:
Planning. M.P.

SCHOOL OF PUBLIC COMMUNICATION:
Public Communication. M.A.

School of Law

Established 1913. Semester system. Law library: 232,800 volumes. Library has LEXIS, NEXIS, WESTLAW, DIALOG, COMPUCLERK, CAMPULEQ, LEGALTRAC, INFOTRAC.

Annual tuition: full-time $2623, residents and American citizens; nonresident, non-American citizens $3500. Nonresidents can attend full-time only. No on-campus housing available. Total average annual additional expense: $5000.

Enrollment: first-year class, full-time 114, part-time 46; total 523 (men 47%, women 53%). Faculty: full-time 33, part-time 23. Degree conferred: J.D.

ADMISSION REQUIREMENTS. LSDAS Law School report, bachelor's degree, two transcripts, LSAT, PAEG required in support of application. Interview not required. Accepts transfer applicants. Graduates of unaccredited colleges not considered. Apply to Office of Admission after September 1, before February 15. Fall admission only. Application fee $45. Phone: (809)767-8580.

ADMISSION STANDARDS. Selective. Accepts 20–25% of total annual applicants.

FINANCIAL AID. Scholarships, tuition waivers, assistantships, loans. Apply to the University's Office of Financial Aid in San Juan after acceptance, before April 15. Use FAFSA. About 10% of students receive aid other than loans from outside sources.

DEGREE REQUIREMENTS. For J.D.: 92 credits minimum, at least 60 in residence, three-year (day) or four-year (evening) program; 92 credit hour program.
Note: School has summer law program at the University of Barcelona (Spain).

Medical Sciences Campus—Division of Graduate Studies

Established 1960. Located in San Juan (00936-5067). Public control. Special facilities: Caribbean Primate Research Center, Puerto Rican Cancer Center, Center for the Study of Sexually Transmitted Disease, Center for Energy and Environmental Research, Clinical Research Center.

Tuition: per credit $75. Enrollment: full-time 509 (men 70%, women 30%). Faculty: full-time 41, part-time 3. Degrees conferred: M.S., M.S.N., M.P.H., Ph.D.

ADMISSION REQUIREMENTS. Transcripts, GRE Subject Tests, interview, two recommendations, proficiency in English and Spanish required in support of application. Accepts transfer applicants. Apply by February 15 (Fall), by November 1 (Spring) to Director of Graduate Studies. Phone: (809)753-2962.

ADMISSION STANDARDS. Selective for most departments. Usual minimum average: 2.75 (A = 4).

FINANCIAL AID. Annual awards from institutional funds: scholarships, assistantships, fellowships, loans. Apply to appropriate department chairman for fellowships, assistantships. Use FAFSA. About 30% of students receive aid other than loans from university and outside sources.

DEGREE REQUIREMENTS. For M.S., M.P.H.: 30–36 credit hours minimum, at least 24 in residence; reading knowledge of one foreign language; thesis/nonthesis; final oral exam. For Ph.D.: 60 credit hours minimum beyond the bachelor's, at least 40 in residence; qualifying exam; reading knowledge of two foreign languages; comprehensive exam; dissertation; final oral exam.

FIELDS OF STUDY.
Anatomy.
Audiology.
Biochemistry.
Biostatistics.
Environmental Health.
Epidemiology.
Health Services Administration.
Microbiology.
Nursing Administration.
Occupational Health.
Pharmacy.
Pharmacology.
Physiology.
Public Health.
Speech Pathology.

School of Medicine
P.O. Box 365067

Established 1949. Located in San Juan (00936-5067). Library: 100,000 volumes. Annual tuition: $5800. Tuition varies for nonresident students according to program, approximately $10,500. Total average figure for all other expenses: $6500.

Enrollment: first-year class 110, total 419 (men 45%, women 55%); Faculty: about 400, full- and part-time. Degree conferred: M.D.

ADMISSION REQUIREMENTS. For M.D. program: transcripts, letters of recommendation, fluency in English and Spanish, MCAT required in support of application. Does not have EDP. Interview by invitation only. Applicants must have completed at least three years of college study. Accepts limited number of nonresidents. Apply to Office of Dean after June 1, before December 15. Application fee $15. Phone: (809)758-2525, ext. 1810; fax: (809)751-3284.

ADMISSION STANDARDS. Selective. Accepts 25–30% of total annual applicants. Approximately 97% are residents.

FINANCIAL AID. Scholarships for resident students only. Apply by April 30 to Financial Aid Office. Use FAFSA. About 50% of students receive some aid from School.

DEGREE REQUIREMENTS. For M.D.: satisfactory completion of four year program.

School of Dentistry

Established 1956. Located in San Juan (00936-5067). Annual tuition: resident $5000, nonresident varies. Limited on-campus housing available for single students only. Average academic year housing costs: $6000. Contact Dean of Students Office for both on- and off-campus housing information. Total average cost for all other first-year expenses: $6129.

Enrollment: D.M.D. programs, first-year class 40 (men 30%, women 70%); graduate program, full-time 16 (men 15, women 1). Faculty: full-time 66, part-time 31. Degrees conferred: D.M.D., M.S.

ADMISSION REQUIREMENTS. For D.M.D. program: AADSAS, official transcripts, three letters of recommendation, DAT (no later than October), proficiency in Spanish required in support of application. Preference given to Puerto Rican students. Interview by invitation only. Applicants must have completed at least three years of college study. Accepts transfer applicants. Apply to Director of Admissions after June 30, before December 15. Application fee $25. Phone: (809)758-2525, ext. 1113. For graduate programs: official transcripts, two letters of recommendation, interview required in support of School's application. Accepts transfer applicants. Enrollment limited to residents. Apply to Chair of Graduate Committee by December 15. Application fee $15.

ADMISSION STANDARDS. For D.M.D. Program: Accepts 65% of total annual applicants. 100% are residents of Puerto Rico. For graduate program: competitive. Usual minimum average: 3.0 (A = 4).

FINANCIAL AID. For D.M.D. program: scholarships, grants, loans for Puerto Rican resident students only; apply to the University's Dean of Students Office; no specified closing date. About 75% of students receive aid from School and outside sources. For graduate program: fellowships for hospital residency. All graduate students receive aid during residency.

DEGREE REQUIREMENTS. For D.M.D.: satisfactory completion of 46-month program. For M.S. (oral surgery): 36 months minimum, at least 2 semesters in hospital residency; thesis; final written exam. For M.S.: 24 months minimum, hospital residency; thesis; final written exam.

FIELDS OF GRADUATE OF STUDY.
General Practice.
Oral and Maxillofacial Surgery.
Pedodontics.
Prothesis.

UNIVERSITY OF PUGET SOUND
Tacoma, Washington 98416-0005

Founded 1888. Coed. Private control. Methodist affiliation. Semester system. Library: 363,000 volumes, 194,000 microforms, 2000 current periodicals, 19 PCs.

Annual tuition: full-time $18,030; per course $2270. No on-campus housing available for graduate students.

Graduate Studies

Enrollment: full-time 144, part-time 98. University faculty: full-time 29, part-time 33. Degrees conferred: M.A.T., M.Ed., M.O.T., M.P.T.

ADMISSION REQUIREMENTS. Official transcripts, three letters of recommendation, GRE/MAT required in support of application. Interview required for Education. Proficiency in English or TOEFL required of international students. Accepts transfer applicants. Graduates of unaccredited institutions not considered. Apply to Office of Admissions one month prior to registration. Application deadline for M.O.T. and M.P.T. is February 1. Rolling admissions process. Application fee $35. Phone: (206)756-3211.

ADMISSION STANDARDS. Selective for all departments. Usual minimum average: 3.0 (A = 4). 50th percentile or higher on tests.

FINANCIAL AID. Scholarships, research assistantships, teaching assistantships, Federal W/S, loans. Approved for VA benefits. Apply to appropriate school for assistantships; to Financial Aid Office for all other programs. Use FAFSA. Phone: (206)756-3214. About 25% of students receive aid from both University and outside sources.

DEGREE REQUIREMENTS. For master's: 8 units (32 semester hours) minimum, at least 6 units in residence; oral/written comprehensive exam; thesis/nonthesis option for some degrees.

FIELDS OF STUDY.
Counselor Education. M.Ed.
Education Administration. M.Ed.

Elementary Education. M.A.T.
Improvement of Instruction. Includes elementary, reading, secondary. M.Ed.
Occupational Therapy. M.O.T.
Pastoral Counseling. M.Ed.
Physical Therapy. M.P.T.
Secondary Education. M.Ed.

PURDUE UNIVERSITY
West Lafayette, Indiana 47907-1968

Founded 1869. Located 65 miles NW of Indianapolis. Coed. State control. Semester system. Special facilities: Agricultural Experiment Station, Animal Science Research Center, Center for Applied Ethology and Human/Animal Interaction, Center for Applied Mathematics, Center for Artistic Endeavors, Center for Asian Studies, Hellenbrand Biomedical Engineering Center, Center for Classical Studies, Center for Comparative Literature, Engineering Research Center for Intelligent Manufacturing Systems, Engineering Experiment Station, Center for Film Studies, Gifted Education Resource Center, Center for Humanistic Studies, Jet Propulsion Center, Center for Leadership Studies, Center for Medieval Studies, Center for AIDS Research, Center for Intelligent Manufacturing Systems, Marriage and Family Center, Center for Paralysis Research, Center for Plant Environmental Stress Physiology, Policy Center for Life Long Learning, Retail Institute, Center for Research on the Aging, Center for Rural Development, Social Research Center, Center for Technology Transfer and Pollution Prevention, University Research Park. Library: 2,107,000 volumes, 2,136,000 microforms, 14,300 current periodicals.

Annual tuition: full-time, resident $3208, nonresident $10,636; per hour, resident $115, nonresident $351. On-campus housing for 1300 married students, 800 graduate men and women. Average annual housing cost: $4200 for married students, $3000 for single students. Apply to Director's Office, Young Graduate House, Purdue University, for graduate housing; Director, Married Student Housing, Nimitz Drive, Purdue University, for married student housing; for off-campus housing, apply to Off-Campus Housing Services, Hovde Hall, Office of the Dean of Students. Phone: (317)494-7045.

Graduate School

Graduate faculty: almost 1690. Degrees conferred: M.A., M.Agr., M.F.A., M.A.T., M.S., M.S.A.A.E., M.S.Ag.E., M.S.C.E., M.S.Ch.E., M.S.Ed., M.S.E.E., M.S.F., M.S.I.A., M.S.I.E., M.S.Met.E., M.S.N.E., Ed.S., Ph.D.

ADMISSION REQUIREMENTS. Official transcripts, three letters of reference required in support of School's application. GRE/MAT/GMAT required by many departments. TOEFL required for international applicants. Accepts transfer applicants. Graduates of unaccredited institutions not considered. Apply to department of major interest one semester in advance and not later than May 1 (Fall), September 1 (Spring), March 1 (Summer). Application fee $30. Phone for general information: (317)494-2600.

ADMISSION STANDARDS. Selective for most departments, very selective for the others. Usual minimum average: 3.0 (A = 4).

FINANCIAL AID. Annual awards from institutional funds: scholarships, fellowships (including minority fellowships), teaching assistantships, research fellowships, administrative assistantships, full and partial tuition waivers, Federal W/S, loans. Approved for VA benefits. Apply by February 1 to appropriate department for fellowships, assistantships; to Financial Aid Office for all other programs. Use FAFSA. About 60% of full-time students receive aid from University and outside sources. No aid for part-time students.

DEGREE REQUIREMENTS. For master's: usually about 33 hours, at least two semesters in residence; thesis/nonthesis option: final written/oral exams for most majors; reading knowledge of one foreign language for some majors. For Ph.D.: usually 50–60 hours minimum beyond the bachelor's, at least one year in residence; qualifying exam for most majors; preliminary exam; reading knowledge of one foreign language for most majors; thesis; final written/oral exam.

FIELDS OF STUDY.
Accounting. M.S., Ph.D.
Aeronautics and Astronautics. M.S., M.S.A.A.E., M.S.E., Ph.D.
Agricultural and Biological Engineering. M.S., M.S.Ag.E., M.S.E., Ph.D.
Agricultural Economics. M.S., Ph.D.
Agronomy. M.S., Ph.D.
American Studies. M.A., Ph.D.
Anatomy. M.S., Ph.D.
Animal Sciences. M.S., Ph.D.
Anthropology. M.S., Ph.D.
Applied Ethology and Human/Animal Interactions. Interdisciplinary.
Applied Optimization. Ph.D.
Applied Statistics. Ph.D.
Art and Design. M.A.
Art Education. M.S.Ed., Ph.D.
Audiology. M.S., Ph.D.
Bacteriology. M.S., Ph.D.
Biochemistry. Interdisciplinary Program. M.S., Ph.D.
Biomedical Engineering and Bioengineering. Interdisciplinary.
Bio-organic Chemistry. Ph.D.
Biophysics. M.S., Ph.D.
Botany and Plant Pathology. M.S., Ph.D.
Cell and Developmental Biology. Ph.D.
Chemical Engineering. M.S., M.S.Ch.E., M.S.E., Ph.D.
Chemistry. Includes analytical, geochemistry, inorganic, organic, physical.
Civil Engineering. M.S., M.S.C.E., M.S.E., Ph.D.
Clinical Pharmacy. M.S., Ph.D.
Communication. M.A., M.S., Ph.D.
Comparative Literature. Interdisciplinary. M.A., Ph.D.
Computer Sciences. M.S., Ph.D.
Consumer Behavior. M.S., Ph.D.
Counseling and Development. M.S., M.S.Ed., Ph.D., Ed.S.
Creative Arts. M.A. or M.F.A. only.
Curriculum Theory. M.S.Ed., Ph.D.
Developmental Biology. M.S.
Developmental Studies. M.S., Ph.D.
Early Childhood Education. Ph.D.
Earth and Atmospheric Sciences. M.S., Ph.D.
Ecology, Evolutionary and Population Biology. M.S., Ph.D.
Economics. Ph.D.
Education of the Gifted. M.S.Ed.
Educational Administration. M.S., M.S.Ed., Ph.D., Ed.S.
Educational Computing. M.S.Ed., Ph.D.
Educational Psychology. M.S., M.S.Ed., Ph.D.
Electrical Engineering. M.S., M.S.E., M.S.E.E., Ph.D.
Elementary Education. M.A.T., M.S.Ed., Ph.D.
English.
Entomology. M.S., Ph.D.
Environmental Health Sciences. Ph.D.
Epidemiology. M.S., Ph.D.
Exercise Physiology. M.S., Ph.D.

Extension Education. M.S.
Family and Consumer Economics. M.S., Ph.D.
Family Studies. M.S., Ph.D.
Finance. M.S., Ph.D.
Food Science. M.S., Ph.D.
Foreign Language Education. M.S.Ed., Ph.D.
Forestry and Natural Resources. M.S., M.S.F., Ph.D.
French. M.A., Ph.D.
French Education. M.A.T.
Geographic Information System and Remote Sensing. Interdisciplinary.
German. M.A., Ph.D.
German Education. M.A.T.
Health Promotion. M.S., Ph.D.
History. M.A., Ph.D.
Horticulture. M.Agr., M.A., Ph.D.
Hospitality Administration.
Human Factors in Industrial Engineering. Interdisciplinary. M.S., M.S.I.E., Ph.D.
Human Resources Management. M.S.
Immunology. M.S., Ph.D.
Industrial Administration. M.S.I.A.
Industrial and Physical Pharmacy. Ph.D.
Industrial Technology. M.S. nonthesis only.
Instructional Development. M.S.Ed., Ph.D., Ed.S.
International Management. M.S.
Language Arts. M.S.Ed., Ph.D.
Linguistics. M.A., Ph.D.
Literature. Includes creative writing. M.A., Ph.D.
Management Information Systems. M.S., Ph.D.
Management Science. M.S.
Manufacturing Engineering. M.S., M.S.I.E., Ph.D.
Manufacturing Management. M.S.
Marketing. M.S., Ph.D.
Marriage and Family Therapy. M.S., Ph.D.
Materials Engineering. M.S., M.S.E., Ph.D.
Mathematics. M.S., Ph.D.
Mathematics/Science Education. M.S.Ed., Ph.D.
Mechanical Engineering. M.S., M.S.M.E., Ph.D.
Medicinal Chemistry. M.S.
Medicinal Chemistry and Pharmacognosy. Ph.D.
Medieval Studies. Interdisciplinary.
Metallurgical Engineering. M.S.Met.E.
Microbiology. Ph.D.
Mineral Resources. Interdisciplinary.
Molecular Biology. Ph.D.
Natural Products. M.S.
Neurobiology. M.S., Ph.D.
Nuclear Engineering. M.S., M.S.N.E., Ph.D.
Nutrition. M.S., Ph.D.
Operations Research. M.S., M.S.I.E., Ph.D.
Organizational Behavior and Human Resource Management. Ph.D.
Pharmacology and Toxicology. M.S., Ph.D.
Philosophy. M.A., Ph.D.
Physics. M.S., Ph.D.
Physiology. M.S., Ph.D.
Plant Physiology. Interdisciplinary. M.S., Ph.D.
Political Science. M.A., Ph.D.
Psychology. Includes educational.
Quantitative Methods. M.S., Ph.D.
Restaurant, Hotel and Institutional and Tourism Management. M.S.
Retail Management. M.S., Ph.D.
Russian. M.A.
Russian Education. M.A.T.
Social Studies Education. M.S.Ed., Ph.D.
Sociology. M.S., Ph.D.
Spanish. M.A., Ph.D.
Spanish Education. M.A.T.
Special Education. M.S. Ed., Ph.D.
Speech and Hearing Science. M.S., Ph.D.
Speech-Language Pathology. M.S., Ph.D.

Sport Biomechanics. M.S., Ph.D.
Sport Psychology. M.S., Ph.D.
Statistics and Computer Science. M.S.
Strategic Management. M.S., Ph.D.
System Engineering. M.S., M.S.I.E., Ph.D.
Textile Science. M.S., Ph.D.
Theater. M.A., M.F.A.
Theoretical Statistics. M.S.
Veterinary Medicine. Includes veterinary anatomy, M.S., Ph.D.,
  thesis; veterinary clinical sciences, M.S. only, thesis; veteri-
  nary pathobiology, M.S., Ph.D., thesis; veterinary physiology
  and pathology, M.S., Ph.D., thesis.

Graduate Study at Other Campuses

Purdue University maintains a system-wide graduate school
under which some courses and/or programs are offered at the regional campuses located at Hammond and Westville, as well as
at the Indiana University–Purdue University campuses at Fort
Wayne and Indianapolis.

School of Veterinary Medicine (47907-1240)

Established 1957. Tuition/fees: resident $8048, nonresident
$19,348. Total living expenses: $4790.
  Enrollment: first-year class 60, total 235 (men 50%, women 50%).
School faculty: 76. Degrees conferred: D.V.M., D.V.M.-Ph.D.

ADMISSION REQUIREMENTS. VMCAS report, two transcripts, GRE, animal/veterinary experience, essay required in
support of application. Interview by invitation only. Applicants
must have completed at least two years of college study. Accepts
transfer applicants on a space available basis only. Preference
given first to Indiana residents, second to residents of states without veterinary schools. Apply to Office of Admissions after July 1
and before November 1. Fall admission only. Application fee:
none. Phone: (317)494-7893.

ADMISSION STANDARDS. Accepts about 12–15% of total annual applicants. Approximately twenty nonresident applications
are accepted.

FINANCIAL AID. Scholarships, assistantships, fellowships, full
and partial tuition waivers, Federal W/S, grants. Apply to Office
of Financial Aid by March 1. Use FAFSA.

DEGREE REQUIREMENTS. For D.V.M.: satisfactory completion of four-year program, at least three years in residence. For
Ph.D., see Graduate School listing above.

FIELDS OF GRADUATE STUDY.
Anatomy.
Embryology.
Epidemiology.
Immunology.
Interdisciplinary. Includes bioengineering, medicinal chemistry,
  molecular biology, neuroscience.
Pathology.
Pharmacology.
Physiology.
Toxicology.

PURDUE UNIVERSITY CALUMET
Hammond, Indiana 46323-2094

Established 1948. Coed. State control. Semester system. Library: 205,000 volumes, 1300 current periodicals.
  Tuition: per credit hour, resident $113, nonresident $257. No
on-campus housing for graduate students. Day care facilities
available.

Graduate Division

Enrollment: full-time 96, part-time 907. Faculty: full-time
140, part-time 16. Degrees conferred: M.A., M S., M.S.E.

ADMISSION REQUIREMENTS. Transcripts required in support of application. GRE/GMAT/MAT required by some departments. TOEFL required for international applicants. Accepts
transfer applicants. Apply to the Office of Graduate Study; no
specified closing date. Application fee $30. Phone: (219)989-
2257.

ADMISSION STANDARDS. Selective. Usual minimum average: 2.75 (A = 4).

FINANCIAL AID. Research fellowships, reaching assistantships, Federal W/S, loans. Apply to appropriate departments for
fellowships, assistantships; to Financial Aid Office for all other
programs. Use FAFSA. Phone: (219)989-2660.

DEGREE REQUIREMENTS. For master's: 33–48 semester
hours; knowledge of one foreign language required by some departments; candidacy; final oral/written exam.

FIELDS OF STUDY.
Applied Mathematics. M.S.
Biology. M.S.
Communications. M.A.
Counseling and Personnel Services. M.S.Ed.
Educational Administration. M.S.Ed.
Elementary Education. M.S.Ed.
Engineering. M.S.E.
English. M.A.
History. M.A.
Instructional Development. M.S.Ed.
Management. GMAT for admission; 48 credits for M.S.
Marriage and Family Therapy. M.S.
Mathematics. M.S.
Media Science. M.S.Ed.
Nursing. M.S.
Secondary Education. Includes biology, English, history, indus-
  trial, mathematics, political science, communication. M.S.Ed.

QUEENS COLLEGE OF THE CITY UNIVERSITY OF NEW YORK
Flushing, New York 11367

Established 1937. Coed. New York State control. Semester
system. Library: 672,000 volumes, 652,000 microforms, 3300
current periodicals.
  Tuition: full-time, state resident $4350, per credit $185; nonresident $7600, per credit $320. No housing available. Day care
facilities available.

Division of Graduate Studies

Graduate study since 1950. Enrollment: full-time 293, part-
time 3086 (men 960, women 2419). Faculty: full-time 637, part-
time 476. Degrees conferred: M.A., M.L.S., M.F.A., M.S.Ed.,
M.A.L.S., Advanced Certificates.

ADMISSION REQUIREMENTS. Transcripts required in support of Divisional application. GRE Subject Test, interview required for some departments. TOEFL required for international
applicants. Accepts transfer applicants. Graduates of unaccredited institutions not considered. Apply to Office of Graduate Admissions by April 1 (Fall), November 1 (Spring). Application fee
$40. Phone: (718)997-5200.

ADMISSION STANDARDS. Selective or very selective. Usual minimum average: 2.75, 3.0 for major (A = 4).

FINANCIAL AID. Fellowships, assistantships, Federal W/S, loans. Approved for VA benefits. Apply by April 1 to appropriate department chair for fellowships, assistantships; to Financial Aid Office for all other programs. Use FAFSA and University's FAF. Phone: (718)977-5100. Aid available to part-time students.

DEGREE REQUIREMENTS. For master's: generally 30 semester hours; thesis and comprehensive exam required for some degrees. For Post-Baccalaureate Certificate (teacher certification): 30 credits beyond the bachelor's degree. For Advanced Certificate: 30 semester hours beyond the master's.

FIELDS OF STUDY.
Administration and Supervision. Includes elementary, secondary. Advanced Certificate.
Art History. M.F.A.
Biochemistry. M.A.
Biology. M.A.
Chemistry. M.A.
Computer Science. M.A.
Education. Includes art, early childhood, elementary, English, foreign languages, mathematics, music, science, secondary, reading, school psychology, special, teaching English to speakers of other languages. Post-Baccalaureate; Advanced Certificate programs: administration and supervision, school psychology, marriage and family counseling. M.S.Ed.
English.
Fine Arts. M.F.A.
Geology. M.A.
History. M.A.
Interdisciplinary-Liberal Arts. M.A.L.S.
Library Science. Includes specializations in school or public, academic and special. M.L.S., Advanced Certificate in Librarianship.
Linguistics. M.A.
Literature/Creative Writing. M.A.
Mathematics. M.A.
Media Studies. M.A.
Music. M.A.
Music Performance. M.A.
Physics. M.A.
Psychology. M.A.
Romance Languages. Includes French, Italian, or Spanish. M.A.
Sociology. M.A.
Speech Pathology. M.A.
Urban Affairs. M.A.

School of Law

Founded 1986. Semester system. Law library: 216,900 volumes. Library has LEXIS, NEXIS, WESTLAW.

Annual tuition: full-time resident $6452, nonresident $9682. No on-campus housing available. Total average annual additional expense: $8300.

Enrollment: first-year class 157; total 444 (men 45%, women 55%). Faculty: full-time 39, part-time 20. Degree conferred: J.D.

ADMISSION REQUIREMENTS. LSDAS Law School report, bachelor's degree, transcripts, LSAT, letters of recommendation required in support of application. Interviews by invitation only. Accepts transfer applicants. Graduates of unaccredited colleges not considered. Apply to School by March 14. Admits Fall only. Application fee $35. Phone: (718)575-4210.

ADMISSION STANDARDS. Selective. Accepts 20–25% of total annual applications.

FINANCIAL AID. Scholarships, tuition waivers, Federal W/S, loans. Apply to Student Aid Office by April 1. Use FAFSA. About 68% of students receive aid other than loans from School.

DEGREE REQUIREMENTS. For J.D.: satisfactory completion of 92 semester hour program.

QUINNIPIAC COLLEGE
Hamden, Connecticut 96518-1904

Founded 1929. Coed. Semester system. Library: 264,800 volumes, 169,000 microforms, 4100 current periodicals, 31 PCs.

Annual tuition: full-time $8760; per semester credit $365. On-campus housing available for single students only. Average academic year housing costs: $5790 (including board), off-campus housing costs: $450–$600 per month. Contact Housing Office for both on- and off-campus housing information. Phone: (203)281-8666.

Graduate Programs

Graduate study since 1965. Enrollment: full-time 659, part-time 322. Graduate faculty: full-time 109, part-time 117. Degrees conferred: M.A.T., M.B.A., M.H.A., M.H.S., M.S.P.T.

ADMISSION REQUIREMENTS. Official transcripts required in support of application. Interviews required for some programs. TOEFL required for international applicants. Accepts transfer applicants. Graduates of unaccredited institutions not considered. Apply to Director of Graduate Admissions at least one month prior to date of registration; for Physician Assistant program apply by December 31, Pathologist program apply by February 15. Rolling admissions process. Application fee $40. Phone: (203)281-8672, (203)281-8749.

ADMISSION STANDARDS. Selective. Usual minimum average: 2.75 (A = 4).

FINANCIAL AID. Annual awards from institutional funds: assistantships, Federal W/S, loans. Approved for VA benefits. Apply to Office of Financial Assistance; no specified closing date. Use FAFSA. Aid available for part-time students.

DEGREE REQUIREMENTS. For master's: 32–60 credits minimum, at least 26–54 in residence; thesis/nonthesis option; no foreign language requirement; final exams/internships in some programs.

FIELDS OF STUDY.
Business Administration.
Health Services Administration.
Medical Laboratory Sciences.
Pathologist Assistant Studies.
Physical Therapy.
Physician Assistant Studies.
Teaching.

School of Law

Founded in 1979 as part of the University of Bridgeport, name change in 1995 and School moved to Hamden, CT. Special program: Pre-Admission Summer Program. Law library: 286,000 volumes. Library has LEXIS, WESTLAW, DIALOG.

Annual tuition: full-time $15,960, part-time per credit: $665. On-campus housing available; room and board: approximately $8000.

Enrollment: first-year class full-time 225, part-time 70, total enrollment 766 (men 64%, women 36%). Faculty: full-time 38, part-time 23. Degrees conferred: J.D., J.D.-M.B.A., J.D.-M.H.A., LL.M. (Taxation, Taxation and Business).

ADMISSION REQUIREMENTS. LSDAS Law School report, LSAT, transcripts, references required in support of application. Graduates of unaccredited colleges not considered. Apply to the Office of Admissions. Admissions on a rolling basis, early applicants given special consideration. Application fee $40. Phone: (203)287-3333.

ADMISSION STANDARDS. Accepts about 40–45% of total annual applicants.

FINANCIAL AID. Scholarships, Federal W/S, loans. Apply to Financial Aid Office by June 1. Use FAFSA and Quinnipiac Financial Aid Application. About 80% of students receive some aid from school.

DEGREE REQUIREMENTS. For J.D.: 86 semester hour program, minimum of two years in residence. For LL.M.: at least 24 credits beyond J.D.

RADFORD UNIVERSITY
Radford, Virginia 24142

Founded 1913. Located 40 miles SW of Roanoke. Coed. State control. Semester system. Special facilities: Center for Brain Research and Informational Sciences, Curriculum Materials Center, Economics Research Center, Geography Research Center, Institute for Engineering Geosciences. Library: 303,000 volumes, 77,000 microforms, 2500 current periodicals.

Annual tuition: resident $3186, nonresident $9060; per credit hour resident $133, nonresident $253. On-campus housing for single students only. Annual academic year housing costs: $5200 for single students, $7000 for married students living off-campus. Contact Director of Residential Life for off-campus housing information. Phone: (703)831-5375.

Graduate College

Enrollment: full-time 424, part-time 268. Graduate faculty: full-time 230, part-time 9. Degrees conferred: M.A., M.B.A., M.F.A., M.S., M.S.W., Ed.S.

ADMISSION REQUIREMENTS. Transcripts, GRE/GMAT/MAT/NTE required in support of College's application. TOEFL required for international applicants. Accepts transfer applicants. Graduates of unaccredited institutions not considered. Apply to Dean of Graduate College by March 1 (Fall), November 1 (Spring), April 1 (Summer). No application fee. Phone: (703)831-5431; fax: (708)831-6061.

ADMISSION STANDARDS. Relatively open. Usual minimum average: 2.75, for candidacy 3.0 (A = 4).

FINANCIAL AID. One hundred and thirty-three teaching assistantships, Federal W/S, loans. Approved for VA benefits. Apply by April 1 to Graduate Office for assistantships; to Financial Aid Office for all other programs. Use FAFSA. Phone: (703)831-5408. About 50% of full-time Graduate students receive aid other than loans from University and outside sources.

DEGREE REQUIREMENTS. For master's: 30 semester hours minimum; thesis for M.A.; NTE, GRE, or MAT required for admission to candidacy; GMAT required for admission to candidacy for business majors in the nonteaching option. For Ed.S.: 30 semester hours beyond master's.

FIELDS OF STUDY.
Art.
Business Administration.
Communication Disorders. Includes audiology, speech, language pathology.
Computational Sciences.
Corporate and Professional Communication.
Counselor Education.
Criminal Justice.
Curriculum and Instruction.
Education. Includes elementary, secondary, leadership.
Educational Media.
Engineering Geosciences.
English.
International Economics.
Leisure Services.
Music.
Music Therapy.
Nursing.
Physical Education.
Psychology. Includes clinical, experimental, industrial/organizational.
Reading.
Science Education.
Social Work.
Special Education. Includes emotionally disturbed and learning disabilities.

UNIVERSITY OF REDLANDS**
Redlands, California 92373-0999

Founded 1907. Located 60 miles E of Los Angeles. Coed. Private control. Modified semester system. Library: 200,000 volumes, 125,000 microforms, 1200 current periodicals.

Tuition: per credit $365. Limited on-campus housing for graduate students. Contact Director of Housing for both on- and off-campus housing information. Phone: (714)793-2121.

Graduate Studies

Enrollment: full-time 36, part-time 200. Faculty: full-time 12, part-time 100. Degrees conferred: M.A., M.M., M.S., M.B.A.

ADMISSION REQUIREMENTS. Official transcripts usually required in support of application. TOEFL required for international applicants. Accepts transfer applicants. Apply to appropriate department; no specified closing. Application fee $30. Phone: (714)793-2121, ext. 2200.

ADMISSION STANDARDS. Selective. Usual minimum average: 2.5 or 3.0, depending on program (A = 4).

FINANCIAL AID. Limited to loans. Approved for VA benefits. Apply to Director of Financial Aid. Use FAFSA. Phone: (714)793-2121.

DEGREE REQUIREMENTS. For master's: 34–36 units minimum; thesis/nonthesis option: final oral/written exam.

FIELDS OF STUDY.
Administrative Services. M.A.
Adult Education. M.A.
Business Administration. M.B.A.
Communicative Disorders. M.S.
Curriculum Leadership. M.A.
Music. M.M.
Pupil Personnel Services. M.A.

REED COLLEGE

Portland, Oregon 97202-8199

http://www.reed.edu

Founded 1911. Coed. Private control. Semester system. Library: 400,000, 120,000 microforms, 80 PCs.

Tuition: $1930 per unit. No housing available for graduate students. Contact the Office of Residential Life for off-campus housing. Phone: (503)777-7536.

Graduate Division

Enrollment: 30 part-time. Faculty: full-time 2 (rotated each semester). Degree conferred: M.A.L.S.

ADMISSION REQUIREMENTS. Transcripts, two letters of recommendation, interview required in support of application. M.A.L.S. applicants must complete two Reed courses before formal candidacy. TOEFL required for international applicants. Accepts transfer applicants. Apply to Graduate Studies Office. Application fee $20. Phone: (503)777-7259; fax: (503)777-7581.

ADMISSION STANDARDS. Very selective.

FINANCIAL AID. Limited to one or two scholarships, loans. Approved for VA benefits. Apply to Financial Aid Office; no specified closing date. Use FAFSA. Phone: (503)777-7224.

DEGREE REQUIREMENTS. For M.A.L.S.: 32 units; final oral exam; degree paper thesis.

FIELD OF STUDY.

Liberal Studies. Interdisciplinary degree. No major within degree.

REGENT UNIVERSITY

Virginia Beach, VA 23464-9831

School of Law

Established in 1976 as O. W. Coburn School of Law of Oral Roberts University. School opened in Virginia Beach in 1986. Semester system Law library: 290,000 volumes. Library has LEXIS, NEXIS, WESTLAW, DIALOG, INFOTRAC, LEGAL-TRAC.

Annual tuition: full-time $12,000. No on-campus housing available. Total average annual additional expense: $8300.

Enrollment: first-year class 137; total 343 (men 73%, women 27%). Faculty: full-time 17, part-time 15. Degrees conferred: J.D.

ADMISSION REQUIREMENTS. LSDAS Law School report, bachelor's degree, transcripts, LSAT, letters of recommendation required in support of application. Interviews by invitation only. Accepts transfer applicants. Graduates of unaccredited colleges not considered. Apply to the Office of Admissions by April 1. Admits Fall only. Application fee $30. Phone: (804)579-4127.

ADMISSION STANDARDS. Selective. Accepts 20–25% of total annual applications.

FINANCIAL AID. Scholarships, tuition waivers, assistantships, Federal W/S, loans. Apply to Student Aid Office by April 1. Use FAFSA. About 60% of students receive aid other than loans from School.

DEGREE REQUIREMENTS. For J.D.: satisfactory completion of 92 semester hour program.

RENSSELAER POLYTECHNIC INSTITUTE

Troy, New York 12180-3590

Founded 1824. Located 10 miles N of Albany. Coed. Private control. Special facilities: Rensselaer Design Research Center, Center for Composite Materials and Structure, Lighting Research Institute, Center for Infrastructure and Transportation Studies, Clean Room, Materials Research Center, Fresh Water Institute, G. M. Low Center for Industrial Innovation, Geotechnical Centrifuge Research Center, Center for Manufacturing Productivity, Center for Integrated Electronics, Scientific Computation Center, Center for Science and Technology Policy. University-affiliated Technology Park. Library: 420,0000 volumes, 1,100,000 microforms, 3800 current periodicals, 47 PCs in all libraries.

Tuition: per credit $570. On-campus housing for 265 married students, unlimited housing for graduate men and women. Average academic year housing costs: $2340–$4473 for single students, per month $355–$660 for married students. Apply to Residence Life and Student Dining. Phone: (518)276-6284. Day care facilities available.

Graduate School

Graduate study since 1826. Enrollment: full-time 1656, part-time 413. Graduate faculty: full- and part-time 348. Degrees conferred: M.E., M.S., M.B.A., M.F.A., M.Arch., D.Eng., Ph.D.

ADMISSION REQUIREMENTS. Two transcripts, two letters of reference in support of School's application. GRE Subject Test required for some programs, recommended for others; GMAT required for M.B.A. TOEFL required for international applicants. Interview not required. Accepts transfer applicants. Graduates of unaccredited institutions not considered. Apply to Director of Graduate Admissions. Application fee $35. Phone: (518)276-6789.

ADMISSION STANDARDS. Competitive to very selective. Usual minimum average: 3.0 (A = 4).

FINANCIAL AID. Sixteen scholarships, 321 teaching assistantships, tuition waivers, Federal W/S, loans. Approved for VA benefits. Apply by February 1 to Department Chair for scholarship, fellowships, assistantships; to Office of Financial Aid for all other programs. Use FAFSA. About 65% of students receive aid other than loans from Institute and outside sources.

DEGREE REQUIREMENTS. For master's: 30 credit hours minimum, except M.B.A. in School of Management, which requires 60 credits; M.S. in Lighting requires 48; M.S. in Environmental Management and Policy requires 45 credits, at least 24 in residence; thesis required by some departments. For Ph.D., D.Eng.: 90 credit hours minimum beyond the bachelor's, at least 45 in residence; candidacy exam; thesis; final oral exam.

FIELDS OF STUDY.

Aeronautical Engineering and Astronautics.

Applied Mathematics. M.S., Ph.D.

Architecture.

Biochemistry.

Biology. M.S., Ph.D.

Biomedical Engineering.

Biophysics.

Building Science.

Business Administration.

Chemical Engineering.

Chemistry. M.S., Ph.D.

Civil Engineering.

Communications and Rhetoric. M.S., Ph.D.

Computer and System Engineering.
Computer Science. M.S., Ph.D.
Decision Sciences. Interdisciplinary. Ph.D. only.
Earth and Environmental Sciences. M.S., Ph.D.
Economics. M.S. only.
Electrical Engineering.
Electric Power Engineering.
Electronic Arts.
Engineering Physics.
Engineering Science. M.S., Ph.D.
Environmental Engineering.
Environmental Management and Policy. Interdisciplinary. Ph.D.
Finance.
Geology.
Geophysics.
Health Administration.
Industrial Management.
Lighting.
Management.
Management Engineering. M.S., M.E. only.
Management Information Systems.
Managerial Economics. Interdisciplinary. Ph.D. only.
Manufacturing Systems Engineering.
Marketing.
Materials Engineering.
Mathematics. M.S., Ph.D.
Mechanical Engineering.
Mechanics. M.S., Ph.D.
Microbiology.
Molecular Biology.
Nuclear Engineering.
Operations Research and Statistics. Interdisciplinary.
Philosophy. M.S. only.
Physics.
Psychology. M.S. only.
Science and Technology Studies. M.S., Ph.D.
Statistics.
System Engineering.
Technical Communication. M.S. only.
Transportation Engineering.
Urban and Environmental Studies. Interdisciplinary.

The Hartford Graduate Center

Hartford, Connecticut 06120-2991

Established 1955. Located in Hartford, Groton, and Waterbury Connecticut. Coed. Library: 30,000 volumes, 535 current periodicals.

Tuition: per credit $460. No on-campus housing. Enrollment: part-time 2100 (men 68%, women 32%). Faculty: full-time 25, part-time 75. Degrees conferred: M.S., M.B.A.

ADMISSION REQUIREMENTS. Transcripts, GMAT/GRE, two letters of recommendation required in support of Center's application. Accepts transfer applicants. Graduates of unaccredited institutions not considered. Apply to Dean of Student Affairs at least 30 days prior to the start of term. Application fee $25. Phone: (800)433-4723, (203)548-2420; E-mail: mstr@hgc.edu.

ADMISSION STANDARDS. Selective. Usual minimum average: 3.0 (A = 4).

FINANCIAL AID. Grants, scholarships, assistantships, loans. Approved for VA benefits. Apply to Office of Student Affairs; no specified closing date. Use FAFSA.

DEGREE REQUIREMENTS. For M.S.: 30–39 credit hours minimum, at least 24 in residence; thesis/nonthesis option. For M.B.A.: 46 credit hours minimum.

FIELDS OF STUDY.
Biomedical Engineering.
Business Management. Includes industrial, commercial, public-sector organization.
Computer and Information Science.
Engineering. Includes biomedical, electrical, mechanical.
Engineering Science.
Management. Includes environmental management and policy, finance, financial institutions, health-care, human resource, international, marketing.
Metallurgy.

RHODE ISLAND COLLEGE
Providence, Rhode Island 02908-1924

Founded 1854. Coed. State control. Semester system. Library: 540,000 volumes, 820,000 microforms, 35 PCs.

Annual tuition: full-time resident $2982, nonresident $5518; per credit, resident $150, nonresident $292. Limited on-campus housing for graduate students. Average academic year housing costs: $2800–$5600. Contact the Director of Housing for both on- and off-campus housing information. Phone: (401)456-8240. Day care facilities available.

Graduate School

Graduate study since 1924. Enrollment: full-time 200, part-time 1500. College faculty teaching graduate students: full-time 40, part-time 8. Degrees conferred: M.A., M.Ed., M.F.A., M.A.T., M.S.W., C.A.G.S., M.S.

ADMISSION REQUIREMENTS. Transcripts, three letters of recommendation, GRE/MAT required in support of School's application. TOEFL required for foreign applicants. Accepts transfer applicants. Graduates of unaccredited institutions not considered. Apply to Graduate Office by April 1 (Fall), November 1 (Spring), February 1 (M.S.W. deadline). Application fee $25. Phone: (401)456-8700; fax: (401)456-8117.

ADMISSION STANDARDS. Selective for most departments. Usual minimum average: 3.0 (A = 4).

FINANCIAL AID. Thirty-six assistantships, five internships, Federal W/S, loans. Approved for VA benefits. Apply by March 1 to Dean of Graduate Studies for assistantships; to Office of Financial Aid for all other programs. Use FAFSA. Phone: (401)456-8700. About 30% of students receive aid other than loans from College and outside sources. Aid sometimes available for part-time students.

DEGREE REQUIREMENTS. For master's: 30 credit hours minimum; final written comprehensive exam. For M.S.W.: 60 credits minimum, at least 30 in residence; individual or group thesis. For C.A.G.S.: 30 credit hours minimum beyond the master's.

FIELDS OF STUDY.
Art.
Bilingual Education.
Biology.
Counseling.
Early Childhood Education.
Educational Psychology.
Elementary Education.
Elementary School Administration.
English.
French.
Health Education.
History.

Industrial Technology.
Mathematics.
Music.
Physical Science.
Psychology.
Reading.
Secondary Education.
Secondary School Administration.
Social Work.
Special Education.
Teaching English as a Second Language (TESL).
Technology Education.
Theater.

RHODE ISLAND SCHOOL OF DESIGN
Providence, Rhode Island 02903-2784

Founded 1877. Coed. Private control. Semester system, Special facility: Museum of Art. Library: 80,000 volumes, 6 PCs.

Annual tuition and fees: full time $17,600, per credit $585. On-campus housing available for single graduate students. Average academic year housing costs: $6618 (including board). Off-campus housing per month: $375. Contact Housing and Residence Life for on- and off-campus housing information. Phone: (401)454-6650.

Graduate Division

Enrollment: full-time 150 (men 50%, women 50%). Faculty: full-time 18, part-time 10. Degrees conferred: M.A.Art.Ed., M.Arch., M.A.T., M.F.A., M.I.D., M.L.A.

ADMISSION REQUIREMENTS. Transcripts, full portfolio required in support of application. TOEFL required for international applicants. Interview not required, but recommended. Accepts transfer applicants. Apply to Division of Graduate Studies by February 1. Fall admission only. Application fee $35. Phone: (401)454-6131; fax: (401)454-6694.

ADMISSION STANDARDS. Competitive. Admission based on talent.

FINANCIAL AID. Grants, scholarships, assistantships, fellowships, Federal W/S, loans. Approved for VA benefits. Apply by February 1 to Graduate Studies Committee. Use FAFSA and CSS Profile. Phone: (401)454-6635; fax: (401)454-5412. About 30% of students receive aid from School and outside sources.

DEGREE REQUIREMENTS. For M.I.D., M.F.A., M.L.A.: 66 semester credits minimum, two years in residence; thesis. For M.A.T.: 34–37 semester credits minimum. For M.A.Art.Ed.: 33–39 semester credits minimum. M.Arch.: 111 credits, three years in residence.

FIELDS OF STUDY.
Architecture.
Art Education.
Ceramics.
Furniture Design.
Glass.
Graphic Design.
Industrial Design.
Jewelry and Light Metals.
Landscape Architecture.
Painting.
Photography.
Printing.
Sculpture.
Textiles.

UNIVERSITY OF RHODE ISLAND
Kingston, Rhode Island 02681

Founded 1888. Located 30 miles S of Providence. Coed. State control. Semester system. Special facilities: Biotechnology Center, Research Center in Business, Child Development Center, Center for Energy Studies, Institute of Human Sciences and Services, Labor Research Center, International Center for Marine Resource Development, Marriage and Family Center, Center for Ocean Management, Robotics Research Center. Library: 955,000 volumes, 1,100,000 microforms.

Annual tuition: full-time, resident $3312, nonresident $9106. On-campus housing for single and married students. Average academic year housing costs: $4800 (including board) for single students; $3500 for married students. Contact Residential Life Office for both on- and off-campus housing information. Phone: (401)792-2935. Day care facilities available.

Graduate School

Enrollment: full-time 1225, part-time 2932. Faculty: full-time 699, part-time 72. Degrees conferred: M.A., M.S., M.P.A., M.C.P., E.M.B.A., M.B.A., M.L.I.S., M.M.A., M.M., Pharm.D., Ph.D.

ADMISSION REQUIREMENTS. Two official transcripts, three letters of recommendation required in support of School's application. GRE or MAT required for most departments, GRE Subject Test for some departments, GMAT for business programs. Interview required in some programs. TOEFL required of international students. Accepts transfer applicants. Graduates of unaccredited colleges not considered. Apply to Dean of Graduate School by April 15 (Fall), November 15 (Spring). Earlier dates in some programs. Application fee $35. Phone: (401)792-2262.

ADMISSION STANDARDS. Very competitive to selective. Usual minimum average: 2.75 (A = 4).

FINANCIAL AID. Scholarships, fellowships, diversity fellowships, teaching/research assistantships, Federal W/S, loans. Approved for VA benefits. Apply by February 15 to Dean for scholarships and fellowships; to appropriate departments for assistantships; to Financial Aid Office for all other programs. Use FAFSA. Phone: (401)792-2314. Aid sometimes available for part-time students.

DEGREE REQUIREMENTS. For master's: 30 credits minimum, at least 24 in residence; thesis with oral defense (6 credits) for most departments, or nonthesis with major paper; comprehensive exam. For Ph.D.: 72 credits minimum beyond the bachelor's, at least 24 in full-time residence or two consecutive semesters in full-time attendance; preliminary exam; proficiency in research tool/foreign language required in some programs; dissertation; final oral exam.

FIELDS OF STUDY.
Accounting. M.S.
Adult Education. M.A.
Applied Mathematical Science. Includes applied mathematics, computer science, statistics, applied probability. Ph.D.
Biochemistry. M.S., Ph.D.
Botany. M.S., Ph.D.
Chemical Engineering. M.S., Ph.D.
Chemistry. M.S., Ph.D.
Clinical Laboratory Science. M.S. only.
Clinical Psychology. Ph.D.
Communicative Disorders. M.A., M.S.
Community and Area Development. M.C.P. only.
Comparative Literature. M.A. only.
Computer Science. M.S., Ph.D.
Design Systems. M.S., Ph.D.
Economics. M.A.

Electrical and Computer Engineering. M.S., Ph.D.
Elementary Education. M.A., M.S.
English. M.A., Ph.D.
Entomology. M.S., Ph.D.
Environmental Engineering. M.S., Ph.D.
Experimental Psychology. Ph.D.
Finance. M.B.A.
Fluid Mechanics. M.S., Ph.D.
Food and Nutrition Science. M.S., Ph.D.
French. M.A.
Geology. M.S.
Geotechnical Engineering. M.S., Ph.D.
Health Education. M.S.
History. M.A.
Industrial Engineering. M.S.
International Business. M.B.A.
International Development Studies.
International Sports Management. M.B.A.
Labor and Industrial Relations. M.S.
Library Science. M.L.I.S. only.
Management. M.B.A.
Manufacturing Engineering. M.S.
Marine Affairs. M.A., M.M.A.
Marketing. M.B.A.
Marriage and Family Therapy. M.S.
Mathematics. M.S., Ph.D.
Medicinal Chemistry. M.S., Ph.D.
Microbiology. M.S., Ph.D.
Nursing. Includes nursing service administration, teaching of nursing. M.S.
Ocean Engineering. M.S., Ph.D.
Oceanography. M.S., Ph.D.
Pharmaceutics. M.S., Ph.D.
Pharmacognosy. M.S., Ph.D.
Pharmacology and Toxicology. M.S., Ph.D.
Pharmacy. Pharm.D.
Pharmacy Administration. M.S.
Philosophy. M.A.
Physical Education. M.S.
Physical Therapy. M.S.
Physics. M.S., Ph.D.
Plant Pathology. M.S., Ph.D.
Political Science. M.A.
Public Administration. M.P.A. only.
Reading. M.A.
Recreation. M.S.
Resource Economics and Marine Resources. M.S., Ph.D.
School Psychology. M.S., Ph.D.
Secondary Education. M.A.
Solid Mechanics. M.S., Ph.D.
Spanish. M.A.
Speech-Language Pathology. M.A., M.S. only.
Structural Engineering. M.S., Ph.D.
Textiles, Fashion Merchandising and Design. M.S.
Transportation Engineering. M.S., Ph.D.
Zoology. M.S., Ph.D.

RICE UNIVERSITY

Houston, Texas 77005-1892
http://riceinfo.rice.edu

Founded 1912. Coed. Private control. Semester system. Library: 1,534,000 volumes, 1,950,000 microforms, 14,800 current periodicals.

Annual tuition: full-time $13,300, part-time per credit $740. On-campus housing available for graduate students. Average academic year housing costs: $2400 (room only) for single students, $3600 (room only) for married students. Contact the Housing Office for both on- and off-campus information. Phone: (713)522-1096.

Graduate Division

Enrollment: full-time 1355 (men 65%, women 35%); part-time 50. University faculty: full-time 454, part-time 30. Degrees conferred: M.A., M.B.A., M.M., M.Arch., M.S., D.M.A., Ph.D.

ADMISSION REQUIREMENTS. Transcripts, three letters of recommendation, GRE or GMAT required in support of application. TOEFL required for foreign applicants. Interview not required. Accepts transfer applicants. Graduates of unaccredited institutions not considered. Apply to Dean by February 1. Most students enter Fall semester. Application fee $25. Phone: (713)527-4002.

ADMISSION STANDARDS. Competitive. Usual minimum average: 3.0 (A = 4).

FINANCIAL AID. Four hundred scholarships, 350 research assistantships, 30 teaching assistantships, Federal W/S, loans. Approved for VA benefits. Apply by February 1 to appropriate department chair for fellowships, assistantships; to Financial Aid Office for all other programs. Use FAFSA. Phone: (713)527-4958. About 90% of all thesis students receive aid other than loans from University and outside sources. No aid for part-time students.

DEGREE REQUIREMENTS. For master's: 30 semester hours minimum, at least 24 in residence; qualifying exam; final oral exam; thesis/nonthesis option. For M.M.: 43–57 semester hours, at least 36 in residence. For M.B.A.: a minimum of two years in residence. For Ph.D.: normally three or more years beyond the bachelor's degree, at least two years in residence; qualifying exam; final oral exam; thesis.

FIELDS OF STUDY.
Accounting
Anthropology.
Architecture.
Art History.
Astronomy.
Astrophysics.
Biochemistry.
Biology.
Biomedical Engineering.
Business Administration.
Chemical Engineering.
Chemistry.
Civil Engineering.
Computational and Applied Mathematics.
Computer Engineering.
Computer Science.
Ecology and Evolutionary.
Economics.
Electrical Engineering.
Engineering and Applied Sciences.
English.
Environmental Science and Engineering.
French Studies.
Geology.
Geophysics.
German and Slavic Studies.
History.
International Business.
Linguistics.
Management.
Materials Science.
Mathematics.
Mechanical Engineering.

Music.
Philosophy.
Physics.
Political Science.
Psychology.
Religious Studies.
Space Physics.
Statistics.
Urban Design.

UNIVERSITY OF RICHMOND
Richmond, Virginia 23173

Founded 1830. Private control. Baptist affiliation. Semester system. Library: 600,000 volumes, 150,000 microforms, 100 PCs.

Annual tuition: full-time $16,670, per credit $285–$995. No on-campus housing available.

Graduate School

Graduate study since 1921. Enrollment: full time 70, part-time 150. Faculty: full-time 105. Degrees conferred: M.A., M.S., M.Ed., M.H., M.S.M.

ADMISSION REQUIREMENTS. Transcripts, three letters of recommendation, statement of purpose, GRE Subject Tests required in support of School's application. TOEFL required of international students. Interview not required. Transfer applicants considered. Graduates of unaccredited institutions not considered. Apply to Graduate School by March 15 prior to beginning of semester for which admission is sought. Application fee $30. Phone: (804)289-8417.

ADMISSION STANDARDS. Selective for most departments. Usual minimum average: 3.0 (A = 4).

FINANCIAL AID. Tuition remission program for full-time students; special tuition rates for part-time students. Fellowships, 35 academic scholarships, Federal W/S, loans. Approved for VA benefits. Apply by March 1 to Dean of Graduate School for assistantships, scholarships; to the Office of Financial Aid for all other programs. Use FAFSA. Phone: (804)289-8438. About 60% of full-time students receive aid other than loans from University and outside sources.

DEGREE REQUIREMENTS. For M.A., M.S.: 27–36 semester hours; thesis; comprehensive exam. For M.Ed.: 31–36 semester hours; comprehensive exam; internship. For M.H.: 30 hours minimum, no thesis. For M.S.M.: 32 semester hours; comprehensive exam; internship.

FIELDS OF STUDY.
Biology.
Education. Includes early childhood, middle education 4–8, secondary education 8–12, reading, special education, supervision.
English.
History.
Humanities.
Physical Education.
Psychology.
Sports Management.

The E. Claiborne Robins School of Business— Graduate Division

Enrollment: full-time 10, part-time 256. Faculty: full-time 40, part-time 6. Degree conferred: M.B.A.

ADMISSION REQUIREMENTS. Transcripts, three letters of recommendation, statement of purpose, GMAT required in support of School's application. TOEFL required of international students. Interview not required. Transfer applicants considered. Graduates of unaccredited institutions not considered. Apply to Graduate Division by July 1 (Fall), November 1 (Spring). Rolling admissions process. Application fee $25. Phone: (804)289-8553; fax: (804)287-6544.

ADMISSION STANDARDS. Selective. Usual minimum average: 2.75 (A = 4).

FINANCIAL AID. Limited to six assistantships, loans. Approved for VA benefits. Apply to Financial Aid Office; no specified closing date. Use FAFSA. Phone: (804)289-8438. About 60% of full-time students receive aid other than loans from University and outside sources.

DEGREE REQUIREMENTS. For M.B.A.: 36–48 semester hours minimum.

FIELD OF STUDY.
Business Administration.

T. C. Williams School of Law

Established 1870. Semester system. Law library: 230,500 volumes. Library has LEXIS, NEXIS, WESTLAW, DIALOG, VU-TEXT. Special facilities: Alternative Dispute Resolution Center.

Annual tuition: $17,170. Limited on-campus housing for single students. Total average annual additional expense: $6500.

Enrollment: first-year class 168; total full-time 467 (men 52%, women 48%). School faculty: full-time 25, part-time 65. Degrees conferred: J.D., J.D.-M.B.A., J.D.-M.H.A., J.D.-M.S.W., J.D.-M.U.S.P.

ADMISSION REQUIREMENTS. LSDAS Law School report, bachelor's degree, transcripts, LSAT required in support of application. Personal interviews optional. Accepts transfer applicants. Graduates of unaccredited institutions not considered. Apply to School after September 1, before January 15. Admits beginning students Fall only. Application fee $35. Phone: (804)289-8189.

ADMISSION STANDARDS. Selective. Accepts 20–25% of total annual applicants.

FINANCIAL AID. Scholarships, assistantships, Federal W/S, loans. Apply to Financial Aid Office by February 25. Phone: (804)289-3438. Use FAFSA. About 15% of students receive aid other than loans from School.

DEGREE REQUIREMENTS. For J.D.: satisfactory completion of three-year program; 86 semester hours minimum. For master's degrees, see Graduate School listing above.
Note: Summer programs in Cambridge (Great Britain) and Caracas (Venezuela).

RIDER UNIVERSITY
Trenton, New Jersey 08602-3001

Founded 1865. Coed. Private control. Semester system. Library: 325,000 volumes, 400,000 microforms, 2000 current periodicals.

Tuition: per credit, Education $305; Business Administration $370; Westminster Choir School $475. On-campus housing for single students available. Contact Graduate Housing Office for both on- and off-campus housing information. Phone: (609)896-5102.

Graduate Studies

Enrollment: full-time 226, part-time 1071. Faculty: full-time 83, part-time 30. Degrees conferred: M.A., M.B.A., M.M.

ADMISSION REQUIREMENTS. Official Transcript, two professional recommendations required in support of application. GMAT and Audition required for some programs. TOEFL required for international applicants. Accepts transfer applicants. Graduates of unaccredited institutions not considered. Apply to Director of Graduate Services at least one month prior to registration. Rolling admissions process. Application fee $35. Phone: (609)896-5036; fax: (609)896-8029.

ADMISSION STANDARDS. Selective. Usual minimum average: 2.5 (A = 4).

FINANCIAL AID. Fellowships, research assistantships, teaching assistantships, Federal W/S, loans. Approved for VA benefits. Apply to the Director of Financial Aid; no specified closing date. Use FAFSA. Phone: (609)896-5360.

DEGREE REQUIREMENTS. For M.A.: 33–36 credit hours minimum, depending on program; thesis/nonthesis option. For M.B.A.: 30–57 credit hours, depending on previous degree and number of foundation courses waived. For M.M.: 30–36 credit hours minimum; thesis/nonthesis option/recital.

FIELDS OF STUDY.
Business Administration. M.B.A.
Business Education. M.A.
Counseling Sciences. M.A.
Curriculum, Instruction and Supervision. M.A.
Education Administration. M.A.
Human Services Administration. M.A.
Music. Includes accompanying, conducting, composition, performance, organ, theory, voice. M.M.
Reading-Language Arts. M.A.

RIVIER COLLEGE
Nashua, New Hampshire 03060-5086

Founded 1933. Located NW of Boston. Coed. Private control. Semester system. Library: 131,000 volumes, 43,000 microforms.
Tuition: per credit $274. No on-campus housing for graduate students.

Graduate School

Enrollment: full-time 89, part-time 983 (men 50%, women 50%). Graduate faculty: full-time 20, part-time 70. Degrees conferred: M.A., M.B.A., M.A.T., M.Ed., M.S.

ADMISSION REQUIREMENTS. Transcripts, interview, required in support of School's application. MAT required for education applicants. TOEFL required for international applicants. Accepts transfer applicants. Apply to Dean, Graduate School by August 1 (Fall), November 30 (Spring). Application fee $25. Phone: (603)888-1311, ext. 8234; fax: (603)888-0237.

ADMISSION STANDARDS. Selective. Usual minimum average: 2.75 (A = 4).

FINANCIAL AID. Limited to loans. Approved for VA benefits. Phone: (603)888-1311, ext. 8510.

DEGREE REQUIREMENTS. For M.A., M.S., M.Ed.: 30 semester hours minimum including thesis, or 33 hours without thesis; final written exam. For M.B.A.: 36–45 semester hours.

FIELDS OF STUDY.
Business Administration. Includes health care administration.
Computer Information System.
Computer Science.
Counseling and Psychotherapy.
Education. Includes elementary, administration, learning disabilities, reading, secondary.
English.
Modern Languages.
Nursing.

ROBERT MORRIS COLLEGE
Coraopolis, Pennsylvania 15108-1189
http://www.robert-morris.edu

Coed. Private control. Semester system. Library: 122,000 volumes, 290,000 microforms, 894 current periodicals, 16 PCs.
Tuition: per credit $303. Limited on-campus housing available. Contact Housing Office for off-campus housing information. Phone: (412)262-8408.

Graduate Studies

Enrollment: 964 all part-time. Faculty: full-time 27, part-time 29. Degrees conferred: M.B.S., M.S.

ADMISSION REQUIREMENTS. Official transcript, two professional recommendations required in support of application. GMAT strongly recommended. Accepts transfer applicants. Apply to Dean, Graduate Studies at least one month prior to registration. Application fee $25. Phone: (412)227-8535; fax: (412)262-4049; E-mail: zimmer@robert-morris.edu.

ADMISSION STANDARDS. Selective. Usual minimum average: 2.5 (A = 4).

FINANCIAL AID. Limited to assistantships, loans. Apply to the Financial Aid Office; no specified closing date. Use FAFSA. Aid available to part-time students.

DEGREE REQUIREMENTS. For M.S.: 33–36 credit hours minimum, depending on program. For M.B.A.: 30–57 credit hours, depending on previous degree and number of foundation courses waived.

FIELDS OF STUDY.
Accounting. M.S.
Business Administration. M.B.A.
Computer Information Systems. M.B.A., M.S.
Finance. M.S.
Management. M.B.A.
Marketing. M.B.A., M.S.
Sport Management. M.B.A., M.S.
Taxation. M.S.

ROCHESTER INSTITUTE OF TECHNOLOGY
Rochester, New York 14623-0887
http://www.rit.edu

Founded 1829. Coed. Private control. Quarter system. Library: 354,000 volumes, 250,000 microforms, 4753 current periodicals.
Annual tuition: $17,259; part-time $485 per quarter hour. On-campus housing for married students on space-available basis. Annual housing costs: $2700–$5034. Apply to Center for Residence Life for on- and off-campus housing information. Phone: (716)475-8815 (on-campus), 475-2575 (off-campus).

Graduate Studies

Graduate study since 1959. Enrollment: full-time 655, part-time 1393. Institute faculty: full-time 500, part-time varies by quarter. Degrees conferred: M.B.A., M.E., M.F.A., M.S., M.S.T., Ph.D.

ADMISSION REQUIREMENTS. Transcripts, letters of recommendation required in support of application. GMAT required for M.B.A.; GRE, MAT for some programs. Evidence of proficiency in English (TOEFL or Michigan Test of English administered at RIT) required of international applicants. Interview required for some departments. Accepts transfer applicants. Apply to Admissions Office. Application fee $35. Phone: (716)475-6631.

ADMISSION STANDARDS. Selective. Usual minimum average varies by department.

FINANCIAL AID. Annual awards from institutional funds: Ninety teaching assistantships, Federal W/S, loans. Approved for VA benefits. Apply at time of admission to appropriate department head; for scholarships, apply to Dean of Graduate Studies; to Financial Aid Office for all other programs. Use FAFSA. Phone: (716)475-2186. Loans are also available under New York State's Supplemental Higher Education Loan Financing Program.

DEGREE REQUIREMENTS. For M.S.: 45–72 quarter hours minimum. For M.F.A.: 85–90 quarter hours minimum. For M.S.T.: 48 quarter hours minimum. For M.B.A.: 76 quarter hours minimum. For M.E.: 48 quarter hours minimum. Thesis required for some programs. Ph.D.: as determined by committee review.

FIELDS OF STUDY.
Accounting. M.B.A.
Applied and Mathematical Statistics. M.S.
Art Education. M.S.T. only.
Business Administration. M.B.A.
Career and Human Resource Development. M.S.
Ceramics and Ceramic Sculpture. M.F.A., M.S.T.
Chemistry. M.S.
Clinical Chemistry. M.S.
Computer Graphics Design. M.F.A.
Computer Integrated Manufacturing. M.S.
Computer Science. M.S.
Finance. M.S.
Fine and Applied Arts. Includes design art, craft. M.F.A., M.S.T.
Imaging and Photographic Science. Includes imaging, color. M.S.
Industrial Engineering. M.E.
Information Technology. M.S.
Instructional Technology. M.S.
International Business. M.B.A.
Manufacturing Management and Leadership. M.S.
Materials Science and Engineering. M.S.
Mechanical Engineering. M.S.
Medical Illustration. M.F.A.
Packaging Science. M.S.
Photography. M.F.A.
Printing. Includes publishing, systems, technology.
School Psychology. M.S.
Secondary Education of Students Who Are Deaf or Hard of Hearing. M.S.
Software Development and Management. M.S.

UNIVERSITY OF ROCHESTER
Rochester, New York 14627-0416
http://www.rochester.edu

The University of Rochester, established in 1850, is independent and coeducational, and operates on a semester system. Three of the University's 6 schools and colleges are on the River Campus. The School of Medicine and Dentistry and the School of Nursing are within a 5-minute walk, and the Eastman School of Music is 2 miles away. Special facilities include a large biology-chemistry-mathematics complex, a nuclear structure research laboratory with a 24-MeV tandem Van Degraaff accelerator, the Mees Observatory (at the highest location in the eastern United States), an atomic energy ERDA project (radiation biology and biophysics), a well-staffed computing center, campus-wide access to the Internet, and several hundred microcomputers linked to the campus network, the Managerial Economics Research Center, Center for Environmental Health Sciences, the New York State Center for Optical Technology, Center for Photoinduced Charge Transfer, Center for Superconductive Circuits, the Center for Visual Science, the Laboratory for Laser Energetics, Center for Research in Government Policy and Business. Library: 2,800,000 volumes, 3,636,000 microforms, 141 PCs in all libraries.

Annual tuition: full-time $19,360 (Simon School $23,364; Eastman School of Music $20,320). On-campus housing available; contact Housing Coordinator. Phone: (716)275-5521.

Graduate Studies

Graduate study since 1851. Enrollment: 2700. Graduate faculty: full-time 1000, part-time 200. Degrees conferred: M.A., M.S., M.B.A., M.H.P., M.M., M.A.T., Ed.D., D.M.A., Ph.D.

ADMISSION REQUIREMENTS. Transcripts, two letters of recommendation required in support of application. GRE Subject Tests, GMAT recommended. TOEFL required for international applicants. Accepts transfer applicants. Graduates of unaccredited institutions not considered. Apply to department offering specific degree program. Application fee $25 (Simon School $75). Phone: (716)275-2121 (general information number).

ADMISSION STANDARDS. Competitive. Usual minimum average: 3.0 (A = 4).

FINANCIAL AID. Most Ph.D. candidates receive grants, assistantships, or fellowships. For M.A., M.S., M.M., D.M.A., M.B.A. candidates: scholarships, Federal W/S, loans. Approved for VA benefits. To be eligible for aid, new students must apply by February 15. Use FAFSA. Phone appropriate department for information regarding assistantships, fellowships.

DEGREE REQUIREMENTS. For M.A., M.A.T., M.S.: 30 semester hours minimum, at least 20 in residence; thesis; final oral exam; for nonthesis option, master's essay for some departments; comprehensive exam. For M.B.A.: 66 semester hours minimum, at least 48 semester hours in residence; comprehensive exam; thesis not required. For Ed.D.: 90 semester hours minimum beyond the bachelor's, comprehensive exam; dissertation; final oral exam. For Ph.D.: 90 semester hours beyond the bachelor's degree or 60 semester hours minimum beyond the master's, at least two consecutive semesters in full-time residence; competence in foreign languages required by some departments; written/oral qualifying exam; dissertation; final oral exam. For D.M.A.: 60 semester hours minimum beyond the master's, at least one year in full-time residence; demonstrated proficiency in performance; oral/written exam; qualifying exam; dissertation; final oral exam. For joint M.D.-Ph.D.: same requirements for both programs individually, although course work and research may overlap.

FIELDS OF STUDY.

THE COLLEGE OF ARTS AND SCIENCE:
Biology. M.S., Ph.D.
Biology-Geology. M.S.
Brain and Cognitive Science. M.A., Ph.D.
Chemistry. M.S., Ph.D.

Computer Science. M.S., Ph.D.
Economics. M.A., Ph.D.
English. M.A., Ph.D.
Geological Sciences. M.S., Ph.D.
History. M.A., Ph.D.
Philosophy. M.A., Ph.D.
Physics. M.A., M.S., Ph.D.
Physics and Astronomy. Ph.D.
Political Science. M.A., Ph.D.
Psychology. Includes clinical, social. M.A., Ph.D.
Public Policy Analysis. M.S.
Statistics. M.A., Ph.D.
Visual and Cultural Studies. M.A., Ph.D.

THE COLLEGE OF ENGINEERING AND APPLIED SCIENCE:
Electrical Engineering. M.S., Ph.D.
Materials Science. M.S., Ph.D.
Mechanical and Aerospace Sciences. M.S., Ph.D.
Optics. M.S., Ph.D.

EASTMAN SCHOOL OF MUSIC:
Conducting. D.M.A.
Conducting (Choral). M.M.
Jazz Studies and Contemporary Media. M.M.
Music Composition. M.A., M.M., D.M.A., Ph.D.
Music Theory. M.A., Ph.D.
Musicology. M.A., Ph.D.
Performance and Literature. M.M., D.M.A.

GRADUATE SCHOOL OF EDUCATION AND HUMAN DEVELOPMENT:
Education. M.S., M.A.T, Ed.D., Ph.D.

SCHOOL OF MEDICINE AND DENTISTRY:
Anatomy. M.S., Ph.D.
Biochemistry. M.S., Ph.D.
Biophysics. M.S., Ph.D.
Dental Science. M.S.*
Environmental Studies. M.S.
Genetics. Ph.D.
Health Services Research. Ph.D.
Industrial Hygiene. M.S.*
Medicine. M.D.
Microbiology and Immunology. M.S., Ph.D.
Neuroscience. M.S., Ph.D.
Pathology. M.S., Ph.D.
Pharmacology. M.S., Ph.D.
Physiology. M.S., Ph.D.
Public Health. M.P.H.
Toxicology. M.S., Ph.D.
Note: Part-time studies only.

SCHOOL OF NURSING:
Nursing. M.S., Ph.D.

WILLIAM E. SIMON GRADUATE SCHOOL OF BUSINESS ADMINISTRATION:
Business Administration. M.B.A., M.S., Ph.D.

JOINT PH.D. DEGREE PROGRAMS:
Biology and Medicine.
Biology and Neurobiology.

School of Medicine and Dentistry (14642)

Founded 1920. Annual tuition: $21,500; student fees $1310. On-campus housing available for married, single students. Apply to the Housing Coordinator, Medical Center. Total average figure for all other expenses: $6964.

Enrollment: first-year class 100; total full-time 703 (men 50%, women 50%); postgraduates 370. Faculty: full-time 800, part-time 72. Degrees conferred: M.D., M.D.-Ph.D., M.S., Ph.D.

Graduate study only in dentistry; no D.D.S. (Medical Scientist Training Program).

ADMISSION REQUIREMENTS. For M.D.: transcripts, letters of recommendation, personal statement, MCAT, required in support of application. Applicants must have completed at least three years of college study. Interview by invitation only. Does not have EDP. Accepts transfer and foreign applicants. Apply to Committee on Admission after June 15, before October 15. Application fee $60. Phone: (716)275-4539; fax: (716)473-1016.

ADMISSION STANDARDS. For M.D.: very competitive. Accepts 5% of total annual applicants. Approximately 35% are state residents.

FINANCIAL AID. For M.D.: scholarships, loans. Apply to Financial Aid Office. MSTP funded by NIH. Use FAFSA. About 80% of students receive some aid from School.

DEGREE REQUIREMENTS. For M.D.: satisfactory completion of four-year program. For M.S., Ph.D., see Graduate Studies above.

FIELDS OF GRADUATE STUDY.
Anatomy.
Biochemistry.
Biomedical Engineering.
Biophysics.
Cell Biology.
Community Health. M.S. only.
Dental Research. M.S. only.
Genetics.
Health Sciences Education. M.S. only.
Immunology.
Microbiology.
Neuroscience.
Pathology.
Pharmacology.
Physiology.
Radiation Biology.
Toxicology.
Note: Joint degree programs in biology and neurobiology, physiology and neurobiology, psychology and neurobiology.

THE ROCKEFELLER UNIVERSITY
New York, New York 10021-6399

Founded 1901. Coed. Private control. Graduate study only. Special facilities: Howard Hughes Medical Institute, Center for Human Genetics, Laboratory Animal Research Center, Research Center for Ecology and Ethology, Center for Research on Alzheimer's Disease, Center for Studies in Physics and Biology. Library: 184,000 volumes, 15 PCs.

No tuition charge. On-campus housing for married and single students. Average academic year housing costs: $2900–$4600. Contact the office of the Dean for all housing information.

Graduate Programs

Established 1954. Enrollment: full-time 120. Faculty: full-time 175. Degree conferred: Ph.D.

ADMISSION REQUIREMENTS. Transcripts, at least two letters of recommendation, letter from applicant, interview required in support of application. GRE strongly recommended; Subject Test useful. TOEFL recommended for international applicants. Applications should be completed by January 15. Address inquiries to Office of the Dean. Application fee $50. Phone: (212)570-8086; fax: (212)327-8505.

ADMISSION STANDARDS. Very competitive.

FINANCIAL AID. All students receive a stipend and tuition remission.

DEGREE REQUIREMENTS. For Ph.D.: Five years of research and study generally required; dissertation; final oral exam.

FIELDS OF STUDY.
Biochemistry.
Biomedical Sciences.
Biophysics.
Cell Biology.
Chemistry.
Developmental Biology.
Experimental High Energy Physics.
Genetics.
Immunology.
Microbiology.
Molecular Biology.
Neuroscience.
Parasitology.
Theoretical Physics.
Virology.

ROCKFORD COLLEGE
Rockford, Illinois 61108-2393

Founded 1847. Located on new campus 90 miles NW of Chicago. Coed. Private control. Semester system. Library: 165,000 volumes, 7400 microforms.

Annual tuition: full-time $14,000, per credit $360. On-campus housing for graduate students; no married student housing. Average academic year housing costs: $4400. Contact the Dean, Student Services for housing information. Phone: (815)226-4045.

Graduate Study

Graduate study since 1950. Enrollment: full-time 51, part-time 300. Faculty: full-time 15, part-time 27. Courses offered evenings and Summer. College does not seek full-time or nonlocal students, although such applicants are considered. Degrees conferred: M.A.T., M.B.A.

ADMISSION REQUIREMENTS. Transcripts, GRE/GMAT for M.B.A., three letters of recommendation required in support of application. TOEFL required for international applicants. Interview sometimes required. Accepts transfer applicants. Apply to Office of Graduate Studies prior to registration. Application fee $35. Phone: (815)226-4013; fax: (815)226-4119.

ADMISSION STANDARDS. Selective. Usual minimum average: 3.0 (A = 4).

FINANCIAL AID. Grants, loans. Approved for VA benefits. Apply to Office of Graduate Studies; no specified closing date. Use FAFSA. Phone: (815)226-3383; fax: (815)226-4119.

DEGREE REQUIREMENTS. For M.A.T.: 32–36 semester hours minimum, at least 24 in residence; GRE for candidacy; no language requirement; thesis required for some programs. For M.B.A.: 36 semester hours minimum; prerequisite courses or competency test, in economics, accounting, finance, statistics, mathematics; ten required courses and two electives required.

FIELDS OF STUDY.
Art.
Economics and Business.
Elementary Education.
English.
Learning Disabilities.
Mathematics.
Reading.
Secondary Education.
Social Studies.

ROLLINS COLLEGE
Winter Park, Florida 32789-4499
http://www.rollins.edu

Established 1885. Located adjacent to Orlando. Coed. Private control. Semester system. Library: 263,000 volumes, 37,400 microforms. No on-campus housing available for graduate students. Contact the Office of Residential Life for off-campus housing information. Phone: (800)866-2405, (407)646-2405.

Roy E. Crummer Graduate School of Business
http://www.crummer.rollins.edu

Graduate study since 1957. Annual tuition: $17,200. Enrollment: full-time 130, part-time 150; Executive M.B.A. 45. Faculty: full-time 17. Degree conferred: A.M.B.A. (applicants must have at least three years of significant work experience), E.A.M.B.A. (for applicants with little or no work experience), P.M.B.A., E.M.B.A.

ADMISSION REQUIREMENTS. Transcripts, GMAT required in support of School's application. TOEFL required for international applicants. Apply by April 1 for Fall admission only. Rolling admissions process. Late applications considered on a space available basis. Application fee for A.M.B.A., E.A.M.B.A., P.M.B.A. $40; E.M.B.A. $50. Phone: (800)866-2405, (407)646-2405; fax: (407)646-1550.

ADMISSION STANDARDS. Selective. Usual minimum average: 3.2 (A = 4).

FINANCIAL AID. Forty-three scholarships, twenty-nine administrative assistantships, loans. Use FAFSA and institutional FAF. Phone: (407)646-2395. About 35% of students receive aid other than loans from College and outside sources.

DEGREE REQUIREMENTS. For A.M.B.A.: Eleven month accelerated program. For E.A.M.B.A.: two year program. For P.M.B.A.: Thirty-two month program. For E.M.B.A.: Twenty month program.

FIELD OF STUDY.
Business Administration. Includes accounting, finance, marketing, management, operation.

Hamilton Holt School—Graduate Division

Tuition: per credit $525. Enrollment: full-time 68, part-time 235. Faculty: full-time 24, part-time 3. Degrees conferred: M.A., M.A.T., M.L.S.

ADMISSION REQUIREMENTS. Transcripts, GRE required in support of School's application. TOEFL required for international applicants. Accepts transfer applicants. Graduates of unaccredited institutions not considered. Apply to Coordinator of Records and Registration; no specified closing date. Rolling admissions process. Late applications considered on a space available basis. Application fee $50. Phone: (407)646-2232; fax: (407)646-1551.

ADMISSION STANDARDS. Selective. Usual minimum average: 2.75 (A = 4).

FINANCIAL AID. Ten scholarships, seven fellowships, ten assistantships, loans. Approved for VA benefits. Apply by April 1 to the Dean for scholarships, fellowships, assistantships; to Financial Aid Office for loans. Use FAFSA and institutional FAF. Phone: (407)646-2395. About 35% of students receive aid other than loans from College and outside sources.

DEGREE REQUIREMENTS. For master's: 30–36 credit hour program; thesis/nonthesis option.

FIELDS OF STUDY.
Elementary Education.
Human Resources.
Liberal Studies.
Mental Health Counseling.
School Counseling.
Secondary Education. Includes English, mathematics, music.

ROOSEVELT UNIVERSITY
Chicago, Illinois 60605-1394

Founded 1945. Coed. Private control. Semester system. Branch campus at Schaumburg, IL (60173). Library: 400,000 volumes, 115,000 microforms.
Tuition: per hour $398. Limit on-campus housing for single students only. Annual housing costs: $3966–$5266. Apply to Office of Residence Life for housing information. Phone: (312)341-2004.

Graduate Division

Enrollment: full-time 388, part-time 1771. Faculty: full-time 89, part-time 76. Degrees conferred: M.A., M.B.A., M.M., M.P.A., M.S., M.S.J., M.G.S.

ADMISSION REQUIREMENTS. Transcripts required in support of application. GMAT required for Business. Accepts transfer applicants. Apply to Coordinator of Graduate Admissions by July 15 (Fall), December 1 (Spring). Application fee $25, $35 for international applicants. Phone: (312)341-3612; fax: (312)341-4316.

ADMISSION STANDARDS. Selective. Usual minimum average: 2.7–3.0 (A = 4) depending on program.

FINANCIAL AID. Fifteen scholarships, eighteen teaching assistantships, Federal W/S, loans. Approved for VA benefits. Apply by February 15 to Graduate Admissions for scholarships; to appropriate department chair for assistantships; to Financial Aid Office for all other programs. Use FAFSA. Phone: (312)341-3565. Limited merit awards available for part-time students.

DEGREE REQUIREMENTS. For master's: 30–60 semester hours of graduate work; thesis/nonthesis option; final written/oral exam; research paper.

FIELDS OF STUDY.
Accounting.
Business Administration. M.B.A.
Chemistry.
Computing and Information Science.
Economics.
Education. Includes early childhood, elementary teacher, secondary teacher, school guidance and counseling, mental health and community counseling, educational supervision and administration, reading.
English.
General Studies. Interdepartmental.
Gerontology.
History.
Information Systems.
International Business. M.S.I.B.
Journalism. M.S.J.
Languages. Includes French, Spanish.
Marketing Communications.
Mathematical Sciences.
Music. Includes performance, theory, composition, musicology, music education.
Political Science.
Psychology.
Public Administration.
Sociology.
Theater and Music Theater.

ROSARY COLLEGE
River Forest, Illinois 60305-1099
http://www.rosary.edu

Founded 1901. Located 10 miles W of the Chicago Loop. Coed. Private control. Roman Catholic. Semester system. Library: 210,000 volumes, 1100 current periodicals.
Tuition: per three-credit course $1280. On-campus housing available for single students only. Annual housing cost: $4740–$5420 (including board). Apply to Housing Office. Phone: (708)524-6237.

Graduate School of Business

Tuition: per 3 credit course $1280. On-campus housing available. Enrollment: full-time 60, part-time 300. Faculty: full-time 18, part-time 24. Degrees conferred: M.B.A., M.S.Acc., M.B.A.-J.D. (with John Marshall Law School), M.S.-M.I.S., M.S.O.M.

ADMISSION REQUIREMENTS. Transcripts, three letters of recommendation, GMAT required in support of School's application. TOEFL required for international applicants. Accepts transfer applicants. Apply to School at least one month prior to registration. Application fee $25. Phone: (708)524-6810; fax: (708)366-5360.

ADMISSION STANDARDS. Selective. Usual minimum average: 2.5 (A = 4).

FINANCIAL AID. Ten scholarships, twenty assistantships, Federal W/S, loans. Approved for VA benefits. Apply by April 15 to Dean for scholarships, assistantships; to the Director of Financial Aid for all other programs. Use FAFSA. Phone: (708)524-6809.

DEGREE REQUIREMENTS. For master's: 30–51 semester hours minimum, at least 24 in residence; practicum (for some programs); computer proficiency for M.B.A.

FIELDS OF STUDY.
Accounting.
Entrepreneurship.
Finance.
General Management.
Health Care Administration.
Human Resource Management.
International Business.
Management Information Systems.
Managerial Communication.
Marketing.
Organization and Management.
Note: Weekend M.B.A. available.

Graduate School of Education

Tuition: per 3 credit course $1280. On-campus housing available.

Enrollment: full-time 11, part-time 129. Faculty: full-time 7, part-time 6. Degrees conferred: M.A., M.A.T., M.S.

ADMISSION REQUIREMENTS. Transcripts, three letters of recommendation required in support of School's application. TOEFL required for international applicants. Accepts transfer applicants. Apply to School by August 15 (Fall), January 10 (Spring). Rolling admissions process. Application fee $25. Phone: (708)524-6924.

ADMISSION STANDARDS. Selective. Usual minimum average: 2.75 (A = 4).

FINANCIAL AID. Seven fellowships, sixteen assistantships, Federal W/S, loans. Approved for VA benefits. Apply by April 15 to Dean for fellowships, assistantships; to the Director of Financial Aid for all other programs. Use FAFSA. Phone: (708)524-6809. Aid available for part-time students.

DEGREE REQUIREMENTS. For master's: 30–36 semester hours minimum, at least 24 in residence; thesis/nonthesis option.

FIELDS OF STUDY.
Early Childhood Education.
Education.
Educational Administration.
Special Education.

Graduate School of Library and Information Science

Graduate study since 1949. Enrollment: full-time 40, part-time 136 (men 22%, women 78%). Faculty: full-time 10, part-time 33. Degrees conferred: M.L.I.S., several Certificates of Special Studies.

ADMISSION REQUIREMENTS. Transcripts of all post-secondary study, two letters of recommendation required in support of School's application. GRE required for some applicants. TOEFL required for international applicants. Accepts transfer applicants. Graduates of unaccredited institutions not considered. Apply to the Graduate School at least one month prior to registration. Application fee $25. Phone: (708)524-6844.

ADMISSION STANDARDS. Selective. Usual minimum average: 3.0 (A = 4).

FINANCIAL AID. Annual awards from institutional funds: thirteen assistantships, Federal W/S, loans. Approved for VA benefits. Apply to Director of Financial Aid by March 15. Use FAFSA. Phone: (708)524-6845.

DEGREE REQUIREMENTS. For M.L.I.S.: 36 semester hours minimum; thesis. Degree must be completed within 5 years or 6 summers.

FIELDS OF STUDY.
Library Information Science.
Management Information System. Combined program with School of Business.
Note: Collaborative programs with College of St. Catherine in St. Paul, MN. Requires courses at Rosary College as well as at CSC.

ROSE-HULMAN INSTITUTE OF TECHNOLOGY
Terre Haute, Indiana 47803-3920

Founded 1874. Coed. Private control. Quarter system. Library: over 150,000 volumes. Special facilities: digital computers, high flux neutron generator, observatory, Center of Applied Optics, Center of Technology Assessment.

Annual tuition: full-time $15,612, per credit $435. On-campus housing for 700 students; none for graduate students. Average academic year housing costs: $2187–$4440. Apply to Dean of Students. Phone: (812)877-8257.

Graduate Studies

Graduate study since 1894. Enrollment: full-time 75, part-time 40. Institute faculty: full-time 120: no part-time faculty. Degree conferred: M.S.

ADMISSION REQUIREMENTS. Transcripts, GRE, three references required in support of application. Interview desirable. TOEFL and GRE required for international applicants. Accepts transfer applicants. Apply to Dean for Research and Graduate Studies; no specified closing dates, though preference is given to those applying by February 1. Application fee: none. Phone: (812)877-8402; fax: (812)877-8895.

ADMISSION STANDARDS. Selective. Usual minimum average: 3.0 (A = 4), TOEFL minimum score 580.

FINANCIAL AID. Annual awards from institutional funds: Nine international fellowships, twenty-seven graduate assistantships, four research assistantships, tuition grants, loans. Apply by April 1 to Dean of Research and Graduate Studies for fellowships, assistantships; to Financial Aid Office for all other programs. Use FAFSA. Phone: (812)877-8403. About 60–80% of students receive aid other than loans from Institute and outside sources.

DEGREE REQUIREMENTS. For M.S.: 51 quarter hours minimum; thesis; final oral exam; no language requirement.

FIELDS OF STUDY.
Applied Optics.
Biomedical Engineering.
Chemical Engineering.
Civil Engineering.
Electrical Engineering.
Environmental Engineering.
Mechanical Engineering.

ROWAN COLLEGE OF NEW JERSEY
Glassboro, New Jersey 08028-1701

Founded 1923. Name changed in 1992. Located 35 miles SE of Philadelphia. Coed. State Control. Semester system. Library: 325,000 volumes.

Annual tuition: full-time resident $4330, nonresident $6864; per credit, resident $190, nonresident $286. No on- or off-campus housing available.

Graduate Studies

Graduate study since 1950. Enrollment: full-time 50, part-time 1438. Graduate faculty: full-time 100, part-time 10. Degrees conferred: M.A., M.B.A., M.S. in Teaching.

ADMISSION REQUIREMENTS. Transcripts, MAT/GRE/GMAT/NTE required in support of application. TOEFL required for international applicants. Interview required by some departments. Accepts transfer applicants. Apply to Graduate Admissions Office prior to registration. Application fee $30. Phone: (609)256-4050.

ADMISSION STANDARDS. Selective. Usual minimum average: 2.8 for last 60 credits (A = 4).

FINANCIAL AID. Annual awards from institutional funds: graduate and residence assistantships (non-teaching), Federal W/S, loans. Apply to Graduate Office. Use FAFSA. Phone: (609)863-6141. About 10% of students receive aid from College.

DEGREE REQUIREMENTS. For master's: 32–48 credit hours minimum; thesis or final project; written comprehensive exam.

FIELDS OF STUDY.
Administration. Includes elementary, secondary.
Business Administration.
Community College Education.
Elementary School Teaching.
Engineering.
Environmental Education and Conservation.
Learning Disabilities.
Mathematics.
Professional Psychology. 60 credit hour Certificate only.
Public Relations. Includes corporate, educational.
Reading Education.
School Psychology.
School and Public Librarianship.
Secondary Teaching. Usual subject fields.
Special Education.
Student Personnel Services. Includes guidance counselor.
Subject Matter Teaching. Includes art, music, mathematics, science, supervision and curriculum development.
Theater.

RUSH MEDICAL COLLEGE OF RUSH UNIVERSITY
Chicago, Illinois 60612-3832

Founded 1837. Closed in 1942. Merged with Presbyterian–St. Luke's Medical Center 1971.

Annual tuition: $22,944; student fees $1536. Limited on-campus housing available. Contact Assistant Dean, Student Services. Total average figure for all other expenses: $9000.

Enrollment: first-year class 120 (EDP 10); total 496 (men 55%, women 45%). Faculty: full-time 370, part-time 1800. Degrees conferred: M.D., M.D.-Ph.D.

ADMISSION REQUIREMENTS. AMCAS report, transcripts, MCAT, three recommendations (one from premedical committee) required in support of application. Interview by invitation only. Preference given to state residents. Has EDP; apply between June 15 and August 1. Apply through AMCAS after June 15, before November 15. Application fee $45. Phone: (312)942-6913; fax: (312)942-2333.

ADMISSION STANDARDS. Competitive. Accepts about 3–5% of total annual applicants. Approximately 85% are state residents.

FINANCIAL AID. Scholarships, loans, grants. Apply to Financial Aid Office after acceptance; before May 15. About 80% of students receive some aid from College.

DEGREE REQUIREMENTS. For M.D.: satisfactory completion of four-year curricular plan.

FIELDS OF GRADUATE STUDY.
Anatomical Sciences.
Biochemistry.
Immunology.
Microbiology.
Neurosciences.

Pharmacology.
Physiology.
Psychology.

RUTGERS, THE STATE UNIVERSITY OF NEW JERSEY, CAMDEN
Camden, New Jersey 08102-1401

Coed. State control. Semester system. Library: 267,000 volumes, 133,000 microforms.

Annual tuition: full-time residents $5734, nonresidents $8406; per credit resident $236, nonresident $349. On-campus housing available. Average academic year housing costs: $3850 for single students, $7440 for married students. Contact the Housing Office for both on- and off-campus housing information. Phone: (609)225-6471.

Graduate School

Enrollment: total full- and part-time 400. Faculty: full-time 24, part-time 1. Degrees conferred: M.A., M.S., M.P.A., M.P.T.

ADMISSION REQUIREMENTS. Transcripts, GRE Subject Tests required in support of School's application. TOEFL required for international applicants. Accepts transfer applicants. Graduates of unaccredited institutions not considered. Apply to Director of Graduate Admissions by July 1 (Fall), December 1 (Spring); for P.T. program, December 15 (Fall admission only). Application fee $25. Phone: (609)225-6056; fax: (609)225-6498.

ADMISSION STANDARDS. Competitive. Usual minimum average: 2.5 (A = 4).

FINANCIAL AID. Annual awards from institutional funds: Eight teaching assistantships, ten research assistantships, Federal W/S, loans. Approved for VA benefits. Apply by March 15 to Dean for assistantships; to Director of Financial Aid for all other programs. Use FAFSA. Phone: (609)225-6149.

DEGREE REQUIREMENTS. Essentially the same as those for main campus.

FIELDS OF STUDY.
American and Public History.
Biology.
English.
Liberal Studies.
Mathematics.
Nursing.
Physical Therapy.
Public Policy and Administration.

School of Law (08102-3650)

Established 1926. Semester system. Law library: 400,000 volumes. Library has LEXIS, NEXIS, WESTLAW.

Annual tuition: residents $8550, nonresidents $12,544; per credit resident $354, nonresident $522. No on-campus housing. Total average annual additional expense: $8000–$10,000.

Enrollment: first year class, 260 (day), 53 (evening); full- and part-time 783 (men 55%, women 45%). Faculty: full-time 37, part-time 60. Degrees conferred: J.D., J.D.-M.A. (Political Science), J.D.-M.B.A., J.D.-M.C.R.P., J. D.-M.P.A.

ADMISSION REQUIREMENTS. LSDAS Law School report, bachelor's degree, transcripts, letters of recommendation, LSAT required in support of application. Interview sometimes required. Accepts transfer applicants. Graduates of unaccredited colleges not considered. Apply to Admissions Office by March 1. Application fee $40. Admits Fall only. Phone: (609)225-6102.

ADMISSION STANDARDS. Selective. Accepts 40–45% of total annual applicants.

FINANCIAL AID. Scholarships, fellowships, Federal W/S, loans, legal employment. Apply to Director of Financial Aid by March 1. Use FAFSA and Institutional financial aid application. About 75% of students receive some aid from School.

DEGREE REQUIREMENTS. For J.D.: 84 credits minimum, at least final two terms in residence. Evening program:Nine9 semesters plus one summer session. For master's degrees, see Graduate School, main campus, below.

RUTGERS UNIVERSITY
New Brunswick, New Jersey 08903
http://www.rutgers.edu

Established 1766. Located 33 miles SW of New York City. Coed. State control. Semester system. Special facilities: Center for Advanced Biotechnology and Medicine, Center for Advanced Food Technology, Center for Agriculture, Center for Alcohol Studies, American Affordable Housing Institute, Center for American Women in Politics, Art Museum, Institute for Biostatistics, Center for Ceramic Research, Center of Cognitive Sciences, Center for Computer Aids for Industrial Productivity, Center for Discrete Mathematics and Theoretical Computer Science, Controlled Drug-Delivery Research Center, Institute for Criminological Research, Center for the Critical Analysis of Contemporary Culture, Eagleton Institute of Politics, Environmental and Occupational Health Sciences Institute, Fiber Optics Materials Research, Institute for Health, Health Care Policy and Aging Research, Center for Historical Analysis, Center for International Conflict Resolution and Peace Studies, Institute of Marine and Coastal Sciences, Center for Materials Synthesis, Center for Operations Research, Laboratory for Surface Modification, Center for Urban Policy Research, Waksman Institute of Microbiology, Wireless Information Network Laboratory, Institute for Research on Women. Library: 5,267,000 volumes, 3,300,000 microforms, 24,000 current periodicals.

Annual tuition: full-time residents $5734, nonresidents $8406; per credit residents $230, nonresidents $349. On-campus housing for 380 married students, 703 single students. Average academic year housing costs: $3750–$6300 for single students; per month $494–$628 for family housing. Contact Graduate and Family Housing Office for both on- and off-campus information. Phone: (908)445-2215.

The Graduate School

Graduate study since 1876. Enrollment: full-time 1854, part-time 3082 (men 2820, women 2116). Graduate faculty: full-time 1842. Degrees conferred: M.A., M.A.T., M.C.R.P., M.S., M.S.T., M.Phil., Dr.P.H., Ph.D.

ADMISSION REQUIREMENTS. Transcripts, GRE, two or three letters of recommendation required in support of School's application. GRE Subject Test required for many programs. TOEFL required for international applicants. Interview not required. Accepts transfer applicants. Graduates of unaccredited colleges not considered. Apply to Admissions Office by July 1 (Fall), December 1 (Spring), March 1 (Summer). Applicants seeking financial support should apply by February 1 for the Fall term. Application fee $40. Phone: (908)932-7711; fax: (908)932-8231.

ADMISSION STANDARDS. Very competitive or selective.

FINANCIAL AID. One hundred academic scholarships, 450 fellowships, 560 teaching assistantships, 525 graduate assistantships, Federal W/S, loans. Approved for VA benefits. Apply by February 1 to appropriate department Chair for assistantships, fellowships; to Admissions Office for all other programs. Use FAFSA and institutional FAF. Phone: (908)932-7755; fax: (908)932-7385. About 80% of students receive aid other than loans from School and outside sources.

DEGREE REQUIREMENTS. For master's: 30 credit hours minimum; thesis required by some departments; final oral/written comprehensive exam. For Ph.D.: 3 years minimum beyond the bachelor's, at least one year in full-time residence required by some programs; reading knowledge of one or two foreign languages required by some programs; qualifying exam; thesis; final oral exam.

FIELDS OF STUDY.
Agricultural Economics. M.S.
Animal Sciences. M.S., Ph.D.
Anthropology. M.A., Ph.D.
Art History. M.A., Ph.D.
Biochemistry. M.S., Ph.D.
Biomedical Engineering. M.S., Ph.D.
Bioresource Engineering. M.S.
Cell and Developmental Biology. M.S., Ph.D.
Ceramic Science and Engineering. M.S., Ph.D.
Chemical and Biochemical Engineering. M.S., Ph.D.
Chemistry. M.S., M.S.T., Ph.D.
Civil and Environmental Engineering. M.S., Ph.D.
Classics. M.A., M.A.T., Ph.D.
Communication, Information and Library Studies. Ph.D.
Comparative Literature. Ph.D.
Computer Science. M.S., Ph.D.
Ecology and Evolution. M.S., Ph.D.
Economics. M.A., Ph.D.
Electrical Engineering. M.S., Ph.D.
English. Ph.D.
Entomology. M.S., Ph.D.
Environmental Sciences. M.S., Ph.D.
Food Science. M.S., Ph.D.
French. M.A., M.A.T., Ph.D.
Geography. M.A., M.S., Ph.D.
Geological Sciences. M.S., Ph.D.
German. M.A., Ph.D.
History. Ph.D.
Industrial and System Engineering. M.S., Ph.D.
Industrial Relations and Human Resources. Ph.D.
Italian. M.A., M.A.T., Ph.D.
Linguistics. Ph.D.
Materials Science and Engineering. M.S., Ph.D.
Mathematics. M.S., Ph.D.
Mechanical and Aerospace Engineering. M.S., Ph.D.
Mechanics. M.S., Ph.D.
Meteorology. M.S.
Microbiology and Molecular Genetics. M.S., Ph.D.
Music. M.A., M.A.T., Ph.D.
Nutritional Sciences. M.S., Ph.D.
Oceanography. M.S., Ph.D.
Operations Research. M.S., Ph.D.
Pharmaceutical Science. M.S., Ph.D.
Pharmacology. Ph.D.
Philosophy. Ph.D.
Physics and Astronomy. M.S., M.S.T., Ph.D.
Physiology and Neurobiology. Ph.D.
Plant Biology. M.S., Ph.D.
Plant Pathology. M.S., Ph.D.
Plant Science and Technology. M.S., Ph.D.
Political Science. M.A., Ph.D.

Psychology. Ph.D.
Public Health. M.P.H., Ph.D., Dr.P.H. (Offered jointly with and
   administered by UMDNJ-RWJMS.)
Social Work. Ph.D.
Sociology. M.A., Ph.D.
Spanish. M.A., M.A.T., Ph.D.
Statistics. M.S., Ph.D.
Toxicology. M.S., Ph.D.
Urban Planning and Policy Development. M.S., M.C.R.P., Ph.D.
Women's Studies. M.A.

Graduate School of Management and Labor Relations

Graduate study since 1950. Located on Newark and New Brunswick campuses. Annual tuition: full-time per term, resident $7948, nonresident $11,850; per credit, resident $329, nonresident $492. On-campus housing for graduate students.

Enrollment: full-time 350, part-time 1200, Ph.D. 150. Degrees conferred: M.B.A., M.B.A. in Professional Accounting, E.M.B.A., M.Acc., M.T., Ph.D.

ADMISSION REQUIREMENTS. Transcripts, two letters of recommendation, two essays, GMAT required in support of School's application. TOEFL required for international applicants. Accepts transfer applicants. Graduates of unaccredited institutions not considered. For M.B.A.: apply to Admissions Office, 92 New Street, Newark, NJ 07102. Deadline for full-time entry: May 15; part-time May 15 and November 15; Professional Accounting (June entry full-time only) March 15; international April 15. For Ph.D., apply to Admissions Office, Graduate School—Newark, 249 University Avenue, Newark, NJ 07102. Application fee $40. M.B.A. phone: (201)648-1234; Ph.D. phone: (201)648-5371.

ADMISSION STANDARDS. Competitive. Average GPA: 3.1 (A = 4), average GMAT: 580, work experience: three years full-time, five years part-time.

FINANCIAL AID. Annual awards from institutional funds: 20 scholarships, 20 fellowships, 10 teaching assistantships (Ph.D. only), 100 internships, Federal W/S, loans. Apply by March 1 to Dean for scholarships, fellowships, assistantships; to Admissions Office for all other programs. Use FAFSA. Phone: (201)648-1234. About 25% of students receive aid other than loans from school. No aid for part-time students.

DEGREE REQUIREMENTS. For M.B.A.: 60–61 credits, at least 49 in residence. For M.B.A. in Professional Accounting: 63 credits. For M. Acc.: 30 credits. For Ph.D.: 72 credits, at least 65 in residence; qualifying exam; dissertation; final oral exam.

FIELDS OF STUDY.
Accounting.
Consultancy.
Finance.
Human Resources Management.
International Business.
Management Information Systems.
Marketing.
Quantitative Studies.
Real Estate.
Small Business/Entrepreneurship.

Graduate School of Education

Graduate study since 1924. Semester system. Annual tuition: full-time resident, $5734, nonresident $8406; per credit, resident $236, nonresident $349.

Enrollment: full-time master's 119, part-time 403; full-time doctoral 56, part-time 310. Faculty: full-time 57, part-time 57. Degrees conferred: Ed.M., Ed.S., Ed.D.

ADMISSION REQUIREMENTS. Transcripts, GRE, three letters of recommendation required in support of School's application. TOEFL required for international applicants. Accepts transfer applicants. Graduates of unaccredited institutions not considered. Apply to Graduate Admissions Office by March 1 (Fall); Counseling Psychology by January 15. Application fee $40. Phone: (908)932-7711/7712; fax: (908)932-8231.

ADMISSION STANDARDS. Selective. Usual minimum average: master 3.0 (A = 4) and 1000 GRE, doctorate 3.5 and GRE 1100.

FINANCIAL AID. Twenty-five academic scholarships, twenty grants, five fellowships, ten research assistantships, ten teaching assistantships, ten internships, Federal W/S, loans. Approved for VA benefits. Apply to appropriate department chair for scholarships, fellowships, assistantships; to Office of Financial Aid for all others; no specified closing date. Use FAFSA and institutional FAF. Phone: (908)932-7755; fax: (908)932-7385. About 20% of students receive aid from School and outside sources. Aid available for part-time students.

DEGREE REQUIREMENTS. For Ed.M.: 30 credit hours minimum; comprehensive written exam/thesis for some departments. For Ed.S.: 64 credit hours minimum beyond the bachelor's, at least 24 in residence; qualifying exam. For Ed.D.: 72 credit hours minimum beyond the bachelor's, at least 42 at Rutgers; qualifying exam; dissertation; final oral exam.

FIELDS OF STUDY.
Administration and Supervision. Includes elementary, general, higher, school business, secondary, urban.
Adult Education.
Bilingual-Bicultural Education.
Counseling Psychology.
Early Childhood Education.
Educational Statistics and Measurement.
English as a Second Language.
English/Language Arts.
Language Education.
Learning/Cognition and Development.
Mathematics.
Reading.
Science.
Social and Philosophical Foundations of Education.
Social Studies.
Special Education.
Vocation-Technical Education.

School of Communication, Information and Library Studies

http://www.scils.rutgers.edu

Graduate study since 1953. Annual tuition: full-time, resident $5734, nonresident $8906, per credit resident $236, nonresident $349. On-campus housing available.

Enrollment: full-time 127, part-time 462 (men 20%, women 80%). Faculty: full-time 29, part-time 14. Degrees conferred: M.L.S., M.C.I.S., Ph.D.

ADMISSION REQUIREMENTS. Transcripts, GRE, three letters of reference, personal statement required in support of School's application. TOEFL required of international students. Interview not required. Accepts transfer applicants. Graduates of unaccredited institutions not considered. Apply to Director of Admissions by May 1. Application fee $35. Phone: (201)932-7711; fax: (908)932-8231.

ADMISSION STANDARDS. Selective. Usual minimum average: 3.0 (A = 4).

FINANCIAL AID. Ten scholarships, six fellowships, fourteen teaching assistantships, Federal W/S, loans. Approved for VA benefits. Apply as part of admission application. Use FAFSA and institutional FAF. Phone: (201)932-7755; fax: (908)932-7385. About 5% of students receive aid other than loans from School and outside sources. Aid sometimes available to part-time students.

DEGREE REQUIREMENTS. For M.L.S.: 36 credit hours. For M.C.I.S.: 36 credit hours, at least 30 in residence. For Ph.D.: essentially the same requirements as for the Graduate School.

FIELDS OF STUDY.
Communication and Information Studies.
Communication and Library Studies.
Library and Information Studies.

School of Social Work

http://www.info.rutgers.edu

Graduate study since 1955. Tuition: per credit, resident $236, nonresident $349.

Enrollment: full-time 308, part-time 410. Faculty: full-time 49, part-time 31. Degrees conferred: M.S.W., Ph.D. (offered through Graduate School).

ADMISSION REQUIREMENTS. Transcripts, personal statement, three letters of recommendation required in support of School's application. GRE required for doctoral applicants. TOEFL required for international applicants. Accepts transfer applicants. Graduates of unaccredited institutions not considered. Apply to Office of Graduate Admissions by May 1 (Fall); March 1 (advanced standing accelerated program). Application fee $35. Phone: (908)932-7711; fax: (908)932-8231.

ADMISSION STANDARDS. Selective. Usual minimum average: 3.0 (A = 4).

FINANCIAL AID. Limited fellowships, research assistantships, field placement, stipends, Federal W/S, loans. Approved for VA benefits. Apply to University Financial Aid Office by March 1. Use FAFSA and institutional FAF. Phone: (908)932-7057; fax: (908)932-7385. About 46% of students receive aid other than loans from School and outside sources.

DEGREE REQUIREMENTS. For M.S.W.: 60 credit hours minimum, at least 36 in residence; research project. For Ph.D., see Graduate School listing above.

FIELDS OF STUDY.
Administration.
Direct Practice.
Policy and Planning.

School of Law–Newark Campus (07102-3192)

Established 1908. Semester system. Library: 404,400 volumes. Library has LEXIS, NEXIS, WESTLAW, DIALOG.

Annual tuition: resident $8550, nonresident $12,544; per credit resident $354, nonresident $522. No on-campus housing available. Total average annual additional expense: $14,000–$16,000.

Enrollment: first-year class 192 (day), 66 (evening); total 800 (men 49%, women 51%). Faculty: full-time 36, part-time 40. Degrees conferred: J.D., J.D.-M.A.(Criminal Justice, Political Science), J.D.-M.C.R.P., J.D.-Ph.D.

ADMISSION REQUIREMENTS. LSDAS Law School report, bachelor's degree, transcripts, LSAT required in support of application. Interview not required. Accepts transfer applicants. Graduates of unaccredited institutions not considered. Minority

Student Program available. Apply to Director of Admissions of School by March 1. Application fee $40. Fall admission only. Phone: (201)648-5557.

ADMISSION STANDARDS. Selective. Accepts 20–25% of total annual applicants.

FINANCIAL AID. Scholarships, fellowships, Federal W/S, loans. Apply to the University's Financial Aid Office by March 1. Use FAFSA and institutional FAF. About 10% of students receive aid other than loans from School.

DEGREE REQUIREMENTS. For J.D.: satisfactory completion of three-year program; 84 credits hours minimum.

THE SAGE COLLEGES
Troy, New York 12180-4115
http://www.sage.edu

Founded 1916. Located 10 miles E of Albany. Coed on graduate level. Private control. Semester system. Library: 350,000 volumes, 1600 current periodicals. Library fully automated.

Tuition: per credit: $340. Limited on-campus housing. Contact the Director of Residence Life for both on- and off-campus housing information. Phone: (518)270-2008.

Sage Graduate School

Graduate study since 1950. Enrollment: full-time 250, part-time 948. Faculty: full-time 23, part-time 33. Degrees conferred: M.A., M.S., M.B.A., M.S.Ed.

ADMISSION REQUIREMENTS. Transcripts, two recommendations, interview, GRE/GMAT required in support of School's application. TOEFL required for international applicants. Accepts transfer applicants. Graduates of unaccredited institutions not considered. Apply to Dean, Sage Graduate School; no specified closing date. Rolling admissions process. Application fee $25. Phone: (518)270-2264.

ADMISSION STANDARDS. Selective. Usual minimum average: 2.75 (A = 4).

FINANCIAL AID. Twenty-four grants, twenty-four teaching assistantships, federal traineeships, Federal W/S, loans. Approved for VA benefits. Apply to Sage Graduate School for assistantships; to Financial Aid Office for all other programs; no specified closing date. Use FAFSA. Phone: (518)270-2341.

DEGREE REQUIREMENTS. For master's: 31–54 credits; thesis/nonthesis option; seminar/comprehensive exam.

FIELDS OF STUDY.
Business Administration. Includes finance, management, human resources. M.B.A.
Community Psychology. Includes general community psychology, alcohol drug abuse, community counseling, child care and children's services. M.A.
Elementary Education. Includes reading, special education. M.S.Ed.
Family Nurse Practitioner. M.S.
Guidance and Counseling. M.S. only.
Health Education. Includes community health education, school health education. M.S.
Health Services Administration. Includes administration, health education. M.S.
Nursing. Includes community health nursing, medical-surgical nursing, psychiatric-mental health nursing. M.S., M.S./M.B.A.

Nutrition. M.S.
Occupational Therapy. M.S.
Public Service Administration. Includes human services administration, public management. M.S.
Reading/Special Education. M.S.Ed.
Secondary Education. Includes usual academic subjects. M.S.Ed.

SAGINAW VALLEY STATE UNIVERSITY
University Center, Michigan 48710
http://www.svsu.edu

Founded 1963. Located 8 miles from Saginaw. State control. Coed. Early semester system. Library: 358,000 volumes, 247,100 microforms, 1639 current periodicals, 25 PCs.

Tuition: per credit hour, resident $147, nonresident $289. Limited on-campus housing available for single students only. Contact Director of Housing for both on- and off-campus housing information. Phone: (517)790-4255. Day care facilities available.

Graduate Program

Enrollment: full-time 41, part-time 820. Faculty: full- and part-time 41. Degrees conferred: M.A., M.A.T., M.B.A., M.Ed.

ADMISSION REQUIREMENTS. Transcripts, GRE/GMAT, letters of recommendation, interview required in support of application. Michigan Teaching Certificate required for M.A.T., M.Ed. TOEFL required for international applicants. Accepts transfer applicants. Graduates of unaccredited institutions not considered. Apply to Director of Admissions; no specified closing date. Rolling admissions process. Application fee $25. Phone: (517)790-4200.

ADMISSION STANDARDS. Selective. Usual minimum average: 3.0 (A = 4).

FINANCIAL AID. Limited to Federal W/S, loans. Approved for VA benefits. Apply to the Office of Financial Aid; no specified closing date. Use FAFSA. Phone: (517)790-4103; fax: (517)790-0180.

DEGREE REQUIREMENTS. For M.A., M.A.T., M.Ed.: 33–39 hours; thesis/nonthesis option/project. For M.B.A.: 36–48 credit hours minimum depending upon previous preparation, 24 in residence.

FIELDS OF STUDY.
Business Administration. M.B.A.
Criminal Justice/Political Science. M.A.
Educational Administration. M.Ed.
Elementary Education. Includes early childhood, learning disabilities, emotionally impaired, reading, classroom teaching.
Secondary Education. Includes English, history, chemistry, mathematics, physics, biology, classroom teaching.

ST. BONAVENTURE UNIVERSITY
Bonaventure, New York 14778-2284

Established 1859. Located 70 miles SE of Buffalo. Coed. Private control. Roman Catholic. Semester system. Library: 300,000 volumes, 539,000 microforms, 1200 current periodicals.

Annual tuition: full-time $7110; per credit $395. On-campus housing for single students only. Average academic year housing costs: $2830–$4556. Contact Coordinator of Residence Living for both on- and off-campus housing information. Phone: (716)375-2512.

Graduate School.

Enrollment: full-time 293, part-time 377 (men 50%, women 50%). Faculty: full-time 111, part-time 13. Degrees conferred: M.A., M.A.T., M.S., M.S.Ed., M.B.A.

ADMISSION REQUIREMENTS. Official transcripts, two letters of recommendation, GRE/GMAT required in support of School's application. GRE Subject Test, interview required by some departments. TOEFL required for international applicants. Accepts transfer applicants. Graduates of unaccredited institutions not considered. Apply to Graduate School at least thirty days prior to registration. Rolling admission process. Application fee $35. Phone: (716)375-2021.

ADMISSION STANDARDS. Selective for many departments. Usual minimum average: 2.5 (A = 4).

FINANCIAL AID. Eight research assistantships, two teaching assistantships, Federal W/S, loans. Approved for VA benefits. Apply by April 1 to School of Graduate Studies for assistantships; to Financial Aid Office for all other programs. Use FAFSA. Phone: (716)375-2528. About 10% of students receive aid from School and outside sources. Aid sometimes available for part-time students.

DEGREE REQUIREMENTS. For master's: 30 semester hours minimum, at least 24 in residence; thesis/nonthesis option; final oral exam for some departments; reading knowledge of one foreign language for some departments; written/oral comprehensive exam.

FIELDS OF STUDY.
Accounting. M.B.A.
Business Administration. M.B.A.
Counseling Psychology. M.S., M.S.Ed.
Educational Administration. M.S., M.S.Ed.
English. M.A.
Franciscan Studies. M.A.
History. M.A.
Management. M.B.A.
Marketing. M.B.A.
Psychology. M.A.
Reading. M.S.Ed.
Special Education. M.S.Ed.
Teacher Education. M.A.T.
Teacher Education—Elementary. M.S.Ed.
Teacher Education—Secondary. M.S.Ed.
Theology. M.A.

ST. CLOUD STATE UNIVERSITY
St. Cloud, Minnesota 56301-4498
http://www.stcloud.msus.edu

Founded 1869. Located 62 miles NW of Minneapolis on Interstate 94. Coed. State control. Quarter System. Library: 775,000 volumes, 1,602,000 microforms, 54 PCs.

Tuition: per credit resident $81, nonresident $127. On-campus housing for single students only. Average academic year housing costs: $2937 (including board). Apply to Director of Housing. Phone: (612)255-2166.

School of Graduate and Continuing Studies

Graduate study since 1953. Enrollment: full-time 332, part-time 927. Graduate faculty: full-time 465, part-time none. Degrees conferred: M.A., M.M., M.S., M.B.A., Specialist program.

ADMISSION REQUIREMENTS. Two transcripts, GRE required in support of application. GMAT required for Business applicants. TOEFL required of international applicants. Interview required for Applied Psychology. Apply to Graduate Studies Office; no specified closing dates. Application fee $15. Phone: (612)255-2113; fax: (612)654-5371.

ADMISSION STANDARDS. Selective for most departments. Usual minimum average: 2.75 (A = 4).

FINANCIAL AID. Twenty-five scholarships, 327 full/part-time assistantships, Federal W/S, loans. Apply by May 1 to appropriate department Chair for scholarships, assistantships; to Financial Aid Office for all other programs. Use FAFSA and University's FAF. Phone: (612)255-2047; fax: (612)654-5424. Aid sometimes available for part-time students.

DEGREE REQUIREMENTS. For master's: Plan A—46 hours minimum, at least 30 in residence; thesis; final written/oral exam. Plan B—48–51 hours minimum, at least 30 in residence; final comprehensive exam; no thesis; starred paper required by some departments. Plan C—54 hours; portfolio/projects; final written/oral exam. For Specialist program: 45 quarter hours beyond master's; field study.

FIELDS OF STUDY.
Accounting.
Applied Economics. M.S.
Art. M.A.
Biology.
Business Administration. GMAT for admission.
Child and Family Studies.
Communication Disorders.
Communication Management.
Computer Science.
Counseling Psychology. Includes community, rehabilitation, school.
Criminal Justice.
Curriculum and Instruction. Includes elementary, middle school/junior high, senior high, reading.
Educational Administration. M.S., Specialist.
English. Includes TES. M.A., M.S.
Exercise Science.
Geography.
Gerontology.
History. M.A.
History—Public History.
Human Relations.
Industrial Studies.
Information Media.
Mathematics.
Music. M.M.
Physical Education.
Psychology: Behavior Analysis.
Public Relations.
Special Education.
Special Education Administration. Specialist.
Speech Communication.
Sport Psychology.
Sports Management.

ST. EDWARD'S UNIVERSITY
Austin, Texas 78704-6489

Founded in 1885. Coed. Independent. Trimester system. Evening sessions. Library: 145,000 volumes, 6,000 microforms, 1800 current periodicals.

Tuition: per credit $366. On-campus housing available for 40–60 single students. Annual academic year costs: $2500–$4200. Phone: (512)448-8400.

Graduate Program

Graduate study since 1970. Enrollment: full-time 10, part-time 501. Faculty: full-time 15, part-time 25. Degrees conferred: M.B.A., M.A.H.S.

ADMISSION REQUIREMENTS. Transcripts, GRE/GMAT required in support of application. TOEFL required for international applicants. Accepts transfer applicants. Graduates of unaccredited institutions not considered. Apply to Graduate admissions office; no specified closing date. Application fee $25. Phone: (512)448-8600; fax: (512)448-8492.

ADMISSION STANDARDS. Selective. Usual minimum average: 2.75 (A = 4).

FINANCIAL AID. Limited to loans. Approved for VA benefits. Apply to Financial Aid Office; no specified closing date. Use FAFSA. Phone: (512)448-8520.

DEGREE REQUIREMENTS. For M.B.A.: 36–60 semester hours. For M.A.H.S.: 36–54 semester hours.

FIELDS OF STUDY.
Business Administration. Five tracks available: business management, general business, public administration, telecommunications, management information systems.
Human Services. Three tracks available: counseling, social/psychological services, administration.

ST. FRANCIS COLLEGE
2701 Spring Street
Fort Wayne, Indiana 46808-3994

Founded 1890. Coed. Private Control. Roman Catholic. Semester system. Library: 82,000 volumes, 478,000 microforms.

Tuition: per hour $320. On-campus housing for 46 men, 170 women; none for married students. Average academic year housing costs: $4600–$5000 (including board). Contact Director of Residence Life for both on- and off-campus housing information. Phone: (219)434-7411.

Graduate School

Graduate study since 1961. Enrollment: full-time 50, part-time 200. Graduate faculty: full-time 40, part-time 35. Degrees conferred: M.A.F.A., M.B.A., M.S., M.S.Ed., M.S.N.

ADMISSION REQUIREMENTS. Transcripts, interview required in support of School's application. GMAT required for business; MAT required for Nursing and Education. Accepts transfer applicants. Apply to Dean of Graduate Studies two months prior to registration. Application fee $20. Phone: (219)434-3250; fax: (219)434-3183.

ADMISSION STANDARDS. Relatively open. Usual minimum average: 2.5 (A = 4).

FINANCIAL AID. Limited to assistantships, Federal W/S, loans. Approved for VA benefits. Apply to Dean of Graduate Studies for assistantships; to Director of Financial Aid for all other programs. No specified closing date. Use FAFSA. Phone: (219)434-3283; fax: (219)434-3183.

DEGREE REQUIREMENTS. Varies according to program.

FIELDS OF STUDY.
Business Administration.
Counseling Psychology.

Education. Includes elementary, secondary, reading, special education (SEH, MIDLS, LD).

Psychology. Includes counseling, general, preclinical, school.

ST. FRANCIS COLLEGE

Loretto, Pennsylvania 15940-060O

Founded 1847. Located 90 miles E of Pittsburgh. Private control. Roman Catholic. Semester system. Library: 188,800 volumes, 725 current periodicals.

Tuition: per credit $385. Limited on-campus housing for single students. Average academic year housing cost: $5910 (including board). Contact the Office of Residence Life for on- and off-campus housing information. Phone: (814)472-3029.

Graduate School of Human Resource and Industrial Relations

Graduate study since 1961. Enrollment: full-time 4, part-time 130. Graduate faculty: full-time 1, part-time 25. Degree conferred: M.A.

ADMISSION REQUIREMENTS. Transcripts, letters of reference required in support of School's application. TOEFL required for international applicants. Accepts transfer applicants. Graduates of unaccredited institutions not considered. Apply to Director of Graduate School by August 1 (Fall), prior to registration for other sessions. Rolling admissions process. Application fee $15. Phone: (814)472-3026; fax: (814)472-3369.

ADMISSION STANDARDS. Selective. Usual minimum average: 2.5 (A = 4).

FINANCIAL AID. Annual awards from institutional funds: Two scholarships, one fellowship, one research assistantship, loans. Approved for VA benefits. Apply by March 31 to Director, Graduate School of Human Resource Management and Industrial Relations for scholarships, fellowships, assistantships; to Financial Aid Office for loans. Use PHEAA. Phone: (814)472-3010. About 3–5% of students receive aid other than loans from School and outside sources. No aid for part-time students.

DEGREE REQUIREMENTS. For M.A.: 30 credit hours minimum, research project.

FIELDS OF STUDY.
Human Resource Management.
Industrial Relations.

ST. JOHN'S COLLEGE

Annapolis, Maryland 21404-2800

Founded in 1696. Located 30 miles from Washington, D.C. Coed. Private control. Library: 85,000 volumes, 8 PCs in library.

Semester tuition: $3960; per credit hour $430. No on-campus housing available. Average off-campus housing cost: $700 per month.

Graduate Institute

Graduate study since 1977. Enrollment: full-time 80. Faculty taken from regular full-time faculty of 60 who teach in both undergraduate and graduate programs. Degree conferred: M.A.

ADMISSION REQUIREMENTS. Transcripts, essay required in support of Institute's application. TOEFL required for interna-

tional applicants. Accepts transfer applicants. Graduates of unaccredited institutions considered. Application fee: none. Phone: (410)263-2371, ext. 241; fax: (410)626-2880.

ADMISSION STANDARDS. Selective. Usual minimum average: 3.0 (A = 4). Essay given more weight than GPA.

FINANCIAL AID. Scholarships, Federal W/S, loans. Apply to Director of Financial Aid; no specified closing date. Use FAFSA.

DEGREE REQUIREMENTS. For M.A.: 36 credit hours minimum; thesis or special project.

FIELDS OF STUDY.
Liberal Arts. Includes literature, mathematics and natural science, philosophy and theology, politics and society.
Western Classics.

ST. JOHN'S COLLEGE

Santa Fe, New Mexico 87501-4599

Founded in 1964. Located 65 miles from Albuquerque, N.M. Coed. Private control. Library: 60,000 volumes, 9 PCs in library.

Semester tuition: $3960; per credit hour $430. On-campus housing available. Average academic year housing costs: $2999 (including board); 8-week summer session $1900 (including board).

Graduate Institute

Graduate study since 1967. Summer session and academic year evening program. Enrollment: full-time 80. Approximately 60 full-time faculty are taken from regular faculty who teach in both undergraduate and graduate programs. Degree conferred: M.A.

ADMISSION REQUIREMENTS. Transcripts, essay required in support of Institute's application. TOEFL required for international applicants. Accepts transfer applicants. Graduates of unaccredited institutions considered. Application fee: none. Phone: (505)984-6083; fax: (505)984-6003.

ADMISSION STANDARDS. Selective. Usual minimum average: 3.0 (A = 4.0). Essay given more weight than GPA.

FINANCIAL AID. Seventy scholarships, loans. Apply to Director of Financial Aid; no specified closing date. Use FAFSA. Phone: (505)984-6058. Approximately 30–35% of all graduate students receive some form of aid.

DEGREE REQUIREMENTS. For M.A.: 36 credit hours minimum; thesis or special project.

FIELDS OF STUDY.
Eastern Classics. Proficiency in Sanskrit or Classical Chinese required for degree.
Liberal Arts. Includes literature, mathematics and natural science, philosophy and theology, politics and society.

ST. JOHN'S UNIVERSITY

Collegeville, Minnesota 56321

Founded 1857. Located 80 miles NW of Minneapolis. Coed on the graduate level. Private control. Roman Catholic. Semester system. Library: 488,000 volumes, 118,000 microforms, 3200 current periodicals, 110 PCs in library.

Tuition: per credit, Summer $180; Fall and Spring $504. On-campus housing for graduate students. Average academic year housing cost: $2386. Apply to Director of Admissions. Phone: (612)363-2102.

Graduate School of Theology

Open to clerical, religious, and lay students. Enrollment: summer full-time 65, part-time 152; academic year, full-time 80, part-time 59. Graduate faculty: full-time 8, part-time 13. Degrees conferred: M.A., M.Div.

ADMISSION REQUIREMENTS. Transcripts, letters of recommendation required in support of application. TOEFL required for international applicant. MAT or GRE required during first semester. Interview not required. Accepts transfer applicants. Apply to Director of Admissions; no specified closing date. Application fee $25. Phone: (612)363-2102.

ADMISSION STANDARDS. Selective. Usual minimum average: 3.0 (A = 4.0).

FINANCIAL AID. Sixty-eight scholarships, Federal W/S, loans. Apply to Director of Admissions; no specified closing date. Use FAFSA. Phone: (612)363-2102. About of 90% of full-time students receive aid other than loans from University and outside sources. Some aid for part-time students.

DEGREE REQUIREMENTS. For M.A. (Theology; Liturgical Studies): 30 credit minimum; reading knowledge of one foreign language; final comprehensive exam. For M.A. (Liturgical Music; Pastoral Ministry), M.Div.. 30 credits minimum; final comprehensive exam.

FIELDS OF STUDY.
Liturgical Music.
Liturgical Studies.
Pastoral Ministry.
Theology. Includes scriptural, systematic, historical, liturgy, monastic studies, pastoral ministry; M.A., M.Div.

ST. JOHN'S UNIVERSITY
Queens Campus
Jamaica, New York 11439
Staten Island Campus
Staten Island, New York 10301

Founded 1870. Coed. Private control. Roman Catholic. Semester system. Library: 1,400,000 volumes, 2,242,000 microforms, 15,000 current periodicals, 154 PCs in libraries.

Tuition: per credit varies between $475 and $650 depending upon program. No on-campus housing for graduate or married students. Contact Dean of Students for off-campus housing information. Phone: (718)990-6161, ext. 6573.

Graduate School of Arts and Sciences

Queens campus only. Enrollment: full-time 480, part-time 716 (men 36%, women 64%). Faculty: full-time 161, part-time 111. Degrees conferred: M.A., M.L.S., M.S., M.Div., M.Phil., M.A.-M.L.S., M.L.S.-M.S., D.A., Ph.D.

ADMISSION REQUIREMENTS. Transcripts, two letters of recommendation required in support of School's application. GRE required for Ph.D. programs, GRE/interview for some departments. TOEFL required for international applicants. Graduates of unaccredited institutions not considered. Accepts transfer applicants. Apply to Office of Dean of Admissions at least three months prior to registration. Application fee $40. Phone: (718)990-6161.

ADMISSION STANDARDS. Selective. Usual minimum average: 3.0 for master's, 3.5 (in major) for doctorates (A = 4).

FINANCIAL AID. Annual awards from institutional funds: doctoral fellowships, graduate assistantships, research assistantships, Federal W/S, loans. Apply by April 1 to the Office of the Dean for fellowships, assistantships; to the Financial Aid Office for all other programs. Use FAFSA. Phone: (718)990-6161. About 19% of students receive aid other than loans from School.

DEGREE REQUIREMENTS. For master's programs: varies between 30 and 60 semester hours, at least one year in residence; research tool for some departments; written/oral comprehensive exam; thesis/nonthesis option. For M.Div.: 99 semester hours required. For program: 45 semester hours minimum beyond the master's; two-year minimum residence; foreign language/research tool required; written comprehensive exam; research essay. For Ph.D.(Biology): minimum of 60 credits beyond the B.S. degree, or 32 hours beyond the master's, at least two years in residence; foreign language/research tool required; written comprehensive exam; dissertation; oral exam. For Ph.D. (Clinical Psychology). 90 semester hours beyond the bachelor's, full-time residency; one-year internship; written/oral comprehensive exam; dissertation; oral exam.

FIELDS OF STUDY.
Asian Studies. M.A.
Biology. M S., Ph.D.
Chemistry. M.S.
Clinical Psychology. Ph.D.
English. M.A., D.A.
General-Experimental Psychology. M.A.
Government and Politics. M.A.
History. M.A.
Library Science. M.L.S.
Mathematics. M.A.
Modern World History. D.A.
Priestly Studies. M.Div.
School Psychology. M.S.
Sociology. M.A.
Spanish. M.A.
Speech-Language Pathology and Audiology. M.A.
Theology. M.A.

Graduate School of Business Administration

Graduate division established 1959. Tuition: per credit $550. Enrollment: full-time 265, part-time 990. Graduate faculty: full-time 55, part-time 6. Degrees conferred: M.B.A., Advanced Professional Certificate.

ADMISSION REQUIREMENTS. Official transcripts, GMAT, two letters of recommendation, written statement of objectives required in support of School's application. TOEFL required for international applicants. Interview not required. Accepts transfer applicants. Graduates of unaccredited institutions not considered. Apply to Office of Dean of Admission and Registrar at least three months prior to registration. Application fee $40. Phone: (718)990-6114; fax: (718)990-1677.

ADMISSION STANDARDS. Selective. Usual minimum average: 3.0 (A = 4).

FINANCIAL AID. Forty research assistantships, tuition awards, stipends, Federal W/S, loans. Approved for VA benefits. Apply to the Financial Aid Office; no specified closing date. Use FAFSA, TAP. Phone: (718)990-6403; fax: (718)969-4773.

DEGREE REQUIREMENTS. For M.B.A.: 39 credits; thesis optional. For A.P.C.: 18 credits beyond the M.B.A.

FIELD OF STUDY. *Business Administrations.* Specializations in accounting, computer information systems, decision science, economics, executive management, finance, international finance, financial services, marketing, marketing management, taxation. The School's center of study in Rome, Italy has a specialization in finance.

School of Education and Human Services

Enrollment: full-time 95, part-time 1016. Faculty: full-time 30, part-time 60. Degrees conferred: M.S. Professional Diploma, Ed.D., Ph.D.

ADMISSION REQUIREMENTS. Transcripts, GRE required in support of School's application. TOEFL required for international applicants. Accepts transfer applicants. Apply to Office of Dean, at least three months prior to registration. Rolling admissions process. Application fee $20. Phone: (718)990-6107; fax: (718)990-1677.

ADMISSION STANDARDS. Very competitive for some departments, selective in others. Usual minimum average: 3.0 (A = 4).

FINANCIAL AID. Annual awards from institutional funds: scholarships, fellowships, assistantships, Federal W/S, loans. Approved for VA benefits. Apply by March 1 to department chair for scholarships, fellowships, assistantships; to Financial Aid Office for all other programs. Use FAFSA. Phone: (718)990-6403; fax: (718)990-4773.

DEGREE REQUIREMENTS. For M.S.: 33 semester hours minimum, at least 27 in residence; comprehensive written exam. For Professional Diploma: 60 semester hours minimum beyond the bachelor's. For Ph.D.: 90 semester hours minimum beyond the bachelor's; reading knowledge of one foreign language or statistics; written comprehensive exam; dissertation; final oral exam. For Ed.D.: 90 semester hours minimum beyond the bachelor's; written comprehensive exam; dissertation; final oral exam.

FIELDS OF STUDY.
Administration and Supervision.
Bilingual/Bicultural Education.
Counselor Education.
Curriculum and Teaching. Includes elementary, early childhood education.
Elementary Education.
Instructional Leadership.
Reading.
Rehabilitation Counseling.
School Counseling.
Secondary Education. Includes most subject fields.
Special Education.

College of Pharmacy and Allied Health Professions

Graduate study since 1929.
Tuition: per credit $600. No on-campus housing available. Contact Student Life Office for off-campus housing information. Phone: (718)990-6783.
Enrollment: full-time 90, part-time 118 (men 60%, women 40%). Faculty: full-time 38, part-time 6. Degrees conferred: M.S., Ph.D., Pharm.D.

ADMISSION REQUIREMENTS. Transcripts, GRE, two letters of recommendation required in support of application. TOEFL required for foreign applicants. Interview required for Pharm.D. only. Accepts transfer applicants. Graduates of unaccredited institutions not considered. Apply to Office of Graduate Admissions at least one month prior to registration. Application fee $40. Phone: (718)990-6114; fax: (718)990-1677.

ADMISSION STANDARDS. Selective. Usual minimum average: 3.0 (A = 4).

FINANCIAL AID. Annual awards from institutional funds: 34 doctoral fellowships, twenty-seven graduate assistantships, Federal W/S, loans. Approved for VA benefits. Apply by May 1 to Dean of Graduate Division of College for fellowships, assistantships; to Financial Aid Office for all other programs. Phone: (718)990-6403; fax: (718)969-4773. Use FAFSA. About 30% of students receive aid other than loans from College and outside sources. No aid for part-time students.

DEGREE REQUIREMENTS. For Pharm.D.: 66 semester hours minimum; comprehensive oral/written exam; thesis. For M.S.: 30–33 semester hours minimum; comprehensive oral/written exam; thesis. For Ph.D.: 36 semester hours beyond the master's, exclusive of dissertation research; dissertation; comprehensive written/oral exam.

FIELDS OF STUDY.
Clinical Pharmacy.
Cosmetic Science.
Drug Information Specialist.
Industrial Pharmacy.
Medical Technology.
Medicinal Chemistry.
Pharmacology.
Pharmacotherapeutics.
Pharmacy Administration.
Toxicology.

School of Law

Located at Jamaica (Queens) campus (11439). Semester system. Law library: 426,000 volumes, 53 PC workstations. Library has LEXIS, NEXIS, WESTLAW, DIALOG.
Annual tuition: $20,000 (day), $15,000 (evening). No on-campus housing available. Total average annual additional expense: $8000.
Enrollment: first-year class, day 270, evening 107; total full- and part-time 1210 (men 64%, women 36%). Faculty: full-time 56, part-time 13. Degrees conferred: J.D., J.D.-M.A. (Government and Politics).

ADMISSION REQUIREMENTS. LSDAS Law School report, bachelor's degree, transcripts, LSAT required in support of application. Accepts transfer applicants. Graduates of unaccredited institutions not considered. Apply to Director of Admissions by March 1 (Fall), October 1 (Spring). Application fee $50. Phone: (718)990-6611.

ADMISSION STANDARDS. Selective. Accepts about 30–35% of total annual applicants.

FINANCIAL AID. Scholarships, assistantships, Federal W/S, loans. Apply to University's Financial Aid Office by April 1. Use FAFSA and institutional financial aid form. Aid available for part-time students.

DEGREE REQUIREMENTS. For J.D.: 84 semester hours minimum, at least 30 in residence.

ST. JOSEPH COLLEGE
West Hartford, Connecticut 06117-2700
http://www.sjc.edu

Founded 1932. Located 3 miles W of Hartford. Coed on graduate level. Private control. Roman Catholic affiliation. Semester system. Special facilities: Athletic Center, Gengras Center for Exceptional Children, Marriage and Family Center, School for Young Children. Library: 120,000 volumes, 6100 microforms, 640 current periodicals.

Annual tuition: per credit $360. On-campus housing for graduate students available. Annual cost: $4810 (including board). Apply to Director, Residential Life. Phone: (860)232-4571, ext. 214.

Graduate Program

Graduate study since 1959. Enrollment: full-time 101, part-time 607 (men 15%, women 85%). College faculty: full-time 32, part-time 10. Degrees conferred: M.A., M.S., M.A.M.F.T., six year certificate.

ADMISSION REQUIREMENTS. Transcripts, two references, interview, GRE or MAT required in support of application. TOEFL required for international applicants. Accepts transfer applicants. Apply to Graduate Office; no specified closing date. Application fee $25. Phone: (860)232-4571, ext. 227; fax: (860)233-5695.

ADMISSION STANDARDS. Selective. Usual minimum average: 3.0 (A = 4).

FINANCIAL AID. Eighteen assistantships, eighteen internships, loans. Approved for VA benefits. Apply to Director of Financial Aid; no specified closing date. Use FAFSA and institutional FAF. Phone: (860)232 4571.

DEGREE REQUIREMENTS. For M.A.: 30 semester hours minimum; thesis optional, may supply 6 credits; final comprehensive evaluation. For S.Y.C.: 32 credits minimum beyond the master's.

FIELDS OF STUDY.
Child Development and Education. Includes early childhood, elementary, secondary, special education.
Natural Sciences. Includes biological science, chemistry, biochemistry, nutrition, science education.
Nursing. Includes psychiatric/mental health, family health.
Religious Studies. Includes pastoral ministry.
Social Sciences. Includes counseling, marriage and family therapy, human development, gerontology.

ST. JOSEPH'S UNIVERSITY
Philadelphia, Pennsylvania 19131-1376

Founded 1851. Coed. Private control. Roman Catholic. Semester system. Library: 323,000 volumes, 711,000 microforms.

Tuition: per credit $410; computer science and M.B.A. $420. No on-campus housing for graduate and married students. Average annual housing cost: $4500. Apply to Residence Life Office for off-campus housing. Phone: (610)660-1063.

Graduate Program

Enrollment: full-time 120, part-time 2900. Graduate faculty: full-time 50, part-time 80. Degrees conferred: M.S., M.B.A.

ADMISSION REQUIREMENTS. Transcripts, two letters of recommendation required in support of application. GMAT for M.B.A. programs. TOEFL required for international applicants. Accepts transfer applicants. Graduates of unaccredited colleges not considered. Apply to appropriate School at least one month prior to registration. Application fee $30. Phone: (610)660-1289 (Art & Science), (610)660-1690 (Business).

ADMISSION STANDARDS. Selective. Usual minimum average: 3.0 (A = 4).

FINANCIAL AID. Annual awards from institutional funds: nine assistantships. Apply by February 15 to Chairman, Chemistry Department, for four teaching assistantships; to Director, Computer Science Graduate Program, for four teaching assistantships; to Chairman, Criminal Justice, for two research assistantships; to Chairman, Education Department, for two assistantships; to Director of M.B.A. Program, for three assistantships. Use FAFSA. Phone: (215)660-1760. About 5–10% of students receive aid other than loans from University.

DEGREE REQUIREMENTS. For M.S. Biology: 36 credits minimum. For M.S. Chemistry: 31 credits minimum. For M.S. Computer Sciences: 31 credits. For M.S. Criminal Justice: 30 credits. For M.S. Education or Health Education: 36 credits. For M.S. Health Administration: 36 credits. For M.S. Gerontological Services: 36 credits. For M.S. Public Safety: 33 credits minimum. For M.S. Training and Development: 36 credits. For M.B.A.: 33 credits minimum.

FIELDS OF STUDY.
Business Administration. Includes accounting, management, food marketing, finance, health administration, information systems, international business, law and court administration, marketing, and medical management.
Chemistry.
Computer Science.
Criminal Justice.
Education. Includes business, chemistry, health, reading, secondary.
Gerontological Services.
Health Administration.
Health Education. Includes employee assistance, nutritional marketing.
Psychology. Includes biopsychology, health psychology, and social psychology.
Public Safety.
Training and Development.

ST. LAWRENCE UNIVERSITY
Canton, New York 13617-1455

Founded 1856. Located 130 miles N of Syracuse, 80 miles S of Ottawa. Coed. Private control. Library: 440,000 volumes, 462,000 microforms, 3291 current periodicals.

Annual tuition: per credit $430.

Graduate Division

Enrollment: full-time 12, part-time 136. Faculty: full-time 6, part-time 7. Degrees conferred: M.A., M.Ed., C.A.S.

ADMISSION REQUIREMENTS. Transcripts, three letters of recommendation, GRE required in support of application. TOEFL required for international applicants. Interview recommended. Accepts transfer applicants. Graduates of unaccredited institutions not considered. Apply to Chair, Education Department; no specified closing date. Application fee $30. Phone: (315)379-5872.

ADMISSION STANDARDS. Selective. Usual minimum average 2.75 (A = 4).

FINANCIAL AID. Resident hall counseling/assistantships, three teaching fellowships, Federal W/S, loans. Approved for VA benefits. Use FAFSA. Phone: (315)379-5265. Apply to Director of Student Services. No aid for part-time students.

DEGREE REQUIREMENTS. For master's: 33–60 semester hours minimum; 6 transfer hours allowed. For C.A.S.: 30 semester hours minimum beyond master's.

FIELDS OF STUDY.
Counseling and Human Development. M.Ed. or 60-hour program leading to Certificate of Advanced Standing (C.A.S.).
Educational Administration. M.Ed. or 60-hour program leading to Certificate of Advanced Standing (C.A.S.).
General Studies. Thesis/nonthesis option for M.Ed.

SAINT LOUIS UNIVERSITY
St. Louis, Missouri 63103-2097

Founded 1818. Coed. Private control. Roman Catholic affiliation. Semester system. Special facilities: Center for Applied Behavior Science, Center for Irish Law, Institute for Molecular Virology, Seismographic Stations Network, Center for Public Policy, Center for Jewish Law, Center for Medieval and Renaissance Studies, Yalem Computing Center, Reis Biological Station, Doisy Hall of Medical Research, Vatican Film Library. Library: 1,500,000 volumes, 1,100,000 microforms, 12,000 current periodicals.

Tuition: per credit $480. On-campus housing for 400 single students. Average academic year housing costs: $5640 (including board) for single students. Contact the Director of Residence Life for both on- and off-campus housing information. Phone: (314)977-2797.

Graduate School

Graduate study since 1832. Enrollment: full-time 509, part-time 1532 (men 682, women 733). Graduate faculty: full-time 450, part-time 98. Degrees conferred: M.A., M.A. in U.A., M.S., M.S. in Dent., M.S. in Diet., M.S.S. in N.R., M.H.A., M.P.A., M.P.H., M.S.D., M.S.N., M.Pr.Gph., M.Pr.Met., Ed.S., Ed.D., Ph.D., Certificates.

ADMISSION REQUIREMENTS. Transcripts, GRE, three references, autobiographical sketch, goals statement required in support of School's application. GMAT required for Business. TOEFL required for international applicants. Accepts transfer applicants. Apply to Dean of Graduate School at least six weeks prior to registration. Application fee $50. Phone: (314)977-2240; fax: (314)977-3943.

ADMISSION STANDARDS. Relatively open to very competitive. Usual minimum average 3.0 in last 60 credits for master's (A = 4).

FINANCIAL AID. Annual awards from institutional funds: 50 fellowships, 120 teaching assistantships, 100 research assistantships, 60 specialized assistantships, Federal W/S, loans. Approved for VA benefits. Apply preferably by February 1 to Dean of the Graduate School for fellowships, assistantships; to Financial Aid Office for all other programs; no specified closing date. Use FAFSA. Phone: (314)977-2350. About 65% of all students receive aid other than loans from University and outside sources.

DEGREE REQUIREMENTS. For master's: 30 semester hours minimum including 6 hours of thesis for research degree; research tool (foreign language, computer literacy, statistics); final oral exam. For Ed.S.: 30 semester hours minimum beyond master's. For Ed.D.: about 75 hours beyond bachelor's degree; research-methods sequences; preliminary exam; culminatory project. For Ph.D.: about 48–60 hours, plus 12 hours research,

beyond the bachelor's degree, minimum one year in full-time residence, preliminary written and oral exams; research tool; dissertation.

FIELDS OF STUDY.
Aerospace Engineering. M.S. only.
Allied Health Administration. M.A. only.
American Studies.
Anatomy.
Biochemistry. Ph.D. only.
Biology.
Business Administration. GMAT for admission. Includes accounting, economics, international business, management and decision sciences, marketing, personnel and industrial relations.
Cell and Molecular Biology. Ph.D. only.
Chemistry. M.S. only.
Communications. M.A. only.
Communication Disorders. M.A. only.
Community Health. M.P.H. only.
Dietetics. M.S. only.
Economics.
Education. M.A., Ed.S., Ed.D., Ph.D.
English.
French. M.A. only.
Geophysics.
Health Services Research. Ph.D. only.
Historical Theology.
History.
Hospital and Health Care Administration. M.H.A. only.
Mathematics.
Meteorology.
Microbiology. Ph.D. only.
Neurobiology. Ph.D. only.
Nursing.
Orthodontics. M.S.D. only.
Pathology.
Pharmacological and Physiological Sciences.
Philosophy.
Physical Therapy. M.S.
Psychology.
Public Policy Analysis and Administration.
Spanish. M.A. only.
Theology. M.A. only.
Urban Affairs. M.A. in U.A. only.

School of Social Service

Graduate study since 1930. Semester system. Tuition: per hour $445.

Graduate enrollment: full-time 150; part-time 100. Faculty: full-time 18, part-time 10. Degree conferred: M.S.W.

ADMISSION REQUIREMENTS. Transcripts, interview, letters of reference, personal statement required in support of School's application. GRE or MAT strongly recommended. TOEFL required for international applicants. Accepts transfer applicants. Apply to Director of Admission by March 1 (Fall), October 1 (Spring). Application fee $50. Phone: (314)977-2722; fax: (314)977-2931.

ADMISSION STANDARDS. Selective. Usual minimum average: 3.0 (A = 4).

FINANCIAL AID. Annual awards from institutional funds: thirty scholarships, two fellowships, two research assistantships, eighteen internships, Federal W/S, loans. Approved for VA benefits. Apply to Director of Admissions. Use FAFSA. Phone: (314)977-2722. About 50% of students receive aid other than loans from School and other sources.

DEGREE REQUIREMENTS. For M.S.W.: 57 semester hours minimum, including 12 in field work.

School of Law (63108)

Founded 1842. Semester system. Law library: 400,000. Library has LEXIS, NEXIS, WESTLAW, DIALOG. Special facilities: Center for Health Law Studies, Center for International and Comparative Law, Center for Employment Law.

Annual tuition: full-time $17,120, part-time $12,787. On-campus housing available. Total average annual additional expense; $7500.

Enrollment: first-year class full-time 175, part-time 75; total full- and part-time 830 (men 58%, women 42%). Faculty: full-time 44, part-time 25. Degrees conferred: J.D., J.D.-M.H.A., J.D.-M.A. (Urban Affairs), J.D.-M.B.A., J D.-M.S.W.

ADMISSION REQUIREMENTS. LSDAS Law School report, transcripts, LSAT (not later than December), letters of recommendation required in support of application. Interview not required. Accepts transfer applicants. Graduates of unaccredited colleges not considered. Apply to Director of Admissions by March 1. Admits first-year students. Fall only. Application fee $30. Phone: (314)658-2800.

ADMISSION STANDARDS. Selective. Accepts 35–40% of total annual applicants.

FINANCIAL AID. Scholarships, full and partial tuition waivers, fellowships, Federal W/S, loans. Apply to the Financial Aid Office by March 1. Use FAFSA. About 55% of students receive aid other than loans from School.

DEGREE REQUIREMENTS. For J.D.: 88 semester hours minimum. For master's degrees, see Graduate School listing above.

School of Medicine

First facility in medicine appointed 1836.

Present school acquired 1903. Tuition: $25,600; student fees $1080. Limited housing available. Contact Director of Housing for information. Total average figure for all other expenses: $9100.

Enrollment: first-year class 150 (EDP 8), total 578 (men 65%, women 35%). Faculty: full-time 584, part-time 800. Degrees conferred: M.D., M.D.-Ph.D.

ADMISSION REQUIREMENTS. AMCAS report, transcripts, recommendations, MCAT, interview required in support of application. Has EDP; apply between June 15 and August 1. Apply to Committee on Admissions after June 15, before December 15. Admits Fall only. Applicants planning to begin medical studies after only three years of college work considered. Application fee $100. Phone: (314)577-8205; fax: (314)577-8214.

ADMISSION STANDARDS. Very competitive. Accepts 5–8% of total annual applicants. Approximately 32% are state residents.

FINANCIAL AID. Scholarships, loans. Apply by May 1 to Financial Aid Office. Use FAFSA. About 5–10% of students receive aid other than loans from School.

DEGREE REQUIREMENTS. For M.D.: satisfactory completion of four-year program.

FIELDS OF GRADUATE STUDY.
Anatomy.
Biochemistry.
Cell Biology.
Genetics.
Immunology.
Molecular Biology.
Neurosciences.
Pathology.
Pharmacology.
Physiology.

SAINT MARY'S UNIVERSITY
Winona, Minnesota 55987-1399

Founded 1912. Private control. Roman Catholic affiliation. Semester system.

Tuition: per credit $205. No on-campus housing available.

Graduate School

Enrollment: full-time 347, part-time 2088. Faculty: full-time 43, part-time 312. Degree conferred: M.A.

ADMISSION REQUIREMENTS. Official transcripts required in support of School's application. Additional requirements vary by program. TOEFL required for international applicants. Accepts transfer applicants. Graduates of unaccredited institutions not considered. Apply to the Graduate Office at least one month prior to registration. Rolling admissions process. Application fee $20. Phone: (612)874-9877; fax: (612)874-7108.

ADMISSION STANDARDS. Selective for most programs. Usual minimum average: 2.75 (A = 4).

FINANCIAL AID. Limited to loans. Apply to the Financial Aid Office; no specified closing date. Use FAFSA. Phone: (800)635-5987.

DEGREE REQUIREMENTS. For master's: 43–48 semester hours depending on program; thesis/nonthesis option; final oral colloquia presentation for most programs.

FIELDS OF STUDY.
Arts Administration.
Counseling and Psychological Services.
Developmental Disabilities.
Education.
Educational Administration.
Human and Health Services Administration.
Human Development.
Management.
Nurse Anesthesia.
Pastoral Ministries.
Philanthropy and Development.
Telecommunications.

ST. MARY'S UNIVERSITY
San Antonio, Texas 78228-8507

Founded 1852. Coed. Private control. Semester system. Library: 525,000 volumes, 17,000 microforms, 1400 current periodicals, 66 PCs.

Tuition: per credit $349. On-campus housing available for single students only. Average academic year housing costs: $2550 (room only). Contact Housing office for both on- and off-campus housing information. Phone: (210)436-3534.

Graduate School

Graduate study since 1936. Enrollment: full- and part-time 1332. Graduate faculty: full-time 50, part-time 25. Degrees conferred: M.A., M.B.A., M.J.A., M.P.A., M.S., Ph.D.

ADMISSION REQUIREMENTS. Transcripts, two letters of recommendation, GRE/GMAT required in support of School's application. TOEFL required for international applicants. Interview not required. Accepts transfer applicants. Apply to Graduate School by August 1 (Fall), two weeks prior to registration for other semesters. Application fee $15. Phone: (210)436-3101; fax: (210)431-2220.

ADMISSION STANDARDS. Selective. Usual minimum average: 3.0 (A = 4).

FINANCIAL AID. Assistantships, Federal W/S, loans. Approved for VA benefits. Apply by March 1 to Dean of the Graduate School for assistantships; to Financial Aid Office for all other programs. Use FAFSA. About 5–10% of students receive aid other than loans from university.

DEGREE REQUIREMENTS. For master's: 30–36 semester hours minimum, at least 24 in residence, thesis; 30–36 hours, nonthesis option for all departments; reading knowledge of 1 foreign language for some departments; final oral/written exam. For Ph.D.: 78 semester hours beyond master's; reading knowledge of one foreign language; comprehensive exam; dissertation; final oral exam.

FIELDS OF STUDY.
Business Administration. GMAT for admission.
Catholic School Leadership.
Clinical Psychology.
Communication Studies.
Computer Information Systems.
Computer Science.
Economics.
Educational Leadership.
Electrical Engineering.
Engineering Systems Management.
English Literature and Language.
History.
Industrial Engineering.
International Relations.
Justice Administration.
Mental Health and Marriage and Family Therapy. 48 credit master's program.
Pastoral/Leadership Administration.
Political Science.
Psychology. 42 credit program.
Public Administration.
Reading.
Theology.

School of Law (78228-8601)

Established 1927. Semester system. Library: 270,000 volumes. Library has LEXIS, NEXIS, WESTLAW, DIALOG. Special facilities: Institute on World Legal Problems, Center for International Legal Studies.

Tuition: per semester hour $500. Limited on-campus housing.

Enrollment: first-year class 260; total 763 (men 54%, women 46%). Faculty: full-time 31, part-time 43. Degrees conferred: J.D., J.D.-M.B.A., J.D.-M.P.A., J.D.- I.R., J.D.-T.H., J.D.- Engineering.

ADMISSION REQUIREMENTS. LSDAS Law School report, bachelor's degree, transcripts, LSAT, recommendations required in support of application. Graduates of unaccredited colleges not

considered. Apply to Chairperson, Faculty Admissions Committee by March 1. Application fee $45. Phone: (210)436-3523.

ADMISSION STANDARDS. Selective. Admits about 30–35% of total annual applications.

FINANCIAL AID. Scholarships, assistantships, Federal W/S, loans. Apply to Director of Financial Aid by April 1. Use FAFSA. About 70% of students receive some aid from School.

DEGREE REQUIREMENTS. For J.D.: satisfactory completion of three-year program; 90 credit hour program.

ST. MICHAEL'S COLLEGE

Colchester, Vermont 05439
http://smcvax.smcvt.edu/www/smc-cwis

Founded 1903. Located near Burlington. Private control. Roman Catholic affiliation. Semester system. Library: 176,000 volumes, 78,000 microforms, 50 PCs.

Tuition: per credit $260. Limited on-campus housing available for single students only. Average academic year housing costs: $3950 (room only). Contact assistant Dean of Students for both on- and off-campus housing information. Phone: (802)654-2566. Day care facilities available

Graduate School

Graduate study since 1940. Enrollment: full-time 142, part-time 741. Faculty: full-time 9, part-time 137. Degrees conferred: M.A., M.Ed., M.S.A.

ADMISSION REQUIREMENTS. Transcripts, letters of recommendation, GRE required in support of School's application. TOEFL required for international applicants. Interview recommended for some programs. Accepts transfer applicants. Apply to Dean at least one month prior to registration. Application fee $25. Phone: (802)654-2100; fax: (802)654-2664.

ADMISSION STANDARDS. Selective. Usual minimum average: 2.8 (A = 4).

FINANCIAL AID. Three assistantships, Vermont loans and scholarships, Federal W/S, loans. Apply to Director of Financial Aid; no specified closing date. Use FAFSA and institutional FAF. Phone: (802)654-3243; fax: (802)654-2591.

DEGREE REQUIREMENTS. For master's: 36–42 semester hours.

FIELDS OF STUDY.
Administration. M.S.A. only.
Clinical Psychology. Sixty semester hours. M.A.
Education.
Teaching English as a Second Language.
Theology and Pastoral Ministry.

THE COLLEGE OF SAINT ROSE

Albany, New York 12203-1419

Founded 1920. Coed. Private control. Semester system. Library: 195,000 volumes, 165,000 microforms, 1000 current periodical, 10 PCs.

Tuition: per credit $321. Limited housing for graduate students. Average monthly housing costs: $3550–$5550. Contact the Director of Residence Life for both on- and off-campus housing information. Phone: (518)454-5295.

Graduate School

Graduate study since 1949. Enrollment: full-time 144; part-time 1132. Graduate faculty: full-time 68, part-time 22. Degrees conferred: M.A., M.S., M.S.Ed., M.B.A.

ADMISSION REQUIREMENTS. Transcripts, two letters of recommendation, GMAT required for Business Administration and Accounting. TOEFL required for international applicants. Accepts transfer applicants. Apply to Dean of Graduate School at least three months prior to registration. Rolling admissions process. Application fee $25. Phone: (518)454-5136; fax: (518)454-2012.

ADMISSION STANDARDS. Selective. Usual minimum average: 2.75 (A = 4).

FINANCIAL AID. Five assistantships, thirty internships, Federal W/S, loans. Approved for VA benefits. Apply by March 1 to appropriate Department for internships, scholarships, assistantships; to Financial Aid Office for all other programs. Use FAFSA and institutional FAF. Phone: (518)454-5168. Some aid for part-time students.

DEGREE REQUIREMENTS. For master's: 30 semester hours minimum, at least 24 in residence; thesis/nonthesis option; written comprehensive exam for some departments.

FIELDS OF STUDY.
Accounting. M.S.
Art Education.
Business Administration.
Communication Disorders.
Counseling.
Education. Includes early childhood, elementary, mental retardation, learning disabilities, emotionally handicapped, secondary, educational psychology, educational administration and supervision.
English.
History and Political Science.
Liberal Studies.
Music Education.
Reading.
School Psychology.

COLLEGE OF ST. SCHOLASTICA
Duluth, Minnesota 55811-4199

Founded 1912. Coed. Private. Church related. Quarter system. Library: 137,000 volumes, 14,500 microforms, 31 PCs.

Tuition: per credit $292. On-campus housing available for single students. Average academic year housing costs: $6100. Contact the Housing Office for both on- and off-campus housing information. Phone: (218)723-6483. Day care facilities available.

Graduate Studies

Graduate study since 1972. Enrollment: full-time 113, part-time 231. Faculty: full-time 19, part-time 22. Degrees conferred: M.A., M.Ed.

ADMISSION REQUIREMENTS. Transcripts, GRE (Nursing, Exercise Physiology program only), two letters of recommendations required in support of application. TOEFL required for international applicants. Accepts transfer applicants. Apply to Graduate Office by March 1 for Physical Therapy, January 31 for Occupational Therapy; apply to all other programs at least one month prior to each quarter. Application fee $50. Phone: (800)447-5444, (218)723-6285; fax: (218)723-6796.

ADMISSION STANDARDS. Selective. Usual minimum average: 3.0 for last two years (A = 4). TOEFL minimum score 575.

FINANCIAL AID. Limited to loans. Approved for VA benefits. Apply to Director of Financial Aid; no specified closing date. Use FAFSA. Phone: (218)723-6397; fax: (218)723-6290.

DEGREE REQUIREMENTS. For M.Ed.: 56 quarter credits. For M.A. Nursing: 52 quarter credits. For M.A. Management: 50 quarter credits. For M.A. Physical Therapy: 77 quarter credits. For M.A. Occupational Therapy: 63 quarter credits. For M.A. Exercise Physiology: 49 quarter credits.

FIELDS OF STUDY.
Education.
Educational Media.
Exercise Physiology.
Health Information Management.
Management.
Nursing.
Occupational Therapy.
Physical Therapy.

UNIVERSITY OF ST. THOMAS
Houston, Texas 77006-4694

Founded 1885. Coed. Private control. Roman Catholic affiliation. Semester system. Library: 189,000 volumes, 428,000 microforms, 899 current periodicals.

Tuition: per credit $362. On-campus housing for single students only. Average academic year housing costs: $3870 (including board). Contact Director of Residence Life for both on- and off-campus housing information. Phone: (713)525-3836.

Graduate Study

Enrollment: full-time 252, part-time 631. Graduate faculty: full-time 106, part-time 38. Degrees conferred: M.A., M.B.A., M.Ed., M.Div., M.A.Th., Ph.D.

ADMISSION REQUIREMENTS. Official transcripts, three letters of recommendation, GMAT (for Business), essay required in support of application. TOEFL required for international applicants. Accepts transfer applicants. Graduates of unaccredited colleges not considered. Apply to Director of Admissions at least two months prior to entrance. Rolling admissions process. Application $25. Phone: (713)525-3505; fax: (713)525-2110.

ADMISSION STANDARDS. Selective. Usual minimum average: 2.75 (A = 4).

FINANCIAL AID. Fellowships, assistantships, tuition waivers, Federal W/S, loans. Apply to the appropriate School for fellowships, assistantships; to the Office of Financial Aid for all other programs. No specified closing dates. Use FAFSA.

DEGREE REQUIREMENTS. For most master's: 32–36 credits minimum final written/oral exam; no thesis or language requirement. For M.B.A.: 36–42 semester credits. For M.Div.: at least two years in residence; thesis; reading knowledge of either Hebrew, Latin, Greek. For Ph.D.: 60 credits minimum beyond the bachelor's degree; qualifying exam; reading knowledge of two foreign languages; dissertation; final oral exam.

FIELDS OF STUDY.
Business Administration.
Education.

Liberal Arts.
Philosophy.
Theology.

UNIVERSITY OF ST. THOMAS
St. Paul, Minnesota 55105-1089

Founded 1885. Coed on the graduate level. Private control. Roman Catholic affiliation. Semester system. Library: 357,935 volumes, 394,371 microforms.

Tuition: per credit $325. No on-campus housing available. Contact Director of Residence Life for both on- and off-campus housing information. Phone: (612)647-5625.

Graduate Study

Graduate study since 1950. Enrollment: full-time 240, part-time 4358. Graduate faculty: full-time 59, part-time 159. Degrees conferred: M.A., M.B.A., M.I.M., M.M., M.B.C., M.M.S.E., M.S.D.D., M.S.W., Ed.S.

ADMISSION REQUIREMENTS. Official transcripts, three letters of recommendation, GMAT (for Business), essay required in support of application. TOEFL required for international applicants. Accepts transfer applicants. Graduates of unaccredited colleges not considered. Apply to Director of Admissions at least two months prior to entrance. Rolling admissions process. Application $35. Phone: (612)647-5000.

ADMISSION STANDARDS. Selective. Usual minimum average: 2.75 (M.A.), 3.0 (M.B.A.), 3.25 (Ed.S.)

FINANCIAL AID. Limited to loans. Apply to the Office of Financial Aid; no specified closing dates. Phone: (612)647-5232.

DEGREE REQUIREMENTS. For most master's: 32–36 credits minimum final written/oral exam; no thesis or language requirement. For M.B.A., M.I.M.: 36–42 semester credits. For Ed.S.: 33 credits beyond the master's; final written/oral exams; final project.

FIELDS OF STUDY.

GRADUATE SCHOOL OF ARTS:
English. M.A.
Kodaly. M.A.
Orff-Schulwerk. M.A.

GRADUATE SCHOOL OF BUSINESS:
Business Administration. M.B.A.
Business Communication. M.B.C.
Finance. M.B.A.
Government Contracts. M.B.A.
Health Care. M.B.A.
Information Systems. M.B.A.
Insurance. M.B.A.
International Management. M.I.M.
Management. M.B.A.
Marketing. M.B.A.
Nonprofit Human Resources. M.B.A.
Public Management. M.B.A.
Sport Management. M.B.A.
Venture Management. M.B.A.

GRADUATE SCHOOL OF EDUCATION, PROFESSIONAL PSYCHOLOGY, SOCIAL WORK:
Curriculum and Instruction. M.A.
Educational Leadership and Administration. M.A., Ed.S.
Gifted, Creative, Talented Education. M.A.

Learning and Human Development Technology. M.A.
Professional Psychology. M.A.
Social Work. M.S.W. Offered jointly with the College of St. Catherine.
Special Education. M.A.
Teaching. M.A., M.A.T.

GRADUATE SCHOOL OF TECHNOLOGY:
Manufacturing System Engineering. M.M.S.E.
Software Design and Development. M.S.D.D.

ST. XAVIER UNIVERSITY
Chicago, Illinois 60655-3105

Founded 1847. Coed. Roman Catholic. Semester system. Library: 153,000, 116,000 microforms.

Annual tuition: $7344; per credit $408. On-campus housing for 285 graduate students. Average academic year housing costs: $4800. Contact the Director of Campus Life for both on- and off-campus housing information. Phone: (312)298-3499.

Graduate Studies

Enrollment: full- and part-time 2050. College faculty teaching graduate students: full-time 77, part-time 6. Degrees conferred: M.A., M.S., M.B.A.

ADMISSION REQUIREMENTS. Transcripts, three letters of recommendation, GRE/GMAT/MAT in support of application. TOEFL required for international applicants. Accepts transfer applicants. Apply to Director of Admissions; no specified closing date. Application fee $35. Phone: (312)298-3050; fax: (312)779-9061; E-mail: admission@sxu.edu.

ADMISSION STANDARDS. Selective. Usual minimum average: 3.0 (A = 4).

FINANCIAL AID. Institutional and need-based scholarships available, Federal W/S, loans. Approved for VA benefits. Apply by July 15 to Director of Financial Aid. Phone: (312)298-7071; fax: (312)779-9061.

DEGREE REQUIREMENTS. For master's: 30 semester hours minimum; research project.

FIELDS OF STUDY.
Business. Includes specialization options in finance, financial trading and practice, health care, generalist/administration, management, management information systems, marketing, or international business.
Counseling Psychology. Includes developmental disabilities, geriatric services, individual and family services.
Education. Includes administration, curriculum and instruction, reading, general studies, learning disabilities.
English. M.S.
Nursing. Includes medical surgical, community health (M.S.-M.B.A.), psychiatric, mental health.
Speech-Language Pathology.

SALEM STATE COLLEGE
Salem, Massachusetts 01970-5353

Founded 1854. Located 20 miles NE of Boston. Coed. State control. Semester system. Library: 230,500 volumes, 100,000 microforms.

Tuition: per credit resident $140, nonresident $230. No on-campus housing available.

Graduate School

Enrollment: full-time 155, part-time 1210 (men 342, women 1023). Graduate faculty: full-time 13, part-time 77. Degrees conferred: M.A., M.A.T., M.B.A., M.Ed., M.S., M.S.N., M.S.W., M.S.N.-M.B.A.

ADMISSION REQUIREMENTS. Transcripts, three letters of reference, GRE/GMAT/MAT required in support of School's application. TOEFL required for international applicants. Interview not required. Accepts transfer applicants. Graduates of unaccredited institutions not considered. Apply to Dean of Graduate School by November 1 (Spring), July 1 (Fall) for M.B.A.; by January 1 for M.S.W.; all others on rolling admissions. Application fee $25. Phone: (508)741-6323.

ADMISSION STANDARDS. Selective. Usual minimum average: 2.5 (A = 4) and 2.7 in major field of study.

FINANCIAL AID. Limited to twenty graduate assistantships, Federal W/S, loans. Approved for VA benefits. Apply by May 1 to the Dean of Graduate School for assistantships; to Financial Aid Office for all other programs. Use FAFSA. Phone: (508)741-6112.

DEGREE REQUIREMENTS. For M.Ed., M.A.T.: 36–39 semester hours minimum, at least 27 in residence; final written/oral exam. For M.A.: 33 semester hours; one foreign language or computer statistics; final written exam. For M.S. in Geo Information, Science: 40 semester hours. For M.S. in Math: 30 semester hours. For M.S.N.: 39 semester hours. For M.B.A.: 54 semester hours; computer proficiency. For M.S.W.: 60 semester hours.

FIELDS OF STUDY.
Biology.
Business Administration.
Chemistry.
Counseling and Psychological Services.
Early Childhood Education.
Elementary Education.
English.
English as a Second Language.
Geo Information Science.
History.
Library and Media Studies.
Mathematics.
Middle School Education.
Nursing.
Reading.
School Administration.
School Counseling.
Secondary Education.
Social Work.
Special Education.

SALISBURY STATE UNIVERSITY
Salisbury, Maryland 21801-6837
http://www.ssu.umd.edu

Founded 1925. Located 125 miles SE of Baltimore. Coed. State control. Semester system. Special facilities: Center for Technology in Education, Research Center for Delmarva History and Culture, Small Business Development Center. Library: 228,000 volumes, 587,000 microforms, 1650 current periodicals, 32 PCs.

Tuition: per credit resident $140, nonresident $210. No on- or off-campus housing for graduate students.

Graduate Program

Graduate study since 1962. Enrollment: full-time 141, part-time 533. Graduate faculty: full-time 125, part-time 17. Degrees conferred: M.Ed., M.A., M.B.A., M.S.

ADMISSION REQUIREMENTS. Official transcripts, GRE/GMAT/MAT/NTE required in support of application. TOEFL required for international applicants. Accepts transfer applicants. Graduates of unaccredited institutions not considered. Apply by August 1 (Fall), January 1 (Spring) to the Graduate Admissions Office. Application fee $30. Phone: (410)543-6161; fax: (410)543-6138.

ADMISSION STANDARDS. Varies by department.

FINANCIAL AID. Limited to graduate assistantships, loans. Approved for VA benefits. Apply to appropriate department chair for assistantships; to the Financial Aid Office for all other programs. Use FAFSA. Phone: (410)543-6165; fax: (410)543-6168.

DEGREE REQUIREMENTS. For M.Ed.: 33 semester hours. For M.S.-Nursing: 39 semester hours. For M.A.-English: 33 credits minimum. For M.B.A.: 30 semester hours.

FIELDS OF STUDY.
Business Administration. M.B.A.
Early Childhood Education. M.Ed.
Elementary Education. M.Ed.
English. M.A.
Middle/Secondary Education. Includes English, history, mathematics, music, science. M.Ed.
Nursing. Includes family nurse practitioner.
Post-Secondary Education. M.Ed.
Psychology. M.A.
Reading. M.Ed.
Teaching. M.A.

SAMFORD UNIVERSITY
Birmingham, Alabama 35229-0002
http://www.samford.edu/

Founded 1941. Coed. Private control. Baptist affiliation. Semester system. Library: 508,000 volumes, 248,000 microforms, 4600 current periodicals, 176 PCs.

Tuition: per credit Business, Divinity, Education, Music $300. Annual cost: Pharmacy $12,000. No on-campus housing available. Monthly housing costs: $300–$500. Contact Director, Residence Life for both on- and off-campus housing information. Phone: (205)870-2932.

School of Graduate Studies

Graduate study since 1965. Enrollment: full-time 1214, part-time 314. Faculty: full-time 107, part-time 51. Degrees conferred: M.S. in Ed., M.S. in Environ. Mgt., M.S.N., M.B.A., M.S., M.Mus., M.Mus.Ed., Ed.S., M.Div., D. Min., M.Mus., Pharm.D.

ADMISSION REQUIREMENTS. Transcripts, photograph required in support of School's application. GRE/NTE required for Education, Liberal Arts majors; GMAT for Business majors; MAT for Music. TOEFL required for international applicants. Interview desirable. Accepts transfer applicants. Graduates of unaccredited institutions not considered. Apply to Graduate Dean at least one month prior to entrance. Application fee $25. Phone: (205)970-2565.

ADMISSION STANDARDS. Selective. Usual minimum average: 2.5 (A = 4).

FINANCIAL AID. Annual awards from institutional funds: ten scholarships, Federal W/S, loans. Approved for VA benefits. Apply to the Financial Aid Office; no specified closing date. Use FAFSA and institutional FAF. Phone: (205)870-2905; fax: (205)870-2171. About 10% of students receive aid other than loans from University and outside sources.

DEGREE REQUIREMENTS. For M.A.: 33 semester hours minimum including thesis, at least 24 in residence; reading knowledge of one foreign language; comprehensive exam. For M.S. in Ed., M.Mus.: 32–33 hours minimum, at least 24 in residence; no thesis or language requirement; comprehensive exam. For M.B.A.: 36–45 hours, depending upon previous preparation, at least 24 in residence. For M.Mus.Ed.: essentially the same as for M.S. in Ed., except 37 semester hours required. Final written/oral exams for all master's. For Ed.S.: 30 semester hours beyond the master's. For Pharm.D.: 65 credits, plus 139 professional credits.

FIELDS OF STUDY.
Accounting.
Business Administration.
Church Music.
Comparative Law.
Early Childhood Education.
Educational Administration.
Elementary Education.
Environmental Management.
Law.
Music.
Music Education.
Nursing.
Pastoral Care.
Pharmacy.
Principalship and Supervision.
Religion.
Secondary Education. Includes English, history, mathematics, biology.
Theological Studies.

Cumberland School of Law

Established 1847. School acquired by Samford University in 1961. Semester system. Library: 200,000 volumes. Library has LEGALTRAC, LEXIS, NEXIS, WESTLAW, OCLC; 23 personal computer workstations.

Annual tuition: $16,480 (flat rate). Limited on-campus housing available.

Enrollment: first-year class 245, full-time 635 (men 62%, women 38%). Faculty: full-time 34, part-time 29. Degrees conferred: J.D., J.D.-M.A.E., J.D.-M.B.A., J.D.-M.P.M., J.D.-M.Div., J.D.-M.S.L. (Environmental Management), M.C.L. (for International Law School graduates).

ADMISSION REQUIREMENTS. LSDAS Law School report, bachelor's degree, transcripts, three references, LSAT degree required in support of application. Interview recommended. Accepts transfer applicants. Graduates of unaccredited colleges usually not considered. Apply to Admission Office after October 1, before May 1 (priority deadline February 28.). Admits Fall only. Application fee $40. Phone: (205)870-2702, (800)888-7213.

ADMISSION STANDARDS. Selective. Accepts 30–35% of total annual applicants.

FINANCIAL AID. Scholarships, Federal W/S, loans. Apply to University's Director of Financial Aid by March 1. Use FAFSA.

DEGREE REQUIREMENTS. For J.D.: 90 semester hours program. For master's degrees, see Graduate School listing above.
Note: School has Summer program in Germany, England, and British Columbia.

SAM HOUSTON STATE UNIVERSITY
Huntsville, Texas 77341-2448

Founded 1879. Located 70 miles N of Houston. Coed. State control. Semester system. Special facilities: Sam Houston Memorial Museum, Texas Regional Institute for Environmental Studies. Library: 775,200 volumes, 539,000 microforms, 3000 current periodicals.

Annual tuition: full-time resident $768, nonresident $5904; part-time per semester, resident $120, nonresident $246. On-campus housing for 102 married students, unlimited for single students. Average academic year housing costs: $3100 (including board) for single students; $2900 for married students. Contact Director of Housing for both on- and off-campus housing information. Phone: (409)294-1812.

Graduate Studies

Graduate study since 1938. Enrollment: full-time 373, part-time 926. College faculty teaching graduate students: full- and part-time 239. Degrees conferred: M.A., M.B.A., M.Ed., M.S., M.F.A., M.L.S., Ph.D.

ADMISSION REQUIREMENTS. Two official transcripts, GRE required in support of application. TOEFL required for international applicants. Accepts transfer applicants. Graduates of unaccredited institutions not considered. Apply to Graduate Office at least four weeks prior to registration. Rolling admissions process. Application fee $15. Phone: (409)294-1401.

ADMISSION STANDARDS. Selective. Usual minimum average: 2.5 (A = 4).

FINANCIAL AID. Annual awards from institutional funds: scholarships, teaching fellowships, research assistantships, internships, Federal W/S, loans. Approved for VA benefits. Apply well in advance of registration to the Graduate Office for assistantships, fellowships; to the Financial Aid Office for all other programs. Use FAFSA. About 10% of students receive aid from College and outside sources.

DEGREE REQUIREMENTS. For M.A., M.L.S.: 30 semester hours minimum including thesis, at least 24 in residence; candidacy; comprehensive exam. For M.Ed., M.S., M.B.A.: 36 semester hours minimum, at least 30 in residence; candidacy; thesis optional for six credits; comprehensive oral/written exam. For Ph.D.: 90 semester hours beyond the bachelor's, at least 30 in residence; two semesters for supervised teaching; written/oral exam; dissertation.

FIELDS OF STUDY.

COLLEGE OF ARTS AND SCIENCES:
Applied Music and Literature. M.M.
Biology. M.A., M.Ed., M.S.
Ceramic. M.A., M.F.A
Chemistry. M.Ed., M.S.
Computing Science. M.Ed., M.S.
Conducting. M.M.
Dance. M.F.A.
Drawing. M.A., M.F.A.
English. M.A., M.Ed.
History. M.A.
Jewelry. M.A.
Kodaly Pedagogy. M.M.
Mathematics. M.A., M.Ed., M.S.
Music Education. M.Ed.
Painting. M.A., M.F.A.
Physics. M.S.
Political Science. M.A.
Printmaking. M.A., M.F.A.

Sociology. M.A.
Theory and Composition. M.M.

COLLEGE OF BUSINESS ADMINISTRATION:
Business Administration. M.B.A.

COLLEGE OF CRIMINAL JUSTICE:
Criminal Justice. M.A., M.S., Ph.D.

COLLEGE OF EDUCATION AND APPLIED SCIENCE:
Agricultural Education. M.Ed.
Agriculture Business. M.S.
Clinical Psychology. M.A.
Counseling. M.A., M.Ed.
Curriculum and Instruction. M.Ed.
Early Childhood Education. M.Ed.
Educational Administration. M.Ed.
Elementary Education. M.Ed.
Health Education. M.Ed.
Industrial Education. M.A., M.Ed.
Industrial Technology. M.A.
Kinesiology. M.A.
Library Science. M.L.S.
Reading. M.Ed.
School Psychology. M.A.
Secondary Education. M.A., M.Ed.
Special Education. M.Ed.
Supervision. M.Ed.

SAN DIEGO STATE UNIVERSITY

San Diego, California 92182
http://www.sdsu.edu

Founded 1897. Coed. State control. Semester system. Special facilities: Center on Aging, Lupinski Institute for Judaic Studies, Production Center for Documentary and Drama, Institute for International Security and Conflict Resolution, Mt. Laguna Observatory, Center for Energy Studies, Molecular Biology Institute, Institute for Public Health. Library: 1,095,000 volumes, 3,554,000 microforms, 5900 current periodicals, 45 PCs in all libraries.

Annual tuition/fees: full-time, resident $1902, nonresident $1128 plus $246 per unit. On-campus housing for 2077 single students; none for married students. Average academic year housing costs: $5172 (including board). Contact the Director of Housing and Residential Life for both on- and off-campus housing information. Phone: (619)594-5742. Day care facilities available.

Graduate Division and Research

Enrollment: full-time 1872, part-time 3476. Faculty: full- and part-time over 1200. Degrees conferred: M.A., M.S., M.B.A., M.C.P., M.F.A., M.M., M.P.A., M.P.H., M.S.W., Ph.D.

ADMISSION REQUIREMENTS. Two transcripts, GRE required in support of application. TOEFL required for international applicants. GRE Subject Test, GMAT, interview required by some departments. Accepts transfer applicants. Graduates of unaccredited colleges not considered. Apply to Admissions Office of the University by July 1 (Fall), December 1 (Spring). Rolling admissions process. Application fee $55. Phone: (619)594-3761; fax: (619)594-4902.

ADMISSION STANDARDS. Selective. Usual minimum average: 2.75 (A = 4).

FINANCIAL AID. Teaching assistantships, graduate assistantships, Federal W/S, loans. Apply by February 15 to appropriate

department chairman for assistantships; to Financial Aid Office for all other programs. Use FAFSA. Phone: (619)594-6323. About 20% of students receive aid other than loans from University and other sources. Aid available for part-time students.

DEGREE REQUIREMENTS. For M.A., M.S., M.M.: 30 units minimum, at least 21 in residence; thesis/comprehensive exam; reading knowledge of one foreign language for some majors. For M.S. (Counseling): 60 units minimum, at least 30 in residence; comprehensive exam. For M.C.P.: 57 units minimum, at least 30 in residence. For M.B.A.: 30–60 units, at least 21 in residence. For M.F.A.: 60 units, at least 30 in residence. For M.P.A.: 36 units, at least 21 in residence. For M.S.W.: 56 units, at least 28 in residence. For M.P.H.: 48–55 units, depending on concentration, at least 39 in residence. For Ph.D. (Biology, Chemistry, Clinical Psychology, Engineering, Public Health): at least two years in full-time residence, one year on the campus of the University of California at San Diego and one year at San Diego State University; preliminary written exam; dissertation; final oral exam. For Ph.D. (Ecology): at least two years in full-time residence, one year at University of California at Davis and one year at San Diego State University; qualifying exam; dissertation; final oral exam. For Ph.D. (Education): 48 semester units of residency, 24 at Claremont Graduate School and 24 at San Diego State University; qualifying exam; dissertation; final oral exam. For Ph.D. (Geography): at least two years in full-time residence, one year at University of California Santa Barbara and one year at San Diego State University; qualifying exam; dissertation; final oral exam.

FIELDS OF STUDY.
Accountancy.
Anthropology. Thesis, one language, final oral exam for M.A.
Applied Mathematics.
Art. Studio art; thesis or creative project for M.A., M.F.A.
Art History. Thesis, final oral exam.
Asian Studies. Interdepartmental.
Astronomy.
Biology. GRE Subject for admission. Thesis, final oral exam for M.A., M.S.; one language for M.A.; joint doctoral program with University of California at San Diego.
Business Administration. GMAT for admission; thesis or comprehensive exam for M.S., M.B.A.
Chemistry. Thesis, final oral exam for M.S.; joint doctoral program with University of California at San Diego.
City Planning.
Communicative Disorders.
Computer Science.
Counseling. M.S. Full-time, Fall admission only. Includes marriage, family and child counseling; school counseling; school psychology.
Drama. Thesis for M.A., M.F.A.
Ecology. Joint doctoral program with University of California at Davis.
Economics.
Education. Includes elementary, secondary, educational technology, special education, administration and supervision, educational research, counseling, reading, multicultural; joint doctoral program with Claremont Graduate School.
Engineering. Includes aerospace, civil, electrical, mechanical; joint doctoral program with University of California at San Diego.
English. One language. M.F.A. in creative writing.
French.
Geography. Joint doctoral program with University of California at Santa Barbara.
Geology. GRE Subject for admission.
History. One language for M.A.
Home Economics.
Latin American Studies. Interdepartmental.
Liberal Arts. Interdepartmental.
Linguistics.

Mass Communication. Interdepartmental.
Mathematics.
Microbiology.
Music. Public recital or thesis for M.A., M.M.
Nursing.
Nutritional Science.
Philosophy.
Physical Education.
Physics. One language for M.A.
Political Science.
Psychology. GRE Subject for admission; thesis, final exam for M.A., M.S.; joint doctoral program in clinical psychology with University of California at San Diego.
Public Administration. M.P.A.
Public Health. Joint doctoral program with the University of California at San Diego.
Radiological Health Physics. Thesis.
Rehabilitation Counseling. Fall admission only.
Social Work. Admits Fall only; apply to Director of School of Social Work between November 1 and April 15; interview required for admission.
Sociology.
Spanish.
Speech Communication.
Statistics.
Telecommunication.

UNIVERSITY OF SAN DIEGO
San Diego, California 92110-2492

Founded 1949. Private control. Roman Catholic. Semester system. Special facilities: Children's Advocacy Institute, Patient Advocacy Clinic, Public Interest Law Center. Library: 825,000 volumes, 1,035,000 microforms, 7600 current periodicals.

Tuition: per credit master's program $505, per credit doctoral programs $525. On-campus for both single and married graduate students. Average academic year housing costs: $6590 (including board) for single students; $6900 for married students. Contact Director of Graduate Housing for both on- and off-campus housing information. Phone: (619)260-4622.

School of Graduate and Continuing Education

Enrollment: full-time 553, part-time 745. Graduate faculty: full-time 121, part-time 25. Degrees conferred: M.A., M.F.A., M.S. (Tax), M.A.T., M.Ed., M.B.A., M.I.B., M.S.N., D.N.Sci., Ed.D.

ADMISSION REQUIREMENTS. Two official transcripts, GRE/MAT/GMAT, three letters of recommendation required in support of School's application. TOEFL and financial information form required for international applicants. Accepts transfer applicants. Graduates of unaccredited colleges not considered. Apply to the Office of Graduate Admissions; for most master's programs May 1 (Fall), November 15 (Spring), March 15 (Summer), other degree programs have specific deadlines consult Graduate Application for those deadlines. Rolling admissions process. Application fee $35 (master's), $40 (doctoral). Phone: (800)248-4873, (619)260-4524; fax: (619)260-2393.

ADMISSION STANDARDS. Selective. Usual minimum average: 3.0 recommended (A= 4); GMAT score minimum of 525; GRE Verbal, Quantitative and Analytical score minimum of 500; TOEFL score minimum of 600.

FINANCIAL AID. Annual awards from institutional funds: assistantships, traineeships, fellowships, Federal W/S, loans. Approved for VA benefits. Apply by May 1 to the Office of Financial Aid. Use FAFSA. Phone: (800)248-4873, (619)260-4514. About 37% of students receive aid other than loans from University and outside sources. Aid available to part-time students.

DEGREE REQUIREMENTS. For M.A.: 30 units minimum, at least 24 in residence; reading knowledge of one foreign language; thesis included; final written exam. For M.A.T., M.Ed., M.S.N.: same as for M.A., except no language requirement. For M.B.A., M.I.B.: 60 units minimum; computer proficiency. For M.S.(Tax): 36-unit program. For D.N.Sc.: 54 units minimum, at least 1 semester in full-time study; written exam; dissertation; oral defense. For Ed.D.: 60 units minimum beyond master's degree, at least two semesters in residence; qualifying exam; candidacy; dissertation; final oral exam.

FIELDS OF STUDY.
Business Administration.
Counseling.
Curriculum and Instruction.
Dramatic Arts. In conjunction with Old Globe Theatre. M.F.A.
Education. Includes most subject fields.
Educational Leadership. Ed.D.
History.
International Business. M.I.B.
International Relations.
Marine Science. M.S.
Marriage, Family and Child Counseling.
Nursing. M.S.N., D.N.Sc.
Pastoral Care and Counseling.
Practical Theology.
Special Education.

School of Law

Established 1954. Semester system. Law library: 345,000 volumes. Library has LEXIS, WEST LAW, CALI.

Annual tuition: $18,940 (day), $13,300 (evening).

Enrollment: first-year class day 255, evening 80, total 1040 (men 60%, women 40%). Faculty: full-time 55, part-time 65. Degrees conferred: J.D., J.D.-M.A., J.D.-M.B.A., J.D.-M.I.B., J.D.-M.I.R. (International Relations), LL.M. (Taxation, Comparative Law).

ADMISSION REQUIREMENTS. LSDAS Law School report, bachelor's degree, transcripts, LSAT required in support of application. Photograph required after admittance. Interview not required. Accepts transfer applicants. Graduates of unaccredited colleges not considered. Apply to Admissions Office after September 1, before March 1 (priority deadline February 1); evening students May 1. Admits first-year students Fall and Summer only. Application fee $35. Phone: (619)260-4528, (800)248-4873.

ADMISSION STANDARDS. Selective. Accepts 20–25% of total annual applicants.

FINANCIAL AID. Scholarships, fellowships, assistantships, Federal W/S, loans. Apply to Office of Financial Aid by March 2. Use FAFSA. About 9% of students receive aid other than loans from School.

DEGREE REQUIREMENTS. For J.D.: 85 credits minimum, three-year (day), four-year (evening) program, at least 55 in residence. For LL.M.: at least 24 credits minimum beyond the J.D.; one-year of full-time study and research.

Note: Summer study abroad programs in England, France, Ireland, Mexico, Poland, and Russia.

SAN FRANCISCO ART INSTITUTE
San Francisco, California 94133-2299

Founded 1871. Coed. Private control. Library: 25,000 volumes.

Annual tuition: full-time $16,416. Per unit $684. No on-campus housing available. Studio space for graduate students. Contact the Student Services Department for off-campus housing information. Phone: (415)749-4525.

Graduate Program

Enrollment: full-time 137, part-time 4. Faculty: part-time 12. Degree conferred: M.F.A.

ADMISSION REQUIREMENTS. Transcripts, portfolio of original art work, statement of purpose required in support of application. TOEFL, TSE required for international applicants. Accepts transfer applicants, but no credits are transferred. Apply to Graduate Program Committee by February 15 (Fall), November 1 (Spring). Application fee $50. Phone: (415)749-4500; fax: (415)749-4590.

ADMISSION STANDARDS. Very competitive. Admission based primarily on portfolio and statement of purpose. TOEFL score minimum 500.

FINANCIAL AID. Fourteen academic scholarships, ninety-five grants, Federal W/S, loans. Approved for VA benefits. Apply to Director of Financial Aid; recommended deadline April 1. Use FAFSA. Phone: (415)749-4500, (415)749-4590. About 67% of students receive aid other than loans from Institute.

DEGREE REQUIREMENTS. For M.F.A.: 60 semester units; final examination of work and an exhibition. No language or thesis requirements.

FIELDS OF STUDY.
Filmmaking.
New Genres.
Painting.
Photography.
Printmaking.
Sculpture Ceramics.

SAN FRANCISCO CONSERVATORY OF MUSIC
San Francisco, California 94122-4411

Founded 1917. Coed. Private control. Semester system. Library: 33,500 volumes, 4,500 individual recordings and tapes.

Annual tuition: $14,500; per credit $650. No on-campus housing. Contact Admission Office for off-campus housing information.

Graduate Division

Graduate study since 1960. Enrollment: full-time 73, part-time 14 (men 41%, women 59%). Faculty: full-time 11, part-time 3, plus private instructors. Degree conferred: M.M.

ADMISSION REQUIREMENTS. Transcripts, two letters of recommendation, audition required in support of application. TOEFL required for international applicants. Accepts transfer applicants. Graduates of unaccredited institutions not considered. Apply to Director of Student Services by March 1 for most majors. Admits Fall and Spring. Application fee $60. Phone: (415)759-3431; fax: (415)759-3499.

ADMISSION STANDARDS. Musical proficiency more important than undergraduate GPA.

FINANCIAL AID. Seventy scholarships, Federal W/S, loans. Apply to Director of Student Services by March 1; preference given to early applicants. Phone: (415)759-3422. Use FAFSA and institutional FAF. About 65% of students receive aid other than loans from School and outside sources.

DEGREE REQUIREMENTS. For M.M.: 30 semester hours minimum, all in residence; two public recitals.

FIELDS OF STUDY.
Chamber Music.
Classical Guitar.
Composition.
Conducting.
Keyboard Instruments.
Orchestral Instruments.
Piano Accompanying.
Voice.

SAN FRANCISCO STATE UNIVERSITY
San Francisco, California 94132-1722

Founded 1899. Coed. State control. Semester system. Library: 900,000 volumes, 2,000,000 microforms, 4300 current periodicals, 200 PCs in all libraries.

Annual fees/tuition: full-time, resident $1982, nonresident and foreign students $1982 plus $246 per unit; part-time, resident $1316, nonresident $1316 plus $246 per unit pro-rata basis. Limited on-campus housing for graduate students. Average academic year housing cost: $4000–$5000 for single students. Contact Housing Office for both on- and off-campus housing information. Phone: (415)338-1067.

Graduate Division

Enrollment: full-time 2015, part-time 2408. Faculty: full-time 475, part-time 236. Degrees conferred: M.A., M.S., M.B.A., M.F.A., M.M., M.P.A., M.P.T., M.S.W., Ed.D., Ph.D.

ADMISSION REQUIREMENTS. Transcripts required in support of application. Interview, GRE/GMAT/MAT/ NTE required for some departments. TOEFL required for international applicants. Accepts transfer applicants. Graduates of unaccredited institutions not considered. Apply to Office of Graduate Admissions at least one month prior to registration. Application fee $55. Phone: (415)338-2233; fax: (415)338-2514.

ADMISSION STANDARDS. Very selective for several departments, competitive for the others. Usual minimum average: 3.0 (A = 4). TOEFL score required 550.

FINANCIAL AID. Annual awards from institutional funds: 24 Graduate Equity Fellowships, 150 assistantships, Federal W/S, loans. Approved for VA benefits. Apply by March 1 to appropriate department chair for fellowships, assistantships; to Financial Aid Office for all other programs. Use FAFSA. Phone: (415)338-1581; E-mail: http://www.finaid@sfsu.edu. About 60% of students receive aid other than loans from University funds. No aid for part-time or foreign students.

DEGREE REQUIREMENTS. For M.A., M.S., M.M.: 30 units minimum, at least 24 in residence; thesis, creative project/final written/oral exam; usually no language requirement. For M.B.A.: 30–57 units minimum, at least 24 in residence; thesis/research project; no language requirement. For M.P.A.: 35–39 units minimum, at least 24 in residence. For M.P.T.: offered jointly with University of California, San Francisco; 64 units in residence. For M.S.W.: 60 units minimum, at least 30 in residence; field work/thesis; no language requirement. For

M.F.A.: 60 units, at least 30 in residence. For Ed.D., Ph.D.: offered jointly in Special Education with University of California, Berkeley; requirements vary with degree program.

FIELDS OF STUDY.
Accounting.
Anthropology.
Art.
Biology. Includes cell, conservation, molecular, ecology and systematic, marine, microbiology.
Business Administration.
Chemistry. Includes biochemistry.
Chinese.
Cinema.
Cinema Studies.
Classics.
Clinical Science.
Communicative Disorders.
Comparative Literature.
Computer Science.
Counseling.
Creative Arts.
Creative Writing.
Drama.
Economics.
Education. Includes administration, adult education, early childhood, education technology, elementary, secondary, special education, special interest program.
Engineering.
English. Includes composition, creative writing, English as a foreign language, literature, linguistics.
Ethnic Studies.
French.
Geography. Includes environmental planning.
Geoscience.
German.
Gerontology.
Health Science.
History.
Home Economics.
Humanities.
Industrial Arts.
International Relations.
Italian.
Japanese.
Marine Science.
Mathematics.
Museum Studies.
Music.
Nursing.
Philosophy.
Physical Education.
Physical Science.
Physical Therapy.
Physics.
Political Science.
Psychology. Includes clinical, developmental, educational, industrial/organizational, physiological, psychological research, social.
Public Administration.
Radio and Television.
Recreation.
Rehabilitation Counseling.
Russian.
Science. Interdisciplinary.
Social Science. Interdisciplinary.
Social Work.
Spanish.
Special Education.
Special Major.
Speech Communication.
Taxation.
Theater Arts.
Women's Studies.

UNIVERSITY OF SAN FRANCISCO
San Francisco, California 94117-1080

Founded 1855. Coed. Private control. Roman Catholic, Jesuit affiliation. Semester system. Library: 720,000, 1,384,000 microforms, 5400 current periodicals, 60 PCs in all libraries.

Tuition: per unit, master's $590, Ed.D. programs $630; $490 for off-campus Education master's. On-campus housing for 1050 men, 580 women, limited number of married students. Average academic year housing costs: $6300–8198 (including board) for single students. Apply to Director of Residence Life. Phone: (415)666-6824.

Graduate Division

Graduate study since 1867. Enrollment: full-time 1430, part-time 719. Faculty: full-time 72, part-time 105. Degrees conferred: M.A., M.S., M.B.A., M.H.R.O.D., M.N.O., M.R.E., M.P.A., Ed.D.

ADMISSION REQUIREMENTS. Two transcripts, two letters of recommendation required in support of application. GRE for M.A. programs; GMAT for M.B.A. TOEFL required for international applicants. Interview not required. Accepts transfer applicants. Graduates of unaccredited institutions not considered. Admissions deadlines vary by program, contact Office of Graduate Admission at least three months prior to desired registration period for specific deadlines. Application fee $40, foreign applicants $50. Phone: (800)CALL-USF (outside of California), or (415)666-6563.

ADMISSION STANDARDS. Competitive. Usual minimum average: 3.0 (A = 4).

FINANCIAL AID. Merit scholarships, research assistantships, teaching assistantships, tuition grants, Federal W/S, loans. Approved for VA benefits. Apply by March 1 to appropriate departmental chair for fellowships, assistantships; to Financial Aid Office for all other programs. Use FAFSA. Phone: (415)666-6303. About 60% of students receive aid other than loans from University. Loans available for part-time students.

DEGREE REQUIREMENTS. For M.A., M.S.: 24–36 units minimum including thesis, at least 20 in residence; reading knowledge of one foreign language for some majors; final written/oral exam. For M.B.A.: 30–48 units minimum including thesis, at least 25 in residence; additional study may be required depending upon previous preparation; final oral exam; no language requirements. For M.H.R.O.D., M.N.O., M.P.A.: 48 credits minimum, at least 30 in residence; final exam. For Ed.D.: 60 semester hours of course work beyond master's degree, at least 48 in residence; qualifying exam; dissertation; final oral exam.

FIELDS OF STUDY.
Asian-Pacific Liberal Studies.
Biochemistry.
Biology. Includes developmental, marine, microbiology.
Business Administration.
Chemistry. Includes analytical, inorganic, organic, physical.
Computer Science.
Ecology.
Economics.
Education. Includes education administration, private school administration, international and multicultural education, education psychology/counseling, school psychology, curriculum

and instruction, early childhood, special education, reading, elementary, secondary, school supervision, counseling, junior college teaching; TESL, religious education; no language for M.A.

Environmental Management.
Finance.
Genetics.
Human Resource and Organizational Development.
International Business.
Nonprofit Organizations Management.
Nursing.
Public Administration.
Rehabilitation Administration.
Sport Fitness Management.
Theology.
Writing.

School of Law (94117-1080)

Established 1912. Semester system. Law library: 260,000 volumes. Library has LEXIS, NEXIS, WESTLAW.

Annual tuition: $18,900 (day), per credit $675 (evening). On-campus housing available. Total average annual additional expense: $9700.

Enrollment: first-year class 175 day, 60 evening; total, full-time 568 (day), part-time 150 (evening) (men 49%, women 51%). Faculty: full-time 29, part-time 65. Degrees conferred: J.D., J.D.-M.B.A.

ADMISSION REQUIREMENTS. LSDAS Law School report, bachelor's degree, transcripts, LSAT, two recommendations required in support of application. Accepts transfer applicants. Graduates of unaccredited institutions not considered. Apply to Director of Admissions by February; June 1 (evening). Admits first-year students September only. Application fee $40. Phone: (415)666-6544.

ADMISSION STANDARDS. Selective. Accepts 30–35% of total annual applicants.

FINANCIAL AID. Scholarships, Federal W/S, loans. Apply by March 2 to Financial Aid Office. Use FAFSA. About 35% of students receive aid other than loans from School. Aid available to part-time students.

DEGREE REQUIREMENTS. For J.D.: satisfactory completion of three-year (day), four-year (evening) program; 86 semester hours program.
Note: School has summer programs in Ireland and Czech Republic.

SAN JOSE STATE UNIVERSITY
San Jose, California 95192-0025

Founded 1857. Located 50 miles S of San Francisco. Coed. State control. Semester system. Library: 800,000 volumes, 700,000 microforms, 11,000 current periodicals.

Annual fees/tuition: full-time, resident $1976, nonresident $1976 plus $246 per unit. On-campus housing for married and single students. Average academic year housing costs: $3500–$4500. Contact Housing Office for both on- and off-campus housing information. Phone: (408)924-6160. Day care facilities available.

Graduate Studies and Research

Graduate study since 1946. Enrollment: full-time 2100, part-time 3167. Faculty: 300 full-time, 124 part-time. Degrees conferred: M.A., M.S., M.B.A., M.S.W., M.P.A., M.U.R., M.P.H., M.F.A.

ADMISSION REQUIREMENTS. Transcripts required in support of application. GRE Subject Tests/GMAT/MAT required or recommended for some programs. TOEFL required for international applicants. Interview not required. Accepts transfer applicants. Graduates of unaccredited institutions not considered. Apply to Graduate Studies Office by November 1 (Fall), August 1 (Spring). Applications considered after above dates on a space-available basis. Application fee $59. Phone: (408)924-2480.

ADMISSION STANDARDS. Selective for most majors. Usual minimum average: 2.5 for last 60 credits (A = 4).

FINANCIAL AID. Limited to Federal W/S, loans. Approved for VA benefits. Apply to Financial Aid Office; no closing date specified. Use FAFSA. Phone: (408)924-6100.

DEGREE REQUIREMENTS. For master's: 30 semester units minimum, at least 24 in residence; final written/oral exam; thesis/nonthesis option; creative project; reading knowledge of one foreign language for some departments.

FIELDS OF STUDY.
Aerospace Engineering.
Art. Includes creative, art history, graphic design.
Biochemistry.
Biological Sciences. Includes marine, toxicology, microbiology.
Business Administration. Includes taxation, accountancy. GMAT for admission.
Chemical Engineering.
Chemistry. Includes analytical, inorganic, organic, physical.
Child Development.
Civil Engineering and Applied Mechanics.
Computer Science.
Criminal Justice Administration.
Economics.
Education. Early childhood, elementary, secondary, special education, administration and supervision, art, higher, counseling and student personnel, instructional technology, speech pathology and audiology, learning handicapped, severely handicapped, teaching credentials.
Electrical Engineering.
English. GRE Subject for candidacy. Includes creative writing; one language for M.A.
Fine Arts. Includes art, theater arts.
Foreign Languages. Includes French, Spanish; GRE General for candidacy; working knowledge of second language for M.A.
Geography.
Geology.
Gerontology.
Health Science.
History.
Human Factor and Ergonomics.
Industrial and Systems Engineering.
Industrial Studies.
Interdisciplinary Major.
Library and Information Science.
Linguistics.
Marine Sciences.
Mass Communication.
Materials Engineering.
Mathematics.
Mechanical Engineering.
Meteorology.
Music. Includes performance, literature, theory and composition, education; GRE Music Subject Tests for Candidacy; thesis project, recital or composition for M.A.
Natural Science.
Nursing.
Occupational Therapy.
Philosophy.
Physical Education.

Physics.

Political Science.

Psychology. Includes counseling, experimental, school; project or thesis for M.A., M.S.

Public Administration.

Public Health.

Radiological Health Physics.

Recreation. Project or thesis for M.S.

Social Science. Interdepartmental program.

Social Work.

Sociology. GRE Subject for candidacy; thesis, one language for M.A.

Software Engineering.

Speech Communication. GRE Subject for candidacy; thesis or project for M.A.

Teaching English as a Second Language. M.A.

Theater Arts. Includes drama, dance.

Urban and Regional Planning. Thesis or project for M.U.P.

Writing.

SANTA CLARA UNIVERSITY

Santa Clara, California 95053-0001

Founded 1851. Located 45 miles S of San Francisco. Coed. Private control. Roman Catholic. Quarter system. Library: 715,000 volumes, 1,162,000 microforms, 8000 current periodicals, 91 PCs in all libraries.

Tuition: per unit College of A&S $274; Business and Administration $406; Division of Psychology $310; Engineering $519. On-campus housing for graduate students on a space-available basis. Contact Director of Housing for off-campus housing information. Phone: (408)554-4900. Day care facilities available.

Graduate Programs

Graduate study since 1951. Enrollment: full-time 1300, part-time 1939. Graduate faculty: full-time 135, part-time 108. Degrees conferred: M.A., M.B.A., M.S. (Engineering), Engineer.

ADMISSION REQUIREMENTS. Two transcripts, three letters of recommendation required in support of application. GRE/GMAT required for some programs. TOEFL required for international applicants. Interview usually not required. Accepts transfer applicants. Graduates of unaccredited institutions not considered. Apply to Dean's Office, School of Engineering June 1 (Fall), January 1 (Spring); Graduate Admissions, School of Business, July 1 (Fall); Graduate Admissions, Division of Counseling Psychology and Education and College of A&S, May 1 (Fall), February 1 (Spring). Application fee $25–$55 (fee varies from division to division), international application fee $75. Phone: College of A&S (408)554-4455; CP&E (408)554-4505; Business (408)554-4500; Engineering (408)554-4600.

ADMISSION STANDARDS. Competitive. Usual minimum average: 2.75 (Engineering), 3.0 (all other departments) (A = 4).

FINANCIAL AID. Scholarships, fellowships, assistantships, Federal W/S, loans. Approved for VA benefits. Apply by February 1 to appropriate Dean's Office for fellowships, assistantships; to Financial Aid Office for all other programs. Use FAFSA. Phone: (408)554-4505.

DEGREE REQUIREMENTS. For M.A.: 45 quarter units minimum; final written/oral exam may also be required. For M.B.A.: minimum of 18 courses beyond basic courses, at least 16 in residence. For Engineer: minimum of 45 units beyond the master's; thesis. For Ph.D. (Engineering, electrical only): 135 units minimum of graduate credit, at least 11 months in full-time residence; 45 units research credit for the master's and doctor's theses; language requirement to be determined; thesis; final oral exam.

FIELDS OF STUDY.

COLLEGE OF ARTS AND SCIENCES:

Catechetics.

Liturgical Music.

Pastoral Liturgy.

LEAVEY SCHOOL OF BUSINESS AND ADMINISTRATION:

Agribusiness.

Business Administration.

DIVISION OF COUNSELING PSYCHOLOGY AND EDUCATION:

Counseling Psychology.

Education.

Educational Administration.

Health Psychology.

Marriage, Family and Child Counseling.

Pastoral Counseling.

Pupil Personnel Services.

Special Education.

SCHOOL OF ENGINEERING:

Applied Mathematics.

Civil Engineering.

Computer Sciences.

Electrical Engineering.

Engineering Management.

Mechanical Engineering.

School of Law

Founded 1912. Semester system. Law library: 224,800 volumes. Library has LEXIS, NEXIS, WESTLAW, OSCAR.

Annual tuition: full-time $19,130/per credit $666. No on-campus housing available. Total average annual additional expense: $8000.

Enrollment: first-year class, full-time 220, part-time 61; total full-time 672, part-time 214 (men 49%, women 51%). Faculty: full-time 34, part-time 31. Degrees conferred: J.D., J.D.-M.B.A.

ADMISSION REQUIREMENTS. LSDAS Law School report, bachelor's degree, transcripts, LSAT required in support of application. Accepts transfer applicants. Graduates of unaccredited colleges not considered. Apply to Office of Admissions after September 1, before March 1. Rolling admissions process. Admits beginning students Fall only. Application fee $40. Phone: (408)554-4800.

ADMISSION STANDARDS. Selective. Accepts about 30–35% of total annual applicants.

FINANCIAL AID. Scholarships, fellowships, assistantships, Federal W/S, loans. Apply to Office of the Dean for Scholarships by February 1; Director of Financial Aid for loans by May 1 for all other aid. Use FAFSA. About 21% of students receive aid other than loans from School.

DEGREE REQUIREMENTS. For J.D.: 86 credit hours minimum, at least three years in residence for day students, at least four years in residence for part-time students.

Note: Summer programs in France, Switzerland, England, Hong Kong, Singapore, Korea, Thailand, and Japan are sometimes available.

SARAH LAWRENCE COLLEGE

Bronxville, New York 10708

Founded 1928. Located 15 miles N of New York City. Coed on graduate level. Private control. Semester system. Library: 288,000 volumes, 1135 current periodicals.

Tuition: per credit $498–$596. No on-campus housing for graduate students. Average monthly costs: $300–$500. Contact Student Affairs Office for off-campus housing information. Phone: (914)395-2373.

Graduate Studies

Graduate study since 1950. Enrollment: full-time 182, part-time 68. Faculty: full-time 25, part-time 20. Degrees conferred: M.A., M.F.A., M.S., M.P.S., M.S.Ed.

ADMISSION REQUIREMENTS. Transcripts, two letters of recommendation required in support of application. Interview sometimes requested. TOEFL required for international applicants. Accepts transfer applicants. Graduates of unaccredited colleges not considered. Apply to Committee on Graduate Studies by February 1. Fall admission. Application fee $45. Phone: (914)395-2373.

ADMISSION STANDARDS. Very selective for most departments, competitive for all others. Usual minimum average: 3.0 (A = 4).

FINANCIAL AID. Annual awards from institutional funds: ten grants, assistantships, loans. Apply by March 1 to Committee on Graduate Studies. Use FAFSA. Phone: (914)395-2570. About 25% of students receive aid other than loans from College and outside sources. Aid sometimes available to part-time students.

DEGREE REQUIREMENTS. For M.F.A. and most M.A., 36 credits, at least two years in residence; thesis or project. For some M.A.'s: 40 credits, at least two years in residence; fieldwork. For M.S., M.P.S.: 40 credits, at least two years in residence; fieldwork. For M.S.: 38 credits; fieldwork.

FIELDS OF STUDY.
Art of Teaching. M.S.Ed.
Child Development. M.A.
Dance. M.F.A.
Education. Includes early childhood, elementary.
Health Advocacy. M.A., M.P.S.
Human Genetics. M.P.S., M.S.
Theater. M.A., M.F.A.
Women's History. M.A.
Writing. M.F.A.

UNIVERSITY OF SCRANTON

Scranton, Pennsylvania 18510-4631
http://www.cds.vots.edu

Founded 1888. Coed. Private control. Catholic affiliation. Semester system. Library: 328,000 volumes, 307,000 microforms, 2000 current periodicals, 96 PCs.

Tuition: per credit $415; M.B.A. $433; Software Engineering $462. No on-campus housing available. Average off-campus housing cost per month: $450. Contact Director, Residence Life for off-campus housing information. Phone: (717)941-6226.

Graduate School

Enrollment: full-time 200, part-time 600. Graduate faculty: full-time 70, part-time 22. Degrees conferred: M.A., M.B.A., M.H.A., M.S.N., M.S.

ADMISSION REQUIREMENTS. Transcripts, letters of recommendation required in support of School's application. GMAT required for business applicants. Software Engineering applicants may submit either the GMAT or GRE. TOEFL required for international applicants. Interview required for some programs.

Accepts transfer applicants. Graduates of unaccredited institutions not considered. Apply to School at least thirty days prior to registration date. Foreign applicants should apply at least three months prior to registration date. Rolling admissions process. Application fee $35. Phone: (800)366-4723, (717)941-7600; fax: (717)941-4252.

ADMISSION STANDARDS. Selective for most departments. Usual minimum average: 2.75 (A = 4).

FINANCIAL AID. Annual awards from institutional funds: Approximately sixty graduate assistantships, Federal W/S, loans. Approved for VA benefits. Apply by March 1 to Graduate Dean. Use FAFSA and University's FAF. Phone: (717)941-7700. No aid for part-time students.

DEGREE REQUIREMENTS. For master's: 30–48 semester credits; thesis/nonthesis option; final written/oral exam.

FIELDS OF STUDY.
Biochemistry.
Business. GMAT for admission. M.B.A. only.
Chemistry.
Clinical Chemistry.
Community Counseling.
Elementary Education.
English.
Health Administration. M.H.A.
History.
Human Resources Administration.
Nursing. M.S.N.
Reading Education.
Rehabilitation Counseling.
School Administration. Includes elementary and secondary.
School Counseling.
Secondary Education.
Software Engineering.
Theology.

SEATTLE PACIFIC UNIVERSITY

Seattle, Washington 98119-1997
http://www.spu.edu

Founded 1891. Coed. Private control. Free Methodist. Quarter system. Library: 200,000 volumes, 300,000 microforms.

Limited on-campus housing for single and married graduate students.

Average academic year housing costs: $5100 (including board) for single students, $6600 for married students. Contact Coordinator of Housing for both on- and off-campus housing information. Phone: (206)281-2099.

Graduate Studies

Tuition: per credit $282, except Business, Information Systems $390; Education $248; Educational Administration $260; M.E.T. $305; Nursing $260; Nurse Practitioner $295; TESOL $225; Ed.D. $319; Psy.D. $350. Enrollment: full-time 114, part-time 475. Graduate faculty: full-time 51, part-time 54. Degrees conferred: M.Ed., M.A., M.I.S.M., M.S., M.S.N., M.B.A., Ed.D., Psy.D.

ADMISSION REQUIREMENTS. Transcripts, two letters of reference, GRE or MAT required in support of application. GMAT for M.B.A. program. Interview required for some departments. TOEFL required for foreign applicants. Accepts transfer applicants. Apply to Graduate School at least six weeks prior to registration. Application fee $35. Phone: (206)281-2021.

ADMISSION STANDARDS. Competitive. Usual minimum average: 3.0. (A = 4), 3.0 in last 45 credits. TOEFL minimum score 550; for M.B.A., I.S.M. 575; TESOL 600.

FINANCIAL AID. Teaching/research assistantships, fellowships for teaching preparation, Federal W/S, loans. Approved for VA benefits. Apply by April 1 to appropriate School for assistantships, fellowships; to Financial Aid Office for all other programs. Use FAFSA. Phone: (206)281-2046.

DEGREE REQUIREMENTS. For master's: 45 quarter hours minimum, last 15 in residence; three credit course in Christian thought; candidacy; comprehensive exam; thesis/nonthesis option/project. For Ed.D., Psy.D.: 90–96 quarter hours beyond master's degree; qualifying exam; comprehensive exam; dissertation; clinical internship for Psy.D.; final oral exam.

FIELDS OF STUDY.

COLLEGE OF ARTS AND SCIENCES:
Clinical Family Psychology. Psy.D.
Marriage and Family Therapy. M.S.
TESOL. M.A.

SCHOOL OF BUSINESS AND ECONOMICS:
Business Administration. M.B.A.
Information Systems Management. M.I.S.M.

SCHOOL OF EDUCATION:
Curriculum and Instruction. M.Ed.
Education. Ed.D.
Reading/Language Arts. M.Ed.
School Administration. M.Ed.
School Counseling. M.Ed.
Teaching. M.A.

SCHOOL OF HEALTH SCIENCES:
Nursing. M.S.

SEATTLE UNIVERSITY
Seattle, Washington 98122
http://www.seattle.edu

Founded 1891. Coed. Private control. Jesuit affiliation. Quarter system. Library: 200,000 volumes, 362,000 microforms, 1429 current periodicals, 26 PCs.

Tuition: per credit hour $317–$411 (depending on program). Limited on-campus housing for graduate single students. Average academic year housing costs: $5721 (including board). Contact Residential Life Office for both on- and off-campus housing information. Phone: (206)296-6274. Day care facilities available.

Graduate School

Graduate study since 1901. Enrollment: full-time 353, part-time 1342. Faculty: full-time 293, part-time 41. Degrees conferred: M.A., M.A.P.S., M.A.T.S., M.S., M.Ed., M.B.A., M.I.B., M.A. in Ed., Ed.D., M.C., M.S.E., M.Div., M.M., M.N.P.L., M.I.T., M.S.N., M.P.A., M.S.F., M.A.E., Ed.S.

ADMISSION REQUIREMENTS. Transcripts required in support of School's application. GRE/GMAT/NTE, interview required for some programs. Accepts transfer applicants. Graduates of unaccredited institutions not considered. Apply to Graduate Admissions Office at least sixty days prior to registration. Application fee $55. Phone: (206)296-5900.

ADMISSION STANDARDS. Selective. Usual minimum average: 2.75 (A = 4).

FINANCIAL AID. Six hundred and seventy-nine grants (based on need); departmental recruiting scholarships also available, Federal W/S, loans. Approved for VA benefits. Apply to Financial Aid Office; no specified closing date. Use FAFSA. Phone: (206)296-5840; fax: (206)296-5656.

DEGREE REQUIREMENTS. For master's: 45–60 quarter hours minimum, at least 25 in residence; thesis; final oral/written exam depending upon program. For Ed.D.: 90 quarter hours minimum; preliminary exam; dissertation; final exam.

FIELDS OF STUDY.
Applied Economics.
Business Administration.
Counseling. Includes school, agency, postsecondary.
Divinity.
Education. Includes administration, curriculum and instruction, special and gifted, leadership, adult education and training, school psychology, student development, teaching English to speakers of other languages.
Finance.
International Business.
Not-for-Profit Leadership.
Nursing.
Pastoral Studies.
Psychology.
Public Administration.
Religious Education.
Software Engineering.
Teaching.
Transforming Spirituality.

School of Law

Formerly Puget Sound School of Law. Semester system. Law library: 312,000 volumes. Library has LEXIS, NEXIS, WESTLAW, DIALOG, BRS, VUTEXT, WILSONLINE, DATATIMES.

Annual tuition: full-time $16,380. No on-campus housing available. Total average annual additional expense: $10,300.

Enrollment: first-year class full-time 250, part-time 40; total 343 (men 54%, women 46%). Faculty: full-time 41, part-time 24. Degree conferred: J.D.

ADMISSION REQUIREMENTS. LSDAS Law School report, bachelor's degree, transcripts, LSAT, letters of recommendation required in support of application. Interviews by invitation only. Accepts transfer applicants. Graduates of unaccredited colleges not considered. Apply to the Office of Admissions by April 1. Admits Fall only. Application fee $50. Phone: (206)591-2252.

ADMISSION STANDARDS. Selective. Accepts 20–25% of total annual applications.

FINANCIAL AID. Scholarships, tuition waivers, assistantships, Federal W/S, loans. Apply to Student Aid Office by April 1. Use FAFSA. About 30% of students receive aid other than loans from School.

DEGREE REQUIREMENTS. For J.D.: satisfactory completion of 90 semester hour program.

SETON HALL UNIVERSITY
South Orange, New Jersey 07079-2697

Founded 1856. Located 20 miles SW of New York City. Coed. Private control. Roman Catholic. Semester system. Walsh Library: 435,000 volumes, 368,000 microforms, 2500 periodicals, 32 PCs and CD-ROMs in libraries.

Tuition: per credit nonbusiness $437, business $470. Limited on-campus housing for graduate students. Average academic year housing costs: $2825. Contact Director of Housing for on- and off-campus housing information. Phone: (201)761-9172.

Graduate Division

Graduate study since 1943. Enrollment: full-time 531, part-time 2673. Faculty: full-time 187, part-time 74. Degrees conferred: M.A., M.B.A., M.S., M.P.A., Ed.S., Ed.D., Ph.D. (Chemistry and Education).

ADMISSION REQUIREMENTS. Two transcripts required in support of application. Interview, MAT/GRE/GMAT required by some departments. TOEFL required for international applicants. Accepts transfer applicants. Graduates of unaccredited institutions not considered. Apply to Graduate Office by July 1 (Fall), November 1 (Spring), May 1 (Summer). Application fee $30. Phone: (201)275-2036.

ADMISSION STANDARDS. Selective for most departments. Usual minimum average: 3.0 (A = 4).

FINANCIAL AID. Annual awards from university funds: 11 academic scholarships, 4 fellowships, 146 administrative assistantships, 38 teaching assistantships, Federal W/S, loans. Approved for VA benefits. Apply by March 1 to appropriate departmental chair for assistantships, fellowships; to Financial Aid Office for all other programs. Use FAFSA. Phone: (201)761-9350; fax: (201)761-7954. About 30% of students receive aid other than loans from University and outside sources.

DEGREE REQUIREMENTS. For master's: 30 credits minimum, qualifying exam/thesis required in some departments; competency in one foreign language required in some programs in the College of Arts and Sciences; comprehensive exam. For Ed.D., Ph.D.: 70 credits minimum beyond the bachelor's degree; matriculation exam; dissertation; final oral exam.

FIELDS OF STUDY.

COLLEGE OF ARTS AND SCIENCES:
Asian Studies.
Biochemistry.
Biology.
Chemistry. Includes analytical, inorganic, organic, physical. M.S., Ph.D.
Church/Religious Organization. M.P.A.
Corporate and Public Communications.
Criminal Justice/Court Administration. M.P.A.
English.
Health Policy and Management.
Jewish-Christian Studies.
Management of Nonprofit Organization. M.P.A.
Mathematics.
Microbiology.
Museum Professions.
Public Service Administration and Policy. M.P.A.

COLLEGE OF EDUCATION AND HUMAN SERVICES:
Bilingual/Bicultural Education. Ed.S.
Clinical Psychology.
Counseling Psychology.
Counselor Preparation.
Educational Administration and Supervision.
Educational Media.
Elementary Education.
Health Professions Education.
Higher Educational Administration.

Human Resources Training and Development.
Marriage and Family Counseling.
Professional Development.
School and Community Psychology.
Secondary Education.
Student Personnel Services (K–12).

W. PAUL STILLMAN SCHOOL OF BUSINESS:
Accounting.
Economics.
Finance.
Financial Planning.
Human Resource Management.
Information Systems.
International Business.
Management.
Management Information Systems.
Marketing.
Professional Accounting.
Quantitative Analysis.
Sports Management.
Taxation.
Note: Evening program requires GMAT for admission; M.B.A., M.S. Taxation, Joint M.B.A.-J.D.

COLLEGE OF NURSING:
Advanced Practice in Critical Care. Includes critical care nurse practitioner.
Advanced Practice in Primary Health Care. Includes adult nurse practitioner, gerontological nurse practitioner, pediatric nurse practitioner, school nurse practitioner, women's health nurse practitioner.
Nursing Administration.
Nursing Education for Advanced Practice Nurses.

SCHOOL OF GRADUATE MEDICAL EDUCATION:
Health Sciences. M.S.
Physician Assistant. M.S.

SCHOOL OF THEOLOGY:
Pastoral Ministry. Includes church management, catechetical health care, liturgical, spirituality, youth.
Theology. Includes biblical studies, ecclesia history, Judaeo-Christian studies, moral theology, systematic.

School of Law

Organized 1951. Located in Newark (07102). Semester system. Law library: 315,500 volumes. Library has LEXIS, NEXIS, WESTLAW, DIALOG.

Annual tuition: $18,900, per credit $630. Total average annual additional expense: $15,000.

Enrollment: first-year class, 300 (day), 108 (evening); total full- and part-time 1342 (men 58%, women 52%). Faculty: full-time 51, part-time 97. Degrees conferred: J.D., J.D.-M.B.A.

ADMISSION REQUIREMENTS. LSDAS Law School report, bachelor's degree, transcript, LSAT letters of recommendation required in support of application. GMAT required for joint degree program. Accepts transfer applicants. Graduates of unaccredited colleges not considered. Apply to the Admissions Office after September 1, before April 1. Application fee $45. Phone: (201)642-8747.

ADMISSION STANDARDS. Selective. Accepts 35–40% of total annual applicants.

FINANCIAL AID. Scholarships, full and partial tuition waivers, assistantships, Federal W/S, loans. Apply to Director of Financial Aid by May 15. Use FAFSA. About 30% of students receive aid other than loans from School.

DEGREE REQUIREMENTS. For J.D.: satisfactory completion of three-year (day), four-year (evening) program; 85 credit hour program.

Note: Summer abroad programs with the University of Parma and University of Milan.

SHIPPENSBURG UNIVERSITY OF PENNSYLVANIA
Shippensburg, Pennsylvania 17257-2299

Founded 1871. Located 40 miles SW of Harrisburg. Coed. State control. Semester credit hour system. Library: 428,000 volumes, 1,599,000 microforms, 1740 current periodicals, 41 PCs in library.

Annual tuition: full-time residents $4030, nonresident $6716, part-time per semester, resident $661 (minimum), nonresident $1108 (minimum). On-campus housing for graduate men and women during Summer sessions only. Average off-campus housing costs: $300 per month. Housing costs for summer: single, on-campus $532 for 5 weeks; $228 for 5 weeks (room only). Contact Dean of Students Office for off-campus housing information. Phone: (717)532-1213.

School of Graduate Studies

Enrollment: full-time 213, part-time 674. College faculty teaching graduate students: full-time 85, part-time 12. Degrees conferred: M.A., M.Ed., M.S., M.P.A.

ADMISSION REQUIREMENTS. Transcripts, GRE/MAT required in support of School's application. TOEFL required for international applicants. Accepts transfer applicants. Apply to Dean of Graduate Studies at least eight weeks prior to registration. Rolling admissions process. Application fee $20. Phone: (717)532-1213.

ADMISSION STANDARDS. Selective for most departments. Usual minimum average: 2.75 (A = 4).

FINANCIAL AID. Annual awards from institutional funds: sixty assistantships, loans. Apply to Dean of the Graduate Studies for assistantships; to the Financial Aid Office for all other programs. Use FAFSA and University's FAF. Phone: (717)532-1131.

DEGREE REQUIREMENTS. For master's: 30–48 semester hours minimum, 24 in residence; thesis/nonthesis option.

FIELDS OF STUDY.
Administration of Justice.
Biology.
Business Education.
Chemistry.
Communication Study.
Computer Education.
Computer Science. GRE required.
Counseling.
Educational Administration.
Elementary Education.
English. GRE Subject for admission.
Geoenvironmental Studies.
History.
Information Systems.
Mathematics.
Psychology.
Public Administration.
Reading.
Special Education.

SIENA HEIGHTS COLLEGE
Adrian, Michigan 49221-1796

Founded 1919. Located 65 miles SW of Detroit. Coed. Private control. Roman Catholic. Semester system. Library: 118,000 volumes, 22,000 microforms, 540 current periodicals.

Tuition: per credit $280. No on-campus housing for graduate students. Contact Director, Residence Life for off-campus housing information. Phone: (517)263-0731.

Graduate Division

Graduate study since 1953. Enrollment: full-time 36, part-time 167. Graduate faculty: full-time 3, part-time 16. Degree conferred: M.A.

ADMISSION REQUIREMENTS. Transcripts, three letters of recommendation required in support of application. TOEFL required for international applicants. Interview recommended. Accepts transfer applicants. Apply to Graduate Office by April 1 (Summer), August 1 (Fall). Application fee $25. Phone: (517)263-0731, ext. 283.

ADMISSION STANDARDS. Selective for most departments. Usual minimum average: 3.0 (A = 4).

FINANCIAL AID. Limited Federal W/S, loans. Approved for VA benefits. Apply to Financial Aid Office; no specified closing date. Use FAFSA. Phone: (517)263-0731, ext. 211.

DEGREE REQUIREMENTS. For M.A.: 36–48 semester hours; thesis/research project.

FIELDS OF STUDY.
Agency Counseling. Forty-eight semester hours.
Early Childhood Education. Thirty-nine semester hours program.
Elementary Education. Thirty-six semester hours program.
Human Resource Development. Thirty-six semester hours program.
Middle School Education. Thirty-six semester hours program.
Reading (K–12). Thirty-six semester hours program.
School Counseling. Thirty-six semester hours program.
Secondary Education. Thirty-six semester hours program.

SIMMONS COLLEGE
Boston, Massachusetts 02115-5898

Founded 1899. Coed on graduate level. Private control. Semester system. Library: 266,000 volumes, 2000 microforms, 2000 current periodicals, 100 PCs.

Tuition: $530 per semester hour. On-campus housing for graduate students. Average academic year housing costs: on-campus $7700, off-campus $12,000. Contact the Office of Student Housing for both on- and off-campus housing information. Phone: (617)521-1102.

Graduate Division

Enrollment: full-time 538, part-time 1513. College faculty: full-time 64, part-time 99. Degrees conferred: M.A., M.S., M.S.Ed., M.B.A., M.A.T., M.Phil., M.S.W., Ph.D., D.A.

ADMISSION REQUIREMENTS. Transcripts, references required in support of application. TOEFL required for international applicants. Interview, GRE/GMAT/MAT sometimes necessary. Apply to Director of appropriate program. Call for information regarding deadlines and application fees; they vary by graduate program. Rolling admissions process. Phone: (617)521-2910; fax: (617)521-3199.

ADMISSION STANDARDS: Selective. Usual minimum average: 2.75 (A = 4).

FINANCIAL AID. Grants, scholarships, assistantships, Federal W/S, loans. Type and amount of aid varies according to program of study. Apply by March 1 to Director of Financial Aid. Use FAFSA. Phone: (617)521-2910. Aid sometimes available for part-time students.

DEGREE REQUIREMENTS. For master's: 32–56 semester hours, dependent upon the program; thesis required in some programs. For Ph.D.: 70 credits minimum beyond bachelor's, at least 32 in residence; competency in 2 foreign languages, or computer tool may be substituted for 1 language; dissertation; final oral exam.

FIELDS OF STUDY.
Children's Literature. M.A.
Communications Management. M.S.
Education. Includes elementary, middle and high school, severe special needs, moderate special needs, integration specialist, teaching English as a second language. M.A.T.
English. Includes English, American, comparative. M.A., M.Phil.
Foreign Languages and Literatures. Includes Spanish, French. M.A.
Health Care Administration. M.S.
Liberal Studies. M.A.
Library and Information Science. M.S.
Management. M.B.A.
Physical Therapy. M.S.
Primary Health Care Nursing. M.S.
Social Work. M.S., Ph.D.

SLIPPERY ROCK UNIVERSITY OF PENNSYLVANIA
Slippery Rock, Pennsylvania 16057
http://www.sru.edu

Located 50 miles N of Pittsburgh. Coed. State control. Library: 600,000 volumes, 1,223,000 microforms, 1700 current periodicals, 22 PCs.

Annual tuition: full-time resident $3368, nonresident $6054; per credit resident $187, nonresident $322. On-campus housing for single students only. Average academic year housing cost: $3928 (including board). Contact Office of Director of Residence Life for both on- and off-campus housing. Phone: (412)738-2082. Day care facilities available.

Graduate Division

Enrollment: full-time 250, part-time 500. Faculty: part-time 200, part-time 10. Degrees conferred: M.Ed., M.A., M.S., M.S.N., M.P.A., D.P.T.

ADMISSION REQUIREMENTS. Transcripts, GRE, interview (Physical Therapy) required in support of application. TOEFL required for international applicants. Interview not required. Accepts transfer applicants. Graduates of unaccredited institutions not considered. Apply to Graduate School Office at least two months prior to registration. Application fee $25, $35 for D.P.T. Phone: (412)738-2051; fax: (412)738-2908.

ADMISSION STANDARDS. Selective. Usual minimum average: 2.75, some programs required 3.0 (A = 4).

FINANCIAL AID. Annual awards from institutional funds: five scholarships, one hundred assistantships, Federal W/S, loans. Apply by January 15 to appropriate department chair for assistantships; to Office of Financial Aid for all other programs. Use FAFSA. Phone: 738-2044; fax: (412)738-2922. About 35% of students receive aid other than loans from College and outside sources.

DEGREE REQUIREMENTS. For master's: 30 credit hours minimum, at least 18 in residence; thesis or final document; final written/oral exam. For D.P.T.: 60 credits beyond the master's degree, at least two years in full-time residence; qualifying exam; dissertation; internship; final oral exam.

FIELDS OF STUDY.
Elementary Education.
English.
Guidance and Counseling.
Health and Physical Education.
History.
Nursing.
Physical Science.
Physical Therapy.
Public Administration.
Reading.
Recreation.
Secondary Education. Includes mathematics, science.
Special Education.
Sustainable Systems.

SMITH COLLEGE
Northampton, Massachusetts 01063

Founded 1871. Located 100 miles W of Boston. Coed on graduate level. Private control. Semester system. Library: 1,100,000 volumes, 84,000 microforms, 3000 current periodicals, 95 PCs. Special facilities: Fine Arts Center, Center for the Performing Arts, Clarke Science Center. Cooperative M.E.D. program with the Clarke School for the Deaf; cooperative Ph.D. program with Amherst, Hampshire, Mount Holyoke, University of Massachusetts.

Annual tuition: $20,380, per credit $640. On-campus housing for 25 graduate students, none for married students. Average annual housing cost: $6920 (including board). Phone: (413)585-3050.

Graduate Study

Graduate study since 1879. Enrollment: full-time 78, part-time 35 (men 10%, women 90%). College faculty: full-time 98, part-time 38. Degrees conferred: M.A., M.A.T., Ed.M., M.E.D. (Teaching of the Deaf), M.F.A. (Dance), M.S. in Exercise and Sport Studies.

ADMISSION REQUIREMENTS. Transcripts, GRE/MAT, three letters of recommendation required in support of application. TOEFL required for international applicants. Interview not required. Apply to Director of Graduate Study by January 15 M.E.D. (April 15 without financial aid); April 1 M.F.A.; March 1 all other programs. Application fee $40. Phone: (413)585-3050; fax: (413)585-2075.

ADMISSION STANDARDS. Competitive for most departments. Usual minimum average: 3.0 (A = 4).

FINANCIAL AID. Fifty academic scholarships, fifteen grants, twenty-six fellowships, Federal W/S, loans. Apply by January 15 to Director of Graduate Study for scholarships, fellowships; to Financial Aid Office for all other programs. Use FAFSA and CSS

Profile. Phone: (413)585-3050; fax: (413)858-2075. About 80% of students receive aid from College and outside sources.

DEGREE REQUIREMENTS. For M.A., Ed.M., M.E.D., M.F.A.: 8 semester courses minimum in residence; thesis or final project. For M.A.T.: 8 semester courses minimum in residence, usually one academic year plus one summer internship. For M.S. in Exercise and Sport Studies: usually two years in full-time residence.

FIELDS OF STUDY.
Art History. M.A.T. only.
Biological Sciences. Includes botany, microbiology, zoology. M.A., M.A.T., Ph.D. Cooperative Ph.D. with five college programs.
Classics. M.A.T. only.
Dance. M.F.A. only.
Education and Child Study. Ed.M., M.A.T., M.A., M.E.D.
English. M.A.T. only.
Exercise and Sport Studies. M.S. only.
French. M.A., M.A.T.
History. M.A.T., M.A.
Italian. M.A.
Music. M.A., M.A.T.
Physics. M.A.T. only.
Religion. M.A. only.
Spanish. M.A.T. only.
Teaching of the Deaf. M.E.D. only.
Theater. M.F.A. only.

School for Social Work

Since 1918. Semester system. Annual tuition: full-time $9352. On-campus housing available.

Enrollment: full-time 396. School faculty: full-time 15, part-time 100. Degrees conferred: M.S.W., Ph.D.

ADMISSION REQUIREMENTS. Official transcripts, MAT required in support of School's application. TOEFL required for international applicants. Accepts transfer applicants. Graduates of unaccredited institutions not considered. Apply by February 15 to the Office of Admissions. Application fee $50. Phone: (413)585-7960.

ADMISSION STANDARDS. Competitive. Usual minimum average: 3.0 (A = 4).

FINANCIAL AID. Scholarships, tuition waivers, internships, loans. Apply by February 1 to the Financial Aid Office. Use FAFSA. About 50% of students receive aid from the School and outside sources.

DEGREE REQUIREMENTS. For M.S.W.: 4 semesters in full-time residence; field work experience; final project. For Ph.D.: three years minimum beyond bachelor's; at least two years in residence; advancement to candidacy; comprehensive exam; dissertation; final oral exam.

SONOMA STATE UNIVERSITY
Rohnert Park, California 94928-3609
http://www.admrec.sonoma.edu

Founded 1960. Located 45 miles N of San Francisco. Coed. State control. Semester system. Library: about 460,000 volumes, 1,380,000 microforms, 1600 current periodicals, 35 PCs.

Annual fee: full-time resident $2130, nonresident $2130 plus $246 per unit. On-campus housing for single students only. Average academic year housing costs: $4744. Contact Housing Of-

fice for both on- and off-campus housing information. Phone: (707)664-2541. Day care facilities available.

Graduate Division

Enrollment: full-time 669, part-time 444. College faculty teaching graduate students: full-time 26, part-time 161. Degrees conferred: M.A., M.S., M.B.A., M.P.A.

ADMISSION REQUIREMENTS. Transcripts, GRE/GMAT/MAT required in support of application. TOEFL required for international applicants. Accepts transfer applicants. Graduates of unaccredited institutions not considered. Apply to Office of Admissions and Records at least two months in advance of registration. Application fee $55. Phone: (707)664-2778.

ADMISSION STANDARDS. Varies by department. Usual minimum average: 3.0 (A = 4).

FINANCIAL AID. Limited to Federal W/S, loans. Apply by April 1 to Financial Aid Office. Use FAFSA. Phone: (707)664-2389.

DEGREE REQUIREMENTS. For master's: 30–60 units minimum, at least 21 in residence; thesis/nonthesis option; final oral exam/projects.

FIELDS OF STUDY.
Biology. Includes environmental.
Business Administration.
Creative Writing.
Education. Includes curriculum and instruction, early childhood, administration, reading, special.
English.
History.
Marriage, Family and Child Counseling.
Nursing.
Physical Education.
Psychology.
Public Administration.
School Counseling.
Special Major.
World Literature.

UNIVERSITY OF THE SOUTH
Sewanee, Tennessee 37375-1000
http://www.sewanee.edu

Founded 1857. Located 50 miles W of Chattanooga. Coed. Private control. Semester system. Library: 453,121 volumes, 246,754 microforms, 20 PCs.

Annual tuition: full-time $8620, per credit $265. On-campus housing for 50 graduate students in apartments only. Average academic year housing costs for single or married seminary students: $4300–$8500. Day care facilities available.

School of Theology

Founded 1872. Enrollment: full-time 72, part-time 5 (M.Dir., and M.A.). Faculty: full-time 12, part-time 5. Degrees conferred: M.Div. (S.T.M. and D.Min. are only in Summer), S.T.M., D.Min., M.A.

ADMISSION REQUIREMENTS. Transcripts, letter of recommendation, GRE, interview required in support of application. TOEFL required for international applicants. Accepts transfer applicants. Apply to Admissions Office before April 15. Application fee $25. Phone: (615)598-1283; fax: (615)598-1852.

ADMISSION STANDARDS. Competitive. Usual minimum average: 3.0 (A = 4).

FINANCIAL AID. 75 grants which are need-based, institutional work program for M.Div., M.A. students only. Contact Financial Aid Office for application deadlines. Phone: (615)598-1312; fax: (615)598-1667.

DEGREE REQUIREMENTS. For M.Div.: 91 credits minimum, at least 30 in residence and two semesters in full-time study. For M.A.: 48 hours including thesis. For S.T.M.: 30 credits minimum beyond the M.Div., four summers in residence; thesis. For D.Min.: 30 credits minimum beyond the M.Div., normally takes four summers in residence.

FIELD OF STUDY.
Theology.

UNIVERSITY OF SOUTH ALABAMA
Mobile, Alabama 366880-0002

Founded 1964. Quarter system. Library: 437,000 volumes, 770,000 microforms, 3600 current periodicals.

Tuition/fees: residents per quarter $62, plus $65 per quarter hour fee; nonresident $100 (1–5), $200 (6–11), $300 (12 or more), plus $65 per quarter hour. On-campus housing available for 502 married students, 1690 single students. Average academic year housing costs: $3322 (including board). Contact Director of Housing for both on- and off-campus housing information. Phone: (334)460-6195.

Graduate School.

Created 1968. Enrollment: full-time 835, part-time 926. Graduate faculty: full-time 231. Degrees conferred: M.A., M.Acct., M.B.A., M.Ed., M.P.A., M.S., M.S.Ch.E., M.S.E.E., M.S.M.E., M.S.N., Ed.S., Ed.D., Ph.D.

ADMISSION REQUIREMENTS. Transcripts required in support of School's application. Standardized test, recommendation required by some programs. TOEFL required for international applicants. Accepts transfer applicants. Graduates of unaccredited institutions considered. Apply to Director of Admissions by September 1 (Fall quarter), December 10 (Winter quarter), March 10 (Spring quarter), June 1 (Summer quarter). Deadlines for all admissions documents for International students are: Fall, June 15; Winter, October 1; Spring, January 1; Summer, April 1. Application fee $20. Phone: (205)460-6141, (800)872-5247.

ADMISSION STANDARDS. Selective. Usual minimum average: 3.0 (provisional 2.5) (A = 4).

FINANCIAL AID. 78 research assistantships, 25 teaching assistantships, 19 fellowships, stipends, Federal W/S, loans. Approved for VA benefits. Apply to appropriate department for fellowships, assistantships; to the Office of Financial Aid for all other programs. Use FAFSA and University's FAF. Approximately 30% of graduate students receive aid other than loans from the University or outside sources.

DEGREE REQUIREMENTS. For master's: 48 quarter hours minimum, at least 3 quarter hours in residence; foreign language may be required by some programs; comprehensive exam; thesis/nonthesis option. For Ed.S.: 45 quarter hours beyond the master's. For doctoral programs: 90 quarter hours minimum, at least 6 quarters in residence; preliminary exam; dissertation; reading knowledge of one language, a research tool or computer technique; final oral exam.

FIELDS OF STUDY.
Accounting.
Basis Medical Sciences. Includes biochemistry, microbiology/immunology, pharmacology, physiology, structural and cellular biology.
Biological Sciences.
Business and Management.
Communications.
Computer and Information Science.
Education. Includes agency counseling, early childhood, educational leadership, educational media, elementary, exercise technology, health, instructional design, middle school, physical education, reading, school counseling, school psychometry, secondary, special, therapeutic recreation.
Engineering. Includes chemical, electrical, mechanical.
English.
History.
Marine Science.
Mathematics.
Medicine.
Nursing. Includes adult health nursing, community-mental health nursing, woman and child health nursing, executive and midlevel administration.
Psychology.
Public Administration.
Sociology.
Speech and Hearing Sciences.

College of Medicine (36688-0002)

Established 1967. Annual tuition: resident $7000, nonresident $14,000, student fees $567.

Enrollment: first-year class 64 (EDP 10), total 254 (men 60%, women 40%). Faculty: full-time 144, part-time 10. Degrees conferred: M.D., M.D.-Ph.D.

ADMISSION REQUIREMENTS. AMCAS report, transcripts, MCAT, recommendations required in support of final application. Interview by invitation. Applicants must have completed at least three years of college study. Has EDP (Alabama residents only); apply between June 15 and August 1. Preference given to state residents. Graduates of unaccredited colleges not considered. Apply after June 15, before November 15. Application fee $25, submitted with supplemental application. Phone: (334)460-7176; fax: (334)460-6761.

ADMISSION STANDARDS. Selective. Admits about 10–15% of total applicants. Approximately 80% are state residents.

FINANCIAL AID. Limited scholarships, medical student summer research program, loans. Apply after acceptance to Office of Financial Aid. About 5% of students receive some aid from School.

DEGREE REQUIREMENTS. For M.D.: satisfactory completion of four-year program; pass step 2 of USMLE. For Ph.D., see Graduate listing above.

FIELDS OF GRADUATE STUDY.
Anatomy.
Biochemistry.
Cell Biology.
Genetics.
Immunology.
Microbiology.
Molecular Biology.

Neurosciences.
Pharmacology.
Physiology.

MEDICAL UNIVERSITY
OF SOUTH CAROLINA
Charleston, South Carolina 29425-0002

Founded 1824. Coed. State control. Semester system. Library: 225,000 volumes, 1704 microforms, 50 PCs. No on-campus housing available.

College of Graduate Studies

Annual tuition/fees: full-time resident $3014, nonresident $3862. Enrollment: full-time 185, part-time 35. Degrees conferred: M.S., Ph.D.

ADMISSION REQUIREMENTS. Transcripts, three letters of recommendation, GRE Subject Tests, interview required in support of application. Accepts transfer applicants. Approximately 90% are state residents.

ADMISSION STANDARDS. Selective. Usual minimum average: 3.0 (A = 4) residents.

FINANCIAL AID. Teaching research/fellowships, teaching assistantships, full and partial tuition waivers, Federal W/S, loans. Apply to appropriate department chair for fellowships; to Office of Financial Aid for all other aid. No specified closing date. Use FAFSA.

DEGREE REQUIREMENTS. For M.S.: 30 semester hours minimum, at least 18 in residence; reading knowledge of one foreign language; thesis; final oral exam. For Ph.D.: 60 credits minimum beyond the bachelor's, at least one year in continuous residence; reading knowledge of two foreign languages; written/oral qualifying exam; dissertation; final oral exam.

FIELDS OF STUDY.
Anatomy.
Biochemistry.
Biometrics.
Biostatistics.
Cell Biology.
Genetics.
Immunology.
Microbiology.
Molecular Biology.
Pathology.
Pharmacology.
Physiology.

Medical School

Annual tuition: full-time, resident $6546, nonresident $18,986, student fees residents $264, nonresident $8672. Total average figure for all other expenses: $10,300.
Enrollment: first-year class 135 (EDP 10); total 538 (men 55%, women 45%). Faculty: full- and part-time 820. Degrees conferred: M.D., M.D.-Ph.D.

ADMISSION REQUIREMENTS. AMCAS report, transcripts, MCAT, recommendations, interview required in support of application. Interview by invitation only. Has EDP (South Carolina residents only); apply between June 15 and August 1. Applicants must have completed at least three years of college study. Preference given to state residents. Accepts transfer applicants. Apply to Registrar after June 15, before December 1 (Fall). Application fee $25. Phone: (803)792-3281; fax: (803)792-3764.

ADMISSION STANDARDS. Selective. Accepts 8–10% of total annual applicants. Approximately 65% are state residents.

FINANCIAL AID. Scholarships, internships, loans. Apply to Office of the Dean by April 24. Use FAFSA. About 35% of students receive aid other than loans from School.

DEGREE REQUIREMENTS. For M.D.: successful completion of four-year program. For Ph.D., see Graduate School listing above.

College of Dental Medicine

First class admitted Fall 1967. Semester system.
Annual tuition: resident $6403, nonresident $18,607. Limited on-campus housing available. Average academic year off-campus housing costs: $10,500. Total average cost for all other first-year expenses: $6038.
Enrollment: first-year class 49; total 182 (men 75%, women 25%); postgraduates 26. Faculty: full-time 50, part-time 49. Degrees conferred: D.M.D., M.S., D.M.D.-Ph.D.

ADMISSION REQUIREMENTS. AADSAS report, transcripts, DAT required in support of College's application. Interview by invitation only. Preference given to state residents. Applicants must have completed at least three years of college study. Apply to Office of Enrollment Services after June 1, before December 1. Application fee $45. Phone: (803)792-3281.

ADMISSION STANDARDS. Selective. Accepts about 15–20% of total annual applicants. Approximately 80% are state residents.

FINANCIAL AID. Scholarships, grants, loans. Apply to Director of Financial Aid after acceptance. Use FAFSA. Phone: (803)792-2536. About 40% of students receive some aid from School and outside sources.

DEGREE REQUIREMENTS. For D.M.D.: satisfactory completion of four-year program. For M.S.: 30 semester hours minimum, at least 24 in residence; thesis; final oral exam. For Ph.D.: see Graduate School listing above.

FIELDS OF GRADUATE STUDY.
General Dentistry.
Oral and Maxillofacial Surgery.
Pediatric Dentistry.
Pedodontics.
Periodontics.

SOUTH CAROLINA STATE COLLEGE
Orangeburg, South Carolina 29117

Founded 1896. Located 50 miles S of Columbia. Coed. State control. Semester system. Library: 273,000 volumes, 686,000 microforms, 1375 current periodicals, 21 PCs.
Tuition: per credit, resident $152, nonresident $200.
Limited on-campus housing. Average academic year housing costs: $1260. Contact Director of Housing for both on- and off-campus housing information. Phone: (803)536-8560.

School of Graduate Studies

Established 1946. Enrollment: full-time 250, part-time 475. Faculty: full- and part-time 76. Degrees conferred: M.A., M.A.T., M.Ed., M.S., Ed.S., Ed.D.

ADMISSION REQUIREMENTS. Transcripts, GRE or MAT, NTE (for M.Ed.) required in support of School's application. Interview not required. Accepts transfer applicants. Apply to Dean of Graduate Studies one month prior to registration. Rolling admissions process. Application fee $15. Phone: (803)536-8809.

ADMISSION STANDARDS. Relatively open for master's, selective for all other degrees. Usual minimum for all master's: 2.5 (A = 4), for Ed.S.: 3.25 GPA, GRE total 850, for Ed.D.: 3.25 GPA, GRE total 1000.

FINANCIAL AID. Ten fellowships, fifteen research assistantships, Federal W/S, loans. Approved for VA benefits. Apply to Director of Financial Aid by June 1. Use FAFSA.

DEGREE REQUIREMENTS. For master's: 36 semester hours minimum, at least 30 in residence; GRE, English Subject Test, NTE for candidacy (M.Ed.); comprehensive exams; thesis/nonthesis option.

FIELDS OF STUDY.
Agribusiness.
Biology Education.
Business Education.
Counseling.
Educational Administration.
Elementary Education.
English Education.
Home Economics.
Industrial Education.
Mathematics Education.
Nutritional Science.
Reading.
Rehabilitation Counseling.
Science.
Secondary Education.
Social Studies.
Special Education.
Speech Pathology and Audiology.

UNIVERSITY OF SOUTH CAROLINA
Columbia, South Carolina 29208

Founded 1801. State control. Coed. Semester system. Special facilities: Ira and Nancy Koger Center for the Arts, Belle W. Baruch Institute for Marine Biology and Coastal Research, Counseling and Human Development Center, Center for Developmental Disabilities, Earth Sciences and Resources Institute, Center for Economic Education, Center for Fracture Mechanics and Nondestructive Evaluation, Center for Industrial Research, Center for Industry Policy and Strategy, International Center for Public Health Research, Center for Machine Intelligence, Center for Science Education, Southeast Manufacturing Technology Center, Institute for Southern Studies, Center for the Study of Suicide and Life Threatening Behavior, McKissick Museum. Library: 2,675,000 volumes, 4,075,000 microforms, 20,722 current periodicals, 219 PCs.

Annual tuition: full-time residents $3340, nonresidents $7368; per credit residents $180, nonresidents $367. On-campus housing for married students, graduate men, graduate women. Average academic year housing costs: $2800–$3600 for married students, $4500–$5500 for single students. Contact Director of Family, Conference & Summer Housing for on- and off-campus housing information. Phone: (803)777-4571. Day care facilities available.

Graduate School

Established 1906. Enrollment: full-time 5300, part-time 6000. Faculty: full- and part-time 1215. Degrees conferred: M.A., M.Acc., M.A.T., M.B.A., M.C.J., M.E., M.Ed., M.E.R.M., M.F.A., M.H.A., M.I.B.S., M.L.I.S., M.M., M.M.A., M.M.Ed., M.N., M.P.A., M.P.E.R., M.S., M.S.W., M.Tax., D.M.A., M.N., Ed.D., Dr.Ph., Ph.D.

ADMISSION REQUIREMENTS. Transcripts, two letters of recommendation, GRE Subject Tests/MAT, GMAT (business majors) required in support of School's application. TOEFL required for international applicants. Interview not required. Accepts transfer applicants. Graduates of unaccredited institutions not considered. Apply to Graduate School with complete credentials by July 1 (Fall), November 15 (Spring), May 1 (Summer). Rolling admissions process. Application fee $35. Phone: (803)777-4243; fax: (803)777-2972.

ADMISSION STANDARDS. Selective for most departments. Usual minimum average: 3.0 (A = 4).

FINANCIAL AID. Annual awards from institutional funds: eighty scholarships, one hundred fellowships, two hundred teaching assistantships, five hundred research assistantships, Federal W/S, loans. Approved for VA benefits. Apply to Dean of Graduate School for scholarships; to appropriate department chairman for assistantships, fellowships; to Financial Aid Office for all other programs; no specified closing date. Use FAFSA. About 55% of students receive aid other than loans from University and outside sources. Aid sometimes available to part-time students.

DEGREE REQUIREMENTS. For M.A., M.S.: 30 semester hours minimum, at least 24 in residence; one language for some programs; thesis/nonthesis option; comprehensive exam. For other master's: usually, language requirement is eliminated and course work is allowed in lieu of thesis. For doctoral programs: 72 hours minimum beyond the bachelor's degree, at least two years in residence; reading knowledge of one foreign language varies by department, research tool, or computer technique; qualifying exam; candidacy; dissertation; final oral exam.

FIELDS OF STUDY.
Accountancy.
Anthropology. M.A. only.
Art. Includes history, fine arts, studio.
Biology.
Biomedical Science.
Biostatistics.
Business Administration.
Chemical Engineering.
Chemistry.
Civil and Environmental Engineering.
Clinical and Community Psychology.
Communicative Disorders.
Comparative Literature.
Computer Engineering.
Computer Science.
Corrections.
Counselor Education.
Criminal Justice Planning.
Curriculum and Instruction.
Early Childhood Education.
Earth Resources Management. M.E.R.M.
Earth Sciences.
Economics.
Education.
Educational Administration.
Educational Psychology.
Educational Research.
Engineering.
English. Includes linguistics, education.
Environmental and Occupational Health.
Epidemiology.
Exercise Science.
Experimental Psychology.

French.
Genetics.
Geography.
Geology.
German.
Health Education.
History.
Hotel, Restaurant and Tourism Administration.
Instructional Media.
International Affairs.
International Business.
Journalism. M.A. only.
Juvenile Services.
Library Science.
Marine Science.
Mathematics.
Media Arts.
Museum Studies.
Music. Includes composition, conducting, education, music history, performance, piano pedagogy.
Natural Science. M.A.T. only.
Nursing. Includes cardiovascular, community health, family nurse practitioner, nursing administration, nursing science, oncology, parent-child.
Personnel and Employment Relations. M.P.E.R.
Pharmacy.
Philosophy. M.A. only.
Physical Education.
Physics and Astronomy.
Psychology.
Public Health.
Public Policy and Administration.
Reading.
Rehabilitation Counseling.
Social Studies. M.A.T. only.
Social Work. M.S.W. only.
Sociology. M.S. only.
Spanish.
Special Education.
Speech Pathology and Audiology.
Statistics.
Taxation.
Teaching English as a Second Language.
Theater and Speech.
Vocational and Technical Education.

School of Law

Established 1867. Semester system. Law library: 326,000 volumes. Library has LEXIS, NEXIS, WESTLAW, DIALOG, RLIN, OCLC.

Annual tuition: full-time, resident $6500, nonresident $12,801. On-campus housing available. Total average annual additional expense: $9000.

Enrollment: first-year class 240; total 765 (men 60%, women 40%); no part-time students. Faculty: full-time 44, part-time 25. Degrees conferred: J.D., J.D.-M.A. (Economics), J.D.-M.B.A., J.D.-M.I.B., J.D.-M.Acc., J.D.-M.P.A., J.D.-M.C.J.

ADMISSION REQUIREMENTS. LSDAS Law School report, bachelor's degree, transcripts, LSAT, personal statement, letters of recommendation required in support of application. Interview not required. Accepts transfer applicants. Preference given to state residents. Graduates of unaccredited colleges not considered. Apply to Director of Admissions after September 1, before February 15; transfer application deadline May 1. Admits beginning students Fall only. Application fee: residents $25, nonresidents $35. Phone: (803)777-6605.

ADMISSION STANDARDS. Selective. Accepts 35–40% of total annual applicants.

FINANCIAL AID. Scholarships, fellowships, Federal W/S, loans. Apply to University's Financial Aid Office after acceptance, before April 15. Use FAFSA. Very few students receive aid from School funds.

DEGREE REQUIREMENTS. For J.D.: 6 semesters minimum, at least two years in residence; 91 semester credit programs. For master's degree, see Graduate School listing above.

School of Medicine

Established 1974. Library: 80,000 volumes. Annual tuition: resident $7290, nonresident $18,620. Enrollment: first-year class 72 (EDP 12); total 270 (men 65%, women 35%). Faculty: full- and part-time 680. Degrees conferred: M.D., M.D.-Ph.D.

ADMISSION REQUIREMENTS. AMCAS report, transcripts, MCAT, recommendations required in support of final application. Interview by invitation only. Personal essay may be requested. Has EDP; apply between June 15 and August 1. Preference given to state residents. Graduates of unaccredited colleges not considered. Apply to Associate Dean for Admissions after June 15, before December 1. Application fee $20. Phone: (803)733-3325; fax: (803)733-3328.

ADMISSION STANDARDS. Admits about 10–12% of total annual applicants. Approximately 75% are state residents.

FINANCIAL AID. Scholarships, loans. Apply after acceptance to Office of Student Affairs. About 90% of students receive aid from School.

DEGREE REQUIREMENTS. For M.D.: satisfactory completion of four-year program. For Ph.D.: see Graduate School listing above.

FIELDS OF GRADUATE STUDY.
Anatomy.
Cell Biology.
Immunology.
Microbiology.
Molecular Biology.
Neurosciences.
Pathology.
Pharmacology.
Physiology.

SOUTH DAKOTA SCHOOL OF MINES AND TECHNOLOGY
Rapid City, South Dakota 57701-3995

Founded 1885. Coed. State control. Semester system. Special facilities: Institute for the Study of Mineral Deposits, Mining and Mineral Resources Institute, Engineering and Mining Experiment Station, Institute of Atmospheric Sciences, Museum of Geology. Library: 98,600 volumes, 206,000 microforms, 916 current periodicals, 15 PCs.

Tuition: per credit, resident $80, nonresident $235. On-campus housing for single students only. Average academic year housing cost: $3120 (including board). Contact Housing Director for both on- and off-campus housing information. Phone: (605)394-2348.

Graduate Division

Graduate study since 1900. Enrollment: full-time 150 (men 74%, women 26%), part-time 108. School faculty: full-time 110, part-time 30. Degrees conferred: M.S., Ph.D.

ADMISSION REQUIREMENTS. Transcripts, three letters of recommendation required in support of application. GRE/Subject Test/GMAT required by some departments. TOEFL required for foreign applicants. Interview not required. Accepts transfer applicants. Graduates of unaccredited institutions not considered. Apply to Dean of Graduate Division at least two months prior to registration. Application fee domestic students $15, foreign students $100. Phone: (605)394-2493; fax: (605)394-5360.

ADMISSION STANDARDS. Selective for most departments. Usual minimum average: 2.75 (A = 4). TOEFL score 560 for admission without tutoring.

FINANCIAL AID. Annual awards from institutional funds: 198 teaching assistantships, 63 research assistantships, 43 fellowships, Federal W/S, loans. Approved for VA benefits. Apply to Dean, Graduate Division at least three months prior to registration. Use FAFSA. About 50% of students receive aid other than loans from School and outside sources. Aid sometimes available for part-time students.

DEGREE REQUIREMENTS. For M.S.: 30 credit hours minimum, at least 18 in residence; thesis; final oral exam; or 32 hours without thesis, at least 18 in residence; final oral exam. For Ph.D.: four years beyond the bachelor's degree, at least 80 credits (includes M.S. allowance); research requirement; qualifying exam; comprehensive exams; thesis; final oral exam.

FIELDS OF STUDY.
Atmospheric, Environmental and Water Resources. GRE for admission. Ph.D. only.
Chemical Engineering. M.S. only.
Chemistry. M.S. only.
Civil Engineering. M.S. only.
Computer Science. GRE for admission. M.S. only.
Electrical Engineering. GRE for admission. M.S. only.
Geological Engineering. GRE Subject for admission.
Geology. GRE Subject for admission.
Materials Engineering and Science. GRE for admission.
Mechanical Engineering. M.S. only.
Metallurgical Engineering. M.S. only.
Meteorology. GRE Subject for international applicants.
Mining Engineering. M.S. only.
Paleontology. GRE Subject for admission. one language for M.S.. M.S. only.
Physics. M.S. only.
Technology Management. GMAT for admission. M.S. only.

SOUTH DAKOTA STATE UNIVERSITY
Brookings, South Dakota 57007

Founded 1881. Coed. State control. Semester system. Library: 495,000 volumes, 695,000 microforms, 3030 current periodicals, 54 PCs.
Tuition: per credit, resident $80, nonresident $235. On-campus housing for 88 married students, 1688 men, 1644 women. Average academic year housing costs: on-campus for single students, $1156 (double room), $2133 (including board). Varies for married students because of off-campus costs. Contact Director of Student Housing for both on- and off-campus housing information. Phone: (605)688-5148.

Graduate School

Graduate study since 1891. Enrollment: full-time 280, part-time 796. Graduate faculty: full-time 286, part-time none. Degrees conferred: M.A., M.S., M.Ed., Ph.D.

ADMISSION REQUIREMENTS. Transcripts, two letters of recommendation required in support of School's application. GRE required for some departments. TOEFL required of international

students. Interview not required. Accepts transfer applicants. Graduates of unaccredited colleges not considered. Apply to Graduate Office at least one month prior to registration. Application fee $15. Phone: (605)688-4181; fax: (605)688-6167; E-mail: Davisd@adm.sdstate.edu.

ADMISSION STANDARDS. Selective for most departments. Usual minimum average: 2.5 (with condition), 3.0 (unconditional) (A = 4).

FINANCIAL AID. Thirty-one scholarships, 204 teaching assistantships, 200 research assistantships. Approved for VA benefits. Apply to appropriate department chair for assistantships, scholarships; to Financial Aid Office for all other programs. Use FAFSA. Phone: (605)688-4695; fax: (605)688-6384.

DEGREE REQUIREMENTS. For M.A.: 30 credit hours minimum, at least 22 in residence; thesis; final oral exam. For M.Ed.: 32 credit hours minimum, at least 22 in resident; final research report; final oral exam; or 35 hours minimum, at least 22 in residence; comprehensive written exam; final oral exam. For M.S.: 30 credit hours minimum, 5-7 credits thesis or 32 credits with research paper; 48 credits required for M.S. in Counseling and Human Resource Development. For Ph.D.: minimum 90 hours (may be reduced to 60 with prior master's degree), at least 50 in residence; preliminary exam; dissertation; final oral exam.

FIELDS OF STUDY.
Agricultural Engineering. M.S., Ph.D. Offered in conjunction with Iowa State University.
Agronomy. M.S., Ph.D.
Animal Science. M.S., Ph.D.
Atmospheric, Environmental and Water Resources. Ph.D. only.
Biological Sciences. Includes animal and range sciences, biology and microbiology, dairy science, plant science, veterinary science, wildlife and fisheries sciences. Ph.D. only.
Biology. M.S.
Chemistry. M.S., Ph.D.
Communication Studies and Theatre. M.A.
Counseling and Human Resource Development. M.S.
Curriculum and Instruction. M.Ed.
Dairy Science. M.S., Ph.D.
Economics. M.S.
Educational Administration. M.S.
Engineering. Includes agricultural, civil and environmental, computer science, electrical, mechanical, physics. M.S., Ph.D.
English. M.A.
Entomology. M.S.
Geography. M.S.
Health, Physical Education and Recreation. M.S.
Home Economics. M.S.
Industrial Management. M.S.
Journalism. M.S.
Mathematics. M.S.
Microbiology. M.S.
Nursing. M.S.
Pharmaceutical Sciences. M.S.
Plant Pathology. M.S.
Rural Sociology. M.S.
Sociology. Ph.D. only.
Wildlife and Fisheries Sciences. M.S.

UNIVERSITY OF SOUTH DAKOTA
Vermillion, South Dakota 57069-2390

Founded 1882. Located 60 miles S of Sioux Falls, S. Coed. State control. Semester system. Special facilities: Business Research Center, Government Research Bureau, Historical Preservation Center, Institute of American Indian, Oral History Center,

South Dakota Geological Society, W. H. Over Museum. Library: 735,000 volumes, 645,000 microforms, 8100 current periodicals, 138 PCs in all libraries.

Annual tuition: full-time resident $3100, nonresident $5700; per credit, resident $80, nonresident $235. On-campus housing for 80 married students. Average annual housing cost: $1850 for married students, $2598 (including board) for single students. Contact Resident Services for both on- and off-campus housing information. Phone: (605)677-5663.

Graduate School

Graduate study since 1889. Enrollment: full-time 833, part-time 390 (men 70%, women 30%). University faculty: full- and part-time 531. Degrees conferred: M.A., M.B.A., M.M., M.M.S., M.P.A., M.S., Ed.S., Ed.D., Ph.D.

ADMISSION REQUIREMENTS. Two official transcripts, GRE Subject Tests/GMAT required in support of School's application. Interview not required. TOEFL, financial statement required for international applicants. Accepts transfer applicants. Graduates of unaccredited institutions not considered. Apply to Dean of Graduate School by July 15. Application fee $15. Phone: (605)677-6498.

ADMISSION STANDARDS. Selective for most departments. Usual minimum average: 3.0 (A = 4).

FINANCIAL AID. Research assistantships, teaching assistantships, Federal W/S, loans. Approved for VA benefits. Apply by March 15 to appropriate department for assistantships; to Financial Aid Office for all other programs. Use FAFSA. Phone: (605)677-5446. About 25% of students receive aid other than loans from School, 40% from all sources. Aid sometimes available for part-time students.

DEGREE REQUIREMENTS. For M.A., M.M.: 30–32 semester hours minimum, at least 20 in residence; thesis/nonthesis option; final oral/written exam. For M.M.S.: 30 hours minimum, at least 20 in residence; thesis; final oral/written exam. For M.B.A., M.P.A.: one calendar year in residence; otherwise same as for M.A. For Ed.S.: 64 semester hours minimum; preliminary exam; research project; comprehensive exam; final oral exam. For Ed.D.: 90 hours minimum beyond the bachelor's degree, at least 30 in residence; preliminary written exam; comprehensive exam; dissertation; final oral exam. For Ph.D.: 84 hours minimum beyond the bachelor's degree, at least two years in residence; preliminary exam; dissertation; final oral exam.

FIELDS OF STUDY.
Accounting. M.P.A.
Administrative Studies. M.S.
Adult and Higher Education. M.A., Ed.S., Ed.D.
Anatomy. M.A., Ph.D.
Biochemistry. Thesis for M.A., Ph.D.
Biology. M.A., Ph.D.
Business Administration. GMAT for admission. M.B.A.
Chemistry. M.A.
Communication. M.A.
Counseling and Guidance. M.A., Ed.S., Ed.D.
Curriculum and Instruction. Ed.S., Ed.D.
Economics. M.A.
Educational Administration. M.A., Ed.S., Ed.D.
Educational Psychology. M.A., Ed.S., Ed.D.
Elementary Education. M.A.
English. M.A., Ph.D.
Health, Physical Education and Research. M.A.
History. M.A.
History of Musical Instruments.
Management Information Systems. M.S., M.B.A.
Mathematics. M.A.

Microbiology. M.A., Ph.D.
Music. Includes literature, education, applied. M.M.
Occupational Therapy. M.S.
Physical Therapy. M.S.
Physiology and Pharmacology. M.A., Ph.D.
Political Science. M.A.
Psychology. Thesis for M.A.; M.A., Ph.D.
Public Administration. M.P.A.
Secondary Education. M.A.
Sociology. M.A.
Special Education. M.A.
Theater. M.A., M.F.A.

School of Law (57069-2390)

Founded 1901. Semester system. Law library: 163,000 volumes. Library has LEXIS, NEXIS, WESTLAW, DIALOG, SDLN.

Annual tuition/fees: resident $3024, nonresident $7506. Limited on-campus housing available. Total average annual additional expense: $7000.

Enrollment: first-year class 83, total 225 (men 65%, women 35%). Faculty: full-time 16, part-time 4. Degree conferred: J.D.

ADMISSION REQUIREMENTS. LSDAS Law School report, bachelor's degree, transcripts, two letters of recommendation, LSAT, two photos, personal statement required in support of application. Accepts transfer applicants. Preference given to state residents. Graduates of unaccredited institutions not considered. Application fee $15. Phone: (605)677-5443.

ADMISSION STANDARDS. Accepts 20–25% of total annual applicants.

FINANCIAL AID. Scholarships, assistantships, Federal W/S, loans. Apply to Financial Aid Office by March 1. Use FAFSA. Phone: (605)677-5446. About 25% of students receive aid other than loans from school.

DEGREE REQUIREMENTS. For J.D.: 90 semester hour program, at least two years residence.

School of Medicine (57069-2390)

Expansion to a degree-granting medical school was approved by the legislature in 1974.

Annual tuition: resident $9098, nonresident $21,479; student fees $2535. Total average figure for all other expenses: $7500. Enrollment: first-year class 50; total full-time 210 (men 58%, women 42%). Faculty: full-time 153, part-time 258. Degrees conferred: M.D., M.D.-Ph.D.

ADMISSION REQUIREMENTS. AMCAS report, transcripts, letters of recommendation, MCAT, supplemental application, interview required in support of application. Applicants must have completed at least three years of college study. Does not have EDP. Preference given to South Dakota residents. Apply after June 15, before November 15. Application fee $15, fee after screening $15. Phone: (605)677-5233; fax: (605)677-5109.

ADMISSION STANDARDS. Selective. Accepts 10% of total annual applicants. Approximately 85% are state residents.

FINANCIAL AID. Tuition waivers, scholarships, fellowships. Apply after Fall classes begin to Office of Student Affairs. Use FAFSA. About 88% of students receive some aid from School.

DEGREE REQUIREMENTS. For M.D.: satisfactory completion of 4-year program and the passing of Step 1 and Step 2 of the USMLE. For Ph.D. see Graduate School listing above.

FIELDS OF GRADUATE STUDY.
Anatomy.
Biochemistry.
Microbiology.
Molecular Biology.
Pharmacology.
Physiology.

UNIVERSITY OF SOUTH FLORIDA
Tampa, Florida 33620-9951

Founded 1956. Coed. State control. Semester system. Special facilities: Florida Institute of Oceanography, Gerontology Center, Center for Nearshore Marine Science, Center for Urban Transportation Research, Center of Microelectronics Research, Center for Engineering Development and Research. Library: 1,600,000 volumes, 4,002,300 microforms, 4678 current periodicals.

Tuition: per semester hour, resident $121, nonresident $392. On-campus housing available for single students only. Average academic year housing costs: $2460–$5150. Contact Director of University Housing for both on- and off-campus housing information. Phone: (813)974-2764.

Graduate Division

Enrollment: full-time 2357, part-time 3916. Faculty: full- and part-time 1400. Degrees conferred: M.A., M.Acc., M.Arch., M.B.A., M.Ed., Ed.S., Ed.D., M.C.E., M.E., M.F.A., M.M., M.P.A., M.P.H., M.S.P.H., M.S.C.E., M.S.C.S., M.S.E., M.S.E.E., M.S.E.M., M.S.E.S., M.S.I.E., M.S.M.E., M.S.W., M.S., Ph.D.

ADMISSION REQUIREMENTS. Transcripts, GRE Subject Tests (GMAT for business only). TOEFL and TSE required for international applicants. Interview required by some departments. Three letters of recommendation required by Natural Science Division. Accepts transfer applicants. Graduates of unaccredited institutions not considered. Apply at least two months prior to registration. Application fee $35. Phone: (813)974-2846.

ADMISSION STANDARDS. Selective for most departments. Usual minimum average: 2.75 (A = 4).

FINANCIAL AID. One hundred and eighty fellowships, approximately 1200 assistantships for teaching/research, Federal W/S, loans. Approved for VA benefits. Apply by February 1 to department chair for fellowships, assistantships; to Director of Financial Aids for all other programs. Use FAFSA. Phone: (813)974-4700.

DEGREE REQUIREMENTS. For master's: 30–36 semester hours minimum, at least 18 credits in residence; reading knowledge of one foreign language for some majors; thesis/nonthesis option; final oral/written exam. For Ed.S.: 30 semester hours beyond the master's. For Ed.D.: essentially the same as for the Ph.D., except no foreign language requirement. For Ph.D.: minimum of 90 credits beyond bachelor's degree; preliminary exam; reading knowledge of two foreign languages or equivalent; dissertation; final oral/written exam.

FIELDS OF STUDY.

SCHOOL OF ARCHITECTURE AND COMMUNITY DESIGN:
Architecture. Joint program with Florida Agricultural and Mechanical University. M.Arch.

COLLEGE OF ARTS AND SCIENCES:
Aging Studies. Ph.D. only.
American Studies. M.A. only.
Applied Anthropology.
Applied Mathematics. Ph.D. only.
Audiology. M.S. only.
Biochemistry.
Biology.
Botany. M.S. only.
Chemistry. Includes analytical, inorganic, organic, physical.
Communication.
Criminology. M.A.
Ecology. Ph.D. only.
Engineering Sciences. Ph.D. only.
English.
French. M.A. only.
Geography. M.A.
Geology. M.S.
Gerontology. M.A.
History. M.A.
Liberal Arts. M.L.A. only.
Linguistics. M.A.
Marine Biology.
Mass Communication. M.A.
Mathematics.
Microbiology. M.S.
Oceanography.
Philosophy.
Physics.
Physiology. Ph.D.
Political Science. M.A.
Psychology. Includes clinical, clinical-community, industrial, organizational.
Public Administration. M.P.A. only.
Rehabilitation Counseling.
Religious Studies. M.A.
Social Work. M.S.W. only.
Sociology. M.A.
Speech Pathology. M.S. only.
TESL. M.A.
Zoology. M.S.

COLLEGE OF BUSINESS ADMINISTRATION:
Accountancy. M.Acc.
Business Administration. M.B.A., Ph.D.
Economics. M.A.
Executive. M.B.A.

COLLEGE OF EDUCATION:
Art Education. M.A.
Business Education.
Curriculum and Instruction. M. Ed., Ph.D.
Educational Leadership. M.Ed.
Elementary Education. M.A.
English Education. M.A.
Exceptional Child Education. Includes emotionally disturbed, gifted, motor disabilities, mental retardation, specific learning disabilities. M.A.
Foreign Language. Includes French, German, Latin, Spanish. M.A.
Guidance and Counseling. M.A.
Humanities Education. M.A.
Industrial Technical Education.
Junior College Teaching. Includes biology, business, chemistry, economics, engineering, English, French, geography, geology, history, mathematics, physics, political science, sociology, Spanish, speech communication.
Library, Media, and Information Studies. M.A.
Measurement and Evaluation. M. Ed.
Music Education. M.A.
Physical Education. M.A.
Reading Education. M.A.

School Library Media.
School Psychology. M.A.
Science Education. Includes biology, chemistry, physics. M.A.
Social Science Education. M.A.
Speech Communication Education. M.A.
Vocational and Adult Education. Includes adult, business and office, distributive, industrial-technical.

COLLEGE OF ENGINEERING:
Chemical Engineering. M.S.C.E., Ph.D.
Civil Engineering. M.C.E., M.S.C.E.
Computer Engineering. M.S.C.S., Ph.D.
Electrical Engineering. M.S.E.E., Ph.D.
Engineering. M.E., M.S.E., M.S.E.S., Ph.D.
Engineering Management. M.S.E.M.
Industrial Engineering. M.S.I.E., Ph.D.
Mechanical Engineering. M.S.M.E., Ph.D.

COLLEGE OF FINE ARTS:
Art. M.F.A.
Art History. M.A.
Choral Conducting.
Composition.
Music. M.M.
Music Education.
Theory.

COLLEGE OF NURSING:
Nursing. M.S.

COLLEGE OF PUBLIC HEALTH:
Public Health. Includes environmental health, epidemiology and biostatistics, health policy and management, industrial hygiene/safety management, maternal and child health, public and community health education. M.S.P.H., Ph.D.

College of Medicine (33612-4799)

Established 1965, first class entered 1971. Annual tuition: resident $8245, nonresident $21,245; student fees none. On-campus housing available. Total average figure for all other expenses $9100.

Enrollment: first-year class 96 (EDP 29); graduate program, first-year class 10; total 420 (men 65%, women 35%). Faculty: full- and part-time 140, graduate, full-time 50. Degrees conferred: M.D., Ph.D.

ADMISSION REQUIREMENTS. For M.D.: transcripts, MCAT, recommendations required in support of application. Has EDP (Florida residents only); apply between June 15 and August 1. Preference given to Florida residents. Graduates of unaccredited colleges not considered. Apply to Assistant Dean for Admissions after July 1, before December 1. For Graduate Program: transcripts, GRE Subject Tests required in support of application. TOEFL required of foreign students. Accepts transfer applicants. Apply before August 15 to Graduate Office. Application fee $20. Phone: (813)974-2229; fax: (813)974-4990.

ADMISSION STANDARDS. For M.D.: selective. Accepts about 10–15%, of total annual applicants. 100% are state residents. For Graduate Program: accepts about 20% of total annual applicants. Usual minimum average 3.0 (A = 4).

FINANCIAL AID. For M.D.: limited scholarships, loans. Apply to Office of Financial Aid after acceptance. Use FAFSA. For Graduate Program: fellowships, assistantships. Apply to Financial Aid Office by March 1. Phone: (813)974-2068.

DEGREE REQUIREMENTS. For M.D.: satisfactory completion of three to four-year program. For Ph.D., see Graduate School listing above.

FIELDS OF GRADUATE STUDY.
Anatomy.
Biochemistry.
Cell and Molecular Biology.
Immunology.
Immunopharmacology.
Medical Microbiology.
Pathology.
Pharmacology and Therapeutics.
Physiology.

SOUTH TEXAS COLLEGE OF LAW
Houston, Texas 77002-7000

Established 1923. Private control. Semester system. Law library: 310,000 volumes, 116,000 microforms, 44 PC workstations.

Annual tuition: full-time $13,800, part-time $9100. No on-campus housing. Total average annual additional expense: $11,380.

Enrollment: first-year class, full-time 325, part-time 135; total full- and part-time 1300 (men 62%, women 38%). Faculty: full-time 55, part-time 40. Degree conferred: J.D.

ADMISSION REQUIREMENTS. LSDAS Law School report, bachelor's degree, transcripts, LSAT, letters of recommendation, personal statement required in support of application. Graduates of unaccredited colleges not considered. Accepts transfer applicants. Transfers admitted Fall and Spring. Apply to Director of Admission by March 15 (Fall), August 15 (Spring), January 15 (Summer). Application fee $40. Phone: (713)646-1810.

ADMISSION STANDARDS. Selective. Accepts 30–35% of total applicants.

FINANCIAL AID. Scholarships, tuition equalization, grants, Federal W/S, loans. Apply to Financial Aid Office before May 1. Use FAFSA. About 20–25% of students receive aid other than loans from College and outside sources.

DEGREE REQUIREMENTS. For J.D.: 90 semester hours, at least 24 semester hours and last 3 semesters in residence.

SOUTHEAST MISSOURI STATE UNIVERSITY
Cape Girardeau, Missouri 63701-4799

Founded 1873. Located 125 miles S of St. Louis. Coed. State control. Semester system. Library: 350,000 volumes, 2800 current periodicals, 50 PCs. Special collection: Faulkner Collection.

Fees: per semester, resident $882, nonresident $1593. On-campus housing for married and single students. Average academic year housing costs: single students $3200 (including board); married students $2500. Contact Residence Life Office for on- and off-campus housing information. Phone: (314)651-2274.

Graduate Study

Graduate study since 1965. Enrollment: full-time 9, part-time 630. Faculty: full-time 190. Degrees conferred: M.A., M.B.A., M.M.E., M.N.S., M.S.A., M.S.N., Ed.S.

ADMISSION REQUIREMENTS. Transcripts required in support of application. GRE required for some programs. TOEFL required for international applicants. Accepts transfer applicants. Graduates of unaccredited institutions not considered. Apply to Dean of Graduate Study by April 1 (Fall), September 1 (Spring),

February 1 (Summer). Rolling admissions process. Application fee $20. Phone: (314)651-2192; fax: (314)651-2001.

ADMISSION STANDARDS. Selective. Usual minimum average: 2.5 (A = 4), 3.0 GPA for some programs.

FINANCIAL AID. Five graduate scholarships, seventy teaching assistantships, ten research assistantships, Federal W/S, loans. Approved for VA benefits. Apply with admission application to appropriate department head for assistantships; to Financial Aid Office for all other programs. Use FAFSA. Phone: (314)651-2253. About 15% of students receive aid other than loans from University and outside sources. No aid other than loans for part-time students.

DEGREE REQUIREMENTS. For master's: 32 semester hours minimum, at least 24 in residence; thesis or final document. For Ed.S.: one year beyond the master's.

FIELDS OF STUDY.
Biology.
Business Administration.
Business Education.
Communication Disorders.
Criminal Justice Administration.
Elementary Administration.
Elementary Education.
English.
Geosciences.
Guidance and Counseling.
History.
Home Economics.
Human Services Administration.
Mathematics.
Music. Includes education.
Nursing.
Psychological Counseling.
Public Administration.
Secondary Administration.
Secondary Education.
Special Education.

SOUTHEASTERN LOUISIANA UNIVERSITY
Hammond, Louisiana 70402

Founded 1925. Located 60 miles N of New Orleans. Coed. State control. Semester system. Special facilities: Center for Regional Studies, Biological Turtle Cove Research Station, Agricultural and Educational Research Station, JFK Assassination Resources Center, Institute for Human Development. Library: 323,000 volumes, 606,000 microforms, 2100 current periodicals, 38 PCs.

Annual tuition: full-time resident $1920, nonresident $3036; per semester, part-time, resident $272, nonresident $272. On-campus housing for 60 married students, unlimited for single students. Average academic year housing costs: $2400 (including board) for single students; $2500 for married students. Contact Director of Housing for both on- and off-campus housing information. Phone: (504)549-2118.

Graduate Studies

Graduate study since 1960. Enrollment: full-time 314, part-time 975. Graduate faculty: full-time 114, part-time 5. Degrees conferred: M.A., M.M., M.Ed., M.S.N., M.B.A., Ed.S.

ADMISSION REQUIREMENTS. Official transcripts, GRE required in support of application. Copy of teaching certificate re-

quired for Education majors. GMAT required for M.B.A. applicants. GRE Subject required by some programs. TOEFL required for international applicants. Interview not required. Accepts transfer applicants. Graduates of unaccredited institutions not considered. Apply to Admissions Office at least 30 days prior to registration. Rolling admissions process. Application fee $10, $25 for international applicants. Phone: (504)549-3872.

ADMISSION STANDARDS. Relatively open. Usual minimum average: 2.5, 3.0 for candidacy (A = 4).

FINANCIAL AID. Fellowships, research assistantships, teaching assistantships, Federal W/S, loans. Apply at least 30 days prior to registration to appropriate department head for fellowships, assistantships; to Financial Aid Office for all other programs. Use FAFSA. Phone: (504)549-2244. About 30% of students receive aid from University and outside sources.

DEGREE REQUIREMENTS. For M.Ed.: 30 semester hours minimum, except Secondary Guidance and Counseling 33 hours, at least 21 in residence; final written/oral exams. For Ed.S.: 30 semester hours minimum, at least 21 in residence; thesis or research project. For M.S.: 30 semester hours minimum; thesis. For M.B.A.: one-year program for students with degree in business, two-year for non–degree holders.

FIELDS OF STUDY.
Biological Sciences. M.S.
Business Administration. M.B.A.
Counselor Education. M.Ed.
Educational Administration. Ed.S.
Elementary Teaching. M.A.
English. M.A.
Health Studies. M.A.
History. M.A.
Kinesiology. M.A.
Music Theory. M.M.
Nursing. M.S.N.
Performance. M.M.
Psychology. M.A.
School Administration and Supervision. M.Ed.
Secondary Teaching. M.Ed.
Special Education. M.Ed., M.S.

SOUTHEASTERN OKLAHOMA STATE UNIVERSITY
Durant, Oklahoma 74701-0609

Established 1909. Located 90 miles N of Dallas, Texas. Coed. State control. Semester system. Library: 160,000 volumes, 300,000 microforms, 1100 current periodicals, 11 PCs.

Annual tuition: full-time resident $1680, nonresident $3960; per hour, resident $58, nonresident $153. On-campus housing for 36 married students, 125 single men, 100 single women. Average academic year housing costs: single students $2619 (including board), married students $2940. Contact Housing Director for both on- and off-campus housing information. Phone: (405)924-0121, ext. 2592.

Graduate School

Graduate study since 1954. Enrollment: full-time 146, part-time 306. Faculty teaching graduate students: full-time 96, part-time 4. Degrees conferred: M.A.S., M.B.S., M.Ed., M.T.

ADMISSION REQUIREMENTS. Transcripts, GRE/GMAT, interview required in support of School's application. TOEFL required for international applicants. Accepts transfer applicants.

Graduates of unaccredited colleges not considered. Apply to Dean of Graduate School at least one month prior to date of registration. Application fee: none. Phone: (405)924-0121, ext. 2428.

ADMISSION STANDARDS. Selective. Usual minimum average: 2.75 (A = 4).

FINANCIAL AID. Scholarships, teaching assistantships, Federal W/S, loans. Apply to the Director of Financial Aid; no specified closing date. Use FAFSA and institutional FAF. Phone: (405)924-0121, ext. 2406; fax: (504)920-7469.

DEGREE REQUIREMENTS. For master's: 33 semester hours minimum, at least 24 in semester hours in residence; thesis/nonthesis option.

FIELDS OF STUDY.
Administrative Studies. Includes business management.
Behavioral Studies. Includes counseling.
Education. Includes secondary education, elementary education, counseling, school administration.
Technology. Includes electronics, design, manufacturing processes, computer science, safety, sciences.

SOUTHERN CALIFORNIA COLLEGE OF OPTOMETRY
Fullerton, California 92631-1615

Founded 1904. Coed. Private control. Quarter system. Library: 15,823 volumes, 360 current periodicals, 13 PCs.
Annual tuition: full-time $16,200, per unit $500. No on-campus housing available.

Graduate Study

Enrollment: full-time 376 (men 122, women 254). Faculty: full-time 37, part-time 35. Degree conferred: O.D.

ADMISSION REQUIREMENTS. Transcripts, bachelor's degree, OAT, three letters of recommendation, interview required in support of application. Accepts transfer applicants. Apply to Admissions Office by March 15. Admits Fall only. Rolling admissions process. Application fee $50. Phone: (714)449-7446; fax: (714)879-0481.

ADMISSION STANDARDS. Selective. Usual minimum average: 2.75 (A = 4).

FINANCIAL AID. Scholarships, Federal W/S, loans. Approved for VA benefits. Apply to Financial Aid Office following registration. Use FAFSA. Phone: (714)449-7447. About 89% of students receive aid other than loans from College.

DEGREE REQUIREMENTS. For O.D.: 4 years and 241 quarter units.

UNIVERSITY OF SOUTHERN CALIFORNIA
Los Angeles, California 90089-0913
http://www.usc.edu

Founded 1880. Coed. Private control. Semester system. Special facilities: USC-Atelier Art Gallery, Arnold Schoenberg Institute, East Asian Studies Center, Center for Feminist Research, Fisher Gallery, Signal and Image Processing Institute, Informa-

tion Science Institute, Hydrocarbon Research Institute, Center for International Business Education and Research, Center for Laser Studies, Alzheimer's Disease Research Center, Gerontology Research Institute, Center for the Management of Engineering Research and Technology, Center for Multiethnic and Transnational Studies, Pacific Center for Health Policy and Ethics, Social Science Research Institute, Center for Future Research, Center for Software Engineering, Center for Urban Affairs, Von Kleinsmid Center for International and Public Affairs. Library: 2,700,000 volumes, 1,500,000 microforms, 16,000 current periodicals, 138 PCs in all libraries.

Tuition: per unit $645. On-campus housing available. Average monthly housing costs: $255–$350 two bedroom, $360–$475 single bedroom. Contact Housing Office for detailed information. Phone: (800)872-4632. Day care facilities available.

Graduate School

Graduate study since 1910. Enrollment: full-time 8374, part-time 3100. Graduate faculty: 2243. Degrees conferred: M.A., M.A.E.D.P., M.F.A., M.P.T., M.P.P., M.P.A.S., M.S., M.S.N., M.S.S., M.S.S.M., M.U.D., Ph.D.

ADMISSION REQUIREMENTS. Official transcripts, an earned bachelor's degree, GRE required in support of School's application. GRE Subject Test required by some departments. TOEFL encouraged for international applicants. Accepts transfer applicants. Graduates of unaccredited institutions not considered. Apply to University Office of Admissions, preferably early in the preceding semester. Application fee $50. Phone: (213)740-5686; fax: (213)740-7577.

ADMISSION STANDARDS. Competitive for most departments, selective or very competitive for the others. Usual minimum average: 3.0 (A = 4).

FINANCIAL AID. Two thousand three hundred and twenty-nine fellowships, 574 research assistantships, 1098 teaching assistantships, Federal W/S, loans. Approved for VA benefits. Apply by February 1 to Dean of Graduate School for scholarships and fellowships, to appropriate department chair for assistantships; to Financial Aid Office for all other programs. Use FAFSA. Phone: (213)740-1111. Most full-time students receive some financial support. About 50% of all students receive aid other than loans from University and outside sources. Aid sometimes available for part-time students.

DEGREE REQUIREMENTS. For master's: 24 units minimum, at least 20 in residence; thesis/nonthesis; final written/oral exam; some departments require language, some permit comprehensive exam in lieu of thesis. For Ph.D.: 60 units minimum beyond the bachelor's, at least three years in residence; preliminary exam; reading knowledge of one foreign language for most programs; dissertation; final oral exam.

FIELDS OF STUDY.
Anatomy and Cell Biology.
Anthropology. Includes social, visual.
Applied Mathematics.
Art History.
Biochemistry.
Biokinesiology and Physical Therapy.
Biological Sciences. Includes marine molecular, neurobiology.
Biometry. Includes applied biometry and epidemiology, epidemiology.
Chemistry. Includes chemical physics.
Cinema-Television. Includes critical studies, film and literature.
Classics.
Communication Arts and Sciences.
Communications Management. M.A. only.

Communication Theory and Research. Ph.D.
Comparative Literature.
Computer Science.
Craniofacial Biology.
East Asian Area Studies. M.A. only.
East Asian Language and Culture. Ph.D.
Economic Development Programming. M.A.E.D.P. only.
Economics.
English.
Epidemiology. Ph.D. only.
Exercise Science.
Fine Arts. M.F.A.
French.
Geography.
German.
Gerontology. Includes public policy.
History.
Human Factors and Ergonomics.
International Relations.
Journalism. Include broadcast, international, print.
Linguistics.
Mathematics.
Microbiology. Ph.D. only.
Molecular Pharmacology and Toxicology.
Museum Studies. M.A. only.
Music.
Neuroscience. Ph.D.
Nursing. M.S. only.
Occupational Sciences. Ph.D.
Occupational Therapy. M.A. only.
Ocean Sciences.
Pathobiology.
Pharmaceutical Economics and Policy.
Pharmaceutical Sciences. Includes toxicology.
Pharmacology and Nutrition.
Philosophy.
Physics.
Physiology and Biophysics. Ph.D. only.
Political Economy and Public Policy. Ph.D. only
Political Science.
Preventive Medicine. Includes health behavior. Ph.D. only.
Professional Writing. M.P.W.
Psychology. Ph.D. only.
Public Policy. M.P.P. only.
Religion. Includes social ethics.
Safety and Health. M.S.
Slavic Languages and Literatures.
Sociology. Includes applied demography, criminology.
Spanish.
Statistics. M.S. only.
Systems Management. M.S. only.
Theater. M.F.A.

School of Architecture

Established 1887. School's library: 60,000 volumes, 200,000 slides.

Annual tuition: $19,140; per credit $645. Enrollment: full-time 40. School faculty: full-time 20, part-time 25. Degrees conferred: M.Arch., M.B.S., M.L.A.

ADMISSION REQUIREMENTS. Transcripts, GRE, design portfolio, three letters of reference required in support of application. TOEFL required for foreign applicants. Graduates of unaccredited colleges not considered. Applicants with nonarchitecture degrees not considered for M.Arch. program. Apply to University Office of Admissions by March 1. Application fee $50. Phone: (213)740-2723.

ADMISSION STANDARDS. Competitive. Usual minimum average: 3.0 (A = 4).

FINANCIAL AID. Four scholarships, seven to eight teaching assistantships, Federal W/S, loans. Apply to Financial Aid Office: no specified closing date. Use FAFSA and University's FAF. Phone: (213)740-1111.

DEGREE REQUIREMENTS. For master's: one to three years minimum, at least one to two in residence; thesis.

FIELDS OF STUDY.
Architecture.
Building Science.
Landscape Architecture.

Graduate School of Business Administration
http://cwis.usc.edu:80/dept/sba

Graduate study since 1920.
Tuition: per semester $8466 (1518 units) M.B.A.
Enrollment: full-time 400, part-time 862. Graduate faculty: full-time 50, part-time 12. Degrees conferred: M.B.A., M.S.B.A., M.S.I.O.M., M.Acc., M.Bus.Tax., Ph.D.

ADMISSION REQUIREMENTS. Transcript, GMAT, introduction to calculus prior to enrollment, letters of recommendation required in support of School's application. Two years of professional work experience preferred. TOEFL required for international applicants. Graduates of unaccredited institutions not considered. Apply to the Graduate School of Business: full-time applicants by April 15, part-time applicants by June 1, April 1 (Fall) October 1 (Spring). Application fee $90 domestic, $125 for international applicants. Phone: (213)740-8846; fax: (213)749-8520.

ADMISSION STANDARDS. Selective. Usual minimum average: 3.2 (A = 4), GMAT 626.

FINANCIAL AID. Annual awards from institutional funds: each year qualified full-time M.B.A. students are offered merit-based fellowships ranging from 12 full tuition, loans. Approved for VA benefits. Apply by April 1 (Fall). Phone: (213)743-1111. About 33% receive aid other than loans from School, outside sources, and interested individuals.

DEGREE REQUIREMENTS. For M.B.A., M.S.I.O.M., M.S.B.A.: contact (213)740-8846; for Accounting contact (213)740-4867; for Ph.D.: contact (213)740-0674.

FIELDS OF STUDY.
Business of Entertainment.
Business Entrepreneurship.
Controllership.
Corporate Finance.
Corporate Financial Reporting.
Designing and Reengineering Management Accounting and Control Systems.
Finance and Marketing.
Financial Analysis.
Information Systems.
Investments.
Management and Organization.
Marketing (Managing Clients).
Marketing (Managing Products).
Operations Management (Manufacturing).
Operations Management (Service).
Real Estate.
Strategic Human Resource Management.
Technology and Innovation Management.
Note: the following dual degree programs are available; J.D. M.B.A., M.B.A.-M.R.E.D., M.B.A.-M.S. in Gerontology, M.B.A.-M.S.I.S.E., M.B.A.-D.D.S., M.B.A.-M.S. Nursing, Pharm.D.-M.B.A., J.D.-M.B.T.

School of Education

Doctoral degrees in education awarded since 1927.

Tuition: $645 per unit. Graduate enrollment: full-time 525, part-time 321. Faculty: full-time 48, part-time 100. Degrees conferred: M.S., M.F.C.C., Ed.D. The Ph.D. is administered by the Graduate School.

ADMISSION REQUIREMENTS. Official transcripts, GRE required in support of Schools application. Interview not required. TOEFL required for international applicants. International students whose first language is English are exempted. Accepts transfer applicants. Graduates of unaccredited institutions not considered. Apply to University Office of Admissions one month prior to registration. Application fee $50. Phone: (213)740-2383.

ADMISSION STANDARDS. Competitive for most departments. Usual minimum average: 3.0 (master's), 3.0 (doctorate) (A = 4).

FINANCIAL AID. Scholarships, 121 fellowships, 2 research assistantships, 25 teaching assistantships, training grants, Federal W/S, loans. Approved for VA benefits. Apply by April 1 to Dean of School of Education for fellowships, assistantships; to Financial Aid for all other programs. Use FAFSA. Phone: (213)740-3495. About 50% of students receive aid other than loans from University and outside sources. Aid sometimes available for part-time students.

DEGREE REQUIREMENTS. For M.S.: 28 units minimum, at least 24 in residence; thesis/nonthesis option or master's seminar. For Ed.D.: 96 units minimum beyond the bachelor's, at least 66 in residence; preliminary review; qualifying exam; dissertation; final oral exam. For Ph.D., see Graduate School listing above.

FIELDS OF STUDY.
Administration and Policy. Ph.D.
College Student Personnel Services. M.S.
Counseling Psychology. M.S., Ph.D.
Curriculum and Instruction. Ed. D. Ph.D.
Curriculum and Teaching. M.S.
Educational Leadership. M.S.
Educational Psychology. M.S., Ph.D.
Instructional Technology. M.S.
International and Intercultural Education. M.S.
Language, Literacy and Learning. Ph.D.
Marriage, Family and Child Counseling. M.F.C.C.
Pupil Personnel Services (K–12). M.S.
Teaching English as a Second Language. M.S.

School of Engineering

http://www.usc.edu

Graduate study since 1931. Semester system.

Annual tuition $11,000, per credit $645. Graduate enrollment: full-time 1400, part-time 550. Graduate teaching faculty: full-time 140, part-time 38. Degrees conferred: M.S., Engineer. The Ph.D. is administered by the Graduate School.

ADMISSION REQUIREMENTS. Two transcripts, GRE required in support of School's application. Some majors also require GRE Subject Test. Interview not required. Accepts transfer applicants. Graduates of unaccredited institutions not considered. Apply to University Office of Admissions at least eight weeks prior to beginning of semester for U.S. citizens and permanent residents, at least three months for international applicants. Application fee $55. Phone: (213)740-5686; fax: (213)740-8493.

ADMISSION STANDARDS. Selective for most departments. Usual minimum average: 3.0 (A = 4) for M.S., 3.5 for Ph.D.

FINANCIAL AID. Annual awards from institutional funds: 510 teaching/research assistantships, Federal W/S, loans. Approved for VA benefits. Apply by February 1 to chair of major department for assistantships; to Financial Aid Office for all other programs. Use FAFSA and University's FAF. Phone: (213)740-5444; fax: (213)740-0680. About 35% of full-time students receive aid other than loans from both School and outside sources. Loans available for part-time students.

DEGREE REQUIREMENTS. For M.S.: 27 units minimum, at least 23 in residence; thesis/nonthesis option. For Engineer: 30 units beyond the master's degree, at least 26 units in residence; Engineer's exam. For Ph.D., see Graduate School listing above.

FIELDS OF STUDY.
Aerospace Engineering. Includes option in ocean engineering.
Biomedical Engineering. Includes options in biomedical imaging, telemedicine.
Chemical Engineering.
Civil Engineering. Includes options in applied mechanics, environmental.
Computer Engineering.
Computer Science. Includes options in computer networks, multimedia and creative technologies, software engineering, robotics and automation.
Earthquake Engineering.
Electrical Engineering. Includes options in systems, electrophysics VLS design, computer networks, multimedia and creative technologies.
Industrial and Systems Engineering. Includes options in operations research, engineering management, manufacturing engineering, and safety engineering.
Materials Science. Includes option in materials engineering.
Mechanical Engineering.
Petroleum Engineering.
Systems Architecture and Engineering.

School of Fine Arts (90089-0292)

http://www.usc.edu/univ/entries/fineart.html

Tuition: per credit $645.

Graduate enrollment: full-time 34, part-time 3. School faculty: full-time 10, part-time 17. Degrees conferred: M.F.A., A.M.

ADMISSION REQUIREMENTS. Two transcripts, three letters of reference (GRE required for Public Art Studies), twenty-slide portfolio for studio M.F.A., supplemental application and materials for A.M. TOEFL required for international applicants. Apply to both School of Fine Arts and Graduate School by February 1. Application fee $50. Phone: (213)740-2787 Art Office, (213)740-7686 Grad Admissions.

ADMISSION STANDARDS. Competitive. Usual minimum average: 3.0 (A = 4).

FINANCIAL AID. Eleven teaching assistantships, eight internships, Federal W/S, loans. Approved for VA benefits. Apply by February 1 to School's Financial Aid Office. Use FAFSA and University's FAF. Phone: (213)740-1111; fax: (213)740-0680.

DEGREE REQUIREMENTS. For A.M.: 40 units; internships. For M.F.A.: 48 credits; thesis/exhibition.

FIELDS OF STUDY.
Public Art Studies. A.M.
Studio Art. M.F.A.

School of Music

Observed its centennial in 1984. Semester system.
Tuition: per credit $645.

Graduate enrollment: full-time 183, part-time 182. Faculty: full-time 54, part-time 75. Degrees conferred: M.M., M.M.Ed., D.M.A. The M.A., Ph.D. are offered through the Graduate School.

ADMISSION REQUIREMENTS. Transcripts, supplementary application required in support of regular University application. Personal or taped performance audition required for all performance majors; original scores for composition majors; research paper or thesis for M.A. or Ph.D. Accepts transfer applicants. Apply to Office of Admission, School of Music preferably well in advance of registration. Application fee $55. Phone: (213)740-8986; fax: (213)740-8995.

ADMISSION STANDARDS. Selective. Talent weighted more heavily than GPA in most programs.

FINANCIAL AID. Tuition awards, scholarships, teaching assistantships. Apply to School's Office of Financial Aid; no specified closing date. Use FAFSA. Phone: (213)740-5444; fax: (213)740-0680. Application details accompany application for admission.

DEGREE REQUIREMENTS. For M.M.: 30 units minimum, at least 26 in residence. For M.M.Ed.: 30 units minimum, at least 26 in residence; Music Graduate Entrance Exam; one or two recitals for performance majors; thesis for music education majors, thesis and recital for composition majors. For D.M.A.: 65 units minimum beyond the bachelor's, at least 35 units in residence and two consecutive semesters in full-time attendance; reading knowledge of one foreign language; qualifying exam; dissertation for composition, music education, and church music majors; two solo recitals and two other appropriate appearances for performance majors; final oral exam. For M.A., Ph.D., see Graduate School listing above.

FIELDS OF STUDY.
Choral Music.
Church Music.
Composition.
Music Education.
Musicology. M.A., Ph.D.
Performance. Includes keyboard collaborative arts, classical guitar, studio guitar, early music, jazz studies, orchestral instruments, keyboard (piano, organ, harpsichord), voice, opera.
Theory. M.A., Ph.D.

School of Pharmacy

Founded in 1905. Semester system.
Annual tuition: full-time $19,660.
Enrollment: professional program 707; graduate program 40. Faculty: full-time 25, part-time and courtesy clinical 300. Degrees conferred: Pharm.D.; M.S., and Ph.D. administered by the Graduate School.

ADMISSION REQUIREMENTS. Pharm.D.: two transcripts documenting completion of required preprofessional courses, written essay; two letters of recommendation, personal interview required in support of School's application. Accepts transfer applicants. Graduates of unaccredited institutions not considered. Apply to Office of Admissions by March 31 (Fall). Graduate program: two official transcripts, three letters of recommendation, GRE required in support of application. Transfer applicants accepted. Apply to Director of Admissions by March 1 (Fall), December 15 (Spring). Application fee $50. Phone: (213)342-2650.

ADMISSION STANDARDS. Selective. Accepts 23% of applicants in professional and graduate programs. Usual minimum average: 2.75 (A = 4).

FINANCIAL AID. Professional program: loans and scholarships based upon financial eligibility and merit. Institutional FAF included with application package. Graduate programs: fellowships, teaching assistantships, loans. Apply by March 1 to Coordinator, Graduate Programs Committee. Phone: (213)342-1466.

DEGREE REQUIREMENTS. Professional program: four-year curriculum following two years of preprofessional undergraduate college study. For M.S. and Ph.D., see the Graduate School listing above.

FIELDS OF STUDY.
Molecular Pharmacology and Toxicology. M.S. Ph.D.
Pharmaceutical Economics and Policy. M.S., Ph.D.
Pharmaceutical Sciences. M.S., Ph.D.
Pharmacy. Pharm.D.

School of Social Work
http://www.usc.edu

Graduate study since 1920. Semester system.
Tuition: per credit $645.
Graduate enrollment: full-time 315, part-time 120. Faculty: full-time 29, part-time 26. Degrees conferred: M.S.W., Ph.D.

ADMISSION REQUIREMENTS. Two transcripts, references, personal statement required in support of School's application. TOEFL, TSE required for international applicants. Accepts transfer applicants. Apply to Office of Admissions by April 1. Fall admission only. Application fee $55. Phone: (213)740-2013.

ADMISSION STANDARDS. Competitive. Usual minimum average: 3.0 (A = 4).

FINANCIAL AID. Annual awards from institutional funds: twenty-five scholarships, twenty-five internships, Federal W/S, loans. Approved for VA benefits. Apply by February 15 to the University Financial Aid Office. Use FAFSA and University's FAF. Phone: (213)740-1111. About 45% of students receive aid other than loans from School and outside sources. No aid for part-time students.

DEGREE REQUIREMENTS. For M.S.W.: 56 units minimum in residence. For Ph.D., see Graduate School listing above.

School of Public Administration

Established 1929. Semester system. Campuses located in Sacramento, California; Washington, D.C.; and home campus in Los Angeles.
Tuition: per credit $645.
Enrollment: full-time 375, part-time 225. Faculty: full-time 28, part-time 70. Degrees conferred: M.P.A., M.H.A., D.P.P., D.P.A., Ph.D.

ADMISSION REQUIREMENTS. USC Graduate Admission Application, School Supplemental Application, two official transcripts, three letters of recommendation, current resume, GRE, GMAT or LSAT test scores required in support of School's application process. TOEFL required for international applicants. Interview not required. Accepts transfer applicants (up to 8 units can be transferred). Apply to School of Public Administration by February 1. Application fee $55. Phone: (213)740-6942.

ADMISSION STANDARDS. Selective. Usual minimum GPA of 3.0 in last 60 semester units or 90 quarter units. GRE (or equivalent GMAT or LSAT) score of 1000 on verbal and quantitative sections.

FINANCIAL AID. Awards from institutional funds: seventy-five partial tuition scholarships, two doctoral fellowships, unlimited graduate internships, tuition waivers, Federal W/S, loans. Approved for VA benefits. Apply to School by February 15 for Fall awards, November 1 for Spring awards. Financial aid application for Federal programs are due March 10. Use FAFSA and University's FAF.

DEGREE REQUIREMENTS. For M.P.A.: 41 units of study. For M.P.P., M.H.A.: 48 units, at least 36 in residence. For Ph.D., D.P.A.: completion of 60 units past the bachelor's degree, at least 30 in residence; qualifying exam; dissertation; systems requirement for D.P.A., a foreign language requirement for Ph.D.

FIELDS OF STUDY.
Ambulatory Care. Certificate program.
Education Policy. M.P.P.
Environmental Policy. M.P.P.
Financial Management. M.P.A.
Governance and Citizenship. D.P.A., Ph.D.
Government-Business-Non-Profit. M.P.P.
Health Policy. M.P.P.
Health Policy and Management. D.P.A., Ph.D.
Human Resource Management. M.P.A., D.P.A., Ph.D.
Intergovernmental Management and Policy. M.P.A., M.P.P.
International and Comparative Policies. D.P.A., Ph.D.
International Policy and Management. M.P.A.
Judicial Administration/Court Management. M.P.A.
Local Government. M.P.A.
Long Term Care. Certificate program.
Media and Communication Policy. M.P.P.
Mental Health. M.H.A.
Non-Profit Management. M.P.A.
Public Management. M.P.P.
Public Management and Policy. D.P.A., Ph.D.
Public Policy. D.P.A., Ph.D.
Social Welfare Policy. M.P.P.
Urban Policy. M.P.P.
Note: Dual master's degrees in conjunction with the USC Schools of Gerontology, Law, Social Work, and Urban and Regional Planning; Hebrew Union College.

Law Center (90089-0071)

Founded 1896. Semester system. Law library: over 330,000 volumes. Library has LEXIS, WESTLAW.

Annual tuition: $22,238. On-campus housing available. Total average annual additional expense: $12,100.

Enrollment: first-year class 200; total 631 (men 55%, women 45%). Faculty: full-time 48, part-time 34. Degrees conferred: J.D., J.D.-M.A. (Economics), J.D.-M.B.A., J.D.-M.P.A., J.D.-M.S.W., J.D.-Ph.D. (Social Sciences with California Institute of Technology), LL.M., M.L.S.

ADMISSION REQUIREMENTS. LSDAS Law School report, bachelor's degree, transcripts, LSAT (not later than December), letters of recommendation required in support of application. Interview not required. Accepts transfer applicants. Graduates of unaccredited colleges not considered. Apply to Admissions Office after September 1, before February 1. Fall admission only. Application fee $60. Phone: (213)740-7331.

ADMISSION STANDARDS. Selective. Accepts 10–15% of total annual applicants.

FINANCIAL AID. Scholarships, fellowships, assistantships, Federal W/S, loans. Apply to Director of Financial Aid, the Law Center by February 1. Use FAFSA. Phone: (213)740-7331.

DEGREE REQUIREMENTS. For J.D.: 88 credits minimum; maximum of 30 units in transfer for study completed at other law schools. For LL.M., M.L.S.: at least 24 credits beyond the J.D.; thesis.

School of Medicine (90033)

Organized 1885. Annual tuition: $27,830; student fees $1172. Total average figure for all other expenses: $9842. Enrollment: first-year class 150, total 808 (men 60%, women 40%). Faculty: full-time 685, part-time 56. Degrees conferred: M.D., M.D.-M.S., M.D.-Ph.D.

ADMISSION REQUIREMENTS. AMCAS report, letters of recommendation, MCAT supplement application required for admission. Interview by invitation only. Applicants must have completed at least three years of college study. Has EDP; apply between June 15 and August 1. Accepts transfer applicants. Graduates of unaccredited colleges not considered. Apply after June 15, before November 1. Application fee $50. Phone: (213)342-2552.

ADMISSION STANDARDS. Very competitive. Accepts 3–5% of total annual applicants. Approximately 50% are state residents.

FINANCIAL AID. Scholarships, loans. Apply to University Financial Aid Office. Use FAFSA. About 75% of students receive some aid from School. Phone: (213)342-2552.

DEGREE REQUIREMENTS. For M.D.: satisfactory completion of four-year program; transfer students from other medical schools may be admitted to advanced standing in second- or third-year class. For M.S., Ph.D., see Graduate School listing above.

FIELDS OF GRADUATE STUDY.
Biochemistry.
Biophysics.
Cell Biology.
Genetics.
Immunology.
Microbiology.
Molecular Biology.
Neurosciences.
Pathology.
Physiology.

School of Dentistry

Founded 1897. Trimester system. Annual tuition: $29,748. Limited on-campus housing available. Average academic year housing costs: $8000. Contact Housing Office in Student Union Building for both on- and off-campus housing information. Total average cost for all other first-year expenses: $8400.

Enrollment: first-year class 130; total 293 (men 60%, women 40%). Degrees conferred: D.D.S., D.D.S.-M.B.A. The M.S., Ph.D. are offered through the Graduate School.

ADMISSION REQUIREMENTS. AADSAS, official transcripts, three letters of reference, DAT (no later than October) required in support of School's application. Applicants must have at least two years of college study. Interview by invitation only. Accepts transfer applicants from U.S. and Canadian dental schools only. Graduates of unaccredited colleges not considered. Apply to Office of Admissions and Student Affairs after June 1, before April 1. Deadline for transfer applicants March 1. Application fee $50. Phone: (213)740-2841.

ADMISSION STANDARDS. Selective. Accepts about 20–25% of total annual applicants.

FINANCIAL AID. Scholarships, grants, loans. Apply to Office of Admissions and Student Affairs; no specified closing date.

Phone: (213)740-2841. Use FAFSA. About 90% of students receive some form of financial assistance.

DEGREE REQUIREMENTS. For D.D.S.: satisfactory completion of 11 consecutive 15 week trimesters. For M.S., Ph.D., see Graduate School listing above.

FIELDS OF GRADUATE STUDY.
Biochemistry.
Cellular Molecular Biology.
Craniofacial Biology.
Experimental Pathology.
Immunology.
Microbiology.
Physiology.

SOUTHERN COLLEGE OF OPTOMETRY

Memphis, Tennessee 38104-2211

Founded 1932. Coed. Accredited by Southern Association of Colleges and Schools and by Council on Optometric Education. Private control. Quarter system. Library: 20,500 volumes, 531 microforms, 25 PCs.

Annual tuition: resident $8900, nonresident $13,900. No on-campus housing available. Contact the Records and Admissions Office for off-campus housing information. Phone: (800)238-0180.

Enrollment, full-time 458. College faculty: full-time 39, part-time 4. Degree conferred: O.D.

ADMISSION REQUIREMENTS. Transcripts showing satisfactory completion of 90 semester hours of prescribed preoptometry courses (bachelor's degree preferred), two letters of recommendation, interview, OAT required in support of College's application. Apply to Admissions Office by March 31 (priority date). Rolling admissions process. Application fee $50. Phone: (901)722-3224, (800)238-0180.

ADMISSION STANDARDS. Competitive. Usual minimum average: 3.0 (A = 4).

FINANCIAL AID. Scholarships, Federal W/S, loans. Approved for VA benefits. Apply by April 1 to Financial Aid Office. Use FAFSA. Phone: (901)722-3207.

DEGREE REQUIREMENTS. For O.D.: 232 quarter hours minimum, at least 180 in residence.

SOUTHERN CONNECTICUT STATE UNIVERSITY

New Haven, Connecticut 06515-1355

Founded 1893. Coed. State control. Semester system. Special facilities: Business and Economic Development Center, Child Abuse Center, Center for Communication Disorders, Center for Computing and Society, Center for Environment, Reading Center, Research in Behavioral Science Center, Urban Studies Center. Library: 463,000 volumes, 411,000 microforms, 5000 current periodicals, 32 PCs.

Annual tuition: full-time, resident $3550, nonresident $8610; per credit $143. Some on-campus housing in summer for single

graduate students. Average academic year housing costs: $5061 (including board). Contact Housing Office for both on- and off-campus housing information. Phone: (203)392-5870.

School of Graduate Studies and Continuing Education

Graduate study since 1947. Enrollment: full-time 608, part-time 2245. Graduate faculty: full-time 154, part-time 70. Degrees conferred: M.A., M.F.T., M.L.S., M.P.H., M.S., M.S.Ed., M.S.N., M.S.W., Sixth Year Professional Diploma.

ADMISSION REQUIREMENTS. Transcripts, GRE (nursing, library science), GRE Subject Test (biology, foreign language departments), GMAT (business economics), departmental interview required in support of School's application. TOEFL required for international applicants. Accepts transfer applicants. Graduates of unaccredited institutions not considered. Apply to Dean of Graduate Studies by July 15 (Fall), November 15 (Spring), May 15 (Summer). Application fee $20. Phone: (203)392-5237.

ADMISSION STANDARDS. Usual minimum average: 2.75 (A = 4) and/or 3.3 in graduate major area.

FINANCIAL AID. Fellowships, assistantships for teaching/research, Federal W/S, loans. Approved for VA benefits. Apply to appropriate department chair for fellowships, assistantships; to Financial Aid Office for all other programs. Use FAFSA. Phone: (203)392-4232. About 10% of students receive aid other than loans from College and outside sources. Aid available for part-time students.

DEGREE REQUIREMENTS. For master's: 30 semester hours minimum, at least 21 credits in residence; comprehensive exam; thesis/nonthesis option. For Professional Diploma: 30 semester hours beyond the master's, all in residence; final comprehensive exam.

FIELDS OF STUDY.
Art.
Bilingual/Bicultural Education.
Biology.
Business Economics.
Chemistry.
Communications Disorders.
Counseling.
Educational Leadership.
Elementary Education.
English.
Environmental Education.
Foreign Languages. Includes French, Spanish, Romance languages.
History.
Instructional Technology.
Library Science and Instructional Technology.
Marriage and Family Therapy.
Mathematics.
Modern Languages. Includes French, Spanish.
Nursing.
Physical Education.
Psychology.
Reading.
Recreation and Leisure.
Research, Measurement, and Evaluation.
School Health Education.
School Nurse-Teacher Studies.
School Psychology.
Science Education.
Social Work.

Sociology.
Special Education.
Urban Studies.

SOUTHERN ILLINOIS UNIVERSITY

Carbondale, Illinois 62901-6806
http://www.siu.edu/gradschl/

Founded 1869. Located 100 miles SE of St. Louis, Mo. Coed. State control. Semester system. Special facilities: Center for Archaeological Investigation, Coal Extraction and Utilization Center, Center for Dewey Studies, Materials Technology Center. Library: 2,000,000 volumes, 2,400,000 microforms, 15,000 current periodicals.

Annual tuition: full-time, resident $3138, nonresident $7218. On-campus housing for married, single graduate students. Average academic year housing costs: $3500 (room and board) for single students; monthly rent $350. Contact University Housing Office for both on- and off-campus housing information. Phone: (618)453-2301. Day care facilities available.

Graduate School

Graduate study since 1944. Enrollment: full- and part-time 2900. Graduate faculty: full-time 1682, part-time 1857. Degrees conferred: M.A., M.S., M.F.A., M.B.A., M.Acc., M.S. in Ed., M.M., M.P.A., Ph.D., Rh.D., D.B.A.

ADMISSION REQUIREMENTS. Official transcripts required in support of School's application. GRE/GMAT/MAT, letters of recommendation required by some departments. TOEFL required for international applicants. Accepts transfer applicants. Graduates of unaccredited institutions not considered. Contact departments directly for admission material and requirements. Rolling admissions process. Application fee $20. Phone: (618)536-7791.

ADMISSION STANDARDS. Selective for most departments, very selective or competitive for others. Usual minimum average: 2.7 (A = 4).

FINANCIAL AID. Annual awards from institutional funds: scholarships, fellowships, teaching assistantships, research assistantships, other grants, Federal W/S, loans. Approved for VA benefits. Apply by November 15 to appropriate department chair for fellowships, assistantships; to Financial Aid Office for all other programs. Use FAFSA. Phone: (618)453-4334; fax: (618)453-7305. Over 90% of full-time students are given some type of financial assistance.

DEGREE REQUIREMENTS. For M.A., M.S.: 30–45 semester hours minimum, at least half in residence; foreign language optional with some departments; thesis for many majors; final written/oral exam. For M.F.A.: 40–60 hours minimum, at least half in residence; thesis; final exhibit of creative work; final exam. For M.B.A., M.P.A., M.Acc.: 30–36 hours minimum, at least half in residence; final written/oral exam. For M.S. in Ed.: same as for M.A., M.S. For M.M.: same as for M.S. in Ed., except recital required in some fields. For Ph.D., Rh.D., D.B.A.: no set hourly requirements (some departments set hourly minimum); at least two semesters in full-time residence; departments establish research tools; dissertation for 24 hours; final written/oral exam.

FIELDS OF STUDY.
Accountancy. M.Acc.
Administration of Justice. M.S.
Agribusiness Economics. M.S.
Agricultural Education and Mechanization. M.S.
Animal Science. M.S.

Anthropology. M.A., Ph.D.
Applied Linguistics. M.A.
Art. M.F.A.
Behavior Analysis and Therapy. M.S.
Biological Sciences. M.S.
Business Administration. M.B.A., D.B.A.
Chemistry. M.S., Ph.D.
Cinema and Photography. M.F.A.
Civil Engineering. M.S.
Communication Disorders and Sciences. M.S.
Computer Science. M.S.
Curriculum and Instruction. M.S. in Ed.
Economics. M.A., M.S., Ph.D.
Education. Ph.D. in 8 concentrations.
Educational Administration. M.S. in Ed., Ph.D.
Educational Psychology. M.S. in Ed., Ph.D.
Electrical Engineering. M.S.
Engineering Science. Ph.D.
English. M.A., Ph.D.
English as a Foreign Language. M.A.
Foreign Languages and Literatures. Includes French, German, Spanish. M.A.
Forestry. M.S.
Geography. M.A., Ph.D.
Geology. M.S., Ph.D.
Health Education. M.S. in Ed., Ph.D.
Higher Education. M.S. in Ed., Ph.D.
Historical Studies. Ph.D.
Journalism. M.A., M.S., Ph.D.
Manufacturing System. M.S.
Mathematics. M.A., M.S., Ph.D.
Mechanical Engineering. M.S.
Microbiology. M.S., Ph.D.
Mining Engineering. M.S.
Music. M.M.
Pharmacology. M.S., Ph.D.
Philosophy. M.A., Ph.D.
Physical Education. M.S. in Ed., Ph.D.
Physics. M.S.
Physiology. M.S., Ph.D.
Plant Biology. M.A., M.S., Ph.D.
Plant and Soil Science. M.S.
Political Science. M.A., Ph.D.
Psychology. M.A., M.S., Ph.D.
Public Administration. M.P.A.
Recreation. M.S. in Ed.
Rehabilitation Administration and Services. M.S., Rh.D.
Rehabilitation Counseling. M.S.
Social Work. M.S.W.
Sociology. M.A., Ph.D.
Special Education. M.S., Ed.D., Ph.D.
Speech Communication. M.A., M.S., Ph.D.
Telecommunications. M.A.
Theater. M.F.A.
Workforce Education. M.S. in Ed., Ph.D.
Zoology. M.A., M.S., Ph.D.

School of Law

Established 1973. Semester system. Library: 310,000 volumes. Library has LEXIS, NEXIS, WESTLAW, LEGALTRAC.

Annual tuition: resident $5253, nonresident $11,980. On-campus housing available. Apply to Housing Office. Phone: (618)453-2301. Total average annual additional expense: $7686.

Enrollment: first-year class 120; total 347 (men 59%, women 41%). Faculty: full-time 24, part-time 8. Degrees conferred: J.D., J.D.-M.B.A., J.D.-M.P.A., J.D.-M.Acc., J.D.-M.D.

ADMISSION REQUIREMENTS. LSDAS Law School report, bachelor's degree, transcripts, LSAT, recommendations required in support of application. Graduates of unaccredited institutions not considered. Apply to Admissions Office; no specified closing date. Rolling admissions process. Application fee $25. Phone: (618)453-8767.

ADMISSION STANDARDS. Selective. Admits about 30–35% of total annual applications.

FINANCIAL AID. Scholarships, grants, full and partial tuition waivers, fellowships, assistantships, loans. Apply to Office of Student Work and Financial Assistance by May 1. Use FAFSA.

DEGREE REQUIREMENTS. For J.D.: satisfactory completion of 90 semester hour program. For combined degree programs: normally requires one additional year; see Graduate School listing above.

School of Medicine

Established 1969. Located at Springfield (62794-9230). Annual tuition: resident $10,920, nonresident $32,760; student fees $1205. On-campus housing available. Total average figure for all other expenses: $8697.

Enrollment: first-year class 72 (EDP 20); total 317 (men 55%, women 45%). Faculty: full-time 254, part-time 22. Degrees conferred: M.D., M.D.-J.D.

ADMISSION REQUIREMENTS. AMCAS report, transcripts, MCAT, recommendations, screening interview required in support of application. Has EDP; apply between June 15 and August 1. Accepts state residents only. Graduates of unaccredited colleges not considered. Apply after June 15, before November 15. Application fee $50. Phone: (217)524-0326; fax: (217)785-5538.

ADMISSION STANDARDS. Competitive. Accepts about 8–10% of total annual applicants. 99% are state residents.

FINANCIAL AID. Limited scholarships, loans. About 88% of students receive some aid from School.

DEGREE REQUIREMENTS. For M.D.: satisfactory completion of four-year program.

School of Dental Medicine (62002)

Established 1969. Located in Alton, Illinois, near St. Louis, Mo. Annual tuition: resident $5200, nonresident $15,600. On-campus housing available. Average academic year housing costs: $9780. Total average costs for all other expenses: $7372.

Enrollment: first-year class 50; total 195 (men 75%, women 25%). Faculty: full-time 45, part-time 38. Degree conferred: D.M.D.

ADMISSION REQUIREMENTS. AADSAS, official transcripts, DAT (October test preferred), three letters of recommendation required in support of School's application. Applicants must have completed at least two years of college study, prefer three years of study. Interview by invitation only. Preference is given to state residents. Graduates of unaccredited colleges not considered. Apply after June 1, before April 1. Application fee $20. Phone: (618)474-7120.

ADMISSION STANDARDS. Selective. Usual minimum average: 2.5 (A = 4). Admits about 25–30% of total annual applicants. Approximately 85% are state residents.

FINANCIAL AID. Limited scholarships, grants, loans. Apply after acceptance to Office of Student Affairs. Use FAFSA. Phone: (618)474-7175. About 81% of students receive aid from School and outside sources.

DEGREE REQUIREMENTS. For D.M.D.: satisfactory completion of forty-six-month program.

SOUTHERN ILLINOIS UNIVERSITY AT EDWARDSVILLE
Edwardsville, Illinois 62026-1046

Located 20 miles from St. Louis, Mo. Coed. State control. Quarter system. Library: 775,000 volumes, 1,200,000 microforms, 6060 current periodicals, 450 PCs in all libraries.

Annual tuition: full-time resident $1859, nonresident $4820; per credit resident $90 (special part-time tuition reduction program for Missouri residents), nonresident $305. On-campus housing available for 248 married students, 1000 single students. Annual academic year housing costs: $2127 (room only) single students; $5400 married students. Contact Housing Office for on- and off-campus housing information. Phone: (618)892-3931.

Graduate School

Enrollment: full-time 1000, part-time 808. Faculty: full-time 250, part-time 115. Degrees conferred: M.A., M.B.A., M.F.A., M.M., M.M.R., M.P.A., M.S.A., M.S.C.E., M.S., M.S. in Ed., M.S.E., M.S.E.E., Specialist, Ed.D.

ADMISSION REQUIREMENTS. Transcripts required in support of School's application. GRE/MAT/GMAT, letters of recommendation required in some programs. TOEFL required for international applicants. Graduates of unaccredited institutions considered. Apply to Graduate Admissions Office at least two months prior to registration. Application fee $20. Phone: (618)692-3010.

ADMISSION STANDARDS. Selective. Usual minimum average: 2.5 (A = 4).

FINANCIAL AID. Annual awards from institutional funds: 19 academic scholarships, 350 assistantships, stipends, tuition remission program, Federal W/S, loans. Approved for VA benefits. Apply by March 31 to appropriate department chair for assistantships; to Office of Financial Aid for all other program deadlines. Use FAFSA.

DEGREE REQUIREMENTS. For master's: minimum 48 quarter hours, at least 32 in residence; thesis/nonthesis option/research project; internships/practicum; exhibitions/recitals; final exam. For Specialist: 45 quarter hours beyond the master's degree, at least 36 in residence; final exam. For Ed.D.: 108 quarter hours, at least two years in residence; qualifying exam, dissertation; final oral exam.

FIELDS OF STUDY.
Accountancy.
Art Education.
Art Studio. Includes ceramic, drawing, fabric, fiber, painting, printmaking, sculpture.
Art Therapy.
Behavioral Science.
Biological Sciences.
Business Administration.
Business Education.
Chemistry.
Community Health Nursing.
Economics.
Educational Administration and Supervision.
Elementary Education.
Engineering. Includes civil, electrical.
English.
Environmental Studies.
Geographical Studies.
History.
Instructional Process.
Instructional Technology.

Management Information Systems.
Marketing Research. M.M.R. only.
Mass Communications.
Mathematical Studies.
Music Education.
Music Performance.
Nursing.
Philosophy.
Physical Education.
Physics.
Political Science.
Psychology.
Public Administration.
Secondary Education. Includes thirteen teaching fields.
Sociology.
Special Education.
Speech Communication.
Speech Pathology.

UNIVERSITY OF SOUTHERN MAINE
Portland, Maine 04103-9300

Founded in 1878 as Gorham State College and in 1970 merged with the University of Maine at Portland to form the University of Southern Maine. Library: 542,000 volumes, 1,140,000 microforms, 8100 current periodicals, 33 PCs in all libraries.

Tuition: per hour, resident $167, nonresident $471. Limited on-campus housing during academic year. On-campus housing available in summer. Contact Resident Life Office for both on- and off-campus housing information. Phone: (207)780-5158. Day care facilities available.

Graduate School

Graduate study authorized in 1964. Enrollment: full-time 430, part-time 320. Graduate programs are evenings, Saturdays and Summer sessions. Graduate faculty: full-time 70. Degrees conferred: M.A., M.B.A., M.O.T., M.S., M.S.Ad.Ed., M.S.Ed.

ADMISSION REQUIREMENTS. Transcripts, three references, GRE/MAT/MAT required in support of application. Additional materials may be required. Interview recommended. TOEFL required for international applicants. Accepts transfer applicants. Apply to Office of Graduate Affairs by April 1 for priority consideration. Departmental deadlines may vary. Rolling admissions process. Application fee $25. Phone: (207)780-4380.

ADMISSION STANDARDS. Competitive. Usual minimum average: 2.75 (A = 4).

FINANCIAL AID. Limited to graduate assistantships, Federal W/S, loans. Approved for VA benefits. Apply to Office of Graduate Affairs by June 1. Use FAFSA. Phone: (207)780-4380.

DEGREE REQUIREMENTS. Variable by program; most master's degree require 32–36 credits; thesis/nonthesis option. Nearly all degree programs are offered at the Portland or Gorham campuses, Occupational Therapy offered at Lewiston-Auburn campus.

FIELDS OF STUDY.
Adult Education. M.S.Ad.Ed.
American and New England Studies. M.A.
Business Administration. M.B.A.
Computer Science. M.S.
Counselor Education. M.S.Ed.
Educational Leadership. M.S.Ed.
Health Policy and Management. M.S.
Immunology. M.S.

Industrial Education. M.S.Ed.
Literary Education. M.S.
Nursing. M.S.
Occupational Therapy. M.O.T.
Public Policy and Management. M.A.
School Psychology. M.S.
Special Education. M.S.

SOUTHERN METHODIST UNIVERSITY
Dallas, Texas 75275

Founded 1911. Coed. Private control. Methodist affiliation. Semester system. Special facilities: university herbarium, Dallas Seismological Observatory, Statistical Research Laboratory, Shuler Museum of Paleontology, Institute for the Study of Earth and Man, Electron Microscopy Laboratory, Fort Burgwin Research Center, The Meadows Collection of Art, Computing Laboratory, Environmental Engineering Science Center. Library: 2,800,000 volumes, 641,000 microforms, 5600 current periodicals.

Annual tuition: per credit $592. On-campus housing for married and single graduate students. Approximate average academic year housing costs: $3500 for married students, $2526 (room only) for single students. Contact Office of Housing for both on- and off-campus housing information. Phone: (214)768-2407. Day care facilities available.

Dedman College

Enrollment: full-time 169, part-time 494. Faculty: full-time 176, part-time 51. Degrees conferred: M.A., M.B.E., M.S., Ph.D.

ADMISSION REQUIREMENTS. Two transcripts, GRE, two to four letters of recommendation required in support of College's application. GRE Subject Test required for some departments. TOEFL required for international applicants. Interview not required. Accepts transfer applicants. Graduates of unaccredited institutions not considered. Apply to Office of Research and Graduate Studies; no specified closing date. Application fee $40. Phone: (214)768-4345.

ADMISSION STANDARDS. Selective. Minimum average: 3.0 or GRE V + Q score of 1100. TOEFL minimum score 550.

FINANCIAL AID. Annual awards from institutional funds: 10 scholarships, 110 teaching fellowships, 6 research fellowships, full and partial tuition waivers, Federal W/S, loans. Apply by May 1 to appropriate department for fellowships, assistantships; to Financial Aid Office for all other aid. Use FAFSA. Phone: (214)768-3314. About 60% of students receive aid other than loans from College and outside sources. Aid available for part-time students.

DEGREE REQUIREMENTS. For M.A., M.S.: 30 semester hours minimum, at least one year or its equivalent in residence for most programs; thesis/nonthesis option; comprehensive written/oral exam. For Ph.D.: generally three years beyond the bachelor's degree, at least one year in residence; qualifying exam; reading knowledge of one foreign language for most programs; dissertation; final oral exam.

FIELDS OF STUDY.
Anthropology. Includes medical anthropology.
Archaeology. M.A., Ph.D.
Bilingual Education. M.B.E.
Biological Sciences. GRE Subject Test in biology required for admission.
Chemistry. GRE Subject Test in chemistry required for admission. M.S. only.

Economics. Includes applied, GRE if GPA is below 3.0.

English. GRE Subject Test in literature required for admission. M.A. only.

Geological Sciences. Includes geology, geophysics, applied geophysics. M.S. only.

History. M.A. only.

Latin American Studies. M.A. only.

Liberal Arts.

Mathematical Sciences. Includes applied (M.S.), mathematics (M.A.).

Physics.

Political Science. GRE for admission. M.A. only.

Psychology. Includes general/experimental, clinical and counseling (M.A. only); MMPI release form required for clinical and counseling.

Religious Studies.

Statistics.

Meadows School of the Arts

Tuition: per credit $592.

Enrollment: full-time 127, part-time 122. Graduate faculty: full-time 60, part-time 25. Degrees conferred: M.A., M.F.A., M.M., M.M.T., M.S.M.

ADMISSION REQUIREMENTS. Transcripts, three letters of recommendation, resume, qualifying audition required in support of School's application. GRE sometimes required. TOEFL required for international applicants. Apply to Director of Admissions and Records by February 1. Application fee $40. Phone: (214)768-3765; fax: (214)768-3272.

ADMISSION STANDARDS. Selective for most departments, competitive for the others. For most programs talent given greater weight than GPA.

FINANCIAL AID. One hundred ten scholarships, thirty fellowships, fifty assistantships for teaching/research, Federal W/S, loans. Apply to Financial Aid Office by May 1. Use FAFSA. Phone: (214)768-3314. About 60% of students receive aid from School and outside sources. Aid sometimes available to part-time students.

DEGREE REQUIREMENTS. For M.A.: 36–48 semester hours; reading knowledge of foreign language for some departments; thesis/internship. For M.F.A.: 60–66 semester hours; project. For M.M., M.M.T., M.S.M.: 30 semester hours minimum; recital/final project.

FIELDS OF STUDY.

Art. Includes ceramics, drawing, painting, photography, printmaking, sculpture. M.F.A.

Art History.

Arts Administration. Joint degree program with Cox School of Business. M.A.-M.B.A.

Music. Includes performance, piano pedagogy, music education, music history and literature, music theory and composition, orchestra conducting, choral conducting, music therapy, sacred music (joint programs with Perkins School of Theology). M.M., M.M.T., M.S.M.

Theater. Includes acting, design. M.F.A. only.

TV/Radio. Includes mass communication. M.F.A., M.A.

Edwin L. Cox School of Business—Graduate Division

Graduate study since 1950. Semester system.

Annual tuition: full-time $11,052; per semester hour $614. Enrollment: full-time 322, part-time 315. Graduate faculty: full-time 57, part-time 21. Degree conferred: M.B.A.

ADMISSION REQUIREMENTS. Official transcripts, recommendation, GMAT, interview required in support of School's application. TOEFL required of international applicants. Accepts transfer applicants. Graduates of unaccredited institutions not considered. Apply by May 1 (Fall), November 1 (Spring) to Graduate Admissions Office. Rolling admissions process. Application fee $40. Phone: (214)768-2630; fax: (214)692-4099.

ADMISSION STANDARDS. Competitive. Usual minimum average: 3.0 (A = 4).

FINANCIAL AID. Merit-based scholarships, seventy-five research assistantships, Federal W/S, loans. Approved for VA benefits. Apply by March 15 to the Office of the Dean for assistantships; to Office of Financial Aid for all other programs. Use FAFSA. Phone: (214)768-3417.

DEGREE REQUIREMENTS. For M.B.A.: 45–60 semester hours, depending upon previous degree program.

FIELDS OF STUDY.

Accounting.

Business Administration.

Entrepreneurship.

Finance.

Management Information Science.

Marketing.

Organizational Behavior and Administration.

School of Engineering and Applied Science—Graduate Division

http://www.seas.smu.edu

Graduate study since 1949. Semester system.

Annual tuition: full-time $10,800; per credit $524. Enrollment: full-time 86, part-time 937. Graduate faculty: full-time 41, part-time 15. Degrees conferred: M.S., D.Eng., Ph.D.

ADMISSION REQUIREMENTS. Official transcripts, GRE required in support of School's application. TOEFL required for international applicants. Interview not required. Accepts transfer applicants with up to 6 hours of transfer credits. Graduates of unaccredited institutions not considered. Apply to Director of Graduate Division, School of Engineering and Applied Science by application deadline on back of form. Application fee $25. Phone: (214)768-3484; fax: (214)768-3883.

ADMISSION STANDARDS. Selective. Usual minimum average: 3.0 (A = 4).

FINANCIAL AID. Annual awards from institutional funds: forty-two research/teaching fellowships, eighty-eight research/teaching assistantships, loans. Approved for VA benefits. Apply by May 1 to Director of Graduate Division for assistantships, fellowship; to Financial Aid Office for all other programs. Use FAFSA. Phone: (214)768-3417; fax: (214)768-3878. About 90% of students receive aid other than loans from School and outside sources.

DEGREE REQUIREMENTS. For M.S.: 30 semester hours minimum, 24 in residence; thesis/nonthesis option. For Ph.D.: 78 semester hours minimum, at least 30 in residence; qualifying exam; dissertation; final exam. For D.Eng.: 78 hours required; essentially the same as for Ph.D., praxis required.

FIELDS OF STUDY.

Computer Engineering.

Computer Science.

Electrical Engineering.

Engineering Management.

Hazardous and Waste Materials Management.

Manufacturing Systems Management.
Mechanical Engineering.
Operations Research.
Software Engineering.
Systems Engineering.
Telecommunication.

School of Law (75275-0116)

Established 1925. Semester system. Law library: 456,000 volumes. Library has LEXIS, WESTLAW.

Annual tuition: full-time $18,424. On-campus housing for 80 single students, 75 married students. Average annual housing costs: $7000–$8000 for single students, $10,000–$12,000 for married students. Apply to Director of Lawyers Inn.

Enrollment: first-year class 248, total full-time 741 (men 57%, women 43%). Faculty: full-time 38, part-time 13. Degrees conferred: J.D., J.D.-M.B.A., LL.M. (Taxation; Comparative and International Law, for International attorneys only), S.J.D.

ADMISSION REQUIREMENTS. For J.D. program: LSDAS Law School report, bachelor's degree, transcripts, letters of recommendation, LSAT, required in support of application. Accepts transfer applicants. Apply to School of Law by March 1; beginning students admitted Fall only. For graduate program: transcripts, letters of recommendation required in support of application. Interview not required. Graduates of unaccredited colleges not considered. Apply to Secretary, Committee on Graduate Studies, School of Law, by March 1. Application fee $45. Phone: (214)768-2550; fax: (219)768-4390.

ADMISSION STANDARDS. For J.D.: selective. Accepts about 30–35% of total annual applicants.

FINANCIAL AID. For J.D. program: scholarships, Federal W/S, loans. Apply to Director of Financial Aid by February 28. Use FAFSA. Phone: (214)768-3417. For graduate program: scholarships, fellowships; apply to Chair of Committee on Graduate Studies by May 1. About 20% of students receive aid other than loans from School. No aid for part-time students.

DEGREE REQUIREMENTS. For J.D.: 90 semester hours minimum, at least last 6 semesters in residence. For LL.M.: at least 24 semester hours minimum, one year in full-time residence. For S.J.D.: one year minimum in residence; thesis; oral exam.
Note: Summer programs available at Oxford University and the University of Edinburgh.

UNIVERSITY OF SOUTHERN MISSISSIPPI
Hattiesburg, Mississippi 39406-0066

Founded 1910. Located 90 miles SE of Jackson. Coed. State control. Semester system. Special facilities: Automation and Robotics Application Center, Bureau of Educational Research, Gulf Coast Research Laboratory, Health Related Sciences Institute, Institute of Environmental Science, the Mississippi Polymer Institute, Physical Fitness Institute. Library: 872,000 volumes, 2,162,000 microforms, 5000 current periodicals, 155 PCs.

Annual tuition: full-time, resident $2518, nonresident $5025. On-campus housing for 296 married and 4700 single students. Average academic year housing cost: $798–$898 for married students, $600–$898 for single students. Contact Resident Life Office for both on- and off-campus housing information. Phone: (601)266-4783. Day care facilities available.

Graduate School

Established 1947. Enrollment: full-time 1233, part-time 865. Faculty: full-time 450, part-time 73. Degrees conferred: M.A., M.S., M.Ed., M.B.A., M.F.A., M.L.S., M.M., M.M.E., M.P.A., M.S.N., M.S.W., Ed.S., Ed.D., Ph.D.

ADMISSION REQUIREMENTS. Two transcripts, GRE/GMAT/MAT/NTE Test, two recommendations required in support of School's application. Interview may be required. TOEFL required for international applicants. Accepts transfer applicants. Apply by August 9 (Fall), November 11 (Winter), February 19 (Spring), May 19 (Summer) to Director of Graduate Admissions. Rolling admissions process. Application fee $0, $25 for international applicants. Phone: (601)266-5137; fax: (601)266-5138.

ADMISSION STANDARDS. Selective for most departments. Usual minimum average: 2.75 (A = 4).

FINANCIAL AID. Annual awards from institutional funds: 2800 scholarships, 604 teaching assistantships, fellowships, internships, tuition waivers, Federal W/S, loans. Apply by March 15 to Dean for assistantships, fellowships; to Financial Aid Office for all other programs. Use FAFSA. Phone: (601)266-4774. About 60% of students receive aid from School and outside sources. Aid available for part-time students.

DEGREE REQUIREMENTS. For master's: 30 semester hours minimum, at least 15 in residence; reading knowledge of one foreign language; thesis required for many majors; final written/oral exam. For M.Ed., M.S. in Teaching: same as above, except no thesis requirement. For Ed.S.: 30 hours minimum beyond the master's, at least one quarter in full-time residence; final written exam. For Ph.D.: 78 hours minimum beyond the bachelor's, at least two consecutive semesters in full-time residence; reading knowledge of two foreign languages or one language and statistics; preliminary exam; dissertation; final written/oral exam. For Ed.D.: essentially same as for Ph.D., except MAT for candidacy, no language requirement; knowledge of statistics required.

FIELDS OF STUDY.
Adult Education. M.Ed.
Anthropology. M.A., M.S.
Art Education. M.A.E.
Biological Sciences. Includes botany, environmental, genetics, marine, microbiology, molecular. M.S., Ph.D.
Business Administration. M.B.A.
Business Education. Includes business teacher, distributive vocational teacher. M.S., M.Ed.
Chemistry. Includes biochemistry. M.S., Ph.D.
Communications. M.A., Ph.D.
Community Health Nursing. M.S.
Computer Science. M.S.
Counseling and Personnel Services. Includes school, college. M.Ed.
Counseling Psychology. M.S., Ph.D.
Criminal Justice. M.C.J.
Economic Development. M.S.
Educational Administration and Supervision.
Educational Curriculum and Instruction. Includes early childhood, elementary, secondary, reading. M.S., M.Ed.
Educational Media and Technology. M.Ed.
English. Includes Creative writing, linguistics, TESOL. M.A., Ed.S., Ph.D.
Family Life Studies. Includes child development, family living, family relations, marriage and family therapy, child life, gerontology. M.S.
Fine Arts. M.F.A.
Geography. M.A.
Geology. M.S.
Health. Ph.D., Ed.D.

Health Education. Includes community health, occupational safety, school health, safety and driver education. M.S.

History. M.A., Ph.D.

Home Economics. Includes family economics and management, food and nutrition. M.S., Ed.S.

Industrial and Vocational Education. M.S.

Institution Management. M.S.

Library Science. Includes archival studies, information studies, media studies. M.L.S.

Manufacturing Technology. M.S.

Marine Science. Ph.D.

Mathematics. M.S.

Medical Technology. M.S.

Music. Includes performance, church, conducting, history and literature, theory and composition, woodwind performance. M.M., D.M.A.

Music Education. M.M.E., D.M.A., Ph.D.

Nursing Service Administration. M.S.

Philosophy. M.A.

Physical Education. Includes exercise, exercise physiology, teaching, coaching, administration. M.S., Ph.D., Ed.D.

Physics. M.S.

Political Science. M.A.

Polymer Science. M.S., Ph.D.

Professional Accountancy. M.P.A.

Psychiatric Nursing. M.S.

Psychology. Includes clinical, experimental, school. M.A., Ph.D.

Public Health. M.Ed.

Public Relations. M.A.

Recreation. Ed.D., Ph.D.

Research and Evaluation. M.S.

Science Education. M.S., M.Ed., Ed.D., Ph.D.

Scientific Computing. Ph.D.

Social Work. M.S.W.

Special Education. M.Ed.

Speech Hearing Sciences. M.A., Ph.D.

Teleprocessing Science. M.S.

Theater. M.F.A.

SOUTHERN NAZARENE UNIVERSITY
Bethany, Oklahoma 73008-2694

From 1920–1955 was known as Bethany-Peniel College; name changed in 1986. Coed. Semester system. Affiliated with Church of the Nazarene. Library: 105,000 volumes, 90,000 microforms, 642 current periodicals, 10 PCs.

Tuition: per semester hour $264. On-campus housing available for 60 married students, limited for single graduate students. Average academic year housing costs: single students $2400 (including board); married students $2700. Contact Dean of Student Services for both on- and off-campus housing information. Phone: (405)491-6316.

Graduate College

Graduate program began in 1963. Enrollment: full-time 168, part-time 102 (men 132, women 139). Faculty: full-time 25. Degrees conferred: M.A., M.S.Mgt., M.Min., M.S.C.P.

ADMISSION REQUIREMENTS. Transcripts, MAT/GMAT required in support of College's application. Interview strongly recommended. TOEFL required for international applicants. Accepts transfer applicants. Graduates of unaccredited institutions considered on a conditional basis. Apply to Director of Graduate Studies by August 1 (Fall), December 1 (Spring). Application fee $25. International application fee $35. Phone: (905)491-6316, (405)491-6302.

ADMISSION STANDARDS. Selective. Usual minimum average: 3.0 (A = 4) on last 60 hours.

FINANCIAL AID. Limited teaching fellowships, loans. Approved for VA benefits. Apply to the Financial Aid Office. Phone: (405)491-6310; fax: (405)491-6381. Use FAFSA.

DEGREE REQUIREMENTS. For master's: 32 semester hours minimum; thesis optional; comprehensive exam.

FIELDS OF STUDY.
Business Administration.
Business Management.
Communication Arts.
Counseling Psychology.
Curriculum and Instruction.
Early Childhood Education.
Elementary Education.
Reading.
Religion.

SOUTHERN OREGON STATE COLLEGE
Ashland, Oregon 97520

Founded 1926. Located 300 miles S of Portland. Coed. State control. Quarter system. Library: 275,000 volumes, 760,000 microforms, 2137 current periodicals.

Annual tuition: full-time, resident $4776, nonresident $8583. On-campus housing: 60 units for married students, 2000 single students. Average academic year housing costs: $3500 for married students, $4000 for single students (includes board). Apply to Director of Student Services for off-campus housing information. Phone: (541)552-6371 (single students), (541)488-4401 (married students).

Graduate Division

Graduate study since 1952. Enrollment: full-time 163, part-time 162. College faculty: full-time 170, part-time 10. Degrees conferred: M.A., M.S.

ADMISSION REQUIREMENTS. Transcripts, GRE/GMAT/NTE required in support of application. TOEFL required for applicants whose native language is not English. Interview may be required for some programs. Accepts transfer applicants. Apply to Admission Office at least one month prior to registration. Application fee $50. Phone: (541)552-6203.

ADMISSION STANDARDS. Selective. Usual minimum average: 3.0 (A = 4).

FINANCIAL AID. Limited to loans. Approved for VA benefits. Apply to Director of Financial Aids. Use FAFSA. Phone: (541)482-6181.

DEGREE REQUIREMENTS. For M.A., M.S.: 45 quarter hours minimum, at least 30 in residence; thesis/nonthesis option; final oral/written comprehensive exam.

FIELDS OF STUDY.
Arts and Letters.
Business Administration.
Elementary Education.
Environmental Education.
Mathematical and Computer Science.
Sciences.
Secondary Education.
Social Sciences.

SOUTHERN UNIVERSITY AND AGRICULTURAL AND MECHANICAL COLLEGE

P.O. Box 9860
Baton Rouge, Louisiana 70813

Founded 1880. Coed. State control. Semester system. Special facilities: Health Research Center, Environmental and Energy Institute, Center for Sickle Cell Disease Research, Center for Social Research. Library: 451,000 volumes.

Annual tuition: full-time, resident $2046, nonresident $3822; part-time varies according to course load. On-campus housing available for single students only. Average academic year housing costs: $2934 (including board). Contact Housing Office for both on- and off-campus housing. Phone: (504)771-3590.

Graduate School

Established 1956. Enrollment: full-time 279, part-time 679. Faculty: full- and part-time 146. Degrees conferred: M.A., M.Ed., M.P.A., M.S.

ADMISSION REQUIREMENTS. Transcripts required in support of School's application. GRE/GMAT recommended. Interview not required. TOEFL required for international applicants. Accepts transfer applicants. Graduates of unaccredited institutions not considered. Apply to Graduate Office by July 1 (Fall), December 1 (Spring), May 1 (Summer). Rolling admissions process. Application fee $5. Phone: (504)771-5390.

ADMISSION STANDARDS. Selective for most departments. Usual minimum average: 2.5 (A = 4).

FINANCIAL AID. Annual awards from institutional funds: teaching assistantships, research assistantships, Federal W/S, loans. Approved for VA benefits. Apply at least thirty days prior to registration to Dean of the Graduate School for assistantships; to the Office of Financial Aid for all other programs. Use either FAFSA. Phone: (504)771-2796. About 10% of students receive aid other than loans from School. Aid sometimes available for part-time students.

DEGREE REQUIREMENTS. For master's: 30–36 semester hours minimum, at least 24 in residence and 18 weeks in full-time attendance; thesis required for M.A., optional for other degrees; final written/oral exam.

FIELDS OF STUDY.
Accountancy. M.P.A.
Administration and Supervision. M.Ed.
Biochemistry. M.S.
Biology. M.S.
Chemistry. Includes analytical, inorganic, organic, physical. M.S.
Counselor Education. M.A.
Elementary Education. M.Ed.
Environmental Sciences. M.S.
Information Systems. M.S.
Mass Communication. M.A.
Mathematics. M.S.
Media. M.Ed.
Mental Health Counseling. M.A.
Micro/Minicomputer Architecture. M.S.
Nursing. M.S.N.
Operating Systems. M.S.
Public Administration. M.P.A.
Rehabilitation Counseling. M.S.
Secondary Education. Includes agriculture, biology, business education, chemistry, English, health and physical education, home economics, industrial arts, mathematics, music, social studies. M.Ed.

Social Sciences. Interdisciplinary. Includes history, political science, sociology. M.A.
Therapeutic Recreation. M.S.

Law Center

P. O. Box 9294

Founded 1947. Semester system. Law library: 349,000 volumes. Library has LEXIS, NEXIS, WESTLAW, DIALOG.

Annual tuition; resident $3088, nonresident $6288. On-campus housing available. Total average annual additional expense: $6900.

Enrollment: first-year class 125; total full-time 323 (men 60%, women 40%). Faculty: full-time 28, part-time 11. Degree conferred: J.D.

ADMISSION REQUIREMENTS. LSDAS Law School report, bachelor's degree, transcripts, LSAT (prior to March test date), two letters of recommendation, narrative on why one selects the field of law required in support of application. Interview may be requested. Accepts transfer applicants. Graduates of unaccredited colleges not considered. Apply to Office of Admissions by March 30. Beginning students admitted Fall only. Application fee: none. Phone: (504)771-5340, (800)537-1135.

ADMISSION STANDARDS. Accepts 70% of total annual applicants.

FINANCIAL AID. Scholarships, assistantships, Federal W/S, loans. Apply Financial Aid Committee by April 15. Use FAFSA. About 20% of students receive aid other than loans from School.

DEGREE REQUIREMENTS. For J.D.: 96 semester hours, 6 semesters in residence.

SOUTHWEST MISSOURI STATE

Springfield, Missouri 65804-0094
http://www.smsu.edu.

Founded 1905. Semester system. State control. Special facilities: Center for Archaeological Research, Center for Business and Research, Center for Cultural Programs and Development, Center for Economic Research, Center for Gerontological Studies, Center for Ozarks Studies, Center for Human Resources and Service, Center for Resource Planning and Management. Library: 583,904 volumes, 844,023 microforms, 4200 current periodicals.

Tuition: per credit resident $100, nonresident $200. On-campus housing available. Average academic year housing costs: $3180 room/suite style (includes 20 meals per week); $2030 apartment style. Contact Residence Life for both on- and off-campus housing information. Phone: (417)836-5536.

Graduate College

Enrollment: full-time 500, part-time 1500. Faculty: full-time 396, part-time 19. Degrees conferred: M.A., M.B.A., M.P.A., M.M., M.S., M.S.Ed., M.S.N., M.S.W., Ed.S.

ADMISSION REQUIREMENTS. Official transcripts required in support of application. TOEFL required for foreign applicants. GRE/GMAT required for some programs. Accepts transfer applicants. Graduates of unaccredited institutions not considered. Apply to Graduate College at least four weeks prior to registration. Rolling admissions process. Application fee $15. Phone(417)836-5335; fax: (417)836-6888.

ADMISSION STANDARDS. Selective. Usual minimum average: 2.75 (A = 4) or satisfactory GRE or GMAT scores.

FINANCIAL AID. Three hundred graduate assistantships available, $5250– $7250 stipend and incidental fee waivers, Federal W/S, loans. Apply to department head for assistantships; to Financial Aid Office for all other programs. No specified closing date. Use FAFSA. Phone: (417)836-5262; fax: (417)836-8392.

DEGREE REQUIREMENTS. For master's: 32–47 semester hours minimum; research project; comprehensive exam. For Ed.S.: 70 semester hours minimum; research project; comprehensive exam.

FIELDS OF STUDY.
Accounting.
Biology.
Business Administration.
Chemistry.
Communication Sciences and Disorders.
Communications.
Defense and Strategic Studies.
Educational Administration.
Educational Specialist.
Elementary Education.
English.
Guidance and Counseling.
History.
Materials Science.
Mathematics.
Music.
Nurse Anesthesia.
Nursing.
Psychology.
Public Administration.
Reading.
Religious Studies.
Resource Planning.
Secondary Education.
Social Work.
Special Education.
Theater
Writing.

SOUTHWEST TEXAS STATE UNIVERSITY

San Marcos, Texas 78666-4605

Founded 1899. Located 28 miles SW of Austin. Coed. State control. Semester system. Library: 1,200,000 volumes, 1,485,000 microforms, 5500 current periodicals, 55 PCs.

Tuition: per credit resident $42, nonresident $246. On-campus housing for 100 married students, 2000 men, 2250 women. Average annual housing cost: $6000 for married students, $4500 (including board) for single students. Contact Director of Residential Life for both on- and off-campus housing information. Phone: (512)245-2382.

Graduate School

Graduate study since 1935. Enrollment: full-time 772, part-time 1570. Graduate faculty: full-time 267, part-time 41. Degrees conferred: M.A., M.Acc., M.A.G., M.A.I.S., M.A.T., M.B.A., M.Ed., M.F.A., M.M., M.P.A., M.S., M.S.C.D., M.S.C.J., M.S.H.P., M.S.T., M.P.A., M.S.I.S., M.S.P.T., M.S.W.

ADMISSION REQUIREMENTS. Transcripts, GRE/GMAT required in support of School's application. Interview not required for most programs. TOEFL, TSE (for M.B.A., M.P.A., History) required for international applicants. Accepts transfer applicants. Graduates of unaccredited institutions not considered. Apply to

Dean of Graduate School by November 15 (Spring), April 15 (Summer), July 15 (Fall). International applicants must submit application at least one month prior to deadlines above. In addition, if applicant is submitting foreign credentials, a $50 evaluation fee accompany application and $25 application fee. Application fee $25. Phone: (512)245-2581; fax: (512)245-8365.

ADMISSION STANDARDS. Selective. Usual minimum average (some programs are higher): 2.75 (A = 4) on last 60 hours of bachelor's degree. Minimum GMAT score 400, minimum TOEFL score 550, minimum TSE score 45.

FINANCIAL AID. Annual awards from institutional funds: ten minority scholarships, fellowships, sixty teaching assistantships, loans. Approved for VA benefits. Apply to Office of Financial Assistance for fellowships, loans; to appropriate department chair for assistantships. Use FAFSA. Phone: (512)245-2315. About 10% of students receive aid other than loans from University and outside sources. Aid sometimes available for part-time students.

DEGREE REQUIREMENTS. For M.A.: 30 semester hours minimum including thesis, at least 24 in residence; final oral/written exams. For M.A.T., M.Ed., M.M.: 36 semester hours minimum, at least 30 in residence; no thesis required. For M.Acc., M.B.A.: 30 semester hours minimum, but usually 36. For M.S.C.J., M.P.A.: 39 semester hours minimum. For M.A.G, M.S.H.P., M.S.I.S., M.S.T.: 39 semester hours minimum; up to 9 hours may be granted for work/life experience in M.S.I.S. program.

FIELDS OF STUDY.
Accounting.
Agricultural Education.
Biology.
Business Administration.
Chemistry.
Communication Disorders.
Computer Science.
Counseling and Guidance.
Creative Writing.
Criminal Justice.
Developmental Education.
Educational Administration.
Elementary Education.
English.
French.
Geography.
German.
Health and Physical Education.
Health Education.
Health Professions. Includes allied health research, health care administration, health care human resources.
History.
Industrial Technology.
Interdisciplinary Studies.
Management of Vocational-Technical Education.
Mathematics.
Music-Music Education.
Music-Performance.
Physical Education.
Physical Therapy.
Physics.
Political Science.
Professional Counseling.
Public Administration.
Reading Education.
School Psychology.
Secondary Education.
Social Work.
Sociology.
Spanish.

Special Education.
Speech Communication.
Theater Arts.

THE UNIVERSITY
OF SOUTHWESTERN LOUISIANA

Lafayette, Louisiana 70504
http://www.usl.edu

Founded 1900. Located 110 miles W of New Orleans. Coed. State control. Semester system. Special facilities: Center for Louisiana Studies, Acadiana Research Laboratory, Center for Crustacean Research, New Iberia Research Center, Center for Advanced Computer Studies, Center for Socioeconomic Education. Library: 720,000 volumes, 1,290,000 microforms, 6850 current periodicals, 30 PCs.

Annual tuition: full-time, resident $1885, nonresident $5485. On-campus housing for 150 married students, 1397 men, 1168 women. Average academic year housing costs: single $2082 (including board); married $2940. Contact Director of Housing for both on- and off-campus housing information. Phone: (318)482-6471.

Graduate School

Graduate study since 1956. Enrollment: full-time 584, part-time 837. Faculty: full- and part-time 300. Degrees conferred: M.A., M.S., M.Ed., M.E., M.M., M.B.A., M.M.Ed., Ph.D.

ADMISSION REQUIREMENTS. Two official transcripts, GRE required in support of School's application. TOEFL required for international applicants. Interview not required. Accepts transfer applicants. Graduates of unaccredited institutions not considered. Apply to Dean one month prior to registration. Application fee $5 (American), $15 (international). Phone: (318)482-6965; fax: (318)482-6195.

ADMISSION STANDARDS. Selective. Usual minimum average: 2.75 (A = 4).

FINANCIAL AID. Fifty fellowships, 93 research assistantships, 211 teaching assistantships, tuition waivers, Federal W/S, loans. Approved for VA benefits. Apply to Dean of Graduate School by May 1. Use FAFSA.

DEGREE REQUIREMENTS. For master's: 30 semester hours minimum, at least 24 in residence; final written/oral exam; reading knowledge of one foreign language in some majors; thesis required for most majors. For M.B.A.: 56 semester hours minimum, at least 30 in residence; computer proficiency. For Ph.D.: 50–60 semester hours beyond the master's, one year in full-time residence; proficiency in one language and research tool; general exam; dissertation; final oral exam.

FIELDS OF STUDY.
Administration and Supervision.
Applied Physics.
Biology. Includes environmental, evolutionary.
Business Administration.
Chemical Engineering.
Civil Engineering.
Communication.
Computer Engineering.
Computer Science.
Counselor Education.
Curriculum and Instruction.
Education of the Gifted.
Engineering Management.

Engineering Systems.
English. One language for M.A.
Environmental Biology.
Francophone Studies.
French.
Geology.
History.
Human Resource Management.
Mass Communication.
Mathematics.
Mechanical Engineering.
Microbiology.
Music.
Music Education.
Petroleum Engineering.
Physics.
Psychology.
Rehabilitation Counseling.
Speech Pathology and Audiology.
Statistics.
Writing.

SOUTHWESTERN OKLAHOMA
STATE UNIVERSITY

100 Campus Drive
Weatherford, Oklahoma 73096-3098

Founded in 1903. Located 70 miles west of Oklahoma City. Coed. State control. Semester system. Library: 250,000 bound volumes, 1,000,000 microforms, 1370 current periodicals, 36 PCs, access to Internet.

Tuition: per credit hour, resident 3000–4000 level—$53.50; 5000 level—$67.50, non-resident 3000–4000 level—$135.00; 5000 level—$162.50. On-campus housing for 64 married students, 1547 single students. Average academic year housing costs: $1860–$2366. Contact the Director of Student Housing for both on- and off-campus housing information. Phone: (405)774-3024.

Graduate School

Graduate study since 1953. Enrollment: full-time 229, part-time 246. Faculty: full- and part-time 215. Degrees conferred: M.Ed., M.S.A.P., M.B.A., M.M.

ADMISSION REQUIREMENTS. Official transcripts, GRE/GMAT required in support of School's application. Letters of reference for some programs. TOEFL required for international applicants. Interview not required. Accepts transfer applicants (maximum transfer credits: 9 hours.). Graduates of unaccredited institutions not considered. Apply to Dean of the Graduate School; no specified closing date. Application fee: none. Phone: (405)774-3769; fax: (405)774-3795.

ADMISSION STANDARDS. Usual minimum average: 2.5 (A = 4). Applicants must meet minimum formula of undergraduate GPA plus GRE or GMAT score.

FINANCIAL AID. Limited to two fellowships, seven research assistantships, twelve teaching assistantships, Federal W/S, loans. Approved for VA benefits. Apply to Director of Financial Aid by March 1. Use FAFSA and institutional FAF. Phone: (405)774-3786; fax: (405)774-3795.

DEGREE REQUIREMENTS. For M.Ed.: 32 semester hours. For M.B.A.: 33 semester hours. For M.S.A.P.: 36 semester hours. For M.M.: 32 semester hours.

FIELDS OF STUDY.
Applied Psychology.
Art.
Business Administration.
Counseling.
Early Childhood.
Educational Administration.
Elementary Education.
English.
Health, Physical Education and Recreation.
Library Media.
Mathematics.
Music.
Natural Sciences.
Psychology.
Reading.
Secondary Education. Includes several subject areas.
Social Sciences.
Special Education.
Teaching.
Technology.

SOUTHWESTERN UNIVERSITY SCHOOL OF LAW
675 South Westmoreland Avenue
Los Angeles, California 90005-3992

Founded 1911. Semester system. Library: 355,000 volumes. Library has LEXIS, WESTLAW, RLIN, WILSONLINE, LEGALTRAC.

Annual tuition: full-time $19,020, part-time $12,046, SCALE program $22,545. No on-campus housing available. Total average annual additional expense: $11,500.

Enrollment: first-year class, full-time 348, part-time 120; total full-time 880, part-time 330 (men 50%, women 50%). Faculty: full-time 47, part-time 42. Degree conferred: J.D.

ADMISSION REQUIREMENTS. LSDAS Law School report, bachelor's degree, transcripts, LSAT required in support of application. Interviews required for SCALE. Letters of recommendation and supplementary essay recommended. Accepts transfer applicants from ABA approved law schools. Apply to Office of Admissions by June 30. Application fee $50. Phone: (213)738-6717.

ADMISSION STANDARDS. Selective. Accepts about 50% of total annual applicants.

FINANCIAL AID. Scholarships, tuition waiver, assistantships, Federal W/S, loans. Apply to Financial Aid Office by June 1. Use FAFSA. About 15–20% of students receive aid other than loans from School or outside sources. Loan forgiveness program available.

DEGREE REQUIREMENTS. For J.D.: 87 semester credits in full- or part-time program; completion of two calendar years in SCALE program.
Note: Summer study abroad in Argentina, Canada, Mexico.

SPALDING UNIVERSITY
Louisville, Kentucky 40203-2188

Founded 1814. Coed. Private control. Roman Catholic. Semester system. Library: 175,000 volumes, 16,000 microforms, 342 current periodicals, 46 PCs.

Tuition: per credit hour $300–$320 (M.A.), $325 (specialist), $350–$430 (doctoral). On-campus housing 20 single graduate

students. Average academic year housing costs: $2980 (including board). Contact Director of Housing for both on- and off-campus housing information. Phone: (502)858-7139.

Graduate Study

Enrollment: full- and part-time 375. College faculty teaching graduate students: full-time 27, part-time 8. Degrees conferred: M.A., M.A.T., M.S.N., Specialist, Psy.D., Ed.D.

ADMISSION REQUIREMENTS. Official transcripts, GRE required in support of application. TOEFL required for international applicants. Accepts transfer applicants. Graduates of unaccredited institutions not considered. Apply to Graduate Admissions Office at least four weeks prior to registration. Application fee $30. Phone: (502)585-7105; fax: (502)585-7158.

ADMISSION STANDARDS. Selective. Usual minimum average: 3.0 (proposed major) (A = 4).

FINANCIAL AID. Eighteen scholarships, forty-three administrative/research assistantships, Federal W/S, loans. Approved for VA benefits. Apply to the Director of Student Financial Aid. Use FAFSA and institutional FAF. Phone: (502)585-9911, ext. 200.

DEGREE REQUIREMENTS. For M.A.: 30 semester hours minimum, at least 24 in residence; written comprehensive exam; research papers. For M.A.T., M.A.L.S.: 36 semester hours minimum. For M.S.N.: 39 semester hours minimum, written comprehensive exam; thesis. For Specialist: 30 semester hours beyond the master's. For Psy.D.: M.A. plus 69 semester hours; internship and dissertation; final oral exam. For Ed.D.: M.A. plus 60 semester hours; dissertation; final oral exam. Limit of eight years to complete doctorate.

FIELDS OF STUDY.
Education. Includes elementary, secondary, administration, computer and reading leadership; Certification and Endorsements (non-degree).
Library Science.
Nursing.
Pastoral Ministries. M.A.
Psychology.
Religious Studies.

SPRINGFIELD COLLEGE
Springfield, Massachusetts 01109-3797

Founded 1885. Located 85 miles W of Boston. Coed. Private control. Semester system. Library: 150,000 volumes, 550 microforms, 620 current periodicals, 100 PCs.

Tuition: per credit hour $416. On-campus housing for limited number of married, single-students. Average academic year housing costs (room only): $5600 for single students. Contact Housing Director for both on- and off-campus housing information. Phone: (413)748-3102.

School of Graduate Studies

Graduate study since 1899. Enrollment: full-time 536, part-time 315. College faculty: full-time 80, part-time 15. Degrees conferred: M.S., MED., M.P.E., M.S.W., C.A.S., D.P.E.

ADMISSION REQUIREMENTS. Transcripts, letter of recommendation required in support of application. GRE required for doctoral applicants. TOEFL required for international applicants. Interview sometimes required. Apply to Office of Graduate Admissions, preferably by July 1 (Fall), November 1 (Spring). Application fee $35. Phone: (413)748-3479; fax: (413)748-6394.

ADMISSION STANDARDS. Selective for most majors. Usual minimum average: 2.5 (A = 4).

FINANCIAL AID. Forty-eight scholarships, seventy teaching fellowships, six research fellowships, fifteen rehabilitation traineeships, ten residence hall directorships, three internships, Federal W/S, loans. Approved for VA benefits. Apply by February 1 to director of appropriate graduate program for fellowships, assistantships; to Financial Aid Office for all other programs. Phone: (413)748-3108. Use FAFSA, Financial Aid transcript. About 60% of full-time students receive aid other than loans from College and outside sources. No aid for part-time students.

DEGREE REQUIREMENTS. For master's: 32 semester hours minimum, at least 26 in residence; may include thesis with final oral/written exam. For C.A.S.: 32 semester hours minimum beyond the master's, at least 26 in residence. For D.P.E.: 90 semester hours minimum, at least 45 in residence and 30 in full-time attendance; preliminary exam; dissertation; final oral exam.

FIELDS OF STUDY.
Adapted Physical Education.
Art Therapy.
Athletic Administration.
Biomechanics.
Counseling and Psychological Services. Interview required.
Health Care Management.
Health Promotion/Wellness Management.
Health Science.
Movement Science.
Occupational Therapy.
Physical Education. Interview for D.P.E.
Physical Therapy.
Recreation and Leisure Services.
Rehabilitation Services. Includes alcohol, substance abuse, developmental disabilities, motor learning.
Social Work.
Teacher Education.

STANFORD UNIVERSITY
Stanford, California 94305-9991
http://www.stanford.edu

Founded 1891. Graduate study since 1891. Located near Palo Alto, 30 miles SE of San Francisco. Coed. Private control. Quarter system. Special facilities: Center for Chicano Studies, Hopkins Marine Station at Pacific Grove, California; Hoover Institution of War, Revolution, and Peace; Humanities Center, Institute for Energy Studies, Center for International Studies, Institute for Research on Women and Gender, Stanford Medical Center, Computation Center; Center for Materials Research; Stanford Linear Accelerator Center; special laboratories for study in high voltage, electronics, nuclear engineering, physics, biophysics, and microwaves. Library: 6,450,000 volumes, 4,200,000 microforms, 47,000 current periodicals, 600 PCs in all libraries.

Annual tuition: full-time $20,490, School of Business $23,100, Engineering $21,885. On-campus housing for graduate 3000 men and women. Average academic year housing costs: $9000 single students (including board), married students $18,000 (including board). Contact the Housing Assignment Services for on-campus housing (415)725-2810 and Community Housing Service for off-campus housing (415)723-3906.

Graduate Study

Graduate study since 1891. Enrollment: full-time 6500. Faculty: full-time 1740. Degrees conferred: A.M., M.S., M.A.T., Engineer, M.F.A., Ed.S., D.M.A., Ed.D., Ph.D.

ADMISSION REQUIREMENTS. Two official copies of all transcripts, GRE, three letters of recommendation in duplicate, statement of purpose required in support of application. Interview not required. TOEFL required for international applicants. Accepts transfer applicants. Graduates of unaccredited institutions not considered. Apply to Office of Graduate Admissions by January 1 (Fall). Admits Fall only. Application fee $65, $75 for international applicants. Phone: (415)723-4291; fax: (415)725-7248.

ADMISSION STANDARDS. Very competitive for most departments, competitive for the others.

FINANCIAL AID. Annual awards from institutional funds: 1000 scholarships, 500 teaching fellowships, 1500 research fellowships, Federal W/S, loans. Most scholarships and fellowships have no teaching or research requirements. Apply to Office of Financial Aid by December 15 for art, history, biological sciences, and biophysics. Apply by January 1 for schools of Education, Earth Science, Humanities and Science, Medicine (non M.D.); and chemical, civil, and electrical engineering, and computer science. Apply by February 15 for all other engineering departments, for scholarships and fellowships; to appropriate department for assistantships. Use FAFSA. Financial Aid. Phone: (451)723-3058. About 72% of students receive aid other than loans from University and outside sources.

DEGREE REQUIREMENTS. For M.A., M.S.: three quarters (36–45 units) minimum in residence, some departments require more; thesis/nonthesis option; written/oral exams in some departments; reading knowledge of one foreign language for some departments. For M.A.T.: three quarters (45 units) minimum in full-time residence; teaching credential. For Engineer: six quarters (71–90 units) minimum, at least three quarters in residence; thesis. For Ed.D.: nine quarters (108–135 units) minimum beyond the bachelor's degree, at least six quarters in residence and two quarters in consecutive full-time attendance; dissertation, final oral exam. For D.M.A.: same as for Ed.D., except final project usually replaces dissertation. For Ph.D.: nine quarters (109–135 units) minimum beyond the bachelor's degree, at least six quarters in residence, full-time attendance requirement for most departments; preliminary/final written exams in most departments; dissertation; final oral exams.

FIELDS OF STUDY.
Anthropology. Apply by January 1.
Applied Physics. Apply by January 1.
Art. Art history, art education, studio; portfolio for admission to studio major; apply by December 15.
Asian Languages. Includes Chinese, Japanese; admits Summer also.
Biochemistry. Apply by January 1. Ph.D. only.
Biological Sciences. Includes biology, botany, zoology; apply by December 15.
Biophysics. Apply by December 15 for Fall. Ph.D. only.
Cancer Biology. GRE Subject in chemistry, biology, or physics for admission. Ph.D. only; apply by January 1.
Chemistry. Apply by January 1. Ph.D. only.
Classics. Includes Greek, Latin. apply by January 1.
Communication. Includes journalism, broadcasting, film, communication research; MAT for Ph.D.; apply by January 1.
Comparative Literature. GRE Subject in English or foreign language; apply by January 1.
Computer Science. Apply by January 1.
Drama. Ph.D. only.
East Asian Studies. A.M. only; apply by January 1.
Economics. Ph.D. only; apply by January 1.
Education. Apply by January 1.
English. GRE Subject in literature; apply by January 1.
Epidemiology.
French and Italian. GRE Subject; tape recording of applicant reading French; apply by January 1.

Genetics. GRE Subject in biology or chemistry; Ph.D. only; apply by January 1.

German. GRE Subject in German; apply by January 1 for Ph.D.

History. Apply by January 1; admits to Summer also.

Humanities. A.M. only.

Immunology. Ph.D. only.

International Policy Studies. A.M. only; apply by January 1.

Latin American Studies. A.M. only. Spanish or Portuguese; apply by January 1.

Linguistics. Apply by January 1.

Mathematics. Apply by January 1.

Medical Information Science. Apply by January 1.

Microbiology and Immunology. GRE Subject in biology or chemistry for admission. Ph.D. only; apply by January 1.

Modern Thought and Literature. GRE Subject in applicant's major field; apply by January 1.

Molecular and Cellular Physiology. GRE Subject Test in biology for admission. Ph.D. only.

Molecular Pharmacology.

Music. Apply by January 1.

Neurosciences Program. GRE Subject in biology or chemistry; apply by January 1.

Pharmacology. GRE Subject in biology or chemistry.

Philosophy. Fall only for Ph.D.; apply by January 1.

Physics. Apply by January 1. Ph.D. only.

Political Science. Apply by January 1.

Psychology. GRE General/Subject for admission; apply by January 1. Ph.D. only.

Religious Studies.

Russian and East European Studies. A.M. only. Apply by January 1.

Scientific Computing and Computational Mathematics. GRE Subject in mathematics; apply by January 1.

Slavic Languages and Literature. Apply by January 1.

Sociology. Apply by January 1. Ph.D. only.

Spanish and Portuguese. GRE Subject in Spanish; apply by January 1.

Statistics. GRE Subject (if applying for financial aid); apply by January 1 for Ph.D.

Structural Biology. GRE subject in biology or chemistry. Ph.D. only; apply by January 1.

Graduate School of Business

http://gsb-www.stamford.edu/gsbhome.html

Graduate study since 1925. Quarter system.

Tuition: full-time $23,100. On-campus housing available. Enrollment: full-time, M.B.A. 790; Ph.D. 98, no part-time students, evening classes, or Summer session. Faculty: full-time 80, part-time 20. Degrees conferred: M.B.A., Ph.D.

ADMISSION REQUIREMENTS. Two official transcripts, three recommendations, GMAT required in support of application for M.B.A., GRE for Ph.D. TOEFL required of international students. Graduates of unaccredited colleges not considered. Apply to Office of Admissions (for first round) by March 29. Application fee $140. Phone: (415)723-2766; fax: (415)725-7831.

ADMISSION STANDARDS. Very competitive.

FINANCIAL AID. Annual awards from institutional funds: 370 fellowships, 100 Ph.D. research assistantships, loans. Approved of VA benefits. Apply to Ph.D. office for Ph.D. financial aid. Apply to Director of Financial Aid, Graduate School of Business for all other programs; no specified closing date. Use FAFSA. Phone: (415)723-3282; fax: (415)725-3328.

DEGREE REQUIREMENTS. For M.B.A.: six quarters (108 units); no thesis or language requirement. For Ph.D.: nine quarters minimum; four comprehensive and one minor field exams; dissertation; final oral exam. Students with recent bachelor's degree or equivalent are encouraged to apply directly to doctoral program. Joint four-year J.D.-M.B.A. program offered in cooperation with Stanford School of Law.

FIELDS OF STUDY.
Accounting.
Economics.
Entrepreneurship.
Finance.
Global Management.
Human Resource Management.
Leadership.
Marketing.
Operations and System Analysis.
Operations, Information and Technology.
Organizational Behavior.
Public Management.
Strategic Management.

School of Earth Science

Graduate study since 1891. Quarter system.

Annual tuition: $20,490. Enrollment: full-time 220, part-time none. Faculty: full-time 37, part-time 41. Degrees conferred: M.S., Engineer, Ph.D.

ADMISSION REQUIREMENTS. Two official copies of all transcripts, GRE, three letters of recommendation, statement of purpose required in support of School's application. Interview not required. TOEFL required for international students. Some departments accept transfer applicants. Graduates of unaccredited institutions not considered. Apply to Department by January 15 (GES and PE) or February 1 (Geophysic). Application fee $55. Phone: (415)723-4291.

ADMISSION STANDARDS. Very competitive for most departments.

FINANCIAL AID. Annual awards from institutional funds; research/teaching assistantships, Federal W/S, loans. Approved for VA benefits. For assistantships apply to appropriate department at time of admission. Use FAFSA. Phone: (415)723-2644. Departments offer teaching/research assistantships to most students who are admitted.

DEGREE REQUIREMENTS. For M.S.: three quarters (36–45 units) minimum in residence, some departments require more; thesis in most cases; written/oral exams in some departments. For Engineer: six quarters (72–90 units) minimum, at least three quarters in residence; thesis. For Ph.D.: nine quarters (108–135 units) minimum beyond the bachelor's, at least six quarters in residence, full-time attendance requirement for most departments; preliminary/final written exams in most departments; dissertation; final oral exams.

FIELDS OF STUDY.
Geological and Environmental Sciences.
Geophysics.
Petroleum Engineering.

School of Education

http://www-leland.stanford.edu/dept/SUSE

Graduate study since 1891. Quarter system.

Annual tuition: $20,490. Enrollment: full-time 380, part-time none. Faculty: full-time 40, part-time none. Degrees conferred: A.M., Ed.S., Ed.D., Ph.D.

ADMISSION REQUIREMENTS. Two official copies of all transcripts, GRE, three letters of recommendation, statement of purpose required in support of application. Interview not required.

TOEFL required for international applicants. Accepts transfer applicants. Apply to Office of Admissions by January 1, some departments have later deadlines. Admits Fall only. Application fee $65, $75 for international applicants. Phone: (415)723-4794; fax: (415)725-7412.

ADMISSION STANDARDS: Competitive for all departments.

FINANCIAL AID. Annual awards from institutional funds: scholarships, fellowships, assistantships, Federal W/S, loans. Approved for VA benefits. Apply with application for admission. Use FAFSA. Phone: (415)723-4793.

DEGREE REQUIREMENTS. For A.M.: three quarters (36–45 units) minimum in residence, some departments require more; thesis/nonthesis option; written/oral exams in some departments. For Ed.D., Ph.D.: 72 units minimum beyond the bachelor's degree, at least nine quarters in residence, full-time attendance requirement; preliminary exams in most departments; dissertation; final oral exams.

FIELDS OF STUDY.
Curriculum and Teacher Education. Includes general curriculum, teacher education, curriculum in art, English, science, social studies. A.M., Ed.D., Ph.D.
Language, Literacy and Culture. Includes bilingual, language policy, second language education, writing, reading and language. A.M., Ed.D., Ph.D.
Learning, Design and Technology. A.M. only.
Psychological Studies in Education. Includes educational psychology, child and adolescent development, counseling psychology. Ed.D., Ph.D.
Social Sciences and Educational Practice. Includes administration and policy analysis, international comparative education, anthropology of education, economics of education, history of education, philosophy of education, sociology of education, interdisciplinary studies. A.M., Ed.D., Ph.D.
Stanford Teacher Education Program (STEP). Includes single subject clear teaching credential in English, languages (Chinese, French, German, Japanese, Latin, Spanish), mathematics, science (biology, chemistry, physics), social studies. A.M. only.

School of Engineering

Graduate study since 1925. Quarter system.
Annual tuition: $21,885. Enrollment: full-time 2551, part-time 281. Faculty: full-time 219, part-time 5. Degrees conferred: M.S., Engineer, Ph.D.

ADMISSION REQUIREMENTS. Two copies of all transcripts, GRE (Subject Test for some programs), three letters of recommendation required in support of School's application. Interview not required. TOEFL required for international applicants. Accepts transfer applicants. Apply to Office of Graduate Admissions by January 1 (Fall), November 1 (Winter), February 1 (Spring), May 1 (Summer); some departments may have later deadlines. Application fee $65, $75 for international applicants. Phone: (415)723-4291.

ADMISSION STANDARDS. Very competitive for most departments, competitive for the others.

FINANCIAL AID. Annual awards from institutional funds: scholarships, fellowships, assistantships, Federal W/S, loans. Approved for VA benefits. Apply to Office of Graduate Admissions by January 1 for chemical, civil and electrical engineering, February 15 all other engineering departments, for scholarships, fellowships; to appropriate department for assistantships. Use FAFSA and institutional FAF. Phone: (415)723-2644. About

60% of students receive aid other than loans from University and outside sources.

DEGREE REQUIREMENTS. For M.S.: three quarters (36–45 units) minimum in residence, some departments require more; thesis in most cases; written/oral exams in some departments; reading knowledge of one foreign language for some departments. For Engineer: six quarters (72–90 units) minimum, at least three quarters in residence; thesis. For Ph.D.: nine quarters (108–135 units) minimum beyond the bachelor's degree, at least six quarters in residence, full-time attendance requirement for most departments; preliminary/final written exams in most departments; dissertation; final oral exams.

FIELDS OF STUDY.
Aeronautics and Astronautics.
Chemical Engineering.
Civil Engineering.
Computer Science.
Electrical Engineering.
Engineering-Economics Systems.
Engineering Management.
Industrial Engineering and Engineering Management.
Manufacturing Systems Engineering.
Materials Science and Engineering.
Mechanical Engineering. Ph.D. only.
Operations Research. Ph.D.; admits Fall only.
Product Design.
Scientific Computing and Computational Mathematics. GRE Subject Test in mathematics; apply by January 1.

School of Humanities and Sciences

Quarter system. Enrollment: full-time 1578, part-time 482. Faculty: full- and part-time 483. Degrees conferred: A.M., M.S., M.A.T, M.F.A., D.M.A., Ph.D.

ADMISSION REQUIREMENTS. Two official copies of all transcripts, GRE and three letters of recommendation required in support of School's application. Subject Test/MAT, statement of purpose required for some programs. Interview not required. TOEFL required for international students. Accepts transfer applicants. Graduates of unaccredited institutions not considered. Apply to Office of Graduate Admissions by January 1 (Fall), November 1 (Winter), February 1 (Spring), May 1 (Summer); some departments have later deadlines. Application fee $65, $85 for international applicants. Phone: (415)723-1572; fax: (415)723-3235.

ADMISSION STANDARDS. Very competitive for most departments, competitive for the others. Accepts approximately 17–20% of applicants.

FINANCIAL AID. Annual awards from institutional funds: scholarships, fellowships, assistantships, full and partial tuition waivers, Federal W/S, loans. Most scholarships and fellowships have no teaching or research requirements. Apply to Office of Graduate Admissions by December 15 for art, history, biological sciences and biophysics fellowships; January 1 for all other humanities and sciences departments scholarships, fellowships; to appropriate department for assistantships; to Financial Aid Office for all other programs. Use FAFSA. Phone: (415)723-3058. About 72% of students receive aid other than loans from University and outside sources.

DEGREE REQUIREMENTS. For A.M., M.S.: three quarters (36–45 units) minimum in residence, some departments require more; thesis in most cases; written/oral exams in some departments; reading knowledge of one foreign language for some departments. For M.A.T.: three quarters (45 units) minimum in full-time residence; teaching credential. For D.M.A.: nine quarters (108–135 units) minimum beyond bachelor's, at least six quarters in residence and two quarters in consecutive full-time attendance; comprehensive exam; final project. For Ph.D.: nine quarters (108–135 units) minimum beyond the bachelor's, at least six quarters in residence, full-time attendance requirement for most departments; preliminary/qualifying written exams in most departments; dissertation; final oral exam.

FIELDS OF STUDY.
Anthropology. A.M., Ph.D.
Applied Physics. M.S., Ph.D.
Art. Includes history, studio portfolio for admission to studio. A.M., M.A.T., M.F.A., Ph.D.
Asian Languages. Includes Chinese, Japanese. A.M., Ph.D.
Biological Sciences. Includes botany, cell, zoology. M.A.T., M.S., Ph.D.
Biophysics.
Chemistry.
Classics. Includes Greek, Latin. A.M., Ph.D.
Communication. Includes broadcasting, communication. Ph.D.
Comparative Literature. Ph.D.
Drama. Ph.D.
East Asian Studies. A.M.
Economics. Ph.D.
English. Includes creative writing. A.M., Ph.D.
Film. A.M.
Food Research Institute. Includes food and agricultural economics. A.M., Ph.D.
French. Includes education (M.A.T. only). A.M., Ph.D.
German Studies. A.M., M.A.T., Ph.D.
History. A.M., M.A.T., Ph.D.
Humanities. A.M.
International Policy Studies. A.M.
Italian. A.M., Ph.D.
Journalism. A.M.
Latin American Studies. A.M., M.A.T.
Linguistics. A.M., Ph.D.
Mathematics. M.A.T., M.S., Ph.D.
Media Studies. A.M.
Modern Thought and Literature. Ph.D.
Music. A.M., D.M.A., Ph.D.
Philosophy. A.M., Ph.D.
Physics. M.A.T., Ph.D.
Political Science. A.M., Ph.D.
Psychology. Ph.D.
Religious Studies. A.M., Ph.D.
Russian. A.M.
Russian and East European Studies. A.M., M.A.T.
Slavic Languages and Literature. M.A.T., Ph.D.
Sociology. Ph.D.
Spanish. A.M., Ph.D.
Statistics. M.S., Ph.D.

Law School (94305-8610)

Established 1893. Semester system. Law library: 450,250 volumes. Library has LEXIS, NEXIS, WESTLAW.

Annual tuition: $23,250. On-campus housing available. Total average annual additional expense: $10,200 (single), $18,700 (married).

Enrollment: first-year class 186; total full-time 556 (men 55%, women 45%); no part-time study. Faculty: full-time 44; part-time 54. Degrees conferred: J.D., J.D.-M.P.A. (Woodrow Wilson School of Public and International Affairs, Princeton), J.D.-M.A. (The Johns Hopkins School of Advanced International Studies), J.D.-M.A.(Economic, History, Political Science), J.D.-M.B.A., J.S.D., J.S.M.

ADMISSION REQUIREMENTS. LSDAS Law School report, bachelor's degree, transcripts, two recommendations, LSAT required in support of application. Interview not required. Accepts

transfer applicants. Graduates of unaccredited colleges not considered. Apply to Director of Admissions and Financial Aid by March 1. Earlier filing strongly advised. Admits Fall only. Application fee $65. Phone: (415)723-4985.

ADMISSION STANDARDS. Very competitive. Accepts 7–10% of total annual applicants.

FINANCIAL AID. Scholarships, teaching fellowships, Federal W/S, loans. Apply by May 15 (scholarships, no closing date for loans) to Director of Admissions and Financial Aid. Use FAFSA. About 73% of students receive aid from School.

DEGREE REQUIREMENTS. For J.D.: satisfactory completion of three-year program. For J.S.M.: one year in full-time study beyond the J.D. For J.S.D.: J.D. required; at least one year in residence; dissertation.

School of Medicine (94304-1677)

Incorporated 1908. Medical library 200,000 volumes. Annual tuition: $25,350 (3-quarter academic year).

Enrollment: first-year class 86 (EDP 2), total 456 (men 58%, women 42%). Faculty: full-time 514, part-time and volunteer 1200. Degrees conferred: M.D., Ph.D. (Medical Scientist Training Program).

ADMISSION REQUIREMENTS. AMCAS report, transcripts, recommendations, MCAT, interview required in support of application. Applicants must have completed at least three years of college. Has EDP; apply between June 15 and August 1. Accepts transfer applicants. Apply to Director of Admission after June 15, before November 15. Graduate program: transcripts, GRE required in support of a supplementary application. Apply by February 1 to chair of appropriate department. Application fee $65. Phone: (415)725-6861; fax: (415)725-4599.

ADMISSION STANDARDS. For M.D.: Very competitive. Accepts 2–4% of total annual applicants. Approximately 55% are state residents.

FINANCIAL AID. Scholarships, research fellowships, loans. MSTP funded by NIH. Apply to Financial Aid Office after admission, as soon as possible after February 1. Use FAFSA. Phone: (415)723-6958. About 80% of students receive some aid from the School.

DEGREE REQUIREMENTS. For M.D.: satisfactory completion of thirteen quarters of academic work and passing USMLE. For Ph.D.: nine quarters minimum beyond the bachelor's, some departments require reading knowledge of one or more languages; preliminary written exam; dissertation; final oral exam.

FIELDS OF GRADUATE STUDY.
Anatomy.
Biochemistry.
Biomedical Engineering.
Biophysics.
Cancer Biology. (MSTP)
Cell Biology.
Genetics.
Health Research & Policy.
Immunology. (MSTP)
Medical Information Science. (MSTP)
Microbiology.
Neurosciences. (MSTP)
Pathology.
Pharmacology. (MSTP)
Physiology.

THE COLLEGE OF STATEN ISLAND OF THE CITY UNIVERSITY OF NEW YORK
Staten Island, New York 10301

Founded 1955. Coed. Municipal control. Semester system. Special facilities: Center for Developmental Neurosciences and Developmental Disabilities, Center for Environmental Science, Center for Immigrant and Population Studies. Library: 190,000 volumes, 706,000 microforms, 1378 current periodicals.

Tuition: per credit, city resident $185, nonresident $320. No on-campus housing. Day care facilities available.

Division of Graduate Studies

Enrollment: full-time 46, part-time 1059. Faculty: full-time 47, part-time 42. Degrees conferred: M.A., M.S., M.S. in Ed., Advanced Certificate.

ADMISSION REQUIREMENTS. Transcripts, GRE (except teacher education), letters of recommendation required in support of divisional application. TOEFL required for international applicants. Accepts transfer applicants. Graduates of unaccredited institutions not considered. Apply to Office of Admissions well in advance of registration. Application fee $40. Phone: (718)982-2010; fax: (718)982-2500.

ADMISSION STANDARDS. Selective. Usual minimum average: 3.0 (A = 4).

FINANCIAL AID. Fifteen fellowships, six research assistantships, nineteen teaching assistantships, Federal W/S, loans. Approved for VA benefits. Apply to Director of Financial Aid; no specified closing date. Use University's FAF. Phone: (718)982-2030.

DEGREE REQUIREMENTS. For master's: 30 semester hours minimum, at least 24 in residence; thesis/final written exam.

FIELDS OF STUDY.
Biology.
Cinema Studies.
Computer Science.
Educational Administration and Supervision.
Elementary Education.
English.
Environmental Sciences.
Liberal Studies.
Physical Therapy.
Polymer Chemistry.
School and Community Counseling.
Secondary Education.
Special Education.

STEPHEN F. AUSTIN STATE UNIVERSITY
Nacogdoches, Texas 75962

Founded 1921. Located 140 miles NE of Houston. Coed. State control. Semester system. Library: 850,000 volumes, 1,102,625 microforms, 3260 current periodicals.

Annual tuition: per credit, resident $32, nonresident $200. On-campus housing for 416 married students, 1661 men, 2343 women. Average annual housing cost: $3800 (including board). Contact Director of Housing. For both on- and off-campus housing information. Phone: (409)568-2601.

Graduate School

Graduate study since 1937. Enrollment: full-time 400, part-time 1200 (men 40%, women 60%). Graduate faculty: full-time 202, part-time 99. Degrees conferred: M.A., M.B.A., M.Ed., M.F., M.F.A., D.F. (Forestry), M.I.S., M.M., M.P.A., M.S., M.S.F., M.S.W., Ph.D. in Forestry (cooperative with Texas A&M University).

ADMISSION REQUIREMENTS. Transcripts, GRE, GMAT (for M.B.A.) required in support of School's application. TOEFL, TWE required for international applicants. Interview not required. Accepts transfer applicants. Graduates of unaccredited institutions not considered. Apply to Graduate School by August 1. Application fee $25 for international students, none for domestic students. Phone: (409)468-2807.

ADMISSION STANDARDS. Selective. Usual minimum average: 2.8 (A = 4).

FINANCIAL AID. Annual awards from institutional funds: twenty-five scholarships, two hundred teaching assistantships, twenty-five research assistantships, Federal W/S, loans. Approved for VA benefits. Apply by March 1 to Director of Scholarships and Loans for scholarships, to head of major department for assistantships, to Financial Aid Office for all other programs. Phone: (409)468-2403. Use FAFSA. About 50% of students receive aid other than loans from College and outside sources. Aid sometimes available for part-time students.

DEGREE REQUIREMENTS. For master's: 30 semester hours minimum including thesis or 36 semester hours minimum without thesis, at least 24 in residence; final oral/written exams.

FIELDS OF STUDY.
Accounting.
Agriculture.
Art. Includes applied, design, fine arts.
Biology.
Business. Includes general business, management. GMAT required for admission; M.B.A. only.
Chemistry.
Communication. Includes speech communication, journalism, organizational, radio-television-film.
Computer Science.
Education. Includes administration, counseling, supervision, early childhood, elementary, secondary, reading, special education.
English.
Forestry. Thesis for M.E., M.S.F., D.F.
Geology.
History.
Human Sciences.
Kinesiology.
Mathematics.
Music.
Natural Science.
Physics. Thesis usually required.
Psychology. Thesis usually required for M.A.
Social Work.
Speech Pathology and Audiology.
Statistics.
Theater.

STETSON UNIVERSITY
De Land, Florida 32720-3781

Founded 1883. Located 40 miles N of Orlando. Coed. Private control. Semester system. Library 491,000 volumes, 149,000 microforms, 1400 current periodicals.

Tuition: per semester hour $315. Limited on-campus housing. Average academic year off-campus housing costs: $500 per month. Contact Dean of Students Office for both on- and off-campus housing information. Phone: (904)822-7000.

Graduate Division

Graduate study since 1902. Enrollment: full- and part-time 250. Faculty: full-time 10, part-time 5. Degrees conferred: M.A., M.S., M.A.T., M.Ed., M.B.A., M.Acc., Ed.S.

ADMISSION REQUIREMENTS. Official transcripts, three letters of references, GRE/GMAT/MAT required in support of application. Interview required for some departments. Accepts transfer applicants. Apply to Chair of Graduate Students at least two months prior to registration. Application fee $25. Phone: (904)822-7120.

ADMISSION STANDARDS. Selective. Usual minimum average: 3.0 (A = 4).

FINANCIAL AID. None from University funds. State scholarships available, Federal W/S, loans. Apply to the Financial Aid Office; no specified closing date. Use FAFSA. Phone: (904)822-7501.

DEGREE REQUIREMENTS. For master's: 30 semester hours minimum, at least 24 in residence; reading knowledge of 1 foreign language for some majors; thesis or final oral exam. For Ed.S.: 30 semester hours beyond master's.

FIELDS OF STUDY.
Accountancy.
Business Administration.
Counseling.
Education. Includes leadership, guidance, elementary education, learning disabilities, counseling, exceptional child.
English.
Marriage and Family Therapy.

College of Law

Founded 1900. Located in St. Petersburg (33707). Semester system. Law Library: 320,000 volumes. Library has LEXIS, NEXIS, WESTLAW.

Annual tuition: $18,175; Summer session $3250. On-campus housing available. Room cost per year: $3000–$4000. Apply to Director, Stetson Inn. Total average annual additional expense: $10,000.

Enrollment: first-year class 235; total full-time 628 (men 48%, women 52%); no part-time study. Faculty: full-time 38, part-time 51. Degrees conferred: J.D., J.D.-M.B.A.

ADMISSION REQUIREMENTS. LSDAS Law School report, bachelor's degree, transcripts, letters of recommendation, LSAT required in support of application. Accepts transfer applicants. Graduates of unaccredited colleges not considered. Apply to Director of Admissions by March 1. Admits new students to Fall, Spring, Summer. Application fee $35. Phone: (813)345-1121, ext. 214.

ADMISSION STANDARDS. Selective. Accepts 25–30% of total annual applicants.

FINANCIAL AID. Scholarships, grants, research/teaching assistantships, Federal W/S, loans. Apply to Financial Aid Office by April 1. Phone: (813)345-1300. Use FAFSA. About 10% of students receive aid other than loans from College.

DEGREE REQUIREMENTS. For J.D.: 88 semester hours minimum; advanced standing for work completed at other accredited law schools considered. For M.B.A.: see Graduate Divisional listing above.

STEVENS INSTITUTE OF TECHNOLOGY
Hoboken, New Jersey 07030
http://www.stevens-tech.edu

Founded 1870. Coed. Private control. Semester system. Special facilities: Automotive Research Laboratory, Davidson Laboratory for Fluids Research, Plastics Institute of America Laboratory, Laboratory of Psychological Studies, Computer Center, Energy Center, Polymer Processing Institute, Center for Surface Engineered Materials, Schacht Management Laboratory, Specialized Department Laboratories. Library: 135,000 volumes, 10,000 microforms, 2600 current periodicals, 11 PCs.

Tuition: per credit $625. Average academic year housing costs: $7000 for married students; $4050–$4900 for single students. Contact Director of Residence Halls for both on- and off-campus housing information. Phone: (210)216-5128.

Graduate School

Enrollment: full-time 403, part-time 1137 (men 75%, women 35%). Faculty: full-time 102, part-time 72. Degrees conferred: M.E., M.Eng., M.S., Engineer (chemical, civil, computer, electrical, mechanical), Ph.D.

ADMISSION REQUIREMENTS. Two official transcripts, two letters of recommendation required in support of School's application. GRE/GMAT for management. TOEFL required for international applicants. Interview not required. Transfer applicants accepted. Graduates of unaccredited institutions not considered. Apply to Graduate School at least one month prior to beginning of semester, for international applicants at least two months prior to beginning of semester. Rolling admissions process. Application fee $40. Phone: (201)216-5234; fax: (201)216-8044.

ADMISSION STANDARDS. Selective. Usual minimum average: 2.5 (A = 4).

FINANCIAL AID. Annual awards from institutional funds: 62 fellowships, 111 teaching assistantships, 39 research assistantships, 10 graduate assistantships, Federal W/S, loans. Approved for VA benefits. Apply to individual department heads for assistantships, fellowships; to Financial Aid Office of all other programs. Use FAFSA. Phone: (201)216-5291. About 30% of full-time students receive aid from Institute.

DEGREE REQUIREMENTS. For master's: 30 credit hours minimum; thesis/nonthesis option. For Ph.D.: equivalent of three years of course work, at least one year in residence; reading knowledge of one foreign language for some departments; preliminary and/or comprehensive exam; dissertation; final oral exam.

FIELDS OF STUDY.
Applied Mathematics. Includes analysis, discrete mathematics, probability and statistics. M.S.
Chemical Biology. M.S.
Chemical Engineering. M.Eng., Ch.E., Ph.D.
Chemistry. M.S., Ph.D.
Civil Engineering. Includes coastal, construction management, technical, structures.
Computer Engineering. M.Eng., C.E., Ph.D.
Computer Sciences. M.S., Ph.D.
Construction Management. Interdisciplinary. M.S.
Design and Production Management. Interdisciplinary. M.S.
Electrical Engineering. M.Eng., E.E., Ph.D.
Engineering. Interdisciplinary. Ph.D.
Engineering Optics. M.S., Ph.D.
Engineering Physics. M.S.

Environmental Engineering. Includes environmental process, groundwater control, inland and coastal environmental hydrodynamics. Ph.D.

Information Management. M.S., Ph.D.

Management. Includes general management, human resources management, management planning, management of technology.

Management Information Systems.

Materials Science. M.S., Ph.D.

Mathematics. M.S., Ph.D.

Mechanical Engineering. M.Eng., M.E., Ph.D.

Physics. M.S., Ph.D.

Telecommunications. M.S., Ph.D.

Telecommunications Management. Interdisciplinary. M.S.

SUFFOLK UNIVERSITY

Boston, Massachusetts 02108

http://www.SUFFOLK.edu

Founded 1906. Coed. Private control. Semester system. Library: 292,000 volumes, 675,000 microforms, 6000 current periodicals.

Annual tuition: full-time $12,800 for M.A., M.S., M.Ed.; $14,900 for M.B.A.; $14,124 for M.P.A., M.H.A.; $16,500 for M.S.A., M.S.F., M.S.T.; $12,840 for M.S.P.S., M.S.I.E.; $17,000 for Ph.D. No on-campus housing for graduate students. Average academic year off-campus housing costs: $600 per month. Contact Dean of Students for off-campus housing information.

Graduate Study

Enrollment: full-time 160, part-time 1465. University faculty: full-time 247, part-time 1254. Degrees conferred: M.S., M.A., M.Ed., M.B.A., M.H.A., M.P.A., M.S.A., M.S.F., M.S.I.E., M.S.C.S., M.S.P.S., M.S.T., C.A.G.S., C.A.P.S., Ph.D., J.D.-M.B.A., J.D.-M.S.I.E., J.D.-M.P.A.

ADMISSION REQUIREMENTS. Official transcripts required in support of application. MAT or GRE, two letters of reference for M.A., M.S., M.S. in Ed., M.Ed., M.S.P.S., Ph.D. applicants. GMAT for M.B.A., M.S.F., M.S.A., M.S.T. applicants. GMAT or GRE for M.S.I.E. applicants. TOEFL required for international applicants. Accepts transfer applicants. Apply to Admissions Office by June 15 (Fall). Application fee $35 for School of Management; $50 Liberal Arts. Phone: (617)573-8302; fax: (617)573-0116.

ADMISSION STANDARDS. Very selective. Usual minimum average: 2.7 (A = 4).

FINANCIAL AID. Annual awards from institutional funds: 42 research fellowships, Federal W/S, loans. Approved for VA benefits. Apply by April 15 to Director of Financial Aid. Use FAFSA and University's FAF. Phone: (617)573-8470. About 10% of students receive aid other than loans from University and outside sources. Aid Available for part-time study.

DEGREE REQUIREMENTS. For M.A., M.S.Ed., M.S.I.E., M.S.P.S., M.S.C.S.: 30–36 hours minimum, at least 24 in residence. For M.B.A.: 30–36 hours, except students without previous training may be required to complete up to 59 hours. For M.P.A.: 36 hours minimum, at least 30 in residence; For M.S.A., M.S.F., M.S.T.: 30 hours beyond M.B.A., 57–60 without master's. For Ph.D.: 60 hours minimum beyond master's degree, at least 45 hours in residence; reading knowledge of two foreign languages for some departments or one language and a research tool; qualifying exam; candidacy; dissertation; final oral exam.

FIELDS OF STUDY.

Accounting. M.S.A. only.

Administration of Higher Education.

Adult and Continuing Education.

Business Administration.

Business Education.

Communication.

Computer Science. M.S.C.S.

Finance. M.S.F. only.

Finance and Human Resources. M.P.A.

Financial Services and Banking. M.S.F.S.B.

Human Resources Development.

International Economics. M.S.I.E.

Mental Health Counseling.

Political Science. M.S.P.S.

Professional Teacher Trainer Development.

Psychology. Ph.D. only.

Public Administration.

Public Administration/Disability Studies. M.P.A.

Public Administration/Health.

Public Administration/Non-Profit Management. M.P.A.

Public Administration/State and Local. M.P.A.

School Counseling.

Secondary Education. Usual subject fields.

Taxation. M.S.T. only.

Law School

Established 1906. Semester system. Law library: 300,000 volumes. Library: has LEXIS, NEXIS, WESTLAW, DIALOG.

Annual tuition: day $17,740, evening $13,306. No on-campus housing available. Total average annual additional expense: $9000–$11,000.

Enrollment: first-year class 336 (day), 170 (evening); total full-time and part-time 1582 (men 49%, women 51%). Faculty: full-time 71, part-time 71. Degrees conferred: J.D., J.D.-M.B.A., J.D.-M.P.A., J.D., M.S.I.E.

ADMISSION REQUIREMENTS. LSDAS Law School report, bachelor's degree, transcript, LSAT (no later than February), two letters of recommendation required in support of application. Interview not required. Accepts limited number of transfer applicants. Graduates of unaccredited institutions not considered. Apply to Director of Admissions by March 1. Application fee $50. Phone: (617)573-8144.

ADMISSION STANDARDS. Selective. Accepts about 20–25% of total annual applicants.

FINANCIAL AID. Scholarships, fellowships, assistantships, Federal W/S, loans. Apply to Financial Aid Office by March 1. Use FAFSA and institutional FAF. About 25% of students receive University aid other than loans.

DEGREE REQUIREMENTS. For J.D.: 90 semester hours minimum, at least the last year in residence. For master's degrees: see Graduate School listing above.

SUL ROSS STATE UNIVERSITY

Alpine, Texas 79832

Founded 1920. Located 300 miles W of San Antonio. Coed. State control. Semester system. Library: 250,000 volumes, 456,000 microforms, 2000 current periodicals, 18 PCs.

Tuition: per credit, resident $30, nonresident $222. On-campus housing for 155 married students, 320 men, 480 women. Average academic year housing costs: $2450 for married students, $2760 (room and board) or $1100 (room only) for single students. Contact Housing Officer for both on- and off-campus housing information. Phone: (915)837-8190.

Graduate Division

Graduate study since 1930. Enrollment: full-time 229, part-time 751 (men 55%, women 45%). Graduate faculty: full-time 60, part-time 20. Degrees conferred: M.A., M.B.A., M.Ed., M.S.

ADMISSION REQUIREMENTS. Two official transcripts, GRE, GMAT required in support of application. TOEFL, interview required for international applicants. Interview not required for domestic applicants. Accepts transfer applicants. Graduates of unaccredited institutions not considered. Apply to Graduate Office by July 15 (Fall), December 1 (Spring), May 1 (First Summer Session), June 25 (Second Summer Session). Application fee: none for domestic applicants, $50 for international applicants. Phone: (915)837-8052; fax. (415)837-8431.

ADMISSION STANDARDS. Relatively open. Usual minimum average: 2.5 (A = 4).

FINANCIAL AID. Annual awards from institutional funds: twelve scholarships, ten research assistantships, twenty-four administrative assistantships, four internships, Federal W/S, loans. Approved for VA benefits. Apply by June 1 to Dean, Graduate Division. Use FAFSA. About 68% of students receive aid other than loans from University. Aid sometimes available to part-time students.

DEGREE REQUIREMENTS. For M.A., M.S.: 30 semester hours minimum, at least 18 in residence; thesis; comprehensive exam. For M.Ed.: 36 semester hours minimum, at least 24 in residence; thesis/nonthesis option; comprehensive exam. For M.B.A.: 56 semester hours minimum, at least 30 hours in residence; computer proficiency; thesis/nonthesis option; comprehensive exam.

FIELDS OF STUDY.
Accounting.
Agriculture-Range Animal Science.
Art. Includes applied, design, education, history.
Bilingual Education.
Biology.
Business Administration.
Communication.
Counseling and Guidance.
Drama.
Economics.
Educational Administration.
Elementary Education.
English.
Geology.
Government.
History.
International Affairs.
International Business.
Music Education.
Physical Education.
Political Science.
Professional Education.
Public Administration.
Range Science.
Reading.
Speech.
Vocational and Technical Education.

SYRACUSE UNIVERSITY
Syracuse, New York 13244-0003
http://cwis.syr.edu

Founded 1871. Coed. Private control. Semester system. Special facilities: Center for Advanced Technology in Computer Application and Software Engineering, Science and Technology Center, Northeast Parallel Architectures Center, Center for Membrane Engineering and Science, Center for the Study of Citizenship, Institute for Energy Research, Institute for Sensory Research, Interdisciplinary Institute for Literacy, Advance Graphics Research Laboratory, Natural Sciences Computing Center, Centro de Estudios Hispanicos, Gerontology Center, Robert H. Brethen Operations Management Institute, Better Audio Laboratory and Archive, George Arents Research Library. Library: 2,200,000 volumes, 2,600,000 microforms.

Tuition: per credit $503. On-campus housing for both married and single graduate students. Average academic year housing costs: $4921 (room only) for single students, $8540 (including board) for married students. Apply to Office of South Campus Housing for both on- and off-campus housing information. Phone: (315)443-2567.

Graduate School

Graduate study since 1876. Enrollment: full-time 2500, part-time 2500. Graduate faculty: full-time 965, part-time 501. Degrees conferred: M.Arch.I., M.Arch.II, M.A., M.S., Ph.D., D.A., Ed.D., C.A.S., E.E., C.E., M.L.S., M.B.A., M.P.A., M.S.C., M.P.S., M.S.W., M.F.A., M.I.D., M.Mus. Combined degree programs: J.D.-M.L.S., J.D.-M.B.A., J.D.-M.S., J.D.-Ph.D., J.D.-M.P.A.

ADMISSION REQUIREMENTS. Two official transcripts, three letters of recommendation, interview (for some programs), GRE General Test most programs, GMAT for Management required in support of School's application. TOEFL required for international applicants. Accepts transfer applicants. Graduates of unaccredited institutions not considered. Apply to Graduate School prior to registration. Application fee $40. Phone: (315)443-9130.

ADMISSION STANDARDS. Very competitive for some departments, competitive or selective for the others. Usual minimum average: 3.0 (A = 4).

FINANCIAL AID. Eighty scholarships, 101 fellowships, 875 teaching/research assistantships, Federal W/S, loans. Approved for VA benefits. Apply by January 10 for fellowships, March 1 for assistantships and scholarships to appropriate department; to Financial Aid Office for all other programs. Submit FAFSA by February 28. Phone: (315)443-1513. About 65% of students receive aid other than loans from University. Aid sometimes available for part-time students.

DEGREE REQUIREMENTS. For most master's: 30 semester hours minimum, at least 24 in residence; thesis/nonthesis option for some departments; comprehensive oral/written exam. For Ph.D., Ed.D.; D.A.: 48–90 credit hours, 50% of program in residence; 1 foreign language and other research tool requirement; qualifying exam; dissertation; final oral exam; recital for D.A.

FIELDS OF STUDY.

SCHOOL OF ARCHITECTURE:
Architecture.

COLLEGE OF ARTS AND SCIENCES:
Applied Mathematics.
Applied Statistics.
Biology.

Biophysics.
Chemistry.
English. Includes creative writing.
Fine Arts. Includes art history, musicology.
Foreign Languages. Includes classics, French, German, Greek, Romance, Spanish.
Geology.
Humanities. Interdisciplinary.
Linguistic Studies.
Mathematics.
Philosophy.
Physics.
Psychology. Includes clinical, experimental, school, social.
Religion.
Science Teaching. Interdisciplinary.

SCHOOL OF EDUCATION:
Art Education.
Audiology.
Counselor Education.
Cultural Foundations of Education.
Curriculum and Instructional Planning.
Educational Administration.
Elementary Education N–6.
English Education.
Health Education.
Higher/Postsecondary Education.
Instructional Design, Development and Evaluation.
Mathematics Education.
Music Education.
Physical Education.
Reading.
Rehabilitation Counseling.
Science Education. Includes biology, chemistry, earth science, physics.
Social Studies Education.
Special Education. Includes educating infants and young children with special needs, learning disabilities, mental retardation.
Speech Education.
Speech-Language Pathology.
Teaching and Curriculum.

C. SMITH COLLEGE OF ENGINEERING AND COMPUTER SCIENCE:
Chemical Engineering and Material Science.
Civil Engineering. Includes environmental, sanitary science.
Computer and Information Science.
Computer Science.
Electrical Engineering. Includes computer engineering.
Hydrogeology.
Mechanical and Aerospace. Includes aerospace, mechanical, manufacturing.
Neuroscience.
Solid State Science and Technology.
System and Information Science.

COLLEGE OF HUMAN DEVELOPMENT:
Child and Family Studies.
Consumer Studies.
Environmental Arts.
Marriage and Family Therapy.
Nutrition Science.

SCHOOL OF INFORMATION STUDIES:
Information Resources Management.
Information Transfer.
Library Science.

SCHOOL OF MANAGEMENT:
Accounting.
Business Administration.

Finance.
Human Resources Management.
International Business.
Management Information Systems.
Managerial Statistics.
Marketing Management.
Operations Management.
Organization and Management.
Transportation and Distribution Management.

MAXWELL SCHOOL OF CITIZENSHIP AND PUBLIC AFFAIRS:
Anthropology.
Economics.
Geography.
History.
International Relations.
Political Science.
Public Administration.
Social Science.
Sociology.

S. I. NEWHOUSE SCHOOL OF PUBLIC COMMUNICATION:
Advertising.
Communications Management.
Magazine.
Mass Communications.
Media Administration.
Newspaper.
Photography.
Public Communications Studies.
Public Relations.
Television-Radio.

SCHOOL OF NURSING:
Nursing.
Nursing/Business Administration.

SCHOOL OF SOCIAL WORK:
Social Work.

COLLEGE OF VISUAL AND PERFORMING ARTS:
Advertising Design.
Art Education.
Art Photography.
Art Video.
Ceramics.
Computer Graphics.
Drama.
Fiber Structure and Interlocking.
Film.
Illustration.
Industrial Design.
Metalsmithing.
Museum Studies.
Music. Includes composition, education, organ, percussion, piano, strings, theory, voice, winds.
Painting.
Printmaking.
Sculpture.
Speech Communication.
Studio Research.
Surface Pattern Design.

College of Law (13244-1030)

Established 1895. Semester system. Law library: 327,000 volumes. Library has LEXIS, WESTLAW.

Annual tuition: full-time $19,660. Housing available for married students. Total average annual additional expense: $10,000.

Enrollment: first-year class 271; total full-time 779 (men 58%, women 42%). Faculty: full-time 40, part-time 41. Degrees conferred: J. D., J.D.-M.B.A., J.D.-M.P.A., J.D.-M.S. J.D.-Ph.D., LL.M.

ADMISSION REQUIREMENTS. LSDAS Law School report, bachelor's degree, transcripts, LSAT (no later than April 1) required in support of application. Interview not required. Accepts transfer applicants. Graduates of unaccredited institutions not considered. Apply to Director of Admissions after September 15, before April 1. Rolling admissions process. Fall admission only. Application fee $40. Phone: (315)443-1962.

ADMISSION STANDARDS. Selective. Accepts 40% of total applicants.

FINANCIAL AID. Scholarships, grants, partial tuition waivers, fellowships, assistantships, Federal W/S, loans. Apply to Office of Admissions and Financial Aid by March 1. Use FAFSA. Approximately 78% of students receive some aid from School.

DEGREE REQUIREMENTS. For J.D.: 6 semesters minimum, at least two years in residence; 87 credit hour program. For LL.M.: at least 24 credits beyond the J.D.; 1 year in full-time residence.
Note: Summer study abroad in England available.

TARLETON STATE UNIVERSITY
Stephenville, Texas 76402

Founded 1899. Located 65 miles SW of Fort Worth. Coed. State control. Semester system. Library: 664,500 volumes, 750,000 Microforms, 2000 current periodicals, 75 PCs.
Tuition: per credit hour, resident $42, nonresident $246. On-campus housing available. Average academic year housing costs: $2800 (including board) single students; $1800 (room only) married students. Contact Dean of Students for both on- and off-campus housing information. Phone: (817)968-9680.

School of Graduate Studies

Graduate study since 1971. Enrollment: full-time 360, part-time 700. Faculty: full-time 0, part-time 99. Degrees conferred: M.A., M.S., M.Ed., M.B.A.

ADMISSION REQUIREMENTS. Official transcripts, GRE/GMAT required in support of School's application. TOEFL required for international applicants. Accepts transfer applicants. Graduates of unaccredited colleges not considered. Apply to Dean prior to first day of registration. Application fee $20, $50 for international applicants. Phone: (817)968-9104; fax: (817)968-9389.

ADMISSION STANDARDS. Relatively open. Usual minimum average: 2.5 (A = 4).

FINANCIAL AID. Annual awards from institutional funds: one scholarship, fourteen teaching assistantships, Federal W/S, loans. Approved for VA benefits. Apply to Graduate Dean; no specified closing date. Use FAFSA and institutional FAF. Phone: (817)968-9070; fax: (817)968-9389.

DEGREE REQUIREMENTS. For master's: 36–48 hours minimum; comprehensive exam; thesis/nonthesis; project for some programs.

FIELDS OF STUDY.
Agriculture. M.S.
Agriculture Education. M.S.

Biology. M.S.
Business Administration. M.B.A.
Counseling. M.Ed.
Elementary Administration. M.Ed.
Elementary Education. M.Ed.
English. M.A.
Government. M.A.
Health and Physical Education. M.Ed.
History. M.A.
Mathematics. M.S.
Reading. M.Ed.
Secondary Education. M.Ed.
Special Education. M.Ed.

TEMPLE UNIVERSITY
Philadelphia, Pennsylvania 19122
http://astro.temple.edu

Founded 1894. Coed. State related. Semester system. Libraries: 2,189,000 volumes, 2,189,000 microforms, 15,000 current periodicals, 300 PCs in all libraries.
Tuition: per semester hour, resident $287; nonresidents $400. On-campus housing available. Average academic year housing cost: $4344 for single students; $6000 for married students. Contact Office of Student Residences for both on- and off-campus housing information. Phone: (215)204-7925.

Graduate School

Enrollment: full-time 3800, part-time 2500. Faculty: full-time 1222, part-time 200. Degrees conferred: M.A., M.B.A., M.Ed., M.F.A., M.J., M.L.A., M.M., M.M.T., M.P.T., M.S., M.S.D., M.S.E., M.S.N., M.S.W., D.M.A., Ed.D., Ph.D.

ADMISSION REQUIREMENTS. Transcripts, letters of recommendation, statement of educational objectives required in support of School's application. GRE General/Subject Tests/MAT/GMAT, auditions, performances, portfolio, and/or interview required by some departments. TOEFL required of all international applicants. Accepts transfer applicants. Apply directly to Academic Department; closing dates vary by department, consult Bulletin. Application fee $30. Phone: (215)787-1380; fax: (215)204-8781.

ADMISSION STANDARDS. Competitive or selective for most departments. Usual minimum average: 3.0 (A = 4).

FINANCIAL AID. One hundred and thirty five fellowships, 175 research assistantships, 500 teaching assistantships, 60 administrative assistantships, 400 graduate assistant, Federal W/S, loans. Approved of VA benefits. Apply by March 1 to appropriate department for scholarships, fellowships, teaching/research assistantships; to Director of Financial Aid for all other programs. Use FAFSA and institutional FAF. Phone: (215)204-1405; fax: (215)204-5897.

DEGREE REQUIREMENTS. For M.A., M.S.: 24 semester hours minimum; thesis for some departments; final oral/written exam usually required. For M.B.A.: 45–60 semester hours minimum, research paper; final oral/written exam. For M.S.E., M.Ed.: 30 semester hours minimum; final written exam; or 24 semester hours minimum; thesis. For M.F.A.: 48–52 semester hours minimum; thesis; final oral exam. For M.L.A.: 30 semester hours minimum; qualifying essay. For M.M.: 30 semester hours minimum, at least 24 in residence; comprehensive exam. For M.J.: 40 semester hours minimum; written exam; written project; oral exam. For M.S.W.: four semesters in full-time residence; field work experience; final project. For D.M.A.: 38 hours minimum beyond the master's; written/oral qualifying exam; final oral exam; dissertation/final project. For Ed.D.: 68 semester hours minimum beyond the bachelor's degree; preliminary written exam; dissertation; final oral/written exam. For Ph.D.: three years minimum beyond the bachelor's; dissertation; final oral exam.

FIELDS OF STUDY.

COLLEGE OF ALLIED HEALTH PROFESSIONS:
Nursing. M.S.N.
Occupational Therapy. M.S. only.
Physical Therapy. M.S. only.

SCHOOL OF BUSINESS AND MANAGEMENT:
Actuarial Science.
Business Administration. Includes accounting, computer and information science, economics, finance, health administration/health care financial management, physical distribution, real estate and urban land studies, risk management and insurance, international business administration, marketing.
Economics.
Management Science/Operations Management.
Statistics.
Taxation.

SCHOOL OF COMMUNICATIONS AND THEATER:
Communications. Includes mass media, speech-language hearing, rhetoric and communication. M.A. only.
Journalism. M.J. only.
Radio-Television-Film. M.F.A. only.
Theater. Includes acting, directing, playwriting, scenic design/tech; admits Fall only; apply by March 1. M.F.A. only.

SCHOOL OF DENTISTRY:
Oral Biology. M.S.D.
Orthodontics. M.S.D.

COLLEGE OF EDUCATION:
Curriculum, Instruction and Technology in Education. Includes Art, early childhood, elementary, language education (Ed.M., Ed.D.), second/foreign language, mathematics/science education (Ed.M., Ed.D.), special education, vocational/technical education. Ed.M.
Educational Leadership and Policy Studies. Includes educational administration, urban education studies. Ed.M., Ed.D.
Psychological Studies in Education. Includes counseling and school psychology, education psychology. Psychoeducational process. Ed.M only.

COLLEGE OF ENGINEERING, COMPUTER SCIENCE AND ARCHITECTURE:
Computer Applications in Systems Engineering. M.S.E. only.
Environmental Health.

COLLEGE OF HEALTH, PHYSICAL EDUCATION, RECREATION AND DANCE:
Community Health Education. M.P.H.
Dance.
Health Education.
Physical Education.
Recreation and Leisure Studies.

SCHOOL OF MEDICINE:
Anatomy.
Biochemistry.
Medicine. Combined M.D./Ph.D. program.
Microbiology and Immunology.
Molecular Biology and Genetics.

Pathology.
Pharmacology.
Physiology.

ESTHER BOYER COLLEGE OF MUSIC:
Music. M.M., D.M.A.
Music Education.
Music Therapy.

TYLER SCHOOL OF ART:
Art. M.F.A. only.

COLLEGE OF ARTS AND SCIENCES:
African American Studies.
Anthropology.
Art History.
Biology.
Chemistry.
Computer and Information Science.
Criminal Justice.
English.
Geography. M.A. only.
Geology. M.A. only.
History.
Master of Liberal Arts.
Mathematics.
Philosophy.
Physics.
Political Science.
Psychology.
Religion.
Sociology.
Spanish.
Urban Studies. M.A. only.
Note: Application deadlines vary by department.

SCHOOL OF PHARMACY:
Pharmaceutical Chemistry.
Quality Assurance and Regulatory Affairs.
Note: Apply by June 1 (Fall).

SCHOOL OF SOCIAL ADMINISTRATION:
Social Work. Includes social administration, social planning, policy, and community organizing, social service delivery. M.S.W. only.
Note: Apply by March 1 (Fall).

School of Law

Founded 1895. Semester system. Law library: 451,600 volumes. Library has LEXIS, NEXIS, WESTLAW, RLN, INNOVAC, DIALOG, CALI.

Annual tuition: resident, day $8182, evening $6300; nonresident, day $14,696, evening $11,500. On-campus housing available. Total average annual additional expense: $10,000.

Enrollment: first-year class full-time 305, part-time 75; total full- and part-time 1240 (men 54%, women 46%). School faculty: full-time 56, part-time 138. Degrees conferred: J.D., J.D.-M.B.A., LL.M. (Taxation, Legal Education).

ADMISSION REQUIREMENTS. LSDAS Law School report, bachelor's degree, transcripts, LSAT (not later than February) required in support of application. Accepts transfer applicants. Graduates of unaccredited colleges not considered. Apply to School Admissions Office, preferably by March 1. Application fee $50. Phone: (215)204-8925.

ADMISSION STANDARDS. Selective. Accepts 20–25% of total annual applicants.

FINANCIAL AID. Scholarships, Federal W/S, loans. Apply to the Office of Financial Aid by March 1. Use FAFSA. About 10% of students receive aid other than loans from School.

DEGREE REQUIREMENTS. For J.D.: satisfactory completion of three-year day or four-year evening program: 83 unit program. For LL.M.: at least 24 credits beyond the J.D.; one year minimum; final research project.
Note: Summer study abroad in Rome, Athens, Tel Aviv, and semester abroad in Tokyo available.

School of Medicine (19140)

Established 1901. Annual tuition: resident $2,182, nonresident $26,286; student fees $358. Total average figure for all other expenses: $7451. Enrollment: M.D. program, first-year class 180 (5 EDP); total 806 (men 59%, women 41%); postgraduates 304. Faculty: full-time 450, part-time 100. Degrees conferred: M.D., M.D.-Ph.D., M.S., Ph.D.

ADMISSION REQUIREMENTS. For M.D. program: AMCAS report, transcripts, letters of recommendation, MCAT, final screening interview required in support of application. Preference given to state residents. Has EDP; apply between June 15 and August 1. Apply to Director of Admissions after June 15, before December 1. Application fee $55. Phone: (215)707-3656; fax: (215)707-6932. For graduate program: transcripts, two letters of Recommendation, GRE Subject Tests, interview required in support of application. Accepts transfer applicants. Graduates of unaccredited colleges not considered. Apply to Associate Dean of Health Sciences Center prior to registration. Application fee $10.

ADMISSION STANDARDS. For M.D. program: very competitive. Accepts about 5% of total annual applicants. Approximately 65% are state residents. For graduate program: selective.

FINANCIAL AID. For M.D. program: scholarships, loans; apply to Director, Health Sciences Center Financial Aid Office, by April 1. Use FAFSA. About 80% of students receive some type of aid. For graduate program: scholarships, fellowships, assistantships for teaching/research. Apply to Associate Dean of Graduate School for scholarships, fellowships, to appropriate department chair for assistantships; no specified closing date. About 20% of graduate students receive aid other than loans from School.

DEGREE REQUIREMENTS. For M.D.: satisfactory completion of four-year program. For M.S., Ph.D., see Graduate School listing above.

FIELDS OF GRADUATE STUDY
Anatomy.
Biochemistry.
Immunology.
Microbiology.
Molecular Biology.
Pathology.
Pharmacology.
Physiology.

School of Dentistry (19140)

Organized 1863. Annual tuition: resident $18,328, nonresident $26,000. No on-campus housing available. Average academic year off-campus housing costs: $10,808. Contact the Office for Housing and Financial Aid Counseling. Phone: (215)707-7663. Total average cost for all other first-year expenses: $5214.

Enrollment: D.D.S. program, first-year class 100; 500 total (men 70%, women 30%); graduate program 60. Faculty: full-

time 79, part-time 79. Degree, conferred: D.D.S., D.D.S.-M.B.A., M.S., Ph.D.

ADMISSION REQUIREMENTS. For D.D.S. program: AAD-SAS, official transcripts, DAT required in support of School's application. Evidence of proficiency in English required of international students. Applicants must have completed at least three years of college study, four years of study preferred. Preference given to state residents. Transfer applicants not considered. Graduates of unaccredited colleges not considered. Apply to Assistant Dean after August 1, before May 1. Application fee $30. Phone: (215)707-7663; fax: (215)707-2802. For graduate program: official transcripts, D.D.S. or D.M.D. degree, interview required in support of School's application. Transfer applicants, graduates of unaccredited institutions not considered. Apply to School by February 1 (Fall). Application fee $30.

ADMISSION STANDARDS. Selective. Usual minimum average: 2.5 (A = 4). Accepts 15–20% of total annual applicants for D.D.S. program. Approximately 50% are state residents. For graduate programs: usual minimum average: 3.0 (A = 4).

FINANCIAL AID. For D.D.S. program: limited to state and federal aid programs. Apply to Assistant Dean after acceptance. Use FAFSA. Phone: (215)707-2667. For graduate program: fellowships, assistantships for teaching/research. Apply by July 1 to Dean of School. Use FAFSA. About 80% of students receive aid other than loans from School and outside sources.

DEGREE REQUIREMENTS. For D.D.S.: satisfactory completion of forty-five-month program. For Postgraduate Certificate Programs: four semesters minimum (two years) in full-time residence. For M.S.: two semesters minimum (one year) in full-time residence; thesis; final exam. For Ph.D.: see Graduate School listing above.

FIELDS OF GRADUATE STUDY.
Endodontology.
General Dentistry.
Oral Biology. M.S.
Oral Surgery.
Orthodontics.
Periodontology.
Physiology. M.S.; Ph.D. from Graduate School.

TENNESSEE STATE UNIVERSITY
Nashville, Tennessee 37209-1561

Founded 1912. Coed. State control. Semester system. Daycare facilities available. Library: 408,000 volumes, 14,400 microforms, 1259 current periodicals, 9 PCs.

Annual tuition: full-time resident $2392, nonresident $6522; per credit resident $125, nonresident $306. On-campus housing for single students. Apply to Dean of Women or Dean of Men.

Graduate School

Graduate study since 1941. Enrollment: full- and part-time 1550. Faculty: full-time 200. Degrees conferred: M.A., M.A.Ed., M.E., M.Ed., M.B.A., M.P.A., M.S., M.S.N., M.C.J., Ed.D.

ADMISSION REQUIREMENTS. Transcripts, GRE required in support of School's application. TOEFL required for international foreign applicants. Accepts transfer applicants. Apply to Dean, Graduate School, at least six weeks prior to registration. Application fee $5. Phone: (615)963-5901.

ADMISSIONS STANDARDS. Relatively open to selective. Usual minimum average: 2.5 (A = 4).

FINANCIAL AID. Limited to assistantships, loans. Approved for VA benefits. Apply to Director of Financial Aid; no specified closing date. Use FAFSA.

DEGREE REQUIREMENTS. For master's: 30–33 semester hours minimum, at least 27 in residence; thesis in some departments. For Ed.D.: 69 hours maximum beyond the master's; comprehensive exam; advancement to candidacy; dissertation or special project; final oral exam.

FIELDS OF STUDY.
Adult Education.
Agricultural Sciences.
Biological Sciences.
Business Administration.
Chemistry.
Counseling Psychology.
Criminal Justice.
Education. Includes elementary, secondary, administration and supervision, counselor, curriculum and instruction, secondary school instruction, usual teaching fields, special.
Engineering.
English.
Health and Physical Education.
Home Economics.
Mathematics.
Music Education.
Nursing.
Psychology.
Public Administration.
Reading.
Recreation.
Speech Pathology and Audiology.

TENNESSEE TECHNOLOGICAL UNIVERSITY
Cookeville, Tennessee 38505
http://www.tntech.edu

Established 1915. Located 80 miles E of Nashville. Coed. State control. Semester system. Library: 1,000,000 items, 50 PCs.

Annual tuition: full-time resident $3600, nonresident $6812. On-campus housing for 300 married students, 2000 men, 1800 women. Average academic year housing costs: $2700 for married students, $5040 (includes board) for single students. Contact Director of Housing for both on- and off-campus housing. Phone: (615)372-3414.

Graduate School

Graduate study since 1958. Enrollment: full-time 371, part-time 637 (men 43%, women 57%). Faculty: full-time 315, part-time 40. Degree conferred: M.A., M.S., M.B.A., Ed.S., Ph.D. (Engineering only).

ADMISSION REQUIREMENTS. Transcripts, letters of recommendation required in support of School's application. MAT required for education majors. GRE required for science and engineering majors. GMAT required for M.B.A. applicants. TOEFL required for international applicants. Accepts transfer applicants. Apply to Dean of Graduate School eight weeks prior to registration, international students six months, in advance. Application fee $5, $30 for international applicants. Phone: (615)372-3897; fax: (615)372-3497.

ADMISSION STANDARDS. Selective. Usual minimum average: 2.75 (A = 4).

FINANCIAL AID. Annual awards from institutional funds: ten scholarships, thirty teaching assistantships, one hundred research assistantships, Federal W/S, loans. Approved for VA benefits. Apply to appropriate department chair for assistantships, scholarships; to Financial Aid Office for all other programs. No specified closing date. Use FAFSA and University's FAF. Phone: (615)372-3073; fax: (615)372-6335. About 50% of students receive aid from University. No aid for part-time students except loans.

DEGREE REQUIREMENTS. For master's: 30 semester credits minimum, at least 24 in residence; thesis; final oral exam. For M.B.A.: 36 hours. For Ed.S.: 30 credits minimum beyond the master's. For Ph.D.: 60 hours minimum; one year in residence; qualifying exam; advancement to candidacy; dissertation; final oral exam.

FIELDS OF STUDY.

COLLEGE OF ARTS AND SCIENCES:
Biology.
Chemistry.
English.
Mathematics.

COLLEGE OF BUSINESS ADMINISTRATION:
Business Administration.

COLLEGE OF EDUCATION:
Administration and Supervision. Includes elementary principal, materials supervisor, secondary principal, superintendent (not available at M.A. level), supervisor of instruction.
Curriculum and Instruction. Includes curriculum, early childhood education, elementary education, reading, secondary education, special education.
Educational Psychology and Counselor Education. Includes educational psychology, elementary counselor, school psychology, secondary counselor, student personnel services.
Health and Physical Education.

COLLEGE OF ENGINEERING:
Chemical Engineering.
Civil Engineering.
Electrical Engineering.
Industrial Engineering.
Mechanical Engineering.

UNIVERSITY OF TENNESSEE AT CHATTANOOGA
Chattanooga, Tennessee 37403-2504

Founded 1886 as University of Chattanooga, merged July 1969 with the University of Tennessee. Coed. State control. Semester system. Special facilities: Center for Economic Education, Cadek Conservatory of Music, Center for Environmental/Energy Education, Institute of Archaeology, Odor Research Center. Library: 404,150 volumes, 1,005,000 microforms.

Tuition: per credit, resident $123, nonresident $300. On-campus housing for limited number of single graduate students; none for married students (except during Summer). Average academic year housing costs: $1600 (excluding board). Contact Dean of Student Affairs Office for both on- and off-campus housing information. Phone: (423)755-4246.

Graduate Division

Enrollment: full-time 331, part-time 985 (men 44%, women 56%). University faculty teaching graduate students: 250. Degrees conferred: M.A., M.B.A., M.Ed., M.M., M.P.A., M.S., M.S.C.J., M.S.N.

ADMISSION REQUIREMENTS. Transcripts, GRE, MAT for M.Ed., M.S.C.J., M.A., M.M., and M.S. in Psychology; GMAT for M.B.A., three letters of reference, required in support of application. Interview sometimes required. TOEFL required for international applicants. Accepts transfer applicants. Apply to Graduate Office by August 1 (Fall), well in advance of registration for other semesters. Application fee $25. Phone: (423)755-4666.

ADMISSION STANDARDS. Relatively open. Usual minimum average: 2.5 (A = 4).

FINANCIAL AID. Forty-seven assistantships, Federal W/S, loans. Approved for VA benefits. Apply to the Financial Aid Office; no specified closing date. Use FAFSA and University's FAF. Phone: (423)755-4677.

DEGREE REQUIREMENTS. For M.A., M.S., M.S.N.: 33 semester hours minimum, at least 27 in residence; thesis/nonthesis option. For M.B.A., M.P.A.: 31–36 semester hours minimum, at least 30 in residence. For M.Ed.: 33 semester hours minimum, at least 24 in residence; final comprehensive exam. For M.S.C.J.: 36 semester hours minimum, at least 30 in residence; qualifying exam; thesis optional; internship. For M.M.: 33 semester hours minimum, at least 30 in residence. Additional requirements depend upon major.

FIELDS OF STUDY.
Accounting.
Business Administration.
Computer Science.
Counseling.
Criminal Justice.
Educational Administration.
Elementary Education.
Engineering.
Engineering Management.
English.
Music.
Nursing. Includes anesthesia, family nurse practitioner.
Psychology. Includes industrial, organizational, school.
Public Administration.
Secondary Education. Includes English, history, mathematics, natural science, physics, social sciences, business, health, physical education.
Special Education.

UNIVERSITY OF TENNESSEE
Knoxville, Tennessee 37996

Founded 1794. Coed. State control. Semester system. Special facilities: Institute of Agriculture, Center for Business and Economic Research, Energy, Environment and Resources Center, Forensic Anthropology Center, Management Development Center, McClung Museum, Measurement and Control Engineering Center, Social Science Research Institute, Space Institute, Stokey Institute of Liberal Arts, Transportation Center, cooperating University in Oak Ridge Associate Universities Program. Library: 2,000,000 volumes, 2,000,000 microforms, 14,000 current periodicals.

Tuition: per credit, resident $151, nonresident $387. On-campus housing for 800 married students, 7500 men, 7500 women. Average annual housing cost: $5300 for single students, $6800 for married students. Apply to Office of Residence Halls or Rental Properties. Phone: (423)974-3411. Day care facilities available.

Graduate School

Graduate study since 1928. Enrollment: full-time 4041, part-time 3084. University faculty: full-time 1289, part-time 185. Degrees conferred: M.A., M.S., M.Arch., M.B.A., M.F.A., M.P.H., M.P.A., M.Acc., M.Math., M.Music., M.S.N., M.S.P., M.S.S.W., Ed.S., Ed.D., Ph.D.

ADMISSION REQUIREMENTS. Official transcripts required in support of School's application. GRE Subject/GMAT required for many departments. TOEFL required for international applicants. Interview not required. Accepts transfer applicants. Graduates of unaccredited institution. Apply to Office of Graduate Admissions and Records prior to registration. Foreign students apply at least six months prior to registration. Application fee $15. Phone: (423)974-3251; fax: (423)974-6541; E-mail: gsinfo@utk.edu.

ADMISSION STANDARDS. Very selective for most departments, competitive or selective for the others. Usual minimum average: 2.7 (A = 4).

FINANCIAL AID. One hundred and sixty-eight scholarships, 562 research assistantships, 970 teaching assistantships, 634 administrative assistantships, Federal W/S, loans. Approved for VA benefits. Apply by February 1 to the Graduate School for fellowships, to appropriate department chairman for assistantships; to Financial Aid Office for all other programs. Use FAFSA. Phone: (423)974-3131. About 65% of students receive aid other than loans from School and outside sources. Aid available to part-time students.

DEGREE REQUIREMENTS. For master's: 30 semester hours minimum; thesis/final project; final oral/written exam. For Ed.S.: 60 semester hours minimum; one to two semesters in full-time attendance; qualifying exam may be required; thesis/nonthesis option; final oral/written exam. For Doctorates: 24 hours minimum beyond the master's, at least one year in full-time residence; comprehensive written exam; reading knowledge of one foreign language or proficiency in research techniques; dissertation; final oral exam.

FIELDS OF STUDY.

INTERDISCIPLINARY PROGRAMS:
Aviation Systems. M.S. only.
Comparative and Experimental Medicine. GRE for admission.
Industrial and Organizational Psychology. GRE/GMAT for admission.

COLLEGE OF AGRICULTURAL SCIENCES AND NATURAL RESOURCES:
Agricultural Economics. GRE for admission.
Agricultural Engineering. GRE Subject for international applicants.
Agricultural Engineering Technology. M.S. only.
Agricultural and Extension Education. M.S. only.
Animal Science. GRE for admission.
Entomology and Plant Pathology. M.S. only.
Food Technology and Science. GRE for Ph.D.
Forestry. GRE for admission; M.S. only.
Ornamental Horticulture and Landscape Design. M.S. only.
Plant and Soil Science. GRE for admission.
Wildlife and Fisheries Science. GRE for admission. M.S. only.

COLLEGE OF BUSINESS ADMINISTRATION:
Accounting. GMAT for admission; M.Acc. only.
Business Administration. GMAT for admission.
Economics. GRE for admission.
Logistics and Transportation.
Management Science. GRE/GMAT for admission. M.S., Ph.D. only.
Statistics. GRE/GMAT for admission. M.S. only.

COLLEGE OF COMMUNICATIONS:
Communications. GRE for admission.

COLLEGE OF EDUCATION:
College Student Personnel. GRE for admission. M.S. only.
Curriculum and Instruction.
Education. GRE for admission. Ph.D. only.
Educational Psychology. GRE for admission.
Educational Psychology and Guidance. GRE for admission. Ed.S. only.
Guidance. GRE for admission; M.S. only.
Human Performance and Sport Studies. GRE for admission.
Leadership in Education. GRE for admission.
Rehabilitation Counseling. M.S. only.
Special Education. GRE for admission. M.S. only.

COLLEGE OF ENGINEERING:
Aerospace Engineering. GRE for international applicants.
Chemical Engineering. GRE for international applicants.
Civil Engineering. GRE for international applicants.
Electrical Engineering. GRE for admission.
Engineering Science.
Environmental Engineering. GRE for international applicants. M.S. only.
Industrial Engineering. M.S. only.
Mechanical Engineering. GRE for international applicants.
Metallurgical Engineering. GRE for international applicants.
Nuclear Engineering. GRE for admission.
Polymer Engineering. GRE for international applicants.

COLLEGE OF NURSING:
Nursing. GRE for admission.

SCHOOL OF BIOMEDICAL SCIENCES:
Biomedical Science. GRE for admission.

COLLEGE OF ARCHITECTURE AND PLANNING:
Architecture. M.Arch. only.
Planning. M.S.P. only.

COLLEGE OF SOCIAL WORK:
Social Work. GRE for Ph.D.

COLLEGE OF HUMAN ECOLOGY:
Child and Family Studies. GRE for admission; M.S. only.
Food Service and Lodging Administration. GRE for admission. M.S. only.
Health Education. GRE for admission. Ed.D. only.
Health Promotion and Health Education. M.S. only.
Human Ecology. GRE for admission; Ph.D. only.
Human Resources and Development. GRE for admission.
Interior Design. GRE for admission; M.S. only.
Nutrition. GRE for admission. M.S. only.
Public Health. M.P.H. only.
Recreation and Leisure Studies. M.S. only.
Safety Education and Service. M.S., Ed.S. only.
Textiles, Retailing and Consumer Sciences. GRE for admission. M.S. only.
Vocational-Technical Education. Ed.S. only.

COLLEGE OF ARTS AND SCIENCES:
Anthropology. GRE for admission.
Art. M.F.A. only.
Audiology. GRE for admission; M.A. only.
Biochemistry. GRE for admission.
Botany. GRE for admission.
Chemistry. GRE for admission.
Computer Science. GRE for admission.
Ecology. GRE for admission.
English. GRE Subject for admission.
French. M.A. only.

Geography. GRE for admission.
Geology. GRE Subject for admission.
German. M.A. only.
History. GRE Subject for admission.
Life Sciences. GRE for admission. Includes ethology.
Mathematics. M.Math.
Microbiology. GRE for admission.
Modern Foreign Languages. Ph.D. only.
Music. Audition required for admission. M.M. only.
Philosophy. GRE for admission.
Physics.
Political Science. GRE for admission.
Psychology. GRE Subject for admission.
Public Administration. GRE for admission. M.P.A. only.
Sociology. GRE for admission.
Spanish. M.A. only.
Speech and Hearing Science. GRE for admission. Ph.D. only.
Speech Pathology. GRE for admission. M.A. only.
Theater. M.F.A. only. GRE for admission.
Zoology. GRE Subject for admission.

SCHOOL OF INFORMATION SCIENCES:
Information Sciences. GRE for admission; M.S. only.

College of Nursing

Founded in 1971. Graduate study since 1977. NLN accredited.
  Tuition: per credit, resident $151, nonresident $387. Enrollment: full-time 82, part-time 62. Faculty: full-time 4, part-time 16. Degrees conferred: M.S.N., Ph.D.

ADMISSION REQUIREMENTS. Transcripts, GRE, bachelor's degree, Graduate Program Data Form, three Graduate Rating Forms required in support of College's applications. TOEFL and TSE required for international applicants. Graduates of unaccredited institution not considered. Preference given to Tennessee residents. Apply by February 1 (Fall), October 15 (Spring). Application fee $15. Phone: (423)974-4151.

ADMISSION STANDARDS. Selective. Usual minimum average: 3.0 (A = 4). GRE scores 1000 minimum.

FINANCIAL AID. Limited to Federal W/S, loans. Approved for VA benefits. Apply to Financial Aid Office by May 1. Use FAFSA and institutional FAF. Phone: (423)974-3131; fax: (423)974-2175.

DEGREE REQUIREMENTS. For M.S.: 36 semester hours; thesis; comprehensive exam. For Ph.D.: 42 semester hours beyond master's; qualifying exam; dissertation; final oral exam.

FIELDS OF STUDY.
Adult Health Nursing.
Mental Health Nursing.
Nurse Practitioner.
Nursing Administration.
Nursing of Women and Children.

College of Architecture and Planning
http://funne/web.utc.edu/"arch/arch/lectures.html

  First students enrolled 1965. Annual tuition full-time resident, $2744, nonresident $7080, per credit resident $151, nonresident $360. Enrollment: Architecture—full-time 27, part-time 3; Planning—full-time 28, part-time 7. School faculty: full-time 24, part-time 6. Degree conferred: M.Arch., M.S.P.

ADMISSION REQUIREMENTS. Transcripts, GRE, three letters of recommendation, statement of career goals, portfolio (Architecture) required in support of College's application. Interview not required. Accepts transfer applicants. Graduates of unaccredited institutions not considered. Apply to Director of Admissions by February 1. Application fee $15. Phone: (423)974-5265; fax: (423)974-0565.

ADMISSION STANDARDS. Selective. Usual minimum average: 3.0 (A = 4).

FINANCIAL AID. Annual awards from institutional funds: eight assistantships, three research assistantships, two internships, loans. Approved for VA benefits. Apply by March 1 to appropriate program head for assistantships; to Financial Aid Office for all other programs. Use FAFSA. Phone: (423)974-3131; fax: (423)974-5341. About 50% of students receive aid other than loans from University and outside sources. Aid sometimes available to part-time students.

DEGREE REQUIREMENTS. For M.Arch.: 102 credit hours for students with non-architectural degree, 60 credit hours for those from accredited degree programs; 6 credits for thesis. For M.S.P.: 72 credit hours minimum; thesis for 9 credits; Summer work internship usually required, except for candidates with previous planning experience; thesis; comprehensive written exam; oral exam.

FIELDS OF STUDY.
Building Technology. M.Arch.
Design. M.Arch.
Economic Development Planning. M.S.P.
History/Theory. M.Arch.
Land-Use Planning. M.S.P.
Real Estate Development Planning. M.S.P.

College of Social Work
http://www.csw.uik.edu

Founded 1942. Centers in Knoxville, Nashville (37203), and Memphis (38103). Dean's Offices in Knoxville. On-campus housing at Knoxville only. Enrollment: full-time 250, part-time 140. Faculty: full-time 35, part-time 11. Degrees conferred: M.S.S.W., Ph.D.

ADMISSION REQUIREMENTS. Transcripts required in support of application. GRE required for Ph.D. applicants. TOEFL required for international applicants. Accepts transfer applicants. Graduates of unaccredited colleges not considered. Apply to Office of Admissions of College by March 1. Fall admission only. Seating fee $30. Phone: (423)974-6697; fax: (423)974-4803.

ADMISSION STANDARDS. Competitive. Usual minimum average: 3.0 (A = 4).

FINANCIAL AID. Limited to seven M.S.S.W. assistantships, eight Ph.D. assistantships, agency internships, Federal W/S, loans. Approved for VA benefits. Apply to Director of Admissions by March 1. Use FAFSA. Phone: (423)974-3131, (423)974-2175.

DEGREE REQUIREMENTS. For M.S.S.W.: 60 semester hours minimum; thesis or elective courses and comprehensive exam. For Ph.D.: 60 semester hours beyond master's degree, including 24 hours of dissertation research; final oral exam.

College of Law

Established 1890. Semester system. Located in Knoxville (37996-1800). Library: 365,000 volumes. Library has LEXIS, WESTLAW, INFOTRAC. Special facilities: Center for Entrepreneurial Law, Center for Advocacy and Dispute Resolution.
Annual tuition: resident $3794, nonresident $9620.
Enrollment: first-year class 158; total full-time 478 (men 57%, women 43%). Faculty: full-time 35, part-time 34. Degrees conferred: J.D., J.D.-M.B.A., J.D.-M.P.A.

ADMISSION REQUIREMENTS. LSDAS Law School report, bachelor's degree, transcripts, LSAT (not later than December), two letters of recommendation, personal statement required in support of application. Interview not required. Preference given to state residents. Accepts transfer applicants. Graduates of unaccredited colleges not considered. Apply to Admissions Office after October 1, before February 1. Application fee $15. Phone: (615)974-4131; fax: (615)974-0681.

ADMISSION STANDARDS. Selective. Accepts about 25–30% of total annual applicants.

FINANCIAL AID. Scholarships, fellowships, Federal W/S, loans. Apply to Financial Aid Office by February 1. Use FAFSA. About 5% of students receive aid other than loans from College.

DEGREE REQUIREMENTS. For J.D.: satisfactory completion of three-year program; 89 credit hour program.

College of Veterinary Medicine (37901-1071)

Annual tuition: resident $4702, nonresident $11,298. Total average cost for all other expenses: $6000–$8000.
Enrollment: first-year class 60, total full-time 235 (men 45%, women 65%); postgraduates 40. Faculty: full-time 83. Degree conferred: D.V.M.

ADMISSION REQUIREMENTS. VMCAS report, transcripts, VCAT, recommendations/evaluations, personal essay, animal/veterinary experience required in support of application. Interview by invitation only. Preference given to state residents. Graduates of unaccredited colleges not considered. Apply to the College after July 1, before November 1. Application packets distributed in October must be completed and returned by January 15. Application fee $15. Phone: (615)974-7263.

ADMISSION STANDARDS. Selective. Accepts 33–50% of qualified state applicants. Accepts 15–20% "at large" nonresident applicants.

FINANCIAL AID. Scholarships, assistantships, loans available. Apply after acceptance to Office of Financial Aid. Use FAFSA.

DEGREE REQUIREMENTS. For D.V.M.: satisfactory completion of four-year program.

UNIVERSITY OF TENNESSEE AT MARTIN
Martin, Tennessee, 38238-1000
http://www.utm.edu

Traces its origin to Hall-Moody Institute founded in 1900. State controlled since 1927. Located 125 miles NE of Memphis. Semester system. Special facilities: Reelfoot Lake Research and Teaching Center, Center for Excellence in Science and Mathematics Education, Center for Environmental and Conservation Education. Library: 309,000 volumes, 504,000 microforms, 1500 current periodicals, 11 PCs. Selected by the Humanities Research Corporation as one of the exemplary institutions of higher education with regard to the use of the computer for learning and teaching.
Annual tuition: full-time, resident $2572, nonresident $6948; per credit resident $139, nonresident $385. On-campus housing for 226 married students, 1155 men, 1427 women. Average annual housing cost: $2800–$3500 for married students, $3250 (including board) for single students. Contact Director of Housing for both on- and off-campus housing information. Phone: (901)587-7730. Day care facilities available.

Graduate School

Enrollment: full-time 60, part-time 254 (men 25%, women 75%). Graduate faculty: full-time 128, part-time 18. Degrees conferred: M.S., M.Acc., M.B.A.

ADMISSION REQUIREMENTS. Two official transcripts, GMAT(business) required in support of School's application. GRE/MAT/NTE required before the completion of 6 semester hours. TOEFL required for international applicants. Interview not required. Accepts transfer applicants. Apply to Graduate Studies Office at ten working days prior to registration. Application fee $25, $50 for international applicants. Phone: (901)587-7012; fax: (901)587-7019.

ADMISSION STANDARDS. Relatively open. Usual minimum average: 2.5 cumulative, or 3.0 in upper divisional work (A = 4).

FINANCIAL AID. Annual awards from institutional funds: fifty-two assistantships, twelve residence hall assistantships, loans. Approved for VA benefits. Apply to Dean of the School for assistantships; to Financial Aid Director for all other programs. No specified closing date. Use FAFSA. Phone: (901)587-7040. About 30% of students receive aid other than loans from University and outside sources. Aid available for part-time students.

DEGREE REQUIREMENTS. For master's: 30–48 semester hours minimum, the equivalent of two semesters in residence unless transferring within the University of Tennessee system; thesis optional in Human Environmental Science, education; final written/oral exam.

FIELDS OF STUDY.
Accountancy.
Business Administration.
Child Development and Family Relations.
Curriculum and Instruction.
Educational Psychology.
Food Science and Nutrition.
Home Management and Family Economics.
Human Environmental Science.
Occupational Home Economics.
Teaching. Includes elementary, secondary.

UNIVERSITY OF TENNESSEE, MEMPHIS
Memphis, Tennessee 38163-0002

Founded 1911. Coed. State control. Semester system. Special facilities: DEC PDP-11/70, 11/34, IBM 370/3031; Stout Neuroscience Mass Spectrometry Laboratory, Memorial Research Center, Clinical Research Center, Molecular Resource Center, Center for Neurosciences, Materials Science Toxicology Laboratory. Library: 263,000 volumes, 300,000 microforms, 23 PCs.

On-campus housing available for 147 single men, 205 single women. Average academic year housing costs: $6500. Contact the Director of Housing for both on- and off-campus housing information. Phone: (901)448-5609.

College of Graduate Health Sciences

Annual tuition: full-time resident $3424, nonresident $9210. per credit, resident $181, nonresident $487. Enrollment: full-time 171, part-time 0. Faculty: full-time 262, part-time 22. Degrees conferred: M.S., Ph.D.

ADMISSION REQUIREMENTS. Official transcripts, three recommendations, GRE Test required in support of College's applications. Interview encouraged. Four-year bachelor's degree or equivalent required. TOEFL required for international applicants. Graduates of unaccredited colleges not considered. Apply to University Director of Admissions, before February 15. Application fee: $25. Phone: (901)448-5560; fax: (901)448-7772.

ADMISSION STANDARDS. Selective. Usual minimum average: 3.0 (A = 4).

FINANCIAL AID. Ten scholarships, thirty-eight teaching assistantships, seventy-eight research assistantships, two fellowships, tuition waiver, loans. Apply to the Financial Aid Office; no specified closing date. Use FAFSA. Most full-time students receive aid from School.

DEGREE REQUIREMENTS. For M.S.: 30 semester hours minimum, at least 18 in residence; thesis; comprehensive oral/written exam for some departments. For Ph.D.: at least one year in residence; oral/written candidacy exam; dissertation; final oral exam.

FIELDS OF STUDY.
Anatomy and Neurobiology.
Biochemistry.
Biomedical Engineering.
Health Sciences Administration.
Immunology.
Medical Microbiology.
Medicinal Chemistry.
Microbiology.
Molecular and Cell Biology.
Pathology.
Pharmaceutics.
Pharmacology.
Physiology and Biophysics.
Virology.

College of Medicine

Founded in 1851, moved to Memphis (38163-2166) in 1911. Annual tuition: resident $8684, nonresident $16,585; student fees $472. Total average figure for all other expenses: $7000.

Enrollment: first-year class 165, total full-time 601 (men 60%, women 40%). College faculty: full-time 693, part-time 97. Degrees conferred: M.D., M.D.-Ph.D.

ADMISSION REQUIREMENTS. AMCAS report, transcripts, letters of recommendation, MCAT, interview required in support of application. Preference given to Tennessee and the eight contiguous state's residents. Does not have EDP. Apply to Director of Admissions after June 15, before November 15. Application fee $25. Phone: (901)448-5559.

ADMISSION STANDARDS. Selective. Accepts about 12–15% of total annual applicants. Approximately 90% are state residents.

FINANCIAL AID. Scholarships, loans. Apply to Director of Admissions after acceptance. Use FAFSA.

DEGREE REQUIREMENTS. For M.D.: satisfactory completion of four-year program; pass step 1 and step 2 of USMLE.

FIELDS OF GRADUATE STUDY.
Anatomy.
Biochemistry.
Cell Biology.
Immunology.
Microbiology.
Molecular Biology.
Neurosciences.
Pathology.

Pharmacology.
Physiology.

College of Dentistry

Founded 1878. Annual tuition: resident $5950, nonresident $14,492. On-campus housing available. Average academic year housing costs: $7574. Contact the Housing Office. Phone: (901)448-5609. Total average for all other first-year expenses: $7250.

Enrollment: first-year class 80; 360 total (men 75%, women 25%); graduate study 22. College faculty: full-time 63, part-time 69. Degree conferred: D.D.S.

ADMISSION REQUIREMENTS. For D.D.S. program: official transcripts, DAT, three letters of recommendation required in support of College's application. Interview by invitation only. Applicants must have completed at least three years of college study, four years of study preferred. Preference given to Tennessee and Arkansas residents. Apply to Assistant Dean after July 1, before December 31. Application fee $25. Phone: (901)448-6201; (800)788-0040. For graduate program: official transcripts, D.D.S. or equivalent degree. Interview by invitation. Transfer applicants, graduates of unaccredited institutions not considered. Apply to College by December 1.

ADMISSION STANDARDS. For D.D.S. program: Selective. Usual minimum average: 2.5 (A = 4); DAT score 16 or better. Accepts 50% of total annual applicants. Approximately 758 are residents of Arkansas and Tennessee. For graduate programs: competitive for most programs.

FINANCIAL AID. Scholarships, grants, loans, Federal W/S; fellowships for periodontics program only. Apply to Financial Aid Office within thirty days of acceptance. Use FAFSA. Phone: (901)488-5609. About 15% of students receive aid from College and outside sources.

DEGREE REQUIREMENTS. For D.D.S.: satisfactory completion of forty-five-month program.

FIELDS OF GRADUATE STUDY.
General Dentistry. Two-year advanced program; no degree conferred.
Oral Surgery. Three-year advanced program; no degree conferred.
Orthodontics. Two-year advanced program; no degree conferred.
Pediatric Dentistry. Two-year advanced program; no degree conferred.
Periodontics. Two-year advanced program; no degree conferred.

College of Nursing
http://utmgopher.utmem.edu/nursing/nurse.html

Graduate study since 1976. Annual tuition: full-time, resident $3490, nonresident $9584; per credit, resident $194, nonresident $533.

Enrollment: full-time 96, part-time 32. Faculty: full-time 18, part-time 2. Degrees conferred: M.S.N., Ph.D.

ADMISSIONS REQUIREMENTS. Official transcripts, bachelor's degree, Graduate Program Data Form, three Graduate Rating Forms required in support of College's application. TOEFL, TSE required for international applicants. Accepts transfer applicants. Graduates of unaccredited colleges not considered. Preference given to Tennessee residents. Apply by January 15 (Fall). Application Fee $25. Phone: (901)448-6125; fax: (901)448-4121.

ADMISSIONS STANDARDS. Selective. Usual minimum average: 3.0 (A = 4).

FINANCIAL AID. Limited to Federal W/S, loans. Approved for VA benefits. Apply to Financial Aid Office by May 1. Use FAFSA and institutional FAF. Phone: (901)448-5568.

DEGREE REQUIREMENTS. For M.S.: 36 semester hours; thesis. For Ph.D.: 42 semester hours beyond master's; qualifying exam; dissertation; final oral exam.

FIELDS OF STUDY.
Adult Critical Care Nursing.
Family Nurse Practitioner.
Neonatal Nurse Practitioner.
Nurse Administration.
Nurse Anesthesia.
Psychiatric Family Nurse Practitioner.
Public/Community Health Nursing.

College of Pharmacy—Graduate Programs in Pharmaceutical Sciences

Established 1928. Located in Memphis (38163).

Annual tuition: resident $3522, nonresident $8500, hour, resident $196, nonresident $481. On-campus housing at Medical Units campus in Memphis for 195 men, 233 women; none for married students. (Note: There is no separation of graduate from undergraduate students.) Apply to Office of Student Housing for both on- and off-campus housing. Phone: (901)448-5609.

Enrollment: full-time 14 (men 12, women 2). College faculty teaching graduate students, full-time 13, part-time 21. Degrees conferred: M.S., Ph.D., Pharm.D.-Ph.D.

ADMISSION REQUIREMENTS. Transcripts, GRE required in support of application. TOEFL required, TSE recommended for international applicants. Accepts transfer applicants. Apply to Office of Dean at least three months in advance of registration. Application fee $25. Phone: (901)448-6026; fax: (901)448-6940.

ADMISSION STANDARDS. Very selective for most departments. Usual minimum average: 3.0 (A = 4), GRE combined score 1500.

FINANCIAL AID. Annual awards from institutional funds: nine teaching assistantships, five research assistantships, tuition waivers, Federal W/S, loans. Approved for VA benefits. Apply to Office of Dean for assistantship, to Financial Aid Office for all other programs. Phone: (901)448-5568. All full-time students receive aid other than loans from College and outside sources.

DEGREE REQUIREMENTS. For M.S.: 30 semester hours minimum; thesis/research project; final written/oral exam. For Ph.D.: minimum of six semesters beyond the B.S.; at least one year in full-time residence; proficiency in designated research tools; dissertation; final written/oral exam.

FIELDS OF STUDY.
Medicinal Chemistry.
Pharmaceutics.

UNIVERSITY OF TENNESSEE AT OAK RIDGE
Oak Ridge, Tennessee 37831-8077

Coed. State control. Graduate only. Semester system. Special facilities: DEC PDP-10, IBM 3031. Associated with Oak Ridge National Laboratory.

Annual tuition: full-time, residents $3939, nonresidents $10,134. No on-campus housing available.

Graduate School of Biomedical Sciences

Enrollment: full-time 22 (men 65%, women 35%) ; part-time 0. School faculty: full-time 4, part-time 24. Degrees conferred: M.S., Ph.D.

ADMISSION REQUIREMENTS. Official transcripts, GRE Subject Tests, three references required in support of School's application. TOEFL required for foreign applicants. Accepts transfer applicants. Apply by April 30 (Fall), November 1 (Spring) to Director of School. Application fee $15. Phone: (615)574-1227; fax: (615)576-4149.

ADMISSION STANDARDS. Very selective. Usual minimum average: 3.0 (A = 4).

FINANCIAL AID. Annual awards from institutional funds: 19 fellowships, research assistantships, loans. Apply to Director of School. About 95% of students receive aid other than loans from University and outside sources.

DEGREE REQUIREMENTS. For M.S.: one year minimum; thesis. For Ph.D.: four years minimum; residence requirements may be reduced by previous graduate study; preliminary exam; reading knowledge of one foreign language; dissertation; final oral exam and public presentation of dissertation.

FIELDS OF STUDY.
Biological Sciences. Includes microbiology, cell physiology, biochemistry, biophysics, cytology, genetics, developmental biology, molecular and cellular biology.
Health Sciences. Includes immunology, radiation biology, virology, carcinogenesis, experimental pathology, mammalian genetics, gerontology.

UNIVERSITY OF TENNESSEE SPACE INSTITUTE

Tullahoma, Tennessee 37388-8897

Located 100 miles SE of Nashville. Coed. State control. Graduate study only. Semester system. Special facilities: Flight Test and Performance Center, Gas Dynamic facilities, Center for Laser Application, Magnetohydrodynamic Coal Field Flow facilities. Library: 19,000 volumes, 189,000 microforms, 175 current periodicals, 2 PCs.

Annual tuition: full-time, resident $2614, nonresident $6950; per credit resident $142, nonresident $378. On-campus housing for single students only. Average academic year on-campus housing costs: $1440; off-campus housing costs: $375 per month. Contact Director of Housing for both on- and off-campus housing information. Phone: (615)393-7218.

Graduate Programs

Enrollment: full-time 99, part-time 163 (men 85%, women 15%). Graduate faculty: full-time 41, part-time 7. Degrees conferred: M.S., Ph.D.

ADMISSION REQUIREMENTS. Two official transcripts, GRE required in support of application. TOEFL required for international applicants. Interview not required. Accepts transfer applicants. Apply to Assistant Dean for Admissions and Student Affairs at least 2 months prior to registration. Rolling admissions process. Application fee $15, $40 for international applicants. Phone: (615)393-7432; fax: (615)393-7346.

ADMISSION STANDARDS. Very selective. Usual minimum average: 3.0 (A = 4).

FINANCIAL AID. Annual awards from institutional funds: ten fellowships, seventy-three research assistantships, full and partial tuition waivers, Federal W/S, loans. Approved for VA benefits. Apply to appropriate department for fellowships, assistantships; to Assistant Dean for Admissions and Student Affairs for all other programs. No specified closing date. Use FAFSA. Aid available for part-time students.

DEGREE REQUIREMENTS. For master's: 30–36 semester hours minimum, the equivalent of two semesters in residence unless transferring within the University of Tennessee system; thesis/nonthesis option; written/oral exam. For Ph.D.: 24 credit hours minimum beyond the master's, at one year in full-time residence; comprehensive written exam; reading knowledge of one foreign language or proficiency in research technique; dissertation; final oral exam.

FIELDS OF STUDY.
Aerospace Engineering.
Applied Mathematics. M.S. only.
Aviation Systems. M.S. only.
Chemical Engineering. M.S. only.
Computer Science. M.S. only.
Electrical Engineering.
Engineering Management. M.S. only.
Engineering Sciences.
Mechanical Engineering.
Mechanics.
Physics.

TEXAS A & M UNIVERSITY

College Station, Texas 77843-1244

Founded 1876. Located 100 miles N of Houston. Coed. Semester system. State control. Special facilities: Institute for Biosciences and Technology, Center for Biotechnology, Policy and Ethnics, Center for International Business Studies, Institute for Scientific Computation, Institute for Nautical Archaeology, Nuclear Science Center, Presidential Studies Center, Public Policy Research Institute, Race and Ethnic Studies Center, Texas Agricultural Experiment Station, Texas Engineering Station, Texas Transportation Institute, oceanographic vessel, Runyon Art Collection, Space Research Center, Cyclotron Institute. Library: 2,068,000, 4,300,000 microforms, 17,300 current periodicals, 400 PCs in all libraries.

Annual tuition and fees (9 hours per semester): resident $2447, nonresident $6299. Limited on-campus housing available. Average academic year housing costs: $184–$290 per month. Contact Director of Campus Housing for both on- and off-campus housing information. Phone: (409)845-1741.

Office of Graduate Studies

Graduate study since 1923. Enrollment: full-time 7500, part-time 300. Graduate faculty: full-time 2000, part-time 500. Degrees conferred: M.A., M.S., M.Agr., M.Arch., M.B.A., M.C.S., M.Ed., M.Eng., M.L.A., M.P.A., M.U.P., D.E.D., Ph.D., Ed.D., D.Eng.

ADMISSION REQUIREMENTS. Official transcripts, GRE/GMAT required in support of application. TOEFL required nonnative English speakers. Interview not required. Accepts transfer applicants. Graduates of unaccredited colleges not considered. Apply to Dean of Admissions and Records at least six weeks prior to registration; international applicants at least six months prior to registration. Application fee $25. Phone: (409)854-1044; fax: (409)845-0727.

ADMISSION STANDARDS. Competitive for some departments, very competitive for the others. Usual minimum average: 3.0 (A = 4).

FINANCIAL AID. Annual awards from institutional funds: scholarships, teaching assistantships, nonteaching assistantships, research assistantships, Federal W/S, loans. Approved for VA benefits. Apply to appropriate department for assistantships; to Financial Aid Office for all other programs. No specified closing date. Use FAFSA. Phone: (409)862-3319; fax: (409)847-9061. About 65% of students receive aid other than loans from College and outside sources. Aid sometimes available to part-time students.

DEGREE REQUIREMENTS. For M.A.: 30 semester hours minimum, 9 credit hours during one semester or two consecutive six-week summer terms in residents; knowledge of one foreign language; thesis; final oral/written exam. For M.S.: 32 semester hours minimum, 9 credit hours during one semester or two consecutive six-week summer terms in residence; thesis; final oral/written exam. For M.Agr.: 36 semester hours minimum, at least 12 hours on Main Campus; balance on-campus to satisfy residence; final project; final oral/written exam. For M.Arch.: 52 hours for nonthesis program, 12 hours on Main Campus; balance on-campus to satisfy residence. For M.B.A.: 36 hours minimum, at least 12 hours on Main Campus; balance on-campus to satisfy residence; final oral/written exam. For M.C.S.: 36 hours minimum, at least 12 hours on Main Campus; balance on-campus to satisfy residence; final comprehensive exam. For M.Ed.: 36 hours minimum, at least 12 hours on Main Campus; balance on-campus to satisfy residence; final oral/written exam. For M.Eng.: 36 hours minimum, at least 16 in residence; written reports; final oral/written exam. For M.L.A.: 40 hours minimum, 12 hours on Main Campus to satisfy residence. For M.P.A.: 36 hours minimum; 12 hours on Main Campus to satisfy residence. For M.U.P.: 48 hours minimum, at least 12 hours on Main Campus; balance on-campus to satisfy residence; comprehensive oral exam. For doctorate (D.ED., Ed.D., D.Eng.): 6 semesters full-time study or its equivalent, at least 9 credit hours during two consecutive semesters or during one semester and one adjacent twelve-week summer session to satisfy residence; reading knowledge of one or two foreign languages depending on department and degree; qualifying exam; dissertation; final oral exam.

FIELDS OF STUDY.
Accounting.
Adult and Extension Education.
Aerospace Engineering.
Agricultural Chemistry.
Agricultural Development.
Agricultural Economics.
Agricultural Education.
Agricultural Engineering.
Agronomy.
Animal Breeding.
Animal Science.
Anthropology.
Architecture.
Biochemistry.
Bioengineering.
Biology.
Biophysics.
Botany.
Business Administration.
Business Analysis.
Business Computing Science.
Chemical Engineering.
Chemistry.
Civil Engineering.
Computing Science.

Construction Management.
Construction Science.
Counseling Psychology.
Crops.
Curriculum and Instruction.
Dairy Science.
Economic Entomology.
Economics.
Educational Administration.
Educational Psychology.
Educational Technology.
Electrical Engineering.
Engineering.
Engineering (Interdisciplinary).
English.
Entomology.
Epidemiology.
Finance.
Fisheries Science.
Floriculture.
Food Science and Technology.
Forestry.
Genetics.
Geography.
Geology.
Geophysics.
Health and Physical Education.
History.
History (American).
Horticulture.
Industrial Education.
Industrial Engineering.
Industrial Hygiene.
Industrial Psychology.
Laboratory Animal Medicine.
Land Development.
Land Economics and Real Estate.
Landscape Architecture.
Management
Marketing.
Mathematics.
Mechanical Engineering.
Mechanized Agriculture.
Meteorology.
Microbiology.
Modern Languages.
Natural Resources Development.
Nuclear Engineering.
Nutrition.
Ocean Engineering.
Oceanography.
Petroleum Engineering.
Physical Education.
Physics.
Physiology of Reproduction.
Plant Breeding.
Plant Pathology.
Plant Physiology.
Plant Protection.
Plant Sciences.
Political Science.
Poultry Science.
Psychology.
Public Administration.
Range Science.
Recreation and Resources Development.
Rural Sociology.
Safety Engineering.
School Psychology.
Sociology.
Soil Science.

Soils.
Statistics.
Urban and Regional Planning.
Urban and Regional Science.
Veterinary Anatomy.
Veterinary Medical Science.
Veterinary Medicine and Surgery.
Veterinary Microbiology.
Veterinary Parasitology.
Veterinary Pathology.
Veterinary Physiology.
Veterinary Public Health.
Veterinary Toxicology.
Vocational Education.
Wildlife and Fisheries Science.
Wildlife Science.
Zoology.

School of Medicine (77843-1114)

Established 1971. Library 75,000 volumes. Annual tuition: resident $6550, nonresident $19,650; student fees $1100. Enrollment: first-year class 48; total 187 (men 60%, women 40%). Faculty: full- and part-time 674. Degrees conferred: M.D., M.D.-Ph.D.

ADMISSION REQUIREMENTS. AMCAS report, transcripts, MCAT, three letters of recommendation required in support of application. Interview by invitation. Preference given to state residents. Does not have EDP. Apply to Office of Student Affairs after May 1, before November 1. Application fee $45. Phone: (409)845-7744; fax: (409)847-8663.

ADMISSION STANDARDS. Competitive. Admits about 8–10% of total annual applicants. Approximately 100% are state residents.

FINANCIAL AID. Scholarships, loans. Apply after acceptance to Student Affairs Office. Use FAFSA. About 90% of students receive some aid from School.

DEGREE REQUIREMENTS. For M.D.: satisfactory completion of four-year program. For Ph.D.: see Graduate College listing above.

FIELDS OF GRADUATE STUDY.
Anatomy.
Biochemistry.
Genetics.
Microbiology.
Neurosciences.
Pathology.
Pharmacology and Toxicology.
Physiology.

College of Veterinary Medicine

Annual tuition: resident $5400, nonresident $16,200. Total average cost for all other expenses: $8645.

Enrollment: first year 120; total 500 (men 50%, women 50%). Faculty: full-time 119, part-time 3. Degrees conferred: D.V.M., M.S., Ph.D.

ADMISSION REQUIREMENTS. VMCAS report, transcripts, MCAT or GRE, 64 undergraduate credits minimum, three evaluations/recommendations, animal/veterinary experience required in support of application. Accepts transfer applicants on a space-available basis only. Accepts state residents only. Apply after July 1, before October 1. Application fee $45. Phone: (409)845-5051.

ADMISSION STANDARDS. Selective. Admits 30% of total annual applicants. Accepts approximately seven nonresident applicants annually.

FINANCIAL AID. Fellowships, assistantships, partial tuition waivers, Federal W/S, loans available. Apply to Director of Student Financial Aid. Use FAFSA.

DEGREE REQUIREMENTS. For D.V.M. : satisfactory completion of three-year program. For M.S., Ph.D.: see Graduate College listings above.

FIELDS OF STUDY.
Epidemiology.
Pathology.
Physiology.
Public Health.
Toxicology.
Veterinary Anatomy.
Veterinary Large Animal Medicine and Surgery.
Veterinary Microbiology.
Veterinary Small Animal Medicine and Surgery.

TEXAS A & M UNIVERSITY— CORPUS CHRISTI
Corpus Christi, Texas 78412-5503

Coed. Semester system. State control. Special facilities: Center for Coastal Studies, Environmental Research Consortium, Wells Gallery. Library: 321,000, 505,000 microforms, 1500 current periodicals, 20 PCs.

Annual tuition and fees (9 hours per semester): resident $1734, nonresident $4362.50, per credit resident $60, nonresident $252. Limited on-campus housing available for single students, none for married students. Average academic year housing costs: $2280; off-campus housing costs: $450 per month. Contact Director of Housing for both on- and off-campus housing information. Phone: (512)994-2707.

Graduate Division

Enrollment: full-time 262, part-time 977. Graduate faculty: full-time 109, part-time 49. Degrees conferred: M.A., M.Acc., M.B.A., M.P.A., M.S., M.S.N., Ed.D.

ADMISSION REQUIREMENTS. Official transcripts, GRE/GMAT required in support of application. TOEFL required nonnative English speakers. Interview not required. Accepts transfer applicants. Graduates of unaccredited colleges not considered. Apply to Director of Admissions by July 15 (Fall), November 15 (Spring). Application fee $10, $30 for international applicants. Phone: (512)994-2624; fax: (512)944-5887.

ADMISSION STANDARDS. Selective. Usual minimum average: 2.75 (A = 4).

FINANCIAL AID. Annual awards from institutional funds: scholarships, assistantships, Federal W/S, loans. Approved for VA benefits. Apply by March 15 to Financial Aid Office. Use FAFSA. About 25% of students receive aid other than loans from College and outside sources. Aid available to part-time students.

DEGREE REQUIREMENTS. For M.A., M.S., M.S.N.: 30–36 semester hours minimum, thesis/nonthesis option; final oral/written exam. For M.B.A., M.Acc.: 36 hours minimum, final oral/written exam. For M.P.A.: 36 hours minimum; comprehensive oral exam. For Ed.D.: six semesters full-time study or its equivalent, at least 9 credit hours during two consecutive semesters or during one semester and one adjacent twelve-week summer session to satisfy residence; qualifying exam; dissertation; final oral exam.

FIELDS OF STUDY.
Accounting.
Biology.
Computer Science.
Consumer Education.
Counselor Education.
Curriculum and Instruction.
Economics.
Education.
Educational Administration.
Elementary Education.
English.
Environmental Sciences.
Interdisciplinary. Includes arts, humanities, social sciences.
Mathematics.
Nursing.
Nursing Administration.
Psychology.
Public Policy and Administration.
Secondary Education.
Vocational and Technical Education.

TEXAS A & M UNIVERSITY
Kingsville, Texas 78363

Founded 1925. Located 40 miles SW of Corpus Christi. Coed. State control. Semester system. Library 460,000 volumes, 520,000 microforms, 38 PCs in all libraries.

Annual tuition: full-time, resident $768, nonresident $5904. On-campus housing for married students. Average academic year housing cost: $2392. Contact Campus Housing Office for both on- and off-campus housing information. Phone: (512)595-3419. Day care facilities available.

College of Graduate Studies

Enrollment: full-time 294, part-time 769. Faculty: full-time 190, part-time 15. Degrees conferred: M.A., M.S., M.M., M.P.A., M.B.A., M.Engineering, M.Ed., Ed.D. (BiLing.Ed., Ed. Admin.), Ph.D. (Wildlife Sciences).

ADMISSION REQUIREMENTS. Transcripts, GRE/GMAT required in support of College's application. TOEFL required for international applicants. Accepts transfer applicants. Apply to Director of Admissions at least two months prior to registration. Application fee of $25 for international applicants. Phone: (512)593-3907.

ADMISSION STANDARDS. Selective. Usual minimum average: 3.0 (A = 4).

FINANCIAL AID. Scholarships, Federal W/S, loans. Apply to Director of Financial Aid; no specified closing date. Use FAFSA. Phone: (512)545-3911.

DEGREE REQUIREMENTS. For master's: 30 semester hours minimum, thesis often required; final written/oral exam. For Ed.D.: 60 semester hours minimum beyond master's degree, at least 48 in residence; qualifying exam; candidacy; dissertation; final oral exam.

FIELDS OF STUDY.
Agriculture. Includes agribusiness, agricultural education, animal science, human sciences, plant and soil sciences, range and wildlife management, wildlife science.

Art.
Biology.
Business Administration.
Chemistry.
Communication Sciences and Disorders.
Education. Includes administration and supervision, counseling, early childhood, elementary, bilingual-bicultural, English as a second language, special education, adult education, reading, kinesiology.
Engineering. Includes chemical, civil, electrical, environmental, industrial, mechanical, natural gas, computer science.
English.
Geology.
History and Politics.
Mathematics.
Music.
Psychology and Sociology.
Spanish.

TEXAS CHRISTIAN UNIVERSITY
Fort Worth, Texas 76129-0002
http://www.tcu.edu

Founded 1873. Coed. Private control. Semester system. Special facilities: Center for Remote Sensing, Experimental Mesocosm Facility, Lake Worth Fish Hatchery, Institute of Behavioral Research, cooperative association with Oak Ridge Institute of Nuclear Studies. Library: 1,138,000 volumes, 425,000 microforms, 3700 current periodicals.

Tuition: per credit $314, M.B.A. $314. Campus housing for married students at Brite Divinity School campus housing; none for graduate single students. Contact the Housing Office for both on- and off-campus housing information. Phone: (817)921-7865.

Graduate School

Enrollment: full-time 535, part-time 629. Faculty: full-time 217. Degrees conferred: M.A., M.B.A., M.Ed., M.F.A., M.L.A., M.M., M.M.Ed., M.S., M.S.E., Certificate program, D.M., Ph.D.

ADMISSION REQUIREMENTS. Official transcripts, GRE/GMAT required in support of graduate application. TOEFL required for international applicants. Interview not required. Accepts transfer applicants. Graduates of unaccredited institutions not considered. Apply to Graduate Office at least six weeks prior to registration. No Application fee. Phone: (817)921-7515, (800)828-3764; fax: (817)921-7134. For M.B.A.: Phone: (817)921-7531; fax: (817)921-7227.

ADMISSION STANDARDS. Very selective for most departments. Usual minimum average: 3.0 (A = 4).

FINANCIAL AID. Annual awards from institutional funds: teaching fellowships, research fellowships, teaching assistantships, research assistantships, internships (approximately 911), Federal W/S, loans. Approved for VA benefits. Apply by February 1 to Graduate School for fellowship, assistantships, internships; to Financial Aid Office for all other programs. Use FAFSA and institution FAF. Phone: (817)921-7858; fax: (817)921-7333. About 77% of students receive aid other than loans from School and outside sources. Limited aid for part-time students.

DEGREE REQUIREMENTS. For master's: 30 semester hours minimum, at least 24 in residence; thesis; final oral exam. For Administrator's Certificate: 60 semester hours beyond the bachelor's degree; special project. For D.M., Ph.D.: three years minimum beyond the bachelor's degree, the second year or its equivalent in full-time residence; reading knowledge of one or two foreign languages, depending upon department; qualifying exam; dissertation; final oral exam.

FIELDS OF STUDY.
Art. Comprehensive exam for candidacy. M.F.A. only.
Ballet–Modern Dance. Final artistic project for degree. M.F.A. only.
Biology.
Business. Includes management statistics; GMAT for admission. M.B.A. only.
Chemistry. German proficiency, cumulative exam required for Ph.D.
Communication in Human Relations. M.S.
Divinity. M.A. only.
Economics. M.A. only.
Education. Includes educational research, administration, general education, special education, physical education; 36 credits, nonthesis option for master's.
Elementary Education.
English. Candidacy exam for M.A.; one modern language, qualifying exam, diagnostic exam for Ph.D.
Environmental Sciences.
Geology. Preliminary exam for M.S.
History. One modern language, qualifying exam for Ph.D.
Liberal Arts. M.L.A. only.
Media Studies. Final written exam for M.S. M.S. only.
Ministry. D.M.
Music. Includes performance, musicology, theory. M.M., M.M.Ed. only.
Physics. One language, qualifying exam for Ph.D.
Psychology. One language, other exams for Ph.D.
Secondary Education.
Software Engineering.
Speech Communication. Final written exam for M.S. M.S. only.
Speech-Language Pathology. Comprehensive exam for M.S.
Theological Studies. M.A. only.
Theater. Final artistic project for M.A., M.F.A.

TEXAS SOUTHERN UNIVERSITY
Houston, Texas 77004-4584

Founded 1947. State control. Semester system. Special facilities: Cancer Prevention Awareness Center, Center for Excellence in Education, Mickey Leland Center on World Hunger and Peace, Research Center for Minority Institutions, Urban Resources Center. Library: 464,300 volumes, 391,800 microforms, 28 PCs.

Annual tuition: full-time, resident $1564, nonresident $4984; per credit resident $43, nonresident $133. On-campus housing for married and single students. Average academic year housing costs: $3800 for married students, $4511 (including board) for single students. Off-campus housing costs: $480 per month. Contact Director of Housing for both on- and off-campus housing information. Phone: (713)527-7205.

Graduate School

Enrollment: full- and part-time 1100. Faculty: full-time 125, part-time 25. Degrees conferred: M.A., M.S., M.Ed., M.B.A., M.Mus.Ed., M.C.R., M.P.A., Ed.D., Ph.D., D.Pharm.

ADMISSION REQUIREMENTS. Official transcripts, GRE/GMAT/MAT required in support of School's application. TOEFL required of international applicants. Accepts transfer applicants. Graduates of unaccredited institutions not considered. Apply to the School at least six weeks prior to registration. Application fee $35, $75 for international applicants. Phone: (713)313-7233.

ADMISSION STANDARDS. Selective. Usual minimum average: 2.5 (A = 4); for M.B.A., 2.75 minimum average (undergrad-

uate GPA plus 200) plus GMAT score = 950; for Ed.D., average GPA for the last 60 semester hours times 100 plus the verbal and quantitative must = at least 1000, minimum average must be at least 2.5.; for Ph.D., 2.75 GPA, GRE score at least 950.

FINANCIAL AID. Assistantships, Federal W/S, loans. Approved for VA benefits. Apply to Graduate School for assistantships; to Financial Aid Office for all other programs. No specified closing date. Use FAFSA and University's FAF. Phone: (713)313-7207. About 25% of students receive aid other than loans from University and outside sources.

DEGREE REQUIREMENTS. For master's: 36 semester hours minimum, at least 30 in residence; thesis/nonthesis option. For M.B.A.: 36 semester hours minimum; 27 in residence. For M.P.A.(Accounting): 36 semester hours minimum, 30 in residence. For M.C.P., M.P.A. (Public Administration), M.A. (Psychology): 48 semester hours minimum; 42 in residence; thesis/no thesis option. For Ed.D.: 72 semester hours minimum, 57 in residence; qualifying exam; dissertation; final oral exam. For Ph.D.: 75 semester hours minimum, at least 66 in residence; candidacy; reading knowledge of one or two foreign languages; dissertation; final oral exam.

FIELDS OF STUDY.
Accounting. M.P.A.
Administrative Management Systems.
Biology.
Business Administration.
Chemistry.
City Planning.
Counseling and Guidance.
Counselor Education.
Education. Includes elementary, secondary (usual subject areas), administration and supervision, higher, curriculum and instruction.
English.
Environmental Toxicology.
History.
Human Performance.
Human Services.
Industrial Technology.
Journalism.
Mathematics.
Music. Includes applied, education, composition, musicology.
Pharmacy.
Psychology.
Public Administration.
Sociology.
Speech Communication.
Telecommunications.
Transportation.

Thurgood Marshall School of Law

Established 1947. Semester system. Law library 300,000 volumes. Library has LEXIS, WESTLAW, DIALOG.

Annual tuition: full-time, resident $4270, nonresident $8620. Limited housing available. Total average annual additional expense: $7500.

Enrollment: first-year class 250, total 540 (men 54%, women 46%). Faculty: full-time 29, part-time 19. Degrees conferred: J.D., J.D.-M.B.A., J.D.-M.P.A., J.D.-M.A. (History).

ADMISSION REQUIREMENTS. LSDAS Law School report, bachelor's degree, two transcripts, LSAT, two letters of recommendation required in support of application. Accepts transfer applicants. Interview not required. Graduates of unaccredited colleges not considered. Preference given to state residents. Admits to Fall semester only. Apply to the Office of Admissions by April 1. Application fee $40. Phone: (713)527-7114.

ADMISSION STANDARDS. Selective. Accepts 30–35% of total annual applicants.

FINANCIAL AID. Scholarships, partial tuition waivers, fellowships, assistantships, Federal W/S, loans. Apply to Director of Financial Aid by May 1. Use FAFSA. About 90% of students receive some of aid.

DEGREE REQUIREMENTS. For J.D.: 90 semester hours minimum, at least 45 in residence. For master's degrees: see Graduate School listing above.

TEXAS TECH UNIVERSITY
Lubbock, Texas 79409
http://www.ttu.edu

Founded 1923. Coed. State control. Semester system. Special facilities: Center for Agricultural Technology, Center for Applied Research in Industrial/Automation and Robotics, Institute for Banking and Financial Studies, Institute for Communications Research, Community Design Center, Institute for Disaster Research, Institute for Ergonomics Research, Center for Feed and Industry Research and Education, Center for Forensic Studies, Center for Historic Preservation and Technology, International Textile Research Center, Plant Stress and Water Conservation Institute, Center of Public Service, Ranching Heritage Center, Center for the Study of the Vietnam Conflict, Texas Wine Marketing Research Center, Turkish Oral Archives, Wildlife and Fisheries Management Institute. Library: 2,750,000 volumes, 8,467,000 microforms, 16,000 current periodicals, 202 PCs in all libraries.

Annual tuition: full-time, resident $600; nonresident $2700; per credit resident $50–$62, nonresident $264. On-campus housing for single students, none for married students. Annual housing costs: $3984. Apply to Director of Housing Reservation: Phone: (806)742-2261; to Student Association off-campus housing information: Phone: (806)742-3631.

Graduate School

Graduate study since 1927. Enrollment: full-time 2720, part-time 1136 (men 2082, women 1774). Faculty: full-time 700, part-time 25. Degrees conferred: M.A., M.B.A., M.Ed., M.F.A., M.Eng., M.Ag., M.A.Ed., M.P.A., M.M.E., M.S.Ch.E., M.S.C.E., M.S.E.E., M.S.I.E., M.S.M.E., M.S.P.E., M.S.H.E., M.S., Ed.D., Ph.D.

ADMISSION REQUIREMENTS. Official transcripts, GRE/GMAT required in support of School's application. Letters of recommendation required for some departments. TOEFL required for international applicants. Interview not required. Accepts transfer applicants. Graduates of unaccredited institutions not considered. Apply to Office of the Dean of Graduate Admissions at least thirty days prior to date of registration. Application fee $25, $50 for international applicants. Phone: (806)742-2787; fax: (806)742-1746.

ADMISSION STANDARDS. Selective for most departments. Usual minimum average: 3.0 (A = 4) or 1000 GRE.

FINANCIAL AID. Annual awards from institutional funds: one hundred scholarships, four hundred teaching assistantships, four hundred research assistantships, out-of-state waivers, Federal W/S, loans. Approved for VA benefits. Apply to appropriate department chairman for assistantships; to Financial Aid Office for all other programs. No specified closing date. Use FAFSA and University's FAF. Phone: (806)742-3681; fax: (806)742-0880. About 20% of students receive aid other than loans from College and outside sources. No aid for part-time students.

DEGREE REQUIREMENTS. For master's: 30–36 semester hours minimum, at least 24 in residence; thesis/nonthesis option; final comprehensive exam; foreign language requirements vary by department. For doctorates: 72 semester hours minimum, at least two consecutive semesters in residence; oral/written preliminary exam; oral/written qualifying exam for candidacy; foreign language requirements vary by department and program; dissertation; final oral exam.

FIELDS OF STUDY.

GRADUATE SCHOOL:
Interdisciplinary Studies. Interdepartmental. Master's only.
Land Use Planning, Management and Design. Doctorate only.

SCHOOL OF AGRICULTURE:
Agricultural Economics.
Agricultural Education. Master's only.
Agriculture. Master's only.
Agronomy, Horticulture and Entomology. Master's only.
Animal Science.
Crop Science. Master's only.
Fisheries Science.
Food Technology. Master's only.
Park Administration and Landscape Architecture. M.L.A. only.
Range and Wildlife Management.
Soil Science. Master's only.

SCHOOL OF ARCHITECTURE:
Architecture. Master's only.

SCHOOL OF ARTS AND SCIENCES:
Anthropology. Master's only.
Art.
Atmospheric Science. Master's only.
Biology.
Chemistry.
Classical Humanities. Master's only.
Communication Studies. Master's only.
Comparative Literature. Interdepartmental.
Economics.
English.
Fine Arts. Interdisciplinary doctorate (art, music, drama).
French. Master's only.
Geosciences.
German. Master's only.
Health, Physical Education and Recreation. Master's only.
History.
Linguistics. Interdepartmental.
Mass Communication.
Mathematics.
Microbiology.
Museum Sciences. Master's only.
Music. Includes applied music.
Philosophy. Master's only.
Physics. Includes applied physics.
Political Science.
Psychology.
Public Administration.
Sociology. Master's only.
Spanish.
Speech Communication. Master's only.
Sports Health. Master's only.
Statistics. Master's only.
Technical Communications.
Theater Arts.
Zoology.

SCHOOL OF BUSINESS ADMINISTRATION:
Accounting.
Business Statistics.

Finance.
Health Organizational Management. Master's only.
Management.
Management Information Systems.
Marketing.
Operations Management.

SCHOOL OF EDUCATION:
Bilingual Education.
Counselor Education.
Curriculum and Instruction.
Educational Psychology and Leadership.
Elementary Education.
Higher Education.
Instructional Technology.
Reading.
Secondary Education.
Special Education.
Supervision. Master's only.

SCHOOL OF ENGINEERING:
Chemical Engineering.
Civil Engineering.
Computer Science.
Electrical Engineering.
Environmental Engineering. Master's only.
Environmental Technology Management. Master's only.
Industrial Engineering.
Mechanical Engineering.
Petroleum Engineering. Master's only.

SCHOOL OF HUMAN SCIENCES:
Clothing, Textiles and Merchandising.
Environmental Design and Consumer Economics.
Family Financial Planning. Master's only.
Food and Nutrition.
Home Economics Education.
Human Development and Family Studies.
Marriage and Family Therapy.
Restaurant, Hotel and Institutional Management. Master's only.

School of Law

Established 1967. Semester system. Library 250,000 volumes. Library has LEXIS, NEXIS, WESTLAW.

Annual tuition: resident $10,800, nonresident $13,501. On- and off-campus housing available. Apply to Housing Office. Total average annual additional expense: $8450.

Enrollment: first-year class 217; total 612 (men 65%, women 35%). Faculty: full-time 22, part-time 12. Degrees conferred: J.D., J.D.-M.B.A., J.D.-M.P.A., J.D.-M.S. (Agricultural Economics).

ADMISSION REQUIREMENTS. LSDAS Law School report, bachelor's degree, transcripts, LSAT, letters of recommendation required in support of application. Accepts transfer applicants. Graduates of unaccredited colleges not considered. Apply to Dean by February 1. Rolling admissions process. Admits Fall only. Application fee $40. Phone: (806)742-3791.

ADMISSION STANDARDS. Selective. Accepts about 30–35% of total annual applicants.

FINANCIAL AID. Scholarships, assistantships, Federal W/S, loans. Apply to Office of the Director of Financial Aid by February 1. Use FAFSA.

DEGREE REQUIREMENTS. For J.D.: satisfactory completion of 90 credit hour program. For master's degree: see Graduate School listing above.

School of Medicine

Established 1969 and is part of University Health Science Center, Lubbock (79430). Annual tuition: resident $6550, nonresident $19,650; student fees $864. Total average cost for all other expenses: $10,206.

Enrollment: first-year class 120 (EDP 3); total 391 (men 70%, women 30%). Faculty: full- and part-time 314. Degrees conferred: M.D., M.D.-Ph.D.

ADMISSION REQUIREMENTS. Transcripts, MCAT, recommendations required in support of application. Interviews by invitation only. Preference given to state residents. 98% of class must be state residents. Has EDP (for Texas, eastern New Mexico and southwestern Oklahoma residents only); apply between June 15 and August 1. Graduates of unaccredited colleges not considered. Apply to Associate Dean for Admissions after June 15, before November 1. Application fee $40. Phone: (806)743-2297; fax: (806)743-3021.

ADMISSION STANDARDS. Selective. Accepts about 15–20% of total annual applicants. Approximately 98% are state residents.

FINANCIAL AID. About 65% of students receive financial assistance. Apply to Office of Student Financial Aid after acceptance. use FAFSA.

DEGREE REQUIREMENTS. For M.D.: satisfactory completion of four-year program. For Ph.D.: see Graduate listings above.

FIELDS OF GRADUATE STUDY.
Anatomy.
Biochemistry.
Microbiology.
Pharmacology.
Physiology.

TEXAS WESLEYAN UNIVERSITY
Irving, Texas 75061

School of Law

Established 1989. Semester system. Library 133,200 volumes. Library has LEXIS, NEXIS, WESTLAW.

Tuition: per credit $370. No on-campus housing available. Total average annual additional expense: $11,500.

Enrollment: first-year class, full-time 87, part-time 100; total full-time 254, part-time 339 (men 50%, women 50%). Faculty: full-time 23, part-time 15. Degree conferred: J.D.

ADMISSION REQUIREMENTS. LSDAS Law School report, bachelor's degree, transcripts, LSAT required in support of application. Letters of recommendation and supplementary essay recommended. Accepts transfer applicants from ABA approved schools. Apply to Office of Admissions by June 30. Application fee $50. Phone: (214)579-5751.

ADMISSION STANDARDS. Selective. Accepts about 50% of total annual applicants.

FINANCIAL AID. Scholarships, Federal W/S, loans. Apply to Financial Aid Office by June 1. Phone: (214)579-5738. Use FAFSA. About 15–20% of students receive aid other than loans from School or outside sources.

DEGREE REQUIREMENTS. For J.D.: 88 semester credits in full- or part-time program.

THE UNIVERSITY OF TEXAS AT ARLINGTON

Arlington, Texas 76019

Founded 1895. Located in the Center of Dallas–Fort Worth. Coed. Public control. Semester system. Special facilities: Automation and Robotics Research Institute, Community Services Research Center, Center for Research in Contemporary Art, Energy Systems Research Center, Center for Rhetorical and Critical Theory, Center for Positron Studies, Center for Social Research, Center for Greater Southwestern Studies and History of Cartography. Library: 1,500,000 volumes, 1,250,000 microforms, 5800 current periodicals.

Annual tuition: full-time, resident $2626, nonresidents $7930. On-campus housing for 330 married students, 800 single students. Annual housing cost: $2800 single students; $4500 for married students. Contact Director of Housing for both on- and off-campus housing information. Phone: (817)272-2791.

Graduate School

Graduate study since 1952. Enrollment: full- and part-time 4200 (men 51%, women 49%). Faculty: full-time 470, part-time 10. Degrees conferred: M.A., M.Arch., M.B.A., M.Engr., M.C.R.P., M.S.N., M.C.S., M.E.T., M.P.A., M.S., M.S.S.W., D.Sc., Ph.D.

ADMISSION REQUIREMENTS. Official transcripts, GRE/GMAT (M.B.A., M.P.A.) required in support of School's application. Portfolio required for M.Arch. TOEFL required of international applicants. Accepts transfer applicants. Graduates of unaccredited colleges not considered. Apply to Director of Admissions 60 days prior to beginning of semester; international applicants should apply at least 120 days prior to beginning of semester. Application fee $25, $50 for international applicants. Phone: (817)272-2681.

ADMISSION STANDARDS. Very selective or selective. Usual minimum average: 3.0 (A = 4).

FINANCIAL AID. Annual awards from institutional funds: one hundred teaching assistantships, two hundred research assistantships (TSE required of those whose primary language is not English), Federal W/S, loans. Apply to Dean for scholarships, to appropriate departmental chair for fellowships/assistantships; to Financial Aid Office for all other programs. No specified closing date. Use FAFSA. Phone: (817)272-3561.

DEGREE REQUIREMENTS. For master's: Plan I—30 semester hours minimum; thesis; final oral exam. Plan II—33 semester hours minimum; internship/project; comprehensive exam. Plan III—36 semester hours minimum; comprehensive exam. For Ph.D., D.Sc.: four years beyond the bachelor's degree minimum, at least one year in residence; qualifying exam; dissertation; final oral exam.

FIELDS OF STUDY.
Accounting. M.P.A.
Applied Chemistry. D.Sc.
Applied Physics. D.Sc.
Architecture.
Archival Administration. Certificate.
Biology. Ph.D.
Biomedical Engineering. Ph.D.
Business Administration. Includes accounting, business administration and administrative science, economics; M.A., M.B.A., Ph.D.
Chemistry.
City and Regional Planning.
Computer Science.
Criminal Justice.

Economics.
Education.
Engineering. Includes aerospace, civil, computer science and engineering, electrical, industrial, materials science and engineering, mechanical, mechanics, software engineering. M.S., M.Eng., Ph.D.
Geology.
Humanities. Includes teaching. Ph.D. only.
Information Systems.
Interdisciplinary Studies.
Landscape Architecture.
Liberal Arts. Includes English, foreign languages, political science, history, linguistics, sociology.
Marketing Research. M.S.
Mathematical Sciences. Ph.D.
Mathematics.
Nursing.
Personnel and Human Resource Management. M.S.
Psychology.
Public Administration. M.P.A.
Public and Urban Administration. Ph.D.
Real Estate.
Science. Includes biology, chemistry, geology, mathematics, physics, radiological physics.
Social Work. Ph.D.
Sociology.
Taxation. M.S.
Urban Affairs.

THE UNIVERSITY OF TEXAS AT AUSTIN

Austin, Texas 78712-7666
http://www.utexas.edu
    //www.utexas.edu/student/giac

Founded 1883. Coed. State control. Semester system. Special facilities: Biochemical Institute, Computation Center, Drug Dynamics Institute, Bureau of Economic Geology, Bureau of Engineering Research, Harry Huntt Ransom Humanities Research Center, Lyndon B. Johnson Library and Museum, Bureau of Business Research, Institute of Latin American Studies, Institute of Marine Science, McDonald Observatory, Population Research Center, Texas Memorial Museum. Library: 6,680,000 volumes, 4,700,000 microforms, 75,000 current periodicals.

Annual tuition and fees: full-time, resident $1536, nonresident $6672. Average academic year housing costs: extremely wide range. Contact Housing and Food Service Division for both on- and off-campus housing information. Phone: (512)471-3136.

Graduate School

Graduate study since 1909. Enrollment: full-time 11,294 (men 55%, women 45%). Faculty: full-time 2398. Degrees conferred: M.A., M.B.A., M.Ed., M.F.A., M.L.I.S., M.M., M.P.A., M.Arch., M.S.Appl.Physics, M.S.Comp & Appl.Math., M.S.Econom., M.S.Sc. & Tech., M.Public Affairs, M.S.S.W., M.S.CRP., M.S.C.S., M.S.N., M.S.Eng., M.S.Pharm., M.S. in Arch. Studies, Pharm.D., Ed.D., D.M.A., Ph.D.

ADMISSION REQUIREMENTS. Official transcripts, GRE/GMAT required in support of School's application. Interview required by some departments. TOEFL required for international applicants. Graduates of unaccredited colleges not considered. Apply to Graduate and International Admission Center. Departmental deadlines vary, contact appropriate department for this information. Application fee $50; $75 for international applicants. Phone: (512)475-7438.

ADMISSION STANDARDS. Selective for most departments. Usual minimum average: 3.0 (A = 4).

FINANCIAL AID. Annual awards from institutional funds: scholarships, assistantships, Federal W/S, loans. Approved for VA benefits. Apply to appropriate Graduate Adviser for scholarships, assistantships; to Financial Services Office for all other aid. No specified closing date. Use FAFSA. Phone: (512)475-6282. "Substantial numbers" of students receive aid other than loans from School and outside sources. Aid available to part-time students.

DEGREE REQUIREMENTS. For most master's: 30 semester hours minimum, at least one year in residence; thesis; comprehensive oral/written exam for some departments. For M.B.A., M.P.A., M.Arch., M.L.I.S, M.S.S.W., M.S.Pharm., M.S.CRP., M.S.C.S.: 30–60 hours depending on previous background, at least 30 hours in residence; thesis/final report. For M.Ed.: 36 hours minimum, at least 30 in residence; final competency exam. For Ph.D.: at least one year in residence; foreign language requirement set by department; oral/written candidacy exam; dissertation; final oral exam. For Ed.D.: comprehensive oral/written exam; other requirements essentially the same as for Ph.D. For D.M.A.: requirements essentially the same as for Ph.D., except original composition/dissertation/performance.

FIELDS OF STUDY.
Aerospace Engineering.
American Civilization.
Anthropology.
Arabic Studies.
Architectural Engineering. M.S. only.
Architecture. M.Arch., M.S.Arch. Studies, Ph.D.
Art. Includes studio, art history, art education; M.A., M.F.A.; Ph.D. in art history.
Asian Cultures and Languages.
Asian Studies. M.A.
Astronomy.
Biochemistry.
Biological Sciences. Includes botany, microbiology, zoology.
Business Administration. Includes accounting, finance, management science and information systems, management, marketing.
Chemical Engineering.
Chemistry.
Civil Engineering.
Classics. Includes Greek, Latin.
Communication. Includes journalism, radio-television-film; speech, advertising.
Community and Regional Planning. M.S.CRP., Ph.D.
Comparative Literature. M.A., Ph.D.
Computer Sciences.
Economics.
Education. Includes curriculum and instruction, educational administration, educational psychology, foreign language education, kinesiology and health education, special education, mathematics and science education.
Electrical and Computer Engineering.
Engineering Mechanics.
English.
Environmental Health Engineering. M.S. only.
French.
Geography.
Geological Sciences.
Germanic Languages.
Government.
Hebrew Studies.
History.
Human Ecology. Includes nutrition, child development. M.A., Ph.D.
Latin American Studies. Interdepartmental.
Library and Information Science.
Linguistics.
Mathematics.
Mechanical Engineering.
Middle Eastern Studies.
Music.
Operations Research and Industrial Engineering.
Persian Studies.
Petroleum Engineering.
Pharmacy. Includes pharmacology, industrial pharmacy, pharmaceutical chemistry.
Philosophy.
Physics.
Post-Soviet and East European Studies. M.A.
Professional Accounting. M.P.A. only.
Psychology.
Public Affairs. Master of Public Affairs only.
Slavic Languages.
Social Work.
Sociology.
Spanish and Portuguese.
Statistics.
Writing.
Zoology.

School of Law (78714-9105)

Founded 1883. Semester system. Law library: 850,000 volumes.

Annual tuition/fees: resident $4820, nonresident $10,200.

Enrollment: first-year class 551; full-time 1549 (men 58%, women 42%); no part-time students. Faculty: full-time 79, part-time 79. Degrees conferred: J.D., J.D.-M.A. (Latin American Studies), J.D.-M.B.A., J.D.-M.P.A., LL.M., M.C.J. (for foreign law school graduates).

ADMISSION REQUIREMENTS. Bachelor's degree, transcripts, LSAT required in support of application. Interview not required. Accepts transfer applicants. Graduates of unaccredited institutions not considered. Apply to University Director of Admissions by February 1 (Fall). Application fee $50, $75 for international applicants. Phone: (512)471-3207.

ADMISSION STANDARDS. Selective. Accepts about 20–25% of total annual applicants.

FINANCIAL AID. Scholarships, research assistantships, Federal W/S, loans. Apply to Financial Aid Office by March 1. Use FAFSA. About 25% of students receive aid other than loans from School. Most aid for second- and third-year students.

DEGREE REQUIREMENTS. For J.D.: satisfactory completion of three-year program. For LL.M.: 32 semester hours minimum; thesis. For M.C.J.: by advisement.

THE UNIVERSITY OF TEXAS SOUTHWESTERN MEDICAL CENTER AT DALLAS

Dallas, Texas 75235-9096
http://www.swmed.edu

Established 1943. Coed. State control. Semester system. Special facilities: Howard Hughes Medical Institute; Zale Lipshy Hospital; Cain Center for Biomedical Research; James M. Collins Center for Biomedical Research; Cecil H. and Ida Green Center for Reproductive Biology Sciences; Robert T. Hayes Center for Mineral Metabolism Research; Erik Jonson Center for Research on Molecular Genetics and Human Disease; Kimberly-Clark Center for Breast Cancer Research; Eugene McDermott

Center for Human Growth and Development; Eugene McDermott Center for Pain Management; Mobility Foundation Center for Rehabilitation Research; W. A. "Tex" and Deborah Moncrieg, Jr., Center for Cancer Genetics; Harry S. Ross Heart Center; Frank M. Ryburn, Jr., Cardiac Center; Harold C. Simmons Arthritis Research Center; Harold C. Simmons Comprehensive Cancer Center; Kent Waldrep Foundation Center for Basic Neuroscience Research; Cancer Immunobiology Center; Center for Basic Research in Transplantation Immunology; the Nuclear Medicine Center. Library: 225,000 volumes, 10,000 microforms, 2000 current periodicals.

Southwestern Graduate School of Biomedical Sciences

Annual tuition: full-time residents $1218, nonresidents $6402; per credit: resident $32, nonresident $246.

Enrollment: full-time 460 (men 50%, women 50%). Faculty: full-time 265, part-time 45. Degrees conferred: M.A., M.S., Ph.D.

ADMISSION REQUIREMENTS. Official transcripts, three recommendations, GRE required in support of School's application. Four-year bachelor's degree or equivalent required. Interviews encouraged. TOEFL required for international applicants. Accepts transfer applicants. Graduates of unaccredited colleges not considered. Apply to Registrar, University of Texas Southwestern Medical Center, deadlines vary by program. Application fee none. Phone: (214)688-3606, Fax: (214)648-3289.

ADMISSION STANDARDS. Selective. Usual minimum average: 3.0 (A = 4). GRE average score 1150.

FINANCIAL AID. Scholarships, assistantships, fellowships for teaching/research, Federal W/S, loans. Approved for VA benefits. Apply to Financial Aid Office; no specified closing date. Use FAFSA. Phone: (214)648-3611; fax: (214)648-3289. Most Ph.D. students receive stipends.

DEGREE REQUIREMENTS. For master's: 30 semester hours minimum, at least 24 in residence; thesis; comprehensive oral/written exam for some departments. For Ph.D.: at least one year in residence; foreign language requirement set by department; oral/written candidacy exam; dissertation; final oral exam.

FIELDS OF STUDY.
Biochemistry and Molecular Biology.
Biomedical Communication. M.A. only.
Biomedical Engineering.
Cell and Molecular Biology.
Cell Regulation.
Clinical Psychology.
Genetics and Development.
Immunology.
Molecular Biophysics.
Molecular Microbiology.
Neuroscience.
Pharmacology.
Physiology.
Radiological Sciences.
Rehabilitation Counseling and Psychology. M.S. only.

Southwestern Medical School (75235-9096)

Established 1943. Medical library 270,000 volumes.

Annual tuition: resident $6550, nonresident $19,650; student fees $534. Enrollment: first-year class 200, total 791 (men 65%, women 35%); total full-time 812. Faculty: full-time 823, part-time 111. Degrees conferred: M.D., M.D.-Ph.D., (Medical Scientist Training Program), M.D.-Ph.D. (medical combined degree program with University of Texas at Arlington).

ADMISSION REQUIREMENTS. Transcripts, letter of recommendation from Premedical Committee, two additional letters of recommendation, MCAT required in support of application. Interview by invitation only. Applicants must have completed at least three years of college study. Accepts transfer applicants. 90% of class must be state residents. Apply to University of Texas System Medical and Dental Application Center at Austin (78701) after April 15, before October 15. Application center fee: residents $45 plus $5 for each additional school, nonresidents $80 plus $10 for each additional school. Phone: (214)648-2670; fax: (214)648-3289.

ADMISSION STANDARDS. Selective. Accepts about 10–12% of total annual applicants. Approximately 88% are state residents.

FINANCIAL AID. Limited to scholarships, loans. MSTP funded by NIH. Apply after acceptance, before July 1 to Office of Student Financial Aid. Use FAFSA.

DEGREE REQUIREMENTS. For M.D.: satisfactory completion of four-year program.

FIELDS OF GRADUATE STUDY.
Biochemistry.
Biophysics.
Cell Biology.
Genetics.
Immunology.
Microbiology.
Molecular Biology.
Neurosciences.
Pharmacology.
Physiology.

UNIVERSITY OF TEXAS MEDICAL BRANCH AT GALVESTON
Galveston, Texas 77555

Established 1891. Coed. State control. Semester system. Special facilities: DEC/VAX11/750, IBM 3081, Biomedical Engineering Center, Marine Biomedical Institute, Molecular Science Institute, Institute for Medical Humanities, Shriner's Burn Institute. Library: 270,000 volumes, 4000 microforms, 47 PCs.

Limited graduate housing available for single students, none for married students. Average academic year housing costs: $2795 (room only).

Graduate School of Biomedical Science
http://www.utmb.edu/gsbs/programs/html

Graduate study since 1969. Annual tuition: full-time, resident $864, nonresident $6642; per credit, resident $32, nonresident $246.

Enrollment: full-time 223, part-time 55 (men 50%, women 50%). Faculty: full-time 263, part-time 6. Degrees conferred: M.A., M.M.S., M.S., M.S.N., Ph.D.

ADMISSION REQUIREMENTS. Official transcripts, three recommendations, GRE required in support of School's application. Four-year bachelor's degree or equivalent required. Interview encouraged. TOEFL required for all international applicants. Accepts transfer applicants. Graduates of unaccredited institutions given consideration. Apply to Dean, Graduate School of Biomedical Science; no specified closing date. Application fee $25, $50 for international applicants. Phone: (409)772-2665; fax: (409)747-0772.

ADMISSION STANDARDS. Selective. Usual minimum average: 3.0 (A = 4).

FINANCIAL AID. Eleven scholarships, eighty-one research assistantships, Federal W/S, loans. Approved for VA benefits. Apply to Financial Aid Office; no specified closing date. Use FAFSA. Phone: (409)722-4955; fax: (408)722-4466. About 35% of students receive aid other than loans from School. Aid sometimes available to part-time students.

DEGREE REQUIREMENTS. For master's: 36 semester hours minimum, at least 24 in residence; thesis; comprehensive oral/written exam for some departments. For Ph.D.: at least one year in residence; foreign language requirement set by department; oral/written candidacy exam; dissertation, final oral exam.

FIELDS OF STUDY.
Anatomy.
Biochemistry.
Cell Biology.
Clinical Gerontology.
Human Genetics.
Immunology.
Medical Humanities.
Molecular Biology.
Neuroscience.
Nursing.
Pathology.
Pharmacology and Toxicology.
Physiology and Biophysics.
Virology.

School of Medicine (77555-1317)

Established 1891. Medical library 90,000 volumes. Annual tuition: resident $6550, nonresident $19,650; student fees $427.

Enrollment: first-year class 200, total 780 (men 53%, women 47%). Faculty: full-time 823, part-time 111. On-campus housing for women; none for married students and men. Average annual housing cost: $3500. Apply to Manager, Dormitories and Apartments. Phone: (409)772-1898. Degrees conferred: M.D., M.D.-Ph.D.

ADMISSION REQUIREMENTS. Transcripts, letter of recommendation from Premedical Committee, two additional letters of recommendation, MCAT required in support of application. Interview by invitation only. Applicants must have completed at least three years of college study. Accepts transfer applicants. 90% of class must be state residents. Apply to University of Texas System Medical and Dental Application Center at Austin (78701) after April 15, before October 15. Application center fee: residents $45 plus $5 for each additional school, nonresidents $80 plus $10 for each additional school. Phone: (409)772-3256.

ADMISSION STANDARDS. Selective. Accepts about 15% of total annual applicants. Approximately 93% are state residents.

FINANCIAL AID. Limited scholarships, loans. Apply after acceptance, before July 1 to Office of Student Financial Aid. About 45% of students receive some aid from School.

DEGREE REQUIREMENTS. For M.D.: satisfactory completion of four-year program.

FIELDS OF GRADUATE STUDY.
Anatomy.
Biochemistry.
Biophysics.
Cell Biology.
Genetics.
Immunology.
Microbiology.
Molecular Biology.
Neurosciences.

Pathology.
Pharmacology.
Physiology.

THE UNIVERSITY OF TEXAS HEALTH SCIENCE CENTER AT HOUSTON
Houston, Texas 77225-0036

Established 1972. Located 2 miles SW of Downtown. The Health Science Center includes the Medical School, the Dental Branch (formerly Texas Dental College), the Graduate School of Biomedical Sciences, the School of Public Health, the School of Allied Health Sciences and the School of Nursing. Library: 259,000 volumes, 2800 current periodicals, 68 PCs.

Graduate School of Biomedical Sciences
http://gsbs.gs.uth.tmc.edu

Established 1963. Coed. Tuition: per credit, resident $32, nonresident $222. Enrollment: full-time 387, part-time 51 (men 228, women 210). Faculty: full-time 394, part-time 11. Degrees conferred: M.S., Ph.D.

ADMISSION REQUIREMENTS. Transcripts, GRE, three letters of recommendation, personal statement background, research interests, and professional goals required in support of School's application. GRE Subject Test recommended. TOEFL and TWE required of international students. Interview optional. Apply to Office of the Registrar, UT Health Science Center, P.O. Box 20036, Houston, Texas 77225, eight weeks prior to registration. Priority deadline for Fall admission is January 15. Application fee $10. Phone: (800)UTH-GSBS, (713)792-4582; fax: (713)794-1601.

ADMISSION STANDARDS. Competitive. Usual minimum average: 3.0 (A = 4).

FINANCIAL AID. Fifty-three scholarships, 323 research assistantships, 11 teaching assistantships, 11 training grants, loans. Nearly all admitted students are awarded financial aid. Use FAFSA for all non-merit aid. Phone: (713)792-4260, (713)795-0364. About 95% of students receive aid from School and outside sources.

DEGREE REQUIREMENTS. For M.S.: 24 hours of course work, two semesters of registration for thesis. For Ph.D.: three tutorial laboratory rotations; four area courses, one ethics course; qualifying exam; dissertation; final oral exam.

FIELDS OF GRADUATE STUDY.
Anatomy.
Biochemistry.
Biomathematics.
Biophysics.
Cancer Biology.
Cell Biology.
Genes and Development.
Genetic Counseling.
Genetics.
Immunology.
Integrative Biology.
Medical Physics.
Microbiology.
Molecular Biology.
Neurosciences.
Oral Biomaterials.
Pathology.
Pharmacology.

Physiology.
Radiation Biology.
Regulatory Biology.
Reproductive Biology.
Sensory Sciences.
Toxicology.
Virology.

Medical School

Established 1969. Annual tuition: resident $6550, nonresident $19,650. Total average cost for all other expenses: $7500. Enrollment: first-year class 201; total 780 (men 54%, women 46%).

Faculty: full- and part-time and volunteers 2000. Degrees conferred: M.D., M.D.-Ph.D.

ADMISSION REQUIREMENTS. Transcripts, MCAT, recommendations required in support of application. Interview by invitation. Preference given to state residents. Graduates of unaccredited colleges not considered. 90% of class must be state residents. Apply to University of Texas System, Medical and Dental Application Center, Austin, Texas 78701, after June 15 before October 15. Application fee $40 (resident) plus $5 for each additional school, $80 (nonresident) plus $5 for each additional school. Phone: (713)792-4711; fax: (713)792-4238.

ADMISSION STANDARDS. Selective. Admits about 10–15% of total annual applicants. Approximately 92% are state residents.

FINANCIAL AID. Scholarships, loans. Apply after acceptance to Office of Financial Aid. About 60% of students receive some aid from School.

DEGREE REQUIREMENTS. For M.D.: satisfactory completion of four-year program.

FIELDS OF GRADUATE STUDY.
Anatomy.
Biochemistry.
Cell Biology.
Genetics.
Immunology.
Microbiology.
Molecular Biology.
Neurosciences.
Pathology.
Pharmacology.
Physiology.

Dental School

Established 1905. Joined University of Texas system in 1972. Located in Houston (77225-0068).

Annual tuition: full-time, resident $7046, nonresident $17,846. No on-campus housing available. Average academic year housing costs: $12,000. For off-campus housing, contact Resident Manager, Texas Medical Center. Total average cost for all other first-year expenses: $4096.

Enrollment: first-year class 62; 393 total (men 50%, women 50%); graduate program 32. Faculty: full-time 232, part-time 21. Degree conferred: D.D.S.

ADMISSION REQUIREMENTS. AADSAS (nonresidents), official transcripts, three letters of recommendation, DAT required in support of School's application. Applicants must have completed at least three years of college study, four years of study preferred. Interview by invitation only. Preference given to state residents. Accepts transfer students. Apply to UT System, Medical and Dental Application Center, Austin, Texas 78701, after April 15, before November 1. Application fee $35 resident, $70

nonresident. Dental School Admissions Office Phone: (713)792-4151.

ADMISSION STANDARDS. Selective. Usual minimum average: 3.0 (A = 4). Accepts about 20–25% of total annual applicants. Approximately 90% are state residents.

FINANCIAL AID. Scholarships, grants, loans. Apply to the Health Science Center's Financial Aid Office; no specified closing date. Use FAFSA. Phone: (713)792-4260. About 84% of students receive some aid from University and outside sources.

DEGREE REQUIREMENTS. For D.D.S.: satisfactory completion of forty-six-month program.

School of Public Health

Founded 1967. Coed. Semester system.
Tuition: per credit, resident $32, nonresident $246.
Enrollment: full-time 292, part-time $482. Faculty: full-time 79, part-time 10. Degrees conferred: M.P.H., M.S., D.P.H., Ph.D.

ADMISSION REQUIREMENTS. Transcripts, two letters of recommendation, GRE Test required in support of application. TOEFL required for international applicants. Accepts transfer applicants. Graduates of unaccredited institutions considered. Apply to Office of Registration by March 1 (Fall), September 1 (Spring). Application fee $10. Phone: (713)792-4425.

ADMISSION STANDARDS. Very selective. Usual minimum average: 3.0 (A = 4).

FINANCIAL AID. Scholarships, traineeships, grants and contracts, loans. Approved for VA benefits. Apply to the Financial Aid Office; no specified closing date. Use FAFSA. Phone: (713)792-4425. About 33% of students receive aid other than loans from School and outside sources.

DEGREE REQUIREMENTS. For master's: satisfactory completion of prescribed course of study, at least one academic year in duration; comprehensive exam or project. For D.P.H.: at least one academic year in preparation for qualifying exam; research project. For Ph.D.: satisfactory completion of prescribed course of study, at least two semesters in residence; qualifying exam; dissertation; final oral exam.

THE UNIVERSITY OF TEXAS HEALTH SCIENCE CENTER AT SAN ANTONIO
San Antonio, Texas 78284

Coed. State control. Semester system. Special facilities: DEC system -20, DEC/VAX 8650, 8700, 11-/785; Center for Research in Reproductive Biology; Scanning Electron Microscope facility. Library: 206,000 volumes, 2500 current periodicals.

Graduate School of Biomedical Sciences

Tuition: per credit, resident $32, nonresident $222. Enrollment: full-time 293, part-time 215 (men 55%, women 45%). Faculty: full-time 225, part-time 36. Degrees conferred: M.S., M.S.N., Ph.D.

ADMISSION REQUIREMENTS. Transcripts, GRE, three letters of recommendation, research interests, and professional goals statement required in support of School's application. GRE Subject Test recommended. TOEFL and TWE required of international applicants. Interview optional. Graduates of unaccredited institutions not considered. Apply to Office of the Registrar,

UT Health Science Center, P.O. Box 20036, Houston, Texas 77225, eight weeks prior to registration. Priority deadline for Fall admission is January 15. Application fee $10. Phone: (210) 567-3709; fax (210) 567-3719.

ADMISSIONS STANDARDS. Selective. Usual minimum average: 3.0 (A = 4).

FINANCIAL AID. Scholarship, assistantships, fellowships for teaching/research, loans. Apply to appropriate department by March 31. Use FAFSA for all non-merit aid. About 35% of students receive aid from school and outside sources.

DEGREE REQUIREMENTS. For M.S.: 30 semester hours minimum, at least 24 in residence; thesis; comprehensive oral/written exam for some departments. For Ph.D.: at least one year in residence; foreign language requirement set by department; oral written exam for candidacy; dissertation; final oral exam.

FIELDS OF STUDY.
Anatomy. Ph.D. only.
Biochemistry.
Cell Biology.
Clinical Pharmacy.
Community Health Nursing. M.S.N. only.
Critical Care Nursing. M.S.N. only.
Dentistry. M.S.
Human Genetics.
Medical-Surgical Nursing. M.S.N. only.
Microbiology.
Molecular Medicine.
Neurobiology.
Nursing Care of Children. M.S.N.
Nursing Service Administration. M.S.N. only
Pharmacology. Ph.D. only.
Physiology.
Psychiatric Mental Health. M.S.N. only.
Radiological Sciences.
Reproductive Biology.
Women's Health. M.S.N.

Medical School (78284-7701)

Established 1891. Medical library 90,000 volumes. Annual tuition: resident $6500, nonresident $19,650.

Enrollment: first-year class 200, total 819 (men 40%, women 40%). Faculty: full-time 823, part-time 111. On-campus housing for women; none for married students and men. Average annual housing cost: $3500. Apply to Manager, Dormitories and Apartments. Degrees conferred: M.D., M.D.-Ph.D.

ADMISSION REQUIREMENTS. Transcripts, letter of recommendation from Premedical Committee, two additional letters of recommendation, MCAT required in support of application. Interview by invitation only. Applicants must have completed at least three years of college study. Accepts transfer applicants. 90% of class must be state residents. Apply to University of Texas System Medical and Dental Application Center at Austin (78701) after April 15, before October 15. Application center fee: residents $45 plus $5 for each additional school, nonresidents $80 plus $10 for each additional school. Phone: (210)567-2665; fax: (210)567-2685.

ADMISSION STANDARDS. Selective. Accepts about 10–15% of total annual applicants. Approximately 90% are state residents.

FINANCIAL AID. Limited scholarships, loans. Apply after acceptance, before July 1 to Office of Student Financial Aid. Use FAFSA. About 45% of students receive some aid from School.

DEGREE REQUIREMENTS. For M.D.: satisfactory completion of four-year program.

FIELDS OF GRADUATE STUDY.
Biochemistry.
Cell Biology.
Immunology.
Microbiology.
Pharmacology.
Physiology.

Dental School (78284-7702)

Established 1969. Annual tuition: resident $5400, nonresident $16,200. No on-campus housing available. Average academic year off-campus housing costs: $14,000. Contact Dean for Student Affairs for housing information. Phone: (210)567-3181. Total average cost for all other first-year expenses: $2850.

Enrollment: first-year class 90; 413 total (men 65%, women 35%). Faculty: full-time 146, part-time 49. Degree conferred: D.D.S.

ADMISSION REQUIREMENTS. AADSAS (nonresidents), official transcripts, DAT (not later than October), three letters of recommendation required in support of School's application. Preference given to state residents and veterans. Interview by invitation only. Graduates of unaccredited institutions not considered. Apply to UT System, Medical and Dental Application Center, Austin, Texas 78701, after April 15, before November 1. Application fee: resident $35, nonresident $70. Dental School's Admissions Office. Phone: (512)567-2674.

ADMISSION STANDARDS. Selective. Accepts about 30–35% of total annual applicants. Approximately 85% are state residents.

FINANCIAL AID. Limited state, federal scholarships, loans. Apply to Student Financial Aid office after acceptance. Use FAFSA. Phone: (210)567-2365. About 95% of students receive aid from School and outside sources.

DEGREE REQUIREMENTS. For D.D.S.: satisfactory completion of thirty-nine-month program.

FIELDS OF GRADUATE STUDY.
Dental Diagnostic Sciences.
Endodontics.
General Dentistry.
Oral and Maxillofacial Surgery.
Pediatric Dentistry.
Periodontics.
Prosthodontics.

THE UNIVERSITY OF TEXAS AT DALLAS
Richardson, Texas 75083-0688
http://www.utdallas.edu

Created 1969. Coed. State control. Semester system. Special facilities: Callier Center for Communications Disorders, Center for Applied Optics, Center for Lithospheric Studies, Center for Quantum Electronics, Center for Space Sciences, Center for Genetic Technology, Institute for Environmental Sciences, Communications and Learning Center, Center for China and U.S. Management Studies, Center for Research and Teaching, Bruton Center for Development Studies, Morris Hite Center for Product

Development and Marketing Science, Center for International Accounting Development, Translation Center. Library: 524,000 volumes, 1,519,000 microforms, 2400 current periodicals.

Tuition: per credit, resident $78.50, nonresident $270.50. On-campus housing available for single and married students. Average academic year housing costs: $4953 (including board); off-campus costs: $375–$700 per month.

Graduate School

Graduate study since 1969. Graduate enrollment: full-time 1201, part-time 2951. Graduate faculty: full-time 221, part-time 104. Degrees conferred: M.A., M.A.T., M.B.A., M.S., M.S.E.E., M.S.E.S., M.P.A., Ph.D., D.Chem.

ADMISSION REQUIREMENTS. Official transcripts, bachelor's degree, GRE, GMAT (School of Management) required in support of School's application. TOEFL required for international applicants. Accepts transfer students. Graduates of unaccredited institutions not considered. Apply to Director of Admissions January 31. Rolling admissions process. Application fee: domestic none, international students $75. Phone: (214)883-2294; information line: (214)883-2341; fax: (214)883-2599.

ADMISSION STANDARDS. Selective. Usual minimum average: 3.0 (A = 4).

FINANCIAL AID. Scholarships, assistantships, internships, partial tuition waivers, Federal W/S, loans. Approved for VA benefits. Apply by November 1 to the appropriate department for scholarships and assistantships; to Financial Aid Office for all other aid. Phone: (214)883-2941; fax: (214)883-2947. Use FAFSA and Institutional FAF. About 65% of students receive aid from University and outside sources. Financial aid is sometimes available for part-time study.

DEGREE REQUIREMENTS. For master's: 36–45 semester credits minimum; at least 30–39 credits in residence; thesis/nonthesis option; comprehensive written/oral exam. For Ph.D., D.Chem.: 60 credits minimum beyond bachelor's, at least one year in full-time study; proficiency in one foreign language for some programs; qualifying exam; advancement to candidacy; dissertation; final oral exam.

FIELDS OF STUDY.
Applied Cognition and Neurosciences.
Biology.
Business Administration.
Chemistry.
Communication Disorders.
Computer Sciences.
Electrical Engineering. Includes telecommunications, microelectronics.
Engineering Sciences. Includes manufacturing sciences.
Geosciences.
Human Development and Communication Sciences.
Human Development and Early Childhood Disorders.
Humanities. Includes aesthetics studies, studies in literature, history of ideas, humanities.
Industrial Chemistry.
Interdisciplinary Studies.
International Management Studies.
Management and Administrative Sciences. Includes accounting.
Mathematical Sciences. Includes applied mathematics, mathematics, statistics.
Molecular and Cell Biology.
Physics.
Political Economy.
Public Affairs.
Science Education.

THE UNIVERSITY OF TEXAS AT EL PASO
El Paso, Texas 79968-0001

Established 1913. Coed. State control. Semester system. Special facilities: NSF Material Science Center, Inter-American and Border Studies, El Paso Centennial Museum, Center for Environmental Resource Management, Center for Entrepreneurial Development, Advancement Research and Support, El Paso Solar Pond Research Station, Institute for Manufacturing and Materials Management, Center for Environmental Resource Management, Oral History Institute, Bureau of Business and Economics Research. Library: 812,000 volumes, 1,090,500 microforms, 2500 current periodicals, 130 PCs.

Annual tuition: full-time, resident $1678, nonresident $6814. On-campus housing for 60 married students, 328 men, 122 women. Average academic year housing costs: $4000 for married students, $2600 for single students. Contact Housing Office for both on- and off-campus housing information. Phone: (915)747-5352.

Graduate School

Graduate study since 1940. Enrollment: full-time 687, part-time 1051. University faculty teaching graduate students: full-time 341, part-time 13. Degrees conferred: M.A., M.Ed., M.B.A., M.M., M.P.A., M.Acy., M.S., M.S.I.S., M.A.T., M.A.I.S., M.S.N., Ph.D.

ADMISSION REQUIREMENTS. Two official transcripts, GRE/GMAT required in support of School's application. MAT may be required for nursing students. Interview not required. TOEFL required for international applicants. Accepts transfer applicants. Graduates of unaccredited institutions not considered. Apply by July 1 (Fall), November 1 (Spring) to Graduate Student Services Office. Application fee none, $65 for international applicants. Phone: (915)747-5491; fax: (915)747-6474.

ADMISSION STANDARDS. Selective. Usual minimum average: 2.75 (A = 4).

FINANCIAL AID. Scholarships, fellowships, research/teaching assistantships, partial tuition waivers, Federal W/S, loans. Approved for VA benefits. Apply to the appropriate department for fellowships, assistantships; to the Office of Student Financial Aid for all other programs. No specified closing date, although applicants are advised to submit their applications before March 1 for the upcoming academic year. Office of Student Financial Aid. Phone: (915)747-5204. Use FAFSA and institutional FAF. Aid is sometimes available to part-time students.

DEGREE REQUIREMENTS. For M.A., M.S.: 30 semester hours minimum, at least 24 in residence; thesis; comprehensive oral/written exam. For M.Ed.: 36 semester hours minimum, at least 30 in residence. For M.B.A., M.Acc.: 36 semester hours minimum, at least 30 in residence; computer proficiency. For M.P.A.: 36 semester hours minimum, at least 30 in residence; internship; comprehensive exam. For M.S.N.: 36 semester hours minimum, at least 30 in residence; practicum; comprehensive exam. For M.S.I.S.: 36 semester hours minimum, at least 30 in residence; report. For M.A.T.: 36 semester hours minimum, at least 30 in residence; comprehensive exam. For M.A.I.S.: 36 semester hours minimum, at least 30 in residence; final project; oral examination. For Ph.D.: 30 semester hours minimum beyond the master's; qualifying exam; proficiency in one foreign language for some programs; dissertation; final oral exam.

FIELDS OF STUDY.
Accountancy. M.Acy.
Adult Health. M.S.N.

Art. M.A.
Biological Sciences. M.S.
Business Administration. M.B.A.
Chemistry. M.S.
Civil Engineering. M.S.
Clinical Psychology. M.A.
Computer Engineering. M.S., Ph.D.
Creative Writing in English. M.F.A.
Creative Writing in Spanish. M.F.A.
Educational Leaderships and Foundations. M.Ed.
Educational Psychology and Special Services. M.Ed.
English. M.A.
Experimental Psychology. M.A.
Geological Sciences. M.S., Ph.D.
Geophysics. M.S.
History. M.A.
Industrial Engineering. M.S.
Interdisciplinary Studies. M.A.I.S., M.S.I.S.
Kinesiology and Sports Studies. M.S.
Linguistics. M.A.
Manufacturing Engineering. M.S.
Mathematical Sciences. M.A.T., M.S.
Mechanical Engineering. M.S.
Metallurgical Engineering. M.S.
Music. Includes music education, performance. M.M.
Nurse Midwifery. M.S.N.
Nursing Administration. M.S.N.
Parent-Child Nursing. M.S.N.
Physics. M.S.
Political Science. M.A.
Psychiatric/Mental Health Nursing. M.S.N.
Psychology. Ph.D.
Public Administration. M.P.A.
Sociology. M.A.
Spanish. M.A.
Speech. M.A.
Speech Language Pathology. M.S.
Statistics. M.S.
Theater Arts. M.A.
Women's Health Care/Nurse Practitioner. M.S.N

THE UNIVERSITY OF TEXAS OF THE PERMIAN BASIN

Odessa, Texas 797621-0001

Coed. State control. Semester system. Special facilities: Center for Energy and Economic Diversification, Center for Behavioral Analysis. Library: 270,000 volumes, 1,074,000 microforms, 723 current periodicals.

Annual tuition: full-time, resident $900, nonresident $3996; per credit resident $50, nonresident $222. On-campus housing for single and married students. Average academic year housing costs: single students $1850, married students $2850. Contact Director of Graduate Housing for both on- and off-campus housing information.

Graduate School

Enrollment: full-time 61, part-time 256. Faculty: full-time 48, part-time 7. Degrees conferred: M.A., M.B.A., M.S.

ADMISSION REQUIREMENTS. Two transcripts, GRE/GMAT required in support of application. TOEFL required for international applicants. Accepts transfer students. Graduates of unaccredited institutions not considered. Applications processed on a rolling basis. Apply to the Registrar by April 1 (Summer), July 1

(Fall), November 1 (Spring) for priority consideration. Application fee none. Phone: (915)552-2640; fax: (915)552-2374.

ADMISSION STANDARDS. Selective. Usual minimum average: 2.5 (A = 4).

FINANCIAL AID. Limited to Federal W/S, loans. Approved for VA benefits. Apply to Director of Financial Aid; no specified closing date. Use FAFSA and Institutional FAF. Financial aid is sometimes available for part-time study.

DEGREE REQUIREMENTS. For M.A., M.S.: 30 semester credits minimum, at least 24 credits in residence; thesis/nonthesis option; comprehensive written/oral exam. For M.B.A.: 36–45 semester credits, at least 30–39 credits in residence; computer proficiency.

FIELDS OF STUDY.
Biology. M.A.
Business Administration. M.A.
Early Childhood Education. M.A.
Educational Administration. M.A.
Educational Supervisor. M.A.
Elementary Education. M.A.
English. M.A.
Geology. M.S.
Guidance and Counseling. M.A.
History. M.A.
Kinesiology. M.A.
Psychology. M.A.
Reading. M.A.
Secondary Education. M.A.
Special Education. M.A.

THE UNIVERSITY OF TEXAS AT SAN ANTONIO

San Antonio, Texas 78249

Founded in 1969. Coed. State control. Semester system. Special facilities: Institute for Studies in Business, Economics and Human Resources; Center for Archaeological Research; Center for Applied Research and Technology. Library: 464,000 volumes, 2,100,000 microforms, 2100 current periodicals.

Annual tuition: full-time resident $2584, nonresident $5860. On-campus housing for both single and married students. Average academic year housing costs: $4200 (including board) for single students; $2600 for married students. Contact Director of Chisholm Hall, Phone: (210)694-6700; or Director of University Oaks Apartments. Phone: (210)561-8699.

Graduate School

Graduate study since 1973. Graduate enrollment: full-time 648, part-time 1806. Graduate faculty: full-time 252, part-time 121. Degrees conferred: M.A., M.B.A., M.P.Acct., M.F.A., M.M., M.S., M.P.A., Ph.D.

ADMISSION REQUIREMENTS. Official transcripts, GRE/GMAT required in support of School's application. Auditions/portfolio review required for music/art applicants. TOEFL required for international applicants. Accepts transfer students. Graduates of unaccredited institutions not considered. Applications processed on a rolling basis. Apply to the Director of Admissions and Registrar April 1 (Summer), June 1 (Fall), November 1 (Spring) for priority consideration. Application fee $20. Phone: (210)691-4530.

ADMISSION STANDARDS. Selective. Usual minimum average for last 60 credits for unconditional admission: 3.0 (A = 4).

FINANCIAL AID. Scholarships, assistantships, Federal W/S, loans. Approved for VA benefits. Apply to the appropriate department for scholarships and assistantships; to Director of Financial Aid for all other forms of aid. No specified closing date. Phone: (210)691-4154. Use FAFSA. Financial aid is sometimes available for part-time study.

DEGREE REQUIREMENTS. For M.A., M.S.: 30 semester credits minimum, at least 24 credits in residence; thesis/nonthesis option; comprehensive written/oral exam. For M.B.A., M.P.Acct.: 36–45 semester credits, at least 30–39 credits in residence; computer proficiency. For M.P.A.: 36 semester credits minimum, at least 30 credits in residence; comprehensive exam. For M.M.: 30 semester credits minimum, at least 24 in residence; recital; written/oral exam. For M.F.A.: 60 semester credits minimum, at least 48 credits in residence; gallery level exhibition/special project; written/oral exam. For Ph.D.: 60 credits minimum beyond the master's degree, at least 48 in residence; foreign language proficiency set by department; qualifying exam; candidacy; dissertation; final oral exam.

FIELDS OF STUDY.
Accounting.
Anthropology.
Archaeology.
Architecture.
Art. Includes art history.
Bicultural-Bilingual Studies.
Biology. Includes cell, molecular.
Biotechnology.
Business Administration.
Chemistry.
Civil Engineering.
Computer Sciences.
Education.
Educational Leadership. Cooperative degree with UT-Austin.
Electrical Engineering.
English.
Environmental Sciences.
Geology.
History.
Human Resources Management.
Information Systems
International Business.
Management Accounting.
Management Science.
Management of Technology.
Mathematics. Includes mathematics education.
Mechanical Engineering.
Music.
Psychology.
Public Administration.
Spanish.
Statistics.
Taxation.
Teaching English as a Second Language.

THE UNIVERSITY OF TEXAS AT TYLER
Tyler, Texas 75799-0001

Coed. State control. Semester system. Special facilities: Zuckerman Electron Microscope Laboratory, University of Texas High Speed Computational Center, Center for Policy Studies,

Child and Family Abuse Clearinghouse. Library: 180,000 volumes, 446,000 microforms, 1500 current periodicals.

Annual tuition: full-time, residents $1764, nonresident $6900. No on-campus housing available.

Graduate Studies

Graduate Enrollment: full-time 286, part-time 1193. Graduate faculty: full-time 115, part-time 33. Degrees Conferred: M.A., M.B.A., M.Ed., M.P.A., M.S.N., M.S.

ADMISSION REQUIREMENTS. Two official transcripts, GRE/GMAT required in support of application. TOEFL required for international applicants. Accepts transfer students. Graduates of unaccredited institutions not considered. Apply to the Director of Admissions and Records by April 1 (Summer), July 1 (Fall), November 1 (Spring) for priority consideration. Rolling admissions process. Application fee none. Phone: (903)566-7201.

ADMISSION STANDARDS. Selective. Usual minimum average: 2.75 (A = 4).

FINANCIAL AID. Scholarships, assistantships, full and partial tuition waivers, Federal W/S, loans. Approved for VA benefits. Apply to the appropriate department for scholarships and assistantships; to Director of Financial Aid for all other programs. No specified closing date. Use FAFSA and Institutional FAF. Financial aid is sometimes available for part-time study.

DEGREE REQUIREMENTS. For M.A., M.S.: 30 semester credits minimum, at least 24 credits in residence; thesis/nonthesis option; comprehensive written/oral exam. For M.Ed.: 36 semester credits minimum, at least 30 in residence. For M.B.A., M.P.A.: 36–45 semester minimum, at least 30–39 credits in residence; computer proficiency. For M.S.N.: 36 semester credits minimum, at least 30 credits in residence; practicum; comprehensive exam.

FIELDS OF STUDY.
Biology. M.S.
Business Administration. M.B.A.
Clinical Exercise Physiology. M.S.
Computer Sciences. M.S.
Early Childhood Education. M.A., M.Ed.
Elementary Education. M.A., M.Ed.
Health Care. M.B.A.
Liberal Studies. Interdisciplinary. M.A., M.S.
Mathematics. M.S.
Nursing. M.S.N.
Psychology. M.A., M.S.
Public Administration. M.P.A.
Reading. M.A., M.Ed.
Secondary Education. M.A., M.Ed.
Special Education. M.A., M.Ed.
Technology. M.S.

THE UNIVERSITY OF TEXAS— PAN AMERICAN
Edinburg, Texas 78539-2999

Founded 1927. Coed. State control. Semester system. Special facilities: Speech and Hearing Clinic, Coastal Marine Biology Laboratory, Rio Grande Valley Archives. Library: 269,000 volumes, 669,000 microforms, 2200 current periodicals.

Tuition/fees: per semester resident $1524, nonresident $6660. On-campus housing for single students only. Annual housing cost: $2482.50 (including board). Contact Director of Student Services for both on- and off-campus housing information. Phone: (210)381-3439.

Graduate Studies

Enrollment: full- and part-time 1169. Graduate faculty: full-time 88, part-time 3. Degrees conferred: M.A., M.B.A., M.Ed., M.S., M.S.I.S.

ADMISSION REQUIREMENTS. Two transcripts, GRE/GMAT required in support of application. TOEFL required for international students. Accepts transfer students. Graduates of unaccredited institutions not considered. Applications processed on a rolling basis. Apply to the Director of Admissions and Records by April 1 (Summer), July 1 (Fall), November 1 (Spring) for priority consideration. Application fee none. Phone: (210)381-2206.

ADMISSION STANDARDS. Selective. Usual minimum average: 2.75 (A = 4).

FINANCIAL AID. Scholarships, assistantships, partial tuition waivers, grants, Federal W/S, loans. Approved for VA benefits. Apply by January 15 to the appropriate department for scholarships and assistantships; to Director of Financial Aid for all other programs. Use FAFSA. Financial Aid is sometimes available for part-time study.

DEGREE REQUIREMENTS. For M.A., M.S., M.S.I.S.: 30 semester credits minimum, at least 24 credits in residence; thesis/nonthesis option; comprehensive written/oral exam. For M.Ed.: 36 semester credits minimum, at least 30 in residence. For M.B.A.: 36–45 semester credits, at least 30–39 credits in residence; computer proficiency.

FIELDS OF STUDY.
Bilingual and Bicultural Studies.
Biology.
Business Administration.
Counselor Education.
Drama.
Education.
Educational Administration.
Educational Psychology.
English.
History.
Interdisciplinary Program. Includes humanities, social sciences.
Mathematics.
Physical Education.
Public Administration.
Reading.
Secondary Education.
Spanish.
Speech and Interpersonal Communication.
Teaching English as a Second Language.

TEXAS WOMAN'S UNIVERSITY
Denton, Texas 76204-0479

Established 1901. Located 35 miles NW of Dallas. Coed on graduate level. State control. Special facilities: Animal Care Facility, CompuPASS Learning Laboratory, Food Testing Laboratory, Speech and Hearing Clinic, Textile Research Laboratory. Library: 788,000 volumes, 652,000 microforms, 2800 current periodicals, 50 PCs in all libraries.

Tuition: resident, per semester hour $52, nonresident $242. On-campus housing for 2880 graduate women, 70 graduate men, 53 married students. Average academic year housing costs:

$2640 (including board) for single students; $3200 for married students. Apply to the Office of University Housing. Phone: (817)989-3676.

Graduate School

Graduate study since 1930. Enrollment: full- and part-time over 4000. Faculty: full-time 306, part-time 10. Degrees conferred: M.A., M.B.A., M.F.A., M.S., M.Ed., M.O.T., M.L.S., M.Ed., Ed.D., Ph.D.

ADMISSION REQUIREMENTS. Official transcript, GRE/GMAT required in support of School's application. Some programs require interview, letters of recommendation. TOEFL required for international applicants. Accepts transfer applicants. Graduates of unaccredited schools not considered. Apply to Graduate Admissions at least ninety days prior to registration. Application fee $25. Phone: (817)898-3073.

ADMISSION STANDARDS. Selective for most departments. Usual minimum average: 3.0 (A = 4).

FINANCIAL AID. Over four hundred scholarships, research assistantships, teaching assistantships, internships, Federal W/S, loans. Approved for VA benefits. Apply to appropriate departmental chair for assistantships; to Director of Financial Aid for all other programs. No specified closing date. Phone: (817)898-3050. Use FAFSA. Aid sometimes available for part-time students.

DEGREE REQUIREMENTS. For master's: 30 semester hours with thesis or 36 semester hours with professional paper or project; additional requirements vary from program to program. For Ph.D.: at least 90 hours beyond the bachelor's; proficiency in two research tools; qualifying exam; dissertation, final oral/written exam. For Ed.D.: essentially the same as Ph.D., but requires a proficiency in statistics as a research tool. Some doctorates require a residency of two consecutive semesters.

FIELDS OF STUDY.

THE COLLEGE OF ARTS AND SCIENCES (M.A., M.B.A., M.F.A., M.S., PH.D.):
Art.
Art Education.
Art History.
Biology.
Biology Teaching.
Business Administration.
Chemistry.
Chemistry Teaching.
Counseling Psychology.
Dance.
Design.
Drama.
English.
Fashion Merchandising.
Fashion and Textiles.
Government.
History.
Mathematics.
Mathematics Teaching.
Molecular Biology.
Music.
Music Therapy.
Psychology.
Rhetoric.
School Psychology.
Sociology.
Studio Art.

COLLEGE OF EDUCATION AND HUMAN ECOLOGY (M.A., M.S., M.ED., ED.D., PH.D.):
Administration.
Child Development.
Consumer Sciences.
Counseling and Guidance.
Early Childhood Education.
Elementary Education.
Family Studies.
Home and Family Life.
Marriage and Family Counseling.
Reading.
Special Education.
Supervision.

SCHOOL OF LIBRARY INFORMATION SCIENCES (M.A., M.L.S., PH.D.):
Library Science.

COLLEGE OF NURSING (M.S., PH.D.):
Community Health.
Maternal-Child Health.
Medical-Surgical.
Nursing.
Pediatric Nurse Practitioner.
Psychiatric-Mental Health.

SCHOOL OF HEALTH SCIENCES (M.A., M.S., ED.D., PH.D.):
Education of the Hearing Impaired.
Food Science.
Health Care Administration.
Health Education.
Health Studies.
Institutional Administration.
Nutrition.
Physical Education.
Speech-Language Pathology.

SCHOOL OF OCCUPATIONAL THERAPY (M.A., M.O.T.):
Occupational Therapy.
Rehabilitation Technology.

SCHOOL OF PHYSICAL THERAPY (M.S., PH.D.):
Physical Therapy.

THOMAS M. COOLEY LAW SCHOOL
P.O. Box 13038
Lansing, Michigan 48901-3038

Established 1972. Private. Trimester system. Morning, afternoon, evening divisions. Library: 326,000 volumes. Library has LEXIS, NEXIS, WESTLAW; 12 PC work stations. Special facilities: Sixty Plus Law Center.

Tuition: per credit $465. No on-campus housing available. Total average annual additional expense: $15,500.

Enrollment: first-year class day and evening 800; total 1700 (men 65%, women 35%). Faculty: full-time 51, part-time 100. Degree conferred: J.D.

ADMISSION REQUIREMENTS. LSDAS Law School report, bachelor's degree, transcripts, LSAT required in support of application. Accepts transfer applicants. Apply to Admissions Office at least one month prior to beginning of trimester. Rolling admissions process. Admits September, January and May. Application fee $100. Phone: (517)371-5140.

ADMISSION STANDARDS. Admits about 60% of total annual applicants.

FINANCIAL AID. Honor scholarships, Federal W/S, loans. Apply to the Financial Aid Office; no specified closing date. Use FAFSA. About 80% of students receive some aid from School.

DEGREE REQUIREMENTS. For J.D.: satisfactory completion of 90 credit hour program.

THOMAS JEFFERSON UNIVERSITY
Philadelphia, Pennsylvania 19107

Founded 1824, Private control. Semester system. Medical library: 170,000 volumes, 10,634 microforms, 2200 current periodicals, 70 PCs.

Annual Graduate School tuition: $11,925; per credit $597. On-campus housing available. Average academic year housing costs: apartments $800/month, dormitory $350/month. Contact the Director of University Housing Office for both on- and off-campus housing information. Phone: (215)955-7665. On-campus daycare facilities available.

College of Graduate Studies

Enrollment: full-time 291, part-time 324 (men 31%, women 69%). Faculty: full-time 200, part-time 0. Degrees conferred: M.S., Ph.D.

ADMISSION REQUIREMENTS. Official transcripts, three letters of recommendation, GRE required in support of College's application. TOEFL required for international applicants. Accepts transfer applicants. Graduates of unaccredited institutions not considered. Apply to Director of admission; no specified closing date. Application fee $30. Phone: (215)955-0155; fax: (215)923-6690.

ADMISSION STANDARDS. Competitive. Usual minimum average: 3.0 (A = 4).

FINANCIAL AID. One hundred and nine fellowships, forty-four research assistantships, Federal W/S, loans. Approved for VA benefits. Apply to the Dean for fellowships, assistantships; to Financial Aid Office for all other programs. Use FAFSA and institutional FAF. Phone: (215)955-1232; fax: (215)923-6690.

DEGREE REQUIREMENTS. For M.S.: minimum 30 credits, maximum 44; final project or thesis. For Ph.D.: minimum of 45 credits beyond the master's, at least one year in full-time residence; qualifying exam; dissertation; final written/oral exam.

FIELDS OF STUDY.
Biochemistry and Molecular Biology.
Biomedical Chemistry. M.S. only.
Developmental Biology and Teratology.
Genetics.
Immunology.
Microbiology. M.S. only.
Microbiology and Molecular Virology.
Molecular Pharmacology and Structural Biology.
Nursing. M.S. only.
Occupational Therapy. M.S. only.
Pathology and Cell Biology.
Physical Therapy. M.S. only.
Physiology.

Jefferson Medical College

Founded 1824. Library: 155,000 volumes.
Annual tuition: $25,235; student fees $850. Total average figure for all other expenses: $9595. Enrollment: first-year class 220 (EDP 30); total full-time 500 (men 65%, women 35%). College

faculty: full-time 666, part-time 33. Degrees conferred: B.S.-M.D. (programs with University of Delaware and Penn State University), M.D., M.D.-M.B.A., M.D.-M.H.A., M.D.-Ph.D.

ADMISSION REQUIREMENTS. AMCAS report, transcripts indicating completion of at least three years of college work, letters of recommendation, MCAT required in support of application. Interview by invitation only. Has EDP; apply between June 15 and August 1. Accepts transfer and foreign applicants: foreign students must have four-year degree from U.S. institution. Apply to AMCAS after June 15, before November 15. Application fee $65. Phone: (215)955-6983; fax: (215)923-6939.

ADMISSION STANDARDS. Competitive. Accepts about 3–5% of total annual applicants. Approximately 40% are state residents.

FINANCIAL AID. Scholarships, loans. Apply to Office of Student Financial Aid after March 15, before April 1. Use FAFSA.

DEGREE REQUIREMENTS. For M.D.: satisfactory completion of four-year program. For Ph.D. requirements see Graduate College listing above.

FIELDS OF GRADUATE STUDY.
Biochemistry.
Cell Biology.
Genetics.
Immunology.
Microbiology.
Molecular Biology.
Pathology.
Pharmacology.
Physiology.

UNIVERSITY OF TOLEDO
Toledo, Ohio 43606-3398

Founded 1872, became a state university in 1967. Coed. State control. Quarter system. Special facilities: VAX-11/785, Humanities Institute, Polymer Institute, Center for International Studies, Center for Institutional Research and Services, Eitel Institute for Silicate Research, Ritter Astrophysical Research, Polymer Institute, Opinion Research Institute, Urban Affairs Center. Library: 1,900,000 volumes, 1,400,000 microforms, 5000 current periodicals, 32 PCs in all libraries.

Annual tuition: full-time resident $5330, nonresident $10,615; per credit, resident $148, nonresident $295. Off-campus housing only. Average monthly housing costs: $140–$260. Contact Coordinator of Commuter and Off-Campus Housing Services. Phone: (419)537-8521. On-campus day-care facilities available.

Graduate School

Graduate study since 1912. Enrollment: full-time 903, part-time 1822. Graduate faculty: full-time 470, part-time 50. Degrees conferred: M.A., M.B.A., M.Ed., M.M., M.S., Ed.S., Ed.D., Ph.D.

ADMISSION REQUIREMENTS. Three official transcripts, three letters of recommendation, GMAT/MAT/GRE Subject Tests required in support of School's application. TOEFL required for international applicants. Accepts transfer applicants. Graduates of unaccredited institutions not considered. Apply to Director of Admissions at least one month prior to registration. All requirements must be completed at least 2 weeks prior to registration. Rolling admissions process. Application fee $30. Phone: (419)537-2669.

ADMISSION STANDARDS. Selective. Usual minimum average: 2.7–3.0 (A = 4).

FINANCIAL AID. Annual awards from institutional funds: 7 scholarships, stipends, 24 internships, 525 teaching assistantships, 120 research assistantships, Federal W/S, loans. Approved for VA benefits. Apply by March 1 to Graduate School for assistantships; to Financial Aid for all other programs. Use FAFSA. Phone: (419)537-2056. About 25% of students receive aid other than loans from School and outside sources. No aid for part-time students.

DEGREE REQUIREMENTS. For master's: 45 quarter hours minimum, at least 36 in residence; thesis/comprehensive exam/one language for some departments. For Ed.D.: 135 quarter hours minimum beyond the bachelor's, at least three consecutive Summers in full-time residence; written comprehensive exam; knowledge of statistics; dissertation; final oral exam. For Ph.D.: 135 quarter hours minimum beyond the bachelor's, at least three quarters in full-time residence; reading knowledge of one foreign language for some departments; comprehensive exam; dissertation; final exam.

FIELDS OF STUDY.
Accounting.
Biology.
Chemical Engineering.
Chemistry.
Civil Engineering.
Economics.
Education.
Electrical Engineering.
Engineering Physics.
Engineering Science.
English.
Foreign Language. Includes French, German, Spanish.
Geography.
Geology.
History.
Industrial Engineering.
Liberal Studies.
Manufacturing Management.
Mathematics.
Mechanical Engineering.
Medicinal Chemistry.
Music. Includes education, performance.
Pharmaceutical Science.
Philosophy.
Physics and Astronomy.
Political Science.
Psychology.
Public Health.
Sociology.
Taxation.

College of Law (43606-3390)

Organized 1906. Semester system. Library: 285,000 volumes. Library has LEXIS, NEXIS, WESTLAW. Special facilities: Legal Institute of the Great Lakes.

Annual tuition: full-time resident $6325, nonresident $12,226; per credit resident $264, nonresident $509. No on-campus housing available. For off-campus housing contact either the Student Bar Association or the University's Off-Campus Living Office. Total average annual additional expense: $10,200.

Enrollment: first-year class 180 (day), 40 (evening); total 625 (men 62%, women 38%). Faculty: full-time 36, part-time 22. Degrees conferred: J.D., J.D.-M.B.A.

ADMISSION REQUIREMENTS. LSDAS Law School report, bachelor's degree, transcripts, LSAT, two letters of recommendation required in support of application. Campus visit encouraged. Evidence of proficiency in English required of foreign students. Interview not required. Accepts transfer applicants. Graduates of unaccredited colleges not considered. Apply to Office of Admissions by March 15 (full-time), May 15 (part-time). Fall admission only. Application fee $30. Phone: (419)537-4131.

ADMISSION STANDARDS. Accepts 45–50% of total annual applicants.

FINANCIAL AID. Scholarships, grants, assistantships, Federal W/S, loans. Apply to Office of Financial Aid by April 1. Use FAFSA. About 10% of students receive aid other than loans from College.

DEGREE REQUIREMENTS. For J.D.: successful completion of three-year program (day), four-year program (evening); 87 credit hour program.

TOURO COLLEGE
300 Nassau Road
Huntington, L.I., New York 11743

Jacob D. Fuchsberg Law Center

Established 1976. Semester system. Library: 325,000 volumes. Library has LEXIS, NEXIS, WESTLAW, DIALOG, AUTO-CITE, OCLC. Special facilities: Institute of Local and Suburban Law.
Annual tuition: full-time $15,940; part-time $12,740. No on-campus housing available. Total average annual additional expense: $8000–$10,000.
Enrollment: first-year class, full-time 170, part-time 89; total 875 (men 55%, women 45%). Faculty: full-time 36, part-time 9. Degrees conferred: J.D., J.D.-M.S. (Tax) with Long Island University, LL.M (for International attorneys only).

ADMISSION REQUIREMENTS. LSDAS Law School report, bachelor's degree, transcripts, LSAT, recommendations required in support of application. Accepts transfer applicants. Graduates of unaccredited colleges not considered. Apply to the Admissions Office by May 1. Rolling admissions process. Application fee $45. Phone: (516)421-2244, ext. 313.

ADMISSION STANDARDS. Admits about 40% of total annual applications.

FINANCIAL AID. Scholarships, grants, fellowships, Federal W/S, loans. Apply to Admissions Office by May 1, priority consideration March 1. Use FAFSA.

DEGREE REQUIREMENTS. For J.D.: satisfactory completion of 84 credit program. For LL.M.: at least 24 credits beyond the J.D., one year in full-time residence.

TOWSON STATE UNIVERSITY
Baltimore, Maryland 21204

Founded 1866. Coed. State control. Semester system. Special facilities: Center for Mathematics and Sciences Education, Center for Suburban and Regional Studies, Center for the Teaching and Research on Women, Center for the Teaching and Study of Writing. Library: 536,000 volumes, 400,000 microforms, 1900 current periodicals, 18 PCs.
Tuition: per credit, $159 resident, nonresident $290. Limited on-campus housing. Average academic year on-campus housing

costs: $2900–$5600; off-campus costs: $610–$750 per month. Contact the Director, Residence for both on- and off-campus housing information. Phone: (410)830-2516.

Graduate School

Graduate study since 1957. Enrollment: full-time 400, part-time 1400. Graduate faculty: full-time 30, part-time 60. Degrees conferred: M.A., M.S., M.Ed., M.F.A., M.M., M.A.T.

ADMISSION REQUIREMENTS. Transcripts required in support of application. GRE, interview required for some programs. TOEFL required for international applicants. Apply to the Graduate School; no specified closing date, some programs have deadlines. Rolling admission process. Application fee $25. Phone: (410)830-2501; fax: (410)830-3434.

ADMISSION STANDARDS. Selective. Usual minimum average: 2.75 (A = 4).

FINANCIAL AID. Annual awards from institutional funds: one hundred research assistantships, nine teaching assistantships, Federal W/S, loans. Approved for VA benefits. Apply to Dean of Graduate School for assistantships; to Financial Aid Office for all other programs. No specified closing date. Use FAFSA and University's FAF. Phone: (410)830-2098.

DEGREE REQUIREMENTS. For master's: 30–60 semester hours; thesis/nonthesis option; final written/oral exam.

FIELDS OF STUDY.
Art Education.
Biology.
Early Childhood Education.
Elementary Education.
Geography and Environmental Planning.
Health Science.
Human Resource Development.
Instructional Technology.
Liberal Studies.
Mass Communication.
Music Education.
Music Performance.
Occupational Therapy.
Professional Writing.
Psychology.
Reading.
Secondary Education.
Speech Language Pathology and Audiology.
Teaching.
Visual Arts.

TRINITY COLLEGE
Hartford, Connecticut 06106

Founded 1823. Coed. Private control. Semester system. Library: 900,000 volumes, 385,000 microforms.
Tuition: per credit $810. No on-campus housing available.

Graduate Program

Graduate study since 1988. Offered in evenings during academic year, and during Summer term. Graduate enrollment: part-time 200. Faculty: full-time 16, part-time 4. Degrees conferred: M.A.

ADMISSION REQUIREMENTS. Transcripts, letters of academic recommendation required in support of application. Accepts transfer applicants. Graduates of unaccredited institutions not considered. Apply to Office of Graduate Studies by April 1 (Fall),

November 1 (Spring). Phone: (860)297-2150; fax: (860)297-5362.

ADMISSION STANDARDS. Relatively open when provisional acceptees are included. Usual minimum average: 3.0 (A = 4).

FINANCIAL AID. Limited to five grants, loans. Apply to Office of Graduate Studies. Use FAFSA and College's FAF.

DEGREE REQUIREMENTS. For M.A.: ten courses, includes thesis or comprehensive exam.

FIELDS OF STUDY.
American Studies.
Economics.
English.
History.
Public Policy Studies.

TRINITY UNIVERSITY
San Antonio, Texas 78212-7200
http://www.trinity.edu

Founded 1869. Coed. Private control. Presbyterian affiliation. Semester system. Special facilities: working agreements with Southwest Research Institute, Southwest Foundation for Research and Education, United States Air Force School for Aerospace Medicine, University of Texas Health Science Center. Library: 793,000 volumes, 286,000 microforms, 2400 current periodicals.
Tuition: per credit $562.50. No housing for graduate students.

Graduate School

Graduate study since 1950. Enrollment: full-time 143, part-time 112. University faculty: full-time 15, part-time 9. Degrees conferred: M.A., M.A.T., M.Ed., M.S.

ADMISSION REQUIREMENTS. Transcripts, letters of recommendation, GRE/GMAT required in support of School's application. TOEFL required of international applicants. Accepts transfer applicants. Apply to Graduate Admissions Office at least one month prior to registration. Phone: (512)736-8201.

ADMISSION STANDARDS. Selective. Usual minimum average: 3.0 (A = 4); 600 TOEFL score for international applicants.

FINANCIAL AID. Annual awards from institutional funds: thirty-six departmental assistantships, Federal W/S, loans. Approved for VA benefits. Apply to department of choice for assistantships, to Financial Aid Office for all other programs. No specified closing date. Use FAFSA. Phone: (512)736-8315. About 20% of students receive aid other than loans from School and outside sources.

DEGREE REQUIREMENTS. For master's: 30-36 semester hours minimum, at least 80% in residence; thesis for some departments; nonthesis option includes research project/comprehensive exam/internship.

FIELDS OF STUDY.
Educational Administration.
Health Care Administration. Two-year program includes one-year residency; external degree (three-year program).
School Psychology.

Teaching.
Urban Administration. Two-year program; includes two-semester internship.

TROY STATE UNIVERSITY
Troy, Alabama 36082

Founded 1887. Located 55 miles SE of Montgomery. Coed. State control. Quarter system. Library: 245,000 volumes, 708,000 microforms, 1675 current periodicals.

Tuition: per quarter hour resident $57, nonresident per quarter hour $114. On-campus housing for 48 married students, 1500 single students. Average academic year housing costs: $3030. Contact Director, University Housing for both on- and off-campus housing information. Phone: (334)670-3346. Day care facilities available.

Graduate School

Graduate study since 1958. Enrollment: full-time 188, part-time 388. Graduate faculty: full-time 202, part-time 147. Degrees conferred: M.S., M.B.A., Ed.S.

ADMISSION REQUIREMENTS. Transcripts, GRE Subject Tests, GMAT/MAT/NTE required in support of School's application. TOEFL required for international applicants. Accepts transfer applicants. Graduates of unaccredited institutions not considered. Apply to Dean of Graduate School at least one month prior to registration. Rolling admissions process. Application fee $20. Phone: (334)670-3188; fax: (334)670-3702.

ADMISSION STANDARDS. Selective. Usual minimum average: 2.5, 3.0 for last two years (A = 4).

FINANCIAL AID. Two thousand and three hundred and fifty-nine scholarships, Federal W/S, loans. Approved for VA benefits. Apply to the Financial Aid Office; no specified closing date. Use FAFSA. Phone: (334)670-3186; fax: (334)670-3702.

DEGREE REQUIREMENTS. For M.S.: 45 quarter hours minimum, at least 36 in residence; thesis/nonthesis option; final written exam. For M.B.A.: 60 quarter hours. For Ed.S.: 50 quarter hours minimum beyond the master's.

FIELDS OF STUDY.
Business Administration.
Computer Science.
Counseling Education.
Criminal Justice.
Education. Includes early childhood, elementary, secondary, administration and supervision, special education (includes ED, MR, MLH).
Foundations of Education.
Human Resource Management.
International Relations.
Nursing.
Police Administration.
Public Administration.

TROY STATE UNIVERSITY AT DOTHAN
Dothan, Alabama 36304-0368

Established 1961. Coed. State control. Quarter system. Library: 80,000 volumes, 178,000 microforms, 697 current periodicals.

Tuition: per hour resident $61; nonresident $122. No on-campus housing available.

Graduate School

Enrollment: full- and part-time 659. Graduate faculty: full- and part-time 70. Degrees conferred: M.S., M.B.A., M.S.Ed., Ed.S.

ADMISSION REQUIREMENTS. Transcripts, GRE/GMAT/MAT/NTE required in support of School's application. Class B Alabama certification or equivalent required for some programs. Accepts transfer applicants. Graduates of unaccredited colleges not considered. Apply to Director of Admissions and Records at least one month prior to registration. Rolling admissions process. Application fee $15. Phone: (334)983-6556; fax: (334)983-6322.

ADMISSION STANDARDS. Selective. Usual minimum average: 2.5, 3.0 for last two years (A = 4).

FINANCIAL AID. Limited to loans.

DEGREE REQUIREMENTS. For M.S., M.S.Ed.: 45 quarter hours minimum, at least 36 in residence; thesis/nonthesis option; final written exam. For M.B.A.: 60 quarter hours, at least 45 in residence; final exam. For Ed.S.: 55 quarter hours minimum beyond the master's.

FIELDS OF STUDY.
Accounting. M.B.A., M.S.
Business Education. M.S.
Computer Information Systems. M.S.
Counseling and Psychology. M.S.
Counselor Education. M.S.
Educational Administration. M.S., M.S.Ed.
Elementary Education. M.S.
Executive M.B.A.
Finance. M.B.A.
History and Social Sciences. M.S.
Human Resource Management. M.S.
Management of Information Systems. M.B.A.
Pre-elementary Education. M.S.
School Administration. Ed.S.
School Counseling. M.S.Ed.
School Psychology. M.S.Ed.
Secondary Education. M.S.

TROY STATE UNIVERSITY IN MONTGOMERY
Montgomery, Alabama 36103-4419

Established 1990. Coed. State control. Quarter system. Library: 22,000 volumes, 1473 microforms, 337 current periodicals.
Tuition: per hour resident $58, nonresident $104. No on-campus housing available.

Graduate School

Enrollment: full-time 226, part-time 318. Graduate faculty: full-time 25, part-time 35. Degrees conferred: M.A., M.S., M.B.A., Ed.S.

ADMISSION REQUIREMENTS. Transcripts, GMAT/MAT/NTE required in support of School's application. Class B Alabama certification or equivalent required for some programs. Accepts transfer applicants. Graduates of unaccredited colleges not considered. Apply to Dean of Graduate Studies at least one

month prior to registration. Rolling admissions process. Application fee $20. Phone: (334)241-9580.

ADMISSION STANDARDS. Selective. Usual minimum average: 2.5, 3.0 for last two years (A = 4).

FINANCIAL AID. Limited to loans.

DEGREE REQUIREMENTS. For M.A., M.S.: 45 quarter hours minimum, at least 36 in residence; thesis/nonthesis option; final written exam. For M.B.A.: 60 quarter hours, at least 45 in residence; final exam. For Ed.S.: 55 quarter hours minimum beyond the master's.

FIELDS OF STUDY.
Adult Education. M.S.
Business Administration. M.B.A.
Computer and Information Systems. M.S.
Counseling and Human Development. M.S., Ed.S.
Educational Administration. Ed.S.
Elementary Education. M.S.
Teaching. M.A.

TRUMAN STATE UNIVERSITY
Kirksville, Missouri 63501-4221

Founded 1897. Formerly Northeast Missouri State University, name changed in 1996. Located 200 miles NW of St. Louis. Coed. State control. Semester system. Library: 661,000 volumes, 1,215,000 microforms, 3300 current periodicals.
Annual tuition: full-time, resident $3192, nonresident $5784; per credit, resident $133, nonresident $241. On-campus housing for 30 married students, 48 men, 48 women. Average academic year housing costs: $3624 (including board); off-campus housing $300 per month. Contact Housing Office for both on- and off-campus housing information. Phone: (816)785-4227.

Graduate Studies

Enrollment: full-time 159, part-time 47. Faculty: full- and part-time 135. Degrees conferred: M.A., M.S., M.Ac., M.A.E.

ADMISSION REQUIREMENTS. Transcripts, GRE/GMAT required in support of application. TOEFL required for international applicants. Accepts transfer applicants. Graduates of unaccredited institutions not considered. Apply by June 15 to Dean for Graduate Studies. Application fee $10. Phone: (916)785-4109; fax: (816)785-7460.

ADMISSION STANDARDS. Selective. Usual minimum average: 2.75 (A = 4).

FINANCIAL AID. Annual awards from institutional funds: twenty-two research assistantships, thirty-six teaching assistantships, Federal W/S, loans. Approved for VA benefits. Apply to the Dean for Graduate Studies; no specified closing date. Use FAFSA. Phone: (816)785-4130. About 13% of students receive aid other than loans from University and outside sources. Aid available for part-time students.

DEGREE REQUIREMENTS. For master's: 30–48 credits minimum, final oral/written comprehensive exam.

FIELDS OF STUDY.
Accountancy. GMAT for admission.
Biology. GRE for admission.
Communication Disorders. GRE for admission.
Comparative Literature. GRE for admission.
Counseling. GRE for admission.

Education. GRE for admission.
English. GRE for admission.
History. GRE for admission.
Mathematics. GRE for admission.
Music.

TUFTS UNIVERSITY

Medford, Massachusetts 02155
http://www.tufts.edu

Founded 1852. Located 5 miles NW of Boston. Coed. Private control. Semester system. Special facilities: Center for Applied Child Development, Electro-Optics Technology Center, Center for Environmental Management, Lincoln Filene Center for Science and Math Teaching, Science and Technology Center. Library: 802,000 volumes, 987,000 microforms, 4700 current periodicals.

Annual tuition: full-time (one-year master's and first year of doctoral program) $21,903; (two-year master's) $15,730, (School Psychology) $18,340; part-time, per course $2738. Limited on-campus housing for single students; none for married students. Average academic year housing costs: $800 per month. Contact Campus Housing Office for both on- and off-campus housing information. Phone: (617)627-3248. Day-care facilities available.

Graduate School of Arts and Science

http://www.tufts.edu/as/gsas/gsashome.hmtl

Graduate study since 1875. Enrollment: full- and part-time 1305 (men 43%, women 57%). University faculty teaching graduate courses: full-time 330, part. time 220. Degrees conferred: M.A., M.A.T., M.F.A., M.S., Ph.D.

ADMISSION REQUIREMENTS. Official transcripts, three letters of recommendation, GRE Subject Tests, personal statement required in support of School's application. TOEFL required for international applicants. Interview sometimes required. Apply to Director of Admission of Graduate School by February 15 (Fall); some departments have other deadlines. Application fee $50. Phone: (617)627-3106.

ADMISSION STANDARDS. Very selective for most departments. Usual minimum average: 3.0 (A = 4).

FINANCIAL AID. Annual awards from institutional funds: 225 scholarships, 160 teaching assistantships, 50 research assistantships, fellowships, Federal W/S, loans. Approved for VA benefits. Apply to the Dean by February 15. Use FAFSA. Phone: (617)627-3528. About 65% of students receive aid other than loans from School and outside sources.

DEGREE REQUIREMENTS. For master's: 8 courses minimum, at least two terms in residence; thesis/nonthesis option; reading knowledge of one foreign language for some majors; final oral exam. For Ph.D.: 30 courses minimum, at least 10 in residence; qualifying exam; reading knowledge of one or more foreign languages, depending upon department; qualifying exam; dissertation; final written/oral exam.

FIELDS OF STUDY.
Biology. M.S., Ph.D.
Chemical/Biochemical Engineering. M.S., Ph.D.
Chemistry. M.S., Ph.D.
Child Study. M.A., M.A.T., Ph.D.
Civil and Environmental Engineering. No language for M.S. M.S., Ph.D.
Classics. Includes Latin, Greek. M.A. only.

Computer Science. M.S.
Drama. Theater arts majors must have practical knowledge of stagecraft; Ph.D. is academic, does not include performance or technical practice.
Economics. M.A.
Education. Includes elementary, secondary, school psychology. M.A., M.A.T. only.
Electrical Engineering. M.S., Ph.D.
Engineering Management. M.S.
English. M.A., Ph.D.
Fine Arts. M.F.A.: thesis is creative project with written discussion. M.A., M.F.A.
French. M.A. only.
German. M.A. study offered at Medford and in Germany. M.A. only.
History. M.A. only.
Interdisciplinary Doctorate.
Mathematics. M.S., Ph.D.
Mechanical Engineering. M.S., Ph.D.
Music. Includes musicology, theory and composition. M.A. only.
Occupational Therapy. M.S., M.A.
Philosophy. M.A. only.
Physics. M.S., Ph.D.
School Psychology. M.S., Ph.D.
Urban and Environmental Policy. M.A., M.S.

The Fletcher School of Law and Diplomacy

http://www.tufts.edu/fletcher

Established 1933. Semester system.

Annual tuition: $18,620. Enrollment: full-time 350 (men 180, women 120), part-time 0. Faculty: full-time 28, part-time 20. Degrees conferred: M.A., M.A.L.D., Ph.D.; J.D.-M.A.L.D. in conjunction with Harvard Law School and U.C. Berkeley–Boalt Hall Law School, M.B.A.-M.A.L.D., Amos Tuck School of Business Administration, Dartmouth College, M.S.J.-M.A.L.D., Medill School of Journalism, Northwestern University.

ADMISSION REQUIREMENTS. Official transcripts, three letters of reference, GRE or GMAT required in support of School's application. Interview recommended. TOEFL required for international applicants. Apply to Director of Admissions of School after September 1, before January 15. Normally admits Fall only. Application fee $65. Phone: (617)627-3040; fax: (617)628-5508.

ADMISSION STANDARDS. Highly competitive. Usual minimum average: 3.0 (A = 4).

FINANCIAL AID. One hundred and twenty scholarships, twenty-five teaching fellowships, twenty-five research fellowships, Federal W/S, loans. Approved for VA benefits. Apply by January 15 to Director of Admissions of School. Use FAFSA and Fletcher's FAF. Phone: (617)627-3528. About 65% of students receive aid other than loans from School and outside sources.

DEGREE REQUIREMENTS. For M.A.: one year in residence including 8 semester courses; reading and oral competency in one foreign language; final oral exam and application limited to midcareer professionals only. For M.A.L.D.: two years in residence; 16 semester courses, thesis; oral competency in one language; final oral exam. For Ph.D.: two and a half years in residence including 20 semester courses; written and oral comprehensive exam; reading and oral competency in one language; dissertation; final oral exam.

FIELD OF STUDY.
International Affairs. Includes programs in international law and organization, diplomatic history and international political relations, international economic relations, political institutions and systems, international business management and finance.

School of Medicine

Established 1893. Located in Boston (02111). Library 110,000 volumes. Annual tuition $30,240, student fees $1839. On-campus housing available. Total average figure for all other expenses: $9248.

Enrollment: first-year class 160 (EDP 3); total 630 (men 54%, women 46%). Faculty: full-time 258, part-time 942. Degrees conferred: M.D., M.D.-M.P.H., M.D.-Ph.D.

ADMISSION REQUIREMENTS. AMCAS report, transcripts, recommendations, MCAT, required in suport of application. A final screening interview may be requested in some cases. Applicants must have completed at least three years of college study. Accepts transfer applicants. Has EDP; apply between June 15 and August 1. Apply to Director of Admissions after June 15, before November 1 (firm). Application fee $75. Phone: (617)636-6571.

ADMISSION STANDARDS. Very competitive. Accepts 3–5% of total annual applicants. Approximately 25% are state residents.

FINANCIAL AID. Limited number of scholarships, loans. Apply to the Committee on Financial Aid after acceptance, before May 1. Use FAFSA or GAPSFAS. About 33% of students receive some aid from School.

DEGREE REQUIREMENTS. For M.D.: satisfactory completion of four-year program.

FIELDS OF GRADUATE STUDY .
Biochemistry.
Cell Biology.
Genetics.
Immunology.
Microbiology.
Molecular Biology.
Neurosciences.
Pharmacology.
Physiology.
Public Health.

School of Dental Medicine

Established 1868 as Boston Dental College, incorporated into Tufts University in 1899. Located in Boston (02111).

Annual tuition: $26,585. Limited on-campus housing available. Average academic year housing costs: $11,500. Total average cost for all other first-year dental related expenses: $5220.

Enrollment: First-year class 131; total 480 (men 65%, women 35%); Postgraduates 60. Faculty: full-time 34, part-time 322. Degrees conferred: B.A.-D.M.D. (Adelphi University), D.M.D.

ADMISSION REQUIREMENTS. AADSAS report, transcripts, three letters of recommendations (one from a biology instructor, one from a chemistry instructor), DAT, interview required in support of School's application. Accepts transfer applicants. Apply to Admissions Office after July 1, before March 1. Application fee $45. Phone: (617)636-6639.

ADMISSION STANDARDS. Selective. Usual minimum average: 3.0 (A = 4). Accepts 25–30% of total annual applicants. Approximately 25% are state residents.

FINANCIAL AID. Scholarships, loans. Apply by May 1 to Admissions, Financial Aid and Housing Office after acceptance. Use FAFSA. About 80% of students receive some aid from School.

DEGREE REQUIREMENTS. For D.M.D.: satisfactory completion of forty-four-month program.

School of Veterinary Medicine

Located in North Grafton (01536).

Annual tuition: contract students $5496–12,496, resident non-contract $22,096; nonresident noncontract $24,496. Total average cost for all other expenses: $9550.

Enrollment: first-year class 75, total full-time 260 (men 50%, women 50%), postgraduates 40. Faculty: full-time 82, part-time 148. Degrees conferred: D.V.M., D.V.M.-M.P.H., D.V.M.-M.S., D.V.M.-Ph.D. The M.S. and Ph.D. are offered through the Graduate College.

ADMISSION REQUIREMENTS. Transcripts, GRE General Test, recommendations, personal essay, animal/veterinary experience required in support of application. Interviews by invitation only. Preference given to state residents. Accepts transfer applicants (apply by June 1 for following September). Graduates of unaccredited colleges not considered. Apply to the School after July 1, before November 1. Application fee $60. Phone: (508)839-7920; fax: (508)839-2953.

ADMISSION STANDARDS. Selective. Accepts 25–30% of qualified applicants.

FINANCIAL AID. Scholarships, assistantships, Federal W/S, loans available. Apply to Office of Financial Aid by March 1. Use FAFSA.

DEGREE REQUIREMENTS. For D.V.M.: satisfactory completion of four-year program. For M.P.H., M.S., Ph.D.: see Graduate College listing above.

FIELDS OF GRADUATE STUDY.
Animals and Public Policy (Fletcher School of Law & Diplomacy). M.P.H.
Applied Biotechnology (with Worcester Polytechnic Institute). M.S.
Biochemistry. Ph.D.
Cell Biology. Ph.D.
Fisheries Biology. M.S.
Immunology. Ph.D.
Livestock Development. M.S.
Microbiology. Ph.D.
Molecular Genetics. Ph.D.
Neurosciences. Ph.D.
Pharmacology. Ph.D.
Physiology. Ph.D.
Public Health. M.P.H.
Wildlife Medicine. M.S.
Note: All Ph.D. programs through Seckler School of Graduate Biomedical Sciences and the University of Massachusetts Medical Center.

TULANE UNIVERSITY
New Orleans, Louisiana 70118-5669
http://www.tulane.edu

Founded 1834. Coed. Private control. Semester system. Special facilities: Center for Archaeology, Roger Thayer Stone Center for Latin American Studies, Southeastern Architectural Archives, William Ranson Hogan Jazz Archives, Center for Research on Women, Delta Regional Primate Research Center, Lindy Boggs Center for Energy and Biotechnology, Murphy Institute of Political Economy, Middle American Research Institute, Tulane Research and Teaching Center, U.S.–Japan Cooperative Biomedical Research Laboratories. Library: 2,003,000 volumes, 2,300,000 microforms, 17,000 current periodicals.

Annual tuition: full-time $20,478, per credit $1200. Limited on-campus housing available. Average academic year housing costs: $6300 and up for married students, $6000 for single students. Apply to Housing Office. Phone: (504)865-5724.

Graduate School

Graduate study since 1883. Enrollment: full-time 1050, part-time 50. Graduate faculty: full-time 350. Degrees conferred: M.A., M S., M.Ed., M.A.T., M.F.A., M.L.A., Ph.D.

ADMISSION REQUIREMENTS. Official transcripts of all undergraduate and graduate work, three recommendation forms, statement of career objective, GRE required in support of application. GRE Subject for some departments. TSE (preferred) or TOEFL required for international applicants. Application deadlines: February 1 (Fall), December 1 (Spring), May 1 (Summer). Application fee $45. Phone: (504)865-5100.

FINANCIAL AID. Fellowships, teaching/research assistantships, scholarships, Federal W/S, loans. Approved for VA benefits. Apply by February 1 (Fall semester) to Office of Financial Aid. Use FAFSA. Phone: (504)865-5723.

DEGREE REQUIREMENTS. For M.A., M.S.: 24 semester hours plus thesis, 30 hours without thesis; reading knowledge of one foreign language for some programs; final written/oral exam. For M.F.A.: 30 hours minimum; creative project or recital; final essay. For M.Ed., M.A.T.: 36 hours minimum; no thesis or foreign language requirement. For Ph.D.: 48 hours minimum; reading knowledge of two foreign languages; preliminary or general exam; dissertation; final oral exam.

FIELDS OF STUDY.
Anatomy.
Anthropology.
Art.
Biochemistry.
Biomedical Engineering.
Biostatistics.
Business Administration.
Cell and Molecular Biology.
Chemical Engineering.
Chemistry.
Civic and Cultural Management.
Civil Engineering.
Classical Languages.
Computer Science.
Ecology, Evolution, and Organismal Biology.
Economics.
Education. Includes early childhood, art, administration, secondary.
Electrical Engineering.
English.
Epidemiology.
French and Italian.
Geology.
German and Slavic Languages.
History.
Human Genetics.
International Health and Development.
Latin American Studies.
Mathematics.
Mechanical Engineering.
Microbiology and Immunology.
Molecular and Cellular Biology.
Music.
Neuroscience.
Paleontology.
Parasitology.
Pharmacology.
Philosophy.
Physics.

Physiology.
Political Science.
Psychology.
Sociology.
Spanish and Portuguese.
Theater.

A. B. Freeman School of Business

http://freeman.sob.tulane.edu/freeman/freeman.html

Accredited by AACSB since 1916. Graduate study since 1940. Special facilities; Goldring Institute of International Business, Levy-Rosenblunt Institute for Entrepreneurship, Burkenroad Institute for the Study of Ethics and Leadership in Management, Computer Integrated Manufacturing Laboratory.

Annual tuition: $19,700; per credit $665. Graduate enrollment: full-time 223, part-time 161. Faculty: full-time 21, part-time 9. Degrees conferred: M.Acct., M.B.A., M.B.A.-I.D., M.B.A.-M.P.H., M.B.A.-M.A. (LAS). Ph.D. offered in conjunction with the Graduate School.

ADMISSION REQUIREMENTS. Official transcripts, two recommendations, GMAT, personal essay, resume of professional experience required in support of School's application. TOEFL required for international applicants. Evaluative interviews required for all applicants living in the U.S. or Canada. Must have baccalaureate degree from an accredited institution. Apply for Fall admission to Director of Admissions by May 1 (domestic), April 1 (international). Spring admission for part-time study only. Application fee $40 (domestic), $50 (international). Phone: (504)865-5410 or (800)223-5402; fax: (504)865-6770.

ADMISSION STANDARDS. Competitive. Usual minimum average 3.2 (A = 4).

FINANCIAL AID. One hundred fellowships, thirty research assistantships, forty administrative assistantships, forty teaching assistantships, Federal W/S, loans. Approved for VA benefits. Apply by April 1 to Office of Financial Aid. Phone: (504)865-5273; fax: (504)862-8750. FAFSA required for FW/S, loans. Phone fellowships are merit based and are awarded to approximately half of the entering class. Research/administrative/teaching assistantships are arranged through faculty and staff.

DEGREE REQUIREMENT S. For M.B.A.: 61 credit hours, 20 courses plus two focus modules; no language or thesis requirement. For M.Acct.: 36 credits minimum.

FIELD OF STUDY.

Business Administration. Areas of concentration in accounting and taxation, finance, marketing, decision, information and operations management, economic analysis, human resources management, management.
Note: International business electives and an innovative study-abroad/internship program are offered. The school has associations with the International Management Center in Hungary, Hautes Eludes Commerciales in France, Czech Management Center in the Czech Republic, Hong Kong University of Science and Technology in Hong Kong, Tsinghua University in the PRC, the Instituto Tecnologico Autonomo de Mexico in Mexico City, and the Institute Tecnologico y de Estudios Superiores de Monterrey in Mexico.

School of Social Work

Founded 1914. Graduate study only. Annual tuition: $13,608, per credit $399. Enrollment: full-time 230, part-time 18. Faculty: full-time 18, part-time 30; clinical instructors 100. Degrees conferred: M.S.W., D.S.W., M.S.W./M. P.H.

ADMISSION REQUIREMENTS. Official transcripts, two academic references, and one current or most recent work reference required in support of School's application. Interview sometimes required. TOEFL required for international applicants. Accepts transfer applicants. Graduates of unaccredited institutions not considered. Apply by April 30 (Fall full-time program), November 15 (Spring part-time program) to Assistant Dean for Admissions and Student Affairs. Application fee $25. Phone: (504)865-5314; fax: (504)865-8727.

ADMISSION STANDARDS. Competitive. Usual minimum average: 2.5 (A = 4).

FINANCIAL AID. 10 merit and need-based scholarships, fellowships, grants, teaching assistantship, Federal W/S, loans. Apply by April 30 to Office of Student Affairs of the School. Use FAFSA. Phone: (504)865-5723.

DEGREE REQUIREMENTS. For M.S.W.: 60 semester hours minimum, at least 30 in full-time residence; no language or thesis requirement. For D.S.W.: (General) 36 hours beyond the M.S.W., (Clinical) 45 hours beyond the M.S.W.; internship; teaching practicum; dissertation; written/oral exams. For M.S.W.-M.P.H.: M.S.W. awarded after four semesters, M.P.H. after fifth semester.

FIELDS OF STUDY.
Clinical Social Work.

School of Law

Established 1847. Semester system. Law library: 474,000 volumes. Library has LEXIS, NEXIS, WESTLAW, DIALOG, EELS, ORBIT, QUICKLAW, VU TEXT, DATATIMES. Special facilities: Tulane Tax Institute, Corporate Law Institute, Admiralty Law Institute.

Annual tuition: $20,540. On- and off-campus housing available. Total average annual additional expense: $10,120.

Enrollment: first-year class 333; total 1000 (men 57%, women 43%); no part-time students. Faculty: full-time 47, part-time 43. Degrees conferred: J.D., J.D.M.A.(Latin American Studies and International Relations), J.D.-M.B.A., J.D.M.H.A., J.D.-M.P.H., J.D.-M.S.P.A., LL.M. (Admiralty, Energy and Environment), M.C.L., M.C.L. (Europegn Legal Practice), S.J.D.

ADMISSION REQUIREMENTS. LSDAS Law School report, bachelor's degree, transcripts, LSAT, letters of recommendation required in support of application. Interview not required. Accepts transfer applicants. Graduates of unaccredited colleges not considered. Apply to Admissions Office after October 1, before May 1 (February 1 strongly recommended). Rolling admissions process. Application fee $45. Phone: (504)865-5930.

ADMISSION STANDARDS. Selective. Accepts about 25–30% of total annual applicants.

FINANCIAL AID. Scholarships, fellowships (advanced students only), Federal W/S, loans. Apply to Director of Financial Aid by February 15; preliminary Financial Aid form due with admissions application. Use FAFSA. About 40% of students receive aid other than loans from School.

DEGREE REQUIREMENTS. For J.D.: 6 semesters minimum, at least 2 in full-time residence; 88 semester credits. For LL.M., M.C.L.: 24 hours minimum beyond the J.D.; one year in full-time residence; thesis; final written exam. For S.J.D.: usually at least two years in full-time resident beyond the J.D.; dissertation; final written exam.

Note: Summer study abroad in England, Israel, The Netherlands, Canada, France, Italy, Germany, Greece.

School of Medicine (70112-2699)

Founded 1834. Annual tuition: $27,000, student fees $1060. On-campus housing for married and single students. Total average figure for all other expenses: $9535. Enrollment: first-year class 148 (EDP 20); total 598 (men 57%, women 43%). Degree conferred: M.D. The M.S., M.P.H., and Ph.D. are offered through other Graduate Schools.

ADMISSION REQUIREMENTS. AMCAS report, transcripts, recommendations, MCAT required in suport of application. Interview by invitation only. Applicants must have completed at least three years of college study. Accepts transfer applicants. Has EDP; apply between June 15 and August 1. Apply to Chair of the Committee on Admissions after June 15, before December 15. Application fee $65. Phone: (504)588-5187.

ADMISSION STANDARDS. Very competitive. Accepts 3–5% of total annual applicants. Approximately 15% are state residents.

FINANCIAL AID. Scholarships, loans. Apply to the Chair, Financial Aid Committee, by April 1. Use FAFSA. About 80% of students receive some aid from School.

DEGREE REQUIREMENTS. For M.D.: satisfacotry completion of four-year program. For M.S., M.P.H. and Ph.D., see Graduate School listing above.

FIELDS OF GRADUATE STUDY.
Anatomy.
Biochemistry.
Biomedical Engineering.
Cell Biology.
Genetics.
Microbiology and Immunology.
Molecular Biology.
Neuroscience.
Parasitology.
Pharmacology.
Physiology.

School of Public Health and Tropical Medicine (70112-2824)

Tuition: per credit hour $380. Enrollment. full-time 300, part-time 125 (men 65%, women 35%). Faculty: full-time 52, part-time 17. Degrees conferred: M.P.H., M.S.P.H., M.H.A., M.S.W.-M.P.H., M.A.-M.P.H., M.P.H.&T.M., D.P.H., Sc.D., M.D.-M.P.H., J.D.-M.P.H. The Ph.D. is offered through the Graduate School.

ADMISSION REQUIREMENTS. Transcripts, three recommendations, GRE required in support of School's application. TOEFL required for international applicants. Interview may be required. Accepts transfer applicants. Apply to the Office of Admissions and Students Affairs by April 1 (Fall) and November 1 (Spring). Admits both semesters. Application fee $40. Phone: (800)676-5398, (504)584-3547; fax: (504)584-1667.

ADMISSION STANDARDS. Very selective. Usual minimum average: 3.0 (A = 4).

FINANCIAL AID. Annual awards from institutional funds: thirty scholarships, five research fellowships, ten research assistantships, Federal W/S, loans. traineeships available to U.S. citizens. Approved for VA benefits. Apply, preferably by April 1, to Director of the School for scholarships, fellowships, assistantships; to Admission Office for all other programs. Use FAFSA. Phone: (504)588-5387. About 75% of students receive aid other than loans from School and outside sources.

DEGREE REQUIREMENTS. For M.P.H., M.S.P.H., M.H.A: 36 credit hours minimum, at least one year in residence. For M.P.H.&T.M.: essentially same as for M.P.H., except candidates must hold the M.D. or equivalent. For Dr.P.H., Sc.D.: at least one and up to three years in full-time residence, depending upon previous preparation and accomplishment; qualifying exam; dissertation; final oral exam.

FIELDS OF STUDY.
Applied Health Sciences.
Biostatistics.
Environmental Health Education.
Epidemiology.
Health Communication.
Health Systems Management.
International Health.
Maternal and Child Health.
Nutrition.
Parasitology.
Population Studies.
Tropical Medicine.

THE UNIVERSITY OF TULSA

Tulsa, Oklahoma 74104-3126

http://www.utulsa.edu

Founded 1894. Coed. Private control. Special facilities: Enterprise Development Center, Venture Capital Exchange, anthropological research sites. Library: approximately 778,000 volumes, 2,381,000 microforms, 7500 current periodicals; special authors collection, U.S. Civil War collection, and American Indian law collection.

Annual tuition: full-time $9140, per credit hour $480. On-campus housing for 632 women, 632 men; 200 married students. Average academic year housing cost: $4360 (including board). Contact Director of University Housing for both on- and off-campus housing information. Phone: (918)631-2378.

Graduate School

Established 1933. Enrollment: full-time 459, part-time 273 (men 55%, women 45%). Faculty: full-time 250. Degrees conferred: M.A., M.S., M.B.A., M.Acc., M.Tax., M.Eng., M.Engineering and Technology Management, M.S.M.S.E., M.S.Eng., M.M.E., M.M., M.T.A., M.F.A., M.N.A., Ph.D., M.N.A.-M.B.A., J.D.-M.S., J.D.-M.A., J.D.-M.B.A.

ADMISSION REQUIREMENTS. Official transcripts required in support of School's application. GRE/GMAT required for most departments. Evidence of English proficiency and TOEFL required for international students. Interview not required. Transfer students accepted. Graduates of unaccredited institutions not considered. Apply to Graduate School at least one month prior to enrollment. Application fee $30. Phone: (800)882-4723 or (918)631-2336; fax: (918)631-2073.

ADMISSIONS STANDARDS. Selective. Usual minimum average: 3.0 (A = 4).

FINANCIAL AID. Scholarships, 239 teaching assistantships, 160 research assistantships, Federal W/S, loans. Approved for VA benefits. Apply by February 1 for Fall term. Use either FAFSA. Phone: (918)631-2526; fax: (918)631-2073. About 63% of graduate students receive aid other than loans from both the University and outside sources.

DEGREE REQUIREMENTS. For master's: 30 semester hours minimum, at least 24 in residence; thesis/nonthesis option; final oral exam in some departments. For Ph.D.: 60 semester hours

minimum beyond the master's; one foreign language and/or computer language may be required; candidacy exam; qualifying exam; dissertation; comprehensive written/oral exam.

FIELDS OF STUDY.
Anthropology. M.A.
Art. M.F.A., M.T.A.
Biological Science. Includes environmental science, genetics, organismic biology. M.S., Ph.D.
Business Administration. GMAT for admission. M.B.A., M.Acc., M.Tax.
Chemical Engineering. M.S. in Engineering, M. of Engineering, Ph.D.
Clinical Psychology. M.A., Ph.D.
Computer Science. M.S., Ph.D.
Education. Includes elementary, secondary, gifted, reading, school counseling. M.A., M.S.M.S.E., M.T.A.
Electrical Engineering. M.S. in Engineering, M. of Engineering.
Engineering and Technology Management. In cooperation with College of Business Administration. M. of Engineering and Technology Management.
English Language and Literature. Includes rhetoric and writing, writing in the professions, and research in and analysis of literature. M.A., Ph.D.
Geosciences. Includes geochemistry, geology, and geophysics. M.S., Ph.D.
History. M.A.
Industrial/Organizational Psychology. M.A., Ph.D.
Mathematical Sciences. M.S.
Mechanical Engineering. M.S. in Engineering, M.Eng., Ph.D.
Music. Includes composition, applied music. M.M., M.M.E.
Nursing. M.N.A.
Petroleum Engineering. M.Eng., M.S. in Engineering, Ph.D.
Speech/Language Pathology. M.S.
Joint Programs. J.D.-M.A., J.D.-M.B.A., J.D.-M.S., J.D.-M.Acc., J.D.M.Tax., M.N.A.-M.B.A.; includes accounting, business administration, taxation, biological science, clinical psychology, industrial/organizational psychology, history, English language and literature.

College of Law

Semester system with 8-week Summer session. Full- and part-time study. Law library: 265,000 volumes. Library has LEXIS, NEXIS, WESTLAW, DIALOG. Special facilities: National Energy Law and Policy Institute.

Tuition: per credit $490. On- and off-campus housing available. Total average annual additional expense: on-campus $7710, off-campus $9050.

Enrollment: first-year class, full-time 155, part-time 70; total full- and part-time 635 (men 65%, women 35%). Faculty: full-time 37, part-time 23. Degrees conferred: J.D., J.D.-M.A.(History, Modern Letters, Industrial and Organizational Psychology), J.D.-M.S. (Anthropology, Biological Sciences, Geosciences), J.D.-M.Acc., J. D.-M.Tax.

ADMISSION REQUIREMENTS. LSDAS Law School report, Bachelor's degree, LSAT required in support of application. Interview not required. Accepts transfer applicants in good standing from accredited law schools. Graduates of unaccredited colleges not considered. Apply to Admissions Office after September 1, before January 15 (flexible). Application fee $30. Phone: (918)631-2709.

ADMISSION STANDARDS. Selective. Accepts about 30–35% of total annual applicants.

FINANCIAL AID. Scholarships mainly for advanced students, Federal W/S, loans. Apply to Office of Dean by February 1 (flexible). Use FAFSA. About 5% of students receive aid other than loans from College and outside sources.

DEGREE REQUIREMENTS. For J.D.: 88 credit hours minimum, at least the last 30 in residence. For master's degree: see Graduate School listing above.

TUSKEGEE UNIVERSITY
Tuskegee, Alabama 36088

Founded 1881. Located 38 miles E of Montgomery. Coed. Private and state-related control. Semester system. Special facilities: George Washington Carver Research Foundation. Library: 301,000 volumes, 269,000 microforms, 1020 current periodicals.

Annual tuition: full-time resident $8020. On-campus housing for 48 married students, 150 men, 150 women. Average academic year housing costs: $4000–$5200 for married students, $3750 (including board) for single students. Apply to Manager of Auxiliary Enterprises by May 1. Phone: (334)727-8915. Day care facilities available.

Graduate Programs

Graduate study since 1944. Enrollment: full-time 241, part-time 133. University faculty teaching graduate students: full-time 128, part-time 11. Degrees conferred: M.Ed., M.S., M.S.E.E., M.S.M.E., M.S.N.E.

ADMISSION REQUIREMENTS. Official transcripts, GRE General Test required in support of application. TOEFL required for international applicants. Interview not required. Accepts transfer applicants. Apply to Admissions Office by July 15 (Fall), November 15 (Spring), April 15 (Summer). Application fee $25, $35 for international applicants. Phone: (334)727-8500; fax: (334)727-8451.

ADMISSION STANDARDS. Selective. Usual minimum average: 2.7 (A = 4).

FINANCIAL AID. Annual awards from institutional funds: thirty-five research assistantships, thirty-seven teaching assistantships, ten graduate assistantships, Federal W/S, loans. Approved for VA benefits. Apply by April 15 to appropriate department chair for assistantships; to Financial Aid Office for all other programs. Use FAFSA. About 35% of students receive aid other than loans from University and outside sources. Aid available to part-time students.

DEGREE REQUIREMENTS. For master's: 30–36 semester hours; thesis/nonthesis option; final oral/written exam.

FIELDS OF STUDY.
Agricultural Economics.
Agricultural Sciences.
Agronomy and Soil Sciences.
Animal Science.
Biology.
Chemistry.
Education. Includes counselor, administration, elementary, science, secondary, vocational and technical.
Electrical Engineering.
Environmental Sciences.
Mechanical Engineering.
Nutrition.
Veterinary Science.

School of Veterinary medicine

Established 1945. Annual tuition: full-time $8580. Total average cost for all other expenses: $5000–$7000.

Enrollment: first-year class 60; total full-time 245 (men 45%, women 55%). Faculty: full-time 55. Degrees conferred: D.V.M., D.V.M.-M.S.

ADMISSION REQUIREMENTS. Transcripts, VCAT, recommendations, animal/veterinary experience required in support of application. Interview by invitation only. Applicants must have completed at least two years of college study. Preference given to state and SREB residents, Apply to Dean of School by April 30. Graduate study: Bachelor's degree, transcripts required in support of application. Apply to Dean of School after July 1, before January 7. Application fee $25. Phone: (205)727-8460.

ADMISSION STANDARDS. Accepts about 35% of total annual applicants, forty to forty-five "at-large" spaces available for non-residents.

FINANCIAL AID. For information and forms write to the University's Director of Financial Aid. Apply by April 15. Use FAFSA.

DEGREE REQUIREMENTS. For D.V.M.: satisfactory completion of four-year program. Students in combined programs take graduate course during summer only. For M.S. requirements: see Graduate School listing above.

FIELDS OF GRADUATE STUDY.
Anatomy and Histology.
Clinical Medicine.
Microbiology.
Pathology and Parasitology.
Physiology and Pharmacology.
Surgery.

UNION COLLEGE
Barbourville, Kentucky 40906-1499

Founded 1879. Located 100 miles S of Lexington. Coed. Private control. Methodist affiliation. Semester system. Library: 80,000 volumes.

Tuition: per hour $190. Limited on-campus housing for 30 married students, 50 men, 50 women. Average academic year housing costs: $3040 (including board) for single students. Contact Dean of Students. Phone: (606)546-1230.

Graduate School

Enrollment: full-time 12, part-time 400. Graduate faculty: full-time 22, part-time 14. Degree conferred: M.A. in Ed.

ADMISSION REQUIREMENTS. Two official transcripts, GRE/NTE, two letters of recommendation, teaching certificates required in support of School's application. TOEFL required for international applicants. Interview desirable. Accepts transfer applicants. Graduates of unaccredited institutions not considered. Apply to Dean of the Graduate School by August 15 (Fall). Application fee $15. Phone: (606)546-1210; fax: (606)546-1217.

ADMISSION STANDARDS. Selective. Usual minimum average: 2.5 (A = 4).

FINANCIAL AID. Limited to loans. Approved for VA benefits. Apply to Financial Aid Office. Use FAFSA. Phone: (606)546-1224; fax: (606)546-1217.

DEGREE REQUIREMENTS. For M.A. in Ed.: 30 semester hours minimum, at least 24 in residence and one semester or Summer session in full-time attendance; thesis optional for 6 hours; final written exam.

FIELDS OF STUDY.
Elementary Education. Includes kindergarten.
Elementary School Principal.

Pupil Personnel Services.
Reading Specialist.
Secondary Education. Includes English, social studies, health, science, secondary principalship.
Supervisor of Instruction K–12.

UNION COLLEGE
Schenectady, New York 12308-2311

Founded 1795. Coed. Private control. Trimester system. Library: 496,000 volumes, 586,000 microforms, 1950 current periodicals.

Tuition: per course $1300-$1555, varies by discipline. No on-campus housing available. Contact Housing Office for off-campus housing information. Phone: (518)388-6061. Day care facilities available near campus.

Graduate Studies

Graduate study since 1904. Enrollment: full-time 130, part-time 400. Faculty: full-time 10, part-time 34. Degrees conferred: M.A., M.A.T., M.S., M.B.A., M.S.T., Ph.D.

ADMISSION REQUIREMENTS. Official transcripts, three letters of recommendation required in support of application. Interview not required except for M.A.T./M.S.T. program. Accepts transfers with one or two courses (depending on program). GMAT scores required for admission to Graduate Management Institute. Apply to Graduate Studies Office by May 1, April 1 for M.A.T.; part-time applicants may apply throughout year. Part-time students may complete between one and three courses (depending on program) at Union before applying for degree status. Application fee $35. Phone: (518)388-6288.

ADMISSION STANDARDS. Selective. Usual minimum average: 3.0 (A = 4).

FINANCIAL AID. Twenty scholarships, twenty-eight fellowships and assistantships available for full-time students in the Graduate Management Institute, occasional assistantship available in engineering departments, loans. Use FAFSA and College's FAF. Phone: (518)388-6642; fax: (518)388-6686. No institutional aid for part-time students.

DEGREE REQUIREMENTS. For M.A., M.A.T., M.S., M.S.T.: 10 full courses (33 credits) required in most departments; thesis for some departments. For M.S. from Graduate Management Institute: 15 full courses; for M.B.A.: 18 full courses; thesis/final oral/written exam. For Ph.D.: 15 courses minimum, 1 year of residency; dissertation; final oral/written exam.

FIELDS OF STUDY.
Accounting. M.B.A.
Administrative and Engineering Systems. Ph.D. only.
Biology. M.S.
Business Administration. Includes health systems management, M.B.A. (Private Sector).
Computer Management Systems. M.S.
Computer Science. M.S.
Engineering. Includes electrical, mechanical.
Health Systems Administration.
Health Systems Management.
Industrial Administration.
Life Sciences and System.
Operations Research.
Science and Mathematics for Secondary School Teachers.
Secondary Education. M.A.T. only.

Albany Law School

Founded 1851. Located in Albany (12208-3494). Semester system. Law library: 450,000 volumes, 847,000 microforms, 7 computer workstations. Library has LEXIS, NEXIS, WESTLAW, DIALOG, VU TEST, WILSONLINE. Special facilities: Government Law Center.

Annual tuition: full-time $17,795, part-time $13,346.

Enrollment: first-year class 245; full-time 807 (men 53%, women 47%). Faculty: full-time 42, part-time 32. Degrees conferred: J.D., J.D.-M.B.A. (Union College, R.P.I., St. Rose college), J.D.-M.P.A. (SUNY at Albany).

ADMISSION REQUIREMENTS. LSDAS Law School report, Bachelor's degree, transcripts, LSAT (prior to March 15), two letters of recommendation required in support of application. Interview not required. Accepts transfer applicants. Graduates of unaccredited colleges not considered. Apply to School by March 15. Fall admission only. Application fee $50. Phone: (518)445-2326; fax: (518)445-2315.

ADMISSION STANDARDS. Selective. Accepts 50% of total applicants.

FINANCIAL AID. Scholarships, partial tuition waiver, assistantships, Federal W/S, loans. Apply to Financial Aid Director by April 15. Use FAFSA and institutional request for Financial Assistance form. About 85% of students receive aid other than loans from School.

DEGREE REQUIREMENTS. For J.D.: satisfactory completion of three-year program; 90 credits hour program.

THE UNION INSTITUTE
Cincinnati, Ohio 45206-1925
http://www.tui.edu

Founded 1964. Coed. Private control. Semester system. External, nonresidential, self-paced, interdisciplinary, independent study program. Library houses approximately 3500 of the Institute's doctoral dissertations only.

Tuition: per semester $3660. No on-campus housing available.

Graduate School

Graduate study since 1969. Enrollment: full-time 1200, part-time 0. Graduate faculty: full- and part-time 89. Degree conferred: Ph.D.

ADMISSION REQUIREMENTS. Master's degree, two official transcripts, three letters of recommendation, three detailed narrative essays (autobiography, statement of current interests, proposed program overview) required in support of School's application. Interview not required. Apply to the Dean at least two months prior to preferred date of enrollment. Application fee $50. Rolling admission process. Phone: (800)486-3116 or (513)861-6400; fax: (513)861-0779.

ADMISSION STANDARDS. Selective. No minimum GPA or test score required. Individualized admission process based on evidence of ability to self-direct, conceptualize define, and carry out a doctoral-level research program.

FINANCIAL AID. Limited to Federal W/S, loans. Apply to the Financial Aid Office; no specified closing date. Use FAFSA and Institutional FAF. Phone: (800)486-3116.

DEGREE REQUIREMENTS. For Ph.D.: at least six semesters (24 months) in continuous full-time enrollment; attendance at a ten-day entry colloquium and three five-day seminars; internship, dissertation.

FIELDS OF STUDY (PROGRAMS ARE INDIVIDUALLY DESIGNED).
Area/Ethnic Studies.
Business.
Communication.
Computer/Information Sciences.
Creative and Performing Arts.
Health Care.
Literature.
Philosophy/Religion.
Psychology.
Public Policy and Administration.
Science/Mathematics.
Social Sciences.
Sociology and Social Work.
Women's Studies.
Note: All fields of study are interdisciplinary, and degree programs are individually prepared for each learner.

UNITED STATES INTERNATIONAL UNIVERSITY

San Diego, California 92131-1799

Founded 1924. Private control. Quarter system. Multicampus institution; graduate study at San Diego, Kenya, Mexico campuses. Library: about 205,000 volumes, 209,000 microforms, 1200 current periodicals, 25 PCs.

Tuition: per unit $230–$325 depending on program. On-campus housing available. Average academic year housing costs: $5700 (private room), $4500 (double occupancy). Contact Director of Housing for both on- and off-campus housing information. Phone: (619)635-4592.

Graduate Schools

Enrollment: full-time 602, part-time 451 (men 30%, women 70%). University faculty teaching graduate students: full-time 56, part-time 64. Degrees conferred: M.A., M.B.A., M.I.B.A., D.B.A., Ed.D., Psy.D.

ADMISSION REQUIREMENTS. Official transcripts; references; GRE, MAT, or GMAT required in support of School's application. Interview not required. International applicants must also submit evidence of proficiency in English or TOEFL and a financial statement. Accepts transfer applicants. Graduates of unaccredited institutions not considered. Apply to Director of Admissions at least six weeks prior to registration. Application fee $25. Phone: (619)635-4772, ext. 980; fax: (619)635-4739.

ADMISSION STANDARDS. Selective. Usual minimum average: 3.0 master's; 3.2 doctorate (A = 4). TOEFL score of at least 500.

FINANCIAL AID. Scholarships, teaching fellowships, teaching assistantships, internships, Federal W/S, loans. Apply to individual schools for fellowships, assistantships; to Financial Aid Office for federal programs. Use FAFSA and institutional FAF. Phone: (619)635-4558.

DEGREE REQUIREMENTS. For master's: 45 quarter units minimum, at least 35 in residence; thesis; final written exam. For D.B.A., Ed.D., Psy.D.: at least 105 quarter units beyond the master's; dissertation; final oral exam.

FIELDS OF STUDY.

COLLEGE OF ARTS AND SCIENCES:
Clinical Psychology.
Counseling Psychology.
Educational Administration.
Industrial/Organizational Psychology.
International Relations. Includes development studies, international communication, peace and conflict studies, leadership studies.
Marriage and Family Therapy.
Multicultural Education.
Teaching English to Speakers of Other Languages.
Technology and Learning.

COLLEGE OF BUSINESS:
Business Administration.
International Business Administration.
Strategic Management.

THE UNIVERSITY OF THE ARTS

Philadelphia, Pennsylvania 19102-4944
http://www.libertynet.org/~uarts/

Founded 1876. Coed. Private control. Semester system. Special facilities: electronic media laboratory, video editing studios, Oxberry Animation Stand, analog and digital electronic music studios, music calligraphy laboratory, Borowsky Center for Publication Arts, laser scanner laboratory, industrial design computer-aided product design center. Merriam, Drake, and Black Box Theaters. Library: 100,992 bound volumes, 395 current periodicals, 11 PCs.

Annual tuition: full-time $13,850; per credit hour $700. No on-campus housing available. Contact the Director of Residential Life for off-campus housing information. Phone: (215)875-2205.

Graduate Program

Enrollment: full-time 90, part-time 32. University faculty teaching graduate students: full-time 15, part-time 12. Degrees conferred: M.A., M.F.A., M.A.T., M.I.D.

ADMISSION REQUIREMENTS. Official transcripts, audition, portfolio, interview required in support of application. TOEFL required for international applicants. Accepts transfer applicants in Music and Art Education. Apply to the Director of Admission at least two month prior to date of registration. Application fee $30, $50 for international applicants. Phone: (215)732-4832; fax: (215)875-5458.

ADMISSION STANDARDS. Selective. Usual minimum average: 3.0 (A = 4). Talent is usual basis for most admissions decisions.

FINANCIAL AID. Scholarships, assistantships, grants-in-aid, Federal W/S, loans. Approved for VA benefits. Apply with application for admission to Director of Admissions. Use FAFSA. Phone: (215)875-4858. About 24–36% of students receive aid other than loans from University and outside sources.

DEGREE REQUIREMENTS. For M.A.: 36 semester hours minimum, at least 24 in residence; thesis; creative project. For M.F.A.: 60 semester hours, all in residence; thesis; four years for completion required. For part-time M.F.A.: 60 semester hours over four six-week summer residencies; eight independent study projects; thesis/exhibition during fifth summer.

FIELDS OF STUDY.
Art Education.
Book Arts/Printmaking.
Ceramics.
Industrial Design.
Museum Education.
Museum Exhibition, Design Planning.
Music Education.
Painting.
Sculpture.
Visual Arts.

UTAH STATE UNIVERSITY

Logan, Utah 84322
http://sticky.usu.edu

Founded 1888. Located 80 miles N of Salt Lake City. Coed. State control. Quarter system. Library: 1,200,000 volumes, 2,300,000 microforms, 14,000 current periodicals.

Annual tuition: full-time, resident $2262, nonresident $6942, international students $6942. On-campus housing for 670 married students, 1058 men, 1002 women. Average academic year housing costs: $2752 (including board), $4980 for married students. Contact Director, Housing and Residential Life, for both on- and off-campus housing information. Phone: (801)797-3113. Day-care facilities available.

School of Graduate Studies

Graduate study since 1914. Enrollment: full-time 1617, part-time 679 (men 70%, women 30%). Faculty: full-time 574, part-time 106. Degrees conferred: M.A., M.Ac., M.A.I., M.B.A., M.C.E.D., M.E., M.Ed., M.E.S., M.F., M.F.A., M.L.A., M.M.T., M.S., M.S.S., Ed.S., C.E., E.E., Ed.D., Ph.D.

ADMISSION REQUIREMENTS. Two official transcripts from each postsecondary institution attended, three letters of recommendation, GRE/GMAT (Business) required in support of School's application. TOEFL required for international applicants. Accepts transfer applicants. Graduates of unaccredited colleges not considered. Apply to Graduate Office 60 days prior to registration for quarter desired. Application fee $30, $35 for international applicants. Phone: (801)797-1189; fax: (801)797-1192.

ADMISSION STANDARDS. Selective. Usual minimum average GPA: 3.0 (A = 4); admission test score in the 40th percentile of above.

FINANCIAL AID. Forty-two research fellowships, 240 teaching assistantships, scholarship tuition waivers and nonresident tuition waivers, Federal W/S, loans. Approved for VA benefits. Apply to appropriate department head for fellowships, assistantships; to Financial Aid Office for all other programs. Use FAFSA. Phone: (801)797-0173; fax: (801)797-0654.

DEGREE REQUIREMENTS. For master's: 45–51 quarter hours minimum, at least 36 in residence; reading knowledge of one foreign language for M.A.; thesis/final report in some departments; final exam. For M.F.A.: generally two-year program. For M.B.A.: one to two-year program, depending on background of candidate. For M.F. (for holders of Bachelor's in field other than forestry): 90 hours minimum. For Ed.S., C.E., E.E.: 45 quarter hours beyond the master's; project. For Ed.D.: 90 credits minimum beyond the master's, at least five quarters in residence; dissertation; comprehensive written exam; final oral exam. For Ph.D.: 90 credits minimum beyond the master's, at least four quarters in residence (three consecutive quarters); dissertation; preliminary exam; comprehensive written exam; final oral exam.

FIELDS OF STUDY.

COLLEGE OF AGRICULTURE:
Agricultural Economics. M.S.
Agricultural Systems Technology and Education. M.A., M.S.
Animal Science. M.A., M.S., Ph.D.
Animal Science and Molecular Biology. M.S., Ph.D.
Biometeorology. M.A., Ph.D.
Bioveterinary Science. M.A., M.S.
Community Economic Development. M.C.E.D.
Dairy Science. M.A., M.S.
Nutrition and Food Science. M.S., Ph.D.
Physical Ecology. M.S., Ph.D.
Plant Ecology. M.S., Ph.D.
Plant Science. M.A., M.S., Ph.D.
Plant Science and Molecular Biology. M.S., Ph.D.
Soil Science. M.S., Ph.D.
Toxicology. M.S., Ph.D.

COLLEGE OF BUSINESS:
Accounting. M.Ac.
Business Administration. M.B.A.
Business Information Systems and Education. M.S., Ed.D., Ph.D.
Economics. M.A., M.S., M.S.S., Ph.D.
Human Resource Management. M.S.S.

COLLEGE OF EDUCATION:
Communicative Disorders. M.A., M.Ed., M.S. Ed.S.
Education. Includes business, information systems and education, communicative disorders, elementary education, research and evaluation, educational audiology; Ed.D., Ph.D.
Elementary Education. M.A., M.Ed., M.S.
Health, Physical Education, and Recreation. M.S., M.Ed.
Instructional Technology. M.S., M.Ed., Ed.S.
Psychology. M.A., M.S., Ph.D.
Secondary Education. M.A., M.Ed., M.S., Ed.S.
Special Education. M.S., M.Ed., Ph.D.

COLLEGE OF ENGINEERING:
Biological and Agricultural Engineering. M.S., M.E., Ph.D.
Civil and Environmental Engineering. M.S., C.E., M.E., Ph.D.
Electrical Engineering. E.E., M.S., M. E., M. E. S., Ph.D.
Industrial Technology and Education. M.S.
Irrigation Engineering. M.S., Ph.D.
Mechanical Engineering. M.S., M.E., Ph.D.

COLLEGE OF FAMILY LIFE:
Family and Human Development. M.S.
Family and Life. Ph.D.
Human Environment. M.S.
Nutrition and Food Sciences. M.A., M.S., Ph.D.
Nutritional Food Sciences and Molecular Biology. M.S., Ph.D.

COLLEGE OF HUMANITIES, ARTS, AND SOCIAL SCIENCES:
American Studies. M.A., M.S.
Art. M.A., M.F.A.
Communication. M.A., M.S.
English. M.A., M.S.
History. M.A., M.S., M.S.S.
Landscape Architecture, Town and Regional Planning. M.S., M.L.A.
Political Science. M.A., M.S.
Social Sciences. M.S.S.
Sociology. M.A., M.S., M.S.S., Ph.D.
Theater Arts. M.A., M.F.A.

COLLEGE OF NATURAL RESOURCES:
Aquatic Ecology. M.S., Ph.D.
Fisheries and Wildlife. M.S., Ph.D.
Forest Ecology. M.S., Ph.D.
Forest Management. M.F.
Forestry. M.F., M.S., Ph.D.

Range Ecology. M.S., Ph.D.
Range Science. M.S., Ph.D.
Recreation Resource Management. M.S., Ph.D.
Watershed Science. M.S., Ph.D.
Wildlife Ecology. M.S., Ph.D.

COLLEGE OF SCIENCE:
Biochemistry. M.S., Ph.D.
Biochemistry and Molecular Biology. M.S., Ph.D.
Biology. M.S., Ph.D.
Biology and Molecular Biology. M.S, Ph.D.
Biology Ecology. M.S., Ph.D.
Chemistry. M.S., Ph.D.
Computer Science. M.S.
Geology. M.S.
Geology Ecology. M.S.
Mathematical Sciences. Ph.D.
Mathematics. M.S., M.Math.
Physics. M.S., Ph.D.
Statistics. M.S.
Toxicology. M.S., Ph.D.
Toxicology and Molecular Biology. M.S., Ph.D.

UNIVERSITY OF UTAH

Salt Lake City, Utah 84112
http.//www.utah.edu

Founded 1850. State control. Quarter system. Special facilities: Advanced Combustion Engineering Research Center, American West Center, Archaeological Center, Center of Architectural Studies, Center for Atmospheric and Remote Sounding Studies, Institute for Biomedical Engineering, Center for Controlled Chemical Delivery, Cosmic Ray Observatory, Center for Excellence in Nuclear Technology, Engineering and Research, Center for Health Care, Hinckley Institute of Politics, Intermountain Burn Center, Obert C. and Grace A. Tanner Humanities Center, Center for Human Toxicology, Garn Institute for Finance, Gerontology Center, Huntsman Cancer Institute, Jon A. Dixon Laser Institute, Middle East Center, Social Research Center, Utah Museum of Fine Arts, Utah Museum of Natural History. Library: 3,089,000 volumes, 3,126,000 microforms, 21,800 current periodicals, 186 PCs.

Annual tuition: full-time, resident $1893, nonresident $5726; part-time per quarter, resident $346, nonresident $1000. On-campus housing for 1092 married students, 102 men and 52 women. Average academic year housing costs: $1800 for single students, $2500 for married students. Contact Director of Residential Living for both on- and off-campus housing information. Phone: (801)581-8667. Day care facilities available.

Graduate School

Enrollment: full-time 3896, part-time 1251. Faculty: full- and part-time 1459. Degrees conferred: M.A., M.Arch., M.A.T., M.B.A., M.E., M.E.A., M.Ed., M.F.A., M.H.R.M., M.Mus., M.Pr.A., M.P.A., M.S., M.S.P.H., M.S.W., M.Phil., M.Stat., Ed.S., Ph.D., Ed.D., Pharm.D., D.S.W., E.E.

ADMISSION REQUIREMENTS. Official transcripts GRE/GMAT/MAT required in support of School's application. GRE Subject required for some programs. TOEFL required for international applicants. Interview may be required. Accepts transfer applicants. Graduates of unaccredited institutions not considered. Apply to the Director of Admissions at least 60 days prior to registration. Application fee $30, $50 for international applicants. Phone: (801)581-7642; fax: (801)585-3034.

ADMISSION STANDARDS. Selective to very competitive. Usual minimum average: 3.0 (A = 4).

FINANCIAL AID. Annual awards from institutional funds: several hundred teaching/research assistantships, teaching/research fellowships, tuition waivers, Federal W/S, loans. Approved for VA benefits. In addition, all departments have established teaching positions for graduate students with stipends. Apply by March 1 to Graduate Fellowship Office for fellowships, to appropriate department chair for assistantships; to Financial Aid Office for all other programs. Use FAFSA. Phone: (801)581-6211. About 20% of students receive aid other than loans from School and outside sources. Aid sometimes available for part-time students.

DEGREE REQUIREMENTS. For master's: 45 quarter hours minimum, at least 36 in residence; foreign language qualifying exam for M.A.; thesis; final oral/written exam. For E.E., Ed.S.: 45 quarter hours beyond master's. For Ph.D.: 81 quarter hours, one of the last two years must be spent in full-time resident study; foreign language requirements vary by department; preliminary exam; thesis; final oral exam. For Ed.D.: language requirements vary from department to department, some have none at all; other requirements essentially the same as for the Ph.D.

FIELDS OF STUDY.

GRADUATE SCHOOL OF BUSINESS:
Accounting. GMAT for admission; includes professional accounting; M.B.A., M.Pr.A., Ph.D.
Business Administration. GMAT for admission; M.B.A., Ph.D.
Finance. GMAT for admission. M.B.A., M.S., Ph.D.
Human Resource Management. GRE for admission. M.B.A., M.H.R.M., Ph.D.
Marketing. GMAT for admission. M.B.A., Ph.D.

GRADUATE SCHOOL OF EDUCATION:
Cultural Foundation. M.Ed., Ph.D.
Educational Administration. M.Ed., Ed.D., Ph.D.
Educational Psychology. M.A., M.Ed., M.S., M.Stat., Ph.D.
Educational Studies. M.A., M.Ed., M.S., Ph.D.
Elementary Education. M.Ed.
Secondary Education. M.Ed.
Special Education. M.Ed., M.S., Ph.D.

COLLEGE OF ENGINEERING:
Applied Mechanics. M.S.
Bioengineering. M.E., Ph.D.
Chemical Engineering. M.E., M.Phil., M.S., Ph.D.
Civil Engineering. M.E., M.S., Ph.D.
Computer Science. M.E., M.Phil., M.S., Ph.D.
Engineering Administration. M.E.A.
Fuels Engineering. M.E., M.S., Ph.D.
Materials Science and Engineering. Interdepartmental. M.E., M.S., Ph.D.
Mechanical Engineering. M.E., M.Phil., M.S., Ph.D.
Nuclear Engineering. M.E., M.S., Ph.D.

COLLEGE OF FINE ARTS:
Art Education. M.A.
Art History. M.A.
Ballet. M.A., M.F.A.
Ceramics. M.F.A.
Drawing. M.F.A.
Film. M.F.A.
Graphic Design. M.F.A.
Illustration. M.F.A.
Metal Sculpture. M.F.A.
Modern Dance. M.F.A., M.A.
Music. M.A., M.Mus., Ph.D.
Painting. M.F.A.
Photography. M.F.A.
Printmaking. M.F.A.

Sculpture. M.F.A.
Theater. M.F.A., Ph.D.

COLLEGE OF HEALTH:
Audiology. M.A., M.S.
Exercise and Sports Science. M.Phil., M.S., Ed.D., Ph.D.
Food and Nutrition. M.S.
Health Education. M.Phil, M.S., Ed.D., Ph.D.
Recreation and Leisure. M.Phil., M.S., Ed.D., Ph.D.
Speech-Language Pathology. M.A., M.S.

COLLEGE OF HUMANITIES:
Communication. M.A., M.Phil. M.S., Ph.D.
Comparative Literature. M.A., Ph.D.
Creative Writing. M.F.A.
English. M.A., Ph.D.
French. M.A.
German. M.A.
History. GRE for admission. M.A., M.S., Ph.D.
Language Pedagogy. Includes French, German, Arabic, Hebrew, Persian, Turkish, Spanish. M.A.T.
Linguistics. Interdepartmental; M.A.
Middle East Studies. M.A., Ph.D.
Philosophy. M.A., M.S., Ph.D.
Spanish. M.A., Ph.D.

COLLEGE OF MINES AND EARTH SCIENCES:
Geological Engineering. M.E., M.S., Ph.D.
Geology. M.S., Ph.D.
Geophysics. M.S., Ph.D.
Meterology. M.S., Ph.D.
Mining Engineering. M.E., M.S., Ph.D.

COLLEGE OF NURSING:
Nursing. M.S., Ph.D.
Note: Apply to Dean of College of Nursing and Graduate School; NLNGNE, GRE, MAT for admission.

COLLEGE OF PHARMACY:
Medical Chemistry. M.S., Ph.D.
Pharmaceutics and Pharmaceutical Chemistry. M.S., Ph.D.
Pharmacology and Toxicology. M.S., Ph.D.
Pharmacy. Pharm.D.
Pharmacy Practice. M.S.

COLLEGE OF SCIENCE:
Biological Chemistry. Ph.D.
Biology. M.Phil.
Cell Biology. Ph.D.
Chemical Physics. Ph.D.
Chemistry. Ph.D.
Ecology and Evolutionary Biology. M.S., Ph.D.
Genetics. M.S., Ph.D.
Mathematics. M.A., M.Phil., M.S., Ph.D.
Molecular Biology. Ph.D.
Physics. M.A., M.Phil., M.S., Ph.D.
Science. M.S.

COLLEGE OF SOCIAL AND BEHAVIORAL SCIENCE:
Anthropology. M.A., Ph.D.
Economics. M.A., M.Phil., M.S., M.Stat., Ph.D.
Geography. M.A., M.S., Ph.D.
Political Science. M.A., M.S., Ph.D.
Psychogy. GRE/MAT for admission; M.A., M.S., M.Stat., Ph.D.
Public Administration. M.P.A.
Sociology. M.A., M.S., Ph.D.

GRADUATE SCHOOL OF ARCHITECTURE:
Architecture. M.Arch., M.S.

GRADUATE SCHOOL OF SOCIAL WORK:
Social Work. M.S.W., D.S.W.

College of Law

Organized 1914. Semester system. Law library: 271,000 volumes. Library has LEXIS, NEXIS, WESTLAW, VU TEXT, PALER. Special facilities: Center for Environmental and Resource Law.

Annual tuition: full-time, resident $4400, nonresident $9850. On- and off-campus housing available for both married and single students.

Enrollment: first-year class 129; total full-time 346 (men 54%, women 46%). College faculty: full-time 29, part-time 36. Degrees conferred: J.D., J.D.-M.B.A., J.D.-M.P.A., LL.M. (Energy, Environmental Law, Natural Resources Law).

ADMISSION REQUIREMENTS. LSDAS Law School report, Bachelor's degree, transcripts, LSAT, personal statement required in support of application. Accepts transfer applicants. Apply to Office of Dean of College by January 15 (for priority consideration). Rolling admission process. Admits Fall only. Application fee $40. Phone: (801)581-7479.

ADMISSION STANDARDS. Selective. Accepts 30–35% of total annual applicants.

FINANCIAL AID. Scholarships, tuition waivers, fellowships, assistantships, Federal W/S, loans. Apply to Financial Aid Office of University by February 15 for priority consideration. Phone: (801)581-6211. Use FAFSA. About 10% of students receive aid other than loans from College.

DEGREE REQUIREMENTS. For J.D.: 88 semester hours minimum. For LL.M.: at least 24 credit hours beyond the J.D.; one year in full-time residence.
Note: Study-abroad program in London available.

College of Medicine (84132)

Founded 1905, expanded to a four-year program in 1943.

Annual tuition: resident and WICHE contact states $6125, nonresident $13,513, student fees $427. Total average figure for all other expenses: $7725.

Enrollment: first-year class 100 (EDP 9), total 408 (men 74%, women 26%). Faculty: full- and part-time 800. Degree conferred: M.D., M.D.-Ph.D. The M.S., Ph.D. are offered through the Graduate School.

ADMISSION REQUIREMENTS. AMCAS, transcripts, letters of recommendation, MCAT required in support of application. Interviews by invitation only. Applicants must have completed at least three years of college study. Preference given to state residents and residents of Idaho. Nonresidents must aply under EDP; apply between June 15 and August 1. Apply to Admissions Office after June 15, before October 15. Application fee: $40. Phone: (801)581-7498; fax: (801)585-3300.

ADMISSION STANDARDS. Selective. Accepts 30% of total annual applicants. Approximately 75% are state residents.

FINANCIAL AID. Limited scholarships, loans. Apply to Financial Aid Office by June 15. Few students receive aid other than loans.

DEGREE REQUIREMENTS. For. M.D.: satisfactory completion of four-year program. For M.S., Ph.D., see Graudate School listing above.

FIELDS OF GRADUATE STUDY.
Anatomy.
Biochemistry.

Cell Biology.
Community Medicine. M.S. only.
Family and Preventive Medicine.
Internal Medicine.
Medical Informatics.
Medical Laboratory Sciences.
Microbiology.
Molecular Biology.
Neurosciences.
Pathology.
Surgery.

VALDOSTA STATE COLLEGE
Valdosta, Georgia 31698

Founded 1906. Located 75 miles NE of Tallahassee, Florida. Coed. State control. Quarter system. Library: 375,000 volumes, 855,000 microforms, 2800 current periodicals, 20 PCs in all libraries.

Annual tuition: resident $2121, nonresident $5350; per credit resident $47, nonresident $132. On-campus housing for 601 graduate men, 1082 graduate women; 12 units for married students. Average academic year housing costs: $1440 board $1785 for graduate men and women; $3468 for married students. Contact Director, Housing and Residence Life for both on- and off-campus housing information. Phone: (912)333-5920.

Graduate Studies

Graduate study since 1968. Enrollment: full time 654, part time 791. College faculty teaching graduate students: full-time 177, part-time 30. Degrees conferred: M.A., M.S., M.B.A., M.Ed., M.P.A., Ed.S., Ed.D.

ADMISSION REQUIREMENTS. Two official transcripts, GRE (for education applicants; M.A., M.S. applicants), GRE or GMAT (for M.P.A. applicants), GMAT (for business) required in support of application. TOEFL required for international applicants. Accepts transfer applicants. Graduates of unaccredited institutions not considered. Apply to Director of Graduate Admissions by August 1 (Fall), November 14 (Winter), February 15 (Spring), May 1 (Summer). Application fee $10. Phone: (912)333-5694; fax: (912)245-3853.

ADMISSION STANDARDS. Relatively open. Usual minimum average: 2.5 (A = 4).

FINANCIAL AID. Two hundred scholarships, ninety-one research assistantships, two teaching assistantships, Federal W/S, grants, loans. Approved for VA benefits. Apply by June 1 to Director of Student Aid. Use FAFSA and institutional FAF. Phone: (912)333-5935; fax: (912)333-5430. About 20% of students receive aid other than loans from College and outside sources.

DEGREE REQUIREMENTS. For M.A.: 45 quarter hours minimum plus thesis, at least 20 in residence; or 50 quarter hours minimum without thesis, at least 25 in residence; reading knowledge of one foreign language; comprehensive/oral exam. For M.Ed.: 50 quarter hours minimum plus thesis, at least 25 in residence; or 60 quarter hours minimum without thesis, at least 30 in residence; comprehensive written/oral exam. For M.S.: 40 quarter hours minimum plus thesis, at least 20 in residence; or 55 quarter hours minimum without thesis, at least 30 in residence; comprehensive written/oral exam. For M.B.A., M.P.A.: 60 quarter hours minimum, at least 30 in residence; comprehensive written/oral exam. For Ed.S.: 45–60 quarter hours beyond the master's; thesis/nonthesis option. For. Ed.D.: at least 73 quarter hours beyond the master's; qualifying exam; candidacy; dissertation; final oral exam.

FIELDS OF STUDY.
Business Administration.
Education. Includes curriculum and instruction, educational leadership, elementary, guidance and counseling, health and physical, instructional technology, music, reading, special education, secondary, physical education, vocational education.
English.
History.
Music.
Nursing.
Psychology.
Psychology, Counseling and Guidance.
Public Administration.
Sociology. Includes anthropology, criminal justice, and social services.
Social Work.

VALPARAISO UNIVERSITY
Valparaiso, Indiana 46383-6493

Founded 1959. Coed. Private control. Lutheran affiliation. Semester system. Library: 529,000 volumes, 333,000 microforms, 3700 current periodicals, 106 PCs.

Tuition: per credit hour $195. No on-campus housing available. For off-campus information contact Director of Housing. Phone: (219)464-5413.

Graduate Studies

Graduate study since 1963. Classes offered in evening and Summer session. Enrollment: full-time 50, part-time 225, Faculty: full-time 35, part-time 5. Degrees conferred: M.A., M.A.A.B.S., M.A.L.S., M.Ed., M.M., M.S.N., M.S. Spec. Ed.

ADMISSION REQUIREMENTS. Official transcripts, interview required in support of application. GRE recommended; required for M.A., M.E., M.S. Spec. Ed. degree. TOEFL required for international applicants. Accepts transfer applicants. Graduates of unaccredited institutions not considered. Apply to Director of Graduate Studies one month prior to registration for Spring, Summer, and Fall. Application fee $30. Phone: (800)349-2611, (219)464-5313; fax: (219)464-5381.

ADMISSION STANDARDS. Selective. Usual minimum average: 3.0 (A = 4).

FINANCIAL AID. Limited to Federal W/S, loans. Approved for VA benefits. Apply to the Office of Financial Aid: no specified closing date. Use FAFSA. Phone: (800)348-2611.

DEGREE REQUIREMENTS. For M.A., M.Ed., M.M., M.S.: 30–36 semester hours minimum, at least 24 in residence; no thesis or language requirement. For M.A.A.B.S.: 42 semester hours minimum, at least 30 in residence; research project.

FIELDS OF STUDY.
Counseling and School Psychology. M.A.A.B.S. only.
Education. Includes elementary, reading, secondary, special education.
English. M.A.L.S. only.
History. M.B.L.S. only.
Human Behavior and Society. M.A.L.S.
Learning Disabilities. M.S. Spec. Ed.
Music. M.M., M.A.L.S.
Nursing. M.S.N.

School of Law

Founded 1879. Semester system. Library: 226,300 volumes. Library has LEXIS, NEXIS, WESTLAW, DIALOG, VUTEXT, QL system.

Annual tuition: full-time $14,360. Total average annual additional expense: $9200.

Enrollment: first-year class 148; total full-time 498 (men 55%, women 45%). Faculty: full-time 25. part-time 17. Degree conferred: J.D.

ADMISSION REQUIREMENTS. LSDAS Law School report, Bachelor's degree, transcripts, LSAT required in support of application. Recommendations strongly suggested. Interview sometimes required. Accepts transfer applicants. Graduates of unaccredited institutions not considered. Apply to Dean by April 15 for priority consideration. Application fee $30. Phone: (219)465-7829; outside Indiana, (800)262-0656; fax: (219)465-7872.

ADMISSION STANDARDS. Accepts 50% of total annual applicants.

FINANCIAL AID. Scholarships, grants, full and partial tuition waivers, assistantships, Federal W/S, loans. Apply to the Financial Aid Office, preferably before April 1. Use FAFSA. About 65% of students receive aid other than loans from School.

DEGREE REQUIREMENTS. For J.D. 90 hours, at least 30 in residence; final written exam.
Note: Summer study abroad in Cambridge (England).

VANDERBILT UNIVERSITY

Nashville, Tennessee 37240-1001

http://vanderbilt.edu

Founded 1873. Coed. Private control. Semester system. Special facilities: Center for Baudelaire Studies, Fine Arts Gallery, Robert Penn Warren Center for the Humanities, Free Electron Laser Center, John F. Kennedy Center for Research on Education and Human Development, Stevenson Center for Natural Sciences, Arthur J. Dyer Observatory, medical research facility, Vanderbilt Institute for Public Policy Studies. Library: 2,000,000 volumes. Joint libraries (with George Peabody and Scarritt colleges) 2,000,000 volumes, 1,800,000 microforms, 16,000 current periodicals.

Annual tuition: full-time $14,994–$18,864; per credit $786. On-campus housing for 140 married students, 110 men, 105 women. Annual housing costs: $4260 single students, $5022 married students. Contact Office of Residential Affairs for both on- and off-campus housing information. Phone: (615)322-2591. Day-care facilities available.

Graduate School

Graduate study since 1875. Enrollment: full-time 1547 (men 877, women 760), part-time 183. University faculty: full-time 1400. Degrees conferred: M.A., M.S., M.A.T., M.L.A.S., Ph.D.

ADMISSION REQUIREMENTS. Official transcripts, three letters of recommendation, GRE required in support of School's application. Interview not required. TOEFL required for international applicants. Accepts transfer applicants. Graduates of unaccredited institutions not considered. Apply to Dean of Graduate School by January 15 (Fall), November 1 (Spring), May 1 (Summer). Application fee $40. Phone: (615)343-272; fax: (615)322-3827.

ADMISSION STANDARDS. Competitive for some departments, selective for others. Usual minimum average: 3.0 (A = 4).

FINANCIAL AID. Seven hundred and fifty teaching fellowships, assistantships; five hundred research fellowships, assistantships; tuition waivers, Federal W/S, loans. Approved for VA benefits. Apply by January 15 to Graduate School for fellowships, assistantships; to Financial Aid Office for all other programs. Use FAFSA. About 70% of students receive aid other than loans from University, 75% from all sources. Aid sometimes available to part-time students.

DEGREE REQUIREMENTS. For M.A., M.S.: 24 semester hours minimum; reading knowledge of one foreign language in some programs; thesis/nonthesis option for some departments. For M.A.T: 30–36 semester hours minimum. For Ph.D.: 72 semester hours minimum beyond the Bachelor's degree, at least one year in residence; reading knowledge of one foreign language in some programs; qualifying exam; dissertation; final exam.

FIELDS OF STUDY.
Anthropology.
Art History. Master's only.
Astronomy. Master's only.
Biochemistry. Ph.D. only.
Biological Sciences. Master's only.
Biology.
Biomedical Engineering.
Cell Biology.
Cellular and Molecular Pathology.
Chemical Engineering.
Chemistry.
Civil Engineering.
Classics.
Comparative Literature.
Computer Science.
Economics.
Education and Human Development.
Electrical Engineering.
English.
Environmental and Water Resources Engineering.
French.
Geology. Master's only.
German.
Hearing and Speech Sciences.
History.
Latin American Studies.
Liberal Arts and Science. Master's only.
Management. Ph.D. only.
Materials Science and Engineering.
Mathematics.
Mechanical Engineering.
Microbiology and Immunology.
Molecular Biology.
Molecular Physiology and Biophysics. Ph.D. only.
Nursing Science. Ph.D. only.
Pharmacology. Ph.D.
Philosophy.
Physics.
Political Science.
Portuguese. Master's only.
Psychology. Includes clinical.
Psychology and Human Development.
Religion.
Sociology.
Spanish.
Spanish-Portuguese. Ph.D. only.

Divinity School

Graduate study since 1875. Coed. Semester system.

Tuition: per credit $561. On-campus housing available.

Enrollment: full- and part-time 190. School faculty teaching professions students: full-time 27, part-time 20. Degrees conferred: M.Div., M.T.S.

ADMISSION REQUIREMENTS. Official transcripts, letters of recommendation, essay required in support of School's application. TOEFL required for international applicants. Interview recommended. Accepts transfer applicants. Apply to Director of Admissions by August I (Fall), December 1 (Spring). Application fee $25. Phone: (615)343-3963; fax: (615)343-9957.

ADMISSION STANDARDS. Selective. Minimum acceptable GPA: 2.9 (A = 4). Minimum TOEFL score: 600.

FINANCIAL AID. Scholarships, tuition grants, Federal W/S, loans. Approved for VA benefits. Apply by February 1 to Director of Admissions. Use FAFSA plus CSS Profile.

DEGREE REQUIREMENTS. For M.Div.: 84 credits. For M.T.S.: 51 credits.

Peabody College of Vanderbilt University (37203)

http://peabody.vanderbilt.edu/GPC/peabody/html

Merged with Vanderbilt in 1979. Coed. Semester system. Tuition: per credit $591. Enrollment: full-time 430, part-time 220. College faculty: full-time 93, part-time 76. Degrees conferred: M.S., M.P.P., M.Ed., Ed.S., Ed.D., Ph.D.

ADMISSION REQUIREMENTS. Official transcripts, GRE/MAT required in support of College's application. TOEFL required for international applicants. Interviews required for doctoral programs. Apply to Director of Admissions by March 1 (Fall). Application fee $35. Phone: (615)322-8410; fax: (615)322-8401.

ADMISSION STANDARDS. Very selective for most departments. Usual minimum average: 3.0 for last two years (A = 4).

FINANCIAL AID. Annual awards from institutional funds: scholarships, research fellowships, research assistantships, teaching assistantships, internships, Federal W/S, loans. Approved for VA benefits. Apply by March 1 to department chair for fellowships, assistantships; to Director of Financial Aid for all other programs. Use FAFSA and CSS Profile. Phone: (615)322-3591. About 60% of students receive aid from College and outside sources.

DEGREE REQUIREMENTS. For master's: 30 credit hours minimum, at least 24 in residence; final oral/written exam. For Ed.S.: 30 credit hours minimum beyond the master's, at least one semester in residence; final project. For Ph.D.: 72 credit hours minimum beyond the bachelor's, at least two semesters in full-time residence; qualifying exam; dissertation; proficiency in appropriate research methods; final oral exam. For Ed.D.: essentially the same as Ph.D. except 84 credit hours minimum.

FIELDS OF STUDY.
Curriculum and Instruction.
Early Childhood Education.
Elementary Education.
English Education.
Health Promotion and Education.
Higher Education Administration.
Human Development.
Human Resource Development.
Language and Literacy.
Mathematics Education.
Policy Development and Program Evaluation.
Psychology and Human Development.
School Administration.
Science Education.
Secondary School Teaching.
Social Studies Education.
Special Education.

Owen Graduate School of Management

Annual tuition: $21,800.

Enrollment: full-time 485. School faculty teaching graduate students: full-time 45, part-time 7. Degrees conferred: M.B.A., Ph.D.

ADMISSION REQUIREMENTS. Official transcripts, letters of recommendation, GMAT required in support of School's application. TOEFL required for international applicants. Interview required. Graduates of unaccredited institutions not considered. Apply to Dean of School by March 15. Application fee $50. Phone: (615)322-6469 or (800)288-OWEN; fax: (615)343-0061.

ADMISSION STANDARDS. Selective. Usual minimum average: 3.2 (A = 4).

FINANCIAL AID. One hundred and nineteen scholarships, six research assistantships, Federal W/S, loans. Approved for VA benefits. Apply by March 1 to Dean of the School for assistantships; to Financial Aid Office for all other programs. Phone: (615)322-3591. Use FAFSA and CSS Profile.

DEGREE REQUIREMENTS. For M.B.A.: 60 semester hours minimum, at least 36 in residence. For Ph.D.: 72 semester hours beyond Bachelor's, at least 2 semesters in residence; comprehensive exam; dissertation; final oral exam.

FIELDS OF STUDY.
Accounting.
Finance.
Management.
Management Information System.
Marketing.
Operations Management.
Organizational Studies.
System.

School of Engineering

Graduate study since 1875. Coed. Semester system.

Annual tuition: full-time $14,148; per credit $841.

Enrollment: full-time 330, part-time 49. School faculty teaching graduate students: full-time 79, part-time 0. Degrees conferred: M.S., M.Eng., Ph.D.

ADMISSION REQUIREMENTS. Official transcripts, letters of recommendation, GRE required in support of application. TOEFL required for international applicants. Interview not required. Accepts transfer applicants. Graduates of unaccredited colleges not considered. Apply to Dean of Graduate School by January 15. Application fee $40. Phone: (615)322-2727; fax: (615)322-3827.

ADMISSION STANDARDS. Selective. Usual minimum average: 3.0 (A = 4).

FINANCIAL AID. Twenty-six fellowships, ninety-six research assistantships, eighty-nine teaching assistantships, Federal W/S, loans. Approved for VA benefits. Apply by January 15 to Dean of the School for fellowships, assistantships; to Financial Aid Office for all other programs. Phone: (615)322-3591; fax: (615)343-8512. Use FAFSA and CSS Profile.

DEGREE REQUIREMENTS. For M.S., M.E.: 30 semester hours minimum, at least 12 in residence; thesis/research project; final oral exam. For Ph.D.: 72 semester hours, at least 24 credits of course work beyond the master's, at least two semesters in residence; comprehensive exam; dissertation; final oral exam.

FIELDS OF STUDY.
Biomedical Engineering.
Chemical Engineering.
Civil Engineering.
Computer Science.
Electrical Engineering.
Environmental and Water Resources Engineering.
Materials Science.
Mechanical Engineering.

School of Law (37240)

Founded 1873. Semester system. Library: 276,000 volumes. Library has LEXIS, NEXIS, WESTLAW, INFOTRAC.
Annual tuition: $20,750. On-campus housing available. Apply to Office of Residential and Judicial Affairs. Total average annual additional expense: $11,125.
Enrollment: first-year class 187; total full-time 550 (men 65%, women 35%). Faculty: full-time 32, part-time 32. Degrees conferred: J.D., J.D.-M.A., J.D.-M.B.A., J.D.-M.Div., J.D.-M.P.P., J.D.-M.T.S., J.D.-Ph.D.

ADMISSION REQUIREMENTS. LSDAS Law School report, bachelor's degree, transcripts, three letters of recommendation, LSAT required in support of application. Accepts transfer applicants. Graduates of unaccredited institutions not considered. Apply to Director of Admissions by February 1 (flexible). Application fee $50. Phone: (615)322-6452.

ADMISSION STANDARDS. Selective. Accepts 10% of total annual applicants.

FINANCIAL AID. Scholarships, loans. Apply to the Office of Financial Aid by March 31 for priority consideration. Use FAFSA. About 30% of students receive aid other than loans from School.

DEGREE REQUIREMENTS. For J.D.: satisfactory completion of three-year program; 88 semester hour program. For master's degree: see Graduate School listing above.

School of Medicine (37232-0685)

Founded 1873. Library: 155,000 volumes; has MEDLINE. Annual tuition: $22,000, student fee $1225. On-campus housing available. Total average cost for all other expenses: $8145.
Enrollment: first-year class 104 (EDP 5); total 393 (men 64%, women 56%); postgraduates 60. Faculty: full-time 887, part-time 700. Degrees conferred: M.D., M.D.-Ph.D. (Medical Scientist Training Program).

ADMISSION REQUIREMENTS. AMCAS report, transcripts, recommendations, MCAT, bachelor's degree required in suport of application. Interview and final application by invitation only. Has EDP; apply between June 15 and August 1. Apply to AMCAS after June 15, before November 1. Application fee $50. Phone: (615)322-2145; fax: (615)343-8397.

ADMISSION STANDARDS. Very competitive. Accepts about 4–6% of total annual applicants. Approximately 14% are state residents.

FINANCIAL AID. Limited scholarships, fellowships, loans. MSTP funded by NIH. Apply to Assistant Dean, Student Services by June 1. Phone: (615)343-6310. Use FAFSA. About 5% of students receive aid other than loans from School.

DEGREE REQUIREMENTS. For M.D.: satisfactory completion of four-year program. For Ph.D.: see Graduate School listing above.

FIELDS OF GRADUATE STUDY.
Biochemistry.
Biomedical Engineering.
Cell Biology.
Immunology.
Microbiology.
Molecular Biology.
Pathology.
Pharmacology.
Physiology.

VASSAR COLLEGE
Box 77
Poughkeepsie, New York 12601
http://www.vassar.edu

Incorporated 1861. Located 75 miles N of New York City. Coed. Private control. Semester system, Library: 750,000 volumes, 634,000 microforms, 3600 current periodicals.
Total tuition for graduate degree: $20,940. On-campus housing available. Average academic year housing costs: $6310 (including board). Contact Director of Residential Life for both on- and off-campus housing information. Phone: (914)437-5862.

Graduate Program

Graduate study since 1869. Enrollment: full-time 1, part-time 7. College faculty: 221. Degrees conferred: M.A., M.S.

ADMISSION REQUIREMENTS. Official transcripts, letters of recommendation, interview required in support of application. GRE recommended. TOEFL required for international applicants. Accepts transfer applicants. Graduates of unaccredited institutions not considered. Apply to Chair of appropriate department by April 1. Application fee $60. Phone: (914)437-7300; fax: (914)437-7063.

ADMISSION STANDARDS. Very competitive.

FINANCIAL AID. Limited to Federal W/S, loans. Use FAFSA, institutional FAF, and CSS Profile. Phone: (914)437-5320; fax: (914)437-5325. About 60% of students receive aid other than loans from College and outside sources. Aid sometimes available for part-time students.

DEGREE REQUIREMENTS. For M.A., M.S.: 8 units minimum, at least 6 units in residence; thesis; reading kowledge of one foreign language; final oral/written exam may be required.

FIELDS OF STUDY.
Biology.
Chemistry.
Drama.

VERMONT LAW SCHOOL
Chelsea Street
South Royalton, Vermont 05506-0096

Established 1976. Semester system. Library: 191,000 volumes. Library has LEXIS, NEXIS, WESTLAW, DIALOG. Special facilities: Environmental Law Center.

Annual tuition: $17,250. Total average annual additional expense: $11,650.

Enrollment: first-year class 164; total 479 (men 54%, women 46%). Faculty: full-time 34, part-time 23. Degree conferred: J.D., J.D.-M.S.L., M.S.L. (Environmental Law).

ADMISSION REQUIREMENTS. LSDAS Law School report, bachelor's degree or equivalent, transcripts, LSAT, recommendations, personal statement required in support of application. Graduates of unaccredited colleges not considered. Apply to Admissions Office by February 15 for priority consideration. Application fee $50. Phone: in Vermont (802)763-8303; (800)227-1395.

ADMISSION STANDARDS. Selective. Accepts about 30–35% of total applications.

FINANCIAL AID. Scholarships, tuition grants, Federal W/S, loans. Apply to Admissions Office by February 15. Use FAFSA. About 85% of students receive some aid from School.

DEGREE REQUIREMENTS. For J.D.: satisfactory completion of 84 semester hour program. For M.S.L.: at least 24 credits beyond the J.D.: one year of full-time study.

UNIVERSITY OF VERMONT
Burlington, Vermont 05405-0160

Founded 1791 Located 95 miles S of Montreal, Canada. Coed. State control, Semester system. Library: 1,100,000 volumes, 851,000 microforms, 8,000 current periodicals, several PC laboratories.

Tuition: per credit, resident $281, nonresident $701. University on-campus housing for married students and for single students. Average academic year housing costs: $4600 for single students; $5200 for married students. Contact Director, Than Allen Housing for both on- and off-campus housing information. Phone: (802)655-0661.

Graduate College

Graduate study since 1807. Enrollment: full- and part-time 1200. Faculty: full- and part-time 500. Degrees conferred: M.A., M.S., M.Ed., M.A.T., M.S.T., M.B.A., M.Ext.Ed., M.P.A., M.S.W., Ed.D., Ph.D.

ADMISSION REQUIREMENTS. Official transcripts, GRE/MAT/GMAT (Business), letters of recommendation required in support of College's application. GRE Subject for some programs. Interview required for some departments. Accepts transfer applicants. Graduates of unaccredited institutions not considered. Apply to Graduate College Admissions Office by April 1 (Psychology, January 15, Civil and Environmental Engineering, Higher Education, and Student Affairs Administration, February 1, Botany, Field Naturalist, February 15; Cell and Molecular Biology, Communication Sciences, Counseling, Historic Preservation, Natural Resources, Natural Resource Planning, March 1), March 1 if applying for scholarships and fellowships. Application fee $25. Phone: (802)656-2699, (802)656-0519.

ADMISSION STANDARDS. Very competitive for most departments. Usual minimum average: 3.0 (A = 4).

FINANCIAL AID. Annual awards from institutional funds: 20 fellowships, 200 research assistantships, 250 administrative assistantships, 50 internships, Federal W/S, loans. Approved for VA benefits. Apply by March 1 to the appropriate Chair for fellowships, assistantships; to Office of Financial Aid for all other programs. Use FAFSA. Phone: (802)656-3156; fax: (802)656-4076. Limited aid available for part-time students.

DEGREE REQUIREMENTS. For M.A., M.S., M.S.T., M.Ed., M.Ext.Ed.: 30 semester hours minimum, at least 22 in residence; thesis/nonthesis option; final oral/written exam. For M.A.T.: same as above, except no thesis. For M.B.A.: 48 semester hours; may be reduced depending upon previous preparation; final written/oral exam. For Ph.D.: 75 semester hours minimum beyond the bachelor's, at least 51 in residence; reading knowledge of one foreign language for some programs; comprehensive exam; dissertation; final oral defense

FIELDS OF STUDY.
Agricultural Biochemistry.
Anatomy and Neurobiology. Ph.D. only.
Animal and Food Sciences.
Biochemistry.
Biology.
Biomedical Engineering. M.S. only.
Biostatistics. M.S. only.
Botany.
Business Administration. M.B.A. only.
Cell and Molecular Biology.
Chemistry. One language for M.S.
Civil and Environmental Engineering.
Communication Sciences. M.S. only.
Computer Science. M.S. only.
Counseling. M.S. only.
Education. M. Ed.; Ed.D. in Educational Administration only.
Electrical Engineering.
Engineering Physics. M.S. only.
English. One language for M.A.; M.A., M.A.T. only.
Extension Education. M.Ext.Ed. only.
Field Naturalist. M.S. only.
Forestry. M.S. only.
French. M.A., M.A.T. only.
Geography. M.A., M.A.T. only.
Geology. M.S., M.A.T., M.S.T. only.
German. M.A., M.A.T. only.
Greek and Latin. M.A., M.A.T. only.
Higher Education and Student Affairs Administration. M.Ed. only.
Historic Preservation. M.S. only.
History. Sample research paper for admission to M.A. M.A., M.A.T. only.
Materials Science.
Mathematical Sciences. Ph.D. only.
Mathematics. M.S. only.
Mechanical Engineering.
Medical Laboratory Science. M.S. only.
Microbiology and Molecular Genetics.
Molecular Physiology and Biophysics.
Natural Resource Planning. M.S. only.
Natural Resources. Ph.D. only.
Nursing. M.S. only.
Nutritional Sciences. M.S. only.
Pathology. M.S. only.
Pharmacology.
Physical Therapy. M.S. only.
Physics. M.S. only.
Plant and Soil Science.

Psychology.
Public Administration. M.P.A. only.
Social Work. M.S.W. only.
Statistics. M.S. only.
Water Resource. M.S. only.
Wildlife and Fisheries Biology. M.S. only.

College of Medicine

Established in 1822, seventh oldest medical school. Library: 100,000 volumes.

Annual tuition: Vermont resident $10,850, Maine resident $13,730, others $25,900, student fees $450. Limited housing available. Total average cost for all other expenses: $8010.

Enrollment: first-year class 93 (EDP 10); full-time 375 (men 50%, women 50%). Faculty: full- and part-time 1091. Degrees conferred: M.D., M.D.-Ph.D.

ADMISSION REQUIREMENTS. AMCAS report, transcripts, MCAT, letters of evaluation required in support of application. Interview by invitation only. Has EDP; apply between June 15 and August 1. Preference given to residents of Vermont, Maine. Apply to Associate Dean for Admission after June 15, before November 1. Application fee $65. Phone: (802)656-2154; fax: (802)656-8577.

ADMISSION STANDARDS. Competitive. Accepts about 4–6% of all annual applicants. Approximately 33% are state residents.

FINANCIAL AID. Limited to scholarships, Federal W/S, loans, grants. Apply to Office of Financial Aid; no specified closing date. Few students receive aid other than loans from College.

DEGREE REQUIREMENTS. For M.D.: satisfactory completion of four-year program.

FIELDS OF GRADUATE STUDY.
Anatomy.
Biochemistry.
Cell Biology.
Genetics.
Microbiology.
Molecular Biology.
Pathology.
Pharmacology.
Physiology.

VILLANOVA UNIVERSITY
Villanova, Pennsylvania 19085-1699

Founded 1843. Located 10 miles W of Philadelphia. Coed. Private control. Roman Catholic. Semester system. Library: 900,000 volumes, 1,694,000 microforms, 4000 current periodicals, 122 PCs in all libraries.

Tuition: per credit Arts $360, Science $410, Nursing $410, Engineering $550, M.B.A. $410. No on-campus housing available. For off-campus housing information, contact housing office. Phone: (610)519-7209.

Graduate School of Liberal Arts and Sciences

Graduate study since 1931. Enrollment: full-time 200, part-time 900 (men 50%, women 50%). Faculty: full-time 210, part-time 46. Degrees conferred: M.A., M.S., Ph.D.

ADMISSION REQUIREMENTS. Two official transcripts required in support of School's application. Recommendations, GRE Subject Tests, interview required for program. TOEFL required for international applicants. Deadlines vary by program.

Contact Dean's office for deadlines. Rolling admission process. Application fee $25. Phone: (610)519-7090; fax: (610)519-7096.

ADMISSION STANDARDS. Competitive for some departments, selective for others. Usual minimum average: 3.0 (A = 4).

FINANCIAL AID. From the University, graduate assistantships, scholarships, fellowships, research assistantships, Federal W/S, loans. Deadline for applications for University aid vary by program. Contact Graduate Dean for specific dates with reference to assistantships, fellowships. Contact Financial Aid Office for all other programs. Use FAFSA and Graduate School FAF. Phone: (610)519-4010.

DEGREE REQUIREMENTS. For master's: 30–48 semester hours; comprehensive exam; reading knowledge of one foreign language for some majors; thesis/nonthesis option; final oral/written exam. For Ph.D.: 60 semester hours beyond the master's, at least two semesters in residence; qualifying exam, candidacy; dissertation; final oral exam.

FIELDS OF STUDY.
Applied Statistics.
Biology.
Chemistry.
Classical Studies.
Community Counseling.
Computer Science.
Criminal Justice Administration.
Elementary Education.
Employee Counseling.
English.
Health Care Administration.
History.
Human Organization Science.
Human Resource Development.
Human Services Administration.
Liberal Studies.
Mathematics.
Philosophy.
Political Science.
Psychology.
Public Administration.
School Counseling.
School Leadership.
Secondary Education.
Spanish.
Teaching of Mathematics.
Theater.
Theology.

College of Commerce and Finance

Enrollment: full-time 60, part-time 826. Faculty: full-time 55, part-time 24. Degrees conferred: M.B.A., M.T.

ADMISSION REQUIREMENTS. Two official transcripts, GMAT required in support of College's application. TOEFL required for international applicants. Apply to Director of Admissions; no specified closing date. Phone: (610)519-4336; fax: (610)519-7864. Rolling admission process. Application fee $25.

ADMISSION STANDARDS. Selective. Usual minimum average: 3.0 (A = 4).

FINANCIAL AID. Limited to assistantships, loans. Approved for VA benefits. Apply to Dean for assistantships, to Financial Aid Office for all other programs. Use FAFSA and institutional FAF. Phone: (610)519-4010.

DEGREE REQUIREMENTS. For M.B.A.: 60 semester hours; comprehensive exam. For M.Tax.: 36 semester hours.

FIELDS OF STUDY.
Business Administration.
Taxation.

College of Engineering

Enrollment: full-time 72, part-time 371. Faculty: full-time 58, part-time 35. Degrees conferred: M.C.E., M.Ch.E., M.S.C.E., M.S.E.E., M.M.E., M.S.T.E.

ADMISSION REQUIREMENTS. Two official transcripts, GRE required in support of College's application. TOEFL required for international applicants. Accepts transfer applicants. Graduates of unaccredited institutions not considered. Apply to Director of Admissions; no specified closing date. Rolling admission process. Application fee $25. Phone: (610)519-4940; fax: (610)519-4941.

ADMISSION STANDARDS. Selective. Usual minimum average: 3.0 (A = 4).

FINANCIAL AID. Eight scholarships, thirteen research assistantships, twenty-six teaching assistantships, Federal W/S, loans. Approved for VA benefits. Apply to Dean for assistantships, to Financial Aid Office for all other programs. Use FAFSA and institutional FAF. Phone: (610)519-4010.

DEGREE REQUIREMENTS. For master's: 30–36 hours; thesis/nonthesis option; comprehensive exam.

FIELDS OF STUDY.
Chemical Engineering.
Civil Engineering.
Computer Engineering.
Electrical Engineering.
Mechanical Engineering.
Transportation Engineering.
Water Resources and Environmental Engineering.

College of Nursing

Enrollment: full-time 20, part-time 158. Faculty: full-time 19, part-time 4. Degrees conferred: M.S.N.

ADMISSION REQUIREMENTS. Two official transcripts, GRE required in support of College's application. TOEFL required for international applicants. Accepts transfer applicants. Graduates of unaccredited institutions not considered. Apply to Director of Admissions; no specified closing date. Rolling admission process. Application fee $25. Phone: (610)519-4934.

ADMISSION STANDARDS. Selective. Usual minimum average: 3.0 (A = 4).

FINANCIAL AID. Five assistantships, Federal W/S, loans. Approved for VA benefits. Apply to Dean for assistantships; to Financial Aid Office for all other programs. Use FAFSA and institutional FAF. Phone: (610)519-4010. Aid sometimes available for part-time students.

DEGREE REQUIREMENTS. For master's: 30–36 semester hours; thesis; comprehensive exam.

FIELDS OF STUDY.
Clinical Case Management.
Community Nurse Service Administration.
Nursing Administration.

Staff Administration.
Teaching of Nursing.

School of Law

Founded 1953. Semester system. Law library: 427,000 volumes. Library has LEXIS, NEXIS, WESTLAW, DIALOG: 58 computer work stations.

Annual tuition: $17,750. No on-campus housing available. Contact Student Bar Association in June for current off-campus housing lists. Total average cost for all other expenses: $12,300.

Enrollment: first-year class 240; total full-time 700 (men 52%, women 48%); no part-time, summer, or evening study. Faculty: full-time 41, part-time 34. Degrees conferred: J.D., J.D.-M.B.A., J.D.-Ph.D. (Law and Psychology), LL.M. (Taxation).

ADMISSION REQUIREMENTS. LSDAS Law School report, bachelor's degree, transcripts, LSAT required in support of application. Interview not required. Transfer applicants considered for admission into second-year class; one full year of superior work at another accredited/approved law school is required. Graduates of unaccredited colleges not considered. Apply to Admissions Office after September 1, before January 31. Application fee $75. Phone: (610)519-7010.

ADMISSION STANDARDS. Accepts 50% of total annual applicants.

FINANCIAL AID. Scholarships, special minority scholarships, partial tuition waivers, resident assistantships, counselorships, Federal W/S, loans. For resident assistantships, apply to Dean of Residence Life. Apply to Financial Aid Office by March 1 for all other programs. Use FAFSA. About 20% of students receive aid from Law School sources.

DEGREE REQUIREMENTS. For J.D.: satisfactory completion of three-year program; 87 semester hour program. For LL.M.: at least 24 credits beyond the J.D.: one year in full-time residence.

VIRGINIA COMMONWEALTH UNIVERSITY
Richmond, Virginia 23284-3051
http://www.vcu.edu

Founded 1838. University formed with merger of Richmond Professional Institute and Medical College of Virginia in 1968. Coed. State control. Semester system. Special facilities: Anderson Art Gallery, Burn Trauma Clinic, Institute of Biotechnology, Business Management Center, Massey Cancer Center, Sickle Cell Anemia Center, Institute of Statistics, Virginia Center on Aging, Virginia Center for Public/Private Initiative. Library: 925,000 volumes, 8300 current periodicals.

Annual tuition: resident $4742, nonresident $11,982; per credit resident $246, nonresident $648. Limited on-campus housing for graduate students. Average academic year housing costs: $2500–$4000. Contact Director of Residence Life for both on- and off-campus hosing information. Phone: (804)828-7666.

School of Graduate Studies
http://www.vcu.edu/gradweb/gradhome.html

Enrollment: full-time 2332, part-time 3349. Faculty: full-time 775. Degrees conferred: M.A., M.Acc., M.A.E., M.B.A., M.Ed., M.F.A., M.H.A., M.I.S., M.M., M.P.A., M.P.H., M.S., M.S.H.A., M.S.N.A., M.S.O.T., M.S.W., M.Tax., M.T., M.U.R.P., Ph.D., J.D.-M.H.A., J.D.-M.U.R.P., J.D.-M.S.W., M.S.-D.D.S., M.S.-M.D., Pharm.D., Ph.D., Ph.D.-D.D.S., Ph.D.-M.D., Ph.D.-Pharm.D., C.Acc., C.A.S., C.A.S.R., C.C.S., C.C.J.A., C.I.S., C.P.I., C.P.C., C.P.M., C.T.

ADMISSION REQUIREMENTS. Transcripts, GRE/GMAT/MAT required in support of School's application. TOEFL required for international applicants. Accepts transfer applicants. Graduates of unaccredited institutions not considered. Apply to Director of Admissions. Application deadlines vary by program. Application fee $25. Phone: (804)828-6916; fax: (804)828-6949.

ADMISSION STANDARDS. Selective. Minimum acceptable GPA: 2.7 (A = 4).

FINANCIAL AID. Annual awards from institutional funds: four hundred teaching/research assistantships, full and partial tuition waivers, Federal W/S, loans. Approved for VA benefits. Apply to appropriate department chair for assistantships, fellowships; to Financial Aid office for all other aid; no specified closing dates. Phone: (804)828-6669; fax: (804)828-6187. Use FAFSA. About 15% of students receive aid other than loans from University and outside sources. Aid sometimes available to part-time students.

DEGREE REQUIREMENTS. Vary by program.

FIELDS OF STUDY.
Accountancy. M.Acc.
Accounting. C.Acc.
Administration and Supervision. Includes administration, supervision, dual major in administration and supervision. M.Ed.
Adult Education. M.Ed.
Aging Studies. C.A.S.
Anatomy. M.S., Ph.D. Includes orthopedic physical therapy track in anatomy. Ph.D.
Applied Social Research.
Art Education. M.A.E.
Art History. Includes architectural history, historical studies, museum studies. M.A., Ph.D.
Biochemistry. Includes biotechnology track in biochemistry and microbiology/immunology. M.S., Ph.D.
Biology. Includes molecular, cellular, and environmental biology; systematics and evolution; physiology and developmental biology. M.S.
Biomedical Engineering. M.S., Ph.D.
Biostatistics. M.S., Ph.D.
Business. Includes decision sciences, economics, finance, information systems, marketing, human resources management, industrial relations, realestate and urban land development, risk management and insurance. M.S.
Business. Ph.D.
Business Administration. Generalist and specialization. M.B.A.
Chemistry. Includes analytical, inorganic, organic, physical, M.S., Ph.D.; chemical physics track, Ph.D.
Clinical Laboratory Sciences. Advanced master's, C.A.S., M.S.
Computer Science. C.C.S., M.S.
Counselor Education. Includes classroom guidance, guidance/counseling, dual certificate in counselor and visiting teacher. M.Ed.
Crafts. Includes ceramics, furniture design, glassworking, jewelry or metalworking, textiles. M.F.A.
Creative Writing. Includes fiction, poetry. M.F.A.
Criminal Justice Administration. Includes corrections, courts, forensic science, law enforcement. M.S., C.C.J.A.
Curriculum and Instruction. Includes instructional technology, library, media; early, middle, and secondary education. M.Ed.
Design. Interior environments, photography/film, visual communications. M.F.A.
Economics. Includes general, financial. M.A.
English. Includes literature, writing, and rhetoric. M.A.
Genetic Counseling. M.S.
Gerontology. M.S.
Health Administration. Executive master's, M.S.H.A.
Health Services Adminstration. Includes hospitals/hospital systems, long-term care facilities, health planning and policy/institutional settings, other areas by permission of graduate program director. M.H.A.

Health Services Organization and Research. Major: health services education, management/information systems, organizational behavior, organizational policy/planning; minor: administration problem areas, health specialty areas. Ph.D.
Human Genetics. M.S., Ph.D.
Information System. C.I.S.
Interdisciplinary Studies. M.I.S.
Mathematical Sciences. Includes applied mathematics, mathematics, operations research, statistics. M.S.
Mathematics Education. M.Ed.
Media Management, Professional Journalism and Advertising. M.S.
Medicinal Chemistry. Includes organic medicinal chemistry, pharmaceutical analysis, physical medicinal chemistry M.S., Ph.D.
Microbiology and Immunology. Includes biotechnology track in biochemistry and microbiology/immunology. M.S., Ph.D.
Music. Includes composition, education, performance, conducting. M.M.
Nurse Anesthesia. M.S.N.A. Also advanced M.S.N.A. for Certified Registered Nurse Anesthetist. M.S.
Nurse Practitioner. Includes adult health (generalist or immunocompetence), child health, family health, women's health. Post Master's Certificate.
Nursing. Includes adult health (generalist or immunocompetence), child health, family health, psychiatric mental health, women's health; M.S. Biology of health and illness, human health and illness, nursing systems; Ph.D.
Nursing Administration. Includes clinical nurse manager, nurse executive, psychiatric mental health, women's health. M.S.
Occupational Therapy Professional. M.S.O.T.
Occupational Therapy Post-Professional. Includes administration, education, gerontology, hand management, pediatrics, physical disabilities, psychosocial dysfunction. M.S.
Painting and Printmaking. M.F.A.
Pathology. M.S., Ph.D.
Patient Counseling.
Pharmacology and Toxicology. M.S., Ph.D.
Pharmacy and Pharmaceutics. Includes Pharmaceutical analysis pharmaceutics, pharmacy administration. M.S., Ph.D.
Physical Education. M.S.
Physical Therapy-Entry Level. (three-year professional) M.S.
Physical Therapy. Includes advanced, orthopedic physical therapy, kinesiology and biomechanics, hand management, neurology, physical therapy, pediatric physical therapy.
Physics. Includes instrumentation, physics of materials, physics research. M.S.
Physiology. M.S., Ph.D.
Planning Information Systems. C.P.I.
Pre-Medical Basic Sciences. Includes anatomy, biochemistry, human genetic, microbiology, pharmacology, physiology. Post Baccalaureate/Graduate Certificate.
Professional Counseling. C.P.C.
Psychology. Includes clinical, counseling, general. Ph.D.
Public Administration. M.P.A., Ph.D.
Public Health. M.P.H.
Public Management. C.P.M.
Reading. M. Ed.
Recreation, Parks, and Tourism. M.S.
Rehabilitation Counseling. Includes alcohol and drug education/rehabilitation program, community resources utilization and development, correctional rehabilitation, individual and group counseling, mental health rehabilitation, services to the severely physically handicapped, vocational evaluation and work adjustment. M.S.
Sculpture. M.F.A.
Social Work. Includes clinical social work practice, social work planning, and administrative practice. M.S.W., Ph.D.
Sociology. M.S.
Special Education. Includes early childhood, emotional disturbance, learning disabilities, mentally retardation, severe/profound disabilities. M. Ed.

Taxation. Includes academic, professional; M.Tax.

Teaching. Five-year program combining undergraduate and graduate study. Includes early education NK–4, middle education 4–8, secondary education 8–12, special education. M.T.

Theater. Acting, costume design, directing, stage design/technical theater, theater education. M.F.A.

Urban and Regional Planning. Includes economic development, environmental planning, housing and community planning, physical land use planning, planning management, urban revitalization. M.U.R.P.

Urban Revitalization Planning Information. C.U.R.P.

Urban Services. Includes adult education and training, educational leadership, instructional leadership, urban services leadership. Ph.D.

COOPERATIVE PROGRAMS:

Cooperative Program with Presbyterian School of Christian Education. First year spent at PSCE, second year at VCU in the M.S.W. program for' M.A. of Christian Education. An additional year at VCU leads to the' M.S.W. degree.

Counselor Education. D.Ed. awarded by the College of William & Mary.

Dual Degree Program in Law and Health Administration with the T. C. William Law School of the University of Richmond. J.D.-M.H.A.

Dual Degree Program in Law and Social Work with the T. C. Williams Law School of the University of Richmond. J.D.-M.S.W.

Dual Degree Program in Law and Urban Planning with the T. C. William Law School of the University of Richmond. J.D.-M.U.R.P.

Engineering Program. M.E. awarded by the University of Virginia and either M.S. or M.E. by Virginia Polytechnic Institute and State (University, Old Dominican University, George Mason University, and Mary/Washington College.

Interdisciplinary Studies with Virginia State University. M.I.S.

Medical College of Virginia—Professional Programs (23248-0565)

Medical College found 1838. Merged with Richmond Professional Institute in 1968 to form Virginia Commonwealth University. Medical library: 304,000 volumes. On-campus housing available.

School of Medicine—Graduate Study

Graduate study since 1934. Annual tuition/fees: full-time, resident $6096, nonresident $15,680; per credit resident $212, nonresident $614.

Enrollment: full-time 290, part-time 30. Graduate faculty: full-time 190, part-time 0. Degrees conferred: M.S., Ph.D., M.D.-Ph.D., specialized master's, certificates.

ADMISSION REQUIREMENTS. Transcripts, three letters of recommendation, interview (for most departments), GRE Subject Tests required in support of application. TOEFL required of all international applicants. Accepts transfer applicants. Graduates of unaccredited institutions not considered. Apply to School of Graduate Studies by April 1 (Fall). Admits Fall only. Application fee $25. Phone: (804)828-6916; fax: (804)828-6949.

ADMISSION STANDARDS. Competitive for most departments. Usual minimum average: 2.75 (A = 4).

FINANCIAL AID. Scholarships, twenty-one NIH traineeships, twelve fellowships, fifty-eight research assistantships, ninety-five teaching assistantships, Federal W/S, loans. Approved for VA benefits. Apply to Office of Dean for assistantships, fellowships, to Financial Aid Office for all other programs. No specified closing date. Phone: (804)828-0523; fax: (804)828-2703.

About 75% of students receive aid other than loans from School and outside sources.

DEGREE REQUIREMENTS. For master's: one year minimum in residence; thesis; final exam. For Ph.D.: two years in residence beyond the master's; comprehensive written; advancement to candidacy; dissertation; final oral exam.

FIELDS OF STUDY.

Anatomy.

Biochemistry and Molecular Biophysics.

Biomedical Engineering.

Biostatistics.

Genetic Counseling. M.S.G.C.

Human Genetics.

Immunology.

Medicinal Chemistry.

Microbiology and Immunology.

Molecular Biology and Genetics.

Neuroscience.

Pathology.

Pharmaceutical Chemistry.

Pharmacology and Toxicology.

Pharmacy and Pharmaceuticals.

Physiology.

Public Health. M.P.H.

Structural Biology.

School of Medicine (23298-0565)

Founded 1838. Library: 600,000 volumes. Annual tuition: resident $9,457, nonresident $23,317, student fees $868. Total average cost for all other expenses: $6000. Enrollment: first-year class 174 (EDP 34); total 670 (men 61%, women 39%). School faculty: full-time 596, part-time and volunteers 1350. Degrees conferred: M.D., M.D.-Ph.D.

ADMISSION REQUIREMENTS. AMCAS report, transcripts, MCAT, recommendations, interview required in support of application. Applicants must have completed at least 90 hours of college study. Interview by invitation only. Preference given to state residents. Accepts transfer applicants. Has EDP; apply between June 15 and August 1. Apply to AMCAS after June 15, before November 15. Application fee $75. Phone: (804)786-9630; fax: (804)371-7628.

ADMISSION STANDARDS. Competitive. Accepts 5–8% of total annual applicants. Approximately 70% are state residents.

FINANCIAL AID. Scholarships, fellowships, loans, Federal W/S. Apply to Financial Aid Office of the School for scholarships, to Dean of the School for fellowships by September 1. Use FAFSA. About 15% of students receive aid other than loans from school.

DEGREE REQUIREMENTS. For M.D.: satisfactory completion of four-year program, at least final two years in residence. See Graduate Division entry for Ph.D. requirements.

School of Dentistry (23298)

Established 1893. Located at the Health Sciences complex. State supported.

Annual tuition: resident $8698, nonresident $20,636. Total average cost for all other first-year expenses: $3490. On-campus housing for married and single students. Average academic year housing costs: $12,000. Phone: (804)282-7666.

Enrollment: first-year class 80, total 314 (men 65%, women 35%); postgraduates 38. School faculty: full-time 74, part-time 111. Degrees conferred: D.D.S., D.D.S.-M.S., D.D.S.-Ph.D.

ADMISSION REQUIREMENTS. AADSAS report, transcripts, DAT (no later than October), recommendations, interview required in support of School's application. Applicants must have completed at least 90 semester hours of college study, School prefers 120 semester hour applicants. Interview by invitation only. Accepts transfer applicants. Preference given to state residents. Apply to Director of Admissions after June 1, before February 15. Application fee $35. Phone: (804)828-9196.

ADMISSION STANDARDS. Selective. Accepts about 25-30% of total annual applicants. Approximately 85% are state residents.

FINANCIAL AID. Limited. Apply to Financial Aid officer of School; no specified closing date. Use FAFSA. Phone: (804)828-9196.

DEGREE REQUIREMENTS. For D.D.S.: satisfactory completion of four-year program, least two years in residence. For D.D.S.-M.S.: satisfactory completion of four to five year program. For D.D.S.-Ph.D.: satisfactory completion of six to seven year program. Offered jointly with School of Graduate Studies.

FIELDS OF GRADUATE STUDY.
Dental Anesthesia.
Endodontics.
Fixed and Maxillofacial Prosthodontics
Oral Pathology.
Oral Surgery.
Orthodontics.
Pediatric Dentistry.
Periodontics.
Prosthodontics.

School of Nursing

Master's study since 1968; doctoral study since 1986. Annual tuition: full-time resident $2296, nonresident 5810; per credit resident $206, nonresident $596. Enrollment: full-time 84, part-time 81. Graduate faculty: full-time 16, part-time 4. Degrees conferred: M.S., Ph.D.

ADMISSION REQUIREMENTS. Official transcripts, GRE, current nursing license, B.S. in nursing from an NLN-accredited school or a baccalaureate, three references required in support of School's application. TOEFL required for international applicants. Accepts transfer applicants. Graduates of unaccredited institutions not considered. Apply to School of Graduate Studies; no specified closing date. Application fee $25. Phone: (804)282-5171; fax: (804)828-7743.

ADMISSION STANDARDS. Competitive. Usual minimum average: 3.0 (A = 4).

FINANCIAL AID. Annual awards from institutional funds. Scholarships, grants, teaching assistantships, Federal W/S, loans. Apply by May 1 to the Office of Enrollment Services. Phone: (804)828-5171. Use FAFSA and institutional FAF. About 68% of students receive aid other than loans from both School and outside sources.

DEGREE REQUIREMENTS. For M.S.: 36–48 semester credits minimum (up to 12 approved credits may be transferred), qualifying exam; thesis option. For Ph.D.: 60 credits minimum (up to 15 approved credits may be transferred); qualifying exam; dissertation; oral exam.

FIELDS OF STUDY.
Adult Health Generalist. M.S.
Adult Health Immunocompetence. M.S.
Adult Nurse Practitioner. Post master's certificate.
Biology of Health and Illness. Ph.D.
Child Health. M.S.
Family Health. M.S.

Family Nurse Practitioner. Post master's certificate.
Human Health and Illness.
Nursing Systems. Ph.D.
Nursing Systems—Clinical Nurse Manager. M.S.
Nursing Systems—Nurse Executive. M.S.
Pediatric Nurse Practitioner. Post master's certificate.
Psychiatric Mental Health. M.S.
Women's Health.
Women's Health Nurse Practitioner. Post master's certificate.

VIRGINIA POLYTECHNIC INSTITUTE AND STATE UNIVERSITY
Blacksburg, Virginia 24061-0202
http://milieu.vt.edu

Founded 1872. Located 40 miles W of Roanoke. Coed. State control. Semester system. Library: 1,545,000 volumes, 3,900,000 microforms, 17,200 current periodicals.

Annual tuition: full-time, resident $4757, nonresident $6986; part-time, per semester minimum resident $755, nonresident $1127. Limited on-campus housing. Average academic year housing costs: $1024 (room only) single students. Contact Manager, Campus Housing, for both on- and off-campus housing information. Phone: (540)231-6204.

Graduate School
http://milieu.grad.vt.edu/rgs.html

Enrollment: full-time 4000, part-time 1800 (men 70%, women 30%). Faculty: full-time 1500. Degrees conferred: M.A., M.Acc., M.B.A., M.F, M.F.A., M.A.Ed., M.S.Ed., M.Arch., M.S., M.Engr., M.P.A., M.I.S., M.L.A., M.U.A., M.U.R.P., C.A.G.S., Ed.D., Ph.D.

ADMISSION REQUIREMENTS. Official transcripts, three letters of recommendation required in support of application. GRE/GMAT, interview required for some departments. GRE/Subject Tests strongly recommended. TOEFL and GRE required for international applicants. Accepts transfer applicants. Graduates of unaccredited colleges not considered. Apply to School by February 15 (for priority consideration), or at least two months prior to registration. Application fee $25. Phone: (540)231-6691; fax: (540)231-3714.

ADMISSION STANDARDS. Very selective for many departments. Usual minimum average: 3.0, 2.7 for provisional (A = 4).

FINANCIAL AID. Annual awards from institutional funds: 50 scholarships, 1500 fellowships, 2000 teaching/research assistantships, 9 internships, Federal W/S, loans. Approved for VA benefits. Apply to appropriate department chairman for scholarships, fellowships, assistantships; to Financial Aid Office for all other programs. Phone: (703)231-5179. Use FAFSA. About 60% of students receive aid other than loans from School and outside sources.

DEGREE REQUIREMENTS. Master's: 30 semester hours minimum, at least 24 in residence; thesis/nonthesis option; final oral/written exam. For C.A.G.S.: 30 semester hours beyond the master's; final written exam. For Ph.D.: 90 semester hours minimum beyond the bachelor's, at least 30 in full-time attendance; reading knowledge of one foreign language in some departments; preliminary exam; dissertation; final oral/written exam. For Ed.D.: essentially the same as for the Ph.D., except no language requirement.

FIELDS OF STUDY.
Accounting.
Aerospace Engineering.
Agricultural Economics.

Agricultural Engineering.
Agronomy.
Anaerobic Microbiology.
Animal Sciences. Includes dairy, poultry.
Architecture.
Biochemistry and Nutrition.
Biology. Includes botany, microbiology, zoology.
Business Administration. Includes finance, management, management science, marketing.
Chemical Engineering.
Chemistry.
Civil Engineering.
Clothing and Textiles.
Computer Science. Includes applications, information systems.
Economics.
Education. Includes administration, administration and supervision of special education, curriculum and instruction, elementary, educational microcomputing, instructional technology and design, reading, secondary (English, mathematics, music, science, social studies), student personnel services, vocational technical (agricultural, business, home economics, marketing, vocational industrial).
Educational Research and Evaluation.
Electrical Engineering.
Engineering Mechanics.
English.
Entomology.
Environmental Design and Planning.
Environmental Engineering.
Environmental Science and Engineering.
Family and Child Development.
Fisheries and Wildlife Sciences.
Food Science and Technology.
Forest Products.
Forestry.
Genetics.
Geography.
Geology.
Geophysics.
History.
Horticulture.
Housing, Interior Design, and Resource Management.
Human Nutrition and Foods.
Industrial Engineering and Operations Research.
Landscape Architecture.
Materials Engineering Science.
Mathematics.
Mechanical Engineering.
Mining and Minerals Engineering.
Physics.
Plant Pathology, Physiology, and Weed Science.
Political Science.
Psychology.
Public Administration/Public Affairs.
Science and Technology Studies.
Sociology.
Statistics.
Systems Engineering.
Theater Arts.
Urban Affairs.
Urban and Regional Planning.
Veterinary Medical Science.

Virginia-Maryland Regional College of Veterinary Medicine (2461-0443)

Annual tuition: full-time resident $8251, nonresident $20,132. Annual housing cost: $10,000–$14,000.

Enrollment: first-year class 80; total full-time 300 (men 45%, women 55%). College faculty: full-time 90. Degrees conferred: D.V.M., D.V.M.-M.S., D.V.M.-Ph.D.

ADMISSION REQUIREMENTS. VMCAS report (nonresidents), transcripts, GRE, Advanced Biology, three recommendations, animal/veterinary experience required in support of application. Interview by invitation only. Applicants must have completed at least two years of college study. Preference given to state and Maryland residents. Accepts transfer applicants on a space-available basis only (Virginia and Maryland residents only). Apply to the Office of Student Services after September 1, before November 15. Application fee $45. Phone: (703)231-5699.

ADMISSION STANDARDS. Accepts 25–30% of total annual applicants. Has up to ten spaces available for non-Virginia/Maryland residents.

FINANCIAL AID. Scholarships, fellowships, assistantships, loans. Apply to Financial Aid Office before February 1. Use FAFSA.

DEGREE REQUIREMENTS. For D. V. M.: satisfactory completion of four-year program. For M.S. and Ph.D.: see Graduate School listing above.

FIELDS OF GRADUATE STUDY.
Microbiology.
Pathology.
Pharmacology.
Physiology.
Toxicology.

VIRGINIA STATE UNIVERSITY
Petersburg, Virginia 23806-0001

Founded 1882. Located 25 miles S of Richmond. Coed. State Control. Semester system. Library: 215,000 volumes, 551,000 microforms, 1080 current periodicals, 7 PCs.

Annual tuition: full-time, resident $3554, nonresident $8149; per credit resident $94, nonresident $286. No on-campus housing available. Average academic year housing costs: $4845 (including board) for single students. Contact Dean of Students Office for both on- and off-campus housing information. Phone: (804)524-5862.

Graduate Division

Enrollment: full-time 101, part-time 504. College faculty teaching graduate students: full-time 48, part-time 5. Degrees conferred: M.A., M.S., M.Ed., M.I.S., C.A.G.S.

ADMISSION REQUIREMENTS: Two official transcripts, GRE required in support of application. TOEFL required for international applicants. Accepts transfer applications. Apply to Graduate School by May 1 (Fall), November 1 (Spring). Application Fee $25. Phone: (804)524-5984; fax: (804)524-5104.

ADMISSION STANDARDS. Selective. Usual minimum average: 2.6 (A = 4) for unconditional admission.

FINANCIAL AID. Annual awards from institutional funds. Fellowships, asistantships, Federal W/S, loans. Approved for VA benefits. Apply by March 1 to Financial Aid Office. Use FAFSA. Phone: (804)524-5990; fax: (804)524-6818. About 10% of students receive aid other than from University and outside sources.

DEGREE REQUIREMENTS. For M.A., M.S.: 24–27 semester hours minimum; thesis for 3–6 hours, 21 semester hours in residence. For M.Ed.: 33 hours including project or 36 hours including statistics and research; comprehensive examination. For C.A.C.S.: 30 semester hours beyond the master's.

FIELDS OF STUDY.
Biology.
Economics.
Educational Administration and Supervision.
Educational Media.
Elementary Education.
English.
Guidance.
History.
Mathematics/Mathematics Education.
Physics.
Psychology.
Special Education.
Vocational Technical Education. Emphasis on either agricultural education, business education, home economics education, or industrial education.
Vocational Technical Education. C.A.G.S.

UNIVERSITY OF VIRGINIA
Charlottesville, Virginia 22906-3196
http://www.virginia.edu

Established 1819. Located 66 miles W of Richmond, 120 miles S of Washington. Coed. State control. Semester system. Special facilities: Olsson Center for Applied Ethics, Center for Biological Timing, Center for Electrochemical Sciences and Engineering, Institute for Environmental Negotiation, Center for High Temperature Composites, Taylor Murphy International Business Studies Center, Institute for Nuclear and Particle Physics, Center for Russian and East European Studies, Center for South Asian Studies, University Transportation Center. Library: 3,200,000 volumes and 4,600,000 microforms.

Annual tuition: full-time, resident $4652, nonresident $14,438; part-time per semester minimum, resident $868, nonresident $2496. Average academic year housing costs: $2030 (including board) for single students; $3000 for married students. Contact Office of Housing, Station 1, Page House, University of Virginia 22904, for both on- and off-campus housing information. Phone: (804)924-6873. Day care facilities available.

Graduate School of Arts and Sciences

Graduate study since 1904. Enrollment: full-time 1844, part-time 70. University faculty teaching graduate students: full-time 575, part-time 78. Degrees conferred: M.A., M.A.T., M.A.P.A., M.F.A, M.S., Ph.D.

ADMISSION REQUIREMENTS. Transcripts, GRE, two letters of recommendation required in support of School's application. TOEFL required for international applicants. Accepts transfer applicants. Graduates of unaccredited institutions not considered. Apply to Office of the Graduate School by July 15 (Fall), December 1 (Spring). Application fee $40. Phone: (804)924-7184.

ADMISSION STANDARDS. Very selective for most departments, competitive for others. Usual minimum average: 3.0 (A = 4).

FINANCIAL AID. Annual awards from institutional funds: 500 teaching assistantships, 100 research assistantships, 350 fellowships, partial tuition waivers, Federal W/S, loans. Approved for VA benefits. Apply by February 1 to individual departments for fellowships, assistantships; to the Office of Financial Aid for all other programs. Use FAFSA. Phone: (804)924-3725. About 60% of students receive aid other than loans from School and outside sources.

DEGREE REQUIREMENTS. For master's: 24 semester hours minimum plus thesis, 30–36 credit without thesis; reading knowledge of one foreign language (by completion of two years of college credit or equivalent) for some programs; final oral/written exam. For Ph.D.: a minimum of 72 semester hours (or 50 beyond the master's); proficiency in one or two foreign languages (if applicable); preliminary/qualifying exam; dissertation; final/oral exam.

FIELDS OF STUDY.
Anatomy. Ph.D.
Anthropology. M.A., Ph.D.
Art History. M.A., Ph.D.
Asian and Middle Eastern Languages and Culture. M.A.
Astronomy. M.A., Ph.D.
Biochemistry. Includes biophysics, molecular biology. Ph.D.
Biology. M.A., M.S., Ph.D.
Cell Biology. M.S., Ph.D.
Chemistry. M.S., Ph.D.
Classics. M.A., M.A.T., Ph.D.
Clinical Psychology. Ph.D.
Creative Writing. M.F.A.
Drama. M.F.A.
Economics. M.A., Ph.D.
Education. M.A., Ph.D. only.
English. M.S., M.A.T., Ph.D.
Environmental Sciences. M.A., M.S., Ph.D.
Foreign Affairs. M.A., Ph.D.
French. M.A., Ph.D.
German Language and Literature. M.A., M.A.T., Ph.D.
Government. M.A., M.A.T., Ph.D.
History. M.A., M.A.T., Ph.D.
Hospital Epidemiology. M.S.
Italian. M.A.
Linguistics. M.A.
Mathematics. M.A., M.A.T., M.S., Ph.D.
Microbiology. M.S., Ph.D.
Molecular Physiology. M.S., Ph.D.
Music. M.A., M.A.T.
Neuroscience. Ph.D.
Pharmacology. M.S., Ph.D.
Philosophy. M.A., Ph.D.
Physics. M.A., M.A.T., M.S., Ph.D.
Physiology. Ph.D.
Psychology. M.S., Ph.D.
Public Administration. M.A.P.A.
Religious Studies. M.A., Ph.D.
Rhetoric and Communication Studies. M.A.
Slavic Languages and Literature. M.A., Ph.D.
Sociology. M.A., Ph.D.
Spanish. M.A., Ph.D.
Spanish Teaching. M.A.T.
Surgery. M.S.
Vascular Biology. Ph.D.

School of Architecture

Enrollment: full-time 210 (men 107, women 103), no part-time students. Faculty: full-time 44, part-time 14. Degrees conferred: M.Arch., M.Arch.H., M.L.A., M.P., Ph.D.

ADMISSION REQUIREMENTS. Transcripts, GRE required in support of application. TOEFL required for international applicants. Accepts transfer applicants. Graduates of unaccredited institutions not considered. Apply to Dean of School; preliminary deadline December 1, final deadline January 15 for Architecture, Architecture History; February 1 for M.L.A., M.P. Application fee $40. Phone: (804)924-6442; fax: (804)982-2678.

ADMISSION STANDARDS. Very selective. Usual minimum average: 3.0 (A = 4).

FINANCIAL AID. Grants and fellowships. Architecture School Financial Aid form should be filed with application. Loans, Federal W/S available through University's Office of Financial Aid, Michie North, Emmet Street, Charlottesville, Virginia 22903. Phone: (804)982-6000. Apply by March 31 for Fall semester. Use FAFSA and School's FAF.

DEGREE REQUIREMENTS. For M.Arch.: Summer session plus 92 semester hours (less for B.S. in Arch. recipients), at least two years in residence. For M.L.A.: Summer session plus 94 semester hours, at least two years in residence. For M.Arch.H.: 36 semester hours, 24 hours in residence; comprehensive exam; one foreign language; thesis; final oral exam. For M.P.: 50 semester hours, summer internship. For Ph.D.: 48 semester hours plus 18 semester hours of nontopical research; written and oral exam; additional foreign language; dissertation; oral defense.

FIELDS OF STUDY.
Architectural History. M.Arch.H., Ph.D.
Architecture. Includes American urbanism, preservation; M.Arch.
Landscape Architecture. M.L.A.
Planning. Includes urban, environmental land use, policy. M.P.
Note: Study abroad available in Venice.

Graduate School of Business Administration (22906-3196)
http://www.darden.virginia.edu

Founded 1954, graduate study since 1955. Annual tuition and fees: full-time, resident $11,819, nonresident $19,627. Limited on-campus housing available to graduate students.

Enrollment: full-time 500, no part-time students. School faculty: full-time 50, part-time 20. Degrees conferred: M.B.A., M.B.A.-M.A., M.B.A.-M.E., M.B.A.-J.D., M.B.A.-M.S.N., Ph.D.

ADMISSION REQUIREMENTS. Official transcripts, recommendations, GMAT required in support of application. TOEFL and TSE required for all international students. Interview recommended. Apply to Office of Admissions of School (P.O. Box 6500) by March 15 (Fall). Admits first-year students Fall only. Application fee $75. Phone: (800)UVA-MBA-1, (804)924-7281; fax: (804)924-4859.

ADMISSION STANDARDS. Very selective. Average GPA: 3.2. Average GMAT: 645.

FINANCIAL AID. All financial aid is "need" based. Apply by March 1 to Director of Financial Aid. Use FAFSA and Darden Scholarship Form. Phone: (804)924-4822; fax: (804)942-4859. About 40% of students receive aid other than loans from School and outside sources.

DEGREE REQUIREMENTS. For M.B.A.: four semesters minimum (eighteen half-semester courses), four in residence; thesis. For Ph.D.: two years minimum study beyond the master's; dissertation; final oral/written exam. Joint degree programs generally add one to one and a half years to M.B.A. program.

The Curry School of Graduate Education

Graduate study since 1905. Semester system.
Annual tuition: full-time resident $4658, nonresident $14,444. Enrollment: full-time 680, part-time 320. Faculty: full-time 100, part-time 26. Degrees conferred: M.Ed., M.T., Ed.S., Ed.D., Ph.D.

ADMISSION REQUIREMENTS. Official transcripts, GRE Subject Tests, three letters of recommendation required in support of School's application. TOEFL required for international applicants. Accepts transfer applicants. Graduates of unaccredited institutions not considered. Apply to Office of School, preferably by April 1. Application fee $40. Phone: (804)924-0741, (804)924-0474.

ADMISSION STANDARDS. Selective. Usual minimum average: 3.0 (A = 4).

FINANCIAL AID. One hundred and sixty scholarships, two hundred grants, one hundred teaching assistantships, fifty internships, Federal W/S, loans. Approved for VA benefits. Apply to Office of the School by April 1. Use FAFSA. Phone: (804)924-6000.

DEGREE REQUIREMENTS. For M.Ed., M.T.: 30–48 semester hours minimum, at least 24 in residence; comprehensive exam. For Ed.S.: 30 semester hours beyond the master's; comprehensive exam. For Ed. D.: at least one semester in full-time residence; preliminary exam; comprehensive exam; final dissertation; final oral exam. For Ph.D.: same as for Ed.D., except research project; proficiency in research methodology and statistics, and two years residency.

FIELDS OF STUDY.
Administration and Supervision.
Clinical and School Psychology.
Communication Disorders.
Counselor Education.
Curriculum and Instruction.
Educational Evaluation.
Educational Psychology.
Educational Research.
Elementary Education.
English Education.
Foreign Language Education.
Higher Education.
Instructional Technology.
Mathematics Education.
Physical Education.
Reading.
Science Education.
Social Foundations.
Social Studies Education.
Special Education.

School of Engineering and Applied Science— Graduate Division

Graduate study since 1946. Semester system.
Annual tuition: full-time resident $6854, nonresident $14,444, per semester resident (1–3 credits) $862, (4–8 credits) $1683, nonresident (1–3 credits) $2425, (4–8 credits) $4837.
Enrollment: full-time 586, part-time 107. Faculty teaching graduate students: full-time 150. Degrees conferred: M.S., M.E., Ph.D.

ADMISSION REQUIREMENTS. Official transcripts, three letters of recommendation, GRE required in support of School's application. TOEFL, financial statement certifying $22,000 available for first year of study required for international applicants. Accepts transfer applicants. Interview not required. Apply to Dean of School by August 1 (Fall), December 1 (Spring); international applicants apply by April 1 (Spring); September 1 (Fall). Application fee $40. Phone: (804)924-3879; fax: (804)982-2734.

ADMISSION STANDARDS. Selective. Usual minimum average: 3.0 (A = 4). TOEFL Score: 600.

FINANCIAL AID. One hundred and thirty-five fellowships, 133 teaching assistantships, 361 research assistantships, 10 traineeships, 40 other awards, Federal W/S, loans. Approved for VA benefits. Apply by February 1 to Dean for fellowships, assistantship; to Financial Aid Office for all other programs. Use FAFSA.

Phone: (804)924-3897. About 85% of students receive aid other than loans from School and outside sources. Aid rarely available to part-time students.

DEGREE REQUIREMENTS. For M.E., M.S.: 24–30 semester hours minimum, at least one semester in residence for M.S.; thesis/research project; final oral thesis exam. For Ph.D.: 48 semester hours, at least 24 credits of research beyond the master's, at least two semesters in residence; comprehensive exam; dissertation; final oral exam.

FIELDS OF STUDY.
Applied Mathematics.
Applied Mechanics.
Biomedical Engineering.
Chemical Engineering.
Civil Engineering.
Computer Science.
Electrical Engineering.
Engineering Physics.
Environmental Engineering.
Materials Science and Engineering.
Mechanical Engineering and Aerospace Engineering.
Nuclear Engineering.
Structural Engineering.
System Engineering.
Transportation Engineering and Management.

School of Law (22901)

Established 1826. Semester system. Law library: 730,000 volumes. Library has LEXIS, NEXIS, WESTLAW.

Annual tuition: full-time, resident $12,030, nonresident $19,178. Total average annual additional expense: $9875.

Enrollment: first-year class 380; total full-time 1142 (men 61%, women 39%); no part-time students. Faculty: full-time 56, part-time 52. Degrees conferred: J.D., J.D.-M.A. (Economics, Government and Foreign Affairs, History, Sociology, Philosophy), J.D.-M.P., (Marine Affairs, Urban Planning), J.D.-M.B.A., J.D.-M.S. (Acc.), J.D.-Ph.D., LL.M., S.J.D.

ADMISSION REQUIREMENTS. For J.D. program: transcripts, LSAT, two recommendations required in support of application. Applicants must have completed four years of college study. Interview not required. Accepts transfer applicants. Graduates of unaccredited colleges not considered. Apply to Admissions Office of School, preferably by January 15 (Fall), Application fee $40. Phone: (804)924-7351. For graduate program: transcripts, GRE required in support of application. Interview may be required. Graduates of unaccredited colleges not considered. Apply to Admissions Office of the School; closing date varies by school.

ADMISSION STANDARDS. Selective. Accepts 20–25% of total annual applicants.

FINANCIAL AID. Scholarships, fellowships, assistantships, Federal W/S, federal and law school loans. Apply to Federal Students Aid Center by February 1 for scholarships and Federal programs. Use FAFSA. Apply to Chair of Graduate Commission for fellowships, assistantships. About 65% of students receive some aid from all sources.

DEGREE REQUIREMENTS. For J.D.: 6 semesters minimum in residence; 86-credit-hour program. For LL.M.: at least 24 credits beyond the J.D.; two semesters minimum in residence; final paper. For J.S.D.: two semesters minimum in residence; dissertation; final oral exam.

School of Medicine (22908)

Established 1824. Annual tuition: full-time, resident $9676, nonresident $22,006, student fees $822. Total average cost for all other expenses: $7500.

Enrollment: first-year class 139 (EDP 6); total 550 (men 58%, women 42%). Faculty: full-time 670, part-time 165. Degrees conferred: M.D. M.D.-Ph.D. (Medical Scientist Training Program).

ADMISSION REQUIREMENTS. AMCAS report, transcripts, letters of recommendation, MCAT, final screening interview required in support of application. Applicants must have completed at least three years of college study. Has EDP; apply between June 15 and August 1. Preference given to Virginia residents. Apply to Director of Admissions after June 15, before November 1. Application fee $50. Phone: (804)924-5571; fax: (804)982-2586.

ADMISSION STANDARDS. Competitive. Accepts about 3–5% of total annual applicants. Approximately 70% are state residents.

FINANCIAL AID. Scholarships, loans. MSTP funded by NIH. Apply to Financial Aid Director by January 1. Use FAFSA. About 80% of students recieve some type of aid.

DEGREE REQUIREMENTS. For M.D.: satisfactory completion of four-year program. Ph.D. is granted through the Graduate School of Arts and Sciences.

FIELDS OF GRADUATE STUDY.
Anatomy.
Biochemistry.
Biomedical Engineering.
Biophysics.
Cell Biology.
Microbiology.
Molecular Biology.
Neurosciences.
Pathology.
Pharmacology.
Physiology.

WAGNER COLLEGE
Staten Island, New York 10301

Founded 1883. Coed. Private control. Receives some support from the Lutheran Church of America. Semester system. Daycare facilities available. Library: 301,000 volumes, 777,000 microforms, 1500 current periodicals.

Tuition: per credit $520. On-campus housing for single students only. Average academic year housing cost: $5800 (including board). Contact Director of Residence Life for both on- and off-campus housing information. Phone: (718)390-3412.

Division of Graduate Studies

Graduate study since 1952. Enrollment: full-time 104, part-time 196. College faculty: full-time 31, part-time 30. Degrees conferred: M.B.A., M.S., M.S.Ed.

ADMISSION REQUIREMENTS. Official transcripts, MAT/NTE/GMAT required in support of application. Interview not required. TOEFL required for international applicants. Accepts transfer applicants. Graduates of unaccredited institutions not considered. Apply to Director of Graduate Admissions at least one month prior to registration. Rolling admission process. Application fee $50; $65 for international applicants. Phone: (718)390-3411.

ADMISSION STANDARDS. Selective for most departments. Usual minimum average: 2.5 (A = 4).

FINANCIAL AID. Fifteen fellowships, fourteen teaching assistantships, tuition waivers, Federal W/S, loans. Approved for VA benefits. Apply by May 1 to Director of Graduate Studies for fellowships, assistantships; to Office of Financial Aid for all other programs. Use FAFSA. Phone: (718)390-3183. About 20% of students receive aid from College. Aid available to part-time students.

DEGREE REQUIREMENTS. For M.S.: 34–42 credits depending upon department. For M.B.A.: 36 credits, at least 30 in residence. For M.S. in Ed.: 34 credit hours minimum; 36 credit hours minimum in special education; thesis/nonthesis option.

FIELDS OF STUDY.
Bacteriology. M.S.
Elementary Education. M.S.Ed.
Executive Management. M.B.A.
Finance. M.B.A.
International Business. M.B.A.
Management. M.B.A.
Marketing. M.B.A.
Nursing. M.S.
Special Education. M.S.Ed.

WAKE FOREST UNIVERSITY
Winston-Salem, North Carolina 27109

Founded 1834. Coed. Private control. Baptist affiliation. Semester system. Library: 1,600,000 volumes, 1,400,00 microforms, 25,000 current periodicals, 100 PCs.

Annual tuition: full-time $15,500. Limited on-campus housing for graduate students. Contact the Director of Residence Life and Housing for both on- and off-campus housing information. Phone: (910)759-5185.

Graduate School

Graduate study since 1866. Enrollment: full-time 275, part-time 136 (men 184, women 227). Faculty: full-time 404. Degrees conferred: M.A.Ed., M.A.L.S., M.S.A., M.S., Ph.D.

ADMISSION REQUIREMENTS. For Arts and Sciences: official transcripts, three letters of evaluation, interview for most departments, GRE Subject Tests/GMAT (accountancy) required in support of School's application. TOEFL required for international applicants. Accepts transfer applicants. Apply to Dean of Graduate School by February 15. Application fee $25. Phone: (800)257-3166; fax: (910)759-6074. For Bowman Gray School of Medicine–Graduate Program: official transcripts, three letters of evaluation, GRE Subject Tests required in support of School's application. TOEFL required for international students. Accepts transfer applicants. Graduates of unaccredited institutions not considered. Apply to Dean of the Graduate School by February 15. Application fee $25. Phone: (910)759-5301, or (800)257-3166; fax: (910)759-6074.

ADMISSION STANDARDS. Very selective for most departments, selective for the others. Usual minimum average: 3.0 (A = 4).

FINANCIAL AID. For Arts and Sciences: annual awards from institutional funds: scholarships, fellowships, assistantships (varies on availability), loans. Apply at the time of application to Dean of Graduate School. Use FAFSA. Phone: (800)257-3166; fax: (910)759-6074. About 85% of students receive aid other than loans from School and outside sources. For Bowman Gray

School of Medicine–Graduate Program: scholarships, teaching/research fellowships, research assistantships. Apply at time of application for admission to Dean of Graduate School. About 34% of students receive aid other than loans from School, 90% for all sources. No aid for part-time students.

DEGREE REQUIREMENTS. For master's: 30 semester hours minimum, at least 24 in residence; reading knowledge of one foreign language for some departments, substitution allowed in others; thesis/nonthesis option; final oral/written exam. For Ph.D.: three years minimum beyond the bachelor's, at least one year in residence; reading knowledge of two foreign languages in some departments, with substitutions allowed in others for one or both; preliminary oral/written exam; dissertation; final exam.

FIELDS OF STUDY.
Accountancy. M.S.A.
Anesthesia. M.S. only.
Anthropology. M.A. only.
Biochemistry.
Biology.
Chemistry.
Communication. M.A. only.
Comparative Medicine. M.S. only.
Education. Includes secondary and school counselors. M.A.Ed. only.
English. M.A. only.
Epidemiology. M.S. only.
Health and Sport Science. M.S. only.
History. M.A. only.
Liberal Studies. M.A.L.S. only.
Mathematics Computer Science. M.A., M.S. only.
Medical Engineering.
Medical Genetics. M.S. only.
Microbiology and Immunology.
Molecular and Cellular Pathobiology. M.S. only.
Molecular Genetics.
Neurobiology and Anatomy.
Neuroscience.
Pastoral Counseling. In conjunction with School of Pastoral Care of North Baptist Hospital. M.A. only.
Physics.
Physiology and Pharmacology.
Psychology. M.A. only.
Religion. M.A. only.

School of Law (P.O. Box 7206)

Established 1894. Semester system. Law library: 250,000 volumes. Library has LEXIS, NEXIS, WESTLAW, DIALOG, EPIC, ACES; 53 computer workstations.

Annual tuition, fees: $18,200. On-campus housing for 56 married students. Apply to Director of Housing. Total average annual additional expense: $6000–$8000.

Enrollment: first-year class 160; total full-time 468 (men 61%, women 39%). Faculty: full-time 33, part-time 31. Degrees conferred: J.D., J.D.-M.B.A.

ADMISSION REQUIREMENTS. LSDAS Law School report, Bachelor's degree, transcripts, LSAT, one academic recommendation, Dean's Certification required in support of application. Interviews are recommended only. Accepts transfer applicants. Graduates of unaccredited institutions not considered. Apply to Admissions Office after September 1, before March 15. Rolling admissions process. Application fee $50. Phone: (910)761-5437.

ADMISSION STANDARDS. Selective. Accepts 25% of total annual applicants. Transfer applicants accepted on a space-available basis only.

FINANCIAL AID. Scholarships, Federal W/S, loans. Apply by May 1 to Financial Aid Office. Use FAFSA. About 78% of students receive aid from School. No aid for part-time students.

DEGREE REQUIREMENTS. For J.D.: 89 semester hours minimum, at least final year in residence.

Bowman Gray School of Medicine (27157-1090)

Established 1902. Library: 110,000 volumes. Annual tuition: $23,000. Total average cost for all other expenses: $8500.

Enrollment; first-year class 108 (EDP 5); total full-time 539 (men 67%, women 33%); postgraduates 156. Faculty: full-time 645, part-time 520. Degree conferred: M.D. The M.S. and Ph.D. are offered through the Graduate School.

ADMISSION REQUIREMENTS. AMCAS report, transcripts, MCAT, recommendations, including premedical advisory committee, required in support of application. Has EDP; apply between June 15 and August 1. Interviews and supplemental application by invitation only. Preference given to state residents. Apply after June 15, before November 1 to Associate Dean for Admissions. Application fee $50. Phone: (910)748-4264, Fax: (910)748-5807.

ADMISSION STANDARDS. Very competitive. Accepts 2–3% of total annual applicants. Approximately 55% are state residents.

FINANCIAL AID. Scholarships, loan funds. Apply to Financial Aid Director. About 85% of students receive some financial aid.

DEGREE REQUIREMENTS. For M.D.: satisfactory completion of four-year program. For M.S., Ph.D., see Graduate School listing above.

FIELDS OF GRADUATE STUDY.
Anatomy.
Anesthesia.
Biochemistry.
Medical Genetics.
Microbiology.
Molecular and Cellular Pathobiology.
Neuroscience.
Pharmacology.
Physiology.
Virology.

WALLA WALLA COLLEGE
College Place, Washington 99324-3000
http://www.wwc.edu

Founded 1892. Located 160 miles SW of Spokane. Coed. Private control. Seventh-Day Adventist. Quarter system. Library: 235,000 volumes, 10,000 microforms, 1000 current periodicals, 20 PCs.

Tuition: per credit $312. On-campus housing for 1480 single students, 110 units for married students. Average academic year housing costs: $1863 (room only) for a single student; $3200 for married students. Contact Rental Properties for on- and off-campus housing information. Phone: (509)527-2109.

Graduate School

Graduate study since 1900. Enrollment: full-time 133, part-time 17. Graduate faculty: full-time 24, part-time 18. Degrees conferred: M.A., M.Ed., M.S., M.S.W.

ADMISSION REQUIREMENTS. Official transcripts, GRE Subject Tests required in support of School's application. Inter-

view not required. TOEFL required for international applicants. Accepts transfer applicants. Apply to Dean of Graduate Studies at least three months prior to registration. Application fee $20. Phone: (509)527-2421; fax: (509)527-2397.

ADMISSION STANDARDS. Selective. Usual minimum average: 2.75 (A = 4).

FINANCIAL AID. Fifteen scholarships, ten teaching assistantships, Federal W/S, loans. Approved for VA benefits. Apply by April 15 to the Financial Aid Office for scholarships, to department chair for assistantships. Use FAFSA and institutional FAF. Phone: (509)527-2315; fax: (509)527-2253. About 30% of students receive aid other than loans from College, 35% from all sources. Aid sometimes available to part-time students.

DEGREE REQUIREMENTS. For master's: 45 credits minimum, at least 30 in residence; thesis required for M.S., M.A.; final oral/written exams.

FIELDS OF STUDY.
Biological Sciences.
Education and Psychology. Includes administration, educational foundations, elementary and secondary guidance.
Social Work.

WASHBURN UNIVERSITY OF TOPEKA
Topeka, Kansas 66621

Founded 1865. Located 65 miles W of Kansas City. Coed. Municipal control. Semester system.

Tuition per hour: resident $126, nonresident $261. On-campus housing for graduate students available. Average academic year housing costs: $3210. Contact Director of Housing for both on- and off-campus housing information. Phone: (913)231-1065. Day care facilities available.

Graduate Program

Enrollment: full-time 59, part-time 295. Graduate faculty: full-time 32, part-time 19. Degrees conferred: M.A., M.B.A., M.Ed., M.S.W.

ADMISSION REQUIREMENTS. Official transcripts, references, GMAT, interview required in support of application. TOEFL required for international applicants. Accepts transfer applicants. Apply to Director of Graduate Programs at least one month prior to registration. Application fee: none. Phone: (913)231-1010, ext. 1307.

ADMISSION STANDARDS. Selective. Usual minimum average: 3.0 (A = 4).

FINANCIAL AID. Scholarships, research fellowships, research assistantships, teaching assistantships, Federal W/S, loans. Approved for VA benefits. Apply by April 1 to Dean's office for fellowships, assistantships: to Financial Aid Office all other programs. Use FAFSA. Phone: (913)231-1010, ext. 1151.

DEGREE REQUIREMENTS. For M.A., M.Ed., M.S.W.: 32 semester hours minimum, at least 24 in residence; final document. For M.B.A.: 30 semester hours minimum; computer proficiency.

FIELDS OF STUDY.
Advanced Clinical Practice. M.S.W. only.
Business Administration.
Clinical Psychology.
Education. Includes administration, curriculum and instruction, reading, special education.

School of Law

Organized 1903. Semester system. Law library: 272,000 volumes. Library has LEXIS, NEXIS, WESTLAW, DIALOG; 30 computer work stations. Special facilities: Rural Law Center.

Annual tuition: residents $6510, nonresidents $9750. On-campus housing available. Annual housing cost: $3250–$4000.

Enrollment: first-year class 152; total 435 (men 57%, women 43%). Faculty: full-time 26, part-time 27. Degree conferred: J.D.

ADMISSION REQUIREMENTS. LSDAS Law School report, bachelor's degree, transcripts, LSAT required in support of application. Interview not required. Accepts transfer applicants. Preference given to state residents. Graduates of unaccredited institutions not considered. Admits to both Fall and Spring semesters. Apply to Admissions Office by March 15 (Fall), September 15 (Spring). Later applications considered on space-available basis only. Application fee $30. Phone: (913)231-1185, (800)332-0291.

ADMISSION STANDARDS. Accepts 40% of total annual applicants.

FINANCIAL AID. Scholarships, Federal W/S, loans. Apply to Financial Aid Office by March 15 for priority consideration. Use FAFSA. About 10% of students receive aid other than loans from School.

DEGREE REQUIREMENTS. For J.D.: 90 credit hours minimum, at least 24 hours and the last year in residence.
Note: Six-week program of international study at Brunel University of West London (Great Britain) available.

WASHINGTON COLLEGE
Chestertown, Maryland 21620-1197

Founded 1782. Located 85 miles NE of Washington, D.C., 55 miles SE of Wilmington, Delaware. Coed. Private control. Semester system. Library: 200 volumes, 8 PCs.

Tuition: per credit $200. No housing available for graduate students. For off-campus housing, contact Business Office of the College.

Graduate Division

Enrollment: approximately 75 (mainly part-time). Faculty: full-time 22, part-time 7. Degree conferred: M.A.

ADMISSION REQUIREMENTS. Transcripts, letters of recommendation, GRE (required for Psychology), appropriate baccalaureate degree required in support of application. Accepts transfer applicants. Apply to Graduate Office at least one month prior to registration. Application fee none. Phone: (410)778-7770.

ADMISSION STANDARDS. Selective. Usual minimum average: 3.0 (A = 4).

FINANCIAL AID. None.

DEGREE REQUIREMENTS. For M.A.: 30 semester hours; thesis/nonthesis option.

FIELDS OF STUDY.
Education. Courses only.
English Literature.
History-Social Science.
Psychology.

WASHINGTON AND LEE UNIVERSITY
Lexington, Virginia 24450

Founded 1849. Located 50 miles NE of Roanoke. Private control.

On-campus housing available. Average annual housing cost: $4300 for single students. Apply to Director of University Services.

School of Law

Established 1849. Semester system. Law library: 306,000 volumes. Library has LEXIS, NEXIS, WESTLAW.

Annual tuition: full-time $16,130. Total average annual additional expense: $6500.

Enrollment: first-year class 128, total 371 (men 60%, women 40%). Faculty: full-time 32, part-time 11. Degree conferred: J.D.

ADMISSION REQUIREMENTS. LSDAS Law School report, bachelor's degree, transcripts, two letters of recommendation, LSAT required in support of application. Interview not required. Accepts transfer applicants. Graduates of unaccredited colleges not considered. Apply to office of Dean of School after July 1, before February 1 for priority consideration. Application fee $40. Admits beginning students to Fall only. Phone: (703)463-8504.

ADMISSION STANDARDS. Selective. Accepts about 20–25% of total applicants.

FINANCIAL AID. Scholarships, grants, fellowships, Federal W/S, loans. Apply to Dean of School by March 1. Use FAFSA. About 52% of students receive financial assistance.

DEGREE REQUIREMENTS. For J.D.: 85 semester hours minimum, at least final four semesters in residence.

WASHINGTON STATE UNIVERSITY
Pullman, Washington 99164
http://www.wsu.edu

Founded 1890. Located 80 miles S of Spokane. Coed. State control. Semester system. Special facilities: Humanities Research Center, Small Business Research Center, Social and Economic Sciences Research Center, Computing Center, Nuclear Reactor Center, Electron Microscope Laboratory, Agricultural Research Centers, College of Engineering Research Division, State of Washington Water Research Center, Bioanalytical Research Center, Laboratory Animal Facility, Molecular Biophysics Laboratory. Library: 1,700,000 volumes, 2,900,000 microforms, 24,500 current periodicals, 72 PCs.

Annual tuition: full-time, resident $4936, nonresident $12,368; per credit, resident $233, nonresident $605. On-campus housing for 648 married students, unlimited for single students. Average academic year housing costs: $3200–$4500 for married students, $4100 (including board) for single students. Contact Program Coordinator Residence Halls (509)335-9574 for on-campus housing information; Program Coordinator Housing Commission (509)355-4577 for off-campus housing information.

Graduate School

Graduate study since 1902. Enrollment: full-time 1600, part-time 700. Graduate faculty: full-time 750, part-time 31. Degrees conferred: M.A., M.S., M.F.A., M.A.T., Ed.M., M.B.A., M.Nurs., M.R.P., Ed.D., Ph.D.

ADMISSION REQUIREMENTS. Two official transcripts, GRE/GMAT/MAT required in support of School's application.

TOEFL required for international applicants. Accepts transfer applicants. Foreign students apply at least six months prior to registration. Apply to the Director of Admissions at least two months prior to registration. Application fee $35. Phone: (509)335-3535; fax: (509)335-1949.

ADMISSION STANDARDS. Very selective for most departments, relatively open to very competitive for others. Usual minimum average: 3.1 (last two years) (A = 4).

FINANCIAL AID. Annual awards from institutional funds: 10 fellowships, 800 teaching assistantships, 350 research assistantships, Federal W/S, loans. Approved for VA benefits. Apply by February 1 to the Dean of Graduate School for assistantships, fellowships; to Financial Aid Office for all other programs. Use FAFSA. Phone: (509)335-9711. About 70% of students receive aid other than loans from University and outside sources.

DEGREE REQUIREMENTS. For M.A., M.S.: 30 credits minimum, at least one year in residence; language requirements vary by department; thesis/nonthesis option; final exam in all departments. For M.A.T.: 30 credits minimum, at least 24 in residence; final oral exam. For Ed.M.: qualifying exam; other requirement, same as for M.A.T. For M.B.A., M.R.P.: 30 credits minimum, no thesis; final oral exam. For M.N.: 45 credits, thesis; final oral exam. For Ed.D., Ph.D.: six semesters minimum beyond the bachelor's, at least four semester, in residences language requirements vary by department; oral/written preliminary exam; thesis; final oral exam.

FIELDS OF STUDY.
Accounting. M.Acct.
Agricultural Economics. M.A., Ph.D.
Agricultural Engineering. M.S.
Agronomy. M.S., Ph.D.
American Studies. M.A., Ph.D.
Animal Sciences. M.S., Ph.D.
Anthropology. M.A., Ph.D.
Architecture. M.S. only.
Art. Includes interior design. M.F.A.
Biochemistry. M.S., Ph.D.
Biology. M.S. only.
Botany. M.S., Ph.D.
Business Administration. M.B.A. Ph.D.
Chemical Engineering. M.S., Ph.D.
Chemical Physics. Ph.D.
Chemistry. Includes analytical, inorganic, organic, physical. M.S., Ph.D.
Civil Engineering. M.S., Ph.D.
Computer Science. M.S., Ph.D.
Criminal Justice. M.A.
Economics. M.A., Ph.D.
Education. M.A., Ed.M. Ed.D. Ph.D.
Electrical Engineering. M.S., Ph.D.
Engineering. M.S only.
Engineering Management. M.Eng.Mgt. only.
Engineering Science. Ph.D. only.
English. M.A., Ph.D.
Entomology. M.S., Ph.D.
Environmental Engineering. M.S.
Environmental Science. M.S.
Fine Arts. M.F.A. only.
Food Science. M.S., Ph.D.
Foreign Language and Literatures. M.A. only.
French. M.A.
Genetics and Cell Biology. M.S., Ph.D.
Geology. M.S., Ph.D.
Geotechnical Engineering.
German. M.A.
History. M.A., Ph.D.
Horticulture and Landscape Architecture. M.S. Ph.D.

Human Development. M.A. only.
Human Nutrition. M.A., M.S. only.
Kinesiology. M.S.
Materials Science and Engineering. M.S.
Mathematics. Includes applied; M.S., Ph.D.
Mechanical Engineering. M.S., Ph.D.
Microbiology. M.S., Ph.D.
Music. M.A.
Natural Resource Sciences. M.S., Ph.D.
Nursing. M.Nurs.
Nutrition. M.S., Ph.D.
Pharmacology and Toxicology. M.S., Ph.D.
Physics. M.S., Ph.D.
Plant Pathology. M.S., Ph.D.
Plant Physiology. M.S., Ph.D.
Political Science. M.A., Ph.D.
Psychology. Includes clinical; M.S., Ph.D.
Regional Planning. M.R.P.
Sociology. M.A., Ph.D.
Soils. M.S., Ph.D.
Spanish. M.A.
Speech and Hearing Science. M.S. only.
Theater Arts and Drama. M.A. only.
Veterinary Science. M.S., Ph.D.
Zoology. M.S., Ph.D.

College of Veterinary Medicine (99164-7012)

Founded 1899.
Annual tuition: full-time resident and contract state residents $8064; nonresidents $20,476. Annual housing cost: $3200–$4000.
Enrollment: first-year class 62, total full-time 260 (men 45%, women 55%). College faculty: full-time 90. Degree conferred: D.V.M.-M.S.

ADMISSION REQUIREMENTS. VMCAS report, transcripts, GRE, three recommendations, animal/veterinary experience required in support of application. Interview by invitation only. Applicants must have completed at least two years of college study. Preference given to state, Idaho, Oregon, and WICHE residents. Accepts transfer applicants under special circumstances only. Apply to the Office of Student Services after August 1, before November 1. Application fee $40. Phone: (509)335-1532.

ADMISSION STANDARDS. Selective. Accepts 10–15% of total annual applicants. Accepted approximately five nonresident "at-large" applicants.

FINANCIAL AID. Scholarships, loans. Use FAFSA before February 1.

DEGREE REQUIREMENTS. For D.V.M.: satisfactory completion of four-year program.

WASHINGTON UNIVERSITY

St. Louis, Missouri 63130-4899
http://www.wustl.edu

Founded 1853. Coed. Private control. Semester system. Special facilities: Center for Air Pollution and Trend Analysis, Center for the Study of American Business, Center for American Indian Studies, Institute for Biomedical Computing, Business, Law and Economics Center, McDonnell Center for Cellular and Molecular Neurobiology, Center for Computational Mechanics, Computer and Communications Research Center, Construction Management Center, Center for the Study of Data Processing, Carolyne Roehm Electronic Media Center, Center for Engineering Computing, Center for Genetics in Medicine, McDonnell Center for Studies of Higher Brain Function, Center for the History of Freedom, Center for Intelligent Computer Systems, International Writers Center, Center for the Study of Islamic Societies and Civilizations, Markey Center for Research in Molecular Biology of Human Disease, Center for Optimization and Semantic Control, Center for Plant Science and Biotechnology, Center for Political Economy, Center for the Study of Public Affairs, Center for Robotics and Automation, Social Work Research Development Center, McDonnell Center for Space Sciences, Center for Technology Assessment and Policy, Urban Research and Design Center, Central Institute for the Deaf. Library: 2,980,000 volumes, 2,420,000 microforms, 18,600 current periodicals.

Annual tuition: full-time $20,000; per unit $833. No oncampus housing available. Average academic year housing costs: $380–$680 per month.

Graduate School of Arts and Sciences

Formal graduate study since 1898. Enrollment: full-time 1365, part-time 25. School faculty: full-time 500, part-time 80. Degrees conferred: A.M., M.S., M.L.A., M.A.Ed., M.A.T., M.M., M.F.A.W., M.S.S.H., A.G.C., Ph.D.

ADMISSION REQUIREMENTS. Official transcripts, GRE Subject Test required in support of application. Official TOEFL or TSE required for international applicants. Interview required in some programs. Accepts transfer applicants. Graduates of unaccredited institutions not considered. Apply to Office of the Dean, preferably by January 15 (January 1 for the Division of Biology and Biomedical Sciences, April 1 for Speech and Hearing). Rolling admission process. Application $35. Phone: (314)935-6880; fax: (314)935-4887.

ADMISSION STANDARDS. Competitive for most departments. Usual minimum average: 3.0 (A = 4).

FINANCIAL AID. Annual awards from institutional funds: 700 scholarships, 120 fellowships, 300 research assistantships, 250 teaching assistantships, 20 internships, grants, Federal W/S, loans. Approved for VA benefits. Apply by January 15 to Dean for scholarships, to appropriate department head for fellowships, internships, assistantships; to the Financial Aid Office for all other programs. Use FAFSA and University's FAF. Phone: (314)935-6821. About 65% of students receive aid other than loans from School and outside sources.

DEGREE REQUIREMENTS. For A.M., M.L.A., M.S., M.S.S.H.: 24 semester hours plus thesis, or 30 hours plus essay, at least one year in residence; 6 hours maximum in transfer; final written exam. For M.A.Ed.; 33 hours minimum, at least 27 in residence; final written exam. For M.M.: 33 hours minimum, at least 27 in residence; includes graduate recital; reading knowledge of two modern languages. For M.F.A.W.: 39 hours minimum, at least 33 in residence, up to 15 hours in workshops or tutorials of directed writing. For A.G.C. (Education): normally 30 hours minimum beyond the master's, at least 24 in residence; qualifying written exam; final written project; final oral exam. For Ph.D.: 72 hours minimum beyond the bachelor's, at least 24 in residence; reading knowledge of one or two languages may be specified by major department; preliminary exam; dissertation; final oral exam.

FIELDS OF STUDY.
Anthropology. A.M.
Art History and Archaeology. One language for A.M., two for Ph.D.
Asian and Near Eastern Languages and Literature. A.M., Ph.D.
Biochemistry. Ph.D.
Bio-organic Chemistry. Ph.D.

Business Administration. M.S., Ph.D.; M.B.A., E.M.B.A. offered through Graduate School of Business Administration.
Chemistry. Includes organic, bioorganic, polymer, physical, biophysical, inorganic, organometallic, bioinorganic, nuclear, radiochemistry. A.M., Ph.D.
Classics. A.M.
Comparative Literature. Includes literary theory, European and American literature, Chinese and Japanese literature.
Developmental Biology.
Drama. A.M.
Earth and Planetary Sciences. Includes sedimentary geology, planetary exploration. A.M., Ph.D.
East Asian Studies. Includes economic development, law, political economic and intellectual history, literature and culture, art history and archaeology. A.M., Ph.D.
Economics. Includes economic history, economic theory, econometrics, industrial organization, monetary economics, political economy, public economics, public finance. A.M., Ph.D.
Education. Includes teacher education preservice and inservice, educational research. M.A.Ed., M.A.T., Ph.D.
English and American Literature. A.M., Ph.D.
European Studies. A.M. only.
Evolutionary and Population Biology.
Germanic Languages and Literatures. GRE for admission; one language in addition to German for A.M., two for Ph.D.
History. A.M., Ph.D.
Immunology. Ph.D.
Islamic and Near Eastern Studies. A.M. only.
Jewish Studies. A.M. only.
Literature and History. A.M. only.
Mathematics. Includes analysis, geometry, algebra. M.S., Ph.D.
Molecular Biophysics. Ph.D.
Molecular Cell Biology. Ph.D.
Molecular Genetics. Ph.D.
Molecular Microbiology and Microbial Pathogenesis. Ph.D.
Movement Science. Ph.D.
Music. Includes musicology, theory, composition; entrance exam for Ph.D.; qualifying exam for master's, two languages for Ph.D. M.M., A.M., Ph.D.
Neurosciences. Ph.D.
Performing Arts. Includes dramatic literature, criticism, theory, modern drama, Renaissance Drama, theater. A.M. only.
Philosophy. A.M., Ph.D.
Philosophy/Neuroscience/Psychology. Ph.D.
Physics. A.M., Ph.D.
Plant Biology. Ph.D.
Political Economy. Includes public choice, international political economy, public policy. A.M.
Political Science. A.M., Ph.D.
Psychology. Includes experimental, development and aging, social. Ph.D.
Romance Languages and Literature. French literature, Spanish literature; two languages in addition to major for Ph.D. A.M., Ph.D.
Social Work. Ph.D. only. M.S.W. offered through School of Social Work.
Speech and Hearing. M.S.S.H., Ph.D.
Technology and Human Affairs. A.M. only.
Writing Program. Includes fiction, poetry, nonfiction, playwriting. Writing samples must be included with application materials. M.F.A.W.

School of Art

Tuition per credit: $692. Enrollment: full-time 40. School faculty: full-time 20, part-time 8. Degree conferred: M.F.A.

ADMISSION REQUIREMENTS. Transcripts, BFA or equivalent, twenty slide portfolio, three recommendations, statement of purpose required in support of application. TOEFL required for international students. Graduates of unaccredited colleges not considered. Apply to Graduate Office by February 1. Application fee $30. Phone: (314)935-4761; fax: (314)935-4862; E-mail: cbaldwin@art.wustl.edu.

ADMISSION STANDARDS. Competitive. Usual minimum average: 3.0 (A = 4).

FINANCIAL AID. Fifty scholarships, two fellowships, twenty teaching assistantships, twenty technical assistantships, Federal W/S, loans. Approved for VA benefits. Apply to Graduate Office; various deadlines in January and February. Use FAFSA and University's FAF. Phone: (314)935-4761, Fax: (315)935-4862. 100% of students receive aid other than loans from both School and outside sources.

DEGREE REQUIREMENTS. For M.F.A.: 60 credits; thesis; exhibition.

FIELDS OF STUDY.
Ceramics. Includes glass.
Painting.
Photography.
Printmaking.
Sculpture.

John M. Olin School of Business (Campus Box 1133)

Annual tuition: $20,000. Enrollment: full-time 300, part-time 300 (men 75%, women 25%). School faculty: full-time 57, part-time 23. Degrees conferred: M.B.A., E.M.B.A., Ph.D.

ADMISSION REQUIREMENTS. Official transcripts, GMAT, two references required in support of School's application. TOEFL, telephone interview required for all international students. Interview may be required. Graduates of unaccredited colleges not considered. Apply to Admissions Office by March 30 (Fall); no specified closing dates for other terms. Application fee $45. Phone: (314)935-7301; fax: (314)935-4465.

ADMISSION STANDARDS. Selective. Average GPA: 3.25 (A = 4). Average GMAT: 603.

FINANCIAL AID. Fifty scholarships, three fellowships, assistantships, Federal W/S, loans. Approved for VA benefits. Apply by March 15 to Director of Financial Aid. Use FAFSA and Olin Supplemental FAF. Phone: (314)935-7301. About 65% of students receive aid other than loans from School. Part-time students are eligible for loans only.

DEGREE REQUIREMENTS. For M.B.A., E.M.B.A.: 67 semester hours minimum, at least 52 in residence. For Ph.D.: see Graduate School listing above.
Note: Summer program in London available.

School of Engineering and Applied Science of Sever Institute of Technology

Founded 1948. Tuition: per credit $795. Graduate enrollment: full-time 330, part-time 460. Institute faculty: full-time 80, part-time 20. Degrees conferred: M.S., D.Sc.

ADMISSION REQUIREMENTS. Official transcripts, letters of recommendation required in support of School's application. Interview desirable. TOEFL required for international applicants. Accepts transfer applicants. Graduates of unaccredited institutions not considered. Apply to Chairman of the Department; no specified closing dates. Application fee $20. Phone: (314)935-6166.

ADMISSION STANDARDS. Selective. Usual minimum average: 2.75 (last 2 years) (A = 4).

FINANCIAL AID. Annual awards from institutional funds: 40 scholarships, 181 research assistantships, Federal W/S, loans. Apply by February 15 to appropriate department for scholarships, assistantships; to Financial Aid Office for all other programs. Use FAFSA. Phone: (314)935-4761. About 48% of students receive aid other than loans from Institute and outside sources.

DEGREE REQUIREMENTS. For M.S.: 30 units minimum, at least 24 in residence; thesis/nonthesis option; final written/oral exam. For D.Sc.: 72 units minimum beyond the bachelor's, at least 24 in full-time residence; qualifying exam; dissertation; final written/oral exams.

FIELDS OF STUDY.
Biomedical Engineering.
Chemical Engineering.
Civil Engineering.
Construction Management.
Economics and Systems Science.
Electrical Engineering.
Engineering and Policy.
Geodetic Science.
Management of Technology.
Materials Science.
Mechanical Engineering.
Structural Design.
Systems Science and Mathematics.

George Warren Brown School of Social Work

Established 1925. Semester system.
Tuition per credit $538. Off-campus housing only. Contact Graduate Housing Office for both on- and off-campus housing information. Phone: (314)935-5092.
Enrollment: full-time 374, part-time 88. School faculty: full-time 26, part-time 40. Degrees conferred: M.S.W., M.S.W-J.D., M.S.W.-M.B.A., Ph.D.

ADMISSION REQUIREMENTS. Transcripts, references required in support of application. interview may be required. TOEFL required for international applicants. Accepts transfer applicants. Graduates of unaccredited institutions not considered. Apply to Director of Admissions and Student Resources at least two months in advance of registration. Earlier application encouraged. Rolling admission process. Application fee $25; $35 for both doctoral and international applicants. Phone: (314)935-6600; fax: (314)935-8511.

ADMISSION STANDARDS. Very selective. Usual minimum average: 3.0 (A = 4).

FINANCIAL AID. One hundred and thirty-seven fellowships, five teaching assistantships, scholarships, tuition remission grants, Federal W/S, loans. Approved for VA benefits. Apply by May 1 to Dean's Office for fellowships, assistantships; to Director of Financial Aid for all other programs. Phone: (314)935-6630. Use FAFSA and Institutional FAF.

DEGREE REQUIREMENTS. For M.S.W.: 45–60 credits minimum, depending on previous academic preparation; 10 of 60 credits are in field practicum, normally in two different social work settings. For Ph.D.: 51 credits beyond the M.S.W. or 72 beyond the baccalaureate; at least one year in full-time residence; qualifying exams; dissertation; final oral exam.

School of Law (63130-4899)

Founded 1867. Semester system. Law library: 500,000 volumes. Library has LEXIS, NEXIS, WESTLAW, LEGI-SLATE.

Annual tuition: full-time $20,350. Limited on-campus housing. For off-campus housing, call (314)935-5050. Total average annual expenses: $9000–$10,000.

Enrollment: first-year class 216, total full-time 637 (men 62%, women 38%). Faculty: full-time 41, part-time 68. Degrees conferred: J.D., J.D.-M.A. (Asian Studies, Political Science), J.D.-M.S.W., J.D.-M.H.A., J.D.-M.B.A., J.D.-M.S. (Environmental Law and Policy), J.D.-M.S.Ec. (Economics), J.D.- M.S.W., LL.M. (Taxation).

ADMISSION REQUIREMENTS. LSDAS Law School report, bachelor's degree, transcripts, LSAT, personal statement, resume, letters of recommendation required in support of application. Interview not required. Accepts transfer applicants. Graduates of unaccredited colleges not considered. Apply to Office of Admissions by March 1 for priority consideration. Admits Fall only. Application fee $50. Phone: (314)935-4525.

ADMISSION STANDARDS. Selective. Accepts 40–45% of total annual applicants.

FINANCIAL AID. Scholarships, grants, Federal W/S, loans. Apply to Office of Financial Aid by March 1. Use FAFSA. About 30% of students receive scholarships from School.

DEGREE REQUIREMENTS. For J.D.: 85 hours minimum, at least two semesters in full-time residence. For LL.M.: at least 24 credits beyond the J.D.; one year in full-time residence; thesis.

School of Medicine (63110)

Formed 1899. Library: 217,000 volumes; has MEDLINE.

Annual tuition: $27,435. Total average cost for all other expenses $7685.

Enrollment: first-year class 120, total 472 (men 60%, women 40%). Faculty: full-time 1100, part-time 1200. Degrees conferred: M.D., M.A.-M.D., M.D.-Ph.D. (Medical Scientist Training Program).

ADMISSION REQUIREMENTS. AMCAS report, transcripts, recommendations, MCAT required in support of application. Interview by invitation only. Applicants must have completed at least three years of college study. Does not have EDP. Apply through AMCAS after June 15, before November 15. Application fee $50. Phone: (314)362-6857; fax: (314)362-4658.

ADMISSION STANDARDS. Very competitive. Accepts 3–4% of total annual applicants. Approximately 8% are state residents.

FINANCIAL AID. Scholarships. MSTP funded by NIH. About 63% of students receive aid other than loans from School. Apply to Financial Aid Officer following acceptance. Use FAFSA.

DEGREE REQUIREMENTS. For M.D.: satisfactory completion of four-year program. For M.A.: satisfactory completion of five-year program. Ph.D.: see Graduate listing above.

FIELDS OF GRADUATE STUDY.
Anatomy.
Biochemistry.
Biophysics.
Cell Biology.
Genetics.
Immunology.
Microbiology.
Molecular Biology.
Neurosciences.
Pathology.
Pharmacology.
Physiology.

UNIVERSITY OF WASHINGTON
Seattle, Washington 98195
http://www.grad.washington.edu

Founded 1861. Coed. State control. Quarter system. Special facilities: Applied Physics Laboratory, arboretum, Bureau of Governmental Research Services, Botanical and Drug Plant Gardens, Burke Memorial Washington State Museum, Center for the Humanities, Center for Social Welfare, Center for Urban Horticulture, Child Development and Mental Retardation Center, Fisheries Research Institute, Friday Harbor Laboratories, Henry Art Gallery, Institute on Aging, Institute for Ethnic Studies in the United States, Laboratory of Radiation Biology, Northwest Center for Research on Women, oceanographic research vessels, Regional Primate Research Center, Washington Mining and Mineral Resources Research Institute. Libraries: 5,350,669 volumes, 6,070,000 microforms, 56,000 current periodicals, 483 PCs in all libraries.

Annual tuition: full-time resident $5044, nonresident $12,475; part-time, per quarter resident $505, nonresident $1212. On-campus housing for 672 married students, 4400 units for men and women. Average academic year housing cost: $4000 for married students; $3300 for single students, $7248 (includes $3948 for board). Contact Student Services Office: (206)543-4059 for on-campus housing information; (206)543-8997 for off-campus housing information. Day care facilities available.

Graduate School

Established 1911. Enrollment: full-time 6260 (men 60%, women 40%), part-time 1661. Graduate faculty: full-time 2400. Degrees conferred: M.A., M.Arch., M.A.I.S., M.A.T., M.B.A., M.Comm., M.Ed., M.F.A., M.Lib., M.O.T., M.P.T., M.S.W., M.S.P.A., M.H.A., M.S., M.S.Aero. & Astro., M.S.B.C.M., M.S.Cer.Eng., M.S.Chem.Eng., M.S.Civ.Eng., M.S.D., M.S.E.E., M.For.Res., M.S.Mech.Eng., M.S.Met.Eng., M.M., M.S.Nuc.Eng., M.N., M.P.A., M.P.H., M.S.P.E., M.S.P.H., M.S.Rad.Sci., M.U.P., Ph.D., Ed.D., D.M.A., D.A.

ADMISSION REQUIREMENTS. Two official transcripts, letters of recommendation, GRE Test required in support of School's application. Satisfactory score on TOEFL required for international students. Accepts transfer applicants. Graduates of unaccredited institutions not considered. Apply to Office of Graduate Admissions by May 15 (Summer), July 1 (Fall), November 1 (Winter), February 1 (Spring). Application fee $45. Phone: (206)543-5929 (request school/program).

ADMISSION STANDARDS. Very competitive for some departments, competitive and selective for the others. Minimum average: 3.0 for last two years (A = 4).

FINANCIAL AID. Six hundred and eighty-two scholarships/fellowships, 2369 teaching/research assistantships, Federal W/S, loans. Approved for VA benefits. Apply by February 15 to appropriate department chair/graduate program coordinator. Use FAFSA. Phone: (206)543-6101. About 35% of students receive aid other than loans from School. Aid sometimes available to part-time students.

DEGREE REQUIREMENTS. For master's: 36 credits minimum, at least three quarters (27 credits) in residence; foreign language and thesis for some departments; final oral/written exam. For doctorates: three years minimum, at least one year in full-time residence; reading knowledge of two foreign languages in some programs for Ph.D.; candidacy exam; dissertation; final exam.

FIELDS OF STUDY.

Accounting. M. Prof. Acc.
Aeronautics and Astronautics. M.S.A.A., Ph.D.
Anthropology. M.A., Ph.D.
Applied Mathematics. M.S., Ph.D.
Architecture. M.Arch.
Art. M.F.A.
Art History. M.A., Ph.D.
Asian Languages and Literature. M.A., Ph.D.
Astronomy. M.S., Ph.D.
Atmospheric Sciences. M.S., Ph.D.
Behavioral Neuroscience. Ph.D.
Biochemistry. M.S., Ph.D.
Bioengineering. M.S., M.S.E., Ph.D.
Biological Structure. M.S., Ph.D.
Biology Teaching. M.A.T.
Biostatistics. M.S., Ph.D.
Botany. M.S., Ph.D.
Building Construction Management. M.S.B.C.M.
Business Administration. M.B.A., Ph.D.
Chemical Engineering. M.S.Ch.E., Ph.D.
Chemistry. M.S., Ph.D.
Civil Engineering. M.S.Civ.E., Ph.D.
Classics. M.A., Ph.D.
Communications. M.A., M.C., Ph.D.
Comparative Literature. M.A., Ph.D.
Comparative Medicine. M.S.
Computer Science and Engineering. M.S., Ph.D.
Dance. M.F.A.
Dentistry. Includes endodontics, oral biology (M.S., Ph.D.), oral medicine, orthodontics, periodontics, pediatric dentistry, prosthodontics. M.S.D.
Drama. Includes acting, costume design, history, lighting design, playwriting, scenic design. M.F.A., Ph.D.
Economics. M.A., Ph.D.
Education. Includes administration, counselor, curriculum and instruction, special, speech. M.Ed., Ed.D., Ph.D.
Electrical Engineering. M.S.E.E., Ph.D.
Engineering. M.S.E., M.Engr., M.S.
English. M.A., M.A.T., Ph.D.
Environmental Health. M.P.H., M.S., Ph.D.
Epidemiology. M.P.H., M.S., Ph.D.
Fisheries. M.S., Ph.D.
Forest Resources. M.F.R., M.S., Ph.D.
Genetics. M.S., Ph.D.
Geography. M.A., Ph.D.
Geological Sciences. M.S., Ph.D.
Geophysics. M.S., Ph.D.
Germanics. M.A., Ph.D.
Health Administration. M.H.A.
Health Services. M.P.H.
History. Includes international studies, M.A. only; comparative religion, East Asian studies, Middle Eastern studies, Russian and East European studies, South Asian studies. M.A., Ph.D.
Immunology. M.S., Ph.D.
International Studies. Includes China studies, comparative religion, Japan studies, Korea studies, Middle Eastern studies, Russian/East European/Central Asian studies, South Asian studies. M.A.I.S. only.
Laboratory Medicine. M.S.
Landscape Architecture. M.L.A.
Law. LL.M., Ph.D.
Library and Information Science. M.Libr.
Linguistics. M.A., Ph.D.
Marine Affairs. M.M.A.
Materials Science and Engineering. M.S.M.S.&E., Ph.D.
Mathematics. M.A., M.S., Ph.D.
Mechanical Engineering. M.S.M.E., Ph.D.

Medical History and Ethics. M.A.
Microbiology. M.S., Ph.D.
Molecular and Cellular Biology. Ph.D.
Molecular Biotechnology. Ph.D.
Museology. M.A.
Music. M.A., M.M., D.M.A., Ph.D.
Near and Middle Eastern Studies. M.A.
Near East Language and Civilization. M.A.
Nursing. M.N., M.S., Ph.D.
Nutritional Sciences. M.S.
Oceanography. Includes biological, chemical, physical; M.S., Ph.D.
Pathobiology. M.S., Ph.D.
Pathology. M.S., Ph.D.
Pharmacology. M.S., Ph.D.
Pharmacy. Includes medicinal chemistry, pharmaceutics. M.S., Ph.D.
Philosophy. M.A., Ph.D.
Physics. M.S., Ph.D.
Physiology and Biophysics. M.S., Ph.D.
Political Science. M.A., Ph.D.
Psychology. Includes clinical, school; M.S., Ph.D.
Public Affairs. M.P.A.
Quantitative Ecology and Resource Management. M.S., Ph.D.
Rehabilitation Medicine. M.R.M., M.S., M.P.T.
Romance Language and Literature. M.A., Ph.D.
Scandinavian Languages and Literature. M.A., Ph.D.
Slavic Languages and Literature. M.A., Ph.D.
Social Welfare. Ph.D.
Social Work. M.S.W.
Sociology. M.A., Ph.D.
Speech and Hearing Sciences. M.S., Ph.D.
Speech Communication. M.A., Ph.D.
Statistics. M.S., Ph.D.
Technical Communication. M.S.
Urban Design and Planning. M.U.P., Ph.D.
Zoology. M.S., Ph.D.

School of Law (98105)

Established 1899. Quarter system. Law library: 430,000 volumes. Library has LEXIS, NEXIS, WESTLAW, DIALOG, DATATIMES.

Annual tuition: resident $4500, nonresident $11,500. Limited on-campus housing available. Total average annual additional expense: $11,000.

Enrollment: first-year class 187; total full-time 498 (men 54%, women 46%); postgraduates 26. Faculty: full-time 44, part-time 25. Degrees conferred: J.D., J.D.-M.B.A., J.D.-M.I.S., LL.M. (Marine Affairs).

ADMISSION REQUIREMENTS. LSDAS Law School report, Bachelor's degree, transcripts, LSAT (not later than December) required in support of application. TOEFL required for foreign students. Interview not required. Graduate of unaccredited colleges not considered. Apply to Admission Office after September 15, before January 15. Admits Fall only. Application fee $35. Phone: (206)543-0199; fax: (206)543-5671. For graduate study, apply to Director, Graduate Program, School of Law.

ADMISSION STANDARDS. Selective. Accepts 25% of total annual applicants.

FINANCIAL AID. Scholarships, partial tuition waivers, fellowships, assistantships, Federal W/S, loans. About 24% of students receive aid other than loans from School. Apply to Assistant Dean of School by March 1. Use FAFSA.

DEGREE REQUIREMENTS. For J.D.: 135 quarter hours minimum, at least 9 quarters in residence. For LL.M.: 36 quarter hours beyond the J.D. or equivalent; Asian Law requires proficiency in Japanese, Chinese, or Korean; thesis. For LL.M. (Law and Marine Affairs): 40–45 quarter hours, 15 in residence; research project.

FIELDS OF GRADUATE STUDY.
Asian Law. Emphasis on China, Japan, Korea.
International Environmental Law.
Law and Marine Affairs.
Law Librarianship.
Law of Sustainable International Development.

School of Medicine

Founded in 1945. Health Sciences Library: 100,000 volumes. Annual tuition: resident $8178, nonresident $20,592. Total average cost for all other expenses $5200.

Enrollment: first-year class 165, total 700 (men 55%, women 45%). Facult: full- and part-time and volunteers 1100. Degrees conferred: M.D., M.D.-Ph.D. (Medical Scientist Training Program). The M.S. and Ph.D. are offered through the Graduate School.

ADMISSION REQUIREMENTS. AMCAS report, transcripts, three letters of recommendation, MCAT, autiobiography, final screening interview required in suport of application. Does not have EDP. Interview and supplemental materials by invitation only. Accepts transfer applicants. Graduates of unaccredited colleges not considered. Preference given to WAMI residents. Apply to Assistant Dean for Admissions after June 15, before November 1. Application fee $35. Phone: (206)543-7212.

ADMISSION STANDARDS. Selective. Accepts about 15–20% of total annual applicants. Approximately 90% are WAMI residents.

FINANCIAL AID. Scholarships, research fellowships, loans. MSTP funded by NIH. Apply to School's Financial Aid Office after acceptance, but before February 28. Phone: (206)685-2520. Use FAFSA. About 80% of students receive some aid from School.

DEGREE REQUIREMENTS. For M.D.: satisfactory completion of four-year program. For M.S., Ph.D., see Graduate School listing above.

FIELDS OF GRADUATE STUDY.
Biochemistry.
Biomedical Engineering.
Biophysics.
Cell Biology.
Genetics.
Immunology.
Microbiology.
Molecular Biology.
Neurobiology.
Pathology.
Pharmacology.
Physiology.

School of Dentistry (98195-6365)

Established 1945. Annual tuition: resident $8178, nonresident $20,592. Total average cost for all other first-year expenses $4352. On-campus housing available. Annual housing costs: $9834.

Enrollment: first-year class 50; total 212 (men 70%, women 30%). Faculty: full-time 69, part-time 48. Degrees conferred: D.D.S., M.S.D., M.S., Ph.D.

ADMISSION REQUIREMENTS. AADSAS report, transcripts, DAT, recommendations required in support of application. Applicants must have completed at least three years of college study. Interview by invitation only. Preference given to state and WICHE residents. Apply through AADSAS after June 1, before December 1. Application fee $35. Phone: (206)543-5840; E-mail: evrgreen@U.washington.edu.

ADMISSION STANDARDS. Selective. Accepts 10–15% of total annual applicants. Approximately 80% are state residents.

FINANCIAL AID. Scholarships, grants, loans. About 20% of students receive aid other than loans from School. Apply to Financial Aid Office by March 1. Phone: (206)543-5840. Use FAFSA.

DEGREE REQUIREMENTS. For D.D.S.: satisfactory completion of 12 quarters of study, including summer quarters after year two, and year three. For M.S.D.: satisfactory completion of one-year program. For M.S., Ph.D.: see Graduate School listing above.

FIELDS OF GRADUATE STUDY.
Endodontics. M.S.D. only.
Oral Biology. M.S. and Ph.D. only.
Oral and Maxillofacial Surgery. Certificate.
Oral Medicine. M.S.D. only.
Orthodontics. M.S.D. only.
Pediatrics Dentistry. M.S.
Periodontics. M.S.D. only.
Prosthodontics. M.S.D. only.

UNIVERSITY OF WEST ALABAMA
Livingston, Alabama 35470

Founded 1835. Name changed from Livingston University in 1995. Located 120 miles SW of Birmingham. Coed. State control. Quarter system. Library: 97,000 volumes, 481,000 microforms, 870 current periodicals.

Tuition: per quarter hour $65. On-campus housing for both single and married students. Average academic year housing costs: $2055 (including board) for single students; $2650 for married students (including board). Contact Director of Housing for both on- and off-campus housing information. Phone: (205)652-3400.

School of Graduate Studies

Graduate study since 1958. Enrollment: full- and part-time 271. Graduate faculty: full-time 39, part-time 2. Degrees conferred: M.Ed., M.S.C.Ed., M.A.T.

ADMISSION REQUIREMENTS. Transcripts, GRE/MAT/NTE, Alabama teaching certificate, or equivalent required in support of School's application. (Certificate not required for master's in Continuing Education or M.A.T.) TOEFL required for international applicants. Interview not required. Accepts transfer applicants. Apply to Director of Admissions; no specified closing dates. Rolling admission process. Application fee $15. Phone: (205)652-3400.

ADMISSION STANDARDS. Selective. Usual minimum average: 2.5 (A = 4).

FINANCIAL AID. Limited to Federal W/S, loans. Apply to Office of Financial Aid by April 1. Use FAFSA and University's FAF. Phone: (205)652-3400. About 10% of students receive aid other than loans from University, 26% from all sources. Aid available for part-time students.

DEGREE REQUIREMENTS. For M.Ed.: 50 hours minimum, 15 in full-time residence, no thesis; final written exam. For M.S.C.Ed.; 50 hours minimum, 15 in full-time residence; final written exam. For M.A.T.: 60 hours minimum, 15 in full-time residence; final written exam. No language requirement for any degrees.

FIELDS OF STUDY.
Continuing Education. M.S.C.Ed. only.
Early Childhood Education.
Elementary Education.
Guidance and Counseling.
Library Media.
Physical Education.
School Administration.
Secondary Education.
Special Education.

WAYNE STATE COLLEGE
Wayne, Nebraska 68787

Founded 1891. Located 100 miles NW of Omaha. Coed. State control. Semester system. Library: 170,000 volumes, 544,000 microforms, 1000 current periodicals, 60 PCs.
Tuition: per credit, resident $69, nonresident $138. On-campus housing available. Average academic year housing costs: $2000 (room only) for single students; $2650 for married students. Contact Housing Office for both on- and off-campus housing information. Phone: (402)375-7318.

Graduate School

Enrollment: full-time 31, part-time 247. Faculty teaching graduate students: full-time 0, part-time 73. Degrees conferred: M.S.E., M.B.A., Ed.S.

ADMISSION REQUIREMENTS. Official transcripts, GRE/GMAT required in support of School's application. Accepts transfer applicants. Apply to Dean of Graduate Studies at least two months prior to date of registration. Rolling admission process. Application fee $10. Phone: (402)375-7232.

ADMISSION STANDARDS. Relatively open. Usual minimum average 2.5 (A = 4).

FINANCIAL AID. Annual awards from institutional funds: thirty-three teaching assistantships, loans. Apply by May 1 to Director of Graduate Studies Office for assistantships, to Financial Aid Office for all other programs. Use FAFSA. Phone: (402)375-7230. About 10% of students receive aid other than loans from College and outside sources. No aid for part-time students.

DEGREE REQUIREMENTS. For master's: 30 semester hours minimum; thesis optional; final oral/written exam. For Specialist: 33 semester hours beyond the master's degree; special project.

FIELDS OF STUDY.
Business Administration. M.B.A.
Business Education. M.S.E.
Counselor Education. M.S.E.
Educational Administration. Ed.S.
Elementary Administration. M.S.E.
Elementary Education. M.S.E.
English Education. M.S.E.
History. M.S.E.
Industrial Education. M.S.E.
Mathematics. M.S.E.
Physical Education. M.S.E.
Science. M.S.E.

Secondary Administration. M.S.E.
Social Sciences. M.S.E.
Special Education. M.S.E.

WAYNE STATE UNIVERSITY
Detroit, Michigan 48202

Founded 1868. Coed. State control. Semester system. Special facilities: Addiction Research Center, Center for the Study of Arts and Public Policy, Center for Urban Studies, Research Institute for Engineering Sciences, Institute of Gerontology, Hilberry Classic Repertory Theater, National Teachers Corps Center, Medical Center, Charles Grosberg Religious Center, FM station, Cryogenics Laboratory, Mass Communications Center (equipped for closed-circuit TV and portable videotaping operation), statistical research laboratory, Computer and Data Processing Center (includes two IBM and one Amdahl mainframe). Library: over 2,830,000 volumes, 3,300,000 microforms, 24,000 current periodicals.
Tuition: per credit, resident $153, nonresident $329. On-campus housing for 800 single students. Average annual housing cost: $750 per semester in dormitory; $450 per month in apartments. Apply to Housing Authority. Phone: (313)577-2116.

Graduate School

Graduate study since 1930. Enrollment: full-time 6013, part-time 7498. Graduate faculty: full- and part-time 1710. Degrees conferred: M.A., M.S., M.Ed., M.A.I.R., M.A.T., M.S.L.S., M.B.A., M.F.A., M.L., M.M., M.P.A., M.U.P., M.S.W., Ed.S., Ed.D., Ph.D.

ADMISSION REQUIREMENTS. Official transcripts required in support of School's application. GRE, MAT, GMAT/other entrance exams, letters of recommendation, interviews required by many departments. TOEFL required for international applicants. Accepts transfer applicants. Graduates of unaccredited institutions not considered. Apply to Office of University Admissions by July 1 (Fall), November 1 (Winter), March 1 (Spring), June 1 (Summer). Application fee $20; $30 for international applicants. Phone: (313)577-3577; fax: (313)577-7536.

ADMISSION STANDARDS. Selective for most departments. Usual minimum average: 2.6 (A = 4).

FINANCIAL AID. Annual awards from institutional funds: 250 scholarships, 55 graduate fellowships, 6–8 minority fellowships, 1013 graduate assistantships, Federal W/S, loans. Approved for VA benefits. Apply in early Winter to Graduate Dean for scholarships and fellowships, to department chair for assistantships; to Financial Aid Office for all other programs. Use FAFSA and University's FAF. Phone: (313)577-2172 (scholarships and fellowships), (313)577-3378 (loans). About 30% of students receive aid other than loans from University and outside sources. Aid available for part-time students.

DEGREE REQUIREMENTS. For most master's: Plan A—24 semester hours minimum plus thesis; Plan B—28 semester hours minimum plus essay; Plan C—30 semester hours minimum without thesis or essay, at least 24 in residence; final written/oral exam; no language for most majors. For Ed.S.: 30 hours minimum beyond the master's, at least 24 in residence; terminal project or field study. For Ed.D.: 100 hours minimum beyond the bachelor's, at least 30 in residence; preliminary, qualifying, final written/oral exam; dissertation. For Ph.D.: 90 hours minimum beyond the bachelor's, including dissertation, at least 30 in residence; preliminary exam for some majors; written/oral qualifying exams; final oral exam; reading knowledge of one or more foreign languages required in some fields.

FIELDS OF STUDY.

SCHOOL OF BUSINESS ADMINISTRATION:
Business Administration. M.B.A.
Taxation. M.S.T.

COLLEGE OF EDUCATION:
Administration and Supervision. Ed.D., Ph.D.
Art Education. M.Ed.
Bilingual/Bicultural Education. M.Ed.
Career and Technical Education. M.Ed., Ed.D., Ph.D.
Counselor Education. M.A., M.Ed., Ed.D., Ph.D.
Curriculum and Instruction. Ed.D., Ph.D.
Education Evaluation and Research. M.Ed., Ed.D., Ph.D.
Educational Leadership. M.Ed.
Educational Psychology. M.Ed., Ed.D., Ph.D.
Educational Sociology. M.Ed., Ed.D., Ph.D.
Elementary Education. M.A., M.A.T., M.Ed.
English Education (Secondary). M.Ed.
Foreign Language Education. M.Ed.
Health Education. M.Ed.
Higher Education. Ed.D., Ph.D.
History and Philosophy of Education. M.Ed., Ed.D., Ph.D.
Instructional Technology. M.Ed., Ed.D., Ph.D.
Mathematics Education. M.Ed.
Physical Education. M.Ed.
Pre-School and Parent Education. M.Ed.
Reading. M.Ed., Ed.D.
Recreation and Park Service. M.A.
Rehabilitation Counseling and Community Inclusion. M.A.
School and Community Psychology. M.A.
Science Education. M.Ed.
Secondary Education. M.A., M.A.T.
Social Studies Education (Secondary). M.Ed.
Special Education. M.Ed., Ed.D., Ph.D.
Sports Administration. M.A.

COLLEGE OF ENGINEERING:
Chemical and Materials Science Engineering. M.S., Ph.D.
Civil and Environmental Engineering. M.S., Ph.D.
Computer Engineering. M.S., Ph.D.
Electrical Engineering. M.S., Ph.D.
Electronic and Computer Control Systems. M.S.
Engineering Management. M.S.
Engineering Technology. M.S.E.T.
Environmental Auditing.
Hazardous Materials Management on Public Lands.
Hazardous Waste Control.
Hazardous Waste Management. M.S.
Industrial Engineering. M.S., Ph.D.
Manufacturing Engineering. M.S.
Mechanical Engineering. M.S., Ph.D.
Operations Research. M.S., Ph.D.
Polymer Engineering.

COLLEGE OF FINE, PERFORMING, AND COMMUNICATION ARTS:
Art. M.A., M.F.A.
Art History. Includes museum practices. M.A.
Communication. Includes general speech, oral interpretation, public relations/organization of communication, radio–TV–film, speech communication, speech communication education. M.A., Ph.D.
Design and Merchandising. M.A.
Music. Includes, composition, choral conducting, music education, performance, theory. M.A., M.M.
Theater. M.A., M.F.A., Ph.D.

GRADUATE SCHOOL:
Alcohol and Drug Abuse Studies.
Archival Administration.
Child and Family Life Studies.

Developmental Disabilities.
Gerontology.
Individual Interdisciplinary. Ph.D.
Infant Mental Health.
Library and Information Science. M.S.
Molecular Biology and Genetics. M.S., Ph.D.
Molecular and Cellular Toxicology. M.S., Ph.D.

COLLEGE OF LIBERAL ARTS:
Anthropology. M.A., Ph.D.
Art History. M.A.
Criminal Justice. M.P.A., M.S.
Economics. M.A., Ph.D.
English. Includes comparative literature. One language for M.A. M.A., Ph.D.
History. M.A., Ph.D.
Languages. Includes classics, French, German, Italian, Modern Languages (Ph.D.), Near Eastern, Spanish; M.A.
Linguistics. M.A.
Philosophy. M.A., Ph.D.
Political Science. M.A., Ph.D.
Public Administration. M.P.A.
Sociology. M.A., Ph.D.

COLLEGE OF LIFELONG LEARNING:
Interdisciplinary Studies. M.I.S.

COLLEGE OF NURSING:
Adult Primary Care Nursing. M.S.N.
Adult Psychiatric Mental Health. M.S.N.
Advanced Medical-Surgical Nursing. M.S.N.
Child and Adolescent Psychiatric Nursing. M.S.N.
Community Health Nursing. M.S.N.
Neonatal Nurse Practitioner.
Nursing. Ph.D.
Nursing Care Administration. M.S.N.
Nursing Education.
Nursing, Parenting, and Families. M.S.N.
Transcultural Nursing. M.S.N.

COLLEGE OF PHARMACY AND ALLIED HEALTH PROFESSIONS:
Allied Health Professions.
Anesthesia. M.S.
Clinical Laboratory Science. M.S.
Clinical Pharmacy. Pharm.D.
Health Systems Pharmacy Management. M.S.
Occupational and Environmental Health Sciences. M.S.
Occupational Therapy. M.S.
Pharmaceutical Sciences. M.S., Ph.D.
Physical Therapy. M.P.T.
Physician Assistant Studies. M.S.

COLLEGE OF SCIENCE:
Audiology and Speech Language Pathology. M.S., Ph.D.
Biological Sciences. Includes molecular biotechnology; GRE for admissions. M.S., Ph.D.
Chemistry. One language for M.S. M.A., M.S., Ph.D.
Communication Disorders and Sciences. M.A., Ph.D.
Computer Science. M.A., M.S., Ph.D.
Geology. M.S.
Mathematics. Includes applied, mathematical statistics. M.A., M.S., Ph.D.
Nutrition and Food Science. M.A., M.S., Ph.D.
Physics and Astronomy. M.A., M.S., Ph.D.
Psychology. Includes human development. M.A., Ph.D.

SCHOOL OF SOCIAL WORK:
Social Work. Includes administration and community, family, children and youth services, health care services, mental health services. M.S.W.

URBAN, LABOR, AND METROPOLITAN AFFAIRS:
Dispute Resolution. M.A.
Economic Development.
Geography. M.S.
Industrial Relations. M.A.I.R.
Urban Planning. M.U.P.

Law School

Founded 1927. Law library: 416,000 volumes. Library has LEXIS, NEXIS, WESTLAW. Special facilities: Intellectual Property Law Institute.

Annual tuition: full-time residents $6050, nonresidents $13,070; part-time resident $3292, nonresident $7036. Total average annual additional expense: $14,700.

Enrollment: first-year class, full-time 220, part-time 64; total 825 (men 54% women 46%), LL.M., 137. Faculty: full-time 33, part-time 34. Degrees conferred: J.D., J.D.-M.A. (History, Public Policy), LL.M. (Taxation, Labor Law, Corporate Planning).

ADMISSION REQUIREMENTS. LSDAS Law School report, bachelor's degree, transcripts, LSAT required in support of application. Interview not required. Accepts transfer applicants. Graduates of unaccredited institutions not considered. Apply to Director of Admissions by March 15. Rolling admissions process. Admits Fall only. Application fee $20. Phone: (313)577-3937.

ADMISSION STANDARDS. Selective. Accepts 40 of total annual applicants.

FINANCIAL AID. Scholarships, Federal W/S, loans. Apply to the Financial Aid Office by April 23. Use FAFSA. About 16% of student receive aid other than loans from School. Aid sometimes available for part-time student.

DEGREE REQUIREMENTS. For J.D.: Three years full-time or four years part-time, with satisfactory completion of 86-semester-hour program. For LL.M.: at least 24 semester hours beyond the J.D.; final essay.
Note: Summer and semester study-abroad programs available at the University of Warwick (Great Britain).

School of Medicine

Founded 1868. Library: 150,000 volumes. Located at Detroit Medical Center (48201). Annual tuition: resident $9709, nonresident $19,489, student fees $350. Total average cost for all other expenses $10,635.

Enrollment: first-year class 256 (EDP 25), total 1044 (men 57%, women 43%). Faculty: full-time 384, part-time 1200, Degree conferred: M.D. The Ph.D. is offered through the Graduate School.

ADMISSION REQUIREMENTS. AMCAS report, transcripts, recommendations, MCAT (prefer Spring results) required in support of application. Interview required of those candidates under serious consideration. Applicants must have completed at least three years of college study. Has EDP; apply between June 15 and August 1. Accepts transfer applicants. Preference given to state residents. Apply to Office of Admissions after June 15, before December 15 (firm). Application fee $30. Phone: (313)577-1466.

ADMISSION STANDARDS. Selective, Accepts 10–12% of total annual applicants. Approximately 92% are state residents.

FINANCIAL AID. Scholarships, loans, college work-study. Summer fellowships. Apply to Committee on Financial Aid and Scholarships after acceptance. Phone: (313)577-1039. About 30% of students receive aid other than loans from School.

DEGREE REQUIREMENTS. For M.D.: satisfactory completion of four-year program; step 1 of USMLE must be passed by end of year III. For Ph.D., see Graduate Division listing above. Combined M.D.-Ph.D. program is available. Apply during first year in medical school.

FIELDS OF GRADUATE STUDY.
Anatomy and Cell Biology. M.S., Ph.D.
Basic Medical Sciences. M.S.
Biochemistry and Molecular Biology. M.S., Ph.D.
Cancer Biology. M.S., Ph.D.
Cellular and Clinical Neurobiology. Ph.D.
Community Health Services. M.S.
Immunology and Microbiology. M.S., Ph.D.
Medical Physics. Ph.D.
Medical Research. M.S.
Pathology. Ph.D.
Pharmacology. M.S., Ph.D.
Physiology. M.S., Ph.D.
Psychiatry. M.S.
Radiological Physics. M.S.
Rehabilitation Sciences. M.S.

WEBSTER UNIVERSITY
Webster Groves, Missouri 63119-3194
http://198.246.0.2

Founded 1915. Located in St. Louis and 60 location worldwide. Coed. Private control. Semester system. Library: 222,000 volumes, 84,000 microforms, 2500 current periodicals.

Tuition: per credit hour $315 at home campus. No on-campus housing available.

Graduate Program

Graduate study since 1963. Enrollment: full-time 2220, part-time 5090. Faculty: full-time 60, part-time 1340. Degrees conferred: M.A., M.B.A., M.A.T., M.M., M.S., D.Mgt.

ADMISSION REQUIREMENTS: Official transcripts, bachelor's degree required in support of application. TOEFL required for international applicants. Accepts transfer applicants. Graduates of unaccredited institutions not considered. Application fee $20. Phone: (314)968-7000 or (800)75-ENROL; fax: (314)968-7166.

FINANCIAL AID. None other than loans. Approved for VA benefits. Financial Aid Office Phone: (324)968-6917; fax: (314)968-7125.

DEGREE REQUIREMENTS. For M.A., M.S.: 36 semester hours; thesis/nonthesis option. For M.B.A.: 36 semester hours. For M.A.T.: 33 semester hours. For M.M.: 32–34 semester hours. For D.Mgt.: 42 semester hours.

FIELDS OF STUDY.
Accounting.
Art.
Business.
Communication.
Computer Resources and Information Management.
Computer Science.
Counseling.
Finance.
Gerontology.
Health Care Management.
Health Services Management.
Human Resources Development.
Human Resources Management.

International Business.
International Relations.
Legal Studies.
Management.
Marketing.
Mathematics.
Media Communications.
Multidisciplinary Studies.
Music. Includes composition, conducting, jazz studies, education, performance, pedagogy.
Nursing.
Procurement and Acquisitions Management.
Public Administration.
Real Estate Management.
Science.
Security Management.
Social Science.
Space Operations. (Colorado Springs location only).
Space Systems.
Telecommunications Management.

WESLEYAN UNIVERSITY
Middletown, Connecticut 06459-0260

Founded 1831. Located 16 miles S of Hartford. Coed. Private control. Semester system. Special facilities: Center for the Arts, Davison Art Center, Freeman Athletic Center, Science Center, Van Vleck Observatory. Library: 2,000,000 volumes, 3500 current periodicals, 15 PCs.

Annual tuition: full-time $20,190, per course $2525. On-campus housing for married students, 93 graduate men, 65 graduate women. Average academic year housing cost: $400–$505 per month for married students, $3820 (room only) for single students. Apply to Graduate Admissions Office in Middletown for both on- and off-campus housing information. Phone: (203)685-2390.

Graduate Program

Graduate study since 1965. Enrollment: full-time 154, part-time 361. University faculty: full-time 109. Degrees conferred: M.A., M.A.L.S., C.A.S., Ph.D.

ADMISSION REQUIREMENTS. Transcripts, three letters of recommendation, GRE required in support of application. GRE Subject Test recommended. TOEFL required for international applicants. Interview often useful. Accepts transfer applicants. Apply to Graduate Admissions Office by March 15 for most programs, by January 15 for music. Application fee, none; $25 application fee for Music program. Phone: (203)685-1390; fax: (203)685-2001.

ADMISSION STANDARDS. Very competitive for some departments, competitive for others. Usual minimum average: 3.0 (A = 4).

FINANCIAL AID. Annual awards from institutional funds: 125 scholarships, 60 grants, 90 teaching assistantships, Federal W/S, loans. Approved for VA benefits. Apply, normally by March 15, to appropriate department chair for assistantships; to Financial Aid Office for all other programs. Use FAFSA and institutional FAF. Phone: (203)685-2800. About 98% of students receive aid from University and outside sources. Aid sometimes available for part-time students.

DEGREE REQUIREMENTS. For M.A.: one year in full-time study or the equivalent, but no more than four years for completion and at least two-thirds of total program in residence; reading knowledge of one foreign language for most majors, more for some programs; thesis or creative project; final written/oral exam. For M.A.L.S.: 30 semester hours, at least 24 in residence; designed for those who want an interdisciplinary education; credit may be earned solely in Summer sessions or in one calendar year of full-time study. For C.A.S. (for those who hold the master's degree): requirements essentially the same as for M.A.L.S. (transfer credits not accepted). For Ph.D.: normally at least 16 semester courses beyond the bachelor's, usually at least three years in residence; reading knowledge of two foreign languages; preliminary/qualifying exams; dissertation; final written/oral exam.

FIELDS OF STUDY.
Astronomy. Qualifying exam, apprenticeships for M.A. M.A. only.
Biology. Two years for M.A.
Chemistry.
Earth Science. M.A. only.
Mathematics. Apply by March 15.
Molecular Biology.
Music. Includes choral conducting and composition in Western music, ethnomusicology; Ph.D. in ethnomusicology only.
Physics. Two years for M.A.
Psychology. Apply by March 15. M.A. only.
Note: Special programs leading to the M.A.L.S. and C.A.S. use the course offerings of several University departments, with specializations in arts, humanities, mathematics, general studies, science, and social science.

WEST CHESTER UNIVERSITY OF PENNSYLVANIA
West Chester, Pennsylvania 19383

Founded 1871. Located 25 miles W of Philadelphia and 17 miles north of Wilmington. Coed. State control. Semester system. Library: 510,000 volumes, 1,033,000 microforms, 3000 current periodicals, 72 PCs in all libraries.

Tuition: per credit, resident $187, nonresident $336. Limited on-campus housing for graduate students. Average academic year housing costs: $4100 (including board). Apply to Director, Residence Life, for on-campus housing information; to the Office of Off-Campus Life for all off-campus housing information. Phone: (610)436-3307.

Division of Graduate Studies

Graduate study since 1959. Enrollment: full-time 357, part-time 1556. Faculty: 125 full- and part-time. Degrees conferred: M.Ed., M.A., M.S., M.M., M.B.A., M.S.A.

ADMISSION REQUIREMENTS. Two official transcripts required in support of application. Some programs require GRE Subject Test, MAT, or GMAT scores, interviews, and recommendations. TOEFL required for international applicants. Apply to Office of Graduate Studies by April 15 for Fall semester admission, October 15 for Spring semester. Application fee $25. Phone: (610)436-2943.

ADMISSION STANDARDS. Vary with program. Usual minimum average: 2.75, 3.00 for full degree status (A = 4).

FINANCIAL AID. Scholarships, awards, one hundred graduate assistantships, loans. Apply by February 1 to Dean of Graduate Studies and department chair for assistantships, scholarships, awards; to Financial Aid for all other programs. Use FAFSA. Phone: (610)436-2943.

DEGREE REQUIREMENTS. For master's: 30 credits minimum plus thesis, or 36 credits minimum without thesis; final written/oral exam in most programs.

FIELDS OF STUDY.
Administration. M.S. only.
Biology. M.A. only.
Business Administration. Includes economics/finance, general business, management. M.B.A.
Chemistry. Includes clinical, general. M.S. only.
Communication Studies. M.A. only.
Communicative Disorders. M.A. only.
Computer Science. M.S. only.
Counselor Education. M.Ed., M.S.
Criminal Justice. M.S. only.
Educational Research. M.S. only.
Elementary Education. M.Ed. only.
English. M.A. only.
Environmental Health. M.S. only.
French. M.A., M.Ed.
Geography. M.A. only.
German. M.Ed. only.
Health Services. M.S.A. only.
Higher Education Counseling. M.S. only.
History. M.A., M.Ed.
Human Resources Management. M.S.A. only.
Instructional Media. M.Ed., M.S.
Latin. M.Ed. only.
Leadership for Women. M.S.A. only.
Mathematics. M.A. only.
Music Education. M.M. only.
Music History. M.A. only.
Music Theory, Composition, and Performance. M.M. only.
Nursing. M.S. only.
Philosophy. M.A. only.
Physical Education. M.S. only.
Physical Science. Includes chemistry, earth science. M.A. only.
Psychology. Includes clinical, general, group psychotherapy, industrial/organizational. M.A. only.
Public Administration. M.S.A. only.
Public Health. M.S. only.
Reading. M.Ed. only.
School Health. M.Ed. only.
Secondary Education. M.Ed. only.
Secondary School Counseling. M.Ed. only.
Spanish. M.A., M.Ed.
Special Education. M.Ed. only.
Sport and Athletic Administration. M.S.A. only.
Training and Development. M.S.A. only.
Urban and Regional Planning. M.S.A. only.

part-time 5. Degrees conferred: M.A., M.S., M.M., M.Ed., M.B.A., M.P.A., M.P.Acc., Ed.S.

ADMISSION REQUIREMENTS. Official transcripts, NTE, GRE/GMAT, MAT, recommendations required in support of School's application. Interview for psychology majors. TOEFL required for international applicants. Accepts transfer applicants. Graduates of unaccredited institutions not considered. Apply to Dean of the Graduate School by August 19 (Fall), December 15 (Winter), March 10 (Spring), June 6 (Summer). Application fee $15. Phone: (770)836-6419; fax: (770)830-2301.

ADMISSION STANDARDS. Selective. Usual minimum average: 2.5 (A = 4).

FINANCIAL AID. Annual awards from institutional funds: 46 graduate assistantships; 208 research assistantships, Federal W/S, loans; varying number of dormitory hosts and hostesses. Approved for VA benefits. Apply to Dean of the Graduate School; no specified closing date. Use FAFSA. Phone: (770)836-6421. About 20% of students receive aid other than loans from University and outside sources.

DEGREE REQUIREMENTS. For M.A., M.S.: 45 quarter hours minimum plus thesis, or 60 hours without thesis, at least 25 or 30 hours minimum on-campus; reading knowledge of one foreign language; final comprehensive, oral exam. For M.M., M.P.A., M.Ed.: 60 quarter hours minimum, at least 30 on-campus; final written/oral exam; no language or thesis requirements. For M.B.A., M.P.Acc.: 50 quarter hours minimum, all on-campus. For Ed.S.: at least 45 quarter hours beyond the master's research project, at least 25 on-campus.

FIELDS OF STUDY.
Biology.
Business Administration.
Education. Includes elementary, secondary, middle school, special, guidance and counseling, art, administration and supervision, early childhood education, media, music, reading, physical education, business education, school home services, speech pathology.
English.
Gerontology.
History.
Mathematics.
Music.
Psychology.
Public Accounting.
Public Administration.
Rural and Small Town Planning.
Sociology.

STATE UNIVERSITY OF WEST GEORGIA
Carrollton, Georgia 30118

Founded 1933. Located 48 miles W of Atlanta. Coed. State control. Quarter system. Library: 314,213 volumes, 910,493 microforms, 1460 current periodicals, 55 PCs.

Annual tuition: full-time, resident $2067, nonresident $6141; per quarter hour, resident $52; nonresident $166. No on-campus housing for married students. Average academic year housing costs: $3345 (including board). Contact Director of Residential Life for off-campus housing information. Phone: (770)836-6426.

Graduate School

Graduate study since 1967. Enrollment: full-time 208, part-time 35. College faculty teaching graduate students: full-time 95,

WEST TEXAS A&M UNIVERSITY
Canyon, Texas 79016-0001

Graduate study since 1909. Located 15 miles S of Amarillo. Coed. State control. Semester system. Special facilities: Drylands Agriculture Institute, Equine Center, Killgore Research Center, Pan Handle Plains Historical Museum, Texas Experiment Station Regional Division. Library: 349,224 volumes, 125,080 microforms, 1815 current periodicals, 17 PCs.

Tuition: per credit resident $42, nonresident $246. On-campus housing costs: $3260 (includes board). Apply to Director of Housing. Phone: (806)656-3300.

Graduate School

Graduate study since 1932. Enrollment: full-time 4428, part-time 220. Graduate faculty: full-time 180, part-time 45. Degrees conferred: M.A., M.B.A., M.Ed., M.S., M.Ag., M.M., M.P.A., M.S.N., M.F.A.

ADMISSION REQUIREMENTS. Official transcripts, MAT/ GRE, GMAT (Business) required in support of School's application. Interview required by some departments. TOEFL required for international applicants. Accepts transfer applicants. Graduates of unaccredited institutions not considered. Apply to Director of Admissions. Rolling admissions process. Application fee for international applications $25. Phone: (806)656-2730; fax: (806)656-2733.

ADMISSION STANDARDS. Relatively open. Usual minimum average: 2.60, 2.85 for last two years (A = 4).

FINANCIAL AID. Annual awards from institutional funds: twenty-eight teaching assistantships, five research assistantships, Federal W/S, loans. Approved for VA benefits. Apply to appropriate department chair for assistantships; to Financial Aid Office for all other programs. Use FAFSA. Phone: (806)656-2055; fax: (806)656-2924. About 10% of students receive financial assistance. Aid sometimes available to part-time students.

DEGREE REQUIREMENTS. For master's: 30 credit hours with thesis or 36 credit hours with nonthesis option (available in most departments); at least 18 hours in residence comprehensive final exam.

FIELDS OF STUDY.
Accounting. M.P.A.
Agricultural Business. M.S.
Agriculture. M.S.
Animal Science. M.S.
Art. Includes studio; M.A.
Business. M.B.A
Chemistry. M.S.
Communication. M.A.
Education. Includes elementary, secondary (usual subjects), administration, counseling, diagnostician studies, health and physical (M.S.), reading specialist studies. M.Ed.
Engineering Technology. M.S.
English. M.A.
Environmental Science. M.S.
Family Nursing. M.S.N.
Finance and Economics. M.S.
History. M.A.
Interdisciplinary Study. M.A.
Mathematics. M.S.
Music. M.A.
Plant Science. M.S.
Political Science. M.A.
Psychology. M.A.
Sports and Exercise Science. M.S.

WEST VIRGINIA GRADUATE COLLEGE
100 Angus E. Peyton Drive,
South Charleston, West Virginia 25303-1600
http://www.wvgc.edu

College authorized and established 1972. Administrative offices located near Charleston, West Virginia. Most courses offered in evenings and on weekend at off-campus sites. Library: 47,000 volumes, 490,000 microforms, 490 current periodicals.

Annual tuition: resident $1614, nonresident $5796, per credit resident $90, nonresident 322. No on-campus housing available.

Enrollment: full-time 225, part-time 2515. Faculty: full-time 55, part-time 85. Degrees conferred: M.A., M.B.A., M.S.I.R., M.S.M., M.S., M.S.E., Ed.S.

ADMISSION REQUIREMENTS. Transcripts, three letters of recommendation, GRE, GMAT (business), MAT (psychology) required in support of College's application. TOEFL required for international applicants. Interview required for some departments. Accepts transfer applicants. Graduates of unaccredited colleges not considered. Apply to Admission Office at least 2 months prior to registration. Application fee none. Phone: (304)766-1901; fax: (304)746-2522.

ADMISSION STANDARDS. Selective. Usual minimum average: 2.5 (A = 4).

FINANCIAL AID. Limited to grants, tuition waivers, loans. Approved for VA benefits. Apply to Financial Aid Office: no specified closing date. Use FAFSA. Phone: (304)746-1906; fax: (304)746-2522.

DEGREE REQUIREMENTS. For master's: 36 semester hours minimum: thesis or problem report for many departments; final oral/written exam. For Ed.S.: 30 semester hours minimum beyond master's; special project.

FIELDS OF STUDY.
Business Administration.
Counseling.
Educational Leadership.
Elementary Education.
Engineering. Includes chemical, control systems, environmental, management.
Environmental Science.
Humanities.
Industrial Relations.
Information Systems.
Management. Includes criminal justice, employee relations, health care, public. M.S.M. only.
Psychology. Includes school (Ed.S.).
Reading Education.
Secondary Education.
Special Education.

WEST VIRGINIA SCHOOL OF OSTEOPATHIC MEDICINE
Lewisburg, West Virginia 24901-1128

College of Osteopathic Medicine

Founded 1974. Coed. State control. Semester system. Library: 38,000 volumes, 520 current periodicals, 12 PCs; has MEDLINE, CANCERLINE, BIOETHIC, HEALTH, PALINET, TOXLINE, DIALOG, OCLC.

Annual tuition: resident $9450, nonresident $24,300. No on-campus housing available. Total of all other first-year expenses $19,511.

Enrollment: first-year class 65, total 258 (men 68%, women 32%). Faculty: full-time 21, part-time 60. Degree conferred: D.O.

ADMISSION REQUIREMENTS. AACOMAS report, bachelor's degree preferred, official transcripts, MCAT, three recommendations (one from premed advisory committee, one evaluation from a physician, preferably a D.O.), supplemental form required in support of application. Interview by invitation only. Graduates of unaccredited colleges not considered. Preference given to state residents, SREB residents, southern Appalachian state residents. Apply by March 1 to the Director of

Admissions and Registrar. Admits first-year students Fall only. Rolling admission process. Application fee $50; $75 for nonresidents. Phone: (800)356-7836 (in state), (800)537-7077 (out of state), (304)645-6270.

ADMISSION STANDARDS. Selective. Accepts approximately 7% of total annual applicants. Usual minimum average: 2.75 (A = 4). Mean GPA: 3.1.

FINANCIAL AID. Scholarships, tuition waivers, loans. Approved for VA benefits. Apply by July 1 to the Financial Aid Office. Use FAFSA and institutional FAF.

DEGREE REQUIREMENT. For D.O.: satisfactory completion of four-year program.

WEST VIRGINIA UNIVERSITY
Morgantown, West Virginia 26506-6009

Established 1867. Located 70 miles S of Pittsburgh, Pennsylvania. Coed. State control. Semester system. Special facilities: Agricultural Experiment Station, Center for Black Culture and Research, Bureau of Business Research, Bureau of Government Resource, Energy Research Center, Concurrent Engineering Research Center, Fluidization Center, Engineering Experiment Station, Gerontology Center, Institute for the History of Technology and Industrial Archeology, Institute for Labor Relations, NASA facility, National Research Center for Coal and Energy, Regional Research Institute, Water Research Institute, Westvaco Natural Resource Center. Women Studies Center. Library: 1,877,000 volumes, 2,612,000 microforms, 13,000 current periodical, 200 PCs in all libraries.

Annual tuition: full-time, resident $2244, nonresident $6774; per credit resident $103, nonresident $358. Limited on-campus housing for single and married students. Annual housing costs: $4400 (including board) for single student; $4800 for married students. Off-campus housing costs: $330–$482 per month. Contact Housing and Residence Life for both on- and off-campus housing information. Phone: (304)293-2812.

Graduate Studies

Enrollment: full-time 2278, part-time 3258. Faculty: full-time 789, part-time 200. Degrees conferred: M.A., M.S., M.Agr., M.M., M.B.A., M.F.A., M.P.A. (Professional Accountancy), M.P.A., M.S.F., M.S.E., M.S.E.E., M.S.A.E., M.S.C.E., M.S.Ch.E., M.S.E.E., M.S.E.M., M.S.F., M.S.I.E., M.S.M.E., M.S.N., M.S.PNGE., M.S.W., M.S.J., M.A.L.S., C.A.S., Ed.D., D.M.A., Ph.D.

ADMISSION REQUIREMENTS. Official transcripts required in support of application. GRE Subject Tests/GMAT, letters of recommendation, interviews required for some departments. TOEFL required for foreign applicants. Accepts transfer applicants. Graduates of unaccredited colleges not considered. Apply to Director of Admissions and Records at least one month prior to general registration. Rolling admission process. Application fee $25. Phone: (800)344-NWUI; fax: (304)293-3080.

ADMISSION STANDARDS. Selective for most departments, very selective or competitive for the others. Usual minimum average: 2.5 (A = 4).

FINANCIAL AID. Annual awards from institutional funds: 50 scholarships/fellowships, 600 teaching assistantships, 450 research assistantships, tuition waivers, Federal W/S, loans. Approved for VA benefits. Apply by March 1 to appropriate department chairman for fellowships, assistantships; to the Of-

fice of Financial Assistance for all other programs. Use FAFSA. Phone: (304)293-5242. Aid available for part-time students.

DEGREE REQUIREMENTS. For master's: 30 semester hours minimum, at least 24 in full-time residence; thesis/nonthesis option; final report for many departments; final oral/written exam in many programs. For C.A.S.: 30 hours minimum beyond the master's, at least 24 in residence including one semester or Summer session in full-time study; research report; final oral exam. For Ed.D.: 72 semester hours minimum beyond the bachelor's, at least two consecutive semesters in full-time residence; advancement to candidacy exams; dissertation; final oral exam. For D.M.A.: three years full-time study, at least one year in full-time residence; written research project; reading knowledge of one foreign language. For D.M.A., Performance: same as above except major solo recital. For D.M.A., Composition: major composition project; final oral exam. For Ph.D.: three years minimum beyond the bachelor's, at least two semesters in full-time residence; foreign language competency required by most departments; dissertation; final oral exam.

FIELDS OF STUDY.

COLLEGE OF AGRICULTURE AND FORESTRY:
Agricultural Education. M.S.
Agricultural and Resources Economics. M.S.
Agricultural Sciences. Ph.D.
Agriculture. M.Agr.
Animal and Veterinary Science. M.S.
Family Resources. M.S.
Forestry. M.S.F.
Natural Resources Economics. Ph.D.
Plant and Soil Sciences. M.S.
Recreation and Parks Management. M.S.
Wildlife and Fisheries Resources. M.S.

COLLEGE OF ARTS AND SCIENCES:
Biology. M.S., Ph.D.
Chemistry. M.S., Ph.D.
Communication Studies. M.A.
Computer Science. M.S., Ph.D.
English. M.A., Ph.D.
Foreign Languages. M.A.
Geography. M.A.
Geology. M.S., Ph.D.
History. M.A., Ph.D.
Mathematics. M.S., Ph.D.
Physics. M.S., Ph.D.
Political Science. M.A., Ph.D.
Psychology. M.A., Ph.D.
Public Administration. M.P.A.
Sociology and Anthropology. M.A.
Statistics. M.A.

COLLEGE OF BUSINESS AND ECONOMICS:
Economics. M.A., Ph.D.
Industrial Relations. M.S.
Professional Accountancy. M.P.A.

COLLEGE OF CREATIVE ARTS:
Art. M.A.
Music. M.M., Ph.D., D.M.A.
Theater. M.F.A.
Visual Arts. M.F.A.

COLLEGE OF ENGINEERING:
Aerospace Engineering. M.S.A.E.
Chemical Engineering. M.S.Ch.E.
Civil Engineering. M.S.C.E.

Electrical Engineering. M.S.E.E.
Engineering. M.S.E., Ph.D.
Engineering of Mines. M.S.E.M.
Industrial Engineering. M.S.I.E.
Mechanical Engineering. M.S.M.E.
Mineral Engineering. Ph.D.
Occupational Hygiene and Occupational Safety. M.S.
Petroleum and Natural Gas Engineering. M.S.PNGE.
Safety and Environmental Management. M.S.

COLLEGE OF HUMAN RESOURCES AND EDUCATION:
Counseling. M.A.
Education. Ed.D.
Education Administration. M.A.
Educational Psychology. M.A.
Elementary Education. M.A.
Reading. M.A.
Rehabilitation Counseling. M.S.
Secondary Education. M.A.
Special Education. M.A.
Speech Pathology and Audiology. M.S.
Technology Education. M.A.

INTERDISCIPLINARY PROGRAMS:
Genetics and Developmental Biology. M.S., Ph.D.
Liberal Studies. M.A.L.S.
Reproductive Physiology. M.S., Ph.D.

PERLEY ISAAC REED SCHOOL OF JOURNALISM:
Journalism. M.S.J.

COLLEGE OF MINERAL AND ENERGY RESOURCES:
Engineering of Mines. M.S.E.M.
Mineral Engineering. Ph.D.
Petroleum and Natural Gas Engineering. M.S. PNGE.
Safety and Environmental Management. M.S.

SCHOOL OF NURSING:
Nursing. M.S.N.

SCHOOL OF PHARMACY:
Pharmaceutical Sciences. M.S., Ph.D.

SCHOOL OF PHYSICAL EDUCATION:
Physical Education. M.S.

SCHOOL OF SOCIAL WORK:
Social Work. Includes aging, community health, mental health, family. M.S.W.

College of Law (26506-6130)

Established 1878. Semester system. Law library: 198,400 volumes, Library has LEXIS, WESTLAW, CALI.

Annual tuition/fees full-time, resident $3994, nonresident $10,254. On-campus housing available. Apply to University Housing office. Total average annual additional expense: $7000–8000.

Enrollment: first-year class 118, total full-time 400 (men 52%, women 48%). No part-time students. Faculty: full-time 26, part-time 9. Degrees conferred: J.D., J.D.-M.B.A., J.D.-M.P.A.

ADMISSION REQUIREMENTS. LSDAS Law School report, bachelor's degree, transcripts, LSAT required in support of application. West Virginia residents given preference. Accepts a limited number of transfer applicants. Graduates of unaccredited colleges not considered. Apply to Office of Admission, after September 1, before February 1. Admits beginning students Fall only. Application fee $45. Phone: (304)293-5304; fax: (304)293-6891.

ADMISSION STANDARDS. Selective. Accepts 25% of total annual applicants.

FINANCIAL AID. Scholarships, Federal W/S, loans. Apply to the Financial Aid Counselor by March 1. Use FAFSA and institutional application (due by April 1). About 15% of students receive aid other than loans from College. No aid for part-time students.

DEGREE REQUIREMENTS. For J.D.: 90-credit-hour program, at least 55 in residence.

School of Medicine

Located at Medical Center. Medical training since 1902. Library 84,000 volumes.

Annual tuition: resident $1710 nonresident $4620; student fees, resident $6670, nonresident $16,094. Housing available for married and single students. Total average cost for all other expenses $7000.

Enrollment: first-year class 88 (EDP 9), total 374 (men 56%, women 44%); postgraduates 206. Faculty: full-time 482, part-time 34. Degrees conferred: M.D., M.D.-Ph.D. The M.S., Ph.D. are offered through the Graduate School.

ADMISSION REQUIREMENTS. AMCAS Report, transcripts, recommendations, MCAT, final screening interview required in support of application. Has EDP (state residents only); apply between June 15 and August 1. Interview by invitation only. Applicants must have completed at least three years of college study for admission. West Virginia residents given preference. Accepts transfer applicants. Graduates of unaccredited colleges not considered. Apply to Chair, Committee on Admissions, after June 15, before December 1. Admits beginning students Fall only. Application fee $30. Phone: (304)293-3521; fax: (301)293-4973.

ADMISSION STANDARDS. Selective. Accepts about 10–12% of total annual applicants. Approximately 90% are state residents.

FINANCIAL AID. Scholarships, loans; fellowships, assistantships for teaching/research. Apply to Financial Aid Officer for scholarships, loans; to appropriate department chair for fellowships, assistantships; no specified closing date. Use FAFSA.

DEGREE REQUIREMENTS. For M.D.: satisfactory completion of four-year program. For Ph.D., see Graduate School listing above.

FIELDS OF GRADUATE STUDY.
Anatomy.
Biochemistry
Biomedical Engineering.
Cell Biology.
Immunology.
Microbiology.
Molecular Biology.
Neurosciences.
Pharmacology and Toxicology.
Physiology.

School of Dentistry

Established 1957. Located at Medical Center.

Annual tuition: resident $5127, nonresident $13,234. Total average cost for all other first-year expenses $7780. Housing available. Contact Director of Housing for both on- and off-campus housing information. Phone: (304)293-4491.

Enrollment: first-year class 40, total full-time 250 (men 70%, women 30%); postgraduates 15. Faculty: full-time 63, part-time 86. Degrees conferred: D.D.S., M.S., D.D.S.-M.S., D.D.S.-Ph.D.

ADMISSION REQUIREMENTS. AADSAS report, transcripts, DAT (not later than November 1) required in support of application. Interview by invitation only. Applicants must have completed at least three years of college study for admission. West Virginia residents given preference. Graduates of unaccredited institutions not considered. Apply to Dean of Admissions after June 1, before March 1 (flexible). Application fee $30. Phone: (304)293-3521.

ADMISSION STANDARDS. Selective. Accepts about 15–20% of total annual applicants. Approximately 50% are state residents.

FINANCIAL AID. Scholarships, loans. Apply to Financial Aid Officer for scholarships and loans; no specified closing date. Use FAFSA. Phone: (304)293-3706.

DEGREE REQUIREMENTS. For D.D.S.: satisfactory completion of three to four-year program. For M.S.: satisfactory completion of one-year program. For Ph.D.: see Graduate School listing above.

FIELDS OF GRADUATE STUDY.
Dental Hygiene. M S.
Endodontics. M.S.
Oral Surgery. Certificate only.
Orthodontics. M.S.

WESTERN CAROLINA UNIVERSITY
Cullowhee, North Carolina 28723-9022

Founded 1889; college work began 1907. Located 52 miles W of Asheville. Coed. State control. Semester system. Special facility: Computer Center with two DEC VAX 4000/700A, Mountain Aquaculture Center, Mountain Heritage Center, Center for Improving Mountain Living. Library: 436,000 volumes, 1,116,000 microforms, 2100 current periodicals.

Annual tuition: full-time, resident $1669, nonresident $8823; per credit, resident $135, nonresident $1029. On-campus housing for 1570 graduate men, 1733 graduate women; 45 units for married students. Average academic year housing costs: single students $2454 (including board), married students $3750 (including board). Contact Director of Housing for both on- and off-campus housing information. Phone: (704)227-7303.

Graduate School

Graduate study since 1951. Enrollment: full-time 294, part-time 396. Graduate faculty: full-time 273, part-time 20. Degrees conferred: M.A., M.A.Ed., M.H.S., M.I.E., M.B.A., M.M.E., M.P.A., M.P.M., M.S., Ed.S., C.A.S.

ADMISSION REQUIREMENTS. Official transcripts, letters of reference in most programs (GRE for M.A., M.A.Ed., M.H.S., M.I.E., M.M.E., M.P.A., M.S., Ed.S., C.A.S.; GMAT for M.B.A., M.P.M.) required in support of School's application. TOEFL required for international applicants. Accepts transfer applicants. Graduates from unaccredited institutions not considered. Apply to and have all credentials at Graduate School at least 2 months prior to registration. Application fee $25. Phone: (704)227-7398; fax: (704)227-7480.

ADMISSION STANDARDS. Selective. Usual minimum average: 3.0 (A = 4).

FINANCIAL AID. Annual awards from institutional funds: 3 Chancellors' fellowships, 175 graduate assistantships, 30 tuition waivers, 16 study grants, Federal W/S, loans. Approved for VA benefits. Apply by March 15 to Dean of Graduate School or department chair for assistantships, fellowships; to the Financial Aid for all other programs. Use FAFSA. Phone: (704)227-7290. About 25% of students receive aid other than loans from University and outside sources. Aid sometimes available to part-time students.

DEGREE REQUIREMENTS. For master's: 30–36 semester hours, at least 24 in residence; comprehensive exam; thesis for M.A., M.H.S., M.S.; some M.A., M.S. programs require one foreign language. For Ed.S.: 30 semester hours beyond the master's; special project.

FIELDS OF STUDY.
American History. M.A.
Applied Mathematics. M.S.
Art Education. M.A.
Biology. M.S.
Business Administration. M.B.A.
Chemistry. M.S.
Communication Disorders. M.S.
Community Counseling. M.S.
Curriculum and Instruction. M.Ed.
Educational Supervision. Includes elementary, middle, curriculum and instruction, instructional technology specialist-computers. M.Ed., Ed.S.
Elementary Education. M.Ed.
English. M.A.
Health Sciences. M.H.S.
Home Economics. M.S.
Human Resources Development. M.S.
Industrial Education. Includes public school, two-year colleges. M.I.E.
Middle grades. M.Ed., Ed.S.
Music. M.A.
Music Education. M.M.E.
Physical Education. Includes public school, two-year colleges; M.Ed.
Physical Therapy. M.P.T.
Project Management. M.P.M.
Psychology. Includes clinical, general, school. M.A.
Public Affairs. M.P.A.
Reading. Includes public school, two-year colleges. M.Ed.
School Administration. M.S.A.
School Counseling. C.A.S.
Secondary Education. Includes biology, business, chemistry, English, mathematics, social sciences, home economics. M.Ed.
Special Education. Includes general (with concentrations in behavioral, learning disabilities, mental retardation). M.Ed.
Studio Art. M.A.
Technology. M.S.
Two-Year College Teaching. Includes biology, chemistry, English, individually approved multidisciplinary studies, mathematics, physical education, social sciences. M.Ed.

WESTERN CONNECTICUT STATE UNIVERSITY
Danbury, Connecticut 06810-6885
http://www.wcsu.edu

Established 1903, Located 60 miles N of New York City. Coed. State control. Semester system. Library: 220,000 volumes, 50,000 microforms.

Tuition: per semester hour, resident $170, nonresident $170. On-campus housing available. Average academic year housing costs: $3950–$4496. Contact Office of Housing for both on- and off-campus housing information. Phone: (203)837-8543.

Division of Graduate Studies

Graduate study since 1955. Enrollment: 1050 (men 400, women 650). College faculty: full-time 40, part-time 10. Degrees conferred: M.A., M.B.A., M.S., M.H.A., M.S.N.

ADMISSION REQUIREMENTS. Official transcripts, interview required in support of application. GRE/MAT/GMAT required for some programs. TOEFL required for international applicants. Accepts transfer applicants. Graduates of unaccredited colleges not considered. Apply to Dean, Division of Graduate Studies; no specified closing dates. Application fee $20. Phone: (203)837-8243; fax: (203)837-8320.

ADMISSION STANDARDS. Selective for some departments, relatively open for others. Usual minimum average: 2.7 (A = 4).

FINANCIAL AID. Limited to assistantships, Federal W/S, loans. Approved for VA benefits. Apply to Director of Financial Aid; no specified closing date. Use FAFSA and University's FAF. Phone: (203)837-8580; fax: (203)837-8320. About 5% of students receive aid other than loans from outside sources.

DEGREE REQUIREMENTS. For M.A., M.S.: 30 semester hours minimum, at least 21 in residence; thesis/nonthesis option. For M.S.N.: 40 semester hours. For M.B.A.: 57 semester hours.

FIELDS OF STUDY.
Biological and Environmental Sciences. M.A.
Business. M.B.A., M.H.A.
Community Counseling.
Earth and Planetary Sciences. M.S.
Education. Includes early childhood curriculum, English curriculum, and instructional technology, mathematical, music, reading, special.
English. M.A.
History. M.A.
Mathematics. Includes computer sciences. M.A.
Nursing. Includes adult. M.S.N.
School Counseling. M.S.

WESTERN ILLINOIS UNIVERSITY
Macomb, Illinois 61455-1390
http://www.wiu.edu

Founded 1895. Located 250 miles SW of Chicago. Coed. State control. Semester system. Library: 1,000,000 volumes, 200 microforms, 3500 current periodicals.

Annual tuition: full-time, resident $2918, nonresident $7214. On-campus housing for 336 married students, 3148 men, 2972 women. Average annual housing cost: $3810 for married students, $4493 (including board) for single students. Contact Graduate and Family Housing Office for on-campus (309)298-2461, off-campus (309)298-3285.

School of Graduate Studies

Graduate study since 1945. Enrollment: full-time 691 (men 352, women 339), part-time 1035. Graduate faculty: full-time 372, part-time 43. Degrees conferred: M.A., M.S., M.S. in Ed., M.B.A., M.Acc., M.F.A., Ed.S., S.S.P.

ADMISSION REQUIREMENTS. Two official transcripts, GRE Subject Test (Psychology, Political Science only), GMAT (M.B.A. and Accounting only) required in support of School's application. Interview required for some departments. TOEFL

required for international applicants. Accepts transfer applicants. Graduates of unaccredited institutions not considered. Apply to Graduate Admissions at least three weeks prior to registration. No application fee. Phone: (309)298-1806; fax: (309)299-2245.

ADMISSION STANDARDS. Relatively open. Usual minimum average: 2.5 (A = 4).

FINANCIAL AID. Annual awards from institutional funds: 5 grants, 346 assistantships, 14 teaching assistantships, Federal W/S, loans. Approved for VA benefits. Apply by March 1 to appropriate chair for assistantships; to Financial Aid Office for all other programs. Use FAFSA. Phone: (309)298-2446; fax: (309)298-2353. About 50% of students receive aid other than loans from University and outside sources.

DEGREE REQUIREMENTS. For master's: 30–36 semester hours minimum, at least 24 in residence; thesis/nonthesis option; final written/oral exam. For Ed.S. (Educational Administration only): 32 hours minimum beyond the master's; 12 credits within a period of three consecutive semesters. For M.F.A. (Theater): 60 hours minimum, two academic years, and one Summer in residence.

FIELDS OF STUDY.
Accountancy. GMAT for admission.
Biological Sciences. Includes botany, zoology.
Business Administration. GMAT for admission.
Chemistry.
College Student Personnel. Interview required for admission.
Communication Sciences and Disorders.
Computer Science.
Economics.
Education. Includes elementary, counseling (interview for admission), educational administration, health, interdisciplinary studies, reading, special education.
English.
Geography.
Gerontology.
History.
Industrial Technology.
Instructional Technology and Telecommunications.
Law Enforcement and Justice Administration.
Mathematics.
Music.
Physical Education.
Physics.
Political Science. GRE Subject for admission.
Psychology. GRE Subject for admission.
Public Communication and Broadcasting.
Recreation, Park, and Tourism Administration.
Sociology.
Theater. Interview required for admission.

WESTERN KENTUCKY UNIVERSITY
Bowling Green, Kentucky 42101-3576

Founded 1906. Located 120 miles S of Louisville, 65 miles N of Nashville. Coed. State control. Semester system. Library: 875,000 volumes, 2,400,000 microforms, 4800 current periodicals, 50 PCs in all libraries.

Annual tuition: full-time resident $2210, nonresident $6050; per credit, resident $120, nonresident $334. On-campus housing available for single students only. Average academic year housing costs: $1600. Off-campus housing costs: $400–$550. Contact Director of Housing for both on- and off-campus housing information. Phone: (502)745-2100.

Graduate Studies

Graduate study since 1931. Enrollment: full-time 400, part-time 1650 (men 35%, women 65%). Graduate faculty: full-time 350, part-time 70. Degrees conferred: M.A., M.S., M.A.E., M.P.A., M.P.Acc., Ed.S.

ADMISSION REQUIREMENTS. Transcripts, GRE/MAT, GMAT (business) required in support of application. TOEFL required for international applicants. Accepts transfer applicants. Graduates of unaccredited institutions not considered. Apply to Office of Graduate Studies at least two month prior to enrollment date. Application fee $20. Phone: (502)745-2446.

ADMISSION STANDARDS. Selective. Usual minimum average: 2.75 (3.0 for some departments) (A = 4).

FINANCIAL AID. Annual awards from institutional funds: 40 teaching assistantships, 160 research assistantships, Federal W/S, loans. Approved for VA benefits. Apply to Office of Graduate Studies for assistantships; to the Office of Financial Aid for all other programs. Use FAFSA. Phone: (502)745-2755, (502)745-6586.

DEGREE REQUIREMENTS. For master's: 30 credit hours minimum; thesis/nonthesis option. For Specialist (Ed.S.), S.S.P.: 30 credit hours beyond the master's degree.

FIELDS OF STUDY.
Accountancy.
Agricultural Education.
Agricultural Sciences.
Art Education.
Biology.
Business Education.
Chemistry.
City and Regional Planning.
Communication.
Communication Disorders.
Computer Science.
Counselor Education.
Economics.
Educational Administration.
Elementary Education.
English.
Exceptional Child Education.
Folklore Studies.
French.
Geography.
German.
Health Education.
History.
Home Economics and Family Living.
Interdisciplinary Early Childhood.
Library Science.
Mathematics.
Mental Health Counseling.
Music.
Music Education.
Nursing.
Physical Education and Recreation.
Psychology.
Public Administration.
Public and Community Health.
Reading.
Secondary Education.
Sociology.
Spanish.
Student Affairs.
Vocational and Technical Education.

WESTERN MARYLAND COLLEGE
Westminster, Maryland 21157-4390

Founded 1867. Located 32 miles NW of Baltimore. Coed. Private control. Semester system. Library: 173,000 volumes.

Tuition: per credit $195. Limited on-campus housing available during academic year and Summer session for single students only. Average academic year housing costs: $5465. Contact Housing Office for both on- and off-campus housing information. Phone: (410)857-2237.

Graduate Program

Enrollment: full-time 76; part-time 1102 (men 30%, women 70%). Graduate faculty: full-time 25, part-time 60. Degrees conferred: M.S., M.L.A.

ADMISSION REQUIREMENTS. Official transcripts, three letters of reference, interview; GRE, MAT, or NTE required in support of application. TOEFL required for international applicants. Accepts transfer applicants. Apply to Dean of Graduate Admissions. Application fee $30. Phone: (410)857-2500; fax: (410)857-2515.

ADMISSION STANDARDS. Selective. Usual minimum average: 2.75 (A = 4).

FINANCIAL AID. Graduate assistantships available in housing, education department, physical education department, grants, loans. Apply to department chair; no specified closing date. Use FAFSA. Phone: (410)857-2233; fax: (410)857-2729. About 5% of students receive aid other than loans from both College and outside sources.

DEGREE REQUIREMENTS. For master's: 30–33 hours; thesis/nonthesis option; comprehensive exam.

FIELDS OF STUDY.
Administration.
Counseling.
Curriculum and Instruction.
Education of the Deaf. Includes the teaching of sign language, the teaching of interpreting.
Elementary Education.
Liberal Arts.
Media/Library Science.
Physical Education.
Reading.
Secondary Education.
Special Education.

WESTERN MICHIGAN UNIVERSITY
Kalamazoo, Michigan 49008-5120

Founded 1903. Located 150 miles W of Detroit. Coed. State control. Semester system. Special facilities: Applied Mechanics Institute, Behavior Research and Development Center, Business Research and Service Institute, Center for Communications Research, Concurrent Computation Research Center, Design Center, Center for Electron Microscopy, Enabling Technology Center, Center for Research on Educational Accountability and Teacher Evaluation, Geographic Information System Research Center, Medieval Institute, Printing and Research Center, Kercher Center for Social Research, Institute for Water Sciences, Women's Center. Library: 1,649,000 volumes, 600,000 microforms, 540 current periodicals, 288 PCs in all libraries.

Tuition: per semester credit hour, resident $133, nonresident $326. On-campus housing available for both married and single students. Average academic year housing cost: $4097 (including board) for single students; $345–$579 per month for married students. Contact Housing Director for both on- and off-campus housing information. Phone: (800)882-9819.

The Graduate College

Enrollment: full-time 1034, part-time 2111 (men 50%, women 50%). University faculty teaching graduate students: full-time 725, part-time 401. Degrees conferred: M.S., M.A., M.F.A., M.B.A., M.D.A., M.M., M.P.A., M.S., M.S.A., M.S.E., M.S.W, Ed.S., Ed.D., D.P.A., Ph.D.

ADMISSION REQUIREMENTS. Transcripts, GRE Subject (doctoral programs only) required in support of application. Interview required for admission to specialist and doctoral programs. TOEFL or MTELP required for international applicants. Accepts transfer applicants. Graduates of unaccredited institutions not considered. Apply by February 15 to Office of Graduate Admissions and Orientation. Rolling admission process. Application fee $25. Phone: (616)387-2000.

ADMISSION STANDARDS. Selective to relatively open. Usual minimum average: 2.75 (A = 4).

FINANCIAL AID. Annual awards from institutional funds: 127 fellowships, 326 teaching assistantships, 88 research assistantships, tuition waivers, Federal W/S, loans. Approved for VA benefits. Apply by February 15 to Graduate College for scholarships, fellowships; to department head for assistantships; to Financial Aid Office for all other programs. Use FAFSA. Phone: (616)387-6000. About 35% of full-time students receive aid from University and outside sources. Aid available for part-time students.

DEGREE REQUIREMENTS. For master's: 30 hours minimum, at least 24 in residence; thesis, one language required for some majors; final written/oral exams, final review. For Ed.S: 30 hours minimum beyond the master's, at least 30 in residence in most cases; final project. For Ph.D.: 90 hours minimum beyond the bachelor's, at least one year in full-time residence, knowledge of two research tools, one of which will normally be a language; qualifying exam; dissertation, for which 15 hours is given; final written/oral exams. For Ed.D., D.P.A.: same as for Ph.D., except only one research tool, which may be a language.

FIELDS OF STUDY.
Accounting. M.S.A.
Anthropology. M.A.
Applied Economics. Ph.D.
Applied Mathematics. M.S.
Art. M.A., M.F.A.
Athletic Training. M.A.
Biological Sciences. M.S., Ph.D.
Biostatistics. M.S.
Business Administration. M.B.A.
Chemistry. M.A.
Clinical Psychology. M.A., Ph.D.
Communication. M.A.
Comparative Religion. M.A., Ph.D.
Computational Mathematics. M.S.
Computer Science. M.S., Ph.D.
Counselor Education and Counseling Psychology. M.A., Ed.D.
Creative Writing. M.F.A.
Development Administration. M.D.A.
Early Childhood Education. M.A.
Earth Science. M.S.
Economics. M.A.
Educational Leadership. M.A., Ed.S., Ed.D., Ph.D.
Electrical Engineering. M.S.E.
Engineering Management. M.S.
English. M.A., M.F.A.
Fine Arts. Sixty credits for M.F.A.

Geography. M.A.
Geology. M.S., Ph.D.
Health Care Administration. M.P.A.
History. M.A., Ph.D.
Home Economics.
Industrial Engineering. M.S.E., Ph.D.
Manufacturing Science. M.S.
Mathematics. M.A., Ph.D.
Mathematics Education. M.A. Ph.D.
Mechanical Engineering. M.S.E., Ph.D.
Medieval Studies. M.A.
Music. M.M.
Occupational Therapy. M.S.
Operations Research. M.S.
Paper Science and Engineering. M.S.
Philosophy. M.A.
Physical Education. M.A.
Physics. M.A., Ph.D.
Political Science. M.A., Ph.D.
Psychology. M.A., Ph.D.
Public Administration. M.P.A., D.P.A.
School Psychology. Ed.S., Ph.D.
Science Education. M.A., Ph.D.
Social Work. M.S.W.
Sociology. M.A., Ph.D.
Spanish. M.A.
Special Education. M.A., Ph.D.
Speech Pathology and Audiology. M.A.
Statistics. M.S., Ph.D.
Teaching in the Elementary School. M.A.
Teaching of Geography. M.A.
Teaching in the Middle School. M.A.
Teaching of Music. M.M.

WESTERN NEW ENGLAND COLLEGE
Springfield, Massachusetts 01119-2654

Founded in 1919. Coed. Semester system. Library: 289,000 volumes, 3,098,000 microforms, 4200 current periodicals, 75 PCs.

Tuition: per credit hour $317. No on-campus housing available for graduate students. For off-campus housing, contact Office of Student Housing.

Graduate Programs

Graduate study since 1978. Enrollment: part-time 841 (men 75%, women 24%). Faculty: full-time 35, part-time 19. Degrees conferred: M.S., M.B.A., M.S.A., M.S.C.J.A., M.S.E.M., M.S.E.E., M.S.M.E.

ADMISSION REQUIREMENTS. Official transcripts required in support of application. GRE recommended; two letters of recommendation for Engineering applicants, GMAT for Business. Apply to Division of Continuing Education at least one month prior to date of enrollment. Application fee $30. Phone: (413)782-1249; fax: (413)782-1779.

ADMISSION STANDARDS. Selective. Usual minimum average: 2.5 (2.75 Engineering Programs) (A = 4).

FINANCIAL AID. Limited to four assistantships, Federal W/S, loans. Approved for VA benefits. Apply Director of Financial Aid. No specified closing date. Use FAFSA. Phone: (413)782-1258.

DEGREE REQUIREMENTS. For M.S.: 30 semester hours required. For M.B.A.: 30–48 semester hours depending upon undergraduate courses.

FIELDS OF STUDY.

SCHOOL OF BUSINESS:
Accounting.
Business Administration.
Business Administration (weekend).
Criminal Justice Administration.
Finance.
Health Care Management.
Information System.
Management of Information System.
Marketing.

SCHOOL OF ENGINEERING:
Electrical Engineering.
Industrial and Manufacturing Engineering.
Mechanical Engineering.

School of Law (01119-2689)

Semester system. Library: 301,000 volumes. Library has LEXIS, NEXIS, WESTLAW, DIALOG, MEDIS, OCLC.

Annual tuition: full-time $14,146, part-time $11,146. Limited on-campus housing available. Total average annual additional expense: $6000–$7500.

Enrollment: first-year class, full-time 185, part-time 64; total 482 (men 52%, women 48%). Faculty: full-time 33, part-time 23. Degree conferred: J.D.

ADMISSION REQUIREMENTS. LSDAS Law School report, bachelor's degree, transcripts, LSAT, two letters of recommendation, personal statement required in support of application. Apply to Admissions Office by April 1 (full-time program), May 1 (part-time program). Rolling admissions process. Application fee $35. Phone: (413)782-1406.

ADMISSION STANDARDS. Selective. Admits about 50% of total annual applicants.

FINANCIAL AID. Scholarships, grants, Federal W/S, loans. Apply to Financial Aid Office by April 4. Use FAFSA. About 65% of students receive some aid from School.

DEGREE REQUIREMENTS. For J.D.: satisfactory completion of three-year (full-time), four-year (part-time) program; 88-credit-hours program.

WESTERN NEW MEXICO UNIVERSITY
Silver City, New Mexico 88061-0680

Founded 1893, Located 200 miles SW of Albuquerque. Coed. State control. Semester system. Library: 141,000 volumes, 372,000 microforms, 900 current periodicals and searchable databases.

Annual tuition: resident $1398, nonresident $4390. On-campus housing for 65 married students, 250 graduate men, 150 graduate women. Average annual housing cost: $2540 (including board) for single students, $2460 for married students. Apply to Director of Residence Life. Phone: (505)538-6629.

Graduate Division

Graduate study since 1950. Enrollment: full- and part-time 350. Graduate faculty: full-time 30, part-time 4. Degrees conferred: M.A., M.A.T., M.B.A.

ADMISSION REQUIREMENTS. Transcripts, GMAT (MBA applicants) required in support of application. GRE required for applicants with a GPA between 2.75 and 3.19. TOEFL required

for international applicants. Interview not required. Accepts transfer applicants. Graduates of unaccredited institutions not considered. Apply to Office of Admissions two weeks prior to registration. Application fee $10. Phone: (505)538-6106; fax: (505)538-6155.

ADMISSION STANDARDS. Selective. Usual minimum average: 3.0 (A = 4).

FINANCIAL AID. Annual awards from institutional funds: twenty-four graduate assistantships, two teaching assistantships, Federal W/S, loans. Approved for VA benefits. Apply to Director of Graduate Division; no specified closing dates. Use either FAFSA. Phone: (505)538-6173. About 10% of students receive aid other than loans from University and outside sources.

DEGREE REQUIREMENTS. For M.A., M.A.T.: 30 semester hours minimum with thesis, at least 30 in residence; or 36 semester hours without thesis, at least 30 in residence. For M.B.A.: 36 semester hours minimum.

FIELDS OF STUDY.
Business Administration.
Education and Counseling. Includes art, elementary, secondary education with concentrations in history, English, mathematics, science, special, administration.

WESTERN OREGON STATE COLLEGE
Monmouth, Oregon 97361

Organized 1882. Located 64 miles SW of Portland. Coed. State control. Semester system. Special facilities: Regional Resource Center on Deafness, Educational Evaluation Center, Teaching Research Center. Library: 167,000 volumes, 530,000 microforms, 1700 current periodicals, 29 PCs.

Annual tuition: full-time resident $4554, nonresident $8136; part-time, resident $502 per semester, nonresident $502. On-campus housing for both single and married students available. Average academic year housing costs: $4179 (including board) for single students; $3285 for married students; off-campus housing costs: $350 per month. Contact Student Affairs Office for both on- and off-campus housing information. Phone: (503)838-8311. Day care facilities available.

Graduate Programs

Enrollment: full-time 62, part-time 233. Faculty: full-time 111, part-time 19. Degrees conferred: M.A., M.A.T., M.S.Ed.

ADMISSION REQUIREMENTS. Transcripts, GRE/MAT required in support of application. Interview required for some programs. TOEFL required for international applicants. Accepts transfer applicants. Graduates of unaccredited institutions not considered. Apply by May 15 (Fall), January 15 (Spring) to Director of Admission. Rolling admissions process. Application fee $50. Phone: (503)838-8211.

ADMISSION STANDARDS. Competitive. Usual minimum average: 2.75 (A = 4).

FINANCIAL AID. Ten research assistantships, seven teaching assistantships, full and partial tuition waivers, Federal W/S, loans. Approved for VA benefits. Apply to Provost for assistantships; to Financial Aid Office for all other programs. Use FAFSA and College's FAF. Phone: (503)838-8475. About 5% of students receive aid from College and outside sources. Aid available for part-time students.

DEGREE REQUIREMENTS. For master's: 30–36 semester hours minimum, at least 24–30 in residence; thesis/nonthesis option; final oral/written exam.

FIELDS OF STUDY.
Correctional Administration. M.A., M.S.
Early Childhood Education. Includes middle school; M.S.Ed.
Information Technology. M.S.Ed.
Learning Disabilities. M.S.Ed.
Multihandicapped Education. M.S.Ed.
Reading Education. M.S.Ed.
Rehabilitation Counseling. M.S.Ed.
Secondary Education. Includes humanities, science, social science, socially and educationally different. M.A.T., M.S.Ed.

WESTERN WASHINGTON UNIVERSITY
Bellingham, Washington 98225-5996
http://www.wwu.edu

Established 1893. Located 85 miles N of Seattle. Coed. State control. Quarter system. Library: 600,000 volumes, 1,900,000, 4800 current periodicals, 150 PCs.

Annual tuition: full-time, resident $3885, nonresident $11,820; per credit resident $130, nonresident $394. On-campus housing for 1460 women, 1164 men; 13 coed units, 1 woman only; 3 apartment buildings, 268 apartment units for single and married students. Average academic year housing costs: $4800 (including board) for single students. Contact Director, University Residences for both on- and off-campus housing information. Phone: (360)650-2950.

Graduate School

Graduate study since 1947. Enrollment: full-time 618, part-time 239. (men 40%, women 60%). Faculty teaching graduate students: full-time 300, part-time 25. Degrees conferred: M.A., M.S., M.Ed., M.B.A., M.Mus.

ADMISSION REQUIREMENTS. Transcripts, letters of recommendation, GRE, GMAT required in support of School's application. Interview required for some programs. TOEFL required for non-native English-speaking applicants. Accepts transfer applicants. Graduates of unaccredited colleges not considered. Apply to Dean of Graduate School by June 1 (Fall), October 1 (Winter), February 1 (Spring), May 1 (Summer). Many programs admit Fall Quarter only; some programs have earlier deadlines. Application fee $35. Phone: (360)650-3170; fax: (360)650-6811.

ADMISSION STANDARDS. Selective. Required average: 3.0 (A = 4) last 90 quarter credits (60 semester hours).

FINANCIAL AID. Fifty-six academic scholarships, ninety-two teaching assistantships, ten research assistantships, fifty fee waivers, Federal W/S, loans. Approved for VA benefits. Early application is encouraged. Contact Graduate School for information on assistantships, fee waivers; the Student Financial Services Office for all other programs. Use FAFSA. Phone: (360)650-3470; fax: (360)650-7291. About 25% of students receive aid other than loans from College and outside sources.

DEGREE REQUIREMENTS. For master's: 45 quarter hours minimum with thesis, or 48 quarter hours minimum without thesis and written comprehensive exam; reading knowledge of foreign language required for some departments.

FIELDS OF STUDY.
Anthropology.
Art.
Biology.
Business Administration.
Chemistry.
Computer Science.
Education.
English.
Environmental Science.
Geography.
Geology.
History.
Mathematics.
Music.
Physical Education.
Political Science.
Psychology.
Sociology.
Speech Pathology and Audiology.
Theater.

WESTFIELD STATE COLLEGE
Westfield, Massachusetts 01086
http:.wsc.mass.edu

Founded 1838. Located 12 miles W of Springfield. Coed. State control. Semester system. Library: 166,721 volumes, 440,000 microforms, 1100 current periodicals, 15 PCs.

Tuition: per semester hour, resident $130, nonresident $140. No on-campus housing available for graduate students. Contact Director, Residential Life, for off-campus housing information. Phone: (413)572-5402.

Graduate Studies and Continuing Education

Graduate study since 1963. Enrollment: full-time 10, part-time 240. Faculty teaching graduate students: 71 full-time, 20 part-time. Degrees conferred: M.A., M.S., M.Ed., C.A.G.S.

ADMISSION REQUIREMENTS. Transcripts required in support of application. TOEFL required for international applicants. GRE, MAT recommended. Interview may be requested. Accepts transfer applicants. Graduates of unaccredited colleges not considered. Apply to Dean, Graduate Studies and Continuing Education prior to registration. Application fee $30. Phone: (413)572-5224; fax: (413)572-5227.

ADMISSION STANDARDS. Selective. Usual minimum average: 2.6 (A = 4).

FINANCIAL AID. Graduate assistantships, grants, New England Regional Student Program, loans. Apply to Dean, Graduate Studies and Continuing Education for assistantships; to Financial Aid Office for all other programs. No specified closing date. Use FAFSA. Phone: (413)572-5407.

DEGREE REQUIREMENTS. For master's: 33 semester hours minimum; comprehensive exam; thesis/nonthesis option in some programs. For C.A.G.S.: 30 semester hours minimum beyond the master's; comprehensive exam.

FIELDS OF STUDY.
American History. M.Ed.
Criminal Justice. M.S.
Early Childhood. M.Ed.
Educational Administration. M.Ed., C.A.G.S.
Elementary Education. M.Ed.
English. M.A.
Middle School Teacher.
Music.
Occupational Education. M.Ed., C.A.G.S.
Psychology. M.A.

School Principal. C.A.G.S.
Secondary Education. Includes biology, chemistry, general science, foreign language (French, Spanish), history, mathematics, social studies. M.Ed.
Special Education. M.Ed.
Teaching of Reading. M.Ed.
Technology for Education. M.Ed.

WESTMINSTER COLLEGE
New Wilmington, Pennsylvania 16142-0001

Founded 1852. Located 60 miles NE of Pittsburgh. Coed. Private control. Presbyterian affiliation. Semester system. Library: 215,000 volumes, 10,250 microforms, 970 current periodicals, 75 PCs.

Annual tuition: $8500, per course $1000. No on-campus housing available.

Graduate Program

Graduate study since 1944. Enrollment: part-time 100. Graduate faculty: Degree conferred: M.Ed.

ADMISSION REQUIREMENTS. Transcripts required in support of application. MAT occasionally required. Graduates of unaccredited colleges not considered. Accepts transfer applicants. Apply to Director of Admissions by August 30 (Fall), January 15 (Spring). Rolling admissions process. Application fee $20. Phone: (412)946-7100.

ADMISSION STANDARDS. Selective. Usual minimum average: 2.75 (A = 4).

FINANCIAL AID. Limited to loans, grants. Apply to Financial Aid Office; no specified closing date. Use FAFSA. Phone: (412)946-7100.

DEGREE REQUIREMENTS. For M.Ed.: 10 courses minimum, at least 8 in residence; final written exam.

FIELDS OF STUDY.
Elementary Education.
Elementary School Principal.
English.
Guidance Counselor-Secondary.
History.
Reading Specialist.
School Superintendent.
Secondary School Principal.
Supervision and Curriculum Studies.

WHEELOCK COLLEGE
Boston, Massachusetts 02215

Founded 1888. Private control. Semester system. Library: 70,000 volumes, 750,000 microforms.

Tuition: per credit $475. On-campus housing available. Apply to Director of Graduate Admissions.

Graduate Division

Graduate study since 1953. Enrollment; full-time 200, part-time 300. Graduate faculty: full-time 15, part-time 40. Degrees conferred: M.S., C.A.G.S.

ADMISSION REQUIREMENTS. Transcripts, three references, interview in support of application. TOEFL required for international applicants. Accepts transfer applicants. Graduates of unaccredited institutions not considered. Apply to Director of Graduate Admissions at least two months prior to semester of entry. Application fee $35, international applicants $30. Rolling admissions process. Phone: (617)734-5200, ext. 198; fax: (617)232-7127.

ADMISSION STANDARDS. Selective. Usual minimum average: 3.0 (A = 4).

FINANCIAL AID. Two Centennial scholarships, twenty grants, twenty to twenty-five assistantships, Federal W/S, loans. Apply by April 15 to Director of Financial Aid, Graduate School. Use FAFSA and institutional graduate FAF. Phone: (800)734-5216, (617)734-5200 ext. 191. About 50% of students receive aid other than loans from College. Limited aid for part-time students.

DEGREE REQUIREMENTS. For M.S.: 32–40 semester hours minimum. For C.A.G.S.: 30 semester hours beyond the master's; thesis required.

FIELDS OF STUDY.
Administration. Includes child care, human, school, teacher leadership.
Child Life: Hospital and Health Care Settings.
Early Intervention: Infants and Toddlers with Special Needs.
Family Studies.
Infant and Toddler Studies.
Intergenerational Studies.
Leaderships in Early Childhood.
Parenting Education and Family Support.
Reading.
Teaching Early Childhood and Elementary Children.
Teaching Young Children with Special Needs.
Teaching Students with Special Needs K–9.

WHITTIER COLLEGE
Whittier, California 90608-0634

Chartered 1901. Located adjacent to Los Angeles. Coed. Private control. Quaker affiliation. Library: 200,000 volumes.

Tuition: per credit $305. No on-campus housing available. Day-care facilities available.

Graduate Program

Enrollment: full- and part-time 550. College faculty teaching graduate students: full-time 40, part-time 8. Degree conferred: M.A.

ADMISSION REQUIREMENTS. Transcripts, GRE or MAT required in support of application. TOEFL required for international applicants. Accepts transfer applicants. Apply to the Graduate Program; no specified closing dates. Rolling admissions process. Application fee $50. Phone: (310)907-4200, ext. 4248.

ADMISSION STANDARDS. Selective. Usual minimum average: 3.0 (A = 4).

FINANCIAL AID. None for graduate students.

DEGREE REQUIREMENTS. For M.A.: 34 credits minimum, at least 18 in residence; thesis.

FIELD OF STUDY.
Education. Includes administration, early childhood, elementary, secondary.

School of Law (90020)

Established 1975. Semester system. Library: 230,000 volumes. Library has LEXIS, NEXIS, WESTLAW, DIALOG.

Annual tuition: full-time $18,900, part-time $11,340. Total average annual additional expense: $12,500.

Enrollment: first-year class, full-time 190, part-time 90; total 750 (men 52%, women 48%). Faculty: full-time 27, part-time 10. Degrees conferred: J.D., J.D.-M.B.A.

ADMISSION REQUIREMENTS. LSDAS Law School report, bachelor's degree, transcripts, LSAT, letters of recommendation, personal statement required in support of application. Apply to Admissions Office by March 15. Rolling admissions process. Application fee $50. Phone: (310)938-3621, ext. 123, 128; (800)808-8188.

ADMISSION STANDARDS. Selective. Admits about 35–40% of total annual applicants.

FINANCIAL AID. Scholarships, grants, Federal W/S, loans. Apply to Financial Aid Office by June 1. Use FAFSA. Aid sometimes available students.

DEGREE REQUIREMENTS. For J.D.: satisfactory completion of three-year (full-time), or four-year (part-time) program; 87-credit-hour program.

WHITWORTH COLLEGE

Spokane, Washington 99251-0001

Founded 1890. Coed. Private control. Presbyterian affiliation. 4-1-4 system. Library: 120,000 volumes, 85,000 microforms, 875 current periodicals, 10 PCs.

Tuition: per credit $205. On-campus housing available for graduate students. Contact Housing Office for both on- and off-campus housing information. Phone: (509)466-3287.

Graduate Study

Enrollment: full- and part-time 426. College faculty teaching graduate students: full-time 15, part-time 45. Degrees conferred: M.A.T., M.Ed., M.I.M.

ADMISSION REQUIREMENTS. Official transcripts, GRE required in support of application. Interview sometimes requested. TOEFL required for international applicants. Accepts transfer applicants. Apply by September 1 (Fall), February 1 (Spring) to Office of Admissions. Rolling admissions process. Application fee $25. Phone: (509)466-1000, ext. 3212.

ADMISSION STANDARDS. Selective. Usual minimum average: 2.75 (A = 4).

FINANCIAL AID. Limited Federal W/S, loans. Apply by April 15 to Office of Financial Aid. Use FAFSA.

DEGREE REQUIREMENTS. For master's: 30–36 semester credits minimum, thesis/nonthesis option, research paper or internship; comprehensive exam.

FIELDS OF STUDY.
Educational Administration. M.Ed.
Gifted and Talented. M.A.T.
International Management. M.I.M.
Physical Education. M.A.T.
Reading. M.A.T.
School Counselor. M.Ed.
Special Education. M.Ed.
Teaching English as a Second Language. M.A.T.

WICHITA STATE UNIVERSITY

Wichita, Kansas 67260-0004
http://twsuvm.uc.twsu.edu

Founded 1895. Coed. State control. Semester system. Special facilities: Administrative Assessment Center, National Institute for Aviation Research, Digital Computing Center, Center for Entrepreneurship, Center for Forensic Science, Center for Urban Studies, Rehabilitation Engineering Center, Gerontology Center, Reading Assessment Center, two low-speed and two supersonic-speed wind tunnels, Water Tunnel. Library: 938,000 volumes, 907,000 microforms, 6300 current periodicals, 60 PCs.

Annual tuition: full-time resident $2600.80, nonresident $7517; per credit, resident $86.70, nonresident $291.50 On-campus housing available. Average academic year housing costs: $6410. Contact Office of Student Housing for both on- and off-campus housing information. Phone: (316)689-3693.

Graduate School

http://twsuvm.us.twsu.edu:80/~admgwww/

Graduate study since 1928. Enrollment: full-time 827, part-time 2237 (men 45%, women 55%). University faculty: full-time 450, part-time 25. Degrees conferred: M.A., M.S., M.A.J., M.B.A., M.Ed., M.S.E., M.F.A., M.M., M.M.Ed., M.C.S., M.S.N., M.P.A., M.P.F., M.P.T., Ed.S., Ed.D., Ph.D.

ADMISSION REQUIREMENTS. Two official transcripts required in support of School's application. GRE/GMAT/MAT may be required by some programs. Portfolio required for M.F.A. applicants. TOEFL required for international applicants. Interview not required. Accepts transfer applicants. Apply to Graduate Office at least three weeks prior to registration. Application fee: none for domestic applicants, $25 for international applicants. Phone: (316)689-3095; fax: (316)689-3253.

ADMISSION STANDARDS. Selective. Usual minimum average: 2.75 for last two years (A = 4).

FINANCIAL AID. Thirty fellowships, 597 assistantships for teaching/research, Federal W/S, loans. Apply by March 15 to appropriate department chair for assistantships and fellowships; to Financial Aid Office for all other programs. Use FAFSA and University's FAF. Phone: (316)689-3430. About 20% of students receive aid other than loans from University and outside sources.

DEGREE REQUIREMENTS. For M.A., M.S.: 30 credit hours minimum; final written/oral exam; reading knowledge of one language for many departments. For M.A.J., M.P.T.: 33 hours minimum including thesis, internships, or practicum. For M.B.A.: 33–54 hours, depending upon previous academic background. For M.Ed., M.S.N.: 30 hours plus thesis or 36 hours without thesis; final written exam. For M.S.E.: 36 hours without thesis, final oral/written exam. For M.F.A.: 60 hours minimum in art, 48 minimum in creative writing, including final creative project or thesis; final written/oral exam. For M.M.: 30 hours minimum, including thesis or recital; final oral exam. For M.M.Ed.: 30 hours including thesis or recital; or 32 hours, including research seminar, final oral exam. For M.P.A.: 39 hours minimum, including urban affairs core and internships or practicum. For Ed.S.: normally 30 hours beyond the master's; final written/oral exam. For Ph.D., Ed.D.: 90 hours beyond the bachelor's; preliminary written exam; foreign languages or research tools; dissertation; final oral exam.

FIELDS OF STUDY.
Accounting. GMAT for admission. M.P.A., M.B.A. only.
Administration of Justice. M.A.J.
Aerospace Engineering. GRE for admission. M.S., Ph.D.
Anthropology. M.A.
Art Education. Portfolio for admission. M.A.

Biology. GRE Subject Test, three letters of recommendation for admission. M.S. only.

Business. GMAT for admission. M.S. only.

Business Administration. GMAT for admission. M.B.A. only.

Chemistry. GRE Subject Test, two letters of reference, statement for goals and research interest. Apply by second Monday in November (Spring), second Monday in April (Fall). M.S., Ph.D.

Communications. Includes communications, theater/drama. GRE for admissions. M.A.C. only.

Communicative Disorders and Sciences. GRE, three letters of recommendation for admission. Apply by March 1 (Summer and Fall), October 1 (Spring). M.A., Ph.D.

Computer Science. GRE taken during first year. M.S. only.

Counseling. Statement of Goals, three letters of recommendation for admission. M.Ed.

Creative Writing. Includes fiction, poetry. M.F.A.

Curriculum and Instruction. GRE/MAT, three recommendations for admission. M.Ed.

Economics. GRE taken during first year. M.A.

Educational Administration and Supervision. GRE, three letters of recommendation. M.S., Ed.D.

Electrical Engineering. GRE for admission. M.S., Ph.D.

English. M.A.

Environmental Science. M.S.

Fine Arts. Includes ceramics, painting, printmaking, sculpture. Portfolio, three letters of recommendation, statement of goals, resume for admission. M.F.A. only.

Geology. M.S.

Gerontology. Names of three references for admission. M.S.

History. One language for M.A. M.A. only.

Industrial Engineering. GRE for admission. M.S., Ph.D.

Liberal Studies. Essay, personal interview for admission. M.A. only.

Mathematics. M.S.

Mathematics—Applied. GRE Subject Test for admission. Ph.D.

Mechanical Engineering. GRE for admission. M.S., Ph.D.

Music. Includes history/literature, instrumental conducting, performance, piano/organ, piano pedagogy, strings/wind/percussion, voice. M.M.

Music Education. Includes choral, elementary, instrumental, music in special education. M.M.Ed.

Nursing. Includes administration, education. M.S.N.

Physical Education, M.Ed.

Physical Therapy. Departmental application, three references for admission. M.P.T.

Physics. M.S.

Political Science. GRE for admission. M.A.

Psychology. Includes community/clinical, human factors. GRE General/Subject required for admission; one language or research tool for M.A. M.A., Ph.D.

Public Administration. GRE desirable. M.P.A.

Public Health. GRE or equivalent test, program application, one year professional experience for admission. M.P.H.

School Psychology. GRE, three reference, Statement of Goals and research interest. Ed.S. only.

Sociology. One language depending upon thesis topic. M.A.

Spanish. One language in addition to Spanish. M.A.

Special Education. GRE, one year teaching experience for admission. M.Ed.

Sport Administration. Three references, personal interview for admission. M.Ed.

Statistics. M.S. only.

WIDENER UNIVERSITY
Chester, Pennsylvania 19013-5792

Founded 1821. Located 15 south of Philadelphia. Coed. Independent. Semester system. Special facilities: CDC CYBER 930, Digital VAX-11/750, Prime 9955, Prime 2555, Child Development Center, Engineering Research Center, University Art Museum. Prime-Medusa Computer Aided Design Laboratory, Center for Computer Assisted Instruction, Business Research Center. Library: 500,000 volumes, 15,000 microforms, 1800 current periodicals.

Tuition: per credit M.B.A. $415; Nursing $395; M.P.A., M.L.A. $325; M.Ed. $320; Engineering $470; doctoral programs $405. No on-campus housing available. Off-campus housing available within walking distance of the campus. Average academic year housing costs $6500 (including board). Contact Director of Housing by May 30 for housing information. Phone: (610)499-4393.

Graduate Study

Enrollment: full-time 477, part-time 1800. Faculty: full-time 156, part-time 216. Degrees conferred: M.A., M.B.A., M.Ed., M.S., M.S.N., M.E., M.H.P., M.P.A., M.S.W., Psy.D., D.N.Sc., Ed.D.

ADMISSION REQUIREMENTS. Transcripts required in support of application. GRE/GMAT required for some departments. TOEFL required of international applicants. Accepts transfer applicants. Graduates of unaccredited institutions not considered. Apply to Assistant Provost at least one month prior to preferred entrance date. Application fee $25–$40. Phone: (610)499-4372.

ADMISSION STANDARDS. Usual minimum average: 2.5 (A = 4) master's level, 3.0 for doctoral programs.

FINANCIAL AID. Limited to assistantships, loans. Approved for VA benefits. Apply by April 15 to Director of Financial Aid for all programs. Use FAFSA and institutional FAF.

DEGREE REQUIREMENTS. For master's: 30–45 semester hours minimum with or without thesis, at least 24 in residence, final written/oral exam in some programs. For D.N.Sc., 60–63 credits; computer literacy, preliminary exam; dissertation; final written/oral exam. For Ed.D., Psy.D.: 60–65 credits beyond master's; preliminary exam; dissertation/project; final written/oral exam.

FIELDS OF STUDY.
Accounting.
Business Administration and Management.
Chemical Engineering.
Civil Engineering.
Clinical Psychology.
Computer and Software Engineering.
Educational Leadership.
Electrical Engineering.
Elementary Education.
Engineering Management.
Environmental Engineering Option.
Health Administration.
Health and Medical Services Administration.
Human Resources Management.
Industrial Administration.
Liberal Studies.
Mathematics Education.
Mechanical Engineering.
Nursing. Includes adult health, emergency critical-care nursing, family nurse practitioner studies.
Physical Therapy.
Public Administration.
Reading.
Social Work.
Software Engineering.
Superintendency.
Taxation.
Telecommunication Engineering.

Delaware Law School (19803-0474)

Established 1971. Branch in Harrisburg, PA (17110-9450). Semester system. Library: 518,000 volumes. Library has LEXIS, NEXIS, WESTLAW, DIALOG, LEGALTRAC, INFOTRAC.

Annual tuition: Day $16,850, Evening $12,640. No on-campus housing available. Total average annual additional expense: $10,500.

Enrollment: first-year class 450 (day), 225 (evening); total 2050 (men 60%, women 40%). Faculty: full-time 104, part-time 105. Degree conferred: J.D., J.D.- M.B.A., J.D.-Psy.D., LL.M. (Taxation).

ADMISSION REQUIREMENTS. LSDAS Law School report, bachelor's degree, transcripts, LSAT, letters of recommendation required in support of application. Accepts transfer applicants. Graduates of unaccredited colleges not considered. Apply to Admissions Office by May 15. Rolling admissions process. Application fee $60. Phone: (302)477-2162.

ADMISSION STANDARDS. Admits about 45–50% of total annual applications.

FINANCIAL AID. Scholarships, Federal W/S, loans. Apply to Office of Admissions by May 1. Use FAFSA. About 50% of students receive some aid from School.

DEGREE REQUIREMENTS. For J.D.: satisfactory completion of three-year (day) or four-year (evening) program; 87-credit-hour program. For LL.M.: at least 24 credits beyond the J.D.; two semesters in full-time residence.
Note: Summer programs in Nairobi (Kenya), Geneva (Switzerland), Paris (France).

WILKES UNIVERSITY

Wilkes-Barre, Pennsylvania 18766-0002

Founded 1933. Located 100 miles NW of Philadelphia. Coed. Private control. Semester system. Library: 210,000 volumes, 700,000 microforms, 1100 current periodicals, 45 PCs.

Tuition: per semester hour $415. Limited on-campus housing for graduate students.

Graduate School

Enrollment: full-time 40, part-time 750 (men 40%, women 60%). Faculty: full- and part-time 80. Degrees conferred: M.S., M.B.A., M.H.A.

ADMISSION REQUIREMENTS. Transcripts, GRE/MAT/GMAT letters of recommendation required in support of School's application. Interview may be required. Accepts transfer applicants. Apply to Dean of Admissions; no specified closing date. Application fee $30. Phone: (717)831-4415; fax: (717)824-2934.

ADMISSION STANDARDS. Selective. Usual minimum average: 2.75 (A = 4).

FINANCIAL AID. Graduate assistantships, counselorships, Federal W/S, loans. Apply to Director of Graduate Studies by March 1; no specified closing date. Use FAFSA and University's form (PHEAA). Phone: (717)831-4345; fax: (717)831-4902.

DEGREE REQUIREMENTS. For master's: 30–39 credit hours minimum, at least 24 in residence. For Ph.D.: at least 60 credits beyond the bachelor's degree, two years in residence; foreign language requirement varies by department; preliminary exam; candidacy; dissertation; final oral exam.

FIELDS OF STUDY.
Biology Education (secondary).
Business Administration. GMAT for admission
Chemistry Education (secondary).
Educational Computing.
Educational Development and Strategies.
Educational Leadership.
Electrical Engineering. GRE for admission. M.S., Ph.D.
English Education (secondary).
Health Administration.
History Education (secondary).
Mathematics.
Mathematics Education (secondary).
Nursing. GRE or MAT for admission.
Physics. M.S., Ph.D.
Physics Education (secondary).
Secondary Education.

WILLAMETTE UNIVERSITY

Salem, Oregon 97301-3931
http://www.willamette.edu

Willamette University was founded in 1842 and consists of a College of Liberal Arts, College of Law, and the Atkinson Graduate School of Management. The University is located 42 miles S of Portland, Oregon. Library: 408,000 volumes, 182,000 microforms, 3100 current periodicals, 45 PCs.

Limited on-campus housing available for graduate students. Average academic year housing costs: $11,350 (including board). Contact Dean of Residence Life for both on- and off-campus housing information. Phone: (503)370-6212.

Atkinson Graduate School of Management
http://www.willamette.edu/agsm

Graduate study since 1974. Coed. Semester system. Special facility: Atkinson School Technology Center includes 23 PCs.

Annual tuition: full-time $14,160; per credit $472.

Enrollment: full-time 155, part-time 28. Faculty: full-time 11, part-time 6. Degrees conferred: M.M., M.M.-J.D.

ADMISSION REQUIREMENTS. Transcripts, GMAT/GRE, letters of reference, application form and essay required in support of School's application. TOEFL required for applicants. Graduates of unaccredited institutions not considered. Apply by April 1 for priority consideration; rolling admissions process after that on a space-available basis only. Application fee $40. Phone: (503)370-6167, Fax: (503)370-3011; E-mail: joneill@willamette.edu.

ADMISSION STANDARDS. Selective. Usual minimum average: 3.0 (A = 4).

FINANCIAL AID. Seventy merit-based scholarships, eleven research assistantships, Federal W/S, loans. Approved for VA benefits. Apply by April 1. Use FAFSA. Phone: (503)370-6273.

DEGREE REQUIREMENTS. For M.M.: 63 semester hours. Joint Law and Management degree requires four years of full-time study.

FIELD OF STUDY.
Management.

College of Law

Founded 1883. Semester system. Library: 225,000 volumes, Library has LEXIS, NEXIS, WESTLAW, CALI. Special facility: Truman Wesley Collins Legal Center.

Annual tuition: full-time $16,300. Housing available for single students only. Annual housing costs: $6500 (including board).

Enrollment: first-year class 165; total full-time 502 (men 61%, women 39%); no part-time study available. Faculty: full-time 28, part-time 16. Degrees conferred: J.D., J.D.-M.M. (Management).

ADMISSION REQUIREMENTS. LSDAS Law School report, bachelor's degree, transcripts, references, LSAT required in support of application. Accepts transfer applicants. Graduates of unaccredited colleges not considered. Apply to Dean after September 1, before February 1 for priority consideration. Rolling admissions process. Application will be accepted as long as space is available. Admits beginning students Fall only. Application fee $40. Phone: (503)370-6282.

ADMISSION STANDARDS. Selective. Accepts 50% of total annual applicants. Approximately 64% of enrolled students are nonresidents.

FINANCIAL AID. Scholarships, partial tuition waivers, Federal W/S, loans. Apply to the Office of Financial Aid by February 1. Use FAFSA. About 10% of students receive aid other than loans from School and outside sources.

DEGREE REQUIREMENTS. For J.D.: 88 semester hours minimum; writing requirements; final exam.
Note: Study-abroad program in Shanghai (China) available.

THE COLLEGE OF WILLIAM AND MARY

Williamsburg, Virginia 23187-8795

http://www.wm.edu

Founded 1693. Located 50 miles SE of Richmond. Coed. State control. Semester system. Libraries of the College are the central Earl Gregg Swem; the chemistry, physics, geology, biology, and music libraries; the Marshall-Wythe Law Library; the School of Marine Science; the Professional Resource Center (School of Business Administration); Learning Resource Center/Curriculum Library (School of Education): 1,200,000 volumes, 1,800,000 microforms, 545,000 government documents, 1,000,000 manuscripts. Special facilities: Institute of Early American History and Culture, Virginia institute of Marine Science (VINIS), Center for Archaeological Research, Archaeological Conservation Center, Institute for the Bill of Rights, Millington Life Sciences Hall, Muscarelle Museum, William Small Physical Laboratory; Research opportunities at Colonial Williamsburg Foundation, Continuous Electron Beam Accelerator Facility (CEBAF), the Eastern State Hospital, the National Center for State Courts, and the Langley Research Center (LARC) of the National Aeronautics and Space Administration. Graduate students work at the national laboratories and accelerator installations throughout the world.

Annual tuition: full-time, resident $4906, nonresident $14,916; per credit, resident $153, nonresident $465. On-campus housing for 122 graduate men and women, and 10 married students' apartments. Average academic year housing costs: $3634–$4824 (including board) single students; $5140 for married students. Contact Office of Residence Life for on-campus information. Phone: (804)221-4314, Office of Off-Campus Housing for off-campus information. Phone: (804)221-3302.

Division of Graduate Studies

Enrollment: full- and part-time 2010. Graduate faculty: full- and part-time 675. Degrees conferred: M.A., M.S., M.Ed., M.B.A., M.L.&T., M.P.P., Ed.D., Psy.D., Ph.D.

ADMISSION REQUIREMENTS. Official transcripts, letters of reference required in support of application. GRE/GMAT, interview required for some departments. TOEFL required for international applicants. Accepts transfer applicants. Apply to appropriate department chair or dean of professional school by May 1 for priority consideration. Application fee varies by school. Phone: (804)221-2467; fax: (804)221-2464.

ADMISSION STANDARDS. Competitive for some departments, selective for all others. Minimum average: 2.5 (A = 4).

FINANCIAL AID. Awards from institutional funds: scholarships, research fellowships, teaching assistantships, internships, Federal W/S, loans. Approved for VA benefits. Apply to appropriate department chair for fellowships, assistantships; to Financial Aid Office for all other programs. Use FAFSA. Phone: (804)221-2420; fax: (804)221-2515. About 50% of students receive aid other than loans from College and outside sources.

DEGREE REQUIREMENTS. For M.A.: 24 semester credits, at least one year in residence; reading knowledge of one foreign language for some departments; thesis; final exam. For M.S.: 32 semester credits minimum; thesis not required. Other requirements same as for M.A. For M.P.P.: 48 semester credits over two years; ten-week internship in summer between first and second years. For M.Ed., M.A. in Ed. 30 semester credits minimum, at least 18 in residence; thesis/final project (except for Secondary School Teaching); comprehensive exam. For M.B.A.: 60 semester credits minimum; thesis optional. For M.L.&T: one year minimum beyond the J.D. or equivalent. For Ed.D.: 90 semester credits minimum, at least 60 in residence; preliminary exam; dissertation; final oral exam. For Psy.D.: three years minimum, three terms per year, at least two years in residence; one year internship, comprehensive exam; final written or oral exam. For Ph.D.: three years minimum, at least one year in residence; reading knowledge of one or two foreign languages in some departments; comprehensive exam; dissertation; final oral exam.

FIELDS OF STUDY.
American Studies. M.A., Ph.D.
Anthropology. Emphasis on historical archeology. M.A. only.
Applied Sciences. Includes applied mathematics and computer science, chemical physics, atmospheric and plasma science, and materials science; thesis optional. M.S., Ph.D.
Biology. M.A. only.
Business Administration. M.B.A. only.
Chemistry. M.A. only.
Computer Science. M.S., Ph.D.
Education. Includes programs for superintendents, guidance counselors, directors of instruction. M.A., M.-Ed., Certificate of Advanced Study, Ed.D.
History. Includes M.A. apprenticeship and Ph.D. internship programs in historical archeology, historical editing, historical libraries.
Law. Program in law and taxation. M.L.&T.
Marine Science. Includes marine biology, fisheries biology. M.A., Ph.D.
Physics. M.S., Ph.D.
Psychology. M.A. in general psychology, Psy.D. in clinical.

Marshall-Wythe School of Law

Established 1779. Semester system. Law library: 315,000 volumes. Library has LEXIS, NEXIS, WESTLAW, DIALOG; 25 computer workstations. Special facilities: Institute of Bill of Rights Law.

Annual tuition: resident $6674, nonresident $17,002. Limited on-campus housing. Total average annual additional expense: $9700.

Enrollment: first-year class 190; total full-time 554 (men 55%, women 45%); postgraduates 12–15. Faculty: full-time 31, part-time 27. Degrees conferred: J.D., J.D.-M.A. (American Studies), J.D.-M.B.A., J.D.-M.P.P., LL.M. (Taxation, American Legal System for foreign students).

ADMISSION REQUIREMENTS. LSDAS Law School report, bachelor's degree, transcripts, LSAT, two letters of recommendation required in support of application. TOEFL required for foreign applicants. Accepts transfer applicants. Graduates of unaccredited colleges not considered. Apply to Admissions Office after September 15, before March 1 for priority consideration. Application fee $30. Phone: (804)221-3785; fax: (804)221-3261.

ADMISSION STANDARDS. Selective. Accepts 20–25% of total annual applicants.

FINANCIAL AID. Scholarships, fellowships, assistantships, Federal W/S, loans. Apply to the Office of Financial Aid by February 1. Use FAFSA. About 20% of students receive aid other than loans from School.

DEGREE REQUIREMENTS. For J.D.: 90 semester credit program, at least final year in residence. For LL.M.: at least 24 credits beyond J.D.; one year in full-time residence.

WILLIAM CAREY COLLEGE

Hattiesburg, Mississippi 39401-5499

Located 125 miles from New Orleans, Louisiana. Coed. Trimester system. Library: 107,000 volumes, 30,000 microforms, 628 current periodicals, 3 PCs.

Tuition: per credit hour $110. Limited on-campus housing available.

Graduate Division

Founded in 1969. Enrollment: full- and part-time 185 (men 13, women 10). Faculty: full-time 21, part-time 11. Degrees conferred: M.Ed., M.B.A.

ADMISSION REQUIREMENTS. Transcripts, letters of recommendation, teaching certificate (for Education) required in support of application. TOEFL required for international applicants. Accepts transfer applicants. Apply to the Chair Graduate Division; no specified closing date. Rolling admissions process. Application fee $10. Phone: (601)582-6144.

ADMISSION STANDARDS. Selective. Usual minimum average: 2.5 (A = 4).

FINANCIAL AID. Limited Federal W/S, loans. Use FAFSA and College's FAF Phone: (601)582-6153. About 10% of students receive aid from College and outside sources. Aid available for part-time students.

DEGREE REQUIREMENTS. For M.B.A., M.Ed.: 30–36 semester hours minimum; evaluation tests; comprehensive exam.

FIELDS OF STUDY.
Business Administration. M.B.A.
Educational Leadership. M.Ed.
Elementary Education. M.Ed.
Secondary Education. M.Ed.

WILLIAM MITCHELL COLLEGE OF LAW

875 Summit Avenue,
St. Paul, Minnesota 55105

Founded 1900. Renamed in 1956. Private control. Semester system. Law library: 210,000 volumes. Library has LEXIS, WESTLAW.

Annual tuition: three-year program $15,333; four-year program $11,130. No on-campus housing. Total average annual additional expense: $7500.

Enrollment: first-year class full-time, day 220; part-time, evening 142; total 1050 (men 53%, women 47%). Faculty: full-time 40, part-time 90. Degrees conferred: J.D., LL.M.

ADMISSION REQUIREMENTS. Bachelor's degree, transcripts, LSAT, writing sample required in support of application. Interview not required. Transfer applicants accepted. Graduates of unaccredited colleges not considered. Apply to Admissions Office by May 1 for priority consideration. Admits Fall only. Application fee $35. Phone: (612)290-6329.

ADMISSION STANDARDS. Selective. Accepts 65% of total annual applicants.

FINANCIAL AID. Scholarships, minority scholarships, Federal W/S, loans. Apply to Financial Aid Office before March 1. Use FAFSA. About 5% of students receive aid other than loans from College. Aid available for part-time, third-, fourth-year students.

DEGREE REQUIREMENTS. For J.D.: 86-semester-hour program; advanced standing considered. For LL.M.: at least 24 credits beyond J.D.

WILLIAM PATERSON COLLEGE OF NEW JERSEY

Wayne, New Jersey 07470-8420
http://www.wilpaterson.edu

Founded 1855. Located 20 miles W of New York City. Coed. State control. Semester system. Special facility: New Sarah Byrd Askew library. Library: 303,000 volumes, 850,000 microforms, 2200 current periodicals, 35 PCs.

Tuition: per credit, resident $187, nonresident $266. On-campus housing available for single graduate students only. Average academic year housing costs: $2500. Contact Director of Residence Life for both on- and off-campus housing information. Phone: (201)595-2714.

Graduate Division

Graduate study since 1966. Enrollment: full-time 162, part-time 1034. Faculty: full-time 238, part-time 3. Degrees conferred: M.A., M.A.T., M.B.A., M.Ed., M.S., M.S.N.

ADMISSION REQUIREMENTS. Official transcripts, interview, GRE or MAT, GMAT (Business) required in support of application. TOEFL, W.E.S. required for international applicants. Accepts transfer applicants. Apply to Office of Graduate Studies and Research by August 1 (Fall), November 1 (Spring) for most departments. Application fee $35. Phone: (201)595-2237; fax: (210)595-2035.

ADMISSION STANDARDS. Selective. Usual minimum average: 3.0 (A = 4).

FINANCIAL AID. Graduate assistantship, internships, loans. Approved for VA benefits. Apply to the Office of Graduate Studies and Research for assistantships, internships; to the Financial Aid Office for all other programs. Use FAFSA. Phone: (201)595-2022.

DEGREE REQUIREMENTS. For master's: 30–42 credit hours minimum, at least 24 in residence; research thesis; project; comprehensive exam. For M.B.A.: 60 credit hours minimum.

FIELDS OF STUDY.

Biological Sciences. Includes biology, biotechnology. M.A., M.S.

Communication Arts. Includes television, theater. M.A. only.

Counselor Services. Includes agency, school. M. Ed.

Education. Includes bilingual/English as a second language, language art, learning technologies, mathematics, science, educational media, early childhood. M.Ed. only.

English. M.A. only.

Finance.

Management.

Marketing.

Reading. M.Ed.

Special Education. Includes mentally retarded, learning disabilities, physically handicapped, emotionally handicapped. M.Ed. only.

Teaching. M.A.T. only.

TESOL.

Visual Arts. Includes painting, sculpture, ceramics, metals, printing, fibers. M.A. only.

Writing.

Note: Certification programs in Education available.

WILLIAMS COLLEGE
Williamstown, Massachusetts 01267

Founded 1793. Located 50 miles E of Albany, New York. Coed. Private control. Semester system. Special facilities: art museum, Clark Art Institute, Adams Memorial Theater. Library: 680,000 volumes.

Annual tuition: Art History full-time $22,859. On-campus housing required for single graduate students. Annual housing cost: $5990. Contact Graduate Housing Office. Phone: (413)458-2303, ext. 403.

Graduate Study

Enrollment: Art History full-time 28, part-time 0. Faculty: full-time 24. Degree conferred: M.A.

ADMISSION REQUIREMENTS. Transcripts, four letters of recommendation, GRE required in support of application. Interview recommended. Accepts transfer applicants. TOEFL required for international applicants. Apply to Director, Graduate Programs for Art History, by January 15. Phone: (413)258-9545. Application fee $35. Phone: (413)458-2303, ext. 403.

ADMISSION STANDARDS. Competitive. Usual minimum average: 3.0 (A = 4).

FINANCIAL AID. Art History full- and partial scholarships. Apply by April 15 to Director, Graduate Programs. Use FAFSA. 100% of students receive some aid from College and outside sources.

DEGREE REQUIREMENTS. For M.A.: 8 credit units, two winter study periods, one year minimum in resident; reading knowledge of two foreign languages; thesis; final oral exam.

FIELD OF STUDY.
Art History.

WINONA STATE UNIVERSITY
Winona, Minnesota 55987-5838

Founded 1858. Located 110 miles SE of Minneapolis. Coed. State control. Quarter system. Library: 244,000 volumes, 831,000 microforms, 1700 current periodicals, 45 PCs.

Tuition: per credit, resident $75.60, nonresident $119.75. Average academic year housing cost: $3100 (including board).

Limited on-campus housing for graduate students. Contact Director of Student Housing for both on- and off-campus housing information. Phone: (507)457-5305. Day-care facilities available.

Graduate Programs

Graduate study since 1953. Enrollment: full-time 29, part-time 587. College faculty teaching graduate students: full-time 75, part-time none. Degrees conferred: M.S., M.A., M.B.A., Specialist Degree in Educational Administration.

ADMISSION REQUIREMENTS. Transcripts GRE/GMAT required in support of application. Interview not required. TOEFL required for international applicants. Accepts transfer applicants. Graduates of unaccredited institutions not considered. Apply to Office of Graduate Studies at least one month prior to registration. Application fee $15. Phone: (507)457-5038; fax: (507)457-5578.

ADMISSION STANDARDS. Selective. Usual minimum average: 2.5 (A = 4).

FINANCIAL AID. Annual awards from institutional funds: sixteen assistantships, Federal W/S, loans. Approved for VA benefits. Apply at least six months prior to registration to appropriate department chair for assistantships; to Financial Aid Office for all other programs. Use FAFSA. Phone: (507)457-5090.

DEGREE REQUIREMENTS. Thesis plan: 45 quarter hours minimum; final written/oral exam. Nonthesis plan: 48–72 quarter hours; final written exam. Specialist: 45 quarter hours beyond the master's; special project.

FIELDS OF STUDY.
Business Administration. GMAT for admission. M.B.A.

Business Education. M.S.

Community Counseling. M.S.

Education. Includes K–12, special education. M.S.

Educational Leaderships. M.S., Ed.S.

Elementary Administration. M.S.

Elementary Counseling.

English. M.A., M.S.

Nursing. M.S.

Secondary Administration. M.S.

Secondary Counseling. M.S.

WINTHROP UNIVERSITY
Rock Hill, South Carolina 29733
http://lurch.winthrop.edu

Founded 1886. Located 25 miles SW of Charlotte, North Carolina. State control. Semester system. Library: 369,149 volumes, 1,099,337 microforms, 2300 current periodicals, 25 PCs.

Annual tuition: full-time, resident $3798, nonresident $6840; per semester hour, resident $159, nonresident $285. On-campus housing available for married and single students; 54 married housing units. Average academic year housing costs: $3498 (including board) for single students; $3800 for married students. Contact Director, Residence Life, for housing information. Phone: (803)323-2260.

Graduate Division

Enrollment: full-time 323, part-time 852. University faculty: full-time 253, part-time 123. Degrees conferred: M.A., M.S., M.F.A., M.M.T.H., M.A.T., M.L.A., M.M., M.Ed., M.B.A., M.M.E., Ed.S., S.S.P.

ADMISSION REQUIREMENTS. Official transcripts from all postsecondary institutions attended, GMAT (business), GRE/MAT, NTE/Class III Professional Teaching Certificate for certain programs required in support of application. TOEFL or ELS Language Center English proficiency level 109 required for international applicants. Accepts transfer applicants. Graduates of colleges not accredited by a regional accrediting agency must be approved by the Graduate Council. Apply to the Office of Graduate Studies; no specified closing date. Application fee $35. Phone: (803)323-2204.

ADMISSION STANDARDS. Selective. Usual minimum average: 3.0 (A = 4).

FINANCIAL AID. Annual awards from institutional funds: research assistantships, graduate assistantships, Federal W/S, loans. Approved for VA benefits. Forms for assistantships available in Office of Graduate Services. Apply to Financial Aid Office for all federal programs. Use FAFSA and institutional FAF. Phone: (803)323-2189; fax: (803)323-4528. Aid sometimes available to part-time students.

DEGREE REQUIREMENTS. For all master's: 30–60 semester hours minimum; M.A., M.S. thesis optional. For Ed.S., S.S.P.: 60–66 semester hours beyond the bachelor's.

FIELDS OF STUDY.
Art Education.
Biology.
Business Administration.
Business Education.
Education. Includes most subject areas.
English.
Family and Consumer Science.
Fine Arts. Slide portfolio for admission.
Food and Nutrition.
Guidance.
History.
Liberal Arts.
Mathematics.
Music. Entrance exam for admission; two recitals for M.M.
Physical Education.
Reading.
School Psychology. Additional special application and interview for admission.
Spanish.

MEDICAL COLLEGE OF WISCONSIN
Milwaukee, Wisconsin 53226-0509

Founded 1913, renamed 1970. Coed. Public, formerly associated with Marquette University. Semester system. Special facilities: National EST Center, MRI Center, Blood Research Institute. Library: 210,000 volumes, 25 PCs. No on-campus housing available. Total average costs for all other expenses beyond tuition: $9058.

Graduate School

Annual tuition: full-time $8611.
Enrollment: full-time 79, part-time faculty: full-time 100, part-time 46. Degrees conferred: M.S., Ph.D.

ADMISSION REQUIREMENTS. Transcripts, GRE Subject Tests/MAT, interview required in support of application. TOEFL required for all foreign students. Accepts transfer applicants. Graduates of unaccredited colleges not considered. Apply to Office of Admissions June 1 (Fall), December 1 (Spring). Application fee $40. Phone: (414)456-8218.

ADMISSION STANDARDS. Competitive. Usual minimum average: 3.0 (A = 4).

FINANCIAL AID. Eighty-five research assistantships, eighteen fellowships, Federal W/S, loans. About 20% of students receive some aid from school and outside sources. Apply to Director of Financial Aid; apply by February 15. Use FAFSA.

DEGREE REQUIREMENTS. For M.S.: 30–36 semester hours minimum; foreign language requirement varies by department; comprehensive exam; thesis. For Ph.D.: six semesters in residence, at least two semesters in full-time study; qualifying exam; dissertation; final oral exam. For M.D.-Ph.D.: satisfactory completion of six to seven-year program.

FIELDS OF STUDY.
Anatomy.
Biochemistry.
Bioethics.
Biophysics.
Genetics.
Immunology.
Microbiology.
Molecular Biology.
Neurosciences.
Pathology.
Pharmacology.
Physiology.

Medical School

Annual tuition: resident $13,811, nonresident $23,909. Total average other expenses: $9058.
Enrollment: first-year class 200 (EDP 40); total 807 (men 62%, women 38%). Faculty: full-time 758, part-time 68. Degrees conferred: M.D., M.D.-Ph.D. (Medical Scientist Training Program).

ADMISSION REQUIREMENTS. AMCAS report, transcripts, MCAT, two letters of recommendation, personal interview required in support of application. Has EDP; apply between June 15 and August 1. Interview by invitation only. Preference given to state residents. Graduates of unaccredited colleges not considered. Apply to Committee on Admissions after June 15, before November 15. Application fee $50. Phone: (414)456-8246.

ADMISSION STANDARDS. Very competitive for nonresidents, selective for residents. Accepts about 4–6% of total annual applicants. Approximately 50% are state residents.

FINANCIAL AID. Scholarships, loans. Apply to Director of Financial Aid after acceptance, before April 24. Use FAFSA. About 20% of students receive some aid from College and outside sources. Apply to Director of Financial Aid, April 24. Use FAFSA.

DEGREE REQUIREMENTS. For M.D.: satisfactory completion of four-year program. For M.D.-Ph.D.: satisfactory completion of six to seven-year program.

UNIVERSITY OF WISCONSIN– EAU CLAIRE
Eau Claire, Wisconsin 54702-4004
http://www.uwec.edu

Founded 1916. Located 85 miles E of St. Paul, Minnesota. Coed. State control. Semester system. Special facilities: Foster Art Gallery, Center for Communication Disorders, Human Development Center, Kate Gill Literary Research Center, S. W.

Casey Observatory, James Newman Clark Bird Museum, Pigeon Lake Field Station, L. E. Phillips Planetarium. Library: 522,536 volumes, 1,221,674 microforms, 1990 current periodicals, 55 PCs.

Annual fees: full-time, resident $3223, nonresident $9870; per credits resident $180, nonresident $549. On-campus housing for single graduate students, none for married students. Average academic year housing costs: $3400 (including board). Contact Director of Housing for both on- and off-campus housing information. Phone: (715)836-3674.

Graduate Studies

Graduate study since 1960. Enrollment: full-time 141, part-time 400. Graduate faculty: full-time 380, part-time 25. Degrees conferred: M.A., M.A.T., M.B.A., M.E., M.M., M.S., M.S.N., M.S.T., M.S.E.

ADMISSION REQUIREMENTS. Official transcripts, GRE/GMAT, interview required in support of application. TOEFL required for international applicants. Accepts transfer applicants. Apply to Director of Admissions at least 30 days prior to registration. Application fee $35. Phone: (715)836-5415; fax: (715)836-2380.

ADMISSION STANDARDS. Relatively open. Usual minimum average for probationary admission: 2.25 (A = 4).

FINANCIAL AID. Annual awards from institutional funds: scholarships, twenty-six graduate assistantships, Federal W/S, loans. Approved for VA benefits. Apply by March 1 to Director of Financial Aids. Use FAFSA. Phone: (715)836-3733, Fax: (715)836-2380. About 40% of full-time students receive aid other than loans from University and outside sources. Aid sometimes available to part-time students.

DEGREE REQUIREMENTS. For master's: 30–36 semester hours minimum, at least 21 in residence; thesis/nonthesis option/final paper; final written/oral comprehensive exam.

FIELDS OF STUDY.
Biology.
Business Administration.
Communicative Disorders.
Elementary Education.
English.
Environmental and Public Health.
History.
History/Social Science.
Mathematics.
Music.
Nursing.
Psychology.
Reading.
School Psychology.
Special Education.

UNIVERSITY OF WISCONSIN– LA CROSSE

La Crosse, Wisconsin 54601-3742
http://www.uwlax.edu

Founded 1909. Located 125 miles W of Madison. Coed. State control. Semester system. Special facilities: Bureau of Business and Economic Research, Center for Education Profession, Rhea Pederson Reading Center, River Studies Center. Library: over 419,000 volumes, 990,000 microforms, 1900 current periodicals, 25 PCs.

Annual fees: full-time, resident $3300, nonresident $9947; per credit, resident $184, nonresident $554. Limited on-campus housing for single graduate students only. Average academic year housing costs: $2270 (including board). Contact Director of Campus Housing for both on- and off-campus housing information. Phone: (608)785-8075. Day care facilities available.

Graduate Studies

Graduate study since 1956. Enrollment: full-time 253, part-time 329. University faculty teaching graduate students: full-time 139, part-time 55. Degrees conferred: M.B.A., M.E.P.D., M.P.H., M.S., M.S.Ed.

ADMISSION REQUIREMENTS. Transcript, GMAT (Business) required in support of application. TOEFL required for international applicants. Accepts transfer applicants. Graduates of unaccredited institutions not considered. Apply to Admissions Office at least one month prior to registration. Rolling admission process. Application fee $35. Phone: (608)785-8939.

ADMISSION STANDARDS. Selective. Required minimum overall GPA of 2.85, or 3.0 in last 60 undergraduate credits.

FINANCIAL AID. Fifty graduate assistantships, Federal W/S, loans. Approved for VA benefits. Apply by March 15 to Director of Financial Aid. Phone: (608)785-8604. Use FAFSA. About 50% of students receive aid from University and outside sources. Aid available to part-time students.

DEGREE REQUIREMENTS. For master's: 30–48 credit hours minimum, at least 24 in residence; thesis/final document; final oral/written exam.

FIELDS OF STUDY.
Adult Fitness–Cardiac Rehabilitation.
Biology. Includes clinical microbiology, nurse anesthetist.
Business Administration.
College Student Personnel.
Community Health Education. M.P.H. only.
Education.
Exercise and Sport Science. Includes pedagogy, sport administration, human performance.
Marine Biology.
Physical Therapy.
Reading.
Recreation Management.
School Health Education.
School Psychology.
Special Education.
Special Physical Education.
Therapeutic Recreation.

UNIVERSITY OF WISCONSIN

Madison, Wisconsin 53706-1380

Founded 1948. Coed. State control. Semester system. Special facilities: Institute on Aging, Biotechnology Center, Biotron, Center for Demography and Ecology, Educational Research and Development Center, Institute for Research in the Humanities, Industrial Relations Research Institute, Institute for Environmental Studies, Sea Grant Institute, Space Science and Engineering Center, McArdle Cancer Research Laboratory, Synchrotron Radiation Center, Waisman Center on Mental Retardation and Human Development, Wisconsin Regional Primate Center, Wisconsin Center for Applied Microelectronics, Wisconsin Clinical Cancer Center, Women's Studies Research Center. Day-care facilities available. University libraries: 5,530,000 volumes, 4,100,000 microforms, 46,100 current periodicals.

Annual tuition: full-time, resident $4375, nonresident 13,296; per semester (minimum), resident $821, nonresident $2494. Limited on-campus housing available for graduate students. Average academic year housing costs: $2150 for single students, $5000 for married students. Contact Director of Residence Halls, Assignment Office of University Housing for both on- and off-campus housing information. Phone: (608)262-2522.

Graduate School

Established 1904. Enrollment: full- and part-time 9684 (men 55%, women 45%). Faculty: full- and part-time about 2400. Degrees conferred: M.A., M.B.A., M.F.A., M.M., M.Acc., A.Mus.D., Ph.D.

ADMISSION REQUIREMENTS. Official transcripts required in support of School's application. GRE Subject Tests, GMAT required by many departments. Evidence of proficiency in English or TOEFL, or MELAB required for international students. Interview not required. Accepts transfer applicants. Graduates of unaccredited institutions not considered. Apply to Dean of Graduate School at least six weeks prior to registration. Application fee $38. Phone: (608)262-2433.

ADMISSION STANDARDS. Very selective for most departments, competitive for others. Usual minimum average: 3.0 (A = 4).

FINANCIAL AID. Scholarships, fellowships, teaching research/project assistantships, Federal W/S, loans. Approved for VA benefits. Apply by January 15 to appropriate department with completed forms, transcripts, and GRE Subject Test. Use FAFSA. Phone: (608)262-3060.

DEGREE REQUIREMENTS. For master's: two semesters minimum, at least one in residence. In addition, each department has its own requirements regarding oral/written exams and thesis/nonthesis option. For M.F.A.: 4 semesters minimum, at least two in residence; final oral exam. For Ph.D.: six semesters minimum, at least three semesters in residence, and one year in full-time attendance; comprehensive preliminary exam; thesis; final oral exam. For A.Mus.D.: essentially the same as for the Ph.D.

FIELDS OF STUDY.
Actuarial Science.
African Languages and Literature.
Afro-American Studies.
Agricultural Economics.
Agricultural Engineering.
Agricultural Journalism.
Agronomy.
Analytical Clinical Chemistry.
Anatomy.
Anthropology.
Art.
Art Education.
Art History.
Astronomy.
Atmospheric Sciences.
Bacteriology.
Biochemistry.
Biometry.
Biomolecular Chemistry.
Biophysics.
Botany.
Buddhist Studies.
Business.
Cartography and Geographic Information Systems.
Cellular and Molecular Biology.
Chemical Engineering.
Chemistry.
Child and Family Studies.
Chinese.
Civil and Environmental Engineering.
Classics.
Communication Arts.
Communicative Disorders.
Comparative Literature.
Computer Science.
Conservation Biology and Sustainable Development.
Consumer Science.
Continuing and Vocational Education.
Counseling Psychology.
Curriculum and Instruction.
Dairy Science.
Developmental Biology.
Development Policy and Public Administration.
Development Studies.
Economics.
Education Administration.
Educational Policy Studies.
Educational Psychology.
Electrical Engineering.
Endocrinology-Reproductive Physiology.
Engineering Mechanics.
English.
Entomology.
Environmental Monitoring.
Environmental Toxicology.
Family and Consumer Journalism.
Food Science.
Forestry.
French.
Genetics.
Geological Engineering.
Geology and Geophysics.
German.
Greek.
Hebrew and Semitic Studies.
History.
History of Science.
Horticulture.
Human Cancer Biology.
Industrial Engineering.
Industrial Relations.
Interior Environment.
Italian.
Japanese.
Journalism and Mass Communication.
Kinesiology.
Land Resources.
Landscape Architecture.
Latin.
Latin American and Iberian Studies.
Legal Institutions.
Library and Information Studies.
Linguistics.
Manufacturing Systems Engineering.
Mass Communications.
Materials Science.
Mathematics.
Meat and Animal Science.
Mechanical Engineering.
Medical Genetics.
Medical Microbiology and Immunology.
Medical Physics.
Metallurgical Engineering.
Music.
Neurophysiology.
Neuroscience.
Nuclear Engineering and Engineering Physics.

Nursing.
Nutritional Sciences.
Oceanography and Limnology.
Oncology.
Pathology.
Pharmacology.
Pharmacy.
Philosophy.
Physics.
Physiology.
Plant Breeding and Plant Genetics.
Plant Pathology.
Political Science.
Portuguese.
Poultry Science.
Preventive Medicine-Administrative Medicine.
Preventive Medicine-Epidemiology.
Psychology.
Public Affairs and Administration.
Public Affairs and Policy Analysis.
Public Policy and Public Administration.
Rehabilitation Psychology.
Rural Sociology.
Scandinavian Studies.
Science Education.
Slavic Languages and Literature.
Social Welfare.
Social Work.
Sociology.
Soil Science.
South Asian Languages and Literature.
South Asian Studies.
Southeast Asian Studies.
Spanish.
Special Education.
Statistics.
Textiles and Clothing.
Theater and Drama.
Therapeutic Science.
Urban and Regional Planning.
Veterinary Science.
Water Chemistry.
Water Resources Management.
Wildlife Ecology.
Zoology.

Law School

Established 1848. Semester system. Law library: 400,000 volumes. Library has LEXIS, NEXIS, WESTLAW.

Annual tuition: full-time, resident $5504, nonresident $14,261.

Enrollment: first-year class 269; total 900 (men 55%, women 45%). Faculty: full-time 60, part-time 15. Degrees conferred: J.D., J.D.-M.A., J.D.-M.B.A., J.D.-M.L.S., J.D.-M.P.A., J.D.-Ph.D. (Philosophy, Sociology), LL.M., S.J.D.

ADMISSION REQUIREMENTS. For J.D. program: LSDAS Law School report, bachelor's degree, transcripts, LSAT, personal statement required in support of application. Interview not required. Accepts a few transfer applicants on space available basis only. Apply to Admissions Committee of School after October 1, before February 1; for transfer applicants June 1. Fall admission only. Application fee: $65. Phone: (608)262-5914. For graduate study: transcripts required in support of application. Apply to Dean of School (attention: Research Committee) by April 1.

ADMISSION STANDARDS. Selective. Accepts 20–25% of total annual applicants. Approximately 70–80% of class are state residents.

FINANCIAL AID. For J.D. program: scholarships, Federal W/S, loans. Apply by March 1 to Financial Aid Office. Use FAFSA. For graduate study: scholarships, research fellowships, teaching assistantships. Apply by March 1 to the Dean (attention: Research Committee). About 20% of students receive aid other than loans from School.

DEGREE REQUIREMENTS. For J.D.: 90-credit-hour program, at least final 30 credits in residence. For LL.M.: at least 24 credits beyond the J.D.; one year in residence; thesis/research project. For S.J.D.: one year minimum in residence; thesis. For master's and doctoral degrees; see Graduate School listing above.

Medical School

Established 1907. Library: 125,000 volumes. Annual tuition and fees: resident $13,722, nonresident $19,966. Housing available. Apply to Office of Housing. Phone: (608)262-2522. Total average costs for all other expenses: $7000.

Enrollment: first-year class 143 (EDP 25); total 604 (men 50%, women 50%). Faculty: full-time 322, part-time 60. Degrees conferred: M.D., M.D.-M.S., M.D.-Ph.D.

ADMISSION REQUIREMENTS. AMCAS report, transcripts, MCAT, three recommendations required in support of application. Final screening interview by invitation only. Preference given to state residents. Has EDP (state residents only); apply between June 15 and August 1. Apply to committee on admissions after June 15, before November 15. Application fee $35. Phone: (608)263-4925; fax: (608)262-2327.

ADMISSION STANDARDS. Selective. Accepts 20–30% of total annual applicants. 85% are state residents.

FINANCIAL AID. Scholarships, grants, loans. Apply to Scholarship Committee by February 15. About 10% of students receive aid other than loans from School.

DEGREE REQUIREMENTS. For M.D.: satisfactory completion of four-year program. For M.D.-M.S.: satisfactory completion of five-year program. For M.D.-Ph.D.: satisfactory completion of six to seven-year program.

FIELDS OF GRADUATE STUDY.
Anatomy.
Biochemistry.
Biophysics.
Cell Biology.
Genetics.
Immunology.
Microbiology.
Molecular Biology.
Neurosciences.
Pathology.
Pharmacology.
Physiology.

School of Veterinary Medicine

Annual tuition: resident $10,060, nonresident $14,586. Total average cost for all other expenses: $8200.

Enrollment: first-year 80, total 340 (men 45%, women 55%). Faculty: full-time 75; part-time 3. Degrees conferred: D.V.M., D.V.M.-M.S., D.V.M.-Ph.D.

ADMISSION REQUIREMENTS. VMCAS report (nonresident), transcripts, GRE, 60 undergraduate credits minimum, three evaluation/recommendations, animal/veterinary experience support of application. Preference given to state resident. Accepts transfer applicants on a space-available basis only. Apply to Dean of School after September 1, before November 15. Application fee $35. Phone: (608)263-2525.

ADMISSION STANDARDS. Admits 40% of total annual applicants. Accepts approximately 60–70% state residents; ten to twenty spaces available for nonresidents.

FINANCIAL AID. Scholarships, assistantships, Federal W/S, loans. Apply to Director of Student Financial Aid. Use FAFSA.

DEGREE REQUIREMENTS. For D.V.M.: satisfactory completion of four-year program. For joint degree programs: see Graduate College listing above.

UNIVERSITY OF WISCONSIN–MILWAUKEE
Milwaukee, Wisconsin 53201-0340
http://www.uwm.edu

Founded 1956. Coed. State control. Semester system. Special facilities: Center for Architecture and Urban Planning Research, Center for Business Competitiveness, Center for Great Lakes Studies/Great Lakes Research facility, Center for Latin American, Center for Nursing Research and Evaluation, Center for Twentieth Century Studies, Field Station, Institute on Race and Ethnicity, Laboratory for Surface Studies, Management Research Center, Center for Urban Transportation Studies, Urban Research Center, Center for Women's Studies. Library: over 4,300,000 cataloged items, PCs in all libraries.

Annual tuition: full-time, resident $4440, nonresident $13,323. Limited on-campus housing available for single students. Average academic year housing costs: $4096–$4197. Contact Director of Residence Life for both on- and off-campus housing information. Phone: (800)622-0287, (414)229-4065.

Graduate School
http://www.uwm.edu/dept/Grad-sch/

Graduate study since 1965. Enrollment: full-time 1293, part-time 3382 (men 35%, women 65%). Faculty: full-time 800. Degrees conferred: M.A., M.S., M.Arch., M.B.A., M.F.A., M.I.L.R., M.M., M.L.I.S., M.P.A., M.S.W., M.U.P., Ph.D.

ADMISSION REQUIREMENTS. Official transcripts required in support of School's application. GRE/GMAT/MAT recommended. Interview required for some programs. TOEFL required for international applicants. Accepts transfer applicants. Graduates of unaccredited institutions not considered. Apply to Graduate School by January 1 (Fall and Summer), September 1 (Spring). Application fee domestic $38, international applicants $68. Phone: (414)229-4982; e-mail: gradschool@csd.uwm.edu.

ADMISSION STANDARDS. Selective. Usual minimum average: 2.75 (A = 4).

FINANCIAL AID. Scholarships, 125 fellowships, 493 teaching assistantships, 114 research assistantships, 118 teaching assistantships, Federal W/S, loans. Approved for VA benefits. Apply by mid-January to the Graduate School Fellowship Office for fellowships; to appropriate department for assistantships; to Financial Aid Office for all other programs. Use FAFSA. Phone: (414)229-4541; fax: (414)229-5689.

DEGREE REQUIREMENTS. For master's: 24–48 semester hours; thesis/nonthesis option for many majors; final written/oral exam for some majors. For Ph.D.: 54 credits minimum beyond the bachelor's; foreign language or research skill for most programs; dissertation; final oral defense.

FIELDS OF STUDY.
Administrative Leadership and Supervision in Education. M.S.
Anthropology. M.S., Ph.D.
Architecture. M.Arch., Ph.D.
Art. M.A., M.F.A.
Art Education. M.S.
Art History. M.A.
Biological Sciences. M.S., Ph.D.
Business Administration. M.B.A.
Chemistry. M.S., Ph.D.
Communication. M.A.
Communications Sciences and Disorders.
Computer Science. M.S. Ph.D. offered through Engineering Department.
Cultural Foundations of Education. M.S.
Curriculum and Instruction. M.S.
Economics. M.A., Ph.D.
Educational Psychology. M.S.
Educational Rehabilitation Counseling. M.S.
Engineering. M.S., Ph.D.
English. M.A., Ph.D.
Exceptional Education. M.S.
Foreign Language and Literature. M.A.
Geography. M.A., M.S., Ph.D.
Geosciences. M.S., Ph.D.
History. M.A.
Industrial and Labor Relations. M.I.L.R.
Library and Information Science. M.L.I.S.
Management. M.S.
Management Science. Ph.D.
Mass Communication. M.A.
Mathematics. M.S., Ph.D.
Music. M.M.
Nursing. M.S., Ph.D.
Performing Arts. Includes film and theatre; M.F.A.
Physics. M.S., Ph.D.
Political Science. M.S., Ph.D.
Psychology. M.S., Ph.D.
Public Administration. M.P.A.
Social Work. M.S.W.
Sociology. M.A.
Urban Education. Ph.D.
Urban Planning. M.U.P.
Urban Studies. M.S., Ph.D.

UNIVERSITY OF WISCONSIN–OSHKOSH
Oshkosh, Wisconsin 54901-3551

Established 1871. Located 85 miles NW of Milwaukee. Coed. State control. Semester system. Library: 439,000 volumes, 127,000 microforms, 29 PCs.

Annual fees: full-time, resident $3174, nonresident $9821; per semester (minimum) resident $529, nonresident $1638. On-campus housing for 50 graduate men, 50 graduate women; none for married students. Average academic year housing costs: $2200 (single room, two semesters). Apply to Director of Residence Life for both on- and off-campus housing information. Phone: (414)424-3212. Day care facilities available.

Graduate School

Established 1963. Total enrollment: 1599 (men 35%, women 65%). University faculty teaching graduate students: full-time 145, part-time 32. Degrees conferred: M.S., M.S.N., M.S.Ed., M.B.A., M.P.A.

ADMISSION REQUIREMENTS. Official transcripts required in support of School's application. GMAT or GRE, interview required by some programs. TOEFL required for international applicants. Accepts transfer applicants. Graduates of unaccredited institutions not considered. Apply to Dean of Graduate School at least three months prior to registration. International applicant at least 6 months prior to registration. Application fee domestic $38, international $68. Phone: (414)424-1223.

ADMISSION STANDARDS. Selective. Usual minimum average: 2.75 (A = 4). Some programs require 3.0 minimum.

FINANCIAL AID. Annual awards from institutional funds: eight academic scholarships, seventy assistantships, ten advanced opportunity grants to minority students. Approved for VA benefits. Apply by March 1 to Graduate Dean. Use FAFSA. Phone: (414)424-3377. About 20% of students receive aid other than loans from University and outside sources. Aid sometimes available to part-time students.

DEGREE REQUIREMENTS. For master's: 30–48 semester hours minimum, at least 21 in residence; thesis/research paper; comprehensive oral/written exam.

FIELDS OF STUDY.
Biology. GRE for admission. M.S. only.
Business Administration. GMAT for admission. M.B.A. only.
Counseling. M.S.Ed. only.
Educational Leadership. M.S. only.
Elementary Education. M.S.Ed. only.
Mathematics Education. M.S. only.
Nursing. M.S.N. only.
Physics. M.S. only.
Psychology. GRE for admission. M.S. only.
Public Administration. M.P.A. only.
Reading. M.S.Ed. only.
Special Education. M.S.Ed. only.
Speech and Hearing Science. GRE for admission. M.S. only.

UNIVERSITY OF WISCONSIN–PLATTEVILLE

Platteville, Wisconsin 53818-3099
http://www.uwplatt.edu

Founded 1866. Located 70 miles SW of Madison. Coed. State control. Semester system. Library: 422,000 volumes, 968,000 microforms, 1550 current periodicals, 25 PCs.

Annual tuition: full-time, resident $3245, nonresident $9892; per semester (minimum) resident $529, nonresident $1648. On-campus housing for single graduate students. Average academic year housing costs: $1500 (room only). Average summer housing cost: $200–300. Contact Director of Student Housing for both on- and off-campus housing information. Phone: (608)342-1845; E-mail: egley@uwplatt.edu. Day care facilities available.

School of Graduate Studies

Graduate study since 1957. Enrollment: full-time 77, part-time 79. Graduate faculty: full-time 3, part-time 124. Degrees conferred: M.S., M.S.Ed.

ADMISSION REQUIREMENTS. Official transcripts required in support of School's application. TOEFL required for international applicants. Interview not required. Accepts transfer students. Apply to the School of Graduate Studies by May 15 (Summer) prior to registration for other semesters. Application fee $38. Phone: (800)362-5515, (608)342-1263; fax: (608)342-1389; E-mail: raimer@uwplatt.edu.

ADMISSION STANDARDS. Selective. Usual minimum average: 2.75; 2.9 for last 60 credits (A = 4).

FINANCIAL AID. Limited to assistantships, Federal W/S, loans. Approved for VA benefits. Apply by July 1 to Dean of the School of Graduate Studies. Use FAFSA. Phone: (608)342-1836; fax: (608)342-1122. About 20% of students receive aid other than loans from all sources. Aid available to part-time students.

DEGREE REQUIREMENTS. For master's: 30–36 semester hours minimum, at least 24 residence; thesis; oral exam/research paper; comprehensive exam.

FIELDS OF STUDY.
Adult Education.
Agricultural Industries.
Counselor Education.
Elementary Education.
Industrial Technology Management.
Management.
Middle School Education.
Secondary Education.
Vocational-Technical Education.

UNIVERSITY OF WISCONSIN–RIVER FALLS

River Falls, Wisconsin 54022-5013

Founded 1874. Located 30 miles SE of St. Paul, Minnesota. Coed. State control. Semester system.

Annual tuition: full-time, resident $3242, nonresident $9889; per semester (minimum) resident $563, nonresident $1671. On-campus housing for single students, limited number of married students. Average annual housing cost: $3500 for single students. Apply to Housing Director.

Graduate Study

Graduate study since 1962. Enrollment: full-time 142, part-time 297 (men 25%, women 75%). University faculty: full-time 243, part-time 5. Degrees conferred: M.A.T., M.S.E., M.S.T., M.E. in Prof.Dev., M.S.

ADMISSION REQUIREMENTS. Official transcripts, bachelor's degree in support of application. Some programs require interview and letters of recommendation. GRE or MAT for counseling program. TOEFL required for international students. Accepts transfer students. Apply to the Office of Graduate study; deadlines vary by department. Application fee $38. Phone: (715)425-3943.

ADMISSION STANDARDS. Relatively open. Minimum average: 2.75 (A = 4).

FINANCIAL AID. Annual awards from institutional funds: ten assistantships, Federal W/S, loans. Approved for VA benefits. Apply to Dean of Graduate School. Use FAFSA. Phone: (715)425-3843. Aid sometimes available for part-time students. About 40% of students receive aid from University and outside sources.

DEGREE REQUIREMENTS. For master's in Teaching: 30–40 credit hours minimum (no more than 9 credits in transfer); thesis/final document; final oral/written exam.

FIELDS OF STUDY.

Agriculture Education.
Communicative Disorders.
Counseling.

Elementary Education.
English.
History.
Learning Disabilities. Certification.
Mathematics/Science.
Professional Development in Education.
Reading.
School Psychology.
School Supervision.
Speech Communication.

English. M.S.T.
Guidance and Counseling. M.S.E.
History. M.S.T.
Human and Community Resources. M.S.
Interpersonal Communication. M.A.
Mass Communication. M.A.
Music. M.M.Ed.
Natural Resources. M.S.
Nutritional Sciences. M.S.

UNIVERSITY OF WISCONSIN–STEVENS POINT

Stevens Point, Wisconsin 54481-3897

Founded 1894. Coed. State control. Semester system. Special facilities: Center Wisconsin Environmental Field Station, Forest and Wildlife Research Station, Planetarium, Museum of Natural History. Library: 351,000 volumes, 743,000 microforms, 1900 current periodicals, 40 PCs.

Annual tuition: full-time, resident $3280, nonresident $9889; part-time per semester resident $589, nonresident $1694. On-campus housing for single students only. Average academic year housing costs: $3150 (including board). Contact Director of Student Housing for both on- and off-campus housing information. Phone: (715)346-3511. Day care facilities available.

Graduate School

Enrollment: full-time 150, part-time 294 (men 20%, women 80%). Full-time faculty teaching graduate students: 423. Degrees conferred: M.A., M.B.A., M.M., M.S.T., M.S., M.S.E., M.M.Ed.

ADMISSION REQUIREMENTS. Official transcripts, GRE required in support of application. TOEFL required for international applicants. Accepts transfer applicants. Graduates of unaccredited institutions not considered. Apply to Dean of Graduate School at least one month prior to registration. Some graduate program may require additional application materials. Rolling admissions process. Application fee $35. Phone: (715)346 2631.

ADMISSION STANDARDS. Selective. Usual minimum average: 2.75 (A = 4). Individual graduate programs may require a higher G.P.A.

FINANCIAL AID. Fifty-two research assistantships, sixty-three graduate assistantships, Federal W/S, loans. Approved for VA benefits. Apply May 1 to Dean of Graduate School for assistantships; to Director of Financial Aid for all other programs. Use FAFSA. Phone: (715)346-4771. Aid sometimes available to part-time students.

DEGREE REQUIREMENTS. For master's: 30–36 credits minimum, including culminating experience, at least 24–30 in residence; thesis/nonthesis option; final written/oral exam for some programs.

FIELDS OF STUDY.
Advertising and Public Relations. M.A.
Business and Economics. M.B.A.
Communicative Disorders. M.S.
Corporate Communication. M.A.
Education. M.S.E.
Educational Administration. M.S.E.
Elementary Education. M.S.E.

UNIVERSITY OF WISCONSIN–STOUT

Menomonie, Wisconsin 54751
http://www.uwstout.edu

Chartered 1893. Located 60 miles E of St. Paul. State control. Semester system. Special facilities: Design Research Center, Manufacturing Technology Transfer Center, Center for Innovation and Development, Center for Excellence in Advanced Technology, Center for Vocational, Technological and Adult Education, Center for Excellence in Tourism, Food and Tourism Industries, Social Science Research Center. Library: 218,000 volumes, 968,000 microforms, 1539 current periodicals, 135 PCs.

Annual tuition: full-time, resident $3283, nonresident $9889. Off-campus housing only. Average academic year room and board costs: $4500 for married students, $2818 for single students. Contact Stout Student Affairs Office. Phone: (715)232-2100.

Graduate College

Graduate study since 1935. Enrollment: full-time 279, part-time 230 (men 50%, women 50%). Graduate faculty: full-time 220, part-time 0. Degrees conferred: M.S., M.S. Ed., Ed.S.

ADMISSION REQUIREMENTS. Official transcripts required in support of College's application. GRE required for Applied Psychology. Interview required for some programs. TOEFL required for international applicants. Accepts transfer applicants. Apply to Graduate Student Evaluator at least one month prior of registration. Application fee $38. Phone: (715)232 1322.

ADMISSION STANDARDS. Selective in some departments, relatively open in others. Usual minimum average: 2.25 (A = 4).

FINANCIAL AID. Annual awards from institutional funds: twenty-one scholarships, fifty-nine teaching/research assistantships, forty-four tuition waivers, Federal W/S, loans. Approved for VA benefits. Apply by April 15 to Financial Aid Director. Use FAFSA. Phone: (715)232-1363; fax: (715)232-5246. About 50% of students receive aid other than loans from University and outside sources. Aid sometimes available to part-time students.

DEGREE REQUIREMENTS. For master's: 30–48 semester hours minimum, at least 6 in residence; thesis or final paper. For Ed.S.: 36 semester hours beyond the master's.

FIELDS OF STUDY.
Applied Psychology.
Education.
Food Science and Nutrition.
Guidance and Counseling. M.S., Ed.S.
Home Economics.
Hospitality and Tourism.
Industrial and Vocational Education. Ed.S. only.
Industrial/Technology Education.

Management Technology.
Marriage and Family Therapy.
Risk Control.
School Psychology.
Training and Development.
Vocational Education.
Vocational Rehabilitation.

UNIVERSITY OF WISCONSIN–SUPERIOR
Superior, Wisconsin 54880-2873

Founded 1893. Coed. State control. Semester system. Special facilities: Halden Fine and Applied Arts Center, Lake Superior Research Institute. Library: 285,000 volumes, 855,000 microforms, 1500 current periodicals.

Annual tuition: full-time, resident $3220, nonresident $9867; part-time per semester, resident $562, nonresident $1670. On-campus housing for single students only. Average academic year housing costs: $3036. Off-campus housing costs: $200–$600. Contact Resident Life Center for both on- and off-campus housing information. Phone: (715)394-8438.

Graduate Division

Established 1949. Enrollment: full-time 117, part-time 360. University faculty: full-time 87; part-time 14. Degrees conferred: M.A., M.S.Ed., Ed.S.

ADMISSION REQUIREMENTS. Official transcripts required in support of application. Interview required for Ed.S. program. TOEFL required for international applicants. Accepts transfer applicants. Apply to Dean of Graduate Division by August 1 (Fall), November 1 (Winter), February 1 (Spring), May 15 (Summer). Rolling admissions process. Application fee $20; $50 for international applicants. Phone: (715)394-8295; fax: (715)394-8107.

ADMISSION STANDARDS. Selective. Usual minimum average: 2.5 (A = 4).

FINANCIAL AID. Annual awards from institutional funds: twelve scholarships, eighteen assistantships, five minority fellowships, Federal W/S, loans. Apply by May 1 to Dean of Graduate Division for assistantships; to the Financial Aid Office for all other programs. Use FAFSA. About 25% of students receive aid other than loans from School and outside sources. Aid available to part-time students.

DEGREE REQUIREMENTS. For M.A., M.S.Ed.: 30–36 credits minimum, at least 24 in residence; MAT for candidacy; thesis/final project; final written/oral exam. For Ed.S.: 30 credits minimum beyond the master's, final written/oral exams; internship may be required.

FIELDS OF STUDY.
Art. Includes education, history, therapy, studio. M.A.
Communicating Arts. Includes mass communication, radio, television, film, speech communication, theater. M.A.
Counselor Education. M.S.Ed.
Educational Administration. M.S.Ed., Ed.S.
Elementary Education.
Emotionally Disturbed Learner. M.S.Ed.
Instruction. M.S.Ed.

Learning Disabilities. M.S.Ed.
Reading. M.S.Ed.
School Psychology. M.S.Ed.

UNIVERSITY OF WISCONSIN–WHITEWATER
Whitewater, Wisconsin 53190-1790

Established 1868. Located 51 miles W of Milwaukee. Coed. State control. Semester system. Library: 387,600 volumes, 950,000 microforms, 1500 current periodicals.

Annual tuition: full-time, resident $3259, $3627 (Business), nonresident $9906, $10,275 (Business); per credit, resident $181, $201 (Business), nonresident $550, $571 (Business). On-campus housing for single students only. Average academic year housing costs: $2850 (including board). Contact Office of Residential Life for both on- and off-campus housing information. Phone: (414)472-1151.

School of Graduate Studies

Enrollment: full- and part-time 1021. Faculty: 307. Degrees conferred: M.A.T., M.S.Ed., M.S., M.B.A., M.E.P.D., M.M.E.

ADMISSION REQUIREMENTS. Official transcripts required in support of School's application. GMAT required for Business. TOEFL required for international applicants. Accepts transfer applicants. Graduates of unaccredited colleges not considered. Apply to School of Graduate Studies at least two months prior to registration. Rolling admissions process. Application fee $20. Phone: (414)472-1006.

ADMISSION STANDARDS. Relatively open. Usual minimum average: 2.5 (A = 4).

FINANCIAL AID. Assistantships, Federal W/S, loans. Approved for VA benefits. Apply by April 15 to Dean, School of Graduate Studies, for assistantships; to the Financial Aid Office for all other programs. Use FAFSA. Aid available for part-time students.

DEGREE REQUIREMENTS. For all master's: 30–36 semester hours minimum; thesis/nonthesis option; final written or oral comprehensive exam option.

FIELDS OF STUDY.
Accounting. M.S.
Business Administration. Includes accounting, decision support systems, finance management, managerial economics, marketing, international business. M.B.A. only.
Communications. Includes speech, communicative disorders, mass; M.S.
Counselor Education. M.S.
Curriculum and Instruction. Includes art education, early childhood, gifted and talented, reading. M.S.
Elementary Education. M.S.
Library Media. M.S.
Music. M.M.E.
Professional Development. Two years teaching experience required for admission. M.E.P.D. only.
Reading. M.Ed.
Safety. Includes occupational, school, traffic. M.S.
School Business Management. M.S.Ed.
School Psychology. M.S.Ed.
Special Education. Includes MR, EM, learning disabilities, early childhood, severely, profoundly handicapped, transitional needs. M.S.Ed.

WORCESTER POLYTECHNIC INSTITUTE

Worcester, Massachusetts 01609-2247

http://www.wpi.edu

Founded 1865. Located 35 miles W of Boston. Coed. Private control. Semester system. Special facilities: Alden Research Laboratories (fluid mechanics), Aluminum Casting Research Laboratory, Applied Bioengineering Center, Computational Electromagnetics and Ultrasonics Systems Design and Development, Center for Crystal Growth in Space, Center for Holographic Studies and Laser Technology, Catalytic Sciences Laboratory, Electron Microscopy Laboratory, Center for Inorganic Membrane Studies, Center for Intelligent Processing of Materials, Magnetic Imaging Center, Manufacturing Engineering Application Center, Nuclear Reactor (pool type), Powder Metallurgy Center, computation facility, Van de Graaff accelerator, Center for Wireless Information Networks Studies. Library: 340,500 volumes, 800,000 microforms, 1273 current periodicals, 51 PCs.

Tuition: per credit hour $590. No on-campus housing for single or married graduate students. Contact Residential Services Office for off-campus housing information. Phone: (508)831-5645.

Graduate Program

Enrollment: full-time 408, part-time 597. Graduate faculty: full-time 205, part-time 81. Degrees conferred: M.B.A., M.Eng., M.S., Ph.D.

ADMISSION REQUIREMENTS. Official transcripts, GRE/GMAT (for some departments), three letters of recommendation required in support of application. GRE recommended. Interview not required. TOEFL required for international applicants. Accepts transfer applicants. Graduates of unaccredited institutions not considered. Apply by March 1 to Office of Graduate Admission. Application fee $50. Phone: (508)831-5301; fax: (508)831-5717.

ADMISSION STANDARDS. Selective for most departments. Usual minimum average: 3.0 (A = 4).

FINANCIAL AID. Annual awards from institutional funds: 15 scholarships, 110 teaching assistantships, 59 assistantships, loans. Approved for VA benefits. Apply by March 1 to Office of Graduate Admissions. Use FAFSA and institutional FAF. Phone: (508)831-5469; fax: (508)831-5743. About 47% of full-time students receive aid other than loans from Institute and outside sources.

DEGREE REQUIREMENTS. For M.S., M.Eng.: 30–36 credit hours minimum, at least 20 in residence; thesis/nonthesis option. For M.B.A.: 45 credits, minimum, at least 30 in residence; computer proficiency. For Ph.D. minimum of three years or about 90 credits beyond the bachelor's, at least 30 credits of research; dissertation; final oral exam.

FIELDS OF STUDY.
Biology and Biotechnology. GRE for admission.
Biomedical/Clinical Engineering. GRE for admission.
Biomedical Science.
Chemical Engineering. GRE for international applicants.
Chemistry and Biochemistry.
Civil and Environmental Engineering.
Computer and Communications Networks. GRE for admission.
Computer Science. GRE for admission.
Electrical and Computer Engineering. GRE for admission.
Fire Protection Engineering.
Management. GMAT for admission. M.B.A., M.S.-M.B.A.
Manufacturing Engineering.
Materials Science and Engineering.
Mathematical Sciences.
Mechanical Engineering.
Physics.

WORCESTER STATE COLLEGE

Worcester, Massachusetts 01602-2597

Founded 1874. Located 30 miles W of Boston. Coed. State control. Semester system. Library: 144,067 volumes, 14,228 microforms, 2100 current periodicals.

Tuition: per credit, resident $118, nonresident $118. No on-campus housing available.

Graduate Studies

Graduate study since 1947. Enrollment: full-time 47, part-time 536. Faculty: full-time 33, part-time 26. Degrees conferred: M.S., M.Ed., Certification Programs.

ADMISSION REQUIREMENTS. Transcripts, two letters of recommendation, GRE or MAT, interview required in support of application. TOEFL required for international applicants. Accepts transfer applicants. Graduates of unaccredited institutions not considered. Apply to Admissions Office. Apply by November 1 (Spring), April 15 (Summer), June 15 (Fall). Application fee $10 MA resident; $40 for nonresidents. Phone: (508)793-8120; fax: (508)793-8191.

ADMISSION STANDARDS. Selective. Usual minimum average: 2.75 (A = 4).

FINANCIAL AID. Limited to research assistantships, internships, Federal W/S, loans. Approved for VA benefits. Apply to Financial Aid Office; no specified closing date. Use FAFSA. Phone: (508)793-8056; fax: (508)793-8194.

DEGREE REQUIREMENTS. For master's: 33–36 semester hours minimum, at least 21 in residence; final written/oral exam.

FIELDS OF STUDY.
Biology. M.S. only.
Education. Includes early childhood, elementary, English, health, history, middle, secondary. M.Ed. only.
Human Services Management. M.S.
Leadership and Educational Administration. Certification only.
Reading. Certification only.
School Principal. Certification only.
Secondary Education.
Speech/Language Pathology. M.S. only.
Supervisor/Director. Certification only.

WRIGHT STATE UNIVERSITY

Dayton, Ohio 45435

Became independent unit in 1967. Coed. State control. Quarter system. Special facilities: Cox Institute, Center for Environmental Quality, Groundwater Management Center, NASA-Lewis Research Center, Intelligent Systems Applications Center, Kettering Research Laboratory, Center for Labor-Management Cooperation, Edison Materials Technology Center, Ohio Aerospace Institute, Center for Urban and Public Affairs. Library:

643,000 bound volumes, 1,200,000 microforms, 5220 current periodicals, 123 PCs.

Tuition: full-time per quarter, resident $1445, nonresident $2588; per quarter hour for less than 10.5 hours, resident $137, nonresident $244. On-campus housing available. Average academic year housing costs: $3900 (including board) for single students; $5470 for married students. Contact Office of Student Development for both on- and off-campus housing information. Phone: (513)873-4172.

School of Graduate Studies

Graduate study since 1965. Enrollment: full-time 819, part-time 1805 (men 45%, women 55%). University faculty teaching graduate students: full-time 646, part-time 40. Degrees conferred: M.A., M.S., M.Ed., M.B.A., M.S.C.E., M.S.E., M.S.T., M.A.T., M.R.C., M.Hum., M.Mus., M.U.A., Ed.S., Psy.D., Ph.D.

ADMISSION REQUIREMENTS. Transcripts required in support of School's application. TOEFL, TSE required for international applicants. GRE required for M.S. in Economics, M.A. in Applied Behavioral Science, M.S.C.E. in computer engineering, M.S. in computer science, M.S. in human factors and industrial/organizational psychology, M.U.A. in urban administration and the Psy.D., Ph.D. programs. The GMAT is required for the M.B.A., M.S. in logistics management. GRE/MAT required for College of Education and Human Services programs. Accepts transfer applicants. Apply to Assistant Dean and Director of Graduate Admissions and Records at least one month prior to registration. Application fee $25. Phone: (513)873-2976; fax: (513)873-3781; E-mail: wsugrad@desire.wright.edu.

FINANCIAL AID. Annual awards from institutional funds: 35 scholarships, 60 research assistantships, 165 teaching assistantships, 170 graduate assistantships, 40 internships, 51 predoctoral and postdoctoral fellowships, Federal W/S, loans. Approved for VA benefits. Apply to School of Graduate Studies for assistantships, fellowships, internships; to Office of Financial Aid for all other programs. No specified closing date. Use FAFSA. Phone: (513)873-2321. About 50% of full-time students receive aid.

DEGREE REQUIREMENTS. For master's: 45 quarter hours minimum, at least 33 in residence; thesis for most M.A. and M.S. programs; final exam. For Ph.D.: two-year minimum in residence beyond the master's; reading knowledge of one foreign language; written/oral exam; dissertation; final oral exam. For Psy.D.: essentially the same as for Ph.D., except a research tool in place of the one foreign language.

FIELDS OF STUDY.

COLLEGE OF BUSINESS ADMINISTRATION:
Accountancy. M.Acc.
Finance. M.B.A.
Financial Administration. M.B.A.
Health Care Management. M.B.A.
International Business. M.B.A.
Logistics Management. M.B.A., M.S.
Management. M.B.A.
Management Information Systems. M.B.A.
Marketing. M.B.A.
Operations Management. M.B.A.
Project Management. M.B.A.
Social and Applied Economics. M.S.

COLLEGE OF EDUCATION AND HUMAN SERVICES:
Classroom Teacher. Includes art, business, computer, early childhood, elementary, mathematics, physical, reading, science secondary, special (developmentally handicapped, multihandicapped, orthopedically handicapped, severe behavior handicapped, specific learning disabilities, gifted). M.A., M.Ed.

Counseling. Includes business and industrial, exceptional children, gerontology, marriage and family, mental health, student personnel services in higher education. M.A., M.S.
Educational Leadership: Administrative Specialist. Includes business management, instruction, pupil personnel, research, special education, school and community relations, staff personnel administration. M.A., M.Ed.
Educational Leadership: Curriculum and Supervision. Includes computer facilitator, media supervisor, special education supervisor, teacher leader, vocational supervisor, assistant superintendent, principalship. M.A., M.Ed.
Educational Specialist and Higher Education/Adult Continuing Education. Includes curriculum and instruction, superintendency. Ed.S.
Rehabilitation Counseling. Includes chemical dependency, severely disabled. M.R.C.
Student Personnel Services. Includes school counseling, school social worker. M.A., M.Ed.

COLLEGE OF ENGINEERING AND COMPUTER SCIENCE:
Biomedical Engineering. M.S.E.
Computer Engineering. M.S.C.E., Ph.D.
Computer Science. M.S.C.S., Ph.D.
Electrical Engineering. M.S.E.
Human Factors Engineering. M.S.E.
Materials Engineering. M.S.E.
Mechanical Engineering. M.S.E.

COLLEGE OF LIBERAL ARTS:
Applied Behavioral Science. Includes criminal justice and social problems.
English. Includes English, English writing and language. M.A.
History. M.A.
Humanities. M.Hum.
Music Education. M.M.
TSOL. M.A.
Urban Administration. M.U.A.

COLLEGE OF NURSING AND HEALTH:
Adult Health and Illness. M.S.
Community Health. M.S.
Family Nurse Practitioner. M.S.
Nursing. M.S.
Nursing Administration. M.S.
Nursing Education. M.S.

COLLEGE OF SCIENCE AND MATHEMATICS:
Anatomy. M.S.
Applied Mathematics. M.S.
Applied Statistics. M.S.
Biochemistry and Molecular Biology. M.S., Ph.D.
Biological Sciences. M.S.
Biomedical Sciences. Ph.D.
Chemistry. M.S.
Earth Science Education. M.S.T.
Geological Sciences. M.S.
Human Factors and Industrial/Organizational Psychology. M.S., Ph.D.
Mathematics. M.S.
Microbiology and Immunology. M.S.
Physics. M.S., M.S.T.
Physiology and Biophysics. M.S.

SCHOOL OF NURSING:
Nursing. M.S.
Nursing Administration. M.S.-M.B.A.

SCHOOL OF GRADUATE STUDIES:
Aerospace Medicine. M.S.
Interdisciplinary Studies. M.A., M.S.

School of Medicine (P.O. Box 1751)

Established 1973. Annual tuition: resident $11,552, nonresident $16,352, student fees $639. Enrollment: first-year class 90 (EDP 10); total 403 (men 50%, women 50%). Faculty: over 1000. Degree conferred: M.D., M.D.-Ph.D.

ADMISSION REQUIREMENTS. AMCAS report, transcripts, MCAT, recommendations required in support of application. Interview and supplementary application by invitation only. Has EDP; apply between June 15 and August 1. Apply to Office of Student Affairs/Admissions after June 15, before November 15. Application fee $30. Phone: (513)873-2934; fax: (513)873-3322.

ADMISSION STANDARDS. Selective. Admits about 8–10% of total annual applicants. Approximately 91% are state residents.

FINANCIAL AID. Limited scholarships, loans, grants. Apply after acceptance to Office of Student Affairs. About 25% of students receive some aid from School.

DEGREE REQUIREMENTS: For M.D.: satisfactory completion of four year program.

FIELDS OF GRADUATE STUDY.
Anatomy.
Biochemistry.
Biophysics.
Cell Biology.
Immunology.
Microbiology.
Neurosciences.
Pathology.
Pharmacology.
Physiology.

UNIVERSITY OF WYOMING

Laramie, Wyoming 82071
http:uwyo.edu

Founded 1886. State control. Semester system. Special facilities: American Heritage Center, Elk Mountain Observatory, Enhanced Oil Recovery Institute, Geological Museum, National Park Service Research Center, Laramie Petroleum Research Center, Natural Resources Research Institute, Red Buttes Research Center, Rocky Mountain Herbarium. Library: 1,900,000 volumes and is depository for federal documents; 2,300,000 microforms, 11,000 current periodicals, 75 PCs in all libraries.

Annual tuition: full-time, resident $2591, nonresident $7325; per credits resident $130.50, nonresident $393.50. On-campus housing for 700 married students; limited for single graduate students. Average academic year housing costs: $2130 for married students, $4151 (including board) for single students. Contact Director of Housing for both on- and off-campus housing information. Phone: (307)766-3179.

Graduate School

http://grad.uwyo.edu

Graduate study since 1897. Enrollment: full-time 1700, part-time 1500. University faculty teaching graduate students: full-time 500, part-time 50. Degrees conferred: M.A., M.S., M.A.E., M.A.T., M.M., M.S.E., M.S.T., M.B.A., M.P.A., M.F.A., M.P., I.M.A., I.M.S., Ed.S., Ed.D., Ph.D., Ph.D.E.

ADMISSION REQUIREMENTS. Transcripts, GRE, GMAT (Business) required in support of School's application. GRE Subject required by some departments. TOEFL required for international applicants. Interview generally not required. Accepts transfer applicants. Graduates of unaccredited institutions not considered. Apply to Admissions Office by June 1. Application fee $40. Phone: (307)766-2287; fax: (307)766-4042.

ADMISSION STANDARDS. Very selective for most departments, selective for the others. Usual minimum average: 3.0 (A = 4).

FINANCIAL AID. Annual awards from institutional funds: 10 scholarships, 15 research fellowships, 365 teaching assistantships, 600 research assistantships, Federal W/S, loans. Approved for VA benefits. Apply by February 15 to appropriate department chair for fellowships, assistantships; to Financial Aid Office for all other programs. Use FAFSA. Phone: (307)766-2116; fax: (307)766-3800. About 75% of students receive aid other than loans from School and outside sources. Aid sometimes available to part-time students.

DEGREE REQUIREMENTS. For master's: 30–52 semester hours minimum; thesis/nonthesis option in some departments; final oral/written exam. For Ed.S.: 30 hours minimum beyond the master's, at least two semesters in residence. For Ed.D.: three years minimum beyond the bachelor's, at least 78 semester hours residence including one and a half consecutive semesters; preliminary exam; final project; reading knowledge of one foreign language or competency in research tool often required; final oral/written exam. For Ph.D.: 72 semester hours minimum beyond the bachelor's, at least 18 semester hours in residence; preliminary exam; thesis; final oral/written exam.

FIELDS OF STUDY.

COLLEGE OF AGRICULTURE:
Agricultural Economics. M.S. only.
Agronomy.
Animal Science.
Entomology. M.S. only.
Family and Consumer Science. M.S. only.
Food Science and Human Nutrition.
Molecular Biology.
Plant Pathology. M.S. only.
Rangeland Ecology and Watershed Management.
Reproductive Biology.
Soils.

COLLEGE OF ARTS AND SCIENCES:
American Studies. Interdepartmental; M.A. only.
Anthropology. M.A. only,
Art. Portfolio for admission; M.A., M.A.T.
Botany. M.S., Ph.D.
Chemistry. M.S., M.S.T., Ph.D.
Communication. M.A. only.
Community and Regional Planning. M.P. only.
Computer Science. M.S., Ph.D.
English. M.A. only.
Geography. M.A., M.S.T.
Geography/Water Resources. M.A.
Geology/Water Resources. M.S., Ph.D.
History. GRE Subject Test for admission; one language for M.A. M.A., M.S.T.
Interdisciplinary master's. Self-designed master's with up to three curricula combined. I.M.A., I.M.S.
International Studies. Interdepartmental; one language, thesis for M.A. M.A. only.
Land Use Planning. M.P. only.
Languages—Modern and Classical. Includes French, German, Spanish. M.A. only.
Mathematics. M.S., M.S.T., Ph.D.
Music. Includes applied music, music history and literature, theory and composition. M.A. only.
Philosophy. M.A. only.

Physics. GRE Subject Test for admission. M.S., M.S.T., Ph.D.
Political Science. M.A., M.P.A.
Psychology. Thesis for M.A. M.A., M.S., Ph.D.
Recreation and Park Administration. M.S. only.
Sociology. Thesis for M.A. M.A. only.
Statistics. M.S., Ph.D.
Zoology and Physiology. M.S., Ph.D.
Zoology and Physiology/Water Resources. M.S.

COLLEGE OF BUSINESS:
Business Administration. GMAT for admission. M.B.A.
Economics. M.S., Ph.D.
Finance. M.S.

COLLEGE OF EDUCATION:
Adult and Postsecondary Education.
Applied Science and Technology.
Counselor Education.
Curriculum and Instruction.
Educational Leadership.
Instructional Technology.
Library Science.
Special Education.

COLLEGE OF HEALTH SCIENCES:
Audiology. M.S.
Nursing. M.S.
Physical and Health Education. M.S.
Speech-Language Pathology. M.S.

COLLEGE OF ENGINEERING:
Atmospheric Sciences. M.S., Ph.D.
Bioengineering. Interdisciplinary; thesis for M.S.
Chemical Engineering. Thesis for M.S. M.S. only.
Civil Engineering. M.S., Ph.D.
Electrical Engineering. M.S., Ph.D.
Environmental Engineering. Interdisciplinary. M.S. only.
Mechanical Engineering. M.S., Ph.D.
Petroleum Engineering. M.S., Ph.D.

College of Law (82071-3035)

Established 1920. Semester system. Law library: 174,000 volumes. Library has LEXIS, NEXIS, WESTLAW, INFOTRAC.

Annual tuition: resident $3328, nonresident $7396. On-campus housing available. Apply to Director of Housing. Total average cost for all other expenses: $6500.

Enrollment: first-year class 81; full-time 232 (men 58%, women 42%). Faculty: full-time 14, part-time 3. Degrees conferred: J.D., J.D.-M.B.A., J.D.-M.P.A.

ADMISSION REQUIREMENTS. LSDAS Law School report, bachelor's degree, transcripts, LSAT (no later than February) required in support of application. Preference given to state residents. Accepts transfer applicants. Graduates of unaccredited institutions not considered. Apply to Director of Admissions after September 1, before April 1. Rolling admission process. Fall admission only for beginning students. Application fee $35. Phone: (307)766-6416.

ADMISSION STANDARDS. Selective. Accepts about 25% of total annual applicants.

FINANCIAL AID. Scholarships, fellowships, Federal W/S, loans. Apply to Director of Financial Aids, April 1. Use FAFSA. About 20% of students receive aid other than loans from College.

DEGREE REQUIREMENTS. For J.D.: satisfactory completion of three-year program, at least two years in residence; 88-semester-hour program.

XAVIER UNIVERSITY
Cincinnati, Ohio 45207-5311

Founded 1831. Coed. Private control. Roman Catholic. Semester system. Library: 307,000 volumes, 493,500 microforms, 1500 current periodicals, 22 PCs in libraries.

Tuition: $357–$397 per credit. No on-campus housing, except on a space-available basis. Contact Director of Residence Life for off-campus housing information. Phone: (513)745-4894.

Graduate School

Graduate study since 1946. Enrollment: full-time 300, part-time 2100. University faculty: full- and part-time 440. Degrees conferred: M.A., M.B.A., M.Ed., M.S., M.H.A.

ADMISSION REQUIREMENTS. Official transcripts required in support of School's application. GRE/MAT/GMAT required for some departments. TOEFL required for international applicants. Accepts transfer applicants. Graduates of unaccredited institutions not considered. Apply to Graduate Services Office at least one month prior to registration. Application fee $25; $35 application fee for M.B.A. applicants. Phone: (800)344-4690, (513)745-3360; fax: (513)745-1048.

ADMISSION STANDARDS. Selective. Usual minimum average: 2.7 (A = 4), varies by program.

FINANCIAL AID. Annual awards from institutional funds: scholarships, assistantships, tuition waivers, Federal W/S, loans. Approved for VA benefits. Apply by April 1 to Graduate Services Office for scholarships, assistantships; to Financial Aid Office for all other programs. Use FAFSA. Phone: (513)745-3142; fax: (513)745-2806. About 5% of students receive aid other than loans from University and outside sources. Aid sometimes available to part-time students.

DEGREE REQUIREMENTS. For M.A.: 30 semester hours minimum, at least 24 in residence; MAT for candidacy; reading knowledge of one foreign language in some programs; thesis; final oral exam. For M.B.A.: 36 semester hours minimum, at least 27 in residence; GMAT for candidacy. For M.Ed.: 30–42 semester hours minimum, at least 24–36 in residence; MAT for candidacy. For M.S.: 30 semester hours minimum, at least 24 in residence; MAT for candidacy; thesis/research paper; final oral/written exam. For M.H.A.: 60 semester hours minimum, at least 45 in residence; GMAT for candidacy; residency requirement.

FIELDS OF STUDY.
Agency and Community Counseling. M.Ed.
Art. M.Ed.
Business Administration. M.B.A.
Classic. M.Ed.
Computer Science. M.Ed.
Criminal Justice. M.S.
Educational Administration and Supervision. M.Ed.
English. M.A., M.Ed.
General Science. M.Ed.
History. M.A., M.Ed.
Human Resource Development. M.Ed.
Humanities. M.A.
Mathematics. M.Ed.
Modern Languages. M.Ed.
Montessori Education. M.Ed.
Multicultural Literature. M.Ed.
Music. M.Ed.
Nursing. GRE or MAT for admission. M.S.
Occupational Therapy. Certificate.
Physical Education. M.Ed.
Psychology. M.A.

School Counseling. M.Ed.
Sciences. Includes biology, chemistry, physics. M.Ed.
Secondary Education. M.Ed.
Special Education. M.Ed.
Sport Administration. M.Ed.
Theology. M.A.

XAVIER UNIVERSITY OF LOUISIANA
New Orleans, Louisiana 70125-1098

Founded 1925. Coed. Private control. Roman Catholic affiliation. Semester system. Library: 100,000 volumes.

Tuition: per credit $200. No on-campus housing for graduate students. Day care facilities available.

Graduate School

Enrollment: full-time 200; part-time 200 (men 35%, women 65%). Graduate faculty: full-time 12, part-time 8. Degrees conferred: M.A., M.S., M.A.T., Pharm.D., M.Th.

ADMISSION REQUIREMENTS. Transcripts, two letters of recommendation, GRE Subject Tests or MAT required in support of application. TOEFL required for international applicants. Interview not required. Accepts transfer applicants. Graduates of unaccredited colleges not considered. Apply to Dean of School by August 15 (Fall), January 1 (Spring). Application fee $25. Phone: (504)483-7487; fax: (504)486-4577.

ADMISSION STANDARDS. Relatively open. Minimum average: 2.5, 3.0 in major field (A = 4).

FINANCIAL AID. Limited to Federal W/S, loans. Approved for VA benefits. Apply to Financial Aid Office; no specified closing date. Use FAFSA. Phone: (504)483-3517; fax: (504)482-6258.

DEGREE REQUIREMENTS. For master's: 33 credits minimum; thesis/nonthesis option.

FIELDS OF STUDY.
Education. Includes administration/supervision in service professions, early childhood, elementary, secondary, guidance and counseling in education and noneducation fields, urban education leadership.
Nurse Anesthesiology.
Pharmacy.
Theology.

YALE UNIVERSITY
New Haven, Connecticut 06520

Founded 1701. Located 80 miles NE of New York City. Coed. Private control. Semester system. Special facilities: Beinecke Rare Book and Manuscript Library; Peabody Museum of Natural History; Art Gallery; Paul Mellon Center for British Art and British Studies; observatory; computer center; Child Study Center, Kline Geology Laboratory; Kline Chemistry Research Laboratory; Josiah Willard Gibbs Research Laboratories for biology, physics, molecular biology, biophysics; Center for International and Area Study; Nuclear Structure Laboratory for "Emperor" tandem electrostatic Van de Graaff accelerator; Kline Biology Tower for research and graduate training in biological sciences; Electron and Heavy Ion Accelerator Laboratories; Becton Engineering and Applied Science Center; Institute of Sacred Music; Institute for Social and Policy Studies; Social Interaction Laboratory; Political Science Research Laboratory. Library: over 10,500,000 volumes, 4,700,000 microforms, 54,600 current periodicals.

Annual tuition: full-time $20,300; modest continuing registration fee after the fourth year. On-campus housing for married students, graduate men and women. Average academic year housing costs: $3000–$5000. Contact University Housing Department for both on- and off-campus housing information. Phone: (203)432-2160.

Graduate School of Arts and Science

Graduate School organized in 1847, graduate study since 1732. Enrollment: full- and part-time 2424. University faculty teaching graduate courses: over 500. Degrees conferred: M.A., M.S., M.Phil., Ph.D. (M.A. as a terminal degree only in International and Developmental Economics, International Relations, African Studies Afro-American Studies, American Studies, Archeological Studies, East Asian Studies, English, German, History, History of Medicine and Life Sciences, Medieval Studies Music, Near Eastern Languages and Civilizations, Soviet and East European Studies, Slavic Languages and Literature, and Statistics. M.S. as a terminal degree only in Engineering and Applied Science, Mathematics, Molecular Biophysics and Biochemistry).

ADMISSION REQUIREMENTS. Transcripts, GRE, three letters of recommendation required in support of application. GRE Subject Test required by astronomy, biology, chemistry, computer science, economics, engineering and applied science, English language and literature, genetics, pharmacology, physics, physiology, statistics. Interview required in some cases. TOEFL required for international applicants. Accepts transfer applicants, usually for Ph.D. only. Apply to Coordinator, Graduate Admissions, P.O. Box 1504A, Yale Station, New Haven, Connecticut 06520, preferably one year prior to desired entrance but no later than January 2. Normally admits Fall only. Application fee $50. Phone: (203)432-2770.

APPLICATION STANDARDS. Competitive to very selective. Usual minimum average: 3.0 (A = 4).

FINANCIAL AID. Scholarships, fellowships, assistantships, Federal W/S, loans. Apply by January 2 to appropriate department chair for fellowships, assistantships; to Director of Financial Aid for all other programs. Use FAFSA. Phone: (203)432-2739. Support for Graduate School students while they are in residence at Yale comes from a great variety of sources. More than 80% of full-time candidates for the Ph.D. degree receive substantial aid from Yale or from other institutions and agencies interested in graduate education.

DEGREE REQUIREMENTS. For master's en route to Ph.D.: completion of first year of Ph.D. program; one academic year in full-time residence; recommendation by the appropriate department for the award of the degree, subject to final review by the Committee on Degrees. For terminal master's: one or two academic years of full-time residence depending on the program; high-pass average with at least one term grade of Honors in one-year program, two term grades of Honors in two-year program; foreign language requirements set by department; master's essay required by some departments. For M.Phil.: completion of all requirements for the Ph.D. except those relating directly to the dissertation. For Ph.D.: three academic years in residence; no more than four years to fulfill foreign language and course requirements as set by individual departments; grade of Honors in at least one year course or two term courses; general written/oral exam; prospectus and dissertation; final oral exam.

FIELDS OF STUDY.
Accounting. Ph.D.
African Studies. Two-year M.A. program; proficiency in one African language.

African-American Studies. Two-year M.A. program. M.A., Ph.D.

American Studies. Reading knowledge of two languages or high level of proficiency in one language required. M.A., Ph.D.

Anthropology. Faculty decides with each student individually the particular requirements in respect to languages, statistics, or other research tools. M.A., Ph.D.

Applied Mechanics and Mechanical Engineering. M.Phil, M.S., Ph.D.

Applied Physics. M.S., Ph.D.

Archaeological Studies. No foreign language required. M.A.

Astronomy. Working knowledge of at least two languages; one French, German, or Russian required. M.S., Ph.D.

Biology. Includes experimental pathology, immunobiology, and plant science. Demonstration of competence in one language (French, German, Russian, or any language containing significant biological literature) required. M.S., Ph.D.

Biophysical Chemistry. Ph.D.

Cell Biology. No foreign language requirement. Ph.D.

Cellular Neurobiology. Ph.D.

Chemical Engineering. M.S., Ph.D.

Classics. Reading knowledge of French and German, good knowledge of Greek and Latin grammar and ability to read representative passages in both languages at sight required. Ph.D.

Comparative Literature. Reading knowledge of two modern languages plus Latin or Greek required. Ph.D.

Computer Science. No foreign language required. Ph.D.

East Asian Languages and Literature. One European language plus Chinese and Japanese required. Ph.D.

East Asian Studies. Two-year M.A. program; Chinese or Japanese plus French or German proficiency required. M.A.

Economics. No foreign language required unless connected with dissertation research. Ph.D.

Electrical Engineering. M.S., Ph.D.

English Language and Literature. Ability to read simple prose in three languages or demonstration of the same level of competence in one language and advanced competence in a second language required; one language must be Latin or Greek. Ph.D.

Environmental Sciences. Ph.D.

French. Reading knowledge of a second Romance language; Latin and non-Romance language (usually German) required. Ph.D.

Genetics. No foreign language required. Ph.D.

Geology and Geophysics. No foreign language required, but students may be assigned foreign-language literature in certain fields of specialization. Ph.D.

Germanic Languages and Literature. Reading knowledge of French and Latin as well as thorough preparation in German required. M.A., Ph.D.

History. Reading knowledge of one foreign language required. M.A., Ph.D.

History of Art. Reading knowledge of German and second language relevant to proposed specialty within the field of art history required. Ph.D.

History of Medicine and Life Sciences. M.S., Ph.D.

Immunology. Ph.D.

Inorganic Chemistry. Proficiency in French, Russian, or preferably German required. Ph.D.

International Relations. Reading knowledge of one foreign language (usually French or German) required for admission; two-year M.A. program. M.A.

Italian Language and Literature. Reading knowledge of a second Romance language, Latin, and a non-Romance language (usually German) required. Ph.D.

Linguistics. Proficiency in French and German. Ph.D.

Mathematics. GRE Subject Test for admission. Reading knowledge of two foreign languages required. M.S., Ph.D.

Medieval Studies. Reading knowledge of simple Latin (medieval prose), French, and German required. M.A., Ph.D.

Meteorology. Ph.D.

Microbiology. Ph.D.

Molecular Biophysics and Biochemistry. No foreign language required. Ph.D.

Music. Reading knowledge of German and French or Italian required. M.A., Ph.D.

Near Eastern Languages and Civilizations. Includes Arabic and Islamic studies, archaeology of the ancient Near East, Assyriology, Egyptology, coptic, northwest Semitic studies. Reading knowledge of French and German required. M.A., Ph.D.

Neurobiology. No foreign language required. Ph.D.

Neuroscience. No foreign language required. Ph.D.

Oceanography. Ph.D.

Operations Research/Management Science. Generally no foreign language requirement. Ph.D.

Organic Chemistry. Proficiency in French, Russian, or preferably German required. Ph.D.

Organizational Behavior. Ph.D.

Paleontology and Stratigraphy. Ph.D.

Petrology. Ph.D.

Pharmacological Sciences. Ph.D.

Philosophy. Reading proficiency in French and German required; Ph.D.

Physical Chemistry. Proficiency in French, Russian, or preferably German required. Ph.D.

Physics. Proficiency in one foreign language required. Ph.D.

Political Science. Demonstration of competence in 1 foreign language required. Ph.D.

Psychology. No language requirement. Ph.D.

Religious Studies. Reading proficiency in French and German required. Ph.D.

Renaissance Studies. Reading exams in Latin prose, Italian, and a third language chosen from French, German, Greek, or Spanish. Ph.D.

Slavic Languages and Literature. Adequate command of the Russian language plus a reading knowledge of French and German required. M.A., Ph.D.

Sociology. Proficiency in statistics, methods, and theory. Reading knowledge of French, German, or Russian required. Ph.D.

Soviet and East European Studies. Reading knowledge of Russian and French or German required for admission; two-year M.A. program. M.A.

Spanish and Portuguese. Reading knowledge of a second Romance language, Latin, and a non-Romance language (usually German) required. M.A., Ph.D.

Statistics. M.S., Ph.D.

Structural Geology. Ph.D.

School of Architecture

Visual arts study since 1832. Library 151,300 volumes.

Annual tuition: $20,212, fees $1500. On-campus housing available.

Enrollment: full-time 154. Faculty: full-time 12, part-time 54. Degrees conferred: M.Arch., M.E.D.

ADMISSION REQUIREMENTS. Transcripts, GRE, portfolio, three letters of reference, personal history required in support of School's application. For M.E.D.: research topics and proposed program of study required. TOEFL required for international applicants. Graduates of unaccredited institutions not considered. Apply by January 4 for postprofessional program, by January 10 for others. Fall admission only. Application fee $70. Phone: (203)432-2296.

ADMISSION STANDARDS. Very competitive. Usual minimum average: 3.5 (A = 4).

FINANCIAL AID. Annual awards from school funds: 104 scholarships, 27 teaching assistantships, Federal W/S, loans. Approved for VA benefits. Apply by February 1 to appropriate department for scholarships, assistantship; to Financial Aid Office for all other programs. Use FAFSA. Phone: (203)432-2291. Some 65% of students receive aid from loan sources and the School.

DEGREE REQUIREMENTS. For M.Arch.: B.A. or B.S. required, completion of three-year program, two years in residence. For M.E.D.: B.A., B.S., B.Arch. or M.Arch. required, completion of two-year program, three semesters in residence. For postprofessionals: B. Arch. or equivalent, two-year residence.

FIELDS OF STUDY.
Architecture.
Environmental Design.

School of Drama

Graduate studies in drama since 1925. Annual tuition: $14,200. Graduate enrollment: 200. No part-time students. Limited number of Special Students for one year. School faculty: 53. Degrees conferred: M.F.A., D.F.A., Certificate in Drama, Technical Internship Certificate.

ADMISSION REQUIREMENTS. Statement of purpose, resume, official transcripts, three letters of recommendation required in support of application. Samples of work, GRE required in Dramaturgy and Dramatic Criticism, Stage Management, Sound Design/Engineering, Technical Design and Production, and Theater Management. TOEFL required for international applicants. Apply to the School of Drama by January 25 for Directing; February 1 for Acting; February 15 for all other departments. Application fee $60 for Acting and Directing; $50 for all other programs; $20 for Technical Internship Program. Phone: (203)432-1507.

ADMISSION STANDARDS. Selective to very competitive.

FINANCIAL AID. 140 scholarships. Apply by February 1 to Financial Aid office. Use FAFSA and CSS Profile. Phone: (203)432-1540. About 87% of students receive aid other than loans from School and outside sources.

DEGREE REQUIREMENTS. For M.F.A. and Certificate in Drama: granted upon completion of three years' residency and successful completion of coursework. For D.F.A.: oral qualifying exam; approved written dissertation within two years after completing Yale M.F.A. For Internship Certificate; awarded upon completion with distinction of the one-year internship program.

FIELDS OF STUDY.
Acting. Audition and interview for admission. M.F.A., Certificate in Drama.
Design. Includes scene, costume, lighting; interview, portfolio for admission (no slides). M.F.A., Certificate in Drama.
Directing Session. Interview for admission.
Dramaturgy and Dramatic Criticism. Interview of qualified applicant for admission, two writing samples; GRE.
Playwriting. One original play. M.F.A., Certificate in Drama.
Sound Design/Engineering. GRE, interview for admission. M.F.A., Certificate in Drama.
Stage Management. GRE, interview for admission. M.F.A.
Technical Design and Production. GRE, interview for admission. M.F.A., Certificate in Drama.
Technical Internship Program. GRE or SAT; interview for admission.
Theater Management. GRE, interview for admission. M.F.A.

Divinity School

Tuition: full-time $11,900. Graduate enrollment: full-time 360. No part-time students. School faculty: full-time 33, part-time 10. Degrees conferred M.A.R., M.Div., S.T.M.

ADMISSION REQUIREMENTS. Official transcripts, three letters of recommendation essays required in support of School's

application. TOEFL required for international applicants. Interview not required. Accepts transfer applicants. Apply to Admissions Office by February 1 (Fall), November 1 (Spring). Rolling admissions process. Application fee $45. Phone: (203)432-5360; fax: (203)432-5756.

ADMISSION STANDARDS. Selective.

FINANCIAL AID. Annual awards from institutional funds 25 renewable academic scholarships, 150 internships, 250 grants (need-based), Federal W/S, loans. Apply to Director of Admissions by February 1. Use FAFSA and CSS Profile. Phone: (203)432-5026; fax: (203)432-5756. About 75% of students receive aid other than loans from School and outside sources.

DEGREE REQUIREMENTS. For M.Div.: 72 credit units in full-time residence. For M.A.R.: 48 credit units in full-time residence. For S.T.M.: 24 credit units, minimum in full-time residence; thesis.
Note: Divinity School preschool available; none for infants, toddlers.

School of Forestry and Environmental Studies

Established 1900. Annual tuition: full-time $16,900. Graduate enrollment: full-time 265, part-time 4. School faculty: full-time 28, part-time 4. Degrees conferred: M.F., M.F.S., M.E.S., M.F., D.F.E.S. The Ph.D. is offered through the Graduate School.

ADMISSION REQUIREMENTS. Official transcripts, GRE, three letters of recommendation required in support of School's application. Interview not required, but encouraged. Graduates of unaccredited institutions not considered. Apply to Director of Admission by February 1. No application fee. Phone: (800)525-0330; fax: (203)432-5942.

ADMISSION STANDARDS. Competitive. Usual minimum average: 3.0 (A = 4).

FINANCIAL AID. One hundred and twenty-five scholarships, 125 grants, 60 teaching assistantships, loans. Approved for VA benefits. Apply to Director of Financial Aid by February 1 for M.F., M.F.S., M.E.S.; by January 1 for Ph.D., D.F.E.S. Use FAFSA and institutional FAF. Phone: (203)432-5105.

DEGREE REQUIREMENTS. For M.F., M.F.S., M.E.S.: usually at least two years in full-time residence; completion of three-week Summer field session; special research projects. For Ph.D.: see Graduate School listing above. For D.F.E.S.: similar to Ph.D. program.

FIELDS OF STUDY.
Biometeorology.
Forest Ecology.
Natural Resource Economics: Policy.
Pathology.
Silviculture.
Social Ecology.
Soils.
Spatial Information System.
Tree Physiology: Anatomy.
Tropical Studies.
Wildlife Ecology.
Note: School has special program with Peace Corps which promotes volunteer service.

School of Music

Tuition: $16,750. Graduate enrollment: full-time 190, part-time 6. School faculty: full-time 17, part-time 37. Degrees conferred: M.M., M.M.A., D.M.A. A Certificate program is offered for those who do not hold a bachelor's degree, and an Artist Diploma is offered to those who hold a master's degree.

ADMISSION REQUIREMENTS. Official transcripts, taped performance, three letters of recommendation, interview, and audition required in support of School's application. GRE, exams required of composers, conductors, organists, and M.M.A. candidates. TOEFL required for international applicants. Apply to Director of Admissions by January 31. Application fee $60. Phone: (203)432-4155.

ADMISSION STANDARDS. Highly selective.

FINANCIAL AID. Annual awards from institutional funds: aid awarded on basis of need, 190 scholarships, Federal W/S, loans. Apply to Financial Aid Officer by January 31. Use FAFSA and institutional FAF. Phone: (253)432-1962. About 90% of students receive aid other than loans from School and outside sources.

DEGREE REQUIREMENTS. For M.M.: 72 semester hours minimum, at least two years in full-time residence; reading knowledge of a modern European language; public presentation of recital/compositions each year of residency. For M.M.A.: 108 semester hours minimum, at least three years in full-time residence; public presentation of recitals/compositions every year. For D.M.A.: awarded to candidates who have earned the M.M.A. at Yale and whose achievements in the music profession in the following two to five years have reached the level of distinction to merit granting the degree.

FIELDS OF STUDY.
Composition.
Conducting. Includes orchestral and choral.
Performance. Includes vocal and instrumental.
Sacred Music. Interdisciplinary; cooperative program with Divinity School.

Law School

Founded in 1824. Semester system. Library: 850,000 volumes. Library has LEXIS, NEXIS, WESTLAW, DIALOG.

Annual tuition: $22,600. Total average annual additional expense; $10,600.

Enrollment: first-year class 210; total 640 (men 56%, women 44%); postgraduates 30. Faculty: full-time 50, part-time 67. Degrees conferred: J.D., J.D.-M.A., J.D.-M.Div., J.D.-M.F.S., J.D.-M.E.S., J.D.-M.P.A., J.D.-M.P.P.M., J.D.-Ph.D., J.D.-M.D., LL.M., J.S.D., M.S.L. (for Professional from field outside of Law).

ADMISSION REQUIREMENTS. LSDAS Law School report, bachelor's degree, transcripts, two letters of recommendation, LSAT, 250-word essay required in support of application. Accepts transfer applicants. Graduates of unaccredited colleges not considered. Apply by February 15 to Office of Admission for J.D. program; to Graduate Committee for graduate programs. Beginning students admitted Fall only. Application fee $50. Phone: (203)432-4995.

ADMISSION STANDARDS. Very competitive. Accepts about 6% of total annual applicants.

FINANCIAL AID. Scholarships, Federal W/S, loans; fellowships, assistantships for graduate law study. Apply to the Office of Financial Aid by March 15. Use FAFSA. Apply to the Secretary of Graduate Financial Aid Committee for fellowships, assistantships, and certain scholarships. About 70% of students receive aid from School.

DEGREE REQUIREMENTS. For J.D.: 81 credit program, at least three years in full-time residence. For LL.M.: at least 24 credit hours beyond the J.D., two semesters minimum in full-

time residence. For M.S.L.: one year in full-time residence. For J.S.D.: two semesters minimum beyond the J.D. in full-time residence; dissertation.

School of Medicine

Established 1810. Library 433,000 volumes. Annual tuition: $24,700, student fees $175. Medical School housing for 35 married students, 217 single students. Total average cost for all other expenses: $8000.

Enrollment: first-year 100 (EDP 5); total 475 (men 55%, women 45%). Faculty: full-time 776; part-time 1032. Degrees conferred: M.D., M.D.-Ph.D., (Medical Scientist Training Program), M.P.H., D.P.H. The Ph.D. is offered through the Graduate School.

ADMISSION REQUIREMENTS. For M.D. program: transcripts, two letters of recommendation, MCAT required in support of application. Interviews arranged by invitation only. Applicants must have completed at least three years of college study. Transfer applicants seldom accepted. Has EDP; apply between June 1 and August 1. Graduates of unaccredited colleges not considered. Apply to Assistant Dean for Admissions after June 1, before November 1. Application fee $55. Phone: (203)785-2696; fax: (203)785-3234. For M.P.H., D.P.H. program: transcripts required in support of application. Applicants must hold either (1) the degree of M.D., D.D.S., Ph.D., or D.V.M. or equivalent, or (2) master's or bachelor's in biological or social sciences plus professional academic qualifications or experience. Graduates of unaccredited colleges not considered. Apply to Department of Epidemiology and Public Health by February 1. Application fee $25.

ADMISSION STANDARDS. Very competitive. Accepts about 3–5% of total annual applicants. Approximately 12% are state residents.

FINANCIAL AID. For M.D. program: scholarships, loans. MSTP funded by NIH. Apply to Financial Aid Office promptly after acceptance. Use FAFSA. About 10% of M.D. students receive scholarships from School.

DEGREE REQUIREMENTS. For M.D.: satisfactory completion of four-year program and passing Part I and Part II of NBME; at least two years in full-time residence for students admitted with advanced standing. For M.P.H.: one year minimum, but usually two years, at least three terms of which are spent in full-time residence; final essay. For D.PH.: one year minimum beyond the M.P.H., at least three years total in full-time residence; dissertation; final written/oral exam.

FIELDS OF STUDY.
Biochemistry.
Biophysics.
Biostatics.
Cell Biology.
Environmental Health.
Epidemiology.
Genetics.
Health Services Administration.
Immunology.
Pathology.
Pharmacology.
Physiology and Membrane Biophysics.

School of Nursing

Established in, and graduate study since 1923. Annual tuition: $17,600. On-campus housing available.

Three programs of study available: Master's program for applicants with R.N. licensure and baccalaureate degree in any discipline; or master's program for non-nurse college graduates.

Graduate enrollment: full-time 184, part-time 65. Teaching faculty: full-time 54, part-time 33. Members of other University faculties also give instruction. Degrees conferred: M.S.N., D.N.Sc.

ADMISSION REQUIREMENTS: Transcripts, three personal references, GRE, admission essay, personal interview. For the R.N. Master's program nursing experience desirable but not required. TOEFL required for international applicants. Transfer applicants usually not accepted. Graduates of unaccredited institutions not considered. Apply to Student Affairs Office by November 30 non–Nurse Program; January 15 for R.N. Master's program; March 1 for D.N.Sc. Program. Rolling admissions process. Full-time, scheduled part-time, and nonmatriculated study available. Fall admission only. Application fee $50. Phone: (203)785-2389; fax: (203)737-5409.

ADMISSION STANDARDS. Competitive.

FINANCIAL AID. Seventy-four traineeships and scholarships, Federal W/S, loans. Approved for VA benefits. Apply by March 1 to Dean of School for traineeships, scholarships; to Financial Aid Office for all other programs. Use FAFSA, NEED ACCESS, and institutional FAF. Phone: (203)785-2389; fax: (203)737-5409.

DEGREE REQUIREMENTS. For M.S.N.: 40 credits for R.N. Master's Program and 82 for Graduate Entry non–Nurse Program; thesis/dissertation; final oral exam.

FIELDS OF STUDY.
Adult Advanced Practice Nursing (CV and Oncology).
ANP/FNP/GNP.
Nurse-Midwifery.
Nursing Management and Policy.
Pediatric Nurse Practitioner (Primary Care and Chronic Illness).
Psychiatric-Mental Health Nursing (Adult and Child).

YESHIVA UNIVERSITY
New York, New York 10033-3201
http://www.yu.edu

Founded 1886. Coed. Private control. Semester system. Special facilities: Yeshiva University Museum, research centers in various diseases, Center for Research in Cancer, Rose Fitzgerald Kennedy Center for Research in Mental Retardation, Jack and Pearl Resnik Gerontology Center, Legal Services Clinic, Center for Psychological Intervention. University libraries: 977,421 volumes, 725,000 microforms, 9000 current periodicals, 173 PCs. No on-campus housing available.

Ferkauf Graduate School of Psychology
http://www.yu.edu/fgs/

Established 1957. Semester system. Annual tuition: $16,200.
Enrollment: full-time 263, part-time 135 (men 106, women 292). School faculty: full-time 25, part-time 20. Degrees conferred: M.A., Psy.D., Ph.D.

ADMISSION REQUIREMENTS. Transcripts, two letters of recommendation, GRE Subject Test (for all programs) required in support of School's application. TOEFL required for international students. Accepts transfer applicants. Graduates of unaccredited institutions not considered. Apply to the Office of Admissions at least three months prior to registration. Application fee $35. Phone: (212)430-4207; fax: (718)430-3252.

ADMISSION STANDARDS. Competitive for most departments. Usual minimum average: 3.0 (A = 4).

FINANCIAL AID. Twenty scholarships; seventy fellowships, five assistantships for teaching/research, Federal W/S, loans. Apply by March 1 to Office of Student Finances. Use FAFSA. Phone: (212)960-5269. Aid sometimes available to part-time students.

DEGREE REQUIREMENTS. For master's: 36 credits; thesis/nonthesis option; comprehensive exam. For Psy.D. and Ph.D.: 78 credits minimum; comprehensive exam, dissertation; final oral exam.

FIELDS OF STUDY.
Applied Psychology. M.A.
Clinical Psychology. Psy.D.
Developmental Psychology. Ph.D.
Health Psychology. Ph.D.
School Psychology. Psy.D.

Bernard Revel Graduate School

Established 1937. Semester system. Tuition: per credit $385.
Enrollment: full-time 4, part-time 48. Harry Fischel School for Higher Jewish Studies (established 1945) is Summer component. Summer enrollment: 21. Faculty: full-time 7, part-time 16. Degrees conferred: M.A., Ph.D.

ADMISSION REQUIREMENTS. Official transcripts; appropriate bachelor's degree; knowledge of Hebrew language, literature, and Judaic studies; GRE required in support of School's application. Interview and entrance exam sometimes required. TOEFL required for international applicants. Accepts transfer applicants. Apply to Office of Admissions at least one month prior to registration. Rolling admissions process. Application fee $25. Phone: (212)960-5277; fax: (212)960-0086.

ADMISSION STANDARDS. Selective. Usual minimum average: 3.0 (A = 4).

FINANCIAL AID. Limited to forty-one scholarships, five fellowships, tuition waivers, loans. Apply by April 1 to Dean of the Graduate School for scholarships, assistantships; to Financial Aid Office for all other programs. Phone: (212)960-5253. Use FAFSA.

DEGREE REQUIREMENTS. For M.A.: 30–36 credits minimum; comprehensive exam; thesis/nonthesis option/research project. For Ph.D.: 75 credits; reading knowledge of two foreign languages; qualifying exam; dissertation; final oral exam.

FIELDS OF STUDY.
Bible.
Jewish History. Classical, medieval, modern.
Jewish Philosophy.
Semitic Languages, Literature, and Culture.
Talmudic Studies.

Wurzweiler School of Social Work

Established 1957. Graduate study only. Annual tuition: full-time $13,520 (M.S.W.); $574 per credit (D.S.W.).
Enrollment: full-time 299, part-time 289. Faculty: full-time 26, part-time 36. Degrees conferred: M.S.W., D.S.W., Certificate in Jewish Communal Services.

ADMISSION REQUIREMENTS. Official transcripts, interview, suitable personality required in support of application. TOEFL required for non–English-speaking applicants. Accepts transfer applicants. Graduates of unaccredited colleges not considered.

Fall admission only, except for Block Plan. June admission. Rolling admissions process. Application fee $35. Phone: (212)960-0810; fax: (212)960-0822.

ADMISSION STANDARDS. Competitive.

FINANCIAL AID. One hundred and ninety-two scholarships; forty grants; forty-five fellowships; two research assistantships; twenty-one internships; Federal W/S; loans; stipends from private, national, and state agencies. Approved for VA benefits. Apply to School's Admissions Officer by March 15 for Block Plan; May 14 for all other programs. Use FAFSA. Phone: (212)960-5269; fax: (212)960-0037.

DEGREE REQUIREMENTS. For M.S.W.: 60 credits including prescribed courses; 1200 hours of field instruction; written essay. For D.S.W.: three years beyond the M.S.W.; prescribed and elective seminars; comprehensive exams; field study; dissertation; final oral exam.

FIELDS OF STUDY.
Community Organization/Administration.
Jewish Communal Services. Certificate only.
Social Casework.
Social Group Work.

Benjamin N. Cardozo School of Law (10003)

Established 1976. Located in Greenwich Village. Semester system. Library 355,000 volumes. Library has LEXIS, NEXIS, WESTLAW, OCLC. Special facilities: Jacob Burns Institute of Advanced Legal Studies, Samuel and Ronnie Heyman Center for Corporate Governance.
Annual tuition: $18,825. No on-campus housing available. Total average annual additional expense: $10,000–$12,000.
Enrollment: first-year class 270; total 930 (men 60%, women 40%). Faculty: full-time 47, part-time 25. Degree conferred: J.D.

ADMISSION REQUIREMENTS. LSDAS Law School report, bachelor's degree, transcripts, LSAT, recommendations, personal statement required in support of application. Accepts transfer applicants. Graduates of unaccredited colleges not considered. Apply by April 1 for priority consideration. Admits September (traditional program), January and May (Accelerated Entry Plan). Application fee $60. Phone: (212)790-0274; fax: (212)790-0203.

ADMISSION STANDARDS. Selective. Admits about 25–30% of total annual applicants.

FINANCIAL AID. Scholarships, assistantships, Federal W/S, loans. Apply to Financial Aid Office by April 1. Use FAFSA. Approximately 70% of students receive some form of Financial Aid.

DEGREE REQUIREMENTS. For J.D.: satisfactory completion of 84-credit program.

Albert Einstein College of Medicine: Sue Golding Graduate Division of Medical Sciences

1300 Morris Park Ave. Bronx, New York 10461

Established 1957. Annual tuition: $20,229. Housing facilities same as for College of Medicine.
Enrollment: full-time 217 (men 55%, women 45%). Faculty: full-time 415; no part-time faculty. Degree conferred: Ph.D.

ADMISSION REQUIREMENTS. Transcripts, letters of recommendation, GRE required in support of application. Accepts transfer applicants. Graduates of unaccredited colleges not considered. Apply to Director of Admissions by January 1. Application fee $25. Phone: (718)430-2345; fax: (718)430-8825.

ADMISSION STANDARDS. Selective. Accepts about 12% of total annual applicants.

FINANCIAL AID. Tuition scholarships and fellowship stipends available in most departments. Two hundred and seventeen fellowships. Apply to appropriate department chairman by February 1. Awards made at time of acceptance.

DEGREE REQUIREMENTS. For Ph.D.: three years minimum of full-time study, at least two years in residence; written/oral exam in foreign language; qualifying exam; thesis; oral exam.

FIELDS OF STUDY.
Anatomy.
Biochemistry.
Cell and Developmental Biology.
Developmental Biology and Cancer. Interdepartmental.
Microbiology and Immunology.
Molecular Genetics.
Molecular Pharmacology.
Neuroscience.
Pathology.
Physiology and Biophysics.

Albert Einstein College of Medicine

Established 1950. Located at Westchester Heights campus (Bronx 10461). Special facilities: Ullmann Research Center for Health Sciences, Hospital, Rose Fitzgerald Kennedy Center for Research in Mental Retardation and Human Development, Chanin Institute for Cancer Research. Library: 160,000 volumes. Annual tuition: full-time $25,450, student fees $1300. Seven hundred housing units on-campus. Apply to Assistant Dean. Total average cost for all other expenses: $8500.

Enrollment: first-year class 176; total 698 (men 50%, women 50%). Faculty: full-time 1000, part-time and volunteers 850. Degrees conferred: M.D., M.D.-Ph.D.

ADMISSION REQUIREMENTS. AMCAS report, transcripts, letters of recommendation, MCAT required in support of application. Has EDP; apply between June 15 and August 1. Interviews by invitation only. Applicants should have completed four years of college study; in exceptional cases, three years. Graduates of unaccredited colleges not considered. Apply after June 15, before November 15. Application fee $70. Phone: (718)430-2106; fax: (718)430-8825.

ADMISSION STANDARDS. Very competitive. Accepts about 2–3% of total annual applicants. Approximately 40% are state residents.

FINANCIAL AID. Scholarships, loans. Apply to Student Finance Officer after acceptance. About 50% of students receive some aid from College.

DEGREE REQUIREMENTS. For M.D.: satisfactory completion of four-year program. For M.D.-Ph.D.: satisfactory completion of six-year program.

FIELDS OF GRADUATE STUDY.
Anatomy.
Biochemistry.
Cell Biology.
Genetics.
Immunology.
Microbiology.
Molecular Biology.
Pathology.
Pharmacology.
Physiology.

YOUNGSTOWN STATE UNIVERSITY

Youngstown, Ohio 44555-0002

http://www.ysu.edu

Founded 1908. Coed. State control. Quarter system. Special facilities: Center for Historic Preservation, Ethics Center, Professional Communication Design and Production Center, Public Service Center. Library: 629,000 volumes, 1,050,000 microforms, 3150 current periodicals, 20 PCs.

Tuition: per credit, resident $83, nonresident $175. On-campus housing available for single students only. Average academic year housing costs: $3900 (including board). Contact Housing Office for both on- and off-campus housing information. Phone: (216)742-3547.

Graduate School

Graduate study since 1935. Enrollment: full-time 306, part-time 811 (men 40%, women 60%). Graduate faculty: full-time 271, part-time 41. Degrees conferred: M.A., M.B.A., M.M., M.S., M.S.E., M.S.Ed., Ed.D.

ADMISSION REQUIREMENTS. Official transcripts required in support of College's application. GRE/MAT/GMAT, interview required for some programs. TOEFL required for international applicants. Accepts transfer applicants. Graduates of unaccredited institutions not considered. Apply to Graduate School Admissions Office at least one month prior to registration. Application fee $30; $65 for international applicants. Phone: (216)742-3091; fax: (216)742-1580

ADMISSION STANDARDS. Selective in some departments, relatively open in others. Usual minimum average: 2.75 (A = 4).

FINANCIAL AID. Annual awards from institutional funds: 196 scholarships, 31 fellowships, 96 research assistantships, 33 teaching assistantships, Federal W/S, loans. Approved for VA benefits. Apply by April 15 to Office of the Dean for fellowships, assistantships; to Financial Aid Office for all other programs. Use FAFSA. About 35% of students receive aid from University and outside sources. Aid available for part-time students.

DEGREE REQUIREMENTS. For master's: 45–60 quarter hours minimum, at least 6 in residence; thesis/nonthesis option or final paper. For Ed.S.: 45 quarter hours beyond the master's; special project. For Ed.D.: 135 quarter hours minimum beyond the master's, at least two years in residence; qualifying exam; research tool; dissertation; final oral exam.

FIELDS OF STUDY.

Biology. Thesis for M.S. M.S.

Business Administration. Includes finance, management, marketing. M.B.A.

Chemistry. Thesis for M.S. M.S.

Civil Engineering. Includes environmental/water resources, structural mechanics. M.S.E.

Counseling. M.S.Ed.

Criminal Justice. M.S.

Economics. M.A.

Educational Administration. M.S.Ed.

Educational Leadership. Admits Fall quarter only. Ed.D.

Electrical Engineering. M.S.E.

English. M.A.

History. M.A.

Master Teacher-Elementary. Includes early childhood, middle grade, reading. M.S.Ed.

Master Teacher-Secondary. Includes the usual subjects. M.S.Ed.

Materials Science. M.S.E.

Mathematics. Includes computer science. M.S.

Mechanical Engineering. M.S.E.

Music Education. M.M.

Music History. M.M.

Music Performance. M.M.

Music Theory. M.M.

Special Education. Includes early childhood, gifted and talented. M.S.Ed.

LOCATION OF INSTITUTIONS, BY STATE

Since the institutional entries in the main body of this book are arranged alphabetically without reference to locations, page numbers are not provided here.

Alabama
Alabama Agricultural and Mechanical University
Alabama, University of
  Birmingham
  Huntsville
Auburn University
Auburn University at (Montgomery)
Jacksonville State University
Montevallo, University of
North Alabama, University of
Samford University
South Alabama, University of
Troy State University
Troy State University (Dothan)
Troy State University (Montgomery)
Tuskegee University
West Alabama, University of

Alaska
Alaska, University of

Arizona
American Graduate School of International Management
Arizona State University
Arizona State University West
Arizona, The University of
Northern Arizona University
Phoenix, University of

Arkansas
Arkansas State University
Arkansas, University of
Central Arkansas, University of
Harding University
Henderson State University

California
Antioch Southern California Los Angeles
Antioch Southern California Santa Barbara
Armstrong University
Azusa Pacific University
California College of Arts and Crafts
California Institute of Technology

California Lutheran University
California State Polytechnic University
  Pomona
  San Luis Obispo
California State University
  Bakersfield
  Chico
  Dominguez Hills
  Fresno
  Fullerton
  Hayward
  Humbolt State University
  Long Beach
  Los Angeles
  Northridge
  Sacramento
  San Bernardino
  San Diego State University
  San Francisco
  San Jose State University
  Sonoma State University
  Stanislaus
California, University of
  Berkeley
  Davis
  Hastings College of Law
  Irvine
  Los Angeles
  Riverside
  San Diego
  San Francisco
  Santa Barbara
  Santa Cruz
California Western School of Law
Chapman University
Claremont Graduate School
Dominican College of San Rafael, The
Golden Gate University
Holy Names College
Humboldt State University
La Verne, University of
Loma Linda University
Loyola Marymount University
Mills College
Monterey Institute of Foreign Studies
Mount St. Mary's College
National University
Naval Postgraduate School
Notre Dame, College of

Occidental College
Osteopathic Medicine of the Pacific, College of
Otis College of Art and Design
Pacific Union College
Pacific, University of
Pepperdine University
Pepperdine University–Culver City
Point Loma Nazarene College
Redlands, University of
San Diego State University
San Diego, University of
San Francisco Art Institute
San Francisco Conservatory of Music
San Francisco, University of
Santa Clara University
Southern California College of Optometry
Southern California, University of
Southwestern University School of Law
Stanford University
United States International University
Whittier College

Colorado
Adams State College
Colorado School of Mines
Colorado State University
Colorado, University of
Denver, University of
Northern Colorado, University of

Connecticut
Bridgeport, University of
Central Connecticut State University
Connecticut College
Connecticut, The University of
Eastern Connecticut State University
Fairfield University
Hartford, University of
Health Center, University of Connecticut
New Haven, University of
Quinnipiac College
St. Joseph College
Southern Connecticut State University
Trinity College
Wesleyan University

Western Connecticut State University
Yale University

Delaware
Delaware, University of
Widener University

District of Columbia
American University, The
Catholic University of America, The
Gallaudet University
Georgetown University
George Washington University, The
Howard University

Florida
Barry University
Central Florida, University of
Florida Agricultural and Mechanical
    University
Florida Atlantic University
Florida Institute of Technology
Florida State University
Florida, University of
Jacksonville University
Miami, University of
North Florida, University of
Nova Southwestern University
Rollins College
South Florida, University of
Stetson University

Georgia
Armstrong State College
Augusta College
Berry College
Clark Atlanta University
Columbus College
Emory University
Fort Valley State University
Georgia College of Milledgeville
Georgia Institute of Technology, The
Georgia Medical College of
Georgia Southern University
Georgia State University
Georgia, The University of
La Grange College
Mercer University
Morehouse School of Medicine
Oglethorpe University
Valdosta State College
West Georgia College

Hawaii
Hawaii Pacific University
Hawaii, University of

Idaho
Boise State University
Idaho State University
Idaho, University of

Illinois
Art Institute of Chicago, The School of the
Bradley University
Chicago State University
Chicago, The University of
Concordia Teachers College
DePaul University
Eastern Illinois University
Governors State University
Health Sciences, University of
Illinois Institute of Technology
Illinois State University
Illinois, University at
    Chicago
    Urbana
John Marshall Law School
Loyola University of Chicago

Midwestern University–Chicago College of
    Osteopathic Medicine
National Louis University
Northeastern Illinois University
Northern Illinois University
Northwestern University
Olivet Nazarene University
Rockford College
Roosevelt University
Rosary College
Rush Medical College
St. Xavier University
Southern Illinois University
    Carbondale
    Edwardsville
Western Illinois University

Indiana
Ball State University
Butler University
Evansville, University of
Indiana State University
Indiana University
Indianapolis, University of
Notre Dame, University of
Purdue University
    Calumet
    West Lafayette
Rose-Hulman Institute of Technology
St. Francis College
Valparaiso University

Iowa
Clarke College
Drake University
Dubuque, University of
Iowa State University of Science
    and Technology
Iowa, The University of
Loras College
Marycrest International University
Morningside College
Northern Iowa, University of
Osteopathic Medicine and Health Sciences,
    University of

Kansas
Emporia State University
Fort Hays State University
Kansas Medical Center, University of
Kansas State University
Kansas, University of
Pittsburg State University
Washburn University of Topeka
Wichita State University

Kentucky
Eastern Kentucky University
Georgetown College
Kentucky, University of
Louisville, University of
Moorhead State University
Murray State University
Salmon P. Chase College of Law of Northern
    Kentucky University
Spalding University
Union College
Western Kentucky University

Louisiana
Louisiana State University and Agricultural
    and Mechanical College
Louisiana State University in Shreveport
Louisiana Tech University
Loyola University
McNeese State University
Medical Center, Louisiana State University
New Orleans, University of
Northeast Louisiana University
Northwestern State University of Louisiana
Southeastern Louisiana University

Southern University and Agricultural
    and Mechanical College
Southwestern Louisiana, The University of
Tulane University
Xavier University of Louisiana

Maine
Maine, University of
Medicine, University of
New England College of Osteopathic
    Medicine, University of
Southern Maine, University of

Maryland
Baltimore, University of
Bowie State University
Frostburg State University
Goucher College
Hood College
Johns Hopkins University, The
Loyola College
Maryland Graduate School Baltimore,
    University of
Maryland Institute College of Art
Maryland, University of
Maryland–Baltimore County, University of
Morgan State University
St. John's College
Salisbury State University
Towson State University
Washington College
Western Maryland College

Massachusetts
Assumption College
Babson College
Boston College
Boston University
Brandeis University
Bridgewater State College
Clark University
Emerson College
Fitchburg State College
Framingham State College
Harvard University
Hebrew Teachers College
Massachusetts College of Art
Massachusetts College of Pharmacy
Massachusetts Institute of Technology
Massachusetts, University of
    Amherst
    Boston
    Dartmouth
    Lowell
Mount Holyoke College
New England Conservatory of Music
New England School of Law
North Adams State College
Northeastern University
Salem State College
Simmons College
Smith College
Springfield College
Suffolk University
Tufts University
Western New England College
Westfield State College
Wheelock College
Williams College
Worcester Polytechnic Institute
Worcester State College

Michigan
Andrews University
Central Michigan University
Cranbrook Academy of Art
Detroit College of Law
Detroit Mercy, University of
Eastern Michigan University
Marygrove College
Michigan State University

Michigan Technological University
Michigan, The University of
Northern Michigan University
Oakland University
Saginaw Valley State University
Siena Heights College
Thomas M. Cooley Law School
Wayne State University
Western Michigan University

Minnesota
Bemidji State University
Hamline University*
Mankato State University
Mayo Medical School
Minnesota, University of
Moorhead State University
St. Cloud State University
St. John's University
St. Mary's College
St. Scholastica, College of
St. Thomas, University of
William Mitchell College of Law
Winona State University

Mississippi
Delta State University
Jackson State University
Mississippi College
Mississippi Medical Center, University of
Mississippi State University
Mississippi State University for Women
Mississippi, The University of
Southern Mississippi, University of
William Carey College

Missouri
Central Missouri State University
Drury College
Health Sciences, University of
Kirksville College of Osteopathic
   Medicine
Lincoln University
Maryville University of St. Louis
Missouri, University of
   Columbia
   Kansas City
   Rolla
   St. Louis
Northwest Missouri State University
Saint Louis University
Southeast Missouri State University
Southwest Missouri State University
Truman State University
Washington University
Webster University

Montana
Montana College of Mineral Science and
   Technology
Montana State University
Montana Tech of the University of Montana
Montana, University of

Nebraska
Chadron State College
Concordia College
Creighton University, The
Nebraska, University of
   Kearney
   Lincoln
   Omaha
Wayne State College

Nevada
Nevada, University of
   Las Vegas
   Reno

New Hampshire
Antioch New England Graduate School
Dartmouth College
Franklin Pierce Law Center
Keene State College
New Hampshire, University of
Plymouth State College
Rivier College

New Jersey
Drew University
Fairleigh Dickinson University
   Madison
   Teaneck
Jersey City State College
Kean College of New Jersey
Medicine and Dentistry of New Jersey,
   University of
Monmouth University
Montclair State College
New Jersey Institute of Technology
Princeton University
Rider College
Rowan College of New Jersey
Rutgers University
Seton Hall University
Stevens Institute of Technology
William Paterson College of New Jersey

New Mexico
Eastern New Mexico University
New Mexico Highlands University
New Mexico Institute of Mining and
   Technology
New Mexico State University
New Mexico, The University of
St. John's College
Western New Mexico University

New York
Adelphi University
Albany Medical College
Albany, The University at
Alfred University
Bank Street College of Education
Brooklyn Law School
Canisius College
City University of New York, The
   Bernard M. Baruch College
   Brooklyn College
   City College, The
   Graduate Center
   Herbert H. Lehman College
   Hunter College
   John Jay College of Criminal Justice
   Queens College
   Staten Island, The College of
Clarkson College of Technology
Colgate University
Columbia University
Cornell University
C. W. Post Center of Long Island
   University
Elmira College
Fordham University
Hofstra University
Insurance, College of
Iona College
Ithaca College
Juilliard School, The
Long Island University (Brooklyn)
Manhattan College
Manhattan School of Music
Manhattanville College
New Rochelle, College of
New School for Social Research, The
New York Institute of Technology
New York Law School
New York Medical College
New York State University of at
   Binghamton
   Buffalo

Health Science Center (Brooklyn)
Health Science Center (Syracuse)
Stony Brook (West Campus)
New York, State University of,
   College at,
   Brockport
   Buffalo
   Cortland
   Environmental Science and Forestry
      at Syracuse
   Fredonia
   New Paltz
   Oneonta
   Oswego
   Plattsburg
   Potsdam
New York University
Niagara University
Pace University
Polytechnic University
Pratt Institute
Rensselaer Polytechnic Institute
Rochester Institute of Technology
Rochester, University of
Rockefeller University, The
Sage Colleges
Saint Rose, The College of
Sarah Lawrence College
St. Bonaventure University
St. John's University
St. Lawrence University
Syracuse University
Touro College—School of Law
Union College
Vassar College
Wagner College
Yeshiva University

North Carolina
Appalachian State University
Campbell University
Duke University
East Carolina University
North Carolina Agricultural and Technical
   State University
North Carolina Central University
North Carolina State University
   at Raleigh
North Carolina, The University of
   Chapel Hill
   Greensboro
Wake Forest University
Western Carolina University

North Dakota
Minot State University
North Dakota State University
North Dakota, University of

Ohio
Air Force Institute of Technology
Akron, University of
Antioch University
Bowling Green State University
Capital University
Case Western Reserve University
Cincinnati, University of
Cleveland State University
Dayton, University of
John Carroll University
Kent State University
Medical College of Ohio at Toledo
Miami University
Northeastern Ohio University
Ohio Northern University
Ohio State University, The
Ohio University
Toledo, University of
Wright State University
Xavier University
Youngstown State University

Oklahoma
Central Oklahoma, University of
East Central Oklahoma State University
Health Science Center, University of Oklahoma
Northeastern State University
Northwestern Oklahoma State University
Oklahoma City University
Oklahoma State University
Oklahoma, University of
Oral Roberts University
Phillips University
Southeastern Oklahoma State University
Southern Nazarene University
Southwestern Oklahoma State University
Tulsa, The University of

Oregon
Eastern Oregon State College
Lewis and Clark College
Oregon Graduate Institute of Science
    and Technology
Oregon Health Sciences University
Oregon State University
Oregon, University of
Pacific University
Portland State University
Portland, University of
Reed College
Southern Oregon State College
Western Oregon State College
Willamette University

Pennsylvania
Bloomsburg University of Pennsylvania
Bryn Mawr College
Bucknell University
California University of Pennsylvania
Carnegie Mellon University
Clarion University of Pennsylvania
Dickinson School of Law, The
Drexel University
Duquesne University
East Stroudsburg University of Pennsylvania
Edinboro University of Pennsylvania
Gannon College
Indiana University of Pennsylvania
Kutztown University of Pennsylvania
Lehigh University
Mansfield University of Pennsylvania
Marywood College
Millersville University of Pennsylvania
Pennsylvania and Hahnemann University,
    Medical College of
Pennsylvania College of Optometry
Pennsylvania State University
Pennsylvania, University of
Philadelphia College of Osteopathic Medicine
Philadelphia College of Pharmacy and
    Science, The
Pittsburgh, University of
Robert Morris College
St. Francis College
St. Joseph's University
Scranton, University of
Shippensburg University of Pennsylvania
Slippery Rock University of Pennsylvania
Temple University
Thomas Jefferson Medical University
University of the Arts
Villanova University
West Chester University of Pennsylvania
Westminster College
Widener University
Wilkes University

Puerto Rico
Inter American University
Ponce School of Medicine
Pontifical Catholic University of Puerto Rico

Puerto Rico, University of
Puerto Rico Mayaguez, University of

Rhode Island
Brown University
Bryant College
Providence College
Rhode Island College
Rhode Island School of Design
Rhode Island, University of

South Carolina
Citadel, The
Clemson University
Converse College
Furman University
South Carolina, Medical University of
South Carolina State College
South Carolina, University of
Winthrop University

South Dakota
Augustana College
Black Hills State University
Northern State University
South Dakota School of Mines and Technology
South Dakota State University
South Dakota, University of

Tennessee
Austin Peay State University
East Tennessee State University
Fisk University
George Peabody College for Teachers of
    Vanderbilt University
Meharry Medical College
Memphis, University of
Middle Tennessee State University
South, University of the
Southern College of Optometry
Tennessee State University
Tennessee Technological University
Tennessee, University of
    Chattanooga
    Knoxville
    Martin
    Oak Ridge
    Space Institute
Vanderbilt University

Texas
Abilene Christian University
Angelo State University
Baylor College of Dentistry
Baylor College of Medicine
Baylor University
Dallas, University of
East Texas State University
Hardin-Simmons University
Houston, University of
Incarnate Word College
Lamar University
Midwestern State University
North Texas, University of
Our Lady of the Lake University
Prairie View Agricultural and Mechanical
    University
Rice University
St. Edward's University
St. Mary's University
St. Thomas, University of
Sam Houston State University
South Texas College of Law
Southern Methodist University
Southwest Texas State University
Stephen F. Austin State University
Sul Ross State University
Tarleton State University

Texas A & I University
Texas Agricultural and Mechanical University
Texas Agricultural and Mechanical
    University–Corpus Christi
Texas Christian University
Texas Southern University
Texas Tech University
Texas, The University of
    Arlington
    Austin
    Dallas
    El Paso
    Health Science Center at Houston
    Medical Branch Galveston
    Pan American
    Permian Basin
    San Antonio
    Southwestern Health Science Center
    Tyler
Texas Woman's University
Trinity University
West Texas State University

Utah
Brigham Young University
Utah State University
Utah, University of

Vermont
Bennington College
Goddard College
Middlebury College
St. Michael's College
Vermont Law School
Vermont, University of

Virginia
Eastern Virginia Medical School
George Mason University
Hampton University
Hollins College
James Madison University
Longwood College
Lynchburg College
Old Dominion University
Radford University
Regent University
Richmond, University of
Virginia Commonwealth University
Virginia Polytechnic Institute and State
    University
Virginia State University
Virginia, University of
Washington and Lee University
William and Mary, The College of

Washington
Antioch University Seattle
Central Washington University
Eastern Washington University
Gonzaga University
Pacific Lutheran University
Puget Sound, University of
Seattle Pacific University
Seattle University
Walla Walla College
Washington State University
Washington, University of
Western Washington University
Whitworth College

West Virginia
Marshall University
West Virginia Graduate College
West Virginia School of Osteopathic
    Medicine
West Virginia University

Wisconsin
Cardinal Stritch College
Marquette University
Milwaukee School of Engineering
Wisconsin, Medical College of
Wisconsin, University of
　Eau Claire
La Crosse
Madison
Milwaukee
Oshkosh
Platteville
River Falls
Stevens Point
Stout
Superior
Whitewater

Wyoming
Wyoming, University of

INSTITUTIONAL
ABBREVIATIONS

A.C.U. *Abilene Christian University*
Adams St. C. *Adams State College*
Adelphi U. *Adelphi University*
A.F. Inst. *Air Force Institute of Technology*
Ala. A&M U. *Alabama Agricultural and Mechanical University*
Albany Med. C. *Albany Medical College*
Albany, U. *The University at Albany*
Alfred U. *Alfred University*
Amer. Grad. Sch. Int'l. Mgmt. *American Graduate School of International Management*
Amer. U. *The American University*
Andrews U. *Andrews University*
Angelo St. U. *Angelo State University*
Antioch N. E. *Antioch New England Graduate School*
Antioch So. Cal. (L.A.) *Antioch Southern California Los Angeles*
Antioch So. Cal. (S. B.) *Antioch Southern California Santa Barbara*
Antioch U. (Seattle) *Antioch University Seattle*
Appal. St. U. *Appalachian State University*
Ariz. St. U. *Arizona State University*
Ariz. St. U. (West) *Arizona State University–West*
Ark. St. U. *Arkansas State University*
Armstrong St. C. *Armstrong State College*
Armstrong U. *Armstrong University*
Art Inst. Chicago *The School of the Art Institute of Chicago*
Assump. C. *Assumption College*
Auburn U. *Auburn University*
Auburn U. (Montgomery) *Auburn University at Montgomery*
Augusta C. *Augusta College*
Augustana C. *Augustana College*
Aus. Peay St. U. *Austin Peay State University*
Azusa Pac. U. *Azusa Pacific University*
Babson C. *Babson College*
Ball St. U. *Ball State University*
Bank St. C. *Bank Street College of Education*
Barry U. *Barry University*
Baruch C. (C.U.N.Y.) *Bernard M. Baruch College of the City University of New York*
Baylor C. Dentistry *Baylor College of Dentistry*
Baylor C. Med. *Baylor College of Medicine*
Baylor U. *Baylor University*
Bemidji St. U. *Bemidji State University*
Bennington C. *Bennington College*
Berry C. *Berry College*
Black Hills St. C. *Black Hills State University*
Bloomsburg U. *Bloomsburg University of Pennsylvania*
Boise St. U. *Boise State University*
Boston C. *Boston College*
Boston U. *Boston University*
Bowie St. U. *Bowie State University*
Bowl. Gr. St. U. *Bowling Green State University*
Bradley U. *Bradley University*

Brandeis U. *Brandeis University*
Bridgewater St. C. *Bridgewater State College*
Brooklyn C. (C.U.N.Y.) *Brooklyn College of the City University of New York*
Brooklyn Law *Brooklyn Law School*
Brown U. *Brown University*
Bryant C. *Bryant College*
Bryn Mawr C. *Bryn Mawr College*
Bucknell U. *Bucknell University*
Butler U. *Butler University*
B.Y.U. *Brigham Young University*
Cal. C. Arts & Crafts *California College of Arts and Crafts*
Cal. Luth. U. *California Lutheran University*
Cal. St. Poly. U. (Pomona) *California State Polytechnic University at Pomona*
Cal. St. Poly. U. (San Luis Obispo) *California Polytechnic State University at San Luis Obispo*
Cal. St. U. (Bakersfield) *California State University at Bakersfield*
Cal. St. U. (Chico) *California State University at Chico*
Cal. St. U. (Dominguez Hills) *California State University at Dominguez Hills*
Cal. St. U. (Fresno) *California State University at Fresno*
Cal. St. U. (Fullerton) *California State University at Fullerton*
Cal. St. U. (Hayward) *California State University at Hayward*
Cal. St. U. (Humboldt) *Humboldt State University*
Cal. St. U. (Long Beach) *California State University at Long Beach*
Cal. St. U. (L.A.) *California State University at Los Angeles*
Cal. St. U. (Northridge) *California State University at Northridge*
Cal. St. U. (Sacramento) *California State University at Sacramento*
Cal. St. U. (San Bernardino) *California State University at San Bernardino*
Cal. St. U. (San Francisco) *San Francisco State University*
Cal. St. U. (San Jose) *San Jose State University*
Cal. St. U. (Sonoma) *Sonoma State University*
Cal. St. U. (Stanislaus) *California State University at Stanislaus*
Cal. Tech. *California Institute of Technology*
Cal. U. (Pa.) *California University of Pennsylvania*
Cal. West. Sch. of Law *California Western School of Law*
Campbell U. *Campbell University*
Canisius C. *Canisius College*
Capital U. *Capital University*
Card. Stritch C. *Cardinal Stritch College*
Carnegie Mellon U. *Carnegie Mellon University*
Case West. Res. U. *Case Western Reserve University*
Catholic U. *The Catholic University of America*
Catholic U. of P.R. *Catholic University of Puerto Rico*
C.C.N.Y. (C.U.N.Y.) *City College of the City University of New York*
Cent. Conn. St. U. *Central Connecticut State University*
Cent. Mich. U. *Central Michigan University*
Cent. Mo. St. U. *Central Missouri State University*
Cent. Wash. U. *Central Washington University*
Chadron St. C. *Chadron State College*

Chapman U.   *Chapman University*
Chase C. Law   *Salmon P. Chase College of Law of Northern Kentucky University*
Chicago St. U.   *Chicago State University*
C. Insurance   *College of Insurance*
Citadel   *The Citadel*
Claremont Grad. Sch.   *Claremont Graduate School*
Clarion U.   *Clarion University of Pennsylvania*
Clark Atl. U.   *Clark Atlanta University*
Clark U.   *Clark University*
Clarke C.   *Clarke College*
Clarkson U.   *Clarkson University*
Clemson U.   *Clemson University*
Cleve. St. U.   *Cleveland State University*
C. N. J.   *The College of New Jersey*
C. N. Rochelle   *College of New Rochelle*
C. Notre Dame   *College of Notre Dame*
Colgate U.   *Colgate University*
Colo. Sch. Mines   *Colorado School of Mines*
Colo. St. U.   *Colorado State University*
Columbia U.   *Columbia University*
Columbus C.   *Columbus College*
C. O. M. Pac.   *College of Osteopathic Medicine of the Pacific*
Concordia Teachers C. (Nebr.)   *Concordia College*
Concordia U. (Ill.)   *Concordia University*
Conn. C.   *Connecticut College*
Converse C.   *Converse College*
Cornell U.   *Cornell University*
Cranbrook Acad. Art   *Cranbrook Academy of Art*
Creighton U.   *The Creighton University*
C. St. Rose   *The College of Saint Rose*
C. St. Scholastica   *College of St. Scholastica*
C. Staten Island (C.U.N.Y.)   *The College of Staten Island of the City University of New York*
C.U.N.Y. (Grad. Cent.)   *The City University of New York*
C. Wm. & Mary   *The College of William and Mary*
C. W. Post (L.I.U.)   *Long Island University, C. W. Post Campus*
Dartmouth C.   *Dartmouth College*
Delta St. U.   *Delta State University*
DePaul U.   *DePaul University*
Detroit C. Law   *Detroit College of Law*
Dickinson Sch. Law   *The Dickinson School of Law*
Dominican C. San Rafael   *Dominican College*
Drake U.   *Drake University*
Drew U.   *Drew University*
Drexel U.   *Drexel University*
Drury C.   *Drury College*
Duke U.   *Duke University*
Duquesne U.   *Duquesne University*
East Car. U.   *East Carolina University*
East Cent. Okla. St. U.   *East Central University*
East. Conn. St. U.   *Eastern Connecticut State University*
East. Ill. U.   *Eastern Illinois University*
East. Ky. U.   *Eastern Kentucky University*
East. Mich. U.   *Eastern Michigan University*
East. N. Mex. U.   *Eastern New Mexico University*
East. Ore. C.   *Eastern Oregon State College*
East Stroudsburg U.   *East Stroudsburg University of Pennsylvania*
East Tenn. St. U.   *East Tennessee State University*
East Tex. St. U.   *East Texas State University*
East. Va. Med. Sch.   *Eastern Virginia Medical School of the Medical College of Hampton Roads*
East. Wash. U.   *Eastern Washington University*
Edinboro U.   *Edinboro University of Pennsylvania*
Elmira C.   *Elmira College*
Emerson C.   *Emerson College*
Emory U.   *Emory University*
Emporia St. U.   *Emporia State University*
Fairfield U.   *Fairfield University*
Fairleigh Dickinson U.   *Fairleigh Dickinson University*
Fisk U.   *Fisk University*
Fitchburg St. C.   *Fitchburg State College*
Fla. A&M U.   *Florida Agricultural and Mechanical University*
Fla. Atlantic U.   *Florida Atlantic University*
Fla. Inst. Tech.   *Florida Institute of Technology*
Fla. St. U.   *Florida State University*
Fordham U.   *Fordham University*
Fort Hays St. U.   *Fort Hays State University*
Fort Valley St. U.   *Fort Valley State University*

Framingham St. C.   *Framingham State College*
Franklin Pierce Law Sch.   *Franklin Pierce Law Center*
Frostburg St. U.   *Frostburg State University*
Furman U.   *Furman University*
Gallaudet U.   *Gallaudet University*
Gannon U.   *Gannon University*
Geo. Mason U.   *George Mason University*
Geo. Peabody C.   *George Peabody College for Teachers of Vanderbilt University*
Georgetown C.   *Georgetown College*
Georgetown U.   *Georgetown University*
George Washington U.   *The George Washington University*
Georgia C. Milledgeville   *Georgia College of Milledgville*
Georgia Inst. Tech.   *The Georgia Institute of Technology*
Georgia So. U.   *Georgia Southern University*
Georgia St. U.   *Georgia State University*
Goddard C.   *Goddard College*
Golden Gate U.   *Golden Gate University*
Gonzaga U.   *Gonzaga University*
Goucher C.   *Goucher College*
Gov. St. U.   *Governors State University*
Hamline U.   *Hamline University*
Hampton U.   *Hampton University*
Hardin-Simmons U.   *Hardin-Simmons University*
Harding U.   *Harding University*
Harvard U.   *Harvard University*
Hastings C. Law   *University of California, Hastings College of Law*
Hawaii Pac. U.   *Hawaii Pacific University*
Hebrew C.   *Hebrew College*
Henderson St. U.   *Henderson State University*
Hofstra U.   *Hofstra University*
Hollins C.   *Hollins College*
Holy Names C.   *Holy Names College*
Hood C.   *Hood College*
Howard U.   *Howard University*
Hunter C. (C.U.N.Y.)   *Hunter College of the City University of New York*
Idaho St. U.   *Idaho State University*
Ill. Inst. Tech.   *Illinois Institute of Technology*
Ill. St. U.   *Illinois State University*
Incarnate Word C.   *University of the Incarnate Word*
Ind. St. U.   *Indiana State University*
Ind. U.   *Indiana University*
Ind. U. Penn.   *Indiana University of Pennsylvania*
Inter American U.   *Inter American University*
Iona C.   *Iona College*
Iowa St. U.   *Iowa State University of Science and Technology*
Ithaca C.   *Ithaca College*
Jackson St. U.   *Jackson State University*
Jacksonville St. U.   *Jacksonville State University*
Jacksonville U.   *Jacksonville University*
James Madison U.   *James Madison University*
Jersey City St. C.   *Jersey City State College*
John Carroll U.   *John Carroll University*
John Jay C. (C.U.N.Y.)   *John Jay College of Criminal Justice of The City University of New York*
John Marshall Law Sch.   *John Marshall Law School*
Johns Hopkins U.   *The Johns Hopkins University*
Juilliard   *The Juilliard School*
Kans. St. U.   *Kansas State University of Agriculture and Applied Science*
Kean C. N.J.   *Kean College of New Jersey*
Keene St. C.   *Keene State College*
Kent St. U.   *Kent State University*
Kirksville C.   *Kirksville College of Osteopathic Medicine*
Kutztown U.   *Kutztown University of Pennsylvania*
LaGrange C.   *Lagrange College*
Lamar U.   *Lamar University*
La. Tech. U.   *Louisiana Tech University*
Lehigh U.   *Lehigh University*
Lehman C. (C.U.N.Y.)   *Herbert H. Lehman College of the City University of New York*
Lewis & Clark C.   *Lewis and Clark College*
Lincoln U.   *Lincoln University*
L.I.U.   *Long Island University, Brooklyn Campus*
Livingston U.   *Livingston University*
Loma Linda U.   *Loma Linda University*
Longwood C.   *Longwood College*
Loras C.   *Loras College*

Loyola C. (Md.)   *Loyola College (Maryland)*
Loyola Marymount U.   *Loyola Marymount University (Los Angeles)*
Loyola U. Chicago   *Loyola University of Chicago*
Loyola U. (La.)   *Loyola University*
L.S.U.   *Louisiana State University and Agricultural and Mechanical College*
L.S.U. Med. Cent.   *Louisiana State University Medical Center*
L.S.U. Shreveport   *Louisiana State University in Shreveport*
Lynchburg C.   *Lynchburg College*
Manhattan C.   *Manhattan College*
Manhattan Sch. Music   *Manhattan School of Music*
Manhattanville C.   *Manhattanville College*
Mankato St. U.   *Mankato State University*
Mansfield U.   *Mansfield University of Pennsylvania*
Marquette U.   *Marquette University*
Marshall U.   *Marshall University*
Marycrest I. U.   *Marycrest International University*
Marygrove C.   *Marygrove College*
Maryville U.   *Maryville University of Saint Louis*
Marywood C.   *Marywood College*
Mass. C. Art   *Massachusetts College of Art*
Mass. C. Pharmacy   *Massachusetts College of Pharmacy*
Mayo Med. Sch.   *Mayo Medical School*
McNeese St. U.   *McNeese State University*
Md. Inst. C. Art   *Maryland Institute College of Art*
Med. C. Georgia   *Medical College of Georgia*
Med. C. Ohio   *Medical College of Ohio at Toledo*
Med. C. Penn.   *Medical College of Pennsylvania and Hahnemann University*
Med. C. Wis.   *Medical College of Wisconsin*
Med. U. So. Car.   *Medical University of South Carolina*
Meharry Med. C.   *Meharry Medical College*
Mercer U.   *Mercer University*
Miami U. (Ohio)   *Miami University (Ohio)*
Mich. St. U.   *Michigan State University*
Mich. Tech. U.   *Michigan Technological University*
Middlebury C.   *Middlebury College*
Mid. Tenn. St. U.   *Middle Tennessee State University*
Midwest U.   *Midwestern University–Chicago College of Osteopathic Medicine*
Millersville U.   *Millersville University of Pennsylvania*
Mills C.   *Mills College*
Milwau. Sch. Eng.   *Milwaukee School of Engineering*
Minot St. U.   *Minot State University*
Miss. C.   *Mississippi College*
Miss. St. U.   *Mississippi State University*
Miss. St. U. Women   *Mississippi University for Women*
M.I.T.   *Massachusetts Institute of Technology*
Monmouth U.   *Monmouth University*
Mont. C.M.S.&.T.   *Montana Tech of the University of Montana*
Mont. St. U.   *Montana State University*
Mont. Tech.   *Montana Tech of the University of Montana*
Montclair St. C.   *Montclair State College*
Monterey Inst.   *Monterey Institute of International Studies*
Moorhead St. U.   *Moorhead State University*
Morehead St. U.   *Morehead State University*
Morehouse Sch. of Med.   *Morehouse School of Medicine*
Morgan St. U.   *Morgan State University*
Morningside C.   *Morningside College*
Mt. Holyoke C.   *Mount Holyoke College*
Mt. Sinai Sch. Med.   *Mount Sinai School of Medicine of The City University of New York*
Mt. St. Mary's C.   *Mount St. Mary's College*
Murray St. U.   *Murray State University*
Nat. Louis U.   *National-Louis University*
Nat. U.   *National University*
Naval PG   *Naval Postgraduate School.*
New Eng. Cons. Music   *New England Conservatory of Music*
New Eng. Sch. Law   *New England School of Law*
N.J.I.T.   *New Jersey Institute of Technology*
N. Mex. Highlands U.   *New Mexico Highlands University*
N. Mex. Inst. M&T   *New Mexico Institute of Mining and Technology*
N. Mex. St. U.   *New Mexico State University*
N. Sch. Social Research   *The New School for Social Research*
Niagara U.   *Niagara University*
No. Adams St. C.   *North Adams State College**
No. Ariz. U.   *Northern Arizona University*
No. Car. Ag. & Tech.   *North Carolina Agricultural and Technical State University*

No. Car. Cent. U.   *North Carolina Central University*
No. Car. St. U. (Raleigh)   *North Carolina State University at Raleigh*
No. Dak. St. U.   *North Dakota State University*
No. E. Ill. U.   *Northeastern Illinois University*
No. E. La. U.   *Northeast Louisiana University*
No. E. Ohio U.   *Northeastern Ohio Universities*
No. E. St. U.   *Northeastern State University*
No. E. U.   *Northeastern University*
No. Ill. U.   *Northern Illinois University*
No. Kent. U.   *Northern Kentucky University*
No. Mich. U.   *Northern Michigan University*
Northrop U.   *Northrop University*
Northwestern U.   *Northwestern University*
Nova U.   *Nova Southwestern University*
No. W. Mo. St. U.   *Northwest Missouri State University*
No. W. Okla. St. U.   *Northwestern Oklahoma State University*
No. W. St. U. La.   *Northwestern State University of Louisiana*
N.Y. I. T.   *New York Institute of Technology*
N.Y. Law Sch.   *New York Law School*
N.Y. Med. C.   *New York Medical College*
N.Y.U.   *New York University*
Oakland U.   *Oakland University*
Occidental C.   *Occidental College*
Oglethorpe U.   *Oglethorpe University*
Ohio No. U.   *Ohio Northern University*
Ohio St. U.   *The Ohio State University*
Ohio U.   *Ohio University*
Okla. City U.   *Oklahoma City University*
Okla. St. U.   *Oklahoma State University*
Old Dom. U.   *Old Dominion University*
Olivet Naz. U.   *Olivet Nazarene University*
Oral Roberts U.   *Oral Roberts University*
Ore. Grad. I. Sci. & T.   *Oregon Graduate Institute of Science and Technology*
Ore. Health Sci. U.   *Oregon Health Sciences University*
Ore. St. U.   *Oregon State University*
Otis Art Inst.   *Otis College of Art and Design*
Our Lady Lake U.   *Our Lady of the Lake University*
Pace U.   *Pace University*
Pac. Luth. U.   *Pacific Lutheran University*
Pac. U.   *Pacific University*
Pac. Union C.   *Pacific Union College*
Peabody Institute of the Johns Hopkins University
Penn. C. Opt.   *Pennsylvania College of Optometry*
Penn. St. U.   *Pennsylvania State University*
Penn. St. U. Harrisburg   *Pennsylvania State University at Harrisburg*
Pepperdine U.   *Pepperdine University*
Pepperdine U. (Culver City)   *Pepperdine University, Culver City*
Phila. C. O. M.   *Philadelphia College of Osteopathic Medicine*
Phila. C. Pharmacy   *The Philadelphia College of Pharmacy and Science*
Phillips U.   *Phillips University*
Pittsburg St. U.   *Pittsburg State University*
Plymouth St. C.   *Plymouth State College*
Point Loma C.   *Point Loma Nazarene College*
Poly U.   *Polytechnic University*
Ponce Sch. Med.   *Ponce School of Medicine*
Portland St. U.   *Portland State University*
Prairie View A&M U.   *Prairie View Agricultural and Mechanical University*
Pratt Inst.   *Pratt Institute*
Princeton U.   *Princeton University*
Providence C.   *Providence College*
Purdue U.   *Purdue University*
Purdue U. (Calumet)   *Purdue University Calumet*
Queens C. (C.U.N.Y.)   *Queens College of the City University of New York*
Quinnipiac C.   *Quinnipiac College*
Radford U.   *Radford University*
Reed C.   *Reed College*
Rhode Island C.   *Rhode Island College*
Rhode Island Sch. Design   *Rhode Island School of Design*
Rice U.   *Rice University*
Rider C.   *Rider College*
R.I.T.   *Rochester Institute of Technology*
Rivier C.   *Rivier College*
Robert Morris C.   *Robert Morris College*
Rockefeller U.   *The Rockefeller University*
Rockford C.   *Rockford College*

Rollins C.   *Rollins College*
Roosevelt U.   *Roosevelt University*
Rosary C.   *Rosary College*
Rose-Hulman Inst. Tech.   *Rose-Hulman Institute of Technology*
Rowan C. N.J.   *Rowan College of New Jersey*
R.P.I.   *Rensselaer Polytechnic Institute*
Rush Med. C.   *Rush Medical College*
Rutgers U.   *Rutgers University*
Sage C.   *The Sage Colleges*
Sag. Val. St. C.   *Saginaw Valley State University*
Salem St. C.   *Salem State College*
Salisbury St. U.   *Salisbury State University*
Samford U.   *Samford University*
Sam Houston St. U.   *Sam Houston State University*
San Fran. Art Inst.   *San Francisco Art Institute*
San Fran. Conserv. Music   *San Francisco Conservatory of Music*
San Fran. St. U.   *San Francisco State University*
Sarah Lawrence C.   *Sarah Lawrence College*
S.D.S.U.   *San Diego State University*
Seattle Pac. U.   *Seattle Pacific University*
Seattle U.   *Seattle University*
Seton Hall U.   *Seton Hall University*
S. F. Austin St. U.   *Stephen F. Austin State University*
Shippensburg U.   *Shippensburg University of Pennsylvania*
Siena Heights C.   *Siena Heights College*
Simmons C.   *Simmons College*
Slippery Rock U.   *Slippery Rock University of Pennsylvania*
Smith C.   *Smith College*
Southeast Mo. St. U.   *Southeast Missouri State University*
Southeastern La. U.   *Southeastern Louisiana University*
Southeastern Okla. St. U.   *Southeastern Oklahoma State University*
So. C. Optometry   *Southern College of Optometry*
So. Cal. C. Optometry   *Southern California College of Optometry*
So. Car. St. C.   *South Carolina State College*
So. Conn. St. U.   *Southern Connecticut State University*
So. Dak. Sch. M&T   *South Dakota School of Mines and Technology*
So. Dak. St. U.   *South Dakota State University*
So. Ill. U.   *Southern Illinois University*
So. Ill. U. (Edwardsville)   *Southern Illinois University at Edwardsville*
So. Meth. U.   *Southern Methodist University*
So. Nazarene U.   *Southern Nazarene University*
So. Ore. St. C.   *Southern Oregon State College*
So. Tex. C. Law   *South Texas College of Law*
So. U. & A&M C.   *Southern University and Agricultural and Mechanical College*
Southwest Mo. St. U.   *Southwest Missouri State University*
Southwest Tex. St. U.   *Southwest Texas State*
Southwestern Okla. St. U.   *Southwestern Oklahoma State University*
Southwestern U. Law   *Southwestern University School of Law*
Spalding C.   *Spalding University*
Springfield C.   *Springfield College*
St. Bonaventure U.   *St. Bonaventure University*
St. Cloud St. U.   *St. Cloud State University*
St. Edward's U.   *St. Edward's University*
St. Francis C. (Ind.)   *St. Francis College (Indiana)*
St. Francis C. (Penn.)   *St. Francis College (Pennsylvannia)*
St. John's C.   *St. John's College (New Mexico)*
St. John's C. (Md.)   *St. John's College (Maryland)*
St. John's U. (Minn.)   *St. John's University (Minnesota)*
St. John's U. (N.Y.)   *St. John's University (New York)*
St. Joseph C. (Conn.)   *St. Joseph College (Connecticut)*
St. Joseph's U. (Penn.)   *St. Joseph's University (Pennsylvannia)*
St. Lawrence U.   *St. Lawrence University*
St. Louis U.   *Saint Louis University*
St. Mary's C.   *St. Mary's College of Minnesota*
St. Mary's U.   *St. Mary's University*
St. Michael's C.   *St. Michael's College*
St. Xavier U.   *St. Xavier University*
Stanford U.   *Stanford University*
Stetson U.   *Stetson University*
Stevens Inst. Tech.   *Stevens Institute of Technology*
Suffolk U.   *Suffolk University*
Sul Ross St. U.   *Sul Ross State University*
S.U.N.Y. (Binghamton)   *State University of New York at Binghamton*
S.U.N.Y (Buffalo)   *State University of New York at Buffalo*
S.U.N.Y. (Stony Brook)   *State University of New York at Stony Brook (West Campus)*
S.U.N.Y.C (Albany)   *University at Albany State University of New York*

S.U.N.Y.C. (Brockport)   *State University of New York College at Brockport*
S.U.N.Y.C. (Buffalo)   *State University of New York College at Buffalo*
S.U.N.Y.C. (Cortland)   *State University of New York College at Cortland*
S.U.N.Y.C. Environ. Sci. & For. (Syracuse)   *State University of New York College of Environmental Science and Forestry at Syracuse*
S.U.N.Y.C. (Fredonia)   *State University of New York College at Fredonia*
S.U.N.Y.C. (Geneseo)   *State University of New York College of Arts and Sciences at Geneseo*
S.U.N.Y.C. (New Paltz)   *State University of New York College at New Paltz*
S.U.N.Y.C. (Oneonta)   *State University of New York College at Oneonta*
S.U.N.Y.C. (Oswego)   *State University of New York College at Oswego*
S.U.N.Y.C. (Plattsburg)   *State University of New York College at Plattsburgh*
S.U.N.Y.C. (Potsdam)   *State University of New York College at Potsdam*
S.U.N.Y. H. Sci. Cent.   *State University of New York Health Science Center at Brooklyn*
S.U.N.Y. H. Sci. Cent.   *State University of New York Health Science Center at Syracuse*
Syracuse U.   *Syracuse University*
Tarleton St. U.   *Tarleton State University*
Temple U.   *Temple University*
Tenn. St. U.   *Tennessee State University*
Tenn. Tech. U.   *Tennessee Technological University*
Tex. A&I U.   *Texas A & I University*
Tex. A&M U.   *Texas Agricultural and Mechanical University*
Tex. A&M U. (Corpus Christi)   *Texas Agricultural and Mechanical University, Corpus Christi*
Tex. Christ. U.   *Texas Christian University*
Tex. So. U.   *Texas Southern University*
Tex. Tech. U.   *Texas Tech University*
Tex. Woman's U.   *Texas Woman's University*
Thom. Cooley Law   *Thomas M. Cooley Law School*
Thom. Jefferson U.   *Thomas Jefferson University*
Touro C.   *Touro College*
Towson St. U.   *Towson State University*
Trinity C.   *Trinity College*
Trinity U.   *Trinity University*
Troy St. U.   *Troy State University*
Troy St. U. (Dorhan)   *Troy State University at Dothan*
Troy St. U. (Mont.)   *Troy State University (Montgomery)*
Truman St. U.   *Truman State University*
Tufts U.   *Tufts University*
Tulane U.   *Tulane University*
Tuskegee U.   *Tuskegee University*
U. Akron   *University of Akron*
U. Ala.   *University of Alabama*
U. Ala. (Birm.)   *University of Alabama at Birmingham*
U. Ala. (Huntsville)   *University of Alabama at Huntsville*
U. Alaska   *University of Alaska*
U. Ariz.   *The University of Arizona*
U. Ark.   *University of Arkansas*
U. Arts   *The University of the Arts*
U. Balt.   *University of Baltimore*
U. Bridgeport   *University of Bridgeport*
U. Cal. (Berkeley)   *University of California at Berkeley*
U. Cal. (Davis)   *University of California at Davis*
U. Cal. (Irvine)   *University of California at Irvine*
U. Cal. (Riverside)   *University of California at Riverside*
U. Cal. (San Diego)   *University of California at San Diego*
U. Cal. (San Francisco)   *University of California at San Francisco*
U. Cal. (Santa Barbara)   *University of California at Santa Barbara*
U. Cal. (Santa Cruz)   *University of California at Santa Cruz*
U. Cent. Ark.   *University of Central Arkansas*
U. Cent. Fla.   *University of Central Florida*
U. Cent. Okla.   *University of Central Oklahoma*
U. Chicago   *The University of Chicago*
U. Cincinnati   *University of Cincinnati*
U.C.L.A.   *University of California, Los Angeles*
U. Colo.   *University of Colorado, Boulder*
U. Conn.   *The University of Connecticut*
U. Conn.   *University of Connecticut Health Center*

U. Dallas   *University of Dallas*
U. Dayton   *University of Dayton*
U. Del.   *University of Delaware*
U. Denver   *University of Denver*
U. Detroit   *University of Detroit Mercy*
U. Dubuque   *University of Dubuque*
U. Evansville   *University of Evansville*
U. Fla.   *University of Florida*
U. Georgia   *The University of Georgia*
U. Hartford   *University of Hartford*
U. Hawaii   *University of Hawaii at Manoa*
U. Health Sc. (Chicago)   *Finch University of Health Sciences/The Chicago Medical School*
U. Health Sci.   *University of Health Sciences*
U. Houston   *University of Houston*
U. Idaho   *University of Idaho*
U. Ill.   *University of Illinois*
U. Ill. (Chicago)   *University of Illinois at Chicago*
U. Indianapolis   *University of Indianapolis*
U. Iowa   *The University of Iowa*
U. Kans.   *University of Kansas*
U. Kans. Med. Ctr.   *University of Kansas Medical Center*
U. Ky.   *University of Kentucky*
U. La Verne   *University of La Verne*
U. Louisville   *University of Louisville*
U. Maine   *University of Maine*
U. Maine (Portland-Gorham)   *University of Maine at Portland-Gorham*
U. Mass.   *University of Massachusetts*
U. Mass. (Boston)   *University of Massachusetts*
U. Mass. (Dartmouth)   *University of Massachusetts Dartmouth*
U. Mass. (Lowell)   *Massachusetts, University of, Lowell*
U. Md.   *University of Maryland*
U. Md. (Baltimore)   *University of Maryland at Baltimore*
U. Md. (Baltimore Cnty.)   *University of Maryland Baltimore County*
U. Med. Dent. N.J.   *University of Medicine and Dentistry of New Jersey*
U. Memphis   *University of Memphis*
U. Miami (Fla.)   *University of Miami*
U. Mich.   *The University of Michigan*
U. Minn.   *University of Minnesota*
U. Miss.   *The University of Mississippi*
U. Miss. (Med. Cent.)   *University of Mississippi Medical Center*
U. Mo. (Columbia)   *University of Missouri at Columbia*
U. Mo. (K.C.)   *University of Missouri at Kansas City*
U. Mo. (Rolla)   *University of Missouri—Rolla*
U. Mo. (St. Louis)   *University of Missouri at St. Louis*
U. Mont.   *University of Montana*
U. Montevallo   *University of Montevallo*
U. N.H.   *University of New Hampshire*
U. N. Mex.   *The University of New Mexico*
U. N. Orleans   *University of New Orleans*
U. N. Orleans (Med. Cent.)   *University of New Orleans Medical Center*
U. Neb.   *University of Nebraska*
U. Neb. (Kearney)   *University of Nebraska at Kearney*
U. Neb. (Omaha)   *University of Nebraska at Omaha*
U. Nev.   *University of Nevada, Reno*
U. Nev. (Las Vegas)   *University of Nevada, Las Vegas*
U. New Eng. C.O.M.   *University of New England College of Osteopathic Medicine*
U. New Haven   *University of New Haven*
U. No. Ala.   *University of North Alabama*
U. No. Car. (Chapel Hill)   *The University of North Carolina at Chapel Hill*
U. No. Car. (Greensboro)   *The University of North Carolina at Greensboro*
U. No. Col.   *University of Northern Colorado*
U. No. Dak.   *University of North Dakota*
U. No. Fla.   *University of North Florida*
U. No. Iowa   *University of Northern Iowa*
U. No. Tex.   *University of North Texas*
U. Notre Dame   *University of Notre Dame*
U. of So.   *University of the South*
U. Okla.   *University of Oklahoma*
U. Okla. Health Sc. C   *University of Oklahoma Health Science Center*
U.O. M.&H.   *University of Osteopathic Medicine and Health*
U. Ore.   *University of Oregon*

U. Osteopathic Med. & Health Sci.   *University of Osteopathic Medicine and Health Sciences*
U. Pac.   *University of the Pacific*
U. Penn.   *University of Pennsylvania*
U. Phoenix   *University of Phoenix*
U. Pitt.   *University of Pittsburgh*
U. Portland   *University of Portland*
U. Puerto Rico   *University of Puerto Rico*
U. Puerto Rico, Mayaguez   *University of Puerto Rico, Mayaguez*
U. Puget Sound   *University of Puget Sound*
U. Redlands   *University of Redlands*
U. Rhode Island   *University of Rhode Island*
U. Richmond   *University of Richmond*
U. Rochester   *University of Rochester*
U.S. I. U.   *United States International University*
U. San Diego   *University of San Diego*
U. San Fran.   *University of San Francisco*
U. Scranton   *University of Scranton*
U. So. Ala.   *University of South Alabama*
U. So. Cal.   *University of Southern California*
U. So. Car.   *University of South Carolina*
U. So. Dak.   *University of South Dakota*
U. So. Fla.   *University of South Florida*
U. So. Maine   *University of Southern Maine*
U. So. Miss.   *University of Southern Mississippi*
U. St. Thomas   *University of St. Thomas*
U. St. Thomas (Tex.)   *University of St. Thomas*
U. Tenn.   *University of Tennessee*
U. Tenn. (Chattanooga)   *University of Tennessee at Chattanooga*
U. Tenn. (Martin)   *University of Tennessee at Martin*
U. Tenn. (Memphis)   *University of Tennessee, Memphis*
U. Tenn. (Oak Ridge)   *University of Tennessee at Oak Ridge*
U. Tenn. Space Inst.   *University of Tennessee Space Institute*
U. Tex. (Arlington)   *The University of Texas at Arlington*
U. Tex. (Austin)   *The University of Texas at Austin*
U. Tex. (Dallas)   *The University of Texas at Dallas*
U. Tex. (El Paso)   *The University of Texas at El Paso*
U. Tex. Health Sci. Ctr. (Houston)   *The University of Texas Health Science Center at Houston*
U. Tex. Med. Br. (Galveston)   *University of Texas Medical Branch at Galveston*
U. Tex. Med. Ctr. (Dallas)   *The University of Texas Southwestern Medical Center at Dallas*
U. Tex. Pan Amer.   *The University of Texas—Pan American*
U. Tex. Perm. Basin   *The University of Texas of the Permian Basin*
U. Tex. (Tyler)   *The University of Texas at Tyler*
U. Toledo   *University of Toledo*
U. Tulsa   *The University of Tulsa*
U. Utah   *University of Utah*
U. Va.   *University of Virginia*
U. Vt.   *University of Vermont*
U. Wash.   *University of Washington*
U. West Ala.   *University of West Alabama*
U. Wis.   *University of Wisconsin*
U. Wis. (Eau Claire)   *University of Wisconsin at Eau Claire*
U. Wis. (La Crosse)   *University of Wisconsin at La Crosse*
U. Wis. (Milwaukee)   *University of Wisconsin at Milwaukee*
U. Wis. (Oshkosh)   *University of Wisconsin at Oshkosh*
U. Wis. (Platteville)   *University of Wisconsin at Platteville*
U. Wis. (River Falls)   *University of Wisconsin at River Falls*
U. Wis. (Stevens Point)   *University of Wisconsin at Stevens Point*
U. Wis. (Stout)   *University of Wisconsin at Stout*
U. Wis. (Superior)   *University of Wisconsin at Superior*
U. Wis. (Whitewater)   *University of Wisconsin at Whitewater*
U. Wyo.   *University of Wyoming*
Union C. (Ky.)   *Union College (Kentucky)*
Union C. (N.Y.)   *Union College (New York)*
Union Inst.   *The Union Institute*
Utah St. U.   *Utah State University*
Va. Commonwealth U.   *Virginia Commonwealth University*
Valdosta St. C.   *Valdosta State College*
Valparaiso U.   *Valparaiso University*
Vanderbilt U.   *Vanderbilt University*
Va. Poly. Inst.   *Virginia Polytechnic Institute and State University*
Vassar C.   *Vassar College*
Va. St. U.   *Virginia State University*
Villanova U.   *Villanova University*
Vt. Law   *Vermont Law School*

Wagner C. *Wagner College*
Wake Forest U. *Wake Forest University*
Walla Walla C. *Walla Walla College*
Washburn U. *Washburn University of Topeka*
Wash. C. *Washington College*
Wash. & Lee U. *Washington and Lee University*
Wash. St. U. *Washington State University*
Wash. U. (Mo.) *Washington University*
Wayne St. C. *Wayne State College*
Wayne St. U. *Wayne State University*
Webster U. *Webster University*
Wesleyan U. *Wesleyan University*
West. Car. U. *Western Carolina University*
West Chester U. Pa. *West Chester University of Pennsylvania*
West. Conn. St. U. *Western Connecticut State University*
West Ga. St. U. *State University of West Georgia*
West. Ill. U. *Western Illinois University*
West. Ky. U. *Western Kentucky University*
West. Md. C. *Western Maryland College*
West. Mich. U. *Western Michigan University*
West. N.E. C. *Western New England College*
West. N. Mex. U. *Western New Mexico University*
West. Oregon St. C. *Western Oregon State College*
West Tex. A&M U. *West Texas A&M University*
West Va. Col. *West Virginia Graduate College*
West Va. U. *West Virginia University*

West. Wash. U. *Western Washington University*
Westfield St. C. *Westfield State College*
Westminster C. *Westminster College*
Wheelock C. *Wheelock College*
Whittier C. *Whittier College*
Whitworth C. *Whitworth College*
Wichita St. U. *Wichita State University*
Widener U. *Widener University*
Wilkes C. *Wilkes University*
Willamette U. *Willamette University*
Williams C. *Williams College*
Winona St. U. *Winona State University*
Winthrop C. *Winthrop University*
Wm. Carey C. *William Carey College*
Wm. Mitchell C. Law *William Mitchell College of Law*
Wm. Paterson C. *William Paterson College of New Jersey*
Worcester Poly. Inst. *Worcester Polytechnic Institute*
Worcester St. C. *Worcester State College*
Wright St. U. *Wright State University*
W. Va. Sch. Osteopathic Med. *West Virginia School of Osteopathic Medicine*
Xavier U. (La.) *Xavier University of Louisiana*
Xavier U. (Ohio) *Xavier University*
Yale U. *Yale University*
Yeshiva U. *Yeshiva University*
Youngstown St. U. *Youngstown State University*

INDEX TO FIELDS OF STUDY

American colleges and universities offer graduate and professional degree programs in a bewilderingly varied number of disciplines and areas of specialization. An indication of the scope of opportunities for advanced study is found in the index that follows, listing major fields of study and the institutions that provide them.

Before turning to the index, it is *very important* that the user read and understand the following explanatory notes. Without knowledge of these caveats, the reader may overlook available educational opportunities.

1. Major and subfields of study are listed under these headings:

Agriculture
Architecture
  Naval Architecture
Area Studies
  African/Afro-American Studies
  Asian Studies
  Brazilian Studies
  Canada Area Studies
  Caribbean Studies
  Egyptology
  European Studies
  Hispanic/Iberian Studies
  Indo-European Studies
  Islamic Studies/Literature
  Latin American Studies
  Mediterranean Studies
  Mexican-American Studies
  Near/Middle Eastern Studies
  New York Area Studies
  North American Studies
  Pacific Area Studies
  Russian/East European Studies
  Uralic Studies
Basic Medical Sciences
  Bacteriology
  Immunology
  Radiological Sciences
  Toxicology
Biological Sciences
  Biochemistry
  Biomathematics/Biostatistics
  Biometry/Biometrics
  Biophysics
  Cancer Biology
  Cell Biology
  Genetics
  Environmental Biology
  Marine Biology
  Molecular Biology
Business
  Actuarial/Insurance Sciences

Hotel/Hospitality Management
Human Resource Management
Information Science
International Business/Economics
Management Science
Public/Nonprofit Management
Quantitative Analysis/Studies
Real Estate
Taxation
Communications
  Creative Writing/Writing
  Film/Television
  Journalism
  Technical Writing
  Telecommunication
Computer Science
Criminal Justice/Corrections/Criminology
Dentistry
Education
  Adult Education
  Art Education
  Audio-visual Education
  Bilingual/Multilingual/Multicultural
    Education
  Community College Teaching
  Computers in Education
  Drug and Alcohol/Substance Abuse
    Counseling
  Education of the Gifted
  English as a Second Language
  Learning Disabilities
  Marriage and Family Counseling
  Recreation/Recreational Administration
  Safety Education
  School Librarianship
  Sex Education
  Teaching of Culturally Disadvantaged
  Teaching of Emotionally Disturbed
  Teaching of Mentally Retarded
  Teaching of Physically Handicapped
  Urban Education

Engineering and Technology
  Architectural Engineering
  Bioengineering/Biomedical Engineering
  Ceramic Engineering
  Engineering Management
  Environmental Engineering
  Geological/Geosciences/Geotechnical
    Engineering
  Manufacturing Engineering
  Marine Science/Engineering/
    Oceanography
  Mineral/Mining Engineering/Technology
  Ocean Engineering
  Paper Engineering/Science/Technology
  Petroleum Engineering
  Polymer Engineering/Science
  Sanitary Engineering/Science
  Software Engineering
  System Engineering
  Tanning Research
  Textile Engineering/Science
  Transportation/Traffic Engineering
Environmental Sciences
  Fish/Wildlife Management
  Landscape Architecture
  Meteorology
  Range Management/Science
  Water Resources Administration
Fine Arts
  Art Management
  Arts Therapy
  Interior Design
  Museum Training/Studies/Historic
    Preservation
  Photography
  Textile Design
Foreign Languages/Literatures
  African Languages
  Akkadian
  Bengali
  Caucasian

Celtic
Chinese/Japanese/Asian Languages
Greek
Hebrew/Arabic/Near and Middle Eastern
   Languages/Literatures
Hindi
Latin
Sanskrit
Scandinavian Languages/Literatures
Translation and Interpretation
Urdu
Home/Consumer Economics, Food Science,
   Food Service, Technology, Child and
   Family Life, Nutrition
Horticulture
Humanities
   Classics
   Comparative Literature
   Folklore
   Linguistics
   Philosophy
Law
Liberal Studies
Library/Informational Studies
Medicine
   Medical Illustration

   Medical Technology
   Tropical Medicine
Music
   Music Therapy
Nursing and Health Professions
   Child-Care/Pediatric Nursing
   Family Nursing
   Gerontological Nursing
   Health Care /Health Services/Hospital
     Administration/Management
   Nurse Anesthesia
   Nurse Midwifery
   Nursing
   Occupational Therapy
   Oncology Nursing
   Physical Therapy
   Prosthetics
   Psychiatric Nursing
   Rehabilitation /Counseling Services
Optometry/Visual Sciences
Osteopathic Medicine
Pharmacy
Physical Sciences
   Analytical Chemistry
   Applied Physics
   Astronomy/Space Science

Geology
Geochemistry
Geophysics
Public Administration
Public and Community Health
   Epidemiology
   International Health
Religion
Social Sciences
   Anthropology
   Archaeology
   Geography
   Medieval Studies
   Peace Studies/Conflict Resolution
   Population Studies
   Urban Studies
   Women Studies
Social Work
Theatre/Drama
   Dance
   Dance Therapy
   Music Theatre
   Play Writing
   Theatre for Deaf
   Theatre Management
Urban Design/City Planning
Veterinary Medicine

2. Each major and subfield heading is followed by the abbreviated names of every institution offering study leading to a degree in even one of the subfields customarily associated with the larger area. Thus, if an institution offers *only* fisheries biology, for example, its name is nevertheless included under BIOLOGICAL SCIENCES. The major fields are complete in listing appropriate institutions as of the time of preparation of this manuscript. Inasmuch as the information presented here is only as accurate as that provided by the institutions, and inasmuch as changes occur rapidly in higher education, some programs may not have been properly credited, or may have been discontinued, modified, or added. It bears repeating that this *Guide* is intended only as a first source of information, and certainty in academic planning information can be assured only by contacting the institution in which one is interested.

3. Subfields listed under the major headings are those of special interest or those sufficiently unusual to justify special notice. The student should bear in mind that nomenclature and departmental organization vary substantially from institution to institution. Using the BIOLOGICAL SCIENCES example again, a *Biology* department may offer majors in botany, zoology, entomology, fisheries biology, cellular biology, and others, but this information may not have been made clear or available. Any one of these may have the status of separately constituted academic departments, so that a graduate school with a biology department offering study in botany may have another department, with a different faculty, in zoology. Entomology, a branch of zoology, may be available through still another department. College catalogs can be unilluminating on such points, and seemingly endless combinations can be constructed. The point is, the major listings can be assumed to be as accurate as possible, but the subfields cannot. A potential student should first determine whether the broad field of study in which he or she is interested is available at a particular institution, *then* look to the subfields for clarification, remembering that the latter may be incomplete.

4. At multidivisional universities, study in a particular field may be offered by two or more divisions. Biochemistry may be a program of the chemistry or biology departments of the graduate school of arts and science and also available in the medical school of the same university. Universities with several campuses may offer the same major at three or more different locations *and* divisions. All divisions of an institution must therefore be checked for a particular program.

5. Since names describing fields of study frequently differ, the most common variations parenthetically follow the labels used in this index. When appropriate, it is noted that certain majors are "typically" or "often" included under any given heading.

6. Historically, a number of areas of study have grown and split, the new parts coming under different jurisdictions within the same institution. The dividing lines often remain vague, however. Home economics and music are examples. Home economics might be offered by a school of agriculture, a school of home economics, and a school of education, all in the same university. For this index, some fields of study have been combined in recognition of this commonality. For instance, although there may be three separate de-

partments providing study in musicology, performance, and music education, in practice it is relatively unusual for an institution to offer one and not the others.

7. The abbreviations used for the institutions are meant to be understandable as they stand. If they are not, the reader can refer to the explanatory table that precedes this index. As a final note, the slash mark means *only* "and/or" in this index, as throughout this book.

Agriculture

(Typically includes Agricultural Economics, Agribusiness, Agricultural Education, Agricultural Engineering, Agronomy, Animal Husbandry, Animal Sciences, Dairy Science, Plant Science, Plant Pathology, Plant Physiology, Poultry Science; may include Agricultural Extension, Crop Science, Soils Sciences)

Ala. A&M U.
Angelo St. U.
Ariz. St. U.
U. Ariz.
Ark. St. U.
U. Ark.
Auburn U.
S.F. Austin St. U.
B.Y.U.
Cal. Poly. St. U. (Pomona)
Cal. Poly St. U. (San Luis Obispo)
Cal. St. U. (Chico)
Cal. St. U. (Fresno)
U. Cal. (Berkeley)
U. Cal. (Davis)
U. Cal. (Riverside)
Cent. Mo. St. U.
Clemson U.
Colo. St. U.
U. Conn.
Cornell U.
Corpus Christi St. U.
U. Del.
Drexel U.
East. Ky. U.
East Tex. St. U.
Fla. A&M U.
Fla. St. U.
U. Fla.
U. Georgia
U. Hawaii
U. Idaho
Ill. St. U.
U. Ill.
Iowa St. U.
Kans. St. U.
Kent St. U.
U. Ky.
L.S.U.
U. Maine
U. Md.
M.I.T.
U. Mass.
Mich. St. U.
U. Minn.
U. Mo. (Columbia)
Miss. St. U. Women
Miss. St. U.
Mont. St. U.
Murray St. U.
U. Neb.
U. Nev. (Reno)

U. N.H.
S.U.N.Y.C. Environ. Sci. & For. (Syracuse)
N. Mex. St. U.
No. Car. A&T C.
No. Car. St. U. (Raleigh)
No. Dak. St. U.
Northwest Mo. St. U.
Ohio St. U.
Okla. St. U.
Ore. St. U.
Penn. St. U.
Prairie View A&M U.
U. Puerto Rico
Purdue U.
U. Rhode Island
Rutgers U.
Sam Houston St. U.
Santa Clara U.
So. Car. St. U.
So. Dak. St. U.
So. Ill. U. (Carbondale)
Southern U.
Southwest Tex. St. U.
Sul Ross St. U.
Stanford U.
Tarleton St. U.
Tenn. St. U.
U. Tenn.
Tex. A&I U.
Tex. A&M U.
Tex. Tech. U.
Tuskegee Inst.
Utah St. U.
U. Vt.
Va. Poly. Inst.
Va. St. U.
Wash. St. U.
U. Wash.
Wayne St. U.
West Tex. St. U.
W. Va. U.
West. Ill. U.
West. Ky. U.
U. Wis.
U. Wis. (River Falls)
U. Wyo.

Architecture

Ariz. St. U.
U. Ariz.
Auburn U.
Ball St. U.
Cal. Poly. St. U. (Pomona)
Cal. Poly. St. U. (San Luis Obispo)
Cal. St. Poly. U. (Pomona)
U. Cal. (Berkeley)
U.C.L.A.
Carnegie-Mellon U.
Catholic U.
C.C.N.Y.(C.U.N.Y.)
U. Cincinnati
Clemson U.
Columbia U.
Cornell U.
Cranbrook Acad. Art

Fla. A&M U.
U. Fla.
Georgia Inst. Tech.
Harard U.
U. Hawaii
Howard U.
U. of Houston
U. Idaho
Ill. Inst. Tech
U. Ill.
U. Ill. (Chicago)
Iowa St. U.
Johns Hopkins U.
Kans. St. U.
U. Kans.
Kent St. U.
L.S.U.
La. Tech U.
U. of Md.
M.I.T.
Miami U. (Ohio)
U. Miami (Fla.)
U. Mich.
U. Minn.
Miss. St. U.
Morgan St. U.
U. Neb.
U. Nev.
N.J.I.T.
U. N. Mex.
S.U.N.Y. (Buffalo)
No. Car. St. U. (Raleigh)
No. Dak. St. U.
U. Notre Dame
Ohio St. U.
Okla. St. U.
U. Okla.
U. Ore.
Penn. St. U.
U. Penn.
Pratt Inst.
Princeton U.
U. Puerto Rico
Rhode Island Sh. D.
R.P.I.
Rice U.
U. So. Cal.
U. So. Fla.
Syracuse U.
Tex. A&M U.
Texas Tech. U.
Tulane U.
Tuskegee Inst.
U. of Arts
U. Tenn.
U. Tex. (Arlington)
U. Tex. (Austin)
U. Utah
Va. Poly. Inst.
U. Va.
Wash. St. U.
Wash. U.
U. Wash.
U. Wis. (Milwaukee)
Yale U.

NAVAL ARCHITECTURE

U. Cal. (Berkeley)
U. Mich.

Area Studies

U. Ala.
U. Ariz.
Ball St. U.
Baylor U.
Boston C.
Boston St. U.
Boston U.
Bowl. Gr. St. U.
Brandeis U.
B.Y.U.
Brown U.
Cal. St. U. (Fullerton)
Cal. St. U. (Long Beach)
Cal. St. U. (L.A.)
Cal. St. U. (San Diego)
U. Cal. (Berkeley)
U.C.L.A.
U. Cal. (San Diego)
Case West. Reserve U.
Catholic U.
U. Chicago
C. C. N. Y. (C.U.N.Y.)
Claremont Grad. Sch.
Columbia U.
U. Conn.
U. Dayton
Fairfield U.
Fisk U.
Fla. St. U.
U. Fla.
Georgetown U.
George Washington U.
Gov. St. U.
Harvard U.
U. Hawaii
Howard U.
Hunter C. (C.U.N.Y.)
U. Ill.
Ind. U.
U. Iowa
John Carroll U.
Johns Hopkins U.
U. Kans.
L.S.U.
U. Md.
U. Miami (Fla.)
Mich. St. U.
U. Mich.
U. Minn.
U. Mo. (Columbia)
Monterey Inst.
N. Mex. Highlands U.
U. N. Mex.
C.U.N.Y.
S.U.N.Y. (Albany)
S.U.N.Y. (Binghamton)
S.U.N.Y (Buffalo)
N.Y.U.
Northeastern Ill. U.
No. Ill. U.
No. W. St. U. La.
U. Notre Dame
U. Ore.
Penn. St. U.
U. Penn.
Pepperdine U.
Princeton U.
U. Puerto Rico

Purdue U.
Queens C. (C.U.N.Y.)
St. John's U. (N.Y.)
St. Louis U.
St. Michael's C.
Seton Hall U.
U. So. Cal
So. Meth. U.
Stanford U.
Stetson U.
Syracuse U.
U. Tex. (Austin)
Tulane U.
Union C. (N.Y.)
Utah St. U.
U. Utah
Vanderbilt U.
Vassar C.
Wash. St. U.
Wash. U.
U. Wash.
Wayne St. U.
West. Car. U.
West. Mich. U.
U. Wis.
U. Wyo.
Yale U.
Yeshiva U.

AFRICAN/ AFRO-AMERICAN STUDIES

U. Albany (S.U.N.Y.)
Boston U.
Brown U.
U.C.L.A.
C.C.N.Y. (C.U.N.Y.)
Clark Atlanta U.
Columbia U.
Cornell U.
Duquesne U.
Emory U.
Fisk U.
U. Fla.
George Washington U.
Howard U.
U. Ill.
U. Iowa
Johns Hopkins U.
U. Md. (Baltimore County)
Morgan St. U.
No. Car. A&T St. U.
Northwestern U.
S.U.N.Y. (Albany)
S.U.N.Y.C. (Brockport)
U. Notre Dame
Ohio St. U.
Ohio U.
Princeton U.
St. John's U. (N.Y.)
Temple U.
U. Tex.
U. Wis..
Yale U.

ASIAN STUDIES

U. Ariz.
B.Y.U.
Cal. St. U. (Long Beach)

U. Cal. (Berkeley)
U.C.L.A.
U. Cal. (San Diego)
U. Cal. (Santa Barbara)
U. Chicago
Columbia U.
Cornell U.
Fla. St. U.
George Washington U.
Harvard U.
U.. Hawaii
U. Ill.
Ind. U.
U. Iowa
Johns Hopkins U.
U. Kans.
U. Mich.
Monterey Inst.
C.U.N.Y. (Grad. Cent.)
U. Notre Dame
N.Y.U.
Ohio U.
U. Ore
U. Penn.
U. Pitt.
Princeton U.
St. John's C. (N.M.)
St. John's U. (N.Y.)
S.D.S.U.
U. San Fran.
U. So. Ca.
Seton Hall U.
Stanford U.
U. Tex.
U. Va.
Wash. U. (Mo.)
U. Wash.
U. Wis.
Yale U.

BRAZILIAN STUDIES
U. Minn.
N.Y.U.

CANADA AREA STUDIES
Johns Hopkins U.

CARIBBEAN STUDIES
Fisk U.
S.U.N.Y. (Binghamton)

EGYPTOLOGY
Brown U.
U. Chicago
Johns Hopkins U.

EUROPEAN STUDIES
George Washington U.
Ind. U.
Johns Hopkins U.
C.U.N.Y. (Grad. Cent.)
U. Mich.
Princeton U.

HISPANIC/IBERIAN STUDIES
Brown U.
Catholic U.
C.U.N.Y. (Grad. Cent.)
Conn. C.
Ind. U.
Johns Hopkins U.
U. Minn.
U. N. Mex.
N.Y.U.
U. Notre Dame
U. Puerto Rico
So. Meth. U.

Vassar C.
U. Wis.

INDO-EUROPEAN STUDIES
U.C.L.A.
U. Chicago

ISLAMIC STUDIES/ LITERATURE
U.C.L.A.
Catholic U.
U. Chicago
Dropsie U.
Johns Hopkins U.

LATIN AMERICAN STUDIES
U. Albany (S.U.N.Y.)
American U.
U. Ala.
U. Ariz.
Brown U.
B.Y.U.
Cal. St. U. (L.A.)
U. Cal. (Berkeley)
U.C.L.A
U. Cal. (San Diego)
U. Cal. (Santa Barbara)
Catholic U. of P.R.
U. Chicago
U. of Conn.
Cornell U.
Duke U.
U. Fla.
Georgetown U.
Geo. Wash. U.
Ind. U.
U. Ill. (Chicago)
Johns Hopkins U.
U. Kans.
L. S. U.
Monterey Inst.
U. N. Mex.
U. Notre Dame
N.Y.U.
Ohio U.
U. of Pac.
U. Pitt.
Princeton U.
Queens C. (C.U.N.Y.)
S.D.S.U.
So. Meth. U.
Stanford U.
U. Tex. (Austin)
Tulane U.
Vanderbilt U.
U. Wis.

MEDITERRANEAN STUDIES
Brandeis U.

MEXICAN- AMERICAN STUDIES
Cal. St. U. (L.A.)
Cal. St. U. (Northridge)
Cal. St. U. (San Jose)

NEAR/MIDDLE EASTERN STUDIES
U. Ariz.
Brandeis U.
Brown U.
B.Y.U.
U. Cal. (Berkeley)
U. Chicago
Columbia U.
Cornell U.
Georgetown U.
George Washington U.

Harvard U.
Ind. U.
Johns Hopkins U.
U. Mich.
Monterey Inst.
N.Y.U.
Ohio St. U.
U. Penn.
Princeton U.
U. Tex. (Austin)
U. Utah
Wash. U.
Yeshiva U.

NEW YORK AREA STUDIES
C.U.N.Y. (Grad. Cent.)

NORTH AMERICAN STUDIES
U. Ala.
U. Alaska
U. Ariz.
Appl. St. U.
Baylor U.
Boston C.
Boston U.
Bow. Gr. St. U.
Brandeis U.
B.Y.U.
Brown U.
Cal. St. U. (Fullerton)
Cal. St. U. (L.A.)
Cal. St. U. (Northridge)
U. Cal. (Berkeley)
U.C.L.A.
Case West. Res. U.
Columbia U.
U. Del.
East Car. U.
East. Mich. U.
Emory U.
Fla. St. U.
George Washington U.
Harvard U.
U. Hawaii
Ind. U.
U. Iowa
Johns Hopkins U.
U. Kans.
U. Md.
U. Mass. (Boston)
Mich. St. U.
U. Mich.
U. Minn.
U. Miss.
N. Mex. Highlands U.
U. N. Mex.
S.U.N.Y. (Buffalo)
S.U.N.Y.C. (Cortland)
N.Y.U.
No. East. St. U.
U. Notre Dame
Penn. St. U.
U. Penn.
Purdue U.
St. Louis
St. Mary's U.
S.D.S.U.
Seton Hall U.
U. So. Maine
Trinity C.
Utah St. U.
Wash. St. U.
C. Wlm. & Mary
U. Wyo.
Yale U.

PACIFIC AREA STUDIES
George Washington U.
U. Hawaii

RUSSIAN/EAST EUROPEAN STUDIES
American U.
Ariz. St. U.
Boston C.
Brown U.
U. Cal. (Davis)
U. Chicago
C.C.N.Y. (C.U.N.Y.)
Columbia U.
Cornell U.
Fla. St. U.
Georgetown U.
George Washington U.
Harvard U.
Hunter C. (C.U.N.Y.)
U. Ill.
U. Ill. (Chicago)
Ind. U.
U. Iowa
Johns Hopkins U.
U. Kans.
Mich. St. U.
U. Mich.
U. Minn.
Monterey Inst.
Ohio St. U.
Princeton U.
U. So. Cal.
Stanford U.
U. Tex. (Austin)
U. Va.
U. Wash.
Wayne St. U.
U. Wis.
Yale U.

URALIC STUDIES
Columbia U.
Ind. U.

Basic Medical Sciences

(Typically includes Anatomy, Microbiology, Pathology, Pharmacology, Physiology; often includes Endocrinology, Neurological Sciences, Parasitology, Virology)

Adelphi U.
U. Ala.
U. Ala. (Birm.)
Albany Med. C.
American U.
Angelo St. U.
Ariz. St. U.
U. Ariz.
U. Ark.
Auburn U.
Ball St. U.
Baylor U.
Boston U.
Bowling Green St. U.
Brandeis U.
B.Y.U.
Brooklyn C. (C.U.N.Y.)
Brown U.
Bryn Mawr C.
Bucknell
Butler U.
Cal. Inst. Tech.
Cal. St. U. (Fresno)
Cal. St. U. (Fullerton)
Cal. St. U. (Long Beach)
Cal. St. U. (L.A.)
Cal. St. U. (San Diego)
U. Cal. (Berkeley)

U. Cal. (Davis)
U. Cal. (Irvine)
U.C.L.A.
U. Cal. (San Diego)
U. Cal. (San Francisco)
Carnegie Mellon U.
Case West. Res. U.
Catholic U.
U. Chicago
U. Cincinnati
C.C.N.Y. (C.U.N.Y.)
Clemson U.
Colo. St. U.
U. Colo.
U. Conn.
Columbia U.
Cornell U.
Creighton U.
Dartmouth C.
U. Dayton
U. Del.
DePaul U.
Drexel U.
Duke U.
Duquesne U.
East Car. U.
East Tenn. St. U.
Emory U.
Fairleigh Dickinson U.
Finch Univ. of Health Sci.
Fla. Inst. Tech.
Fla. St. U.
U. Fla.
Fordham U.
George Mason U.
Georgetown U.
George Washington U.
Georgia Inst. Tech.
Med. C. Georgia
U. Georgia
Harvard U.
U. Hawaii
U. Health Sci. (Chicago)
Howard U.
Hunter C. (C.U.N.Y.)
Idaho St. U.
U. Idaho
Ill. Inst. Tech.
U. Ill. (Chicago)
Ind. St. U.
Ind. U.
Iowa St. U.
U. Iowa
James Madison U.
Johns Hopkins U.
Kans. St. U.
U. Kans.
Kent St. U.
U. Ky.
Lehigh U.
Loma Linda U.
L.I.U.
L.S.U. Med. Cent.
La. Tech. U.
U. Louisville
Loyola U. Chicago
U. Maine
Marquette U.
Mayo Grad. Sch.
U. Md.
U. Md. (Baltimore)
M.I.T.
U. Mass.
McNeese St. U.
Meharry Med. C.
Miami U.
U. Miami
Mich. St. U.
Mich. Tech. U.
U. Mich.
U. Minn.

U. Chicago
U. Cincinnati
C.C.N.Y. (C.U.N.Y)
Clarion U. Pa.
Clark Atlanta U.
Clark U.
Clemson U.
Cleve. St. U.
Colo. St. U.
U. Colo.
U. Colo. Health Sci. C.
Columbia U.
U. Conn.
U. Conn. Health Sci. C.
Cornell U.
Creighton U.
Dartmouth C.
U. Dayton
U. Del.
Del. St. U.
Delta St. U.
U. Denver
DePaul U.
U. Detroit Mercy
Drake U.
Drexel U.
Duke U.
Duquesne U.
East Car. U.
East Stroudsburg U. Pa.
East Tenn. St. U.
East. Ill. U.
East. Ky. U.
East. Mich. U.
East. N. Mex. U.
East Tex. St. U.
East. Va. Med. C.
East. Wash U.
Edinboro U. Pa.
Emory U.
Emporia St. U.
Fairleigh Dickinson U.
Fisk U.
Fla. Ag. Mech. U.
Fla. Atlantic U.
Fla. Inst. Tech.
Fla. St. U.
U. Fla.
Fordham U.
Fort Hays St. U.
Framingham St. U.
Frostburg St. U.
George Mason U.
Georgetown U.
George Washington U.
Med. C. Georgia
Georgia C.
    (Milledgeville)
Georgia Inst. Tech.
Georgia So. C.
Georgia St. U.
U. Georgia
Governors St. U.
Hampton U.
U. Hartford
Harvard U.
U. Hawaii
U. Health Sci. (Chicago)
Hofstra U.
U. Houston
Howard U.
Humboldt St. U.
Hunter C. (C. U.N.Y.)
Idaho St. U.
U. Idaho
Ill. Inst. Tech.
Ill. St. U.
U. Ill.
U. Ill. (Chicago)
Incarnate Word C.
U. Indianapolis
Ind. Cent. U.
Ind. St. U.

Ind. U.
Ind. U. Penn.
Iowa St. U.
U. Iowa
Jackson St. U.
Jacksonville St. U.
J. Madison U.
John Carroll U.
Johns Hopkins U.
Kans. St. U.
U. Kans.
Kent St. U.
U. Ky.
Lamar U.
Lehigh U.
Lehman C. (C.U.N.Y.)
Loma Linda U.
L.I.U.
L.S.U.
L.S.U. Med. C.
La. Tech. U.
U. Louisville
Loyola U. Chicago
Loyola U. (La.)
U. Maine
Manhattan C.
Mankato St. U.
Marquette U.
Marshall U.
U. Md. (Baltimore)
U. Md. (Baltimore
    County)
Marywood C.
M.I.T.
U. Mass.
Mayo Grad. Sch.
McNeese St. U.
Meharry Med. C.
U. Memphis
Miami U. (Ohio)
U. Miami (Fla.)
Mich. St. U.
Mich. Tech. U.
U. Mich.
Mid. Tenn. St. U.
Midwest St. U.
Millersville U. Pa.
Miss. C.
U. Minn.
Miss. St. U.
U. Miss.
U. Mo. (Columbia)
U. Mo. (K.C.)
U. Mo. (St. Louis)
Mont. St. U.
U. Mont.
Montclair St. U.
Morehead St. U.
Mt. Sinai Sch. of Med.
    (C.U.N.Y.)
Murray St. U.
U. Neb. (Omaha)
U. Nev.
U. Nev. (Reno)
U. N.H.
U. New Haven
U. Med. & Dent. N.J.
N. Mex. Highlands U.
N. Mex. St. U.
U. N. Mex.
U. N. Orleans
U. N. Orleans (Med.
    Cent.)
N. Sch. Social Research
Pittsburgh St. U.
S.U.N.Y. (Albany)
S.U.N.Y. (Binghamton)
S.U.N.Y. (Buffalo)
S.U.N.Y. (Stony Brook)
S.U.N.Y.C. (Brockport)
S.U.N.Y.C. (Buffalo)
S.U.N.Y.C. (Fredonia)
S.U.N.Y.C. (Geneseo)

S.U.N.Y.C. (New Paltz)
S.U.N.Y.C. (Oneonta)
S.U.N.Y.C. (Plattsburg)
S.U.N.Y.C. Environ. Sci.
    & For. (Syracuse)
N.Y. Inst. Tech.
N.Y. Med. C.
N.Y.U.
U. No. Alabama
No. Car. Ag. & Tech.
No. Car. Cent. U.
No. Car. St. U. (Raleigh)
U. No. Car. (Chapel Hill)
U.N.C. (Charlotte)
U. No. Car. (Greensboro)
U. No. Colo.
No. Dak. St. U.
U. No. Dak.
U. No. Fla.
U. No. Tex.
Northeastern U.
Northeastern Ill. U.
Northeast La. U.
No. E. Mo. St. U.
No. Ariz. U.
U. No. Colo.
No. Ill. U.
U. No. Iowa
No. Mich. U.
Northwest Mo. St. U.
Northwestern St. U. La.
Northwestern U.
U. Notre Dame
Oakland U.
Occidental C.
Med. C. Ohio
Ohio St. U.
Ohio U.
Okla. St. U.
U. Okla.
U. Okla. Health Sci. C.
Old Dom. U.
Oreg. Grad. Inst. Sci. &
    Tech.
Oregon Health Sc. U.
Ore. St. U.
U. Ore.
Pac. U.
U. Pac.
Med. C. Penn.
Penn. St. U.
U. Penn.
Pittsburg St. U.
U. Pitt.
Portland St. U.
Prairie View A&M U.
Princeton U.
U. Puerto Rico
Purdue U.
Purdue U. (Calumet)
Queens C. (C.U.N.Y.)
Quinnipiac C.
R.P.I.
Rhode Island C.
U. Rhode Island
Rice U.
U. Richmond
U. Rochester
Rockefeller U.
Rockford C.
Rollins C.
Roosevelt U.
Rutgers U.
Rush U.
St. Cloud St. U.
St. John's U. (N.Y.)
St. Joseph C. (CT.)
St. Louis U.
St. Mary's U.
Sam Houston St. U.
San Fran. St. U.
U. San Fran.
S.D.S.U.

San Jose St. U.
Seton Hall U.
Shippensburg U. Pa.
Smith C.
Sonoma St. U.
U. So. Ala.
Med. U. So. Car.
So. Car. St. U.
U. So. Car.
So. Dak. St. U.
U. So. Dak.
U. So. Fla.
Southeast Conn. St. U.
Southeast Mo. St. U.
Southeastern Mass. U.
U. So. Cal.
So. Conn. St. U.
So. Ill. U.
So. Ill. U. (Edwardsville)
So. Meth. U.
U. So. Miss.
So. U. A&M C.
Southwest Mo. St. U.
Southwest Tex. St. U.
U. Southwestern La.
Stanford U.
S.F. Austin St. U.
Stevens Inst. Tech.
Sul Ross St. U.
Syracuse U.
Temple U.
Tenn. St. U.
Teachers C.
    (Columbia U.)
Tenn. Tech. U.
U. Tenn.
U. Tenn. (Memphis)
Tex. A&I U.
Tex. A&M U.
Tex. Christ. U.
Tex. So. U.
Tex. Tech. U.
U. Tex. (Arlington)
U. Tex. (Austin)
U. Tex. (Dallas)
U. Tex. (El Paso)
U. Tex. (San Antonio)
U. Tex. (Southwestern
    Med. Sch. Dallas)
U. Tex. (Tyler)
Tex. Woman's U.
Thom. Jeff. U.
U. Toledo
Towson St. U.
Tufts U.
Tulane U.
U. Tulsa
Tuskegee U.
Utah St. U.
U. Utah
U. Vt.
Vanderbilt U.
Villanova U.
Va. Commonwealth U.
Va. Poly. Inst.
Va. St. U.
U. Va.
Wake Forest U.
Walla Walla C.
Wash. St. U.
Wash. U. (Mo.)
U. Wash.
Wayne St. U.
Wesleyan U.
West Chester U. Pa.
West Tex. St. U.
W. Va. U.
West. Car. U.
West. Ill. U.
West. Ky. U.
West. Mich. U.
West N. Mex. U.
West. Wash. U.

Wichita St. U.
Wilkes C.
C. Wm. & Mary
Wm. Patterson C. N.J.
Winona St. U.
Med. C. Wis.
Wis. St. U. (Oshkosh)
Wis. St. U. (Platteville)
U. Wis.
U. Wis. (Eau Claire)
U. Wis. (La Crosse)
U. Wis. (Milwaukee)
U. Wis. (Stevens Point)
U. Wis. (Stout)
Worcester Poly. Inst.
Worcester St. U.
Wright St. U.
U. Wyo.
Yale U.
Yeshiva U.
Youngstown St. U.

BIOCHEMISTRY
Adelphi U.
U. Akron
U. Ala. (Birmingham)
U. Albany (S.U.N.Y)
U. Ak.
Albany Med. C.
Ariz. St. U.
U. Ariz.
U. Ark.
Baylor C. Med.
Baylor U.
Boston C.
Boston U.
Brandeis U.
B.Y.U.
Brown U.
Bryn Maw C.
Cal. St. U. (Fullerton)
Cal. St. U. (Hayward)
Cal. St. U. (Long Beach)
Cal. St. U. (L.A.)
U. Cal. (Berkeley)
U. Cal. (Davis)
U. Cal. (Irvine)
U. C. L.A.
U. Cal. (Riverside)
U. Cal. (San Diego)
U. Cal. (San Fran.)
U. Cal. (Santa Barbara)
Carnegie Mellon U.
Case West. Res. U.
C.C.N.Y. (C.U.N.Y.)
U. Chicago
U. Cincinnati
Clemson U.
Colo. St. U.
U. Colo.
Columbia U.
U. Conn. Health Cent.
Cornell U.
Creighton U.
Dartmouth C.
U. Del.
Duke U.
East. Car. U.
East Tenn. St. U.
Emory U.
Finch U. of Health Sci.
Fla. St. U.
U. Fla.
Georgetown U.
George Washington U.
Med. C. Georgia
Georgia Inst. Tech.
Georgia St. U.
U. Georgia
Harvard U.
U. Hawaii
U. Health Sci. (Chicago)
U. Houston

Howard U.
U. Idaho
Ill. Inst. Tech.
U. Ill.
U. Ill. (Chicago)
Ind. U.
Iowa St. U.
U. Iowa
Johns Hopkins U.
Kans. St. U.
U. Kans.
Kent St. U.
U. Ky.
Loma Linda U.
L.S.U. Med. Cent.
U. Louisville
Loyola U. Chicago
U. Maine
U. Md.
U. Md. (Baltimore)
U. Md. (Baltimore County)
M.I.T.
U. Mass.
U. Mass. (Lowell)
U. Mass. (Med. C. Worcester)
Mayo Grad. Sch.
Meharry Med. C.
Miami U.
U. Miami
Mich. St. U.
U. Mich.
U. Minn. (Duluth)
Miss. St. U.
U. Miss. Med. C.
U. Mo. (Columbia)
U. Mo. (K.C.)
Mont. St. U.
U. Mont.
Mt. Sinai Sch. Med. (C.U.N.Y.)
U. Neb.
U. Neb. Med. Ctr.
U. Nev. (Reno)
U.N.H.
U. Med. & Dent. N.J.
N. Mex. Inst. M&T
N. Mex. St. U.
U. N. Mex.
S.U.N.Y. (Buffalo)
S.U.N.Y. (Stony Brook)
S.U.N.Y. Health Sci. Cent. (Brooklyn)
S.U.N.Y. Health Sci. Cent. (Syracuse)
New York Med. C.
N. Y. U.
No. Car. St. U.
U. No. Car. (Chapel Hill)
No. Dak. St. U.
U. N. Dak.
U. No. Tex.
Northwestern U.
U. Notre Dame
Med. C. Ohio
Ohio St. U.
Okla. St. U.
U. Okla. Health Sci. C.
Old Dominion U.
Ore. Grad Inst. Sci. Tech
Ore. Health Sci.
Ore. St. U.
U. Ore.
U. Pac.
Med. C. Penn.
Penn St. U.
U. Penn.
U. Pitt.
U. Puerto Rico
Purdue U.

Queens U. (C.U.N.Y.)
R.P.I.
U. R.I.
Rice U.
U. Rochester
Rush U.
Rutgers U.
St. Louis U.
U. San Fran.
San Jose St. U.
U. Scranton
Seton Hall U.
U. So. Cal.
Med. U. So. Car.
So. Dak. St. U.
U. So. Dak.
So. Ill. U.
U. So. Miss.
So. U. A & M.C.
Stanford U.
Stevens Inst. Tech.
Temple U.
U. Tenn.
U. Tenn. (Memphis)
Tex. A&M U.
Tex. Tech. U.
U. Tex. (Austin)
U. Tex. Health Sci. C. (Dallas)
U. Tex. Health Sci. C. (Houston)
U. Tex. Health Sci. C. (San Antonio)
U. Tex. Med. Branch (Galveston)
Tho. Jeff. U.
U. Toledo
Tufts U.
Tulane U.
Utah St. U.
U. Utah
Va. Commonwealth U.
Va. Poly. Inst.
U. Va.
Vanderbilt U.
Villanova U.
U. Vt.
Wake Forest U.
Wash. St. U.
U. Wash.
Wayne St. U.
Wesleyan U.
W. Va. U.
Med. C. Wis.
U. Wis.
Wright St. U.
Yale U.
Yeshiva U.

BIOMATHEMATICS/ BIOSTATISTICS

U. Ala. (Birmingham)
Boston U.
U. Cal. (Berkeley)
U.C.L.A.
Case West. Res. U.
U. Cinn.
Columbia U.
Drexel U.
Emory U.
Geo. Mason U.
Georgetown U.
Geo. Wash. U.
U. Hawaii
Harvard U.
Johns Hopkins U.
U. Ill. (Chicago)
U. Iowa
Loma Linda U.
U. Mass.
Med. U. of So. Ca.
U. Mich.
U. Minn.

N.Y. Med. C.
N.Y.U.
S.U.N.Y. (Buffalo)
S.U.N.Y. (Stony Brook)
No. Car. St. U. (Raleigh)
U. N.C. (Chapel Hill)
Ohio St. U.
U. Okla. Health Sci. C.
U. Pitt.
S.D.S.U.
Med. U. So Car.
U. So. Car.
Tulane U.
U. Utah
Vanderbilt U.
Va. Commonwealth U.
U. V.
West. Mich. U.
U. Wash.
Med. C. Wis.
Yale U.

BIOMETRY/ BIOMETRICS

U. Ala.
U. Albany (S.U.N.Y.)
U.C.L.A.
Case West. Res. U.
U. Cincinnati
U. Colo. Health Sci. C.
Columbia U.
Cornell U.
L. S. U. Med. Ctr.
U. Minn.
Mt. Sinai Sch. Med. (C.U.N.Y.)
U. Neb.
No. Car. St. U. (Raleigh)
U. N.C. (Chapel Hill)
U. N. Orleans Med. C.
S.U.N.Y. (Buffalo)
Oregon St. U.
U. So. Cal.
Med. U. So. Car.
Temple U.
U. Tex. Health Sc. Houston
Va. Commonwealth U.
Med. C. Wis.
U. Wis.

BIOPHYSICS

U. Ala.
Ariz. St. U.
U. Ark.
Baylor C. of Med.
Boston U.
Brandeis U.
Cal. Inst. Tech.
Carnegie Mellon U.
Case West. Res. U.
U. Cal. (Berkeley)
U. Cal. (Davis)
U. Cal. (Irvine)
U. Cal. (San Diego)
U. Cal. (San Fran.)
U. Chicago
U. Cincinnati
Clemson U.
Colo St. U.
U. Colo.
Columbia U.
U. Conn.
Cornell U.
Duke U.
Emory U.
Fla. St. U.
Georgetown U.
Harvard U.
U. Hawaii
U. Houston
Howard U.
U. Ill.

U. Ill. (Chicago)
Ind. U.
Iowa St. U.
U. Iowa
Johns Hopkins U.
U. Ky.
U. Louisville
L. S. U. Med. Ctr.
U. Md. (Baltimore)
Mayo Grad. Sch.
U. Miami
Mich. St. U.
U. Mich.
M.I.T.
U. Minn.
U. Miss.
U. Mo. (Kansas City)
U. Neb.
U. Med. & Dent. N.J.
S.U.N.Y. (Buffalo)
S.U.N.Y. (Stony Brook)
S.U.N.Y. Health Sci. Cent. (Brooklyn)
N.Y.U.
Northwestern U.
U. Notre Dame
Med. C. Ohio
Ohio St. U.
U. Okla. Health Sci. Cent.
Ore. St. U.
Med. C. Penn./ Hahnemann Med. C.
U. Penn.
U. Pitt.
Princeton U.
Purdue U.
R.P.I.
U. Rhode Island
U. Rochester
U. So. Cal.
U. So. Fla.
Stanford U.
Syracuse U.
U. Tenn. (Memphis)
Tex. A&M U.
U. Tex. (Houston)
U. Tex. (Southwestern Med. Sch. Dallas)
U. Tex. Med. (Galveston)
U. Vt.
Va. Commonwealth U.
U. Va.
Vanderbilt U.
Wash. St. U.
Wash. U.
U. Wash.
Med. C. Wis.
U. Wis.
Wright St. U.
Yale U.
Yeshiva U.

CANCER BIOLOGY

U. Ariz.
Harvard U.
Northwestern U.
Stanford U.
Wayne St. U.
Yeshiva U.

CELL BIOLOGY

U. Ala.
Albany Med. C.
U. Albany (S.U.N.Y.)
Ariz. St. U.
U. Ariz.
Auburn U.
Baylor C. Med.
Boston U.
Brandeis U.
Brown U.
Cal. Inst. Tech.
U. Cal. (Berkeley)

U. Cal. (Davis)
U. Cal. (Irvine)
U.C.L.A.
U. Cal. (San Diego)
U. Cal. (San Fran.)
Carnegie Mellon U.
Case West. Res. U.
Catholic U.
U. Chicago
U. Cincinnati.
Colo. St. U.
U. Colo.
U. Colo. Health Sci. Cent.
Columbia U.
U. Conn.
U. Conn. Health C.
Cornell U.
Creighton U.
Dartmouth C.
Duke U.
East Car. U.
East Tenn. St. U.
Emory U.
Emporia St. U.
Finch U. Health Sci.
Fla. St. U.
U. Fla.
Geo. Mason U.
Geo. Wash. U.
Georgetown U.
U. Georgia
Harvard U.
U. Hawaii
Ill. Inst. Tech.
U. Ill.
U. Ill. (Chicago)
Ind. St. U.
Ind. U.
Iowa State U.
U. Iowa
James Madison U.
Johns Hopkins U.
Kansas St. U.
U. Kans.
Kent St. U.
L. I. U.
L. S. U. Med. Cent.
Loyola U. (Chicago)
U. Md.
U. Md. (Baltimore)
U. Md. (Baltimore C.)
Marquette U.
M.I.T.
U. Mass.
U. Mass. Med. Cent. (Worcester)
Med. C. Ga.
U. Memphis
U. Miami
Mich. St. U.
U. Mich.
U. Minn.
Mt. Sinai Sch. Med. (C.U.N.Y.)
U. Mo. (Kansas City)
U. Neb.
U. Nev. (Reno)
U. Med. & Dent. N.J.
U. N. Mex.
S.U.N.Y. (Buffalo)
S.U.N.Y. (Stony Brook)
S.U.N.Y. Health Sci. Cent. (Brooklyn)
S.U.N.Y. Health Sci. Cent. (Syracuse)
N.Y. Med. C.
N.Y.U.
No. Car. St. U.
U. No. Car. (Chapel Hill)
No. Dak. St. U.
U. No. Tex.
No. East Ohio U. Col. Med.

Northwestern U.
U. Notre Dame
Oakland U.
Med. C. Ohio
Ohio St. U.
Ohio U.
U. Okla.
Oregon Health Sci. U.
Ore. St. U.
Med. C.
   Penn./Hahnemann U.
Penn. St. U.
U. Penn.
U. Pitt.
Purdue U.
R.P.I.
Rice U.
U.R.I.
U. Rochester
Rush U.
Rutgers U.
St. Louis U.
S.D.S.U.
San Fran. St. U.
U. So. Ala.
U. So. Cal.
Med. U. So. Car.
U. So. Car.
U. So Fla.
Stanford U.
Temple U.
U. Tenn.
U. Tenn. (Memphis)
Tex. A&M U.
Tex. Tech. U.
U. Tex. (Dallas)
U. Tex. (San Antonio)
U. Tex. Health Sci. Cent.
   (Houston)
U. Tex. Health Sci. Cent.
   (San Antonio)
U. Tex. Med. Br.
   (Galveston)
U. Tex.(Southwest. Med.
   Cent., Dallas)
Thom. Jeff. U.
Tufts U.
Tulane U.
U. Tulsa
Utah St. U.
U. Utah
Vanderbilt U.
U. Vt.
U. Va.
Va. Commonwealth U.
Va. Poly. Inst. & St. U.
Wash. St. U.
Wash. U.
U. Wash.
Wayne St. U.
Wesleyan U.
W. Va. U.
Med. C. Wis.
U. Wis.
Yale U.
Yeshiva U.

**ENVIRONMENTAL
BIOLOGY**
Frostburg St. U.
Governors St. U.
Hood C.
U. Mass. (Boston)
S.U.N.Y.C. Environ. Sci.
   For.
N.Y.U.
U. No Dak.
Ohio U.
San Fran. St. U.
Sonoma St. U.
U. So. Miss.
U. Southwestern La.

Tulane U.
Wash. U.

GENETIC
U. Ala.
Albany Med. C.
U. Albany (S.U.N.Y.)
Ariz. St. U.
U. Ariz.
Baylor C. of Med.
Brandeis U.
Brown U.
B.Y.U.
Cal. Inst. Tech.
Cal. St. U. (Dominguez
   Hills)
U. Cal. (Berkeley)
U. Cal. (Davis)
U. Cal. (Irvine)
U.C.L.A.
U. Cal. (San Diego)
U. Cal. (San Fran.)
Carnegie Mellon U.
Case West. Res. U.
Catholic U.
U. Chicago
U. Cincinnati
Clemson U.
Colo. St. U.
U. Colo. Health Sci. Cent.
Columbia U.
U. Conn.
Cornell U.
Creighton U.
U. Del.
Duke U.
Emory U.
Fla. St. U.
U. Fla.
Geo. Wash. U.
U. Georgia
Harvard U.
Howard U.
U. Hawaii
Ill. St. U.
U. Ill. (Chicago)
Ind. U.
Iowa St. U.
Johns Hopkins U.
Kans. St. U.
U. Kans. Med. Cent.
L.S.U. Med. Ctr.
U. Md. (Baltimore)
Marquette U.
U. Mass. Med. Cent.
   (Worcester)
U. Miami
M.I.T.
Mich. St. U.
U. Mich.
U. Minn.
Miss. St. U.
U. Mo. (Columbia)
Mont. St. U.
U. Med. & Dent. N.J.
S.U.N.Y. (Buffalo)
S.U.N.Y. (Stony Brook)
U. N.H.
N.Y.U.
U. No. Car. (Chapel Hill)
U. No. Tex.
U. Notre Dame
Northwestern U.
Med. C. Ohio
Ohio St. U.
Okla. St. U.
Ore. Health Sci. U.
Ore. St. U.
U. Ore.
Penn. St. U.
U. Penn.
U. Pitt.

Purdue U.
U. Rochester
Rockefeller U.
Rutgers U.
Sarah Lawrence C.
U. So. Cal.
Med. U. So. Car.
U. So. Car.
Stanford U.
Temple U.
U. Tenn.
Tex. A&M U.
U. Tex.
U. Tex. Health Sci. Cent.
   (Houston)
U. Tex. Health Sci. Cent.
   (San Antonio)
U. Tex. Health Sci. Cent.
   (Dallas)
Thom. Jeff. U.
Tufts U.
Tulane U.
U. Utah
Va. Commonwealth U.
Va. Poly. Inst.
Wake Forest U.
Wash. St. U.
Wash. U.
U. Wash.
Wayne St. U.
W. Va. U.
U. Wis.
Yale U.
Yeshiva U.

MARINE BIOLOGY
U. Alaska
U. Houston
U. Md.
U. Miami
Nova U.
U. So. Fla.

**MOLECULAR
BIOLOGY**
U. Ala.
Albany Med. C.
U. Albany (S.U.N.Y.)
Ariz. St. U.
U. Ariz.
Auburn U.
Baylor C. of Med.
Brown U.
Cal. Inst. Tech.
U. Cal. (Berkeley)
U. Cal. (Irvine)
U.C.L.A.
U. Cal. (San Diego)
U. Cal. (San Francisco)
Carnegie Mellon U.
Case West. Res. U.
U. Chicago
U. Cinn.
Clark U.
Colo. St. U.
U. Colo.
U. Colo. Health Sci. Cent.
Columbia U.
U. Conn.
U. Conn. Health Cent.
Cornell U.
U. Del.
Drexel U.
Duke U.
Emory U.
Fla. St. U.
U. Fla.
Geo. Mason Univ.
Geo. Wash. Univ.
Georgetown U.
U. Georgia
Harvard U.

U. Hawaii
U. Ill.
U. Ill. (Chicago)
Iowa St. U.
U. Iowa
Johns Hopkins U.
Kans. St. U.
U. Kans.
Med. Cent.
Kent St. U.
L.S.U. Med. Cent.
Loyola U. (Chicago)
U. Md. (Baltimore)
U. Md. (Baltimore Co.)
Marquette U.
U. Mass. Med. Cent.
   (Worcester)
Mayo Grad. Sch.
U. Miami
Mich. St. U.
U. Mich.
U. Minn.
U. Mo. (Columbia)
Mt. Sinai Sch. Med.
   (C.U.N.Y.)
U. Nev. (Reno)
U. Med. & Dent. N.J.
N. Mex. St. U.
U. N. Mex.
S.U.N.Y. (Buffalo)
S.U.N.Y. (Stony Brook)
S.U.N.Y. Health Sci.
   Cent. (Brooklyn)
S.U.N.Y. Health Sci.
   Cent. (Syracuse)
N.Y. Med. C.
N.Y.U.
U. No. Car. (Chapel Hill)
Northeastern Ohio U.
U. No. Tex. C. Med.
Northwestern U.
U. Notre Dame
Ohio St. U.
Ohio U.
Ore. Health Sci. U.
U. Oregon
Penn. St. U.
U. Penn.
U. Pitt.
Princeton U.
Purdue U.
R.P.I.
U. Rochester
Rutgers U.
St. Louis U.
S.D.S.U.
San Fran. St. U.
U. So. Cal.
U. So. Car.
So. Ill. U.
U. So. Miss.
Stanford U.
Temple U.
U. Tenn.
U. Tenn. (Memphis)
Tex. A&M U.
U. Tex. (Dallas)
U. Tex. (San Antonio)
U. Tex. Health Sci. Cent.
   (Houston)
U. Tex. Health Sci. Cent.
   (San Antonio)
U. Tex. Med. Br.
   (Galveston)
Tex. Woman's U.
Thom. Jeff. U.
Tufts U.
Tulane U.
Utah St. U.
U. Utah
Vanderbilt U.
U. Vt.

Va. Poly. Inst.
U. Va.
Wake Forest U.
Washington U.
U. Wash.
Wayne St. U.
West. Va. U.
U. Wis.
U. Wyo.
Yale U.
Yeshiva U.

**RADIOLOGICAL
SCIENCES**
U. Cal. (Irvine)
Colo. St. U.
Geo. Wash. U.
Georgetown U.
U. Iowa
U. Okla. U.
U. Tex. (Houston Health
   Sci. C.)
U. Tex. (Southwest. Med.
   Cent.)

Business

(Business Administration,
Commerce, Management:
typically includes specializations in Accounting,
Finance, Marketing; often
includes Advertising, In-
dustrial Administration,
Industrial and Labor relations, Insurance, Opera-
tions Research, Public
Relations, Quality Con-
trol, Real Estate, Taxa-
tion; majors in Economics
are also common in grad-
uate schools of business
as well as in graduate
schools of arts and science)

A.C.U.
Adelphi U.
U. Akron
Ala. A&M U.
Ala. St. U.
U. Ala.
U. Ala. (Birm.)
U. Ala. (Huntsville)
U. Alaska
U. Albany (S.U.N.Y.)
Am. Grad. Sch. Intl. Mgt.
Amer. U.
Andrews U.
Angelo St. U.
Antioch N.E.
Appal. St. U.
Ariz. St. U.
Ariz. St. U. (West)
U. Ariz.
U. Ark.
Ark. St. U.
Armstrong U.
Assump. C.
Auburn U.
Auburn U. (Montgomery)
Augusta C.
Aus. Peay St. U.
Azusa Pac. U.
Babson C.
Ball St. U.
U. Baltimore
Barry U.
Baruch C. (C.U.N.Y.)
Baylor U.
Black Hills St. U.
Bloomsburg U. of Pa.
Boise St. U.

Troy St. U. (Dorthan)
Troy St. U. (Montgomery)
Tufts U.
Tulane U.
U. Tulsa
Union C.
U.S. I. U.
Utah St. U.
U. Utah
Valdosta St. U.
Vanderbilt U.
U. Vt.
Villanova U.
Va. Commonwealth U.
Va. Poly. Inst.
Va. St. U.
U. Va.
Wagner C.
Wake Forest U.
Washburn U.
Wash. St. U.
Wash. U. (Mo.)
U. Wash.
Wayne St. U.
Wayne St. U.
Webster U.
West Chester U. Pa.
West Ga. C.
West Tex. St. U.
W. Va. Grad. C.
W. Va. U.
West. Car. U.
West. Conn. St. U.
West. Ill. U.
West. Ky. U.
West. Mich. U.
West. New Eng. C.
West. N. Mex. U.
West Tex. A&M U.
West Va. Grad. C..
W. Va. U.
West. Wash. St. U.
Wichita St. U.
Widener U.
Wilkes U.
Williamette U.
C. Wm. & Mary
William Carey C.
William Pat. C. N. J.
Winona St. U.
Winthrop U.
U. Wis. (Eau Claire)
U. Wis. (La Crosse)
U. Wis.
U. Wis. (Milwaukee)
U. Wis. (Oshkosh)
U. Wis. (Stevens Point)
U. Wis. (Stout)
U. Wis. (Whitewater)
Worcester Poly. Inst.
Wright St. U.
U. Wyo.
Xavier U. (Ohio)
Yale U.
Youngstown St. U.

ACTUARIAL SCIENCE/ INSURANCE SCIENCES

Ball St. U.
Cent. Conn. St. U.
U. Fla.
Georgia St. U.
U. Hartford
C. Insurance
Ind. U.
U. Mich.
U. Minn.
U. Neb.
N.Y.U.
U. No. Tex.
Penn. St. U.

U. Penn.
Roosevelt U.
Temple U.
Va. Com. U.
U. Wis.
Youngstown St. U.

HOTEL/ HOSPITALITY MANAGEMENT

U. Ala.
Black Hills St. U.
Cent. Mich. U.
Colo. St. U.
Cornell U.
U. Denver
Fairleigh Dickinson U.
Geo. Washington U.
U. Hawaii
U. Houston
Iowa St. U.
Kans. St. U.
U. Md.
U Mass..
Mich. St. U.
U. Nev. (Las Vegas)
U. New Haven
N.Y.U.
U. No. Car. (Greensboro)
U. No. Tex.
Ohio St. U.
Okla. St. U.
Penn. St. U.
Purdue U.
U. So. Cal.
U. So. Car.
Roch. Inst. Tech.
Va. Poly I.
U. Wis. (Stout)

HUMAN RESOURCE MANAGEMENT
(Typically includes Career Management, Personnel Management, Industrial and Labor Relations)

Adelphi U.
U. Ala.
U. Albany (S.U.N.Y)
American U.
Antioch N.E.
Auburn U.
Auburn U. (Mont.)
Baruch C. (C.U.N.Y.)
Boston C.
Bowie St. U.
Cal. St. U. (Hayward)
Chapman U.
Clarkson U.
Cleveland St. U.
U. Conn.
U. Dallas
DePaul U.
Drexel U.
East. Cent. U.
Fairleigh Dickinson U.
U. Fla.
Framingham St. U.
George Washington U.
Georgia St. U.
Golden Gate U.
U. Hartford
Hawaii Pac. U.
U. Houston
U. Ill. (Chicago)
Ind. U.
Inter. Am. U.
Iona C.
Johns Hopkins U.
Loyola U. (Chicago)
Marygrove C.

Mich. St. U.
Moorhead St. U.
National U.
New Sch. Soc. Res.
N.Y.I.T.
N.Y.U.
U. No. Fla.
Ohio St. U.
U. Pitt.
Purdue U.
Rutgers U.
Sage Grad. Sch.
St. Francis (PA)
U. St. Thomas
St. Xavier U.
U. Scranton
U. So. Cal.
So. East Mo. St. U.
Suffolk U.
Temple U.
Tex. A&M U.
Towson St. U.
Troy St. U.
U. Utah
Webster U.
U.W. Va. C. Grad Studies
Widener U.

INFORMATION SCIENCE/SYSTEMS

U. Ala.
U. Albany (S.U.N.Y.)
U. Ark.
American U.
U. Baltimore
Ball St. U.
B.Y.U.
Cal. St. U. (Fresno)
U. Cal. (Irvine)
U.C.L.A.
U. Cal. (San Francisco)
U. Cal. (Santa Cruz)
Carnegie Mellon U.
U. Cent. Okla.
U. Chicago
Claremont Grad. Sch.
Columbia U.
U. Del.
DePaul U.
Drexel U.
East Tenn. St. U.
U. Evansville
U. Fla.
Geo. Mason U.
George Wash. U.
Georgia Inst. Tech.
Georgia St. U.
U. Hawaii
U. Houston
U. Ill.
Ind. U.
Kans. St. U.
Kutztown U. Pa.
L.I.U. (C.W. Post campus)
U. Louisville
U. Md.
U. Md. (Baltimore Co.)
Marquette U.
U. Mass.
Mercer U.
U. Miami
U. Minn.
U. Mo. (Columbia)
U. Nev. (Reno)
U. N. Haven
N.J.I T
S.U.N.Y. (Albany)
S.U.N.Y. (Buffalo)
N.Y.U.
No. Car. Cent. U.
U. No. Car. (Chapel Hill)
U. No. Car. (Greensboro)
U. No. Tex.

Northeastern U.
Nova U.
Ohio St. U.
Okla. St. U.
U. Oregon
Pace U.
U. Penn.
U. Pitt.
Poly. U.
Pratt Inst.
Princeton U.
Roch. Inst. Tech.
U. Rochester
Roosevelt U.
Rutgers U.
St. John's U. (N.Y.)
St. Mary's U. (Tex.)
Salem St. U.
Seton Hall U.
Shippensburg U. Pa.
Simmons C.
U. So. Ala.
U. So. Car.
U. So. Fla.
So. Ill. U.
Syracuse U.
Temple U.
U. Tenn.
U. Tex. (Austin)
U. Toledo
Troy St. U.
U. Utah
W. Va. Grad. C.
Vanderbilt U.
Va. Poly. Tech.
W. Va. U.
West. New Eng. C.
Wichita St. U.
U. Wis.
U. Wis. (Milwaukee)

INTERNATIONAL BUSINESS/ ECONOMICS

U. Akron
Am. Grad Sch. Intl. Mgt.
American U.
Armstrong U.
Azusa Pac. U.
Babson C.
Baruch C. (C.U.N.Y.)
Baylor U.
Boston U.
Brandeis U.
U. Bridgeport
Cal. St. U. (Fullerton)
Cal. St. U. (Hayward)
Cal. St. U. (L.A.)
U. Cal. (Berkeley)
Card. Stritch C.
Catholic U.
U. Chicago
U. Cinn.
Claremont Grad. Sch.
U. Colo.
Columbia U.
U. Conn.
U. Dallas
U. Denver
DePaul U.
Dominican C. San Rafael
Drury C.
East Mich. U.
Fairleigh Dickinson U.
Geo. Wash. U.
Georgia St. U.
Golden St. U.
U. Hartford
Hawaii Pac. U.
Hofstra U.
U. Houston
Ind. U.
Kans. St. U.

U. Ky.
L.I.U.
L.I.U. (C. W. Post)
U. Md.
U. Memphis
U. Miami
U. Mich.
U. Minn.
Monterey Inst.
Morgan St. U.
National U.
U. N. Haven
U. N. Mex.
N.Y.U.
Nova U.
Okla City U.
Oral Roberts U.
U. Oregon
Pace U.
Penn. St. U.
U. Penn.
Pepperdine U. (Culver City)
Portland St. U.
Quinnipiac C.
Rice U.
U. R.I.
Roosevelt U.
Rutgers U.
St. Joseph U.
St. Louis U.
U. St. Thomas
St. Xavier U.
S.D.S.U.
U. San Diego
U. San Fran.
Seton Hall U.
U. So. Cal.
U. So. Car.
Sul Ross St. U.
Syracuse U.
Temple U.
U. Tex. (Dallas)
U. Toledo
U.S.I.U.
Wagner C.
Wash. U.
Webster U.
U. Wis.
Wright St. U.

MANAGEMENT SCIENCE

Boston U.
U.C.L.A.
Carnegie-Mellon U.
Case West. Res. U.
Dartmouth C.
Fairleigh Dickinson U.
U. Fla.
Frostburg St. U.
Ill. Inst. Tech.
Ind. U.
U. Ky.
Lehigh U.
L.I.U.
L.S.U.
La. Tech. U.
Loyola C. (Md.)
Marshall U.
M.I.T.
U. Mass. (Lowell)
U. Memphis
Miami U. (Ohio)
U. Miami (Fla.)
Mich. St. U.
U. Mich.
Mid. Tenn. St. U.
U. Mo. (Columbia)
Morgan St. U.
S.U.N.Y. (Binghamton)
S.U.N.Y. (Buffalo)
N.Y.U.

...bia U.
...ell U.
.. Denver
DePaul U.
East. Mich. U.
East. Wash. U.
Emerson C.
Fla. St. U.
Ga. St. U.
George Mason U.
Goddard C.
Hollins C.
U. Houston
Ill. St. U.
U. Ill. (Chicago)
Ind. U.
U. Iowa
Johns Hopkins U.
Kans. St. U.
L.I.U.
U. Louisville
L.S.U.
Manhattanville C.
U. Mass.
U. Mass. (Dartmouth)
U. Md.
Miami U.
Mich. St. U.
U. Mich.
Mills C.
Miss. St. U.
U. Mont.
National Louis U.
U. Nev.
N. Mex. St. U.
S.U.N.Y. (Binghamton)
N.Y.U.
U. No. Car. (Greensboro)
Northeastern U.
U. Ore.
Penn. St. U.
U. Penn.
Purdue U.
Queens C. (C.U.N.Y.)
R.P.I.
San Fran. St. U.
U. San Fran.
Sarah Lawrence C.
Sonoma St. U.
So. Meth. U.
U. So. Cal.
U. So. Car.
So. W. Tex. St. U.
U. Southwest La.
Syracuse U.
Temple U.
U. Tenn.
U. Utah
U. Va.
Va. Commonwealth U.
Wash. U.
West. Ill. U.
West. Mich. U.
Wichita St. U.

FILM/TELEVISION
(Broadcasting, Cinema,
Motion Pictures)
U. Ala.
Amer. U.
Art Inst. Chicago
Auburn U.
Ball St. U.
Boston U.
Brooklyn C.
(C.U.N.Y.)
Butler U.
Cal. C. Arts & Crafts
U.C.L.A.
Carnegie Mellon U.
Catholic U.
Cent. Mich. U.
U. Cent. Okla.

U. Cinn.
C.C.N.Y. (C.U.N.Y.)
Claremont Grad. Sch.
U. Colo.
Columbia U.
DePaul U.
Drake U.
East. Ill. U.
Emerson C.
Emory U.
Fairfield U.
Fla. St. U.
U. Fla.
Ind. U.
U. Iowa
Kans. St. U.
U. Kans.
Marquette U.
U. Md.
U. Memphis
Miami U.
U. Miami (Fla.)
Mich. St. U.
U. Mich.
U. Minn.
U. Neb. (Omaha)
U. N. Mex.
N.Y.U.
U. No. Car. (Chapel Hill)
U. No. Car. (Greensboro)
U. No. Tex.
Northwestern U.
Ohio St. U.
Ohio U.
U. Ore.
Penn. St. U.
U. Pitt.
Rhode Island Sch. Design
S.D.S.U.
San Fran. Art. Inst.
San Fran. St. U.
U. So. Cal.
U. So. Car.
So. Ill. U.
So. Meth. U.
Stanford U.
S.F. Austin St. U.
Syracuse U.
Temple U.
U. Tenn.
U. Tex. (Austin)
U. Tex. (El Paso)
Tulane U.
U. Utah
Va. Commonwealth U.
U. Va.
U. Wash.
Wayne St. U.
W. Va. U.
U.Wis. (Superior)

JOURNALISM
A.C.U.
U. Ala.
American U.
Ariz. St. U.
U. Ariz.
Ark. St. U.
U. Ark.
Ball St. U.
Baylor U.
Boston U.
Cal. St. U. (Fullerton)
Cal. St. U. (Northridge)
U. Cal. (Berkeley)
Cent. Mich. U.
Colo. St. U.
U. Colo.
Columbia U.
East Tex. St. U.
Emerson C.
U. Fla.
U. Georgia

U. Ill.
Ind. U.
Iowa St. U.
U. Iowa
Kans. St. U.
U. Kans.
Kent St. U.
L.S.U.
U. Md.
Marquette U.
Marshall U.
U. Memphis
U. Miami (Fla.)
Mich. St. U.
U. Mich.
U. Miss.
U. Mo. (Columbia)
U. Mont.
Murray St. U.
N.Y.U. U. Neb.
U. Nev. (Reno)
U. No. Car.
(Chapel Hill)
U. No. Tex.
Northeastern U.
Northwestern U.
Ohio St. U.
Ohio U.
U. Okla.
U. Ore.
Penn. St. U.
U. Portland
Roosevelt U.
San Jose St. U.
U. So. Cal.
U. So. Car.
So. Dak. St. U.
So. Ill. U.
Stanford U.
Syracuse U.
Temple U.
U. Tenn.
Tex. So. U.
U. Tex. (Austin)
W. Va. U.
U. Wis.

TECHNICAL WRITING
Colo. St. U.
Drexel U.
Miami U.
Mich. Tech. U.
U. Minn.
No. Car. St. U.
Northeastern U.
Ore. St. U.
R.P.I.

TELE-COMMUNICATION
U. Ala.
Barry U.
Cal. St. U. (Fresno)
U. Colo.
U. Dallas
DePaul U.
Geo. Mason U.
Geo. Wash. U.
Golden Gate U.
Ind. U.
Iona C.
Kutztown U. PA.
U. Md.
U. Miami (Fla.)
Mich. St. U.
U. Mich.
N.Y.U.
Ohio U.
U. Pitt.
Poly U.
R.I.T.
U. San Fran.

So. Ill. U.
So. Meth. U.
Tex. So. U.
U. Tex. (Dallas)
Webster U.

Computer Science
(Typically includes Computer Systems, Computer Information Systems, Management Information System)

A.F. Inst.
Ala. A&M U.
U. Ala.
U. Ala. (Birm.)
U. Alaska
American U.
Andrews U.
Angelo St. U.
Ariz. St. U.
U. Ariz.
Ark. St. U.
U. Ark.
Auburn U.
Azusa Pac. U.
Ball St. U.
Baruch C. (C.U.N.Y.)
Baylor U.
Bemidji St. U.
Boston C.
Boston U.
Bowie St. U.
Bowl. Gr. St. U.
Bradley U.
Brandeis U.
B.Y.U.
U. Bridgeport
Brooklyn C. (C.U.N.Y.)
Cal. Inst. Tech.
Cal. Poly St. U. (Pomona)
Cal. Poly. St. U. (San
Luis Obispo)
Cal. St. U. (Chico)
Cal. St. U. (Fresno)
Cal. St. U. (Fullerton)
Cal. St. U. (Northridge)
Cal. St. U. (Sacramento)
U. Cal. (Berkeley)
U. Cal. (Davis)
U. Cal. (Irvine)
U.C.L.A.
U. Cal. (Riverside)
U. Cal. (San Diego)
U. Cal. (Santa Cruz)
Cal. U. Pa.
Carnegie Mellon U.
Case West. Res. U.
Cent. Conn. St. U.
Cent. Mich. U.
U. Chicago
U. Cinn.
City C. (C.U.N.Y.)
Clark Atlanta U.
Clarkson U.
Clemson U.
Cleve. St. U.
Colorado St. U.
U. Colo.
Columbia U.
U. Conn.
Cornell U.
Creighton U.
Dartmouth C.
U. Dayton
U. Dela.
U. Denver
DePaul U.
U. Detroit Mercy
Drexel U.
Duke U.

East Stroudsburg U. of Pa.
East Tenn. St. U.
East Tex. St. U.
East. Wash. U.
Emory U.
Fairleigh Dickinson U.
Fla. Atlantic U.
Fla Inst. Tech.
Fla. St. U.
U. Fla.
Fort Hays St. U.
Geo. Mason U.
Geo. Washington U.
Georgia Inst. Tech.
U. Georgia
Gov. St. U.
Hofstra U.
U. Houston
Howard U.
U. Idaho
Ill. Inst. Tech.
Ill. St. U.
U. Ill.
Ind. U.
Iona C.
Iowa St. U.
U. Iowa
Jackson St. U.
James Madison U.
Johns Hopkins U.
Kansas St. U.
U. Kans.
Kittztown U.
Lamar U.
Lehigh U.
Lehman C. (C.U.N.Y.)
L.S.U.
La. Tech. U.
U. Louisville
Loyola C. (Md.)
Loyola Marymount U.
Loyola U. (Chicago)
U. Maine
Manketo St. U.
Marquette U.
U. Md.
U. Md. (Baltimore)
M.I.T.
U. Mass.
U. Mass. (Boston)
U. Mass (Lowell)
Memphis St. U.
Mercer U.
U. Miami
Mich. St. U.
U. Mich.
Mich. Tech. U.
Mid. Tenn. St. U.
U. Minn.
Miss St. U.
U. Mo.
U. Mo. (K.C.)
U. Mo. (Rolla)
Mont. St. U.
U. Mont.
Montclair St. U.
Moorhead St. U.
U. Neb.
U. Nev. (Les Vegas)
N.J.I.T.
U. N.H
N. Mex. Inst. M&T
N. Mex. St. U.
U. N. Mex.
S.U.N.Y. (Albany)
S.U.N.Y. (Buffalo)
S.U.N.Y. (Stony Brook)
N.Y.U.
No. Car. St. U. (Raleigh)
U. No. Car. (Chapel Hill)
No. Dak. St. U.
U. No. Dak.
U. No. Fla.

Criminal Justice/Corrections/ Criminology

(Includes Law Enforcement, Police Science)

Dentistry

Education

(Typically includes Administration and Supervision, Curriculum and Instruction, Elementary and Secondary Teaching, Evaluation and Research, Foreign Language Education, Foundations and Philosophy of Education, Guidance and Counseling, Health/Physical Education, History and Philosophy of Education, Home Economics Education, Reading Specialist, Recreation, School Psychology, Special Education, Speech Pathology and Audiology, Vocational/Distributive/Occupational Education; often includes Business Education, Early Childhood Education, Extension Education, Middle School Education, Student Personnel Services; offered by over five hundred institutions in all fifty states, so individual institutions are not listed here)

ADULT EDUCATION (ADULT AND COMMUNITY EDUCATION)

U. So Miss.
Syracuse U.
Temple U.
Tenn. St. U.
U. Tenn.
Tex. A&I U.
Tex. A.&M.U.
Tex. Woman's U.
Troy St. U.
(Montgomery)
Va. Commonwealth U.
Va. Poly. Inst.
Wayne St. U.
U. West Ala.
West. Wash. U.
U. Wis.
U. Wis. (Platteville)
U. Wyo.

ART EDUCATION
U. Ala. (Birm.)
Alfred U.
U. Ariz.
Ball St. U.
Boise St. U.
B.Y.U.
Brooklyn C. (C.U.N.Y.)
Cal St. U. (Long Beach)
Case West. Res. U.
Cent Conn. St. U.
U. Cincinnati
City C. (C.U.N.Y.)
Columbia U. (Teachers
C.)
East. Ky. U.
East. Mich. U.
Fla. St. U.
Ga. St. U.
U. Ga.
Howard U.
U. Ill.
Ind. U.
Jersey City St. U.
U. Kans.
Kutztown U. PA.
U. Ky.
L.I.U. (C.W. Post)
Mansfield U. PA
Md. InSt. U. Art
Marywood C.
Mass. C. Art
U. Mass. (Dartmouth)
Miami U.
U. Minn.
Moorhead St. U.
U. N. Mex.
C. New Rochelle
S.U.N.Y.C. (New Paltz)
N.Y.U.
No. Car. A&T St. U.
U. No. Iowa
Ohio St. U.
Penn. St. U.
U. Pitt.
Queens C. (C.U.N.Y.)
R.I. Sch. Design
R.I.T.
Rutgers U.
San Jose St. U.
U. So. Miss.
Syracuse U.
Temple U.
U. Tex. (Austin)
Tex. Wom. U.
U. The Arts
Towson St. U.
Tulane U.
Va. Commonwealth U.
Wayne St. U.
West Ga. C.
West. Car. U.
West. Ky. U.

Wichita St. U.
Winthrop U.
U. Wis.
U. Wis. (Milwaukee)
U. Wis. (Superior)

AUDIO-VISUAL EDUCATION
(Typically includes Educational/Instructional Technology and Media)

Ala. St. U.
Appal. St. U.
Ariz. St. U.
U. Ariz.
U. Ark.
Auburn U.
Bank St. U. Ed.
Bloomsburg U. Pa.
Boise St. U.
Boston U.
Bridgewater St. U.
Cal. St. U. (Chico)
Cal. St. U. (L.A.)
Canisius C.
Catholic U.
Cent. Conn. St. U.
U. Cent. Okla.
Columbia U. (Teachers
Clarke C. (IA)
U. Conn.
U. Dubuque
East Car. U.
East Tex. St. U.
Fairfield U.
Fla. St. U.
Gallaudet U.
Geo. Wash. U.
Georgia So. C.
Georgia St. U.
U. Georgia
Gov. St. U.
Harvard U.
U. Hawaii
Howard U.
Ill. St. U.
Ind. U.
Iona C.
Iowa St. U.
Jackson St. U.
Jacksonville St. U.
James Madison U.
Jersey City St. U.
U. Kans.
U. Ky.
Kent St. U.
L.I.U. (C. W. Post)
Lehigh U.
Mankato St. U.
U. Mass. (Boston)
Marywood C.
McNeese St. U.
Mich. St. U.
U. Neb.
N.Y.U.
No. Car. A&T St. U.
No. Car. Cent. U.
U. No Car. (Chapel Hill)
U. No. Colo.
No. Ill. U.
Northeast Okla St. U.
Nova U.
Ohio U.
Okla. St. U.
Old Dom. U.
U. Oregon
Our Lady of Lake U.
Penn. St. U.
U. Pitt.
Portland St. U.
Prairie View A&M U.

Purdue U.
Radford U.
R.I.T.
St. Cloud St. U.
S.D.S.U.
San Fran. St. U.
San Jose St. U.
Seton Hall U.
U. So. Cal.
U. So. Car.
So. Conn. St. U.
U. So. Fla.
U. So. Ill. (Edwardsville)
U. So. Miss.
Southwest. Okla St. U.
Syracuse U.
Towson St. U.
Temple U.
U. Tenn.
Tex. Tech. U.
U.S.I.U.
Utah St. U.
Va. Commonwealth U.
Va. Poly. Inst.
Va. St. U.
Wash. St. U.
Wayne St. U.
West Car. U.
West. Md. U.
Westfield St. U.
U. Wis.
U. Wis. (La Crosse)
U. Wis. (Stout)
Xavier U. (Ohio)

BILINGUAL/ MULTILINGUAL/ MULTICULTURAL EDUCATION
Adelphi U.
U. Alaska
U. Ariz.
Bank St. U. Ed. Boston
U.
U. Bridgeport
Brooklyn C. (C.U.N.Y.)
Cal. St. U. (Bakersfield)
Cal. St. U. (Sacramento)
Cal. St. U. (San
Bernardino)
U. Cal. (Irvine)
Chicago St. U.
City C. (C.U.N.Y.)
U. Colo.
Columbia U. (Teachers
C.)
U. Conn.
U. Dela.
U. East Mich. U.
Fairleigh Dickinson U.
Fla. St. U.
Fordham U.
Geo. Mason U.
U. Georgia
Hofstra U.
U. Houston
Hunter C. (C.U.N.Y.)
U. Ill.
Jersey City St. U.
L.I.U.
Mankato St. U.
U. Md.
U. Mass. (Boston)
U. Mich.
U. N. Mex.
U. N. Rochelle
S.U.N.Y. (Buffalo)
S.U.N.Y.C. (Brockport)
N.Y.U.
Northern Ariz. U.
U. No. Tex.
Our Lady of Lake

U. Pac.
Penn. St. U.
Point Loma C.
U. Puerto Rico
Rhode Island C.
Rutgers U.
St. John's U. (N.Y.)
U. San Fran.
Sam Houston St. U.
S.D. S. U.
Seton Hall U.
So. Conn. U.
Stanford U.
St. U. Sul Ross
Tex. A & I U.
Tex. Tech. U.
U. Tex. (San Antonio)
U. Tex. (Pan American)

COMMUNITY COLLEGE TEACHING
Columbia U. (Teachers
C.)
U. Conn.
East Car. U.
East. Wash. U.
U. Fla.
Geo. Mason U.
Mich. St. U.
No. Car. St. U.
No. Mich. U.
Ore. St. U.
Pittsburg St. U.
Rowan C. N.J.
Va. Poly. Inst.
West. Mich. U.

COMPUTERS IN EDUCATION
Ariz. St. U.
Augustana College
Azusa Pac. U.
Barry U.
Bank St. U. Ed.
Bemidji St. U.
Brooklyn C.
U. Bridgeport
Brooklyn C. (C.U.N.Y.)
Cal. Poly. San Luis
Obispo
Cal. St. U. (Dominguez
Hills)
Cal. St. U. (L.A.)
Canisius C.
Card. Stritch C.
U. Cent. Ark.
Cleveland St. U.
Columbia U. (Teachers
C.)
DePaul U.
East Wash. U.
Fairfield U.
Fla. Inst. Tech.
Fort Hays St. U.
Gonzaga U.
U. Geogia
Hampton U.
Hofstra U.
Jacksonville U.
L.I.U.
L.I.U. (C.W. Post)
U. Mich.
National Louis U.
U. No. Iowa
U. No. Tex.
No. West. Mo. St. U.
Nova U.
Oakland U.
Ohio U.
Oka. St. U.
U. Penn.

Rivier C.
R.I.T.
Rowan C. N.J.
Sam Houston St. U.
Shippensburg U. PA.
Teikyo Marycrest U.
U. Tex. (Austin)
Trinity C.
U.S.I.U.
Webster U.
Wilkes U.

DRUG AND ALCOHOL/ SUBSTANCE ABUSE COUNSELING
Antioch N.E. Grad. Sch.
Gov. St. U.
L.I.U.
U. No. Fla.
Sage Grad Sch.
Springfield C.

EDUCATION OF THE GIFTED
U. Ala.
Appal. St. U.
Ariz. St. U.
U. Ariz.
Ark. Tech. U.
U. Ark.
Barry U.
Cal. St. U. (L.A.)
Cal. St. U. (Northridge)
Cal. St. U. (Sacramento)
Chicago St. U.
Clark Atlanta U.
Cleveland St. U.
Columbia U. (Teachers
C.)
Converse C.
U. Denver
Drury C.
East. Ky. U.
Emporia St. U.
Georgia St. U.
U. Georgia
Grand Valley St.U.
U. Houston
Hunter C. (C.U.N.Y.)
Idaho St. U.
Ind. U.
Ind. U. Pa.
Jacksonville U.
U. Kans.
Kent St. U.
Mankato St. U.
Mansfield U. Pa.
Millersville U. Pa.
U. Neb. (Kearney)
U. Nev.
C. N. Rochelle
U. No. Colo.
U. No. Iowa
Northeast. Ill. U.
Ohio U.
Okla. City U.
U. Oregon
Purdue U.
St. Cloud St. U.
U. St. Thomas.
Shippensburg U. Pa.
U. So. Ala.
U. So. Fla.
U. So. West. La.
Stetson U.
U. Tenn.
Tex. A&M U.
U. Tulsa
West. Car. U.
C. William & Mary
U. Wis. (Whitewater)

Northeastern U.
Northeastern Ill. U.
Old Dom. U.
U. Pitt.
Radford U.
Syracuse U.
U. Tex. (Austin)
Va. Commonwealth U.
Valdosta St. U.
West. Ore. St. U.
U. Wis. (Superior)

TEACHING OF MENTALLY RETARDED
Ala. A.&M. U.
Appal. St. U.
U. Ark.
Ball St. U.
Bloomsburg St. U.
Bowl. Gr. St. U.
Cal. U. (Pa.)
Card. Stritch C.
Cent. St. U.
Chicago St. U.
Cleveland St. U.
Columbia U. (Teachers C.)
Duquesne U.
East Tex. St. U.
East. Mich. U.
East. Mont. C.
Fort Hays Kans. St. U.
Georgia C. Milledgeville
Georgia St. U.
U. Georgia
Glassboro St. U.
Hampton Inst.
Hofstra U.
Kent St. U.
Lehman C. (C.U.N.Y.)
L.I.U.
Mankato St. U.
Marygrove C.
Millersville U. Pa.
Minot St. U.
U. Mo. (St. Louis)
U. Neb. (Omaha)
U. N. Rochelle
Northeastern U.
Northeastern Ill. U.
Old Dom. U.
U. Pitt.
Roosevelt U.
St. Francis C. (Ind.)
C. St. Rose
U. So. Fla.
U. So. Conn.
So. U. A&M C.
Syracuse U.
Va. Commonwealth U.
Va. St. U.
Valdosta St. U.
West. Car. U.
Winona St. U.

TEACHING OF PHYSICALLY HANDICAPPED
U. Ala.
U. Ariz.
U. Ark.
Ball St. U.
Cal. U. (Pa.)
Cleveland St. U.
Columbia U. (Teachers C.)
Duquesne U.
East. Mont. St. U.
East Tex. St. U.
Georgia St. U.
U. Georgia
Hofstra U.

Kent St. U.
Lehman C. (C.U.N.Y.)
U. Maine
Mankato St. U.
Memphis St. U.
Minot St. U.
U. Neb. (Kearney)
Old Dom. U.
Seton Hall U.
U. So. Conn.
U. Tex. (Austin)
Valdosta St. U.
West. Ore. St. U.

URBAN EDUCATION
Cal. St. U. (Los Angeles)
U. Chicago
City C. (C.U.N.Y.)
Cleveland St. U.
Columbia U. (Teachers C.)
Harvard U.
Ind. U.
Iona C.
Jersey City St. U.
L.I.U.
Morgan St. U.
U. Neb. (Omaha)
Northeastern Ill. U.
Old Dom. U.
U. Penn.
Rhode Island C.
Syracuse U.
Temple U.
Tex. So. U.
Wm. Paterson C. N.J.
Wash. U.
U. Wash.
U. Wis. (Milwaukee)

Engineering and Technology

(Typically includes Applied Sciences, Chemical Engineering, Civil Engineering, Computer Science/Engineering, Construction Engineering, Electrical Engineering, Energy Engineering, Engineering and Applied Sciences, Industrial Engineering, Mechanical Engineering; often includes Aeronautical/ Astronautical Engineering, Engineering Management/ Science, Materials Engineering/Science, Mechanics, Metallurgy/ Metallurgical Engineering, Nuclear Engineering/Science, Operations Research, Structural Engineering, Systems Engineering/Science)

A.F. Inst.
U. Akron
Ala. A&M U.
U. Ala.
U. Ala. (Birm.)
U. Ala. (Huntsville)
U. Alaska
Alfred U.
American U.
Andrews U.
Angelo St. U.
Ariz. St. U.
U. Ariz.
U. Ark.
Auburn U.

Azusa Pac. U.
Ball St. U.
Baylor U.
Boston C.
Boston U.
Bow. Gr. St. U.
Bradley U.
U. Bridgeport
B.Y.U.
Brown U.
Bucknell U.
Cal. Inst. Tech.
Cal. Poly. St. U. (San Luis Obispo)
Cal. St. Poly U. (Pomona)
Cal St. U. (Chico)
Cal. St. U. (Dominguez Hills)
Cal. St. U. (Fresno)
Cal. St. U. (Fullerton)
Cal. St. U. (Hayward)
Cal. St. U. (Long Beach)
Cal. St. U. (L.A.)
Cal. St. U. (Northridge)
Cal. St. U. (Sacramento)
Cal. St. U. (San Bernardino)
U. Cal. (Berkeley)
U. Cal. (Davis)
U. Cal. (Irvine)
U.C.L.A.
U. Cal. (San Diego)
U. Cal. (San Fran.)
U. Cal. (Santa Barbara)
Cal. U. Pa.
Carnegie Mellon U.
Case West. Res. U.
Catholic U.
Cent. Conn. St. U.
U. Cent. Fla.
Cent. Mich. U.
Cent. Mo. St. U.
U. Cincinnati
C.C.N.Y. (C.U.N.Y.)
Clarkson U.
Clemson U.
Cleveland St. U.
Colo. Sch. Mines
Colo. St. U.
Colo. Tech. C.
U. Colo.
Columbia U.
U. Conn.
Cornell U.
Creighton U.
U. Dallas
Dartmouth C.
U. Dayton
U. Del.
U. Denver
DePaul U.
U. Detroit Mercy
Drexel U.
Duke U.
East Car. U.
East. Ill. U.
East. Mich. U.
East. Tenn. St. U.
Emory U.
U. Evansville
Fairleigh Dickinson U.
Fitchburg St. U.
Fla. A&M U.
Fla. Atlantic U.
Fla. Inst. Tech.
Fla. St. U.
U. Fla.
Gannon U.
Geo. Mason U.
Georgetown U.
Geo. Wash. U.
Georgia Inst. Tech.

Georgia So. U.
Georgia St. U.
U. Georgia
Golden Gate U.
Gonzaga U.
Gov. St. U.
U. Hawaii
Hofstra U.
U. Houston
Howard U.
Idaho St. U.
U. Idaho
Ill. Inst. Tech.
U. Ill.
U. Ill. (Chicago)
Ind. St. U.
Ind. U.
Iowa St. U.
U. Iowa
Johns Hopkins U.
Kans. St. U.
U. Kans.
Kent St. U.
Kutztown U. Pa.
U. Ky.
Lamar U.
Lehigh U.
L.I.U.
L.S.U.
L.S.U. Shreveport
La. Tech U.
U. Louisville
Loyola C.
Loyola Marymount U.
Loyola U. (Chicago)
U. Maine
Manhattan C.
Mankato St. U.
Marquette U.
U. Md.
U. Md. (Baltimore Co.)
M.I.T.
U. Mass.
U. Mass. (Dartmouth)
U. Mass. (Lowell)
McNeese St. U.
U. Memphis
Mercer U.
Miami U.
U. Miami (Fla.)
Mich. St. U.
Mich. Tech. U.
U. Mich.
Mid. Tenn. St. U.
Milwaukee Sch. Eng.
U. Minn.
Miss. St. U.
U. Miss.
U. Mo. (Columbia)
U. Mo. (K.C.)
U. Mo. (Rolla)
Monmouth U.
Mont Tech.
Mont. St. U.
Montclair St. U.
Morgan St. U.
National U.
Naval P.G. Sch.
U. Neb.
U. Nev.
U. Nev. (Reno)
Newark C. Eng.
U.N.H.
U. N. Haven
N.J.I.T.
N. Mex. Inst. M&T
N. Mex. St. U.
U. N. Mex.
U. N. Orleans
C.U.N.Y. (Grad. Cent.)
N.Y.I.T.
S.U.N.Y. (Buffalo)
S.U.N.Y. (Stony Brook)

S.U.N.Y.C. Environ. Sci. & For. (Syracuse)
N.Y.U.
No. Car. A.&T.C.
No. Car. St. U. (Raleigh)
U. No. Car. (Charlotte)
U. No. Car. (Chapel Hill)
No. Dak. St. U.
U. No. Dak.
Northeastern U.
N. Ill. U.
U. No. Iowa
U. No. Tex.
Northwestern U.
U. Notre Dame
Nova U.
Oakland U.
Ohio St. U.
Ohio U.
Okla. St. U.
U. Okla.
Old Dom. U.
Ore Grad. Inst. Sci. Tech.
Ore. St. U.
Pace U.
U. Pac.
Penn. St. U.
U. Penn.
U. Phoenix
Pittsburg St. U.
U. Pitt.
Poly U.
Portland St. U.
U. Portland
Prairie View A&M U.
Pratt Inst.
Princeton U.
U. Puerto Rico
Purdue U.
Queens C. (C.U.N.Y.)
R.P.I.
R.P.I. Conn.
U. Rhode Island
Rice U.
Rochester Inst. Tech.
U. Rochester
Roosevelt U.
Rose-Hulman Inst. Tech.
Rutgers U.
St. John's U. (N.Y.)
St. Louis U.
St. Mary's U. (Texas)
S.D.S.U.
San Fran. St. U.
San Jose St. U.
Santa Clara U.
U. Scranton
Seattle U.
U. So. Ala.
U. So. Car.
So. Dak. Sch. M&T
So. Dak. St. U.
U. So. Fla.
U. So. Cal.
So. Ill. U.
So. Ill. U. (Edwardsville)
So. Meth. U.
U. Southwestern La.
Stanford U.
Stevens Inst. Tech.
Suffolk U.
Syracuse U.
Temple U.
Tenn. St. U.
Tenn. Tech. U.
U. Tenn.
U. Tenn. (Chattanooga)
U. Tenn. (Memphis)
U. Tenn. (Space Institute)
Tex. A&I U.
Tex.. A&M U.
Tex. Christ. U.
Tex. Tech. U.

U. Tex. (Arlington)
U. Tex. (Austin)
U. Tex. (Dallas)
U. Tex. (El Paso)
U. Tex. (San Antonio)
U. Tex. (Permian Basin)
U. Tex. (Tyler)
U. Toledo
Troy St. U. (Montgomery)
Tufts U.
Tulane U.
U. Tulsa
Tuskegee U.
Union C. (N.Y.)
Utah St. U.
U. Utah
Vanderbilt U.
U. Vt.
Vilanova U.
Va. Commonwealth U.
Va. Poly. Inst.
U. Va.
Wash. St. U.
Wash. U. (Mo.)
U. Wash.
Wayne St. U.
West Chester U. Pa.
West. Ill. U.
West. Ky. U.
W. Va. C. Grad. Studies
W. Va. U.
West. Ill. U.
West. Mich. U.
West. N. E. C.
Wichita St. U.
Widener U.
Wilkes U.
C. Wm. & Mary
U. Wis.
U. Wis. (Milwaukee)
Worcester Poly. Inst.
Wright St. U.
U. Wyo.
Yale U.
Youngstown St. U.

ARCHITECTURAL ENGINEERING
U. Colo.
U. Fla.
Ill. Inst. Tech.
Kans. St. U.
U. Kans.
U. Memphis
U. Miami
No. Car. A&T St. U.
Okla. St. U.
Penn. St. U.
R.P.I.
U. So. Cal.
Tex. A&M U.
U. Tex. (Austin)
U. Wyo.

BIOENGINEERING/ BIOMEDICAL ENGINEERING
U. Akron
U. Ala. (Birm.)
Ariz. St. U.
Boston U.
Brown U.
Cal. St. U. (Northridge)
Cal. St. U. (Sacramento)
U. Cal. (Berkeley)
U. Cal. (Davis)
U. Cal. (Irvine)
U.C.L.A.
U. Cal. (San Diego)
U. Cal. (San Fran.)
Carnegie Mellon U.
Case West. Res. U.
Catholic U.

Clemson U.
Colo. St. U.
Columbia U.
U. Conn.
Cornell U.
Dartmouth C.
Drexel U.
Duke U.
Geo. Wash. U.
Georgia Inst. Tech.
U. Georgia
Harvard U.
U. Hawaii
U. Houston
U. Ill.
U. Ill. (Chicago)
Iowa St. U.
U. Iowa
Johns Hopkins U.
Kans. St. U.
U. Ky.
La. Tech. U.
Marquette U.
M.I.T.
U. Memphis
Mercer U.
U. Miami
U. Mich.
Milwaukee Sch. Eng.
U. Minn.
Miss. St. U.
N.J.I.T.
U. Nev. (Reno)
S.U.N.Y. (Buffalo)
No. Car. St. U.
U. No. Car. (Chapel Hill)
Northwestern U.
U. Notre Dame
Ohio St. U.
Penn. St. U.
U. Penn.
U. Pitt.
Poly. U.
Purdue U.
U. Rochester
R.P.I./
Rice U.
Rose-Hulman Inst.
Rutgers U.
U. So. Cal.
Stanford U.
U. Tenn.
U. Tenn. (Memphis)
Tex. A&M U.
U. Tex. (Arlington)
U. Tex. (Austin)
U. Tex. (Southwest. Med. Cent.)
Tulane U.
U. Utah
Vanderbilt U.
Va. Commonwealth U .
Va. Poly Inst.
U. Va.
U. Vt.
Wash. U.
U. Wash.
U. Wis.
Worcester Poly. Inst.
Wright St. U.
U. Wyo.

CERAMIC ENGINEERING
Alfred U.
U. Cal. (Berkeley)
U.C.L.A.
Case West. Res. U.
U. Cincinnati
Clemson U.
U. Fla.
Georgia Inst. Tech.
U. Ill.

U. Mo. (Rolla)
Ohio St. U.
Penn. St. U.
R.P.I.
Rutgers U.
U. Wash.

ENGINEERING MANAGEMENT
A. F. Int.
U. Ala. (Huntsville)
U. Alaska
Ariz. St. U.
B.Y.U.
Cal. Poly. San Luis Obispo
Cal. St. U. (Northridge)
Case West. Res. U.
Catholic U.
Cent. Mich. U.
Colo. St. U.
U. Dallas
Dartmouth C.
U. Dayton
U. Denver
U. Detroit Mercy
Drexel U.
U. Evansville
U. Fla.
Fla. Inst. Tech.
George Wash. U.
Ga. Inst. Tech.
Ill. Inst. Tech.
U. Kans.
Lamar U.
Lehigh U.
L.S.U.
U. Md.
U. Md. (Baltimore Co.)
Mercer U.
U. Miami
Mich. Tech. U.
U. Mich.
Milwaukee Sch. Eng.
U. Minn.
U. No. (Rolla
N.J.I.T.
Northeastern U.
Northwestern U.
Oakland. U.
Old Dom. U.
Ore. Grad. Inst. Sc. & Tech.
Penn St. U.
U. Penn
U. Pitt.
Poly U.
R.P.I.
Roc. Inst. Tech
St. Mary's U. (Tex)
Santa Clara U.
U. So. Cal.
So. Dak. Sch. Mines
U. So. Fla.
S. Meth. U.
U. Southwestern La.
Stanford U.
Stevens Inst. Tech.
U. Tenn.
U. Tenn (Space Institute)
Tex. A&M U.
U. Tex. (Austin)
U. Tex (San Antonio)
Tufts U.
U. Toledo
U. Tulsa
U. Utah
Vanderbilt U.
Va. Poly. Inst.
Wash. U.
West Mich. U.
West. Va. Grad. C.
Wichita St. U.

Widener U.
Worcester Poly Inst.

ENVIROMNEMTAL ENGINEERING
U. Ala.
U. Alaska
U. Ariz.
U. Ark.
Auburn U.
Cal. Inst. Tech.
Cal. Poly. (San Luis Obispo)
U. Cal. (Berkeley)
U. Cal. (Irvine)
U.C.L.A.
Carnegie Mellon U.
Case West. Res. U.
Catholic U.
U. Cincinnati
Clemson U.
Colo. Sch. Mines
Colo. St. U.
U. Colo.
U. Conn.
Cornell U.
Dartmouth C.
U. Dayton
Drexel U.
Duke U.
Fla. Inst. Tech.
U. Fla..
Geo. Wash. U.
Georgia Inst. Tech.
U. Hawaii
U. Houston
Humboldt St. U.
Ill. Inst. Tech.
U. Ill.
U. Iowa
Iowa St. U.
Johns Hopkins U.
U. Kans.
Lamar U.
L.S.U. A&M
U. Louisville
Loyola Marymount U.
U. Maine
Manhattan C.
Marquette U.
M.I.T.
U. Mass.
U. Mass. (Lowell)
U. Memphis
Mich. St. U.
Mich. Tech. U.
U. Mich.
Milwaukee Sch. Eng.
Miss. St. U.
U. Mo. (Rolla)
Mont. C. Min. Sci & Tech.
Mont. St. U.
Mont. Tech.
U. Nev.
U.N. Haven
N.J.I.T.
S.U.N.Y. (Buffalo)
S.U.N.Y.C. Environ. Sci. & For. (Syracuse)
U. N. Car. (Chapel Hill)
No. Dak. St. U.
U. No. Dakota
Northeastern U.
Northwestern U.
Ohio U.
Okla. St. U.
U. Okla.
Old Dom. U.
Ore. Grad. Inst. & Tech.
Ore. St. U.
Penn. St. U.
U. Penn.
Poly U.

R.P.I.
U.R.I.
Rice U.
Rose-Hulman Inst.
Rutgers U.
U. So. Cal.
So. Dak. Sch. M&T
So. Dak. St. U.
So. Ill. U.
Stevens Inst. Tech.
Syracuse U.
U. Tenn.
Tex. A&M U.
Tex. Tech. U.
U. Tex (Austin)
Tulane U.
Utah St. U.
Vanderbilt U.
Va. Poly. Inst.
U. Va.
Villanova U.
Wash. St. U.
Wash. U.
U. Wash.
U. Wis.
Youngstown St. U.

GEOLOGICAL/ GEOSCIENCES/ GEOTECHNICAL ENGINEERING
U. Alaska
Ariz. St. U.
U. Ariz.
Auburn U.
U. Cal. (Berkeley)
Colorado Sch. Mines
Colo. St. U.
U. Colo.
Drexel U.
Fla. Inst. Tech.
U. Idaho
Iowa St. U.
Mich. Tech. U.
U. Minn.
U. Mo. (Rolla)
Mont. Tech
U. Nev. (Reno)
N. Mex. St.
Ohio U.
U. Okla
R.P.I.
So. Dak. Sch. of M&T
Tex. A&M U.
U. Utah
Wash. St. U.
U. Wash.

MANUFACTURING ENGINEERING
Auburn U.
Boston U.
B.Y.U.
U.C.L.A.
U. Detroit Mercy
Lehigh U.
U. Mass. (Lowell)
N.J.I.T.
No. Car. St. U.
U. Pitt.
Poly U.
U. R. I.
So. Ill. U.
So. Meth. U.
Stanford U.
Syracuse U.
U. Tex. (El Paso)
Wayne St. U.
U. Wis.

MARINE SCIENCE/ ENGINEERING/ OCEANOGRAPHY

U. Alaska
Boston C.
Cal. St. U. (Hayward)
Cal. St. U. (Sacramento)
U. Cal. (San Diego)
U. Cal. (Santa Cruz)
Columbia U.
U. Conn.
U. Dela.
Fla. Inst. Tech.
Fla. St. U.
U. Hawaii
Johns Hopkins U.
L.I.U.
L.S.U.
U. Maine
U. Md. (Baltimore Co.)
M.I.T.
U. Miami
U. Mich.
Naval P.G.
S.U.N.Y. (Stony Brook)
U. N. H.
No. Car. St. U. (Raleigh)
U. No. Car. (Chapel Hill)
Nova U.
Old Dom. U.
Ore. St. U.
Princeton U.
U. Puerto Rico
U. R. I.
San Jose St. U.
U. So. Ala.
U. So. Car.
U. So. Fla.
U. So. Miss.
Tex. A&M U.
U. Va.
U. Wash.
West. Conn. St. U.
C. Wm. & Mary
U. Wis.
Yale U.

MINERAL/MINING ENGINEERING TECHNOLOGY

U. Ala.
U. Alaska
U. Ariz.
U. Cal. (Berkeley)
Colo. Sch. Mines
Columbia U.
U. Idaho
U. Ky.
Mich. Tech. U.
U. Mich.
U. Minn.
U. Mo. (Rolla)
Mont. Tech.
U. Nev. (Reno)
New Mex. Inst. M&T
U. No. Dak.
Ohio St. U.
Penn. St. U.
U. Pitt.
So. Dak. Sch. M&T
So. Ill. U.
U. Utah
Va. Poly. Inst.
U. Wash.
W. Va. U.
U. Wis.
U. Wyo.

OCEAN ENGINEERING

U. Cal. (Berkeley)
U. Cal. (San Diego)
U. Conn.
U. Del.
Fla. Atlantic U.
Fla. Inst. Tech.

U. Fla.
Geo. Wash. U.
U. Hawaii
U. Miami (Fla.)
U. Mich.
M.I.T.
U. N. H.
Old Dom. U.
Ore. St. U.
U. R. I.
U. So. Cal.
Stevens Inst. Tech.
Tex. A&M U.
Va. Poly. Inst.

OPTICAL SCIENCES

Ala. A&M U.
U. Ariz.
Cleveland St. U.
U. Dayton
U. Houston
U. N. Mex.
Ohio St. U.
U. Roch.

PAPER ENGINEERING/ SCIENCE/ TECHNOLOGY

Georgia Inst. Tech.
U. Mass. (Lowell)
Miami U. (Ohio)
S.U.N.Y.C. Environ. Sci.
   & For. (Syracuse)
No. Car. St. U.
U. Wash.
West. Mich. U.

PETROLEUM ENGINEERING

U. Alaska
U. Cal. (Berkeley)
Colo. Sch. Mines
U. Houston
U. Kans.
L.S.U.
La. Tech. U.
Miss. St. U.
U. Mo. (Rolla)
Mont. Tech.
New Mex. Inst.
U. Okla.
Penn. St. U.
U. Pitt.
U. So. Cal.
U. Southwestern La.
Stanford U.
U. Tenn.
Tex. A&I U.
Tecx. A&M U.
Tex. Tech. U.
U. Tex (Austin)
U. Tulsa
U. Utah
W. Va. U.
U. Wyo.

POLYMER ENGINEERING/ SCIENCE

U. Akron
Carnegie Mellon U.
Case West. Res. U.
U. Cincinnati
Clemson U.
U. Conn
Cornell U.
U. Detroit Mercy
East Mich. U.
U. Fla.
Georgia Inst. Tech..
Lehigh U.
U. Mass.

U. Mass. (Lowell)
M.I.T.
U. Mich
U. Mo. (K.C.)
No. Dak. St. U.
Penn. St. U.
Poly U.
Princeton U.
R.P.I.
U. So. Miss.
U. Tenn.
Wayne St. U.

SANITARY ENGINEERING/ SCIENCE

Cent. Mo. St. U.
Georgia Inst. Tech.
U. Md.
U. Maine
Mich. St. U.
U. Mo. (Columbia)
N.J.I.T.
Penn. St. U.
Tex. A&M

SOFTWARE ENGINEERING

Cal. St. U. (Sacramento)
Carnegie Mellon U.
U. Conn.
Geo. Mason U.
Miss. St. U.
Monmouth U.
National U.
U. N. Haven
Roch. Inst. Tech.
San Jose St. U.
Seattle U.
U. So. Cal.
Tex. Christ. U.
Wayne St. U.
Widener U.

SYSTEM ENGINEERING

A. F. Inst.
U. Ariz.
Boston U.
Cal. Inst. Tech.
Cal. St. U. (Fullerton)
Case West. Res. U.
Geo. Mason U.
Geo. Wash. U.
G. Inst. Tech.
Howard U.
Kans. St. U.
L.S.U.
U. Mass. (Lowell)
U. Neb.
Oakland U.
Okla. St. U.
Poly. U.
Purdue U.
R.P.I.
Rutgers U.
U. So. Cal.
Temple U.
U. Tenn (Space Inst.)
Va. Poly. Inst. St. U.
U. Va.
Wash. U.
W. Va. Inst. Tech.

TANNING RESEARCH

U. Cincinnati

TEXTILE ENGINEERING/ SCIENCE

Auburn U.
Clemson U.

Cornell U.
Georgia Inst. Tech.
U. Mass. (Dartmouth)
No. Car. St. U. (Raleigh)
Purdue U.

TRANSPORTATION/ TRAFFIC ENGINEERING

A. F. Inst.
U. Cal. (Berkeley)
Cent. Mo. St. U.
U. Dayton
U. Dela.
U. Fla.
Iowa St. U.
Morgan St. U.
N.J.I.T.
Northeastern U.
Northwestern U.
U. Okla.
Penn. St. U.
U. Penn.
Poly. U.
Princeton U.
R.P.I.
U. So. Cal.
U. Tenn.
Tex. A&M U.
Tex. So. U.
U. Tex. (Austin)
U. Va.
Villanova U.
Wash. U.
U. Wash.

Environmental Sciences/Studies

(Typically includes Ecology, Forestry, Forest Science, Wood Science/Technology

Ala. A&M U.
U. Ala.
U. Alaska
Antioch N.E.
U. Ariz.
Auburn U.
Baylor U.
B.Y.U.
Brown U.
Cal. Poly. St. U. (San Luis Obispo)
Cal. Poly. St. U. (Pomona)
Cal. St. U. (Fullerton)
Cal. St. Poly. U. (Pomona)
Cal. St. U. (Fresno)
Cal. St. U. (Hayward)
U. Cal. (Berkeley
U. Cal. (Davis)
U. Cal. (Irvine)
U.C.L.A.
Case West. Reserve U.
Chapman U.
U. Cincinnati
Clemson U.
Colo. Sch. Mines
Colo. St. U.
U. Colo.
Columbia U.
U. Conn.
Cornell U.
Drexel U.
Duke U.
Duquesne U.
East Tenn. St. U.
Fla. Inst. Tech.
Fla. St. U.
U. Fla.

Geo. Mason U.
Geo. Wash. U.
U. Georgia
U. Hawaii
Harvard U.
Humbolt St. U.
Hunter C. (C.U.N.Y.)
U. Idaho
U. Ill.
Ind. St. U.
Ind. U.
Iowa St. U.
Jackson St. U.
Johns Hopkins U.
Kans. St. U.
U. Kans.
U. Ky.
L.I.U. (C.W. Post)
L.S.U.
Loyola Marymount U.
U. Maine
Mankato St. U.
U. Md. (Baltimore Co.)
U. Md.
M.I.T.
U. Mass.
U. Mass. (Boston)
U. Mass. (Lowell)
McNeese St. U.
Miami U. (Ohio)
U. Miami (Flà.)
Mich. St. U.
Mich. Tech. U.
U. Mich.
U. Minn.
Miss. St. U.
U. Mo. (Columbia)
Mont. St. U.
U. Mont.
U. Neb.
U. Nev. (Reno)
U.N.H.
U.N. Haven
N.J.I.T.
N. Mex. St. U.
C.U.N.Y. (Grad Ctr.)
S.U.N.Y. (Stony Brook)
S.U.N.Y.C. Environ. Sci.
   & For. (Syracuse)
No. Car. St. U. (Raleigh)
U. No. Car. (Chapel Hill)
No. Ariz. U.
No. Dak. St. U.
U. No. Tex.
Nova U.
Ohio St. U.
Ohio U.
Okla. St. U.
U. Okla.
Old Dom. U.
Ore. Grad. Inst. Sci & Tech.
Ore. St. U.
Penn. St. U.
U. Penn.
U. Pitt.
Poly. U.
Portland St. U.
Princeton U.
Purdue U.
R.P.I.
U. R. I.
Rice U.
Richmond C. (C.U.N.Y.)
Rutgers U.
S.D.S.U.
Shippensburg U. Pa.
Med. C. So. Car.
U. So. Conn.
So. Ill. U.
So. Ill. U. (Edwardsville)
S. F. Austin St. U.

Sul Ross St. U.
Temple U.
U. Tenn.
Tex. A&M U.
Tex. Christ. U.
Tex. Tech. U.
U. Tex. (San Antonio)
U. Tulsa
Tufts U.
Tuskegee U.
Utah St. U.
U. Vt.
Va. Poly. Inst.
U. Va.
Wash. St. U.
U. Wash.
W. Va. U.
West. Wash. U.
C. Wm. & Mary
U. Wis.
U. Wyo.
Yale U.

FISH/WILDLIFE
MANAGEMENT
U. Alaska
U. Ariz.
Auburn U.
B.Y.U.
U. Cal. (Berkeley)
Clemson U.
Colo. St. U.
Cornell U.
U. Fla.
Frostburg St. U.
Humboldt St. U.
U. Idaho
Iowa St. U.
L.S.U. A&M C.
U. Maine
U. Md.
U. Mass.
U. Miami (Fla.)
Mich St. U.
U. Minn.
Miss. St. U.
U. Mo. (Columbia)
Mont. St. U.
U. Neb.
U. N.H.
N. Mex. St. U.
S.U.N.Y.C. Environ. Sci.
  & For. (Syracuse)
U. No. Dak.
U. Okla.
Ore St. U.
Penn. St. U.
So. Dak. St. U.
Sul Ross. St. U.
Tenn. Tech. U.
U. Tenn.
Tex. A&M U.
Tex. Tech. U.
Utah St. U.
Va. Poly Inst.
U. Vt.
U. Wash.
W. Va. U.

LANDSCAPE
ARCHITECTURE
U. Ariz.
Ball St. U.
Cal. Poly St. U. (Pomona)
U. Cal. (Berkeley)
U.C.L.A.
Clemson U.
U. Colo.
Cornell U.
U. Fla.
U. Georgia
Harvard U.
U. Ill.

Iowa St. U.
Kans. St. U.
L.S.U.
U. Mass.
Mich. St. U.
U. Mich.
U. Minn.
Morgan St. U.
S.U.N.Y.C. Environ. Sci.
  & For. (Syracuse)
No. Car. St. U. (Raleigh)
Ohio St. U.
U. Okla.
U. Ore.
Penn St. U.
U. Penn.
U. So. Cal.
Tex A&M U.
Tex. Tech. U.
U. Tex. (Arlington)
U. Tenn.
Utah St. U.
U. Va.
Va. Poly Inst.
U. Wash.
U. Wis.

METEOROLOGY/
ATMOSPHERE
SCIENCES
U. Alaska
U. Albany (S.U.N.Y.)
U. Ariz.
U. Cal. (Davis)
U.C.L.A.
U. Chicago
Clemson U.
Colo. St. U.
Columbia U.
U. Del.
Drexel U.
Fla. St. U.
Georgia Inst. Tech.
U. Hawaii
Iowa St. U.
Johns Hopkins U.
U. Kansas
U. Md.
M.I.T.
U. Miami
U. Mich.
U. Mo. (Columbia)
Mont. St. U.
Naval P.G. Sch.
New Mex. Inst.
  of M&T
S.U.N.Y. (Stony Brook)
N.Y.U.
No. Car. St. U.
Ohio St. U.
U. Okla.
Ore. St. U.
Penn. St. U.
Poly U.
Princeton U.
Purdue U.
Rutgers U.
St. Louis U.
San Jose St. U.
So. Dak. Sch. M&T
Tex. A&M U.
Tex. Tech. U.
Utah St. U.
U. Utah
U. Va.
U. Wash.
U. Wis.
U. Wyo.
Yale U.

RANGE
MANAGEMENT/
SCIENCE

U. Ariz.
B.Y.U.
U. Cal. (Berkeley)
Colo. St. U.
U. Fla.
U. Idaho
Mont. St. U.
N. Mex. St. U.
No. Dak. St. U.
Okla. St. U.
Ore. St. U.
Sul Ross St. U.
Tex. A&I U.
Tex. A&M U.
Tex. Tech. U.
Utah St. U.
U. Wyo.

WATER RESOURCES
ADMINISTRATION
U. Ariz.
Cal. St. U. (Bakersfield)
U. Cal. (Berkeley)
U. Cal (Davis)
U.C.L.A.
Colo. St. U.
U. Colo.
U. Del.
Fla. Inst. Tech.
U. Fla.
Geo. Wash. U.
Humboldt St. U.
U. Idaho
U. Ill. (Chicago)
Iowa St. U.
U. Kans.
L.S.U.
Marquette U.
U. Mich.
U. Mo. (Rolla)
Mont. Tech.
U. Nev.
U. Nev. (Reno)
U.N.H.
N. Mex. Inst.
U. Okla.
S.U.N.Y.C. Environ. Sci
  & For. (Syracuse)
Ore. St. U.
Penn. St. U.
Princeton U.
Rutgers U.
U. So. Cal.
So. Dak. Sch. Mines
U. Tenn.
Tex. A&M U.
U. Tex. (Austin)
Tufts U.
Utah St. U.
U. Va.
Vanderbilt U.
Villanova U.
Wash. St. U.
U. Wis.
U. Wyo.

Fine Arts

(Typically includes Art
History, Studio Arts; of-
ten includes Commercial
Art, Applied Art, Crafts,
Design, Graphic Design,
Industrial Design)

Adelphi U.
Adams St. U.
U. Ala.
Albany (S.U.N.Y.)
Alfred U.
American U.
Appalachian St. U.
Ariz. St. U.

U. Ariz.
Ark. St. U.
U. Ark.
Art. Inst. Chicago
Auburn U.
Ball St. U.
U. Baltimore
Bennington C.
Bloomsburg U. Pa.
Boise St. U.
Boston U.
Bowl. Gr. St. U.
Bradley U.
B.Y.U.
Brooklyn C. (C.U.N.Y.)
Brown U.
Bryn Mawr C.
Cal. C. A&C.
Cal. Poly St. U. (San Luis
  Obispo)
Cal. St. U. (Fresno)
Cal. St. U. (Fullerton)
Cal. St. U. (Long Beach)
Cal. St. U. (L.A.)
Cal. St. U. (Northridge)
Cal. St. U. (Sacramento)
U. Cal. (Berkeley)
U. Cal. (Davis)
U. Cal. (Irvine)
U.C.L.A.
U. Cal. (Riverside)
U. Cal. (San Diego)
U. Cal. (Santa Barbara)
U. Cal. (Santa Cruz.)
Carnegie-Mellon U.
Case West. Res. U.
Catholic U.
Cent. Conn. St. U.
Cent. Mich. St. U.
Cent. Mo. St. U.
Cent. Wash. U.
U. Chicago
U. Cincinnati
C.C.N.Y. (C.U.N.Y.)
Claremont Grad. Sch.
Clemson U.
Cleveland St. U.
Colo. St. U.
U. Colo.
Columbia U.
Conn. C.
U. Conn.
Cornell U.
Cranbrook Acad. Art
U. Dallas
U. Del.
U. Denver
Drake U.
Drexel U.
Duke U.
East Car. U.
East Tenn. St. U.
East Tex. St. U.
East Ill. U.
East. Ky. U.
East. Mich. U.
East. Wash. U.
Edinboro U. Pa.
Emory U.
Emporia St. U.
Fla. St. U.
U. Fla.
Fort Hays St. U.
Frostburg St. U.
Geo. Mason U.
Geo. Wash. U.
Georgia So. U.
Georgia St. U.
U. Georgia
Gov. St. U.
U. Hartford
Harvard U.

U. Hawaii
U. Houston
Howard U.
Humboldt St. U.
Hunter C. (C.U.N.Y.)
Idaho St. U.
U. Idaho
Ill. Inst. Tech.
Ill. St. U.
U. Ill.
U. Ill. (Chicago)
Ind. St. U.
Ind. U.
Ind. U. Pa.
U. Indianapolis
Iowa St. U.
U. Iowa
Jacksonville U.
James Madison U.
Jersey City St. U.
Johns Hopkins U.
Kans. St. U.
U. Kans.
Kent St. U.
U. Ky.
Lamar U.
Lehman C. (C.U.N.Y.)
L.I.U. (C.W. Post)
L.S.U.
La. Tech. U.
U. Louisville
Mankato St. U.
Marshall U.
Md. InSt. U. Art
U. Md.
U. Md. (Baltimore
  County)
Marywood C.
Mass. C. Art.
U. Mass.
U. Mass (Dartmouth)
McNeese St. U.
U. Memphis
Miami U. (Ohio)
U. Miami (Fla.)
Mich. St. U.
U. Mich.
Mills C.
U. Minn.
Miss. C.
Miss. St. U.
U. Miss.
U. Mo. (Columbia)
U. Mo. (K.C.)
Mont. St. U.
U. Mont.
Montclair St. U.
Moorhead St. U.
Morehead St. U.
Morgan St. U.
Murray St. U.
U. Neb.
U. Neb. (Kearney)
U. Neb. (Omaha)
N. Mex. Highlands U.
N. Mex. St. U.
U. N. Mex.
U. N. Orleans
C. New Rochelle
New Sch. Soc. Res.
  (Parson Sch.)
C.U.N.Y. (Grad. Cent.)
S.U.N.Y. (Binghamton)
S.U.N.Y. (Buffalo)
S.U.N.Y. (Stony Brook)
S.U.N.Y.C. (Brockport)
S.U.N.Y.C. (New Paltz)
S.U.N.Y.C. (Oneonta)
S.U.N.Y.C. (Oswego)
N.Y.U.
No. Ariz. U.
No. Car. St. U. (Raleigh)
U. No. Car. (Chapel Hill)

623

...SKRIT
U. Chicago
Harvard U.

SCANDINAVIAN LANGUAGES/ LITERATURES
B.Y.U.
U. Cal. (Berkeley)
U.C.L.A.
U. Chicago
Columbia U.
Harvard U.
U. Minn.
U. Wash.
U. Wis.

TRANSLATION AND INTERPRETATION
U. Ark.
Gallaudet U.
Monterey Inst.
U. Puerto Rico

URDU
U. Chicago

Home/Consumer Economics Food Science, Food Service, Technology, Child and Family Life, Nutrition
A.C.U.
U. Akron
Ala. A&M U.
U. Ala.
Andrews U. Ariz. St. U.
Appal. St. U.
U. Ariz.
U. Ark.
Auburn U.
Azusa Pac. U.
Ball St. U.
Boston U.
Bowie St. U.
Bowl. Gr. St. U.
U. Bridgeport
B.Y.U.
Brooklyn C. (C.U.N.Y)
Cal. Poly. St. U. (San
   Louis Obispo)
Cal. St. Poly. U.
   (Pomona)
Cal. St. (Chico)
Cal. St. U. (Fresno)
Cal. St. U. (Long Beach)
Cal. St. U. (L.A.)
Cal. St. U. (Northridge)
U. Cal. (Berkeley)
U. Cal. (Davis)
U.C.L.A.
Carnegie-Mellon U.
Catholic U.
Cent. Mich. U.
Cent. Mo. St. U.
U. Cent. Okla.
Cent. Wash. U.
Chapman U.
Chicago St. U.
U. Chicago

U. Cinn.
Colo. St. U.
Columbia St. U.
U. Conn.
Cornell U.
U. Dayton
U. Del.
U. Denver
U. Detroit Mercy
Drexel U.
East Car. U.
East. Tex. St. U.
East. Ill. U.
East. Ky. U.
East. Mich. U.
Emory U.
Fairleigh Dickinson U.
Fitchburg St. U.
Fla. St. U.
Framingham St. U.
Geo. Wash. U.
Georgia C. Milledgeville
Georgia So. C.
U. Georgia
Gov. St. U.
Harvard U.
Hampton U.
U. Hawaii
Hood C.
Howard U.
Humboldt St. U.
U. Idaho
Ill. St. U.
U. Ill.
Incarnate Word C.
Ind. St. U.
Ind. U.
Ind. U. Pa.
Iowa St. U.
U. Iowa
Johns Hopkins U.
Kans. St. U.
U. Kans.
Kent St. U.
U. Ky.
Lamar U.
U. LaVerne
Lehman C. (C.U.N.Y)
Loma Linda U.
L.S.U.
La. Tech U.
U. Louisville
Loyola U. (Chicago)
U. Maine
Mankato St. U.
Mansfield U. Pa.
Marshall U.
U. Md.
Marywood C.
U. Mass.
U. Memphis
Mercer U.
Miami U. (Ohio)
Mich. St. U.
U. Minn.
Miss St. U.
U. Miss.
U. Mo. (Columbia)
Mont. St. U.
Montclair St. U.
Moorhead St. U.
Morehead St. U.
Murray St. U.
U. Neb.
U. Nev. (Reno)
U.N.H.
N. Mex. St. U.
U. N. Mex.
S.U.N.Y.C. (Buffalo)
S.U.N.Y.C. (Oneonta)
S.U.N.Y.C. (Plattsburg)
N.Y.U.
N. Car. A. & T. C.

N. Car. Cent. U.
N. Car. St. U.
U. No. Car. (Greensboro)
No. Dak. St. U.
Northeastern U.
N. Ill. U.
U. No. Iowa
U. No. Tex.
Northwestern St. U. La.
Nova U.
Ohio St. U.
Ohio U.
Okla. St. U.
U. Okla.
Ore. St. U.
Penn. St. U.
U. Pitt.
Prairie View A&M U.
U. Puerto Rico
Purdue U.
Queens C. (C.U.N.Y.)
U.R.I.
Rutgers U.
Sage Grad. Sch.
St. John's U. (N.Y.)
St. Louis U.
St. Mary's U. (Minn.)
Sam Houston St. U.
S.D.S.U.
San Jose St. U.
S. Car. St. U.
So. Dak. St. U.
So. East. Mo. St. U.
So. Ill. U.
U. So. Miss.
Southern U.
U. Southwestern La.
Stanford U.
Syracuse U.
Tenn. St. U.
U. Tenn.
U. Tenn. (Martin)
Texas A&M U.
Tex. Christ U.
Tex. So. U.
Tex. Tech. U.
U. Tex. (Austin)
U. Tex. (Dallas)
Tex. Woman's U.
Tufts U.
Tuskegee U.
Utah St. U.
U. Utah
U. Vt.
Wash. St. U.
U. Wash.
Wayne St. U.
W. Va. U.
West. Car. U.
West Ky. U.
West. Mich. U.
Winthrop U.
U. Wis.
U. Wis. (Stevens Point)
U. Wis. (Stout)
U. Wyo.

Horticulture
U. Ark.
Auburn U.
B.Y.U.
U. Cal. (Davis)
Clemson U.
Colo. St. U.
Cornell U.
U. Dela.
U. Fla.
U. Georgia
U. Hawaii
U. Ill.
Iowa St. U.
Kans. St. U.

U. Ky.
L.S.U.
U. Md.
Mich. St. U.
U. Minn.
Miss. St. U.
U. Mo.
U. Neb.
N. Mex. St. U.
No. Car. St. U. (Raleigh)
No. Dak. St. U.
Ohio St. U.
Okla. St. U.
Oregon St. U.
Penn. St. U.
U. Puerto Rico
Purdue U.
U.R.I.
Rutgers U.
So. Ill. U.
U. Tenn.
Tex. A&M U.
Tex. Tech U.
Va. Poly. Inst.
Wash. St. U.
U. Wash.
W. Va. U.
U. Wis.

Humanities
(Typically includes English and History; offered by nearly four hundred institutions in all fifty states, so individual institutions are not listed here)

CLASSICS
U. Albany (S.U.N.Y.)
U. Ariz.
Ball St. U.
Boston C.
Boston U.
B.Y.U.
Brown U.
Bryn Mawr C.
U. Cal. (Berkeley)
U. Cal. (Davis)
U. Cal. (Irvine)
U.C.L.A.
U. Cal. (Santa Barbara)
Catholic U.
U. Chicago
Cincinnati
U. Colo.
Columbia U.
U. Conn.
Cornell U.
Duke U.
Fla. St. U.
U. Fla.
Fordham U.
Georgia St. U.
U. Georgia
Gonzaga U.
Harvard U.
U. Hawaii
Hunter C. (C.U.N.Y.)
U. Ill.
Ind. St. U.
Ind. U.
U. Iowa
John Carroll U.
Johns Hopkins U.
U. Kans.
Kent St. U.
U. Ky.
Loyola U. (Chicago)
Marquette U.
U. Md.
U. Mass.

U. Mich.
U. Minn.
U. Miss.
U. Mo. (Columbia)
U. Neb.
C.U.N.Y. (Grad. Cent.)
S.U.N.Y. (Buffalo)
N.Y.U.
U. No. Car. (Chapel Hill)
U. No. Car. (Greensville)
Northwestern U.
Ohio St. U.
U. Okla.
Old Dom. U.
U. Ore.
Penn. St. U.
U. Penn.
U. Pitt.
Princeton U.
Rutgers U.
San Fran. St. U.
U. So. Cal.
Stanford U.
Syracuse U.
U. Tex. (Austin)
Trinity C.
Tufts U.
Tulane U.
U. Utah
Vanderbilt U.
Villanova U.
U. Va.
U. Vt.
Wash U. (Mo.)
U. Wash.
Wayne St. U.
C. Wm. & Mary
U. Wis.
Yale U.

COMPARATIVE LITERATURE
American U.
Ariz. St. U.
U. Ariz.
U. Ark.
Brandeis U.
B.Y.U.
Brown U.
Cal. St. U. (Fullerton)
U. Cal. (Berkeley)
U. Cal. (Davis)
U. Cal. (Irvine)
U.C.L.A.
U. Cal. (Riverside)
U. Cal. (San Diego)
U. Cal. (Santa Barbara)
U. Cal. (Santa Cruz)
Case West. Res. U.
Catholic U.
U. Chicago
U. Cincinnati
C.C.N.Y. (C.U.N.Y.)
U. Colo.
Columbia U.
U. Conn.
Cornell U.
U. Dallas
Duke U.
Emory U.
Fla. Atlantic U.
U. Georgia
Harvard U.
Hofstra U.
U. Ill.
Ind. U.
U. Iowa
Johns Hopkins U.
Kent St. U.
L.S.U.
U. Md.
U. Mass.
Mich. St. U.

U. Okla.
U. Ore.
Pace U.
U. Pac.
U. Penn.
Pepperdine U.
Port. Cath. U. of P.R.
U. Pitt.
U. Puerto Rico
U. Puget Sound
Quinnipiac C.
U. Richmond
Rutgers U. (Camden)
Rutgers U. (Newark)
St. John's U. (N.Y.)
St. Louis U.
St. Mary's U.
St. Thomas U.
Samford U.
U. San Diego
U. San Fran.
Santa Clara U.
Seattle U.
Seton Hall U.
U. So. Cal.
U. So. Car.
U. So. Dak.
So. Ill. U. (Carbondale)
U. So. Maine
So. Meth. U.
So. Tex. C. Law
So. U. A&M C.
Southwestern U. Law
Stanford U.
Stetson U.
Suffolk U.
Syracuse U.
Temple U.
U. Tenn.
Tex. So. U.
Tex. Tech. U.
U. Tex. (Austin)
Thomas M. Cooley L.
  Sch.
Touro C.
U. Toledo
Tulane U.
U. Tulsa
U. Utah
Valparaiso U.
Vanderbilt U.
Vermont Law Sch.
Villanova U.
U. Va.
Wake Forest U.
Washburn U. Topeka
Wash. & Lee U.
Wash. U. (Mo.)
U. Wash.
Wayne St. U.
West. New Eng. C.
W. Va. U.
Whittier C.
Widener U.
Willamette U.
C. Wm. & Mary
Wm. Mitchell C. Law
U. Wis.
U. Wyo.
Yale U.
Yeshiva U.

Liberal Studies

A.C.U.
U. Albany (S.U.N.Y.)
Antioch N. E. Grad Sch.
Auburn U.
Boise St. U.
Boston U.
Bradley U.
Brooklyn C. (C.U.N.Y.)
B.Y.U.

Cal. St. U. (Chico)
Cal. St. U. (Dominguez
  Hills)
Cal. St. U. (Fullerton)
Cal. St. U. (Long Beach)
U. Cal. (Irvine)
Cent. Wash. U.
Clark U.
U. Dallas
Dartmouth C.
DePaul U.
U. Detroit Mercy
Drew U.
Duke U.
Duquesne U.
East. Wash. U.
Emory U.
Fitchburg St. U.
Frostburg St. U.
Geo. Mason U.
Geo Wash. U.
Hamline U.
Harvard U.
Hofstra U.
Hollins C.
U. Idaho
Ind. U.
Jacksonville St. U.
Johns Hopkins U.
Kean C. N.J.
Keene St. U.
Lincoln U.
L.S.U. (Shreveport)
U. Maine
Manhattanville C.
U. Miami
Mills C.
Miss. C.
U. Mont.
Moorhead C.
N. Mex. St. U.
New Sch. Soc. Res.
S.U.N.Y. (Stony Brook)
S.U.N.Y.C. (Brockport)
S.U.N.Y.C. (Buffalo)
N.Y.U.
No. Car. St. U.
U. No. Car. U. (Charlotte)
U. No. Car. U.
  (Greensboro)
U. No. Colo.
Northwestern U.
C. Notre Dame
Nova U.
Ohio St. U.
Ohio U.
Okla. City U.
Okla. St. U.
U. Okla.
Old Dom. U.
U. Penn.
Queens C. (C.U.N.Y.)
Reed C.
U. Richmond
Rutgers U.
St. John's C. (MD)
St. John's C. (NM)
S.D.S.U.
San Fran. St. U.
Simmons C.
So. Ore St. U.
Stanford U.
Syracuse U.
Temple U.
Tex. Christ. U.
U. Tex. (Arlington)
U. Tex. (Dallas)
U. Tex. (El Paso)
U. Tex. (Pan American)
U. Tex. (Tyler)
U. Toledo
Towson St. U.
Va. Commonwealth U.

Vanderbilt U.
Villanova U.
Wayne St. U.
Wesleyan U.
W. VA. U.
Wichita St. U.
Widener U.
Wright St. U.
Xavier U.

Library/
Information
Studies

U. Ala.
U. Albany (S.U.N.Y.)
Appal. St. U.
U. Ariz.
U. Cal. (Berkeley)
U.C.L.A.
Catholic U.
U. Cent. Ark.
Cent. Mich. St. U.
Cent. Mo. St. U.
Chicago St. U.
Clarion U. Pa.
Clark Atlanta U.
Columbia U.
Drexel U.
East Car. U.
East Tenn. St. U.
Emporia St. U
Fla. St. U.
U. Georgia
U. Hawaii
U. Ill.
Ind. St. U.
Ind. U.
U. Iowa
Jersey City St. U.
Kent St. U
U. Ky.
Kutztown U. Pa.
L.I.U. (C. W. Post)
L.S.U.
Marshall U.
U. Md.
U. Mich.
U. Mo. (Columbia)
U. Nev.
S.U.N.Y. (Buffalo)
No. Car. Cent. U
U. No. Car. (Chapel
  Hill)
U. No. Car.
  (Greensboro)
U. No. Tex.
No. Ill. U.
U. No. Iowa
U. Okla.
Phillips U.
U. Pitt.
Pratt Inst.
U. Puerto Rico
Queens C. (C.U.N.Y.)
U. R. I.
Rosary C.
Rutgers U.
St. John's U. (N.Y.)
Sam Houston St. U.
San Jose St. U.
Simmons C.
U. So. Car.
U. So. Fla.
So. Conn. St. U.
U. So. Miss.
Spalding U.
Syracuse U.
U. Tenn.
U. Tex. (Austin)
Tex. Woman's U.
U. Wash.
Wayne St. U.

West Ky. U.
West. Md. C.
U. Wis.
U. Wis. (Milwaukee)

Medicine

U. Ala. (Birm.)
Albany Med. Sch.
U. Ariz.
U. Ark.
Baylor Col. Med.
Boston U.
Brown U.
U. Cal. (Davis)
U. Cal. (Irvine)
U.C.L.A.
U. Cal. (San Diego)
U. Cal. (San Francisco)
Case West. Res. U.
U. Chicago
U. Cincinnati
U. Colo. Health
  Sci. C.
Columbia U.
U. Conn.
Cornell U.
Creighton U.
Dartmouth C.
Duke U.
E. Car. U.
E. Tenn. St. U.
East. Va. Med. Sch.
Emory U.
Finch U. Health Sci.
  (Chicago)
U. Fla.
Georgetown U.
Geo. Wash. U.
Med. C. Georgia
Georgia St. U.
Harvard U.
U. Hawaii
Howard U.
U. Ill.
U. Ill. (Chicago)
Ind. U.
U. Iowa
Johns Hopkins U.
U. Kans.
U. Ky.
Loma Linda U.
L.S.U. Med. Cent.
L.S.U. Shreveport
U. Louisville
Loyola U. (Chicago)
U. Md.
U. Mass. (Worcester)
Marshall U.
Mayo Med. Sch.
Meharry Med. C.
Mercer U.
U. Miami (Fla.)
Mich. St. U.
U. Mich.
U. Minn. Duluth
U. Minn. Minneapolis
U. Miss. Med. C.
Morehouse Sch. Med.
U. Mo. (Columbia)
U. Mo. (K.C.)
Mt. Sinai Sch. Med.
  (C.U.N.Y.)
U. Neb. Med. C.
U. Nev. Reno
C. Med. & Dent. N.J.
  Newark
C. Med. & Dent. N.J.
  Piscatway
U. N. Mex.
N.Y. Med. C.
S.U.N.Y. (Buffalo)

S.U.N.Y. (Stony Brook)
S.U.N.Y. Health Sci. Cent
  (Brooklyn)
S.U.N.Y. Health Sci.
  Cent. (Syracuse)
N.Y.U.
U. No. Car. (Chapel Hill)
U. No. Dak.
No. East. Ohio U.
Northwestern U.
Ohio St. U.
Med. C. Ohio (Toledo)
U. Okla.
Ore. Health Sci. U.
Med. C. Penn/
  Hahnemann U.
Penn. St. U.
U. Penn.
U. Pitt.
Ponce Sch. Med.
U. Puerto Rico
U. Rochester
Rush U.
St. Louis U.
U. So. Ala.
Med. U. So. Car.
U. So. Car.
U. So. Dak.
U. So. Cal.
U. So. Fla.
So. Ill. U.
Stanford U.
Temple U.
U. Tenn. (Memphis)
Tex. A&M U.
Tex. Tech. U.
U. Tex. (San Antonio)
U. Tex. (Southwestern
  Med. Sch. Dallas)
U. Tex. (Med. Branch
  Galveston)
U. Tex. (Houston)
Thom. Jefferson U.
Tufts U.
Tulane U.
U. Utah
Vanderbilt U.
U. Vt.
Va. Commonwealth U.
U. Va.
Wake Forest U.
Wash. U. (Mo.)
U. Wash.
Wayne St. U.
W. Va. U.
Med. C. Wis.
U. Wis.
Wright St. U.
Yale U.
Yeshiva U.

MEDICAL
ILLUSTRATION

U. Cal. (San Francisco)
Med. C. Georgia
Johns Hopkins U.
U. Mich.
U. Tex. (Southwestern
  Med. Sch. Dallas)

MEDICAL
TECHNOLOGY

Andrews U.
Ball St. U.
B.Y.U.
Cal. St. U. (Fullerton)
Cal. St. U. (Long Beach)
Catholic U.
East. Wash. U.
Fairleigh Dickinson U.
Georgia St. U.
Hahnemann U.
U. Health Sci. (Chicago)

TROPICAL MEDICINE

Music

(Typically includes Composition, Music Education, Musicology, Performance, Theory; may include Ethnomusicology)

MUSIC THERAPY

Nursing and Health Professions

CHILD CARE/ PEDIATRIC NURSING

FAMILY NURSING

(Typically includes Adult, Geriatric, Maternity, Parent Child)

Marquette U.
U. Miami
U. Mich.
U. Mo. (K.C.)
U. N. Mex.
S.U.N.Y. (Buffalo)
S.U.N.Y. (Stony Brook)
N.Y.U.
Oakland U.
Ore. Health Sci. U.
U. Penn.
U. Pitt.
Rutgers U.
St. Louis U.
U. San Fran.
Seton Hall U.
Med U. So. Car.
U. So. Maine
U. Tenn. (Memphis)
U. Tex. Health Cent.
  (Houston)
U. Tex. Health Cent. (San
  Antonio)
Vanderbilt U.
Va. Commonwealth U.
Wayne St. U.
Wichita St. U.
U. Wyo.

GERONTOLOGICAL NURSING
Case West. Res. U.
Emory U.
Hunter C. (C.U.N.Y.)
Loma Linda U.
U. Mass. (Lowell)
N.Y.U.
U. Penn.
Seton Hall U.

HEALTH CARE/HEALTH SERVICES/ HOSPITAL ADMINISTRATION/ MANAGEMENT
U. Ala. (Birm.)
Am. Grad. Sch. Intl. Mgt.
American U.
Ariz. St. U.
U. Ark. (Little Rock)
Barry U.
Baruch C. (C.U.N.Y.)
Baylor U.
Boston U.
Brooklyn C. (C.U.N.Y.)
B.Y.U.
Cal. St. U. (Bakersfield)
Cal. St. U. (Chico)
Cal. St. U. (Fresno)
Cal. St. U. (Los Angeles)
Cal. St. U. (Northridge)
Cal. St. U. (San
  Bernardino)
U. Cal. (Berkeley)
U.C.L.A.
Card. Stritch C.
Case West. Res. U.
Chapman U.
U. Chicago
U. Cincinnati
Clark U.
Cleveland St. U.
U. Colo.
Columbia U. (Teachers
  C.)
Columbus C.
U. Conn.
Cornell U.
U. Dallas
DePaul U.
U. Detroit Mercy Duke U.
East. Ky. U.

East. Wash. U.
U. Evansville
F.D.U.
Fla. Inst. Tech.
U. Fla.
Framingham St. U.
Gannon U.
Geo. Wash. U.
Georgia Inst. Tech.
Georgia St. U.
Golden Gate U.
Gov. St. U.
U. Hartford
U. Hawaii
Harvard U.
Hofstra U.
Howard U.
Hunter C. (C.U.N.Y.)
Idaho St. U.
U. Ill. (Chicago)
Ind. St. U.
Ind. U.
Ind. U. Pa.
Iona C.
U. Iowa
Jersey City St. U.
Johns Hopkins U.
U. Kansas
U. Ky.
Kean C. N.J.
U. La Verne
Loma Linda U.
L.I.U.
L.I.U. (C. W. Post)
Marywood C.
U. Md. (Baltimore Co.)
M.I.T.
U. Mass. (Lowell)
U. Memphis
Med. U. So. Car.
Mercer U.
U. Miami
U. Mich.
U. Minn.
Miss. C.
U. Mo. (Columbia)
U. Mo. (Kansas City)
U. Miss.
National U.
U.N.H.
U. N. Haven
U. New Mex.
Northeastern U.
New Sch. Soc. Res.
New York Med. C.
S.U.N.Y. (Buffalo)
S.U.N.Y. (Stony Brook)
N.Y.U.
U. No. Car. (Chapel Hill)
U. No. Fla.
U. No. Tex.
Northwestern U.
Nova U.
Ohio St. U.
Ohio U.
U. Okla.
U. Ore.
U. Osteopathic Med &
  Health Sci.
Our Lady of the Lakes
Pace U.
Penn. St. U.
U. Penn.
U. Pitt.
Portland St. U.
Quinnipiac C.
R.P.I.
Robert Morris C.
Rush U.
Sage Grad. Sch.
Rutgers U.
St. John's U. (N.Y.)
St. Joseph's U.

St. Louis U.
St. Mary's U. (Minn.)
S.D.S.U.
Seton Hall U.
Simmons C.
U. So. Cal.
U. So. Car.
So. East. Mo. St. U.
Southwest Texas St. U.
Springfield C.
Stanford U.
Suffolk U.
Temple U.
U. Tenn.
Tex. Woman's U.
Towson St. U.
Trinity U.
Tufts U.
Tulane U.
Union C.
Va. Commonwealth U.
Villanova U.
Wash U.
U. Wash.
Webster U.
West Chester U. Pa.
West Car. U.
U. W. Va. Grad. Studies
Widener U.
U. Wis.
U. Wis. (Oshkosh)
Wilkes U.
Wright St. U.
Xavier U. (OH)
Yale U.

NURSE ANESTHESIA
U. Ala. (Birm.)
Cal. St. U. (Long Beach)
U.C.L.A.
Case West. Res. U.
U. Cincinnati
Columbia U.
DePaul U.
U. Detroit Mercy
Gannon U.
Geo. Wash. U.
Gonzaga U.
U. Kans.
U. Mich.
U. No. Car. (Greensboro)
Med C. Penn.
U. Pitt.
Med. U. So. Car.
U. Tex. Health Sci Cent.
  (Houston)
Va. Commonwealth U.
Wake Forest U.
Wayne St. U.
Xavier U. La

NURSE MIDWIFERY
Case West Res. U.
U. Colo. Health Sci C.
Columbia U. (Teachers
  C.)
Emory U.
Georgetown U.
U. Ill. (Chicago)
U. Med. & Dent. N.J.
U. Miami
U. Penn.
U. So. Cal.
Med. U. So. Car.
U. Tex. (El Paso)
Va. Commonwealth U.

NURSING
(Typically includes Nurse
Practitioner, Administra-
tion, Education, Medical
Surgical)

Adelphi U.
U. Akron
U. Ala. (Birm.)
U. Ala. (Hunt.)
U. Alaska
Andrews U.
Ariz. St. U.
U. Ariz.
Ark. St. U.
U. Ark.
Armstrong St. U.
Auburn U. (Mont.)
Azusa Pac. C.
Ball St. U.
Baylor C. Med.
Bloomsburg U. Pa.
Bowie St. U.
Boston C.
Bradley U.
B.Y.U.
Cal. St. (Bakersfield)
Cal. St. U. (Chico)
Cal. St. U. (Domiguez
  Hills)
Cal. St. U. (Fresno)
Cal. St. U. (Long Beach)
Cal. St. U. (L.A.)
Cal. St. U. (Sacramento)
U.C.L.A.
U. Cal. (San Fran.)
Capital U.
Case West. Res. U.
Catholic U.
U. Cent. Ark.
Cent. Conn. St. U.
U. Cincinnati
Clemson U.
U. Colo. Health Sci. Cent.
Columbia U. (Teacher C.)
U. Conn.
Creighton U.
U. Del.
DePaul U.
U. Detroit Mercy
Drake U.
Duke U.
Duquesne U.
East Car. U.
East. Wash. U.
Edinboro U. Pa.
Emory U.
U. Evansville
Fla. Atlantic U.
Fla. St. U.
U. Fla.
Fort Hays St. U.
Gannon U.
Geo. Mason U.
Georgetown U.
Geo. Wash. U.
Georgia C.
Med. C. Georgia
Georgia St. U.
Gonzaga U.
Gov. St. U.
Hampton U.
U. Hartford
U. Hawaii
Howard U.
Hunter C. (C.U.N.Y.)
Idaho St. U.
U. Ill. (Chicago)
Incarnate Word C.
Ind. St. U.
Ind. U.
Ind. U. Pa.
U. Iowa
Johns Hopkins U.
Kent St. U.
U. Kans. Med. C.
U. Ky.
Lehman C. (C.U.N.Y.)
Loma Linda U.

L.S.U. Med. Cent.
La. Tech. U.
U. Louisville
Loyola U. Chicago
U. Maine
Marquette U.
Marshall U.
U. Md.
U. Md. (Baltimore)
U. Mass.
U. Mass. (Boston)
U. Mass. (Dartmouth)
U. Mass. (Lowell)
U. Miami
Mich. St. U.
U. Mich.
Miss. U. Women
U. Minn.
U. Miss.
U. Mo. (Columbia)
U. Mo. (K.C.)
Mont. St. U.
Murray St. U.
U. Neb.
U. Nev. (Las Vegas)
U. Nev. (Reno)
U.N.H.
U. Med. & Dent. N.J.
U. N. Mex.
U. N. Orleans Med. Cent.
C. N. Rochelle
N. Y. Med. C.
S.U.N.Y. (Binghamton)
S.U.N.Y. (Buffalo)
S.U.N.Y. (New Paltz)
S.U.N.Y. (Stony Brook)
S.U.N.Y. Health Sci.
  Cent. (Brooklyn)
S.U.N.Y. Health Sci.
  Cent. (Syracuse)
N.Y.U.
U. No. Car. (Chapel Hill)
U. No. Car. (Charlotte)
U. No. Car. (Greensboro)
U. No. Colo.
U. No. Dak.
No. Ill. U.
No. Mich. U.
Northwestern St. U. La.
Oakland U.
Med. C. Ohio
Ohio St. U.
Old Dom. U.
U. Okla. Health Sci. Cent.
Ore. Health Sci. U.
U. Ore.
Pace U.
Pac. Luth. U.
Med. C. Penn./
  Hahnemann U.
Penn. St. U.
U. Penn.
U. Phoenix
U. Pitt.
U. Portland
Purdue U. (Calumet)
Radford U.
U.R.I.
U. Rochester
Rush U.
Rutgers U.
Sage Grad. Sch.
St. Joseph's C.
St. Louis U.
C. St. Scholastica
St. Xavier U.
Salem St. U.
S.D.S.U.
U. San Diego
San Fran. St. U.
U. San Fran.
San Jose St. U.
Seattle Pac. U.

stitutions are not listed here; also often includes Statistics, Applied Mathematics)

ANALYTICAL CHEMISTRY
Boston C.
Cleveland St. U.
Governor St. U.
U. Houston
Howard U.
Mich. St. U.
Miss. St. U.
U. Mo. (Kansas City)
Northeastern U.
Purdue U.
San Jose St. U.
Seton Hall U.
Wash St. U.
U. Wis.

APPLIED PHYSICS
Appal. St. U.
Brooklyn C. (C.U.N.Y.)
Cal. Inst. Tech.
U. Cent. Okla.
Colo. Sch. Mines
Cornell U.
Geo. Mason U.
Harvard U.
U. Mass. (Boston)
U. Mich.
N.J.I.T.
U. New Orleans
S.U.N.Y. (Buffalo)
U. Southwest. LA.
Stanford U.
Tex. Tech. U.
Va. Commonwealth U.
U. Wash.

ASTRONOMY/ PLANETARY SCIENCES/SPACE SCIENCES
U. Alaska
Ar. St. U.
U. Ariz.
Boston U.
Bowl. Gr. St. U.
Brown U.
B.Y.U.
Cal. Inst. Tech.
U. Cal. (Berkeley)
U.C.L.A.
U. Cal. (Santa Cruz)
Case West. Res. U.
Catholic U.
U. Chicago
Clemson U.
Colo. St. U.
Columbia U.
Cornell U.
Creighton U.
Dartmouth C.
U. Dela.
Fla. Inst. Tech.
U. Fla.
Georgia St. U.
Harvard U.
U. Hawaii
U. Ill.
Ind. U.
Iowa St. U.
U. Iowa
Johns Hopkins U.
U. Kans.
U. Ky.
L.S.U.
U. Maine
U. Md.

M.I.T.
U. Mass.
Mich. St. U.
U. Mich.
U. Minn.
U. Neb.
N. Mex. Inst. M&T
N. Mex. St. U.
U. N. Mex.
S.U.N.Y. (Buffalo)
S.U.N.Y. (Stony Brook)
U. No. Car. (Chapel Hill)
Northwestern U.
Ohio St. U.
U. Okla.
Ore. St. U.
Penn. St. U.
U. Penn.
U. Pitt.
Princeton U.
Rice U.
U. Rochester
R.P.I.
S.D.S.U.
U. So. Cal.
U. So. Car.
U. Tex. (Austin)
Tufts U.
Utah St. U.
Vanderbilt U.
U. Va.
U. Wash.
Wesleyan U.
U. Wis.
U. Wyo.
Yale U.

GEOCHEMISTRY
Cal. Inst. Tech.
U.C.L.A.
Colo. Sch. Mines
Ind. U.
Mont. Tech.
N. Mex. Inst. M&T
U. Nev. (Reno)
Penn. St. U.
U. Tulsa

GEOLOGY
U. Akron
U. Ala.
U. Alaska
U. Albany (S.U.N.Y.)
Ariz. St. U.
U. Ariz.
U. Ark.
Auburn U.
Ball St. U.
Baylor U.
Boise St. U.
Boston C.
Boston U.
Bowl. Gr. St. U.
B.Y.U.
Brooklyn C. (C.U.N.Y.)
Brown U.
Bryn Mawr C.
Cal. Inst. Tech.
Cal. St. U. (Bakersfield)
Cal. St. U. (Chico)
Cal. St. U. (Fresno)
Cal. St. U. (Hayward)
Cal. St. U. (Long Beach)
Cal. St. U. (L.A.)
Cal. St. U. (Northridge)
U. Cal. (Berkeley)
U. Cal. (Davis)
U.C.L.A.
U. Cal. (Riverside)
U. Cal. (Santa Barbara)
Case West. Res. U.
Cent. Mich. U.
U. Cincinnati

C.C.N.Y. (C.U.N.Y.)
Clemson U.
Colo. Sch. Mines
Colo. St. U.
U. Colo.
Columbia U.
U. Conn.
Cornell U.
Dartmouth C.
U. Del.
Duke U.
East Car. U.
East. Ky. U.
East. Wash. U.
Fla. Atlantic U.
Fla. St. U.
U. Fla.
Fort Hays St. U.
Geo. Wash. U.
Georgia St. U.
U. Georgia
Harvard U.
U. Hawaii
U. Houston
Idaho St. U.
U. Idaho
U. Ill.
U. Ill. (Chicago C.)
Ind. St. U.
Ind. U.
Iowa St. U.
U. Iowa
Johns Hopkins U.
Kans. St. U.
U. Kans.
Kent St. U.
U. Ky.
Lehigh U.
Loma Linda U.
L.S.U.
La. Tech. U.
U. Maine
U. Md.
M.I.T.
U. Mass.
U. Memphis
Miami U. (Ohio)
U. Miami
Mich. St. U.
Mich. Tech. U.
U. Mich.
U. Minn.
Miss. St. U.
U. Miss.
U. Mo. (Columbia)
U. Mo. (K.C.)
U. Mo. (Rolla)
Mont. Tech.
Mont. St. U.
U. Mont.
Montclair St. U.
U. Neb.
U. Nev.
U. Nev. (Reno)
U. N. H.
N. Mex. Inst. M&T
N. Mex. St. U.
U. N. Mex.
S.U.N.Y. (Binghamton)
S.U.N.Y. (Buffalo)
S.U.N.Y. (Stony Brook)
S.U.N.Y.C. (Fredonia)
S.U.N.Y.C. (New Paltz)
No. Car. St. U. (Raleigh)
U. No. Car. (Chapel Hill)
U. No. Dak.
No. Ariz. U.
No. Ill. U.
Northwestern U.
Ohio St. U.
Ohio U.
Okla. St. U.
U. Okla.

Old Dom. U.
Ore. St. U.
U. Ore.
Penn. St. U.
U. Penn.
U. Pitt.
Portland St. U.
Princeton U.
Purdue U.
Queens C. (C.U.N.Y.)
R.P.I.
U.R.I.
Rice U.
U. Rochester
Rutgers U.
S.D.S.U.
San Jose St. U.
U. So. Car.
So. Dak. Sch. M&T
U. So. Cal.
U. So. Fla.
So. Ill. U.
So. Meth. U.
U. So. Miss.
U. Southwestern La.
Stanford U.
S. F. Austin St. U.
Sul Ross St. U.
Syracuse U.
Temple U.
U. Tenn.
Tex. A&I U.
Tex. A&M U.
Tex. Christ. U.
U. Tex. (Arlington)
U. Tex. (Austin)
U. Tex. (Dallas)
U. Tex. (El Paso)
U. Tex. (San Antonio)
U. Tex. (Permian Basin)
U. Toledo
Tulane U.
U. Tulsa
Utah St. U.
U. Utah
Vanderbilt U.
U. Vt.
Va. Poly Inst.
Va. St. U.
U. Va.
Wash. St. U.
Wash. U.
U. Wash.
Wayne St. U.
W. Va. U.
West. Mich. U.
West. Wash. St. U.
Wichita St. U.
U. Wis.
U. Wis. (Milwaukee)
Wright St. U.
U. Wyo.
Yale U.

GEOPHYSICS
U. Alaska
Boise St. U.
Boston C.
Cal. Inst. Tech.
U. Cal. (Berkeley)
U.C.L.A.
U. Cal. (Santa Barbara)
U. Chicago
U. Conn.
Colo. Sch. Mines
U. Colo.
U. Conn.
Fla. St. U.
Georgia Inst. Tech.
U. Georgia
U. Hawaii
U. Houston
Ind. U.

Johns Hopkins U.
U. Ill. (Chicago)
U. Kans.
L.S.U.
M.I.T.
U. Memphis
U. Miami
Mich. Tech. U.
U. Minn.
U. Mo. (Rolla)
N. Mex. Inst. M&T
S.U.N.Y. (Stony Brook)
No. Car. St. U. (Raleigh)
U. Okla.
Ore. St. U.
Penn. St. U.
U. Pitt.
Princeton U.
R.P.I.
Rice U.
St. Louis U.
So. Meth. U.
Stanford U.
Tex. A&M U.
U. Tex. (Austin)
U. Tex. (Dallas)
U. Tex. (El Paso)
U. Tulsa
U. Utah
Va. Poly. Inst.
Wash. U.
U. Wash.
U. Wis.
U Wyo.
Yale U.

Public Administration
(Typically includes Energy Management and Policy, Public Policy, Public Management, Public Affairs)

Alfred U.
U. Akron
U. Ala.
U. Ala. (Birm.)
U. Ala. (Huntsville)
U. Alaska
U. Albany (S.U.N.Y.)
Amer. U.
Angelo St. U.
Appal. St. U.
Ariz. St. U.
U. Ariz.
Ark. St. U.
U. Ark.
Auburn U.
Auburn U. (Montogermy)
Ball St. U.
U. Baltimore
Baruch C. (C.U.N.Y.)
Baylor U.
Boise St. U.
Boston C.
Bowie St. U.
Bowl. Gr. St. U.
Brandeis U.
Brooklyn C. (C.U.N.Y.)
Bryant C.
B.Y.U.
Cal. Luth. U.
Ca. St. (Bakersfiled.)
Cal. St. U. (Chico)
Cal. St. U. (Dominguez Hills)
Ca. St. U (Fresno)
Cal St U (Fullerton)
Cal. St. U. (Long Beach)

Cal. St. U. (L.A.)
Cal. St. U. (Northridge)
Cal. St. U. (Sacramento)
Cal. St. U. (San
  Bernardino)
Cal. St. U. (Stanislaus)
U. Cal. (Berkeley)
U. Cal. (Davis)
Canisius C.
Carnegie Mellon U.
Cent. Mich. U.
Cent. Mo. St. U.
U. Chicago
U. Cincinnati
Claremont Grad. Sch.
Clark Atlanta U.
Clark U.
Cleveland St. U.
Colo. Sch. Mines
Columbia U.
U. Colo.
U. Conn.
Cornell U.
U. Dayton
U. Del.
DePaul U.
U. Detroit Mercy
Drake U.
Duke U.
Duquesne U.
East Car. U.
East Ky. U.
East. Mich. U.
East Tenn. St. U.
East. Wash. U.
Fairleigh Dickinson U.
Fla. Atlantic U.
Fla. St. U.
U. Fla.
Framingham St. U.
Gannon U.
Geo. Mason U.
Georgetown U.
Geo. Wash. U.
Georgia C.
  (Milledgeville)
Georgia So. C.
Georgia St. U.
U. Georgia
Golden Gate U.
Gov. St. U.
C.U.N.Y. (Grad. Cent.)
Hamline U.
U. Hartford
Harvard U.
U. Hawaii
Hood C.
U. Houston
Howard U.
Idaho St. U.
U. Idaho
Ill. Inst. Tech.
U. Ill.
U. Ill. (Chicago)
Ind. U.
Iowa St. U.
U. Iowa
Jackson St. U.
Jacksonville St. U.
James Madison U.
John Jay C. (C.U.N.Y.)
Johns Hopkins U.
U. Kans.
Kean C. NJ.
Kent St. U.
Kutztown U. Pa.
U. Ky.
Lamar U.
U. LaVerne
Lewis & Clark
U. Louisville
L.I.U.
L.S.U.

U. Maine
Mankato St. U.
Marywood C.
U. Mass.
U. Mass. (Boston)
U. Md.
U. Md. (Baltimore Co.)
U. Memphis
U. Miami
Mich. St. U.
U. Mich.
Mid. Tenn. St. U.
U. Minn.
Miss. St. U.
U. Miss.
U. Mo. (Columbia)
U. Mo. (K.C.)
U. Mo. (St. Louis)
Mont. St. U.
U. Mont.
Murray St. U.
National U.
U. Neb. (Omaha)
U. Nev. (Las Vegas)
U. Nev. (Reno)
U.N.H.
U. N. Haven
New Mex. Highlands U.
N. Mex. St. U.
U. N. Mex.
U. N. Orleans
S.U.N.Y. (Albany)
S.U.N.Y. (Binghamton)
S.U.N.Y. (Buffalo)
S.U.N.Y.C. (Brockport)
N.Y.I.T.
N.Y.U.
No. Ariz. U.
No. Cal. Cent. U.
No. Car. St. U. (Raleigh)
Northeastern U.
U. No. Car. (Chapel Hill)
U. No. Car. (Charlotte)
U. No. Car. (Greensboro)
U. No. Dak.
U. No. Fla.
No. Ill. U.
No. Mich. U.
U. No. Tex.
Northwestern U.
C. Notre Dame (Cal.)
Nova U.
Oakland U.
Ohio St. U.
Ohio U.
Okla. City U.
U. Okla.
Old Dom. U.
U. Ore.
Pace U.
Pac. Luth. U.
Penn. St. U.
U. Penn.
U. Pitt
Portland St. U.
Princeton U.
U. Puerto Rico
Purdue U.
Rice U.
U. Rochester
Roosevelt U.
Rosary C.
U.R.I.
Rutgers U.
Sage Grad. Sch.
St. Edward's U.
St. John's U. (N.Y.)
St. Louis U.
St. Mary's U.
S.D.S.U.
San Fran. St. U.
U. San Fran.
San Jose St. U.

Seton Hall U.
Seattle U.
Shippensburg U. Pa.
Sonoma St. U.
U. So. Ala.
U. So. Cal.
U. So. Car.
U. So. Dak.
U. So. Fla.
So. E. Mo. St. U.
So. Ill. U.
U. So. Maine
So. Meth. U.
Southwest Mo. St. U.
Southwest Tex. St. U.
Suffolk U.
Sul Ross St. U.
Syracuse U.
Temple U.
Tenn. St. U.
U. Tenn.
U. Tenn. (Chattanooga)
Tex. A&M U.
Tex. So. U.
Tex. Tech. U.
U. Tex. (Arlington)
U. Tex. (Austin)
U. Tex. (Dallas)
U. Tex. (Pan American)
U. Tex. (San Antonio)
U. Toledo
Trenton St. U.
Troy St. U.
Union C.
Utah St. U.
U. Utah
Valdosta St. U.
U. Vt.
Villanova U.
Va. Commonwealth U.
Va. Poly Inst.
U. Va.
Wash. U.
U. Wash.
Wayne St. U.
Webster U.
West Chester U. Pa.
West. Car. U.
West. Conn. U.
West. Ga. C.
West. Ky U.
West. Mich. U.
W. Va. Grad. C.
W. Va. U.
Wichita St. U.
Widener U.
U. Wis.
U. Wis. (Milwaukee)
U. Wis. (Oshkosh)
U. Wyo.
Yale U.

Public and Community Health

U. Ala. (Birm.)
U. Albany (S.U.N.Y.)
U. Ark.
Ball St. U.
Boston U.
Ca. St. U (Fresno)
Cal. St. U. (Long Beach)
Cal. St. U. (Northridge)
Cal. St. U. (Sacramento)
U. Cal. (Berkeley)
U. Cal. (Davis)
U. Cal. (Irvine)
U.C.L.A.
U. Cincinnati
Clemson U.
Colo. St. U.
U. Colo. Health Sci. Cent.
Columbia U.

U. Conn.
Duke U.
E. Car. U.
E. Ky. U.
E. Tenn. St. U.
Emory U.
Georgetown U.
Geo. Wash. U.
Harvard U.
U. Hawaii
Hunter C. (C.U.N.Y.)
U. Ill.
U. Ill. (Chicago)
Ind. U.
U. Iowa
Johns Hopkins U.
U. Kans.
U. Ky.
L.I.U.
Loma Linda U.
Loyola U. (Chicago)
Mankato St. U.
Marshall U.
M.I.T.
U. Mass.
U. Med. & Dent. N.J.
Meharry Med. C.
Mich. St. U.
U. Mich.
U. Minn.
U. Mo. (Columbia)
S.U.N.Y. (Buffalo)
N.Y. Med. C.
N.Y.U.
U. No. Car. (Chapel
  Hill)
No. Ill. U.
U. No. Colo.
U. No. Tex.
Northwestern U.
Med. C. Ohio
Ohio St. U.
Okla. St. U.
U. Okla. Health Sci. Cent.
Old Dominion U.
Ore. St. U.
U. Ore.
Med. C. Penn.
Penn. St. U./Hahnemann
  U.
U. Penn.
U. Pitt
U. Puerto Rico
Purdue U.
R.P.I.
U.R.I.
U. Rochester
Rutgers U.
St. Louis U.
St. Mary's U.
S.D.S.U.
San Fran. St. U.
San Jose St. U.
U. So. Cal.
Med. U. So. Car.
U. So. Car.
Temple U.
U. Tenn.
Tex. A&M U.
Tex. Woman's U.
U. Tex. (Arlington)
U. Tex. (Med. Branch
  Galveston)
U. Tex. Health Sci. Cent.
  (Houston)
Tufts U.
Tulane U.
U. Utah
U. Va.
Va. Commonwealth U.
Wake Forest U.
U. Wash.
Wayne St. U.

U. Conn.
Duke U.
E. Car. U.
E. Ky. U.
E. Tenn. St. U.
Emory U.
Georgetown U.
Geo. Wash. U.
Harvard U.
U. Hawaii
Hunter C. (C.U.N.Y.)
U. Ill.
U. Ill. (Chicago)
Ind. U.
U. Iowa
Johns Hopkins U.
U. Kans.
U. Ky.
L.I.U.

West. Ky. U.
West. Wash. U.
W. Va. U.
Med. C. Wis.
U. Wis.
U. Wis. (Eau Claire)
U. Wyo.
Yale U.

EPIDEMIOLOGY

U. Ala. (Birm.)
Baylor U.
Boston U.
U. Cal. (Berkeley)
U. Cal. (Davis)
U.C.L.A.
U. Cal. (San Diego)
Case West. Res U.
Columbia U.
Cornell U.
Duke U.
Emory U.
Harvard U.
U. Hawaii
U. Ill. (Chicago)
U. Iowa
Johns Hopkins U.
Loma Linda U.
U. Md. (Baltimore)
M.I.T.
U. Mich.
U. Minn.
N. Y. Med. C.
S.U.N.Y. (Buffalo)
N.Y.U.
U. No. Car. (Chapel Hill)
Northwestern U.
Ohio St. U.
U. Okla.
Ore. Health Sci, U.
U. Penn.
U. Pitt.
Purdue U.
Rutgers U.
U. So. Cal.
U. So. Car.
Tex. A&M U.
U. Tex. Health Sci. Cent.
  (Houston)
Tulane U.
Utah St. U.
U. Va.
Wake Forest U.
Wayne St. U.
Med. C. Wis.
U. Wis.
Yale U.
Yeshiva U.

INTERNATIONAL HEALTH

Am Grad. Sch. Intl. Mgt.
Emory U.
Harvard U.
Johns Hopkins U.
U. Mich.
Tulane U.

Religion

(Bible Studies, Religious
Studies, Theology; often
includes Religious Educa-
tion)

A. C. U.
Amer. U.
Andrews U.
Ariz. St. U.
Assumption C.
Augustana C.
Azusa Pac. U.
Barry U.

Baylor U.
Boston C.
Boston U.
Brown U.
U. Cal. (Berkeley)
U. Cal. (Santa Barbara)
Card. Stritch C.
Catholic U.
U. Chicago
Claremont Grad. Sch.
Colgate U.
U. Colo
Columbia U.
Concordia C. (Ill.)
U. Dallas
U. Dayton
U. Denver
U. Detroit Mercy
Drake U.
Drew U.
Duke U.
Dunquesne U.
Emory U.
Fairfield U.
Fla. St. U.
U. Fla.
Fordham U.
Gannon U.
Geo. Wash. U.
U. Georgia
Gonzaga U.
Hardin-Simmons U.
Harvard U.
U. Hawaii
Hebrew C.
Holy Names C.
Incarnate Word C.
Ind. U.
U. Iowa John Carroll U.
U. Kans.
Loma Linda U.
Loyola U.
Loyola &. (Chicago)
Loyola U. (La.)
Marquette U.
Marygrove C.
Marywood C.
Miami U. (Ohio)
U. Miami (Fla.)
Mt. St. Mary's C.
N.Y.U.
U. No. Car. (Chapel Hill)
Northwestern U.
C. Notre Dame
U. Notre Dame
Okla. City U.
Olivet Naz. U.
Oral Roberts U.
U. Pac.
U. Penn.
Pepperdine U.
U. Pitt.
Point Loma Naz. C.
U. Portland
Princeton U.
Providence C.
Rice U.
St. Bonaventure U.
St. John's U. (Minn.)
St. John's U. (N.Y.)
St. Joseph C. (Conn.)
St. Louis U.
St. Mary's C.
St. Mary's U.
St. Michael's C.
St. Xavier U.
Samford U.
U. San Diego
U. San Fran.
Santa Clara U.
Seattle Pac. U.
Seattle U.
Seton Hall. U.

Smith C.
U. So. Cal.
U. So. Car.
So. Meth. U.
So. Naz. U.
Spalding C.
Stanford U.
Syracuse U.
Temple U.
U. Tenn.
Tex. Christ. U.
Trinity U.
Vanderbilt U.
Villanova U.
U. Va.
Wake Forest U.
U. Wash.
U. Wis.
Xavier U. (Ohio)
Yale U.
Yeshiva U.

Social Sciences

(Typically includes Economics, Environmental and Occupational Health, Political Science, Psychology, Sociology)

A.C.U.
Adelphi U.
U. Akron
Ala. A&M U.
U. Ala.
U. Ala. (Birm.)
U. Alaska
U. Albany (S.U.N.Y.)
Alfred U.
Amer. U.
Andrews U.
Angelo St. U.
Antioch N. E.
Antioch L. A.
Antioch Santa Barbara
Antioch Seattle
Appal. St. U.
Ariz. St. U.
U. Ariz.
U. Ark.
Assump. C.
Auburn U.
Auburn U. (Montgomery)
Augusta C.
Auston Peay St. U.
Azusa Pac. U.
Ball St. U.
U. Baltimore
Baruch C. (C.U.N.Y.)
Barry U.
Baylor U.
Bemidji St. U.
Bloomsburg U. Pa.
Boston C.
Boston U.
Bowie St. U.
Bowl, Gr. St. U.
Bradley U.
Brandeis U.
U. Bridgeport
Bridgewater St. U.
B.Y.U.
Brooklyn C. (C.U.N.Y.)
Brown U.
Bryn Mawr C.
Bucknell U.
Butler U.
Cal. Inst. Tech.
Cal. Luth. U.
Cal. St. Poly U. (Pomona)
Cal. St. U. (Chico)
Cal. St. U. (Dominguez Hills)

Cal. St. U. (Fresno)
Cal. St. U. (Fullerton)
Cal. St. U. (Hayward)
Cal. St. U. (Long Beach)
Cal. St. U. (L.A.)
Cal. St. U. (Northridge)
Cal. St. U. (Sacramento)
Cal. St. U (San Bernardino)
Cal. St. U. (Stanislaus)
Cal. U. Pa.
U. Cal. (Berkeley)
U. Cal. (Davis)
U. Cal. (Irvine)
U.C.L.A.
U. Cal. (Riverside)
U. Cal. (San Diego)
U. Cal. (San Francisco)
U. Cal. (Santa Barbara)
U. Cal. (Santa Cruz)
Carnegie Mellon U.
Case West. Res. U.
Catholic U.
U. Cent. Ark.
Cent. Conn. St. U.
U. Cent. Fla.
Cent. Mich. U.
Cent. Mo. St. U.
U. Cent. Okla.
Cent. Wash. U.
Chapman U.
Chicago St. U.
U. Chicago
U. Cincinnati
Citadel
C.C.N.Y. (C.U.N.Y.)
Claremont Grad. Sch.
Clark U.
Clark Atlanta U.
Clemson U.
Cleveland St. U.
Colgate U.
Colo. St. U.
U. Colo.
Columbia U.
Concordia U.
Conn. C.
U. Conn.
Cornell U.
Creighton U.
C.U.N.Y. (Grad. Cent.)
U. Dallas
Dartmouth C.
U. Dayton
U. Del.
Delta St. U.
U. Denver
DePaul U.
U. Detroit Mercy
Dominican C. San Rafael
Drake U.
Drew U.
Drexel U.
Drury C.
Duke U.
Duquesne U.
East Car. U.
East Stroudsburg U. Pa.
East Tenn. St. U.
East Tex. St. U.
East. Ill. U.
East. Ky. U.
East. Mich. U.
East. N. Mex. U.
East. Wash. U.
Edinboro U. Pa.
Emory U.
Emporia St. U.
U. Evansville
Fairfield U.
Fairleigh Dickinson U.
Finch U. Health Sci. (Chicago)

Fisk U.
Fitchburg St. U.
Fla, A&M U.
Fla. Atlantic U.
Fla. Inst. Tech.
Fla. St. U.
U. Fla.
Fordham U.
Fort Hays St. U.
Framingham St. U.
Frostburg St. U.
Gallaudet U.
Gannon U.
Geo. Mason U.
Geo. Wash. U.
Georgetown U.
Georgia C.
Georgia Inst. Tech.
Georgia So. U.
Georgia St. U.
U. Georgia
Goddard C.
Golden Gate U.
Gonzaga U.
Gov. St. U.
U. Hartford
Harvard U.
U. Hawaii
U. Health Sci. (Chicago)
Henderson St. U.
Hofstra U.
Holy Names C.
Hollins C.
Hood C.
U. Houston
Howard U.
Humbolt St. U.
Hunter C. (C.U.N.Y.)
Idaho St. U.
U. Idaho
Ill. Inst. Tech.
Ill. St. U.
U. Ill.
U. Ill. (Chicago)
Ind. St. U.
Ind. U.
Ind. U. Penn.
Inter American U.
Iowa St. U.
U. Iowa
Jackson St. U.
Jacksonville St. U.
James Madison U.
Jersey City St. U.
John Carroll U.
Johns Hopkins U.
John Jay C. (C.U.N.Y.)
Kans. St. U.
U. Kans.
Kean C. N.J.
Kent St. U.
U. Ky.
Kutztown U. Pa.
Lamar U.
U. LaVerne
Lehigh U.
Lewis and Clark C.
Lincoln U.
Loma Linda U.
L.I.U.
L.I.U. (C. W. Post)
L.S.U.
L.S.U. (Shreveport)
La. Tech. U.
Loras C.
U. Louisville
Loyola C.
Loyola Marymount U.
Loyola U. (Chicago)
U. Maine
Mankato St. U.
Mansfield U. Pa.
Marquette U.

Marshall U.
U. Md.
U. Md. (Baltimore)
Marywood C.
M.I.T.
U. Mass.
U. Mass. (Boston)
U. Mass. (Lowell)
McNeese St. U.
U. Memphis
Mercer U.
Miami U. (Ohio)
U. Miami (Fla.)
Mich. St. U.
U. Mich.
Mid. Tenn. St. U.
Midwestern St. U.
Millersville U. Pa.
U. Minn.
Miss. C.
Miss. St. U.
U. Miss.
U. Mo. (Columbia)
U. Mo. (K.C.)
U. Mo. (St. Louis)
Mont. St. U.
Mont. Tech.
U. Mont.
Montclair St. U.
Moorhead St. U.
Morehead St. U.
Morgan St. U.
Mount Holyoke C.
Murray St. U.
National Louis U.
U. Neb.
U. Neb. (Kearney)
U. Neb. (Omaha)
Naval P.G.
U. Nev.
U. Nev. (Las Vegas)
U.N.H.
U. N. Haven
N. Mex. Highlands U.
N. Mex. St. U.
U. N. Mex.
U. N. Orleans
C. New Rochelle
N. Sch. Social Research
S.U.N.Y. (Binghamton)
S.U.N.Y. (Buffalo)
S.U.N.Y. (Stony Brook)
S.U.N.Y.C. (Brockport)
S.U.N.Y.C. (Cortland)
S.U.N.Y.C. (New Paltz)
S.U.N.Y.C. (Oswego)
S.U.N.Y.C. (Plattsburg)
N.Y.U.
No. Car. Cent. U.
No. Car. St. U. (Raleigh)
U. No. Car. (Chapel Hill)
U. No. Car. (Charlotte)
U. No. Car. (Greensboro)
No. Dak. St. U.
U. No. Dak.
U. No. Fla.
Northeast La. U.
No. E. Mo. St. U.
Northeastern U.
Northeastern Ill. U.
No. Ariz. U.
U. No. Colo.
No. Ill. U.
U. No. Iowa
U. No. Tex.
U. No. Tex. Health Sci. Ctr.
No. W. Mo. St. U.
No. W. St. U. La.
No. West. Okla. St. U.
Northwestern U.
C. Notre Dame
U. Notre Dame

U. Denver
East Car. U.
East Tenn. St. U.
East. Ky. U.
East. Mich. U.
Fla. Atlantic U.
Fla. St. U.
U. Fla.
Gannon U.
Geo. Mason U.
Geo. Wash. U.
Georgia St. U.
U. Georgia
U. Hawaii
Hunter C. (C.U.N.Y.)
U. Idaho
Ill. St. U.
U. Ill.
U. Ill. (Chicago)
Ind. St. U.
Ind. U.
Ind. U. Penn.
U. Iowa
Johns Hopkins U.
Kans. St. U.
U. Kans.
Kent St. U.
U. Ky.
L.S.U.
La. Tech. U.
Mankato St. U.
Marshall U.
U. Md.
U. Mass.
U. Memphis
Miami U. (Ohio)
U. Miami
Mich. St. U.
U. Minn.
U. Mo. (Columbia)
U. Mont.
Montclair St. U.
Murray St. U.
U. Neb.
U. Neb. (Omaha)
N. Mex. St. U.
U. N. Mex.
S.U.N.Y. (Albany)
S.U.N.Y. (Binghamton)
S.U.N.Y. (Buffalo)
No. Ariz. U.
U. No. Car. (Chapel
  Hill)
U. No. Car. (Charlotte)
U. No. Dak.
Northeastern Ill. U.
U. No. Colo.
No. Ill. U.
U. No. Iowa
Northwestern U.
Ohio St. U.
Ohio U.
Okla St. U.
U. Okla.
Ore. St. U.
U. Ore.
Penn. St. U.
U. Penn.
Portland St. U.
U. R. I.
Rutgers U.
St. Cloud St. U.
S.D.S.U.
San Fran. St. U.
San Jose St. U.
U. So. Cal.
U. So Car.
So. Dak, St. U.
U. So. Fla.
So. Ill. U.
So. Ill. U. (Edwardsville)
U. So. Miss.

Southern U.
Syracuse U.
Temple U.
U. Tenn.
Tex. A&M U.
U. Tex. (Austin)
U. Toledo
Towson St. U.
U. Utah
Valparaiso U.
Va. Poly Inst. & St. U.
U. Va.
U. Vt.
U. Wash.
Wayne St. U.
W. Va. U.
West Chester U. Pa.
West. Ill. U.
West. Ky. U.
West. Mich. U.
West. Wash. U.
W. Va. U.
U. Wis.
U. Wis. (Milwaukee)
U. Wyo.

MEDIEVAL/
RENAISSANCE
STUDIES
Ariz. St. U.
Boston C.
Catholic U.
U. Conn.
Cornell U.
Duke U.
Harvard U.
Ind. U.
Marquette U.
U. Mo. (Columbia)
C.U.N.Y. (Grad. Cent.)
S.U.N.Y. (Binghamton)
U. Notre Dame
Rutgers U.
West. Mich. U.
Yale U.

PEACE
SCIENCE/CONFLICT
RESOLUTION
Cal. St. U. (Dominguez
  Hills)
Cornell U.
Geo. Mason U.
U. Mass (Boston)
Nova U.
U. Notre Dame
U. Penn.
Wayne St. U.

POPULATION
STUDIES
Ariz. St. U.
Bowl. Gr. St. U.
Brown U.
U. Cal. (Berkeley)
Cornell U.
Duke U.
Fla. St. U.
Fordham U.
Georgetown U.
Harvard U.
Howard U.
U. Ill.
Johns Hopkins U.
U. Mich.
U. Penn.
Princeton U.
U. So. Cal.
Tulane U.
U. Wash.
Wesleyan U.

URBAN STUDIES
U. Akron
Ala. A&M U.
U. Ala.
U. Albany (S.U.N.Y.)
Boston U.
Brooklyn C. (C.U.N.Y.)
Cleveland St. U.
U. Del.
East Tenn. St. U.
Georgia St. U.
Hunter C. (C.U.N.Y.)
Ind. U.
Jersey City St. U.
L.I.U.
U. Louisville
Mankato St. U.
Marquette U.
U. Md.
M.I.T.
U. Memphis
Mich. St. U.
U. Mo. (Kansas City)
Montclair St. U.
U. N. Orleans
C.U.N.Y. (Grad. Cent.)
New Sch. Soc. Res.
N.Y.U.
Old Dom. U.
U. Penn.
Portland St. U.
R.P.I.
U.R.I.
So. Conn. St. U.
St. Louis U.
So. Meth. U.
Temple U.
U. Tex. (Arlington)
Trinity U.
Tufts U.
Va. Commonwealth U.
Va. Poly Inst.
Wash. U.
Wright St. U.
U. Wis. (Milwaukee)

WOMEN'S/
FEMINIST STUDIES
U. Ala.
Ariz. St. U.
U. Cinn.
Clark Atlanta U.
Duke U.
East. Mich. U.
Emory U.
Geo. Wash. U.
Goddard C.
Mankato St. U.
New Sch. Soc. Res.
S.U.N.Y. (Buffalo)
C.U.N.Y. (Grad. Cent.)
N.Y.U.
Ohio St. U.
U. Okla.
Rutgers U.
San Fran. St. U.
Sarah Lawrence C.
So. Ill. U. (Edwardsville)

Social Work

(Includes Human Services,
Social Service, Social
Welfare)

Adelphi U.
U. Ala.
Ariz. St. U.
U. Ark.
Barry U.
Boise St. U.
Boston C.

Boston U.
Brandeis U.
B.Y.U.
Bryn Mawr C.
Cal. St. U. (Fresno)
Cal. St. U. (Long Beach)
Cal. St. U.
  (Sacramento)
Cal. St. U. (San
  Bernardino)
U. Cal. Berkeley
U.C.L.A.
Case West. Res. U.
Catholic U.
Cent. Mich. U.
U. Chicago
U. Cincinnati
Clark Atlanta U.
Colo. St. U.
Columbia U.
Columbia U. (Teachers
  C.)
U. Conn.
U. Dayton
U. Denver
East Car. U.
East. Mich. U.
East. Wash. U.
Fla. St. U.
Fordham U.
Gallaudet U.
Georgia St. U.
U. Georgia
Gov. St. U.
U. Hawaii
Henderson St. U.
Hofstra U.
U. Houston
Howard U.
Hunter C. (C.U.N.Y.)
U. Ill.
U. Ill. (Chicago)
Ind. U.
U. Iowa
Jackson St. U.
John Carroll U.
U. Kans.
Keene St. U.
U. Ky.
L.S.U.
La. Tech. U.
U. Louisville
Lincoln U.
Loyola U. (Chicago)
U. Maine
U. Md.
U. Md. (Baltimore)
Mankato St. U.
Marywood C.
U. Mass (Boston)
Mich. St. U.
U. Mich.
U. Minn.
Miss. St. U.
U. Mo. (Columbia)
U. Mo. (St. Louis)
Moorhead St. U.
National Louis U.
U. Neb. (Omaha)
U. Nev.
U. Nev. (Reno)
N. Mex. Highlands U.
N. Mex. St. U.
C.U.N.Y. (Grad. Cent.)
S.U.N.Y. (Buffalo)
S.U.N.Y. (Stony Brook)
S.U.N.Y.C. (Brockport)
S.U.N.Y.C. (Oswego)
N.Y.U.
No. Car. A&T St. U.
U. No. Car. (Chapel
  Hill)

U. No. Dak.
Northeastern U.
Nova U.
Ohio St. U.
Okla. St. U.
U. Okla.
Our Lady Lake C.
U. Penn.
U. Pitt.
Portland St. U.
U. Puerto Rico
Radford U.
Rhode Island C.
Rutgers U.
Sage Grad. Sch.
St. John's U.
St. Mary's U. (Tex)
St. Louis U.
Salem St. U.
S.D.S.U.
San Fran. St. U.
San Jose St. U.
Simmons C.
Smith C.
So. Conn. St. U.
U. So. Car.
U. So. Cal.
U. So. Fla.
So. Ill. U.
U. So. Miss.
Southern U.
Springfield C.
Syracuse U.
Temple U.
U. Tenn.
U. Tex. (Arlington)
U. Tex. (Austin)
Tulane U.
U. Utah
Valdosta St. U.
Va. Commonwealth U.
U. Vt.
Villanova U.
Walla Walla C.
Wash. U. (Mo.)
U. Wash.
Wayne St. U.
W. Va. U.
West. Mich. U.
Widener U.
U. Wis.
U. Wis. (Milwaukee)
Worcester St. U.
Wright St. U.
Yeshiva U.

Theater/Drama

(Speech/Drama, Speech
Arts, Theater Arts; typi-
cally includes Acting, Directing; often includes
Children's Theater, Criticism, Theater/Costume
Design, Technical Pro-
duction)

U. Akron
U. Ala.
U. Albany (S.U.N.Y.)
Ariz. St. U.
U. Ariz.
Ark. St. U.
U. Ark.
Baylor U.
Bennington C.
Boston U.
Bowl. Gr. St. U.
Brandeis U.
B.Y.U.
Brooklyn C. (C.U.N.Y.)
Butler U.
Cal. Inst. Arts

DANCE

DANCE THERAPY

MUSIC THEATER

PLAYWRITING

THEATER FOR THE DEAF

THEATER MANAGEMENT

Urban Design/City Planning.

(Community Planning, City Planning, Environmental Design, Urban and Regional Planning, Urban Design)

Veterinary Medicine